DATE DUE

DE 1 6 88			

DEMCO 38-296

INTERNATIONAL ENCYCLOPEDIA OF DEVELOPMENTAL AND INSTRUCTIONAL PSYCHOLOGY

Resources in Education

This is a new series of Pergamon one-volume Encyclopedias drawing upon articles in the acclaimed *International Encyclopedia of Education, Second Edition*, with revisions as well as new articles. Each volume in the series is thematically organized and aims to provide complete and up-to-date coverage on its subject. These Encyclopedias will serve as an invaluable reference source for researchers, faculty members, teacher educators, government officials, educational administrators, and policymakers.

The *International Encyclopedia of Developmental and Instructional Psychology* intends to provide a research-based overview in an educational perspective of the present state-of-the-art of our knowledge and understanding of the conditions, processes, and modifiabilities of human development and learning. The Encyclopedia focuses on both developmental and instructional psychology.

Over the past decade the boundaries between these two separate research domains have become increasingly obscure. Indeed, developmental psychologists have shown a growing interest in the impact of environmental factors on development. This has led to the study of education and instructional variables, the predominantly environmental factors. Meanwhile, instructional psychology has become a major subdomain of research on human cognition and development. A substantial contribution to the synergy between both domains derives from the robust research finding that developmental changes are very important conditions, as well as consequences, of the acquistion of knowledge and (meta) cognitive strategies. The resulting changes have inspired the decision to combine both developmental and instructional psychology into one single volume.

Other titles in the series include:

POSTLETHWAITE (ed.)
International Encyclopedia of National Systems of Education, Second Edition

CARNOY (ed.)
International Encyclopedia of Economics of Education, Second Edition

ANDERSON (ed.)
International Encyclopedia of Teaching and Teacher Education, Second Edition

TUIJNMAN (ed.)
International Encyclopedia of Adult Education and Training, Second Edition

PLOMP & ELY (eds)
International Encyclopedia of Educational Technology, Second Edition

KEEVES (ed.)
Educational Research, Methodology, and Measurement, An International Handbook, Second Edition

INTERNATIONAL ENCYCLOPEDIA OF DEVELOPMENTAL AND INSTRUCTIONAL PSYCHOLOGY

Edited by

ERIK DE CORTE

University of Leuven, Leuven, Belgium

and

FRANZ E. WEINERT

Max-Planck-Institut für Psychologische Forschung, München, Germany

PERGAMON

The Boulevard, Langford Lane,
X5 1GB, UK

60 White Plains Road, Tarrytown, New

JAPAN   Elsevier Science Japan, 9-15 Higashi-Azabu 1-chome, Minato-
                 ku, Tokyo 106, Japan

Copyright © 1996 Elsevier Science Ltd

First edition 1996

Library of Congress Cataloging in Publication Data
International encyclopedia of developmental and
instructional psychology / edited by Erik De Corte, Franz E.
Weinert. — 1st ed.
    p.   cm.
  Includes index.
  1. Developmental psychology — Encyclopedias.
I. Corte, Erik de.   II. Weinert, Franz E., 1930–.
BF712.7.I58   1996
155'.03—dc20   96-17900

British Library Cataloguing in Publication Data
A catalogue record for this book is available from the
British Library.

ISBN 0–08–042980–7

Printed and bound in Great Britain by BPC Wheatons Ltd, Exeter.

Contents

Preface   xvii

Introduction   xix

**Section I: A General Framework of Human Development, Learning, and
Instruction in Educational Perspective**   1

History of Developmental Psychology   1
S. WEINERT

Human Development in the Lifespan: Overview   8
F. E. WEINERT

Education and Development   17
L. J. SAHA AND I. FÄGERLIND

Human Development, Learning, and Instruction   25
F. E. WEINERT

History of Instructional Psychology   29
R. E. MAYER

Instructional Psychology: Overview   33
E. DE CORTE

Translating Research into Practice   43
F. E. WEINERT AND E. DE CORTE

Section II: General Issues of Human Development   51

Cross-cultural Approaches to Human Development   51
H. J. KORNADT AND G. TROMMSDORFF

Human Development: Research Methodology   55
A. VON EYE AND C. SPIEL

Human Development: Research and Social Policy   59
S. L. KAGAN

Human Development: Research and Educational Practice   63
A. DEMETRIOU

Developmental Psychopathology   67
A. F. KALVERBOER

Contents

Developmental Disabilities: Severe   73
D. L. Ferguson

**Section III: Basic Cultural Conceptions and Scientific Theories of
Human Development**   77

Cultural and Religious Concepts of Human Development   77
R. M. Thomas

Ecological Models of Human Development   82
U. Bronfenbrenner

Humanistic Models of Human Development   86
N. Groeben

Behaviorist Approaches to Human Development   89
S. W. Bijou

Information-processing Theories of Human Development   92
R. Kail

Piaget's Theory of Human Development   97
A. de Ribaupierre and L. Rieben

Social Learning Theory of Human Development   101
A. Bandura

Socio-biological and Ethological Approaches to Human Development   107
W. Charlesworth

Psychodynamic Theories of Human Development   112
E. Jaeggi

Section IV: Periods, Stages, and Sequences of Human Development   117

Stages in Human Development   117
K. W. Fischer and R. Hencke

Infancy   121
L. P. Lipsitt

Childhood   125
D. F. Bjorklund and W. S. Cassel

Adolescence   130
R. M. Lerner and F. A. Villarruel

Children and Youth at Risk   136
W. E. Davis and E. J. McCaul

Children and Youth with Special Needs, Diagnosis and Classification of   142
B. Algozzine, B. Wong and F. E. Obiakor

Children and Youth with Special Needs, Education of   150
M. C. Reynolds and M. Ainscrow

Lifespan Development   161
J. HECKHAUSEN

Adulthood and Old Age   163
K. W. SCHAIE

Section V: Biological Approaches to Human Development   169

Brain Development and Human Behavior   169
H. J. MARKOWITSCH

Genetics and Human Development   171
P. BORKENAU

Prenatal Development   174
G. GOTTLIEB AND D. E. HUTCHINGS

Physical Growth and Development: Universal Changes and Individual Differences   178
A. F. ROCHE

Sex Differences in Behavior and Development   184
M. STEMMLER AND A. C. PETERSEN

Temperament Development   187
G. A. KOHNSTAMM AND R. P. MARTIN

Section VI: Personality Development in Social Context   193

Socialization   193
A. STURMAN

Self-related Cognition, Learned Helplessness, Learned Optimism,
and Human Development   199
J. P. EISNER AND M.E.P. SELIGMAN

Development and Socialization of Aggression   202
D. G. PERRY

Development of Prosocial Behavior   206
N. EISENBERG

Development of Motivation   209
G. D. HEYMAN AND C.S. DWECK

Emotional Development   213
R. PEKRUN

Social Development   217
J. B. ASENDORPF

Moral Development   222
G. NUNNER-WINKLER

Development of the Self-concept   228
A. HELMKE

Contents

Personality Development   233
D. MAGNUSSON AND B. TÖRESTAD

Gender Roles   239
C. L. MARTIN AND G. LEVY

Early Experience and Human Development   243
J. BROOKS-GUNN AND F. LIAW

Family Influences on Human Development   250
K. A. SCHNEEWIND

Peer Relations and Development   254
C. F. M. VAN LIESHOUT

Problems and Crises in Human Development   258
L. MONTADA

Section VII: Cognitive Development   263

An Overview of Cognitive Development   263
J. PERNER

Cognitive Development: Individual Differences   268
F. E. WEINERT

Cognitive Development and the Acquisition of Expertise   273
G. HATANO

Development of Gifted Children   277
F. J. MÖNKS AND E. J. MASON

Motor Development and Skill Acquisition   280
C. von HOFSTEN

Perceptual Development   284
F. WILKENING

Language Development   288
H. GRIMM

Memory Development   294
W. SCHNEIDER

Development of Reasoning Competences in Early and Later Childhood 297
M. BULLOCK

Development of Social Cognition   304
M KELLER AND M. KILLEN

Play: Developmental Stages, Functions, and Educational Support   306
K. H. RUBIN AND R. J. COPLAN

Development of Learning across the Lifespan   313
M. J. A. HOWE

Section VIII: Theories and Models of Learning in Educational Settings   317

Paradigms in Instructional Psychology   317
A. KNOERS

Learning Theories: Historical Overview and Trends   322
T. J. SHUELL AND K. A. MORAN

Models of Learning   327
R. B. BURNS

Human Learning: Evolution of Anthropological Perspectives   334
B. BOGIN

Constructivism and Learning   338
P. COBB

Situated Learning   341
L. RESNICK

Learning Activity   347
J. LOMPSCHER

Cooperative Learning   351
R. E. SLAVIN

Discovery Learning and Teaching   355
P. TAMIR

Mastery Learning   362
T. R. GUSKEY

Section IX: Processes and Outcomes of Learning   369

Architecture of Cognition   369
J. ELSHOUT

Attention and Learning   372
A. HARNISCHFEGER

Bilingualism   375
K. HAKUTA

Cognition and Learning   377
L. B. RESNICK AND A. COLLINS

Concept Learning   381
R. D. TENNYSON

Concept Learning: Teaching and Assessing   385
R. D. TENNYSON

Creativity   391
J. ELSHOUT

Contents

Declarative and Procedural Knowledge   394
S. OHLSSON

Feedback in Learning   396
R. E. MAYER

Implicit Memory and Learning   399
G. d'YDEWALLE

Knowledge Representation and Organization   402
S. VOSNIADOU

Language and Learning in Education   406
J. U. OGBU

Learning Processes and Learning Outcomes   409
V. J. SHUTE

Learning Strategies and Learning to Learn   419
C. E. WEINSTEIN AND G. VAN MATER STONE

Learning Strategies: Teaching and Assessing   423
C. E. WEINSTEIN AND D. K. MEYER

Literacy   428
D. R. OLSON

Memory: Teaching and Assessing   431
M. PRESSLEY AND P. VAN METER

Metacognition   436
P. R-J. SIMONS

Metacognitive Strategies: Teaching and Assessing   441
P. R-J. SIMONS

Motivation and Learning   445
W. LENS

Visual Perception   451
J. WAGEMANS

Preconceptions and Misconceptions   455
R. DUIT

Prior Knowledge and Learning   459
F. J. R. C. DOCHY

Reasoning   464
J. F. VOSS

Self-regulation in Learning   467
J. KUHL AND K. KRASKA

Student Cognitive Processing and Learning   471
P. H. WINNE AND D. L. BUTLER

Task Analysis   478
G. ROWLAND AND C. M. REIGELUTH

Learning Transfer   483
D. N. PERKINS AND G. SALOMON

Section X: Curriculum and the Psychology of Learning and Instruction   489

Attitudes and Values, Acquiring   489
F. K. OSER

Comprehension: Teaching and Assessing   492
W. SCHNOTZ AND S.-P. BALLSTAEDT

Educational Psychology: Impact on Curriculum   498
G. D. HAERTEL

Expert Knowledge and Performance   505
C. M. ZEITZ AND R. GLASER

Foreign Language Acquisition, Process of   511
M. H. LONG

Learning from Text   519
E. KINTSCH AND W. KINTSCH

Learning Strategies in Second Language Learning   525
J. M. O'MALLEY AND A. U. CHAMOT

Linguistics and Language Learning   531
B. SPOLSKY

Mathematics, Learning and Instruction of   535
E. DE CORTE, L. VERSCHAFFEL AND B. GREER

Mathematics and Language   538
D. PIMM

Mathematics Education, Affective Issues in   543
P. KLOOSTERMAN

Motor Skills: Learning and Instruction   547
J. M. M. VAN DER SANDEN

Development of Learning Skills in Problem-solving and Thinking   550
R. E. MAYER

Problem-solving: Teaching and Assessing   555
R. E. MAYER

Contents

Reading, Learning and Instruction of   559
C. A. PERFETTI

Reading Comprehension, Learning of   562
W. SCHNOTZ

Reading Comprehension in Second and Foreign Language   564
E. BIALYSTOK

Science, Learning and Instruction of   568
M. C. LINN AND B.-S. EYLON

Social Sciences, Learning and Instruction of   572
J. F. VOSS

Visual and Performing Arts, Learning and Instruction of   575
K. FREEDMAN

Writing, Learning and Instruction of   577
A. HILDYARD

Written Composition: Teaching and Assessing   580
S. W. FREEDMAN

Section XI: Social, Cultural, and Affective Aspects of Learning   585

Affect, Emotions, and Learning   585
M. BOEKAERTS

Culture, Cognition, and Education   590
E. J. JACOB

Home Environment and School Learning   597
A. J. FULIGNI AND H. W. STEVENSON

Learning in School, Sociology of   601
P. BROADFOOT

Peer Relations and Learning   607
W. DAMON

Personality, School, and Social Environment as Learning Determinants   611
H. J. WALBERG

Social and Communication Skills   615
C. PONTECORVO

Social Interaction and Learning   619
V. V. RUBTSOV

Coping with Stressful Situations in a Learning Context   623
M. BOEKAERTS

Teachers' Expectations 626
T. L. GOOD

Section XII: Individual Differences and Learning and Instruction 633

Abilities and Aptitudes 633
J. W. PELLEGRINO

Cognitive Styles and Learning 638
S. MESSICK

Gender and School Learning: Mathematics 642
S. F. CHIPMAN

Gender and School Learning: Science 645
M. C. LINN

Individual Differences, Learning, and Instruction 649
R. E. SNOW

Intelligence, Learning, and Instruction 660
D. F. LOHMAN

Student Diversity and Classroom Teaching 665
M. C. WANG

Teaching: Aptitude–Treatment Interaction Model 670
R. E. SNOW

Section XIII: Classroom Learning Environments 675

Academic Learning Time 675
C. W. FISHER

Classroom Environments 679
B. J. FRASER

Group Processes in the Classroom 683
N. BENNETT

Environments for Learning 687
A. COLLINS, J. G. GREENO AND L. B. RESNICK

Time, Allocated and Instructional 691
L. W. ANDERSON

Section XIV: Computers, Media, and Learning 695

Computers and Learning 695
E. DE CORTE, L. VERSCHAFFEL AND J. LOWYCK

Contents

Computer Assisted Learning   700
D. M. WATSON

Computer-managed Learning   704
P. K. KOMOSKI

Computer Networking for Education   708
L. M. HARASIM

Computer Programming, Learning and Instruction of   713
R. E. MAYER

Instructional Design Theories   715
C. M. REIGELUTH

Instructional Psychology   721
J. LOWYCK AND J. ELEN

Media and Learning   725
R. E. CLARK

Problem-solving and Learning: Computer Modeling   730
K. OPWIS AND H. SPADA

Programmed Learning   733
M. ERAUT

Section XV: Learning in Adults   743

Adult Learning: Overview   743
S. D. BROOKFIELD

Experiential and Open Learning for Adults   749
R. H. PAUL

Group Learning   752
G. G. DARKENWALD

Learning in Industrial Settings   755
J. LOWYCK

Learning to Learn: Adult Education   760
R. M. SMITH

Lifespan Learning: Implications for Educators   764
D. MACKERACHER AND A. C. TUIJNMAN

Self-directed Adult Learning   771
R. HIEMSTRA

Section XVI: Learning in Children with Special Needs   779

Cognitive Strategy Instruction: Special Education   779
Y. M. DAVID AND A. S. PALINCSAR

Learning Characteristics of Students with Special Needs   786
M. C. WANG AND E. HABELOW

Neurological Bases of Learning Problems   792
G. S. COLES

Specific Learning Disability   797
D. J. PALMER AND A. CALERO-BRECKHEIMER

Section XVII: Assessment and Learning   805

Assessment in the Service of Learning   805
S. LANE AND R. GLASER

Classroom Assessment   809
P. W. AIRASIAN

Learning Potential and Learning Potential Assessment   813
A. J. J. M. RUIJSSENAARS AND J. H. M. HAMERS

List of Contributors   817

Name Index   825

Subject Index   847

Preface

This *International Encyclopedia of Developmental and Instructional Psychology* is a spinoff volume from the successful second edition of the *International Encyclopedia of Education*, edited by Torsten Husén and T. Neville Postlethwaite and published in 1994. Consequently, the contents of this *Encyclopedia* derive from the entries that were published in the sections entitled "Developmental Psychology" (edited by Franz Weinert) and "Instructional Psychology" (edited by Erik De Corte) of the 12-volume parent *Encyclopedia*.

During the preparatory stage of this volume a systematic framework for organizing the materials was designed, and the authors of the entries that were published in the parent *Encyclopedia* were asked to update their contribution. In addition, about ten new articles were commissioned. Finally, we wrote an introductory section in an attempt to evoke and illustrate the developmental process of the relationship during the twentieth century between developmental psychology and instructional/educational psychology: starting as two quite separate subdomains of psychology with a distinct orientation and approach in the early part of the century, they have gradually drawn together, and the frontiers between them have become more and more blurred. It is precisely this integrative trend over the past decades that has led to the idea of bringing both sections from the parent *Encyclopedia* together in the present volume.

Preparing and realizing this *Encyclopedia* is a major endeavor that can only be achieved thanks to the contribution and help of many people. First of all, we would like to thank the Editors-in-Chief of the parent *Encyclopedia*, Torsten Husén and Neville Postlethwaite, for their expert advice and professional support during the preparation of our sections for the parent *Encyclopedia*, and for their encouragement to prepare and produce this spinoff volume.

Working together with the other Section Editors of the parent *Encyclopedia*—a group of about 20 scholars representing more or less the highest level of expertise in the field of educational research—was a very interesting and rewarding professional experience, but resulted also in new, cordial personal relationships. We are especially grateful to those fellow Editors from whose sections we could borrow relevant entries for this volume.

All the authors who contributed the entries for this *Encyclopedia* deserve our special thanks and appreciation. The coverage and quality of this volume could only be achieved on the basis of their thorough expertise and broad experience relating to the topics discussed, as well as their skills in translating and communicating this expertise at the appropriate level for the intended audience of this volume.

We are very grateful to the wonderful crew at Elsevier Science Ltd, especially to Barbara Barrett and Michele Wheaton for their stimulating encouragement and kind support experienced at meetings and over luncheons in various places on both sides of the Atlantic, but also to Angela Greenwell who has guided and followed up the whole production process conscientiously behind the scenes in Oxford.

Finally, each of us would like to acknowledge a few people in Leuven and München, respectively. Erik De Corte wants to thank warmly his wife Rita for her patience and support not only during work on this *Encyclopedia* but especially during the preparation of the section on Instructional Psychology for the parent *Encyclopedia*, which had to be started from scratch, and which chained him to his desk for innumerable hours during many weekends. He is also grateful to his secretary at Leuven University, Ann Paredis, for her valuable administrative help. Franz Weinert wants to thank his wife Anna for her patience, encouragement, and help throughout the preparation of this volume. He is also particularly grateful to Mariele Kremling of the Max Planck Institute for Psychological Research in München. She handled the enormous mass of administrative and secretarial work perfectly.

ERIK DE CORTE
Leuven, Belgium

FRANZ WEINERT
München, Germany

July 1996

Introduction

E. De Corte and F. E. Weinert

1. Developmental and Instructional Psychology: Two Different Lines of Research and Theory Building

Many psychologists and lay persons are convinced that developmental and instructional psychology are closely linked. This was, however, not so in the past. Admittedly there were programmatic demands and some empirical efforts in this direction around the beginning of the twentieth century (Baldwin 1885). But in the following years the two fields of research developed as distinctly separate disciplines.

Developmental psychologists were primarily interested in developmental processes that had a universal character, were sequential ordered, and directed toward final states (level of mature thinking). They considered rendering a highly precise description of natural development (in a normative frame of reference) to be their most important scientific task. This descriptive–normative orientation, of course, also had an effect upon the role ascribed to education and in particular to instruction. Developmental psychologists at this period of time exhibited "(a) an emphasis on 'respecting' the course of children's development rather than shaping it, (b) a nearly complete absence of theory of how environments, including educational environments, influence development, and (c) a mistrust of instruction as incapable of profoundly influencing human development" (Resnick 1981b p. 2).

A good example of the traditional gap between developmental and instructional psychology is the well-known work of Piaget and his epistemological theory of cognitive development. According to Piaget in 1972 development is identical to "learning in the broader sense." As a rule, however, he differentiated between the concepts of development and learning in that whereas development deals with general mechanisms of acting and thinking, learning in its stricter sense is mainly concerned with the acquisition and memorizing of specific skills and knowledge. Piaget frequently emphasized that this form of learning plays a subordinate role to the laws of development. Cognitive development is not just a successive accumulation of small steps of learning but is governed by the laws of structuring that have both a logical and a biological nature. According to Piaget and Piagetian theorists instruction plays a completely subordinate role in reaching the goal of highly advanced development of thinking.

In contrast to Piaget's skeptical view of instruction as a means of promoting cognitive development, for Vygotsky (1978) instructional processes play a major role in cognitive development. The active internalization of social–cultural tools that is made possible through social interaction, learning, and instruction is, according to Vygotsky, precisely what is necessary for the acquisition of higher mental functions.

Based on Vygotsky's ideas, stimulated by many findings in cross-cultural research, fascinated by the self-regulated acquisition of cognitive competencies in the preschool years, and guided by the principles of some new theories of learning (Brown 1994), there is in recent years a *rapprochement* between developmental and instructional psychology.

1.1 Developmental Psychology: An Evolution-based Descriptive Approach

A scientific-based developmental psychology has only existed since the late nineteenth century. Although this discipline was built on rich experiential sources of knowledge about development and education, it is nonetheless a typical product of the time. Among the many roots of present day developmental psychology, there are two that continue to have an especially important influence: the theory of evolution and the founding of psychology as an empirical science of human behavior.

Today it is hard to imagine that the ideas of evolution and development had such a strong impact in shaping nineteenth-century thought. The term "development" dominated not only such divergent disciplines as astronomy, biology, geology, embryology, psychology, history, and linguistics, but was also to become a central basis for conceptualizations in philosophy and in theories of science. This inspired and led to the continual exchange of facts and ideas between one scientific discipline and another (e.g., between evolutionary biology and developmental psychology). Moreover, it stimulated theorizing about phenomena and general laws of development. Herbert Spencer (1870), for instance, understood development to be each and every change from indefinite, incoherent homogeneity to definite, coherent heterogeneity.

Thus, Heinz Werner characterized the scientific agenda of developmental psychology as follows:

> Every type of theoretical psychology, for example the general psychology of the normal individual, the natural history of man, animal psychology and child psychology, psychopathology and the psychology of abnormal states

of consciousness may all be considered under the aspect of mental development and is, therefore, developmental psychology. Over and above these specialized developmental psychologies there is a general developmental psychology, a comparative science that is just in its infancy, whose task is to compare the results of these various sub-specialities of developmental psychology with each other and to extract the general laws of human mental development (Werner 1926 p. 2).

Wilhelm Wundt (1916), one of the most prominent founders of psychology as a behavioral and social science, doubted that this broad agenda could be accomplished. Even in 1921 he cynically predicted that perhaps 90 percent of all psychologists of that time would confuse developmental psychology with child psychology. He was probably right; in the first half of the twentieth century child psychology did indeed dominate developmental laboratories and textbooks around the world. Nonetheless, even with this more limited scope developmental psychology achieved and maintained an especially unique research perspective within the whole discipline of psychology. In contrast to experimental and differential psychology, child psychology emphasized its own descriptive and normative research approach. This approach demanded broad, exact, and comparative observations and led to the construction of normative developmental scales. With the help of such scales it was possible to diagnose whether an individual child was developing faster (acceleration) or slower (retardation) than the average. Given the fact that such individual differences remain stable over long periods of life this approach had and still has enormous practical importance.

In the second half of the twentieth century there was a major change in the field of developmental psychology which extended it from a science focused almost exclusively on childhood to a lifespan psychology. The inclusion of adulthood and old age in developmental psychology demanded a new conceptualization of human development and initiated a revolution in developmental theories. Although theoretical models of child development differed in many respects, an implicit and dominant assumption was that development is directed by processes of biological maturation. According to Flavell (1970), the fundamental developmental changes during childhood are species-specific, uniform, unavoidable, inevitable, irreversible, and directed toward achieving the mature adult state.

Lifespan psychology attempted to replace or at least expand this strongly biological orientation with a more open, liberal, and pluralistic concept of psychological development. If one considers psychological changes across the lifespan the following characterization (according to Baltes 1987) emerges:

(a) Development is a lifelong process. No age-level, even in early childhood, totally determines subsequent development.

(b) Psychological development is multidirectional. There are increases and decreases in behavioral dispositions at all age-levels (even when growth processes dominate in childhood and processes of decline dominate in old age).

(c) The lifespan approach assumes lifelong individual plasticity.

(d) Most proponents of lifespan developmental psychology also prefer a contextual concept of development. They assume that human development is a complex, dynamic phenomenon in which biological and intrapsychological factors, mechanisms, and tendencies interact dialectically with social, cultural, educational, historical, and ideosyncratic events and experiences.

(e) Last but not least within the context of this introductory chapter there is now a strong awareness in lifespan developmental research of the great importance of learning and instructional processes for human development.

1.2 Instructional Psychology: A Learning-based Prescriptive Approach

The roots of instructional psychology—a domain of inquiry that largely covers mainstream educational psychology—can be traced back to ancient times, but are especially evident from the beginning of the modern era when well-known scholars like Juan Luis Vives (1492–1540), Comenius (1592–1671), and Johann Friedrich Herbart (1776–1841) developed concepts and ideas that today would be considered as part of instructional psychology (Berliner 1993). However, the formal initiation of the field is commonly placed at the beginning of the twentieth century, more precisely in 1903 with the publication of Edward Lee Thorndike's first textbook entitled *Educational Psychology*.

From its origin the field differed in two ways from developmental psychology; namely in its orientation toward learning as opposed to development, and in its prescriptive instead of descriptive approach. For instance, Thorndike conceived educational psychology as the straightforward application of the psychological laws of learning to the design of classroom instruction and teaching materials. On the basis of laboratory experiments with animals, he postulated that in any situation the action performed depends on the strengths of the "bonds" between the situation and the various actions possible. Learning takes place through the differential strengthening of bonds, by reinforcement. Consequently, teaching should be organized in such a way that the correct bonds are strengthened. Thorndike (1922) applied this theory of learning and instruction in a systematic way to the teaching of arithmetic in his book *The Psychology of Arithmetic*. Programmed instruction based on the behaviorist tradition introduced by Skinner (1957) in the middle of the twentieth century is probably the most representative example of the prescriptive approach: it was the straightforward application of the principles of operant conditioning to the design of self-instructional materials (Skinner 1968). Of course, instructional psychology has also always had a descriptive component, in the sense that the laws or principles of learning embody a description of the mechanisms and processes of knowledge acquisition. However, while in developmental psychology the ultimate aim has been the description of universal patterns of evolution and growth, in instructional psychology the final goal has always been to elaborate prescriptions for classroom teaching based on the descriptive laws of learning.

Interestingly, mainstream instructional psychology in the former Soviet Union—while based on a totally different theoretical framework about learning, namely Vygotsky's activity theory—has also from its inception been oriented toward the design of prescriptions for the improvement of educational practice (Vygotsky 1978). A major strategy applied to develop and test optimal instructional conditions for school learning was the use of so-called teaching experiments, as illustrated, for example, in the work of Gal'perin (see De Corte 1977). However, at least two important differences between Western and Russian instructional psychology need to be mentioned. First, from a methodological perspective Russian studies are generally more ecologically valid, but experimentally less rigorous. Second, in Vygotskyan theory learning and development—while still distinguished—are closely related in that the child develops by learning general concepts and principles that can be applied afterwards to a variety of new tasks and problems (Vygotsky 1978). While this latter idea is in line with the view of the Gestalt psychologists, it is in contrast, for instance, with Piaget's conception that learning is constrained by development (see Strauss 1993 for a brief overview of the different perspectives on the relationship between learning and development; see also Liben 1987).

Both contrasting features of instructional as compared to developmental psychology—the orientation toward learning and the prescriptive nature—have continued to characterize the field. For instance, Robert Glaser (1981), a leading scholar in this domain of inquiry since the 1960s, has stated that the psychology of instruction "must have the characteristics of a prescriptive science of design. It will rely upon the traditional sciences to describe how things are and how they function. But its unique activity is to prescribe and design conditions for learning based upon its information" (p. 119). This point of view converges with Lauren Resnick's (1983) idea that a cognitive theory of instruction "must be both descriptive, explaining why instruction works and why it does not, and prescriptive, suggesting what to do the next time for better results" (p. 5–6). Therefore, she distinguishes three

components in a theory of instruction: (a) specification of the capabilities to be acquired; (b) description of the learning processes; and (c) principles of intervention.

Notwithstanding this continuity in the basic orientation of instructional psychology, the field has also undergone major changes, some of which can only be briefly mentioned here. First of all, the initial conception of educational psychology as the application of basic psychology to education, as reflected in the work of Thorndike, has been abandoned. During the third quarter of the twentieth century this "middleman" role of educational psychology as merely carrying psychology to education, was increasingly considered to be unproductive and irrelevant from an educational perspective (Berliner 1993). Wittrock (1967) made a plea for a new conceptualization of the field as the scientific study of human behavior in educational settings. Resnick (1981a) wrote that instructional psychology had become fundamental research on the processes of learning and instruction and Glaser and Bassok (1989) claimed that it had "become a vigorous part of the mainstream of research on human cognition and development" (p. 631).

The latter development of instructional psychology was facilitated by a second major change that originated in the United States, but was influenced by European schools in psychology, especially the Gestalt tradition and the Piagetian school: the shift from behaviorism to cognitive psychology. Because the focus of interest in this new approach was on the processes of human information processing in complex cognitive tasks, the research became more and more directed to educationally relevant areas and problems (as compared to the artificial and knowledge-lean tasks involved in most previous research).

Third, while in the behavioristic era the study of learning was prominent in educational psychology, learning processes were rather pushed to the background in the early days of cognitive instructional psychology when the focus was on the structures and processes of human competence (Glaser and Bassok 1989). However, since the 1980s researchers have gradually shown a renewed interest in investigating acquisition processes. At the same time the conception of learning as a constructive and interactive process has become widely accepted. This growing interest in children's active knowledge construction and meaning building has been paralleled by a development that is of great importance in view of the elaboration of a research-based prescriptive design science for the improvement of educational practices. Instructional psychologists have increasingly left their laboratories to study learning and instruction in real classrooms. The underlying idea behind this is that a strong test of the available descriptive theory of learning processes can be made through attempts at application based on the derivation of guidelines and principles for the design of complex instructional interventions (see, e.g., Brown 1992).

A final trend to be mentioned here is the *rapprochement* between developmental and instructional psychology. Indeed, over the past decades developmentalists have become more and more interested in instruction. There are at least two major reasons for this trend. First, in contrast to the view which prevailed for many years among developmental psychologists, research has yielded compelling evidence that knowledge is a very important component of cognitive development, and that schooling has substantial impact on the growth of children's cognitive abilities (see, e.g., Weinert and Helmke 1995a). Second, Vygotsky's theoretical stance discussed above, that learning and culture are the major vehicles of development, has become widely accepted among developmental psychologists (Liben 1987).

2. Early Efforts to Bridge the Gap Between Developmental and Instructional Psychology

2.1 The Concept of Readiness for Learning

If developmental psychologists proceed from the assumption that development can be damaged by environmental influences but cannot be promoted by instruction, education can only be a matter of protecting the healthy growth of the child, and making use of the individual readiness for learning reached as a function of cognitive development (often indicated by children's chronological or mental age). According to such maturity theories of development, readiness can be tested but not taught.

Advocates of this position assume that spontaneous age-correlated cognitive and behavioral dispositions develop during childhood as a consequence of endogeneous processes (e.g., increase in working memory capacity, or a natural sequence of developmental stages, such as those of Piaget). Of course, such improvements in working memory capacity or the achieved structural level of thinking cannot themselves be explained from a learning perspective but allow and require concrete learning opportunities in the child's environment. Under this perspective learning and instruction have only a supporting role. "All the evidence says: Readiness comes as a healthy child grows and matures. Time is the answer—not special drill or special practice" (Hymes 1958, p.10).

Despite many efforts, however, it was not possible to provide the readiness concept with a theoretical foundation or with valid empirical indicators. All attempts to isolate and/or to combine chronological age, mental age, and various specific developmental indicators of motor, perceptual, or intellectual characteristics have failed to come up with a valid predictor of success and failure in classroom learning. Thus, the application of general states of readiness in the school setting and in many other institutionalized learning opportunities remain vague. Even though the readiness concept has not been validated it is still used in many countries, particularly when children enter school.

2.2 The Concept of Adaptive Instruction

Adaptive education involves the notion that learning environments are designed to take into account differences in student aptitudes that are relevant to the processes and outcomes of learning. Implicitly the concept of adaptive or individualized education has a long history. For instance, in his well-known dialogue with the slave Meno, Socrates tried to adapt his instruction to his student. Nevertheless, in the past educational systems have mostly neglected to take into account the individual differences among students. Indeed, even until the middle of the twentieth century, as argued by Glaser (1977), schooling was generally characterized by a selective and fixed mode of instruction, offering only minimal variations in the conditions under which pupils had to learn by absorbing passively the presented information. This educational practice reflected the psychological conception of the learner's abilities and aptitudes as global, stable, and unchangeable entities which were predictive of future achievement; of development as genetically predetermined; and of learning as a passive process of knowledge acquisition. This view was entirely in accordance with the prevailing idea in mainstream developmental psychology that individual differences in cognitive abilities are stable, and insensitive to environmental influences.

The shift from selective to adaptive education has been driven by changing conceptions of the learner that derive from more recent research on learning and development which began in the 1960s. Evidence has been accumulated which shows that human beings are highly adaptive to environmental conditions and demands, that continuous interactions with the environment are essential for optimum learning and development, that learning is an active process of knowledge construction, and that cognitive abilities and aptitudes can be modified through learning and development (Glaser 1977). Based on this modern view of the learner, adaptive education involves two complementary approaches: the first being that the instructional environment can be adapted to the individual characteristics of the learner and the second that the aptitudes required as preconditions for successful learning can be taught directly. For instance, it has been shown that for students with a high level of fear of failure learning can be improved by providing a highly structured form of teaching. However, one could consider looking for a strategy that aims at decreasing students' fear of failure (see Corno and Snow 1986). It is obvious that in order to match properly the instructional conditions with the student's aptitudes, it is necessary to assess accurately those aptitudes.

In the United States especially there was a proliferation of programs for adaptive education from the mid-1960s till the early 1970s. Among the most well-known were Individually Guided Education (IGE), Mastery Learning, Personalized System of Instruction (PSI), Program for Learning in Accordance with Needs (PLAN), and Adaptive Learning Environments Model (ALEM) (Corno and Snow 1986). Both instructional and developmental psychologists have been involved in research and developmental work relating to the design of such adaptive school environments. However, as observed by Anderson (1994), adaptive education was on the decline by the late 1970s, and faded out worldwide in the 1980s.

2.3 The Concept of Compensatory Education

Compensatory education consists in "the provision of altered or additional education programs and services in the form of cultural and instructional enrichment, educational rehabilitation, and expanded educational opportunities to disadvantaged or deprived school failures who do not receive or profit from normal educational opportunities or provisions" (Flaxman 1985 p. 887). Compensatory education was organized in the mid-1960s in the United States as part of an attempt to fight poverty at the material as well as the mental level. The most famous program, Head Start (for 3- and 4-year olds), started in 1965. Similar programs were subsequently organized throughout the Western world.

The main reasons for the disadvantages which were commonly shared by deprived youngsters throughout the world were: (a) restricted early experiences in the home which did not allow them to develop the necessary intellectual ability to meet the demands of formal schooling; and (b) restricted educational resources and unfavorable social conditions during the early school years which had a negative impact on their school achievement.

Important scientific results of psychological research underlying the efforts to provide compensatory education programs were: (a) the finding—already referred to in the previous subsection—that intellectual ability is greatly malleable and can be improved through external intervention (a finding that was also contested by scholars like Jensen); and (b) the related outcome put forward by Bloom (1964), that the first years of life are very influential in determining cognitive development, since about 50 percent of the variance in adult intelligence can already be accounted for by the age of four.

Instructional as well as developmental psychologists participated in the development and evaluation of compensatory education programs that can be characterized as a form of positive discrimination for socially and educationally deprived children. The programs themselves aim either at enrichment of cognitive development of deprived children during the preschool period, or at remediation and prevention of school failure during formal schooling. Most enrichment programs combine components of the Head Start and Project Follow Through programs (the latter one intended as a follow up program after Head Start for children from kindergarten until Grade 3): a component focusing on elementary language and mathematics skills; a component concentrating on the development of learning readiness and problem-solving skills; and a component stressing social and emotional developmental aspects such as self-concept.

Overall the results of the compensatory education programs show that they have been only moderately successful. It has even been argued sometimes that the programs had nothing more than a "cosmetic" effect, leaving the underlying basic social and domestic environmental conditions of disadvantaged children unchanged. The available evaluation results certainly show that the programs have not succeeded in significantly increasing the average level of intellectual ability of the participants. However, the better programs have been successful in decreasing the cumulative academic failure of those children who were treated in a consistent and concentrated way from childhood through the elementary years of schooling (Flaxman 1985). Just like adaptive education, compensatory intervention programs largely faded out in the 1980s.

3. New Approaches to Bridge the Gap Between Developmental and Instructional Psychology

3.1 Development, Learning, and Instruction: The New Synthesis in Theory Building

In the history of psychology the theoretical gap between developmental and instructional approaches remained for a very long time. The two disciplines developed and maintained different research paradigms—each associated with "imperialistic" attitudes. Developmental psychologists believed that cognitive development is the necessary prerequisite and even the final goal of education: "The first principle is that education for development is not achieved through direct teaching and instruction. Our research evidence indicates that the child generates his own level of thinking. The task of the teacher is to facilitate the process of change . . . In summary, to be effective, the teacher must . . . help the child experience the type of (cognitive) conflict that leads to awareness of the greater adequacy of the next stage" (Kohlberg 1971, p. 92). Contrary to this developmental perspective, learning and instructional psychologists believed for a long time that cognitive development in general is not the prerequisite but the result of education. "The stage in which any individual learner finds himself with respect to the learning of any given new capability can be specified by describing (a) the relevant capabilities he now has; and (b) any of a number of hierachies of capabilities he must acquire in order to make possible the ultimate combination of subordinal entities which will achieve the to be learned task ... In an oversimplified way it may be said that the stage of intellectual development depends upon what the learner knows already and how much he has yet to learn in order to achieve some particular goals. Stages of development are not related to age, except in the sense that learning takes time ... They are not related to logical structures, except in the sense that the combining of prior capabilities into new ones carries its own inherent logic" (Gagné 1968, p. 189).

In contrast to the extreme positions of developmental and instructional psychologists in the 1960s and 1970s there is now a strong movement for a theoretical synthesis of the concepts of development, learning, instruction, and the interactive mind.

Four sources of information play an important role in this new orientation: (a) Cross-cultural studies on development, learning, and teaching in non-Western societies (Rogoff 1990); (b) the acquisition of a variety of competencies and knowledge in early childhood (Gardner 1991); (c) comparisons of learning within and outside the school (Resnick 1987); and (d) the development and evaluation of creative instructional models (Cognition and Technology Group at Vanderbildt 1993).

When looking for the common theoretical spirit of the "new learning theory" (Brown 1994, p. 6) and its various instructional tools (e.g., community of learners, community of practice, cognitive apprenticeship, reciprocal teaching, situated and contextual cognitions), an understanding of learning as an active, constructive, self-directed, situated, and social interactive process emerges. Learning is further seen as the acquisition of socially shared knowledge through guided participation, cooperative work in communities of learners and/or self-regulated learning activities. This position stands in direct opposition to traditional cognitive theories of learning and development.

3.2 First Example: Training Studies

In his book *Intelligence and Experience*, Hunt (1961) proposed "to discover ways to govern the encounters the children have with their environments ... to achieve a substantially faster rate of intellectual development and a substantially higher adult level of intellectual capacity" (p. 363). A good way to investigate this psychological assumption and the "principle of hope" behind it is to use theoretically-based training studies. In a training study one can test the specific promotion of particular characteristics of cognitive development under precisely defined learning and instructional conditions. This type of developmental, learning, and instructional research has become very popular in the last four decades.

Hundreds or maybe thousands of separate studies have been undertaken, of which only a small part meet methodological standards allowing theoretically valid interpretations of the empirical results. In a historical review Brainerd (1983) identified three phases of research: an early phase from 1954 to 1963 ("You can't train it"), a middle phase running from 1964 to 1971 ("Yes, you can train it"), and a later phase from 1973 onwards ("What can you train and how can you train it?"). The last phase mentioned by Brainerd remained until 1996 and its message seems very generalizable. Analyzing the results of the many different training studies, five conclusions can be drawn:

(a) Young children seem more competent under favorable learning and instructional conditions ("zone of proximate development") than their performance on standardized tests and in many everyday situations would suggest. This is true both for the acquisition and the use of concepts, rules, strategies, and heuristics.

(b) Many studies showed that by appropriate measures some aspects of cognitive development can be influenced and even accelerated within specific limits and in specific domains. Nevertheless, a short-term training of general intellectual abilities, learning capacities or problem-solving competencies may increase performance scores of psychometric tests but does not have a long-lasting impact on the quality of thinking, learning or memory in general.

(c) In many cases it remains unclear whether the competence inferred from the performance of trained younger children is really identical to that of older untrained children. Similar questions can be asked about the relation between training results with persons who have different levels of intelligence but similar levels of performance. In training studies there are frequently pretraining as well as posttraining differences in learning speed, encoding strategies, and in transfer capabilities.

(d) Training in the use of cognitive strategies (e.g., rehearsal, organizational strategies, elaboration) is particularly successful if additional special metaknowledge about the use of these strategies and self-regulatory skills (e.g., monitoring) are taught. The use of training packages (multicomponential treatments) and self-controlled techniques in the context of the acquisition of content specific knowledge are especially effective. Such instructional strategies are not only useful in experimental training settings but also in promoting classroom teaching and learning.

(e) What kind of training setting and what form of instruction are chosen to support learning depends on the learning and/or developmental goals. To the extent that skill or knowledge acquisition and academic achievement are the goals, instructor-controlled methods of students' active learning are superior, especially for younger pupils and in well structured knowledge-domains. In contrast, if the goal is to help all students "to learn to become independent thinkers and learners rather than simply become able to perform basic competencies and retrieve simple knowledge facts" (Cognition and Technology Group at Vanderbilt, 1993, p. 15) then methods in which students have opportunities to learn more independently; to identify, define, and solve problems in different ways; and to use acquired insights to overcome novel tasks are more likely to be successful.

3.3 Second Example: The Zone of Proximal Development

Vygotsky's notion of the zone of proximal development has played a major role in the *rapprochement* between developmental and instructional psychology. Since the 1970s this concept has also become increasingly recognized in Western instructional and developmental psychology as an important construct (Van Parreren 1973, Vygotsky 1978), and has strongly influenced our view of the relationship between learning and development, and of the role of social and cultural factors in cognitive development.

Vygotsky (1978) introduced the concept of the zone of proximal development as a fundamentally new approach to the problem that "learning should be matched in some manner with the child's level of development" (p. 85). However, he argued that in order to fully understand the relationship of the developmental process to learning capabilities, we must distinguish between two developmental levels: the actual and the potential levels of development. The actual developmental level refers to those performances that a child can perform independently; they are the result of "already *completed* developmental cycles" (p. 85). Traditional Western intelligence tests are typical measures of this actual level of development: the child has to solve autonomously the items of the test which are presented in a very standardized way. But, according to Vygotsky, children can do more if they receive some help or support. The zone of proximal development is then "the distance between the actual developmental level as determined by independent problem-solving and the level of potential development as determined through problem-solving under adult guidance or in collaboration with more capable peers" (p. 85). "The actual developmental level characterizes mental development retrospectively, while the zone of proximal development characterizes mental development prospectively" (p. 86–87). Therefore, Vygotsky considers the zone of proximal development —what children can do with the support of others—as a better indicator of their cognitive development than what they can do alone.

This conception of cognitive development has important implications for education. Indeed, it is not effective to orient learning and instruction toward the actual developmental level, because in this way one lags behind what has already been achieved. To the contrary, learning and instruction must be oriented toward the zone of proximal development. This involves helping the child to master independently those performances that constitute this zone of proximal development and stimulating cognitive development by provoking and creating a new zone of proximal development. As stated by Vygotsky himself (1978): "the only 'good learning' is that which is in advance of development" (p. 89).

In theoretical perspective Vygotsky's position implies that learning from instruction is an essential condition for development. However, learning and development are not identical, but "learning is a necessary and universal aspect of the process of developing culturally organized, specifically human, psychological functions" (p. 90).

This notion of the zone of proximal development underlies a substantial amount of research undertaken since the 1980s at the crossroad of developmental and instructional psychology (see Liben 1987). As examples we mention Strauss' (1987) model of educational–developmental psychology, and the work of Brown on the design of supportive contexts for learning and development (Brown and Reeve 1987).

3.4 Third Example: The Apprenticeship Model of Instruction

The apprenticeship model of instruction has been presented by Collins et al. (1989) as an alternative to traditional schooling based on an information-transmission approach to learning. The theoretical background of the model is the so-called situated cognition paradigm: in reaction to the cognitive–psychological view that knowledge acquisition is more or less a purely cognitive process taking place in the head, and consisting in the acquisition of mental representations, this paradigm stresses that learning essentially occurs in interaction with social and cultural contexts and artefacts, and especially through participation in cultural activities and practices (Brown et al. 1989). This new conception is strongly influenced by ethnographic and cross-cultural research showing that effective learning out of school is much more contextualized and collaborative as compared to learning in school (Resnick 1987), and is convergent with Vygotskian theory in which the importance of social and cultural factors in learning and development is also stressed.

The cognitive apprenticeship model of instruction has been derived from traditional apprenticeship, in which a learner concludes a contract with a master in a certain craft to learn the tasks in the domain through direct observation of, and participation in authentic activities. Brown et al. (1989) define the approach as follows: "Cognitive apprenticeship methods try to enculturate students into authentic practices through activity and social interaction in a way similar to that evident—and evidently successful—in craft apprenticeship" (p. 37). In other words, processes of knowledge and skill acquisition should be embedded in situations and contexts that are rich in resources and learning materials, that offer ample opportunities for social interaction, and that are representative of the kinds of tasks and problems to which the learners will have to apply their knowledge and skill in the future.

Based on an analyses of a number of successful intervention studies, Collins et al. (1989) have elaborated their apprenticeship model of instruction in a framework for the design of ideal learning environments consisting of four dimensions: contents to be taught, teaching methods, sequencing of learning tasks, and social context of learning. Assuming that one agrees with the modern viewpoint that learning and culture play a crucial role in cognitive development, apprenticeship-like environments offer appropriate contexts for unravelling learning and developmental processes and their interactions, as well as for studying effective intervention strategies for fostering learning and development.

3.5 Fourth Example: Beyond Classroom Teaching— Cooperative Learning and Self-instruction

Since the beginning of schools, there have been various pedagogical movements for de-schooling the schools. Examples of the results of these movements are open classrooms, cooperative learning, student teams, partner work, recursive teaching, self-directed learning, the use of stimulating projects from the children's experiential world, and independent work during the entire school career to name but a few. All these are attempts by educational reformers to overcome the traditional classroom with its active teachers, passive students, and tedious content to be learned.

Largely independent of such reform ideas, educational research was focused on traditional classroom teaching and learning for a very long time. A prototype of this orientation is the process–product–paradigm. The main goal of this research program is "to define relationships between what teachers do in the classroom (the process of teaching) and what happens to their students (the products of learning) . . . Research in this tradition assumes that greater knowledge of such relationships will lead to improved instruction" (Anderson et al. 1979, p. 193).

The situation changed completely in the 1980s and 1990s as cognitive anthropologists, psychologists, and sociologists began to study learning processes and performances in settings outside the school. Lauren Resnick (1987, p. 13ff) summarized these studies and identified four characteristics of learning outside schools that stand in strong contrast to typical school learning:

(a) Individual cognition in school versus shared cognition outside;

(b) pure mentalism in school versus tool manipulation outside;

(c) symbol manipulation in school versus contextualized reasoning outside school;

(d) generalizing learning in school versus situation-specific competencies outside.

Learning takes place everywhere. School learning is only a small but important part in a world of permanent learning. What then can schools learn from research on learning outside the schools? First of all, schools should integrate some features from learning under everyday life conditions. Two features among many others are particularly important in this respect:

(a) *Cooperative learning*. It is characterized by the cooperation of small groups of learners in order to achieve a common goal. Therefore, learning tasks and projects should be designed in a way that enables and necessitates cooperation between students. From a social constructivist's view, such a setting is not only a social context in which students learn academic lessons, and it is not only a social context in which students learn social lessons. It is more than these:" . . . social interaction is considered as essential for learning, with individual knowledge construction occurring through processes of interaction, negotiation and collaboration through which learners become acculturated members of a . . . community and culture . . . As a result, common meanings, knowledge, and practices are developed by the community members (De Corte et al. 1996).

(b) *Self-instruction*. Not in opposition to, but rather as a complement for cooperative learning, self-instruction is in and out of the classroom one of the most recommended techniques for improving intrinsic motivation, deep understanding, and a broad transfer of what is learned. Self-initiated, self-generated, self-organized, self-governed, or self-controlled learning (in contrast to learning that is directed and controlled by the teacher) is an important aspect in the educational reform movement of the twentieth century and is now interpreted by many cognitive, developmental, and instructional psychologists as an essential prerequisite for the acquisition of meaningful and useful knowledge.

Does a reliance on self-instruction as the most efficient mode of teaching increase the likelihood of substantial deficits in acquired knowledge? As the available literature attests, such deficits do indeed occur under the condition of self-organized learning—particularly in younger pupils. Deficits in the systematic construction of knowledge, in the appropriate level of abstraction of learned information, in the acquisition and use of efficient learning strategies and sometimes in the correctness of learned information have been reported (Weinert and Helmke, 1995b).

As a consequence of the advantages and disadvantages of self-instructed learning, it seems necessary to combine self-controlled and teacher-controlled learning. Learning, of course, seems to lead to an especially deep understanding and to an especially flexible use of learned information when learners are intrinsically motivated by the content of what is to be learned and/or by the learning goals, when their own activity is high, and when errors can be overcome by personal effort. However, these statements are only part of the truth. A variety of studies—both in the classroom and under experimental conditions—have shown that in many cases instruction in which the teacher activity presents information to students and supports individual learning processes is more effective than self-instruction. This is especially true for young children. Thus, learning itself underlies developmental changes related to the increasing availability and accessibility of ever more sophisticated learning strategies.

4. Concluding Remarks: What can Instructional Psychologists Learn from Developmental Psychology and What can Developmental Psychologists Learn from Instructional Psychology?

At the beginning of the twentieth century Ament (1906) remarked rigorously "Pure scientific research in child psychology to the psychologists and their results to the pedagogues." Of course, this statement was and still is completely wrong. As mentioned elsewhere in this volume (see Weinert and De Corte: Translating Research into Practice), there is a strong need for partnership between developmental psychologists, instructional psychologists, and educational practitioners if the goal is not only to bridge the gap between developmental and instructional psychology but also to translate psychological research into educational practice.

What can developmental and instructional psychologists learn from each other? First of all, there is convincing theoretical and empirical evidence that not only the relationship between development and learning but also the relationship between instruction and learning is very complicated. Maturational precursors, implicit learning, and self-organizing processes that spontaneously integrate new information with already available knowledge all mean that cognitive development always entails more than the sum of explicit learning processes. In addition, more must be learned than can be taught. These restrictions on the importance of explicit learning do not mean that school learning and deliberate practice are unimportant for cognitive development. Quite the opposite: to a considerable degree cognitive development consists in the acquisition of expertise in a variety of different content domains. Nevertheless, instructional psychologists have to accept species-specific, age-related, and aptitude-dependent constraints which restrict the ontogenetic possibilities whether, when, and how an individual can acquire knowledge in a given field.

References

Ament W 1906 *Fortschritte der Kinderseelenkunde*. G. Fischer Verlag, Jena

Anderson L W 1994 Individualized instruction. In: Husén T, Postlethwaite T N 1994 *The International Encyclopedia of Education, 2nd edn*. Pergamon Press, Oxford, UK

Anderson L, Evertson C, Brophy J 1979 An experimental study of effective teaching in first-grade reading groups. *Elem. Sch. J.* 79: 19–223

Baldwin J M 1885 *Mental Development in the Child and the Race*. Macmillan, New York

Baltes P B 1987 Theoretical propositions of life-span developmental psychology: On the dynamics between growth and decline. *Dev. Psychol.* 23: 611–26

Berliner D C 1993 The 100-year journey of educational psychology: From interest, to disdain, to respect for practice. In: Fagan T K, VandenBos G R (eds.) 1993 *Exploring Applied Psychology: Origins and Critical Analysis*. American Psychological Association, Washington, DC

Bloom B S 1964 *Stability and Change in Human Characteristics*. Wiley, New York

Brainerd C J 1983 Varieties of strategy training in Piagetian concept learning. In: Pressley M, Levin J R (eds.), *Cognitive Strategy Research—Educational Applications*. Springer, New York

Brown A L 1992 Design experiments: Theoretical and methodological challenges in creating complex interventions in classroom settings. *Journal of the Learning Sciences* 2: 141–78

Brown A L 1994 The advancement of learning. *Educ. Researcher* 23(8): 4–12

Brown A L, Reeve R A 1987 Bandwidths of competence: The role of supportive contexts in learning and development. In: Liben L S (ed.) 1987

Brown J S, Collins A, Duguid P 1989 Situated cognition and the culture of learning. *Educ. Researcher* 18(1): 32–42

Cognition and Technology Group at Vanderbilt 1993 Designing learning environments that support thinking: The Jasper Series as a case study. In: Duffy T M, Lowyck J, Jonassen D H (eds.) *Designing Environments for Constructive Learning*. Springer-Verlag, Berlin

Collins A, Brown J S, Newman S E 1989 Cognitive apprenticeship: Teaching the crafts of reading, writing and mathematics. In: Resnick L B (ed.) 1989 *Knowing, Learning, and Instruction. Essays in Honor of Robert Glaser*. Lawrence Erlbaum Associates, Hillsdale, New Jersey

Corno L, Snow R E 1986 Adapting teaching to individual

differences among learners. In: Wittrock M C (ed.) 1986 *Handbook of Research on Teaching*. Macmillan, New York

De Corte E 1977 Some aspects of research on learning and cognitive development in Europe. *Educ. Psychol.* 12: 197–206

De Corte E, Greer B, Verschaffel L 1996 Mathematics teaching and learning. In: Berliner D, Calfee R (eds.) *Handbook of Educational Psychology*. Macmillan, New York

Flavell J 1970 Cognitive change in adulthood. In: Goulet R, Baltes P B (eds.) 1970 *Lifespan Developmental Psychology: Research and Theory*. Academic Press, New York

Flaxman E 1985 Compensatory education. In: Husén T, Postlethwaite T N (eds.) 1985 *The International Encyclopedia of Education*. Pergamon Press, Oxford, UK

Gagné R M 1968 Contributions of learning to human development. *Psychol. Rev.* 75: 177–91

Gardner H 1991 *The Unschooled Mind—How Children Think and How Schools Should Teach*. Basic Books, New York

Glaser R 1977 *Adaptive Education: Individual Diversity and Learning*. Holt, Rinehart and Winston, New York

Glaser R 1981 Instructional psychology: Past, present, and future. *Pedagogische Studien* 58: 111–22

Glaser R, Bassok M 1989 Learning theory and the study of instruction. *Annu. Rev. Psychol.* 40: 631–66

Hunt J McV 1961 *Intelligence and Experience*. The Ronald Press, New York

Hymes J Jr 1958 *Before the Child Reads*. Row, Peterson & Co., Evanston, Illinois.

Kohlberg L 1971 The concept of developmental psychology as the central guide to education. In: *Proceedings of the Conference in Psychology and the Process of Schooling in the Next Decade: Alternative Conceptions*. University of Minnesota, Department of Special Education, Leadership Training Institute, Minneapolis, Minnesota

Liben L S (ed.) 1987 *Development and Learning: Conflict or Congruence?* Lawrence Erlbaum Associates, Hillsdale, New Jersey

Resnick L B 1981a Instructional psychology. *Annu. Rev. Psychol.* 32: 659–704

Resnick L B 1981b Social assumptions as a context for science: Some reflections on psychology and education. *Educ. Psychol.* 16: 1–10

Resnick L B 1983 Toward a cognitive theory of instruction. In: Paris S G, Olson G M, Stevenson H W (eds.) 1983 *Learning and Motivation in the Classroom*. Lawrence Erlbaum Associates, Hillsdale, New Jersey

Resnick L B 1987 Learning in school and out. *Educ. Res.* 16(9): 13–20

Rogoff B 1990 *Apprenticeship in Thinking. Cognitive Development in Social Context*. Oxford University Press, New York

Skinner B F 1957 *Verbal Behavior*. Appleton-Century-Crofts, New York

Skinner B F 1968 *The Technology of Teaching*. Meredith Corporation, New York

Spencer H 1870 *The Principles of Psychology*, Vol. I. Williams & Norgate, London

Strauss S 1987 Educational–developmental psychology and school learning. In: Liben L S (ed.) 1987

Strauss S 1993 Theories of learning and development for academics and educators. *Educ. Psychol.* 28: 191–203

Thorndike E L 1903 *Educational Psychology*. Science Press, New York

Thorndike E L 1922 *The Psychology of Arithmetic*. Macmillan, New York

Van Parreren C F 1973 De relatie onderwijs-cognitieve ontwikkeling in de Russische psychologie (The relation of education–cognitive development in Russian psychology). In: De Wit J, Bolle H, Jessurun Cardozo-van Hoorn R (eds.) 1973 *Psychologen over het kind. Kinderpsychologische opstellen 3*. Tjeenk Willink, Groningen

Vygotsky L S 1978 *Mind in Society. The Development of Higher Psychological Processes*. Harvard University Press, Cambridge, Massachusetts

Weinert F E, Helmke A 1995a Interclassroom differences in instructional quality and interindividual differences in cognitive development. *Educ. Psychol.* 30: 15–20

Weinert F E, Helmke A 1995b Learning from wise mother nature or big brother instructor: The wrong choice as seen from an educational perspective. *Educ. Psychol.* 30: 135–42

Werner H 1926 *Einführung in die Entwicklungspsychologie (Introduction to Developmental Psychology)*. J A Barth, Leipzig

Wittrock M C 1967 Focus on educational psychology. *Educ. Psychol.* 4: 7–20

Wundt W 1916 Völkerpsychologie und Entwicklungspsychologie (Cultural and developmental psychology). *Psychologische Studien* 10: 189–239

A General Framework of Human Development, Learning, and Instruction in Educational Perspective

History of Developmental Psychology

S. Weinert

Every science has many ancestors, roots, and research traditions. This is also true of developmental psychology, which is concerned with one of the basic facts of human existence: the fact that there are typical age differences and age-related changes in most aspects of human functioning.

Throughout all history, poets, philosophers, educators, and physicians have applied themselves to developmental issues. A rich but culture- and time-specific lay psychology has provided us with (often contradictory) generalizations and explanations about human development along with (sometimes incompatible) advice on how to facilitate development and how to avoid developmental problems.

Although every society differentiates between various "ages," their significance, their duration, and the "set of cultural definitions which ascribe to each age grouping its basic characteristics" (Eisenstadt 1956 p. 22) vary widely across cultural, historical, and societal contexts.

A scientifically-based developmental psychology has only existed for little more than 100 years. Thus, in parallel with the progression of psychology in general, developmental psychology has a long tradition but only a brief history.

It is obviously beyond the scope of this entry to give a comprehensive historiographical description of the various themes, important persons, theoretical ideas, and lines of empirical research spanning developmental psychology's first century as a formal science. Instead, only a few particularly important roots, milestones, and changes concerning (a) the subject matter of developmental psychology and (b) the theoretical conceptions of development will be presented.

For a long period of time, the focus of developmental psychology research concentrated on only those changes in infancy and childhood that were species specific, uniform, unavoidable, significant, and irreversible. Yet, the change in perspective from child psychology towards a lifelong developmental psychology (e.g., Baltes et al. 1980, Baltes 1987) is largely responsible for the expansion of the initially narrow and biologically-oriented concept of development into a more comprehensive and liberal one. In its broader conception, developmental psychology is able to encompass such changes that are multidirectional, reversible, and not necessarily typical for all human beings and that are brought about by societal, cultural, historical, and idiosyncratic events and experiences.

One especially conspicuous feature revealed by a retrospective glance at the one-hundred-year history of scientific developmental psychology is the persisting coexistence of highly contradictory notions. It is precisely this wealth of different theoretical convictions and empirical research methods that possibly favoured the transformation of developmental psychology from being a primarily descriptive science characterized by monocausal explanatory concepts to being an increasingly process-oriented science whose main concern became the explanation of change and constancy during the course of the lifetime by delineating the psychological prerequisites, relevant environmental conditions, dynamic processes, and moderating variables of developmental change.

1. Historical Roots: The Emergence and Consolidation of Developmental Psychology as an Empirical Science

The nineteenth century is often seen as the formative period in the emergence of developmental psychology. Among the many roots of present-day developmental psychology, there are at least two that continue

1

to have an especially important impact: (a) the theory of evolution, and (b) the founding of psychology as an empirical science of human behavior.

1.0.1 Theory of Evolution. One of the "most distinctive features of nineteenth-century thought was the widespread interest evinced in history" (Mandelbaum 1971 p. 41). Scientists and scholars in almost every discipline believed that an adequate understanding of any biological, psychological, or philosophical phenomena requires a consideration of their place and role in a historical or developmental sequence or process. This basic idea was even more general, pervasive, and far reaching than the special contents of Charles Darwin's (1859) epochal work on the origin of species. The programmatic ideas of Jean Baptiste Lamarck (1744–1829), Ernst Haeckel (1834–1919), Herbert Spencer (1820–1903), and Charles Darwin (1809–1882) had important and varied direct or indirect influences on developmental psychology. To mention just three of these:

(a) The "biogenetic law" or "recapitulation hypotheses," which exerted an enormous fascination on developmental psychologists in America and in Europe, specified that "ontogenesis is the abbreviated and speedy recapitulation of phylogenesis" (Haeckel 1866 p. 300). In the second half of the twentieth century this vague analogy is no longer given scientific credibility.

(b) Influenced by the idea of evolutionary continuity, comparative studies of all sorts were fostered in developmental psychology—across human and nonhuman species, across cultures, and across age-groups. This comparative orientation considerably enriched the knowledge base available to developmental psychology and is still important in the 1990s. In sociobiological and evolutionary research traditions, comparative animal studies and comparative cultural studies attempted and still attempt to describe the universality, variability, adaptation, and specificity of human behavior.

(c) The functional perspective of adaptation to environmental constraints as well as the idea of the significance of a good fit between environmental characteristics and the individual is to be found in many developmental theories. Yet, precisely this approach has shown that "different people took different messages from evolutionism and occasionally those messages could come into conflict" (White 1968 p. 187).

1.0.2 Psychology as empirical science. From the beginning, developmental psychology has been conceived as a subdiscipline of psychology, embedded in its scientific and institutional framework. Most would trace the birthdate of scientific psychology as a discipline independent of physiology and philosophy to the year 1879 when Wilhelm Wundt established the first experimental laboratory in Leipzig. However, Wilhelm Wundt (1907 p. 336) argued against the necessity of considering child development for reaching an understanding of phenomena such as the mental life of adults. He was also sceptical about the possibilities of an experimental child psychology. Even though early research disproved this scepticism, it may explain why developmental psychology took its own paths in its formative years by outlining its own descriptive and normative research approach. Nevertheless, the course taken by psychology as a scientific discipline shaped developmental psychology in at least two important ways: (a) by a constant (although often selective) exchange of scholars, theories, concepts, and models that allowed developmental psychology to import many new ideas and useful variables; and (b) by the adoption of the methodological standards of scientific psychology.

Between 1890 and 1915, developmental psychology was consolidated as an empirical discipline and experienced a tremendous worldwide growth. In these 25 years, no fewer than 21 child psychology journals and 26 university institutes were founded around the world (Bühler and Hetzer 1929). Despite a general orientation towards a descriptive–normative approach in the early days of developmental psychology, considerable heterogeneity existed in terms of theoretical orientations, research questions, and research methods. This diversity will be sketched below by briefly describing a few special roots that continue to be important.

1.1 Early Biological Perspectives on Child Development and the Systematic Observation of Child Behavior

The pioneering work of the physiologist Wilhelm Preyer (1841–1897) is regarded as one of the cornerstones in developmental psychology's most important empirical research paradigm: the explicit, systematic, methodologically controlled observation of child behavior and age-related changes. Many developmental psychologists followed the path taken by Preyer and developed improved strategies, controls, and methods for behavioral observation. One of the most important of these was Arnold Gesell (1880–1961). As the director of the well-known Yale Clinic of Child Development, he developed and improved upon methods, systematized behavioral observation, introduced technical devices (e.g., films), amassed a huge archive of behavioral data from children of all ages, and outlined regular developmental sequences for many behavioral domains. This work provided the scientific prerequisites for the construction of developmental assessment tests that allowed the comparison of children's observed developmental states with empirically derived behavioral age norms.

The assumption that age-related changes in the child's physical and psychological functioning were biologically predetermined was implicitly or explicitly contained in many of these descriptive approaches. It was widespread among researchers and expressed in many different forms. G Stanley Hall (1840–1924) for example, was profoundly influenced by the idea that ontogeny recapitulates phylogeny. His descriptive approach to (lifelong) human development was based on comprehensive cross-sectional studies that employed extensive questionnaires. Gesell, in contrast, a former student of Hall, emphasized maturation-based changes but distanced himself from the ideas of recapitulation.

1.2 Early Constructivist Perspectives on Cognitive Development and the Study of Individual Differences

Alfred Binet (1857–1911) was one of the founders of scientific child psychology who did not believe in a strong maturation-based conception of development. To the contrary, he stressed the importance of the child's activity in constructing his or her own development. In his view, the purpose of cognitive development lay in the adaptation to the social and physical world. The child was seen as actively assimilating new experiences to existing ways of thinking.

Despite his manifold research interests, Binet's name is primarily associated with the construction of the first intelligence test and the concept of "mental age" as a global quantitative measure of intelligence that differentiates between the developmental levels of individuals. The standardized assessment of intelligence was viewed as a diagnostic instrument used to distinguish objectively between normal and retarded children in order to provide them with the appropriate type of instruction (regular or special classes). The Binet and Simon (1905) intelligence test for children became the worldwide standard model for countless similar testing procedures.

Less known or even forgotten is Binet's constructive conception of cognitive development, which predated Jean Piaget by more than three decades, as well as his experimental approach to child psychology, which preceded Watson's famous experiments on conditioning of emotion by nearly two decades (see Siegler 1992 for an interesting discussion of this point). Binet's research on prose memory, eyewitness testimony, intrinsic motivation, expertise in chess, cognitive style—to name just a few of his research interests—foreshadowed the results obtained in more recent studies and provided "convincing evidence for the proposition that a *science* of human development was possible" (Cairns 1983 p. 51).

In a similar vein, the genetic epistemology of James Mark Baldwin (1861–1934) anticipated important theoretical ideas, themes, and developmental concepts to be elaborated later on by Piaget and Vygotsky.

Nevertheless, both Binet and Baldwin did not have many scholars, and the mechanisms of development they proposed were too vague and outside the dominating trends to be acknowledged by the prevailing mainstream research (Siegler 1992, Cairns 1983).

1.3 Early Behavioristic Perspectives on Child Development and Experimental Child Research

John B Watson (1878–1958), the intensely criticized and alternately admired founder of radical behaviorism, held the basic laws of learning to be valid independent of age and to account for developmental change. As a demonstration, he used classical conditioning procedures to show that even infants could acquire a new emotional response to a previously neutral stimulus (e.g., fear of an object) when this stimulus (e.g., a piece of fur) was frequently paired with a stimulus that already elicited anxiety of its own accord (e.g., a very loud noise).

Watson believed that most human behavior and attitudes were acquired during development by expanding a few inborn reflexes and instincts with such conditioned learning. This belief was expressed in his famous, if controversial statement: "Give me a dozen healthy infants, well-formed, and my own specified world to bring them up in and I'll guarantee to take any one at random and train him to become any type of specialist I might select—doctor, lawyer, artist, merchant-chief, and yes, even beggar-man and thief, regardless of his talents, penchants, tendencies, abilities, vocations, and race of his ancestors" (Watson 1924 p. 104).

Even Watson agreed that this statement went far beyond the results of infant learning experiments. Today, the assumption that developmental change can be reduced to elementary learning processes is held to be scientifically untenable by most developmental psychologists. Nevertheless, Watson's introduction of the experimental method to infant research and his empirical demonstrations that learning processes are important not only for cognitive, but also for socioemotional development are still important in modern developmental psychology. These ideas were later reemphasized and substantiated by Skinner (1938), and in a modern way by Bandura's (1989) social-cognitive learning theory.

1.4 The Psychoanalytic Perspective on Child Development and Research on Socialization

The Viennese neurologist Sigmund Freud (1856–1939) developed his psychoanalytical model of personality and personality development as well as his ideas about the origins and treatments of neurotic diseases and symptoms outside of and in sharp contrast to the "academic psychology" founded by Wilhelm

Wundt. Contrary to behavioristic views, "Freud focused on unconscious processes, clinical contexts and subjective methods, while espousing a discontinuous stage and critical period view of development" (Parke et al. 1994 p. 172).

For Freud, the motor of psychic development was a set of psychosexual drives. These drives dominate behavior, appear in a regular sequence over childhood and adolescence, and are expressed physically through specific preferred sources of sexual satisfaction and object attachments, for instance, the oral phase (birth to one year) is characterized by a dominance of the mouth region and oral activities such as sucking.

Freud and many of his followers believed that excessive satisfaction or frustration (or a mixture of excessive satisfaction and frustration) of the latent impulses dominating a particular phase of development would lead to premature personality fixation at that phase and that especially traumatic experiences occurring in a specific phase could be the basis of later neurotic development. Freud himself believed that personality was often fixed by the first four or five years of life and that later developments only gradually expressed what was already in existence.

2. Aspects of Continuity and Change in Developmental Psychology in the Twentieth Century

In modern history of developmental psychology there is a great variety of lines of empirical research and theory construction. Nevertheless, four of them are of special interest and of lasting influence to recent trends in basic and applied developmental psychology.

2.1 From Biological Determinism to the Search for Biological Foundations of Human Development

Many theoretical conceptions of development as well as empirical results have contributed to the downfall and exclusion of radical maturational theories, with their interpretation of development as being biologically predetermined. It is widely accepted now (a) that the child is active from birth and increasingly able to direct and control his/her (information processing) activities, and (b) that the environment (e.g., learning opportunities, attachment figures, and so on) significantly contributes to developmental change.

This is not to say that maturation or biologically predetermined prerequisites do not play a significant role in child development. To the contrary, the biological foundations of development and their interaction with environmental variables are increasingly receiving attention in present day research. To name just four examples:

(a) Maturation is assigned a central role in the explanation of developmental changes in some more recent developmental theories. Case's (1986) neo-Piagetian conception of development, for example, attributes a key position in cognitive development to the limited capacity of the short-term memory story. Although this capacity is assumed to remain stable over time, Case suspects that the functional capacity of short-term memory grows with the increasing efficiency and speed of basic memory operations. Maturation is given an important role at this point.

(b) Research outlining the influence of, for example, early deprivation (no or only limited visual stimulation) on the development of the visual system in cats along with findings on synaptogenesis (cf. e.g., Siegler 1989) indicated that biologically driven processes, far from being environmentally independent, are influenced decisively by the environment. In contrast to experience-dependent learning processes, they can be viewed as experience-expectant, but not as completely independent of experiences.

(c) Over the past 20 years, infant research, more than any other subdiscipline, has witnessed an intensified search for innate skills or skills that are available from an early age in an effort to determine their significance for further development. Thus, it appears that infants already possess conceptual knowledge (e.g., knowledge of physics) and are especially receptive to certain kinds of information (e.g., to the prosodic characteristics of speech).

(d) In present day psychological research, the grand dichotomies of nature and nurture, maturation and learning, self-regulation and social influence, universal and culture-specific determinants, no longer express the same ideological controversy as they did. Rather they are seen as sets of complementary forces that interact to explain human development and the development of individual differences in behavior. In fact "the diversity of explanatory processes of development is one of the hallmarks of the 1980s and 1990s" (Parke et al. 1994 p. 18).

2.2 From Early Constructivist Perspectives to Elaborate Models of Self-regulation, Interiorization, and Special Models of Information Processing

Although Binet's and Baldwin's constructive conceptions of development foreshadowed the work of Piaget (1896–1980) and Vygotsky (1896–1934), it is the combination of elaborated theoretical ideas and new methodological approaches that allows the theories of these two significant scientists to be viewed as belonging to the most important milestones in twentieth-century developmental psychology. Despite the many differences between these two theoretical positions, there are at least four important similarities: (a) For both theorists, the goal of developmental research consisted of gaining a better understanding of the higher cognitive processes by looking at their sources and developmental changes. The study of developmental changes was thus given a central role in the construction of psychological theories; (b) both stressed the importance of activity and action for cognitive development; (c) in addition, both believed that development entails more than a change in external forms of behavior. Rather, it is characterized by qualitative changes in basic cognitive structures (Piaget) or in mental functions (Vygotsky); and (d) we owe to them a wide range of nonobvious, even counterintuitive observations that have become an important part of our current store of general knowledge of mental development in childrn.

2.2.1 Piaget and the concept of self-regulation. Piaget's perspective stems from a combination of epistemological considerations and a biological science orientation. He believed that the types of knowledge a child had constructed at a particular point in time determined how that child would perceive a new problem, what kinds of problem-solving activities were possible, and which errors were most likely to occur. In other words, the child's cognitive structures (which developed in a regular, i.e., invariant, unidirectional, irreversible, and universal sequence of qualitative changes) determined what and how he/she could think about the world.

Piaget (1970) interpreted the results of his empirical studies as support for the idea that knowledge states and such basic and (to adults) obvious concepts as space, time, speed, and causality developed slowly over the course of cognitive development. For example, infants do not yet know what is obvious to older children and adults: that an object (e.g., a toy) continues to exist and occupy space when it is no longer perceptible because it is covered by a cloth (object permanence); similarly, young children do not know that the amount, number, and volume of objects do not change when they are simply rearranged in space (conservation). These concepts are neither innate nor simply learned from adults but rather the result of the child's active confrontation with his/her environment. According to Piaget, the development of cognitive structures—which become increasingly flexible and allow the child to process increasingly unobservable, complex information, that is, to represent information symbolically and to manipulate it mentally—is driven by an innate tendency to adapt to new experiences on the basis of available knowledge structures. From birth onwards, the child actively uses his/her knowledge structures to understand the world (assimilation). As these structures confront the constraints and demands of the external world, they, in turn, slowly adapt (accommodation). The innate tendency to search

continuously for a better balance between the two processes of assimilation and accommodation is the foundation of the fundamental mechanism of self-regulation, which directs and maintains cognitive development.

It is hard to portray how important Piaget's theoretical perspective and his empirical evidence were for the history of developmental psychology in the twentieth century. In the early 1960s, when his work became well-known in America, it caused a revolution in developmental theory and stimulated an enormous number of empirical studies and critical theoretical debates. In fact, some of the empirical results obtained in these studies led theorists to question seriously whether a general structural perspective as the one taken by Piaget could fully account for developmental changes. These were:

(a) The development of concepts that were formally and logically similar seemed more heterogeneous and domain specific than a general developmental model would predict.

(b) Children's thinking and problem-solving skills were more task specific than a structuralist theory would predict.

The research carried out from an information-processing perspective has caused a transition from domain-general theories of cognitive development (which posit only general competencies and competence deficits, independent of task, content, and function) to a variety of more specific models of developmental change. This has led to a considerably more complex picture of what it is that develops, namely a diverse set of competencies, rather than only a single entity or overarching structure.

2.2.2 L S Vygotsky and the interiorization of social–cultural means. Most developmental theories, especially Piaget's universalistic theory, portray child development as an individual, intrapsychic process that is largely independent of social interaction and social–cultural contexts. This was not so for Vygotsky, who stressed the social and dialectic aspects of human development. His analysis of the social origin of higher mental functions has received increased attention since the 1980s.

According to Vygotsky, higher mental functions such as conscious attention, consciously controlled memory, and volition do not develop in the isolated individual, but in the social interaction that provides sociocultural means (e.g., speech as a social tool for controlling social exchange) that are actively taken up by the child, slowly internalized, and thus transformed into newly available means for problem-solving. In his view, the most important qualitative change in ontogeny that leads to higher, consciously controlled mental functions is the interiorization of such social control by cultural means, and thus the transition from social to self control. This interiorization was not conceived simply as a change from external to internal processes. Rather, it is a qualitative developmental process in which the structures and functions of the respective psychological means change. In addition, with the acquisition of new psychological means, all higher mental processes are fundamentally and qualitatively changed.

In this perspective, higher psychological functions are neither "implanted" in the child through social transmission nor developed independently of social–cultural contexts. Instead, social interactions and instruction in shared, goal-directed action contexts provide the tools for change that the child must then actively interiorize and transform.

The implication of this view is that the analysis of developmental changes in terms of cognitive functions requires more than isolated studies of single children. More attention should be given to the child's social interactions with experienced members of its society. This consideration has had both important theoretical as well as practical and diagnostic consequences that are especially evident in the now well-known concept of the "zone of proximal development." It marks out the difference between the levels of shared and interiorized functions, that is, between the "actual developmental level as determined by independent problem-solving" and the higher level of "potential development as determined through problem-solving under adult guidance or in collaboration with more capable peers" (Vygotsky 1978 p. 86). The (individually different) zone of proximal development has acquired importance as a diagnostic tool in developmental psychology as well as being a useful concept in instruction.

The difference between Piaget's and Vygotsky's developmental positions is clearly visible in their treatment of the role of instruction in development. Both agree that the effectiveness of teaching and learning depends on the developmental level of the child. For Piaget, instructional processes cannot induce any essential developmental changes but are dependent on developmental changes. In contrast, for Vygotsky, instructional processes play a major role in the development of higher mental processes.

2.3 From Psychoanalytic Approaches to a Broad Study of Socioemotional Development

Psychoanalysis has clearly transcended its traditional horizons. Two lines of development can be discerned: (a) Freud's psychoanalytic model of development and some important later modifications were combined with behaviorist learning theories and/or social–anthropological findings to become the theoretical basis of psychological research on socialization. Research included the study of how children develop within specific societies, and the effects of cultural mores, social belief-value systems, and particular parental practices on the developing personality. (b) Freud's research has stimulated a more general interest both in socioemotional development and in the issue of isolating the most important social and psychological conditions that determine the future mental health of a child. In this field, the works of John Bowlby (1907–1990) and Mary J Ainsworth (1913–) represent a milestone in the history of developmental psychology.

In his report for the World Health Organization (WHO) in 1951, John Bowlby heavily emphasized the importance of early experience for later personality development. He outlined the pervasive ill effects of early childhood separation and deprivation, and expressed the conviction that successful parenting is a principal key to the mental health of the next generation.

An obvious question concerned explaining the significance of early interpersonal relationships and early childhood separation on the child's subsequent development. In Bowlby's opinion, neither the psychoanalytic perspective prevailing at the time nor the social learning theories that dominated developmental psychology could adequately explain the existing empirical facts. In both perspectives early social relationships were regarded as a derivative of primary need satisfaction, feeding in particular, and the infant was seen as a passive, narcissistic recipient. Despite his psychoanalytic training, Bowlby took a very different stance: ". . .he conceived of attachment behavior as a major component of human behavioral equipment, on a par with eating and sexual behavior, and as having protection as its biological function, not only in childhood but throughout life" (Ainsworth and Bowlby 1991 p. 336). Bowlby's theoretical conception of infant–parent attachment was strongly influenced by ethological research, and also by evolutionary biology, cybernetic system theory, and cognitive psychology, particularly information-processing theories.

From a psychological point of view, attachment was thought to describe the emotional bond that develops between a child and his or her caretaker. From a functional point of view, this emotional bond should serve as the key element in balancing the infant's need for safety and the need for exploration and varied learning experiences. Attachment was seen as the mechanism that keeps interest and fear in balance and that protects children: if a situation is strange or frightening or if the distance between the attachment figure and the child threatens to become too large, attachment behaviors are initiated by the mother or the child to keep the system within bounds.

Despite its biological roots, the attachment system was conceived as being neither innate nor entirely predetermined; instead, its course is determined by social interaction, that is, it grows through feedback in response to active behavior.

John Bowlby's and Mary Ainsworth's ethologically-oriented attachment theory has stimulated a large amount of subsequent research, ranging from the examination of the stability of early attachment patterns and their predictive power for later socioemotional and cognitive development, the investigation of cultural similarities and differences in attachment patterns, to the analysis of attachment patterns in adolescence and adulthood.

2.4 From Child Research to Lifespan Developmental Psychology

As mentioned previously, another milestone in the history of developmental psychology in the twentieth century is the result of a collective effort by many scientists to redefine developmental psychology to include the entire lifespan, from birth to death (see Baltes et al. 1980, Baltes 1987).

Of course, earlier attempts to include at least old age in developmental research had been made because it was believed that development during the latter part of the lifespan may mirror development during childhood.

The focus of the new conceptualization did not dwell solely on expanding the range of developmental research to include adulthood and old age. Rather, it presented a fundamentally new theoretical orientation: lifespan psychology (exemplified by Baltes 1987 and many others) attempted to replace or at least enlarge the strongly biological orientation of child psychology with a more open, liberal, and pluralistic concept of psychological development that views development as a lifelong, multidirectional process. Most proponents of lifespan developmental psychology also espouse a contextualized concept of development. They assume that human development is a complex, dynamic phenomenon in which biological and intrapsychological factors, mechanisms, and tendencies interact dialectically with interpersonal, societal, cultural, historical, and nonnormative events and experiences (see Baltes et al. 1980).

References

Ainsworth M D, Bowlby J 1991 An ethological approach to personality development. *Am. Psychol.* 46: 333–41
Baltes P B 1987 Theoretical propositions of life-span developmental psychology: On the dynamics between growth and decline. *Dev. Psychol.* 23: 611–26
Baltes P B, Reese H W, Lipsitt L P 1980 Life-span developmental psychology. *Annu. Rev. Psychol.* 31: 65–110

Bandura A 1989 Social cognitive theory. *Annals of Child Development* 6: 1–60
Binet A, Simon T 1905 Application des méthodes nouvelles au diagnostic du niveau intellectuelle chez des enfants normaux et anormaux d'hospice et d'ecole primaire. *L'année Psychologique* 11: 245–336
Bowlby J 1951 *Maternal Care and Mental Health.* World Health Organization, Geneva
Bühler C, Hetzer H 1929 Zur Geschichte der Kinderpsychologie. In: Brunswik E (ed.) 1929 *Beiträge zur Problemgeschichte der Psychologie.* Verlag von Günter Fischer, Jena
Case R 1986 The new stage theories in intellectual development: Why we need them; what they assert. In: Perlmutter M (ed.) 1986 *Perspectives on Intellectual Development—The Minnesota Symposia on Child Psychology.* Erlbaum, Hillsdale, New Jersey
Cairns R B 1983 The emergence of developmental psychology. In: Mussen P H (ed.) 1983 *Handbook of Child Psychology,* Vol.1, 4th edn. Wiley, New York
Darwin C 1859 *Origin of Species by Means of Natural Selection.* John Murray, London
Eisenstadt S N 1956 *From Generation to Generation.* The Free Press, New York
Haeckel E 1866 *Generelle Morphologie der Organismen,* Vol.1. Reimer, Berlin
Mandelbaum M 1971 *History, Man, and Reason.* Johns Hopkins University Press, Baltimore, Maryland
Parke R D, Ornstein P A, Rieser J J, Zahn-Waxler C 1994 The past as prologue: An overview of a century of developmental psychology. In: Parke R D, Ornstein P A, Rieser J J, Zahn-Waxler C (eds.)
Piaget J 1970 Piaget's theory. In: Mussen P H (ed.) 1970 *Carmichael's Manual of Child Psychology,* Vol.1. Wiley, New York
Siegler R S 1989 Mechanisms of cognitive development. *Ann. Rev. Psychol.* 40:353–79
Siegler R S 1992 The other Alfred Binet. *Dev. Psychol.* 28: 179–90
Skinner B F 1938 *The Behavior of Organisms.* Prentice-Hall, Englewood Cliffs, New Jersey
Vygotsky L S 1978 *Mind in Society: The Development of Higher Psychological Processes.* Harvard University Press, Cambridge, Massachusetts
Watson J B 1924 *Behaviorism.* People's Institute Publishing Co., New York
White S H 1968 The learning-maturation controversy: Hall to Hull. *Merrill-Palmer-Q.* 14:187–96
Wundt W 1907 *Outlines of Psychology.* Stechert, New York

Further Reading

Dixon R A, Lerner R M 1992 A history of systems in developmental psychology. In: Bornstein M H, Lamb M E (eds.) 1992 *Developmental Psychology, An Advanced Textbook,* 3rd edn. Erlbaum, Hillsdale, New Jersey
Parke R D, Ornstein P A, Rieser J J, Zahn-Waxler C (eds.) 1994 *A Century of Developmental Psychology.* American Psychological Association, Washington, DC

Human Development in the Lifespan: Overview

F. E. Weinert

The focus of this entry is not on human development in general, but on psychological studies of the phenomena, mechanisms, and determinants of human development.

In the traditional knowledge base of all cultures and in the works of many philosophers, educators and physicians spanning different historical periods, there are observations, speculations, and considerable areas of knowledge about human development; developmental psychology as a scientific discipline, however, began only after the last third of the nineteenth century. Between 1890 and 1914 more than 20 journals and 25 research institutes devoted to child psychology were founded (Bühler and Hetzer 1929). Since then, scientific work on human development has expanded enormously and in the 1990s, developmental concerns are among the most prolific questions in the field of psychology. An overview of developmental theories and empirical research can therefore be only very selective and condensed.

This entry will begin with a description of some of the historical roots of scientific thinking about human development. This will be followed by a brief outline of some of the most central theoretical orientations, controversies and perspectives in modern developmental psychology. This overview will serve as the basis for a consideration of cognitive development and personality development in a social context. The entry will end with a discussion of relations among the study of human development, child rearing, and education.

1. Historical Roots of Modern Developmental Psychology

The roots of developmental psychology can be traced to the application of evolutionary theory to scientific psychology at the end of the nineteenth century. At that time, ideas about evolution influenced not only biology, but also philosophy and science in general. It was generally accepted that every living system developed " . . . from an indefinite, incoherent homogeneity to a definite, coherent heterogeneity" (Spencer 1881 p. 189).

Developmental psychology was accordingly understood to include not just child psychology, but also the psychology of animals, cultures and mankind. The task set by this broad-based approach was to compare developmental variations systematically across different systems and to formulate general developmental laws of biological and mental life (Werner 1940). However, even then one of the founders of modern psychology, Wilhelm Wundt, had no doubt that, in contrast to his own theoretical position, "at least nine-tenths" of all psychologists would equate developmental psychology with child psychology (Wundt 1916 p. 196). This concern was soon evident in research activities, as childhood and adolescence became the primary subject matter of developmental psychology. However, some important elements of evolutionary theory remained central to the study of human development, even to the end of the twentieth century.

The concept of "biogenic law," which stemmed entirely from the philosophical spirit of the nineteenth century, strongly influenced the thinking of many developmental psychologists. This "law" refers to the doctrine that ontogeny recapitulates phylogeny. Briefly, development within an individual is postulated to follow a sequence of stages that correspond to the evolutionary history of the species.

The extent to which the theory of evolution and its metaphorical extensions contributed to this doctrine is well illustrated by W. Stern's characterization of human development:

> In the first months of life, dominated by the lower senses and the dark and musty pull of drives and reflexes, the human infant is at the mammalian stage; in the second half year, with the acquisition of grasping and complex imitation, the infant reaches the highest mammalian level, that of the apes; the essential evolution into mankind occurs during the second year, with the acquisition of upright locomotion and speech. In the next 5 years of play and fantasy, the child is at the level of primitive natives. After this follows entry into school, a tighter integration into a social field with strict duties, and a sharp division between work and leisure—this is the ontogenetic parallel of man's entry into a civilized culture with its state and economic organizations. In the first years of school the simple behaviors of classical antiquity and Old Testament times are more suited to the child's mind; the middle years bring the visionary characteristics of the Christian culture; a mental differentiation appropriate to the culture of the present times is achieved only around the time of puberty. Certainly, puberty is described often enough as the Enlightenment of the individual (Stern 1906 p. 299).

Despite considerable fascination among North American and European turn-of-the century developmental psychologists with this idea of a condensed recapitulation of phylogeny in ontogeny, the superficial parallels did not withstand empirical scrutiny and theoretical critique. Nonetheless, some of the basic ideas underlying this philosophical and scientific tradition have remained, and are evident in modern versions of evolutionary theory, in sociobiology, in human ethology, and in cultural anthropology.

The roots of developmental psychology in the ideas of evolution are expressed even more strongly in the basic theories and methodological paradigms that have dominated the field since its beginnings. For example, a typical assumption is "that cognitive changes during childhood have a specific set of formal 'morphogenetic' properties that presumably stem from the biological-maturational growth process underlying these changes. Thus, childhood cognitive modifications are largely inevitable, momentous, directional, uniform and irreversible" (Flavell 1970 p. 247).

The biological perspective in psychological theories of childhood development is complemented by similar explanations for typical changes in old age. The "maturation-degeneration-hypothesis" (patterns of decline in old age are the mirror image of growth processes in childhood) in animal and human development is one example. Thus, developmental psychologists are primarily interested in the age at which basic cognitive dispositions or behavioral competencies first appear, the cognitive prerequisites for these behaviors, how they change ("grow") over the course of time, when a mature form is achieved, and when these dispositions or competencies decrease in quantity or quality as a function of aging.

This theoretical orientation has been supported by the most common methodology used to empirically study developmental phenomena: cross sectional studies. In these studies, behavior or performance is measured in samples of different aged subjects, and observed age group differences are used to infer how individuals develop over time. In addition, data are generally aggregated within age groups; thus, mean differences in the performance of different age groups are used as indicators of universal developmental patterns, and intraindividual and interindividual variations from mean age group performance are rarely attended to. There are only a very few longitudinal studies in which development is assessed by repeated measurements of the same individuals at different ages.

This one-sided methodological approach has meant that most theories of development are universal (they are held to be valid for all humans) and naturalistic–descriptive (they promise to describe those developmental processes that cannot be produced by environmental factors, although they may be modified by them). With such an orientation it is clear why the study of the origins of individual differences and the study of the contents of developing cognitive competencies have generally been ignored historically.

An interesting attempt to relate universal models of development to observed individual differences was undertaken by Binet and Simon (1905), who constructed the first developmental test to measure intelligence. They interpreted variations in the rate at which children's intelligence increased as an indication of stable individual differences in intellectual abilities, and thus founded the psychometric approach for describing cognitive development.

The impact of experimental psychology, which also began to establish itself as a science at the end of the nineteenth century, was much smaller than the enormous influence of evolutionary theory on subsequent developmental research. Although developmental psychologists adopted the same formal criteria for methodological and theoretical rigor as those used in experimental psychology, the function of experimental designs varied: in developmental psychology, they provided standardized conditions for observing "natural behavior" at different ages, rather than conditions for studying behavior (or its acquisition) as a function of stimulus variation.

Radical behaviorism provided an exception to this generalization. In this research tradition, individual behavioral development was seen primarily as a function of learning under appropriate environmental conditions, although species-specific inherited characteristics and maturational processes were not denied. An example (never empirically supported) of this position is Watson's famous statement: "Give me a dozen healthy infants, well-formed, and my own specified world to bring them up in and I'll guarantee to take any one at random and train him to become any type of specialist I might select—doctor, lawyer, artist, merchant-thief and, yes, even beggar-man and thief, regardless of his talents, penchants, tendencies, abilities, vocations, and race of his ancestors" (Watson 1970 p. 104; orig. 1925).

This utopian expectation of infinite, arbitrary human malleability was contradicted even by Skinner (1966) because of the demonstrable effects of inherited characteristics on ontogenesis. Nonetheless, the importance of learning for the development of animal and human behavior was consistently and emphatically stressed in behavioristic theories.

The precise conceptual relation between development and learning has always been somewhat controversial. However, there is no debate that the environment, individual experiences, and child care practices play important roles in the inception and shaping of human behavior. This view is in principle also accepted by those developmental psychologists who ascribe an important role to species-specific genetic factors, biological maturation, and the spontaneous unfolding of cognitive abilities (Chomsky 1959, Piaget 1947).

A stronger learning-centered perspective on human development appears in a variety of the different developmental theories described below.

In Freud's (1917) psychoanalytic interpretation of development, a sequence of natural stages in the development of psychosexual drives in childhood (oral, anal, phallic, and genital phases) was assumed. However, he also gave a decisive role to the social environment and argued that the individual personality characteristics were shaped by specific destiny of innate drives. This theoretical perspective became an essential principle underlying socialization research (Zigler and Child 1969).

Sociological interpretations of development (Goslin

1969) focus on the role of culture, the family milieu, socio-economic status and interpersonal relations in development. These aspects, that is the totality of informal and institutional social learning opportunities (as well as constraints), are taken as the significant conditions that shape human development.

The cognitive approach to human development concentrates primarily on diverse changes in information processing. One result of work from this perspective has been to recognize the acquisition of domain specific knowledge as important for the development of competent thinking and acting. Learning, practice, and instruction are given a key role in cognitive development (Ericsson and Crutcher 1990).

The contrastive pairs, development and socialization, maturation and learning, universal developmental stages and individual developmental patterns represent two different theoretical traditions that have existed since the beginning of developmental psychology. The contrast expressed to by these pairs refers to a scientific task that is still not solved: "It is precisely the convergence of those two theoretical developments which constitutes a major challenge and promise for the future of research in developmental psychology" (Bronfenbrenner 1963 p. 538).

2. Theoretical Orientations, Controversies, and Perspectives in Modern Developmental Psychology

It is difficult to make general statements about significant research directions and scientific progress when one considers the state of developmental psychology in the 1990s. The phenomena and age ranges that are studied are diverse, and the empirical questions, methodological paradigms, and underlying theoretical models are varied. This gives the impression that developmental psychology is not at all a unitary research tradition that addresses some comprehensive and common questions spanning heterogeneous issues, topics, and tasks. It seems to be more a collection of many different and separate research directions that have in common only the fact that they are somehow concerned with the description or explanation of age-related differences or changes over the course of the human lifespan. The time of overarching theories and theoretical controversies in developmental psychology has ended, and has been replaced by an inflation of micromodels and some theories of medium breadth. Scientific discourse about general issues has shifted to the level of metamodels. These metamodels concern systems of relatively general assumptions about what changes and how change occurs in the development of human behavior.

2.1 Mechanistic and Organismic Models of Development

A dichotomous classification of developmental models as mechanistic or organismic that was suggested by

Reese and Overton (1970, see also Overton and Reese 1973) is not concerned with psychological theories in the narrow sense, but rather with the basic philosophical and anthropological world views that underlie psychological models in general.

The mechanistic metamodel of development treats behavioral change as the complex outcome of more elementary, mechanistically functioning, quantifiable processes. Prototypical for these models are behavioristic learning explanations of developmental change. Not only do they explain the acquisition of motor skills, factual knowledge, or emotional reactions as the cumulative result of stimulus–response connections, they also claim that elementary learning processes and combinations of their effects can explain such complex developmental events as language development, the acquisition of creativity and the genesis of a reflexive self concept. The units of scientific analysis are elementary learning processes and their conditions (e.g., contiguity between stimulus and response, practice, reinforcement).

All in all, the importance of mechanistic models has not been very large in the history of developmental psychology; presently, they play a completely subsidiary role as metatheories, although mechanistic explanations are used in many areas of developmental research.

In contrast to mechanistic models, organismic metamodels adopt a holistic world view; that is, the organism is portrayed as an integrated and internally differentiated whole. The development of this dynamic organism is characterized by qualitative, discontinuous, and stage-like changes that give rise to "novel" properties. A frequent metaphor for this process is the developmental sequence from egg to larva to butterfly.

An organismic metamodel characteristically underlies universalistic theories that treat individual development as an epiphenomenon of species-specific inherited qualities that can be influenced, but not directed by environmental conditions. Piaget's (1947) stage theory of cognitive development and Erikson's (1959) stage model of personality development are two familiar examples of this approach. The many variants of organismic metamodels have traditionally had an important role in developmental psychology.

The theoretical restrictions related to the organismic model, that psychological development seems simply "a prisoner of age and stage" (Dannefer 1988 p. 7) led theorists to extend Reese and Overton's (1970) classification to further metamodels in the 1970s and 1980s. Two metamodels especially stimulated subsequent theoretical discussion and empirical research.

The first was a contextual metamodel. The emphasis in this model is on a life-long

  . . . reciprocal, or dynamic, influence of biological and psychological (or organism) processes and environmental (or contextual) conditions. In these conceptions, the reciprocal relation between the interrelated features of the person and his or her context are held to not merely 'interact' in the linear sense used in analysis of variance. Instead, person and context transact . . . or 'dynamically interact'. . . . By virtue of their reciprocal relation, each of the features is transformed by the other (Ford and Lerner 1992 p. 11).

As a metamodel, contextualism, in connection with systems theory and probabalistic explanatory models, has provided an important and varied framework for research in developmental psychology.

A second additional variant of the organismic world view is the attempt to formulate a metamodel to characterize specifically human attributes of development. This variant is deeply rooted in the philosophical spirit of the Enlightenment and in phenomenological and existential philosophical traditions. The anthropological roots of such a humanistic model of development can be described as follows: "As self-aware entities, human beings are intentional creatures. That means that they place meanings on things" (Kenyon 1988 p. 7). This model addresses development in a human organism that is seen as active from birth on, productively structuring its own information processing activities, and becoming increasingly more skillful in the self-organization of behavior and in self-reflective thinking.

Although the humanistic model is very important for understanding certain aspects of human development, it is not suited to the description or explanation of many other aspects of behavioral change.

2.2 Variable-centered Approach and Person-centered Approach

If one studies developmental psychology textbooks, it is possible to learn a great deal about the origins of motor behavior, perception, memory, intelligence, anxiety, achievement motives, the self concept, or social behavior; however, little mention (and in many cases no mention!) is made of the developing person.

The variable-centered approach is dominant in developmental research, as it is in psychological research in general. This approach dictates the preferred theoretical constructs and methodological units used in the collection, analysis, and interpretation of empirical data. At this subpersonal level, it is typical for psychological variables to be analyzed separately and related functionally. In large, this is because of an assumption that lawful, domain-specific regularities concerning the "behavior of variables" (Wohlwill 1973 p. 359) are valid independent of the behaving person. Although this assumption has been supported in many, but not all cases, it does not allow statements about thinking, action, or development of the individual. Psychological functions and traits (e.g., motives, memory, intelligence, or temperament) are themselves neither conscious, intentional, nor self-reflective, despite what their descriptions in textbooks sometimes suggest. These qualities are properties only

of individuals, not of processes or traits. Thus, it seems necessary and would be productive to extend (not replace!) the variable-centered approach with a person-centered approach.

In this case, the person is the unit of analysis in empirical research and related theoretical interpretations. Sufficient numbers of appropriate theoretical, methodological and statistical models are currently available to carry out this task.

"The issue about person versus variable approaches is reflected in the debate over ideographic versus nomothetic, typological versus dimensional, and clinical versus statistical approaches to empirical psychological research. Most of the time, the two approaches have been regarded as contradictory. . . . (We have) argued that they are compatible, and that what superficially seems to be contradictory in methodology and empirical results is often the result of inadequacies in theoretical distinctions and in methodological sophistication" (Magnusson 1988 p. 23).

2.3 Unidirectional Up-and-down Models and Multidirectional, Pluralistic Models of Development

As mentioned above, models in developmental psychology are dominated by a theoretical orientation toward the biological concepts of growth (in childhood) and decline (in old age). A typical example was expressed by Denney, who wrote:

The data . . . clearly indicate that there is an increase in cognitive ability during childhood until a peak is reached in late adolescence or early adulthood; after that age there appears to be a decline in cognitive ability. . . . Although there are not enough data on structural change to draw any strong conclusion, these data suggest that older adults may be similar to younger children not only in their level of performance . . . but also in the structure of their abilities. This evidence suggests again that development during the latter part of the life span may mirror development during childhood (Denney 1982 p. 818).

In contrast to this restrictive growth–decline concept of development, life-span models offer a considerably more open, liberal, and pluralistic picture of development. In these models, human development is perceived as a life-long process. This process is polymorphic; that is, it is always composed of many, diverse changes in behavior that are combined or separate, continuous or discontinuous, and that can vary considerably in direction. There are developmental gains at all age levels (even in old age) and developmental losses at all age levels (even in childhood). This perspective assumes a large degree of plasticity in psychological development. Developmental processes are determined by biological factors (genetics, maturation, degenerative processes), historical–cultural life conditions, individual life histories, social contexts and nonnormative life events.

The life span approach is closely related to the contextualistic world view (Baltes 1987, Baltes et

11

al. 1980). Although a monolithic growth model is predominant in child research, pluralistic life span models increase in influence on studies of other age populations.

2.4 Nature and Nurture as Determinants of Development

An especially controversial scientific issue is the relative influence of inherited factors (nature) and environmental conditions (nurture) in human development and in the development of individual differences in psychological characteristics. In discussions of this issue, the fact that two different questions are actually meant is often ignored.

One question concerns species-specific inheritance characteristics of all normal humans, that is, the genetic information that allows physical and psychological development to occur. For this type of inheritance to be expressed, some particular conditions must be met in the child's social–cultural environment. According to Scarr (1992), the relation between internal and external developmental conditions is expressed in the following ways:

(a) Preadaptation: children are preadapted to react appropriately to a certain range of environmental conditions, to adapt, to process relevant information, and to acquire knowledge on the basis of their species-specific genetic inheritance.

(b) Variation: there are large variations in the stimulation and caretaking conditions within genetically specified areas in the natural environment that support normal development. These very different patterns of stimulation are "functionally equivalent opportunities for people to construct their own experiences" (Scarr 1992 p. 5).

(c) Limits: environments that fall outside the range of appropriate species-specific variations do not support normal development. "Thus, normal development does occur in a wide variety of human environments, but not in those lacking 'average expectable' conditions under which the species has evolved" (Scarr 1992 p. 5).

The second question in the nature–nurture discussion concerns the relative weight given to individual inheritance and environmental conditions in the development of interindividual differences in cognitive competencies and personality traits. The largest problem for research addressed to inherited factors is that it has not yet been possible to determine the genotype at the molecular level. Thus, genetic influences on development must be indirectly estimated. This is typically achieved by the comparison of related and nonrelated children (monozygotic twins, siblings, adopted children) that are raised together or apart. This method allows an estimation of the relative weight of genetic

factors and environmental conditions that operate in a particular population in a particular historical period on variation in the development of psychological characteristics. However, it is not possible to make general statements about the importance of genetic influences for single individuals or for the species in any possible environment. This restriction is often ignored or misunderstood.

When one strictly acknowledges the methodological possibilities and constraints of estimates of heritability, the empirical results, despite public controversies, are relatively uniform and consistent. Whereas about half of the variance in the development of cognitive competencies in industrialized nations is determined by genetic differences, the genetic component in personality characteristics seems somewhat lower (Plomin 1990).

However, it is important to recognize that the influences of genetic and environmental factors are not independent of each other. There is a covariation between genetic and environmental influences that increases over the lifespan. This occurs because the environment that parents provide for their children corresponds to the parents' genetic makeup and older children and adolescents actively seek out those environments that correspond to their own genotype. It is also important to note that genetic factors do not influence the development of psychological differences directly, but through genetically determined learning processes.

Whether or not early childhood learning experiences have long term effects that are highly resistant to change, as many socialization theories suppose, is a controversial issue not resolved by the available empirical data. This controversy arises in personality development with respect to the effects of excessive gratification or frustration of early needs, or loss of an attachment figure, and in cognitive development with respect to the consequences of sensory or intellectual deprivation.

3. Cognitive Development

Everyday observations provide direct and convincing testimony of the extent to which children's understanding of physical, psychological and social phenomena, memory for new information, and complex problem solving improves over the first 15 years of life.

There is no doubt that Jean Piaget made the largest contribution to the scientific understanding of such cognitive changes. In his monumental scientific work, Piaget assumed that human intelligence allows the highest forms of both stable and flexible adaptation between an organism and its environment. Every healthy child is naturally equipped to acquire the necessary adaptive cognitive structures through a process of interaction with the environment and active processing of environmental information. This acquisition follows a universal sequence of qualitative changes in the structural base of logical thinking. According to Piaget, there are four major stages: sensory-motor, preoperational, concrete-operational, and formal-operational.

Sensory-motor stage (birth to age 2): the main activities concern perceptual-motor coordinations. During this stage children acquire the knowledge that people and objects still exist, even when they are out of sight–knowledge that requires the mental representation of the external world. During this stage, children also learn that they can produce desired effects by their own actions and begin to show productive use of tools.

Preoperational stage (ages 2 to 7): where as a sensory-motor child can only solve problems for which direct sensory input and direct actions are possible, a preoperational child can achieve the same outcome mentally. The acquisition of language, man's most important symbol system, is one important means for symbolic action. The functional value of play lies in the exploration, experimentation and practice of diverse action possibilities in various "as-though" situations. During such activities, the child primarily has an egocentric perspective, that is, the world is not evaluated as it is, but as it is perceived from the child's point of view.

Concrete-operational stage (ages 7 to 11): during the preoperational stage, children shift from a perceptual to a more conceptual orientation. During the concrete operational stage, it becomes possible to reason in terms of more than one dimension at a time and to represent reversible object transformations. Whereas the thought of the preoperational child is generally egocentric, centered on one dimension, and not reversible, the thought of the concrete operational child is nonegocentric, multidimensional, and reversible. These achievements are only possible with concrete contents, not with abstract symbols, but they do concern more than single acts "because the central feature of the operations is that they are joined in systems" (Piaget 1972 p. 41).

Formal-operational stage (age 11 to adulthood): the ability to access a flexible system of formal, abstract operations gained around the time of adolescence allows the child to reflect and think about abstract and hypothetical contents, to search for systematic and flexible novel problem solutions and to reason according to internalized laws of logic.

According to Piaget this universal and general sequence of stages of cognitive development is the result of the complex processes of assimilation (adjustment of external information to fit internally available cognitive schemes) and accommodation (adjustment of internally available cognitive schemes to fit increasingly complex external information) that serve to keep the entire cognitive system in a dynamic state of balance (equilibrium).

Piaget's scientific work has become universally known and respected. However, the structural-genetic theory has been criticized and its empirical support has been questioned. What is at issue is not so much the epistemological value of the theory, but rather its psychological implications. Piaget has been especially criticized by scientists from an information processing approach (Siegler 1991).

In this approach, it is assumed that cognitive development can be described as improvement in more or less domain specific information processing skills. These changes are explained both as age-related growth in working memory capacity and as the cumulative acquisition of declarative and procedural knowledge. In addition, processes of empirical and reflective abstraction are postulated to lead to the construction of metacognitive knowledge and skills that allow considerable improvement in the self-control of thinking and acting.

Arguments made for the importance of knowledge in the development of thinking are at times quite radical and in strict contradiction of Piagetian theory. For example, Carey (1984) wrote: "Children differ from adults only in the accumulation of knowledge (p. 37). . . . Children know less than adults; children are novices in almost every domain in which adults are experts" (p. 64).

This extreme knowledge-based explanation of cognitive development has led in part to a large degree of educational optimism (Ericsson and Crutcher 1990); however, it cannot be empirically supported in its radical version. What is not considered in this approach, and what is not considered in the Piagetian approach, are stable individual differences in intelligence and cognitive development that are partially genetically determined. The available empirical data suggest not only that all humans of all ages possess large intraindividual plasticity and untapped reserves for cognitive learning and performance, but also that interindividual differences in cognitive abilities are relatively stable. For example, when one provides children with the same optimal learning opportunities, all children improve their performance considerably, but the interindividual differences remain or increase.

Results from research on mastery learning provide a good example. Mastery learning approaches attempt to have the majority of students (80–95%) reach demanding learning goals (90–95% correct answers) by giving extra optimal instructional time. The empirical results are, however, rather disappointing.

> Mastery theorists suggest an equilibrium of high and equal achievement accompanied by low and equal learning time. But equality of learning time and of achievement appear to be mutually exclusive. If equal learning time is desired, as in many current forms of schooling, the inequalities of achievement outcome appear to be an inevitable concomitant. If equality of achievement out-

come is chosen as an end, as in mastery learning, the inequality of time seems necessary as a means (Arlin 1984 p. 82f).

4. *Personality Development in Social Context*

Cognitive development and personality development have frequently been treated as two separate research domains in psychology. Their conceptual and thematic separation makes it more difficult to perceive that there are many basic relations between changes in cognitive functioning and the development of personality traits (Thomae 1970).

Examples are the areas of motivational and moral development. Complex information from personal experiences, achievement demands, and social expectancies must be processed to set realistic behavioral goals and levels of aspiration, to specify causes for success and failure, and to construct a concept of the self. A sufficiently advanced cognitive developmental level is usually assumed to be a prerequisite condition for accomplishing these tasks.

That causal attributions for action outcomes, realistic self concepts and personal standards are closely related to the acquisition of judgment, evaluation, and decision skills during childhood, is an assumption made by theorists such as Piaget (1932), Kohlberg (1981/1984) and many others who postulate strong parallels between cognitive and moral development, and who claim that moral judgments play a key role in moral behavior.

A similar pattern was noted by Heckhausen (1982) for achievement motivation where theories

have been based largely on the study of adult achievement behavior. Here we have attempted to extract developmental characteristics for these findings and to search for scattered empirical evidence to support a developmental theory. A logical structure of cognitive developmental steps has become visible that outlines the unfolding of achievement-oriented behavior between the ages 3 and 13 (Heckhausen 1982 p. 661).

Similar conclusions can be made concerning theories and data for the acquisition of other motivational systems governing the self concept and social behavior.

Although the demonstration of cognitive prerequisites is very convincing, a pressing question is whether these cognitive prerequisites are necessary and sufficient conditions for the acquisition of personality features or not, that is, whether "preferences need no inferences" (Zajonc 1980). It is very difficult to answer this question, because the differential development of behavioral dispositions is often lost in the scientifically inaccessible early childhood. Nonetheless, there is some evidence: for example, studies show that some even quite young children show behavioral reactions characteristic of learned helplessness after they have had clear experiences of failure (Dweck

1991). Such vulnerability in motivational states is apparently possible even when children do not have the cognitive skills to process an elaborated relation between failure and their own abilities.

Do early, endogenous temperament differences, early personal experiences, or experienced reactions from the social environment lead to such a dispositional asymmetry between positive and depressive attributional styles for success and failure? It is not yet clear either theoretically or empirically why a relatively large group of people from early childhood on

"should disparage their own effectiveness, abilities, and competence in their own eyes and in the eyes of others, even when there is no compelling reason—when the same achievement outcomes could have been attributed so that subjects can retain a much higher sense of self-esteem without diminishing attributional plausibility. The question then is, whether such persons have acquired a negative self-image in which they intend to adhere, even after having had more positive experiences.... Recent findings are surprising, they show the degree to which individuals will hold to a preconceived notion even though it has been disproved by the facts ... " (Heckhausen 1987 p. 146).

This citation raises the central question in personality research. This question concerns stability, variability and change in personality characteristics—regardless of whether they are plausible or implausible, functional or dysfunctional, helpful or hurtful to the individual. Of course, in many psychological theories personality is defined as what does not change over the life course, especially when one would expect changes.

In this definition, two types of stability are meant: the similarity of behavior across different situations (situational consistency) and the similarity of behavior across longer time spans (temporal persistency). When temporal stability is at issue, it does not imply that individual behavior always remains identical, but instead that interindividual differences in a psychological characteristic remain constant over time, that is, that the relative position of an individual in his or her reference group remains constant over time.

The dominant model used to describe human personality and the temporal stability of individual differences is the Five-Factor model ("Big Five"). The single dimensions in this model are characterized as follows: Factor I, extraversion versus introversion (surgency); Factor II, friendly compliance versus hostile noncompliance (agreeableness); Factor III, conscientiousness (will); Factor IV, neuroticism versus emotional stability; Factor V, openness to experience (intellect, culture) (Digman 1990).

The Five-Factor model (primarily assessed with questionnaires) has been demonstrated to be very useful for describing personality with both self ratings and other ratings (e.g., from teachers). By combining values on the five dimensions, it is possible to characterize individual personality, to describe individual differences, and to predict behavior, even for school age children (Halverson et al. 1993). From adolescence on, the stability of the five personality dimensions appears relatively high, and is quite high in longitudinal studies of adults (e.g., correlations of 0.8 over a six-year span [see Costa and McCrae 1988]). On the other hand, it is difficult to evaluate the individual stability of personality characteristics in childhood because there are enormous differences between the temperamental factors measured in early childhood and the dimensions measured by the Five-Factor model. Whether these discrepancies are related to instability in personality characteristics in early childhood, to the different measures used, or to developmental transformations in personality characteristics is presently an open question.

What underlies the high stability of personality characteristics in later childhood and adulthood? At first glance, they seem to support "the conclusion most of us make with surprise upon seeing a good friend after many years of separation: He is just the same as he always was" (Digman 1990 p. 434).

However, beyond some stability in general personality characteristics, it often also seems that individuals show substantial changes in personal opinions, beliefs, problems, and patterns of reactions to developmental tasks. An important question is whether individual reactions to critical life events (e.g., unemployment, death of a close person, severe illness) are really predictable from the "Big Five." It appears that this is not the case. Rather, what seems to determine these reactions is much more a person's subjective interpretation of the event, the style of coping, and the degree to which social support is available (Montada et al. 1992).

Thus, to understand the relation between stability and change, an ecological model of personality development (Bronfenbrenner 1989) may be very productive and necessary. This sort of model is not concerned so much with change in single psychological variables, but with an interaction between the individual (an idiosyncratic pattern of variables) and his or her social environment.

It is without a doubt scientifically important that significant effects from genetic factors, family background, peer relations, the school experiences, social reference groups, work life, and critical life events are assessed in longitudinal studies. However, there is as yet no theoretical model that would allow assessment of the cumulative, compensatory and/or trade-off effects of these multiple factors on the development of personality. This problem is presently an issue in the many studies on the origins of sex and gender differences (Hyde and Lynn 1986) as well as in studies on the identification of individuals at risk (Kohlberg et al. 1972). Given the current state of knowledge in the field, a comprehensive model based on behavior genetics and social cognitive learning theory would seem to

be the most appropriate for describing and explaining personality development in a sophisticated way.

5. Conclusion: Development and Education

Psychological development without education is an abstract fiction that does not occur in reality. The human is biologically incomplete at birth and needs intensive care, social interaction, and learning, especially in infancy and childhood. Thus, the question for the social sciences is not whether education is necessary, but rather which different social conditions and educational interventions affect personality development and how they do so.

When education is discussed in this connection, it is generally not conscious teaching and intentional instruction that is meant, but rather the incidental learning that arises from living experiences and interactions in a sociocultural community, the many forms of learning from observation and imitation of others, as well as the countless behavioral directions, suggestions, supports, and corrections provided by adults and peers. Over the course of development, a good deal must be learned that cannot be explicitly taught.

If one defines psychological development as those changes in individual patterns of behavior that occur over the life course, then the concept of "education" refers both to those sociocultural conditions and interventions that are explicitly directed to foster desired behavior and inhibit or correct undesired behavior (intentional education) as well as to those behaviors and events in the child's environment that have the effect of strengthening or inhibiting behavior, but that are not planned or intentionally presented (functional education). The boundaries between unplanned socialization and planned educational interventions are fluid and cannot be sharply distinguished.

There are three different theoretical positions concerning the relation between development and education. First, development as the result of education. Proponents of this perspective (Watson 1925, Skinner 1966) assume that except for some sensory and motor abilities present at birth and some biologically preprogrammed maturational processes in the first years, all human behavior must be learned. What is meant by psychological development from this perspective is the complex outcome of many single, related and embedded processes of learning. Unplanned and planned behavioral shaping by environmental factors are relevant educational mechanisms.

> The child is born with certain reflex mechanisms that ensure that he will acquire and reflect the content inherent in the environmental agents that stimulate and shape his behavior. . . . Growth is a continuous process of learning behavior . . .; . . .the environment gradually shapes the behavior of the child. Consequently, the theoretical focus is upon the child's behavioral achievements, particularly

those that bring him into increasing conformity with his physical and social milieu (Langer 1969 p. 159f).

Second, development as a prerequisite of education. In contrast to a learning theoretical explanation of human development, advocates of this position assume that spontaneous age-typical cognitive and behavioral disposi ons develop during childhood as a consequence of endogenous processes (e.g., maturationally directed increases in working memory capacity). This improvement in learning capacity that cannot itself be explained from a learning theory perspective, allows and requires concrete learning opportunities in the child's environment. According to this view, the child is reliably able to take advantage of such learning opportunities, because humans are naturally outfitted with mechanisms for active information search and processing that are appropriate for the systematic construction of cognitive structures. Under this perspective, education has only a supporting role. Spontaneous psychological development is in any case a necessary prerequisite for an explicit acquisition of cultural knowledge (Gesell and Ilg 1943).

Third, development as the goal of education. According to this view, more advanced cognitive structures cannot be directly taught; however, the processes of spontaneous development need support and facilitation from the social environment, so that they do not remain at a relatively immature stage (concrete operations) or regress to an earlier stage. Kohlberg and Mayer (1972) explicitly promote the "ideology" that it is especially important for the individual to attain the most advanced stage of cognitive development possible because personal autonomy, self responsibility, and moral action are stage-dependent. They criticize both behaviorists and advocates of an antiauthoritarian movement because in their opinion "it is better for the child to be a happy pig than an unhappy Socrates" (Kohlberg and Mayer 1972 p. 472).

The most important task of education according to this view is thus not to shape behavior or to transmit specific knowledge, but to provide optimal stimulation to foster cognitive development, that is, stage transformation. But how, for example, can education for development proceed in the school?

The task of the teacher is to facilitate the process of change. In summary: To be effective, the teacher must have a knowledge of the child's level of thought; match the child's level by communicating at the level directly above; focus on reasoning; and help the child experience the type of cognitive conflict that leads to awareness of the greater adequacy of the next stage (Kohlberg no date p. 42f).

These three different views of the relation between development and education are not currently advocated in their most radical forms, but only in more liberal interpretations. Many empirical studies have shown that different facets of human development require different concepts of education. This conclusion is not a simple eclectic compromise, but rather the pragmatic outcome of the current state-of-the-art of theory in developmental psychology.

See also: Human Development: Research Methodology; Ecological Models of Human Development; Lifespan Development

References

Arlin M 1984 Time, equality, and mastery learning. *Rev. Educ. Res.* 54(1): 65–86
Baltes P B 1987 Theoretical propositions of life-span developmental psychology: On the dynamics between growth and decline. *Dev. Psychol.* 23(5): 611–26
Baltes P B, Reese H W, Lipsitt L P 1980 Life-span developmental psychology. *Annu. Rev. Psychol.* 31: 65–110
Binet A, Simon T 1905 Application des méthodes nouvelles au diagnostic du niveau intellectuelle chez des enfants normaux et anormaux d'hospice et d'école primaire. *Annee Psychol.* 11: 245–336
Bronfenbrenner U 1963 Developmental theory in transition. *Child Psychology. The Sixty-second Yearbook of the National Society for the Study of Education. Part 1.* Chicago Press, Chicago, Illinois
Bronfenbrenner U 1989 Ecological systems theory. *Annals of Child Development* 6: 187–249
Bühler Ch, Hetzer H 1929 Zur Geschichte der Kinderpsychologie. In: Brunswik E et al. (ed.) 1929 *Beiträge zur Problemgeschichte der Psychologie.* Verlag von Günter Fischer, Jena
Carey S 1984 Cognitive development. The descriptive problem. In: Gazzaniga M S (ed.) 1984 *Handbook of Cognitive Neuroscience.* Plenum Press, New York
Chomsky N 1959 Review of Skinner's verbal behavior. *Language* 35: 26–58
Costa P T Jr, McCrae R R 1988 Personality in adulthood: A six year longitudinal study of self-reports and spouse ratings on the NEO personality inventory. *J. Pers. Soc. Psychol.* 54(5): 853–63
Dannefer D 1988 What's in a name: An account of the neglect of variability in the study of aging. In: Birren J E, Bengtson V L (eds.) 1988 *Emergent Theories of Aging.* Springer, New York
Denney N W 1982 Aging and cognitive changes. In: Wolman B B (ed.) 1982 *Handbook of Developmental Psychology.* Prentice Hall, Englewood Cliffs, New Jersey
Digman J M 1990 Personality structure: Emergence of the five-factor model. *Annu. Rev. Psychol.* 41: 417–40
Dweck C S 1991 Self theories and goals: Their role in motivation, personality, and development. In: Dienstbier R A (ed.) 1991 *Nebraska symposium on motivation*, Vol. 36. University of Nebraska Press, Lincoln, Nebraska
Ericsson K A, Crutcher R J 1990 The nature of exceptional performance. In: Baltes P B, Featherman D L, Lerner R M (eds.) 1990 *Life-span Development and Behavior*, Vol. 10. Erlbaum, Hillsdale, New Jersey
Erikson E H 1959 Identity and the life cycle. *Psychol. Iss.* 1(1): 18–164
Flavell J 1970 Cognitive change in adulthood. In: Goulet R, Baltes P B (eds.) 1970 *Life-span Developmental Psychology: Research and Theory.* Academic Press, New York
Ford D H, Lerner R M 1992 *Developmental Systems*

Theory: An Integrative Approach. Sage, Newbury Park, California

Freud S 1917 *Vorlesungen zur Einführung in die Psychoanalyse.* Heller Verlag, Leipzig

Gesell A, Ilg F L 1943 *Infant and Child in the Culture of Today.* Harper & Row, New York

Goslin D A 1969 *Handbook of Socialization, Theory and Research.* Rand McNally, Chicago, Illinois

Halverson C F, Kohnstamm G A, Martin R P 1993 *The Five Factor Model and its Roots in Childhood.* Erlbaum, Hillsdale, New Jersey

Heckhausen H 1982 The development of achievement motivation. In: Hartup W H (ed.) 1982 *Review of Child Development Research*, Vol. 6. The University of Chicago Press, Chicago, Illinois

Heckhausen H 1987 Causal attribution patterns for achievement outcomes: Individual differences, possible types and their origins. In: Weinert F E, Kluwe R H (eds.) 1987 *Metacognition, Motivation, and Understanding.* Erlbaum, Hillsdale, New Jersey

Hyde J S, Linn M C (eds.) 1986 *The Psychology of Gender.* The Johns Hopkins University Press, Baltimore, Maryland

Kenyon G M 1988 Basic assumptions in theories of human aging. In: Birren J E, Bengtson V L (eds.) 1988 *Emergent Theories of Aging.* Springer, New York

Kohlberg L 1981/1984 *Essay on Moral Development*, Vols. 1–2. Harper and Row, San Francisco, California

Kohlberg L no date The concepts of developmental psychology as the central guide to education. In: *Proceedings of the Conference in Psychology and the Process of Schooling in the Next Decade: Alternative Conceptions.* University of Minnesota, Minneapolis, Minnesota

Kohlberg L, LaCrosse I, Ricks D 1972 The predictability of adult mental health from childhood behavior. In: Wolman B B (ed.) 1972 *Manual of child psychopathology.* McGraw-Hill, New York

Kohlberg L, Mayer R 1972 Development as the aim of education. *Har. Educ. Rev.* 42(4): 449–96

Langer J 1969 *Theories of development.* Holt, Rinehart & Winston, New York

Magnusson D 1988 *Individual Development from an Interactional Perspective: A Longitudinal Study.* Erlbaum, Hillsdale, New Jersey

Montada L, Filipp S H, Lerner M J (eds.) 1992 *Life Crisis and Experiences of Loss in Adulthood.* Erlbaum, Hillsdale, New Jersey

Overton W F, Reese H W 1973 Models of development: Methodological implications. In: Nesselroade J R, Reese H W (eds.) 1973 *Life-span Developmental Psychology: Methodological Issues.* Academic Press, New York

Piaget J 1932 *The Moral Judgement of the Child.* Pinguin Books, Harmondsworth

Piaget J 1947 *La Psychologie de l'Intelligence.* Colin, Paris

Piaget J 1972 Development and learning. In: Lavatelli C S, Stendler F (eds.) 1972 *Readings in Child Behavior and Development*, 3rd edn. Harcourt Price, New York

Plomin R 1990 *Nature and Nurture.* Brooks/Cole Publishing Comp, Pacific Grove, California

Reese H W, Overton W F 1970 Models of development and theories of development. In: Goulet L R, Baltes P B (eds.) 1970 *Life-span Developmental Psychology: Research and Theory.* Academic Press, New York

Scarr S 1992 Developmental theories for the 1990s: Development and individual difference. *Child Dev.* 63(1): 1–19

Siegler R S 1991 *Children's Thinking.* Prentice Hall, Englewood Cliffs, New Jersey

Skinner B F 1966 The phylogeny and ontogeny of behavior. *Science.* 153: 1205–13

Spencer H 1881 *The Principles of Psychology*, Vol. I, 3rd edn. Williams & Norgate, London

Stern W 1906 *Person und Sache. System der philosophischen Weltanschauung. I. Ableitung und Grundlehre.* Barth, Leipzig

Thomae H 1970 Theory of aging and cognitive theory of personality research. *Hum. Dev.* 12: 1–16

Watson J B 1925. *Behaviorism.* Kegan Paul, Trench, Trubner, London

Werner H 1940 *Comparative Psychology of Mental Development*, 3rd edn. Int. Universities Press, New York

Wohlwill J F 1973 *The Study of Behavioral Development.* Academic Press, New York

Wundt W 1916 Völkerpsychologie und Entwicklungspsychologie. *Psychologische Studien* 10: 189–239

Zajonc R B 1980 Feeling and thinking: Preferences need no inferences. *Am. Psychol.* 35(2): 151–75

Zigler E, Child I L 1969 Socialization. In: Lindzey G, Aronson E (eds.) 1969 *The Handbook of Social Psychology*, 2nd. edn., Vol. 3. Addison-Wesley, Reading, Massachusetts

Education and Development

L. J. Saha and I. Fägerlind

The relationship between education and development has been the center of much discussion and controversy since the 1950s. Since that time, the conviction that education, in its formal form, makes a positive, and indeed an essential, contribution to the development of countries has shifted from unbridled optimism during the 1950s and 1960s to guarded hope and even despair in the 1990s (Fägerlind and Saha 1989). What was once thought to be a simple cause-and-effect relationship is now seen to be a highly complex one, and contingent upon many factors, not the least being the very understanding of education and of development.

This entry will define education and development and discuss the changing nature of opinion about these two concepts. This will be followed by an examination of the various dimensions of national development and how education is related to each. Finally, some of the main issues in the understanding of the link between education and development will be addressed.

1. Education as an Agent of Change and Development

In the debates about whether and how education contributes to the development of a society there is often a neglect of what specifically the two concepts mean. With regard to development, the word is most often understood as economic development. For example, economists such as Psacharopoulos and Woodhall (1985) and Todaro (1989) define development as the improvement of a country's productive capacity. Although they acknowledge the importance of political and social factors in addition to the economic, these are seen as important primarily insofar as they help or hinder economic development.

Todaro (1989) added that development, particularly in the 1950s and 1960s, has "traditionally meant the capacity of a national economy, whose initial economic condition has been more or less static for a long time, to *generate and sustain* an annual increase in its gross national product at rates of perhaps 5 to 7% or more"(p. 86). Other writers, however, have argued that development is multifaceted, and includes changes in social structures and institutions, changes in social attitudes, values, and behaviors, and finally changes toward social and political equality and the eradication of poverty.

1.1 Definition of Development

Notions of how societies change and develop are not new or novel to current debates. From Classical Antiquity, through the Enlightenment, right up to modern times, there have always been ideas and theories about how societies change and develop. At the least, notions of development have included the realization of potential, irrespective of what that potential might be.

In the following discussion, development is defined in terms of three dimensions: (a) economic, (b) social/cultural, (c) political. As used here, economic development means the increase in the efficiency of the production system of a society. Social/cultural development includes changes in attitudes, values, and behaviors. Finally, political development is understood to mean the equal distribution of power and the absence of domination of any one group over another. Political development thus includes political participation, access to political positions, and the development of national integration, cohesion, and identity (Fägerlind and Saha 1989).

1.2 Definition of Education

In this broader definition of development it is important to emphasize first the distinction between formal,

informal, and nonformal education. Each of these is related differently to the process of development, and each type of education requires different types of policies in terms of education and development goals and strategies. Second, it is also important to distinguish between basic literacy, primary, secondary, and tertiary education. The strength of the relationship between these different levels of education and the development of a society requires specification. Finally, an enduring debate in formulating education policies for development is whether academic or vocational education programs are more appropriate for development strategies. The following sections most often refer to primary and secondary education with respect to development outcomes, but do not intend to preclude other forms of education from being considered in the development context. Some of these other forms of education and their relevance for development are addressed later in this entry.

2. Education and Economic Development

2.1 The Neoclassical View

The most common understanding of education and development is in terms of economic development. Models of economic growth have been dominant since the emergence of the eighteenth-century theories of progress of Adam Smith, John Stuart Mill, and others. Theories of economic progress agree that one, but not the main, component of progress is the human dimension, for example, the quality of the workforce and the skills that it possesses.

The underlying assumptions in the link between education and economic development are those of human capital theory, whereby any improvement in the health, skills, or motivation of the workforce are seen to improve the productivity of workers. Insofar as education brings about improvements in the quality of the human population, it is seen as a contribution to the economic growth of a country.

The economists who hold this view cite considerable evidence which they regard as supportive. For example, a review of 31 studies of rural areas showed that farmers with an educational attainment of four years increased their productivity by 8.7 percent (Lockheed et al. 1980). Although it is difficult to locate studies of the impact of education on the productivity of factory workers in single countries, the evidence available reported by Haddad et al. (1990) also points out that one consequence of higher levels of education is the opportunity to change to jobs with higher skill demands and incomes.

At an aggregate level Psacharopoulos (1985) has provided perhaps the most comprehensive evidence that investment in education does result in forms of economic growth. If one assumes that economic development can be defined in terms of rates of return, then his studies since the early 1970s merit attention. Beginning with a study of 32 countries in 1973, Psacharopoulos, by the mid-1980s, was able to demonstrate rates-of-return to investment in education for 60 countries. His findings show that in developing countries the rates of return to primary schooling was 27 percent, compared to 16 percent and 13 percent for secondary and higher education respectively.

However, in assessing the contribution of education to economic development it is necessary to take into account the difference between individual rates of return and social rates of return. Education may benefit the careers of individuals more than the careers of countries. In this respect Psacharopoulos's findings are even more interesting, for the rates of return to individuals are on the whole greater than those to society, and the discrepancies are greater for the higher education level than for the primary school level. Therefore, while it is appropriate to focus attention on the social rates of return to investment in education, it is also important to keep in mind the individual rates of return, as the latter may occur partly at the expense of the former.

The implications, according to Psacharopoulos (1985), of his rates-of-return analysis of investment in education are as follows: (a) education is underfunded, as the rates of return are higher than the social discount used in project evaluation; (b) primary schooling should be the paramount priority for educational investment; (c) higher education is oversubsidized, (d) the expansion of the participation of women in education results in returns comparable to those of men; (e) investment in general curricula is as good as investment in vocational curricula.

2.2 Alternative Views

There are some economists who suggest that the relationship between education and development is not as straightforward as is implied by the neoclassicists. In the late 1960s Coombs (1968) argued that the expansion of educational facilities would not necessarily lead to economic growth, but rather to an economic crisis brought about by the costs of sustaining larger but inappropriate educational structures. More than a decade later Coombs's (1985) argument was more complex but not appreciably different.

In the late 1970s Weiler (1978) called into question the priorities that the classical and neoclassical models of education and economic growth assumed. He questioned the notion that educational expansion would automatically lead to economic growth. He suggested that issues of equity, the relationship between education and work, and educational reform were among the three most important issues related to choice in educational policy-making, and that it is misleading to assume that investment in education will necessarily lead to economic growth.

The criticisms continued into the late 1980s and early 1990s. Blaug (1985) argued that the "golden years" of the economics of education ended in the early 1970s; since then there has been a realization that other factors besides the market affect changes in society. Blaug suggested that economists should direct their attention to the "screening hypothesis," the "incomplete employment contract," and labor market segmentation for explanations as to why educational expansion had not resulted in the level, or type, of economic growth desired. In essence, he argued that explanations about the link between education and development should include institutional and sociological factors in addition to economic factors.

Klees (1989) and Easton and Klees (1990) have argued that there are at least two alternatives to the human capital perspective in conceptualizing the relationship between education and economic development. The first is the institutionalist approach, whereby attention is directed to the patterns of social behavior that shape supply and demand for education (rather than the reverse), and the use to which it is put. In this context labor market segmentation and internal labor markets have been seen as important explanatory variables for the failure of investment in education to bring about the desired results (Easton and Klees 1990). The second is the radical economic perspective, or neo-Marxist political economy, which focuses on the ways that education leads to the reproduction of social inequalities, and the detrimental effects that these processes have on economic growth. Authors such as Bowles and Gintis (1976) and Carnoy and Levin (1985) have suggested that investment in education can and does have negative effects on economic growth. The failure of economists to take these factors into account leads to educational policies that result in more problems than are solved. In other words, educational expansion does not necessarily lead to economic growth.

2.3 Conclusions on Education and Economic Development

The belief that educational expansion will necessarily lead to economic growth is problematic. Although the notion of investment in education as human capital has dominated policy and planning since the 1960s, there is an emerging consensus that education may also have negative effects on economic growth. The problem is one of perspective and the resulting policies and plans, not of whether education has effects on the economy. Clearly the issues are related to questions of what kind of education, what kind of economic growth, and economic growth for whom? In spite of much research and debate, the links between education and the economy are not fully understood, and it would be erroneous to assume that consensus on this issue exists among academics and policymakers.

3. Education and Social Development

A preoccupation with the economic dimensions of development overlooks other ways in which education contributes to the development of a country. Social aspects of development may, in many respects, equal the economic in importance. Social dimensions of development include factors such as quality of life, modernity in attitudes, values, and beliefs, and the satisfaction of basic human needs. When these are not met, the effects of economic development on a country may be attenuated or blocked altogether. It is essential to take into account the ways in which education may or may not influence these factors to obtain a broader perspective on the overall relationship between education and development.

3.1 Education and Modernization

Although there is disagreement about the meaning and usefulness of the concept of modernization, largely because it is thought to be imprecise, multidimensional, and oriented toward the West, it has nevertheless been the object of much research. Furthermore, much of the policy and planning in the area of education and development, at least implicitly, assumes a modernization perspective.

Much of the research on modernization has been based on the definitions and measures of Inkeles, who first attempted to operationalize the notion of the "modern man" (Inkeles and Smith 1974). Following Inkeles and Smith, a modern person is characterized by the following: (a) openness to new experience; (b) readiness for social change; (c) awareness of diversity in attitudes and opinions, but the disposition to hold one's own views; (d) being fact-oriented in forming opinions; (e) focusing on the present and the future rather than the past; (f) possessing a sense of personal efficacy; (g) orientation to long-term planning; (h) trust in social institutions and in individuals; (i) placing a premium on technical skill; (j) showing high regard for education; (k) respect for the dignity of others; (l) understanding the logic underlying production and industry.

The basic thesis of Inkeles and others is that the path to modern development cannot occur without modern citizens. Furthermore, modernization theorists hold that people do not become modern except by participating in modern institutions, the chief of which are education (schools) and industry (factories).

There is evidence to support the notion that schools are important and effective modernizing institutions. People who attain higher levels of education (or who achieve at higher levels), also have higher levels of educational and occupational aspirations, less adherence to traditional customs and beliefs, an openness to new experiences, a willingness to migrate, and a reduction of family ties.

One of the early studies of modernization in which

education played a part is found in Lerner (1964), who argued that that adults in the Middle East who had attained at least a secondary school education had higher levels of psychic empathy, that is, the ability to adjust efficiently to continually changing environments. Similar relationships between education and modernization were found in Mexico and Brazil. If one includes the notion of political interest and awareness as an indicator of modernization, Almond and Verba (1965) found that higher levels of education resulted in higher levels of political interest among respondents in the United States, United Kingdom, Germany, Italy, and Mexico. Inkeles and Smith (1974) found strong correlations between educational attainment and individual modernity in their study of adults in Argentina, Chile, East Pakistan (Bangladesh), India, Israel, and Nigeria. The correlations were consistently higher than those between modernity and both exposure to mass media and occupational experience. In other words, education was the strongest modernizing agent of the three factors. Subsequent studies have reinforced these earlier findings.

Finally, in a study of the comparative effects of education and the mass media (in particular the Western cinema) on modernization, Delacroix and Ragin (1978) argued that the school is a domestically based modernizing institution while the mass media may or may not be. In their study of 49 less-developed countries, they concluded that the school had the potential to modernize without Westernizing, and that countries with strong state-sponsored programs (mobilizing regimes) used education as a modernizing agent more effectively than states with weaker programs.

3.2 Education and Modernization: A Critique

One of the important critiques of modernization as related to education is whether schooling inevitably leads to modernity. Armer and Youtz (1971) were among the first to suggest that under certain circumstances, schooling could have a traditionalizing rather than modernizing effect, and that it is the school curriculum rather than the school organization that accounts for this effect. Studies of Koranic schools have supported this notion; Wagner and Lofti (1980) found that Koranic schools actually inhibit the acquisition of modern values. Schools seem most successful as traditionalizing mechanisms in countries that have most strongly resisted foreign domination, such as Morocco, Nigeria, and Indonesia (Wagner 1985).

A further criticism of the modernization hypothesis is that many studies of modernity are based on attitude and value questionnaire items which are themselves similar to those espoused by Western-style schools. Thus studies of educational attainment and modernization are in fact studies of school learning generally. Second, because the school is a selective institution, it may be that the acquisition of modern values is due to factors other than the school itself. Persons already predisposed to the acquisition of modern values are the same as those predisposed to acquire more schooling.

Finally, the schooling and modernity thesis rests on the assumption that modernization inevitably leads to development. However, modernization can be detrimental to development. The "brain drain" of educated and skilled persons from developing countries, the disruption of social relationships as a result of the modernizing process, the destruction of useful traditional social institutions, and the creation of a modernized elite who are out of touch with the general population are but a few of the negative consequences of modernization on social development. When education produces a negative form of modernization in a society, then education can also have a negative impact on the social development of a country.

3.3 Education, Quality of Life, and Basic Human Needs

Another aspect of social development is quality of life and the meeting of basic human needs. When there are major disparities in the distribution of material goods —the lack of adequate food, shelter, and clothing— large proportions of populations are unable to contribute to the development process. Although education may not have a direct effect on the redistribution of resources, it can inhibit this process. For example, a study of the 32 states of Mexico concluded that literacy level was related to the provision of basic needs such as the eradication of infant mortality, nutrition, clean water, and healthcare. Furthermore it was argued that Mexico would lag behind other less developed countries in per capita income until these basic needs were met (Wood 1988).

The relationship between education and quality of life, and the meeting of basic human needs, parallels that of modernization in that both focus on changing people. However, they differ in that modernization involves social–psychological changes whereas a focus on quality of life and the meeting of basic human needs involves change in the physical and social conditions of the population. The impact of education on physical and social conditions is less direct than its impact on attitudes and values. It is not clear how an increase in educational level will necessarily result in more equitable distribution of physical and social conditions, particularly if higher levels of educational attainment are concentrated in a small selective elite group in society. In this respect, the improvement in quality of life and the meeting of basic human needs may depend on the level of political development in a country.

4. Education and Political Development

Political development can be defined in terms of high levels of political integration (i.e., high solidarity and low levels of conflict) and political participation (i.e., high levels of mobilization, such as voting and other forms of decision-making). These processes include political socialization, the preparation for political leadership, and political integration and the development of national political consciousness. Political development, in the form of political participation and the sharing of political power, may provide the "sufficient cause" for the link between education and economic and social development to occur.

4.1 Education, Political Socialization, and Citizenship

The importance of education for the inculcation of political attitudes, values, and behavior has been extensively researched (e.g., Renshon 1977). However, there are other important agents of political socialization which also merit attention, such as the media and the family. Research on the relative effects of these three agents of political socialization is not clear. Also unclear is the extent to which learning about politics and citizenship may occur differently in developed and less developed countries, or in different cultural settings.

While it is generally assumed that political socialization is functional for system maintenance (i.e., maintaining the status quo), it may be more correct to assume system persistence, that is, system maintenance plus change (Nathan and Remy 1977). Torney-Purta and Schwille (1986) have argued that no industrialized country has had complete success in imparting coherent and consistent civic values, partly because many desired values are in fact incompatible, such as democratic values (tolerance and equality) and support for the national government (national patriotism and trust in government). Furthermore, in some industrialized countries (the United States and United Kingdom) there is emphasis on individual success while in others (Japan, Greece, and Germany) security is seen as important. Ichilov (1991) reported that in Israel the effects of the school on knowledge about politics and democratic citizenship orientations are not uniform. Students who participate in class discussions, who are in academic rather than vocational programs, who are males of eastern ethnic origin, and who are members of disadvantaged groups are more affected by school experiences in the acquisition of these characteristics.

Ultimately, the effect of education on political socialization explains how societies change as well as how they persist. Because political learning occurs differently in countries with different structural characteristics, schools in some less developed countries socialize students toward political change rather than political stability, in spite of the official curriculum of the school or national ideology. This was the case in Kenya and Tanzania, where students rated developmental and modernizing problems as more important than the preservation of customs and tradition. Likewise in a comparative study of Colombia and the

United States, it was found that American students held favorable political dispositions toward their government, while the opposite was true for Colombian students (Nathan and Remy 1977). Finally, it can happen that the political values taught in school may openly conflict with those of the political leadership, as Harber (1984) found in his study of the Hausa in Nigeria.

Thus education plays an important role in the political socialization of young people. However, the outcomes of that socialization process may support tradition or it may favor change and development.

4.2 Education and Political Leadership

One aspect of political socialization concerns the selection and preparation of political leaders. Sometimes political leaders are conservative and act to maintain the economic, social, and political system; at other times, they are major agents of change.

Although education systems are the normal avenue to political leadership, there are other avenues, such as the military, religion, or tradition. In many countries certain schools are known as the training grounds for elites, as in the United Kingdom and the United States.

In less developed countries the recruitment and training of political leadership are more problematic. Latukefu (1988) argued that in Papua New Guinea the traditional elite existed before the formal education system was established, and selection was based on knowledge about deities, mythology, and folklore. The modern elite, on the other hand, are products of the education system and follow a lifestyle very different from that of most of the population. But elite schools, by transmitting modern knowledge, ensure a claim to future elite status (Smith and Bray 1988).

However, if the gap between the elite and the general population is too great, there is a greater possibility of political instability. Thus the role of education in the preparation of political leadership includes both recruitment and selection for elite status; at the same time it ensures that elites maintain contact with the general population and helps to determine whether the elite is conservative or change-oriented. These aspects of the relationship between education and the development of political leadership are less well-known.

4.3 Education and Nation-building

The third aspect of political development to which education contributes concerns nation-building. Nation-building, in particular, refers in part to the development of a national identity and national consciousness. This process is closely linked to the legitimation of center-formation and the creation of a national culture. This requires the establishment of a national consensus regarding the political system itself. In addition to political socialization, education promotes citizenship and loyalty through the use of national symbols such as the flag, a national song or anthem, or a constitution, a monarch or other highly visible political leader (real or symbolic). The formation of the nation-state requires the breaking down of regional loyalties and identities, and their replacement with national loyalties and identities.

To the extent that less developed societies often experience weak levels of political consensus, high levels of regional or tribal loyalties, and high levels of tension and conflict, the importance of political development may enjoy equal priority to that of economic and social development. In such societies the expansion of education often serves to incorporate members into the state through the bestowal of citizenship. To this extent, the emergence of, and participation in a mass education system has been called a baptism "in a national history, a written language, national culture, and the mysteries of technical culture" (Meyer and Rubinson 1975 p. 146). By incorporating the individual into the nation-state, education strengthens the state and its institutions.

However, while education can serve as an agent for nation-building, it can also bring about divisions and conflict in society. Some writers have focused attention on education as a commodity that has often been unequally distributed in society, and thus has served as a source of advantage, of exclusion from social goods, and of social division rather than social integration and national consensus. Examples of this disintegrative effect of education have been documented in Nigeria, Kenya, and other developing countries.

Likewise, if education operates as an agent of political consensus and nation-building, then the most educated members of society should also be the most loyal and the most well-integrated. However, the pervasiveness of student activism in many societies, and the oppositional nature of many student movements, suggests that the integrative effect of education may be more problematic than is sometimes acknowledged. Nevertheless, as members of the educated elite, students are often nationalistic in their opposition to governments, particularly where those governments are totalitarian or controlled by outside interests, such as many former colonial regimes were. Thus, even student movements, either of the left or the right, can be seen as agents in the process of political development (Altbach 1991).

Like other aspects of education and political development, education may be a necessary but not sufficient condition for development to occur. One factor not often taken into account in the relationship between education and political development is the extent to which political systems actually control and structure the nature of the educational system.

4.4 Education as a Political Product

Political systems can shape the curriculum, the forms of assessment, discipline, and also the extent to which young people participate or leave the school system. In all societies decisions about education are made on the basis of what is expected from the schools. Whether vocational or academic programs are emphasized often depends on the skills desired or required by government decree in response to needs of the economic system.

The development status of a country is an important determinant of the shape of an educational system. The amount of funding available, the strength of traditional values, the extent to which the economy is based on agriculture or industry, are important inputs into what is expected of schools. Another important determinant is whether the economy is capitalist or socialist. Although the rapid collapse of many socialist economies in the early 1990s might suggest that socialism is not a viable economic form, it nevertheless made unique demands on educational systems, as does capitalism. Socialist education has been identified as more collectivity-oriented, more vocational, and more ideological than its capitalist counterpart.

While education can contribute to the development of a country in the ways described above, it can also be controlled by many aspects of the system. The interrelationship between education and its political, economic, and social system remains an important area for further research attention.

5. Issues in Education and Development

There are a number of issues that are likely to dominate education and development policies and strategies well into the twenty-first century. These will be briefly described in the final section of this entry.

5.1 Literacy

Literacy has always been associated with levels of development. Bowman and Anderson (1973) argued that a literacy rate of 40 percent is necessary but not sufficient for economic growth. Furthermore, high levels of industrialization are thought to require literacy levels of 70 to 80 percent. Although literacy rates remain low in many less developed countries, literacy campaigns and programs received high priority during the 1970s and 1980s in many newly independent countries such as Mozambique and Angola, and postrevolutionary countries such as Cuba and Nicaragua. These campaigns have served both developmental and ideological purposes, for the process of learning to read and write has often also involved learning about the social and economic goals of the new governments.

The problems related to literacy programs are those of sustaining effort until literacy goals are achieved for all members of society and literacy reaches a level where the gains will not be lost. A second problem concerns the maintenance of a literate environment, which includes the availability of newspapers and other reading materials. Finally, the priorities in literacy

programs are such that often females and rural dwellers are the last to be targeted, the result being that in many less developed countries they remain the least literate and the most disadvantaged.

5.2 Gender Inequality

Women and girls have lagged behind men in literacy and educational attainments in virtually all developing countries. Furthermore, the disparity between women and men is increasing. According to Stromquist (1990), of the 154 million new illiterates in the world between 1960 and 1985, 133 million, or 86.4 percent were women. Women constitute one-third of the world's official paid labor force, they grow almost half the world's food, they perform most of the world's domestic work, and they provide more healthcare than all health services combined. Yet, in many countries, women cannot own land, they often work a double day, and in many countries they do not enjoy equal political participation (Fägerlind and Saha 1989).

In spite of unequal educational participation and attainments, Psacharopoulos (1985) argued that "expanding the provision of school places to cover women is not only equitable but socially efficient as well" (p. 592). There are in many societies, however, cultural and institutional obstacles to the attainment of gender equality, against females as participants in the process of development and as recipients of the gains from development. The reasons for this inequity are described by Stromquist (1990), as follows: (a) a patriarchical ideology, which argues that women's roles are complementary to men's roles; and (b) the control that men have over women's sexuality, such as norms relating to virginity, limited physical mobility, the stigmatization of abortion, and the association of contraception with promiscuity. This control can include physical violence and the separation of women from men upon reaching puberty, either symbolically or physically.

The equal education of women in all countries represents an important development objective, but one that has often been neglected. Although important gains continue to be made, the inequalities are sometimes subtle. Both as a development resource, and also in terms of justice, gender equity remains a major issue in educational issues that purport to promote development.

5.3 Vocational and Academic Education

The controversy about the advantages of vocational or academic secondary school curricula for development is largely related to attempts to match schooling with the needs of developing economies. The topic had its origins in Foster's (1966) contention that vocational schooling would never contribute to development goals as long as the academic curriculum was preferred for its employment prospects. Thus an enduring difficulty in many countries is the establishment of a curriculum that will provide needed labor force skills, and one that is also consistent with popular social demand.

The major difficulty with the coexistence of vocational and academic curricula is that they relate to two occupational sectors. They therefore tend to institutionalize and maintain inequalities in a society. While it is generally agreed that technical skills at all levels are needed in both agricultural and industrial economies, as long as the modern industrial sector is disproportionally rewarded, attempts to establish and promote vocational education will encounter difficulty.

Between 1950 and 1975, Benavot (1983) found that vocational education had declined on a global scale, a trend he associated with increasing emphasis on egalitarian ideologies. However, Psacharopoulos (1985) found that the rate of return for vocational education is lower (12%) than the rate of return for general education (16%). In a survey of 21 studies, a World Bank report concluded that vocational education is not only more expensive than general education, but may not be the most cost-effective way of imparting desired technological skills (Haddad et al. 1990). For the latter, short-term training programs in institutes and firms may be the better alternative.

Vocational education remains an attractive, if not controversial, solution to the production of skills needed by many developing economies. Furthermore, it appears suitable for students not equipped for academic educational programs. However, in terms of social inequalities and adaptability to rapid change, it remains unclear which type of education contributes most to economic, social, and political development.

5.4 Equity and Efficiency

An issue facing all countries concerns decisions regarding equity and efficiency. Should emphasis be placed on keeping as many young people in school as long as possible, or should attention be directed mainly to those with proven ability to succeed to higher levels of schooling? The two processes are interrelated. At a global level, about 15 percent of all primary and secondary school students are repeaters, and as much as 20 percent of education budgets is spent on repeaters and future dropouts (Haddad et al. 1990).

The efficiency of schooling can be raised by improving inputs. Studies have shown that factors such as teacher quality, textbooks, homework, and time spent in school can improve student achievement (Saha 1983, Fuller 1987). However, it is not clear as to which inputs are most cost-effective, and because the teaching-learning process is complex, no one input alone will make a large impact on improvement on student performance. Nevertheless, the variation between schools in less developed countries is great enough to justify raising the quality of any of the inputs

in order to raise performance substantially (Haddad et al. 1990).

6. Conclusion

The evidence for the impact of education on economic, social, and political development is sufficient to dispel the skepticism that occurred in the late 1970s. However, the relationship is too complex to assume that any investment in education will produce the desired results. It is possible to overinvest in education, or to invest in the wrong kind of education. Because of expanding technologies and knowledge, it is virtually impossible for a country to pursue development policies without providing for an educated population. Education is a major agent for development, but only if it is adapted and used in a manner appropriate to the development needs of a particular country.

References

Almond G A, Verba S 1965 *The Civic Culture: Political Attitudes and Democracy in Five Nations: An Analytic Study*. Little, Brown & Co., Boston, Massachusetts
Altbach P G 1991 Student political activism. In: Altbach P G (ed.) 1991 *International Higher Education: An Encyclopedia*, Vol. 1. Garland, New York
Armer M, Youtz R 1971 Formal education and individual modernity in an African society. *Am. J. Sociol.* 76 (4): 604–26
Benavot A 1983 The rise and decline of vocational education. *Sociol. Educ.* 56 (2): 63–76
Blaug M 1985 Where are we now in the economics of education? *Econ. Educ. Rev.* 4 (1): 17–28
Bowles S, Gintis H 1976 *Schooling in Capitalist America: Educational Reform and the Contradictions of Economic Life*. Basic Books, New York
Bowman M J, Anderson C A 1973 Human capital and economic modernization in historical perspective. In: Lane F C (ed.) 1973 *Fourth International Conference of Economic History*. Mouton de Gruyter, Paris
Carnoy M, Levin H 1985 *Schooling and Work in the Democratic State*. Stanford University Press, Stanford, California
Coombs P H 1968 *The World Educational Crisis: A Systems Analysis*. Oxford University Press, New York
Coombs P H 1985 *The World Crisis in Education: The View From the Eighties*. Oxford University Press, New York
Delacroix J, Ragin C 1978 Modernizing institutions, mobilization, and Third World development: A cross-national study. *Am. J. Sociol.* 84 (1): 123–50
Easton P, Klees S 1990 Education and the economy: Considering alternative perspectives. *Prospects* 20 (4): 413–28
Fägerlind I, Saha L J 1989 *Education and National Development: A Comparative Perspective*, 2nd edn. Pergamon Press, Oxford
Foster P 1966 The vocational school fallacy in development planning. In: Anderson C A, Bowman M J (eds.) 1965 *Education and Economic Development*. Frank Cass, London

Fuller B 1987 What school factors raise achievement in the Third World? *Rev. Educ. Res.* 57: 255–92

Haddad W D, Carnoy M, Rinaldi R, Regel O 1990 *Education and Development: Evidence For New Priorities.* World Bank Discussion Paper No. 95, World Bank, Washington, DC

Harber C R 1984 Development and political attitudes: The role of schooling in northern Nigeria. *Comp. Educ.* 20 (3): 387–403

Ichilov O 1991 Political socialization and schooling effects among Israeli adolescents. *Comp. Educ. Rev.* 35(3): 430–46

Inkeles A, Smith D H 1974 *Becoming Modern: Individual Change in Six Developing Countries.* Heinemann Educational, London

Klees S J 1989 The economics of education: A more than slightly jaundiced view of where we are now. In: Caillods F (ed.) 1989 *The Prospects For Educational Planning.* UNESCO, Paris

Latukefu S 1988 The modern elite in Papua New Guinea. In: Bray M, Smith P (eds.) 1988 *Education and Social Stratification in Papua New Guinea.* Longman Cheshire, Melbourne

Lerner D 1964 *The Passing of Traditional Society: Modernizing the Middle East.* Free Press, New York

Lockheed M E, Jamison D T, Lau L J 1980 Farmer education and farm efficiency: A survey. In: King T 1980 *Education and Income.* World Bank Staff Working Paper No. 402, World Bank, Washington, DC

Meyer J, Rubinson R 1975 Education and political development. In: Kerlinger F (ed.) 1975 *Review of Research in Education.* Peacock, Itasca, Illinois

Nathan J A, Remy R C 1977 Comparative political socialization: A theoretical perspective. In: Renshon S A 1977 *Handbook of Political Socialization: Theory and Research.* Free Press, New York

Psacharopoulos G 1985 Returns to education: A further international update and implications. *J. Hum. Resources* 20: 583–604

Psacharopoulos G, Woodhall M 1985 *Education for Development: An Analysis of Investment Choices.* Oxford University Press, New York

Renshon S A (ed.) 1977 *Handbook of Political Socialization.* Free Press, New York

Saha L J 1983 Social structure and teacher effects on academic achievement: A comparative analysis. *Comp. Educ. Rev.* 27(1): 69–88

Smith P, Bray M 1988 Educating an elite: Papua New Guinea enrolment in international schools. In: Bray M, Smith P (eds.) 1988 *Education and Social Stratification in Papua New Guinea.* Longman Cheshire, Melbourne

Stromquist N P 1990 Women and illiteracy: The interplay of gender subordination and poverty. *Comp. Educ. Rev.* 34(1): 95–111

Todaro M P 1989 *Economic Development in the Third World,* 4th edn. Longman, London

Torney-Purta J, Schwille J 1986 Civic values learned in school: Policy and practice in industrialized nations. *Comp. Educ. Rev.* 30(1): 30–49

Wagner D A 1985 Islamic education: Traditional pedagogy and contemporary aspects. In: Husén T, Postlethwaite T N (eds.) 1985 *International Encyclopedia of Education,* 1st edn. Pergamon Press, Oxford

Wagner D A, Lofti A 1980 Traditional Islamic education in Morocco: Socio-historical and psychological perspectives. *Comp. Educ. Rev.* 24(2 Pt. 1): 238–51

Weiler H N 1978 Education and development from the age of innocence to the age of scepticism. *Comp. Educ.* 14(3): 179–98

Wood R H 1988 Literacy and basic needs satisfaction in Mexico. *World Dev.* 16(3): 405–17

Human Development, Learning, and Instruction

F. E. Weinert

Different theoretical perspectives provide a historical background for contemporary scientific discussions about the relations between development, learning, and instruction. This entry will first describe the significance of learning for cognitive development. Next, the influence of schooling and instruction on learning, and thus on cognitive development, will be considered. This will be followed by a discussion of the role that individual ability differences play in cognitive development, learning, and instruction. Finally, some relevant conclusions for education will be drawn.

Concepts such as development, learning, and instruction cannot be precisely or usefully defined without explicit reference to psychological theory. For example, from one theoretical perspective, only those changes in competence over the lifespan that are not themselves the result of learning are considered to be examples of development, even though they may constitute psychological or physiological prerequisites for learning specific knowledge and skills. From another theoretical perspective, maturation and experience are seen to interact in the acquisition of cognitive structures, so that a good deal must be learned over the course of cognitive development, even though it cannot be directly taught. This assumption, although it takes very different forms, can be found in the theories of Piaget (1952) and Vygotsky (1978). Both stressed the importance of a child's spontaneous cognitive activities when encoding and processing information. However, whereas Piaget's theory takes the individual construction of cognitive competencies as its focus, for Vygotskian theory it is the development of "socially shared cognition" that is the basis for the development of mental functioning in the individual. These socially shared cognitions are also seen to influence the "zone of proximal development," which refers to the difference between a currently achieved developmental level and potential development (Vygotsky 1978 p.86), a concept many believe should direct the design of instruction (e.g., Newman et al. 1989). From yet another theoretical perspective, cognitive development—with the exception of maturational processes in early childhood—can be seen as entirely due to learning processes that can be systematically optimized through appropriate instruction. This perspective is shared by both behavioristic and some cognitively oriented theorists.

1. The Significance of Learning for Cognitive Development

From the late nineteenth century onward, modern psychology concentrated on studying the structure and output of cognitive functions without regard to content; for example, in perception, thinking, memory, and learning. Largely influenced by progress in cognitive science, the significance of content-specific knowledge and, thus, of the effects of learning for the processing of new information and for cognitive functions in general was first given appropriate weight in psychological theories in the late 1970s and early 1980s.

1.1 The Influence of Domain-specific Learning and Knowledge on Cognitive Development

In models of human information-processing, both general world knowledge and domain-specific knowledge (e.g., about chess, physics, computer programming, medicine) provide partly necessary and partly facilitating conditions for learning, understanding, and problem-solving. The term "knowledge" is more precisely defined in cognitive science than in everyday use. In addition to the quantity of content-specific knowledge, qualitative features are also specified, such as the structural organization of knowledge (e.g., hierarchically organized or organized in lists), the ways in which information is mentally represented (e.g., iconic, symbolic, or enactive), the ease with which stored knowledge can be accessed, and the cognitive operations that can be performed on the knowledge base.

The extraordinary importance of an accessible knowledge base for learning and thinking is demonstrated by the so-called expert–novice paradigm. If one compares the performance of people with similar intelligence levels but different amounts of domain-specific knowledge, individuals with greater domain-specific knowledge (experts) outperform novices on all knowledge-dependent cognitive tasks. The performance differences rest on the fact that, compared with novices, experts are more likely to judge problems according to relevant and important features rather than according to superficial aspects, they are more likely to have available many automatized processing routines that serve to free short-term memory capacity, they can quickly switch between analytic–featural and synthetic–holistic strategies, depending on task demands, and they can process extensive clusters of information simultaneously (Chi et al. 1988). However, the experts' performance advantage occurs only in those areas for which they have comprehensive, specialized knowledge. For example, chess masters demonstrate extraordinary memory performance for complex chess positions, but show average memory performance when they are asked to remember random groupings of chess pieces or other equally complex material not related to chess.

The convincing results from comparisons of novice–expert differences are not limited to adults: they have also been replicated in developmental studies. Thus, in contrast to the typical developmental findings, younger children perform better than older children when they are given tasks in a content domain for which, in contrast to the usual case, the younger children have a better knowledge base (e.g., Chi 1978). These and other findings led Carey to make the following assumption: "Children know less than adults. Children are novices in almost every domain in which adults are experts" (1984 p.64). Given such a theoretical position, learning naturally assumes a key role, and a large degree of educational optimism is often the result. Instruction is thus regarded as deliberately and systematically supporting the acquisition of expertise. Good examples of this are learning to read, learning to write, and learning in mathematics and science.

1.2 The Acquisition of General Cognitive Competencies

Fostering cognitive development through the transmission and acquisition of domain-specific knowledge is a slow process requiring effort. Many, therefore, have attempted to develop ways to encourage the development of cognitive skills in a more general form through teaching and learning general strategies and skills. Learning to learn, learning to think, intelligence training, and the maximization of nonspecific transfer are some key concepts in this area. Large numbers of programs directed to these skills have been developed. They range from very broad enrichment or training programs for fostering intelligence (e.g., Feuerstein et al. 1980), to specialized teaching concepts to train thinking strategies, to complex programs from both

Piagetian and information-processing perspectives for stimulating cognitive development. The results from evaluation studies of these programs are quite varied, but can be summarized by the following trends.

(a) Learning and thinking are not fundamentally improved by short-term, programs that focus on formal, content-free cognitive functions. This conclusion is especially true when performance on demanding school-related or everyday tasks is used as a criterion for success (Blagg 1991).

(b) There are, however, a large number of learning and thinking skills, strategies and techniques that can be effectively trained. Important among these are metacognitive competencies; that is, the acquisition of intelligent strategies for information-processing, better reflective understanding of one's learning and problem-solving, and the automatization of effective self-monitoring techniques (Prawat 1989).

(c) Such training can be used to "cultivate" thinking and learning in the context of the acquisition of content-specific knowledge in many domains and disciplines. In general, the following conclusion can be drawn: the more general a rule or strategy is (that is, the more it can be used across many situations), the smaller is its importance in solving highly demanding content-specific tasks (Siegler 1983).

2. The Influence of Schooling and Instruction on Cognitive Development

In contrast to the Piagetian perspective, in which schooling and instruction are seen to have a small, or even detrimental effect on cognitive development, a good deal of empirical research suggests that the quality of instruction is important for learning in school (Weinert et al. 1989), that the quality of school learning influences the systematic acquisition of knowledge, skills, and abilities, and that the quality of acquired knowledge broadly determines cognitive development.

Whether one compares cognitive development in schooled versus unschooled populations, or analyzes the effects of cross-national differences in schooling and teaching standards on performance in various school subjects, or looks at differences in students as a function of teaching quality in relatively homogeneous school systems, there is always at least a trend—usually constituting substantial evidence—showing that the quality of schools, teachers, and instructional methods "make a difference."

However, the theoretical and empirical relations between instruction, learning, and cognitive devel-

opment should not be portrayed in too simple, too direct or too linear a fashion. Shulman (1982), for example, called differences between research results on cognitive learning and school teaching a paradox, and noted:

> Although the research on learning has taught us the importance of the active, transforming role of the learner, the research on teaching continues to demonstrate the importance of direct instruction, an approach which seems to suggest a passive view of the learner. But it is important to recognize that direct instruction does not put knowledge in the heads of learners but creates the conditions under which students will use the academic learning time fruitfully. (Shulman 1982 p.97)

The relation between learning and development is similarly complex and complicated. Maturational precursors, especially in early childhood, implicit learning, specific and unspecific transfer of learning, and self-organizing processes that integrate new information with already available knowledge all mean that cognitive development always entails more than the sum of observable learning processes. In addition, more is always learned than can be taught. This is true both for the acquisition of factual world knowledge and for the development of such abilities as creativity.

These restrictions on the importance of explicit learning processes do not mean that school learning and deliberate instruction are unimportant for the development of cognitive competencies. Quite the opposite: to a considerable degree, cognitive development consists in the acquisition of expertise in a variety of different content domains, and this expertise is a necessary prerequisite for the solution of all demanding problem-solving tasks. To acquire this expertise, systematic, cumulative learning that is directed to deep understanding and the acquisition of highly automatized routines is indisputably important.

3. Developmental Change, Stable Individual Differences in Cognitive Abilities, and Learning

Learning influences cognitive development and is influenced by cognitive development. This complex, ever-changing relation is, however, moderated by stable individual differences in ability. The theoretical assumption that the rate of intellectual development depends on intellectual abilities was already evident in Binet and Simon's (1905) first intelligence tests for children. This assumption has, in principle, been confirmed by a variety of empirical studies. Although long-term facilitative effects on the cognitive development of disadvantaged children have been shown in well-planned compensatory stimulation programs, the stability of individual differences in achievement and ability tests is high even in grade school, as long as all students are provided with equally good learning environments. A good example of this is the resistance of individual achievement differences in programs of mastery learning and mastery teaching. The attempt to introduce achievement equalizing teaching strategies into classrooms generally does not obviate performance differences: they remain the same or even increase when one compensates for learning rate. When uniform achievement levels are attained, individual cognitive differences are reflected in large differences in the time required to learn the material (Slavin 1987). This presents another theoretical paradox. Although the influence of prior domain-specific knowledge on learning and understanding new information is larger than that of intelligence, stable individual ability differences nonetheless determine how quickly and intelligently knowledge can be acquired. Thus, the equalization of ability differences and related differences in cognitive development cannot, at least given the current state of the field, be a realistic goal for school learning or instruction.

4. Conclusion

There are three requirements for influencing development through instruction and learning:

(a) learning tasks and instruction that are compatible with children's developmental level and with their available domain-specific and domain-general learning prerequisites ("zone of proximal development"; see Newman et al. 1989);

(b) deliberate stimulation of cognitive development by systematically designed teaching programs that confront the learners with cognitive challenges that can be mastered with effort and support from the teacher—through such programs both cognitive competencies and learning motivation can be improved;

(c) the guarantee of possibilities for overcoming individual students' knowledge gaps, false concepts and learning blocks through remedial instruction (Weinert et al. 1989).

See also: Cognitive Development and the Acquisition of Expertise; Development of Learning across the Lifespan; Expert Level of Understanding; Human Development: Research and Educational Practice; Individual Differences and Instruction; Knowledge Representation and Organization; Prior Knowledge and Learning

References

Binet A, Simon T 1905 Application de méthodes nouvelles au diagnostic du niveau intellectuel chez des enfants normaux et anormaux d'hospice et d'école primaire. *Année Psychologique* 11: 245–336
Blagg N 1991 *Can We Teach Intelligence?* Erlbaum, Hillsdale, New Jersey
Carey S 1984 Cognitive development: The descriptive problem. In: Gazzaniga M S (ed.) 1984 *Handbook of Cognitive Neuroscience*. Plenum Press, New York
Chi M T H 1978 Knowledge structure and memory development. In: Siegler R S (ed.) 1978 *Children's Thinking: What Develops?* Erlbaum, Hillsdale, New Jersey
Chi M T H, Glaser R, Faro M J (eds.) 1988 *The Nature of Expertise*. Erlbaum, Hillsdale, New Jersey
Feuerstein R, Rand Y, Hoffman M, Miller R 1980 *Instrumental Enrichment: An Intervention Program for Cognitive Modiability*. University Park Press, Baltimore, Maryland
Newman D, Griffin P, Cole M 1989 *The Construction Zone: Working for Cognitive Change in Schools*. Cambridge University Press, New York
Piaget J 1952 *The Origins of Intelligence in Children*. International University Press, New York
Prawat R S 1989 Promoting access to knowledge, strategy, and disposition in students: A research synthesis. *Rev. Educ. Res.* 59(1): 1–41
Shulman L S 1982 Educational psychology returns to school. In Kraut A G (ed.) 1982 *The G. Stanley Hall Lecture Series*, Vol. 2. American Psychological Association, Washington, DC
Siegler R S 1983 Five generalizations about cognitive development. *Am. Psychol.* 38(3): 263–77
Slavin R E 1987 Mastery learning reconsidered. *Rev. Educ. Res.* 57(2): 175–213
Vygotsky L S 1978 *Mind in Society: The Development of Higher Psychological Processes*. Harvard University Press, Cambridge, Massachusetts
Weinert F E, Schrader F W, Helmke A 1989 Quality of instruction and achievement outcomes. *Int. J. Educ. Res.* 13(8): 895–914

Further Reading

Resnick L B 1987 *Education and Learning to Think*. National Academy Press, Washington, DC
Resnick L B (ed.) 1989 *Knowing, Learning, and Instruction: Essays in Honor of Robert Glaser*. Erlbaum, Hillsdale, New Jersey
Rogoff B 1990 *Apprenticeship in Thinking: Cognitive Development in Social Context*. Oxford University Press, New York, Oxford

History of Instructional Psychology

R. E. Mayer

Instructional psychology is the scientific study of how instructional manipulations affect changes in the learner. It is a part of education psychology, concerned with the relation between instruction and learning. Examples include the issue of whether a phonics or whole word approach is more effective in helping students learn how to read, or how to design mathematics instruction in order to maximize students' success in transferring what they have learned to new problems. Instructional psychology is an interdisciplinary field that draws mainly on psychology and education and an international field that has benefited from the contributions of scholars of many nations.

The purpose of this entry is to provide an overview of the history of instructional psychology during the twentieth century. During the past century, instructional psychology has developed as a truly international venture, has sought the appropriate relation between psychology and education, and has grappled with the question of how best to characterize the process of learning and instruction. This entry addresses the historic role of international scholars in shaping today's field of instructional psychology, three phases in the relation between psychology and instruction, and three metaphors of learning and instruction that have evolved.

1. Instructional Psychology as an International Field of Study

The development of today's field of instructional psychology has been a true international effort, with the discipline's most influential figures representing an array of nations. For example, in Germany, in spite of claims that high level cognitive processes could not be directly studied, Ebbinghaus (1964) produced the world's first experimental study of human learning and memory. Later, Gestalt psychologists (Dunker 1945, Wertheimer 1959) and their contemporaries, such as Selz (Frijda and DeGroot 1982)—many of whom migrated from Germany—empirically established a distinction between learning by memorizing and learning by understanding. Their search for an account of how people understand and transfer solutions from one problem to another remains as one of instructional psychology's most important issues (Mayer 1995).

In France, when educators needed a way to predict school success, Binet (see Wolf 1973) developed the world's first empirically validated test of mental ability and provided a theory of how cognitive skills could be taught. In Britain, while his colleagues around the world studied the learning behavior of laboratory animals in contrived settings, Bartlett (1932) produced the world's first empirical study of meaningful learning from prose by humans. A generation later, his revolutionary theory of learning based on assimilation to schema helped shape the rebirth of modern cognitive psychology and its implications for education. Similarly, in Switzerland, while his colleagues chronicled the physical and behavioral development of children, Piaget (see Flavell 1963) produced the world's most comprehensive body of research and theory on cognitive development. Piaget's view of humans as sense makers who assimilate new experiences to existing schemas eventually became a driving force in the rebirth of cognitive theories of learning and development.

In Russia, Vygotsky's (1978) landmark studies of the social construction of learning laid the groundwork for exciting innovations in current educational practice and became the centerpiece of an emerging theory of social constructivism. In the Netherlands, De Groot's (1965) classic study of expert chess players served as model for contemporary research on expertise, which is a central theme in cognitive science research on education. Overall, from the first educational intervention study based on the "Wild Boy of Aveyron" in France in the early 1800s (see Lane 1976) to today's international comparisons of educational achievement (Robitaille and Garden 1989), the field of instructional psychology has been enriched by the international diversity of perspectives of its contributing scholars.

Over the course of the twentieth century, North America has contributed the majority of instructional psychologists, and for this reason histories of instructional psychology may tend to underemphasize developments elsewhere in the world. Yet, the theoretical and methodological influences on instructional psychology have come and continue to come from a variety of nations. As it enters its second century as a scientific discipline, instructional psychology continues as a truly international discipline.

2. Three Phases in the Relation Between Psychology and Instruction

The history of instructional psychology during the twentieth century can be viewed as a search for the appropriate relation between psychological theory and instructional practice. Three phases in the relation over the course of the twentieth century can be characterized as a one-way street, a dead-end street, and a two-way street (Mayer 1992).

2.1 One-way Street

During the first half of the twentieth century, the appropriate relation between psychology and instruction was optimistically thought to be a one-way street in which advances in psychology would be applied to improve instructional practice. In his classic book, *The Principles of Teaching Based on Psychology*, Thorndike (1906 p. 257) eloquently presented his faith and confidence that the science of psychology could be used to improve the practice of education:

> The efficiency of any profession depends in large measure upon the degree to which it becomes scientific. The profession of teaching will improve. . .in proportion as its members direct their work by the scientific spirit and methods, that is by honest, open-minded consideration of the facts, by freedom from superstitions, fancies or unverified guesses, and. . .in proportion as the leaders in education direct their choices of methods by the results of scientific investigation rather than by general opinion.

Thus, as America's premier educational psychologist, Thorndike viewed educational psychology as what Cubberly (1920 p. 755) called a "guiding science of the school."

Similarly, in his famous lectures to American school teachers in the 1890s—later published as *Talks to Teachers*—William James (1958 p. 22) offered a vision of how to apply psychology to teaching:

> The desire of the schoolteachers for a completer professional training, and their aspiration toward the professional spirit in their work, have led more and more to turn to us for light on fundamental principles. And in the few hours which we are to spend together you look to me, I am sure, for information concerning the mind's operation, which may enable you to labor more easily and effectively in the several classrooms over which you preside.

In summary, at the turn of century hopes were high that the "proper application of psychological findings might lead the way to better instruction in all schools" (Woodring 1958 p. 6).

2.2 Dead-end Street

Unfortunately, proponents of the one-way-street approach underestimated the difficulties in applying psychology to education. First, the psychology of the early 1900s lacked a sufficient database about how people learn. For example, James (1958 p. 23) noted in the 1890s that "there is no new psychology worthy of the name." Second, even if there had been a research-based theory of human cognition, it could not have been directly applied to education because, as Bruner (1964) later noted, descriptive theories about how people learn do not translate directly into prescriptive theories about how to teach. James (1958 p. 23) warned teachers against thinking "that psychology, being a science of the mind's laws, is something from which you can deduce definite programmes and

schemes and methods of instruction for immediate classroom use."

By the middle of the twentieth century, the optimistic period of the one-way-street view had come to an end. It was replaced by the pessimism of a dead-end street view in which the relation between psychology and instruction was largely terminated. Psychologists busied themselves in conducting well-controlled studies of highly simplified learning situations, often involving the behavior of laboratory animals in contrived laboratory settings. Educators focused on the practical day-to-day problems of teaching without concern for basing educational decisions on research-based theory. Resnick (1983 p. 12) notes that during this period educational psychologists failed to clarify the provocative ideas of European scholars such as Wertheimer or Piaget: "Despite some elegant examples of the kinds of instructional goals that might be promoted, neither Gestaltist nor Piagetian analyses have proceeded very far in specifying these outcomes."

Grinder (1989) summarizes three reasons for the change: the withdrawal of psychologists from a commitment to contributing to educational policy, the irrelevance of psychological research that failed to study educational problems in natural settings, and the fractionation of psychological theory into a collection of unrelated doctrines. In short, during the dead-end-street period of the mid-twentieth century, the discipline of instructional psychology had lost its claim to being a guiding science for education.

2.3 Two-way Street

Beginning in the 1960s and accelerating in the 1980s and 1990s, psychology and instruction entered a new phase in their relationship—a two-way street in which the two fields contribute mutually to one another. Educational settings provide psychology with challenging issues to address, thus helping to bring psychological theories closer to the real world. In contrast to the failed attempts at building general theories of learning during the first half of the twentieth century (Bower and Hilgard 1981), the psychological theories of the 1990s focus on learning and cognition in subject matter domains. The emerging psychologies of subject matter represent a productive advance in psychological theory that is attributable to the demands of educators. Thus, instead of solely being a recipient of psychology's ideas, education has been a driving force in moving psychology from the fruitless search for general theories of learning in contrived settings to the fruitful study of cognition in more realistic academic settings (Neisser 1976). Similarly, as psychology has finally begun to generate theories that are relevant to education, educators have begun to find ways to apply psychological research in schools.

This third phase in the rocky relation between psychology and instruction has engendered a spirit of guarded optimism once again. For example, Wittrock

(1989 p. 75) predicts that "recent advances in the study of cognition will lead to a useful and prescriptive theory of instruction and teaching." Simon (1979) has shown how the emergence of cognitive psychology as a productive approach had its roots in European traditions including the Gestalt, Wurzburg, and Piagetian schools.

3. Three Metaphors of Learning and Instruction

Philosophers and historians of science have emphasized the role of metaphors and shown how "research in. . .scientific fields. . .is guided by a somewhat motley collection of models or metaphors" (Sternberg 1990 p. 3). Similarly, the development of instructional psychology can be viewed as a search for the most appropriate metaphor of learning. During the twentieth century three metaphors of learning have vied for dominance in guiding the discipline of instructional psychology: learning as response strengthening, learning as knowledge acquisition, and learning as knowledge construction (Mayer 1992). These are summarized in Table 1.

3.1 Learning as Response Strengthening

During the first half of the twentieth century the dominant metaphor was that learning involves the strengthening or weakening of responses, or more precisely, the strengthening or weakening of associations. For example, based largely on studies of animal learning in laboratory settings, Thorndike (1965) proposed the law of effect—the idea that a response that was followed by satisfaction to the learner would be more likely to be repeated under the same circumstances in the future whereas a response that was followed by dissatisfaction would be less likely to be produced in the future. In short, rewarding a response led automatically to a strengthening of the association between the situation and the response whereas punishing a response led automatically to a weakening of the association. The response-strengthening view has its roots in the philosophical tradition of associationism, as articulated by British empiricists such as Hobbes, Locke, Berkeley, and Hume (see Humphrey 1963, Mandler and Mandler 1964).

According to this view learners are passive recipients of rewards and punishments whereas teachers are dispensers of rewards and punishments. Under the response-strengthening metaphor drill-and-practice became a preferred method of instruction. In an extreme version of drill-and-practice called recitation, teachers ask a simple question requiring a short (usually one-word) answer and call on a student to produce an answer. A correct answer is rewarded with praise whereas an error is punished by criticism (or even physical punishment). Cuban (1984 p. 28) describes an early 1900s classroom in which "the teacher. . .had acquired a habit of conducting recitations at the rate of from 100 to 200 questions and answers per classroom period of 45 minutes." By taking the response-strengthening metaphor to an extreme, teachers who relied on recitation had become "drillmasters instead of educators" (Cuban 1984 p. 29).

3.2 Learning as Knowledge Acquisition

The response strengthening view was challenged on the grounds that it focused mainly on rote learning while ignoring meaningful learning, or to put it another way, that it explained retention but not transfer (Katona 1967, Wertheimer 1959). For example, (Katona 1967 p. 4–5) argued that "the main objection to the prevailing theory, which makes one kind of the connection the basis of all learning, is not that it may be incorrect but that in the course of psychological research it has prevented an unbiased study of other possible kinds of learning." The Gestalt psychologists offered a vision that included two kinds of learning: learning by rote, which led to retention but not transfer, and learning by understanding, which led to retention and transfer (Mayer 1995, Wertheimer 1959).

Following the rebirth of modern cognitive psychology in 1956 (see Gardner 1985), the dominance of the response strengthening view came to an end. Although the gestaltists were the first to offer a coherent alternative to the response-strengthening view, their vision of learning as a search for understanding was not widely accepted. The Gestalt vision failed to become the consensus metaphor of learning because

Table 1
Three metaphors of learning

Dominant period:	Learning is:	Learners are:	Teachers are:	Typical instructional methods are:
1900s to 1950s	Response strengthening	Recipients of rewards and punishments	Dispensers of rewards and punishments	Recitation and worksheets, drill-and-practice
1960s to 1970s	Knowledge acquisition	Information processors	Dispensers of knowledge	Lecturing and textbooks
1980s to 1990s	Knowledge construction	Sense makers	Cognitive guides	Discussion, guided discovery, guided participation in academic tasks

"they were right but they lacked a language to make their ideas clear" (Johnson-Laird 1988 p. 19). Instead, cognitive psychologists of the 1960s and 1970s based their new metaphor of learning on an emerging new technology—the electronic digital computer.

In comparing humans to computers, the symbolic format of information in computers becomes equated with knowledge in humans, and performing computations on symbols in computers becomes equated with human cognition (Lachman et al. 1979). Although the underlying organization of the digital computer differs greatly from that of the human brain, both computers and humans take in information and process it (Newman and Simon 1972). It follows that when information processing replaced behaviorism as the dominant approach to cognition, the knowledge-acquisition metaphor replaced the response-strengthening metaphor as the dominant metaphor of learning.

Based largely on research involving human learning in laboratory settings, the dominant view of the 1960s and 1970s became learning as knowledge acquisition. According to this view learners are information processors who take in information, perform mental operations on it, and store it in memory. Correspondingly, teachers are viewed as dispensers of information. In the most extreme forms of the knowledge-acquisition view, teachers are viewed as full of knowledge, students as empty vessels, and knowledge is seen as a commodity that is transmitted from the teacher to the student. Under the knowledge-acquisition metaphor the preferred methods of instruction involved lecturing and requiring students to read textbooks. Each discipline is broken into courses, each course into lessons, each lesson into specific pieces of information. Achievement tests are used to determine how much is learned.

3.3 Learning as Knowledge Construction

As researchers moved from studying human cognition in contrived laboratory settings to studying human cognition in more realistic settings, the information-processing view of learning as knowledge acquisition became increasing under attack. For example, Neisser (1976 p. xi) criticized information-processing research of the 1960s and 1970s on the grounds that it had become "disappointingly narrow, focusing inward on the analysis of specific experimental situations rather than outward toward the world beyond the laboratory." As researchers conducted research in more realistic settings—including educational settings—the constructivist nature of human learning became more apparent. Moving the venue of study to educationally-relevant settings enabled the revitalization of both cognitive psychology and instructional psychology.

By the 1980s and 1990s, the constructivist view of learning as knowledge construction emerged as a dominant metaphor. Constructivism has a long history in psychology, including the work of Piaget(see Flavell 1963) and Bartlett (1932) on assimilation to schema, the Gestalt psychologists' work on learning by understanding (Wertheimer 1959), and Dewey's (1902) classic arguments for a child-centred approach to education; yet, the knowledge-construction metaphor has become the consensus view only recently. According to this view, learning involves an active, self-guided search for understanding in which learners construct their own knowledge. Learners become sense makers and teachers become cognitive guides who help learners. The preferred modes of instruction include learner participation in meaningful academic tasks in which the teacher provides needed support and guidance. In addition, discussions of meaningful academic tasks replace lecturing as the dominant form of teacher–student interaction.

Like its predecessors, the cognitive–constructivist metaphor of 1980s and 1990s is subject to revision, including the incorporation of the social and cultural contexts of learning. Building on the landmark work of Vygotsky (1978), an emerging framework of social constructivism has the potential to yield a fourth metaphor of learning as social negotiation. Within the last decade, extensions of Vygotsky's ideas have influenced educational reform in his native Russia, and around the world (Das and Gindis 1995, Davydov 1995). Similarly, educational researchers have highlighted the cultural context of learning by demonstrating that children do not use school-taught procedures in carrying out mathematical computations outside of school (Nunes et al. 1993).

4. Conclusion

In summary, this historical overview of instructional psychology during the twentieth century reflects three themes. First, instructional psychology has been an international discipline that has been enriched by theoretical and methodological contributions from scholars around the world. Second, the relation between the fields of psychology and instruction has progressed from a one-way street in which psychology was applied to instruction, to a dead-end street in which psychology and instruction did not communicate, to a two-way street in which the two fields mutually benefit one another. Third, the dominant metaphor of learning underlying psychological theory and educational practice has progressed from response strengthening in which learners are passive recipients of rewards and punishments, to knowledge acquisition in which learners are recipients of information, to knowledge construction in which learners are sense makers who actively build their own knowledge.

Instructional psychology shows every sign of continued accomplishments in the future, including advancements in psychologies of subject matter, in the assessment of individual differences, in the fostering of learning strategies, and in understanding the social, cultural, and motivational contexts of learning.

References

Bartlett F C 1932 *Remembering* Cambridge University Press, Cambridge

Bower G H, Hilgard E R 1981 *Theories of Learning*, 5th edn. Prentice-Hall, Englewood Cliffs, New Jersey

Bruner J S 1964 Some theorems on instruction illustrated with reference to mathematics. In Hilgard E (ed.) 1964 *The Sixty-third Yearbook of the National Society for the Study of Education. Part 1: Theories of Learning and Instruction*. National Society for the Study of Education, Chicago, Illinois

Cuban L 1984 *How Teachers Taught*. Longman, New York

Cubberly E P 1920 *The History of Education*. Houghton Mifflin, Boston, Massachusetts

Das J P, Gindis B (eds.) 1995 Lev S. Vygotsky and contemporary educational psychology (special issue) *Educ. Psychol.* 30: 55–104

Davydov V V 1995 The influence of L.S. Vygotski on education theory, research, and practice. *Educ. Researcher* 24(3): 12–21

De Groot A D 1965 *Thought and Choice in Chess*. Mouton, The Hague

Dewey J 1902 *The Child and the Curriculum*. University of Chicago Press, Chicago, Illinois

Duncker K 1945 On problem solving. *Psychological Monographs* 58:5 Whole No. 270

Ebbinghaus H 1964 *Memory*. Dover, New York

Flavell J H 1963 *The Developmental Psychology of Jean Piaget*. Van Nostrand, Princeton, New Jersey

Frijda N H, De Groot A D (eds.) 1982 *Otto Selz: His Contribution to Psychology*. Mouton, The Hague

Gardner H 1985 *The Mind's New Science*. Basic Books, New York

Grinder R E 1989 Educational psychology: The master science. In: Wittrock M C, Farley F (eds.) 1989 *The Future of Educational Psychology*. Erlbaum, Hillsdale, New Jersey

Humphrey G 1963 *Thinking: An Introduction to its Experimental Psychology*. Wiley, New York

James W 1958 *Talks to Teachers*. Norton, New York

Johnson-Laird P N 1988 *The Computer and the Mind*. Harvard University Press, Cambridge, Massachusetts

Katona G 1967 *Organizing and Memorizing*. Hafner, New York

Lachman R, Lachman J L, Butterfield E C 1979 *Cognitive Psychology and Information Processing: An Introduction*. Erlbaum, Hillsdale, New Jersey

Lane H 1976 *The Wild Boy of Aveyron*. Harvard University Press, Cambridge, Massachusetts

Mandler J M, Mandler G 1964 *Thinking: From Association to Gestalt*. Wiley, New York

Mayer R E 1992 Cognition and instruction: Their historic meeting within educational psychology. *J. Educ. Psychol.* 84: 405–12

Mayer R E 1995 The search for insight: Grappling with Gestalt psychology's unanswered questions. In Sternberg R J, Davidson J E (eds.) 1995 *The Nature of Insight*. MIT Press, Cambridge, Massachusetts

Neisser U 1976 *Cognition and Reality*. Freeman, New York

Newell A, Simon H A 1972 *Human Problem Solving*. Prentice-Hall, Englewood Cliffs, New Jersey

Nunes T, Schliemann A D, Carraher D W 1993 *Street Mathematics and School Mathematics*. Cambridge University Press, Cambridge

Resnick L B 1983 Toward a cognitive theory of instruction. In: Paris S G, Olson G M, Stevenson H W (eds.) 1983 *Learning and Motivation in the Classroom*. Erlbaum, Hillsdale, New Jersey

Robitaille D F, Garden R A (eds.) 1989 *The IEA Study of Mathematics II: Contexts and Outcomes of School Mathematics*. Pergamon Press, Oxford

Simon H A 1979 Information processing models of cognition. *Annu. Rev. Psychol.* 30: 363–96

Sternberg R J 1990 *Metaphors of Mind*. Cambridge University Press, Cambridge

Thorndike E L 1906 *The Principles of Teaching Based on Psychology*. Mason-Henry Press, Syracuse, New York

Thorndike E L 1965 *Animal Intelligence*. Hafner, New York

Vygotsky L S 1978 *Mind in Society*. Harvard University Press, Cambridge, Massachusetts

Wertheimer M 1959 *Productive Thinking*. Harper & Row, New York

Wittrock M C 1989 Educational psychology and the future of research in learning, instruction, and teaching. In: Wittrock M C, Farley F (eds.) 1989 *The Future of Educational Psychology*. Erlbaum, Hillsdale, New Jersey

Wolf T H 1973 *Alfred Binet*. University of Chicago Press, Chicago, Illinois

Woodring P 1958 Introduction. In: James W 1958

Instructional Psychology: Overview

E. De Corte

Instructional psychology is defined here as the study of the processes and outcomes of human learning in a variety of educational and instructional settings, and of the nature and the design of environments that are appropriate to elicit and keep going those learning processes aiming at the attainment of competence, and of a disposition toward skilled learning, thinking, and problem solving in a given domain. The term "instructional psychology" was introduced in 1969 by Gagné and Rohwer (1969) as the title of their literature review in the *Annual Review of Psychology* of a field of inquiry indicated until then as "educational psychology." Today one can say that while educational psychology is somewhat broader in scope than instructional psychology—involving, for instance, psychological aspects of childrearing in the family—both terms cover largely the same domain of research, because most work has been done on studying knowledge and skill acquisition in instructional settings. A major reason for this state-of-the-art is that since the 1960s there has been a growing convergence between the psychology of learning and instruction, on the one hand, and cognitive science, on the other. Indeed as a result of this convergence the mainstream of theory and research has focused on the analysis of knowledge, performance, and competence in a variety of complex cognitive task domains. And, as a consequence instructional psychology has during the 1980s "become a vigorous part of the mainstream of research on human cognition and development" (Glaser and Bassock 1989 p. 631).

A comprehensive review of this extensive field of research is outside the scope of this entry. Snow and Swanson (1992 p. 584) have distinguished five essential components in a theory of learning from instruction: "(a) description of desired end states or goals of instruction in a domain; (b) description of goal-relevant initial states of learners prior to instruction; (c) explication of the transition processes from initial to desired states; (d) specification of instructional conditions that promote this transition; and (e) assessment of performance and instructional effects." After a short historical overview of major trends in research on learning and instruction during the twentieth century, this entry will selectively focus on recent work relating mainly to three of these components, namely desired end states, transition processes, and instructional conditions. The entries in Parts VIII to XVI of this *Encyclopedia* provide complementary information on those and also the remaining two components (initial states of learners and assessment). For an even broader and more thorough overview of the field, especially from an Anglo-Saxon perspective, the reader is referred to the series of review articles in the *Annual Review of Psychology* (especially those from 1981 onwards: Resnick 1981, Gagne and Dick 1983, Pintrich et al. 1986, Glaser and Bassok 1989, Weinstein 1991, Snow and Swanson 1992, Voss et al. 1995), and to the first *Handbook of Educational Psychology* (Berliner and Calfee 1996). To get a more comprehensive idea of European research one can consult the series of edited volumes that involve a selection of reviewed chapters reporting work presented at the first three European Conferences for Research on Learning and Instruction (De Corte et al. 1987, Mandl et al. 1990, Carretero et al. 1991, and the periodicals *European Journal of Psychology of Education* (published since 1986), and *Learning and Instruction. The Journal of the European Association for Research on Learning and Instruction* (since 1991).

1. The History of Instructional Psychology in a Nutshell

The history of research on learning and instruction can be traced back to the beginning of the twentieth century. At that time the whole field of psychology was dominated by the associationist approach with Thorndike as the main representative. This was followed in the middle of the century by the behaviorist tradition led by Skinner. Within these two traditions a tremendous amount of research on learning has been carried out, but mainly in laboratory situations using nonacademic, often very artificial and even meaningless learning tasks and materials such as nonsense words or syllables. Nevertheless, the principles derived from those experiments were generalized to meaningful learning in the classroom, taking for granted the universal validity of the so-called laws of learning. And these laws in turn constituted the basis for instructional interventions. In other words, associationism as well as behaviorism gave rise to the elaboration of a comprehensive theory of instruction, encompassing three out of the five components distinguished by Snow and Swanson (1992), namely methods for specifying desired end states, a general theory of transition or learning processes, and methods and conditions for instruction (Resnick 1983).

The European counterparts of associationism and behaviorism in the first part of this century were the Gestalt psychology and the Würzburg school of psychology. Both schools strongly disagreed with the behaviorist conception of psychology as a science of behavior, and were instead interested in the structure of knowledge and the processes of thinking. For instance, Selz analysed thinking as a dynamic event, and showed that it entails organized structures (see Frijda and De Groot 1981).

Although behaviorism became well-known also in Europe, this school has never been as dominant as in the United States. To the contrary, the typical European ideas remained more influential, especially in connection with education. Moreover, somewhat later in the century two other theories have had a great impact on educational psychology, namely Piaget's (1950) developmental psychology, and Vygotsky's (1978, see also Davydov 1995) activity theory.

While the Gestaltists, the Würzburgers, and Piaget made interesting contributions to our better understanding of the kinds of cognitive skills that education should pursue, they had not much to offer with respect to a theory of learning and of instructional intervention (Resnick 1983). To the contrary, the Vygotskyan school elaborated a more comprehensive instructional theory, based on investigations that—in comparison to the behaviorist studies—score high in terms of ecological validity, but rather low in terms of methodological rigor. Major contributions within the Vygotskyan tradition have been made by scholars like Gal'perin (see De Corte 1977) and Davydov (1990).

Meanwhile, American psychology had undergone a major change, namely the shift from behaviorism toward cognitive psychology. In this latter view, man is no longer conceived of as a collection of responses toward external stimuli but essentially as an information processor. This important development in American psychology was initiated in the late 1950s, and was influenced by Würzburg and Gestalt psychology (Simon 1979). This so-called information-processing approach has since the 1960s become also dominant in instructional psychology. In this approach one is no longer satisfied with studying externally observable behavior, but instead tries to analyze the mental processes and cognitive structures that underly performance. This is attended with a fundamentally changed conception of the nature of human cognition, namely a shift from an atomistic toward a Gestalt view that considers the organization of knowledge as the central characteristic of cognition. In contrast to behaviorism, this approach has strongly influenced Western European research on learning and instruction (see e.g., De Corte et al. 1987). Of special significance in this regard was the NATO International Conference on Cognitive Psychology and Instruction, held in Amsterdam in 1977 (see Lesgold et al. 1978). Interestingly, during the 1970s the Vygotskyan activity-oriented view became also influential in some other parts of Europe than the socialist countries, especially The Netherlands and the Nordic countries (see e.g., Hedegaard et al. 1984).

An additional trend in instructional psychology in Europe has to be mentioned here, namely the phenomenographic approach initiated by Marton at the University of Gothenburg, and applied especially in Sweden, the United Kingdom, and Australia. Phenomenography is a qualitative approach to learning based on in-depth interviews with students in which their own learning intentions and experiences while learning complex materials, are systematically explored and analyzed (Marton 1981).

Finally, in the late 1980s an important new development emerged in cognitive science in the United States under the impulse of scholars like John Seely Brown, Allan Collins, and Jim Greeno (Brown et al. 1989, Collins et al. 1989, Greeno 1989). To overcome some shortcomings of the then prevailing information-processing view, they called for the adoption of the situated cognition and learning paradigm. Remarkably, this new framework for the study of cognition was strongly influenced by constructs and ideas of activity theorists like Vygotsky and Leontiev, and also by ethnographic anthropological research (Rogoff and Lave 1984). The major criticism of the information-processing approach is that it considers thinking as a process that takes place within the mind (Greeno 1989), and knowledge as a self-sufficient substance, independent of the situations in which it is acquired and applied (Brown et al. 1989). In contrast, in the new paradigm thinking is conceived of as an interactive activity between the individual and a situation, and knowledge is situated, "being in part a product of the activity, context, and culture in which it is developed and used" (Brown et al. 1989 p. 32). In between the situated cognition model has been elaborated somewhat differently by several theorists (Gruber et al. in press), and it raises many questions

that need further research in view of verifying the paradigm's validity and applicability for learning in educational settings. Nevertheless, it looks as if the situated cognition and learning model involves the potential to usher in a unifying trend in research on learning and instruction not only overarching the information-processing and activity-oriented approaches but also the phenomenographic viewpoint (Entwistle and Marton 1989).

2. Toward a Dispositional View of Competence as Desired End State

While during the behaviorist era learning was a prominent issue in psychological research, with the advent of cognitive science the focus shifted toward the study of the structures and processes of human competence and expertise in an attempt to answer questions concerning the representation and organization of knowledge, the nature and characteristics of understanding, and the knowledge and cognitive skills involved in competent problem solving. Representative of this domain of inquiry is the vast amount of research in which expertise in a large variety of content domains was analyzed by comparing the performance of experts and novices (see e.g., Chi et al. 1988, *Expert Level of Understanding*). This work has resulted in the identification of critical aspects of expert performance which generalize over the domains that were studied. These findings are at the same time relevant from an educational perspective, because they contribute to the clarification and definition of the primary goals of learning in different instructional and training settings. Indeed, taking into account the results of the analyses of expertise, there is now a fairly broad consensus that becoming skilled in a given domain requires the integrated acquisition of the following four categories of aptitudes (for a more detailed discussion see Bruer 1993, De Corte 1995, Perkins and Salomon 1989, Pintrich et al. 1993):

(a) A well-organized and flexibly accessible domain-specific knowledge base, involving the facts, formulas, concepts, rules, principles, etc., that constitute the substance of a subject-matter field.

(b) Heuristic methods, i.e., search strategies for problem analysis (such as decomposing a problem into subgoals) that do not guarantee but significantly increase the probability of finding the right solution, because they induce a systematic approach to the problem.

(c) Metacognition which involves knowledge and beliefs about one's own cognitive functioning, on the one hand (e.g., believing that one's cognitive ability can be developed and improved through learning and effort), and skills and strategies relating to the self-regulation of one's own cognitive processes, on the other (e.g., monitoring an ongoing problem-solving process).

(d) Affective components such as beliefs, attitudes, and emotions relating to a subject-matter field (e.g., believing that solving a problem is a mindful and effortful activity versus believing that it is a matter of being lucky).

Notwithstanding the rather broad consensus about the importance of those four categories of aptitudes in skilled performance, several related issues and questions have been and are still under dispute in the literature. Major examples are: What is the relative importance of domain-specific knowledge versus general cognitive skills in expert performance? How do affective components relate to and interact with the cognitive aspects involved in learning and performance? How can the phenomenon of inert knowledge be explained; in other words, why do students fail to use and apply their acquired knowledge—which can be recalled on request—in situations where it is relevant and appropriate to do so? The latter issue is narrowly related to the issue of transfer: To what degree can knowledge acquired in one context be transferred to novel learning tasks and problem situations?

In the early days of cognitive science investigations in laboratory settings using mainly knowledge-lean tasks showed the important role of general cognitive skills, such as heuristic strategies, in skilled problem solving (Newell and Simon 1972). But starting in the mid-1970s a large series of expert–novice studies in semantically rich content domains demonstrated the significant role of domain-specific knowledge in expert performance (Chi et al. 1988). Yet, continued research in the 1980s evidenced that domain-specific knowledge could not fully account for human expertise, and showed that metacognitive, self-regulatory skills are a major determinant of successful learning and skilled thinking (Brown et al. 1983, Wang et al. 1993). Disputes about the relative importance of domain-bound knowledge versus domain-general strategies and skills accompanying this development (see e.g., Perkins 1995), seem to come more or less to an end. Indeed, it has become obvious that it is a false dichotomy (Sternberg 1989), because domain-specific knowledge and more general heuristic and metacognitive strategies play a complementary and interactive role in competent learning, thinking, and problem solving. Therefore, most scholars now endorse the viewpoint that "we should combine the learning of domain-specific subject matter with the learning of general thinking skills, while also making sure that children learn to monitor and control their thinking and learning" (Bruer 1993 p. 52; see also Alexander and Judy 1988, Perkins 1995, Perkins and Solomon 1989, Pressley et al. 1989). Furthermore, research on conceptual change has shown that knowledge and skill acquisition, for instance in the physical sciences, can be constrained by presuppositions and beliefs involved in children's naive theories of the physical world (Vosniadou 1994).

The available evidence shows that the integrated acquisition of domain-related knowledge and general cognitive skills is certainly a necessary, but not yet a sufficient condition to overcome the well-known phenomenon of inert knowledge (see e.g., Bransford and Stein 1993, Perkins 1995). In other words, expert performance entails more than the sum of the different categories of aptitudes mentioned above; it requires in addition a disposition toward skilled learning, thinking, and problem solving. According to Perkins (1995, see also Perkins et al. 1993) the notion of a disposition involves besides ability and motivation two other crucial components, namely sensitivity and inclination. Sensitivity refers to the feeling for and alertness to task and problem situations in which it is relevant and useful to apply acquired knowledge and skills, while inclination is the tendency to do so whenever appropriate. This dispositional conception of expertise accounts for the phenomenon of inert knowledge: students often possess the ability to perform certain tasks or to solve problems, but they do not exercise them because of lack of spontaneous inclination and sensitivity.

Especially since the beginning of the 1990s it has been properly observed by several authors, that due to the dominance of the information-processing approach instructional psychology has studied cognition and learning too one-sidedly from a cognitive perspective. As a consequence, researchers have begun to pay more and more attention to building connections between the affective, emotional and motivational aspects of learning on the one hand, and the cognitive components on the other (see e.g., Boekaerts 1992, Helmke 1989, Pintrich et al. 1993). In this respect the dispositional view of skilled learning and thinking offers a useful framework for the integration of both kinds of aptitudes, in the sense that the sensitivity and inclination aspects of the disposition can be conceived of as interfaces or mediators between the cognitive and the affective components. There is no doubt that this view needs validation in future research; however, drawing on the available literature, several illustrations can already be given. For instance, Dweck (1989) has introduced the already well-known distinction in motivational theory between two types of goal orientation: learning goals (aiming at increasing one's competence and mastering new tasks) versus performance goals (aiming at validating one's competence and obtaining favorable judgments of one's ability). Correlational research has shown that these two kinds of goal orientation can lead to differences in students' cognitive approach to and involvement in tasks and problems (Pintrich et al. 1993). It is plausible that this can be accounted for by the fact that a different goal orientation induces a distinct inclination to use one's cognitive potential. A second example is that students' inclination and sensitivity to apply available knowledge can be blocked by emotional barriers. As argued by Boekaerts (1992), confronted with a task or a problem that evokes negative expectations and/or feelings, students will develop a coping intention rather than a learning intention: they are not oriented toward learning or mastery, but primarily concerned about restoring their well-being. It is only after regaining their well-being that a learning intention can emerge, and, consequently, the sensitivity and inclination aspects of the disposition can mediate the application of the cognitive potential.

Being able to transfer acquired knowledge and skills to new learning tasks and problem situations is widely considered as an important goal of education. therefore, it is not surprising that since the early days of instructional psychology the issue of transfer has repeatedly been in the main focus of research on learning and instruction. As shown, for instance, by the publication of a series of books in the 1980s and 1990s, there has recently been a strong upsurge in the interest in the topic among researchers (Cormier and Hagman 1987, Detterman and Sternberg 1993, McKeough et al. 1995, Singley and Anderson 1989). This literature shows that transfer is a very complex phenomenon, that transfer effects do not occur spontaneously, and are even difficult to obtain deliberately. The latter findings have been accounted for by some scholars by the robust result of the analysis of expertise referred to above, namely that competence in a domain depends largely on the availability of a well-organized domain-specific knowledge base. This interpretation was reinforced by the recent view that learning is situated (Brown et al. 1989), and, thus, context-bound. Yet, another explanation does not deny the significance of domain-related knowledge for skilled performance, but stresses that the lack of transfer in many studies is mainly due to the absence of the appropriate conditions needed for transfer to occur (Perkins and Salomon 1989). These conditions relate to characteristics of the learners (subject variables) to features of the tasks (task variables), and to the nature of instruction (instructional variables) (De Corte in press). With respect to the subject variables, it is plausible that the acquisition of the sensitivity and inclination aspects of a disposition to competent learning and thinking is of crucial importance in view of facilitating and mediating transfer of knowledge and skills in students. It is interesting in this respect to mention that lately Bereiter (1995) has elaborated a dispositional view of transfer. With regard to teaching variables, recent studies in which appropriate instructional conditions were designed and implemented, have shown that significant transfer can occur (see e.g., Adley and Shayer 1993, Campione et al. 1995). For a more detailed discussion of the transfer issue, the reader is referred to *Transfer of Learning*.

3. Constructive Learning as Lever for the Transition from Initial to Desired End State

Due to the strong emphasis of cognitive psychological research on the analysis of performance, the study of learning was largely depressed in the early days of the information-processing approach (Glaser and Bassok 1989). But the scene has changed since then, and at present many researchers in the field of instructional psychology show an active interest in learning processes (see e.g., the special issue of the *Review of Educational Research* edited by Iran-Nejad et al. 1990). Moreover, their work has been enriched by contributions from research on learning in nonschool settings, such as anthropological studies of apprenticeships and investigations in corporate and industrial contexts. From this research a series of characteristics of effective and meaningful learning processes have emerged that constitute building blocks for what Bereiter (1990) has called an educational learning theory. Those characteristics about which there is nowadays a rather broad consensus in the literature (see e.g., Brown and Campione 1994, Shuell 1992) can be summarized in the following definition of learning: it is a constructive, cumulative, self-regulated, goal-directed, situated, collaborative, and individually different process of meaning construction and knowledge building.

3.1 Learning is Constructive

Research in the 1980s and 1990s has convincingly shown that learning is an effortful and mindful process, in which students actively construct their own knowledge and skills through reorganization of their already acquired mental structures in interaction with the environment (Steffe and Gale 1995). This overarching characteristic of learning is, for instance, evidenced in a negative way in the misconceptions and defective procedures that many learners acquire in a variety of content domains, such as mathematics, physics, computer programming, history, etc. (see *Preconceptions and Misconceptions*, Perkins and Simmons 1988). Some scholars take an extreme or radical position in this respect claiming that all knowledge is a subjective and purely idiosyncratic cognitive construction, whereas others represent a more moderate or realistic point of view that allows for the possibility of mediating learning through appropriate intervention and guidance (see *Constructivism and Learning*). Notwithstanding the large variety in theoretical perspectives along the radical–moderate dimension, the constructivist view certainly implies that acquiring knowledge and skills requires active cognitive processing from the side of the learner.

3.2 Learning is Cumulative

This characteristic stresses the important impact of student's formal as well as informal knowledge on subsequent learning (see *Prior Knowledge and Learning, Preconceptions and Misconceptions,* Dochy 1992). In fact, this feature is implied in constructive nature of learning. Indeed, it is on the basis of what they already know and can do that students select and process actively the information they encounter, and, as a consequence, build new meanings and acquire new skills. Due to the fact that—as mentioned above—students are sometimes afflicted by misconceptions, the influence of prior knowledge on learning can be negative and inhibitory instead of positive and facilitating.

3.3 Learning is Self-regulated

This feature refers to the metacognitive nature of effective learning, and is also implied in the constructive perspective. Indeed, self-regulation means that students manage and monitor their own processes of knowledge building and skill acquisition (see *Self-regulation in Learning,* Schunk and Zimmerman 1994). Skilled self-regulation facilitates appropriate decision-making during learning (e.g., looking up a formula, a concept, or a principle; reconsidering or restructuring a problem situation; making a tentative estimation of the expected outcome), as well as the monitoring of an ongoing learning process by providing one's own feedback and performance evaluations, and by keeping oneself concentrated and motivated. The more students become self-regulated, the more they assume control and agency over their learning; consequently they are less dependent on external, instructional support for performing those regulatory activities.

An additional argument for promoting students' self-regulation of their learning derives from the finding, that high levels of metacognition facilitate the transfer of acquired knowledge and skills to new learning tasks and problems. In other words, students having good metacognitive awareness and strategies seem to be more able at using what they have learned in multiple ways to approach unfamiliar problems and situations (Brown 1989).

3.4 Learning is Goal-oriented

Notwithstanding the occurrence of incidental learning, it is generally agreed upon that effective and meaningful learning is facilitated by an explicit awareness of, and orientation toward a goal (Bereiter and Scardamalia 1989). Because of its constructive and self-regulated nature, it is plausible to assume that learning will be most productive when students choose and determine their own objectives. Therefore, it is desirable to stimulate and support goal-setting activities in students, or—in the terms of Dweck (1989) referred to in the previous section—to promote in them an orientation toward learning goals. But, learning can also be successful and productive when objectives are

put forward by a teacher, a textbook, or a computer program, on the condition, however, that those goals are accepted and adopted by the students so that they generate in them a real learning intention.

3.5 Learning is Situated and Collaborative

As mentioned already in the historical section, the conception that learning and cognition are situated emerged in reaction to the mentalistic view of learning and thinking as highly individual and purely cognitive processes occurring in the head, and resulting in the construction of mental representations. In contrast, situativity theory proposes a contextualized and social conception of learning and thinking: learning is enacted essentially in interaction with the social and cultural context and artefacts, and especially through participation in cultural activities and contexts (Lave and Wenger 1991). In other words, learning is not a purely "solo" activity, but essentially a distributive one, i.e. the learning effort is distributed over the individual student, his partners in the learning environment, and the resources and tools that are available (Salomon 1993). This situated perspecitive obviously implies the necessity to anchor learning into authentic, real-life social and physical contexts. It also involves clearly the importance of collaboration in productive learning, reflected in such activities as exchanging ideas, comparing solution strategies, and discussing arguments. Of special significance is that interaction and cooperation induce and mobilize reflection, and, thus, foster the development of metacognitive knowledge and strategies, and the self-regulation of learning. Of course, productive interaction and collaboration suppose mastery of social and communication skills which in themselves have to be acquired (see *Social and Communication Skills*).

3.6 Learning is Individually Different

The processes and outcomes of learning vary among students due to individual differences in a diversity of aptitudes that affect learning, such as conceptions of and approaches to learning, learning potential, prior knowledge, cognitive styles, learning strategies, interest, motivation, self-efficacy, self-worth, etc. (see Part XII of this volume on Individual Differences and Learning and Instruction). In order to induce productive learning in students instruction should take these differences into account. For instance, using the phenomenographic theoretical framework and methodology, Marton and his colleagues identified different conceptions of and approaches to learning in university students (Marton et al. 1984, Entwistle et al. 1993). A basic distinction in this respect is between a deep and a surface approach to learning. Students adopting a deep approach intend to understand the learning material; they try to relate new information to previous knowledge and search for relations within it. In contrast, surface learners focus on memorizing information in view of mere reproduction. Not surprisingly, the investigators found that in terms of learning outcomes students having a deep approach outperformed the surface learners.

Especially relevant in the framework of a modern theory of learning from instruction are differences in students' learning potential which reflect the variability in their zone of proximal development (Vygotsky 1978). This latter concept refers to those activities and performances that a child cannot yet carry out autonomously, but can achieve with the support of an adult or a peer (in other words, as a distributed activity). The relevance of this notion lies herein that instead of linking up instruction to students' current level of development—as measured by traditional intelligence and achievement tests—one should focus on their zone of proximal development. This means that instruction should: (a) help learners to master independently the performances that constitute this zone at a given moment; (b) stimulate cognitive growth by creating new zones of proximal development. Learning potential tests are a new type of assessment instrument to diagnose students' zone of proximal development (see *Learning Potential and Learning Potential Tests*).

Stressing the preceding features of productive learning processes does not imply that all learning at all times can or should involve all those characteristics. For instance, accentuating the importance of social interaction and collaboration does not exclude the possibility that students also acquire new knowledge individually. On the other hand, if one intends to foster in students the disposition toward competent learning and thinking outlined in the previous section, it will be necessary to elicit in them acquisition processes that embody to a substantial degree and in a variety of combinations those aspects of effective learning.

4. Powerful Teaching–Learning Environments to Promote the Transition to the Desired End State

Powerful teaching–learning environments create the appropriate instructional conditions to evoke in students learning activities and processes that facilitate the transition from their initial state toward the disposition to productive learning, thinking, and problem solving. Therefore, a challenging task for instructional psychology research consists of elaborating and validating a coherent framework of principles for the design of such powerful learning environments. Starting from our current knowledge and understanding of skilled performance in a variety of content domains (as described in Sect. 2) and of the characteristic of effective acquisition processes (see Sect. 3), but also based on observation of the practice of excellent teachers, over the past years researchers have begun to address this challenge. A promising approach in

this respect seems to consist in the creation and evaluation in real classrooms of complex instructional interventions guided by design principles that embody this present understanding of competence, of effective learning processes, and of successful teaching. Major examples of such orienting principles for the design of powerful learning environments are the following (De Corte 1995):

(a) Learning environments should initiate and support constructive and self-regulated acquisition processes in all students, thus, also in the more passive learners. However, from a realistic constructivist perspective students' construction of knowledge and skills can be mediated through appropriate guidance by teachers, peers, and educational media such as educational software. In other words, the claim that productive learning requires good teaching still holds true. But, this first principle also implies that systematic interventions should gradually be removed, so that students become progressively agents of their own learning.

(b) Complementary to the first principle, learning environments should allow for the flexible adaptation of instructional support, especially the balance between self-regulation and external regulation, to take into account individual differences in cognitive as well as in affective and motivational aptitudes. Moreover, the crucial influence on learning of motivated factors points to the necessity of balancing instructional interventions and affective support (Boekaerts 1992).

(c) Taking into account the situated and collaborative nature of effective learning, powerful learning environments should embed students' constructive acquisition processes as much as possible in authentic, real-life contexts that have personal meaning for the learners, that offer ample opportunities for distributed learning through social interaction and cooperation, and that are representative of the tasks to which students will have to apply their knowledge and skills in the future. Acquisition of a disposition to skilled learning and thinking, especially the inclination and sensitivity aspects of this disposition, will require extensive experience and practice with the different aptitudes involved in it in a large variety of situations.

(d) Because domain-specific knowledge and domain-general heuristic and metacognitive strategies play a complementary role in competent learning and problem solving, learning environments should create opportunities to acquire general cognitive skills embedded in different subject-matter domains.

Cognitive apprenticeship (Collins et al. 1989) and developmental instruction (Van Parreren 1988) are two models for the design of learning environments that are largely in accordance with those principles. For instance, cognitive apprenticeship—the model that has become most influential in the early 1990s—describes four dimensions that constitute a learning environment: content, teaching methods, sequence of learning tasks, and social context of learning. With respect to content an ideal learning environment should focus on the acquisition of all categories of knowledge that experts master and apply, namely domain-specific knowledge, heuristic methods, metacognitive skills, and learning strategies. To help students to acquire those different categories of knowledge and skills, the teacher can apply six different teaching methods: modelling, coaching, scaffolding, articulation, reflection, and exploration. The model specifies three principles for sequencing the learning tasks: increasing complexity, increasing diversity, and performing global before local skills. Finally, five guidelines are given for creating a favorable social context for learning: situated learning, opportunities for observation of experts, enhancing intrinsic motivation, fostering cooperative learning, and comparing problem-solving processes and strategies.

Although further research is needed to validate the design principles described above, a series of intervention studies in a variety of content domains that embody those guidelines to some degree, have already reported supporting empirical evidence. In many cases these investigations also attempt to integrate educational technology, especially computer programs and, more recently, multi-media systems, in their learning environments. Space restrictions do not allow here an extensive review of the major examples of such intervention studies. Therefore, the most well-known projects will be mentioned briefly, and one program will be discussed in some detail, namely Brown and Campione's (1994) "Fostering Communities of Learners" project (see also Bruer 1993).

In the domain of mathematics several successful investigations with students of different age levels have been carried out (see also De Corte et al. 1996): Schoenfeld's (1985) heuristic teaching of problem solving in geometry at the college level; anchored instruction of mathematical problem solving in the higher grades of the primary school, designed by the Cognition and Technology Group at Vanderbilt (1992); Cobb's second-grade mathematics project (see Wood et al. 1995); and, Realistic Mathematics Education in the primary school (Streefland 1991). Anchored instruction is an example of technology-based program: instruction is anchored in videodisc-based complex problem spaces that provide a richer, more authentic, and more dynamic presentation of information than textual material; the videodisc (such as *The Adventures of Jasper Woodbury* which relates to planning journeys) creates an environment for cooperative learning and discussion in small groups, as well as for individual and whole-class problem solving. Although Realistic Mathematics Education was founded in the early 1970s, it clearly involves a number of features of effective acquisition processes and design principles for powerful learning environments that emerged from more recent research.

ThinkerTools is a computer-supported curriculum to teach Newton's laws about force and motion to sixth-graders (White 1993). The computer part of the curriculum is a microworld that allows children to simulate physical phenomena, and to design experiments to discover the laws that describe those phenomena. As such the microworld offers opportunities for active learning based on everyday experience and prior knowledge, and it stimulates group cooperation and group discussion. White has shown that sixth-graders taught with ThinkerTools acquired a better understanding of Newton's laws than high school students in a traditional curriculum.

CSILE (Computer-Supported Intentional Learning Environment) has grown out of research by Scardamalia, Bereiter, and their co-workers in the mid-1980s on computer-based learning and teaching of writing, focussing on enhancing primary school children's metacognitive activities during the planning and revising phases of text production (Scardamalia et al. 1984). Building on the positive results of that work they have elaborated their system into a domain-independent hypermedia environment that can be used as an educational medium throughout the curriculum (Scardamalia and Bereiter 1992). The system allows students to build and elaborate their own, common database consisting of text and graphical material relating to problems and topics under study. All students have access to the database and they can comment on each others notes. This latter feature of the environment aims at inducing collaborative problem solving and knowledge construction in the classroom.

The "Fostering Communities of Learners" project initiated by Brown, Campione and their co-workers is certainly one of the most representative examples of a research-based attempt at totally changing the classroom environment. While their approach intends to contribute to the optimization of classroom practices, the primary goal is to advance theory building. Basic components of the learning environment are: reciprocal teaching, the jigsaw method of cooperative learning, and the creation of a new classroom culture (Brown and Campione 1994, Campione et al. 1995).

Reciprocal teaching creates a learning environment in which a small group of students is provided guided practice in acquiring four cognitive strategies in view of enhancing reading comprehension: asking questions, summarizing, clarifying comprehension difficulties, and making predictions about the future content of a text. A major feature of reciprocal teaching is that it takes the form of a dialogue in which the teacher and the pupils take turns in leading the discussion. Initially the teacher uses modeling to show how the strategies can be applied in reading a text. As the pupils progress in mastering the strategies, they gradually take a greater share and more responsibility in the dialogues; the teacher continues to provide coaching and scaffolding whenever necessary, and stimulates articulation of and reflection on the ongoing reading activities.

The jigsaw method implies that small *research* groups of pupils first study each a subtopic of a broader theme (e.g., developments in Central and Eastern Europe); afterwards they regroup into *learning* groups in which each pupil is the expert in one subtopic, so that by combining their knowledge they all learn about the whole theme.

A new classroom culture is created based on four qualities: an atmosphere of individual responsibility coupled with communal sharing; mutual respect between students and between students and teachers; establishment of a community of discourse that facilitates constructive discussion, questioning, and criticism; and a restricted number of participant structures (reciprocal teaching being one of them) that are frequently practised. Brown and Campione have already reported positive effects of their learning environment on the acquisition of domain-specific knowledge, on critical thinking about the content of a domain, on reading comprehension, and on the transfer of explanation and argumentation skills (Brown and Campione 1994, Campione et al. 1995).

5. Conclusion

The preceding selective, and, thus, incomplete review shows that in the 1980s and 1990s research in the field of instructional psychology has made substantial progress toward the elaboration of a theory of learning from instruction. Indeed, we have now a fairly good understanding of what skilled performance in a large variety of content domains involves. At the same time the related research in which performance of experts and novices at different stages of competence was compared, has contributed to clarify one of the components of a theory of learning from instruction that was not explicitly addressed in this article, namely the description of goal-relevant initial states of learners prior to instruction. Considerable advances have also been made in unravelling major characteristics of effective learning processes. And, a series of intervention studies has started to address basic questions relating to the design and evaluation of powerful teaching–learning environments to elicit and maintain acquisition processes that are conducive to the attainment of a disposition to competent learning, thinking, and problem solving. The progress that has been achieved is documented in further detail in the articles in this volume that review and discuss the research results relating to

specific topics. However, these entries also raise many problems and issues that have emerged from past research, and need to be addressed in future inquiry.

References

Adey P, Shayer M 1993 An exploration of long-term far-transfer effects following an extended intervention program in the high school science curriculum. *Cognition and Instruction* 11: 1–29

Alexander P A, Judy J E 1988 The interaction of domain-specific and strategic knowledge in academic performance. *Rev. Educ. Res.* 58: 375–404

Bereiter C 1990 Aspects of an educational learning theory. *Rev. Educ. Res.* 60: 603–24

Bereiter C 1995 A dispositional view of transfer. In: McKeough A, Lupart J, Marini A (eds.) 1995

Bereiter C, Scardamalia M 1989 International learning as a goal of instruction. In: Resnick L B (ed.) 1989 *Knowing, Learning, and Instruction. Essays in Honor of Robert Glaser.* Erlbaum, Hillsdale, New Jersey

Berliner D C, Calfee R C (eds.) 1996 *Handbook of Educational Psychology.* Macmillan, New York

Boekaerts M 1992 The adaptable learning process: Initiating and maintaining behavioural change. *Appl. Psychol.* 41: 377–97

Bransford J D, Stein B S 1993 *The Ideal Problem Solver: A Guide for Improving Thinking, Learning, and Creativity.* W H Freeman and Company, New York

Brown A L 1989 Analogical learning and transfer: What develops? In: Vosniadou S, Ortony A (eds.) 1989 *Similarity and Analogical Reasoning.* Cambridge University Press, Cambridge

Brown A L, Bransford J D, Ferrera R A, Campione J C 1983 Learning, remembering, and understanding. In: Mussen P H, Flavell J H, Markman E M (eds.) 1983 *Child Psychology, Volume III: Cognitive Development.* John Wiley, New York

Brown A L, Campione J C 1994 Guided discovery in a community of learners. In: McGilly K (ed.) 1994 *Classroom Lessons: Integrating Cognitive Theory and Classroom Practice.* MIT Press/Bradford Books, Cambridge, Massachusetts

Brown J S, Collins A, Duguid P 1989 Situated cognition and the culture of learning. *Educ. Researcher* 18(1): 32–42

Bruer J T 1993 *Schools for Thought: A Science of Learning in the Classroom.* MIT Press, Cambridge, Massachusetts

Campione J C, Shapiro A M, Brown A L 1995 Forms of transfer in a community of learners: Flexible learning and understanding. In: McKeough A, Lupart J, Marini A (eds.) 1995

Carretero M, Pope M, Simons R J, Pozo J I (eds.) 1991 *Learning and Instruction: European Research in an International Context*, Vol. 3. Pergamon Press, Oxford

Chi M T, Glaser R, Farr M J (eds.) 1988 *The Nature of Expertise.* Erlbaum, Hillsdale, New Jersey

Cognition and Technology Group at Vanderbilt 1992 An anchored instruction approach to cognitive skills acquisition and intelligent tutoring. In: Regian J W, Shute V J (eds.) 1992 *Cognitive Approaches to Automated Instruction.* Erlbaum, Hillsdale, New Jersey

Collins A, Brown J S, Newman S E 1989 Cognitive apprenticeship: Teaching the crafts of reading, writing and mathematics. In: Resnick L B (ed.) 1989 *Knowing, Learning, and Instruction. Essays in Honor of Robert Glaser.* Erlbaum, Hillsdale, New Jersey

Cormier S M, Hagman J D (eds.) 1987 *Transfer of Learning. Contemporary Research and Applications.* Academic Press, San Diego, California

Davydov V V 1990 *Types of Generalization in Instruction: Logical and Psychological Problems in the Structuring of School Curricula.* National Council of Teachers of Mathematics, Reston, Virginia

Davydov V V 1995 The influence of L.S. Vygotsky on education theory, research, and practice *Educ. Researcher* 24(3): 12–21

De Corte E 1977 Some aspects of research on learning and cognitive development in Europe. *Educ. Psychol.* 12: 197–206

De Corte E 1995 Fostering cognitive growth: A perspective from research on mathematics learning and instruction. *Educ. Psychol.* 30: 37–46

De Corte E in press Learning theory and instructional science. In: Reimann P, Spada H (eds.) in press *Learning in Humans and Machines: Towards an Interdisciplinary Learning Science.* Elsevier Science Ltd, Oxford

De Corte E, Greer B, Verschaffel L 1996 Mathematics teaching and learning. In: Berliner D C, Calfes R C (eds.) 1996

De Corte E, Lodewijks H, Parmentier R, Span P (eds.) 1987 *Learning and Instruction. European Research in an International Context*, Vol. 1 Leuven University Press, Leuven/Pergamon Press, Oxford

Detterman D K, Sternberg R J (eds.) 1993 *Transfer on Trial: Intelligence, Cognition, and Instruction* Ablex, Norwood, New Jersey

Dochy F J R C 1992 *Assessment of Prior Knowledge as a Determinant for Future Learning.* Lemma, Utrecht

Dweck C S 1989 Motivation. In: Lesgold A Glaser R (eds.) 1989 *Foundations for a Psychology of Education.* Erlbaum, Hillsdale, New Jersey

Entwistle N, Entwistle A, Tait H 1993 Academic understanding and contexts to enhance it: A perspective from research on student learning. In: Duffy T M, Lowyck J, Jonassen D H (eds.) 1993 *Designing Environments for Constructive Learning.* NATO ASI Series F: Computer and Systems Sciences, Vol. 105. Springer-Verlag, Berlin

Entwistle N, Marton F 1989 Introduction: The psychology of student learning. *Eur. J. Psychol. Educ.* 4: 449–52

Frijda N H, De Groot A D (eds.) 1981 *Otto Selz: His Contribution to Psychology.* Mouton, the Hague

Gagné R M, Dick W 1983 Instructional psychology. *Ann. Rev. Psychol.* 34: 261–95

Gagné R M, Rohwer W D Jr 1969 Instructional psychology. *Ann. Rev. Psychol.* 20: 381–418

Glaser R, Bassok M 1989 Learning theory and the study of instruction. *Annu. Rev. Psychol.* 40: 631–66

Greeno J G 1989 A perspective on thinking. *Am. Psychol.* 44: 134–41

Gruber H, Law L C, Mandl H, Renkl A in press Situated learning and transfer: State-of-the-art. In: Reimann P, Spada H (eds.) in press *Learning in Humans and Machines: Towards an Interdisciplinary Learning Science.* Elsevier Science Ltd, Oxford

Hedegaard M, Hakkarainen P, Engestrom Y (eds.) 1984 *Learning and Teaching on a Scientific Basis: Methodological and Epistemological Aspects of the Activity Theory of Learning and Teaching.* Psykologisk Institut, Aarhus Universitet, Aarhus

Helmke A 1989 Affective student characteristics and cognitive development. *Int. J. Educ. Res.* 13: 915–32

Iran-Nejad A, McKeachie W J, Berliner D C (eds.) 1990 Toward a unified approach to learning as a multisource phenomenon. *Rev. Educ. Res.* 60: 509–624

Lave J, Wenger E 1991 *Situated Learning. Legitimate Peripheral Participation.* Cambridge University Press, Cambridge

Lesgold A M, Pellegrino J W, Fokkema S D, Glaser R (eds.) 1978 *Cognitive Psychology and Instruction.* Plenum Press, New York

Mandl H, De Corte E, Bennett S N, Friedrich H F (eds.) 1990 *Learning and Instruction. European Research in an International Context. Vol. 2:1 Social and Cognitive Aspects of Learning and Instruction. Vol. 2:2 Analysis of Complex Skills and Complex Knowledge Domains.* Pergamon Press Oxford

Marton F 1981 Phenomenography: Describing conceptions of the world around us. *Instructional Science* 10: 177–200

Marton F, Hounsell D J, Entwistle N J 1984 *The Experience of Learning.* Scottish Academic Press, Edinburgh

McKeough A, Lupart J, Marini A (eds.) 1995 *Teaching for Transfer: Fostering Generalization in Learning.* Erlbaum, Mahwah, New Jersey

Newell A, Simon H A 1972 *Human Problem Solving.* Prentice Hall, Englewood Cliffs, New Jersey

Perkins D N 1995 *Outsmarting IQ: The Emerging Science of Learnable Intelligence.* The Free Press, New York

Perkins D N, Salomon G 1989 Are cognitive skills context-bound? *Educ. Researcher* 18(1): 16–25

Perkins D N, Simmons R 1988 Patterns of misunderstanding: An integrative model of science, math, and programming. *Rev. Educ. Res.* 58: 303–26

Perkins D N, Jay E, Tishman S 1993 Beyond abilities: A dispositional theory of thinking. *Merrill-Palmer Q.* 39: 1–21

Piaget J 1950 *The Psychology of Intelligence.* Routledge and Kegan Paul, London

Pintrich P R, Cross D R, Kozma R B, McKeachie W J 1986 Instructional Psychology. *Annu. Rev. Psychol.* 37: 611–51

Pintrich P R, Marx R W, Boyle R A 1993 Beyond cold conceptual change: The role of motivational beliefs and classroom conceptual factors in the process of conceptual change. *Rev. Educ. Res.* 63: 167–99

Pressley M, Borkowski J G, Schneider W 1989 Good information processing: What it is and how education can promote it. *Int. J. Educ. Res.* 13: 857–67

Resnick L B 1981 Instructional Psychology. *Annu. Rev. Psychol.* 32: 659–704

Resnick L B 1983 Toward a cognitive theory of instruction. In: Paris S, Olson G, Stevenson H (eds.) 1983 *Learning and Motivation in the Classroom.* Erlbaum, Hillsdale, New Jersey

Rogoff B, Lave J (eds.) 1984 *Everyday Cognition: Its Development in Social Context.* Harvard University Press, Cambridge, Massachusetts

Salomon G (ed.) 1993 *Distributed Cognition. Psychological and Educational Considerations.* Cambridge University Press, Cambridge

Scardamalia M, Bereiter C 1992 An architecture for collaborative knowledge building. In: De Corte E, Linn M

C, Mandl H, Verschaffel L (eds.) 1992 *Computer-based Learning Environments and Problem Solving*. NATO ASI Series F: Computer and Systems Sciences, Vol. 84. Springer-Verlag, Berlin

Scardamalia M, Bereiter C, Steinbach R 1984 Teachability of reflective processes in written composition. *Cognit. Sci.* 8: 173–90

Schoenfeld A H 1985 *Mathematical Problem Solving*. Academic Press, New York

Schunk D H, Zimmerman B J (eds.) 1994 *Self-regulation of Learning and Performance: Issues and Educational Applications*. Erlbaum, Hillsdale, New Jersey

Shuell T J 1992 Designing instructional computing systems for meaningful learning. In: Jones M, Winne P H (eds.) 1992 *Adaptive Learning Environments: Foundations and Frontiers*. NATO ASI Series F: Computer and Systems Sciences, Vol. 85. Springer-Verlag, Berlin

Simon H A 1979 Information processing models of cognition. *Annu. Rev. Psychol.* 30: 363–96

Singley M K, Anderson J R 1989 *The Transfer of Cognitive Skill*. Harvard University Press, Cambridge, Massachusetts

Snow R E, Swanson J 1992 Instructional psychology: Aptitude, adaptation, and assessment. *Annu. Rev. Psychol.* 43: 583–626

Steffe L P, Gale J (eds.) 1995 *Constructivism and Education*. Erlbaum, Hillsdale, New Jersey

Sternberg R J 1989 Domain-generality versus domain-specificity: The life and impending death of a false dichotomy. *Merrill-Palmer Q.* 35: 115–30

Streefland L (ed.) 1991 *Realistic Mathematics Education in Primary School. On the Occasion of the Opening of the Freudenthal Institute*. University of Utrecht Freudenthal Institute, Utrecht

Van Parreren C F 1988 *Ontwikkelend onderwijs* Acco, Leuven

Vosniadou S 1994 Capturing and modeling the process of conceptual change. *Learning and Instruction* 4: 45–69

Voss J F, Wiley J, Carretero M 1995 Acquiring intellectual skills. *Annu. Rev. Psychol.* 46: 155–81

Vygotsky L S 1978 *Mind in Society. The Development of Higher Psychological Proceses*. Harvard University Press, Cambridge, Massachusetts

Wang M C, Haertel G D, Walberg H J 1993 Toward a knowledge base for school learning. *Rev. Educ. Res.* 63: 249–94

Weinstein C S 1991 The classroom as a social context for learning. *Annu. Rev. Psychol.* 42: 493–525

White B Y 1993 ThinkerTools: Causal models, conceptual change, and science education. *Cognition and Instruction* 10: 1–100

Wood T, Cobb P, Yackel E 1995 Reflections on learning and teaching mathematics in elementary school. In: Steffe L P, Gale J (eds.) 1995

Translating Research into Practice

F. E. Weinert and E. De Corte

After 100 years of systematic research in the fields of education and educational psychology, there is, in the early 1990s, still no agreement about whether, how, or under what conditions research can improve educational practice. Although research and educational practice each have changed substantially since the beginning of the twentieth century, the question of how science can actually contribute to the solution of real educational problems continues to be controversial.

Because there are no general rules or strategies for translating research into practice, the first part of this entry focuses briefly on some of the basic problems concerning the relation between theory and practice in education. Next, six different approaches that attempt in various ways to make research findings relevant to education, particularly in schools, are discussed. These approaches concern: (a) using theoretical knowledge to improve technology for teaching and learning; (b) facilitating teacher expertise as a practical application of research on teaching; (c) using studies on classroom learning to provide the scientific basis for ability grouping, mastery learning and adaptive teaching; (d) using research on cognitive development and learning as a source of scientific

information about how to train student's learning competencies and self-instructional skills; (e) using educational research to design, implement and evaluate new models of schooling and instruction; and (f) using research findings as a source of background knowledge for practitioners. Suggestions for how research can be made more relevant to educators and for ways in which educational practice can be more research-based are proposed on the basis of these different approaches.

1. The Gap Between Research and Educational Practice

Most research in education and educational psychology is conducted with the explicit or implicit goal of directly or indirectly improving educational practice. As Anderson and Burns (1985) stated, "the primary purpose of classroom research is to help educators to improve the conditions of learning and the quality of learning of increasingly large numbers of students" (p. IX). The kinds of necessary research, the required theoretical insights, and the ways that scientific findings should be translated into practice to attain this goal are issues that have not as yet been resolved.

When empirical and experimental research on educational phenomena began, there was a widespread vision, conviction, and expectation that it would generate a scientifically informed basis for educational practice. In 1893, for example, Rein (1893) stated that "there is only one way in teaching that corresponds to nature; to follow carefully the laws of the human mind and to arrange everything according to these laws. The attainment of adequate instructional procedures follows from knowledge of and insight into these laws" (p. 107).

When these ambitious hopes did not seem to be realized, there was substantial disappointment among both scientists and practitioners. It was not clear how teachers could use such very general and vague recommendations as those, for example, based on a synopsis of classical learning theories by Thorpe and Schmuller (1954). They concluded that instruction was especially effective when learners were motivated; when task demands matched learners' aptitudes; when learners received sufficient opportunities to relate elements of the learning task to the learning goal; when learners could use external criteria to judge their progress; and when the learning process occurred under conditions that facilitated adaptation to the total situation. Although these conclusions are probably valid, it is not surprising that such nonspecific psychological statements and such obvious educational recommendations led the educational community to the cynical conclusion that learning theorists were perhaps the only ones who could derive personal benefit from learning theory.

Dissatisfaction was not limited to problems in finding practical applications for learning theory. The results from research on teaching also seemed unproductive in providing educators with practical guidance. This can be seen, for example, in Bloom's (1966) resigned summary of the state of research: "large class, small class, TV instruction, audiovisual methods, lecture, discussion, demonstration, team teaching, programmed instruction, authoritarian and non-authoritarian instructional procedures, etc. all appear to be equally effective methods in helping the student learn more information or simple skills" (p. 217).

The limited applicability of educational science for educational practice has resulted in several metatheoretical debates that have contributed only a little to improving the research situation or to solving practical problems. Some examples of the debated issues are:

(a) Is the gap between scientific and practical work the result of a production deficit in research, a reception deficit in the practitioners, or deficits in translating theoretical knowledge into practical suggestions? This debate has led at least to the insight that scientists and practitioners have different ways of perceiving the world, prefer to define their problems in different ways, and thus speak different "languages".

(b) How relevant is basic, as opposed to applied research, for education? This debate is especially unproductive, both theoretically and practically. On the one hand, it is difficult to differentiate pure or basic research from applied research; on the other hand, it has become clear that findings from both research prototypes have specific advantages and disadvantages with respect to their practical applications.

(c) Is it more appropriate to use quantitative or qualitative methods in educational research? This debate has almost become a religious war for many, even though the theory of science convincingly teaches that both approaches are necessary and complementary components of any system of research in the social sciences.

2. Theory and Research

These metatheoretical debates and the many concrete attempts to derive practical applications from research findings have led to a variety of different proposals for solving the research–practice problem. Two positions are especially characteristic of these proposals: the first is that theory should take precedence; the second is that empirical work should take precedence.

The first characteristic position, that theory should be pre-eminent, can be captured by a quotation from Mook (1983), who, in agreement with many other scientists, recalled the truth of the classical adage that nothing is more useful than a good theory.

> Ultimately, what makes research findings of interest is that they help us in understanding everyday life. That understanding, however, comes from theory or analysis of the mechanisms; it is not a matter of generalizing the findings themselves. . . The validity of those generalizations is tested by their success and predictions and has nothing to do with their naturalness, representativeness or even non-creativity of the investigations on which they rest (p. 386).

Examples of the ways in which theoretical models have aided in the solution of practical problems include the use of attribution theory to provide a better understanding of students' intuitive explanations for their success and failure; the use of findings from the expert–novice research paradigm to estimate the relative importance of general abilities and domain specific knowledge in the solution of demanding tasks; and the use of theories of prejudice in the analysis of social conflicts.

The second characteristic position, focused on empirical research, is invoked in instances where there are competing theories, where context conditions determine psychological processes, or where descriptive or causal models must be transposed into prescriptive statements. Sequential research strategies are proposed to solve such problems. One example is the description of "six steps on the road from pure learning research to technological research and development in the classroom" suggested by Hillgard (1964): step 1—research on learning with no regard for its educational relevance; step 2—pure research on learning with content that is similar to school subject matter; step 3—research on learning that is relevant to education because the subjects are students, the material learned is school subject matter and/or the learning conditions are similar to classroom situations; step 4—research on learning and instruction in special laboratory classrooms; step 5—use of experimentally tested learning and teaching strategies in normal classrooms; step 6—developmental work related to advocacy and adoption, for a wider use of the research based educational strategies (p. 405–11).

These and similar sequential research strategies are followed in many research and development centers around the world. The differences among the programs are, however, too large to allow conclusions about the success of such a strategy. In principle, the possibilities and limits of this approach also depend on the basic relation between educational research and educational practice. Good educational practice is not simply applied science, nor does it consist in the correct use of findings from applied research. Science can at best only provide an important and useful, but always limited, theoretical basis for the planning, analysis, control, support, reflection and better understanding of educational practice.

The limits of scientific prediction and explanation of educational outcomes are expressed in the conclusions reached by Haertel et al. (1983) based on a comparison of different psychological models of educational performance. They concluded that:

> Classroom learning is the multiplicative, diminishing-returns function of four essential factors—student ability and motivation and quality and quantity of instruction—and possibly four supplementary or supportive factors—the social-psychological environment of the classroom, education-stimulating conditions in the home and peer group, and exposure to mass media. Each of the essential factors appears to be necessary but insufficient by itself for classroom learning; that is all four of these factors appear required at least at minimum levels for classroom learning to take place. It also appears that the essential factors may substitute, compensate, or trade-off for one another in diminishing rates of return. (p. 75f)

3. Models for Bridging the Gap between Research and Educational Practice

There is no general rule that specifies correct, expedient or appropriate ways to use scientific findings to solve the practical tasks of education. More importantly, there can in principle be no such rule. There are, however, various approaches available that show how research can be used in different ways and the strategies that can be used to translate research into practice.

3.1 From Learning Theories to Teaching Technologies

Educational technology consists of systems of rules, tools and activities designed to bring students to the point where they can achieve specific learning goals systematically, effectively and economically. Even more, Glaser and Cooley (1973) perceive technology "as a vehicle for making available to schools what psychologists have learned about learning" (p. 855). Such standardized technologies should of course be derived from explicit and tested scientific theory. Although not a necessary component of educational technology, technical devices are frequently used with the purpose of minimizing the negative consequences of fluctuation in attention to errors or mistakes, whether by students or teachers.

The first researcher who, from theoretical grounds, wanted to replace normal instruction in the classroom with almost revolutionary mechanical teaching techniques was Skinner (1954). In the early 1950s Skinner argued that the behaviorist models of learning and conditioning and the psychological laws specifying how to shape behavior through contingent reinforcement of desired reactions were the scientific prerequisites for successful and effective instruction. It was his belief that these principles could not be used in classroom teaching because teachers were not able to present the material to be learned in sufficiently elementary components and were not able to provide the requisite number of reinforcements in the necessary contiguity to learners' behavior, verbal or nonverbal. Thus, he recommended programmed instruction and the use of teaching machines.

Beyond Skinner's initial attempts, the development of educational technologies made dramatic progress in the 1970s and 1980s. Computer-assisted instruction, integrated learning systems, intelligent tutoring systems, instructional media and intelligent learning environments are some of the key concepts referring to the development, study and use of modern technical aids for improving educational practice (for a review see Niemiec and Walberg 1992, Scott et al. 1992).

In particular, modern computer technology offers a variety of possibilities for the technical design of controlled, but flexible, adaptive, and intelligently guided instructional systems and learning processes. The prerequisite for these systems are general learning theories and domain specific models of knowledge acquisition that allow the following:

(a) analysis of the learning goal in terms of competent performance (specification of the learning task);

(b) description of the initial state of the learner (specification of individual differences in relevant skills and knowledge);

(c) determination of the methods that effectively lead to knowledge acquisition (specification of instructional methods);

(d) assessment of the effects of these instructional methods (specification and measurement of learning progress).

Although there is no disagreement that educational technologies provide an up-to-date tool for education as well as an excellent opportunity for employing research results in a practical way, we have to recognize the relative failure of educational computing in general, and in mathematics in particular. The high expectations supported by research, that rose in the early 1980s—with respect to the potential of the computer as a lever for the innovation and improvement of schooling, have not been redeemed. Elsewhere De Corte (1994) has argued that a major reason for this relative failure of computers in education is that the machine has been mainly introduced as a add-on to an existing, largely unchanged classroom setting. In addition, due to a lack of good communication, teachers usually had only low expectations about computer support for their teaching (see e.g., Kaput 1992). Also, there was in most cases no question at all of an orientation toward modifying teachers' conceptions about educational goals and their beliefs about learning.

3.2 Research on Teaching and the Acquisition of Teacher Expertise

A large part of educational research is directed toward investigating educational productivity, teacher effectiveness and the relation between instructional quality and learning outcomes. Although the empirical findings are very impressive, they are also quite diverse and are not stable across different studies. In a synthesis of the effects of instructional variables on learning, the following rank ordering of noncontent related factors was found (with decreasing effect strength): reinforcement, accelerated learning programs, cues and feedback, cooperation programs, personalized instruction, adaptive instruction, tutoring, higher order questions (Fraser et al. 1987).

If one considers that the effects of single instructional variables can be masked or mediated by combined, compensatory and interactive effects from other teaching, student and context variables (Weinert et al. 1989), it becomes apparent that training single teaching skills can not be a practical implication of these research results.

It seems considerably more effective to provide a combined training program for teachers that uses the results from research on teaching (Tillema and Veenman 1987). The paradigm of the expert teacher provides an interesting theoretical perspective for the practical application of such research findings. Prompted by work in cognitive psychology, this paradigm investigates how experienced and successful teachers differ from inexperienced and/or unsuccessful teachers in their knowledge about education and in their teaching activities (Berliner 1992). The research results from this paradigm have already been applied in the design of teacher training.

This paradigm allows the integration of two research traditions that have been portrayed as alternative approaches (Stolurow 1965): "Model the master teacher or master the teaching model?" (see also Weinert et al. 1992). In the expert teacher paradigm, it is possible to directly and systematically relate research on teaching and learning in the classroom to teacher training. Such training should not be directed toward producing a uniform type of "expert teacher," but should explicitly assume that there are interindividual differences in the teacher competencies to be trained (Anderson and Burns 1985).

3.3 Studies of Classroom Learning

In contrast to the subject pools used in experimental investigations of learning, the classroom is best described as a group of students with very different learning prerequisites who are to be instructed at the same time in the same place. Massive interindividual differences in cognitive abilities, knowledge, skills, motivation, interests, attitudes, and study habits affect both students' learning behavior and their learning achievements. The relevant research concerning these factors is very extensive. It has led to a large number of psychological theories about how personality states and traits are relevant to learning, and has contributed to the development of measurement models and measurement instruments for diagnosing individual differences in learning prerequisites and learning outcomes.

Carroll (1963) provided an important contribution to the practical application of this psychological research with his "model of school learning". Described simply, Carroll proceeded from the assumption that, given equivalent learning time, students with different aptitudes would diverge in their learning performance: that is, some students would not attain the required performance goal. To avoid this outcome, each learner must be allowed the learning time he or she needs to attain a specific learning goal.

This model has had a strong influence on subsequent research; in many respects it has been further specified, broadened and extended, and it has also been used for a variety of different practical applications (see Anderson 1984). For example, the following concepts and procedures can be traced to Carroll's original model: time on task (the time during which a student is actually involved in a learning task); the personalized system of instruction; individually prescribed instruction; mastery learning; and, largely independent of Carroll's model of school learning, the aptitude–treatment interaction (ATI) research program (Snow 1989). All these approaches have been concerned with the question of whether and to what extent undesired effects of individual student aptitude differences on learning outcomes can be reduced by variations in instruction.

Research on the dependence of school achievement on aptitude differences and instructional conditions has led to important practical applications. Three of these are grouping students for learning, mastery learning, and adaptive teaching.

The educational benefits of grouping students for learning are controversial and seem to depend on the effects of a variety of factors. Furthermore, these benefits are both student- and criterion-specific (Slavin 1990). A successful practical application of ATI research has not been made.

Mastery learning is the attempt to ensure that as many students in a class as possible (90–95%) meet a required learning criterion (90–95% correct items in a criterion test). This goal is achieved by a limited increase in learning time (about 20%) and optimal instructional use of the learning time. Although what one can actually expect from mastery learning in normal school instruction is somewhat controversial (Slavin 1987, Kulik et al. 1990), there is no doubt that this is a fruitful model that allows productive research and practical applications.

Adaptive teaching is based on many ideas from Carroll's model of school learning and ATI research. Adaptive teaching

> involves both learner adaptation *to* the environmental conditions presented and teacher adaptation *of* the environmental conditions to the learners' present state, to effect changes in that state. The teacher's goal, in other words, is to make environmental variations 'nurtured' rather than merely 'natural' for each learner of concern (Corno and Snow 1986, p. 607).

"Adaptive teaching" is thus an omnibus term covering a large number of different standardized and informal procedures for adapting teaching in variable, flexible and dynamic ways to students' individual differences, so that optimal learning conditions can be provided for each student.

3.4 Fostering Students' Learning Competencies and Self-instructional Skills

In the above characterization of adaptive teaching it was noted that the optimization of individual learning requires not only that instruction be compatible with the cognitive and motivational demands of the student, but also that students' learning competencies and learning motivation be explicitly fostered. There is considerable research in cognitive psychology, developmental psychology and educational psychology that addresses how to promote competencies and motivation. At the forefront are investigations on transfer of training, learning to think, the promotion of metacognitive skills, and the development of self-instructional skills.

Much of the theoretically oriented research also includes suggestions for applying the findings. Relevant support programs have been tried for elementary, secondary and university students. Although these programs have demonstrated that intellectual skills and thinking performance cannot be arbitrarily trained, they have also convincingly shown that the training of metacognitive competencies and self-instructional skills can result in lasting improvements (Blagg 1991). When such programs have realistic goals, are provided over an extensive time frame, and, if possible, are directed toward the acquisition of domain specific knowledge, all students can profit.

3.5 The Use of Research Findings for New Models of Schooling

Research can be used not only to improve existing educational institutions, school organizations and instructional conditions, but also to plan new models for schooling. Such an approach to change is needed when it is unclear whether an educational goal can be reached by gradual and piecemeal changes in current activities or whether fundamental reform is more necessary. Both theoretical discussion and practical experiences are available for using research findings in this way (Salisbury 1993). Such change requires considerations of the factors that must be considered in planning a new educational system, the strategies that should be employed, the problems that must be addressed, and the implementation tasks that must be performed.

3.6 Research as a Source of Background Knowledge for Practitioners

The practical application of research consists in more than the instrumental use of research findings. In addition, science and research have an educational function; that is, they provide individuals with knowledge about themselves and the world, and allow individuals to act rationally.

Because people think, decide, and act primarily on the basis of their available knowledge (whether it is correct or incorrect, complete or incomplete, objective or biased), it is important and necessary for those involved in the educational process (politicians, administrators, principals, teachers, parents, students, and researchers) to be able to change or replace their personal beliefs, intuitive knowledge, prejudices and suppositions with reliable and valid information. Such a replacement is not only a prerequisite for reflective, responsible, and effective individual action, but also a condition for rational communication and discourse among educational practitioners. Although it is not possible to measure the effectiveness of this function of research, it nonetheless seems plausible and important to translate as many research results as possible into the language of the practitioner.

A potentially very promising strategy for bridging the theory–practice gap is a combination of the last two strategies; namely using research for the design, implementation, and evaluation of new models of education and schooling on the one hand, and research as a source of background knowledge for teachers on the other. This strategy consists in the creation and evaluation in real classrooms of complex instructional interventions that embody our present (hypothetical) understanding of effective learning processes and powerful learning environments. In order to have a reasonable chance of success, such attempts at totally changing the classroom environment and culture should be undertaken in partnership between researchers and knowledgeable practitioners. Such partnership is essential not only to promote good two-way communication, but also with a view to modifying and reshaping teachers' beliefs about education, learning, and teaching. The positive effects of this partnership idea have, for instance, been shown by Huberman (1990). In a qualitative study of the linkages between researchers and practitioners, he has shown that contacts between both parties during a research project can result not only in better applications of the outcomes of a single study, but also in the establishment of more enduring forms of collaboration.

A specific approach which is in line with this holistic strategy is represented by scholars who advocate the use of so-called design experiments, and who aim at the development of a design science of education (Brown 1992, Collins 1992). According to Collins (1992 p. 15) "a design science of education must determine how different designs of learning environments contribute to learning, cooperation, motivation, etc." As a result a design theory would emerge that can guide the implementation of educational innovations by identifying the variables influencing their success or failure. This intervention approach has a twofold goal: it intends to advance theory building, while at the same time contributing to the optimization of classroom practices. In this respect, Brown (1994) argued that theory building is crucial for conceptual understanding as well as for practical dissemination. In fact, Brown's project "Fostering communities of learners" is one of the most representative examples of the design experiment approach (Brown 1994, Brown and Campione 1994). In this project the classroom is fundamentally redesigned using innovative components such as reciprocal teaching, the "jigsaw method" of cooperative learning, and the creation of a new classroom culture. Reciprocal teaching establishes a learning environment in which a small group of students is provided with guided practice in acquiring

four cognitive strategies with a view to improving their skill in reading comprehension. These strategies are: asking questions, summarizing, clarifying comprehension difficulties, and making predictions about the future content of a text. A major feature of reciprocal teaching is that it takes the form of a dialogue, in which the teacher and the pupils take turns in leading the discussion; gradually the pupils' share and responsibility in the dialogues increases.

The "jigsaw method" implies that small *research* groups of pupils first study each a subtopic of a broader theme (e.g., developments in Central and Eastern Europe). Afterwards they regroup into *learning* groups in which each pupil is the expert in one subtopic, so that by combining their knowledge they all learn about the whole topic. A new classroom culture and climate is created based on four qualities, namely individual responsibility, mutual respect, establishment of a community of discourse, and a restricted number of participant structures (such as reciprocal teaching).

In the perspective of the further dissemination of this new kind of learning environment it is necessary to keep in mind that they should be realizable in existing classrooms. In this respect the notion of a partnership between researchers and practitioners is also crucial in the light of the necessity of the reach–practice reciprocity. Whereas practitioners can help in translating theory into practice, and, thus, in making classroom teaching more research-based, their partner role can also contribute to make research more practice-driven.

Finally, the orientation of this intervention approach to theory building raises a major challenge for the researchers, namely the development of an appropriate methodology for designing experiments in complex classroom settings in such a way that sound and theoretically valid conclusions can be drawn from a wide range of quantitative and qualitative empirical data.

4. Conclusion

While the effectiveness of these six different approaches to the problem of bridging the theory–practice gap has not been systematically studied, it is plausible that each of them has not only some merits but also some weaknesses. Moreover, much will depend on how each approach is used in translating research results into practice. In this respect, we like to argue here that to be successful in making psychological theory and research applicable to education one should develop a strategy that combines the following basic characteristics:

(a) Good communication with practitioners which means that the relevant outcomes are translated in such a way that they are palatable, accessible, and usable for teachers.

(b) An orientation toward a fundamental change of

teachers' belief systems about the goals of education and about good teaching and effective learning (in line with the view described above).

(c) A holistic (as opposed to a partial) approach to the teaching–learning environment, i.e., all relevant aspects of the learning environment should be addressed.

The relation between research and practice is complex and difficult. As a consequence, there is no simple, uniform solution to the problem of translating scientific results into practical suggestions. Nonetheless, some general conclusions can be drawn.

First, many different types of research are applicable to educational practice. The value of a scientific study for educational practice is not in any way directly related to the extent to which it mirrors typical features of an applied educational setting.

Second, research results can be used in educational practice in different ways. Six typical examples have been noted: the development of educational technologies, teacher training, the optimization of instruction, fostering students' learning competencies, the design of new models of schooling, and the use of scientific information as background knowledge for practitioners.

Third, these different strategies for applying research results are not mutually exclusive. Rather, it is desirable to combine several variants to improve the practical situation.

Finally, exploring the processes by which theoretical knowledge can be transformed into practical action must itself be an important domain of educational research.

References

Anderson L W (ed.) 1984 *Time and School Learning.* Croom Helm, London

Anderson, L W, Burns R B 1985 *Research in Classrooms.* Pergamon Press, Oxford

Berliner D C 1992 The nature of expertise in teaching. In: Oser F K Oser, Dick A, Patry J L (eds.) 1992 *Effective and Responsible Teaching.* Jossey-Bass, San Francisco, California

Blagg N 1991 *Can We Teach Intelligence?* Erlbaum, Hillsdale, New Jersey

Bloom B S 1966 Twenty-five years of educational research. *Am. Educ. Res. J*, 3(3): 211–21

Brown A L 1992 Design experiments: Theoretical and methodological challenges in creating complex interventions in classroom settings. *Journal of the Learning Sciences* 2: 141–78

Brown A L 1994 The advancement of learning. *Educ. Researcher* 28(8): 4–12

Brown A L, Campione J C 1994 Guided discovery in a community of learners. In: McGilly K (ed.) 1994 *Classroom Lessons: Integrating Cognitive Theory and Classroom Practice.* MIT Press, Cambridge, Massachusetts

Carroll J B 1963 A model of school learning. *Teach. Coll. Rec.* 64: 723–33

Collins A 1992 Toward a design science of education. In: Scanlon E, O'Shea T (eds.) 1992 *New Directions in Educational Technology.* NATO-ASI Series F: Computers and Systems Sciences, Vol. 96, Springer-Verlag, Berlin

Corno L, Snow R E 1986 Adapting teaching to individual differences among learners. In: Wittrock M C (ed.) 1986 *Handbook of Research on Teaching*, 3rd edn. MacMillan Inc., New York

De Corte, E 1994 Toward the integration of computers in powerful learning environments. In: Vosniadou S, De Corte E, Mandl H (eds.) 1994 *Technology-based Learning Environments: Psychological and Educational Foundations.* NATO-ASI Series F: Computer and Systems Sciences, Vol. 137, Springer-Verlag, Berlin

Fraser B J, Walberg H J, Welch W W, Hattie, J A 1987 Synthesis of educational productivity research. *Int. J of Educ. Res.* 11: 145–252

Glaser R, Cooley W 1973 Instrumentation for teaching and instructional management. In: Travers R M W (ed.) *Second Handbook of Research in Teaching.* Rand McNally, Chicago, Illinois

Haertel G D, Walberg H J, Weinstein T 1983 Psychological models of educational performance: A theoretical synthesis of constructs. *Rev. of Educ. Res.* 53(1): 75–91

Hilgard E R 1964 A perspective on the relationship between learning theory and educational practice. In: Hilgard E R (ed.) 1964 *Theories of Learning and Instruction.* The National Society for the Study of Education, Chicago, Illinois

Huberman M 1990 Linkage between researchers and practitioners: A qualitative study. *American Educational Research Association* 27: 363–91

Kaput J J 1992 Technology and mathematics education. In: Grouws D A (ed.) 1992 *Handbook of Research and Mathematics Teaching and Learning.* Macmillan Inc., New York

Kulik C L C, Kulik J A, Bangert-Drowns R L 1990 Effectiveness of Mastery Learning Programs: A meta-analysis. *Rev. Educ. Res.* 60: 265–99

Mook D A 1983 In defense of external invalidity. *Am. Psychol.* 38(4): 379–87

Niemiec R P, Walberg H J 1992 The effect of computers on learning. *Int. J. Educ. Res.* 17(1): 99–108

Rein W (1993) *Pädagogik im Grundriß*, 2nd edn. Göchen, Stuttgart

Salisbury D F 1993 Designing and implementing new models of schooling. *Int. J. Educ. Res.* 19(2): 99–195

Scott R, Cole M, Engel M 1992 Computers and education: A cultural constructivist perspective. In: Grant G (ed.) 1992 *Rev. Res. Educ.* 18: 191–251

Skinner B F 1954 The science of learning and the art of teaching. *Harv. Educ. Rev.* 24(2): 86–97

Slavin R E 1987 Mastery learning reconsidered. *Rev. Educ. Res.* 57(2): 175–213

Slavin R E 1990 Achievement effects of ability grouping in secondary schools: A best-evidence synthesis. *Rev. Educ. Res.* 60(3): 471–99

Snow R E 1989 Aptitude–treatment interaction as a framework for research on individual differences in learning. In: Ackerman P L, Sternberg R J, Glaser R (eds.) *Learning and Individual Differences* Freeman, New York

Stolurow L M 1965 Model the master teacher or master the

teaching model. In: Krumbholtz J D (ed.) 1965 *Learning and the Educational Process*. Rand McNally, Chicago, Illinois

Thorpe L P, Schmuller A M 1954 *Contemporary Theories of Learning*. Wiley, New York

Tillema H H, Veenman S A M (eds.) 1987 Development in training methods for teacher education. *Int. J. Educ. Res.* 2(5): 517–600

Weinert F E, Helmke A, Schrader F W 1992 Research on the model teacher and the teaching model. In: Oser F K, Dick A, Patry J L (eds.) *Effective and Responsible Teaching—The New Synthesis*. Jossey-Bass, San Francisco, California

Weinert F E, Schrader F W, Helmke A 1989 Quality of instruction and achievement outcomes. *Int. J. Educ. Res.* 13(8): 895–914

Further Reading

Bloom B S 1976 *Human Characteristics and School Learning*. McGraw-Hill, New York

Glaser R 1977 *Adaptive Education: Individual Diversity and Learning*. Holt, Rinehart, and Winston, New York

Snow R E, Federico P A, Montague W E (eds.) 1980 *Aptitude, Learning, and Instruction*, vols. 1, 2. Erlbaum, Hillsdale, New Jersey

SECTION II

General Issues of Human Development

Cross-cultural Approaches to Human Development

H. J. Kornadt and G. Trommsdorff

Findings from psychological research on human development carried out primarily in Western cultures may not be universally valid. Research in other cultures reveal hitherto unknown facts and processes. Thus, a cross-cultural approach provides an essential contribution to the understanding of developmental processes and the influence of genetic and environmental factors, for example universals as well as cultural specification can be found in cognitive, emotional, and motivational development.

1. Main Topics and Controversies

Historically, the course of physical and psychological development was first studied as child psychology. Later, developmental psychology concentrated increasingly on factors influencing the development of individual differences in personality characteristics and on the basic regularities as postulated by various theories. Only later was the scope extended to life-span development. Systematic cross-cultural research began relatively late, although Wundt and Freud had already referred to the importance of psychological phenomena in foreign cultures.

Most research findings, methods, and theoretical approaches have hitherto originated mainly in Western cultures, and a Euro- or ethnocentric viewpoint has prevailed. Consequently, one important objective of cross-cultural research consists in obtaining a broader empirical basis including non-Western cultures. The first question is whether the course of development is similar or different in various cultures and whether different phenomena occur.

A more ambitious objective of cross-cultural comparison is the testing of theoretical assumptions. A classic example concerns the observations made by Malinowski (1927) about the Oedipus complex. From a psychoanalytical viewpoint, a boy's object of love is his mother, and his father is therefore his rival; that is why the boy develops aggression toward his father. However, the Trobriander's aggression is not directed against the father, who is only the mother's lover, but against the uncle, who is the male authority figure. Here cross-cultural comparisons make it possible to disentangle the two functions of the father, which are confounded in Western culture.

In this sense, systematic cross-cultural research uses cultures differing in theoretically relevant variables as "natural experiments" to investigate theoretical assumptions: factors that cannot be manipulated experimentally (e.g., living conditions, child-rearing techniques, values) can thus be studied.

Of course, specific methodological problems arise: the functional equivalence in sampling, instruments, and data analysis has to be ascertained. If a concept, a question, or a mode of behavior has a different meaning in one culture than in another, the results cannot be interpreted easily. It is often difficult to exclude with certainty nonobvious differences of meaning.

The central research issue is the nature–nurture problem, that is, the question of whether biologically determined hereditary factors or learning experience (e.g., socialization) is more important for development. This has become a major controversy in psychology, even affecting political ideologies.

In the 1930s and 1940s the culture-and-personality school examined the relations between "basic personality" in a culture and the common cultural conditions of its development. This idea, starting from a combination of learning and psychoanalytical assumptions, was less oriented to the nature–nurture controversy than earlier anthropological studies. Another approach mainly dealt with separate characteristics. Here, some authors tried to demonstrate biological universalities; others believed that cultural experiences are more important (cultural relativism).

Both approaches are limited in scope. In the early 1990s, it is believed that development is the result of interactions between biological factors and experience during socialization. More attention has also been given to the child's own activity in structuring these interactions and thereby in partly structuring its own development, aspects which can preferably be studied cross-culturally.

Finally, "cultural psychology" must be mentioned as a special approach that is distinctly different from cross-cultural psychology. Cultural psychology pursues the ambitious goal of understanding how cultural traditions, institutions, symbolic systems, and social practices interact and, as a whole, direct psychological development, so that differences in cognitions, motives, self, and so on, seen as a result of culture, are the focus of research. At the same time, culture and the external world are conceived of as intentionally constructed, so that in the end the complex interactions become the object of research (Boesch 1991, Shweder 1991).

2. Nature–Nurture Controversy

An important impetus for cross-cultural research came from Mead's study (1929) on childhood and youth in Samoa. She described cheerful, nonaggressive, free and easy people who showed no conflicts. She explained this by the particular form of socialization in Samoa, that was sexually permissive, "free of constraints," and free of severe and painful punishment or pressure.

Mead's central message was that the problems typical of Western cultures, especially during puberty (such as aggression, rivalry, jealousy, and feelings of guilt) do not originate from biological heritage, but from socialization. She was convinced of the plasticity of human beings; namely, that the personality is, to a great extent, a product of the culture. This was in line with the cultural relativism of her teacher Boas and the early behaviorism which arose as a radical reaction to the previous biological determinism.

Until the 1970s, Mead's work, which obviously accorded with the *Zeitgeist*, considerably influenced theoretical reasoning in social science. But Mead's one-sided milieu-theoretical position has proved to be untenable, as the careful study by Freeman (1983) in Samoa has shown. Mead's report was based on insufficient observations and unjustified conclusions and generalizations. Even in those early days there were no such cheerful, free, and unaggressive personalities; at least they did not differ substantially from other cultures.

It is also the case that the simple dichotomy that portrays personality characteristics as either genetically or environmentally determined, is insufficient; the question regarding the extent to which these two factors determine the development, for example, of intelligence, is posed incorrectly. It is known that both factors play a decisive role in a complicated interaction during development. The real task for research is to clarify this interaction; here, cross-cultural research has made essential contributions.

Another major topic in cross-cultural research is the question of biologically determined universalities on the one hand and culture-specific developments on the other. One example of the search for biologically rooted universals is the extensive series of ethological studies by Eibl-Eibesfeldt (1976). He assumes that, in human development, factors which are phylogenetically inherited are of special importance. By observing children in different cultures he showed, for example, that special forms of rivalry and aggression occur everywhere, even in cultures that are considered to be nonaggressive (e.g., Bushmen). Also territoriality, courting behavior, and some facial expressions and gestures are universal.

In the same way, many studies (e.g., Ekman 1972) showed that certain emotions (joy, fear, anger, etc.) are expressed and recognized universally. However, cross-cultural investigations have also shown that the further development of emotional expression, in particular its perception and impact on behavior, are not universal to the same degree. Culturally determined learning processes obviously play a role; for example, in societies where the expression of anger is inappropriate, children develop the ability to control the expression of anger, and even to diminish the experience of anger (e.g., by reinterpreting a frustrating situation). These processes still have not been sufficiently investigated but cross-cultural results indicate that emotions are not simply innate reactions to specific situations but are mediated by cultural learning.

3. Cross-cultural Studies on the Development of Specific Functional Areas

3.1 Achievement Motive

The concept of achievement motivation (to strive for success in competition with a standard of excellence) has been accepted as a universal motive and as the driving force for economic and academic success. Early cross-cultural studies demonstrated that the achievement motive and economic success (in individuals, as well as in society) were positively correlated (McClelland 1961). The development of the motive was assumed to be influenced by certain child-rearing techniques: early independence training is related to high achievement motive. From further cross-cultural studies, it became clear that it is not the age but the appropriateness to the child's development that is crucial.

Furthermore, cross-cultural studies have shown that a specifically Western interpretation of the motive that makes a functional distinction between achievement and affiliation motives is ethnocentric. Although this distinction appears valid in the West, both motives are related in other cultures (e.g., Japan). In Japan, striving for individual achievement and success is not approved because achievement should serve the group. These findings have also led to the insight that functional criteria have to be derived from development in order to differentiate motives and to allow for their transcultural identification.

3.2 Attachment

Cross-cultural research in various cultures has shown that infants are universally motivated to develop affective bonds with a person with whom they can feel secure (e.g., in case of danger). Different types of attachment (secure, avoidant, resistant) emerge depending on the care-giver's responsiveness. These forms of attachment are also the basis for the development of prosocial and antisocial motives and of cognitive schemata about the self and the world ("working models") in further personality development.

From cross-cultural research it is known that infants can have affective bonds with a variety of people. Cultural differences in the frequency of various forms of attachment are of special interest. In Japan, the number of securely attached infants is significantly higher than in the United States and Germany (Grossmann and Grossmann 1992). This reflects a special kind of caretaking which is deeply rooted in the culture (Kornadt and Trommsdorff 1990).

3.3 Aggression

Many cross-cultural studies have shown that cultures differ significantly with regard to aggression (Kornadt et al. 1980). Because aggressive reactions in early childhood are universal, culture-specific forms of socialization should influence the development of aggressiveness. Whereas results concerning the effects of punishment are contradictory, it is known that neglect and rejection and a positive evaluation of aggression promote aggressiveness. However, the function of these factors is not clear. An investigation in five cultures based on motivation theory demonstrated that the cultures differed in the strength of the aggression motive. Interestingly, in all cultures a certain sequence of internal processes led to aggressive action (frustration—anger—malevolent interpretation—activation of aggression motive—goal setting—decision for aggressive action) indicating a possibly universal motive system. However, this pattern is not inevitable.

In East Asian cultures, where aggressive behavior is disapproved of, frustration is often interpreted as harmless (so that no anger occurs). One culture-specific reaction to anger is regret for the situation and guilt about it (Kornadt et al. 1992).

These characteristics in East Asian cultures are connected with culture-specific socialization. Especially in Japan, mothers establish a very close attachment with the child. If the mother requires acquiescence from the child, she avoids risking the harmony between herself and the child. However, she does not generally give up or question any of the rules she had set up before (Kornadt and Trommsdorff 1990). This behavior is embedded in a much wider cultural context in which several factors have a similar effect on development. The fact that such functional systems, different from those in the West, can develop underscores the importance of considering complex interaction processes in development.

3.4 Prosocial Behavior

According to psychobiological approaches, prosocial behavior (altruism), like aggression, results from a built-in motivation promoting survival. The observation of prosocial behavior in infancy also indicates a universal predisposition. Universal tendencies to help family members rather than strangers have been demonstrated by comparing Chinese and English samples. Despite contradictory results within United States samples, cross-cultural studies have shown that empathy induces helping. However, cultural differences exist in the quality and frequency of helping: this has been shown by Whiting and Whiting (1975) for children from cultures of different complexity and household structure, and by Trommsdorff (1995) for children from individualistic and collectivistic cultures. Data on socialization show that the mother's responsiveness fosters the child's empathy, and that "individualistic social responsibility" training fosters helping.

3.5 Cognitive Development

Many studies have investigated whether the sequence of stages of cognitive development and its age-specific occurrence as postulated by Piaget, who assumed a genetic basis, is universal. It has become clear that cultural differences in cognitive development do exist for the later developmental stages; also, the development of formal operations is domain specific. One explanation is that although cognitive competence has developed, the corresponding performance lags behind (e.g., because a behavior is not culturally valued). Another assumption is simply that growing up in a specific culture determines cognitive development. However, although there is evidence that fundamental processes in cognitive development are universal, it is still not clear how they are genetically determined (Jahoda 1986). At the same time, the local cultural and interpersonal context is important.

3.6 Moral Development

Proceeding from Piaget's stage theory, Kohlberg postulated six transculturally invariant stages of moral development. Again, the lower but not necessarily the highest stages appear to be universal. For example, it was found in India that interpersonal obligations are given priority over competing justice obligations. This can be seen as a culture-specific alternative of a postconventional moral code. Whether this implies another structure of moral judgment or only that a different principle than that of abstract justice is used is still an open question (Eckensberger 1993).

3.7 Self

The nature–nurture controversy appears to be obsolete; obviously, both factors interact with each other. A child is born in a certain ecocultural environment and already has capabilities. In the course of development, in which both sides influence one another, the child gradually starts to develop individual functional systems, which must be adaptive in his or her environment.

If processes of development are conceived not as passive reactions to the external world, nor as biologically predetermined internal processes, but rather as an active interaction between the individual and the environment, it is insufficient to study the development of single variables. These are interrelated within the personality. Thus, the self as an integrating factor gains importance.

In developmental psychology, it is usually assumed that children strive to become independent and autonomous. This implies the development of a corresponding concept of self. However, cross-cultural research has recently shown how ethnocentric this view is. In Asian cultures, interconnectedness with others characterizes the self-concept. Here, the self is seen as part of a social network in which the individual is embedded. The differences between an independent and an interdependent self have consequences for cognitive, emotional, and motivational processes: a stronger other-orientedness prevents ego-focused emotions (e.g., anger, pride) and promotes other-focused emotions (e.g., shame, indebtedness). Abstract principles are less important for behavior than the social context (Markus and Kitayama 1991).

3.8 Holistic Approaches

Some cross-cultural approaches analyze the complex influences of culture. In the famous work by Whiting and Whiting (1975) children from six cultures were observed in their daily activities. It was shown that basic forms of social behavior (e.g., helping, hurting, dominating) are universal, but that they vary according to characteristics of the particular culture. In cultures with a relatively simple (as opposed to complex) socioeconomic structure, children were more "nurturant-responsible" and less egoistic. Similarly, cultures with nuclear, rather than extended, families showed more prosocial behavior.

Another theoretical approach distinguishes between individualistic and collectivistic cultures (Triandis 1990). Some cultural differences mentioned here (e.g., those concerning achievement, aggression, child-rearing, self) are partly related to this dimension;

others are social values, rules, control orientation (Trommsdorff 1989, 1995). However, because concepts of individualistic/collectivistic orientation are still rather general, further studies of their function are needed.

4. Outlook: Trends and Tasks

An increasing tendency to include different cultures in empirical research can be observed. This allows optimistic expectations that ethnocentric biases will be reduced. However, several shortcomings have to be overcome. Often, the methods used in cross-cultural research have been tested only in Western cultures and their appropriateness for non-Western cultures is not ascertained. The ecological validity of verbal measures and their relation to behavior are seldom clear. Also, results are often generalized for an entire culture without discussing what aspect of the culture is represented by the sample. In the same way, intra-cultural comparisons are often neglected in favor of intercultural comparisons. Furthermore, single variables are studied without taking into account possible functional relations between these and other variables relevant to development. Here, cross-cultural research has an important task: to discover functional units of development and functional relationships which are yet unknown in Western culture. To summarize, cross-cultural research can be very useful for studying development as a process of complex interactions between the self and the environment, including the role of individuals who actively structure parts of these interactions and who thus influence their own developmental processes and outcomes.

See also: Human Learning, Evolution of Anthropological Perspectives; Perspectives on Culture, Cognition and Education; Development of Motivation

References

Boesch E E 1991 *Symbolic Action Theory and Cultural Psychology*. Springer-Verlag, New York

Eckensberger L H 1993 Moralische Urteile als handlungsleitende normative Regelsysteme im Spiegel der kulturvergleichenden Forschung. In: Thomas A (ed.) 1993 *Einführung in die kulturvergleichende Psychologie*. Hogrefe, Verlag für Psychologie, Göttingen

Eibl-Eibesfeldt I 1976 *Menschenforschung auf neuen Wegen*. Molden, Vienna

Ekman P 1972 Universals and culture differences in facial expression of emotion. In: Cole J K (ed.) 1972 *Nebraska Symposium on Motivation 1971*. University of Nebraska Press, Lincoln, Nebraska

Freeman D 1983 *Margaret Mead and Samoa: The Making and Unmaking of an Anthropological Myth*. Harvard University Press, Cambridge, Massachusetts

Grossmann K, Grossmann K 1992 Attachment behavior of Japanese toddlers before and after separation from their mothers. Paper presented at the 2nd conference of German–Japanese Society for Social Sciences, Saarbrücken

Jahoda G 1986 A cross-cultural perspective on developmental psychology. *International Journal of Behavioral Development* 9(4): 417–37

Kornadt H J, Eckensberger L H, Emminghaus W B 1980 Cross-cultural research on motivation and its contribution to a general theory of motivation. In: Triandis H C, Lonner W (eds.) 1980 *Handbook of Cross-cultural Psychology. Vol. 3: Basic Processes*. Allyn and Bacon, Boston, Massachusetts

Kornadt H J, Hayashi T, Tachibana Y, Trommsdorff G, Yamauchi H 1992 Aggressiveness and its developmental conditions in five cultures. In: Iwawaki S, Kashima Y, Leung K (eds.) 1992 *Innovations in Cross-cultural Psychology*. Swets and Zeitlinger, Amsterdam

Kornadt H J, Trommsdorff G 1990 Naive Erziehungstheorien japanischer Mütter. *Zeitschrift für Sozialisationsforschung und Erziehungssoziologie* 2: 357–76

Malinowski B 1927 *Sex and Repression in Savage Society*. Kegan Paul, London

Markus H R, Kitayama S 1991 Culture and the self: Implications for cognition, emotion and motivation. *Psychol. Rev.* 98 (2): 224–53

McClelland D C 1961 *The Achieving Society*. Van Nostrand, Princeton, New Jersey

Mead M 1929 *Coming of Age in Samoa: A Psychological Study of Primitive Youth for Western Civilisation*. Cape, London

Shweder R A 1991 *Thinking through Cultures: Expeditions in Cultural Psychology*. Harvard University Press, Cambridge, Massachusetts

Triandis H C 1990 Cross-cultural studies of individualism and collectivism. In: Berman J J (ed.) 1990 *Cross-cultural Perspectives* (Nebraska Symposium on Motivation 1989, Vol. 37). University of Nebraska, Lincoln, Nebraska

Trommsdorff G (ed.) 1989 *Sozialisation im Kulturvergleich*. Enke, Stuttgart

Trommsdorff G 1995 Empathy and prosocial action in cultural environments. A cross-cultural analysis. In: Kindermann T, Valsiner J (eds.) 1995 *Development of Person–context Relations*. Erlbaum, Hillsdale, New Jersey

Whiting B B, Whiting J W M 1975 *Children of Six Cultures: A Psycho-cultural Analysis*. Harvard University Press, Cambridge, Massachusetts

Further Reading

Munroe R L, Munroe R H 1994 *Cross-cultural Human Development*. Waveland Press, Prospect Heights, Illinois

Segall M H, Dasen P R, Berry J W, Poortinga Y H 1990 *Human Behavior in Global Perspective: An Introduction to Cross-cultural Psychology*. Pergamon Press, New York

Human Development: Research Methodology

A. von Eye and C. Spiel

Developmental research investigates constancy and change in behavior and learning across the human life course. This entry discusses the methods used to arrive at clear-cut statements concerning human development and adult learning, specifically, methods for data collection, data analysis, and interpretation. Examples are drawn from educational and psychological research of relevance to adult education.

1. Fundamental Methodological Paradigms

1.1 The Univariate Developmental Paradigm

One of the simplest methodological paradigms in social science research (Baltes et al. 1977) involves the mechanistic or deterministic assumption that observed behavior depends on or can be predicted from causal or independent variables. In brief, this assumption is that D = f(I) where D denotes the dependent variable, for example, adults' progress in learning, and I denotes the independent variable, for example, social climate in the study groups.

From a developmental perspective the prediction of constancy and change is important. Dynamic variants of the univariate developmental paradigm predict a variable, observed at later points in time, from the same variable, observed at earlier points in time. For example, a typical question is whether high achievement motivation at the start of an adult class allows one to predict high achievement motivation in later classes. Developmental changes are inferred if prediction equations, for example, regression equations, involve parameters that indicate change, for example, average increases.

Other variants of this paradigm predict changes in behavior from variables other than the dependent ones. For example, changes in behavior in menopause are predicted from changes in hormone levels (Paikoff et al. 1992). To be able to depict changes in behavior within individuals, at least two observations of the dependent variable are required.

1.2 The Multivariate Developmental Paradigm

In a most general sense, multivariate research involves two or more variables on the dependent variable side and two or more variables on the independent variable side (Baltes et al. 1977). In developmental research, one observes two or more variables and predicts constancy or change in these variables from earlier observations of the same variables (dynamic modeling) and/or from other variables.

There has been an intense debate as to what design for data collection is the most suitable. The following sections present the basic research designs, give an overview of this discussion, and summarize the conclusions with relevance for adult education research.

2. Designs for Human Development Research

There are three basic designs for developmental research: the cross-sectional, the longitudinal, and the time-lag designs. The advantages and drawbacks of each of these will be discussed. The basic assumption that underlies each of these designs is that individuals who participate in investigations are not systematically different from the population under study.

2.1 The Cross-sectional Research Design

In cross-sectional designs, researchers observe one or more variables at one point in time and in two or more groups of individuals differing in age. The use of cross-sectional designs is by far the most popular research strategy in developmental psychology, for the following reasons: most importantly, only one observation point is necessary, so that studies using cross-sectional observations take little time compared to studies using repeated observations. In addition, financial costs are typically relatively low. There are also benefits on the interpretational side. Because observations are made at only one point in time, sample fluctuations are, by definition, not a problem. Researchers can assume that samples are constant. Many adult education surveys employ this cross-sectional design.

However, cross-sectional research also has a number of specific deficiencies, most of which result from using only one observation point. Specifically, for conclusions from cross-sectional research to be valid one has to accept a number of assumptions. Some of these assumptions are strong, that is, they are difficult to satisfy, for the following reasons: (a) age samples ("cohorts") are drawn from the same parental population at birth. If this is not the case there is no way to discriminate between developmental processes and cohort differences; (b) differences in behavior that are related to age, that is, differences between individuals from different age groups, are stable over historical time. Again, if this is not the case there is no way to discriminate between changes in development that are caused by secular, historical changes, or by cohort differences; (c) differences between individuals from different age cohorts can be interpreted as indicating developmental changes that would occur within individuals as they move from one age group to the other.

If these assumptions do not hold, there is no reasonable way to assign developmental changes to such causes as age, adult learning, or historical time in a clear-cut way. Indeed, there is an abundance of literature showing that cohorts are different from each other (see Baltes et al. 1978). For example, researchers have suggested that the phenomenon of mid-life crisis may be less prevalent in the cohorts born around 1950 than in cohorts born in the time around the Great Depression (see Rybash et al. 1991). Thus, the development of a mid-life crisis may be viewed as a secular phenomenon rather tha a ubiquitous developmental phenomenon.

Selection of methods for statistical data analysis depends on the type and distribution of data. Classical statistical methods for analysis of quantitative cross-sectional data include analysis of variance, multivariate analysis of variance, and discriminant function analysis. For qualitative data chi-square decomposition, log-linear analysis, prediction analysis, and configural frequency analysis are often recommended (see von Eye 1990a, 1990b, Rovine and von Eye 1991).

2.2 The Longitudinal Research Design

In longitudinal designs, researchers observe one or more variables at two or more points in time and in one cohort. Variation over time occurs when individuals grow older during the course of the investigation.

Longitudinal studies have a number of advantages over cross-sectional studies (Schaie 1983, Baltes et al. 1977, de Ribaupierre 1989). One of the most important advantages is that only longitudinal investigations allow one to describe intra-individual development, that is constancy and change within the individual across time. In cross-sectional research intra-individual development must be inferred under strong assumptions. However, results from cognitive studies suggest that growth curves derived from cross-sectional data do not necessarily have the same shape as curves derived from longitudinal data (Salthouse 1991).

In addition, interindividual differences in intra- individual development, that is, differences between individuals' developmental patterns, can be depicted only by observing the same individuals more than once. A typical research question is whether adult learners from disadvantaged social backgrounds derive greater benefit from attempts to teach learning strategies than students from other social backgrounds. The description of such differences is important for a researcher interested in homogeneity of development. Homogeneity of development can be investigated at the variable level; for instance, by asking whether certain cognitive abilities decline in adulthood more rapidly than others. Homogeneity can also be investigated at the differential level; for example, by asking whether (and why) individuals display different developmental trajectories.

Another major advantage of longitudinal studies is that the constancy and change in relationships among variables can be investigated. For example, one could ask whether the relationship between adult learning and cognitive capacity changes over the adult life course. One of the most important preconditions for age, cohort, and time comparisons is what has been termed "dimensional identity" (Schmidt 1977). A set of variables is considered to show dimensional identity if the interrelations among variables remain unchanged over all observation points. When variable interrelations change in cross-sectional studies, it is impossible to determine whether these changes are due to age or group differences. When variable interrelations change in longitudinal studies they reflect developmental processes. However, in both cases changes in variable interrelations render comparisons of results from different age groups or cohorts difficult.

A last advantage of longitudinally collected data concerns the investigation of causes for constancy and change. A general assumption is that causes occur prior to effects. Thus, causes for development must be observed before developmental changes occur. This observation is obviously possible only in longitudinal research. Causal analysis is of concern in adult education, because of interaction among the factors that influence participation. For example, it has been found in longitudinal studies that schooling predicts first-time participation in adult education, but that this effect diminishes with time, so that experience of adult education becomes an increasingly powerful predictor of participation at a subsequent point in the life course (Tuijnman 1991).

The desirable properties of longitudinal research are offset by a number of shortcomings. The first of these is that the wrong choice of the number and spacing of observations may prevent researchers from adequately assessing underlying processes of change. Thus, researchers may miss critical periods or events, may fail to depict validly the dynamics of change, or may even completely misrepresent the shape of a growth curve.

A second shortcoming concerns serial effects of repeated measurements, such as "testing effects." For example, when individuals score higher in a particular test (e.g., an adult literacy test) in a second measurement, one cannot be sure that the increase in performance reflects an increase in ability rather than an increase due to remembering test items or familiarization with the test situation.

Similar to cross-sectional designs, sample selection may play a critical role in longitudinal studies. There may be specific selection effects, because longitudinal studies require more effort from participants than cross-sectional studies. In addition, longitudinal studies may suffer from attrition; that is, loss of participants due to moving, loss of interest, illness, or, in particular in studies including older adults, death. Each of these problems can lead to invalid description of developmental processes.

Another important shortcoming of longitudinal research is that the costs are higher than in cross-sectional research. In addition, there are interpretational problems. Most important is that of generalizability over samples. Because of cohort differences, growth curves may not be the same for samples from different cohorts (see Baltes et al. 1977). The same applies if selection effects are taken into account.

Selection of statistical methods for analyzing longitudinal data must consider data quality, distributional characteristics, and sample size. Latent class models and structural equation models that allow the explanation of patterns of relationships among variables in nonexperimental environments are becoming increasingly popular (see Bartholomew 1987, Rovine and von Eye 1991). These methods can also be useful for estimating development and change in continuous or categorical data. (For a more detailed overview of statistical methods for analysis of longitudinal data see von Eye 1990a, 1990b.)

2.3 The Time-lag Design

In time-lag designs, researchers observe one or more variables at two or more points in time and in two or more groups of individuals that belong to different cohorts but are of the same age. Variation over time results from the spacing between observation points. Although time-lag designs are far less popular than cross-sectional and longitudinal designs, they are useful in many respects. For example, the finding that there has been a considerable variation in Standard Achievement Test performance in the United States over the last 50 years could only come from a time-lag investigation.

Time-lag investigations are selected when researchers are interested in comparing cohorts. However, time of measurement and historical time are confounded. Therefore, generalizations to other cohorts, other historical times, or even other age groups are problematic. As far as costs are concerned, time-lag designs exhibit the same problems as longitudinal designs. As far as sampling is concerned, there are similarities with cross-sectional studies. As far as interpretability is concerned, there are strong constraints resulting from the focus on only one age group. For these reasons, time-lag designs have been the least popular in research on human development and adult learning.

2.4 The Age × Time of Measurement × Cohort Design

This is the only developmental research design that varies the three aspects of time: age (A), time of measurement (T), and year of birth (cohort—C). However, there is no way to vary these three aspects independently, which would be necessary to separate their effects. The reason is that the three time variables are linearly dependent on each other. Each can be expressed as a linear combination of the other two, as is shown in the following formulas. (For the following formulas, T and C are expressed in calendar years, e.g., 1951, A is expressed in years, e.g., 40.)

(a) $A = T - C$

(b) $C = T - A$

(c) $T = C + A$

Therefore, research designs have been developed that vary only two of the three variables, A, C, and T. The following designs result: $A \times C$, $A \times T$, and $C \times T$. (For a more detailed description see Baltes et al. 1977, Schaie 1983.)

With regard to $A \times C$, researchers observe two or more cohorts over three or more observation points. At the beginning of the observation of each cohort, the cohorts are of the same age. Thus observations of the younger cohorts begin when they reach the age the older cohorts were when they were first observed. To carry out a study a minimum of three observation points and two cohorts are necessary. At least two age levels must be covered. Schaie and Baltes (1975) argue that the $A \times C$ arrangement is the most useful for ontogenetic research, because this design allows one to depict constancy and change with age; that is, intra-individual change. In addition, it allows one to depict interindividual differences in intra-individual change. However, the authors also claim that using any of the two-dimensional designs is defensible, depending on the purpose of research.

The main problem with treating A, C, and T as explanations for development is that one has to make strong assumptions when one applies the two-dimensional designs. Specifically, when applying the $A \times C$ design one must assume that the effects of T are negligible; for $A \times T$ one must assume that the effects of C are negligible; and for $C \times T$ one must assume that the effects of A are negligible.

3. Special Methods

This section covers a selection of special methods, including intervention studies, microdevelopmental studies, single case studies, and training studies.

3.1 Intervention Studies

The designs discussed above are typically applied to observe natural behavior. Intervention does not take place. In contrast, research on specific kinds of intervention, for example through adult education, and its effects is often done using randomized experiments. For example, experiments examine the effects of systematic variations in teaching behavior on learner achievement. For studying intervention effects, researchers observe one or more variables in two or more groups of students, who are randomly assigned to treatments, at one or more points in time. Whenever they can be realized, randomized experiments are the preferred designs because causal inferences can be drawn from the results. Methods for statistical analysis of data from randomized experiments most often include analysis of variance.

Examples of designs for intervention studies include reversal designs and multiple baseline designs (see Baltes et al. 1977). In reversal designs researchers first establish the rate of spontaneous behavior; that is, the baseline. Then they introduce some treatment (experimental condition) that constitutes the first reversal, and assess the rate of behavior again. The second reversal occurs at the end of the treatment, and so forth. All later assessments are compared with the first, the baseline.

Reversal designs typically are applied in learning studies. One of the basic assumptions of such studies is that it is, in principle, possible that behavior rates return to the baseline after the treatment. If behavior changes are irreversible, as is often assumed of developmental changes, reversal designs become less useful.

3.2 Single Case Studies

Single case studies, also referred to as "single subject studies," involve the detailed investigation of one individual. The primary goals pursued with single case studies include the detailed description of specific processes (e.g., language development) in individuals, the development of skills in individuals with specific deficits, and treatment of behavior disorders. For analysis of single case studies time series analysis, trend analysis, or spectral analysis are most often applied.

3.3 Training Studies

In training studies researchers often combine reversal with multiple baseline designs. Multiple behaviors are trained, assessments occur before and after training periods, but there is no assumption that training affects only one type of behavior. Goals pursued with training studies include the development of skills (e.g., learning skills), the compensation of losses (e.g., memory in old age), and the reversal of decline (e.g., achievement motivation in midlife). A large number of training studies have been concerned with intellectual development (Willis and Schaie 1986, Baltes et al. 1988). Researchers were able to show that intellectual decline in adulthood can typically be compensated by appropriate training (for a detailed discussion see Salthouse 1991).

Statistical analysis of data from training studies typically involves analysis of variance with repeated observations.

3.4 Microdevelopmental Studies

Typically, longitudinal and sequential studies span several years. For instance, Schaie's Seattle Longitudinal Study observes individuals in a 7-year rhythm.

However, development also takes place in shorter time frames. Relatively short-term development is termed "microdevelopment." Studies investigating microdevelopment typically are longitudinal in nature and involve a relatively large number of observation points that are spaced in short intervals so that points in time where changes occur will not be missed (see Siegler and Crowley 1991).

An example of a microdevelopmental study is reported by Fischer and Lamborn (1989) who investigated the development of honesty and kindness in adolescents. They reported a sequence of stages. Development that carries individuals from one stage to the next is termed "macrodevelopment." Progress within stages is termed "microdevelopment." The authors specified transformation rules that describe development at the microdevelopmental level.

Statistical methods for analysis of microdevelopment include trend analysis, time series analysis, and structural equation modeling.

See also: Lifespan Development; Human Development in the Lifespan: Overview; Development of Learning across the Lifespan

References

Baltes P B, Cornelius S W, Nesselroade J R 1978 Cohort effects in behavioral development: Theoretical orientation and methodological perspectives. In: Collins W A (ed.) 1978 *Minnesota Symposium on Child Psychology*, Vol. 11. Erlbaum, Hillsdale, New Jersey

Baltes P B, Kliegl R, Dittmann-Kohli F 1988 On the locus of training gains in research on the plasticity of fluid intelligence in old age. *J. Educ. Psychol.* 80: 392–400

Baltes P B, Reese H W, Nesselroade J R 1977 *Life-span Developmental Psychology: Introduction to Research Methods.* Brooks/Cole, Monterey, California

Bartholomew D J 1987 *Latent Variable Models and Factor Analysis.* Oxford University Press, Oxford

de Ribaupierre A 1989 Epilogue: On the use of longitudinal research in developmental psychology. In: de Ribaupierre A (ed.) 1989 *Transition Mechanisms in Child Development: The Longitudinal Perspective.* Cambridge University Press, Cambridge

Fischer K W, Lamborn S D 1989 Mechanisms of variation in developmental levels: Cognitive and emotional transitions during adolescence. In: de Ribaupierre A (ed.) 1989 *Transition Mechanisms in Child Development: The Longitudinal Perspective.* Cambridge University Press, Cambridge

Paikoff R L, Buchanan C M, Brooks-Gunn J 1992 Methodological issues in the study of hormone–behavior links at puberty. In: Lerner R M, Petersen A C, Brooks-Gunn J (eds.) 1992 *Encyclopedia of Adolescence*, Vol 2. Garland, New York

Rovine M J, von Eye A 1991 *Applied Computational Statistics in Longitudinal Research.* Academic Press, Boston, Massachusetts

Rybash J W, Roodin P A, Santrock J W 1991 *Adult Development and Aging*, 2nd edn. Brown and Benchmark, Dubuque, Iowa

Salthouse T A 1991 *Theoretical Perspectives on Cognitive Aging.* Erlbaum, Hillsdale, New Jersey

Schaie K W 1983 What can we learn from the longitudinal study of adult psychological development? In: Schaie K W (ed.) 1983 *Longitudinal Studies of Adult Psychological Development.* Guilford, New York

Schaie K W, Baltes P B 1975 On sequential strategies in developmental research: Description or explanation. *Hum. Dev.* 18(5): 384–90

Schmidt H D 1977 Methodologische Probleme der entwicklungspsychologischen Forschung. *Probleme und Ergebnisse der Psychologie* 62: 5–27

Siegler R, Crowley K 1991 The microgenetic method: A direct means for studying cognitive development. *Am. Psychol.* 46(6): 606–20

Tuijnman A C 1991 Lifelong education: A test of the accumulation hypothesis. *Int. J. Lifelong Educ.* 10(4) 275–85

von Eye A (ed.) 1990b *Statistical Methods in Longitudinal Research. Vol. 1: Principles and Structuring Change.* Academic Press, Boston, Massachusetts

von Eye A (ed.) 1990a *Statistical Methods in Longitudinal Research, Vol. 2: Time Series and Categorical Longitudinal Data.* Academic Press, Boston, Massachusetts

Willis S L, Schaie K W 1986 Training the elderly on the ability factors of spatial orientation and inductive reasoning. *Psychology and Aging* 1(3): 239–47

Human Development: Research and Social Policy

S. L. Kagan

In many nations, recent years have presaged remarkable policy advancements for children and adults. Despite these accomplishments, the marginality of effective knowledge utilization in the creation of productive social policy is evident. Taking this issue as its focus, this entry explores the role that human development research has played in improving the quality of life worldwide. It suggests that the historically tenu-

ous connection between research and policy is in the process of being strengthened (Horowitz and O'Brien 1989). Such relationships are often hallmarked by an increasingly thoughtful search for definitions, mechanisms, and strategies that will maximize the synergy of research and policy interactions. This entry also suggests that if the application of research to policy is to move beyond incrementalism, scholars, practitioners, and policymakers must take stock of the persistent challenges that have impeded the research-to-policy link, and the research–policy synergy must be recontextualized.

1. Research and Policy Schism: Reality or Rhetoric?

Writing in *The Care and Education of Young Children In America*, Lazar (1980) recalled "only three studies that directly changed policies and actions" (p. 61). He cited Spitz's (1945) work on the short- and long-term effects of institutional care on infant development, Clark and Clark's (1952) work on racial differentiation in preschool children, and the Consortium for Longitudinal Studies' (1977) work on the long-term effects of preschool programs. In questioning the viability of applying social science for policy-making, Lazar was joined by others, even more skeptical: Cohen and Garet (1975 p. 19) noted that "there is little evidence to indicate that government planning offices have succeeded in linking social research and decision-making"; Wholey et al. (1971 p. 46) concluded more vehemently that "the recent literature is unanimous in announcing the general failure of evaluation to affect decision-making in a significant way" and Weiss (1972) summarized the thinking of the time by suggesting that the results of evaluation research have exerted little, if any, significant influence on program decisions.

Despite the prevailing concern that social science —broadly construed—had limited effect on programs and policy, many researchers, believing that such a link would advance child and family well-being and that such a link was indeed possible, have explicitly called for more collaboration between research and policy (Bronfenbrenner 1974, National Research Council 1978, Takanishi et al. 1983). Indeed, as Caldwell and Ricciuti (1973) noted, "it is our conviction that there should be a symbiotic relationship between social policy and social action on the one hand and child development research and its underlying theory on the other" (p. viii).

During the 1980s, efforts to link research to policy gained currency. Centers proliferated (Policy Studies Organization 1978), foundation support grew, and professional organizations began to consider social policy as an important component of their efforts. Scientists, concerned about having their findings applied to policy, sought nontraditional outlets for their work and devoted more energy to dissemination and popularization of their research findings.

2. Challenges of Linking Research and Policy

Despite these encouraging advancements and an emerging receptivity to social science research in general, the challenges inherent in applying research

to social policy formulation remain abundant. Four challenges characterize the difficulty: (a) challenges related to differing values; (b) challenges related to the lack of definitional clarity; (c) challenges related to process and context; and (d) challenges related to measuring policy-relevant outcomes.

2.1 Challenges Related to Differing Values

While numerous value considerations have impeded the effectiveness of the link between research and policy, two of these are particularly notable. The first is generic, unearthing value differences regarding the role of scientists in general policy formulation; the second is more specifically related to human services and questions the appropriate role of government in involving itself in child and family life.

The first challenge, commonly referred to as the "philosopher-king" issue, suggests that the reputation of scientists as bearers of "truth" and "ultimate knowledge" may be overexalted in the policy domain. Reflecting a general dissatisfaction with the leading role played by social scientists in influencing policy-making, Rossi and Wright (1985) noted that in a truly democratic society, "social scientists must be content with an advisory but not dominating role" (p. 331). Such positions have gained currency and have been amplified by realistic appraisals that explode the myth of the neutrality of science (Cronbach et al. 1980, Lindblom and Cohen 1979, Mark and Shotland 1985). As the construct of the philosopher-king has been dethroned, other knowledge-makers have ascended in the policy hierarchy, including the media and the funding agencies. Moreover, the receptiveness of the policy-making body itself is now more of an issue (Pettigrew 1985).

In some countries, the utilization of research for the creation of social policy is clouded by historic values that disavow the role of government in family matters. Where primacy and privacy are accorded the family and/or national ambivalence characterizes the value accorded human services, policy discourse is often derailed from empiricism to ideology. While debate about the value of policy typically precedes debate about the nature of policy, sometimes the reverse is true, with carefully honed policy stances serving as proxies for deeply held beliefs about the relationship between family and government (Woolsey 1977). In nations where politically explosive issues remain unresolved, the most elegant and socially relevant research is often forced to withstand ideological litmus tests. Moreover, research utility can be further marginalized when human service policies are considered ancillary or are subordinated to broader societal needs (e.g., tax equity or defense policy).

2.2 Challenges Related to the Lack of Definitional Clarity

Fostering a research–policy connection can be further

impaired by the lack of agreed-upon definitions of the following: policy research and analysis; policy-related research; and basic, applied, and evaluation research. One school of thought suggests that many of the terms can be used interchangeably (Maccoby et al. 1983, Nagel 1990). Conversely, another school of thought suggests that policy analysis is a distinct domain of inquiry. Moroney (1981) indicated that policy analysis is distinguished from conventional research by the way in which questions are formulated as well as by the specific purposes of the analysis. Distinguishing policy analysis from policy evaluation, Greenberger et al. (1976) suggested that policy evaluation is used to discern how well an existing program is achieving its intended outcomes, while policy analysis detects whether there are conceivable combinations of programs that might achieve desired ends. Classified by intention, others have suggested a four-tiered research to policy continuum, moving from basic, through applied, through policy-relevant, to policy-dominant research (Kagan 1993). Despite many attempts to clarify distinctions among research types, ambiguity persists and may impede the effective production and utilization of research.

2.3 Challenges Associated with Process and Context

Advancing policy-relevant research is further complicated by the fact that to be optimally relevant to the policymaker, social science research must be adequately contextualized. It must transcend pristine laboratory conditions and take real-life environments into account. Research must be ecologically valid, considering the human organism within the context of multiple environments and cultural backgrounds. But to contextualize research appropriately means that issues must be reframed and neglected questions addressed. For example, research that has focused exclusively on the relationship between interventions and child cognitive outcomes must be reset within a broadened economic, political, and institutional context (Gormley 1991, Grubb 1991, Young and Nelson 1973). Social scientists need to ask questions that have a direct bearing on policy: What is the relationship between maternal self-sufficiency, family stability, and program stability on child development? What is the relationship between program regulations, cost, and quality? Such questions may necessitate new research strategies.

Exploring the effect of treatment variables may require, for example, a combination of holistic research strategies that may include qualitative and quantitative approaches (e.g., unstructured observations, case studies, open-ended interviews, observational checklists). Such combined strategies have been labeled as "multiplism," an approach to social science research that takes as its premise the fact that no single research methodology, measure, or manipulation is perfect (Cook 1985).

2.4 Challenges Related to Measuring Policy-relevant Outcomes

Through a better understanding of the array of treatment variables and their interactions, research will be better prepared to respond to policy-relevant issues. Unanswered questions will become part of the research agenda. A nonequivalent situation exists regarding outcome data. Policymakers, anxious to obtain results that are clear and simple to understand, have been more than content to use IQ or employability results as primary expressions of program efficacy (Zigler and Trickett 1978, Zigler 1991). Expanding horizons to embrace additional dimensions—cognitive, physical, and socio-emotional development—is one important step. Further, researchers need to use outcome categories (e.g., delinquency, welfare dependence, referral to special education, and attendance) that have relevance for policymakers and are easily understood by the public. Such efforts both to broaden the range of outcomes and to make them more tangible might also be beneficial in derailing mounting concerns regarding the nongeneralizability of research findings. More research on typical programs using broader outcome indices should produce information that will be more appropriate for policymakers.

3. Implications of the Challenges

The factors discussed above help to clarify why effective links between research and policy are not more numerous. They suggest important strategies to be considered over the 1990s if the field is to maximize the application of its knowledge to improve the quality of life for children and their families. First, researchers need to be clear about the aims of their research before they embark on it. If research is to have policy utility, it must be conceptualized so that its methods and measures will have that aim in mind. Second, researchers may need to recognize the limitations of policymakers' time and promulgate their research in more easily digestible forms. Third, helping policymakers understand research tractability and complexities will encourage them to be competent users of empirically based knowledge. Fourth, policymakers need to understand that, while not yielding all answers to complex social problems, research provides a solid base from which to construct policy. As such, research deserves financial attention. Finally, researchers should not have unrealistic expectations for their research; research is just one tool—albeit an important one—within an entire range of information used by those who construct policy. The researcher's purpose is to assure its optimal utilization.

See also: Knowledge Representation and Organization; Human Development: Research & Educational Practice

References

Bronfenbrenner U 1974 Developmental research, public

policy and the ecology of childhood. *Child Devl.* 45: 1–5

Caldwell B, Ricciuti H (eds.) 1973 *Child Development and Social Policy: Review of Child Development Research*, Vol. 3. University of Chicago Press, Chicago, Illinois

Clark K B, Clark M P 1952 Racial identification and preference in Negro children. In: Swanson G E, Newcomb T M, Hartley E R (eds.) 1952 *Readings in Social Psychology*, 2nd edn. Holt, New York

Cohen D K, Garet M S 1975 Reforming educational policy with applied social research. *Harv. Educ. Rev.* 45 (1): 17–41

Consortium for Longitudinal Studies 1977 *The Persistence of Preschool Effects: A Long-term Follows-up of Fourteen Infant and Preschool Experiments*. Final Report for ACYE Grant No. 18–76–07843. Cornell University, Community Services Laboratory, Ithaca, New York

Cook T 1985 Postpositivist critical multiplism. In: Shotland R L, Mark M M (eds.) 1985 *Social Science and Social Policy*. Sage, Beverly Hills, California

Cronbach L J et al. 1980 *Toward Reform of Program Evaluation*. Jossey-Bass, San Francisco, California

Gormley W T Jr. 1991 State regulations and the availability of child care services. *Journal of Policy Analysis and Management* 10 (1): 78–95

Greenberger M, Crenson M A, Crissey B L 1976 *Models in the Policy Process: Public Decision-making in the Computer Era*. Russell Sage Foundation, New York

Grubb N 1991 Choosing wisely for children: Policy options for early childhood programs. In: Kagan S L (ed.) 1991 *The Care and Education of America's Young Children: Obstacles and Opportunities (Ninetieth Yearbook of the National Society for the Study of Education)*. University of Chicago Press, Chicago, Illinois

Horowitz F D, O'Brien M 1989 In the interest of the nation: A reflective essay on the state of our knowledge and the challenges before us. *Am. Psychol.* 44 (2): 441–45

Kagan S L 1993 The research-policy connection: Moving beyond incrementalism. In: Spodek B (ed.) 1993 *Handbook of Research on the Education of Young Children*. Macmillan, New York

Lazar I 1980 Social research and social policy: Reflections on relationships. In Haskins R, Gallagher J J (eds.) 1980 *Care and Education of Young Children in America. Policy, Politics, and Social Science*. Ablex, Norwood, New Jersey

Lindblom C E, Cohen D K 1979 *Usable Knowledge: Social Science and Social Problem-solving*. Yale University Press, New Haven, Connecticut

Maccoby E, Kahn A, Everett B A 1983 The role of psychological research in the formation of policies affecting children. *Am. Psychol.* 38 (1): 85–90

Mark M M, Shotland R L 1985 Toward more useful social science. In: Shotland R L, Mark M M (eds.) 1985 *Social Science and Social Policy*. Sage, Beverly Hills, California

Moroney R M 1981 Policy analysis within a value theoretical framework. In Haskins R, Gallagher J (eds.) 1981 *Models for Analysis of Social Policy: An Introduction*. Ablex, Norwood, New Jersey

Nagel S S 1990 Introduction: Bridging theory and practice in policy/program evaluation. In: Nagel S S, Dunn W (eds.) 1990 *Policy Theory and Policy Evaluation Concepts, Knowledge, Causes, and Norms*. Greenwood Press, New York

National Research Council 1978 *The Federal Investment in Knowledge of Social Problems, Vol. 1*. National Academy Press, Washington, DC

Pettigrew T 1985 Can social scientists be effective actors in the policy arena? In: Shotland R L, Mark M M (eds.) 1985 *Social Science and Social Policy*. Sage, Beverly Hills, California

Policy Studies Organization 1978 *Policy Research Centers Directory*. Policy Studies Organization, Urbana, Illinois

Rossi P H, Wright J D 1985 Social science research and the politics of gun control. In: Shotland R L, Mark M M (eds.) 1985 *Social Science and Social Policy*. Sage, Beverly Hills, California

Spitz R A 1945 Hospitalization. *Psychoanalytic Study of the Child* 1: 53–74

Takanishi R, DeLeon P H, Pallak M S 1983 Psychology and public policy: Affecting children, youth, and families. *Am. Psychol.* 38: 67–69

Weiss C H 1972 *Evaluation Research: Methods of Assessing Program Effectiveness*. Prentice-Hall, Englewood Cliffs, New Jersey

Wholey J S, Scanlon J W, Dugfy H G, Fikumotos J S, Vogt E M 1971 *Federal Evaluation Policy: Analyzing the Effects of Public Programs*. The Urban Institute, Washington, DC

Woolsey S 1977 Piedpiper politics and the child-care debate. *Daedulus* 106, 127–45

Young D R, Nelson R R 1973 *Public Policy for Day Care of Young Children*. Lexington Books, Lexington, Massachusetts

Zigler E 1991 Using research to inform policy: The case of early intervention. In: Kagan S L (ed.) 1991 *The Care and Education of America's Young Children: Obstacles and Opportunities (Ninetieth Yearbook of the National Society for the Study of Education)*. University of Chicago Press, Chicago, Illinois

Zigler E, Trickett P 1978 IQ, social competence, and evaluation of early childhood intervention programs. *Am. Psychol.* 33 (9): 789–98

Further Reading

Cohen D K, Weiss J A 1977 Social science and social policy: Schools and race. In: Weiss C H (ed.) 1977 *Using Social Research in Public Policymaking*. Lexington Books, Lexington, Massachusetts

Gallagher J 1981 Models for policy analysis: Child and family policy. In: Haskins R, Gallagher J (eds.) 1981 *Models for Analysis of Social Policy: An Introduction*. Ablex, Norwood, New Jersey

McLaughlin M 1985 Implementation realities and evaluation design. In: Shotland R L, Mark M M (eds.) 1985 *Social Science and Social Policy*. Sage, Beverly Hills, California

Weiss C H 1977 Introduction. In: Weiss C H (ed.) 1977 *Using Social Research in Public Policymaking*. Lexington Books, Lexington, Massachusetts

Human Development: Research and Educational Practice

A. Demetriou

Research on human development and educational practice are inextricably intertwined because they share common goals and objectives. This convergence is particularly apparent in the relations between cognitive or moral development, on the one hand, and educational practice, on the other. These issues are discussed in turn in this entry. A general framework for integrating different approaches and some general suggestions for future research will also be proposed.

1. Common Goals and Objectives

The foremost aim of the study of human development has always been the specification of human competence or characteristics at successive phases of development. Most major systems in developmental psychology involve descriptions of successive stages or levels, characterizing the gradual transformation of the human infant into an adult able to cope efficiently with the demands of the physical and social environment.

Education also deals with the developing person. Education aims, of course, not to describe but to support, shape, and enhance the person's development. The means to this end are the teaching of different fields of knowledge and the transmission of values and skills in such a way that they are assimilable by the person at the age at which they are taught. Therefore, the knowledge offered by the developmentalist can direct educators in the development of curricula and teaching materials matching the assimilatory capabilities of the learner. This would maximize the efficiency of the transmission of knowledge from the educational system to the student.

The second major focus of the study of human development is the understanding of the dynamics of change; that is, the innate mechanisms and processes that cause and enable progress to ever higher levels of competence. Education also capitalizes on cognitive change. The transmission of knowledge presupposes effective teaching methods. To be effective, teaching methods have to enable the student to move from a lower to a higher level of understanding or abandon less efficient skills for more efficient ones. Therefore, an understanding of the dynamics of development might assist educators in their attempt to develop effective teaching methods.

Finally, developmental psychology studies individual differences in the structure, rate, and mechanisms of development. It is a truism that education deals with intra- and interindividual variation. To achieve its aims, education has to be able both to meet the special needs and proclivities of different individuals as well as to provide them with the opportunity to cultivate their particular talents. Therefore, education would become more flexible in catering for the needs of different learners if it could be guided by an accurate map of the different structures of competence and possible alternative change mechanisms leading to maturity.

In conclusion, education can draw upon the study of human development in order to decide what to teach and how to teach different people at different ages. However, the road between the study of human development and educational practice is bidirectional. In fact, educational practice is part of development. This is so because education sets the frame in which development occurs, it provides the nutrients that keep the motor of development running, and it shapes the goals that development must attain. Thus, in a sense, what the student of human development is investigating is to a large extent the product of educational practice. In other words, the competence, skills, and values of different age phases may to a large extent reflect what is provided by education at these phases. The change mechanisms that govern development may reflect the learning practices adopted by education at different educational levels. Individual differences in development may mirror the various alternatives made available to the developing person by the educational system. This intertwining of human development research with educational practice is highlighted by abundant evidence showing that students who lag behind in cognitive development have inferior school performance and vice versa (see Weinert 1987).

2. Cognitive Development and Educational Practice

Curriculum analysts try to work out how different courses should be structured so as to induct students into a given field of knowledge efficiently and permanently. In physics, for example, when should concepts such as force, heat, energy, and entropy first be introduced? How is each to be decomposed into subconcepts? How can scientific thinking itself be taught? When should hypothesis testing and theory construction activities be introduced? Regarding mathematics, when and how must the concepts of number, arithmetic operations, fractions, and proportions be introduced? These questions can be answered from the point of view of two epistemological traditions in developmental psychology; namely, the structural –constructive tradition initiated by Piaget and the empiricist tradition.

2.1 The Constructivist Tradition

According to Piaget's theory, thought develops along a sequence of stages. Specifically, the stages of sensorimotor, preoperational, intuitive, concrete operational, and formal operational intelligence. The stages are not mere descriptive conventions. They represent the general constructive possibilities of the human mind at successive phases of development. Thus, on the one hand, each stage is characterized by a whole structure that governs the general quality of the person's understanding of the world. On the other hand, a higher stage cannot be attained unless the preceding stages have been consolidated. This is so because each successive stage is built on the structure of the previous stage.

Progression through the hierarchy of stages is the result of an equilibration process which gradually removes contradictions between concepts or between the person's representation of reality and reality itself. This process is self-directed and constructive; that is, the contradictions need to be actively discovered by the person and reflected upon if they are to be resolved at a higher level of understanding. It is not sufficient for them simply to be demonstrated by somebody else. It needs to be stressed that activity in Piaget's theory is not tantamount to overt activity. It may be solely mental activity that is directed to the reconstruction of a given representation of reality in order to grasp the relations involved. Activity, then, is the basis of reflexive abstraction which is one of the main causes of cognitive change.

The detailed description of changes in the understanding of most fields of knowledge on which the school focuses, together with his general theory of cognitive organization and change, have led many scholars to apply Piaget's ideas in education. Most notable is the impact of Piaget's theory on the teaching of science and mathematics, but it has affected the teaching of practically every field of knowledge, including sociology, history, poetry, and religion, and has been considered relevant to every level, from preschool to college education. In fact, the spirit of Piagetian theory has affected educational curricula and methods in many subtle ways all over the world, although a systematic investigation of these influences has not yet been attempted (see Shayer and Adey 1981).

The foremost assumption of this approach is that any scientific concept will be developed through the Piagetian sequence of stages and substages. Thus, the curriculum engineer must specify how the concepts concerned are understood at each stage.

The next step is to design curricula that would implement the results of this analysis in coursework and materials that would make each target concept understandable at each level. The teaching addressed to a given age should always start with those components of each hierarchy that match the developmental level of this age. It should then gradually expand to expose the student to higher modes of thinking.

However, this expansion should not go far ahead of the student's present level. Teaching at remote levels might cause the student either to ignore or to distort the concept taught. This may be one of the reasons underlying the presence of so many misconceptions in students' minds.

Individual evaluation is an important component of this approach because not all individuals or groups in a population of the same age function at the same level. Stage attainment in underprivileged populations may be considerably delayed. Therefore, individual evaluation is necessary in order to adapt teaching to different students or groups. This necessitates the development of valid and reliable tests which would be able to reveal the student's level of understanding separately for each concept.

An important aspect of educational practice stemming from the constructivist tradition is its reliance on the student's activity. Thus a good portion of time should be spent in activities and related reflection that enable students to build their own models of the concepts concerned. For instance, students could be provided with a balance and several weights to experiment with in order to discover the proportional relations involved in this physical equilibrium system.

2.2 The Empiricist Tradition

The approach to curriculum development stemming from the Piagetian tradition has been criticized by scholars affiliated to the so-called empiricist tradition in developmental psychology. Among the various criticisms two figure most prominently. First, the assumption that there is a general structural level for each age to which teaching must be adapted causes teaching to lag behind development instead of pulling it ahead. In fact, there is evidence indicating that all kinds of concepts and abilities can be found in some germinal or skeletal form from as early as the first months of life. This evidence lends credibility to Bruner's controversial view that "any subject can be taught effectively in some intellectually honest form to any child at any stage of development" (Bruner 1960 p. 33). The second criticism disputes the assumption that the quality of understanding at a given moment in development can be reduced to a whole structure. According to this view, development in one field may occur independently of development in other fields.

These views have become popular under the flag of the novice–expert paradigm. The core assumption of this paradigm is that development is equivalent to learning; that is, once one is given the chance and the time to master a certain body of knowledge or acquire a certain kind of skill, one is able, in principle, to become an expert irrespective of age (Chi and Rees 1983). Thus, according to this criticism, the design of curricula for different school subjects should take into account the peculiarities of the different thought structures they presuppose. However, researchers in this tradition do recognize some general principles under-lying the transformation of a novice into an expert. These include: (a) the employment of metacognitive skills (e.g., problem decomposition, construction of alternative problem representations); (b) the modeling of experts; (c) cooperative learning situations. Under these conditions, rich and situated learning environments may be created that would enable a student to go from previous knowledge to new knowledge and from simple skills to complex skills within a domain.

3. Moral and Social Development and Educational Practice

Understanding the rules and principles that govern the functioning of a person's community in particular and of human culture in general, and the acquisition of the moral and social values that enable a person to function adaptively in society are as important as the acquisition of the knowledge and skills discussed above. There have been many attempts since around 1970 to develop programs that would enhance the person's moral and social development. These attempts have been influenced extensively by Kohlberg's theory of moral development.

Kohlberg's theory shares many common assumptions with that of Piaget. Starting from Piaget and based on about 30 years of research, Kohlberg proposed a six-stage sequence of moral development. In line with Piaget's concept of activity, Kohlberg maintained that moral development is the result of social interaction that produces moral conflicts. Resolution of moral conflicts gradually orients the person from himself or herself (the stage of preconventional morality) to others, from a person's narrow group to the concerns of the broader community (the stage of conventional morality), and from the specifics of the present and the transient to general values and permanent principles (the stage of principled morality).

The theory advanced by Kohlberg was seen as the frame that would direct educators in how to educate citizens according to the most valued goals and aspirations of civilization. The Vietnam War, the rise in the crime rate, and social conflicts and upheavals precipitated the application of this theory to education. The first application was attempted by Kohlberg himself in a women's prison. It was then extended to the normal school context. These programs attempted to implement the following principles: (a) students should be exposed to and discuss real moral conflicts (e.g., what has to be done if a student has stolen money from another student?); (b) students should be encouraged to take the role of all persons involved in a moral conflict, increasing their understanding of the problem under discussion and inducing the student to adopt the concepts of fairness and human rights; (c) discussions should take the students' present level into account and should lead to conflict resolution one stage above this

level; (d) finally, students should participate actively in the formation of the rules and principles governing the functioning of a particular group and even the school as a whole (Wasserman and Garrod 1983). These programs were also extended to professional settings, with the aim of providing workers and professionals with a clear sense of the implications that their decisions and activities may have for the community, humanity in general, and even the entire planet.

If they succeeded, such programs would be important for the development of social stability and cohesion as well as harmony between the individual and society. As a result, considerable energy and resources were spent on evaluating them. According to the results of this evaluation, it appears that sensitivity to issues of morality and higher human values does improve. However, major stage changes do not seem to occur; that is, the way moral conflicts are resolved does not alter considerably as a result of participation in these programs. Finally, even changes in the quality of moral reasoning do not necessarily result in changes in moral behavior (Wonderly and Kupfersmid 1980).

The limited success of these programs may be due to the fact that Kohlberg's theory, like Piaget's, is too inflexible and global. Morality might indeed involve the concepts of fairness and consistency but it also involves dimensions such as personal ideals, beliefs, and goals, and, of course, the quest for personal satisfaction and happiness. According to Turiel (Turiel et al. 1987), the development of social understanding evolves within three distinct domains: the moral, the social conventional (forms of address, modes of dress, forms of greeting, etc.), and the personal (issues of privacy, adoption of goals or behaviors that are harmless to others, etc.). Educational programs that involve the other two domains may prove more successful than the programs that only involve the moral domain.

4. Conclusion

The different approaches discussed above are complementary rather than incompatible. This section will highlight points of agreement and suggest directions for future research (see Demetriou et al. 1992).

It is now accepted that different fields of knowledge are differentially organized and represented. Therefore, they pose different challenges for learning. Demetriou et al. (1993) have identified five systems of thought organization: categorical, quantitative, causal, propositional, and spatial. Gardner (1983) added musical, bodily, and social intelligence to this list. These systems are differentially related to different school subjects depending upon their conceptual similarities to them. Instruction across fields has to be adapted to the processing and representational requirements of the cognitive structures to which they are related. The investigation of how this adaptation may be effected has barely started.

It is also accepted that there are general constraints that set an upper limit on the complexity of any skill or concept that can be constructed at a particular age level. These constraints depend on the structural characteristics of the human mind and they can be defined, according to Case (1985), in terms of working memory capacity and efficiency of information processing (see relevant literature in Demetriou et al. 1992). There is considerable agreement that major changes in these upper limits broadly coincide with major stage shifts in the Piagetian system.

Although, therefore, the optimum potentials of each age constrain what can be learned, instruction is needed to transform the potentialities associated with each optimum level into real skills and knowledge within different domains. Learning in one domain does not automatically generalize to other domains. At the extreme, it cannot be expected that there will be automatic transfer from the moral to the cognitive domain or vice versa. However, the employment of general management strategies facilitates the acquisition and consolidation of skills in particular domains. At the same time, the acquisition of domain-specific skills provides experiences about cognitive functioning that can be transformed into general metacognitive strategies. In this sense, reflection on moral issues may shape strategies that can be transferred into the domain of learning complex scientific concepts and vice versa. Research on these issues is very sparse.

The relation between the development of general potentialities and learning in specific domains is very complex. School performance until early adolescence is more dependent on general rather than domain-specific cognitive skills. Thereafter the role of general abilities diminishes and the role of domain-specific abilities increases. However, the more remote from everyday experience and the more symbolically idiosyncratic a domain is (mathematics being a prime example), the more learning will be dependent on the state of general abilities (compare Demetriou et al. 1992).

The construction of these skills is greatly facilitated by both the person's active involvement with different tasks, as Piaget maintained, and by interpersonal scaffolding, as Vygotsky suggested. However, learning at different ages is facilitated by different teaching methods. Before the age of 10, personal exploration together with teacher's explication or peer interaction is more effective in producing change than any of these methods alone. Later, any single method may be equally efficient. This is the case because at later stages the mind is characterized by representational and symbolic fluency such that it can easily translate concepts from one representational system or code into another (Karmiloff-Smith 1992). How this translation occurs and how it can be facilitated by education are as yet unclear.

Finally, it is now accepted that students with different cognitive styles learn better under different methods. For instance, field-independent persons prefer an analytic approach to problem-solving whereas field-dependent persons prefer a holistic approach (Globerson 1989). To be successful, teaching should provide learners with different styles the opportunity to learn via their preferred style, even if they operate on the same developmental level. It is only gradually that students may be induced into other learning styles so as to build multiple and yet integrated and flexible knowledge strategies and stores.

References

Bruner J S 1960 *The Process of Education.* Harvard University Press, Cambridge, Massachusetts

Case R 1985 *Intellectual Development: Birth to Adulthood.* Academic Press, Orlando, Florida

Chi M T H, Rees E T 1983 A learning framework for development. *Hum. Dev.* 9: 71–107

Demetriou A, Efklides A, Platsidou M 1993 The architecture and dynamics of developing mind: Experiential structuralism as a frame for unifying cognitive developmental theories. *Monographs of the Society for Research in Child Development* 58(5) no. 234

Demetriou A, Shayer M, Efklides A (eds.) 1992 *Neo-Piagetian Theories of Cognitive Development: Implications and Applications for Education.* Routledge, London

Gardner H 1983 *Frames of Mind: The Theory of Multiple Intelligence.* Basic Books, New York

Globerson T 1989 What is the relationship between cognitive style and cognitive development? In: Globerson T, Zelniger T (eds.) 1989 *Cognitive Style and Cognitive Development.* Ablex, Norwood, New Jersey

Karmiloff-Smith A 1992 *Beyond Modularity.* MIT Press, Cambridge, Massachusetts

Shayer M, Adey P 1981 *Towards a Science of Science Teaching: Cognitive Development and Curriculum Demand.* Heinemann, London

Turiel E, Killen M, Helwig C C 1987 Morality: Its structure, functions, and vagaries. In: Kagan J, Lamb S (eds.) 1987 *The Emergence of Morality in Young Children.* University of Chicago Press, Chicago, Illinois

Wasserman E, Garrod A 1983 Application of Kohlberg's theory to curricula and democratic schools. *Educational Analysis* 5(1): 17–36

Weinert F E 1987 Developmental processes and instruction. In: De Corte E, Lodewjiks H, Parmentier R, Span P (eds.) 1987 *Learning and Instruction: European Research in an International Context*, Vol. 1. Pergamon Press, Oxford

Wonderly D, Kupfersmid J H 1980 Kohlberg's moral judgment program in the classroom: Practical considerations. *Alberta Journal of Educational Research* 26(2): 128–41

Further Reading

Bergowitz M W, Oser F (eds.) 1985 *Moral Education: Theory and Application.* Erlbaum, Hillsdale, New Jersey

Biggs J, Collis K 1982 *Evaluating the Quality of Learning: The SOLO Taxonomy* (Structure of the Observed Learning

Outcome). Academic Press, New York
Furth H G, Wachs H 1975 *Thinking Goes to School: Piaget's Theory in Practice.* Oxford University Press, New York
Gardner H 1991 *The Unschooled Mind: How Children Think*

and How Schools Should Teach. Basic Books, New York
Newman D, Griffin P, Cole M 1989 *The Construction Zone: Working for Cognitive Change in School.* Cambridge University Press, Cambridge

Developmental Psychopathology

A. F. Kalverboer

1. Introduction

The term "developmental psychopathology," originally coined by Sroufe and Rutter (1984), covers a great diversity of deficits and abnormalities. Their common characteristic is that they emerge during early or later childhood (rarely in late adolescence) and are thought to be a consequence of a complex interplay between biological, psychological, and social factors (Lewis and Miller 1990). The pathogenesis and etiology of developmental psychopathology can only be understood if there is a clear insight into possible risk and protective factors. In particular, the interplay between the structural and functional development of the central nervous system and the mechanisms that play a role in the development of ontogenetic adaptations of functions is a field of growing interest that is of utmost importance for improving understanding of the determinants of developmental abnormalities and deficits. It is one of the crucial challenges of this "decade of the brain" to gain more insight into these processes.

1. Diagnostic Systems of Mental Disorders

Sroufe and Rutter (1984) emphasize how the study of normal and deviant development has to go hand in hand, so that pathology can be understood in terms of basic mechanisms. This approach has been largely lacking. Clinicians (child psychiatrists, clinical and developmental psychologists) have strongly focused on the description and diagnosis of pathological conditions: as a result an elaborated diagnostic system has been developed, namely the American Psychiatric Association's diagnostic manual, known as DSM-III-R (1987). In this system, the "psychiatric and clinical nomenclature" is continuously refined but without attention being paid to the developmental principles that may underlie normal and pathological development. The manual has great value for clinicians, as it offers internationally applied descriptions of the phenomenology of all mental disorders and gives diagnostic criteria for each disorder. However, it does not make any attempt to offer a theoretical basis for the etiology and pathogenesis of deviance. In the long run, insight

into mechanisms is a prerequisite for improving clinical diagnostics and treatment. This should be attained by theory building based on empirical research of an interdisciplinary and longitudinal character.

As well as the American Psychiatric Association's DSM-III-R, there is another internationally recognized system: the World Health Organization's ICD (the International Classification of Diseases, the latest version of which is ICD-9-CM, 9th revision, clinical modification, 1979). The ICD-9-CM classification has been the official system for recording "all diseases, injuries, impairments, symptoms and causes of death" since January 1979, both internationally and in the United States. Internationally, the DSM system is the more influential concerning mental disorders. As far as possible, DSM has been made compatible with the general ICD system, using similar codes for diseases. Almost all the diagnostic terms in the DSM-III-R system are also included in the mental section of the ICD-9-CM system.

In the following section, the DSM-III-R system's treatment of developmental disorders will be briefly discussed.

2. The DSM-III-R Classification System of Mental Disorders

Each mental disorder is conceptualized in the Manual as:

> a clinically significant behavioral or psychological syndrome or pattern that occurs in a person and that is associated with present distress (a painful symptom) or disability (impairment in one or more important areas of functioning) or with a significant increased risk of suffering death, pain, disability, or an important loss of freedom. . . . Whatever its original cause, it must currently be considered a manifestation of a behavioral, psychological, or biological dysfunction in the person. (DSM-III-R 1987 p. xxii)

The general approach to classification is descriptive and atheoretical, justified by widely varying theoretical orientations with respect to etiology. Where possible, explicit diagnostic criteria, based on up-to-date empirical research, have been included. DSM-III-R is a multiaxial system for evaluation to ensure that certain information that may be of value in planning treatment and predicting outcomes for each person is recorded on each of the following five axes: Axis 1: Clinical syndromes, Axis 2: Developmental disorders and personal disorders, Axis 3: Physical disorders and conditions, Axis 4: Severity of psychosocial stressors, and Axis 5: Global assessment of functioning.

In the view of the manual's authors this implies that "in its entirety this multiaxial system provides a biopsychosocial approach to assessment" (p. xxv)

A separate chapter in the manual is devoted to "disorders usually first evident in infancy, childhood or adolescence." These are roughly the sorts of syndromes covered by the term "developmental psychopathology." The main classes of disorders under this heading are:

(a) *Mental retardation.* The essential features of this disorder are: significant subaverage general intelligence (i.e., roughly an IQ below 70), accompanied by significant deficits or impairments in adaptive functioning, and onset before 18 years of age (DSM-III-R p. 28).

(b) *Pervasive developmental disorders.* These disorders are characterized by: "qualitative impairment in the development of reciprocal social interaction, in the development of verbal and nonverbal communication skills, and in imaginative activity. Activities are frequently markedly restricted, stereotyped and repetitive" (p. 33). This class has only one specified subgroup, namely autistic disorder or infantile autism (see Howlin and Yule 1990, Hertzig and Shapiro 1990), the remaining disorders being known as pervasive developmental disorder not otherwise specified (PDDNOS). Detailed diagnostic criteria are given for autistic disorder. Examples of characteristics are: no or abnormal seeking of comfort, lack of awareness of the existence of feelings of others, no mode of communication, stereotyped body movements, and persistent preoccupation with parts of objects.

(c) *Specific developmental disorders.* These are "disorders that are characterized by inadequate development of specific academic, language, speech, and motor skills and that are not due to demonstrable physical or neurological disorder, a pervasive developmental disorder, mental retardation, or deficient educational opportunities" (p. 39). The main subgroups are:

  (i) *academic skills disorders,* for example, developmental arithmetic disorder and developmental reading disorder;
  (ii) *language and speech disorders,* for ex-

ample, developmental articulation disorder, developmental expressive disorder, and developmental receptive language disorder;
  (iii) *motor skills disorder,* with the main subgroup "developmental coordination disorder" or "clumsiness."

(d) *Other developmental disorders.* Here the important subclasses are the following:

  (i) *disruptive behavior disorders,* characterized by behavior that is socially disruptive and is often more distressing to others than to the people with the disorders. Subcategories are:
  (ii) *attention-deficit hyperactivity disorder* (ADHD), characterized by "inappropriate degrees of inattention, impulsiveness, and hyperactivity" (p. 50);
  (iii) *oppositional defiant disorder,* characterized by negativistic, hostile, and defiant behavior;
  (iv) *conduct disorder,* essential feature: "a persistent pattern of conduct in which basic rights of others and major societal rules are violated" (p. 53).

(e) *Anxiety disorders of childhood or adolescence.* Here anxiety is the predominant clinical feature. Subcategories are:

  (i) *separation anxiety disorder*: "excessive anxiety concerning separation from those to whom the child is attached" (p. 60);
  (ii) *avoidant disorder of childhood and adolescence*: "an excessive shrinking from contact with unfamiliar people" (p. 61);
  (iii) *overanxious disorder*: with the essential feature of "excessive or unrealistic anxiety or worry for a period of 6 months or longer," which is generalized to a variety of situations (p. 63).

(f) *Eating disorders,* including anorexia nervosa ("intense fear of gaining weight"), bulimia nervosa "recurrent episodes of binge eating," and Pica "persistent eating of a nonnutritive substance") (p. 65ff).

(g) *Gender identity disorders,* with the essential feature of "an incongruence between assigned sex and gender identity." Subtypes are among others: *gender identity disorder of childhood,* "persistent and intensive distress in a child about his or her assigned sex and the desire to be, or insistence that he or she is, of the other sex); and *transsexualism,* "a persistent preoccupation to acquire the sex characteristics of the other sex") (p. 71ff).

(h) *Tic disorders,* the best known subcategory of

which is *Tourette's disorder*, characterized by multiple motor and one or more vocal tics.

(i) *Elimination disorders*, with two subgroups of "functional encopresis" and "functional enuresis."

(j) *Speech disorders not elsewhere classified*, for example, *cluttering* ("a disturbance of fluency involving an abnormally rapid rate and erratic rhythm of speech that impedes intelligibility") and *stuttering* ("a marked impairment in speech fluency characterized by frequent repetitions or prolongations of sounds or syllables")

(k) *Other disorders of infancy, childhood, or adolescence*. Subcategories are: *elective mutism* ("persistent refusal to talk in one or more major social situations, despite the ability to comprehend spoken language and to speak"; p. 88), *reactive attachment disorder of infancy or childhood* ("a disturbance in social relatedness, presumed to be due to grossly pathogenic care that preceded the onset of the disturbance"; p. 91), and *stereotype/habit disorder* ("intentional and repetitive behaviors that are nonfunctional," such as body-rocking and head-banging; p. 93).

3. Etiological Models

Titles of books such as *Psychopathology: An Interactional perspective* (Magnusson and Ohman 1987) indicate that simple main effects and linear models for normal and deviant development are not sufficient. Transactional models (Sameroff and Chandler 1975) in which the developmental outcome is seen as a result of an interplay in the course of development between biological and environmental factors are required to account for the complex determination of developmental disorders. On the one hand, social deprivation models have not been supported by empirical studies; early social and emotional deprivation (in particular, inadequate or inconsistent mothering) does not seem to have the dramatic consequences for human social development that has been claimed on the basis of these models. On the other hand, consequences of early somatic complications (e.g., hypotonia, anoxia, prematurity, early growth retardation) for cognitive and social development are also evidently much less severe than was once suggested by clinicians (Sameroff and Chandler 1975, Kalverboer 1979). Dunn (1976) discusses the effects for later development of early mother–infant relations. She stresses the adaptibility of the developmental process, indicating that effective development can be obtained in many different ways: mothers do not have to be "tuned in" to every phase of their children's development. Children can also develop properly (as is shown in Kibbutz studies) in conditions where the mother does not spend more than 2 hours a day with the child. Quality of interaction is more important than quantity.

Children who had lived all their early lives in nurseries lagged temporarily behind in language, but not in nonverbal development, and at the age of 4 their verbal and nonverbal skills were at age level and they did not show signs of behavioral disturbance (Tizard and Rees 1975). Evidently the organism possesses a large self-righting tendency, which is in agreement with the model proposed by Waddington (1975). He postulated a largely genetically based capacity to maintain a certain "optimal" pathway of development and overcome disturbing factors. He "provides a way of thinking about developmental pathways and on the astonishing capacity of the system to right itself after a perturbation and return to its former track" (Bateson 1976 p. 403).

Empirical studies by Werner and her colleagues give support to these notions. Not only do they show that all kinds of prenatal and perinatal complications have adverse effects on children's later development only if they grow up in poor social conditions, they also pay attention to the capacity of many children to achieve an optimal development even though they live in unfavorable conditions. In their book *Vulnerable but Invincible* Werner and Smith (1982) discuss a large number of "protective" factors in the child and the environment which may compensate for or counteract risk conditions. Protective factors within the child are, for example: "high activity level; good-natured; affectionate disposition; ability to focus attention and control impulses; and internal locus of control" (Werner and Smith 1982 p. 134). Such characteristics may contribute to the self-righting qualities of the child and positively interact with sources of support in the caregiving environment. (Such factors are e.g., close peer friends, much attention paid to infant during first year, and so on.)

4. Levels of Explanation

Rose (1976) has presented a model in which various domains of functioning have been circumscribed as different levels of explanation. In Table 1 a modification of the Rose model is given.

Models of the etiology or causation (pathogenesis) of disorders can be developed within each level of functioning, focusing particularly on either anatomical structures, biochemical or physiological processes, or neurological/behavioural functions. Rose stresses how little is understood of how mechanisms at various levels of explanation may relate to each other. The evidence rarely goes further than to suggest a certain parallelism between phenomena at different levels of the "hierarchic scheme."

The sorts of disorders covered by the term developmental psychopathology always contain phenomena related to different levels of functioning, such as the

Table 1
"Levels" of explanation[a]

	"Levels"	Specification
In context (holistic)	1 Sociological	Social institutions: family, neighborhood, school, health services, etc.[b]
	2 Psychological	(a) Relationship systems: parent-child, child-group, etc
		(b) Social interaction processes: in family, school, etc.
		(c) Behavioral systems: adaptive behavioral patterns, like (complex) skills, play behavior, exploratory activity, contact behavior, etc.
		(d) Psychological basic functions: attention, long- and short-term memory, perceptuomotor and cognitive functions; in general: structural and energetic aspects of information processing, including psychophysiology
	3 Neurological/ neurophysiological	Sensory and motor systems: optimality of the central nervous system; EEG, EMG, etc.
Out of context (reductionist)	4 Biochemical	Neurotransmission
	5 Anatomical	Functionally organized systems in the CNS/Mechanical characteristics of the organism

Source: Adapted by Kalverboer (1990) from Rose (1976).
a The term "levels" is in quotation marks as the author does not completely agree with Rose's notion of a hierarchy of levels of explanation (the term "aspects" is preferable, but Rose's terminology is followed nevertheless)   b At these levels, perceptions, expectations, and value systems play an important role and should be included in the explanatory models.

anatomical, biochemical, physiological, neurological, psychological, or social level. A point in case is attention-deficit hyperactivity disorder (ADHD). This condition may serve to illustrate how mechanisms at various levels may coincide in one particular clinical syndrome (see also Kalverboer 1990). In ADHD the following sorts of disorders are frequently reported:

(a) *Neuroanatomical.* A large variety of possible involvements are suggested, concerning deeper or more surface areas of the brain, or various cortical areas such as frontal, parietal, and temporal areas (in particular frontal areas are frequently mentioned). Often, however, there is not any clear indication of structural brain disorder in ADHD. Sometimes there is some indirect evidence of structural brain disorder, specifically when there are factors in the child's life history that are known to affect brain development, such as severe encephalitis.

(b) *Biochemical.* A lack of balance among various neurotransmission systems, which affect the functions of the autonomous nervous system, is postulated as a crucial factor in ADHD as well as in autism. Porges (1976) gave evidence for an imbalance between sympathetic (excitatory) and parasympathetic (inhibitory) systems in the brain in conditions such as hyperactivity, autism, and what he calls "psychopathy." Various frequently used psychopharmacological substances (such as methylphenidate in ADHD) are thought to influence the functioning of these systems and eventually restore the balance among them. Important in this respect is the study on differential effects of drug doses on learning and social inter-

action. However, there are many pitfalls in such studies and the data are still controversial (Gadow 1989). How such disorders on the biochemical level may affect brain function and ultimately adaptive behavior is largely unclear. There is much speculation (e.g., concerning effects of drugs on specific mechanisms of information processing or on energetic processes) but hardly any hard evidence for such specific relationships is available.

(c) *Neurophysiological.* Disorders in electrophysiological processes in the brain of a general or more specific kind are frequently thought to be present in ADHD. Well-known statements based on electroencephalographical (EEG) recordings, such as: "mild signs of immaturity," "generalized imbalance," or "incoherence between brain activity in the two hemispheres." More specific phenomena are suggested in evoked potential studies, in which attempts are made to relate aspects of information processing (such as "decision-making") to specific evoked potential changes. In other developmental disorders, such as mental retardation, autism, and developmental reading or speech disorders, the situation is rather similar. How such physiological dysfunctions may affect the child's cognitive functions is again largely unclear, although in some instances attempts are made to develop some theory about these connections (e.g., the lack of left-hemisphere dominance hypothesis with respect to dyslexia).

(d) *Neurological.* Hard neurological evidence for brain damage is almost exclusively found in those cases of ADHD in which mental problems are present in combination with specific somatic diseases, such as spasticity/hemiplegia. Much more widespread are reports on so-called "soft" neurological signs (a better term is "minor neurological dysfunctions" or MND) in relation to developmental disorders. Such signs are thought to indicate a less optimally functioning nervous system which may contribute to problems in adaptive behavior. Only occasionally such signs of MND are specifically linked to particular brain areas (such as problems in the timing of movements to the cerebellum). Such signs may indicate that there is some diffuse brain impairment, but generally they are nonconclusive with respect to the presence or absence of a structural brain defect. Detailed neurological assessment procedures for infants and children have been worked out by Prechtl and Beintema (1968), and by Touwen (1979). Such procedures may be useful in that they present a profile of neurological dysfunctions which can be meaningfully related to developmental (adaptive) problems (e.g., choreiform dyskinesia to writing disorder). Needless to say, there is a likelihood of circular reasoning in the attempt to relate minor neurological signs to disorders in behavioral functions and skills, as both may be just different aspects of the same functional repertoire.

(e) *Psychological*. Disorders in information processing have been the target of much experimental research in ADHD. The general finding is that many children with ADHD are slower and less consistent in all aspects of information processing, without showing any specific defect in selective or sustained attention or in memory processes (Sergeant and Van der Meere 1990). In particular, "unadaptive" variability in perceptual and motor processes is characteristic of conditions such as ADHD and clumsiness (i.e., Developmental Coordination Disorder). Most evidence suggests that there are problems at the "energetic" level (see Sanders' 1983 information processing model) in such children; they are not able or not inclined to maintain the proper behavioral state or motivation, which would allow them to show consistent and flexible adaptive behavior. Problems in maintaining, and flexibility varying rhythmic patterns may be a core phenomenon, underlying many of the behavioral and learning difficulties reported in such children (Geuze 1990).

Again, such phenomena are also found in other developmental disorders, such as autism and mental retardation. They may of course be accompanied by specific functional disorders, for example, those concerning perceptual discrimination (auditory, visual), spatial organization, or comprehension. This may be particularly the case in specific developmental disorders, such as developmental arithmetic or reading disorders, or

language and speech problems. Again, insight is largely lacking in how problems at the level of basic functions may influence more complex skills.

(f) *Social*. Many children with ADHD have problems in their social relationships and communicative functions (see Kalverboer et al. 1990b). In the peer group they are more often considered as "bulliers," whereas clumsy children are more often the bulliers' victims (Kalverboer et al. 1990a). In this social domain other categories of developmentally disturbed children may show quite different patterns. For example, severe antisocial behavior is frequently found in conduct-disordered children whereas extreme problems in communicative functions characterize autistic children.

5. *Longitudinal and Interdisciplinary Approaches*

To obtain futher insight into the mechanisms that may play a role in normal and deviant development, longitudinal studies are required in which interactional and cognitive processes are closely followed and in which individual pathways of development can be traced. Such studies should account for the complex transactions that play a role in interactional and learning processes. An example is a study on cognitive and social development in preterm infants which focuses on the detection of risk mechanisms. (Kalverboer and Wijnroks 1992). In this study the behavioral organization in preterm infants (aspects such as "overstretching"; impairments in postural control and visual orienting behavior, which may affect their adaptive qualities), is continuously monitored during the first year of life and related to the caretakers' capacities to react sensitively to the child's actions. Such a study may reveal why some preterm children develop behavioral disorders, whereas others do not. Close follow-up studies are indispensable for designing proper strategies for early guidance and treatment.

Refined longitudinal studies on individual development have made methodological and theoretical contributions to the study of early risk for developmental psychopathology. However, sophisticated techniques also have their limitations, especially if their use is not guided by a thorough knowledge of the data. Using such techniques, one can easily lose direct contact with the clinical phenomena from which the data were derived. Brown et al. (1991) state:

> It is highly desirable for a worker to give him or herself the opportunity of arriving at the same insight from as many different directions as possible. And this may only come at times from muddling through data, moving from one thing to another as ideas occur, and reworking analyses over and over again as new factors emerge. (p. 68)

Interdisciplinary studies, in which a problem-centered approach is adopted, are still rare, but absolutely necessary for gaining more insight into the complex "biopsychosocial" determination of disorders, as defined in DSM-III-R. There is still not much understanding of the mechanisms that may underlie clinical problems. Such knowledge is required for the improvement of diagnostic tools and procedures for optimizing children's development. Only in exceptional cases, such as metabolic diseases like phenylketonuria (PKU) and Congenital Hypothyroidism (CH), are (biochemical) mechanisms sufficiently known to develop treatments that may prevent children from developing severe clinical dysfunctions. However, in the domain of "developmental psychopathology" this is more the exception than the rule.

6. Conclusion

The field of "developmental psychopathology" is still largely ruled by clinical approaches, which may be a barrier to more fundamental, theory driven research on the mechanisms that play a role in the etiology and pathogenesis of a disease.

Interdisciplinary and longitudinal study programs are required to obtain insight into the complex biopsychosocial determinants of developmental problems. Such insight is required for the development of the proper tools for the early diagnosis of risk conditions, the prevention of (severe) psychopathology, and the guidance of problem children and their social environment. The development of tools for the interdisciplinary study of developmental processes over a larger age range is essential. The continuity/discontinuity issue requires special scientific attention. A better understanding of the "laws" underlying developmental deviance is needed. Natural histories as well as experimental studies are required to obtain insight into these processes.

See also: Brain Development and Human Behavior; Genetics and Human Development

References

American Psychiatric Association 1987 *Diagnostic and Statistic Manual of Mental Disorders*, 3rd rev. edn. The American Psychiatric Association, Washington, DC

Bateson P P G 1976 Rules and reciprocity in behavioral development. In: Bateson P P G, Hinde R A (eds.) 1976 *Growing Points in Ethology*. Cambridge University Press, Cambridge

Brown G W, Harris T O, Lemyre L 1991 Now you see it, now you don't—some considerations on multiple regression. In: Magnusson D, Bergman L R, Rudinger G, Törestad B (eds.) 1991 *Problems and Methods in Longitudinal Research: Stability and Change*. Cambridge University Press, Cambridge

Dunn J 1976 How far do early differences in mother-infant relations affect later development? In: Bateson P P G, Hinde R A (eds.) 1976 *Growing Points in Ethology*. Cambridge University Press, Cambridge

Gadow K D 1989 Dose-response effects of stimulant drugs: A clarification of issues. In: Bloomingdale L M, Swanson J M (eds.) 1989 *Attention Deficit Disorder*, Vol. 4. Pergamon Press, Oxford

Geuze R H 1990 Variability of performance and adaptation to changing task demands in clumsy children. In: Kalverboer A F (ed.) 1990

Hertzig M E, Shapiro T 1990 Autism and pervasive developmental disorders. In: Lewis M, Miller S M (eds.) 1990

Howlin P, Yule W 1990 Taxonomy of major disorders in childhood. In: Lewis M, Miller S M (eds.) 1990

Kalverboer A F 1979 Neurobehavioural findings in preschool and school-aged children in relation to pre- and perinatal complications. In: Shaffer D, Dunn J (eds.) 1979 *The First Year of Life*. Wiley, New York

Kalverboer A F (ed.) 1990 *Developmental Biopsychology: Experimental and Observational Studies in Children at Risk*. University of Michigan Press, Ann Arbor, Michigan

Kalverboer A F, De Vries H, Van Dellen T 1990a Social behaviour in clumsy children as rated by parents and teachers. In: Kalverboer A F (ed.) 1990

Kalverboer A F, Overbeek B, Vaessen W 1990b Social behaviour in hyperactive children, as rated by parents and teachers. In: Kalverboer A F (ed.) 1990

Kalverboer A F, Wijnroks L 1992 Early intervention programs focusing on the parent–child system. In: Nakken H, van Gemert G H, Zandberg T (eds.) 1992 *Research on Intervention in Special Education*. Edwin Mellen, Lampeter

Lewis M, Miller S M (eds.) 1990 *Handbook of Developmental Psychopathology*. Plenum Press, New York

Magnusson D, Ohman A (eds.) 1987 *Psychopathology: An Interactional Perspective*. Academic Press, New York

Porges S W 1976 Peripheral and neurochemical parallels of psychopathology: A psychophysiological model relating autonomic imbalance to hyperactivity, psychopathy, and autism. *Advances in Child Development and Behavior* 11: 35–65

Prechtl H F R, Beintema D J 1968 *Die neurologische Untersuchung des reifen Neugeborenen*. Georg Thieme Verlag, Stuttgart

Rose S 1976 *The Conscious Brain*, rev. edn. Penguin, Harmondsworth

Sameroff A J, Chandler M J 1975 Reproductive risk and the continuum of caretaking casualty. In: Horowitz F D (ed.) 1975 *Review of Child Development Research*, Vol. 4. University of Chicago Press, Chicago, Illinois

Sanders A F 1983 Toward a model of stress and human performance. *Acta Psychol.* 53(1): 61–97

Sergeant J A, Van der Meere J J 1990 Attention deficit disorder: A paradigmatic approach. In: Kalverboer A F (ed.) 1990

Sroufe L A, Rutter M 1984 The domain of developmental psychopathology. *Child Dev.* 55(1): 17–29

Tizard B, Rees J 1975 The effect of early institutional rearing on the behavior problems and affectional relationships of 4-year-old children. *J. Child Psychol. Psychiatry Allied Discip.* 16(1): 61–73

Touwen B C L 1979 Neurological examination of the child with minor nervous dysfunction. *Clinics in Developmental Medicine, No. 1*. Heinemann, London

Waddington C H 1975 *The Evolution of an Evolutionist.* Edinburgh University Press, Edinburgh
Werner E E, Smith R S 1982 *Vulnerable but Invincible: A Longitudinal Study of Resilient Children and Youth.* McGraw-Hill, New York
World Health Organization (WHO) 1979 *International Classification of Diseases*, 9th revision. World Health Organization, Geneva

Developmental Disabilities: Severe

D. L. Ferguson

There seems to be a remarkable similarity in the history of experience of persons with severe developmental disabilities in many parts of the world. If they survive at all, the social response toward such individuals has tended to be one of essentially benign neglect, although some countries' neglect has been more benign than others' (Blatt and Kaplan 1966). The presence of obvious sensory, cognitive, or physical disability was thought to render people by definition beyond repair, and consequently beyond any expectation of hope or help.

However, most societies developed some effort to "test" this conclusion of chronicity, usually with some professionally guided attempt at remediation. Once the attempt failed to achieve whatever social standard held for the majority of the population, the service of choice was custodial care, most often in segregated settings (Ferguson 1989), if care was officially provided at all.

With the advent of compulsory education laws in the United States, schools repeated this pattern of attempted remediation, followed by official exclusion on the basis of chronic ineducability (Ferguson 1987). This process of benign neglect and exclusion in both schools and community services has been gradually revised through a series of policy reforms, beginning with normalization and mainstreaming, followed by integration, and now reconceptualized as "supported inclusion." This entry describes how each policy shift emerged and was then replaced by subsequent reform agendas. Supported inclusion, the current guiding concept, is also described in terms of its implications for practice in schools, communities, and universities.

1. Defining Persons with Severe Developmental Disabilities

Persons with severe disabilities are historically identifiable as those consistently excluded from the preferred service agenda of the period for achieving economic productivity and self-reliance for people with less severe disabilities (Ferguson 1987). Since the emergence of modern special education in Europe, beginning in France at the start of the nineteenth century, an incrementalism of increased expectations, fueled by improving medical, assistive, and instructional technologies, has characterized reform initiatives in the United States and a number of other Western countries (Ferguson 1987). This social nature of the definition of disability creates a pattern of continuity across different cultural examples over time. Thus, the specific population of persons considered severely disabled, the policies and practices applied, and the lives experienced by persons with severe disabilities in North America, might vary in time or sequence from those in some other Western or developing countries, but the broad pattern remains consistent.

Persons with severe disabilities are generally found among those members excluded from service by their failure to meet the varying requirements of reform, rather than by some immutable set of individual traits and abilities. In the most recent past, this residual population in many Western countries has come to mean those defined as severely mentally retarded. Thus, included in the designation "severely developmentally disabled" are those individuals identified by The Association for Persons with Severe Handicaps (TASH) as severely intellectually and or multiply disabled. Previous categorical designations for this group of individuals included moderate, severe, and profound mental retardation, in combination with medical conditions such as visual and hearing impairment, dual sensory impairment, cerebral palsy, autism, serious emotional disturbance, and epilepsy. Current preferred definitions follow the lead of the World Health Organization and other international groups in emphasizing the noncategorical, functional need for extensive ongoing support in more than one major life activity (including mobility, communication, self-care, and learning as required for independent living, employment, and self-sufficiency).

2. Normalization

The term "normalization" was first used in 1959 by Nils Bank-Mikkelsen, then head of the Danish Mental Retardation Service. His influence led to the Danish Act of 1959, the stated purpose of which was to enable mentally retarded people to live in a manner as close to normal living conditions as possible. Focusing on outcome, Bank-Mikkelsen hoped to combat what he called the "dogma of protectionism" and bring retarded people the same legal and human rights that all others have (1969).

By 1969, Bengt Nirje of Sweden had formulated a principle of normalization, based on extending to mentally retarded people patterns and conditions of everyday life as similar as possible to those of society's mainstream. Focusing on "normal means" of providing care and service, Nirje (1976) described eight normal rhythms of life that should not be denied disabled persons. These included normal rhythms of the day, week, year, and life cycle, and normal opportunities to receive the respect of others, live with the opposite sex, live in typical housing, and experience financial security.

By 1972, Wolf Wolfensberger had offered another formulation of the principle of normalization, incorporating the Danish emphasis on normal outcomes with the Swedish one on normal means. In addition, he broadened the concept to include any disabled or "devalued" person. Wolfensberger's (1972) principle of normalization refers to the use of culturally valued means to help people to live lives that are culturally valued; its implications have been the subject of much debate and misunderstanding, both in the literature and among service professionals. Some criticize normalization as ignoring real individual differences, as attempting to make people normal, or denying people relationships with their disabled peers. Others feel normalization is unrealistic, places an undue burden on people to change, is only really applicable to the most mildly disabled, or, finally, is empirically unverified.

Despite ongoing debate over the misconceptions and implications of normalization, for persons with severe disabilities the discussion might be described as resulting in a new respect for their humanity. The "out of sight, out of mind" segregation into homes and institutions too often discharged social responsibility in the form of custodial care without looking deeply into the quality and adequacy of that care.

3. Mainstreaming

Strictly speaking, "mainstreaming" did not apply to persons with severe disabilities, yet the debates over the term's application to other students with learning and sensory disabilities stretch back to the 1850s. More recently, in the 1960s, the term was used as special educators began to question the practice of segregated special classes for students with mild learning disabilities (Dunn 1968). Mainstreaming emerged in part as an argument against separate remediation classes, in favor of "mainstreaming" remediation support into the general education context.

Much of the early controversy regarding mainstreaming resulted in part from the term itself. New legal emphasis in the United States on "regular

educational environments," combined with normalization's reference to a person functioning "in the mainstream of society," resulted in two misconceptions: first, mainstreaming as physical placement in a regular class, followed by mainstreaming only for the appropriately eligible, that is, students with mild disabilities.

In the service of mainstreaming, thousands of students previously labeled as "educable mentally retarded" were declassified and returned to regular classes. In response, educators attempted to restrict mainstreaming to those few disabled students who were "most nearly normal." The confusion and debates about mainstreaming have not been short-lived, nor have they been confined to the United States. Similar discussion about the location of remedial education, and the necessary changes in the curriculum and teaching strategies employed by mainstream teachers, continues in several European countries, including the United Kingdom, Finland, and Italy (e.g., Hargreaves 1983).

If normalization brought a new respect for the humanity of persons with disabilities, mainstreaming maintained and reinforced the discourse about disability as different and in need of repair. The mainstreaming debate was essentially over where the repair would occur and which persons and methods should be used to accomplish it. Britain's *Warnock Report* and 1981 Education Act, which extend a medically based, individualistic deficit model of disability to 20 percent of British schoolchildren, is one example of mainstreaming logic articulated as national policy that resulted in fewer students learning in the "mainstream" of public education (Fulcher 1989).

4. Integration

Unlike mainstreaming, integration draws much more on social and political discourse. The United States' Education of the Handicapped Act of 1975 (now the Individuals with Disabilities Education Act, IDEA) is perhaps the most detailed example of the merging of civil rights and professional conceptualizations of disability. From a democratic perspective, any child has a civil right to public education. For students previously excluded from schooling as too disabled to benefit, the application of a civil rights framework accorded them the status of a widely disenfranchised and discriminated against minority group (Gliedman and Roth 1980). The essential intent of integration was to remediate social discrimination by ending stigmatizing and discriminatory educational exclusion and segregation. Since students with severe developmental disabilities were most often numbered among those excluded and segregated because of professional assessment of limited or absent learning potential, calls for integration promised to result in substantial changes in their schooling experiences.

The negative and deleterious effects of separate education inspired new education policies in countries other than the United States (e.g., Commonwealth Schools Commission 1985), that also principally focused on a democratic ideal of schooling access for all students. In other places, where the mainstreaming discussions were already well-advanced, the word "integration" seemed simply to replace the word "mainstreaming," with little real change. Essentially a policy about not excluding or segregating students with disabilities, integration came to dominate discussions about appropriate educational remediation of student learning and ability deficits. Since, however, the concept of integration did not specify what exactly was to be done instead of exclusion and segregation, many different interpretations and examples resulted. Some interpretations emphasized a more political agenda (Booth 1988), others a matching of provision to need, but most failed to change the schooling experiences of students with significant disabilities from more to less segregated, while increasing the number of special education students receiving segregated schooling (Fulcher 1989, Singer and Butler 1987).

The efforts of educational professionals to balance the rights of students to be educated with a highly individualized, medically dominated, deficit/remediation model of disability most often resulted in educational services (and other disability services) delivered along some continuum of services and locations. Similarly, in other disability services the demand for less segregation and the continuing need to remediate disability-based deficits resulted in an analogous continuum in other service spheres. One consequence of this continuum was that the power of integration was never realized for many of the students or adults it was intended to aid. Integration's promise, of a mainstream that tolerated and perhaps incorporated more differences in abilities, remained largely unfulfilled. Even those persons who found themselves physically integrated in general education classrooms, group homes, and community workplaces often did not reap the promised rewards of full membership, giving rise to the call for functional, social, community, and organizational integration as well as simple physical presence.

5. Supported Inclusion

Previously segregated schooling and community services for children, youth, and adults with severe disabilities became newly justified as appropriate and "least restrictive," giving rise by the late 1980s to calls for educational inclusion and supported community life. Inclusion, unlike integration, did not depend on being segregated in the first place. Rather than separating students on the basis of disability, according to this concept all students should from the beginning of their schooling careers be included, by right, in the opportunities and responsibilities of public schooling, community living, and employment.

More than ceasing to segregate in the first place, the concept of inclusion in the late 1980s and early 1990s is really a call for a substantial reconceptualization of special education, disability services, and the mainstream. If integration accorded persons with disabilities the right to be a minority group, supported inclusion argues for their right to be active, fully contributing members of their communities. The mainstream thus becomes a norm characterized by maximum diversity rather than organized according to the statistical symmetry of the bell curve.

At the same time, the focus of services to achieve that end are characterized by the concept of support rather than remediation. Smull and Bellamy (1991 pp. 528–29) identify five emphasis shifts of this reconceptualization of service focus:

(a) in the view of disability, from an emphasis on individual limitations to a focus on environmental constraints;

(b) in the public role, from providing community readiness programs to guaranteeing access and providing support;

(c) in the individualized assessment and planning process, from diagnostic-prescriptive approaches to choice-based approaches;

(d) in service location, from separate programs to integrated settings;

(e) in service strategy, from formal to informal supports.

The implications for supported educational inclusion are only beginning to emerge in many places. Perhaps one of the most promising new policies is that of the Danish Ministry of Education, which rejects the usefulness of disability designations in favor of an emphasis on curriculum and teaching as a more productive way to achieve student competence and eventual community participation and contribution.

The history of reform efforts in both education and disability services encourages, at the very least, modesty about any new initiative. Nevertheless, supported inclusion seems particularly promising because, unlike earlier reform efforts, it attempts to strike new balances between the experience of disability and the professional response to disability; between repairing disability and incorporating people as members of a diverse community despite their disability; and between the importance of personal and family preferences and the recommendations of experts. At the very least, supported inclusion seems an important and appropriate legacy of the increased presence of persons with severe disabilities in schools and communities as a consequence of earlier normalization, mainstreaming, and integration initiatives.

References

Bank-Mikkelsen N 1969 A metropolitan area in Denmark: Copenhagen. In: Kugel R, Wolfensberger W (eds.) 1969 *Changing Patterns in Residential Services for the Mentally Retarded*. President's Committee on Mental Retardation, Washington, DC

Blatt B, Kaplan F 1966 *Christmas in Purgatory: A Photographic Essay on Mental Retardation*. Allyn and Bacon, Boston, Massachusetts

Booth T 1988 Challenging conceptions of integration. In: Barton L (ed.) 1988 *The Politics of Special Education Needs*. Falmer Press, London

Commonwealth Schools Commission 1985 *Report of the Working Party on Special Education on Commonwealth Policy and Directions in Special Education*. Commonwealth Schools Commission, Canberra

Dunn L 1968 Special education for the mildly retarded: Is much of it justifiable? *Excep. Child.* 35(1): 5–22

Ferguson D L 1987 *Curriculum Decision Making for Students with Severe Handicaps: Policy and Practice*. Teachers College Press, New York

Ferguson P M 1989 Abandoned to their fate: A history of social policy and practice toward severely retarded people in America, 1820–1920. *Dissertation Abstracts International, 50*, 661A–662A

Fulcher G 1989 Integrate and mainstream? Comparative issues in the politics of these policies. In: Barton L (ed.) 1989

Gliedman J, Roth W 1980 *The Unexpected Minority: Handicapped Children in America*. Harcourt Brace Jovanovich, New York

Hargreaves D H 1983 *The Challenge for the Comprehensive School: Culture, Curriculum and Community*. Routledge and Kegan Paul, London

Nirje B 1976 The normalization principle. In: Kugel R, Shearer A (eds.) 1976 *Changing Patterns in Residential Services for the Mentally Retarded*. President's Committee on Mental Retardation, Washington, DC

Singer J D, Butler J A 1987 The Education for All Handicapped Children Act: Schools as agents of social reform. *Harv. Educ. Rev.* 57(2): 125–52

Smull M W, Bellamy G T 1991 Community services for adults with disabilities: Policy challenges in the emerging support paradigm. In: Meyer L H, Peck C A, Brown L (eds.) 1991 *Critical Issues in the Lives of People with Severe Disabilities*. Paul H. Brookes, Baltimore, Maryland

Wolfensberger W 1972 *The Principle of Normalization in Human Services*. National Institute for Mental Retardation, Toronto

Further Reading

Barton L (ed.) 1989 *Integration: Myth or Reality?* Falmer Press, London

Kiernan W E, Schalock R L (eds.) 1989 *Economics, Industry, and Disability: A Look Ahead*. Paul H. Brookes, Baltimore, Maryland

Lipsky D K, Gartner A 1989 *Beyond Separate Education: Quality Education for All*. Paul H. Brookes, Baltimore, Maryland

Meyer L H, Peck C A, Brown L (eds.) 1991 *Critical Issues in the Lives of People with Severe Disabilities*. Paul H. Brookes, Baltimore, Maryland

Porter G L, Richler D (eds.) 1991 *Changing Canadian Schools: Perspectives on Disability and Inclusion*. G. Allan Roeher Institute, Ontario

Taylor S J, Bogdan R, Racino J A (eds.) 1991 *Life in the Community: Case Studies of Organizations Supporting People with Disabilities*. Paul H. Brookes, Baltimore, Maryland

Villa R A, Thousand J S (eds.) 1995 *Creating an Inclusive School*. Association for Supervision and Curriculum Development, Alexandria, Virginia

Basic Cultural Conceptions and Scientific Theories of Human Development

---

Cultural and Religious Concepts of Human Development

R. M. Thomas

The term "culture" in one of its popular uses, refers to the broad array of beliefs and activities shared by members of a group. Such an array typically includes concepts about human development—about how and why people develop as they do (descriptive beliefs) and about how people should develop in order to grow up properly (prescriptive beliefs). The array forms a kind of commonsense theory of development, since the beliefs are held in common by the group members who have come to view their shared convictions as being obviously true. The word "group" in this context can mean a nation, a religious denomination, a social class or caste, an ethnic body, a tribe, an extended family, or the like.

The subcategory of culture entitled "religion" typically includes people's beliefs about the origin of the universe, the purpose of life, supernatural forces that may influence life's events, important characteristics of human personality, the nature of the lifespan, how and why people develop over their lifespan, and more. These aspects together can form the conception of human development held by dedicated adherents of a particular faith.

Whereas traditional cultural and religious concepts have evolved since prehistoric times, those beliefs about human development that are termed scientific or scientifically based are of recent origin, hardly more than a century or two old. For at least two reasons, studying connections between traditional beliefs and scientific views can prove enlightening. First, what is referred to as "scientific" has been derived from earlier cultural beliefs, and the resulting scientific concepts have now become part of modern culture. Second, traditional beliefs and scientific views now coexist today side by side, sometimes in conflict and sometimes in mutual support. As a means of demonstrating such relationships, this entry describes five types of cultural beliefs about human development and then identifies links between traditional cultural concepts and scientific views.

1. Diverse Cultural and Religious Concepts

Typical human-development issues on which cultural and scientific beliefs focus include: (a) how the human species originated; (b) the purpose of human development; (c) personality structure; (d) the nature of the lifespan; and (e) causal forces that determine how an individual develops. The following examples illustrate a variety of beliefs held by different groups about such matters.

1.1 Human Origins

Nearly all major cultures offer an explanation of how the human species began. The belief system extending from Judaism through Christianity into Islam holds that a supreme being—Jehovah, God, or Allah—in a period of six days created the entire universe, including all living things in the forms in which they appear today. On the sixth day the first man, Adam, was produced, and from one of Adam's ribs the first woman, Eve, was created. These two became the progenitors of all the people who have ever lived on earth.

In the Shinto tradition of Japan, a pair of male and female ancestors, Izanagi and Izanami, gave birth to the 14 islands that were thought to make up the earth's geography, and the pair subsequently bore 35 deities to rule over such elements as the sky, lands, and fire. All members of the Japanese race are descended from the issue of such dieties (Philippi 1968).

One version of Hindu lore from India holds that before the beginning of time a Cosmic Soul generated a golden egg from which sprang Brahman, the Cosmic Soul's operational form. The original egg divided into two halves, one forming heaven and the other earth. All beings on the earth have since been derived from Brahman through the existing beings subdividing themselves to produce the world's continually growing population (Renou 1961). In another version, the Cosmic Soul began in the shape of a person, born of the golden egg. When the person reflected on his condition, he realized he was alone and afraid, so he "became the size of a man and wife in close embrace. He divided this body in two. From that division arose husband and wife . . . . From that union human beings were born" (Nikhilananda 1956 pp. 115–17).

The Taoist Tao (meaning "The Way") tradition in China has pictured human origins as arising through a four-stage process. The universe at first was nothingness. From nothingness there appeared the One. Soon the One became the Two. Then the Two generated "the ten thousand," a phrase referring to all of humanity.

In summary, over the centuries varied accounts of human origins have been popular in different cultures.

1.2 The Purpose of Human Development

From the viewpoint of most religions, the two most common purposes of human development have been: (a) to grow up in ways that match the dictates of the gods and (b) to prepare the individual for what the soul will experience after physical death. In effect, life on earth is seen as a preparation for the soul's eternity of existence after death.

In contrast to these spiritual goals, common sense has often cast purposes of development in more immediate and mundane terms, such as maintaining good health, acting maturely (behaving like an adult), gaining skills for survival, and achieving happiness.

1.3 Personality Structure

The term "personality structure" refers to the components that make up a human being. Some definitions of personality include an individual's body as well as those nonphysical aspects that may be referred to as mental, psychological, or spiritual. However, other conceptions of personality limit their focus to nonphysical features. The following text will illustrate conceptions of personality structure that have been held in various societies.

During the Middle Ages and Renaissance in Europe, philosophers evolved a conception of personality in which each human was composed of a body and a soul. Sometimes the division was tripartite—body, mind, and soul. The mind or soul segment was divided into a diversity of capacities or attributes called faculties. Typical faculties were those of reason, imagination, memory, laughter, reverence, will, loyalty, sympathy, and faith. A particular individual's personality depended on how much of each faculty was present. Some people had superior memories, others were especially reverent, and still others surpassed in loyalty and faith. Vestiges of faculty psychology are still prominent today in Western societies, as reflected in such comments as: "She has a great capacity for sympathy" and "He was completely irrational; he seemed to have lost his faculties."

In belief systems that include both mind and soul, the distinction between the two is often obscure and difficult to demonstrate. The characteristic most often used to differentiate the two is that the mind continues to exist only as long as the body is alive, but the soul lives on after death.

A variant of the soul-mind combination is found among the Gurung people of Nepal. In Gurung belief, a person is composed of the four natural elements of Hindu tradition (earth, water, fire, air) plus a soul (*plah*, comprised of nine constituent parts in men and seven in women) and a conscious mind (*sae*). People are unaware of their soul, even though it is the essential life force that keeps the body intact. The *plah* is socially dependent, relying on the nurturance of the community to prevent the constituent parts from flying apart and causing illness or death. The *sae* is a person's conscious individuality and observable personality attributes.

> An individual's *sae* can be bigger or smaller. A person with a big *sae* . . . has an inner equilibrium, manifested as generosity, friendliness, dignity, and evenness of temper. A small *sae* involves a tendency to be easily angered or hurt and is expressed as withdrawal and selfishness, an unwillingness to respond to the demands of others, and a reluctance to share . . .. The idea of the *sae* describes an interactive process between an individual's inner condition and the outer events of the world. Misfortune or humiliation causes the *sae* to shrink, and a small *sae*, in turn, leads to bad judgment, incorrect behavior, and unfortunate event. (McHugh 1989 pp. 81–82)

Zulu culture in southeast Africa pictures humans as consisting of body and spirit. At the time of death the spirit or soul leaves the body and goes to live in the spirit world, which is not the heaven or hell of the Judeo–Christian–Islamic tradition but, rather, exists in parallel with the physical world thereby making the spirit available to influence the development of people who are still alive. Each spirit is thought to leave the body with its earthly personality intact. Hence, the soul of a person who was irascible in life will continue to be ill-tempered in the spirit world. Zulus further believe that people differ in the amount of power they wield in their interactions with nature and with other humans. This power is not lost at the time of death. Instead, it increases after death, as a result of the soul's increased proximity to the sources of power that reside in the spirit world (M'Timkulu 1977).

1.4 The Lifespan

Modern books about human development envisage the lifespan as extending from the moment of biological conception (male sperm uniting with female ovum) until the moment of physical death. In this sense, the average life span extends over 60–80 years. However, in many cultural traditions, calculating the life span is not such a simple matter. In Judeo–Christian–Islamic doctrine, the lifespan differs for each person's physical and spiritual aspects. The physical self starts with biological conception and ends when the heart stops pumping. However, the spiritual self—the soul—has been inserted into the unborn fetus sometime during the mother's pregnancy and will then continue to exist eternally after physical death.

In Hindu tradition, the physical life span is from conception until death. However, the soul is eternal. Each particular soul was created in the primordial past, when it separated from the Cosmic Soul. Over aeons of time, an individual soul has inhabited innumerable different bodies. It has left one body when that body expired, has then transferred itself to a newly born body, inhabiting it until that one also expired. This transmigration of the soul from body to body can continue over infinite time until the individual spirit can once more merge into the Cosmic Soul whence it originated.

1.5 Causal Forces in an Individual's Development

The forces that are assumed to determine why individuals develop as they do can differ from one belief system to another. For many people in present-day societies, causality involves two major sources of influence: heredity and environment. These interact in complex ways to fashion each person's pattern of growth. In addition, most religious doctrines propose that the predominant causal influence is supernatural power wielded either by a single god in monotheistic religions or by a panoply of spirits in polytheistic traditions. A further proposed causal factor can be a person's own free will, which is typically presumed to be under the conscious control of that individual and not manipulated by forces outside the person. Finally, some conceptions of causality include chance (luck or fate), a factor people cite whenever they are unwilling to attribute an aspect of development to a person's genetic endowment, the environment, supernatural forces, or free will. The following examples illustrate the patterns that such conceptions of cause can assume in three cultures.

On the west coast of the United States, Chumash Indian tradition holds that all humans possess the ability to influence others' lives. In addition, all other units of nature besides people—animals, plants, rocks, and bodies of water—are endowed with such human qualities as will, intelligence, and emotionality. Supernatural spirits also display these qualities. Furthermore, each unit is invested with its own degree of power, with that power more often negative in effect than positive. How any individual will develop is the result of the interaction of these myriad forces. Because there are so many units—each with a particular amount of power and guided by its own will, thought, and feelings—there is no way to predict how a given individual will grow up. This condition of unpredictability cannot properly be labeled "chance" or "luck," since in Chumash belief such concepts do not exist; everything is caused. Instead, unpredictability derives

from too many units interacting on the basis of their individual wills and feelings.

> The universe is thus subject to sudden changes that are neither foreseeable nor predictable. A good deed may be repaid by evil, or an evil deed by good; a winner may inexplicably lose, or an ineffectual man succeed. behavior is uncertain. . . . The universe, in short, is fraught with peril, full of dangers that one can only hope to avoid through a judicious combination of knowledge and prudence. (Blackburn 1975 pp. 70–71)

Although in most societies the act of sexual intercourse is believed to be the cause of pregnancy, such a conviction is not universal. Among traditional Trobriand Islanders of the South Pacific, pregnancy is believed to result from one ancestral spirit inserting another ancestral spirit into the mother's womb. This action, they contend, is most readily accomplished if the opening has been enlarged by intercourse, hence explaining why women who have frequent intercourse become pregnant more often than those who do not (Malinowski 1948).

In some cultures environmental conditions at the time a child is conceived are thought to determine certain of the child's characteristics. The Chenchu in the Hyderabad hill country of India believe that a child conceived in the rain will cry a great deal and one conceived in total darkness will be born blind. To prevent such misfortunes, parents refrain from copulating in the rain or darkness (Oswalt 1972). In effect, proposed causes of development can differ markedly from one culture to another. With these examples of cultural traditions in mind, the next section will consider how such commonsense beliefs can relate to scientific views of human development.

2. Comparing Cultural and Scientific Beliefs

The term "science" is generally used to identify both a general method of seeking the truth and a body of information compiled by the use of that method. Observations of scientists at work reveal no single, specific scientific method. Rather, what scientists hold in common is a set of general precepts or attitudes that guide their efforts.

One precept is that conclusions about human development should be founded on empirical evidence; that is, on evidence derived from the direct study of people's appearance and behavior. Thus the source of scientific knowledge is neither cultural tradition nor religious authority; instead, the source is empirical data and their logical interpretation.

A second precept is that all conclusions are subject to revision as the result of additional empirical evidence and its analysis. Consequently, from a scientific perspective, no answers to questions about development should be regarded as final and definitive. Each answer is assumed to be no more than an approximation of the truth, an approximation that requires further testing and refinement.

What, then, is the connection between cultural and scientific concepts? The connection is quite intimate, since the matters scientists study derive from cultural beliefs. Hence, scientific endeavors can be conceived as activities designed to systematize, confirm, illuminate, replace, refine, extend, and set aside common sense. These seven functions are illustrated by the following examples.

2.1 Systematization

Two intellectual exercises that humans are prone to pursue are those of classifying and theorizing. Classifying involves establishing categories into which observations of phenomena can be placed. Theorizing, in one of its forms, consists of proposing why changes in one phenomenon produce particular changes in others. Classifying and theorizing both serve to systematize life; to impose order on events so as to make them understandable. One of the principal functions of science has been to improve cultural and religious classes and theories by means of extensive empirical observations, the rigorous application of logic, and the creation of novel ways to perceive development.

The classifying function can be illustrated with the case of children's physical or psychological handicaps that are judged worthy of special educational treatment. In Great Britain in the 1880s, traditional cultural conceptions regarding which handicaps warranted special educational provisions were limited to two levels of mental retardation, imbecile and idiot. By 1913 six more categories had been added—moral imbecile, mental defective (feeble-minded), blind, deaf, epileptic, and physically defective. Over the next seven decades, as empirical investigations of handicaps rapidly mounted, further distinctions were added. By 1981 the list included: learning difficulties (severe and mild forms), blind, partially sighted, deaf, partially hearing, epileptic, maladjusted, disruptive, physically handicapped, speech defective, delicate, dyslexic, autistic, neuropathic, inconsequential, psychiatrically crippled, aphasic, and more (Tomlinson 1982).

An example of science's theorizing function is the explanation of human development advanced by the Russian psychologists Vygotsky and Elkonin, who proposed that children's intellectual growth derives from the activities in which children engage. In this theory, each stage of life is identified with a leading activity which represents a person's main goal-oriented, genuinely industrious interaction with the world. The activity serves to alter the structure of the child's intellect. In other words, the child's actions produce changes in thought patterns. Vygotsky and Elkonin identified the following learning activities for six stages of development from birth through adolescence: (a) engaging in emotional contact with adults (birth to

age 1); (b) manipulating objects (ages 1–3); (c) playing games (ages 3–7); (d) learning in school (ages 7–11); (e) improving social communication (ages 11–15); and (f) learning a vocation (ages 15–17) (Thomas 1992).

2.2 Confirm Action

In the nineteenth and twentieth centuries, as societies have sought to provide universal formal education for the young, children throughout the world have usually been admitted to primary school between the ages of 5 and 7. This policy was originally founded on commonsense observations of when children can first learn to read, write, and calculate. The appropriateness of such a policy has subsequently been confirmed by hundreds of formal empirical studies. Most children's neurological maturity and background of experience do prepare them to profit from instruction in reading, writing, and calculating at this age.

2.3 Refinement

In all literate societies, common sense has always shown that people of the same chronological age do not all learn to read and write equally well. However, in past centuries the extent to which different individuals' literacy skills deviated from the average was little more than vaguely recognized. One of the major contributions of researchers in the twentieth century is the precision with which they have described individual differences in literacy and have explained why they occur. Similar advances in knowledge of human differences have been achieved in all other aspects of development as well.

2.4 Illumination

People always knew from their commonsense observations that young children and adults differ in the way they think about events in the physical world. However, common sense did not make clear the nature of these differences. During the twentieth century, the understanding of such differences was significantly advanced by the Swiss developmentalist Jean Piaget. One phenomenon of child development that he explicated was centration, which is the tendency of children under age 5 or 6 to focus attention on one aspect of an event and overlook other important aspects. As an illustration, young children cannot consider two dimensions, such as height and width, at the same time. If there is the same amount of water in two glasses of identical size and shape, the typical 4-year old will agree that both contain the same amount of water. But if the child sees the water from one glass poured into a taller and thinner glass, he will center exclusively on the height dimension and thus conclude that the taller glass contains more water, thereby providing an example of centration. Piaget explained that other characteristics of immature logic also contribute to such an error of judgment. For instance, the young child also fails to comprehend the principle of compensation; that is, that the dimensions of an object can operate in coordination so that one dimension compensates for another. The greater width of the original glass compensates for its lack of height (Piaget and Inhelder 1969).

2.5 Extension

In many present-day societies, as well as past ones, a popular belief has been that the most fundamental secular purpose of development is to equip people to survive. Typically this purpose extends beyond bare survival, so that the aim of development is for people to thrive in health, longevity, physical comfort, and personal satisfaction.

In its commonsense version, belief in a survival motive has sometimes been limited to the survival of the individual (self-interest) and, perhaps, of the immediate group (family, clan, tribe). According to other versions, the survival aim encompasses all of humanity—that is, the human species. But in recent times, sociobiologists have extended the concept to a more fundamental level. After citing studies of altruistic behavior (e.g., sacrificing one's own welfare for the welfare of others), scientists have postulated that the most natural purpose of life is not the survival of the species, since species are eliminated or altered with the passing of time. Rather, the basic aim is the survival of the genes, which are the carriers of life itself (Wilson 1975).

2.6 Replacement

Perhaps the most dramatic instance of a scientific conception replacing a traditional cultural view is found in the case of Charles Darwin's nineteenth-century proposal about human origins. Darwin's precise observations of hundreds of animal species living in diverse environments led him to conclude that humans had not suddenly been created in their present form a few thousand years ago. Instead, he theorized that humans were the product of an evolutionary process which started many aeons ago and linked together all forms of the earth's animal life in a complex developmental network. Although many religious fundamentalists continue today to deny this view of human origins, nearly all members of the international scientific community and a large portion of the informed public subscribe to some form of Darwinism.

2.7 Avoidance

Not all cultural concepts are seriously addressed by the scientific community. Some are simply ignored. Typical examples are soul, spirit world, and life after death.

These matters rarely, if ever, appear in scientific discourse because they cannot be operationally defined or empirically confirmed or disconfirmed, at least not by the investigative methods presently available. It is true that developmentalists do study how and why people come to hold such beliefs. However, researchers generally do not include soul or spirit world as components of their own conceptions of either personality or the environment, since belief in soul and spirit world depend too much on faith in tradition and on appeals to divine authority to suit the standards of empirical science.

See also: Attitudes and Values, Acquiring

References

Blackburn T C (ed.) 1975 *December's Child: A Book.* University of California Press, Berkeley, California

Malinowski B 1948 *Magic, Science, and Religion and Other Essays.* Doubleday, Garden City, New York

McHugh E L 1989 Concepts of the person among the Gurungs of Nepal. *American Ethnologist* 11(1): 75–86

M'Timkulu D 1977 Some aspects of Zulu religion. In: Booth N S (ed.) 1977 *African Religions.* NOK, New York

Nikhilananda S 1956 *The Upanishads: Aitareya and Brihadaranyaka,* Vol. 3. Harper, New York

Oswalt W H 1972 *Other Peoples, Other Customs.* Holt, Rinehart and Winston, New York

Philippi D L 1968 *Kojiki.* Princeton University Press, Princeton, New Jersey

Piaget J, Inhelder B 1969 *The Psychology of the Child.* Routledge and Kegan Paul, London

Renou L 1961 *Hinduism.* Braziller, New York

Thomas R M 1992 *Comparing Theories of Child Development,* 3rd edn. Wadsworth, Belmont, California

Tomlinson S 1982 *A Sociology of Special Education.* Routledge and Kegan Paul, London

Wilson E O 1975 *Sociobiology: The New Synthesis.* Harvard University Press, Cambridge, Massachusetts

Further Reading

National Geographic Society 1973 *Primitive Worlds: People Lost in Time.* National Geographic Society, Washington, DC

Parrinder G 1975 *African Mythology.* Hamlyn, New York

Peel R 1988 *Spiritual Healing in a Scientific Age.* Harper & Row, San Francisco, California

Stevenson H, Azuma H, Hakuta K (eds.) 1986 *Child Development and Education in Japan.* Freeman, New York

Terrell J U 1979 *The Arrow and the Cross: A History of the American Indian and the Missionaries.* Capra Press, Santa Barbara, California

Thomas R M (ed.) 1988 *Oriental Theories of Human Development: Scriptural and Popular Beliefs from Hinduism, Buddhism, Confuicianism, Shinto, and Islam.* Lang, New York

Ecological Models of Human Development

U. Bronfenbrenner

Ecological models encompass an evolving body of theory and research concerned with the processes and conditions that govern the lifelong course of human development in the actual environments in which human beings live. Although most of the systematic theory-building in this domain has been done by Bronfenbrenner, his work is based on an analysis and integration of results from empirical investigations conducted over many decades by researchers from diverse disciplines, beginning with a study carried out in Berlin in 1870 on the effects of neighborhood on the development of children's concepts (Schwabe and Bartholomai 1870). This entry consists of an exposition of Bronfenbrenner's theoretical system, which is also used as a framework for illustrating representative research findings.

1. The Evolution of Ecological Models

Bronfenbrenner's ecological paradigm, first introduced in the 1970s (Bronfenbrenner 1974, 1976, 1977, 1979), represented a reaction to the restricted scope of most research then being conducted by developmental psychologists. The nature of both the restriction and the reaction is conveyed by his oft-quoted description of the state of developmental science at that time: "It can be said that much of developmental psychology is the science of the strange behavior of children in strange situations with strange adults for the briefest possible periods of time" (Bronfenbrenner 1977 p. 513).

In the same article, Bronfenbrenner presented a conceptual and operational framework (supported by the comparatively small body of relevant research findings then available) that would usefully provide the basis and incentive for moving the field in the desired direction. During the same period, he also published two reports pointing to the challenging implications of an ecological approach for child and family policy (1974) and educational practice (1976).

Within a decade, investigations informed by an ecological perspective were no longer a rarity. By 1986, Bronfenbrenner was able to write:

> Studies of children and adults in real-life settings, with real-life implications, are now commonplace in the research literature on human development, both in the United States and, as this volume testifies, in Europe as well. This scientific development is taking place, I believe, not so much because of my writings, but rather because the notions I have been promulgating are ideas whose time has come. (1986b p. 287).

At the same time, Bronfenbrenner continued his work on the development of a theoretical paradigm. What follows is a synopsis of the general ecological model as delineated in its most recent reformulations (Bronfenbrenner 1989, 1990, Bronfenbrenner and Ceci 1993).

2. The General Ecological Model

Two propositions specifying the defining properties of the model are followed by research examples illustrating both.

Proposition 1 states that, especially in its early phases, and to a great extent throughout the life course, human development takes place through processes of progressively more complex reciprocal interaction between an active, evolving biopsychological human organism and the persons, objects, and symbols in its immediate environment. To be effective, the interaction must occur on a fairly regular basis over extended periods of time. Such enduring forms of interaction in the immediate environment are referred to as *proximal processes*. Examples of enduring patterns of proximal process are found in parent–child and child–child activities, group or solitary play, reading, learning new skills, studying, athletic activities, and performing complex tasks.

A second defining property identifies the threefold source of these dynamic forces. Proposition 2 states that the form, power, content, and direction of the proximal processes effecting development vary systematically as a joint function of the characteristics of the developing person; of the environment—both

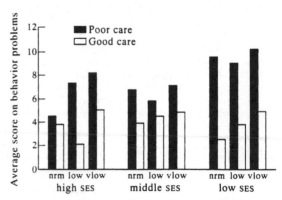

nrm = normal birth rate; low = between normal and 5.5 lbs;
vlow = 5.5 lbs. or less

Figure 1
Problem behavior at age 4 (by birth weight, mother's care, and social class)

immediate and more remote—in which the processes are taking place; and the nature of the developmental outcomes under consideration.

Propositions 1 and 2 are theoretically interdependent and subject to empirical test. A research design that permits their simultaneous investigation is referred to as a process–person–context model. A first example illustrating the model is shown in Fig. 1. The data are drawn from a classic longitudinal study by Drillien (1963) of factors affecting the development of children of low birth weight compared to those of normal weight. The figure depicts the impact of the quality of mother–infant interaction at age 2 on the number of observed problem behaviors at age 4 as a joint function of birth weight and social class. As can be seen, a proximal process, in this instance mother–infant interaction across time, emerges as the most powerful predictor of developmental outcome. In all instances, good maternal treatment appears to reduce substantially the degree of behavioral disturbance exhibited by the child. Furthermore, as stipulated in Proposition 2, the power of the process varies systematically as a function of the environmental context (in this instance, social class) and of the characteristics of the person (in this case, weight at birth). Note also that the proximal process has the general effect of reducing or buffering against environmental differences in developmental outcome; specifically, under high levels of mother–child interaction, social class differences in problem behavior become much smaller.

Unfortunately, from the perspective of an ecological model the greater developmental impact of proximal processes in poorer environments is to be expected only for indices of developmental dysfunction, primarily during childhood. For outcomes reflecting developmental competence (e.g., mental ability, academic achievement, social skills) proximal processes are posited as having greater impact in more advantaged and stable environments throughout the life course. An example of this contrasting pattern is shown in Fig. 2, which depicts the differential effects of parental monitoring on school achievement for high school students living in the three most common family structures found in the total sample of over 4,000 cases. The sample is further stratified by two levels of mother's education, with completion of high school as the dividing point. Parental monitoring refers to the effort by parents to keep informed about, and set limits on, their children's activities outside the home. In the present analysis, it was assessed by a series of items in a questionnaire administered to adolescents in their school classes.

Once again, the results reveal that the effects of proximal processes are more powerful than those of the environmental contexts in which they occur. In this instance, however, the impact of the proximal process is greatest in what emerges as the most advantaged ecological niche, that is, families with two biological parents in which the mother has had some education beyond high school. The typically declining slope of the curve reflects the fact that higher levels of outcome are more difficult to achieve so that at each successive step, the same degree of active effort yields a somewhat smaller result.

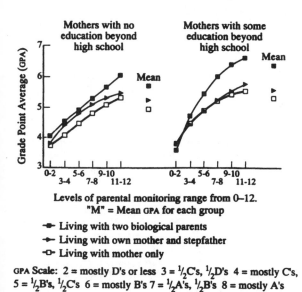

Levels of parental monitoring range from 0–12.
"M" = Mean GPA for each group

- ➡ Living with two biological parents
- ➡ Living with own mother and stepfather
- ➡ Living with mother only

GPA Scale: 2 = mostly D's or less 3 = ½C's, ½D's 4 = mostly C's, 5 = ½B's, ½C's 6 = mostly B's 7 = ½A's, ½B's 8 = mostly A's

Figure 2
Effect of parental monitoring on grades in high school by family structure and mother's level of education

3. Environments as Contexts of Development

The foregoing example provides an appropriate introduction to another distinctive feature of the ecological model, its highly differentiated reconceptualization of the environment from the perspective of the developing person. Based on Lewin's theory of psychological fields (Bronfenbrenner 1977; Lewin 1917, 1931, 1935), the ecological environment is conceived as a set of nested structures, each inside the other like a set of Russian dolls. Moving from the innermost level to the outside, these structures are defined as described below.

3.1 Microsystems

A microsystem is a pattern of activities, social roles, and interpersonal relations experienced by the developing person in a given face-to-face setting with particular physical, social, and symbolic features that invite, permit, or inhibit engagement in sustained, progressively more complex interaction with, and activity in, the immediate environment. Examples include such settings as family, school, peer group, and workplace.

It is within the immediate environment of the

microsystem that proximal processes operate to produce and sustain development, but as the above definition indicates, their power to do so depends on the content and structure of the microsystem. Specific hypotheses regarding the nature of this content and structure, and the as yet limited research evidence on which they are based are documented in the work of Bronfenbrenner (1986a, 1986b, 1988, 1989, 1993). Most of the relevant studies of proximal processes have focused on the family, with all too few dealing with other key developmental settings, such as classrooms and schools. A notable exception in this regard is the work of Stevenson and his colleagues (Stevenson and Stigler 1992, see also Ceci 1990).

3.2 Mesosystems

The mesosystem comprises the linkages and processes taking place between two or more settings containing the developing person (e.g., the relations between home and school, school and workplace, etc.). In other words, a mesosystem is a system of microsystems.

An example in this domain is the work of Epstein (1983a, 1983b) on the developmental impact of two-way communication and participation in decision-making by parents and teachers. Elementary school pupils from classrooms in which such joint involvement was high not only exhibited greater initiative and independence after entering high school, but also received higher grades. The effects of family and school processes were greater than those attributable to socioeconomic status or race.

3.3 Exosystems

The exosystem comprises the linkages and processes taking place between two or more settings, at least one of which does not contain the developing person, but in which events occur that indirectly influence processes within the immediate setting in which the developing person lives. (e.g., for a child, the relation between the home and the parent's workplace; for a parent, the relation between the school and the neighborhood peer group).

Especially since the early 1980s, research has focused on three exosystems that are especially likely to affect the development of children and youth indirectly through their influence on the family, the school, and the peer group. These are the parents' workplace (e.g., Eckenrode and Gore 1990), family social networks (e.g., Cochran et al. 1990), and neighborhood–community contexts (e.g., Pence 1988).

3.4 Macrosystems

The macrosystem consists of the overarching pattern of micro-, meso-, and exosystems characteristic of a given culture or subculture, with particular reference to the belief systems, bodies of knowledge, material resources, customs, life-styles, opportunity structures, hazards, and life course options that are embedded in each of these broader systems. The macrosystem may be thought of as a societal blueprint for a particular culture or subculture.

This formulation points to the necessity of going beyond the simple labels of class and culture to identify more specific social and psychological features at the macrosystem level that ultimately affect the particular conditions and processes occurring in the microsystem (see Bronfenbrenner 1986a, 1986b, 1988, 1989, 1993).

3.5 Chronosystems

A final systems parameter extends the environment into a third dimension. Traditionally in the study of human development, the passage of time was treated as synonymous with chronological age. Since the early 1970s, however, an increasing number of investigators have employed research designs in which time appears not merely as an attribute of the growing human being, but also as a property of the surrounding environment not only over the life course, but across historical time (Baltes and Schaie 1973, Clausen 1986, Elder 1974, Elder et al. 1993).

A chronosystem encompasses change or consistency over time not only in the characteristics of the person but also of the environment in which that person lives (e.g., changes over the life course in family structure, socioeconomic status, employment, place of residence, or the degree of hecticness and ability in everyday life).

An excellent example of a chronosystem design is found in Elder's classic study *Children of the Great Depression* (1974). The investigation involved a comparison of two otherwise comparable groups of families differentiated on the basis of whether the loss of income as a result of the Great Depression of the 1930s exceeded or fell short of 35 percent. The availability of longitudinal data made it possible to assess developmental outcomes through childhood, adolescence, and adulthood. Also, the fact that children in one sample were born eight years earlier than those in the other permitted a comparison of the effects of the Depression on youngsters who were adolescents when their families became economically deprived with the effects on those who were still young children at the time.

The results for the two groups presented a dramatic contrast. Paradoxically, for youngsters who were teenagers during the Depression years, the families' economic deprivation appeared to have a salutary effect on their subsequent development, especially in the middle class. As compared with the nondeprived who were matched on pre-Depression socioeconomic status, deprived boys displayed a greater desire to achieve and a firmer sense of career goals. Boys and girls from deprived homes attained greater satisfaction in life, both by their own and by societal standards. Though more pronounced for adolescents from middle-class backgrounds, these favorable outcomes were evident among their lower-class counterparts as well. Analysis of interview and observation protocols enabled Elder to identify what he regarded as a critical factor in investigating this favorable developmental trajectory: the loss of economic security forced the family to mobilize its own human resources, including its teenagers, who had to take on new roles and responsibilities both within and outside the home and to work together toward the common goal of getting and keeping the family on its feet. This experience provided effective training in initiative, responsibility, and cooperation.

4. Genetic Inheritance in Ecological Perspective

The most recent extension of the ecological paradigm involves a reconceptualization of the role of genetics in human development (Bronfenbrenner and Ceci 1993). The new formulation calls into question and replaces some of the key assumptions underlying the established "percentage-of-variance" model employed in behavior genetics. Specifically, in addition to incorporating explicit measures of the environment conceptualized in systems terms, and allowing for non-additive, synergistic effects in genetics–environment interaction, the proposed "bioecological" model posits proximal processes as the empirically assessable mechanisms through which genotypes are transformed into phenotypes. It is further argued, both on theoretical and empirical grounds, that heritability, defined by behavioral geneticists as "the proportion of the total phenotypic variance that is due to additive genetic variation" (Cavalli-Storza and Bodmer 1971 p. 536), is in fact highly influenced by events and conditions in the environment. Specifically, it is proposed that heritability can be shown to vary substantially as a direct function of the magnitude of proximal processes and the quality of the environments in which they occur, potentially yielding values of heritability that, at their extremes, are both appreciably higher and lower than those hitherto reported in the research literature.

If this bioecological model sustains empirical testing, this would imply that many human beings may possess genetic potentials for development significantly beyond those that they are presently manifesting, and that such unrealized potentials might be actualized through social policies and programs that enhance exposure to proximal processes in environmental settings providing the stability and resources that enable such processes to be maximally effective.

Certainly, thus far it has by no means been demonstrated that this latest extension of the ecological paradigm has any validity. Nor is the validation of hypotheses the principal goal that ecological models are designed to achieve. Indeed, their purpose may be better served if the hypotheses that they generate are found wanting, for the primary scientific aim of the ecological approach is not to claim answers, but to provide a theoretical framework that, through its application, will lead to further progress in discovering the processes and conditions that shape the course of human development.

However, beyond this scientific aim lies a broader human hope. That hope was expressed in the first systematic exposition of the ecological paradigm:

> Species *Homo sapiens* appears to be unique in its capacity to adapt to, tolerate, and especially to create the ecologies in which it lives and grows. Seen in different contexts, human nature, which I had once thought of as a singular noun, turns out to be plural and pluralistic; for different environments produce discernible differences, not only across but within societies, in talent, temperament, human relations, and particularly in the ways in which each culture and subculture brings up the next generation. The process and product of making human beings human clearly varies by place and time. Viewed in historical as well as cross-cultural perspective, this diversity suggests the possibility of ecologies as yet untried that hold a potential for human natures yet unseen, perhaps possessed of a wiser blend of power and compassion than has thus far been manifested. (Bronfenbrenner 1979 p. xiii)

See also: Socialization

References

Baltes P B, Schaie W 1973 *Life-span Developmental Psychology: Personality and Socialization.* Academic Press, New York

Bronfenbrenner U 1974 Developmental research, public policy, and the ecology of childhood. *Child Dev.* 45(1): 1–5

Bronfenbrenner U 1976 The experimental ecology of education. *Teach. Coll. Rec.* 78(2): 157–204

Bronfenbrenner U 1977 Toward an experimental ecology of human development. *Am. Psychol.* 32: 515–31

Bronfenbrenner U 1979 *The Ecology of Human Development: Experiments by Nature and Design.* Harvard University Press, Cambridge, Massachusetts

Bronfenbrenner U 1986a Ecology of the family as a context for human development: Research perspectives. *Dev. Psychol.* 22 (6): 723–42

Bronfenbrenner U 1986b Recent advances in the ecology of human development. In: Silbereisen R K, Eyferth K, Rudinger G (eds.) 1986 *Development as Action in Context: Problem Behavior and Normal Youth Development.* Springer-Verlag, Berlin

Bronfenbrenner U 1988 Interacting systems in human development: Research paradigms, present and future. In: Bolger N, Caspi A, Downey G, Moorehouse M (eds.) 1988 *Persons in Context: Developmental Processes.* Cambridge University Press, Cambridge

Bronfenbrenner U 1989 Ecological systems theory. In: Vasta R (ed.) 1989 *Six Theories of Child Development: Revised Formulations and Current Issues*, Vol. 6. JAI Press, Greenwich, Connecticut

Bronfenbrenner U 1990 The ecology of cognitive development. *Zeitschrift fur Sozialisationsforschung und Evziehungssoziologie (ZSE]* 10(2): 101–14

Bronfenbrenner U 1993 The ecology of cognitive development: Research models and fugitive findings. In: Wozniak R H, Fischer K (eds.) 1993 *Thinking in Context.* Erlbaum, Hillsdale, New Jersey

Bronfenbrenner U, Ceci S J 1993 Heredity, environment, and the question "how?": A new theoretical perspective for the 1990s. In: Plomin R, McClearn G E (eds.) 1993 *Nature, Nurture, and Psychology*. APA Books, Washington, DC

Cavalli-Storza L L, Bodmer W F 1971 *The Genetics of Human Populations*. W H Freeman, San Francisco, California

Ceci S J 1990 *On Intelligence . . . More or Less: A Bioecological Treatise on Intellectual Development*. Prentice-Hall, Englewood Cliffs, New Jersey

Clausen J A 1986 *The Life Course: A Sociological Perspective*. Prentice-Hall, Englewood Cliffs, New Jersey

Cochran M, Larner M, Riley D, Gunnarsson L, Henderson C R Jr. 1990 *Extending Families: The Social Networks of Parents and their Children*. Cambridge University Press, New York

Drillien C M 1963 *The Growth and Development of the Prematurely Born Infant*. E and S Livingston Ltd, Edinburgh

Eckenrode J, Gore S (eds.) 1990 *Stress between Work and Family*. Plenum Press, New York

Elder G H Jr. 1974 *Children of the Great Depression: Social Change in the Life Experience*. University of Chicago Press, Chicago, Illinois

Elder G H Jr., Modell J, Parke R D 1993 *Children in Time and Place: Individual, Historical and Developmental Insights*. Cambridge University Press, New York

Epstein J L 1983a *Effects on Parents of Teacher Practices of Parent Involvement*. Center for the Social Organization of Schools, Johns Hopkins University, Baltimore, Maryland

Epstein J L 1983b Longitudinal effects of family–school–person interactions on student outcomes. *Research in Sociology of Education and Socialization* 4: 101–27.

Lewin K 1917 Kriegslandschaft. *Zeitschrift fur Angewandte Psychologie* 12: 440–47

Lewin K 1931 Environmental forces in child behavior and development. In: Murchison C (ed.) 1931 *A Handbook of Child Psychology*. Clark University Press, Worcester, Massachusetts

Lewin K 1935 *A Dynamic Theory of Personality*. McGraw-Hill, New York

Pence A R (ed.) 1988 *Ecological Research with Children and Families: From Concepts to Methodology*. Teachers College, Columbia University, New York

Schwabe H, Bartholomai F 1870 Der Vorstellungskreis der Berliner Kinder beim Eintritt in die Schule. In: *Berlin und seine Entwicklung: Städtisches Jahrbuch für Volkswirthschaft und Statistik Vierter Jahrgang*. Guttentag, Berlin

Stevenson H W, Stigler J W 1992 *The Learning Gap: Why Our Schools are Failing and What We Can Learn from Japanese and Chinese Education*. Summit Books, New York

Humanistic Models of Human Development

N. Groeben

All traditions within psychology ascribe certain characteristics to their object of study, namely human beings. Among these traditions, humanistic psychology stands out in making this anthropological perspective explicit by attempting to model those characteristics that are regarded as specifically human, particularly the capacity for self-actualization. In this entry, various models within humanistic psychology and their application to education are discussed.

1. The Program of Humanistic Psychology

Humanistic psychology is frequently called the "third force" by its representatives, thus distinguishing it from the two classical traditions within psychology, behaviorism and psychoanalysis. Humanistic psychologists criticize both of these traditions for their reductionism. In behaviorism it is the idea that human beings are controlled by their environment which is regarded as reductionist, leading to alienation and dehumanization (Shaffer 1978 p.6f.); within psychoanalysis, the biologism of the Freudian model is similarly thought to result in depersonalization. Humanistic

psychologists oppose these reductionisms by taking into account phenomenological and existentialist traditions within philosophy and psychology (Misiak and Sexton 1973). They therefore focus on those characteristics and capacities that are constitutive for human beings (in contrast to machines and animals), such as authenticity, wholeness and integrity, intentionality and the "search for meaning," freedom and "being-in-the world," and so on. In conceptualizing all these characteristics, they take as their starting point the central idea of the self-actualizing person, that is, the person who fully uses and develops his or her own capabilities and potentialities.

2. Central Assumptions and Models

As a consequence, humanistic psychologists believe that the study of human beings in their wholeness, freedom, integrity, autonomy, and so on, requires a dissociation from the traditional scientific conception of psychology. Thus, humanistic psychology takes as its programmatic starting point the conscious experience of human beings which it attempts to study in a strictly phenomenological and experiential manner; at the same time, humanistic psychologists believe that human nature will never fully be known (Shaffer 1978). On this basis, three models can be distinguished within humanistic psychology (Becker 1982 p. 145): models of the search for meaning, models of self-actualization, and models of self-regulation. Whereas models of the search for meaning and of self-actualization primarily concentrate on values and goals, that is, on the product, models of regulation tend to emphasize the process, that is, the means toward reaching these goals (Quitmann 1991).

2.1 Models of Self-actualization

Among models of self-actualization, those put forward by Maslow and Rogers have become most widely known. Within his motivational hierarchy, Maslow (1954, 1968) distinguished between deficiency needs and growth needs which he regarded as being hierarchically based upon each other. Among the deficiency needs he included physiological needs, safety needs, needs for belonging and love, and esteem needs (in this hierarchical order); among the growth needs, self-actualization needs occupy the highest rank. On the basis of a qualitative-empirical study of living and historical personalities, Maslow arrived at 18 characteristics of psychologically "healthy" self-actualization, such as "better perception" of reality, and mystical borderline experiences (peak experiences). He further postulated (at least toward the end of the development of his theory) that self-actualization is something that cannot be reached by aiming at it directly, but only as a "by-product of actions directed towards other goals" (Becker 1982 p.111).

In this respect, Rogers appears to be more naive, or at least more direct. He regarded the need for self-realization as an "organismic tendency" that is inherent in all human beings and that can at most be hampered by the environment. If such restraints arise, psychotherapy is necessary in order to remove them, as far as possible. This is also the reason why Rogers initially developed his theory (similar to psychoanalysis) as a theory of psychotherapy (Rogers 1951). In the course of further elaborations, Rogers, however, also came to regard the basic attitudes of congruence, empathy, and positive regard (which are central in the therapeutic context) as helpful for the development of interpersonal relationships and the individual's relation to him- or herself (Rogers 1959). Thus he finally arrived at a developmental theory of the "fully functioning person" (Rogers 1963).

2.2 Search for Meaning and Self-regulation

This perspective of self-realization has also been extended to the "experiential horizon of transcendence," a concept that has been placed partly within neo-psychoanalysis with its orientation toward the psychology of the ego (e.g., Frankl), but within humanistic psychology most of all by Allport (1961). His characteristics of the "mature personality" differ in their degree of abstraction: "extension of the sense of self; warm relating of the self to others; emotional security (self-acceptance); realistic perception, skills, and assignments; self-objectification; insight and humor; unifying philosophy of life" (Allport 1961 p.275). Under the perspective of "philosophy of life" Allport also took into account conceptions from within the German phenomenological tradition by distinguishing between six value orientations.

As regards the practical effectiveness of humanistic psychology, however, those approaches that point out ways and means toward the realization of self-actualization have been particularly relevant. The approaches in this context all start from a therapeutic perspective that is then extended to include educational and interpersonal relationships in general. This applies to Rogers as well as to the Gestalt therapy of Perls (1969) and in particular to Cohn's (1972) theme-centered interactional method. Cohn postulated ground rules for interaction (such as: "Be your own chairman!" and "Disturbances take precedence!") which she regards as "existential postulates of being" (cf. Quitmann 1991). Within a humanistically oriented social psychology and technology, these maxims, together with related subsidiary rules are widely accepted in the early 1990s.

3. Applications: Humanistic Education and the Human Potential Movement

Cohn's method has also played an important part in the application of humanistic psychology to education, both in the classroom as well as in adult education. Representatives of humanistic education (Patterson 1973, Simpson and Gray 1976) advocate a group-oriented approach to a far greater extent than proponents of traditional (teacher-oriented) instruction. They greatly stress group teaching and the responsibility of the group for its own actions. In the context of this group-centered educational approach, Cohn's theme-centered rules constitute one method that allows the group members to work together democratically as equals, thereby supporting the autonomy and responsibility of the individual. Humanistic education (as an application of humanistic psychology to the area of education) aims above all to foster the self-actualization of the learner; this implies, in particular, that the learner is able to experience learning per se as meaningful, comprising not merely the content of what is learned but also its personal meaning to the learner (Shaffer 1978).

"Significant learning" in this sense is also the focus of the nondirective, person-centered approach (developed from Roger's theory), aimed at the learners' self-initiation, self-control, and self-evaluation, their personal involvement on both cognitive and emotional levels, and so on (Karmann 1987).

Within the Gestalt approach, the integration of cognitive and affective learning is taken even further by including physical and social dimensions; the goal of this approach is to foster physical and psychological relaxation, physical training, improvement of one's vital sense, improvement of communication and social skills (Karmann 1987). These goals of learning and personal development cannot be directly taught (as Maslow had already postulated). Only indirect support can be given; this, however, requires that (too) strict institutional structures be dismantled. One of the most striking consequences for the institution of the school is the conception of the open classroom. An atmosphere of informality permits each child to learn at his or her own pace; in small groups, different subjects can be pursued and various learning activities take place simultaneously (Shaffer 1978). The principle behind this—that learning works best if it is not forced, but arises out of the learners' natural, spontaneous curiosity—is also the basis for the Summerhill Model (Neill 1960) which contains no institutional obligations for the child at all.

These same goals and methods have also been applied to adult education and business. Within this "human potential movement," various models of humanistic psychology have been employed in order to further personal growth, such as t-labs (sensitivity groups), psychodrama, meditation, and so on (Shaffer 1978), including contributions to the humanization of the working world (job enlargement, job enrichment, partially autonomous working groups, and so on).

4. Controversial Perspectives

4.1 Antieducation?

The application of humanistic psychology to the educational and the social area illustrates the problems inherent in the humanistic models. As one might expect on the basis of the criticisms raised against behaviorism and psychoanalysis by humanistic psychology itself, it is the (remaining) organismic implications that especially lead to conceptual inconsistencies and related difficulties. This applies in particular to the Rogerian postulate of an organismic tendency toward self-actualization. Quitmann (1991) regards this postulate as a form of "unconditional trust in the human organism" (p.171). This unconditional trust is one of the reasons why humanistic psychology and the antieducational movement are so closely related: because the organismic "omnipresence of the good makes any form of education obsolete" (Herzog 1991 p. 31; see also the criticism by Winkler 1982).

In addition, the fact that the Rogerian approach for instance originated in a therapeutic context has a certain deleterious effect, particularly with respect to the postulate of positive regard. Because positive regard is seen as constituting the central path toward self-acceptance, self-acceptance is seen as the basis for making a realistic perception and processing of one's own existence possible in the first place. From outside the client-centered therapeutical approach, however, this appears as a purely hedonistic form of self-acceptance, because from a moral point of view a mature personality must also be able realistically to perceive his or her own actions, habits, and dispositions, even if this leads to a negative evaluation. Partial inconsistencies or paradoxes of this kind occur even more frequently within "transpersonal psychology." This approach is termed the "fourth force" by its advocates who place their focus on human consciousness, including processes that enlarge or alter consciousness, such as spiritual experiences, ecstasy, borderline experiences and experiences of dying.

4.2 Neglect of the Social Dimension?

Leaving aside the problem that humanistic psychology tends to stray into nonscientific realms, it appears that it has so far primarily provided starting points for correcting a socialization history overly controlled from the outside, and for overcoming or avoiding an unnecessarily negative self-concept. This is due to the therapeutic origin of a majority of the approaches within humanistic psychology, and to the fact that most models advocate an individualistic understanding of self-actualization (Karmann 1987). The social dimension is considered by humanistic approaches only very indirectly, primarily by regarding the "self" as the individual manifestation of the human in general, and thus of the social dimension of the human. However, this can hardly be accepted as a sufficient model of the social integration and interaction of human beings (Quitmann 1991). Among the humanistic theorists, it is Fromm who comes closest to overcoming this weakness. His reconstruction of nonproductive orientations (receptive masochist orientation; exploitative sadistic orientation; hoarding destructive orientation; marketing and indifferent orientation [1980 Vol. II]) constitutes a critique of the individual as well as of the social developments in the modern age. These he counters with a productive orientation of creative work, love, and rational thinking; creative activity allows human beings to take in the world, love to overcome their isolation without losing their individuality. Recent discussions of these issues include, in particular, the ethical aspects in the development of individuals and society, ranging from the question of gender differences in moral development (cf. Blasi 1988; Edelstein et al. 1993) to proposals for an ecologic ethics of responsibility for future generations (Jonas 1985).

5. Conclusion

Humanistic psychology thus elaborates the anthropological perspective of the autonomous, responsible human being who is capable of determining the direction and structure of his or her lifelong development by self-reflection and self-actualization. It thus offers a starting point toward the realization of values and means that avoids excessive control and direction by others on all levels, including social norms and structures, educational and business institutions, group and community interactions. When applied to classroom education, humanistic psychology has focused on developing approaches that are aimed at breaking up autocratic structures, to make it possible to learn in a personally meaningful way, that includes affective as well as physical dimensions.

See also: Ecological Models of Human Development

References

Allport G W 1961 *Pattern and Growth in Personality*. Holt, Rinehart and Winston, New York
Becker P 1982 *Die Psychologie der seelischen Gesundheit. Vol. 1: Theorien, Modelle, Diagnostik*. Hogrefe, Göttingen
Blasi A 1988 Identity and the development of the self. In: Lapsley D K, Power F C (eds.) 1988 *Self, Ego, and Identity. Integrative Approaches*. Springer, New York
Cohn R 1972 Style and spirits of the theme-centered interaction method. In: Sager C, Kaplan H S (eds.) 1972 *Progress in Group and Family Therapy*. Brunner/Mazel, New York
Edelstein W, Nunner-Winkler G, Noam G 1993 *Moral und Person*. Suhrkamp, Frankfurt
Fromm E 1980 *Gesamtausgabe*, Vols. I-X. Deutsche Verlags-Anstalt, Stuttgart
Herzog W 1991 *Das moralische Subjekt*. Huber, Bern
Jonas H 1985 *Das Prinzip Verantwortung. Versuch einer Ethik für die technologische Zivilisation*, 4th edn. Insel, Frankfurt
Karmann G 1987 *Humanistische Psychologie und Pädagogik*. Klinkhardt, Bad Heilbrunn
Maslow A H 1954 *Motivation and Personality*. Harper and Row, New York
Maslow A H 1968 *Toward a Psychology of Being*. Van Nostrand, Princeton, New Jersey
Misiak H, Sexton V S 1973 Phenomenological, Existential, and Humanistic Psychologies. Grune and Stratton, New York
Neill A S 1960 *Summerhill: A Radical Approach to Child-Rearing*. Hart, New York
Patterson C H 1973 *Humanistic Education*. Prentice-Hall, Englewood Cliffs, New Jersey
Perls F S 1969 *Gestalt Therapy Verbatim*. Real People Press, Moab, Utah
Quitmann H 1991 *Humanistische Psychologie: Zentrale Konzepte und philosophischer Hintergrund*, 2nd edn. Hogrefe, Göttingen
Rogers C R 1951 *Client-centered Therapy: Its Current Practice, Implications, and Theory*. Constable, London
Rogers C R 1959 A theory of therapy, personality, and interpersonal relationships. In: Koch S (ed.) 1959 *Psychology: A Study of a Science*, Vol. 3. McGraw-Hill, New York
Rogers C R 1963 The concept of the fully functioning person. *Psychotherapy: Theory, Research, and Practice* 1(1): 17–26
Shaffer J B P 1978 *Humanistic Psychology*. Prentice-Hall, Englewood Cliffs, New Jersey
Simpson E L, Gray M A 1976 *Humanistic Education: An Interpretation*. Ballinger, Cambridge, Massachusetts
Winkler M 1982 *Stichworte zur Antipädagogik*. Klett-Cotta, Stuttgart

Further Reading

Bühler C, Allen M 1972 *Introduction to Humanistic Psychology*. Brooks/Cole, Monterey, California
Frankl V E 1963 *Man's Search for Meaning: An Introduction to Logotherapy*. Washington Square, New York
Fromm E 1970 *To Have or to Be?* Harper and Row, New York
Jourard S M, Landsman T 1980 *Healthy Personality: An Approach from the Viewpoint of Humanistic Psychology*. Macmillan, New York
Rogers C R 1969 *Freedom to Learn: A View of What Education Might Become*. Merrill, Columbus, Ohio

Behaviorist Approaches to Human Development

S. W. Bijou

Behaviorist approaches to human development are a legacy of decades of experimental research on learning and conditioning. They have always formed part of a psychological system that adheres to a philosophy of science based exclusively on natural science; that is, a science that deals exclusively with observable events, such as biology, chemistry, and physics.

These approaches came into existence in the early twentieth century with the founding of behaviorism by Watson (1919). Watson's new "school" was a protest against the dominant view at that time, which held that psychology is the study of inner experiences or feelings, by subjective, introspective methods. Although Watson contended that psychology should be the study of observable behavior (or responses) in relation to the environment (or stimuli) by direct experimental procedures, he did not deny the existence of inner experiences. He firmly believed, however, that they could not be studied by scientific procedures since they were not observable.

Watson's treatment of human development was too piecemeal and too skewed in the direction of young children to be considered a theory of human development. His research with infants initially focused on handedness and emotional behavior, particularly the development and elimination of fears. His conceptual system was restricted to the classical conditioning model of Pavlov, the famous Russian physiologist. Nonetheless, he speculated widely on practical problems, particularly problems related to child-rearing practices.

1. Emergence of Formal Theories of Development

The first set of formal theories of human development emerged in the 1940s. Based on Clark L Hull's motivational theory of learning, they embraced the principles of both Pavlovian conditioning and Thorndikian trial-and-error learning (as elaborated by E L Thorndike). Leading figures in this approach, called social learning theory, were John Dollard, Neal H Miller, and, in particular, Robert R Sears (1947). This group stressed the importance of parent–child relations in a child's personality development, supporting some of their views by research on dependency, identification, imitation, sex-typing, neurotic behavior, and child-rearing patterns.

As the popularity of the Hullian learning theory waned during the 1960s, a second version of social learning theories surfaced, led then by Bandura and Walters (1963) and continued by Bandura (1977). This version of social learning theory stimulated considerable research on children, particularly on aggression, modeling (or imitation), and learning through observation. In the successive revisions of this view, there was a gradual shift away from motivational variables and toward cognitive processes. Consequently, by the early 1980s social learning theories were now called "social cognitive theories" (Bandura 1989).

At about the same time as the emergence of a second wave of social learning theories, the behavior analysis theory of development was advanced by Bijou and Baer (1961). Based essentially on Skinner's (1953) philosophy of science and the science of behavior, it also incorporated features from Kantor's (1959) interbehavioral psychology. Since the behavior analysis theory of development is currently the only systematic behavior theory in use (Bijou 1993), the following sections will be devoted to a description of its paradigm, theory and principles of development, methods of research, influence, limits, and continuing merits.

2. Paradigm of Behavior Analysis Theory

Briefly stated, behavioral psychology is concerned with the interaction between behavior (verbal and nonverbal) and the environment. From this perspective, human development consists of the changes that occur in the relationships between the behavior of a biological evolving or devolving person with his or her hereditary potential and environmental conditions, past (history) and present. The changes in relationships, or the different ways in which a person responds to objects, persons, and events are usually progressive (e.g., a child first speaks in one-word sentences and gradually progresses to full sentences). However, they may also be regressive, particularly in old age and senility (e.g., memory loss). Such changes occur in accordance with the principles derived from experimental studies of individual animals and humans.

3. Principles of Development

The basic principles of development have been derived from research in classical and operant conditioning and learning. Those stemming from classical conditioning center on changes in feelings and emotions and their elaboration into complex reactions, such as sympathy and affection. Basic principles pertain to the attachment, detachment, and generalization of feelings and emotions in relation to persons, objects, and situations.

Operant principles apply to changes in purposeful or goal-seeking behavior, ranging from the simplest forms of behavior (e.g., an infant grasping a rattle and bringing it to his or her mouth) to the most complex behavior (e.g., decision-making and problem-solving). They describe the strengthening and weakening of behavior on the basis of consequences, which are referred to as positive and negative reinforcers, punishment, and extinction.

Other principles apply to the variations in operant behavior, such as: (a) the occurrence of behavior not specifically reinforced, such as saying "hello" to a stranger (generalization); (b) the development of highly skilled behavior, such as hitting a baseball with a bat (shaping); (c) the development of acquired tastes and motivations (conditioned reinforcers); (d) the development of behavior similar to the behavior seen in another person (modeling or imitation); and (e) decision-making and problem-solving behavior (self-management).

The many varieties of operant behavior come about through the consequences of responses, as described by the above principles. Some, however, happen on the basis of rules; for example, following directions and instructions, or assimilating information (Hayes 1989). Here the person must of course be able to understand and follow the rules in order to respond properly.

4. Research Methods

Behavioral developmental psychologists prefer to study their subject matter—behavior in relation to the environment—by experimental methods involving one subject at a time. The setting in which the work is conducted may be either a laboratory or any number of field situations, such as a lounge-like room, play yard, playroom, classroom, home, clinic room, or a work situation. The procedures used, termed "experimental designs," may vary, but essentially they consist of taking measures at the following times: (a) before experimental intervention, or at a baseline; (b) during experimental intervention; and (c) again under baseline conditions to see whether there are differences that can be attributed to the intervention. These procedures are repeated to evaluate the reliability of the data.

In studies requiring evaluations of skills, abilities, and personality traits, measures are based on verbal and nonverbal responses to real-life tasks and situations. For example, measures may be taken on whether a person—child or retarded adult—can eat with a spoon, take off and put on his or her clothes, greet a stranger, or write his or her name. The devices employed are checklists, surveys, and inventories, rather than tests with scores yielding a mental age and IQ.

5. Influence of the Behavioral Approach

Books on the behavior analysis of development have been translated from English into Spanish, Italian, Portuguese, and Japanese. Together with the original English-language versions, they have served as textbooks in colleges and universities in the United States, Canada, Mexico, Venezuela, Peru, Spain, Italy, and the United Kingdom.

The approach has also been the basis of applied research and a wide range of practical applications in the same countries. Its influence is seen in early childhood education, elementary education ("Direct Instruction" and "Precision Teaching"), and special education. Since it offers detailed guidance for parents, this approach has had an influence on child-rearing practices. Finally, it has significantly contributed to procedures for treating personal adjustment problems, notably the clinical treatment of eating and toileting disorders, excessive aggression, shy and withdrawn behavior, and autism.

6. Limits and Extent of Remediation

The following criticisms have been leveled at the behavioral approach: (a) it postulates that the developing person is passive; (b) the research focuses too much on processes; (c) it is inadequate for dealing with language behavior, mental processes, and complex behavior such as problem-solving and creativity.

While the criticism about passivity may be valid for Watson's classical behaviorism, which considered psychological and physiological behavior to be one and the same, this is not true of modern behaviorism. The view in the 1990s is that behavior and stimuli are always reciprocally interrelated—the developing person is always active and changing in some way (even when he or she appears passive) and the environment, too, is always active (Kantor 1959).

Behavioral research has undeniably focused on universal principles of behavior change and has devoted insufficient attention to principles applicable to particular sets of circumstances. This imbalance should be corrected if the approach is to arrive at both a descriptive and an explanatory account of development (e.g.; Hart and Risley 1995).

The criticism that behavioral psychology cannot deal with language behavior presupposes that behavioral psychology is unable to account for how a person can make a language response that had not ever previously been reinforced. It is more accurate for critics to claim that behaviorists do not deal with language behavior in the same way that linguists and cognitive psychologists do. Language behavior is treated functionally by behaviorists, that is, as operant behavior with principles that do indeed account for behavior that has never been directly reinforced (see Sect. 3).

The claim that behavioral psychology is inadequate for dealing with mental activities may also be interpreted to mean that it does not deal with them in the same way that mentalistic psychology does. Mentalistic psychology deals with mental activities by postulating unobservable terms, such as cognitive structures and processes inferred from observation and research. In contrast, behavioral psychology studies inner experiences ("private events") by self-observational reports, to learn about their nature and the reliability of the observations.

The criticism that behavioral psychology cannot deal with complex behavior is justified since in the past it has given relatively little attention to such behavior. The tendency has, however, developed to study all classes of behavior, as evidenced by the increasing research activity on perceptual behavior, the development and subsequent variations of moral behavior, and problem-solving (e.g; Hayes 1989).

7. Continuing Merits of Behavioral Psychology

Although cognitive approaches to human development dominate the psychological landscape, behavioral approaches continue to advance and mature. Attempts are being made to integrate Kantor's interbehavioral psychology further into the system, which features the interrelationship of all events in an interaction, and also Skinner's experimental analyses of behavior, thereby accentuating a contextual philosophy of science and a more detailed unit of analysis.

At the same time, the behavioral approach continues to extend its research contributions to applied developmental problems and to practical application. Moreover, the emergence of new journals, namely, the *Journal of Behavior Education* (1992–) and *Behaviorism and Social Issues* (1991–) attest to the continuing viability of the behavioral approach to human development.

See also: Human Development: Research Methodology; Childhood

References

Bandura A 1977 *Social Learning Theory*. Prentice-Hall, Englewood Cliffs, New Jersey

Bandura A 1989 Social cognitive theory. In: Vasta R (ed.) 1989 *Annals of Child Development*, Vol. 6. Jessica Kingsley, London

Bandura A, Walters R H 1963 *Social Learning and Personality Development*. Holt, Rinehart, and Winston, New York

Bijou S W 1993 *Behavior analysis of child development*. Context Press, Reno, Nevada

Bijou S W, Baer D M 1961 *Child Development: A Systematic*

and Empirical Theory. Prentice-Hall, Englewood Cliffs, New Jersey

Hart B, Risley T R 1995 *Meaningful Differences in the Everyday Experiences of Young Children*. Paul H. Brookes, Baltimore, Maryland

Hayes S C (ed.) 1989 *Rule-governed Behavior: Cognition Contingencies and Instructional Control*. Plenum Press, New York

Kantor J R 1959 *Interbehavioral Psychology*, 3rd edn. Principia Press, Bloomington, Indiana

Sears R R 1947 Child psychology. In: Dennis W (ed.) 1947 *Current Trends in Psychology*. Pittsburgh Press, Pittsburgh, Pennsylvania

Skinner B F 1953 *Science and Human Behavior*. Free Press, New York/Collier-Macmillan, London

Watson J B 1919 *Psychology from the Standpoint of a Behaviorist*. Lippincott, Philadelphia, Pennsylvania

Further Reading

Schlinger H D Jr. *Behavior–Analytic View of Child Development*. Plenum Press, New York

Skinner B F 1957 *Verbal Behavior*. Prentice-Hall, New York

Thomas R M 1979 *Comparing Theories of Child Development*. Walsworth Publishing, Belmont, California

Information-processing Theories of Human Development

R. Kail

The modern study of cognitive development is dominated by the information-processing perspective, which draws heavily on an analogy with computer operations to explain the development of mental activities. Information processing is not a unified theory but instead denotes a collection of concepts that provides a unique lens with which to view cognitive development. This entry begins with a description of some of the core assumptions of this approach, then illustrates how the approach has been used to understand human development, and finally examines differences between the information-processing model and other models of development.

1. Core Assumptions

At the core of information-processing research is a shared view of how psychological activities are best understood. Generally, information-processing psychologists seek to understand relations between observable stimuli (input) and observable responses (output) by describing activities that intervene between input and output. They typically proceed by devising models of cognition in specific domains on the assumption that these models will converge in

a way that reveals general principles of cognition. The components of these models consist of internal representations of information and of processes that operate on these representations. A complete model of cognition for a particular task or domain would include specific mechanisms for all cognitive activities that underlie performance, including perceptual mechanisms for encoding information, processes for manipulating and storing information, processes for selecting and retrieving stored information, and processes that decide among alternative actions. The resulting model would characterize cognition in individuals at a particular age. Extended to the problem of development, information-processing psychologists have the following additional goals: (a) describing features of information processing that are associated with different ages; (b) identifying properties of the information-processing system that both enable and constrain change.

This general account of the information-processing approach actually includes a number of individual assumptions that need to be stated explicitly, as they define a commonly shared, if minimal, view of this perspective.

The first assumption is that cognitive phenomena can be described and explained in terms of mental processes and representations that intervene between observable stimuli and responses. Information processing is primarily an approach to understanding cognition, defined broadly as psychological acts of knowing. Information-processing theorists assume that information is represented internally and manipulated by mental processes. The aim of research is to determine how information is represented and organized, and to identify the specific processes used in achieving particular cognitive aims. This account of human thought in terms of internal codes and processes is the essence of the computer metaphor that forms the core of the information-processing approach. Humans and computers engage in many similar activities: they must interpret symbolic information, perform operations on the interpreted information, and emit a response. Thus humans, like computers, can be considered as symbol manipulators (Newell et al. 1958).

A second assumption is that a relatively small number of elementary processes underlie all cognitive activity. Information-processing psychologists contend that acts of knowing can be decomposed into distinct, component processes. In turn, these components can also be decomposed, a process that can, in principle, be repeated until a set of fundamental cognitive operations has been identified. This organization means that most cognitive phenomena can be analyzed at many levels. For example, reading might be considered as a single process at one level of analysis, but at another it might be viewed in terms of such components as decoding and comprehension. These components might then themselves be decomposed into even more fine-grained operations, such as specific memory-manipulation processes (Kail and Bisanz 1992).

A third assumption is that individual processes operate in concert. The fundamental operations of a computer become useful only when they are combined with other operations to form routines that may, in turn, be combined with other routines to form higher-order programs. According to the information-processing view, the same is true of human cognition. A critical goal of psychological research is to understand how fundamental processes are combined and organized to produce performance on different tasks. Moreover, it is generally assumed that higher levels of organization may have emergent properties that are qualitatively different from the properties of lower-level operations (Palmer and Kimchee 1986).

It should be noted that, although the second assumption emphasizes the need to identify microscopic components of cognition, the third assumption makes it clear that reductionism of this sort is not the sole aim of research. Instead, identifying fundamental processes *and* determining their organization in performance in particular domains are both essential goals (Kail and Bisanz 1982).

A fourth and final assumption is that cognitive development occurs by means of self-modification. In information-processing theories, thinking is to be understood through an account of the representation of information and of the processes that manipulate this information. These accounts focus on internal factors rather than external, environmental factors such as reward or punishment. In like manner, when information-processing psychologists seek to explain how thinking changes with development, they focus on internal factors. The mechanisms that underlie development are thought to be internal to the system itself, rather than imposed by the environment; hence developmental change is construed as self-modification. This orientation does not deny the importance of environmental events for cognitive change, but simply claims that "whatever the form of the external environment, the information-processing system itself must ultimately encode, store, index and process that environment" (Klahr 1989 p.138).

2. Analyses of Developmental Change

The assumptions described in Sect. 1 have provided the basis for information-processing analysis of developmental change in a number of domains, including perception, problem-solving, language, motor control, and social cognition. This section begins with an example of an information-processing approach in a particular domain, then describes some general mechanisms of developmental change.

2.1 An Illustrative Example: Information-processing Analysis of the Development of Arithmetic Skills

In many societies mastering arithmetic skills is an important objective in the early years of schooling. The processes underlying acquisition of these skills have been described in a number of information-processing theories; work by Siegler and his colleagues is representative (Siegler and Shrager 1984, Siegler and Jenkins 1989). Siegler's account of the steps involved in solving a simple addition problem is illustrated in Fig. 1. A child or adult begins by encoding the problem and then attempting to retrieve an answer directly from a knowledge base consisting of stored facts. These facts are represented mentally in terms of associations between problems (e.g., what is $2 + 5$?) and candidate answers (6, 7, 8, etc.), associations that vary in strength. If the associative strength between the retrieved answer and the problem ($Act [A_n]$) exceeds a preset confidence criterion (C), then the answer is stated. If this associative strength does not exceed the confidence criterion, then retrieval is attempted again. This retrieval cycle is repeated until an answer is retrieved that has an associative strength exceeding the confidence criterion or the number of retrieval attempts exceeds a preset limit (*max*). In the latter case, retrieval is abandoned and an answer is generated using a backup procedure such as counting on one's fingers or counting mentally.

The general process illustrated in Fig. 1 does not change with age. However, a problem becomes more strongly associated with the correct answer through repeated exposure. In other words, children's answers to problems are frequently confirmed or disconfirmed by parents, teachers, peers, or self-discovery. The associative strength between a problem and an answer increases every time the child responds with that answer. Frequency of exposure to arithmetic problems is moderately correlated with age, which means that correct answers gradually increase in associative strength as children get older.

Of course, children do not experience all simple addition problems equally often. Problems with smaller addends are presented by parents and in textbooks more often than problems with larger addends (Hamann and Ashcraft 1986). Consequently, answers to problems with small addends develop associative strength more rapidly, which means that a child may well use retrieval for these problems while at the same time using backup strategies for problems with larger addends.

Siegler's work exemplifies the information-processing perspective in many ways. Observed behaviors—in this case, the speed and accuracy with which children answer addition problems—are explained in terms of a relatively small set of processes that operate in certain ways on internal representations of knowledge. The processes are represented by the retrieval cycle shown in Fig. 1 and knowledge of arithmetic facts is represented by the associative strengths that are acquired as children develop. Performance is determined by the interaction of these processes and knowledge representations as the child is attempting to solve a problem. The environment, and particularly the frequency with which a child experiences certain types of problems, has an important influence on development, but this influence is mediated by the way in which information is processed.

2.2 Mechanisms of Development

Many developmental psychologists view human development as a series of discrete states connected by transitions. This view has led to two primary goals for research: (a) to describe each developmental state precisely; (b) to explain transitions from one developmental state to the next. Information-processing analyses of the sort typified by Siegler's work have yielded much evidence pertinent to both of these goals. Hypotheses about specific mechanisms are still somewhat speculative, but some consensus is beginning to emerge about the general functions and characteristics of developmental mechanisms. The remainder of this section focuses on mechanisms of development suggested by the information-processing approach.

2.2.1 Change in procedures and rules. As children develop, their approaches to problems become more sophisticated and more efficient. For example, when reasoning about scientific concepts, adolescents typically use more sophisticated rules than children. In like manner, when trying to remember information, adolescents use more powerful mnemonics than do younger children. These insights about cognitive development are not unique to the information-processing view. The important contribution of the information-processing perspective has been to explain the transition toward more sophisticated and efficient procedures. In Siegler's work, for example, exposure to addition problems gradually increases associative strength, ultimately to the point where the correct answer exceeds the confidence criterion; the result is that answers are no longer calculated (using backup strategies such as counting) but are retrieved instead.

Another method by which more advanced procedures may emerge is through generalization. Consider the following, simplified example. Suppose that

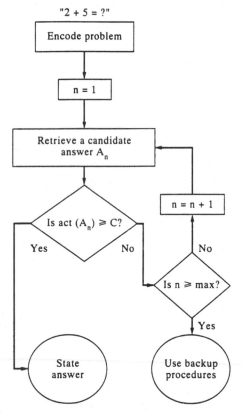

"2 + 5 = ?"

Figure 1
Simplified model of mental arithmetic processes[a]
Source: Kail and Bisanz (1992), after Siegler and Shrager (1984)
a The number of retrieval attempts is indexed by n, and *max* represents an upper limit on this number. *Act(A_n)* refers to the activation level of the candidate answer retrieved on attempt n, and C refers to the confidence criterion for accepting a retrieved answer

children just learning to add sometimes use the following rule:

Rule 1: *If* the goal is to add (1 + 2), *then* count 1 finger, followed by 2 fingers, and say the result.

Suppose that children also have the rule:

Rule 2: *If* the goal is to add (3 + 4), *then* count 3 fingers, followed by 4 fingers, and say the result.

A generalized version of these results would replace the constants—(2 + 3) and (3 + 4)—with variables, producing a new, generalized rule:

Rule 3: *If* the goal is to add two numbers, m and n, *then* count m fingers, followed by n fingers, and say the result.

Generalization is thought to occur because new rules are compared to existing rules. If a new rule differs from an existing rule only in the constants included in the conditions, then a more general rule is created by replacing the constants with variables (Anderson 1983).

Of course, children sometimes learn rules that are too general and they must learn appropriate boundary conditions. "Discrimination" refers to the process by which more specific conditions are associated with rules. Continuing the examples with simple addition, children might attempt to apply Rule 3 to problems such as 8 + 11 and 6 + 7. Upon discovering that they lack enough fingers for these problems, the situations associated with successful use of Rule 3 are compared with those associated with unsuccessful use. The result is a narrowing of the conditions that elicit Rule 3:

Rule 4: *If* the goal is to add two numbers, m and n, each of which is 5 or less, *then* count m fingers, followed by n fingers, and say the result.

Changes such as generalization and discrimination require self-modification processes that examine existing rules and their output, examine the adequacy of the outputs, and modify existing rules. Most information-processing theorists assume that the human cognitive system comes equipped with many or most of the basic processes for self-modification, although the precise nature of these processes remains primarily a matter of speculation (Kail and Bisanz 1982).

2.2.2 Development caused by change in mental effort. All people are limited in the amount of mental activity they can perform at one time. People can usually concentrate their efforts on one or two activities; if they try to do more, performance deteriorates rapidly. This limit on mental activity has been referred to as a limitation in processing resources or mental effort. Common to both terms is the idea that most intellectual tasks require effort and that all individuals are limited in the effort available to them.

Applied to development, the resources available for mental activity may simply increase with age. Adolescents may have more processing resources than children, who have more resources than preschoolers and infants. Just as additional random-access memory allows a computer to run more complex software, a gradual age-related increase in processing resources may be responsible for developmental change in the complexity of thought.

Processing resources may be implicated in developmental change in a second way. As individuals acquire more experience on a particular task, fewer resources may be required for successful performance. Performance may become so refined that ultimately the task is performed without effort. Automatization has occurred when a process can be performed without using processing resources at all. For example, beginning drivers are instructed to avoid talking with passengers and listening to the radio; both activities would take resources needed for driving. However, with more experience behind the wheel, fewer resources are needed for safe driving, so drivers can converse while maintaining the same level of driving skill.

Applied to development, children are seen as "universal novices." Whatever the task, their experience is limited compared with that of adults. With age, children gain greater experience, so that processing requires fewer resources. Thus, although the total amount of resources may not change with age, greater experience means that children gradually have more resources available for allocation to novel or particularly challenging tasks.

2.2.3 Increased speed of processing. As children develop, they complete most mental processes more rapidly. A useful rule of thumb is that 4- and 5-year olds will respond three times as slowly as adults; 8-year olds will respond twice as slowly. These age differences apparently reflect a global mechanism that limits the speed with which children and adolescents can execute cognitive processes (Kail 1991). The impact of this global mechanism on the speed of mental processing is most evident on tasks where the response speed is measured, but is not limited to them. On the contrary, speed of processing may play a role whenever a specified number of actions must be completed in a fixed period of time. Thus, for any task where children must answer in a specified period, age differences in performance may be due to the fact that younger children could not complete all of the processes responsible for successful task performance in the time allotted.

3. Comparison with Other Approaches

Further insights into the nature of the information-processing framework come from comparisons with two other major theoretical approaches—Piaget's theory and the contextual viewpoint. These approaches are examined in detail elsewhere (see *Piaget's Theory of Human Development*), but a brief description here will set the stage for comparisons with information processing.

The Piagetian approach emphasizes general theoretical principles that govern intellectual growth and change. Intellectual growth is described as a set of states that are qualitatively different, reflecting major changes in cognitive structure. Performance on individual tasks is of interest only insofar as it sheds light on general principles of cognitive development.

The contextual approach emphasizes that human development is inseparable from the environmental contexts in which a child develops. That is, theories cannot consider development in a vacuum but must instead examine it in the multiple interactive contexts in which it occurs, including institutions (e.g., families and schools), culture, and history. In Rogoff's words, "the individual child, social partners, and the cultural milieu inseparable contributors to the ongoing activities in which child development takes place." (Rogoff 1990 p. 18)

When contextual theory is the reference point, information-processing and Piagetian theory have many similarities. Unlike contextual theory, both information-processing and Piagetian theory focus primarily on an individual's mental development. Both approaches agree that the outward manifestations of cognition may depend strongly on context but that the underlying developmental principles should be relatively unaffected by contextual variation. In Piagetian theory, for example, the functional invariants (adaptation, organization) are thought to be invariant across cultures. Similarly, information-processing theories hold that mental processes can be understood in terms of organized sets of basic processes regardless of the specific context in which children develop. Furthermore, although Piagetian and information-processing psychologists would agree that cultural context (at many different levels) can have a profound impact on cognitive development, the impact is always mediated by the developing individual's mental structures.

Although the Piagetian and information-processing frameworks emphasize the primacy of individual mental development, their approaches differ considerably. The remainder of this section focuses on two related issues that illustrate differences in these approaches.

3.1 Homogeneity of Mind

Traditional stage theories of development, such as Piaget's, are often criticized for their monolithic approach to the phenomenon. In other words, at each stage in development, a unified mental structure—a homogeneous mind—is presumed to be responsible for all cognition, which leads to the prediction of considerable consistency in performance across tasks.

This viewpoint is unable to account for the fact that children sometimes solve tasks successfully at younger ages than those expected by Piaget's theory or that performance on some tasks improves more rapidly with age than performance on other tasks that are equally demanding.

Information-processing theories adopt a less homogeneous approach to the mind. The transition mechanisms described above—increased processing resources, increased processing speed, and more frequent automatization—are not mutually exclusive; all could be involved in development. Combined, they yield a steady age-related increase in cognitive skill. However, unlike Piaget's concept of disequilibrium, the process of change is continuous. There are no abrupt or qualitative changes in development. Instead, increased resources, automatization, and processing speed result in constant but gradual cognitive change. In addition, they allow for variations across tasks because a child's performance may be automatic on some tasks but not on others. This approach even allows for variation on different versions of the same task: in Siegler's model, for example, a child should solve familiar addition problems with retrieval but less familiar problems by counting.

3.2 Task Specificity

Piaget's theory "has been concerned with pervasive, abstract structures that apply to a broad range of tasks . . . and to long-term temporal phenomena in the form of structural change . . . .. A task is only of interest insofar as it does require a certain concept for its solution" (Breslow 1981 p. 348). Thus, the emphasis is on general principles of development which are wide ranging and not specific to particular tasks. In contrast, information-processing psychologists argue that cognitive structures cannot be studied independently of specific tasks or domains. Most methods for studying cognition require that inferences be made from performance on specific behavioral tasks. Consequently, understanding of cognitive development is necessarily linked to an understanding of performance on cognitive tasks of interest.

This orientation does not mean that information-processing theories have no general components. Modern information-processing theories often include such general components because detailed analyses of separate tasks have pointed to common components of performance (Kail 1991).

4. Conclusion

Information-processing approaches have led to greater understanding in many domains of cognitive development. These advances have begun to converge on a number of conclusions concerning the nature of cognitive–developmental change in infancy, childhood, and adolescence, and the mechanisms responsible for this change. The view that emerges from the approach is one that combines Piaget's search for general principles of development with an appreciation for the importance of the acquisition of skill in particular domains.

See also: An Overview of Cognitive Development; Cognitive Development; Individual Differences; Cognition and Learning

References

Anderson J R 1983 *The Architecture of Cognition.* Harvard University Press, Cambridge, Massachusetts
Breslow L 1981 Reevaluation of the literature on the development of transitive inferences. *Psych. Bull.* 89(2): 325–51
Hamann M S, Ashcraft M H 1986 Textbook presentations of the basic arithmetic facts. *Cognition and Instruction* 3: 173–92
Kail R 1991 Development of processing speed in childhood and adolescence. In: Reese H W (ed.) 1991 *Advances in Child Development and Behavior*, Vol. 23. Academic Press, San Diego, California
Kail R, Bisanz J 1982 Information processing and cognitive development. In: Reese H W (ed.) 1982 *Advances in Child Development and Behavior*, Vol. 17. Academic Press, New York
Kail R, Bisanz J 1992 The information-processing perspective on cognitive development in childhood and adolescence. In: Sternberg R J, Berg C A (eds.) 1992

Klahr D 1989 Information-processing perspectives. In: Vasta R (ed.) 1989 *Annals of Child Development*, Vol. 6. JAI Press, Greenwich, Connecticut
Newell A, Shaw J G, Simon H A 1958 Elements of a theory of human problem solving. *Psychol. Rev.* 65: 151–66
Palmer S E, Kimchee R 1986 The information-processing approach to cognition. In: Knapp T J, Robertson L C (eds.) 1986 *Approaches to Cognition: Contrasts and Controversies.* Erlbaum, Hillsdale, New Jersey
Rogoff B 1990 *Apprenticeship in Thinking: Cognitive Development in Social Context.* Oxford University Press, New York
Siegler R S, Jenkins E 1989 *How Children Discover New Strategies.* Erlbaum, Hillsdale, New Jersey
Siegler R S, Shrager J 1984 Strategy choices in addition and subtraction: How do children know what to do? In: Sophian C (ed.) 1984 *Origins of Cognitive Skills.* Erlbaum, Hillsdale, New Jersey

Further Reading

Bjorklund D (ed.) 1990 *Children's Strategies: Contemporary Views of Cognitive Development.* Erlbaum, Hillsdale, New Jersey
Klahr D, Langley P, Neches R (eds.) 1987 *Production System Models of Learning and Development.* MIT Press, Cambridge, Massachusetts
Siegler R S 1983 Information processing approaches to development. In: Mussen P H (ed.) 1983 *Carmichael's Manual of Child Psychology.* Wiley, New York
Sternberg R J, Berg C A 1992 (eds.) *Intellectual Development.* Cambridge University Press, Cambridge

Piaget's Theory of Human Development

A. de Ribaupierre and L. Rieben

One of the most influential and enduring theories of cognitive development was proposed by Jean Piaget (1896–1980), a Swiss epistemologist and psychologist. Piaget was trained as a biologist. However, he very soon oriented his research toward the study of the mechanisms governing the development of human knowledge. He developed the discipline of genetic epistemology which, because of its grounding in empirical studies, he considered to be independent from philosophy.

This entry reviews the concepts of Piaget's epistemology and psychology that are most important from an educational point of view. It also indicates some of the more recent models of development that have suggested extensions to or revisions of Piaget's original approach.

1. The Classical Piagetian Approach

1.1 Piaget as Epistemologist

Piaget's epistemology should not be confused with his psychology, the latter being defined as the theory of intellectual development in ontogeny. Genetic epistemology and genetic psychology are nevertheless very close, because Piaget's aim was to define mechanisms that are common to phylogeny and ontogeny.

Genetic epistemology is the study of the mechanisms of the growth of knowledge (Piaget 1970); more specifically, it consists of studying the "roots of the various sorts of knowledge from their most elementary forms on and to follow their development in ulterior levels including scientific thinking" (translated by the authors, Piaget 1970 p. 6). Piaget's epistemology is genetic, not only because it is interested in the development of knowledge, but also because of its method, based both on historico-critical and psychogenetic approaches. In contrast to empiricist perspectives, it does not consider knowledge as a mere copy of external realities, and emphasizes the role of action versus sensory apperception of objects. Knowledge is constructed through the actions exerted by the subject on physical, social, and conceptual objects. In opposition to nativist perspectives, genetic epistemology rejects the hypothesis of pre-existing structures of the mind. Genetic epistemology is essentially constructivist and interactionist; it is also fundamentally interdisciplinary.

The aim of Piaget's empirical work was to demonstrate that a given level of knowledge always results from a reorganization of the preceding one. Reconstruction means more than an addition of more elements of a lower type in order to attain a higher level. One direct consequence of a constructivist perspective is that an epistemologist or a psychologist studying any level of development will ask what characterized the preceding level, and will stress developmental progression toward higher levels. An essential mechanism for this reconstruction is "reflective abstraction," that is, a process by which the child extracts characteristics or coordinations from actions or operations; it is called "reflective" both because it consists of a mental reorganization and because it implies a reflection or a transfer onto a higher level of what was established at a lower level. Reflective abstraction is contrasted with empirical or simple abstraction which bears mainly on observable characteristics of objects or classes of objects.

1.2 Piaget as Psychologist

Piaget's psychology deals mainly with cognitive operations, and their successive forms. Intelligence is defined as the most general form of coordination of the actions and operations that characterize the various developmental levels, and not as a mental faculty or an entity in itself (e.g., Piaget 1947). Intelligence develops through a succession of general stages, defined by overall structures. Piaget was not interested in individual or task-specific performances, but in the generic behavior of subjects in classes of situations. Hierarchies of behaviors reflect cognitive operations specific to each developmental level, as well as their organization in overall general structures.

The number of stages defined in Piaget's publications varies from three to five. Most often, he referred to four stages: sensorimotor, preoperational, concrete operational, and formal operational. Piaget used mathematical formalization to define the underlying structures of the stages: a group of displacements for the sensorimotor stage, groupings for the concrete operational stage, and a group of four operations (INRC group) for the formal operational stage. He also attempted to formalize the preoperational stage by means of the logic of functions. The order of the stages is considered to be constant and necessary due to the dynamics of mental activity. Other cognitive activities such as mental imagery, perception, memory, or language are always dealt with by Piaget in relation to the development of operational structures. They are termed "figurative" because they attempt to represent reality as it appears. Figurative activities are contrasted with (and subordinated to) "operative" activities which attempt to transform reality. The sequence of stages described by Piaget concerns only the operative activities.

Although Piaget grew increasingly less interested in the description of these general stages, this is probably the feature of his theory that has been most often retained and criticized. In particular, the generality of the stages was questioned by the existence of *décalages*, that is, temporal lags between the acquisition of concepts supposed to pertain to the same level. Readers of Piaget have often overestimated the necessity of synchronism in acquisitions across situations as implied by the theory. It should be stressed that Piaget did not postulate that the generality of structures meant strict synchronism, even though some of his writings were admittedly ambiguous with respect to this issue.

Piaget himself put more emphasis on the mechanisms accounting for the transition from one stage to the next. Like other authors, he considered that development is influenced by maturation, experience, and social factors; however, he often paid little more than lip service to these three factors. He was indeed more interested in demonstrating the necessity of a fourth factor, "equilibration," which he regarded as accounting for the direction of development (Piaget 1975). Improving equilibration (*équilibration majorante*) is seen as the causal mechanism underlying the progression of cognitive development. It is a dynamic sequence of states of disequilibrium–equilibrium and embodies the organism's striving toward a more general equilibrium. Equilibration is the only mechanism, according to Piaget, that can account for the emergence of novel behavior, even though work since the 1980s has disputed the idea that Piaget's theory can really account for the emergence of novel behaviors. Equilibration is based on the interplay of two essential functions: assimilation (incorporation of new information into an existing system) and accommodation (modification of existing schemes or structures by newly assimilated elements, in order to respond to the demands of the environment). Cognitive structures are put into disequilibrium by perturbations which resist the assimilatory process and lead to errors or failures of action. Re-equilibration is made possible by regulations, which entail the modification of an action as a function of feedback regarding its previous outcomes, ultimately leading to compensatory reconstructions. Equilibration is thus necessary when contradictions and cognitive conflicts arise, hence the importance given by Piaget to cognitive conflict as a source of cognitive development.

1.3 Piaget as Educational Thinker

Piaget published several papers on educational topics (see, e.g., Piaget 1972), most of which were written in response to requests linked to his position in the International Bureau of Education and in UNESCO. These papers can be schematically classified into four broad domains: educational rights, teaching methods, teacher education, and curriculum problems, especially in mathematics and science teaching. On the whole, they contain general principles that often reflect his personal system of values rather than precise implications of his theory for education. Many practical consequences of his theory had already been advocated by earlier educational innovators (such as Montessori, Freinet, or Dewey). Piaget's model thus provides an *a posteriori* theoretical justification for a number of educational perspectives.

Overall, Piaget defended three principles. First, education should focus on the development of general schemes rather than teach specific skills, and should be more process- than content-oriented. Second, from a constructivist viewpoint, teaching methods should give more place to the child's action. Third, curriculum designs should take into consideration developmental sequences and the fact that the learning of a given notion is tied to the child's cognitive level. This last principle has often been misinterpreted as a "waiting position," implying that teachers should wait until children have reached a certain developmental level before teaching the corresponding notions.

1.4 Early Educational Applications

Piaget's theory has had a considerable influence on educational theory and there have been a number of attempts to apply it in the classroom. Generally, it has been used to promote active methods of teaching. It has also encouraged teachers to pay attention to the child's own way of thinking and to adopt a positive interpretation of errors in reasoning. However, there have also been biases, particularly by educators who have attempted to apply isolated parts of the theory. For instance, the principle of adapting to the child's developmental sequence has too often, as already mentioned, resulted in a *laissez-faire* attitude. In application of a neo-behavioristic perspective, on the other hand, the acceleration of stages has become a major goal. Piagetian tasks have also been used as components of the curriculum, which has led, for example, to direct teaching of conservation tasks in the classroom.

2. Unsolved Issues in the Piagetian Theory

A number of problems related to the possible implications of Piagetian theory for education remain open. Piagetian theory has been subjected to heavy criticism

by developmental psychologists for various reasons, especially since most critics have addressed only isolated elements of the theory or failed to take into account the fact that Piaget's project was essentially epistemological. The criticisms may be outlined as follows:

(a) Numerous *décalages*, which cannot be predicted by the theory, have been observed between notions which are supposed to belong to the same structural level; between-task correlations have often been observed to be rather low. This has led a number of researchers to claim that development is domain-specific.

(b) Piaget's portrait of the child appeared too universal and focused on the subject, independent of his or her cultural environment. This in part explains why Vygotsky's theory of socially mediated learning has gained an increasing audience within the educational world.

(c) The description of stage transition is not sufficiently detailed. Despite Piaget's recommendation that teaching be adapted to the developmental sequence, his account of this developmental sequence is not fine-grained enough to be useful for educational practice and to allow for a precise assessment of a child's developmental level.

(d) The theory places too much emphasis on the development of logico-mathematical thinking; its explanatory power for other acquisitions, such as reading and writing, is therefore very limited.

(e) Piagetian theory does not provide sufficient information on learning mechanisms and on the effects of training. Consistent with his epistemological project, Piaget was interested in demonstrating that the general mechanisms governing learning and development are similar. More recently, Inhelder et al. (1974) have dealt directly, but very partially, with learning issues.

(f) Like many general psychological theories, Piaget did not take individual differences into consideration.

At this point, it should be stressed that most of these criticisms concern Piaget's specific models as they have been applied to psychology or to education. Altogether, however, the questions raised by Piaget and his general, epistemological model remain fully relevant to psychology in the early 1990s.

3. Beyond Piaget

3.1 Neo-Piagetian Models

In the late 1970s, there was a strong resurgence of structuralist approaches in developmental psychology (Reuchlin 1995), exemplified by neo-Piagetian models (e.g., Case 1985, Fischer 1980, Pascual-Leone

1987). The objective of these models is to provide a response to some of the questions left open in Piagetian theory, while preserving most of its core postulates. They have in common the search for isomorphisms or invariants across different classes of situations. As a consequence, the notion of general stages has been maintained by most neo-Piagetian authors. Nevertheless, the structuralist features of these models are quite different from those postulated by Piaget. First, the hypothesis of a unique, general, logical structure underlying the organization of all behaviors at a given moment of development has been abandoned. The structures that are defined in the early 1990s are more local. This amounts to assigning a much greater role to context. Second, isomorphisms across domains are thought to result from common constraints or "strictures" rather than from a common structure. There is a certain consensus in favor of postulating the existence of general limits in information-processing or attentional capacity, which impose a ceiling on cognitive performances while allowing for situational and individual variability. As a consequence, qualitative changes can be considered to result from a quantitative increase in general resources (e.g., Pascual-Leone et al. 1978). Third, the importance given to context has as its corollary a much stronger emphasis on task analysis, that is, on an analysis of the characteristics of external situations together with an analysis of the strategies that children adopt when confronted with these situations, and of the processing load that these strategies entail. Fourth, some neo-Piagetians also grant more importance to individual differences, which are no longer considered as mere quantitative variations around a single norm, but also as qualitative differences; consequently, they claim that there can be different developmental paths for different types of subjects.

3.2 Educational Implications

Most neo-Piagetian models embody interesting potential applications to education, even though they have not been fully spelled out. Generally, they all retain the emphasis placed by Piaget on the child's activity. They also suggest at least three consequences for the design of curricula. First, they stress the necessity of finer grained analyses of situations and provide, at least partly, a method of task analysis which may prove worthwhile for education (Siegler and Jenkins 1989). Second, empirical results demonstrate that the child's information-processing capacity places constraints on what can be taught; nevertheless, some studies (e.g., Case 1985) also show that tasks can be simplified in terms of their informational load and can thus be taught earlier than the age at which they would spontaneously be mastered. Third, the stages defined in these models are of shorter duration and may thus be more relevant in terms of the instructional sequence. However, although these models enhance the significance

of Piaget's theory for educational practice, their relevance is generally restricted—as was that of the initial theory—to the acquisition of general reasoning skills such as logical or scientific thinking, their contribution being much less obvious with regard to reading or writing.

There are other direct prolongations of Piaget's theory that convey interesting educational implications, in particular with respect to instructional methods. For instance, the Piagetian model has been extended to analyze the role of the environment and the effectiveness of various types of educational practices (Lautrey 1980). Social–psychological approaches have stressed the importance for cognitive development not only of cognitive conflict but also of sociocognitive conflicts (Doise et al. 1975).

Finally, it should be noted that the Piagetian theory has indubitably had some influence, albeit indirect, on the trend in education to teach thinking and higher-level reasoning (e.g., Resnick 1987). These approaches, like the classical Piagetian approach, are process-oriented rather than content-oriented.

See also: An overview of Congnitive Development; Sociobiological and Ethological Approaches to Human Development; Cognition and Learning

References

Case R 1985 *Intellectual Development: Birth to Adulthood.* Academic Press, Orlando, Florida

Doise W, Mugny G, Perret-Clermont A N 1975 Social interaction and the development of cognitive operations. *European Journal of Social Psychology* 5(3): 367–83

Fischer K W 1980 A theory of cognitive development: The control and construction of hierarchies of skills. *Psychol. Rev.* 87(6): 477–531

Inhelder B, Sinclair H, Bovet M 1974 *Apprentissage et Structures de la Connaissance.* Presses Universitaires de France, Paris

Lautrey J 1980 *Classe Sociale, Milieu Familial, Intelligence.* Presses Universitaires de France, Paris

Pascual-Leone J 1987 Organismic processes for neo-Piagetian theories: A dialectical causal account of cognitive development. *International Journal of Psychology* 22(5–6): 531–70

Pascual-Leone J, Goodman D R, Ammon P, Subelman I 1978 Piagetian theory and neo-Piagetian analysis as psychological guides in education. In: McCarthy Gallagher J, Easley J A (eds.) 1978 *Knowledge and Development,* Vol. 2. Plenum, New York

Piaget J 1947 *La Psychologie de l'Intelligence.* Colin, Paris

Piaget J 1970 *L'Epistémologie Génétique.* Presses Universitaires de France, Paris

Piaget J 1972 *Où Va l'Education.* Denoël, Paris

Piaget J 1975 *L'Equilibration des Structures Cognitives.* Presses Universitaires de France, Paris

Resnick L B 1987 *Education and Learning to Think.* National Academy Press, Washington, DC

Reuchlin M 1995 *Totalités, Éléments, Structures en Psychologie.* Presses Universitaires de France, Paris

Siegler R S, Jenkins E 1989 *How Children Discover New Strategies.* Lawrence Erlbaum, Hillsdale, New Jersey

Further Reading

Case R 1992 Neo-Piagetian theories of intellectual development. In: Beilin H, Pufall P B (eds.) 1992 *Piaget's Theory: Prospects and Possibilities.* Erlbaum, Hillsdale, New Jersey

Chapman M 1988 *Constructive Evolution: Origins and De-velopment of Piaget's Thought.* Cambridge University Press, Cambridge

Piaget J 1970 Piaget's theory. In: Mussen P H (ed.) 1970 *Carmichael's Manual of Child Psychology,* Vol. 1, 3rd edn. Wiley, New York

Piaget J, Inhelder B 1966 *La Psychologie de l'Enfant.* Presses Universitaires de France, Paris

Resnick L B (ed.) 1989 *Knowing, Learning, and Instruction: Essays in Honor of Robert Glaser.* Lawrence Erlbaun, Hillsdale, New Jersey

Vuyk R 1981 *Overview and Critique of Piaget's Genetic Epistemology 1965–1980,* 2 Vols. Academic Press, London

Social Learning Theory of Human Development

A. Bandura

Theories of human development differ in their conceptions of human nature and what they regard as the basic determinants and mechanisms of personal adaptation and change. This entry analyzes human development from the perspective of social cognitive theory (Bandura 1986). Development is not a monolithic process. Human capabilities vary in their psychobiologic origins and in the experiences needed to develop and maintain those capabilities. Human development, therefore, includes many different types and patterns of changes. Diversity in social practices produces substantial individual differences in the competencies, interests, and values that are cultivated and those that remain underdeveloped.

1. Model of Causation

Prior to an analysis of the capabilities that govern human development, the model of causation on which social cognitive theory is founded is reviewed briefly. This theory explains human adaptation and change in terms of triadic reciprocal causation. In this causal model, environmental influences, behavior, and cognitive, biological, and other personal factors operate as interacting determinants that alter each other. Through this process of two-way causation, people are both producers and products of their environment.

When human development is viewed from a lifespan perspective, the influential determinants include a varied succession of life events that differ in their power to affect the direction lives take (Brim and Ryff 1980). Many of these determinants include age-graded social influences that are provided by custom within familial, educational, and other institutional systems. Some life events involve biological conditions that contribute to the course of human development. Other life events are unpredictable occurrences in the physical environment. Still others involve irregular life events such as career changes, divorce, migration, accidents and illnesses.

Social and technological changes alter, often considerably, the kinds of life events that become customary in the society. Major sociocultural changes that make life markedly different, such as economic adversities that alter livelihoods and opportunity structures, military conflicts, cultural upheavals, new technologies, and political changes that modify the character of the society can have strong impact on life courses. Life experiences under the same sociocultural conditions at a given time will differ for people who encounter them at different points in their lifespan (Elder 1981).

Whatever the social conditions might be, there is still the task of explaining the varied directions that personal lives take at any given time and place. This requires a personal, as well as a social, analysis of life paths. In addition to the prevailing sociocultural influences, people are often brought together through a fortuitous constellation of events that can shape the course of their lives (Bandura 1982). There are many fortuitous elements in the events people encounter in their daily lives. Indeed, some of the most important determinants of life paths often arise through the most trivial of circumstances.

Psychology does not have much to say about the occurrence of fortuitous encounters, except that personal attributes and particular social affiliations and milieus make some types of encounters more probable than others. However, psychology can provide the basis for predicting the nature, scope, and strength of the impact that fortuitous encounters will have on human lives. Many chance encounters touch people only lightly, others leave more lasting effects, and still others thrust people into new trajectories of life. The power of fortuitous influences to initiate enduring personal changes is determined by the reciprocal influence of personal attributes and social factors. These interactive determinants have been extensively analyzed elsewhere (Bandura 1982).

In social cognitive theory, people are neither driven by inner forces nor shaped and controlled by the environment. As already seen, people function as influential contributors to their own development and psychosocial functioning within a network of reciprocally interacting influences. Individuals are characterized within this theoretical perspective in terms of a number of basic capabilities, which are reviewed next.

2. Symbolizing Capability

Social cognitive theory assigns a central role to cognitive, vicarious, self-regulatory, and self-reflective processes in human development and functioning. The remarkable capacity for symbolization provides humans with a powerful tool for comprehending their environment and for creating and regulating environmental conditions that touch virtually every aspect of their lives. Most environmental influences operate through cognitive processes. Cognitive factors partly determine which environmental events will be observed, what meaning will be conferred on them, whether they leave any lasting effects, what emotional impact and motivating power they will have, and how the information they convey will be organized for future use. It is with symbols that people process and transform transient experiences into cognitive models that serve as guides for reasoning and action. With the aid of symbols, people give structure, meaning, and continuity to their experiences.

People gain understanding and expand their knowledge by operating symbolically on the information derived from personal and vicarious experiences. The remarkable flexibility of symbolization enables people to create ideas that transcend their sensory experiences. Through the medium of symbols they can communicate with others at any distance in time and space. However, in keeping with the interactional perspective, social cognitive theory devotes much attention to the social origins of thought and the mechanisms through which social factors exert their influence on cognitive functioning.

3. Vicarious Capability

Psychological theories have traditionally emphasized learning through the effects of exploratory actions. If knowledge and skills could be acquired only by direct experience, human development would be greatly retarded, not to mention exceedingly tedious and hazardous. A culture could never transmit its language, mores, social practices, and adaptive competencies if they had to be shaped laboriously in each new member by response consequences without the benefit of models who exemplify the cultural patterns. The abbreviation of the acquisition process through modeling is vital for survival as well as for human development because natural endowment provides few inborn skills, and errors can be hazardous. Moreover, the constraints of time, resources, and mobility impose severe limits on the situations and activities that can be directly explored for the acquisition of new knowledge and competencies.

3.1 Primacy and Scope of Modeling Differences

Humans have evolved an advanced capacity for observational learning that enables them to expand their knowledge and skills rapidly on the basis of information conveyed by modeling influences. Indeed, virtually all behavioral, cognitive, and affective learning resulting from direct experience can occur vicariously by observing people's behavior and its consequences for them (Bandura 1986, Rosenthal and Zimmerman 1978).

Much learning occurs either deliberately or inadvertently by observation of people in one's environment. However, a vast amount of information about human values, thinking skills, and behavior is gained from models in the mass media. A major significance of symbolic modeling lies in its wide-reaching influence. Unlike learning by doing, which requires shaping the actions of each individual through repeated trial-and-error experiences, in observational learning a single model can transmit new ways of thinking and behaving simultaneously to many people in widely dispersed places. People's conceptions of social reality depend heavily on vicarious experiences, by what they see and hear (Adoni and Mane 1984, Signorielli and Morgan 1990). The more their images of reality rely upon the media's symbolic environment, the greater is its social impact (Ball-Rokeach and DeFleur 1976).

Most psychological theories were formulated long before the advent of the enormous advances in the technology of communication. As a result, they ignore the increasingly powerful role the symbolic environment plays in present-day human lives. Whereas previously, modeling influences were largely confined to the behavior patterns exhibited in a person's immediate environment, televised modeling has vastly expanded the range of models to which members of society are exposed day in and day out. By drawing on these modeled patterns of thought and behavior, observers transcend the bounds of their immediate environment. New ideas and social practices are now being rapidly diffused by symbolic modeling within a society and from one society to another (Bandura

1986, Rogers 1982). Because television occupies a large part of people's lives, the study of acculturation in the present electronic era must be broadened to include electronic acculturation.

3.2 Subfunctions of Observational Learning

Observational learning is governed by four subfunctions. *Attentional processes* determine what is observed and extracted from the profusion of modeling influences. People cannot be greatly influenced by models if they do not remember what they have seen. A second major subfunction governing observational learning involves cognitive *representational and memory processes*. In the third subfunction in modeling—the *behavioral production process*—symbolic conceptions are translated into appropriate courses of action. This is achieved through a conception-matching process in which conceptions guide the construction and execution of behavior patterns. Skills are then perfected by corrective adjustments until actions match conceptions. The fourth subfunction in modeling concerns *motivational processes*. People do not perform everything they learn. Performance of observationally learned behavior is influenced by three major types of incentive motivators: *direct outcomes*, *vicarious outcomes* of observed consequences of others, and *self-evaluative outcomes* toward one's own conduct.

Modeling is not a process of behavioral mimicry. Rather, modeling influences convey rules for generative and innovative behavior. This higher-level learning is achieved through abstract modeling in which observers extract the rules governing the modeled judgments and action. Through abstract modeling, people acquire linguistic rules of communication, standards for categorizing and judging events, thinking skills on how to gain and use knowledge, gender role conceptions and personal standards for regulating one's own motivation and conduct (Bandura 1986, Rosenthal and Zimmerman 1978).

3.3 Diverse Effects of Modeling

The discussion thus far has centered on the acquisition of knowledge, cognitive skills, and new styles of behavior through observational learning. Modeling has diverse effects, each governed by different determinants and underlying mechanisms. In addition to cultivating new competencies, modeling influences can strengthen or weaken restraints over behavior patterns that have been previously learned. Modeling affects restraints by the information it conveys about the probable rewarding or punishing consequences of modeled courses of action (Walters 1968).

People are easily aroused by the emotional expressions of others. What gives significance to vicarious emotional arousal is that observers can acquire lasting attitudes, emotional reactions, and behavioral proclivities toward persons, places, or things that have been associated with modeled emotional experiences. Individuals learn to fear the things that frightened others, to dislike what repulsed them, and to like what gratified them (Bandura 1986). The actions of models can also serve as social prompts that activate, channel, and support previously learned behavior. Thus, the types of models that prevail within a social milieu partly determine which human qualities, from among many alternatives, are selectively encouraged. In sum, modeling influences serve diverse functions as tutors, inhibitors, disinhibitors, social prompters, emotion arousers, and shapers of values and conceptions of reality.

4. Forethought Capability

Another distinctive human characteristic is the capability for forethought. People do not simply react to their immediate environment, nor are they steered by their past. Most human behavior, being purposive, is regulated by forethought. The future time perspective manifests itself in many different ways. People anticipate the likely consequences of prospective actions, they set goals for themselves, and they plan courses of action that are likely to produce desired outcomes and avoid detrimental ones. Through exercise of forethought, people motivate themselves and guide their actions anticipatorily. The capacity for intentional and purposive action is rooted in symbolic activity. Future events cannot be causes of current motivation and action because they have no actual existence. However, by being represented cognitively in the present, foreseeable future events are converted into current motivators and regulators of behavior.

Human behavior is extensively regulated by its effects. Behavior patterns that produce positive outcomes are readily adopted and used, whereas those that bring unrewarding or punishing outcomes are generally discarded. However, external consequences are not the only kind of outcomes that influence human behavior. People profit from the successes and mistakes of others as well as from their own experiences. As a general rule, they do things they have seen succeed and avoid those they have seen fail. However, observed outcomes exert their influence through perceived similarity that one is likely to experience similar outcomes for similar courses of action and that one possesses the capabilities to achieve similar performances (Bandura 1986). People also influence their own motivation and behavior by the positive and negative consequences they produce for themselves. This mode of self-regulation will be considered later.

Because outcomes exert their influence through forethought, they have little or no impact until people discover how outcomes are linked to actions in their environment. This is no easy matter. In everyday life, actions usually produce mixed effects, they may occur immediately or far removed in time, the same behavior may produce different effects depending on where, when, and toward whom it is performed, and many situational factors influence how actions affect the environment. Such causal ambiguity provides a fertile ground for misjudgment. When belief about the effects of actions differs from actuality, behavior is weakly controlled by its actual consequences until repeated experience instills realistic beliefs. Yet it is not always one's beliefs that change in the direction of social reality. Acting on erroneous beliefs can alter how others behave, thus shaping the social reality in the direction of the misbeliefs (Snyder 1981).

5. Self-regulatory Capability

People are not simply knowers and performers. They are also self-reactors with a capacity for self-direction. Successful development requires the gradual substitution of internal regulation and direction for external sanctions and mandates. Once the capability for self-direction is developed, self-demands and self-sanctions serve as major guides, motivators, and deterrents. In the absence of internal standards and self-sanctions, individuals would behave like weather vanes, constantly shifting direction to conform to whatever momentary influence happened to impinge upon them.

The self-regulation of motivation, affect, and action operates partly through internal standards and evaluative reactions to one's own behavior (Bandura 1991a). The anticipated self-satisfaction gained from fulfilling valued standards provides one source of incentive motivation for personal accomplishments. Self-dissatisfaction with substandard performances serves as another incentive motivator for enhanced effort. The motivational effects do not stem from the standards themselves, but rather from the fact that people respond evaluatively to their own behavior.

5.1 Motivational Standards

Most theories of self-regulation are founded on a negative feedback system. In this view discrepancy between one's perceived performance and an adopted standard motivates action to reduce the disparity. However, self-regulation by negative discrepancy tells only half the story and not necessarily the more interesting half. In fact, people are proactive, aspiring organisms. Human self-regulation relies on discrepancy production as well as discrepancy reduction. People motivate and guide their actions by setting themselves challenging goals and then mobilizing their skills and effort to reach them. After people attain the goal they have been pursuing, those with a strong sense of efficacy set higher goals for themselves. Adopting further challenges creates new motivating discrepancies to be mastered.

5.2 Social and Moral Self-regulatory Standards

In areas of functioning involving achievement strivings and cultivation of competencies, the internal standards that are selected as a mark of adequacy are progressively raised as knowledge and skills are acquired and challenges are met. In many areas of social and moral behavior the internal standards that serve as the basis for regulating one's conduct have greater stability. In other words, people do not change from week to week what they regard as right or wrong or good or bad. After they adopt a standard of morality, their self-sanctions for actions that match or violate their personal standards serve as the regulatory influences (Bandura 1991b). People do things that give them self-satisfaction and a sense of self-worth. They refrain from behaving in ways that violate their moral standards because it will bring self-disapproval. Self-sanctions thus keep conduct in line with internal standards.

Moral standards do not function as fixed internal regulators of conduct. Self-regulatory mechanisms do not operate unless they are activated, and there are many processes by which moral reactions can be disengaged from inhumane conduct (Bandura 1986, 1991b). Selective activation and disengagement of internal control permits different types of conduct with the same moral standards. One set of mechanisms disengages moral control by moral justification. What is culpable is made personally and socially acceptable by portraying it in the service of moral purposes. Self-deplored acts can also be made righteous by advantageous comparison with more flagrant inhumanities. Euphemistic language provides another convenient device for masking reprehensible activities or even conferring a respectable status upon them.

Self-sanctions are activated most strongly when personal causation of detrimental effects is apparent. Another set of disengagement practices operates by obscuring or distorting the relationship between actions and the effects they cause. This is achieved by displacement of responsibility for detrimental conduct to others, or by diffusing responsibility through division of labor, group decision-making and group action. Additional ways of weakening deterring self-sanctions operate through disregard or distortion of the consequences of action. As long as the detrimental results of one's conduct are ignored, minimized, distorted, or disbelieved there is little reason for self-censure to be activated.

The final set of disengagement practices operates on how perpetrators view the people they harm. Self-sanctions against cruel conduct can be disengaged or blunted by dehumanization, which divests people of human qualities or invests them with bestial qualities. Attribution of blame to victims is still another expedient that can serve self-exonerative purposes. By blaming victims or circumstances, not only are one's own actions excusable but one can even feel self-righteous in the process. Because internalized controls can be selectively activated and disengaged, marked changes in moral conduct can be achieved without altering people's personality structures, moral principles or self-evaluative systems.

6. Self-reflective Capability

The capability for self-reflection concerning one's own thinking and personal efficacy is another attribute that receives prominent attention in social cognitive theory. Effective cognitive functioning requires ways of distinguishing between accurate and faulty thinking. In verifying thought by self-reflective means, people monitor their ideas, act on them or predict occurrences from them, then judge from the results the adequacy of their thoughts, and change them accordingly. Judgments concerning the validity and functional value of one's thinking are formed by comparing how well thoughts match some indicator of reality. Four different modes of thought verification can be distinguished: *enactive, vicarious, persuasory*, and *logical* forms.

6.1 Modes of Verifying the Adequacy of Thought

Enactive verification relies on the adequacy of the fit between thought and the results of one's actions. Good matches verify their reasoning; mismatches tend to refute it. In the vicarious mode of thought verification, observing other people's behavior and its effects serves as a way of checking the correctness of one's own thinking about what leads to what. The persuasory mode of thought verification relies on comparing one's thoughts to the judgments of other. When experiential verification is either difficult or impossible, people evaluate the soundness of their views by checking them with what others believe. This mode of verification often arises in matters involving specialized knowledge or beliefs concerning things with which one has little or no contact. In the course of development, people acquire rules of inference. This enables them to detect certain erros in thought by logical verification. By reasoning from what is already known, they can derive knowledge about things that extend beyond their experience and check the validity of their reasoning.

Self-reflectivity entails shifting the perspective of the same agent rather than reifying different internal agents or selves regulating each other. Thus, in their daily lives people act on their thoughts and later analyze how well their thoughts have served them in managing events. But it is the one and the same person who is doing the thinking and later evaluating the adequacy of his or her knowledge, thinking skills, and action strategies. The shift in perspective does not transform a person from an agent to an object; one is just as much an agent reflecting on one's experiences as in executing the original courses of action.

6.2 Self-efficacy Appraisal

Among the types of thoughts that affect human development and functioning, none is more central or pervasive than people's judgments of their capabilities to exercise control over their own functioning and over events that affect their lives. The self-efficacy mechanism plays a central role in human agency (Bandura 1986). People's beliefs in their efficacy influence how they think, feel, act, and motivate themselves. Such beliefs influence what people choose to do, how much effort they invest in activities, how long they persevere in the face of obstacles and failure experiences, whether their thought patterns are self-hindering or self-enhancing, and how much stress and despondency they experience during anticipatory and actual transactions with the environment. A high sense of self-efficacy pays off in performance accomplishments and personal well-being.

Beliefs of personal efficacy are based on four principal sources of information. These are: (a) performance mastery experiences; (b) vicarious experiences for judging capabilities in comparison with performances of others; (c) verbal persuasion and related types of social influences that lead to the belief that one possesses certain capabilities; and (d) physiological states and reactions from which people partly judge their capableness, strength, and vulnerability. These different sources of efficacy information must be cognitively processed, weighted, and integrated into self-beliefs of efficacy.

Different periods of life present certain prototypic competency demands for successful functioning. Changing aspirations, time perspectives, and cultural variations over the course of the lifespan alter how people structure, regulate, and evaluate their lives. Normative changes in required competencies with age do not represent lock-step stages through which everyone must inevitably pass. There are many pathways through life and, at any given period, people vary substantially in how efficaciously they manage their lives.

Each of the distinctive human capabilities reviewed in the preceding sections requires certain conditions for its development and undergoes characteristic developmental changes over the course of the lifespan. Analysis of the developmental determinants and mechanisms of these capabilities falls beyond limits of this entry, but are reviewed elsewhere in considerable detail (Bandura 1986).

7. Characteristics of Human Nature

Viewed from the social cognitive perspective, human nature is characterized by a vast potentiality that can be developed by direct and vicarious experience into a variety of forms within biological limits. To say that a major distinguishing mark of humans is their endowed plasticity is not to say that they have no nature or that they come structureless. The plasticity, which is intrinsic to the nature of humans, depends upon specialized neurophysiological mechanisms and structures that have evolved over time. These advanced neural systems, which are specialized for processing, retaining, and using coded information, provide the capacity for the very characteristics that are distinctly human, that is, generative symbolization, forethought, evaluative self-regulation, reflective self-consciousness, and symbolic communication.

Most patterns of human behavior are organized by individual experience and retained in neural codes, rather than being provided ready-made by extensive inborn programming. Although human thought and conduct may be developed largely through experience, innate endowments enter into every form of behavior to some degree. Genetic factors and neural systems affect behavioral potentialities and place constraints on capabilities. Because behavior contains mixtures of inborn elements and learned patterns, dichotomous thinking, which separates activities into innate and acquired categories, is seriously inaccurate.

Humans have an unparalleled capability to become many things. As lifespan theorists have observed (Baltes and Reese 1984), human development is a heterogeneous phenomenon that encompasses different types of abilities that follow different trajectories of change and are modifiable throughout the life course. The human qualities that are cultivated and the life paths that realistically become open to members of a society are partly determined by the nature of the cultural agencies to which their development is entrusted. Social systems that cultivate competencies, create opportunity structures, provide adequate resources, and permit leeway to develop diverse aspects of personal potentialities, increase the likelihood that people will realize what they wish to become.

See also: Lifespan Development; Learning Theories: Historical Overview and Trends; Learning Process and Learning Outcomes

References

Adoni H, Mane S 1984 Media and the social construction of reality: Toward an integration of theory and research. *Commun. Res.* 11(3): 323–40

Ball-Rokeach S, DeFleur M 1976 A dependency model of mass media effects. *Commun. Res.* 3(1): 3–21

Baltes P B, Reese H W 1984 The life-span perspective in developmental psychology. In: Bornstein M H, Lamb M E (eds.) 1984 *Developmental Psychology: An Advanced Textbook*. Erlbaum, Hillsdale, New Jersey

Bandura A 1982 The psychology of chance encounters and life paths. *Am. Psychol.* 37(7): 747–55

Bandura A 1986 *Social Foundations of Thought and Action: A Social Cognitive Theory*. Prentice-Hall, Englewood Cliffs, New Jersey

Bandura A 1991a Self-regulation of motivation through anticipatory and self-regulatory mechanisms. In: Dienstbier R A (ed.) 1991 *Perspectives on Motivation: Nebraska Symposium on Motivation*, Vol. 38. University of Nebraska Press, Lincoln, Nebraska

Bandura A 1991b Social cognitive theory of moral thought and action. In: Kurtines W M, Gewirtz J L (eds.) 1991 *Handbook of Moral Behavior and Development Vol. 1: Theory*. Erlbaum, Hillsdale, New Jersey

Brim O G Jr., Ryff C D 1980 On the properties of life events. In: Baltes P B, Brim O G Jr (eds.) 1980 *Life-Span Development and Behavior*, Vol. 3. Academic Press, New York

Elder G H 1981 History and the life course. In: Bertaux D (ed.) 1981 *Biography and Society: The Life History Approach in the Social Sciences*. Sage, Beverly Hills, California

Rogers E M 1982 *Diffusion of Innovations*, 3rd edn. Free Press, New York

Rosenthal T L, Zimmerman B J 1978 *Social Learning and Cognition*. Academic Press, New York

Signorielli N, Morgan M (eds.) 1990 *Cultivation Analysis: New Directions in Media Effects Research*. Sage, Newbury Park, California

Snyder M 1981 On the self-perpetuating nature of social stereotypes. In: Hamilton D L (ed.) 1981 *Cognitive Processes in Stereotyping and Intergroup Behavior*. Erlbaum, Hillsdale, New Jersey

Walters R H 1968 Some conditions facilitating the occurrence of imitative behavior. In: Simmel E C, Hoppe R A, Milton G A (eds.) 1968 *Social Facilitation and Imitative Behavior*. Allyn and Bacon, Boston, Massachusetts

Further Reading

Bandura A (ed.) 1995 *Self-efficacy in Changing Societies*. Cambridge University Press, New York

Rosenthal T L 1984 Cognitive social learning theory. In: Endler N S, Hunt J M (eds.) 1984 *Personality and the Behavioral Disorders*, Vol. 2, 2nd edn. Wiley, New York

Schwarzer R (ed.) 1992 *Self-Efficacy: Thought Control of Action*. Hemisphere, Washington, DC

Zimmerman B J 1989 A social cognitive view of self-regulated academic learning. *J. Educ. Psychol.* 81(3): 329–39

Socio-biological and Ethological Approaches to Human Development

W. Charlesworth

There is no longer any question that evolutionary theory has come to play a major role in the understanding of human nature and its origins. The theory has not only become indispensable to such biological disciplines as genetics, ecology, sociobiology, and ethology (Mayr 1982), but has also become relevant for disciplines ranging from anthropology, philosophy, epistemology, through psychology and culture anthropology, to political science and law.

Traditionally, the theory's greatest empirical relevance has been for disciplines that deal with phylogeny; that is, with the evolution of populations of plants and animals over vast periods of geological time. However, the theory has become relevant for those dealing with much shorter periods of time—for example, researchers who are engaged in the empirical study of ontogeny, the development of individuals over their lifespan (Immelmann et al. 1981), as well as for learning theorists who view evolutionary theory as a conceptual tool for understanding the nature and adaptive functions of learning (Bolles and Beecher 1987). The relevance of development and learning for education is well-recognized. It is only a matter of time before education and culture are viewed more fully as part of the larger picture of human evolutionary change.

1. Education, Evolution, and Culture

Education and evolution share several general features. Like evolution, the process of education entails the transmission of information across generations. This transmission is achieved in the form of specifiable units. Evolution involves genes or units of DNA (deoxyribonucleic acid) drawn through various processes of natural selection and random drift from a population gene pool. Once in place as part of a fertilized cell (zygote), DNA (deoxyribonucleic acid) initiates and orchestrates the construction of physical structures (brain, bones, muscles, endocrine glands, etc.) that make physical survival possible.

Education likewise involves specifiable units. These units, labeled "memes" by Dawkins (1989) and "culturgens" by Lumsden and Wilson (1981), are defined as ideas, words, percepts, and material artifacts such as tools, structures, and written materials that give rise to them; in short, everything that can be defined as cultural artifacts. These units are drawn by various selection and random processes from cultural pools and transmitted across generations in the form of traditions, skills, and useful knowledge. This transmission is achieved through informal processes of socialization and enculturation as well as through the formal process of education. However, unlike DNA, cultural units are generated by, and stored in, the human brain. Also, unlike DNA which is transmitted instantaneously by parents to offspring at the moment of conception, cultural units are transmitted over the individual's lifespan. Most of developmental early transmission is carried out by parents, family members, peers, and teachers.

1.1 Mind, Culture, and Evolution

The main proximate mechanisms for the transmission of cultural information in human behavior are cognitive, historically summed up in the more general concept of "mind." Beginning with Darwin (1871), evolutionists have had no doubt that human evolution was influenced by the human mind and that culture is its chief product. Such an influence was seen as distinctively human since evolution in all other species appears to have taken place in the realm of physical structures.

As a member of the primate order, humans share many physical similarities with apes and monkeys, so many that, from fossil evidence alone, there is no question where humans belong in the evolutionary scheme of things. However, from such evidence there is no way to predict that the evolutionary future of the human species would have been so different from its primate relatives. Similarities between humans and other primates begin at the level of the physical and fade out at the level of the psychological. The differences between them lies in the realm of the psychological and cultural. As Dobzhansky et al. (1977) note, "Without doubt, the human mind sets our species apart from nonhuman animals" (p. 453).

Whether this division between humans and other species is merely quantitative, as Darwin was wont to argue, or whether it is qualitative, is debatable. The crucial point is that the human mind and the functional utility of consciousness makes culture possible (Crook 1980). Because it can change itself so often to meet new challenges, the human mind (unlike gene pools which require generations to change) is the main adaptational tool for altering culture within and across generations.

While sharing with DNA the function of transmitting useful information cross-generationally, education differs from evolution in at least one critical respect. Education involves conscious intent. Being devoid of conscious goal-directedness, the major processes of gene mutation, selection, and retention move inexorably along a plane of blind causality. The processes of education are very different. As educators are well aware, education as a cultural task is carried out with mindful intent towards pre-established goals, no matter how precisely or vaguely envisioned.

1.2 Culture in Other Species

While it is recognized that no other species appears to engage in the process of education in the same premeditated, goal-directed manner that humans do, there is no longer any question that nonhuman species have some form of culture. Behavior and its artifacts that emerge in different ways in separated populations of the same species are used as evidence for cultural (rather than physical) adaptation. Such behavior and artifacts are cultural in the sense that they are invented by and transmitted across population members. While the invention process in other species is unknown, observational evidence suggests that the process of transmission involves the passing on of information from one generation to another through such learning processes as modeling and imitation. As Bonner (1980) notes, ample empirical evidence of the social transmission of adaptive information is achieved by a wide range of animal species: chimpanzees copy from each other the use of various foraging tools and socially relevant communication signals; Japanese macaques imitate others in washing potatoes in salt water; various species of birds learn from others how to identify and follow traditional migration routes; English blue tits learn from each other how to pierce milk bottle tops with their beaks.

2. Development as the "Evolutionary Site" of Education

The processes of evolution take place across generations of population as well as within the developmental lifespan of individuals. In other words, generational changes and development changes are not independent (Gould 1977). Education for adaptation takes place in the brains of human individuals who are in a constant process of developing across the span of time allotted to them as a member of a particular species.

After a long and unproductive history of attempting to view evolution as a Lamarckian product (i.e., children inherit the habits their parents developed over their lifetime), evolutionary theorists have begun to address the mutual relationships between phylogeny and ontogeny by emphasizing development as the paramount site for the epigenetic operation of genetic (nature) and environmental (nurture) factors (Lumsden and Wilson 1981). Attempts to strengthen this much more realistic and productive view of the interactive nature of evolution and ontogeny are well under way. MacDonald (1988), for example, has developed an evolutionary synthesis of human development. As he conceives it, phylogenetically evolved rules interact epigenetically with local environmental factors to constrain and facilitate the development of various social and personality phenotypes characterizing the human individual.

2.1 Intelligence and Individual Differences

The main physical site of changes during development being recognized as the central nervous system, it was clear for Darwinians that intelligence (and its product, culture) was clearly implicated in human evolution. The work of Galton and others on measuring intelligence was inspired by this notion. Since intelligence was associated with learning, it was not long before researchers began developing tests to measure educability. Valid measures of such a capacity, it was hoped, would allow educators to place children properly in the kind of schools that would benefit them most. For the most part, the initial focus was upon children who were mentally retarded. Later, attention was focused on the gifted and on the general population.

Darwin's notions of natural selection and survival being connected to differences in certain traits (such as intelligence), quickly led to invidious comparisons between cultures, ethnic groups, social classes, and in some cases families. Such comparisons were socially explosive and aroused concern among social scientists and educators. Because of fears of the consequences of believing in genetic determinism, evolutionary theory, especially as it applied to human intelligence, fell into disrepute for many decades after Darwin (Degler 1991). As a partial consequence of this, there has been a considerable delay in conceptual attempts to forge what must be necessary connections between culture, evolution, intelligence, education, and individual development.

3. Ethology

The significant contribution of evolutionary theory to understanding education and human development, however, does not lie in finding analogies and dependencies between them and evolution. It lies rather in those empirical disciplines that deal directly with human nature and its origins. Two such disciplines are ethology and sociobiology.

3.1 Animal Ethology

Historically, modern ethology as a biological discipline has its roots in the method of naturalistic observation and theory of Darwinian evolution as applied to the study of animal behavior. Three eminent ethologists, Konrad Lorenz, Niko Tinbergen, and Karl von Frisch, were awarded the Nobel Prize in 1972. Their achievement was the culmination of decades of effort observing, describing, and explaining the natural behavior of animals, and laboriously constructing extensive, detailed inventories of behavior (ethograms).

Their goal was to answer four questions about behavior: its causes, its functions, its ontogeny, and its evolutionary history.

3.2 Instinct and Learning

A principal theme of early ethological research was the relationship between instinct and learning (Tinbergen 1969), a theme analogous to the nature–nurture issue —historically the focus of much thinking on human development and education. Ethologists, like other evolutionary biologists, naturally focused on instinct and nature. However, contrary to popular belief among many English-speaking behavioral scientists, Lorenz, Tinbergen, and other early ethologists did not see instinct as the only important determinant of animal behavior (Lorenz 1981). Learning was clearly implicated in animal adaptation; for example bees have to learn the locations of flowers, squirrels how to forage and crack nuts efficiently, goslings how to attach themselves to a protective mother. Innate and learned elements of behavior were seen as being woven together by experience (frequently over early development) into adaptive, instrumental behavior patterns.

3.3 Human Ethology

While early ethologists' focus was on animal behavior and making cross-species comparisons to investigate its evolutionary origins, they were not unmindful of the applications of their ideas and findings to human behavior. Consistent with evolutionary theory, they viewed the complexities of human behavior as located on the continuum of numerous and interesting ways that species adapt to their environments.

In the 1960s, humans gradually became the subject of research interest as a result of the work of ethologists such as Eibl-Eibesfeldt (1989) and others, who applied the methods and concepts already developed by ethologists to the study of human children and adults. Conducting extensive observations and film documentations of human behavior, these pioneers concentrated their interest on human nonverbal social signals (facial expressions and gestures) across cultures (using the classical ethological comparative approach), as well as on dominance hierarchies, aggression, altruistic behavior, and social behavior of young children.

In the early 1990s, the field of human ethology is well-established and growing (Eibl-Eibesfeldt 1989). Nevertheless, its specific contribution to understanding education has so far consisted mostly of concepts and methodological advice. Charlesworth (1979), for example, proposes that intelligence should be observed ethologically, as behavior (cognitively driven and guided) and not just conceptualized as a disposition to be measured with tests. Naturalistic observation conducted in problem (educational) settings would not only give better estimates of individuals' cognitive capacities relevant for education, but also shed direct light on the educational process itself.

Some of the conceptual and empirical focuses of human ethologists of relevance for educational researchers include:

(a) Educability as an important, genetically determined, and universal, species-typical adaptation of humans;

(b) Early experience, critical periods of heightened sensitivity to certain stimuli, and learning experiences with consequences for later development;

(c) The significant role played by curiosity, exploration, and play in human learning, and the retention of such activities into later life even when sexual maturity plays a major role;

(d) The role of motivational, emotional, and nonverbal behavior in influencing social interactions that take place in the classroom and other educational settings (Bernhard 1988);

(e) The value of conducting cross-species, as well as cross-cultural, studies of education for enlarging understanding of educational functions and processes;

(f) The importance of direct naturalistic observation and permanent documentation (film and videotape) of education in action.

4. Sociobiology

Sociobiological thinking does not direct itself specifically to the acquisition of culture through education. Nevertheless, it does deal with the infrastructure of socially motivated needs, motives, and emotions that influence human behavior and consequently have an impact upon the educational process.

The central principle of sociobiology is that there is a strong causal relationship between social adaptation in individuals and success in genetic reproduction (fitness) (Wilson 1975). The scope encompassed by this principle reflects much of Darwin's interest in sex and reproduction. It includes: cost–benefit analyses of reproductive strategies (thus introducing economics into human social behavior); parental investment in offspring and potential parent–child conflict over this investment; reproductive strategies that are offspring-prodigious and uneconomical, contrasted with strategies that are offspring-limited and economical; differences between male and female strategies; family structure; nepotism; inclusive fitness; reciprocity; cheating; and deception in communication and its ultimate effects on reproduction.

In the early 1990s there exists no single, comprehensive, and empirically established method of connecting such topics to education and individual development. In the spirit of the potential that sociobiological thinking currently offers to the understanding of human nature, the following is presented as a modest start in the direction of an increasing understanding of the education process from the sociobiological point of view.

4.1 The Individual's Tasks

Given that all environments have limited resources, individuals must constantly compete against the environment and frequently between each other for survival. Successful competition is driven by selfish motives and achieved by acquiring and employing the knowledge and means for satisfying them. In a highly social species such as *Homo sapiens*, successful competition requires the relatively rapid acquisition of appropriate competitive as well as cooperative skills; that is, those skills necessary in order to interact with others without being exploited in the process. In other words, everyone must learn how to balance selfish and altruistic motivations in social interactions. In contrast, to survive physically and economically, every individual must acquire work skills as part of job and career preparation. Without such socially useful skills, individuals are usually destined to some form of slavery or antisocial behavior.

Acquisition of both sets of skills is initially achieved with the help of parents and family and later with the support of social institutions such as schools. Culturally appropriate education (i.e., education that contributes to the individual's successful adaptation) is especially crucial for the individual and can be seen as the source of much social conflict over the role of educational institutions in society.

The importance of appropriate education, from the sociobiological point of view, is that it is causally related to the degree to which the individual ultimately contributes genes to the next generation. However, having genetic offspring is not sufficient. Offspring have to be provided with adequate resources until they, in their turn, can reproduce. Such provisions depend on socially acceptable work which requires adequate education.

4.2 Parents and Teachers

Parents invest time, energy, and resources in their genetic offspring and teachers teach because they are rewarded (usually indirectly) to help offspring become competent adults. Since costs are involved, parents, according to sociobiological reasoning, aim to minimize the cost of raising their children and having them educated. In the process, parents may attempt to maximize the teachers' efforts while teachers, on the other hand, attempt to maximize the benefits they receive for their efforts. If they are idealists who are prepared to educate for little reward, teachers run

the risk of being exploited materially by the parents. Conversely, parents may feel they are being exploited by teachers when evidence of improvements in the childrens' adaptive capacity is difficult or impossible to obtain.

Such sociobiological reasoning is a reminder of some of the possible reasons behind the depth of emotion that results when parents feel teachers are not working hard enough to educate their children and teachers are convinced that parents are not preparing their children with the right attitudes toward education. In societies where teachers have little social or economic status, relative to other professions, the conflict between teachers and parents and public officials can be intense and protracted. In such societies teacher unions are formed to advance the cause of teachers. Parent–teacher organizations are usually formed to advance the cause of both.

The main point here is that such an important cultural task as education, that of transmitting information vital for every individual's (and hence culture's) survival, is not free of individual motives based on powerful biological predispositions to survive and reproduce.

4.3 Peers

Potential conflict involving selfish behavior and the need to control it through socially acceptable means does not only exist between the teachers, parents, and public officials involved in education. Peers, inside and outside the classroom, also participate in this conflict. Fighting, cheating, and rivalries between groups of schoolchildren are facts of school life. They, of course, reflect social, political, and economic factors. But they also reflect human biological heritage (Bernhard 1988). The struggle for daily satisfactions associated with self-esteem, good grades, and social status are reflected in dominance behavior, classroom disruption, posturing with special clothes and behavior, and ingratiation; as well as in hard work, conformity, willingness to cooperate with the teacher, and good behavior.

Recognizing the "biological inevitability" of the need of each child to succeed socially and/or academically requires teachers (as well as the whole educational system) to deal with each child on an individual basis and at the same time as a member of a cultural collective. Balancing both is one of the most difficult problems that educators face. The claim maintained by evolutionary biologists is that self-maximizing behavior is natural, since it is a product of motivational mechanisms that rest on evolved genetic programs. From their viewpoint, parents and educators have to recognize that such behavior characterizes all individuals regardless of their age and level of education. To assume that such behavior is caused by the child's family, socioeconomic, and cultural/ethnic status alone, is an oversimplification which, if overemphasized in educational planning, inevitably leads to the failure of most attempts to ameliorate problem situations. Sociobiological reasoning maintains that socially and individually destructive behavior can be controlled if the child's self-interests are taken into consideration. Instructing the child to relinquish self-interest in order to conform, sacrifice, and act altruistically for the good of the collective has, at best, only a temporary effect.

4.4 Global Consequences

Because sociobiology focuses on reproduction, and its demographic consequences, it provides an opportunity of developing a global perspective of education and its effect on human behavior. Education conceivably has an effect not only on children's future reproductive behavior, but also upon their social interactions as adults. Such interactions, as is well-known, can lead to the enhancement, or gradual destruction, of the human species. Education also has an effect upon childrens' future habits toward their environments and its resources. In short, the survival of the human species (as well as that of thousands of other species), and all the ecological niches that serve life, depends on education as the only acceptable alternative to avoiding disaster. As evolutionists long recognized, the result of humans entering on the evolutionary scene has been massive and irreversible global changes. Controlling these changes is fully the responsibility of that species which caused them.

5. Conclusion

Evolutionary theory, as it is expressed in the disciplines of ethology and sociobiology, can be viewed as putting education into three contexts:

(a) An evolutionary, biologically historical, context which makes it possible to view education comparatively across species and within the context of brain evolution and functioning.

(b) The context of current adaptation as a naturally occurring process characterizing all humans under all conditions (not only institutional) thereby requiring a broad conceptualization to include the concepts of educability, the recognition of needs for play and exploration as part of education, the importance of competition and cooperation in human relations, and the concepts of selfishness and altruism as guiding social interactions and how they are related to reproductive strategies.

(c) A global context, both present and future, that regards education as a distinctively human process having enormous implications for current human adaptation and future human populations as well

as for the world's ecology upon which all life depends.

(d) Finally, education must be put into a methodological context which requires that education be observed objectively in action as an ethologist would observe the activities of any species.

At this point, a cautionary note should be sounded: while evolutionary theory expands the understanding of education as well as of human development, it cannot hope to offer a complete understanding. For instance Darwin had no pretensions to psychological insight. Evolutionary theory was not formulated to deal with the nature of psychological functions (conscious, symbolic, linguistic) nor with the nature and function of education as a cultural task that makes possible much of what is significant about being human. Expansion of empirical knowledge about development and education has to depend on the efforts of educational and developmental psychologists. Ethology and sociobiology can, at best, serve to place these processes within a wider conceptual framework, thereby expanding the research domain and allowing for a greater synthesis of knowledge about education.

See also: Genetics and Human Development; Physical Growth and Development: Universal Changes and Individual Differences

References

Bernhard J G 1988 Primates *in the Classroom: An Evolutionary Perspective on Children's Education.* University of Massachusetts Press, Amherst, Massachusetts

Bolles R C, Beecher M D (eds.) 1987 *Evolution and Learning.* Erlbaum, Hillsdale, New Jersey

Bonner J T 1980 *The Evolution of Culture in Animals.* Princeton University Press, Princeton, New Jersey

Charlesworth W 1979 Ethology: Understanding the other half of intelligence. In: von Cranach M, Foppa K, Lepenies W, Ploog D (eds.) 1979 *Human Ethology: Claims and Limits of a new Discipline.* Cambridge University Press, Cambridge

Crook J H 1980 *The Evolution of Human Consciousness.* Clarendon Press, Oxford

Darwin C 1871 *The Descent of Man and Selection in Relation to Sex* (numerous editions)

Dawkins R 1989 *The Selfish Gene.* Oxford University Press, Oxford

Degler C N 1991 *In Search of Human Nature: The Decline and Revival of Darwinism in American Social Thought.* Oxford University Press, Oxford

Dobzhansky T, Ayala F J, Stebbins G L, Valentine J W 1977 *Evolution.* Freeman, San Francisco, California

Eibl-Eibesfeldt I 1989 *Human Ethology.* Aldine de Gruyter, New York

Gould S J 1977 *Ontogeny and Phylogeny.* Belknap Press, Cambridge, Massachusetts

Immelmann K, Barlow G W, Petrinovich L, Main M (eds.) 1981 *Behavioral Development: The Bielefeld Interdisciplinary Project.* Cambridge University Press, Cambridge

Lorenz K 1981 *The Foundations of Ethology.* Springer
    Verlag, New York
Lumsden C J, Wilson C O 1981 *Genes, Mind, and Culture:
    The Co-evolutionary Process.* Harvard University Press,
    Cambridge, Massachusetts
MacDonald K B 1988 *Social and Personality Development:
    An Evolutionary Synthesis.* Plenum Press, New York

Mayr E 1982 *The Growth of Biological Thought: Diversity,
    Evolution, and Inheritance.* Harvard University Press,
    Cambridge, Massachusetts
Tinbergen N 1969 *The Study of Instinct.* Clarendon Press,
    Oxford
Wilson E O 1975 *Sociobiology: The New Synthesis.* Harvard
    University Press, Cambridge, Massachusetts

Psychodynamic Theories of Human Development

E. Jaeggi

This entry addresses the following areas: (a) how psychodynamic and psychological theories of development differ; (b) how Freudian psychodynamic theory has been further developed with regard both to drive theory and to the entire lifespan; and (c) the pragmatic consequences of Adler's theory of human development.

1. Characteristics of Psychodynamic Developmental Psychology

There are a number of important differences between psychodynamic and psychological developmental approaches, which are outlined briefly below.

Initially, psychodynamic developmental psychology was conceptualized retrospectively. Freud himself inferred particular early childhood experiences almost exclusively from reports given by his adult patients and used these observations to construct a comprehensive theory of development on the basis of his theoretical assumptions. This remained the generally accepted method for a considerable time. Only in the 1950s and 1960s did psychoanalysts first turn their attention to direct observations of children. Beginning in the late 1970s, a methodically sophisticated program of psychoanalytic research on infancy emerged, that was partly experimental in nature. In contrast, models in mainstream developmental psychology were based from the beginning on observation and experimentation.

Because of the retrospective approach, a relation between childhood and adulthood (although almost exclusively restricted to disturbed development) was given precedence in psychoanalytic models of development.

The concept of the unconscious—an integral part of all psychodynamic theories—played a much greater role in psychoanalytic theories than in mainstream developmental theories. The unconscious fantasies of both children and their parents were included in the construction of developmental models. According to

psychoanalytic theory, it is not only actual experience that determines later events but, perhaps even more strongly, the related unconscious and conscious fantasies.

Related to the focus on the unconscious is a strong orientation in psychodynamic models of development toward motivational–emotional factors and a weaker interest in the development of cognitive competencies, which are usually considered by mainstream theories of development. Each discipline occasionally suffers from the absence of consideration of the other dimension.

2. Freud and the First Phase

During the first years of the psychoanalytic movement, the sequence of psychosexual development proposed by Freud (1905, 1923) and based on his drive theory claimed universal validity.

According to this theory, the child is born with an instinctive energy that seeks release of tension through various erogenous zones. Over the course of the first 5 years, the erogenous zones undergo characteristic shifts. These shifts are linked to physiological maturity. The dominant erogenous zones, (to which, of course, the child's activities are directed) are the mouth in the first year, the anus from the second to the fourth year, and the genitals in the fourth and fifth year. This established sequence was described as comprising the oral, anal, and phallic phases. In addition, an aggressive tendency—probably innately determined—is present from the very beginning. This tendency also proceeds according to set phases (and varies with early interactions), providing the child with the possibilities for a wide range of experience and behavior. Passing through the phallic phase is a prerequisite for overcoming, more or less successfully, the Oedipal crisis (sexual/affectionate desire for the parent of the opposite sex and the accompanying sense of guilt). For Freudian psychoanalysts this step occupies a prominent position in human development.

The innovative aspect of the theory of phases is the claim that developmental progression or stagnation is determined by the ways in which drives are gratified (between desire and denial).

The preferred experiential and behavioral modes in each of the respective steps (giving/taking in the oral; withholding and secreting in the anal; showing one's strength, or seeking admiration, in the phallic; competing in the Oedipal) provide a model for behavior and experience outside the realm of instinct-determined activities. According to this model, psychological disorders occur when a life event or situation recall an unsatisfactorily resolved conflict in one of the early childhood phases. This recollection triggers a regression to the specific childhood phase with its related means of conflict resolution which is rarely suitable for an adult.

In each phase, there are specific conflicts which are countered by age-specific defense mechanisms. These different modes of defense can also be repeated when conflicts arise later in life. These points were further differentiated by the ego psychologists.

3. Ego Psychology and Object-relation Psychology: Modification of the Psychoanalytic Developmental Theory

Ego psychologists (e.g., Anna Freud, Heinz Hartmann, René Spitz; see the synopsis by Drews and Brecht 1975) stressed new aspects of child development. Most importantly, developmental considerations were extended to include ego functions (usually called perception, thinking, motor activity, etc.). These ego functions, to some extent independent of instinct development, guarantee the child's adaptation to the environment through auto- and alloplastic activities (i.e., the capability of changing either oneself or the environment if necessary) in a "conflict-free" zone. The concept of the primary autonomy of ego functions (a developmental process that proceeds independently of instinct development) should, according to Hartmann, help fill the gap between the psychological and psychoanalytical developmental theories. However, Hartmann's work was mostly conducted and expanded within the field of psychoanalysis.

Anna Freud's great achievement should be mentioned in this context. Her theoretical work, based on practical experience with children in the orphanage for war children (The Hampstead Clinic) that she cofounded with Dorothy Burlingham, took her father's drive theory of development a step further by connecting it with ego development. The "Hampstead Index," a psychoanalytically oriented measurement, was developed to define the developmental state of a child with regard to its instinct development and ego functions (A. Freud 1965). The developmental sequence Freud outlined describes age-specific interactions of ego development, instinct development, and object-relation development. Anna Freud's work has also been of interest to educational psychology. Numerous children's homes and guidance agencies (such as the child guidance clinics) use the psychoanalytical–pedagogical considerations she and Burlingham developed.

The psychoanalytical theory of development further stresses the development of social relations (object relations) as well as the ego performances related to the process of adaptation. Stored libidinous and aggressive energies are shifted from the instinctual to the noninstinctual sphere and become available to the ego in the form of neutralized energy, resulting in an important contribution to the development of ego functions (reality testing, perception, thinking, mobility). Here ego analysts' considerations overlap with the modern psychoanalytic infant research described below.

Object-relation theorists (Fairbairn, Guntrip, Mahler, Winnicott, and later, Kernberg; see synopsis by Minden 1988, Kernberg 1993) are of the opinion that Anna Freud placed too much emphasis on the pleasure principle (aggressive and libidinous elements), writing as though caregivers were only recipients of libidinous input. For this reason they stress the reciprocal interaction between child and mother which exists from the start. In newer psychoanalytic work this interaction has been examined closely, in part through selective observation of children. This research is oriented toward the development of emotional relationships to the environment. Consequently, modern psychoanalytic theories of disorder pay great attention to successful or unsuccessful relationships.

According to Mahler's theory (Mahler et al. 1975) which, while controversial, is of great significance to modern psychoanalytic theories of development (including the accompanying theory of abnormal psychology), the child's quest for autonomy is considered the dominant feature in development. Development takes place in phases where the child seeks independence from the primary caregiver and experiences resulting fears. As with drive theory-oriented psychoanalysis, every unsatisfactorily completed phase can drastically hinder development and lead to typical disorders later in life when situations arise that are similar to the original experience.

Mahler and her colleagues (1975) proposed an important sequence of phases with regard to this striving for autonomy. The so-called autistic phase in which the child perceives no separation from the mother is followed by the symbiotic phase. Here the first object differentiation begins, even though the child still imagines himself or herself linked to the mother in an all-powerful state.

Starting in the fourth month, the first subphase of what Mahler termed "separation-individuation" begins, when the child discovers his or her separation from the mother. (Modern psychoanalytic infant researchers, however, assume that children experience themselves as separate beings from the start.) In the following two phases, the child experiences the new possibility of moving away from the mother, first by crawling and climbing, then by walking. This introduces another mother–child interaction phase. How the mother reacts to the child's new independence is of the utmost importance. Her reaction creates a model of experience that will set a pattern for later life. The nature of the emotional experience of interchanging between the unknown environment and the protective shelter provided by the mother determines the proximity–distance pattern for the future. Walking provides a means of moving even farther away from the mother. It thereby generates the great fear that one may have ventured too far. In this highly sensitive phase, the mother's behavior is of particularly great importance.

If the alternating desires between autonomy and proximity are fulfilled in an optimal way, the child can proceed to the next stage: attainment of the consolidation of individuality and object-constancy. This is based on the assurance that an absent loved one will repeatedly be available without having changed, thereby providing a first constant mental image.

An unsatisfactory transition from these two phases can lead to severe disorders such as psychosis. If the reconciliation crisis is inadequately resolved, borderline disorders and narcissistic neuroses can arise (Rohde-Dachser 1979). Individual authors have proposed different ways of connecting developmental psychology based on object-relation theory with developmental drive theory. However, both the idea that illness is triggered by a situation resembling an early childhood source of disorder and the importance of conscious and unconscious fantasies are maintained by all authors. Later disorders can be traced back to specific developmental phases responsible for conflict, and also provide clues for therapeutic interventions. For Freud, priority was given to creating consciousness of infantile conflict. His followers have made some modifications with regard to a specific relationship model in which the early childhood deficit is not only to be interpreted but also, to some extent, to be corrected in various ways through a close therapeutic relationship.

4. Modern Psychoanalytic Infant Research

Using the concept of object relations and modern, partly psychophysiological methods, psychoanalytic infant researchers have studied the first mother–child interactions. The emphasis in this research, in contrast to the older psychoanalytic view, is placed on the newborn (and very young) child's activity in this interaction on the motivational systems (which are seen as more varied than in the older psychoanalytic view) and on the emotions (Stern 1985, Lichtenberg 1983, Emde 1989, Krause 1983). Many psychoanalysts consider

Freud's belief in a dual-drive theory (i.e., libidinous and aggressive goals as the impetus for development) to be outdated.

Many observations and experiments have pointed to the existence of a wide variety of motivational systems. Lichtenberg (1983), for example, presents the following systems: (a) the preservation of psychological equilibrium, (b) bonding-attachment, (c) exploration and self-assertion, (d) aversion, (e) sensual pleasure and sexual excitement.

Innate emotions such as despair, anger, happiness, surprise, aversion, and curiosity (Emde 1989, Krause 1983) allow the infant a much wider scope of action and experience than previously believed. The degree to which these research results will affect abnormal psychology remains to be seen as of the early 1990s, but it is already known that unsatisfactory mother–child interactions can lead to a much wider range of possible developmental disorders than was once thought to be the case.

5. The Entire Lifespan

Erikson (1959), a neo-psychoanalyst, made an important addition to the first psychoanalytical theories of development by extending the concept of development to include the entire life span. For Erikson, human development is not completed, as for Freud, with the Oedipal phase (all further experience being merely a diversified repetition of previous experience). Erikson postulated an eight-stage model of development continuing into old age. For his theory, the dominant factor is not psychosexuality but an ego-dominated confrontation with the given culture and environment, which inevitably leads to crisis.

Within a psychoanalytical framework, adolescence is less frequently studied than early childhood stages. Freud did, however, point to the fact that psychosexuality manifests itself in two phases, so that in adolescence, the earlier stage themes (especially the Oedipal) are revived. Between the early stages and adolescence lies a period of rest called the "latency phase," which is relatively free of instinctual developmental conflict. Other authors (A Freud, Eisler, Bernstein, Blos) believe that adolescence offers a second chance to correct developmental damage that occurred in childhood (see the synopsis by Erdheim 1984).

6. The Theory of Narcissism and Human Development

Among psychoanalysts, a hotly contested newer developmental approach is Kohut's (1971) theory that narcissism is the dominant developmental event. Unlike

Sigmund Freud, Kohut defines narcissism as a feeling of self-esteem, an affective attitude toward oneself. The regulation of feelings of self-esteem is, together with the regulation of pleasure/pain, a major principle of development. A very early feeling of insecurity arises when the primarily harmonious state of the fetus is jeopardized by the unavoidable frustration of extra-uterine existence. At the same time, this insecurity is an opportunity for development. It is through this frustration that the child learns that he or she is a being separate from the environment. The first internal images of the self and the environment are formed. This learning, however, is repeatedly frustrated by age-specific defense mechanisms such as regression to the state of intra-uterine existence (or whatever one considers it to be), denial, and idealization. A person's own helplessness is thereby time and again briefly balanced and negated. The later development of a healthy feeling of self-esteem is dependent on the degree of frustration (without a certain amount of frustration, serious disturbances would result), and on the primary caregiver's way of handling these defense mechanisms. On the one hand, children should be supported in their denial through idealizing themselves and their parents (all children must feel that their "ideal" parents consider them to be particularly attractive, lovable, intelligent, etc.: according to Kohut, the child needs the "glow in his mother's eye") but on the other hand, children must also attain a realistic assessment of themselves and others appropriate to their age.

Along with instinct development and its connected stages of maturity, Kohut postulates another independent developmental system, namely that of narcissism.

Kohutian developmental psychology has gained enormous popularity. The popular books on the theory of narcissism by Miller (1981) and Schmidbauer (1977) have helped foster a better understanding of this theory among both laypeople and professionals in German-speaking countries.

Theories of disorders have also been strongly influenced by the concept and the importance of narcissistic development. The "narcissistic personality disorder" has become a generally accepted concept, although there is an increasing danger that the concept is used too broadly (Hoffmann and Hochapfel [1987] stressed in their theory of neurosis that a distorted feeling of self-esteem can be observed in every neurotic disorder).

Kohut's concept of development has attained particular significance for the psychoanalytic therapy technique. For many disorders (i.e., the narcissistic ones), he required that the analyst somehow make up for the missing empathy and omit the interpretation of many early childhood transference phenomena (such as idealizing).

Blanck and Blanck's well-known books (1974, 1979) provide an integration of ego psychology. In these books, the main approaches of developmental psychoanalytic theory are applied to both the etiological and therapeutic domains.

7. Adler's Considerations of Development and Prevention

The model proposed by Alfred Adler, first a student and then an opponent of Freud, stresses the practical application of the theory of development to educational matters. In contrast to Freud, Adler considered the damages and dangers in childhood as avoidable. He therefore attributed great importance to the area of prevention (Adler 1982).

For Adler, human development is guided by an inherent striving for power that must fight against an innate feeling of inferiority (real, as in the case of actual organ inferiority, or imaginary). Each person develops his or her own "style" to cope with this conflict. This "life-style" is usually completed within the first 5 years of life, and all subsequent experiences are devoted to the maintenance of this style. The "life-style" is refined in the course of one's life through the so-called biased apperceptions (selective perception and bestowal of meaning).

The conflict between power assertion and a feeling of inferiority instigates both developmental crises and opportunities that can, in the case of unsatisfactory outcomes, result in neurosis. Adler was mainly concerned with the (conscious and unconscious) goals that a person pursues through his or her life-style. Thus Adler's developmental psychology has a strong teleological character. For Adler an important factor in social development is sibling relationships, a form of relationship in which rivalry and the resulting problems are particularly strong, and a type of relationship generally neglected by psychoanalysts.

This developmental model is not well-suited to the elaboration of a differential theory of neurosis because the concepts of power striving and inferiority feelings are ubiquitous and applied to nearly all disorders. Adler assumes that a child can be effectively helped in this natural struggle between feelings of inferiority and the drive for power because a natural superiority should enable the adult to comprehend the child and to steer him or her clear of mistakes. Adler also believes that mistakes can be corrected during the school years. Consequently, he counsels teachers and educators on how to compensate for mistakes made by the parents. Adler's optimism with regard to education stems from the great importance he accords to reason and will. He implicitly assumes that much can be achieved through insight and willpower, an assumption quite close to that of everyday or common-sense psychology.

Adler had a large influence in Austria and Germany, and later also in the United States. Child guidance services, preschools, and experimental schools were originally based on his concepts of education. His advice is not only directed to the problem child, but also to the family and the school environment. As a result, some family therapists consider him to be a forerunner of this form of counseling. One of his best-known students, Rudolf Dreikurs (see Dreikurs and Soltz 1964), contributed to the wide dissemination of Adlerian ideas, especially in the United States, with his popular book on education.

See also: Lifespan Development; Emotional Development; Personality Development

References

Adler A 1982 (ed. Ansbacher H, Antoch R) *Psychotherapie und Erziehung. Ausgewählte Aufsätze.* Fischer, Frankfurt
Blanck G, Blanck R 1974 *Ego Psychology: Theory and Practice.* Columbia University Press, New York
Blanck G, Blanck R 1979 *Ego Psychology Two: Developmental Psychology.* Columbia University Press, New York
Dreikurs R, Soltz V 1964 *Children: The Challenge.* Duell, Sloan, and Pearce, New York
Drews S, Brecht K 1975 *Psychoanalytische Ich-Psychologie.* Suhrkamp, Frankfurt
Emde R 1989 Towards a psychoanalytic theory of affect, I/II. In: Greenspan S, Pollock G (eds.) 1989 *The Course of Life: Psychoanalytic Contributions Towards Understanding Personality Development.* Mental Health Study Center, Washington, DC
Erdheim M 1984 *Die gesellschaftliche Produktion von Unbewu[beta]theit.* Suhrkamp, Frankfurt
Erikson E H 1959 Identity and the life cycle: Selected papers. *Psychol. Iss.* 1(1): 18–171
Freud A 1965 *Normality and Pathology in Childhood. Assessments of Development.* International University Press, New York
Freud S 1905 Drei Abhandlungen zur Sexualtheorie. In: Freud S 1986 *Gesammelte Werke*, Vol. 5. Fischer, Frankfurt
Freud S 1923 Die infantile Genitalorganisation. In: Freud S 1986 *Gesammelte Werke*, Vol. 8. Fischer, Frankfurt
Hoffmann S, Hochapfel G 1987 *Einführung in die Neuro-senlehre und Psychosomatische Medizin*, 3rd edn. UTB Schattauer, Stuttgart
Kernberg O 1993 Psychoanalytische objektbeziehungstheorien. In: Mertens W (ed.) 1993 *Schlüsselbegriffe der Psychoanalyse.* Verlag Internationale Psychoanalyse, Stuttgart
Kohut H 1971 *The Analysis of the Self.* International Universities Press, New York
Krause R 1983 Zur Onto-phylogenese des Affektsystems und ihrer Beziehungen zu psychischen Störungen. *Psyche* 37(11): 1016–43
Lichtenberg J 1983 *Psychoanalysis and Infant Research.* Analytic Press, Hillsdale, New Jersey
Mahler M, Pine F, Bergman A 1975 *The Psychological Birth of the Human Infant.* Basic Books, New York
Miller A 1981 *Prisoners of Childhood.* Basic Books, New York
Minden G von 1988 *Der Bruchstück-Mensch. Psychoanalyse der frühgestört-neurotischen Menschen in der technokratischen Gesellschaft.* Ernst Reinhardt Verlag, Munich
Rohde-Dachser C 1979 *Das Borderline-Syndrom.* Verlag Hans Huber, Bern
Schmidbauer W 1977 *Die hilflosen Helfer. Über die seelische Problematik der helfenden Berufe.* Rowohlt, Hamburg
Stern D 1985 *The Interpersonal World of the Infant: A View from Psychoanalysis and Developmental Psychology.* Basic Books, New York

Further Reading

Baumgart M 1991 Psychoanalyse und Säuglingsforschung: Versuch einer Integration unter Berücksichtigung methodischer Unterschiede. *Psyche* 45(9): 780–809
Dornes M 1993 *Der Kompetente Säugling.* Fischer Verlag, Frankfurt
Heigl-Evers A, Weidenhammer B 1985 Die Freud'sche Theorie der Entwicklung der weiblichen Persönlichkeit aus heutiger psychoanalytischer Sicht. *Forum der Psychoanalyse* 1(3/4): 201–22
Laplanche J, Pontalis J B 1967 *Vocabulaire de la Psychoanalyse.* Presses Universitaires de France, Paris
Mertens W 1992 *Entwicklung der Psychosexualität und der Geschlechtsidentität.* Kohlhammer, Stuttgart

Periods, Stages, and Sequences of Human Development

Stages in Human Development

K. W. Fischer and R. Hencke

Although the concept of sequential, qualitatively different stages of development has been central in explaining how infants grow into adults, educators have been ambivalent about the concept of stage. The wide variability that teachers encounter in their students' skills, talents, and interests has led them to resist a concept that seems to imply uniformity across children. In addition, educators believe that education makes a difference in children's development, and stage concepts are sometimes taken to mean that experience has little role in development (Bidell and Fischer 1992).

Theories of developmental stages since the 1980s promise to eliminate these problems for educators by dealing directly with the variability and diversity in children's behavior. Children are viewed as moving through diverse developmental pathways, not one monolithic sequence. Stages take different specific forms in different pathways, although they share key qualitative changes or discontinuities across pathways (Case et al. 1991, Fischer and Farrar 1987). Environmental influences such as education, family, and culture shape the variations in pathways of individual children. Teachers can potentially analyze a child's specific pathway and use developmental analysis to help individualize the education of that child.

1. Classic Stage Theories

These modern stage theories have grown from disputes among traditional theories that dealt with stages as primarily maturational, environmental, or interactional (Kohlberg and Meyer 1978). Each of these types of theories emphasizes different aspects of development and has different implications for educators.

In *maturational models*, the stages of development are seen as discrete steps in the emergence of innate qualities or structures, comparable to the egg, caterpillar, pupa, and adult stages in the development of butterflies. Maturational models emphasize the genetic bases of development and are used especially to describe development of the body and brain and the relations between these physical changes and behavior. In education, maturational models such as that of Arnold Gesell (Gesell et al. 1938) have promoted the concept of readiness, that is, readiness for school in general or for specific academic tasks such as reading. Later critiques of early schooling indicate that educators still often neglect children's developmental readiness for the school experience and thus engender both learning difficulties and emotional problems (Elkind 1987).

Environmental theories stress the relation of qualitative changes in the individual to changing environmental demands, especially landmark events such as the onset of crawling, entry into school, and the start of puberty. Such far-reaching events produce stagelike changes in people's behavior and learning. The most extreme learning-based models, such as behaviorism, eschew the notion of stages entirely. A wide variety of enrichment programs in education, such as preschools for disadvantaged children and programs for children with special needs or talents, are based upon the principle that major environmental changes produce major shifts in development.

Interactional theories of development analyze how heredity and environment work together in development. Jean Piaget built an influential theory that emphasized interaction and stimulated consideration of the relevance of stages to education. However, Piaget's stage hypothesis was mostly maturational, based on the theory that all children progress through a universal sequence of cognitive—developmental stages. Many educators have been frustrated by this Piagetian stage notion, which seems to require that they direct their instruction primarily to the crucial moment when each student is about to enter a new Piagetian stage (Duckworth 1987).

New, more thoroughly interactional theories build upon one of Piaget's more interactional concepts: that children's central goal is to learn to act in the specific environments where they live. The action systems they build combine the children's own biological properties with characteristics of their specific environments, including their culture(s). These theories offer more complex and detailed accounts of the processes producing development and the relations between environmental conditions and stagelike shifts in behavior, especially in cognitive development (Case et al. 1991, Fischer and Farrar 1987) but also in social–emotional development (Selman and Schultz 1990).

2. Characteristics of Developing Behavior

Children's developing behavior shows four key stage-relevant characteristics. Behavior develops in a specific *sequence* in a content domain. At some points in that sequence, there are *discontinuities* in the behavior. At certain points, there are also substantial *synchronies* across tasks and domains. A given child does not always perform at the same developmental level but shows a *developmental range*, variation in level as a function of context and emotional state.

2.1 Sequence

The most fundamental characteristic of development is its sequentiality. Traditional methods of assessing developmental sequences have relied upon presentation of a single task to either children of different ages (cross-sectional designs) or one child at a variety of ages (longitudinal designs). Sequence is then inferred from variations in children's task performance at different ages. Piaget's descriptions of the preoperational and concrete operational stages of thinking are one example. Both stages are detected through a single task, such as conservation of an amount of liquid (i.e., explaining how a quantity of liquid will remain constant when it is poured from a container of one shape into a container of a different shape). Preoperational thinking is indicated when the child assumes that the amount changes with the shape, whereas concrete operational thinking occurs when the child explains that the amount remains constant even with changes in shape.

Traditional models of developmental sequence, building upon the findings from single-task methods, have assumed that development involves a unitary hierarchy, in which separate actions at an early stage are all integrated to form a unified understanding at a later stage. This kind of hierarchy has been proposed for phenomena as diverse as moral judgment (Kohlberg 1969) and scientific reasoning (Inhelder and Piaget 1958).

Unitary hierarchical models of development predict that all people show essentially the same stages of development, climbing the same universal developmental ladder. Such portraits of development have been sharply criticized as ethnocentric, gender-biased,

and fundamentally wrong. They fail to capture the diversity of human development, and the methods used to test these models in research and assessment have typically been so limited that it has been virtually impossible to detect any developmental sequences other than simple linear ones.

The single-task method illustrates the problems with traditional assessment techniques in both the classroom and the laboratory. Because it does not sample behavior widely, it provides a narrow view of a child's skills and a poor test of sequence. For example, a change in the complexity of a task will usually alter what a child does in the task. A child who can explain conservation of liquid when dealing with one glass of juice being poured into another will often fail in the more complex task of explaining conservation when faced with several different glasses being poured. The single-task method ignores the effects of factors like complexity and treats the child as if he or she had a single, unitary competence.

What is needed instead are methods that build upon the fact that task and context affect children's understanding and skill, such as Guttman scales (Guttman 1944), which use separate tasks to assess each stage or step in a developmental sequence. Good teaching requires both assessing how variation in task and context affects understanding and using that variation to facilitate generalization of important concepts across tasks. Teachers and researchers need to sample tasks broadly to get a full portrait of children's developing skills and concepts.

Recent stage theories posit great diversity in developmental pathways (Bidell and Fischer 1992). Children construct specific actions and understandings from diverse experiences in diverse contexts and cultures. There is no single unitary hierarchy or pathway but instead complex multiple-strand pathways forming a developmental web instead of a ladder.

2.2 Discontinuity and the Dynamics of Developing Behavior

A primary argument for developmental stages is discontinuity in growth between stages, such as growth spurts. Methods for demonstrating discontinuity use a near-continuous measure of sequence, such as the scalogram, in combination with a measure of time, such as age (Fischer et al. 1984). Spurts appear when performance on a large number of sequential tasks jumps abruptly during a brief period.

Traditional arguments about stages have typically assumed that development must be either mostly discontinuous or mostly continuous. For example, behaviorists and many information-processing theorists have argued that nearly all learning occurs as a result of gradual accumulation of skills and that stages reflect imposition of arbitrary divisions upon this continuity. Later work has moved beyond this dichotomous argument to determine the conditions under which development is continuous and those under which it is discontinuous.

Most modern theories of development assume that an action arises from multiple components in the person and the context, and that the ways the components combine in a given instance determine the form of the action. The form will therefore vary dynamically as there are significant variations in the components. Among the characteristics that vary are the discontinuity or continuity of development. As a result, the same action can show strongly discontinuous stages under some conditions and completely continuous growth under others (van Geert 1991, van der Maas and Molenaar 1992).

The traditional way of dealing with such variations in an action is to distinguish competence from performance (Flavell and Wohlwill 1969). Even when the "true" competence is discontinuous, according to this argument, the performance may not demonstrate the competence, and so development may appear to be continuous. Thus performance which appears continuous is simply a poor reflection of the underlying discontinuities in competence.

An alternative model, inspired in part by the work of the Russian scientist Vygotsky (1978), is that action varies throughout a *developmental range*. There is not one true competence but a range in the limits on behavior in which the level of skill truly varies for an individual child (Fischer et al. 1993). When a child's action approaches the upper limit on performance, termed the "optimal level," development shows discontinuities such as spurts. When the action occurs lower down in the range, a child operates at her or his functional level and development is gradual and continuous. That is, at optimal level shifts between stages tend to be abrupt, but under most assessment conditions, children do not perform optimally. When they are not given practice, instruction, and contextual support for a skill, they perform at their functional level, which shows continuous change, not discontinuity. Most instruction deals with understanding at functional level.

2.3 Synchrony in Development

Within stage theories, the mechanisms assumed to underlie discontinuities in performance are both general and powerful, and so they affect a variety of behaviors within and across developmental pathways in different domains, leading to some synchronized developmental changes. While the precise point synchrony predicted by Piaget's notion of the *structure d'ensemble* has proven to be nonexistent, a looser interval form of synchrony has been found often and remains characteristic of developmental stages. Two new developments emerge within a short interval, although not at precisely the same point in time.

Of course, synchrony does not occur for all tasks that link to a concept. Only through consideration of the many factors that cause variability in developmental level, such as task complexity, familiarity, motivation, and contextual support, is it possible to detect the kinds of synchrony that occur with development of a new stage. For example, synchrony for a given child will come and go depending upon where the child is operating in the developmental range.

Synchrony can be explained as resulting from the process of skill generalization, first across tasks within a domain and then across domains (Fischer and Farrar 1987). Children learn a concept or skill in one task and context, and they have to work to generalize it gradually to more and more distant tasks. One straightforward prediction from this explanation is that the degree of synchrony obtained between tasks depends upon their similarity to one another. Another prediction is that children will keep extending a powerful concept to new contents over weeks, months, or even years, thus producing higher and higher synchrony across tasks over time.

Although synchrony across tasks is not so powerful or unitary as Piaget's theory predicted, there do seem to be some relatively general understandings that apply across a fairly large number of tasks. These central conceptual structures can be taught to children and can rapidly affect their skill in a number of related tasks. For example, there appears to be a central conceptual structure for number that underlies how young children deal with many tasks involving quantity. When they are taught a more effective understanding of number, their skill in an array of quantity tasks improves relatively rapidly (Case and Griffin 1990).

3. Techniques for Modeling and Testing Development

Modern mathematical and statistical techniques allow precise modeling of the dynamic phenomena of development, including complex branching pathways, discontinuities, developmental range, and generalization of concepts across domains. Traditional statistical techniques focused on linear changes, but nonlinear changes are readily depicted in newer, more developmentally appropriate techniques.

One class of techniques is based on the mathematics of dynamic systems (van Geert 1994). Changes in a grower (anything that develops) are modeled in terms of a few simple variables, including a starting point, a growth rate, a basic capacity for growth, and feedback about the level of the grower. Forms of growth are described by straightforward mathematical equations, which have been shown to fit developmental patterns shown by real children for early language, cognitive development, and brain growth. Virtually all these functions show stagelike growth under many conditions and continuous growth under other conditions. The same is true for growth of many aspects of brain activity and anatomy, which frequently show spurts and plateaus in development that seem to parallel some of the discontinuities in behavior (Thatcher 1994).

Statistics are also available for inferring complex developmental patterns, including both discontinuities and complex, branching pathways. For example, longitudinal growth analysis permits the testing of different predicted patterns of growth for any repeated-measures data (longitudinal design or Guttman scale) (Willett 1989). Catastrophe-theory analysis provides tests of whether developmental changes fit a set of criteria for catastrophes, which are an especially powerful type of discontinuity (van der Maas and Molenaar 1992).

Partially ordered scaling, which generalizes the logic of Guttman scaling to complex developmental sequences, describes nonlinear, branching developmental pathways in children's behaviors (Fischer et al. 1993). Detection of this variation and diversity in children's skills requires the use of multiple tasks and contexts for assessment. Series of tasks are administered that are designed to detect possible sequences including branching. A sequence can then be tested through the task orderings obtained for each child. Children's performance profiles can show either unitary sequences, branching pathways, or independent strands. Research using this technique to study reading in young children found several distinct developmental pathways in different children. Skilled young readers integrated initially separate strands of skills into an integrated sequence, while less successful readers developed reading skills along several independent strands simultaneously. With this sort of measurement technique, educators can determine more exactly what a child understands, and researchers can test stage and sequence with precision both within and across children.

4. The Usefulness of Stage Concepts

The traditional concept of stage was not especially useful to educators because it implied that children all learned and developed in the same, uniform way. Newer concepts of stage assume that behavior is dynamic, arising from multiple interacting components and therefore showing diverse forms of development, not a single ladder of stages.

Children develop through orderly sequences of skills or concepts, showing abrupt stagelike discontinuities under some circumstances, and demonstrating some synchronies across tasks and contexts. However, different children often develop along different pathways, and their pathways are complex and branching. In addition, children operate in a developmental range along each branch, not at a single point. Models and assessment techniques available for understanding these complex developmental pathways provide new ways for educators to analyze children's diverse approaches to learning and to understand how

to facilitate individual children's developing skills and understandings.

See also: Physical Growth and Development: Universal Changes and Individual Differences; An Overview of Cognitive Devolopment; Social Development

References

Bidell T R, Fischer K W 1992 Cognitive development in educational contexts: Implications of skill theory. In: Demetriou A, Shayer M, Efklides A (eds.) 1992 *Neo-Piagetian Theories of Cognitive Development: Implications and Applications for Education.* Routledge & Kegan Paul, London

Case R et al. 1991 *The Mind's Staircase: Exploring the Conceptual Underpinnings of Children's Thought and Knowledge.* Erlbaum, Hillsdale, New Jersey

Case R, Griffin S 1990 Child cognitive development: The role of central conceptual structures in the development of scientific and social thought. In: Hauert C A (ed.) 1990 *Developmental Psychology: Cognitive, Perceptuo-Motor, and Neuropsychological Perspectives.* Elsevier, Amsterdam

Duckworth E 1987 *The Having of Wonderful Ideas and Other Essays on Teaching and Learning.* Teachers College Press, New York

Elkind D 1987 *Miseducation: Preschoolers at Risk.* Knopf, New York

Fischer K W, Farrar M J 1987 Generalizations about generalization: How a theory of skill development explains both generality and specificity. *International Journal of Psychology* 22(5–6): 643–77

Fischer K W, Knight C, Van Parys M 1993 Analyzing diversity in developmental pathways: Methods and concepts. In: Edelstein W, Case R (eds.) 1993 *Constructivist Approaches to Development.* S Karger, Basel

Fischer K W, Pipp S, Bullock D 1984 Detecting developmental discontinuities: Methods and measurements. In: Emde R N, Harmon R J (eds.) 1984 *Continuities and Discontinuities in Development.* Plenum Press, New York

Flavell J H, Wohlwill J F 1969 Formal and functional aspects of cognitive development. In: Elkind D, Flavell J H (eds.) 1969 *Studies in Cognitive Development: Essays in Honor of Jean Piaget.* Oxford University Press, New York

Gesell A, Thompson H, Amatruda C S 1938 *The Psychology of Early Growth Including Norms of Infant Behavior and a Method of Genetic Analysis.* Macmillan, New York

Guttman L 1944 A basis for scaling qualitative data. *Am. Sociol. Rev.* 9: 139–50

Inhelder B, Piaget J 1958 (trans. Parsons A, Seagrim S) *The Growth of Logical Thinking from Childhood to Adolescence.* Basic Books, New York

Kohlberg L A 1969 Stage and sequence: the cognitive – developmental approach to socialization. In: Goslin D (ed.) 1969 *Handbook of Socialization Theory and Research.* Rand McNally, Chicago, Illinois

Kohlberg L A, Meyer R 1978 Development as the aim of education. In: Kuhn D (ed.) 1978 *Stage Theories of Cognitive Development: Criticisms and Application.* Harvard Educational Review, Cambridge, Massachusetts

Selman R L, Schultz L H 1990 *Making a Friend in Youth: Developmental Theory and Pair Therapy.* University of Chicago Press, Chicago, Illinois

Thatcher R W 1994 Cyclic cortical reorganization: Origins of human cognitive development. In: Dawson G, Fischer K W (eds.) 1994 *Human Behavior and the Developing Brain.* Guilford, New York

van der Maas H, Molenaar P 1992 A catastrophe-theoretical approach to cognitive development. *Psychol. Rev.* 99: 395–417

van Geert P 1991 A dynamic systems model of cognitive and language growth. *Psychol. Rev.* 98(1): 3–53

van Geert P 1994 *Dynamic Systems of Development: Change between Complexity and Chaos.* Harvester Wheatsheaf, London

Vygotsky L 1978 *Mind in Society: The Development of Higher Psychological Processes.* Harvard University Press, Cambridge, Massachusetts

Willett J 1989 Some results on reliability for the longitudinal measurement of change: Implications for the design of studies of individual growth. *Educ. Psychol. Meas.* 49(3): 587–602

Infancy

L. P. Lipsitt

Infancy is the developmental period immediately following birth, and is distinguished by the extent to which unconditioned or congenital responses, which are essentially "gifts of the species," are especially evident as determinants of the baby's reactions to stimulation. Very soon, the superimposition of experiential conditions shapes those responses in new directions depending upon the culture, family practices, and individual dispositions of the baby's caretakers. The context comes to have an increasing influence on the behavioral repertoire of the baby, while the initial substrate of responses remains as a core to which the response tendencies of the baby will return, especially under stressful conditions.

1. Issues

Among the significant issues surrounding the nature of infancy are:

(a) The question of relative influences of organismic and environmental factors;

(b) The role of early experience in determining later behavior and development, an issue which includes consideration of the durability of early influences, the reversibility of the effects of early trauma, and the effects of early intervention on the physical maturation and behavioral development of the young;

(c) The question of individual differences, as in temperament, and the extent to which these can be altered through training regimens or interventions;

(d) The processes through which behavior change is effected and emotional development is promoted in the early months of life.

1.1 The Nature–Nurture Issue

Many studies have sought to establish how much of an individual's life destiny and the personality characteristics of individuals, like intelligence levels, can be accounted for by genetic factors, and how much by the environment. Both domains of influence are relevant and in fact affect one another. The assumption of a dichotomy is misguided. Just as the manifestation of specific behaviors may await the development of neuromotor "permissions," so the neuromorphological characteristics of the organism are themselves affected by the experience to which the organism is subjected (Hubel and Wiesel 1979, Larsson 1944, Rosenzweig and Bennett 1978).

1.2 Infantile Experience and Later Development and Behavior

The assumption that there is a primary influence of early infantile experience on behavior and development of the child relates both to the learning potential of the young organism and to psychodynamic theories about the enduring intensity of the early mother–child relationship. The early experience supposition derives some of its strength from neurobiological data, and from lasting influences of either severe deprivational conditions (e.g., maternal smoking, drug use, or abuse) during pregnancy or the perinatal period which may have neurobehavioral consequences for the offspring (Nyberg et al. 1993). In general, and in the absence of exceptionally severe infantile deprivation or handicapping experiences, the evidence points to deleterious effects of infantile experience mostly in interaction with later conditions of abuse, constraint, or sensory limitation (Buka et al. 1993, Sameroff and Chandler 1975). This view of the resiliency of youngsters is supported by Garmezy and Rutter (1983), who find that handicapping conditions of early life are often attenuated by the introduction of positive experiences at later ages.

1.3 Mental Development

The study of mental age in relation to chronological age has yielded procedures for calculating, for individual children, the developmental quotient (DQ), an index derived similarly to that of the intelligence quotient (IQ). Ascertainment of "mental age" has been at the core of developmental psychology for many years, and can be said to have been the major passion of students of developmental psychology until the 1950s when a new fascination for experimentalism emerged. The early studies of behavioral and mental attributes of infants and children, based on an anthropometric model which sought to measure physical growth as a function of age, were essentially normative investigations. Researchers observed the behaviors of children from different cultures and family backgrounds at progressive chronological ages and sought to find the "universals" of development (Spiker and McCandless 1954, Nugent et al. 1989). Achievement of milestone behaviors was the criterion, historically, of "good development," and the success of parents and their children was in remaining "within normal limits" with respect to milestone behaviors like crawling, creeping, walking, pulling to standing, walking alone, making a mark with a crayon, uttering two-word sentences, and so on.

This approach tended to ignore the processes through which children achieved these milestones. The field eventually gave way to a new orientation which emphasized these mechanisms and processes of infant development, rather than merely describing the achievement platforms in relation to chronological age (Spiker and McCandless 1954). Interestingly, Piaget (1959) combines both facets of concern: achievement and process. On the one hand, his theory tags ages by or at which specific behavioral achievements are seen (the descriptive aspects) but, on the other hand, his theory is about the ontogenetic processes, indigenous to age groups, which enable the traversal from one platform to the next. An emerging emphasis by developmentalists on cognitive processes in development, is testimony that the solely descriptive or normative studies of the past have been supplanted by psychological experimentalism.

1.4 Behavior Change Processes

Changes in behavior with increasing age are seen to be a joint and synergistic function of both constitutional factors and experiential conditions. Learning processes have been studied in rather great detail, with the result that it is commonly acknowledged by developmentalists in the early 1990s that babies come into the world with all of their sensory systems functioning, and that their capacity for sensing the world and for responding reflexively to a variety of

stimuli enables them to be stimulated systematically and cumulatively. The natural world of the infant usually provides rather orderly sets of repetitive stimuli, such as in feeding, and the environment capitalizes on the baby's approach and avoidance tendencies to provide nourishment and to avoid hazards. The baby's apparent appreciation of pleasure and annoyance results in the baby being rewarded (reinforced) for engaging in some behaviors and for refraining from others. Thus the infant is ready for learning even at birth, and both classical and operant conditioning techniques (and combinations of these) have been useful in demonstrating the capacity of very young babies to acquire new behaviors or intensify some which already exist in their response repertoire. Both types of learning are seen in the everyday changes of babies' behavioral adaptations, and can be demonstrated in laboratory situations (Papousek 1959, Rovee-Collier and Lipsitt 1982).

2. Reflexes in Infancy

Normal infants come into the world with a capacity, essentially as a gift of the species, for responding to a variety of stimuli in somewhat stereotyped ways. They blink their eyes at bright lights and puffs of air, grasp objects with their fingers when something presses against their palms, and can even carry their own suspended weight. When held horizontally and prone in water, infants alternate arm and leg movements as if swimming, turn their head in the direction of a tactile stimulus to the cheek, and make rhythmic stepping movements when supported upright with their legs touching a surface below. All of these behaviors are clearly adaptive at the moment, such as when the infant turns its head away from a stimulus which would cause respiratory occlusion.

2.1 Reflexes as Preparation for Later Behavior

Perhaps as interestingly and importantly, these behaviors are preludes to behaviors which are yet to be organized and developed in more mature ways. For example, the swimming reflex which is seen in the newborn infant (McGraw 1943) undergoes a transformation to voluntary control at around 4–6 months of age—with the transitional period at 2–4 months of age (which McGraw characterizes as a period of "disorganized behavior")—and becomes the eventual voluntary or learned swimming behavior which is seen in mature humans. Practicing these early-manifested reflexes can speed the appearance of their more mature forms. Babies whose alternating reflexive leg movements are practiced tend to walk earlier. Some ingenious studies of "imitative" behaviors in babies in the first month of life (Meltzoff and Moore 1983) suggest that infants are predisposed or constitutionally set to engage in some rather mature-looking behaviors, seemingly foreshadowing the dynamic interactions which will enable children eventually to acquire the rhythms and styles of their families, and the rules and mores of their cultures.

2.2 Behavioral Organization in Infancy

Among the infantile behaviors that have been extensively studied by experimentalists since the early 1950s are looking, sucking, and crying (Lipsitt 1969, Rovee-Collier and Lipsitt 1982). These three response systems provide the opportunity to observe the hedonic control of infant behavior. Just as later human behavior is under strong incentive control, so the infant's behavior seems to derive its impetus from the pleasures and annoyances of sensation (Pfaffmann 1960).

Babies appear in the world with tendencies to engage in approach and avoidance behavior, and these features of behavior seem to be under hedonic control, which is to say that pleasure and annoyance mediate approach and avoidance. No learning is required to cause the newborn baby to turn its head away from an object that blocks respiration. By the same token, no learning is required for sucking to occur in response to stimulation around the mouth. Initially, these responses seem to be largely under subcortical control. However, the environment and experience begin to affect the manner or style in which these responses are exercised even within hours or days of birth. With successive experiences of feeding from the mother's breast over the first five days of life, for example, babies recognize or discriminate their mothers by their odors from other breast-feeding mothers (Rovee-Collier and Lipsitt 1982). Similarly, they adjust their feeding posture to the feeding environment in the first few days, much as other mammals do (Rheingold 1963), and show remarkable organization of head adjustment at the breast to accommodate to the mother's unique physique and postural idiosyncrasies.

2.3 Approach–Avoidance Behavior, and Hedonic Mediation

Of special importance in the understanding of infant behavior is the fact that normal newborns, with exceptions occurring in children born at risk, are equipped with a variety of congenital responses which are instrumental in enabling them to approach satisfying stimuli and avoid annoying conditions. Thus they will turn their heads toward and suck on something that enters their mouths, and will turn from or avoid any stimulation around the face that threatens respiratory occlusion. This hedonic basis of infantile responsivity is of evolutionary heritage and serves the infant well in promoting its survival by facilitating acquisition of nutriment and escape from oxygen deprivation.

2.4 Unresolved Issues

As in any emerging scientific activity, there are disputes in the field of child development regarding infant

capacities, particularly as to what the newborn baby senses, appreciates, processes, remembers, uses in its subsequent behavior, and so on (Rovee-Collier 1987). There is a plethora of opinion based upon relatively limited data. For example, the question arises as to whether the sounds a newborn heard as a fetus had any effect whatsoever on its subsequent behavior. While it has been known for many years that the fetus hears sounds, only in the late twentieth century has the discovery been made that the newborn baby may behave discriminatorily to sounds heard before birth and after. DeCasper and Fifer (1980) used an ingenious study methodology to investigate the question. Capitalizing on the burst-pause rhythmicity of newborn sucking, for half of their subjects they made the baby's own mother's voice contingent on pauses longer than their no-stimulus average, and strangers' voice contingent on shorter-than-average pauses. For the other half, they reversed the conditions. They found a significant effect of the mother's voice. The same did not occur to the father's voice. The father's voice may be of a different quality coming from the "outside" as opposed to the mother's voice which resonates in her internal body cavity. The babies even adjusted their sucking pattern depending on whether the sound which was made contingent on sucking was a story (or not) read during pregnancy to the fetus. The results clearly point to the need for a large research investment in this area. While it is well-known that nutritional and other physiological conditions greatly affect fetal and later development, little is known of the effects of experiential conditions on the well-being or the eventual educational achievement of the child based upon very early experiences.

3. Sensory Capacities

While all sensory systems of the normal, full-term newborn are functioning at birth, recovery from the stress of birth, physical maturation, and the gradual experiencing of the environment through specific sensory channels affords the infant opportunity to increase its acuity in all modalities and to experience the pleasures and annoyances associated with sensory stimulation (Aslin 1987).

3.1 The Visual Capacities of Human Infants

The best information available thus far is that although even newborns can see, visual acuity does not approach adult ability until about one year of age. At birth, babies are especially attracted to light–dark contrasts. Between 2 and 3 months of age, a period in which a great deal of cortical maturation is evident, babies show special interest in organizations of visual stimulation and the internal components, especially the eyes, of the human face. Babies detect depth at around 2–3 months of age, but fear depth only at around the time they begin to crawl.

4. *Piaget's Theory of Cognitive Development in Infancy*

Piaget's theory of infant development is perhaps the broadest of blankets (Piaget 1959), though it lacks important specifics, covering our knowledge of infancy. His first of four major stages of development, which is known as the "sensorimotor period," is based upon the presumption that the infant's actions on the environment, and the effects these have, are of great importance in setting the stage for later development. The individual comes to understand object permanence, and the separation of self from others, through observations and manipulations of objects in his or her world. This first stage of human development is divided into six substages:

(a) Exercising of reflexes, birth to 1 month;

(b) Developing "schemes" like sucking and grasping, from 1 to 4 months, usually involving basic pleasures of sensation (Piaget seems to be calling attention to learned accommodations without using learning terminology);

(c) Discovering procedures for relating to the outside world, from 4 to 8 months of age, and seeming to know, as indicated by its repetitious behavior, that its own behavior produces simple results;

(d) Engaging in intentional behavior, at 8 to 12 months, at which stage the infant seems to have a representational plan, recognizing from memory that a certain behavior may produce a specific result, then trying it, and confirming the hypothesis;

(e) Exploring novelty, 12 to 18 months, trying out behaviors to note their effects and either continuing or discontinuing them based on their efficacy or reward value;

(f) Engaging in truly mental representation, rultidimensioning past experiences to instigate new events.

5. *Implications for Parenting and Education*

Advances in the study of infant behavior and development indicate clearly that human babies are rather more capable of sensing and learning in the first days and weeks of life than they were presumed to be in the nineteenth and early twentieth centuries. This new awareness has led to, or is coincident with, a changing pattern of parenting practices, involving closer contact on the part of both parents with their babies, greater interest and involvement of the father in infant development and the care of the baby, a new sensitivity to the baby's consciousness, and the infant's potential for being influenced by experience.

With the great strides that have been made in public health measures, and pediatric care including immunizations, especially in developed countries, there has been a concomitant shift in the factors most responsible for death and debility in infants in the first year of life. After the first few days of life in which respiratory distress and other effects of prematurity or low birth weight are the principal hazards, the major risks are essentially behavioral, primarily accidents and other conditions of life which are in principle environmentally controllable. The major threats to survival and development of infants in less developed countries are hunger and insufficient medical care which, too, are controllable with shifts in global and geopolitical conditions.

See also: Stages in Human Development; Genetics and Human Development; Piaget's Theory of Human Development

References

Aslin R 1987 Visual and auditory development in infancy. In: Osofksy J (ed.) 1987
Buka S L, Tsuang M T, Lipsitt L P 1993 Pregnancy and delivery complications and psychiatric diagnosis. *Archives of General Psychology* 50: 151–56
DeCasper A J, Fifer W P 1980 Of human bonding: Newborns prefer their mother's voices. *Science* 208(4498): 1174–76
Garmezy N, Rutter M (eds.) 1983 *Stress, Coping and Development in Children.* McGraw-Hill, New York
Hubel D H, Wiesel T N 1979 Brain mechanisms of vision. *Sci. Am.* 241(3): 130–39
Larsson K 1994 The psychobiology of parenting in mammals. *Scand. J. Psychol.* 35: 97–143
Lipsitt L P 1969 Learning capacities of the human infant. In: Robinson R J (ed.) 1969 *Brain and Early Behavior: Development in the Fetus and Infant.* Academic Press, New York
McGraw M 1943 *The Neuromuscular Maturation of the Human Infant.* Columbia University Press, New York
Meltzoff A, Moore M K 1983 The origins of imitation in infancy: Paradigm, phenomena, and theory. In: Lipsitt L P, Rovee-Collier C (eds.) 1983 *Advances in Infancy Research*, Vol. 2 Ablex, Norwood, New Jersey
Nugent J K, Lester B M, Brazelton T B 1989 *The Cultural Context of Infancy, Vol I. Biology, Culture, and Infant Development.* Ablex, Norwood, New Jersey
Nyberg K, Allebeck P, Eklund G, Jacobson B 1993 Obstetric medication versus residential area as perinatal risk factors for subsequent adult drug addiction in offspring. *Pediatric and Perinatal Epidemiology* 7: 23–32
Papousek H 1959 A method of studying conditioned alimentary reflexes in infants up to six months of age. *Pavlov Journal of Higher Nervous Activity* 9: 143–48
Pfaffmann C 1960 The pleasures of sensation. *Psychol. Rev.* 67: 253–68
Piaget J 1959 *La naissance de l'intelligence chez l'enfant.* DeLachaux et Niestlé, Neuchâtel

Rheingold H L 1963 *Maternal Behavior in Mammals*. Wiley, New York

Rosenzweig M R, Bennett E L 1978 Experimental influences on brain anatomy and brain chemistry in rodents. In: Gottlieb G (ed.) 1978 *Studies on the Development of Behavior and the Nervous System, Vol 4: Early Influences*. Academic Press, New York

Rovee-Collier C 1987 Learning and memory in infancy. In: Osofsky J (ed.) 1987 *Handbook of Infant Development*, 2nd edn. Wiley, New York

Rovee-Collier C, Lipsitt L P 1982 Learning, adaptation, and memory in the newborn. In: Stratton P (ed.) 1982 *Psychobiology of the Human Newborn*. Wiley, New York

Sameroff A J, Chandler M J 1975 Rultidimensiontive risk and the continuum of caretaking casualty. In: Horowitz F D (ed.) 1975 *Review of Child Development Research*, Vol. 4. University of Chicago Press, Chicago, Illinois

Spiker C C, McCandless B R 1954 The concept of intelligence and the philosophy of science. *Psychol. Rev.* 61: 255–66

Further Reading

Elkonin D B 1957 The physiology of higher nervous activity and child psychology. In: Simon B (ed.) 1957 *Psychology in the Soviet Union*. Routledge and Kegan Paul, London

Haith M, Campos J J (eds.) 1983 Infancy and developmental psychobiology In: Mussen P H (ed.) 1983 *Handbook of Child Psychology*, 4th edn. Wiley, New York

Haith M M, Hazan C, Goodman G S Expectation and anticipation of dynamic visual events by 3.5 month-old babies. *Child Dev.* 59(2): 467–79

Osofsky J D 1987 *Handbook of Infant Development*, 2nd edn. Wiley-Interscience, New York

Childhood

D. F. Bjorklund and W. S. Cassel

In this entry, important changes that occur during childhood are examined. Included in the survey are changes in: (a) physical growth; (b) social and emotional development; (c) language; and (d) cognition.

Childhood begins when infancy ends, and this, for the purposes of this entry, is with the advent of children's first two-word sentences, usually between the ages of 16 and 20 months. The word "infancy" derives from the Latin and translates roughly as "without language," or more literally, "no speech." Childhood is followed by adolescence, and the onset of puberty is used here as the endpoint of childhood. Thus, the period of childhood to be reviewed here ranges from the beginning of true productive language, at approximately 18 months, to the beginning of puberty, at about 12 or 13 years.

1. Physical and Motor Development

Different organs and physical systems develop at different rates. The head and the central nervous system grow most rapidly during the neonatal and early childhood periods, with the head and brain reaching about 90 percent of their adult size by age 5. The reproductive system grows the slowest, with sexual maturity being achieved at puberty. Although adolescence begins with the enlargement of the reproductive organs, there is a one- to two-year period of low fertility in both boys and girls, thus extending the period humans spend as nonreproductive (Tanner 1978).

Generally, boys and girls grow taller at about the same rate until approximately 11 to 12 years of age. At the same age, girls have a growth spurt for approximately two years that gives them a temporary height and strength advantage over boys. Thereafter, boys grow more rapidly than girls until about age 14 or 15, at which time children are practically fully grown (Tanner 1978).

By early childhood, children are walking, although the toddling 2-year old lacks the gross-motor skills of older children and adolescents. Children's gross-motor skills are refined over the preschool years, with children walking and running in a way that is qualitatively similar to adults by age 6. Fine-motor skills develop gradually over the preschool years. For example, children are not able to copy accurately a visual design until about 5 years of age, with substantial improvements in drawing skills still developing over the school years (Goodenough 1926). Such fine-motor skills are important in technological societies for writing and for many activities in traditional societies, such as weaving.

2. Social and Emotional Development

2.1 Parents' Influence on Children's Behavior

Social development of children follows a general pattern from home/self-centered to external/other-centered behavior. As children grow more physically capable, they become increasingly independent of their parents and experience the broader world outside of their homes. Contemporary behavioral genetics theories hold that genetic factors (a child's genotype) become increasingly influential with age in determining what environments children will experience, thus affecting greatly their social and intellectual development. In other words, with increasing age, children actively choose which activities they engage in, with these choices being heavily influenced by genetically determined dispositions (Scarr 1992).

However, children's relationships with their parents continue to influence their behavior outside the home. For example, emotional relationships between children and their parents tend to be stable from late infancy through childhood, with securely attached infants becoming securely attached children (Main et al. 1985). Moreover, quality of attachment in infancy (secure, insecure, or disorganized) has been found to be related to later social and intellectual development, with children who were rated as securely attached as infants or toddlers developing a better self-image, being more effective problem solvers, and being better liked by peers than children who were insecurely attached (e.g., Cohn 1990).

Parenting style also affects children's behavior. The children of authoritarian parents, who establish firm rules and frequently enforce them by use of physical punishment, often tend to be withdrawn, discontented, aggressive, and distrustful of others. Children of permissive parents, who generally exert little control over their children, often lack self-reliance, self-control, and explorative tendencies. Children of authoritative parents, who set clear standards and enforce rules with warmth and explanations, often are independent, socially responsive, self-controlled, explorative, and self-reliant (Baumrind 1967).

2.2 Development of Peer Relations

During the preschool years (ages 2 to 5), children's social interaction with peers increases substantially. As their interaction increases, so also do conflicts. Preschoolers who are friends fight with one another just as much as preschoolers who are only acquaintances. Conflicts are less intense between friends than between nonfriends and are more likely to result in nearly equal outcomes for the involved children (Hartup et al. 1988).

Many preschoolers take part in parallel play, two or more children playing near each other, possibly involved in similar activities but not engaged in mutual, or cooperative play. This semisocial parallel play may be a precursor to more social forms of interaction and truly cooperative play, which increases over early childhood as children become more able to take the perspective of others.

Throughout childhood, children segregate themselves into same-sex groups for play and other social activities; this same-sex segregation is universal and increases during the early school years (Maccoby and Jacklin 1987). Boys and girls play differently, with boys engaging in more rough-and-tumble play and centering their interactions on movable toys, whereas girls tend to engage in dramatic play and table activities. During the preschool years, and through adolescence, girls are more apt to play in smaller groups than boys.

Dominance hierarchies, or "pecking orders," in children's groups are established as a result of children testing each other in games and activities that produce clear winners and losers. Dominance hierarchies serve to reduce antagonism within the group, distribute scarce resources, and focus division of labor. Younger children are more apt to establish dominance hierarchies based upon their physical abilities to control other children. As children grow older, and most especially at puberty, other factors such as sexual maturity tend to become important in the establishment of a dominant position in the peer group (see Shaffer 1994).

2.3 Prosocial Behavior

The development of prosocial behavior, behavior that is intended to benefit others, is based on the development of empathy. Beginning at about age 2, children begin to understand that others have needs and feelings that are different from their own. Their empathic abilities improve as they become less egocentric (that is, less self-centered in their perspective-taking abilities) and as their role-taking abilities improve. By about age 11, children have developed a capacity for empathy with another person's life experience rather than simply with a single event in the person's life.

Sharing is seen in toddlers, but is more common in older children. Older preschool children are more prone to try to "help," such as assisting a parent or other adult accomplish some task. These forms of prosocial behavior increase over the school years to about 9 years of age when "helping" activities seem to level off (see Shaffer 1994).

2.4 Aggression in Children

Aggression is not limited to one gender or one age group of children, although boys, on average, are physically more aggressive than girls. The frequency and nature of aggressive behavior change with age. Aggressive behavior is common among young preschoolers, but decreases in frequency from ages 2 through 5. Levels of aggression are fairly stable over childhood, with aggressive toddlers becoming aggressive school age children (Cummings et al. 1989).

2.5 Development of the Self

The development of the concept of the self is very important for social development. About 75 percent of children show some form of self-recognition (such as recognizing themselves in the mirror) by the age of 18–24 months. Late in their second year, children begin using pronouns in their language (*I, me, my*, and *mine*) that indicate a differentiation between themselves and others (Lewis and Brooks-Gunn 1979).

Initially, children's verbal references distinguishing themselves from others are centered on physical characteristics ("I'm stronger," "I'm bigger"). Only when children approach adolescence do they begin making more psychological, or abstract, references distinguishing themselves from others ("I'm happy," "I'm smart") (Montemayor and Eisen 1977).

3. Language Development

Beginning with their first combination of words into simple sentences at about 18 months, children's utterances become longer and more complex. Over the preschool years, children of all cultures learn the grammatical rules of their language, often applying them when not appropriate. This is reflected by overregularization, in which children use rules in situations where they do not apply (e.g., in English, saying "goed," "runned," or "mouses"). Children's syntax (the grammatical structure of their sentences) increasingly comes to resemble that of adults in their culture, as reflected by their formation of language constructions such as negatives, questions, and the use of relational terms. At all ages, children's receptive language (i.e., what they can understand) is more advanced than their productive language (i.e., what they can produce). By age 5, children's language greatly resembles that of adults. Although the structure of children's language does increase in complexity over the school years (e.g., in English, use of passive tense, more consistent noun/verb agreement), the differences between the grammar used by 6- and 7-year olds and by adults are subtle and minor (de Villiers and de Villiers 1978).

The ability to learn a new language is greatest in early childhood and wanes until adolescence, when second-language learning often becomes especially difficult. Adolescents and adults who successfully learn the syntax of a second language rarely sound like native speakers but continue to have decided accents, unlike children, who can master both the syntax and phonology of a new language "like a native."

Semantics (the meaning of language terms) also develops markedly through childhood. The number of words children have in their productive vocabularies grows rapidly beginning at about 2 years of age, increasing to between 8,000 and 14,000 words by the first grade, with individual words becoming more elaborately encoded and associations with other words in memory becoming stronger and more numerous (see Bjorklund 1995).

Over childhood, children learn to categorize word concepts into natural language categories, first acquiring concepts at a basic level (e.g., chairs, cars) before learning to categorize according to superordinate categories (e.g., furniture, vehicles).

Children's representations can be expressed in terms of scripts, which are a form of schematic organization, with real-world events arranged in terms of temporal and causal relations between components of the event (e.g., who did what to whom and when). Preschool children's attempts at remembering sequences of events are based on scripts. Moreover, parents help young children form narratives in remembering events by asking them questions that focus on the important things to remember about events, such as who was involved, what was done, where did it occur, and what was the sequence of acts (see Fivush and Hudson 1990).

4. Cognitive Development

4.1 Representation

Developing alongside language late in the second year of life are imagery, fantasy play, and the ability to delay, or defer imitation. Piaget (1962) proposed that the representations of young children were symbolic but intuitive and illogical (preoperational period), becoming logical at some stage between the ages of 5 and 7 years, although still tied to concrete objects (the stage of concrete operations). Beginning in early adolescence, children's thinking was described by Piaget as abstract, with "hypothetico-deductive reasoning" characterizing thought (formal operations).

Experiments by Flavell and his colleagues have shown the limits of symbolic representation in young children by investigating their knowledge about the distinction between appearance and reality (e.g., Flavell et al. 1986). For example, in some experiments, children watched as white milk was poured into a filtered glass to appear red, or they were shown objects that had uncharacteristic sounds or smells (e.g., socks that smelled like peanut butter). Questions to the children then focused on two areas: what the objects looked like, "how they look to your eyes right now"; and the actual identity of the objects, "how they really and truly are." Somewhat surprisingly, Flavell et al. (1986) reported that most 3-year olds could not solve these apparently simple problems, even with explicit training, causing the authors to conclude that 3-year olds did not have even a minimal understanding of the appearance—reality distinction. Flavell et al. (1986) speculated that 3-year olds are unable to represent an object in more than one form at a time (dual encoding) and so base their answers on either the appearance (the milk looks red, so it really and truly *is* red) or the actual identity (the rock-like sponge is a sponge, so it *looks* like a sponge) of an object. With age, children become more adept at dual encoding, although it is not until late childhood or early adolescence before truly abstract distinctions can be made between the appearance and the reality of things.

During childhood, children develop naive "theories" of how the world works, and these theories reflect, in part, their representational abilities. For example, they learn what is animate and what is not, and what characteristics are attributed to the living and the nonliving. Children aged 3 and 4 develop theories of number, learning the one-to-one correspondence between count words and objects counted, that the last word in a count series reflects the total number of objects in the set (cardinal principle), and that anything, tangible or intangible, can be counted (Gelman and Gallistel 1978). They also develop a "theory of mind," which is a causal-explanatory framework to explain why people behave as they do, More specifically, they can understand that other people's behavior is governed by their wants, wishes, hopes, and goals (i.e., their desires), and by their ideas, opinions, and knowledge (i.e., their beliefs) (Perner 1991, Wellman 1990).

4.2 Learning and Remembering

Although most learning and memory tasks are mastered more easily by older than by younger children, there are some exceptions, notably in implicit memory. Implicit memory refers to memory for information that the individual did not explicitly set out to learn but was acquired in the process of performing related cognitive activity. For example, implicit memory is reflected in tasks where subjects are asked to make decisions about the perceptual characteristics of words (e.g., CHERRY: "Does it have an H in it?" or "Is it written in lower-case letters?") and later, unexpectedly, asked to recall the words or to complete word fragments (che——y). Because subjects do not explicitly attend to the meaning of words, performance on these tasks, when compared to proper controls, reflects the amount of information people acquire implicitly. Unlike explicit, or intentional, memory tasks, there are no age differences in implicit memory over childhood, suggesting that the processes of implicit memory are fully functional in school-age children (Naito 1990).

Age differences are dramatic, however, for explicit learning and memory tasks, where children intentionally attempt to solve problems. One popular approach to studying children's problem-solving behavior has been to evaluate strategies, usually defined as goal-directed, effortful, cognitive operations that are potentially available to consciousness.

Children aged 2 and 3 will use simple strategies to solve problems, such as staring at the place where a toy was hidden before they are allowed to retrieve it. Young children fail to use more complex strategies spontaneously, such as rehearsing or grouping items by meaning in a memory test; however, they can often be trained to use such strategies with corresponding improvements in their performance, a phenomenon referred to as "production deficiency." Research has found that when children are just learning to use a strategy there is a phase when they spontaneously produce the strategy without enhancing their task

performance. Miller (1990) has referred to this as a "utilization deficiency," and describes it as a transition phase between nonstrategy use and effective strategic behavior.

Young children usually require more explicit training before they benefit from a strategy than older children, although even preschoolers will use a strategy when provided with familiar materials and clear instructions. Young children behave strategically only under highly favorable tasks conditions; with age, children broaden the situations in which they will use effective strategies (see Bjorklund 1995).

Age differences in explicit learning and memory tasks have been attributed to many different factors. For example, with age, children process information more quickly and experience less interference from both external sources (e.g., task-irrelevant stimuli) and internal sources (e.g., task-irrelevant thoughts) (Harnishfeger and Bjorklund 1993). Also, older children typically have more world knowledge than younger children, with the knowledge advantage influencing how information is processed (see Bjorklund 1995).

A particularly effective demonstration of the effect of knowledge on children's cognitive performance comes from an experiment by Schneider et al. (1989). In their study, third-, fifth-, and seventh-grade children were classified as either experts or novices for the game of soccer, and further classified, within each expertise group, as high or low IQ. The children were then given a text comprehension test on a soccer-related story. Soccer experts, regardless of their level of IQ, performed better than soccer novices. In short, having detailed background knowledge for the story overrode the effect of IQ on text comprehension.

Young children's problem-solving is often done "out loud" or by using physical prompts, and only in later childhood becomes covert. For example, preschool children will initially solve simple addition problems by physically counting their fingers or other external markers. They later count or add out loud, and only at the age of 7 or 8 years begin to solve problems of arithmetic mentally. Berk (1986) reported that the amount of "private speech" (i.e., children talking to themselves) while solving arithmetic problems was positively related to intelligence at Grade 1 but not at Grade 3, demonstrating that brighter children internalize their problem-solving sooner than less bright children.

Another factor that develops gradually over childhood and influences children's problem-solving is metacognition, namely, the knowledge a person has of his or her cognitive skills and the ability to monitor task performance and make adjustments toward achieving a goal. Older children are more aware of both endogenous and exogenous factors that influence attention, communication, imitation, memory, and reading than younger children and are better at evaluating the effectiveness of their attempts at task performance (see Bjorklund 1995). Young children generally overestimate their performance on cognitive tasks, thinking that they will remember more items on a memory test or achieve more in school than they actually will (Stipek and MacIver 1989).

Children's poor metacognition is generally viewed as a detriment to effective cognition, and understandably so. However, because young children are out of touch with their actual cognitive and physical abilities, they are less apt to be discouraged by their low levels of performance and thus tend to persist at tasks and attempt new ones where a better informed child, with a more realistic assessment of his or her performance, may not. This, and other aspects of young children's immature cognitive abilities may actually be adaptive and should not be viewed as simply ineffective thinking that must be overcome by instructions (Bjorklund and Green 1992).

4.3 Culture, Schooling, and Cognitive Development

Humans have evolved certain cognitive abilities to deal with problems encountered over thousands of years, and it can be assumed that children worldwide possess the same basic neurological hardware for developing these cognitive skills. However, which skills develop and how they are expressed will vary with cultural experience. Different cultures will value and foster different cognitive skills. Cognition always occurs within a cultural context and can never be evaluated out of that context.

Perhaps the most dramatic differences in cognitive development are observed between children from schooled and nonschooled cultures. Children who attend school learn to divorce their thinking from specific contexts. They more readily classify information on the basis of abstract criteria, reason about things for which they have no prior knowledge, and use strategies to learn and remember information (Rogoff 1990). However, when given the proper contextual supports, unschooled children perform comparably to schooled children. For example, nonschooled children are much less apt to use memory strategies and thus they perform poorly on tasks in which they are asked to remember unrelated pieces of information (such as words). Performance differences disappear, however, when children are asked to remember contextually relevant information (Rogoff 1990).

5. The Significance of Childhood

Childhood in humans is longer than that of any other mammal. This extended childhood has great significance for the species. Humans, more than any other animal, depend on learning for survival. Moreover, human development cannot be understood out of the cultural context in which it occurs. Children require time to learn the complicated procedures and the social web of relationships at the center of all cultures, and the extended childhood provides the time needed

to learn what must be learned. Humans are not the only species with complex social organization, but the variety of human cultures is far greater than that of any other species. The diversity of cultures in which any particular child may find himself or herself necessitates that learning be flexible. Unlike the social insects, children are not genetically programmed for certain social roles. Slow growth and prolonged childhood equips a person not only with time to learn the ways of their specific culture but also with mental and social flexibility, so that a given child can become a weaver, hunter, navigator, or computer programmer, depending on the cultural apprenticeship provided.

See also: Stages in Human Development; Piaget's Theory of Human Development; Physical Growth and Development: Universal Changes and Individual Diifferences; Human Development: Research Methodology

References

Baumrind D 1967 Child care practices anteceding three patterns of preschool behavior. *Genet. Psychol. Monogr.* 75(1): 43–88

Berk L E 1986 Relationship of elementary school children's private speech to behavioral accompaniment to task, attention, and task performance. *Dev. Psychol.* 22(5): 671–80

Bjorklund D F 1995 *Children's Thinking: Developmental Function and Individual Differences*, 2nd edn. Brooks/Cole, Pacific Grove, California

Bjorklund D F, Green B L 1992 The adaptive nature of cognitive immaturity. *Am. Psychol.* 47(1): 46–54

Cohn D A 1990 Child—mother attachment of six-year-olds and social competence at school. *Child Dev.* 61(1): 152–62

Cummings E M, Iannotti R J, Zahn-Waxler C 1989 Aggression between peers in early childhood: Individual continuity and developmental change. *Child Dev.* 60(4): 887–95

de Villiers J G, de Villiers P A 1978 *Language Acquisition.* Harvard University Press, Cambridge, Massachusetts

Fivush R, Hudson J A (eds.) 1990 *Knowing and Remembering in Young Children.* Cambridge University Press, Cambridge

Flavell J H, Green F L, Flavell E R 1986 The development of children's knowledge about the appearance—reality distinction. *Monographs of the Society for Research in Child Development* 51(1): 1–68

Gelman R, Gallistel C 1978 *The Child's Understanding of Number.* Harvard University Press, Cambridge, Massachusetts

Goodenough F L 1926 *The Measurement of Intelligence through Drawing.* Holt Publishing, Yonkers, New York

Harnishfeger K K, Bjorklund D F 1993 The ontogeny of inhibition mechanisms: A renewed approach to cognitive development. In: Howe M L, Pasnak R (eds.) 1993 *Emerging Themes in Cognitive Development. Vol. 1: Foundations.* Springer-Verlag, New York

Hartup W W, Laursen B, Stewart M I, Eastenson A 1988 Conflict and the friendship relations of young children. *Child Dev.* 59(6): 1590–1600

Lewis M, Brooks-Gunn J 1979 *Social Cognition and the Acquisition of Self.* Plenum Press, New York

Maccoby E E, Jacklin C N 1987 Gender segregation in childhood. In: Reese H W (ed.) 1987 *Advances in Child Development and Behavior*, Vol. 20. Academic Press, San Diego, California

Main M, Kaplan N, Cassidy J 1985 Security in infancy, childhood, and adulthood: A move to the level of representation. In: Bretherton I, Waters E (eds.) 1985 *Growing Points of Attachment Theory and Research.* University of Chicago Press, Chicago, Illinois

Miller P H 1990 The development of strategies of selective attention. In: Bjorklund D F (ed.) 1990 *Children's Strategies: Contemporary Views of Cognitive Development.* Erlbaum, Hillsdale, New Jersey

Montemayor R, Eisen M 1977 The development of self-conceptions from childhood to adolescence. *Dev. Psychol.* 13(4): 314–19

Naito M 1990 Repetition priming in children and adults: Age-related dissociation between implicit and explicit memory. *Journal of Experimental Child Psychology* 50(3): 462–84

Perner J 1991 *Understanding the Representational Mind.* MIT Press, Cambridge, Massachusetts

Piaget J 1962 *Play, Dreams, and Imitation in Childhood.* Norton, New York

Rogoff B 1990 *Apprenticeship in Thinking: Cognitive Development in Social Context.* Oxford University Press, New York

Scarr S 1992 Developmental theories for the 1990s: Development and individual differences. *Child Dev.* 63(1): 1–19

Schneider W, Körkel J, Weinert F E 1989 Domain-specific knowledge and memory performance: A comparison of high- and low-aptitude children. *J. Educ. Psychol.* 81(3): 306–12

Shaffer D R 1994 *Social and Personality Development*, 3rd edn. Brooks/Cole, Pacific Grove, California

Stipek D, MacIver D 1989 Developmental change in children's assessment of intellectual competence. *Child Dev.* 60(3): 521–38

Tanner J M 1978 *Fetus into Man: Physical Growth from Conception to Maturity.* Harvard University Press, Cambridge, Massachusetts

Wellman H M 1990 *The Child's Theory of Mind.* MIT Press, Cambridge, Massachusetts

Adolescence

R. M. Lerner and F. A. Villarruel

In this entry the characteristics of development in the adolescent period, that is, the second decade of life, are discussed. Adolescence may be defined as the period within the lifespan when most of a person's biological, psychological, and social characteristics are changing from what is considered childlike to what is considered adult. For the adolescent—the person experiencing this set of transitions—this period is a dramatic challenge, one requiring adjustment to changes in the self, in the family, and the peer group. In many societies, adolescents typically experience institutional changes as well, such as a change in school setting, or a transition from school to either the world of work or to college. For both adolescents and their parents, adolescence is a time of excitement and of anxiety, of happiness and of troubles, of discovery and of bewilderment, of breaks with the past and yet of continuations of childhood behavior.

Adolescence is a period about which much has been written, but until the 1970s, little was known. Until the early 1970s when medical, biological, and social scientists began intensive studies of the adolescent period, there was relatively little sound scientific information available to verify or refute the romantic, literary characteristics of adolescence typical of the older literature. In the early 1990s, however, such information does exist, and it is not consistent with the idea that early adolescence is necessarily a stormy and stressful period.

Unfortunately, however, there is a major limitation in the status of the contemporary scientific literature about adolescent development. Most studies in the literature have involved the study of European or United States middle-class samples. There are only a few high-quality investigations that have studied adolescents from natural or cultural settings outside North America or Europe.

1. Key Generalizations about Adolescent Development

In the early 1990s, there is an increasingly more voluminous and sophisticated scientific literature about adolescence. The aforementioned limitations of this literature notwithstanding, it is possible to indicate several key generalizations that may be made about this period of life.

1.1 Multiple Levels of Context are Influential During Adolescence

Individual differences in adolescent development may be found throughout the world, involving different combinations of biological, psychological, and societal factors; no single influence (e.g., biology) acts alone or as the "prime mover" of change (Brooks-Gunn and Petersen 1983, Lerner 1987, Lerner and Foch 1987, Petersen 1988).

Accordingly, although adolescence is a period of extremely rapid transitions in such characteristics as height, weight, and body proportions (apart from infancy no other period of the life cycle involves such rapid changes) and although hormonal changes are part of the development of early adolescence, hormones are not primarily responsible for psychological or social developments taking place during this period (Petersen and Taylor 1980). The quality and timing of hormonal or other biological changes influence and are influenced by psychological, social, cultural, and historical factors (Elder 1980, Stattin and Magnusson 1990, Tanner 1991).

Global and pervasive effects of puberty do not seem to exist. When biological effects are found they interact with contextual and experiential factors (Stattin and Magnusson 1990). Accordingly, there is no evidence for general cognitive disruption over adolescence. Indeed, cognitive abilities increase over this period. Moreover pubertal timing is not predictive of gender differences on such tasks as spatial cognition. Girls' earlier maturation does not result in general sex differences in cognition (Graber and Petersen 1991).

1.2 Changing Relations Between Adolescents and Their Contexts Produce Development

The period of adolescence is one of continual change and transition between individuals and their contexts (Lerner 1987). These changing relations constitute the basic process of development in adolescence; they underlie both positive and negative outcomes during this period (Lerner 1984, 1995).

Accordingly, when the multiple biological, psychological, and sociocultural changes of adolescence occur simultaneously (e.g., when menarche occurs at the same time as a school transition), there is a greater risk of problems occuring in youth's development (Simmons and Blyth 1987). Indeed, in adolescence bad decisions (e.g., involving school, grades, sex, and drugs) have more negative consequences than in childhood, and the adolescent is more responsible for those consequences than in childhood (Petersen 1988). Nevertheless, most developmental trajectories across this period involve good adjustment on the part of the adolescent, and the continuation of positive parent–child relationships. Put simply, young adolescents are strongly tied to the family (e.g., Offer 1969).

Thus, adolescence is a good time for interventions involving the family. For instance, whereas minor parent–child conflicts (e.g., regarding chores and privileges) are normal in adolescence, major conflicts should be of concern to parents. However, the salience of the family in the adolescent period makes such conflicts an appropriate intervention target.

1.3 Individual Differences and Diversity

There are multiple pathways through adolescence. Inter-individual (between-person) and intra-individual (within-person) differences in development are the "rule" in this period of life.

Accordingly, there is diversity between and within each ethnic, racial, or cultural minority group. Therefore, general rules that confound class, race, and/or ethnicity do not apply (Lerner 1991). In regard to policies and programs, then, any intervention must be tailored to the specific target population, and in particular, to a group's developmental and environmental circumstances. However, because adolescents are so different from each other, no single policy or intervention can be expected to reach all of a given target population or to influence everyone in the same way (Lerner 1995).

Furthermore, normal adolescent development involves variability within the person as well as between people. Temperamental characteristics involving mood and activity level are good examples. There are differences among adolescents in such characteristics. In addition, individual adolescents may change over the course of their life in the quality of the temperament they manifest.

Thus, the breadth and depth of the high-quality scientific information available about development in adolescence underscores the diversity and dynamics of this period of life. The theoretically interesting and socially important changes of this period constitute one reason why the field of adolescence has attracted an increasing degree of scientific attention.

2. Biological Changes During Adolescence

The physical and physiological changes of adolescence typically span the second decade of life, involving early adolescence (around years 10–14 or 15), middle adolescence (years 15–17), and late adolescence (years 18–20). Within these stages of adolescence bodily and psychological changes do not proceed uniformly; however, a general sequence for these changes applies to most people (Katchadourian 1977, Tanner 1991).

It is useful to speak of phases of bodily changes in adolescence in order to draw important distinctions among various degrees and types of change. Bodily changes affect height, weight, fat and muscle distribution, glandular secretions, and sexual characteristics. When some of these exchanges have begun, but most are yet to occur, the person is said to be in the *prepubescent* phase (Schonfeld 1969). When most of those bodily changes that will eventually take place have been initiated, the person is in the *pubescent* phase. Finally, when most of those bodily changes have already occurred the person is in the *postpubescent* phase; this period ends when all bodily changes associated with adolescence are complete (Schonfeld 1969).

2.1 Problems Associated with Pubertal Change

Although the sequence of the bodily changes of puberty is fairly uniform among individuals, there is considerable variation in the rate of change (Marshall and Tanner 1986). Some adolescents mature more rapidly or more slowly than their peers. Variations in the rate of bodily change in adolescence often affect psychological and social development.

For instance, *delayed puberty* and *precocious puberty* are related to insufficient production or the early production of hormones, respectively (Cutler 1991). Some physical problems may be known only to the adolescent initially. Painful menstruation, known as "dysmenorrhea," and the failure to menstruate, which is termed "amenorrhea," affect females and may have medical and/or emotional causes. Other physical disorders are externally noticeable: acne is an example of a problem which causes great concern to adolescents, since it is visible to others and is the most common disorder of medical significance during this period of life.

Moreover, because variations in height, weight, and muscle and fat distributions arise as a consequence of pubertal change, adolescents often become preoccupied with their own bodies (Lerner 1987). This focus is promoted by the character of thought processes during this period, and in some cases, adolescents' concerns with their own bodily changes can result in problems.

Moreover, the role of social context in shaping the behavioral effects of puberty helps explain why bodily changes among adolescents can also differ in relation to sociocultural and historical factors (e.g., Katchadourian 1977, Tanner 1991). The age of menarche, for example, varies among countries and even among different cultures within one country. Moreover, there has been a historical trend downward in the average age of menarche. Among European samples of youth there was a decrease of about four months per decade from about 1840 to about 1950 (Tanner 1991). This rate seems to have slowed down, but has not stopped (Marshall and Tanner 1986, Tanner 1991). Within United States samples, however, the decline in the age of menarche seems to have stopped about 1940; since that time 12.5 years has been the expected value for menarche among middle-class European–Americans. The most dramatic downward trend in the average age of menarche was evident in Japan. This trend in the average age of menarche is generally ascribed to the improved health and nutrition of children and adolescents, influences which are moderated by historical, cultural, and socioeconomic variables affecting a given society or group.

In sum, puberty both influences and is influenced by the adolescent's social world (the socioeconomic and nutritional characteristics of the nation, the family, the school, and peer group) and also by the other features of his or her development, such as cognitive changes (Elkind 1967, Keating 1991, Overton and Byrnes 1991).

3. Changes in the Social World of Adolescents

The adolescent's social world is broader and more complex than that of the infant and the child. The most notable social phenomenon of adolescence is the emergence of the marked importance of peer groups. The adolescent comes to rely heavily on the peer group for security and guidance; this is a time when such support is urgently needed, and perhaps only others undergoing the same transition can be relied upon to understand what is being experienced. Contrary to cultural stereotype, however, the family is also quite influential for adolescents (Steinberg 1991). It is useful to discuss, then, the relative influence of parents and peers in the development of adolescents.

3.1 The Influence of Parents and Peers

No social institution has a greater influence throughout development than the family. Most studies indicate that most adolescents have few, if any, serious disagreements with parents. Indeed, during adolescence very few families experience a major deterioration in the quality of the parent–child relationship (Steinberg 1991). Moreover, in choosing their peers, adolescents typically gravitate toward those who exhibit attitudes and values consistent with those maintained by the parents; these opinions are the beliefs ultimately adopted by the adolescents themselves (Guerney and Arthur 1983).

For instance, while peers affect adolescents in regard to such issues as educational aspirations and performance, in most cases there is convergence between family and peer influences. While it is the case that adolescents and parents have somewhat different attitudes about issues of contemporary social concern (e.g., politics, drug abuse, and sexuality), most of these differences reflect contrasts in the intensity of attitude rather than its direction. In other words, adolescents and parents are rarely diametrically opposed on a particular issue; rather, most generational differences simply involve different levels of support for the same position.

In sum, there is considerable diversity in the nature of parent–child relations in adolescence, and diversity related to the particular context within which youth and families develop. Whereas some of this diversity represents patterns of behavior that may be undesirable to both parents and their children (e.g., dropping out of school), for most youth there is a convergence between the attitudes and behaviors in which they engage and the views, desires, or expectations of their parents.

3.2 Pathways of Development Through Adolescence

Several studies have documented that, for most youth, adolescence is *not* a period of "storm and stress"; it is neither a period of wrenching oneself away from parents nor of frequent and inevitable problem behaviors.

For instance, Bandura (1964) observed that by adolescence most children had so thoroughly adopted parental values and standards that parental restrictions were actually reduced. In addition, Bandura noted that although the storm and stress idea of adolescence implies a struggle by youth to free themselves of dependence on parents, parents actually begin to train their children in childhood to be independent. Finally, Bandura found that the adolescent's choice of friends was not a major source of friction between adolescents and parents. Adolescents tended to form friendships with those who shared similar values. As such, the peers tended to support those standards of the parents that already had been adopted by the adolescents themselves.

Bandura points out, however that these observations do not mean that adolescence is an unstressful, problem-free period of life. Of course no period of life is devoid of crisis or adjustment problems, and any period of life may present particular adjustment problems for some people and not for others. Thus, caution must be exercised in attributing problems observed in one group of adolescents to all adolescents, or in generalizing from one culture to another.

From Bandura's (1964) study it may be concluded that: (a) even when storm and stress is seen in adolescence, it is not necessarily the result of events in adolescence, but instead may be associated with prior developments; and (b) storm and stress is not necessarily characteristic of the adolescent period: many possible types of adolescent development can occur.

The existence of such different paths through adolescence is supported by the results of other studies. Offer (1969) found three major routes through the adolescent period. He noted that there is a *continuous-growth* type of development that involves smooth changes in behavior. Young adolescents showing such development were not in any major conflict with their parents and did not feel either that parental rearing practices were inappropriate or that parental values were ones that they themselves did not share. Most adolescents fell into this category. A second type of pattern is *surgent growth*, where development involves abrupt change. Such rapid change does not necessarily involve the turmoil associated with storm and stress. Finally, however, Offer did identify a *tumultuous-growth* type of adolescent development, characterized by crisis, stress, and problems.

Thus, the belief that adolescence is a period of general disruption of parent–child ties, or the belief in the emergence of problematic social behaviors among virtually all youth, do not find support in the contemporary scientific literature. The facts of adolescent development allow the study of the social problems which do occur during this period to be put in an appropriate perspective. Problems such as drug and alcohol abuse and delinquency are quite significant; but these problems do not occur with a majority of contemporary youth, irrespective of racial, ethnic, or socioeconomic status. Nevertheless, it is important to highlight the nature of the social problems which do exist within this period of life. Although only a minor-ity of youth exhibit these problems, on a population basis this frequency translates into millions of people. (Lerner 1995)

3.3 Social Problems of Adolescence

Juvenile delinquency is defined in the United States as the violation of a law committed by a person prior to his or her 18th birthday, a violation which would have been a crime committed by an adult. In turn, a status offense is a violation of the law which involves a behavior which would not have been illegal if engaged in by an adult.

Some of the problems of adolescence which are classified as delinquent because, for instance, they involve a status offense, really signify more of an issue of poor social relationships than of criminality. For example, running away from home is technically considered a delinquent act, but it is really more than that. Between 750,000 and one million adolescents in the United States run away from home each year (Adams 1991). Home environments that involve rejection, neglect, disinterest, hostile control, parent–child conflict, inadequate supervision, and lack of family organization are associated with adolescents' running away (Adams 1991).

Thus, running away is a sign of a young person's inability to tolerate the social setting in which he or she resides. Leaving home may also be a way of telling parents that the home situation has become seriously intolerable, or it may be a way of indicating that help is needed.

Other problematic behaviors also skirt the borderlines between status offenses, social relationship issues, and actual illegality. Problems of teenage sexuality—unsafe sex, pregnancy, and childbearing— pertain both to status offenses and social relationships. In turn, issues of tobacco, alcohol, and drug abuse cross the borderlines between status offenses and illegality.

In regard to teenage sexuality, adolescents are not usually contraceptively protected when they begin sexual activity, and a large proportion are inadequately protected throughout adolescence. As an illustration of this point, about two-thirds of sexually active United States adolescent females either use no contraceptives at all or use only nonbarrier methods, such as withdrawal (Boyer and Hein 1991). As a result of such practices, there are hundreds of thousands of cases of sexually transmitted diseases and of pregnancies among adolescents each year in the United States. Between 30 and 40 percent of adolescent mothers have been impregnated by males who have not yet reached their 20th birthday (Elster 1991). About 15 percent of all Black males have, by the age of 19 years, fathered a child; corresponding rates among similarly aged Latino and European–American males are 11 percent and 6.5 percent respectively (Elster 1991).

Illicit use of drugs has been decreasing among

youth in the United States. At the end of the 1970s, 60 percent of high school seniors reported having used marijuana; by the end of the 1980s the corresponding statistic was 44 percent. However, 51 percent of American high school seniors have tried at least one illicit drug (Kandel 1991). Moreover, almost all American high school seniors—92 percent—report some experience with alcohol. While 19 percent of the group report smoking cigarettes daily (Rauch and Huba 1991), and 66 percent have had at least some experience with cigarettes (Kandel 1991). Tobacco, alcohol, and drug use is initiated in early adolescence. Parents and teachers may model such behaviors to adolescents. If parents or teachers smoke, the probability of an adolescent doing so is increased significantly. Moreover, many "early users" of tobacco, alcohol, and drugs eventually develop habits of regular use.

Thus, there is a high proportion of adolescents for whom early use leads to continued adult use. Nevertheless, for many adolescents there is only a brief experimentation with such substances. Indeed, most adolescents recognize the dangers of drug, alcohol, and tobacco abuse, and it is still the case that for most youth problems of addiction do not arise.

Unfortunately, as noted above, given the proportion of adolescents who are involved in this and other risk behaviors, and the absolute number of youth that these proportions involve, there should be no complacency about this conclusion. Accordingly, at the very least there should be an examination of the individual and contextual factors that appear to put adolescents at risk of exhibiting the problem behaviors prominent during this period. In addition, it would be appropriate to study the individual and contextual factors that, when combined in intervention programs, appear to prevent the actualization of risk.

4. Risk And Prevention

Dryfoos (1990) has discussed the contrasting sets of individual and contextual factors that are associated with both the actualization and the prevention of risk behaviors in adolescence, that is, with substance use and abuse; with unsafe sex, adolescent pregnancy, and childbearing; with school failure and dropping out; and with crime and delinquency. Dryfoos found that there are six common characteristics involved in the occurrence during adolescence of one or more of these risk behaviors, and identified three individual and three contextual factors:

(a) *Age.* The earlier the initiation of any of the risk behaviors of adolescence, the more likely it is that the individual will engage in the behavior to a great extent and that he or she will suffer negative consequences.

(b) *Expectations for education and school grades.*

All risk behaviors are associated with the adolescent's sense of self, especially insofar as self-perceived academic/scholastic competence is concerned (Harter 1983). Young people who do not expect to do well in school, and who do not in fact do well, are at risk for all the problem behaviors studied by Dryfoos (1990).

(c) *General behavior.* Inappropriate behaviors and inadequate conduct (e.g., acting out, truancy, and conduct disorders) are related to the appearance of risk behaviors.

(d) *Peer influences.* As noted by Stattin and Magnusson (1990), an individual's likelihood of engaging in problem behaviors is not simply due to individual factors (such as early pubertal maturation). In addition, contextual factors (e.g., the nature of the peer group within which the youth is embedded) are involved. Similarly, Dryfoos (1990) found that having peers who engage in risk behaviors, and having a low resistance to participating with peers, are factors associated with an adolescent's exhibiting such behaviors.

(e) *Parental influences.* Particular styles of parenting —that is, authoritarian or permissive styles, as compared to an authoritative one—place a youth "at-risk" for problem behaviors. Similarly, if parents do not monitor their children, or do not supervise, guide, or communicate with them effectively, there is a strong likelihood that an "at-risk" status will be actualized. In addition, if adolescents are not affectively tied to their parents by those positive ties which have been noted as being normal during this period (e.g., Douvan and Adelson 1966), risk behaviors are also likely to occur.

(f) *Neighborhood influences.* The community context also plays a role in the actualization of risk. A neighborhood characterized by poverty, or by urban, high-density living, is involved with risk actualization.

Dryfoos (1990) noted that a particular set of integrations among individual, familial, peer, and community "levels of organization" is involved in the actualization of risk behaviors among adolescents. In turn, however, there are other integrations, involving these several levels, that are involved in the design and delivery of successful prevention programs for "at-risk" youth.

In essence, then, there are multiple features of person and context that should be combined to design and deliver a successful program preventing the actualization of risk in adolescence. Building on the general developmental characteristics of the period, these programs, when attuned as well to the specific characteristics and needs of youths and their settings, will help adolescents avoid the development of risk behaviors.

In sum, Dryfoos (1990) indicated that there are grounds for optimism regarding the likely success of prevention efforts if these programs are designed and delivered sensitively. Above all, it must constantly be borne in mind that no one, single or isolated, effort is apt to succeed, given that risk behaviors are interrelated and influenced by a host of individual and contextual factors.

5. Conclusion

Adolescence is a double-edged sword. It is a period potentially harboring myriad social problems. Yet the scientific evidence indicates that individual differences are prominent throughout adolescence, and that conditions exist or can be created to allow most young people to pass through this period with few, if any, major traumas. There is great resilience among youth (Werner and Smith 1982), and for most adolescents the period is one of quite favorable physical and mental health. Most adolescents can successfully meet the challenges of this transition period; they can assimilate in a coherent way the biological, cognitive, emotional, and social changes they are experiencing, and can form a useful (if sometimes provisional) self-definition. This sense of self, or identity, will allow youth to make decisions and commitments, first to educational paths, and then to careers and to other people. These decisions and commitments can eventuate in the adoption of roles (e.g., worker, spouse, and parent) beneficial to the advancement of society.

In sum, it may be concluded that, insofar as one limits one's generalizations to the samples studied within the contemporary scientific literature, young people have or can be given the personal, emotional, and social context resources necessary to meet successfully the biological, psychological, and social challenges of this period of life, leaving it with a developmentally new, but nevertheless useful, sense of self. Parents, educators, and other caregivers can be confident, then, that if a social context attuned to the developmental changes and individuality of youth is present, healthy and successful people will emerge from the period of adolescence.

References

Adams G R 1991 Runaways, negative consequences for. In: Lerner R M, Petersen A C, Brooks-Gunn J (eds.) 1991, Vol. 1

Bandura A 1964 The stormy decade: Fact or fiction? *Psychol. Sch.* 1 (3): 224–31

Boyer C B, Hein K 1991 AIDS and HIV infection in adolescents: The role of education and antibody testing.

In: Lerner R M, Petersen A C, Brooks-Gunn J (eds.) 1991, Vol. 1

Brooks-Gunn J, Petersen A C 1983 *Girls at Puberty: Biological and Psychosocial Perspectives.* Plenum Press, New York

Cutler G B Jr. 1991 Puberty, precocious, treatment of. In: Lerner R M, Petersen A C, Brooks-Gunn J (eds.) 1991, Vol. 2

Douvan E, Adelson J 1966 *The Adolescent Experience.* Wiley, New York

Dryfoos J G 1990 *Adolescent at Risk: Prevalence and Prevention.* Oxford University Press, New York

Elder G H Jr. 1980 Adolescence in historical perspective. In: Adelson J (ed.) 1980 *Handbook of Adolescent Psychology.* Wiley, New York

Elkind D 1967 Egocentrism in adolescence. *Child Dev.* 38: 1025–34

Elster A 1991 Fathers, teenage. In: Lerner R M, Petersen A C, Brooks-Gunn J (eds.) 1991, Vol. 1

Graber J A, Petersen A C 1991, Cognitive changes at adolescence: Biological perspectives. In: Gibson K R, Petersen A C (eds.) 1991 *Brain Maturation and Cognitive Development: Comparative and Cross-cultural Perspectives.* Aldine de Gruyter, New York

Guerney L, Arthur J 1983 Adolescent social relationships. In: Lerner R M, Galambos N L (eds.) 1983 *Experiencing Adolescence: A Sourcebook for Parents, Teachers, and Teens.* Teachers College Press, Columbia, New York

Harter S 1983 Developmental perspectives on the self-system. In: Mussen P H (ed.) 1983 *Handbook of Child Psychology. Vol. 4: Socialization, Personality, and Social Development* 4th edn. Wiley, New York

Kandel D 1991 Drug use, epidemiology and developmental stages of involvement. In: Lerner R M, Petersen A C, Brooks-Gunn J (eds.) 1991, Vol. 2

Katchadourian H 1977 *The Biology of Adolescence.* Freeman, San Francisco, California

Keating D P 1991 Cognition, adolescent. In: Lerner R M, Petersen A C, Brooks-Gunn J (eds.) 1991, Vol. 1

Lerner R M 1984 *On the Nature of Human Plasticity.* Cambridge University Press, New York

Lerner R M 1987 A life-span perspective for early adolescence. In: Lerner R M, Foch T T (eds.) 1987

Lerner R M 1991 Changing organism-context relations as the basic process of development: A developmental contextual perspective. *Dev. Psychol.* 27: 27–32

Lerner R M 1995 *America's Youth in Crisis: Challenges and Options For Programs and Policies.* Sage, Thousand Oak, California

Lerner R M Foch T T (eds.) 1987 *Biological-psychosocial Interactions in Early Adolescence: A Life-span Perspective.* Erlbaum, Hillsdale, New Jersey

Marshall W A, Tanner J M 1986 Puberty. In: Falkner F, Tanner J M (eds.) 1986 *Human Growth. Vol. 2: Postnatal Growth, Neurobiology,* 2nd edn. Plenum Press, New York

Offer D 1969 *The Psychological World of the Teenager: A Study of Normal Adolescent Boys.* Basic Books, New York

Overton W F, Byrnes J P 1991 Cognitive development. In: Lerner R M, Petersen A C, Brooks-Gunn J (eds.) 1991, Vol. 1

Petersen A C 1988 Adolescent development. In: Rosenzweig M R (ed.) 1988 *Annual Review of Psychology,* Vol. 39. Annual Reviews, Inc., Palo Alto, California

Petersen A C, Taylor B 1980 The biological approach to adolescence: Biological change and psychological adaptation. In: Adelson J (ed.) 1980 *Handbook of Adolescent Psychology*. Wiley, New York

Rauch J M, Huba G J 1991 Drug use, adolescent. In: Lerner R M, Petersen A C, Brooks-Gunn J (eds.) 1991, Vol. 1

Schonfeld W A 1969 The body and the body image in adolescents. In: Caplan G, Lebovici S (eds.) 1969 *Adolescence: Psychosocial Perspectives*. Basic Books, New York

Simmons R G, Blyth D A 1987 *Moving into Adolescence: The Impact of Pubertal Change and School Context*. Aldine, Hawthorne, New Jersey

Stattin H, Magnusson D 1990 *Pubertal Maturation in Female Development*. Erlbaum, Hillsdale, New Jersey

Steinberg L 1991 Parent—adolescent relations. In: Lerner R M, Petersen A C, Brooks-Gunn J (eds.) 1991, Vol. 2

Tanner J 1991 Menarche, secular trend in age of. In: Lerner R M, Petersen A C, Brooks-Gunn J (eds.) 1991, Vol. 2

Werner E E, Smith R S 1982 *Vulnerable but Invincible*. McGraw-Hill, New York

Further Reading

Coleman J S, Husén T 1985 *Becoming Adult in a Changing Society*. OECD, Paris

Dornbusch S M et al. 1981 Sexual development, age, and dating: A comparison of biological and social influences upon one set of behaviors. *Child Dev.* 52(1): 179–85

Feldman S, Elliott G 1990 *At the Threshold: The Developing Adolescent*. Harvard University Press, Cambridge, Massachusetts

Hagen J W, Paul B, Gibb S, Wolters C 1990 Trends in research as reflected by publications in *Child Development*: 1930–1989. Paper presented at the Biennial Meeting of the Society for Research on Adolescence, Atlanta, Georgia

Kennedy R E 1991 Delinquency. In: Lerner R M, Petersen A C, Brooks-Gunn J (eds.) 1991, Vol. 1

Lerner R M Petersen A C, Brooks-Gunn J(eds.) 1991 *Encyclopedia of Adolescence*, 2 Vols. Garland, New York

Petersen A C 1985 Pubertal development as a cause of disturbance: Myths, realities, and unanswered questions. *Genet. Psychol. Monogr.* 111: 207–31

Silbereisen R 1992 Adolescent behavior in context: Comparative analyses of beliefs, daily contexts, and substance use in West Berlin and Warsaw. In Featherman D L, Lerner R M, Perlmutter M (eds.) 1992 *Life-span Development and Behavior*, Vol. 11. Erlbaum, Hillsdale, New Jersey

Villarruel F A, Lerner R M 1994 *Promoting Community-based Programs for Socialization and Learning. (New Directions for Child Development,* No 63). Jossey-Bass, San Francisco, California

Whiting B B, Whiting J W M 1991 Preindustrial world, adolescence in. In: Lerner R M, Petersen A C, Brooks-Gunn J (eds.) 1991, Vol. 2

Children and Youth at Risk

W. E. Davis and E. J. McCaul

Throughout history, children have endured countless hardships. They have been exposed to cruel mistreatment, excessive and brutal varieties of work, as well as physical and emotional abuse. In fact, until relatively modern times, children were considered chattel and treated as such (Hart 1991). Although the twentieth century has experienced marked changes in attitudes toward children, even in 1990 a quarter of a million children died every week from preventable illnesses and malnutrition. A UNICEF report, entitled *The State of the World's Children 1990*, indicated that "in many countries, poverty, child malnutrition and ill health are advancing again after decades of steady retreat" (Committee on Foreign Relations 1990 p. 128). According to the report, every new day witnesses 6,000 children dying of pneumonia, 7,000 children dying of diarrhoeal dehydration, and 8,000 children dying of measles, whooping cough, or tetanus (p. 130). These facts have led to considerable concern over the status of the world's children, and in 1989 the United Nations held a Convention on the Rights of the Child. The articles developed at the convention outlined basic, fundamental rights for the world's children and provided a focal point for international child advocacy. While the United States was not one of the initial 54 countries to sign the articles, United States educators have become increasingly concerned over at-risk children and are engaging in considerable discussion of the many relevant issues involving this population. This entry summarizes the discourse regarding children and youth in at-risk circumstances.

1. Background

Since 1980, shifting political, social, and economic forces have dramatically changed conditions for the world's children. A war in the Middle East, the fall of the Soviet Union, an end to statutory apartheid in South Africa, and other events have reshaped the global educational landscape and left children and youth in a variety of at-risk situations (Glenn 1992, Murphy 1992, New 1992, Rust 1992). Educational systems must respond to these changing circumstances if they are to address the unique, individual needs of these children.

The 1980s were a period of social change and educational upheaval in the United States. Public schools reverberated from the aftershocks created by the publication of *A Nation At Risk* (National Commission on Excellence in Education 1983). Soon after the publication of this report, school reform packages were introduced in many states. These packages included raising academic standards, increasing graduation requirements, and evaluating schools through statewide assessment. The expressed intent of the reform efforts was to produce students with the skills and knowledge that would allow them to be competitive with their counterparts from countries such as Germany and Japan in the modern, technological, and global workplace.

At some point during this decade of school reform, another movement gradually gathered momentum. At first only a few educators expressed concern over the possible negative consequences of reform efforts for some children. Soon, however, hardly a day passed without a headline proclaiming that not only schools, but children and youth in the United States were at risk —from increasing levels of poverty, homelessness, substance abuse, or youth violence. International comparisons began to include not only achievement test scores, but also such factors as infant mortality rates, maternal health indicators, and incidences of teenage pregnancy.

In spite of this sudden proliferation of information about at-risk children, many United States educators of the 1990s are seeking guidance in developing effective policies and implementing successful programs. Besides, the relevant issues encompass ethical, cultural, and political dimensions; many United States educators feel overwhelmed, paralyzed into inaction, and are asking the question: "What do we mean by a child being 'at risk'?"

2. Definitions of "At Risk"

Definitions of "at risk" must take into account the social, economic, and cultural environment of the particular child. The term "at risk" may refer to the stress experienced by a Turkish immigrant child in a Scandinavian country (Glenn 1992); it may refer to the adjustments demanded of a South African child in a postapartheid society (Murphy 1992); or it may refer to the low self-esteem and cultural devaluation experienced by an Alaskan Eskimo child (New 1992). The term "at risk" is necessarily culture bound, and in the broader sense, may refer to any child or youth whose own beliefs, values, or cultural norms conflict with the dominant culture's social and educational environment (Davis and McCaul 1990).

Not surprisingly then, most definitions of "at risk" in the literature tend to be broad and inclusive. For example, Catterall and Cota-Robles (1988) described three common conceptions of at risk: (a) children from poor families; (b) children with different cultural backgrounds or minorities; and (c) children from limited English-speaking families. Levin (cited in NSBA Monograph 1989) defined at-risk students as "those who lack the home and community resources to benefit from traditional schooling practices. Because of poverty, cultural obstacles, or linguistic differences, these children tend to have low academic achievement and high dropout rates. Such students are heavily concentrated among minority groups, immigrants, non-English speaking families, and economically disadvantaged populations" (p. 6).

Natriello et al. (1990) delineated four perspectives that underlie most common definitions of at risk: (a) culturally deprived/socially disadvantaged; (b) educationally deprived; (c) at risk according to indicators or predictors of educational difficulty; and (d) at risk as the general population of children and youth. The first perspective has its roots in the reform movements of the mid-1960s and emphasizes the relative disadvantage with which some students begin their public school experience. The disadvantage may entail some family "shortcomings" such as low socioeconomic status or lack of a stimulating environment. Proponents of this view stressed early childhood intervention in order to compensate for experiential deficits of early childhood. In addition, the funding for federal programs aimed at remedial education in the United States public schools, such as the federal Chapter 1 and Migrant Education programs, are based on this perspective. Chapter 1 funds are allocated to economically disadvantaged schools but, at the school level, any child with the potential to benefit from remedial instruction may be served by the program and receive individualized or small group instruction aimed at raising his or her educational attainment. The Migrant Education Program also provides small group or individualized instruction for the children of migrant agricultural workers.

The second perspective, that of the disadvantaged as "educationally deprived," focuses upon the school program and the social, cultural, or political factors contributing to educational deprivation. Proponents of this perspective argue that the cultural differences should not be viewed as cultural deficiencies and that proponents of the culturally deprived/socially disadvantaged perspective have thus inadvertently promoted prejudicial treatment of minority groups such as African Americans. Further, the cultural difference/deprivation perspective tends to "blame the victim" instead of focusing upon school reform and restructuring.

The third perspective utilizes the term "at risk" to refer to children who have certain characteristics which point to possible educational problems in the future. Hence, the presence of certain individual and/or environmental characteristics place a child at risk and may serve as a predictor of later educational outcomes such as low educational achievement, dropout behavior, or social problems in the school environment. Interventions are then tailored toward identified students. This approach resembles the special education process of identifying students and then providing them with specially designed instruction. Nevertheless, from this perspective, many students other than those with disabilities are now considered as at risk. For example, it is well-established that characteristics such as being male, being a member of an ethnic minority group, or being from a family of low socioeconomic status are correlated with higher rates of dropping out of school. While the future-orientation of this perspective allows for intervention strategies, labeling a student as at risk may lead to problems of stigmatizing students or creating lowered teacher expectations, particularly for children from minority groups.

The final perspective, that of youth in general being at risk, is the broadest and most encompassing. "This perspective essentially defines the entire population or at least the entire youth population as potentially disadvantaged. By not identifying any one segment of the population as being disadvantaged, this conceptualization of at risk places the whole burden of addressing the problems of disadvantaged youth on an examination of the institutions that are intended to support and develop young people" (Natriello et al. 1990 p. 11). This perspective also emphasizes the impact on the youth of the United States of social and demographic changes such as the rise in single-parent families, youth criminal activity, alcohol and drug use, sexually transmitted disease, and the increasing number of children living in poverty. It is a perspective that focuses upon the need for broad, national attitudinal and political changes as a precursor to addressing the problem of youth at risk.

Each of the perspectives outlined above has potential strengths and weaknesses in terms of its implied intervention strategies. The culturally deprived perspective, for example, suggests active early intervention to remediate experiential deficits. Clearly, many early intervention efforts with students determined to be at risk of educational failure—for example, the Headstart Program—have enjoyed considerable success. As noted by proponents of the educational deprivation perspective, however, there is an inherent danger in cultural deprivation approaches of assuming that culturally different is culturally deficient. Similarly, each perspective has an implicit intervention strategy with its accompanying strengths and weaknesses.

3. Circumstances of At-risk Students

As with definitions of at risk, a variety of theories and perspectives exist regarding the circumstances of children at risk. Further, the circumstances of at-risk children vary widely from culture to culture. Circumstances may vary from the stress experienced by a South American youth adjusting to Swedish society (Ehn 1990) to the abject poverty and starvation facing some children in South Africa (Murphy 1992). In the United States, considerable concern has arisen over the increasing number of children experiencing problems such as substance abuse, teenage pregnancy, alcohol or drug effects as babies, and youth violence. Nevertheless, five key indicators are commonly associated with educationally at-risk children: (a) living in an economically poor household; (b) having minority/racial group identity; (c) living in a single-parent family; (d) having a poorly educated mother; and (e) having a non-English-language background. All of these indicators are correlated with poor performance in school, although not always for commonly understood or agreed upon reasons. Moreover, the indicators are not independent, and children with several indicators are at the greatest risk of educational failure. In discussing these indicators, there is a clear danger of stereotyping and stigmatizing specific groups of children. Not all poor children, for example, are educationally disadvantaged, and neither are all minority children, nor all children living in single-parent households. Many students are survivors and manifest remarkable resilience. Further, the individual circumstances of children need to be taken into account—students may be at risk because their value systems may be in conflict with the established norm for the school or community. Their diversity from the norm may not be valued, respected, or tolerated; therefore, they too are at a high risk for poor overall adjustment to school. Nevertheless, each of the five key indicators cited above clearly is associated with low levels of educational achievement. These are discussed below.

3.1 Poverty

Children represent the largest and fastest growing group of the poor in the United States. It is estimated that there are more than 12.6 million poor children presently living in that country—nearly 20 percent of all children under the age of 18 (Children's Defense Fund 1990, Reed and Sautter 1990). More United States citizens are poor in the 1990s than before the War on Poverty was initiated in 1964, despite the fact that the official United States' poverty rate for all citizens in 1989 edged slightly downward to 13.1 percent. Nearly 40 million people of all ages live in families that fall below the official poverty line (US$7,704 for a family of two; US$9,435 for a family of three; and US$12,092 for a family of four). Again, 40 percent of this population are children (Hodgkinson 1991, Reed and Sautter 1990).

Further, in the United States of the 1990s, the younger a child is the greater are his or her chances of being poor. Of all children age 3 and under, over four million children, 23 percent are poor; nearly 22 percent of 3 to 5-year olds are poor; and more than 20 percent (over 4 million) of 6 to 11-year old children are poor. Very young children who live in poor households are especially vulnerable and face threats to their health, safety, and psychological development that can have long-term effects on their chances of becoming healthy, productive adults. In fact, poverty increases the risk of infant mortality. As Zill and Rogers (1988) pointed out, "when the U.S. infant mortality rate is compared with that of other industrialized countries, the United States ranks only seventeenth, behind countries like Japan, the Scandinavian countries, France, Australia, and Britain" (pp. 55–56).

3.2 Race/Ethnicity

Of all of the factors associated with educational disadvantage, racial/ethnic minority status probably is the most commonly cited. In particular, African American and Hispanic children and youth have traditionally performed less well than White children on various standardized academic achievement tests. For example, in the National Assessment of Educational Progress (NAEP), the reading, writing, and mathematics skills of African American and Hispanic children are substantially below those of White children at ages 9, 13, and 17 (Davis and McCaul 1991). Although some data exist which suggest that this academic performance gap between ethnic/racial minority youth and White youth may be narrowing, there continues to be a significant discrepancy between the groups. Further, because African American and Hispanic children are far more likely to drop out of school than are White children in the United States, the educational achievement gap between the two groups may be underestimated. Data from the October 1986 Current Population Survey indicated that 17.3 percent of African American respondents and 38.2 percent of Hispanic respondents aged 22 to 24 were neither enrolled in school nor high-school graduates, as compared with only 13.9 percent of White respondents within the same age group. In some inner cities the dropout rate for African American and Hispanic youth exceeds 60 percent (Natriello et al. 1990 p. 18).

3.3 Living in Single-parent Homes

Family structure in the 1990s United States is vastly different from what it was in the 1950s and 1960s. Hodgkinson (1991) reported that over one-third of all marriages performed in 1988 were second marriages for at least one partner. Divorce is more common than it was. Hodgkinson also estimated that over one-half of all new marriages in the 1990s will end in divorce and that 23 percent of all children born in this period will be born outside of marriage. Children living in single-parent households, estimated to be one in four children, are far more likely to be impoverished than children living in two-parent households. Among children who grew up in the 1970s, nearly three-quarters of those who spent at least some time in a single-parent family lived in poverty at least part of the time. More than one-third (37.8%) of these children spent at least 4 years of their first decade in poverty, and one in five (21.8%) lived in poverty for 7 or more of their first 10 years. Conversely, children living continuously in a two-parent, male-headed family have but a 20 percent chance of living in poverty for at least 1 year in their first 10, and only a 2 percent chance of being poor continuously from birth to age 10 (Natriello et al. 1990).

3.4 Educational Level of Mother

Children of poorly educated mothers (a) perform worse academically and (b) leave school earlier than children of better educated mothers. According to 1986 NAEP test results, children of poorly educated mothers scored lower than children of better educated mothers in both reading and mathematics at every age level measured, with the most pronounced difference occurring in mathematics. For example, of the third-grade children participating in the 1986 NAEP, only 46 percent of those whose mothers had not completed high school scored above the level of beginning skills and understanding on the mathematics proficiency test, while 73 percent of those children whose mothers were at least high-school graduates attained that level of mastery (Natriello et al. 1990). Maternal education is also related to the likelihood of dropping out of school. Barro and Kolstad's 1987 study found that children in families where the mother has not completed high school are two to three times more likely to drop out of high school themselves than are children in families where the mother has obtained more schooling (Barro and Kolstad 1987).

The educational level of the mother is especially important because it is the mother who usually is the primary caretaker in single-parent households. Many of these mothers either do not work or hold low-paying jobs. Clearly, children living in single-parent households are much more likely to be poor than children who live in two-parent families.

3.5 Limited English Proficiency

Students whose primary language is other than English (PLOTE) or who have limited English proficiency (LEP) are generally at a distinct disadvantage in United States public schools. These students not only often encounter academic barriers, but many are forced to deal with emotional and social obstacles too. For example, children with limited English proficiency are also more likely to drop out of school than are children from homes in which English is spoken exclusively. In a study reported in 1987, those students from homes where only a non-English language was spoken were more than twice as likely to drop out of high school as students from homes where English was the sole or primary language (Salganik and Celebuski 1987).

Further, ethnic and cultural customs of these students are often not understood by their peers and teachers. For example, children from some cultures tend to be more passive in group settings. Thus, a child's "lack of verbal responsiveness" could be misinterpreted by teachers as lack of interest or motivation. Likewise, children from other cultural backgrounds may manifest behaviors in the classroom or in the community which are perceived as being verbally or physically aggressive. In reality, these verbalizations and physical behaviors may not represent overt acts of defiance or disrespect but rather they may more accurately be reflective of cultural or subcultural norms.

4. Estimated Size of the Population

Despite the broad and imprecise nature of the available indicators of the educationally disadvantaged population, it is clear that substantial numbers and troubling proportions of United States' children may be classified as educationally at risk. A conservative estimate is that at least 40 percent of these children are at risk of failure in school on the basis of at least one of the five factors cited above. Other estimates indicate large percentages of United States children are at risk. A national study using a large, representative sample of youth indicated that 22 percent of eighth graders had one "risk factor" and 20 percent had two or more (Hafner et al. 1990). Another estimate indicated that approximately 33 percent of young children in the United States could be considered at risk before they even began formal schooling (Hodgkinson 1991). Demographic projections suggest that the birth rate is highest for populations that have traditionally suffered from poverty and low educational levels, thus suggesting that a greater percentage of students will be at risk in the near future.

5. Programming for Children in At-risk Circumstances

Traditionally, many children considered to be at risk of educational failure received services through the federal special and compensatory education programs. However, research on effective practices with many of these children at risk suggests that traditional approaches have not worked successfully. Neither retaining lower achieving students nor separating students for pull-out programs (the traditional approach employed in compensatory and special education programs) has demonstrated effectiveness. Moreover, pull-out programs have been criticized as stigmatizing (Lipsky and Gartner 1989, Slavin and Madden 1989, Stainback and Stainback 1985, Wang et al. 1988). A final criticism of pull-out programs is that the eligibility requirements for compensatory and special education have led to many at-risk students "falling through the cracks" of the two systems and thereby failing to receive needed services.

In determining what is effective programming with at-risk students, Slavin and Madden (1989) identified three broad categories for intervention: (a) prevention, (b) classroom change, and (c) remediation. With regard to the latter two categories, several attributes have been identified as characteristics of effective programs for at-risk students: comprehensiveness, intensity, flexibility, accessibility, and adaptability to specific student needs (Schorr 1989, Slavin and Madden 1989).

One of the more recent and promising reform approaches for at-risk students is that of accelerated schools. Proponents of accelerated schools argue that compensatory and remedial programs "institutionalize" students at risk as slow learners, thus reducing teacher expectations. They slow down the pace of instruction so that students at risk fall farther and farther behind. Teachers may fail to motivate students at risk, may not close the achievement gap between at-risk and mainstream students, and may not help students at risk to develop effective learning strategies. Four premises underlie these accelerated education projects: (a) high expectations and high status for the participants; (b) a specific deadline for closing the achievement gap of at-risk children; (c) a fast-paced curriculum that includes concepts, analysis, problem-solving, and interesting applications; and (d) the involvement of parents, the use of community resources, and the extensive use of parents and volunteers (Levin 1988).

At the secondary level, several authors (Hahn et al. 1987, Hamilton 1986) have suggested that schools need to individualize their instruction and curriculum for those students who are at risk of academic failure and who suffer from low self-esteem. Schools should, therefore, consider providing students with flexible options for completing their education. Some students, for example, may need a program of less concentration but a longer duration—a 5 or 6-year program with work-study options. Indeed, Hamilton (1986) argued that many at-risk students would benefit from more out-of-school experiences and more intensive work-related training. Community-based learning, he suggested, leads to enhanced positive attitudes as well as increased achievement for at-risk students.

In a related vein, Wehlage and Rutter (1986) offered three suggestions for schools interested in providing positive educational experiences for at-risk youth: (a) a sense of responsibility on the part of teachers and administrators toward the education of at-risk youth; (b) an effort to establish fair and respected discipline practices; and (c) a reconceptualization of schoolwork which allows at-risk students to achieve satisfaction and continue their schooling. Other research supports the notion that school climate and organization can substantially affect student engagement with schooling. Therefore, a school's atmosphere must emphasize positive teacher–student contact and support. Schools with considerable social disorganization, characterized by high truancy rates and substantial discipline problems, can work to change the school atmosphere by improving staff–administrator relationships and by instituting fair and consistent discipline policies. Establishing a positive ethos in which faculty and students share a sense of mission lessens student alienation as evidenced by absenteeism and dropout behavior. Further, schools that experience lower dropout rates are those in which face-to-face contact between students is the rule rather than the exception, in which there is an emphasis on academic pursuits, and in which the environment is safe and orderly. Teachers in these effective programs tend to see themselves as having a counseling role with students and encourage students toward trust relationships and social bonding with adults. Also there is some evidence that community support and involvement are key factors in establishing a positive school climate for at-risk youth. In addition, it was found that teacher commitment was a necessary ingredient for the effective education of at-risk youth (Bryk and Thum 1989).

6. Conclusion

The importance of establishing a positive school climate, characterized by teachers' active involvement and nurturing support of students, permeates the literature on children in at-risk circumstances. The same spirit infused the 1989 United Nations Convention at which the rights of the world's children were delineated. These included rights commonly afforded adults—freedom of movement, association, and belief —in addition to rights to nurturance, protection, and care (Hart 1991).

Clearly, these rights transcend the boundaries of individual classrooms and extend to the family, community, and society at large. Nevertheless, educators are in a unique position to recognize children's problems, advocate for solutions, and facilitate the provision of necessary services using resources from the school, family, and community. Further, research has indicated the value of formal education in enhancing the human capital of a nation (Husén and Tuijnman 1991). With the advent of a global economy and international interdependence, lifelong education becomes a primary consideration and educating children in at-risk circumstances has become not a luxury, but a necessity.

See also: Social and Communication Skills

References

Barro S, Kolstad A 1987 *Who Drops Out of High School? Findings from High School and Beyond*. National Center for Education Statistics, US Department of Education, Washington, DC

Bryk A, Thum Y M 1989 The effects of high school organization on dropping out: An exploratory investigation. *Am. Educ. Res. J.* 26(3): 353–83

Catterall J, Cota-Robles E 1988 The educationally at-risk: What the numbers mean. In: Conference on Accelerating the Education of At-risk Students 1988 *Accelerating the Education of At-risk Students*. Center for Educational Research at Standford University, Stanford, California

Children's Defense Fund Staff 1990 *Children 1990: A Report Card, Briefing Book, and Action Primer*. Children's Defense Fund, Washington, DC

Committee on Foreign Relations, United States Senate 1990 *State of the World's Children*. US Government Printing Office, Washington, DC

Davis W E, McCaul E J 1990 *At-risk Children and Youth: A Crisis in Our Schools and Society*. College of Education, University of Maine, Orono, Maine

Davis W E, McCaul E J 1991 *The Emerging Crisis: Current and Projected Status of Children in the United States*. Institute for the Study of At-risk Students, Orono, Maine

Ehn B 1990 The rhetoric of individualism and collectivism. In: Swedish Immigration Institute (ed.) 1990 *The Organization of Diversity in Sweden*. Invandrarminnesarkivet, Helsingborg

Glenn C L 1992 Educating the children of immigrants. *Phi Del. Kap.* 73(5): 404–08

Hafner A, Ingels S, Schneider B, Stevenson D, Owings J A 1990 *National Educational Longitudinal Study of 1988: A Profile of the American Eighth Grader* National Center for Education Statistics, Washington, DC

Hahn A, Danzberger J, Lefkowitz B 1987 *Dropouts in America: Enough is Known for Action*. Institute for Educational Leadership, Washington, DC

Hamilton S F 1986 Raising standards and reducing dropout rates. In: Natriello G (ed.) 1986 *School Dropouts: Patterns and Policies*. Teachers College Press, New York

Hart S N 1991 From property to person status: Historical perspective on children's rights. *Am. Psychol.* 46(1): 53–9

Hodgkinson H L 1991 Reform versus reality. *Phi Del. Kap.* 73(1): 9–16

Husén T, Tuijnman A 1991 The contribution of formal schooling to the increase in intellectual capital. *Educ. Researcher* 20(7): 17–25

Levin H M 1988 *Accelerated Schools for At-risk Students*. Center for Policy Research Education, New Brunswick, New Jersey

Lipsky D K, Gartner A (eds.) 1989 *Beyond Separate Education: Quality Education for All*. Paul H Brookes, Baltimore, Maryland

Murphy J T 1992 Apartheid's legacy to Black children. *Phi Del. Kap.* 73(5): 367–74

National Commission on Excellence in Education 1983 *A Nation At Risk: The Imperative for Educational Reform*. US Department of Education, Washington, DC

National School Boards Association (NSBA) 1989 *An Equal Chance: Educating At-risk Children to Succeed*. NSBA, Alexandria, Virginia

Natriello G, McDill E L, Pallas A M 1990 *Schooling Disadvantaged Children: Racing Against Catastrophe*. Teachers College Press, New York

New D A 1992 Teaching in the Fourth World. *Phi Del. Kap.* 73(5): 396–98

Reed S, Sautter R C 1990 Children of poverty: The status of 12 million young Americans. *Phi Del. Kap.* 71(10): K1–K12

Rust V D 1992 Educational responses to reforms in East Germany, Czechoslovakia, and Poland. *Phi Del. Kap.* 73(5): 386–89

Salganik L, Celebuski C 1987 *Educational Attainment Study: Preliminary Tables*. Pelavin Associates, Washington, DC

Schorr L B 1989 *Within Our Reach: Breaking the Cycle of Disadvantage*. Doubleday & Co, New York

Slavin R E, Madden N A 1989 What works for students at risk: A research synthesis. *Educ. Leadership* 46(5): 4–13

Stainback W, Stainback S 1984 A rationale for the merger of special and regular education. *Excep. Child.* 51(2): 102–11

Wang M C, Reynolds M C, Walberg H J 1988 Integrating the children of the second system. *Phi Del. Kap.* 70(3): 248–51

Wehlage G, Rutter R 1986 Dropping out: How much do schools contribute to the problem? In: Natriello G (ed.) 1986 *School Dropouts: Patterns and Policies*. Teachers College Press, New York

Zill N, Rogers C C 1988 Recent trends in the well-being of children in the United States and their implications for public policy. In: Cherlin A J (ed.) 1988 *The Changing American Family and Public Policy*. University Press of America, Washington, DC

Further Reading

Kozol J 1991 *Savage Inequities: Children in America's Schools*. Crown Publishing, New York

Children and Youth with Special Needs, Diagnosis and Classification of

B. Algozzine, B. Wong and F. E. Obiakor

Assessment is the process of gathering information for purposes of making decisions on educational programs for certain children and youth. Diagnosis and classification are part of this decision-making process. Because special education services are not universally accessible, decisions on students' eligibility for special education services and type of appropriate service are part of the special education process. Teachers participate in making these diagnosis and classification decisions and these practices are applicable across the existing categories of students with special needs.

1. Purposes of Diagnosis and Classification

Diagnostic decisions result in the classification of students with special education needs, but the ultimate purpose is improved instruction that results from altered intervention practices (McLoughlin and Lewis 1990, Salvia and Ysseldyke 1995, Ysseldyke et al. 1992). Cromwell et al. (1975) described four categories of information and their relations in diagnostic practices (see Table 1). Category A represents historical and/or etiological information—the precursors of observable behaviors and characteristics used in making diagnostic decisions. Category B is comprised of information from current assessments of an individual's behavior and characteristics—test scores, observations, and data from structured and unstructured interviews. Category C represents specific treatments and interventions and Category D contains information about outcomes of interventions. Diagnostic practices that include categories C and D are considered more accurate because they include treatment and evaluation information. Gathering information simply to classify and group individuals is useful in calling attention to new diagnostic categories. However, most professionals agree that the process of making diagnostic and classification decisions is justifiable largely on grounds that improved intervention will result.

2. Legal Considerations in Diagnosis and Classification

Rules and regulations established by education laws greatly influence special education. This is partially due to the dissatisfaction many parents and professionals experienced with early special education practices. For example, there was a time when a special education classification meant the end to normal educational experiences. Students in special classes lost contact with their regular class peers and often remained in special education for their entire school careers. Parents and professionals argued that such educational segregation of students with special needs was not sound pedagogy and legal action was required to ensure that practices changed. There was also a time when diagnostic decisions were grounded in the recommendations of a single teacher or on the results of a single test. Such ill-founded decision-making resulted in special class enrollments in which minority students were overrepresented. Parents and professionals protested against such insensate educational policy and legal action was mandated to ensure that these unsound practices changed.

In the 1990s, special education is a disabled student's right. In 1975, President Ford signed into law the Education for All Handicapped Children Act (Public Law 94–142). The law was reauthorized with the passage of the Individuals with Disabilities Education Act (IDEA) amendments in 1990. Written to improve services provided to individuals with disabilities, the

Table 1
Diagnostic practices

Type	Nature of practices
AB	Describes relation between historical events or causes and current pupil characteristics or behavior without considering treatment or outcomes.
AC	Describes relation between historical events or causes and particular treatments and interventions without concern for effects.
AD	Describes relation between historical events or causes and outcomes without considering pupil or treatment differences.
ABC	Describes relation between interventions and historical events, causes, and student characteristics without considering outcomes.
ABCD	Treatments with predictable outcomes are prescribed based on historical information and student characteristics—complete model.
BC	Describes relation between student characteristics and particular treatments and interventions without concern for effects.
BCD	Describes relation between student characteristics, treatments, and outcomes without considering historical information.
CD	Describes relation between treatments and outcomes without concern for causes or student characteristics.
BD	Describes relation between characteristics and outcomes without considering historical information and interventions.

Source: Adapted from Cromwell et al. 1975

law provided parents (and their children) with specific rights related to diagnosis and classification practices.

By law, students with disabilities and their families are guaranteed rights of due process. This means that these students and their families have the same rights as any other person. Educational diagnoses and classifications cannot be changed without the informed consent (e.g., written permission) of parent(s) or guardian(s). Parents are also entitled to independent assessments and impartial hearings when decisions about their children are being made.

Students with disabilities and their families are also entitled by law to protection in evaluation activities that are part of the educational experience. This means that students cannot be classified for special programs in an arbitrary and capricious manner. Students with disabilities and their families are entitled to have diagnostic decisions made about them using individually administered tests. It is assumed that these tests are appropriate for students with disabilities and that the decisions will be made in an unbiased fashion (e.g., without regard to ethnic, cultural, or racial characteristics).

School personnel by law must prepare an individualized education program (IEP) for every student enrolled in a special education program. Teachers must have clearly documented plans for how instructional time will be spent. The IEP is a written document that specifies educational plans and objectives and serves as a management tool for implementing recommendations derived during this stage of the diagnostic process. Again, the ultimate purpose of diagnosis and classification is improved educational experiences.

Students with disabilities must be educated in the least restrictive environment. The education of students with disabilities must parallel as much as possible the education of nondisabled students. Many students with disabilities are enrolled full-time in general education classes and receive only indirect services from special education personnel. Others leave their general education classes periodically to go to other classes for special education services (pull-out programs). Still others are enrolled primarily in special education classes but, to the maximum extent possible, attend general education classes for part of the school day. For example, a student might be enrolled in special education but attend a general education class for instruction in mathematics, music, art, or physical education.

3. Models of Diagnosis and Classification

Traditional models of diagnosis are test driven and focus on identifying problems in individuals. Within this model, the diagnostic process consists of several stages of decision-making.

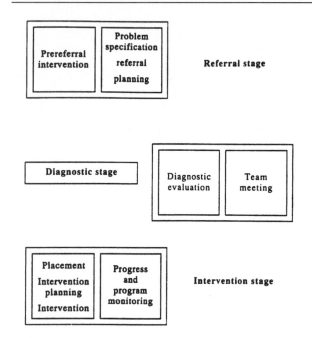

Figure 1
Steps in diagnostic process

During the referral stage, teachers identify problems and try interventions before deciding formally to refer a student. When these interventions fail, teachers refer the student for formal evaluation and participate in planning the diagnostic assessment (e.g., supply anecdotal records, complete checklists).

A diagnostic evaluation and team meeting take place during the diagnostic stage. The purpose of the diagnostic evaluation is to gather information on current levels of functioning in areas related to the suspected disability, classify the individual, and make a decision about the appropriateness of special education services. This evaluation must be conducted by personnel representing multidisciplinary perspectives (e.g., school psychologists, social workers, school nurses, speech and language pathologists, special education teachers, learning disabilities specialists, reading specialists, regular classroom teachers, principals, physicians, or parents). The written report typically includes the following information:

(a) the extent to which the student is eligible for special education (e.g., whether current classification criteria have been met);

(b) the basis for the decision (e.g., current levels of functioning);

(c) observed behavior supporting the diagnostic decision;

(d) relation of behavior to current levels of functioning;

(e) educationally relevant findings from other disciplines;

(f) other findings (e.g., environmental, cultural, or economic influences).

Following the written report, a team meeting is held to discuss the findings of the diagnostic evaluation and plan interventions to meet the student's special learning needs. Typically parents, teachers, students, and representatives from agencies that participated in the diagnostic evaluation take part in this team meeting. Participants also discuss the content of the student's IEP at this meeting.

Arguing that special education exists because generalized education programs fail to educate a portion of the students assigned to them, Deno (1989) presented an alternative model for improving current diagnostic practices using curriculum-based methods of

Table 2
Curriculum-based decision-making model

Stages	Activities	Purpose
Problem identification	Observing and recording of student performance during instruction	Determining that a problem exists
Problem definition	Describing of discrepancies between expected and actual performance	Determining that discrepancies are important
Problem exploration	Identifying potential improvements and costs associated with them	Selecting a solution to be tested
Solution implementation	Implementing a solution and monitoring progress	Determining that solution should be continued or revised
Problem resolution	Identifying discrepancies between expected and actual performance	Determining that discrepancies are acceptable and special program may be discontinued

Source: Deno 1989

assessment. The steps in the curriculum-based measurement (CBM) decision-making model are illustrated in Table 2.

During the problem identification (screening/referral) step, observations and performance records are gathered in educationally relevant domains (e.g., basal readers, district-wide mathematics textbooks). Deciding if discrepancies between expected and actual performance are large enough to require special education is central to the problem definition (eligibility/classification) step. During the problem exploration (intervention planning) step, treatment alternatives, probable performance improvements, and associated costs are identified. In the solution implementation (progress monitoring) step, decisions are made about continuing or modifying interventions. During the problem resolution (program monitoring) step, differences between expected and actual performance are evaluated and decisions are made related to continuing an intervention program.

When using curriculum-based procedures to diagnose students with special needs, school district personnel develop local norms by identifying a representative sample of curriculum materials for each grade level, establishing a sampling plan, and training people to gather assessment information and summarize performances. After teams identify specific referral problems, gather assessment information, and determine if additional intervention is necessary, curriculum-based decision-making takes one of two general forms.

In single-step models, referred students are compared to local grade-level norms on appropriate curricular materials. In some districts, discrepancy ratios are calculated by dividing normative performance by referred student's performance and decisions are made based on local cutoff scores (e.g., −2.0 or greater discrepancy ratio). In other districts, percentile scores derived from local norms are used in establishing cutoff scores and making eligibility decisions (Shinn 1989).

In multiple-step models, teachers or parents first refer a student. Evidence is then collected illustrating performance outside the range of regular classroom peers. The performance of referred students is evaluated to determine if it is outside the range that can be accommodated in regular classrooms. This approach closely approximates the decision-making process described by Salvia and Ysseldyke (1995) and others (McLoughlin and Lewis 1990, Ysseldyke and Algozzine 1994).

4. Diagnostic Procedures

Teachers gather diagnostic information using tests, observations, and interviews; the three provide complementary information on a student (Ysseldyke and Algozzine 1994). Tests are sets of questions designed to provide information about an individual's knowledge of content; they vary by administration, content, and form. Observations are records of an individual's performance of a specified behavior; they vary by form, content, and count. Interviews are sets of questions about past life experiences, current performance, characteristics, or future plans. Interviews vary by administration, content, and form.

4.1 Application

School personnel answer the following questions when conducting diagnostic evaluations and team meetings:

(a) What are the student's current levels of functioning?

(b) What multidisciplinary information is available?

(c) Does the student have an achievement discrepancy?

(d) Does the student have a disability?

(e) What goals, objectives, and placements are appropriate?

(f) What special education services should be provided?

(g) How will progress be monitored?

Formal and informal tests, observations, and interviews are used to gather this information during diagnostic evaluations for students suspected of having special learning needs (Hammill et al. 1989, McLoughlin and Lewis 1990, Salvia and Ysseldyke 1995). These measures may be administered to groups or individuals to provide information about most academic subjects as well as other areas of special learning needs. Some group-administered tests of intelligence include the Test of Cognitive Skills, the Otis-Lennon School Ability Test, and the Cognitive Abilities Test (McLoughlin and Lewis 1990, Salvia and Ysseldyke 1995). Popular individually administered intelligence tests include the Wechsler Intelligence Scale, for Children—Revised and the Stanford-Binet Intelligence Scale. Cognitive abilities are also measured as part of the Woodcock-Johnson Psychoeducational Battery and the Kaufman Assessment Battery for Children (McLoughlin and Lewis 1986, Salvia and Ysseldyke 1995). The Peabody Individual Achievement Test and the Wide Range Achievement Test are examples of popular achievement tests (McLoughlin and Lewis 1990, Salvia and Ysseldyke 1995). Names of these and other commonly used individual assessment devices are presented in Table 3.

5. Issues in Diagnosis and Classification

No area of special education has generated more critical analysis or controversy than diagnosis and classification. This is largely due to problems associ-

Table 3
Tests commonly used in diagnosis and classification

Cognitive Abilities and Intelligence
    Cognitive Levels Test
    Kaufman Assessment Battery for Children
    Learning Potential Assessment Device
    Peabody Picture Vocabulary Test—Revised
    Stanford-Binet Intelligence Scale
    Test of Nonverbal Intelligence
    Wechsler Intelligence Scale for Children—Revised

Adaptive Behavior
    AAMD Adaptive Behavior Scale
    Scales of Independent Behavior
    Vineland Adaptive Behavior Scales

Problem Behaviors
    Behavior Rating Profile
    Behavior Evaluation Scale
    Behavior Problem Checklist—Revised
    Burks' Behavior Rating Scale
    Devereux Behavior Rating Scales
    Walker Problem Behavior Identification

General School Achievement
    BRIGANCE Diagnostic Comprehensive Inventory of Basic Skills
    Kaufman Test of Educational Achievement
    Peabody Individual Achievement Test
    Wide Range Achievement Test

Reading Achievement
    Diagnostic Reading Scales
    Gray Oral Reading Tests
    Stanford Diagnostic Reading Test
    Woodcock Reading Mastery Tests

Mathematics Achievement
    Diagnostic Test of Arithmetic Strategies
    ENRIGHT Diagnostic Inventory of Basic Mathematics Skills
    KeyMath Diagnostic Arithmetic Test
    Test of Early Mathematics Ability

Language Abilities
    Boehm Test of Basic Concepts
    Diagnostic Spelling Test
    Test of Language Development
    Test of Written Language
    Test of Written Spelling
    Woodcock Language Proficiency Battery

ated with defining disabilities, developing operational criteria for use in identifying students, and assigning labels to individuals as an indication of a diagnosis (Ysseldyke and Algozzine 1994).

Substantial variation exists across states and even across districts in the definitions and operational criteria used to make diagnostic decisions in special education. This flexibility, although regulated by the federal government, unfortunately encourages underidentification of students with some special needs, such as emotional disturbances. It also allows school personnel to avoid identification of students when it is expedient to do so. The situation also creates a problem for the student who qualifies for services in one locale, but who moves across state or even district lines and finds himself/herself not qualified for those same services in the new location.

Diagnosing and classifying students may also have adverse effects upon other school experiences by encouraging educators to:

(a)   direct attention to supposed etiological factors that are either child specific or outside the school setting, thus alleviating educators of responsibility for instigating or exacerbating a child's difficulties;

(b) pursue causes of maladaptive child behavior in the realm of nonobservable, intrapsychic events, instead of analyzing student behavior in the context in which it is dysfunctional;

(c) cease to work toward solving problems as a result of discovering causal factors that are perceived as too deeply imbedded in the personality to respond to intervention;

(d) employ indirect interventions (e.g., non-behavioral therapies) to change overt behavior patterns (e.g., aggression, withdrawal).

Although the process of diagnosing and classifying students seems to be grounded more in the need to secure monies for specific populations rather than to influence programming decisions, the impact of labeling students cannot be ignored. For example, research has demonstrated that educators have a more negative attitude toward students with behavior problems, as a group, than toward most other exceptionalities. It has also been shown that teachers have conceptions associated with different labels. The effects of these ideas remain even after the label has been removed or some conflicting or neutral information about the student has been provided. (International concerns emerge when tests developed in the United States are translated into foreign languages for use in other countries.)

5.1 Diagnosis and Classification of Culturally Diverse Students

Observation shows that diagnosis and classifications of special needs students have not measured up to acceptable standards when culturally diverse students are involved. It is assumed that teachers teach, judge, and evaluate students based on their personal perceptions, values, and idiosyncrasies. If this supposition is correct, questions of accountability, psychological hazards, privacy invasion, and test bias must also be addressed. In addition, questions of appropriateness of assessment tools and procedures, accuracy of differential diagnosis, appropriateness of placement, and effectiveness of pedagogical strategies are important.

Many scholars (Obiakor 1991, 1994, Ogbu 1988, Salvia and Ysseldyke 1995, Samuda 1975, 1976, Ysseldyke and Algozzine 1994) agree that tests that produce consistent results may not measure what they purport to measure. Minority students are likely to differ as much as their nonminority peers in test-taking skills (Minton and Schneider 1980). This makes it difficult to justify using methods and instruments that have been standardized to a middle-class, European–American sample. According to Samuda (1975), standardized tests "preserve the status quo" and relegate "Blacks and other minorities to an inferior position in

the larger society" (p. 3). A logical extension is that tests and other assessment activities create labels and categories which have far-reaching social, economic, psychological, and educational implications. Samuda noted that tests lead to "mislabeling and poor learning environments that divert the education of Blacks and other minorities into a barely elementary and functional level" (p. 13).

Assessor bias is a critical factor, Dent (1976) and Johnson (1976, 1981) challenged assessors and teachers who failed to consider the culture of their students. The initial referral process must be properly investigated because of the cognitive, cultural, and learning styles that minority students bring into school programs. Cummins (1989) explained that "psychological assessment has served to legitimize the educational disabilities of minority students by locating the academic 'problems' within the students themselves" (p. 116). The endemic problem of looking "within" the student buttresses the theory of biological determinism that assumes that intelligence cannot be improved in spite of compensatory education programs. Gould (1981) remarked that biological determinism subscribes to the principle that "worth can be assigned to individuals and groups by measuring intelligence as a single quantity" (p. 20). This view was espoused by Goddard (1912), Hernstein (1971), and Jensen (1969), whose conclusions have particularly attracted the critical attention of many scholars (Obiakor 1991, Ogbu 1987, 1988, 1990, Rueda 1989). For example, Gelb et al. (1986) wrote:

> One cannot examine the relevant historical material without concluding that mental testers promoted eugenic and racist interests and that they sought to, and to some degree succeeded in, providing those interests with a mantle of scientific respectability. (p. 30)

5.1.1 The African Experience. In Africa, where the cultures are extremely diverse, there are no standardized tests or even educational programs designed with respect to cultural values, language symbols, and cognitive styles. In Nigeria, for example, there are problems with admitting exceptional individuals into school programs because of the lack of mandates. Educational programs are indiscriminately integrated without consideration for the specific needs of special students. Those students with serious integrative problems are admitted into residential programs and institutions; no systematic screening facility is available for exceptional children. As Ogbue (1975) pointed out, there is only one assessment center—the Child Guidance Center in Lagos. The lack of federal mandatory laws in special education has hindered efforts to identify instruments to assess the strengths and weaknesses of students. Classes are mainstreamed without consideration for the specific exceptionalities. In fact, severely disabled individuals are institutionalized and placed in residential settings. As Obiakor et al. (1991) explained:

The borderline or at-risk cases are not easily identifiable which makes the whole idea of special education to be nonexistent in Nigeria. Most exceptional students are indiscriminately integrated into mainstream classes. It becomes a matter of "survival of the fittest" for these individuals. (p. 15)

In Nigeria, as in much of Africa, there are only a few poorly defined categories of special needs students. According to Ogbue (1975, 1981) the categories include (a) the blind and partially sighted, (b) the deaf and partially hearing, (c) the physically disabled, (d) the mentally retarded, (e) the hospitalized children, and (f) the gifted. The high illiteracy rate in Nigeria and other parts of Africa makes it difficult for citizens to be aware of their fundamental rights. Most educational programs are intensively politicized to the detriment of participants (Obiakor and Maltby 1989). Section 8 of the National Policy on Education (Federal Ministry of Education 1975), which was expected to ameliorate the plight of exceptional individuals, has not had the expected effect (Obiakor 1991). It is reasonable to conclude that diagnosis and classification in Nigeria have not materialized to instructional intervention.

5.1.2 Call for nontraditional focus. There is a lack of assessment tools that respond to all the needs of diversity in Africa and the United States. For example, there is the question of how assessment tools used by the Child Guidance Center in Lagos respond to Nigerian values, symbols, and styles. This same issue has been reiterated by minority group members in the United States. Samuda (1975) argued that:

If it is our purpose to serve the mass of citizens and if it is our goal to use measurement to facilitate the education of the poor, of the minority student, and of the atypical individual, then we will need to expand our research endeavors. Psychometric technology must become the handmaiden of educational innovation in optimizing the individual's competence through qualitative analysis of achievement and weaknesses so as to point the way toward the modification of instruction matched to the individual needs of individual students. (pp. 156–57)

Samuda's statement suggests that assessment of culturally diverse students must respond to the needs of these students and their parents. The "shared enterprise" phenomenon must prevail as interaction is enhanced within the classroom setting. According to Duran (1989), "assessment will serve a more effective role if it is able to assist teachers and resource specialists in guiding the everyday instruction of pupils" (p. 158). Tests should lead to new learning. Culturally diverse students should be tested, trained, and retested to see if they have acquired new skills. The Midwestern National Origin Desegregation Assistance Center (1982) suggested (a) parental consent and involvement in psycho-educational assessment, (b) nonbiased assessment that considers culture, race,

gender, and language, and (c) multidimensional assessment. Minton and Schneider (1980) concluded:

We cannot limit ourselves to the identification of trait dimensions or typological classifications across individuals without also considering the characteristics of the environments within which individuals function. Nor can we limit ourselves to an analysis of the environmental determinants of human differences without also considering the hereditary determinants. Finally, we have to ask ourselves what kind of society is most desirable for the expression of human diversity—for the opportunity for each of us to grow as individuals and at the same time not infringe on the rights of others to develop their own individuality. (p. 489)

6. Perspective on Diagnosis and Classification

Those who work with students with special learning needs use assessment information on a daily basis. Different types of tests are used to assess different skills, abilities, and characteristics of students. Intelligence tests measure various verbal and nonverbal abilities. Achievement tests measure performance in academic areas of instruction. Differences between performance scores on intelligence and achievement tests are the basis for deciding whether a student should be classified as learning disabled, mentally retarded, emotionally disturbed, or some other category. Observations of behavior and interviews are used to corroborate test results from diagnostic evaluations and support discussion presented at team meetings where professionals discuss placement issues of particular students.

While the diagnostic process appears straightforward, significant controversy continues to revolve around decision-making on the eligibility for special education for a student. The controversy is based largely on inconsistent use of diagnostic criteria. If states and local school districts are free to decide what tests, methods, and criteria can be used to assign students to classifications, decision-making will necessarily be varied. When decision-making is varied, the same student may be "learning disabled" in one school district and not in another. This apparent inconsistency can only cause problems for professionals trying to diagnose and serve students with special needs.

See also: Children and Youth with Special Needs, Education of

References

Cromwell R L, Blashfield R K, Strauss J S 1975 Criteria classification systems. In: Hobbs N (ed.) 1975 *Issues in The Classification of Children.* Jossey-Bass, San Francisco, California

Cummins J 1989 A theoretical framework for bilingual special education. *Excep. Child.* 56 (2): 111–19

Deno S L 1989 Curriculum-based measurement and special education services: A fundamental and direct relationship. In: Shinn M (ed.) 1989 *Curriculum-based Measurement: Assessing Special Children.* Guilford Press, New York

Dent H E 1976 Assessing Black children for mainstream placement. In: Jones R L (ed.) 1976 *Mainstreaming and the Minority Child.* Council for Exceptional Children, Reston, Virginia

Duran R P 1989 Assessment and instruction of at-risk Hispanic students. *Excep. Child.* 56(2): 154–58

Gelb S A, Allen G E, Futterman A, Mehler B 1986 Rewriting mental testing history: The view from the American psychologist. *Sage Race Relations Abstracts* 11(2): 18–31

Goddard H H 1912 *The Kallikak Family, a Study in the Heredity of Feeble-mindedness.* MacMillan, New York

Gould S J 1981 *The Mismeasurement of Man.* W W Norton & Company, New York

Hammill D D, Brown L, Bryant B R 1989 *A Consumer's Guide to Tests in Print.* Pro-Ed Austin, Texas

Hernstein R 1971 I. Q. *Atlantic Monthly* 43–64

Jensen A R 1969 How much can we boost IQ and scholastic achievement? *Harv. Educ. Rev.* 39: 1–123

Johnson J L 1976 Mainstreaming Black children. In: Jones R L (ed.) 1976 *Mainstreaming and the Minority Child.* Council for Exceptional Children, Reston, Virginia

Johnson J L 1981 Priorities for Black exceptional children in the 1980s. Paper presented at the Council for Exceptional Children (CEC) Topical Conference, New Orleans, Louisiana

McLoughlin J A, Lewis R B 1990 *Assessing Special Students,* 3rd edn. Macmillan Inc., New York

Midwestern National Origin Desegregation Assistance Center 1982 *Special Education for Exceptional Bilingual Students: A Handbook for Educators.* MNODAC, Milwaukee, Wisconsin

Minton H L, Schneider F W 1980 *Differential Psychology.* Waveland Press Inc., Prospect Heights, Illinois

Nigerian Federal Ministry of Education 1975 Section 8 of the National Policy on Education. Federal Ministry of Education, Lagos

Obiakor F E 1991 African–American quandaries in school programs. Paper presented at the General Meeting of the National Black Caucus of Special Educators, Council for Exceptional Children, Atlanta, Georgia

Obiakor F E 1994 *The Eight Step Multicultural Education.* Kendal/Hunt, Dubuque, Iowa

Obiakor F E, Aramburo D, Maltby G P, Davis E 1991 Comparison of special education in Nigeria and the United States. Paper presented at the 69th Annual International Convention of the Council for Exceptional Children (CEC), Atlanta, Georgia

Obiakor F E, Maltby G P 1989 *Pragmatism and Education in Africa: Handbook for Educators and Development Planners.* Kendall Hunt Publishing Co., Dubuque, Iowa

Ogbue R M 1975 *A Survey of Special Education Facilities in Nigeria.* Federal Ministry of Nigeria, Lagos, Nigeria

Ogbue R M 1981 Experiments in integration: The Nigerian experience. *Educafrica* 135–52

Ogbu J U 1987 *Types of Cultural Differences and Minority School Adjustment and Performance.* Distinguished Visiting Professor Lecture Series No. 1, New Mexico State University, Las Cruces, New Mexico

Ogbu J U 1988 Human intelligence testing: A cultural ecological perspective. *Nat. Forum* 68(2): 23–29

Ogbu J U 1990 Understanding diversity: Summary comments. *Educ. Urb. Soc.* 22(4): 425–29

Rueda R 1989 Defining mild disabilities with language-minority students. *Excep. Child.* 56(2): 121–28

Salvia J, Ysseldyke J E 1995 *Assessment in Special and Remedial Education,* 6th edn. Houghton Mifflin, Boston, Massachusetts

Samuda R J 1975 *Psychological Testing of American Minorities: Issues and Consequences.* Harper & Row Publishers, New York

Samuda R J 1976 Problems and issues in assessment of minority group children. In: Jones R L (ed.) 1976 *Mainstreaming and the Minority Child.* Council for Exceptional Children, Reston, Virginia

Shinn M R 1989 Identifying and defining academic problems: CBM screening and eligibility procedures. In: Shinn M (ed.) 1989 *Curriculum-based Measurement: Assessing Special Children.* Guilford Press, New York

Ysseldyke J E, Algozzine B, Thurlow M L 1992 *Critical Issues in Special and Remedial Education.* Houghton Mifflin, Boston, Massachusetts

Ysseldyke J E, Algozzine B 1994 *Introduction to Special Education,* 3rd edn. Houghton Mifflin, Boston, Massachusetts

Further Reading

Deno S L 1985 Curriculum-based measurement: The emerging alternative. *Excep. Child.* 52: 219–32

Deno S L 1986 Formative evaluation of individual programs: A new role for school psychologists. *School Psychology Review* 15(3): 358–74

Figueroa R A 1989 Psychological testing of linguistic minority students: Knowledge gaps and regulations. *Excep. Child.* 56(2): 145–52

Gickling E, Havertape J 1981 *Curriculum-based Assessment (CBA).* National School Psychology Inservice Training Network, Minneapolis, Minnesota

McLoughlin J A, Lewis R B 1986 *Assessing Special Students.* Merrill, Columbus, Ohio

Ysseldyke J E, Algozzine B 1984 *Introduction to Special Education.* Houghton Mifflin, Boston, Massachusetts

Children and Youth with Special Needs, Education of

M. C. Reynolds and M. Ainscrow

The topics considered in this entry are generally related to fields such as history, policy development, administrative arrangements, personnel preparation, research, international activities, and major trends in the education of children and youth with special needs. For more detailed treatment of special education topics, see other entries under such headings as diagnosis and classification of children and youth with special needs or learning characteristics of students with special needs. A complete story about education for disabled children and youth would tell mainly of neglect. The field of special education has developed only quite recently and unevenly in the various parts of the World. What is described here is mainly a positive story of developing efforts by educators to serve disabled students, but many disabled children are isolated and still lacking the special education they need.

1. Definitions

The specialized forms of education provided for disabled or handicapped children and youth comprise the field of special education. Sometimes special education is provided as a supplement to general or regular education; other times it totally replaces regular education.

1.1 Disabilities

The term "handicapped" is often used interchangeably

Table 1
Students aged 6-21 enrolled in special education programs in the United States by category of disability 1988-89

Disability category	Number	Percentage
Learning disabled	1,998,422	47.7
Speech or language impaired	968,908	23.1
Mentally retarded	581,465	13.9
Emotionally disturbed	377,295	9.0
Multihandicapped	84,870	2.0
Hard of hearing and deaf	57,555	1.4
Orthopedically impaired	47,392	1.1
Other health impaired	50,349	1.2
Visually handicapped	22,743	0.5
Deaf blind	1,516	0.04
Total	4,190,515	100.0

Source: US Department of Education 1990

with other terms such as "disabled" or "impaired." A useful distinction is to use "impairments" in reference to direct defects or deficiencies of individual persons, such as torn ligaments or misshapen eyes. "Disabilities" refer to functions of the individual which are limited or distorted because of impairments; for example, the torn ligaments may cause inability of the individual to run or jump, the misshapen eyes may cause blurred vision. The term "handicapped" is used in a broader way to indicate a clear disadvantage in the person's life such as exclusion from employment, denial of entrance to a training program, or exclusion from certain forms of social life. The term "handicapped" encompasses social arrangements which operate to the disadvantage of disabled persons. Traditionally the term handicapped has been used in defining special education, but the term "disabled"—as defined here—might often be more appropriate.

1.2 Categories of Disability

The disabilities which lead to placement in special education programs vary greatly, both qualitatively and in degree. A common approach in delineating the disabilities of individuals and in organizing programs in the schools is to use a set of categories. Three special education categories which often receive attention are: students who are visually disabled, deaf, or mentally retarded. It should not be assumed that these categories are easily defined (*see Children and Youth with Special Needs, Diagnosis and Classification of*). Additional categories of special education are used in many places. In the United States, school districts throughout the nation are required to report enrollments in special education programs, using the categories listed in Table 1. In recent years an apparent trend is to make noncategorical approaches to special education, but few data are available to document this trend.

Also included in Table 1 are data showing the numbers and percentages of disabled students in the various categories for the school year 1988–89 (US Department of Education 1990). By far the largest category was learning disability (LD) in which about 48 percent of the special education students were enrolled. The LD category came into common use in the United States only in the 1960s and has grown very rapidly, though it is unused as a category in most of the world. In an important sense LD is not a distinct category; the methods for classifying students vary greatly from one school district to another. LD identifies a broad range of students who are not learning well in existing programs.

2. Numbers of Disabled Children

Attempting to define the numbers of children who need special education presents considerable difficulty. Care must be taken in considering any data that are presented since terminology and categorization vary considerably from country to country. Furthermore in some countries it is very difficult, even impossible, to obtain reliable and recent data. An estimated 10 percent of the world's children are disabled. Table 1 shows that in the United States 4.2 million children received special education in 1988–89. That is 9.4 percent of the total population of children and youth aged six to seventeen. Eighty percent of children live in developing countries and few receive special services of any kind (Hegarty 1990).

Despite the fact that it has been more than 40 years since the Universal Declaration of Human Rights asserted that "everyone has a right to education," many children in the world do not receive adequate education, including those who have disabilities. The text of the 1990 World Conference on Education for All, held in Thailand, pointed out that the following realities persist:

(a) More than 100 million children, including at least 60 million girls, have no access to primary schooling.

(b) More than 960 million adults, two-thirds of whom are women, are illiterate and functional illiteracy is a significant problem in industrialized and developing countries.

(c) More than one-third of the world's adults have no access to the printed knowledge, new skills, and technologies that could improve the quality of their lives and help them shape, and adapt to, social and cultural change.

(d) More than 100 million children and countless adults fail to complete basic education programs; millions more satisfy the attendance requirements but do not acquire essential knowledge and skills.

The contribution of special education, therefore, has to be considered against this background of international crisis with respect to education in general.

Probably the most helpful source of data with respect to special educational provision internationally arises out of a survey of 58 countries conducted in 1986–87 (UNESCO 1988b). The information provided by this survey illustrates the discrepancies in the level of progress among the various regions and countries. For example, 34 of the countries had fewer than one percent of pupils enrolled in special educational programs and 10 of these countries had special education available for less than one-tenth of one percent of pupils.

Precise figures for developing countries are particularly difficult to establish but the studies that are available confirm the disturbing scale of the problem. For example, Ross (1988) summarized data gathered from 13 countries in eastern and southern Africa indicating that virtually all these countries had special education enrollments for approximately 0.1 percent or fewer of the school age population. Such data led Hegarty (1990) to conclude: "The stark reality underlying these figures is that the great majority of children and young people with disabilities do not receive an appropriate education—if indeed they are offered any education. In many countries, less than one child in a hundred receives the special educational provision that s/he needs" (p. 4).

3. Historical Developments

3.1 Early Developments

It is possible to detect certain patterns in the historical development of special education across different countries. The pace of these developments varies from country to country. It is also important to note that the field of special education is of relatively recent origin. In its early stages the emphasis was on provision for children with distinct disabilities but with the expansion of public education, broader forms of special education have been introduced.

In the United Kingdom the first schools for the blind and deaf were founded toward the end of the eighteenth century. The first separate education provision for children with physical disabilities was made in 1851; before the middle of the nineteenth century so called mentally defective children were often placed in workhouses and infirmaries. Special provision for pupils with milder forms of disability came much later.

As with ordinary education, education for children with disabilities in many countries began with individual and charitable enterprise. Then the government intervened first to support voluntary efforts, and finally to create a national framework in which public and voluntary agencies could act in partnership to see that all children received a suitable education. In many developing countries such a national framework has still to be established (UNESCO 1988a).

3.2 Developments since 1960

Many current practices in special education have been developed since the early 1960s. This period has been marked by significant shifts in beliefs within the field and this process of change is still apparent in many parts of the world.

During the early part of that period there was a marked emphasis on making provision for children with particular disabilities. In many countries provision of special education depended on assessing a child with respect to a perceived handicapping category or condition. Thus, over the years, special education became a separate world catering to that small percentage of children perceived as disabled. Those involved in special education had relatively little contact with mainstream schools. This isolation was reinforced in some countries by the fact that many of the providers of special education were voluntary organizations and that some special schools were located in accommodations away from the community.

The emphasis changed in the later 1960s and early 1970s. A concern with equal opportunities in a number of Western countries heightened awareness of children in ordinary schools who were perceived as making unsatisfactory progress. Consequently there was a substantial growth in various forms of remedial education, including the establishment of special classes within or attached to mainstream schools.

3.3 Trends since the 1970s

Further changes occurred in the 1970s in several areas of the world, including the United States, Canada, Australia, and several Western European countries. New ideas emerged that challenged the basis of existing provisions for pupils having special educational needs. Adams (1986) summarized six trends that were particularly important. These were:

(a) a growing understanding that handicapping conditions are much more widely spread, more varied, and more complex than categorization systems based largely on medical criteria tended to indicate;

(b) greater awareness that not only does the incidence of handicap and the recognition of it alter over time as a result of medical, economic, and social changes, but also that the difficulties encountered by young people in their educational and general development are likely to arise as much from disadvantaged circumstances as from individual characteristics;

(c) more general acceptance of the fact that parents, however much in some cases they may be "part of the problem," not only have rights in relation to their children which must be respected but also have a unique and valuable contribution to make to their children's development which must be more effectively exploited by the professionals;

(d) a growing recognition of the value of early intervention to help children with special needs and of the need for continuing attention with regular review and appropriate modification of support programs to meet their changing needs;

(e) a better appreciation of the fact that there is no sharp divide between the "handicapped" and the "normal" but rather a range of individual needs across a continuum;

(f) wider understanding and acceptance of the fact

that every young person has a right to as full, independent, and "normal" life as possible and that therefore the aim of the community in relation to young people with more severe difficulties must be as much integration as possible into mainstream school and community life.

3.4 National Legislation

As a result of these trends significant legislation to change the basis of special education was introduced in a number of countries. Possibly the most influential of these was Public Law 94–142, the Education for All Handicapped Children Act (1975), in the United States. This sought a legislative solution to educational inequities in that it was designed to redress the denial of rights to education of the handicapped (Yanok 1986). The key provision was the requirement that public schools throughout the United States should provide appropriate education for every school-age handicapped child irrespective of the nature of the child's disability. More specifically the legislation mandated that all students with disabilities be provided with appropriate instruction in the least restrictive environment possible, which for most would be in the regular classroom. It also specified an elaborate set of procedures and timelines for referral, assessment, classification, and placement of students, and extended to students and parents certain constitutional rights and procedural safeguards (Skrtic 1991). In years following 1975, provisions of PL 94–142 were amended to extend the right to education to younger disabled children, mandatorily from age three and permissively from the moment of birth.

The United States legislation has subsequently inspired similar developments in other Western countries. For example, the 1981 Education Act in England and Wales sought to establish a new framework for children requiring special provision. Its main strategy was the introduction of the Statement of Special Educational Need, an extensive reporting procedure used to monitor the progress of individual pupils and, where necessary, provide them with additional resources. This legislation has broadly similar approaches to those required by the United States legislation.

Evidence of new legislation internationally is provided by a UNESCO survey (1988b). Two-thirds of the respondents in the survey (i.e., 38 out of 58 countries) made reference to new legislation under discussion or being introduced. This ranged from loosely formulated discussions of the need for various legislative developments to definite plans to introduce regulations governing specific aspects of educational provision.

4. Administrative Arrangements and Policies

Special education is provided through a variety of administrative arrangements. As noted above, in many parts of the world a first arrangement made for special education is in the form of specialized residential schools. This involves bringing disabled children together not only for schooling, but for a total living experience. For example, children who are blind may be collected from a whole province, state, or region for placement in a residential school where they live in dormitories and attend school, usually on campus. Sometimes the students remain in the residential school on a year-round basis; in other instances, they return to their homes for occasional weekends and for vacation periods. Residential schools are common for students who are blind, deaf, or mentally retarded; but the trend is downward for such placements in industrialized nations, especially for children who are mentally retarded (Zappolo et al. 1990, Lakin et al. 1982).

A second common type of arrangement is the specialized day school. In this case an entire school is staffed and equipped to serve a given category of students with disabilities, but it operates only during school hours. Students live at home or occasionally in foster homes or specialized community facilities. Usually this involves individualized arrangements to transport the students to and from the school. Such schools may employ physical and occupational therapists, remedial physical education teachers, speech therapists, nurses, and part-time medical physicians, in addition to specialized teachers.

Evidence from the UNESCO survey (1988b) indicates that the predominant form of provision for special education in many parts of the world is in separate special schools. Such schools often serve very limited numbers of children, leaving many children with disabilities with little or no education. These observations led the participants in UNESCO's consultation in special education (1988a) to make the following statement: "Given the size of the demand and the limited resources available, the education and training needs of the majority of disabled persons cannot be met by special schools and centres" (p. 15). Consequently, a way forward will require changes in both special and mainstream schools. Mainstream schools have to develop forms of organization and teaching that cater to greater pupil diversity; while those special schools that do exist must develop an outward looking stance and take on significantly new roles (Hegarty 1990).

Another arrangement is the special class. In this case an entire classroom, usually located in a regular school, is used to serve disabled children. For example, there may be a special class for children who are mentally retarded or learning disabled. By this arrangement, disabled pupils often attend the same school as the nondisabled children of their neighborhood. There may be some degree of mainstreaming or integration of the disabled and nondisabled students at the school; for example, in shared use of a lunchroom and playground, or perhaps more widely through other forms of integration. Usually enrollments in special classes are lower in number of students per class than in regular or general education classes. Limits in special class enrollments are often imposed by government rules or regulations in return for special financial subsidies to the program. Because special classes can be distributed widely geographically, less specialized transportation is needed than in special day school arrangements.

Still other arrangements include part-time specialized classes and resource rooms managed by teachers who provide part-time services to disabled pupils. A student might be enrolled in a general education class for most of the school day but go for part-time help each day, perhaps an hour or two, to the resource room. The resource room teacher offers intensive help in specific areas of need, such as remedial reading instruction. A student who is blind may go to a specialized resource room for limited periods of instruction in braille, mobility, and orientation. The resource room arrangement involves a degree of integration and has grown rapidly in recent years in some nations, most notably in the United States. Teachers who work in resource rooms may spend some of their work time in consultation with regular classroom teachers as a way of extending and coordinating programs for disabled students.

Some disabled students can be served while fully enrolled in regular education programs if they and/or their teachers are given extra help through contact with itinerant specialists or consultants. Speech therapists often work on an itinerant basis, perhaps serving students in several schools. Students with speech and language problems may be called out of their regular classes for short periods of help each day or several times each week by the itinerant speech therapist. Similarly, itinerant teachers of braille and/or mobility and orientation may teach for brief periods in school hours pupils who are blind; others add help in afterschool and vacation periods in their special fields.

4.1 A Continuum of Placement Options

The full set of special education arrangements and policies concerning school placements for students with disabilities can be represented in chart form as in Figure 1 (Reynolds 1962). The continuum of placements is ordered according to the degree of separation or integration provided for disabled students. As one moves up the continuum, programs become more specialized, expensive, and segregated; at the top of the continuum, in residential schools, the student studies only with specialized teachers and lives only with other disabled students, most often with those who bear the same categorical labels.

The continuum is intended to convey the idea that most disabled students can be served in regular school placements, if supportive help is provided. To the side of the triangle, a policy is expressed to the effect that students should receive no more specialized placement than is required and that, if placed in a special educa-

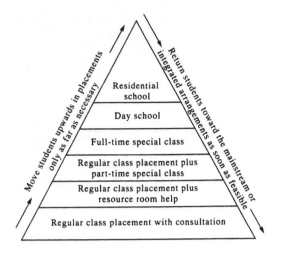

Figure 1
A continuum of special education arrangements

made between social and curricular integration.

Developed countries are experiencing their own difficulties in establishing effective policies for integration. The existence of well established separate provision in special schools and classes creates complex policy dilemmas leading many countries to operate what Pijl and Meijer (1991) refer to as "two tracks." In other words, these countries have parallel, but separate, segregation and integration policies.

In some countries integration represents an aspiration for the future. In Germany, for example, while some pilot initiatives based on the idea of integration are underway, students who are declared eligible for special education must be placed in a special school; statistics for 1986 showed that 4.2 percent of all students between six and sixteen years of age were in separate schools for special education. On the other hand, Denmark and Norway have shown considerable progress in implementing the integration principle. Here the local community school is seen as the normal setting for pupils with special needs.

Discrepancies between stated policy and actual practice are evident in many countries. For example, Pijl and Meijer (1991) note that despite the fact that special schools were abolished in Italy in 1977 most of the so-called integrated pupils are "integrated outside the classroom." Often this means that they are taught by support teachers in separate classrooms. It is reported that the reasons for these problems in implementing a policy of integration are that regular school teachers still do not regard the teaching of pupils with special needs as their responsibility and are often not equipped (by training or materials) to do so.

A problem reported from a number of industrialized countries is that, despite national policies emphasizing integration, there is evidence of a significant increase in the proportions of pupils being categorized and given separate placements in order that their schools can earn additional resources (Ainscow 1991). As a result of her analysis of policies in Australia, the United Kingdom, Scandinavia, and the United States, Fulcher (1989) suggests that the increased bureaucracy that is often associated with special education and the inevitable struggles that go on for additional resources have the effect of escalating the proportion of school children labeled as disabled. As an illustration of this process she describes how in Victoria, Australia, 3,000 students in regular schools are now labelled as "integration children," a category of disability that did not exist prior to 1984.

Dissatisfaction with progress toward integration has caused demands for more radical changes in policy in a number of countries (Ainscow 1991). In the United States this has led to the Regular Education Initiative, a movement calling for the merger of special and regular education (Wang et al. 1986, Will 1986, Stainback and Stainback 1984b). A thorough critical analysis of this development and the heated debate that it has

tion program, a goal should be to return pupils toward the mainstream as rapidly as is feasible.

In some industrialized nations, perhaps most notably in North America and Europe, there is criticism of the continuum idea for suggesting the possibility that any segregated form of special education, such as residential schools, is a suitable arrangement. Such critics assert that only fully integrated or mainstreamed arrangements of special education are acceptable (Meyer et al. 1991, Taylor 1988).

4.2 The Worldwide Movement for Integration

In many countries throughout the world integration is a central element in planning special education (e.g., Ainscow 1990, Pijl and Meijer 1991, UNESCO 1988b). Such an emphasis seems sensible for Third World countries given the extent of the need and the inevitable limitations of available resources. It is also important to note that in many developing countries substantial "casual" integration of children with disabilities in ordinary schools occurs (Miles 1989).

In considering the current scene internationally with respect to integration there is again the problem of differences of definition. Pijl and Meijer (1991) use the term "integration" as a collective noun for all attempts to avoid a segregated and isolated education for pupils with disabilities. As a result of their survey of policies for integration in eight Western countries they suggest that its scope can range from the actual integration of regular and special schools (or classes) to measures for reducing the outflow of students from regular education to special education. Consequently it becomes very difficult to quantify the numbers of pupils with special needs who receive their education in integrated settings, particularly if the important distinction is created in the United States is provided by Skrtic (1991).

5. Classification

A traditional first step in the practical operation of most special education programs is the identification of students as disabled and in need of specialized instruction. This usually involves the classification of students in accord with a prevailing system of categories in the state or other political entity. Such classification can result in a public and stigmatic labeling of the child. Severely disabled children are usually identified in preschool years, by parents in collaboration with physicians, and can be enrolled in special education programs at an early age. Early education programs are increasingly available for disabled children. In the case of milder disabilities, needs often are not clear until after the children have been enrolled in regular schools. Then teacher observations cause referrals for special study, classification, and possibly special placement.

5.1 Extending the Categories

A pervasive trend in classification practices is to enlarge or extend the inclusiveness of the categories. For example, programs initiated to serve students who are blind tend to be extended to serve those who are partially sighted. Programs first designed to serve students who are deaf tend gradually to include more who are hard of hearing. The category "mental retardation" tends, at first, to include only students with severe and obvious degrees of attenuation in cognitive abilities, but then expands to include those described as "educable" and perhaps "borderline." Speech therapists initially prepared to deal with speech and language disorders may later be expected to deal with problems of tongue thrust and eating. Programs organized to serve disabled pupils may later serve others who are judged to be "at risk" of becoming disabled. New categories of disability tend to emerge quite regularly in relatively affluent communities, as in the current proposals in the United States of programs for children born to AIDS-infected mothers, students with attention deficit disorders (with or without hyperactivity), and children born to heroin-addicted mothers.

The proliferation and extension of categories complicates the challenges of diagnosis, classification, and placement in special education and of program administration. This in turn has added to the criticism of programs, for ills such as disjointedness and proceduralism (Reynolds et al. 1987). Disjointedness refers to the problems of coherent administration of many separate programs within the schools, when each has its own rules, bureaucratic managers, advocacy system, funding arrangement, and accountability procedures. Proceduralism refers to the tendency for procedural norms and rules to assume primacy over substantive matters when details and paperwork require much time and energy.

5.2 Educational Classification

Presumably the classification and placement of students in special education programs should have enhancing effects on the instruction and learning of those who are classified. This proposes that classification in the schools should be related to distinctly educational decisions. Accordingly, a student is blind for educational purposes when instruction in braille reading methods is clearly indicated, in preference over clear print reading. Blindness thus may have a somewhat different meaning in the schools than in the medical clinic or in a social services office. Similarly, a pupil is deaf for educational purposes when special communications techniques not involving audition must be taught. A pupil is appropriately classified as mentally retarded in the schools only when a distinctive prescription for educational procedures is indicated for the child and when there is evidence that such a classification and placement is likely to have enhancing effects on the child's learning. This use of the mental retardation classification may not coincide fully with sociolegal classifications or approaches used in nonschool agencies.

Student classification and placement is often a problem because of failure to adhere to a strictly educational orientation. The problem is associated with the fact that a range of professionals, such as psychologists and physicians, are often involved in classification, some of them having little experience in school-related decisions. It appears that a trend toward wider use of curriculum-based assessment practices may be replacing diagnostic and classification procedures that have little relevance to instruction (Tucker 1985). A related development is the increasing use of noncategorical approaches to program organization.

5.3 Labeling and Stigma

Some categorical classifications tend to result in a degree of public labeling of students. Terms such as "mentally retarded" and "emotionally disturbed" appear to be especially stigmatic. Some parents of children given such labels resent and resist the labels and occasionally use legal procedures to express their resistance. In the United States, a number of such legal cases have been pursued by parents, resulting in court-ordered revisions of classification and labeling practices (Larry P v Riles 1972). A further complication in such controversies is that stigmatic labels have been used more often for children of families that are in minority status on the basis of race, ethnicity, linguistic status, or socioeconomic level than for others. A study by a special panel of the US National Academy of Science showed, for example, that children of African-American heritage were classified as mentally retarded at about three times the rate for the generality of pupils in American schools (Heller et al. 1982). Such a disproportion is considered by many to be biased and prejudicial.

Classification concerning mildly disabled pupils is controversial in many ways. Procedures tend to be unreliable and unrelated to needed instruction. Large discrepancies exist in use of categories in various political jurisdictions. These difficulties and inconsistencies are one cause for the belief held by significant numbers of educators that most mildly disabled pupils should be served in strengthened regular classes and schools and not be classified as disabled (Will 1986) (see *Children and Youth with Special Needs, Diagnosis and Classification of*).

6. Special Education Personnel

Often the earliest leadership in initiating special education programs in a country is provided by physicians. Correspondingly, earliest forms of special education are often conducted in hospitals, clinics, or other facilities separate from schools. Later, teachers and schools take increasing responsibility.

6.1 Teacher Preparation

In the most developed nations increasing numbers of special education teachers are prepared in colleges and universities in tracks that overlap with programs for preparation of regular class teachers. Much of the development of specialized teacher preparation in institutions of higher education has occurred since the Second World War. The rate of special education program development was very rapid in this same period and, even with the increasing number of teacher preparation programs, the number of specialized teachers available has always and virtually everywhere, lagged behind program developments and needs in the schools.

In the United States, for example, 84,000 specialized teachers of disabled students were employed in 1968–69; but it was estimated that an additional 237,000 special educators would have been required to completely serve disabled students aged five to seventeen (US Office of Education 1969). The number of colleges offering sequences of preservice preparation for special education teachers in the United States increased from a mere handful in the 1940s to about 350 in 1968. By 1988–89, the number of special education teachers employed in the United States increased to about 300,000; but at least 20 percent of them were judged to be underprepared for their work. The shortage of fully prepared specialized teachers is one cause of the increasing emphasis upon preparing regular teachers to accommodate disabled pupils in regular classrooms and increasing use of specialists in consultation with regular class teachers as an alternative to the direct instruction of disabled pupils by special educators.

The UNESCO survey (1988b) presents a gloomy picture with respect to the international scene in teacher preparation. Only a minority of the 58 countries reported coverage of disability issues in preservice training programs for all teachers. Inservice training opportunities for teachers in regular schools were similarly limited. A wide range of training opportunities was reported for teachers specializing in special education —a five-year course in a teachers college at one extreme, to on-the-job instruction offered on an ad hoc basis at the other. While it is difficult to generalize, it seems clear that the main thrust of training is directed at specialists who will work in segregated special schools. However, it can be argued that the vast majority of children with disabilities could be helped in mainstream schools by relatively minor adjustments to the teaching that is provided (Hegarty 1990). Thus an investment in the preservice preparation of teachers with respect to strategies for accommodating pupil diversity could bring about major improvements in the special education provision offered by schools.

6.2 Auxiliary Professional Staff

In addition to teachers, special education programs involve a variety of other specialists such as psychologists, audiologists, social workers, physical therapists, ocupational therapists, and speech–language therapists who spend much of their time working with disabled students. In addition, a large number of paraprofessionals are employed in special education programs. Relatively little attention has been given to the preparation of paraprofessionals, but this is a likely area for increasing attention. Some paraprofessionals perform quite specialized functions, such as mediating communications between deaf and hearing persons. Such persons require specific skills and some vocational/technical schools are now offering the necessary training.

6.3 Burnout

Problems of supplying special education teachers are enlarged by relatively high rates of teacher "burnout" or withdrawal from the field. "Burnout" rates are especially high for teachers of students who are emotionally disturbed or mentally retarded. One proposal for addressing the "burnout" problem is to rotate special education teachers into regular classes for work with nondisabled pupils for a year or two after a period of service in special education. Better preservice preparation and stronger inservice supports for the special education teachers are also believed to be helpful.

6.4 Curricula for Specialized Teacher Preparation

Curricula for preparation of special education teachers who serve blind or deaf pupils involve some distinct elements, such as teaching braille in the case of blindness, or manual forms of communication in the case of the deaf. For most other categories of disability, general principles of instruction that apply in the instruction of nondisabled pupils appear to be important in special education as well; however, the disabled pupils probably need more intensive instructional help over longer periods of time and with more structure than do nondisabled pupils. Attention to individual differences among students is always important. Some curricular elements in special education teacher preparation which may require special emphasis are: understanding and working with families, methods for creating positive interdependencies among students (e.g., using cooperative groups of disabled and nondisabled pupils), individualized assessment practices, consultation, modifying curriculum and materials to meet individual needs, behavioral methods and direct instruction, teaching for self-regulation and strategic (meta-cognitive) behavior, teaching social skills, teaching basic literacy skills, and use of technology (including prostheses, computers, etc.).

7. Research

The field of special education tends to rely heavily on psychologists and others from outside the field to conduct most of the relevant research. An exception to this observation is the subcategory of severe and profound mental retardation (or developmental disabilities) which has produced a good supply of longterm researchers (Meyer et al. 1991). This seems to be associated with the strong preference of researchers in this field for use of behavioral methods of analysis, instruction, and research. A second exception is in the field of language and speech disorders which has produced a significant number of career-oriented researchers. In both of these exceptional areas, major professional and scientific organizations exist which have provided publication outlets for research in the several fields.

7.1 Problems of Research

A number of practical difficulties make research in special education difficult. One such difficulty concerns cohort changes over time. For example, a large number of children became blind in the 1940s and early 1950s because of overconcentrated use of oxygen in incubators for infants with low birth weights. The cause was discovered in 1954 and the incidence rate for blindness decreased sharply in areas with good medical communications and services. A number of blind children appeared in the 1960s, many of them showing multiple disabilities, who had suffered German measles during an intrauterine period. Thus, the causes of blindness in children from each period were remarkably different. In many characteristics they vary markedly, not only individually but also as time cohorts.

A second difficulty concerns the increasing dispersal of disabled pupils. With the increased emphasis on an integration policy, it is becoming less common to find large numbers of disabled pupils in a single location. More of them attend regular schools in a highly dispersed way and under increasingly diverse circumstances. Doing research under such conditions involves more travel and time, more expense, and more difficulties in interpretation.

A third difficulty arises from unreliable classification practices, so that a researcher who wishes to study students with learning disabilities, for example, cannot be certain that the students found in one situation with that label bear much resemblance to students with the same label in other situations. The same difficulties offer complications for the researcher who wishes to do meta-analyses in special education; data on research subjects and other features of investigation are often lacking or ambiguous. Increasingly, the case is made that the field of special education needs a "marker variable" system to facilitate better communications among researchers and with practitioners. Use of more rigorous standards by editors of research journals in the field would also help to make clear the characteristics of subjects and other matters of research, thus facilitating meta-analyses and generalization of findings.

In addition to these practical difficulties it is possible to identify evidence of a growing theoretical discourse about the nature of research in the field of special education (Barton 1988, Stainback and Stainback 1984a). Specifically, researchers in a number of countries have drawn attention to the limitations of psychological perspectives that emphasize quantitative methodologies. Their analysis leads them to argue for a move towards a greater use of qualitative methods of inquiry. Stainback and Stainback (1984a) suggest that such a move could lead to the development of better-grounded theories and more attention being given to the social and educational relevance of research activities. It would also be welcomed, they argue, by teachers who would find this orientation less intimidating and more relevant to their day-to-day concerns.

7.2 Support for Research

Only rarely has significant support been provided for research on special education topics. The UNESCO survey found that approximately one-third of countries responding allocated separate national funds for research and development in special education. The research topics cited with greatest frequency were integration, early intervention, the organization of special education, the transition from school to adult life, and incidence surveys. The United States government launched a limited program of research in 1957 that has grown steadily in succeeding years. The program operates mainly on an extramural basis:

the federal government gives grants and contracts to outside agencies such as universities, public schools, and state departments of education that compete for funds within priority areas targeted by federal officers. Even in the most prosperous environments, however, support for research is minimal.

7.3 Evaluation

The field of special education has so far failed to provide impressive data concerning merits of its programs. For example, efficacy studies concerning special classes for students who are mentally retarded have had equivocal outcomes, but reviewers uniformly find faults with the research methods and discount findings accordingly. However, more recent meta-analytic studies offer little more convincing evidence for the value of special educational programs. In a 1979 review of efficacy research, Semmel et al. concluded that the evidence does not show advantages for special education placements as compared with results when disabled students remain in regular school programs. A summary report by Dunn (1968) under the title "Special education for the mildly retarded: Is much of it justifiable?" was very negative about outcomes of some special education and caused a broad flow of criticism in the United States.

Broadly framed evaluation studies are very difficult to conduct with precision. In cases of severe disability, special education programs often represent the only opportunity available for education. Whether programs for mildly disabled pupils which involve separation from regular classes and schools are distinctly beneficial for students is a cause of widespread debate in the United States (Will 1986).

8. International Activities

Since the International Year of Disabled Persons (1981) there has been considerable international collaboration with respect to the development of special education policies and programs. Agencies such as UNESCO, UNICEF, and OECD have acted to encourage collaborative developments and many national agencies have invested resources to give them support. The World Declaration on Education for All that arose as a result of the 1990 conference in Jomtien, Thailand, gives further impetus to these efforts. In Article 3.5, it states: "The learning needs of the disabled demand special attention. Steps need to be taken to provide equal access to education to every category of disabled persons as an integral part of the education system."

This challenge is enormous, particularly in developing countries.

Preferred ways of conducting international efforts remain a matter of debate. For example, Miles (1989) questions the value of introducing Western models of special education into countries such as Pakistan and India. He suggests that the reasons they often do not seem to work are complex and include "conceptual blockage." He notes that Western special education is constructed on views of children and the purposes of schooling that may be largely alien to much of the population of the Indian subcontinent. Furthermore, he is critical of the work of advisers visiting Third World countries as part of what he characterizes as the "Western conceptual crusade" that seems to ignore the realities of Third World situations.

At the International Consultation on Special Education (UNESCO 1988a) participants reviewed and assessed international developments related to special education over the previous decade. They also made suggestions concerning the focus of actions to be taken. Conscious of the magnitude of the problems, and committed to the principles of normalization, integration, and participation, they recommended that the complementary approaches of community-based rehabilitation (CBR) and integrated education represented the most effective ways forward.

Community-based rehabilitation is being used by an increasing number of developing countries as a strategy to eliminate the constraints of institution-based rehabilitation. Its implementation in a particular context will depend to a large extent upon a country's strategies for socioeconomic development. Countries often start by setting up a CBR project in a selected district, which provides the basis for gaining national experience and expertise. This is followed by the launching of a wider program, possibly as part of a national plan. Werner (1987) provides an impressive manual of suggestions for setting up such initiatives in rural communities including examples of child-to-child activities. These are intended to encourage school-aged children to help their disabled peers. Approaches developed for use in Third World contexts mirror some of the techniques now being used to create inclusive schools in the West (e.g., Lipsky and Gartner 1989). Both emphasize collaboration, including cooperative learning approaches, as a means of utilizing existing resources for problem solving in educational contexts.

With respect to international efforts to encourage integrated education, a number of interesting initiatives exist. For example, Freeze and Rampaul (1991) describe a development project in Trinidad and Tobago involving the Ministry of Education, the University of Manitoba, and the Canadian International Development Agency. Their approach involves training administrators and teachers in a consultative–collaborative model for providing support to teachers in regular schools. As a result many schools have established resource programs resulting in the integration of previously segregated students.

The UNESCO project "Special Needs in the Classroom" aims to develop and disseminate ideas and materials that can be used by teacher educators to support teachers in mainstream schools (Ainscow 1990). The project materials have been developed through a process of international collaboration and are contained in a resource pack intended to be used as part of pre- and inservice staff development programs. Emphasis is placed on approaches to teaching whole classes that accommodate pupil diversity. During 1990 and 1991 the resource pack was tested in pilot projects by an international team in eight countries (Canada, Chile, India, Jordan, Kenya, Malta, Spain, and Zimbabwe). UNESCO intends to widen this project by using the existing resource team to mount regional initiatives throughout the world.

Additional assistance to the process of international collaboration is provided by a number of professional organizations. The division of International Special Education and Services of the Council for Exceptional Children (in Reston, Virginia, USA) serves as a catalyst for international sharing of promising practices, research, and technology. The International Association of Special Education, through its publications and biannual conferences, fulfills a similar role.

9. Problems and Issues

From this survey of international developments it is possible to draw out a number of important problems and issues that require urgent attention. While the field of special education has made much progress, an analysis of the scene around the world presents a disturbing picture. Hegarty (1990) states: "Those with disabilities, who ironically have the greatest need of education, are the least likely to receive it. This is true of developed and developing countries alike" (p. 2). In developed countries many pupils with disabilities, and others who fail to achieve satisfactory progress in school learning, are formally excluded from the mainstream education system or receive less favorable treatment within it than other children. On the other hand, in many developing countries the continuing struggle to achieve compulsory education for a majority of children takes precedence over meeting the needs of those with disabilities.

The UNESCO Consultation on Special Education (1988a) outlined a number of general obstacles to improvement. These are:

(a) inadequate perceptions and thus policy formation, which is linked to attitudes (cultural, religious, political, or ideological);

(b) rigid legislative and administrative provision, especially as related to characterization of disability and categorical allocation of resources often not matched to individual needs;

(c) the discrepancy between what exists and present knowledge of what should exist due to poor dissemination of knowledge.

(d) the fact that special education in some countries is still perceived as a charitable venture—a welfare program—and responsibility for special education is not always with educational authorities;

(e) administrative and professional separation that continues to divide the educational community into "special" and "regular" components isolated from each other.

As the international field of special education continues to move forward, there has emerged a new set of voices arguing for further reform. These voices reflect developments in different parts of the world. While inevitably they are not in full agreement with respect to their analysis and recommendations, they all adopt a critical perspective, seeking to question the field's theories and assumptions. Examples of writers sharing this perspective include in Australia, Fulcher (1989); in the United Kingdom, Tomlinson (1982); in New Zealand, Ballard (1990); and in the United States Skrtic (1991) and Reynolds et al. (1987). They all draw on theories from outside special education, such as sociology, politics, philosophy, and organizational analysis. Their work, and that of others adopting similar stances, offers a more radical analysis of the policy and practice of special education and points to new possibilities for reform.

One of their concerns is with the way pupils within schools come to be designated as having special needs. They see this as a social process that needs to be continually challenged. More specifically, they argue that the continued emphasis on explaining educational difficulties in terms of child-centered characteristics has the effect of preventing progress in the field. The argument is summed up by Dyson (1990) who states: "The fact remains that the education system as a whole, and the vast majority of institutions and teachers within it, are approaching the twenty-first century with a view of special needs the same as that with which their counterparts approached the present century. That view, for all its avowed concern for the individual child, promotes injustice on a massive scale. It demands to be changed" (pp. 60–61). This radical perspective leads to a reconceptualization of the special needs task (Ainscow 1991). This suggests that progress in the field is dependent upon a general recognition that difficulties experienced by pupils come about as a result of the way schools are organized and the forms of teaching that are provided. In other words, as Skrtic puts it, students with special needs are artifacts of the traditional curriculum.

The way forward must be to reform schools in ways that will make them respond positively to pupil diversity, seeing individual differences as something to be nurtured and celebrated. Within such a conceptualization, a consideration of difficulties experienced by pupils and teachers can provide an agenda for reform and insights as to how this might be accomplished. However, this kind of approach is only possible where there exists a respect for individuality and a culture of collaboration that encourages and supports problem-solving. Such cultures are likely to facilitate the learning of all pupils and, with them, the professional learning of all teachers. Ultimately, therefore, increasing equity is the key to improvements in schooling for all.

See also: Children and Youth with Special Needs, Diagnosis and Classification of

References

Adams F (ed.) 1986 *Special Education.* Councils and Education Press, Harlow

Ainscow M 1990 Special needs in the classroom: The development of a teacher education resourse pack. *International Journal of Special Education* 5(1): 13–20

Ainscow M (ed.) 1991 *Effective Schools for All.* Paul H Brookes, Fulton, London

Ballard K D 1990 Special education in New Zealand: Disability, politics and empowerment. *International Journal of Disability, Development and Education* 37(2): 109–24

Barton L 1988 Research practice: The need for alternative perspectives. In: Barton L (ed.) 1988 *The Politics of Special Education.* Falmer, Lewes

Dunn L 1968 Special education for the mildly retarded—Is much of it justifiable? *Excep. Child.* 35(1): 5–22

Dyson A 1990 Special educational needs and the concept of change. *Oxford Rev. of Educ.* 16(1): 55–66

Freeze D R, Rampaul W 1991 Consultative–collaborative resource teaching as a means of improving special education service delivery. In: Upton G (ed.) 1991 *Staff Training and Special Educational Needs.* Fulton, London

Fulcher G 1989 *Disabling Policies? A Comparative Approach to Education Policy and Disability.* Falmer Lewes

Hegarty S 1990 *The Education of Children and Young People with Disabilities: Principles and Practice.* UNESCO, Paris

Heller K A, Holtzman W H, Messick S (eds.) 1982 *Placing Children in Special Education: A Strategy for Equity.* National Academy Press, Washington, DC

Lakin K L, Krantz G C, Bruininks R H, Clumpner J L, Hill B K 1982 One hundred years of data on populations of public residential facilities for mentally retarded people. *Am. J. Mental Deficiency* 87(1): 1–8

Larry P v Riles 1972 495 Supp 926, US District Court for Northern District of California

Lipsky D K, Gartner A 1989 *Beyond Separate Education: Quality Education for All.* Paul H Brookes, Baltimore, Maryland

Meyer L, Peck C, Brown L (eds.) 1991 *Critical Issues in the Lives of People with Severe Disabilities.* Paul H Brookes, Baltimore, Maryland

Miles M 1989 The role of special education in information based rehabilitation. *International Journal of Special Education* 4(2): 111–18

Pijl S J, Meijer C J W 1991 Does intergration count for much? An analysis of the practices of integration in eight countries. *European Journal of Special Needs Education* 6(2): 100–11

Reynolds M C 1962 A framework for considering some issues in special education. *Except. Child.* 28(7): 367–70

Reynolds M C, Wang M C, Walberg H W 1987 The necessary restructuring of special and regular education. *Excep. Child.* 53(5): 391–98

Ross D H 1988 *Educating Handicapped Young People in Eastern and Southern Africa in 1981–88.* UNESCO, Paris

Semmel M I, Gottlieb J, Robinson N M 1979 Mainstreaming: Perspectives on educating handicapped children in the public schools. In: Berliner D C (ed.) 1979 *Review of Research in Education 7: 223–79.* American Educational Research Association, Washington, DC

Skrtic T M 1991 *Behind Special Education: A Critical Analysis of Professional Culture and School Organization.* Love, Denver, Colorado

Stainback S, Stainback W 1984a Broadening the research perspective in special education. *Excep. Child.* 50(5): 400–408

Stainback W, Stainback S 1984b A rationale for the merger of special and regular education. *Excep. Child.* 51: 102–111

Taylor S J 1988 Caught in the continuum: A critical analysis of the principles of the least restrictive environment. *Journal of the Association for Persons with Severe Handicaps* 13(1): 41–53

Tomlinson S 1982 *A Sociology of Special Education.* Routledge, London

Tucker J A (ed.) 1985 Curriculum-based assessment. *Except. Child.* 52(3)

UNESCO 1988a UNESCO *Consultation on Special Education: Final Report.* UNESCO, Paris.

UNESCO 1988b *Review of the Present Situation in Special Education.* UNESCO, Paris.

US Department of Education 1990 *Twelfth Annual Report to Congress on the Implementation of the Education of the Handicapped Act.* US Department of Education, Washington, DC

US Office of Education 1969 *The Education Professions.* US Government Printing Office, Washington, DC

Wang M C, Reynolds M C, Walberg H J 1986 Rethinking special education. *Educ. Leadership* 44(1): 26–31

Werner D 1987 *Disabled Village Children.* The Hesperian Foundation, Palo Alto, California

Will M 1986 *Educating Students with Learning Problems —A Shared Responsibility.* US Department of Education, Washington, DC

Yanok J 1986 Free appropriate public education for handicapped children: Congressional intent and judicial interpretation. *Remedial and Special Education* 72: 49–53

Zappolo A, Lakin K C, Hill B K 1990 Persons in institutions and special residential settings. In: Fitzgerald I, Thompson S (eds.) 1990 *Disability in the United States.* Springer, New York

Further Reading

Ainscow M 1989 *Special Education in Change.* Fulton Cambridge Institute of Education, London

British Journal of Special Education

Exceptional Children

International Journal of Special Education

Journal of Special Education

Scheerenberger R C 1983 *A History of Mental Retardation.* Paul H Brookes, Baltimore, Maryland

Special Children

Wang M C, Reynolds M C, Walberg H J 1987–91 *Handbook of Special Education: Research and Practice.* Pergamon, Oxford

Williams P 1991 *The Special Education Handbook.* Open University, Milton Keynes

Lifespan Development

J. Heckhausen

The scope and potential of ontogenetic change in humans is larger than in any other species. During childhood and adolescence, but also throughout adulthood and old age, humans show impressive capacity for adaptation to new life ecologies and challenges (see, e.g., Brim and Kagan 1980). It is the unique human adaptive capacity that enables children as well as adults to learn from their parents, teachers, mentors, and other socialization agents. Only by way of human capacity for ontogenetic change can knowledge and skills be transferred from generation to generation. Lifespan developmental potential, thus, is the foundation of human culture and civilization.

1. From Child Psychology to Lifespan Psychology

Traditional and everyday conceptions view development as a unidirectional process toward improvement or growth, which produces long-term and not easily reversible outcomes. Such unidirectional growth conceptions of development stem from a preoccupation of developmental research with infancy and childhood, which has been typical of scientific research and commonsense conceptions. However, pioneers of a view encompassing lifespan development existed even in the eighteenth and nineteeth centuries (see review in Baltes et al. 1980) and early in the twentieth century (e.g., Bühler 1933, Jung 1933).

More recently, a number of research streams in different social sciences disciplines have converged to generate a new and interdisciplinary field of scientific inquiry: lifespan development (see Sørensen et al. 1986). Pioneers of a lifespan developmental perspective in the early and mid-twentieth century included both European and United States scholars, but their impact was limited until multiple institutions and disciplines joined forces. Institutional support came from a number of research centers (e.g., the universities at Bonn, Chicago, Pennsylvania State, Southern California, Syracuse, West Virginia, Wayne State) that devoted programs to lifespan development, which led to a series of conferences, conference proceedings, and annual series, such as *Life-span Development and Behavior* (see overview in Baltes et al. 1980). An important impetus was provided by a number of longitudinal studies, which had begun with large samples of children before the Second World War, and were able to target these populations in their adult years by the 1960s and 1970s (see review in Honzik 1984).

Another influential factor in the evolution of a lifespan developmental approach was the shift in population demographics toward an increasing proportion of old and very old individuals. This shift gave rise to gerontology as a new field of scientific inquiry (e.g., Birren 1964). Although gerontology took a stance against negative stereotype views of aging, the empirical evidence conveys a different message. In contrast to child-developmental research, gerontological research predominantly demonstrated age-related processes of decline in psychological functioning (e.g., Salthouse 1985).

Converging movements in other social sciences fields were particularly salient in sociology and social history (see historical review in Featherman 1983). First, the age stratification model (Riley 1987) in sociology interrelates dynamics on two levels: individual life-course processes and societal changes. The interface of typically asynchronic processes of individual aging and social change bring about new patterns of aging and change in social structure. Age stratification is conveyed by societal institutions (e.g., state-regulated entry age for school, seniority-based promotion rules) and age-normative conceptions internalized by the members of a given society (Hagestad and Neugarten 1985, Neugarten and Datan 1973).

Second, research on family history emerged from an interface of social demography and social history traditions. Such research made use of archive data to identify links between historical changes, birth cohorts, individuals' age at the time of a historical shift, and subsequent life courses, personality, and family structure (e.g., Elder 1980). In addition, long-term societal changes in life-course and family patterns were identified.

Third, socialization is a joint research arena for sociology and developmental psychology. Socialization refers to the processes involved in individuals' acquisition and modification of those values, beliefs and behavior regarded as appropriate by a given community or society. During the mid-1960s socialization research was extended beyond childhood to encompass adolescence and the adult lifespan (Brim and Wheeler 1966). Moreover, differences in social class were accounted for by class-differential successions of roles and role sequences (Clausen 1972), and differential impacts of work environments and activities on personality change (Kohn and Schooler 1983).

2. Basic Concepts of Lifespan Psychology

In contrast to unidirectional models of development, lifespan developmental psychology views development as a process involving both growth and decline (see also Bühler 1933, Erikson 1959, Levinson et al. 1978), thus yielding a multidirectional conception of

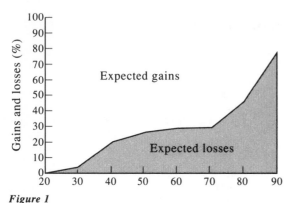

Figure 1
Age-related shifts in expected gains (increase in desirable attitudes) across the adult lifespan
Source: Heckhausen et al. 1989

development (Baltes 1987). According to the lifespan perspective, developmental growth and decline are not merely age-period-specific phenomena of change (e.g., growth in childhood, decline in old age), but instead occur concurrently (Baltes 1987). Decline on one dimension might be accompanied by growth on another dimension (gain–loss dynamic).

Advances in lifespan developmental theory have taken the notion of gain–loss dynamic one step further, in proposing that even a single event of developmental change typically involves aspects of growth as well as decline (Baltes 1987). In language acquisition, for instance, articulation skills in a given language are acquired at the expense of losing the ability to utter sounds that are not part of the language learned (Levelt 1989). This example illustrates selectivity as a fundamental causal mechanism in developmental gain–loss dynamics. Precisely because the scope of human behavior and development is extensive, developmental processes have to be selective in fostering growth in some, but not other, domains of functioning. Growth can occur only if resources are selectively invested at the expense of options that are not chosen. Therefore, gains in one aspect will always imply losses in others. The fundamental characteristic of lifespan development can, therefore, be captured in the concept of "selective optimization" (Baltes and Baltes 1990).

Processes of selective optimization can be identified not only as active choices on the part of the individual, but also operate on the societal level. Society provides age-graded and age-sequential structures of opportunities and constraints, which channel individuals along certain life-course patterns (Hagestad and Neugarten 1985, Kohli and Meyer 1986, Mayer and Huinink 1990). Age-normative challenges in development are captured by Havighurst's (1952) concept of "developmental task."

Along with biological processes of maturation and aging these societal influences comprise the set of *age-graded* conditions of development (Baltes 1987). Age-graded conditions also depend on cultural and historical factors, and are thus subject to *history-graded* influences. Finally, *nonnormative* events, which are irregular in their occurrence and timing represent a third class of important influences on individual development.

3. Lifespan Development and Lifespan Education

The process of aging brings about a continuous decrease in reserve capacity. While the chances for growth decrease with age, the risks for decline increase. This shifting ratio between gains and losses is also reflected in laypersons' conceptions about development in adulthood (Heckhausen et al. 1989). Figure 1 displays the expectations of young, middle-aged, and old adults about desirable and undesirable changes at various age levels. While mostly developmental gains are expected during early adulthood, increasing risks for losses are anticipated in old age.

With increasing age, the individual has to compensate actively to maintain previous levels of functioning in the face of aging-related decline. Compensation can be achieved in two ways. First, the individual can sharpen the selectivity of resource investment by focusing more exclusively on a certain domain. In this way, more resources can be invested and thus the level of functioning may be maintained. Second, the individual can resort to specific compensatory means, such as technical aids or other people's help. Baltes and Baltes (1990) have captured the fundamental strategies of selection and compensation in their model of "selective optimization with compensation."

The concept of "developmental reserve capacity" (Baltes 1987, Kliegl et al. 1989) plays a key role in the interface between models of lifespan development and lifespan education. Developmental reserve capacity determines the range of plasticity in performance, and thus demarcates the potential of instructional interventions. Cognitive training research with older adults has shown that, although there are important interindividual differences (Weinert et al. 1988), and although older individuals can improve their performance substantially, there are clear limits of functioning (Kliegl et al. 1989). In fluid intelligence tasks old adults never attained the level of performance achieved by young adults, especially under conditions of severe time constraints. Similar "testing-the-limits" approaches may be used to gauge the developmental potential in children (Brown and French 1979), and thus help to design appropriate curricula, age-related timetables, and strategies for instruction in formal (e.g., school) as well as more informal (e.g., family) contexts.

See also: Human Development in the Lifespan: Overview; Development of Learning across the Lifespan; Human Development: Research Methodology

References

Baltes P B 1987 Theoretical propositions of life-span developmental psychology: On the dynamics between growth and decline. *Dev. Psychol.* 23(5): 611–26

Baltes P B, Baltes M M 1990 Psychological perspectives on successful aging: The model of selective optimization with compensation. In: Baltes P B, Baltes M M (eds.) 1990 *Successful Aging: Perspectives from the Behavioral Sciences*. Cambridge University Press, New York

Baltes P B, Reese H W, Lipsitt L P 1980 Life-span developmental psychology. *Annu. Rev. Psychol.* 31: 65–110

Birren J E 1964 *The Psychology of Aging*. Prentice-Hall, Englewood Cliffs, New Jersey

Brim O G Jr., Kagan J (eds.) 1980 *Constancy and Change in Human Development*. Harvard University Press, Cambridge, Massachusetts

Brim O G Jr., Wheeler S (eds.) 1966 *Socialization After Childhood: Two Essays*. Wiley, New York

Brown A L, French L A 1979 The zone of potential development: Implications for intelligence testing in the year 2000. *Intelligence* 3(3): 255–77

Bühler C 1933 *Der menschliche Lebenslauf als psychologisches Problem*. Psychologische Monographien 4. Hirzel, Leipzig

Clausen J 1972 The life course of individuals. In: Riley M W, Johnson M, Foner A (eds.) 1972 *Aging and Society. Vol. 3: A Sociology of Age Stratification*. Russell Sage Foundation, New York

Elder G H Jr. 1980 History and the life course. In: Bertaux D (ed.) 1980 *Biography and Society: The Life History Approach in the Social Sciences*. Sage, Beverly Hills, California

Erikson E H 1959 Identity and the life cycle. *Psychol. Iss.* 1(1): 167–71

Featherman D L 1983 Life-span perspectives in social sciences research. In: Baltes P B, Brim O G Jr. (eds.) 1983 *Life-span Development and Behavior*, Vol. 5. Academic Press, New York

Hagestad G O, Neugarten B L 1985 Age and the life course. In: Binstock R H, Shanas E (eds.) 1985 *Handbook of Aging and the Social Sciences*. Van Nostrand Reinhold, New York

Havighurst R J 1952 *Developmental Tasks and Education*. Mckay, New York

Heckhausen J, Dixon R A, Baltes P B 1989 Gains and losses in development throughout adulthood as perceived by different adult age groups. *Dev. Psychol.* 25(1): 109–21

Honzik M P 1984 Life-span development. *Annu. Rev. Psychol.* 35: 309–31

Jung C G 1933 *Modern Man in Search of a Soul*. Harcourt, Brace & World, New York

Kliegl R, Smith J, Baltes P B 1989 Testing-the-limits and the study of adult age differences in cognitive plasticity of a mnemonic skill. *Dev. Psychol.* 25(2): 247–56

Kohli M, Meyer J W (eds.) 1986 Social structure and social construction of life stages. *Hum. Dev.* 29(3): 145–80

Kohn M L, Schooler C 1983 *Work and Personality: An Inquiry into the Impact of Social Stratification*. Ablex, Norwood, New Jersey

Levelt W J M 1989 *Speaking: From Intention to Articulation*. MIT Press, Cambridge, Massachusetts

Levinson D J et al. 1978 *The Seasons of a Man's Life*. Knopf, New York

Mayer K-U, Huinink J 1990 Age, period, and cohort in the study of the life course: A comparison of classical APC analysis with event history analysis or farewell to lexis. In: Magnusson D (ed.) 1990 *Data Quality*. Cambridge University Press, Cambridge

Neugarten B L, Datan N 1973 Sociological perspectives on the life cycle. In: Baltes P B, Schaie K W (eds.) 1973 *Life-span Developmental Psychology: Personality and Socialization*. Academic Press, New York

Riley M W 1987 On the significance of age in sociology. *Am. Sociol. Rev.* 52: 1–14

Salthouse T A 1985 *A Theory of Cognitive Aging* Advances in Psychology Vol. 28. North-Holland, Amsterdam

Sørensen A B, Weinert F E, Sherrod L R (eds.) 1986 *Human Development and the Life Course*. Erlbaum, Hillsdale, New Jersey

Weinert F E, Schneider W, Knopf M 1988 Individual differences in memory development across the life span. In: Baltes P B, Featherman D L, Lerner R M (eds.) 1988 *Life-span Development and Behavior*, Vol. 9. Erlbaum, Hillsdale, New Jersey

Adulthood and Old Age

K. W. Schaie

The marked prolongation of the human lifespan in the twentieth century has led to an increased interest in the educational needs of adults and aging individuals. This entry discusses some of the demographic issues arising from greater aging within industrialized societies, describes major themes of psychological development from young adulthood to old age, and considers the resulting educational implications.

1. Historical Overview

The study of human aging is of relatively recent vintage within the developmental sciences. Although James McKeen Cattell published his treatise *Senescence* in 1922, very little serious work in adult development appeared prior to the 1950s. Many developmental researchers were primarily interested in discovering how individual behavior is acquired early in life. Only slowly did interest in behavioral growth advance from childhood into adolescence; there remains some reluctance to tackle the complexities of behavioral maintenance, change, and decline in adulthood. It was common to suppose that age-related changes in adulthood would be few. Personality was thought to be firmly set as maturity was reached. For, as long as divorce and mid-life career changes were rare phenomena, family and career decisions were made early in life and then maintained. Intellectual abilities were believed to peak early and decline with age; sexual prowess was thought to wane. Yet until the twentieth century few people survived into old age, so these matters could not be examined in depth.

Advances in sanitation, nutrition, and medical knowledge have changed life expectancy dramatically throughout the world. In the industrialized countries, a child born in 1900 could not have expected to reach the age of 50; now average life expectancy in the same countries is approaching 80 years. While at the beginning of the twentieth century fewer than 5 percent of the population attained the age of 65 (often considered as the threshold of old age), comparable figures now range from 12 to 20 percent. These population shifts are not simply due to improvement in medical care and life-styles but also to substantial declines in fertility rates. These rates have not only been affected markedly by the introduction of reliable methods of family planning but also by periods of war, economic expansion, and economic declines. Thus "baby boom" generations are often followed by "baby bust" generations, causing alterations in many behavioral patterns. For example, saving practices in Japan in the 1980s may well have been a function of a "baby boom" generation at its highest earning potential; this may be followed by increased consumption as these baby boomers age. The succession of a baby bust generation following the baby boomers in the United States is likewise thought to threaten the viability of the social insurance system.

The acceleration of technological change has made it quite likely that most persons will experience many job and career changes during their working lives. The rise in both the proportion and the absolute number of older persons in the population will engender a number of structural changes in society. These individuals will have to be better integrated into the social fabric so that more of them can continue to participate actively. Better health and higher levels of education will increase pressures for greater availability of educational opportunities throughout the adult lifespan (Schaie 1982).

2. Adult Cognitive Development

Most cognitive skills reach a peak by early or middle adulthood, maintain a plateau until the late fifties or early sixties, and then begin to show decline. The decline is slow at first but accelerates as the late seventies are reached. Some individuals, however, retain their behavioral competence well into advanced old age, while others show early decline (Cunningham 1987, Labouvie-Vief 1985, Schaie 1996, Willis 1985). Although the applicability of laboratory and academic tests to everyday problems has been questioned, strong

relationships between these measures and competence on everyday tasks have been demonstrated (Willis and Schaie 1986).

Five major questions can be asked about the course of adult cognitive development for which well-supported answers can be provided. These questions are as follows: (a) Do cognitive skills change uniformly through adulthood or are there different life-course ability patterns? (b) At what age is there a reliably detectable age decrement in ability, and what is the magnitude of that decrement? (c) What are the patterns of generational differences, and what is their magnitude? (d) What accounts for individual differences in age-related change in adulthood? (e) Can cognitive decline in old age be reversed? Each of these questions has educational implications which will also be considered.

2.1 Differential Patterns of Change

Age-related changes are not uniform across all cognitive skills: studies of overall IQ or of particular aspects of memory have therefore been found insufficient to monitor age changes and age differences over the adult life course for either individuals or groups. Verbal abilities continue to increase into late mid-life and are maintained well into old age, while novel tasks of an abstract nature (sometimes called "fluid" abilities) show at an early stage age differences favoring younger adults (Horn 1982, Schaie 1996, Siegler 1983). Patterns differ, however, by gender and specific cognitive skill. For example, fluid abilities begin to decline earlier, but verbal abilities appear to show steeper decrement once the late 70s are reached (Schaie 1996). Older learners are consistently better at recognition of information than at its recall. Well-established knowledge structures often tend to compensate for the disadvantages incurred by the perceptual and motor slowing that gradually affect the performance of most individuals past mid-life.

2.2. Age Level and Magnitude of Age-related Cognitive Decline

Cross-sectional studies with the Wechsler Adult Intelligence Scale (WAIS) suggest that significant age differences favoring young adults can be found by the thirties for performance tests and by the sixties for verbal tests (Matarazzo 1972). By contrast, longitudinal studies rarely find reliable age decrement prior to age 60, but observe average decline for all cognitive skills at least by age 74 (Schaie 1996). Analyses of individual differences in intellectual change, however, demonstrate that even at age 81 less than half of all observed individuals showed reliable decremental change over the preceding seven years (Schaie 1984).

Average age-related decrement until age 60 amounts to less than 20 percent of a population standard deviation (a relatively trivial amount), but by age

81 average decrement amounts to at least 1 standard deviation for most intellectual abilities (i.e., all but a small number of persons of this age perform at a level below the average of young adults.

2.3 Generational Differences

The existence of generational (cohort) differences in intellectual abilities has been conclusively demonstrated (Flynn 1984, Willis 1989). Almost linear positive cohort-shifts have been observed for inductive reasoning, with more spasmodic positive shifts for verbal ability and spatial orientation. A curvilinear cohort pattern has been found for number skills, which in the studies reported by Willis (1989) reached a peak for birth cohorts born in the 1920s and then followed a largely negative slope. A similar curvilinear cohort pattern has also been observed for word fluency (Schaie 1996). As a consequence, cross-sectional studies of intellectual aging tend to underestimate age changes prior to age 60 for abilities with negative generational trends and to overestimate age changes for abilities with positive generational trends.

2.4 Individual Differences in Age-related Change in Adulthood

Individual differences in cognitive skills are, of course, large at all ages, such that substantial overlap among different age groups can be found from young adulthood into the mid-1970s (Schaie 1988). Very few individuals decline on all or most abilities. Indeed, maintenance of functioning on one or more abilities is characteristic for most individuals well into advanced old age (Schaie 1989a).

A number of factors have been identified that account for individual differences in age-related change, some of which have been shown to be amenable to experimental intervention. Variables found to be predictive of favorable cognitive aging include: (a) absence of cardiovascular and other chronic disease; (b) favorable environment as indicated by high socioeconomic status (SES); (c) involvement in a complex and intellectually stimulating environment; (d) flexible personality style at mid-life; (e) high cognitive status of spouse; and (f) maintenance of level of perceptual processing speed.

2.5 Reversibility of Cognitive Decline

Unless neurological pathology is present, cognitive interventions may serve to remediate known intellectual decline, and reduce generational differences in those individuals who have remained stable in their own performance over time but who have become disadvantaged when compared to younger persons. The effectiveness of educational interventions has been demonstrated in various laboratory studies (Schaie and Willis 1986, Willis 1987). Cognitive decline in many older people may well be due to disuse of specific skills and can be reversed by appropriate training regimens. In one of the studies by Schaie and Willis, five hours of cognitive strategy training resulted in significant improvement for two-thirds of experimental subjects over age 65, and about 40 percent of those who had declined significantly over 14 years were returned to their predecline level (Schaie and Willis 1986). Further studies are needed to assess whether educational intervention would be most effective by teaching cognitive strategies on basic ability skills or by training on specific everyday tasks. Cognitive training has been shown to be ability-specific. Because most everyday tasks involve components of basic abilities, training on multiple abilities might therefore be required. On the other hand, it is unlikely that training on specific everyday tasks would generalize to substantively different tasks (see Willis 1987, 1992 for further discussion).

3. Personality Development in Adulthood

In contrast to the age changes observed in cognitive skills across the lifespan, the evidence on personality development is one of remarkable stability. With few exceptions, observed age differences in personality traits turn out to be primarily differences between generations. In other words, societal shifts in early socialization and childrearing practices tend to contribute more to observed personality differences between young and old adults than do normative experiences encountered in adulthood.

There are several reasons why personality remains stable throughout adulthood for most persons. Traits, habits, modes of thinking, and the ways by which people cope and interact are all patterned in a unique fashion for each individual. Like any organized system, the adult personality resists change, since change in one aspect would require realignment in other interrelated parts. However, broad societal changes will also impact personality styles (Schmitz-Scherzer and Thomae 1983).

Once formed, adult personality is unlikely to change radically, even when stressful circumstances such as divorce, retirement, or impending death are encountered. Instead, personality traits established early in life determine how persons will respond to adult life stresses. For example, different reactions to retirement reflect earlier adjustment patterns. Individuals with well-integrated personalities experience little difficulty in what they see as the final stage of a series of successful life transitions. On the other hand, those with poorly integrated personalities may encounter the same event with despair and hostility; turning "sour" in the last stages of their life (Erikson 1982).

3.1 Personality Traits

Questionnaire-based studies of personality traits have been based primarily on cross-sectional studies; hence the age differences reported for them probably reflect primarily generational differences. Studies with the Minnesota Multiphasic Personality Inventory (MMPI) suggest that older age cohorts are more introverted. Both older men and women described themselves as more "masculine" than young adults. Young adults described themselves as more energetic, with attitudes that are more unusual and unconventional (Culligan et al. 1983). Questionnaire studies with other instruments, such as the California Personality Inventory (CPI), the Sixteen Personality Factor Questionnaire (16PF), the Guilford–Zimmerman Temperament Survey (GZTS), and the NEO (Neuroticism, Extraversion, and Openness) Personality Inventory show similar findings; traits tend to remain quite stable across adulthood. Most age differences represent generational shifts; and only few traits such as excitability and sociability increase with age (Gough 1969, McCrae and Costa 1987, Siegler et al. 1979, Schaie and Parham 1976). The limited observable change seems to occur largely in young adulthood, during the shift from student to employed status, and not during middle or old age (Kogan 1990).

3.2 The Self-concept

Although personality trait structure remains stable across adulthood, there have been reports of subtle changes in the self-concept. These changes involve the relative importance attributed to various life domains, in the elaboration of possible selves, and the strategies employed to preserve stability (Markus and Herzog 1992).

Traditional sex differences in self-concept are less evident as people get older. Young adult males describe themselves as more aggressive than older males, but older males were higher in cooperation and nurture. Younger women scored higher than younger men in cooperativeness, docility, and dependence. However, these differences disappeared with age; older men were only slightly more dominant than older women (Ryff 1984).

As people age, they tend to change the timing and methods of attaining a goal, they lower their expectations, and they are more ready to abandon an unattainable goal (Brim 1988). Assimilative strategies that involve active adjustment to current circumstances may be chosen in aversive situations in order to avoid depression and disappointment. Alternatively, accommodative strategies are selected in which the individual modifies desired outcomes to match current circumstances. These strategies are increasingly adopted by older adults and represent flexible adjustment to the realistic losses of old age (Brandstädter and Renner 1990).

Most would expect that body image—how a person feels about his or her physical sense—would shift across adulthood as persons age. Contrary to popular opinion, research findings suggest remarkable stability of body image, and the stereotype that older people consider themselves unattractive appears to be inaccurate (Crockett and Hummert 1987, Montepare and Lachman 1989).

Related to changes in self-concept is the maintenance of a sense of psychological well-being. This includes a sense of continued development over the life course, the capacity to maintain goals and a sense of purpose, as well as to maintain high-quality relationships with others. Empirical research on well-being in the later period of life suggest both gains and losses. There is an increase in self-acceptance and self-esteem, but a decline in the sense of personal growth and purpose in life. However, the latter may be offset by many by their capacity to accept change and by possessing a sense of humor (Ryff and Essex 1992).

3.3 Locus of Control

Considerable attention has been devoted to this construct since the 1980s because many mental and physical outcome variables have been identified that depend largely on the extent to which the individuals actually are and—even more importantly—perceive themselves to be in control of their lives and of the resources needed to make meaningful decisions about their life circumstances (Rodin et al. 1990). It has been argued that as adults age they experience an increasing number of life events over which they have little or no control. As a consequence, one might expect a decline with age in the belief in the possibility of control with a corresponding increase in the attribution of control to external factors. Lachman (1989) found changes in control beliefs to be quite domain-specific. Higher levels of belief in external control were found with respect to health and intelligence but not for generalized measures of control. This difference is important, since low internal control beliefs have been related to a depressive outlook in personality, and unfavorable appraisal of personal development and the attainment development of developmental goals (Brandstädter et al. 1987). Changes in control belief with age may also be implicated in age-related changes in coping strategies. Older adults have been found to use more passive and emotion-focused coping strategies in contrast to young adults, who use more active and problem-focused strategies. However, it is possible that the nature of stresses changes with age rather than the coping strategies used. In fact, situationally appropriate reduction in the number of coping strategies used by older persons seems to result in greater coping effectiveness (Meeks et al. 1989).

4. The Adult Learner

In a society marked by rapid technological change, education must continue throughout life for professional updating, inevitable career changes, and the maintenance of competence to deal with a changing society (Willis and Dubin 1990). The forms of postsecondary and adult education change over time, but some of the principles that distinguish the mature and older learner from the traditional young student clearly emerge from the psychological literature (Willis 1985).

First, it is most likely that older learners have had quantitatively less education than contemporary young adults (Willis 1989). Qualitative changes in methods of instruction may also place the re-entrant into formal education at some disadvantage. Second, cumulative physiological injuries to the central nervous system will result in slower response speed (Schaie 1989b), requiring greater redundancy in the exposure to educational materials and in the acquisition of new skills. Third, older learners often do not spontaneously use encoding strategies to process new information. Fourth, accumulated knowledge structures can often be used by older learners to compensate for age-related deficits, particularly when information is to be applied to everyday circumstances with which the older learner may have greater familiarity.

Educators can greatly enhance formal and informal learning in older individuals by understanding these principles and applying them to their practice. For example, although older learners hesitate to employ encoding strategies spontaneously, they are quite capable of using such strategies. Instructors can provide mnemonics to assist the recall of technical terms. Rehearsal may be used when the goal is to retain information in short-term memory, and organization strategies may be useful for encoding into long-term memory. It is particularly important that reading materials be well-organized for older learners. Research on text recall shows that older learners remember the gist of a well-organized text as well as younger people, but that age differences increase when key points in text are hard to identify (Hultsch and Dixon 1990). The increased use of examples in instructional material has also been found to be helpful. In assessing what has been learned, older persons are likely to be at less disadvantage when tests are based on recognition rather than recall.

Cognitive training studies of older persons (Schaie and Willis 1986, Willis 1987) have found that specific ability training (such as on the ability domains of inductive reasoning or spatial orientation) may enhance basic skills in those who have not declined but who are at a disadvantage when compared to younger learners because of the lesser educational experience they received in youth (cohort differences), as well as in those who have declined from previous levels due to disuse or lack of relevant intellectual stimulation. Cognitive training efforts are now being expanded to specific domains of everyday tasks or what is sometimes termed "practical intelligence" (Willis 1992).

Of course, older learners may be anxious about undertaking new learning, in part because of stereo-types that suggest older persons have poor memories and are poorer learners. Pretraining involving anxiety reduction may therefore be helpful for accelerated learning (Yesavage et al. 1989). Finally, gradual sensory losses in vision and hearing need to be compensated for by use of materials in larger print, by improving the acoustic environment, and by reduction in the speed of presentation, to compensate for slower rates of information processing.

Adulthood and old age represent three-fourths of the life span, a period to which educators have not devoted as much attention as it deserves. The increase in average lifespan as well as educational levels among the elderly, have created great opportunities for educational interventions throughout the course of life. These opportunities can be maximized by adapting the educational process to the changing needs and attributes of the mature and older learner.

See also: Lifespan Development; Adult Learning: An Overview; Development of Learning across the Lifespan

References

Brandstädter J R, Krampen G, Grewe W 1987 Personal control over development: Effects on the perception and emotional evaluation of personal development in adulthood. *International Journal of Behavioral Development.* 10(1): 99–120

Brandstädter J R, Renner G 1990 Tenacious goal pursuit and flexible goal adjustment: Explication and age-related analyses of assimilative and accommodative strategies of coping. *Psychology and Aging* 5(1): 58–67

Brim O G 1988 Losing and winning. *Psychol. Today* 34: 48–51

Crockett W H, Hummert M L 1987 Perceptions of aging and the elderly. In: Schaie K W (ed.) 1987

Culligan R C, Osborne D, Swenson W M, Offord K P 1983 *The MMPI: A Contemporary Normative Study.* Praeger, New York

Cunningham W R 1987 Intellectual abilities and age. In: Schaie K W (ed.) 1987

Erikson E H 1982 *The Life Cycle Completed: A Review.* Norton, New York

Flynn J R 1984 The mean IQ of Americans: Massive gains 1932–1978. *Psych. Bull.* 95(1): 29–51

Gough H G 1969 *Manual for the California Psychological Inventory.* Consulting Psychologists Press, Palo Alto, California

Horn J L 1982 The theory of fluid and crystallized intelligence in relation to concepts of cognitive psychology and aging in adulthood. In: Craik F I M, Trehub S (eds.) 1982 *Aging and Cognitive Processes.* Plenum Press, New York

Hultsch D F, Dixon R 1990 Learning and memory in aging. In: Birren J E, Schaie K W (eds.) 1990

Kogan N 1990 Personality and aging. In: Birren J E, Schaie K W (eds.) 1990

Labouvie-Vief G 1985 Intelligence and cognition. In: Birren J E, Schaie K W (eds.) 1985

Lachman M F 1989 Personality and aging at the crossroads: Beyond stability vs. change. In: Schaie K W, Schooler C (eds.) 1989 *Social Structure and Aging: Psychological*

Processes. Erlbaum, Hillsdale, New Jersey

Markus R L, Herzog A R 1992 The role of the self-concept in aging. In: Schaie K W (ed.) 1992

Matarazzo J D 1972 *Wechsler's Measurement and Appraisal of Adult Intelligence*, 5th edn. Williams and Wilkins, Baltimore, Maryland

McCrae R R, Costa P T Jr 1987 Validation of the five-factor model of personality across instruments and observers. *J. Pers. Soc. Psychol.* 52(1): 81–90

Meeks S, Carstensen L L, Tamsky B F, Wright T L, Pellegrini D 1989 Age differences in coping: Does less mean worse? *International Journal of Aging and Human Development.* 28(2): 127–40

Montepare J M, Lachman M E 1989 "You're only as old as you feel": Self-perceptions of age, fears of aging, and life satisfaction from adolescence to old age. *Psychology and Aging* 4(1): 173–78

Rodin J, Schooler C, Schaie K W (eds.) 1990 *Self-directedness: Cause and Effects Throughout the Life Course.* Erlbaum, Hillsdale, New Jersey

Ryff C D 1984 Personality development from the inside: The subjective experience of change in adulthood and aging. In: Baltes P B, Brim O G Jr (eds.) 1984 *Life-span Development and Behavior*, Vol. 6. Academic Press, New York

Ryff C D, Essex M J 1992 Psychological well-being in adulthood and old age: Descriptive markers and explanatory processes. In: Schaie K W (ed.) 1992

Schaie K W 1982 The aging in the coming decade. In: Schaie K W, Geiwitz J (eds.) 1982 *Reading in Adult Development and Aging.* Little, Brown & Co., Boston, Massachusetts

Schaie K W 1984 Midlife influences upon intellectual functioning in old age, *International Journal of Behavioral Development* 7(4): 463–78

Schaie K W 1988 Variability in cognitive function in the elderly: Implication for social participation. In: Woodhead M, Bender M, Leonard R (eds.) 1988 *Phenotylic Variation in Populations: Relevance to Risk Assessment.* Plenum Press, New York

Schaie K W 1989a The hazards of cognitive aging. *Gerontologist* 29(4): 484–93

Schaie K W 1989b Perceptual speed in adulthood: Cross-sectional and longitudinal studies. *Psychology and Aging* 5(2): 171

Schaie K W 1996 Intellectual development in adulthood. In: Birren J E, Schaie K W (eds.) 1996

Schaie K W, Parham I A 1976 Stability of adult personality traits: Fact or fable? *J.Pers. Soc. Psychol.* 34(1): 146–58

Schaie K W, Willis S L 1986 Can decline in adult intellectual functioning be reversed? *Dev. Psychol.* 22(2): 223–32

Schmitz-Scherzer R, Thomae H 1983 Constancy and change of behavior in old age: Findings from the Bonn longitudinal study. In: Schaie K W (ed.) 1983 *Longitudinal Studies of Adult Psychological Development.* Guilford Press, New York

Siegler I C 1983 Psychological aspects of the Duke Longitudinal Studies. In: Schaie K W (ed.) 1983 *Longitudinal Studies of Adult Psychological Development.* Guilford Press, New York

Siegler I C, George L K, Okun M A 1979 Cross-sequential analysis of adult personality. *Dev. Psychol.* 15(3): 350–61

Willis S L 1985 Towards an educational psychology of the older adult learner: Intellectual and cognitive bases. In: Birren J E, Schaie K W (eds.) 1985

Willis S L 1987 Cognitive training and everyday competence. In: Schaie K W (ed.) 1987

Willis S L 1989 Cohort differences in cognitive aging: A sample case. In: Schaie K W, Schooler C (eds.) 1989 *Social Structure and Aging: Psychological Processes.* Erlbaum, Hillsdale, New Jersey

Willis S L 1992 Cognition and everyday competence. In: Schaie K W (ed.) 1992

Willis S L, Dubin S S (eds.) 1990 *Maintaining Professional Competence.* Jossey-Bass, San Francisco, California

Willis S L, Schaie K W 1986 Practical intelligence in later adulthood. In: Sternberg R J, Wagner R K (eds.) 1986 *Practical Intelligence: Origins of Competence in the Everyday World.* Cambridge University Press, Cambridge

Yesavage J A, Lapp D, Sheick J A 1989 Mnemonics as modified for use by the elderly. In: Poon L W, Rubin D, Wilson B (eds.) 1989 *Everyday Cognition in Adulthood and Late Life.* Cambridge University Press, New York

Further Reading

Birren J E, Schaie K W (eds.) 1990 *Handbook of the Psychology of Aging*, 3rd edn. Academic Press, San Diego, California

Birren J E, Schaie K W (eds.) 1996 *Handbook of the Psychology of Aging*, 4th edn. Academic Press, San Diego, California

McCrae R R, Costa P T Jr 1984 *Emerging Lives, Enduring Dispositions: Personality in Adulthood.* Little, Brown & Co., Boston, Massachusetts

Oswald W D (ed.) 1991 *Handbuch der Gerontologie*, 2nd edn. Kohlhammer, Stuttgart

Schaie K W (ed.) 1987 *Annual Review of Gerontology and Geriatrics*, Vol. 7. Springer-Verlag, New York

Schaie K W (ed.) 1992 *Annual Review of Gerontology and Geriatrics*, Vol. 11. Springer-Verlag, New York

Schaie K W, Willis S L 1996 *Adult Development and Aging*, 4th edn. Harper Collins, New York

SECTION V

Biological Approaches to Human Development

Brain Development and Human Behavior

H. J. Markowitsch

The brain constitutes the principal tool for human existence and behavior. Its appropriate development depends on genetic prerequisites and on appropriate environmental stimulation throughout the growth period of the individual. From a number of investigations in nonhuman mammals, the following statement emerges as a permissible generalization, applicable also to human subjects: A particularly limited or biased stimulation may lead to irreparable damage or maladaptation of the brain, whereas a particularly well-arranged milieu may induce an outstandingly well-adapted individual.

1. The Neuronal Bases

At the earliest phase after birth the human central nervous system already contains all the necessary requirements for an optimal adaptation to the environment. Nonetheless, it is definitely not mature, that is, not in a final stage of function. Rather, in interaction with the environment, a number of necessary and important adaptations take place. The processes of neuronal shaping, brain tissue growth, axonal sprouting and synaptic contact formation need an adequate external stimulation, as has been found from a multitude of animal experiments.

For the layperson, probably the greatest surprise is that there is not only growth and expansion during the development of the nervous system, but—to a considerable degree—the opposite also, that is, an elimination of cellular elements. This elimination can be found for entire neurons as well as for cellular parts such as axons or synapses (Jessell 1991a, 1991b; Pritzel 1991). The mechanism of collateral pruning in particular, "defined as the loss of divergent branched projections without the death of the parent neuron, and also referred to as collateral or axon elimination"

(O'Leary 1992 p. 70) seems to be important for establishing the functional diversity of the mammalian neocortex.

Generally, brain development in mammals is characterized by numerous, in part precisely timed changes which start within the embryo, but continue during postnatal life. For humans, these alterations and adaptations continue for years and sometimes even for more than a decade during postnatal life, but have their major impact during the first months and years, when a number of critical periods exist which require a specific environmental input for an optimal development of the brain. The process of myelination is a good illustration of the continuous shaping of the neuronal network necessary for communication within the brain. As early as 1920, Flechsig investigated the process of myelination in detail; that is, the formation of isolating glial substance around axons that allows them to become functionally effective. Myelination is consequently regarded as an index of the maturity of structures from which axons project and to which they project.

While one inference to be drawn from this description is that the developing nervous system is in a quite labile and influenceable condition, another fundamental law governing the developing nervous system— the Kennard principle—has had a major impact since its formulation in the 1930s. Kennard studied and compared the effects of unilateral motor cortex lesions in infant and adult monkeys and found that early brain damage resulted in less severe behavioral deterioration than later damage (e.g., Kennard 1940). Although this principle received frequent support right up to the recent past, its relevance in a number of situations has been questioned (Kolb and Whishaw 1990, Kornhuber et al. 1985, Schneider 1979) so that it seems fair to state that early interventions may have beneficial or detrimental consequences on the brain's ability to control behavior. Whether the scales tip to one side or the other depends on the particular set of conditions prevailing at a given time.

2. Environment–Brain Interactions During Development

While the importance of adequate environmental stimulation, or conversely, the detrimental effects of environmental isolation for socialization have been described in a large number of sources ("Kaspar Hauser experiments"), the relevance and contribution of the environment for the functional integrity of the nervous system were demonstrated in the past mainly by animal experimentation especially in the visual modality.

Hubel and Wiesel (see Hubel 1988) and others described the anatomical and functional consequences of early visual deprivation in cats and monkeys (e.g., by dark rearing, or by suturing the eyelids shut). The spectrum of their results can be summarized by stating that whereas the visual system is genetically programmed to make normal connections and to respond normally, these programs do need adequate stimulation during early life to become functionally effective and stable. Deprivation, including selective environmental stimulation may permanently alter the neuronal responses and responsiveness to the environment. For instance, rearing kittens in an environment consisting exclusively of vertical stripes may later block their ability adequately to process horizontally arranged stimuli. Occasionally, even only hours of biased stimulation may have life-long effects (Kolb and Whishaw 1990). Deprivation, of course, may include nutritional deficiencies. Palti et al. (1985) found that early iron deficiency may have long-lasting effects on cognitive functioning.

Results from recent work with monkeys and human patients suggest that cortical plasticity is a lifelong process; thus stimulation of single fingers (Jenkins et. al. 1990) as well as surgical intervention to reinstablish finger-like limbs from webbed fingers (syndactyly) alters the cortical representation (Mogliner et al. 1993). These findings will be of special relevance for handicapped children, growing up with missing limbs, as they indicate that experience is crucial for brain adaption and that even the adult brain is capable of modification in accordance with environmental stimulation.

There is also considerable evidence that an "enriched" environment may have especially beneficial effects on brain development. Rosenzweig and coworkers (e.g., Rosenzweig 1984), among others, have found that providing rats with a socially and physically "luxurious" environment leads to a thickened cortical mantle, to more numerous synaptic contact areas and to further morphological changes which are indicative of more efficient information processing by the nervous system. For human beings, especially, it might

be appropriate to add the idea that enrichment should not simply be a diversification of the environment, but an appropriately structured and organized environment that enhances the likelihood of inducing relevant effects on the brain and the intellect.

On the other hand, if the necessary prerequisites on the neuronal level have failed to develop appropriately, as in cases of genetic deviations such as Down's Syndrome or fragile-X syndrome or in the case of patients who probably suffered from hypoxia during birth (Prior et al. 1984), even an extraordinarily superior environment will fail to induce a proper intellectual or social development.

Data combining modern brain-imaging techniques with neuropsychological tests have demonstrated that there is frequently a covariance between brain and behavior. As an example, some language- and learning-impaired children may have volume reductions in cortical and subcortical structures (Jernigan et al. 1991).

3. Conclusion

The mammalian and especially the human central nervous system has a considerable degree of plasticity which is greatest immediately postnatally. The nervous system requires constant interaction with the environment for proficient and effective activity during later life (Kolb and Whishaw 1989). This interaction extends from proper nutrition to appropriate sensory input and adequate social stimulation. Environmental stimulation influences processing capacities, including cognitive, intellectual, and social functions especially during critical periods and growth spurts (which occur up to puberty or even longer). Consequently, the effects of proper early stimulation on the child's brain cannot be overestimated.

References

Flechsig P 1920 *Anatomie des menschlichen Gehirns und Rückenmarks auf myelogenetischer Grundlage.* Georg Thieme, Leipzig

Hubel D H 1988 *Eye, Brain, and Vision.* Scientific American Library, New York

Jenkins W M, Merzenich M M, Ochs M T, Allard T, Guic-Robles E 1990 Functional reorganization of primary somatosensory cortex in adult owl monkey after behaviorally controlled tactile stimulation. *Journal of Neurophysiology* 63 (1): 82–104

Jernigan T L, Hesselink J R, Sowell E, Tallal P A 1991 Cerebral structure on magnetic resonance imaging in language-impaired and learning-impaired children. *Arch. Neurol.* 48 (5): 539–45

Jessell T M 1991a Cell migration and axonal guidance. In: Kandel E R, Schwartz J H, Jessell T M (eds.) 1991 *Principles of Neural Science*, 3rd edn. Elsevier, New York

Jessell T M 1991b Neuronal survival and synapse formation. In: Kandel E R, Schwartz J H, Jessell T M (eds.)

1991 *Principles of Neural Science*, 3rd edn. Elsevier, New York

Kennard M A 1940 Relation of age to motor impairment in man and sub-human primates. *A. M. A. Arch. Neurol. Psychiatry 44*: 377–97

Kolb B, Whishaw I Q 1989 Plasticity in the neocortex: Mechanisms underlying recovery from early brain damage. *Progr. Neurobiol.* 32: 235–76

Kolb B, Whishaw I Q 1990 *Fundamentals of Human Neuropsychology*, 3rd edn. W H Freeman, New York

Kornhuber H H, Bechinger D, Jung H, Sauer E 1985 A quantitive relationship between the extent of localized cerebral lesions and the intellectual and behavioral deficiency in children. *European Archives of Psychiatry and the Neurological Sciences* 235 (3): 129–33

Mogilner A et al. 1993 Somatosensory cortical plasticity in adult humans revealed by magnetoencephalography. *Proc. Nat. Acad. Sci. USA* 90 (4): 3593–3597

O'Leary D D M 1992 Development of connectional diversity and specificity in the mammalian brain by the pruning of collateral projections. *Current Opinion in Neurobiology* 2 (1): 70–77

Palti H, Meijer A, Adler B 1985 Learning achievement and behavior at school of anemic and non-anemic infants. *Early Human Development* 10 (3–4): 217–23

Prior M R, Tress B, Hoffman W L, Boldt D 1984 Computed tomographic study of children with classic autism. *Arch. Neurol.* 41 (5): 482–84

Pritzel M 1991 Neuronale Plastizität und Verhalten. In: Andre K (ed.) 1991 *Psychologisch-pädagogische Beiträge*. Verlag Dr. Kovac, Hamburg

Rosenzweig M R 1984 Experience, memory, and the brain. *Am. Psychol.* 39 (4): 365–76

Schneider G E 1979 Is it really better to have your brain lesion early? A revision of the "Kennard principle." *Neuropsychologia* 17 (6): 557–83

Further Reading

Alvarez-Buylla A, Kirn J R, Nottebohm F 1990 Birth of projection neurons in adult avian brain may be related to perceptual or motor learning. *Science* 249: 1444–46

Chalupa L M, Dreher B 1991 High precision systems require high precision "blueprints": A new view regarding the formation of connections in the mammalian visual system. *Journal of Cognitive Neuroscience* 3 (3): 209–19

Löwel S, Singer W 1992 Selection of intrinsic horizontal connections in the visual cortex by correlated neuronal activity. *Science* 255: 209–12

Murthy K D, Desiraju T 1991 Synapses in developing cingulate and hippocampal cortices in undernourished rats. *NeuroReport* 2 (8): 433–36

Rosenzweig M R, Bennett E L, Diamond M C 1972 Brain changes in response to experience. *Sci. Am.* 226 (2): 21–29

Zuccarello M, Facco E, Zampieri P, Zanardi L, Andrioli G C 1985 Severe head injury in children: Early prognosis and outcome. *Child's Nervous System* 1 (3): 158–62

Genetics and Human Development

P. Borkenau

The importance of the relationship between genetics and human development should be apparent, because information about this subject helps parents, teachers, and counselors to set reasonable expectations for the outcomes of interventions. Moreover, such information provides clues as to what kinds of interventions are likely to promote the desired developments.

There are two paradigms in human genetics: Gregor Mendel's and Sir Francis Galton's. Mendel's paradigm is useful for identifying the mode of transmission, the chromosomal basis, and the biochemical mediation of characteristics that are determined by single genes. The goal of Mendelian analysis is to identify the location of effective genes on the chromosomes and biochemical pathways from the immediate chemical effects of genes to observable phenotypes (e.g., blood groups).

In contrast, Galton's paradigm of quantitative–genetic research is useful for investigating the genetic basis of continuous human characteristics that tend to be normally distributed (e.g., stature, intelligence), because they are influenced by many genes. The basic goal of Galton's approach was to estimate the importance of genes for individual differences in personal traits; that is, their heritability. In addition, more elaborate quantitative–genetic research distinguishes among various sorts of genetic effects as well as among two varieties of environments: environments that do or do not contribute to the similarity of children being reared in the same family.

Whereas the genotypes of organisms are fixed from the moment of conception, the effects of the genes change during an individual's lifespan. For example, whereas an embryo's chromosomal sex is fixed with the fertilization of the ovum, many sex characteristics do not develop before puberty. Genetic influences on human development may be analyzed using both Mendel's and Galton's approach. Analyses of the second type usually focus on the heritability of individual differences at various ages, and upon the extent of genetic continuity, that is, the temoral stability of genetic effects (Plomin 1986).

Although relevant to many areas of psychology, the role of human genetics in psychological functioning is most evident in the behavioral consequences of genetic abnormalities. Therefore, this entry begins by considering this topic. The second part then focuses on the methods and some of the findings of quantitative behavior genetics. Finally, the third part addresses developmental behavior genetics; that is, "the study of genetic and environmental influences on individual differences in behavioral development" (Plomin 1983 p. 253).

1. Behavioral Consequences of Genetic Abnormalities

Although many genetic abnormalities are lethal, others produce viable but impaired individuals. The consequences of genetic abnormalities differ in severity, but there are some general rules: (a) because the brain tends to be affected, mental retardation is one symptom of most genetic abnormalities; (b) an abnormal number of chromosomes has more severe consequences than structural aberrations in chromosomes; and (c), as long as there is one intact X-chromosome, an abnormal number of sex chromosomes has less severe consequences than an abnormal number of other chromosomes (autosomes).

Whereas too few autosomes are always lethal, individuals with additional autosomes may survive. The most widespread example is Trisomy 21 (Down's syndrome). Affected individuals have three instead of two exemplars of chromosome 21 and are, along with other characteristics, mentally retarded; the range of intelligence quotients (IQ) of Down's patients is between 20 and 60 (Vogel and Motulsky 1986).

Genetic research was particularly successful in uncovering the genetic sources and biochemical pathways of phenylketonuria (PKU), a hereditary disease with somatic as well as behavioral symptoms, such as severe mental retardation and personality disorders. Due to a defective gene, the enzyme phenylalaninhydroxylase is not produced. This enzyme is necessary to metabolize phenylalanin to tyrosin. Phenylalanin is a toxic component of ordinary food, but it is harmless so long as it is metabolized to tyrosin at a normal rate. In individuals with PKU, however, this metabolism does not occur, and the organism is flooded with phenylalanin and the ensuing symptoms of PKU. Consequently, a successful prevention of the somatic and behavioral symptoms of PKU consists of feeding children who have the deleterious gene with a special diet that is free of phenylalanin. The case of PKU illustrates that the consequences of genetic defects can be counteracted by special environments, and that knowledge of genetic mechanisms may be helpful in creating such environments.

Not all symptoms of deleterious genes can be observed in childhood. For example, Huntington's chorea generally does not become manifest before the fifth decade of life. Huntington's chorea is a hereditary disease that results in a chronic degeneration of the central nervous system and ensuing mental and motor deficiencies.

2. Principles of Quantitative Genetics

Mendelian approaches have been highly successful in uncovering the origins of many diseases that are caused by single deleterious genes (McKusick 1992), but they have not yet provided satisfactory explanations of the normal variation in such human characteristics as stature, IQ, and anxiety. This is the branch of quantitative–genetic research that is still indebted to Galton's ideas. The major purpose of quantitative genetics is to estimate the contribution of various sources of variance to the normal phenotypic variation of a trait in a population (Fisher 1918).

Quantitative–genetic studies investigate the similarity of relatives that have either been reared apart or reared together. If relatives reared apart are phenotypically similar, this indicates some influence of the genes. Correspondingly, if unrelated persons reared together are phenotypically similar, this indicates some influence of the family environment. The most powerful designs for studying the relative importance of genes and environments are studies of monozygotic twins (MZ twins) reared apart and adoption studies. Because MZ twins have identical genes, any difference within pairs reflects nongenetic influence, either environmental effects or error of measurement.

Because error of measurement can be estimated by measuring the same individuals twice, the difference between the short-term stability correlation of each twin's test score and the correlation between MZ twins reared together estimates the contribution of nonshared environment to the variance of the trait. The influence of peers on personality development seems to be a powerful nonshared environmental factor (Daniels 1986, Baker and Daniels 1990). Correspondingly, the difference between the correlation of MZ twins reared together and MZ twins reared apart estimates the influence of shared environment. Thus the study of MZ twins is a powerful design, but it suffers from the scarcity of MZ twins reared apart.

Adoption studies compare first-degree relatives reared apart and unrelated persons reared together. They can therefore make use of a larger number of subjects. If the adoptive parents also have natural children or have adopted more than one child, there are unrelated children reared together in the adoptive home. The correlation between them is a direct estimate of the importance of family environment for the psychological development of these children. Note, however, that adoptive parents are a selected group because not everybody is permitted to adopt children.

Due to the availability of appropriate subjects, most quantitative–genetic studies compare the similarity of MZ twins and dizygotic twins (DZ twins). The rationale is that MZ twins share all their genes whereas DZ twins share 50 percent of their genes. The correlation between DZ twins is therefore subtracted from the correlation between MZ twins, and the doubled difference is used as an estimate of heritability (Falconer 1960). This approach assumes that the trait-relevant environment of MZ twins is not more similar than that of DZ twins. There is indeed some evidence that supports this claim (Scarr and Carter-Saltzman 1979).

Obviously, it would be nice if twin and adoption studies yielded similar results. More recent quantitative–genetic analyses therefore analyze data from various groups of subjects simultaneously, using structural equation modeling. This approach has three advantages over simple heritability estimates: (a) it makes separate estimates of more sources of variance feasible; (b) it yields more dependable estimates of the importance of genes and environments; (c) it allows some of the assumptions that underlie heritability estimates to be tested.

2.1 Some Findings about Intelligence

Bouchard and McGue (1981) reviewed the world literature on familial studies of IQ and reported the mean correlations shown in Table 1. It is clear that the similarity of persons reared together or apart increases with their genetic relatedness. This points to the importance of genes for individual differences in IQ. Moreover, at all levels of genetic relatedness, persons reared together have more similar IQs than persons reared apart. This points to the importance of family environment. Finally, the environments of dizygotic twins are more similar than those of ordinary siblings.

Chipuer et al. (1990) used structural equation modeling to analyze the correlations shown in Table 1. A good fit was obtained for a model that allowed for additive and nonadditive genetic as well as shared and nonshared environmental effects. Moreover, it was

necessary to assume particularly similar twin environments. Additive gene effects accounted for 32 percent, nonadditive gene effects for 19 percent, and effects of the common environment for 35 percent (twins) or 22 percent (siblings) of individual differences in IQ. Thus genetic sources explained about 50 percent of individual differences in IQ. Studies on older subjects suggest even higher heritability estimates (Brody and Crowley 1995).

These findings show that genetic factors contribute substantially to the individual differences in IQ that are observed in modern societies. What they do *not* show, however, is that education has no effect. Rather, the mean IQs in modern societies have risen sharply since the Second World War (Flynn 1987), and longer and better education has certainly contributed to this development. But despite the massive gains in mean intelligence, substantial individual differences persist and are likely to reflect predominantly genetic factors.

2.2 Findings about Personality Traits

Extraversion and neuroticism are the personality traits that have been most extensively studied. Studies that measured these traits by questionnaire found that genes account for about 50 percent of their variance. In contrast to intelligence, however, only environmental factors of the nonshared variety seem to be important (Loehlin 1989, Nichols 1978). This suggests a reconceptualization of those environmental factors that shape individual differences in personality: those parental behaviors that affect all their children in a similar way seem to be of minor importance.

3. Developmental Behavioral Genetics

As early as 1949 Skodak and Skeels reported a direct relation between the age of adopted children and the extent that they resembled their biological mothers with regard to IQ: the correlation between the IQs of biological mothers and their natural children who had been adopted rose from r=0.04 when the children were 2 years old to r=0.31 when the children were 13 years old. In contrast, the IQ-correlations between adopted children and their adoptive parents remained at a low level (below r=0.10). This indicates that it is mainly the genetic blueprint that directs the course of children's cognitive development whereas the learning experiences in the family seem to be of minor importance for individual differences in IQ.

A major longitudinal twin project, the Louisville Twin Study, has suggested similar conclusions. Whereas measures of cognitive development were equally similar for MZ twins and DZ twins in the first year of their lives, indicating no heritability at this age, the correlations increased for MZ twins and decreased for DZ twins. Among 15-year old twins, the correlations were r=0.88 for MZ twins and r=0.54 for DZ twins, indicating a heritability of 0.68 (Wilson 1983).

Table 1
Familial correlations of intelligence

Persons compared	Mean correlation
Monozygotic (MZ) twins reared together	0.86
Monozygotic (MZ) twins reared apart	0.72
Dizygotic (DZ) twins reared together	0.60
Siblings reared together	0.47
Parent-offspring reared together	0.42
Siblings reared apart	0.24
Parent-offspring reared apart	0.22
Half-siblings reared together	0.31
Natural and adopted children reared together	0.29
Two adopted children reared together	0.34
Adopted child and adoptive parent	0.19

Moreover, pre- and perinatal factors such as gestational age and weight at birth correlated substantially with the level of cognitive development among infants but not among school children (Wilson 1978). Thus the effects of these factors are transitory. Finally, the spurts and lags in cognitive development were more synchronized among pairs of MZ twins than among pairs of DZ twins. This shows directly that cognitive developmental change and stability are influenced by genetic factors.

An example of a longitudinal adoption study is the Colorado Adoption Project. Here, the correlation between biological parents and their adopted-away offspring rose from r=0.14 for 1-year olds to 0.28 for 7-year olds, whereas the correlations between adoptive parents and their adopted children were uniformly low (Fulker et al. 1988). This replicates the findings by Skodak and Skeels (1949). Note, however, that two factors may contribute to the rising correlation between biological parents and their adopted-away offspring: (a) the heritability of the trait may rise; or (b) the same genes may produce changing effects during ontogenesis. This can be clarified by considering twin or sibling correlations in addition to parent–offspring correlations. A relevant study by Plomin et al. (1988) showed that the genetic continuity of IQ is high in contras to the genetic continuity of more specific components of intelligence. Thus it is likely that the same genes are important for individual differences in the IQs of infants and adults, but the overall importance of genes for the level of cognitive development increases with age.

References

Baker L A, Daniels D 1990 Nonshared environmental influences and personality differences in adult twins. *J. Pers. Soc. Psychol.* 58(1): 103–110

Brody N, Crowley M J 1995 Environmental (and genetic) influences on personality and intelligence. In: Saklofske D H, Zeidner M (eds.) *International Handbook of Personality and Intelligence.* Plenum, New York

Bouchardæ T J, McGue M 1981 Familial studies of intelligence: A review. *Science* 212(4498): 1055–59

Chipuer H M, Rovine M, Plomin R 1990 LISREL-modeling: Genetic and environmental influences on IQ revisited. *Intelligence* 14(1): 11–29

Daniels D 1986 Differential experiences of siblings in the same family as predictors of adolescent sibling personality differences. *J. Pers. Soc. Psychol.* 51(2): 339–46

Falconer D S 1960 *Introduction to Quantitative Genetics.* Ronald Press, New York

Fisher R A 1918 The correlation between relatives on the supposition of Mendelian inheritance. *Transactions of the Royal Society of Edinburgh* 52: 399–433

Flynn J R 1987 Massive IQ gains in 14 nations: What IQ tests really measure. *Psych. Bull.* 101(2): 171–91

Fulker D W, DeFries J C, Plomin R 1988 Genetic influence on general mental ability increases between infancy and middle childhood. *Nature* 336(6201): 767–69

Loehlin J C 1989 Partitioning environmental and genetic contributions to behavioral development. *Am. Psychol.* 44(10): 1285–92

McKusick V A 1992 *Mendelian Inheritance in Man*, 10th edn. Johns Hopkins University Press, Baltimore, Maryland

Nichols R C 1978 Twin studies of ability, personality, and interests. *Homo* 29: 158–73

Plomin R 1983 Developmental behavioral genetics. *Child Dev.* 54(2): 253–59

Plomin R 1986 *Development, Genetics, and Psychology.* Erlbaum, Hillsdale, New Jersey

Plomin R, DeFries J C, Fulker D W 1988 *Nature and Nurture During Infancy and Early Childhood.* Cambridge University Press, Cambridge, Massachusetts

Scarr S, Carter-Saltzman L 1979 Twin method: Defense of a critical assumption. *Behavior Genetics* 9(6): 527–42

Skodak M, Skeels H M 1949 A final follow-up study of one hundred adopted children. *J. Genet. Psychol.* 75: 85–125

Vogel F, Motulsky A G 1986 *Human Genetics: Problems and Approaches.* Springer Verlag, New York

Wilson R S 1978 Synchronies in mental development: An epigenetic perspective. *Science* 202(4371): 939–48

Wilson R S 1983 The Louisville Twin Study: Developmental synchronies in behavior. *Child Dev.* 54(2): 298–316

Prenatal Development

G. Gottlieb and D. E. Hutchings

This entry describes features of normal and abnormal development of the human fetus, especially those that pertain to the psychological functioning of the newborn and older infant. It begins with a discussion of normal prenatal sensory development, and goes on to describe some congenital defects and their causes.

1. Sensory Development: General Aspects

While the motor or neuromuscular immaturity of the human infant at birth makes it an "altricial" mammal (one whose needs must be ministered to by an adult caregiver), the human newborn is the only altricial species in which all of the sensory systems become capable of functioning before birth (see Fig.1).

The precocious nature of human sensory development is characteristic of "precocial" animals, ones which are born in such an advanced neurosensory and neuromuscular state that they can stand, move about, and feed or search out nourishment for themselves at birth (Gottlieb 1971). This remarkable state of affairs means that, with the exception of vision, all of the newborn infant's sensory–perceptual development has been influenced, for good or ill, by events during the

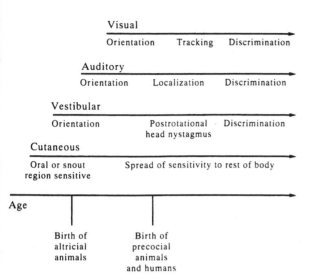

Figure 1

Ontogenetic sequence of development of four sensory systems in human fetus and other animals

Source: Based on Gottlieb 1968, 1971

prenatal period. While only the sequence of cutaneous, vestibular, auditory, and visual sensory systems are depicted in Fig. 1, based on extrapolation from other species (Alberts 1984), it seems highly probable that gustation or taste becomes competent in the human fetus after vestibular onset and before auditory functioning, that is, some time between 90 and 140 days of a normal gestation period of 265 days.

An overt response to tactile stimulation is present in the human fetus around day 49 after fertilization, consisting of bending the head away from the site of stimulation when the oral region is touched lightly (Hooker 1952). The correlative trigeminal anatomy of this and other cutaneous responses was worked out in detail by Humphrey (1964). Minkowski (1928) had observed what appeared to be vestibular righting reflexes in human fetuses between days 90 and 120, and Humphrey (1965) maintained that the lateral vestibular nucleus is almost certainly functional between 12 to 16 weeks of prenatal development, if not earlier. Since the human newborn is barely able to right its head, Humphrey (1965) pointed out that the increase in the size of the head prior to birth may not be matched by a comparable increase in muscle tonus, so vestibular righting reflexes might be absent in the newborn for this reason rather than insufficient vestibular development.

2. Auditory Sensitivity

At about 6 to 7 months the human fetus is capable of responding to auditory stimulation. At this time the organ of Corti is comparable to the adult (Bredberg 1968), and Wedenberg (1965) recorded fetal heart rate changes to sound stimulation in utero. During the 7th month, the fetus's bodily reaction to sound is of sufficient magnitude so that objective behavioral recordings can be made via a pneumograph attached to the mother's body. Actually, 2 to 7 weeks before term it is frequently possible to observe indirectly the fetus's response to sound by merely watching the maternal abdomen and noting the extent to which strong abdominal deformations coincide with repeated applications of the stimulus (e.g., Wedenberg 1965). Since it is known that auditory function, as well as other sensory functions, can occur prior to the complete maturation of the receptor, there is good reason to believe that human auditory sensitivity may begin earlier than is indicated in the early 1990s. This supposition is supported by the report of auditory evoked cortical responses in human infants born prematurely after 21 to 27 weeks of gestation (Weitzman and Graziani 1968). Since a response was obtained from the youngest preterm infant tested (21 weeks), the onset of auditory sensitivity is still not known.

To determine whether the prenatal onset of audition has consequences for the newborn's early social attachment to its mother, DeCasper and Spence (1986) had pregnant mothers read nursery rhymes to their fetus during the last month of gestation. Not only did these fetuses respond in a behaviorally selective way to the voice of their own mother after birth, they also responded in a selective way to the story their mother had read to them when the story was spoken by another mother in the study. These findings suggest that prenatal acquaintance with their mother's voice not only helps to establish the early postnatal social relationship with their mother but may also be the beginning of the process of becoming selectively (perceptually) responsive to features of their native language, a process that continues over the first year of postnatal life (Werker 1989).

3. Visual Sensitivity

While the earliest onset of the capacity for visual function in the human fetus is not known, Ellingson (1960) recorded evoked cortical responses to light flashes in a premature infant as early as day 182 (26 weeks) or thereabouts, and Engel (1964) recorded a similar response in a premature infant around day 154 (22 weeks). In comparison with the auditory receptor, which is completely differentiated several months before birth, the human visual receptor is not completely developed even at birth (Yakovlev and Lecours 1967). Also, myelinated auditory projection fibers reach the cerebral cortex earlier than visual fibers.

4. Congenital Malformations and Their Causes

Most infants—some 95 percent or more—are perfectly normal at birth. A small percentage, however, are

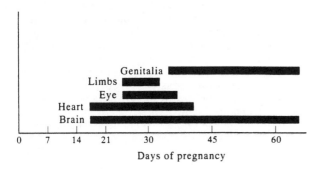

Figure 2
Critical periods in embryonic development

born with defects that range from very minor to those that are so severe as to adversely affect the quality of life or that are life-threatening.

Teratology is the study of congenital malformations. These are structural or anatomical abnormalities present at birth (e.g., cleft palate, cleft lip, missing or extra fingers and toes, spina bifida) and are also referred to as "birth defects." A teratogen is a chemical, drug, or other agent (e.g., virus) that causes congenital malformations (Shepard 1985). The abnormalities produced by teratogens almost always occur during the first trimester of pregnancy when the major organs of the embryo are forming. Different organ systems have specific "critical periods" when they are most sensitive to damage, and those for humans are shown in Fig. 2. Developmental toxicology is the study of chemically induced adverse effects that are produced during development (Schardein 1985).

Approximately 3 percent of newborns have one or more significant malformations at birth and, by the end of the first postnatal year, an additional 3 percent are found to have a developmental abnormality. Another group, whose size cannot be estimated, is born with functional abnormalities of the nervous, respiratory, gastrointestinal, and immune systems.

Very little is known of the specific causes of these effects. It is estimated that 10 to 15 percent of allhuman congenital malformations are due to environmental agents and another 10 to 15 percent to hereditary factors, such as genetic mutations and abnormalities of the chromosomes. The remainder are considered to result from unknown causes that might be related to some poorly understood combination of hereditary susceptibilities and environmental factors.

5. Human Teratogens: Drugs and Chemicals that Produce Congenital Malformations

That X-irradiation is a teratogen has been known since the early part of the twentieth century and it is well-established that the developing brain is particularly sensitive to irradiation-induced injury. Studies of the effects of in utero exposure to atomic radiation in Hiroshima and Nagasaki revealed that such exposure can cause mental retardation.

Thalidomide, a drug marketed in Europe in the 1950s to treat morning sickness, is one of the most potent teratogens known. Before being withdrawn from the market in the early 1960s, it was found to produce a wide variety of malformations, the most debilitating being severe limb reduction, that is the absence or incomplete formation of arms and legs.

Alcohol, consumed in large amounts (approximately 6 oz. of pure alcohol per day), produces the fetal alcohol syndrome (FAS) characterized by growth retardation, defects of the joints and facial skeleton, and mild to moderate mental retardation. Of mothers consuming these large amounts of alcohol, about 10 to 15 percent give birth to infants with FAS.

Diethylstilbesterol (DES) is a synthetic nonsteroidal estrogen used during the 1950s and 1960s to prevent spontaneous abortion, a treatment later proven to be ineffective. It produces vaginal cancer in female offspring, but the symptoms do not appear until the teenage years.

Compounds in the vitamin A family, including palmitate and retinoic acid, are potent teratogens. One form, isotretinoin, marketed as "Accutane" in the United States, a prescription drug for the treatment of cystic acne, causes malformations of the brain and external ear. It was marketed with clear and explicit warnings to both physicians and consumers of its action as a teratogen.

6. Developmental Neurotoxicants

There are several chemicals, called "developmental neurotoxicants," that are known to produce toxic or adverse effects on the developing brain, both during the prenatal and postnatal periods of growth. These agents do not produce anatomical defects as described above, but instead adversely influence the way in which the brain functions (Riley and Vorhees 1986).

What has become known as "fetal Minamata disease" resulted from the maternal ingestion of methylmercury-contaminated food. Mercury pollutants contained in waste water and discharged from a chemical plant in Minamata, Japan, accumulated in fish and shellfish, an important staple of the local inhabitants' diet. Even though most of the exposed mothers did not show symptoms of mercury poisoning, exposure of the fetus during the third trimester produced widespread brain injury.

Of all the developmental neurotoxicants, lead has been the most extensively studied and is viewed as a serious pediatric public health problem. Pregnant women and children living in major urban centers where soils and dusts become contaminated with lead-based paint are at risk of high exposure. Increases in blood levels of lead are known to occur in children as soon as they begin to crawl and place contaminated hands and toys in their mouth. Behavioral processes of learning and problem-solving are known to be adversely affected in exposed children.

The polychlorinated biphenyls (PCBs), first introduced in the 1930s, are a group of synthetic hydrocarbons that had widespread commercial use as electrical insulating fluid, in heat exchangers, plastics, transformers, capacitors, and carbonless copy paper. As a result of their largely uncontrolled disposal and exceptional persistence, they became a major environmental pollutant in the air, water, and soil of industrialized countries. Accidental ingestion of high concentrations of PCBs in combination with other compounds (i.e., polychlorinated dibenzofurans, terphenyls, and quaterphenyls) via contaminated cooking oil in Japan and Taiwan produced chronic poisoning in some 3,000 individuals. Contamination in the United States is known to have occurred through the food chain, particularly in Great Lakes fish, although the route of exposure for the general population remains unknown. Children of women prenatally exposed to PCBs show adverse effects on learning and behavior.

Diphenylhydantoin (DPH) is one of several prescription medications used to treat epileptic seizures. It has been implicated as a human teratogen but the data remain inconclusive. Although only a relatively small number of children prenatally exposed to DPH have been assessed for neurobehavioral effects, results tentatively suggest a reduction in IQ scores.

Heroin is a drug of abuse and methadone is a drug used to treat heroin addiction. Exposure to either of these drugs during pregnancy causes the newborns to show withdrawal symptoms of irritability, tremulousness, hyperactivity, and digestive disturbance. These symptoms gradually subside and disappear over several weeks to a few months and there do not appear to be any long-term effects that persist into later life.

Because many of the causes of birth defects are unknown, not all can be prevented. But many chemicals have been identified as being hazardous to the fetus, newborn, and developing child and this information should be used to provide the safest environment possible so that each child has the best possible beginning.

See also: Brain Development and Human Behavior

References

Alberts J 1984 Sensory–perceptual development in the Norway rat: A view toward comparative studies. In: Kail R, Spear N S (eds.) 1984 *Comparative Perspective on Memory Development*. Erlbaum, Hillsdale, New Jersey
Bredberg G 1968 Cellular pattern and nerve supply of the human organ of Corti. *Acta Oto-Laryngol.* Suppl. 236: 1–135
DeCasper A, Spence M J 1986 Prenatal maternal speech influences newborns' perception of speech sounds. *Infant Behavior and Development* 9:135–50
Ellingson R J 1960 Cortical electrical responses to visual stimulation in the human infant. *Electroencephalographs in Clinical Neurophysiology* 12: 663–77
Engel R 1964 Electroencephalographic responses to photic stimulation, and their correlation with maturation. *Annals of the New York Academy of Science* 117: 407–12
Gottlieb G 1968 Prenatal behavior of birds. *Quarterly Review of Biology* 43: 148–74
Gottlieb G 1971 Ontogenesis of sensory function in birds and mammals. In: Tobach E, Aronson L R, Shaw E (eds.) 1971 *The Biopsychology of Development*. Academic Press, New York
Hooker D 1952 *The Prenatal Origin of Behavior*. University of Kansas Press, Lawrence, Kansas
Humphrey T 1964 Some correlations between the appearance of human fetal reflexes and the development of the nervous system. *Progr. Brain Research* 4: 93–133
Humphrey T 1965 The embryologic differentiation of the vestibular nuclei in man correlated with functional development. *International Symposium on Vestibular Oculomotor Problems* 51–56
Minkowski M 1928 Neurobiologische Studien am menschlichen Foetus. In: Abderhalden E (ed.) 1928 *Handbuch der biologischen Arbeitsmethoden*, Sect. 5. Urban und Schwarzenberg, Berlin
Riley E P, Vorhees C V (eds.) 1986 *Handbook of Behavioral Teratology*. Plenum Press, New York
Schardein J L 1985 *Chemically Induced Birth Defects*. Dekker, New York
Shepard T H 1989 *Catalog of Teratogenic Agents*, 6th edn. Johns Hopkins University Press, Baltimore, Maryland
Wedenberg E 1965 Prenatal tests of hearing. *Acta Oto-Laryngol.* 206: 27–32
Weitzman E D, Graziani L J 1968 Maturation and topography of the auditory evoked response of the prematurely born infant. *Developmental Psychobiology* 1: 79–89
Werker J 1989 Becoming a native listener. *Am. Sci.* 77: 54–59
Yakovlev P I, Lecours A R 1967 The myelinogenetic cycles of regional maturation of the brain. In: Minkowski A (ed.) 1967 *Regional Development of the Brain in Early Life*. Blackwell, Oxford

Further Reading

Gottlieb G (ed.) 1973 *Behavioral Embryology*. Academic Press, New York

Physical Growth and Development: Universal Changes and Individual Differences

A. F. Roche

Physical growth and development are important in planning physical education curricula and setting goals for physical performance. This account begins at birth and is restricted to individuals born at term and free of pathological conditions. Body size and proportions, physical maturation, and body composition are considered, together with their determinants and their relationships to physical performance.

1. Methods of Assessment

The choice of methods is important in considering the literature, the assessment of students, and the design and implementation of research. Growth implies change. When data are recorded at only one age, only change from conception can be evaluated. More precise information about change is provided if the measurement of a child or a group of children is repeated after an interval, thus providing the increment during the interval. Incremental data are conceptually satisfying, but it is difficult to interpret increments for individuals by comparison with reference data. The errors of measurement may differ from those in the reference data. The intervals between measurements commonly vary from those in the reference population.

Tracking is an important aspect of growth. This is the tendency for individuals to retain rank order for a variable across time. Tracking is commonly judged from: (a) age-to-age correlations, (b) the ability to fit parametric models to serial data, or (c) the extent to which there is parallelism of curves fitted to serial data for individuals. Tracking is similar to "canalization," which is the extent to which the serial data for an individual remain in the same canal (zone) on a growth chart. In this sense, a zone is the space between adjacent percentile lines.

The most obvious changes in body proportions during growth are the decreases in head size relative to weight and recumbent length and the increases in leg length relative to recumbent length during infancy. Weight increases relative to stature during pubescence; this is indexed by weight/stature^2 which is called the Body Mass Index with units of kg/m^2. This index, and closely similar indices (relative weight, weight-for-stature) will be referred to as BMI in this entry.

Growth is closely associated with maturation, which is the monotonic part of development in which all individuals reach the same level when young adults. Skeletal maturity can be assessed from radiographs of the hand-wrist. The FELS method is preferred because it is based on objective grading of maturity indicators that were tested extensively (Roche et al. 1988). The statistical method used provides confidence limits for each assessment that reflect the amount of useful information available from the radiograph.

Between 10 and 16 years the rate of maturation can be judged from ages at menarche and at the development of secondary sex characters. Age at menarche can be obtained prospectively; for example, by return of postcards or by using probit analysis of responses to retrospective questions about whether menstruation has occurred. The grading of secondary sex characters is assisted by the excellent color photographs and textual descriptions in van Wieringen et al. (1971 pp. 35–47). Age at the maximum rate of pubescent growth in stature (peak height velocity) indicates the rate of maturation; this age can be approximated from increments and identified exactly from models fitted to growth data. The term "pubescence" will be used in reference to the period of development of the ability to reproduce sexually and to changes during the next few years. In combination, the pubescent and postpubescent periods constitute adolescence.

The increases in the size and maturity of the body during growth are associated with important changes in total and regional body composition. Total body composition is described in terms of the percentage of body weight that is fat (percent body fat) and fat-free mass.

2. Satus At Birth

Mean birth weights are about 3.5 kg for boys and 3.4 kg for girls in many European groups, but slightly lower means have been reported from Latin America. The means for many other groups are about 3.0 kg, but there is considerable variation probably reflecting differences in nutrition and the prevalence of diseases and preterm births. The larger birth weights of boys are associated with slightly greater lengths and skinfold thicknesses (Johnston 1986). These sex differences, with minor exceptions, persist throughout the growth period. Important determinants of size at birth include maternal factors (age, size, nutritional status, socioeconomic status, smoking behavior, parity, interpregnancy interval), and altitude. Maternal smoking has a large effect on weight and a lesser effect on recumbent length.

3. Infancy

Infancy (i.e., from birth to age 2) is a critical period, particularly in less developed countries where there are high rates of infant morbidity and mortality and large fluctuations in growth rates. Growth during infancy is an important index of current health and nutritional status.

3.1 Size

In the presentation of size during infancy, the sequence followed is: status at a particular age, increments, growth patterns, and changes in proportions. The same sequence is followed in later sections relating to size during childhood and pubescence.

After birth, there is a loss of weight that is usually regained in about one week. Infants who do not regain their birth weight by 15 days lag in size and skinfold thicknesses throughout the first year. Growth in weight, recumbent length, and head circumference is characterized by rapid increases, rapid decelerations, and increasing variability. Birth weight is doubled at about 4 months in developed countries and slightly later in less developed countries.

Increments for weight, recumbent length, and head circumference have been reported for intervals ranging from one to six months. A short interval is important clinically because it could lead to early recognition of unusual growth. Caution is necessary, particularly for very short intervals, because errors will be a major component of the observed increments if the data are not of high quality. Birth weight must be considered in the judgment of increments because it is related to the rate of growth during infancy. Despite this association, there is considerable individual variation in growth patterns during infancy.

Infant growth patterns explain only a small fraction of the variance at 10 years or in adulthood in general populations, but moderate infant malnutrition affects weight and stature though not skinfold thicknesses, arm muscle areas, or skeletal maturity at 7 years (Johnston et al. 1984).

During infancy, there is relatively rapid growth of the legs and slow growth of the head. There are some ethnic differences in proportions. For example, Africans tend to have small values for the ratio shoulder breadth–hip breadth and the distal parts of the limbs are long relative to stature.

3.2 Maturation

Because of the lack of metric units for measuring the changes involved, it is difficult to prove that maturation is rapid during infancy. This can be inferred, however, from the rapid changes in grades of skeletal maturity indicators. As in other growth periods, girls are in advance of boys by amounts that increase with chronological age in a near-linear fashion during infancy (Roche 1968).

3.3 Body Composition

The percentage of body fat increases from about 12 percent at birth to about 22 percent at 1 year; there are corresponding increases in skinfold thicknesses and BMI (Rolland-Cachera et al. 1984). All these measures decrease markedly from 1 to 2 years. Fat-free mass increases during infancy at similar rates in breast-fed and formula-fed infants, but bone mineral density (a regional measure of bone mineral per unit area) decreases in breast-fed infants but does not change in formula-fed infants (Rutledge et al. 1976).

3.4 Determinants

There are significant familial effects on weight and recumbent length that increase from birth to 6 months and then decrease until 2 years. Path analyses show that transmitted effects, which combine genetic and environmental influences, are more important for recumbent length than for weight, but nontransmitted environmental effects are more important for weight (Byard et al. 1991).

The different growth patterns shown by breast-fed and formula-fed infants may be due to the lack of random assignment and variations among studies in the criteria for the allocation of infants to these groups, though this is difficult to establish. The rate of growth in weight decreases at about 4 months in exclusively breast-fed infants. While breast-fed and formula-fed infants do not differ in recumbent length, skinfold thicknesses are larger in the formula-fed (Whitehead and Paul 1984). Maternal smoking reduces weight and recumbent length but these effects decrease with age and are small by 5 years (Elwood et al. 1987).

Reports of differences in growth within countries between urban and rural babies generally show more growth in urban babies. The differences are greater in less developed countries. Studies of these differences are difficult to interpret in the absence of information about migration. They also tend to obscure differences between local regions, and few provide information about the specific influences responsible for the observed differences. The important influences are likely to include hygiene, nutrition, and the availability of health services.

4. Childhood

Growth during childhood (i.e., ages 2 to 10) is nearly linear except for a small spurt at about 6 years that is more of biological than of practical interest. Tracking is marked during childhood.

4.1 Size

Boys exceed girls by about 2 cm in stature but the differences in weight and in head circumference are slight. The sex differences in weight decrease toward the end of childhood, but those in head circumference increase (Sempé et al. 1979 pp. 28–61). During childhood, the rate of growth in stature decreases but there is an increase in the rate of growth in weight (Roche and Himes 1980). Increments in stature are almost the same in each sex but those for weight are slightly higher in girls, particularly near the end of childhood.

Size during childhood is associated with the timing of the pubescent spurt; large children tend to have early spurts. There are high correlations between childhood statures and stature at 17 years that do not change with age during childhood (Ashizawa et al. 1977), and there are moderate but significant correlations between skinfold thicknesses from early childhood to late childhood and early adulthood. Tracking of skinfold thicknesses is similar for trunk and extremity sites but is greater for girls than boys. There is no sex difference in tracking for BMI; these correlations increase rapidly as older childhood ages are considered until the correlations between values in childhood and in young adulthood reach about 0.6 at 7 years (Rolland-Cachera et al. 1989).

It has been postulated that there are concurrent spurts in brain growth (head circumference) and mental growth (Piagetian stages, mental age, IQ) during childhood and pubescence. Several of the postulated spurts are not present in serial data and the observed spurts in head circumference and mental age are not related (McCall et al. 1983).

Body Mass Index values decrease slightly from 2 to 6 years when increases begin that continue int pubescence. The change to increasing values ("rebound") occurs at about 6 years (Rolland-Cachera et al. 1984, Siervogel et al. 1991). The age at rebound is an important predictor of adult BMI values; early rebounds, independently of BMI at 1 year and of rate of maturation, are associated with large adult values. The ratio trunk length–stature decreases during childhood in each sex because the legs are growing more rapidly than the trunk, but the ratio hip breadth–shoulder breadth increases in each sex to 6 years after which there is little change in boys but a continuing decrease in girls.

4.2 Maturation

During childhood, skeletal maturation is more rapid in girls than boys, consequently the sex difference increases with age (Roche et al. 1976 p.15).

4.3 Body Composition

Fat-free mass increases linearly during childhood and is slightly larger in boys than girls. Triceps and subscapular skinfold thicknesses tend to be larger in girls than boys. They decrease from 2 to 5 years, reaching a nadir at about 7 years (Johnston 1986); these thicknesses are significantly correlated with stature during childhood (Himes and Roche 1986). Skinfold thicknesses on the trunk are similar to those on the limbs in each sex; a centripetal pattern, with excess adipose tissue on the trunk, is not established until pubescence.

4.4 Determinants

The differences in size, proportions, and maturity during childhood do not appear to be determined by hormone levels but they may reflect receptor sensitivity or genetic differences. Parent–child correlations for stature increase with age and are larger for boys than girls. These correlations allow assessments of childhood stature taking parental stature into account (Himes et al. 1981). The BMI may be influenced by x-linked genes and there may be a major gene for this index in boys (Byard et al. 1989). This suggestive evidence does not necessarily imply there are controlling genes on the x-chromosome; an alternative explanation is that genetic factors may act differently in male and female environments.

Changes in environmental influences are indicated by secular changes. This term refers to changes over time in a population that is not affected by migration. Because of migratory effects, many reports of national secular trends are spurious and those for subgroups (e.g., students at one school) must be evaluated carefully since demographic changes may have occurred in the school population. The need for caution is shown by some findings from the Fels Study. When all the data are considered, a secular trend in stature is not evident, but when the data are analyzed within families, there are definite increases across generations for individuals measured at the same ages (Bock and Sykes 1989). This intrafamilial increase is evident by 1 year of age and does not increase as older ages are considered. Positive secular trends reflect improvements in the environment but associations with specific aspects of the environment (e.g., diet) are rarely possible.

4.5 Relationships with Physical Performance

Measures of body size have low positive correlations with speed and strength and there are low negative correlations between weight and activities in which the body or an object is projected (e.g., jumping). Both growth and performance measures tend to track during childhood.

5. Pubescence

During pubescence (i.e., 10–16 years), growth rates change markedly and there are slight decreases in the extent to which status values at young ages predict status values at older ages. Pubescence is not a unitary event even at the physical level. Almost all organs and tissues are involved, but they differ in the extent and type of the changes that occur and there are individual variations in the timing and sequence of spurts even within the skeleton (Roche 1974).

5.1 Size

Plotted status medians for stature accelerate at 11 years for boys and 9 years for girls in developed countries. This marks the beginning of the pubescent spurt, which tends to occur later in less developed countries. During pubescence, the sex difference for stature increases by about 2 cm and the sex difference for weight decreases by about 9 kg. From 10 through 12 years, girls are slightly taller than boys and they are heavier until 13 years due to their earlier pubescent spurts. The age range when girls exceed boys in stature and weight occurs later in populations with delayed pubescence.

The peak rates of growth occur at about 14 years in boys and 12 years in girls for stature and at slightly older ages for weight. Due to differences in the timing of pubescence, girls exceed boys in stature increments from 9 through 13 years and in weight increments from 11.5 through 13.5 years. Despite differences in timing, the percentage who achieve adult stature at peak height velocity is similar in each sex (Prader 1984). After peak height velocity, there are decreases in the rates of growth that are more rapid for stature than for weight.

The patterns of growth in stature during pubescence are the same in all normal individuals, but the timing of the maximum rates of growth and the maximum rates themselves vary among and within groups.

Tracking coefficients during pubescence are greater for stature and fat-free mass than for percent body fat (Pařízková 1976). Due to tracking, adult stature can be predicted from the stature, weight, and skeletal age of a child and the mean of the statures of both parents (Roche et al. 1975, 1988). The median absolute prediction errors are 3 cm at 1 year, 2 cm at 7 years, and 2.5 cm at 14 years. This level of accuracy holds on cross validation when the method is applied to those free of diseases that affect adult stature. Reduced tracking of stature, weight, and skinfold thicknesses during pubescence is, in part, responsible for concurrent decreases in the accuracy of adult stature predictions.

The ratio trunk length–stature decreases until 13 years in boys and 11 years in girls after which there are small increases. The ratio hip breadth–shoulder breadth changes little in boys to 11 years but then decreases; it increases until 15 years in girls. The narrow hips and long limbs of Africans, noted during childhood, persist through pubescence to adulthood. BMI values show spurts at 13.6 years (boys) and 13.0 years (girls) in United States children; similar timing has been reported from Egypt (El-Nofely et al. 1988, Siervogel et al. 1991).

Correlations between BMI values during pubescence and those in adulthood are about 0.6 (Rolland-Cachera et al. 1989). The patterns of change in BMI values during childhood and pubescence, but not those during infancy, are related to BMI and percent body fat in adulthood (Cronk et al. 1982a, 1982b). These relationships allow estimates of the risk that children and adolescents, grouped by current BMI values, will have values in middle age that exceed the recommended ranges (Guo et al. 1992). Values beyond these ranges

are associated with increased risks of some cardiovascular and metabolic diseases.

5.2 Maturation

In each sex, secondary sex characters begin to develop about one year after the commencement of the pubescent spurt; menarche occurs about 1 year after peak height velocity. At the time of peak height velocity, secondary sex characters are fully mature in boys but not in girls. The female advancement in skeletal maturity increases during early pubescence until the maximum sex difference, about 33 months of male skeletal age, is reached at 12 years.

Most testicular growth occurs during pubescence. Early in pubescence, there are histological changes that lead to the development of spermatozoa before sexual maturation is complete. Ovarian follicles are present in very young girls but larger and more numerous follicles are present during pubescence (Brook and Stanhope 1989).

5.3 Body Composition

Large sex differences in fat-free mass develop during pubescence; the total increment from 10 to 20 years is about 33 kg in males and 16 kg in females. In boys, rapid increases continue throughout pubescence but there is little increase in girls after 14 years. In each sex, the maximum increments in fat-free mass coincide with peak height velocity. Arm muscle area and skeletal mass are similar in the two sexes until 12 years, after which there are marked accelerations in boys but only slight increases in girls. By 16 years, values for arm muscle area and skeletal mass are about 40 percent larger for boys than for girls.

Percent body fat is greater in girls than boys; this sex difference is small from 10 to 12 years but it increases markedly from then to 16 years as percent body fat decreases in boys but increases in girls. Part of the increasing fatness of girls is due to the pubescent accumulation of fat in the breasts and near the hips. In boys, skinfold thicknesses, particularly those at abdominal and arm sites, increase prior to and early in pubescence and decrease markedly during pubescence. In girls, skinfold thicknesses increase throughout pubescence and these changes are rapid after 13 years (Cronk et al. 1983). The correlations between skinfold thicknesses at various sites are low during childhood but increase during pubescence, especially in boys (Siervogel et al. 1982). As a result, measures at one or a few sites are more representative during pubescence than at younger ages.

5.4 Determinants

Parent–child correlations for stature decrease slightly from 10 to 13 years and then increase for parent–daughter pairs but not parent–son pairs. Parent–

child correlations for weight decrease gradually to 16 years (Chrzastek-Spruch 1984). The transmissible sibling resemblance for BMI does not change with age during pubescence but the nontransmissible sibling resemblance decreases. The variability in serial weight percentile levels from 2 to 17 years within individuals is based on the same genetic architecture in each sex, but the genetic control of the mean percentile level appears to differ between the sexes (Towne et al. 1992).

Testosterone (boys) and estradiol (girls) may initiate pubescence; adrenal androgens in girls are unlikely to be important, partly because the timing of changes in their serum concentrations does not coincide with changes in growth rates (Prader 1984). The increased growth hormone concentrations during pubescence in each sex are probably due to stimulation by sex steroids. Growth hormone probably stimulates the secretion of somatomedins and it is necessary for the direct effects of sex steroids on growth.

The term "catch-up growth" refers to an acceleration that occurs when a retarding influence such as disease is removed. As a result, the child's growth status returns to about the same percentile level as that prior to the disease. During pubescence, the normal growth patterns of slowly maturing children may be mistaken for catch-up growth when these children have delayed spurts at ages when growth has decelerated in most children. Malnutrition retards growth in all aspects of body size and body composition, but with rehabilitation "catch-up growth" can occur up to the age of 5 years (Martorell and Habicht 1986). In the absence of catch-up growth, low fat-free mass (largely muscle) persists into adulthood leading to reductions in work capacity, productivity, and, perhaps, immunocompetence. Catch-up can occur in brain size but it is unclear as to what extent the increases in size are due to the accumulation of fluid or histological changes (Roche 1980).

In boys the early increases in testis size are dependent on gonadotrophins and testosterone, and the development of the penis and pubic hair is dependent on androgens. The breast and pubic hair changes in girls are largely dependent on estrogens while changes in the ovary are dependent on gonadotrophin and luteinizing hormone. Cyclical production of gonadotrophins and ovarian hormones in girls leads to endometrial hyperplasia which breaks down when estrogen support is reduced. Menarche occurs when there is sufficient hyperplasia prior to breakdown.

Marked physical activity or loss of weight may delay menarche and its timing may be influenced by androgenic effects of adipose tissue on estrogen metabolism and gonadotrophin-releasing hormone. Menarcheal timing is also influenced by genes, socioeconomic status, urban/rural residence, altitude, family size, and birth order. It has been claimed that menarche occurs when a critical body weight or a critical amount of body fat is reached, but there is little supporting evidence. Weight, total body fat, and skinfold thicknesses are no less variable at menarche than at other times.

Environmental influences are evident in the marked secular changes in growth during the twentieth century in many countries; these probably reflect improvements in nutrition and health care (Roche 1979, Roede and van Wieringen 1985). The increases involve size, rates of maturation, and proportions; most of the increase in stature has been in leg length. In many developed countries, the secular trend has ceased or slowed, presumably because the environment is not continuing to improve. There are some groups, however, in which a secular trend has not occurred, indicating that the environment has not improved (e.g., the Zapotes in Mexico; see Malina et al. 1980).

5.5 Relationships to Physical Performance

Correlations of stature, weight, and fat-free mass with motor performance are generally low, but those for strength are moderate, particularly at 13 to 15 years in boys. Body fatness is negatively correlated with performance on tasks for which the body has to be projected. Rapidly maturing boys exceed slowly maturing boys on speed and strength measures until late adolescence when slow maturers perform better than rapid maturers (Lefevre et al. 1990).

As in childhood, boys have greater maximum working capacity and more upper limb and trunk strength per unit weight and fat-free mass than girls, but there are no corresponding sex differences for lower limb strength (Docherty and Gaul 1991). Maximum work capacity is positively related to body size and it is larger, relative to weight, in slow maturers than in rapid maturers, probably on account of differences in body composition (Kemper et al. 1986). Variations in the timing of pubescence and the large pubescent changes in size and body composition cause considerable changes in serial performance data during pubescence, which reduce the tracking coefficients.

6. After Pubescence

After pubescence there is rapid deceleration in the rates of growth in stature and weight. Increases in fat-free mass and arm muscle area continue until the early 20s; these increases are more rapid in males than females. During this time, there are similar increases in percent body fat and skinfold thicknesses in each sex.

Adult stature is reached at median ages of about 21 years in males and 17 years in females (Roche 1989). In United States groups the median amounts of growth in stature after 16 years are about 1.2 cm in males and 0.9 cm in females. The median total growth in stature after menarche is 7.4 cm and that after peak height velocity is 17.8 cm in males and 15.8 cm in females. About half of each total increase occurs in the first year after menarche or after peak height velocity, and growth has almost stopped five years after these events. The amounts of growth in stature after menarche and peak height velocity are inversely related to the ages at which these events occur. In the postpubescent period, weight increases more in males than in females, and there are marked decelerations in each sex.

7. Reference Data

A single set of reference data is essential for international comparisons but a recent national set can be used within a country if it was developed in an appropriate way. The data should be from a large sample of healthy children, with documentation of sampling, measurement procedures, age grouping, and data management and analysis. Ideal reference data would have correction factors for important variables such as parental size. The case for a single set is based on the small differences in size among upper socioeconomic groups from various countries. The minor differences noted may be environmental. It is important to stress that reference data are not targets for individuals but the reference distributions are targets when intervention programs are applied to groups.

See also: Genetics and Human Development

References

Ashizawa K, Takahashi C, Yanagisawa S 1977 Stature and body weight growth patterns from longitudinal data of Japanese children born during World War II. *J. Human. Ergol.* 6(1): 29–40

Bock R D, Sykes R C 1989 Evidence for continuing secular increase in height within families in the United States. *Am. J. Hum. Biol.* 1(2): 143–48

Brook C G D, Stanhope R 1989 Normal puberty: Physical characteristics and endocrinology. In: Brook C G D (ed.) 1989 *Clinical Paediatric Endocrinology*, 2nd edn. Blackwell Scientific, Oxford

Byard P J, Siervogel R M, Roche A F 1989 X-linked pattern of inheritance for serial measures of weight/stature². *Am. J. Hum. Biol.* 1(4): 443–49

Byard P J, Guo S, Roche A F 1991 Family resemblance for patterns of growth in early childhood. *Am J. Hum. Biol.* 3(4): 332–37

Chrzastek-Spruch H M 1984 Share of genetic factors in growth and development of children based on longitudinal studies. In: Borms J, Hauspie R, Sand A, Susanne C, Hebbelinck M (eds.) 1984 *Human Growth and Development*. Plenum Press, New York

Cronk C E, Roche A F, Chumlea W C, Kent R 1982a Longitudinal trends of weight/stature² in childhood in relationship to adulthood body fat measures. *Hum. Biol.* 54(4): 751–64

Cronk C E et al. 1982b Longitudinal trends and continuity in weight/stature² from 3 months to 18 years. *Hum. Biol.* 54(4): 729–49

Cronk C E, Mukherjee D, Roche A F 1983 Changes in triceps and subscapular skinfold thickness during adolescence. *Hum. Biol.* 55(3): 707–21

Docherty D, Gaul C A 1991 Relationship of body size, physique, and composition to physical performance in young boys and girls. *Int. J. Sports Med.* 12(6): 525–32

El-Nofely A A, Abou-Zeid A W, Tawfik W A 1988 The influence of some socio-demographic factors on weight/height² in Egyptian children aged 6–14 years. *Int. J. Anthrop.* 3: 131–38

Elwood P C, Sweetnam P M, Gray O P, Davies D P, Wood P D P 1987 Growth of children from 0–5 years: with special reference to mother's smoking in pregnancy. *Ann. Hum. Biol.* 14(1): 543–57

Guo S, Roche A F, Siervogel R M, Chumlea W C, Jennings A 1992 Risk analysis of body mass index (BMI): Prediction of adult overweight from childhood. Part II. Risk estimates and their practical application. *Am. J. Phys. Anthrop.* S14: 85

Himes J H, Roche A F, Thissen D 1981 *Parent-specific Adjustments for Assessment of Recumbent Length and Stature*. Monographs in Paediatrics, Vol. 13, pp. 1–88. Karger, Basel

Himes J H, Roche A F 1986 Subcutaneous fatness and stature: relationship from infancy to adulthood. *Hum. Biol.* 58(5): 737–50

Johnston F E 1986 Somatic growth of the infant and preschool child. In: Falkner F, Tanner J M (eds.) 1986 *Human Growth: A Comprehensive Treatise*, 2nd edn. *Vol. 2: Postnatal Growth, Neurobiology*. Plenum Press, New York

Johnston F E, Sharko J, Cravioto J, DeLicardie E 1984 Growth and skeletal maturation of Mexican children 4 to 7 years, with and without diagnoses of chronic protein-energy malnutrition. In: Borms J, Hauspie R, Sand A, Susanne C, Hebbelinck M (eds.) 1984 *Human Growth and Development*. Plenum Press, New York

Kemper H C G, Verschuur R, Ritmeester J W 1986 Maximal aerobic power in early and late maturing teenagers. In: Rutenfranz J, Mocellin R, Klimt F (eds.) 1986 *Children and Exercise XII*. Human Kinetics Publishers, Champaign, Illinois

Lefevre J, Beunen G, Steens G, Claessens A, Renson R 1990 Motor performance during adolescence and age thirty as related to age at peak height velocity. *Ann. Hum. Biol.* 17(5): 423–35

Malina R M, Himes J M, Stepick C D, Gutierez Lopez F, Buschang P H 1980 Growth of rural and urban children in the Valley of Oaxaca, Mexico. *Am. J. Phys. Anthrop.* 55(2): 269–80

Martorell R, Habicht J P 1986 Growth in early childhood in developing countries. In: Falkner F, Tanner J M (eds.) 1986 *Human Growth: A Comprehensive Treatise*, 2nd edn. *Vol. 3: Methodology, Ecological, Genetic and Nutritional Effects on Growth*. Plenum Press, New York

McCall R B, Meyers E D Jr, Hartman J, Roche A F 1983 Developmental changes in head-circumference and mental-performance growth rates: A test of Epstein's phrenoblysis hypothesis. *Dev. Psychobiol.* 16(6): 457–68

Pařízková J 1976 Growth and growth velocity of lean body mass and fat in adolescent boys. *Pediat. Res.* 10: 647–50

Prader A 1984 Biomedical and endocrinological aspects of normal growth and development. In: Borms J, Hauspie

R, Sand A, Susanne C, Hebbelinck M (eds.) 1984 *Human Growth and Development*. Plenum Press, New York

Roche A F 1968 Sex-associated differences in skeletal maturity. *Acta Anat. (Basel)* 71: 321–40

Roche A F 1974 Differential timing of maximum length increments among bones within individuals. *Hum. Biol.* 46(1): 145–57

Roche A F (ed.) 1979 Secular trends in human growth, maturation and development. *Monogr. Soc. Res. Child Dev.* 44(3–4): 3–120

Roche A F 1980 Possible catch-up growth of the brain in man. *Acta Med. Auxol.* 12(3): 165–79

Roche A F 1989 The final phase of growth in stature. *Growth, Genetics and Hormones* 5: 4–6

Roche A F, Wainer H, Thissen D 1975 *Predicting Adult Stature for Individuals*. Monographs in Paediatrics, Vol. 3, pp. 1–114. Karger, Basel

Roche A F, Roberts J, Hamill P V V 1976 *Skeletal Maturity of Youths 12–17 Years: United States Vital and Health Statistics*. National Center for Health Statistics, Series 11, No. 160, United States Government Printing Office, Washington, DC

Roche A F, Himes J H 1980 Incremental growth charts. *Am. J. Clin. Nutr.* 33: 2041–52

Roche A F, Chumlea W C, Thissen D 1988 *Assessing the Skeletal Maturity of the Hand-Wrist: FELS Method*. C C Thomas, Springfield, Illinois

Roede M J, van Wieringen J C 1985 Growth diagrams 1980: Netherlands third nation-wide survey. *Tijdeschrift voor Sociale Gezondheidszorg* 63: 1–34

Rolland-Cachera M-F et al. 1984 Adiposity rebound in children: A simple indicator for predicting obesity. *Am. J. Clin. Nutr.* 39(1): 129–35

Rolland-Cachera M-F, Bellisle F, Sempé M 1989 The prediction in boys and girls of the weight/height² index and various skinfold measurements in adults: A two-decade follow-up study. *Int. J. Obesity* 13(3): 305–11

Rutledge M M, Clark J, Woodruff C, Krause G, Flynn M A 1976 A longitudinal study of total body potassium in normal breastfed and bottle-fed infants. *Pediatr. Res.* 10(2): 114–17

Sempé G, Pédron G, Roy-Pernot M-P 1979 *Auxologie: Méthode et séquences*. Laboratorie Théraplix, Paris

Siervogel R M, Roche A F, Himes J H, Chumlea W C, McCammon R 1982 Subcutaneous fat distribution in males and females from 1 to 39 years of age. *Am. J. Clin. Nutr.* 36(1): 162–71

Siervogel R M, Roche A F, Guo S, Mukherjee D, Chumlea W C 1991 Patterns of change in weight/stature² from 2 to 18 years: Findings from long-term serial data for children in the FELS Longitudinal Growth Study. *Int. J. Obesity* 15(7): 478–85

Towne B, Guo S, Siervogel R M, Roche A F 1992 Genetic analysis of percentile body weight variation from ages 2 to 17. *Proc. Annual Meeting of the American Society for Clinical Nutrition*, No. 131

van Wieringen J C, Wafelbakker F, Verbrugge H P, De Haas J H 1971 *Growth Diagrams 1965 Netherlands: Second National Survey on 0–24 Year Olds*. Wolters-Noordhoff, Groningen

Whitehead R G, Paul A A 1984 Growth charts and the assessment of infant feeding practices in the western world and in developing countries. *Early Hum. Develop.* 9(3): 187–207

Further Reading

Lohman T G, Roche A F, Martorell R (eds.) 1991 *Anthropometric Standardization Reference Manual*, Abridged edition. Human Kinetics Publishers, Champaign, Illinois

Malina R M, Bouchard C 1991 *Growth, Maturation, and Physical Activity*. Human Kinetics Publishers, Champaign, Illinois

Malina R M, Roche A F (eds.) 1983 *Manual of Physical Status and Performance in Childhood. Vol. 2: Physical Performance*. Plenum Press, New York

Roche A F, Malina R M (eds.) 1983 *Manual of Physical Status and Performance in Childhood. Vol. 1: Physical Status*. Plenum Press, New York

Shephard R J 1991 *Body Composition in Biological Anthropology*. Cambridge University Press, Cambridge

Roche A F 1992 *Growth, Maturation and Body Composition: The Fels Longitudinal Study 1929–1991*. Cambridge University Press, Cambridge

Sex Differences in Behavior and Development

M. Stemmler and A. C. Petersen

The controversy regarding the topic of sex differences ranges from a discussion of the nature and importance of these differences to a discussion of their causes and consequences. Common themes of the controversy are questions such as whether nature or nurture plays a stronger role in accounting for the observed differences, whether men and women share more similarities than dissimilarities, and whether the study of sex differences is reduced to the measurement of women's deviations from a well-established male norm (Petersen et al. 1982, Gilligan 1982).

Because of the magnitude of findings on sex differences relative to space limitations, this entry will only sample the relevant areas with brief summaries of: the history of the study of sex differences; the status in the early 1990s of some traditional areas in the study of sex differences (i.e., cognition and achievement, personality and social behavior, and biology); and the development of sex differences, an emerging area in the field.

1. History of Research on Sex Differences

The history of research on sex differences is marked by personal beliefs of researchers and the prevailing *Zeitgeist* of particular eras. The study of sex differences in the United States can be traced to the turn of the twentieth century, when female researchers such as Helen Bradford Thompson, Leta Stetter Hollingsworth, and Helen Thompson Wooley tried to prove that women were not inferior to men (Shields 1975); an unsuccessful battle against scientific beliefs in substantial psychological sex differences. Until the 1960s, most of the findings of sex difference research confirmed popular stereotypes and, according to Bernard (1976) and Shields (1975), even helped to prolong women's inferior status.

The study of sex differences in the 1970s was largely influenced by the women's movement. A growing number of women in the field challenged traditional research by pointing out shortcomings and methodological flaws. Further, women became increasingly interested in the study of female abilities and their implications for female psychology and development.

In the 1980s, this field focused on understanding female behavior apart from male behavior. Researchers like Gilligan (1982) argued that major theories of development are androcentric. The concepts and constructs used in empirical research most often represented the interests, competence, and worldviews of men, with the consequence that documented sex differences portrayed women in an unfavorable way.

By the mid-1980s, two new trends within the study of sex differences evolved. The use of meta-analysis to analyze and summarize studies on specific sex differences (e.g., Hyde and Linn 1986, Linn and Petersen 1986) reduced the likelihood of bias in reviews. The use of a lifespan perspective and prospective studies of normative samples permit identification of different developmental tracks for men and women together with their underlying biological, social, and psychological causes (e.g., Petersen et al. 1991).

2. Observed Differences in Behavior

2.1 Cognition and Achievement

The study of sex differences in cognitive functioning can be divided into four domains: (a) intelligence, (b) cognitive abilities, (c) cognitive development, and (d) academic achievement (Dubas and Petersen 1993).

Research on general intelligence measured by IQ tests has not found any significant sex differences (e.g., Maccoby and Jacklin 1975). It is important to note that the inventors of IQ tests, Binet and Terman, did not believe that there were sex differences (Dubas

and Petersen 1993). As a consequence, IQ tests have been carefully constructed to yield no sex differences; items which show a sex bias are deleted.

Thurstone's notion of "primary mental abilities" (1938) permitted a comparison of females and males on different cognitive abilities. In their classic review of the literature on sex-related differences, Maccoby and Jacklin (1975) identified three cognitive abilities showing reliable sex differences: in spatial and mathematical abilities males have an advantage over females, whereas females score consistently higher than males on tests of verbal abilities. In general, studies using data collected after 1974 show a decrease in sex differences in cognitive abilities (Hyde and Linn 1986). This decrease happened faster than could be explained by any biological changes in the population.

Studies on cognitive sex differences using Piaget's model of stage development of intelligence concluded that the stage of formal operation is achieved by boys two to four times more often than girls. However, studies that use sex-neutral stimuli, and not the science experiments used by Piaget, find no differences.

The United States achievement indicators such as course grades, years of education, and occupational aspirations portray females in a more egalitarian way. For instance, girls receive higher grades than boys at all grade levels and in all academic areas (National Science Foundation 1988). In 1990, women earned over 50 percent of the bachelor's and master's degrees but only 36 percent of the doctorates. Despite no differences between males and females in college completion, women are still not as successful as men in the world of work (Dubas and Petersen 1993).

In sum, there are now only a few cognitive abilities on which there are consistent but small sex differences. Jacklin (1989) even concluded that "gender is not an important variable in the measurement of intellectual abilities" (p. 131). Yet attainments by women as adults still lag behind those of men.

2.2 Personality and Social Behaviors

In considering gender differences in personality and social behavior, research has focused on aggression, comformity, empathy, and causal attributions of success and failure.

In their landmark review of sex differences, Maccoby and Jacklin (1975) concluded that there is clear evidence for sex differences in aggression, with males being more aggressive than females. Whereas there is little discussion about the existence of a sex difference, there is more dispute about the possible causes of such a difference (Deaux 1985). In their follow-up review on sex differences in aggression, Maccoby and Jacklin (1980) concluded that both socialization and biological factors cause the observable sex differences in aggression. One biological variable accounting for these differences is activity level (Block 1976).

In their extensive review of ability to be influenced and conformity, Eagly and Carli (1981) concluded that sex differences do not exist except in situations involving group problems. However, only 1 percent of the variance in these behaviors is accounted for by the "variable" sex (Eagly and Carli 1981).

In their summary of sex differences in empathy, Petersen et al. (1982) stated that "there appears to be evidence of greater empathic response from females, but the results are somewhat less consistent than with other characteristics, such as aggression" (p. 1703). Sex differences in empathy are primarily attributable to the ability to decode nonverbal behavior (Rosenthal and DePaulo 1979) and to traditional feminine role behavior.

Causal attributions of success and failure can be considered with three models: general externality, self-derogation, and low expectancy. All three models predict that women are unlikely to attribute their success to ability. Whereas former investigations supported the externality model, a recent meta-analysis of studies on causal attributions revealed that none of the models is well-supported empirically (Whitley et al. 1986). However, the authors stated that the results of the studies on causal attribution indicate two consistent sex differences: men make stronger ability attributions and weaker luck attributions than women, regardless of the outcome.

2.3 Biological Differences

Within the study of biological characteristics of males and females, three areas have received high attention: (a) hormonal differences, particularly sex-steroid hormones; (b) differences in brain development; and (c) gender-differential vulnerability.

Differences in kind and amount of hormones are frequently cited as causing differences in the behavior of males and females, based on results of research with animals. Sex hormones differ even prenatally and there is some evidence that these hormones might be associated with sex differences in cognitive abilities (e.g., Petersen 1976). Recent technical developments made it possible to study hormone–behavior linkages in humans using nonintrusive measures and normal populations of children and adolescents (Jacklin 1989). The results of large-scale studies of adolescents show that the simple models of hormone–behavior relationships developed from animal research are not able to explain the data satisfactorily. Studies with young children revealed that a particular hormone may be related to behavior in different ways for boys and girls (Jacklin 1989). Because there are few replicated results, caution in inferring hormonal causation for these sex differences is suggested.

There is evidence that the brains of male and female rats differ anatomically (e.g., Goy and McEwen 1980). Animal research has shown that the sexual differentiation of the brain is mainly driven by hormones and it is hypothesized that prenatal hormones have an organizing effect on sex-specific postnatal behavior (Susman and Petersen 1992). One way in which hormones can organize behavior is through sensitization; that is, hormones may sensitize individuals in such a way that males and females differ in readiness for certain types of emotional responses (Susman and Petersen 1992).

Studies on the human brain have been less successful in providing evidence for anatomical differences between males and females. Further, brain development is also influenced by experience.

Studies of sex differences in brain organization have focused on the link between brain lateralization and cognitive abilities, where complete lateralization was associated with better spatial ability. However, the results have been inconsistent and more recent research examines specific locations of function and myelinization of the brain (Gibson and Petersen 1991).

Vulnerability is another area of well-documented sex differences. Males are more physically vulnerable than females, a difference more pronounced at the beginning and end of the lifespan (Jacklin 1989).

3. Biopsychosocial Development

The study of sex differences can profit from longitudinal studies on normative samples where biological, psychological, and social factors are taken into consideration to explain the development of males and females. Instead of comparing males and females on a number of outcomes, the different developmental tracks for boys and girls are identified. One example of such an approach is the Adolescent Mental Health Study by Petersen (1984). She found that developmental differences between boys and girls in depressed affect can be explained by experiential factors like relative timing of pubertal changes, transition to secondary school, and the number of stressful life events experienced (Petersen et al. 1991); also important is the way in which ups and downs in psychological well-being during the life course are integrated into a person's life history. Sex differences in observed behavior cannot be fully understood until the influences on male and female developmental trajectories are examined.

4. Conclusion

There are only a few areas in research where sex differences are well-established. The declining differences in cognition suggest that sex differences result less from biological, and especially inherited, differences than from different life circumstances. Differences in life circumstances for males and females are less obvious than in the past though they still exist in the early 1990s in superficially equal-looking contexts like school. For reasons of gender equity, the idea of single-sex schools have become more popular. The study of different developmental tracks for males and females can provide further information for such discussions.

References

Bernard J 1976 *Sex Differences: An Overview (Module 26).* MSS Modular Publications, New York

Block J H 1976 Issues, problems, and pitfalls in assessing sex differences: A critical review of "The Psychology of Sex Differences." *Merrill-Palmer Q.* 22(4): 283–308

Deaux K 1985 Sex and gender. *Annu. Rev. Psychol.* 36: 49–81

Dubas J S, Petersen A C 1993 Differential cognitive development and achievement in adolescent girls. In: Sugar M (ed.) 1993 *Female Adolescent Development.* Brunner/Mazel, New York

Eagly A H, Carli L L 1981 Sex of researchers and sex-typed communications as determinants of sex differences in influenceability: A meta-analysis of social influence studies. *Psych. Bull.* 90: 1–20

Gibson K R Petersen A C 1991 *Brain Maturation and Cognitive Development: Comparative and Cross-cultural Perspectives.* Aldine de Gruyter, New York

Gilligan C 1982 *In a Different Voice: Psychological Theory and Women's Development.* Harvard University Press, Cambridge, Massachusetts

Goy R W, McEwen B S 1980 *Sexual Differentiation of the Brain.* MIT Press, Cambridge, Massachusetts

Hyde J S, Linn M C 1986 *The Psychology of Gender: Advances Through Meta-analysis.* Johns Hopkins University Press, Baltimore, Maryland

Jacklin C N 1989 Female and male: Issues of gender. *Am. Psychol.* 44(2): 127–33

Linn M C, Petersen A C 1986 A meta-analysis of gender differences in spatial ability: Implications for mathematics and science achievement. In: Hyde J S, Linn M C (eds.) 1986

Maccoby E E, Jacklin C N 1975 *The Psychology of Sex Differences.* Stanford University Press, Stanford, California

Maccoby E E, Jacklin C N 1980 Sex differences in aggression: A rejoinder and reprise. *Child Dev.* 51(4): 964–80

National Science Foundation 1988 *Women and Minorities in Science and Engineering.* National Science Foundation, Washington, DC

Petersen A C 1976 Physical androgyny and cognitive functioning in adolescence. *Dev. Psychol.* 12(6): 524–33.

Petersen A C 1984 The early adolescence study: An overview. *Journal of Early Adolescence.* 4(2): 103–06

Petersen A C, Sarigiani P A, Kennedy R E 1991 Adolescent depression: Why more girls? *Journal of Youth and Adolescence* 20: 247–71 (Special issue: The emergence of depressive symptoms during adolescence)

Petersen A C, Tobin-Richards M H, Crockett L 1982 Sex differences. In: Mitzel H E (ed.) 1982 *Encyclopedia of Educational Research*, Vol. 4. The Free Press, New York

Rosenthal R, DePaulo B M 1979 Sex differences in eavesdropping on nonverbal cues. *J. Pers. Soc. Psychol.* 37: 273–85

Shields S A 1975 Functionalism, Darwinism, and the psychology of women: A study in social myth. *Am. Psychol.* 30(7): 739–54

Susman E J, Petersen A C 1992 Hormones and behavior. In: McAnarney E R, Kreipe R E, Orr D P, Comerci G D (eds.) 1992 *Textbook of Adolescent Medicine.* W P Saunders, Philadelphia, Pennsylvania

Thurstone L L 1938 *Primary Mental Abilities.* University of Chicago Press, Chicago, Illinois

Whitley B E, McHugh M C, Frieze I H 1986 Assessing the theoretical models for sex differences in causal attributions of success and failure. In: Hyde J S, Linn M C (eds.) 1986

Further Reading

Eagly A H 1986 Some meta-analytic approaches to examining the validity of gender-difference research. In: Hyde J S, Linn M C (eds.) 1986

Rosenthal R, Rubin D C 1982 Further meta-analytic procedures for assessing cognitive gender differences. *J. Educ. Psychol.* 74(5): 708–12

Temperament Development

G. A. Kohnstamm and R. P. Martin

In the opinion of most authors who write on the subject, temperament is considered to be a trait related to the emotional, motivational, and social aspects of personality rather than to the cognitive, intellectual, cultural, and moral aspects. Furthermore, within the emotional, motivational, and social domain, temperament refers to inborn rather than acquired sources of behavior, to those individual differences that are assumed to be constitutional and should thus have at least some stability over the course of life. Many

authors also contend that a certain degree of heritability is a requirement for calling a trait a matter of temperament.

This discussion of temperament begins with the history of the study of temperamental differences, followed by a description of the major conceptual approaches in use in the early 1990s. The entry continues with an inspection of the relevance of temperament studies for classroom behavior, for the processes of teaching, and for the development of skills and knowledge. Finally, an extremely interesting new development is mentioned in which theories of childhood temperament and adult personality are related: the "Big Five" or Five Factor Model in personality psychology.

1. History and Conceptual Approaches

Whereas the study of temperament in adulthood has a long international history, the study of temperament in childhood is rather new and is only beginning to be internationally oriented in the early 1990s.

Thomas and Chess (1977) and their colleagues in the New York Longitudinal Study (NYLS) are generally credited for the wave of interest in temperament in infancy and childhood which became manifest in the 1970s and 1980s. The sudden increase of temperament research in childhood since the 1980s bears witness to this renewed interest in an old concept.

However, there were also other reasons for the new interest in the phenomena collected under the umbrella term "temperament" in infancy and childhood. In the United States the work *Personality and Temperament* by the psychologist Diamond appeared in 1957. Diamond gave evidence for the view that individuation of temperament takes place very early, so that within the first year of life it is possible to identify behavioral characteristics which the individual is likely to retain into adolescence. Diamond's book, although not widely read or quoted, led to another seminal volume by Buss and Plomin (1975).

The new popularity of thinking about individual differences in temperament among infants and children led to a steadily growing research literature in the 1980s. This new interest in basic individual differences is probably related to the equally new general interest in the biological roots of behaviour and the fascination with progress in biogenetics and psychopharmacology. The results from some extensive twin studies caused many to rethink their position on the nature–nurture controversy. Accepting constitutional propensities for a particular behavioral style was no longer synonymous with a racist or sexist attitude.

There are four major approaches to temperament in childhood and adolescence. The first is the clinically oriented approach of the United States psychiatrists Thomas and Chess (1977) and the pediatrician Carey with all its related endeavors, including the work of Lerner and Lerner (1986) and of the educationists Keogh (1989) and Martin (1989). Whereas the originators of this approach discerned nine separate temperament dimensions, many of the people who chose to work in this framework have reduced the number of dimensions because of the results of factor analyses. The second approach is the theoretical approach of the psychologists Buss and Plomin, who originally discerned four separate dimensions but subsequently reduced their set to three: emotionality, activity,

and sociability/shyness. The third approach is the theoretically oriented scheme mainly directed at infancy, originated by Escalona (1968), Rothbart and Derryberry, and by Goldsmith and Campos (Rothbart and Goldsmith 1985).

Finally, there is the European approach. The interest of early German educators in individual differences in temperament, which arose in the nineteenth century, was continued in Poland by Strelau (1985). His main temperament concept, derived from Pavlov, is the strength of the nervous system. According to Strelau's "regulative theory," individuals differ in their capacity to regulate exitatory and inhibitory processes. Strelau also refers to Gray's concept of arousability as a key notion of temperament. In addition to standardized laboratory observations, this group also uses questionnaires to measure the strength of excitation (Strelau 1989).

Because the majority of studies of temperament and development which have relevance for education belong to the first group mentioned above, this entry devotes less attention to the other three. Eventually these others may also become important for the processes of education.

2. Temperament and Education

The relevance of temperamental differences for the process of education was probably first explicitly recognized by the nineteenth-century German writer Herbart, for the practical purpose of fitting teaching methods to these individual differences. However, most early twentieth-century educational reformers did not share this interest. For example, in the writings of Maria Montessori, individual differences in temperament-like characteristics are generally not treated as a matter of concern for teachers. On the other hand, Downey (1923), believed temperament to be determined by: (a) the amount of nerve energy possessed by the individual; and (b) the tendency for such energy to express itself immediately in motor reactions. More specifically, she held that in schooling "Disciplinary problems demand a broader view of personality than merely an IQ-rating. If at various stages in development (e.g., adolescence) different temperamental patterns prevail, it may be necessary to modify educational methods to meet these differences" (Downey 1923 p. 306).

The instructional environment in which school teaching ordinarily takes place favors the pupil who can sustain attention, who can persist in a task—even when difficult or boring—and who can remain seated for hours in succession (Martin 1989). One can easily think of certain temperamental characteristics that facilitate coping with the ordeals of learning and performing in the classroom. The same may apply to doing homework. High levels of gross motor activity are not adaptive in this context, unless regulated (Strelau 1989) and controlled. The capacity to persist in focused attention, on the other hand, is highly adaptive. Regulation and control is also important if strong tendencies for expressing negative reactions to unpleasant social and physical stimuli are present. Students also need to be tolerant of changes in routines, teachers, environments, temperatures, noise levels, and other pupils. Finally, it is adaptive to be liked by others, both peers and teachers. Looking back at the nine NYLS dimensions of Thomas and Chess (1977), it is easy to predict that children who score high on the negatively valued poles of many of these dimensions will have a difficult time in school. This is exactly what has been found in several studies (for overviews, see Keogh 1989 and Martin 1989).

However, there are some problems with temperament assessments. First, in most studies comparing temperament ratings by parents and by teachers, the agreement is not high. One reason for this discrepancy is that the situations at home and at school are so different that the behavioral expression of underlying temperamental traits is different in both situations. Because temperament inferences are made from observed behavioral characteristics in specific day-to-day situations, two different groups of observers, say parents and teachers, produce different "perceived" temperaments in children and pupils. If this is true, is it possible to know what the "real" temperament is?

Another problem is that the behavioral expressions of high activity level, inattentiveness, and uncontrolled negative reactions are also the main components of the familiar syndrome known as "attention deficit disorder with hyperactivity". What advantage is there in recasting this well-known diagnostic category into temperamental terms?

One clear advantage of thinking in terms of individual differences in temperament is found in school counselors talking with both parents and teachers, and in teachers regulating their own negative reactions to the behavior of some of their pupils. To be able to see particular types of behavior patterns as expressions of inborn characteristics of temperament can relieve both parents and teachers of feelings of inadequacy, guilt, and frustration, and can thus be helpful in improving relations. This function of improving mental health was what Thomas and Chess had in mind when they launched their crusade in the behavioristic and psychoanalytically oriented 1950s and 1960s in the United States.

Keogh and Kornblau (Keogh 1989) have shown that teachers have firm views about the temperamental attributes that constitute a global cluster named "teachability," whereas Feurstein and Martin (Keogh 1989) found that teachers value children's behaviors that contribute to "manageability" and sociability.

One kind of data that provides some insight into those temperamental characteristics that teachers find most salient for their work with students come from the results of factor analyses of teacher ratings of temperament. Keogh et al. (1982), who factor analyzed

the items of the Teacher Temperament Questionnaire of Thomas and Chess (1977), and Presley and Martin (1994), who factor analyzed the items of the Teacher Form of the Temperament Assessment Battery for Children (Martin 1988), obtained three factors. The first and strongest factor was heavily loaded with items dealing with attention to schoolwork. This factor was labelled "Task Persistence," and a child achieving a high score on this factor would be characterized as being not easily distracted while engaged in seatwork, as persistent even when forced with difficult tasks, and as being able to control his or her motor activity level. The second factor, termed "Social Inhibition," consisted primarily of items dealing with a shy or withdrawing response when faced with a new social situation, and a slowness in engaging in a new school task, or a new learning activity. The underlying psychological process seems to be a fearful, tentative reaction to novel situations. Finally, the third factor, known as "Reactivity," deals primarily with an over-reaction in stressful situations. For example, a child scoring high on this dimension would overreact if teased by others, or if the teacher had to correct his or her behavior. Further, children scoring high on this dimension are characterized as being loud, extremely active, and disruptive of ongoing classroom activity. This factor has much in common with the characteristic that is sometimes labeled "emotional intensity."

Martin et al. (1983) have shown that teachers have a more positive attitude, and more affectionate feelings, toward students who are task-persistent, and who are socially approaching in interactions with their teacher and other children. Many other researchers (Brophy and Good 1974) have shown that highly active, and overreactive students are disruptive of ongoing classroom activities, and tend to engender negative teacher attitudes. The results of recent factor analyses of temperament scales seem to support these studies, and demonstrate that the characteristics of persistence, social inhibition, and emotional reactivity or intensity are the temperamental characteristics that are most salient for teachers, at least in elementary schools.

It is important for teachers and school counselors to realize that there are clear average sex differences in temperament, notably with regard to the dimensions motor activity and emotionality. Boys of all ages tend to be motorically more active than girls, whereas girls after puberty generally tend to rate themselves as more emotional (Kohnstamm 1989). For motor activity the difference between the means of the two separate normal distributions is about half a standard deviation. Although such a difference may not mean much for the total proportion of explained variance in the common distribution, boys outnumber girls considerably in the upper "hyperactive" tail of that distribution, as every teacher knows. For emotionality the results are less consistent. However, in self-ratings after puberty the means for the two sexes also differ by about half a standard deviation. Although these sex differences probably have biological roots, cultural effects enlarge the basic sex differences into stereotypical gender differences. The effects of culture are also different on males and females occupying the same position on specific dimensions. School-age boys and girls in the seventh decile of the common distribution of inhibition or of externalizing reactivity following frustration elicit quite different reactions, dependent upon the culture in general and on social class in particular. The more rigidly the sex roles in a culture or social class are fixed, the more different are the reactions.

Further, the reactions differ according to the situation in which the behavior is exhibited and observed. The fact that teacher ratings produce larger sex differences than parent ratings in some of the studies can probably be explained in several ways. One reason certainly is that the school environment, with its limited space, its many behavioral restrictions, and its intensive social interactions of the two sexes, elicits behavior patterns that parents may not always see at home. So rather than thinking that teachers are more sex-stereotyped in their perceptions than parents, it is more likely that school life elicits more sex-stereotyped behaviors than life at home.

3. A New Development: The Five Factor Model

In adult personality psychology, support for a five factor model or FFM (also known as the Big Five) is expressed in many publications based on studies undertaken in the United States, the Netherlands, and Germany. The FFM claims that, at least in Western cultures and languages, the perceptions of individual differences in personality by groups of perceivers (parents, teachers, peers), have an underlying structure of five basic dimensions. These five dimensions are usually labeled as follows: (a) extraversion—introversion; (b) agreeableness; (c) conscientiousness; (d) neuroticism versus emotional stability; and (e) intellect, culture, or openness to experience (John et al. 1988, Digman 1990, Goldberg 1993). Digman (1963) was the first to demonstrate the operation of the FFM in teacher ratings of first- and second-grade children in Hawaii. More recently, studies done with schoolchildren in the Netherlands, Belgium, and the United States seem to indicate that at least from early adolescence onward the best model for categorizing individual differences among pupils is the Five Factor Model (Halverson et al. 1994). Developmental psychologists from several countries have posed the question of how these dimensions develop (in the perception of individual differences) from childhood into adulthood: what are the roots of the Big Five? The structure of perceived temperament in early childhood as described above seems to differ considerably from a FFM structure, but in late childhood the correspondence seems to grow considerably. Thus, from early adolescence onward, parents and teachers alike—as groups, individuals may differ from these group trends—

unconsciously seem to use a five-dimensional scheme to perceive, judge, and evaluate the temperaments and personalities of their children and pupils. More studies are required to confirm the results found thus far. However, it is already clear that the Five Factor Model is a powerful tool, and serves as a unifying framework in a field hampered by so many divergent views on individual differences in temperament and personality.

See also: Emotional Development

References

Brophy J, Good T 1974 *Teacher—Student Relationships: Causes and Consequences.* Holt, Rinehart and Winston, New York
Buss A H, Plomin R 1975 *A Temperament Theory of Personality Development.* Wiley Interscience, New York
Diamond S 1957 *Personality and Temperament.* Harper & Row, New York
Digman J M 1963 Principal dimensions of child personality as inferred from teacher's judgments. *Child Dev.* 34: 43–60
Digman J M 1990 Personality structure: Emergence of the five-factor model. *Annu. Rev. Psychol.* 41: 417–40
Downey J E 1923 *The Will-temperament and Its Testing.* World Book Company, Yonkers-on-Hudson, New York
Escalona S 1968 *The Roots of Individuality: Normal Patterns of Development in Infancy.* Tavistock Publications, London
Goldberg L R 1993 The structure of phenotype personality traits. *Am. Psychol.* 40(1): 26–34
Halverson C F, Kohnstamm G A, Martin R P 1994 *Development of the Structure of Temperament and Personality from Infancy to Adulthood.* Erlbaum, Hillsdale, New Jersey
John O P, Angleitner A, Ostendorf F 1988 The lexical approach to personality: A historical review of trait taxonomic research. *European Journal of Personality* 2(3): 171–203
Keogh B K 1989 Applying temperament research to school. In: Kohnstamm G A, Bates J E, Rothbart M K (eds.) 1989 *Temperament in Childhood.* Wiley, Chichester
Keogh B K, Pullis M E, Cadwell C 1982 A short-form of the Teacher Temperament Questionnaire. *J. Educ. Meas.* 19(4): 323–29
Kohnstamm G A 1989 Temperament in childhood: Cross-cultural and sex differences. In: Kohnstamm G A, Bates J E, Rothbart M K (eds.) 1989 *Temperament in Childhood.* Wiley, Chichester
Lerner J V, Lerner R M (eds.) 1986 *Temperament and Social Interaction in Infants and Children.* Jossey-Bass, San Francisco, California
Martin R P 1988 *Temperament Assessment Battery for Children.* Clinical Psychology Publishing, Brandon, Vermont
Martin R P 1989 Activity level, distractability, and persistence: Critical characteristics in early schooling. In: Kohnstamm G A, Bates J E, Rothbart M K (eds.) 1989 *Temperament in Childhood.* Wiley, Chichester
Martin R P, Nagel R, Paget K 1983 Relationship between temperament and classroom behavior, teacher attitudes, and academic achievement. *Journal of Psychoeducational Assessment* 1: 377–86

Presley R, Martin R P 1994 Toward a structure of preschool temperament: factor structure of the temperament assessment battery for children. *J. Pers.* 62: 415–448

Rothbart M K, Goldsmith H H 1985 Three approaches to the study of infant temperament. *Dev. Rev.* 5(3): 237–60

Strelau J 1985 *Temperament Bases of Behavior: Warsaw Studies on Individual Differences*. Swets and Zeitlinger, Lisse

Strelau J 1989 The regulative theory of temperament as a result of East—West influences. In: Kohnstamm G A, Bates J E, Rothbart M K (eds.) 1989 *Temperament in Childhood*. Wiley, Chichester

Thomas A, Chess S 1977 *Temperament and Development*. Brunner/Mazel, New York

Further Reading

Kohnstamm G A, Mervielde I 1996 Personality and emotional development. In: Demetriou A, Doise W, van Lieshout CFM (eds.) 1996 *Life-span Developmental Psychology: A European Perspective*. Wiley, Chichester

Personality Development in Social Context

Socialization

A. Sturman

Socialization, in its broadest sense, is the process whereby individuals become members of society or members of sectors of society. It is concerned with how individuals adopt, or do not adopt, the values, customs, and perspectives of the surrounding culture or subcultures.

The interactive nature of socialization, that is, the interaction of values, customs, and perspectives on individuals as well as the adaptation of those values, customs, and perspectives as a result of negotiation among members of groups, has made it fertile ground for the social sciences, but especially for psychologists and sociologists either working alone or in combination as social psychologists. Each discipline, however, has tended to approach the subject from a different angle. Psychologists have focused on how individuals learn and, in particular, on stages of development, whereas sociologists have focused on the relationships into which individuals move.

The first section in this entry elaborates on the brief definition of socialization provided in this introduction. This is followed by a review of the antecedents to current theories of socialization and how they relate to more general sociological theory, a review of current theory and research on socialization, and an overview of the issues raised by research into the different contexts in which socialization takes place. Section 5 is an examination of the application to the field of education of studies into socialization, both in the sense of schooling as a socializing context and as regards the effects on schooling of other contexts such as the family.

While the discussion of the antecedents to current theory embraces psychological, anthropological, and sociological theory, most of the discussion of current theory and its application to education draws upon the sociological tradition.

1. An Elaboration of the Concept of Socialization

Bush and Simmons (1981) comment that distinctions between the concepts of maturation, development, and socialization are stressed in sociological work on socialization. Research into maturation processes and developmental stages has, however, contributed to research and theory on socialization.

Bush and Simmons also comment that maturation is depicted as entailing a more or less automatic unfolding of biological potential in a predictable sequence, while development is viewed as a set of sequential changes from simple to more complex structures within the boundaries set by both biological and social structures. Both the concepts of development and socialization stress an interaction between individual behavior and the environment, but socialization does not necessarily entail sequential change from simple to complex structures.

Wentworth (1980 p. 83) has defined socialization as: "the activity that confronts and lends structure to the entry of nonmembers into an already existing world or a sector of that world."

As described by Musgrave (1987), embodied in this definition of the concept of socialization are the implications that it is a crucial link between the existing culture of a group and its members, that it can refer to processes at many levels, and that there is no assumption that the norms learned are believed or must be obeyed, that is, the norms are not necessarily internalized and change is therefore possible. This final implication allows for resistance to socializing forces, acknowledges that individuals may construct their own norms and, consequently, makes central to the study of socialization the issue of deviance, that is, behavior which does not meet existing norms.

Socialization is therefore interactive: the values, customs, and perspectives of cultures and subcultures influence how individuals behave but do not necessarily determine that behavior. Cultural influences and individual patterns of development both require consideration.

Related to this, Gecas (1981) notes that the concept of socialization has two fairly distinct meanings in sociology, both of which are valid and necessary for an adequate conceptualization. One stresses the individual's adaptation and conformity to societal requirements, and the other emphasizes the individual's development into a self-assertive, distinct human being. Gecas comments that the changes that individuals undergo become sociologically relevant in the context of organized social relationships and, in this sense, there is a "membership" component to socialization:

> This component of socialization is most evident in the concept of identification, one of the key processes in socialization. Two aspects of socialization are relevant here: identification *of* and identification *with* . . . Identification *of* deals with the establishment of identities, that is, the determination of who one is and who the others are in the situation. Identification *with* refers to the emotional and psychological attachment that one has with some person or group. (Gecas 1981 p. 166)

Musgrave (1987 p. 3) has also referred to socialization as forward looking and to the effects of prior socializing experiences:

> The outcomes are important to those involved, both to those responsible for the continuity of groups, that is those with some power, and to those being socialised, whether unconsciously or because they hope to become members of some group. Sociologists often speak of anticipatory socialisation to highlight this forward-looking aspect. What has, however, to be noted is that prior socialisation may prepare potential members of groups well or less well for further experiences.

Individuals, during the course of their lives, do not experience one process of socialization but are subjected to many. Agents of socialization include wider cultural influences, families, and the formal organizations in which individuals work or learn (schools, military academies, prisons, public service bureaucracies, and the like). Sieber and Gordon (1981) categorize these socializing organizations into "total institutions," such as prisons, military academies, and boarding schools, and organizations that are less total in their regimes such as schools, summer camps, and the like. Goffman (1961) discusses the pervasive socializing influences of institutions with long duration and high intensity compared with other less pervasive or intensive institutions, of which schools are one example. Focusing on the contexts in which socialization takes place requires that special attention be given to the social structural features of these situations, such as patterns of interaction, group composition, and other group features like size and boundary permeability (see Gecas 1981).

Gecas comments that contexts of socialization vary in scope and duration. After Wheeler (1966), a distinction can be made between "developmental socialization systems" whose purpose is the training, education, or further socialization of individuals, and "re-socialization systems" whose purpose is to correct some deficiency in earlier socialization. A distinction has also been made (see Brim and Wheeler 1966) between "primary" and "secondary" socialization: the former refers to roles learned earlier in life and the latter to those that occur later. While the temporal distinction has some usefulness, Musgrave (1987) warns against the belief that primary socialization is necessarily more permanent than secondary and has warned that these distinctions can lead to a deterministic view, in that actors are seen to be socialized and cannot create patterns of behavior to meet needs.

2. Antecedents to Current Theories of Socialization

Bush and Simmons (1981) have traced the historical antecedents to current theory on socialization and have referred to the classical works of Freud, Piaget, Cooley, George Herbert Mead, Margaret Mead, Benedict, Erikson, and Mannheim.

Freud's (1961, originally published in 1930) psychosexual stage theory, and in particular his theory of the three inborn structures of the mind or personality (the id, the ego, and the superego), provided one of the most influential interpretations of the socialization process. The development of the ego and the superego are seen as the basic tasks of socialization, and identification, that is, the act of becoming like something or someone is the key process. Each psychosexual stage identified by Freud is defined by where and upon whom an individual's libidinal energy is cathected at a given time.

Piaget's (1970) theory of development, which is concerned with the progressive construction and reconstruction of cognitive structures as the child develops, has also been influential in the field of socialization. According to Piaget, the child actively assimilates and organizes new information according to existing cognitive structures, and this produces the cognitive reorganization that constitutes the various stages of development outlined in his theory.

The work of Cooley (1964) and Mead (1934) on the emergence of the self through social interaction, and in particular their distinction of the "I" and "me," is also central to socialization, as is the work of Mead (1928) and Benedict (1938) on the ways in which the culture of a society can affect the character and outcomes of life transitions.

Erikson (1950), who conceived of eight ages of man, with each stage having its specific development task that must be accomplished for individuals to progress to the next stage, provides one of the most influential frameworks to deal specifically with the issue of socialization over the whole lifespan. Mannheim (1952) focuses on the effects of generations as a source of social change and as a potential influence on the socialization process.

Bush and Simmons (1981) argue that these very diverse classical theories have shaped the themes or raised points of contention that continue to pervade the study of socialization. In particular, they refer to the issues of continuity or discontinuity of processes of socialization and the universality of socialization processes over time and space.

Musgrave (1987), from a sociological perspective, has also reviewed past theories of socialization. He has argued that sociological theory, as applied to socialization, has followed two main paths. The first is the "organic" approach, which sees society as a network of interrelated positions filled by individuals who are in agreement about how they should interact. The key concept in this approach is structure, which is analyzed in terms of roles and statuses within institutions. The second is the "conflict" approach, which analyzes society in terms of groups whose interests conflict. The key concepts are logically conflict and interests, but power is also important. Both of these approaches have been used to analyze social behavior and, in particular, socialization at the societal and interpersonal levels.

Musgrave comments that until the 1960s the major tradition in considering socialization was the organic approach at the societal level. Sociologists examined how individuals became social beings by learning the different roles attached to positions they were expected to move through. As examples of this approach, Musgrave refers to the classical work of Margaret Mead, Durkheim, and Parsons. As Musgrave has reported, this approach has been criticized on the grounds that the logic tends to be teleological (a particular effect implies a particular cause), there is scant attention paid to issues of conflict and change, and, mainly because of this, the approach, knowingly or not, supports a conservative ideology.

Musgrave notes that since the 1960s some sociologists have worked at the societal level but from a conflict approach. The main emphasis of these writers has been on the way social groups with different interests come into conflict and on the results of that conflict. Musgrave refers to the work of sociologists both within the Marxist tradition and outside that tradition. Musgrave comments that there have been difficulties with both arms of this approach. He notes the internecine squabbles of the Marxist sociologists about what is true doctrine and the fact that Marxist predictions have not come to pass, and he notes theoretical and methodological problems with the approach of the non-Marxist sociologists.

Musgrave argues that it was also in the 1960s that greater emphasis was placed on interpersonal interaction, and he refers to the pioneering works of Goffman, Weber, Husserl, Schutz, and Berger and Luckman. Like societal theories, the interpersonal approach developed in both the organic and conflict traditions. Musgrave notes in fact that the work on symbolic interactionism, which focuses on the ways actors construct meanings in interaction, work usually associated with George Herbert Mead, has been applied to both organic and conflict theories.

Examples of work in the organic tradition alone include the culture and personality theorists such as Margaret Mead, whose work examined the links between societal structure and personality, and the

ethnomethodologists such as Garfinkel, who studied the ways in which people come to perceive and produce everyday interaction (see, e.g., Garfinkel 1967). Examples of work at the interpersonal level described by Musgrave and conducted within the conflict tradition include the work of Blau (1964) and Homans (1961) on exchange theory. In the view of these theorists, society is a network of transactions or exchanges carried out by explicit or implicit bargaining.

Musgrave comments that work at the interpersonal level has also been subjected to criticism at the theoretical and methodological level.

Musgrave concludes that each of the four approaches has helped the gradual clarification of ideas about social interaction but each has theoretical weaknesses. He argues therefore that there is a need for a unifying approach:

> In it emphasis is put upon the actor as a potentially creative subject who, depending upon how power is structured within his career, constructs rather than reconstructs sometimes cognitive, but particularly moral knowledge, as this is communicated to him both through language and other cues. (Musgrave 1987 p. 23)

3. Current Theory and Research into Socialization

Bush and Simmons (1981) have reviewed current theory and research into socialization and have argued that underlying virtually all of the contemporary sociological views is the assumption that socialization is a continuing, lifelong process, although some writers would argue that change over time is anomalous, while others see it as a logical extension of values, norms, and the like that are formed in childhood and adolescence.

Bush and Simmons refer to the contemporary work that has revolved around the processes of role acquisition, role conflict, and role transitions, including role loss. Among the issues that have been addressed in this research have been an investigation of the stressful effects of role discontinuity, the effects on stress reduction of anticipatory socialization, the effects of the nature of role changes (do role changes that involve gains have the same effects as those involving losses?), the effects on role transition of rites of passage and being "off-time," the effects of lack of clarity on role consensus, and the effects on individuals of role conflict.

Bush and Simmons also refer to three general perspectives to socialization throughout the lifetime that have emerged: life-stage theories, lifespan developmental psychology, and life-course orientation.

4. Contexts of Socialization

Gecas (1981), while acknowledging that the number of contexts of socialization in a complex society is almost limitless, examines in some detail five contexts: the family, school, peer group, occupational setting, and radical resocialization settings. Zimmer and Witnov (1985) referred to a number of agents of socialization: culture, nations, family, formal organization, technology (television and computers), literature, and leaders. They examined in some detail three of these agents: culture, the family, and formal organization.

In Sect. 4 below a brief reference is made to the major themes that are present in theory and research with respect to three of these contexts: the family, peer groups, and occupational organizations. Section 5 deals separately with issues concerned with education and socialization.

4.1 The Family Context

Both Gecas and Zimmer and Witnov comment that the family is the context most closely associated with the topic of socialization because as an institution its major function is the socialization and care of children, both for membership of the family group and membership of the larger society. They argue that, because relationships within a family are usually intimate, intensive, and relatively enduring, socialization which takes place there is usually the most pervasive and consequential.

The issues raised in research and theory concerning socialization in the family have referred both to relationships within families and to the place of the family in society. Among the issues raised in the former are: the effects of the social organization of the family and in particular of the distribution of power within it; the processes of socialization, such as modeling, role-playing, and reinforcement, and the outcomes of these processes; the development in children of sex role identity, aggression, morality, and achievement; and the effects on socialization of different parental styles, family size and configuration, and single-parent families. With regard to the place of the family in the larger system of social institutions, one of the most common issues addressed in research and theory is the location of the family in the social class system.

4.2 The Childhood Peer Group Context

Gecas (1981) notes that the most important feature of the peer group is that it is a voluntary association, which means that boundaries of such groups are fluid. The peer group is also relatively independent of parental control, and consequently can be the context for the development of deviant or delinquent behavior. Gecas notes that association in peer groups is between status equals, and interaction is therefore more likely to be based on egalitarian norms, although informal status hierarchies, typically based on achievement in activities valued by the group, do develop. A third feature of such groups, noted by Gecas, is that they are typically segregated by sex.

Gecas argues that socialization in peer groups is

characterized by its effect on three broad areas of the child's development: the development and validation of the self, the development of competence through role taking, and the acquisition of knowledge not gained in the family. The key to the importance of the peer group in these areas lies in the friendship bonds that are formed.

4.3 The Occupational Context

While the primary role of occupational organizations is not socialization, the structure of occupational settings can affect individual attitudes and values. Moreover, most large organizations have processes of induction and orientation which are designed to socialize new recruits into that organization.

Robbins et al. (1986) have described the process of occupational socialization as one of adaptation which takes place when an individual passes from outside the organization to the role of an inside member. Organizational socialization attempts to adapt the new employee to the organization's culture by conveying how things are done. From the perspective of the organization, acceptance by the employee of the organization's pivotal standards is imperative for individual performance and organizational stability. Nevertheless individuals vary in the degree to which they conform totally to the traditions and customs of the organization.

Gecas (1981) notes that occupational settings vary considerably with regard to a wide range of features such as power and authority relationships, worker participation, bureaucratization, and work complexity. One important distinction which tends to emerge in large organizations is between labor and management: workers in management are more likely to identify with the organization and nonmanagerial workers are more likely to identify with each other and may come into conflict with those in management.

It has been suggested that the conditions experienced in work can affect attitudes and values of workers. Kohn and his associates argue that certain structural features of work, such as the amount of autonomy or complexity, can give rise to values of autonomy or conformity (see, for example, Kohn and Schooler 1978). Kanter (1977) argues that the adaptation of individuals to their work situation and their degree of commitment to work is a function of their location on three structural dimensions: the opportunity structure, the power structure, and the social composition of peer clusters.

As Gecas (1981) comments, work settings, like other socialization contexts, are affected by the larger society within which they exist. He notes that much of the sociological literature has dealt with the alienating effects of capitalism and he draws attention to the pioneering work of Marx and the research of Bowles and Gintis (1976).

5. *Socialization and the School Context*

The school, like the family, has an explicit socialization function. The extent of this function in the context of schooling is, however, more controversial and touches on the very nature of schooling. While it is accepted that schools have responsibilities in the affective domain as well as the academic domain, the extent of the former responsibilities are unclear and in constant flux. These responsibilities are not only controversial in the sense that they overlap with the responsibilities of the other agencies, particularly the family, but it is often argued that society loads schools with a range of responsibilities that go well beyond their academic mandate and ultimately detract from that mandate. The delicacy of these issues is not new. For example, the place of religious education in schools proved one of the most controversial issues in the development of schooling in many countries, and in the late twentieth century the teaching of sex education in schools has evoked mixed responses. There are parents who hold that this is an area of responsibility for the family, not the school.

5.1 *Schooling and Other Socialization Contexts*

While schooling is viewed as the major educational context for children, a great deal of education takes place outside school, and in particular in the family. In fact, the publication of the Coleman Report in the United States (Coleman et al. 1966) and subsequent confirmatory reports or reviews (see Averch et al. 1972, Jencks et al. 1972) led to the belief that schools make little difference in educational achievement, and it is the social status of the students' families that account for most of the difference in achievement levels. Subsequently, these findings have been challenged both on methodological and theoretical grounds and it is generally accepted that schooling has a greater effect on student achievement than was originally acknowledged. Research into the characteristics of effective schools has been one of the growth areas of educational research in the late 1980s and the 1990s.

Nonetheless, by the time children go to school they will have learned a great deal that will affect their schooling experience. Kerckhoff (1986) notes, for example, that families contribute greatly to the motivational and cognitive skill levels exhibited by their children, and they continue to influence those qualities throughout schooling. Important aspects of the family that contribute to these influences include parental expectations, cultural differences, social status differences, and parent–child interactions.

The cultural differences are evident both from within-nation studies and cross-nation studies. For example, research in Australia (see Sturman 1986) has consistently shown the higher educational aspirations of students whose backgrounds are from non-English-speaking countries. Similarly, Fuller et al. (1986) have argued that some of the differences between educational achievement levels in Japan and the United States can be attributed to the fact that elements of socialization in the Japanese family are more deeply agreed upon, less variable across parents, and more tightly coupled with the educational system.

Kerckhoff also draws attention to the important influence of peer groups on schooling, in particular because the organization of schooling ensures that students spend a great deal of time with their peers. He notes that friendship relations in school can affect educational aspirations and other aspects of the schooling process.

5.2 *The Socializing Processes of Schooling*

The socializing processes of schools can be overt or hidden. For example, teachers, because they tend to come from a similar social background, may unknowingly pass on to students certain attitudes and values. Other aspects of schooling may be more open.

Gecas (1981) argues that the most conspicuous socialization process in the classroom is social reinforcement such as praise, blame, privileges, and particularly the allocation of grades. From a review of the research, Gecas suggests that teachers reward students who conform to the social order of the school with higher grades. Thus, personality characteristics such as drive to achieve, citizenship, dependability, perseverance, and punctuality may be rewarded more highly than actual achievement. Gecas also refers to the research which suggests that teacher expectations of students can become important predictors of student achievement.

Gecas commented that students are, however, not necessarily passive recipients of the pressures they experience. They may engage in activities that alter these experiences to make them more favorable to their interests, such as the avoidance of failure by nonparticipation in certain activities, or participating but using the minimum of effort.

5.3 *Schooling and the Larger Social Setting*

One of the more influential theories that has been applied to education and which touches on the socialization effects of schooling is the idea that the educational system reproduces a system of knowledge based on the class relations which exist outside schools (Bourdieu and Passeron 1977). However, as Musgrave (1987) reports, critics argue that the theory does not explain how the process occurs at the interpersonal level and that, in fact, reproduction does not always take place. Musgrave comments that one way of conceptualizing this failure has been to examine resistance in education: both teachers and students can become alienated from a system where they are asked to do what they may not wish to do and the result of the alienation can be resistance.

Analysis of the links between education and the economy has tended to argue a structural correspondence, that is, that the educational system perpetuates the economic order (see Bowles and Gintis 1976). However, Musgrave (1987) notes that the critics of the correspondence theory point, to the difficulty in establishing the direction of causation and hence to the failure of the theory to address the mechanism of influence.

6. Conclusion

Research and theory on socialization covers a very wide area, ranging from micro studies of interpersonal relationships to macro studies of societal structures and cultural influences. The contexts of socialization range from the wider culture to the family, peer group, and occupational settings. This entry has attempted to map the area and draw attention to the complexity of the subject matter.

References

Averch H S, Carroll J, Donaldson T S, Kiesling H J, Pincus J 1972 *How Effective is Schooling?* Rand Corporation, Santa Monica, California

Benedict R 1938 Continuities and discontinuities in cultural conditioning. *Psychiatry* 1: 161–67

Blau P 1964 *Exchange and Power in Social Life.* Wiley, New York

Bourdieu P, Passeron J C 1977 *Reproduction in Education, Society and Culture.* Sage, London

Bowles S, Gintis H 1976 *Schooling in Capitalist America.* Routledge and Kegan Paul, London

Brim O G, Wheeler S (eds.) 1966 *Socialization After Childhood: Two Essays.* Wiley, New York

Bush D M, Simmons R G 1981 Socialization processes over the life course. In: Rosenberg M, Turner R H(eds.) 1981 *Social Psychology: Sociological Perspectives.* Basic Books, New York

Coleman J S et al. 1966 *Equality of Educational Opportunity.* US Government Printing Office, Washington, DC

Cooley C H 1964 *Human Nature and the Social Order.* Scribner's, New York

Erikson E H 1950 *Childhood and Society.* Norton, New York

Freud S 1961 *Civilization and Its Discontents.* Dorsey, New York

Fuller B, Holloway S D, Azuma H, Hess R D, Kashiwagi K 1986 Contrasting achievement rules: Socialization of Japanese children at home and in school. In: Kerckhoff A C(ed.) 1986 *Research in Sociology of Education and Socialization: A Research Annual*, Vol. 6. JAI Press, Greenwich, Connecticut

Garfinkel H 1967 *Studies in Ethnomethodology.* Prentice-Hall, Englewood Cliffs, New Jersey

Gecas V 1981 Contexts of socialization. In: Rosenberg M, Turner R H (eds.) 1981 *Social Psychology: Sociological Perspectives.* Basic Books, New York

Goffman E 1961 *Asylums: Essays on the Social Situation of Mental Patients and Other Inmates.* Doubleday/Anchor, New York

Homans G C 1961 *Social Behavior: Its Elementary Forms.* Harcourt, Brace and World, New York

Jencks C et al. 1972 *Inequality: A Reassessment of the Effect of Family and Schooling in America.* Basic Books, New York

Kanter R M 1977 *Men and Women of the Corporation.* Basic Books, New York

Kerckhoff A C 1986 Family position, peer influences, and schooling. In: Richardson J G (ed.) 1986 *Handbook of Theory and Research for the Sociology of Education.* Greenwood Press, New York

Kohn M L, Schooler C 1978 The reciprocal effects of the substantive complexity of work and intellectual flexibility: A longitudinal assessment. *Am. J. Sociol.* 84: 24–52

Mannheim K 1952 The problem of generations. In: Mannheim K (ed.) 1952 *Essays in the Sociology of Knowledge.* Routledge and Kegan Paul, London

Mead G H 1934 *Mind, Self, and Society*, University of Chicago Press, Chicago, Illinois

Mead M 1928 *Coming of Age in Samoa.* Morrow, New York

Musgrave P W 1987 *Socialising Contexts: The Subject in Society.* Allen and Unwin, Sydney

Piaget J 1970 *Structuralism.* Basic Books, New York

Robbins S P, Low P S, Mourell M P 1986 *Managing Human Resources.* Prentice-Hall, Sydney

Sieber R T, Gordon A J (eds.) 1981 *Children and Their Organizations: Investigations in American Culture.* Hall, Boston, Massachusetts

Sturman A 1986 *Immigrant Australians and Education.* Australian Education Review No. 22. ACER, Hawthorn

Wentworth W M 1980 *Context and Understanding: An Inquiry into Socialization Theory.* Elsevier, New York

Wheeler S 1966 The structure of formally organized socialization settings. In: Brim O G, Wheeler S (eds.) 1966

Zimmer J M, Witnov S J 1985 Socialization. In: Husén T, Postlethwaite T N (eds.) 1985 *The International Encyclopedia of Education*, 1st edn. Pergamon Press, Oxford

Further Reading

Goslin D A (ed.) 1973 *Handbook of Socialization Theory and Research.* Rand McNally, Chicago, Illinois

Kerckhoff A C (ed.) 1983 *Research in Sociology of Education and Socialization: A Research Annual*, Vol. 4. JAI Press, Greenwich, Connecticut

Self-related Cognition, Learned Helplessness, Learned Optimism, and Human Development

J. P. Eisner and M.E.P. Seligman

Explanatory style—that is, the habitual manner in which a person explains the causes of events—is the topic of this entry. The entry first reviews the theoretical basis of explanatory style in learned helplessness theory. It then explores the deleterious effects of a pessimistic explanatory style. Finally, the entry discusses the development of explanatory style and then provides a detailed review of the origins of individual differences in explanatory style.

1. Explanatory Style and the Reformulated Theory of Learned Helplessness

Learned helplessness arises when a person expects that his or her responses cannot control outcomes (Seligman and Maier 1967, Overmier and Seligman 1967). Certain deficits spring from this expectation of uncontrollability. A helpless person fails to attempt responses that may control outcomes. When he or she inadvertently does control outcomes with an action, the helpless person fails to learn that this action had an effect. These failures of action and learning are the characteristic deficits of learned helplessness in both animals and humans. Depressed mood, an emotional deficit, is also found in helpless humans but cannot be measured in animals.

According to the reformulated theory of learned helplessness (Abramson et al. 1978), individuals will try to explain why their actions fail to control outcomes. Causal explanations for their failure fall along three dimensions: the stable–unstable, global–specific, and internal–external dimensions. First, causes can be described as permanent (stable) or transient (unstable). Persons who explain their failure with a stable cause will expect future failures and will experience chronic helplessness deficits. Second, causes can be construed as affecting many aspects of a person's life (global) or only few areas (specific). When a person believes that the cause of the failure globally effects his or her life, that person will expect failure in many areas of life. This expectation will result in helplessness deficits across many areas in his or her life. Third, causes can be viewed as internal or external to the individual. Persons who explain their failure with an internal cause will lose self-esteem.

The reformulated theory argues that a person's vulnerability to helplessness stems directly from his or her explanatory style, the habitual manner in which that person explains the causes of events. Explanatory style ranges from pessimistic to optimistic in quality. A person who tends to explain the causes of bad events as stable, global, and internal in nature and the causes of good events as unstable, specific, and external in nature has a pessimistic explanatory style. Conversely, a person who habitually explains bad events by unstable, specific, and external causes and good events by stable, global, and internal causes has an optimistic explanatory style. The reformulated theory asserts that, compared to individuals with an optimistic explanatory style, those with a pessimistic explanatory style are more likely to experience pervasive and chronic symptoms of helplessness when faced with uncontrollable negative events.

2. Effects of Explanatory Style Across the Lifespan

A pessimistic explanatory style has a wide array of negative effects. Compared to those with an optimistic explanatory style, individuals who typically explain negative events with internal, stable, and global attributions are more likely to grow depressed in the face of bad events. This finding holds true for both adults (see Peterson and Seligman 1984) and for children ranging from ages 8 to 13 (Seligman et al. 1984, Nolen-Hoeksema et al. 1986).

Individuals with a pessimistic explanatory style achieve less than do optimists. Nolen-Hoeksema et al. (1986) found that third-, fourth-, and fifth-graders with pessimistic explanatory styles will have lower achievement test scores than children with optimistic styles. Other work indicates that young adults with an optimistic explanatory style will earn higher grades than those with a pessimistic style (Seligman et al. 1992). Finally, among adults in the workplace, those with an optimistic explanatory style evidence greater work productivity than their pessimistic counterparts (Schulman and Seligman 1990, Seligman and Schulman 1986).

Explanatory style has other effects as well. In adults, pessimistic explanatory style predicts poorer athletic performance and illness (see Seligman 1992). Research has not yet examined how explanatory style affects these areas of performance and health in children.

3. Developmental Differences in Explanatory Style

Before the age of 7 or 8, children do not manifest helplessness deficits when they fail. Studies suggest that young children may not experience help-lessness because they attribute negative events to external, unstable, and specific causes (see Seligman et al. 1988). Nolen-Hoeksema's (1986) cross-sectional study of developmental differences in explanatory style provides the most direct evidence. She found that 7- and 8-year old children were more likely than 4- and 5-year old children to attribute negative events to internal and global causes.

4. Origins of Individual Differences in Explanatory Style

At about age 8, some children begin to show signs of a pessimistic explanatory style. Why do some children develop such a style while others remain optimistic? Previous work suggests several different determinants of individual differences in explanatory style. Very little, however, is known about the relative contribution that each of these determinants makes to explanatory style. Consequently, this entry considers each proposed determinant of individual differences separately.

4.1 Teachers' Differential Performance Feedback

Unlike boys, girls tend to blame lack of ability, a stable characteristic, for poor performance. Boys, by contrast, are likely to ascribe their poor performance to an unstable cause, namely, lack of effort (Dweck and Repucci 1973, Nicholls 1975). Dweck et al. (1978) argued that differential performance feedback in the classroom is responsible for these sex differences in explanatory style. Dweck et al. examined teachers' performance feedback to fourth-grade children. They found that teachers focused their praise on different aspects of children's work, according to a child's sex. Over 90 percent of praise for boys' work related to intellectual competence. By contrast, significantly less of the praise for girls focused on intellectual aspects of their work (80.9%). Sex differences in teachers' negative evaluations were also evident. Only 54.4 percent of teachers' criticisms of boys' work referred to intellectual incompetence; whereas for girls, 88.9 percent of teachers' negative evaluations were directed at intellectual performance.

To establish that these differential feedback patterns actually cause sex differences in explanatory style, Dweck et al. (1978) conducted a laboratory study in which they reproduced the two feedback patterns found for teachers' criticism of children's work. When both boys and girls received the girls' feedback pattern, they most often ascribed their failure on a subsequent task to lack of ability. Children who received the boys' feedback pattern, however, attributed their failure to lack of effort. These results, then, strongly suggest that differential performance feedback is one factor responsible for individual differences in explanatory style.

4.2 Modeling

A child may learn his or her explanatory style by modeling a parent's style. This hypothesis predicts a positive correlation between children's and parents' explanatory styles. Some preliminary support for the hypothesis was offered by Seligman et al. (1984), who found that a mother's explanatory style for bad events correlated with her child's style for bad events. Pessimistic mothers had pessimistic children. Fathers' explanatory styles, however, were unrelated to those of their children.

4.3 Adults' Attributions for Children's Behavior

The attributions that adults make for a child's behavior may determine his or her explanatory style. The most obvious empirical finding that this hypothesis suggests is a positive correlation between children's attributions for failure and parents' attributions for their child's failure. Fincham and Cain (1986) failed to find this expected relationship.

Dweck et al. (1978), however, provided some evidence that adults directly teach children to make certain attributions. As was noted previously, boys tend to ascribe failures to an unstable cause (poor motivation) while girls more often attribute their failures to a stable cause (poor ability). Dweck et al. found that teachers give boys and girls equal amounts of failure feedback and that they invoke motivation, not ability, as the cause of failure for both sexes. However, teachers more often give boys, rather than girls, failure feedback that is accompanied by a motivation attribution. Compared to a girl, a boy more often hears teachers attribute his failures to poor motivation. Perhaps, then, a boy will attribute his failures to poor motivation because he has learned to do so directly from his teachers.

4.4 Differential Exposure to Noncontingency

As a direct extension of the reformulated theory of learned helplessness, Abramson et al. (1978) proposed that repeated experience with uncontrollable events will lead a person to develop a pessimistic explanatory style, whereas exposure to controllable events will foster an optimistic explanatory style.

Some supporting evidence for this view has been found. Children who experience their parents' divorce or separation, both significant uncontrollable events, subsequently develop a more pessimistic explanatory style for negative events than do children whose parents remain together (Nolen-Hoeksema et al. 1991).

4.5 Interpersonal Trust

Erikson (1950) suggested that basic trust is the corner-stone of a healthy personality. When mistrust takes precedence over trust, other aspects of personality development will be disrupted. Elaborating on this notion, Eisner (in press) argued that dispositional mistrust of others close to a person spawns a pessimistic explanatory style, whereas trust fosters an optimistic style. Preliminary evidence helps to support this claim. Among college students, mistrust of intimate others predicts a pessimistic explanatory style, while trust predicts an optimistic style over time.

4.6 Childhood Depression

Nolen-Hoeksema et al. (1992) found that when third-grade children experience an episode of depression they are likely to develop a pessimistic explanatory style for negative events. This pessimistic style endures even after children's depressive symptoms begin to diminish.

Depression may create a pessimistic explanatory style in two ways (Nolen-Hoeksema et al. 1992). First, the behavioral and cognitive symptoms of depression could cause repeated academic and social failures in school. These failures may convince depressed children that negative events stem from stable, global, and internal causes. Second, depressed mood may bias children's cognitive processes so that negative interpretations of events are more accessible than positive ones. If negative interpretations are most accessible as explanatory style develops, a child will be at risk of developing a pessimistic explanatory style.

4.7 Genetic Influences

Other work provides evidence for the genetic transmission of explanatory style. Schulman et al. (1991) found an intraclass correlation of 0.48 for explanatory style in monozygotic twins. By contrast, the explanatory styles of dizygotic twins were uncorrelated. The results suggest that the quality of one's explanatory style may have a genetic component.

5. Conclusion

Explanatory style affects many domains of functioning. In the areas of achievement and mental health, a pessimistic explanatory style can have detrimental effects across the lifespan. Given these effects, a thorough understanding of the origins of explanatory style will help inform educational policies and child-rearing practices.

While research points to several possible causes of a pessimistic explanatory style, little is known about the relative importance of each cause. Current knowledge suggests that explanatory style has a genetic component. Some combination of nongenetic factors, however, seems to play an equally important causal role in the development of individual differences in explanatory style. Further research is necessary to determine which factors have the greatest influence on a child's developing explanatory style.

See also: Development of Self-concept; Human Development: Research and Educational Practice

References

Abramson L Y, Seligman M E P, Teasdale J D 1978 Learned helplessness in humans: Critique and reformulation. *J. Abnorm. Psychol.* 87: 49–74

Dweck C S, Davidson W, Nelson S, Enna B 1978 Sex differences in learned helplessness: II. The contingencies of evaluative feedback in the classroom and III. An experimental analysis. *Dev. Psychol.* 14(3): 268–76

Dweck C S, Repucci N D 1973 Learned helplessness and reinforcement responsibility in children. *J. Pers. Soc. Psychol.* 25(1): 109–16

Eisner J P in press The Origins of Explanatory Style: Interpersonal Trust as a Determinant of Optimism and Pessimism

Erikson E H 1950 *Childhood and Society.* Norton, New York

Fincham F D, Cain K M 1986 Learned helplessness in humans: A developmental analysis. *Dev. Rev.* 6(4): 301–33

Nicholls J G 1975 Causal attributions and other achievement-related cognitions: Effects of task outcomes, attainment value, and sex. *J. Pers. Soc. Psychol.* 31(3): 379–89

Nolen-Hoeksema S 1986 Developmental differences in explanatory style and its relationship to learned helplessness. (Doctoral dissertation, University of Pennsylvania)

Nolen-Hoeksema S, Girgus J S, Seligman M E P 1986 Learned helplessness in children: A longitudinal study of depression, achievement, and explanatory style. *J. Pers. Soc. Psychol.* 51(2):435–42

Nolen-Hoeksema S, Girgus J S, Seligman M E P 1991 Individual differences in the course of depression in children of divorce. Unpublished manuscript

Nolen-Hoeksema S, Girgus J S, Seligman M E P 1992 Consequences of depressive symptoms in childhood: The possible origins of dysthymia. Unpublished manuscript

Overmier J B, Seligman M E P 1967 Effects of inescapable shock upon subsequent escape and avoidance responding. *J. Comp. Physiol. Psychol.* 63(1): 23–33

Peterson C, Seligman M E P 1984 Causal explanations as a risk factor for depression: Theory and evidence. *Psychol. Rev.* 91(3): 347–74

Schulman P, Keith D, Seligman M E P 1991 Is optimism heritable? A study of twins. Paper submitted for publication

Schulman P, Seligman M E P 1990 Explanatory style predicts productivity among life insurance agents. Unpublished manuscript, University of Pennsylvania

Seligman M E P 1992 *Helplessness: On Depression, Development, and Death,* Freeman, San Francisco, California

Seligman M E P Kamen L P, Nolen-Hoeksema S 1988 Explanatory style across the lifespan: Achievement and health. In: Hetherington E M, Lerner R M, Perlmutter M (eds.) 1988 *Child Development in lifespan Perspective.* Erlbaum, Hillsdale, New Jersey

Seligman M E P, Maier S F 1967 Failure to escape traumatic shock. *J. Exp. Psychol.* 74(1): 1–9

Seligman M E P, et al. 1984 Attributional style and depressive symptoms in children. *J. Abnorm. Psychol.* 93(2): 235–38

Seligman M E P, Schulman P 1986 Explanatory style as a predictor of productivity and quitting among life insurance sales agents. *J. Pers. Soc. Psychol.* 50: 832–38

Seligman M E P, Schulman P, Butler R P, Priest R F, Burke W P 1992 Explanatory style predicts grades and retention among West Point cadets. Unpublished manuscript, University of Pennsylvania

Further Reading

Dweck C S 1975 The role of expectations and attributions in the alleviation of learned helplessness. *J. Pers. Soc. Psychol.* 31(4): 674–85
Dweck C S, Wortman C B 1982 Learned helplessness, anxiety, and achievement motivation: Neglected parallels in cognitive, affective, and coping responses. In: Krohne H W, Laux L (eds.) 1982 *Achievement, Stress, and Anxiety.* Hemisphere, New York
Eisner J P, Seligman M E P 1991 Learned helplessness. In: Dulbecco R (ed.) 1991 *Encyclopedia of Human Biology*, Vol. 4. Academic Press, London
Kovacs M 1989 Affective disorders in children and adolescents. *Am. Psychol.* 44: 209–15
Rutter M 1986 The developmental psychopathology of depression: Issues and perspectives. In: Rutter M, Izard E, Read P B (eds.) 1986 *Depression in Young People: Developmental and Clinical Perspectives.* Guilford Press, New York
Seligman M E P 1990 *Learned Optimism: The Skill to Conquer Life Obstacles, Large and Small.* Random House, New York

Development and Socialization of Aggression

D. G. Perry

Aggression—that is, behavior aimed at harming another person—is a social problem of growing importance. This entry discusses developmental patterns in aggression, theories of aggression, the roles of biology, socialization, and cognition in aggressive development, and intervention with aggressive children.

1. Developmental Patterns in Aggression

Three issues will be discussed in this section: developmental changes in the forms and elicitors of aggression, the stability of aggression, and sex differences in aggressive development.

1.1 Developmental Changes in the Forms and Elicitors of Aggression

Surprisingly little is known about how the forms and elicitors of aggression change with age. Over the preschool years, physical aggression decreases and verbal aggression increases (Parke and Slaby 1983). Much of the aggression of younger preschoolers is "instrumental" (aimed at retrieval of an object or privilege); "hostile" aggression (aimed at restoring self-esteem) develops later, presumably because it rests on the ability to infer the intentions and motives of an attacker (Hartup 1974). At any given age, there exists considerable trait-like cross-situational consistency in aggression: children who are the most (or least) aggressive in one context, such as the home, tend also to be the most (or least) aggressive in other contexts, such as the school (Perry and Bussey 1984).

1.2 Stability of Aggression

Aggression is highly stable over time, indeed about as stable as intelligence (Olweus 1979). The degree of stability varies inversely with both the length of the interval covered and the subjects' age at the time of first assessment. In one study, assessments of aggression among 10-year olds predicted their aggressiveness 22 years later (Eron et al. 1991). Aggressive children may remain aggressive because of biological factors, because they continue to live in environments conducive to aggression, because they retain cognitions conducive to aggression (e.g., the belief that aggression is successful), or because they elicit from the environment certain reactions (e.g., rejection from normal peers) that reinforce their aggression (Perry and Bussey 1984).

1.3 Sex Differences in Aggressive Development

At all ages males are more aggressive than females, and this is true for verbal as well as physical aggression (Maccoby and Jacklin 1974). Aggression is about equally stable in boys and in girls, however (Olweus 1984). Reasons for the sex difference in aggression are unclear, but may involve biological factors (e.g., muscularity, temperament, hormones) as well as environmental ones (e.g., more physical punishment and encouragement of aggression for boys). Nature–nurture interplays may also be important. For example, boys' more active and resistant-to-control temperaments may elicit physical punishment from parents, which teaches the boys aggressive styles of interpersonal influence.

2. Theories of Aggressive Development

This section outlines three theories of aggression: ethological theory, psychoanalytic theory, and social cognitive theory.

2.1 Ethological Theory

Ethologists (e.g., Lorenz 1966) view aggression as instinctive behavior. In animals as well as human beings, aggressive energy is thought to build up within the organism independently of external stimuli but to be periodically discharged or released by appropriate environmental elicitors, especially frustrations (goal blockages) and threats (e.g., territorial infringement). The theory emphasizes the importance of behavior patterns that have adaptive (survival) value for a species. Thus, the role of aggression in mate and resource selection and defense is emphasized. Moreover, within a species, groups often form dominance hierarchies, allowing group members to settle conflicts by exchanging signals of dominance and submission rather than by overt aggression. Thus, dominance hierarchies curb intragroup aggression.

Although the ethological perspective has yielded interesting data about the stimuli that regulate aggression in natural settings, the theory has been criticized for: (a) viewing aggression as a product of biologically programmed stimulus–response links that are minimally influenced by learning; (b) the absence of evidence to support the notion of an accumulating reservoir of aggressive energy; (c) the failure to acknowledge the role of higher cognition (e.g., values) in regulating aggression; and (d) the absence of data to support the "catharsis hypothesis," or the idea that observing and performing aggression depletes one of aggressive energy and reduces the inclination to further aggression.

2.2 Psychoanalytic Theory

Freud (1940) viewed people as biologically endowed with an aggressive drive that is aroused by frustrating and other ego-threatening events. When the drive is aroused, aggression may be expressed directly toward the provocateur (if no punishment is expected), or may be displaced, turned toward the self, suppressed, repressed, or otherwise defensively handled (especially if the aggressive impulses meet resistance from real-world or superego sources). If drive is aroused but not expressed, it accumulates. Moreover, if aggressive impulses are repressed rather than discharged, when the individual later encounters persons and events that are symbolically reminiscent of the originally frustrating circumstances, aggressive drive may be subconsciously aroused and motivate aggressive actions.

Although this theory recognizes the role of cognition (especially in the form of defensive transformations of aggressive drive), there exists little scientific evidence for the hypothesized defensive and subconscious processes. Also, like ethological theory, psychoanalytic theory has been criticized for its "hydraulic" properties, especially the idea that aggression springs from an invisible internal reservoir of energy that accumulates if unexpressed and is reduced through acts of vicarious and direct aggression (catharsis).

2.3 Social Cognitive Theory

According to social cognitive theory (Bandura 1986), children's social experiences influence how they mentally represent their social worlds and process social information; in turn, children's cognitions guide their social behavior. Much aggression is acquired through observing the aggression of others: by watching the behavior of playground bullies, television villains, and even their own parents acting as disciplinarians, children learn how to engage in a wide variety of harmful acts. Children are most likely to enact aggression, however, when they expect valued outcomes for it and believe they are capable of performing the requisite responses. Children learn about the likely consequences of aggression and about their ability to perform it partly through observation and partly through personal experiences. Children who see others rewarded for aggression, for example, may attempt aggression and, if successful, perceive themselves as capable aggressors.

In this theory, aggression comes under the control of internal self-regulatory processes. When children clearly see that society frowns on (or rewards) certain actions, they may internalize the standard, coming to experience guilt (or pride) for the behavior. For example, if children see that certain forms of aggression in certain situations or toward certain targets are inappropriate (e.g., physical aggression toward females, or aggression against someone whose frustrating behavior is unintentional), they may avoid acting aggressively under these circumstances for fear of self-censure. Not all children learn the same rules. Members of delinquent gangs, for example, may internalize the norm that violence and destruction are worthy of self-praise rather than self-blame.

Social cognitive theorists shun the concept of aggression as a reflexive reaction to frustration, but they do not deny the importance of frustrating and other aversive events in aggression. Indeed, they believe that aggression is often a response children learn to make when deprived, threatened, or hurt, especially if the children find aggression to be successful at improving their plight. Reactions to frustration and other arousing events are cognitively mediated, or depend on the individual's cognitive evaluation of the arousing event. For example, children who develop a style of blaming others for their mishaps and believe that aggression is an effective way to eradicate frustrations should be more likely to perform aggression than children who do not pin their misery on others or who can think of effective, nonaggressive solutions to conflicts. Considerable evidence supports the social cognitive perspective, as reviewed below.

3. Biological Bases of Aggression

Several biological factors affect aggressive development. First, body size, muscularity, and strength are correlated with aggression (Feshbach 1970). Second, physically unattractive children are more aggressive than attractive children (Langlois and Stephan 1981). Third, hormones influence aggression: injecting male hormones prenatally or early in development into animals of certain species enhances later aggressive reactions to certain stimuli (Parke and Slaby 1983, Reinisch 1981). Moreover, circulating levels of male hormones in adult men predict aggressive reactions to provocation and threat (Olweus et al. 1980). Fourth, children born with difficult, hot-headed, or oppositional temperaments are at risk of aggressive development (Bates et al. 1991, Olweus 1980, Thomas et al. 1968). Finally, identical twins are more similar than fraternal twins in aggressiveness (Plomin 1990).

The impacts of these biological factors upon aggression, however, are neither direct nor inevitable. Most biological factors interact with environmental ones to influence aggressive development. Muscular, strong children probably develop aggressive habits mainly when their forceful attempts to remove frustrations or to control others are allowed to succeed (Perry and Bussey 1984). Physically unattractive children may develop aggression mainly because adults and peers expect and elicit negative behavior from unattractive children (Langlois and Stephan 1981). Children with problem temperaments may elicit inept parental behaviors (e.g., erratic and harsh discipline, poor monitoring of the child) that promote child aggression. Even hormonal influences hinge on social conditions (Cairns 1979).

4. Socialization Influences on Aggression

This section discusses influences of the family, the peer group, and the media on aggressive development.

4.1 Family Influences on Aggression

When children do not enjoy positive and emotionally satisfying relationships with their parents, or when the parents are inept at family management practices, the risk of aggressive development increases. These influences are discussed here.

Parental hostility and rejection are associated with child aggression (McCord 1979, Olweus 1980). It has also been suggested that the security of the child's attachments to caregivers figures in aggressive development (Ainsworth 1979, Sroufe 1983). Insecurely attached children are ones who have experienced an insensitive and emotionally unavailable caregiver and have come to display one of two styles of defensive coping to deal with the caregiver's unpredictability: excessive emotional dependence on the caregiver or excessive avoidance of the caregiver. Compared to securely attached children (who have experienced emphatic caregiving and can count on the caregiver's sensitive response at times of stress), insecurely attached children are expected to distrust others, to start fights, and to oppose others. Indeed, insecurely attached children are less compliant and more oppositional, with both parents and peers, than securely attached children. However, there is little evidence that insecurely attached children are actually more aggressive than securely attached children (Perry et al. 1992).

Inept family management practices can promote aggressive development. Among the parental practices that cause aggression are: (a) failure by the parents to monitor the child's whereabouts (Patterson and Stouthamer-Loeber 1984); (b) displays of violent behavior by at least one parent toward the child, toward siblings, or toward others outside the home (McCord 1979); (c) permissiveness in child-rearing (Baumrind 1973); (d) interparent or intraparent inconsistency in discipline (Martin 1975); and (e) ineffectual management of parent–child conflicts. The final item listed above requires elaboration. Patterson (1982) has shown that parents of aggressive children tend to be irritable and conflict-prone, in that they: (a) instigate numerous everyday family conflicts (e.g., by teasing, humiliating, or bossing their children); (b) have a low threshold for responding aversively to the moves of other family members; (c) allow family conflicts to escalate; and (d) respond unpredictably to escalated conflicts, by occasionally allowing their children to have their way, while at other times angrily assaulting them.

These findings support the hypothesis of social cognitive theory that environmental factors promote cognitions that encourage aggression. Parents who are aggressive, erratic, rejecting, and blaming not only teach their children to expect hostility and unpredictability in others but also communicate the message that aggression is an acceptable way of influencing others. Moreover, parents who intermittently allow their child to prevail during escalated conflicts teach the child that high-intensity coercion may succeed when lower-intensity efforts fail.

4.2 Peer Influences on Aggression

Children who acquire aggressive habits at home tend to take their aggression to the playground and school, where they often face rejection by normal peers, acceptance by deviant peers, and academic failure (Cairns and Cairns 1991, Patterson et al. 1991). Moreover, previously nonaggressive children may acquire aggressive habits from their peers, especially if they are frequently victimized by more aggressive children, try to defend themselves with counterattacks, and find these counterattacks to be successful (Patterson et al. 1967).

The fact that aggressive children are rejected by normal peers is important. Such rejection reduces the child's opportunities for normal socialization. Moreover, because normal peers treat aggressive children with open distrust and dislike, aggressive children's expectations that others are treating them with hostility are strengthened. This leads them to perceive hostility even when it is not there (e.g., when they are accidentally provoked) and therefore to behave aggressively when circumstances do not warrant it (Dodge 1986).

4.3 Media Influences on Aggression

Contrary to the catharsis hypothesis of ethological and psychoanalytic theories, but consistent with social cognitive theory, media violence increases rather than decreases children's aggressive tendencies (Bandura 1986, Perry et al. 1990). Evidence of this has been provided by both laboratory experiments and field studies. Field studies show that the relation between television violence and children's aggression is not readily explained by other variables (e.g., social class or a child's temperament).

Television violence has several effects, including: (a) teaching new styles of aggression; (b) teaching that aggression is effective; (c) desensitizing the viewer to violence and suffering, thereby decreasing the chance the viewer will aid others in distress; and (d) teaching the idea that aggression is commonplace, thereby making the viewer feel that aggression is acceptable and strengthening the viewer's tendency to perceive hostile intentions in others. Harmful effects of television violence are greater for, but not limited to, children who already possess favorable attitudes toward aggression, who have aggressive fantasies, or who are emotionally aroused when exposed to the violence (Perry et al. 1990).

5. Social Cognition and Aggression

As suggested by social cognitive theory, aggression is influenced by cognition. When responding to certain stimuli (e.g., provocation), aggressive children reveal deficits and biases in social information processing that lead them to respond aggressively (Dodge 1986, Perry et al. 1990). For example, compared to nonaggressive children, aggressive children tend to interpret ambiguously motivated provocations by others as acts of deliberate hostility, they have trouble thinking of nonaggressive solutions to conflicts, and they expect positive outcomes (control over a victim, increased self-esteem) for performing aggression. As reviewed above, inept family management, poor peer relations, and media violence are all implicated in the learning of cognitions that promote aggression. Discovering how cognitive factors interact with emotional factors to affect aggressive behavior is one important area for future study.

6. Intervention with Aggressive Children

According to the catharsis principle of ethological and psychoanalytic theories, intervention should involve activities that drain children of aggressive urges. This approach is not recommended, however, because encouraging children to enact (even in play) or to observe aggression increases rather than diminishes their aggressive tendencies (Parke and Slaby 1983).

As suggested by social cognitive theory, altering the environmental conditions that support aggression is a more promising approach to intervention. Intervention programs have been developed for both family and school settings. One successful family intervention idea involves teaching parents to reduce their aversive treatment of the child, to monitor the child, to resist the escalation of conflicts, to punish aggression consistently with time out (isolation), and to reward the child for acceptable social behavior (Patterson 1982). A successful school intervention idea involves increasing teachers', peers', and parents' awareness of bully/victim problems, developing clear rules against aggressive behavior, and providing support and protection for victimized children (Olweus 1978).

Coaching aggressive children in cognitive strategies designed to reduce aggression (teaching them to avoid assuming that others are acting with hostile intent, to be aware of the harmful consequences of aggression, to think of nonaggressive solutions to conflict, etc.) may also be helpful, but such cognitive retraining may not generalize to the natural environment unless real changes are also made in the environment to support the newly trained cognitions (Pepler and Rubin 1991). For example, aggressive children may continue to believe that peers are hostile unless peers can be induced to change their rejecting behavior, and aggressive children may not change their perceptions of the consequences of their actions unless consistent sanctions (e.g., time out) are actually applied to their behavior. Finally, training aggressive children in social skills (e.g., how to make friends, how to join a group of children at play) and tutoring them in academic skills may provide them with positive means of obtaining desired rewards, thereby reducing the need for antisocial behavior (Patterson 1982).

References

Ainsworth M D S 1979 Infant–mother attachment. *Am. Psychol.* 34(10): 932–37

Bandura A 1986 *Social Foundations of Thought and Action: A Social Cognitive Theory*. Prentice-Hall, Englewood Cliffs, New Jersey

Bates J E, Bayles K, Bennett D S, Ridge B, Brown M M 1991 Origins of externalizing behavior problems at eight years of age. In: Pepler D J, Rubin K H (eds.) 1991

Baumrind D 1973 The development of instrumental competence through socialization. In: Pick A D (ed.) 1973 *Minnesota Symposium on Child Psychology*, Vol. 7. University of Minnesota Press, Minneapolis, Minnesota

Cairns R B 1979 *Social Development: The Origins and Plasticity of Interchanges*. Freeman, San Francisco, California

Cairns R B, Cairns B D 1991 Social cognition and social networks: A developmental perspective. In: Pepler D J, Rubin K H (eds.) 1991

Dodge K A 1986 A social information processing model of social competence in children. In: Perlmutter M (ed.) 1986 *Minnesota Symposium on Child Psychology*, Vol. 18. Erlbaum, Hillsdale, New Jersey

Eron L D, Huesmann L R, Zelli A 1991 The role of parental variables in the learning of aggression. In: Pepler D J, Rubin K H (eds.) 1991

Feshbach S 1970 Aggression. In: Mussen P H (ed.) 1970 *Carmichael's Manual of Child Psychology*, Vol. 2, 3rd edn. Wiley, New York

Freud S 1940 *The Ego and the Mechanisms of Defense*. Hogarth, London

Hartup W W 1974 Aggression in childhood: Developmental perspectives. *Am. Psychol.* 29(5): 336–41

Langlois J H, Stephan C 1981 Beauty and the beast: The role of physical attractiveness in the development of peer relations and social behavior. In: Brehm S S, Kassin S M, Gibbons F X (eds.) 1981 *Developmental Social Psychology: Theory and Research*. Oxford University Press, New York

Lorenz K 1966 *On Aggression*. Methuen, London

Maccoby E E, Jacklin C N 1974 *The Psychology of Sex Differences*, 2 Vols. Stanford University Press, Stanford, California

Martin B 1975 Parent–child relations. In: Horowitz F D (ed.) 1975 *Review of Child Development Research*, Vol. 4. University of Chicago Press, Chicago, Illinois

McCord J 1979 Some child-rearing antecedents of criminal behavior in adult men. *J. Pers. Soc. Psychol.* 37(9): 1477–86

Olweus D 1978 *Aggression in the Schools: Bullies and Whipping Boys*. Hemisphere, Washington, DC

Olweus D 1979 Stability of aggressive reaction patterns in males: A review. *Psychol. Bull.* 86(4): 852–75

Olweus D 1980 Familial and temperamental determinants of aggressive behavior in adolescent boys: A causal analysis. *Dev. Psychol.* 16(6): 644–66

Olweus D 1984 Development of stable aggression reaction patterns in males. In: Blanchard R, Blanchard C (eds.) 1984 *Advances in the Study of Aggression*, Vol. 1.

Academic Press, New York

Olweus D, Mattson A, Schalling D, Low H 1980 Testosterone, aggression, physical and personality dimensions on normal adolescent males. *Psychos. Med.* 42(2): 253–69

Parke R D, Slaby R G 1983 The development of aggression. In: Hetherington E M (ed.) 1983 *Handbook of Child Psychology. Vol. 4: Socialization, Personality, and Social Development*. Wiley, New York

Patterson G R 1982 *Coercive Family Processes*. Castilia Press, Eugene, Oregon

Patterson G R, Capaldi D, Bank L 1991 An early starter model for predicting delinquency. In: Pepler D J, Rubin K H (eds.) 1991

Patterson G R, Littman R A, Bricker W 1967 Assertive behavior in children: A step toward a theory of aggression. *Monogr. Soc. Res. Child Dev.* 32(5) Serial No. 113: Whole issue

Patterson G R, Stouthamer-Loeber M 1984 The correlation of family management practices and delinquency. *Child Dev.* 55(4): 1299–307

Pepler D J, Rubin K H (eds.) 1991 *The Development and Treatment of Childhood Aggression*. Erlbaum, Hillsdale, New Jersey

Perry D G, Bussey K 1984 *Social Development*. Prentice-Hall, Englewood Cliffs, New Jersey

Perry D G, Perry L C, Boldizar J P 1990 Learning of aggression. In: Lewis M, Miller S (eds.) 1990 *Handbook of Developmental Psychopathology*. Plenum, New York

Perry D G, Perry L C, Kennedy E 1992 Conflict and the development of antisocial behavior. In: Shantz C U, Hartup W W (eds.) 1992 *Conflict in Child and Adolescent Development*. Cambridge University Press, Cambridge

Plomin R 1990 *Nature and Nurture: An Introduction to Behavioral Genetics*. Brooks/Cole, Pacific Grove, California

Reinisch J M 1981 Prenatal exposure to synthetic progestins increases potential for aggression in humans. *Science* 211(4487): 1171–73

Sroufe L A 1983 Infant–caregiver attachment and patterns of adaptation in preschool: The roots of maladaptation and competence. In: Perlmutter M (ed.) 1983 *Minnesota Symposium in Child Psychology*, Vol. 16. Erlbaum, Hillsdale, New Jersey

Thomas A, Chess S, Birch H 1968 *Temperament and Behavior Disorders in Children*. New York University Press, New York

Development of Prosocial Behavior

N. Eisenberg

Until about 1970, there was relatively little research on the development of prosocial behavior (i.e., voluntary, intentional behavior intended to benefit others), including altruism (sympathetically or morally motivated prosocial behavior). However, psychologists and educators have increasingly turned their attention to the positive side of morality, with the consequence that there is a substantial body of research on the development and socialization of prosocial behavior,

as well as on the personal characteristics associated with children's prosocial responses.

1. The Emergence of Prosocial Behavior

For a long time, most philosophers and psychologists —as well as many laypersons—considered infants and young children to be very self-interested and amoral.

It is now clear that young children are capable of prosocial behavior oriented toward others. However, the nature of prosocial responding seems to change somewhat during the first few years of life.

Even 6-month olds respond to distressed peers with actions such as leaning or gesturing toward them, and touching them. Whether infants respond in this manner because of concern or out of mere curiosity is unclear. By 10 to 14 months of age, infants frequently express agitation and disturbance in reaction to viewing others in distress (Eisenberg 1992, Radke-Yarrow and Zahn-Waxler 1984).

Self-distress as a response to the distress of others decreases in frequency during the second year of life (Radke-Yarrow and Zahn-Waxler 1984). At about 1 year of age, children begin to exhibit reactions that suggest some understanding that their own distresses and those of others are not one and the same (Hoffman 1984). In the second year of life, children sometimes make focused efforts to interact positively with victims in distress. Often these efforts consist initially of positive physical contact such as patting the victim; by 18 to 24 months of age, the child's interventions include more controlled and positive acts of assistance. At this age, children may not fully distinguish between their own and another person's inner states and are apt to confuse them with their own; thus, their attempts to help others often consist of giving the other person what they themselves find most comforting (Hoffman 1984).

It is likely that 3-year olds' responses to the distresses of others are more appropriate and competent than are those of 18-month olds. However, despite the fact that preschool children can and do respond to others in distress on some occasions, comforting of distressed others is still a relatively infrequent act, particularly outside of the home (see Eisenberg and Mussen 1989).

The sharing of objects in social interactions not involving distress is relatively common among 1- to 2-year olds, having grown during the first year of life. However, such sharing by young children may not be motivated primarily by concern for the other person; giving and cooperative exchanges of objects seem to be effective ways for young children to sustain positive social interchanges. In addition, young children frequently try to help with household chores (Eisenberg and Mussen 1989, Radke-Yarrow et al. 1983), although children's motives for such helping are unknown.

It is not clear whether naturally occurring sharing and helping behaviors directed toward people in their social world increase with age during the preschool and school years, and little is known about school-age children's comforting behaviors. However, older children are more likely to share objects or money with unknown others (e.g., with charities) and older children are more skilled in their comforting communications than are younger children (see Eisenberg

1992, Eisenberg and Mussen 1989, Radke-Ya al. 1983).

Although the increase in prosocial behavior with age generally is small or even nonexistent (depending on the type of prosocial behavior), older and younger children may differ greatly in their reasons for helping. In general, older children are more likely than younger children to assist for altruistic or other-oriented motives whereas younger children are more likely to assist in order to obtain material or social rewards (Bar-Tal 1982, Eisenberg 1986).

The consistency of children's prosocial behavior across settings and time seems to increase with age. In the first few years of life, consistency in prosocial responding across settings and time is low. In contrast, moderate consistency in the prosocial behavior of preschoolers, elementary schoolchildren, and adolescents has been observed (see Eisenberg and Mussen 1989, Savin-Williams 1987).

2. Cultural Influences

Vast differences in people's typical levels of prosocial functioning have been observed across societies. In some cultures, aggression, ridicule, and cruelty are commonplace, whereas in others social interactions are characterized by caring, helping, and support (see Eisenberg 1992, Rohner 1975).

Differences among subcultures and cultures are also evident in studies of children's cooperative behavior. Children reared in traditional rural subcultures and traditional, semiagricultural settlements cooperate more than do children reared in modern, urban settings. In addition, children who are in the process of assimilating, or who are exposed to the dominant, urban culture in their school tend to be less cooperative than children from the same cultural group with less exposure to the urban culture (see Eisenberg and Mussen 1989, Radke-Yarrow et al. 1983).

There is limited research on the precise reasons for the apparent cross-cultural and subcultural differences in prosocial and cooperative behavior. Nonetheless, the existing research is consistent with the conclusion that cross-cultural differences in warm, supportive parenting may account in part for the differences (Rohner 1975). In addition, cultures vary in the degree to which they specifically teach and reinforce positive or negative values and behaviors (see Eisenberg 1992). Moreover, in traditional cultures, the survival of the group is often dependent on cooperation and helping among kin and neighbors. Consequently, the child's everyday experiences and chores involve cooperation and prosocial actions because they are part of the routine of daily life (Graves and Graves 1983, Whiting and Whiting 1975). Indeed, cultural variation in the degree to which children are assigned chores that significantly contribute to the well-being of the family has been associated with cross-cultural differences in

207

children's prosocial behavior (Whiting and Whiting 1975). In this and other ways, the structure of traditional, nonurban, subsistence cultures seems to promote a cooperative, prosocial orientation, at least in regard to other members of the community.

3. The Socialization of Prosocial Behavior

Although there is probably a genetic component to individual differences in empathy and altruism (Rushton et al. 1986, see also Eisenberg and Mussen 1989), differences among people in prosocial behavior *within* a culture appear to be due, in part, to the effects of socialization within the home and the larger community. Specifically, prosocial children tend to have parents who model prosocial actions and value prosocial behaviors, use reasoning in disciplinary interactions rather than primarily punishment or threats, provide opportunities for their children to engage in prosocial actions, and encourage their children to take perspectives and show empathy and sympathy (Eisenberg and Mussen 1989, Radke-Yarrow et al. 1983). For example, parents of people who rescued Jews from the Germans during the second World War tended to model and teach their children prosocial values, emphasized caring for others and applying ethical principles to a wide spectrum of humanity, used reasoning rather than punitive discipline, and had warm and respectful relationships with their children (Oliner and Oliner 1988).

Parental practices that promote the development of sympathy in their children are perhaps most clearly associated with the development of children's altruism. This is not surprising because sympathetic people are more prosocial than are other people (Eisenberg and Miller 1987). It appears that parents can facilitate sympathetic and altruistic responses even in young children if they encourage their children to consider the consequences of their behaviors for others (see Radke-Yarrow et al. 1983).

In addition, teachers and schools influence children's prosocial development. For example, school-based programs that emphasize rational discipline, cooperation, and prosocial values, and that provide activities designed to enhance children's sympathy and understanding of others, appear to foster elementary schoolchildren's prosocial behavior (Solomon et al. 1988). Moreover, television appears to be a socializer; children's viewing of prosocial television programming is modestly associated with the level of children's prosocial behavior (see Eisenberg and Mussen 1989).

4. Personal Characteristics Associated with Children's Prosocial Behavior

Prosocial children appear to differ from less prosocial children on a variety of personal dimensions. Most notably, children who engage in more prosocial behavior, especially behaviors that appear to be altruistically motivated, tend to exhibit a relatively high level of perspective-taking (i.e., the ability to understand others' thoughts, feelings, and point of view) and moral reasoning (reasoning about moral conflicts), and are emotionally responsive to other people in need or distress. This is not surprising; understanding others' perspectives, feeling their distress and concern for their distress, and thinking about the validity of other individuals' needs and relevant moral principles have frequently been cited as the basis of moral behavior, including altruism (Eisenberg 1986, Hoffman 1984, Underwood and Moore 1982). However, sympathy, higher-level moral reasoning, and perspective-taking are probably not relevant to (and do not predict) prosocial behaviors that are enacted for egoistic reasons or are performed habitually or without much thought.

In addition, sociable, assertive, socially competent children seem especially likely to engage in some types of prosocial acts, including those that require social initiative (e.g., prosocial behaviors that are emitted spontaneously, without being requested) and are performed outside of the home. In contrast, nonassertive children seem to assist primarily when asked, and often they may comply with a request because they have difficulty asserting themselves and coping with social conflicts. In addition, the expression of positive emotion is associated with spontaneous prosocial actions, whereas high levels of aggression tend to be associated with low levels of children's prosocial behavior (Eisenberg and Mussen 1989).

Intelligent children exhibit somewhat more prosocial behavior than less intelligent children, probably because they feel more competent than other children, are better able to discern others' needs and use higher-level moral reasoning. Finally, girls and boys may prefer to engage in different types of prosocial behavior; for example, girls may prefer giving physical or psychological comfort to other people whereas boys may feel more comfortable providing instrumental assistance. Sex differences in children's prosocial behavior are small, although when they occur they generally favor girls (Eisenberg and Mussen 1989, Radke-Yarrow et al. 1983).

5. Conclusion

It appears that the development of prosocial behavior is associated with a combination of personal factors, which in turn are influenced by cognitive and emotional development, biological factors, and socialization. However, there is relatively little research on the complex interplay of these factors, particularly in settings outside the home and in non-Western cultures.

See also: Social Development; Socialization; Cross-cultural Approaches to Human Development; Moral Development

References

Bar-Tal D 1982 Sequential development of helping behavior: A cognitive-learning approach. *Dev. Rev.* 2(2): 101–24

Eisenberg N 1986 *Altruistic Emotion, Cognition and Behavior.* Erlbaum, Hillsdale, New Jersey

Eisenberg N 1992 *The Caring Child.* Harvard University Press, Cambridge, Massachusetts

Eisenberg N, Miller P A 1987 The relation of empathy to prosocial and related behaviors. *Psych. Bull.* 101(1): 91–119

Eisenberg N, Mussen P H 1989 *The Roots of Prosocial Behavior in Children.* Cambridge University Press, Cambridge

Graves N B, Graves T D 1983 The cultural context of prosocial development: An ecological model. In: Bridgeman D L (ed.) 1983 *The Nature of Prosocial Development: Interdisciplinary Theories and Strategies.* Academic Press, New York

Hoffman M L 1984 Interaction of affect and cognition in empathy. In: Izard C E, Kagan J, Zajonc R B (eds.) 1984 *Emotions, Cognition, and Behavior.* Cambridge University Press, New York

Oliner S P, Oliner P M 1988 *The Altruistic Personality: Rescuers of Jews in Nazi Europe.* Free Press, New York

Radke-Yarrow M, Zahn-Waxler C 1984 Roots, motives, and patterns in children's prosocial behavior. In: Staub E, Bar-Tal D, Karylowski J, Reykowski J (eds.) 1984 *Development and Maintenance of Prosocial Behavior: International Perspectives on Positive Behavior.* Plenum Press, New York

Radke-Yarrow M, Zahn-Waxler C, Chapman M 1983 Prosocial dispositions and behavior. In: Mussen P (ed.) 1983 *Manual of Child Psychology. Vol. 4: Socialization, Personality, and Social Development.* Wiley, New York

Rohner R P 1975 *They Love Me, They Love Me Not: A Worldwide Study of the Effects of Parental Acceptance and Rejection.* HRAF Press, New Haven, Connecticut

Rushton J P, Fulker D W, Neale M C, Nias D K B, Eysenck H J 1986 Altruism and aggression: The heritability of individual differences. *J. Pers. Soc. Psychol.* 50: 1192–98

Savin-Williams R C 1987 *Adolescence: An Ethological Perspective.* Springer-Verlag, New York

Solomon D, Watson M S, Delucchi K L, Schaps E, Battistich V 1988 Enhancing children's prosocial behavior in the classroom. *Am. Educ. Res. J.* 25(4): 527–54

Underwood B, Moore B 1982 Perspective-taking and altruism. *Psych. Bull.* 91(1): 143–73

Whiting B B, Whiting J W M 1975 *Children of Six Cultures: A Psychocultural Analysis.* Harvard University Press, Cambridge, Massachusetts

Development of Motivation

G. D. Heyman and C.S. Dweck

Motivation drives and directs behavior; achievement motivation governs behavior relevant to achievement and learning. An understanding of achievement motivation has implications for many aspects of human life, including how individuals develop new skills, and how or whether they make use of existing skills. Consequently, issues concerning the nature and development of achievement motivation take on great theoretical and practical significance.

Many approaches have been taken to explain achievement motivational processes. Some approaches have included the examination of global achievement "motives" or broad self-concepts such as self-esteem. However, researchers have become aware of the need to examine specific concepts that illuminate motivational processes. One such approach, the "goals" approach, has begun to provide answers to the basic questions in the field.

In this entry, the goals approach to achievement motivation will be described. Next, motivation will be discussed from a developmental perspective. Finally, ways to develop adaptive achievement motivation will be examined.

1. The Goals Approach

The goals approach grew out of research on adaptive and maladaptive motivation (see, e.g., Ames 1984, Diener and Dweck 1978). Findings from this research indicate that children of comparable ability often respond very differently when they encounter academic obstacles. Some children (including many with high levels of ability) interpret their difficulties to mean that they have low ability. They seem to lose hope that their efforts will lead them to success, and their performance tends to deteriorate. This constellation of responses, sometimes referred to as a "helpless" pattern, is considered maladaptive because it prevents individuals from reaching potentially attainable, valued goals. In contrast, other children respond to obstacles as challenges to be mastered. These children do not appear to be upset by their difficulties, and sometimes report feeling excited by the challenge. They typically focus their attention on modifying their effort and strategy, and they maintain or improve their level of problem-solving. These reactions, which are frequently called "mastery-oriented" responses, are

Table 1
Relation between beliefs about intelligence, goals, and response to obstacles in achievement situations

Theory of intelligence	Goal orientation	Response to obstacles
Entity (intelligence is fixed)	Performance (goal is to demonstrate competence)	Vulnerability to helpless pattern (low persistence; performance deterioration)
Incremental (intelligence is malleable)	Learning (goal is to increase competence)	Mastery-oriented pattern (high persistence; performance maintenance or improvement)

considered to be adaptive because they allow individuals the time that is often necessary to overcome difficulties and to progress toward valued goals.

Converging research results now suggest that these adaptive and maladaptive motivational responses can result from different goals (see Table 1); that is, from the different aims children pursue in achievement situations. Achievement motivation researchers have examined two classes of achievement goals (see, e.g., Ames 1984, Dweck and Leggett 1988, Nicholls 1984). One class of goals, sometimes referred to as "performance goals," centers on issues of performance and adequacy. When individuals hold performance goals they are concerned with documenting their competence, and they tend to view achievement situations as tests of their competence. Another set of goals, termed "learning goals," revolves around learning and task mastery. When individuals hold learning goals they strive to master new tasks and develop competencies.

Justifiably, children tend to be concerned with both learning and appearing competent. Which of these goals predominates, however, has important motivational consequences. When the focus is on performance goals, task performance is readily seen as measuring ability level. Poor performance is viewed in terms of low ability (particularly when individuals have low confidence about their abilities) and motivational helplessness may result. In contrast, when learning goals are emphasized, difficulties do not provide information about competency; rather, they guide task mastery and learning and indicate the points at which greater effort or new strategies are required. In this way, learning goals facilitate a mastery-oriented motivational stance in the face of difficulty.

These findings concerning achievement goals are consonant with other research in the field, including the work of Kuhl (1983). This research shows that individuals who focus more on such factors as outcomes (state orientation) show greater motivational vulnera-

bility when encountering difficulties than those who concentrate on such factors as learning processes (action orientation).

In summary, results of a great deal of research on achievement goals suggest that when individuals place an emphasis on measuring or proving their ability, they tend to show motivational vulnerability in the face of difficulties. Conversely, when individuals focus their attention on thinking about ways to learn or develop skills, they are more resilient.

Why might different individuals pursue different goals even in identical situations? One reason for this seems to be that they hold different theories of intelligence (see Dweck and Leggett 1988, Faria and Fontaine 1989, Stevenson et al. 1990). Some children tend to view intelligence as a relatively fixed and measurable quality ("entity theory"); other children believe that intelligence is a malleable quality that can be increased through effort ("incremental theory"). Findings from research on these theories suggest that when individuals view their intelligence as a fixed capacity, they are more likely to enter achievement situations pursuing performance goals, looking for ways to demonstrate that this capacity is adequate. In contrast, when individuals believe that their intelligence is malleable they are more likely to pursue learning goals, seeking ways to develop their intelligence.

In short, the entity view of intelligence and performance goals are associated with vulnerability to helplessness. Conversely, the incremental view of intelligence and learning goals are associated with the maintenance of adaptive motivational patterns in the face of difficulty.

2. Motivation and Development

There is growing recognition that motivational processes are dynamic systems that have the potential to change over the course of development. Systematic research has been undertaken in order to understand the nature of the development of achievement motivation.

Several researchers have examined the impact of obstacles on the motivation of children in first grade and younger. In some of this work, young children, after facing obstacles, reported substantial optimism about their chances for future success and displayed motivational resilience. They did not exhibit responses characteristic of the helpless pattern.

Consistent with this notion of children's motivational resilience, some researchers have found developmental differences in the way children reason about effort and ability in relation to achievement outcomes (Nicholls 1984). This work indicates that young children do not understand or measure ability in the same manner as older children, and that young children are more likely to expect effort to lead to desired outcomes. This emphasis on effort rather than ability is characteristic of the mastery-oriented motivational response. These results suggest that young children are less likely to view effort as having negative implications for their abilities and are less apt to question the usefulness of effort. Thus, this developmental research on children's responses to obstacles and on their motivationally relevant thinking supports the idea that children start off with relative motivational resilience and become less adaptively motivated as they grow older.

2.1 Developmental Issues: A New Look

Although previous research has painted a picture of young children as a motivationally homogeneous group who think and respond like mastery-oriented older children, research in the early 1990s suggests a rather different picture. This work demonstrates that when tasks are meaningful and failures are salient, some young children, like their older counterparts, respond to difficulties with negative emotional reactions (Stipek et al. 1992) and also display the thoughts and behaviors characteristic of the helpless pattern (Dweck 1991).

How can findings of children's motivational vulnerabilities be reconciled with findings that children lack concern with or understanding of ability? One possibility is that children think about their performance not in terms of how it reflects on their ability, but on other important aspects of themselves. If failure in achievement situations does have implications for aspects of the self early in life, it would most likely hold meaning in terms of concepts that are familiar to young children. One set of such concepts relates to goodness and badness. Since teaching children what is right and wrong is a major goal of socialization, children are likely to receive numerous messages regarding these issues. Thus, young children may develop ideas about goodness or badness that they can apply to a variety of situations, including achievement contexts (Dweck 1991).

There is some evidence to suggest that children just starting school may indeed think about what achievement outcomes mean about their goodness and badness. Heyman et al. (1992) found that kindergarten children who exhibited responses characteristic of the helpless pattern were more likely to report feeling "bad" after they made mistakes.

Just as young children are not completely protected from motivational difficulties, they are not necessarily doomed to greater risk as they age. As indicated above, children's thinking about achievement situations often becomes increasingly conductive to the helpless pattern as they get older (Nicholls 1984). However, cross-cultural research suggests that such trends in motivationally relevant thinking are not inevitable. For example, Salili et al. (1976) found that Iranian children emphasize effort more as they get older, and Hau and Salili (1990) found that emphasis on learning goals increases with age among Chinese students in Hong Kong.

In summary, research has suggested that there may be meaningful differences in the ways in which younger and older children process ability information and respond to some achievement situations. However, findings indicate that in the context of salient failure, some young children tend to show motivational responses that are very similar to those of older children. Research also suggests that for young children, differences in motivational patterns may be more closely related to conceptions of goodness and badness than to specific conceptions of intellectual competence.

2.2 The Intrinsic Motivation Approach: Parallel Findings

The intrinsic motivation approach to achievement motivation also focuses on the ways in which individuals perceive achievement situations. This approach is primarily concerned with task interest and enjoyment.

As in the goals framework, in the intrinsic motivation framework children often appear less adaptively motivated across development. In other words, children seem to find schoolwork to be less enjoyable as they progress through school. However, to describe young children as full of intrinsic motivation which slowly dissipates is to give an incomplete picture. Lepper et al. (1973) found that even preschoolers lose interest in activities for which their participation has been externally rewarded. In addition, Harter (1986) demonstrated that some children maintain the same level—or even show increases—in intrinsic motivation upon entering junior high school, when most students show the greatest decline.

3. Promoting Adaptive Achievement Motivation

How can the development of adaptive achievement motivation be encouraged? Several approaches that focus on changing achievement contexts and individuals' perceptions of these contexts have met with a good deal of success.

One general approach has focused on changing the explanations children make when they fail. As described earlier, an important aspect of the helpless motivational pattern is that it involves explaining difficulties in terms of personal deficiencies. In contrast, individuals exhibiting mastery-oriented motivation do not explain their difficulties in this way. When they do give such explanations they tend to remain focused on effort and strategy (Diener and Dweck 1978). Researchers have found that when children are taught to provide explanations in terms of factors over which they have control, adaptive motivational consequences are likely to result. Specifically, these positive effects have been demonstrated in situations in which children are taught to focus attention on their effort or strategy, rather than their ability, when they are having difficulties (Dweck 1975, Andrews and Debus 1978).

Another general approach to enhancing achievement motivation has involved a focus on goals. Researchers consistently have demonstrated that a variety of factors that emphasize performance goals often tend to be associated with negative motivational consequences, and that factors that elicit learning goals are associated with adaptive motivation. For example, Butler (1987) found that children who received information about their performance or ability level through normative grades or praise (performance goal manipulation) on a divergent thinking task showed less intrinsic motivation than children who received feedback of task-relevant comments or no feedback. In another goal manipulation, Ames (1984) gave children problems to solve in a competitive context that emphasized performance relative to a peer, as compared to an individualistic structure in which self-improvement was emphasized. She found that children who worked in the individualistic (learning goal) context were less likely to attribute failure to ability and more apt to engage in self-instruction than were children working in the competitive (performance goal) context.

More comprehensive programs are being implemented that utilize research from both the goals and intrinsic motivation frameworks. One such program emphasizes learning goals through enhancing children's interest in learning and providing them with skills to meet learning goals (Ames 1990). Students with motivational difficulties who were involved in this program showed motivational benefits in comparison to a control group of children with motivational difficulties. These benefits included higher levels of intrinsic motivation and higher perceived ability.

Adaptive motivation may also be promoted by influencing motivationally relevant theories about intelligence. Indeed, Stevenson et al. (1990) argued that the Japanese and Chinese cultural beliefs that people are very malleable help to account for the high levels of academic success achieved by many children in these countries. Preliminary research suggests that one can influence children's goal choices by influencing their beliefs about intelligence (see Dweck and Leggett 1988). Specifically, when incremental (malleable) beliefs about intelligence were emphasized, as opposed to entity (fixed) beliefs, children were more likely to endorse learning goals. Although further research is needed, it seems likely that more adaptive motivation will result if individuals can be taught to think about their abilities as malleable.

In summary, adaptive motivation can be promoted at multiple levels, incorporating individuals' explanations of their difficulties, the goals they hold for achievement situations, their beliefs about intelligence, and their intrinsic interest in achievement situations.

References

Ames C 1984 Achievement attribution and self-instructions under competitive and individualistic goal structures. *J. Educ. Psychol.* 76(3): 478–87

Ames C 1990 Achievement goals and classroom structure: Developing a learning orientation. Paper presented at the annual meeting of the American Educational Research Association, Boston, Massachusetts

Andrews G R, Debus R 1978 Persistence and causal perceptions of failure: Modifying cognitive attributions. *J. Educ. Psychol.* 70(2): 154–66

Butler R 1987 Task-involving and ego involving properties of evaluative situations: Effects of different feedback conditions on motivational perceptions, interest, and performance. *J. Educ. Psychol.* 79(4): 474–82

Diener C, Dweck C S 1978 An analysis of learned helplessness: Continuous changes in performance, strategy, and achievement cognitions following failure. *J. Pers. Soc. Psychol.* 36: 451–61

Dweck C S 1975 The role of expectations and attributions in the alleviation of learned helplessness. *J. Pers. Soc. Psychol.* 31(4): 674–85

Dweck C S 1991 Self-theories and goals: Their role in motivation, personality and development. In: Dienstbier R (ed.) 1991 *Nebraska Symposium on Motivation: Perspectives on Motivation*, Vol. 38. University of Nebraska Press, Lincoln, Nebraska

Dweck C S, Leggett E 1988 A social-cognitive approach to motivation and personality. *Psychol. Rev.* 95(2): 256–73

Faria L, Fontaine A M 1989 Conceptions personelles d'intelligence: Elaboration d'une echelle et études exploratoires. *Cadernos de Consulta Psicologica* 5: 19–30

Harter S 1986 The relationship between perceived competence, affect, and motivational orientation within the classroom: Process and patterns of change. In: Boggiano A K, Pitman T (eds.) 1986 *Achievement and Motivation: A Social-Developmental Perspective*. Cambridge University Press, Cambridge

Hau K, Salili F 1990 Examination result attribution, expectancy and achievement goals among Chinese students in Hong Kong. *Educ. Stud.* 16(1): 17–31

Heyman G D, Dweck C S, Cain K M 1992 Young children's vulnerability to self-blame and helplessness: Relationship to beliefs about goodness. *Child Dev.* 63(2): 401–15

Kuhl J 1983 *Motivation, Konflikt und Handlungskontrolle.* Springer-Verlag, Berlin

Lepper M R, Greene D, Nisbett R E 1973 Undermining children's intrinsic interest with extrinsic rewards: A test of the "overjustification" hypothesis. *J. Pers. Soc. Psychol.* 28(1): 129–37

Nicholls J G 1984 Achievement motivation: Conceptions of ability, subjective experience, task choice, and performance. *Psychol. Rev.* 91(3): 328–46

Salili F, Maehr M L, Gilmore G 1976 Achievement and morality: A cross-cultural analysis of causal attribution and evaluation. *J. Pers. Soc. Psychol.* 33(3): 327–37

Stevenson H W et al. 1990 Contexts of achievement: A study of American, Chinese and Japanese children. *Monogr.* *Soc. Res. Child Dev.* 55 (1–2) (221): 123

Stipek D, Recchia S, McClintic S 1992 Self-evaluation in young children. *Monogr. Soc. Res. Child Dev.* 57 (1) (226): 100

Further Reading

Covington M V, Beery R G 1976 *Self-worth and School Learning.* Holt, Rinehart, and Winston, New York

Stipek D, MacIver D 1989 Developmental change in children's assessment of intellectual competence. *Child Dev.* 60(3): 521–38

Weiner B 1985 An attributional theory of achievement motivation and emotion. *Psychol. Rev.* 92(4): 548–73

Emotional Development

R. Pekrun

Emotions are basic psychological systems regulating adaptation to important environmental and personal demands. They are closely interrelated with physiological, cognitive, and behavioral processes, and are thus of great importance for teaching, learning, and educational achievement. However, because psychological research has been dominated by behaviorist and cognitive approaches, scientific knowledge about emotional development is still rather limited.

1. Conceptualizations of Emotion

1.1 Definition and Classification

Emotions are often broadly defined as systems of interacting processes including emotional feelings, cognitive appraisals, physiological processes, expressive behavior, and motivational tendencies (Kleinginna and Kleinginna 1981). More specific definitions restrict emotions to one or more core components (like emotional feelings and emotion-specific appraisals). For example, current conceptions of test anxiety imply that this emotion consists of: (a) "emotionality," comprising uneasy feelings of apprehension and nervousness along with perceptions of anxiety-specific bodily changes; and (b) "worry" cognitions (e.g., about possible failures or a lack of competence; Hembree 1988).

Classifications of emotion follow dimensional or typological principles. Dimensional approaches identify basic qualities that are common to all emotions, although to varying degrees. Two such dimensions are activation and hedonic tone (positive vs. negative subjective value). Typological approaches classify emotions into discrete categories (Izard and Malatesta

1987). Resulting taxonomies often differentiate discrete "primary" emotions (including joy, interest, sadness, fear, anger, disgust, shame, contempt, and surprise) characterized by emotion-specific, universally found patterns of facial expression. Other emotions are conceptualized as blends or derivatives of primary emotions. One advantage of the discrete emotions approach is that it makes it possible to account for the specific functions of different emotions for specific somatic and psychological processes.

1.2 Theories and Research Traditions

Models of the origins and functions of emotion have largely followed the major paradigms of psychology and related fields of biology and sociology. Developmental theory and empirical research within these approaches has concentrated on emotions in infancy and childhood. Research on adolescent and adult emotional development is, in the early 1990s, still in its early stages.

Psychobiological approaches. Biologically oriented emotion research dates back to Darwin's pioneering work. Central assumptions underlying these approaches are that somatic processes and facial, vocal, and postural expressions constitute the core of emotion; that emotions serve behavioral functions by regulating social communication and instrumental behavior; and that the components of primary emotions are innate. Emphasis is put on the early sequential maturation of components of primary emotions (Izard and Malatesta 1987).

Psychoanalytic theories. Freud assumed that emotions are closely related to the satisfaction or frustration of drives. He regarded emotions as functions of the ego that signal drive states and that give rise to cognitive and behavioral action. One example is anxiety stemming from undesirable sexual impulses which, according to Freud (1926), serves to mobilize defense mechanisms. Early and modern psychoanalytic models relate emotions to stages of psychosexual development and to the development of psychopathology.

Cognitive theories. These assume that emotions are induced by cognitive appraisals. Examples are attributional theory, which explains emotions such as pride and shame as being elicited by causal attributions (Weiner 1985); expectancy theories, which assume that future-related emotions (like anxiety) are induced by event- and coping-related expectancies (e.g., Pekrun 1992); or multifaceted models, which address larger sets of both cognitions and emotions (e.g., Scherer 1984). Cognitively oriented research on emotional development either analyzes the developmental implications of cognitive emotion theories, or it explores the emotional implications of Piagetian approaches. In both cases, the development of emotions is viewed as being closely tied to, or even dependent on, the development of cognitive capacities.

Social learning conceptualizations. Social learning approaches tend to emphasize the influence of social and cultural environments and the resulting cultural and individual specifity of emotions. Typically, social influences are assumed to be mediated by cognitive processes involved in observing and interpreting the behavior of significant other persons (such as primary caregivers).

Integrative approaches. Different approaches to emotional development can be assumed to complement rather than contradict each other. Some authors therefore try to combine elements of different origins. One important example is attachment theory, which uses psychoanalytical, ethological, and social-cognitive learning assumptions to explain patterns of attachment in intimate relationships, their development and their implications for emerging emotions like social anxiety, sadness, and anger (Parkes et al. 1991).

2. General Principles of Emotional Development

Because newborns largely lack cognitive and motoric response capabilities, it is assumed that their psychological life is primarily characterized by sensory and emotional processes. Emotions function to facilitate the infant's environmental adaption, for example by communicating internal states to the caregivers.

Not all primary emotions are available at birth. The sequence in which primary emotions emerge seems

to be universal across cultures and conditions of rearing, indicating that early emotional development is largely a function of maturation, based on species-specific genetic programs (Izard and Malatesta 1987). However, from birth on there are striking individual differences, often conceptualized under the rubric of "temperament." Behavioral genetics research suggests that some portion of these differences may be due to interindividual genetic differences. Additionally, environmental factors play a role, with social influences probably being highly important even in the first months of life. Together, genetic and environmental factors produce relatively high stability in interindividual differences in basic emotional traits (e.g., emotional irritability) at least for the time span from the first year of life to the elementary school years (Campos et al. 1989).

After their emergence, primary emotions are differentiated and connected to new eliciting conditions and instrumental behaviors. Two important influences on such changes are cognitive development and socialization. There is some dispute concerning cognitive development, specifically whether emotion precedes cognition developmentally, cognition precedes emotion, or both develop in parallel. Most probably the relation is interactive: emotions instigate cognitive development (e.g., interest motivates explorative behavior which fosters cognition), and the development of specific cognitive capabilities is necessary for more complex emotions to emerge (Case et al. 1988).

Mechanisms of social influence include the following (see also Lewis and Saarni 1985): (a) exposing the individual to emotion-eliciting situations, thus inducing habitual emotional reactions; (b) displaying emotions which can lead to congruent emotions and situation-related appraisals in the receiver ("emotion contagion," "social referencing," cf. Campos et al. 1989); (c) providing other types of information about emotion-relevant characteristics of situations (e.g., by inducing expectancies relating to significant events), thus building up emotion-eliciting cognitive structures; (d) teaching rules for communicating emotions (e.g., "display rules" for socially acceptable emotion expression); and (e) giving information about coping with emotions. Because such influences may vary greatly across cultures, subcultures, and individuals, they provide a large degree of diversity and variability of human emotional life, despite the relative constancy of its basic elements (such as primary emotional feelings, their expression, and their neurophysiological basis).

3. Development of Specific Emotions

3.1 Primary Emotions

Judging from emerging facial expressions, three emotions present in the newborn are interest, distress, and disgust (see overview in Izard and Malatesta 1987). Three to four weeks after birth, enjoyment indicated by stimulus-induced ("exogenous") smiling emerges. From the beginning, these emotions have specific antecedents and functions. Interest is elicited by human faces and by novelty, thus facilitating social interaction as well as exploration and cognitive growth. Distress is caused by physical discomfort and pain, and serves to summon the help of caregivers. Specific olfactory and gustatory stimuli elicit disgust, which aids in rejecting offensive substances and also functions to alert caregivers. Joy is elicited first by the human voice and later by human faces. Expressed by social smiling, it elicits reciprocation by caregivers and is therefore important for continuous, affectively positive interactions that foster infant–caregiver attachment. Furthermore, after approximately two months, the capacity to enjoy cognitive stimulation gradually develops. Thus, like interest, joy also serves functions of social interaction and of cognitive growth facilitation.

Surprise, sadness, anger, and fear do not appear to arise before the third month of life. The emergence of these emotions is congruent with the development of cognitive capabilities (such as anticipating events, appraising the degree to which they are expected, perceiving their causes, and differentiating the known from the unknown), and of emotion-related instrumental behavior (such as locomotive action necessary for fight, flight, and avoidance) during the first year of life.

Fear in infancy has been researched extensively. At some point in time between the sixth and twenty-fourth month, nearly all infants display negative emotional reactions to adult strangers and to separations from the caregiver in unfamiliar situations. These reactions seem primarily to be related to fear, although other emotions (such as anger) may also play a role. Stranger-related and separation-related fearfulness gradually vanish during the following two years of life and are replaced by fears of different kinds (such as fear of animals and of natural disasters), which are typical of childhood (Marks 1987).

The further development of emotions is characterized by the emergence of socially referenced, cognitively more complex emotions such as shame and contempt (probably during the second year of life), and by the differentiation and cognitive elaboration of emotions. In line with changes in cognitive development during childhood, capacities emerge which imply that both the elicitors and the contents of emotion may derive from abstract rather than concrete phenomena, and to past or future events rather than of the present.

3.2 Self-evaluative Emotions

The self-evaluative emotions of pride, shame, and guilt are of special educational importance because of their functions for self-regulated achievement and moral behavior (see the review in Geppert and Heckhausen 1990). In the domain of achievement, early precursors of pride and shame are joy following mastery and sadness following nonmastery of actions. Emerging in the second year of life, these emotions are closely connected to the early development of the motivation to produce self-controlled actions and outcomes. Whereas joy and sadness may imply intentional striving for mastery, achievement-contingent pride and shame require additional cognitive competencies to attribute success and failure to one's own proficiencies.

During the preschool and elementary years, global concepts of the child's own proficiency are differentiated into the concepts of ability and effort, resulting in a further differentiation of self-evaluation following achievement. Specifically, in older children and adults, failure in ability-centered tasks tends to produce shame, whereas failure in effort-centered tasks can lead to feelings of guilt. However, because naturalistic studies on achievement-related emotions beyond infancy are largely lacking, knowledge about the further development of achievement-related pride and shame and about their factual educational relevance is virtually absent.

In the domain of moral behavior, pride may be elicited by behavior that is beneficial for others or that exceeds moral standards, whereas shame and guilt are induced by behavior that violates moral norms or causes damage to another person. More is known about shame and guilt than about moral pride. Both shame and guilt presuppose a clear concept of the self as an agent independent of the social environment. Therefore, they probably do not emerge earlier than during the second year of life.

Furthermore, guilt requires an understanding that damage to another person is caused by oneself. Such an understanding is first developed by feeling empathy with another person's negative emotions, which are then attributed to one's own faults. Therefore, the development of empathy may precede the development of guilt. In early stages (i.e., during the second and third years of life), guilt may be induced by mere spatial or temporal contiguity between one's own behavior and another's bad feelings. Later in childhood, development of more differentiated insights about the differences between one's own and another's emotional life and about the causes and effects of one's own action leads to feelings of guilt independent of close contiguity and of another's expressed emotions.

3.3 Academic Emotions: The Case of Test Anxiety

Achievement-related emotions in academic settings can be assumed to influence students' motivation, achievement, and well-being. Students' test anxiety is the only academically relevant emotion that has been researched intensively (see the review in Hembree 1988). Early developmental precursors of this culture- and institution-specific emotion may lie in social anxiety related to the consequences of failure or in self-evaluative achievement emotions as described above.

In current systems of schooling in Western societies, test anxiety seems to develop primarily during the elementary years. A number of studies document a sharp increase in mean frequency and intensity from Grades 1 to 4, resulting in a high prevalence in late childhood. This developmental trend accompanies a decrease in average self-concepts of academic abilities found for this time period.

Beyond elementary school, there are no universal developmental trends. Instead, there is differential development, dependent, for example, on group membership if academic tracking occurs, and on individual achievement. Specifically, students changing from lower to higher tracks often experience a decrease in their relative achievement status within their class, which may be accompanied by frequent failures and, therefore, the development of more test anxiety. The reverse seems to hold for changes from higher to lower tracks.

On an individual level, students' test anxiety is developmentally related to their academic achievement. Negative correlations between test anxiety and achievement have been found in a large number of studies. These correlations are relatively weak in the beginning and get stronger during the elementary years. Such relations are probably the product both of influences of achievement failures on the development of anxiety, and of negative reverse effects of anxiety on problem-solving, learning, and achievement (Pekrun 1992).

Test anxiety has also been shown to be correlated with teacher, parent, and peer behavior. Variables that correlate positively with test anxiety are pressure for achievement, punishment after failure, and competition within the classroom, indicating that such behaviors may induce anxiety in students. The role of social support, on the other hand, is less clear. Typically, correlations between teacher or parent support and students' test anxiety are near zero. This may be due to ambiguous effects of different types of support conveying both help in alleviating anxiety and high achievement expectancies that induce anxiety. Another possibility would be feedback mechanisms implying anxiety-reducing effects of support, but support-provoking effects of students' expressed anxiety, thus producing overall zero correlations.

4. Directions for Future Research

Because it is still in its infancy, research on emotional development is largely characterized by fragmentization of single research efforts based on narrow theoretical perspectives, and by a focus almost exclusively on infant and childhood development. Thus, two general requirements for future research are:

(a) the integration of theoretical perspectives and interdisciplinary collaboration, and (b) the extension of research into adolescence and adulthood, that is, the adoption of a lifespan perspective on emotional development.

Furthermore, more extensive research into emotions with direct educational relevance is needed. First, current knowledge about emotions related to learning and achievement is largely restricted to test anxiety. More research is needed about, for example, epistemological emotions underlying exploratory behavior and intrinsic motivation to learn, and about positive emotions related to achievement. Second, more studies are necessary concerning the development of social emotions regulating the formation of values, identity, and social behavior.

5. Educational Implications

Two domains in which current knowledge makes it possible to derive practical advice are infant-caregiver attachment and test anxiety in students. A secure attachment to the caregiver(s) seems to be a favorable condition for positive affective development (specifically, concerning social emotions in intimate relationships). Two conditions that foster the development of secure attachment are: (a) stable caregiver-infant relations, and (b) immediate and sensitive responses to the infant's needs and social signals.

Concerning test anxiety, a number of efficient therapeutic procedures are available today (Hembree 1988). Below the level of therapeutic measures, prevention and modification may take place in educational settings themselves. Suitable strategies are to reduce negative, failure-related expectancies as well as to reduce the high subjective values of achievement that underlie test anxiety. Reduction of negative expectancies can be achieved by raising competencies, by lowering externally set goals, and by altering standards of achievement. Specifically, individually referenced standards of evaluation may be more beneficial for low-achieving, anxiety-prone students than socially referenced norms implying competition. Reduction of excessive subjective importance of failure can be attained by devaluation of success and failure, by avoiding achievement-related punishment, and by reducing negative academic career consequences as far as possible. All these measures can be assumed to be beneficial for motivational development as well, and most of them might be adopted by both parents and teachers.

On a school and societal level, changes intended to influence students' affective development positively might be achieved by creating normative school cultures and organizational structures that focus more on individually referenced challenges and mastery goals than on interindividual competition. However, before firm suggestions for restructuring schools can be made, more school-wide empirical research into viable strategies is needed (Covington 1992).

See also: Personality Development; Social Development; An Overview of Cognitive Development

References

Campos J J, Campos R G, Barrett K C 1989 Emergent themes in the study of emotional development and emotion regulation. *Dev. Psychol.* 25(3): 394–402

Case R, Hayward S, Lewis M, Hurst P 1988 Toward a neo-Piagetian theory of cognitive and emotional development. *Dev. Rev.* 8(1): 1–51

Covington M V 1992 *Making the Grade. A Self-worth Perspective on Motivation and School Reform.* Cambridge University Press, New York

Freud S 1926 *Hemmung, Sympton und Angst.* Internationaler Psychoanalytischer Verlag, Leipzig [1936 *Inhibitions, Symptoms and Anxiety.* Hogarth Press/Institute of Psychoanalysis, London]

Geppert U, Heckhausen H 1990 Ontogenese der Emotionen. In: Scherer K R (ed.) 1990 *Psychologie der Emotion. Enzyklopädie der Psychologie*, Series IV, Vol. 3. Hogrefe, Göttingen

Hembree R 1988 Correlates, causes, effects, and treatment of test anxiety. *Rev. Educ. Res.* 58(1): 47–77

Izard C E, Malatesta C Z 1987 Perspectives on emotional development I: Differential emotions theory of early emotional development. In: Osofsky J D (ed.) 1987 *Handbook of Infant Development*, 2nd edn. Wiley, New York

Kleinginna P R, Kleinginna A M 1981 A categorized list of emotion definitions, with suggestions for a consensual definition. *Motivation and Emotion* 5(4): 345–79

Lewis M, Saarni C 1985 *The Socialization of Emotions.* Plenum Press, New York

Marks I M 1987 The development of normal fear: A review. *J. Child Psychol. Psychiatry Allied Discip.* 28(5): 667–697

Parkes C M, Stevenson-Hinde J, Marris P (eds.) 1991 *Attachment Across the Life Cycle.* Routledge, London

Pekrun R 1992 Expectancy-value theory of anxiety. In: Forgays D G, Sosnowski T, Wrzesniewski K (eds.) 1992 *Anxiety: Recent Developments in Cognitive, Psychophysiological and Health Research.* Hemisphere, Washington, DC

Scherer K R 1984 On the nature and function of emotion: A component process approach. In: Scherer K R, Ekman P (eds.) 1984 *Approaches to Emotion.* Erlbaum, Hillsdale, New Jersey

Weiner B 1985 An attributional theory of achievement motivation and emotion. *Psychol. Rev.* 92(4): 548–73

Further Reading

Fogel A, Thelen E 1987 Development of early expressive and communicative action: Reinterpreting the evidence from a dynamic systems perspective. *Dev. Psychol.* 23(6): 747–61

Fox N A, Davidson R J (eds.) 1984 *The Psychobiology of Affective Development.* Erlbaum, Hillsdale, New Jersey

Grossmann K 1991 Emotional development. In: Lerner R M, Peterson A C, Brooks-Gunn J (eds.) 1991 *Encyclopedia of Adolescence.* Garland, New York

Pekrun R, Frese M 1992 Emotions in work and achievement. In: Cooper C L, Robertson I T (eds.) 1992 *International Review of Industrial and Organizational Psychology*, Vol. 7. Wiley, Chichester

Sarason I G (ed.) 1980 *Test Anxiety: Theory, Research, and Applications.* Erlbaum, Hillsdale, New Jersey

Scherer K R, Ekman P (eds.) 1984 *Approaches to Emotion.* Erlbaum, Hillsdale, New Jersey

Sroufe L A 1989 Socioemotional development. In: Osofsky J D (ed.) 1989 *Handbook of Infant Development.* Wiley, New York

Social Development

J. B. Asendorpf

This entry will focus on stability and change in individual differences in social behavior in the period between preschool age and adulthood. It will consider behavioral problems and implications for educational practice.

1. Age-related Changes in Social Behavior

In contrast to the study of cognitive development, there are only a few broad theories of developmental stages in social development (e.g., Erikson 1980), and they have had little impact on the current understanding of social behavior. Age-related changes in social behavior between preschool and adulthood are better described as smooth trends rather than as distinct steps, and cannot be fully captured within an individual-centered framework. This is because many changes in individual behavior are intimately linked to changes in social relationships and to changes in the larger social environment. Consequently, social behavior is addressed here from three perspectives: an individual, an interactional, and an ecological perspective.

1.1 Growing Social-cognitive Competence

From an individual perspective, many changes in social behavior can be understood as a consequence of increasing social-cognitive competence which, in turn, is partly acquired through social interaction. Among the social competencies that are of major importance for educational settings are empathy, self-awareness, and control beliefs.

Empathy refers to sharing the cognitions and/or emotions of others. Hoffman (1987) proposed a developmental sequence for empathy. An early form of spontaneous empathy enables children to react with sympathy and assistance to the distress of others. A later form of empathic awareness of others' feelings rests on the capacity to take deliberately the perspective of others. In late childhood, children become aware of others' general life conditions beyond immediate situations and become concerned with entire groups of people (e.g., the poor, the oppressed).

Observational studies have demonstrated that 18-month-old children are already capable of empathic behavior and that perspective-taking ability, as shown in social problem-solving, emerges around 4 years of age. Older studies that relied upon interviewing children about the intentions and emotions of others have seriously underestimated the ability of young children to take perspectives, because they studied how children reason about empathy rather than empathic behavior itself. The same critique applies to studies of moral cognition based on analyses of children's reasoning about hypothetical situations of moral conflict.

These changes in awareness of others are accompanied by parallel changes in public self-awareness (the awareness of oneself as a social object that is evaluated by others), which gives rise to self-conscious emotions such as embarrassment, shame, and pride, and to self-presentational behavior (Buss 1980). Studies have shown that children as young as 18 months of age can react in an embarrassed manner when they are the center of others' attention, and 2-year olds can react with shame when they fail a task in public. Self-consciousness reaches a peak in adolescence and then declines with increasing age. The self-presentational function of social behavior becomes most salient in lying, cheating, and deceiving —behaviors that require deliberate perspective taking and thus emerge around the age of 4 years.

Control beliefs refer to a broad class of self-related cognitions that support competent patterns of social behavior (Bandura 1986, Ford 1985). Two important types of belief refer to the responsiveness of the environment, or the social support received from particular persons, and to one's ability to achieve desired social outcomes ("self-efficacy expectations"). These beliefs appear to be rooted in experiences of contingency in social interaction that are first acquired in infancy and that are reflected in different patterns of attachment to caregivers. The extent to which these early acquired control beliefs serve as "working models" for other social relationships later in life (e.g., with peers and spouses) is a controversial issue (see Bretherton 1985). The degree to which later experiences of support and self-efficacy in specific relationships can modify such early acquired working models, and the extent to which control beliefs become increasingly specific to particular social settings (e.g., school versus family), particular people, and particular types of social competence (e.g., initiating contact with peers or maintaining friendship), remain open empirical questions. Despite these controversies concerning the continuity and domain-specificity of control beliefs, it is clear that these beliefs become integrated into the self-concept and continue to serve as important motivating functions for social interaction through adulthood.

1.2 Changing Importance of Relationships

Beginning with their entry into large groups of peers in preschool, children in Western cultures show an increasing orientation to peers and a decreasing orientation to parents. The central role of peer relationships for adolescents has been recognized for a long time (a field study of United States adolescents found that they spent 52 percent of their time with classmates and friends but only 18 percent of their time with family members; see Csikszentmihalyi and Larson 1984). The importance of experiencing early peer relationships for the development of social skills and self-confidence has been increasingly recognized, and developmental changes in children's interactions with unfamiliar peers, classmates, and friends have been studied in detail.

Psychologists have now begun to integrate findings on children's relationships with parents, siblings, friends, and other significant persons such as teachers within a common framework: the child's social network (see Belle 1989). Research focuses on the social support that children receive from different members of their network and on possible compensatory effects for poor relationships with particular network members (e.g., can good relationships with siblings compensate for poor relations with classmates?).

1.3 Changes in the Social Environment

From an ecological perspective, individual development proceeds within a culturally structured environment, but even ecological views rarely account for the fact that the environment changes with the developing person. There are culturally regulated, normative changes such as school entry, transitions from one school type to the next, or entry into the job market, and nonnormative changes due to "critical life events" such as illness, moving to another city, divorce from a spouse, and birth of a child. These changes usually lead to a major alteration in people's social network by deleting members, adding new members, and redefining the function of the remaining members (e.g., in terms of their social support; see Belle 1989).

Just as important as these obvious environmental changes are more subtle changes in the behavior of significant members of the network toward the child. For example, parents change their attitudes and behavior toward children as both grow older, based on culturally shared beliefs about timetables for child development (Sigel 1992). In such ways parents, but also teachers, try to make sure that children fulfill certain developmental tasks at certain ages (Havighurst 1972).

Ecological developmental models stress the reciprocity of the relationship between individual development and environmental change. Individuals can select, modify, and even construct their social environment to some extent. Thus, individuals and their social environment can mutually influence each other. For example, particular teacher behaviors promote or undermine students' school motivation, but these behaviors also appear to be partly controlled by students' school motivation; students who show signs of rebelliousness or boredom are often responded to by teachers with increasingly more noncontingent and controlling behaviors (Skinner 1990).

2. Individual Differences in Social Behavior

Whereas differences in cognitive abilities can be explained to a great extent by spurts or delays in general development in early childhood, this approach is less viable in the social domain. From early on, there are many individual differences in social behavior that cannot be explained by a maturity concept, but that rather reflect qualitative differences in behavior and can be viewed as personality characteristics (traits) because they show considerable stability over time.

2.1 Social Traits

Since the 1980s there has been a growing consensus among personality psychologists that traits rated by the self or by knowledgeable informants vary on five independent dimensions in Western cultures. The best evidence on children's social traits comes from research on teachers' judgments by Digman (1989), who labeled the five factors as: extraversion, friendly compliance, will to achieve, emotional stability, and intellect. Most relevant for the social domain are extraversion, emotional stability, and friendly compliance. Extraversion and emotional stability correspond closely to the psychologist Eysenck's concepts of extraversion and neuroticism. Friendly compliance versus hostile noncompliance is a factor characterized by disruptive-aggressive behavior at the low end and cooperative, friendly but also submissive behavior at the high end. Will to achieve is characterized by high carefulness, conscientiousness, and concentration ability and is most relevant for school motivation.

Most of the existing findings on social traits in childhood, including temperamental traits, can be easily related to these three dimensions or combinations of them. Often, extraversion and emotional stability are not distinguished but represented by a single factor, sociability versus withdrawal. It is important for a proper understanding of these "personality factors" to note that they are, in fact, not characteristics of the personality of individuals but characteristics of samples of questionnaire items and people judged on these items. Which factors are identified in a study depends strongly on the set of items used as well as on the sample of subjects. Furthermore, broad factors such as sociability versus withdrawal lump together many traits that are only loosely related to each other.

To illustrate, more detailed studies of children's social behavior have identified at least three different types of social withdrawal among children (see Rubin and Asendorpf 1993). Among children who do not often interact with peers there are active–withdrawn children who often engage in solitary sensorimotor-functional activity or solitary–dramatic play; these children are judged by their teachers to be high in hostile aggression. A completely different group includes children who frequently play alone in a quiet, constructive way without signs of social anxiety; it seems that these children are simply less interested in peers, but do not have problems with them. A third group of children also often plays constructively, but exhibits signs of inhibition and anxiety in peer interaction.

More generally, broad traits can be differentiated into lower-order traits that are more specific in terms of the behavior, its social functions, or the situations where it occurs, and these lower-order traits may be once more differentiated at an even lower level of generality. Thus, individual differences in social behavior can be described by a hierarchy of traits rather than by a few broad traits.

2.2 Social Competence

Similar hierarchical conceptions have been proposed for a differentiated view of social competence (e.g., Waters and Sroufe 1983). Social competence refers to the ability to achieve goals in social interaction while simultaneously using and maintaining positive relationships with others. Goals can be short-term, situation or relationship-specific goals, or long-term, general goals such as "maintaining friendship." Depending on the specificity of the goals involved, the broad construct of social competence can be increasingly specified when one considers lower-level competencies.

Social competence can be related to high values on the broad traits of emotional stability, friendly compliance, will to achieve, and intellect, but research on social competence has focused less on a trait perspective than on a functional analysis of the various cognitive, emotional, and motivational components that contribute to social competence. Individual differences in empathy, perceived social support, means–ends thinking, goal directedness, interest in social goals, and self-efficacy expectations, but also individual differences in IQ and grade point average, have been shown to contribute to social competence (see Ford 1985).

The relations between social competence and these components can be situation-specific. For example, Asendorf and van Aken (1994) showed that children's social competence with peers was strongly related to their IQ only in the first year of a three-year preschool education program—with increasing familiarization with the setting in general, and the peer group in particular, the influence of IQ on social competence decreased. Whereas high IQ seems to be helpful for social adaptation to an unfamiliar group of peers, social competence in a familiar peer group appears to be due more to the quality of the relationships with group members.

2.3 Stability and Change of Individual Differences

At the level of broad factors, social traits already show considerable stability over time in childhood. Stability in this context means constancy of individual differences over time, not absence of change in individual characteristics. For example, social competence as an individual difference variable may be very stable over age although older children solve social problems more competently than younger children. High stability means that the rank order of individuals in a trait remains constant over time in a particular population. Thus, stability is a concept that refers to populations and not to individuals, and is age- and culture-specific.

Digman (1989) reported a mean stability of 0.58 over four years of elementary school for extraversion and friendly compliance, and 0.45 for emotional stability (with different teachers serving as raters at different points in time). These figures are attenuated by the unreliability of each measurement at the two points in time. After correction for unreliability, Olweus (1979) found a "true" average five-year stability of 0.69 in a meta-analysis of 24 studies on children's and adolescents' aggressivity.

Although these figures may appear high, a meta-analysis of the literature on the stability of extraversion and neuroticism in adults resulted in a much higher average "true" five-year stability of 0.90 (Conley 1984). This discrepancy is consistent with the frequent observation in longitudinal studies of personality that the stability of individual differences over a constant retest interval increases with the age of the subjects. Four major factors contribute to this stabilization of individual differences during development (see Asendorpf 1992), as follows.

First, it is often impossible to assess the same construct (e.g., social competence) with the same method at different ages because the meaning of behavior changes with age. The younger the subjects, the

greater this difficulty, and the more probable it is that observed instability of individual differences is due to nonequivalent measurement over age. Second, different individuals grow up in different environments, and to the extent that the environmental differences are stable, this gives rise to systematically different experiences which, in turn, stabilize individual differences in behavior. Third, genetic differences give rise to an accumulation of genetic effects on behavior because the genotype is constant throughout life. Fourth, when children grow older they become more able to control their environment according to their individual preferences, and the resulting increase in personality–environment fit may contribute to the stabilization of personality differences.

3. A Person-oriented View of Social Development

Most knowledge about individual differences in social development is derived from studies of particular behaviors or traits that are analyzed in isolation. If the focus is on personality differences, one person is contrasted with many other agemates. An insufficiently explored alternative is to study personality patterns instead of isolated variables: many traits are contrasted within one person. Different individuals can then be compared with regard to the similarity of their personality patterns, and the stability and change of these individual patterns over age can be studied.

Asendorpf and van Aken (1991) found large individual differences in the stability of such personality patterns (based on dozens of traits per person) over age. Using German and Dutch samples of children, they replicated the finding that the stability of children's personality patterns could be predicted by their social competence. Even stronger findings later emerged when the social competence of German preschoolers was related to the consistency of their personality patterns between teacher judgments at age 4 and parental judgments at age 10: a correlation of 0.76 between early competence and the consistency of personality was found. Because social competence is a highly valued trait, this finding also indicates that socially desirable personality patterns are more stable than undesirable ones.

Three different mechanisms may have contributed to this finding. First, competent children may buffer their personality against disturbing environmental influences by selecting or shaping their environment more according to their needs, whereas noncompetent children may be more a victim of their environment. Second, a high consistency in personality judgments across teachers and parents implies a high consistency in the views of these important partners in social interaction which, in turn, may promote social competence because the social environment is more predictable for these children. Third, children who grow up in a more stable, predictable social environment may find it easier to adapt to specific environmental demands during development; consequently, they may act more competently and may be more stable in their personality.

4. Behavior Problems

In a large representative sample of United States children between 4 and 16 years who had been referred to mental health services and a matched control group of children, Achenbach et al. (1991) identified three major syndromes of behavior problems: internalizing problems (withdrawn, anxious/depressed, somatic complaints), externalizing problems (aggressive and delinquent behavior), and attention problems. Internalizing problems are related to low emotional stability and low extraversion, externalizing problems to low friendly compliance, and attention problems to low will to achieve in Digman's (1989) five-factor model of childhood personality.

The discussion of stability and change in individual differences in social behavior in the normal range can be extended to behavior problems (see Rutter and Garmezy 1983). As rules of thumb, (a) the stability of behavior problems increases with increasing age, and (b) the stability of problem behavior is lower than the stability of normal behavior and depends strongly on the stability of the environment. Furthermore, "looking backward" often results in stronger prediction of behavior problems than "looking forward." For example, the great majority of delinquent adults were already delinquent or antisocial as children but only a minority of delinquent juveniles become adult sociopaths. Finally, the stability of behavior problems varies considerably with the type of problem. It appears that externalizing problems show an earlier stabilization and a higher level of stability than internalizing problems.

The mechanisms that may underlie the causes and stabilization of behavior problems have been studied in a broader context than before. For example, the role of peer acceptance and rejection in the stabilization of behavior problems has been increasingly emphasized, not only for externalizing problems but also for internalizing problems (see Asher and Coie 1990). Whereas peers are already sensitive to externalizing problems in preschool, and peer rejection is a major reason for the stability of aggressive-disruptive behavior from early on, it seems that peers do not begin to recognize withdrawn peers as deviant before middle childhood, which may be one reason why passive-withdrawn behavior does not become a risk factor for internalizing problems before mid-childhood. It is important to note that this peer reinforcement of social problems depends upon cultural norms and values. For example, Chen et al. (1992) showed that, contrary to Western findings, Shanghai fourth-graders preferred passively withdrawn peers as friends—in accordance with Confucian philosophy, which considers emotional inhibition and self-restraint to be indicators of accomplishment and maturity.

5. Implications for Educational Practice

Three implications of findings on social development for educational practice will be discussed (see Minuchin and Shapiro 1983 for an overview of social development in the school context): implications of the role of peer reputation, of the social network perspective, and of the reciprocity between individual and environmental change.

Research has shown that aggressiveness is not the only major reason for peer rejection; beginning in mid-childhood, passive withdrawal from peers seems to be another major risk factor for peer rejection, followed by internalizing problems. Because withdrawn peers do not interfere with teaching, and often represent models of proper school decorum, their emotional difficulties are less often recognized by teachers. Teachers, but also peers, should be made more aware of the social-emotional difficulties of these children and adolescents.

Educators, particularly school psychologists, can profitably enlarge their view of children's social networks. Although it is natural to focus primarily on the social context of a child in class, research has begun to show that there are important compensatory effects among a child's relationships with peers in school, friends outside school, and family members. Of those children who have problems with classmates, the ones most in need of help are those who do not receive social support from other relationships outside school. Thus, increasing the social support from such relationships, particularly with nonschool peers, can be one important type of intervention.

Finally, the increasing recognition of the reciprocity of the relationship between individual development and environmental change questions the implementation of educational programs that focus exclusively on the teacher. Teachers' behavior is partly under the control of pupils' behavior, and the linkage between the behavior of both parties is certainly one important source of resistance to changing pupils' behavior. Classroom intervention may be more effective if it focuses not only on teachers, but also on established feedback loops between teachers' and pupils' behavior.

See also: Personality Development; Development of Social Cognition; Socialization; Social and Communication Skills; Development of Prosocial Behavior; Personality Development

References

Achenbach T M, Howell C T, Quay H C, Conners C K 1991 National survey of problems and competencies among four- to sixteen-year-olds. *Monogr. Soc. Res. Child Dev.* 56(3): 225

Asendorpf J B 1992 Beyond stability: Predicting inter-individual differences in intraindividual change. *Eur. J. Pers.* 6(2): 103–17

Asendorpf J B, van Aken M A G 1991 Correlates of the temporal consistency of personality patterns in childhood. *J. Pers.* 59(4): 689–703

Asendorpf J B, van Aken M A G 1994 Traits and relationship status. *Child Dev.* 65(6): 1786–1798

Asher S J, Coie J 1990 *Peer Rejection in Childhood*. Cambridge University Press, Cambridge

Bandura A 1986 *Social Foundations of Thought and Action*. Prentice-Hall, Englewood Cliffs, New Jersey

Belle D (ed.) 1989 *Children's Social Networks and Social Supports*. Wiley, New York

Bretherton I 1985 Attachment theory: Retrospect and prospect. In: Bretherton I, Waters E (eds.) 1985 Growing points of attachment theory and research. *Monogr. Soc. Res. Child Dev.* 50(1) No. 209: 3–35

Buss A H 1980 *Self-consciousness and Social Anxiety*. Freeman, San Francisco, California

Chen X, Rubin K H, Sun Y 1992 Social reputation and peer relationships in Chinese and Canadian children: A cross-cultural study. *Child Dev.* 63(6): 1336–43

Conley J J 1984 The hierarchy of consistency. *Pers. Ind. Diff.* 5(1): 11–25

Csikszentmihalyi M, Larson R 1984 *Being Adolescent*. Basic Books, New York

Digman J M 1989 Five robust trait dimensions: Development, stability, and utility. *J. Pers.* 57(2): 195–214

Erikson E H 1980 *Identity and the Life Cycle*. Norton, New York

Ford M E 1985 The concept of competence. In: Marlowe H A, Weinberg R B (eds.) 1985 *Competence Development*. Thomas, Springfield, Illinois

Havighurst R J 1972 *Developmental Tasks and Education*. McKay, New York

Hoffman M L 1987 The contribution of empathy to justice and moral judgement. In: Eisenberg N, Strayer J (eds.) 1987 *Empathy and its Development*. Cambridge University Press, Cambridge

Minuchin P P, Shapiro E K 1983 The school as a context for social development. In: Hetherington E M (ed.) 1983 *Handbook of Child Psychology*, Vol. 4. Wiley, New York

Olweus D 1979 Stability of aggressive reaction patterns in males: A review. *Psych. Bull.* 86(4): 852–75

Rubin K H, Asendorpf J B (eds.) 1993 *Social Withdrawal, Inhibition and Shyness in Childhood*. Erlbaum, Hillsdale, New Jersey

Rutter M, Garmezy N 1983 Developmental psychopathology. In: Hetherington E M (ed.) 1983 *Handbook of Child Psychology*, Vol. 4. Wiley, New York

Sigel I E 1992 *Parental Belief Systems: The Psychological Consequences for Children's Development*. Erlbaum, Hillsdale, New Jersey

Skinner E A 1990 Development and perceived control: A dynamic model of action in context. In: Gunnar M, Sroufe L A (eds.) 1990 *Minnesota Symposium on Child Psychology*, Vol. 23. University of Minnesota Press, Minneapolis, Minnesota

Waters E, Sroufe L A 1983 Social competence as a developmental construct. *Dev. Rev.* 3(1): 79–97

Further Reading

Van Hasselt V B, Hersen M (eds.) 1992 *Handbook of Social Development*. Plenum Press, New York

Whiting B B, Edwards C P 1988 *Children of Different Worlds: The Formation of Social Behavior*. Harvard University Press, Cambridge, Massachusetts

Moral Development

G. Nunner-Winkler

This entry begins with definitional issues. The major theoretical perspectives on moral development are then introduced, followed by a review and critique of the dominant model of moral development. Finally, educational implications will be briefly discussed.

1. Definition of Morality

Although there is no unanimous agreement on the exact delimitation of the moral domain, there is nonetheless some consistency in both philosophical and everyday considerations of the minimal definitional requirements for the characteristics of moral rules and for the moral evaluation of behavior.

1.1 Moral Rules

Some social rules reflect cultural traditions only. People follow them from habit but are free to do otherwise without particularly severe sanctions (e.g., "ties should be worn at work"). Moral rules are those social rules that are considered categorically binding for all (universal rules), or for the incumbents of specific roles or for members of specific societies only (specific rules). Universal rules forbid direct harm to others (e.g., by killing or hurting them); specific rules forbid indirect harm to others by not fulfilling their legitimate expectations (e.g., by breaking a promise or failing to perform a duty). These rules can be derived from assumptions about universal physical and social features of humankind. Physically, humans are vulnerable and no instinct keeps them from killing or hurting one another. If humans were immortal or saints there would be no need for a (universal) rule against direct harm. Socially, humans need institutions for survival and thus are dependent on others to do their duty, that is, to follow specific rules and avoid indirect harm.

Beyond this universal core of morality there is widespread divergence. The content of specific duties varies with roles and cultures. It is controversial whether and under what conditions exceptions to (universal and specific) moral rules are justifiable. Although transgression is always considered immoral when done to serve the interests of the wrongdoer, it may be considered justifiable if transgressing avoids greater harm. There is no consensus, however, on what constitutes "greater harm": some cultures include transcendental costs (e.g., offending gods) and some people give greater weight to consequences for concrete individuals, others to consequences that affect the social order. Disagreement also arises from the fact that as social institutions change, so do socially derived duties, but only gradually. Finally—as illustrated by debates on abortion or animal rights—there is disagreement on what are considered "moral objects" (i.e., those toward whom moral rules have to be kept): all living creatures, all members of the human species, or rational agents only.

1.2 Moral Evaluation

Being moral implies morally evaluating behavior. This is based on several underlying considerations:

(a) There is a categorical difference between acknowledging the existence of a norm from an observer's perspective (e.g., "in this culture slavery is considered to be wrong"), and claiming validity for a norm from a participant's perspective (e.g., "slavery is wrong!"). Moral evaluation is based on the claim of normative validity.

(b) In utilitarianism, morality is judged from consequences: "Good" is whatever (impartially) maximizes welfare. In deontological ethics, morality is judged on intention: "moral" is acting from duty or "right" intentions. Everyday moral evaluation considers both. This can be read from people's spontaneous emotional reactions. People react to the same act of carelessness (e.g., failure to have the brakes on one's car checked) with either indignation or indifference depending on the consequences (e.g., whether someone gets run over). This illustrates utilitarian thinking. The same objective harm (e.g., someone having stepped on one's toe) is treated with indignation or forgiveness depending on intentions. This illustrates deontological thinking.

(c) There is some "freedom of will." Only acts that are committed voluntarily and consciously —not those done under hypnosis, intoxication, or physical threat—are responded to with moral indignation or sanctions.

In summary, universal and specific moral rules forbid direct and indirect harm to others. The content of specific rules differs between roles and cultures, and people differ in judging whether exceptions to moral rules are justifiable. In making moral evaluations people claim normative validity for the moral rules, take consequences and intentions into account, and presuppose freedom of will.

2. Theories of Moral Learning

Three aspects of morality: behavior, motivation, and judgment have been considered to greater or lesser degree by three different theoretical traditions: social learning theory, psychoanalytic theory, and cognitive theories. These approaches differ widely in their basic assumptions concerning human nature, relevant learning mechanisms, and their methodology.

2.1 Classical Social Learning Theories

Classical social learning theories focus on the origin and expression of behavior and explain it in terms of conditioning and modeling. For example, in a variety of experimental studies, children have been shown to suppress behavior that is punished, to perform behavior that is—concretely or symbolically—rewarded, and to imitate behavior that is displayed by a (powerful) role model. Generally, social learning theorists have restricted themselves to observing behavior under experimentally manipulated conditions and to describing the factors that inhibit or promote behavior that conforms to existing norms usually as defined by the experimenter. Subjects' intentions and their contextualized moral judgments are not assessed; the difference between factually existing and justifiable norms is not addressed; and the conditioning paradigm considers only self-serving motives. This tradition has often been criticized as missing the very definition of morality by ignoring subjects' normative appraisals and truly moral motives.

2.2 Psychoanalytic Theories

According to psychoanalytic theories, moral behavior and evaluation is determined by super-ego functions (an incorporation of societal norms, represented by the parents). They focus on motivation as the primary mechanism. Due to fear of the powerful (potentially castrating) father, boys come to suppress an awakening sexual desire for the mother and internalize parental expectations ("identification with the aggressor"). The desire to avoid super-ego sanctions (e.g., feelings of guilt or shame) then motivates norm conformity. (Because women cannot be threatened by fear of castration their super-ego will, according to Freud, "never become as inexorable, impersonal . . . as we demand of men.") A further motive for conformity arises from "anaclitic identification": children invest emotional energy into their relationships with persons who satisfy their primary needs, and thus become dependent on their responses. From fear of losing their love, or simply to restore the original symbiotic bliss, children develop a need to conform to their caretakers' expectations. Even though psychoanalytic theories are not limited to observations but focus on internal thoughts and fantasies, they are subject to the same criticism as social learning theories: moral norms are identified with existing norms, and moral motivation is reduced to fulfilling self-serving needs. Both approaches conceptualize subjects as passively shaped products of external socialization influences and do not consider autonomous agency.

2.3 Cognitive Theories

Cognitive theories focus on moral judgment. The child is seen as actively making sense of the world by reconstructing the rules underlying the natural or social order in a continuous process of hypotheses testing. The methodology and epistemology in this tradition are complex: children's behavior in experimental situations is observed, and the reasoning processes behind their behavior are assessed in clinical interviews; changes in reasoning are reconstructed in the form of a "developmental logic," a sequence of increasingly more differentiated and better integrated cognitive structures that allow increasingly more adequate ("objectively true") solutions to problems. This conceptual framework is considered by many to be more adequate for describing moral development. Humans are seen as active, truth-seeking agents; the subjective understanding of a situation is considered; reason and insight are included as motivating forces; the distinction between "better" or "worse" solutions to problems is seen as justifiable.

Within this framework two main theorists have been most influential: the Swiss psychologist Piaget (1896–1980) laid the foundations on which Kohlberg (1927–1987) built his theory of moral development.

3. Cognitive Theories of Moral Development

3.1 Piaget

Piaget (1932) studied moral development by questioning 5- to 13-year old children about their understanding of rules, punishment, justice, and bad acts. He proposed two stages: the first (heteronomous morality) is characterized by children's egocentrism, that is, their inability to take the point of view of others, and their one-sided affectionate respect for adults. In this stage children judge the badness of acts by their consequences rather than the actor's intentions ("objective responsibility"); they see rules as objective, absolute, and unalterable, and interpret any accident happening to a wrongdoer as punishment ("immanent justice").

Children come to attain the second stage (autonomous morality) through two mechanisms: egalitarian interactions with peers characterized by mutual re-

spect and the acquisition of an increasingly decentered cognitive capacity. Now they begin to understand the function of rules as flexible instruments for human purposes and values, the function of punishment in reparation, and the importance of intentions in evaluating actions.

Piaget's description has been qualified by later research. Children have been shown to have a more differentiated understanding of rules (Turiel 1983) and an earlier comprehension of intentions and their relevance for moral judgments. Also, Piaget's two-stage model has been expanded by a more refined, multistage sequence.

3.2 Kohlberg

Kohlberg's theory of moral development, first advanced in 1958 and later considerably enlarged and revised, has dominated the field since the early 1960s. This theory has inspired international research and debates on the meaning of morality, on processes of moral learning, and on moral education.

Kohlberg described moral development as deriving from changes in the reasoning structures that allow one to justify moral norms and that motivate moral action. These changes follow a sequence of three levels with two stages each, based on a structural core that consists in a widening of the child's sociomoral perspective. The theory entails several postulates.

(a) *Developmental logic:* Each stage is a structured whole that is qualitatively different from the others; the sequence of stages is invariant, irreversibly progressive without stage skipping; the stages form a hierarchy: higher stages are better differentiated and integrated structures that allow the agent to handle more considerations or perspectives and that provide the basis for increasingly more adequate solutions to moral dilemmas.

(b) The *prerequisite postulate*: Piaget's stages of operational thinking are necessary but not sufficient prerequisites for the attainment of increasingly sophisticated levels of perspective-taking that, in turn, are necessary though not sufficient prerequisites for the attainment of higher levels of moral understanding.

(c) *Cognitive conflict postulate*: Cognitive conflict is seen as the primary developmental mechanism.

(d) *Universality postulate*: The sequence of stages is claimed to be universal.

(e) *Cognitive-affective parallelism*: There is a structural identity in stage-specific justifications for the validity of moral norms and stage-specific reasons motivating norm conformity.

(f) *Judgment action consistency*: The readiness to act in accordance with moral judgments increases with moral developmental stage.

The stages are defined as follows. At the *pre-conventional level* (typical of most children under 9) situations are judged from a concrete individual perspective: children have not yet come to understand and uphold shared moral norms, and consider rules to be external to the self. "Right" is defined as obeying rules and authority, avoiding punishment, and not doing physical harm (stage 1) or as meeting one's own interests and letting others do the same (stage 2); the reasons for doing right are to avoid punishment and to bow to the superior power of authorities (stage 1), or to serve one's own needs or interests (stage 2).

At the *conventional level* (typical of most adults) morality is judged from a "member-of-society" perspective and is identified with socially shared, internalized norms. "Right" means living up to the expectations of one's group (stage 3), or doing one's duty in society (stage 4); the reasons for doing right are the need to be "good" in one's own or others' eyes and caring for others (stage 3), or the need to maintain a good conscience by meeting defined obligations (stage 4).

At the *postconventional level* (reached by only a few adults) moral values are defined from a "prior-to-society" perspective in terms of self-chosen universal principles. "Right" is upholding legal contracts (stage 5) or is defined in terms of universal ethical principles, such as equality and respect for the dignity of human beings as individuals (stage 6); the reasons for doing right are obligations to the social contract (stage 5) or a commitment to principles that have been rationally understood and accepted as valid (stage 6).

Like Piaget, Kohlberg used clinical interviews as his main research method. Subjects were confronted with hypothetical moral dilemmas. In these, a protagonist must resolve competing moral demands for which there is no "right" answer (e.g., "should a man steal a drug to save his dying wife if there is no other solution?"). Subjects are first to decide what the protagonist ought to do ("uphold the law or preserve life?") and then to justify and defend this decision against moral counterarguments advanced by the interviewer with the intention of eliciting the subject's competence level. To score responses, subject's justification arguments are matched to structurally similar criterion judgments listed for each stage in the scoring manual (see Colby and Kohlberg 1987).

Objective tests have also been developed in which subjects rank their preferences for a set of standardized responses that express stage-specific moral considerations. The most widely used among these is Rest's Defining Issues Test (DIT). Gibbs et al. (1992) developed a brief interview and coding manual that can be used with younger children. It has been shown that preference measures produce scores that are consistently higher (about one stage) than spontaneously produced answers.

4. Empirical Support and Criticism

Kohlberg's basic postulates have been widely tested. The results will briefly be discussed.

4.1 Developmental Logic

Age and stage have been shown to correlate in cross-sectional studies (Snarey 1985) indicating support for the developmental sequence of Kohlberg's stages. Regression or stage skipping have rarely been found in longitudinal studies (Snarey 1985, Walker 1986) and have not been induced in experimental studies designed to produce moral development (see Sect. 4.3), supporting the claim of an invariant order.

There is conceptual and empirical support for Kohlberg's theory of hierarchy. Conceptually, the stage sequence comprises an increasing universalization of perspectives, with stage 1 articulating the perspective of an isolated individual, stage 2 of a dyad, stage 3 of a group, stage 4 of a society, and stages 5 and 6 of humanity at large. It also implies an expansion of the factors considered morally relevant with stage 1 focusing on negative, stage 2 on positive consequences to the individual, stage 3 on intentions and role obligations, and stage 4 on societal institutions and legality. At the postconventional level these different factors are integrated and weighed in a flexible and context-sensitive manner. Empirically, it has been found that subjects prefer higher, and reject lower stage reasoning (Walker 1986). Thus, commonsense intuitive moral judgments reflecting acknowledgement of the greater adequacy of higher stages support Kohlberg's claim.

4.2 The Prerequisite Postulate

Because the structural core of moral stages is defined by perspective-taking levels, the claim of the "necessary" prerequisite of role-taking is analytically true. The further claim that cognitive prerequisites are necessary—with moral stage 2 presupposing concrete, stage 3 beginning formal, stage 4 basic formal, and stage 5 consolidated formal operations—and that neither cognitive, nor perspective-taking development are sufficient for moral development has been supported empirically (cf. Kuhn et al. 1977; Walker 1986).

4.3 Cognitive Conflict

In contrast to social learning and psychoanalytic theories, which assume identification or modeling as the primary developmental mechanisms, cognitive theories see development as a result of cognitive conflict. There is some experimental evidence to suggest that cognitive conflict may be a sufficient condition for moral development. In studies where subjects were exposed to moral arguments designed to induce cognitive conflict by being discrepant either in reasoning structure (i.e., one or two stages above the subject's own stage), or in the content of the action decision, or in both, development of about one-third to one-half stage could be induced, with two sources of conflict producing greater change than one, supporting the cognitive conflict mechanism. Listening to arguments two stages above one's own or justifying contrary action decisions has been shown to stimulate development so that arguments one stage higher (arguments that had not been heard) are produced. This finding is not compatible with modeling theories.

4.4 The Universality Postulate

Kohlberg has been accused of ethnocentrism (Simpson 1974) and gender bias (Gilligan 1982) in his claim of universal validity for the stage model that was initially developed from interviews with United States males only. The debate about universalism in morality involves two issues: (a) whether there are universal norms, and (b) whether Kohlberg's stage sequence is universal. The first issue has been discussed (see Sect. 1). The second has been widely researched, although almost exclusively in terms of Kohlberg's understanding of morality.

Concerning ethnocentrism, the universal presence of stages 1–4 is reported in a review of 45 studies from 27 widely diverse cultures involving over 5,000 subjects. Postconventional thinking was found in urban samples only, not in traditional tribal or village societies either in Western or non-Western cultures (Snarey 1985). Thus, the principled quality of the postconventional level might be seen as a characteristic of a "metalevel" that will develop only when norms characterizing socially differentiated subsystems conflict, a situation that does not occur in normatively integrated cultures.

Concerning gender bias, Gilligan (1982) claimed that there are two moralities: a rigid justice orientation more typical for men (corresponding to stage 4) and a flexible morality of care and responsibility more typical for females (corresponding to stage 3). This critique has not stood up: Walker (1986) reviewed 80 studies using Kohlberg's interview, including 152 samples and more than 10,000 subjects and found sex differences in fewer than 15 percent of the studies, and these, moreover, tended to disappear when education and employment were controlled for. Thoma (1986) reported a meta-analysis of 56 samples involving about 6,000 subjects using Rest's DIT and found a negligible difference *favoring* women. Lind et al. (1987) found no sex differences in an intercultural study involving 3,000 students from West Germany, Austria, and Poland. Thus, empirical findings clearly refute Gilligan's criticism of a sex bias in Kohlberg's stage model. Nevertheless, Gilligan's work refocused attention on care, a moral concern that had been central in utilitarian ethics and somewhat neglected in Kohlberg's deontological theory.

4.5 Cognitive–Affective Parallelism and Preconventional Morality

According to Kohlberg, external sanctions are seen as constitutive for norms, and conformity is motivated by self-serving interests at the preconventional level; the intrinsic validity of moral principles is understood and has motivating force only at the postconventional level. Kohlberg's picture of the preconventional child as an egotistic, cost-benefit calculator has been criticized. Turiel (1983) showed that children as young as 5 years understand that some rules, specifically those that forbid direct harm to others, have a universal and intrinsic validity, independent of authorities and sanctions. Research on altruism has shown that from early on children spontaneously behave nonegotistically: they help, share, and console others. Nevertheless, young children cannot be considered to be competent moral actors. Nunner-Winkler and Sodian (1988) found that although they truly understood the intrinsic validity of moral rules, a majority of 5-year olds (and even some 8-year olds) expected hypothetical wrongdoers to feel good when transgressing these rules to satisfy their own needs. Children of 5–7-years old who attributed amoral emotions (wrongdoer feels "good") have been shown to be more likely to transgress in real-life moral conflicts . This finding suggests that younger children's emotion attributions to a hypothetical wrongdoer can be interpreted as an indicator of moral motivation. (Once children grow capable of self-reflexive role-taking their responses may be confounded by social desirability concerns.) Children's justifications for their attributions of moral emotions (wrongdoer feels "bad") show that for the most part neither fear of external or internal sanctions nor empathy and compassion are seen to motivate moral action, but rather an intrinsic formal motive to do what is right because it is right (Nunner-Winkler in press).

The seemingly contradictory claims about the moral status of preconventional children can be integrated: Turiel drew upon rule understanding, which even young children possess. Kohlberg asked for action decisions. Before having acquired moral motivation, children will act as cost-benefit calculators or follow their spontaneous inclinations. As research on altruism has shown, these may well be prosocial—children will do nice things if they feel like it. A moral problem however arises when their spontaneous desires conflict with moral rules. Young children will then expect to feel happy about satisfying their own needs, even if by transgressing. This interpretation (which still requires further empirical substantiation) suggests that moral development is based on three types of learning processes: (a) an early and universal acquisition of knowledge of the intrinsic validity of moral norms, (b) a later, differential development of moral motivation, and (c) a continuously increasing understanding of the complexity of human relations and social institutions required to apply adequately abstract rules to concrete situations.

4.6 Judgment–Action Consistency

From a careful review of 74 studies concerned with the relationship between moral reasoning scores and behavioral measures of moral actions (e.g., delinquency, cheating behavior, altruistic behavior, resistance to conformity pressures) involving more than 5,000 subjects, Blasi (1980) reported considerable support for the consistency hypothesis. The claim of increasing consistency between reasoning and behavior at higher moral stages is supported by studies showing that those persons who behaved morally in extreme situations (e.g., who resisted in the classic Milgram experiments or who refused to partake in the My Lai massacre) had attained postconventional thinking. Nevertheless, more recent research does not support Kohlberg's assumption of a fundamental unity of moral judgment, motivation, and action. Rather, it seems that a more adequate perspective is to treat cognitive understanding and an internal motivational anchoring of morality as separate issues (see Sect. 4.5). For example, Colby and Damon (1993) report that moral "exemplars," that is, people for whom caring about morality has become the core of their identity, and who follow their moral convictions even at extreme personal costs (i.e., people with a high level of moral motivation) are found at all stages of moral development, not just at the postconventional level. On the other hand, Nisan (1993) found that "normal" subjects at all stages will strike a compromise between moral and personal values in moral conflicts.

Moral behavior, of course, is not determined solely by moral understanding, moral motivation, and other value orientations. There are further personality characteristics and situational variables that influence whether people will actually do what they know to be the right thing to do. For example, research on helping behavior in emergency situations has consistently found that the likelihood of helping decreases with increasing numbers of bystanders, although self-confident and knowledgeable people are more likely to help. Also, people may make use of defense mechanisms to rationalize self-serving behavior in severe moral conflicts.

5. Educational Implications

There are natural context variables that are indirectly (via cognitive and sociocognitive development) or directly conducive to the development of moral understanding and commitment: attending a formal school system, experiencing friendship (Keller and Edelstein 1993), egalitarian styles of intrafamilial conflict resolution, and parental disciplinary techniques that combine warmth and argumentative reasoning (Hoffman and Saltzstein 1967).

There have also been efforts directly to influence moral development. One method has been to offer moral discussion courses in which students are confronted with higher stage arguments. Substantial increases in moral development have been reported in a majority of studies of such intervention programs (Enright et al. 1983, Rest 1979).

A more ambitious intervention is the construction of "just communities": these are attempts to organize schools or prisons democratically, that is, to have conflictual issues publicly debated and voted upon. It has been shown that just communities not only increase individual moral development but—and this may be even more important—change the "moral atmosphere," so that members begin to feel more responsible for each other (Power et al. 1989, Kohlberg 1981/1984, Oser and Althof 1992).

See also: Social Development; Socialization

References

Blasi A 1980 Bridging moral cognition and moral action: A critical review of the literature. *Psych. Bull.* 88(1): 1–45
Colby A, Damon W 1993 The uniting of self and morality in the development of extraordinary moral commitment. In: Noam G, Wren T (eds.) 1993 *Morality and Self.* MIT Press, Cambridge, Massachusetts
Colby A, Kohlberg L 1987 *The Measurement of Moral Judgement.* Cambridge University Press, Cambridge
Enright R D, Lapsley D K, Levy V M 1983 Moral education strategies. In: Pressley M, Levin J R (eds.) 1983 *Cognitive Strategy Research: Educational Applications.* Springer Verlag, New York
Gibbs J C, Basinger K S, Fuller D 1992 *Moral Maturity: Measuring the Development of Sociomoral Reflection.* Erlbaum, Hillsdale, New Jersey
Gilligan C 1982 *A Different Voice: Psychological Theory and Women's Development.* Harvard University Press, Cambridge, Massachusetts
Hoffman M L, Saltzstein H D 1967 Parent discipline and the child's moral development. *J. Pers. Soc. Psychol.* 5: 45–57
Keller M, Edelstein W 1993 The development of a moral self from childhood to adolescence. In: Noam G, Wren T (eds.) 1993 *Morality and Self.* MIT Press, Cambridge, Massachusetts
Kohlberg L 1981/1984 *Essays on Moral Development,* Vols. 1 and 2. Harper and Row, San Francisco, California
Kuhn D, Langer J, Kohlberg L, Haan N S 1977 The development of formal operations in logical and moral judgment. *Genet. Psychol. Monogr.* 95(1): 97–188
Lind G, Grochelewsky K, Langer J 1987 Haben Frauen eine andere Moral? In: Unterkircher L, Wagner I (eds.) 1987 *Die andere Hälfte der Gesellschaft.* Verlag des Österreichischen Gewerkschaftsbundes, Vienna
Nisan M 1993 Balanced identity: Morality and other identity values. In: Noam G, Wren T (eds.) 1993 *Morality and Self.* MIT Press, Cambridge, Massachusetts
Nunner-Winkler G in press Moral development. In: Weinert F E, Schneider W (eds.) *The Longitudinal Study on the*

Genesis of Individual Competencies (LOGIC). Cambridge University Press, New York

Nunner-Winkler G, Sodian B 1988 Children's understanding of moral emotions. *Child Dev.* 59: 1323–38

Oser F, Althof W 1992 *Moralische Selbstbestimmung.* Klett-Cotta, Stuttgart

Piaget J 1932 *The Moral Judgment of the Child.* Routledge and Kegan Paul, London

Power F, Higgins A, Kohlberg L 1989 *Lawrence Kohlberg's Approach to Moral Education.* Columbia University Press, New York

Rest J R 1979 *Development in Judging Moral Issues.* University of Minnesota Press, Minneapolis, Minnesota

Simpson E L 1974 Moral development research: A case study of scientific cultural bias. *Hum. Dev.* 17(2): 81–106

Snarey J R 1985 Cross-cultural universality of socio-moral development: A critical review of Kohlbergian research. *Psych. Bull.* 97(2): 202–32

Thoma S J 1986 Estimating gender differences in the comprehension and preference of moral issues. *Dev. Rev.* 6(2): 165–80

Turiel E 1983 *The Development of Social Knowledge. Morality and Convention.* Cambridge University Press, Cambridge

Walker L J 1986 Cognitive processes in moral development. In: Sapp G L (ed.) 1986 *Handbook of Moral Development: Models, Processes, Techniques, and Research.* Religious Education Press, Birmingham, Alabama

Further Reading

Turiel E in press Morality. In: Damon W (series ed.), Eisenberg N (volume ed.) in press *Handbook of Child Psychology: Social, Emotional, and Personality Development.* Wiley, New York

Development of the Self-concept

A. Helmke

"Self-concept" can be understood as the relatively stable picture people have of themselves and their own attributes. Two features of self-concept are of particular theoretical and practical relevance: the *content* of self-concept and the *evaluation* of attributes. This entry focuses on the development of these two aspects of self-concept. Special emphasis will be placed on its evaluative (or affective) component, in particular on the self-concept of ability.

1. The Diversity of "Self"-constructs

An overview of research on the development of self-concept must take into account the considerable diversity of "self"-constructs (such as self, self-concept, self-schema, self-understanding, self-knowledge, self-system, self-evaluation, self-esteem, and so on) and closely related constructs (e.g., ego, identity), which are sometimes used interchangeably. Although a semantic analysis of all these self-related constructs is beyond the scope of this entry (see Wylie et al. 1979 for details), it is necessary to make at least the following distinctions to avoid further conceptual confusion (see also Fig. 1).

1.1 Self as Subject and Object

A time-honored distinction originates in James (1892), who differentiated between the self as "I" (= existential self) and as "Me" (= categorical self)—

see Level 2 in Fig. 1. For example, in a phrase such as "I think about me," the "I" refers to the self as thinker, that is, as a *subject*, whereas the "me" refers to the self as an *object* of thinking. The vast majority of empirical research studies have focused on the second aspect.

1.2 Structural versus Evaluative Aspect of Self-concept

The concept of the self as an object has two components: a *descriptive* component, that is, the content and the structure of the self's attributes, and an *evaluative* or affective component, that is, the worth or value that persons attach to their attributes or to themselves as a whole (Level 3 in Fig. 1).

1.3 Global Self-esteem versus Domain-specific Self-evaluations

The affective component takes as its focus either the person as a whole (self-esteem), various particular domains, such as cognitive, physical, or social competence (Level 4 in Fig. 1), or even specific subdomains, such as mathematical ability, artistic ability, or swimming skill (Levels 5 and 6).

2. Theoretical View of the Nature of Self-concept

Various theorists have emphasized different aspects of the structure, function, and determinants of self-concept. A particularly influential approach to the

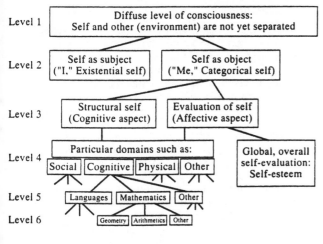

Level 1

Level 2

Level 3

Level 4

Level 5

Level 6

Figure 1
A Hierarchical model of self-concept and its development

object (the categorical self). To analyze when and through what cues infants develop self-representation, Lewis and Brooks-Gunn (1979) conducted a series of studies on infant self-recognition. In a frequently used technique (known as the "Rouge test"), a dot of rouge is surreptitiously placed on the infant's nose by the mother and then the infant is placed in front of a mirror. If the infant touches its own nose rather than the one in the mirror, this is judged as an indicator of self-recognition and shows that the child has acquired a mental image of the self that allows the dot of rouge to be perceived as abnormal. Other experiments have used photographs and videotapes. By 18–24 months infants can distinguish between the self and others in mirrors, pictures, and video playbacks. Recognition of features and the attachment of the appropriate personal pronoun or name to their mirror images and other pictorial representations represent the successful accomplishment of a basic developmental task in self-concept development; namely, the separation of the self as subject and the self as object (Harter 1983).

origin of self-concept was "symbolic interactionism." Cooley (1902) introduced the concept of the "looking-glass self," to represent the idea that a person's self-concept is in large part the result of interactions with significant others.

A comprehensive theory dealing with the *function* of the self-concept was suggested by Epstein (1973), who integrated a variety of positions on the nature of self-concept. According to Epstein, self-concept serves two basic functions: (a) hedonic, that is, to maximize pleasure and minimize pain; (b) structuring or integrating, that is, to organize and assimilate the data of experience. Whereas the first function is equivalent to the enhancement of self-esteem, the second focuses on the need to maintain the conceptual system and consistency. Epstein regarded self-concept as a subjective theory that serves similar functions (especially the structuring or integrating function) as a scientific theory, and therefore can be evaluated like a scientific theory, for example, by criteria such as testability, internal consistency, external validity, and parsimony.

3. Precursors and Early Development of Self-concept

A necessary precondition for the development of a self-concept is the ability to differentiate the self from the surrounding environment; that is, to develop a sense of the self as *subject* (the existential self)—see Levels 1 and 2 in Fig. 1. Lewis and Brooks-Gunn (1979) have provided a highly detailed analysis of the development of the existential self.

The second developmental task of the infant is to learn the particular attributes that define the self as

4. Changes in the Structure of Self-concept

The investigation of the development of the content of self-concept beyond infancy has largely been based on verbal rather than behavioral criteria, in particular, on clinical interviews or content analyses of standardized response data. For example, in the "Who am I?" technique, children are asked to describe themselves or to complete sentences of the type "I am a . . . " or "I am a boy or girl, who . . . ." The results of these studies (for overviews see Damon and Hart 1988, Rosenberg 1986) show that the development of the self as object can be characterized by two main features. First, whereas preschoolers typically dwell on their physical characteristics, their possessions, and their likes or dislikes, with increasing age psychological traits, attitudes, beliefs, fears, and wishes come to predominate. This increasing focus on the internal world rather than on overt and visible elements also reflects a growing capacity for, and interest in, reflecting on personal feelings and thoughts (Rosenberg 1986). Second, self-concept also becomes more differentiated with development. An infant's classification and definition of the self starts with basic dimensions such as age, size, and gender, and is extended by global psychological characteristics which become increasingly more finely tuned and complex over time. Not only does the mere number of psychological characteristics applied to the self increase with age, but the structural organization also changes—from arbitrary and isolated behavioral attributes to stable dispositions.

In contrast to this unidimensional description of the development of self-concept, Damon and Hart (1988) proposed a comprehensive theory of the development of self-understanding. They argued that the main developmental change is not a shift from physical to psychological conceptions of the self. Rather, they stated that there are systematic developmental trends *within* each of the physical, the active, social, and psychological selves. Development in each of these four areas of the self as object is claimed to progress through the same four stages: (a) categorical identifications, (b) comparative assessments, (c) interpersonal implications, and (d) systematic beliefs and plans. Likewise, Damon and Hart postulated that the development of the self as subject (with its aspects of continuity, distinctness, and agency) is also hallmarked by four developmental stages: (a) categorical identifications, (b) permanent cognitive and active capabilities and immutable self-characteristics, (c) ongoing recognition of the self by others, and (d) relations between past, present, and future selves.

5. Changes in the Evaluative Aspect of Self-concept

The following sections of this entry deal with the affective aspect of the self-concept. Thus, the meaning of the term "self-concept" should be understood as its evaluative component (see Fig. 1). Two issues are of particular importance: dimensionality and stability.

5.1 Dimensionality

Can the (evaluative) self-concept be regarded as a unidimensional construct, as Coopersmith (1967) supposed, or are there multiple selves that are more or less independent of each other? Harter's research on this topic (1983) has been particularly influential in developmental psychology because it was concerned from the beginning with the construction of psychometrically sound measurement devices for children of different ages and with systematic empirical research. Her results, based on factor analyses, showed that children of 8 and over distinguish five separate domains; scholastic competence, athletic competence, social acceptance, physical appearance, and conduct. In contrast, younger children distinguish fewer domains; for example, they define cognitive and athletic skills as one factor.

Shavelson and Bolus (1982) suggested a hierarchical model of self-esteem, which has become particularly prominent in educational psychology. Below the highest level—general self-concept—there are three content areas of self-esteem: academic (cognitive), social, and physical, which are then further broken down into various subareas (see Fig. 1, Levels 4–6). The academic self-concept, for example, comprises the self-concepts of reading, mathematics and other subjects; and social self-esteem is differentiated into relationships with peers and parents.

5.2 Stability

How stable is the evaluative aspect of self-concept? There is controversy in the literature, with some researchers arguing that self-concept is totally governed by situational influences (and is therefore only as stable as the situations themselves) and others maintaining that self-concept is a highly stable personality trait. The issue of stability versus lability of self-concept is difficult to analyze because very different concepts of stability have been used in the literature (e.g., ipsative vs. normative). Also, only a few longitudinal studies on this topic are available. Given these restrictions, there is some empirical evidence for the following trends. During the period of the construction of self-concept (i.e., infancy), self-concept becomes increasingly stable. Periods of destabilization may occur after crucial life-events such as changing school or repeating a class, which are usually accompanied by changes in the reference group and/or the standard of evaluation. A second phase of destabilization is typically found during adolescence (see Rosenberg 1986).

6. Development of the Self-concept of Ability

The self-concept of academic ability, that is, school-related competencies and activities, is of particular interest for educational practice and has been a field of very active research. The following issues will be discussed: a developmental trend from overestimation toward more realism in self-evaluation; the role of the classroom context as a moderator variable; and the dynamics of the interplay between academic achievement and academic self-concept.

6.1 From Optimism to Realism?

Young children tend strongly to overestimate their own ability when it is measured against objective tests of performance or their actual standing relative to others in the classroom. An unrealistically high self-concept of ability has been found in many areas of competence, especially those related to academic achievement. Children's self-concepts do not begin to correlate with actual classroom performance before the second grade (age 7). To explain this, developmental researchers have pointed to the cognitive deficiencies of young children, in particular to their difficulties in integrating past performance information correctly, comparing their own performance to those of others, and differentiating between effort and ability as determinants of achievement outcomes (Stipek 1984). These problems, in conjunction with a strong tendency toward wishful thinking and a great need for self-enhancement, foster an unrealistically positive self-evaluation.

These individualistic explanations have been complemented by investigations of environmental factors that might explain young children's tendency to overestimate themselves (see Sect. 6.2). From a long-term perspective, research on the functionality of under- versus overestimation has shown that moderate overestimation of one's academic ability, rather than realistic self-perception, seems to be a support factor associated with favorable cognitive and affective development, whereas underestimation must be regarded as a risk factor (Helmke 1992).

6.2 *The Role of the Classroom Context*

The impact of school and teacher variables on students' self-concept has been analyzed from various perspectives (for an overview see Pekrun 1985). Starting from the finding that there are substantial classroom differences not only in the level of self-concept, but also in the degree to which students under- or overestimate their abilities, two sets of data—one from the research program on ability formation (Marshall and Weinstein 1984) and one using the classroom context approach (Helmke 1992)—have shown that an individualistic explanation is insufficient. Rather, the relation between objective performance and the corresponding self-evaluation is moderated by classroom composition, the quality of instruction, and the teacher–student relationship. For example, differential treatment (such as calling on or criticizing some students less frequently, or assigning tasks of varying difficulty) that reflects achievement-related teacher expectations can be informative to students about their ability and thus affect their self-concept of ability. Furthermore, classroom organization has been shown to affect the ease and the salience of self-evaluation of one's abilities: there is a high congruence between performance and the corresponding self-concept in classrooms characterized by ability grouping, low student autonomy, high competition, and high salience of success and failure, and highly public feedback. Finally, the style of evaluating students' achievement also influences the comparability of intraclass performance differences: comparability is high when the evaluation is normative (i.e., based on social comparison) and low when the standard of evaluation is mastery or intraindividual changes in achievement.

6.3 *Causal Ordering of Self-concept and Ability*

The direction of causality between academic achievement and academic self-concept has been the subject of considerable interest in educational psychology (for an overview see Marsh 1990). The theoretical perspective of symbolic interactionism suggests that the academic self-concept more or less accurately mirrors past achievement-related successes and failures. This consideration underlies the skill-development approach, which maintains that self-concept is primarily the *result* of past achievement rather than a cause of subsequent achievement. The opposite position is held by the self-enhancement model, which claims that academic self-concept is primarily a cause rather than an effect of academic achievement: a high self-concept is regarded as a precondition for effort and persistence and as a protective buffer against self-doubts and other "worry-cognitions" that impair achievement in achievement situations.

The empirical evidence for the two models (for an overview see Helmke 1992) is scarce, since longitudinal studies and causal modeling techniques are required for a sound treatment of the causal ordering. The state of research can be summarized by two points. First, there is considerable stability in both academic achievement and the self-concept of ability. Second, when cross-lagged effects are found at all, the pattern of causation is mostly reciprocal, indicating that the academic self-concept is (at least partially) a cause and a consequence of academic achievement.

There are, however, several unresolved issues in this research area. For example, does the causal pattern also depend on classroom and instructional contexts? Is the relation between academic self-concept and academic achievement general or specific within academic domains? What mediational processes can explain correlations between self-concept and achievement? Does it make a difference if complex models, including both test achievement *and* grades are used as indicators of achievement? (For a discussion of these points see Helmke 1992.) A longitudinal 4-year study (Helmke and van Aken 1996) has shown that in elementary school the pattern of the relation between achievement (in mathematics) and self-concept (of mathematics ability) clearly supports the skill development model, indicating that self-concept in elementary school does not have motivational properties. Furthermore, the impact of *grade* on later self-concept increased, which was not the case for the impact of *test achievement* on later self-concept.

The best answer to emerge thus far is that the self-concept of ability must be regarded as both a cause and a consequence of achievement. As Markus and Wurf (1987) have emphasized, this reciprocal perspective is also valid for the transaction between the self-concept and the environment: on the one hand, environmental factors influence the self-concept (see Sect. 6.2 and 7); on the other, both the *choice* of an adequate environment and the *shaping* of that environment according to one's needs and expectations are affected by one's self-concept.

7. *Parental Impact on the Development of Self-concept*

For infants, a secure emotional attachment to their caregivers is the crucial prerequisite for the development of a favorable self-concept. According to Lewis and Brooks-Gunn (1979), a key to the development of a favorable self-concept is the experience of regular consistencies between actions and outcomes in the external environment, which allow the infant to establish generalized expectancies about control of the world. Particularly important behaviors are caregivers' attempts to meet the infant's homeostatic needs and parental imitation of infants' actions.

For older children, self-concept has been linked to patterns of child-rearing. One of the most prominent studies was by Coopersmith (1967), who found that the parenting style used by parents of boys with high self-esteem was characterized by high acceptance of their children, clearly defined limits on their children's activities, and, within the limits set by parents' standards and social norms, respect for individuality.

8. Implications for Educational Strategies

Attempts to foster the development of a favorable self-concept of ability must consider that self-concept is affected and determined by many factors, including external influences from the family, school and classroom environments, and internal factors related to individual cognitive and affective prerequisites. A central requirement of *parental* behavior is that it fosters the child's sense of controllability and predictability, especially of the caregiver's behavior, within both a climate of warmth and unconditional acceptance and clear standards. In the *school* context, the development of a positive self-concept seems to be facilitated when teachers' standards for evaluating student achievement are based on individual reference norms and on mastery rather than social comparison. Also useful is a multitask environment that offers children varied opportunities to capitalize on their strengths and to compensate for failures in one area by successes in others. At the *individual* level, it is important to note that a necessary (but often not sufficient) element for fostering a positive self-concept of ability is the acquisition of the underlying actual competencies (i.e., a sufficient knowledge base, efficient study habits, good learning strategies, etc.). It is also important to take into account the nomological network of the self-concept of ability; that is, a high self-concept of ability can also be fostered by increasing intrinsic motivation, reducing test anxiety, or changing attributions of failure from internal stable causes to external or controllable causes.

See also: Social Development; Emotional Development; Socialization; Self-related Cognition, Learned Helplessness, Learned Optimism, and Human Development; Development of Motivation

References

Cooley C H 1902 *Human Nature and the Social Order.* Scribner, New York
Coopersmith S 1967 *The Antecedents of Self-Esteem.* Freeman, San Francisco, California
Damon W, Hart D 1982 The development of self-understanding from infancy through adolescence. *Child Dev.* 53(4): 841–64
Epstein S 1973 The self-concept revisited: Or a theory of a theory. *Am. Psychol.* 28(9): 405–16
Harter S 1983 Developmental perspectives on the self-system. In: Mussen P H (ed.) 1983 *Handbook of Child Psychology. Vol 4: Socialization, Personality, and Social Development.* Wiley, New York
Helmke A 1992 *Selbstvertrauen und schulische Leistungen.* Hogrefe, Göttingen
Helmke A, van Aken M 1996 The causal ordering of academic achievement and self-concept of ability during elementary school: A longitudinal study. *J. Educ. Psychol.* 88 (1)
James W 1892 *Psychology: Briefer Course.* Fawcett, New York
Lewis M, Brooks-Gunn J 1979 *Social Cognition and the Acquisition of Self.* Plenum Press, New York
Markus H, Wurf E 1987 The dynamic self-concept: A social psychological perspective. *Annu. Rev. Psychol.* 38: 299–337
Marsh H W 1990 Causal ordering of academic self-concept and academic achievement: A multiwave, longitudinal panel analysis. *J. Educ. Psychol.* 82(4): 646–56
Marshall H, Weinstein R S 1984 Classroom factors affecting students' self-evaluation: An interactional model. *Rev. Educ. Res.* 54(3): 301–25
Pekrun R 1985 Schulischer Unterricht, schulische Bewertungsprozesse und Selbstkonzeptentwicklung. *Unter Wiss.* 13: 220–48
Rosenberg M 1986 Self-concept from middle childhood through adolescence. In: Suls J, Greenwald A G (eds.) 1986 *Psychological Perspectives on the Self*, Vol. 3. Erlbaum, Hillsdale, New Jersey
Shavelson R J, Bolus R 1982 Self-concept: The interplay of theory and methods. *J. Educ. Psychol.* 74(1): 3–17
Stipek D J 1984 Young children's performance expectations: Logical analysis or wishful thinking? *Advances in Motivation and Achievement* 3: 33–56
Wylie R C, Miller P, Cowles S, Wilson A 1979 *The Self-Concept. Vol. 2: Theory and Research on Selected Topics.* University of Nebraska Press, Lincoln, Nebraska

Further Reading

Damon W 1983 *Social and Personality Development: From Infancy Through Adolescence.* Norton, New York
Epstein S 1990 Cognitive-experiential self theory: Implications for developmental psychology. In: Gunnar M R, Sroufe L A (eds.) 1990 *Minnesota Symposium on Child Psychology: Self Processes and Development*, Vol. 23. Erlbaum, Hillsdale, New Jersey
Harter S 1986 Processes underlying the construction, maintenance, and enhancement of the self-concept in children. In: Suls J, Greenwald A G (eds.) 1986 *Psychological Perspectives on the Self*, Vol. 3. Erlbaum, Hillsdale, New Jersey
Rosenberg M 1979 *Conceiving the Self.* Basic Books, New York

Personality Development

D. Magnusson and B. Törestad

"Personality" is a concept which is commonly used both in everyday language and in psychological research and practice to epitomize other persons' observable behaviors in terms of the differential ways they relate to, interact with, and adjust to their social and physical surroundings. The emphasis is most often on cognitive, emotional, and behavioral styles, which are apt to change across the lifespan. Personality is thus a hypothetical construct that has no existence of its own; it is inferred from behavior and used to characterize individuals. As Pervin stated:

> The study of personality focuses not only on a particular psychological process but also on the relationships of different processes. Understanding how these processes act together to form an integrated whole often involves more than an understanding of each of them separately. People function as organized wholes, and it is in the light of such organization that we must understand them. (Pervin 1984 p. 3)

Much personality research is oriented toward single aspects (variables and traits) of individual development. In this entry, however, the emphasis is on the dynamics underlying human ontogeny. Such a view must necessarily address many interdependent aspects both in the individual and in the environment.

1. The Concept of Personality Development

Personality development refers to progressive or regressive changes in the structure and/or functioning of the personality across the entire lifespan from conception to death.

Two concepts are central when defining personality development: time and change. Although the passage of time is not equivalent to development, development always has a temporal dimension. If a person's distinctive pattern of characteristics remains unchanged across time no development has occurred. For example a salient personality characteristic, such as a phobic fear of snakes that originated at the age of 8 and that remains unaltered at the age of 12, has not "developed" only because a certain amount of time has elapsed. However, if the disorder becomes more severe from age 8 to 12, a negative, or regressive, development (change) has taken place. A positive, or progressive development could occur if the phobic symptoms decrease in frequency and/or in intensity.

Consequently, processes that continue in an unchanged manner, within existing structures, do not constitute development. Thus, developmental models must be distinguished from models that analyze and explain why individuals function as they do only in terms of their current psychological and biological dispositions.

1.1 Basic Propositions for a Holistic View of Personality Development

The present definition of personality takes a holistic view of personality development. The individual is a psychological, social, and biological being in continuous interaction with the environment. A holistic stand rests on three major propositions:

(a) The individual develops and functions as a total, integrated organism. Development does not take place in single aspects per se, that is, in isolation from the totality.

(b) The individual develops and functions in a dynamic, continuous, and reciprocal process of interaction with the environment.

(c) The characteristic way in which the individual develops, in interaction with the environment, depends on and influences the continuous reciprocal process of interaction among subsystems of psychological and biological factors. (Magnusson 1988 p. 21)

1.2 The Mental System

The individual is not simply a passive recipient of stimulation from the environment; he or she is also an active, purposeful agent in the person–environment interaction process (Endler and Magnusson 1976). Thus, an individual's inner and outer life is guided by the functioning of the perceptual-cognitive system (including world-views and self-perceptions) with related emotions, motives, needs, values, and goals. This can be briefly summarized as the "integrated mental system."

By selecting and interpreting information from the external world and transforming this information into internal and external actions, the mental system plays a crucial role and serves as a leading edge for adaptation in individual development in that it mobilizes neurobiological and physiological modifications and environmental changes.

Congenital factors (including genetic factors) set the stage for the development of an individual's mediating mental system. Within the restrictions, and using the potentialities of these biological factors, the structure and functioning of an individual's mediating mental system is formed. This system changes slowly in a process of maturation and experience that takes place in the continuous, bidirectional interaction between the individual and the environment. Thus, the mediating system is both a function of the individual's interaction with the environment in the course of individual development and it plays a crucial, guiding role in the interaction process at each stage of the development process.

1.3 Biological Factors

Two issues concerning biological factors are of interest in this connection: nature versus nurture, and the role of physiological factors.

An issue debated since ancient times concerns nature versus nurture, the relative role of hereditary and environmental factors in current individual functioning, and in the development of individual functioning.

The role of genetic factors has been a central issue since the beginning of differential psychology. An emphasis on hereditary factors in individual development, characterized by Hunt (1961) as a belief in "predetermined development" and "fixed intelligence" formed the theoretical basis for the first standardized intelligence tests and constituted a basic element in developmental research for many decades. After an interim period (beginning in the 1960s) in which genetic factors were virtually ignored there has been a renewed interest, instigated by new developments in human genetics. That various aspects of individual development are, to some extent, determined by inherited properties of the body is supported by much empirical research (Buss and Plomin 1984).

The traditional view of the role of genetic factors has been a unidirectional cause–effect relation. At a most basic level, the onset and course of certain developmental sequences may be determined genetically to the extent that they are common to all individuals. However, even such developmental sequences as the onset of the menstrual cycle in girls and the regulation of growth in height are somewhat modifiable by environmental factors. Within the limits set by inherited factors, the potential for variability and change is large because of interplay with environmental factors.

This means that a hereditary predisposition for a certain type of behavior does not mean that it cannot be changed by environmental influences (cf. Angoff 1988). In his evaluation of the role of heredity and environment in individual differences in aggression, Cairns (1979) concluded that the differences obtained by selective breeding show strong environmental specificity and can be modified by environmental social conditions to such an extent that the inherited differences no longer matter. In longitudinal studies, Meyer-Probst et al. (1983) demonstrated that favorable social conditions acted as protective factors for later social development among children identified at birth as biologically at risk.

In this perspective, current individual functioning is the result of a history of person–environment interaction. It is not possible to disentangle the relative role of environmental and inherited factors in this process at the individual level. The outcome of the process, at a particular stage of development, depends both on the initial potential resources and limitations of the individual and on the properties of the environment with which the individual interacts.

The process by which an individual interacts with the environment can be described as an active adaptation process. In this adaptation process, physiological factors, in constant interaction with cognitive-emotional factors, play an important role. Biologically, the endocrine system, in particular the sympathetic-adrenal and pituitary-adrenal systems, are of special importance. Cannon (1914) pointed to the role of the sympathetic-adrenomedullary system in emergency situations and demonstrated that adrenaline and noradrenaline are released as an adjustment mechanism to prepare the body for fight and flight as an effect of sympathetic innervation in response to threatening stimuli.

Rapid developments in neuropsychology, endocrinology, and pharmacology have provided new knowledge about the role of physiological factors in the way individuals think, feel, act, and react (Hockey et al. 1986). The role of individual differences in biological maturation during adolescence was reviewed by Stattin and Magnusson (1991). The involvement of physiological factors in the developmental process has been empirically demonstrated in a number of studies on antisocial behavior (cf. Magnusson et al. 1993).

1.4 The Role of Environment in Personality Development

Environmental factors play a decisive role in the developmental process of all individuals. The main concern of the behavioral sciences is with the social environment.

Contact with others is necessary for the development of speech and language as a tool for thought and for communication; for the development of adequate world-views and self-perceptions; and for the development of well-functioning, integrated norm and/or moral systems. The importance of contact with others for physical health has been emphasized in the increasing number of reports from research on social networks.

Aspects of the environment influence the individual's current behavior and developmental course at all levels. A distinction should be made between the environment as a source of sensory stimulation and the environment as a source of information.

In important respects physical environment acts upon the individual and can be reacted to without intermediate interpretation processes. This view of the environment as a source of stimulation that elicits and releases individual responses was bluntly expressed by B.F. Skinner: "A person does not act upon the world, the world acts upon him" (Skinner 1971 p. 211). This conception of the environment is inherent in much developmental research in which various aspects of the upbringing environment in the home and at school have been regarded as "causes" in the development process of individuals with reference to a one-direction cause–effect model.

The assumption that the environment is a source of information contributes to understanding the way an individual interacts with the environment at various levels of complexity. This view is reflected in modern social learning theory, which assumes that an individual's way of dealing with the external world develops through a process of learning in which two types of perceived contingencies are formed. These are: (a) situation–outcome contingencies (certain situational conditions will lead to certain outcomes), and (b) behavior–outcome contingencies (certain actions by the individual will have certain predictable consequences) (cf. Bolles 1972). The formation of situation–outcome and behavior–outcome contingencies constitutes one source of stability and continuity of individuals' functioning in current situations and contributes to the development of well-functioning mental systems in the individual.

1.5 Significant Events

There are large individual differences in the type and degree of environmental influences on the development process. Of particular interest in this connection is the occurrence of significant single events that may have profound impact on the life-course of an individual. Some occur seemingly randomly, but are rather a consequence of the individual's readiness for a certain type of action or reaction (e.g., marriage or a new job) and an opportunity offered by the environment (e.g., meeting another person, receiving a job offer) (cf. Bandura's 1982 discussion of "chance events"). In other cases, a significant event may be the result of deliberate action by an individual or by influencing others. Buying a new house in a particular area with specific characteristics in terms of neighbors, opportunities or jobs, schooling, cultural and leisure-time activities, and so on, instead of in an area with other characteristics, may have decisive effects on the direction of the future life-course of all family members. Significant single events may occur over the entire lifespan. Their character depends on the physical and mental readiness of the individual to act and react to the opportunities and restrictions offered by the environment.

Significant events have the effect of changing the direction of the life-course. Sometimes this effect is not immediately visible, but grows slowly and has decisive effects on an individual's life in a way that is characteristic of the so-called "butterfly effect" in chaos theory. In other cases, the effect is more direct and leads to what has been discussed in terms of "turning points" (Pickles and Rutter 1991).

2. Dynamic Interaction

A central concept in an interactionistic view of individual functioning is the concept of "dynamic interaction." This concept refers to person-bound dynamic processes. In order to avoid confusion it is necessary to distinguish between dynamic interaction, on the one hand, and statistical interaction in designs for the study of interindividual differences, on the other.

Dynamic interaction is a characteristic of individual functioning at all levels of physiological and psychological processes. An example of the interplay of mental, physiological, and environmental factors may be illustrative. If a person encounters a situation that he or she experiences as threatening or demanding, for example, an examination or a work task, the cognitive act of interpreting the situation stimulates, via the hypothalamus, the excretion of adrenaline from the adrenal glands, which in turn triggers other physiological processes. This cognitive-physiological interplay is accompanied by emotional states of fear and/or anxiety and/or by generally experienced arousal. In the next stage of the process these emotions affect not only the individual's behavior and handling of the environment, but also his or her interpretation of the sequence of changes in the situational conditions, and thereby his or her physiological reactions in terms of autonomous reactivity. Thus, the perceptual-cognitive system and the biological system of an individual are involved in a continuous loop of reciprocal interaction. The way this process functions is among other things contingent upon the environment as it is perceived and given meaning by the individual. The outcomes of such situation–individual encounters will set the stage for subsequent reactions and actions to psychologically similar situations, as interpreted by the individual in his or her perceptual-cognitive system. In the developmental process, this interaction process affects both the mental system, for example, in its interpretation of certain types of situations, the response to such situations, and the physiological system. One possible effect of frequent encounter of stressful situations is that it may affect the immune system and lead to psychosomatic symptoms (Öhman and Magnusson 1987).

"Dynamic interaction" refers to the functioning of an individual and can be contrasted to statistical interaction in the study of interindividual differences. In investigating the hypothesis that females are more often relation-oriented and males more often achievement-oriented, it is possible to examine this hypothesis in experimental situations. A possible result would be that females choose the more "relational" situations and males prefer the more achievement-eliciting ones. Such a finding would point to a statistical interaction between sex and type of orientation.

Dynamic interaction can best be described by means of six fundamental and interrelated principles: multidetermination, interdependence, reciprocity, temporality, nonlinearity, and integration (Magnusson and Törestad 1993)

(a) *Multidetermination.* Multiple background factors underly all manifestations of personality. Consequently, what is observed and labeled as "personality" and "personality development" has multiple, often interacting, causes.

(b) *Interdependence.* Very often two or more factors are mutually dependent upon the existence of another factor without their influencing the other one(s) in a direct way. One example is shyness and social competence. In the course of long-term development, shyness may disappear and be replaced with social skills but they cannot very well exist side by side.

(c) *Reciprocity.* The reciprocal character of the processes involved in personality development implies that the common assumption of a unidirectional causal relationship between biological and environmental factors on the one hand, and mental and behavioral aspects of individual functioning on the other hand, is no longer a useful model. Biological factors can be both causes and outcomes. The same goes for the environment: it is both a cause and an outcome of the individual's interaction with the environment. The individual both influences and is influenced by the environment at each stage of development. The best illustration of the reciprocity in person–environment interactions can be drawn from person–person interaction, particularly parent–child interaction (cf. Bell 1968, Peterson 1979). A child influences the behavior of the parents and other family members who form an important aspect of its own developmental environment; the child is both the creation of and the creator of his or her environment.

(d) *Temporality.* The description of personality development as a process is fundamental to understanding and explaining the inner core of personality and its development. A process can be characterized as a continuous flow of interrelated, interdependent events. This definition introduces time as a basic ingredient in every model to be applied to individual functioning and change.

(e) *Nonlinearity.* The nonlinearity principle principally refers to the interrelationships among variables within the individual and on the individual's interaction with the environment. This principle implies, for example, that the impact of hormone A on hormone B is not necessarily linear, that is, the simple function "the more of A, the more of B" is not valid; the relationship may take on any function. The same is true for the interplay between a single individual and his or her environment.

(f) *Integration.* At all levels of personality, component processes are coordinated in their functions to serve the goal of the total personality. Integration reflects the principle that the total is more than the sum of its parts.

3. A Holistic, Dynamic View of Individual Development

The view of individual development as a dynamic, holistic process relates to a long tradition in psychology (cf. Allport 1937, Lewin 1935, Murray 1938, Stern 1911). For research on psychological functioning in a developmental perspective, different, holistic views have been advocated by Block (1971), Cairns (1983), Magnusson (1990), Sameroff (1983), and Wapner and Kaplan (1983), among others.

A holistic view emphasizes an approach which sees the individual as an organized whole, that functions as a totality and is characterized by the partly specific patterning of relevant aspects of structures and processes. The totality has properties that go beyond those belonging to the parts. It gets its characteristic features and properties from the interaction among the operating elements involved, not from the effect of each part on the totality. An individual functions as a totality at each stage of development, and each aspect of the structures and processes involved (perceptions, plans, values, goals, motives, biological factors, conduct, etc.) takes on meaning from the role it plays in the total functioning of the individual. The whole picture has an information value that goes beyond what is contained in the separate parts.

An individual's current way of functioning reflects the influence of his or her past course of development. The individual's readiness to respond to a particular situation in a particular way has been formed in a process of continuous interaction with various situations in the past. In the developmental process, the environment provides information and offers feedback for the building of valid conceptions of the outer world as a basis for further interaction. In this continuous interaction with the environment in its physical and social manifestations, individuals develop an integrated system of mental structures and contents that shape and constrain the modes of functioning. On the basis of and within the limits of inherited dispositions, affective tones become attached to specific contents and actions, and strategies are developed for coping with various kinds of situations and environments.

3.1 The Total Person–Environment System Changes Over Time

A fundamental characteristic of the process of individual development is that the total system of operating factors—biological, psychological, and social—changes across time as a result of maturation, experience, and learning (Gottlieb 1991). The total system is in continuous transition into new states across the lifespan. Over time both environments and individuals change and interact as totalities; the individual as a result of biological changes (e.g., growth, myelinization of the brain) and cognitive and emotional experiences, and the environment as a consequence of individuals' direct and indirect actions in and on it, among other things. The fact that both persons and environments change across the lifespan leads to changes in the character of the interaction between them. The interaction process per se will thus precipitate development. For example, the character of the interactive process within a family changes across time.

A consequence of the perspective applied here is that changes do not take place in single aspects isolated from the totality. The extent to which different aspects of individual functioning are influenced by environmental factors in this process varies. For example, in sexual development, some features, such as gonadal structure and function, are strongly regulated by biological factors. On the other hand, other aspects of individual functioning, such as choice of peers and type of sexual relations, may be strongly open to experiential influences (Cairns 1991). This perspective, of course, also has methodological implications.

3.2 Stability and Change in the Developmental Process

Much debate has been centered in the issues of stability versus change and continuity versus discontinuity in individual development. Characteristics of most of the studies addressed to these issues are (a) that they deal with data for single variables, one at a time, for example, aggressiveness, intelligence, hyperactivity; and (b) that they express the temporal consistency of single variables in terms of relative stability, that is, in terms of stable rank orders of individuals across time for the variable under consideration.

As emphasized above, a fundamental characteristic of individual functioning as a holistic, dynamic process is that individuals do not develop in terms of single variables but as total integrated systems. In this perspective, all changes during the lifespan of an individual are characterized by lawful continuity (Magnusson and Törestad 1992); the functioning of an individual at a certain stage of development is lawfully related to the functioning of the individual at earlier and later stages, but is not necessarily predictable.

In this perspective, each change in the process of human ontogeny is understandable and explainable in the light of the individual's previous life history and the functioning of the environment at the time for the change. This is true even for changes that are so abrupt that they seem to break a stable direction of development, for example, such changes that have been characterized as "turning points," sometimes appear as a result of "chance events" or "significant events" (Bandura 1982, Magnusson and Törestad 1992, Pickles and Rutter 1991).

3.3 Traits and Levels of Analysis

Individual functioning and interindividual differences can be analyzed at two levels: (a) in terms of the structures and processes involved at a particular moment in time under certain situational conditions, that is, in terms of states; and (b) in terms of more enduring dispositions to think, act, and react in certain ways, that is, in terms of traits.

The notion that the total functioning of an individual in relation to various aspects of the environment reflects latent dispositions to act and react in certain ways is a fundamental assumption behind the view of lawful continuity. It is compatible with an interactionist stand. Such dispositions underlie and guide an individual's selection of situations, the selection of stimuli and events to attend to in the situation, and the way information about the external world is treated and transformed into inner thoughts and outer actions. Individual differences in such dispositions, which are both general and differential, explain individual differences in the partly idiosyncratic cross-situational patterns of behavior that characterize individuals.

From a temporal perspective, the latent dispositions to act and react in certain ways change as a result of the development of the totality, as described and discussed in a previous section. It should be noted that traits are discussed in terms of aspects of the functioning of an individual. Traits in such terms are fuzzy concepts and do not exist per se. "Intelligence" and "aggressiveness" do not exist as separate entities: they are aspects of the total functioning of individuals who can behave more or less intelligently, more or less aggressively.

4. Implications

An interactional view of personality development, as summarized briefly above, has consequences for both society and research.

The extent to which the social environment is meaningfully structured and how it is structured (i.e., the system of values, norms, rules, and roles guiding the behavior of significant persons in the environment) is essential for the development of the child's conceptions of the external world and his or her role in it. It is the patterning and consistency of other people's demands, rewards, and punishments, that help the child develop a sense of order and lawfulness which can be used to assign meaning to the environment and to make valid predictions about situation–outcome contingencies and behavior–outcome contingencies in the external world. Such valid contingencies enable the individual to make predictions about the external world, and to exert predictive control. In addition, the formation of such contingencies allows the individual to foresee the outcomes of different lines of action and to use that knowledge as a basis for effective purposive action and to exert action control. The individual's ability to predict and take active control of the environment forms the fundamental basis for goal-directed activity and for the experience of meaningfulness.

This view of individual development emphasizes the importance of maintaining clear norms and rules for children in the rearing environments as well as for adults in society. This proposition was supported by Olofsson (1973), who found that lack of such clear norms and rules in the family background was the strongest single factor underlying adult criminality among males.

Most generalizations about the individual developmental process are made from cross-sectional research on individual differences. The limitations of this way of investigating development were discussed by Weinert and Schneider (1993). Their conclusion is that to understand a developmental process in which psychological and biological factors in the individual and environmental factors interact to produce functioning at a certain point in time, it is necessary to follow the same individuals across time, that is, to conduct longitudinal research.

As emphasized above, an individual's mental system develops in the process of interaction with the environment. Thus, environmental factors play a direct and central role in the development of the structure, content, and functioning of an individual's mental system and directly influence the ways in which the individual deals with the environment.

The environment constantly changes in various respects at all levels. This implies that there are systematic differences between generations, within the same culture, in respects that affect the individual's development process. The study of generational cohort effects is essential for two reasons. First, it enables the investigation of whether and to what extent results obtained on one cohort are also valid for other cohorts. Second, information about systematic differences in individual functioning as a result of changing societal conditions contributes to understanding and explaining the individual development process.

Cross-cultural differences appear at all levels of environments, between urban and rural cultures within countries, as well as between countries. This factor naturally has to be considered when interpreting results from single studies performed in a particular culture with its particular conditions. It also underscores the need for cross-cultural research to determine what is variant and what is invariant across cultures in individual functioning and development (cf. Lonner 1980). Such knowledge contributes to the understanding of the lawful principles underlying individual development.

From the present perspective, information on single aspects of an individual's personality, derived in isolation from the totality, has limited value for understanding and explaining the dynamic processes of change and development. Whenever major or minor changes in an individual's way of functioning are observed (e.g., the sweeping changes that often occur in the transition to the teenage period) they are seldom described or explained in terms of isolated variables. One or two salient aspects might be emphasized as typical of the changes, but the central focus is the development of new behavior patterns; that is, changes that involve several aspects of individual development. Thus, when discussing personality development, the appropriate complement to a pronounced variable- (or trait-) orientated stand is a person-oriented approach to describe the patterning of relevant factors operating in the development process. Such attempts have been made (e.g., Bergman 1993, Magnusson 1993) and they have turned out to be a fruitful tool for describing personality both from a current as well as from a developmental perspective.

See also: Development of Self-concept; Moral Development; Social Development; Socialization

References

Allport G W 1937 *Personality: A Psychological Interpretation.* Holt, Rinehart, and Wilson, New York
Angoff W H 1988 The nature–nurture debate, aptitudes and group differences. *Am. Psychol.* 43(9): 713–20
Bandura A 1982 The psychology of chance encounters and life paths. *Am. Psychol.* 37(7): 747–55
Bell R Q 1968 A reinterpretation of the direction of effects in studies of socialization. *Psychol. Rev.* 75(2): 81–95
Bergman L R 1993 Some methodological issues in longitudinal research: Looking forward. In: Magnusson D, Casaer P (eds.) 1993 *Longitudinal Research on Individual Development: Present Status and Future Perspectives.* Cambridge University Press, Cambridge
Block J 1971 *Lives through Time.* Bancroft Books, Berkeley, California
Bolles R C 1972 Reinforcement, expectancy and learning. *Psychol. Rev.* 79(5): 394–409
Buss A H, Plomin R 1984 *Temperament: Early Developing Personality Traits.* Erlbaum, Hillsdale, New Jersey
Cairns R B 1979 Toward guidelines for interactional research. In: Cairns R B (ed.) 1979 *The Analysis of Social Interactions: Methods, Issues, and Illustrations.* Erlbaum, Hillsdale, New Jersey
Cairns R B 1983 The emergence of developmental psychology. In: Mussen P H (ed.) 1983 *Handbook of Child Psychology*, Vol. 1, 4th edn. Wiley, New York
Cairns R B 1991 Multiple metaphors for a singular idea. *Dev. Psychol.* 27(1): 23–26

Cannon W B 1914 The emergency function of the adrenal medulla in pain and the major emotions. *Am. J. Physiol.* 33: 356–72

Endler N S, Magnusson D 1976 Toward an interactional psychology of personality. *Psych. Bull.* 83(5): 956–79

Gottlieb G 1991 Experiential canalization of behavioral development: Theory. *Dev. Psychol.* 27: 4–13

Hockey G R, Gaillard A W K, Coles M G H (eds.) 1986 *Energetics and Human Information Processing.* Martin Nijhoff, Dordrecht

Hunt J M 1961 *Intelligence and Experience.* Ronald Press, New York

Lewin K 1935 *A Dynamic Theory of Personality.* McGraw-Hill, New York

Lonner N 1980 The search for psychological universals. In: Triandis H et al. (eds.) 1980 *Handbook of Cross-cultural Psychology,* Vol. 6. Allyn and Bacon, Boston, Massachusetts

Magnusson D 1988 Individual development from an inter-actional perspective. In: Magnusson D (ed.) 1988 *Paths Through Life,* Vol. 1. Erlbaum, Hillsdale, New Jersey

Magnusson D 1990 Personality development from an inter-actional perspective. In: Pervin L (ed.) 1990 *Handbook of Personality: Theory and Research.* Guilford Press, New York

Magnusson D 1993 Human ontogeny: A longitudinal perspective. In: Magnusson D, Casaer P (eds.) 1993 *Longitudinal Research on Individual Development: Present Status and Future Perspectives.* Cambridge University Press, Cambridge

Magnusson D, Klinteberg B, Stattin H 1993 Juvenile and persistent offenders: Behavioral and physiological characteristic. In: Ketterlinus R, Lamb M (eds.) 1993 *Adolescent Problem Behaviors.* Erlbaum, Hillsdale, New Jersey

Magnusson D, Törestad B 1992 The individual as an interactive agent in the environment. In: Walsh B, Craig K, Price R (eds.) 1992 *Person–Environment Psychology: Models and Perspectives.* Erlbaum, Hillsdale, New Jersey

Magnusson D, Törestad B 1993 A holistic view of personality: A model revisited. *Annu. Rev. Psychol.* 44

Meyer-Probst B, Rösler H-D, Teichmann H 1983 Biological and psychosocial risk factors and development during childhood. In: Magnusson D, Allen V (eds.) 1983 *Human Development: An Interactional Perspective.* Academic Press, Orlando, Florida

Murray H A 1938 *Explorations in Personality: A Clinical and Experimental Study of Fifty Men of College Age.* Oxford University Press, New York

Öhman A, Magnusson D 1987 An interactional paradigm for research on psychopathology. In: Magnusson D, Öhman A (eds.) 1987 *Psychopathology: An Interactional Perspective.* Academic Press, Orlando, Florida

Olofsson B 1973 *Unga lagöverträdare III. Hem, uppfostran, skola och kamratmiljö i belysning av intervju- och uppföljningsdata.* Statens Offentliga Utredningar 1973: 25, Stockholm

Pervin L A 1984 *Personality: Theory and Research.* Wiley, New York

Peterson D R 1979 Assessing interpersonal relationships by means of interaction research. *Behavioral Assessment* 1: 221–76

Pickles A, Rutter M 1991 Statistical and conceptual models of "turning points" in developmental processes. In: Magnusson D, Bergman L R, Rudinger G, Törestad B (eds.) 1991 *Problems and Methods in Longitudinal Research: Stability and Change.* Cambridge University Press, Cambridge

Sameroff A J 1983 Developmental systems: Contexts and evolution. In: Mussen P H (ed.) 1983 *Handbook of Child Psychology, Vol. 1: History, Theory and Methods.* Wiley, New York

Skinner B F 1971 *Beyond Freedom and Dignity.* Knopf, New York

Stattin H, Magnusson D 1991 Stability and change in criminal behavior up to age 30. *British Journal of Criminology* 31(4): 327–46

Stern W 1911 *Die differentielle Psychologie in ihren metodischen Grundlagen.* Verlag von Hohann A. Barth, Leipzig

Wapner S, Kaplan B 1983 *Toward a Holistic Developmental Psychology.* Erlbaum, Hillsdale, New Jersey

Weinert F E, Schneider W 1993 Cognitive, social, and emotional development. In: Magnusson D, Casaer P (eds.) 1993 *Longitudinal Research on Individual Development: Present Status and Future Perspectives.* Cambridge University Press, Cambridge

Gender Roles

C. L. Martin and G. Levy

As children grow older they learn about the areas in which their culture assigns meaning to gender. These beliefs about gender have implications for children's behavior, interactions, and aspirations. This entry addresses how children develop gender roles. The first section discusses definitions of terms. The second section summarizes the major theories. Section 3 describes developmental changes in gender roles and Sect. 4 outlines the ways in which social and familial conditions contribute to gender role development. The final section describes implications for education.

1. Definitions of Terms

Gender roles are the characteristics that are culturally defined as appropriate for one sex or the other. Gender roles are multidimensional: they cover many domains including biological gender, activities and interests, personal–social attributes, social relationships, and symbolic characteristics (e.g., gestures). Within each domain it is necessary to examine individuals' concepts, self-perceptions, preferences, and behaviors (Huston 1983).

Self-perceptions have been a popular area of study, particularly ideas about masculinity and femininity. Masculinity and femininity were traditionally defined as opposite poles of one dimension. Researchers have since shown that they are two independent dimensions. From this research emerged a new concept, psychological androgyny, which represents a combination of feminine and masculine traits. Androgynous individuals have a wide repertoire of behaviors available to them and are able to adapt to a broader range of situations than sex-typed individuals (i.e., those having masculine traits or feminine traits, see Huston 1983).

2. Theories of Gender Role Development

A number of different theories have been proposed to account for gender-role development. This section addresses the most influential of these theories and evaluates their contributions.

2.1 Psychoanalytic Theory

Freud (1960) proposed one of the earliest theories of gender-role development. In his psychoanalytic theory, individuals pass through five psychosexual stages: oral, anal, phallic, latency, and genital. At each stage, "libidinal energies" (i.e., strong pleasurable feelings) are focused on specific bodily zones.

During the oral and anal stages, children become attached to their mothers. During the phallic stage (3–6 years), gender-role development of boys and girls diverges as a function of identification with the same-sex parent. Identification derives primarily from children's realization that they either have, or lack, a penis. Boys grow anxious that the father might perceive them as competition for the mother's love. Consequently, boys identify with the same-sex parent, fearing that the father might otherwise castrate him.

Girls envy possession of a penis, blame their mothers for their lack of a penis, and begin to shift love toward their fathers. Once realizing that yearnings for their fathers are futile, girls identify with their mothers. The desire for a penis is supplanted by the wish to have a male child. Little empirical support exists for psychoanalytic premises, although they have been influential in the development of new theories.

2.2 Social Learning Theories

According to traditional social learning theory (Mischel 1970), gender-typed behaviors are acquired and preserved through reinforcement, punishment, and generalization to different contexts. In these ways, in-

dividuals learn what types of behaviors are appropriate in different types of situations.

Contemporary cognitive social learning theory has concentrated on the role of observational learning: learning by watching the behaviors of others (e.g., Bussey and Bandura 1984). Rather than acquiring gender-typed behaviors solely as a function of reinforcement and punishment, children are credited with possessing the cognitive abilities needed to form expectations regarding behavior by observing the reactions to others' behavior. These expectations then influence children's own behavior.

Social learning theories have enhanced understanding as to how social agents (such as parents and teachers) influence gender-role development. The theories have been less effective in accounting for developmental changes in gender-role development (Ruble and Martin in press).

2.3 Cognitive Developmental Theories

Kohlberg (1966) proposed that gender-role development is dependent on children's intellectual level, particularly their understanding of gender categories. Children go through stages in understanding gender. First, children learn to identify people by sex (3 years). Second, they acquire the knowledge that sex will not change over time (gender stability, 4 years). Third, they learn that sex remains constant even if appearance changes (gender constancy, 4–6 years). Research has affirmed that children from the United States (Slaby and Frey 1976), Kenya, Nepal, Belize, and American Samoa (Munroe et al. 1984) follow this sequence. Once they understand gender constancy, children become strongly motivated to learn about their own sex and to behave like others of their own sex.

Although research has supported the ideas that children acquire information about gender in stages and level of intellectual ability relates to learning about gender, the relation between gender constancy and behavior has not been consistently supported (see Ruble and Martin in press). However, cognitive developmental theory has been extremely influential in defining the child's role in gender-role development.

2.4 Gender Schematic Processing Theories

Gender schematic processing theory is concerned with how children's beliefs about males and females influence their behavior and thinking (Bem 1981, Martin and Halverson 1981). Gender schemas are networks of mental associations representing knowledge about the sexes. Gender schemas develop because children have inborn tendencies to categorize and simplify information. Because most societies strongly emphasize gender, it becomes a salient classification dimension.

When children discriminate the sexes and recognize their own gender group, they quickly learn gender schemas and become motivated to carry out sex-appropriate roles. Once acquired, children's behavior and thinking are guided by gender schemas: most children pay attention to, play with, and learn more about sex-appropriate than sex-inappropriate objects. Furthermore, because gender schemas simplify information, they also lead to information loss and distortion. Several United States studies have shown that children change their memories for information that does not match their gender schemas (e.g., a boy cooking) into information that does (e.g., a girl cooking).

Gender schematic processing theory has provided new insights about the powerful nature of gender-related beliefs and has been effective in explaining how gender beliefs are maintained. The theory has been less effective in explaining very early gender-related behavior and the inconsistent relation between behavior and knowledge.

3. Developmental Changes

Children's preferences for sex-typed toys appear as early as 1½ years old. Children can identify their own sex and that of others by 2 to 3 years. By 3, they possess rudimentary stereotypes about the activities and appearance of females and males and their preferences for same-sex friends and sex-appropriate toys becomes stronger. By 5, children develop stereotypes about occupations, and evidence from Western cultures shows that children hold extensive and rigid gender stereotypes (Ruble and Martin in press, Zammuner 1987).

During middle childhood, two developmental patterns become evident. First, children's knowledge about gender-related traits increases such that, by age 10, they reflect adults' gender stereotypes. Second, with age, children show flexibility in beliefs about gender. For example, older German children believed that some girls may prefer trucks whereas younger ones did not (Trautner et al. 1989). Despite increasing flexibility, children's same-sex preferences for playmates increase throughout childhood (Ruble and Martin in press).

An important issue has been the relation between children's understanding of gender and their behaviors and preferences. Early researchers were guided by Kohlberg's ideas that children's understanding of gender constancy motivated adherence to sex-appropriate roles. However, little support has been found for the idea that gender constancy influences preferences or behavior (Levy and Carter 1989).

Recent evidence suggests that children's ability to label themselves and others as female or male, regardless of the completeness of their understanding of such labels, provides a basis for early gender-role development. For instance, children's ability to gender label at an early age relates to gender-typed toy play at 27 months of age, and greater gender-role awareness at 4 years of age (Fagot and Leinbach 1989).

4. Societal Influences

Most societies provide numerous and redundant sources of information about gender roles. Children learn about gender roles by observing regularities in the appearance and activities of males and females. In most cultures, adult females and males dress differently and a child's sex is often marked through the use of hairstyles, adornment, or clothing. In Mexico, Mixtecan mothers pierce the ears of daughters in the first weeks of life (Whiting and Edwards 1988). Every known society has a division of labor by sex, although the kinds of work assigned to women and men varies by culture. Parents may reinforce the societal division of labor by assigning different chores to sons and daughters. Moreover, gender information is socially transmitted through language: social agents label gender groups and describe the characteristics associated with the sexes for children.

4.1 Media

In television, movies, and books, children are exposed to traditional gender roles. Because of its popularity, television is a particularly potent information source. Television has a strong impact because it changes the kinds of activities children engage in as well as presenting traditional gender roles. For example, when television was introduced in a Canadian town, community and sport activities decreased and gender-role stereotypes increased (Kimball 1986).

The content of television programs and advertisements is frequently gender-biased. Females are outnumbered by males by about two to one and both sexes are often shown in traditional gender roles. Men are more likely than women to be shown as problem-solvers, educated professionals, and powerful. Women are typically shown in the home (Ruble and Martin in press). Children's books display similar gender biases. Central characters are more likely to be males than females and both sexes tend to be shown in traditional domestic and occupational roles.

4.2 Peers

As children grow older, peers act as central agents of gender-role socialization. Peers provide children with feedback about their behaviors. Research in the United States, Canada, and Australia indicates that children who behave in gender-appropriate ways are played with more frequently, are better liked, and are less likely to be teased than children who behave in gender-inappropriate ways (Hartup 1983).

Another facet of peer influence concerns gender segregation. This preference for playing in same-sex groups is apparent in Western and non-Western cultures, as well as in other primates (Carter 1987).

The sex of playmates influences the qualities of play such as where children play, the activity level of play, and the kinds of reinforcement contingencies that are available (Carter 1987). Same-sex peer preference begins around age 3 and remains at least until early adolescence, resulting in boys and girls growing up in distinct subcultures (Whiting and Edwards 1988).

4.3 Family Influences

Families are primary sources of information about gender roles. In many families, parents' occupations expose children to gender roles and associated inequities because mothers are likely to be employed in less prestigious jobs than fathers. Family structure, such as whether both parents live at home, influences who is available in the home to serve as role models for gender-roles.

Parental beliefs about the characteristics of sons and daughters also influence gender-role development. For example, although there were no physical differences, United States parents rated sons as being bigger and stronger than daughters, even within 24 hours of birth. Furthermore, parents expose girls and boys to different physical environments by providing them with different types of toys.

The answer to the question of whether parents treat boys and girls differently depends on which area of behavior is examined. Few consistent differences have been found in Western parents' encouragement or discouragement of personality characteristics or social behaviors, whereas consistent differences have been found across many cultures in the assignment of chores and in the encouragement of sex-appropriate activities. For instance, in Ngeca, Kenya, girls routinely engage in daily childcare whereas boys do not (Whiting and Edwards 1988).

Adults' encouragement of sex-appropriate activities may be partly in response to differences between girls and boys. However, adults also respond to the sex of the child even when no other differences exist. Experimental studies have shown that adults who interact with an infant labeled a boy treat the infant differently than others who believe the same infant is a girl (Huston 1983). Parents' encouragement of certain activities in children may result in boys and girls learning different skills.

4.4 School Influences

Many aspects of the school environment, including instructional materials, curricula, and teachers influence children's gender-role development. The school environment may foster cultural messages concerning gender (Ruble and Martin in press).

Gender biases are apparent in instructional materials. In United States elementary school readers and textbooks, male characters outnumber female characters, and are more frequently portrayed as dominant, active, and adventurous whereas female characters are often portrayed as passive and helpless. Women (and minorities) are also less often mentioned as significant historical figures.

Course curricula and course participation also influence gender-role development. Boys outnumber girls in mathematics and science courses, whereas girls outnumber boys in courses on homemaking and office skills. Course selections negatively influence performance of high school girls on quantitative tests, as well as dampening expectations of academic achievement (Minuchin and Shapiro 1983).

In the United States, a hierarchy of gender-typed roles is typically presented in elementary schools, with male administrators and principals and female teachers. Moreover, teachers respond to boys and girls in different ways. Preschool and elementary teachers tend to direct more disapproval to boys than girls (Ruble and Martin in press). However, teachers also direct more positive attention to boys than girls, especially for masculine behaviors (i.e., assertiveness). Girls receive attention for being quiet and compliant. These patterns occur at all levels of education, in many cultures, and by teachers of both sexes (Minuchin and Shapiro 1983).

5. Implications for Education

The values concerning the adoption of traditional roles have changed, particularly in Western cultures. No longer are traditional roles considered the goal of socialization efforts. Instead, more emphasis is placed on ensuring that individuals embrace a wide variety of behaviors, activities, and traits. Furthermore, researchers have shifted the focus from emphasizing parents as the major socialization agents to consideration of other socialization forces (i.e., schools, peers) and emphasis on children's self-socialization into gender roles.

Educational systems have been responsive to these changes in values. Educators have adopted various strategies to decrease gender biases. For instance, teachers' use of reinforcement has been successful in increasing mixed-sex play (Serbin et al. 1977). Open schools using nonsexist materials have been successful in decreasing gender segregation and sex-appropriate play. Educators and researchers strive to develop effective methods to decrease gender biases.

References

Bem S L 1981 Gender schema theory: A cognitive account of sex typing. *Psychol. Rev.* 88(4): 354–64
Bussey K, Bandura A 1984 Influence of gender constancy and social power on sex-linked modeling. *J. Pers. Soc. Psychol.* 47(6): 1292–1302
Carter D B 1987 The roles of peers in sex role socialization. In: Carter D B (ed.) 1987
Fagot B I, Leinbach M D 1989 The young child's gender schema: Environmental input, internal organization. *Child Dev.* 60(3): 663–72

Freud S 1960 Some psychical consequences of the anatomical distinctions between the sexes. In: Strachey J (ed. and trans.) 1960 *The Complete Psychological Works of Sigmund Freud*. Hogarth Press, London

Hartup W W 1983 Peer relations. In: Mussen P H (ed.) 1983 *Handbook of Child Psychology. Vol. 4: Socialization, Personality, and Social Development*. Wiley, New York

Huston A C 1983 Sex-typing. In: Mussen P H (ed.) 1983 *Handbook of Child Psychology. Vol. 4: Socialization, Personality, and Social Development*. Wiley, New York

Kimball M M 1986 Television and sex-role attitudes. In: Williams T M (ed.) 1986 *The Impact of Television: A Natural Experiment in Three Communities*. Academic Press, New York

Kohlberg L A 1966 A cognitive-developmental analysis of children's sex role concepts and attitudes. In: Maccoby E (ed.) 1966 *The Development of Sex Differences*. Stanford University Press, Stanford, California

Levy G D, Carter D B 1989 Gender schema, gender constancy, and gender-role knowledge: the roles of cognitive factors in preschoolers' gender-role stereotype attributions. *Dev. Psychol.* 25(3): 444–49

Martin C L, Halverson C F 1981 A schematic processing model of sex typing and stereotyping in children. *Child Dev.* 52(4): 1119–34

Minuchin P P, Shapiro E K 1983 The school as the context for social development. In: Mussen P H (ed.) 1983 *Handbook of Child psychology. Vol. 4: Socialization, Personality, and Social Development*. Wiley, New York

Mischel W 1970 Sex typing and socialization. In: Mussen P H (ed.) 1970 *Carmichael's Handbook of Child Psychology*, Vol. 2. Wiley, New York

Munroe R H, Shimmin H S, Munroe R L 1984 Gender understanding and sex role preferences in four cultures. *Dev. Psychol.* 20(4): 673–82

Ruble D N, Martin C L in press Gender development. In: Damon W (series ed.), Eisenberg N (volume ed.) *Handbook of Child Psychology: Social development*. Wiley, New York

Serbin L A, Tonick I J, Sternglanz S H 1977 Shaping cooperative cross-sex play. *Child Dev.* 48(5): 924–29

Slaby R G, Frey K S 1976 Development of gender constancy and selective attention to same-sex models. *Child Dev.* 46(4): 849–56

Trautner H M, Helbing N, Sahm W B, Lohaus A 1989 Langschnittliche Analyse von Entwicklungsmerkmalen der Geschlechtstypisierung im Kindesalter. Paper presented at the meetings for the Society for Research in Child Development, Kansas City, Kansas

Whiting B B, Edwards C P 1988 *Children of Different Worlds: The Formation of Social Behavior*. Harvard University Press, Cambridge, Massachusetts

Zammuner V L 1987 Children's sex-role stereotypes: A cross-cultural analysis. In: Shaver P, Hendrick C (eds.) 1987 *Sex and Gender*. Sage, Newbury Park, California

Further Reading

Carter D B (ed.) 1987 *Current Conceptions of Sex Roles and Sex Typing: Theory and Research*. Praeger, New York

Liben L S, Signorella M L (eds.) 1987 *Children's Gender Schemata*. Jossey-Bass, San Francisco, California

Maccoby E E 1990 Gender and relationships: A developmental account. *Am. Psychol.* 45(4): 513–20

Maccoby E E, Jacklin C N 1974 *The Psychology of Sex Differences*. Stanford University Press, Stanford, California

Martin C L 1991 The role of cognition in understanding gender effects. In: Reese H (ed.) 1991 *Advances in Child Development and Behavior*. Academic Press, San Diego, California

Early Experience and Human Development

J. Brooks-Gunn and F. Liaw

The ways in which developmental and educational psychologists study children and families have altered dramatically since the 1970s. This is due, in part, to accumulating evidence about the flexibility of both children and their parents to respond to environmental changes and to reorganize behavior in response to internal and external challenges. While theoretical writings have always reflected plasticity of the organism in the face of environmental variations, the methodologies used, the topics chosen, and the conceptual models offered were constrained by the following beliefs about development (Brooks-Gunn 1987, Scarr and McCartney 1983, Weinberg 1989).

First, early experiences were believed to shape the young child in such a way that once a change was made, it would be sustained beyond the early years of life (Bloom 1964, Hunt 1961). Second, development was portrayed as essentially a within-the-person phenomenon, with contextual features having a relatively small impact, or having an impact on a limited set of behaviors. Less attention was paid to environmental factors. Third, development was thought to proceed in a fairly standard sequence for all persons, rendering the study of individual differences unnecessary (Brooks-Gunn and Furstenberg 1987).

All of these premises have been challenged, the end results being that development is more likely to be characterized as an interaction between the organism and the environment and as a process with elements of both continuity and discontinuity. Some evidence exists that behavioral change during the infancy and preschool years is not sustained unless aspects of the environment are structured to foster changes or unless family circumstances are altered (Brim and Kagan 1980).

1. Development and Well-being

Development encompasses the social, emotional, cognitive, and health well-being of both child and parent. The dual focus on children and parents implies that each group is important in its own right. Parental well-being can influence child well-being both directly and indirectly. For example, the ability to find and hold a job provides the family with economic resources which may influence the child by the quality of schooling and childcare received, or neighborhood resided in, all of which affect child well-being (Baydar and Brooks-Gunn 1991, Brooks-Gunn et al. (in press a). Likewise, child well-being may influence the parent. This may be demonstrated by the effect on parental work decisions and emotional health of having a low birth weight child or a developmentally delayed child. A study which looked at mothers' entrance into the work force in the Infant Health and Development Program—an eight-site randomized clinical trial testing the efficacy of early intervention services upon low birth weight children's cognitive and emotional functioning—showed that mothers with lighter low birth weight infants entered the work force later than mothers with heavier low birth weight infants (Brooks-Gunn et al. (in press b).

2. Enhancement and Change

The term "enhancement" implies change in development. However, rarely is change in child and environment studied simultaneously. One of the best examples is a 20-year follow-up of a sample of Baltimore teenage mothers and their firstborn children. The dyads were seen when the mother was pregnant, and when their firstborns were aged approximately 1, 4, 16, and 20 (Furstenberg et al. 1987). The study found that effects of changes depended upon specific maternal characteristics, specific child outcomes, and specific ages. For example, the mother's change in welfare status (i.e., moving off welfare after the child's preschool years) significantly reduced the likelihood of the child's subsequent grade failure. By contrast, the mothers' early fertility behavior negatively affected preschoolers' performance, but later fertility did not affect adolescents' school achievement.

3. Models to Study Change

Changes in child and environment are no better illustrated than by the models which are used to study individuals and environment. Three of the most influential models are briefly summarized (Brooks-Gunn and Chase-Lansdale 1991). The ecological perspectives of Bronfenbrenner (1979, 1989) since the late 1960s focused not only on reciprocal influences of individual and environment upon one another, but upon the different contexts in which individuals reside. Ecological models also take seriously the notion that interactions occur among the different contexts and that individuals alter contexts such that change in the environment must be taken into account as well as changes in an individual's behavior.

Family system models (Hinde and Stevenson-Hinde 1988) are complementary to the ecological ones as they look at how the family operates as a system as well as a collection of individuals. Not only are reciprocal effects examined, but the functioning of the family as a whole is considered.

The final model focuses on risk and vulnerability. Vulnerability implies that a particular child or group of children who are at risk in a probablistic sense for manifesting a certain behavior or set of behaviors are susceptible to decrements in well-being; risk factors are those biological and environmental conditions known to be associated with decrements in well-being (Brooks-Gunn 1990a, Garmezy and Rutter 1983, Werner and Smith 1982). Environmental conditions include parenting behavior, parental characteristics (emotional and physical health, drug use, cognitive ability, maternal beliefs about childrearing), coparenting between mothers and grandmothers, and parental time and resource allocation to children. Biological conditions include neonatal status and health (i.e., low birth weight, respiratory distress), temperament, congenital conditions (e.g., Down Syndrome, cerebral palsy), and early developmental delays of unknown etiology. Research has focused on these conditions, both independently and in concert with one another, that influence young children's well-being. There is some evidence that many of the conditions known to be associated with decrements in children's well-being are interrelated (e.g., low birth weight is associated with low maternal education, poverty, smoking or drug use, lack of healthcare; Brooks-Gunn 1990a), and that the effect of risk factors is cumulative (Sameroff et al. 1987). The opposite of vulnerability and risk factors is resilience and protective factors.

Figure 1, which integrates models focusing on risk and resilience, family systems, and ecological factors, illustrates a simple model including child, familial and extrafamilial influences upon children's development. The literature is reviewed in the following sections on how these factors are associated with young children's outcomes, particularly in the cognitive and emotional realms.

4. Background Characteristics of the Family

The first set of influences (labeled (a) in Fig. 1) is background characteristics of the family. This category would include maternal age at the birth of the child, ethnicity, education, and characteristics of the parent's family of origin.

Maternal education is the background characteristic most often studied. It is almost always associated with young children's outcomes. This is true even when differences in factors such as family income, family size, presence of father, and employment are controlled. Education itself is associated with the mother's experiences in her family, typically studied as intergenerational transmission of educational attainment (Featherman and Hauser 1987). The mother's commitment to education might be as important as her actual educational attainment. In the Baltimore study, maternal aspirations for children's education in their first year of life were associated with the children's educational attainment 20 years later, controlling for the actual level of education the mother attained as well as welfare use, father presence, and preschool ability (Furstenberg et al. 1987, Baydar et al. 1993). The mechanisms for the maternal education effect are not only family income, but the provision of learning and reading experiences and probably the importance of such activities (Bradley et al. 1989, Duncan et al. in press).

5. Child Characteristics at Birth

The second set, labeled (b) in Fig. 1 involves those individual characteristics with which the child is endowed. These include gender, birth order, prenatal and neonatal health conditions. Also included are characteristics which, although subject to change, are believed to be influenced heavily by birth conditions and genetics: temperament, health conditions in the infant and toddler years, maternal perceptions of child's health, early attention, arousal and affect, as elicited by different levels and types of environmental stimulation (these differences being particularly pronounced in children at biological risk due to conditions such as low birth weight, fetal exposure to drug use, and intrauterine growth retardation).

6. Parent Characteristics

The next three sets of characteristics involve the parent. These are divided into parental resources, parenting practices, and parental social and psycho-

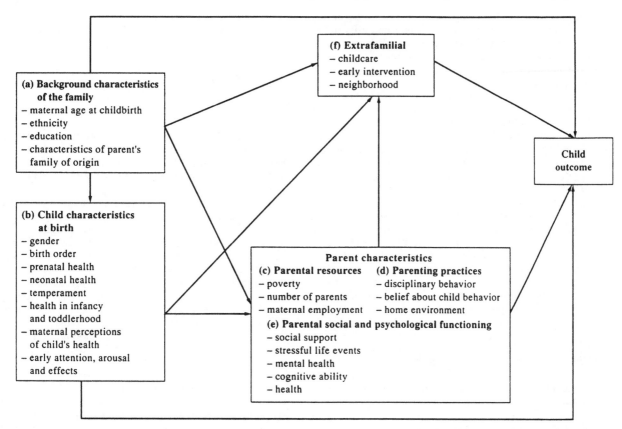

Figure 1
Model of early experience and child development

logical functioning, and are labeled (c), (d), and (e) respectively in Fig. 1.

6.1 Parental Resources

Parental resources focus on family income as well as time available to spend with the child. The two are often associated in complex ways. For example, children in single-parent households often have only one parent with whom to interact. Single parents, especially if working, have little time to invest in their children. The birth of a sibling alters the time available to spend with older children; spacing, hence, is particularly important (Furstenberg et al. 1985). Poverty may be the most influential factor of resources. In 1990, almost one in four preschoolers in the United States lived in a poor household at any point in time (US Bureau of the Census 1991, Duncan et al. in press).

Poverty is strongly associated with young children's well-being, with poor children usually displaying poorer cognitive and socioemotional development than the economically advantaged (Parker et al. 1988). It has been argued that poverty affects children by its negative effects on parents, such that poor parents are more likely to experience social and psychological distress, which in turn impair the quality of parenting skills and consequently increases the probability of adverse behavior in children (e.g., Huston 1991, McLoyd 1989, Brooks-Gunn and Chase-Lansdale 1991).

The number of parents available in the household is another resource factor that influences young children's well-being. Research shows that children who are reared in single-parent families are associated with poorer cognitive performance and school achievement (Garfinkel and McLanahan 1986), and are less likely to graduate from high school. In some cases where a father is absent, grandmothers may play a significant parenting role. This is particularly true for young, unmarried mothers (Brooks-Gunn and Chase-Lansdale 1991). Grandmothers have been found to be a protective factor for Black preschoolers whose mothers are single parents (Furstenberg 1976). It is believed that the availability of a second committed parent figure may be more important than who that adult is (Chase-Lansdale et al. 1991).

Maternal employment is associated with resources, since it increases financial resources but decreases time resources available for the child. A substantial amount of research has focused on effects of maternal employment upon children, stimulated by the theoretical writing of Bowlby on the untoward effects of maternal separation (Phillips and Howes 1987). Several small-scale studies have reported that White middle-class children are more likely to exhibit avoidant or anxious attachment during brief laboratory separation from their mothers around 12 to 15 months of age if their mothers were employed in their first year of life (Hock 1980, Pedersen et al. 1982). Results of a large national sample (the children of the National Longitudinal Survey of Youth) show small negative effects on preschoolers' verbal ability and behavior problems if their mothers were employed in the first year of life (Baydar and Brooks-Gunn 1991). Maternal employment that was more than 10 hours a week, and maternal employment that began between the child's fourth and eighth month accounted for these effects; no effects of employment in the second or third year, nor whether employment was continuous or not were found in these analyses (Baydar and Brooks-Gunn 1991). Of particular interest is the fact that these effects were most pronounced in poor families, who presumably are less likely to be able to purchase high-quality child care. Furthermore, grandmother care buffered children from negative effects, speaking to the earlier point about the availability of committed adult figures for optimal development.

As mentioned earlier, child development is the result of an interaction between the organism and the environment. Research on low birth weight children is a good example of this transactional process. Accumulating evidence shows that low birth weight children, who are at risk for developmental delays and behavior problems, develop normally and experience less school difficulties if their social and familial environments are benign (e.g., high income, high parental education, positive parent–child interactions, and a responsive and intellectually stimulating environment); their development is more likely to be in jeopardy when reared in an adverse environment (Brooks-Gunn et al. 1992, 1993b; Sigel 1983).

6.2 Parenting Practices

Parenting practices include behaviors directed toward the child. Dimensions of interest include parenting behavior, parental beliefs about child development, and provision of learning experience. Disciplinary practices that emphasize reasoning, consistency, and child self-direction are more associated with more intellectual competence, self-autonomy, and internal locus of control in children than practices that are permissive, authoritarian, or conformity-oriented (Baumrind 1989, Maccoby and Martin 1983, Osofsky 1979). Consistent significant associations have been found between parental beliefs about childrearing and a child's cognitive competence, even controlling for socioeconomic status and maternal mental illness (Sameroff and Feil 1985, Sigel 1985). Differences in parental beliefs about child development are related to age, maternal education, and social class, with parents of higher socioeconomic status giving more sophisticated explanations of behavior.

Maternal interactive behavior, such as positive affective involvement and developmentally appropriate stimulation and instructions have been associated with child cognitive and social outcomes (Maccoby and Martin 1983, Sroufe 1983). A mother's provision of a stimulating and responsive physical and learning home environment for her children has been associated with cognitive gains made by the child (Bradley et al. 1989, Elardo et al. 1975, Gottfried 1984). Some researchers suggest that the importance of the home environment in relation to children's intelligence shifts with age such that its effect is most important in early life up to the end of the preschool period, and progressively decreases when children enter school and other environmental factors increase their influence (Luster and Dubow 1992).

6.3 Parental Social and Psychological Functioning

Parental social and psychological functioning include factors such as social support, stressful life events, parental mental health, cognitive abilities, and health. Some evidence shows causal links between maternal depressive symptoms and children's well-being (Richter and Pelligrini 1989). Maternal depression has been strongly associated with early impairments in mother–infant interaction and in later child behavior problems (Field et al. 1979, McLoyd 1989, Sameroff and Seifer 1983). Life stress, health problems, social support, and depression are interrelated. Such stressors may affect children via mother–child interaction, organization of the home environment, and time spent with the child (Huston 1991, McLoyd 1989).

Parental cognitive ability is highly associated with child intelligence and achievement (Ramey et al. 1989). The influence of parental cognitive ability may be via its influence on the type of the intellectual, physical, and learning environment provided for the child, which in turn has a positive relationship with children's development, as mentioned earlier.

7. Extrafamilial Circumstances

The final set of factors focus on extrafamilial circumstances (labeled (f) in Fig. 1). They include childcare, early intervention, and neighborhood. They are grouped together because, while important, they play a smaller role in young children's development than do familial factors on the young child's development.

7.1 Childcare

With more than 50 percent of mothers with young children in the workforce in the United States, use of extrafamilial care for children becomes common, although its effect on child development is inconclusive. Earlier research provides no evidence that daycare has negative effects on children's intellectual development. Instead, participation in high-quality childcare programs was associated with greater social competence, and to a lesser extent, positive relationships with peers in young children (Clarke-Stewart 1989, Clarke-Stewart and Fein 1983, Rutter 1981). Some researchers, however, caution about the extensive use of full-time extrafamilial childcare, especially low-quality care for more than 20 hours a week in the first year of life.

More recent research in the United States shows that early entry into daycare does not in itself result in adverse child development, be it short-term or long-term; rather, it is low quality of childcare that does (Hayes et al. 1990, Howes 1988). High ratings of center quality, smaller group size, higher adult–child ratio, more child-related training of caregivers, and more social interactions between children and caregivers have been associated with positive cognitive and social outcomes in children from toddlerhood through preschool years (Hayes et al. 1990), and has been used as criteria for high quality of childcare. When high quality of care is assured, as is the case in Sweden, no adverse effect of infant day care or any type of child care were found. Children entering day care as infants performed significantly better on cognitive tests, having more positive school achievement and socioemotional development at 28 and 40 months, and at ages 8 and 13 than children entering daycare at later ages and those in home care (Anderson 1989, Sternberg et al. 1991).

7.2 Early Intervention

Early intervention programs have been provided for biologically and environmentally disadvantaged children to enhance their resilience. The best study of the effect of early intervention on children's development may be that conducted by the Consortium for Longitudinal Studies. Integrating data from 11 well-designed and research-oriented preschool programs for disadvantaged (mostly low-income, Black) children in the United States, the Consortium reported immediate IQ and academic gains of the program children, but these gains tended to diminish one or two years later (Lazar and Darlington 1982). However, children from the intervention programs were less likely than their no-preschool counterparts to be retained in grade, to fail in school requirement, or to be placed in special educational services. A few long-term studies indicate that children attending high quality preschool programs are also more likely to graduate after high school and less likely to engage in delinquent behavior (Berrueta-Clement et al. 1984). This suggests that initial effects of the intervention on IQ may have given the disadvantaged children early school success and self-esteem to maintain their motivation and efforts in the later grades (Brooks-Gunn 1990b, Woodhead 1988, Zigler 1992).

Intervention studies for biologically at-risk children (including handicapped and low birth weight children) reported similar findings. The best evidence for the success of early intervention for disabled children comes from Shonkoff and Hauser-Cram's (1987) meta-analysis of 31 evaluations. They reported positive effects of early intervention on children's intelligence, language ability, and motor development.

Intervention was more effective for children with mild cognitive delays, and greater effects were found in programs with extensive parental involvement. Similar early intervention programs have been developed for low birth weight children (usually begun at an earlier age). Many small-scale studies reported positive effects on children's cognitive functioning, social competence, parent–child interactions, and home environment (Brooks-Gunn 1990a, 1990b; Meisels et al. in press). Results from the Infant Health and Development Program, the largest multisite early intervention for low birth weight children, show that intervention children had higher IQ scores and fewer behavior problems than follow-up children at age 3 (Infant Health and Development Program 1990). Children received home visiting and center-based care. Moreover, the intervention was more effective for mothers with low educational attainment than those with high educational attainment, more effective for Black than for White children, and more effective for most at-risk children (Brooks-Gunn et al. 1993a).

Reviews of the efficacy of intervention programs show that early interventions have positive effects on children's well-being if they have the following characteristics: (a) intervention begun as early as possible, (b) services provided to parents as well as to the child, (c) frequent contacts, (d) higher level of parental involvement, and (e) lower child–teacher ratio (Bryant and Ramey 1987, McKey et al. 1985, Lazar and Darlington 1982, Schorr 1988).

8. Conclusion

All of these sets of factors interact with one another in complex ways. In a classic two-decade study of the children of Kauai, an interaction between child perinatal problems and family poverty status was found, such that perinatal problems were associated with much lower IQ scores at age 2 in low than high socioeconomic status families (Werner et al. 1971). Similar findings were found at ages 10 and 18 (Werner and Smith 1977, 1982). Other studies with premature infants also support the mediating effect of the rearing environment, such that significantly poorer child outcomes would occur when children with biological or perinatal risks were reared in an adverse (or less responsive) environment (Liaw and Brooks-Gunn in press a).

The fact that some children in poor families do well and some children in more advantaged families do not do well indicates the inadequacy of using a single factor in explaining development. Instead, developmental delays may be accounted for by a cumulative risk model, which posits that the cumulation of risk factors, rather than the individual risk factors per se, accounts for developmental delays seen in young children (Sameroff et al. 1987). Two groups of researchers studied the cumulative effect of risk factors

and reported that multiple risk factors had more of an effect than would be expected looking at each singly, and that as the number of risks increased, the child and family functioning decreased (Liaw and Brooks-Gunn in press b, Sameroff et al. 1987).

Finally, it must be stressed that development continues past the young childhood years. While early experience may influence developmental trajectories, later experiences may alter them. The policy question is how to help families overcome circumstances such as low education, poverty, lack of access to childcare and health care, given that such changes will enhance children's functioning.

See also: Ecological Models of Human Development

References

Anderson B 1989 Effects of public day-care: A longitudinal study. *Child Dev.* 60: 857–66

Baumrind D 1989 Rearing competent children. In: Damon W (ed.) 1989 *Child Development Today and Tomorrow.* Jossey-Bass, San Francisco, California

Baydar N, Brooks-Gunn J 1991 Effects of maternal employment and child-care arrangements on preschoolers' cognitive and behavioral outcomes: Evidence from the children of the National Longitudinal Survey of Youth. *Dev. Psychol.* 27(6): 932–45

Baydar N, Brooks-Gunn J, Furstenberg F F Jr. 1993 Early warning signs of functional illiteracy: Predictions in childhood and adolescence. *Child Dev.* 64(3): 815–29

Berrueta-Clement J R, Schweinhart L J, Barnett W S, Epstein A E, Weikart D P 1984 *Changed Lives: The Effects of the Perry Preschool Programs on Youths through Age 19.* High/Scope Press, Ypsilanti, Michigan

Bloom B S 1964 *Stability and Change in Human Characteristics.* Wiley, New York

Bradley R H et al. 1989 Home environment and cognitive development in the first three years of life: A collaborative study involving six sites and three ethnic groups in North America. *Dev. Psychol.* 25(2): 217–35

Brim O G Jr., Kagan J (eds.) 1980 *Constancy and Change in Human Development.* Harvard University Press, Cambridge, Massachusetts

Bronfenbrenner U 1979 Contexts of child rearing: Problems and prospects. *Am. Psychol.* 34: 844–50

Bronfenbrenner U 1989 Ecological systems theory. *Annals of Child Development* 6: 187–249

Brooks-Gunn J 1987 Pubertal processes: Their relevance for psychological research. In: Van Hasselt V B, Hersen M (eds.) 1987 *The Handbook of Adolescent Psychology.* Pergamon Press, New York

Brooks-Gunn J 1990a Identifying the vulnerable child. In: Rogers D E, Ginzberg E (eds.) 1990 *Improving the Life Chances of Children at Risk.* Westview Press, Boulder, Colorado

Brooks-Gunn J 1990b Promoting healthy development in young children: What educational interventions work? In: Rogers D E, Ginzberg E (eds.) 1990 *Improving the Life Chances of Children at Risk.* Westview Press, Boulder, Colorado

Brooks-Gunn J, Chase-Lansdale P L 1991 Children having

children: Effects on the family system. *Pediatric Annals* 20(9): 467–81

Brooks-Gunn J, Duncan J, Klebanov P, Sealand N in press a Do neighborhoods influence child and adolescent behavior? *Am. J. Sociol.*

Brooks-Gunn J, Furstenberg F F Jr. 1987 Continuity and change in the context of poverty: Adolescent mothers and their children. In: Gallagher J J, Ramey C T (eds.) 1987 *The Malleability of Children.* Brookes, Baltimore, Maryland

Brooks-Gunn J, Gross R T, Kraemer H C, Spiker D, Shapiro S 1992 Enhancing the cognitive outcomes of low birth-weight premature infants: For whom is the intervention most effective? *Pedia.* 89(8): 1209–15

Brooks-Gunn J, Guo G, Furstenberg F F Jr. 1993a Who drops out and who continues beyond high school: A 20-year follow-up of Black urban youth. *Journal of Research in Adolescents*

Brooks-Gunn J, Klebanov P K, Liaw F, Spiker D 1993b Enhancing the development of low birth weight, premature infants: Changes in cognition and behavior over the first three years. *Child Dev.* 64(3): 736–53

Brooks-Gunn J, McCormick M C, Benasich A A, Shapiro S, Black G in press b Effects of early education intervention on maternal employment, public assistance, and health insurance. *American Journal of Public Health*

Bryant D M, Ramey C T 1987 An analysis of the effectiveness of early intervention programs for environmentally high-risk children. In: Guralnick M, Bennett C (eds.) 1987 *The Effectiveness of Early Intervention for At-risk and Handicapped Children.* Academic Press, San Diego, California

Chase-Lansdale P L, Mott F L, Brooks-Gunn J, Phillips D H 1991 Children of the National Longitudinal Survey of Youth: A unique research opportunity. *Dev. Psychol.* 27(6): 918–31

Clarke-Stewart K A 1989 Infant day-care: Maligned or malignant? *Am. Psychol.* 44(2): 266–73

Clarke-Stewart K A, Fein G G 1983 Early childhood programs. In:Mussen L P H (ed.) 1983 *Handbook of Child Psychology,* Vol. 2. Wiley, New York

Duncan G J, Kebanuv P K, Brooks-Gunn J in press Economic deprivation and early childhood development. *Child Dev.*

Elardo R, Bradley R, Caldwell B M 1975 The relation of infants' home environments to mental test performance from six to thirty-six months: A longitudinal analysis. *Child Dev.* 46: 71–76

Featherman D L, Hauser R M 1987 *Lifespan Development and Change.* Academic Press, New York

Field T M, Dempsey J R, Shuman H H 1979 Developmental assessments of infants surviving the respiratory distress syndrome. In: Field T M, Sostek A M, Goldberg S, Shuman H H (eds.) 1979 *Infants born at Risk: Behavior and Development.* Spectrum, New York

Furstenberg F F Jr. 1976 *Unplanned Parenthood: The Social Consequences of Teenage Childbearing.* Free Press, New York

Furstenberg F F Jr., Brooks-Gunn J, Morgan P 1987 *Adolescent Mothers in Later Life.* Cambridge University Press, New York

Furstenberg F F Jr., Daniels D, Denn J, Plomin R 1985 Environmental differences within the family and adjustment differences within pairs of adolescent siblings. *Child Dev.* 56(3): 764–74

Garfinkel I, McLanahan S 1986 *Single Mothers and their Children: A New American Dilemma.* Urban Institute Press, Washington, DC

Garmezy N, Rutter M (eds.) 1983 *Stress, Coping, and Development in Children.* McGraw-Hill, New York

Gottfried A W (ed.) 1984 *Home Environment and Early Cognitive Development.* Academic Press, New York

Hayes C D, Palmer J L, Zaslow M E 1990 *Who Cares for America's Children? Child Care Policy for the 1990s.* National Academy Press, Washington, DC

Hinde R A, Stevenson-Hinde J 1988 *Relationships within Families: Mutual Influences.* Clarendon Press, Oxford

Hock E 1980 Working and non-working mothers and their infants: A comparative study of maternal care-giving characteristics and infant social behavior. *Merill-Palmer Q.* 46: 79–101

Howes C 1988 Relations between early child care and schooling. *Dev. Psychol.* 24: 53–57

Hunt J V 1961 *Intelligence and Experience.* Roland Press, New York

Huston A (ed.) 1991 *Children in Poverty: Child Development and Public Policy.* Cambridge University Press, Cambridge

Infant Health and Development Program 1990 Enhancing the outcomes of low birthweight, premature infants: A multisite randomized trial. *Journal of the American Medical Association* 263(22): 3035–42

Lazar I, Darlington R 1982 Lasting effects of early education: A report from the Consortium for Longitudinal Studies. *Monogr. Soc. Res. Child Dev.* 47(2–3): 1–151

Liaw F, Brooks-Gunn J in press a Patterns of low birth-weight children's cognitive development. *Dev. Psychol.*

Liaw F, Brooks-Gunn J in press b Effects of cumulative risks and poverty on low birth-weight children's cognitive and behavioral problems. *Journal of Clinical Child Psychology*

Luster T, Dubow E 1992 Home environment and maternal intelligence as predictors of verbal intelligence: A comparison of preschool and school-age children. *Merill Palmer Q.* 38: 151–75

Maccoby E E, Martin J A 1983 Socialization in the context of the family: Parent–child interaction. In: Hetherington E M (ed.) 1983 *Handbook of Child Psychology: Vol. 4. Socialization, Personality and Social Development.* Wiley, New York

McKey R H et al. 1985 *The Impact of Head Start on Children, Family, and Communities: Head Start Synthesis Project.* DHHS Publication No. (ODHS) 85–31193. US Government Printing Office, Washington, DC

McLoyd V 1989 The impact of economic hardships on Black families and children: Psychological distress, parenting, and socioemotional development. *Child Dev.* 61(2): 311–64

Meisels S J, Dichtelmiller M, Liaw F R in press A multidimensional analysis of early childhood intervention programs. In: Zeanah C (ed.) in press *Handbook of Infant Mental Health.* Guilford Press, New York

Osofsky J D (ed.) 1979 *Handbook of Infant Development.* Wiley, New York

Parker S, Greer S, Zuckerman B 1988 Double jeopardy: The impact of poverty on early child development. *The Pediatric Clinics of North America* 35: 1227–40

Pedersen F A, Cain R Jr., Zaslow M, Anderson B 1982 Variation in infant experience associated with alternative family roles. In: Laosa L, Siegel I (eds.) 1982 *Families* as *Learning Environments for Children*. Plenum Press, New York

Phillips D, Howes C 1987 Indicators of quality in child care. Review of research. In: Phillips D A (ed.) 1987 *Quality in Child Care: What does Research Tell Us?* National Association for the Education of Young Children, Washington, DC

Ramey C, Lee M W, Burchinal M R 1989 Developmental plasticity and predictability: Consequences of ecological change. In: Bornstein M H, Krasnegor N A (eds.) 1989 *Stability and Continuity in Mental Development: Behavioral and Biological Perspectives*. Erlbaum, Hillsdale, New Jersey

Richter J, Pelligrini D 1989 Depressed mothers' judgments about their children: An examination of the depression-distortion hypothesis. *Child Dev.* 60(5): 1068–75

Rutter M 1981 Social-emotional consequences of daycare for preschool children. *American Journal of Orthopsychiatry* 51(1): 4–28

Sameroff A J, Feil L A 1985 Parental concepts of development. In: Siegel I E (ed.) 1985 *Parental Belief Systems*. Erlbaum, Hillsdale, New Jersey

Sameroff A J, Seifer R 1983 Familial risk and child competence. *Child Dev.* 54(5): 1254–68

Sameroff A J, Seifer R, Barocas R, Zax M, Greenspan S 1987 Intelligence quotient scores of 4-year-old children: Social environmental risk factors. *Pedia.* 79(3): 343–50

Scarr S, McCartney K 1983 How people make their own environments: A theory of genotype—environment effects. *Child Dev.* 54: 424–35

Schorr L 1988 *Within Our Reach: Breaking the Cycle of Disadvantage*. Anchor, New York

Shonkoff J P, Hauser-Cram P 1987 Early intervention for disabled infants and their families: A quantitative analysis. *Pedia.* 80(5): 650–58

Sigel L S 1983 Correction for prematurity and its consequences for the assessment of the very low birthweight infants. *Child Dev.* 54(4): 1176–88

Sigel I E 1985 A conceptual analysis of beliefs. In: Sigel I E (ed.) 1985 *Parental Belief Systems*. Erlbaum, Hillsdale, New Jersey

Sroufe L A 1983 Infant—caregiver attachment and patterns of adaptation in the preschool: The roots of maladaption and competence. In: Perlmutter M (ed.) 1983 *Development and Policy Concerning Children with Special Needs*. Erlbaum, Hillsdale, New Jersey

Sternberg K J et al. 1991 Does out-of-home care affect compliance in preschoolers? *International Journal of Behavioral Development* 14(1): 45–65

US Bureau of the Census 1991 Current Population Reports, Series P-60, No. 175, *Poverty in the United States: 1990* US Government Printing Office, Washington, DC

Weinberg R A 1989 Intelligence and IQ: Landmark issues and great debates. *Am. Psychol.* 44(2): 98–104

Werner E E, Bierman J M, French F E 1971 *The Children of Kauai: A Longitudinal Study from the Prenatal Period to Age Ten*. University of Hawaii Press, Honolulu, Hawaii

Werner E E, Smith R S 1977 *Kauai's Children Come of Age*. University of Hawaii Press, Honolulu, Hawaii

Werner E E, Smith R S 1982 *Vulnerable But Not Invincible: A Longitudinal Study of Resilient Children and Youth*. McGraw Hill, New York

Woodhead M 1988 When psychology informs public policy: The case of early childhood intervention. *Am. Psychol.* 43: 443–54

Zigler E F 1992 Early childhood intervention: A promising preventive for juvenile delinquency. *Am. Psychol.* 47: 997–1006

Family Influences on Human Development

K. A. Schneewind

From a systems-oriented perspective, individual development within the family is conceived as a coevolutionary process. Although the family as a special group of persons and the individual family member each have their own developmental paths both mutually influence each other. Based on a rather broad psychological definition of the family, some selected topics and research findings including behavior genetics, health, relationships on different system levels, and family intervention will be presented.

1. Defining the Family

In a time when sociologists—at least in the Western world—contend that disintegration and deinstitutionalization of the family has led to a growing pluralization of family forms, defining the family is not an easy task. Many solutions have been proposed to solve this definitional dilemma. They range from conceiving of the family as a legalized two-generational unit of coresiding persons related by blood and/or adoption, to viewing it as a widely unspecified constellation of persons who of their own volition call themselves a family. For the purposes of this entry, families are defined as special variants of intimate relationship systems for which the maintenance of boundaries, privacy, closeness, and permanence are crucial, albeit empirically more or less variable, defining elements. This definition not only includes nontraditional family forms found in modern society but also focuses on a genuine psychological perspective; that is, how and to what extent people influence each other and are influenced by the relationship context in which they are living. In addition, it takes into account the dynamic nature of the codeveloping individual–family unit by explicitly considering the possibility that a person might be part of a series of quite different intimate relationship systems across his or her life course.

2. Heredity and Health in Family Life

2.1 Behavior Genetics

The fact that, unlike adopted children, consanguineous children are genetically related to their parents and siblings is of fundamental importance for the explanation of individual differences and commonalities within the family context. Quantitative behavior genetics, including developmental behavior genetics, have made great progress since the early 1980s. Based on large data sets mainly from Anglo-American and Scandinavian countries, the following general conclusions can be drawn (Plomin and Rende 1991): (a) the variation of cognitive and socioemotional personality variables has a substantial genetic component; (b) in a developmental perspective genetic influences become increasingly more important as individual differences are determined by an active genotype–environment covariation; (c) family-related experiences such as perceived parental warmth can partially be attributed to genetic influences; (d) nonshared environmental influences (e.g., specific treatment of a child by parents or siblings) contribute to individual differences to a larger extent than family variables that are common to all offspring (e.g., socioeconomic status, generalized parenting style). The latter finding partially explains why siblings raised in the same family are so different from one another, although the siblings' specific genetic endowment may also contribute to phenotypic differences. The importance of nonshared environments has led—ironically within a behavior genetic research program—to a more detailed exploration of specific environmental influences inside and outside the family that are linked to the development of individual differences.

2.2 The Family and Health

There is ample evidence that people living in a long-term (usually marital) relationship are, on average, physically and psychologically healthier than single, divorced, or widowed persons. For instance, the data suggest that in the United States the death rates of unmarried people are up to 50 percent (females) or even 250 percent (males) higher than for married people. Causes of death with a strong behavioral component (e.g., lung cancer, suicide, accidents) have a particularly high incidence rate for unmarried people. Moreover, clinically diagnosed personality dysfunctions (e.g., anxiety, depression) are also more likely to be found among this group. Attempts to explain these differences range from mate selection (i.e., healthy people are more likely to find a partner) to the special social and emotional support provided in long-term intimate relationships (e.g., less risky life-styles, more preventive and health-enhancing activities are practiced, especially by women). It should be stressed, however, that these findings are based on sample means and thus do not account for differential effects. There are some indications, for example, that the beneficial effects of living in a marriage can only be found in rewarding and nondistressed relationships.

Although living in a long-term relationship tends to be a protective factor for a person's well-being this is not the case for parenthood. On average, parents do not fare better than childless people and can even be expected to encounter somewhat higher health risks. However, differential influences must again be taken into account. Among these are the following factors: sufficient financial resources of the family, available childcare services, support from spouse or kin in sharing childcare and household chores (Ross et al. 1990).

2.3 Family Violence

In some cases the family itself may become a health risk. In Western societies this is especially true for children and women, increasingly also for older family members, whose personal integrity can be violated by physical maltreatment and sexual abuse. The expression and definition of domestic violence is different from country to country; the same holds true for corresponding laws, criminal statistics, and estimated numbers of unknown cases. Despite these differences, there is consistent evidence that domestic violence is rapidly increasing in the Western industrialized nations, quite apart from the growing neglect of children in economically deprived Third World countries. The causes and consequences of family violence and neglect are in general well-researched, suggesting a multidimensional pattern of causes among which variables like economic hardship, social and personal stress, low self-esteem, unrealistic expectations of child-rearing, and a history of experience of violence in one's own family of origin are especially salient. Several reviews concerning the consequences of child maltreatment lead to similar conclusions; that is, maltreated children tend to be more aggressive, show more internalizing and externalizing behavior problems, are less empathetic, have more troubled peer relationships, and perform lower on cognitive tasks. Preventive action seems to be imperative in view of these findings, although so far the results of corresponding programs have yielded mixed results (Gelles and Conte 1990).

3. Family Relations

The number of possible relationships within a family increases exponentially with the number of individual family members. In a four-person family, for example, there are 11 groupings of family members (i.e., six dyads, four triads, and one tetrad). In addition, relations among relationships (e.g., between the couple and the parent–child system) must be taken into account, not to mention the relationships connecting the family and its subsystems with other social units (e.g., extended family, peers). These complex patterns of relationships should be kept in mind as some of the major types of relationships within the family are briefly reviewed.

3.1 Couple Relations

Because couples are the architects of the family system, the quality of their relationship greatly influences their personal well-being, couple satisfaction, and the way they handle their children—and vice versa. One way to gain a better understanding of the concomitants of the spouses' relationship quality is to analyze the communication experiences and corresponding behavior of distressed and nondistressed couples. Research clearly indicates that distressed couples can be characterized by a number of negative relationship skills (e.g., lack of active listening and self-disclosure, escalating conflict behavior, maintenance of irrational beliefs). Strained couple relationships and interparental conflict also seem to have a negative impact on childrens' personality development, especially for boys, although more prospective longitudinal studies are needed to disentangle causes and effects.

It should also be mentioned that the quality of couple relationships varies depending on the meaning that the spouses attach to their relationship. Fitzpatrick (1988), for instance, has found three marital types (i.e., traditionals, independents, and separates) that differ according to their preferred connectedness and autonomy, which in turn differentially influences their sense of marital satisfaction. More research is needed to determine the long-term developmental outcome of couple types both on the spouse and on the parent–child level.

3.2 Parent–Child Relations

The care and socialization of children are among the most important societal tasks that, to a great extent, are entrusted to the family. Theoretical models to explore the determinants, concomitants, and consequences of parenthood have increasingly become more complex by addressing not only specific parent–child interactions per se, but also by looking at contextual and systemic influences such as heredity, child temperament, the parents' personality and relationship history, couple relationship, workplace, social support, and economic resources. In addition, theoretical advances, especially using attachment and social-learning approaches, have shown some convergence concerning the development of competent behavior in children and adolescents. In summary, parents raising their children in a climate of affection

and responsiveness, using clear and explicable rules, providing developmentally enhancing and autonomy-granting environments, are more likely to have children with a positive self-concept who are emotionally stable, socially competent, well-accepted by their peers, academically successful, and intrinsically self-responsible (Belsky 1990).

However, this general developmental pattern needs to be qualified in view of the aforementioned moderating influences, thus giving each individual developmental path its very special and unique gestalt. In addition, it should be realized that these conclusions are only valid for a pattern of societal and personal values that is typical for the Western world. It has been argued that, in contrast to the West, the value system of the Eastern world is quite different, centering more on sociability, calmness, and passive contemplation. Accordingly, parental socialization practices have been shown to differ markedly from Western standards to ensure an appropriate transmission of these values.

3.3 Sibling Relations

Despite declining birthrates in industrialized countries, the sibling relationship still contributes substantially to the process of individual and family development. Beside the more structural properties of sibling constellations (i.e., spacing, distribution of sexes) and their impact on intra- and extrafamilial relationships, more fine-grained behavioral analyses have shown that differential parental treatment is strongly related to the quality of sibling relationships. Siblings who are treated differently by their parents tend to develop poorer and more conflictual relationships among themselves and also show more adaptational problems as adolescents (Dunn and Stocker 1989). This might impede the fulfillment of developmental tasks across the sibling life-cycle (e.g., caring for elderly parents, mutual support with health and financial problems). Although siblings tend to develop a closer and less competitive relationship in later life, much more knowledge is required about differential developmental paths of siblingship in a lifespan perspective.

3.4 Intergenerational Relations

With increasing life expectancies, it is becoming more probable that three or even four generations coexist. Relationships between grandparents or great-grandparents and their grandchildren or great-grandchildren are usually perceived as being rather positive by both sides. Again, differential effects seem to moderate these relationships suggesting specific systemic influences. Thus, it has been shown that, on average, grandchildren report a close relationship with their grandparents only if they also feel that the relationship between their parents and grandparents is emotionally satisfying.

However, intergenerational relations can also be less rewarding and even harmful. The experience of family violence and divorce, for example, seems to have a strong component that is transmitted from generation to generation. The work by Elder et al. (1984) is especially revealing as to the mechanisms of this intergenerational transmission process. By linking the life courses of four generations, these authors were able to demonstrate that insensitive, controlling, and hostile parenting behavior has a detrimental impact on the personality and marital relations of the offspring, which in turn leads to inadequate parenting on their part when they have children of their own. In the same vein, Rutter's (1988) work comparing the parenting behavior of home-reared and institution-reared mothers, showed that mothers who, as children, had to be placed into an institution because of their parents' severe marital discord displayed much poorer parenting, especially if the placement happened before their fourth birthday. These results accord well with increasing research evidence stemming from an attachment theoretical approach. Nevertheless, it should be noted that there are also internal and external resources (e.g., strong personal interests, support from relatives, friends, or spouses) that serve as protective factors in coping with adverse life conditions.

4. Family Intervention

Whereas the research on family–individual codevelopment reviewed so far was noninterventive in nature, there are strong pleas for more intervention-oriented approaches for studying the individual within the family. Since the advent of family therapy as a special systemic treatment method, many hopes have been placed in this approach. Although family therapy has become a more salient example of therapeutic intervention, it needs to be complemented by other nontherapeutic, albeit interventive approaches, especially family counseling, family prevention, and family policy. All four of these approaches will be briefly commented on in the following paragraphs.

4.1 Family Therapy

Family therapy is not a monolithic treatment approach. Rather there are many different models and schools expanding almost all theoretical approaches that have been used in individual therapy by adding a systemic or relationship component to the core belief system. For family therapy in its narrower sense, it is indispensable to use sound diagnostic assessment of clinically relevant individual and/or familial dysfunctions on which family treatment can be based. Depending on the preferred theoretical orientation, research evidence on effective treatment outcomes is still scarce, although in some comparative studies it was shown that family therapy was equal or even superior to other (usually individual-oriented) treatment approaches. However, more specific research on the indication,

treatment process, and outcome are clearly needed to determine their long-term impact on individual and family relations (Piercy and Sprenkle 1990).

4.2 Family Counseling

Whereas family therapy is basically aimed at therapeutic change, family counseling usually does not imply the treatment of more or less severe individual or familial dysfunctions. Instead, family counseling is a method of helping people by providing relevant information, encouraging them to clarify possible courses of action and assisting them in solving problems by themselves. Thus, family counseling is not confined only to psychosocial problems, but also extends to contexts that connect families with the outer world (e.g., school, workplace, neighborhood, and community). Although the ingredients of the counseling process such as strengthening personal and family resources or enhancing self-exploration have been shown to be beneficial for further individual and family development, more and better research on evaluation in counseling is called for.

4.3 Preventive Family Intervention

Family prevention refers to the optimization of developmental processes in nonclinical families (primary prevention) and to the prophylactic support or aftercare of high-risk families (secondary and tertiary prevention). These approaches are mainly based on providing information and imparting social skills to enhance communication and problem-solving capabilities. Research on family enrichment, divorce counseling, or families with a schizophrenic member attest to the importance and effectiveness of preventive measures for the benefit of the individual and the family alike.

4.4 Family Policy

Although at a different level, family policy is another interventive approach to helping families better cope with their lives. The quality and diversity of governmental measures taken to ensure family well-being vary greatly from country to country. Governmental intervention concerning issues such as financial transfers, support of extrafamilial child care services, parental leave, legislation on divorce, or child custody exemplifies how important family policy measures are in structuring the family's life course. It is here that the knowledge base of family psychology has much to contribute to the initiation and evaluation of programs aimed at strengthening family resources and self-regulation.

5. Conclusion

From a systemic and contextualistic point of view, it has been argued here that individual development within the family is a coevolutionary process. Elsewhere an integrative family systems model has been proposed (Schneewind 1992) that takes into account developmental stressors and resources on both a vertical axis (comprising biographically accumulated experiences) and a horizontal axis (referring to momentary and future life events). Moreover, the model relates these stressors and resources to different interconnected systems (i.e., person, couple/family, multigenerational, and extrafamilial systems). It is hoped that a conceptional framework such as this will help to instigate more interventive and noninterventive research with special emphasis on differential paths of individual development within the context of intimate relationship systems.

See also: Home Environment and School Learning

References

Belsky J 1990 Parental and nonparental child care and children's socioemotional development: A decade in review. *J. Marriage Fam.* 52(4): 885–903

Dunn J, Stocker C 1989 The significance of differences in siblings' experiences within the family. In: Kreppner K, Lerner R M (eds.) 1989

Elder G H, Liker J D, Cross C 1984 Parent–child behavior in the great depression: Life course and intergenerational influences. In: Baltes P B, Brim O G (eds.) 1984 *Lifespan Development and Behavior*, Vol. 6. Academic Press, New York

Fitzpatrick M A 1988 *Between Husbands and Wives: Communication in Marriage.* Sage, Newbury Park, California

Gelles R J, Conte J R 1990 Domestic violence and sexual abuse of children: A review of research in the eighties. *J. Marriage Fam.* 52(4): 1045–58

Piercy F P, Sprenkle D H 1990 Marriage and family therapy: A decade in review. *J. Marriage Fam.* 52(4): 1116–26

Plomin R, Rende R 1991 Human behavioral genetics. *Annu. Rev. Psychol.* 42: 161–90

Ross C E, Mirowsky J, Goldsteen K 1990 The impact of the family on health: The decade in review. *J. Marriage Fam.* 52(4): 1059–78

Rutter M 1988 Functions and consequences of relationships: Some psychopathological considerations. In: Hinde R A, Stevenson-Hinde J (eds.) 1988

Schneewind K A 1992 Familien zwischen Rhetorik und Realität: Eine familienpsychologische Perspektive. In: Schneewind K A, von Rosenstiel L (eds.) 1992 *Wandel der Familie.* Hogrefe, Göttingen

Further Reading

Booth A (ed.) 1991 *Contemporary Families: Looking Forward, Looking Back.* National Council on Family Relations, Minneapolis, Minnesota

Cowan P A, Hetherington M (eds.) 1991 *Family Transitions.* Erlbaum, Hillsdale, New Jersey

Hinde R A, Stevenson-Hinde J (eds.) 1988 *Relationships within Families: Mutual Influences.* Clarendon Press, Oxford

Kreppner K, Lerner R M (eds.) 1989 *Family Systems and Life-span Development.* Erlbaum, Hillsdale, New Jersey

Peer Relations and Development

C. F. M. Van Lieshout

A peer system refers to the interactions, relationships, and group structures involving persons in a group of nearly the same developmental level. Age level is often used as an indicator for peer status. However, in many instances age mates are not peers. For example, in most school achievement domains mentally retarded persons are not peers of intellectually normal individuals. Furthermore, age mates may not be peers in every developmental domain. In athletics physically handicapped persons are not peers of nonhandicapped individuals, although they may be peers in intellectual competence. Class groups are often homogeneous on a number of characteristics, such as age level, achievement level, learning difficulties, and so on. The goal of this entry is to describe the relevance of peer relations in school classes for children's social, emotional, and personality development.

Peer relations in schools require attention for several reasons. First, for a substantial number of children peer problems lead to long-term disturbances, such as early school dropout, delinquent behavior in adolescence, and psychopathology in adulthood (Parker and Asher 1987). There is no obvious reason for schools to restrict their mission to teaching and learning of cognitive skills. Many children are victimized by aggressive peers, and tolerance of aggression in school offers for some children systematic instruction that goals in peer relations can be achieved in an aggressive way and that peers can be involved in their aggression. Because school is usually obligatory, some theorists consider that children have a basic right not to be systematically exposed to peer aggression in school, and to learn prosocial interactive and problem-solving skills (see Olweus 1991). Second, positive peer relations facilitate instruction and learning in class and peer problems disturb these activities (Elton Report 1989). Schools have an obligation to eliminate factors that hinder children's effective learning and teachers' instruction.

Third, the class group and the school are excellent settings for the support of children and adolescents with peer problems.

It is estimated that 10 to 20 percent of all children are chronically rejected, isolated, or victimized by others or suffer major repercussions from their own aggressive behavior and from bullying others (see Newcomb et al. 1993, Olweus 1991). Although similar percentages are found in studies in several Western countries and Japan, numbers in individual groups may differ considerably. A more accurate estimate of this general percentage is hard to make because some of these behavioral problems overlap. In addition, this percentage may vary from study to study depending on assessment methods and the composition of investigated groups.

1. Peer Competence and the Peer System

In a conceptual framework for the understanding of social relationships in groups, Hinde (1976) has distinguished three hierarchic levels: interactions, relationships, and group structure. Interactions between individuals are seen as basic elements for social relationships. Relationships are the basis for group structure. Description of an interaction requires specification of the content, that is, what individuals are doing together (e.g., A does X to B and B responds with Y), and the quality of an interaction. An essential aspect of the quality of an interaction is its valence. Whether an interaction is positive/prosocial or negative/antisocial is an important determinant of the meaning of an interaction for a relationship. However, existing relationships also affect the quality of specific interactions. For example, a mutual friendship or enemy relationship determines whether a child eventually considers a harsh or even painful competition as positive or as negative. Relationships involve a succession of interactions between two individuals. Description of a relationship requires specification of the content and quality of the interactions as well as their patterns with respect to each other and over time. Mutual friendships (Hartup 1992) and a bully/victim relationship (Olweus 1991) are examples of influential types of relationship in school classes. However, numerous spontaneous and organized, short- and long-term relationships may be distinguished in a class group. They may concern curricular activities, such as peer teaching, as well as extracurricular domains, for example, sports or class play. The group structure is to be described by the nature, quality, and patterning of relationships. Patterns of relationships determine the structure of the group but are, in turn, influenced by group dynamics resulting from explicit or implicit group goals and norms or from subgroup coalitions (see Hartup 1983).

The peer system in a class does not operate in a vacuum. Children in a class also interact with teachers. Different compositions of school classes in secondary schools may result in shifting peer systems. Furthermore, children participate in relationships and groups outside school. Finally, children have their longest and most influential relationships with their parents and siblings at home. All these relationships, especially the latter, affect children's peer interactions and relationships in class.

The quality of children's peer behavior is reflected by peer competence. Peer competence can be defined as children's ability to affect interpersonal outcomes or goals, taking into account the frame of reference of other peer group members (see Renshaw and Asher 1982). In positive or prosocial interactions children are able to take into account their partners' interests in pursuing their own goals. In negative or antisocial interactions children pursue their own goals without considering those of their partners or even at the cost of their partners' interest. The first are instances of prosocial behavior, the second of aggression. Peer competence reflects several different component capacities, such as social encoding and information-processing skills, social interactive skills, affective responding, and children's social motives. During sequences of social interactions these capacities are used over and over very rapidly in real time and often at a nonconscious level (see Dodge 1986). Deficiencies in peer competence may result from deficiencies in each of these component capacities. For example, when children misinterpret their partners' intentions, motives, and affective states or when they do not evaluate the potential consequences of their actions, peer competence may be low.

2. Assessment

Relationships and group structure in peer groups are assessed using sociometric procedures. In sociometric procedures, group members evaluate each other on one or more criteria, resulting in received scores for each group member on each criteria. Since the early 1980s two-dimensional sociometric models have been used for classification of group members in five sociometric status groups: popular, rejected, neglected, controversial, and average sociometric status. Sociometric status classification involves several steps.

First, the number of "most liked" and "least liked" nominations each child in a group receives are used to derive scores for acceptance and rejection. Second, two independent dimensions are constructed: social impact, as the sum of acceptance plus rejection nominations, and social preference as the result of acceptance minus rejection nominations. Social impact or social visibility is a measure of social salience or the relative degree that children are noticed by their peers, either as liked or as disliked. Social preference or likability reflects the relative extent to which children are liked or disliked by their peers. Third, children are assigned to sociometric groups. Popular children have high acceptance and low rejection scores, rejected children have high rejection and low acceptance scores, neglected children have low impact, and controversial children have high impact scores. Other children have an average status; they have intermediate scores on acceptance and rejection as well as on social preference and social impact. Two different procedures are used: the standard score model is based on standardized scores (Coie et al. 1982) and the probability model is based on binomial probability theory (Newcomb and Bukowski 1983). Both methods have highly similar psychometric performance characteristics and result in convergent classifications. Both methods tend to identify about 15 percent popular, 15 percent rejected, 10 percent neglected, 5 percent controversial, and 55 percent average children. These percentages may vary from group to group depending on group composition and group atmosphere.

Assessment of peer competence can be derived from several sources, such as self and peer evaluations, parent or teacher judgments, observations of children's interactive behavior, assessments of children's social cognitions, and so on. These assessments are typically related, with correlations between 0.30 and 0.40. There are several reasons for such moderate interrelations (see Newcomb et al. 1993). First, the accessibility of each of these informants sources to peer relations varies. Second, the informants sources are constrained by potential cognitive biases and limitations. Third, the nature of the relationship with a child leads to different interests in evaluating children's peer behavior. For example, teachers' evaluations reflect their primary interest in instruction and learning and effective class group management. Parents' evaluations reflect their affective–emotional relationship with their children and children's self evaluations reflect their private feelings and experiences with classmates. Such experiences and feelings are often inaccessible to others. Therefore, depending on assessment purposes, a specific informant has to be used or different perspectives from several informants have to be considered.

3. Sociometric Status, Peer Competence, and Developmental Pathways

In a meta-analysis of 41 studies, Newcomb et al. (1993) investigated sociometric group differences on several aspects of aggression, sociability, withdrawal, and academic/intellectual ability. Information was moderately consistent over four different sources: observation, and peer, adult, and self reports. Popular children are most liked by peers and best friends, and show higher levels of sociability and cognitive abilities and lower levels of aggression and withdrawal. They have the social abilities to achieve interpersonal goals and to maintain positive relationships. Although

popular children are able to be assertive/aggressive, their behavioral repertoire primarily leads to positive social outcomes for themselves and for others and they score low on measures of general aggression, negative affect, and disruption. Rejected children provide a nearly polar opposite to the behavior patterns of popular children. They are more aggressive and withdrawn and less sociable and cognitively skilled than average children. In contrast to controversial children, who have the highest level of aggressive behavior, rejected children lack positive qualities that balance out their aggressive behavior. Rejected children are at risk in their social development.

Controversial children represent a combination of characteristics found among rejected and popular children. They compensate for their high level of aggressive behavior with significantly better cognitive and social abilities. Neglected children also experience some adjustment difficulties. They have been found to be less aggressive and exhibit less sociability. They are not more withdrawn. However, the lack of stability of the neglected status classification and the limited extent and magnitude of behavioral problems do not make them an at-risk group. They seem to opt for a lower level of involvement in the peer group and they do not experience depression. Extensive involvement in the peer group does not seem to be a developmental necessity. Neglected children often have a reciprocal best friend and, in general, they have average friendship skills (Newcomb et al. 1993).

A growing number of longitudinal studies provide support for at least four developmental pathways by which early peer relationships and peer competence are related to later personality development. First, the behavioral repertoire of popular children is primarily made up of socially skilled behaviors that also lead to positive social outcomes in the long run. These children sustain stable peer relationships and friendships that are mutually beneficial. Friendships provide several functions for children, involving (a) emotional resources, both for "having fun" and adapting to stress; (b) cognitive resources both for problem-solving and knowledge acquisition; (c) contexts in which basic social skills are acquired and elaborated (e.g., social communication, cooperation, and group entry skills); and (d) forerunners of subsequent relationships (Hartup 1992). Social skills and friendships that protect popular children against social–emotional adjustment problems are similarly beneficial for the majority of average and neglected children. There are no data for the small group of controversial children to indicate whether their aggressive behavior makes them an at-risk group in the long run, or whether they are protected by their social and cognitive abilities. Those skills enable them to initiate aggressive group behavior, to profit from it, and to avoid negative consequences.

The second and third pathway concern rejected children. Cillessen et al. 1992 suggest that the rejected status group is not homogeneous. Nearly half of the rejected children, especially boys, are also aggressive children; a smaller but substantial subgroup, more often girls, show high levels of withdrawal; and a third subgroup is not very deviant from average status. Patterson et al. (1989) have specified the developmental pathway of aggressive rejected children (the second pathway). In early childhood, ineffective parenting practices with temperamentally difficult or irritable infants may lead to childhood conduct disorders. In elementary school, the conduct-disordered behaviors lead to academic failure, peer rejection, and low self-esteem. These failures lead, during adolescence, to increased risk for depressive mood and involvement in a deviant peer group. Finally, these adolescents are at high risk for engaging in chronic delinquent behavior.

The third developmental pathway concerns children who are consistently rejected, avoided, and excluded from peer interactions but who are not very aggressive. Chronic rejection, paired with high levels of withdrawal and low social and cognitive abilities may lead to feelings of loneliness and symptoms of depression.

A fourth developmental pathway concerns a mixed group of children, especially early adolescents, who as a consequence of contextual circumstances or as a result of risk-taking behavior temporarily or for a longer period of time experience behavior problems such as drug use, concomitant problems in school, and delinquent behavior (see Loeber 1988).

4. Intervention and Treatment Programs

Numerous treatment programs have been developed, although most of them have been limited in scope and in time, in theoretical background, and in setting. For example, specific behavioral or social–cognitive responses have been trained during a few weeks or months outside the class or home in child-focused approaches. Although such programs have often been effective, they do not provide adequate long-term maintenance of improvement. Peer problems often have functional meaning for children and are not restricted to a single setting of school, home, or peer group. A child who is aggressive toward peers is often also aggressive at home and toward teachers. Treatments are only effective when they use multiple methods, aim at clearly specified but broad behavioral domains, and are maintained across settings for a long period of time. Therefore, the introduction of treatment programs in schools requires extensive preparation.

First, clearly specified socioemotional goals and outcome expectancies have to be formulated and adopted by individual teachers and teacher teams, by school authorities and, eventually, by parents and class groups. Adoption of such goals by the school district facilitates availability of teacher training and guidance services in the district. Second, a long-term assessment program has to be adopted with specific screening and assessment procedures involving multiple information sources such as teacher, peer, and parental evaluations and self-reports. Initial assessments estimate the extent of peer problems; later assessments control maintenance of improvement may have a preventive signaling function for individual children. Third, treatments should involve individual children, their parents, the class group, and the parents as a group. Treatment should be directed at separate interactions, enhance peer and teacher–child relationships, and support the class group structure. Programs should be supported by the school and continue over children's school career. Fourth, teachers should be given training in appropriate effective child and class group management skills and be able to communicate openly and effectively with individual parents and parents as a group. Fifth, programs have to be based on three components of social support: (a) nurturant and warm working relations and avoidance of hostility; (b) coregulation of behavior, that is, clear rules and limit setting balanced with respect for autonomy; and (c) open communication and avoidance of misleading information. Warm working relations and avoidance of hostility have to be fostered among children in class, between teachers and children, between teachers and parents, and within the teacher team. Clear and acceptable rules and limits to unacceptable behavior are paired with respect for autonomy, and fostering self-control, that is self-goal setting, self-monitoring, and self-reinforcement for individual children as well as group control in terms of group goal setting, group monitoring, and group reinforcement for the class. Working relations and responsibilities for parents, teachers, and schools should be clearly defined and mutually supporting. Schools have to consider, and should know how to deal with, adverse effects of parents' personal problems, such as low self-esteem, parental depression and other psychopathology, marital discord, and effects of delinquency and drug use. Open communication and avoidance of misleading information should be maintained within the team, between teachers and children and the class, and with individual parents and parents as a group.

In Europe two national programs have been proposed. In England and Wales the Elton Report (1989) focused on discipline in schools and recommended numerous activities congruent with the ones proposed here. However, by the end of 1992 proposals had not yet been systematically introduced in schools. In Norway a national campaign against bully/victim problems in schools has resulted in substantial immediate and long-term reduction of bully/victim problems and of general antisocial behavior (e.g., vandalism), as well as in increasing student satisfaction with school life (Olweus 1991).

See also: Social Development; Development and Socialization of Aggression; Individual Differences and Instruction

References

Cillessen A H N, Van Ijzendoorn H W, Van Lieshout C F M, Hartup W W 1992 Heterogeneity among peer rejected boys: Subtypes and stabilities. *Child Dev.* 63: 893–905

Coie J D, Dodge K A, Coppotelli H 1982 Dimensions and types of social status: A cross-age perspective. *Dev. Psychol.* 18(4): 557–70

Dodge K A 1986 A social information-processing model of social competence in children. In: Perlmutter M (ed.) 1986 *Minnesota Symposia on Child Psychology*, Vol 18. Erlbaum, Hillsdale, New Jersey

Elton Report 1989 *Discipline in Schools: Report of the Committee of Inquiry.* HMSO, London

Hartup W W 1983 Peer relations. In: Mussen P H (ed.) 1983 *Handbook of Child Psychology: Vol.4 Socialization, Personality, and Social Development.* Wiley, New York

Hartup W W 1992 Friendships and their developmental significance. In: McGurk H (ed.) 1992 *Contemporary Perspectives.* Erlbaum, Hove

Hinde R A 1976 Interactions, relationships, and social structure. *Man* 11: 1–17

Loeber R 1988 Natural histories of conduct problems, delinquency and associated substance use. Evidence for developmental progression. In: Lahey B B, Kazdin A E (eds.) 1988 *Advances in Clinical Child Psychology*, Vol. 11. Plenum Press, New York

Newcomb A F, Bukowski W M 1983 Social impact and social preference as determinants of children's peer group status. *Dev. Psych.* 19(6): 856–67

Newcomb A, Bukowski W M, Pattee L 1993 Children's peer relations: A meta-analytic review of popular, rejected, neglected, controversial, and average sociometric status. *Psych. Bull.* 113: 99–128

Olweus D 1991 Bully/victim problems among school children: Basic facts and effects of a school based intervention program. In: Pepler D J, Rubin K H (eds.) 1991

Parker J G, Asher S R 1987 Peer relations and later personal adjustment: Are low-accepted children at risk? *Psych. Bull.* 102(3): 357–89

Patterson G R, DeBarsyshe B D, Ramsey E 1989 A developmental perspective on antisocial behavior. *Am. Psychol.* 44(2): 329–35

Renshaw P D, Asher S R 1982 Social competence and peer status: The distinction between goals and strategies. In: Rubin K H, Ross H S (eds.) 1982 *Peer Relationships and Social skills in Childhood.* Springer Verlag, New York

Further Reading

Asher S R, Coie J D 1990 *Peer Rejection in Childhood*, Cambridge University Press, Cambridge

Berndt T J, Ladd G W (eds.) 1989 *Peer Relationships in Child Development.* Wiley, New York

Hartup W W 1970 Peer interaction and social organization. In: Mussen P H (ed.) 1970 *Carmichael's Manual of Child Psychology*, Vol. 2. Wiley, New York

Pepler D J, Rubin K H (eds.) 1991 *The Development and Treatment of Childhood Aggression.* Erlbaum, Hillsdale, New Jersey

Problems and Crises in Human Development

L. Montada

Most problems in human development belong to one of three categories: (a) a desired or prescribed goal cannot be reached by using well-established routines, and new solutions, new insights, new skills, or new knowledge are required; (b) goals that have been pursued must be abandoned because of losses, failures, or constraints, and alternative goals must be chosen or established; and (c) two goals are incompatible and a decision that the less favored goal has to be abandoned is required. In short, many developmental problems can be conceptualized as discrepancies or incompatibilities between goals, opportunities, demands, capacities, and resources. A special case is the lack of or loss of goals to motivate commitments. The concept of "crisis" is used when a person is not easily able or prepared to do what is required in a situation, but is also emotionally affected by the existing problem.

Developmental problems and crises are those that affect a person's life-course and life plans. These problems or crises are frequently remembered as major challenges or turning points, or as traumatic events that demand a readjustment, perhaps requiring new goal decisions, the reorganization of life plans, the acquisition of new competencies, or a change of the self-concept and of views about the world. The changes may result in developmental gains or in disorders. Gains are expected to result from the mastery of problems and crises. It is a common idea that major changes and growth in human development result from struggling with problems and crises and that a new level of intellectual, social, and personal organization will be gained by overcoming them.

Most of the relevant knowledge is documented in the literature concerning developmental tasks, normative life crises, and critical life events. While the sequence of developmental tasks is conceived of as being more or less age normative (i.e., a majority of individuals in a population are confronted with the same class of tasks within a specific period of life), critical life events occur more or less incidentally or accidentally at various points within a lifetime, although they may have a decisive impact on future life and development.

1. Age-normative Crises and Tasks

1.1 Stage Models

Stage models of human development usually entail the metaphor of a crisis of transition from one level to the next, with the transition triggered by problems or conflicts that cannot be solved at the lower stage. The organismic assumption is that problems result from universal maturational or developmental changes within the organism allowing new cognitions, experiences, and interactions. Piaget's stages of cognitive development in 1970 and Freud's sequence of psychosexual conflicts in childhood and adolescence (Freud 1938) are classic examples. In contrast, in dialectic, interactional, or transactional approaches, both the subjects and the various life contexts contribute to the generation and solution of problems and crises, and, because both subjects and contexts exhibit large differences and are continuously changing, neither a universal sequence of problems nor a universal sequence of outcomes is expected.

Erikson's theory of personality development (1968) is a prominent example of the organismic tradition. There are eight major stages throughout the life-course, each characterized by a specific conflict or crisis. The central issues of the crises or the stage-specific conflicts are trust versus mistrust (first year of life), autonomy versus shame and doubt (third year), initiative versus guilt (fourth and fifth year), industry versus inferiority (middle childhood), identity versus role diffusion (adolescence), intimacy versus isolation (early adulthood), generativity versus stagnation (middle adulthood), and ego integrity versus despair (later adulthood). The crisis in adolescence concerning the issue of identity versus role diffusion is well-known. The adolescent has to build up facets of a self concerned with gender, familial background, religion, moral values, educational and professional aspirations and capacities, political attitudes, and so forth and to integrate them into a consistent personal identity. Failures to construct an identity result in "role diffusion," characterized by an imbalance of attitudes and values, goal instability, and sometimes ideological one-sidedness, unrealistic expectations, superficial and unstable commitments, or drug abuse. Failure to master the stage-typical crises results in lasting personality disorders. The postulated universality of these stages is, however, open to question.

1.2 Developmental Tasks

Like Erikson, Havighurst structured the life-course along a sequence of problems that he labeled developmental tasks. However, he adopted a more explicit dialectical perspective, bridging biological, sociological, and psychological approaches. Taxonomies list numerous specific developmental tasks in each life period that may be subsumed under some general concerns like "making the most of disengagement" in the seventh decade. Developmental tasks for the elderly, for instance, are mastering retirement from professional roles, health problems, or loss of partners, and accepting one's own life history, a decline in physical and mental abilities, and the finiteness of human life.

Havighurst's sequence of developmental tasks was considered widespread in Western societies. There are other tasks that are not statistically normal and age bound, which, nevertheless, may have a decisive influence on the future course of life. In fact, in life retrospectives focusing on major turning points, milestones, transitions, and stressful or traumatic experiences, the postulated age-normative tasks and crises do not constitute the majority of reported memories (Thomae and Lehr 1986).

Havighurst (1972) suggested three broad sources of developmental tasks throughout the life course: biological changes within the organism such as puberty and menopause, tasks set by society (e.g., in education and professional life), and values, aspirations, and goals of the developing individual. For instance, upward mobility depends on biological factors such as mental and physical health; on psychological factors such as individual aspirations, capacities, and education; on social context factors such as job aspirations of the family; on societal factors such as availability of occupational positions, possibly affirmative actions for hitherto underpriviledged subpopulations; and on cultural factors such as the general valuation of upward mobility or informal normative constraints for subpopulations. Thus, the chances for optimal development may vary considerably between birth cohorts, families, and individuals.

This is the view of modern conceptions of human development (e.g., Lifespan Developmental Psychology, see Baltes et al. 1980) that use interactional models and postulate reciprocal influences between individuals, members of social networks, and cultural and societal opportunities, demands, and resources, and assume that subjects are active agents in their own development who have long-term commitments, and select goals, settings, and contexts. Development is expected to take differential and individual trajectories. One example of the differential impact of the same context conditions illustrates this conception. According to Elder's studies, the Great Depression of the 1930s had greatly varying effects on children depending on their age. For younger children of unemployed fathers the experience of familial conflict and poor parenting caused by the economic problems had long-lasting negative effects on personality and achievement. For the adolescent sons, however, this was an opportunity to assume some responsibility for the support of the family and the experience had long-lasting positive effects on their personality, and social and professional development (Elder 1974).

2. Critical Life Events

Events such as the birth of a sibling; parents' divorce; moving to another school or residence; marriage; becoming a parent; getting, changing, or losing a job; serious health problems; becoming a victim of crime; the death of a close one; accidents; a natural catastrophe; or economic losses are breaks in the course of life that require (or permit) changes in roles, goals, or the organization of one's life, and that quite frequently lead to the acquisition of new abilities, knowledge, attitudes, or affiliations. Such events generate problems, which either constitute challenges for growth or risks of maladjustment and disorders.

A broad range of criteria have been used to assess the consequences of critical life events and of struggling with their associated problems. The risk of pathogenetic stress that resulted in mental or psychosomatic illness has been investigated from a clinical perspective. Effect variables such as negative emotions (e.g., strong fears following traumatic threats, resentment toward a victimizer, or mourning following bereavement), loss of self-esteem and help-lessness following failure, loss of interpersonal trust following betrayal, and loss of belief in a just world following uncompensated and unpunished victimization are specific types of problems. The continuation of these effects for a prolonged period of time is an indicator of impaired mental health or personality disorder. Developmental gains may include a positive self-concept including self-efficacy, acquired belief in one's own invulnerability, the capacity to cope with loss, and various problem-solving strategies and skills.

Early research was focused on the impact of critical life events on mental and physical health. The hypothesis was—in analogy to the stress concept—that the number and amount of life changes caused by an event would be the most important risk factor. Therefore, an accumulation of events was expected to increase the risk of failing to solve the multiple associated problems. After extensive research through the 1970s and 1980s it became evident that for the population as a whole, the impact of events is not as large as was expected and explains no more than 10 percent of the variance of health scores and mortality. Whereas most people recover and adjust quite quickly after having experienced a critical event, some do not. This has been shown for a variety of event types, even including the death of a close one, serious injuries, and illnesses. Research is required to identify the factors that explain or predict both successful problem-solving and adjustment and failures to adjust adequately. Specifically, can dimensions be identified along which an event risk varies? Are strategies and interventions available to prevent poor adjustment? What are the major differences between people who show good and poor adjustment?

2.1 Relevant Dimensions of Events

The hedonistic value of events varies considerably. Some events are generally experienced as desirable (e.g., marriage, birth of a child, getting a job), others as undesirable, implying adversity or losses. However, the evaluation of the same class of events typically varies among individuals. The birth of a child, for instance, might be a burden for some, interfering with a professional career; the death of a spouse might mean liberation for some; injuries and illness might serve as an excuse for professional failure or as an atonement for guilt. What is relevant is the subjective valuation, not the normative one. Life changes that are caused by an event may be more or less appreciated, taken for granted, regretted, resented, or hated. Negative effects are more likely with negatively valued changes. The extent of change per se is not necessarily distressing, but may, instead, be challenging.

A significant factor is how many members of a population are confronted with a critical event. If many members of a population are affected, as is the case with some historically graded events such as major economic depressions, wars, or natural or technical catastrophes, the psychological and social experience is different from cases where only single individuals are affected, such as accidents, criminal victimizations, or bereavements. Problems and losses that are widespread within a population are presumably less likely to be perceived as unjust, society is more inclined to respond with sympathy to victims and to provide support, and negative social reactions are less probable because ascriptions of responsibility to victims are less likely. For the same reasons, transitions (such as pregnancy, retirement, marriage) which are "in-time" (that is, within the normal age range) are easier to cope with than "off-time" transitions that bear a higher risk of social critique and subjective shame.

2.2 Subjective Interpretations

The psychological impact of events is largely derived from their subjective interpretation. For instance, the impact of becoming physically handicapped as a result of an event varies widely depending on subjective views of the event. Two categories of interpretation are particularly relevant: (a) attributions of causation and responsibility, and (b) views about the meaning.

For instance, the distress caused by serious injury depends a good deal on whether it was considered to be caused by natural processes, to be simply one's fate, to be caused by a responsible agent, or to be personally caused. These different views elicit different emotional responses: guilt if the subject feels personally responsible, outrage if others are responsible. In many cases, victims may ascribe some causal responsibilities to themselves which might help them to avoid feelings of resentment against others and feelings of helplessness or lack of control in similar situations. For some victims it might be easier to find an emotional balance if nobody is to blame, because the injury is viewed simply as the result of bad luck.

Yet this is not true for all those who consider the question "Why me?". They are searching for meaning, explanations, or responsibilities. Bad luck makes the injury meaningless, and undeserved bad luck undermines their belief in a just and controllable world. Injuries resulting from intentional attacks, a suicide attempt, or risky adventures are not meaningless because reasoned actions which resulted in the injury can be perceived. A second category of meaning may be found in positive consequences of events such as the experience of mastering serious problems, the experience of solidarity by members of a social network, or the reordering of life priorities. The search for meaning, and explanations and attributions of responsibility, can be considered as ways of coping with an event and with associated problems.

2.3 Ways of Coping

Research on coping has identified a variety of ways to deal with adversity, for instance, ruminations about threats and losses, positive illusions about the future, palliative views (such as "downward" comparisons with those who are still worse off, minimization of problems, positive illusions about the future), seeking help and support, efforts to find concrete solutions for problems, and so on.

The various ways of dealing with problems are not uniform in their effectiveness; rather, the effectiveness depends on the particular case, perhaps with the exception that continuous contemplation neither solves the problem nor changes its perception, but merely stabilizes the awareness of adversity. Moreover, continuing to ruminate will frequently reduce the readiness of social network members to extend social support.

Palliative views reduce negative emotions such as fear, resentment, and depression. They seem to be a good choice for instances such as illnesses where a realistic appraisal is neither helpful in solving the problem nor in avoiding further negative consequences. There are, however, cases when a realistic appraisal is needed to motivate decisions which might be adequate to solve the problem (e.g., in the case of unemployment by either applying for jobs or starting a training for a new career).

Constructive problem-solving is widely considered to be the ideal coping strategy. This may be true in cases when problems can be solved without exhausting all resources, without interfering with other important goals, without producing strain, and without bearing the risk of side-effects. In some cases a better strategy may be to accept losses, or to reorganize goal priorities to make them fit the opportunities, capacities, and resources. Brandtstädter and Renner (1992)

made an important distinction between tenacious goal pursuit and goal accommodation. They found that elderly people who used an accommodative strategy in coping with age-bound losses had less depressive symptoms than those using a goal pursuit that might eventually fail.

2.4 Protective Factors

Research on the issue of critical events has addressed the question of whether vulnerability or protective factors exist beyond effective ways of coping. This research has identified biological, psychological, and sociological factors.

On a psychobiological level is Dienstbier's concept of toughness. Toughness can be trained (e.g., by aerobic training or by engaging in a reasonable number of challenging tasks). "Toughening up" means a relative strengthening of the "softer" peripheral catecholamine-bound arousal system as compared to the more "aggressive" central cortisol-bound arousal system. Toughened individuals are therefore better equipped to meet stressors without undue physiological arousal (Dienstbier 1992).

On the psychological level, traitlike personality features like Kobasa's concept of hardiness (Kobasa 1982), as well as the experience-based confidence to cope with critical situations, are noteworthy, as are self-efficacy or internal control beliefs and a broad repertoire of possible approaches to problems.

On the social level, a large body of research suggests that social support is a protective factor and negative social reactions are risk factors. Received social support is helpful in many cases, but can also interfere with the development of self-efficacy and competence in problem-solving. While the effects of social support are not always positive, the effects of negative social reactions like derogating and blaming victims constitute secondary problems and are consistently related to maladjustment.

3. Implications for Education and Counseling

Taking an interactional perspective implies taking several possible sources of the generation of problems and crises into account: individuals with their goals, aspirations, and abilities; social networks with their aspirations, normative constraints, and resources; and society with its demands, opportunities, and subserviences. Problems are constituted as incongruencies and incompatibilities between goals, aspirations, demands, resources, and so on. Consequently, the prevention or the solution of problems may take different approaches, focusing on different sources. The choice of an approach in actual cases depends not only on its feasibility but, within an educational perspective, has to be based on criteria for optimal development. Priority should be given to approaches that give individuals opportunities to build up abilities, protective traits, and convictions that will help them to cope better with future problems and crises (see *Student Counseling*). The experience of mastering crises may strengthen confidence in self-efficacy. Building up a repertoire of coping strategies and of rules for adequately using them in different situations may contribute to stress immunization. Since the life-course may be conceived of as a series of problems it seems appropriate to perceive every problem (from daily hassles to big losses) as a potential challenge and an occasion for learning and gaining new insights.

See also: Development of Learning across the Lifespan

References

Baltes P B, Reese H W, Lipsitt L P 1980 Life-span Developmental Psychology. *Annu. Rev. Psychol.* 31: 65–110

Brandtstädter J, Renner G 1992 Coping with discrepancies between aspirations and achievements in adult development: A dual process model. In: Montada L, Filipp S H, Lerner M J (eds.) 1992 *Life Crises and Experiences of Loss in Adulthood.* Erlbaum, Hillsdale, New Jersey

Dienstbier R A 1992 Mutual impact of toughening on crises and losses. In: Montada L, Filipp S H, Lerner M J (eds.) 1992

Elder G H Jr 1974 *Children of the Great Depression.* University of Chicago Press, Chicago, Illinois

Erikson E H 1968 *Identity, Youth and Crises.* Norton, New York

Freud S 1938 *Abriss der Psychoanalyse.* Fischer, Frankfurt

Havighurst R J 1972 *Developmental Task and Education.* McKay, New York

Kobasa S C 1982 Commitment and coping in stress resistance among lawyers. *J. Pers. Soc. Psychol.* 42: 707–17

Thomae H, Lehr U 1986 Stages, crises, and life span development. In: Sorensen A B, Weinert F E, Sherrod L R (eds.) 1986 *Human Development and the Life Course.* Multidisciplinary Perspectives. Erlbaum, Hillsdale, New Jersey

Further Reading

Brandtstädter J, Gräser H (eds.) 1983 *Entwicklungsberatung.* Hogrefe, Göttingen

Datan N, Ginsberg L H (eds.) 1975 *Life Span Developmental Psychology, Normative Life Crises.* Academic Press, New York

Filipp S H (ed.) 1990 *Kritische Lebensereignisse.* Psychologie Verlags Union, Munich

Fisher S, Reason J (eds.) 1988 *Handbook of Life Stress, Cognition and Health.* Wiley, New York

Kessler R C, Price R H, Wortman C B 1985 Social Factors in Psychopathology: Stress, Social Support, and Coping Processes. *Annu. Rev. Psychol.* 36: 531–72

Montada L, Filipp S H, Lerner M J (eds.)1992 *Life Crises and Experiences of Loss in Adulthood.* Erlbaum, Hillsdale, New Jersey

Cognitive Development

An Overview of Cognitive Development

J. Perner

Cognitive development has traditionally been understood as the study of how cognition develops, where cognition is conceived of as one part within the tripartite division of the mind into cognition, conation, and affection. The field has been dominated since its inception by Piaget's theory. However, growing dissatisfaction with Piaget's methods, in particular by Anglo-American experimentalists, led to increasing assimilation of the field to the information-processing paradigm of cognitive psychology. This brought about great improvements in experimental control for alternative determinants of children's performance on Piagetian tasks, for example, memory limitations and communication problems between experimenter and child (Donaldson 1978). It also brought clearer formulation of and greater precision in identifying the mental structures underlying children's problem-solving strategies. Also, disenchantment with the deductive intractability of Piaget's fundamental developmental concepts (e.g., assimilation and accommodation) led to attempts to make these notions more precise within computer models of cognitive change (Klahr 1984).

Despite these advances Piaget remains influential in the early 1990s in at least two respects. Most cognitive developmentalists are still investigating the developmental phenomena that Piaget discovered, and the deeper problems that he raised remain unsolved. Although becoming a subdiscipline of cognitive psychology brought better methods and better conceptual tools for studying cognition, it did not provide a cogent alternative to Piaget in accounting for development. The reason for this failure is related to the foundational problems of cognitive science at large, which are under debate by philosophers of mind and cognitive scientists, and which are fueled by controversy between the traditional symbolic account of cognition and the new connectionist paradigm.

1. Concept Acquisition

One of the most serious problems of cognitive science in the late twentieth century is the inability to explain how concepts can be acquired. An important theoretical approach to solving some of these problems is the idea that the mind is like a computer program. This is the governing idea behind Fodor's (1975) proposal of a "language of thought." Of course, the proposal is not that human thoughts are exactly like language but that they share some of the critical properties of languages. One of these properties is *compositionality*, by which the meaning of complex expressions (sentences) are systematically related to the meaning of its component expressions (e.g., words). This is a crucial property because without it, it is difficult to see how people could know the meaning of an infinite variety of sentences. Compositionality explains this because it is necessary to learn only the meaning of a finite set of words and rules of composition and with that the meaning of all possible, meaningful sentences can be constructed.

This approach is now known as the "classical view," in which a set of basic symbolic expressions are combined into new and complex expressions. There is a severe developmental limitation inherent in this view because it can account for knowledge change only in terms of a change in combinations of basic, preformed expressions. In other words, learning is conceived as the formation of mental sentences out of a given mental vocabulary (basic concepts). Since the starting point is a given vocabulary, traditional cognitive science finds it difficult to explain where that basic vocabulary comes from. The traditional empiricist answer to this, as demonstrated in the concept formation experiments pioneered by Ach (1925) and known to developmental psychologists through Vygotsky (1965), is that concepts (corresponding to all the words in a dictionary) can be decomposed into perceptual features. However, attempts to flesh out this theory (e.g., Miller and Johnson-Laird 1976) and to design concept-learning computer programs were largely unconvincing (e.g., Winston 1975). Fodor explains that lack of success.

Fodor (1981) argued that because attempts to give definitions have persistently met with failure for the vast majority of words to be found in the dictionary, all these words must reflect basic concepts; that is, concepts that cannot be reduced to a much smaller set of just a few basic perceptual concepts. Furthermore, since there is no conceivable explanation within the framework of cognitive science of how basic concepts could be acquired, he concludes that they must be innately given. Experience is required only in order to trigger these preformed concepts.

These are not philosophers' esoteric ideas. Rather they bring into the open the tacit assumptions underlying most post-Piagetian research in cognitive development. This research, therefore, stands in this respect in contrast to Piaget's theory which is centrally based on the emergence of new concepts through the organism's interaction with its environment. Take Piaget and Inhelder's (1974) conservation experiments. For Piaget, the ability to conserve quantity over changing perceptual appearances signals the construction of a genuinely new form (concept) of quantity out of an older, more primitive one. There has been much research on this topic but without providing an alternative explanation of how these conceptual changes occur. Rather, the more outstanding research results are based on smarter, more child-adequate methods, so that one could demonstrate earlier correct performance on conservation tasks than described by Piaget. But these results leave open the question as to when these concepts are acquired. The implicit message, though, is that smarter experimenters will devise even smarter experiments to demonstrate understanding of quantity invariance at ever younger ages until the neonate stage is reached. In a word, this research tradition tacitly assumes that knowledge is really innately specified.

Moreover, the main theoretical proposals for the observed improvement with age on Piaget's original tasks have—as far as concepts are concerned—a nativist flavor, since these theories are silent on the origin of concepts. The existence of requisite concepts seems to be tacitly assumed and the young child's failure on diagnostic tasks is purported to be explained in terms of an inability to apply these concepts due to insufficient memory or information-processing limitations (Pascual-Leone 1970, Case 1978). Thus it seems ironic that Pascual-Leone and Case describe their theories as "neo-Piagetian," when from the point of view of conceptual development which is close to the heart of Piagetian theory, they would be better described as "anti-Piagetian." Few researchers in this tradition have recognized this nativist implication of their research enterprise. Only more recently have infancy researchers, who have been able to demonstrate quite remarkable cognitive abilities at very early ages, argued for innateness of at least the very basic conceptual framework (Spelke 1990).

So Fodor (1981) seems to be right about cognitive development as practiced within late-twentieth-century cognitive science: it assumes—in most cases tacitly—the pre-existence of concepts. But does this mean that Fodor's nativist claim about concept acquisition

is right, or is his claim rather an indication of a flaw in the theoretical basis of cognitive science as currently practiced? Fortunately, as Samet (1986) points out, empiricists (who want to grant experience more of a role in concept acquisition) have several defences against Fodor's argument. In particular, they can deny that concept acquisition is through "learning" in the specific sense used by Fodor as rational change through testing hypotheses. Instead, it could proceed by nonrational, physical changes. Fodor considered that possibility but only in the absurd-sounding instance of being knocked on one's head. There is, however, a very popular and certainly less absurd alternative of a nonrational, physical change: connectionist learning (see Rumelhart et al. 1988, McClelland et al. 1986).

Since connectionist models give hope for genuine concept formation they might soon play an important role in cognitive development. Enthusiasm must, however, remain guarded. It is necessary to ask whether what connectionists call concepts really are concepts. For Fodor one essential feature of concepts is that they provide the basic vocabulary in a compositional symbolic system (language of thought). Fodor and Pylyshyn (1988) have argued that connectionism is not compositional and, hence, falls short of the conceptual abilities of the human mind. Connectionists have responded to this challenge. Van Gelder (1990) argues that Fodor and Pylyshyn's argument applies only to a certain version of compositionality but not to a more abstract conception of it. So, the dispute continues and it is too early to make predictions about the eventual success of connectionist theory. Consequently it is also too early to talk in terms of the educational implications of this newly opening research area.

2. Children's Theories

Connectionism may eventually only be part of an explanation of how genuine conceptual change can occur, because the concepts acquired in the connectionist models' nets reflect only statistical regularities across input patterns. In philosophy of science it has become clear that scientific concepts cannot be reduced to logical combinations of perceptual categories. The same also seems to be true for our everyday concepts. Although infants may initially base their concepts solely on perceptual similarity (Keil 1989), they soon transcend that stage and base their concepts on causal relations (Carey 1985b). When based on causal relations concepts are usually considered to be theoretical terms in a (causal) theory.

Carey (1985b) explored how children's biological concepts, such as "living thing," "animal," "baby," and so on, change as a function of children's growing understanding of how the body works. For instance, young children of 4 to 7 years have an essentially behavioral theory of internal organs (lungs are for breathing). Later, by about 10 years, they understand that organs interact for the purpose of maintaining life (metabolism). The important point is that this growth in their biological theory prompts a change in their concepts in this domain. For instance, younger children do not have a concept of "living thing" as it is usually understood. They only consider animals as "alive" in distinction to inanimate objects. Plants are, therefore, grouped with inanimate objects because on a "behavioral theory" they are more similar in distinction to animals. By age 10 this changes, because by this stage children have the theoretical prerequisite for understanding that plants and animals share the essential necessity of life sustenance.

Keil (1989) provides evidence for this view of conceptual change being tied to theory change in terms of a shift from characteristic to defining features which occurs for all domains of knowledge. For instance, kindergarten children will judge "a man of daddy's age who visits often and brings presents but is not related to your father or mother" to be an uncle but deny that status to "a 2-year old brother of your mother." From about age 7 onwards most children make the opposite judgment.

Keil interprets this shift as a consequence of the child's acquisition of the appropriate theory of kinship. In other words, the younger children pin down their concept of uncle on the surface similarities of all the typical instances of uncles that they have encountered, whereas the older children embed their concept in a theory of family relationships. In support of this interpretation, Keil reports that the shift is observed at about the same age for concepts that belong to the same theoretical domain but at different times for different domains, for example, for cooking terms the shift occurs well after the age of 9 years.

Carey (1985a) pointed out that the "theory view" of cognitive development provides an interesting compromise between two extreme views about the generality of developmental constraints. There is, on the one hand, Piaget's theory that postulates the development of completely overarching logical constraints on what children at a particular developmental stage can learn. These constraints pertain to any domain of knowledge. Unfortunately for Piagetian theory, the correlations between tasks from different domains do not bear out this prediction (e.g., Brainerd 1978). The opposite view is that children can develop any level of expertise within a particular domain if they are given enough time and opportunity to practice the relevant skills. This is exemplified in Chi's (1978) research with young chess experts. It demonstrates that there is not a uniform increase in memory capacity with age. Rather, memory depends on level of expertise, as 10-year old chess experts have a considerably better memory for chess positions, but not for other spatial patterns, than mediocre adult players.

Carey (1985a) emphasizes that the "theory view" cautions against interpreting such results to mean that children at any age can become experts in any field if they just spend enough time and effort on it. The reason for this caution is that a domain like chess is not independent from other bodies of knowledge. Each domain is based on a groundwork of more general theories. Thus there is a clear educational implication. Contrary to what Piaget's (1971) theory suggests, one can do more than wait until the child matures and reaches formal operations before he or she can become a chess master. Training on any task, whatever the domain, should be valuable at any age. However, one must not forget that for training to be successful it has to build from the bottom up and so, depending on how extensive the groundwork is before the target domain is reached, there may be a practical limit as to when a child can become a chess expert even under optimal conditions. Chess expertise is just the tip of a large iceberg of hidden knowledge, because chess is not just the moving of pieces around a board according to certain rules. To even understand the point of it children have to be able to appreciate the interpersonal motivation of the players for moving the pieces. That is, they need the foundation of what is called a "theory of mind" (Perner 1991). For instance, children need to appreciate that both their opponents and themselves want to win and that their opponents may sometimes not realize the implication of a move, and so on.

People take all this required social background knowledge for granted by the time they start to learn chess, and so are not aware that it was a necessary prerequisite for playing chess. It is well-known, however, that it takes some years before young children develop their theory of mind to the level at which they can appreciate the point of competitive games (Sodian 1991). Thus a naive approach to training may be actually harmful because premature preoccupation with chessboards may not be a good way of acquiring the prerequisite theory of mind. Putting pressure on a 1-year old to play with chess pieces may be quite counterproductive and have a quite different effect than it would have for a 6-year old who is already endowed with the necessary understanding of the opponent's mind.

All this, however, does not mean that one simply has to wait for a "theory of mind" to mature, as Leslie (1987) seems to imply. Training a theory of mind may not be an easy thing to do but there is suggestive evidence that under, as it were, permanent training conditions in conducive family conditions substantial gains can be obtained. Perner et al. (1994) found that children with two siblings achieve a particular level of performance on theory-of-mind tasks almost one year earlier than children without siblings, and Dunn et al. (1991) found that 2-year old children who show certain interaction patterns with their mothers concerning their siblings tend to do better on theory-of-mind tasks a year later.

So, to follow through with the logic of the "theory view" on the hypothetical chess training example, it appears that in principle one could produce younger and younger chess experts, but because at increasingly younger ages more and more prerequisite theories need to be built up there are severe practical limits as to what could possibly be achieved at a very young age.

3. Consciousness and the Distinction between Implicit and Explicit Knowledge

Since the 1980s there has been greater critical comment that cognitive psychology needs an account of the difference between unconscious and conscious and of related distinctions like that between *knowing how* (to do something) and *knowing that* (something is the case), procedural and declarative, inaccessible and accessible, which different theorists relate in different ways.

In the developmental literature it is primarily Karmiloff-Smith (1992) who has drawn attention to these distinctions. In an example from language development (1991), she points out that by 5 years children are competent users and interpreters of the articles "a" and "the." Their knowledge about the use of these articles is, however, purely implicit because this knowledge is entirely embedded in the procedures by which children produce and interpret articles. After the age of 5, children acquire a more explicit understanding of the conditions of use as indicated by their spontaneous corrections. This means that their knowledge cannot be purely implicit, embedded in their procedures of use, because for corrections to occur there must be explicit knowledge about the correct use by which to measure the performance of the currently executed procedure. Around 9 or 10 years, children have an even more explicit understanding, in fact, they have elaborate theories about the conditions of use. Their knowledge about these conditions is explicit in the strongest sense of being conscious and verbally expressible.

Mandler (1983) used the distinction between implicit and explicit mental representation to bring Piaget's distinction between sensorimotor intelligence and "mental representation" in line with terminology in cognitive science. More recently the distinction has found another application in an intriguing finding by Goldin-Meadow and her colleagues (e.g., Goldin-Meadow et al. 1992). They investigated the transitional phase in coming to understand Piagetian conservation tasks. Nonconservers say that when liquid is poured from a wider bowl into a thinner beaker it becomes more, because the column of the liquid in the thinner beaker is higher than in the original bowl. Conservers understand that the amount of liquid stays the same and they can justify this in view of the increase in level in the thin beaker by pointing out that this increase is compensated for by a decrease in width. What Goldin-Meadow and her colleagues discovered was that for a few months before they become conservers,

nonconservers, who fail to take width of the containers into account in their judgment of quantity and show no sign of awareness of its relevance in their verbal justifications, nevertheless start to gesture about width with their hands. It seems as if their gestures express some implicit knowledge of its relevance.

Admittedly the understanding of the nature of the distinction between implicit and explicit knowledge is far from perfect. But until the early 1980s it was still heresy in some circles to think that there was implicit, unconscious knowledge. By the early 1990s it has become an intensively researched field.

Research on implicit learning is probably of most relevance to developmental concerns because it aims at finding the basic mechanism by which implicit knowledge is acquired. This has been studied in two paradigms. Broadbent (1991) adopted a paradigm for studying complicated systems interactions to demonstrate that people can learn to control such a system without any explicit, conscious knowledge of the rules which they must be using to achieve their level of performance.

Reber (1989) studied implicit knowledge of artificial grammars. Subjects were given a list of letter strings (which had been generated by some grammar) to memorize. By letting them later sort new strings according to whether they thought they belonged to the old set or not, Reber was able to demonstrate that subjects must have abstracted the structure of the grammar, and yet his subjects were unable to describe the basis of their judgments with any degree of accuracy (i.e., no conscious, explicit awareness). The theoretical framework that grew out of this work on implicit learning of artificial grammars has been used to explain the language learning problems of dysphasic children (Weinert 1991).

The area with perhaps the most intense focus on the implicit–explicit distinction is research on memory. This also offers promising links with developmental research. For instance, Tulving (1985) proposed a threefold distinction of levels of consciousness and types of memory. Implicit or procedural memory involves no consciousness of knowing (anoetic consciousness). A paradigm example is priming experiments, for example, presentation of the word "butter" increases the probability that the word fragment "b–t–er" is completed as "butter" rather than "bitter," "butler," or "bother," without any awareness (inability to recognize or recall) that the word "butter" had been presented. The effect of presenting "butter" can be explained as an effect on the procedures that are later used in thinking of a suitable completion of the word fragment, but no explicit representation that the word "butter" had been encountered is formed. Infants' memory may be predominantly of this kind (Mandler 1983).

Tulving's second level of consciousness relates to semantic memory, which involves awareness that one knows (noetic consciousness), for example, that the word "butter" was part of a list of words. Tulving, however, distinguishes this level of consciousness from a further level of autonoetic consciousness which is required for true remembering which is accompanied by the recollective experience that, for example, one knows that "butter" was on the word list because one has experienced it being there.

Perner (1991) argued that if recollective experiences are based on the understanding that one knows something because one has experienced it then children should not have this type of memory until they can understand the origin of their knowledge. Theory of mind research indicates that children cannot do this before the age of about 4 years. And indeed, Perner and Ruffman (1995) reports a correlation between children's free recall (an indicator of episodic memory) and their ability to distinguish knowledge from lucky guesses and their understanding that senses inform about particular properties only (e.g., the eyes about color, lifting by hand about weight).

This finding illustrates the wider role that research on children's theories of mind will play in explaining how children come to reflect on their own knowledge, how they can make their implicit knowledge explicit and accessible to consciousness. Although theory-of-mind research focused initially on children's difficulty in understanding other people's minds, as it partly grew out of the Piagetian research on perspective taking, it has since become increasingly clear that there is as much for children to learn about their own minds.

The educational implications of this research can potentially be quite significant. By finding systematic ways to foster children's theory of mind there would be a way to increase their understanding of their own minds with beneficial effects on, for example, their episodic memory and, perhaps most significant, on their ability to gain self-control. As Perner (1991) speculated, the ability to conceptualize their own desires and intentions ought to be a first step towards children's ability to gain control over these internal states.

See also: Cognitive Development: Individual Differences; Cognitive Development and the Acquisition of Expertise

References

Ach N 1925 *Über die Begriffsbildung: Eine experimentelle Untersuchung zur Psychologie und Philosophie und Pädagogie.* Cälvor, Göttingen

Brainerd C J 1978 *Piaget's Theory of Intelligence.* Prentice-Hall, Englewood Cliffs, New Jersey

Broadbent D E 1991 Recall, recognition, and implicit knowledge. In: Kessen W, Ortony A, Craik F I M (eds.) 1991 *Memories, Thoughts, and Emotions: Essays in Honor of George Mandler.* Erlbaum, Hillsdale, New Jersey

Carey S 1985a Are children fundamentally different kinds of thinkers and learners than adults? In: Chipman S F, Segal J W, Glaser R (eds.) 1985 *Thinking and Learning Skills*, Vol. 2. Erlbaum, Hillsdale, New Jersey

Carey S 1985b *Conceptual Change in Childhood.* MIT Press, Cambridge, Massachusetts

Case R 1978 Intellectual development from birth to adulthood: A neo-Piagetian interpretation. In: Siegler R S (ed.) 1978 *Children's Thinking: What Develops?* Erlbaum, Hillsdale, New Jersey

Chi M T H 1978 Knowledge structures and memory development. In: Siegler R S (ed.) 1978 *Children's Thinking: What Develops?* Erlbaum, Hillsdale, New Jersey

Donaldson M 1978 *Children's Minds.* Fontana, London

Dunn J, Brown J, Slomkowski C, Tesla C, Youngblade L 1991 Young children's understanding of other people's feelings and beliefs: Individual differences and their antecedents. *Child Dev.* 62(6): 1352–66

Fodor J A 1975 *The Language of Thought.* Harvard University Press, Cambridge, Massachusetts

Fodor J A 1981 The present status of the innateness controversy. In: Fodor J A 1981 *Representations.* Harvester Press, Brighton

Fodor J A, Pylyshyn Z W 1988 Connectionism and cognitive architecture: A critical analysis. *Cog.* 28 (1–2): 3–71

Goldin-Meadow S, Alibali M W, Church R B 1992 Transition in concept acquisition: Using the hand to read the mind. Unpublished manuscript, University of Chicago, Chicago, Illinois

Karmiloff-Smith A 1991 Beyond modularity: Innate constraints and developmental change. In: Carey S, Gelman R (eds.) 1991 *The Epigenesis of Mind.* Erlbaum, Hillsdale, New Jersey

Karmiloff-Smith A 1992 *Beyond Modularity: A Developmental Perspective on Cognitive Science.* MIT Press, Cambridge, Massachusetts

Keil F C 1989 *Concepts, Kinds, and Cognitive Development.* MIT Press, Cambridge, Massachusetts

Klahr D 1984 Transition processes in quantitative development. In: Sternberg R J (ed.) 1984 *Mechanisms of Cognitive Development.* W H Freeman, New York

Leslie A M 1987 Pretense and representation: The origins of "Theory of Mind." *Psychol. Rev.* 94(4): 412–26

Mandler J M 1983 Representation. In: Flavell J H, Markman E M (eds.) 1983 *Manual of Child Psychology. Vol 3: Cognitive Development.* Wiley, New York

McClelland J L, Rumelhart D E the PDP Research Group 1986 *Parallel Distributed Processing: Explorations in the Microstructure of Cognition Vol. 2: Psychological and Biological Models.* MIT Press, Cambridge, Massachusetts

Miller G A, Johnson-Laird P N 1976 *Language and Perception.* Cambridge University Press, Cambridge

Pascual-Leone J 1970 A mathematical model for the transition rule in Piaget's developmental stages. *Acta Psychol.* 32(4): 301–45

Perner J 1991 *Understanding the Representational Mind.* MIT Press, Cambridge, Massachusetts

Perner J, Ruffman T 1995 Episodic memory and autonoetic consciousness: Developmental evidence and a theory of childhood amnesia. *Journal of Experimental Child Psychology.* 59: 516–48

Perner J, Ruffman T, Leekam S R 1994 Theory of mind is contagious; you catch it from your sibs. *Child Dev.* 64: 1224–34

Piaget J 1971 *Biology and Knowledge.* University of Chicago Press, Chicago, Illinois

Piaget J, Inhelder B 1974 *The Child's Construction of*

Quantities: Conservation and Atomism. Basic Books, New York

Reber A 1989 Implicit learning and tacit knowledge. *J. Exp. Psychol. Gen.* 118(3): 219–35

Rumelhart D E, McClelland J L, the PDP Research Group 1988 *Parallel Distributed Processing: Explorations in the Microstructure of Cognition, Vol. 1: Foundations.* MIT Press, Cambridge, Massachusetts

Samet J 1986 Troubles with Fodor's nativism. *Midwest Studies of Philosophy* 10: 575–94

Sodian B 1991 The development of deception in young children. *British Journal of Developmental Psychology* 9(1): 173–88

Spelke E S 1990 Principles of object perception. *Cognit. Sci.* 14(1): 29–56

Tulving E 1985 Memory and consciousness. *Canadian Psychology* 26(1): 1–12

Van Gelder T 1990 Compositionality: A connectionist variation on a classical theme. *Cognit. Sci.* 14(3): 355–84

Vygotsky L S 1965 *Thought and Language.* MIT Press, Cambridge, Massachusetts

Weinert S 1991 *Spracherwerb und implizites Lernen.* Hans Huber, Bern

Winston P H 1975 Learning structural descriptions from examples. In: Winston P H (ed.) 1975 *The Psychology of Computer Vision.* McGraw-Hill, New York

Cognitive Development: Individual Differences

F. E. Weinert

Mainstream cognitive development research is based on a universalistic model of the ontogenesis of mental abilities and intellectual competencies. It is assumed "that cognitive changes during childhood have a specific set of formal 'morphogenetic' properties that presumably stem from the biological–maturational growth process underlying these changes. Thus, childhood cognitive modifications are largely inevitable, momentous, directional, uniform, and irreversible." (Flavell 1970 p. 247).

Consistent with this conceptual orientation, most theories of cognitive development can be characterized by four typical features. Specifically, more or less similar to the Piagetian approach, these theories are:

(a) universal: theories intended as valid for all humans,

(b) general: theories addressed, in principle, to the development of all cognitive functions and phenomena,

(c) structural: theories that, in principle, pertain only to changes in basic cognitive competencies and generally ignore the acquisition of knowledge and skills that can or must be learned as a consequence of attaining a particular developmental level, and

(d) naturalistic–descriptive: theories that attempt to encompass those developmental processes that cannot be produced by environmental conditions, although they can be modified.

The dominance of universal and general theories of development since the scientific beginnings of developmental psychology in the nineteenth century has led to a persistent lack of descriptions and explanations of individual differences in cognitive development.

Although intra- and interindividual differences in cognitive development have been addressed in educationally directed research since the scientific beginnings of psychology, they have generally played a marginal role in theory construction. This one-sided orientation is also one important reason why developmental psychology has been less important for educational theory and practice than it could be, given its scientific potential.

The situation is changing in dramatic ways. Comprehensive and diverse efforts to study both universal changes and individual differences systematically began only in the 1970s. Nonetheless,

the research evidence is clear: many studies have documented that cognitive development demonstrates some general stage-like properties and some consistency across domains. At the same time, research also shows that environmental and organismic factors have powerful effects on levels, and individual differences in development seem to be common. Different children show different developmental patterns as a function of both environmental and organismic factors. (Fischer and Silvern 1985 p. 624)

Different approaches for conceptualizing individual differences in cognitive development are described below, followed by a brief review of the influence of genetic and environmental factors on the emergence, stability, and change in cognitive differences. Finally, some conclusions concerning the necessity of matching instruction to individual differences in cognitive development will be drawn.

1. Conceptualization of Individual Differences in Cognitive Development

If one observes a large number of children over a long enough period of time, several types of differences

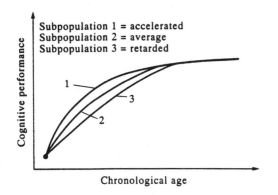

Figure 1
Rate differences in cognitive development with no predictive value

in cognitive dispositions and performances can be ascertained.

First, there are some developmental differences that are not stable. For example, particular linguistic competence criteria are achieved by some young children sooner than others, but these differences do not necessarily have an effect on later language achievement in childhood or adulthood (individual differences in developmental rate).

Second, one can observe individual differences in intellectual abilities in early and middle childhood (e.g., in nonverbal reasoning, inductive and deductive thinking, spatial reasoning) that remain relatively stable over long periods of life and that can only marginally be influenced by variations in education or by intensive training (stable individual differences in cognitive capabilities).

Third, there are great individual differences in knowledge and skills among children, adolescents, and adults with comparable intellectual abilities. For example, whereas some individuals have specialized expertise in chess, others have equally good knowledge of biology, and yet others have exceptional computer skills. These differences, and changes in such differences throughout life, are primarily dependent on the quantity and quality of content-specific learning (individual differences in domain-specific knowledge).

1.1 Individual Differences in Developmental Rate

The empirical fact that the cognitive development of individuals can be faster or slower than the mean development of their age group is common knowledge, and has been replicated in countless scientific studies. Motor development in infancy, language development in early childhood, and logical thinking in schoolchildren are well-known examples.

What is scientifically interesting is not so much the existence of such phenomena, but rather the question

of the causes, stability, and long-term consequences of individual variability in developmental rate. However, the theory-based knowledge about causes, stability, and consequences of such differences still remains unsatisfactory.

Nonetheless there is sufficient empirical evidence to suggest that genetic (e.g., from mentally retarded and gifted populations), organismic (e.g., prematurity), and environmental conditions (e.g., severe sensory deprivation) can have considerable influence on the emergence and stability of developmental differences. When a developmental difference is classified according to the extent to which it deviates from the norm, its persistence, and its long-term consequences, it is possible to differentiate two types of differences in developmental rate.

The first type includes variations in the rate at which particular competencies and performances are attained that are more or less specific, within the range of broadly defined population norms, and not predictive of later cognitive development. As is seen in Fig. 1, for example, moderate interindividual age differences in the acquisition of particular motor, linguistic, and intellectual skills can be observed, but they are not correlated with later performance differences in these individuals. Compensatory education for this type of retarded development is thus not necessary.

A particular variant of such nonpredictive, unstable developmental differences are those that Piaget called horizontal *décalages* in his stage model of cognitive development. This refers to the fact that children often display a cognitive operation of a lower structural level in unfamiliar contexts, although they have acquired the general competence of a higher level. In other words, "cognitive structures are consolidated and integrated through generalized use. The entire cognitive system is consequently distinguished by increasing invariability and stability" (Edelstein et al. 1990 p. 528). Temporary intra-individual variability in cognitive performance level thus has no special significance. However, despite Piaget's skepticism concerning attempts to systematically facilitate development through instruction, practice with variable content-related contexts designed to overcome horizontal *décalage* in the structural level of cognitive development nonetheless seems effective and useful (Aebli 1970).

The second type of variations in the rate at which particular competence and performance criteria can be achieved are severe, more or less general, and are predictive of later cognitive development (see Fig. 2).

For differences in developmental rate that lie outside of broadly defined population norms (means above or below two standard deviations) and that concern more general cognitive functions (e.g., intellectual abilities, severe language disorders), it must be assumed that there is a significant correlation between the developmental tempo and the maximum achievable developmental level. This means that early and

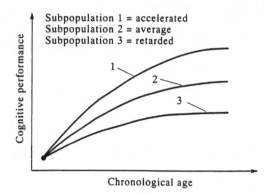

Subpopulation 1 = accelerated
Subpopulation 2 = average
Subpopulation 3 = retarded

Figure 2
Rate differences in cognitive development with predictive value

massive delays in cognitive development frequently indicate large and persistent handicaps in cognitive competencies and, complementarily, that early and massive accelerations in cognitive development frequently indicate giftedness with related educational opportunities. There are empirical suggestions that both very delayed and very accelerated developmental rates reflect not only quantitative differences, but usually also qualitative differences in the development of information processing capabilities. This has been shown both for mentally retarded (Weiss et al. 1986) and for highly gifted individuals (Waldmann and Weinert 1990).

As noted above, despite some similarities in their behavioral manifestations, the two types of differences in developmental rate are fundamentally different. Whereas the first type primarily refers to transitory acceleration or retardation within a "normal" developmental range, the second type refers to developmental differences that are early and significant indicators of stable individual differences in cognitive abilities.

1.2 Individual Differences in Cognitive Capabilities

Since Binet and Simon's (1905) pioneering work, it has been assumed that the rate of intellectual development in childhood allows a valid prognosis of adult intelligence. This hypothesis has been generally supported from the eighth year of life by the demonstration of an increase in the stability of performance differences on unfamiliar and complex intelligence test tasks with increasing chronological age. This has provided an important theoretical basis for the psychometric approach to the differential description of cognitive development and for the construction of intelligence tests for children.

Originally the measure used to characterize the level of intellectual development was "mental age." This was based on the observation that intelligence test performance regularly improved over childhood and adolescence. One can determine the mean standardized intellectual performance level achieved at each age level, and use this empirical norm to judge whether an individual is accelerated, retarded, or normal in development. In the last case, chronological age and mental age are identical.

Although this measurement technique was adopted and used with enthusiasm in Europe and North America, it was also criticized. For example, a delay or acceleration of two mental age years in a 4-year old clearly means something completely different from the same delay or acceleration in a 10-year old. Stern (1911) therefore proposed the intelligence quotient (IQ) as a relatively stable measurement. This measure has been primarily calculated by dividing the mental age by chronological age and multiplying the result by 100. An individual with an age-typical intelligence level would thus have an IQ of 100. The range of interindividual variability in developmental and ability differences is from about 40 to 160; IQs under 70 are frequently interpreted as an indication of mental retardation and IQs over 130 are frequently interpreted as an indication of giftedness.

Throughout the twentieth century, the methods for measuring intelligence have been greatly improved, the reliability of the testing procedure has increased, and the underlying psychological and statistical models have become extremely sophisticated. Psychometric methods are presently useful tools for measuring individual differences in intellectual development and cognitive abilities, despite continuing theoretical and pragmatic critiques, some of which are justified, and some not.

It is important to note that although the intelligence quotient is very useful, it is in principle a highly aggregated and global measure of intellectual ability that reflects a variety of abilities, knowledge, and skills. More specifically, as both everyday experience and many empirical studies have shown, the IQ masks intra-individual differences in cognitive abilities. This shortcoming has led to the development of models of multiple intelligence. For example, Thurstone (1938) differentiated the following types of primary mental abilities that are relatively independent in strength: verbal understanding, verbal fluency, memory, inductive and deductive reasoning, spatial visualization, and mathematical aptitudes. Similar classifications of cognitive abilities are also included in more modern theories of intelligence (Sternberg 1985).

1.3 Individual Differences in Content-specific Knowledge

The focus on the study of cognitive functions and formal skills in the psychometric approach led to a preference for tests that can be solved with a combination of everyday knowledge and logical reasoning. This meant that the importance of content-specific knowledge for the quality of intellectual performance was not considered in developmental and differential psychology. This began to change in the 1970s because of input from cognitive psychology. Investigations of behavior and performance on difficult tasks from different content areas (e.g., chess, physics, medicine, social sciences) showed that high intellectual ability cannot compensate for a lack of content-specific knowledge. This knowledge refers not only to the amount of information about a specific content area, but also to its organization (e.g., unorganized vs. hierarchically organized), its mental representation (e.g., iconic, verbal-declarative, procedural) and its accessibility across situational variations.

The extraordinary importance of content-specific knowledge for productive thinking has been especially vividly demonstrated by the expert–novice paradigm. If one compares people similar in intelligence but differing in content-specific knowledge on problem-solving tasks, those who possess extensive knowledge (experts) outperform novices in all regards (Ericsson and Crutcher 1990). Superior performance by experts is only found for tasks for which content-specific knowledge is available and necessary. For example, chess masters show extraordinarily good memory for complex chess configurations, but show only average performance for random chess configurations or for material irrelevant to chess knowledge.

The expert–novice paradigm has also been successfully applied in developmental studies (Carey 1984, Chi 1978). It has been shown that the typical performance superiority of older versus younger children arises not only from their advanced cognitive developmental level, but is also related to age-typical differences in knowledge. For example, if a comparison is made of the performance of younger experts and older novices, the younger children with more expert knowledge show superior performance. Although children acquire a large storehouse of culturally and socially shared knowledge over the course of development, there are nonetheless relatively early intra- and interindividual differences in content-specific knowledge that increase with increasing age, and that contribute significantly to variations in cognitive performance.

2. Determinants of Individual Differences in the Development of Cognitive Competencies

The relative contribution of inherited factors and environmental conditions to the development of individual differences in cognitive abilities is a controversial theme in scientific psychology. Nevertheless, a review of the results from studies of identical twins and adopted children leads to the relatively unambiguous inference that at least half or somewhat more of the variance in IQ in industrial countries is determined by genetic differences. Such a statement of course also means that close to half of the variance in IQ is not genetically determined (Plomin 1990). This conclusion has frequently led to misunderstanding and false interpretations in public opinion. Bouchard and his colleagues have phrased the fundamental problem in the following way:

> The proximal cause of most psychological variance probably involves learning through experience, just as radical environmentalists have always believed. The effective experiences, however, to an important extent are self-selected, and that selection is guided by the steady pressure of the genome (a more distal cause) (Bouchard et al. 1990 p. 227).

The genetic determination of cognitive competencies is larger for variations in IQ and primary mental abilities than for interindividual differences in knowledge, skills, and school achievement (Plomin 1990, Scarr 1992). However, this does not mean that all students can acquire the same quantity and quality of knowledge, given that they are equally motivated and invest the necessary time in learning. Although many social scientists appear to believe in such an educational utopia (Ericsson and Crutcher 1990), empirical studies show that: (a) more intelligent students can acquire and process more new information than less intelligent students, even with equivalent prerequisite knowledge; (b) students with higher learning prerequisites achieve better performance outcomes with the same learning time, or require less learning time to achieve the same performance outcomes (Slavin 1987); and (c) there are greater possibilities for compensating for lower abilities (above a minimal threshold) by increased learning effort in the acquisition of knowledge and skills than in the acquisition of formal cognitive operations (Blagg 1991).

In addition to genetic differences, environmental conditions also play a substantial role in the emergence of and change in individual differences in cognitive development. Important environmental conditions are the influence of the cultural–historical context, the family, the school (Weinert 1989), and work-related activities. In contrast to many skeptical claims, recent studies show that the school plays an especially important role in the development of cognitive competencies and in the emergence of individual differences:

> Of course, schooling is not the complete story in the formation and maintenance of IQ-scores and IQ-related cognitive processes[.]. Children differ in IQ and cognitive processes prior to entering school, and within a given classroom there are sizeable individual differences despite an equivalence of schooling . . . Thus, the conclusion seems fairly clear: Even though many factors are responsible for individual and group differences in the intellectual development of children, schooling emerges as an extremely important source of variance, notwithstanding historical and contemporary claims to the contrary. (Ceci 1991 p. 719).

3. Conclusion

Psychological models for describing, explaining, and changing individual differences in cognitive development have direct importance for instructional theories and educational practice. If educational goals are to provide motivating challenges for students, they must represent realistic discrepancies from the current level of cognitive performance (dispositions). If teachers want to facilitate students' learning, they must consider individual learning prerequisites. If remedial instruction is to help students overcome learning difficulties, individual differences in general skills, content-specific knowledge and information processing skills must be considered.

The prerequisites for appropriately using psychological models to solve educational problems are the availability of standardized aptitude, learning, and achievement tests, teachers with the professional skills to construct informal tests, and instructors and students who can intuitively diagnose (or self-diagnose) learning progress and learning difficulties. It is empirically certain that a combination of such diagnostic competencies and effective instructional skills is a necessary and favorable precondition for successful teaching (Helmke and Schrader 1987).

Instructional strategies that take account of individual differences in cognitive development include adaptive teaching, individualized instruction, ability grouping, teaching for mastery learning, aptitude–treatment–interaction, and training programs to enhance students' cognitive skills, as well as their self-instructional skills (Corno and Snow 1986, Slavin 1987).

See also: An Overview of Cognitive Development

References

Aebli H 1970 Piaget—and beyond. *Interchange* 1: 12–24
Binet A, Simon T 1905 Application des méthodes nouvelles au diagnostic du niveau intellectuelle chez des enfants normaux et anormaux d'hospice et d'école primaire. *Année Psychol.* 11: 245–336
Blagg N 1991 *Can We Teach Intelligence?* Erlbaum, Hillsdale, New Jersey
Bouchard T J Jr, Lykken D T, McGue M, Segal N L, Tellegen A 1990 Sources of human psychological differences: The Minnesota study of twins reared apart. *Science* 250: 223–28
Carey S 1984 Cognitive development. The descriptive problem. In: Gazzaniga M S (ed.) 1984 *Handbook of Cognitive Neuroscience.* Freeman, New York

Ceci S J 1991 How much does schooling influence general intelligence and its cognitive components? A reassessment of the evidence. *Dev. Psychol.* 27: 703–22
Chi M T H 1978 Knowledge structure and memory development. In: Siegler R (ed.) 1978 *Children's Thinking: What Develops?* Erlbaum, Hillsdale, New Jersey
Corno L, Snow R E 1986 Adapting teaching to individual differences among learners. In: Wittrock M C (ed.) 1986 *Handbook of Research on Teaching*, Vol. 3. Macmillan, New York
Edelstein W, Keller M, Schröder E 1990 Child development and social structure: A longitudinal study on individual differences. In: Baltes P B, Featherman D L, Lerner R M (eds.) 1990 *Life-span Development and Behavior*, Vol. 10. Erlbaum, Hillsdale, New Jersey
Ericsson K A, Crutcher R J 1990 The nature of exceptional performance. In: Baltes P B, Featherman D L, Lerner R M (eds.) 1990 *Life-span Development and Behavior*, Vol. 10. Erlbaum, Hillsdale, New Jersey
Fischer K W, Silvern L 1985 Stages and individual differences in cognitive development. *Annu. Rev. Psychol.* 36: 613–48
Flavell J 1970 Cognitive change in adulthood. In: Goulet R, Baltes P B (eds.) 1970 *Life-span Developmental Psychology: Research and Theory.* Academic Press, New York
Helmke A, Schrader F W 1987 Interactional effects of instructional quality and teacher judgement accuracy on achievement. *Teaching and Teacher Education* 3: 91–98
Plomin R 1990 *Nature and Nurture.* Brooks/Cole, Pacific Grove, California
Scarr S 1992 Developmental theories for the 1990s: Development and individual difference. *Child Dev.* 63: 1–19
Slavin R E 1987 Mastery learning reconsidered. *Rev. Educ. Res.* 56: 175–213
Stern W 1911 *Intelligenzproblem und Schule.* Teubner, Leipzig
Sternberg R J 1985 *Beyond IQ: A Triarchic Theory of Human Intelligence.* Cambridge University Press, Cambridge
Thurstone L L 1938 *Primary Mental Abilities.* University of Chicago Press, Chicago, Illinois
Waldmann M, Weinert F E 1990 *Intelligenz und Denken—Perspektiven der Hochbegabungsforschung.* Verlag für Psychologie, Göttingen
Weinert F E (ed.) 1989 The relation between education and development. *Int. J. Educ. Res.* 13: 827–948
Weiss B, Weisz J R, Bromfield R 1986 Performance of retarded and nonretarded persons on information processing tasks: Tests of the similar structure hypotheses. *Psych. Bull.* 100: 157–75

Further Reading

Ackerman P L, Sternberg R J, Glaser R (eds.) 1989 *Learning and Individual Differences.* Freeman, New York

Cognitive Development and the Acquisition of Expertise

G. Hatano

Are children less competent than adults in the abilities of thinking and problem-solving primarily because they lack rich experience and knowledge, or primarily because their basic processes of storing and retrieving information and/or general problem-solving and reasoning skills are inferior? Are cognitive differences between adults and children similar to expert–novice differences? Is the process of cognitive development analogous to that of gaining expertise? To address these questions, this entry, after briefly reviewing research on expertise, examines the relationship between cognitive development and the acquisition of expertise, and attempts to derive a few educational implications.

1. Research on Expertise

Typical studies on expertise follow three steps: (a) identifying experts who reveal outstanding performance on a criterion task; (b) analyzing how they perform on a set of variants of the criterion task, often in comparison with novices or intermediates; and (c) proposing and examining learning mechanisms for their performances. The first step can easily be implemented in any domain where an external system of evaluation or qualification exists. For example, expert chess or tennis players can be identified by their success at tournaments, or by the high ratings they attain through an acknowledged organization of players. Experts can also be identified by their outstanding performance on an experimental task that has been administered to a large number of people, as in the case of memory experts (e.g., how many digits can be repeated immediately after presentation). Yet another method is to select experts according to their status (e.g., to accept university professors in physics as experts in physics).

The second step involves using outcome measures such as the percentage correct for solving different kinds of tasks or the time needed for solution. Ideally, in order to help provide exact characterizations of experts' strength, some of the variant tasks should reveal marked differences between experts and novices or intermediates, whereas others should show only negligible or even reversed differences. An early successful example of this is provided by Chase and Simon (1973), who demonstrated that the more accurately certain chessboard positions (taken from actual games and presented for a short period of time) were recalled the greater the expertise of the player, although the difference disappeared for random board positions.

Even stronger evidence for the effect of expertise on the memory of relevant pieces of information was obtained by Chi's (1978) study which showed better memory of board positions by children already experienced in playing chess, who averaged 10 years of age, than by novice graduate students.

Outcome measures are not sufficient to illuminate the cognitive processes involved in experts' task performance. Therefore, protocol analysis (typically of subjects' utterances while performing the task under instructions of "thinking aloud") is often undertaken in this step. Through the use of protocol analysis, De Groot's (1965) pioneering work showed that chess masters could pick out good candidate moves without extensive search. Other verbal techniques (e.g., asking for justifications) and nonverbal techniques (e.g., classification, solving the target task with an additional task or constraint) are also used.

The third step is to give an explanation for the outstanding performance of experts in terms of acquisition or learning. As with expertise in the real world, most studies can only propose models of gaining expertise from the comparison of subjects differing in the extent of mastery, because observing the actual process involved takes a long time. Many such explanations take the formation of chunks, namely, higher-order units that often serve as conditions for specific actions as critical. Perceptual chunks allow chess experts to choose a good move without extensive search. Similar but more abstract problem schemas enable physics experts to solve a variety of physics problems without relying on weak heuristics. As for expertise in the laboratory, in very small, artificial domains like digit memory or the Tower of Hanoi puzzle, proposed mechanisms can be examined by the observation and fine-grained analysis of the process of gaining expertise, for example, by describing how a rich repertoire of strategies is accumulated (Anzai 1987).

An important contribution to the understanding of human competence presented by investigators of expertise is the innovative view of individual differences (e.g., Chi et al. 1982). These researchers attribute the outstanding performance of experts primarily to what has been acquired, that is, to a well-organized body of domain-specific knowledge and skill, rather than IQ or genetically given talents. Another contribution is their demonstration that knowledge acquisition and problem-solving are mutually facilitative, that is, knowledge acquired through problem-solving tends to enhance later problem-solving.

However, it must be pointed out that there are inadequacies in studies on expertise undertaken thus far:

They have failed to consider sociocultural contexts of gaining expertise (Brown et al. 1989); have ignored qualitative changes in the acquisition process, treating expertise as if it were linearly incremental (Carey 1985); and have often neglected the fact that there are different courses of expertise as well as different types of experts (Hatano and Inagaki 1986, Sloboda 1991).

2. Commonalities and Differences Between Cognitive Development and Gaining Expertise

Is the process of acquiring expertise described above similar to that of cognitive development? Are studies on expertise informative for investigators of cognitive development? Answers to these questions vary even among leading cognitive developmentalists. Some give affirmative answers and argue that developmental or adult–child differences are similar to expert–novice differences, because children are "universal novices" (e.g., Brown and DeLoache 1978). This implies that adults and children differ primarily in the amount of their knowledge; in other words, what develops is domain-specific knowledge. Moreover, they take the acquisition of knowledge through repeated experiences of problem-solving as most important in cognitive development.

Others offer negative answers. They assert that the characterization of the child in this way oversimplifies what develops (Keil 1989), and hence that many models of novice–experts shifts have little relevance for cognitive development.

The two research traditions, one on expertise and the other on cognitive development, started with studies of very different sorts of phenomena (playing chess in the former and solving problems of a logicomathematical nature in the latter), and therefore their typical studies have been very different. Moreover, the process of cognitive development surely involves something more than the acquisition of expertise in narrow and artificial domains like chess. However, it can still be asserted that the process of cognitive development is similar to that of gaining expertise, and that theories as well as data on expertise are informative for understanding cognitive development for the following reasons: (a) both processes are conceptualized primarily in terms of the acquisition of knowledge available in the society; and (b) some similar phenomena, for example, the acquisition of naive theories, have recently been studied in the two streams. The differences between them lie in their characterizations of the acquisition of knowledge, and are often matters of emphasis on one point over another.

Below, five frequently mentioned characterizations of knowledge acquisitions are offered. For each, it will be investigated whether and how these characteristics are shared by accounts of the processes of gaining expertise and of cognitive development; that

is, the extent to which adult novices and children acquire a body of knowledge in similar ways.

2.1 Knowledge is Constructed

Human beings are active agents in information processing and action, and often construct knowledge as a by-product of their problem-solving or comprehension activity. However, the claim that knowledge is acquired by construction does not deny that knowledge is to some extent transmitted, as in the case of a recipe or a manual of instructions. Because the transmission of knowledge usually relies on verbal communication, adult novices seem to acquire knowledge by transmission, whereas children almost always do so by construction.

However, transmission cannot be perfect, because human language is able to describe only part of the target knowledge, involves some ambiguity, and allows for different interpretations, especially when the sender and receiver do not share much common knowledge. More importantly, active agents, whether adults or children, often try to interpret and enrich what is transmitted, that is, to supplement it by construction. Therefore the difference between adult novices and children with regard to the construction of knowledge is a matter of degree; they do not seem qualitatively or fundamentally different.

2.2 Knowledge Acquisition Involves Restructuring

The process of knowledge acquisition involves restructuring as well as enrichment. Studies on cognitive development have been concerned with conceptual change, a radical form of restructuring, and have found that some of the concepts found in children cannot readily be translated into adult "vocabulary" (Carey 1988). In contrast, studies on expertise have demonstrated that knowledge becomes richer and better organized as students gain expertise, but have often neglected restructuring or reorganization of knowledge.

However, in principle, reorganization of knowledge may take place in adults as they go through the process of gaining expertise. For example, constituent pieces of knowledge, and/or concepts included, may change (e.g., naive misconceptions may be replaced by scientific conceptions). Thus differences between cognitive development and expertise are more apparent than real with regard to restructuring of knowledge.

2.3 Process of Knowledge Acquisition is Constrained

Knowledge acquisition can concisely be described as the process of constructing and reorganizing knowledge under a variety of constraints. Here the term "constraints" refers to conditions that facilitate the process of acquisition as well as restrict its possible range. The process of knowledge construction and restructuring is constrained both internally (by cognitive constraints) and externally (by sociocultural constraints). The former includes innate tendencies and acquired pieces of knowledge. Young children are more competent than previously believed (Gelman 1979), because, due to innate constraints, they can learn quickly and solve problems in several specific areas, for example, naive physics, psychology, and biology (Wellman and Gelman 1992). In addition, children exhibit more advanced modes of reasoning in a domain where they possess fairly rich acquired knowledge and can use it. Domain-specific knowledge can help problem-solvers to represent aptly a given problem so that they can readily handle it.

Although those who investigate expertise emphasize the role of acquired knowledge, and those who investigate cognitive development take innate tendencies to be more critical, it can reasonably be assumed that both types of internal constraints apply to both expertise and cognitive development. In other words, the two processes do not seem very different in terms of cognitive constraints.

Sociocultural constraints can be divided into cultural constraints such as shared artifacts (e.g., tools, social organizations, symbols, beliefs) and social constraints such as behavior of other people, interactions with them, and social contexts created by them. These constraints serve to eliminate a great number of possible hypotheses and interpretations in advance, so that it is usually easy for people, including children, to find what they should do in everyday situations.

2.4 Knowledge Acquisition is Usually Domain-specific

Recent cognitive studies have demonstrated that individual competence varies considerably from domain to domain. Investigators of expertise, as pointed out above, have asserted that the most critical determinant of problem-solving competence is not general intelligence but the relevant domain-specific knowledge and also that people accumulate knowledge only in the domain within which they solve problems repeatedly. In research on cognitive development, Piaget's stage theory, which assumed that subject's competence depended on their logicomathematical structures applicable across domains, has been challenged or even rejected by many investigators. Thus investigators in the two research streams apparently agree that knowledge is usually acquired separately for each domain.

However, there exist a few differences in interpreting this characterization. First, the notion of domain is not the same in the two traditions: whereas it denotes a narrow, often artificially defined range of an activity in the expertise tradition, in the cognitive development tradition it typically refers to a body of knowledge representing some aspect of the world. Second, the expertise tradition emphasizes the self-contained nature of a domain, whereas the cognitive development tradition supposes that analogical transfer of knowledge or skill across domains is not only possible but also occurs quite often. Third, cognitive developmentalists stress that some domain-general skills (e.g., literacy and measurement or quantification as well as general reasoning and metacognitive skills) are used in the acquisition of domain-specific knowledge, and that adult novices and children differ markedly in their repertoire of domain-general skills and in how promptly they can retrieve them. Fourth, many cognitive developmentalists believe that the course and process of development vary from domain to domain, because each domain is expected to embody a different set of innate constraints (Carey and Gelman 1991). These differences between the two research streams probably reflect the corresponding differences between adult novices and children.

2.5 Knowledge Acquisition is Situated in Contexts

Human knowledge acquisition is conceptualized as a process of representing experiences with an object, event, conceptual entity, or the like, so that the resulting representation (i.e., knowledge) can readily be used in future problem-solving and understanding. As such, it is situated in and influenced by various features of contexts. Acquired knowledge is also situated in the sense that it reflects the history of its acquisition and use, including associations with contexts. Although textbooks of a given domain summarize a body of knowledge as a set of propositions, the knowledge which individuals "possess" in their heads includes representations of a more personal, concrete nature.

However, as humans gain expertise, knowledge underlying their performances becomes decontextualized (or "desituated") in the sense that it is no longer inextricably associated with the situation in which it was originally acquired. The problem-solving competence of experts is no longer context-bound in the same sense as that of novices; they are able to achieve their goals across contexts, and to solve various novel problems in the domain.

A debatable point here is whether cognition and knowledge of an adult who is a local novice and those of a child who is a universal novice are situated to the same extent. Adults may have an advantage in this point because of their more efficient and solid basic processes, for example, ability to verbalize and grasp rules more firmly, larger working memory capacity, and proficiency in performing operations.

3. Educational Implications

The implications for educating children that can be derived from the preceding discussion are summarized below:

(a) If cognitive development is taken as a form of acquisition of expertise, it suggests the possibility of a more flexible choice of subject-matter content. Educators can choose any content insofar as children are deeply involved in it and recognize the significance of learning it. This is because theories of expertise do not give priority to the age of students (or the total amount of general experience, logicomathematical structure, or anything that is closely correlated with age), and assume that learning becomes easier, irrespective of age, as students accumulate relevant pieces of knowledge, which work as internal constraints.

(b) If cognitive development is approximated by the acquisition of expertise, this suggests that educators use students' prior knowledge as a constraint. Although the body of their acquired domain-specific knowledge is internal and not directly subject to educators' control, modifying it prior to the target lesson is often not too difficult. Theories of expertise indicate that acquired rich and well-organized knowledge in a specific domain enables students both to acquire new pieces of knowledge easily and to reason in advanced modes.

(c) Although the view of cognitive development which regards it as the acquisition of expertise has advantages such as those mentioned above, educators should pay due attention to those aspects of cognitive development that cannot be grasped by expert–novice shift models. For example, they should consider what students possess prior to formal instruction, more specifically, their informal knowledge that may be used as a source for analogical learning of school subjects, and weak heuristics that can be relied on in the beginning phases of instructed learning. Children's competence should not be underrated, as suggested by investigators of expertise, but neither should the magnitude of labor and time needed for cognitive growth be underestimated.

See also: An Overview of Cognitive Development; Cognitive Styles and Learning

References

Anzai Y 1987 Doing, understanding, and learning in problem solving. In: Klahr D, Langley P, Neches R (eds.) 1987 *Production System Models of Learning and Development.* MIT Press, Cambridge, Massachusetts

Brown A L, DeLoache J S 1978 Skills, plans and self-regulation. In: Siegler R S (ed.) 1978 *Children's Thinking: What Develops?* Erlbaum, Hillsdale, New Jersey

Brown J S, Collins A, Duguid P 1989 Situated cognition and the culture of learning. *Educ. Researcher* 18: 32–42

Carey S 1985 *Conceptual Change in Childhood.* MIT Press, Cambridge, Massachusetts

Carey S 1988 Conceptual differences between children and adults. *Mind and Language* 3: 167–81

Carey S, Gelman R (eds.) 1991 *The Epigenesis of Mind: Essays on Biology and Cognition.* Erlbaum, Hillsdale, New Jersey

Chase W G, Simon H A 1973 The mind's eye in chess. In: Chase W G (ed.) 1973 *Visual Information Processing.* Academic Press, New York

Chi M T H 1978 Knowledge structures and memory development. In: Siegler R S (ed.) 1978 *Children's Thinking: What Develops?* Erlbaum, Hillsdale, New Jersey

Chi M T H, Glaser R, Rees E 1982 Expertise in problem solving. In: Sternberg R (ed.) 1982 *Advances in the Psychology of Human Intelligence,* Vol. 1. Erlbaum, Hillsdale, New Jersey

De Groot A D 1965 *Thought and Choice in Chess.* Mouton, The Hague

Gelman R 1979 Preschool thought. *Am. Psychol.* 34(10): 900–05

Hatano G, Inagaki K 1986 Two courses of expertise. In: Stevenson H, Azuma H, Hakuta K (eds.) 1986 *Child Development and Education in Japan.* Freeman, New York

Keil F C 1989 *Concepts, Kinds, and Cognitive Development.* MIT Press, Cambridge, Massachusetts

Sloboda J 1991 Musical expertise. In: Ericsson K A, Smith J (eds.) 1991

Wellman H M, Gelman S A 1992 Cognitive development: Foundational theories of core domains. *Annu. Rev. Psychol.* 43: 337–75

Further Reading

Chi M T H, Glaser R, Farr M J (eds.) 1988 *The Nature of Expertise.* Erlbaum, Hillsdale, New Jersey

Ericsson K A, Smith J (eds.) 1991 *Toward a General Theory of Expertise: Prospects and Limits.* Cambridge University Press, Cambridge

Osherson D N, Smith E E (eds.) 1990 *An Invitation to Cognitive Science. Vol. 3: Thinking.* MIT Press, Cambridge, Massachusetts

Development of Gifted Children

F. J. Mönks and E. J. Mason

The need for extraordinarily talented and capable people who can deal with complex issues facing modern society—for example, the global economy, advancing technology, national security, and increasing population size with its attendant problems of feeding, waste disposal, and overcrowding—is forcing governments to invest in the gifted (Pendarvis et al. 1990; Williams and Mitchell 1989). The development of the gifted can be approached in two ways. The first represents a concern for the manner in which the attribute of giftedness is acquired, and how one develops into a gifted person. Giftedness might result from genetics, experience, parents' level of attainment, or it might be the result of the interaction between the genetic make-up and a supportive social environment. The first approach emphasizes theoretical explanation and research activities. The second approach stresses the nurture of giftedness through programs, policies, and educational innovations.

1. Definitions of Giftedness

In general, four main groups of definitions of giftedness can be found in the literature. Two refer to psychological constructs (trait-oriented models and cognitive component models), a third focuses on achievement and accomplishment, while the fourth takes an environmental view.

Representatives of the trait-oriented model approach consider giftedness to be a relatively stable personal trait, not dependent on the environment, historical period, or socioeconomic condition. Lewis Terman, the pioneer of psychological testing, saw intelligence as a unitary inherited trait, and identified giftedness with an IQ score of 135 or higher. The Marland definition (cited in Pendarvis et al. 1990 p. 6) reflects this position, emphasizing that gifted "children . . . by virtue of outstanding abilities are capable of high performance." In 1978, the United States government identified gifted children as " . . . youth who are identified . . . as possessing demonstrated or potential abilities that give evidence of high performance capabilities in . . . intellectual, creative, specific academic, or leadership ability, or in the performing and visual arts, and who by reason thereof, require services or activities not ordinarily provided by the school" (cited in Pendarvis et al. 1990 p. 6).

In cognitive component models, the quality of information processing is more important than the quantifiable results of testing. One representative of this orientation, Rüppell et al. (1986), proposes replacing IQ by the QI index (Quality of Information processing).

Authors in the achievement-oriented model category consider achievements as observable output of giftedness. For the purpose of gifted programs, a distinction is made between potential and realized capacities. Knowledge about what is potential and what is realized provides the opportunity for intervention.

The economic situation, political climate, and public opinion determine to a great extent whether the study of giftedness is seen as a priority (Williams and Mitchell 1989). The sociocultural or psychosocial model approach takes the pragmatic position that giftedness is defined and determined in the context of the availability of programs and the presence of concern for extraordinary ability (see Gallagher and Coleman 1992).

From the research and program literature it is clear that definitions in the first and third categories predominate. However, as cognitive information-processing models become more advanced, these approaches will probably become more prominent. The fourth kind of definition, with its reliance on socioeconomic and political concerns, seems to affect the availability and planning of programs for the gifted more than it has affected research on the gifted.

2. Research on the Development of Gifted Children

Reflecting the influence of the trait- and achievement-oriented definitions, most of the research has been conducted in a psychological or an educational context or a combination of the two. The beginning of interest in research on giftedness has frequently been credited to Terman's longitudinal study with the early Stanford-Binet Intelligence Test and his publication of the book, *Genetic Studies of Genius* (see Grinder 1990). Much of the research on giftedness has concerned theories of intelligence, intelligence testing, and psychometric approaches to identification of giftedness. However, more recent analyses have challenged the assumption that high IQ scores and general intelligence are necessarily required for, or reflective of, gifted performance (Heller 1992).

Since the 1980s an increasing number of studies addressing the value of IQ tests in identifying present and future gifted performance in specific academic and skill areas has appeared in the research literature. Other studies have focused on identification of giftedness in groups that had been previously ignored in gifted research, such as the handicapped, the underprivileged, and ethnically divergent minority groups within a particular national setting (Sekowski 1992). Partly fueled by this search for the gifted in nontraditional settings, criteria for identification are being broadened. For example, Schack and Starko (1990) reported that teachers emphasized creativity, learning speed and ease, curiosity, and initiative in seeking one's own learning experiences as essential for academic giftedness, although teachers with more experience emphasized the IQ score as well. Further, teachers of the gifted indicated that classroom performance was a less reliable criterion because these students do not always do well in classrooms designed for more typical children.

A continuing theme in the research concerns the long-term or lifespan performance of gifted children. Most of this research from small- and large-scale longitudinal studies conducted in the United States, Germany, the Netherlands, and other countries suggests certain consistent findings. For example, it appears that children who are identified as gifted at a young age tend to continue to be identified as having high ability later in life (Mönks 1992). Accelerated readers seem to maintain an edge over other students, although the difference decreases with age; boys are more likely to sustain gifted performance and interest in science and mathematics than girls in Western cultures. In addition, experience with the contents of educational curricula prior to formal schooling (e.g., through involvement with preschool or after-school programs, hobbies, etc.), family characteristics such as parents' educational level and attitudes toward education, students' interests and attitudes toward learning, and access to experiences all seem to contribute to being identified as gifted.

Research has been directed at understanding how to teach gifted students. For example, programs which are designed to take gifted children out of the regular classroom for part of the day (called "pull-out" programs) have been shown to have small positive effects on achievement, critical thinking, and creativity and show no negative effects on self-concept (Vaughn et al. 1991). Other research has addressed the learning processes, environment, and teacher behavior in the gifted classroom. It has been found, for example, that outstanding teachers of gifted students were higher in such traits as enthusiasm, self-knowledge, ability to act as a facilitator and to apply knowledge when compared to normal class teachers (Whitlock and DuCette 1989).

Another theme in gifted research is the role played by the culture and cultural opportunity (Merenheimo 1991). This literature suggests that, because of cultural expectations and related reasons, females are often neglected in programs for the gifted (Ayles 1992). In addition, research suggests that diversity of cultural background and opportunity results in certain children not being readily identified as gifted, or being excluded from opportunity for gifted expression and performance.

Technology has been influential in gifted research in cognitive psychology. In addition to presenting complex stimulus and problem-solving situations and providing for increased accuracy in the study of such variables as response time, computers have provided a useful model for human information processing. Study of such topics as the nature of expert thinking, and elements and structures of productive mental processing have been useful for understanding giftedness. Taking this approach, for example, research by Dark and Benbow (1990) has shown that mathematically gifted students are able to express mathematically verbal statements of quantity and relationship more readily than their peers or college students taking mathematics courses, and Borland (1989) found that divergent thinking was associated with a "strict percept-strict concept" mental processing cognitive style.

The research literature on development of the gifted has been characterized as tending toward the applied and methodologically simple (Carter and Swanson 1990). In addition, it tends to emphasize programming for the gifted rather than development of theory-guided explanations and knowledge (Gallagher 1986). A large segment of the research on the gifted appears to be in the area of experimental programming.

3. Programs for Development of the Gifted

A variety of programs have been developed to meet the needs of the gifted. Programs can be clustered into enrichment and acceleration, and heterogeneous and homogeneous ability groupings. In England and Wales, Her Majesty's Inspectorate published in 1992 a review of the gifted entitled: *The Education of Very Able Children in Maintained Schools*, which emphasized both enrichment and ability grouping. This report acknowledged four main approaches to gifted education: (a) giving a common task designed to elicit different levels of response; (b) allowing a pupil to proceed through a course at his or her own pace; (c) enriching through supplementary tasks designed to broaden or deepen skills or understanding; and (d) setting educational tasks which require different levels of sophistication within a common theme or topic (pp. 19–20).

Enrichment means that the student studies material that is not usually part of the regular curriculum (e.g., ancient history, foreign language, etc.), or that a deeper treatment is given to regular subjects in the curriculum. Enrichment may be provided as part of the school program or in weekend or summer camp experiences. The main intention of enrichment programs is to reduce boredom and increase motivation for school. The central goal of an enrichment program is to allow the child to progress at his or her own pace and ability. Such a program can only be effective if it matches the child's interests, needs, and capabilities.

In an *accelerated* program, the pupil works at a higher level and/or faster pace than others in the peer group, or is given early admission to primary, secondary, or higher education, or possibly skips grades.

Grade skipping requires care in application to avoid social and emotional adjustment difficulties for the child. For example, in China there are programs for acceleration which could result in a child entering university at the age of 14 years. This kind of radical acceleration has many opponents who foresee adverse effects on the child's emotional adjustment. Comparing enrichment and acceleration, Daurio (1979) came to the conclusion that "No studies have shown enrichment to provide superior results over accelerative methods. Enrichment at best may only defer boredom until a later time . . . Most resistance (to acceleration) stems from concerns about the socioemotional development of the accelerated student. When the facts are studied, however, we find that such adjustment problems generally are short lived" (p. 53). While it is clear that very able pupils frequently require curriculum enrichment and extension, some can only be served appropriately with a faster pace. Parents and teachers must play responsible roles in these decisions.

In contrast to enrichment and acceleration, grouping methods do not directly affect the nature of the instruction, but serve the child's needs by organization of the classroom and learning environment. The most extreme grouping approach is the special school for very able students.

In *homogeneous grouping*, children are sorted by ability. These groups may form whole classes, or subgroups within a self-contained classroom. Further, the groupings may apply to the whole or part of the school day in which the child is "pulled out" to study with other very able peers. Another approach to grouping involves nongraded classes in which instruction is adapted flexibly to match individual student capabilities and learning pace. Grouping within a class can be done with individualized instruction designed to meet the exceptional learner's needs and abilities. In addition, small groups within the class can be formed to accommodate instructional needs, pace, and ability.

A major advantage of homogeneous grouping is that the pupil can interact with his or her high ability peers. A significant feature of this approach is that it is often viewed as nondemocratic and elitist (Williams and Mitchell 1989). Yet opponents of homogenous grouping tend to overlook the other side of the issue: to require very able students to adhere to standards they may have already surpassed may itself be undemocratic and harmful to a significant number of students. A special issue of *Gifted Child Quarterly* (Benbow 1992) was devoted to matters of grouping and acceleration.

Heterogeneous grouping also creates opportunities to serve the special needs of gifted pupils through early entrance to school and college, grade skipping, allowing the child to move at his or her own pace, and compacting the curriculum (reducing the time required to study a subject thus allowing time for expanded study). Another technique, grouping by interest, can be organized between classes and grades.

4. Conclusion

Research seems to suggest that a differentiated curriculum, which is responsive to individual students' needs and capabilities, seems more desirable than any single approach. Although the argument has been presented that heterogeneous ability grouping and cooperative learning are "the most effective means of serving the needs of all students, even the 'gifted'" (Mills and Durden 1992 p. 13) such a statement is not warranted because comparisons between cooperative learning and other instructional approaches have yet to be scientifically evaluated. Cooperative learning and ability grouping are both useful educational practices when used appropriately either alone or in combination. In addition, interaction with peers is regarded as a prerequisite for human development. A very able child needs interaction with developmentally and intellectually similar persons.

How all the elements of an effective gifted education program can be meshed into an appropriate educational experience is not yet clear from the literature. In view of the research and programs discussed in this entry, the design and structure of the Montessori schools may provide a potential model for ideal gifted education.

Maria Montessori (1870–1950) was prominent in the educational reform movement in Europe during the 1920s. The reform movement abandoned the traditional view that a student had to adjust to the school and argued that schools should serve the needs of the child for optimal development to occur. In 1905 Montessori established the first "Children's House" to serve the retarded and extremely poor. Her educational methods, quite revolutionary at the time, continue to be provocative.

In a Montessori education, development of the child's concentration, independence, and sense of responsibility are emphasized. The role of the teacher is unique in the Montessori classroom. A teacher is a partner of the child who observes needs, intentions, and abilities in an ongoing process of identification. Montessori believed the child innately recognizes his or her own abilities, and thus the role of the teacher is as facilitator, providing what the child requires as the child is observed in activities.

In the primary school all children are responsible for their work environment. They select their own tasks and work pace. A feeling of security and respect is frequently reported in such an environment. The Montessori elementary school is organized at three levels rather than grades. As a result, all classes are mixed-grade (or nongraded) permitting children to be in groups with different ability levels within the same classroom. This arrangement provides opportunity for cooperative learning, individualized instruction, ability grouping and other options. With its flexibility and conception of the teacher's role as observer and facilitator of the child's optimal development, the

Montessori School suggests a promising model for effective gifted education.

See also: Cognitive Development: Individual Differences

References

Ayles R 1992 Gifted girls: A case of wasted talent? In: Mönks F J, Katzko M W, van Boxtell H W (eds.) 1992 *Education of the Gifted in Europe: Theoretical and Research Issues.* Swets and Zeitlinger, Amsterdam

Benbow C A (ed.) 1992 Challenging the gifted and acceleration. *Gifted Child Quarterly* 36(2): 59–117

Borland J H 1989 Cognitive controls, cognitive styles, and divergent production in gifted preadolescents. *Journal for the Education of the Gifted* 11 (4): 57–82

Carter K R, Swanson H L 1990 An analysis of the most frequently cited gifted journal articles since the Marland Report: Implications for researchers. *Gifted Child Quarterly* 34 (3): 116–23

Dark V, Benbow C P 1990 Enhanced problem translation and short-term memory: Components of mathematical talent. *J. Educ. Psychol.* 82 (3): 420–29

Daurio S P 1979 Educational enrichment versus acceleration: A review of the literature. In: George W C, Cohn S J, Stanley J C (eds.) 1979 *Educating the Gifted: Acceleration and Enrichment.* Johns Hopkins University Press, Baltimore, Maryland

Gallagher J J 1986 A proposed federal role: Education of gifted children. *Gifted Child Quarterly* 30 (1): 43–46

Gallagher J J, Coleman M R 1992 *State Policies on the Identification of Gifted Students from Special Populations: Three States in Profile.* Gifted Education Policy Studies Program, University of North Carolina, Chapel Hill, North Carolina

Grinder R E 1990 Sources of giftedness in nature and nurture: Historical origins of enduring controversies. *Gifted Child Quarterly* 34 (2): 50–55

Heller K A 1992 Giftedness research and education of the gifted in Germany. In: Mönks F J, Katzko M W, van Boxtel H W (eds.) 1992 *Education of the Gifted in Europe: Theoretical and Research Issues.* Swets and Zeitlinger, Amsterdam

Her Majesty's Inspectorate 1992 *The Education of Very Able Children in Maintained Schools.* HMSO, London

Merenheimo J 1991 Cultural background and experience controlling the manifestation of giftedness. *Scand. J. Educ. Res.* 35 (2): 115–29

Mills C J, Durden W G 1992 Cooperative learning and ability grouping: An issue of choice. *Gifted Child Quarterly* 36 (1): 11–16

Mönks F J 1992 General introduction: From conception to realization. In: Mönks F J, Katzko M W, van Boxtel H W (eds.) 1992 *Education of the Gifted in Europe: Theoretical and Research Issues.* Swets and Zeitlinger, Amsterdam

Pendarvis E D, Howley A A, Howley C B 1990 *The Abilities of Gifted Children.* Prentice Hall, Englewood Cliffs, New Jersey

Rüppell H, Hinnersmann H, Wiegand J 1986 QI instead of IQ: New tests for the prediction of exceptional problem solving abilities in mathematical-scientific-technological areas. Paper presented at the 6th World Conference on Gifted and Talented Children, Hamburg

Schack G D, Starko A J 1990 Identification of gifted students: An analysis of criteria preferred by preservice teachers, classroom teachers, and teachers of the gifted. *Journal for Education of the Gifted* 13 (4): 346–63

Sekowski A 1992 Problems of the education of the gifted in the countries of Middle East Europe. In: Mönks F J, Katzko M W, van Boxtel H W (eds.) 1992 *Education of the Gifted in Europe: Theoretical and Research Issues.* Swets and Zeitlinger, Amsterdam

Vaughn V L, Feldhusen J F, Asher W J 1991 Meta-analyses and review of research on pull-out programs in gifted education. *Gifted Child Quarterly* 35 (2): 92–98

Whitlock M S, DuCette J P 1989 Outstanding and average teachers of the gifted: A comparative study. *Gifted Child Quarterly* 33 (1): 15–21

Williams W G, Mitchell B G 1989 *From Afghanistan to Zimbabwe: Gifted Education in the World Community.* Peter Lang, New York.

Further Reading

Bloom B S (ed.) 1985 *Developing Talent in Young People.* Ballantine Books, New York

John-Steiner V 1985 *Notebooks of the Mind: Explorations of Thinking.* Harper & Row, New York

Radford J 1990 *Child Prodigies and Exceptional Early Achievers.* Harvester Wheatsheaf, New York

Supplee P L 1990 *Reaching the Gifted Underachiever: Program, Strategy and Design.* Teachers College Press, New York

Motor Development and Skill Acquisition

C. von Hofsten

After a long dormant period, renewed interest in motor development arose during the 1980s. New approaches were developed, which emphasized action systems rather than just motor mechanisms and paid attention to the fact that movements are guided rather than elicited. This entry discusses the new trends and how they are applied to the nature–nurture problem, early expressions of motor ability, and skill acquisition.

1. Background

Motor development was the main focus of interest of some of the early pioneers in developmental psychology, especially McGraw (1943) and Gesell (1946). They were both convinced that a detailed description of movements and their changes in form with age would yield important insights into the developmental process. The well-known and comprehensive studies of posture and movement in normal children which they undertook to test this hypothesis are widely cited. However, the importance of these studies for a general understanding of development has mostly been forgotten.

In the 1980s and early 1990s there was considerable renewed interest in the area of motor development. Both *Developmental Psychology* (1989) and *Child Development* (1992) devoted special issues to the topic. The reasons for this renaissance are both methodological and theoretical. First, techniques for recording movements and muscle activities have become very sophisticated. Movements can be recorded and analyzed to millisecond resolutions, which enables researches to obtain detailed and revealing views into the split-second world of movements. Second, there have been important advances in the understanding of the theoretical issues involved in motor development, based on the pioneering work of Bernstein (1967) and Gibson (1966, 1979). It has become evident that motor development cannot be understood as an autonomous, encapsulated phenomenon—clearly it is not simply driven by neuromuscular maturation; indeed, any study of it has to take perception into account. Every coordinated act involves the whole organism and can only be understood as a dynamic interaction involving both the organism and its environment.

2. Development as the Development of Dynamic Systems

What distinguishes a living organism from dead matter is not the kind of molecules involved but the fact that the molecules in a living organism form a dynamic system. Any dynamic system will tend to organize itself and produce stable patterns with many fewer degrees of freedom than are potentially possible. As the parameters of a system change, in whatever way, the stability may be lost and "chaos" introduced until the system finds a new stability into which to settle. This model is clearly attractive to theorists of motor development, for seveal reasons. It can deal with the complexity of the motor system, handle the many determinants of development including genetics, and describe appropriately the process of change with age. Futher, it can account for the phenomena of stability within developmental stages, as well as the dramatic changes that often occur between stages. System approaches are certainly not new in developmental psychology.

The approaches of Gesell (1946) and Piaget (1953) to the study of development were systems approaches.

Current concerns in systems theory are derived from contemporary physics. The principles of nonlinear dynamics (see, e.g., Haken 1983) supply a precise mathematical model for describing how new forms may arise in complex dynamic systems, irrespective of scale. In other words, it is able to deal with both micro and macro levels at the same time, which is a great advantage. However, it is difficult to specify many of the variables that feed into a developing biological system. It is therefore too early to tell how useful this model will be for the study of motor development. It has, however, already provided new insights into the developmental process. For instance, it has shown that variability may serve an important function rather than being a nuisance. According to the model, high variability signifies reorganization leading to a qualitative change, and variability may also be a necessary component in creating opportunities for developmental change.

3. Organizing the Neural System

There can be no genetic blueprint for the neural system. It is far more complex than the genotype itself. At all stages of its development, there is an element of self-organization leading to globally ordered states of brain structures. These ordered states cannot be predicted from any single factor feeding into the system and there are many external and internal determinants in addition to the genotype. However, the genotype has a privileged role in the developmental process. It determines the boundary conditions and sets the interaction rules guiding the organization of the nervous system for optimal biological utility (von der Malsburg and Singer 1988).

Studies of the developing brain point to two basic phases in the mapping of neural systems. First, there is a stage of crude mapping characterized by an overproduction of cells, axons, and synapses. This is followed by a second stage of self-organizing activity, characterized by the strengthening of useful connections and elimination of less useful ones. In the first phase, axons, guided by chemical attractors, migrate from the sending toward the receiving structure. Axons are scattered indiscriminately; but the chemical attractors will ensure that there will be important preferences in their distribution. This will result in crude correspondence between the sending and the receiving arrays. However crude, this would appear to be a necessity: computer simulations have shown that if separate regions of a network organize themselves independently of each other, the resulting maps may be out of register along their boundaries or may have conflicting orientations (Linsker 1990). This is avoided if a crude map is given at the outset that guides the subsequent self-organizing processes.

In the second phase, the system organizes itself through spontaneous activity in the circuits themselves and through interactions with the rest of the body and the outer world. Therefore, the structuring of the brain is tailored to the environment surrounding the organism. The similarity in appearance of the brain in different individuals is dependent not only on the similar genotypes among humans, but also on the invariances both in the environment and in activities performed.

4. The Origin of Movements

Voluntary movements have traditionally been regarded as originating in reflexes defined as innate, low-level organized neural loops eliciting specific responses to key stimuli. The reflex hypothesis can, however, be questioned, for several reasons. First, it is unclear how reflexes evolved to become building blocks for action. Evolution works by solving action problems, which suggests that the simpler and more basic component systems are also action systems and that actions originate from actions (von Hofsten 1989). Second, ultrasound studies of movements in prenatal infants have demonstrated that the first movements performed are spontaneous rather than elicited (de Vries et al. 1985). Finally, studies by Thelen and associates (see, e.g., Thelen 1985, 1986, 1990, Thelen et al. 1984) on the development of walking in infants, and by von Hofsten and associates (von Hofsten 1980, 1982, 1983, von Hofsten and Rönnqvist 1988) on the development of reaching cast further doubt on the reflex hypothesis.

In an excellent series of studies, Thelen and associates (Thelen 1985) asked questions about the origin of walking in children. According to the reflex hypothesis, walking begins as a reflex which is inhibited as neonate stepping disappears and which finally comes under voluntary control as real walking emerges. Thelen and associates found that the kicking of infants who performed no steps when held upright showed the same temporal patterning as newborns who were stepping. When they submerged the legs of young infants in water (Thelen et al. 1984), they found that these infants would indeed step. The stepping of 3-month old infants, who normally step very little or not at all, would be about equal to newborn rates in a comparable group. Furthermore, when weights were applied to the legs (Thelen et al. 1984), newborn stepping disappeared earlier. These results do not support the idea of an inhibited reflex at all. Rather, they indicate that a specific biomechanical constraint —namely, the dramatic postnatal increase in weight of the infant's legs—determines the disappearance of newborn stepping.

Both these and other results (Thelen 1986) show that the appearance of walking in development is dependent on multiple constraints. It is the expression of a self-organizing system, the outcome of which is a function of a number of different factors, including pattern generation, tonus control, articulator differentiation, extensor strength, postural control, visual flow sensitivity, body constraints, and motivation.

The same is true for arm movements. Neonates are known to direct reaching movements towards a seen target in front of them (von Hofsten 1982). What is common with these early reaching movements is their convergence on a common goal and not their form or starting position. The reflex nature of some of the postures involving the arms of the infant has also been studied recently. Van der Meer et al. (1995) studied the assymetric tonic neck postures in 2-week-old infants. They attached strings to the wrists of the infants which could be pulled gently in the direction of their feet. With their head turned to one side they resisted the pull of the string on the arm on that side. The other hand, which they could not see, was pulled down by the string. The same result was obtained when the baby's arms were visually switched using video cameras and monitors. It was the seen arm that resisted the pull of the strings and not the arm that the infant was turned towards. These studies show that young infants move their arms into the visual field and keep them there in order to explore the environment and the visual correlates of self-produced movement rather than as the result of rigid reflexes

A remarkable ability of infants to coordinate their action relative to an external event has been demonstrated in early catching behavior. In a series of studies, von Hofsten (1980, 1983) found that by the time infants start to master reaching for stationary objects, they can also reach successfully for fast-moving ones. Infants aged 18 weeks were found to catch an object moving at 30 cm/sec. von Hofsten (1983) found that 8-month old infants successfully caught objects moving at 120 cm/sec. The initial aiming of these reaches was within a few degrees of the meeting point with the target, and the variable timing error was only between 50 and 60 milliseconds. In these studies, infants maintained predictive and precise coordination with the targets in spite of much variability in starting position, speed of the reach, form of the reaching trajectory, position of target at encounter, and so on. These findings accord far more closely with the idea of an action system than the idea of a reflex.

In the act of reaching for an object there are several problems that must be resolved in advance if the encounter with the object is to be smooth and efficient. The reaching hand needs to adjust to the orientation, form, and size of the object. Furthermore, securing the target must be timed in such a way that the hand starts to close around it in anticipation of, and not as a reaction to, the object encounter. Von Hofsten and Rönnqvist (1988) found that this occured from the very onset of successful reaching and grasping around 5 months of age. In other words, when an infant encounters an object in the act of reaching for it, the grasping is not a tactually elicited reflex but a planned action.

5. Skill Acquisition

In all actions, future oriented control of movement is of crucial importance for skillful performance. There are several reasons for this. First, there is a lag between the time when information enters into a system and the time when adjustments are made. Even if there were no transmission lag in the system, however, knowing about a problem only when it occurs is too late because it takes time before the contraction of a muscle has an effect. Both such lags will introduce interruptions in the flow of action if adjustments are prepared only after problems arise. If this happens, movements will become discontinuous. Finally, some events are irreversible and simply have to be dealt with ahead of time. As the foot is lowered toward the ground in a stepping movement, the nature of the ground—whether hard, soft, or slippery—has to be anticipated. Otherwise the smoothness of walking will be disrupted.

However, it is not only interaction with the external world that requires prospective control. Smoothness and continuity of movements cannot be accomplished without prediction. Several different forces act on the limb or body segment during a movement. There are, of course, torques originating from muscle contractions aimed at moving the segment in question, but because the body is a mechanically linked system, torques are also generated from other moving segments coupled to it. The form of movement is also affected by the pull of gravity which will be different for different orientations of the limb in space. The visco-elastic properties of muscles, joints, and tendons will also affect the final form of movement. To be able to produce an intended movement, all these passive forces must be kept under control by the adjustments of active muscular contractions ahead of time.

Another set of problemes requiring prospective control has to do with the fact that coordination and regulation of purposeful movements are only possible in relation to a stable context; that is, the posture of the body. To be able to act purposefully, a person must be able to maintain the balance and equilibrium of the body and a stable orientation relative to the environment. However, movements themselves will affect the equilibrium of the body. When a body part is moved, the point of gravity of the whole body is displaced; if the movement is forceful, it will create a momentum that will push the body out of equilibrium unless it is counterbalanced.

The fact that smooth and continuous movements are controlled prospectively has been realized for a long time. In the literature, such movements are known as "feedforward-controlled" or "open-loop movements." Less continuous movements are considered to be controlled through information acquired during execution and are known as "feedback-regulated." Feedforward control and feedback control have traditionally been considered as qualitatively different from each other. However, the role of feedback is not primarily to evaluate the past but to predict the future, as with feedforward. The difference is merely a question of how far into the future the prediction extends. As the smoothness of movements increases with skill acquisition, so too does the span of predictive control.

6. Development of Prospective Control

Motor development involves acquiring knowledge about the possibilities for and limitations of movement, about the external world, and about how one moves in the external world. It is a matter of finding out about the contextual opportunities and constraints of the task, detecting its local contingencies, and being prepared for difficulties and problems that may arise. It can also be described as exploring and familiarizing oneself with the task space, defined by the different dimensions of the task. Getting to know the task space can best be achieved by exercising the task and systematically varying its different parameters. This is exactly what young infants do when they learn to act. Piaget (1953) was so impressed by the fact that infants stubbornly repeat newly acquired action in this way that he named several of his sensorimotor stages as stages of circulatory behaviors.

When the task space is known, the subject can both develop a plan to work through it and at the same time be aware of the problems that may be encountered while doing so. However, it is insufficient simply to be aware of potential problems. They also need to be detected and dealt with. Bernstein (1967) showed that it is impossible to preprogram a movement totally because of the number of degrees of freedom involved. Thus, perhaps the most important aspect of skill acquisition is to learn to extract the right kind of information that will guide the movement through the task space. In other words, developing movement skills is very much a question of developing perception. Perception is needed throughout the execution of a movement and its task is always prospective: it has to inform the actor about upcoming problems so that they can be dealt with ahead of time or at an early stage, when they are harmless. If this is done, flexibility of movements can be preserved while maintaining their smoothness and continuity. According to Reed, "the importance of practice and repetition is not so much to stamp in patterns of movement, but rather to encourage the functional organization of action systems. This principle is constant throughout life: the achievement of an action is not the agent's coming to possess an immutable program, but rather the development of a skill. This means the ability to use perceptual information so as to coordinate movements and postures in a flexible manner that serves to accomplish a desired task" (Reed 1990 p. 15).

See also: Perceptual Development

References

Bernstein N 1967 *The Coordination and Regulation of Movements*. Pergamon Press, Oxford

Child Development 1992 Vol. 63 (6) (issue devoted to Developmental Biodynamics)

Developmental Psychology 1989 Vol. 25(6) (issue devoted to Motor Development)

de Vries J I P, Visser G H A, Prechtl H F R 1985 The emergence of fetal behavior, II: Quantitative aspects. *Early Human Development* 12(2): 99–120

Gesell A 1946 The ontogenesis of infant behavior. In: Carmichael L (ed.) 1946 *Manual of Child Psychology*. Wiley, New York

Gibson J J 1966 *The Senses Considered as Perceptual Systems*. Houghton Mifflin, Boston, Massachusetts

Gibson J J 1979 *The Ecological Approach to Visual Perception*. Houghton Mifflin, Boston, Massachusetts

Haken H 1983 *Synergetics: An Introduction*, 3rd edn. Springer-Verlag, Berlin

Linsker R 1990 Perceptual neural organization: Some approaches based on network models and information theory. *Annual Review of Neuroscience* 13: 257–81

McGraw M B 1943 *The Neuromuscular Maturation of the Human Infant*. Columbia University Press, New York

Piaget J 1953 *The Origin of Intelligence in the Child*. Routledge, New York

Reed E S 1990 Changing theories of postural development. In: Woollacott M, Shumway-Cook A (eds.) 1990 *Development of Posture and Gait Across the Life Span*. University of South Carolina Press, Columbia, South Carolina

Thelen E 1985 Developmental origins of motor coordination: Leg movements in human infants. *Developmental Psychobiology* 18(1): 1–18

Thelen E 1986 Development of coordinated movement: Implications for early human development. In: Wade M G, Whiting H T R (eds.) 1986 *Motor Development in Children: Aspects of Coordination and Control*. NATO/ASI Series D, No. 34. Nijhoff, Dordrecht

Thelen E 1990 Coupling perception and action in the development of skill: A dynamic approach. In: Bloch H, Bertenthal B (eds.) 1990 *Sensory-motor Organization and Development in Infancy and Early Childhood*. Klumer, Dordrecht

Thelen E, Fisher D M, Ridley-Johnson R 1984 The relationship between physical growth and a newborn reflex. *Infant Behavior and Development* 7: 479–93

von der Malsburg C, Singer W 1988 Principles of cortical network organization. In: Rakic P, Singer W (eds.) 1988 *Neurobiology of Neocortex*. Wiley, London

Van der Meer A L H, vand der Weel F R, Lee D N 1995 The functional significance of arm movements in neonates. *Science*, 267:693–95

von Hofsten C 1980 Predictive reaching for moving objects by human infants. *Journal of Experimental Child Psychology* 30(3): 369–82

von Hofsten C 1982 Eye—hand coordination in newborns. *Dev. Psychol.* 18: 450–61

von Hofsten C 1983 Catching skills in infancy. *J. Exp. Psychol. Hum. Percept. Perform.* 9(1): 75–85

von Hofsten C 1989 Motor development as the development of systems: Comments on the special issue of *Developmental Psychology* on motor development. *Dev. Psychol.* 25(6): 950–53

von Hofsten C, Rönnqvist L 1988 Preparation for grasping an object: A developmental study. *J. Exp. Psychol. Hum. Percept. Perform.* 14(4): 610–21

Perceptual Development

F. Wilkening

Psychological research on perceptual development has many facets. Much weight has been placed on theoretical issues, which have proven to be most relevant in the first year of a child's life. This entry outlines the main approaches to clarifying the basic theoretical issues and also discusses practical implications, such as the effects of specific perceptual interventions and environments.

1. Lay View and Scientific Approach

Perception is at the core of all psychological processes by which people experience and interpret the world. It would be meaningless to study higher cognitive processes without knowing how the senses function and how perception works. This is especially true if one wants to understand changes in the cognitive systems from infancy through childhood. Thus it is important to look at perceptual development.

A 1-year old baby does not think and reason in the same way as an adult. Virtually all data and theories in psychology agree on this point. But what about perception? To a lay psychologist, it seems conceivable that a baby sees the world in essentially the same way as an adult—that it sees the same colors, the same distances in space, and hears the same tones. Only when higher-order "knowledge" is involved (e.g., when trying to interpret letter signs in a street or trying to make sense of the sounds of a language) might it reasonably be expected that the baby's perception differs from that of older children and adults.

This lay view of perceptual development is not really wrong. On a general level, it reflects surprisingly well what research has found, and it may also help in understanding why, unlike in any other field of psychology, research has concentrated on the first months of life. In the years after infancy, the child rapidly accumulates a vast amount of knowledge, and the role of that knowledge in interpreting the incoming sensory information often becomes so strong that "pure" perception is hard, if not impossible, to investigate. Nevertheless, the interwoven nature of perception and cognition in later years is an important topic in itself that deserves serious study. This issue will be considered at the end of the entry—when it will be evident how the lay view has to be elaborated and specified.

2. Perception in Infancy

Since the 1960s about 90 percent of the published studies on perceptual development have dealt with young infants. This is explained not only by the reason given above, but also by the empiricism–nativism controversy about the origins of human knowledge, a debate related to a long-standing concern in philosophy. Here the question of whether all knowledge comes through the senses and grows only with experience (empiricist view), or whether there are some kinds of knowledge that cannot be learned (implying that humans have to be born with an intelligent, "knowing" sensory apparatus—nativist view), gave rise to much speculation and theoretical argumentation. Over centuries, however, the two conflicting ideas could not be subjected to an experimental test.

What was needed to settle the issue was information about how the newborn child perceives the world, but there is no straightforward access to that information. No researcher remembers what he or she saw at birth. Moreover, perception is private, and therefore it is necessary to rely in some way on what the perceiving person communicates. This is relatively easy with children and adults, who understand instructions and can tell, for example, whether two tones sound different or the same, or can report that they see a yellow ball. With young infants, their perceptions have to be inferred from their behavior. It was not until the middle of the twentieth century that psychologists invented ingenious experiments for this purpose—methods have since become more and more sophisticated. The hope, at the outset of this scientific enterprise, was to reveal the perceptual capabilities of the newborn and thus to resolve the nature–nurture debate from hard data. The most prominent field of investigation has been space (or depth) perception, which will be treated here in some detail, to illustrate typical methods and important conceptual findings. In many ways, these experimental approaches can be taken as exemplary for other investigative fields in perceptual development.

2.1 Depth Perception

Humans perceive a three-dimensional world, although the crucial stimulus in the head, the image on the retina being only two-dimensional. How is this pos-

sible? Do people gradually learn to "construct" the third dimension from various experiences of moving in space (empiricist view), or are they equipped with an innate computational mechanism that automatically gives information about depth (nativist view)? Both positions are logically possible. If the latter were true, one should expect the ability to perceive a three-dimensional space to be present at birth—or very soon thereafter.

In a now classic experiment, Gibson and Walk (1960) studied depth perception in infancy, using a novel apparatus termed the "visual cliff." Babies were placed at the edge of what appeared to be a cliff. In fact, the precipitous drop was covered with plexiglass that prevented the babies from falling down. Gibson and Walk found that virtually all babies investigated—infants between 6 and 14 months—did not crawl over the edge of the cliff, not even to reach their mothers. The conclusion was that perception of depth must be present as early as 6 months after birth.

Unfortunately, this method is limited to infants who can move around. To study depth perception in precrawling infants, Campos et al. (1970) used the visual cliff but monitored a different behavior: heart rate. They put the babies face-down on the apparatus and suddenly exposed them to either the deep or the shallow side. By 2 months of age, babies on the deep side showed changes in heart rate, mostly a slowing down, which suggests that they make some discrimination related to depth. Interestingly, heart rates in 9-month-old babies also change when placed on the deep side of the cliff, but they speed up rather than slow down. This discrepancy suggests that although the ability to perceive depth appears to be present by 2 months of age, the fear of depth may not develop before the infant has experience in crawling.

Bower and his colleagues developed another technique that allowed them to study depth perception in even younger babies in a highly functional way (Bower et al. 1970). Children were placed in front of a rear-projection screen onto which a shadow of an optically approaching cube was cast. This projection technique cleverly avoided the air changes and acoustic cues that an actual object would have caused. Infants only 2 weeks of age showed an avoidance response when the approaching object was on a hit pass—apparently about to strike them in the face. They threw back their heads and tried to shield their faces. Bower et al. took this avoidance response as evidence for depth perception in babies only a few days old. However, Yonas (1981) objected that the upper contour of the approaching cube image always moved upward. If infants simply tracked the rapidly changing upper contour of the cube, so Yonas argued, the throwing back of their heads might only give an impression of avoiding an impending collision—and thus not necessarily signify depth perception. In a series of control experiments, Yonas tested his alternative hypothesis and found that, when the upper contour of the approaching object remained at a constant level, the avoidance response could not be reliably demonstrated before the age of approximately 4 months.

Converging data came from experiments using a very different method, based on the principle of stereopsis. This refers to the fact that each eye registers separate, slightly different images of the world, and that this binocular disparity provides information about depth. Fox et al. (1980) showed infants a slightly different series of random-dot stereograms to each eye. Only the fusion of these images created the illusion of a three-dimensional solid object moving across the screen. The question was whether infants would take advantage of these depth cues and follow the imaginary movement with their eyes. This behavior did not emerge until the fourth month after birth.

These studies, taken together, suggest that babies as young as 4 months are capable of perceiving depth. The ingenious techniques developed in this field greatly advanced knowledge about the visual capacities of the infant. However, it is not known if depth perception emerges at some point of development before 4 months, or if it is present even at birth.

2.2 Other Visual Capacities in Infancy: A Summary

If other fields of early perceptual development are considered they suggest conclusions similar to those advanced about depth perception. By applying ingenious new experimental techniques, researchers have shown that the old belief that babies are perceptually incompetent is incorrect. It is now safe to state that after a few months infants' visual systems are well-developed. Clearly before the end of the first year they have the visual capacities for seeing the world virtually as an adult does.

2.2.1 Acuity. The visual acuity of the newborn child is relatively poor but it improves rapidly. A 6-month old infant can probably see as clearly as an adult. One way to demonstrate this is by using the "preferential looking" method, a paradigm developed and extensively used by Fantz and his colleagues (see Fantz 1969). In this the infant is presented with a pair of stimuli. In studies on acuity, one stimulus was a homogeneous gray, the other a set of stripes that varied in width. The overall brightness of the two stimuli was held constant. It was found that infants at all ages look longer at—and so appear to prefer—heterogeneous patterns. However, the younger the babies were, the wider the stripes had to be in order to evoke a preference response. Apparently, newborns see a pattern with fine stripes (which can be discriminated by 6-month olds) as homogeneous gray.

2.2.2 Perception of colors. By 4 months, babies probably perceive colors as adults do (Bornstein 1981). A powerful method for demonstrating this is the "habituation technique," which has been very widely used. In a typical habituation experiment, an infant is shown a stimulus, say green. If the infant attends to the initial presentation, that attention response is monitored. After a certain time, the attention will normally decrease; habituation occurs. Then another stimulus is introduced; the green changes, say, to blue. If the child can make this discrimination, the new color will re-excite attention.

2.2.3 Scanning. From the first days of life infants actively orient themselves to visual information. In the first two months, however, their inspection of the world is quite limited; they tend to fixate on certain, often relatively uninformative, aspects. In the next few months their scanning becomes wider and wider, and soon it is virtually as effective as in adults. This has also been shown for infants' perception of the human face.

The data in this field come from the "corneal reflection technique" developed in the 1960s. The reflection of the stimulus in the baby's eye is photographed; this is taken as an indicator of what he or she looks at. As is the case with other methods sketched here, this technique is now used for a variety of research questions and has greatly advanced knowledge about visual perception in infancy.

2.3 Auditory Perception

Sound is a very important source of information for the infant. Perhaps one of the greatest challenges presented to any newborn child is to discriminate and make sense of the sounds of language. Since Eimas et al. (1971) made their pioneering study, a growing body of data has clearly shown that by the age of 6 months infants can discriminate virtually any acoustic difference that is phonologically relevant in natural languages. Moreover, infants' processing of speech sounds seems to follow principles of categorical perception—as is the case with adults. This means, for example, that infants do not hear a continuous transition from a "ba" to a "pa," but either a "ba" or a "pa." Such discrimination can be made by infants as young as 1 month. The phenomenon of categorical perception of speech in early infancy, incidentally, has led to some interesting speculation about the existence of a specialized module of language perception.

It seems safe to conclude from field studies that auditory capacities—and those that enable speech discrimination—are quite mature in early infancy. Of course, there is much room for development when it comes to higher levels of perceiving and cognitive functioning, especially in processing language in ordinary contexts. As was indicated above, however, in those contexts perception and higher-order cognition cannot—and perhaps should not—be separated in scientific study. Nevertheless, attention will now be given to perception in childhood, a large age range much less studied than the short period of infancy.

3. Perceptual Changes in Childhood

Is has been a long-standing assumption in developmental psychology that children's perception becomes more and more differentiated as they become older. Among all the conceptual issues related to perceptual development in the postinfancy years, this notion has received the greatest attention in scientific inquiry. A popular view is that young children's perception is generally holistic, and that this mode of perception changes into an analytic one only around the end of the preschool years. This view can be traced back to the German *Ganzheitspsychologie* in the 1920s. It experienced a revival at the end of the 1970s, and has since been intensively studied under the name of the "separability hypothesis" (Shepp et al. 1980). One reason for the enormous interest in this issue was that, if it were true that the ability to analyze stimuli perceptually is missing in early childhood, this might have important educational implications, particularly for teaching reading and writing.

After a decade of research, it became evident in the late 1980s that the separability hypothesis is no longer tenable. This had to be conceded even by its early proponents (e.g., Smith 1989). They first attenuated the strong version of the claim, by arguing that the young child may not be generally incompetent at perceiving analytically, but may just have a stronger tendency than older children to process incoming information holistically. A series of experiments by Wilkening and Lange (1989) has shown, however, that even this liberalized notion cannot account for the data. With various factors controlled for, they found no holistic-to-analytic developmental trend. The ability to decompose multidimensional stimuli perceptually was already found in the youngest children investigated: 4-year olds. This result corresponds to theories of cognitive development (e.g., Piaget's), which see the major difficulty of younger children as being their tendency to focus "overanalytically" on one aspect of the stimulus.

The fate of the holistic-to-analytic notion can be taken as an instructive example of the problems of studying perceptual development after the first years of life, when more and more higher-level cognition develops. The different classification behavior of younger children was mistakenly seen as a phenomenon of (holistic) perception. In fact, as research suggests, young children's behavior was a result of their cognitive interpretation of ambiguous instructions. In general, if cognitive factors are controlled for, there seems to be much less developmental change in perception in childhood than was once thought.

4. Perceptual Disorders, Deprivation, and Enrichment in Development

Practitioners are often interested in exceptions to normal perceptual development. In general, educationalists ask: What are the effects of perceptual disorders and of specific forms of stimulation? This question can be refined into at least three variants. The first asks whether an impairment in one system (e.g., blindness) affects perceptual functioning in the other sensory systems. Second, how does such an impairment affect psychological development beyond perception (e.g., in cognition)? Third, and for nonhandicapped children with normal perceptual functioning, how can development be modified by environmental stimulation?

With regard to the first question, one common view is that deprivation in one perceptual system leads to a higher level of functioning in one or more of the other systems. This compensation view would assume, for example, that congenitally blind children develop better perceptual capabilities in the senses of hearing, smell, and/or touch. In considering this issue, it is important to distinguish between perceptual functioning per se and attentional factors. The data from studies that have made this distinction—by applying adequate psychophysical methods—allow the following general conclusion. It seems that a handicap in one system, whether blindness or deafness, does not raise another, unimpaired system to a higher level of perceptual functioning. What is often the case, however, is that attention and awareness in one or more of the other systems are enhanced, compared to attention and awareness in nonhandicapped children. There is good evidence for this kind of compensation, concerning attention, but not for perception per se. To complete this way of addressing the issue, it should be added as a summary statement that there is no support for the opposite, pessimistic view that a deficit in one perceptual function might lead to losses in the other, originally unimpaired, sensory systems.

There has been much interest in the more general question of how psychological development in general, both cognitive and social, is affected by specific perceptual disorders. What kind of problems, for example, are to be expected in blind children, and how do they relate to their specific perceptual experience (and deprivation)? Clear answers to these questions are very hard to give. Severe handicaps, such as blindness and deafness, are associated with so many other variables in the course of development that it seems impossible to attribute later problems—if they arise—to the basic peculiarity in perception. These questions thus lie outside the field of perceptual development.

Turning to perceptually nonhandicapped children, there have been relatively few attempts to assess the effects of perceptual modification in this "normal" population. The question of whether cognitive development can be enhanced in certain perceptual environments and/or with perceptual interventions has been of particular interest. As to training programs, most notable is the AGAM project developed in Israel (Razel and Eylon 1990). There it has been found that training with two-dimensional patterns can have positive effects on intellectual functioning in preschool and early school age. Other studies have focused on the effects of physical stimulation in the first year of life on later cognitive development. In general, it seems safe to say that a perceptual environment that provides neither overstimulation nor understimulation is the best for a child's cognitive—and social—development. Almost all findings converge on such an "optimal match hypothesis" (Wachs 1979). Summarizing this line of research, Bornstein (1984 p. 123) cogently concluded that "our physical and perceptual experiences seem to be sufficiently common to render most perceptions nearly the same for everyone, everywhere."

See also: Perception and Learning; An Overview of Cognitive Development

References

Bornstein M H 1981 Psychological studies of color perception in human infants: Habituation, discrimination and categorization, recognition, and conceptualization. In: Lipsitt L P (ed.) 1981 *Advances in Infancy Research*, Vol 1. Ablex, Norwood, New Jersey

Bornstein M H 1984 Perceptual development. In: Bornstein M H, Lamb M E (eds.) 1984 *Developmental Psychology: An Advanced Textbook*. Erlbaum, Hillsdale, New Jersey

Bower T G R, Broughton J M, Moore M 1970 Infant response to approaching objects: An indicator of response to distal variables. *Perception and Psychophysics* 9(2–3): 193–96

Campos J J, Langer A, Krowitz A 1970 Cardiac responses on the visual cliff in prelocomotor human infants. *Science* 170(3954): 196–97

Eimas P D, Siqueland E R, Jusczyk P, Vigorito J 1971 Speech perception in infants. *Science* 171(3968): 303–06

Fantz R L 1969 Studying visual perception and the effects of visual exposure in early infancy. In: Gelfand D (ed.) 1969 *Social Learning in Childhood*. Books-Cole, Belmont, California

Fox R, Aslin R, Shea S L, Dumais S 1980 Stereopsis in human infants. *Science* 207(428): 323–24

Gibson E J, Walk R D 1960 The "visual cliff." *Sci. Am.* 202(4): 64–71

Razel M, Eylon B S 1990 Development of visual cognition: Transfer effects of the AGAM Program. *J. Applied Developmental Psychology* 11: 459–85

Shepp B E, Burns B, McDonough D 1980 The relation of stimulus structure to perceptual and cognitive development: Further tests of a separability hypothesis. In: Wilkening F, Becker J, Trabasso T (eds.) 1980 *Information Integration by Children*. Erlbaum, Hillsdale, New Jersey

Smith L B 1989 A model of perceptual classification in children and adults. *Psychol. Rev.* 96(1): 125–44

Wachs T D 1979 Proximal experience and early cognitive–intellectual development: The physical environment. *Merrill-Palmer Q.* 25(1): 3–41

Wilkening F, Lange K 1989 When is children's perception holistic? Goals and styles in processing multidimensional stimuli. In: Globerson T, Zelniker T (eds.) 1989 *Cognitive Style and Cognitive Development*. Ablex, Norwood, New Jersey

Yonas A 1981 Infants' responses to optical information for collision. In: Aslin R N, Alberts J R, Peterson M R (eds.) 1981 *Development of Perception: Psychobiological Perspectives*. Academic Press, New York

Further Reading

Aslin R N, Smith L B 1988 Perceptual development. *Annu. Rev. Psychol.* 39: 435–73

Gibson E J, Spelke E S 1983 The development of perception. In: Flavell J H, Markman E (eds.) 1983 *Handbook of Child Psychology: Cognitive Development*. Wiley, New York

Hoemann H W 1978 Perception by the deaf. In: Carterette E C, Friedman M P (eds.) 1978 *Handbook of Perception*, Vol. 10. Academic Press, New York

Rosinski R R 1977 *The Development of Visual Perception*. Goodyear, Santa Monica, California

Salapatek P, Cohen L (eds.) 1987 *Handbook of Infant Perception Vol 2: From Perception to Cognition*. Academic Press, Orlando, Florida

Warren D H 1978 Perception by the blind. In: Carterette E C, Friedman M P (eds.) 1978 *Handbook of Perception*, Vol. 10. Academic Press, New York

Language Development

H. Grimm

Language is a complex system consisting of at least six components: phonology, morphology, syntax, lexicon, speech acts, and discourse. The major landmarks in the process of acquiring the categories and rules of these components will be outlined in this entry. Perceptual and social prerequisites for this process will then be discussed in order to look more closely at the critical and still unresolved question of how it is possible that children are able to acquire and master structural knowledge of considerable formal complexity at a very early and immature stage in their cognitive development. About 7–8 percent of preschoolers are, however, seriously impaired in their language development. Possible causal explanations and implications for diagnosis and therapy will be briefly discussed.

1. Landmarks in Language Development

1.1 From Speech Sounds to Word Production

Children's first words are celebrated by parents as one of the most important events in the first two years of development. These words do not appear suddenly out of the void, but are the result of the early and rapid development of phonology. The seemingly speechless infant has turned out to be linguistically more competent than ever imagined (Golinkoff and Hirsh-Pasek 1990).

Productive phonological development comprises at least four major landmarks (Menyuk 1988, Hoff-Ginsberg 1993). The first perceptible landmark is reached when the 6- to 8-week old infant starts to coo. Subsequent to the appearance of laughter and an increase in vowel and consonant sounds, the 6- to 9-month old attains the babbling stage. The production of consistent consonant–vowel series (such as "dada") may be taken as an indication of the infant's increasing control over the vocal mechanism (Menyuk 1988). Deaf infants do not produce canonical babbling and thus may be differentiated from hearing children at this early developmental stage. The prelinguistic sound production may also be a useful predictor for later developmental language disorders. Jensen et al. (1988) reported that at-risk infants who showed significant reductions in some reduplications and consonants later had low scores in a preschool language test.

The period of prespeech phonological development ends between 10 and 14 months with the production of the first words. In contrast to the continuity view, Jakobson (1968) claimed a discontinuity between babbling and speech. According to his view, the babbling stage does not represent a genuine stage of language development, because the child produces a variety of different sounds that are not found together in any single language. After this stage he postulated an interim silent stage in which the child nearly loses his or her ability to produce sounds. Only at the end of this period would the child's true language acquisition process begin. However, the empirical findings that children produce only a small number of sounds during the babbling stage and that they continue to babble after producing their first words clearly argue against Jakobson's view and, rather, tend to corroborate a continuity view from sounds to first words (e.g., Roug et al. 1989).

At around 18 months of age, children attain the fourth landmark; that is, the magical 50-word vocabulary mark. Henceforth they learn new words far more quickly than before, so that at age 2 they can produce over 200 words. Interestingly, children may start to pronounce certain words less accurately than they did before. This temporary "regression" in pronunciation actually marks a step forward, in that children no longer produce words as isolates but rather assimilate them into a phonological system which they have begun to induce from the given data base (see, e.g., Bowerman 1982).

As is generally the case in language development, children are also able to perceive more distinctions than they are able to produce in phonological development. Thus, children can comprehend words with phonological characteristics that they cannot produce. Already in the first weeks of life they categorically discriminate all major phonemic contrasts and are sensitive to intonation and stress cues. Between 3 and 5 months, they are able to "lip-read," and a few months later they can use phonetic features to distinguish foreign from native languages (for summary see, e.g., Jusczyk 1994).

1.2 From Words to Sentence Production

The noticeable spurt of vocabulary growth after the 50-word mark reflects a functional shift from interpersonal language (social words and specific names) to intrapersonal language (cognitive relational words and names). Children now appear to be primarily interested in using words to categorize the objects they see. This naming explosion depends upon the development of: (a) cognitive ability to break events down into components, and (b) the insight that all things can be named. Mothers who often play labeling games certainly help their children in the task of learning names for things (e.g., Bruner 1986).

Children's meaning representations are different from the meanings that adults convey with words. Of special interest are overextensions whose bases include perceptual similarity to the original referent (e.g., dog for cat), functional similarity (e.g., hat for spectacles pushed up on top of the head) and contextual association (e.g., child points to bag and says "mommy"). When a child first overextends the word "dog" to cover not only dogs but also cats, sheep, and other four-legged mammals and subsequently learns the word "cat," the child will at the same time stop overextending "dog" to cover cats. Markman and Wachtel (1988) explained this sequence by the assumption of mutual exclusivity: children assume that each object can have only one category label and that each label can refer to only one category of objects. That this one-to-one mapping principle indeed guides children's first hypotheses about a word's meaning was also shown by experiments. The authors demonstrated that 3-year olds treated a novel term as a label for a novel object but rejected the term as a label for an already familiar object.

The comprehension vocabulary differs not only in size—the most obvious asymmetry—but also in content from the productive vocabulary. Children are capable of understanding adverbs, syntactic connectives, terms that indicate causal relationships, and so on before they are able to use these productively. Correspondingly, children already comprehend sentences before they produce word combinations. Basic aspects of grammar are comprehended prior to their appearance in spontaneous speech. Thus, for example, 16- to 19-month old infants already seem to be sensitive to meaning carried by word order (Golinkoff et al. 1987).

The emergence of word combinations coincides with the vocabulary spurt around 18 to 24 months. The first word combinations are frequently described as "telegraphic," since only high information-bearing words are included and words marking grammatical structure are omitted. The analogy between word combinations and a telegram is, however, not quite accurate: the content of children's early combinations is highly context-bound, whereas a telegram is usually clearly comprehensible without contextual knowledge.

It is important to note that children who fail to produce 50 words and first-word combinations at 24 months should be considered as being at risk in expressive language development. This is true for about 13 to 20 percent of 2-year olds. Researchers are consistent in reporting that 40–50 percent of these children at risk do not "outgrow" their language delays but instead start a career as language-impaired children (e.g., Paul 1991).

The second landmark in grammatical development is characterized by the beginning of the acquisition of the inflectional system and the appearance of linguistic means for marking negation and asking questions. In languages such as German with a rich inflectional system, the flexibility of word order is related to the production of grammatical morphemes. However, this is only true for normal language acquisition. The word order used by language-impaired children remains rigid even though the children have acquired some morphology (e.g., Grimm 1987, 1993).

Children attain the third landmark around the age of 2½ years when they produce sentences with more than one clause and an increasing number of morphological markers. Only 18 months later, by the age of 4 years, do children use most of the major types of complex constructions (for summary, see Menyuk 1988). This rapid and dramatic change in grammatical knowledge is governed by important reorganization processes. The child works hard in order to induce the complex latent structure of language. Incomplete and invalid utterances (e.g., "That play I it"), wrong sentence interpretations, as well as morphological overextensions make it possible to understand the nature of children's qualitatively different representations. In the mid-1960s Brown (1965 p. 297) formulated the dictum that "the clearest evidence that a very young child can give that he is working at the latent structure of language is, paradoxically enough, the production of an unlawful utterance." Before children are capable of a full analysis of linguistic structures, they make use of a variety of strategies for the interpretation of complex sentences. The "order of mention" strategy leads to misinterpretation of sentences such as "Mary went out after John came in," because the child interprets the order in which the elements are mentioned as the order in which these elements occurred. When applying the "event probability strategy" children arrive at a correct understanding of passive sentences and of sentences with embedded relative clauses that describe irreversible relations (e.g., "The dog is fed by the boy") but misinterpret the same sentence constructions that describe reversible relations (e.g., "The girl is chased by the boy"). Morphological errors demonstrate even more impressively how children successively uncover more abstract levels of structure and regularity. Bowerman (1982) differentiated three stages of reorganization. The first stage is designated the "rote stage," because the child recalls correctly from rote memory both the regular form (e.g., foot) and the irregular (e.g., feet) as unanalyzed units. Thus, the language knowledge is superficial. Later on, at the "rule stage," overextensions occur. These errors of overregularization (e.g., "foots," "breaked," "mans") give clear evidence that the child has now realized that the forms are composed of units. The child starts to extend the regular pattern to irregulars. At the third stage the child produces correct irregular forms again. However, these forms are now of a different theoretical status, because they no longer represent unanalyzed isolates, but are integrated in the newly acquired morphological rule system.

Karmiloff-Smith (1986) drew special attention to a fourth important milestone of grammatical development, reached at age 5 when the internal linguistic representations of already-used forms change. The use of pronouns, for example, was up to this point only deictic; that is, they referred to extralinguistic referents. The child now starts to use pronouns anaphorically; that is, to organize cohesive texts. Accordingly, the period from 5 to about 8 years of age is most aptly described as the development from intuitive knowledge to conscious knowledge. Children of this age range are in the process of developing a metalinguistic awareness of categories and rules, which represents a necessary prerequisite for reading and writing. As Menyuk correctly pointed out, those experiences that lead to metaprocessing of language knowledge are of great interest to teachers. "These experiences, then, could be replicated early for those children who appear not to be getting them in the natural course of events" (Menyuk 1988 p. 187).

1.3 From Sentences to Conversational Exchange

Research in pragmatics concentrates on the two questions of how children organize their conversational exchanges and how they organize their narrative discourse. Space in this entry only allows for a few remarks (for a review see, e.g., Menyuk 1988, Shatz 1983). Communication precedes language: in the dawning of communication from 9 months on, children use gestures symbolically and intentionally in the sense of protoimperatives and protodeclaratives

(Bates et al. 1988). As children's language skills develop, they also start to refer to the communication itself when they request information. True social conversation among peers seems to emerge around the age of 3. Most important, young children at this early age already adjust their language to the age, state, and informational need of their partners and are not egocentric communicators as is postulated by the well-known egocentrism hypothesis first formulated by Piaget.

The organization of narrative discourse is usually mastered between 5 and 7 years; children are able clearly to indicate old and new information by linguistic devices and to perform anaphoric mappings. This is of special interest to teachers because "the child's mental representations of the organization of narratives can have a profound effect on the child's reading and writing abilities" (Menyuk 1988 p. 113).

2. Precursors of Language Acquisition

How is it possible that very young children manage to acquire the formally complex rule-system of language, even though they are unable to solve other cognitive problems of similar or even distinctly lesser complexity? This as yet unresolved question has elicited various answers. In spite of the variety of the theoretical positions, consensus exists on at least three aspects: (a) language is a "problem space per se" (Karmiloff-Smith 1986); (b) the child must perform distributional analyses in order to discover the grammatically relevant units and subunits and their rules of combination; (c) for a ready and undisturbed functioning of the process of implicit learning, there must be an optimal interplay between the child's predispositions and information-processing capabilities and characteristics of the language environment that are specific to the language-learning process (e.g., Morgan 1986).

2.1 Predispositions

The infant has an original cognitive endowment that is very systematic and surprisingly abstract in character (Bruner 1985). From birth onward, infants are active in processing information, in that they attend only to certain aspects of sensory stimuli and seek regularities; they have the ability to imitate and to memorize seen or heard stimuli. However, these general cognitive prerequisites cannot be sufficient for the language acquisition task. Rather, very specific perceptual abilities that enable the child to recognize some coherent internal structure in the incoming stream of speech are also needed. Some studies have demonstrated that infants only a few days old are able to differentiate the prosodic characteristics of their maternal language from those of a foreign language and to discriminate a variety of phonetic contrasts. Further, 4-month old infants prefer infant-directed speech that is prosodically enriched and distinctly interrupted at phrase boundaries as compared to adult-directed speech (for a review, see Jusczyk 1994).

2.2 Social Factors

The acoustic features in parental speech are optimally adjusted to the infant's speech perception capacities for organizing the linguistic input into categories (Papoušek and Papoušek 1991). This is why infants prefer infant-directed speech or baby talk, which is exaggerated in its pitch levels and intonation contours, and consists of short utterances with long pauses in between (see Snow and Ferguson 1977). From the start, baby talk is a component of parent–infant communication; it is not just a "shower of spoken language but a highly interactive affair" (Bruner 1985 p. 36). Parents are guided by an implicit pedagogy when they repeatedly produce situations that provide infants with opportunities to practice their own communicative behavior and to detect contingencies between their behavior and their parents' responses. Bruner considers these situations as "regularized formats" that furnish a scaffold for "teaching" reference; during little games or request patterns, the mother "reduces the degree of freedom with which the child has to cope, concentrates his attention into a manageable domain, and provides models of the expected dialogue from which the child can extract selectively what he needs for fulfilling his role in discourse" (Bruner 1978 p. 254). With the child's developmental progress, the mother increasingly extends the formats and more restrictively plays the role of a "communicative ratchet" when insisting on optimal responses. For example, when the name of a referent is mastered, she will no longer accept a babble.

Parents continue to support the language acquisition process by using a special speech style often called "motherese." Although empirical findings support conflicting sides in the question of whether certain types of features are conducive to language growth or not, the data from longitudinal studies suggest that at least some features of the maternal input language exert an influence on the child's rate of language acquisition. Thus, for example, mothers' use of auxiliaries in inverted yes/no questions reliably influences the rate at which their children develop the auxiliary system. Similarly, language teaching strategies such as repetitions, extensions, and corrections of children's utterances have proved to be very helpful for the child's language acquisition process (for a review see, e.g., Grimm and Weinert 1993).

3. Language Development Disorders

Although there are many consistencies in the routes children follow in normal language, there is also much variation from child to child due to different environmental and educational experiences and to differences in the way in which children cognitively act on the world. However, differences in the rate and the strategies of language learning culminate in normal language learning. In contrast, language-disordered children fall outside the variation observed in normal language children.

3.1 Specifically Language Impaired (SLI) Children

SLI children are characterized by late and slow development. They exhibit delays of one year or more in language production, but are usually less retarded in language comprehension. Although there is great variation, the formal morpho-syntactic aspects of their language are more disturbed, and also more profoundly disturbed, than the semantic and pragmatic aspects. The language of these children is fragmentary and contains many syntactic and morphological errors (e.g., Leonard 1987). The production of idiosyncratic sentence forms as well as the children's tendency to plateau clearly indicates that SLI children do not follow the same language acquisition sequence as normal children do. Grimm (1987, 1993) assumed that the SLI children's underlying representations of phrases and clauses are different from those of normally developing children. That these insufficient underlying representations are related to insufficient underlying representations of texts is further proposed by the finding that SLI children also show significant deficits in their narrative skills (e.g., Grimm 1993, Paul 1991).

When SLI children reach school age, reading and writing deficits accompany the still-existing oral language deficits. Because of their difficulty in deriving the relevant information from spoken and written language, and because of additional academic problems, SLI children can develop generalized intellectual and also motivational problems. The more serious the children's language problems are the more pronounced they are and the more likely to be accompanied by psychiatric disturbances (e.g., Howlin and Rutter 1987).

3.2 What Are the Causes?

SLI children must be clearly differentiated from mentally retarded, autistic, hearing impaired, and aphasic children since they do not show mental deficiency, severe personality disorder, hearing impairment or neurological causes that could account for their severe language impairment. This lack of obvious causes has led to various explanatory hypotheses (e.g., Leonard 1987 for a summary). On theoretical and empirical grounds, at least three explanations can be ruled out: (a) that the children experience a deficient language input; (b) that they are suffering from an overall slow maturation of the brain; and (c) that their symbolic representational ability is severely disturbed. Observational and experimental studies are, however, supportive of the notion that SLI children are slow in processing auditory stimuli, have problems with

rhythmic sound patterns, show deficits in short-term memory, and are unable to process language in a gestalt-like manner.

On the basis of these findings, Grimm (1993) proposed the following theoretical explanation. Because of their memory limitations and their problems in processing the rhythmic structure of incoming speech, SLI children are prevented from following a gestalt-like strategy of language processing and are thus prevented from memorizing longer speech units that may form the basis for the inductive acquisition of formal linguistic regularities. Because the children predominantly adopt only single words from the input language, their data base is very restricted and thus does not allow them to perform distributional analyses successfully in order to induce the latent structure of language.

3.3 Necessity of Early Diagnosis and Therapy

After having read the seminal volume on baby talk edited by Snow and Ferguson (1977), Brown formulated the following insightful and delicate advice for a mother concerned about how she could facilitate her young child's learning of language:

> Believe that your child can understand more than he or she can say, and seek, above all, to communicate. To understand and to be understood. To keep your minds fixed on the same target. In doing that, you will, without thinking about it, make 100 or maybe 1000 alterations in your speech and action. Do not try to practice them as such. There is no set of rules of how to talk to a child that can even approach what you unconsciously know. If you concentrate on communicating, everything will follow. (Brown 1977 p. 26)

On the basis of the reported data, it is unquestionable that without intervention SLI children's language deficits will persist and will not be "outgrown." Longitudinal data show that the gap between SLI children and their normal age group even increases over time (Grimm 1993). If it is further correct that SLI children are not only delayed in their language development but also process incoming speech in a different way, then the assumption that the normal sequence of language development is somehow the right sequence for those children to follow can be seriously challenged. Therefore, not only is an early intervention required but also a specific one. But which abilities and mechanisms are modifiable? Is it possible to train the speed of processing auditory stimuli or memory for speech clauses? Research is urgently needed to find answers to these and related questions. However, theoretical and empirical results already allow the conclusion that the use of the gestalt-like strategy of language processing could be a "first step of language-teaching programs that teach language rules" (Connell 1987 p. 11).

Thus, Connell (1987) has experimentally demonstrated that for SLI children an imitation teaching procedure is more effective than a modeling–teaching procedure with regard to the acquisition of a non-English, invented language rule. And most interestingly, Brown and Palincsar (1987) proposed teaching poor readers an integrative form of processing of written materials instead of the analytic word-by-word reading.

If it is correct that SLI children's language disorder and their reading and writing problems are manifestations of the same underlying deficits (e.g., Tallal 1988), then an early diagnosis and therapy (or intervention) to treat the language disorder could prevent the occurrence of reading and writing problems at later points in development. Although the problem of early identification of language acquisition deficits is far from resolved, the use of parental checklists appears very promising. Thus, quite impressive positive correlations ($r>0.70$) could be established between the estimated and measured lexical and syntactical abilities in 2-year olds (Dale 1991). That parental estimations may also have a satisfactory predictive validity was shown in several follow-up studies (e.g., Camaioni et al. 1991).

References

Bates E, Bretherton I, Snyder L 1988 *From First Words to Grammar: Individual Differences and Dissociable Mechanisms.* Cambridge University Press, Cambridge

Bowerman M 1982 Reorganizational processes in lexical and syntactic development. In: Wanner E, Gleitman L R (eds.) 1982 *Language Acquisition: The State of the Art.* Cambridge University Press, Cambridge

Brown A L, Palincsar A S 1987 Reciprocal teaching of comprehension strategies: A natural history of one program for enhancing learning. In: Day J D, Borkowski J G (eds.) 1987 *Intelligence and Exceptionality: New Directions for Theory, Assessment, and Instructional Practices.* Ablex, Norwood, New Jersey

Brown R 1965 *Social Psychology.* Free Press, New York

Brown R 1977 Introduction. In: Snow C E, Ferguson C A (eds.) 1977

Bruner J S 1978 The role of dialogue in language acquisition. In: Sinclair A, Levelt J M, Jarvella R J (eds.) 1978 *The Child's Conception of Language.* Springer-Verlag, Berlin

Bruner J S 1985 The role of interaction formats in language acquisition. In: Forgas J P (ed.) *Language and Social Situations.* Springer-Verlag, New York

Bruner J S 1986 The inspiration of Vygotsky. In: Bruner J S (ed.) 1986 *Actual Minds, Possible Worlds.* Harvard University Press, Cambridge, Massachusetts

Camaioni L, Castelli M C, Longobardi E, Volterra V 1991 A parent report instrument for early language assessment. *First Language* 11: 345–59

Connell P J 1987 An effect of modeling and imitation teaching procedures on children with and without specific language impairment. *Journal of Speech and Hearing Research* 30: 105–13

Dale P S 1991 The validity of a parent report measure of vocabulary and syntax at 24 months. *Journal of Speech and Hearing Research* 34(3): 564–71

Golinkoff R M, Hirsh-Pasek K 1990 Let the mute speak: What infants can tell us about language acquisition. *Merrill-Palmer Q.* 36(1): 67–92

Golinkoff R M, Hirsh-Pasek K, Cauley K, Gordon L C 1987 The eyes have it: Lexical and syntactic comprehension in a new paradigm. *Journal of Child Language* 14(1): 23–45

Grimm H 1987 Developmental dysphasia: New theoretical perspectives and empirical results. *The German Journal of Psychology* 11(1): 8–22

Grimm H 1993 Syntax and morphological difficulties in German-speaking children with specific language impairment (developmental dysphasia): Implications for diagnosis and intervention. In: Grimm H, Skowronek H (eds.) 1993 *Language Acquisition Problems and Reading Disorders: Aspects of Diagnosis and Intervention.* De Gruyter, New York

Grimm H, Weinert S 1993 Patterns of interaction and communication in language development disorders. In: Blanken G, Dittmann J, Grimm H, Marshall J C, Wallesch C -W (eds.) 1993 *Linguistic Disorders and Pathologies. An International Handbook.* De Gruyter, Berlin

Hoff-Ginsberg E 1993 Lndmarks in children's language development. In: Blanken G, Dittmann J, Grimm H, Marshall J C, Wallesch C-W (eds.) 1993 *Linguistic Disorders and Pathologies. An International Handbook.* De Gruyter, Berlin

Howlin P, Rutter M 1987 The consequences of language delay for other aspects of development. In: Yule W, Rutter M (eds.) 1987 *Language Development and Disorders.* MacKeith, London

Jakobson R 1968 (trans. Keilor A R) *Child Language, Aphasia and Phonological Universals.* Mouton, The Hague

Jensen T S, Boggild-Andersen B, Schmidt J, Ankerhus J, Hansen E 1988 Perinatal risk factors and first-year vocalizations: Influence on preschool language and motor performance. *Developmental Medicine and Child Neurology* 30(2): 153–61

Jusczyk P W 1994 Infant speech perception and the development of the mental lexicon. In: Goodman J C, Nusbaum H C (eds.) 1994 *The Transition from Speech Sound to Spoken Words.* MIT Press, Cambridge, Massachusetts

Karmiloff-Smith A 1986 Some fundamental aspects of language development after age 5. In: Fletcher P, Garman M (eds.) 1986 *Language Acquisition*, 2nd ed. Cambridge University Press, Cambridge

Leonard L B 1987 Is specific language impairment a useful construct? In: Rosenberg S (ed.) 1987 *Advances in Applied Psycholinguistics, Vol. 1: Disorders of First-language Development.* Cambridge University Press, Cambridge

Markman E M, Wachtel G F 1988 Children's use of mutual exclusivity to constrain the meanings of words. *Cognit. Psychol.* 20(2): 121–57

Menyuk P 1988 *Language Development. Knowledge and Use.* Scott, Foresman and Co., Glenview, Illinois

Morgan J L 1986 *From Simple Input to Complex Grammar.* MIT Press, Cambridge, Massachusetts

Papoušek M, Papoušek H 1991 Preverbal vocal communication from zero to one: Preparing the ground for language acquisition. In: Lamb M E, Keller H (eds.) 1991 *Infant Development: Perspectives from German-speaking Countries.* Erlbaum, Hillsdale, New Jersey

Paul R 1991 Profiles of toddlers with slow expressive language development. *Topics in Language Disorders* 11(4): 1–13

Roug L, Landberg I, Lundberg L-J 1989 Phonetic development in early infancy: A study of Swedish during the first 18 months of life. *Journal of Child Language* 16(1): 19–40

Shatz M 1983 Communication. In: Flavell J H, Markman E M (eds.) 1983 *Handbook of Child Psychology. Vol. 3: Cognitive Development.* Wiley, New York

Snow C, Ferguson C A (eds.) 1977 *Talking to Children: Language Input and Acquisition.* Cambridge University Press, Cambridge

Tallal P 1988 Developmental language disorders. In: Kavanagh J, Truss T (eds.) 1988 *Learning Disabilities: Proceedings of the National Conference.* York Press, Parkton, Maryland

Further Reading

Bruner J S 1983 *Child's Talk: Learning to use Language.* Norton, New York

Kessel F S (ed.) 1988 *The Development of Language and Language Researchers: Essays in Honor of Roger Brown.* Erlbaum, Hillsdale, New Jersey

Kuhl P 1987 Perception of speech and sound in early infancy. In: Salapatek P, Cohen L (eds.) 1987 *Handbook of Infant Perception. Vol. 2: From Perception to Cognition.* Academic Press, Orlando, Florida

Miller J (ed.) 1990 *Research on Child Language Disorders: A Decade of Progress.* Pro-Ed, Austin, Texas

Piatelli-Palmarini M (ed.) 1980 *Language and Learn ing: The Debate between Jean Piaget and Noam Chomsky.* Harvard University Press, Cambridge, Massachusetts

Memory Development

W. Schneider

Since the 1970s, a new interest in the development of memory has stimulated numerous research activities. These have led to a complex pattern of findings. Although the majority of studies address memory development in children, use of a lifespan perspective has also attracted much attention. This entry will present the most important outcomes of research on memory processes, in both children and adults.

1. Sources of Memory Development in Children

According to most researchers, changes in basic capacities, memory strategies, metacognitive knowledge, and domain knowledge all contribute to children's memory development (Bjorklund 1990, Schneider and Pressley 1989, Siegler 1991). There is also broad agreement that some of these sources of development contribute more than others, and that some play an important role in certain periods of childhood but not in others.

1.1 The Role of Basic Capacities

One of the earliest views of memory development relied heavily on the concept of "capacity." In its simplified version, memory development was exclusively seen as a function of memory capacity: according to this model, what develops in memory is the hardware of the memory system conceptualized as absolute capacity, rather than its software, that is, specific processes or procedures to memorize materials. Of course, such a simplified view is incompatible with the memory data.

Dempster (1985) reviewed in detail potential sources of development for short-term capacity. Taken together, the data from numerous studies show that age-correlated performance increases in memory span should not be interpreted as enlargement of some biologically determined capacity, particularly when memory development during the preschool years and thereafter is considered. It is only during early infancy that the effects of structural changes and basic processes seem to be large and direct contributors to memory performance (Siegler 1991). Factors that may contribute to developmental increases in memory span from the preschool years onward include: (a) speed of information processing; (b) automatic item processing.

In sum, then, it appears that *intra-individual* changes in children's memory capacity contribute little to memory development. As was pointed out by Siegler (1991), these basic processes are present at a very early age and function well even in very young children. Although basic processes are essential for memory, they do not contribute much to improvements in memory with age.

1.2 Effects of Memory Strategies

"Memory strategies" have been defined as mental or behavioral activities that achieve cognitive purposes and are effort-consuming, potentially conscious and controllable (Flavell 1985).

Since the early 1970s numerous studies have investigated the role of strategies in memory development. Particularly in the 1970s individual differences in the use of memory strategies were conceived of as the major source of developmental differences in memory development (Weinert and Perlmutter 1988). The majority of studies on the development of strategies investigated children's use of rehearsal, organization, and elaboration strategies in laboratory tasks. Typically, these strategies were not observed in children younger than 6 or 7. This absence of strategic behavior was attributed to a "production deficiency" (Flavell 1985). That is, young children do not engage in memory strategies because they simply do not know how and when to do so. However, more recent research has shown that the ages of strategy acquisition are relative, and variable between and within strategies. Even preschoolers and kindergarten children are able to use intentional strategies, both in ecologically valid settings such as hide-and-seek tasks, and in the traditional context of a laboratory task (see Schneider and Pressley 1989).

In general, the use of creative, natural-tasks settings in studies conducted mainly in the 1980s and early 1990s has clearly shown that young children's strategic competencies have been underestimated for a long time. Despite this recent change in perspective, there seems little doubt that the most dramatic developmental changes in children's strategy use can be observed during the elementary school years.

Taken together, the findings from studies demonstrate that strategy development in children is more continuous than was originally assumed. They also show that use of encoding and retrieval strategies must be considered in interaction. New methodologies (e.g., mathematical modeling) permit sophisticated analyses of encoding versus retrieval (for a review see Brainerd 1985). Even more importantly, there is now an increasing realization that the use of encoding and retrieval strategies largely depends on children's strategic as well as nonstrategic knowledge. There is impressive evidence that individual differences in metacognitive and domain-specific knowledge may have a strong impact on how well strategies are executed, and on how much children recall in a memory task. Given these findings, the earlier belief that individual differences in memory strategies represent the most important source of memory development no longer seems tenable. There is now broad consensus that the narrow focus on developmental changes in strategy use should be replaced by an approach that takes into account the effects of various forms of knowledge on strategy execution.

1.3 The Role of Metacognitive Knowledge

One knowledge component that has been systematically explored since the early 1970s concerns children's knowledge about memory. Flavell and Wellman (1977) coined the term "metamemory" to refer to a person's potentially verbalizable knowledge about memory storage and retrieval, and developed a taxonomy that parsed metamemory into two main categories, "sensitivity" and "variables." The sensitivity category included knowledge of when memory activity is necessary (i.e., memory monitoring). The variables category included a person's mnemonic self-concept, characteristics of a task relevant to memory, and knowledge about potentially applicable memory strategies (see Schneider and Pressley 1989 for an overview of conceptualizations of metacognitive knowledge).

Empirical research exploring the development of different aspects of metacognitive knowledge revealed that children's knowledge of facts about memory increases considerably over the primary-grade years, but is incomplete by the end of childhood. Most studies showed impressive increases in knowledge about strategies with increasing age, a finding that was paralleled by the development of strategic skills. Thus an important aim of most empirical studies was to demonstrate that there are close relationships between metamemory and memory behavior.

Evaluating the outcomes of research dealing with metamemory–memory behavior relationships is a complicated task. Whereas the first generation of studies found only weak relationships between knowledge about strategies and strategy use, a second generation of studies indicated a more positive pattern of results. In a meta-analysis of studies containing metamemory–memory relationship data, Schneider and Pressley (1989) reported an overall correlation of 0.41 based on a large set of studies. Accordingly, a significant statistical association between metamemory and memory was found, particularly when the relationship between knowledge about strategies and the use of memory strategies was concerned. What children know about their memory obviously influences how they attempt to remember. Given the diversity of findings, however, much more needs to be known about the interplay between metacognitive knowledge and strategic behavior in various memory situations.

1.4 The Impact of Domain Knowledge

Since the late 1970s, there has been increasing evidence for the striking effects of domain knowledge on performance in many memory tasks. In numerous studies, it has been shown that domain knowledge influences how much as well as what children recall (Chi and Ceci 1987). Research on the interaction of domain knowledge and specific memory strategies indicates that there are at least three ways in which the knowledge base relates to strategy use (Pressley et al. 1987): knowledge can (a) facilitate the use of particular strategies, (b) generalize strategy use to related domains, or (c) even diminish the need for strategy activation.

1.4.1 Knowledge and the use of particular strategies.

The assumption that rich knowledge enables competent strategy use has been confirmed in numerous studies. Most of these studies focused on the effects of conceptual or semantic knowledge on the use of organizational strategies in sort–recall tasks. Experimental manipulations concerned children's knowledge of categorical relationships among items in terms of "category typicality" or "interitem associativity." Taken together, this research clearly showed that differences in the meaningfulness of words considerably influences strategic processing, particularly in young school children. Strategic effects of the knowledge base are not restricted to categorization tasks but have been observed in other memory paradigms as well (Pressley et al. 1987).

1.4.2 Knowledge strategy use and related domain.

Several researchers (e.g., Best and Ornstein 1986, Bjorklund 1987) have proposed that semantic organization initially seen in the recall of young school children is mediated not by a deliberately imposed strategy but by the relatively automatic activation of well-established semantic memory relations. As they automatically process highly related items in a categorical fashion, children may notice categorical relations in their recall. They may then realize that categorization is a good learning strategy.

1.4.3 Nonstrategic effects of the knowledge base.

Evidence that rich domain knowledge can diminish the need for strategy activation has been convincingly demonstrated in developmental studies using the expert–novice paradigm. Studies comparing experts and novices in a given domain (e.g., chess or soccer) on a memory task related to that domain provided evidence that rich domain knowledge enables a child expert to perform much like an adult expert and better than an adult novice—thus showing a reversal of usual developmental trends. Moreover, these studies also confirmed the assumption that rich domain knowledge can compensate for low overall aptitude on domain-related cognitive tasks, as no differences were found between high- and low- aptitude experts on the various recall and comprehension measures.

Taken together, these findings indicate that domain knowledge increases greatly with age, and is clearly related to how well children remember. Domain knowledge also contributes to the development of other competencies that have been proposed as sources of memory development, namely basic capacities, memory strategies, and metacognitive knowledge. Accordingly, it seems evident that changes in domain knowledge play a large role in memory development.

2. Memory Development in Adults and the Elderly

Assessments of memory development between late adolescence and late adulthood have not revealed any substantial changes in memory performance as a function of capacity, strategies, or knowledge. Obviously, interindividual performance differences remain stable, and intra-individual changes over time seem

negligible during this time period. On the other hand, numerous studies have identified declines in memory performance in the elderly. Attempts to locate the sources of memory losses in old age have relied on the four components already outlined above.

2.1 The Influence of Basic Capacities

Study of memory in the elderly is made difficult by the problem of recruiting representative subjects. This makes it difficult to judge the importance of cognitive capacity as an explanatory factor. However, even studies that used healthy and intelligent old people as subjects generally found that information–processing speed was generally reduced in the elderly (see reviews by Knopf 1987, Light 1991). Training studies focusing on "developmental reserve capacity" (e.g., Baltes and Kliegl 1992, Kliegl et al. 1989) revealed that although elderly persons could considerably increase their memory performance as a function of cognitive training, none of the older adults reached a level of performance approaching the average of (trained) young adults. There is reason to assume that the negative age difference found in these studies is due to neurobiological constraints leading to a reduction of mental capacity.

2.2 The Impact of Memory Strategies

According to the often invoked "disuse hypothesis," older people should use memory strategies less frequently than young adults because they are no longer capable of complex memory tasks. By and large, however, there is little evidence to support this assumption. For example, Knopf (1987) did not find any differences between young adults and the elderly in the use of grouping strategies. Regardless of age, most subjects were able to use organizational strategies facilitating the recall of long wordlists. On the other hand, effects of strategy use on memory performance seemed to decrease with increasing age. Whereas these and many other findings provide strong evidence against the "disuse hypothesis," they are in accord with the assumption that memory loss in old age is related to decreases in mental capacity and information-processing speed.

2.3 The Role of Knowledge Components

The results of most studies assessing age differences in metacognitive and domain-specific knowledge do not indicate any decline in these knowledge components as a function of age. Although metacognitive knowledge seems to remain stable in old age, its relation to memory performance decreases with increasing age (see Knopf 1987). Regarding the impact of domain-specific knowledge, several findings support a "compensation hypothesis" in that older subjects can use their particularly rich knowledge in many domains to compensate for deficiencies resulting from slower information-processing (Salthouse 1991).

3. Conclusion

Generalizations in the field of memory research are difficult given the great variability of memory phenomena, attributes, modalities, and contents. Given the evidence of several studies, however, it appears that the knowledge base and metacognitive knowledge are major sources of interindividual differences in memory performance, regardless of chronological age. Remarkable intraindividual changes in memory development are apparent during the elementary school years and in old age. Young children's memory gains can be attributed to the joint development of strategies and knowledge. Decreases in memory functions observable in very old adults point to neurobiological constraints that could be due to both a genetically determined program of biological aging as well as to a neurophysiological substrate resulting from a lifetime of experience and cognitive activity (Baltes and Kliegl 1992).

See also: Adult Learning: An Overview; Development of Learning across the Lifespan

References

Baltes P B, Kliegl R 1992 Further testing of limits of cognitive plasticity in old age: Negative age differences in a mnemonic skill are robust. *Dev. Psychol.* 28(1): 121–25

Best D L, Ornstein P A 1986 Children's generation and communication of mnemonic organizational strategies. *Dev. Psychol.* 22(6): 845–53

Bjorklund D F 1987 How age changes in knowledge base contribute to the development of children's memory: An interpretive review. *Dev. Rev.* 7(2): 93–130

Bjorklund D F (ed.) 1990 *Children's Strategies: Contemporary Views of Cognitive Development.* Erlbaum, Hillsdale, New Jersey

Brainerd C J 1985 Model-based approaches to storage and retrieval development. In: Brainerd C J, Pressley M (eds.) 1985 *Basic Processes in Memory Development.* Springer- Verlag, New York

Chi M T H, Ceci S J 1987 Content knowledge: Its role, representation, and restructuring in memory development. In:

Reese H W (ed.) 1987 *Advances in Child Development and Behaviour.* Academic Press, San Diego, California

Dempster F N 1985 Short-term memory development in childhood and adolescence. In: Brainerd C J, Pressley M (eds.) 1985 *Basic Processes in Memory Development.* Springer-Verlag, New York

Flavell J H 1985 *Cognitive Development*, 2nd edn. Prentice-Hall, Englewood Cliffs, New Jersey

Flavell J H, Wellman H M 1977 Metamemory. In: Kail R Hagen J W (eds.) 1977 *Perspectives on the Development of Memory and Cognition.* Erlbaum, Hillsdale, New Jersey

Kliegl R, Smith J, Baltes P B 1989 Testing-the-limits and the study of adult age differences in cognitive plasticity of a mnemonic skill. *Dev. Psychol.* 25(2): 247–56

Knopf M 1987 *Gedächtnis im Alter.* Springer-Verlag, Berlin

Light L L 1991 Memory and aging: Four hypotheses in search of data. *Annu. Rev. Psychol.* 42: 333–76

Pressley M, Borkowski J G, Schneider W 1987 Cognitive strategies: Good strategy users coordinate metacognition and knowledge. In: Vasta R (ed.) 1987 *Annals of Child Development*, Vol. 5. JAI Press, New York

Salthouse T A 1991 *Theoretical Perspectives on Cognitive Aging.* Erlbaum, Hillsdale, New Jersey

Schneider W, Pressley M 1989 *Memory Development Between 2 and 20.* Springer-Verlag, New York

Siegler R S 1991 *Children's Thinking*, 2nd edn. Prentice-Hall, Englewood Cliffs, New Jersey

Weinert F E, Perlmutter M (eds.) 1988. *Memory Development: Universal Changes and Individual Differences.* Erlbaum, Hillsdale, New Jersey

Further Reading

Charness N (ed.) 1985 *Aging and Human Performance.* Wiley, Chichester

Kail R V 1990 *The Development of Memory in Children*, 3rd edn. Freeman, New York

Kausler D H 1991 *Experimental Psychology, Cognition, and Human Aging*, 2nd edn. Springer-Verlag, New York

Schneider W, Körkel J, Weinert F E 1990 Expert knowledge, general abilities, and text processing. In: Schneider W, Weinert F E (eds.) 1990 *Interactions among Aptitudes, Strategies, and Knowledge in Cognitive Performance.* Springer-Verlag, New York

Development of Reasoning Competences in Early and Later Childhood

M. Bullock

The term "reasoning" refers to the human capacity for drawing conclusions or making inferences on the basis of known or assumed facts, in accordance with rational rules or principles. Investigations of how children of different ages reason, the extent to which their reasoning extends beyond simple inferences based on immediate stimulus information, and the complementary roles played by specific content knowledge and content-independent inference processes and strategies in reasoning performance have long been among the central issues in cognitive development. An understanding of developmental differences in reasoning and of the sources of reasoning errors is important for educational practice in general, because educational material can be more effective when it matches children's reasoning skills, and for curricula addressed to facilitating reasoning skills in particular.

Several themes have characterized research on the development of reasoning in the late twentieth century. First, the demonstration of more sophisticated cognitive competence in young preschoolers than was previously claimed has led researchers to step away from stage-structural models that confined systematic reasoning to late childhood and adolescence, and to ask *what* aspects of *what types* of reasoning processes are available to children at different ages, as a means of specifying more closely what it is that develops. Second, increased attention has been paid to analyzing the conditions that facilitate or hinder performance on reasoning tasks, and to suggest how children's reasoning may be fostered. Third, researchers have begun to address a long-standing issue in cognitive development: the extent to which age-related changes in reasoning performance should be understood as arising from domain-general and content-independent cognitive changes, or as arising from increased domain-specific knowledge. Fourth, there has been renewed interest in the extent to which a general logic model (e.g., propositional logic as described by Inhelder and Piaget 1958, or inference schemata as described by Braine and O'Brien 1991) can serve as the basis for describing reasoning competence.

1. Definitions

Broadly defined, reasoning can be taken to include all cognitive activities in which inference plays a role; that is, where a conclusion is derived from information, not directly perceived. However, this broad definition has been differentiated in the literature in at least two different ways. In one approach, what is studied is the ability to make inferences *about* objects, events, or processes in different content domains (e.g., social reasoning, mathematical reasoning, spatial reasoning, biological reasoning, mechanical reasoning). Here, the developmental questions concern when children's reasoning within a content domain begins to be determined by (domain-specific) definitional principles or causal relations rather than by surface features such as perceptual similarity, or by association. In the other approach, reasoning is defined as the ability to make inferences *according to* different, specific types of inferential systems (e.g., logical reasoning, analogical reasoning, transitive reasoning). Here, the developmental questions concern whether and when children come to apply and understand these inferential systems.

A second distinction is important for addressing the question of when children demonstrate reasoning of either type. This concerns the difference between implicit and explicit reasoning. When an individual makes an inference, but this inference is automatic and direct, the reasoning is implicit: it is a feature of the reasoning system, not goal-directed, involves little intentional mental effort, is probably not available to conscious awareness, and it is probably not amenable to intentional modification or strategy use. In contrast, reasoning is explicit when an inference is purposefully or consciously made while solving a problem or task, when it involves mental effort, or when an individual can strategically manipulate or articulate the processes of reasoning, or knows why and how an inference is justified.

These two distinctions (reasoning about versus reasoning according to; implicit versus explicit reasoning) are important in considerations of how to characterize developmental changes in reasoning: studies have demonstrated that even quite young children have an impressive array of implicit and explicit reasoning skills when they reason *about* events in a variety of domains. Reasoning *according to* different sorts of inferential systems shows a more complicated picture: although younger children show some implicit use of inferential systems, they only demonstrate explicit goal-directed reasoning under limited conditions.

In this entry, recent trends in the study of the development of reasoning *about* will first be described, followed by developmental accounts of two characteristic types of reasoning *according to* that are particularly important for educational activities and which have each been studied extensively in the developmental literature, deductive reasoning (logical inferences) and analogical reasoning (reasoning with relations).

2. Reasoning About Objects, Events, and Processes

2.1 Early Competencies

Traditionally, age-related changes in children's reasoning about events, objects, and processes were characterized as a general and universal shift from inferences based on direct, perceptually based cues or associations to inferences based on more abstract underlying categories or principles or logical structure. This shift was considered to arise from global changes in mental structure (e.g., Inhelder and Piaget 1958) or from increases in information-processing capacity (e.g., Case 1985) that allowed more powerful and coherent inferences across content domains. This view was extensively challenged by research which showed strong content effects on reasoning and by research showing surprisingly sophisticated inferential competence in preschoolers (see Wellman and Gelman 1992 for a review). For example, children as young as 4 years infer the properties and actions of novel objects on the basis of such fundamental category distinctions as animate–inanimate, rather than on the basis of perceptual similarity (Gelman and Spelke 1981, but see Keil 1989); they infer the causes of physical events on the basis of causal mechanism rather than temporal contiguity or cause–effect similarity (Bullock 1985, Shultz 1982); they infer the existence of unseen mental states such as belief and desire and reason about how these will affect behavior (see Astington et al. 1988 for a review); and they can reason about number transformations on the basis of quantitative, not perceptual cues (Gelman and Gallistel 1978). These and related findings have led to the suggestion that young children possess a variety of rich domain-specific knowledge systems that support inferential reasoning, and that age-related change in reasoning performance occurs more because of changes in the content and organization of this knowledge, often referred to as "implicit theories," than because of changes in basic inferential processes (Carey 1985). Such changes in domain-specific knowledge are not simply quantitative, adding more and more knowledge. Rather, knowledge change can involve restructuring of the central concepts in a domain, increased hierarchical organization, and differentiation of central and peripheral concepts that can then support new or more powerful inferences.

2.2 Later Developments in Reasoning About

The findings of robust, implicit reasoning about objects, events, and transformations within a variety of core domains in preschoolers does not imply that there is no important developmental change. There are well-documented age-related changes in reasoning performance that arise when the task involves explicitly assessing inferential processes justifying conclusions, manipulating inferences, generalizing inferential processes to novel or abstract content, or when inferences require integrating information over time or stimulus dimensions. For example, in text comprehension tasks, school-children in the younger grades are less likely to make or modify the inferences necessary to link a series of events into a coherent story, especially when the content is unexpected or unfamiliar (Ackerman et al. 1991). However, because age differences are minimized when concepts are made salient, or when they are embedded within rich domain-specific knowledge contexts, it is likely that these differences arise from an increasing ability to access and use available concepts or from more focused attention (younger children are more likely to fail to make appropriate inferences when the relevant information is embedded in other, irrelevant filler material).

Age differences that are more difficult to explain in terms of processing limitations occur when the task involves explicitly testing or modifying inferences. For example, when asked to generate evidence to support a conclusion, younger children are typically unsystematic; and when given new information that is not entirely compatible with their prior knowledge or

hypotheses, younger children are more likely to distort or ignore information or fail to make an appropriate inference. To illustrate: several researchers (see, e.g., Linn 1986, Kuhn et al. 1988) have shown in science contexts that children do not change their incorrect prior beliefs, even when given direct feedback or contradiction training. Skills in systematically justifying inferences and in testing conclusions improve throughout middle childhood and adolescence (Kuhn et al. 1988).

3. Reasoning According to Inferential Systems

Research showing substantial age differences has generally addressed children's ability to reason according to inferential systems, assessing the use of reasoning strategies and knowledge about reasoning itself. The large majority of these studies have looked at deductive, or logical, reasoning.

3.1 Deductive Reasoning

Deductive reasoning is unique among reasoning processes because valid inferences that follow the rules of deduction are necessarily true, not merely plausible or likely or empirically true. Moreover, justifying the validity of a deduction involves addressing the form of a statement, not its content. Deductive reasoning underlies such activities as identifying contradictions, testing hypotheses, or evaluating the logical soundness of an explanation.

The area most widely studied in the assessment of deductive reasoning is logical problem-solving. Children are typically asked to make inferences about a set of statements that follow a particular logical form (e.g., a syllogism such as: "All a's are b. This is an a. Therefore it is b."; or a conditional if–then sentence such as: "if p then q. p is true. Therefore q.") Researchers have asked three related developmental questions: do children make logically valid inferences, and if so when? What conditions support or hinder logically valid inferences? Do children understand that deductive inferences are logically (as opposed to empirically) true, and if so when?

The evidence in the early 1990s on age differences in deductive–inference performance presents a complicated picture. Even preschoolers can make some logically valid inferences under some circumstances, yet most adults make errors on some problem types under most circumstances. Such findings suggest that, in contrast to many developmental accomplishments, deductive reasoning is not a unitary competence and is not universally acquired (at least in its more complex forms). The literature on age-related changes can be summarized briefly as follows: a rudimentary ability to make direct, implicit deductive inferences about well-known or easily represented concrete material (of the form: "If it is sunny, we will take a walk. It is sunny. Therefore, we will take a walk.") is available before children enter school. Many, if not most children, at least in Western cultures, will then acquire the competence to make explicit deductive inferences, even for abstract forms, during adolescence, though this competence may not always be evident in performance, for example, when a logical conclusion is factually untrue (see Braine and Rumain 1983 for a review).

Findings of a consistent age-related pattern in the kinds of inferences children make accurately will be illustrated here with inferences about conditional rules ("If p then q."; e.g., "If it rains, then the grass is wet."). From a logician's point of view, there are two determinate (i.e., necessary) inferences one can validly make from such a rule: (a) given p (it rains) one can infer that q (the grass is wet) must be the case, and (b) given *not-q* (the grass is not wet) one can infer that p is not the case (it did not rain). No other inferences are valid because they are indeterminate: that is, the state of q (the grass is/is not wet) is indeterminate given *not-p* (it did not rain), and the state of p (raining/not raining) is indeterminate given *not-q* (the grass is wet) (the grass could be wet for other reasons, e.g., it snowed, it was watered, and so on). A variety of studies have shown that younger children can make the two determinate inferences, but do not distinguish indeterminate from determinate inferences. Rather, they treat all inferences as determinate, and thus make invalid deductions such as "the grass is not wet" when told "it did not rain." Older children (adolescents) are more likely to distinguish determinate and indeterminate inferences, especially when given facilitating conditions or training. Adolescents are better at other kinds of deductive reasoning as well, including the use of falsification strategies to test an inference, and integrating inferences together to construct a deductive argument.

3.1.1 Explanations of Age-related Changes in Deductive Reasoning. Most researchers conclude from age differences in deductive reasoning that accurate logical reasoning performance is unlikely before adolescence except for the most elementary of inferences. However, the explanation for age-related changes in reasoning and for younger children's difficulties with logical tasks has become a matter of some controversy. Developmental explanations are focused on three, not necessarily mutually exclusive issues: whether (and how) domain-general inference schemes develop; whether (and how) nonlogical mediating variables affect reasoning performance; and whether (and how) metacognitive understanding of deduction as a separate knowledge domain develops.

Inference schemes. Claims about the existence and development of domain-general deductive inference schemes can be ordered along a continuum in terms of when and how such schemes might be acquired. At one extreme are Inhelder and Piaget (1958), who claimed that logical reasoning reflects the structure of the mind: that is, the organization of the mind can be modeled as a logical network (which Piaget described as 16 binary operations). According to this claim, once the logical network is acquired, it automatically leads to logical competence independent of content. This abstract structure is fully acquired only in adolescence after a long period of observation of and reflection on concrete transformations in the physical world. Piaget's characterization has been criticized because there is more variability in logical reasoning performance than his competence model would predict, and because the particular logic he used to describe mental structure seems incomplete. However, the legacy of this view is strong, and is evident in many current models (e.g., Overton 1990) that restrict true logical reasoning to adolescence.

Braine (1990) presented a second claim about domain-general deductive reasoning schemes. He argued that there are two types of domain-general inference schemes. The first he called a natural logic: it is a set of elementary reasoning schemes, based on such natural language terms as "if," "or," "and," "not," "all," "any," and "some," that is universally acquired, used without error and automatically, and is necessary for comprehending everyday discourse and practical reasoning. This natural logic is available early (at least by school age), and is independent of content as long as the content is empirically available and concrete. Braine claimed that the performance of younger children can be explained by their mastery of this natural logic. Later developments arise from secondary inference schemes (which are also domain-general), which allow analytic processing of the form of a statement rather than its content. These skills are not universal, but are rather the result of literacy and schooling.

The view that there are universal deductive reasoning schemes (whether acquired in adolescence or much earlier) is challenged by researchers who propose that all reasoning that looks like logical inference is actually a generalization from domain-specific pragmatic reasoning schemes (e.g., Cheng and Holyoak 1985). Pragmatic reasoning schemes are sets of expectations that arise from repeated experiences with everyday events, such as those involving permission or obligation. These specify the necessary and possible relations between premises (e.g., "*If* you are over 18 you may drink beer."; "If you drink beer, you *must be* over 18."). The data used to justify the claim that deductive reasoning is based on pragmatic reasoning contexts come from studies showing that deductive inferences are more accurate when embedded in such contexts. There has been a lively debate in the literature about whether this approach can explain the broad range of inferential competence, and whether it can explain understanding of necessity and implication.

Mediating performance factors. A second developmental focus is on the role of performance factors that facilitate or hinder deductive reasoning. Most researchers here assume that logical competence is masked because extralogical factors related to the encoding or processing of logical problems interfere. For example, pragmatic conversational rules (or information-processing limitations) may lead children to encode a logical statement incorrectly, causing them to reason about a rule different from the one intended (e.g., "if" may be encoded as "if and only if," Braine and O'Brien 1991); they may fail to represent a relationship in a way that allows thinking about the possible situations to which a rule can apply and thus fail to draw a correct inference (e.g., Johnson-Laird et al. 1986); or they may be unwilling to give "can't tell" answers to indeterminate situations (Braine and Rumain 1983). According to this focus, children's logical reasoning performance can be facilitated in several ways: by minimizing processing demands, by providing content that facilitates accurate encoding and representation of the propositions, and by the use of training designed to focus attention on the form rather than the content of the material. For example, several studies (summarized in Braine and Rumain 1983) have shown that it is possible to facilitate children's distinction between determinate and indeterminate inferences when additional information is presented. For example, given the statement "If it rains, the grass is wet.", children who are also told "But the grass could also get wet if someone waters it." are more likely to avoid the false inference that "the grass is wet" means "it rained." It is also possible to facilitate reasoning by manipulating the content of reasoning problems. For example, children's performance improves when tasks are related to everyday pragmatic reasoning schemes (e.g., Light et al. 1989) or to familiar activities (Sophian and Somerville 1988), or when the child is asked to reason about fantasy content that allows a focus on the form, not the empirical truth of a statement (Markovits and Vachon 1989).

Metacognitive factors. Researchers from this perspective argue that although children have the structural competence to reason logically, they do not do so because they lack an explicit metacognitive understanding of logic as a unique domain (a "metalogic"), and thus (a) do not understand that logical reasoning is concerned with validity, not empirical truth, and (b) do not consciously employ reasoning strategies to coordinate or compare inferences, to generate and test counterexamples, or to construct a line of argument (Moshman 1990). The first signs of such metacognitive awareness are shown at the end of the preschool period when children understand that inferential access is a valid source of knowledge (Sodian and Wimmer 1987), and can distinguish those inferences that are necessarily true from those that are merely plausible for simple concrete situations (Fabricius et al. 1987). However, this elementary understanding is not robust and is consolidated over middle childhood, as is shown by increasing understanding that there are different rules of validity for logical and empirical conclusions, and that logical rules form a unique domain. For example, in a classic study, Osherson and Markman (1975) gave children statements such as "The chalk in my hand is either yellow or it is not yellow." and asked whether they would have to check to know if the statement was true or not. Whereas preschoolers and young children in grade school said one would have to check (not distinguishing empirical from logical truth), older schoolchildren could evaluate the logical validity of the sentence without reference to empirical truth. Komatsu and Galotti (1986) showed that it is not until late grade school that children understand that logical rules are different from physical and social conventional rules (e.g., that logical rules must hold under all circumstances at all times).

An explanation for these age-related changes is suggested by Moshman (1990) who proposed three developmental levels. First, until the age of 6 or 7 children do not yet have a concept of logical necessity, although their deductive inferences follow logical norms. At the next step, during middle childhood, conclusions that are logically necessary are distinguished from those that are empirically likely, but only for premises that are assumed to be true. That is, the insight about logical necessity is not content-free, and children are unable to reason about the validity of an argument independent of the truth of its constituent premises. For example, given the statements "Elephants are either plants or animals. Elephants are not animals." children of middle school age will not accept the conclusion "elephants are plants" as valid. That is, they do not understand logical inference as using content-independent relations. This next and third step, a concept of inferential validity, is achieved only in adolescence, and only by some individuals. What it allows is an ability to reason about the possible, not just the actual; that is, to apply logical inference rules to abstract or contra-intuitive content.

3.2 Analogical Reasoning

In analogical reasoning, relational information from a known system (the source) is identified and transferred or mapped onto a new system (the target). The ability to reason analogically is central for problem-solving in new content domains for which there is no ready solution, for transferring knowledge, and for acquiring new knowledge.

Classical research looked at age differences in the ability to reason analogically by presenting tasks modeled on the traditional four-term verbal analogy taken from intelligence tests: $a:b::c:d$ ("a is to b as c is to d"). In a typical test, the subject's task is to supply the last term in the series; for example: "Black is to white as hard is to steel/stone/solid/soft/blue." To solve such a problem, one must extract the relation suggested by the $a:b$ terms (opposites) and apply it to the c term to find the unknown d term. Analogy has also been studied in problem-solving tasks in which a solution process for one problem must be mapped onto a second problem. Generally, it has been claimed from such tasks that analogical reasoning develops late: performance shows a steady increase until adolescence, with younger children providing solutions based on associative (hard/stone) or similarity (hard/solid) relations.

The view that younger children do not reason analogically has been challenged by studies that have shown that even young preschoolers demonstrate the ability to use relational structure to reason analogically when their performance is supported by two factors: (a) when the relations are ones about which they have sufficiently rich understanding, and (b) when they are given explicit hints to look for relations (see Goswami 1991 for a review).

However, despite early competence, there are still age-related differences in analogical reasoning, even when familiar content is used. These differences arise when children must apply analogical reasoning spontaneously (e.g., without hints or feedback) or when the analogical mapping is not readily apparent and concerns underlying abstract relations. For example, Gentner (1989) looked at the ability to go beyond surface similarity between analogies and to detect and use higher-order structural relations (what she termed systematicity). To demonstrate age differences in the use of systematicity, Gentner asked 4–6-year-olds and 8–10-year-olds to reason analogically from one story plot to another. She varied the surface similarity of characters in the source and transfer stories, and whether the plot was organized by an underlying causal or moral relationship or not (systematicity). Although increased similarity facilitated performance at all ages, only the older children benefited from increased systematicity, leading Gentner to conclude that there is a shift in middle childhood from reliance on surface-level object relations, to the use of underlying, more abstract relational structure. The reasons for this shift are controversial: some (e.g., Brown 1990) have argued that it can be explained in terms of increasing domain-specific knowledge (because with increasing knowledge the structure of concepts becomes organized according to underlying relations rather than surface-level features); others have argued that there is a more general "characteristic to defining" shift (Keil 1989); and yet others (e.g., Goswami 1991) have proposed a metacognitive account whereby children increasingly reflect on the demands of an analogical reasoning task and spontaneously and explicitly seek out relational similarity.

3.3 Nondevelopmental Factors that Affect Reasoning

There is considerable interest in identifying both personality and experiential factors that influence reasoning performance. For example, cognitive style may affect reasoning performance: individuals who are characterized as reflective (rather than impulsive) are more likely to perform accurately, and reflectiveness training improves performance, although only for children classified as impulsive (Baron et al. 1986, Overton 1990). Experiential factors present a complex picture. Although most researchers agree that complex forms of reasoning are facilitated by schooling, it is not clear what aspects of instruction are important. Direct instruction in logic does not seem to facilitate performance on typical inferential errors (Cheng et al. 1986), although there is some suggestion that a combination of subject-matter training combined with reasoning training has facilitatory effects (Linn 1986). Specification of noncognitive factors that affect reasoning and of the educational and life experiences that foster the development of reasoning skills is a challenge for future research.

4. Conclusion

Age-related changes in performance across different reasoning types suggest the beginnings of a new coherent developmental picture. Preschoolers show an ability to use inferential reasoning processes to reach accurate and valid conclusions in a variety of domains for which they have rich conceptual knowledge when they are asked to reason *about* objects, events, and processes. They can also make simple, direct deductive inferences, and can reason analogically when the content about which they reason makes direct use of their knowledge base. Developmental differences seem to arise from two changes: an increasing ability to apply inferential abilities to novel, abstract, or contra-intuitive content, and an increasing understanding of inference as a mode of thinking in which the form, not the content, takes precedence. These developments seem to be gradual rather than stage-like: whereas younger children can make valid inferences under some circumstances, they do not do so consistently, they do not yet understand the unique status of inference as a source of knowledge, and they are less likely to separate empirical reality from logical or inferentially derived validity. What becomes increasingly available through adolescence (and beyond) is an ability to apply inferential processes regardless of content, and an ability to reflect on and evaluate the products of reasoning.

The educational implications of research on reasoning skills are summarized by Scholnick (1990 p. 179): "children need multiple redundant sources of input . . . meaningful input to support logical processing . . . logic to support meaning to detect failures of comprehension." In other words, both increased domain-specific knowledge and increased use of reasoning strategies can facilitate reasoning. A challenge for research is to determine the interacting roles of domain-specific knowledge, the acquisition of new and more powerful inference schemes, and the acquisition of more specific and explicit knowledge about inference as a mode of thinking.

See also: Childhood; Piaget's Theory of Human Development; Cognition and Learning; An Overview of Cognitive Development

References

Ackerman B P, Jackson M, Sherrill L 1991 Inference modification by children and adults. *Journal of Experimental Child Psychology* 52(2): 166–96

Astington J, Olson D, Harris P 1988 *Developing Theories of Mind*. Cambridge University Press, Cambridge

Baron J, Badgio P, Gaskins I W 1986 Cognitive style and its improvement: A normative approach. In: Sternberg R J (ed.) 1986 *Advances in the Psychology of Human Intelligence*, Vol 3. Erlbaum, Hillsdale, New Jersey

Braine M D S 1990 The "natural logic" approach to reasoning. In: Overton W F (ed.) 1990

Braine M D S, O'Brien D P 1991 A theory of IF: A lexical entry, reasoning program, and pragmatic principles. *Psychol. Rev.* 98(2): 182–203

Braine M D S, Rumain B 1983 Logical reasoning. In: Flavell J H, Markman E M (eds.) 1983 *Handbook of Child Psychology. Vol 3: Cognitive Development*. Wiley, New York

Brown A L 1990 Domain-specific principles affect learning and transfer in children. *Cognit. Sci.* 14(1): 107–33

Bullock M 1985 Causal reasoning and developmental change over the preschool years. *Hum. Dev.* 28(4): 169–91

Carey S 1985 *Conceptual Change in Childhood*. MIT Press, Cambridge, Massachusetts

Case R 1985 *Intellectual Development: Birth to Adulthood*. Academic Press, New York

Cheng P W, Holyoak K J 1985 Pragmatic reasoning schemas. *Cognit. Psychol.* 17(4): 391–416

Cheng P W, Holyoak K J, Nisbett R E, Oliver L M 1986 Pragmatic versus syntactic approaches to training deductive reasoning. *Cognit. Psychol.* 18(3): 293–328

Fabricus W V, Sophian C, Wellman H M 1987 Young children's sensitivity to logical necessity in their inferential search behavior. *Child Dev.* 58(2): 409–23

Gelman R, Gallistel C R 1978 *The Child's Understanding of Number*. Harvard University Press, Cambridge, Massachusetts

Gelman R, Spelke E 1981 The development of thoughts about animate and inanimate objects: Implications for research on social cognition. In: Flavell J H, Ross L (eds.) 1981 *Social Cognitive Development: Frontiers and Possible Futures*. Cambridge University Press, Cambridge.

Gentner D 1989 The mechanisms of analogical learning. In: Vosniadou S, Ortony A (eds.) 1989

Goswami U 1991 Analogical reasoning: What develops? A review of research and theory. *Child Dev.* 62: 1–22

Inhelder B, Piaget J 1958 *The Growth of Logical Thinking from Childhood to Adolescence: An Essay on the Construction of Formal Operational Structures*. Basic Books, New York

Johnson-Laird P, Oakhill J, Bull D 1986 Children's syllogistic reasoning. *Quarterly Journal of Experimental Psychology* 38A: 35–58

Keil F C 1989 *Concepts, Kinds and Cognitive Development*. MIT Press, Cambridge, Massachusetts

Komatsu L K, Galotti K M 1986 Children's reasoning about social, physical, and logical regularities: A look at two worlds. *Child Dev.* 57(2): 413–20

Kuhn D, Amsel E, O'Loughlin M 1988 *The Development of Scientific Thinking Skills*. Academic Press, San Diego, California

Light P, Blaye A, Gilly M, Girotto V 1989 Pragmatic schemas and logical reasoning in 6- to 8-year-old children. *Cognitive Development* 4(1): 49–64

Linn M C 1986 Science. In: Dillon R F, Sternberg R J (eds.) 1986 *Cognition and Instruction*. Academic Press, Orlando, Florida

Markovits H, Vachon R 1989 Reasoning with contrary-to-fact propositions. *Journal of Experimental Child Psychology* 47(3): 398–412

Moshman D 1990 The development of metalogical understanding. In: Overton W F (ed.) 1990

Osherson D N, Markman E 1975 Language and the ability to evaluate contradictions and tautologies. *Cog.* 3(3): 213–26

Overton W F 1990 Competence and procedures: Constraints on the development of logical reasoning. In: Overton W F (ed.) 1990

Scholnick E 1990 The three faces of if. In: Overton W F (ed.) 1990

Shultz T R 1982 Rules of causal attribution. *Monogr. Soc. Res. Child Dev.* 47(1): 1–51

Sodian B, Wimmer H 1987 Children's understanding of inference as a source of knowledge. *Child Dev.* 58(2): 424–33

Sophian C, Somerville S C 1988 Early developments in logical reasoning: Considering alternative possibilities. *Cognitive Development* 3(2):183–222

Wellman H M, Gelman S A 1992 Cognitive development: Foundational theories of core domains. *Annu. Rev. Psychol.* 43:337–75

Further Reading

Lunzer E A 1978 Formal reasoning: A reappraisal. In: Presseisen B Z, Goldstein D, Appel M H (eds.) 1978 *Topics in Cognitive Development. Vol. 2: Language and Operational Thought*. Plenum Press, New York

Overton W F (ed.) 1990 *Reasoning, Necessity, and Logic: Developmental Perspectives*. Erlbaum, Hillsdale, New Jersey

Sternberg R J (ed.) 1982 *Handbook of Human Intelligence*. Cambridge University Press, Cambridge

Vosniadou S, Ortony A (eds.) 1989 *Similarity and Analogical Reasoning*. Cambridge University Press, Cambridge

Development of Social Cognition

M Keller and M. Killen

The field of developmental social cognition emerged during the 1970s (see Chandler 1976, Shantz 1983 for overviews). It originated in the framework of theories of cognitive development, particularly Piaget's theory of cognitive–structural development, and in social psychological theories of person perception.

Piaget characterized children's understanding of the physical and the social world as egocentric, which means a fusing of self's and others' perspectives. Only with the achievement of concrete operations are the perspectives of the self and others gradually differentiated, a process that reaches into adolescence. Mead (1934), on the other hand, had defined the ability to take the perspective of others as a fundamental process in socialization.

The concept of egocentrism and the definition of stages of perspective taking became a first predominant focus in social cognitive research (Flavell et al. 1968). This includes cognitive and affective processes such as the affective sharing of others' worlds as captured in the concept of empathy (Hoffman 1977).

Since the mid-1980s the variety of measures used in the field and the heterogeneous results with regard to what children can and cannot understand at the same age has contributed to a systematic analysis of the structure and content dimensions involved in social cognition. Structure has been defined as the coordination of components of knowledge within circumscribed domains (Turiel 1983) and as the ability to differentiate and coordinate the perspectives of self and others (Edelstein et al. 1984, Selman 1980). Action theory has been proposed as an integrative framework for defining structure and content components as well as social and moral cognition (Keller and Edelstein 1991).

1. Processes of Social Cognition

Perspective-taking was analyzed by cognitive psychologists with regard to specific types of content, such as visual–spatial or social inferences. The prototypical perspective-taking tasks refer to the question of when in development a person understands that knowledge about a situation is based on the particular access one has to reality, be it visual or conceptual. How different social perspectives are interpreted and coordinated has been described as a sequence of levels of perspective-taking (Selman 1980). Dimensions such as intentions, feelings, and expectations have been used as different content aspects of the perspectives. Since the mid-1980s the false-belief paradigm has become one way to examine perspective-taking

abilities (Perner 1988). Understanding false beliefs requires the knowledge that a person may act on beliefs that can be diametrically opposed to perceptual reality. This paradigm has become part of a more general representational theory of mind as a set of mental concepts among which desires and beliefs are central. Although 3-year olds can understand that actions are based on desires, there is a debate about whether they understand the function of beliefs. Yet it has been shown that children younger than 3 can represent alternative models of reality in pretend play and in the appearance–reality distinction.

In the social-psychological tradition (Higgins 1981), causal or attribution schemata, biases, and scripts have gained importance in social cognitive research. Even 3-year olds have some knowledge about typical events which is stable, schematic, general, and temporally/causally structured. Such shared event knowledge provides a context for children's play and mother–child discourse.

2. Domains and Categories of Social Cognition

Three general areas of research in social cognition have been distinguished: (a) psychological judgment of the self and others in terms of motives, intentions, beliefs, and feelings; (b) the different types of social and moral rules governing actions and interactions; and (c) relations between persons and the role of culture.

2.1 Understanding Situations and Persons

In the social-psychological tradition of perception research, age-related social inferences—with a more recent interest in scripts and causal attribution schemata—have attracted considerable interest. With increasing age children begin to draw inferences about the psychological meaning of situations in terms of the motives, intentions, and feelings of the person involved. Furthermore, more central and more implicit information about situations is processed and actions are explained with regard to multiple causes, including external-situational and internal-dispositional determinants. Understanding of motives and intentions and the coordination of consequences and intentions was a predominant topic in early research. Understanding emotions has become increasingly important since the mid-1980s. Whereas early research was concerned with the understanding of basic emotions in prototypical situations, later research has looked at more complex emotions such as pride, guilt, or mixed emotions. A new line of research has connected the understanding of emotions with the theory of mind research (Wellman 1990) and has touched on topics such as the understanding of surprise, hiding of emotions, and the distinction between real and apparent emotion.

2.2 Understanding Relationships and Moral Rules

Given familiar everyday problems, preschool children have a sense of self and are capable of understanding intentions, emotion, and motives (Damon 1983). In addition, they recognize the necessity of fairness and understand social conventions.

Turiel's (1983) domain distinction research has shown that all children make conceptual distinctions between moral and social-conventional rules. Within the moral category, they also make distinctions between physical harm and property damage.

Research on social and moral concepts in middle childhood and adolescence has covered a large range of topics from understanding authority and peer relationships to complex societal issues, such as abortion and drug use (see Killen and Hart 1995). These studies have shown that with increasing age, individuals weigh and coordinate a number of different components embedded within complex dilemmas in order to make judgments about the best course of action.

Research has shown that different types of relationship provide different sources of experiences for children's developing social cognition. Thus, parent–child relations have been characterized as ones of authority and child–child relations as ones of equality. Research has examined the nature of these relationships and their influence on development, as well as children's conceptions of these types of relations (Damon 1983, Krappmann 1989, Youniss 1980). Parents' statements to children about psychological, moral, and social-conventional rules influence how children conceptualize these relations by providing ways of pointing to relationships between actions and their consequences. Through peer interaction, children develop reciprocal and mutual ways of interaction.

Research on children's concepts of authority has shown that children do not make unilateral judgments about authority but make judgments based on the jurisdiction, legitimacy, and experience of an individual in a position of power, and that they differentiate between parental and child authority (Laupa 1991, Tisak 1994). Research on friendship is another important domain. It shows that concepts of friendship emerge during the preschool years and are transformed in middle childhood and adolescence (Corsaro 1985).

2.3 The Role of Culture in Social-cognitive Development

On a broader level, cultural messages influence children's acquisition of social concepts. How culture plays a role in the acquisition of social concepts has received much attention (Turiel et al. 1987). This involves identifying different types of cultural beliefs, and analyzing how such beliefs mediate judgments about social categories such as morality, convention, and the self. Research on the role of cultural influences has revealed several general findings: (a) universal patterns exist with reference to the understanding of social and moral rules (Shweder et al. 1987); (b) universal patterns are apparent in the child's ability to make inferences about the mental states of others (Avis and Harris 1991); and (c) universal patterns exist regarding the ability to understand cultural norms and rituals. At the same time, several culturally specific patterns emerge, pertaining to concepts of the self, understandings of the natural order and biological knowledge, and views of social roles and customs (see Turiel 1994). Thus, there is a heterogeneity of social orientations and social-cognitive abilities that are not solely determined by a person's cultural membership (Wainryb 1991).

3. Acquisition of Social and Moral Knowledge

Investigating cultural beliefs and their relation to social-cognitive categories raises the important issue of the acquisition of social and moral knowledge. This is a complex question for which there are many different answers. In the field of social cognition, there is a consensus that the process of meaning-making is based on knowledge structures derived from social interaction. Individuals make judgments about their experiences and these judgments form their social categories of the world (Keller and Edelstein 1991, Killen 1991, Turiel 1983). How children acquire these knowledge categories has been examined from several different perspectives. Much work has been done on parent–infant interaction, which has shown that infants take the initiative in engaging in exchanges with others, and that reciprocity is a part of early social exchanges. The importance of these findings is to show that the young child is active, not passive, and that there are indications of an early social predisposition. Through a complex set of interactions throughout the lifespan, individuals develop a growing understanding of the social world that is multifaceted and heterogeneous.

References

Avis J, Harris P 1991 Belief-desire reasoning among Baka children: Evidence for a universal conception of mind. *Child Dev.* 62(3): 460–67

Chandler M 1976 Social cognition: A selected review of current research. In: Furth H, Overton W, Gallagher J (eds.) 1976 *The Yearbook of Developmental Epistemology*, Vol. 1. Plenum Press, New York

Corsaro W 1985 *Friendship and Peer Culture in the Early Years.* Ablex, Norwood, New Jersey

Damon W 1983 *Social and Personality Development: Infancy through Adolescence.* Norton, New York

Edelstein W, Keller M, Wahlen K 1984 Structure and content in social cognition: Conceptual and empirical analyses. *Child Dev.* 55(4): 1514–26

Flavell J H, Botkin P T, Fry C L Jr, Wright J W, Jarvis P E 1968 *The Development of Role-taking and Communication Skills in Children.* Wiley, New York

Higgins E T 1981 Role taking and social judgment: Alternative developmental perspectives and processes. In: Flavell J, Ross L (eds.) 1981 *Social Cognitive Development.* Cambridge University Press, Cambridge

Hoffman M L 1977 Empathy, its development and prosocial implications. In: Keasey C B (ed.) 1977 *Nebraska Symposium on Motivation*, Vol. 25. University of Nebraska Press, Lincoln, Nebraska

Keller M, Edelstein W 1991 The development of socio-moral meaning making: Domains, categories, and perspective-taking. In: Kurtines W, Gewirtz J (eds.) 1991 *Handbook of Moral Behavior and Development*, Vol. 2. Erlbaum, Hillsdale, New Jersey

Killen M 1991 Social and moral development in early childhood. In: Kurtines W, Gewirtz J (eds.) 1991 *Handbook of Moral Behavior and Development*, Vol. 2. Erlbaum, Hillsdale, New Jersey

Killen M, Hart D (eds.) 1995 *Morality in Everyday Life: Developmental Perspectives.* Cambridge University Press, Cambridge

Krappmann L 1989 Family relationships and peer relationships in middle childhood. In: Kreppner K, Lerner R M (eds.) 1989 *Family Systems and Life-span Development.* Erlbaum, Hillsdale, New Jersey

Laupa M 1991 Children's reasoning about three authority attributes: Adult status, knowledge and social position, *Dev. Psychol.* 27: 321–329

Mead G H 1934 *Mind, Self and Society.* University of Chicago Press, Chicago, Illinois

Perner J 1988 Higher-order beliefs and intentions in children's understanding of social interaction. In: Astington J W, Harris P O L, Olson D R (eds.) 1988 *Developing Theories of Mind.* Cambridge University Press, Cambridge

Selman R L 1980 *The Growth of Interpersonal Understanding.* Academic Press, New York

Shantz C U 1983 Social cognition. In: Mussen P H, Flavell J H, Markman E (eds.) 1983 *Handbook of Child Psychology*, Vol. 3. Wiley, New York

Shweder R A, Mahapatra M, Miller J G 1987 Culture and moral development. In: Kagan J, Lamb S (eds.) 1987 *The Emergence of Morality in Young Children.* University of Chicago Press, Chicago, Illinois

Tisak M 1994 Domains of social reasoning and beyond. *Annals of Child Development* 11: 95–130

Turiel E 1983 *The Development of Social Knowledge: Morality and Convention.* Cambridge University Press, Cambridge

Turiel E 1994 Morality, authoritarianism, and personal agency in cultural contexts. In: Sternberg R J, Ruzgis P (eds.) 1994 *Personality and Intelligence.* Cambridge University Press, Cambridge

Turiel E, Killen M, Helwig C 1987 Morality: Its structure, functions, and vagaries. In: Kagan J, Lamb S (eds.) 1987 *The Emergence of Morality in Young Children.* University of Chicago Press, Chicago, Illinois

Wainryb C 1991 Understanding differences in moral judgments: The role of informational assumptions. *Child Dev.* 62: 840–851

Wellman H M 1990 *The Child's Theory of Mind.* MIT Press, Cambridge, Massachusetts

Youniss J 1980 *Parents and Peers in Social Development. A Sullivan-Piaget Perspective.* Chicago University Press, Chicago, Illinois

Play: Developmental Stages, Functions, and Educational Support

K. H. Rubin and R. J. Coplan

For centuries, children have been observed to spend much of their time engaged in play. It has not been until recent years, however, that play as a topic of serious empirical pursuit has received scientific attention (Rubin et al. 1983). Historically, several factors have inhibited the study of play. For example, many writers have assumed that play is a trivial and inconsequential activity; also, play has been difficult—if not impossible—to define. Nevertheless, despite these problems, social scientists and educators have been so struck by this historically pervasive phenomenon that for this reason alone they have voraciously pursued the study of children's play. The developmental and educational significance of play in childhood is discussed in this entry.

1. Classical Theories of Play

Contemporary research on the topic of children's play draws heavily from early theoretical accounts about the functional significance of the phenomenon (for a review see Rubin et al. 1983). These early theories are briefly discussed below.

The "surplus energy" theory characterized play as "blowing off steam." Schiller (1954), an eighteenth-century poet and philosopher, defined play as the "aimless expenditure of exuberant energy." He wrote that work satisfied the primary needs of the human species. Once these needs were met, the superfluous energy that remained resulted in play. Because children were not responsible for their own survival, they were thought to have a total energy "surplus," which they depleted through play.

According to the "relaxation theory," the purpose of play is to restore energy expended in work. Thus, labor was viewed as consuming human energy and as resulting in an energy deficit. This deficit could be replenished through rest or sleep, or by engaging in play.

"Recapitulation" theorists believed that cultural

epochs in human history were repeated sequentially in children's play: the animal stage (children's climbing and swinging); the savage stage (hunting, tag, hide-and-go-seek); the nomad stage (keeping pets); the agricultural/patriarchical stage (playing with dolls, digging in sand); and the tribal stage (team games). They also believed that play served as an outlet for the catharsis or release of unnecessary primitive instincts, thereby preparing individuals for the intellectually advanced activities of the modern era.

According to "preexercise" theorists, the period of childhood existed so that the organism could play. Humankind's relatively long period of immaturity was considered necessary to allow for children to practice the instinctively based complex skills that would be essential for survival in adulthood. Thus, the adaptive function of play was to prepare children to perfect skills they would require in adulthood.

Each of these four classical theories has serious limitations. For example, the surplus energy theory offers no reason why children continue to play even when exhausted; the recreation theory cannot explain why children play (since they do not suffer the stresses of work); and the recapitulation theory cannot explain why many "occupations" of earlier races are omitted and "regressions" occur from time to time in children's play.

Despite these limitations, these early theories continue to have an impact on how many people think about play. For example, parents and teachers of young children are often heard to express reservations about poor weather conditions that might keep children indoors all day. The traditionally held belief is that such restriction constrains the expenditure of energy waiting to be "burned off."

2. Modern Theories of Play

Several common themes run through twentieth-century interpretations of children's play. These include the following beliefs: (a) that children need to play in order to express themselves or to relieve themselves of anxieties and fears; (b) that play results, in part, from wish fulfillment.

2.1 Psychoanalytic Theory

Freud (1961) believed that play provided children with important avenues for the expression of wish fulfillment and the mastery of traumatic events. For example, he argued that play allowed the child to transcend the rigid sanctions of reality, and therefore served as a safe context for the child to vent socially unacceptable (e.g., aggressive) impulses.

Freud addressed the mastery aspect of play through the repetition compulsion, a psychic mechanism that allows individuals to cope with traumatic events through a compulsive repetition of components of the disturbing events. Since children were believed to be more susceptible to trauma than adults, they were thought to use play to become the active masters of situations in which they were once passive victims. For example, if a young child has been scolded by her mother for spilling a glass of milk, the child may reenact the scene numerous times with a doll, casting herself in the role of angry mother.

2.2 Piaget's Theory

Piaget (1962) suggested that play represents the purest form of assimilation. In assimilation, children incorporate events, objects, or situations into existing ways of thinking. Thus, as "pure assimilation," play was not considered an avenue to cognitive growth, but rather a reflection of the child's present level of cognitive development.

Piaget described three stages in the development of play. First, practice play appeared in infancy; it consisted of sensorimotor actions (e.g., clapping hands). Through this "functional exercise," Piaget believed that children acquired and honed the basic motor skills inherent in their everyday activities. Second, symbolic play, appearing around the second year, required an implied representation of absent objects (e.g., pretending to bake a cake while in the sand box). As opposed to practice play, where actions are exercised and elaborated for their functional value, symbolic play allows the exercise of actions for their representational value. The last structural category to develop was games-with-rules. This type of play activity necessarily incorporates social coordination and a basic understanding of social relationships. In the case of games, rules and regulations are imposed by the group, and the overriding structure results from collective organization.

2.3 Vygotsky's Theory

Like Piaget's theory, Vygotsky's (1967) discussion of play was framed within a larger psychological theory of children's cognition. Vygotsky argued that children used symbolic play as an essential link in the association of abstract meanings and their associated concrete objects. Repetitive symbolic play was useful in allowing the child to conceive of meanings independently of the objects that they may represent. For example, by pretending that a wooden block is a car, and driving it around the room, a young child gains experience in understanding the abstract meaning of the concept of "car." Thus, play provided children with a self-controlled context in which they could explore the relation between words, names, objects, and concepts.

2.4 Other Modern Theories

"Drive modulation" theorists have proposed that excessively high and excessively low levels of stimulation are aversive, and play is used as a means of modulating the arousal associated with this aversion (Berlyne 1960). For example, when confronted with a novel object, "specific exploration" allows the child to explore its features and relieve arousal through increasing familiarity with the object. Following specific exploration an optimal level of arousal is sought through "diverse exploration" or stimulus-seeking activity. This latter form of exploration, or play, increases stimulation when children are "bored" and continues until arousal reaches an optimal level. Thus play is viewed as a stimulus producing activity that is generated by low levels of arousal.

Bateson (1956) proposed a theory of play that focused on its "metacommunicative" aspects. Accordingly, children establish a context, or "frame," for play (e.g., by laughing or smiling), and this "frame" allows for the incorporation of pretend roles and a focus on make-believe meanings of objects and actions. Developmentally, these contexts allow for the children to learn not so much about the roles they are playing, but rather about the processes of framing and reframing roles.

Cognitive theorists (e.g., Bruner 1972) have emphasized the creativity and flexibility that are promoted by children's play. Accordingly, play allows the individual to explore new combinations of behaviors and ideas within a psychologically safe milieu. Through play, children develop behavioral "prototypes" that may be used subsequently in more "serious" contexts. For example, a young girl may dress and undress her doll many times, and later incorporate her accomplishments from this play session when dressing herself. As such, the means become more important than the ends, and since accomplishing goals is not important in play, children are free to experiment with new and unusual combinations of behavior. The experience of this type of play provides children with additional flexibility in solving "real-life" problems.

Finally, theoretical accounts from the 1980s onward have focused on the regulation and understanding of emotions. For example, Fein (1989) has suggested that children pretend in an effort to reconstruct and gain mastery over emotionally arousing experiences. When children come to realize that others have similar affect-regulatory needs and that others (peers) share with them similar emotion-arousing experiences, they begin to direct their pretense activities toward peers. From this conceptual perspective, social pretense has an affective origin: children engage in social pretense to share emotionally significant experiences with their peers.

3. Issues in Defining Play

It is one thing to think about why play exists in the human repertoire; it is something else altogether to define it. According to Rubin et al. (1983), the following characteristics, when taken together, define play.

(a) Play is not governed by appetitive drives, compliance with social demands, or inducements external to the behavior itself; instead play is intrinsically motivated.

(b) Play is spontaneous, is free from external sanctions, and has self-imposed goals.

(c) Play asks "What can I do with this object or person?" This question differentiates play from exploration, which asks "What is this object (or person) and what can I do with it (him or her)?"

(d) Play is not a serious rendition of an activity or a behavior it resembles; instead it consists of activities that can be labeled as pretense.

(e) Play is free from externally imposed rules—this characteristic distinguishes play from games-with-rules.

(f) Play involves active engagement—this distinguishes play from daydreaming, lounging, and aimless loafing.

4. Developmental Progressions in Children's Play

Between the periods of infancy and middle childhood, children's play undergoes an evolution in both form and content. Numerous theorists have suggested that the structural properties of play change with and reflect development. These progressions are reviewed briefly below.

4.1 Infant and Toddler Play

Observations of very young children at play provide researchers with a window into the development of representational thinking. In the first year of life, most play with objects is sensorimotor in structure and function. For example, babies tend to act on objects with little regard for their physical features (e.g., banging a plastic cup on the floor). By the end of the first year, infants become more discriminating and representational in their play. Objects are combined in "appropriate" and meaningful ways (e.g., a plastic cup is placed on a saucer; an empty cup is brought to the mouth as if the child is drinking from it). These latter developments reveal the critical components that reflect rapid growth in representational thinking. These components include: (a) decontextualized behavior; (b) self–other relationships; (c) object substitutions; and (d) sequential combinations.

Decontextualized behavior is first observed at the end of the first year of life. Basically, it involves the "out of context" production of familiar behavior.

For example, the infant may close his or her eyes, put head on pillow, and lie in a curled position at a time of day (e.g., mid-morning) and in a context (e.g., a playground) that is detached from the situational context when and where sleeping or napping occurs (Fenson 1984). By the middle of the second year, the toddler coordinates the use of several objects in his or her demonstrations of decontextualized behavior (e.g., a teddy bear is fed from an empty cup).

This latter use of objects in pretense captures the essence of the second developmental component of play, self–other relationships. (McCune 1986). When pretense appears at about 12 months, it is centered around the child's own body (e.g., the child feeds itself). Roughly between 15 and 21 months, play becomes other referenced; however, the "other" is typically an inanimate object as in the teddy bear example noted above. Moreover, during this period, when others are involved in pretense activities they are passive recipients of the child's behavior. Beyond 20 months, and increasingly so up to about 30 months, the child gains the ability to "step out" of the play situation and to manipulate the "other" as if it were an active agent (e.g., the teddy bear "feeds" a doll with a plastic spoon). The developmental significance of these accomplishments should not be underestimated. Advances in maturity of play reflect the young child's increasing ability to represent symbolically things, actions, roles, and relationships.

A third component of play is the use of substitute objects. The ability to identify one object with another (e.g., a stick is used as a laser gun) is paradigmatic of symbolic representation.

Finally, the fourth component of play is the coordination and sequencing of pretense. Between the ages of 12 and 20 months, toddlers' pretend acts become increasingly coordinated into meaningful sequences. At first, the child produces a single pretend gesture (drinking from a plastic cup); later, the child relates, in succession, the same act to the self and then to others (drinks from the cup, feeds the teddy bear from the cup). Subsequently, in a multischeme combination, the young child is able to coordinate different sequential acts (pours tea, feeds the teddy bear, puts bear to sleep). By the end of the second year, children indicate verbally that these coordinated sequences are planned prior to execution (child self-verbalizes sequence of pretense behavior prior to acting).

4.2 The Play of Preschoolers and Elementary School-age Children

The above noted constituents of play are mastered prior to or near the child's second birthday. These elements of play become increasingly shared with others as children mature. Indeed, many psychologists suggest that one of the essential "tasks" of early childhood is to master the means to share and coordinate decontextualized and substitutive activities (e.g., Goncu 1989).

Why is shared or social pretense important? According to Howes (1992), there are essentially three functions of sociodramatic play. First, it creates a context for mastering the communication of meaning. Second, it provides opportunities for children to learn to control and compromise; these opportunities arise during discussions and negotiations concerning pretend roles and scripts and the rules guiding the pretend episodes. Third, social pretense allows for a "safe" context in which children can explore and discuss issues of intimacy and trust.

During the preschool period (3 to 5 years), social pretense increases in quantity and becomes qualitatively more sophisticated. Thus by 36 months children are generally able to communicate pretend scripts to adults and peers; by 5 years they can discuss, assign, and enact play themes while continuing to add novel components. Finally, by the middle years of childhood, social pretend becomes a venue for self-disclosure and the sharing of confidences. This is especially true for pretend play in the company of close friends.

5. Correlates and Outcomes of Play

Since the 1970s researchers have investigated the relationships between children's play and the development of a diverse range of cognitive, social, social-cognitive, and linguistic skills.

5.1 Play and Cognitive Development

Children (3- to 5-year olds) who engage frequently in sociodramatic and constructive play tend to perform better on tests of intelligence than their age-mates who are more inclined to play in a sensorimotor fashion. Children who frequently play in a constructive fashion (e.g., building things, constructing puzzles) are likely to be proficient at solving convergent problems (problems with a single solution). Those who frequently play in a dramatic fashion are likely to be proficient at solving divergent problems (problems with multiple solutions; Pepler 1982).

Given that pretense is thought to play a significant role in the development of cognitive skills, it is not surprising to find that researchers have attempted to improve cognitive prowess by providing children with training in pretense play. It has been reported that training children to engage in sociodramatic play (group make-believe) improves children's IQ scores, and the effects are relatively long-lasting (Smith et al. 1981). Results from other training studies indicate that imaginative play is a significant causal force in the development of creativity, quantitative invariance or reversibility, and sequential memory.

5.2 Play and Social Development

Because successful participation in social pretend play requires many of the skills theorized to be associated with the achievement of competent peer relationships, this type of play is viewed as a marker of social competence from toddlerhood to the middle and late childhood years. Specifically, researchers have found that preschoolers who frequently engage in sociodramatic play are more socially skilled and socially competent than their age-mates who infrequently engage in such activity. Moreover, results from various training studies indicate that instruction in sociodramatic play is associated with increases in cooperation, social participation, and role-taking skills (for a review see Rubin et al. 1983).

5.3 Play and Language Development

The mechanisms by which play may aid in the development of linguistic competencies are straightforward. Children frequently play with the different forms and rules of language. This play may take the form of repeating strings of nonsense syllables (phonology), substituting words of the same grammatical category (syntax), or intentionally distorting meaning through nonsense and jokes (semantics). As a result, language play may help children perfect newly acquired language skills and increase conscious awareness of linguistic rules, as well as provide a superior context in which the child may gain valuable language practice (Garvey 1974).

Generally speaking, particular phases in the development of symbolic play and language tend to co-occur. For example, sociodramatic play appears to be an important factor in the development of oral language and vocabulary, story production, story comprehension, communication of meaning, and the early development of literacy (for a review see Christie 1991).

6. Factors Influencing the Play of Children

Some children are more likely to play than others; moreover, play styles and preferences vary from individual to individual. Researchers have begun to investigate factors that may influence the development of individual differences in play styles.

6.1 Personality and Environmental Contributions to the Development of Children's Play

Individual differences in the quality and quantity of children's play are thought to develop, in part, because of traits internal to the child. For example, in infancy, attention to novel stimuluses and habituation efficiency (the amount of time to habituate, or "get used to" novel stimuluses) is predictive, not only of subse-quent attentional skills and cognitive competence, but also of infant and toddler play competence (Tamis-LeMonda and Bornstein 1989). During the preschool years, playfulness (Barnett 1991) and a preference for interacting with people versus objects (Jennings 1975) are stable traits that contribute to the form and content of children's play.

Although play behaviors may be influenced by internal, dispositional characteristics, it seems clear that family factors play a significant role as well. Socialization experiences and family relationships influence not only the rate by which children progress through the stages of play development, but also individual differences in play styles and expression. For example, maternal stimulation during the infant's first year of life is associated concurrently with infants' visual and tactile exploration, with play competence at 1 year, pretense play and representational competence at 13 months, and cognitive competence at 1 and 2½ years of age (see Tamis-LeMonda and Bornstein 1989).

Two of the more critical parenting ingredients, in infancy, appear to be the modeling of action and the solicitation of activity. For example, a mother of an infant may dial a toy telephone (modeling) and then move the toy toward the baby suggesting that the infant dial the telephone. The significance of such maternal behavior is underscored by the finding that parental modeling and solicitation of play behavior predicts subsequent play competence (Tamis-Le Monda and Bornstein 1989).

Parents who are responsive and sensitive to their infants provide a secure context within which their babies can explore novel objects and people (Sroufe 1983). In turn, exploration facilitates the growth of early representational or symbolic play. Children who have an insecure relationship with their parents may be less explorative of their environments in infancy and in the toddler period. Thus it is not surprising that infants with insecure attachment relationships engage in less social pretend play as preschoolers (Bretherton 1989).

From about the age of 3, symbolic or representational play increasingly becomes a social activity. Thus those parenting behaviors (modeling, reinforcement, instruction, induction accompanied by warmth) that encourage children's prosocial, cooperative activity are likely to influence the extent to which children play in a sociodramatic fashion.

Although it would be reasonably safe to conclude that the quality of children's play behaviors is the product of the interaction between internal, dispositional characteristics and the types of socialization experiences received, it is likely that other environmental factors may prove influential as well. For example, family stress such as that caused by marital separation and divorce appears to elicit aberrations or regressions in children's normal play patterns (Hetherington et al. 1979).

Another environmental factor that influences the quantity and quality of play is social class. Middle-class children engage in significantly more sociodramatic play than their lower-class age-mates (for a review see Rubin et al. 1983). Some psychologists have suggested that these findings reflect differences in the processes of emotion regulation and cognitive development. Given that middle-class children are more likely than lower-class children to use language to express emotions, and given their greater facility in language, the consistent social class difference in the production of social pretense is unsurprising (Fein 1989).

Nevertheless, it is important to note that several researchers have not found social-class differences in the production of sociodramatic play (e.g., von Zuben et al. 1991). These findings have been attributed to the ameliorative effects of positive social and educational experiences such as access to a reinforcing peer group, and the availability of a high-quality school program.

Relatedly, researchers indicate that peers use reinforcement, punishment, and modeling to influence play. This is especially true for the demonstration and development of sex-typing in play. Researchers have also investigated how other factors such as age, sex, and familiarity of play partners influence children's play behaviors (Hartup 1983). In general, children play more, and at higher cognitive levels, when in the company of an acquaintance than when alone or with an unfamiliar child; moreover, children prefer friends, as opposed to a familiar partner (not a friend), for engaging in fantasy play, and play between friends is longer and richer in content (Werebe and Baudonniere 1991).

6.2 Ecological Influences

There is a rich and lengthy history of research concerning the effects of ecological factors, such as types of material, toys, equipment, and venue (indoor versus outdoor) on the social and cognitive characteristics of children's play. For example, group and dramatic play is especially encouraged by the availability of dress-up clothes, dolls and "action figures," vehicles, and housekeeping props. Paints, crayon, and art materials evoke nonsocial but constructive activities, while clay, :nd, and water tend to elicit functional-sensorimotor play (for reviews of ecological influences on play see Bergen 1988).

Researchers have focused also on more general ecological factors such as indoor versus outdoor play and the density of play space. Generally, outdoor play is the preferred choice of older preschoolers, and is more likely than indoor play to take on a pretense character (Striniste 1989). Decreased play space results in a decrease in running and rough-and-tumble play and an increase in physical contact, onlooking behavior, and imaginative play (Smith and Connolly 1980).

6.3 Media and Curriculum Influences

The average North American child watches over 3 hours of television a day, or more than 25 hours in a single week (Nielsen Television Services 1985). It should, therefore, not be surprising that researchers have investigated the effects of television watching on children's play. Several studies indicate that children who frequently watch television are less playful and less imaginative in their play (e.g., Singer and Singer 1979). The content of children's television also has important implications on their play behaviors. While children's watching of action-adventure programs is associated with less dramatic play and more aggressiveness, programs with educational underpinnings and positive social messages have been found to increase imaginative free play in young children (Huston-Stein et al. 1981).

A more familiar influence on children's play is the school curriculum. For example, highly structured (e.g., largely teacher-directed) preschool programs tend to reduce the range, diversity, and performance level of young children's play. Moreover, imaginative play is more common in less structured programs, while highly structured programs encourage constructive use of materials and goal-oriented activity. Some researchers, however, have reported that structured preschool programs positively influence the demonstration of pretend activities (e.g., Johnson et al. 1980). A possible explanation for these findings is that when structure is imposed during nonfree play periods, and when it involves features such as small group instruction stressing language arts and abstract thinking, the influences on sociodramatic activities during free play may be positive. Therefore, when evaluating curriculum effects, it may be important to consider not only the amount of structure in a curriculum, but also how this structure is integrated and applied on a day-to-day basis.

7. Conclusion

It is clear that play is a developmental phenomenon of significant proportion. Not only does it seem to provide a window into the child's cognitive and socioemotional being, it also appears to a propelling force for the development of cognitive, language, and socioemotional skills. Thus play should no longer be viewed as simply a "filler" for early education curriculum innovators; instead, it should be considered an informal, enjoyable, and relatively stress-free way of providing children with intellectual and social stimulation.

See also: Piaget's Theory of Human Development; Human Development in the Lifespan: Overview; Social Development; Social Interaction and Learning

References

Barnett L A 1991 The playful child: Measurement of a disposition to play. *Play and Culture* 4: 51–74

Bateson G 1956 The message "This is play". In: Schaffner B (ed.) 1956 *Group Processes.* Macy, New York

Bergen D 1988 *Play as a Medium for Learning and Development.* Heinemann, Portsmouth, New Hampshire

Berlyne D E 1960 *Conflict, Arousal, and Curiosity.* McGraw-Hill, New York

Bretherton I 1989 Pretense: The form and function of make-believe play. *Dev. Rev.* 9(4): 383–401

Bruner J S 1972 The nature and uses of immaturity. *Am. Psychol.* 27: 687–708

Christie J F (ed.) 1991 *Play and Early Literacy Development.* State University of New York Press, Albany, New York

Fein G G 1989 Mind, meaning, and affect: Proposals for a theory of pretense. *Dev. Rev.* 9(4): 345–63

Fenson L 1984 Developmental trends for action and speech in pretend play. In: Bretherton I (ed.) 1984 *Symbolic Play.* Academic Press, New York

Freud S 1961 *Beyond the Pleasure Principle.* Norton, New York

Garvey C 1974 Some properties of social play. *Merrill-Palmer Q.* 20(3): 163–80

Goncu A 1989 Models and features of pretense. *Dev. Rev.* 9(4): 341–44

Hartup W W 1983 Peer relations. In: Hetterington E M, Mussen P H (eds.) 1983 *Handbook of Child Psychology. Vol. 4: Socialization, Personality and Social Development.* Wiley, New York

Hetherington E M, Cox M, Cox R 1979 Play and social interaction among children following divorce. *J. Soc. Issues* 35(4): 26–49

Howes C 1992 *The Collaborative Construction of Pretend.* State University of New York Press, Albany, New York

Huston-Stein, Fox S, Greer D, Watkins B A, Whitaker J 1981 The effects of TV action and violence on children's social behavior. *J. Genet. Psychol.* 138: 183–91

Jennings K D 1975 People versus object orientation, social behavior, and intellectual abilities in preschool children. *Dev. Psychol.* 11(4): 511–19

Johnson J E, Ershler J, Bell C 1980 Play behavior in a discovery-based and a formal education preschool program. *Child Dev.* 51(1): 271–74

McCune L 1986 Symbolic development in normal and atypical infants. In: Fein G, Rivkin M (eds.) 1986 *The Young Child at Play: Reviews of Research*, Vol 4. National Association for the Education of Young Children, Washington, DC

Nielsen Television Services 1985 *Nielsen Report on Television.* Nielson, Northbrook, Illinois

Pepler D J 1982 Play and divergent thinking. In: Pepler D J, Rubin K H (eds.) 1982 *The Play of Children: Current Research and Theory.* Kargen, Basel

Piaget J 1962 *Play, Dreams, and Imitation in Childhood.* Norton, New York

Rubin K H, Fein G G, Vandenberg B 1983 Play. In: Hetherington E M, Mussen P H (eds.) 1983 *Handbook of Child Psychology. Vol. 4: Socialization, Personality and Social Development.* Wiley, New York

Schiller F 1954 *On the Aesthetic Education of Man.* Yale University Press, New Haven, Connecticut

Singer D G, Singer J L 1979 Television viewing and aggressive behavior in preschool children: A field study. Paper presented at the Conference on Forensic Psychology, New York

Smith P K, Connolly K J 1980 *The Ecology of Preschool Behavior.* Cambridge University Press, Cambridge

Smith P K, Dagleish M, Herzmark G 1981 A comparison of the effects of fantasy play tutoring and skills tutoring in nursery classes. *International Journal of Behavioral Development* 4(4): 421–41

Sroufe L A 1983 Infant-caregiver attachment and patterns of adaptation in preschool: The roots of maladaptation and competence. In: Perlmutter M (ed.) 1983 *Minnesota Symposium in Child Psychology*, Vol. 16. Erlbaum, Hillsdale, New Jersey

Striniste N A 1989 Early childhood outdoors: A literature review related to the design childcare environments. *Children's Environments Quarterly* 6(4): 25–31

Tamis-LeMonda C S, Bornstein M H 1989 Habituation and maternal encouragement of attention in infancy as predictors of toddler language, play, and representational competence. *Child Dev.* 60(2): 738–51

von Zuben M V, Crist P A, Mayberry W 1991 A pilot study of the differences in play behavior between children of low and middle socioeconomic status. *American Journal of Occupational Therapy* 45(2): 113–18

Vygotsky L S 1967 Play and its role in the mental development of the child. *Soviet Psychology* 5(3): 6–18

Werebe M J G, Baudonniere P M 1991 Social pretend play among friends and familiar preschoolers. *International Journal of Behavioral Development* 14(4): 411–28

Further Reading

Doyle A B, Connolly J, Rivest L P 1980 The effect of playmate familiarity on the social interactions of young children. *Child Dev.* 51: 217–23

Lamb M E, Roopnarine J L 1979 Peer influence on sex-role development in preschoolers. *Child Dev.* 50(4): 1219–22

Development of Learning across the Lifespan

M. J. A. Howe

There can be few if any days in a person's life in which no learning takes place. Throughout an individual's life, learning provides important functions. It is important to bear in mind that the single term "learning" covers a range of diverse phenomena, many of which have little in common with one another beyond the fact that they all involve some kind of broadly adaptive change occurring. In the case of most varieties of learning developmental improvements are observed in the speed or efficiency with which learned capabilities are acquired, but there are exceptions. For example, in some kinds of simple conditioning it is hard to discern differences between young children and adults (Estes 1970). It would be an oversimplification to say that development directly causes improved learning, and more accurate to state that increased age merely provides time for events or processes to take place which make certain kinds of learning more likely. With the onset of adulthood, most people do not experience sudden or sharp changes in learning ability, but some decline may be observed in old age.

1. Timing and the Notion of Critical Periods

Contrary to a widely held belief, there are no sharply defined "critical periods" during which particular skills or abilities have to be acquired if they are to be gained at all. Even in the case of language acquisition, which is thought by most psychologists to depend to a considerable extent on innate characteristics that are unique to humans, it has been found that full recovery may take place following the most severe deprivation of learning experiences (Koluchova 1976). And early deprivation of opportunities for social learning does not, on its own, render impossible the eventual normal development of social skills and abilities (Schaffer 1990).

Moreover, critics of Piagetian theories have gone beyond challenging the notion of critical developmental periods in learning and have increasingly questioned the view that learning capabilities are closely tied to the stage of intellectual development that a child has reached. For some researchers (Brainerd 1977), the valid uses of such stages are restricted to ones that simply describe children's performance rather than claiming to identify the underlying structures that constrain and account for the observed level of performance. There is evidence to show that some of the children's errors which a Piagetian interpretation would ascribe to childlike or restricted reasoning processes are actually caused by specific deficits in linguistic and semantic knowledge (Donaldson 1978).

That is not to say that the developmental phasing and sequencing of learning experiences is by any means unimportant. On the contrary, it can be vital. A good illustration of the crucial nature of the sequence in which different subskills are gained is provided by some experiments on learning in infants that were conducted by White (1971). He was interested in trying to accelerate the kinds of learning that result in young babies becoming able to reach out for objects and pick them up. His first efforts succeeded in improving visual attending skills, which he knew to be an important component of the reaching behavior he wished to accelerate. However, to White's surprise, that intervention delayed rather than brought forward the infants' ability to reach out for objects. Further investigations established that the reason for this apparently paradoxical finding was that White's successful efforts to improve visual attending had the additional, unanticipated, effect of distracting infants from a crucial behavior which normally occurs at around the same time, that of simply observing one's own hands. It turned out that the latter behavior makes a key contribution to the learning of reaching skills, and that the reason for the failure of White's attempt to accelerate reaching was that his intervention disrupted the sequence in which the subskills which lead to that ability are normally gained.

Even when the precise timing and sequencing of learned skill elements is not an issue and no age-related differences in learning ability are involved, age-related factors can still exert a large influence on what a learner actually achieves. For example, in order to reach the highest levels of excellence as a musical performer it may be highly advantageous to begin learning before the end of childhood, if only because an individual who commenced learning as an adult would find it extremely difficult to devote the time and sustain the high level of motivation and concentration necessary in order to achieve the highest levels of performance as an instrumentalist. This may demand as much as 20,000 or 30,000 hours, or around eight hours per day for 10 years. Similarly large amounts of time are needed to reach the highest levels of ability at other areas of achievement, such as chess (Simon and Chase 1973, Howe 1990). And in the case of the skill of composing music, it has been established that no musical works that are now regarded as being of major importance have been produced prior to the composer having devoted around 10 years to concentrated training in composing, typically following many years devoted to the acquisition of basic musical abilities (Hayes 1981).

A number of investigations have examined the

relationships between age and achievement at various abilities. Intellectual achievements tend to peak around the third, fourth, and fifth decades of life, earlier in some areas of achievement, such as mathematics, and later in others (Simonton 1992). But this does not necessarily mean that ability to learn as such is closely related to age: in most instances a more likely explanation is that the age-related variations in achievements are largely accounted for by other reasons. One is the simple fact that it can take many years to gain the skills necessary for the highest levels of performance. A second reason is that the circumstances and commitments of an older person's life may make it hard to maintain the single-mindedness and the concentrated effort directed to a specialized sphere of excellence that is usually necessary for reaching the highest peaks of human achievement.

2. Developmental Learning Differences

Although learning does not exhibit the kinds of clear developmental changes that would be found if there were universal age-related changes in the kinds of learning or the rate of learning that are possible at different ages, learning and age are by no means unrelated. Older children and adults outperform younger children at a wide range of learning activities, including most of the kinds of learning that receive prominence in school curricula, and especially those learning tasks that are relatively complex or abstract, or which necessitate the learner depending to a marked extent on previously acquired knowledge or skills.

Why is it that, compared with adolescents and adults, young children are often at a disadvantage when confronted with learning tasks? Simply to say that learning ability has or has not "developed" does not really answer the question: it is necessary to know what changes, and how it changes, in order to bring about the age-related improvements. One possibility is that physical development provides the explanation, via, for example, improved conductance of chemico-electrical impulses in the cortex as a result of increased myelinization. Alternatively, changes in the number or size of brain cells, or in their physical structure, could account for the older child's greater success as a learner.

However, although physical changes in the brain do play a part in the development of learning during the very earliest years, from toddlerhood onward such changes cease to be a cause of age-related variability in learning, and therefore other causes must be found. The kinds of changes that do continue to affect learning, and largely account for the improvements in learning and remembering that are observed as children get older form three broad (and overlapping) categories. These are, first, increases in knowledge; second, the increased use of skills, strategies, and metaskills; and third, a range of influential habits

and attributes that are broadly related to motivation, personality, and the directing of attentional resources.

2.1 The Influence of Existing Knowledge

A crucial influence on many kinds and forms of learning is exerted by the learner's existing knowledge, that is to say, what the person already knows. Simply as a result of having lived longer, older people know more than young children, and their increased knowledge may facilitate learning in any situation in which the information or skills that are to be acquired are in any way related to information or skills which the learner already possesses.

A good way to demonstrate the influence of a person's existing knowledge on new learning is to compare children and adults in situations where, in contrast to what is usual, the children happen to be more rather than less knowledgeable than the adults within the domain of knowledge relevant to the task. For example, Chi (1978) has found that 10-year olds are comparable with adults at tasks involving their retaining lists of verbal and numerical information. However, when the information to be retained takes the form of chess pieces arranged on a chessboard in legitimate positions that might occur in a game of chess, and the children are good chess players whereas the adults are merely competent at the game, the 10-year olds consistently outperform the adults. Similarly, Ceci and Howe (1978) found that in a study of word learning, 13-year olds were initially much more successful than 10-year olds, who in turn were better than children aged 7. However, when the experimenters carefully adapted the task to ensure that all the words were familiar to even the youngest children, so that they were capable of perceiving the relationships between the words to be learned and some other words that were provided as "cues" to guide recall, the age differences completely disappeared. In other words, the outcome of ensuring that the youngest participants possessed all the relevant knowledge about the task items that was available to the oldest participants completely eradicated (in the latter study) or reversed (in the previous study) the usual age-related difference in performance.

Knowledge may be an important cause of developmental differences in learning even in situations where it appears that many causes are involved. For instance Carey (1985) studied children's understanding of the concept of "being alive." Traditionally, confusions in relation to this are assumed to reflect a fundamental limitation in "animistic reasoning," but Carey found that, contrary to this belief, children's ability to understand the concept—as it relates to humans and other species—depends very heavily on the knowledge they have acquired. Their confusions about the concept, which young children may regard as being a property of children but not of animals, follow directly from their lack of biological knowledge concerning processes such as sleeping, breathing, and eating. As far as the ability to learn is concerned, these findings clearly contradict the view by which "mere knowledge" is seen as having only limited importance.

Even in situations where it at first seems very unlikely that difference between people could be the cause of differences in performance at tasks which involve learning, it may nevertheless turn out that people's existing knowledge is very important. For instance, even when the materials used in a study of learning are chosen to be highly familiar to all participants, there may be differences between participants in the way in which their knowledge in relation to the materials is actually represented, structured, and connected. That is so in the case of simple items such as digits, for example. Although all digits may be familiar to even the younger children in a learning experiment, individuals of different ages still differ in their knowledge about various aspects of the digits that make them meaningful and have implications for learning. Thus, although the number 2 may be highly familiar to younger children as well as older people, learning that involves that number may also be facilitated by knowledge about the digit which is possessed by older but not by younger learners, such as the facts that 2 is a prime number and the square root of 4 and the cube root of 8 (Chi and Ceci 1987).

2.2 Learning Skills and Strategies

Even when there is no conscious intention to learn, the extent to which a person retains new information is strongly affected by the kinds of mental processing that occur at the time the new information is perceived (Craik and Lockhart 1972, Craik and Tulving 1975). As young people get older, partly but not wholly as an outcome of schooling, they become increasingly adept at a range of mental activities and strategies that have the effect of magnifying a person's ability to profit from learning. In the case of certain skills, such as reading, the effect of mastering it is radically to transform the learner's potential for new learning, by opening windows onto experiences that were previously inaccessible and making numerous new opportunities available. With narrower skills and strategies the effects are more specific and circumscribed, but the possibility of magnifying the power of learning activities and opening up previously unavailable opportunities to gain new capabilities still remains.

Each of a large variety of skills and strategies can contribute to learning. Some strategies, such as rehearsal and self-testing, exert a positive influence on learning by ensuring that information to be learned is effectively repeated a sufficient number of times to ensure that it can be adequately processed. Other strategies, such as ones that necessitate the learner organizing or elaborating or categorizing new material, are effective largely because they ensure that there are adequate conceptual links between the new material and existing knowledge or by forming stronger links

and connections within the body of information that is to be acquired. Yet other strategies, such as ones that incorporate rhythms or rhymes or the meaningful verbal narratives that are sometimes introduced to facilitate the learning of otherwise unrelated lists of items (such as the initial-letter mnemonic *R*ichard of *Y*ork *G*ave *B*attle *I*n *V*ain, which is introduced in order to help English schoolchildren learn the colors of the rainbow), are effective partly because they provide connections between items which are otherwise separate. (People find it hard to learn large numbers of entirely separate items of information, and a strategy that effectively reduces the number of separate elements to be acquired will often make learning easier.) Other strategies which are often effective involve the learner forming visual images that represent items to be learned and sometimes link them together. The (learned) skills, strategies, and other devices that can be introduced to facilitate learning vary considerably in their complexity and in their range of application. The word "mnemonic" is sometimes introduced as a descriptive term for strategies and devices designed to help the learner recall new or unfamiliar information.

Generally speaking, as they get older young people become increasingly prone to making use of appropriate strategies for learning, and also increasingly adept at using strategies, and they develop a widening repertoire of learning skills. They also gain more sophisticated metaskills. That is, they become better at being aware when new learning is necessary, knowing when it is appropriate to introduce a skill or strategy that will facilitate learning, and choosing a strategy that is maximally effective for a particular task, or, if necessary, adapting an existing strategy in order to deal with an unfamiliar situation.

2.3 Motivational and Other Influences

Both knowledge and mental skills form distinctly cognitive influences upon learning, but it would be wrong to assume that all the important determinants that contribute to age-related differences in the effectiveness of individuals' efforts to learn are exclusively cognitive ones. Throughout life, learning is also affected by a variety of factors that are either not cognitive at all or cognitive only in the broadest sense. These form a mixed bag, and include influences that have more to do with motivation and personality than with cognition as such. They include temperament, attentiveness, perseverance, determination, fatigue, distractibility, enthusiasm for learning, self-confidence, impulsiveness, sense of being in control, feelings of autonomy, feelings of success and optimism, as against fear of failure, independence, and self-directedness. The precise effects of these can be highly specific to the particular learning task involved, and in any person each of them alter from one day to the next.

There is no straightforward developmental progression in the manner in which these extracognitive factors exert an influence on learning, although there are some general trends. For example, compared with children, older individuals are often, but not always, less impulsive and distractible, and better at maintaining their concentration. However such changes are largely the result of a person's experiences and educational history than of any universal developmental change. Some individuals never gain the habit of giving the concentrated attention to verbal materials that is necessary for the kinds of successful learning that enable a child to become an educated adult. Some of the above factors are fairly closely linked to particular phases of life. For example, it is clear that, while motivational influences on learning are important throughout the lifetime, the direction and form of motivational influence changes between childhood and adulthood. And compared with older people adolescents seem to experience particular difficulties with sustaining the relatively solitary learning activities that form a necessary part of life as a successful student (Csikszentmihalyi and Larson 1984).

3. Learning in the Older Person

Following early adulthood, although continued cognitive development can and does occur, its form and direction in any person depends very largely on the particular circumstances of the particular individual (Labouvie-Vief and Chandler 1978).

With old age, there may be some deterioration in the physical variables that can affect learning (e.g., hearing and eyesight) and in the motivational influences (e.g., reduced incentives to learn or, in some people, deteriorating self-confidence as a learner), and some forms of learning may be hampered by changes in mental processing activities. Some investigations have reported decrements in old age in recall and learning of verbal information. However, for many older learners, their effectiveness at utilizing existing knowledge and learning strategies will compensate in full or in part for any negative changes that take place. Consequently, when the information is highly meaningful, researchers undertaking experiments on learning and remembering have observed no deterioration in the performance of older people, compared with young adults (Hultsch and Dixon 1984). Age differences favoring younger people are either small or nonexistent when the learner has prior knowledge about the topic, is well-motivated, and when the material to be acquired is well-organized.

See also: Lifespan Development; Self-directed Adult Learning

References

Brainerd C J 1977 Cognitive development and concept learning: An interpretative review. *Psych. Bull.* 84(5): 919–39
Carey S 1985 Are children fundamentally different kinds of thinkers and learners than adults? In: Chipman S F, Segal J W (eds.) 1985 *Thinking and Learning Skills. Vol. 2: Research and Open Questions.* Erlbaum, Hillsdale, New Jersey
Ceci S J, Howe M J A 1978 Semantic knowledge as a determinant of developmental differences in recall. *Journal of Experimental Child Psychology* 26(2): 230–45
Chi M T H 1978 Knowledge structures and memory development. In: Siegler R (ed.) 1978 *Children's Thinking: What Develops?* Erlbaum, Hillsdale, New Jersey
Chi M T H, Ceci S J 1987 Content knowledge: Its role, representation, and restructuring in memory development. *Advances in Child Development* 20: 91–142
Craik F I M, Lockhart R S 1972 Levels of processing: A framework for memory research. *J. Verbal Learn. Verbal Behav.* 11(6): 671–84
Craik F I M, Tulving E 1975 Depth of processing and the retention of words in episodic memory. *J. Exp. Psychol. Gen.* 104(3): 268–94
Csikszentmihalyi M, Larson R 1984 *Being Adolescent: Conflict and Growth in the Teenage Years.* Basic Books, New York
Donaldson M 1978 *Children's Minds.* Fontana, London
Estes W K 1970 *Learning Theory and Mental Development.* Academic Press, New York
Hayes J R 1981 *The Complete Problem Solver.* Franklin Institute Press, Philadelphia, Pennsylvania
Howe M J A 1990 *The Origins of Exceptional Abilities.* Blackwell, Oxford
Hultsch D F, Dixon R A 1984 Memory for text: Materials in adulthood. In: Baltes P B, Brim O G (eds.) 1984 *Life-span Development and Behavior 6.* Academic Press, New York
Koluchova J 1976 Severe deprivation in twins: A case study. In: Clarke A M, Clarke D B (eds.) 1976 *Early Experience: Myth and Evidence.* Open Books, London
Labouvie-Vief G, Chandler M J 1978 Cognitive development and life-span developmental theory: Idealistic versus contextual perspectives. In: Baltes P B (ed.) *Life-Span Development and Behavior 1.* Academic Press, New York
Schaffer H R 1990 *Making Decisions about Children: Psychological Questions and Answers.* Blackwell, Oxford.
Simon H A, Chase W G 1973 Skill in chess. *Am. Sci.* 61(4): 394–403
Simonton D K 1992 Leaders of American psychology, 1879–1967: Career development, creative output, and professional achievement. *J. Pers. Soc. Psychol.* 62(1): 5–17
White B L 1971 *Human Infants: Experience and Psychological Development.* Prentice-Hall, Englewood Cliffs, New Jersey

Further Reading

Coles G 1987 *The Learning Mystique: A Critical Look at Learning Disabilities.* Fawcett Columbine, New York
Ericsson K A, Smith J (eds.) 1991 *Toward a General Theory of Expertise: Prospects and Limits.* Cambridge University Press, Cambridge
Howe M J A (ed.) 1977 *Adult Learning: Psychological Research and Applications* Wiley, London

Theories and Models of Learning in Educational Settings

Paradigms in Instructional Psychology

A. Knoers

A paradigm is a theory framework within a science, constructed and used in a given period of time. This entry gives an overview of the major paradigms that have guided research on learning and instruction, mainly since the beginning of the twentieth century.

1. Behaviorism

During the second decade of the twentieth century E L Thorndike developed a theory of learning known as "connectionism." It assumed that specific responses become linked with specific contiguous stimuli, in a so-called "S–R bond" or connection. According to Thorndike, behavior is controlled by application of different laws of learning. His two most important laws are well-known: the law of effect and the law of exercise. According to the law of effect, when responses to a stimulus are followed by a positive, rewarding effect they are strengthened or reinforced. For example: "How much is 12 times 4?" Answer: "48." Reinforcement: "That is correct, John!" The law of exercise states that the connection between S and R becomes stronger by use, exercise, or repetition. "Drill-and-practice" instructional programs are based on this law. Thorndike's influence on education has been great, especially through his book *Psychology of Arithmetic* (1922). The S–R paradigm also became the keystone of J B Watson's *Behaviorism* in the 1920s.

Skinner (1953) was the first psychologist after the 1930s to develop a scientific behavioristic learning theory. He distinguished two kinds of behavior: respondent and operant behavior. Respondent behavior follows on a stimulus from "outside," as in the case of a reflex or a conditioned reflex in the sense described by I P Pavlov (e.g., when a dog salivates at a bell signal, having learnt to associate the bell with the the provision of food). Operant behavior is more spontaneous: it is initiated by the organism, animal, or human being. When it is reinforced in a positive or a negative way it can be considered as conditioned behavior. This means that it will be strengthened and will be repeated as soon as the reinforcer, that is the rewarding or aversive stimulus, appears.

Discrimination learning is established by presenting a reinforcer immediately after an intended behavior has taken place. Another procedure is that of shaping, which involves the stepwise approach of the intended complex behavior by building upon diverse partial behaviors. This procedure underlies Skinnerian programmed instruction. (Task analysis is used to discover the correct order of the steps in a learning hierarchy.) Two other applications of Skinner's approach are mastery learning and behavior modification, the latter being a technique that is also used in psychotherapy.

According to behavioristic theory, only behavior that has been reinforced is under control. "Learning" means developing correct behavior in a situation in which reinforcing stimuli are presented by a teacher or by a machine. The theory says nothing about the processes that take place within the individual during learning. Therefore behaviorism can be considered as a noncognitive theory.

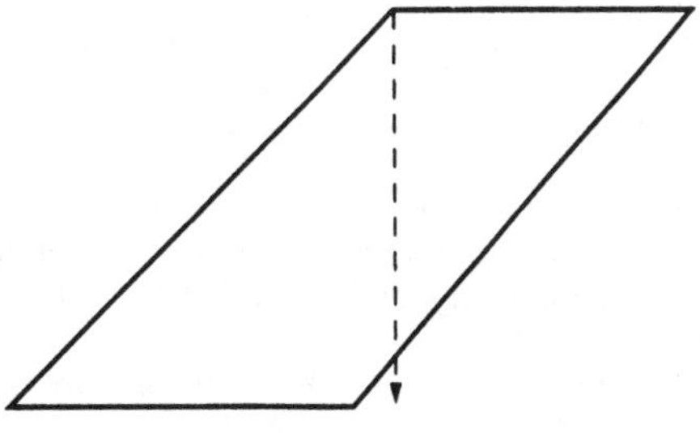

Figure 1
Wertheimer's parallelogram problem

2. Gestalt Psychology

Early European Gestalt psychology (as developed by K Koffka, W Köhler, and M Wertheimer) is based on the principle that a figure or a configuration—in German, a *Gestalt*—can only be seen, because it stands out against a background. This spontaneously observed global Gestalt is gradually given structure. A rose window in a cathedral, for instance, is at first seen as a many-colored whole, but gradually it acquires structure and sense; the whole is more than the sum of its parts. According to the Gestaltists there is no essential difference between observing, thinking, and learning. Learning means getting insight, discovering a structure. Problems are suddenly solved by an "Aha" experience, albeit on the basis of prior learning experiences. Creative problem-solving and learning imply switching from an approach that does not lead to a solution to an approach that does by means of forming a good Gestalt.

As a consequence of their global approach to learning phenomena, the Gestaltists, unlike the behaviorists, have said little about instruction. Only Wertheimer (1945) has applied the paradigm of Gestalt construction to problems in school subjects, especially in mathematics and science. For instance, he once attended a lesson of pupils who had learned to find the area of a parallelogram by drawing a perpendicular line and then multiplying the base of the parallelogram by the perpendicular. Wertheimer then asked them to find the area of a parallelogram in a different position, as in Fig. 1. No pupil noticed that the figure had simply been inverted. Consequently, their response was: "We haven't had that yet." Wertheimer used this example to show that in education rote learning of procedures should not be used.

3. The Würzburg School, Selz, and Duncker

The Würzburg School (Kulpe, Bühler, Ach) was a reaction against the associationist psychology in Germany. According to adherents of this school, thinking operates with ordering categories such as means–aims, cause–effect. Ach held the opinion that there is a "determinating tendency" in thinking which means that it is goal-directed and controlled by the thinking task, an idea that was taken up by Selz (at Mannheim). The problem of how thinking takes place was investigated by Selz using Külpe's method of the so-called "experimental introspection." Introspection is the observation of phenomena occurring in one's own conscience. The disadvantage of this method is that the natural development of phenomena is changed if they are consciously and intentionally observed. The Würzburgers thought that this could be prevented through the inquiry of the thinking process by means of a controlled thinking task. The tasks given were: subordination, coordination, whole, part, definition (Selz 1924). An example of such a task is:

Task:	Part?
Stimulus word:	Branch
Reaction:	Tree
Reaction time:	1.8 sec.

After completion of the task the subject was asked what he had thought when given the task. Thus instead of introspection, immediate retrospection was used.

Selz found that there are special thinking operations or methods that are used to solve a particular thinking task. They may be regarded as schemes that anticipate the thinking process (schematic anticipation). Therefore it is possible to acquire thinking methods that are most appropriate for the solution of different kinds of problems. The educational implication of this paradigm of schematic anticipation is that teachers can help students to use the correct thinking methods in solving different kinds of problems.

Duncker's (1935) accurate analysis of problem situations has exerted strong influence, not only on the work of some Gestaltists, but also on that of more recent problem-solving psychologists. He demonstrated the important role in problem-solving processes played by heuristic methods such as goal analysis, situation analysis, and conflict analysis.

4. Piaget and Vygotsky

The Swiss epistemologist Piaget is one of the most famous precursors of cognitive psychology. He had a great interest in the development of intelligence (Piaget 1947), and essential to his developmental theory is the idea that the individual plays an active role in acquiring knowledge about reality. A person learns something by doing, by action. This may be a real action or a mental one: an interiorized action, which Piaget calls "operation" (the paradigm of interiorization). Piaget distinguished four stages in the development of intelligence. In each stage the activity of the individual is directed toward removing the disturbance of an original balance which is caused by an unknown phenomenon (the conflict). For instance, how is it that the same amount of water has a higher level in a narrow glass than in a broader one? Learning is an active process in the individual, a process of discovery, based upon assimilation or "the integration of any sort of reality into a structure" (Piaget 1964 p. 195). Development, however, is the basis of all possible learning processes.

This position differs markedly from the theory of Vygotsky. In Vygotsky's paradigm of interiorization, cultural influence and education play a greater part. Learning is based upon the guidance and the transmission of culture by a teacher, who stimulates the student to explore what Vygotsky (1929) calls the "zone of proximal development" (ZPD). This means that the teacher, after having assessed the actual development of a student (as seen in what the student can do

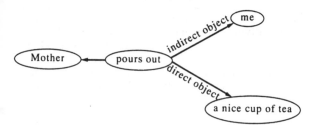

Figure 2
Network structure of a sentence

independently), can help him by adequate instruction to attain better and unexpected results. Guided by the teacher, the student can attain a higher level of learning than his or her own actual development seemed to make possible.

The ideas of discovery learning developed by Piaget and that of guidance in learning developed by Vygotsky are of great importance to education. The paradigms of interiorization and of ZPD mentioned above were among those elaborated by the Russian psychologist Gal'perin.

5. Cognitive Psychology

The term "cognitive psychology" refers to an approach that attempts to describe and explain the underlying cognitive processes of behavior. In contrast with the S–R or "black box" paradigm of behaviorism, cognitive psychology postulates that clear inferences are possible about the inner transforming process between "inputs" and "outputs" (the "white box" paradigm). Following Mayer (1981), cognitive psychology can be defined as the scientific analysis of human mental processes and memory structures in order to find out more about human behavior. The analysis considers the human being as an information-processing system, and focuses on the cognitive processes, the cognitive structures, and strategies employed. The analysis of processes starts by giving students and intellectual task, for instance an arithmetic problem. The researcher observes accurately the way in which a student solves the problem, asks questions about the solution activities, and tries to find out what the knowledge acquired looks like. Analysis of cognitive structures tries to unravel knowledge and to look for a structure into which the component parts of this knowledge are fitted. For instance, a "network structure" of the sentence "Mother pours me out a nice cup of tea" is given in Fig. 2.

In addition to cognitive processes there are also "executive control processes," which are a kind of self-regulating activity, also known as "metacognitive capabilities." They plan, regulate, and control the cognitive processes that take place in the mind. When used

in more difficult problem-solving tasks, metacompetencies can intensify the effectivenes of domain-specific knowledge (Weinert 1989). Self-regulating skills are cogenitive as well as socioemotional by nature (Boekaerts 1994).

6. The Phenomenographic Approach

This approach is in some respects a reaction against the lack of attention in research to the question of how learners themselves experience their learning. Indeed, the basic principle of research according to the phenomenographic approach is that it focuses on apprehended or experienced processes and content. This research "aims at descriptions, analysis and understanding of experiences" (Marton 1981 p. 177) of different students. For instance, students are interviewed after having read a scholarly article. The transcripts "reveal qualitative differences in the levels of understanding" (Entwistle 1987). Marton emphasized that they do not indicate individual differences between students. His rigorous analyzing procedure revealed that there are different categories of approaches to learning. Marton and Säljo (1976) demonstrated in an experiment that simple factual questions induced a surface approach. Students, commenting on what they experienced in their own everyday studies, reported different learning strategies. These approaches are comparable to the "depth of processing" approach of Craik and Lockhart (1972) and to other well-known learning strategies. The difference between these approaches lies mainly in the different intentions of the students: being able merely to reproduce at the given moment what has been learned as opposed to forming a personal opinion built upon what has been learned in this and in former cases. The phenomenographic approach has formed the basis of fruitful research on several approaches to learning.

7. The Situated Cognition and Learning Paradigm

This paradigm involves a reaction against the cognitive psychology approach, especially against the neglect in cognitive psychology of the impact of situational and contextual factors on learning and cognition (De Corte 1989). It draws upon ethnographic and anthropological research but is also influenced by the Russian activity theorists Vygotsky and Leontiev. The paradigm emphasizes that knowledge should not be abstracted from the context or the situations in which it is embedded; children, for instance, should not learn words in a foreign language without the context of ordinary communication (Brown et al. 1989). The analysis of cognition and learning by the initiators of this approach has resulted in a general model for designing ideal learning environments involving four dimensions: content, method, sequence, and sociology. This learning through what is called "cognitive apprenticeship" is considered to be a promising approach. In authentic activity and in social interaction with other students and with the teacher as an expert practitioner (e.g., as a mathematician solving a real problem) students acquire knowledge as a set of tools. Major teaching methods are modeling, coaching, scaffolding, multiple practice in collaboration, and articulation of and reflection on one's performance, knowledge, and thinking (Collins 1991).

A major aim of schooling is that students can use their knowledge of a domain outside the school culture in which it has been learned (transfer). However, if situated cognition and learning are taken to the extreme, transfer becomes almost impossible. A good deal of research has yet to be done to support this speculative paradigm. If it can be supported it should form a significant theoretical link between American cognitive psychology, Russian activity psychology, and the ethnographic and phenomenographic approaches.

8. Trends and Developments in Instructional Psychology

While instructional psychology studies the way in which learning can be improved, the original learning theorists intended to describe and explain learning as accurately as possible. Therefore, they investigated learning in a controllable laboratory situation. The experimental settings in which learning tasks are arranged in the laboratory are characterized by internal validity, which means that the outcomes of (the) learning (experiment) can only be attributed to the manipulated independent variables. All other independent variables are under control.

A weak point of this approach was the lack of external validity or the so-called "ecological validity," which must be provided if research results are to be appropriate for real classroom settings. Since the 1970s instructional psychologists have tried to use so-called quasi-experiments. The difference between these quasi-experiments and laboratory experiments consists in the structure of the research groups. In laboratory experiments groups are composed at random. Quasi-experiments work with real groups such as school classes.

9. Toward Integration

There are at least two reasons why integration of instructional psychology, developmental psychology, and the study of individual differences is desirable. First, while in instructional psychology the research literature often refers to groups of students, it goes without saying that there are no average learners but only individual students. Second, it is a well-known principle that instruction, in order to be effective, has to be contingent on the learning behavior of the students. This learning behavior is in turn greatly dependent on the developmental level of the students. School structure is based upon age and developmental level: primary, secondary, or tertiary education. Therefore "school tasks are a specific type of developmental tasks" (van Lieshout 1987 p. 54).

A well-known paradigm in the research on individual differences is the aptitude–treatment–interaction (ATI) paradigm. This paradigm proposes that groups of students differing in certain aptitudes should be approached with different educational treatments, because special treatments appear to fit (interact with) particular aptitudes of students. Modern research emphasizes the process analysis of aptitudes (Snow 1989). The most important discovery with regard to integration, however, is that knowledge is the prime component of cognitive development, and that the availability of knowledge is a primary condition for individuals to achieve performance in different domains.

10. Changes in Research Designs and Techniques

Pioneers in instructional psychology such as Thorndike and Skinner dreamt of a real "science" of teaching. Like the natural sciences, this "science" was intended to be quantitative, objective, and experimental. Experiments were devised to enable the causes of changes in student behavior to be discovered. Process–product studies tried to determine a linear relation between teacher behavior (process) and learning outcomes in students (product).

In the 1960s and 1970s correlational research flourished alongside experimental research. In quasi-experimental educational settings the effect of teaching in "experimental" groups was compared with that in control groups.

Advanced statistical methods helped to calculate the exact chance of certain changes taking place under the influence of certain educational conditions. During the 1970s other approaches in educational research became popular: interpretative, critical, and qualitative approaches. Interpretative research stressed the fact that there cannot be a "causal connection between teacher behavior and student learning" (Gage 1989), because human beings are not "billiard balls" but creatures with intentions, plans, goals, and purposes, and who have a view about their own and others' behavior, which influences their activity. Critical theorists stressed the fact that learning, like any other human activity, is influenced by the social and political context in which it takes place.

Qualitative research of an interpretative and critical nature makes use of descriptive and analytical methods, as used, for example, by historians. Educational researchers have described, classroom processes in terms of actions and meaning perspectives. ("Meaning perspective" is a term that denotes the immediate meaning of action from the actor's point of view.) Researchers have used methods such as introspection, thinking aloud, individual interviews, and analyses of protocols of student behavior and problem-solving proceses. According to Gage (1989), there is "no necessary antagonism between the objectivists, the interpretivists, and the critical theorists." Their approaches supplement one another. Process–product studies can be enriched by case and interview studies that stress the meaning-perspectives of teachers and students.

See also: Teaching: Aptitude-Treatment Interaction Model; Architecture of Cognition; Cognition and Learning; Human Development, Learning, and Instruction; History of Instructional Psychology; Individual Differences and Instruction; Learning Processes and Learning Outcomes; Historical Overview and Trends of Learning Theories; Mastery Learning; Models of Learning; Piaget's Theory of Human Development; Learning Strategies and Learning to Learn

References

Boekaerts M 1994 Affect, emotions and learning. In: Husén T, Postlethwaite T N (eds.) 1994 *The International Encyclopedia of Education*, 2nd edn. Pergamon Press, Oxford

Brown J S, Collins A, Duguid P 1989 Situated cognition and the culture of learning. *Educ. Researcher* 18(1): 32–42

Collins A 1991 Cognitive apprenticeship and instructional technology. In: Idol L, Jones B F (eds.) 1991 *Educational Values and Cognitive Instruction: Implications for Reform*. Erlbaum, Hillsdale, New Jersey

Craik F I M, Lockhart R S 1972 Levels of processing: A framework for memory research. *J. Verbal Learn. Verbal Behav.* 11: 671–84

De Corte E 1989 Acquiring and teaching cognitive skills: A state-of-the-art of theory and research. In: Drenth P J D, Sergeant J A, Takens R J (eds.) 1989 *European Perspectives in Psychology. Vol. 1: Theoretical Psychometrics. Personality, Developmental, Educational, Cognitive, Gerontological*. Wiley, Chichester

Duncker K 1935 On problem solving. *Psychological Monographs* 58(5): (Whole No. 270)

Entwistle N 1987 Explaining individual differences in school learning. In: De Corte E, Lodewijks H, Parmentier R, Span P (eds.) 1987 *Learning and Instruction: European Research in an International Context*, Vol. 1. Pergamon Press, Oxford

Gage N L 1989 The paradigm wars and their aftermath: A "historical" sketch of research on teaching since 1989. *Educ. Researcher* 18(7): 4–10

Marton F 1981 Phenomenography: Describing conceptions of the world around us. *Instructional Science* 10(2): 177–200

Marton F, Säljo R 1976 On qualitative differences in learning, II: Outcome as a function of the learner's conception of the task. *Br. J. Educ. Psychol.* 46(2): 115–27

Mayer R E 1981 *The Promise of Cognitive Psychology*. Freeman, San Francisco, California

Piaget J 1947 *La psychologie de l'intelligence*. Colin, Paris

Piaget J 1964 Development and learning. In: Ripple R E (ed.) 1964 *Readings in Learning and Human Abilities: Educational Psychology*. Harper and Row, New York

Selz O 1924 *Die Gesetze der produktiven und reproduktiven Geistestätigkeit*. Cohen, Bonn

Skinner B F 1953 *Science and Human Behavior*. Macmillan Inc., New York

Snow R E 1989 Aptitude–treatment interaction as a framework for research on individual differences in learning. In: Ackerman P L, Sternberg R, Glaser R (eds.) 1989 *Learning and Individual Differences: Advances in Theory and Research*. Freeman, New York

van Lieshout C F M 1987 Learning and instruction: A part of development. In: De Corte E, Lodewijks H, Parmentier R, Span P (eds.) 1987 *Learning and Instruction: European Research in an International Context*, Vol. 1. Pergamon Press, Oxford

Vygotsky L S 1929 The problem of the cultural development of the child. *J. Genet. Psychol.* 36: 415–34

Weinert F 1989 The impact of schooling on cognitive development: One hypothetical assumption, some empirical results, and many theoretical speculations. *EARLI News* 8: 3–7

Wertheimer M 1945 *Productive Thinking*. Harper and Row, New York

Further Reading

Collins A, Brown J S, Newman S E 1989 Cognitive apprenticeship: Teaching the craft of reading, writing and mathematics. In: Resnick L B (ed.) 1989 *Knowing, Learning, and Instruction: Essays in Honor of Robert Glaser*. Erlbaum, Hillsdale, New Jersey

Corno L, Snow R E 1986 Adapting teaching to individual differences among learners. In: Wittrock M C (ed.) 1986 *Learning and Instruction: European Research in an International Context*, Vol. 1. Pergamon Press, Oxford *Handbook of Research on Teaching*, 3rd edn. Macmillan Inc., New York

De Corte E, Verschaffel L 1989 Teaching word problems in the primary grades: What research has to say to the teachers. In: Greer B, Mulhern G (eds.) 1989 *New Directions in Teaching Mathematics Education*. Routledge, London

Erikson F 1986 Qualitative methods in research on teaching. In: Wittrock M C (ed.) 1986 *Handbook of Research on Teaching*, 3rd edn. Macmillan Inc., New York

Glaser R 1987 Learning theory and theories of knowledge. In: De Corte E, Lodewijks H, Parmentier R, Span P (eds.) 1987 *Learning and Instruction: European Research in an International Context*, Vol. 1. Pergamon Press, Oxford

Merrill M D 1987 Component display theory. In: Reigeluth C M (ed.) 1987 *Instructional Theories in Action*. Erlbaum, Hillsdale, New Jersey

Van der Veer, Valsiner J 1991 *Understanding Vygoksky: A Quest for Synthesis*. Basis Blackwell, Oxford

Vygotsky L S 1978 *Mind in Society: The Development of Higher Psychological Processes*. Harvard University Press, Cambridge, Massachusetts

Learning Theories: Historical Overview and Trends

T. J. Shuell and K. A. Moran

Learning theories have changed dramatically since the 1960s. Traditional theories (based largely on stimulus-response views of behavior) have been superseded by newer theories based on cognitive psychology and a concern for social, cultural, and developmental factors. Traditionally, learning has been defined as a change in behavior or performance resulting from experience and practice. Although a concern for change is still evident, the emphasis has shifted to the restructuring of knowledge and changes in understanding rather than changes in behavior. "Problem-solving" rather than "memorization" has become the prevailing metaphor.

Over the years, various theoretical and philosophical differences regarding learning have existed, although some convergence of thinking has occurred. This entry discusses the continuing evolution of learning theory and research, especially as it relates to learning in an educational setting. As understanding of learning evolved, several transitions can be identified. Behavioral theories of learning dominated the field prior to the 1960s, when the "cognitive revolution" began to influence thinking about human behavior. Although cognitive psychology seldom focused on learning per se, it influenced the way psychologists thought about the acquisition of knowledge (Shuell 1986). During the 1980s, limitations of research in cognitive psychology (e.g., the use of laboratory rather than real-world tasks and a failure to consider noncognitive factors such as motivation, interest, and emotion) led to new and sometimes controversial theories such as situated cognition and cognitive apprenticeship. Constructivism and mental models are also receiving increased attention. The following discussion is organized in terms of these major eras.

1. Early Research on Learning

Research on learning flourished during the first half of the twentieth century, especially in the United States where it was heavily influenced by the behaviorism that dominated American psychology during this period and by the work of such seminal figures as E L Thorndike and B F Skinner. Learning was conceptualized as something that occurs from the outside-in: environmental stimuli impinge on an individual who makes a response, and the consequences of this response (i.e., reinforcement) determines the probability of that response occurring again when the same or a similar situation is encountered. This United States research consisted largely of laboratory studies (often with animals) using simplistic tasks for the purpose of identifying universal laws of learning.

In contrast to the functional orientation of United States research, European research during this period focused more on the structural characteristics of mental functioning. The principal aim of this research was an understanding of the mental processes responsible for thinking and other mental activities; this focus of research interest was evident in the studies of perception by Gestalt psychologists and the studies of cognitive development by Piagetian researchers. These studies were based on a philosophical concern for understanding the human mind, and unlike the United States interest in identifying factors responsible for educational change, there was little European concern for investigating how mental processes could be altered through instructional intervention (Resnick 1987). Vygotsky's action psychology existed during this period, but several decades elapsed before it had a major impact on learning theory in either the United States or Europe.

The behavioral explanations of learning that emerged from research in the United States were considered too mechanistic by European psychologists, while European approaches were criticized by American psychologists for ignoring the "change" they considered so central to learning and for producing studies that lacked methodological soundness. Following the First World War, however, a variety of social and philosophical changes, along with certain technological advances, set the stage for new conceptions of the human mind. Theories of information processing and the advent of computers began to influence United States psychology, as did changing beliefs about the individual's role and responsibility in society. The spirit of this age—reflecting the individual's ability to influence the course of events both historically and personally—became most pronounced during the 1960s, when a strong egalitarian philosophy began to influence both United States psychology and social action. These factors made it possible to reconcile some of the differences between American and European research.

Influenced by German Gestalt psychology and the Würzburg school in Europe, cognitive scientists began to view the learner as an active information processor analogous to computers and proposed conceptions of learning from the perspective of cognitive psychology. Consistent with European interest in mental processes, these early cognitive psychologists focused on the internal mediation that occurs between the originating stimulus and the learner's response, for example, how the individual interprets the stimulus and processes it before making a response. This focus on the internal and active processes of the individual generated new conceptions of what constitutes learning. It should be noted, however, that while prevailing theories focus primarily on complex, meaningful forms of learning, other types of learning also exist. At times, for example, students learn information via operant and classical conditioning in spite of a reluctance by cognitive psychologists to acknowledge this fact. As Robert Gagné has convincingly argued for many years, (e.g., 1985), there are several different types of learning, and a comprehensive understanding of learning must include both behavioral and cognitive theories. Nevertheless, the following discussion focuses on meaningful learning, as this type of learning is generally accepted to be the primary goal of education, and since it better represents thinking about learning in the early 1990s.

2. Cognitive Conceptions of Meaningful Learning

The meaningful learning of complex material is an active, constructive, cumulative, self-regulated, and goal-oriented process (Shuell 1986, 1992). The learner interprets the information to be acquired and the task in which it is embedded (e.g., reading a book, listening to an explanation, analyzing a picture, writing a critique) and constructs a mental representation of the task and material based on these perceptions and relevant prior knowledge. As essential information is always missing from the physical stimulus, the learner adds information in order to make sense of the situation. Thus, the learner's representation is unique, and it may or may not be consistent with similar representations formed by other individuals (e.g., a teacher). In fact, the learner's perceptions of the instructional situation and the type of psychological processing in which the learner engages is the single most important factor in determining what the individual learns. The teacher or instructional agent (e.g., book, computer) plays an important role, by ensuring that the learner is engaged appropriately with the instructional materials, but it is the learner who determines what is actually learned. Before elaborating further, it may be helpful to consider the nature of meaningful learning and how it differs from simpler forms of learning.

2.1 The Nature of Meaningful Learning

References to "meaningful learning" are common, although the exact nature of what is meant by the term is often vague. One major difference between meaningful, cognitive learning and simpler forms of learning is that the former is usually concerned with understanding, while the latter is usually concerned with behavioral change. Although "understanding" is difficult to define in a rigorous manner, certain characteristics of the concept can be identified. In order for a body of knowledge to be meaningful and capable of being understood, it must be structured and organized. Few people would claim, for example, that it is possible to understand a telephone number, although most would agree that it is possible to learn, know, or remember one. Therefore, understanding a body of knowledge involves the establishment of relationships among the concepts and facts that comprise that body of knowledge, and such understanding can be assessed by paraphrasing, summarizing, or answering questions about the material and/or by performing a transfer task (Shuell 1992).

Another difference is that meaningful learning involves the acquisition of a complex body of knowledge while simpler forms of learning typically involve a collection of separate and isolated facts. Meaningful learning is also more likely to extend over a prolonged period and to involve different phases of learning (Shuell 1990). For example, during the initial phase of learning, the acquisition of more or less isolated facts may provide the conceptual glue necessary for an initial structure; later in learning, however, organizational strategies may provide the relationships necessary for synthesis and high-level understanding.

Although definitions of learning by cognitive psychologists are similar to more traditional definitions (Shuell 1986), cognitive scientists talk about learning in very different ways, as when Brown (1990) suggests that "Learning is much more an evolutionary, sense-making, experiential process of development than of simple acquisition" (p. 268).

For educational purposes, it should be borne in mind that the meaning does not reside in the material being learned, or depend on the manner in which it is presented to the student. The material may possess a potential for being meaningful, but it is the learner who makes it meaningful by processing it in a meaningful way. It is not sufficient for the teacher to explain or demonstrate how various concepts and facts are related, since this activity can occur without meaningful learning taking place on the part of the student. The five characteristics of meaningful learning previously identified contribute to an understanding of the concept and are treated below.

(a) Active—the learner must carry out various cognitive operations on the information being learned for it to be acquired in a meaningful manner. The emphasis, of course, is on mental rather than physical activity.

(b) Constructive—knowledge is not an entity that can be passed intact from one person (teacher, book, etc.) to another (the learner). Each learner perceives and interprets new information in a unique manner (based on factors such as prior knowledge, interest, motivation, attitude toward self, etc.) and then elaborates this information by relating it to existing knowledge and/or other aspects of the material being learned. Consequently, no two students end up with exactly the same understanding of the concepts and facts being studied.

(c) Cumulative—new learning builds upon the individual's prior knowledge and mental models, although prior knowledge can inhibit as well as facilitate new learning. The large body of literature on prior conceptions and the difficulty involved in overcoming misconceptions illustrate the potent influence that prior knowledge has on learning.

(d) Self-regulated—as learning progresses, the learner must make decisions about what to do next (e.g., rehearse a particular piece of information, seek an answer to a question that comes to mind, look for similarities among various pieces of information). Effective learners also monitor the learning process, making periodic checks of how well the material is understood. The self-regulation of learning involves a number of factors, including metacognition, self-efficacy, and studying.

(e) Goal-oriented—meaningful learning is more likely to be successful if the learner has at least a general idea of the goal being pursued and holds appropriate expectations for achieving the desired understanding. Providing instructional objectives is one of many ways to establish goals, although in many instructional situations it is more appropriate for students to develop or discover goals independently. In any case, it is the *student's* goal that is critical. The mere statement of objectives or goals by a teacher is not sufficient; they must be adopted as the learner's personal goals if they are to impact the learning process.

2.2 Learning Functions

The preceding discussion described the nature of meaningful learning, but it provided little information on how learning actually occurs. Various psychological principles of learning (drawn from a large body of theory and research) are summarized in Table 1 (Shuell 1992). These learning functions are relevant for different types of learning, although the extent of their applicability depends on the particular type under consideration. Although these processes occur within the individual, they can be performed in a number of equally valid and effective ways, that is, various methods are functionally equivalent for eliciting the relevant cognitive processes in the learner.

These learning functions, along with the characteristics of meaningful learning outlined above, provide a summary of cognitive conceptions of learning. The assumption that the individual is an active processor of new information guides the majority of research on learning in the early 1990s and has, to a large extent, reconciled some of the differences among earlier

approaches. Nevertheless, limitations in the explanatory power of research in cognitive psychology have prompted new questions and insights.

3. Beyond Cognitive Conceptions: Toward New Understandings of Learning from Instruction

Although cognitive psychology and the information-processing model continue to dominate research on learning, critics have argued that important considerations are ignored by focusing strictly on cognitive processes. These considerations include concerns for: (a) the social/cultural nature of learning; (b) "authentic" (real world) rather than artificial tasks; (c) the role of motivation, interest, and affect; (d) the domain-specific nature of learning; and (e) the constructive nature of learning. In addition, instructional psychology has been concerned largely with describing the nature of expertise rather than with clarifying how this expertise is acquired. Consequently, cognitive psychology has not contributed significantly to a theory concerned with the instructional interventions necessary to help students achieve expertise. These concerns represent emerging areas of investigation and extensions of existing cognitive theories of learning and illustrate a transition in thinking about meaningful learning.

3.1 Social and Situational Factors

Concern for learning in a social/cultural context has been heavily influenced by the writings of Vygotsky, work in cultural psychology, and calls for "authentic learning" (e.g., Brown et al. 1989). Cognitive psychology's strict focus on mental processes has been criticized for its failure to consider social and cultural mediators that affect learning.

Cultural psychology in particular has investigated the learning of mathematical or other daily living skills in non-Western and less school-dominated cultures, suggesting that Western studies of learning and developmental psychology have been by the structure of school. Furthermore, Brown et al. (1989) suggest that learning and cognition are situated in a particular cultural context (culture on a small, not large, scale) and that knowledge evolves by being used in "authentic" activities. This concern for authentic learning argues that substantial differences exist between learning as it typically occurs in school and learning as it occurs in the real world.

These notions of situated cognition and authentic learning have suggested a model of teaching and learning known as "cognitive apprenticeship" (see Brown et al. 1989). This model provides a framework for designing learning environments in which students learn to model performance through a system of conceptual scaffolding that is gradually eliminated.

The theory of learning proposed by Russian psychologist Gal'perin has received attention in Europe

Table 1
Twelve learning functions[a]

Expectations	Meaningful learning is most effective when the learner has at least a general idea of what is to be accomplished from the learning task. Expectations change as learning progresses, and include affective (emotional, self-efficacy, etc.) as well as cognitive goals. Providing an overview or the student identifying the purpose of a lesson are examples of ways in which expectations can be initiated.
Motivation	The learner must persist and contribute effort if meaningful learning is to occur. Motivation and expectations are interrelated--e.g., expectations regarding self-efficacy may affect one's motivation.
Prior knowledge activation	Both cognitive and affective prerequisites must be activated so that relevant attitudes and appropriate knowledge structures in the learner's memory are available for use. This function can be initiated by reminding students of prerequisite information or by asking oneself what is already known about the topic being learned.
Attention	The material being studied always contains a large amount of information, and the learner must focus on relevant information, disregarding (at least for the moment) the irrelevant information that is available.
Encoding	Information in short-term memory must be encoded before further processing. The learner adds personal meaning to the new information, such as seeing a stimulus and interpreting it as a car, although the same information might be encoded in various ways by different individuals or under different conditions. The use of mnemonics and/or diagrams are examples of how encoding can be initiated.
Comparison	A body of potentially meaningful knowledge contains many interrelated facts and concepts. In order for it to be acquired in a manner that involves understanding rather than rote memorization, the learner must make many comparisons in searching for similarities and differences that permit the formation of higher-order relationships characteristic of understanding.
Hypothesis generation	Hypotheses about the material/task being learned are generated as part of the active, constructive nature of meaningful learning. This function can be initiated by encouraging students to try alternate courses of action or by the learner generating alternative solutions.
Repetition	Rarely is something learned in a single exposure. The nature of repetition in meaningful learning is different from repetition in simpler forms of learning, but it is still necessary. Meaningful learning takes time; going over the material more than once provides opportunities for new relationships to emerge. The inducement of multiple perspectives and engaging in systematic reviews are two ways this function can be initiated.
Feedback	Feedback on the adequacy and accuracy of the learner's understanding is necessary for learning to progress. Without adequate and instructionally relevant feedback, the learner is likely to flounder or practice inappropriate behaviors.
Evaluation	Feedback is necessary but not sufficient; the learner must interpret and evaluate the feedback to determine its reliability and how to make best use of it.
Monitoring	The learning process needs to be monitored, preferably by the learner, to determine if reasonable progress is being made. Self-testing to determine if understanding has been achieved is an example of how this function can be initiated.
Combination, integration, synthesis	As learning progresses, isolated pieces of information must be combined in ways that permit the integration and synthesis of information from various sources. Developing organizational schemes such as tables and diagrams is an example of how this function can be initiated.

a Source: Shuell 1992

(for a good summary of Gal'perin's work, see De Corte 1977). This theory, based on Vygotsky's social action theory, suggests that there are three stages or levels of action (material, verbal, and mental) between the interaction with external objects and the development of higher-order mental processes.

As a result of the increased recognition of cultural and social influences, most of the educationally relevant work in cognitive psychology has moved away from what are perceived as sterile laboratory settings derived from earlier behavioral approaches, to more naturalistic classroom situations and beyond to the real world. This emphasis on naturalistic settings has also supported the development of ethnographic and phenomenographic approaches to studying students' perspectives and activities during learning.

3.2 Motivation and Emotion

Historically, research on learning has demonstrated a marked lack of concern for motivational and affective aspects of learning, especially within cognitive psychology's information-processing approach. These factors are beginning to receive increased attention in thinking about meaningful learning in the early 1990s. In relating studies on motivation to the educational context, Pintrich and De Groot (1990) posit three ways in which motivation influences learning: (a) the individual's belief about his or her ability to accomplish a task, a concern related to the expectation function discussed in Table 1; (b) the learner's reasons or purpose for engaging in a task, as illustrated by research on interest (see Schiefele 1991); and (c) the learner's affective reactions to the task (e.g., anxiety, anger, pride, shame, and guilt). Research on motivation is also beginning to investigate motivation for specific tasks rather than more general traits or indirect influences such as achievement motivation.

3.3 Domain-specific Learning

Learning theories have traditionally been concerned with general laws that hold across virtually all situations. The concern for expert–novice differences that began to appear in the late 1970s resulted in new ideas about the nature of competence. These ideas, along with a concern for social/cultural factors, led to theories that stress the domain-specific nature of learning. Transfer across domains began to be questioned, although debate continues about the balance between the domain-specific and domain-general aspects of learning.

3.4 Instructional Intervention

The relationship between learning and teaching is not always as obvious as it might appear. The proper balance between student learning (studying, discovery, etc.) and didactic teaching has been debated for centuries, and the two have typically been studied as separate entities rather than an integrated process. After many years of being more concerned with describing the nature of expertise than with the means by which that expertise is acquired, cognitive psychology is beginning to address issues of instructional intervention (Glaser 1991; Shuell 1986, 1992). The cognitive apprenticeship model, reciprocal teaching, and cooperative learning (the latter two of which grew out of concerns for the social nature of learning) are examples of efforts in the early 1990s to develop appropriate ways to facilitate learning. To the extent that meaningful learning is a self-regulated process of discovery, then the role of the instructional agent (teacher, book, computer, etc.) poses a challenging question for those interested in understanding learning in educational settings (Shuell 1992). Some of the most promising research on the relationship between specific learning experiences and various instructional activities in actual classroom settings is contained in the work of Nuthall and Alton-Lee (1990) in New Zealand.

4. Conclusion

Learning is no longer viewed merely as the acquisition of behaviors or isolated facts. The restructuring of a person's prior knowledge is now acknowledged as a more appropriate way of thinking about meaningful learning, although other forms of learning also exist. In addition, the relationship between learning and development, the likelihood of phases in complex learning (Shuell 1990), and learning from cases are all receiving increased attention. These new views expand the understanding of learning by focusing on factors often ignored in previous research. Future research, however, must not lose sight of how learning occurs, the various types of learning involved in school learning, and ways in which learning can be influenced by education.

See also: Adult Learning: Overview; Constructivism and Learning; Expert Level of Understanding; Feedback in Learning; Learning Environments; Learning Processes and Learning Outcomes; Instructional Psychology; Metacognition; Models of Learning; Motivation and Learning; Preconceptions and Misconceptions; Prior Knowledge and Learning; Self-regulation in Learning

References

Brown J S 1990 Toward a new epistemology for learning. In: Frasson C, Gauthier G (eds.) 1990 *Intelligent Tutoring Systems: At the Crossroads of Artificial Intelligence and Education.* Ablex, Norwood, New Jersey
Brown J S, Collins A, Duguid P 1989 Situated cognition and the culture of learning. *Educ. Researcher* 18(1): 32–42
De Corte E 1977 Some aspects of research on learning and cognitive development in Europe. *Educ. Psychol.* 12(2): 197–206

Gagné R M 1985 *The Conditions of Learning and Theory of Instruction*, 4th edn. Harcourt, Brace, Jovanovich, New York

Glaser R 1991 The maturing of the relationship between the science of learning and cognition and educational practice. *Learning and Instruction* 1(2): 129–44

Nuthall G, Alton-Lee A 1990 Research on teaching and learning: Thirty years of change. *Elem. Sch. J.* 90(5): 547–70

Pintrich P R, De Groot E V 1990 Motivational and self-regulated learning components of classroom academic performance. *J. Educ. Psychol.* 82(1): 33–40

Resnick L B 1987 Instruction and the cultivation of thinking. In: De Corte E, Lodewijks H, Parmentier R, Span P (eds.) 1987 *Learning and Instruction: European Research in an International Context*, Vol. 1. Pergamon Press, Oxford

Schiefele U 1991 Interest, learning, and motivation. *Educ. Psychol.* 26(3–4): 299–323

Shuell T J 1986 Cognitive conceptions of learning. *Rev. Educ. Res.* 56(14): 411–36

Shuell T J 1990 Phases of meaningful learning. *Rev. Educ. Res.* 60(4): 531–47

Shuell T J 1992 Designing instructional computing systems for meaningful learning. In: Jones M, Winne P H (eds.)

1992 *Adaptive Learning Environments*: Foundations and Frontiers. Springer-Verlag, New York

Further Reading

Bandura A 1986 *The Social Foundations of Thought and Action: A Social Cognitive theory*. Prentice-Hall, Englewood Cliffs, New Jersey

De Corte E et al. (eds.) 1987 *Learning and Instruction: European Research in an International Context*, 2 Vols. Pergamon Press, Oxford

Marshall H H (ed.) *Redefining Student Learning: Roots of Educational Change*. Ablex, Norwood, New Jersey

Resnick L B (ed.) 1989 *Knowing, Learning, and Instruction: Essays in Honor of Robert Glaser*. Erlbaum, Hillsdale, New Jersey

Riesbeck C, Schank R 1989 *Inside Case-Based Reasoning*. Lawrence Erlbaum, Hillsdale, New Jersey

Steffe L P, Gale J (eds.) 1995 *Constructivism in Education*. Erlbaum, Hillsdale, New Jersey

Zimmerman B J, Schunk D H (eds.) 1989 *Self-Regulated Learning and Academic Achievement: Theory, Research, and Practice*. Springer-Verlag, New York

Models of Learning

R. B. Burns

Models are heuristics for theorists and researchers. They guide thinking by simplifying and representing complex phenomena as a set of relationships among a few important variables. Models of learning represent the most important learner and instructional variables influencing school learning. This entry discusses models of learning and related concepts, and describes five historically important models of learning.

1. Models of Learning

One outcome of educational and instructional psychology has been the development of models of learning. Generally, models of learning organize into a theoretical system a small set of learner and instructional variables that have a conceptual or empirical link to student learning. Such models are usually represented pictorially in such a way that the interrelationships among the learner and instructional variables and their relationship to student learning are made explicit in some form of causal diagram. It is partly because of such pictorial representations that the term "model" is used in place of the term "theory."

While models of learning are theoretical in nature, their content is inherently practical. Models of learning focus on the salient instructional conditions influencing school learning. Because of their content, models of learning can have direct implications for the design of school curriculum and instruction, and some of them have generated specific instructional models for implementation in schools.

Since models of learning carry a dual role, being both theoretical and practical, theoretical validity and practical relevance are two fundamental criteria for evaluating models of learning. Theoretical validity refers both to the extent to which empirical findings support the relationships specified by the model, and to the ability of the model to stimulate new thinking about school learning. Practical relevance refers to the ability of the model to generate concepts and principles capable of guiding classroom practice.

1.1 Models and Theories of Learning

Models of learning are distinct from theories of learning. Theories of learning describe the behavioral and cognitive processes involved when learners change as a result of experience in some situation. Experimental psychology has a rich history in the development of theories of learning, and work on such theories continues. While learning theorists sometimes develop different "models" of the learning process, as when learning is viewed as information processing and modeled as a series of cognitive structures regulating and modifying the flow and organization of information, these are descriptions of the process of learning in individuals and do not generally focus on the external conditions that might optimize the learning process. This latter domain is the domain of models of learning.

Models of learning differ from theories of learning in at least two further ways. First, because models of learning deal with school learning, where groups of learners are brought together for extended periods of time, there is sometimes a concern for the distributional properties of the group of learners making up a class. The range of ability in a classroom, for example, is as important to the understanding of classroom learning phenomena as short-term memory processes are to the understanding of complex cognitive performance. Second, the time frame is different for models and theories of learning. Models of learning consider learning as it unfolds over weeks, months, and years of schooling, whereas learning theory deals with processes which are often measured in seconds and minutes. As a result, models of learning tend to be macro rather than micro models, and their constructs are molar ones like motivation and prior knowledge, on the learner side, and quality of instruction and curriculum structure on the instructional side. The variables common to learning theories characterize the more molecular processes of learning like encoding, short-term memory, attention, retrieval, and the like.

Moreover, the extended time frame in models of learning requires attention to at least two questions not typically considered by theories of learning:

(a) What are the natural curricular or instructional units that serve to break long periods of school time into psychological chunks? The learning task and the learning unit have been two common choices, and their organization over the course of a semester or school year naturally leads to issues of curricular sequence, instructional design, and the accumulative nature of learning.

(b) What are the relationships between learner characteristics and learning outcomes over time? Models of learning typically deal with the constructs of aptitude and achievement, among others, raising important issues about the influence of prior learning on new learning and how to conceptualize and model their interrelationships over time.

Models of learning, then, are macro models of molar constructs that predict learning outcomes over relatively long periods of time for groups of learners in classrooms. In contrast, theories of learning are more molecular descriptions of the processes of learning that occur in individual learners during relatively short periods of time. However, having presented this division as a sharp dichotomy, a caveat is in order.

Research in cognitive science has begun to blur the distinction between theories and models of learning by providing detailed descriptions of competent performance on school tasks and the instructional conditions needed to move a learner from a novice state with respect to the task to one of expertise. Thus, contrary to the emphasis placed on the description of learning processes by past theories of learning, cognitive science is focusing more attention on the outcomes of learning and the instructional conditions necessary to support and develop expert performance (Glaser and Bassok 1989). This work may eventually bridge theories and models of learning.

1.2 Related Concepts

Terms closely related to models of learning include "theories of teaching," "models of teaching," "theories of instruction," and "models of instruction." These terms are used loosely and interchangeably in the literature, depending on the writer's background and orientation.

One reason for their overlap is that these terms have been in use only since the mid-1960s. At that time, a concern developed over the relevance of theories of learning for the design of classroom instruction. In Hilgard (1964), both Gage and Bruner argued that theories of learning needed to be transformed into theories of teaching (Gage) or theories of instruction (Bruner) if they were to benefit practice. A burgeoning literature on theories and models of teaching and instruction followed, and along with it there arose some confusion over how to delimit and define these areas. Even the emergence of the field of instructional psychology during the 1970s has not helped the problem of definition appreciably; a perusal of the eight *Annual Review of Psychology* chapters on instructional psychology to date reveals a field that is still evolving with fluid boundaries.

The various connotations of the concept of "model" contribute to the lack of clarity. The most common use of models in educational and instructional psychology is as formal, symbolic representations of relationships among variables, similar to the way models of learning are defined in this entry. Others, however, see models differently. Nuthall and Snook (1973) reject this view and consider models as well-developed points of view that guide research. Joyce and Weil (1992), in describing some "models of teaching," use the term "model" in its natural language sense as an example or prototype to be emulated or copied.

1.3 Models of Learning and Instructional Practice

Theories and models of learning are inherently connected to theories and models of teaching and instruction by virtue of the fact that any example of the former can generate an instance of the latter simply by asking a prescriptive question.

When the prescriptive question is asked of theories of learning, it takes the following form: if this is a description of learning, then what are the concepts and principles for instruction that *support these processes* of learning? The answer is usually a variety of instructional design models and theories of instruction that vary according to the language system used in the original learning theory (see Gagné and Dick 1983). For models of learning, the prescriptive question takes a slightly different form: If this is what predicts learning, then what constructs and variables *optimize the outcomes* of learning? Here the propensity is to develop a more specific model of instruction that instantiates the learning model and that can be emulated for classroom practice (see Wang and Walberg 1985).

It should be understood, however, that the translation of theories and models of learning into practice is not merely a one-to-one mapping from one domain to another. The process of translating a theory or model of learning into practice usually requires additional concepts, grounded in practical knowledge of how classrooms operate, that are necessary to make the theory or model "workable" in real classroom settings. Thus, the distance between a model of learning and classroom practice can be great, and issues of teacher and school change and fidelity of implementation clearly become relevant.

Moreover, theories and models of learning are not the sole source of theories and models of teaching and instruction. Theories and models of teaching and instruction can arise from philosophical (e.g., Lamm 1976), conceptual (e.g., Klauer 1985), and empirical (e.g., Anderson et al. 1989) analyses. The translation process might, perhaps, be better characterized in the following way: theories and models of learning, supplemented with additional knowledge about classrooms, contribute to an amalgam of concepts, principles, constructs, and variables that are combined into practical theories and models of teaching and instruction.

1.4 Summary

The distinctions presented above are summarized in Fig. 1. Theories and models of learning are represented on the left. Both are empirical, but theories of learning describe the learning process while models of learning focus on variables that impact the outcomes of school learning directly.

When prescriptive questions about practice are asked, theories and models of teaching or instruction result, represented by the four boxes to the right in Fig. 1. Theories of teaching focus on explanations of teacher interactions with learners, while models of teaching typically prescribe practice. Theories of instruction tend to be general, acting to integrate derived principles and concepts from theories of learning, while models of instruction are usually more specific and instantiate a particular theory or model of learning.

2. Some Examples of Models of Learning

Five models of learning which originated in the 1960s and 1970s are described in this section, and their relationship to more recent models of learning is considered.

2.1 Carroll's Model of School Learning

Perhaps the most well-known model of school learning is that of Carroll (1963). Carroll's basic notion was that the degree of learning was a simple function of the time spent by a learner relative to the time needed for learning, represented as a ratio with time spent in

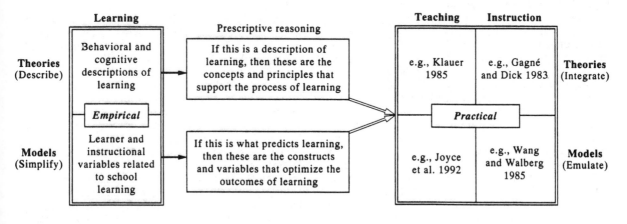

Figure 1
Theories and models of learning, teaching, and instruction

the numerator and time needed in the denominator. If both were the same, then learning would be complete; if the numerator was less than the denominator, learning would be less than complete. Carroll identified three variables that determine time spent and three variables that interact in a relatively complicated way to determine time needed.

Considering the numerator first, time spent learning was defined as the shortest of three time variables: perseverance (the amount of time a learner was willing to spend on a task, basically a proxy variable for motivation), opportunity to learn (the amount of time allowed for learning in the instructional setting), and time needed, the denominator of the model. Time needed was defined by three variables: aptitude (the time needed to learn under ideal instructional conditions), and two additional variables that interact potentially to increase the time needed to learn beyond that required by aptitude: ability to understand instruction and quality of instruction.

Ability to understand instruction was defined as a combination of general intelligence and verbal ability. The former comes into play when instruction requires learners to reason or figure out tasks themselves and the latter comes into play whenever the language of the instructional environment is beyond the verbal ability of learners. Quality of instruction was conceptualized as interacting with ability to understand instruction as follows: when the quality of instruction was high, little additional time beyond that required by aptitude would be needed. Yet as the quality of instruction decreased—when learners were required to figure out the concepts themselves or the verbal demands increase—then the time needed to learn would be a function of both aptitude and the additional time required by the lower quality of instruction. The lower quality of instruction, however, might not affect all learners equally. Learners with greater general intelligence, verbal ability, or both might be able to supply what the instruction lacked and not need much additional time beyond that required by aptitude. Learners with less general intelligence and/or verbal ability, however, would experience relatively greater hardship as the quality of instruction decreased and require additional time beyond that required by aptitude. In extreme cases, they might not be able to learn the task because the additional time required was beyond what they were willing to spend or exceeded what was provided by the instructional situation.

Carroll's model is significant for a number of reasons. First, it has spawned a large and diverse theoretical and empirical literature (Carroll 1989). Second, in one succinct statement, the model organized several of the most important school learning variables: aptitude, intelligence, verbal ability, prior learning, motivation, opportunity to learn, quality of instruction, and learning tasks. Third, conceptualizing aptitude in terms of individual differences in time needed to learn directed attention away from the

limiting notion of aptitude as fixed capacity for learning, and stimulated more optimistic thinking about how instructional conditions might be arranged to take such differences into account.

Finally, the use of time as a metric in Carroll's model generated an enormous amount of thinking about time as a variable in learning and instruction. For example, time has been used to define student characteristics, such as the concept of learning rate that underlies many views of individualized instruction or the concepts of engaged time and active learning time brought to fruition in the Beginning Teacher Evaluation Study (Fisher et al. 1980). More importantly, the concept of time has been used conceptually to link student and instructional variables. Bennett (1978) and Wiley and Harnischfeger (1974), for example, define the total amount of time available for instruction and then embed the student variables of engaged and active learning time within these extra-student temporal parameters.

2.2 Dahllöf's Steering Group Model

A model of class achievement that is superficially similar to Carroll's is that of Dahllöf (1971). Dahllöf was concerned that the extant studies on the effect of ability grouping on student achievement failed to take into account relevant teaching process variables. He argued that the lack of achievement differences between low ability and heterogeneously grouped classes found in some grouping studies could be explained by a "theory of steering."

Dahllöf hypothesized that teachers use a steering group of students as a criterion to decide on instructional pacing, the steering group being a subgroup of the class roughly between the 10th and 25th percentile in ability. Such a steering group could explain the lack of achievement differences between heterogeneous and low-ability classes because the distribution of low-ability students would be about the same in both types of classes and thus the steering groups would be about the same. With similar steering groups, the two types of classes would progress at about the same pace and cover about the same curriculum, resulting in similar achievement despite different grouping configurations.

Although Dahllöf's model gives attention to time spent on learning, curriculum difficulty, and teaching methods, the key variable is the steering group. The steering group directly impacts teacher pacing, which in turn influences curriculum coverage and ultimately student achievement. The steering group itself is indirectly affected by whatever administrative policy is in place for assigning students to classrooms, establishing what Dahllöf called a "frame factor." Frame factors act broadly to restrict or limit the options available to teachers during the teaching process.

The Dahllöf model and its development by Lundgren (1972) explicitly takes into account the group nature of school learning, and that feature alone sets this model apart from others discussed in this entry. The group focus of the model also places it in the context of more sociological approaches to instruction like that of Barr et al. (1983). While the steering group hypothesis has neither generated much research nor produced any instructional models, the theoretical significance of group compositional effects for models of learning is great and is being treated in research.

2.3 Bloom's Model of School Learning

Bloom's (1976) model of school learning features only three variables affecting student learning—cognitive entry behaviors, affective entry characteristics, and quality of instruction—but the model includes a characterization of the process of instruction as it unfolds in time. The three variables in Bloom's model are organized around the concept of a learning unit, defined as several weeks of curriculum. It is significant that aptitude is not among Bloom's student variables, one reason why he is often considered an extreme environmentalist. Instead, Bloom chose to focus on task-specific learner characteristics because they are more alterable than aptitude and thus more under the control of educators.

The significant feature of Bloom's model is his characterization of what occurs to learners as they progress through sequential learning units. Bloom argued that the cognitive and affective outcomes of one unit of instruction act as the cognitive entry behaviors and affective entry characteristics for the next unit of instruction. Under conditions of low quality of instruction, relatively few students experience successful learning on any given learning unit, and as they progress through the curriculum, fewer students approach subsequent units with the necessary prerequisites. Under these conditions, individual differences in learning can be expected to widen as learning problems compound over time, and only a relatively few students, those with high aptitude, can be expected to learn to high levels.

Under conditions of high quality of instruction, where most students are taken to high levels of learning on each unit before moving to the next, more students will begin each subsequent unit of instruction with the necessary learning prerequisites and will therefore be in a better position to profit from instruction. Over a series of learning units, the model postulates that learning successes will build on each other and that individual differences in learning will lessen as more students begin each new learning unit with the appropriate prerequisites. Moreover, student success will spawn more positive affective entry characteristics and students will approach new learning with more confidence and motivation. Under such conditions, Bloom estimated that perhaps as much as 90 percent of the achievement variation could be accounted for by the three variables in his model.

Bloom's model raises two important issues. First, Bloom substitutes high-quality instruction, which he characterizes as teaching similar to that which occurs during tutoring, for student aptitude. To make this substitution, however, requires that some students spend additional time on each learning unit. Under normal group instructional conditions, the additional time required raises two questions: are faster learners held back to wait for their slower classmates, and is as much curriculum covered? Proponents of the Bloom model claim that valuable learning experiences can be designed for faster learners and that the additional time requirements do not constrict the curriculum, especially since the additional time spent at an early stage in instruction can be made up later as learning becomes more efficient. Critics of the model claim that faster students are not provided with quality learning experiences as they wait for their slower classmates, and question whether in fact learning becomes more efficient under high quality of instruction.

A second issue raised by Bloom's model of school learning concerns the nature of individual differences. Bloom suggested the possibility that individual differences in learners will eventually vanish under high quality of instruction. This notion has been met with much skepticism. Bloom distinguished between individual differences in *learners* and individual differences in *learning*, suggesting that the former are often invoked to explain the latter. By arguing that high quality of instruction can substitute for student aptitude, Bloom's model offers the possibility that individual differences in learners need not contribute to individual differences in learning as much as they do. His model is, in part, an attempt to describe the limits under which individual differences in school learning are exhibited.

Although closely related, Bloom's model of school learning and the mastery learning approach to instruction are not the same. Bloom's model is a theoretical attempt to explain individual differences in school learning; mastery learning is an instructional model that prescribes carefully delineated learning outcomes, organizes the curriculum into a series of learning units, and provides periodic feedback-correction and additional time to take most students to high levels of learning on a learning unit before the class proceeds to the next unit. Bloom's model and mastery learning perhaps illustrate best the empirical and practical sides of Fig. 1.

Mastery learning can be viewed, however, as a special case of high quality of instruction in the Bloom model and the empirical findings on the effectiveness of mastery learning can be taken as evidence for or against the validity of Bloom's theory. While the evidence generally shows mastery learning to have positive effects, just how effective it is, and under what conditions, is still the subject of debate.

2.4 *Bruner's Theory of Instruction*

Bruner's (1966) theory of instruction is different in form from the previous models in three respects. First, Bruner called his model a "theory of instruction" rather than a model of learning. Bruner did this to highlight the difference between descriptive theories of learning and instructional practice, arguing that theories of instruction should identify conditions that improve and even optimize learning outcomes. Second, individual differences, while clearly recognized, are not the focus of Bruner's model of learning. Finally, his theory was not represented as a pictorial diagram with relationships specified between variables. Rather, Bruner outlined four features of instruction that need to be considered in making prescriptive decisions about teaching and the design of instruction. The four features are:

(a) Learner predispositions—the motivational factors that influence learners' desire for learning, for example, "exploration of alternatives."

(b) Structure of knowledge—how the knowledge to be learned is represented, how much information is presented, and how well the structure generates useful connections to other knowledge or allows connections to other knowledge to be seen by the learner.

(c) Sequence—the ordering of curriculum presented to learners.

(d) Timing and nature of reinforcement—the use of corrective information about how learning is proceeding.

Despite these differences, Bruner's "theory of instruction" fits the definition of a model of learning given earlier in this entry. He identifies a few important classes of learner and instructional variables that are thought to optimize learning. Furthermore, these are molar variables that affect learning over long periods of instructional time.

Two aspects of Bruner's theory, briefly described below, have been particularly important in the development of "discovery learning" models and more recent cognitive approaches to instruction—namely, his description of intrinsic motivation in students and his characterization of the structure of knowledge.

According to Bruner, the natural propensity in humans for learning is self-rewarding and self-sustaining. He described a number of important intrinsic motives, including curiosity, a desire for competence, the aspiration to identify with and emulate human models, and a commitment to work jointly with others, what he labeled "reciprocity." Much of school learning, Bruner suggests, is taken out of the context of real activity and relevant social action, and consequently fails to enlist the intrinsic energy derived from these motives. Challenging and meaningful activities, teachers acting as day-to-day "competence models," and cooperative group activities can help to foster this natural motivational energy.

Bruner also attended to the structuring of knowledge, both in terms of how it is to be presented to students as well as in the way students come to represent knowledge cognitively. Knowledge can be represented in three ways: by actions necessary to achieve a given result (enactive), by summary images that depict a concept without completely defining it (iconic), and by a set of orderly propositions governed by rules, such as language (symbolic). Each of these three modes of representation—actions, pictures, and symbols—has implications for the characterization of knowledge in terms of its economy (how much information must be held in memory) and to its generative power (its ability to connect to other knowledge). Bruner argues for diversity and "opportunism" in curriculum and instruction, suggesting that students be provided with different ways of becoming engaged in and working with materials to develop greater understanding and integration of knowledge and skills.

More recent work in "cognitive apprenticeship" and "situated learning" approaches to instruction (Collins et al. 1989) have much in common with Bruner. These approaches, grounded in a model of learning that recognizes the social and contextual nature of learning in naturalistic settings, attempt to engage students in "authentic" activity and social interaction similar to that engaged in by a skilled expert and apprentice. Among other techniques, these approaches focus on the explicit, visible modeling of the desired target performance by the teacher, the use of group activities to provide a supportive learning context for less skilled students and to "distribute" work across the group, and the gradual fading of external support as learners assume more responsibility for their learning. The reciprocal teaching model of Brown and Palincsar (1989), for example, helps students develop self-monitoring reading comprehension skills through modeling, coaching, and cognitive scaffolding techniques undertaken with small groups of learners.

2.5 *Gal'perin's Stage-by-Stage Theory*

Gal'perin's (1969) theory of stage-by-stage formation of mental actions is more a theory of learning than a model of learning. Nevertheless, the heart of his theory, a series of five stages of learning, has provided a "model" for the design of instructional practice and is thus treated here.

Action is central to Gal'perin's theory. Learning involves the transformation of initially external, manual actions toward an object or representation of that object to internal, mental actions. This transformation process is characterized by a series of qualitative changes in cognitive activity that ultimately result in the internalization of new knowledge and ability. The five stages are: (a) an orienting stage where learners become familiarized with the whole object or activity to be learned, but have yet to carry it out, (b) a material stage where the activity is carried out with real objects or models, (c) an external speech stage where the activity is verbalized or written out, (d) an unvoiced external speech where the activity is silently verbalized, and (e) an internalized speech stage where the activity becomes entirely mental action. Actions at each of these stages can be characterized by four parameters of form, generalization, abbreviation, and mastery, and much of the theory develops these parameters at each stage of action.

Talyzina (1981) has derived a set of instructional design principles from Gal'perin's theory, proposing a kind of cognitive task analysis of the desired learning activity that provides the basis for developing a teaching program progressively carrying the learner through each of the five stages of learning. Her program includes some features similar to those of mastery learning, including check tests, provisions for systematic feedback, close monitoring of learning, and learner orientation to and modeling of the complete activity to be performed.

3. Conclusion

Because models of learning attempt to predict or explain individual differences in school learning, it is not surprising that they are closely associated with attempts to adapt instruction to student diversity. The models of Carroll and Dahllöf underlie approaches to instruction that vary the pacing of instruction, and the models of Bloom, Bruner, and Gal'perin underlie approaches that vary the method of instruction. Given the ubiquity of student diversity, there is every reason to believe that future models of learning and the instructional approaches they spawn will continue to direct attention to both the quantity (pacing) and quality (method) of instruction.

See also: Learning Environments; Learning Processes and Learning Outcomes; Historical Overview and Trends of Learning Theories; Paradigms in Instructional Psychology; Teaching: Aptitude-Treatment Interaction Model; Computers and Learning

References

Anderson L, Ryan D, Shapiro B 1989 *The IEA Classroom Environment Study*. Pergamon Press, Oxford
Barr R, Dreeben R, Wiratchai N 1983 *How Schools Work*. University of Chicago Press, Chicago, Illinois
Bennett N 1978 Recent research on teaching: A dream, a belief and a model. *Brit. J. Educ. Psychol.* 48(2): 127–47

Bloom B 1976 *Human Characteristics and School Learning*. McGraw-Hill, New York
Brown A, Palincsar A 1989 Guided, cooperative learning and individual knowledge acquisition. In: Resnick L (ed.) 1989 *Knowing, Learning, and Instruction*. Erlbaum, Hillsdale, New Jersey
Bruner J 1966 *Toward a Theory of Instruction*. Harvard University Press, Cambridge, Massachusetts
Carroll J 1963 A model of school learning. *Teach. Col. Rec.* 64: 723–33
Carroll J 1989 The Carroll model: A 25-year retrospective and prospective view. *Educ. Res.* 18(1): 26–31
Collins A, Brown J, Newman S 1989 Cognitive apprenticeship: Teaching the crafts of reading, writing, and mathematics. In: Resnick L (ed.) 1989 *Knowing, Learning, and Instruction*. Erlbaum, Hillsdale, New Jersey
Dahllöf U 1971 *Ability Grouping, Content Validity, and Curriculum Process Analysis*. Teachers College Press, New York
Fisher C et al. 1980 Teacher behaviors, academic learning time, and student achievement: An overview. In: Denham C, Lieberman A (eds.) 1980 *Time To Learn: A Review of the Beginning Teacher Evaluation Study*. National Institute of Education, Washington, DC
Gagné R, Dick W 1983 Instructional psychology. *Annu. Rev. Psychol.* 34: 261–95
Gal'perin P Y 1969 Stages in the development of mental acts. In: Cole M, Maltzman I (eds.) 1969 *A Handbook of Contemporary Soviet Psychology*. Basic Books, New York
Glaser R, Bassok M 1989 Learning theory and the study of instruction. *Annu. Rev. Psychol.* 40: 631–66
Hilgard E (ed.) 1964 *Theories of Learning and Instruction*. University of Chicago Press, Chicago, Illinois
Joyce B, Weil M 1992 *Models of Teaching*, 4th edn. Allyn and Bacon, Boston, Massachusetts
Klauer K 1985 Framework for a theory of teaching. *Teaching and Teacher Education* 1(1): 5–17
Lamm Z 1976 *Conflicting Theories of Instruction: Conceptual Dimensions*. McCutchan, Berkeley, California
Lundgren U 1972 *Frame Factors and the Teaching Process: A Contribution to Curriculum Theory and Theory on Teaching*. Coronet Books, New York
Nuthall G, Snook I 1973 Contemporary models of teaching. In: Travers R (ed.) 1973 *Second Handbook of Research on Teaching*. Rand McNally, Chicago, Illinois
Talyzina N 1981 *The Psychology of Learning: Theories of Learning and Programmed Instruction*. Progress, Moscow
Wang M, Walberg H (eds.) 1985 *Adapting Instruction to Individual Differences*. McCutchan, Berkeley, California
Wiley D, Harnischfeger A 1974 Explosion of a myth: Quantity of schooling and exposure to instruction, major educational vehicles. *Educ. Res.* 3(4): 7–11

Further Reading

Harnischfeger A, Wiley D 1978 Conceptual issues in models of school learning. *J. Curric. St.* 10: 215–31
Laing G 1986 *Building Scientific Models*. Gower, Aldershot
Talyzina N 1973 Psychological bases of programmed instruction. *Instr. Sci.* 2(3): 243–80

Human Learning: Evolution of Anthropological Perspectives

B. Bogin

The human capacity to learn, both in formal school settings and in informal social settings, has a biological basis. This basis, which evolved during the past 100 million years or more, includes: (a) the mammalian central nervous system, especially the brain; (b) the primate pattern of infant care and juvenile growth; and (c) the uniquely human stages of childhood and adolescent growth and development. This entry discusses the evolution of human learning with respect to these three components.

1. Definition of Evolution

Biological evolution is the continuous process of genetic adaptation of organisms to their environments. Natural selection determines the direction of evolutionary change and operates by differential mortality between individual organisms (i.e., the carriers of genetic variation prior to reproductive maturation), and by differential fertility of mature organisms. Thus, genetic adaptations that enhance survival of individuals to reproductive age and increase the production of similarly successful offspring will increase in frequency in the population.

2. Mammalian Foundations

"Learning is a very basic property of nervous systems, not an unusual or costly evolutionary adaptation" (Tierney 1986 p.340). All animal species have some capacity for association learning. Mammals, and some birds, evolved a new capacity, learning by observation and imitation (Bonner 1980). This adaptation required brains that are both larger and more complex than the brains of nonmammals. The fossil record shows that the mammalian brain has undergone repeated selection for increases in size relative to total body weight (Jerison 1976). Mammals have also evolved complex and functionally diversified brain structures (Kaas 1987). Jerison showed that mammalian brains have a system of neurological pathways that bring together, at various locations, information from the visual, auditory, and olfactory senses. This "integrative neocortical system" allows "sensory information from various modalities as information about objects in time and space" (Jerison 1976 p.101).

Mammals do not just react to environmental stimuli; they perceive, store, retrieve, and evaluate information and adjust behavior responses according to the present situation and past experience. Larger, more complex brains allow for a greater capacity for learning and more flexible behavior, because learned behavior may be constantly modified by further learning. Mammals successfully rear a higher percentage of their offspring to reproductive age than do reptiles and other "lower" animals with less complex brains. Thus, mammalian types of brains, and learning, were favored by natural selection.

3. Primate Foundations

The primates are a mammalian order that includes prosimians, monkeys, apes, and people. Primates have, on average, the largest brains relative to body weight, the most complex brains, and the greatest capacity for learning of all mammalian orders. Brain anatomy alone, however, cannot account for primate learning skills. Other biological and behavioral changes, related to brain evolution, are required. One example is the biology of lactation. Many mammalian species sequester their young in nests and nurse them infrequently. This pattern of periodic feeding, coupled with sensory deprivation during infancy, works well for species with limited brain growth after birth and limited learning potential.

In neurologically more advanced mammals, especially primates, mother and infant remain in virtually constant physical contact for several weeks or months after birth. The norm for primates is one infant per pregnancy, which facilitates intimate physical contact since there is no competition between siblings for the mother. Suckling is done "on demand," 24 hours a day. The primate infant travels with its mother, sensing many of the things that the mother experiences and developing motor and sensory skills in the process. This type of early sensory stimulation is known to be conducive to further learning (Jolly 1985).

In addition to a more intimate mother–infant bond, the Old World monkeys, apes, and humans follow a pattern of growth that differs from most other mammals in two major ways. The first difference is that neurological development, especially growth of the brain, is about 90 percent complete before sexual maturity is achieved. The second difference is that sexual development is deferred until a time well after the infancy period of postnatal growth takes place. Most mammals, for example, the rat (see Fig. 1), show an advancement of brain growth relative to body growth in general and reproductive tissue growth in particular. However primates, progressively from monkeys to humans, delay body growth and reproductive development, but do not delay brain growth (see Fig. 2).

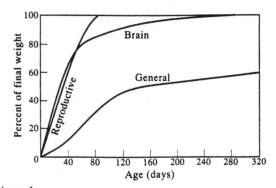

Figure 1
Growth of the body in general, the brain, and the reproductive system in the rat
Source: Timiras P S 1972

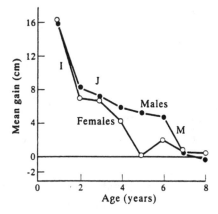

Figure 3
Baboon crown-rump length velocity. The letters indicate the stages of growth: I—infancy, J—juvenile, M—sexual maturity. Age "B" indicates birth
Source: Coelho A M 1985

Primate evolution added a new stage of delayed growth between infancy and sexual maturation called the "juvenile growth period" (see Fig. 3). Juveniles are "prepubertal individuals that are no longer dependent on their mothers (parents) for survival" (Periera and Altmann 1985 p.236). Juvenile primates learn skills that are essential for reproductive success, including identification and utilization of food, predator avoidance, and the behavioral dynamics of their social group.

Some examples of juvenile primates as learners are descriptions of the development of insect "fishing" skills in chimpanzees (Goodall 1968) and predator alarm calls in vervet monkeys (Seyfarth et al. 1980). In both cases, the juveniles must observe and imitate adults performing these behaviors for many months before their own performance is reasonably error-free. Juvenile primates may also learn new behaviors that are passed on to the social group. Field studies of

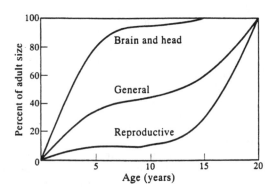

Figure 2
Growth of the body in general, the brain, and the reproductive system in the human being
Source: Harris J A et al. 1930

Japanese macaques showed that a juvenile monkey introduced both the washing of food to clean it of grit and swimming into her social group (Jolly 1985).

Laboratory studies help clarify the biological basis, extent, and flexibility of primate learning. Language experiments, for instance, reveal that apes can learn more than 100 symbolic meanings for objects and concepts. However, there is no consensus that apes learn the rules of grammar or sentence construction (Terrace et al. 1979, Savage-Rumbaugh et al. 1990). Matsuzawa (1985) trained a chimpazee named Ai to use symbols to identify 11 colors and 14 object names. Ai also learned to use Arabic numerals to identify the numbers 1 through 6. It was easiest for Ai to learn the symbols for colors and hardest to learn the symbols for numbers. When presented with items from all three conceptual groups, for example, three yellow gloves, Ai spontaneously ordered her answers into color/object/number or object/color/number. Matsuzawa notes that human children also display this ordering in ease of learning and response. This suggests that specific components of learning, and specific brain centers responsible for each component, evolved at different rates in primates. From an ecological and behavioral perspective this makes some sense. Selection for learning numbers would be less important than for learning objects and colors related to food, predators, and sociosexual signaling.

4. Human Foundations

4.1 Childhood and Adolescence as Unique Growth Stages

Human beings expand upon the general primate capacity for learning by adding two new stages of growth

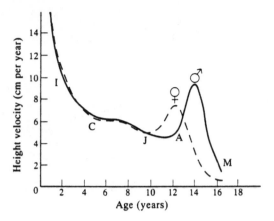

Figure 4
Human growth velocity in height. The letters indicate stages of
growth: I—infancy, C—childhood, J—juvenile, A—adolescence,
M—sexual maturity
Source: Prader A 1984

—childhood and adolescence (Bogin 1988, 1990,
1994, 1995). These stages are defined biologically by
changes in growth rate (see Fig. 4). In people, there is
a rapid decrease in growth rate from birth to about the
age of 2. This is the infant stage and it is shared by
other primates. Only in humans, however, is infancy
followed by a more gentle decrease and then a leveling
off in the rate of growth to about age 7 or 8. This is the
childhood stage. In a behavioral sense, childhood is the
period of time following weaning when the youngster
is still dependent upon older individuals for feeding
and protection. The juvenile stage follows and growth
rates decrease a bit until about age 10 for girls and
age 12 for boys. Then comes another uniquely human
stage of growth: adolescence. Its onset is marked by a
sudden and rapid increase in growth rate, the adolescent growth spurt, which peaks at a growth velocity
unequaled since early infancy. Only the human species
has a growth spurt in both weight and length that
occurs in both boys and girls (Bogin 1988, 1994).
Following the peak growth velocity of the spurt there
is the constant decrease in growth rate that ends with
the attainment of adult stature.

4.2 Learning During Childhood and Adolescence

There is some evidence, based on the study of growth
rates in extinct prehuman fossil species, that childhood
and adolescence evolved during the last 2 million
years of human history (Bogin 1988, 1995, Smith
1991). While there are many possible reasons for the
evolution of new stages of growth in any species
(Bonner 1965), two interrelated aspects of this issue
are pertinent to this discussion of the evolution of
learning. One is the human dependence on learning
complex technical and social skills for survival, and

the second is the behavior of parents and other
adults toward children and adolescents that facilitates
extensive learning.

Higher primates can learn by both imitation and
teaching, but purposeful teaching is probably more important for human beings than for nonhuman primates.
Throughout evolutionary history, people survived by
having available to themselves a fund of detailed
knowledge of a habitat for the location of food,
raw materials, and avoidance of predators or disease.
Survival still requires knowledge of intricate technical
procedures for hunting and gathering, agriculture, or
using the machines of modern industrial societies.
Finally, a myriad of social facts, including knowledge of kinship organization and ritual behavior, are
required. All living humans depend for survival on
these complex technologies, social systems, and ideological belief systems or, more simply, culture. Due
to the sheer volume of cultural information, purposeful teaching is required for a newborn to become a
competent adult.

The prolongation of the growth period by the addition of childhood and adolescence is crucial to the
human learning process, not only because there is so
much to learn, but also because maturation differences
between teachers and students are maximized. Most
cultural information is usually passed from an older,
more experienced individual to a younger individual.
The greater the maturation status difference between
teacher and pupil, the more likely that the transmission
of this type of detailed technical knowledge will be
one-way, older to younger (Jolly 1985). The physical
features of the child, including a small body with
relatively large head (due to a big brain), relatively
short extremities in proportion to stature, and the lack
of secondary sexual characteristics (e.g., conspicuous
body hair or breasts), also facilitate nurturing behavior
and teaching by adults toward children (Bogin 1988,
1990, 1995).

Appropriate social behaviors for adult roles must
also be learned, including those relating to mating
and child rearing. In this regard, the course of adolescent sexual maturation followed by girls and boys
is enlightening. The first outward sign of puberty in
girls is the development of the breast bud, followed by
increased fat deposition on the lower trunk (hips, but-
tocks, thighs), an increase of body hair, the adolescent
growth spurt, and finally menarche. Menarche is usually followed by a period of 1 to 3 years of adolescent
sterility (anovulatory menstrual cycles). Thus, female
fertility is achieved toward the end of the adolescent
growth stage.

The physical changes that girls experience during
adolescence advertise to the larger group their sexual
and social maturation. The appearance of reproductive
maturation of adolescent girls, and the inability of mature adults to detect adolescent sterility, may stimulate
women and men to include the girls in adult social
behavior. Adolescent, but infertile girls begin learning

and practicing adult social interactions, such as male–female bonding, sexual intercourse, and "aunting" type childcare behavior. The net result is that as a primiparous mother, the mature young woman has considerable social and parental experience, increasing the likelihood of survival of her new offspring.

In contrast to the adolescent development of girls, boys achieve fertility well before they assume adult size and the physical characteristics of men. The sequence of development that boys follow begins with enlargement of the testes, followed by an increase in the growth of pubic hair and growth of the penis, sperm production, the adolescent growth spurt, and finally an increase in muscle mass and strength. Hormonal changes occuring early in adolescence are correlated with heightened interest in adult roles and activities. Thus, adolescent "boy–men" are able to learn and practice some adult behavior, including subsistence techniques, adult sociocultural roles, and sexual behavior before they attain adult physical features and are perceived as adults by others. With full maturation, young men are able to perform at adult levels in economic activities and in competition with older men in courtship for women.

4.3 The Social Basis of Human Learning and Schooling

The majority of human learning takes place in a social context, for in virtually all cultures infants, children, juveniles, and adolescents are always in the company of others. Groups of adults with youngsters and age-graded play groups among the young are typical social associations (Herzog 1984, Bogin 1988). Cross-cultural research demonstrates that most human learning takes place in these social groups by means of guided participation and informal apprenticeships (Rogoff 1990, Lave 1990). The social basis for human learning provides for "relaxed nonstressful situations" that promote the acquisition of technological skills and language (Beckoff 1989). The typical style of social learning for the human species is as much a product of evolutionary biology as are the brain and the human stages of growth. A minority of industrialized societies, however, segregate people by age, especially in formal school systems and at work. This practice ignores human biology and behavior and may "reduce the most intelligent primate to a bored and alienated creature" (Washburn 1973 p. 131).

5. Conclusion

Biologists usually measure evolutionary success in reproductive terms and by most criteria the human species is highly successful. Even people without the benefits of modern medicine raise about 50 percent of their infants to adulthood, while our closest relatives, the chimpanzees, rear less than 36 percent to adulthood, and social carnivores (e.g., lions) rear about 12 percent (Lancaster and Lancaster 1983). Much of this success lies in the human capacity for learning complex behaviors. The evolution of the human brain, childhood, and adolescence facilitate a unique style of human social and cultural learning that is part of the reason for the evolutionary success of our species.

References

Beckoff M 1989 Tools, terms, and telencephelons: Neural correlates of "complex" and "intelligent" behavior. *Behav. Brain Sci.* 12(3): 591–93

Bogin B 1988 *Patterns of Human Growth.* Cambridge University Press, Cambridge

Bogin B 1990 The evolution of human childhood. *BioScience* 40(1): 16–25

Bogin B 1994 Adolescence in Evolutionary Perspective. *Acta Paediatr. Suppl.* 406:29–35

Bogin B 1995 Growth and development: Recent evolutionary and biocultural research. In: Boaz N T, Wolfe L D (eds.) 1995 *Biological Anthropology: The State of the Science.* International Institute for Human Evolutionary Research, Bend, Oregon, Ohio

Bonner J T 1965 *Size and Cycle: A Essay on the Structure of Biology.* Princeton University Press, Princeton, New Jersey

Bonner J T 1980 *The Evolution of Culture in Animals.* Princeton University Press, Princeton, New Jersey

Coelho A M 1985 Baboon dimorphism: Growth in weight, length, and adiposity from birth to 8 years of age. In: Watts E S (ed.) 1985 *Nonhuman Primate Models for Human Growth.* Alan R Liss, New York

Goodall J van Lawick 1968 Behavior of free-living chimpanzees of the Gombe Stream area. *Animal Behavior Monographs* 1: 161–311

Harris J A, Jackson C M, Paterson D G, Seammon R E 1930 *The Measurement of Man.* University of Minnesota Press, Minneapolis, Minnesota

Herzog J D 1984 The socialization of juveniles in primate and foraging societies: Implications for contemporary education. *Anthropol. Educ. Q.* 15(1): 70–79

Jerison H S 1976 Paleoneurology and the evolution of mind. *Sci. Am.* 234(1): 90–101

Jolly A 1985 *The Evolution of Primate Behavior,* 2nd edn. Macmillan, New York

Kaas J H 1987 The organization of the neocortex in mammals: Implications for theories of brain function. *Annu. Rev. Psychol.* 38: 129–51

Lancaster J B, Lancaster C S 1983 Parental investment: The hominid adaptation. In: Ortner D J (ed.) 1983 *How Humans Adapt: A Biocultural Odyssey.* Smithsonian Institution Press, Washington, DC

Lave J 1990 The culture of acquisition and the practice of understanding. In: Stiegler J W, Shwewder R A, Herdt G (eds.) 1990 *Cultural Psychology.* Cambridge University Press, Cambridge

Matsuzawa T 1985 Use of numbers by a chimpanzee. *Nature* 315: 57–59

Periera M E, Altmann J 1985 Development of social behavior in free-living nonhuman primates. In: Watts E S (ed.) 1985 *Nonhuman Primate Models for Human Growth and Development.* John Wiley and Sons, New York

Prader A 1984 Biomedical and endocrinological aspects of normal growth and development. In: Borms J et al. (eds.) 1984 *Human Growth and Development*. Plenum, New York

Rogoff B 1990 *Apprenticeship in Thinking: Cognitive Development in Social Context*. Oxford University Press, New York

Savage-Rumbaugh S, Sevcik R A, Brakke K E, Rumbaugh D 1990 Symbols: Their communicative use, comprehension, and combination by bonobos (*Pan paniscus*). *Adv. Infancy Res.* 6: 221–78

Seyfarth R M, Cheney D L, Marler P 1980 Monkey responses to three different alarm calls: Evidence for predator classification and semantic communication. *Science* 210: 801–03

Smith B H 1991 Dental development and the evolution of life history in Hominidae. *Amer. J. Physical Anthropol.* 86(2): 157–74

Terrace H S, Pettito L A, Sanders R J, Bever T G 1979 Can an ape create a sentence? *Science* 206(4421): 891–902

Tierney A J 1986 The evolution of learned and innate behavior: Contributions from genetics and neurobiology to a theory of behavioral evolution. *Animal Learning and Behavior* 14(4): 339–48

Timiras P S 1972 *Developmental Physiology and Aging*. Macmillan, New York

Washburn S L 1973 Primate field studies and social science. In: Nader L, Maretzki T (eds.) 1973 American Anthropological Association, Washington, DC

Further Reading

Cole M, Gay J, Glick J A, Sharp D W 1971 *The Cultural Context of Learning and Thinking: An Exploration in Experimental Anthropology*. Basic Books, New York

Rumbaugh D 1990 Comparative psychology and the great apes: Their competence in learning, language, and numbers. *Psychol. Rec.* 40(1): 15–39

Smuts B B, Cheney D L, Seyfarth R M, Wrangham R W, Struhsaker T T (eds.) 1987 *Primate Societies*. University of Chicago Press, Chicago, Illinois

Whiting B B, Whiting J W M 1975 *Children of Six Cultures: A Psycho-cultural Analysis*. Harvard University Press, Cambridge, Massachusetts

Constructivism and Learning

P. Cobb

The idea that learning is a constructive process is widely accepted; learners do not passively receive information but instead actively construct knowledge as they strive to make sense of their worlds. Empirical support for this position is provided by numerous studies that demonstrate that the understandings that students acquire in instructional situations are frequently very different from those that the teacher intended. Three general instructional implications that follow from constructivism are: (a) priority should be given to the development of meaning and understanding rather than the training of behavior, (b) researchers and teachers should assume that students' actions are rational given the way that they currently make sense of things, and (c) students' errors and unanticipated responses should be viewed as occasions to learn about students' understanding (von Glasersfeld 1989).

Although the basic notions and implications of constructivism are generally supported, it is possible to distinguish between realist and radical positions. The key issue that differentiates the two positions concerns the general function of cognition. From the realist perspective, cognition is the process by which learners eventually construct mental structures that correspond to or match external structures located in the environment. In contrast, radical constructivists consider that cognition serves to organize the learner's experiential world rather than to discover ontological reality.

1. Realist Constructivism

1.1 Assumptions and Tensions

The assumption that students learn by reorganizing their mental structures while interacting with the physical and symbolic environment is common to the various theoretical accounts of cognitive functioning proposed by realist constructivists. A philosophical dilemma arises because learners do not have direct access to the external environment; they can only interpret it in terms of their current knowledge structures. Consequently it is impossible, in principle, to explain how they can construct internal knowledge structures that correspond to the structure of the environment. At a deeper level, the dilemma can be traced to the Cartesian dualism that is created by separating the knower from the environment to be known. In practice, most realist constructivists ignore the philosophical dilemma by making the working assumption that it is useful to treat true or correct knowledge as a reflection of ontological reality. Cognitive research can then pursue the task of specifying increasingly sophisticated knowledge structures, culminating with those that are assumed to match the structure of the environment.

1.2 Implications

A wide variety of instructional approaches have been proposed and studied by realist constructivists. In general, approaches that characterize thinking as a sequence of cognitive behaviors that manipulate incoming information to generate responses have fallen from favor since the 1980s. The more influential approaches of the 1990s instead focus explicitly on the development of conceptual understanding and attempt to ensure that this understanding guides the performance of skills and procedures. For example, analyses conducted in this tradition lead to the recommendation that the construction of procedures for adding and subtracting multidigit numbers should be related to the development of place value understanding. One instructional strategy is to use Dienes blocks that represent 1, 10, 100, and 1,000, and to develop instructional tasks so that students' actions with the blocks will inform their paper and pencil procedures (Fuson 1990). The results of a series of studies conducted by Fuson demonstrate that the computational performance of 7- and 8-year old students taught in this way is significantly superior to that of students who received traditional United States textbook-based instruction. Fuson's work also illustrates the more general strategy of designing external instructional representations that are said to embody the structures or relationships to be learned in a transparent or readily apprehensible way. In the course of the learning process, students construct mental representations that accurately mirror the structure of the instructional materials in their environment.

Other realist approaches concentrate on the teachers' knowledge rather than instructional tasks. For example, Carpenter et al. (1989) reasoned that teachers who understand research-based models of students' conceptual development will make more informed interpretations of their students' thinking. These interpretations would then guide the teachers' selection of developmentally appropriate tasks. Carpenter and his colleagues have used this approach in the area of elementary addition and subtraction word problems with promising results. A working hypothesis of this work is that students construct internal cognitive structures that mirror the semantic structure of increasingly complex arithmetical word problems.

1.3 New Challenges

The basic assumption that viable mental structures mirror the structure of ontological reality implies that what counts as correct or true knowledge does not depend on social or cultural circumstance. Vygotsky (1934) argued that knowing is relative to the situations in which knowers find themselves and numerous more recent studies have demonstrated that cognition is both socially and culturally situated. This is true even of the seemingly most objective type of knowledge, namely mathematics (Carraher et al. 1987). These findings have led several prominent researchers to reconsider the assumption that a fixed, given physical and symbolic environment is the primary source of knowledge.

Increasingly, the view of isolated students interacting with the environment is being displaced by the notion that students are members of classroom communities. Knowing then becomes a social as well as an individual activity in which students explain and justify their thinking as the teacher guides their enculturation into the intellectual practices of their society. The challenge that lies ahead for realist constructivism is to reconcile the characterization of knowing as the ability to participate in the intellectual practices of their society, with the view that it involves the construction of cognitive structures which mirror an environment that exists independently of human activity, culture, and history.

2. Radical Constructivism

2.1 Assumptions and Tensions

Radical constructivism has its roots in a variety of disciplines, but has been most profoundly influenced by the theories of the Swiss psychologist Jean Piaget as interpreted and extended by von Glasersfeld (1989). In general, radical constructivists believe that learners construct increasingly sophisticated ways of knowing solely on the basis of their personal experiences as they attempt to achieve their goals by resolving situations that they find problematic.

Radical constructivists have repeatedly challenged realist constructivists' working hypothesis that true knowledge mirrors ontological reality. However, in stressing that each person lives in the world of his or her own personal experience, radical constructivists have implicitly accepted the Cartesian dualism between ontological reality and the knower. Realist constructivists locate the knowledge to be learned at one pole of the dualism, ontological reality, and radical constructivists locate it at the other pole, subjective experience. Realists have argued that the radical position is solipsistic in that it implies each person inhabits their own private world. In addition, they contend that the notions of truth and certainty thereby have to be relinquished. Radical constructivists typically refute the first charge but usually accept the second.

In practice, radical constructivists necessarily assume that certain aspects of their experiential worlds are given, fixed, and shared with others when they conduct their investigations. For example, when conducting a study of university students' learning of, say, calculus, radical constructivists typically assume without question that students share their understanding of whole number arithmetic. Implicit working hypotheses of this type are, however, subject to revision if a student's activity calls them into question.

2.2 Implications

Given the emphasis on personal experience, radical constructivists initially tended to derive general instructional aphorisms from analyses of individual students' learning. However, since 1987 an increasing number of researchers have used radical constructivism as a general orienting framework within which to develop instructional approaches, frequently in collaboration with teachers. In addition, several approaches developed by researchers working outside the radical constructivist framework are highly compatible with this theoretical position. For example, an approach called Realistic Mathematics Education (RME) described by Treffers (1987) reflects the view that mathematics is an experientially based human activity. Treffers and his colleagues at the Freudenthal Institute in the Netherlands argue that learning occurs as students develop effective ways to solve problems, and involves the reorganization of thinking at increasingly sophisticated levels. One of the characteristics of RME is its contention that the first phase of the learning process should involve an extensive exploration of a range of specific situations drawn from everyday life or from students' physical or imagined reality. This view can be contrasted with the instructional representation approach advocated by some realist constructivists. There, the knowledge to be learned is embodied in physical materials, diagrams, or computer graphics in ways designed to make it readily apprehensible to students. From the perspective of RME, the instructional challenge is to develop sequences of tasks that support students' reorganization of their initially informal activity at increasingly sophisticated levels. Textbooks based on this approach have been used widely in the Netherlands at a range of age levels with considerable success.

In addition to considering the design of instructional tasks, radical constructivists have broadened their focus from the individual student by analyzing the role that social interaction plays in learning. As a consequence, instructional approaches that emphasize small group collaborative work and whole class discussions in which students are expected to justify their thinking have become increasingly prominent since the 1980s. In these approaches, great emphasis is placed on the teacher and students openly negotiating their interpretations of and solutions to instructional tasks. One of the teacher's responsibilities is then to guide the classroom community's establishment of consensual meanings. These meanings in turn become part of the basis for further discussions. Human et al. (1989) have implemented such an approach to elementary school mathematics on a wide scale with promising results. In developing their approach, these researchers have questioned whether it is necessary for students to learn the standard procedures for arithmetical computation. They argue instead that students should be encouraged to construct their own personally meaningful computational algorithms. This approach can be contrasted with the program developed by Fuson. There, the objective is to help students learn the standard computational algorithms in a meaningful way. This difference between the two programs brings to the fore a more general issue, namely, to what extent students' constructions in school should conform to those currently institutionalized in wider society in this era of rapid technological change.

2.3 New Challenges

Like realist constructivists, radical constructivists have been influenced by studies that demonstrate that knowing is socially and culturally situated. On the one hand, the finding that intellectual practices in subject-matter areas differ from one cultural community to another is consistent with radical constructivists' rejection of knowledge as a mirror of ontological reality. On the other hand, the relative homogeneity of these practices within a community sits uncomfortably with radical constructivists' emphasis on the personal experiences of the individual. In particular, it would seem that social interaction is not merely a catalyst for individual cognitive development, but that knowing is, in some sense, intrinsically social. Radical constructivists are therefore faced with the challenge of elaborating their theoretical orientation so that it encompasses both collective activity and individual experience. In this regard, analyses that relate cognitive development to either didactical situations (e.g., Brousseau 1986) or to classroom social interaction patterns (e.g., Bauersfeld 1988) would appear to be of great relevance.

3. Emergent Trends and Issues

Realist and radical constructivists' developing views of the teacher and students as members of a classroom community indicates that a rapprochement could be possible. However, each group will have to transcend the Cartesian dualism it has erected between ontological reality and subjective experience if this possibility is to be realized. For their part, realist constructivists would need to question their working hypothesis that knowledge can be given fixed, ahistorical foundations. The view that what counts as true or certain knowledge evolves historically and differs from one cultural group to another is now widely accepted in a variety of disciplines ranging from literary criticism to the philosophy of mathematics. It is also becoming increasingly clear that this view does not lead to an intellectual anarchy in which any interpretation or opinion is as good as any other. In contrast, radical constructivists might come to the conclusion that their rejection of the possibility of true and certain knowledge both feeds on the realist position and contradicts personal, common sense experience. They would therefore have to develop ways to rehabilitate the notions of truth and certainty.

The theoretical problem of transcending the

Cartesian dualism has its correlate in the activity of teachers. The view that true knowledge corresponds to the structure of a pregiven environment carries with it the risk that the adult's view of the world might be imposed on students at the expense of their individual needs and interests. Conversely, a view which focuses solely on students' personal experiences might downplay the teacher's obligation to enculturate students into the intellectual practices of their society. According to Lampert (1985), this tension between accommodating students' interests and pushing them to act in accordance with institutionalized intellectual practices is an endemic aspect of teaching. Perhaps constructivists who transcend the Cartesian dualism will be in a better position to help teachers cope with this deep-seated tension that pervades their attempts to help students learn with understanding.

See also: Learning Theories: Historical Overview and Trends; Preconceptions and Misconceptions;

References

Bauersfeld H 1988 Interaction, construction, and knowledge: Alternative perspectives for mathematics education. In: Grouws D, Jones D (eds.) 1988 *Effective Mathematics Teaching*. National Council of Teachers of Mathematics and Lawrence Erlbaum Associates, Reston, Virginia

Brousseau G 1986 Fondements et methodes de la didactique des mathematiques. *Recherches en Didactique des Mathematiques* 7(2): 33–115

Carpenter T P, Fennema E, Peterson P L, Chiang C, Loef M 1989 Using knowledge of children's mathematics thinking in classroom teaching: An experimental study. *Am. Educ. Res. J.* 26(4): 499–532

Carraher T N, Carraher D W, Schliemann A D 1987 Written and oral mathematics. *Journal for Research in Mathematics Education* 18(2): 83–97

Fuson K C 1990 Conceptual structures for multiunit numbers: Implications for learning and teaching multidigit addition, subtraction, and place value. *Cognition and Instruction* 7(4): 343–403

Human P G, Murray J C, Olivier A I 1989 *A Mathematics Curriculum for the Junior Primary Phase*. University of Stellenbosch, Research Unit for Mathematics Education, Stellenbosch

Lampert M L 1985 How do teachers manage to teach? Perspectives on problems in practice. *Harv. Educ. Rev.* 55(2): 178–94

Treffers A 1987 *Three Dimensions: A Model of Goal and Theory Description in Mathematics Instruction—The Wiskobas Project*. Reidel, Dordrecht

von Glasersfeld E 1989 Constructivism in education. In: Husén T, Postlethwaite T N (eds.) 1989 *The International Encyclopedia of Education*, 1st edn., Supplementary Vol. 1. Pergamon Press, Oxford

Vygotsky L S 1934 Voprocy detskoi vozrastnoi psikhologii. In: El'konin D B (ed.) 1984 *L. S. Vygotskii. Sobranie Sochineni: Detskaia Psikhologiia*. Pedagogika, Moscow

Further Reading

Davis R B, Maher C A, Noddings N (eds.) 1990 *Constructivist Views on the Teaching and Learning of Mathematics*. Journal for Research in Mathematics Education Monograph No. 4. National Council of Teachers of Mathematics, Reston, Virginia

Piaget J 1970 *Genetic Epistemology*. Columbia University Press, New York

Saxe G B 1991 *Culture and Cognitive Development: Studies in Mathematical Understanding*. Erlbaum, Hillsdale, New Jersey

Steffe L P, Wood T (eds.) 1990 *Transforming Children's Mathematics Education: International Perspectives*. Erlbaum, Hillsdale, New Jersey

von Glasersfeld E (ed.) 1991 *Radical Constructivism in Mathematics Education*. Kluwer, Dordrecht

Situated Learning

L. Resnick

The human sciences can be characterized as a working out of two sets of tensions in interpreting human experience: tensions between the biological and the social and between the particular and the general. This entry examines the relations between two lines of thinking, each commanding increasing attention among psychologists and social scientists, that appear to be contradictory. The first, a position known as *conceptual rationalism*, seeks biological foundations for specific concepts that are central and, perhaps, universal in human development. The second, a position that has come to be known as *situated cognition*, argues that knowledge is acquired in and attuned to specific social and historical situations and that conceptual development can be understood only in terms of the situational contexts of action. It is argued here that the rationalist and situationist views, far from being contradictory, share important epistemological assumptions and can—perhaps must—be combined to provide a theory of cognitive development and functioning. In this entry a view of learning and development called *situated rationalism* is elaborated. This view is illustrated with some examples from mathematics and science learning, and its implications for education are considered.

1. The Conceptual Rationalist Argument: Biological Preparedness

In recent years, there has been a reassertion of interest in the biological basis of human learning and thinking (e.g., Gelman and Carey 1991). This new line of thinking grows out of recent research on language development, concept development in infancy and early childhood, and animal cognition and learning. The core proposal of those pursuing this line of thinking is that there exists a set of biological constraints on learning and cognitive development. This hypothesis leads to a search for evidence that certain aspects of knowledge, although learned in the sense that interaction with the environment over time is required, are nevertheless biologically preferred or "prepared." These highly specific *prepared schemas* or *skeletal structures* are the foundation for the development of mature knowledge by individuals. The argument is, roughly, that each species is specialized for certain forms of knowledge. This biologically preferred knowledge is tuned to the adaptive requirements of the species. It is, thus, situational in the sense that it prepares the young of the species to enter productively into the situations they are most likely to encounter as they grow and to learn from behaving in those situations. Most elaborated until recently as a theory of language acquisition, the argument for biological or "hard-wired" structures that guide and constrain infants as they interpret their earliest experience is now being put forth for basic mathematical, physical, and social concepts as well.

Following philosophical traditions, this can usefully be termed a *rationalist* position; it is reflected in the epistemologies of Plato and Kant, for example. Rationalists differ from associationists and other empiricists not only in postulating a biological basis for specific knowledge, but also in postulating wholes—sets of relationships that accumulate to something more than the sum of their parts—as the fundamental units of cognition. This is captured in the notion of a *schema*—an organizing "design" that superimposes a structure on the pieces. Among the great rationalists who had something to say about education and learning were Wertheimer, for whom the organizing designs were perceptual gestalts, and Piaget, for whom the organizing designs were logical structures.

Today's rationalists are *conceptual rationalists*, because they are more interested in conceptual than in either perceptual or purely logical foundations for thinking. Conceptual rationalists claim that biological preparation is highly domain specific, that infants are biologically prepared to take advantage of very specific affording features of the environment. They believe that the preparedness of the species reaches beyond perceptions (supposedly minimally processed recognitions—cf. Neisser 1976) yet is more specific than the grand logical design of Piaget. They are interested in preparedness for reasoning about number and quantity; for concepts of causality; for notions of weightedness, movement, and rigidity; and for basic psychological and social ideas.

Today's conceptual rationalists do not claim that hard-wired concepts simply mature. Rather, for the biological endowment to be realized, particular environmental conditions must be met. Prepared structures do not substitute for learning but rather make learning possible by constraining and guiding attention, so that, from among the many stimuli children encounter, they select for attention those that will support the formation of particular concepts. Conceptual rationalism is a theory that says children can teach themselves if the right kinds of affordances are present in their environments. Children appear to choose for themselves the kind of stimuli to attend to and to engage in forms of practice that eventually establish a stable and useful concept. Learning and development occur when individuals prepared for certain concepts encounter environments with the kinds of affordances they need to elaborate these prepared structures.

Although conceptual rationalists search for biological foundations for specific concepts, they are, in another sense, generalists. The prepared concepts they study are thought to be universal for the species. They give relatively little attention to social processes (although these are admitted as part of the environmental surround that allows children to elaborate their prepared schemas) or to variations in elaborated conceptual structures that may result from different kinds of experience. On the other hand, conceptual rationalists are individualists in the sense that biologically prepared structures are carried by each individual member of the species and each individual must interact with the environment to produce personal elaborations of the prepared structures. This is the essence of the constructivist argument, which is more or less assumed by the conceptual rationalists.

2. The Situated Cognition Argument: Sociocultural Preparedness

The term *situated cognition* has come to refer to a loose collection of theories and perspectives that propose a contextualized (and, therefore, particularist) and social view of the nature of thinking and learning. Students of situated cognition take as a starting point the distributed nature of cognitive activity—the fact that, under normal circumstances, mental activity involves social coordination. Getting a job done or working something out is almost always done in coordination with others. What makes an individual competent is not just what he or she knows but also how his or her knowledge fits in with that of others with whom activity must be coordinated. Furthermore, activity is often shared with tools (e.g. Hutchins 1991) and even with the everyday physical material about which people reason (Lave 1988). There is, thus, a distribution of cognitive work not only among people but also between people and tools. Being competent means being able to use particular tools in particular ways. The tools themselves embody a portion of the intelligence that is needed to accomplish any particular task. The distributed nature of competent performance means that competence is highly situation specific. One must be good at behaving in a particular situation, with particular tools, and with particular other people. The situated cognition perspective, then, tends to lead away from a search for general structures of knowledge and towards the study of particular environments for cognitive activity and the knowledge attuned to those environments. At the same time, it stresses the social nature of cognitive activity and cognitive development.

In the situated cognition view, the social invisibly pervades even situations that appear to consist of individuals engaged in private cognitive activity. Social constructs of the situation (e.g., What are the rules of the game? Who is in charge? What are the stakes?) influence the nature and course of thinking. And the tools of thought (ranging from external memory devices and measuring instruments to tables of arithmetic conversions and dictionaries, thesauruses, and maps) embody a culture's intellectual history. Tools have theories built into them, and users accept these theories—albeit often unknowingly—when they use these tools. This point is made dramatically by Latour (1987) in his constructed account of the process of challenging a scientific conclusion. Like biologically prepared structures, the tools that one uses not only enable thought and intellectual progress but also constrain and limit the range of what can be thought. In these invisible ways, the history of a culture, an inherently social history, is carried into each individual act of cognition (Cole 1985).

Theories, implicit and explicit, both enable and constrain thinking, just as physical tools do. This observation has become commonplace in cognitive science. What individuals reason about, the knowledge they bring to a cognitive task, provides the interpretive frames or schemas that allow reasoning and problem solving to proceed. These beliefs, individuals' schemas for reasoning, are not purely individual constructions. Instead, they are heavily influenced by the kinds of beliefs and reasoning schemas available in the individuals' surrounding culture.

Not only theories but even ways of reasoning are themselves socially determined. Cognitive tools also include the forms of reasoning and argumentation that are accepted as normative in given cultures. Both Mead (1934) and Vygotsky (1978) proposed that mechanisms of thought are best conceived as internalizations of behaviors first engaged in externally

interacting with others. Mead called thought a "conversation with the generalized other," implying that, as we think individually, we attempt to respond—internally and vicariously—to the imagined responses of others to our ideas and arguments. Vygotsky's central claim was that, to understand individual psychological development, it is necessary to understand the system of social relations in which the individual lives and grows. This system is itself a product of generations of development over time, so that the individual is, in effect, historically situated, an heir to a long cultural development. Primary among the tools that, for Vygotsky, are each individual's patrimony is language, which mediates all thinking (cf. Wertsch 1985).

3. Situated Rationalism

Conceptual rationalists and situated learning theorists can each assemble convincing evidence in support of their views. Each appears, within its own terms, to offer a coherent account of human intellectual development. But each maintains its coherence by limiting the range of questions it is willing to address. Conceptual rationalists search for concepts that appear to be universal and focus their attention on the earliest emergence of these concepts. There is little attention to the varied forms that adult knowledge might take or to how more particular *cultural domains* of knowledge might develop out of biologically prepared structures.

Situationists, on the other hand, are interested in the ways that culture, history, and immediate social contexts shape cognitive activity. Although the language of domains rarely appears, there is much interest in different cultural systems of knowledge. They offer theories, such as Vygotsky's, of how participation in particular forms of social activity leads to personal cognitive competence. But these cultural *sociohistorical* theories of cognition have little or nothing to say about the contributions that the individual might make to development. They do not consider the biological starting point of development, the constraints that biological endowment might place on the directions of socially-shaped cognitive development. The issue generally is not discussed, but sociohistorical theories could just as well accept a *tabula rasa* basic theory of learning as a biologically constrained one—although there is no incompatibility with the idea of biological constraints either.

The lack of attention to the individual's contribution by situationists is not limited to a failure to attend to biological constraints on learning and development. On the whole, today's students of situated cognition are more interested in mapping details of how people coordinate cognitive activity in particular social and tool situations than they are in accounting for personal structures of knowledge. A problem within situated cognition theory is that the individual seems to disappear. Individual competence is replaced by social and institutional forms of behavior. Individual knowledge and skill—characteristics of individuals that can be carried with them from one situation to another—are replaced by *emergent cognition* that belongs to no one and disappears when the moment of emergence has passed.

This contrast is meant to suggest how situated cognition and conceptual rationalism together might be able to do what neither appears able to do alone: provide an account of how individuals learn both the universal concepts for which they appear to be biologically prepared and the much greater variety of culturally specific knowledge and ways of acting that characterize mature people. The issue addressed here is how to understand the relations between the prepared structures and the cultural domains; it is assumed that there are cultural elaborations of conceptions initially founded on the biologically prepared structures. Education—interpreted broadly, not just in terms of institutionalized schooling—is clearly part of the cultural elaboration process.

The remainder of this entry can be viewed as either reintroducing the individual into a radical theory of situated cognition or introducing the social into a theory of biological constraints on learning. Either way, the first task is to expand the notion of prepared structures beyond the biologically prepared, to include the socially prepared. Next, a theory of contextually specific learning that takes into account the idea of prepared structures brought into the situation by participating individuals.

4. Learning as Tuning of Prepared Structures

The conceptual rationalists argue that learning occurs when prepared structures are elaborated in the course of interaction with the environment. The prepared structures direct and constrain attention to particular environmental features that will support elaborations of particular concepts. They render the individual sensitive to particular affordances of situation. With our view of socioculturally prepared structures, it is an easy extension to think of structures resulting from past engagements in culturally specific situations as similarly constraining the way in which individuals enter new situations. Once in a situation of engagement with the environment, prepared structures are modified and elaborated by that engagement. Engagement in a situation thus modifies the structures that prepare one for the next situation. It is this process of elaboration that we call learning.

The work of conceptual rationalists has focused on those elaborations that result in relatively permanent new structures, that is, those that will turn out to be tuned to the affordances of many future situations over an extended period of time. The situated rationalist argument calls for just a slight shift in perspective, one that in no way challenges the underlying argu-

ment of learning on the basis of elaborating prepared structures. It suggested that, in each situation of engagement, what is actually elaborated is only what is needed to act successfully in that particular situation. The new conceptual elaborations are "general" or permanent only to the extent that future situations afford their use. On any particular occasion, one tunes one's behavior and, thus, one's knowledge to the demands of the occasion.

Learning, for the situated rationalist, is a matter of tuning to one's immediate situation, of becoming good in the situation in which one practices. The situation is inclusively defined. It refers to everything in the physical surroundings, and the material used; to the social, institutional, and personal purposes at play; to the other people engaged; and to the language used. In short, much of what is traditionally viewed as context for learning is viewed in a theory of situated practice as an essential part of learning and, thus, of what is learned.

The heart of the argument, then, is that learning is a matter of passing through successive situations in which the individual becomes competent. Individuals develop this situated competence in each situation on the basis of their prepared structures. These prepared structures have both biological and sociocultural roots, with the biological predominating in the earliest months and years and the sociocultural taking increasing control thereafter as each individual's personal history of situations grows and initial biologically prepared structures are successively modified. (Gardner 1991 and Johnson 1987 for convincing arguments that earlier, more purely biologically based schemas do not wholly disappear from adults.)

The learning processes are the same, whether the prepared structures are, in a given instance, primarily biological or primarily sociocultural. In fact, because socialization into a culture begins at birth, there is probably no instance thereafter that can be categorized as purely biological or purely sociocultural in its preparation. In each new situation, learning is a matter of beginning to act in the environment on the basis of the particular affordances of that environment. One's initial actions are either successful or not. If they are dramatically unsuccessful, that is, if there is no match at all between one's prepared structures and the affordances of the environment, the most likely response is to leave the environment, either physically, if possible, or by "tuning out" when actual physical departure is not possible. If the match is complete, there is no learning to take place. One just acts.

But if the match is partial—enough to keep one engaged, but not enough to provide a ready-made set of actions—a process of tuning to the affordances of the environment sets in. This tuning is what is meant here by learning. It produces an ability to act "perfectly" in the environment. But, because it is a tuning process, it results in a specifically situated competence. The competence developed will not be perfect for any other specific environment. An effort to specify the mechanisms of tuning would reach beyond what either situated cognition or conceptual rationalism has attempted to study until now. Connectionist models of cognition (Rummelhart et al. 1986), however, suggest a metaphor, at least, for what the process might be like. In connectionist models, a cognitive system learns by spreading activation across multiple nodes simultaneously. No single node embodies meaning or knowledge; rather, meaning is emergent, the result of ongoing activity in the network. The state of the network (its nodes, the strength and directionality of its links) at the beginning of an episode interacts with new stimuli in the situation to produce a particular pattern of acitivity. This activity can be thought of as the tuning process. It produces a change in the network. The changed network will react somewhat differently—even to similar stimuli—at the start of the next episode and will again tune itself, in a more or less continuous cycle of situation-specific learning.

5. *From Skeletal Structures to Scientific Concepts*

This section discusses briefly how the idea of situated rationalism plays out in two well-studied knowledge domains. Personal histories will not be explored, nor will details of the tuning process be described, because the necessary research—macrolongitudinal and microlongitudinal combined—has not been much pursued until now. But it is possible, on the basis of an assembled body of research, to lay out some plausible hypotheses about the relations between biologically prepared and culturally elaborated knowledge structures in different domains.

There are, logically and empirically, at least two kinds of relations between biologically prepared and culturally elaborated structures of knowledge:

(a) The culturally accepted forms may be *coherent* with biologically prepared structures. For example, certain core concepts of number and algebra can be grown by elaboration of basic principles of counting, plus knowledge about physical material, that there is reason to believe are among the biologically prepared structures available to all human infants.

(b) Culturally accepted or scientific concepts may *contradict* beliefs that are rooted in biologically prepared structures. This appears to be the case for many concepts in physics, where the contradictions give rise to systematic misconceptions and difficulties in learning scientific concepts. It may also be the case for certain mathematical concepts, such as fractions or proportions.

The nature of learning can be expected to be quite different for cultural concepts that are coherent with

biologically prepared structures than for those that are contradictory. At the very least, we should expect to find differences between the two in simple ease of learning. Such differences would be reflected in the ages at which children in a given society acquire the cultural concepts of interest; in the ways in which knowledge of and mastery of the concepts are distributed in the population; and in the extent to which mastery of the concepts appears to depend on formal instruction. For the concepts used as examples here, all three of these indicators distinguish well between the coherent and the contradictory. Non-Newtonian forms of thinking about the physical world predominate among all but the best educated; formal physics is learned relatively late; primarily in formal institutions of instruction, and with considerable difficulty by most students. By contrast, core mathematics concepts that are derivable from knowledge about counting and physical material are learned easily, young, and by nearly everyone who participates in any kind of market economy.

The examples mentioned from physics and mathematics are prototype cases—instances in which enough research has been done to make it clear whether we are dealing with a coherent or a contradictory relationship between the prepared and the culturally elaborated. In other instances (e.g., religion, biology), it is not clear what kind of transformation—whether an elaboration of a biologically prepared concept or its replacement by a new idea—must take place to reach a culturally accepted concept. For many of the most important learned concepts, a mixture of coherent and contradictory relations with several different prepared structures is likely.

6. *Situated Rationalism and Education*

The distinction between concepts that are coherent with biologically prepared structures and those that contradict them suggests the need for two different approaches to teaching and instruction. For coherent concepts, "teaching" is largely a process of helping children elaborate their initial, biologically guided concept into particular cultural forms. It is more a matter of guided exposure to new opportunities for using concepts than of directly telling them about new ideas, although experience with a culture's conceptual language and tools must be considered a key part of this exposure (see Resnick and Greeno 1992). Most educators who espouse a "constructivist" philosophy— a clear majority today—are, apparently, acting on an implicit assumption that what children already know as they enter an instructional situation is coherent with the new concepts to be learned. On this assumption, it is reasonable to conclude that children's own cognitive constructions will move without much resistance toward the culturally accepted forms to which they are exposed.

In the case of cultural knowledge that contradicts biologically preferred concepts, however, education must follow a different path: still constructivist in the sense that simple telling will not work, but much less dependent on untutored discovery and exploration. For these contradictory concepts, ways of helping children replace rather than elaborate initial beliefs need to be found. We have not yet found very good ways of doing this. In physics education, for example, where the phenomenon of resistance to scientific concepts has been recognized for some time, an early idea was that confronting students empirically with the inadequacy of their initial concepts would stimulate rejection of the old and openness to new ideas. This has not worked very well. Students mostly find ways of reinterpreting the empirical data to fit their initial conceptions (Champagne et al. 1980, Joshua and Dupin 1987). Even when they accept the inadequacy of their initial ideas, physical experience and data do not directly suggest new, scientific concepts.

Some researchers have experimented with the use of analogies, usually embodied in special physical models, as a way of teaching the new concepts. Their reported successes (e.g., Brown and Clement 1989, Sayeki et al. 1991,White 1992) have always involved very large investments of time (for students and teachers alike) for learning very limited concepts. In another proposed approach (Chi 1992, Chi and VanLehn 1991, Ohlsson 1992), students would be directly taught certain core scientific concepts and then guided through a process of applying those concepts to many cases. The idea is that students might at first apply the concepts rather mechanically but would eventually come to believe in them because they yielded intellectual power. At that point, but not earlier, it might be profitable to pit the new concepts against the initial, biologically rooted ones. This attractive idea still requires empirical testing.

Beyond the problems involved in teaching specific concepts, the situated rationalist view of learning and development suggests some new perspectives on traditional problems in education. In particular, *individual differences* and *transfer*, both central constructs in educational psychology, can be usefully reconstrued. Both of these constructs have been classically defined in terms of bundles of relatively stable skills. Over the decades, debate has focused on how to describe these skills and how they bundle together. The situated rationalist framework suggests that, instead of decontextualized skills, it would be helpful to think of *personal histories* as the important determinants of the way individuals will act in a particular situation.

When individuals move from situation to situation, they carry histories of prior experience with them. These are histories of ways of behaving. They include the elaborated knowledge structures, along with affective and social propensities, developed in the course of tuning to prior situations. The way one enters a new situation is influenced by one's history of past situations. Situations experienced as similar to a past situation will initially evoke (although not necessarily consciously) ways of behaving that developed through practice and tuning in the previous situation. If these ways of behaving work—that is, if they result in successful behavior in the new situation—they will be further practiced and elaborated. On this analysis, "transfer" would be a case in which a prepared structure and the new situation's affordances interact to produce a situated performance in accord with what educators have defined as the "right" response. Lack of transfer would be a case in which affordances and prepared structures produce a tuned performance not in accord with educators' expectations.

Two features distinguish this notion of personal histories from traditional views of transfer of skills and knowledge. First, what one carries with one to a new situation is much more complex and organic than a collection of skills. It is a whole set of dispositions, interpretations, and representations that, together and interactively, produce an initial response. Second, one's personal history is determinative only as one enters the new situation. Thereafter, all of the people, tools, and material resources of the new situation shape a new situated practice. Cognition is emergent in the situation and specific to it. Yet the individual is not lost, for he or she leaves the encounter with a residue of preparation for the next situation.

The idea of personal histories as a way of thinking about individual differences and transfer suggests that we might profitably think of education as an effort to organize sequences of designed situations that are likely to prepare individuals to tune adaptively to the kinds of natural situations they will encounter outside designated institutions of learning. Current formal education does this very poorly (see Resnick 1987). The special situation of the classroom—calling for private rather than socially shared work and isolating mental activity from engagement in the social and physical world—builds skills and knowledge that allow students to function in school but often fail to transfer to the worlds of work, civic, and personal life. To change this thoughtfully and productively will require a form of theory that is now largely absent from psychological thinking and only loosely developed in other fields of social science, *a theory of situations.* Such a theory would define the dimensions—social, cognitive, and physical—of situations with an eye to how activity in one situation might prepare individuals to enter another. Developing such a theory, taking into account both biological and social constraints on learning, represents a major challenge for those who would apply the concepts of situated rationalism to education.

See also: Cognition and Learning; Instructional Psychology: Overview; Paradigms in Instructional Psychology; Learning Theories: Historical Overview and Trends

References

Brown D E, Clement J 1989 Overcoming misconceptions via analogical reasoning: Abstract transfer versus explanatory model. Paper presented at the American Educational Research Association, San Francisco

Champagne A B, Klopfer L E, Anderson J H 1980 Factors influencing the learning of classical mechanics. *American Journal of Physics* 48: 174

Chi M T H 1992 Conceptual change within and across ontological categories: Examples from learning and discovery in science. In: Giere R (ed.) 1992 *Cognitive Models of Science: Minnesota Studies in the Philosophy of Science*. University of Minnesota Press, Minneapolis, Minnesota

Chi M T H, VanLehn K A 1991 The content of physics self-explanations. *Journal of the Learning Sciences* 1: 69–105

Cole M 1985 The zone of proximal development: Where culture and cognition create each other. In: Wertsch J V (ed.) 1985 *Culture, Communication, and Cognition: Vygotskian Perspectives*. Cambridge University Press, Cambridge

Gardner H 1991 *The Unschooled Mind: How Children Learn, How Schools Should Teach*. Basic Books, New York

Gelman R, Carey S (eds.) 1991 *The Epigenesis of Mind: Essays on Biology and Cognition*. Erlbaum, Hillsdale, New Jersey

Hutchins E 1991 The social organization of distributed cognition. In: Resnick L B, Levine W M, Teasley S D (eds.) 1991 *Perspectives on Socially Shared Cognition* American Psychological Association, Washington, DC

Johnson M 1987 *Body in the Mind: The Bodily Basis of Meaning, Imagination, and Reason*. University of Chicago Press, Chicago, Illinois

Johsua S, Dupin J J 1987 Taking into account student conceptions in a didactic strategy: An example in physics. *Cognition and Instruction* 4: 117–135

Latour B 1987 *Science in Action*. Harvard University Press, Cambridge, Massachusetts

Lave J 1988 *Cognition in Practice: Mind, Mathematics and Culture in Everyday Life*. Cambridge University Press, Cambridge

Mead G H 1934 *Mind, Self, and Society*. University of Chicago Press, Chicago, Illinois

Neisser U 1976 *Cognition and Reality: Principles and Implications of Cognitive Psychology*. W H Freeman, San Francisco, California

Ohisson S 1992 The cognitive skill of theory articulation: A neglected aspect of science education? *Sci & Educ.* 1: 181–192

Resnick L B 1987 Learning in school and out. *Educ. Researcher* 16(9): 13–20

Resnick L B, Greeno J G 1992 Conceptual growth of number and quantity. Unpublished manuscript

Rumelhart D E, McClelland J L, PDP Research Group 1986 *Parallel Distributed Processing: Explorations in the Microstructure of Cognition*, 2 Vols. Bradford Books/MIT Press, Cambridge, Massachusetts

Sayeki Y, Ueno N, Nagasaka T 1991 Mediation as a generative model for obtaining an area. *Learning and Instruction* 1: 229–242

Vygotsky L S 1978 *Mind in Society*. Harvard University Press, Cambridge, Massachusetts

Wertsch J V 1985 *Vygotsky and the Social Formation of Mind*. Harvard University Press, Cambridge, Massachusetts

White B 1992 ThinkerTools: Causal models, conceptual change, and science education. *Cognition and Instruction* 10: 1–100

Learning Activity

J. Lompscher

The concept of learning activity is part of the approach of activity theory to learning elaborated in the framework of the cultural–historical tradition (as developed by Vygotsky, Luria, Leontiev, and others). Activity (German, *Tätigkeit*; Russian, *dejatel' nost*) is understood as a fundamental form of human existence, as interaction between humans and the world presupposing an active, goal-oriented, conscious, societal person. Using certain means under certain conditions the person performs actions on different material and mental levels, directed toward the modification or generation of activity objects which may also be human beings. Interrelations between person and object are mediated by other persons, just as interrelations between persons are mediated by objects. Activity results may not coincide with the intended goals of an activity results consists in modifications of

the person often unintended and unnoticed by himself or herself.

1. Essence and Structure of Learning Activity

Learning activity is a special kind of human activity. It is directed toward the acquisition of social knowledge and competence, by reproducing them individually under conditions of societal, and especially pedagogical, guidance, and conditions of social communication and cooperation (Davydov 1988a, 1988b; Lompscher 1989). In this context the notion of acquisition means the transformation of objective societal values, norms, methods, knowledge, and so on into subjective, psychic structures and features.

Learning effects are produced, on the one hand, by activities directed toward other goals (such as play, work, and communication) and, on the other hand, by activity especially directed toward learning goals. Therefore a distinction can be made between learning through activity and learning as a special activity. From a historical perspective, learning activity has developed from work activity, but ontogenetically it emerges from play and everyday activity.

As a special activity learning has to be acquired by the individual concerned—in other words, learning has to be learned. Learning activity therefore assumes a predominat position in a person's activity system over a certain period—as a rule, under conditions of schooling. When it has been acquired in some measure, it loses this position, but not its significance in personality development: acquisition of knowledge and competence remains an important task throughout life (through extensions of general education, vocational training, and the acquisition of further or higher qualifications).

Learning activity differs from other kinds of activity, by being directed toward a person's self-modification or self-improvement; namely, toward the formation of the subjective prerequisites necessary to accomplish new, and ever more complex and difficult classes of tasks. In this activity the whole person is involved and develops as a whole. Learning results are, as a rule, broader than learning goals directed toward knowledge and competence. In this process the interrelations with the social and material worlds become increasingly indirect and complicated—entailing the formation of a theoretical approach toward the world. New motivational and emotional characteristics develop, and cognitive and metacognitive structures and strategies are elaborated. The psychic activity regulation operates as a whole and must be analyzed and formed in all its complexity and interrelations.

The macrostructure of learning activity consists of the following elements.

First, there are the learners themselves, who at a specific level of personality development perform learning actions in order to reach certain learning goals. Individual activity is embedded in social interaction (coordination, communication, cooperation). Learning results depend principally on the quality and intensity of the learners' activity, which in turn is influenced by cognitive, motivational, emotional, volitional, and social capacities interacting with the social and material conditions of activity.

Second, there are the learning objects to be acquired. When an aspect of the world becomes the object of learning activity, it is in many ways transformed by the level of societal knowledge and ideology applied to it, by theoretical and political principles of selection and preparation, by didactic methods and means of presentation, by psychological views of learning, and the learners. Learning results are not obtained by the actions of learning objects upon learners, but, on the contrary, by the learners' own actions upon the objects.

Third, there are the learning tools necessary for attaining certain learning goals. The main tools are the learner's actions, which have to be in accordance with the content and structure of the learning object in order to make acquisition possible. Therefore, these actions must be acquired; only then can they serve as tools for learning. Material or other objects become learning tools only by including them in the structure of appropriate learning actions.

Fourth are the conditions under which activity takes place. Political, institutional, and familial conditions, social climate, and material situations, may promote or hinder the activity process and its results. Indeed, the optimization of learning conditions is the real aim and object of research and of practical efforts relating to learning and instruction, directed toward the promotion of personality (i.e., cognitive, motivational) development by learning activity as well as other activities.

2. Major Principles of Analysis and Formation of Learning Activity

Although analysis and formation of learning activity require different methods and means, they are mutually connected and presuppose each other. The causal –genetic methodology of activity theory analyzes the genesis of an object and tries to reveal the causes and conditions of its development as well as the modifications of its content and structure. However, the identification of a given state, structure, or feature —though necessary—is insufficient for understanding learning activity. Learning results must be related to the processes and conditions affecting them. If a certain learning effect can be produced or generated by creating and organizing activity conditions according to theoretically and empirically founded hypotheses, and if the development and structure of this learning effect can be analyzed in the process of formation, it can then be explained and recommendations can be offered for educational practice. As a rule, this is a process of gradual approximation involving different trials and steps.

2.1 Unity of Learning Activity and Learning Object

A certain level and structure of learning activity are the prerequisites for the acquisition of a certain particular learning object. If a person is confronted with new subject domains or higher-level tasks in the course of learning activity, appropriate learning actions have to be elaborated or raised to a higher level. Deficits in cognitive, motivational, and other components of activity regulation need to be overcome. However, this cannot be done without consideration of the learning object which is being sought. The learning activity necessary for the acquisition of a certain learning object must be formed in the process of acquiring that object; in other words, what is required is the promotion of development through organization and formation of activity according to the demands of learning objects.

2.2 *Unity of Zone of Actual Performance and Zone of Proximal Development*

A Zone of Actual Performance (ZAP) involves the tasks mastered independently by the learner as a result of previous acquisition processes. Such a zone opens up a Zone of Proximal Development (ZPD) consisting of actions performed with support and under guidance, or by using a model. Learning tasks aimed at promoting the learners' development should be oriented toward this ZPD, because in this zone psychic structures and features not yet fully developed are required and therefore must be intensively promoted. In this process the ZPD is changed into a new ZAP, opening up a new ZPD and so forth. Determining a certain ZPD requires the analysis of the interrelations between three factors:

(a) the objective demands of the learning object in terms of the material and mental activity aiming at acquisition (content and task structure);

(b) the individual conditions necessary for satisfying these demands (knowledge, strategies, attitudes, etc.);

(c) the individual conditions actually available in the learner.

The discrepancy between the necessary and actual prerequisites of learning opens up directions and possibilities for the next steps to be carried out, and for the conditions that must be created to achieve this aim. If there is no discrepancy at all, no learning and developmental effect is possible. If the discrepancy is too large and the learner cannot bridge the gap, no learning and developmental effect is possible, or the activity will be too strenuous mentally and/or physically.

2.3 *Unity of Learning Activity and Teaching Activity*

Learning activity emerges and develops in permanent interaction with teaching activity under instructional conditions. In this interaction learners and teachers are both subjects and objects of activity and of mutual influence. Their actions must be coordinated in order to reach their goals, which are not identical in learners and teachers. Both are mutually dependent: learning takes place under conditions created and organized by teachers (in fact by the whole society), who are in turn depending on the learners' preexisting cognitive and motivational qualities and their realization in the activity process.

The decisive matter is how the teacher is able to analyze the level and structure of the learning activity and to organize conditions for its further formation and development. Therefore, teachers' main orientation cannot be toward the learning object and their own instructional actions and strategies for transmitting the object to the learners ("into their heads"). Rather, teachers have to focus on the activity necessary for the acquisition of that object and toward the learners' facility for this activity. Only in this way will the teacher be able to find and to organize conditions under which zones of proximal development can be transformed into zones of actual performance. To achieve this goal it is insufficient to provide opportunities for spontaneous activity under given conditions. It is necessary to form systematically the required learning activity —not in the sense of affecting a more or less passive object, but in the sense of creating conditions for self-development of active subjects. The starting point here is determined by the learners' developmental needs, existing shares, and potentialities.

3. *Main Conditions of the Formation of Learning Activity*

The following sections will describe one variant of the activity theory approach referred to as ascending from the abstract to the concrete. In this framework the following conditions for the formation of learning activity are emphasized.

3.1 *Learning Goal Formation*

Objects and tasks corresponding to learners' needs and motives produce concrete learning goals under the following conditions: if the learning abilities are sufficient to understand the demands and if the learners' actions in this task situation are directed not only toward attempts to solve the task but also toward the analysis of the demand structure in relation to their own abilities. Evaluation of and reflection on this interrelationship makes a learner aware of what "I do not yet know or what I am not yet able to do, but what I want to know or to be able to do." The unknown can be formulated only in general, global terms. As such, the direction of search and effort is determined. A more or less broad learning perspective is formed which can be subdivided into partial goals and which serves as a basis for orientation, planning, control, and evaluation of learning progress.

3.2 *Formation of Learning Actions*

When actions necessary for attaining certain learning goals are unavailable to the learner, or when quality does not correspond with new learning demands, then they must be systematically formed. Action patterns are given and conditions must be created for their acquisition. In accordance with the concrete learning abilities this may be done in a more or less systematic step-by-step formation oriented toward the acquisition of as yet insufficiently formed abilities, beginning—if necessary—with movement from material or materialized actions via verbalization to mental actions (internalization in interrelation with externalization as proposed by Galperin 1969). In this process complex actions may have to be subdivided first into partial actions, in order to form them separately and then to integrate them into complex actions.

3.3 Formation of Initial Abstractions and Learning Models

Since they operate with concrete objects or situations and trying to discover the essential features and relations that underlie the phenomena and their modifications, learners need a form of crystallization of what they have found out. An appropriate form for this purpose is a learning model that embodies only the most essential features and relations of the learning object, analyzed so far in a simple graphic, verbal, or other format. Thus, an initial abstraction can be generated that is different from the concrete phenomena and contains only the most essential constituting attributes. Such learning models, representing initial abstractions, are significant results of learning activity; at the same time they are starting points and tools of further activity. The ascent from the abstract to the concrete has its fundamental basis in the analysis of concrete phenomena.

3.4 Formation of Concretizations

Initial abstractions are used for penetrating the richness and multifaceted nature of concrete objects, processes, and situations in a learning domain. This process can be organized in such a way that ever more complex learning tasks are tackled. Concrete phenomena are analyzed by means of abstractions which are in turn permanently enriched and further developed by their interaction with the concrete.

4. From Theory to Practice

Other main conditions of the formation of learning activity in the framework of activity theory can only be mentioned briefly; namely, problem-solving, cooperation, communication, reflection, and social relations. This activity and formation approach was formulated in different subject-matter domains (e.g., mathematics, learning of native and foreign languages, history, geography, biology, and physics) and at different educational levels (mainly in elementary education, but also in preschool and in secondary education—and in some cases in vocational training and higher education). Research data reported in the literature show that, when applied, it has produced strong effects with respect to the formation of learning motivation, of concepts and strategies, of theoretical thinking and of domain-specific competence.

The learning activity approach corresponds to other approaches to learning and instruction in such crucial points as orientation toward the active learner and the creation of situations appropriate for active learning (see Boekaerts 1992, De Corte 1990, Engeström 1991, Resnick 1989, Van Oers 1990). A productive synthesis of different approaches may promote scientific understanding and practical effectiveness in learning and instruction.

See also: Learning Potential and Learning Potential Tests; Learning Theories: Historical Overview and Trends; Models of Learning; Learning Processes and Learning Outcomes; Learning to Learn: Adult Education

References

Boekaerts M 1992 The adaptable learning process: Initiating and maintaining behavioural change. *Applied Psychology: An International Review* 41(4): 375–97

Davydov V V 1988a Problems of developmental teaching: The experience of theoretical and experimental psychological research. *Soviet Educ.* 30(8): 15–97; 30(9): 3–83; 30(10): 3–77

Davydov V V 1988b Learning activity: The main problems needing further research. *Multidisciplinary Newsletter for Activity Theory* 1: 29–36

De Corte E 1990 Acquiring and teaching cognitive skills: A state-of-the-art of theory and research. In: Drenth P J D, Sergeant J A, Takens R J (eds.) 1990 *European Perspectives in Psychology*, Vol. 1. Wiley, London

Engeström Y 1991 Non scholae sed vitae discimus: Toward overcoming the encapsulation of school learning. *Learning and Instruction* 1(3): 243–59

Gal'perin P Y 1969 Stages in the development of mental acts. In: Cole M, Maltzman I (eds.) 1969 *A Handbook of Contemporary Soviet Psychology*. Basic Books, New York

Lompscher J 1989 Formation of learning activity in pupils. In: Mandl H, De Corte E, Bennett N, Friedrich H F (eds.) 1989 *Learning and Instruction: European Research in an International Context Vol. 2.2: Analysis of Complex Skills and Complex Knowledge Domains*. Pergamon Press, Oxford

Resnick L B (ed.) 1989 *Knowing, Learning, and Instruction: Essays in Honor of Robert Glaser*. Erlbaum, Hillsdale, New Jersey

Van Oers B 1990 The development of mathematical thinking in school: A comparison of the action-psychological and information-processing approaches. *Int. J. Educ. Res.* 14(1): 51–66

Further Reading

Bol E, Haenen J P P, Wolters M A (eds.) 1985 *Education for Cognitive Development: Proceedings of the Third International Symposium on Activity Theory*. Stichting voor Onderzoek van het Onderwijs (SVO), The Hague

Glaser R 1991 The maturing of the relationship between the science of learning and cognition and educational practice. *Learning and Instruction* 1(2): 129–44

Hedegaard M, Hakkarainen P, Engeström Y (eds.) 1984 *Learning and Teaching on a Scientific Basis: Methodological and Epistemological Aspects of the Activity Theory of Learning and Teaching*. Psykologisk Institut, Aarhus University, Aarhus

Cooperative Learning

R. E. Slavin

Organizing students to work together in small groups is an ancient practice in education throughout the world. While practice varies widely within the various countries, there is a sharp distinction between the approaches to cooperative learning prevalent in the United States and those prevalent in Europe, Israel, and the British Commonwealth. In the United States cooperative learning most frequently takes the form of relatively structured programs focused on mastery of skills, concepts, and information. These programs are likely to involve four-member, heterogeneous learning groups which remain together over a period of several weeks or more. In most cases, the groups receive recognition or occasionally grades based on their learning or performance as a group. In contrast, cooperative learning outside of the Unites States is more likely to focus either on relatively unstructured discussions or on group projects. Group membership is more likely to change from discussion to discussion and project to project. Furthermore, the purpose of the activity is at least as much socialization and general higher-order thinking or problem-solving skills as it is the learning of specific subject matter content.

Research on these different approaches to cooperative learning also differs sharply. Research on approaches developed in the United States (including that conducted in other countries) emphasizes experiments comparing cooperative and traditional methods, with a primary focus on academic achievement as the outcome of interest. Group Investigation, a structured technique based on Dewey's project method that was developed in Israel, has also been studied in experiments of this kind (e.g., Sharan and Shachar 1988). In contrast, there is far less research done on more informal cooperative learning approaches, and that which does exist tends to provide rich descriptions of the cooperative activities rather than any assessment of the outcome of those activities (e.g., Barnes and Britton 1969).

This entry presents a review of research on cooperative learning involving comparisons of cooperative and traditional approaches. With the exception of Group Investigation, all of these programs were developed in the United States. However, research on these and other closely related programs has also been conducted in Canada, Israel, Germany, the Netherlands, and Nigeria.

1. Cooperative Learning Methods

While social psychological research on cooperative learning dates back to the 1920s (see Slavin in press), research on specific applications of cooperative learning to the classroom did not begin until the early 1970s. At that time, three independent groups of researchers in the United States and one in Israel began to develop and research the use of cooperative learning methods in classroom settings. In the early 1990s, there are researchers all over the world studying practical applications of cooperative learning principles, and there are many cooperative learning methods in use. The most widely researched are described in the following sections.

1.1 Student Team Learning

Student team learning methods are cooperative learning techniques developed and studied at Johns Hopkins University. More than half of all experimental studies of practical cooperative learning methods involve student team learning methods.

All cooperative learning methods share the idea that students work together to learn and are responsible for one another's learning as well as their own. In addition to the idea of cooperative work, student team learning methods emphasize the use of team goals and team success which can only be achieved if all members of the team learn the objectives being taught. In student team learning, therefore, the students' tasks are not to do something as a team but to learn something as a team.

Three concepts are central to all student team learning methods: "team rewards," "individual accountability," and "equal opportunity for success." In these techniques, teams may earn certificates or other team rewards if they achieve at or above a designated standard. The teams are not in competition to earn elusive rewards; all (or none) of the teams may achieve the standard in a given week. Individual accountability means that the team's success depends on the individual learning of all team members. Thus, the activity of the team members is focused on tutoring one another and making sure that everyone on the team is ready for a quiz or other assessment which students will be expected to complete without teammate help. Equal opportunity for success means that students contribute to their teams by improving over their own past performance. This ensures that high, average, and low achievers are equally challenged to do their best, and the contributions of all team members will be valued.

Research on cooperative learning methods has indicated that team rewards and individual accountability are essential elements for producing basic skills achievement (Slavin 1983a, 1983b, in press). It is not enough simply to tell students to work together. They must have a reason to take one another's achievement seriously. Further, research indicates that if students are rewarded for doing better than they have in the past, they will be more motivated to achieve than if they are rewarded based on their performance in comparison to others, because rewards for improvement make success neither too difficult nor too easy for students to achieve (Slavin 1980).

There are four principal student team learning methods that have been extensively developed and researched. Of these, two are general cooperative learning methods adaptable to most subjects and grade levels: Student Teams–Achievement Divisions (STAD) and Teams–Games–Tournament (TGT). The remaining two are comprehensive curricula designed for use in particular subjects at particular grade levels: Team Assisted Individualization (TAI) for mathematics in grades 3–6, and Cooperative Integrated Reading and Composition (CIRC) for reading and writing instruction in grades 3–5.

1.1.1 Student Teams–Achievement Divisions (STAD).

In STAD (Slavin 1986), students are assigned to four-member learning teams that are mixed in performance level, sex, and ethnicity. The teacher presents a lesson, and then students work within their teams to make sure that all team members have mastered the lesson. Finally, all students take individual quizzes on the material, at which time they may not help one another.

Students' quiz scores are compared to their own past averages, and points are awarded based on the degree to which students can meet or exceed their own earlier performance. These points are then summed to form team scores, and teams which achieve certain standards may earn certificates or other rewards. The whole cycle of activities, from teacher presentation to team practice to quiz, usually takes from three to five class periods.

This method has been used in a wide variety of subjects, from mathematics to language arts to social studies, from Grade 2 through college. It is most appropriate for teaching well-defined objectives with single right answers, such as mathematical computations and applications, language usage and mechanics, geography and map skills, and science facts and concepts.

1.1.2 Teams–Games–Tournament (TGT).

Teams–Games–Tournament (DeVries and Slavin 1978, Slavin 1986) was the first of the Johns Hopkins cooperative learning methods. It uses the same teacher presentations and teamwork as in STAD, but replaces the quizzes with weekly tournaments in which students compete with members of other teams to contribute points to their team scores. Students compete at three-person "tournament tables" against others with similar past records in mathematics. A "bumping" procedure keeps the competition fair. The winner at each tournament table brings the same number of points to his or her team, regardless of which table it is. Thus, low

achievers (competing with other low achievers) and high achievers (competing with other high achievers) have equal opportunities for success. As in STAD, high-performing teams earn certificates or other forms of team rewards.

1.1.3 Team Assisted Individualization (TAI).

Team Assisted Individualization (TAI) (Slavin et al. 1986) shares with STAD and TGT the use of four-member mixed ability learning teams and certificates for high-performing teams, but where STAD and TGT use a single pace of instruction for the class, TAI combines cooperative learning with individualized instruction. Also, where STAD and TGT apply to most subjects and grade levels, TAI is specifically designed to teach mathematics to students in Grades 3–6 (or older students not ready for a full algebra course).

In TAI, students enter an individualized sequence according to a placement test and then proceed at their own rates. In general, team members work on different units. Teammates check each others' work against answer sheets and help one another with any problems. Final unit tests are taken without teammate help and are scored by student monitors. Each week, teachers total the number of units completed by all team members and give certificates or other team rewards to teams which exceed a criterion score based on the number of final tests passed, with extra points given for perfect papers and completed homework.

Because students take responsibility for checking each others' work and managing the flow of materials, the teacher can spend most of the class time presenting lessons to small groups of students drawn from the various teams who are working at the same point in the mathematics sequence. For example, the teacher might call up a decimals group, present a lesson on decimals, and then send the students back to their teams to work on decimal problems. The teacher might next call the fractions group, and so on.

1.1.4 Cooperative Integrated Reading and Composition (CIRC).

The newest of the student team learning methods is a comprehensive program for teaching reading and writing in the upper elementary grades called Cooperative Integrated Reading and Composition, or CIRC (Stevens et al. 1987). In CIRC, teachers use basal readers and reading groups, much as in traditional reading programs in the United States. However, students are assigned to teams composed of pairs of students from two different reading groups. While the teacher is working with one reading group, students in the other groups are working in their pairs on a series of cognitively engaging activities including reading to one another; making predictions about how narrative stories will come out; summarizing stories to one another; writing responses to stories; and practicing spelling, decoding, and vocabulary. If the reading class is not divided into homogeneous reading groups, all students in the teams work with one another. Students work as a total team to master main idea and other comprehension skills. During language arts periods, students engage in writing drafts, revising and editing one another's work, and preparing for publication of team books.

In most CIRC activities, students follow a sequence of teacher instruction, team practice, team pre-assessments, and quiz. That is, students do not take the quiz until their teammates have determined that they are ready. Certificates are given to teams based on the average performance of all team members on all reading and writing activities.

1.2 Jigsaw

Jigsaw was designed by Elliot Aronson and his colleagues (Aronson et al. 1978). In the original Jigsaw method, students are assigned to six-member teams to work on academic material which has been broken down into sections. For example, a biography might be divided into early life, first accomplishments, major accomplishments, major setbacks, later life, and impact on history. Each team member reads his or her section. Next, members of different teams who have studied the same sections meet in "expert groups" to discuss their sections. Then the students return to their teams and take turns teaching their teammates about their sections. Since the only way students can learn sections other than their own is to listen carefully to their teammates, they are motivated to support and show interest in one another's work.

Slavin (1986) developed a modification of Jigsaw at Johns Hopkins University and then incorporated it in the Student Team Learning program. In this method, called Jigsaw II, students work in four- or five-member teams as in TGT and STAD. Instead of each student being assigned a unique section, all students read a common narrative, such as a book chapter, a short story, or a biography. However, each student receives a topic on which to become an expert. Students with the same topics meet in expert groups to discuss them, after which they return to their teams to teach what they have learned to their teammates. Then students take individual quizzes, which result in team scores based on the improvement score system of STAD. Teams which meet preset standards may earn certificates.

1.3 Learning Together

Researchers at the University of Minnesota developed the Learning Together model of cooperative learning (Johnson and Johnson 1987). The methods they have developed and studied involve students working in four- or five-member heterogeneous groups on assignments. The groups complete a single assignment and receive praise and rewards based on the group product. Their methods emphasize team building activities before students begin working together and regular discussions within groups about how well they are working together.

1.4 Group Investigation

Group Investigation, developed by Shlomo Sharan at the University of Tel-Aviv (Sharan and Sharan 1992), is a general classroom organization plan in which students work in small groups using cooperative inquiry, group discussion, and cooperative planning and projects. In this method, students form their own two- to six-member groups. After choosing subtopics from a unit being studied by the entire class, the groups further break their subtopics into individual tasks and carry out the activities necessary to prepare group reports. Each group then makes a presentation or display to communicate its findings to the entire class.

2. Research on Cooperative Learning

More than 90 high-quality studies have evaluated various cooperative learning approaches over periods of at least four weeks in regular elementary and secondary schools; 96 of these have measured effects on student achievement. These studies all compared effects of cooperative learning to those of traditionally taught control groups on measures of the same objectives pursued in all classes. Teachers and classes were either randomly assigned to cooperative or control conditions, or they were matched on pretest achievement and other factors.

2.1 Academic Achievement

Of the 96 studies of the achievement effects of cooperative learning, 60 (63%) have found significantly greater achievement in cooperative than in control classes; 31 (32%) found no differences; and in five studies did control groups outperform the experimental groups. However, the effects of cooperative learning vary considerably according to the particular methods used.

As noted earlier, two elements must be present if cooperative learning is to be effective: group goals and individual accountability (Slavin 1983a, 1983b, in press). That is, groups must be working to achieve some common goal and the success of the group must depend on the individual learning of every group member. In studies of approaches which include these elements, effects on achievement have been consistently positive; 47 out of 61 such studies (77%) found significantly positive achievement effects. In contrast, only 13 out of 35 studies (37%) lacking group goals and individual accountability found positive effects on student achievement (Slavin in press).

Cooperative learning generally works equally well for all types of students. While occasional studies find particular advantages for high or low achievers, boys or girls, and so on, the great majority find equal benefits for all types of students. Sometimes a concern is expressed that cooperative learning will hold back high achievers. The research provides absolutely no support for this claim; high achievers gain from cooperative learning (relative to high achievers in traditional classes) just as much as do low and average achievers (Slavin in press).

2.2 Intergroup Relations

Social scientists have long advocated interethnic co-operation as a means of ensuring positive intergroup relations in desegregated settings. Contact theory (Allport 1954), the dominant theory of intergroup relations in the United States, predicts that positive intergroup relations will arise from school desegregation if, and only if, students are involved in cooperative, equal-status interaction sanctioned by the school. Research on cooperative learning methods has borne out these predictions. Specifically, students were asked to list their best friends at the beginning of the study and again at the end. The number of friendship choices students made outside their own ethnic groups was the measure of intergroup relations. Positive effects on intergroup relations have been found for STAD, TGT, TAI, Jigsaw, Learning Together, and Group Investigation models (Slavin 1985, in press).

Two of these studies, one on STAD (Slavin 1979) and one on Jigsaw II (Ziegler 1981), included followups of intergroup friendships several months after the end of the studies. Both found that students who had been in cooperative learning classes still named significantly more friends outside their own ethnic groups than did students who had been in control classes. Two studies of Group Investigation (Sharan et al. 1984, Sharan and Shachar 1988) found that students' improved attitudes and behaviors toward classmates of different ethnic backgrounds extended to classmates who had never been in the same groups. Similarly a study of TAI (Oishi 1983) found positive effects of this method on cross-ethnic interactions outside as well as in class.

The United States studies of cooperative learning and intergroup relations involved Black, White, and (in a few cases) Mexican–American students. A study of Jigsaw II by Ziegler (1981) took place in Toronto, where the major ethnic groups were Anglo-Canadians and children of recent European immigrants. The Sharan (Sharan et al. 1984, Sharan and Shachar 1988) studies of Group Investigation took place in Israel and involved friendships between Jews of European and Middle Eastern backgrounds.

2.3 Mainstreaming and Integration

Although ethnicity is a major barrier to friendship, it is not so large as the one between physically or mentally handicapped children and their normal-progress peers. The movement called "mainstreaming" in North America and "integration" in Europe seeks to place as many children as possible in regular classrooms. This movement has created an unprecedented opportunity for handicapped children to take their place in the mainstream of society. It has also created enormous practical problems for classroom teachers, however, and thus often leads to social rejection of handicapped children. Cooperative learning has been used to increase the social acceptance of the mainstreamed student.

The research on cooperative learning and mainstreaming has focused on the academically handicapped child. In one study, STAD was used to attempt to integrate students performing two years or more below the level of their peers into the social structure of the classroom. The use of STAD significantly reduced the degree to which the normal-progress students rejected their mainstreamed classmates, and increased the academic achievement and self-esteem of all students, mainstreamed as well as normal-progress (Madden and Slavin 1983). Other research using cooperative teams has also shown significant improvements in relationships between mainstreamed academically handicapped students and their normal-progress peers (Cooper et al. 1980, Slavin et al. 1984, Slavin in press).

2.4 Self-esteem

Students in cooperative learning classes have been found to have more positive feelings about themselves than do students in traditional classes. These improvements in self-esteem have been found for TGT and STAD (Slavin 1983a), for Jigsaw (Blaney et al. 1977), and for the three programs combined (Slavin and Karweit 1981). Improvements in student self-concepts have also been found for TAI (Slavin et al. 1984).

2.5 Other Outcomes

In addition to effects on achievement, positive intergroup relations, greater acceptance of mainstreamed students, and self-esteem, effects of cooperative learning have been found on a variety of other important educational outcomes. These include liking of school, development of peer norms in favor of doing well academically, feelings of individual control over the student's own fate in school, cooperativeness, and altruism (see Slavin in press). In addition, TGT (DeVries and Slavin 1978) and STAD (Janke 1978) have been found to have positive effects on students' time on-task. Finally, a remarkable study in the Kansas City (Missouri) schools found that lower socioeconomic-status students at risk of becoming delinquent who worked in cooperative groups in sixth grade had better attendance, fewer contacts with the police, and higher behavioral ratings by teachers in seventh through eleventh grades than did control students (Hartley 1976).

3. Conclusion

Research on cooperative learning supports its usefulness for improving such diverse outcomes as student achievement at a variety of grade levels and in many subjects, intergroup relations, relationships between mainstreamed and normal-progress students, and student self-esteem. The widespread and growing use of cooperative learning demonstrates that, in addition to its effectiveness, cooperative learning is practical and attractive to teachers.

References

Allport G 1954 *The Nature of Prejudice*. Addison-Wesley, Cambridge, Massachusetts

Aronson E, Blaney N T, Stephan C, Sikes J, Snapp M (eds.) 1978 *The Jigsaw Classroom*. Sage, Beverly Hills, California

Barnes D, Britton J 1969 *Language, the Learner, and the School*. Penguin, Harmondsworth

Blaney N T, Stephan S, Rosenfeld D, Aronson E, Sikes J 1977 Interdependence in the classroom: A field study. *J. Educ. Psychol.* 69(2): 121–28

Cooper L, Johnson D W, Johnson R, Wilderson F 1980 Effects of cooperative, competitive and individualistic experiences on interpersonal attraction among heterogeneous peers. *J. Soc. Psychol.* 111: 243–52

DeVries D L, Slavin R E 1978 Teams–Games–Tournament (TGT): Review of ten classroom experiments. *J. Res. Dev. Educ.* 12: 28–38

Hartley W 1976 Preventive outcomes of small group education with school children: An epidemiologic follow up of the Kansas City School Behavior Project. Education Report. National Institute of Mental Health, Rockville, Maryland

Janke R 1978 The Teams–Games–Tournament (TGT) method and the behavioral adjustment and academic achievement of emotionally impaired adolescents. Paper presented at the annual convention of the American Educational Research Association, Toronto, April

Johnson D W, Johnson R T 1987 *Learning Together and Alone*, 2nd edn. Prentice-Hall, Englewood Cliffs, New Jersey

Madden N A, Slavin R E 1983 Cooperative learning and social acceptance of mainstream academically handicapped students. *J. Spec. Educ.* 17: 171–82

Oishi S 1983 Effects of team assisted individualization in mathematics on cross-race interactions of elementary school children. Doctoral dissertation, University of Maryland, College Park, Maryland

Sharan S et al. 1984 *Cooperative Learning in the Classroom: Research in Desegregated Schools*. Erlbaum, Hillsdale, New Jersey

Sharan S, Shachar C 1988 *Language and Learning in the Cooperative Classroom*. Springer-Verlag, New York

Sharan Y, Sharan S 1992 *Expanding Cooperative Learning Through Group Investigation*. Teacher's College Press, New York

Slavin R E 1979 Effects of biracial learning teams on cross-racial friendships. *J. Educ. Psychol.* 71(3): 381–87

Slavin R E 1980 Effects of individual learning expectations on student achievement. *J. of Educational Psychology* 72: 520–24

Slavin R E 1983a *Cooperative Learning*. Longman, New York

Slavin R E 1983b When does cooperative learning increase student achievement? *Psych. Bull.* 94(3): 429–45

Slavin R E 1985 Cooperative learning: Applying contact theory in desegregated schools. *J. Soc. Issues* 41(3): 45–62

Slavin R E 1986 *Using Student Team Learning*, 3rd edn. Center for Research on Elementary and Middle Schools, Johns Hopkins University, Baltimore, Maryland

Slavin R E in press *Cooperative Learning: Theory, Research, and Practice*, 2nd edn. Allyn and Bacon, Boston

Slavin R E, Karweit N 1981 Cognitive and affective outcomes of an intensive student team learning-experience. *J. Exp. Educ.* 50:29–35

Slavin R E, Leavey M B, Madden N A 1984 Combining cooperative learning and individualized isntruction: Effects on student mathematics achievement attitudes and behaviors. *Elem. Sch. J.* 84:408–22

Slavin R E, Leavey M B, Madden N A 1986 *Team Accelerated Instruction—Mathematics*. Mastery Education Corporation, Watertown, Massachusetts

Stevens R J, Madden N A, Slavin R E, Farnish A M 1987 Cooperative integrated reading and composition: Two field experiments. *Read. Res. Q.* 22(4): 433–54

Ziegler S 1981 The effectiveness of cooperative learning teams for increasing cross-ethnic friendship: Additional evidence. *Human Organization* 40:264–68

Discovery Learning and Teaching

P. Tamir

"Let him not be taught science; let him discover it" (Rousseau 1773). As can be seen in Rousseau's citation the concept of discovery learning is not new. Discovery learning was a major focus of research and development during the curriculum reform movement of the 1960s. Its central role in this educational reform may be traced to the Woods Hole conference convened by the National Academy of Science in the United States, chaired by Jerome Bruner of Harvard.

The discovery approach, as conceived in Woods Hole, was succinctly summarized in *The Process of Education* (Bruner 1960). Twenty to thirty years later the virtues and limitations of discovery learning are still debated in educational journals (Harris and Taylor 1983, Wellington 1981). Discovery learning has also been mentioned in association with the constructivist approach to learning (Driver 1989). In this entry the nature of discovery learning will be described, various interpretations of the role of the teacher and the student in discovery learning will be examined, findings of selected relevant research will be reported, the relationship between the discovery, inquiry, and constructivist approaches will be explored, and the future of discovery learning and teaching will be considered.

1. The Meanings of Discovery Learning and Teaching

A major problem with the concept of discovery has been its use in different contexts to describe different attributes. With regard to the process of learning it refers to the unique individual experience by which concepts evolve in the mind of the learner rather than being transmitted ready made. "Discovery applies so long as a specific rule or generalization is not mentioned by a teacher. It is usually confined to hierarchically arranged subject matter in which the learner has considerable background. With instructions he has a fairly high probability of deriving by himself correct answers and generalizations" (Wittrock 1966 p. 44). Discovery learning is the opposite of "reception" or "being told" or "being passive" (Shulman and Tamir 1973 p. 1111).

Discovery learning is commonly equated with inductive learning when the subject proceeds from the specific to the general. It is just as plausible, however, to assume that the learner begins with a high-order generalization from which he or she derives more specific conclusions and thus discovers answers and even generalizations (Wittrock 1966 p. 42). "Discovery is something that the student does beyond merely sitting in his seat and paying attention . . . Discovery is a process of search and selection . . . What is sought for and selected varies with the kind of learning that is taking place" (Gagné 1966 pp. 149–50). As far as teaching is concerned "the discovery method of teaching is a frequent description of modes of instruction that are contrasted with other forms of instruction called 'traditional', 'expository', 'guided', 'didactic', 'teacher centered', 'deductive' or 'dogmatic'" (Shulman and Tamir 1973 p. 1111).

2. Presumed Advantages of the Discovery Method

Four major advantages have been attributed by Bruner (1960) and others to the method of discovery:

(a) Discovery learning is more meaningful and hence results in better retention. "To be amenable to learning by discovery what is taught can never be meaningless, useless, or arbitrary. Instead, it must be somehow rational and structured" (Wittrock 1966 p. 29). "Instead of mechanically memorizing isolated bits of information, the student discovers the very principles which connect them" (Tamir and Goldminz 1974 p. 25).

(b) Discovery learning enhances motivation, interest, and satisfaction. Satisfaction is associated with intrinsic motivation which is derived from a drive towards competence.

(c) Discovery learning enhances the development of intellectual capacities, information, and problem-solving skills. Students learn how to discover, how to learn, and how to organize what they have learned.

(d) A generalized heuristics of discovery which has been developed enables the students to solve problems in new contexts, thus increasing transfer of learning.

3. Presumed Disadvantages of Discovery Learning

Discovery learning has not gained easy access in most schools. Several reasons may have accounted for reservations and reluctance on the part of many teachers to adopt it (Harris and Taylor 1983, Wellington 1981). These include:

(a) unfamiliarity and lack of experience on the part of teachers;

(b) time pressure to cover the mandated curriculum;

(c) difficulties encountered by students, especially by slow learners;

(d) failure of teachers to recognize and exercise flexibility in dimensions such as guidance, sequence, and source of direction;

(e) many of the expected benefits from discovery learning do not show up in regular achievement tests;

(f) discovery learning can arouse feelings of uncertainty in both students and teachers, shaking the self-confidence of both;

(g) the image of science often conveyed through students' activities in class is mechanistic, distorted, and false;

(h) the challenge of discovery learning, especially in physics when many concepts, laws, and theories are counterintuitive, may be too high and lead to failure and dissatisfaction.

4. Dimensions of Discovery Learning

In the mid-1960s it was said about discovery learning that there was "precious little substantiated knowledge about the advantages it offers and under what conditions these advantages accrue" (Cronbach 1966 p. 77). Stated somewhat differently, "many claims for learning by discovery are made in educational psychology

Table 1
Levels of openness in the teaching of inquiry

	Problem	Ways/means	Answers
Level 0	given	given	given
Level 1	given	given	open
Level 2	given	open	open
Level 3	open	open	open

but almost none of these claims has been substantiated or even clearly tested in an experiment" (Wittrock 1966 p. 33). In the 1990s there are much more data to support certain positions, even though these positions may remain controversial. Major progress in this respect has become possible as people realize that discovery learning is not an "all or none" phenomenon, and that reception and discovery should be looked upon as opposites on a continuum.

Three dimensions have been frequently used to distinguish discovery from nondiscovery learning, each of which constitutes an independent continuum. These dimensions will be described following Shulman and Tamir (1973 pp. 1111–16).

4.1 Guidance

A useful framework for viewing the question of guidance has been suggested by Schwab (1962). In describing the use of an enquiring laboratory for the teaching of biology, Schwab first distinguishes among three components of the learning situation:(a) problems, (b) ways and means for discovering relations, and (c) answers. As can be seen in Table 1, there are a number of possible ways to permute these components to arrive at different levels of guidance or "openness and permissiveness" in Schwab's terms.

"The manual can pose problems and describe ways and means by which the student can discover relations he does not already know from his books. At a second level, problems are posed by the manual but methods as well as answers are left open. At a third level, problem, as well as answer and method,

are left open: the student is confronted with the raw phenomenon . . ." (Schwab 1962 p. 55).

Herron (as reported by Shulman and Tamir 1973) added the most highly guided dimension where all three levels are given and designated it as Level O, namely, discovery is missing altogether. Herron analyzed the proposed laboratory exercises in the manuals of two secondary science programs, Physical Science Study Curriculum (PSSC) and Biological Science Curriculum Study (BSCS), using the framework proposed by Schwab. He reports that of the 52 PSSC laboratory activities, 39 (nearly 80 percent) are at the zero level of total guidance. Eleven are at Level 1, two at Level 2, and none at Level 3. The data for BSCS are hardly more impressive. The BSCS Blue version laboratory materials show 45 out of 62 laboratory exercises at the zero level, thirteen at Level 1, four at Level 2 and, once again, none at Level 3. Thus, although reading the theoretical literature would surely lead to an anticipation that the new curricula would be filled with discovery teaching, Herron's analysis finds that there is a massive difference between philosophy and practice, despite the claim that the laboratory had changed from a verification-demonstration activity under traditional programs to an inquiry activity under new programs.

4.2 Sequence of Instruction

Although degree of guidance or openness in instruction is the most intuitively sensible meaning for discovery, it is by no means the most widely employed in studies of discovery teaching. Most often the more easily manipulated experimental dimension of "instructional sequence" serves as independent variable. An "inductive sequence," wherein examples or observations precede generalizations, is inevitably dubbed the discovery treatment, while a "deductive sequence," in which generalizations are provided first to be followed by illustrations, is labeled the expository or nondiscovery treatment. The facile manner in which inductive sequencing is identified with discovery reflects a prevalent misunderstanding of how science is conducted. It reflects the pervasive influence of a tradition usually attributed to Bacon and Mill

Table 2
Variations of guidance and sequence in science instruction

	Inductive	Deductive
Guided	Examples of different organisms are given before names of phyla and principles of classifications are given (example-rule sequence).	Names of phyla and principles of classification are given. Subsequently, specific organisms are given as illustrations (rule-example sequence).
Unguided	Examples of organisms are left to students to characterize and then classify. After students have done their own classifications they may be given conventional phyla.	Principles of classification are given. Students are then confronted with an array of organisms which they must classify.

with a little help from generations of science textbook writers who managed to compound the problem by badly misinterpreting Dewey on scientific method. It should be noted that contemporary philosophy and history of science has rejected characterizing science as an objective inductive process. The analyses of scientific thought by Popper, Schwab, Kuhn, Medawar, and others have amply demonstrated the hypothetico-deductive character of modern science. This implicit allegiance to the Baconian inductive myth may reflect how far from current thinking about science are many of those who conduct empirical studies of teaching and learning science.

Table 2 illustrates the interdependence of the guidance and sequence versions of discovery as independent variable. A guided sequence can be inductive or deductive. An inductive presentation can be highly guided or very open. The research on the effects of sequence has not been very productive. One of the reasons for this may be the limited way in which it has been experimentally manipulated. There are at least four different levels at which one can look at the educational consequences of instructional sequence:

(a) the order in which the elements of instruction are presented within a single lesson;

(b) the order in which lessons are sequenced within an instructional unit;

(c) the order in which units are sequenced within an instructional term (may be of several months, half-year, full academic year, or even several years' duration);

(d) the order in which instructional programs are sequenced and/or correlated across a multiyear curriculum.

In the early 1970s, the experimental studies of sequence in science learning, and school learning generally, were almost exclusively of the first type—manipulations of within-lesson sequence. The remaining three levels remained relatively free of empirical trammeling albeit extremely important for educational planning and curriculum development.

Since the 1970s the place of the laboratory in the sequence has received considerable attention. Thus in an inquiry-oriented course the laboratory should lead and take place prior to the theoretical study of the topic in class, or to the presentation of its findings in the textbook (Schwab 1962). Certain particular sequences have been employed and found to be particularly effective. A good example is the "learning cycle," which has been described in detail and its effectiveness confirmed experimentally (Lawson et al. 1989).

4.3 Source and Direction of Classroom Transactions

A different quality often attributed to the inquiring classroom or the discovery method of teaching is the active and initiatory role of the learner. Though this role may be influenced by the degree of guidance, it can be more readily indexed by identifying who initiates and controls the transactions in a learning situation—the teacher or the student.

An example of a student-controlled transaction is the inquiry-training approach to the teaching of science developed by Suchman around 1960. After being shown a brief film clip of an intrinsically anomalous event, the students must conduct the ensuing inquiry through interrogation of the teacher in a format much like "Twenty Questions." This is quite different from what is classically called the "Socratic Method." In Socratic teaching, students are encouraged to formulate principles to account for some phenomenon or to resolve an apparent problem. The teacher then takes control through a series of skillful questions to confront the student with contradictions or internal inconsistencies in the student's position. The teacher usually makes use of a variety of examples, analogies, or metaphors in Socratic teaching. The control of the transaction is clearly in the hands of the teacher.

Ironically, although the control and direction of communications are exactly opposite in the two examples, both are usually classified toward the discovery/inquiry end of the pedagogical continuum. This is probably because both methods employ a great deal of discussion and this characteristic is usually associated with the inquiring classroom. Schwab has always made a great deal of the role of discussion as an instructional technique, both in his earlier "Eros and education" (Schwab 1954) and in his later work on science teaching (Schwab 1962). The lecture, characterized by high levels of guidance (problems, ways and means, and answers all given), typically deductive sequencing, and teacher control of transactions with little or no pupil participation, stands firmly as the epitomization of traditional teaching method. Its diametric opposite would be minimum guidance (problems, methods, and answers all left to student invention or discovery) and undetermined sequences left to student control. Examples of such minimum guidance and a great deal of students' interdependence are the exploration phase in the "learning cycle" (Lawson et al. 1989), the BSCS Second Course *Interaction Between Ideas and Experiments*, and individual research projects carried out by students, usually after school hours.

It should be emphasized that between the two extremes of method just delineated lie an impressive variety of pedagogical procedures. Even though more research on discovery learning is available in the 1990s than in the 1970s, it is still difficult to make sense of the data and apply them in teaching, since few researchers bothered to define their instruction in terms of the dimensions described above. It is hoped that future research will fare better in this respect.

5. Discovery and Inquiry

Learning by discovery is often considered to be identical to learning by inquiry. Indeed there are many similarities between inquiry and discovery, yet they are different. Bruner's conception of the structure of the disciplines implies that any learner, if guided properly, can discover that structure. Schwab's conception of structure is fundamentally different. For Schwab structure such as that of science is not an existing entity to be discovered, but rather a framework imposed by the scientist on the subject matter. Hence, one can talk about inquiry as a property of science or as an instructional method which is similar to discovery. As already observed by Shulman and Tamir (1973 p. 1104) Schwab's distinction between "science as enquiry" and "teaching–learning as enquiry" is an important one. The first defines the substantive focus of the classroom—what is taught and learned. The second refers to the syntax of the classroom and its consequences, the nature of the transactions that will be conducted, the enquiry skills that will be mastered, and the attitudinal "metalessons" that will be learned. In this definition of teaching–learning as enquiry, the activity in which the student participates is not scientific enquiry per se but the critical analysis, interpretation, and evaluation of reports of scientific enquiry. Although this simulates many of the processes in which the scientist engages reflectively during enquiry, it does not require the student to conduct original enquiries in a laboratory.

Schwab (1962) proceeds to contrast the "dogmatic classroom" and the "enquiring classroom" in terms of the ends they seek and the means they employ to achieve those ends. The aim of the enquiring classroom "is not only the clarification and inculcation of a body of knowledge but the encouragement and guidance of a process of discovery on the part of the student" (p. 66). After Schwab (1962) characterizes the full range of activities and purposes of the enquiring classroom, he observes that it is "by no means the only version nor necessarily the most desirable version in all schools for all students. Of the two components—science as enquiry and the activity of enquiring—it is the former which should be given first priority as the objective of science teaching in the secondary school" (p. 71). Criticism and reservations have usually alluded to inquiry as a teaching method, namely discovery learning. The desirability of the conception of "science as inquiry" rather than "rhetoric of conclusions" has reached a high level of consensus among science educators.

6. Discovery and Constructivism

There is now extensive research that shows that "what pupils learn from lesson activities, whether these involve talk, written text, or practical work, depends not only on the nature of the tasks set but on the knowledge schemes that pupils bring to these tasks . . .Learning involves progressive development and restructuring of learners' knowledge schemes" (Driver 1989 p. 84). Since it is assumed that knowledge schemes are constructed by the student, this process of learning has been broadly termed constructivist.

Since knowledge construction is an active process of the learner, the learning process appears to be very similar to discovery learning. However, whereas discovery learning refers to construction done by individual students based on their direct experiences, the constructivist approach realizes that the socially and culturally constructed ideas, principles, theories, and models "cannot all be discovered by individuals through their empirical enquiry . . . Learning involves being initiated into the culture of science . . . Learners need to be given access not only to physical experiences but also to the concepts and models of conventional science" (Driver 1989 p. 85). Thus the construction process involves all kinds of input including discovery and reception inputs, and the role of the teacher is to help pupils process the inputs and construct their knowledge as well as appreciate and apply it.

7. Research Findings

Shulman and Tamir (1973) concluded their review by cautiously stating that "although it has repeatedly been noted that no firm evidence in support of the superiority of discovery learning exists, there are enough suggestive studies and strong advocates, such as Schwab, to maintain the seriousness of the hypothesis that under certain conditions, such as those in which highly transferable problem-solving proficiencies and attitudes toward inquiry in science are the objectives of instruction, those sorts of activities advocated by Bruner or Schwab are more likely to be fruitful than those so strongly supported by Gagné or Ausubel" (p. 1118). The following review of 20 years of subsequent research supports that conclusion. Unfortunately, empirical research carried out since the early 1970s on discovery learning has been scarce. The studies described in the following sections represent a variety of methodologies and were carried out in different countries.

7.1 Meta-analysis

A special issue of the *Journal of Research in Science Teaching* (1983) reports results of several meta-analyses which reflect findings of about 20 years of research. Three of these analyses are relevant to this entry's topic. Shymansky et al. found that the performance of the average student exposed to the discovery-oriented curricula of the 1960s exceeded the performance of 65 percent of the students who studied traditional curricula (pp. 387–404). Wise and Okey found that the average effect size for cognitive achievement was 0.41, whereas the effect size for other outcomes was only 0.15—both in favor of discovery learning (pp. 405–17). Finally, Lott found no difference (effect size 0.06) between inductive or deductive instruction in terms of student achievement.

7.2 Theoretical Analysis and Synthesis of Research Findings

Chi (1991) discusses the relationship between the process of making scientific discoveries and the process of learning science. She notes that the comparisons which are often made between scientific thinking and scientific discovery lead to the metaphor of the lay adult or the child as an intuitive scientist. Since it seems to be impossible to capture the actual process of discovery, she suggests that research should focus on the structure of the mental representation at the time that such discovery was made. Hence research on the first two steps in the discovery process, sensing anomalies and formulating a problem, appear to be more profitable than the common focus on the final steps, formulating and testing the hypotheses. Since the first two steps depend on and stem from a conceptual change, teaching for conceptual change is an essential component of scientific discovery and consequently of learning by discovery as well. "The processes of discovery by medieval students and the processes of learning by naive students must be similar because they both require this radical conceptual shift" (Chi 1991 p. 10). An important implication of this statement for teaching is that "to have students find out themselves would be . . .too difficult for students to undertake" (Chi 1991 p. 14). Instead, it is preferred to teach the correct scientific theory as a prerequisite for discovery. Finally, it is not necessary to "refute students' naive conceptions, since there is evidence that naive and scientific theories can and do co-exist in the minds of expert physicists . . . People are capable of maintaining two separate domains of knowledge analogous to two microworlds" (Chi 1991 p. 2).

7.3 Retrospection

In *The Process of Education*, Bruner (1960) hypothesized the existence of four major advantages to discovery learning (see Sect. 2 above). Tamir and Goldminz (1974) attempted to test these hypotheses empirically by asking science student teachers in Israel to recall from their student days one occasion of learning by discovery and to describe it in as much detail as they could. This description would serve as empirical evidence about the extent of retention. In addition they were requested to indicate their present judgment as to the effect of this learning experience regarding the presumed advantages. The following findings were made:

(a) Retention: 55 percent of the experiences described related to the college level, 45 percent to the high school and 5 percent to the elementary school. In all the cases the subjects described clearly the problem, the technical details, the process of inquiry, and the conclusions. Thus, these data serve as direct evidence for the high rate of retention obtained as a result of discovery learning. Further support for the high level of retention was given by the explicit reference of the subjects to this effect.

(b) Motivation, interest, and satisfaction: most students reported the contribution of discovery learning to be an increase in motivation, curiosity, and interest.

(c) Intellectual capabilities, information, and problem-solving skills: most students mentioned two cognitive outcomes, acquisition of new knowledge and getting insight to new relationships. Very few mentioned either application, correcting misconceptions, or developing reasoning skills.

(d) Heuristic of discovery: few students mentioned learning how to discover.

A replication of the study in a subsequent year supported the previous results and reconfirmed that for close to half of the students the major contribution of discovery learning had been a higher level of understanding and retention.

7.4 Comparative Studies Using Discovery and Non-discovery Instruction

Selim and Shrigley (1983) compared the effectiveness of discovery and expository instruction on science achievement and attitudes of fifth-grade pupils in Egypt. The results indicated that pupils taught by discovery scored higher in science achievement, both recall and application, and had a more positive attitude toward science than their counterparts who were taught by expository instruction. This was equally true for male and female pupils. Discovery learning included the following components: role playing, improvisation, conformity, discrepancy, and satisfaction. In addition to experiencing firsthand the processes of science, the pupils also played the role of inanimate objects or science concepts. For example, seven students wearing different colors of the spectrum were expected to order themselves into the sequence of the rainbow colors. It seems unclear which components of the treatment can be accounted for the results. Perhaps experiential learning in small groups is a better description of the independent variable than discovery learning.

Mulopo and Fowler (1987) compared the outcomes of Grade 11 students in Zambia learning chemistry by discovery and their counterparts taught by a traditional approach. The discovery approach resulted in higher scores of formal reasoners in understanding the nature of science and all the students in attitudes. The traditional approach resulted in higher achievement scores. Overall formal reasoners scored higher than the concrete reasoners.

8. A Look Toward the Future

Several reviews juxtaposing advantages and possible weaknesses of the discovery approach have been published (Harris and Taylor 1983, Wellington 1981). These reviews usually base their criticism of the discovery approach on arguments associated with doubts about the purported similarity between scientific discovery and teaching by discovery. These critics make no attempt to find what happens in science classrooms and how undesirable are the common alternatives which may be characterized as "rhetoric of conclusions." Tamir's observation of many science classes indicates that in spite of their limitations the discovery–inquiry modes of instruction generally bring about better outcomes, both cognitive and affective. There exist various sources which provide circumstantial support to this conclusion. For example, as may be seen in a special issue of *The Gifted Child Today* (1989) many science museums, like that of Ann Arbor, Michigan, "encourage the natural curiosity of young people to explore, participate, and get involved in exhibits, demonstrations and activities." Similarly, "goals of the Children's Museum in Boston are to encourage curiosity, skepticism, and realism while providing opportunities for discoveries and new insights."

It has been posited that the social shift from rural to urban life has created a youth population richer in information than in experience. The implication is that the school has to provide more opportunities to learn from experience. Discovery learning has an important role in this respect. It is not suggested that discovery learning should dominate school learning. However, it is recommended that a substantial portion of learning will employ discovery approaches, provided that the necessary adjustments are made in guidance, sequence, and source of direction.

References

Bruner J S 1960 *The Process of Education*. Harvard University Press, Cambridge, Massachusetts

Chi M T M 1991 Conceptual change within and across ontological categories: Examples from learning and discovery in science. In: Giere R (ed.) 1991 *Cognitive Models of Science—Minnesota Studies in the Philosophy of Science*. University of Minnesota Press, Minneapolis, Minnesota

Cronbach L 1966 The logic of experiments on discovery. In: Shulman L S, Kieslar E R (eds.) 1966 *Learning by Discovery: A Critical Appraisal*. Rand McNally, Chicago, Illinois

Driver R 1989 The construction of scientific knowledge in school classrooms. In: Millar R (ed.) 1989 *Doing Science: Images of Science in Science Education*. Falmer Press, Lewes

Gagné R M 1966 Varieties of learning and the concept of discovery. In: Shulman L S, Kieslar E R (eds.) 1966 *Learning by Discovery: A Critical Appraisal*. Rand McNally, Chicago, Illinois

Gifted Child Today 1989 (special issue)

Harris D, Taylor M 1983 Discovery learning in school science: The myth and the reality. *J. Curric. St.* 15(3): 277–89

Journal of Research in Science Teaching 1983 20(5): 379–509 (special issue)

Lawson A, Renner J, Abraham H 1989 *The Learning Cycle*. NARST Special Publication, No. 1

Mulopo M M, Fowler H S 1987 Effects of traditional and discovery instructional approaches on learning outcomes for learners of different intellectual development: A study of chemistry students in Zambia. *J. Res. Sci. Teach.* 24(3): 217–27

Schwab J J 1954 Eros and education. *Journal of General Education* 8: 54–71

Schwab J J 1962 The teaching of science as enquiry. In: Schwab J J, Brandwein P (eds.) 1962 *The Teaching of Science*. Harvard University Press, Cambridge, Massachusetts

Selim M A, Shrigley R L 1983 The group dynamics approach: A sociopsychological approach for testing the effect of discovery and expository teaching on the science achievement and attitudes of young Egyptian students. *J. Res. Sci. Teach.* 20(3): 213–24

Shulman L S, Tamir P 1973 Research on teaching in the natural sciences. In: Travers R M W (ed.) 1973 *Second Handbook of Research on Teaching*. Rand McNally, Chicago, Illinois

Tamir P, Goldminz E 1974 Discovery learning as viewed in retrospect by the learners. *Journal of College Science Teaching* 1: 23–26

Wellington J J 1981 "What is supposed to happen, Sir?" Some problems with discovery learning. *School Science Review* 63(222): 167–73

Wittrock M C 1966 The learning by discovery hypothesis. In: Shulman L S, Kieslar E R (eds.) 1966 *Learning by Discovery: A Critical Appraisal*. Rand McNally, Chicago, Illinois

Further Reading

Ausubel D P 1968 *Educational Psychology: A Cognitive View*. Holt, Reinhart and Winston, New York

Henson K T 1980 Discovery learning. *Contemporary Education* 51(2): 101–03

Shulman L S, Kieslar E R (eds.) 1966 *Learning by Discovery: A Critical Appraisal*. Rand McNally, Chicago, Illinois

Mastery Learning

T. R. Guskey

Programs based on the ideas of "mastery learning" have excited educators since the early 1970s. In addition, few strategies have been implemented as broadly or evaluated as thoroughly. Mastery learning programs operate in nations around the world at every level of education, from preschool to graduate and professional schools. More importantly, evaluations of these programs show that students in mastery learning classes consistently learn better, reach higher levels of achievement, and develop greater confidence in their ability to learn and in themselves as learners (Guskey and Pigott 1988, Kulik et al. 1990a).

Accompanying the excitement about mastery learning, however, has been confusion and misinterpretation (Guskey 1994). Questions are frequently raised about the essential elements of mastery learning, how those elements are applied, and the extent of change mastery learning requires of teachers interested in implementing the process. This entry will shed light on these and other related issues.

1. The Development of Mastery Learning

Although the basic tenets of mastery learning can be traced to such early educators as Comenius, Pestalozzi, and Herbart (Bloom 1974), most modern applications stem from the writings and research of Benjamin S Bloom of the University of Chicago. In the mid-1960s, Bloom began a series of investigations on how the most powerful aspects of tutoring and individualized instruction might be adapted to improve student learning in group-based classes. He observed that while students learn at different rates, virtually all learn well when provided with the necessary time and appropriate learning conditions. Under these more appropriate conditions, Bloom believed nearly all students could reach the same high level of achievement that usually is attained by only a few, top students under more traditional forms of instruction.

To determine how this result might be practically achieved, Bloom first considered how teaching and learning take place in typical group-based classroom settings. He observed that most teachers begin their teaching by dividing the material they want students to learn into smaller learning units. These units often are sequentially ordered and correspond, in many cases, to chapters in the textbook used in teaching. Following instruction on the unit, a quiz or test is administered to students covering the unit material. To the teacher, this test is an evaluation device, used to determine who learned the material well and who did not. Then, based on the results from this test, students are sorted into categories and assigned grades. To the students, however, this test signifies the end of instruction on the unit and the end of the time they need to spend working on the material. It also represents their one and only chance to demonstrate what they learned. After the test is administered and scored, marks are recorded in the grade book, and instruction begins on the next unit where the process is repeated.

When teaching and learning proceed in this manner, only a small number of students usually learn well and receive the highest marks. Bloom found only about 20 percent of the students in a class generally learn excellently what the teacher set out to teach. Under these conditions, the distribution of achievement among students at the end of the instructional sequence looks much like a normal or bell-shaped curve.

Seeking a strategy that would produce better results, Bloom drew upon two sources of information. The first was knowledge of the ideal teaching and learning situation where an excellent tutor is paired with an individual student. In other words, Bloom tried to determine what critical elements in one-to-one tutoring might be transferred to group-based instructional settings. The second source from which he drew was descriptions of the learning strategies employed by academically successful students. Here Bloom sought to identify the activities of high achieving students in group-based learning environments that distinguish them from their less successful counterparts.

Bloom saw dividing the material to be learned into units and checking on students' learning with a quiz or test at the end of each unit as useful instructional techniques. He believed, however, that the tests used by most teachers did little more than show for whom the initial instruction was or was not appropriate. If, alternatively, these checks on learning were accompanied by a "feedback and corrective" procedure, they could serve as valuable learning tools. That is, instead of using these checks solely as evaluation devices marking the end of each unit, Bloom recommended they be used to diagnose individual learning difficulties (feedback) and to prescribe specific remediation procedures (correctives).

This type of feedback and corrective procedure is precisely what takes place when a student works with an excellent tutor. If the student makes an error, the tutor first points out the error (feedback), and then follows up with further explanation and clarification (corrective). Similarly, academically successful students typically follow up the mistakes they make on quizzes and tests, seeking further information and greater understanding so that their errors are not repeated.

With this in mind, Bloom outlined a specific instructional strategy to make use of this feedback and corrective procedure. He labeled the strategy "Learning for Mastery" (Bloom 1968), and later shortened it to simply "Mastery Learning" (Bloom 1971). In this strategy, the concepts and material students are to learn are first organized into instructional units. For most teachers, a unit is composed of the concepts presented in about a week or two of instructional time. Following initial instruction on the unit, a quiz or assessment is administered to students. Instead of signifying the end of the unit, this assessment is used primarily to give students information, or feedback, on their learning. In fact, to emphasize its new purpose Bloom suggested it be called a "formative assessment," meaning "to inform or provide information." A formative assessment identifies for students precisely what they have learned well to that point, and what they need to learn better.

Also included with the formative assessment are explicit suggestions to students as to what they might do to correct the learning difficulties identified on the assessment. Because these suggested corrective activities are specific to each item or set of prompts within the assessment, students need to work on only those concepts not yet mastered. In other words, the correctives are "individualized." They may point out additional sources of information on a particular topic, such as the page numbers in the course textbook or workbook where the topic is discussed. They may identify alternative learning resources such as different textbooks, alternative materials, learning center activities, or computerized instructional lessons, or they may simply suggest sources of additional practice, such as study guides, independent practice, or guided practice activities. With the feedback and corrective information gained from a formative assessment, each student has a detailed prescription of what more needs to be done to master the concepts or desired learning outcomes from the unit.

When students complete their corrective activities, usually after a class period or two, they are administered a second, parallel formative assessment. There are two major reasons for this second assessment. First, it is necessary to check on the effectiveness of the correctives in helping students overcome their individual learning difficulties. Second, and more important, a second formative assessment offers students a second chance at success. Hence, it serves as a very powerful motivational device.

Through this process of formative assessment, combined with the systematic correction of individual learning difficulties, Bloom believed all students could be provided with a more appropriate quality of instruction than is possible under more traditional approaches to teaching. He recognized that with careful planning, a teacher's initial approach to teaching is likely to be appropriate for many, and perhaps even most, of the students in the class. Because of the individual differences among students, however, that approach is also likely to be inappropriate for some. Corrective procedures make other, hopefully more appropriate, approaches available to those students so that a much larger portion of students learn well and reach high levels of achievement. Bloom believed that by providing students with these more favorable learning conditions, nearly *all* could learn excellently and truly master the subject (Bloom 1971).

2. The Essential Elements of Mastery Learning

Since Bloom first set forth his ideas, much has been written about the theory of mastery learning and its accompanying instructional strategies (e.g., Block and Anderson 1975, Levine et al. 1985). Still, programs labeled "mastery learning" are known to vary greatly from setting to setting (Burns 1987). As a result, educators interested in applying mastery learning often have found it difficult to get a clear and concise description of the essential elements of the process and the specific changes required for successful implementation.

Two elements have been defined as essential to the implementation of mastery learning (Guskey 1987a). Although the actual appearance or format of these elements may vary, they serve a very specific purpose in a mastery learning classroom and most clearly differentiate mastery learning from other instructional approaches. These two essential elements are the "feedback, corrective, and enrichment process"; and "congruence among instructional components."

2.1 Feedback, Correctives, and Enrichment

To use mastery learning, a teacher must offer students regular and specific information on their learning progress. Furthermore, that information must be both diagnostic and prescriptive. That is, the information or "feedback" students regularly receive should: (a) reinforce precisely what was most important to learn in each unit of instruction, (b) recognize what was learned well, and (c) identify to what students need to devote more time. This feedback also must be appropriate for students' level of learning if it is to be effective.

By itself, however, feedback will not help students greatly improve their learning. For significant improvement to occur, the feedback they receive must be paired with specific corrective activities. These "correctives" offer students explicit guidance and direction on how they can correct their learning errors and remedy their learning problems. Most important, the correctives must be different from the initial instruction. Simply having students go back and repeat a process that has already proven unsuccessful is unlikely to yield any better results the second time. Therefore, corrective activities must offer students an instructional alternative. Specifically, they must *present* the material differently and *involve* students differently than did the initial teaching. This means the correctives should incorporate different learning styles or learning modalities. In addition, corrective activities should be effective in improving performance. A new or alternative approach that does not help students overcome their learning difficulties is inappropriate as a corrective and ought to be avoided.

In most group-based applications of mastery learning, correctives are accompanied by "enrichment" or "extension" activities for students who attain mastery from the initial teaching. Enrichment activities provide these students with exciting opportunities to broaden and expand their learning. To be effective these enrichments must be both rewarding and challenging. In general they are related to the subject area being studied, but need not be tied directly to the content of a particular unit. Hence, enrichments offer an excellent means of involving students in challenging, higher level activities such as those designed for gifted and talented students.

This feedback, corrective, and enrichment process can be implemented in a variety of ways. In many mastery learning classes, teachers use short, paper-and-pencil quizzes as formative assessments to give students feedback on their learning progress. However, a formative assessment can be any device teachers use to gain evidence on the learning progress of their students. Thus, essays, compositions, projects, reports, performance tasks, skill demonstrations, and oral presentations can all serve as formative assessments.

Following a formative assessment, some teachers divide the class into separate corrective and enrichment groups. While the teacher directs the activities of students engaged in correctives, enrichment students work on self-selected, independent learning activities that provide opportunities for them to extend and broaden their learning. Other teachers team with colleagues in order to exchange students, so that while one oversees corrective activities the other monitors the enrichment activities. Still other teachers engage students in cooperative learning activities in which corrective and enrichment students work together in teams to ensure all reach the mastery level. If all attain mastery on the second formative assessment, the entire team receives special awards or credit (Guskey 1990a).

Feedback, corrective, and enrichment procedures are crucial to the mastery learning process, for it is through these procedures that mastery learning "individualizes" instruction. In every unit taught, students who need extended time and opportunity to remedy learning problems are offered these through correctives. Furthermore, students who learn quickly and for whom the initial instruction was highly appropriate are provided with an opportunity to extend their learning through enrichments. As a result, all students are provided with favorable learning conditions and more appropriate, higher quality instruction.

2.2 Congruence Among Instructional Components

While feedback, correctives, and enrichment are extremely important, they alone do not constitute mastery learning. To be truly effective, they must be combined with the second essential element of the mastery learning process: congruence among instructional components.

The teaching and learning process generally is perceived as having three major components. To begin one must have some idea of what students are to learn, or the "learning outcomes." This is followed by "instruction" that is intended to result in "competent learners"—students who have learned well and whose competence can be assessed through some form of "evaluation." Mastery learning adds an additional component, the "feedback and corrective" component, that allows teachers to determine for whom the initial instruction was appropriate and for whom an alternative must be planned.

Although essentially neutral with regard to what is taught, how it is taught, and how resultant learning is evaluated, mastery learning does demand there be consistency and alignment among these instructional components. For example, if students are expected to learn higher level skills such as those involved in application or analysis, mastery learning stipulates that instructional activities be planned to give students opportunities to engage actively in those skills. It also requires that students be given specific feedback on their learning of those skills, coupled with directions on how to correct any learning errors. Finally, procedures for evaluating students' learning should reflect those skills as well.

While congruence among instructional components is essential for mastery learning, it is an essential component of effective teaching and learning in general. Suppose, for example, a language arts teacher offered students feedback on their learning through short, multiple-choice quizzes on grammar and punctuation, but then evaluated their learning in terms of the clarity and precision with which they organized ideas in written compositions. In this case, although students received regular feedback, that feedback clearly was not congruent with the procedures used to evaluate their learning. Students may know the rules of grammar and punctuation, but be unable to apply those rules in their writing. Or, they may prepare a composition with perfect grammar and punctuation, but receive a low grade because of inadequate content or poor organization.

In a mastery learning class, the feedback students receive should always be congruent with the specified learning outcomes and the procedures used to evaluate their learning. If students' writing skill, their organization of ideas, and the content of their writing are the criteria by which their learning is to be evaluated, they should receive diagnostic feedback based on those criteria, and prescriptive guidance to correct whatever learning difficulties they may be experiencing.

This element of congruence among instructional components has led some to criticize mastery learning as simply "teaching to the test." The important issue in this regard, however, is what forms the basis for teaching. If a test is the basis of teaching, and if what is taught is determined primarily by that test then, indeed, one is "teaching to the test." Under these conditions, the content and format of the test dictate not only what is taught but also how it is taught. With mastery learning, it is the desired learning outcomes that are the basis of teaching and these, generally, are determined by the teacher. In using mastery learning, teachers simply ensure their instructional activities and the procedures they use to evaluate students' learning match what they have determined to be important for students to learn. Thus, instead of "teaching to the test," mastery learning teachers are more accurately "testing what they teach."

Admittedly, identifying the desired learning outcomes requires teachers to make some crucial decisions. They must decide, for example, what concepts or skills are most important for students to learn and most central to students' understanding of the subject. It is also important, however, for all teachers to recognize that they are already making these decisions. Every time a test is administered, a paper is graded, or any evaluation of learning is made, teachers communicate to their students what they consider to be most important. The use of mastery learning simply compels teachers to confront these decisions more thoughtfully and to make them more intentionally than is often done.

3. Misinterpretations of Mastery Learning

Some early attempts to implement mastery learning were based on very narrow and, in a few instances, inaccurate interpretations of Bloom's ideas. These programs attempted to break learning down into extremely small segments and insisted students "master" each segment before being permitted to move on. Many focused exclusively on lower level cognitive skills and were based on strict adherence to a rigid "scope and sequence" of learning objectives. Teachers were regarded in these programs as little more than managers of materials and record-keepers of student progress.

Unfortunately, similar misinterpretations of mastery learning still exist in the 1990s. The narrowness and rigidity of these early programs were never Bloom's intent, however. Nowhere in his writings can even the suggestion of such be found. Bloom always considered thoughtful and reflective teachers to be essential to the successful implementation of mastery

learning. In fact, in his earliest descriptions of mastery learning, Bloom stressed flexibility in the process:

> There are many alternative strategies for mastery learning. Each strategy must find some way of dealing with individual differences in learners through some means of relating the instruction to the needs and characteristics of the learners . . . . The nongraded school . . . is one attempt to provide an organizational structure that permits and encourages mastery learning. (Bloom 1968 pp. 7–8)

Bloom also emphasized the need to focus instruction in mastery learning classrooms on higher level learning outcomes, not simply basic skills. He noted:

> I find great emphasis on problem solving, applications of principles, analytical skills, and creativity. Such higher mental processes are emphasized because this type of learning enables the individual to relate his or her learning to the many problems he or she encounters in day-to-day living. These abilities are stressed because they are retained and utilized long after the individual has forgotten the detailed specifics of the subject matter taught in the schools. These abilities are regarded as one set of essential characteristics needed to continue learning and to cope with a rapidly changing world. (Bloom 1978 p. 578)

Research studies show that mastery learning is highly effective when instruction focuses on high-level outcomes such as problem-solving, drawing inferences, deductive reasoning, and creative expression (Arredondo and Block 1990, Mevarech 1985, Soled 1987).

Although Bloom considered mastery learning to be neutral with regard to curricular focus and teaching methodology, he believed it could be a powerful supplement to any teacher's instructional procedures. Mastery learning was designed to give teachers a practical and efficient tool better to meet the needs of individual students within the demanding environment of a group-based classroom. As such, it also presents teachers with a means to provide their students with the kinds of experiences educators now recognize as essential to the development of thinking skills and other complex cognitive processes.

4. Implications and Research Results

Several important implications stem from this description of mastery learning. The first is that mastery learning is quite flexible in its application. It is possible, for example, for two teachers to implement mastery learning successfully in identical courses or grade levels using very different approaches. Both would employ the same essential elements of the mastery learning process, but the way they conduct their initial teaching, the type of formative assessments they use, the kind of corrective activities and enrichments in which their students engage, all could be different. In other words, there is no one best way to implement mastery learning. Successful applications depend, to a large extent, on teachers' ability to adapt the essential elements of mastery learning to the particular context in which they teach and the unique characteristics of their students.

A second implication is that mastery learning is broadly applicable. It is apparent to most how mastery learning might be used to teach subjects that are structured and hierarchical, such as mathematics, but the mastery learning process is equally effective when applied to instruction in less structured subjects such as language arts and social studies.

In teaching creative writing, for example, the first thing the teacher must be able to do is describe, in some detail, the differences between a composition that is creative and one that is not; for if these differences cannot be described, what is the teacher to teach? Describing these differences is an essential prerequisite to teaching the higher level skills associated with creative writing. As soon as these differences are described, however, a basis is established for offering students feedback on their writing, as well as guidance in correcting their errors and making revisions, so a composition that is not creative becomes more like one that is.

In a writing class, students' compositions serve as the formative assessments. They are submitted to the teacher and evaluated in terms of criteria the teacher has taught and discussed with students. In some cases, fellow students may offer evaluative feedback, with directions for doing so provided by the teacher. Compositions are then returned to their writers with suggestions for revision based upon the specified criteria. Corrective activities would involve helping students to make their revisions, using different techniques from those employed in the initial teaching. Once completed, revised compositions are submitted to the teacher again as the second formative assessment.

A third implication of the essential elements of mastery learning is that most teachers need not drastically alter what they are doing to use the process. Unlike many new ideas and strategies that are designed to replace teachers' current teaching methods, mastery learning builds upon those techniques. Rather than having to abandon the practices they have developed and refined over the years, mastery learning provides teachers with a means for improving those practices. It empowers teachers to make the best use of the skills they already have. Most excellent teachers are undoubtedly using some form of mastery learning already. Others are likely to find the mastery learning process blends well with many of their present teaching strategies. Given the demanding nature of teaching and the difficulties generally associated with approaches that require major changes or extensive revisions in teaching procedures, this is an exciting prospect.

Finally, although implementing the essential elements of mastery learning does not require drastic change, extensive research evidence shows the use of these elements can have very positive effects on student learning (Guskey and Pigott 1988, Kulik et al. 1990a). Providing feedback, correctives, and enrichments, and ensuring congruence among instructional components can be accomplished by most teachers with relatively little time or effort, especially if tasks are shared among teaching colleagues. Furthermore, evidence gathered in the United States (Walberg 1984), Asia (Kim et al. 1969), Australia (Chan 1981), Europe (Dyke 1988, Langeheine 1992, Mevarech 1985), and South America (Cabezon 1984) shows that the careful and systematic use of these elements can lead to significant improvements in student learning.

Equally important is the fact that the positive effects of mastery learning are not restricted only to measures of student achievement. The process also has been shown to yield improvements in students' school attendance rates, their involvement in class lessons, and their attitudes toward learning (Guskey and Pigott 1988). This multidimensional impact has been referred to as the "multiplier effect" of mastery learning (Guskey et al. 1982), and makes it one of the most cost-effective means of educational improvement in the 1990s.

One review of the research on mastery learning, contrary to all previous reviews, indicated that the process had essentially no effect on student achievement (Slavin 1987). This finding surprised not only scholars familiar with the vast research literature on mastery learning, showing it to yield very positive results, but also large numbers of practitioners who had experienced its positive impact first hand. A close inspection of this review shows, however, that it was conducted using techniques of questionable validity (Hiebert 1987), employed capricious selection criteria (Kulik et al. 1990b), reported results in a biased manner (Walberg 1988), and drew conclusions not substantiated by the evidence presented (Guskey 1987b). Most importantly, two much more extensive and methodologically sound reviews published since (Guskey and Pigott 1988, Kulik et al. 1990a) have verified mastery learning's consistently positive impact on a broad range of student learning outcomes and, in one case (i.e., Kulik et al. 1990b), showed clearly the distorted nature of this earlier report.

5. Conclusion

The future for mastery learning looks particularly bright from the perspective of both educational practitioners and researchers. Although strikingly different from their personal educational experiences, many classroom teachers in the 1990s recognize the value of the essential elements of mastery learning. Increasing numbers are coming to see the importance of using assessments as learning tools, rather than simply as devices to categorize students and assign grades. Many are also offering corrective activities to students who may need a little more time or another instructional approach to learn well. They are providing enrichment activities for fast learners who can benefit from the opportunity to extend and broaden their learning. Many, too, are working hard to ensure their instructional methods, feedback and corrective procedures, and assessment strategies are congruent with the learning outcomes they most value. For these teachers, mastery learning offers the tools they need to have a more powerful influence on the learning of their students. It empowers them to be more effective and, as a result, makes teaching more rewarding and enjoyable (Guskey 1986).

Researchers have also come to recognize the value of the essential elements of mastery learning and the importance of these elements in effective teaching at any level. As a result, fewer studies are being conducted on the mastery learning process per se. Instead, researchers are looking for ways to enhance results further, adding to the mastery learning process additional elements that positively contribute to student learning in hopes of attaining even more impressive gains. Work on the integration of mastery learning with other innovative strategies appears especially promising (Arredondo and Block 1990; Guskey 1990a, 1990b).

Mastery learning is not an educational panacea and will not solve all the complex problems facing educators at the end of the twentieth century. It also does not reach the limits of what is possible in terms of the potential for teaching and learning. Exciting work is continuing on new ideas designed to attain results far more positive than those typically derived through the use of mastery learning (Bloom 1988). Careful attention to the essential elements of mastery learning will, however, allow educators at all levels to make great strides toward the goal of all children learning excellently.

References

Arredondo D E, Block J H 1990 Recognizing the connections between thinking skills and mastery learning. *Educ. Leadership* 47(5): 4–10

Block J H, Anderson L W 1975 *Mastery Learning and Classroom Instruction*. MacMillan, New York

Bloom B S 1968 Learning for mastery. Instruction and Curriculum. *Evaluation Comment* 1(2): 1–12

Bloom B S 1971 Mastery learning. In: Block J H (ed.) 1971 *Mastery Learning: Theory and Practice*. Holt, Rinehart and Winston, New York

Bloom B S 1974 An introduction to mastery learning theory. In: Block J H (ed.) 1974 *Schools, Society and Mastery Learning*. Holt, Rinehart and Winston, New York

Bloom B S 1978 New views of the learner: Implications for instruction and curriculum. *Educ. Leadership* 35(7): 563–76

Bloom B S 1988 Helping all children learn well in elementary school—and beyond. *Principal* 67(4): 12–17

Burns R B 1987 *Models of Instructional Organization: A Casebook on Mastery Learning and Outcome-based Education*. Far West Laboratory for Educational Research and Development, San Francisco, California

Cabezon E 1984 The effects of marked changes in student achievement patterns on the students, their teachers, and their parents: The Chilean case. Doctoral dissertation, University of Chicago, Chicago, Illinois

Chan K S 1981 The interaction of aptitude with mastery versus non-mastery instruction: Effects on reading comprehension of grade three students. Doctoral dissertation, University of Western Australia, Perth

Dyke W E 1988 The immediate effect of a mastery learning program on the belief systems of high school teachers. Paper presented at the annual meeting of the American Educational Research Association, New Orleans, Louisiana

Guskey T R 1986 Staff development and the process of teacher change. *Educ. Researcher* 15(5): 5–12

Guskey T R 1987a The essential elements of mastery learning. *J. Classroom Interaction* 22(2): 19–22

Guskey T R 1987b Rethinking mastery learning reconsidered. *Rev. Educ. Res.* 57(2): 225–29

Guskey T R 1990a Cooperative mastery learning strategies. *Elem. Sch. J.* 91(1): 33–42

Guskey T R 1990b Integrating innovations. *Educ. Leadership* 47(5): 11–15

Guskey T R 1994 Bloom's "Learning for Mastery" revisited: Modern perspectives and misinterpretations. *Outcomes* 13(1): 16–39

Guskey T R, Barshis D, Easton J Q 1982 The multiplier effect: Exploring new directions in community college research. *Community and Junior College Journal* 52(8): 22–25

Guskey T R, Pigott T D 1988 Research on group-based mastery learning programs: A meta-analysis. *J. Educ. Res.* 81(4): 197–216

Heibert E H 1987 The context of instruction and student learning: An examination of Slavin's assumptions. *Rev. Educ. Res.* 57(3): 337–40

Kim H et al. 1969 *A Study of the Bloom Strategies for Mastery Learning*. Korean Institute for Research in the Behavioral Sciences, Seoul

Kulik C C, Kulik J A, Bangert-Downs R L 1990a Effectiveness of mastery learning programs: A meta-analysis. *Rev. Educ. Res.* 60(2): 265–99

Kulik J A, Kulik C C, Bangert-Downs R L 1990b Is there better evidence on mastery learning? A response to Slavin. *Rev. Educ. Res.* 60(2): 303–07

Langeheine R 1992 State mastery learning: Dynamic models for longitudinal data. Paper presented at the annual meeting of the American Educational Research Association, San Francisco, California

Levine D U et al. 1985 *Improving Student Achievement through Mastery Learning Programs*. Jossey-Bass, San Francisco, California

Mevarech Z R 1985 The effects of cooperative mastery learning strategies on mathematical achievement. *J. Educ. Res.* 78(6): 372–77

Slavin R E 1987 Mastery learning reconsidered. *Rev. Educ. Res.* 57(2): 175–213

Soled S W 1987 Teaching processes to improve both higher and lower mental process achievement. Paper presented at the annual meeting of the American Educational Research Association, Washington, DC

Walberg H J 1984 Improving the productivity of America's schools. *Educ. Leadership* 41(8): 19–27

Walberg H J 1988 Response to Slavin: What's the best evidence? *Educ. Leadership* 46(2): 28

Processes and Outcomes of Learning

Architecture of Cognition

J. Elshout

Around 1970 cognitive psychologists of diverse theoretical and methodological backgrounds found themselves in agreement on a global view of the architecture of cognition—what the basic cognitive functions are and how they work together. This agreement on what one pioneer of the field, Herbert Simon, has called the "standard model of cognition" (Simon and Kaplan 1989) has unified, first cognitive psychology, then psychology as a whole. Since the 1970s the mainstream of psychology, from clinical psychology to educational psychology, has been cognitive in its basic stance. Adherence to the standard model of the architecture of cognition is at the core of this orientation. In this entry the standard model will be described. A much more detailed discussion of the architecture of cognition is found in Posner (1989); a textbook by Anderson (1995), is an example of how the standard model can be developed into a detailed, empirically based account of cognition in its many manifestations.

1. The Central Function: Learning and Memory

The central function within cognition is memory. Information that is attended to is recorded as a memory structure. This process is automatic, nonintentional, and effortless. All information attended to has an equal chance of being recorded in the memory store. Learning is not dependent on a decision to learn, but on a decision to pay attention. Evidence for the attention dependent character of learning comes from, among others, studies of "state-dependent memory," where it is shown that a learner picks up, in addition to what he or she wants to learn, information about feelings and mood, bodily state, the lighting of the room, and so on. Not only is such information also recorded, it is connected to the information that was intentionally studied. Information that was purposefully studied is better recalled if the learner is in the same mood, bodily state, and so forth, as at the time of study (Bower et al. 1978).

2. Momentary Strength and Long-term Strength

Memory structures vary in their momentary strength and their long-term strength. The momentary strength of an item of information in memory is also called its level of activation. When a memory structure is active it can be used. Because the total supply of activation is severely limited, at any given moment only a very small number of memory structures can have sufficient momentary strength to be used. The rest lies dormant. When a memory structure is no longer attended to, the activation level of the structure quickly reverts to the level of dormancy.

A memory structure that is active passes on activation to other structures to which it is connected. When such other structures are dormant, such incoming activation may reawaken them, provided it is strong enough and the receiving structures have sufficient long-term strength. A phenomenon that is explained by the notion of activation being passed along associative pathways is semantic priming. A word, presented for a very short moment, stands a better chance of being recognized when preceded by a semantically related word than by an unrelated word. For instance, "nurse" is recognized more easily when it follows "doctor" than when it follows "lawyer." This is because the memory structure corresponding to "nurse," activated by the stimulus, passes along activation to related information, such as "doctor" and "hospital."

The long-term strength of a memory structure increases with use, the increase diminishing as practice proceeds. The loss of accessibility we observe as a result of disuse, or forgetting, also conforms to a negatively accelerated function. The long-term strength of a memory structure determines how easily it can be awakened from dormancy and also how much activation it can pass along itself.

3. Working Memory and Long-term Memory

Information that is attended to is often said to be in short-term memory or in working memory, a repository distinct from long-term memory (Baddeley 1986). It is useful to think of memory structures as varying along a continuum in their state of accessibility. At one end is a structure that is attended to; its accessibility then is at a maximum. At the other end are the structures in a state of dormancy. In between are memory structures that are not attended to now, but that have been attended to some moments ago, and consequently still have many associative ties of sufficient strength to the present situation. Memory structures in this in-between state can be reaccessed without a great deal of searching. The information that is momentarily in focus, together with the information attached to it, that can be readily reaccessed, may be said to be in working memory. It is difficult to obtain precise measurement of how many units of information (also known as "chunks") a person can attend to at the same time. It is certainly less than the famous estimate of "seven plus or minus two" by the pioneer George Miller (1956). Three plus or minus one is a more realistic value (Wickelgren 1976).

4. Mental Operations

Mental operations of thinking (e.g., attending, ordering) are performed acting upon the information in the structures in working memory. Mental operations take attention and a basic feature of a person's mental architecture is that attention is a very limited resource. The speed and the accuracy of the thinking processes depend on the long-term strength of the mental operations involved. Like that of all stored information, the strength of mental operations increases with practice. Greater strength corresponds to more automatic execution, demanding less and less attentional resources. Processes that have to be supervised are called "controlled." Flexible adaptation to the demands of complex and changing situations calls for a high degree of automatization of mental operations, and a high long-term strength of the memory structures involved.

5. The Organization of Information in Memory

In addition to strength and degree of automatization, two other determinants of successful adaptation are the validity of representation and the organization of information in memory. It is clear that if the representation of the situation is incorrect, adaptation will fail (all the more surely the greater the strength of the misconception). Given sufficient validity a major determinant of successful adaptation is the efficiency of the organization of the contents of memory. Efficiency of organization refers to the degree to which good use is made of two fundamental tendencies of cognition. The first is the tendency to associate, to form clusters of information that then tend to be activated as a whole. Pieces of information that

have been in the focus of attention together become associatively connected, so that when at a later moment one part of this new structure is activated, activation also spreads to the dormant part. One part evokes the other parts; the whole evokes the missing parts (Otto Selz called this *Komplexergänzung*). The new associative relation between pieces of information may have content (e.g., "superordinate of") or may be quite arbitrary (pure contiguity). All links, however, help activation to spread. This associative principle underlies several important phenomena of memory. Memory performance improves when information committed to memory is elaborated with additional material. Elaboration provides additional paths to access the new memory structure. Spreaded study or practice leads to better long-term results because the contexts of learning and therefore the elaborations performed will be more diverse. The fact that memory performance is better the more the test situation (both internal and external) resembles the study situation is also explained by this fundamental associative tendency of the memory function.

Effective study anticipates future use of learned material. Effective study is transfer-appropriate processing. The less the learner knows about the future situation (e.g., about the format of the test questions), the more a strategy of rich elaborative processing at the time of study will pay off. The greater the knowledge about future conditions, the more faithfully they should be simulated at the time of study.

The second fundamental tendency of human cognition is to structure information into hierarchically organized schemata. This ubiquitous tendency shows itself in perception, imagery, language production, recall, motor performance, problem-solving, and many other domains (Anderson 1995). Such hierarchical schemata efficiently organize the information about a great number of different instances of some generic concept of an event (e.g., visiting the dentist), object, (a house) or activity (adding numbers). In the top nodes of such a tree-like schematic structure information of a more general kind is stored, each branch and lower branch containing information of greater specificity and detail. This can be illustrated by the notion of a house. A house is an artificial object (top node). A house among other things (branches) provides shelter. One of the ways a house provides shelter is by having a roof (a lower branch), of which there are several types (still lower branches), and so on.

The formation of hierarchical structures is a fundamental tendency. It is important, therefore, to arrange the sequencing of material in such a way that the formation of correct and efficient schematic structures has the competitive edge over other possible structurings. Hierarchical schemata may allow for inferential recall. Recall is inferential when it is based on deduction from a schema rather than on retrieval from memory (e.g., the house I visited probably had a roof, though I did not notice it). Schemata are also highly useful as guides for structured elaboration of information that is to be learned (e.g., studying the layout of a house). Finally, hierarchical and schematic ordering is a major instrument for achieving attentional economy while processing complex new information. Having formed a good schema, a person knows in general terms what to expect and what to look for.

6. Perception

The gateway to reality is perception. Information entering the system through the senses is first registered in sense-specific sensory memories, that can store a great deal of information for a very brief period of time. This brief storage provides the opportunity to analyze a complex pattern into a set of primitive features and to associate the present combination of features to memory ("it is a book"). This is called "pattern recognition." Pattern recognition in principle requires attention, although it can become highly automatized. Learning to recognize patterns also follows the law of practice.

Apart from pattern recognition, an important function of perception is to form and continually update a representation of the spatial relations between objects, and of our own location and movement in the world. Perception is theoretically interesting because it involves the integration of sensory information received here and now (bottom-up processing), with information about the perceptual context and information from our general store of knowledge, including expectations, schemata, and so on (top-down processing). This process of integration is, as yet, only imperfectly understood. Much about perception (e.g., the perception of depth) may be best understood when we think of it as having been shaped by biological evolution to guide our locomotion and other motor activity. Perception and action are closely entwined.

7. Emotion and Motivation

Human cognition is not indifferent. Emotion and motivation are important functions within the architecture of cognition; the occurrence of an emotion is itself a piece of information, that may be remembered and be associated with other information. Humans have concerns (for survival, etc.) and seem automatically to appraise incoming information to discover whether these concerns are touched. If so, a readiness for a certain type of action (e.g., escape) ensues, of which our feelings (e.g., fear) are part (Frijda 1986). The influence of emotion and motivation on cognition (learning, problem-solving) seems to be mostly mediated through the allocation of attention. It has been amply demonstrated that the intention to learn has no influence upon the amount learned. However, observation of an unmotivated learner might appear to refute this conclusion. The simple answer is that everybody, even the unmotivated student, learns constantly and commits to memory what is in the focus of attention. As mentioned above, it is not this automatic recording activity that is selective, but a person's controlled attention. The learner in question has probably divided attention between the lesson and rebellious thought, and will probably partially remember both. However, more complex mental activity will break down under the influence of strong emotion. Presumably, in such cases the feeling itself and the associated thoughts monopolize all attentional resources.

8. The Executive Function

While it is clear that in full-fledged cognition several executive functions have to be performed, such as monitoring the ongoing operations or deciding to stop or continue an activity, it is far from obvious where in the architecture such functions are to be located. One option is to think of them as being concentrated in one subsystem: the "Executive," overseeing the proceedings. There are, however, problems with this option. One is that to behave intelligently such a supervisor should have a high degree of complexity that itself would necessitate an excutive to control it, and so on. This is known as the "homunculus problem." It has been shown that, in order to function properly, supervisory activities have to be trained (Brown 1975). This points to a second architectural option, which is to think of the control of cognition as a function distributed across all the specific memory structures that guide mental activity in actual detail: strategies, plans, and schemata.

See also: Attention and Learning; Cognition and Learning; An Overview of Cognitive Development; Perception and Learning

References

Anderson J R 1995 *Cognitive Psychology and its Implications*, 4th edn. W H Freeman, New York
Baddeley A D 1986 *Working Memory*. Clarendon Press, Oxford
Bower G H, Monteiro K P, Gilligan S G 1978 Emotional mood as a context for learning and recall. *J. of Verbal Learn. Verbal Behav.* 17(5): 573–85
Brown A L 1975 The development of memory: Knowing, knowing about knowing, and knowing how to know. In: Reese H W (ed.) 1975 *Advances in Child Development and Behavior*, Vol. 10. Academic Press, New York
Frijda N H 1986 *The Emotions*. Cambridge University Press, Cambridge
Miller G A 1956 The magical number seven, plus or

minus two: Some limits on our capacity for processing information. *Psychol. Rev.* 163: 81–97

Posner M I 1989 *Foundations of Cognitive Science.* MIT Press, Cambridge, Massachusetts

Simon H A, Kaplan C A 1989 Foundations of cognitive science. In: Posner M I (ed.) 1989 *Foundations of Cognitive Science.* MIT Press, Cambridge, Massachusetts

Wickelgren W A 1976 Memory storage dynamics. In: Estes W K (ed.) 1976 *Handbook of Learning and Cognitive Processes*, Vol. 4. Erlbaum, Hillsdale, New Jersey

Attention and Learning

A. Harnischfeger

"Attention" is a term used daily by teachers:

> Everyone knows what attention is. It is the taking possession by the mind, in clear and vivid form, of one out of what seem several simultaneously possible objects or trains of thought. Focalization, concentration, of consciousness are of its essence. It implies withdrawal from some things in order to deal effectively with others.... (James 1890 pp. 403–04).

1. Background

Psychologists of the nineteenth century were well aware of the importance of attention in choosing and directing perception and learning. Yet for most of the twentieth century, attention was of little interest to the predominant schools of research, Gestalt and behaviorism. Gestalt psychologists, mostly focusing on perception, had no need of a concept like attention, because they assumed isomorphism between the environmental stimuli and their cortical representations. Behaviorists, although quite interested in learning, focused on stimulus–response research with quite simple learning tasks, mainly involving memorization. They disregarded internal psychological processes, as they assumed that behavioral changes occurred as a consequence of learners' relatively passive responses to environmental stimuli. The only active behavior required of the learner for subsequent reinforcement was an overt response.

In contrast, the new field of cognitive science that evolved from neuropsychology and cognitive psychology from the early 1970s onward realized that the learner's internal cognitive activity is of central importance in learning and that learner-selected stimuli are sometimes perceived in ways not intended by the experiment (anticipated by Underwood 1963 as functional versus nominal stimulus). This selection of stimuli is referred to as "attention."

During the late 1980s, the role of motivation in attentional processes was addressed. Even volition, a concept abandoned by motivational psychology in the 1930s, was rediscovered as relevant for focus and intensity of attention (Heckhausen 1988).

2. Conceptual Models

Neurophysiological studies indicate that attentional processes occur in many areas of the brain, but certain areas appear to be of special importance: attended sensory information is processed in the parietal lobe; the hypocampus seems to play a role in short-term attention; and the frontal lobes play a central role in attentionally directed behavior. However, little is known about how complex attentional processes, such as those required in reading, are linked to underlying neural functions (Friedman et al. 1986).

Attention may involve selection of stimuli either entering the sensory system or coming from memory. Conceptual models of attention assume that selection of stimuli occurs either at entry into the sensory system or in a central system of information analysis. Selection is required, because stimuli seek access to the same information-processing structures, creating a bottleneck effect (structural interference model) or because stimuli compete over limited attentional resources (resource-competition model). The prevailing assumption in cognitive science is to conceive of attention as a resource capacity (Kahneman 1973, Posner 1978). It is also assumed that individuals differ in attentional capacity and that attention can be insufficient as a consequence of resource limitation— that is, low attentional capacity or low allocation of capacity to a specific activity, or as a consequence of data-limitation such as insufficient relevant task information.

The powerful role that attention plays as an input and processing selector in short-term or working memory has been emphasized in a model that locates attention in a central executive system controlling the "visuospatial" and the phonological systems (Baddeley 1986). Whether such a central system should be conceived of as a unitary general processor or as multiple subprocessors with distinct capabilities is disputed (Barber 1989). This conception has implications for the number and kinds of tasks that can be attended to simultaneously.

Two components of attention have been identified: (a) involuntary, phasic attention, also called "arousal" or "orienting response" (Sokolov 1990), which is primarily a short-term response to stimuli; and (b) voluntary, tonic attention, which requires greater activity of the attending individual and tends to be of longer duration. Cognitive and instructional psychology are primarily concerned with voluntary attention, especially of a sustained nature, but arousal plays a role in activating sustained attention.

In the late 1980s models of attention were linked with concepts of motivation and ability. For example, Kanfer and Ackerman (1989) defined all individual differences in ability as differences in attentional resources. They identified three ways in which motivation affects attention: thus, motivation (a) directs behavior and controls (b) intensity and (c) persistence of effort. More attentional resources are required for more difficult tasks, and sustained attentional effort is necessary for complex skill acquisition. Motivational and volitional forces support such long-term attentional resource allocation.

3. Measurement

Although the models of attention are specified in psychological terms, neuroscience has aided in defining and measuring attention through recording of electrical brain waves, cerebral blood flow, and heart rate. Psychological measurements of attention have employed observation of individuals and recall by an individual. In classroom settings, observation of learners by the teacher or observers, who rate attentiveness by means of a rating scale, is a widely used procedure. Eye contact is considered a strong indicator of attention. The other widely used procedure is recall of attentional processes by an individual through questions or stimuli intended to facilitate self-observation. Such measures are only gross indicators of attention, with inaccuracies resulting from feigning and lack of sensitivity due to differences in intensity of attention.

4. Empirical Research in Teaching–Learning Settings

Empirical research on attention outside the laboratory, that is, in instructional settings, has focused heavily on the teaching and learning of reading and on children with learning disabilities and attention deficits.

Much research has focused on comparison of sustained voluntary attention and short-term voluntary

and involuntary attention, especially as these vary between normal learners and learning-disabled, mentally retarded, and hyperkinetic learners. No differences in short-term response were found between the groups, but mentally retarded learners and learners with learning disabilities, behavior and hyperkinetic problems were found to have a lower sustained voluntary attention span, generally referred to as "attention deficit" or "distractability." However, these differences in attention were more pronounced in school learning than in nonacademic out-of-school settings. Sustained attention was also found to be task-specific. This points to the importance that motivation and volition play in learning.

Empirical research in reading has indicated that working memory capacity is an important aspect in the development of reading skills. Selecting relevant information seems to be more difficult for younger readers and for poor readers, as was also shown in studies where visual or phonological distractors such as words between the lines were used. Readers with better recall and comprehension seemed to employ more effective "selective attention strategies." Wittrock (1986) reported that text comprehension can be increased by directing the reader's attention with orienting stimuli such as questions inserted into text. Questions inserted before a related text facilitate verbatim learning, indicating that they help focus attention on relevant details. Questions at the end of a text require recall and reprocessing in working memory and tend to direct attention more broadly. Prior statement of learning objectives seems to focus attention on relevant information. Poor readers benefit more from such guidance than good readers.

How much attention a certain task requires or how fast information can be processed is also dependent on individuals' relevant prior knowledge and skills. Task demands and familiarity with the task are important determinants of speed of task completion. With increasing practice tasks require fewer attentional resources. They become increasingly "resource-insensitive." Research on automaticity in cognitive processes also indicates that well-practiced tasks require fewer attentional resources (i.e., less working memory) than new ones, thus making it possible to attend to multiple tasks simultaneously (Beech 1989). Self-regulation of attentional processes, including self-efficacy, was found to be an important aspect of attentional effort and consequently of school achievement (Bandura 1988, Zimmerman and Schunk 1989).

5. Implications of Findings for Teaching and Learning

Varied cognitive teaching strategies that enhance sustained voluntary attention have been developed.

The most commonly employed approach to increasing involuntary attention or arousal is through instructional materials that are appealing to the learner. Illustrations and layout may create interest, and so initiate attention.

A widely used strategy to increase attention, following the behaviorist tradition, is to reward attentional behavior. Many studies of behavior modification report positive results. Other strategies attempt to increase attention through restricting the amount of stimuli presented. Task-irrelevant information and distracting sensory stimuli are minimized. Often this stimulus reduction is combined with a focus on structuring the learning task clearly.

While the above strategies conceive of the learner as passive, cognitive strategies focusing on the learner as active teach self-help in building selective attentional strategies and sustained voluntary attention. The most widely used selective attention strategy is perhaps speed reading. Strategies building sustained voluntary attention use predominantly self-verbalization, often a variation of "stop, look, and listen."

In general, cognitive strategies have been more successful in increasing sustained voluntary attention in classroom settings than approaches that assume a passive learner. Research on active learning, motivation, cognitive strategies for stimuli selection, and self-control has produced effective tools for classroom teaching and learning.

6. Possible Directions for Research

Research on attentional processes has gained importance in cognitive science. Significant advances have been made in model-building and basic research. Research applicable to school learning has not yet absorbed these advances. Although some relevant and potent findings have reached the classroom, attentional processes need to be studied in actual classroom settings on the basis of recent conceptual models of attention. Further, most of applied research has focused on learning-disabled learners. Outside the area of reading, the study of typical learners has hardly advanced beyond observation of time on task and time off task.

Research on attention also needs to be integrated into more broadly defined conceptual models of teaching and learning (Wittrock 1991) and school learning (Harnischfeger and Wiley 1977, 1985). This would allow the study of attention within the framework of important aspects of instruction and the study of heterogeneous groups of learners who differ in ability, prior knowledge, learning style, and motivation. Cognitive psychology has been moving strongly in the direction of reconceptualizing ability and relating it to motivation and working memory processes, assigning attention a central role.

References

Baddeley A 1986 *Working Memory*. Clarendon Press, Oxford

Bandura A 1988 Self-regulation of motivation and action through goal systems. In: Hamilton V, Bower G H, Frijda N H (eds.) 1988 *Cognitive Perspectives on Emotion and Motivation*. Kluwer, Dordrecht

Barber P J 1989 Executing two tasks at once. In: Colley A M, Beech J R (eds.) 1989 *Acquisition and Performance of Cognitive Skills*. Wiley, New York

Beech J R 1989 The componential approach to learning reading skills. In: Colley A M, Beech J R (eds.) 1989 *Acquisition and Performance of Cognitive Skills*. Wiley, New York

Friedman S L, Klivington K A, Peterson R W (eds.) 1986 *The Brain, Cognition, and Education*. Academic Press, San Diego, California

Harnischfeger A, Wiley D E 1977 Kernkonzepte des Schullernens. *Zeitschrift für Entwicklungspsychologie und Pädagogische Psychologie* 9: 207–28 (1978 Conceptual issues in models of school learning. *J. Curric. Studies* 10 (3): 215–31)

Harnischfeger A, Wiley D E 1985 Origins of active learning time. In: Fisher C W, Berliner D C (eds.) 1985 *Perspectives on Instructional Time*. Longman, New York

Heckhausen H 1988 *Motivation und Handeln*. Springer-Verlag, Berlin (1991 *Motivation and Action*. Springer-Verlag, Berlin)

James W 1890 *The Principles of Psychology*, Vol. 1. Dover, New York

Kahneman D 1973 *Attention and Effort*. Prentice-Hall, Englewood Cliffs, New Jersey

Kanfer R, Ackerman P L 1989 Dynamics of skill acquisition: Building a bridge between intelligence and motivation. In: Sternberg R J (ed.) 1989 *Advances in the Psychology of Human Intelligence*. Erlbaum, Hillsdale, New Jersey

Posner M I 1978 *Chronometric Explorations of Mind*. Erlbaum, Hillsdale, New Jersey

Sokolov E N 1990 The orienting response and future directions of its development. *Pavlov J. Biol. Sci.* 25(3): 142–50

Underwood B J 1963 Stimulus selection in verbal learning. In: Cofer C N, Musgrave B S (eds.) 1963 *Verbal Behavior and Learning: Problems and Processes*. McGraw-Hill, New York

Wittrock M C 1986 Education and recent research on attention and knowledge acquisition. In: Friedman S L, Klivington K A, Peterson R W (eds.) 1986 *The Brain, Cognition, and Education*. Academic Press, San Diego, California

Wittrock M C 1991 Generative teaching of comprehension. *Elem. Sch. J.* 92: 169–84

Zimmerman B J, Schunk D H (eds.) 1989 *Self-regulated Learning and Academic Achievement: Theory, Research, and Practice*. Springer-Verlag, New York

Bilingualism

K. Hakuta

Bilingualism has been investigated from the perspectives of language acquisition, cognition, and social psychology. An important additional perspective comes from the sociological circumstances where bilingualism may be found: the learning of the majority language by a minority group (e.g., Turkish immigrants learning Dutch in Amsterdam); the learning of the minority language by the majority group (e.g., anglophone Canadians learning French); and the study of a foreign language (e.g., Japanese students learning English in Japan). This entry addresses understanding of bilingual development, bilingual cognition, individual differences, and language attrition.

1. Development of Bilingualism

The early literature on the language development of bilingual children was dominated by the study of immigrant children in the United States, and was steeped in the question of whether bilingualism was a handicap. In his textbook on child psychology, Thompson summarized the early literature as follows: "there can be no doubt that the child reared in a bilingual environment is handicapped in his language growth. One can debate the issue as to whether speech facility in two languages is worth the consequent retardation in the common language of the realm" (Thompson 1962 p.367). The literature to which he referred stemmed from the psychometric movement of the early part of the century, coupled with empiricist characterizations of language learning, such as those of Watson and Skinner.

More recent theory about the development of bilingualism is found in the literature of second language acquisition, and parallels that of first language acquisition in being deeply influenced by Chomsky's characterization of language as a generative and universal form of human competence. The complexity and abstractness of this characterization has often led to the conclusion that these aspects of language are not learnable, and therefore are innate. Although researchers in bilingualism draw a distinction between whether the two languages are learned simultaneously (such as through family environments in which the two parents speak different languages) or learned successively (such as through exposure to immigration to another country after the first language is established), the assumption is that both types of bilingual development are guided by similar principles of development. Emphasis is placed on the structure, particularl those structures with levels of abstractness significant enough to constitute evidence of innate constraints on learning. Empiricist factors such as frequency and intensity of exposure, or even surface characteristics of the particular languages that coexist within the learner, are viewed as marginally relevant.

Empirical evidence generally supports this view of the importance of abstract characterizations of language. There is broad agreement on major weaknesses in early studies that compared the effects of specific, concrete aspects of the native language on the way in which the second language is learned (e.g., whether it matters that the word-order patterns of the native language are the same as, or different from, that of the target language). Many second language learners of a given language who differ in these characteristics in their native languages nevertheless make similar errors; furthermore, many errors predicted by such comparisons are not found. Current research focuses on the question of whether second language acquisition is guided by more abstract properties of language, known as "universal grammar" (White 1989). This approach is yielding greater promise for understanding ways in which properties of the native language influence the learning of the second language.

A major area of inquiry is whether the process of second language learning is constrained by the age of the learner. This question was provoked by early speculations in the context of arguments for a nativist view of language. The question can further be divided into whether age effects, if any, are describable as quantitative or qualitative in nature. Most of the work has focused on the question of overall quantitative differences, such as on performance tests or judgments on scales by native speakers of the language. The literature was reviewed by Long (1990), who concluded that there were indeed age effects, particularly in pronunciation. However, there are major methodological issues in the conduct of such research, not the least of which is the natural confounding between age of initial exposure and length of exposure that occurs whenever age of observation is held constant. The qualitative question has centered on whether certain aspects of language, particularly those related to the abstract properties of language, become inaccessible for older learners. This question is still unanswered.

Another area of contention is the nature of the relationship of bilingual development with the development of other domains such as general cognition and the social functioning. Paralleling the study of language acquisition from Chomskyan perspectives, and often in conflict, the 1980s saw the revival of the characterization of language as a social act. This conception defined the study of language development as consisting of units larger than the utterance, that is, social interaction. Additionally, movements within cognitive psychology witnessed the rise of general cognitive models, such as connectionist theory and related interpretations of language acquisition. The question then becomes one of the degree to which bilingual development can be viewed as a self-encapsulated phenomenon (which the views of the current second language acquisition literature implies), or as something that must be understood within a broader sociolinguistic framework. As of 1995 the answer to this question is less a matter of data than one of theoretical orientation.

2. *Bilingualism and Cognition*

The question of the relationship between bilingualism and cognition, much like the question of the nature of bilingual development, was raised in the United States in the early part of the twentieth century as a central question in the study of IQ differences between immigrants (who were bilingual) and citizens (who were presumably monolingual). Unless one took a genetic interpretation, this implied that bilingualism affected cognition (Hakuta 1986). This literature, which argued for negative consequences of bilingualism on general mental processes, was discredited on methodological grounds by Peal and Lambert (1962) who found positive effects of bilingualism on factors that they interpreted as "cognitive flexibility" in their Canadian bilingual sample. Their findings have been replicated and extended in a variety of international contexts, with the additional generalization that the effects of fully developed bilingualism is positive while the effects of partial bilingualism is harmful (Cummins 1976). A general weakness in this literature is the absence of sophisticated theories. There are major differences of opinion about the definition of cognition, ranging from information processing to Vygotskyan social interactional models.

Bialystok offers the most promising view of bilingualism from the cognitive perspective through her model of analyzing effects with regard to the parameters of knowledge and cognitive control. These parameters may be varied independently in experimental settings. This analytic scheme can be applied to the more cognitive aspects of language as well as to its communicative aspects (Bialystok 1990). If this model is correct, then the research strategy shifts from one of looking for main effects between domains (i.e., differences between language and cognition) to one of seeking main effects within domains (i.e., differences between processing parameters) and their interactions with domains.

Another large area of research under this heading is the nature of bilingual memory. The key questions are whether the two languages are organized independently or interdependently, and what relationship there is between verbal and visual memory. The literature generally points to support for interdependence, but not without convincing demonstrations of independence. It is also generally difficult to separate out the effects from the specific experimental tasks used and the criteria employed for selecting bilingual subjects.

3. *Individual Differences*

Questions of individual differences arise both in bilingual development and in the nature of bilingual cognition. With respect to bilingual development, the major issues are the roles of aptitude, attitude, motivation, and personality factors. In the area of bilingual cognition, a persistent question is whether there are different organizations of memory as a function of experience.

The main conclusion regarding individual differences in the likelihood of becoming bilingual is that aptitude, attitude, and personality can all play a role, but that their contribution to the total variance depends on the learning situation. Put another way, there is considerable generality of findings that can be made across similar settings. For example, Gardner (1985) has demonstrated robustness in his findings showing relatively strong contributions of attitude and motivation in the learning of French among high school students in English-speaking parts of Canada. However, attitude is usually not a predictor of the learning of a new language by immigrants, presumably because their motivation for learning the new language is very high. In such settings, much of the variance is predicted by aptitude in the native language. The contributions of personality and learning style are quite a bit more tentative, in large measure due to the fragility of the constructs and measures.

The question of different memory organization for different types of bilinguals was first introduced by a linguist, Weinreich (1968). The major distinction he highlighted was between compound and coordinate bilingualism, in which compound bilingualism entails a single concept being associated with the lexical representations in the two languages, whereas coordinate bilingualism entails different concepts for each lexical representation. The difference in organization is theorized to be a function of distinct histories of exposure, such as being exposed to both languages at home (compound) versus being exposed to one language at home and another at school (coordinate). The empirical evidence for this distinction is not promising, despite vigorous effort. The failure of such an obviously appealing idea may be an instance where a reasonable conclusion might be the acceptance of the null hypothesis that such a distinction, appealing as it might be, does not exist.

4. *Language Attrition*

Finally, a relatively new area of investigation is the phenomenon of attrition in either of the two languages. This situation is usually found in the loss of a foreign language (Weltens 1987) or of the native language in the case of immigrants (Extra and Verhoeven 1993). In the case of foreign language attrition, the major contributing factor is the level of proficiency attained. For immigrants, the situation is somewhat more complex because of large variations in sociolinguistic settings, including attitude toward the native language. Most studies of native language attrition in immigrants focus not just on intraindividual language loss, but on loss in the ethnolinguistic community across generations as well. Communities vary a great deal in their approaches toward language maintenance, and seem to provide the greatest source of variance in degree of language loss.

See also: Cognition and Learning

References

Bialystok E 1990 *Communication Strategies: A Psychological Analysis of Second-Language Use.* Blackwell, Oxford

Cummins J 1976 The influence of bilingualism on cognitive growth: A synthesis of research findings and explanatory hypotheses. *Working Papers on Bilingualism 9.* Ontario Institute for Studies in Education (OISE), Toronto

Extra G, Verhoeven L 1993 *Immigrant Languages in Europe.* Multilingual Matters, Clevedon

Gardner R C 1985 *Social Psychology and Second Language Learning: The Role of Attitudes and Motivation.* Edward Arnold, London

Hakuta K 1986 *Mirror of Language: The Debate on Bilingualism.* Basic Books, New York

Long M H 1990 Maturational constraints on language development. *Studies in Second Language Acquisition* 12(3): 251–85

Peal E, Lambert W E 1962 The relation of bilingualism to intelligence. *Psychological Monographs* 76: 1–27 (Whole No. 546)

Thompson G G 1962 *Child Psychology: Growth Trends in Psychological Adjustment,* 2nd edn. Houghton Mifflin, Boston, Massachusetts

Weinreich U 1968 *Languages in Contact: Findings and Problems.* Mouton, The Hague

Weltens B 1987 The attrition of foreign-language skills: A literature review. *Applied Linguistics* 8(1): 22–38

White L 1989 *Universal Grammar and Second Language Acquisition.* Benjamins, Amsterdam

Further Reading

Bialystok E, Hakuta K 1994 *In Other Words: The Science and Psychology of Second-Language Acquisition.* Basic Books, New York

Hamers J F, Blanc M H A 1989 *Bilinguality and Bilingualism.* Cambridge University Press, Cambridge

McLaughlin B 1984 *Second-Language Acquisition in Childhood: Volume 1. Preschool Children,* 2nd edn. Erlbaum, Hillsdale, New Jersey

McLaughlin B 1987 *Theories of Second-Language Learning.* Edward Arnold, London

Romaine S 1995 *Bilingualism,* 2nd edn. Blackwell, Oxford

Cognition and Learning

L. B. Resnick and A. Collins

What does it mean to know something? How do people use what they know? How do they learn it? Answers to these questions—central to a broadly defined field of cognitive research—will deeply influence choices about what is taught, how classrooms and other environments for learning are organized, and what is expected for educational institutions. This entry examines the implications of three major themes in cognitive theory. It begins with constructivism, a point of broad consensus among cognitive researchers with profound and still unresolved implications for what and how to teach. It turns next to recent conceptions of learning and cognitive change, considering especially how learning abilities arise, whether and how they can be taught. Finally, there is a discussion of the idea that thinking may need to be understood not just as an individual act but also as a process that is distributed among people and between people and tools.

1. Constructivist Dilemmas

Students of cognition generally agree on the *constructive* character of learning. The theoretical framing varies—from Piaget (1970) to Vygotsky (1978), from social discourse to schema theory, from symbolic processing to situated cognition—but virtually all concur that learners are the builders of their own knowledge. The implications of the constructivist turn for education are profound. Put most simply, teaching cannot be construed as putting information into students' heads. Rather it must be construed as arranging for students to construct knowledge for themselves.

For many years, particularly under the influence of Piagetian interpretations of cognitive development, constructivism was taken to mean that there should be no "didactic" teaching. Instead it was proposed that educators should arrange rich exploratory environments for children. In such environments, students would discover or invent knowledge for themselves. It is now known that arranging for students to construct their own knowledge is a far more complex matter, filled with challenges that derive from the nature of expertise and learning.

1.1 Thinking and Learning are Knowledge-dependent

Cognitive research has focused heavily on mapping the nature of problem-solving and the knowledge that supports it. From chess-playing to radiology, and in every school curriculum subject that has been researched, it has been discovered that good thinkers and problem-solvers possess large amounts of problem-specific knowledge (Glaser 1984). Experts call on that knowledge (more heavily than on general cognitive capabilities) to produce skilled, efficient performance. Nevertheless, it appears that educators cannot build expertise by having their students memorize experts' knowledge. Such a method of learning appears to produce "inert" knowledge, which is unlikely to be usable in complex performances. Instead, expert knowledge must be constructed by each individual.

But therein lies a dilemma, for what people are able to construct in the way of new knowledge is itself heavily dependent on what they already know. People need organizing schemas in order to understand and retain new information. The richer and more appropriate to the new knowledge these schemas are, the faster and more fully the new ideas will be assimilated. Research in several subject matters shows that students have substantial knowledge when they enter school, but that this knowledge is rarely built upon while they are there. Moreover, informally acquired knowledge is as likely to interfere with school learning (as in the case of scientific "misconceptions") as to enhance it. Recognition of this problem has begun to produce theory-driven experimentation on how to use and adapt to students' knowledge. Such research is necessarily subject-matter specific, and the way in which old and new knowledge interact apparently varies substantially among subjects and even specific concepts.

1.2 Expert Learners are Strategic Knowledge Constructors

Knowledge is undoubtedly more influential for future learning than "general learning skills." Nevertheless, successful learners also apply certain generic strategies more often and more effectively than those who are less successful (e.g., Chi et al. 1989). These strategies have been studied under many labels, all pointing to the importance of self-conscious management of one's own learning and thinking processes (e.g., Brown et al. 1983). A good deal is now known about what these strategies are, but very little about how to teach them effectively. Efforts to teach metacognitive

skills and other deliberate learning strategies directly have been disappointing. The taught skills often do not "stick," are not applied independently by students, or take a brittle form that does not seem to enhance other learning, even when the new strategies themselves are performed to specification. A repeated finding is that strategies directly taught to students tend not to be spontaneously used under conditions different from those in which they were initially practiced.

1.3 Cognitive Equity: The "Rich Get Richer" Problem

Those already rich in knowledge and in school-valued learning strategies are most likely to benefit from the new opportunities for learning offered in school. Their informally acquired knowledge of concepts relevant to school subject matters gives them a head start on the formal curriculum. Their habits of language, questioning, and elaboration allow them to understand what is wanted and to engage easily in what school asks of them. As long as cognitive research focuses mainly on these "already rich" students, it will fail to provide a foundation for educating the diverse student bodies now in many schools.

Although there exists a long history in psychology of attending to *individual* differences in cognition, a new challenge for cognitive research is to attend to *cultural* differences in cognition. Substantial evidence indicates that some students' cultural knowledge and habits differ significantly from those expected at school and that these differences can limit their *de facto* opportunity to learn in school (Laboratory of Comparative Human Cognition 1983). Until now, however, those who have led the most influential cognitive research programs on school subject-matter learning generally have not attended to group and cultural differences in knowledge and learning; whereas those who have concentrated on such differences —coming often from anthropological, linguistic, and sociological rather than psychological research traditions—have not attended deeply to the content of learning or to the details of the cognitive processes involved. The result has been two largely independent bodies of research knowledge.

The two lines of research are now beginning to converge, most often in the context of instructional development programs in which researchers and teachers jointly assume responsibility for entire programs of teaching and learning (e.g., Brown and Campione 1990). One issue is how to develop general learning habits among students who do not bring them to school on their own: Is it by engaging students in metacognitive processes of analyzing school tasks to see where their own knowledge might apply? Is it by changing the classroom environment to provide a better match to students' out-of-school learning habits? Is self-attribution in learning important? How does it interact with specific forms of knowledge and learning strategy?

Another approach has concentrated on identifying the knowledge that apparently underprepared students do have. Some surprises are emerging. For example, research on the entering mathematics knowledge of various groups of poor children has shown they have most of the basic understanding that more favored students have. Furthermore, some instructional experiments suggest that, contrary to older theories in which prerequisites supposedly needed to be firmly in place before more complex problems were posed, it now seems possible to overcome weak preparation by engaging children in intellectually challenging problem-solving while providing supporting "scaffolding" (e.g., Resnick et al. 1992).

1.4 Knowledge Construction is Time-consuming

The personal mental elaboration necessary for successful learning takes time, much more time than is typically allowed for the study of any topic in the school curriculum. This means that efforts to "cover" an extensive body of knowledge are bound to fail to produce significant learning. In response to this understanding, several leading thinkers have been promoting a philosophy of "less is more." Their idea is that learning a few important ideas and concepts well is more educationally powerful than is a curriculum of extensive but superficial exposure. This has begun to engender a research agenda concerned with identifying powerful, generative concepts —the ones to include in the "less" curriculum— and with figuring out how to teach them so that they are, in fact, generative. This research on the generative curriculum is being pursued subject matter by subject matter, most often in collaborative teams that include cognitive researchers and subject matter experts.

2. Learning and Cognitive Change

From about 1960 to the mid-1980s, cognitive research was concerned primarily with the nature of knowledge and skill, and only peripherally with its acquisition. Cognitive science was, in other words, a science more of knowing than of learning. What was learned about the nature of knowing and about the differences between experts and novices has been extremely valuable in helping to map what is to be learned in ways that reflect the complexity of human thought. But that research did not show how people became expert, much less how others could help them do so, which is, of course, the central problem for education. For the most part, efforts to teach difficult concepts with more directness and clarity, or to train students in the metacognitive or problem-solving strategies that characterize expert thinking, have not worked.

Students practiced what they were taught but did not seem to learn when or how to apply the new ideas or skills. On the other hand, in relatively unstructured "discovery" or "exposure" programs, the "rich get richer" phenomenon was encountered repeatedly: that is, initially strong students often prospered, but the weaker ones did not and sometimes even lost ground when compared with students taught in more traditional supervised practice and memorization approaches. None of this is surprising from the constructivist perspective. Nevertheless, it has been disappointing to find that studies on cognitive expertise did not translate directly into successful instruction.

In the second half of the 1980s, the earlier interest of a few cognitive scientists in learning processes began to spread to more of the cognitive research community. The new focus is on learning as cognitive change. There is little orthodoxy in the new cognitive learning research. Various approaches and methodologies are being developed. They range from intensive microgenetic analyses of individuals' conceptual learning to connectionist-inspired research on skill and knowledge change to analyses of biological constraints on conceptual development. Analytic and descriptive methods coexist with classical experiments. Various kinds of formal modeling—rule-based and connectionist—are used. Instructional interventions play a role as a research tool.

2.1 New Conceptions of Transfer

A century or so of research on transfer from school to out-of-school learning, or even between school subject matters, has produced disappointing results. There has not been much evidence that what is learned in one setting is spontaneously or easily "applied" in another. Some studies (e.g., Nisbett et al. 1987) suggest that a reconceptualization of the Thorndikian "common elements" theory of transfer to focus on higher level rules of reasoning, together with direct instruction in how to apply those rules in apparently disparate situations, may produce substantial generalization. An alternative view revives a neglected concept of transfer as a process of learning in specific domains rather than as a direct application of what has already been learned. In these interpretations (e.g., Brown 1990, Greeno et al. 1992, Resnick in press), the search is not for how knowledge or skill is transported "whole" from one setting to another, but for how learning and performance in one setting prepare one to learn the rules, habits, and knowledge appropriate to a new setting.

2.2 Intentional Learning and Habits of Mind

Although direct training of learning strategies has had limited success in actual practice, there is a broader conceptualization of learning strategies that, in early experiments, looks promising. According to this view, learning skill is construed as a set of habits: of questioning, of elaboration, of exerting deliberate personal effort to understand and to communicate to others. In this conception, emphasis on specific learning strategies gives way to a broad emphasis on putting the management of learning in the hands of learners themselves (e.g., Bereiter and Scardamalia 1989). There are several established research traditions that inform this conception: personality theories suggest that self-concepts are at stake; social psychology offers elaborated theories of attribution by which people explain success and failure and thereby direct their future energies; child development tells us how children are socialized into characteristic roles and ways of behaving. The suggestion is that cognitive habits and ways of behaving might be shaped in ways that are analogous to the ways in which other personal traits are developed. This conception is engendering research on how to create environments for learning that will promote the habits of active mental elaboration and self-management associated with effective learning.

3. Distributed Cognition

Cognitive research has begun to move out of the laboratory and toward a concern with more naturalistic learning environments. Cognitive scientists are beginning to study learning in all kinds of situations, from the workplace to sports teams to museums and scouting groups. This research carries forward many elements of older traditions of human factors research, but it is much broader in scope and orientation, including ethnographic, ethnomethodological, and cultural psychology traditions. A theory of cognitive situations is beginning to emerge that takes the *distributed* nature of cognition as a starting point (Brown et al. 1989, Pea 1993, Resnick 1987). In these theories, cognition is assumed to be shared both with other individuals and with tools and artifacts. This means that thinking is situated in a particular context of intentions, social partners, and tools.

3.1 Tools and Artifacts as Partners in Cognitive Activity

Studies of cognitive performance in complex work situations show that thinking is both enabled and constrained by tools and artifacts that share the load with human beings. In navigation, for example, measuring instruments, charts and graphs, and specialized computational tools embody some of the knowledge that is needed for deciding where to steer a ship. These tools extend human intelligence, enabling people to perceive and think in ways they could not manage unassisted. At the same time, the tools constrain thinking, forcing performances that accord with the theories of measurement that are built into the tools. Not only physical tools but also culturally established conventions for reasoning, such as those built into the practice of science and scientific reporting, function both to extend human cognitive capacity and to limit

individuals' likelihood of imagining solutions that fall far outside the norms of a profession.

3.2 Social Partners in Cognition

Cognition also can be socially distributed, that is, shared across several individuals (Levine et al. 1993, Resnick et al. 1991). Two aspects of socially distributed cognition are of great potential significance for instruction and teaching. The first is learning via interaction: the idea that learning is a matter of internalizing processes initially practiced in interaction with others. This formulation is derived from Vygotsky (1978) and from Mead (1967). It suggests that interacting with others—for example, to solve a mathematics problem, to manage a complex piece of machinery, or to read and interpret a text—is the foundation for eventually being able to perform these tasks on one's own. This suggests that a crucial part of the educator's job is carefully to design interactions that promote the internalization of particular strategies, forms of reasoning, and conceptual stances (Rogoff 1990).

The second theme of importance to education is learning to interact. Outside the classroom, most intellectual work is done in direct interaction with others. In these situations—on the job, in civic life, inside families—one's cognitive competence is judged not only by what one knows, but also by how smoothly one uses this knowledge in joint activity with others. Employers increasingly count on schools to develop these cognitive interaction competencies in students. A new community of scholars with diverse backgrounds—in cognitive science, social psychology, linguistics, anthropology, and sociology—is beginning to assemble a body of data and theory on shared discourse and interactive cognition. A feature of this work is the attention paid to cultural variations in discourse and cognition, variations influenced both by the organizations and institutions in which people function and by the personal and familial habits of interaction that individuals bring with them.

See also: Architecture of Cognition; Expert Level of Understanding; Learning Environments; Metacognition; Transfer of Learning; An Overview of Cognitive Development; Cognitive Styles and Learning

References

Bereiter C, Scardamalia M 1989 Intentional learning as a goal of instruction. In: Resnick L B (ed.) 1989 *Knowing, Learning, and Instruction: Essays in Honor of Robert Glaser*. Erlbaum, Hillsdale, New Jersey
Brown A L 1990 Domain-specific principles affect learning and transfer in children. *Cognit. Sci.* 14(1): 107–33
Brown A L, Bransford J D, Ferrara R A, Campione J C 1983 Learning, remembering, and understanding. In: Flavell J H, Markman E M (eds.) 1983 *Mussen's Handbook of Child Psychology*, 4th edn., Vol. 3 . Wiley, New York

Brown A L, Campione J C 1990 Communities of learning and thinking, or a context by any other name. *Contributions to Human Development* 21:108–26

Brown J S, Collins A, Duguid P 1989 Situated cognition and the culture of learning. *Educ. Researcher* 18(1):32–42

Chi M T H, Bassok M, Lewis M W, Reimann P, Glaser R 1989 Self-explanations: How students study and use examples in learning to solve problems. *Cognit. Sci.* 13:(2)145–82

Glaser R 1984 Education and thinking: The role of knowledge. *Am. Psychol.* 39(2): 93–104

Greeno J G, Smith D R, Moore J L 1992 Transfer of situated learning. In: Detterman D, Sternberg R J (eds.) 1992 *Transfer on Trial: Intelligence, Cognition, and Instruction.* Ablex, Norwood, New Jersey

Laboratory of Comparative Human Cognition 1983 Culture and cognitive development. In: Kessen W (ed.) 1983 *Mussen's Handbook of Child Psychology*, 4th edn., Vol. 1. Wiley, New York

Levine J M, Resnick L B, Higgins E T 1993 Social foundations of cognition. *Annu. Rev. Psychol.* 44:585–612

Mead G H 1967 *Mind, Self, and Society from the Standpoint of a Social Behaviorist.* University of Chicago Press, Chicago, Illinois

Nisbett R E, Fong G T, Lehman D R, Cheng P W 1987 Teaching reasoning. *Science* 238: 625–31

Pea R W 1993 Practices of distributed intelligence and designs for education. In: Salomon G (ed.) 1993 *Distributed Cognitions: Psychological and Educational Considerations.* Cambridge University Press, New York

Piaget J 1970 *L'epistemologie genetique.* Presses Universitaires de France, Paris

Resnick L B 1987 The 1987 Presidential Address: Learning in school and out. *Educ. Researcher* 16(9): 13–20

Resnick L B in press Situated rationalism: Biological and social preparation for learning. In: Hirschfeld L, Gelman S (eds.) in press *Cultural Knowledge and Domain Specificity.* Cambridge University Press, Cambridge

Resnick L B, Bill V, Lesgold S 1992 Developing thinking abilities in arithmetic class. In: Demetriou A, Shayer M, Efklides A (eds.) 1992 *Neo-Piagetian Theories of Cognitive Development: Implications and Applications for Education.* Routledge, London

Resnick L B, Levine J M, Teasley S D (eds.) 1991 *Perspectives on Socially Shared Cognition.* American Psychological Association, Washington, DC

Rogoff B 1990 *Apprenticeship in Thinking: Cognitive Development in Social Context.* Oxford University Press, New York

Vygotsky L S 1978 *Mind in Society: The Development of Higher Psychological Processes.* Harvard University Press, Cambridge, Massachusetts

Concept Learning

R. D. Tennyson

Concepts form the basic elements of human knowledge, and the learning of concepts includes the cognitive processes of: (a) acquisition of newly encountered concepts, (b) elaboration of existing concepts, and (c) development of cognitive strategies to employ concepts in previously encountered and unencountered situations. Concepts are defined as classes of instances that represent objects, symbols, or events and can be characterized as either having well-defined dimensions (i.e., constant) or ill-defined dimensions (i.e., variable). Acquisition of concepts occurs by abstracting information from examples and forming prototypes within memory based on a given situational or contextual culture. Employment or application of concepts occurs through the cognitive strategies of generalization and discrimination.

This entry reviews the nature of concept learning and integrates such learning within the context of a cognitive system model. The cognitive system model is presented as a foundation for the design of instruction to improve concept learning. Implications of concept learning for teaching are twofold: first, learners acquire concepts within meaningful contexts associated with their existing knowledge; and, second, the development of the cognitive strategies can be improved by instruction that provides opportunities for learners to contribute to their own construction of the knowledge base.

1. The Nature of Concept Learning

1.1 Nature of Concepts

Concepts can range from one-of-a-kind elements (e.g., the Hope diamond) to a whole set or class of specific objects, symbols, or events. In this latter situation, a concept may have a finite set of members or an infinite set. Regardless of type of class (i.e., finite or infinite), the members are grouped together on the basis of shared characteristics and can usually be referenced by a particular name or symbol. In addition to class membership, concepts can exhibit either well-defined dimensions or ill-defined dimensions. Well-defined concepts have characteristics that are constant within any situation or context and can be transferred across situations without changes in their definitions (e.g., mathematical concepts, physical science concepts, etc.). On the other hand, ill-defined concepts have characteristics that are variable according to given situations and are not easily transferable from one context to another without being embedded within the different situation (e.g., humanities concepts, language concepts, etc.).

For the purposes of understanding concept learning, the three types of concept classes (objects, symbols, and events) are defined as follows: object concepts exist in time and space and can easily be represented by drawings, photographs, models, or the object itself. Many object concepts can be found by merely scanning the pages of a school textbook. Symbol concepts consist of particular kinds of words, numbers, marks, and numerous other items that represent or describe objects, events, or their relationships, either real or imagined. Many of the concepts learned in school are symbol concepts (e.g., in mathematics and science). Event concepts are interactions of objects, either living or inorganic, in a particular period of time (e.g., history and literature). Event concepts are difficult to learn in the abstract because they require the interaction of previously known object concepts. As stated above, each of these three classes can contain concepts that are either constant in definition or variable according to context. The classification of a given concept is then based on the type of class and definitional structure (i.e., well-defined or ill-defined).

1.2 Nature of Instances

The word "instance" is a general term used to refer to both members and nonmembers of a concept class. There are two kinds of instances: examples and nonexamples. An example is an instance which is a member of the concept under consideration. Members of a given concept class are sometimes called by other names, such as exemplar, positive instance, and positive example. A nonexample, on the other hand, is any instance which is not a member of the concept under consideration but is a member of any other concept; it can also be referred to as a negative instance or negative example.

Examples are the primary or initial element of information learned about concepts. In early childhood, all concepts are actually examples of a given concept: each dog that a child sees is an object concept. In memory, the child is storing each example as a separate concept. As the child matures, the separate example-concepts become increasingly associated and start forming abstractions (prototypes) of given concepts. From the initial formation of a concept from a single example, the child learns that specific examples are only instances of a class of objects, symbols, or events. Thus, over time the child forms in memory prototypes that are abstractions from the examples encountered in the environment.

1.3 Classification Behavior

A concept has been learned when a person can correctly identify the class membership of a specific object, symbol, or event. This type of cognition is termed "classification behavior."

Classification behavior occurs when, given a specific object, symbol, or event, the learner can name or point to the general word that refers to a class to which the specific instance belongs; or, when given the general name of the class and shown representations of specific instances of this and other classes, the learner will be able to identify those objects, symbols, or events which are members of the class and those which are not members of the class. Classification behavior does not occur if the learning task is to state a definition or make an association.

There are two cognitive strategies involved in classification behavior: generalization and discrimination. Generalization occurs when a learner exhibits a particular response in one situation which was acquired in a similar situation. All learners have general cognitive strategies to generalize both within and between concept classes. Knowledge which is learned in one situation can usually be tried again in similar situations. It is this transfer process (combined with discrimination) which enables a learner to adapt to new circumstances.

Discrimination occurs when a learner exhibits a particular response in one situation but a different response in another, similar situation. Discrimination allows the learner to make distinctions between very similar situations. Discrimination provides the cognitive strategy for the learner to differentiate between changes in situations, to communicate precisely, and to deal with the complexity of the environment.

2. Cognitive System Model of Learning

An important aspect in understanding the learning of concepts is the way concepts are formed and employed in memory. Because concepts form the basic knowledge elements in memory, this section will describe a cognitive system model of learning that deals with both concept formation and employment. The importance of such an understanding of a cognitive learning system is that prescriptive models of instruction can be developed that take into account internal cognitive processing as well as the usual teaching methods that manipulate the instructional environment.

2.1 Concept Learning Model

The basic components of the cognitive system model include the following processes: sensory receptors, executive control, affective variables, working memory, and long-term memory. The model also indicates two primary sources for concept formation: external and internal. External concepts enter the cognitive system through the standard sensory mechanisms, while internal concepts are constructed by the exchange between the various system components. External classification behavior is exhibited through the output of the executive control component.

This cognitive system model differs from information-processing models because it is a highly dynamic, interactive system that assumes constant integration of the various components. Each of the components is now discussed in a linear fashion although this is not an accurate representation of how the system operates. For the purposes of this entry, direct reference to the psychomotor domain is not included; other sources present that domain in a more explicit manner (see, e.g., Tennyson and Breuer 1984).

2.2 Sensory Receptors

This component includes the various ways in which external information is entered into the cognitive system. Conceptual information is conveyed through the sensory component and is passively registered in sensory buffers in more or less complete analogical form. These sensory registers are sometimes referred to as "primary memory." Information in these registers decay rapidly and are easily interrupted. Attention and perception-driven processes in the executive control component determine which subset of this information is selected for further processing, as far more information is registered than can be processed and acquired.

External stimuli include those aspects of instruction referred to as "delivery systems," such as text materials, visuals, audio/verbal sources, graphics, illustrations, and drawings. Instructional theory is especially influenced by research dealing with the manipulation of the environment to improve concept learning. For example, computer-based technology has had an effect on how concepts can be represented in visual form. Also, techniques for analyzing concepts for the purposes of improving higher cognitive processing contribute to the importance of this component (Tennyson et al. 1992).

2.3 Executive Control

Control of the cognitive system is usually referenced by some form of an executive processor that regulates the various components of the system by either active or automatic means. Although cognitive theories differ on specific functions and their distribution in the complexity of the system, for the purposes of this entry it is convenient to consider three executive functions: perception, attention, and resources.

Conceptual information coming from either external or internal sources passes through the perception function which performs the processes of being aware of, and assessing the potential value of, the external and/or internal information. In this function, the perception component services the cognitive system for the purposes both of directing attention and of determining effort. The attention function maintains an active interaction with the processes associated with the working memory component. Resources assist in the coordination of the various components of the entire system. Evaluation of effort associated with a given concept learning situation is important in this function. For example, in most situations, there is an abundance of resources available, so determination is made on allocation of necessary resources.

2.4 Working Memory

There is considerable debate as to the divisions or architecture of memory, but in a broad sense, the exact details are not important as regards the instructional implications of the theories (Shuell 1990). In general, there is agreement that memory comes in two forms, a store for previously learned concepts and a store for concepts which are currently being processed. This latter form, working memory, is defined with these salient aspects:

(a) It is limited in capacity.

(b) Concepts in working memory are subject to manipulations such as rehearsal, comparison, or matching and reordering by the processes that operate in working memory.

(c) Concepts are selected for inclusion in working memory either by some consciously active process or by automatic action of well-developed processes in such activities as reading, processing of verbal discourse, and imagery-evoking processes.

The exact processes which operate in working memory vary from theory to theory, but there are a set of processes which most theories have in common. These include the following four processes:

(a) encoding processes which, in concert with the executive control component, deposit incoming concepts into working memory for purposes of employment;

(b) storage processes which interact with long-term memory to create permanent prototypes and increase the strength of existing prototypes;

(c) retrieval processes to obtain necessary existing knowledge (i.e., prototypes, skills, and strategies) from long-term memory;

(d) maintenance processes that keep concepts in working memory so that they are not lost before they are stored in long-term memory.

2.5 Long-term Memory

Long-term memory is the repository for all previously acquired concepts and other information. In contrast to the limited capacity of working memory because of its role of dealing with immediate concerns of concept processing, long-term memory focuses on the nature of knowledge representation in terms of concepts, skills, and strategies. There is agreement among researchers in the field that long-term memory has no capacity limits and that knowledge is considered permanent, although it may become difficult to retrieve.

Within long-term memory there are various types of conceptual knowledge: declarative, procedural, and contextual (Tennyson and Rasch 1988). Declarative knowledge implies an awareness of knowledge and refers to "knowing that," for example, understanding that the concept of underlining keywords in a text will help recall. Procedural knowledge implies a "knowing how" to use given concepts. Contextual knowledge implies an understanding of "knowing why, when, and where" to employ specific concepts. This knowing of why, when, and where, is governed by selection criteria embedded within the organization of the knowledge base. Selection criteria are integrated within the knowledge base because of the interaction with the affective variables component during the learning process. The term "contextual" implies direct association with cognitive skills, which are defined below as domain-dependent cognitive strategies.

The value of conceptual knowledge is its employment in the classification behaviors of generalization and discrimination. The cognitive strategies of generalization and discrimination can be distinguished as either domain-dependent or domain-independent. The concept of cognitive skill describes a specific application of a cognitive strategy within a given situation (or context) whereas cognitive strategy implies domain-free abilities. The cognitive strategies of generalization and discrimination include three primary cognitive abilities (although skills are further refined to specific situations and embedded in contextual knowledge): differentiation, integration, and construction. Differentiation is defined as the twofold ability to understand a given situation and to apply appropriate contextual criteria (i.e., the standards, situational appropriateness, and/or values) by which specific concepts can be selectively retrieved from storage. Integration is the ability to elaborate or restructure existing concepts and/or conceptual networks in the service of previously unencountered problem situations. Construction is the ability to both discover and create new concepts in novel or unique situations.

2.6 Affective Variables

Just as cognitive theories differ in details but have many common features, the same is true of the affective variables component. Given the complexity of the affective domain, and the space limitations of this entry, only some of the more identifiable affective variables that may have implications for concept learning will be addressed. Also, because of their interactive nature and variability, the various types of affect are described without reference to the hierarchy or value of each.

The list includes such variables as motivation, feelings, attitudes, emotions, anxiety, and values. The immediate interaction of this component within the cognitive system is with the executive control component which interfaces with the working memory. For example, motivation influences both attention and maintenance processes. On the other hand, values and feelings would influence the criteria associated with acquisition of contextual knowledge. Anxiety as an affect variable influences both the acquisition and employment processes (e.g., test anxiety may interfere with both generalization and discrimination). Together with emotions, anxiety can be a serious interfering variable in concept learning.

3. Conclusion

Concept learning includes both acquisition of concepts and employment through the classification behaviors of generalization and discrimination. Because of the central dominance of concepts in the content of a knowledge base, and given the complexity of the cognitive system, instructional strategies for concept learning should expand beyond the standard format of definition, example, and practice. Additional instructional variables would improve the organization of new concepts by presentation within a meaningful context. Thus, concepts could be more readily connected with existing networks and prototypes. Second, acquisition of contextual knowledge would be improved by instruction that requires the learner to solve complex problems that would employ knowledge of why, when, and where. Too often learners fail to receive instruction that goes beyond the simple per concept declarative and procedural knowledge.

Additionally, the presented cognitive system model emphasizes the role of cognitive strategies as an integral condition in concept learning. These cognitive strategies can be improved by instruction that provides an environment for learners to engage in dynamic and complex problem situations. The purpose of such instruction is twofold. First, learners will further develop the cognitive abilities of differentiation, integration, and construction. Second, learners will expand and elaborate their knowledge base (i.e., declarative, procedural, and contextual knowledge).

This entry has presented a model of concept learning that describes both the internal processes of learning and the external. The purpose is to establish the construct that learning is more than mere reaction to reinforced responses: that is, learners have the cognitive capability to participate in the constructing of their own knowledge base. Learning occurs in part through the development of internal cognitive strategies and abilities as well as through the manipulation of the environment. Another entry in this *Encyclopedia* describes the variables and conditions that are needed to design a learning environment which would improve the acquisition and employment of concepts (see *Concept Learning: Teaching and Assessing*).

See also: Architecture of Cognition; Attention and Learning; Concept Learning: Teaching and Assessing; Declarative and Procedural Knowledge; Learning Processes and Learning Outcomes; Perception and Learning; Perconceptions and Misconceptions

References

Shuell T J 1990 Phases of meaningful learning. *Rev. Educ. Res.* 60(4): 531–47
Tennyson R D, Breuer K 1984 Cognitive-based design guidelines for using video and computer technology in course development. In: Zuber-Skerritt O (ed.) 1984 *Video in Higher Education.* Kogan Page, London
Tennyson R D, Elmore R, Snyder L 1992 Advancements in instructional design theory: Contextual module analysis and integrated instructional strategies. *Educ. Tech. Res. Dev.* 40(2): 9–22

Tennyson R D, Rasch M 1988 Linking cognitive learning theory to instructional prescriptions. *Instr. Sci.* 17(4): 369–85

Further Reading

Bransford J D, Sherwood R, Vye N, Rieser J 1986 Teaching thinking and problem solving. *Am. Psychol.* 41: 1078–89
Clark R E 1989 Current progress and future directions for research in instructional technology. *Educ. Tech. Res. Dev.* 37(1): 57–66
Fleming M L 1987 Displays and communication. In: Gagné R (ed.) 1987 *Instructional Technology: Foundations.* Erlbaum, Hillsdale, New Jersey
Merrill M D, Tennyson R D, Posey L 1992 *Teaching Concepts: An Instructional Design Guide,* 2nd edn. Educational Technology, Englewood Cliffs, New Jersey
Tennyson R D, Cocchiarella M J 1986 An empirically based instructional design theory for teaching concepts. *Rev. Educ. Res.* 56(1): 40–71
Tennyson R D, Park O 1980 The teaching of concepts: A review of instructional design research literature. *Rev. Educ. Res.* 50(1): 55–70
Winn W D 1989 Towards a rationale and theoretical basis for educational technology. *Educ. Tech. Res. Dev.* 37(1): 35–46

Concept Learning: Teaching and Assessing

R. D. Tennyson

Concepts represent the fundamental elements of all content areas. In formal content situations, concepts are classes of objects, symbols, and events that are grouped together in some fashion by shared characteristics. An important purpose of education is to provide a learning environment in which students can both readily learn new concepts and improve the use of acquired concepts. The purpose of this entry is to present the instructional design guidelines for the preparation of instruction to improve concept learning and employment.

1. Overview of Design Guidelines

The learning of concepts involves three basic cognitive behaviors: (a) understanding the characteristics of a given concept and the association of that concept within a content area; (b) applying a given concept; and (c) knowing when, where, and why to employ a given concept. These cognitive behaviors are best learned when acquired within meaningful contexts. That is, teaching of concepts is more than a mere presentation of information. Where possible, the instruction should draw upon students' exist-

ing knowledge to put the concepts into a context that has meaning and employment potential. For example, historical (i.e., event) concepts are meaningful when viewed within the context or culture of the current environment. When designing concept lessons, the rule of thumb is to include learning objectives that integrate behaviors of content acquisition with improving and extending cognitive strategies for employment (e.g., recall, problem-solving, creativity).

Like the learning of concepts, instructional design as it applies to concepts involves three main activities: (a) the identification of the goals and objectives of the learning environment; (b) the analysis and sequence of the concepts to be learned; and (c) the development of the instruction, which includes selecting the appropriate instructional strategies and means of delivery (e.g., lecture, print materials, electronic). Given the scope of this entry, the design process of selecting the delivery system will not be addressed.

2. Preparing Goals and Objectives

Goals are broad statements that reflect the overall educational outcomes usually associated with a curricular

Table 1
The Instructional Design (ID) model[a]

Model components	Educational goals				
	Acquisition of knowledge			Employment of knowledge	
Memory systems	Declarative knowledge	Procedural knowledge	Contextual knowledge	Cognitive complexity	Cognitive constructivism
Learning objectives	Verbal information	Intellectual skills	Contextual skills	Cognitive strategies	Creative processes
Instructional times	10%	20%	25%	30%	15%
Instructional prescriptions	Expository strategies	Practice strategies	Problem-oriented strategies	Complex-dynamic strategies	Self-directed experiences

a Tennyson 1992

area. Goals can be classified as either statements dealing with acquisition of concepts or the improvement in cognitive strategies for employment of concepts. From these two broad categories, objectives can be directly referenced that specify the type of behavior to be learned and improved. Because behaviors vary according to the complexity of outcomes, objectives are usually labeled to reflect the type of behavior desired. The labeling scheme selected for this entry is influenced by contemporary educational goals associated with improving higher-order cognitive skills and strategies. By directly linking the goals and objectives of the learning environment, it is also possible directly to link the objectives to instructional prescriptions.

In Table 1, an instructional design (ID) model is presented that shows the direct integration of cognitive learning theory with prescribed instructional strategies. In addition to the direct linkages between the various memory systems and instructional strategies, the model includes direct reference to formal classroom instructional time. The times presented in the model focus on goals dealing with acquiring and employing knowledge. The suggested times should be manipulated by the individual curricular situation based upon focus of the goals. The major components of the ID model are: memory systems, learning objectives, instructional time, and instructional prescriptions.

2.1 Memory Systems

The proposed ID model is directly associated with cognitive theories of learning. Because the goals of the ID model include both the acquisition and the employment of knowledge, the memory systems reference the long-term memory subsystems of storage and retrieval. The storage system is composed of three basic forms of knowledge:

(a) declarative knowledge, knowing *that* about the information;

(b) procedural knowledge, knowing *how* to use information; and,

(c) contextual knowledge, knowing *when, where,* and *why* to use given concepts and associated cognitive skills.

The retrieval system is composed of cognitive strategies associated with the processes of recall, problem-solving, and creativity.

2.2 Learning Objectives

The purpose of learning objectives is to elaborate further the curricular goals of knowledge acquisition and employment. Objectives are important in the planning of concept teaching because they provide the means of both allocating instructional time and identifying specific instructional strategies. Five learning objectives can be identified: verbal information, intellectual skills, contextual skills, cognitive strategies, and creative processes.

Verbal information deals with the learner acquiring an awareness and understanding of the concepts within a specified domain of information (i.e., declarative knowledge).

Intellectual skills involve the learner acquiring the skill to use correctly the concepts of a specified domain of information (i.e., procedural knowledge).

Contextual skills focus on the learner's acquisition of a knowledge base's organization and accessibility (i.e., contextual knowledge). The organization of a knowledge base refers to the modular structure of the information, whereas the accessibility refers to the complex cognitive skills that provide the means necessary to employ the knowledge base in the service of recall, problem-solving, and creativity. Contextual knowledge includes the criteria, values, feelings, and appropriateness of a given content domain's modular structure. For example, simply knowing how to classify examples or knowing how to use a concept does not imply that the learner knows when, where, and why to employ specific concepts.

Cognitive strategies deal with both the improvement and development of cognitive strategies and the extension of such strategies to domain-specific cognitive skills. Thus, this learning objective deals with two important issues in education. The first is the elaboration of cognitive strategies that will arm the students with increased domain-specific contextual knowledge (i.e., cognitive skills). The second is the development of the cognitive abilities of differentiation and integration. These abilities provide the cognitive tools to employ and improve the knowledge base effectively; therefore, they are integral to any educational goals seeking to improve higher-order cognition.

Creative processes deal with the most elusive goal of education: the development and improvement of creative abilities. Creativity is a twofold ability: (a) constructing knowledge to solve a problem from the external environment, and (b) constructing the problem as well as the knowledge to solve the problem. Integral to the construction of both the problem and knowledge are the criteria by which consistent judgment can be made. There are two sets of criteria. The first consists of criteria that are known and which can be applied with a high level of consistency. In contrast are those criteria that are developed concurrently with the problem and/or knowledge, and are consistently applied across a high level of productivity. Students should be informed of the criteria in the former and, in the latter, of the necessity to develop criteria.

2.3 Instructional Time

A key factor in implementing the cognitive goals of knowledge acquisition and employment is the allocation of learning time to defined objectives. For example, Tennyson and Rasch (1988) suggest that if improvements in problem-solving and creativity are to occur, there needs to be a significant change in how instructional time is allocated. They recommend that the conventional instructional time allocation for learning be altered so that, instead of 70 percent of instruction being aimed at the declarative and procedural knowledge levels of learning, 70 percent should be devoted to learning situations that involve acquisition of contextual knowledge and development of cognitive strategies.

Using Tennyson and Rasch's recommended figures on instructional time allocation, learning time can be divided into the two main subsystems of long-term memory: storage and retrieval. Within the guidelines illustrated in Table 1, time is assigned according to the cognitive objectives defined in the section

above. In the storage system, learning time is allocated among the three memory systems making up a knowledge base as follows: declarative knowledge 10 percent, procedure knowledge 20 percent, and contextual knowledge 25 percent.

Contextual knowledge learning time should be about equal to the other two knowledge forms because of the necessity to both organize a knowledge base and develop accessibility to it once organized. The value of a knowledge base is primarily in the functionality of its organization and accessibility. Without a sufficient base of contextual knowledge, the opportunity for employment, future elaborations, and extension of the knowledge base is severely limited.

For knowledge acquisition goals, the focus of learning time allocation is on contextual knowledge, and away from the usual practice of heavy emphasis on amount of information. Declarative and procedural knowledge acquisition is believed to be an interactive process that is improved when employing the knowledge base in the service of higher-order thinking situations (i.e., those involving problem-solving and creativity). Time allocated for declarative and procedural knowledge focuses on establishing an initial base of necessary conceptual knowledge that can be used within a context of a problem situation. That is, learning time should include the opportunity for the learner to gain experience in employing the learned concepts.

The learning times presented in Table 1 do not imply a linear sequence of knowledge acquisition going from declarative to contextual. Rather, they represent total amounts in an iterative learning environment where learners are continuously acquiring each form of knowledge. For example, students may engage in contextual knowledge acquisition prior to declarative knowledge acquisition if they currently have sufficient background knowledge (i.e., a discovery method of instruction as contrasted to a structured method) (see *Discovery Learning and Teaching*).

3. Concept Analysis

An important component of instructional design is the analysis of the concepts to be learned. There are two basic types of analysis: (a) a content (task) analysis that focuses on defining the critical characteristics of the concepts and the relationship of those characteristics according to superordinate and subordinate organizations; and (b) a contextual analysis that focuses on the memory or knowledge base organization of the concepts. The first analytic method identifies the external structure of the concepts (either a taxonomy or hierarchy) but does so independently of how it might actually be stored in human memory. However, research in cognitive psychology on human memory suggests that the internal organization of concepts in a knowledge base is based more on employment needs than by attribute characteristics or taxonomic/hierarchical connections (Fodor 1983). That is, the utility of the knowledge base is attributed to its situational organization, not necessarily the amount of information. The implication of knowledge base organization is the need for a contextual analysis of the concepts better to understand their possible internal organization (Garner 1990). Better organization in memory may also imply better accessibility within the knowledge base for such higher order cognitive activities as problem-solving and creativity (Harré 1984).

To understand the nature of knowledge base organization, cognitive psychologists analyze problem complexity and the way individuals try to solve given problems (Klahr et al. 1987). By analyzing problems, it is possible to identify the concepts employed; and, by analyzing the solutions, it is possible to identify the associations of those concepts within given problem situations. The implication for concept teaching is that the sequence of concepts for instruction should be based in part on internal situational associations as well as external structures (Bereiter 1990). The assumption is that because external structures are independent of employment needs, an analysis of possible internal associations would improve the initial organization of the new concepts, resulting in better employment.

A second analytical method, contextual analysis, is proposed when the goals of the curriculum include employment and improvement of cognitive skills and strategies, such as problem-solving, decision-making, and trouble-shooting. Contextual analysis includes five basic steps:

(a) Define the context for the employment of the concepts to be learned. A context is a meaningful application of the concepts. For example, a simulation, a game, a role-playing situation, or a case study provides an instructional vehicle for presenting a meaningful context.

(b) Define the complex problems (problems requiring more than one concept for solution) associated with the context. This step follows a knowledge engineering approach where problems associated with a given context are identified.

(c) For each problem, identify concepts employed for the solution or decision-making.

(d) Identify possible clusters of concepts employed in the solution of the various problems. That is, within a context certain concepts may be employed for a certain set of problems while other concepts may be employed in other sets.

(e) Sequence the clusters according to increasing complexity. For example, the first cluster may involve only two concepts while more complex clusters may have additional concepts. Analyzing problems within a context and then identifying

the concepts and their employment organization (i.e., cluster) provides a means for sequencing the instruction to improve higher order cognition. In other words, the sequence of the instruction is based on the objective of improving employment of knowledge in addition to improvement in acquisition.

4. Instructional Prescriptions

This section describes instructional strategies found through empirical research to improve concept learning. Selection of the various strategies is based upon the learning objectives and the prerequisite knowledge of the students. For students with minimal prerequisite knowledge, an instructional program would probably utilize all of the strategies to insure adequate declarative and procedural knowledge. However, for students with a good knowledge base within the targeted curriculum area, an instructional program would emphasize more of the discovery type of instruction.

4.1 Expository Strategies

The category of expository strategies represents those instructional variables designed to provide an environment for learning of declarative knowledge (see Table 1). The basic instructional variables provide a context for the concepts to be learned. That is, advance organizers are used to provide a meaningful context for the concepts as well as a mental framework of the given domain's abstract structure. In addition to providing a context for the information, meaning can be further enhanced by adapting the context to individual student background knowledge.

The context establishes not only the initial organization of the domain, but also introduces both the "why" of the theoretical nature of the concepts and the "when and where" of the criterion nature of the domain's standards, values, and appropriateness (Bereiter and Scardamalia 1989). Personalizing the context to student background knowledge improves understanding of the information by connecting, within working memory, knowledge that is easily retrieved. Thus, the new knowledge becomes directly connected or associated with existing knowledge.

Following the contextual introduction of the concepts, five additional expository instructional variables are used to present the concepts in forms that extend existing knowledge and that aid in establishing new knowledge. These are as follows:

(a) *Label*. Although a simple variable, it is often necessary to elaborate on a label's origin so that the student is not just trying to memorize a nonsense word.

(b) *Definition*. The purpose of a definition is to connect the new concepts with existing knowledge in long-term memory; otherwise the definition may convey no meaning. That is, the student should already know the critical attributes of the concept. To improve understanding of the new concepts further, definitions may, in addition to presentation of the critical attributes (i.e., prerequisite knowledge), include information linked to the student's background or personal knowledge.

(c) *Best example*. To help students establish initial prototypes or abstractions of a domain's concepts, expository examples that are clear representations should be provided first.

(d) *Expository examples*. Additional examples should provide increasingly divergent representations of the concepts, perhaps also in alternative contexts.

(e) *Worked examples*. This variable provides an expository environment in which the examples are presented to the student in statement forms that elaborate application. The purpose is to help the student in becoming aware of the application (i.e., intellectual skill) of the concept within the given context(s). For example, to learn a mathematical operation, the student can be presented with the steps of the process in an expository problem while concurrently being presented with explanations for each step. In this way, the student may more clearly understand the procedures of the mathematical operation without developing possible misconceptions or overgeneralizations.

4.2 Practice Strategies

The category of practice strategies contains a rich variety of variables and conditions which can be designed into numerous teaching methods to improve learning of procedural knowledge. The term "practice" is used because the objective is for the student to learn how to use procedural knowledge correctly; therefore, it requires constant interaction between student learning (e.g., problem-solving) and instructional system monitoring. Practice strategies should attempt to create an environment in which (a) the student learns to apply procedural knowledge to previously unencountered concepts, while (b) the instructional system carefully monitors the student's performance so as both to prevent and correct possible misconceptions of procedural knowledge.

The basic instructional variable in this strategy is the presentation of problems that have not been previously encountered. Other variables include means for evaluation of learner responses (e.g., pattern recognition), advice (or coaching), elaboration of basic information (e.g., text density), format of information, number of problems, use of expository information, error analysis, and lastly, refreshment and remediation of prerequisite information.

4.3 Problem-oriented Strategies

Problem-oriented strategies involve problem-oriented techniques (e.g., simulations). Simulations improve the organization and accessibility of concepts within a knowledge base by presenting problems that require students to search through their memory to locate and retrieve the appropriate knowledge to propose a solution. Within this context, a simulation is a problem rather than an expository demonstration of some situation or phenomenon (Breuer and Kummer 1990).

Basically, problem-oriented strategies focus on the students trying to use their declarative and procedural knowledge in solving domain-specific contextual problems. Problem-oriented simulations present problem situations that require the student to (a) analyze the problem, (b) work out a conceptualization of the problem, (c) define specific goals for coping with the problem, and (d) propose a solution or decision. Unlike problems in the practice strategies that focus on acquiring procedural knowledge, problem-oriented simulations present situations that require employment of the domain's declarative and procedural knowledge. Thus, the student is in a problem-solving situation that requires establishing cognitive skills (i.e., contextual knowledge) among the concepts of specific domains of information.

4.4 Complex-dynamic Problem Strategies

Complex-dynamic strategies require students to employ their knowledge in the generation of solutions to complex, dynamic problems. Such learning processes are expected to improve the cognitive abilities of students (i.e., differentiation and integration; see Table 1). Five basic features should be considered in the design of instruction for improving cognitive complexity:

(a) The context is meaningful and of interest to the student.

(b) The context permits the student to construct concepts through his or her own cognitive efforts and employ this knowledge in proposing solutions and making decisions.

(c) The context provides a responsive, changing environment in which the student can receive feedback relevant to his or her evolving cognitive skills and strategies.

(d) The context permits the student to move from knowledge employment and improvement to knowledge acquisition, back to knowledge employment, and so on. It is this movement from one process (employment) to another (acquisition), from the employment of discrepant information to the combination of concepts in cognitive strategies that helps overcome boredom and creates interest.

(e) The context measures the degree of cognitive strategy employment independently from the knowledge acquisition.

Complex-dynamic simulations within such domains as politics and economics have been developed. Each simulation starts from a complex scenario that allows individual information searches and decision-making processes. The simulations are responsive as they reflect the decision-making processes of students by changing the status of the variables and conditions that represent the situation. The simulations are open-ended, as all decisions entered bring about a different and usually new status of the depicted situation, which can be "improved" or "optimized" by the student again. The simulation features create steady involvement of students and the repeated need for movement between knowledge and cognitive strategies. Additionally, the need for cognitive activity is supported by organizing the learning and thinking processes within cooperative learning groups. These groups provide opportunities for explanation, argumentation, justification, and adaptation.

4.5 Self-directed Experiences

An important goal of education is the development of learners who can be responsible for not only employing their existing knowledge but for the creating of new knowledge. The purpose of this instructional strategy category is to provide an environment in which students have instructional opportunities to improve their abilities to construct new knowledge.

For the most part, this process of cognitive constructivism can be improved by instruction that is self-directed. That requires a learning environment that is rich in resources and time for the student to seek out answers to both predefined and self-defined problems. Although cognitive constructivism may occur under unplanned environments, planned instructional environments can help create spheres of domain focus. For example, if the area of interest is social studies, the environment may include resources that would benefit creation of knowledge in that area as opposed to domains in the physical sciences.

Several programs of research in writing have shown improvements in basic writing skills as well as creativity through the use of computer-based word-processing systems (Reed 1992). In less planned environments, such as computer-based interactive games, there are findings that individuals construct the necessary concepts to continue improving their performances. For example, computer-based programs provide rich facilities that are under control of the student and, with intelligent systems, allow students to query the system.

A mixed initiative learning environment simulates the interaction between a domain expert and a novice learner. Thus, the student can artificially alter the time necessary to create new knowledge. Interest in virtual reality techniques is especially high in this area because of the total landscape of the artificial environment. Students may have the opportunity to explore just about any avenue of the domain without constraints that may be inherent in the real environment.

5. Concept Evaluation

Evaluation of concepts should take place within four stages of student assessment, ranging from preinstruction (for the purpose of evaluating entry behavior) to postcurriculum (for the purpose of evaluating educational goals). Thus, teachers should view evaluation as an integral component of classroom instruction.

5.1 Pre-instruction Evaluation

Before teaching concepts to students, the teacher should evaluate student entry knowledge. Where possible, the ideal evaluation plan would include assessing two types of knowledge: prior knowledge and prerequisite knowledge. A pretest that measures prior knowledge would identify what concepts to teach and whether any remediation for misconceptions is necessary. A pretest that measures prerequisite knowledge would identify the amount of remedial instruction required before formal instruction of the concepts to be learned begins. Additionally, preinstructional evaluation of aptitude and general achievement would help teachers to establish appropriate levels of difficulty.

5.2 During-instruction Evaluation

A major concern in concept teaching is the amount of instruction required for mastery (i.e., successful employment of learned concepts). Assessment of learning during instruction will help in determining the amount of instruction needed. Methods of evaluation should focus on products that make it possible to assess progress and effort. This type of evaluation can be integrated with the instructional prescriptions for problem-oriented and complex–dynamic strategies.

5.3 Post-instruction Evaluation

In most cases, students should not be required to take a posttest unless the teacher can assume mastery of concept employment. Students and the teacher should be well aware of progress and effort such that post-instruction measures truly evaluate the student at his or her highest level of achievement. Testing methods for learning objectives include final products and criterion-referenced objective tests. Norm-referenced tests may be useful for evaluation of curricular goals (e.g., school district outcome-based goals).

5.4 Postcurriculum Evaluation

Student success in schools is often measured by performance on standardized tests that evaluate students across curricular settings. In such testing individual student knowledge is compared to a large population; rarely does this information identify specific concept knowledge. Rather, postcurriculum evaluation informs the students of their relative level of general achievement in reference to their peers.

6. Conclusion

Teaching and evaluation of concepts can be enhanced when viewed within an integrated instructional program, that is, an instructional program planned to provide both acquisition and employment of concepts. Concepts are valuable when the learner can employ them in future situations. The instructional design (ID) model for concept teaching and evaluation described in this entry meets the educational goals of acquisition and employment. The guidelines presented are flexible and can be manipulated by teachers in reference to their given environment. As such, the guidelines are tools to be controlled by the teacher and, for the most part, improved with experience in their use.

References

Bereiter C 1990 Aspects of an educational learning theory. *Rev. Educ. Res.* 60: 603–24

Bereiter C, Scardamalia M 1989 Intentional learning as a goal of instruction. In: Resnick L B (ed.) 1989 *Knowing, Learning, and Instruction: Essays in Honor of Robert Glaser*. Erlbaum, Hillsdale, New Jersey

Breuer K, Kummer R 1990 Cognitive effects from process learning with computer-based simulations. *Comput. Hum. Behav.* 6: 69–81

Fodor J A 1983 *The Modular Theory of Mind: An Essay on Faculty Development*. Bradford Books, Lexington, Massachusetts

Garner R 1990 When children and adults do not use learning strategies: Toward a theory of settings. *Rev. Educ. Res.* 60: 517–29

Harré R 1984 *Personal Being: A Theory for Individual Psychology*. Harvard University Press, Cambridge, Massachusetts

Klahr D, Langley P, Neches R (eds.) 1987 *Production System Models of Learning Development*. MIT Press, Cambridge, Massachusetts

Reed W M 1992 The effects of computer-based writing tasks and mode of discourse on the performance and attitudes of writers of varying abilities. *Comput. Hum. Behav.* 8: 97–120

Tennyson R D 1992 An educational learning theory for instructional design. *Educ. Technol.* 32(1): 36–41

Tennyson R D, Rasch M 1988 Linking cognitive learning theory to instructional prescriptions. *Instr. Sci.* 17: 369–85

Further Reading

Alexander P A, Judy J E 1988 The interaction of domain-specific and strategic knowledge in academic performance. *Rev. Educ. Res.* 58: 375–404

Merrill M D, Tennyson R D, Posey L 1992 *Teaching Concepts: An Instructional Design Guide*, 2nd edn. Educational Technology, Englewood Cliffs, New Jersey

Tennyson R D 1990a Cognitive learning theory linked to instructional theory. *J. Struct. Learn.* 10: 249–58

Tennyson R D 1990b Computer-based enhancements for the improvements of learning. In: Dijkstra S, van Hout Wolters B H A M, van der Sijde P C (eds.) 1990 *Research on Instruction: Design and Effects*. Educational Technology, Englewood Cliffs, New Jersey

Wertsch J (ed.) 1985 *Culture, Communication, and Cognition: Vygotskian Perspectives*. Cambridge University Press, Cambridge, Massachusetts

Creativity

J. Elshout

Creativity is an important but elusive concept. This entry is concerned with the three focuses of the scientific study of creativity: the person, the product, and the creative process.

Most of the scientific disciplines concerned with humans, from neuropsychology to economics, have been called upon to contribute to an understanding of creativity. From whatever perspective creativity is regarded, there are heated contests among alternative theories, and between the disciplines (e.g., between psychology and sociology) the coordination often leaves much to be desired. In addition, the subject matter itself seems to inspire an individualistic approach that hampers communication and the steady accumulation of warranted fact and understanding. To bring order into such a poorly unified field, a useful first step is to select a kind of prototypical creativity. Scientific creativity fits this role best. The greater part of the literature concerns scientific creativity. When scientific creativity was compared to other kinds (e.g., in architecture or writing) typically more commonalities than differences were found (Taylor and Barron 1963).

A second unifying principle is that the study of creativity has three focuses also known as the "three Ps": the creative person, the creative product, and the creative process. These three aspects of creativity will be discussed in order.

1. The Creative Person

The basic question about the creative person (e.g., scientist) is what characteristics distinguish more creative people from their less creative peers. Research interest may then fan out to encompass matters such as social background effects, home environment, education, developmental patterns, career, personality (temperament), and interests. It is important to realize that the personal characteristic of being creative is merely one component of what is called "eminence," or "importance." The other components of this multidimensional "summing-up concept" are productivity, scholarship, and organizational contribution. The fact that being creative is a separable aspect of eminence is often obscured due to a tendency to select only the most eminent for consideration. The most eminent are statistically likely to score highly on all four contributing traits, even though these are only moderately correlated among each other. However, when a random sample of the complete population of working scientists in a certain field (e.g., psychologists) is taken, a multidimensional picture clearly emerges. There is the phenomenon of, for example, the highly productive scientist who is seldom cited, or the scholar, much appreciated for fine reviews, but who does no original research, and so on. All four components of eminence have their own set of predictive personal characteristics associated with them. In the psychometric tradition much correlational work has been done relating tests of intelligence and data from questionnaires with creativity ratings of scientists obtained from peers and supervisors. The results are clear-cut. The scientists judged more creative are very intelligent but not much more so than their less creative peers. They are characterized by a deeply felt interest in their subject matter, often going back to their childhood. Another striking feature is their independence of mind, their strong liking for the challenge of uncharted areas of investigation, and their persistence. Most distinctive, however, is their seemingly unshakable professional self-confidence. Though the correlations are clear, this approach leaves important aspects of the creativity of a person untouched. It is easy to see how creative potential translates into long hours (50 or more a week) of concentrated intelligent work on the frontiers of science and also to see how those hours result in success; but this will only happen if the environment, as a support system, provides the opportunity for the potential to become actual. Every person, whether they are creative or not, may be viewed as the ward of an informal support system that codetermines the level of performance reached by the individual. Thus, when judging a person to be highly creative on the basis of their scientific work, the researcher into creativity is bound to realize that this judgment pertains not to a self-contained individual but to a person interacting with an environment.

For the assessment of the creative potential of students and young scientists, multipurpose tests of intelligence and aptitude (e.g., the SAT) and temperament have proved to be of limited value. More appropriate are biographical inventories that aim to measure specific correlates of the complex of contributing traits described above. An example is the question of what the respondent prefers: a research position, a teaching position, or a combination of the two (see Taylor 1988).

2. The Creative Product

When can a product be called "creative"? In science, more than in the arts where matters of taste dominate, it is in the interest of all that creative work is universally recognized as such. The creative scientific product solves an important problem, answers an important question, or poses an important new problem or question. Consequently, the creative scientific product is, by definition, important and novel. However, it is in the nature of science that the creative product will eventually be fully accepted and followed. In science creativity is leadership. Defined in this way, the creativity of scientific products hinges on the judgment by peers, namely the recognized experts in the field, whose status is itself a matter of peer judgment. In intellectual domains that lack the institutionalized peer-review structure of science, such as architecture and literature, a similar structure can and has been temporarily established for research purposes: using nominations by peers to select a forum of acknowledged experts and then using this forum to obtain ratings of creativity of products or persons (Barron 1969). Research of this kind brings to the fore striking commonalities between scientific creativity and creativity in other domains.

According to the definition given, creativity is measured on an absolute scale. However, for educational and pedagogical purposes a relative point of view might sometimes be more useful. The comparison is then not between the given product and the absolute best there is, but between the product and the best to be found in a chosen reference group (e.g., the group of children of the same age). For the purpose of clarity in the discussion, it is important never to confound the two perspectives. In particular, creative children should not be thought of as junior, scaled-down versions of adult creative scientists, writers, architects, and so on. There is an important qualitative difference between the promising child and the creative adult, because creative production in the absolute sense is only to be expected from experts who have built up an extensive store of knowledge of their domain. Such expertise invariably takes years and much personal investment to realize (Ericsson and Smith 1991). It is certain that the creative scientist has "what it takes"; the creative child or student still has to prove it.

3. The Creative Process

Two schools of thought exist on the creative process. One regards creating as a process of goal-directed production; the other, Darwinian view, stresses the three processes of random production, goal-directed selection, and retention. Underlying this dispute is the philosophical question of how something novel can ever purposefully be created. Only accidental production of novelty would seem possible; the unknown cannot direct its own production. Psychological theories that start from this point of view stress fast random production of new combinations of already available elements, followed by rigorous evaluation to test whether the combinations generated fit the demands. A vast store of available elements (knowledge), and the opportunity and learning ability to fill this store, are considered prerequisites for creative production. The more elements available, the more new combinations are possible and the higher the level of complexity that can be achieved. Although, according to this view, the generation of new ideas is haphazard, the process itself is a deterministic one. The generation of ideas follows laws of association, and so the inventor/creator has some degree of control (e.g., via the selective filling of the knowledge store and through influencing the contents of working memory). From these ideas, one arrives at the now prevailing theoretical position on creative thought. This claims that, although the creative product striven for is novel and thus unknown, it need not be, and indeed rarely is, totally unknown; otherwise the proposals generated could not be evaluated. The starting point of this theory is that the goal does indeed direct the process of its creation because it is partially and/or schematically known. This view essentially reduces creative production to problem-solving. Both are seen as a process of search that is directed and restricted by approximation (or anticipation) of the end results and of the way to achieve them. To know, for example, that one wants to compose a fugue constrains the search enormously, and each partial result (lines written) constrains this space even further. The schematic approximations or anticipations of the road to the goal are called "heuristic methods." Many different heuristic methods have been described, among them random "generate and test." However, the latter is seen as one method

among others, and not as the basic nature of creative production. Indeed, humans have been shown to be incapable of random generation (try to write a random string of digits; a statistical test for randomness will always show your biases.

Both accounts of the creative process must be amended. As is typical for the psychological approach to human affairs, both stress the short term, the here and now of creation. The history of science, however, shows that actual creation is most commonly a process lasting many years, and taking place in a scientific environment that itself evolves. Nevertheless, mental search may be thought of as a core element of creative production.

4. Education and Creativity

The strong relationship between creativity and expertise has implications for how to go about educating *for* creativity. Many programs have been put on the market that aim at raising problem-solving ability and creativity in general. Both, however, are always particular: productive thinking is domain-specific. Such programs therefore miss the point. When the aim is to foster creativity there are two recommendations. The first is to orient the entire standard curriculum as far as possible toward problem-solving. The second is to help students of greater promise find or construct avenues of accelerated intellectual development in the domain of their choice.

See also: Development of Learning Skills in Problem-solving and Thinking

References

Barron F 1969 *Creative Person and Creative Process*. Holt, Rinehart and Winston, New York
Ericsson K A, Smith J (eds.) 1991 *Toward a General Theory of Expertise: Prospects and Limits*. Cambridge University Press, Cambridge, Massachusetts
Taylor C W 1988 Various approaches to and definition of creativity. In: Sternberg R J (ed.) 1988 *The Nature of Creativity: Contemporary Psychological Perspectives*. Cambridge University Press, Cambridge
Taylor C W, Barron F (eds.) 1963 *Scientific Creativity: Its Recognition and Development*. Wiley, New York

Further Reading

Ochse R 1990 *Before the Gates of Excellence: The Determinants of Creative Genius*. Cambridge University Press, Cambridge
Sternberg R J (ed.) 1988 *The Nature of Creativity: Contemporary Psychological Perspectives*. Cambridge University Press, Cambridge

Declarative and Procedural Knowledge

S. Ohlsson

The distinction between declarative and procedural knowledge is a modern formulation of a long-standing distinction between knowing *that* and knowing *how*; between science and craft; between theory and practice; between understanding and know-how. A central question is: how learners move from one type of knowledge to the other.

1. Background

Although Aristotle distinguished between theoretical (declarative) and practical (procedural) logic, philosophers and logicians have traditionally equated knowledge with declarative knowledge. Polanyi (1958) and Ryle (1949) are important exceptions. The invention of symbolic computer programming in the 1950s led to the first powerful formalizations of procedural knowledge and the declarative–procedural distinction became a topic of debate within artificial intelligence (Winograd 1975). Miller et al. (1956), using the terms *image* and *plan*, wrote that the main task before cognitive psychology was to elucidate the plan, that is, procedural knowledge. Since then, procedural knowledge has been extensively studied under such diverse labels as action analysis, cognitive skills, expertise, planning, problem-solving, procedural learning, and situated cognition. This emphasis has recently been tempered by attempts to analyze the relationship between the two types of knowledge (Aebli 1980, Anderson 1983, Ohlsson and Rees 1991). Although the distinction is latent in early pedagogical thinkers such as John Dewey and Maria Montessori, it only became a topic of research in education in the 1980s (Hiebert 1986).

2. Defining the Two Types of Knowledge

Declarative knowledge consists of (more or less accurate) assertions about the world, while procedural knowledge consists of (more or less efficient) methods for achieving goals.

2.1 Examples and Characteristics of Declarative Knowledge

Declarative knowledge includes assertions about specific events (e.g., "it is raining today"), facts ("Mount Everest is the world's highest mountain"), empirical generalizations ("smoking causes lung cancer"), as well as deeper principles about the nature of reality. The latter include scientific principles (Newton's laws of motion; the principle of evolution through natural selection) and the central tenets of political and religious belief systems. Familiar codifications of declarative knowledge include biographies, expositions of scientific theories, newspaper reports, and travelogues.

Declarative knowledge is *descriptive* (as opposed to imperative or prescriptive). The cognitive unit of declarative knowledge is the proposition. Propositions are expressed in statements. A proposition is true or false; or, more pragmatically put, more or less accurate in describing the world. Declarative knowledge is also called conceptual, descriptive, or propositional knowledge. Various types of declarative knowledge are referred to as autobiographical, episodic, factual, narrative, and theoretical knowledge.

2.2 Examples and Characteristics of Procedural Knowledge

Procedural knowledge includes heuristics, methods, plans, practices, procedures, routines, strategies, tactics, techniques, and tricks. Common instances of procedural knowledge include how to drive a car, how to balance a bank account, and how to arrange a birthday party. Procedural knowledge in technical domains is exemplified by mathematical proof methods and strategies for medical diagnosis. Cooking recipes, instructions for how to fill out tax forms, medical prescriptions, and software manuals are familiar codifications of procedural knowledge.

Procedural knowledge is *prescriptive* rather than descriptive. The cognitive unit of procedural knowledge is often taken to be a *rule* of the general form:

$$\text{Goal, Situation} \rightarrow \text{Action.}$$

Such a rule, sometimes called a "heuristic," states that if a person is pursuing the Goal in the type of context specified by Situation, then the Action is likely to be effective, appropriate, or useful. For example: "If you want to read (= Goal), and the room is too dark (= Situation), then switch on a lamp (= Action)." Rules are expressed in exhortations, instructions, and other types of imperative sentences. Rules are not true or false, because they do not assert propositions but prescribe actions. The value of a rule is a function of the effectiveness of the action it recommends. Procedural knowledge is also referred to by the following terms: ability, expertise, know-how, and skill.

2.3 Instructional Example

Compare the geometric proposition "if two sides a and b in a triangle are congruent, then the two angles A and B opposite those sides are also congruent" with the proof-finding heuristic "if two angles A and B are to be proved congruent (= Goal), and if they are part of the same triangle (= Situation), then try to prove that the opposite sides a and b are congruent (= Action)." The proposition is a true statement about triangles. It does not refer to goals, nor does it prescribe actions. The heuristic, on the other hand, does not describe triangles. It recommends a particular action in a particular context, where the latter is defined by a student's goal and the situation he or she is facing. The proposition is valuable because it is true; the heuristic is valuable because it enables effective problem-solving. The heuristic derives from the principle but is not identical with it. Mastery of geometry requires knowledge of both geometric propositions (theorems) and heuristics for solving geometry problems.

2.4 Reason for the Existence of Two Types of Knowledge

Because declarative knowledge is independent of particular goals or situations, it can be applied in any context in which it might be useful. The price of this generality is the need to derive its implications at the time of action. For example, in the context of sports the principle "whenever two objects slide by each other, there is friction" implies the rule "if you want to skate fast, sharpen your skates" (to lessen friction); in the context of home safety, the same principle implies the rule "if you want to prevent a rug from slipping, put a nonskid pad underneath it" (to increase friction). The principle is general, but to derive either rule from it would require complex reasoning. The rules themselves, on the other hand, are simple to apply but each rule is only applicable in one context. Declarative knowledge provides generality, while procedural knowledge enables rapid action. Intelligent behavior requires both types of knowledge. This argument was first formulated within Artificial Intelligence (Winograd 1975) but it was soon imported into psychology (Anderson 1983).

2.5 Summary

Declarative knowledge refers to a person's environment, while procedural knowledge refers to his or her goals and actions. Declarative knowledge is true or false, while procedural knowledge is more or less effective. Declarative knowledge is general but complicated to apply, while procedural knowledge is easy to apply but restricted to particular contexts. The totality of a person's declarative knowledge is sometimes referred to as the "epistemic structure," while the totality of his or her procedural knowledge is referred to as the "heuristic structure" (Dorner 1976). Intelligence—whether in humans, higher mammals, or in computers, which have yet to be invented—requires both types of knowledge (and possibly other forms of knowledge as yet undiscovered).

3. Research

Most instructional topics consist of both declarative and procedural knowledge. Mastery of a topic requires the ability to convert knowledge from one form to the other (Aebli 1980). For example, a geometry theorem remains inert unless it is converted into problem-solving heuristics.

3.1 Conversion from Declarative to Procedural Knowledge

Theories for the declarative-to-procedural conversion have been proposed by Anderson (1983) and by Ohlsson and Rees (1991). Both theories imply that the conversion is likely to impose high cognitive strain and take considerable time. Consistent with this conclusion, early claims about strong effects of instruction in the underlying declarative rationale on the learning of a skill are only partially supported by subsequent studies (e.g., Kieras and Bovair 1984). Both theory and data thus argue against limiting instruction to the *theory* of a topic. To solve problems on their own, students may need help to convert the theory (declarative knowledge) into problem-solving procedures (procedural knowledge). Research should concentrate on the factors that affect the difficulty of this conversion.

3.2 Conversion from Procedural to Declarative Knowledge

Jean Piaget has proposed that knowledge is acquired through the gradual *internalization* of actions (Piaget and Inhelder 1969). The related theory proposed by Bruner (1966) claims that knowledge first appears in enactive (procedural) form and goes through an intermediate iconic (visual) form before taking on symbolic (declarative) form. This action-to-knowledge principle has been applied extensively to arithmetic instruction in the form of embodiments (manipulatives), namely, sets of physical objects designed to exemplify mathematical concepts and principles, and in so-called "hands-on" science instruction. The empirical evidence for the idea that conceptual understanding is constructed by the internalization of actions is weak (see, e.g., Sowell 1989). Further research on internalization would benefit from a precise theory of this process.

4. Miscellaneous Issues

Some researchers identify procedural knowledge with implicit knowledge, that is, tacit and unreportable knowledge, and define declarative knowledge as conscious and reportable. This view is not universally accepted, primarily because data indicate that people can be governed by declarative principles—so-called "theorems-in-action" (Vergnaud 1988)—which they cannot report or express.

Metacognitive knowledge can be either declarative (as in the proposition "I can't remember names") or procedural (as in the heuristic "if you want to remember something, then rehearse it").

Students are likely to differ with respect to their ability to learn and to use the two types of knowledge, but this type of individual difference has not been investigated.

See also: Cognition and Learning; Knowledge Representation and Organization; Learning Processes and Learning Outcomes

References

Aebli H 1980 *Denken: Das Ordnen des Tuns. Vol. 1: Kognitive Aspekte der Handlungstheorie.* Klett, Stuttgart

Anderson J R 1983 *The Architecture of Cognition.* Harvard University Press, Cambridge, Massachusetts

Bruner J S 1966 Notes on a theory of instruction. In: Bruner J S (ed.) 1966 *Toward a Theory of Instruction.* Harvard University Press, Cambridge, Massachusetts

Dorner D 1976 *Problemlösen als Informationsverarbeitung.* Kohlhammer, Stuttgart

Hiebert J (ed.) 1986 *Conceptual and Procedural Knowledge: The Case of Mathematics.* Erlbaum, Hillsdale, New Jersey

Kieras D E, Bovair S 1984 The role of a mental model in learning to operate a device. *Cognit. Sci.* 8(3): 255–73

Miller G A, Galanter E, Pribram K H 1986 *Plans and the Structure of Behavior.* Adams, Bannister, Cox, New York

Ohlsson S, Rees E 1991 The function of conceptual understanding in the learning of arithmetic procedures. *Cognition and Instruction* 8(2): 103–79

Piaget J, Inhelder B 1969 *The Psychology of the Child.* Routledge and Kegan Paul, London

Polanyi M 1958 *Personal Knowledge: Towards a Post-critical Philosophy.* Routledge and Kegan Paul, London

Ryle G 1949 *The Concept of Mind.* Hutchinson, London

Sowell E J 1989 Effects of manipulative materials in mathematics education. *J. Res. Math. Educ.* 20(5): 498–505

Vergnaud G 1988 Multiplicative structures. In: Hiebert J, Behr M (eds.) 1988 *Number Concepts and Operations in the Middle Grades.* NCTM, Reston, Virginia

Winograd T W 1975 Frame representations and the declarative–procedural controversy. In: Bobrow D G Collins A (eds.) 1975 *Representation and Understanding: Studies in Cognitive Science.* Academic Press, New York

Feedback in Learning

R. E. Mayer

Feedback is information provided to a learner concerning the correctness, appropriateness, or accuracy of the learner's actions (Mayer 1982). This definition has three components: (a) feedback occurs after a learner exhibits behavior of some kind, (b) feedback is observable by the learner, and (c) feedback describes the effects of the learner's behavior. In short, feedback is information about a learner's performance.

1. Educational Uses of Feedback

Feedback is pervasive in education. In academic learning tasks, feedback refers to information concerning the correctness of a student's performance, such as praising a student for giving the correct answer to a teacher's question during classroom discussion, giving a grade on a student's test, or having a smiling face appear on a computer screen whenever a student selects the right answer in a computerized drill-and-practice program. In behavior management tasks, feedback provides information concerning the appropriateness of a student's behavior, such as scolding a student for disruptive classroom behavior or giving a student a prize for engaging in constructive classroom behavior. In skill learning tasks, feedback provides information concerning the accuracy of a student's behavior, such as allowing a student to throw a ball and see whether or not it lands on a target.

2. Behaviorist and Cognitive Views of Feedback in Learning

The behaviorist and cognitive approaches to educational psychology offer alternative interpretations of the role of feedback in learning (Mayer 1987). Behaviorists view feedback as reward or punishment that automatically strengthens or weakens, respectively, the tendency to give a particular response. According to Thorndike's (1911, 1913) classic law of effect, a response that leads to satisfaction is more likely to recur in the same situation and a response that leads to discomfort is less likely to recur in the same situation.

In Skinner's (1968) reinforcement theory, a reinforcer that is contingent on a learner's response increases the frequency of that response in the future whereas a punishment administered after a learner's response decreases the frequency of responding. In both versions of behaviorist theory, the rewards and punishments operate automatically on the learner's specific responses, that is, without the need for conscious interpretation by the learner. Feedback that reinforces a response automatically increases or strengthens the tendency to repeat that response, whereas feedback that punishes a response automatically decreases or weakens the tendency to repeat the response. However, behaviorist theory has been revised to emphasize the use of reinforcement as a more effective method of changing behavior than punishment. According to the behaviorist view, feedback is a central mechanism in learning; learning cannot occur without feedback and the effects of feedback are automatic and specific.

In contrast, cognitive psychologists view feedback as information that the learner interprets and uses to alter his or her knowledge (Mayer 1987). Feedback provides learners with knowledge of results that guides their construction of knowledge; this newly constructed knowledge can generate more successful behavior in the future. Thus, feedback does not automatically change behavior; instead, learners' interpretation of feedback is used to change their knowledge, which in turn can affect their behavior. As in behaviorist theories of learning, feedback is viewed as a central mechanism in learning; however, in contrast to behaviorist theories, the impact of feedback depends on the way that the learner interprets the feedback.

In summary, the behaviorist and cognitive interpretations of feedback differ with respect to what is learned (change in specific behavior versus change in knowledge) and how it is learned (passive and automatic versus active and effortful).

3. Behaviorist and Cognitive Views of Feedback in Instruction

The two views also suggest different instructional prescriptions, as can be seen within the context of three traditional uses of feedback: programmed instruction in academic learning tasks, contingency contracting for classroom management tasks, and drill-and-practice in skill learning tasks.

First, behaviorist and cognitive views of feedback suggest conflicting prescriptions for the design of programmed instruction for academic learning. For example, the behaviorist view holds that programmed instruction should be designed to elicit frequent simple responses that are followed immediately by feedback and are usually correct (Skinner 1968).

According to this view, instruction should allow many opportunities for the learner to produce specific responses that are rewarded. On the other hand, cognitive theory holds that students need detailed feedback that will help in the construction of new knowledge and that they learn from receiving negative feedback after an incorrect or incomplete response. In contrast to the prescriptions of behaviorist theory, studies of concept learning demonstrate that making errors is indispensable for learning, concepts are often learned in all-or-none manner rather than gradually, and students actively test hypotheses (Bruner et al. 1956, Trabasso and Bower 1968). For example, the cognitive approach provides the basis for cognitive process instruction, in which beginning students describe their learning and thinking processes for a given task and then receive feedback in the form of descriptions of the corresponding strategies used by successful learners (Lochhead and Clement 1979, Pressley 1990).

Second, behaviorists and cognitivists hold conflicting views of how feedback serves to decrease unwanted behaviors or increase desired behaviors in a classroom management task. For example, in contingency contracting the teacher and student make a formal agreement that if a student engages in a certain specific behavior there will be a specific consequence. According to behaviorist theory, the rate of responding should change gradually when the contingency is put into effect; for example, a disruptive behavior should gradually decrease if it is punished each time it occurs. This prediction conflicts with the finding that when the teacher simply tells a student that the contingency contract is effect, the student's behavior changes immediately, a result that is consistent with the cognitive view of the learner as an active interpreter of information (Sulzbacher and Houser 1968).

Similarly, there is conflict between the behaviorist and cognitive views of how rewards such as verbal praise or awards serve to increase certain desired classroom behaviors. For example, Lepper et al. (1973) rewarded some preschoolers for drawing a picture during their free time; some students (expected reward group) were told they would receive an award if they drew a picture whereas other students were not told in advance that they would receive the award (unexpected reward group). According to behaviorist theory, both groups should increase their rate of drawing activity on subsequent days because both were rewarded. In contrast, the expected reward group showed a decrease in drawing behavior as compared to a control group, whereas the unexpected reward group showed an increase. This pattern is consistent with cognitive theory: the expected reward children could mentally justify their drawing in terms of the reward they expected, whereas the unexpected reward children could only justify their drawing behavior in terms of their enjoyment. The potentially negative effects of rewarding students for doing something they already like to do has been called "the hidden costs of reward" (Lepper and Greene 1978).

Finally, the two views offer different prescriptions concerning the use of feedback for drill-and-practice in skill learning tasks. In conflict with behaviorist theory, presenting detailed feedback about a person's performance—such as how many inches away from a target the learner's response was—results in faster learning than presenting simple feedback about whether or not the response was successful (Trowbridge and Cason 1932, Adams 1968). This pattern is consistent with the cognitive view that the learner uses feedback as information that can be interpreted, so better quality feedback allows for more efficient changes in the learner's knowledge (Mayer 1987). In order to explore the role of feedback within cognitive theory, Brown and Burton (1978) developed a test that can diagnose the incorrect procedure that a student may be using for multicolumn subtraction. For example, one common bug in an otherwise correct subtraction procedure is always to subtract the smaller number from the larger number in each column, such as:

$$\begin{array}{r} 463 \\ -398 \\ \hline 135 \end{array}$$

Feedback concerning the specific bug(s) in a student's procedure can form the basis for individualized computer tutoring systems. For example, a student who makes errors on subtraction problems because of this bug could receive feedback specifying the need to subtract the bottom from the top number rather than the smaller from the larger number in each column.

4. Conclusion

In summary, feedback is a critical component in effective instruction, and its use in education is changing as behaviorist theory gives way to cognitive theory. Educational practice through the 1950s was dominated by the behaviorist view of feedback as a reinforcer that automatically stamps in responses. The result was an emphasis on drill-and-practice in which a teacher asks a question, a student gives an answer (usually one word), and the teacher indicates whether or not the answer was correct. For example, in some high school classrooms teachers asked questions at the rate of two to four or per minute over the course of a 45-minute class period (Cuban 1984).

In contrast, as cognitive theory has dominated psychology since the 1960s, educational practice has begun to reflect new ways of using feedback. When learners are viewed as active processors of information who construct knowledge rather than as response acquisition machines, educators provide feedback about the learner's cognitive processes used to arrive at an answer rather than feedback solely about the answer produced by the learner. In these classrooms, for example, students describe their thought processes for solving a problem, listen to the thought process described by an expert, and then compare what they did to what the expert did. In short, a continuing shift in the educational use of feedback involves emphasizing feedback about process rather than product.

See also: Learning Theories: Historical Overview and Trends; Paradigms in Instructional Psychology

References

Adams J A 1968 Response feedback and learning. *Psych. Bull.* 70:486–504

Brown J S, Burton R R 1978 Diagnostic models for procedural bugs in basic mathematical skills. *Cognit. Sci.* 2(2):155–92

Bruner J S, Goodnow J J, Austin G A 1956 *A Study of Thinking.* Krieger, Huntington, New York

Cuban L 1984 *How Teachers Taught: Constancy and Change in American Classrooms 1890–1980.* Longman, New York

Lepper M R, Greene D 1978 *The Hidden Costs of Reward.* Erlbaum, Hillsdale, New Jersey

Lepper M R, Greene D, Nisbett R E 1973 Undermining children's intrinsic interest with external rewards: A test of the overjustification hypothesis. *J. Pers. Soc. Psychol.* 28:129–37

Lochhead J, Clement (eds.) 1979 *Cognitive Process Instruction: Research on Teaching Thinking Skills.* Franklin Institute Press, Philadelphia

Mayer R E 1982 Learning. In: Mitzel H E (ed.) 1982 *Encyclopedia of Educational Research*, 5th edn. Free Press, New York

Mayer R E 1987 *Educational Psychology: A Cognitive Approach.* Scott, Foresman and Co., New York

Pressley M 1990 *Cognitive Strategy Instruction that Really Improves Children's Academic Performance.* Brookline Books, Cambridge, Massachusetts

Skinner B F 1968 *The Technology of Teaching.* Prentice-Hall, Englewood Cliffs, New Jersey

Sulzbacher S I, Houser J E 1968 A tactic to eliminate disruptive behaviors in the classroom: Group contingent consequences. *American Journal of Mental Deficiency* 73:88–90

Thorndike E L 1911 *Animal Intelligence.* Hafner, New York

Thorndike E L 1913 *Educational Psychology.* Columbia University Press, New York

Trabasso T R, Bower G H 1968 *Attention in Learning: Theory and Research.* Wiley, New York

Trowbridge M H, Cason H 1932 An experimental study of Thorndike's theory of learning. *J. Gen. Psychol.* 7:245–58

Implicit Memory and Learning

G. d'Ydewalle

While implicit memory refers to the ability of people to unconsciously retrieve and use memories in carrying out performance in some tasks, implicit learning is about people unconsciously acquiring new, abstract knowledge that can be used to help them perform tasks. Both phenomena have been established for quite some time but systematic research has only emerged in recent years. The findings do shed some light on the nature of the memory trace and emphasize that much more is acquired than what is shown in traditional explicit tests of recall and recognition.

In research on memory and learning, it is critically important to distinguish three stages: the encoding and acquisition, the memory trace (what is retained), and finally the use of the memory trace in performing other tasks. The distinction is of course obvious, but it is important to keep it in mind when presenting research on implicit memory and learning. Indeed, the central issues in implicit learning are focused on the acquisition stage, while in implicit memory research the interest is directed to the performance on tasks using unconsciously acquired information. Accordingly, the two research fields are to be separated clearly. In fact, research and publications seldom deal with the two types of phenomena together. Both phenomena also originate from different research traditions, with almost no interaction. This is perhaps a pity as a single study could easily be designed involving the two phenomena, simultaneously investigating the unconscious nature of the acquisition of new rules (implicit learning), and its unconscious retrieval (implicit memory).

1. Origins of Implicit Memory Research

Explicit or direct memory tasks are those tasks in which the instructions at the time of a memory test make reference to a target event in the personal history of the subject. The subject is deemed successful in such tasks when she/he gives behavioral evidence of knowledge concerning that event. Implicit or indirect memory tests are tests requiring the subject to engage in some cognitive or motor activity, where the instructions refer only to the task at hand, and do not make reference to prior events. The facilitation on an implicit memory test by recently encountered information is also called priming.

One can take a broader definition of implicit memory as any transfer that a person exhibits from a prior situation to a current one without awareness that the transfer is occurring. Given such a broad definition, one could encompass such things as Ebbinghaus's measure of savings through relearning, or Freud's

study of slips. Therefore, one could claim that implicit memory is a new term for an old idea: the notion that people can demonstrate the after-effects of experiences in their behavior without being able to consciously recollect the experiences themselves.

However, the current use of the term "implicit memory" is instead applied to a relatively more circumscribed area of research that has grown up from neuropsychological work. In 1889, the Russian physician Korsakoff (1889) described an amnesic patient who received some electric shocks. While the patient could not remember having received shocks, he expressed his anxiety about receiving further shocks each time he saw the equipment which delivered the shocks. Claparède (1911) reports on how when he shook hands with an amnesic woman, there was a needle in his hand which provoked a pain sensation on handshaking. The next day, the woman refused to shake hands, although she did not remember the painful experience of the preceding day.

It is perhaps the neuropsychological work of Warrington and Weiskrantz (1968) which helped to start the systematic research on implicit memory. In their study, amnesic and control patients had to recognize pictures of figures and words. In the first trial, the pictures were very incomplete, whilst on subsequent trials the pictures became more complete until the subjects were able to identify the pictures. The procedure was repeated one and two days later and it was noted that the recognition speed was obviously faster on the following days for both groups of subjects. More importantly, the amnesic patients claimed never to have seen the pictures before; their improved performance was therefore independent from a conscious recollection of the previously seen pictures. That is, the amnesic patients showed a good ability to name a fragmented figure or word if its intact form had recently been presented in the list, even under conditions in which they displayed no conscious recollection for the event's occurrence. In later studies (e.g., Warrington and Weiskrantz 1974), amnesic and control patients had to learn a list of words. The words were chosen such that the three initial letters were shared with other words in English. After a short time interval, two tests followed; one was a recognition test (an explicit memory test) and the other was an implicit memory test. In the implicit memory test, subjects received the first three letters of the words from the learning list and they had to complete the words. While the amnesic patients performed more poorly in the recognition test than the control subjects, there was no difference in the word-completion test.

2. The Nature of the Dissociation between Implicit and Explicit Memory

Experiments such as those by Warrington and Weiskrantz, and many others subsequently, helped create interest both in neuropsychology and in cognitive psychology as to the causes of preserved memory in amnesic patients. Interest was heightened when studies began showing the same sorts of dissociations between implicit and explicitly memory tests in normal subjects. Researchers manipulated independent variables that had powerful effects on measures of explicit memory, but found that they had little or no effect on measures of implicit memory or even had an opposite effect. These dissociations were taken by some as evidence for the existence of two memory systems, whilst other authors suggested that different factors operated in tests of explicit and implicit memory.

Among proponents of the multiple memory system approach, there is agreement that the brain damage of the amnesic patients selectively affects the memory system for conscious recollection, but leaves the system responsible for other forms of memory relatively intact. A distinction has been made between a declarative/explicit and a nondeclarative/implicit memory system with the former referring to verbalizable knowledge and the latter to the execution of skilled behavior without the need for conscious recollection. Performance on explicit memory tests is said to rely primarily on the declarative memory system that is affected in amnesia, whereas the nondeclarative system is said to underlie performance on implicit memory tests. The latter system is not influenced by amnesia.

Roediger (1990) has argued against the separate memory systems. He explains memory dissociations as reflecting differences in the types of processing required by implicit and explicit tests in that there is a unitary memory that can be used in different ways. According to a transfer appropriate processing view, the level of performance on memory tasks will be positively related to the extent that the cognitive operation that are tested are similar to those engaged during initial learning. Explicit and implicit tests typically require different retrieval operations and consequently benefit from different types of processing during the learning phase. Explicit memory tasks require mainly conceptual/semantic processes and implicit tasks are principally based on perceptual processes. This distinction, made by Jacoby (1983), refers to the difference between data-driven and conceptually-driven processing. Data-driven processing involves the analysis of perceptual characteristics, conceptually-driven processing entails analysis of meaning.

In the late 1980s, some new experimental findings led to a reconsideration of the dichotomy between explicit and implicit measures of memory. Some researchers (e.g., Blaxton 1992) reported experimental dissociations that do not respect the boundaries between implicit and explicit memory tasks. In light of these data, it is suggested that the contribution of data-driven processes involving perceptual analysis and conceptually driven, subject-initiated processes varies within different implicit memory or priming tasks. According to Roediger (1990), the basic characteristics of perceptual priming are (a) to be dependent on the modality of presentation of stimuli, and (b) the insensitivity to the level of semantic elaboration. The features of conceptual/semantic priming are (a) the lack of a modality effect, and (b) an effect of the level of processing. The latter means that semantically processed stimuli show more priming than perceptually processed stimuli in a task involving conceptual priming.

It is almost universally accepted that amnesic patients perform at a normal level on implicit memory tasks mainly relying on perceptual processing (e.g., normal performance on word identification tests by Korsakoff patients, see Cermak et al. 1985) but at reduced levels in conceptual priming tasks (e.g., impaired performance on stem completion tests for new associations, see Cermak et al. 1988 for Korsakoff patients and Mayes and Gooding 1989 for a mixed group of amnesic patients).

Therefore, the critical dissociation in amnesic patients is perhaps not between implicit and explicit memory tasks, but between data-driven and conceptually-driven tasks. There are however results that contrast with this view. For instance, Graf and Schacter (1985) found normal priming in amnesic patients in tasks that are generally regarded as conceptual priming tasks. However, in a re-analysis of the data from Graf and Schacter, it was observed that the associative effect was obtained only in patients with relatively mild disorders (Bowers and Schacter 1993).

Brunfaut and d'Ydewalle (in press) explored the contribution of perceptual and conceptual/semantic processes. The performance of Korsakoff and alcoholic patients was compared in three implicit memory tasks (stem completion, word identification, and free association) and one explicit memory task (cued recall). This allowed the authors to examine which was more important: the nature of the task (implicit or explicit), or the underlying processes (perceptual or conceptual/semantic). The results showed only semantic priming in the free association and cued recall tasks of the alcoholic patients, suggesting that Korsakoff patients have particular problems with conceptually-driven processing. The implicit or explicit nature of the memory task does not seem to be critical.

3. Implicit Learning Research

Implicit learning has been investigated in different ways. In a typical sequence learning experiment, subjects report the location of a target item as quickly as possible on each of many trials. Unknown to the subjects, the location of most target items is determined by a complex set of rules. The typical finding (e.g., Cleeremans 1993) is that subjects gradually get faster on rule governed trials, showing that they are taking advantage of the stimulus structure imposed by the rules. Yet they are often unaware of the existence of the rules or that the stimulus is anything other than random sequences. There are of course many other types of implicit learning experiments: control of complex systems (e.g., controlling the output of a sugar factory, see Berry and Broadbent 1988), artificial grammar learning (Reber 1989), and various forms of serial pattern learning (Lewicki et al. 1987).

A simpler implicit learning experiment involves the unconscious detection of a hidden covariation. For example, Lewicki et al. (1989) provided the subjects with a series of digitized brain scans from more-intelligent and less-intelligent people. The stimuli are constructed in such a way that a larger proportion of the brain scans of the more-intelligent people include a particular graphical sign. Thus, there is a correlation between the presence of the graphical sign and being more intelligent. While nobody consciously detected the covariation, the intelligence ratings of new brain scans showed that the subjects unconsciously used the presence of the sign to rate the scans.

While the majority of the research in the field provides conclusive evidence that implicit rule learning is real, powerful, and does not require centralized conscious control, there are some doubts about the existence of an unconscious detection of covariation. Perruchet and Amorim (1992), for example, have cast considerable doubts over the value of the postexperimental questions in many implicit learning experiments which are directed to detect the unconscious nature of the covariation learning. Hendrickx et al. (in press), in a lengthy series of experiments, failed to replicate the covariation findings of Lewicki.

4. Characterizations of Implicit Learning

The unconscious nature of implicit learning needs to be qualified. Cleeremans (1993) suggests that there is sometimes simultaneous development of implicit and explicit knowledge of sequences, subjects often becoming aware of "chunks" they use to recognize familiar patterns. It should be clear that consciousness is not an all or nothing issue. It is often futile to try to establish behavioral tests that will determine unequivocally whether or not any given mental function or content is conscious; different measurement techniques will always yield different answers. However, there is ample evidence that implicit knowledge does indeed exceed what one can verbalize. That is, the cognitive unconscious usually contains more knowledge than is consciously available at any point in time.

Is implicit learning abstract? It all depends on our understanding of abstractness. If we consider capturing the relationship between stimuli as an abstract process, the conclusion is surely positive (except with covariation learning). If abstract is defined as knowledge that is neither based on memory for specific exemplars, nor based on processes that operate on the common relevant features of these exemplars but that is rule-like (such as in reasoning), then the answer is likely to be negative.

5. Implicit Memory and Implicit Learning: Their Relevance for Instructional Psychology

What is now the relevance and significance of the notions of implicit memory and implicit learning for instruction and training? It should be stated clearly that both phenomena have been studied mainly in laboratory settings, with only theoretical issues at stake. Only seldomly is a reference to the educational relevance of the findings reported. Nevertheless, the theoretical issues could have major influence on instructional research and practice. For example, when children are assessed as to their acquisition of new knowledge, most existing assessment tools are using various forms of explicit memory tests. Such a practice may underestimate the amount of acquired knowledge.

In the field of learning a language, it is commonly accepted that a distinction must be made between language learning and language acquisition. Language learning refers a situation where adults systematically learn a new (foreign) language. Language acquisition implies no formal teaching and is the typical situation where the young child absorbs the mother tongue simply by interacting with adults. While it is now generally accepted that the underlying processes in language acquisition and learning are quite different, there is not yet much evidence allowing a more precise description of the underlying processes in language acquisition. Mastering a language implies not only knowledge of a vocabulary but also knowledge of the implicit rules which generate the correct syntactic construction of a sentence. Much could be gained by applying the methodologies of implicit learning research in order to unravel the underlying processes of language acquisition. This is particularly the case when considering the research on implicit learning of artificial grammar (see Reber 1989).

References

Berry D C, Broadbent D E 1988 Interactive tasks and the implicit–explicit distinction. *Br. J. Psychol* 79: 251–72
Blaxton T A 1992 Dissociations among memory measures in memory-impaired subjects: Evidence for a processing account of memory. *Memory and Cognition* 20: 549–62
Bowers J, Schacter D L 1993 Priming of novel information in amnesic patients: Issues and data. In: Graf P, Masson

MEJ (eds.) *Implicit Memory: New Directions in Cognition, Development and Neuropsychology*. Erlbaum, Hillsdale, New Jersey

Brunfaut E, d'Ydewalle G in press A comparison of implicit memory tasks in Korsakoff and alcoholic patients. *Neuropsychologia*

Cermak L S, Bleich R P, Blackford S P 1988 Deficits in the implicit retention of new associations by alcoholic Korsakoff patients. *Brain and Cognition* 7: 312–23

Cermak L S, Tarbot N, Chandler K, Wolbarst, L R 1985 The perceptual priming phenomenon in amnesia. *Neuropsychologia* 23: 615–22

Claparède E 1911 *Psychologie de l'Enfant et Pédagogie Expérimentale* Kundig, Genève

Cleeremans A 1993 *Mechanisms of Implicit Learning: Connectionist Models of Sequence Processing*. MIT Press, Cambridge, Massachusetts

Graf P, Schacter, D L 1985 Implicit and explicit memory for new associations in normal and amnesic subjects. J. Exp. Psychol. Learn. Mem. Cognit. 11: 501–18

Hendrickx H, De Houwer, J, Baeyens F, Eelen P, Van Avermaet E in press Hidden covariation detection might be very hidden indeed. *J. Exp. Psychol. Gen.*

Jacoby L L 1983 Remembering the data: Analyzing interactive processes in reading. *J. Verbal Learn. Verbal Behav.* 22: 485–508

Korsakoff S 1889 Etude médico-psychologique sur une forme de maladies de mémoire. *Revue Philosophique* 28: 501–30

Lewicki, P, Czyzewska M, Hoffman H 1987 Unconscious acquisition of complex procedural knowledge. *J. Exp. Psychol. Learn. Mem. Cognit.* 13: 523–30

Lewicki P, Hill T, Sasaki I 1989 Self-perpetuating development of encoding biases. *J. Exp. Psychol. Gen.* 118: 323–37

Mayes A R, Gooding P 1989 Enhancement of word completion priming in amnesics by cueing with previously novel associates. *Neuropsychologia* 27: 1057–72

Perruchet P, Amorim M-A 1992 Conscious knowledge and changes in performance in sequence learning: Evidence against dissociation. *J. Exp. Psychol. Learn. Mem. Cognit.* 18: 785–800

Reber A S 1989 Implicit learning and tacit knowledge. *J. Exp. Psychol. Gen.* 118: 219–35

Roediger H L III 1990 Implicit memory: Retention without remembering. *Am. Psychol.* 45: 1043–56

Warrington E K, Weiskrantz L 1968 New method of testing long-term retention with special reference to amnesic patients. *Nature* 217: 972–4

Warrington E K, Weiskrantz L 1974 The effect of prior learning on subsequent retention in amnesic patients. *Neuropsychologia* 12: 419–28

Further Reading

Berry D C, Dienes Z 1993 *Implicit Learning: Theoretical and Empirical Issues*. Erlbaum, Hove

Reber A S 1993 *Implicit Learning and Tacit Knowledge: An Essay on the Cognitive Unconscious*. Oxford University Press, New York

Richardson-Klavehn A, Bjork R A 1988 Measures of memory. *Annu. Rev. Psychol.* 39: 475–543

Roediger H L III, Guynn M J, Jones T C 1994 Implicit memory: a tutorial review. In: d'Ydewalle G, Eelen P, Bertelson P (eds.) 1994 *International Perspectives on Psychological Sciences. Vol. 2: The State of the Art.* Erlbaum, Hove

Schacter D L 1994 Priming and multiple memory systems: Perceptual mechanisms of implicit memory. In: Schacter DL, Tulving E (eds.) 1994. *Memory Systems 1994* MIT Press, Cambridge, Massachusetts

Knowledge Representation and Organization

S. Vosniadou

It is generally assumed that people divide the world into concepts which are organized in larger conceptual structures. One of the aims of psychological research is to specify how concepts are represented and to describe the processes that operate on them to produce performance in different cognitive tasks. This entry describes some of the main proposals regarding the organization and representation of concepts and the nature of conceptual change that is brought about by learning and the acquisition of expertise.

1. Knowledge Organization

1.1 Concepts

One of the earliest proposals regarding the nature of concepts, known as the "classical view," describes concepts in terms of a set of necessary and sufficient defining attributes which clearly specify which instances belong to a given conceptual category and which do not. For example, it can be argued that the defining attributes of the concept "bird" are that it is an animal, that it has wings, that it has feathers, and that it can fly.

The classical view of concepts has been challenged on the ground that some concepts cannot be described in terms of necessary and sufficient attributes. For example, Wittgenstein (1958) showed that the concept "game" is characterized by a different set of attributes depending on what kind of game is being talked about, and that there is hardly any attribute that applies equally well to all members of this category. In addition, certain important assumptions and predictions of the classical view of concepts (e.g., that the boundaries between categories should be well-defined and rigid, and that all members of a category should be equally representative of it), have been shown to be wrong. It appears that people differ in their judgments as to whether a given object is a member of a category or not, or on how typical they think a given object is of a certain category.

One attempt to modify the classical view so that it accords more closely with the results of the experimental findings is to consider that concepts consist not only of certain defining attributes but also of certain characteristic attributes. Defining attributes can be thought to constitute the core definition of a concept, while characteristic attributes determine how typical or representative a member of a category is. Other researchers propose to dispense with defining attributes altogether and to assume that concepts consist only of characteristic attributes which have different degrees of importance, or that concepts are organized around certain prototypes or exemplars.

Several research findings have challenged the above-mentioned views as well. For instance, it appears that it is impossible to organize all concepts around prototypes or characteristic attributes and that there is a great deal of variability in the way concepts are represented by different individuals or by the same individual in different contexts.

Another limitation of the prototype view is its reliance on similarity to explain how concepts are grouped together in categories—that is, the notion that categories are formed because certain objects are perceived to be more similar to each other than others. A number of experiments (see Rips 1989) have shown that it is possible to alter similarity judgments without affecting category performance and to alter category judgments without affecting similarity. Rips concluded that category decisions are better viewed as being based on inferences as to the best explanation rather than on similarity of putative members to category prototypes.

Other researchers have also come to similar conclusions. Murphy and Medin (1985) argued that similarity cannot be the only mechanism by which categories are formed, because categories are often formed that are not based on similarity and which nevertheless cohere —for example, the biblical category of clean and unclean animals. They proposed that what determines category membership is not similarity but some complex explanatory framework or theory within which concepts are interpreted. The view that theories determine category membership is an interesting reversal of the commonsense approach that people start by forming atomistic concepts which are then connected to create more complex knowledge structures.

1.2 Conceptual Structures

One of the earliest attempts to characterize the structure in which concepts are organized within memory is found in the idea of the semantic network. In a se-

mantic network, concepts are organized in hierarchical structures, in which some concepts are superordinate to others, and others are subordinate. (For example, the concept "animal" is a superordinate and the concept "canary" is a subordinate of the concept "bird.") In a semantic network each concept has a number of defining attributes which are inherited by its subordinate concepts. In other words, if the concept "bird" has the defining attributes "it can fly," "it has wings," "and it has feathers," these attributes are also the attributes of its subordinate concepts "canary" and "robin." This approach is based on the classical view of concepts and therefore it is subject to all the criticisms that apply to this theoretical position.

A different line of research, concerned mainly with the way in which people comprehend complex sequences of events, has proposed that knowledge is organized in structures known as "schemas," "scripts," and "frames." The term "schema" was originally used by Bartlett (1932), who proposed that people represented in some schematic form their remembrances of events and that these schemas create strong expectations which influence their interpretations of information. Schemas attempt to capture the generic knowledge of the world that people use to solve problems, to comprehend language, and to engage in conversation. The information contained in a schema may be organized in various kinds of relations, from simple class-inclusion to complex causal relations. In addition, schemas themselves can be organized in a hierarchical fashion and may contain other schemas, scripts, or frames. "Scripts" and "frames" are special kinds of schemas. Scripts are specialized and stereotypical schemas, such as the restaurant script, which includes knowledge about the kinds of things that take place when someone goes to eat in a restaurant. Frames represent knowledge about the properties and locations of objects.

There is considerable experimental support, mainly in the context of story comprehension, for the idea that schema-like structures influence the way people understand and remember information. Schemas have also been used to account for the ability to make inferences in complex situations, and to generate predictions about the future.

Other researchers have argued for the necessity of more complex, explanatory, theory-like conceptual structures. The term "theory" is used by these researchers to refer to a complex, relational framework, which includes explanations of phenomena, and not necessarily to a well-formed scientific theory. Indeed, some developmental psychologists have proposed that infants organize their observations around certain basic principles and a notion of causality, which form the foundations of a small number of naive theories. In the process of development and with the acquisition of expertise these become differentiated and restructured.

The above-mentioned proposals regarding the organization of concepts in memory refer to the kind of knowledge known as declarative. Declarative knowledge, or "knowing that," contrasts with procedural knowledge, or "knowing how." Procedural knowledge is the kind of knowledge that allows us to perform skilled actions, from solving a problem and playing chess, to driving a car or playing the piano. Procedural knowledge has been modeled in terms of production systems.

Production systems consist of a large number of production rules, which are "if . . . then" rules. These rules usually operate on some piece of declarative knowledge. For example, our knowledge of chess includes the information that there are several pieces, such as pawns, castles, knights, and bishops, which can move in particular ways. It also includes procedural knowledge, which can be expressed in production rules, such as: "If a piece is threatened, then try to protect it."

2. Knowledge Representation

2.1 Propositions

Concepts and conceptual structures such as the ones discussed above are usually assumed to be represented in a propositional format. Propositional representations are made up of discrete, language-like symbols, which are organized according to a set of rules, and which are usually expressed in the language of the predicate calculus. In the notation of the predicate calculus, objects are represented as predicates and relations as arguments. For example, the sentence "The cat is under the bed" is represented as "UNDER (CAT, BED)." Propositional representations are abstract, in the sense that they characterize information that bears no direct relationship to a given form of perception (e.g., visual, auditory, tactile), unlike pictures, which are strongly associated with the visual modality.

2.2 Mental Images

Mental images are picture-like representations which operate in a special, usually spatial medium, and in that respect are distinct from propositional representations. Thus, the sentence "The cat is under the bed" is represented by the mental picture of a prototypical cat located under a bed.

There has been considerable debate regarding the necessity of mental images as a form of representation. The question of interest is whether mental images can function as knowledge representations independent from some more general, propositional-type representation. A more general type of representation is needed to explain how mental images are interpreted by the mind and related to other types of information coming through the verbal code. It is now generally accepted that although mental images may involve partial reliance on propositional representations, they

are a unique and distinct form of representation, one that deserves to be investigated in its own right.

2.3 Mental Models

Mental models are analog representations that are assumed to preserve the structure of the thing (perceived or conceived) they represent (Johnson-Laird 1983). Mental models may be spatial models, capturing aspects of the physical world, or may represent in an analogical fashion the structure of a sequence of events. Unlike images, mental models are not limited to capturing the specific perceptual properties of real-world objects. Rather, they are high-level constructs, such as beliefs and theories, which can represent the structure of things that may have never been actually seen, such as the mental model of the solar system or the mental model of the atom.

2.4 Connectionist Networks

Propositional representations, mental images, and mental models are all based on the presupposition that human cognition depends on the manipulation of symbols—either language-like or picture-like. Connectionist networks, or parallel distributed processing models, attempt to represent information without making use of symbolic entities. These models consist of elementary, neuron-like processing units which affect other units by exciting or inhibiting them. The elementary units are connected together in different structures, which characterize the nature of the network as a whole. In such a connectionist network, a concept is not represented by a particular unit but is distributed over several units and is expressed by their pattern of activation.

The connectionist approach has captured the imagination of many cognitive scientists and has suggested new answers to many central questions in cognitive psychology. At the same time it has generated new problems which have not yet been resolved. One important question centers around the relationship between symbolic and distributed representations. Some researchers think that the two types of representation are complementary; that is, that mental images and propositions can be conceptualized as higher-order representations that are generated out of lower-level distributed representations. Others, however, do not believe in the complementarity between symbolic and distributed representations.

3. Conceptual Change

Conceptual structures are modified continuously as new knowledge is acquired. Psychologists must understand not only how knowledge is organized and represented, but also the ways in which existing knowledge structures change during the knowledge-acquisition process. A theory of conceptual change is fundamental for any comprehensive account of learning and has important implications for instruction.

One very common kind of conceptual change is known as "enrichment." This term refers to the addition or deletion of concepts in an existing conceptual structure. A great deal of the knowledge that people acquire during life enriches knowledge already possessed. Other kinds of conceptual change involve the differentiation, coalescence, and increased hierarchical organization of existing conceptual structures.

In an important paper on learning in the context of schema theory, Rumelhart and Norman (1978) argued that existing schemata can be modified by new experience through "accretion," "tuning," and "restructuring." Accretion is very much like enrichment. It refers to the gradual accumulation of information within an existing schema. Tuning describes evolutionary changes in the way a schema is applied to interpret a piece of data. It involves generalizing or constraining a schema's applicability, determining its default values, or otherwise improving the accuracy of a schema. Restructuring refers to the creation of new structures, which are constructed either to re-interpret old information or to account for new.

Psychologists differentiate among different kinds of restructurings (see Vosniadou and Brewer 1987). One distinction is between weak and radical restructuring. Weak restructuring refers to reorganizations in the internal structure of a concept or a set of concepts. For example, Chi et al. (1981) proposed that differences in problem-solving and categorization behavior between expert and novice physicists can be described in terms of differences in the hierarchical organization of physics knowledge. Novices treat as superordinate the concepts that for the expert have become a basic category.

Radical restructuring is thought to involve a change in theory, similar in kind to theory changes observed in the history of science. Radical restructuring occurs when an individual has acquired a new theory which is different from the old theory in its structure, in the phenomena it explains, and in the nature of the individual concepts that comprise it.

The weak and radical forms of restructuring described above refer to the reorganization of domain-specific theories, and are known as "domain-specific restructurings." There is another kind of restructuring, which has been referred to as "global restructuring." Global restructuring is most prominent in Piaget's attempts to characterize the changes in the knowledge structures of the child during the process of development.

Piaget argued that the development of the child's thought is characterized by global types of restructurings known as "stages." For Piaget, restructuring requires a change in the structures that determine the nature of the representational format available to the child. According to this view, infants operate on the basis of action schemas and lack the representational ability of the preschool child, while preschoolers operate on the basis of concrete, imagistic, similarity-based conceptual structures lacking the reversibility and transitivity that characterize the conceptual structures of the school-age child. This kind of restructuring affects children's ability to acquire knowledge in all domains; because of that it is known as global restructuring.

Most of the work in the area of conceptual change is descriptive. Little is known about the mechanisms that produce conceptual change, particularly the mechanisms that can bring about the radical restructuring of existing knowledge structures. Considerable attention needs to be paid to the roles of similarity and analogy as mechanisms that promote conceptual change. Recognition of the errors and anomalies that can arise through Socratic types of dialogues is also an important factor.

See also: Cognition and Learning; Concept Learning; Declarative and Procedural Knowledge; Expert Level of Understanding; Piaget's Theory of Human Development; Preconceptions and Misconceptions

References

Bartlett F C 1932 *Remembering: A Study in Experimental and Social Psychology.* Cambridge University Press, Cambridge

Chi M, Feltovich P J, Glaser R 1981 Categorisation and representation of physics problems by experts and novices. *Cognit. Sci.* 5(2): 121–52

Johnson-Laird P N 1983 *Mental Models.* Cambridge University Press, Cambridge

Murphy G L, Medin D L 1985 The role of theories in conceptual coherence. *Psychol. Rev.* 92: 289–316

Rips L R 1989 Similarity, typicality, and categorization. In: Vosniadou S, Ortony A (eds.) 1989 *Similarity and Analogical Reasoning.* Cambridge University Press, New York

Rumelhart D E, Norman D A 1978 Accretion, tuning and restructuring: Three Modes of Learning. In: Cotton J W, Klatzky R (eds.) 1978 *Semantic Factors in Cognition.* Erlbaum, Hillsdale, New Jersey

Vosniadou S, Brewer W F 1987 Theories of knowledge restructuring in development. *Rev. Educ. Res.* 57(1): 51–67

Wittgenstein L 1958 *Philosophical Investigations,* 2nd edn. Blackwell, Oxford

Further Reading

Carey S 1985 *Conceptual Change in Childhood.* MIT Press, Cambridge, Massachusetts

Kosslyn S M 1980 *Image and Mind.* Harvard University Press, Cambridge, Massachusetts

Rumelhart D E, McClelland J L (eds.) 1986 *Parallel Distributed Processing. Vol. 1: Foundations.* MIT Press, Cambridge, Massachusetts

Schank R C, Abelson R P 1977 *Scripts, Plans, Goals and Understanding: An Inquiry into Human Knowledge.* Erlbaum, Hillsdale, New Jersey

Smith E E, Medin D L 1981 *Categories and Concepts.* Harvard University Press, Cambridge, Massachusetts

Vosniadou S, Ortony A (eds.) 1989 *Similarity and Analogical Reasoning.* Cambridge University Press, Cambridge

Language and Learning in Education

J. U. Ogbu

Interest in the relationship between language and thinking in the context of education has grown since the 1960s as a result of concerns over the dismal school performance of "disadvantaged children." The term "disadvantaged children" in the United Kingdom and the United States refers to lower-class and minority children from poor backgrounds. Researchers from different persuasions, "nativists" and "environmentalists," have explained the problem and proposed remedies. This entry will review the differing explanations and remedies.

1. Nativist Perspectives

Reacting to earlier evolutionary models of language development, nativists posit that children are born with natural devices and capabilities for acquiring language from three perspectives: linguistic, biogenetic, and psycholinguistic.

Chomsky (1965), presenting the linguistic version, hypothesizes that a child possesses an inborn language acquisition device. The device permits the child to analyze incoming data and to produce messages. The principles of language acquisition are inborn, enabling the child to discover the underlying system of grammatical rules. Psycholinguists share a similar view. From a biogenetic point of view, Lennenberg (1967) argues that human language is a species-specific phenomenon and its development depends on physical maturation.

Nativists do not directly address the school language problem of disadvantaged children; nor do they suggest remedies for the problem. Indeed, it has been suggested that Lennenberg's views are similar to those of Jensen (1969), who argues that learning is genetically determined (Williams 1970).

2. Environmentalists

Environmentalists believe that language is learned in sociocultural context. Some attribute disadvantaged children's learning problems to "language deficiency," others to "language difference," and a third group to sociocultural factors.

2.1 Deficit Language Perspective

Some psychological and educational studies in the 1960s resulted in designating poor children, especially poor minority children, as linguistically deficient or deprived (Osser 1970). Disadvantaged children were said to lag in language development because of their poor home environment which did not provide adequate "language stimulation" or opportunities to talk with adults. As a result the children did not develop basic English grammar and therefore the cognitive basis to learn the school curriculum (Bereiter and Engelmann 1966).

The language deprivation position has been substantially modified, due to criticisms and the failure of the intervention programs it generated. A cautious version still survives in the notion that disadvantaged children come to school lacking in discourse skills.

2.2 Different Language Perspective

The relativistic view of language goes back to Boas (1940) who believed that every time people use a language they select an aspect of reality. Building on Boasian relativism, Whorf (1941) argued that language is not a way of expressing thoughts but rather an attribute that shapes thoughts. The language people learn as children directs the way they structure and see the world. Anthropologists have also long observed a close relationship between language and cognition. For example, people tend to codify their environment as well as their experiences within that environment in their language (e.g., the vocabulary of fishing people who live near the ocean) (Sapir 1912).

In the 1960s, the application of the language difference perspective to education began to counter the language deficit argument. Its proponents argued that disadvantaged children learned and possessed normal and well-developed languages or dialects, but that they differed from the standard English of the school. The two variants of English language are structurally equal because each is a verbal system used by a speech community and is therefore a well-ordered system with predictable sound patterns, grammatical structure, and vocabulary (Williams 1970). Studies of Black American English dialect, for example, concluded that it was separate but equal to the standard English language (Labov 1970).

From the different language perspective, minority children failed in school—especially in learning to read—because schools forced them to perform in an alien linguistic system. The problem was not that disadvantaged children lacked linguistic or grammatical knowledge or inadequate language socialization but one of interferences (Labov 1970).

Initial remedial efforts focused on eliminating structural interference; that is, eliminating a mismatch between the children's syntax and the syntax of the standard English of the text and the teacher (Baratz 1970) by using texts written in their dialect. When the problem persisted, another remedy assumed that it was due to phonological interference, yet that did not work, either. The conclusion was therefore drawn that failure to learn to read was not due to language differences per se (Simons 1976). It was at this point that the sociolinguistic perspective became important.

3. Beyond Language: Sociolinguistics

Sociolinguists go beyond differences in language per se to examine language usage in a sociocultural context. They emphasize the significance of the social use of language. Therefore, a child learns not only the structural rules of a language but also the rules of the language use or the speech community's theory of speaking: when to speak, when to remain silent, which linguistic code to use and to whom one speaks (Hymes 1967). It was noted that disadvantaged children did not have language problems in their speech communities but only at school where they had to meet the demands of another speech community, namely, the speakers of standard English.

3.1 The Bernstein Paradigm

A pioneer in the study of differences in language usage is Basil Bernstein. Influenced by Whorfian hypothesis, Bernstein argued that different forms of speech codes characterized the English working class and the English middle class, and that these forms of speech significantly influenced the school learning experience of the two classes (1961,1970).

More specifically, Bernstein distinguished between *restricted codes*, associated with working-class family structure, and *elaborated codes*, fostered by the structure of the middle-class family. He suggested that working-class people use fewer passive tenses or verbs and more words with particularistic meanings. The lower class, in other words, has a culturally different way of viewing the world. In contrast, middle-class people use elaborated codes. Middle-class mothers use language more often to socialize and communicate with children. This dominant role of language in socialization helps middle-class children to develop elaborated codes which are more suitable for schooling and for participation in higher levels of contemporary bureaucratic economy and political order (Plumer 1970).

Bernstein's paradigm, like the deficit language theory, attributed disadvantaged children's language problems to their families and their linguistic codes. Similarly, the remedies to the language and learning problems lie in the family, not in the school.

3.2 United States Sociolinguistics

United States sociolinguistics was a part of the language difference movement which began in the 1960s. However, this group went beyond differences in language per se to study differences in language use, especially after the failure of interventions based on assumed interference or mismatch between standard and nonstandard English. Unlike Bernstein, the United States researchers did not attribute the language and learning problems to the family but to the school. However, their initial study of classroom interaction did not focus on language, but on the dynamics of teacher–student interaction and how interaction misunderstanding (or mismatch) adversely affected minority children's learning. Nevertheless, these studies in classroom social interaction promoted the sociolinguistic approach, because they suggested close examination of the "discourse strategies" of disadvantaged children to see if these were expressions of their identity. It was reasoned that if the children's discourse strategies were expressions of their identity and thereby constituted a barrier to learning, classroom instruction could be reorganized to incorporate the children's strategies.

This speculation led to detailed studies of classroom practices (Philips 1972), which both revealed and clarified differences in classroom "participant structures" of the teacher and of disadvantaged children. A participant structure is defined as a constellation of norms, mutual rights, and obligations that shape social relations, determine participants' perceptions about what is going on, and influence learning (Simons 1976). Misunderstandings of linguistic messages and implicit cues in the participant structures affect instruction and learning.

In the 1980s, sociolinguists went beyond the classroom to study the school organization and functioning (Mehan 1979). Their findings led them to argue that there is a distinct school discourse with the structure of the initiation/response/evaluation sequence. This structure constitutes the task of schooling and is evaluative. In other words, schools reward students more for how they present what they learn rather than for what they actually learn. Subsequent research documented the unintended effects of this mode of evaluation on students' performance, providing some clue about changes in teaching styles to promote learning.

Increasingly, sociolinguistic research has focused on how teachers and students jointly construct the learning environment in a way that hinders or enhances learning, with more studies emphasizing hindrance. One major finding is that disadvantaged children's learning problems are socially constructed through a combination of discourse strategies and the social organization of the classroom, especially grouping. This emerging knowledge about linguistic interaction in the classroom is also being used to improve learning by disadvantaged students. It is, however, disappointing that remedial efforts generated by sociolinguistic studies have not produced significant positive results.

4. Implications

The relationship between language and learning has been actively studied since the 1960s by linguists of various persuasions. A lot has been learned about language and education of the disadvantaged from this research. However, no body of commonly accepted findings has yet emerged; nor are there as yet any findings that provide conclusive answers to the primary problem—the failure of disadvantaged children to learn to read. Sociolinguistic research seems to hold some promise but needs a theoretical framework that would take into account the effects of the coping mechanisms which minorities have developed in their subordinate positions in society (Ogbu 1993).

See also: Social and Communication Skills; Linguistics and Language Learning; Socialization

References

Baratz J 1970 Teaching reading in an urban Negro school system. In: Williams F (ed.) 1970 *Language and Poverty: Perspectives on a Theme*. Markham, Chicago, Illinois

Bereiter C, Engelmann S 1966 *Teaching Disadvantaged Children in the Preschool*. Prentice-Hall, Englewood Cliffs, New Jersey

Bernstein B 1961 Social class and linguistic development: A theory of social learning In: Halsey A et al. (eds.) 1961 *Education, Economy, and Society: A Reader in the Sociology of Education*. Free Press, New York

Bernstein B 1970 A sociolinguistic approach to socialization: with some reference to educability. In: Williams F (ed.) 1970 *Language and Poverty: Perspectives on a Theme*. Markham, Chicago, Illinois

Boas F 1940 *Race, Language and Culture*. Macmillan, New York

Chomsky N 1965 *Aspects of the Theory of Syntax*. MIT Press, Cambridge, Massachusetts

Hymes D 1967 On linguistic theory, communicative competence, and the education of disadvantaged children. In: Wax M L, Diamond S, Gearing F O (eds.) 1967 *Anthropological Perspectives On Education*. Basic Books, New York

Jensen A R 1969 How much can we boost IQ and scholastic achievement? *Harv. Educ. Rev.* 39: 1–123

Labov W 1970 The logic of non-standard English. In: Williams F (ed.) 1970 *Language And Poverty: Perspectives on a Theme*. Markham, Chicago, Illinois

Lennenberg E H 1967 *Biological Foundations of Language*. Wiley, New York

Mehan H 1979 *Learning Lessons: Social Organization in the Classroom*. Harvard University Press, Cambridge, Massachusetts

Ogbu J U 1993 From cultural differences to differences in cultural frame of reference. In: Greenfield P, Cocking R (eds.) 1993 *The Development of the Minority Child: Culture and Cognition In and Out of Context*. Erlbaum, Norwood, New Jersey

Osser H 1970 Biological and social factors in language development. In: Williams F (ed.) 1970 *Language And Poverty: Perspectives on a Theme*. Markham, Chicago, Illinois

Philips S 1972 Participant structure and communicative competence: Warm Springs children in community and classroom. In: Cazden C, John V, Hymes D (eds.) 1972 *Functions of Language in the Classroom*. Teachers College Press, New York

Plumer D 1970 A summary of environmentalist views and some educational implications. In: Williams F (ed.) 1970 *Language And Poverty: Perspectives on a Theme*. Markham, Chicago, Illinois

Sapir E 1912 Language and environment. *American Anthropologist* 14: 226–42

Simons H D 1976 Black dialect, reading interference and classroom interaction. Unpublished manuscript. Learning Research and Development Center, University of Pittsburgh, Pittsburgh, Pennsylvania

Whorf B 1941 The relation of habitual thought and behavior to language. In: Sapier L (ed.) 1941 *Language, Culture and Personality*. Free Press, Menasha, Wisconsin

Williams F 1970 Some preliminaries and prospects. In: Williams F (ed.) 1970 *Language And Poverty: Perspectives on a Theme*. Markham, Chicago, Illinois

Learning Processes and Learning Outcomes

V. J. Shute

Learning, the acquisition of new knowledge and skills, is generally regarded as a constructive activity. The construction, however, can assume many forms. Individuals differ in *how* they learn (processes) as well as *what* they learn (outcomes). Bower and Hilgard (1975 p. 1) have summarized this relationship: "as a process is to its result, as acquiring is to a possession, as painting is to a picture." Yet painters differ: they have diverse experiences, use different techniques, and thus produce quite different pictures. The same is true of learners; different outcomes of learning (e.g., propositional knowledge, procedural skills) reflect differences in learning processes (e.g., encoding skills, attention allocation). This entry examines the roots of our understanding of learning processes and outcomes, surveys the state of knowledge, and depicts a model of learning based on this information.

1. Historical Background

Philosophers and psychologists have debated the issue of how humans learn for centuries. This controversy can be reduced to two perspectives: empiricism (i.e., experience is the sole source of learning) and rationalism (i.e., reasoning is the basis of learning). While both positions agree that learning is basically constructive in nature, explanations differ greatly as to how the construction occurs.

1.1 Empiricism

Empiricism posits that learning results from sensory experiences in the world. Complex conceptions can be reduced to simple ideas, which arise from the association of contiguous experiences. Associative "bonds" connect simple ideas, and the bonds can reflect temporal or causal relations. Furthermore, bonds may be strengthened or weakened as a result of additional experiences. The strength of a bond is dependent on the intensity and meaningfulness of the experience, as well as its frequency, duration, and recency of occurrence.

In addition to association-building, empiricists propose a second fundamental learning process, reflection. This relates to the collection and comparison of several ideas at once. With reflection, it is possible to abstract general information from related concepts, enabling inferences and deductions to be made about events and ideas. The philosophy of empiricism (supported by Hobbes, Locke, Hume, and Mill), spawned psychological research on associative learning and behaviorism.

Associative learning processes were first objectively measured in the laboratory established by Wilhelm Wundt in 1879 at the University of Leipzig in Germany. The German psychologist Hermann Ebbinghaus also investigated associative learning phenomena, and is credited with starting the verbal learning tradition in 1885 when *Uber das Gedächtnis* (Memory) was first published (Ebbinghaus 1913). Ebbinghaus additionally demonstrated that statistical analyses could be used to make assertions about the significance of different learning variables. E L Thorndike's landmark research on connectionism in the late nineteenth and early twentieth century further advanced associative-learning research and laid the foundation for the behaviorists.

During the first half of the twentieth century psychological research in the United States was dominated by "behaviorism," initiated by John Watson. The behaviorists argued that psychological research should focus on specific stimuli and observable responses. This movement was influenced by the work of Ivan Pavlov in Russia before the First World War, then by B F Skinner, in the United States (starting in the 1930s). Building on the findings of both Pavlov and Thorndike, Skinner proceeded to study more complex forms of behavior. In general, behaviorism asserted that learning outcomes (i.e., observable behaviors) were solely accounted for by the processes of forming associations and reflection. Thus, they saw no need to postulate intervening, cognitive operations.

1.2 Rationalism

Rationalism disagrees with the basic premise of empiricism that all knowledge is reducible to elementary inputs and associations. Rationalist philosophers (e.g., Descartes, Leibniz, and Kant) held that incoming sensory data merely provided the raw material for use by "interpretive mechanisms," postulated to be part of our innate endowment. These mechanisms serve to impose structure or constraints on learning.

Rationalists cited a wide range of mental phenomena that could not be accounted for by empiricism. For instance, empiricism offered no provision for the organization of information. Also, the solution of novel problems (e.g., "insight" problems) could not be adequately explained by simply applying existing knowledge to new situations. Other phenomena, such as language acquisition, infants' perception of depth, and a predisposition to ascribe "causality" to events, imply some innate or emergent property that goes beyond the reductionist view underlying empiricism. Rationalism inspired Gestalt psychology.

During the early twentieth century when behaviorism was gaining momentum in the United States, Gestalt psychology was being developed by three German psychologists: Max Wertheimer, Kurt Koffka, and Wolfgang Köhler. They disagreed with behaviorists on the issue that psychology should be limited to observable behavior. Rather, they believed that learning involved "emergent" properties not derivable from additive combinations of the properties of its elements. Through carefully designed laboratory experiments (e.g., the solution of problems in which there was no prior experience to draw on), they were able to show that learning required an analysis of the entire situation, not just repeating a specific learned response. In general, Gestalt psychology believed that learning was a derivative of innate perceptual and problem-solving processes. Incoming data from the world would be filtered by these processes and then organized into a structure.

1.3 Empiricism and Rationalism

Psychology soon began to integrate theories derived from the empiricist and rationalist traditions. In Britain Frederic Bartlett developed the notion of storing "schemas" (*interpretations* of experiences) rather than exact representations of items or events (Bartlett 1932). Subsequently, Jean Piaget, a Swiss psychologist, worked on the idea that schemas undergo fundamental changes from infancy to adolescence (Piaget 1954). Cognitive psychology arose in the 1950s, employing established approaches in conjunction with newer ideas and techniques to examine mental processes and learning. In particular, cognitive psychology benefited from computers that were beginning to appear at this time. Computers enabled precise measurements to be obtained within controlled learning environments and provided the basis for the metaphor of the human mind as an information-processing device. During the 1970s and 1980s cognitive research focused on the analysis of expertise, mostly in the areas of memory, problem-solving, and language.

1.4 Instructional Psychology

Starting in the 1980s, instructional psychology became an important and separate part of mainstream cognitive psychology. This new research stream highlighted the issue of transitioning novices to experts, which gained increased attention with the advent of intelligent computer-assisted instruction (Mandl and Lesgold 1988). The critical question within this field is: what characteristics of the learner should be assessed in order to contribute to a science of instruction?

According to prominent researchers in the field

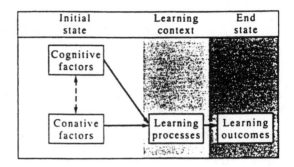

Figure 1
Simple Model of learning

(e.g., Glaser and Bassok 1989, Snow 1990), there are three main elements to a theory of instruction: (a) analysis of the initial state of knowledge and skill; (b) description of the desired or end state of knowledge and skill (learning outcome); and (c) explanation of the learning processes that serve to take a learner from the initial state to the desired state accomplished in instructional settings.

2. Theoretical Framework of Learning

A simple theoretical framework to guide research in this field is shown in Fig. 1. The initial state of the learner influences learning processes (within some learning context or "environment") and these processes affect learning outcome. The influence of learning contexts may be direct or may interact with characteristics of the learner to affect the learning outcome. The main components of learning will now be discussed.

2.1 Initial States

Two basic determinants of learning and performance are cognitive and conative aptitudes. Cognitive aptitudes refer to mental processes and structures associated with knowledge and skill acquisition, such as working-memory capacity and general knowledge (Anderson 1983). Conative aptitudes refer to mental conditions or behaviors directed toward some event (Kanfer 1989). One main difference between these two factors is that the conative aptitudes, in general, are more malleable than the cognitive aptitudes, which tend to represent more stable abilities (Baron 1985). Figure 2 represents an elementary depiction of the initial states with arrows implying possible direction of influence.

2.1.1 Cognitive factors. Learning depends on a person's prior knowledge and cognitive skills. These

Cognitive factors

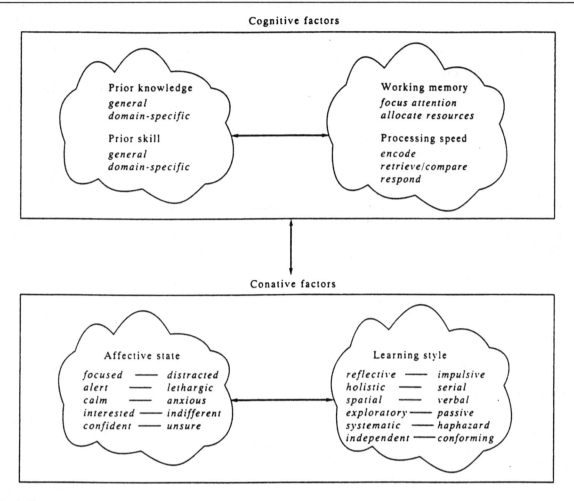

Conative factors

Figure 2
Initial States of the learner

mental characteristics comprise the cognitive factors that govern knowledge and skill acquisition. Kyllonen and Christal (1989) have differentiated these cognitive factors into two main categories: "enablers" and "mediators" of learning.

Enablers consist of what a person already knows and can transfer to new situations (i.e., the depth, breadth, accessibility, and organization of knowledge possessed by a learner). In fact, some researchers have argued that an individual's knowledge structure is the primary determinant of new learning (e.g., Chi et al. 1982, Dochy 1992).

The degree to which an individual's knowledge structure is organized influences both the speed and accuracy by which new knowledge and skills are acquired and retrieved. Glaser and Bassok (1989 p. 26) argued that "structured knowledge enables inference capabilities, assists in the elaboration of new information, and enhances retrieval. It provides potential links between stored knowledge and incoming information, which facilitate learning and problem solving."

Mediators represent limits on the maintenance, storage, and retrieval of information, thus governing the quality and rate of knowledge and skill acquisition. Examples of mediators include working-memory capacity and information-processing speed.

Working memory, in general, is defined as the temporary storage, or activation level, of information being processed (Baddeley 1986). Two processes associated with this measure are (a) focusing attention, and (b) allocating cognitive resources. Working-memory capacity has repeatedly been shown to be a strong predictor of learning across many and varied learning tasks (Anderson 1987, Kyllonen and Christal 1990).

Information-processing speed refers to the rate at which learners acquire and apply new knowledge or skills. The affiliated processes for this cognitive measure include: encoding, storing, retrieving, comparing, and responding to information. While these processes tend to be independent, they are relatively stable across content areas. That is, fast encoders may be slow retrievers, but fast encoders on a word task tend to be fast encoders on a numeric task (Kyllonen and Christal 1989). While enablers are consonant with empirical learning, mediators tend to reflect the rationalist view of innate mechanisms.

2.1.2 Conative factors. In order to learn, individuals need to focus their attention and persist in a new learning task, despite difficulties they may encounter. Individual differences in these behaviors reflect affective as well as learning style differences. These two categories are clustered together under the heading of "conative factors" representing separate but correlated learner attributes.

Affective state, generally, describes an individual's feelings, attitudes, and emotions. Affective states may be altered by external conditions (e.g., a pending exam affecting anxiety) or internal conditions (e.g., sleep deprivation affecting arousal). The affective state of the learner can have a profound influence on learning or performance. For example, Yerkes and Dodson (1908) found a relationship between arousal/anxiety and performance. Foot shocks were administered to subjects while they were learning a visual discrimination task, which ranged from easy to difficult. When the task was easy, increasing the shock level (and thus the anxiety level) actually increased performance on the task. But when the task became more difficult, a negative relation was found between shock level and performance. Optimal performance was associated with moderate levels of foot shocks.

Another set of studies examined the relationship between arousal and learning processes during performance on various learning tasks (Revelle 1989). A memory-search task was used and an individual's affective state (arousal) was manipulated by the administration of caffeine. Learning processes were shown to be differentially affected by arousal. Some processes were facilitated by caffeine intake (e.g., reduced reaction times to respond to items) while other were impaired (e.g., increased latencies associated with processing items in short-term memory, such as encoding and comparing stimuli).

Learning styles refer to "general behavioral dispositions that characterize performance in mental tasks" (Baron 1985 p.366). They can be viewed as parameters of thinking (under voluntary control) with optimum levels for a particular situation. For instance, being "reflective" is often a positive mental trait, but in some cases (e.g., a vigilance task requiring rapid responses), persisting in this style can be detrimental to performance. Whereas affective states are manipulable and transitory, learning styles are comparatively more stable. However, style does imply a preferred orientation toward learning, so it should also be manipulable through instruction or other situational influences.

Probably the most researched learning style measure is reflectivity–impulsivity, the tendency to be accurate at the expense of speed in learning or problem-solving situations. Slower, more accurate processing is equated with a reflective style, while faster, less accurate processing is associated with an impulsive style. Messer (1976) found a negative correlation between impulsivity and IQ: when IQ was held constant, an inverse relationship still held between impulsivity and school performance. Impulsive individuals may not allocate sufficient time for processing information during the learning process, thereby negatively impacting learning outcome. Thus, learning styles may be associated with different learning processes, and learning processes differentially affect learning outcome.

2.2 Learning Processes

The operational definition of learning used in this entry is that learning is a process of constructing relations. These relations can become progressively more complex with increased experience. Learning processes may therefore be defined as any series of mental actions directly responsible for this construction (or learning outcome). This broad definition encompasses a wide range of mental actions, differing in nature as well as in scope of application. To organize the many and varied processes cited in the literature, a framework will be employed, consisting of four learning-type categories, each with its own constituent processes. Three categories are arrayed along a dimension of increasing complexity, from basic associative learning processes (constructing simple relations), followed by procedural learning processes (constructing relations among simple relations) and ending with the more complex processes involved with inductive reasoning (organizing relations into a coherent structure). Furthermore, these three categories of learning are believed to be influenced, or controlled, by a fourth category: metacognition. Figure 3 shows the organization of the learning processes as presented in this entry.

2.2.1 Associative learning. As was discussed in the historical review section, the idea that associative learning processes are important to knowledge and skill acquisition has been held for a long time. Furthermore, contemporary studies continue to offer ample support for this proposition (e.g., Kyllonen and Tirre 1988). The processes affiliated with associative learning are believed to represent fundamental learning abilities, involving the rate and quality of forming associations or links between new and old knowledge. These processes include: encoding and storing information from the environment and retrieving information from memory.

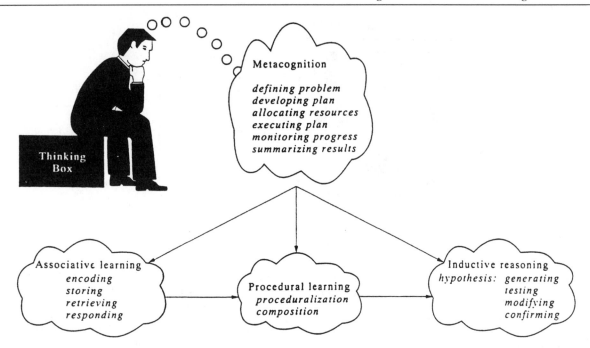

Figure 3
Learning processes

An individual's existing knowledge base greatly affects the construction of new associations. Broader knowledge bases make it easier to establish new associations and also contribute to more distinctive and memorable associations being formed. Consider the following facts: (a) the atomic number of Nitrogen is 7, (b) force = mass × acceleration; and (c) two angles whose sum is 90 degrees are "complementary angles." Learning these items in isolation, without related knowledge, is difficult, requiring studied rehearsing or elaborative processing. However, if some related knowledge existed, new knowledge could be attached to it. For instance, knowing other geometry principles would aid the acquisition of the new fact concerning complementary angles.

Thus, basic associative learning processes facilitate the formation of relationships between novel and existing knowledge; they constitute the mortar for the building blocks of knowledge. The quantity and quality of associated knowledge influence learning outcome as well as the rate at which these developing associations may be stored and accessed. In short, an individual's ability to encode, store, and retrieve information reflects the efficacy of the associative learning processes. These processes are directly influenced by the cognitive and conative factors discussed earlier. For instance, the speed and accuracy of encoding a new unit of information are constrained by an individual's processing speed and working-memory capacity.

2.2.2 Procedural learning. While associative learning processes serve to establish simple relations between facts or concepts, procedural learning processes go a step further to establish relations between relations or "rules." Any unit of knowledge may be represented in the form of "if–then" rules (also known as procedures). Procedures may be general (e.g., how to work backward from a goal) or specific (e.g., how to measure the diameter of a circle). Furthermore, procedural learning can be characterized by the processes related to compiling rules into efficient skills. This is called "knowledge compilation" in the psychological literature.

According to Anderson (1987), knowledge compilation consists of two related processes: proceduralization and composition. Proceduralization is the process that takes a general rule and modifies it into one specialized for a particular task. The general procedure thus serves as a template for the formation of a more domain-specific production or rule. For example, the general rule of working backward from a goal could be applied to a computer programming problem. Given a particular programming problem (or goal state), a programmer could decompose the larger problem into subgoals and attempt to solve each in turn. This general rule could be applied across various domains (e.g., electronics troubleshooting, medical diagnosis) or within a domain (e.g., within a computer programming problem, knowing the procedure for

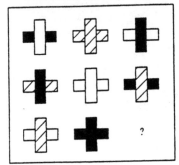

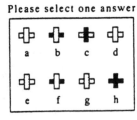

Figure 4
Example inductive reasoning test item

creating an output function could serve as a template for learning the procedure for creating an input function).

The second procedural learning process, composition, pertains to the collapse of a sequence of lower-level rules into a larger, more complex rule. After applying a series of connected rules over and over again, eventually they merge into one large rule. When that particular procedure has to be undertaken again, it can be executed at once, in contrast to the step-by-step character of the procedure evidenced during the early learning. To illustrate, when a person is learning how to play a musical instrument, initial learning consists of acquiring knowledge about notes, sharps and flats, proper hand positions, and scales. But with sufficient experience with the instrument, the player can simply look at some music and play. Rules become strengthened as a result of sustained and successful practice in applying them.

2.2.3 Inductive reasoning. While both associative and procedural learning involve the acquisition of some information at hand (i.e., simple propositions or rules), inductive reasoning transcends given information. It involves the discovery of rules and principles. Although inductive reasoning is a complex learning process, it has been argued that it represents a primary mental ability (e.g., Thurstone 1938).

Typically, inductive reasoning processes are invoked to deal with a set of problems or examples from which specific rules must be derived and applied in the solution of subsequent problems. For example, these processes are needed to solve the problem shown in Fig. 4. The task characteristics require the learner to generate and test hypotheses fitting a given set of data (e.g., progressions of geometric stimuli), as well to modify hypotheses if the test is not confirmed.

The processes of developing and testing hypotheses can be decomposed into lower-level processes. First, various attributes of the data or stimuli must be encoded (e.g., vertical bar shadings in Fig. 4). After that, it is necessary to analyze systematically or compare the ways in which individual stimuli relate to each other. Only then may a hypothesis be generated, establishing a possible relationship among attributes. One of the most difficult aspects of inductive reasoning is maintaining a growing number of relationships or rules in working memory. Thus there is a direct relationship between working-memory capacity and inductive reasoning skills (Kyllonen and Christal 1990). Finally, individual differences in inductive reasoning exist both developmentally as well as within comparable age groups (Goldman et al. 1982).

2.2.4 Metacognition. Metacognition is an "executive learning process"; in other words, personal knowledge of one's learning abilities and limitations, including skills that enable the acquisition and application of knowledge and skills. The processes underlying metacognition include: (a) defining the problem or goal in one's own words; (b) developing a plan to attain that goal; (c) allocating resources for enacting the plan (e.g., time on task); (d) executing the plan; (e) monitoring progress (or identifying problem areas and thus modifying the plan); and (f) summarizing and integrating results (new knowledge or skill) into the existing knowledge structure. This whole series of actions may be performed over and over again because most learning tasks can be decomposed into smaller, more manageable problems.

Metacognition is an emergent process, starting to appear between the ages of 6 and 10 (Kuhl and Kraska 1989). Moreover, not all of the processes arise at the same time. For instance, it is cognitively easier to define a particular problem than to be able to design an effective plan for solving the problem. Flavell et al. (1970) presented a set of items for children (kindergarten to fourth grade) to memorize. Findings showed that older children knew when they had succeeded in memorizing the set; their recall

414

Declarative

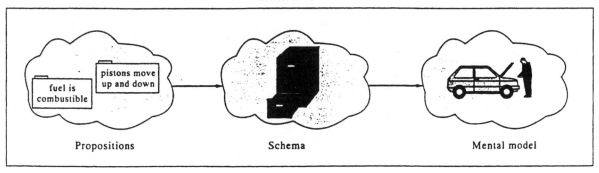

Procedural

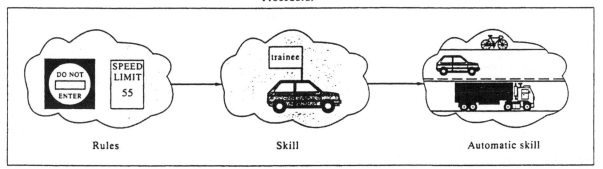

Figure 5
Learning outcomes

performance supported their perceptions. In contrast, when younger children indicated they had memorized the items, their actual recall performance was faulty. Younger children could specify the goal of the task, but were mostly unsuccessful in applying the other metacognitive processes and thus unsuccessful in their outcome performance.

In summary, four types of learning with their associated processes have been postulated to influence learning outcome: associative learning, procedural learning, inductive reasoning, and metacognition. Individual differences in the application of these processes constitute a major determinant of learning outcome and will be discussed below.

2.3 Learning Outcomes

The outcome of learning refers to any change within an individual's knowledge structure that results from a learning situation. Outcomes of learning can be quite diverse, differing in magnitude (e.g., learning a simple fact versus a complex technical skill) as well as content area (e.g., affective and social skills, motor skills, procedural knowledge).

One way of characterizing the wide assortment of learning outcomes can be seen in Fig. 5. The distinction between declarative and procedural outcomes is fundamental but refinements are possible within each of these two categories: declarative knowledge and procedural skills can both be arrayed by complexity.

2.3.1 Declarative knowledge outcomes. The basic unit of information underlying declarative knowledge outcomes is the proposition. It is represented by a single, isolated postulate (e.g., gasoline is a volatile mixture of liquid hydrocarbons). A collection of related postulates comprises a concept—any general, abstract idea constructed from experiences in the world (e.g., gasoline: is a fuel for automobiles, derived from crude petroleum; is used in liquid form; has a distinctive odor; is highly combustible, etc.). Infants begin learning concepts from sensory inputs (i.e., associative bonding and rudimentary reflection). Later, more abstract concepts are formed, such as the notion of the permanence of objects and invariant properties of numbers. Concepts are stored in memory along with their defining characteristics. They are always subject to revision and extension as a result of new experiences in the world.

The next level of declarative knowledge outcome

415

is the schema, defined as an interconnected set of propositions and concepts representing a situation. Schemas form the basis for comparing and interpreting incoming data. They also shape individuals' expectations and hence what is perceived. Yet schemas, based on prior knowledge and beliefs, can lead to erroneous inferences if the foundation is deficient or contains misconceptions. For instance, John's prior experiences were limited to full-service gas stations, then the first time he drove into a self-service gas station, his "gas station schema" would dictate a wait in the car until the attendant arrived. Observing other drivers filling up their gas tanks may prompt him to follow suit. In that case, John would have learned some important new information causing the modification of the existing schema.

The most organized declarative knowledge structure is the mental model, a highly organized set of propositions, concepts, and rules for relating them to one another. Together, these represent an integrated system (e.g., electrical circuit, human respiratory system). A mental model is structured hierarchically; different levels of analysis are possible. At each level of analysis, one can know: information about component parts, how they are connected, and how the system functions as a whole. As an example, the following is a mental model (mid- to high-level) of how mechanical energy is used to drive a car. Fuel lines feed gasoline to the area of the spark plugs. Spark plugs receive energy from the distributor (or electronic ignition) causing a spark to occur. The spark ignites the fuel causing it to explode in a controlled manner. The explosion drives the piston down, and the descending piston drives another piston up and also creates a vacuum causing more fuel to enter the area. Pistons going up and down rotate the crankshaft and this mechanical energy is used to drive the car. In this example, more detailed levels of analysis are possible. This mental model can also be extended for use in understanding other mechanical systems with similar components (e.g., motorcycle engine, lawn mower, outboard motor).

In summary, declarative knowledge outcomes are arrayed from simple to complex (propositions, schemas, mental models). Furthermore, newly acquired declarative knowledge outcomes can be stored in the long-term memory for use in subsequent acquisition of declarative knowledge or procedural skills, constituting a feedback loop. The learning processes responsible for declarative knowledge outcomes are mostly associative, with some inductive reasoning required for the acquisition of complex schemas and mental models.

2.3.2 Procedural skill outcomes. While declarative learning outcomes relate to knowledge *about* something, procedural learning outcomes relate to knowledge of *how to do* something. A rule is the basic unit of action underlying procedural skill outcomes. Rules are typically represented by condition–action pairs. The condition may be defined as the "if" part of a rule, while the action may be defined as the "then" part, consisting of the associated steps of some procedure. If, for example, you want to bake a potato, then place the potato in the microwave oven and set the timer for 6 minutes.

The next level of procedural outcome is a skill, defined as a collection of related rules. A skill may be cognitive (e.g., computing the square root of a number), motor (e.g., typing), social (e.g., using the proper fork at a formal dinner), or even creative (e.g., composing a poem). For example, if you wanted to add two two-digit numbers, such as $49 + 33$, then first add digits in the "ones" column ($9 + 3 = 12$). If the sum exceeds 10, then write what remains under the "ones" column (2) and carry a 1 to the "tens" column. Next, add all digits in the "tens" column ($1 + 4 + 3 = 8$). The final sum is 82.

Finally, a skill may become automatic after considerable practice applying that skill in many and varied situations. Eventually an automatic skill requires little or no conscious effort. For instance, after years of practice driving a car (involving a complex coordination of skills), a person can drive the car in traffic while listening to the radio and planning the evening meal. The execution of this procedure is almost unconscious, compared to the step-by-step manner of invoking procedures, outlined above.

In summary, learning outcomes may be declarative or procedural in nature, and may further be distinguished by level of complexity. Moreover, the learning processes are believed to affect outcomes differentially. Associative learning processes directly affect declarative knowledge outcomes (but can also affect simple rule-learning), procedural learning processes primarily affect skill acquisition. Inductive reasoning processes affect both declarative and procedural outcomes. Metacognitive processes influence learning outcome indirectly, through the other learning processes.

3. A Model of Learning

The purpose of this entry was to examine possible relations among initial states, learning processes, and learning outcomes in order to devise a model of learning. To benefit instructional psychology, a model of learning requires empirically derived information concerning which of the initial states and learning processes affect which outcome measures, how they exert their influence, and what instructional techniques may be used to enhance the processes (and hence the outcome). In addition, each outcome measure requires detailed information about how to test for the presence and quality of various knowledge types. Over time, sufficiently detailed information could be assembled

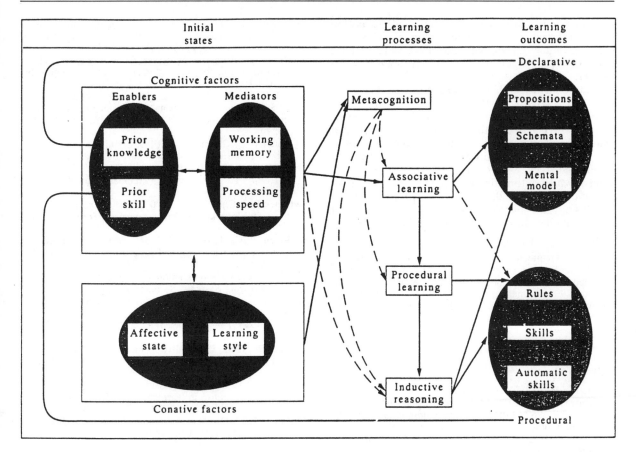

Figure 6
Model of learning

to guide the development of principled instruction across a wide range of curriculum goals.

An attempt at outlining such a model appears in Fig. 6, integrating the components discussed in this entry and representing an expansion of the simple model depicted in Fig. 1. Arrows in the figure represent both real and hypothetical relationships among initial states, learning processes, and learning outcomes. Solid lines denote direct relations and dashed lines represent less direct relations.

This model shows the two initial states (cognitive and conative factors) influencing the learning processes. In particular, the cognitive factors directly impact metacognition, associative learning, procedural learning, and inductive reasoning. These relations have been documented in the literature. The conative factors, however, are depicted as only impacting metacognition, but other relationships are possible (e.g., reflective learning style may facilitate associative learning processes, which enhance declarative knowledge outcomes).

Metacognitive processes monitor the efficacy of the three learning processes and, if necessary, invoke different processes during the solution of a particular problem. However, the three learning processes (associative, procedural, and inductive) ultimately impact what is learned. An analogy can be made with a conductor and musicians performing during a symphony. The conductor directs the musicians but does not actually play any music. The quality of the conducting affects the musicians and thus the musical outcome.

Associative learning processes influence declarative knowledge outcomes, but another possible (dashed-line) relationship can be made to procedural learning. That is, rule-learning could be accomplished via associative learning processes where, for instance, a rule could be learned by rote memorization. Next, procedural learning processes influence procedural outcomes. For example, facility in proceduralizing knowledge leads to the development and acquisition of skills. Inductive reasoning processes exert their influence both on declarative

417

outcomes (e.g., formation of mental models) and on procedural outcomes (e.g., induction of rules). Finally, each newly acquired declarative or procedural outcome feeds back to the initial state of the learner.

Additional research is needed on both the direction and strength of the arrows depicted in the proposed model of learning. Another fertile area of research involves examining relationships between instructional environments and learning outcomes. For instance, the acquisition of a mental model may be enhanced by exploratory or discovery environments, while automatizing a perceptual skill may be facilitated in a drill-and-practice environment. In conclusion, the puzzle parts have been presented and an attempt has been made to relate the pieces together.

See also: Architecture of Cognition; Concept Learning; Constructivism and Learning; Declarative and Procedural Knowledge; Feedback in Learning; Learning Activity; Learning Environments; Learning Theories: Historical Overview and Trends; Metacognition; Models of Learning; Self-regulation in Learning

References

Anderson J R 1983 *The Architecture of Cognition.* Harvard University Press, Cambridge, Massachusetts
Anderson J R 1987 Skill acquisition: Compilation of weak-method problem solutions. *Psychol. Rev.* 94: 192–210
Baddeley A 1986 *Working Memory.* Oxford University Press, Oxford
Baron J 1985 What kinds of intelligence components are fundamental? In: Chipman S F, Segal J W, Glaser R (eds.) 1985 *Thinking and Learning Skills.* Erlbaum, Hillsdale, New Jersey
Bartlett F C 1932 *Remembering: A Study in Experimental and Social Psychology.* Cambridge University Press, London
Bower G H, Hilgard E R 1975 *Theories of Learning.* Prentice-Hall, Englewood Cliffs, New Jersey
Chi M T H, Glaser R, Rees E 1982 Expertise in problem solving. In: Sternberg R (ed.) 1982 *Advances in the Psychology of Human Intelligence,* Vol. 1. Erlbaum, Hillsdale, New Jersey
Dochy F J R C 1992 *Assessment of Prior Knowledge as a Determinant of Future Learning.* Lemma, Utrecht
Ebbinghaus H (trans. Ruger H A, Bussenius C E) 1913 *Memory: A Contribution to Experimental Psychology.* Teachers College Press, New York
Flavell J H, Friedricks A G, Hoyt J D 1970 Developmental changes in memorization processes. *Cognit. Psychol.* 1: 324–40
Glaser R, Bassok M 1989 *Learning Theory and the Study of Instruction.* Technical Report No. 11, University of Pittsburgh, Pittsburgh, Pennsylvania

Goldman S R, Pellegrino J W, Parseghian P E, Sallis R 1982 Developmental and individual differences in verbal analogical reasoning. *Child Dev.* 53: 550–59
Kanfer R 1989 Conative processes, dispositions, and behavior: Connecting the dots within and across paradigms. In: Kanfer R, Ackerman P L, Cudeck R (eds.) 1989
Kuhl J, Kraska K 1989 Self-regulation and metamotivation: Computational mechanisms, development, and assessment. In: Kanfer R, Ackerman P L, Cudeck R (eds.) 1989
Kyllonen P C, Christal R E 1989 Cognitive modeling of learning abilities: A status report of LAMP. In: Dillon R, Pellegrino J W (eds.) 1989 *Testing: Theoretical and Applied Perspectives.* Freeman, San Francisco, California
Kyllonen P C, Christal R E 1990 Reasoning ability is (little more than) working-memory capacity?! *Intelligence* 14: 389–433
Kyllonen P C, Tirre W C 1988 Individual differences in associative learning and forgetting. *Intelligence* 12: 393–421
Mandl H, Lesgold A (eds.) 1988 *Learning Issues for Intelligent Tutoring Systems.* Springer-Verlag, New York
Messer S B 1976 Reflection-impulsivity: A review. *Psych. Bull.* 83: 1026–52
Piaget J 1954 *The Construction of Reality in the Child.* Routledge and Kegan Paul, London
Revelle W 1989 Personality, motivation, and cognitive performance. In: Kanfer R, Ackerman P L, Cudeck R (eds.) 1989
Snow R E 1990 Toward assessment of cognitive and conative structures in learning. *Educ. Researcher* 18: 8–14
Thurstone L L 1938 *Primary Mental Abilities.* Psychometric Monographs No. 1, University of Chicago Press, Chicago, Illinois
Yerkes R M, Dodson J D 1908 The relation of strength of stimuli to rapidity of habit-information. *J. of Comparative Neurology and Psychol.* 18: 459–82

Further Reading

Cronbach L J, Snow R E 1977 *Aptitudes and Instructional Methods: A Handbook for Research on Interactions.* Irvington, New York
Kanfer R, Ackerman P L, Cudeck R (eds.) 1989 *Abilities, Motivation, and Methodology.* Erlbaum, Hillsdale, New Jersey
Kyllonen P C, Shute V J 1989 A taxonomy of learning skills. In: Ackerman P L, Sternberg R J, Glaser R (eds.) 1989 *Learning and Individual Differences.* Freeman, New York
Shute V J 1995 SMART: Student Modeling Approach for Responsive Tutoring. *User Modeling and User-Adapted Interaction* (Special issue on student modeling)
White B Y, Frederiksen J R 1986 *Progressions of Quantitative Models as a Foundation for Intelligent Learning Environments.* Technical Report No. 6277, Bolt, Beranak and Newman, Cambridge, Massachusetts

Learning Strategies and Learning to Learn

C. E. Weinstein and G. Van Mater Stone

Learning-to-learn strategies and skills include any thoughts, emotions, or behaviors that facilitate studying, understanding, knowledge, or skill acquisition, or the reorganization of one's knowledge base. This is particularly important for students at risk of academic failure. The reason for teaching or learning these strategies and skills is to help students become more strategic learners who can take significant responsibility for their own learning. Strategic learners are able to set realistic yet challenging learning goals. They can use knowledge about: (a) themselves as learners; (b) the tasks they must perform; (c) their repertoire of learning strategies and skills; (d) their prior content knowledge; and (e) their knowledge of the context in which they will be expected to use new learning, both in the present and in the future, to help them select effective ways to study and learn new information and skills. Strategic learners can also use executive control processes to create a learning plan, select methods to implement it, use the plan, monitor their progress, and, if necessary, modify their goal or the approach that they are using. Each of these components will be discussed in this entry.

1. The Importance of Becoming a Strategic Learner

Students who want to and are able to take much of the responsibility for regulating their own learning will be in a better position to succeed in a world with rapid technological and social change where lifelong learning will be required. In the United States, for example, people now change jobs on average more than seven times in their lifetime. In addition, at least three of these changes involve shifting career categories. Models of general education that assume the purpose of higher education to be primarily that of job preparation are inadequate. Students must not only increase their knowledge and skills while they are in college, they must also learn how to manage their own learning. Strategic learners can take responsibility for optimizing their learning in both academic and nonacademic contexts (Pintrich 1991, Weinstein and Van Mater Stone in press, Zimmerman and Schunk 1989).

2. Characteristics of Strategic Learners

What does it mean to be an expert strategic learner? First, expert learners have a variety of different types of knowledge that can be classified into five basic categories: (a) knowledge about themselves as learners; (b) knowledge about different types of academic tasks; (c) knowledge about strategies and tactics for acquiring, integrating, and applying new learning; (d) prior content knowledge; and (e) knowledge of both present and future contexts in which their knowledge could be useful. However, these different types of knowledge are not sufficient for expertise. Expert learners must also know how to use these various types of knowledge to meet their learning goals and how to monitor their own progress so that they are sufficiently flexible to alter what they are doing if a problem occurs. They need to know how to use self-assessment or self-testing to determine if they are meeting their learning goals or not.

Students must also want to learn. Effective learning requires the integration of the components of skill and will. Motivation and positive affect for learning derive from many components, and interact with and result from many factors. These factors include things such as the setting, analysis, and use of goals, efficacy expectations, outcome attributions, interest, valuing, instrumentality, and utility value.

Finally, strategic learners have the metacognitive awareness and control strategies to orchestrate and manage their own studying and learning. This involves a number of activities which interact and dynamically impact all other components. These activities include: creating a plan to reach a goal; selecting the specific strategies or methods to use to achieve a goal; implementing the methods selected to carry out the plan; monitoring progress on both a formative and a summative basis; modifying the plan, the methods, or even the original goal, if necessary; and evaluating what was done to decide if this would be a good way to go about meeting similar goals in the future. Evaluating this whole process helps students to build up a repertoire of strategies that can be called upon in the future when a similar situation arises.

3. Knowledge Required For Strategic Learning

Strategic learners have a variety of different knowledge bases that they call upon and integrate to help meet educational or performance goals. The five primary types of knowledge used by students are: (a) knowledge about themselves as learners, (b) the tasks they must perform, (c) their repertoire of learning strategies and skills, (d) their prior content knowledge, and (e) their knowledge of the context in which they will be expected to use new learning, both immediately and in the future. Although it is the integration of these knowledge bases that results in strategic learning, for the purposes of discussion, they will first be discussed individually.

3.1 Knowledge About Oneself as a Learner

Strategic learners know a lot about themselves. For example, they are aware of their academic strengths and weaknesses. Which subjects are harder or easier for them to learn? What are their interests? Where do their talents lie? They also know a great deal about their learning preferences (Biggs 1987, Entwistle 1992, Marton 1988). How do they prefer to study? What are the best times of day for them to concentrate on their work? What are their current study habits and practices?

It is important for students to know about themselves as learners so that they can manage the internal and external resources necessary for attaining their learning goals. It is noteworthy that this knowledge includes personal resources such as emotions, as well as knowledge of cognitive or study strategies. Using all of these information sources helps students to make decisions that will increase their probability of meeting a learning goal. For example, a hypothetical student—Susan—in a course that she has found difficult might need to organize extra study hours, meet with a tutor, and set up an extra session with her study group. However, if the test is in a course in a subject area that Susan has found very easy to learn, she would probably not have to arrange extra study aids.

3.2 Knowledge About Different Types of Academic Tasks

Another type of knowledge needed by strategic learners is knowledge about the different types of academic tasks they will need to perform, such as reading textbooks, listening to lectures, watching demonstrations, writing papers, taking notes, preparing for tests, and so on (Brown et al. 1983, Weinstein and Mayer 1986). It is difficult to set educational or study goals if the student is not clear about the appropriate outcomes for a given task. For example, students must understand the difference between reading a science textbook and reading a novel for an English literature course. They must know how to prepare for different types of tests, such as multiple-choice and essay examinations. Without this type of knowledge, students would find it difficult to set clear goals and optimize their study or learning activities (Pressley et al. 1987).

3.3 Knowledge of Learning Strategies and Study Skills

The acquisition, integration, organization, and storage of new knowledge are all facilitated by the use of effective and efficient learning strategies and study skills (Pressley et al. 1987, Zimmerman 1990, Weinstein

and Mayer 1986, Weinstein and Van Mater Stone in press). A variety of processes and methods are included in this category, each of which is designed to help either organize the study environment, generate and maintain motivation, create positive affect toward learning goals and tasks, make new information more meaningful, help organize new information into more meaningful forms, integrate new information with old knowledge, or reorganize existing knowledge so that it can be intergrated with new understandings and information.

A number of different strategies and skills for studying and learning have been identified in the research literature. The most common study skills described include time management methods, listening techniques, reading strategies, test-taking skills, and dealing with study anxiety. Cognitive learning strategies include generating and maintaining motivation, eliminating negative self-talk and debilitating anxiety, generating positive affect toward learning, building relationships among parts of the material being studied, relating new information to existing knowledge through various forms of elaboration, using cognitive monitoring to focus attention and to facilitate concentration, using comprehension monitoring to check on understanding, and using executive control strategies to organize and orchestrate learning activities.

Students need to learn about different learning strategies and study skills, they need to practice using them, and they need to learn under what conditions they are and are not appropriate to use (Paris et al. 1983, Pressley et al. 1987). Another potential by-product of this practice is the development of well-informed preferences for ways of processing and studying school-related materials (Biggs 1987, Entwistle 1992, Marton 1988). Many students enter higher education settings without a clear sense of their learning preferences, or as prisoners of learning methods they have come to use over time but which may not be the most effective and efficient ways for them to process and learn new information and skills. Learning about a variety of different strategies can help them to make intelligent choices about the strategies that work best for them, as well as providing a resource of alternative strategies that can be used when learning problems occur and their preferences do not work.

3.4 Knowledge of Content

Strategic learners are able to use the prior knowledge they possess about different content areas to help them make sense of new information they are trying to learn and to help store the new information with related knowledge so that it will be easier to retrieve for future use (Alexander and Judy 1988). Thinking about prior content knowledge can increase understanding by providing a knowledge structure in which to place new information. It also helps students to establish relationships to the new information so that it might become more memorable. The more prior knowledge one has in any given area, the easier it becomes to make sense of new information in that area. This is why study in a new area is often more difficult than in one where the student already has some prior knowledge.

3.5 Knowledge of Context

An important aspect of strategic learning is setting and using goals. In order to set realistic yet challenging learning goals, students must be able to appreciate the importance or utility value of what they are trying to learn. Knowledge of context helps students to think about the contexts in which they might apply what they are trying to learn presently or in the future in meeting either their academic, personal, social, or occupational goals. It is not enough simply to want to learn; students must also value the outcomes sufficiently to translate their motivations into actions (Corno 1989.) At any given point in time, the decisions that individuals make about what they will think about or do is the result of a compromise among competing motivations. Which motivations become translated into actions, rather than simple wishes or dreams, is partly a function of the perceived utility values of the different anticipated outcomes.

4. Metacognitive Aspects of Learning to Learn

The act of thinking about one's own thinking, both to decide on processes to implement and to evaluate the outcomes of using those processes, is a crucial aspect of learning to learn. Basically, metacognition involves awareness of one's thinking processes, knowledge about these processes and associated cognitive products, and the ability to evaluate and control these processes. Metacognition is intimately related to the executive, or management, component of learning to learn.

Awareness of one's thinking processes is a critical step in the acquisition and improvement of a learning strategies repertoire, as well as the implementation of the strategies in one's repertoire. Without the ability to reflect upon the processes used to learn new material, students would have difficulty selecting appropriate processes to use, checking on the success of those processes, and modifying them, if necessary, to attain their learning goals effectively and efficiently. This is most clearly seen in comprehension monitoring (Brown et al. 1983). Comprehension monitoring is a subset of metacognitive processing that helps students ascertian whether they are reaching their learning goals on a formative and summative basis. On a formative basis, comprehension monitoring involves checking periodically during the study sessions to ensure that progress is being made toward reaching the learning goal. As a result of these checks, comprehension problems can be identified in good time,

and addressed. The control aspects of comprehension monitoring help the student to identify the problem, consider alternative learning strategies or study skills, and select a potentially optimal new approach. The success of this new method would then be monitored in a similar fashion. On a summative basis, comprehension monitoring involves checking to see if a learning goal has been reached. While this form of monitoring does not have the diagnostic power of formative monitoring, it does help students to determine whether they have acheived the overall goal. It is possible to pass all of the formative checks and still miss the final target. Understanding each paragraph in a text does not necessarily mean that a student has grasped the entire chapter or section. Comprehension monitoring at this level focuses on understanding at the level of integration, organization, analysis, and evaluation.

Strategic learners monitor their comprehension in a variety of ways. What is common to all of these methods is that they involve some form of self-assessment. Common methods used include summarizing, paraphrasing, generating and answering potential test questions, practicing, and attempting to teach the material to another person. The particular method used is not as important as the process. The goal of comprehension monitoring is to help the student identify whether a comprehension error or problem has occurred. The actual method used is relatively unimportant—what matters is that any method used will help the student to detect problems or errors in comprehension. Again, it is useful for students to have a repertoire of methods available so that they have the tools they need for a variety of different learning tasks and goals.

5. Motivational and Affective Components in Learning to Learn

Although strategic learners may know what strategies to use to accomplish a variety of learning tasks, know how to use these strategies, and even know when and why to use different strategies, all this is not enough. Students must also want to learn and they must value the learning enough to persist until they reach their learning goals (Pintrich 1991).

There are a number of factors that impact a student's motivation to reach a particular learning goal. For example, the degree to which students perceive that a particular learning goal fits in with other learning or life goals will affect their level of motivation toward reaching the learning goal. A student who wants to be an engineer may be more motivated to do well in a mathematics course required for engineers than someone who is just taking the course to fulfill a general mathematics requirement. Beliefs and attitudes also have a tremendous impact on directing and maintaining motivation for learning. For example, students' self-efficacious beliefs regarding their capabilities to organize and implement thoughts and actions necessary to achieve a certain performance level affect whether they will even attempt to reach a learning goal, as well as the degree to which they will persist in the face of difficulty (Pintrich 1991). In addition, self-efficacy beliefs about strategy use may indirectly influence performance by impacting the types of methods students select to reach a learning goal (Pintrich and De Groot 1990). Students may believe that a particular strategy is very useful in the abstract but that it would not work if they applied it practically.

Causal attributions are another type of belief that affects students' motivation to select and use effective learning strategies (Weiner 1985). If students attribute learning outcomes primarily to external or uncontrollable sources, such as the difficulty level of the task or innate ability, they will not have the sense of empowerment necessary to take an active role in their own learning. However, if students learn to attribute learning outcomes primarily to their own efforts and developed abilities, then they will be more likely to take an active approach to reaching learning goals. Internal and controllable attributions lead to higher levels of motivation.

6. Executive Control Processes in Learning to Learn

Executive control processes are used by strategic learners to manage the learning process and to orchestrate their use of learning strategies and study skills. These processes take into account the level of students' knowledge in each of the five areas previously discussed, their motivations and emotions, and their goals for a particular learning task. Using all of this information, students are able to create a plan for each learning goal, select the specific strategies or methods they will use to meet the goal, implement the methods selected, monitor their progress, modify either the goal or the methods if necessary, and evaluate their overall approach to the task.

The final step, evaluating their overall approach to the task, is crucial for optimizing future learning (Anderson 1980). The human information-processing system seems unlimited in its capacity to store information but has clear limits to its ability to process information. One of the ways individuals can expand this processing capacity is by "chunking," or creating mental subroutines. These subroutines subsume a number of different steps under a single process, thereby reducing the load on working memory and releasing processing capacity to focus on other aspects of the task or other tasks. Fundamentally, these subroutines reduce the need for conscious attention to the planning, selecting, and implementing steps in the executive control of learning to learn. Once students have established and learned a number of subroutines for performing typical academic tasks, they can approach these tasks in a much more efficient manner. Only if the learning goal changes, or if a comprehension problem is detected, will they have to give much additional thought to how they are going to reach the goal. It takes a lot of time and effort to learn these routines, but once students develop a repertoire they can be both effective and efficient.

See also: Affect, Emotions, and Learning; Learning Activity; Learning Processes and Learning Outcomes; Learning Strategies: Teaching and Assessing; Metacognition; Motivation and Learning; Prior Knowledge and Learning; Self-regulation in Learning; Transfer of Learning

References

Alexander P A, Judy J E 1988 The interaction of domainspecific and strategic knowledge in academic performance. *Rev. Educ. Res.* 58(4): 375–404

Anderson J R 1980 *Cognitive Pyschology and its Implications.* Freeman, San Francisco

Biggs J B 1987 *Student Approaches to Learning and Study.* Australian Council for Educational Research, Melbourne

Brown A L, Bransford J D, Ferrara R A, Campione J C 1983 Learning, remembering, and understanding. In: Flavell J H, Markman E M (eds.) 1983 *Handbook of Child Psychology. Vol. 3: Cognitive Development.* Wiley, New York

Corno L 1989 Self-regulated learning: A volitional analysis. In: Zimmerman B J, Schunk D H (eds.) 1989

Entwistle N J 1992 Student learning and study strategies. In: Clark B R, Neave G (eds.) 1992 *The Encyclopedia of Higher Education.* Pergamon Press, Oxford

Marton F 1988 Describing and improving learning In: Schmeck R B (ed.) 1988 *Learning Strategies and Learning Styles.* Plenum Press, New York

Paris S G, Lipson M Y, Wixson K K 1983 Becoming a strategic reader. *Contemp. Educ. Psychol.* 293–316

Pintrich P R (ed.) 1991 Special issue: Current issues and new directions in motivational theory and research. *Educ. Psychol.* 26(3, 4)

Pintrich P R, De Groot E V 1990 Motivational and self-regulated learning components of classroom academic performance. *J. Educ. Psychol.* 82(1): 33–40

Pressley M, Borkowski J G, Schneider W 1987 Cognitive strategies: Good strategy users coordinate metacognition and knowledge. In: Vasta R, Whitehurst G (eds.) 1987 *Annals of Child Development*, Vol. 4. JAI Press, Greenwich, Connecticut

Weiner B 1985 An attributional theory of achievement motivation and emotion. *Psychol. Rev.* 92(4): 548–73

Weinstein C E, Mayer R E 1986 The teaching of learning strategies. In: Wittrock M (ed.) 1986 *Handbook of Research on Teaching.* Macmillan, New York

Weinstein C E, Van Mater Stone G in press *Broadening our Conception of general Education: The Self-regulated learner.* New Direction Series. Jossey-Bass, San Francisco, California

Zimmerman B J (ed.) 1990 Special issue: Self-regulated learning and academic achievement: An overview *Educ. Psychol.* 25(1)

Zimmerman B J, Schunk D H 1989 *Self-regulated Learning and Academic Achievement: Theory, Research, and Practice.* Springer-Verlag, New York

Further Reading

Jones B F, Idol L 1990 *Dimensions of Thinking and Cognitive Instruction*. Erlbaum, Hillsdale, New Jersey
Weinstein C E 1988 Executive control processes in learning: Why knowing about how to learn is not enough. *Journal of College Reading and Learning* 21: 48–56
Weinstein C E, Goetz E, Alexander P A 1988 *Learning and Study Strategies: Issues in Assessment, Instruction, and Evaluation*. Academic Press, San Diego, California

Learning Strategies: Teaching and Assessing

C. E. Weinstein and D. K. Meyer

Learning strategies can include thoughts, emotions, and behaviors that facilitate the acquisition of knowledge and skills, or the reorganization of one's knowledge base. These strategies are taught and assessed in order to help students become more strategic learners; that is, learners who are willing and able to take significant responsibility for their learning.

Two primary methods are used in teaching strategic learning. The adjunct approach involves creating some adjunct or addition to a course or the general curriculum. These adjuncts can range from a seminar or workshop focusing on a specific strategy to semester- or year-long courses focusing on a broad range of strategies and skills. The metacurriculum approach involves integrating learning strategies instruction into regular content instruction. This approach can focus on strategies specific to the content covered in the course, a broad range of strategies, or a combination of the two.

Assessments of strategic learning primarily involve using self-report methods as diagnostic screening devices to identify students' strengths and weaknesses in a variety of areas related to academic success. These assessments can be used to help students become more aware of their current state of academic self-regulation. They also can contribute to the creation of interventions or programs designed to enhance students' strategic learning. This entry focuses on issues and methods in the teaching and testing of learning strategies.

1. The Importance of Becoming a Strategic Learner

Education involves more than increasing content knowledge and skills. Students also must learn how to manage their learning. Strategic learners want to and know how to take responsibility for optimizing their learning in both academic and nonacademic contexts (Biggs 1987, Entwistle 1992, Pintrich 1991, Weinstein and Van Mater Stone 1993, Zimmerman and Schunk 1989). Strategic learning has tremendous implications for lifelong learning in a rapidly changing, increasingly technological world.

2. What Are the Characteristics of a Strategic Learner?

What does it mean to be an expert strategic learner? First, strategic learners have at least five different knowledge bases they call upon and integrate to help meet educational or performance goals. They are: knowledge about themselves as learners; knowledge about different types of academic tasks; knowledge about strategies and tactics for acquiring, integrating, and applying new learning; prior content knowledge; and knowledge of both present and future contexts in which the knowledge could be useful. However, knowledge alone is not sufficient for expertise. Expert learners also must know how to integrate and use their knowledge and skills to meet their learning goals and how to monitor their progress so they can adjust what they are doing if a problem occurs.

In addition to knowing what to learn and how to learn, students also must want to learn. Effective learning requires the integration of skill and will components. Motivation and positive affect for learning interact with and result from many factors. These factors include goal setting, goal analysis, and goal using; efficacy expectations; outcome attributions; interest; valuing; instrumentality; and utility value.

Finally, strategic learners have the metacognitive awareness and control strategies needed to integrate, orchestrate, and manage their studying and learning. This self-regulation involves a number of interacting activities, which dynamically impact each other. These activities include: creating a plan to reach a goal; selecting the specific strategies or tactics to use to achieve the goal; implementing the methods selected to carry out the plan; monitoring progress on both a formative and a summative basis; modifying the plan, the methods, or even the original goal, if necessary; and evaluating what was done to decide if this would be a good way to go about meeting similar goals in the future. Evaluating this entire process helps students build a repertoire of effective strategies that can be used in the future when similar situations arise.

3. Teaching Learning Strategies

Instruction designed to enhance students' strategic learning takes a variety of forms. Generally, these forms fall into two categories, adjunct instruction and the metacurriculum.

3.1 Adjunct Instruction

Adjunct instruction involves freestanding interventions that can last from an hour to a year. The shorter forms, such as one-hour seminars on textbook reading strategies, usually focus on a specific strategy or related set of strategies. Often these programs are sponsored by learning assistance centers, an administrative unit responsible for student affairs, or taught as supplementary programs through academic departments or units.

A second type of adjunct intervention involves offering strategy instruction as part of the formal instruction in a content course. Usually this instruction is provided in special supplementary or laboratory sessions focusing on strategic learning and studying, or as part of the method called supplemental instruction. For example, many introductory-level college mathematics courses in the United States offer special sessions focusing on how to study and learn mathematics.

The third type of adjunct instruction is the most extensive. It involves long-term interventions designed to help students become more strategic learners in a variety of areas. Often these interventions take the form of a semester- or year-long course, possibly for academic credit. A case study describing a semester-long intervention is described in Sect. 3.2.

3.2 A Case Study: A Course to Teach Strategic Learning

A semester-long course in strategic learning is taught in the Department of Educational Psychology at the University of Texas at Austin. It is a three-credit course, taken for a grade, which meets on a Monday–Wednesday–Friday schedule for one hour each day. The skill, will, and self-regulation components described at the beginning of this entry are addressed in the course.

3.2.1 Student population. A variety of students register for this course, including students predicted at entry to be vulnerable to academic failure, students who experience academic difficulties after entry, and students who simply want to improve their grades. Students meet in classes of 25.

3.2.2 Instructors. The class is taught by graduate students who receive advanced training either through prior experience with similar courses or by auditing the course the semester before they teach it. All new instructors are assigned to a mentor. Weekly meetings are held with all instructors to consider the next week's curriculum, review and critique the past week's classes, and discuss any problems.

3.2.3 Curriculum. The content focuses on all three components of strategic learning: skill, will, and self-regulation. The first three days of the course are used for introductions and pretesting. The pretest data help both instructors and students to identify students' strengths and weaknesses. The measures are used for diagnostic purposes and help create a baseline against which to measure future growth and achievement. (The specific measures used will be described in Sect. 3.2.4.)

The first week is devoted to presenting a model of strategic learning. The metaphor used describes students as managers of their learning. The knowledge, metacognitive, motivation, and executive control components of strategic learning are introduced. The students are told that they will learn how to generate management and implementation plans for common academic tasks such as taking notes in a lecture or from a book, listening in class, completing projects, giving presentations, preparing for and taking examinations, and completing semester projects.

As a part of this process, it is explained that strategic learners are goal directed and use strategies in pursuit of their studying and learning goals. To help them get started, the next topic is setting, using, and analyzing goals. The discussion about establishing and using goals leads into other topics related to motivation and positive affect toward learning. For example, efficacy expectations, valuing, attributions, and utility value are all discussed as components of motivation that are under the students' control.

After a few weeks a semester-long project is introduced. For this project students are asked to choose another class they are taking and select a goal for one of the tasks assigned in the class. The goals usually include things like getting a certain grade on a test, paper, or laboratory project. After setting the goal, the students develop, implement, and monitor a plan for reaching their goal. The purpose of the project is to encourage students to integrate the topics covered already in the course, and topics to be presented. Several class periods are devoted to helping students devise, use, and revise their plans.

Throughout the course all topics are related back to the model of strategic learning. Thus, students are given a schema they can use to make sense of new information and which they can refine as their understanding deepens. Specific topics covered in the second half of the course include: knowledge acquisition strategies; the relationship between understanding and long-term memory; pre-, during-, and post-reading strategies; time management and dealing with procrastination; attention and concentration; note taking; listening skills; preparing for and taking tests; and dealing with academic stress.

The final week of the class is devoted to assessment so that students can see where they have improved. Students also receive feedback about areas they might want to continue working on through the university's learning skills center or other special help programs in some of the individual colleges.

3.2.4 Assessment.

The specific measures used depend on research needs or course development needs being addressed in any given semester. However, a measure of strategic learning and a reading comprehension measure are always used. The measure of strategic learning used is the Learning and Study Strategies Inventory (LASSI) (Weinstein et al. 1987). The LASSI is a 77-item diagnostic/prescriptive self-report measure of strategic learning that focuses on thoughts and behaviors that can be changed and enhanced through educational interventions.

Reading comprehension is assessed using the Nelson-Denny Reading Comprehension Test, Forms E and F (Brown et al. 1981). Half of the students are chosen at random to receive one form at pretest and the parallel form at posttest. National norms are available for each college level (e.g., freshman, sophomore).

3.2.5 Course evaluation.

A variety of means are used to evaluate the course, including course instructor surveys, students' performance in the course (e.g., class tests, selected homework assignments, the semester-long project), students' performance in other classes in the semesters following the course, and changes in the pretest measures at posttesting. Both the instructors and the course receive high ratings from most students.

On the average, students who register for the course have grade-point-averages (GPAs) that are one-half grade point (on a 4-point scale) below other students at the same college level. In the semester after taking the course their GPAs are indistinguishable from other students at their level. Furthermore, this change is maintained over the succeeding semesters. In fact, for freshmen and sophomores, their improvement increases over time. Significant changes are also found for students' scores on the LASSI and Nelson-Denny Reading Comprehension Test, and for measures of self-concept and metacognitive awareness.

3.3 The Metacurriculum

Delivering content without instruction in how to learn the material is like giving someone a state-of-the-art personal computing system without any instructions on how to assemble and use it. Effective instruction includes assuming responsibility for helping students learn how to learn the course material (Entwistle and Tait 1992, Svinicki 1991, Weinstein and Meyer 1991). Just as strategic learners take responsibility for their learning, good teachers provide many opportunities for students to develop and assume this role. When the instruction of learning strategies is integrated with the regular curriculum of a course, then strategy instruction becomes the "metacurriculum."

The metacurriculum includes strategy instruction for all facets of strategic learning: skill, will, and control. For example, teachers may demonstrate learning strategies for understanding and remembering the content. They also can help students develop motivational strategies for initiating, maintaining, and intensifying interest in and self-efficacy for the course content. They may teach abstract concepts by asking students to apply them to situations in their lives.

Teachers can help students set personal goals for the course. In addition, they may require students to monitor their goals and reflect on their degree of success. They also can help students take control of their learning strategies by providing them with organizational tools for planning their course study and assessing their progress.

Teaching students how to learn the course material is a critical aspect of transferring responsibility to the learner because this process involves teaching the skills necessary for assuming responsibility. As Wang and Peverly (1986) argued, if good students are defined as motivated, active, planful, and resourceful, then they should be taught the skills for assuming these roles. In addition, teaching learning strategies as an integrated part of a course allows for course-specific and domain-specific strategies to be applied in meaningful ways. Many of the learning skills students acquire as part of a course also may be transferred to other courses and work situations. (See Entwistle and Tait 1992 for a collection of examples of implementing a metacurriculum approach.)

Finally, the benefits for students of being provided with strategy support while they are learning course topics also extends to teachers. Teachers become more aware of how students learn and of the effectiveness of specific learning strategies for their particular courses.

3.4 A Case Study: The Metacurriculum in a Finance Class

Professor Keane teaches an introductory course in finance. In addition to teaching her students about the various governmental economic regulations and agencies, she also teaches them how to learn the course material. Professor Keane begins her metacurriculum by being very explicit about her goals for the course. After her introduction to the course, she requires that each student (there are 70 students on the course) submit a one-page description of how the course can help them achieve their academic and professional goals.

Professor Keane consistently addresses possible motivational strategies for maintaining interest in the course. She challenges students to present interesting applications of the course topics (e.g., newspaper or magazine articles, cartoons) that can help the class enjoy learning the material. During lectures, Professor Keane makes a point of asking students how they see the current topic helping them in their chosen career (context knowledge).

She also elicits student volunteers to explain basic concepts or review previous topics to check prior knowledge before beginning a new topic (content knowledge). At the same time, she is explicit in asking the entire class to reflect on how much of this information they knew already, and where they might go for extra background information. In addition, students are asked to reflect on why they did not know the information (self-knowledge). For example, were they confused about the topic, were they behind in course readings, or were they disinterested in the class and had been daydreaming?

Professor Keane's lectures are integrated with instruction on how to make sense of content (strategy knowledge). For example, a difficult set of government regulations is reviewed by providing students with meaningful ways to memorize the regulations. Professor Keane is explicit about what information students should highlight in their notes, or suggests note-taking strategies such as, "You might want to number the regulations in your handout for reference in your notes."

Finally, Professor Keane shares her organizational plans for the course with the class so that they can plan the best way to study for examinations, use the textbook and ancillary readings, and pursue their course project. One midterm assignment that she requires is that each student obtains the business card of the person they must interview for their final class project. After collecting all the cards, she asks, "So how has this assignment helped you with your project?" Many students talk about how it helped them avoid procrastinating, or that getting an interview was not as easy as they first thought and they are glad they did not wait until the end of the semester. The session always ends with a discussion of how this experience can be used to help them be more effective in future assignments.

4. Assessment of Learning Strategies

Assessment of students' learning strategies can take a number of forms, most of which involve some type of self-report (Garner 1988). Because it is impossible to observe cognitive processes directly, multiple assessments are often used to obtain converging evidence of students' strategy use.

4.1 Methods Used to Assess Learning Strategies

Three major methods are used to help externalize cognitive and metacognitive strategies: think-aloud procedures, interviews, and strategy-use inventories. Think-aloud procedures require students to describe what they are thinking or doing while completing an actual task. Their verbalizations are concurrent with the activity, which is only interrupted long enough for the verbal report. Students' verbal reports are elicited by instructions or probes that vary in generality (Garner 1988). For example, the students may be asked to "Say everything that you think or do while you complete this reading assignment."

Interviews are used to elicit retrospective reports about what students have thought or done with respect to a recent task or at some time in the past. These reports focus on the cognitive and metacognitive activities that have been completed. This method is also sometimes used to obtain data about hypothetical or prototypical situations that the student has not experienced directly. Interviews are more structured than think-aloud procedures in that at least some questions or probes are planned in advance. Other materials, such as the student's notes or a videotape of the learning situation can be used to stimulate recall (Garner 1988).

Strategy-use inventories are similar to interviews in that they ask students to respond to past, hypothetical, or prototypical situations. They differ, however, in that they are usually administered in written form. An advantage of the written format of strategy-use inventories is that they can be administered individually or to groups of students.

All three forms of assessment should be administered with caution. Students should not report strategies they cannot demonstrate; students should report strategies they would use, not those they think they *should* use; and students should be encouraged to report strategies they might think too obvious or unimportant to mention (Garner et al. 1983). The most important way of authenticating self-report is to gather multiple sources (Ericsson and Simon 1984), especially combining a self-report with a product such as student lecture notes, an examination, or written assignment (Garner 1988).

4.2 A Sample Strategy-use Inventory: The Learning and Study Strategies Inventory (LASSI)

The LASSI is a diagnostic assessment that is used to help students (and their teachers) identify their strengths and weaknesses in 10 different areas related to the skill, will, and self-regulation components of strategic learning. It has been used in about 1,500 post secondary institutions in the United States in a variety of ways, including as a pretest or pretest/posttest measure in learning strategies courses. The LASSI provides standardized scores (percentile score equivalents) and national norms for each of the following 10 scales: Attitude, Motivation, Time Management, Anxiety, Concentration, Information Processing, Selecting Main Ideas, Study Aids, Self Testing, and Test Strategies.

The Attitude Scale contains items addressing students' attitude toward and interest in college, and their general motivation for succeeding in school (sample item: I feel confused and undecided as to what my educational goals should be). The Motivation Scale addresses students' diligence, self-discipline, and willingness to work hard at academic tasks (sample item: When work is difficult I either give up or study only the easy parts). Time Management Scale items address students' use of time management principles and methods to help them organize and control their time (sample item: I only study when there is the pressure of a test). Anxiety Scale items address the degree to which students worry about school and their performance (sample item: Worrying about doing poorly interferes with my concentration on tests). The Concentration Scale items address students' ability to direct their attention to academic tasks, including study activities (sample item: I find that during lectures I think of other things and don't really listen to what is being said). Items on the Information Processing Scale address how well students can use imaginal and verbal elaboration, organization strategies, and reasoning skills to help build bridges between what they already know and what they are trying to learn and remember (sample item: I translate what I am studying into my own words). The Selecting Main Ideas Scale items measure students' skills at selecting important information to concentrate on for further study (sample item: Often when studying I seem to get lost in details and can't see the forest for the trees). Items on the Study Aids Scale measure students' ability to use or create study aids that support and increase meaningful learning (sample item: I use special helps, such as italics and headings, that are in my textbooks). The Self Testing Scale items address comprehension monitoring methods such as reviewing and practicing (sample item: I stop periodically while reading and mentally go over or review what was said). Items on the last scale, Test Strategies, address students' use of test preparation and test-taking strategies (sample item: I have difficulty adapting my studying to different types of courses).

An example of an inventory designed to measure strategic learning as well as approaches to studying can be found in Entwistle's (1992) monograph on student learning.

5. Conclusion

Strategic learners can take responsibility for their learning and they know how to help themselves reach their learning goals. Given the importance of strategic learning for success in education and for meeting lifelong learning goals, it is important for every student to learn how to learn effectively and efficiently. It is also the responsibility of teachers to help their students become more strategic learners.

References

Biggs J B 1987 *Student Approaches to Learning and Study.* Australian Council for Educational Research, Melbourne

Brown J I, Bennett J M, Hanna G 1981 *Nelson-Denny Reading Test, Forms E and F.* Riverside Publishing, Chicago, Illinois

Entwistle N J 1992 Student learning and study strategies. In: Clark B R, Neave G (eds.) 1992 *The Encyclopedia of Higher Education.* Pergamon Press, Oxford

Entwistle N J, Tait H 1992 Promoting effective study skills. In: Cryer P (ed.) 1992 *Learning Actively on One's Own.* CVCP Universities' Staff Development and Training Unit, Sheffield

Ericsson K A, Simon H A 1984 *Protocol Analysis: Verbal Reports as Data.* MIT Press, Cambridge, Massachusetts

Garner R 1988 Verbal-report data on cognitive and metacognitive strategies. In: Weinstein C E, Goetz E T, Alexander P A (eds.) 1988 *Learning and Study Strategies: Issues in Assessment, Instruction, and Evaluation.* Academic Press, San Diego, California

Garner R, Wagoner S, Smith T 1983 Externalizing question-answering strategies of good and poor comprehenders. *Read. Res. Q.* 18(4): 439–47

Pintrich P R (ed.) 1991 Special issue: Current issues and new directions in motivational theory and research. *Educ. Psychol.* 26(3 and 4)

Svinicki M D 1991 Practical implications of cognitive theories. In: Menges R J, Svinicki M D (eds.) 1991 *College Teaching: From Theory to Practice. New Directions for Teaching and Learning.* Jossey-Bass, San Francisco, California

Wang M C, Peverly S T 1986 The self-instructive process in classroom learning contexts. *Contemp. Educ. Psychol.* 11(4): 370–404

Weinstein C E, Palmer D R, Schulte A C 1987 *LASSI: Learning and Study Strategies Inventory.* H and H Publishing, Clearwater, Florida

Weinstein C E, Meyer D K 1991 Cognitive learning strategies and college teaching. In: Menges R J, Svinicki M D (eds.) 1991 *College Teaching: From Theory to Practice. New Directions for Teaching and Learning* (45). Jossey-Bass, San Francisco, California

Weinstein C E, Van Mater Stone G 1993 *Broadening Our Conception of General Education: The Self-regulated Learner*, New Directions Series. Jossey-Bass, San Francisco, California

Zimmerman B J, Schunk D H 1989 *Self-regulated Learning and Academic Achievement: Theory, Research, and Practice.* Springer-Verlag, New York

Literacy

D. R. Olson

This entry is concerned with the uses of writing systems or scripts, specifically who uses them and what they are used for. Literacy may be defined as competence in the use of a script for a particular purpose or range of purposes. Different scripts are based on different principles and involve different competencies. Logographic scripts, such as the one invented by the Chinese almost four millennia ago, employ distinctive characters to represent different morphemes or meaning units. Syllabaries such as those used by the Cree Indians of North America use signs to represent syllables. Alphabets use distinctive signs to represent the phonemes of the language. The choice of unit determines the number of signs required. Logographic scripts may employ thousands of distinctive characters and consequently require a long period of learning. Syllabaries may employ perhaps a hundred signs, alphabets between 20 and 30 signs (Sampson 1985). Although scriptal differences influence the ease or difficulty of becoming literate, cultural attitudes to literacy and the availability of schooling tend greatly to outweigh such differences (Stevenson et al. 1982).

General familiarity with the nature and function of a script is referred to as basic literacy; familiarity with the use of a script for a specified set of functions is referred to as functional literacy. Competence with the formation and interpretation of specialized texts in a domain of expertise is sometimes referred to as elite literacy. As scripts have evolved and as the functions a script serves have changed culturally and historically, literacy as a form of human competence has also acquired a history. The forms this competence takes is a second concern of this entry.

1. Literacy and History

Havelock, a foremost scholar of the implications of literacy, has claimed: "Literacy, though dependent on the technology deployed in inscriptions, is not to be defined in terms of that technology. It is a social condition which can be defined only in terms of readership" (Havelock 1976 p.19). An important dimension of the development of literacy is the invention of scripts which were readily learned and which could be exploited for a broad range of functions. Although all currently functioning scripts or writing systems or orthographies are thought to be adequate to all of the functions they are designed to serve, two properties of scripts are important in understanding the growth of literacy, namely, learnability and expressive power. Learnability refers to the ease with which the script can be acquired. Expressive power refers to the script's ability to express unambiguously the full range of meanings available in the oral language. These two factors are inversely related to each other. Simple, restricted codes or scripts are readily learned but express a limited range of meanings. Pictographic signs such as those used in "environmental writing," including brands, crests, hallmarks, and logos are readily learned even by the youngest children. Full scripts, whether logographic scripts such as those used by the Chinese or alphabetic scripts familiar in the West or mixed scripts such as those used by the Japanese, are more difficult to acquire but once acquired can serve a much broader range of functions.

Alphabets are sometimes claimed to be ideal scripts but more recently this has been shown to be a form of ethnocentrism. Needham (1954–59), an authority on Chinese science, has concluded that the Chinese script was not a significant factor in the failure of the Chinese to develop modern science nor is it an inhibiting factor in modern Chinese scientific work. High levels of literate competence, therefore, have more to do with such factors as the availability of reading materials, availability of instruction in reading and writing, and the perceived relevance of literacy to social and cultural life (Harris 1989). Even in so-called literate societies, most readers learn to read only a select range of written materials; specialized materials, such as those pertaining to religion, science, and government, tend to remain the domain of an elite whose members require several years of education.

Changes in literacy are related to cultural changes but whether literacy produces social change or accompanies social change remains controversial. Historically, the rise of cities coincided with the development of a script suitable for serving bureaucratic purposes. Later, the scientific and philosophical tradition that originated in classical Greece and which has prevailed in the West until this day, developed along with the alphabet. Many writers, including Havelock, maintain that the alphabet was a decisive factor (Gelb 1963, Diringer 1968). McLuhan (1962) and Ong (1982) have claimed that the rise of literacy and the decline of "orality" in the later Middle Ages were fundamental to the Renaissance.

Writers such as Harris (1986) and Gaur (1984) have pointed out that no writing system completely represents speech. Stress and intonation as well as tone of voice convey important aspects of meaning which scripts capture only with difficulty, if ever. For example, how is a script to represent a sneering intonation? The fact that writing systems capture primarily lexical and syntactic properties of speech has the consequence that problems of interpretation are markedly more severe in reading a text than in listening to speech.

There is wide agreement with the more limited claim that literacy has an important effect on consciousness of speech. People familiar with an alphabet perceive speech to be composed of segmentable phonemes; those familiar with a syllabary perceive it as composed of syllables; those familiar with a logography perceive it as composed of morphemes. Consciousness of the language in terms of the properties of the script also induces a certain blindness; namely, the belief that what is written is a complete representation of what the writer meant or intended. Aspects of language and meaning not explicitly represented in a script (i.e., how the writer intended the utterance to be taken—whether seriously, facetiously, ironically, literally, metaphorically—clues to which are often carried by intonation in speech) have been the most difficult to infer in reading and have, historically, provided the most serious obstacles to interpretation. Medieval theologians, for example, debated whether Jesus spoke literally or metaphorically when, taking a piece of bread, he said "This is my body." This has led some writers to suggest that the history of Western thought can be explained in part in terms of the history of reading and interpreting texts (Olson and Torrance 1991, Olson 1994).

2. Functions of Literacy

As writing serves many functions, literacy takes many forms. One of literacy's most important functions in Western culture is that associated with the uses of writing to develop an accumulative research tradition (Eisenstein 1979). Writing permits the accumulation of information collected by many hands over many lifetimes so that "what is known" is no longer identifiable with what anyone knows. But the form of literate competence required to exploit and contribute to that archival form has become highly specialized. It depends not only on literacy skills themselves but on a deeper understanding of the domains represented by those texts. Consequently, literacy trails off into forms of specialized knowledge; at higher levels of competence, literacy and specialized knowledge have become indistinguishable. The popular assumption that literacy training will compensate for this specialized knowledge is misguided. On the other hand, the attempt to use writing for these specialized purposes has contributed to the development of particular literate artifacts such as lists, tables, recipes, indexes, pattern books, dictionaries, thesauri, as well as diagrams, maps, and charts, each of which calls for particular literate competencies. Similarly, the invention of certain literary forms, such as the novel, depended on the existence of a broad-based reading public.

Although social functions such as religion, government, administration as well as the applied arts of agriculture, navigation, and the like exist both in cultures with and without writing, and therefore, with or without literacy, literacy does seem to give these activities a distinctive set of properties. During the Middle Ages, as European societies became more literate, writing came to be used for functions that had earlier been carried out by oral language and ritual. Clanchy (1992) and Stock (1983) have shown how the indenture of servants, deeding of property, evidence at trials, and the preservation of accounts of the lives of the saints, all came to rely increasingly on the use of written texts. As literacy became the dominant means of communication in bureaucratic societies, oral language came to be seen as "loose and unruly" and lacking in authority. People who could not read or write came to be regarded as rude, ignorant, and "illiterate." Street (1984) questions whether the increased reliance on writing was in the service of justice, suggesting rather that it was a means of consolidating power and authority.

Rising levels of literacy were closely related to the great social transformations, the Protestant Reformation and the rise of modern science. The ability to read the Bible for oneself and to discover its meaning was a fundamental basis of Protestantism and the private study, criticism, and updating of objective accounts on the basis of observation were important to the rise of modern science. Both of these functions were enormously facilitated by the rise of printing with movable type in the fifteenth and sixteenth centuries and the translation of important books from scholarly Latin into ordinary vernacular languages. With more material available to be read and with writing playing a prominent role in official business, writing came to take on increased authority and significance. Knowledge came to be identified with the content of books. In the eighteenth and nineteenth centuries in Western Europe and America, even before the establishment of public schooling, more than half of the population had some level of literate competence. Compulsory schooling at the end of the nineteenth century made this level of competence more or less universal.

3. Literacy and Illiteracy

Because of the close association between schooling and literacy, literacy levels are often defined exclusively in terms of length of attendance at school. Three levels of literacy are frequently distinguished: no schooling whatever ("illiteracy"); elementary schooling lasting some four to six years ("basic literacy"); and completion of high school ("high" or "functional literacy"). Such categories are useful for demographic reports that require an indication of the educational levels in particular countries or their regions, but they have little scientific value. Indeed, the appeal to notions of literacy in such contexts is inappropriate and misleading. Arbitrarily identifying "functional literacy" with the completion of secondary school, as was done by the Adult Education Act passed by the United States Congress in 1966, has allowed some writers to claim that "somewhere between 54 and 64 million" Americans, that is, some 25 percent of American adults, are functionally illiterate (Hunter and Harman 1979). Some see in such figures a social problem of great significance and insist on programs of educational reform that would result in higher levels of literacy. However, most scholars criticize both such figures and the resulting claims about "illiteracy".

First, such figures reflect experience with a single institution, the school, rather than with the relevant contexts of application. A person could be highly literate, say in Bible reading or in reading automotive-parts manuals, even if opportunities for schooling were limited. Secondly, the appellation "illiterate" has pejorative connotations implying serious human failing when in fact it merely means the inability to read. It is extremely rare to encounter an individual in a predominantly literate society who cannot read anything and the ability to read in a predominantly "oral" culture may have extremely limited utility.

As an alternative to simply identifying levels of literacy with years of schooling, some scholars have distinguished levels of literacy in another way. Environmental or lay literacy is thought of as the form of unspecified competence involved in dealing generally with a literate environment. Such literacy need never be taught. It is the type of literacy that is acquired through living in an environment organized by written signs, labels, sports scores, and trademarks and in which literate experts aid people in dealing with complex written documents. Almost everyone in a literate society is literate in this sense. Everyone knows the nature, uses, and functions of writing even if they do not personally practice literate skills.

Functional literacy is the degree of literate competence required for dealing with the variety of literate forms encountered in daily life. Employers frequently cite the lack of literate skills of workers as causes of loss of productivity. Closer inspection, however, has indicated that when reading failures occur they are more often a matter of failing to understand the workings of a system than the ability to read. The bottleneck in "reading" is now understood to be a problem of comprehension. That in turn is a function of the depth of knowledge that the reader brings to a text being read rather than a simple familiarity with words and letters. While some attempts have been made to design a test of functional literacy by selecting items that measure the ability to interpret an invoice or to interpret an advertisement correctly, such tests are bedeviled by the fact that no particular literate activities are functional for everyone. To be literate in Reformation Germany in the sixteenth century meant to possess the ability to read the Bible; to be literate in nineteenth-century Boston meant being able to read Henry Thoreau and Oliver Wendell Holmes; to be literate on a twentieth-century building

site means having the ability to read blueprints and materials catalogs. No single skill is functional for everyone.

A literate society is also dependent on the development of elite literacy, a high level of literate competence in specialized domains such as law, science, or theology. Such high levels of literate competence involve learning not only to read and write but also to acquire the specialized vocabulary and the basic principles fundamental to the domain in question. It is estimated that ordinarily literate people have a "reading" vocabulary based on the words they encounter only in reading and writing. This is more than double the size of their speaking and listening vocabulary. In becoming "scientifically literate," for example, a person must acquire not only the concepts specific to a particular scientific domain, concepts such as molecule or gene, but also epistemological concepts, such as assumption, hypothesis, inference and conclusion. In addition the person must learn specialized grammatical forms appropriate to the form of argument, such as setting out claims relative to the evidence for the claims, and learn to distinguish specialized genres such as the descriptions, explanations, arguments, and narratives appropriate to particular literary undertakings. These specialized skills, dependent on high levels of literate competence, require years of formal schooling often accompanied by appropriate apprenticeships.

Part of the significance of literacy comes from the fact that once particular literary forms have been mastered they can be employed equally well in speech as in writing. Consequently, literacy cannot simply be identified with reading and writing. One can write in an essentially oral style or one can speak in a manner characteristic of a book. Literacy makes it possible to speak a written language. In this way literacy has been associated with the evolution of a particular form of thought. As Goody has written: "The advent of a simpler writing system and a larger reading public were clearly factors of great social and intellectual importance in the Mediterranean world and it is not accidental that at the present day so much stress is laid on literacy in programmes of social development" (Goody 1975).

References

Clanchy M T 1992 *From Memory to Written Record: England 1066–1307*, 2nd edn. Blackwell, Oxford
Diringer D 1968 *The Alphabet: A Key to the History of Mankind*, 3rd edn. Funk and Wagnalls, New York
Eisenstein E 1979 *The Printing Press as an Agent of Change: Communication and Cultural Transformations in Early Modern Europe*, Vols. 1–2. Cambridge University Press, New York
Gaur A 1984 *A History of Writing*. British Museum, London
Gelb I J 1963 *A Study of Writing*. University of Chicago Press, Chicago, Illinois

Goody J 1975 *Literacy in Traditional Societies.* Cambridge University Press, Cambridge

Harris R 1986 *The Origin of Writing.* Duckworth, London

Harris W V 1989 *Ancient Literacy.* Harvard University Press, Cambridge, Massachusetts

Havelock E 1976 *Origins of Western Literacy,* Four lectures delivered at the Ontario Institute for Studies in Education, March 1974. Monograph Series 14. OISE Press, Toronto (Reprinted in: Havelock E 1982 *The Literate Revolution.* Princeton University Press, Princeton, New Jersey)

Hunter C St J, Harman D 1979 *Adult Illiteracy in the United States.* McGraw-Hill, New York

McLuhan M 1962 *The Gutenberg Galaxy: The Making of Modern Man.* University of Toronto Press, Toronto

Needham J 1954–59 *Science and Civilization in China,* 3 Vols. Cambridge University Press, Cambridge

Olson D R 1994 *The World on Paper.* Cambridge University Press, Cambridge

Olson D R, Torrance N (eds.) 1991 *Literacy and Orality.* Cambridge University Press, Cambridge

Ong W 1982 *Orality and Literacy: The Technologizing of the Word.* Methuen, London

Sampson G 1985 *Writing Systems: A Linguistic Introduction.* Hutchinson, London

Stevenson H W et al. 1982 Reading disabilities: The case of Chinese, Japanese, and English. *Child Dev.* 53: 1164–81

Stock B 1983 *The Implications of Literacy: Written Language and Models of Interpretation in the Eleventh and Twelfth Centuries.* Princeton University Press, Princeton, New Jersey

Street B 1984 *Literacy in Theory and Practice.* Cambridge University Press, Cambridge

Further Reading

Coulmas F 1989 *The Writing Systems of the World.* Blackwell, Oxford

de Francis J 1989 *Visible Speech: The Diverse Oneness of Writing Systems.* University of Hawaii Press, Honolulu, Hawaii

Tuijnman A C, Kirsch I, Wagner D A (eds.) 1995 *Adult Basic Skills: Advances in Measurement and Policy Analysis.* Hampton Press, New York

Memory: Teaching and Assessing

M. Pressley and P. Van Meter

Students are required to remember great amounts of material in school. Sometimes the demand is explicit, resulting in students intentionally attempting to memorize material; at other times memory is incidental, as when students remember information in text that was read for some other purpose or recall information related to a science or mathematics problem that was solved as part of school work. In general, two factors are cited most frequently as affecting memory of new material: whether the new information is consistent with or can be related to prior knowledge, and how the new information is processed (e.g., whether and which cognitive strategies are applied to the material). Information that is consistent with or can be related to prior knowledge is more easily remembered than information that is not consistent with or relatable to prior knowledge. With respect to information processing, both encoding processes (i.e., activities during study) and retrieval processes (i.e., activities during testing) are known to be critical determinants of how information is organized in long-term memory and how much of it is remembered.

In short, "what the head knows ... has an enormous effect on what the head learns and remembers" (Flavell 1985 p. 213). Whether a person uses the strategies that they possess and coordinates the use of these strategies with other knowledge, however, depends on a third factor, metacognitive competence.

Metacognitive competence refers to the awareness of when, where, and how to use and adapt (i.e., self-regulate) strategies and various types of knowledge (see *Metacognitive Strategies: Teaching and Assessing*).

A critical issue with respect to memory is whether assessments of it are sensitive to all that has been learned. The amount and type of information detected as "remembered" varies with the type of test administered and the degree to which this test stimulates processing compatible with the processing that occurred during study. For example, the amount remembered is likely to be higher if tests stimulate retrieval processes that complement the student's encoding processes while studying. Although most memory tests have focused on the memory product (i.e., what can be remembered), there has been increasing emphasis in the 1970s and 1980s, on measuring the processes that produce remembered information.

The scientific study of memory is an extremely technical field with more than a century of tradition, dating back to Ebbinghaus's classical work in late nineteenth-century Germany. The art of memory enhancement through strategies and the relating of new knowledge to prior knowledge is much older, with important memorization techniques known to have been used by the ancient Greeks (Yates 1966). The study of memory continues to be prominent with experimental and cognitive psychologists, and interventions to enhance memory of educationally relevant content are regularly reported in mainstream educational psychology journals. Although it is impossible to provide anything approaching an exhaustive discussion of a field with such a long history, what follows is a brief discussion of some of the most prominent educationally relevant issues in contemporary memory research.

1. Incidental Versus Intentional Memory

Incidental learning is said to occur when students are not aware that material being covered will be tested for memory. When they are aware of an upcoming memory test, learning is said to be intentional. Even preschoolers are more likely to exert effort and attempt to use memory strategies to remember material when learning is intentional rather than incidental (Baker-Ward et al. 1984). Other things being equal, intentional memory usually exceeds incidental memory. Simply informing students of an upcoming memory test will usually improve memory by increasing cognitive activities that enhance memory.

2. Role of Prior Knowledge in Determining Memory

Memory is often affected by the relationship between incoming information and information already stored in long-term memory (i.e., prior knowledge). If, for example, children have learned about the culture of Indonesia, and are then exposed to a new story about Indonesia, memory of the new story will be affected by what had been learned previously about Indonesia. The encoding of the new story sometimes may be distorted to be consistent with prior knowledge (Brown et al. 1977). Students are more likely to be able to learn material which is related to prior knowledge than material not related to prior knowledge. For example, music students learn sentences about music easily; baseball fans are able to rapidly encode information about baseball. Only music students who are baseball fans have an easy time encoding both types of content (Kuhara-Kojima and Hatano 1991).

One of the most important findings is that even preschoolers rely on well-organized prior knowledge to facilitate their encoding and retrieval of information. For example, preschoolers use their knowledge of birthday parties and eating at fast-food restaurants to remember stories about these events. It has been found that their recall often includes information consistent with prior knowledge that was not included in the to-be-learned stories (Hudson and Nelson 1983).

Whether and how well material is encoded and retrieved depends much more on the compatibility of the material with prior knowledge than on other characteristics of the learners, such as intelligence. For example, highly intelligent children with little soccer knowledge remember less about a soccer story than less intelligent students who are extremely knowledgeable about the game (Schneider et al. 1989).

3. Role of Strategic Processing in Determining Memory

During the 1970s and 1980s, Jenkins (1974) and Flavell (1985) advanced the position that what is remembered is determined by what the learner does while studying. Thus, if given a list of words and instructed to count the number of consonants in each word, a learner will later be unable to recall the words, but will remember if words with five consonants occurred with greater frequency on the list than words with three or seven consonants. In contrast, a person asked to construct an image depicting the referent of each noun on the list (e.g., an image of a cat if "cat" is on the list) will remember many of the specific words later but would probably have difficulty deciding the relative frequencies of words on the list with three, five or seven consonants.

The contention that the specific cognitive processing carried out by a person determines what they remember has inspired two lines of research. The first is work related to determining the processes people use as they attempt to learn material. The second is research to determine whether children and adults can be taught to use more efficient strategies than they inherently do. Studies addressing the former question have produced documentation showing that a variety of memory strategies are more likely to be used naturally with increasing age and education during the childhood and adolescent years (Schneider and Pressley 1989 Chap. 3). Even so, adolescents and adults often fail to use efficient memory strategies, although they are quite capable of carrying out such procedures when taught how to do so (Pressley et al. 1983).

What is a strategy? A strategy is composed of "cognitive operations over and above the processes that are natural consequences of carrying out the task, ranging from one such operation to a sequence of interdependent operations. Strategies achieve cognitive purposes (e.g., comprehending, memorizing) and are potentially conscious and controllable activities" (Pressley et al. 1985 p. 4). Thus, a person can read a book once, carrying out the processes that are a natural consequence of reading, or they can supplement such reading with specific strategies to remember what is being read. An important point to make here is that for younger students such memory-enhancing strategies during reading seem to increase with development, although many adults benefit from explicit instruction in use of the strategies cited below as well as other strategies during reading (Pressley et al. 1992).

Although many variations exist, relatively few

different types of encoding strategies have been studied systematically by researchers. (For reviews, see Pressley et al. 1982, Pressley et al. 1989b.)

3.1 Rehearsal Strategies

When given lists of information to learn, 10-year olds are more likely to repeat the listed material over and over than are 5-year olds. Rehearsal is a common strategy among older children and adults for learning materials that can be listed easily.

3.2 Organization and Reorganization Strategies

When to-be-remembered material contains semantic elements which can be related to prior knowledge, a reorganization strategy can increase the ease of encoding. For example, if a learner is presented with a list of items in random order, but which can be categorized as vehicles, furniture, toys, and foods, reorganization into these categories can enhance learning.

3.3 Elaboration Strategies

The learner can often elaborate to-be-learned material by relating this new information to what is already known. If given a long list of paired associates such as needle–balloon, table–chair, and dog–hamburger, memory for the pairings can be improved by thinking about meaningful relationships between the paired items. For example, the learner could think, "A needle can pop a balloon," "The chairs go under the table," and "Dogs love to eat hamburger."

New facts also can be learned through elaborative processes, Canadian students presented with a great deal of information about one of their provinces (e.g., there are more union members in British Columbia than in any other province) were able to remember the information by asking themselves why the facts are sensible based on their prior knowledge (e.g., Why does it make sense that there are a lot of unions in British Columbia? Well, there certainly are a lot of strikes, and there are a large number of longshoremen serving the west coast fishing and shipping industries). Adults often fail to make such linkages to their prior knowledge unless explicitly instructed to use elaboration strategies to learn to-be-acquired information (Pressley et al. 1992).

3.4 Prior Knowledge Activation Strategies

When people activate knowledge related to to-be-learned content before processing it, their memory of the material is affected. Thus, if asked to activate prior knowledge about burglaries before reading a description of a house, memory of information in the passage relevant to burglary is encoded more effectively. If prompted to activate information relevant to home buying before reading, information pertinent to the purchase of the house is more likely to be remembered from the description (Anderson et al. 1977).

3.5 Imagery

Since Paivio's (1971) seminal work on dual coding theory, it has been recognized that constructing both visual (i.e., imagery) and verbal encodings of to-be-learned material facilitates learning and memory. This effect has been observed with both laboratory tasks (such as list learning) and more ecologically valid tasks (such as learning from connected text).

3.6 Summarization

Attempting to identify the main idea of meaningful material increases memory of the main points of such content. This strategy may occur naturally or be prompted by teacher directions.

3.7 Transformational Mnemonics

There are a variety of memory "tricks" for learning various types of materials. Thus, when remembering a list of items in order, the English learner can use words that rhyme with one, two, three, and so on to facilitate memory. For example, the learner can imagine the first list item in an interaction with a bun, the second in interaction with a shoe, the third with a tree. Then, at recall the learner can retrieve the poem "One is a bun, two is a shoe, three is a tree" along with the images of the bun, shoe, and tree. This retrieval permits the recall of the first three list items. A second transformational mnemonic is the keyword mnemonic, which has been studied extensively since the late 1970s. Keyword mnemonics are useful for learning vocabulary. So to learn the meaning of an unfamiliar vocabulary item (e.g., malachite is a green mineral), the learner thinks of a familiar word or phrase that sounds like the new word (e.g., Mel's kite). The learner then constructs an image containing the referent for this "keyword" and elements of the meaning of malachite. Mel can be seen flying a green kite, with the tail of the kite made of pieces of green ore. (See Levin 1983 for many other examples of keyword mnemonic applications.)

3.8 Retrieval Strategies

In addition to encoding strategies, memory can also be affected by the strategies employed at retrieval. Thus, a person who has read a description of a house remembers it differently if cued at testing to think back to the passage from the perspective of a burglar than if cued at testing to recall from the perspective of a home buyer (Anderson and Pichert 1978). Sometimes children encode information in the form of images but "forget" at testing to think back to the images they created. Their memory for this information can be greatly improved by explicit instruction to retrieve and use the images created at encoding (Pressley and Levin 1980). In general, the use of various retrieval strategies increases with development during the elementary-school years (Kobasigawa 1977).

3.9 Learning Memory Strategies

Children and adults can be taught to use memory strategies. Although execution of strategies is at first slow and deliberate, with practice, strategies can be executed with much less effort than required during this initial acquisition. In other words, with practice, strategy execution becomes automatic (Anderson 1983). Such automatization is essential if strategies are to be used to mediate complex tasks which require coordinated application of a number of strategies. When these strategies are used in combination with other prior knowledge, the result is effective learning of new content.

4. Coordination of Strategies and Other Knowledge

Any complex memory task, for example, remembering the content of a history chapter on the colonization of Africa, requires that a variety of strategies be used in conjunction with prior knowledge activation. How much such learning involves the use of strategies and how much the activation of prior knowledge depends in part on the extent of development of each capacity.

A student with extensive knowledge about African colonization would be able to use that background to quickly understand and relate the new material in the chapter to prior knowledge. As suggested earlier, however, the student might need to be prompted to use his or her prior knowledge as completely as possible (e.g., by cuing of elaboration strategies). Explicit, extensive use of other strategies might be unnecessary for this student. For another student, who lacked knowledge of the colonization of Africa, memory of the material included in the chapter might be much more dependent on use of strategies such as imagery, summarization, and reorganization.

Although there are theorists who continue to argue that memory and memory enhancement are comprehensible in terms of either strategies or knowledge, the prevalent view is that memory, at its best, inevitably involves both strategies and prior knowledge. These two processes must be orchestrated and combined in complementary ways (Baron 1985, Brown et al. 1983, Pressley et al. 1989a).

5. Metacognition and Self-regulation

Although students can execute many strategies when given explicit instructions to do so, they typically fail to continue to use these strategies once the cues have been removed. These failures can take the form of both maintenance (i.e., use of the strategy on similar tasks) and transfer (i.e., generalization to new tasks) failures.

Thus, having taught a student to use a strategy in no way assures continued use of the strategy in either similar or new contexts.

Many theorists and researchers believe that durable use of strategies will be achieved only when students are provided with considerable practice on diverse tasks in diverse settings. This type of practice allows the students to develop understanding about when and where to use the strategies taught as well as how to adapt these strategies to new situations. Good strategy users have extensive and detailed metacognitive knowledge (stored in long-term memory) about the appropriate use of their strategies. Unfortunately, however, many adults do not have detailed metacognitive understanding about the strategies they have acquired, understanding that could be used to guide the effective application of strategies (Dixon and Hertzog 1988).

Critical though such long-term understanding is for the regulation of strategies and other knowledge as part of skilled comprehension and memorization, other types of metacognition also are critical. Awareness of whether what is being studied is actually being learned (termed self-monitoring) can be a critical determinant of strategy use. Awareness that current efforts are not leading to learning should motivate attempts to use different strategies. Substantial data suggest, however, that neither children nor adults are always accurate in monitoring the effectiveness of their current strategies or other cognitive processes (for reviews, see Ghatala 1986, Pressley and Ghatala 1990).

In short, at a theoretical level it is easy to make a case for the criticality of both long- and short-term metacognition in regulating strategies and cognition in general. That gaps in metacognitive knowledge and difficulties in monitoring are common is consistent with the frequent observation that adult learning and cognition often is anything but effectively strategic (Pressley et al. 1992).

6. Assessment of Memory

The traditional way that memory has been measured is to provide a learner with a memory task and subsequently administer a memory test on the content presented during the task. For example, there have been many laboratory studies in which learners have been presented lists of words (e.g., dog, peach, radio, car, lamp, ... stone, book). A recall test for such a list would require that the learner remember the items on the list. A serial recall test would require the items to be remembered in order. A recognition test would involve presentation of another list of items, and learners would be required to recognize items from the first list (e.g., Was "cat" on the list? Was "car?" How about "rock?" Was "peach?").

In general, the more demanding the memory test, the more completely the learner must encode the information during study in order to do well on the test. That is, a serial recall test requires more complete encoding of information than a simple recall test. Recognition generally requires less encoding than recall, although there are exceptions, for example, when distracters on the recognition test are very similar to items on the original study list.

The specific items that are remembered and how they are remembered can often reveal the way in which the information was processed. Thus, if words on a list are presented in a random order but recall occurs in a categorical fashion (e.g., all of the foods recalled together, all of the vehicles recalled together), the inference can be made that reorganization occurred. It is often not clear, however, whether the reorganization took place at encoding or at retrieval (Lange 1978). If semantic associates of original list items are reported as occurring on a recognition test (e.g., "rock" is reported as occurring on a list that actually contained "stone"), there is evidence that coding of study list items stimulated "spreading activation" in the memory system. That is, reading "stone" activated the associated knowledge, "rock," in the long-term knowledge base (Anderson 1983).

Many have argued that using test performance data to make inferences about study processes is relying on indirect measures of processing. More direct measures of processing have been developed and validated in the 1970s and 1980s. If learners are given a list of items to study, the length of time spent on each item can be measured and study strategies can be inferred from the pattern of study times (Belmont et al. 1978). For example, if there is a short pause after the first item on the list, a slightly longer pause after the second, a longer pause still after the third, and so on, the inference can be made that the learner is cumulatively rehearsing the items on the list as they are presented (e.g., saying "dog" after presentation of "dog," saying "dog, peach" after presentation of "peach," saying "dog, peach, radio" after "radio"). Verbal protocol analysis (Ericsson and Simon 1983) is another method now being used to examine processing during study. With this method of measurement, the learner is asked to think aloud, verbally reporting what he or she is doing while studying to-be-learned material.

In summary, several methods are now available for determining the memory processes used by a learner. These methods range from more indirect measures, such as analyses of memory test performance data, to more direct measures, such as time analysis and verbal protocols. The most compelling evidence that the processing involved during a memory task is understood is when the results of several measures converge to support a process interpretation, for example, when the memory test performance (e.g., categorizable items on a list are remembered together) and verbal protocol analyses (e.g., reports of sorting list items into categories during study) coincide. These various methods of testing have permitted insights about the processing of many different types of material, from laboratory lists to connected text.

7. Conclusion

The various topics in this entry are interrelated. Active use of strategies and attempts to relate new material to prior knowledge are more common when a memory task directs intentional learning than when the need to learn is unclear (i.e., memory is incidental). The role of prior knowledge and strategies in memory have only become apparent because of substantial increases in the sophistication of memory assessment, with the procedures for the analysis of test performances and study patterns expanding greatly since the early 1970s. There has been progressively less reliance on indirect measures (i.e., analyses of what was remembered) as psychologists have refined more direct measures (e.g., protocol analyses, pause-time analyses).

What both the indirect and direct analyses have revealed is that memory, at its very best, involves sophisticated articulation of a repertoire of strategies and diverse prior knowledge. Additionally, sophisticated learners are aware of when the use of particular strategies is appropriate. These learners also monitor accurately when strategies and prior knowledge currently in use are permitting effective memorization of new content.

Unfortunately, with increasing sophistication of memory processing assessment, deficiencies in memory processing have also become more apparent. Fully effective, self-regulated use of memory strategies and prior knowledge to enhance the memorization of important new content is rare. More positively, however, many memory strategies can be taught to children and adults. There is growing understanding of the extensive, long-term instruction and practice required for learners to automatize strategies and use them appropriately.

See also: Learning Strategies: Teaching and Assessing

References

Anderson J R 1983 *The Architecture of Cognition.* Harvard University Press, Cambridge, Massachusetts
Anderson R C, Reynolds R E, Schallert D L, Goetz E T 1977 Frameworks for comprehending discourse. *Am. Educ. Res. J.* 14(4): 367–82
Anderson R C, Pichert J W 1978 Recall of previously unrecallable information following a shift in perspective. *J. Verbal Learn. Verbal Behav.* 17(1): 1–12
Baker-Ward L, Ornstein P A, Holden D J 1984 The expression of memorization in early childhood. *Journal of Experimental Child Psychology* 37(3): 555–75
Baron J 1985 *Rationality and Intelligence.* Cambridge University Press, Cambridge
Belmont J M, Butterfield E C, Borkowski J G 1978 Training retarded people to generalize memorization methods across tasks. In: Gruneberg M M, Morris P E, Sykes R M (eds.) 1978 *Practical Aspects of Memory.* Academic Press, London
Brown A L, Smiley S S, Day J D, Townsend M A R, Lawton S C 1977 Intrusion of a thematic idea in children's

comprehension and retention of stories. *Child Dev.* 48: 1454–66

Brown A L, Bransford J D, Ferrara R A, Campione J C 1983 Learning, remembering, and understanding. In: Flavell J H, Markman E M (eds.) 1983 *Handbook of Child Psychology. Vol 1: Cognitive Development*. Wiley, New York

Dixon R A, Hertzog C 1988 A functional approach to memory and metamemory development in adulthood. In: Weinert F E, Perlmutter M (eds.) 1988

Ericsson K A, Simon H A 1983 *Verbal Protocol Analysis*. MIT Press, Cambridge, Massachusetts

Flavell J H 1985 *Cognitive Development*. Prentice-Hall, Englewood Cliffs, New Jersey

Ghatala E S 1986 Strategy-monitoring training enables young learners to select effective strategies. *Educ. Psychol.* 21: 43–54

Hudson J, Nelson K 1983 Effects of script structure on children's story recall. *Dev. Psychol.* 19(4): 625–35

Jenkins J J 1974 Remember that old theory of memory? Well, forget it! *Am. Psychol.* 29(11): 785–95

Kobasigawa A 1977 Retrieval strategies in the development of memory. In: Kail R V, Hagen J W (eds.) 1977

Kuhara-Kojima K, Hatano G 1991 Contribution of content knowledge and learning ability to the learning of facts. *J. Educ. Psychol.* 83(2): 253–63

Lange G 1978 Organization-related processes in children's recall. In: Ornstein P A (ed.) 1978 *Memory Development in Children*. Erlbaum and Associates, Hillsdale, New Jersey

Levin J R 1983 Pictorial strategies for school learning: Practical illustrations. In: Pressley M, Levin J R (eds.) 1983 *Cognitive Strategy Research: Educational Applications*. Springer-Verlag, New York

Paivio A U 1971 *Imagery and Verbal Processes*. Holt, Rinehart, and Winston, New York

Pressley M, Levin J R 1980 The development of mental imagery retrieval. *Child Dev.* 51(2): 558–60

Pressley M, Heisel B E, McCormick C G, Nakamura G V 1982 Memory strategy instruction with children. In: Brainerd C J, Pressley M (eds.) 1982 *Verbal Processes in Children: Progress in Cognitive Development Research*, Vol 2. Springer-Verlag, New York

Pressley M, Levin J R, Bryant S L 1983 Memory strategy instruction during adolescence: When is explicit instruction needed? In: Pressley M, Levin J R (eds.) 1983 *Cognitive Strategy Research: Psychological Foundations*. Springer-Verlag, New York

Pressley M, Forrest-Pressley D L, Elliott-Faust D J, Miller G E 1985 Children's use of cognitive strategies, how to teach strategies, and what to do if they can't be taught. In: Pressley M, Brainerd C J (eds.) 1985 *Cognitive Learning and Memory in Children*. Springer-Verlag, New York

Pressley M, Borkowski J G, Schneider W 1989a Good information processing: What it is and what education can do to promote it. *Int. J. Educ. Res.* 13: 668–78

Pressley M, Johnson C J, Symons S, McGoldrick J A, Kurita J A 1989b Strategies that improve children's memory and comprehension of text. *Elem. Sch. J.* 90(1): 3–32

Pressley M, Ghatala E S 1990 Self-regulated learning: Monitoring learning from text. *Educ. Psychol.* 25: 19–34

Pressley M, El-Dinary P B, Brown R 1992 Skilled and not-so-skilled reading: Good information processing and not-so-good information processing. In: Pressley M, Harris K R, Guthrie J T (eds.) 1992 *Promoting Academic Competence and Literacy: Cognitive Research and Instructional Innovation*. Academic Press, San Diego, California

Schneider W, Körkel J, Weinert F E 1989 Domain-specific knowledge and memory performance: A comparison of high- and low-aptitude children. *J. Educ. Psychol.* 81(3): 306–12

Schneider W, Pressley M 1989 *Memory Development Between 2 and 20*. Springer-Verlag, New York

Yates F A 1966 *The Art of Memory*. Routledge and Kegan Paul, London

Metacognition

P. R-J. Simons

This entry will distinguish three kinds of metacognition: metacognitive beliefs, metacognitive knowledge, and executive control. They will be discussed in relation to learning performance. Their interrelations will also be considered.

1. Metacognition

The concept of metacognition has been used with different meanings. Sometimes the term is used to refer to knowledge about one's own and other people's cognitive processes (e.g., Flavell 1976). Sometimes, however, the concept of metacognition is used in the sense of steering one's cognitive processes (e.g., Brown 1981). Although these two (knowledge and steering) might be closely related, it is important to disentangle them (Lawson 1983, Garner 1987), to distinguish between metacognitive knowledge and executive control. Metacognitive knowledge refers to the knowledge people have of their own (and other people's) cognitions. Executive control is the active monitoring and steering of ongoing cognitive processes. Simon (1979) defined an executive control process as: "The control structure governing the behavior of thinking man is a strategy or program that marshals cognitive resources for performance of a task" (p. 42). Furthermore, a third concept may be discerned: metacognitive beliefs.

Metacognitive beliefs refer to broader, general ideas and theories people have about their own (and other people's) cognitions. They are supposed to be closely connected to their affective, motivational, and volitional convictions. Two kinds of these metacognitive beliefs will be discussed: conceptions of intelligence and conceptions of learning.

2. Metacognitive Beliefs

2.1 Conceptions of Intelligence

Metacognitive beliefs about intelligence (conceptions of intelligence) were studied by Dweck (1988). She found out that people have two kinds of theories of intelligence: the entity theory and the incremental theory. According to the entity theory, intelligence is a fixed commodity and resistant to change through effort or mastery of new skills. According to the incremental theory, however, intelligence is not a fixed capacity. Instead, it is something malleable, that can be increased through effort and learning. Thus, some people see intelligence as "a dynamic, growing quality" and others as "a fixed, static entity." There is a developmental progression from the entity toward the incremental view of intelligence.

Conceptions of intelligence probably determine the kind of goals students (especially learning disabled students) will adopt (Nicholls 1984). Students with an entity conception of intelligence tend to adopt performance goals, whereas students with the incremental view tend to choose learning goals. Performance goals center around concerns about validating one's competence. Learning goals, in contrast, aim at increasing one's competence, at understanding, at figuring out something new. Having learning goals is only possible when one has the incremental view of intelligence. Thus, changing learning strategies is only possible when a child has learning goals. Therefore, efforts to change learning strategies will only be successful when children have an incremental theory of intelligence. In learning strategy research, therefore, important problems include how to change people's conceptions of intelligence and how to induce learning goals instead of performance goals.

2.2 Learning Conceptions

As was shown by Säljö (1979), students differ in the way they see the fundamentals of learning. Five kinds of conceptions could be discerned, with two fundamental underlying ideas. On the one hand, there are students who see learning as having to copy ideas and information into their own heads ("surface conceptions"). On the other hand, there are students who see learning in essence as the construction of knowledge, which one can only do oneself ("deep conceptions").

Learning conceptions correlate with conceptions of instruction. Surface conceptions concur with a view on teaching accentuating that it is the teacher who has to structure, analyze, personalize the learning content through his or her presentations and assignments. Students with deep learning conceptions, on the other hand, believe that teachers can only help the construction process. Vermunt (1992) developed and evaluated an inventory of learning conceptions (and learning and regulation styles) for students in higher education. Three different kinds of learning conceptions could be measured reliably: the surface and deep conceptions mentioned before and a third conception, called the "use-oriented" conception. Students with this last conception of learning stressed that learning is selecting information that can be applied in work or real life contexts. Students with deep and use-oriented conceptions perform better in Open University examinations than students holding reproductive conceptions. Furthermore, Vermunt's studies suggest that students often fail to engage in deep learning when invited to do so because they interpret assignments within their "surface" framework. Learning conceptions are more than simple ideas about learning. They fulfill the criteria of mental models or mini-theories (Claxton 1984) in that they structure a person's predictions, explanations, descriptions, and actions related to the phenomenon of learning.

3. Metacognitive Knowledge

Research on metacognitive knowledge started in the 1970s in the context of developmental psychology. Before then it appeared that children's development of knowledge of memory ("metamemory development") was completed somewhere around 12 years. Now it is less certain that metacognitive development is complete at 12. Instead, even adults may differ in metacognitive knowledge, depending on the domains and problems studied.

Later, research and theory expanded and changed into five new directions. Metamemory became metacognition. Instead of simple memory tasks, complex tasks such as reading, text-processing, and problem-solving came into focus. Executive control was studied instead of metacognitive knowledge. Attention shifted from individual differences toward training. Finally, relations with affective and volitional variables were studied. The first two changes are discussed in this section, while executive control is the topic of the next section. The last two changes are treated in the final section.

3.1 From Metamemory to Metacognition

Flavell (1976) defined metacognition as: "one's knowledge concerning one's own cognitive processes and products or anything related to them, e.g., the learning-relevant properties of information or data" (p.

232). Thus, not only people's knowledge of memory processes were considered to be important, but also their knowledge of thinking, problem-solving, attention, and so on. Miller and Bigi (1979), for instance, studied children's knowledge of attention. Through interviews they found that children differ in the knowledge they have of the role of temptation, noise, breaks, motivation, and deep concentration in attentional processes. For example, first-grade children do not know that television disrupts concentration or that a child absorbed in reading a book might not hear a mother calling. There are developmental differences between first-, third- and fifth-grade children on these and other aspects of meta-attentional knowledge.

Garner summarized the results of studies on metacognitive knowledge as follows: "Younger children in grades 1 and 2 know substantially less than older children in grades 5 and 6 about themselves, the tasks they face, and the strategies they employ in the areas of memory, reading and attention" (Garner 1987 p. 36). Zimmerman (1990), however, showed that there are also large individual differences in older children (12 to 14) in what they know about their self-regulation strategies, such as rereading, help-seeking, reorganizing, orientation, and self-rewarding.

Cross and Paris (1988) discerned three kinds of metacognitive knowledge: declarative metacognitive knowledge (knowing what factors influence human cognition), procedural metacognitive knowledge (knowing how certain skills work or how they should be applied), and conditional metacognitive knowledge (knowing when certain strategies are needed and why they influence cognition).

3.2 Studying More Complex Tasks

A second change in research focus was that knowledge of new areas of human cognition, such as reading and problem-solving, were studied. Myers and Paris (1978), for instance, found that second-grade students know less about reading as a cognitive activity than do sixth-grade students. Differences in metacognitive knowledge of reading refer to: knowing that silent reading is faster than reading aloud; knowing that verbatim retelling is more difficult than paraphrasing; knowing that rereading is an important strategy for resolving comprehension failures; knowing that there is a difference between the meaning of a word and what it "says"; knowing that self-test-strategies help in getting ready for a test; knowing that different strategies are important for reading for study than for reading for fun. Poor readers see reading mainly as a decoding process, whereas good readers focused on comprehension processes. The same subjects who focused on decoding failed to detect investigator-inserted comprehension obstacles in a text.

Thus, there are differences in metacognitive knowledge of reading between younger and older children

and between poor and good readers that are directly related to reading performance.

4. Executive Control

A third change of focus in research was the shift from metacognitive knowledge to executive control. Sternberg (1984), for instance, discerned the following executive control processes that might be used in problem-solving: deciding on the nature of the problem, deciding on performance components relevant for solving tasks, deciding on how to combine performance components strategically, selecting a mental representation for information, allocating resources for problem solution, monitoring solution processes and being sensitive for external feedback. Executive control processes were studied in different domains. Schoenfeld (1985), for instance, studied executive control of mathematical problem-solving. Dörner (1973) studied executive control of complex management decisions. As examples, executive control in the domains of reading and reading for study are treated below.

4.1 Executive Control during Reading

Brown (e.g., 1981) studied executive control processes such as the allocation of study time in reading, judging the importance of ideas, and summarization strategies. For Brown, it is the voluntary control people have over their own cognitive processes that is important. She assumed that the coordination of four factors is especially essential: the learner's characteristics, learning activities, the kind of learning material, and task characteristics.

Four kinds of executive control processes have been studied most extensively (Garner 1987): error detection (comprehension monitoring), text reinspection, allocation of reading time, and summarization.

In comprehension-monitoring research, the error detection paradigm has frequently been used. At certain points inconsistencies or errors are placed in a text deliberately. Error detection rates are low at all age levels studied. Even many adults fail to notice errors that were included deliberately in texts. Some kinds of errors are noticed more easily than others (for instance, logical inconsistencies are detected less easily than false statements). Even when there are explicit hints that the text should be processed analytically and reinspected, a high percentage of errors go unnoticed. There are clear developmental differences and some evidence exists to show that executive control relates both to metacognitive knowledge and performance. A three-stage developmental sequence is consistent with the available evidence. In the first stage, readers or listeners assume that all comprehension problems reside with themselves. In the second stage, the reader or listener focuses on the truth value of the information. It is only in the third phase that readers and listeners look for internal consistency.

Research on text reinspection investigates whether students look back at certain parts of a text when they conclude that they do not understand or remember (parts of) it. At first, however, one should read further to see whether the text becomes comprehensible later on. In general, there are positive relations between text reinspection and reading performance.

Research on the allocation of study time analyzes whether students spend more time on difficult parts of a text or on text they find uncomprehensible. Young students (first and second graders) and also poor students in higher grades (three to six) generally do not allocate extra reading time to the difficult parts.

Finally, in summarization research, subjects are asked to judge the importance of text parts or to write a summary. Summarization skills involve judging the importance of data, condensing information, and writing an abbreviated text. Young children are not aware of the differences in importance. Still they remember the more important parts better than the unimportant ones. Summarization skills are "late developing skills." Clear developmental differences show up. As in the other areas studied, there are positive relations between executive skills and (reading) performance.

The research on executive control of reading had converging findings, which can be summarized as follows: young children and poor readers are not nearly as adept as older ones and better readers in comprehension monitoring and deciding on strategic actions (Garner 1987).

4.2 Executive Control of Reading for Study and Learning

In reading for study as compared to "just" reading, some new aspects come into play, such as having a certain learning goal, choosing certain learning activities, tuning learning activities to the goal, testing and checking in line with the goal, and taking on-line decisions when learning fails to occur. De Jong (1992) discerned seven kinds of executive control: orientation, planning, monitoring, testing, repairing, evaluating, and reflecting.

The category of orientation includes processes that aim at gathering information about the learning task (orientation before learning) or the problem situation during learning in order to select, allocate, or change (ongoing) learning activities. Examples of orientation processes are: glancing through the task, thinking of one's normal study strategy, reflecting on positive or negative characteristics, and reflecting on (gaps in) the foreknowledge. Processes covered by the category of planning express management of the learning behavior by the student. One can think of the choice of learning activities or learning goals and decisions about study time. Monitoring processes function as the finger on the pulse: keeping an eye on the progress of one's own learning processes. Examples of monitoring processes are: noting positive or negative interim results, task characteristics, uncomprehended words, sentences or text fragments, and remaining study time and making an interim evaluation.

Testing is checking whether one has acquired information or reached comprehension, and checking whether learning goals have been reached. Processes such as paraphrasing, summarizing, drawing conclusions, solving exercises, recalling and comparison of text fragments, and asking oneself questions are covered by the category of testing. The category of repairing refers to on-line decisions a student takes during learning. Three kinds of decisions can be discerned: reorientation, on-line planning (now during learning), and diagnosing (finding the causes of problems that occur during learning). Evaluating learning processes refers to judging whether the learning goals have been reached and whether the learning processes proceeded as had been planned. Reflecting, finally, is finding the general in the specifics: thinking about the general things that can be learned from this specific learning experience for next learning. This thinking can focus on all aspects of learning, such as the kinds of goals chosen and reached; the kinds of learning activities executed and the problems experienced; the time needed; the cooperation with other students and teachers; and strengths and weaknesses as a learner. Reflection sets the stage for the next learning episodes and may lead to changes in metacognitive knowledge and beliefs.

The first main conclusion from research done is that good learners are more active in all executive control processes than weak learners (De Jong 1992). At the age level of 12 to 14 years, the better students are more active in monitoring, testing, and planning their own learning than weaker students. Sets of executive control processes explain very high percentages of variance in learning performance. These sets explain more variance than classical learner characteristics such as motivation, test anxiety, and concentration (De Jong 1992, Wang et al. 1990).

A second main conclusion is that executive control processes relate to task characteristics in a complicated way. Different patterns of executive control processes show up in different tasks. Moreover, some executive control processes differentiate between students who perform well or badly on certain tasks, but not on others. In vocabulary learning, for instance, the total quantity of testing processes discriminates between good and weak students, whereas in problem-solving the main differences are orientation, monitoring, and repairing.

The third set of results concerns specific executive control processes: orientation, planning, monitoring, and testing. Students in the beginning phase of secondary education do not orientate before tasks at all; few examples of reorientation were noticed during tasks; better-performing students did not orientate themselves more than weaker ones.

As was the case with orientation, students fail to plan ahead. Planning only shows up on-line when there is a problem or obstacle. One aspect of planning that has been studied is whether students plan different learning activities when learning for recall and multiple-choice questions and when preparing for comprehension or open-ended questions. Three groups of students have been discerned: those who do not plan at all; those who plan extra activities, such as drilling for recall; and those who plan extra activities for learning for comprehension, such as paraphrasing and self-questioning.

Monitoring shows up in many thinking-aloud protocols as an important executive control process. It makes a difference between good and poor learners. It not only matters whether one monitors, but also how one does it and on what states of mind one focuses.

Finally, some conclusions concerning testing are worth mentioning. Weak performers tend to test whether they can reproduce certain information, whereas better-performing students test whether they understand that information by paraphrasing it or by self-questioning.

A fourth and last set of conclusions about executive control processes can be deduced from the work of Vermunt (1992). He found that there are three ways of executive control of learning used by adult students: external control, self-control, and lack of control. This last scale predicts performance quite well. Students stating that they experience problems in executing control over their learning perform less well than other students.

5. Further Research

There is a lack of knowledge about the relations between metacognitive beliefs, metacognitive knowledge, and executive control. Few studies have looked into these relations directly. Yet these relations are often assumed implicitly in training studies. From the fact that teaching metacognitive knowledge is a factor in successful training studies (De Jong 1992), it may be deduced indirectly that there is a relationship between metacognitive knowledge, executive control, and performance. However, more direct research is needed. One assumption is that metacognitive knowledge and/or beliefs form necessary (but insufficient) conditions for executive control. For instance, only someone who intends to be responsible for the correct execution of a certain task will use adequate testing or monitoring processes. Another plausible relation may be (see also Lawson 1983) that metacognitive knowledge arises from reflection (being an executive control process itself) on executive control processes or cognitions. Finally, the three kinds of metacognition may play important roles in explaining transfer.

Three trends in the focus of researchers have been treated above: from metamemory toward metacognition, from simple toward more complex tasks, and from metacognitive knowledge toward executive control. Two further trends have only been briefly mentioned. One of these is the shift of attention from individual and developmental differences toward training. The good results of the metacognitive training programs of, for instance, Palincsar and Brown (1984), led to a new pedagogical optimism and renewed interest in training studies, and contributed at the same time to a decline in research in individual differences. The other trend is a growing interest in affective, motivational variables. It has become increasingly clear that there are close connections between metacognitive knowledge and beliefs and affective, volitional, and motivational variables.

More research on individual differences in metacogniton and executive control is needed. Although training studies are important and have great practical and theoretical value, they need a firmer empirical base of data concerning individual and developmental differences. There are still many unresolved questions concerning the relations between the three kinds of metacognition discerned. Furthermore, there are still a number of undiscovered areas of metacognitive knowledge and executive control. There is a need for a better theory of the developing individual differences and their interrelations so as to be able to produce better training programs.

See also: Affect, Emotions, and Learning; Cognition and Learning; Constructivism and Learning; Expert Level of Understanding; Memory Development; Metacognitive Strategies, Teaching and Assessing; Development of Learning Skills in Problem Solving and Thinking; Self-regulation in Learning; Transfer of Learning

References

Brown A L 1981 Metacognitive development and reading. In: Spiro R J, Bruce B C, Brewer W F (eds.) 1981 *Theoretical Issues in Reading Comprehension.* Erlbaum, Hillsdale, New Jersey
Claxton G 1984 *Live and Learn: An Introduction to the Psychology of Growth and Change in Everyday Life.* Taylor Francis, New York
Cross D R, Paris S G 1988 Development and instructional analyses of children's metacognition and reading comprehension. *J. Educ. Psychol.* 80(2): 131–42
De Jong F P C M 1992 Zelfstandig leren: regulatie van het leerproces en het leren reguleren: een procesbenadering. Doctoral dissertation, Tilburg University
Dörner D 1978 Kognitive Merkmale erfolgreicher und erfolgloser Problemlöser beim Umgang mit sehr

komplexen Systeme. In: Ueckert H, Rhenius D (eds.) 1978 *Komplexe Menscheiche Informationsverarbeitung*. Huber, Bern

Dweck C S 1988 Motivation. In: Lesgold A, Glaser R (eds.) 1988 *Foundations for a Psychology of Education*. Erlbaum, Hillsdale, New Jersey

Flavell J H 1976 Metacognitive aspects of problem solving. In: Resnick L B (ed.) 1976 *The Nature of Intelligence*. Erlbaum, Hillsdale, New Jersey

Garner R 1987 *Metacognition and Reading Comprehension*. Ablex, Norwood, New Jersey

Lawson M J 1983 Being executive about metacognition. In: Kirby J R (ed.) 1983 *Cognitive Strategies and Educational Performance*. Academic Press, New York

Miller P H, Bigi L 1979 The development of children's understanding of attention. *Merrill-Palmer Q*. 25(4): 235–50

Myers M, Paris S G 1978 Children's metacognitive knowledge about reading. *J. Educ. Psychol*. 70(5): 680–90

Nicholls J G 1984 Achievement motivation: Conceptions of ability, subjective experience, task choice and performance. *Psychol. Rev*. 91(3): 328–46

Palincsar A S, Brown A L 1984 Reciprocal teaching of comprehension-fostering and comprehension-monitoring activities. *Cognition and Instruction* 1(2): 117–75

Säljö R 1979 *Learning in the Learners' Perspective: I. Some Common Sense Conceptions. Report No. 16*. Institute of Education, University of Gothenburg

Schoenfeld A H 1985 *Mathematical Problem Solving*. Academic Press, New York

Simon H A 1979 Information processing models of psychology. *Annu. Rev. Psychol*. 30: 363–96

Sternberg R J 1984 What should intelligence tests test? Implications of a triarchic theory of intelligence for intelligence testing. *Educ. Researcher*. 13(1): 5–15

Vermunt J D H M 1992 Leerstijlen en sturen van leerprocessen in het hoger onderwijs. Doctoral dissertation, Tilburg University

Wang M C, Haertel G D, Walberg H J 1990 What influences learning? A content analysis of review literature. *J. Educ. Res*. 84(1): 30–43

Zimmerman B J 1990 Self-regulated learning and academic achievement: An overview. *Educ. Psychol*. 25: 3–17

Metacognitive Strategies: Teaching and Assessing

P. R-J. Simons

Metacognition is primarily concerned with those human reasoning processes that are necessary to solve problems for which no completely developed or automated procedures are available. Both knowledge of these processes and their control or regulation are typically subsumed in the concept of metacognition. This entry addresses a series of six questions related to teaching and assessing metacognition. These questions are:

(a) What aspects of metacognition should be taught?

(b) Who is likely to benefit from metacognitive instruction?

(c) What are the basic principles of metacognitive instruction?

(d) What is an appropriate amount of time for metacognitive instruction?

(e) What tasks should be used to teach metacognition?

(f) Where should metacognition be taught?

The answers to these questions are based primarily on the results of a series of related research studies (De Jong 1987, De Jong and Simons 1988, Simons and De Jong in press, Simons 1989, Simons and Lodewijks 1987, Vermunt and Van Rijswijk 1988). Additional research studies are cited in support of answers to some of the questions. Several methodological issues are then discussed and a series of guidelines for future studies of metacognitive instruction is offered.

1. What Aspects of Metacognition Should Be Taught?

The selection of content to include in metacognitive instruction is not an easy task. Appropriate content can be chosen by examining the differences in metacognition of groups of students: high performing and low performing. Ideally, a diagnosis of the kinds of metacognitive processes not used by low-performing students would be made to corroborate this initial evidence obtained from the comparison.

A second source of content is the information contained in the theoretical and empirical literature. From this literature, three kinds of strategies and skills emerge: awareness of relevant regulatory processes, the possession of regulatory skills, and the availability and use of processing skills. These strategies and skills can form the basis for metacognitive instructional programs.

441

2. Who Is Likely to Benefit from Metacognitive Instruction?

Teaching students skills and strategies they already possess is not likely to be very effective, but if students lack some basic cognitive skills and affective dispositions, the success of metacognitive instruction also may be impaired. Students who lack essential reading skills, for example, can hardly be expected to benefit from instruction aimed at the improvement of study skills or self-regulatory reading skills. Similarly, students who do not believe that it is possible to regulate their own learning or who dislike the strategies being taught to them are not likely to benefit from metacognitive instruction.

Ideal students, then, are those who lack metacognitive skills and strategies, but who are not deficient in other respects. As a consequence, some diagnosis of the students' knowledge and emotional base seems necessary to the success of metacognitive instruction.

3. The Basic Principles of Metacognitive Instruction

Several principles can be derived from current research on metacognitive teaching and learning. Among the most important are the following:

(a) Learning activities and processes, rather than learning outcomes, must be emphasized (Process Principle).

(b) Learning is "thematized" and students are helped to become aware of their learning strategies, self-regulation skills, and the relationship of these strategies and skills to learning goals (Reflectivity Principle).

(c) The interaction of cognitive, metacognitive, and affective components of learning is central (Affectivity Principle).

(d) Students must be made constantly aware of the use and function of knowledge and skills (Functionality Principle).

(e) Teachers and students should strive for transfer and generalization, without expecting either to occur without practice in context (Transfer Principle).

(f) Learning strategies and self-regulation skills need to be practiced regularly, with sufficient time provided and with practice occurring in appropriate contexts (Context Principle).

(g) Students should be taught how they can regulate, diagnose, and revise their own learning (Self-Diagnosis Principle).

(h) Instruction should be designed in such a way that there is an optimal balance between the quality and quantity of learning activity (Activity Principle).

(i) The responsibility for learning should be shifted gradually to the students (Scaffolding Principle).

(j) Especially with younger students, relationships with parents and other adults should be emphasized so that initial attempts at self-regulated learning can be supervised (Supervision Principle).

(k) Cooperation and discussion among students is necessary (Cooperation Principle).

(l) Higher cognitive learning goals which require deeper cognitive processing should be emphasized (Goal Principle).

(m) New subject matter is learned as it becomes anchored to existing knowledge and preconceptions (Preconception Principle).

(n) Instruction should be tailored to the current conceptions of students (Learning Conception Principle).

Not all programs need to include all principles. At the same time, however, programs which adhere to more of these principles are likely to be more effective.

4. Time Needed for Metacognitive Instruction

In general, too little time is allocated to metacognitive instruction in most programs. This assertion does not mean that short training programs cannot have effects. In a study with adult students learning a foreign language vocabulary, impressive results were attained within one hour (Simons and De Jong in press). At the same time, however, short programs generally are not effective with younger children, less able students, and learning-disabled students. Longer programs are more likely to be effective than shorter ones, although research on the optimal length of instructional programs for teaching metacognition is clearly needed.

5. Tasks Needed to Teach Metacognition

The tasks used to teach metacognition should be ecologically valid. That is, they should resemble those tasks that students frequently encounter in and outside of school. If possible, the tasks should be those that students are expected to master in school and on which their performance is systematically monitored and evaluated. Tasks not meeting these criteria are often seen as irrelevant to students.

In addition, tasks assigned to students should be of appropriate difficulty. If the tasks are too easy, students can rely on routine, automatic procedures, and there is no need for regulatory processes. Overly difficult tasks are also problematic. For example, when high and low performing students were given a very difficult task, low performing students stopped working on the task, while high performing students kept trying to accomplish the task despite the fact that their efforts were ineffective, inefficient, and not improving (Simons and Liew-On 1991).

Finally, tasks assigned to students should be similar to those they are likely to be assigned in the "real world." While dissimilar tasks are appropriate from an experimental research perspective to examine issues of transfer and generalizability, it must be realized that the likelihood of transferring learning from tasks used in instruction to very dissimilar tasks is extremely small for most students (Salomon and Perkins 1989).

6. The "Where" of Teaching Metacognition

Since tasks used to teach metacognition should be as ecologically valid as possible, the most appropriate placement of these tasks is in the school curriculum. This embedding of metacognitive instruction in schools is not without its problems, however. Embedding often confuses students. Instead of only having to study and solve problems, students are asked to regulate the processes involved in studying and solving problems.

Prawatt (1991) has offered a resolution to this dilemma. He proposed that "immersion" approaches be developed. In immersion approaches the regulation skills are activated by the teacher without much attention from students. As a consequence, they initially are not viewed by the students as competing requirements. Only after they have been practiced by students and shown to be beneficial to them do they receive attention in the classroom.

7. Methodological Issues in Research on Metacognition

There are several methodological issues that need to be resolved in order to gain a substantially greater understanding of metacognition during the decade of the 1990s. They fall into three categories: experimental design, fidelity of implementation, and assessment of the effects of metacognition.

7.1 Experimental Design

One important question is the composition of a proper control group. Since only students who lack certain strategies and skills should receive instruction, the best control group consists of students who also lack the strategies and skills being taught, but who are not selected for treatment. Of course, random assignment to groups is essential in this case.

When random assignment is not possible, high achieving students who already possess the skills can be used as a "control group." Although these students do not comprise a control group in the traditional sense, they are better than no control group at all. The goal of metacognitive instruction is to give poorer students the strategies and skills used regularly by better students. In this regard, successful metacognitive instruction should be expected to reduce or remove the initial differences between poorer students who are provided with metacognitive instruction and better students left unaided.

7.2 Fidelity of Implementation

A second methodological issue concerns whether the metacognitive instruction envisioned by the designer of the instructional program actually occurs in the form intended in the experimental classrooms and does not occur in the control classrooms. There have been many instances in which intended interventions were distorted completely. In other cases students in control groups have been given the treatment, despite requests by researchers not to do so. Finally, students themselves can also distort interventions by failing to engage in or complete assigned work or failing to use materials or instructional aids offered to them.

7.3 Assessment of Metacognition

A third methodological problem occurs in the area of assessing the effects of metacognitive instruction. Most often, the goals of metacognitive instruction are stated in process terms. That is, instruction is expected to change the ways in which students process information (e.g., summarize information, monitor their acquisition of information). Only indirectly is this instruction expected to influence student learning outcomes. Process measures are not always easy to design, efficient to use, or effective in terms of their technical qualities (e.g., validity, reliability). Nonetheless, the availability and use of adequate assessment techniques are the keys to understanding metacognition and improving metacognitive instruction.

8. Guidelines for Future Studies of Metacognitive Instruction

Based on the foregoing discussion, a set of guidelines pertaining to the design of studies attempting to increase or improve metacognition can be offered.

(a) Develop an instructional program which has

the greatest likelihood of producing the desired results, and examine the effectiveness of the components of the program after its implementation by systematically dismantling it.

(b) Derive the content of the instructional program by looking at studies of the differences between high and low performers, experts and novices, and writings in a variety of theoretical frameworks.

(c) Develop an instructional program which includes at least the following goals or objectives: metacognitive awareness, regulatory skills, learning skills, and affective–motivation skills.

(d) In evaluating the effectiveness of the program, use students who lack the strategies and skills which are included as program goals or objectives. This will quite likely require some diagnosis of the current metacognitive levels of students.

(e) Extend the length of the program to ensure that the students have a reasonable chance of acquiring the metacognitive strategies and skills being taught.

(f) Evaluate the effectiveness of the program both during the program and after its completion.

(g) Incorporate into the program tasks that are ecologically valid and are of appropriate and varied levels of difficulty.

(h) Use effectiveness measures that estimate immediate achievement, "near transfer" of learning, and "far transfer" of learning. "Near transfer" can be facilitated by contextualizing the instruction; "far transfer" can be enhanced by decontextualizing the strategies and skills. Make sure that the learning process, rather than or in addition to learning products or outcomes are monitored.

(i) Embed instruction and immerse students in metacognitive learning in real school settings.

(j) Use control groups that either are composed of similar students (who are randomly assigned to treatment or control groups) or high performing students who serve as benchmarks for program success.

(k) Monitor the program to ensure that it is being implemented as intended; also, monitor the control group to check on the strategies and skills, if any, that they are being taught.

9. Conclusion

Understanding and being able to regulate what and how human beings think is central to teachers' ability to improve substantially how they teach their students.

Providing students with metacognitive strategies and skills enables them to negotiate and meet the demands of a wide variety of educational settings and situations. While some students appear to use such strategies and skills almost naturally, most students can be taught to acquire and use them if the principles of effective metacognitive instruction are followed.

References

De Jong F P C M 1987 Differences in the self-regulation processes between successful and less successful students and the prediction of learning performances in the case of comprehension and learning of text. In:Simons P R J, Beukhof G(eds.) 1987 *Regulation of Learning*. svo-Selecta, The Hague

De Jong F P C M, Simons P R J 1988 Self-regulation in text processing. *European Journal of Psychology of Education* 3(2): 177–90

Prawatt R 1991 The immersion approach to learning to think. *Educ. Researcher*

Salomon G, Perkins D N 1989 Rocky roads to transfer: Rethinking mechanisms of a neglected phenomenon. *Educ. Psychol.* 24(2): 113–42

Simons P R J 1989 Modifying the regulation processes of learning: Two exploratory training studies. *Canadian Journal of Educational Communication* 18(1): 29–48

Simons P R J, Lodewijks J G L C 1987 Regulatory cognitions during learning from text. In: De Corte E, Lodewijks H, Parmentier R, Span P (eds.) 1987 *Learning and Instruction: European Research in an International Context*, Vol. 1. Leuven University Press/Pergamon Press, Oxford

Simons P R J, Liew-On M 1991 Breadth of orientation: Individual differences and training. In:Carretero M, Pozo M, Pope M, Simons P R J(eds.) 1991 *Research on Learning and Instruction*. Pergamon Press, Oxford

Simons P R J, De Jong F P C M in press Self-regulation and computer-aided learning. *Appl. Psychol.*

Vermunt J D H M, Van Rijswijk F 1988 Analysis and development of students' skill in self-regulated learning. *High. Educ.* 17(6): 647–82

Further Reading

Bereiter C, Scardamalia M 1989 Intentional learning as a goal of instruction. In: Resnick L B(ed.) 1989 *Knowing, Learning, and Instruction: Essays in Honor of Robert Glaser*. Erlbaum, Hillsdale, New Jersey

Collins A, Brown J S, Newman S E 1989 Cognitive apprenticeship: Teaching the crafts of reading, writing, and mathematics. In: Resnick L B (ed.) 1989 *Knowing, Learning, and Instruction: Essays in Honor of Robert Glaser*. Erlbaum, Hillsdale, New Jersey

Flavell J H 1979 Metacognition and cognitive monitoring: A new area of cognitive-developmental inquiry. *Am. Psychol.* 34: 906–11

Palincsar A S, Brown A L 1989 Instruction for self-regulated learning. In: Resnick L B, Klopfer L E (eds.) 1989 *Toward the Thinking Curriculum: Current Cognitive Research*. Association for Supervision and Curriculum, Arlington, Virginia

Motivation and Learning

W. Lens

Motivation is an important determinant of learning and its outcomes, as expressed in academic performances. It explains why some students enjoy school life and make the most of their school career, preparing them for a professional career and for life in general. It also explains why so-called demotivated students hate an important part of their daily life and why most of them underachieve, so harming themselves for the rest of their lives. Student motivation is a complex psychological process. There may be many personal and situational reasons why students are motivated or demotivated. This entry discusses the most important aspects of this complex situation and explicitly suggests different avenues that can be taken by teachers and parents to affect the motivation of their students and children.

1. Learning is Overdetermined

Learning and doing well in school are intentional, goal-oriented activities. As such, they are a function not only of cognitive skills and other abilities, but also of affective and motivational variables. Individual differences in the efficiency of learning processes and in their outcomes are explained by differences in abilities or capacities and in motivation. They result from an interaction between cognitive and motivational variables. Whether students learn or not, what they learn, how much time they devote to it, how efficient they are at it, and the level of proficiency they reach are all partly determined by how strongly they are motivated for their school work. The intentionality of school learning can be very complex. Students may have many and varied reasons for studying. They do it to develop their cognitive abilities; they want to know more. They do their best because they want to please the teachers and/or their parents, to be rewarded by them. They want to be successful and not to fail. They may even be highly motivated for their studies because they want to have a particular type of job or profession as adults. It is not unreasonable to assume that for most pupils and students school learning serves many purposes. Learning, then, is "overdetermined." It is instigated and sustained by different types of motivation.

In psychology there is no global theory of motivation that can explain all aspects of student motivation. Basic and more applied research has resulted in a series of more limited minitheories. Each of these theoretical approaches explains some aspect(s) or component(s) of the total motivation to learn and excel at school. This complexity or variety may be confusing for practitioners. They should consider the different theories as different glasses through which they can look at the same rich reality in the classroom or in the study. Each theory reveals different aspects of that reality and offers alternative ways to prevent or cure motivational problems. From such a practical perspective, it is important that educators—based on knowledge of individual students and their histories and family backgrounds—should be creative enough to borrow distinct elements from different theoretical approaches.

2. Motivation as a Psychological Process

Theories of human motivation can be roughly classified in two broad categories: content theories and process theories. Content theories view motivation as a more or less stable, inborn or acquired, personality characteristic (e.g., instincts, drives, needs, motives). They follow a more Aristotelian type of causal explanation: the movement (behavior is a kind of psychological movement) is attributed solely to characteristics of the moving object, in this case the acting individual, and not to the environment in which the movement takes place.

Process theories of motivation follow a Galilean type of explanation. The movement of objects is attributed to characteristics of the objects and of their environment. These theories consider motivation as a psychological process in which personality traits (e.g., needs, motives, abilities) interact with characteristics of the environment, as perceived by the individual (e.g., content and difficulty of the learning task, teachers and parents, the classroom environment). Lewin's conceptualization of behavior as resulting from the interaction between the individual personality and the perceived environment is extended to motivational processes. This implies that there are no students who will be very highly motivated for all types of subject matters or teachers, and that it is fruitless to attempt to create a learning environment in which all pupils will be optimally motivated (Atkinson 1978). Process theories suggest that both traits within the individual and situational circumstances should be taken into consideration in trying to understand, explain, and cure motivational problems and learning difficulties (Snow 1989, Snow and Swanson 1992).

3. Motivation: Explaining or Describing Behavior

Motivational theories intend to offer theoretical explanations for particular behavioral characteristics, such as the intentionality, initiation, persistence, degree of activity, and, for achievement tasks, the level of performance or efficiency. A motivational explanation requires a measure of motivation that is not based on the behavioral differences that need explanation. There is a considerable risk, certainly in daily practice, in failing to observe this rule. Parents and teachers alike often explain pupils' behavior by referring to motivational variables or processes as causes. However, the only empirical basis they have for talking about motivation are the behavioral characteristics themselves. In other words, they offer a pseudoexplanation and produce an unscientific circular argument. In such cases, motivation is not used as an explanatory concept but as a descriptive label. A teacher may, for example, observe that some students often arrive late for classes, do not do their homework, do not pay much attention to what the teacher says, that they try to disrupt the class and underperform in tests. The teacher may wonder why this should be the case, and arrive at the conclusion that they are not motivated for their studies. However, this inference does not explain the students' behavior; it only labels it. A causal explanation must prove that the students are demotivated and for what reasons, independently of the observed behavioral manifestations. Cause and effect should not be confused.

4. Motivation and Persistence in Study

Persistence in study or devoting much time to schoolwork is an important determinant of learning outcomes: practice makes perfect. Persistence is most often understood as being caused by a strong motivation to learn and to do well in school. Motivational psychology assumes a positive linear relationship between strength of motivation and persistence: the stronger the motivation to study, the more time spent studying. Schoolwork, however, should not be considered as an isolated, episodic activity, but as part of a continuous stream of behavior (Atkinson and Birch 1970). In other words, children are engaged in other activities both before and after they study. According to Atkinson and Birch's *The Dynamics of Action* (1970)—taken as a more general motivational theory—it is not only motivation that should be examined when attempting to explain persistence. The initiation and the persistence of learning activities are also dependent on the number and the strength of competing alternative motivational tendencies. Students who have a relatively strong motivation to study but who also have many and/or absorbing extracurricular interests may in fact spend less time learning (in class during lessons and at home in their study) than other students who are less motivated but who have fewer competing motivational interests. Motivational researchers and practitioners need to devote more attention to this important insight. The amount of time spent studying can be increased by enhancing the

motivation to study and by decreasing the number and strength of competing motivational tendencies. Many students do not have enough time to learn because they have too many other interests.

Rollett (1987) introduced the concept of "effort-avoidance motivation" as an alternative explanation for low persistence or low "time on task." She distinguishes this type of negative motivation from low-achievement motivation and from high fear of failure or test anxiety. Rollett found that frustrating experiences during the first contacts with a particular domain may cause a domain-specific tendency to avoid effort. The goal of effort-avoiders becomes an exercise in convincing teachers and parents that they are no good as students. Rollett developed a questionnaire to measure effort-avoidance and a training program to help effort-avoiders.

The time spent on task and how efficiently it is used depend also on metamotivational skills such as volition or will. Volitional processes shield action intentions from hedonically or emotionally more tempting alternatives. They help ensure that such intentions are enacted (Halisch et al. 1987). Salomon and Globerson (1987) introduced the concept of mindfulness in learning contexts. Mindful learning requires sustained mental effort and concentration. Students can be distracted from the learning task by situational provocations and by covert cognitions. In general, it seems easier to control external distractions than internal cognitions that interfere with learning activities. The latter are dependent on rather stable personality traits. The less than optimal performances of failure-threatened or highly test-anxious students, for example, are mostly due to such interfering cognitions (when studying and taking tests). Success-oriented individuals are much less distracted by such task-irrelevant thoughts. The same difference can be found between action-oriented and state-oriented individuals (Kuhl 1986). Action-oriented individuals focus their attention on the actions that are necessary to reach an intended goal (e.g., learning or achievement goals). They persist longer in learning activities because they can more easily control internal and external difficulties and temptations. State-oriented individuals are more preoccupied with existing or desired internal or external states rather than with how to achieve or avoid those states. Such students are preoccupied with what they do not know or cannot yet do and with what they should be able to understand and master, rather than with how to bridge the gap between the two states. For them, it is more difficult to persist in a goal-oriented action. They are easily distracted.

5. Learning Goals and Performance Goals

Dweck (1989) makes a motivationally important distinction between two types of student goals: learning goals and performance goals. These correspond to the two main categories of activities that are expected from students in school: learning and performing. Most of the time students should be involved in learning activities. Their goal must then be to increase their knowledge and competencies, to understand more, and to master more complex issues. With such tasks individuals cannot fail but only improve or grow. Learning tasks offer teachers many opportunities to give positive feedback, enhancing the intrinsic motivation to learn (see Sect. 6) Consequently, there is no room for inhibitory test anxiety or fear of failure. Learning tasks arouse a task-orientation. Students are only occupied by the intellectual problem at hand, wanting to understand it and to find out how to solve it. They may well be attracted by challenging tasks. Even the less intelligent students can improve their knowledge and problem-solving strategies. This gives them feelings of competence, which stimulate their intellectual curiosity.

At other times students have to take tests or exams. Such activities are organized in order to find out how much and how efficiently students have learned. The students' goal now becomes that of proving to themselves and to others (teachers, parents, friends, and peers) how good they are or that of concealing how bad they are. Performance tasks arouse an ego-orientation. The student is less occupied with the task than with how good or how bad he or she will look, and thus strives for success and tries to avoid failure. Performance tasks arouse achievement motivation and fear of failure (test anxiety). Failure-threatened students tend to be inhibited and defensive. Their main concern is to avoid a perception of incompetence (in their own eyes and in the eyes of important others). They avoid challenging tasks.

A potentially important problem for the intrinsic motivation to learn results from the fact that many students (and teachers) perceive learning tasks as performance tasks (Dweck 1989). They are self-oriented rather than task-oriented when they learn. Their goal is not to learn and improve their intellectual abilities, but to demonstrate to themselves and to others their high ability (or to conceal it). In a self-defensive reaction, many students therefore do not seek out challenging tasks or they invest little effort in tasks because the possible combination of high effort and low results would lead to the inference of low ability.

The perception of learning tasks as such or as performance tasks seems to be related to students' and teachers' implicit theory of intelligence (Dweck 1989). Students who conceive intelligence as a stable trait are inclined to show how much they possess. They turn learning tasks into achievement tasks. Such students and teachers believe that a person can have a high or low level of intelligence but also that intelligence cannot develop or grow. A more favorable implicit theory holds that intelligence is a cognitive ability that can be developed through exercise. Students who hold this theory are not afraid of challenging learning

tasks. They want to learn, to enhance their intellectual abilities and knowledge. Learning tasks can only lead to growth, not to failure and the negative emotions that go with it. Such an attitude has a positive effect on the intrinsic motivation to learn.

6. Intrinsic Student Motivation

The total motivation to learn is a combination of intrinsic and extrinsic motivation. Children are *intrinsically* motivated when learning and performing at school are goals in themselves. They are *extrinsically* motivated when the activity is done for the sake of material or other rewards that are not intrinsically related to school learning. In this case, learning and performing well in tests and exams are instrumental activities to earn those rewards. Parents and teachers make much use of such rewards to motivate children. The behavioral effects of extrinsic rewards have been mainly studied in learning psychology (e.g., Skinnerian operant conditioning). Research on student motivation has been concerned predominantly with the different types of intrinsic motivation (Malone and Lepper 1987), even to the neglect of extrinsic motivation. (This has been much less so in research on work motivation.) Educational psychologists seem to assume that extrinsic motivation is far less important than intrinsic student motivation, but this is not the case. Most students—even those with a strong intrinsic motivation—are highly motivated by extrinsic rewards and goals.

6.1 Curiosity

Intellectual or epistemic curiosity is probably the most typical type of intrinsic motivation to learn. The desire to know and to understand intellectual problems is aroused by moderately discrepant, complex, and novel information. Familiar or simple information arouses only satiation and boredom. But learning tasks that are too complex or totally new instigate anxiety and withdrawal. A need for knowledge and information is very strong among young children, but seems to decrease with age. It is very low in many pupils from the end of primary school or the beginning of secondary education onward (about 12 years old), certainly for the type of intellectual problems and information offered in formal education. It is unclear as to what causes this decline in intrinsic curiosity. One potentially important explanation is the frequent use of extrinsic rewards in educational settings (see Sect. 7).

Teachers' own intrinsic interest in subjects and the way in which they present or introduce them have a strong effect on students' intellectual curiosity. From a motivational point of view, the common practice of punishing students for asocial or disruptive classroom behavior by giving them additional reading, writing, or mathematic assignments as home work is highly objectionable: it tells the students quite explicitly that such activities are not intrinsically interesting. By definition, a punishment is an unpleasant experience or activity.

6.2 *Competence and Efficacy*

The need for mastery, or at least competence and efficiency in solving challenging tasks is a second type of intrinsic motivation that is highly relevant for schoolwork. Perceptions and feelings of "self-efficacy" ("I am good at it"; "I can do it") are intrinsically motivating (Bandura 1986). People in general like to do things they are good at. (They usually also become good at things that they like to do.) Students are motivated and invest considerable effort when they expect that they can master a task. That is why challenging tasks can be more motivating. Tasks that are either too easy or too difficult do not arouse motivation. In such tasks, a person cannot expect to feel competent and efficient. Success in very easy tasks is not attributed to abilities or competence, but to the low degree of difficulty. When the task is too difficult a person does not expect to be successful. The probability of failure and hence the perception and feelings of incompetence are then very high. Students need positive feedback contingent upon good performance in order to feel competent (Weinert 1987). Success experiences require that the level of performance in the learning or achievement task is equal to or higher than the level of aspiration or the goal that was strived for, and that the outcome can be internally attributed to abilities and/or effort. Therefore, the use of an individual criterion (e.g., better than the previous performance) rather than a social criterion (e.g., other students' level of performance) in the evaluation of learning outcomes should be recommended. It permits more frequent positive feedback. With this type of criterion, a given learning or achievement task can be challenging for all students in a class, whatever the level of their cognitive abilities. Moreover, the less able students can experience growth in ability and knowledge, which will stimulate their feelings of competence and hence their intrinsic motivation. Students must learn to set realistic learning and achievement goals for themselves. Unrealistically high or low goals do not motivate.

This type of intrinsic motivation is closely related to the positive component of achievement motivation, namely, the motivation to strive for success (Atkinson 1983). Atkinson's theory of achievement motivation holds that success-oriented individuals are most motivated for achievement tasks with a medium degree of difficulty (probability of success around 0.5). For such tasks, the product of the probability of success (Ps) times the incentive value of success (1-Ps) is maximal.

Basic research on epistemic curiosity, on the need for competence or efficacy, and on achievement motivation suggests that these types of intrinsic motivation are strongly aroused in intellectually homogeneous classes. In such groups of students, teachers can set learning and achievement tasks that are optimally discrepant from what is already known and that are moderately difficult for all students. However, meta-analysis of research on the motivational and behavioral effects of homogeneous versus heterogeneous classes shows that this inference does not always hold, certainly not for low-ability groups (Slavin 1990). An alternative is to work, as often as possible, with individualized goals. This can easily be applied by parents when commenting upon their children's school results. Yet it is, of course, not easy for teachers to do so in large and very heterogeneous classes. Computer-assisted learning can be very helpful in this regard, when students do not proceed to the next level until they have mastered tasks of the previous degree of difficulty. That means that they all receive the same amount of positive feedback (although not within the same period of time). With such programs the less able will be able to feel good about correctly solving intellectual problems. Such feelings motivate people. In many regular classes, students have to move on to more difficult tasks before they are able to handle the previous, less difficult ones.

6.3 *Achievement Motivation and Test Anxiety*

Traditional research on achievement motivation in educational settings has studied the positive motivation to strive for success and the negative, inhibitory tendency to avoid failure (test anxiety). Commentators have related preferences for achievement tasks of different degrees of difficulty and individual differences in persistence to individual differences in strength of achievement motivation or to the motivation to strive for success minus the motivation to avoid failure (Atkinson 1983). The resultant achievement motivation is only one component of the total task motivation, besides other sources of intrinsic and extrinsic motivation.

Important research on test anxiety has concentrated on the processes that can explain its negative effects on task performance. Research on the distinction between the cognitive (worry) and the emotional component (emotionality) of anxiety shows that the debilitating effects are mostly due to the worry aspect (interfering cognitions). Such process analyses have shown ways to treat test anxiety, to cope with it, and to avoid its negative consequences. This line of research however, has not taken into account individual differences in the need for achievement or in positive achievement motivation. Research indicates that combining measures of test anxiety and achievement motivation explains more variance than test anxiety (or the motive to achieve) by itself. Students with a high test anxiety and a low need for achievement differ from students with a high test anxiety and a high need for achievement. The latter group suffers less from their high anxiety and they perform better because their resultant achievement motivation is higher (Rand et al. 1991).

6.4 Control and Self-determination

Another type of intrinsic motivation has to do with perceptions of control and self-determination. Human beings want to control their environment and the outcomes of their actions. They want to be at the origin of what happens to them. Lack of control or choice causes demotivation. To feel like a pawn moved by external forces does not motivate (DeCharms 1984). Traditional learning environments in the classroom do not make much allowance for perceptions of control or self-determination; the teacher decides what the pupils have to do and when, and children have little choice. For many pupils this is in strong contrast with their experiences outside school, where they may enjoy considerable autonomy.

7. Attribution Theory

Students spontaneously try to explain their results, especially when a particular result was unexpected: "Why did I fail?" or "Why was I so successful in math?" They look for causes (causal attribution): "I failed because the test was much too difficult," or "I did well because I am very good in math." Such explanations are not always rational. They may be very biased in a self-defensive or self-enhancing way, attributing successes to themselves and failures to external factors. Educational research on Weiner's theory of causal attribution (Weiner 1986) has shown how students' causal explanations of successes and failures affect their emotional reactions to those outcomes, their expectations of future successes and failures, and their further motivation.

7.1 Causal Dimensions

Successes and failures can be explained by a broad variety of causal agents. Weiner developed a three-dimensional taxonomy. The first dimension concerns the locus of causality: internal versus external. The perceived or anticipated cause can be situated within the individual (e.g., abilities, effort) or in the external situation (e.g., luck, task difficulty, help from others). The second dimension concerns the temporal stability: stable versus unstable. Some causes are unstable. They may be present at one time and affect the outcome but absent the next time the same (type of) task has to be performed (e.g., luck, effort). Other causes are perceived as stable over time (e.g., abilities, task difficulty). The third dimension distinguishes controllable versus uncontrollable causes, but the question remains, controllable by whom? By me or by anyone? Weiner (1986 p.50) accepts "controllable by anyone" as the definition of controllability. Most other researchers, however, prefer to define it as "controllable by me." A student may think that a teacher's mood has an important effect on his or her marks; that the teacher can control his or her own mood, but that the student cannot control the teacher's mood. For Weiner, mood is then a controllable cause of good and bad marks.

From a motivational point of view, it is better to consider it as an uncontrollable cause. Controllable causes are only motivating when they can be controlled by the individual performers themselves. In 1978 Abramson et al. introduced a motivationally very relevant fourth dimension, the globality dimension. Causes can be more global or more specific. Global causes have an effect on success and failure in a broad variety of tasks, while specific causes only affect the outcome in a particular type of task. For example, general intelligence is a much more global cause of success and failure in intellectual tasks than is, say, the knowledge of a second language.

For the cognitive, emotional, and motivational consequences of causal attribution of successes and failures, it is not important to know if the perceived causes are objectively internal or external, stable or unstable, controllable or uncontrollable, and global or specific. What matters is how the individual perceives this.

7.2 Attributional Consequences

The affective reactions to success and failure depend on the type of outcome and on the locus dimension. Success arouses a positive affect, failure a negative affect. The emotions that are intrinsically related to success (pride) and failure (shame) require an internal causal attribution of success or failure. However, other emotional reactions are possible after an external causal attribution: success which is attributable to another's help may engender feelings of gratitude; failure attributable to someone else may lead to anger.

The stability or instability of the perceived causes affects future outcome expectancy. After an outcome (success or failure) is attributed to an unstable cause, it can be expected that the outcome in the next trial may be different from or be the same as in the previous trial. Causal attribution to a stable factor typically leads to the expectation that the outcome will be repeated and that its probability will increase: after attributing success to a stable cause, a person will expect to be successful again in the next trial and imagine that the subjective probability of success will be higher than in the previous trial. From a motivational point of view it is more optimal to attribute successes to internal, stable causes, and failures to external, unstable causes. It is always more motivating for a person if he or she can attribute outcome (success or failure) to causes under his or her control. Causal attribution theory provides a conceptual framework that can easily be used to change students' motivation via the cognitive processes of explaining success and failure.

8. Extrinsic Student Motivation

Extrinsic rewards and incentives are frequently used to increase student motivation. For students without any intrinsic interest, these are the only reasons for studying. Basic experimental research has shown that promised and salient extrinsic rewards that are exogenous to the nature of the learning and achievement task and that are given for activities for which there is already intrinsic motivation may undermine the intrinsic motivation to learn and perform well in school. They do so because they cause a shift in the locus of causality from internal to external. Students motivated only by intrinsic concerns perceive their interest in the subject matter to be the sole but important reason for studying it. When they then repeatedly receive extrinsic (material or immaterial) rewards, those rewards progressively become the perceived external reasons for learning. Thereafter the extrinsic rewards and not the intrinsic interest control the learning activities. The intrinsic interest disappears (Lepper and Greene 1978). For example, after experimental subjects received financial rewards for solving intrinsically interesting puzzles, they became less motivated to solve additional puzzles (without being paid) than subjects in a control condition who solved as many puzzles but who were not paid. Originally, subjects solved puzzles because it was fun to do so. When they then received extrinsic rewards, the rewards and not the fun become the reason or motive for doing it. It may be that the low level of intrinsic motivation among many high-school pupils is partly because of this undermining effect of the many extrinsic rewards they receive for doing their best at school and for obtaining high marks.

However, extrinsic rewards do not have this negative effect on intrinsic motivation when they are given in such a way that their controlling aspect is much less salient than their informative aspect. Extrinsic rewards can also be given in such a way that they tell students how good they are at the tasks for which the rewards are given. This can be done by making it very clear to the pupil that the quality or quantity of the reward follows from the skilled performance level and, in addition, by using rewards that are endogenous to the content or type of task that is rewarded. The rewards strengthen perceptions and feelings of competence, enhancing the intrinsic motivation (Deci and Ryan 1985). However, the ecological validity of this important empirical and theoretical work—started in the 1970s by Deci and his collaborators—needs more empirical research in real classroom settings.

Extrinsic incentives for learning may be immediate or delayed. Many students are motivated in their schoolwork by important goals they want to reach in the distant future. They are future-oriented. For them, a successful school career is highly instrumental for a successful career in life in general, and for a successful professional career in particular. The creation of a deep future time perspective by elaborating long, well-structured, and detailed behavioral plans and projects—composed of specific and challenging intermediate and final goals—can have a positive effect on early motivation (Lens 1987, Raynor and Entin 1982, Van Calster et al. 1987).

9. Conclusion

Research on student motivation reflects the complexity of this phenomenon as an interactional process with many aspects, each of which can be approached from different angles. This explains why there is no global theory of motivation for learning but several more partial approaches or "minitheories." It also explains why psychologists cannot offer a series of tailor-made solutions for the specific motivational problems of particular individual students in particular classrooms or learning environments.

However, the heterogeneity of the different approaches is less than it may seem at first sight. In almost all theoretical models, much motivational importance is given to individual cognitions or perceptions (e.g., the perception of competence and efficacy; the subjectively perceived probability of success or failure; the perceived locus, stability, and controllability of causes for success and failure). Therefore, it can be anticipated that the different theories will progressively converge around this common element, which may be labeled with Bandura's (1986) concept of "self efficacy." The motivational and behavioral effects of such cognitions are well-documented. More research is needed on their personal and situational determinants or antecedents. Such research is also a prerequisite for developing more practical training programs to prevent or cure motivational problems in learning situations.

Much research on motivation for learning has emphasized intrinsic motivation. Motivational research in educational psychology should devote more attention to the important role of extrinsic motivation for learning and to how it interacts with the different types of intrinsic motivation.

See also: Affect, Emotions, and Learning

References

Abramson L Y, Seligman M E P, Teasdale J D 1978 Learned helplessness in humans: Critique and reformulation. *J. Abnorm. Psychol.* 87: 49–74

Atkinson J W 1978 Motivational determinants of intellective performance and cumulative achievement. In: Atkinson J W, Raynor J O 1978 *Personality, Motivation and Achievement.* Hemisphere, Washington, DC

Atkinson J W 1983 *Personality, Motivation and Action.* Praeger, New York

Atkinson J W, Birch D 1970 *The Dynamics of Action.* Wiley, New York

Bandura A 1986 *Social Foundations of Thought and Action: A Social Cognitive Theory.* Prentice-Hall, Englewood Cliffs, New Jersey

DeCharms R 1984 Motivation enhancement in educational settings. In: Ames R E, Ames C (eds.) 1984

Deci E L, Ryan R M 1985 *Intrinsic Motivation and Self Determination in Human Behavior.* Plenum Press, New York

Dweck C S 1989 Motivation. In: Lesgold A, Glaser R (eds.) 1989 *Foundations for a Psychology of Education.* Erlbaum, Hillsdale, New Jersey

Halisch F, Kuhl J, Heckhausen H (eds.) 1987 *Motivation, Intention and Volition.* Springer-Verlag, Berlin

Kuhl J 1986 Motivation and information processing: A new look at decision making, dynamic change, and action control. In: Sorrentino R M, Higgins E T (eds.) 1986 *Handbook of Motivation and Cognition: Foundations of Social Bahavior,* Vol. 1. Wiley, New York

Lens W 1987 Future time perspective, motivation, and school performance. In: De Corte E, Lodewijks H, Parmentier R, Span P (eds.) 1987 *Learning and Instruction: European Research in an International Context,* Vol. 1. Leuven University Press, Leuven

Lepper M R, Greene D (eds.) 1978 *The Hidden Costs of Reward.* Erlbaum, Hillsdale, New Jersey

Malone T W, Lepper M R 1987 Making learning fun: A taxonomy of intrinsic motivations for learning. In: Snow R E, Farr M J (eds.) 1987 *Aptitude, Learning, and Instruction. 3: Conative and Affective Process Analyses.* Erlbaum, Hillsdale, New Jersey

Rand P, Lens W, Decock B 1991 Negative motivation is half the story: achievement motivation combines positive and negative motivation. *Scand. J. Educ. Res.* 35: 13–30

Raynor J O, Entin E E 1982 *Motivation, Career Striving, and Aging.* Hemisphere, Washington, DC

Rollett B A 1987 Effort avoidance and learning. In: De Corte E, Lodewijks H, Parmentier R, Span P (eds.) 1987 *Learning and Instruction: European Research in an International Context,* Vol. 1. Leuven University Press, Leuven

Salomon G, Globerson T 1987 Skill may not be enough: The role of mindfulness in learning and transfer. *Int. J. Educ. Res.* 11: 623–37

Slavin R E 1990 Achievement effects of ability grouping in secondary schools: A best-evidence synthesis. *Rev. Educ. Res.* 60: 471–99

Snow R E 1989 Cognitive-conative aptitude interactions in learning. In: Kanfer R, Ackerman P L, Cudeck R (eds.) 1989 *Abilities, Motivation, and Methodology.* Erlbaum, Hillsdale, New Jersey

Snow R E, Swanson J 1992 Instructional psychology: Aptitude, adaptation, and assessment. *Annu. Rev. Psychol.* 43: 583–626

Van Calster K, Lens W, Nuttin J 1987 Affective attitude toward the personal future: Impact on motivation in high school boys. *Am. J. Psychol.* 100: 1–13

Weiner B 1986 *An Attributional Theory of Motivation and Emotion.* Springer-Verlag, New York

Weinert F E 1987 Metacognition and motivation as determinants of effective learning and understanding. In: Weinert F E, Kluwe R H (eds.) 1987 *Metacognition, Motivation, and Understanding.* Erlbaum, Hillsdale, New Jersey

Further Reading

Ames R E, Ames C (eds.) 1984 *Research on Motivation in Education. Vol. 1: Student Motivation.* Academic Press, Orlando, Florida

Ames C, Ames R E (eds.) 1985 *Research on Motivation in Education. Vol. 2: The Classroom Milieu.* Academic Press, Orlando, Florida

Ames C, Ames R E (eds.) 1989 *Research on Motivation in Education. Vol. 3: Goals and Cognition.* Academic Press, Orlando, Florida

Covington M 1992 *Making the Grade: A Self-worth Perspective on Motivation and School Reform.* Cambridge University Press, Cambridge

Hastings N, Schwieso J (eds.) 1987 *New Directions in Educational Psychology. 2: Behaviour and Motivation in the Classroom.* Falmer Press, London

Stipek D J 1993 *Motivation to Learn: From Theory to Practice* (2nd edn.). Allyn, Bacon, W Lens, Massachusetts

Visual Perception

J. Wagemans

Perception—that is, the acquisition of information about the environment through the senses—is essential for adaptive behavior to occur. Moreover, much of what humans learn comes through the senses. Without seeing, hearing, tasting, smelling, and feeling, humans could not learn anything. This entry provides the necessary background for understanding perception as a psychological problem and as an important "input system" that enables a living organism to learn. Want of space precludes an explicit discussion of the link with learning and digression into the important domain of perceptual learning or perceptual development (i.e., the improvement in perceptual tasks, such as discrimination, as a result of practice or development, respectively). The entry will concentrate on visual perception, because the visual modality has been by far the one most frequently studied. The main ideas of two conflicting theoretical approaches will be introduced

451

and specific topics such as object recognition and eye movements briefly considered.

1. Perception as a Psychological Problem

Looking and seeing are activities that most humans can easily engage in fairly soon after birth and which persist uninterruptedly for the human lifespan. The only problems that occur for some people seem to be purely physical (short-sightedness, color-blindness, blindness). At first it might seem strange that so much psychological research has been devoted to visual perception and so many psychological theories have been formulated to try to capture its essence. A closer look reveals why this is so: although looking and seeing may be easy, explaining how these activities work is not.

The process of visual perception is incorporated in a system that can be described anatomically and physiologically. Humans have eyes with pupils, lenses, retinas, and so on. They also have a central nervous system with cells responsible for the capturing of light rays (i.e., receptors), neurons, and connections transmitting the impulses to the brain. The brain itself comprises many parts, each responsible for processing aspects of the incoming stimuli (e.g., color, form, motion). However, the functioning of this system can also be explained in a fundamentally different way. The process can be regarded as information-processing with incoming light rays containing the information that has to be transmitted to a central processing unit to be interpreted. Between "input" (the light) and "output" (the interpretation of what is seen) many processing steps intervene that are in a sense psychological.

One example of a typically psychological process is recognition. To recognize an object a person needs a description, stored somewhere in memory, of how that object looks. The image processed at each instant in time then has to be compared with this description in memory. If the brain can make a match, the object is recognized. However, in theory it is also possible to look at an object without seeing what it is. There is a distinction to be made between looking and seeing, which is not only a matter of terminology. Consider the case of someone who has lost their way when walking in the countryside during the night. Perhaps the person looks to heaven in despair, staring at the stars. If the person happens to be looking at the pole star, this will not help the person if they do not recognize it as such (based on its clarity or its position).

Another example related to the difference between looking and seeing is eye movements. Because only the center of the human retina is sensitive enough to distinguish fine detail, humans have to move their eyes several times each second to bring new information into view. This sequence of eye movements (called saccades) does not scan different parts of the visual field at random. By contrast, very systematic "scan paths" are produced as a function of the stimulus itself and as a result of the observer's personal interest and strategy. Sometimes attention is automatically pulled to a certain location that is essential for survival (e.g., when crossing a road). In sum, a closer examination reveals many different psychological aspects in the process of looking and seeing: memory, interpretation, information-processing, interest, attention, and so on. The domain of psychology devoted to these processes is perceptual psychology.

During the first decades of scientific psychology (1880–1950), visual perception was studied quite frequently, but all research remained within the same general framework. There were, of course, some theoretical controversies; for example, about the importance of "elementary building blocks" (such as points and lines). The "elementarists" argued that the whole percept (e.g., a red triangle) results from the combination of different elementary attributes (e.g., color and form), some of which are even further composed of more elementary features (e.g., three oriented line segments with particular positions and relative angles). In contrast, the "Gestaltists" argued that the whole is more than the sum of its parts and that global aspects of the input are sometimes processed more rapidly than its local elements. However, only in quite recent times have major evolutions in the field of perceptual psychology resulted in striking conflicting approaches of the problem of visual perception. It is possible to distinguish between two major categories of theories: cognitive or "indirect," on the one hand, and ecological or "direct," on the other.

2. The Cognitive or "Indirect" Approach to Visual Perception

The basic idea underlying all theories within this framework is that perception is a complex process which elaborates and enriches the available "input" stimulation so as to produce a meaningful "output" interpretation. Visual perception delivers information about objects, scenes, and events in a three-dimensional world on the basis of a rapid succession of different retinal images ("snapshots"), which are only two-dimensional and also inverted. Therefore, between "input" and "output" the perceiver has to contribute a considerable amount of knowledge in order to add, for example, the third dimension or to integrate the different images into an impression of a continuous world. Because perception cannot be the direct response to a stimulus but depends on intermediate processes to enrich the information, this approach is called "indirect." In fact, the cognitive perceptual psychologist is most interested in this contribution of the perceiver to the process of perception: the influence of memory, the role of expectations and reasoning, and of general as well as specific knowledge.

As an example, consider the case of "size constancy"; that is, the fact that an object is perceived as being of constant size, despite differently sized images on the retina when the object is viewed from different distances. According to cognitivists, this results from the perceiver's ability to "calculate" the real size of an object based on the retinal size and some subtle cues about distance (e.g., perspective or retinal disparity). It is as if the perceiver unconsciously solves an arithmetic puzzle so as to achieve size constancy. Sometimes even specific knowledge of the object might help. For example, if a person can determine that a certain object in view has to be an elephant (a view, for example, based on the trunk), the person will also know approximately how large it is and that it is definitely larger than some objects that might have a larger retinal projection (e.g., a mouse in the foreground of a scene with an elephant at the background).

Some theories go far along this line of thought and regard perception as a kind of "problem-solving" or "hypothesis-testing." Given particular elements in the image (e.g., a right angle), perceivers automatically and quickly generate a hypothesis about what the object can be (e.g., a chair) and try to establish a correspondence between the image of that object stored in the memory with the image on the retina. If this does not fit (e.g., there is no back), new hypotheses have to be generated and tested until the object is recognized. Perceptual psychologists within this cognitive approach are really attempting to study the intelligence of the eye (Gregory 1970) or the logic of perception (Rock 1983).

A characteristic of this approach is that the researcher studies perception with poor stimuli presented in less than desirable conditions. For example, typical equipment consists of a tachistoscope, by which an image can be flashed very briefly, a screen to reduce the visual field, and a head- and chinrest to avoid eye movements. All this is used to restrict the available stimulus information so that the perceiver's own contribution becomes much clearer.

Another typical research "tool" consists of visual illusions; that is, images in which what is perceived does not agree with what is physically real. For example, in the "Ponzo illusion" (Fig. 1), line A is perceived as longer than line B, although they are physically identical. These illusions are explained by the perceiver's own contribution. For example, this illusion might be caused by the perceiver's automatic addition of depth which "fools" the "calculation" of size based on distance (as if the oblique lines represent railway tracks receding in depth). That perception occasionally fails is not considered strange according to the cognitive approach. After all, the viewer's knowledge and reasoning capacity are presented with tremendous challenges, especially given the usual poor state of stimulus information at the outset.

3. The Ecological or "Direct" Approach

Until the 1970s the cognitive approach was the dominant theoretical framework. This changed with the work of Gibson (1979), who argued that this approach was only relevant to explaining curiosities from a perceptual laboratory, not for explaining the ordinary process of perception by which humans and animals adapt to their environments. What every theory of perception has to explain is not why it sometimes fails, but why it ordinarily succeeds in offering a firm basis for adaptive behavior. The fact that humans are not even aware that perception constitutes an important problem is revealing of its normal efficiency.

In normal circumstances the perceiver has much more information available than is assumed by the cognitive approach. An object is usually not isolated but is embedded in the context of a scene in which the ground's surface texture (e.g., pebbles, sand, tiles) provides information about the distances and relative sizes of objects. When viewing distance changes, the size of objects in the retinal image changes too, but some higher-order relations remain unchanged or invariant. For example, the number of texture elements of the ground's surface covered by an object remains constant with changing distance.

Invariants under transformations are an important source of information because motion is the rule rather than the exception. For example, if one drives a car, one sees a flow of elements in the near visual field (e.g., surface of the road) moving in the opposite direction. The direction of this so-called "optic flow" provides information about the direction of movement. The relative velocities of the elements in this optic flow provide information about the distances of objects (i.e., slow = far). The point in the field where there is no motion indicates the direction towards which one is heading. The expansion rate provides information about the speed of approach. The fact that lower animals use these sources of information (e.g., birds diving to catch fish) suggests that a living entity does not need advanced knowledge or the ability to

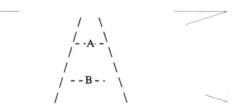

Figure 1
The Ponzo illusion

achieve complex inferences. In contrast, it appears that the human visual system has, in the course of its evolution, developed a special sensitivity for this kind of information. On the basis of these observations, Gibson concluded that perception is not this process of enriching poor information by knowledge, memory, and reasoning, as is assumed by cognitive or indirect theories of perception, but is rather the "direct" pickup of the information that is abundantly present for the perceiver moving about in his normal environment.

The major task for this approach of perception—the "ecological approach" (Gibson 1979)—is to discover the sources of information available for a particular perceptual task. For these purposes, the classic theory of light as a simple ray stimulating a local patch on the retina has to be abandoned. This requires an "ecological optics," studying complex structures in the optic array of reflected light. The ecological research about the perception of human movement patterns (initiated in the 1950s by Johansson) provides a clear example of the major difference between static, point-like stimulation and dynamic, higher-order sources of information(see Johansson 1994). An actor dressed in black with light patches attached to his most important joints (neck, shoulders, elbows, wrists, hip, knees, and ankles) was filmed in the dark. As long as the actor keeps stationary, one sees nothing but a random collection of dots. However, as soon as the actor moves (walks, runs, dances, climbs a stair, etc.), it becomes immediately clear that the dots are attached to a human body and that particular movements are made. This example clearly shows that the critical stimulus information is not in the separate static light points but in the complex spatial relations between the lights and their specific patterns of change over time. The sensitivity of the visual information to these spatiotemporal relations becomes even clearer if one considers that it is easy to see the difference between a male and a female body walking, to estimate the weight of a lifted box, and even to notice the difference between lifting a very heavy box and just faking the action, all from a collection of moving light patches attached to the joints.

Another important characteristic of the ecological approach is that perception is studied in a functional relationship with behavior. For example, what is seen first when looking at objects is their function—what can be done with them. The cognitive theory of object recognition as the process of finding a match between processed retinal images and previously stored image descriptions is found to be untenable, because a person can often say immediately whether they have seen a particular object before or not. This would be much more difficult if the visual memory had to be searched serially to retrieve all possible items contained in it. On the other hand, it is possible to see immediately what a particular object implies for behavior because that is supposed to be specified in the higher-order

relations in the optic array. For example, when one looks at a chair, one does not reconstruct its form on the basis of its retinal image to try to find a corresponding item in the catalogue of known objects, but one immediately notices that it is something to sit on (its "sit-on-ability"). These functional properties of objects were called "affordances" by Gibson (1979). Empirical research has since shown that they are indeed perceptually relevant, especially for describing infant object recognition or tool use. When crawling infants are confronted with a set of different stairs, they all choose the one that has the highest "climb-ability" for them, depending on the relation between step-height and leg-length.

4. Conclusion

Perceptual psychology has grown rapidly since the 1950s and is becoming one of the most vivid sub-disciplines in psychology. The diversity of approaches is considered to be a major advantage because they are complementary. The cognitive or indirect approach has stimulated detailed research about phenomena such as perceptual constancies and visual illusions in tightly controlled laboratory conditions. However, the weak point of this approach is that there are as many theories as there are theorists because each has their own ideas about the specific intermediate processes such as memory, expectations, hypothesis-testing, problem-solving, and so on. The ecological approach, on the other hand, has shown that there is much more information in the real world for moving observers. It is tempting to believe that invariants under transformations are specifying objects, scenes, and events. However, if it has been shown that particular sources of information are available, it still has to be demonstrated that they are used and, if possible, how. A vague formulation of perception as direct pick-up is unsatisfactory. It is clear, however, that there is still much to be done before anyone can claim that perception is understood and that it is known how it functions as an input system for learning.

See also: Perceptual Development; Learning Activity

References

Gibson J J 1979 *The Ecological Approach to Visual Perception*. Houghton Mifflin, Boston, Massachusetts

Gregory R L 1970 *The Intelligent Eye*. Weidenfeld and Nicholson, New York

Johansson G 1994 Configurations in event perception: An experimental study. In: Jansson G, Bergström S S, Epstein W (eds.) 1994 *Perceiving Events and Objects*. Erlbaum, Hillsdale, New Jersey

Rock I 1983 *The Logic of Perception*. MIT Press, Cambridge, Massachusetts

Further Reading

Boff K R, Kaufman L, Thomas J P (eds.) 1986 *Handbook of Perception and Human Performance*, 2 vols. Wiley, New York

Bruce V, Green P R 1990 *Visual Perception: Physiology, Psychology, and Ecology*, 2nd edn. Erlbaum, Hillsdale, New Jersey

Gordon I E 1989 *Theories of Perception*. Wiley, Chichester

Humphreys G W, Bruce V 1989 *Visual Cognition: Computational, Experimental, and Neuropsychological Approaches*. Erlbaum, Hillsdale, New Jersey

Wade N J, Swanston M 1991 *Visual Perception: An Introduction*. Routledge, London

Watt R J 1991 *Understanding Vision*. Academic Press, New York

Preconceptions and Misconceptions

R. Duit

It is an old pedagogical maxim that instruction has to take students' preinstructional knowledge into consideration. Ausubel (1968 p. vi) spelled out this insight in the following way: "The most important single factor influencing learning is what the learner already knows. Ascertain this and teach him accordingly." Since then, this dictum has become the motto for research on the significance of preinstructional conceptions carried out in fields such as reading, writing, mathematics, and science. Educators now have a much better idea of the preinstructional knowledge students possess in various academic and nonacademic fields and of how teaching interacts with this knowledge. It became obvious that students' preinstructional conceptions are frequently in sharp contrast to the notions taught. Such conceptions have proved to be very resistant to change in instruction. Research has revealed a disappointing situation: namely, that instruction often fails to guide students from their preinstructional knowledge to the subject matter intended. Such results have challenged instructional theory and practice, and prompted both a reassessment of instructional aims and the development of new instructional designs.

This entry reviews: (a) findings of empirical studies on students' preinstructional conceptions and (b) new ways of overcoming related learning difficulties. Its focus is on science and mathematics education, as most research has been carried out in these areas.

1. Preconceptions and Misconceptions

The term "conception" in this entry denotes a mental representation of some features of the external world or of theoretical domains. The preinstructional conceptions (i.e., the conceptions students hold prior to instruction) may be divided into two groups: preconceptions and misconceptions. Preconceptions are those conceptions that result from informal experiences in everyday life, whereas misconceptions are misunderstandings that are induced through prior formal teaching.

In the research field under review here, there are many different terms in use. In science and mathematics, the term misconception, for instance, not only stands for faulty conceptions formed by students during prior instruction but for faulty preconceptions in general (seen from the perspective of science or mathematics). This use of misconception is often found in conjunction with the opinion that the faulty conceptions must be erased and replaced by the "correct" ones. The antithesis of this standpoint uses the term "alternative frameworks," indicating that students' preconceptions are viewed as conceptions in their own right, and that they are reasonably successful in many everyday situations.

1.1 Sources of Preconceptions

There are many sources of preconceptions. First, language is a very important source; it contains a large stock of worldviews, some of which are outdated in the light of modern knowledge and which may therefore cause misunderstandings. For example, the sentence "The sun rises" suggests an image of the sun moving in the skies and not the "modern" one of the earth revolving around the sun. Language also provides many general schemata (e.g., thinking in the cause–effect schema) that are helpful in everyday situations, but which may be deeply misleading if used in new fields.

A second important source is provided by interactions with family members, friends, other adults, and peer groups. Such interactions have been shown to generate particular forms of "everyday science" and "everyday mathematics" which flatly contradict some of the main tenets of true science and mathematics.

A third important source is the mass media. And finally, in the case of science, there is yet another highly significant source: sense impressions. The preconceptions of many students concerning such scientific topics as heat, motion, forces, and vision are shaped to a great extent by sense impressions and by physical actions in daily life.

1.2 Sources of Misconceptions

There are three main reasons for misunderstandings induced through instruction. First, empirical studies have shown that teachers themselves sometimes hold faulty conceptions because they were not well-trained and are unfamiliar with their subject-matter area. Second, there is a less obvious reason for faulty conceptions presented by teachers. Several cases are documented where faulty ideas survived for generations simply because they were taken for granted and passed on, without any critique, from one generation of teachers and/or textbooks to another. For instance, there was for many years an exhibit in a leading German science museum which provided a completely false illustration of Newton's Third Law of Motion. The third reason may be regarded as even more subtle than the first two. Research cites many cases in which misconceptions were induced because students interpreted what the teacher presented to them (on the basis of their preinstructional conceptions) in a totally different way from the one the teacher intended. These misconceptions appear to be the most difficult ones to modify in instruction. Often, teachers use the "correct" language (from their point of view) and students give "correct" answers that also make sense from the teachers' perspective, but that are really meant in a quite different way.

2. Theoretical Perspectives of Research

Research in the field of preconceptions and misconceptions has been carried out from different perspectives. On the one hand, there is the predominant group of subject-matter educators (e.g., mathematics and science educators) and, on the other hand, a group of researchers from cognitive science (including affiliated fields such as information-processing theories and artificial intelligence). Accordingly, various theoretical perspectives are in use. Of course, within these, Piagetian ideas (Lawson et al. 1989) and Ausubelian ideas (Novak and Gowin 1984) play important roles. Furthermore, cognitive science and associated fields are of major significance. Phenomenological and hermeneutic perspectives are also employed; for instance, symbolic interactionism (see Bauersfeld 1988), Marton's (1981) phenomenographic approach, and early constructivist approaches such as Kelly's (1955) constructivist alternativism.

The common denominator of the various evolving perspectives is the "constructivist view," in which initially radical constructivism (von Glasersfeld 1990) was the key reference position. According to the constructivist view, learning is not seen as information transmission or filling empty vessels, but rather as an active construction process on the basis of the existing conceptions (i.e., preconceptions and misconceptions). More recently there has been a growing interest in the ideas of social constructivism that has reduced the bias of radical constructivist perspectives which tended, for example, to underestimate the significance of the social construction of knowledge in the learning process (Roth 1995).

3. Major Findings on Students' Preconceptions and Misconceptions

3.1 General Findings

Research has demonstrated that preconceptions and misconceptions significantly guide students' learning. They influence students' attempts to make sense of the information presented in textbooks and in the classroom; moreover they shape the whole learning process. Many preconceptions and misconceptions are highly resistant to change. Quite often, only limited progress in the direction of the intended outcome has been observed, or only minor parts of the new conceptions are formed and integrated by students into their existing knowledge. Their preinstructional conceptions are not merely "fuzzy" ideas, but are consistent to an astonishing degree. Research has also shown the range of application of newly acquired conceptions to be very restricted. In science, students make limited or even no use of the conceptions taught in school outside science classrooms. Moreover, in science classrooms they are employed only if the context of a task or problem is similar to the context used when they were introduced, and if the task or problem is simple enough. As soon as it becomes a little more difficult, most students appear to rely more on their intuitive everyday conceptions than on taught scientific conceptions.

3.2 Findings Concerning Experiments in Science Instruction

Science instruction is a domain in which experiments play a major role in teaching–learning processes. It is normally assumed that students observe the features that are visually obvious from the view point of the teacher. Research shows, however, that students' observations are strongly influenced by their conceptions, and that there are no "objective" observations. Evidence from demonstrations is frequently used in science classes to highlight the differences between students' conceptions and scientific conceptions, showing students that their conceptions are wrong. However, several studies have found that a single counterexample does not convince students that their conceptions are wrong. Rather, they tend to explain an unexpected observation by pointing to specific features of the particular situation.

4. Conceptions beyond Subject-matter Content

The preconceptions and misconceptions discussed so far refer to particular items of subject-matter content (e.g., to the process of vision in science).

Research focusing on these "content-specific" conceptions started in the 1970s. Most studies carried out by subject-matter educators are still similar in approach. But the constructivist view led to the insight that many other preinstructional conceptions determine learning. The following are some of the major conceptions beyond subject matter content.

Metaknowledge, i.e., conceptions of the nature of the content knowledge, is an important yet often neglected issue. In science and mathematics, students' difficulties in understanding science and mathematics conceptions appear to be due in part to misunderstandings of the status of these conceptions. Studies are available that indicate, for instance, that most students and also many teachers are "naive realists"; they view scientific knowledge as a faithful reproduction of the world and not as a tentative human construction.

Teachers' and students' conceptions about the aims of instruction in general and the purpose of a particular teaching event are often not in accord with one another. Whereas teachers tend to take a long-term view, which involves a single event having its place within a structured sequence of related events, students appear to lack such a long-term perspective. As an example of this they might view an experiment as a single event unrelated to others, and so fail to identify an appropriate framework that could guide their investigations.

From a constructivist perspective metacognition is a key issue. The conceptions of the learning process determine how something is taught and learned. Teachers' and students' views of learning and their actual teaching and learning have been investigated. It became obvious that a "filling vessel" view of learning is still the prevalent one, and that a constructivist view, as outlined above, is held only by a small number of teachers and students.

On the teacher's part another kind of conception is of the utmost importance, and may be designated as "conceptions of conceptions" (Marton 1981). It suggest that teachers construct their conceptions of students' conceptions against the background of their own conceptions. This aspect is also of significance for the researcher: what research reports record as preconceptions or misconceptions are, in fact, researchers' conceptions of students' conceptions.

5. Patterns of Misunderstanding

Perkins and Simmons (1988) sought to discern which "frames of understanding" are responsible for misconceptions that are familiar from science, mathematics, and programming. They claimed that the frames they isolated are also valid for understanding misconceptions in other content domains. Perkins and Simmons distinguished four frames:

(a) content frame, or aspects that are usually attribu-

ted to subject-matter content (e.g., facts, definitions, algorithms, content-oriented metacognitive knowledge);

(b) problem-solving frame, or domain-specific and general problem-solving strategies, beliefs about problem-solving, and autoregulative processes to keep oneself organized during problem-solving;

(c) epistemic frame, or domain-specific and general norms and strategies concerning the validation of claims in the domain;

(d) inquiry frame, or domain-specific and general beliefs and strategies that work to extend and challenge the knowledge within a particular domain.

Perkins and Simmons argued convincingly that major learning difficulties result from the one-sided emphasis in traditional instruction on the content frame while hardly any attention is paid to the epistemic and inquiry frames. They also developed ideas for new approaches, ones that address all four frames.

6. New Orientations of Instruction

The "alternative" conceptions of students in grammar, spelling, and arithmetic resulting from instruction are totally unacceptable to teachers. Yet in science, the situation appears to be somewhat different. Research demonstrates that instruction may often fail to "erase" students' preinstructional conceptions, and to "replace" them by scientific ones. Therefore a view is rapidly gaining ground that tolerates the coexistence of both students' "alternative" preconceptions and scientific conceptions. According to this standpoint, students should learn that their "alternative" conceptions may be valuable in many everyday situations, but will fail in other cases where the scientific view is required. The debate on this issue continues, but these research results demand that educators, teachers, and educational decision-makers rethink entrenched positions.

7. Consequences for Instructional Design

In attempting to address learning difficulties arising from preconceptions and misconceptions, several consequences for instructional design have been drawn and evaluated in school practice. Principally, the traditional instructional materials have to undergo fundamental revision. Teachings aids, such as textbooks, have to be evaluated. There must also be attempts to address learning difficulties caused by students' preconceptions and misconceptions, by designing materials using new media, most notably computer-based media such as interactive videodisks or computer-assisted laboratory work. The difference between these attempts and more traditional ones would appear to be that the development of new media forms an integral part of a comprehensive constructivist approach and does not aim at improving learning just by providing a single new item.

The greatest emphasis by far is usually given to the development of new teaching strategies to guide students from their preconceptions and misconceptions to scientific conceptions. Such strategies may be subdivided into two groups: "conceptual growth" and "conceptual change." Conceptual growth approaches start from aspects of students' preinstructional conceptions that are generally in accordance with the conceptions to be taught. Step by step, the core of already appropriate ideas is enlarged; in the main, uninterrupted transition from students' preinstructional conceptions to the new conceptions is assumed. In contrast, conceptual change strategies view the learning process—at least in part—as discontinuous, in that major restructuring of existing conceptions still has to take place. Accordingly, these strategies usually employ some kind of cognitive conflict.

Research results on the effect of approaches that address students' preconceptions and misconceptions are usually in favor of the new approaches. Guzzetti and Glass (1992) carried out a meta-analysis on conceptual change studies. They concluded that teaching and learning arrangements that offend preconceptions and misconceptions, and hence create some sort of cognitive dissonance (for instance, by use of refutational texts or by the strategies presented below) are effective. However, learning process studies have also shown that students have severe difficulties in experiencing the arranged cognitive dissonance (see below).

7.1 The Conceptual Change Model

This model (see Posner et al. 1982) is rooted in information-processing theory and in Kuhnian ideas of paradigm shifts. At the center of the model are the following four conditions of conceptual change: (a) dissatisfaction with existing ideas; (b) the new conception must be intelligible; (c) the conception must appear initially plausible; (d) the new conception must be fruitful. Conditions (a) and (d) have proven to be the most difficult ones for teachers to create. It is difficult to create dissatisfaction with existing ideas. Students are often unable and unwilling to change their conceptions, because they are pleased with them and fail to see the benefit of the new conceptions. Critiques of this model may be summarized thus: conceptual change has to be embedded in conditions that support change such as students' motivation and interests, students' learning strategies, the classroom climate, and the power structures in the classroom.

7.2 Constructivist Teaching Sequences

Constructivist teaching sequences (e.g., Driver 1989) involve a period in which students' preinstructional conceptions are discussed explicitly. In a classroom discussion resembling negotiation, the teacher introduces the conceptions to be learned and promotes them. Cognitive conflict strategies tend to play a major role when students' preconceptions are contrasted with the conception the teachers "advertises," or when predictions on the basis of students' conceptions are shown to be in conflict with empirical evidence. There are two main difficulties with such teaching models, according to the research. First, a large number of students do not like to "play around" with different ideas, but want to learn the right one. Second, students often do not experience the conflict from the teacher's point of view because, within the framework of their own conceptions, there is no such conflict.

7.3 Strategies to Develop Metacognitive Abilities

Several approaches focus on developing students' metacognitive abilities (see Novak and Gowin 1984, Lawson et al. 1989). They are normally not restricted to the development of thinking skills but aim at changing students' views of learning in general. The PEEL project (Baird and Northfield 1992) attempted to guide students toward the constructivist view of learning in which active construction, and not a predominantly passive intake of knowledge, is the key issue. This study uncovered a major difficulty of such approaches. A considerable number of students were unwilling to change their learning behavior toward a constructivist approach, because it was too demanding and, in their view, the payoff from the extra effort was not worthwhile.

8. Recommendations for Research

The trend that emerged in research throughout the 1980s, namely of taking into consideration various kinds of conceptions beyond subject-matter content, is a promising direction for future research. Many issues need much more theoretical analysis and empirical investigation, such as the impact of conceptions about the nature of the particular subject-matter knowledge and the influence of beliefs concerning the learning process. Another important task derives from the lack of learning process studies. Moreover, the study of students' preconceptions and misconceptions should be expanded to embrace other subject-matter fields. Many studies are now available in the areas of science education and mathematics education, but there are still major domains of the school curriculum that warrant attention, such as geography, history, and economics. One final requirement of utmost importance relates to attempts to make teachers familiar with the research findings reviewed in this entry; much greater emphasis than hitherto should be given to bridging the gap between research and practice.

See also: Constructivism and Learning; Knowledge Representation and Organization; Prior Knowledge and Learning; Instructional Design Theories

References

Ausubel D 1968 *Educational Psychology: A Cognitive View.* Holt, Rinehart, and Winston, New York

Baird J R, Northfield J R 1992 *Learning from the PEEL Experience.* Monash University Printery, Melbourne

Bauersfeld H 1988 Interaction, construction, and knowledge: Alternative perspectives for mathematics education. In: Grouws D A, Cooney T J, Jones D (eds.) 1988 *Perspectives on Research on Effective Mathematics Teaching,* Vol. 1. National Council of Teachers in Mathematics (NCTM), Reston, Virginia

Driver R 1989 Changing conceptions. In: Adey P (ed.) 1989 *Adolescent Development and School Science.* Falmer Press, London

Guzzetti B J, Glass G V 1992 Promoting conceptual change in science: A comparative meta-analysis of instructional interventions from reading education and science education. Paper presented at the annual meeting of the American Educational Research Association, San Francisco, California

Kelly G A 1955 *The Psychology of Personal Constructs,* 2 Vols. Norton, New York

Lawson A E, Abraham M R, Renner J W 1989 *A Theory of Instruction: Using the Learning Cycle to Teach Science Concepts and Thinking Skills.* National Association for Research in Science Teaching (NARST), University of Cincinnati, Cincinnati, Ohio

Marton F 1981 Phenomenography: Describing conceptions of the world around us. *Instructional Science* 10(2): 177–200

Novak J, Gowin D B 1984 *Learning how to Learn.* Cambridge University Press, Cambridge, Massachusetts

Perkins D N, Simmons R 1988 Patterns of misunderstanding: An integrative model for science, math, and programming. *Rev. Educ. Res.* 58(3): 303–26

Posner G J, Strike K A, Hewson P W, Gertzog W A 1982 Accommodation of a scientific conception: Toward a theory of conceptual change. *Sci. Educ.* 66(2): 211–27

Roth W-M 1995 *Authentic School Science: Knowing and Learning in Open-inquiry Laboratories.* Kluwer, Dordrecht

von Glasersfeld E 1990 An exposition of constructivism: Why some like it radical. In: Davis R, Maher C, Noddings N (eds.) 1990 *Constructivist Views on the Teaching and Learning of Mathematics.* National Council of Teachers in Mathematics (NCTM), Reston, Virginia

Further Reading

Steffe L, Gale J (eds.) 1995 *Constructivism in Education.* Lawrence Erlbaum, Hillsdale, New Jersey

Treagust D F, Duit R, Fraser B (eds.) 1995 *Improving Teaching and Learning in Science and Mathematics.* Teacher College Press, New York

Vosniadou S 1994 Conceptual change in the physical sciences. *Learning and Instruction* 4 (special issue)

Prior Knowledge and Learning

F. J. R. C. Dochy

The work of Ausubel was certainly not the first to direct attention to the importance of prior knowledge. However, Ausubel highlighted an important moment in the development of instructional psychology. In his basic text *Educational Psychology: A Cognitive View* he unequivocally identified the crucial role of prior knowledge in learning: "If I had to reduce all of educational psychology to just one principle, I would say this: The most important single factor influencing learning is what the learner already knows. Ascertain this and teach him accordingly" (Ausubel 1968). This involves a tripartite assumption:

(a) that prior knowledge is a very important variable in educational psychology;

(b) that the degree (of content and organization) of prior knowledge of a student must be known or measurable for the achievement of optimal learning;

(c) that a learning situation is optimal to the degree to which it is in accord with the level of prior knowledge.

Also more recent investigations into human cognition (Alexander et al. 1992, Dochy and Alexander 1995) showed that prior knowledge is an important student variable in learning. The central finding of investigations of the past fifteen years is that a key to developing such an integrated and generative knowledge base is to build upon the learner's prior knowledge. "Indeed new learning is exceedingly difficult when prior informal as well as formal knowledge is not used as a springboard for future learning. It has also become more and more obvious that in contrast to the traditional meas-

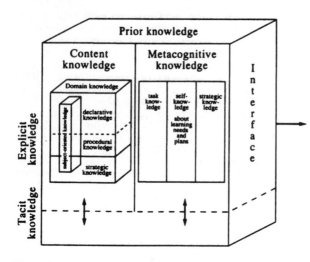

Figure 1
A map of prior knowledge
Source: Adapted from Dochy 1992

ures of aptitude, the assessment of prior knowledge and skill is not only a much more precise predictor of learning, but provides in addition a more useful basis for instruction and guidance" (Glaser and De Corte 1992 p. 1).

After a definition of the concept "prior knowledge," the entry provides a summary of representative and well-known studies supporting the impact of prior knowledge on study results and processes. Some of the main theories that account for the facilitative effect of prior knowledge on learning are then reviewed. Finally, implications for instructional design and classroom teaching are highlighted and emergent issues for further research indicated.

1. The Concept of Prior Knowledge

Definitions of the concept of prior knowledge, such as "what the learner knows in advance," are often too general and vague to be of much use. An exception to this is Bloom's (1982) concept "cognitive entry behaviors," used as a synonym for prior knowledge and defined as "those prerequisite types of knowledge, skills, and competencies which are essential to the learning of a particular new task or set of tasks" (p. 175). In the English-speaking world various terms are used interchangeably. "Prior knowledge" is widely used, but there are also terms such as "knowledge store," "prior knowledge state," "expertise," "expert knowledge," "preknowledge," and "personal knowledge," which are used as synonyms (Dochy and Alexander 1995). For the purposes of empirical research, prior knowledge is mostly defined as the whole of a person's actual knowledge that: (a) is available

before a certain learning task, (b) is structured in schemata, (c) is declarative and procedural, (d) is partly explicit and partly tacit, (e) contains content knowledge and metacognitive knowledge, and (f) is dynamic in nature (see Fig. 1) and stored in the prior knowledge base (Dochy 1992). Research has shown that content knowledge, especially domain-specific knowledge, has most influence on learning (Alexander and Judy 1988, Weinert 1989a). In the past, most research on prior knowledge has focused on domain-specific knowledge.

Figure 1 portrays the previous definition by means of a conceptual map of prior knowledge as a snapshot or "slice-out-of-time" representation. It should be noted that some basic assumptions about prior knowledge underlie this map, that is, forms of knowledge are fluid and dynamic and all forms of knowledge are interactive, which means that the presence or activation of one form of knowledge can influence any other form, directly or indirectly.

2. The Effect of Prior Knowledge on Learning Outcomes

In psychological models of educational performance, prior knowledge plays a major role (for an overview, see Haertel et al. 1983, Johanssen and Grabowski 1993). The effect of prior knowledge on learning outcomes has been shown in studies that attempt to explain the variance in test scores, as well as in research that focuses on the construction of causal models.

2.1 Prior Knowledge and Variance in Post-test Scores

The fact that prior knowledge has been demonstrated to be a potentially important educational variable in the sense of contribution to post-test variance has been raised in several investigations (Tobias 1994). Knowledge measured prior to a course explained, on average, no less than 50 per-cent of the variance in the post-test scores. Comparable results were reported by Bloom (1982), who found correlations of 0.50 to 0.90 between pre-test and post-test scores. From these correlations, Bloom deduced the amount of explained variance. Investigations by Dochy (1992) in ecologically more valid settings (real-life classroom settings), using prior knowledge state tests, revealed that up to 42 percent of variance was explained by prior knowledge.

The results of these investigations into the effect of variables on study results indicates that prior knowledge explains between 30 and 60 percent (or more) of the variance in study results and that prior knowledge overrules all other variables.

2.2 Prior Knowledge and Research Using Causal Modeling Techniques

Attempts to explore causal models of educational achievement have resulted in "complex models," with a good overall fit and a multitude of significant structural coefficients, which stress once more the importance of prior knowledge. There is considerable evidence that "domain-specific" prior knowledge is usually the type of prior knowledge that affects the learning process and results. Above all, domain-specific prior knowledge should not be confused with the overall general ability called "intelligence." In the 1950s, it was still believed that more intelligent people could learn things that less intelligent people could not. A careful scrutiny of empirical findings casts doubt on this for various reasons. First, the correlation between intelligence and achievement is highly variable. Statistical meta-analyses have yielded overall coefficients that range between 0.34 and 0.51. Second, if one partials out the influence of prior knowledge, the correlation between intelligence and study result is drastically reduced to values ranging between 0.0 and 0.30 (Weinert 1989a).

Furthermore, the results from studies on meta-cognition show remarkable parallels with the results from intelligence studies that considered predictors of learning outcomes (r was between 0.07 and 0.20). Contrary to expectations, past research has shown that motivational variables and instructional characteristics contribute very little to the prediction of study performance.

The correlations between prior knowledge and performance remained significant even with intelligence scores partialed out. The conclusion may also be drawn that domain-specific knowledge can compensate for low intellectual ability, but high intellectual ability cannot compensate for low prior knowledge (Weinert 1989b Walker 1987).

The most important finding to emerge from causal models is the superior explanatory power of prior knowledge, the most significant path in the models. Overall, it may be concluded that the past is in fact the best predictor for the future. Differences in the knowledge base are the main source of intra-individual and interindividual differences in cognitive achievement, irrespective of chronological age or the specific domain of knowledge.

3. Effects of Prior Knowledge on the Learning Process

Effects of prior knowledge on the learning process, either positive or negative (support or hindrance), can be classified in three categories: (a) an overall facilitating effect of learning leading to better study results; (b) inherent qualities of prior knowledge (i.e., completeness, accessibility, amount, structure) influencing the facilitating effect (sometimes described as independent effects); and (c) the effects of interaction between the first two types of effect.

3.1 Direct and Indirect Effects

The overall facilitating effect of prior knowledge is generally recognized as being the most important

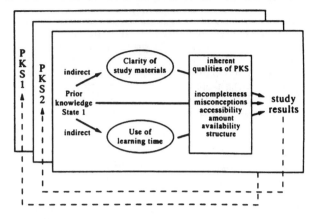

Figure 2
Interaction effects involving inherent quality effect and the facilitating effect

positive effect on learning. Some theories that give an explanation of this finding will be discussed later. Nevertheless, it should be borne in mind that not all facilitating effects are the "direct" results of prior knowledge. For the purpose of this review, a distinction can be made between:

(a) a direct effect of prior knowledge facilitating the learning process and leading to better study results;

(b) an indirect effect of prior knowledge, optimizing the clarity of study materials;

(c) an indirect effect of prior knowledge, optimizing the use of instructional and learning time.

The different relationships can be illustrated when causal modeling is used to analyze the overall relational pattern of variables.

3.2 Inherent Qualities of Prior Knowledge Influencing the Facilitating Effect

The generally accepted facilitating effect of prior knowledge emerges from the implicit assumption that the subject has a high-quality knowledge base. In other words, the subject's prior knowledge state (PKS) has certain characteristics (i.e., qualities) as follows— it is reasonably complete and correct, of reasonable amount, of good accessibility and availability, and well-structured. Consequently, if the prior knowledge state is considered as the independent variable, and study results as a dependent variable, these qualities must be seen as intervening variables, causing interference (Fig. 2). When prior knowledge is used during learning a study task, as shown in Fig. 2, the learning results are added to the original prior knowledge state

(PKS 1) and designated "prior knowledge state 2" (PKS 2), which is used to start a second learning task.

Six inherent qualities of prior knowledge can be distinguished: incompleteness, misconceptions, accessibility, availability, amount, and structure. If these qualities differ from the assumed perception, the facilitating effect of prior knowledge (direct or indirect) will increase or decrease.

3.3 Interaction Effects Between Facilitating Effect and Inherent Qualities

Interaction effects occur between the inherent quality effects (IQE's) and the main facilitating effect (Fig. 2). For example, it was found that subjects from a high-knowledge group (with a high amount of relevant domain-specific knowledge) have several advantages over those with low knowledge when the other inherent qualities differ. Although the overall effect remained significant and dominant, high-knowledge students did not suffer so much from the effects caused by incompleteness and misconceptions in prior knowledge.

Such examples of interactions do suggest that there is a certain hierarchy in prior knowledge effects, in which effects with a higher classification overrule those with a lower classification. It seems obvious that the facilitating effect is at the top of this hierarchy, irrespective of whether the hierarchy is regarded as being based on the average occurrence or the average impact. There is, however, no evidence in past research to suggest a certain ranking in the lower levels.

4. Explaining the Effect of Prior Knowledge

In instructional psychology, many research attempts have been made to exclude the effect of prior knowledge as far as possible, for example by using nonsense syllables in experimental research situations. This was done in the hope—which has since been demonstrated as futile—that fundamental patterns in the learning process could thus be studied in isolation. When prior knowledge eventually did surface within this artificial and restricted framework, it was in a transfer experiment which investigated the influence of learning a series of syllable pairs on learning a second series.

However, a number of attempts have been made to manipulate prior knowledge actively or to apply it in the learning process. These attempts show that the activation of existing cognitive structures generally exerts a facilitating influence on the learning task. This empirically demonstrated phenomenon awaits a full explanation from more applied research. Among other things, it is unclear which cognitive process or processes are to be held responsible for this, and further research is necessary on how to use this facilitating effect in actual educational situations where increased return and improvement of quality are the objectives.

Nevertheless, a number of explanatory theories have been advanced, primarily on the basis of experimental research (see Dochy 1990). According to the restructuring theory, information is structured in a different way in the long-term memory (LTM). The accessibility theory states that prior knowledge increases the accessibility of knowledge and consequently reduces the load on the working memory so that more information per time unit can be processed. The selective attention hypothesis argues that attention is directed selectively at passages relevant to prior knowledge, which are subjected to a deeper level of processing. The retrieval-aid theory proclaims that prior knowledge and access to relevant cognitive structures increases retrieval. The elaboration theory states that the production of elaborations leads to multiple redundant retrieval paths in the cognitive representation.

The different theories are not necessarily mutually exclusive; they are primarily concerned with phases that follow one another during information processing. Accordingly, prior knowledge is said to influence each of these phases: the direction of attention, the encoding of information, its processing in working memory, storage in the long-term memory, and retrieval of information from long-term memory. The different theories or approaches recognize the positive influence of prior knowledge on the selection process from the knowledge base, the capacity of working memory, the elaborations carried out on new information, the storage of new information in long-term memory, and the retrieval of new information.

However, some remarks about the investigations discussed are in order. Some of the studies are characterized by a limited ecological validity. In other words, the experimental situation does not allow the generalization of the findings to real educational situations. This applies to the use of nonsense syllables and to experiments that use lists of words or one or two short sentences as the information that the student must learn. The activation of prior knowledge by short passages of text might also be given as an example here. Sometimes the information to be learnt deals with fictional subjects or non existent situations. Finally, the nature of the test (general questions or specific questions on the text, recognition or remembering, etc.) is seldom taken into account in the interpretation of the results.

5. Conclusion

The explanatory theories related to the effect of prior knowledge can mainly be situated at the knowledge-acquisition components level of information processing. This means that sifting out relevant new information, maximizing internal coherence of knowledge structures, and comparing knowledge structures are the processes where prior knowledge plays a major role. Most of the explanatory theories are strongly linked to the structure of prior knowledge. This implies that the different components of the prior knowledge should be taken into account and can be helpful in educational settings for diagnosis and as a basis for educational support. Further, the possibilities of using prior knowledge state tests (i.e., domain-specific tests measuring students' prior knowledge state) and knowledge profiles (i.e.,plotting as a graph the raw or standardized test scores of a group or an individual on certain parameters) appear to be promising: they provide a rational basis for flexible learning, that is, for adaptation to different entry levels of students, for individualizing learning materials, and for providing individual support (see Dochy 1992, 1994).

It is clear that instruction is to be reconsidered on the basis of a new educational model of the learning process in which the overall assessment takes a central place and the students' prior knowledge state is the starting point (Glaser and De Corte 1992). According to this model (see Fig. 3), the students start by stating their learning goals. These relate to a certain part of the knowledge base (the content or the whole of a university course). After having taken a prior knowledge state test, the learning goals are reformulated (if necessary) and the students start with the appropriate learning tasks. During the learning process the students take progress tests regularly to check their progress, to determine the amount of guidance required, and to identify subsequent learning tasks (Frederiksen et al. 1990).

The trend in education to increase output and to raise student inflow creates new problems. The problem of pursuing two conflicting aims—a high output of student flow (minimum dropout) and more open access—can only be solved by taking the prior knowledge state of students into account. In this way, what appears to be a dilemma can be used to advantage.

In order to take the prior knowledge state of students fully into account, more research is required that allows flexible adaptations in the course materials to students' knowledge profiles, for example by using electronic learning systems. In the near future, research as well as educational practice, will have to focus on:

(a) refining the assessment procedures to grasp the full nature of a student's prior knowledge state;

(b) incorporating prior knowledge state tests as a recurrent feature in courses and curricula;

(c) extending the feedback function of support provisions by making use of the information obtained by prior knowledge state tests and knowledge profiles.

References

Alexander P A, Judy J E 1988 The interaction of domain-specific and strategic knowledge in academic performance. *Rev. Educ. Res.* 58: 375–404

Alexander P A, Kulikowich J A, Schulze S K 1992 How subject-matter knowledge affects recall and intertest. Paper presented at the XXV International Congress of Psychology, Brussels

Ausubel D P 1968 *Educational Psychology: A Cognitive View.* Holt, Rinehart and Winston, New York

Bloom B S 1982 *Human Characteristics and School Learning.* McGraw-Hill, New York

Dochy F J R C 1990 Instructional implications of recent research and empirically based theories on the effect of prior knowledge on learning. In: Pieters J M, Breuer K, Simons P R J (eds.) 1990 *Learning Environments* (Recent Research in Psychology Series) Springer-Verlag, Berlin

Dochy F J R C 1992 *Assessment of Prior Knowledge as a Determinant for Future Learning: The Use of Prior Knowledge State Tests and Knowledge Profiles.* Lemma, Utrecht and Jessica Kingsley, London

Dochy F J R C 1994 Investigating one use of knowledge profiles in a flexible learning environment: Analysing students' prior knowledge states. In: Vosinadou S (ed.) 1994 *Psychological and Educational Foundations of Technology-based Learning Environments.* (NATO ASI Series F Special Program AET) Springer-Verlag, Berlin

Dochy F J R C, Alexander P A 1995 Mapping prior knowledge: A framework for discussion among researchers. *Eur. J. Psychol. Educ.* 10(1)

Frederiksen N, Glaser R, Lesgold A, Shafro M G 1990 *Diagnostic Monitoring of Skill and Knowledge Acquisition.* LEA, Hillsdale, New Jersey

Glaser R, De Corte E 1992 Preface to the assessment of prior knowledge as a determinant for future learning. In: Dochy F J R C 1992 *Assessment of Prior Knowledge as a Determinant for Future Learning: The Use of Prior Knowledge State Tests and Knowledge Profiles.* Lemma, Utrecht and Jessica Kingsley, London

Haertel G D, Walberg H J, Weinstein T 1983 Psychological models of educational performance: A theoretical synthesis of constructs. *Rev. Educ. Res.* 53(1): 75–91

Johanssen D H, Grabowski B L 1993 *Handbook of Individual Differences Learning and Instruction.* LEA, Hillsdale, New Jersey

Tobias S 1994 Interest prior knowledge and learning. *Rev. Educ. Res.* 64(1) 37–54

Walker C H 1987 Relative importance of domain knowledge

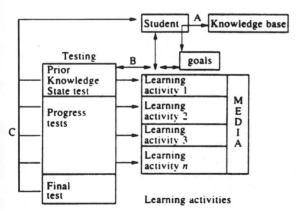

Figure 3
Components of the new model of the learning process

and overall attitude on acquisition of domain-related information. *Cognition and Instruction.* 4(1): 25–42

Weinert F 1989a The impact of schooling on cognitive development: One hypothetical assumption, some empirical results, and many theoretical implications. EARLI News 8: 3–7

Weinert F (ed.) 1989b The relation between education and development. *Int. J. Educ. Res.* 13(8): 827–948

Further Reading

Alexander P A, Dochy F J R C 1994 Adults' views about knowing and believing. In: Garner R, Alexander P A (eds.) 1994 *Beliefs about Text and about Instruction*

with Text. Lawrence Erlbaum Associates, Hillsdale, New Jersey

Alexander P A, Dochy F J R C in press Conceptions of knowlege and beliefs: A Euro–American comparison. *Educ. Psychol.*

Praivat R S 1989 Promoting access to knowledge strategy and disposition in students: A research synthesis. *Rev. Educ. Res.* 59: 1–41

Schneider W 1985 Developmental trends in the metamemory memory behavior relationship: An integrative review. In: Fouest-Piessley D L, Mackinnon G E, Waller T G (eds.) 1985 *Cognition Metacognition and Human Performance* Vol 1. Academic Press, New York

Wagemans L J J M, Dochy F J R C 1991 Principles in the use of experimental learning as a source of prior knowledge *Distance Educ.* (12)85–108

Reasoning

J. F. Voss

This entry presents an overview of research conducted on reasoning. It focuses upon what is probably the most significant trend in reasoning research, the shift from tasks employing the structures of formal logic to tasks involving either particular academic subject matter or thinking in everyday situations. The entry has three sections: the first addresses definitional matters, the second presents a summary of selected research findings, and the third raises some conceptual issues in reasoning research.

1. Issues of Definition

1.1 The Concept of Reasoning

The term "reasoning" refers to the process by which an individual, given particular information, infers some other information from what has been given. The inference may yield a conclusion or, given a conclusion, the inference may be a reason or premise supporting the claim or conclusion. The term also denotes the process of going through a series of inferential steps, as in the "reasoning" involved in solving a mathematical problem or describing the causes of the Second World War. Each step, however, requires some type of justification.

The term "informal reasoning" is not currently common (see Voss et al. 1991). Essentially following a distinction made by Aristotle, formal reasoning refers to reasoning that employs the structures of formal logic, such as the categorical and the conditional syllogism, while informal reasoning refers to reasoning involving the use of discourse structures that have probabilistic contents and often involve opinion, since they are

concerned with "probable truth." The basic structural unit of an informal argument is the enthymeme, that is, a conclusion supported by a reason. Thus it is the task employed, not the reasoning per se, that delineates "formal" and "informal" reasoning.

2. Research Findings

2.1 Reasoning in an Argumentation Context

There has been increasing research interest in argumentation. In the field of rhetoric, for example, writers have argued that formal logical structures have little real-world applicability, and the focus has moved away from the idea of rhetoric as style and delivery to that of rhetoric as the analysis of sound argumentation. With respect to instructionally related research, the study of argumentation, while slow to be addressed, is growing. The child's development of argumentation usage constitutes one aspect of such work. Dunn and Munn (1987), for example, found that approximately one-third of children observed in an age range of 1.8 to 3 years were able to justify their position by the age of 3 when having disputes with their mothers. Further, Stein and Miller (1991) have noted that much of the social interaction of children aged 4–5 involves assertion, defense, and negotiation. Moreover, Miller (1987) in an interesting chapter on collective argumentation, has distinguished three principles involved in cooperative argumentation, namely, generalizability, objectivity, and consistency (or truth). Generalizability refers to the conditions, in a group context, that need to be fulfilled in order for a statement to be justified. Objectivity refers to the acceptance of a statement as collectively valid if it is not denied. Consistency holds that contradictories cannot enter into, or remain in, contents that are collectively valid. Miller further argues that arriving at what is collectively valid begins as early as age 2 and progresses through a number of stages, with knowledge development occurring as an outcome.

Stein and Miller (1991), concerned with children's argument in conflict situations, state that such arguments mostly arise from disagreements about possessions and social goals. Resolution, moreover, takes place hierarchically. The lowest level is maintaining one's own opinion, with the occasional use of physical force and shouting matches. A higher level involves becoming aware of the other person's preferences and attempting to accommodate them. On the third level there is the full realization of the vulnerability of one's own claim and a more extensive resolution may occur. In similar work, Genishi and DiPaolo (1982) found that children's arguments are described by two goals: controlling the behavior of others and asserting one's self. Hofer et al. (1990) studied argumentation between mothers and daughters; the work was cast in a motivational framework placing a mother's desire for control against the daughter's desire for independence. The authors examined the argumentation in detail, showing that the arguments were goal-driven, and demonstrating that argumentative exchanges were relatively short and resolution infrequent.

Another line of argumentation research has considered how effectively individuals are able to generate and evaluate arguments about issues of social concern. In *The Skill of Argument*, Kuhn (1991) presents the results of interviews held with individuals ranging in age from 14 to 69, in which they were asked for the reasons why prisoners return to jail, children drop out of school, and people become unemployed. The results indicated that individuals with a college education demonstrate better reasoning skill than those without, while age and gender had little effect. Reasoning skill measures included the statement and justification of arguments, the statement of alternative causal theories, and the use of counterarguments and rebuttals. Only approximately 20 percent of the 160 people interviewed could be regarded as "good reasoners," a result similar to those obtained by other investigators.

One of the most important facets of informal reasoning is that argumentation can be influenced not only by the individual's knowledge but by the person's beliefs and attitude toward the topic in question. While this fact has long been recognized, research in the informal reasoning context has only begun to address the issue. Of particular importance is that while the evaluation of arguments in formal logic consists of determining whether the argument is valid according to the rules of logic, and while analysis is typically conducted by placing the argument in a content-free canonical form, informal arguments are evaluated on the basis of soundness, determined by the criteria of the ac-

ceptability or plausibility of the supporting reason, and the extent to which the reason supports the claim, sometimes termed "relevance." In addition, strength of counterarguments can be considered as a third criterion. Most importantly, these criteria emphasize that, as opposed to formal arguments, the contents of a given informal argument are critical to its evaluation.

A summary of results indicating that evaluation of informal arguments is indeed influenced by each of these criteria is presented by Voss and Means (1991). In addition, the authors provide results indicating that a person's attitude acts as a weighting factor in judging argument strength. The authors also refer to a model postulating that argument evaluation is influenced by the relation of the claim and to the relation of the supporting reason to particular values activated by that reason. The role of attitude in argumentation has also been addressed by Zammuner (1987), who, in asking individuals to write arguments regarding abortion, described differences in argument structure and language expression in relation to the person's position on the topic.

2.2 Argumentation and Instruction

Advocacy of the idea that argumentation can produce learning can be traced back to Ancient Greece. Orsolini and Pontecorvo (1992) studied the instructional function of argumentation in a classroom context. Following previous research involving textual analysis of group discussions, 5-year-old children were observed in a guided classroom situation, and the discussion was recorded. The authors distinguished three types of conversational sequences, mutual continuations, cycles of contingent queries–answers, and disputes, each facilitating children's talk in a different way. Interestingly, explanations and justifications were most likely to occur during disputes, when children needed to defend a position or when they were requested to give an explanation. The important point, however, is that knowledge construction can be shown to take place in such a context, with argumentation as an important factor.

From an instructional perspective, an important question is the extent to which informal reasoning skill is acquired in school. Research by Perkins (1985) has provided evidence suggesting that informal reasoning is related to a person's ability level, and that schooling does little to develop a person's informal reasoning skills. Similarly, Säljö and Wyndhamna (1990) had students aged 12 and 13 solve a postage stamp problem, where the students were able to draw upon school-acquired knowledge. High-ability students performed better, apparently being more facile in drawing upon their knowledge. These and other findings indicate that the best predictor of informal reasoning performance is general level of intellectual ability, that such individuals are better able to utilize their knowledge in an informal reasoning task, and that experience (including school experience) does little to improve informal reasoning skill. These findings strongly urge that schools develop instructional procedures that will facilitate the acquisition of informal reasoning skill.

Although experience seems to have little influence in developing informal reasoning skill, the fact that such skill can be acquired by students of various ability levels is suggested by the findings of Schliemann and Acioly (1989). These authors have shown that individuals, including children, with little or no formal schooling, are able to make complex mathematical computations in selling Brazilian lottery tickets. While mathematical calculations of this type may differ from argumentation skill, the rather surprising proficiency of the children does suggest that the potential informal reasoning skill of individuals having what appears to be an average or lower-than-average general intellectual ability may enable such individuals to perform better than results have thus far shown.

At a higher academic level, Lehman et al. (1988) found that graduate training had a positive effect upon a particular type of reasoning performance. In the employment of law and medical students, as well as graduate students in psychology and chemistry, it was found that training in law, medicine, and psychology yielded better performance than training in chemistry with respect to reasoning about confounded variables and statistical considerations. While these populations were quite select in relation to general academic abilities, the findings nevertheless do suggest that reasoning skills acquired in one subject matter domain can be transferred to another domain, depending quite likely upon the similarity of the domain requirements.

2.3 Reasoning in Formal Logic Tasks

Because the focus of this entry is upon informal reasoning and especially argumentation, research employing more traditional deductive and inductive tasks is only briefly considered. The study of deduction has been largely marked by the development of models and their testing. The work includes models of reasoning involving "if ... then" conditionals, as well as the categorical syllogism. Research on induction has included considerable work on analogy, as well as the study of covariation, heuristics, and the use and generalizability of mental models and rules (see Sternberg and Smith 1988 for summaries of this work.)

3. Conceptual Issues

3.1 Reasoning, Knowledge, and Subject Matter

Stein and Miller (1991) argued that in studies examining reasoning skill, a factor that must be taken into account is the knowledge a person has about the topic in question. This is because a failure to demonstrate reasoning skill may reflect either a knowledge

deficiency or a lack of reasoning skill (or both). On the other hand, as previously mentioned, knowledge of subject matter does not necessarily mean than an individual will be able to reason effectively using such knowledge. Thus, an "expert reasoner" would be a person who is able to use knowledge and argumentation skills to state and evaluate arguments. Moreover, expert reasoners are able to apply such skills even when their knowledge of a given subject is limited, since, even within the constraints of their knowledge base, they can extract the elements that are susceptible to reason. In any event, research on reasoning requires consideration of the interaction of reasoning skill and knowledge.

One of the most significant questions requiring study is the extent to which reasoning is similar or different in various subject matter domains. While the definition of what constitutes evidence may vary with domain, it is not clear how the reasoning per se may vary with different subject matter. This is a question requiring study. The issue takes on greater significance when its relevance to instruction is considered. The familiar question of whether reasoning can be taught in a generic sense, essentially independent of subject matter, or whether it is best taught in the context of a particular subject, is still a matter of debate. What does seem to be the case is that particular reasoning heuristics may be taught as "think of counterfactuals," and that these heuristics may be applied in various domains. Yet being able to actually think of counterfactual arguments in various domains is dependent upon the individual's knowledge of the domain; the experience is essentially futile unless a person has knowledge of the germane subject matter. Moreover—and this is probably the crux of the issue —it seems that individuals probably need experience in using that knowledge, namely in reasoning with it, or it will lie dormant and retrieval will be relatively difficult. In this sense, informal reasoning involves selective and constrained search that permits the individual to retrieve information which allows for appropriate "reasoning" performance.

3.2 "Logical" Reasoning

Intuitively a good reasoner is thought of as a person who "thinks logically." However, in informal reasoning, especially in relation to topics such as social issues, arguments may be evaluated differently by individuals varying in their beliefs, thus pointing to the fact that appropriate informal reasoning does not yield "truth." However, as Aristotle noted, such reasoning helps individuals make the best decisions and/or draw or support the most justifiable conclusions. Indeed, it would seem that efforts in schooling, where appropriate, need to be directed toward arriving at the "most reasonable conclusion" rather than at the "correct answer," and that great importance should be attached to the student's ability to justify the conclusion.

See also: Development of Learning Skills in Problem-solving and Thinking; Social Sciences, Learning and Instruction of; Cognition and Learning

References

Dunn J, Munn P 1987 Development of justification in disputes with mother and sibling. *Dev. Psychol.* 23(6): 791–98

Genishi C, DiPaolo M 1982 Learning through argument in a preschool. In: Wilkinson L C (ed.) 1982 *Communicating in the Classroom*. Academic Press, New York

Hofer M, Pikowsky B, Fleischmann T 1990 The differential use of arguments in mother–daughter conflicts. Paper presented at the Third International Conference on Dialogue Analysis, Bologna

Kuhn D 1991 *The Skill of Argument*. Cambridge University Press, New York

Lehman D R, Lempert R O, Nisbett R E 1988 The effects of graduate training on reasoning: Formal discipline and thinking about everyday life events. *Am. Psychol.* 43: 431–42

Miller M 1987 Argumentation and cognition. In: Hickman M (ed.) 1987 *Social and Functional Approaches to Language and Thought*. Academic Press, Orlando, Florida

Orsolini M, Pontecorvo C 1992 Children's talk in classroom discussions. *Cognit. Inst.* 9(2): 113–36

Perkins D N 1985 Postprimary education has little impact on informal reasoning. *J. Educ. Psychol.* 77(5): 562–71

Säljö R, Wyndhamna J 1990 Problem solving, academic performance, and situated reasoning: A study of joint cognitive activity in a formal setting. *Br. J. Educ. Psychol.* 60(3): 245–54

Schliemann A D, Acioly N M 1989 Mathematical knowledge developed at work: The contribution of practice versus the contribution of schooling. *Cognition and Instruction* 6(3): 185–221

Stein N, Miller C A 1991 I win -you lose: The development of argumentative thinking. In: Voss J F, Perkins D N, Segal J W (eds.) 1991

Sternberg R J, Smith E E (eds.) 1988 *The Psychology of Human Thought*. Cambridge University Press, Cambridge

Voss J F, Means M L 1991 Learning to reason via instruction in argumentation. *Learning and Instruction* 1(4): 337-50

Voss J F, Perkins D N, Segal J W (eds.) 1991 *Informal Reasoning and Education*. Erlbaum, Hillsdale, New Jersey

Zammuner V L 1987 For or against: The expression of attitudes in discourse. *Text* 7: 411–34

Further Reading

Antaki C (ed.) 1988 *Analyzing Everyday Explanation: A Casebook of Methods*. Sage, London.

Baron J B, Sternberg R (eds.) 1987 *Teaching Thinking Skills: Theory and Practice*. Freeman, New York

Caverni J P, Fabre J M, Gonzalez M 1990 *Cognitive Biases*. North-Holland, Amsterdam

Evans J S B T 1989 Problem solving, reasoning, and decision making. In: Baddeley A, Bernsen N O (eds.) 1989 *Cognitive Psychology—Research Directions in Cognitive Science: European Perspectives*, Vol. 1. Erlbaum, Hillsdale, New Jersey

Holland J H, Holyoak K J, Nisbett R E, Thagard P R 1986 *Induction: Processes of Inference, Learning, and Discovery*. MIT Press, Cambridge, Massachusetts

Johnson-Laird P N, Byrne R M J 1991 *Deduction*. Erlbaum, Hillsdale, New Jersey

Keane M T 1988 *Analogical Problem Solving*. Horwood, Chichester

Resnick L B 1989 *Knowing, Learning, and Instruction: Essays in Honor of Robert Glaser*. Erlbaum, Hillsdale, New Jersey

Self-regulation in Learning

J. Kuhl and K. Kraska

Self-regulation can be defined as the ability to behave according to one's own intentions in a flexible way. With respect to learning, self-regulation bridges the gap between academic performance and two of its determinants, namely cognitive abilities and achievement motivation. Some students are sufficiently capable and motivated to perform well on a learning task, but they have problems in initiating and maintaining the required task-relevant behavior. Many findings from neurophysiological, cognitive, and clinical research support the assumption that this nonmotivational type of underachievement can be attributed to an impairment of a separate mental function or subsystem that mediates the flexible and context-sensitive initiation, maintenance, and termination of self-generated intentions. There is general agreement on the kinds of situations that involve self-regulation, for example postponing an immediate reward in order to obtain a more valuable delayed reward, or accepting small immediate negative consequences in order to avoid substantial long-term negative consequences. Comprehensive theoretical approaches, however, are sparse. This entry describes several historical and current theories of self-regulation and methodological approaches to the assessment of self-regulatory competencies.

1. Three Theoretical Approaches

It was mainly the Soviet psychologists Luria, Vygotsky, and Leontief (1932) who established the tradition of psychological conceptualizations centered around the notion of the ontogenetic development of self-regulation, including its social and cultural origins. This tradition was taken up comparatively late by United States psychologists (Diaz et al. 1990, Meichenbaum 1977). Although Soviet accounts of the child's transition from "impulsive" to voluntary behavior as a result of cultural progress to systematic and organized forms of labor do not play a substantial role in psychological theory in the early 1990s, their ontogenetic perspective has had a considerable impact. According to this perspective, each human being has to acquire voluntary behavior during the course of the socialization process. Basic psychological mechanisms are transformed into signs within a series of social interactions. After a process of internalization, these signs form independent higher forms of psychological functioning.

One unresolved problem concerns the deeper meaning of the concept of internalization. It is often simply equated with subvocalization of others' expectations and norms. Kopp (1982) describes a similar "immature" form of internalization in terms of "self-control" as opposed to "self-regulation." According to Kopp, self-control refers to an intermediate developmental step characterized by behavior strictly in accordance with a cognitive representation of the absent caregiver's commands or directives. True self-regulation, however, requires "taking over effectively the caregiver's regulating role" (Diaz et al. 1990 p. 10). This distinction by Kopp and Diaz will be taken up again in a later section.

In clinical psychology, Kanfer and his associates developed several models of self-regulation and behavioral techniques to alleviate self-regulatory deficits (Kanfer and Schefft 1988). Starting from the point of a disruption in the regular smooth flow of behavior, Kanfer elaborated an information-processing model of self-regulation which focused on the triad of self-monitoring, self-evaluation, and self-reinforcement. This model has been extended and refined in many ways (see Kanfer and Schefft 1988) and can be judged—apart from its concrete influences on clinical practice—as a major contribution to an understanding of therapeutic problem-solving in information-processing and systemic terms. From an educational point of view, Kanfer's emphasis on attributional and self-reinforcing processes is particularly relevant, since functional self-regulatory deficits can result from a lack of appreciation of oneself as a powerful agent.

A third major theoretical approach to self-regulation stems from Ach's (1910) work on willpower. This approach has been elaborated by Kuhl (1992) and reformulated in terms of a computational process model that overcomes the traditional shortcomings of volitional theories.

Although each of the three theories mentioned has a somewhat different focus, all of them contribute to a deeper understanding of students' inability to maintain their plans and defend them against temptations.

Despite the small number of elaborated theories, many researchers have elaborated specific aspects of self-regulation or developed well-designed experimental paradigms which can be integrated in a comprehensive theoretical framework. Especially relevant in this context are Mischel's experiments that contain operationalizations of the basic components of self-regulation such as induction of a conflict between a cognitive decision (e.g., to wait for a more attractive reward) and an emotional temptation (e.g., to obtain a smaller reward immediately), and the use of strategies children employ to resist temptation (Mischel and Mischel 1983).

2. A Theory of Self-regulation

The assumption of conflicts between current intentions and emotional preferences or habitual response tendencies is not as unproblematic as it would seem from the perspective of commonsense psychology. On closer inspection, the assumption raises some complex philosophical problems. What does it mean when a client seeking therapy complains that he wants to stop drinking alcohol, but that he cannot stay away from it? Isn't the fact that he continues drinking evidence enough that he wants to drink? Does a child who has expressed an intention to finish her homework before joining her friends display a self-regulatory deficit when she starts playing with them before finishing her homework, or has she simply changed her intention?

If a change of behavior (e.g., to drinking or playing) occurs without hesitation, regret, attempts to make up for counterintentional behavior, or other signs of conflict, there is no reason to assume a self-regulatory deficit. One would rather assume that the individual has simply changed his or her intention. By contrast, a self-regulatory deficit (what is traditionally called a case of "weakness of will") is usually inferred from evidence for a perseverating conflict between the intention the individual regards as the best choice and an emotional preference for an attractive alternative activity.

Theoretically this conflict can be accounted for on the level of "subpersonal" psychology. This conceptualization involves distinguishing more or less autonomous subsystems within a person. According to this view, several "subpersons" or subsystems may arrive at conflicting decisions on the basis of different information sources, or decision rules, or both. They will therefore compete for the control of overt action since there is no automatic conflict resolution despite continuous and intensive interactions among them.

As for self-regulation, there are three subsystems to be considered: (a) acquired action schemas ("habits"), (b) emotionally supported action tendencies ("emotional preferences"), and (c) deliberately selected action alternatives ("cognitive preferences," or "intentions").

If a cognitive decision is to be enacted, the actual strength of action schemas compatible with the decision has to be made dominant. This may be a difficult task, when there is a persisting conflict between cognitive and emotional preferences. This is due to the "impulsive nature" of strong habits and emotional preferences. The assumption of impulsivity implies that emotional and procedural subsystems have a more direct impact on behavior than higher cognitive processing. The resulting *difficulty of enactment* of cognitive intentions encompassing counteremotional or counterhabitual behavior must be overcome by effortful self-regulatory strategies.

Self-regulatory mechanisms are processes that modulate the interaction between an organism's subsystems. The most important self-regulatory mechanisms which are presumed to serve this purpose are: (a) encoding control, (b) action control, (c) emotion control, (d) motivation control, (e) attention control, (f) intention control, (g) coping with failure, and (h) self-reflective thinking. An additional function called "freezing" will be discussed separately.

Ideally, each of these processes would be characterized by its developmental and learning preconditions, its immediate trigger conditions, and its implementation in terms of mechanisms. Knowledge about the first and second of these aspects is still very limited (see Kuhl and Kraska 1989 for a more detailed discussion).

3. Development and Strategies

3.1 Basics

The development of self-regulatory functions depends on the acquisition of metacognitive and metamotivational knowledge and skills. In the course of their development, individuals will detect regularities between their behavior and internal and external states. For instance, someone who experiences repeated failure after having made impulsive decisions may at some point form a metarule like "fast decisions produce bad results."

According to Kuhl and Kraska's (1989) developmental theory of self-regulation, children have to acquire the following developmental precursors: (a) representation of ongoing action tendencies, (b) concept of impulsivity, (c) self-congruent commitment, and (d) difficulty of enactment. For example, a child who decides to finish her homework can maintain this intention through self-regulatory support, if she has a cognitive representation of the following facts: "I want to do my homework although I don't feel like it at the moment. Finishing my task tends to be more difficult when I'm in the mood to play. But I do not want to go to school tomorrow with unfinished homework, therefore I have to finish this worksheet . . .." The four

precursors are usually met by the time children enter elementary school, whereas self-regulatory strategies seem to develop during elementary school years (Kuhl and Kraska 1989).

3.2 Strategies

This section gives a brief characterization of the different self-regulatory strategies. First, there is the freezing function which creates a "time window" for the operation of the remaining self-regulatory mechanisms by blocking the execution of currently dominant action schemas that are not compatible with the cognitive intention.

Whereas formerly the focus was predominantly on strategies that serve to maintain a chosen intention (e.g., Kuhl and Kraska 1989), strategies that mediate a task shift or the deliberate initiation of planning and self-reflective thinking are emphasized to a similar degree in the early 1990s (Kuhl 1992). This is reflected in the inclusion of self-reflection as a self-regulatory strategy. Frequently, the enactment of an intention requires a high degree of metacontrol over one's own thought processes. For instance, a student preparing for an exam must decide what to learn, how to learn, when to stop learning about one particular topic, and so on. The adequate implementation of the intention to prepare for the exam ideally requires much self-reflective activity directed at one's own thinking, and specific impairments may result from deficient metacontrol (Kuhl and Kraska 1989).

The remaining strategies all consist of the selective activation or inhibition of elements in the different subsystems in order to increase the probability that a chosen intention will be realized. Regarding the developmentally crucial period of elementary school years, there are four main strategies, which are of the greatest importance and will be described in some detail. Children's knowledge concerning these four basic self-regulatory strategies can be assessed by a newly developed standardized test (Kuhl and Christ 1992).

Motivation control is the attempt to generate action-related emotions that increase the evaluative strength of an intention. This can mainly be achieved by imagining positive outcomes of the cognitively chosen action.

Attention control facilitates the maintenance of a difficult intention by means of the selective activation of representations that support the intention and by inhibiting irrelevant aspects. This can be done by selective inhibition of external intention-relevant information (e.g., disregarding potentially conflicting postdecision information) or by the selective activation of action-related information (e.g., activating knowledge about various actions consistent with the current intention).

Emotion control refers to the strengthening of emotions that facilitate the initiation, maintenance, or termination of a difficult intention. For instance, sometimes sadness reduces self-regulatory efficiency, as exemplified by the difficulty of sticking to a dietary intention when one is unhappy. In other situations, a happy mood may have a debilitating effect, because it widens the scope of attention (resulting in an increased awareness of temptations in the environment), and because it creates a positive attitude toward self-gratification and generosity.

Coping with failure refers to an attitude which encourages analysis of one's shortcomings insofar as this is useful for improving one's ability for the next occasion, but discourages analysis when there is no possibility of amending the failure.

3.3 Mature Self-regulation

The development of self-regulation does not end, however, with the acquisition of the ability to maintain one's goal in the face of various distractions. Kuhl and Kraska (1989) included in their developmental theory a final step of volition–emotion integration which was characterized by a more mature form of resolving the conflict between commitment and emotional preference. At this stage of development, persisting conflicts between volitionally supported intentions and emotional preferences are avoided by finding new ways to develop emotional support for difficult intentions. Intentions that cannot obtain emotional support are abandoned after some time.

A crucial and often neglected point related to the stage of cognition–emotion integration concerns the notion of flexibility. The immature form of internalization associated with "self-control" (Kopp 1982) seems to be related to a rigid and literal adherence to internal representations of others' expectations that are not fully assimilated into the self. Research on a related personality disposition towards "state orientation" has shown that the tendency toward incomplete or even "false" internalization of others' beliefs, wishes, and expectations can explain the occurrence of uncontrollable and intrusive cognitions that interfere with efficient processing of information related to an individual's current intentions (Kuhl 1992). State-oriented cognitions can, in turn, help explain several behavioral paradoxes, such as the co-occurrence of high motivation and performance deficits in states of learned helplessness, the co-occurrence of rigid perseveration and distractibility, and the co-occurrence of overcommitment and procrastination (Kuhl 1992, Kuhl and Beckmann 1994). In the late 1990s, state orientation could be related to inhibited access to self-representations and other volitional resources that are assessed by the Volitional Components Checklist (VCC) constructed for adolescents and adults (Kuhl and Fuhrmann 1995).

4. Assessment

The self-regulation test for children (SRTC) (Kuhl and Kraska 1992) is designed to assess self-regulatory performance during standardized temptation episodes generated by a computer. This test is based on performance deficits indicated by decreased speed and/or increased variance in speed of performance during these "temptation episodes." Temptation is evoked by occasionally displaying interesting but distracting information on the upper right-hand part of the computer screen while the subjects are working on a task. In the children's version of this test, subjects are persuaded to commit themselves to a choice–reaction–time task, in order to earn money to buy some desirable toy at the end of the experiment. They are instructed to push one key when one bar appears in the lower left quarter of the screen and another key when two bars appear. Sometimes, a contest between two monkeys climbing a tree is shown on the screen. If the good monkey wins the race, it climbs down and adds a variable amount of money to the child's account shown on the lower right-hand quarter of the screen. If the bad monkey wins, it withdraws a variable amount of money from the account. Children readily understand that they cannot control the race, but that they do not earn money when they interrupt their task to watch the race. Consequently, virtually all the children studied formed an intention to avoid watching the race.

The test is based on an attempt to solve or reduce several difficulties traditionally involved in the measurement of self-regulation (Kuhl and Kraska 1989, 1992). These difficulties relate to the standardization of incentive values of distractors across subjects, induction of a conflict between a deliberate commitment to the task and an emotional temptation to shift attention to the interesting distractor, separation of attentional and self-regulatory deficits, and discrimination between explicit and implicit strategies mediating self-regulatory maintenance of task-related behavior. The SRTC has been administered to a sample of about 1,000 children whose age range was between 5 and 12. Norms exist for elementary school grades 1 to 4. The most striking findings confirming its construct validity include significant correlations with teachers' ratings of self-regulatory behaviors in the classroom (Kraska 1993), theoretically expected interactions with a test assessing self-regulatory strategy knowledge (Kuhl and Christ 1992), and theoretically consistent relationships between SRTC-indices and personality ratings obtained two and four years prior to SRTC-measurement.

5. Training

Some children are in principle capable of resisting temptation but they do so in a rigid way. These children do not show any deficit during temptation episodes. On the contrary, some children supposedly characterized as rigidly self-controlled rather than self-regulated display superior performance during distractor episodes compared to baseline performance. These children seem to overcompensate for the self-regulatory conflict. The extent to which these children are characterized by rigid self-control rather than flexible self-regulation can be identified in the final part of the SRTC. Here contingencies change, in that the children can earn considerably more "money" by watching the monkey competition in order to reach their goal. Several indicators are combined to show whether or not children have been able to adjust their behavior to the changed contingencies. Obviously, intervention must be different for students who fail this part of the test, that is, students who could be characterized as state oriented, as described above. While these children—unlike those with deficits in self-regulatory knowledge—often master the maintenance of an intention, they fail to enter the true self-regulatory stage in terms of a flexible balance between maintenance and change. Intervention in this kind of problem has to center around increasing self-responsibility, acknowledging the personal choice between maintaining an intention and decision for motivational change. Differential training programs designed to alleviate each of the different self-regulatory disorders have been successful according to various criteria (Kraska 1993).

See also: Affect, Emotions, and Learning; Metacognition; Emotional Development; Social Development

References

Ach N 1910 *Über den Willensakt und das Temperament.* Quelle und Meyer, Leipzig

Diaz R M, Neal C J, Amaya-Williams M 1990 The social origins of self-regulation. In: Moll L (ed.) 1990 *Vygotsky and Education: Instructional Implications and Applications of Sociohistorical Psychology.* Cambridge University Press, Cambridge

Kanfer F H, Schefft B K 1988 *Guiding the Process of Therapeutic Change.* Research Press, Champaign, Illinois

Kopp C B 1982 Antecedents of self-regulation: A developmental perspective. *Dev. Psychol.* 18(2): 199–214

Kraska K 1993 *Selbstregulationsförderung: Evaluation eines differentiellen Interventionsansatzes.* Hogrefe, Göttingen

Kuhl J 1992 A theory of self-regulation: Action versus state orientation, self-discrimination, and some applications. *Appl. Psychol.* 41: 95–173

Kuhl J, Beckmann J (eds.) 1994 *Volition and Personality: Action Versus State Orientation.* Hogrefe, Göttingen

Kuhl J, Christ E 1992 *Der Selbstregulations-Strategien-Test für Kinder (SRST-K): Test zur Erfassung Selbstregulatorischen Strategiewissens im Grundschulalter.* Hogrefe, Göttingen

Kuhl J, Kraska K 1989 Self-regulation and metamotivation: Computational mechanisms, development, and assessment. In: Kanfer R, Ackerman P L, Cudeck R (eds.) 1989 *Abilities, Motivation, and Methodology: The Minnesota Symposium on Learning and Individual Differences.* Erlbaum, Hillsdale, New Jersey

Kuhl J, Kraska K 1992 *Der Selbstregulations- und Konzentrationstest für Kinder (SRKT-K): Computerunterstützter Test zur Prozessdiagnostik verschiedener Aspekte der Ablenkungs- und Versuchungsresistenz.* Hogrefe, Göttingen

Kuhl J, Fuhrmann A 1995 *Decomposing Self-control and Self-regulation. The Theoretical and Empirical Basis of the Volitional Components Checklist.* Submitted manuscript. University of Osnibrück, Germany

Leontiev A N 1932 The development of voluntary attention in the child. *J. Genet. Psychol.* 40: 52–83

Meichenbaum D 1977 *Cognitive Behavior Modification: An Integrative Approach.* Plenum, New York

Mischel H N, Mischel W 1983 The development of children's knowledge of self-control strategies. *Child Dev.* 54(3): 603–19

Student Cognitive Processing and Learning

P. H. Winne and D. L. Butler

In the mid-twentieth century conceptions about learning and about how instructional events help students learn underwent a transition. A new view of learning—that the learner adapts to events as they unfold in an instructional environment—replaced one that saw the learner's behavior as controlled by instructional stimuluses (Anderson and Gates 1950). Research into this adaptive process aimed to discover principles for designing instructional environments that could specify "the experiences which most effectively implant in the individual a disposition to learn . . . the ways in which a body of knowledge should be structured so that it can be most readily grasped by the learner . . . the most effective sequences in which to present the materials to be learned . . . the nature and pacing of rewards and punishments in the process of learning and teaching" (Bruner 1964 pp. 307–08). A rapprochement between psychology and instructional research was underway that would sweep up the field of educational psychology within the larger cognitive revolution (Glaser 1982). As research accumulated over the next 40 years, perspectives on learning, instruction, and the learner would evolve significantly.

The view of learning that came to guide theory and research characterizes the learner as an active inquiring agent. Classifying the learner as "active" implies that he or she is continuously involved in cognition about self and environment. Elements interacting in cognition are the learner's mental structures of knowledge and the learner's current perceptions of events, people, and objects in the environment, which are developed in terms of the student's existing knowledge. Thus this conception emphasizes the intrinsic and central role of the learner's prior knowledge as a background for interpreting instruction and as a resource with which to construct new achievements in school subjects.

Characterizing the learner as "inquiring" emphasizes the central role played by hypothesis-framing and testing as the student takes part in the instructional environment. Theoretically, the student creates provisional models and theories about matters at hand; for example, how to participate in a discovery lesson, how to explain why some heavy objects float, how to gain acceptance by peers, and how to achieve personal satisfaction. Means for inquiring into phenomena, models of systems, and theories are themselves learned and can become objects of inquiry.

Finally, acknowledging the learner as an "agent" recognizes that the student does not merely observe surroundings and receive information available therein. Beyond observational and receptive qualities, the student also steps forward to define goals and to seek specific information from peers, a text, or the teacher. Thus, the learner shapes and takes actions in the instructional environment. These acts, mental and physical, elicit information which the student seeks for the purpose of guiding subsequent thinking and acting. In this way, students co-create events that comprise instructional tasks and generate their own learning-from-instruction.

1. A Framework Describing Cognition and Instruction

Many models have been proposed to characterize forms of cognition and the kinds of information that are cognitively manipulated as learners participate in instruction. Literature that predates this entry is summarized in Winne (1985, 1991a, 1991b) and Wittrock (1986). Figure 1 presents a model which describes a learner's cognitive participation in instruction. It involves three broad classes of variables: characteristics of the learner, characteristics of the instructional tasks, and events that transpire as the learner interacts with instructional tasks. Other contemporary models of instructional cognition differ primarily in the variables they assign to these different classes. Variables in Fig. 1 are representative of those in other models and, obviously, are not exhaustive.

Figure 1 should not be interpreted as suggesting that values for variables or relationships among variables are static. Over time, variables are reciprocally determined and interact. That is, changes in a variable in one class can affect other variables within that same class, and may influence variables in other classes

as well. In turn, the affected variable(s) may induce changes in other variables, including the one focused on initially. In this reciprocally determined system, identifying a single "cause" is difficult because choosing the slice in time within which to observe change is arbitrary. For instance, consider the case of a section heading within a textbook chapter. At the time the student is reading the chapter, it seems that the heading (a characteristic of the task environment) induces the student to retrieve (an event transpiring when the learner interacts with the text) some particular prior knowledge (a characteristic of the student). Earlier, however, when the textbook author was writing the chapter, the decision to insert the heading (a characteristic of the task environment) was probably based on a prediction about the prior knowledge that an average reader would possess (a characteristic of the student), and on the author's understanding about how inducing students to retrieve that prior knowledge might help them to construct an understanding of information in the chapter (an event transpiring when the learner interacts with the text). At this earlier time, then, the character of learners' prior knowledge affected the task environment by causing the author to include the heading in the text.

2. Characteristics of the Learner

Characteristics of the learner provide resources for and set limits on how a student reciprocally interprets and shapes instructional tasks. In information-processing models there are two main divisions of these characteristics: (a) features of the cognitive system that processes information; (b) kinds of knowledge (information) represented in the student's mind, both as products of information processing and as vehicles for processing information.

2.1 The Information-processing System

The mind is a biological and physical system and, hence, its functioning is influenced in part by its physical architecture (Newell 1990). While learning is partly a function of characteristics of human biological systems, those characteristics rarely have a direct, observable impact on learning in a classroom or in self-study situations. Two exceptions are notable, however.

Working memory, the metaphorical mental location where information is processed, has a limited channel capacity or span. This capacity is a joint function of the brain's neurophysiological properties and characteristics of the information being processed. Approximately 5 ± 2 information-processing events, such as maintaining conceptual knowledge in memory or performing a routine based on procedural knowledge, can be carried out simultaneously. The more structured knowledge is—chunked or schematized, in the case of conceptual knowledge; composed and automated, in the case of procedural knowledge—the

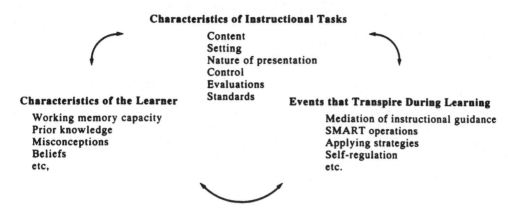

Characteristics of Instructional Tasks

Content
Setting
Nature of presentation
Control
Evaluations
Standards

Characteristics of the Learner

Working memory capacity
Prior knowledge
Misconceptions
Beliefs
etc,

Events that Transpire During Learning

Mediation of instructional guidance
SMART operations
Applying strategies
Self-regulation
etc.

Figure 1
Contextual model of instructional information processing

greater the apparent capacity of working memory. This explains how experts can appear to have huge capacity relative to novices when the fact is that experts use highly structured or automated forms of information in approximately the same "mental volume" in which a novice processes considerably less "dense" information. In general, the interaction of properties of working memory and of information's structure jointly influence information processing during learning from instruction.

The second area where physical properties of the mind clearly influence information processing in instruction arises in cases of learners with a typical neurological conditions (e.g., specific learning disabilities).

2.2 Knowledge

Terms for and theories about knowledge are legion (Alexander et al. 1991). Figure 2 revises Alexander et al.'s model by distinguishing two forms for representing knowledge—declarative and procedural; two levels of awareness about knowledge—tacit and explicit; and three kinds of information in knowledge—conceptual, metacognitive, and sociocultural.

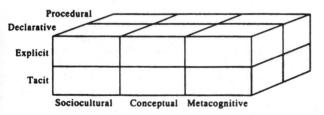

Figure 2
Facets of knowledge

Declarative knowledge is descriptive information, or "knowledge that." It remains static until changed by learning. Hosts of terms describe organizations in which declarative knowledge is organized or stored in memory. Some of the more common are analogy, chunk, concept, frame, image, metaphor, proposition, and schema.

Procedural knowledge is rules, often called condition–action rules or if–then rules, because only if particular conditions are satisfied is this knowledge invoked. One type of procedural knowledge classifies situations based on their properties. It is typically referred to as conditional knowledge because it defines when, where, and why declarative knowledge or a rule is relevant. Conditional knowledge plays a central role in students' use of cognitive strategies. A second type of procedural knowledge, referred to simply as a rule, acts on information to transform knowledge, such as translating information into a visual image. Procedural knowledge underlies the processes that students perform, such as organizing materials and the surrounding environment in preparation for studying. The certainty of the output obtained by applying procedural knowledge can vary. Thus algorithms, which yield reliable outcomes, are distinguished from heuristics, which are predictive but do not assure a determinate result. Sets of rules, in which the conditions of some are satisfied by the output of other rules' actions, are called production systems.

Tacit knowledge (Polanyi 1966) is knowledge the learner possesses which influences cognitive processing but of which the learner is not really aware. It is proposed to exist because, so far, it has not been possible to account fully for information processing and achievements in terms of explicit, reportable forms of knowledge. Iran-Nejad (1990) hypothesized the existence of cognitively local and relatively independent units of procedure-like knowledge that students accumulate through experience. These units are "dynamic," that is, they process information automatically and in parallel with processing that occurs in working memory, but lie "outside" working memory itself. Such dynamic components of knowledge may constitute tacit knowledge and, because of their independence from working memory, explain the apparent impenetrability of tacit knowledge.

Explicit knowledge is knowledge a learner can consciously inspect, including tacit knowledge that converts to explicit form by becoming an "object of thought" (Prawat 1989). Alexander et al. (1991) distinguish two kinds of explicit knowledge, conceptual and metacognitive knowledge, each of which is further divided.

Conceptual knowledge, according to Alexander et al. has two major divisions. The first, content knowledge, is information a student has about his or her physical, social, and mental world. It can be used informally or, especially in the context of schooling, it can be formalized into domains of study such as spelling, science, music, gymnastics, and art. Discourse knowledge, the second main kind of conceptual knowledge, represents information about common forms and functions of language, as well as other symbol systems used to represent and convey conceptual knowledge. In formalized domains of study, discourse knowledge may be unique to the domain and undergird procedures for developing new knowledge in that domain. In science, for instance, a mixture of text structures, mathematical formalisms, and graphic symbol systems are found in academic textbooks. These same discourse structures are used generatively by scientists as tools to extend knowledge of their domain.

As described above, students' extant or prior content knowledge has a powerful influence on information processing and resulting achievements (Perkins and Simmons 1988). Misconceptions may block accurate perceptions of information presented in instruction. Also, students can have difficulty translating and integrating information presented in different discourse systems, such as words and mathematical expressions (Dee Lucas and Larkin 1991), because they lack knowledge about how the two systems correspond. With instruction about what such structures are and how they can be used as schemata for building and monitoring comprehension benefits are observed in recall, problem solving, and transfer (Cook and Mayer 1988, Fuson and Willis 1989).

Metacognitive knowledge is the knowledge that provides the means by which learners actively inquire about knowledge. It is a second-order construct that represents reflections on or knowledge about knowledge, and the procedures by which a student regulates cognition and action. Since metacognition is effortful, conscious cognition, the cells in Fig. 2 where metacognitive and tacit knowledge intersect are shaded to indicate that the model's factors are not fully independent. Alexander et al. (1991) differentiate four interrelated facets of metacognitive knowledge: task knowledge, self-knowledge, strategy knowledge, and goals and plans.

Task knowledge is information a student perceives about the circumstances in which a task is situated and about features of the task itself. It is a composite of the student's prior knowledge about tasks similar to the one now being addressed, plus information provided by the teacher, peers, or directions on assignments. Typical aspects of task knowledge include the number and clarity of criteria by which progress and final products of the task will be evaluated, time allocated for the task, resources that can be acquired to assist with work on the task, whether the student or someone else controls the processes by which the task can develop, and the timing and nature of feedback about performance. These kinds of information create elements of a stable backdrop for performance and, in the case of accessible resources and feedback, new and updated information about how to work on the task and how that work is progressing relative to criteria.

Students may have misconceptions about tasks that interfere with achieving the goals of instruction. For example, Anderson et al. (1991) observed that low-achieving first-grade students often approached seatwork tasks in reading with the understanding that they were to "get the work done" rather than understand information in the task, and develop strategies for accomplishing tasks such as those assigned. In this instance, the students' views of criteria by which the tasks' processes and products would be evaluated were antithetical to developing conceptual knowledge from reading and enhancing procedural knowledge for reading with comprehension.

Self-knowledge consists of a student's idiosyncratic motivational orientations to topics and instructional tasks, plus the student's characteristic beliefs about learning. This knowledge has a fundamental impact on the goals and plans a learner adopts. Winne (1991b) described four constituents of motivational orientation. Incentives are the values—positive, neutral, and negative—that a student perceives to be associated with goals to be accomplished in a specific task. Efficacy judgments are the student's beliefs about skills, abilities, and power to achieve those goals in relation to resources and constraints in the task environment. Outcomes are the results the student predicts will follow from engaging with the task by applying knowledge and skills considered in making the efficacy judgment. Attributions identify reasons, such as a person's ability or the difficulty of a task, that explain why work on the task yields the predicted (or realized) outcomes. All four kinds of motivational knowledge combine in a descriptive profile of the task's utility relative to other approaches to this task or to other tasks.

Strategy knowledge is knowledge about how to process information in tasks to promote comprehension, learning, remembering, and transfer. More specifically, strategy knowledge consists of cognitive procedures that students can use to construct and refine conceptual knowledge, and to develop and elaborate strategy knowledge itself. Four main categories of cognitive strategies, each subclassified at two levels of tasks, basic and complex, can be identified (Weinstein and Mayer 1986). Rehearsal strategies, such as mentally repeating information or copying text, enhance remembering. Elaboration strategies, such as developing mnemonics or assembling new material with prior knowledge using analogies, construct links for encoding knowledge. Organizing strategies—for instance, developing categories or translating and extending newly presented information as spatial maps—promote the assembly of new information into chunks and schemata. Monitoring strategies identify shortcomings in performance and point toward repairs that improve it.

To use strategy knowledge productively, students need to blend several kinds of knowledge. First, they require conceptual knowledge about the subject that is the focus of the task, plus conceptual knowledge about the strategy. The latter includes knowledge of the parts or steps that comprise the strategy (declarative component), knowledge about how to perform those steps (procedural component), and knowledge about which strategies are appropriate given present circumstances surrounding particular tasks (conditional component). Finally, they need metacognitive knowledge about the task, themselves as learners, the implementation of strategies in the context of tasks, and the probable impact of each strategy on performance.

Goals and plans are mental constructions that students, as active inquiring agents, create. Goals are multifaceted representations of states to be achieved that inherently fuse affects (information that represents feelings and emotions) with the various kinds of knowledge previously discussed. Plans are mental structures that range from small, focused, one-step rules to grand and encompassing orchestrations of events. Plans give shape to a student's information processing, constituting how the student addresses instructional tasks. Metaphorically, goals are the "reason qua motive" for engaging in a task, and plans provide instrumental knowledge on which the student calls to realize goals.

Sociocultural knowledge is the accumulated collection of attitudes and beliefs that a student has acquired as a result of experiences in a social and cultural milieu. In relation to instruction, it is about the forms, content, and functions of instruction that have developed from students' previous participation in a variety of instructional tasks. Sociocultural knowledge typically resides at the tacit level; it can, however, be addressed directly, thus becoming explicit. As tacit knowledge, however, sociocultural knowledge can influence information processing without students being aware of it.

A study by Ortony et al. (1985), for example, indicated that Afro–American children who engaged often in a turn-taking verbal riposte called "playing the dozens" are in a stronger position to understand figurative language in literary tasks. More generally, students' differential experiences involving social and cultural conventions influence their abilities to recognize narrators' or speakers' use of literary devices and characters' departures from social conventions that emphasize unusual events (Beach and Hynds 1991). These differences in tacit sociocultural knowledge thus affect what students can glean from tasks and how they judge accomplishments in tasks.

3. Instructional Tasks and Student Cognition

Instructing students is an intentional act in which an instructor strives to improve the cognitive resources that students need to perform tasks. If instruction is effective, students develop more knowledge than they would develop if they were left entirely on their own. That is, the instructor presumes that, by managing students' encounters with curricular information and by guiding them in cognitively processing the subject matter, educational objectives can be achieved more effectively than if they were left to their own devices. Thus, from the point of view of an instructor, instruction consists of (a) deliberately arranging (b) features of the instructional environment (c) to guide (d) the student's modification of aptitudes (e) for performing (f) specified tasks that reflect instructional objectives. From the student's point of view, participating in instruction has three main facets: mediating instruction, learning, and demonstrating achievements.

Corresponding to elements (b) and (c) of instruction, the student perceives features of the instructional environment and decides whether and how to make use of them. The match between students' perceptions and the instructor's guidance is a first step toward instructional effectiveness. For example, an author may mark sections of a text by headings, or a teacher may use transition statements to close segments of a lesson and introduce upcoming content or activity structures. These kinds of information or mediating instruction are features of the environment by which the instructor is attempting to improve what the student might learn from a text.

For the instructor's intentions to be realized, the student must perceive these communications as a particular kind of information, namely, information about what is to be learned and the means for learning it. Moreover, the student must elect to apply particular cognitive processes to that information so that prior knowledge becomes integrated with new subject matter that will be presented in the next moments. In addressing this task, the student determines whether and how to participate in instructional events as the instructor created them.

Corresponding to part (d) of instruction is the

student's processing of information—or learning—available in the instructional environment in concert with prior knowledge. To learn from the text or the lesson, the student must construct temporary structures of knowledge in working memory, such as a hypothesis about schemata useful for understanding information that will be presented next in the text or in an upcoming segment of the lesson. Then, as new information comes available, the student must integrate it with prior knowledge to modify and extend it. The dynamic events comprising students' engagements in information processing form the topics of Sect. 5.

Corresponding to parts (e) and (f) of instruction is the student's job of demonstrating learning by attempting to perform tasks that reflect instructional objectives. For example, having read a text or engaged in a lesson's activities, the student might be invited to discuss issues raised, solve problems posed by the teacher, or design an activity that requires applying information recently presented.

4. Task Characteristics

Because features of tasks are relatively much easier to manipulate and control than are characteristics of students, thousands of research articles have described thousands of experiments in which task characteristics have been investigated as independent variables. To organize this immense variety, five facets of tasks can be identified: conditions under which the task is performed; operations that carry out the task; products that result from operations; evaluations that feed back information about products; standards by which achievement is gauged (Winne 1991b).

Winne and Marx (1989) suggest that there are three conditions under which classroom tasks are performed. These include the content to be learned (declarative and procedural knowledge), the setting (resources available, social features, time allocation), and the nature of the presentation (the medium, goals, and performance cues). Students confronted with academic tasks develop a tentative model representing their interpretation of these conditions, and these perceptions mediate the students' development of goals, plans, and cognitive processing in response to those conditions.

Task conditions interact with the student's information processing to determine the "cognitive load" of a task. Cognitive load can be thought of as a ratio of the demands placed on the student's information-processing system relative to its capacity. Optimum load is a value less, but not greatly less, than 1. A combination of variables, such as rate of presentation, permanence of information display, and the meaningfulness, amount, and complexity of information, operationally define the cognitive load of a task. As noted in Sect. 2.1, there is a relation between information-processing capacity and the degree of organization or automaticity of a student's prior knowledge.

Another important facet of a task is the location of control of the operations needed to carry out the task. Models of instruction vary from discovery environments, in which the student controls most of the task operations, to strongly didactic environments, in which the instructor controls instructional events. When control is vested with the student, cognitive load increases, because the student must regulate most of the information processing. Under most conditions, when learners are granted control, they often exit tasks before they fully achieve knowledge of the subject.

5. Dynamics of Learning from Instruction

This section examines the dynamic interplay among variables and classes of variables in Fig. 1. It is divided into two parts: learning operations and the promotion of self-regulation.

5.1 Learning Operations

Winne (1991a) has described five primitive cognitive operations in which students engage while completing tasks: *s*timulating, *m*onitoring, *a*ssembling, *r*ehearsing, and *t*ranslating. In combination, they form the SMART operations. Stimulating transfers information from long-term memory into working memory, making it "the object of thought". Monitoring matches or compares features of items which are active in working memory. Assembling forms new relations between items of information. Rehearsing maintains information in working memory and can transfer it into long-term memory. Finally, translating recodes information.

Typically, these SMART operations are combined in a learning task to create three main kinds of strategies (Zimmerman 1989). Behavioral strategies lead to choices about overt behavior for pursuing a task. For example, a student might seek feedback by looking up answers after working problems in a text. Environmental strategies are those where the learner modifies conditions of a task to make them more favorable. For instance, a learner might move closer to the teacher to receive more attention. Finally, covert strategies are sequences of cognitions by which a learner guides learning. For example, a learner might mentally summarize a section in a text to improve comprehension.

Although highly automated strategies are tacit, as when an expert engages in tasks that do not challenge expertise, deliberate use of strategies is associated with greater gains in achievement when learners address new material or engage in transfer tasks. Thus, while education aims to help students acquire a large repertoire of automatic–tacit strategies, effective learners also must consciously regulate learning in response to challenging instructional tasks. Such learners are called self-regulated (Paris and Byrnes 1989, Zimmerman 1989) or self-instructive (Wang and Palincsar 1989).

In models of self-regulated learning, students first interpret a task's conditions. Next, perceptions about the values of a task's goals (incentives), judgments of competence and control over learning (efficacy judgments), and beliefs about the roles of effort and ability in learning (attributions) mediate between the student's understanding of task demands and the goals he or she adopts for learning. For example, in the face of low expectation for success, a student may choose task avoidance. In contrast, if a task's goals have high incentive and the student is moderately confident that success can be achieved with effort, setting a goal to understand is probable.

Based on the goals they adopt, self-regulated learners then develop a plan for action, grounded in prior knowledge. A central feature of this plan is obtaining feedback by monitoring intermediate products against goals. Incrementally, the learner modifies knowledge, motivational beliefs, goals, and strategies in response to that feedback. Thus, interaction with the task evolves "strategically" based on dynamic engagements involving the learner, the task and the events that transpire during learning.

Rumelhart and Norman (1978) describe three mechanisms by which new learning is acquired and integrated with prior knowledge in this process. Accretion involves monitoring new information in terms of an existing general schema and encoding the new material as a particular instantiation of that general structure. Tuning is undertaken when new information does not correspond to an existing schema and the student reorganizes elements of prior knowledge to accommodate the new information. For example, a child who has overgeneralized the concept "dog" to include all furry, four-legged animals tunes a schema to differentiate cats from dogs. Finally, restructuring is necessary when no schema adequately encompasses new information or when existing schemata are inadequate for making sense of new knowledge. Here, students construct entirely new knowledge structures by assembling existing knowledge or by inducing a new schema.

Perkins and Simmons (1988) described three classes of misconceptions that parallel Rumelhart and Norman's learning mechanisms. Naive misconceptions are characteristic of insufficient background knowledge. These misconceptions can be remedied by accretion. Ritual misconceptions arise when students have formalized knowledge but can not apply it easily or transfer it. Tuning schemata, for example, by developing analogies, can remedy this problem. Finally, Gordian misconceptions are those where complex formalized knowledge is faulty. Repairing these misconceptions requires the entire conceptual frame to be restructured, producing a personal paradigm shift.

5.2 Promoting Self-regulated Learning

To assist students in developing self-regulated learning, explicit instruction about cognitive strategies should be integrated with subject matter. In this format, subject matter knowledge grows in parallel with declarative and procedural knowledge about strategies, and with conditional knowledge that can guide choices about when to apply particular strategies under specific conditions. To promote transfer and students' independent use of strategies following instruction, metacognitive strategies can be taught that can guide students in planning how to approach tasks and in monitoring progress (Wang and Palincsar 1989). Teaching students positive motivational beliefs, such as refocusing attributions toward effortful use of strategies (Borkowski et al. 1988), is another critical element in promoting self-regulation (Paris and Byrnes 1989).

An assumption underlying students' independent use of strategies is that they consciously and reflectively choose strategies. Salomon and Perkins (1989) highlighted the importance of consciously chosen strategies in their distinction between two kinds transfer. "Low-road transfer" can be promoted by repeated experiences that involve using knowledge in a variety of contexts. It results in automatic transfer across the range of task conditions the student has experienced. "High-road transfer," in contrast, requires the student deliberately to abstract principles about applying strategies. Promoting such reflection in instruction invites the student to decontextualize principles, extending their range of application beyond past experiences. In this analysis, the process of approaching high-road transfer equates to independent use of cognitive strategies.

6. Conclusion

By viewing the student as an active, inquiring agent who constructs knowledge, rather than a mere receiver of information, theories of information processing have come to emphasize the role of a student's prior knowledge and of processes that create achievements through the student's participation in instruction. To realize these theories, researchers have devised and tested systems that characterize prior knowledge and that describe information-handling processes. Modern theories also view instruction as an interaction between features in a teaching environment and each student's prior knowledge, rather than as a unidirectional effect of instruction on students. The student's mediation of instructional events and self-regulation of approaches to learning are recognized as potent factors that influence the development of achievements. An important advance has been a gain in knowledge about ways of guiding students in mediating instruction and in regulating information processes that build knowledge. Continued research in these areas promises gains in theoretical and practical understandings about how instruction can be optimized for effectiveness relative to each student's individual differences.

See also: Cognitive Styles and Learning

References

Alexander P A, Schallert D L, Hare V C 1991 Coming to terms: How researchers in learning and literacy talk about knowledge. *Rev. Educ. Res.* 61(3): 315–43

Anderson G L, Gates A I 1950 The general nature of learning. In: Henry N B (ed.) 1990 *Learning and Instruction*, 49th Yearbook of the National Society for the Study of Education, Pt 1. University of Chicago Press, Chicago, Illinois

Beach R, Hynds S 1991 Research on response to literature. In: Barr R, Kamil M L et al. (eds.) 1991 *Handbook of Reading Research*, Vol. 2. Longman, New York

Borkowski J G, Wehing R S, Carr M 1988 Effects of attributional retraining on strategy-based reading comprehension in learning-disabled students. *J. Educ. Psychol.* 80: 46–53

Bruner J S 1964 Some theorems on instruction illustrated with reference to mathematics. In: Hilgard E R (ed.) 1964 *Theories of Learning and Instruction*, 63rd Yearbook of the National Society for the Study of Education, Pt 1. University of Chicago Press, Chicago, Illinois

Cook L K, Mayer R E 1988 Teaching readers about the structure of scientific text. *J. Educ. Psychol.* 80(4): 448–56

Dee Lucas D, Larkin J H 1991 Equations in scientific proofs: Effects on comprehension. *Am. Educ. Res. J.* 28(3): 661–82

Fuson K C, Willis G B 1989 Second graders' use of schematic drawings in solving addition and subtraction word problems. *J. Educ. Psychol.* 81(4): 514–20

Glaser R 1982 Instructional psychology: Past, present, and future. *Am. Psychol.* 37: 292–305

Iran-Nejad A 1990 Active and dynamic self-regulation of learning processes. *Rev. Educ. Res.* 60(4): 573–602

Newell A 1990 *Unified Theories of Cognition.* Harvard University Press, Cambridge, Massachusetts

Ortony A, Turner T, Larson-Shapiro N 1985 Cultural and instructional influences on figurative language comprehension by inner-city children. *Research in the Teaching of English.* 19(1): 25–36

Paris S G, Byrnes J P 1989 The constructivist approach to self-regulation in classrooms. In: Zimmerman B J, Schunk D H (eds.) 1989 *Self-regulated Learning and Academic Achievement.* Springer-Verlag, Berlin

Perkins D N, Simmons R 1988 Patterns of misunderstanding: An integrative model for science, math, and programming. *Rev. Educ. Res.* 58: 303–26

Polanyi M 1966 *The Tacit Dimension.* Anchor Press, Garden City, New York

Prawat R S 1989 Promoting access to knowledge, strategy, and disposition in students: A research synthesis. *Rev. Educ. Res.* 59: 1–41

Rumelhart D E, Norman D A 1978 Accretion, tuning, and restructuring: Three modes of learning. In: Cotton J W, Klatzky R (eds.) 1978 *Semantic Factors in Cognition.* Erlbaum, Hillsdale, New Jersey

Salomon G, Perkins D N 1989 Rocky roads to transfer: Rethinking mechanisms of a neglected phenomenon. *Educ. Psychol.* 24: 11–142

Wang M C, Palincsar A S 1989 Teaching students to assume an active role in their learning. In: Reynolds M C (ed.) 1989 *Knowledge Base for the Beginning Teacher.* Pergamon Press, Oxford

Weinstein C E, Mayer R E 1986 The teaching of learning strategies. In: Wittrock M C (ed.) 1986 *Handbook of Research on Teaching*, 3rd edn. Macmillan Inc., New York

Winne P H 1985 Cognitive processing in the classroom. In: Husén T, Postlethwaite T N (eds.) 1985 *The International Encyclopedia of Education* 1st edn. Pergamon Press, Oxford

Winne P H 1991a Instructional psychology and a model of teaching. In: Short R H, Stewin L L, McCann S J (eds.) 1991 *Educational Psychology: Canadian Perspectives.* Copp Clark Pittman, Toronto

Winne P H 1991b Motivation and teaching. In: Waxman H, Walberg H A (eds.) 1991 *Effective Teaching: Current Research.* McCutchan, Berkeley, California

Winne P H, Marx R W 1989 A cognitive–processing analysis of motivation within classroom tasks. In: Ames C, Ames R (eds.) 1989 *Research on Motivation in Education: Goals and Cognitions.* Academic Press, San Diego, California

Wittrock M C 1986 Students' thought processes. In: Wittrock M C (ed.) 1986 *Handbook of Research on Teaching*, 3rd edn. Macmillan Inc., New York

Zimmerman B J 1989 A social cognitive view of self-regulated academic learning. *J. Educ. Psychol.* 81: 329–39

Task Analysis

G. Rowland and C. M. Reigeluth

Task analysis is a process used to develop understanding of what is involved in performing and/or learning to perform a task: either a skill, a procedure, or an area of content. In most cases its purpose is to help determine appropriate methods for improving performance of that task, primarily by helping an instructional designer to decide what to teach (content) and how best to teach it (methods). The present entry defines task analysis and describes various purposes it can serve. Major techniques, key questions, and important research issues are discussed.

1. What is Task Analysis?

In a general sense, task analysis determines what is involved in meeting a given goal or need. It follows the process of needs assessment, through which the designer determines where learning or some other form of performance enhancement is required. Thus, task analysis is a process used to develop understanding of what is involved in performing and/or learning to perform a task. This includes the skills and knowledge that are relied upon, the thought processes engaged in, and/or the actions taken in performing the task. Task analysis can also provide information on such factors as the environment where performance takes place, the criticality of the task, typical errors, and the consequences of good or poor performance. In a general sense, the task analyst asks what has to be done by whom, how, when, where, and with what level of skill. Task analysis results in a representation of the task—for example, a list of visual map of task elements and their relationships—that is useful in facilitating performance and/or designing instruction.

The term "task analysis" is often used rather broadly to include analysis of subject matter or content. Related processes that are sometimes considered types of task analysis include job analysis, skills analysis, goal analysis, and instructional analysis.

2. Purposes of Task Analysis

Jonassen et al. (1989) have identified five functions for task analysis, the last three of which are instructional purposes: inventorying tasks, describing tasks, selecting tasks for instruction, sequencing tasks (and subtasks) in instruction, and analyzing task and content level (for selecting instructional strategies). Task analysis information can be useful in such areas as worker selection, training selection, performance appraisal, job design, instructional design, and others. For worker selection, workers can be selected for a job based on their preparation in terms of the skills and knowledge identified by the task analysis. For training selection, a worker might be required to complete only those aspects of a training program that match task elements where his or her skills are lacking. For performance appraisal, results of the task analysis can be used as criteria for evaluating performance, making it easier to identify areas of deficiency. For job design, it is frequently possible to find ways to improve the person–job system (e.g., the task environment or the way the task is performed). For example, the task representation can serve as a job aid, placing knowledge in the world rather than in performers'

heads. As this implies, task analysis often eliminates the need for further work; learning simply to use the aid rather than to remember task steps may be all that is required. For instructional design, designers of courses and curricula use information from a task analysis primarily to identify what individuals need to learn, how instruction should be sequenced, and what instructional strategies and tactics should be used.

Task analysis offers the potential benefit of helping a designer to avoid (or eliminate) content that is irrelevant to achieving the goal. This can decrease costs by reducing training time and reducing the need for learning on the job. On the other hand, it is possible that omitted content could have had unanticipated benefits, say in helping the learner understand other aspects of a job. Therefore, while benefits can be great, task analysis has potential to limit the designer's thinking to those aspects of performance which can be observed and explicitly stated. It is prudent to view task analysis as an aid rather than a prescription in designing, and to analyze problems logically and pose solutions creatively. Further areas where task analysis information is useful include troubleshooting, resource allocation, manual development, and test construction. Task analysis is also a powerful tool used by engineers to increase reliability and reduce error. This entry will focus on task analysis for purposes of instructional design.

3. How Is Task Analysis Carried Out?

Techniques for carrying out task analysis can be grouped into at least five major categories: those which identify subordinate learning skills; those which identify procedural steps; those which identify causal models underlying complex cognitive tasks; those which identify content elements; and those which help the designer to select appropriate instructional strategies. Each of the first four techniques seeks to determine the elements of the task or content area, the relationships among those elements, and the organizing principle that ties all elements together. The fifth technique seeks to determine the kind of learning involved so that appropriate instructional strategies and tactics can be selected. Selection of a particular technique depends primarily on the type of goal involved or the purpose of the analysis, and such classification is typically the first step in conducting the analysis.

Task analysis of subordinate skills assumes that learning a complex skill involves mastery of a number of more simple subskills. If those subskills can be identified and sequenced according to learning prerequisite relations, then learning should be more effective and efficient. The most widely used technique is the learning hierarchy (Gagné 1968), a representation of the task as a visual map of prerequisite skills. Learning entry-level skills at the base of the hierarchy is expected to lead, or "positively transfer," to learning intermediate skills (enabling objectives) in the middle, and to learning the goal (terminal objective) at the top. This technique is especially useful in criterion testing, selection, and placement, and in sequencing instruction. It is often selected when the goal involves performance of an intellectual skill. A disadvantage is that the hierarchy does not show procedural relationships.

Procedural task analysis assumes that tasks are performed as sequences of specific cognitive processes and actions. Hence, task acquisition and performance can be facilitated by identifying steps and representing them in algorithmic form, for example, in a flowchart or decision table. There are two major kinds of procedural task analysis: that which merely identifies the order of steps in a procedure (see e.g., Merrill 1976), and that which also arranges different versions of the task in order of complexity, such as Merrill's (1976) path analysis technique or the Elaboration Theory's simplifying conditions method for procedural content (Reigeluth 1992). Procedural task analysis is often selected when the goal is a physical action or psychomotor task, or an intellectual skill with a fairly limited number of ways it can be performed by experts. It is not appropriate for complex cognitive tasks that vary greatly from one performance to another.

Task analysis of complex cognitive tasks assumes that such tasks are not performed by experts as a sequence of steps; rather experts have an underlying body of knowledge—a set of principles or causal models—that they use to generate an appropriate performance for each particular situation. Therefore, such tasks require a type of task analysis that identifies the underlying principles or causal models that experts use to perform them. There are also two major kinds of complex-cognitive-task analysis: that which merely identifies the underlying principles, and that which also arranges different versions of the task in order of complexity (see e.g., the Elaboration Theory's simplifying conditions method for causal models —Reigeluth 1992). This technique is selected only when the goal is a complex cognitive task.

Task analysis of content elements assumes that some important knowledge is not tied to any one specific task (or goal), such as an understanding of some basic principles of economics or biology. This technique results in some sort of visual map of content, such as an outline, a content taxonomy, or a chart. A content map can provide a powerful tool for a designer to sequence instruction and for a learner to grasp relationships, but it does not identify what the learner should be able to do as a result of learning. That is, the skills or learning outcomes are not made explicit by the map. In carrying out an analysis of content (and in using most other techniques), analysts often employ a card sort method, writing elements on

cards, sorting, selecting, and organizing the cards, and then linking them together.

Task analysis of kinds of learning differs from the above kinds of task analysis in that it does not break down a task into parts; rather it classifies the parts in order to select appropriate instructional tactics. It is based on the assumption that different kinds of learning are best taught with different kinds of instructional tactics. This intact classification of task elements is based on a taxonomy, such as Bloom's or Gagné's (1986) or Merrill's (1983). After a task element has been classified as to the type of learning involved or desired, a set of tactics is assigned for teaching that kind of learning for that element. The most common categories include cognitive, affective, and psychomotor learning, and, within the cognitive domain, memorizing information, understanding relationships, applying skills, and using generic (domain independent) skills (Leshin et al. 1992). The strategy or tactics are then adapted and supplemented based on the learning situation (content, learners, and learning environment).

Often, the learning goal leads to selection of a certain task analysis technique. For example, a psychomotor task such as operating a machine can be expressed as an algorithm fairly easily. Just as often, however, the nature of the goal is not so easily classified, and several different techniques are candidates. Also, the analyst can select one technique, but one technique provides a single perspective. It is often wise to use more than one technique or to combine several. For example, algorithmic elements could be identified for a subordinate skill, or subordinate skills could be identified for a procedural step. Content elements might be attached to either. Reigeluth and Merrill's (1984) extended task analysis procedure represents such a combination.

The techniques described above are representative. Other techniques include path, critical incident, fault tree, pattern noting, and matrix analysis. See Jonassen et al. (1989), Zemke and Kramlinger (1982), and Carlisle (1986) for descriptions of these and many other techniques, and for sample task representations.

The selection of a task analysis technique or techniques will be influenced greatly by the purpose of the analysis. A variety of purposes was listed in the previous section of this entry, but even within the instructional design focus selected here, purpose can include selecting and sequencing the course content (which is the purpose of most of the above-described techniques) or selecting instructional strategies and tactics.

Regardless of the purpose within the instructional design focus, the role of task analysis is to provide information needed for good instructional design decisions. Thus, selection of methods of task analysis should be driven by the information needs at each point in the design process. Task analysis should not be viewed as an activity totally independent from design. In many cases, the instructional theories that a designer selects will specify what those information needs are, because the theories prescribe methods for different situations, particularly for different types of tasks. In effect, theories of instruction require the analyst to seek certain types of information about the tasks in order to select appropriate content, sequences, strategies, and tactics. Therefore, theories of instruction can be seen as having corresponding task analysis methods (although those methods can also be used independently of a given instructional theory). In cases where instructional theory is driving the design, the goal of task analysis becomes not just identification of elements and relationships, but doing so in a manner which supports designing instruction according to the theory.

After a task analysis technique (or combination of techniques) has been chosen, information about the task must be collected. Sources of information for task analysis include various levels of job performers (e.g., novices and experts), supervisors, instructors, content experts, and learners. Also useful are reference guides, training materials, manuals, logs, and other documents, and potentially anything that exists in the physical environment. Data are gathered using unobtrusive participant observation of the job, individual interviews, structured or unstructured group interviews, surveys, and study of documents (Jonassen et al. 1989).

Task analysis tools have been developed that reveal some information on processes that previously remained implicit in performance. For example, cognitive task analysis (Roth and Woods 1989) requires performers to think aloud as they perform tasks. Analysis of the resulting think-aloud protocols gives at least partial evidence of the thought processes performers engage in during performance of the task. These data are believed superior to retrospective reports. That is, the performer describing task performance after the fact often constructs a hypothetical argument of what he or she may have done, as opposed to what really occurred. Of course, skill components that cannot be verbalized, for example, procedures that are performed "automatically" and are no longer consciously controlled, will not appear in a protocol.

4. Key Questions

Perhaps the most difficult questions to answer in conducting a task analysis are where to start and where to stop. When task analysis is employed for creating instruction, the first question, where to start, is difficult but manageable. The analysis should begin with the goal, the broadest statement of what learning is sought, and move to progressively greater levels of detail. This goal is never completely clear, and is much less clear at the outset, but it can at least tentatively be stated and agreed upon.

The second question, where to stop, is more challenging. What to include and what to exclude and how much detail to add or cut are rarely easy decisions. Generally, the learners' abilities and prior knowledge are the major basis for making these decisions. That is, the instruction should start at the learners' current level of skill and knowledge. Ultimately, it is a question of risk management, which must assess the tolerance for error and the consequences of including too much or too little content.

5. Issues and Directions

It is important to recognize that the types of task elements that are identified—for example, subskills, steps in a procedure, underlying principles or causal models, or content elements—and the processes used in breaking the task down, are based on theories of human performance, knowledge, or learning. As those theories advance, new methods of task analysis are developed. Furthermore, different methods of task analysis are compatible with, and useful for, different kinds of learning and different approaches to learning. Thus, analysts break a task down in a particular way because they believe it will be most useful for their situation and philosophy of learning and instruction.

For example, techniques based on a behavioral tradition identify types of behaviors or kinds of learning outcomes (Gagné 1986). In contrast, techniques based on cognitive psychology attempt to describe mental processes that underlie those outcomes. In the case of procedural tasks, the two traditions may often identify the same elements, but in the case of complex cognitive tasks, the differences are great.

Techniques such as cognitive task analysis appear to have much potential. Task analysts or "knowledge engineers" seek to describe the knowledge of experts and to express that knowledge in computer software programs known as expert systems. Significant progress has been made in this area, and expert systems have been developed which do a fair job of solving some problems as experts do. However, a number of constraints on development of expert systems remain, including a primitive understanding of cognitive processes underlying performance, the domain-specificity of expertise, and—as a major consequence of these two factors—the great amount of time needed to develop a single system.

Efforts to understand performance in terms of the mental processes involved include Sternberg's (1983) componential analysis and Rasmussen's SRK or skills, rules, and knowledge (see Goodstein et al. 1988). However, intellectual performance may also be influenced by such things as beliefs and social processes. Furthermore, although general characteristics of experts have been described, there is the clear notion that much of the knowledge and skill of an expert in one domain does not transfer to another. As a result, task analysis or "knowledge acquisition" processes must be repeated for each and every domain. It is also important to note that these techniques, while appropriate to building systems that imitate the behavior of an expert, are not necessarily appropriate as pedagogical tools. The gap between an expert and a novice may be made clear, but how best to help a novice become an expert remains a matter of instructional design.

Since the mid-1980s, increasing credence has been given to a "constructivist" epistemology which views learning as the active development of meaning on the basis of experience. Learning is seen as a constructive act, and the designer should provide for rich experiences by situating activities in authentic contexts and provide for exploration and sharing of multiple perspectives. The implication of this view for task analysis is that, for some learning situations, the learning environment should not be limited to specific task elements and relationships. The analyst may still seek a core of information to make available to all learners, but should avoid setting boundaries on what information is deemed relevant and included for such learning situations. The goals and methods of task analysis from this perspective, and how results can be implemented in instructional systems, are not entirely clear, but efforts are under way in this area.

A second issue concerns when task analysis should be conducted. Task analysis can be seen as a process engaged in after needs assessment and before design. But the costs of performing a task analysis are often high and, therefore, resources are infrequently committed before a clear goal or performance gap is identified. Nevertheless, an iterative process may yield better results. That is, task analysis can inform needs assessment, and design can inform both needs assessment and task analysis. A cyclical approach with feedback and feedforward is implied. A rapid prototyping methodology such as that offered by the Elaboration Theory's simplifying conditions method (Reigeluth 1992) may offer a key to managing such a cyclical process, particularly with a large project and a large design team.

A final issue relates to the potential for computers to assist the analyst, for example, in reducing the amount of time and effort needed to develop an expert system. An example of a computer program designed to help the task analyst is SNOWMAN, or System for Knowledge Management. The potential for computers to assist designers in these and other processes have been explored. Gayeski (1991) raises some questions regarding the nature of such programs, that is, where and for what types of problems such systems, at least as conceived at that time, are appropriate and useful.

See also: Constructivism and Learning; Problem-solving and Learning: Computer Modeling; Instructional Design Theories; Instructional Psychology; Learning Processes and Learning Outcomes; Models of Learning

References

Carlisle K E 1986 *Analyzing Jobs and Tasks*. Educational Technology Publications, Englewood Cliffs, New Jersey
Gagné R M 1968 Learning hierarchies. *Educ. Psychol.* 6(1): 3–6
Gagné R M 1986 *The Conditions of Learning*, 4th edn. Holt, Rinehart, and Winston, New York
Gayeski D M 1991 Software tools for empowering instructional developers. *Performance Improvement Quarterly* 4(4): 21–36
Goodstein L P, Andersen H B, Olsen S E (eds.) 1988 *Tasks, Errors, and Mental Models*. Taylor and Francis, London
Jonassen D H, Hannum W H, Tessmer M 1989 *Handbook of Task Analysis Procedures*. Praeger, New York
Leshin C, Pollock J, Reigeluth C M 1992 *Instructional Design Strategies and Tactics*. Educational Technology Publications, Englewood Cliffs, New Jersey
Merrill M D 1983 Component display theory. In: Reigeluth C M (ed.) 1983 *Instructional Design Theories and Models: An Overview of their Current Status*. Erlbaum, Hillsdale, New Jersey
Merrill P F 1976 Task analysis: An information-processing approach. NSPI *Journal* 15(2): 7–11
Reigeluth C M 1992 Elaborating the elaboration theory. *Educ. Tech. Res. Dev.* 40(3): 80–86
Reigeluth C M, Merrill M D 1984 *The Extended Task Analysis Procedure: User's Manual*. University Press of America, Lanham, Maryland
Roth E M, Woods D D 1989 Cognitive task analysis: An approach to knowledge acquisition for intelligent system design. In: Guida G, Tasso C (eds.) 1989 *Topics in Expert System Design: Methodologies and Tools*. North Holland, Amsterdam
Sternberg R J 1983 Components of human intelligence. *Cog.* 15 (1–3): 1–48
Zemke R, Kramlinger T 1982 *Figuring Things Out: A Trainer's Guide to Needs and Task Analysis*. Addison-Wesley, Reading, Massachusetts

Further Reading

Duffy T M, Lowyck J, Jonassen D H (eds.) 1993 *Designing Environments for Constructive Learning*. Springer-Verlag, Berlin

Learning Transfer

D. N. Perkins and G. Salomon

Transfer of learning occurs when learning in one context or with one set of materials impacts on performance in another context or with other related materials. For example, learning to drive a car helps a person later to learn more quickly to drive a truck, learning mathematics prepares students to study physics, learning to get along with one's siblings may prepare one for better interaction with others, and experience in playing chess might conceivably make a person a better strategic thinker in politics or business. Transfer is a key concept in education and learning theory because most education and training aspires to transfer. Usually the context of learning (classrooms, exercise books, tests, simple streamlined tasks) differs markedly from the ultimate contexts of application (in the home, on the job, within complex tasks). Consequently, the ends of education and training are not achieved unless transfer occurs. Transfer is all the more important in that it cannot be taken for granted. Abundant evidence shows that very often the hoped-for transfer from learning experiences does not occur. Thus, the prospects and conditions of transfer are crucial issues for school and adult education.

1. Transfer Defined

1.1 Transfer versus Ordinary Learning

In a sense, any learning requires a modicum of transfer. To say that learning has occurred means that the person can display that learning later. Even if the subsequent situation is very similar, there will be some differences, perhaps time of day or the physical setting. Thus, no absolute line can be drawn between ordinary learning and transfer.

However, transfer only becomes interesting as a psychological and educational phenomenon in situations where the transfer would not be thought of as ordinary learning. For example, an adult learner may show certain grammar skills on an English test (ordinary learning) but not in everyday speech (the hoped-for transfer). The student may solve the problems at the end of the chapter (ordinary learning) but not similar problems when they occur mixed with others at the end of the course (the hoped-for transfer). In other words, talk of transfer is always at least implicitly contrastive: it assumes learning within a certain context and asks about impact beyond that context.

1.2 Positive versus Negative Transfer

Positive transfer occurs when learning in one context improves performance in some other context. For instance, speakers of one language find it easier to learn related than unrelated second languages. Negative transfer occurs when learning in one context impacts negatively on performance in another. For example, despite the generally positive transfer among related languages, contrasts of pronunciation, vocabulary, and syntax generate stumbling blocks. Learners commonly assimilate a new language's phonetics to crude approximations in their native tongue and use word orders carried over from their native tongue.

While negative transfer is a real and often problematic phenomenon of learning, it is of much less concern to education than positive transfer. Negative transfer typically causes trouble only in the early stages of learning a new domain. With experience, learners correct for the effects of negative transfer. From the standpoint of education in general, the primary concern is that desired positive transfers occur. Accordingly, the remainder of this entry focuses on positive transfer.

1.3 Near versus Far Transfer

Near transfer refers to transfer between very similar contexts, as for instance when distance learners taking an exam face a mix of problems of the same kinds that they have practiced separately in their homework, or when a garage mechanic repairs an engine in a new model of car, but with a design much the same as in prior models. Far transfer refers to transfer between contexts that, on appearance, seem remote and alien to one another. For instance, a chess player might apply a basic strategic principle such as "take control of the center" to investment practice, politics, or a military campaign. It should be noted that "near" and "far" are intuitive notions that resist precise codification. They are useful in broadly characterizing some aspects of transfer but do not imply any strictly defined metric of "closeness."

2. Prospects of Transfer

As noted above, transfer is especially important to learning theory and educational practice, since very often the kinds of transfer hoped for do not occur. The classic investigation of this phenomenon was conducted by the renowned educational psychologist E L Thorndike in the first decades of the twentieth century. Thorndike examined the proposition that studies of Latin disciplined the mind, preparing people for better performance in other subjects. Comparing the performance in other academic subjects of students who had taken Latin with those who had not,

Thorndike (1923) found no advantage whatsoever in Latin studies. In other experiments, Thorndike and Woodworth (1901) sought, and generally failed to find, positive impact of one sort of learning on another. Thorndike concluded that transfer depended on "identical elements" in two performances and that most performances were simply too different from one another for much transfer to be expected. In terms of the rough near–far distinction, near transfer is much more likely than far transfer.

Thorndike's early disturbing findings have resurfaced repeatedly in other investigations. For instance, the advent of computer programming gave rise to the notion that computer programming developed general problem-solving skills, much as Latin was thought to cultivate mental discipline. Unfortunately, several experiments seeking a positive impact of learning to program on problem-solving and other aspects of thinking yielded negative results (see Pea and Kurland 1984, Salomon and Perkins 1987).

Another learning experience that might be thought to impact broadly on cognition is literacy, the mastery of reading and writing. Wide-ranging transfer might be expected from experience with the cognitive demands of reading and writing and the cognitive structures that text carries. However, Scribner and Cole (1981) reported a study of an African tribe, the Vai, with an indigenous form of writing not accompanied by schooling. Using a variety of general cognitive instruments, they found no differences between Vai who had mastered this script and others who had not. They argued that the impact of literacy depends on immersion in diverse activities surrounding literacy, not on acquisition of reading and writing per se. The Vai only employed their script in a very specific way, in contrast with the diverse uses of literacy apparent in many cultures.

For yet another example, researchers have looked for transfer effects between puzzles or games that are isomorphs of one another, sharing the same logical structure but presented or described in very different physical terms. For example, some research has focused on the well-known Tower of Hanoi puzzle, which requires moving three (or more) rings of different sizes between three pegs according to certain rules. One isomorph involves a story about three extraterrestrial monsters, each holding a crystal globe of a different size. The rules for the monsters passing the globes to one another are logically equivalent to the rules for moving the disks from peg to peg.

It is not clear whether study of problem isomorphs should be regarded as near or far transfer, because isomorphs are nearly identical structurally but very different in external trappings. In any case, subjects usually do not recognize the connection between one isomorph and the other and hence do not carry over strategies they have acquired while working with one to the other. However, if the relationship is pointed out, then the learners can transfer strategies fruitfully (Simon and Hayes 1977).

While the preponderance of results concerning transfer appears to be negative, it is important to recognize that occasional positive findings have appeared. For instance, Clements and Gullo (1984) and Lehrer et al. (1988) achieved positive transfer from engagement in LOGO computer programming to certain cognitive measures, including measures of divergent thinking. Brown (1989) reported a series of studies showing positive transfer by preschool children of abstract concepts, for instance the idea of stacking objects to climb on to reach something, or the idea of mimicry as a defense mechanism in animals. Campione et al. (1991) report that when children are taught to self-monitor and self-direct themselves during reading in what has been called "reciprocal teaching," this transfers also to learning in other text-mediated areas of learning such as social studies and mathematics. Salomon et al. (1989) showed that students can transfer from a computer program designed to make them more strategic readers to their performance a while later on in writing, suggesting that what the students acquired was transferable tendencies to self-monitor and self-direct.

3. Transfer and Local Knowledge

Near transfer seems to have much better prospects than far transfer. Not only does this trend appear in the empirical findings, but it also makes sense in terms of contemporary research on "expertise." Since the 1970s, a number of investigators have built a case for the importance of "local knowledge" (with knowledge taken in a broad sense to include skills, concepts, propositions, etc.). In areas as diverse as playing chess, problem-solving in physics, and medical diagnosis, expert performance has been shown to depend on a large knowledge base of a rather specialized kind (see Ericsson and Smith 1991). General cross-domain principles, it has been argued, play a rather weak role. In the same spirit, some investigators have urged that learning is highly situated, that is, finely adapted to its context (Brown et al. 1989, Lave 1988).

A strong local knowledge position would predict little far transfer under any conditions, because knowledge in one context would not be very relevant to others. However, the research on expertise does not really bear this assumption out: the importance of local knowledge does not imply the unimportance of rather general knowledge that works in conjunction with local knowledge (Perkins and Salomon 1989). Moreover, the idea of situated learning does not necessarily imply that the prospects of transfer are limited. Greeno et al. (1993) offer a situated learning view of transfer in which transfer depends on similar opportunities for action across situations that may be very different superficially. In sum, a monolithic local knowledge position is difficult to sustain.

4. Conditions of Transfer

Positive findings of transfer, both near and far, suggest that it is too simplistic merely to ask whether transfer occurs. It can, but often does not; the important question is under what conditions transfer appears.

4.1 Thorough and Diverse Practice

The question of literacy may be considered once more. In a classic study of the impact of literacy and education in the former Soviet Union, Luria (1976) found major influence on a number of cognitive measures. His results concerned a population where reading and writing played multiple roles. The contrast between Luria's and Scribner and Cole's findings suggests that transfer may depend on extensive practice of the performance in question in a variety of contexts. This yields a flexible, relatively automatized bundle of skills easily evoked in new situations.

4.2 Explicit Abstraction

Transfer sometimes depends on whether learners have abstracted critical attributes of a situation. In one demonstration, Gick and Holyoak (1980, 1983) presented subjects with a problem story that allowed a particular solution. From subjects who solved the problem, they elicited what the subjects took to be the underlying principle. They then presented the subjects with another, analogous problem that invited a similar approach. Those subjects who had the fullest and soundest basic grasp of the principle for the first puzzle were most successful with the second. These and other results suggest that explicit abstractions of principles from a situation foster transfer.

4.3 Active Self-monitoring

Similarly, metacognitive reflection on one's thinking processes appears to promote transfer of skills. This contrasts with the explicit abstraction category above, in that abstraction focuses on the structure of the situation whereas self-monitoring focuses on one's own thinking processes. Belmont et al. (1982) undertook a synthesis of a number of efforts to teach retarded persons simple memory strategies and to test whether they would apply these in slightly different contexts. Many of these studies showed no transfer, while a few revealed some. The researchers isolated the factor that appeared to account for success: teaching the subjects not just to apply the strategy but to monitor their own thinking processes in simple ways. Presumably, this activation of self-monitoring helped them later to recognize when they might apply the strategy they had learned.

4.4 Arousing Mindfulness

Mindfulness refers to a generalized state of alertness to the activities one is engaged in and to one's surroundings, in contrast with a passive reactive mode in which cognitions, behaviors, and other responses unfold automatically and mindlessly (Langer 1989). Mindfulness is more encompassing than either explicit abstraction or active self-monitoring, but would have the effect of fostering both.

4.5 Using a Metaphor or Analogy

Transfer is facilitated when new material is studied in the light of previously learned material that serves as an analogy or metaphor. Things known about the "old" domain of knowledge can now be transferred to a "new" domain, thereby making it better understood and learned. For example, students may initially understand the idea of an atom better by thinking of it as a small solar system, or how the heart works by thinking of it as a pump. Of course, most such analogies are limited and need elaboration and qualification.

5. Mechanisms of Transfer

Why do factors of the kind identified above encourage transfer? An answer can best be provided by an examination of the mechanisms of transfer, the psychological paths by which transfer occurs.

5.1 Abstraction

It is still possible to concede Thorndike's point that identical elements underlie the phenomenon of transfer. However, research suggests a more complex picture of how identical elements figure in the process of transfer. An identity that mediates transfer can reside at a very high level of abstraction. Phenomena such as the branching of arteries and that of electrical power networks can evince the same deep principle (the need to deliver something to a region point by point) with great differences in what constitutes a conduit (arteries versus wires) and in what is being carried (blood versus electricity). Such a degree of abstraction helps to account for far transfer, because highly abstract identical elements can appear in very different contexts.

5.2 Transfer by Affordances

Writing from the perspective of situated cognition, Greeno et al. (1993) argue that transfer need not depend on mental representations that apply to the learning and target situations. Rather, during initial learning, the learner may acquire an action schema responsive to the affordances—the action opportunities—of the learning situation. If the potential transfer situation presents similar affordances and the person recognizes them, the person may apply the same or a somewhat adapted action schema there. External or internal representations may or may not figure in the initial learning or the resulting action schema.

5.3 High Road and Low Road Transfer

Two studies (Salomon and Perkins 1989, Perkins and Salomon 1987) synthesized findings concerned with transfer by recognizing two distinct but related mechanisms, the "low road" and the "high road." Low road transfer happens when stimulus conditions in the transfer context are sufficiently similar to those in a prior context of learning to trigger well-developed semiautomatic responses. In keeping with the view of Greeno et al. (1993), these responses need not be mediated by external or mental representations. As a relatively reflexive process, low road transfer figures most often in near transfer. For example, when a person moving house rents a small truck for the first time, they find that the familiar steering wheel, shift, and other features evoke useful car-driving responses. Driving the truck is almost automatic, although it is a different task in several minor ways.

High road transfer, in contrast, depends on mindful abstraction from the context of learning or application and a deliberate search for connections: What is the general pattern? What is needed? What principles might apply? What is known that might help? Such transfer is not in general reflexive. It demands time for exploration and the investment of mental effort. It can easily accomplish far transfer, bridging between contexts as remote as arteries and electrical networks or strategies of chess play and politics. For instance, a person new to politics but familiar with chess might carry over the chess principle of control of the center, pondering what it would mean to control the political center.

In particular cases of transfer, the two roads can work together: some connections can occur reflexively, while others are sought out. In principle, however, the two mechanisms are distinct.

This framework accords well with a number of the points made above. It acknowledges that transfer is sometimes stimulus driven, occurring more or less automatically as a function of frequent and diverse practice (the low road). On the other hand, transfer sometimes involves high levels of abstraction and challenges of initial detection of possible connections (the high road). The framework allows for identical elements in Thorndike's original sense—identities that the organism simply responds to (the low road)—but insists on the importance of identities discovered and exploited by mindful exploration (the high road).

This analysis, along with the views and findings of Luria, Scribner and Cole, Greeno, and others, emphasizes that the conditions for transfer are stringent. Reflexive (low road) transfer requires well-automatized patterns of response that are thus easily triggered by similar stimulus conditions, and it requires stimulus conditions sufficiently similar to prior contexts of learning to act as triggers. Many learning situations offer practice only for a narrow range of examples and not enough practice to achieve significant automaticity, providing a poor basis for reflexive transfer. Mindful (high road) transfer requires active abstraction and exploration of possible connections. Many learning situations do not encourage such mental

investments, although people more inclined to mindfulness or metacognition are by definition more likely to make them.

6. Teaching for Transfer

The observations above about mechanism clarify why transfer does not occur as often as would be wished. They also provide guidelines for establishing conditions of learning that encourage transfer.

In many situations, transfer will indeed take care of itself: situations where the conditions of reflexive transfer are met more or less automatically. For example, instruction in reading literacy normally involves extensive practice with diverse materials to the point of considerable automaticity. Moreover, when students encounter reading situations outside of the literacy class—newspapers, books, assembly directions, and so on—the printed page provides an overt stimulus to evoke reading skills.

In contrast, in many other contexts of learning, the conditions for transfer are less propitious. For example, social studies are normally taught with the expectation that history will provide a lens through which to see contemporary events. Yet the instruction all too commonly does not include any actual practice in considering current events from a historical perspective. Nor are learners encouraged to reflect upon the eras they are studying and extract general widely applicable conclusions, or even questions. In other words, the conventions of instruction work against both automatic (low road) and mindful (high road) transfer.

In response to such dilemmas, two broad instructional strategies to foster transfer may be defined: hugging and bridging (Perkins and Salomon 1988). Hugging exploits reflexive transfer. It recommends that instruction directly engage the learners in approximations to the performances desired. For example, a job counselor might engage students in simulated interviews rather than just discussing good interview conduct. The learning experience thus "hugs" the target performance, maximizing the later likelihood of automatic low road transfer.

Bridging exploits the high road to transfer. In bridging, the instruction encourages the formulation of abstractions, searches for possible connections, mindfulness, and metacognition. For example, a job counselor might ask students to reflect on their strengths and weaknesses and devise a plan to highlight the former and downplay the latter in an interview. The instruction thus would emphasize deliberate abstract analysis and planning. Of course, in the example of the job interview, the teachers might employ both hugging and bridging. Instruction that incorporates the realistic experiential character of the former and the thoughtful analytic character of the latter seems most likely to yield rich transfer.

In summary, a superficial look at the broad conclusions drawn by research on transfer is discouraging: the great majority of studies suggest that transfer is not easily achieved. However, a closer examination of the conditions under which transfer does and does not occur and the mechanisms at work presents a more positive picture: education can achieve abundant transfer if it is designed to do so.

See also: Individual Differences, Learning, and Instruction; Learning to Learn: Adult Education

References

Belmont J M, Butterfield E C, Ferretti R P 1982 To secure transfer of training instruct self-management skills. In: Detterman D K, Sternberg R J (eds.) 1982 *How and How Much can Intelligence be Increased?* Ablex, Norwood, New Jersey

Brown A L 1989 Analogical learning and transfer: What develops? In: Vosniadou S, Ortony A (eds.) 1989 *Similarity and Analogical Reasoning*. Cambridge University Press, New York

Brown J S, Collins A, Duguid P 1989 Situated cognition and the culture of learning. *Educ. Res.* 18(1): 32–42

Campione J C, Brown A L, Reeve R A, Ferrara R A, Palincsar A S 1991 Interactive learning and individual understanding: The case of reading and mathematics. In: Landsmann L T (ed.) 1991 *Culture, Schooling, and Psychological Development*. Ablex, Norwood, New Jersey

Clements D H, Gullo D F 1984 Effects of computer programming on young children's cognition. *J. Educ. Psychol.* 76(6): 1051–58

Ericsson K A, Smith J (eds.) 1991 *Toward a General Theory of Expertise: Prospects and Limits*. Cambridge University Press, Cambridge

Gick M L, Holyoak K J 1980 Analogical problem solving. *Cognit. Psychol.* 12(3): 306–55

Gick M L, Holyoak K J 1983 Schema induction and analogical transfer. *Cognit. Psychol.* 15(1): 1–38

Greeno J G, Smith D R, Moore J L 1993 Transfer of situated learning. In: Detterman D, Sternberg R (eds.) 1993 *Transfer on Trial*. Ablex, Norwood, New Jersey

Langer E J 1989 *Mindfulness*. Addison-Wesley, Reading, Massachusetts

Lave J 1988 *Cognition in Practice: Mind, Mathematics and Culture in Everyday Life*. Cambridge University Press, New York

Lehrer R, Guckenberg T, Sancilio L 1988 Influences of Logo on children's intellectual development. In: Mayer R E (ed.) 1988 *Teaching and Learning Computer Programming: Multiple Research Perspectives*. Erlbaum, Hillsdale, New Jersey

Luria A R 1976 *Cognitive Development*. Harvard University Press, Cambridge, Massachusetts

Pea R D, Kurland D M 1984 On the cognitive effects of learning computer programming. *New Ideas in Psychology* 2(2): 137–68

Perkins D N, Salomon G 1987 Transfer and teaching thinking. In: Perkins D N, Lochhead J, Bishop J (eds.) 1987 *Thinking: The Second International Conference*. Erlbaum, Hillsdale, New Jersey

Perkins D N, Salomon G 1988 Teaching for transfer. *Educ. Leadership* 46(1): 22–32

Perkins D N, Salomon G 1989 Are cognitive skills context bound? *Educ. Researcher* 18(1): 16–25

Salomon G, Globerson T, Guterman E 1989 The computer as a zone of proximal development: Internalizing reading-related metacognitions from a Reading Partner. *J. Educ. Psychol.* 81(4): 620–27

Salomon G, Perkins D N 1987 Transfer of cognitive skills from programming: When and how? *Journal of Educational Computing Research* 3(2): 149–69

Salomon G, Perkins D N 1989 Rocky roads to transfer: Rethinking mechanisms of a neglected phenomenon. *Educ. Psychol.* 24(2): 113–42

Scribner S, Cole M 1981 *The Psychology of Literacy*. Harvard University Press, Cambridge, Massachusetts

Simon H A, Hayes J R 1977 Psychological differences among problem isomorphs. In: Castelan N J, Pisoni D B, Potts G R (eds.) 1977 *Cognitive Theory*, Vol. 2. Erlbaum, Hillsdale, New Jersey

Thorndike E L 1923 The influence of first year Latin upon the ability to read English. *School Sociology* 17: 165–68

Thorndike E L, Woodworth R S 1901 The influence of improvement in one mental function upon the efficiency of other functions. *Psychol. Rev.* 8: 247–61

Further Reading

Cormier S M, Hagman J D (eds.) 1987 *Transfer of Learning: Contemporary Research and Applications*, Academic Press, New York

Detterman D, Sternberg R (eds.) 1993 *Transfer on Trial*. Ablex, Norwood, New Jersey

Vosniadou S, Ortony A (eds.) 1989 *Similarity and Analogical Reasoning*. Cambridge University Press, Cambridge

Curriculum and the Psychology of Learning and Instruction

Attitudes and Values, Acquiring

F. K. Oser

In her book *A Philosophy of Morals*, Heller (1990) included a chapter on how to live an honest life. She adopted the distinction (and then criticized its limits) between the moralist and the moral philosopher, the former analyzing a given moral situation or language, the latter describing, in a teleological sense, how morality should be achieved. She then outlined the "decent person," who needs both value description and normativity in the field of values. The decent person expresses values by facing moral dilemmas, even against their own will, by living a norm-oriented life, and by realizing an existential decision to strive for the good. Decent people set their value standards, express values in their social interactions, and sense a kind of necessity in conforming to values.

Heller's distinction resembles the situation in value education. Whereas sociologists have theories about the origins of general changes in value orientations (including generational effects; e.g., Inglehart 1977), educational psychologists discuss in which directions change should go and what conditions are required for the transformation of an individual value structure. Whereas in many sociological studies, including poll-type and secondary statistical inquiries, values are defined by a more or less determined approval of some action, person, object, norm, rule, or system, and these analyses can reveal to what degree certain values, including moral values, are shared by a society or on some subcultural level, educational psychology is more interested in inner mechanisms of acquisition and change.

1. Two Psychological Approaches to Value Acquisition

The issue of value acquisition and change has been addressed by two major theoretical approaches: social learning theory and cognitive developmentalism. In social learning theory, the focus is on learning: external influences lead to reactions of a cognitive, emotional, and behavioral nature, which in turn contribute to a person's total repertoire of capacities and the willingness to perform value-based actions in the social, moral, or aesthetic domain (e.g., Mischel and Mischel 1976). The structuralist tradition of cognitive–developmental psychology emphasizes not learning but construction. It is suggested that the understanding of values and the significance given to them are strongly dependent on active processes of construction and reconstruction of normative features of reality, which in turn always start from given levels of social understanding and sociomoral reasoning competence. According to this line of thought, understanding is not a matter of transmission of factual knowledge but a product of active reflection of experience in the interpersonal sphere. If values are to become properly integrated within a person, he or she needs experiences in solving value conflicts, in participating in a value-oriented (particularly moral) discourse, and involvement in deliberate attempts at establishing normative rule systems on an interpersonal or group level (e.g., Kohlberg 1985).

Various structural theories have attempted to describe and explain developmental change in different domains of cognitive understanding and reasoning that all have some value dimension. Against the background of Piaget's and Baldwin's theories, stage schemes have been suggested by Kohlberg for the development of moral judgment competence, by Selman, Damon, Turiel, Youniss, and others for the domain of social understanding (including, e.g., the understanding of friendship), by Loevinger, Kegan, Noam, and others for the domain of self-development, and by Oser and Fowler for the domain of religious judgment and faith. This has leds to a distinction between different types of values. Philosophers and lay people distinguish between moral and nonmoral (e.g., aesthetic) values, the latter being characterized by the fact that subscribing to one or other value is of only personal rather than social or societal relevance. One major feature of moral values is their universal existence and justifiability. This marks a crucial difference from many other types of values, such as aesthetic, political, work-oriented, cultural, or religious values, which are all to a much higher degree multifaceted and context-related. Children as young as 3 or 4 years of age can distinguish between social–conventional and moral values, the first being arbitrary and a matter of social agreement, the second being perceived as unimpeachable in their validity (Turiel 1983).

2. The Interplay of Factors

While the two streams of thought mentioned so far used to be treated as opposites, it can be argued that their propositions must not be considered controversial (Gibbs and Schnell 1985). Social learning theory and research programs informed by this line of thought (e.g., most social psychological studies of prosocial behavior) start with overt behavioral stimuli and observe overt reactions; the focus of description is on interindividual differences under specific contextual conditions. Cognitive developmentalism, with its focus on structure, starts with the individual and with the person's internal modes of meaning-making and motivation; the focus is on covert competences of information processing ("the reason behind the reason given") and on interindividual similarities at universal developmental levels. In theory and research, and especially in terms of pedagogical implications, an interplay of both approaches with their ability to explain different aspects of the processes of values learning and change could be fruitful. One empirical example may illustrate this interplay and the processes that are in need of further clarification.

In an intervention study, Oser and Schlaefli (1985) attempted to influence the personal value hierarchies of apprentices. As means of intervention they designed a course involving the clarification of values and highlighting their significance (all this in accordance to social learning theory). They also sought to bring out moral dilemmas and conflicts between values in role-play situations and discussions. Results showed a general change in value hierarchies from a more hedonistic or materialist orientation (characterized by concern for salary and pleasure in sports and leisure time) to concern for more fundamental, interpersonal, or idealistic values such as health, family, self-confidence, and freedom. These changes remained relatively stable in follow-up testing after six months. The six most highly ranked values (in order of decreasing significance: love, friendship, health, tolerance, success in the profession, family) remained the same; yet interestingly, the following two values (freedom and self-confidence) were replaced by values of a more materialistic nature: money and travel.

Referring back to the two major theoretical approaches outlined above, it can be assumed that both environmental factors and processes of active reconstruction of values and their meaning play a role in this ordering and reordering of personal value hierarchies.

Cherishing a value and being ready to express it publicly thus presupposes an experiential awareness of its significance—something that can certainly be supported and encouraged by social models, by the experience that the value is ascribed high significance in a reference group, and by vivid forms of instruction. On the other hand, a full understanding of certain values, particularly immaterial values, and the ability to check their respective importance in cases of value conflicts require cognitive capacities that cannot simply be taught but, rather, must be constructed in a stepwise sequence. The meaning of the notion "freedom," for example, undergoes dramatic changes when the sociomoral perspective becomes broader (and begins to include a conception of the interdependency of human beings in groups and society), when moral thought adopts logical and social reciprocity as a leading principle in the solution of moral conflict, when the understanding of psychological processes allows the individual to understand that vulnerability exists not only on a physical level, and when experience has made clear that freedom is a highly complex political category interpreted in different ways by different people.

3. Attitudes versus Values

What about attitudes? An attitude, it has been proposed (e.g., by McGuire), is a response locating an object of thought along some dimension of judgment. Unlike the first attitude concepts (e.g., those of Allport 1935), attitudes are now usually thought of as: (a) systems with structures, including relationships within one attitude between several objects, relationships between several attitudes with regard to the same object; and (b) belief systems, that is, those involving relationships between several attitudes without necessarily referring to one single object. These systems, in turn, are in specific relationships to other personal subsytems, including affect and behavior. The inclusion of the latter makes up what is usually referred to as the "tripartite definition" of attitude: cognitive, affective, and conative.

This systems or structural approach has some resemblance to the approach used to analyze value systems, which also deal with evaluative or value judgments. The concepts of attitude and value are highly interconnected (see Tesser and Shaffer 1990 p. 488); because the concept of value is broader than the concept of attitude, values have sometimes been seen as "causing" attitudes (Rokeach 1968). For instance, everyday problems typically involve coping with dilemmas, that is, situations characterized by the presence of opposing values (Billing et al. 1988), which leads to more complex attitude or belief systems (Tetlock 1986).

Comparing the tripartite conception of attitudes to

what has been said above about value systems, it turns out that attitude systems and value systems have the same structure and must be measured in similar ways. If people are said to have particular values and particular attitudes, then it is probably accepted that both are similar and have been similarly influenced. Applying the principles presented above means, then, that to change a moral attitude one can change a set of moral values, which can be done through desequilibration of people's value structure, by evaluative judgments, by "consider the opposite" techniques, or by participation and role-taking exercises (see Klauer 1991). Knowledge transformation is only a necessary, not a sufficient condition, for attitude and value change.

4. Central Issues in Value and Attitude Education

When focusing the issue of values and attitudes acquisition on the question of how they are acquired, particular conditions of moral learning have to be addressed. Five topics seem to be of crucial importance.

First is the issue of indoctrination versus value relativism. Indoctrinative approaches hold that strong normative standpoints have to be considered necessary for societal stability and are transmitted by means of example, persuasion, or authority. Relativistic approaches reject the possibility of justifying universal criteria and emphasize the contextuality of values.

The second issue is the autonomy of persons with respect to moral norms. This refers, in philosophical terms, to the issue of freedom and determination; in psychological terms, the discussion refers to the question of whether the growing person is a passive recipient of influences or plays an active, (re)constructive role in development.

Third is the issue of defining the goals of moral education. Reflection of concrete values and value priorities, attitudes, and attitude priorities, and the demands of living up to personal, (sub)cultural, and societal standards are only formally consensual dimensions of various programs in value and moral education. The understanding of goals—as well as of appropriate educational means—differs heavily from one approach to the other (see Hersh et al. 1980).

The fourth issue is the inner mechanisms of moral learning. These have to be distinguished from the learning of attitudes that are much more open to change. (See above for further discussion.)

Finally, there is the issue of content and specificity of concrete values emphasized by the subject, given a specific age, context, and particular situational and cultural conditions. There are two positions concerning contextuality: (a)one in which knowledge handling as such is, in terms of orientations manifested in actions, rather irrelevant, as has been shown in many studies since the classical investigation of Hartshorne and May (1928); (b)one in which in real-life moral decision-making is believed to be always embedded

in a specific reality which creates sex differences with respect of the content (not the stages) and the orientation (justice versus care) of a moral decision. New research shows also that cultural differences are larger than psychologists in general assume.

Much more research still needs to be done. It is not known how knowledge handling and structural competence are related, nor how experienced events lead to different value conceptions. Also unknown are the absolute conditions for optimal age-related development to a cognitive and performative structural level.

From a structural point of view there is no single value that can be induced by education; it always transmits a balance of contradictory values. Therefore the sociological approach in which a subject is asked about one value at a time is unhelpful for educational matters. Anyone can express a view about a value in general, but then act against the view in a conflict situation. We may all oppose stealing but how would we react when confronted by the situation where a man has to steal to save his wife's life (Kohlberg 1984)? Thus, reconciling different theories must in future deal with many more different sources of our subjective value judgment.

A holistic approach of acquiring values and attitudes that comprehends both mentioned theoretical methods is the so-called Just Community approach. Students and teachers learn to decide on school matters in a democratic procedure which enables them to build up a highly shared value system (see Power et al. 1989). This value system is more stable than any other form of value reflection, value clarification, or value arousal. The problem with such a holistic concept is how to measure success. In the future, educational researchers must give more attention to Heller's "decent person" and to what she calls the "moralist position."

See also: Moral Development

References

Allport G W 1935 Attitudes. In: Murchison C (ed.) 1935 *A Handbook of Social Psychology*. Clark University Press, Worcester, Massachusetts

Billing M et al. (eds.) 1988 *Ideological Dilemmas: A Social Psychology of Everyday Thinking*, 2nd edn. Sage, London

Gibbs J, Schnell S V 1985 Moral development "versus" socialization: A critique. *Am. Psychol.* 40(10): 1071–80

Hartshorne H, May M A 1928 *Studies in Deceit. Studies in the Nature of Character*, Vol. 1 Macmillan, New York

Heller A 1990 *A Philosophy of Morals*. Blackwell, Oxford

Hersh R H, Miller J P, Fielding G D 1980 *Models of Moral Education: An Appraisal*. Longman, New York

Inglehart R 1977 *The Silent Revolution: Changing Values and Political Styles among Western Publics*. Princeton University Press, Princeton, New Jersey

Klauer K C 1991 *Einstellungen: Der Einfluß der affektiven Komponente auf das kognitive Urteil*. Hogrefe, Göttingen

Kohlberg L 1984 *Essays on Moral Development. Vol. 2: The Psychology of Moral Development, The Nature and*

Validity of Moral Stages. Harper & Row, San Francisco, California

Kohlberg L 1985 The just community approach to moral education in theory and practice. In: Berkowitz M W, Oser F K (eds.) 1985 *Moral Education: Theory and Application.* Erlbaum, Hillsdale, New Jersey

Mischel W, Mischel H N 1976 A cognitive social-learning approach to morality and self-regulation. In: Lickona T (ed.) 1976 *Moral Development and Behavior: Theory, Research, and Social Issues.* Holt, Rinehart and Winston, New York

Oser F K, Schlaefli A 1985 But it does move: The difficulty of gradual change in moral development. In: Berkowitz M W, Oser F K (eds.) 1985 *Moral Education: Theory and Application.* Erlbaum, Hillsdale, New Jersey

Power F C, Higgins A, Kohlberg L 1989 *Lawrence Kohlberg's Approach to Moral Education.* Columbia University Press, New York

Rokeach M 1968 *Beliefs, Attitudes, and Values: A Theory of Organizational Change.* Jossey-Bass, San Francisco, California

Tesser A, Shaffer D R 1990 Attitudes and attitude change. *Annu. Rev. Psychol.* 41: 479–523

Tetlock P E 1986 A value pluralism model of ideological reasoning. *J. Pers. Soc. Psychol.* 50(4): 819–27

Turiel E 1983 *The Development of Social Knowledge: Morality and Convention.* Cambridge University Press, Cambridge

Further Reading

Feather N T 1975 *Values in Education and Society.* Free Press, New York

Gergen K J 1982 *Toward Transformation in Social Knowledge.* Springer-Verlag, New York

Kohlberg L 1981 *Essays on Moral Development. Vol. 1: The Philosophy of Moral Development—Moral Stages and the Idea of Justice.* Harper & Row, San Francisco, California

Modgil S, Modgil C (eds.) 1986 *Lawrence Kohlberg: Consensus and Controversy.* Falmer Press, Philadelphia, Pennsylvania

Oser F, Althof W 1992 *Moralische Selbstbestimmung: Modelle der Entwicklung und Erziehung im Wertebereich, Ein Lehrbuch.* Klett-Cotta, Stuttgart

Comprehension: Teaching and Assessing

W. Schnotz and S.-P. Ballstaedt

This entry is about comprehension as a central aspect of meaningful learning in the context of teaching. First, basic characteristics of human comprehension are described. Comprehension is considered as a mental construction process. Based on these considerations, possibilities for educational guidance of these construction processes through teaching are discussed. Then, methods for testing and evaluating certain aspects of comprehension are described. Finally, perspectives for further research activities are pointed out.

1. Components of Human Comprehension

Understanding human comprehension requires an understanding of the major components of comprehension. Five primary components are addressed in this section.

1.1 Effort after Meaning

A central task of education is to help people orientate themselves in a complex real and symbolic world and understand its various phenomena. Comprehension can be considered as the most demanding human mental activity since it can encompass perception, memory, thinking, and problem solving. Humans principally assume that information about the world

is understandable. Bartlett (1932) has called this basic anthropological attitude an "effort after meaning." Within interpersonal communication a distinction can be made between comprehension on the content level and comprehension on the communication level. One can understand the conveyed information about the content and one can understand the intention of the message.

1.2 Mental Construction

Findings from hermeneutics, psycholinguistics, cognitive psychology, and artificial intelligence since the early 1980s gave rise to a constructive theory of comprehension (Bransford 1979, Hörmann 1978). The theory's basic assumption holds that comprehension is an active and goal-oriented construction of coherent mental representations based on newly acquired information and prior knowledge. In most cases, comprehension of verbal information has served as a paradigm for the analysis of comprehension. Other forms of comprehension as, for example, comprehension of situations or social behavior have received only little attention.

1.3 Interaction Between External and Internal Influences

Comprehension is not a single act. It results from a

complex interaction between different levels of information processing influenced by external and internal conditions (Engelkamp 1984). On the one hand, comprehension activities are usually triggered by external information which provides the material for mental constructions. Teaching can influence these mental construction processes by presenting certain verbal or pictorial information in an appropriate learning environment. On the other hand, comprehension is being controlled by internal conditions, especially prior knowledge, aims, interests, and expectations. In order to comprehend then, a student must assimilate the new information into pre-existing cognitive structures and/or accomodate these structures according to the new information. Trying to make new information as meaningful as possible by forming coherence with already existing knowledge can sometimes lead to misunderstandings (as when a learner comprehends the presented information in his or her own way but misinterprets the teacher's meaning). The integration of old and new information into a coherent whole requires knowledge-based inferences and can be controlled by metacognitive processes.

1.4 Open-ended Processes

Comprehension is principally an open-ended process. Neisser (1976) has developed a comprehension cycle to explain comprehension. New information enlarges prior knowledge which influences subsequent processing, leading again to a knowledge modification, and so on. Depending on the number of processing cycles, comprehension can be deeper or more superficial. An individual can break off further comprehension efforts for practical reasons. Nevertheless, already understood material can be put into a new context and then be comprehended again in a new way or at a deeper level.

1.5 Context Dependency

Information is always embedded in a context which influences its meaning (Bransford 1979). Actions, for example, are embedded in social situations, words are embedded in sentences and these again are embedded in texts, and so on. The respective context serves to avoid ambiguity and misunderstandings. The context dependency of comprehension is a central issue in situated learning and cognitive apprenticeship.

2. Teaching for Comprehension

Teaching can only lead to comprehension by stimulating an individual to engage in certain mental construction processes. On the one hand, the learner needs sufficient guidance to interrelate new information into prior knowledge. On the other hand, mental construction processes require a certain degree of

individual freedom which should not be unnecessarily limited. A balance has to be found between necessary instructional guidance and the required cognitive independence of the learner.

2.1 Activation of Prior Knowledge

In meaningful learning an individual is expected not only to pick up information about isolated facts but to assemble pieces of knowledge to coherent higher order structures. Coherence formation requires the activation of prior knowledge. According to the theory of cognitive subsumption by Ausubel (1968), a teacher should activate clear, stable, and distinct concepts which allow anchoring of the new information in the learner's knowledge structure. This activation, using advance organizers, provides a general framework which can then be further elaborated through progressive differentiation. A similar notion can be found in the elaboration theory of instruction (Reigeluth 1983). According to this theory, prior knowledge is activated through a preceding epitome which provides a conceptual framework for the integration of new information. Such an epitome contains a few simple central concepts and interconnects them using semantic relations. The subject matter is then described first in a crude, general way. Subsequently, more detailed descriptions follow step by step.

Activation of prior knowledge can also be achieved by the use of examples. On the one hand, examples can help to illustrate general statements and to make instructions more lively by personally affecting the learner. On the other hand, learners often consider an example in isolation without recognizing its relationship to the more general content (Marton and Wenestram 1978). Examples often have a stronger influence on comprehension than explicitly conveyed general information. A frequent recommendation, therefore, is to start with typical examples and then gradually to reduce typicality.

2.2 Triggering of Comprehension Activities

There frequently exists a gap between what learners can do and what they actually do. Many students think that comprehension is a passive reception of knowledge from a teacher or textbook rather than a generative constructive process. Therefore, the question arises how to stimulate learners to engage in the appropriate comprehension activities. Instead of simply presenting ready-made knowledge structures with the help of advance organizers or epitomes, teachers can use genetic or inquiry-oriented teaching. Here, the learner is being stimulated to discover essential coherence relations on his or her own. The teacher requires students to structure problem situations independently, to infer global interrelations from presented examples, to generate hypotheses and to test them (Wagenschein 1989). Epistemic motivation is stimulated through inducing cognitive conflicts (Berlyne 1960). In these less structured learning situations, however, the correlation between general intelligence of the learner and learning outcome usually becomes higher than in highly structured learning environments.

Comprehension activities can also be triggered by adjunct aids like the explication of educational objectives or adjunct questions. A teacher can make educational objectives explicit through providing information about tasks which will have to be solved later on. On the one hand, such information gives learners an orientation basis for directing their processing. On the other hand, however, there is the danger of learners being too selective with regard to the conveyed information. They might then only concentrate on seemingly goal-relevant contents and neglect the other information with the consequence that higher order relations are not recognized.

Well-suited adjunct questions can stimulate reflection or deeper-level processing, evoke cognitive conflicts, or demand an application of what has been understood. Rothkopf (1970) has used the term "mathemagenic activities" for such deeper processing initiated by adjunct questions. In order to support coherence formation, such questions should aim especially at establishing higher order relations. Questions can either precede each instructional section and therefore enhance mainly intentional learning of question-relevant contents, or can follow each instructional section. Then they initiate, on the one hand, intentional learning through recapitulation of the conveyed content, and on the other, incidental learning through generating a specific cognitive orientation. The learner comes to expect similar questions in the following instructional sections and organizes his or her processing activities accordingly (Rickards and Denner 1978).

The application of such adjunct aids has to be well-measured and matched with the cognitive-processing capacity of the learner. Too many educational objectives and adjunct questions can be quite confusing instead of being supportive for the learner. The efficiency of such aids seems to follow a u-inverse function. In the case of very favorable conditions (for example, good individual learning prerequisites, well-structured teaching materials, and sufficient learning time), studies often show no effect since such aids are actually not needed. Under very unfavorable conditions there is again no effect since the aids cannot be utilized appropriately. However, a supportive effect with regard to comprehension and learning can be expected in case of average processing conditions (Hartley and Davies 1976).

2.3 Metacognitive Control and Self-regulation

Comprehension as a mental construction is a goal-directed process. Learners are capable of adapting their cognitive processing to context conditions and expected demands. In order to achieve flexible and adaptive cognitive processing, metacognitive strategies concerning comprehension monitoring and control of one's own processing are necessary. Flavell (1979) has emphasized the importance of metacognitive knowledge (i.e., knowledge about human cognition) for monitoring and controlling one's own processing. However, the role of this metacognitive knowledge is being disputed; even experts often have difficulties in verbalizing their metacognitive self-regulation. Furthermore, existing metacognitive knowledge is often not used.

The regulation of cognitive processing is usually automatized. Only in the case of comprehension problems which cannot be solved with automated procedures is cognitive processing consciously controlled through metacognitive knowledge (Brown et al. 1986). However, learners frequently have inadequate standards for evaluating their comprehension. They often do not realize that they do not really understand. They establish coherence only at the local level and not at the global level or they ignore inconsistencies but are nevertheless under the asumption that they understand well. Glenberg et al. (1982) have called this the "illusion of knowing."

2.4 Strategy Training

Various methods exist aimed at preventing learners from superficial comprehension by teaching them certain processing strategies (Mandl and Friedrich 1992). Some of these strategy training programs, for example, instruct the learner to emphasize central information through self-questioning and to connect this information with other information. Learners can also be supported in independently summarizing what they have understood with the help of certain techniques, such as mapping procedures. Using mapping procedures, the learner graphically depicts the superordinate structure of the learning content. The results are two-dimensional maps which represent the basic structure of a subject area in the form of a diagram and which can be considered as graphical summaries (Anderson 1979). These procedures require the learner to go beyond local coherence and to direct his or her attention also to the higher-order global relations. The techniques usually require many hours of intensive training until they can be mastered and used relatively efficiently. Other strategy training programs emphasize time-planning, concentration management, self-perception, motivational–affective factors, individual learning styles, and social–psychological aspects of learning in groups (e.g., McKeachie et al. 1985, Weinstein 1988).

Studies on the effectiveness of strategy training programs frequently show positive effects with inexperienced learners whereas experienced learners often either profit little or show a decline in comprehension and learning performance. Experienced learners usually follow certain habits in their processing which are relatively resistant to change. If a training program is to have positive effects on learning it must first dismantle these old learning habits before it can establish a new regulatory system. Furthermore, the learner has to concentrate during strategy training on the subject matter and, simultaneously, on the learning techniques to be acquired. Due to this division of attention the cognitive capacity available for the subject matter itself is reduced, which can result in temporarily impaired learning performance. Strategy training programs are probably most efficient when they aim at global coherence formation with less experienced learners.

Newly acquired strategies are often dropped under the pressure of a specific learning situation. The learner then returns to his or her usual processing style. This finding suggests the need to engage in indirect promotion of strategies. The learner is placed in a learning situation and given certain tasks which stimulate the desired processing activities. Such indirect training makes the acquisition of strategies a by-product of subject matter learning. Strategies should not just be practiced. Rather, learners should be convinced of their usefulness in order to increase their willingness to apply them. Furthermore, strategy application depends on motivational transfer, attributional beliefs, and on the learner's self-concept (Borkowski et al. 1988). Comprehension strategies need to be supplemented through socioemotional coping strategies in order to help less efficient learners overcome the negative emotions associated with learning (Lehtinen 1992).

2.5 Situatedness

Context dependency of comprehension implies that the cognitive processes are embedded into situations of everyday life. Therefore, the social aspect of comprehension must be considered. This view has been emphasized by Palincsar and Brown (1984) in what they have called "reciprocal teaching" which supports comprehension activities by embedding them into a social context. Teachers and learners alternately conduct dialogues on instructional text-sections and summarize, make predictions, ask questions, and clarify where necessary. This interaction provides many possibilities to uncover misunderstandings on the part of the individual learner.

The context dependency of comprehension is especially emphasized in the situated learning approach. According to this view, comprehension is best supported in authentic situations with meaningful goal-oriented activities which provide the possibility for a cognitive apprenticeship. The teacher shows the learners, for example, a specific action (modeling) and conveys an orientation base for its execution (scaffolding). The learners then carry out the action themselves while the teacher observes and supports them (coaching). The more the learners become able to master the task, the less help they receive (fading out). Comprehension is viewed here as a process of enculturation whereby the learner adopts knowledge, abilities, and beliefs of social groups (Collins et al. 1989).

3. Testing for Comprehension

Comprehension cannot be measured directly. It is only possible to measure performances which require comprehension as a prerequisite. These indicators can be measured during comprehension (on-line) or after comprehension (off-line). The methods used for testing comprehension only address aspects of these complex comprehension processes (Anderson 1972, Ballstaedt and Mandl 1988).

3.1 Questions

Answering questions is probably the oldest and the most versatile method for testing comprehension (Graesser and Black 1985). Such questions require not only the retrieval of facts, but also additional processing which goes beyond the previously presented information. There is a distinction between open questions which allow answers to be constructed and closed questions which allow only a choice among various possible answers. Multiple-choice questions have proved very efficient in testing. Several variants of such questions are distinguished depending on how many possible answers are being provided and how many of them are correct. The difficulty of constructing multiple-choice questions lies in finding optional answers which require higher order cognitive processing to check their correctness.

3.2 Free Recall

The free recall of a previously learned content using one's own words is also a common method for testing comprehension. The corresponding evaluation can take into account both the quantity and the quality of the response, especially the coherence of recall. The basic assumption that comprehension allows correct reproduction assumes that the learner has created a conceptual representation of the presented information which he or she can then verbalize if required. Different learners will, of course, produce different sequences of the content, use different words, and generate different sentences. This creativity is considered as proof of the integration into prior knowledge. The connection between comprehension and remembering, however, is sometimes rather weak. There are contents which learners understand and then forget and there are contents which they do not understand but can nevertheless remember.

495

3.3 Summarizing

The task of summarizing the most important elements from a large amount of information is especially well-suited for written testing. Here as well, the quantity and quality of the summary can be of interest; the most important information has to be included and the summary has to be coherent. Summaries are quite valid indicators for comprehension since their mental construction requires higher order coherence formation processes. The reduction processes involved in summarizing have been analyzed in detail and a list of macro-operations such as deletion, selection, integration, and generalization has been produced (van Dijk 1980).

3.4 Thinking Aloud

This method requires the verbalization of ongoing cognitive processes while solving a task. Recording and transcribing a protocol are necessary to preserve the material for further evaluation. Thinking aloud is only possible in a single learner situation. Furthermore, it requires that systematic quantitative and qualitative evaluation criteria be developed according to the respective goals of the analysis. The method usually costs a great deal of time, but it allows on-line insight into the actual development of comprehension or misunderstanding (Graesser 1981).

The protocols provide qualitatively rich and distinctive material which reflects various comprehension processes: knowledge activation, inferences, establishment of coherence, and metacognition. Nevertheless, thinking aloud brings only the tip of the iceberg of all the processes of comprehension into view. Much more is going on in the head of a learner than he or she can verbalize. Furthermore, the central assumption that ongoing mental processes can be verbally expressed without distortions has repeatedly been doubted. The objection is that the unusual task of continually verbalizing actually interferes with the comprehension processes.

3.5 Cloze Procedures

The standard form of a cloze procedure consists in a text presented to the subject in which one word out of five is missing. The learner has to fill in the missing words. The percentage of correctly filled blanks is used as the measure of comprehension. There are numerous variants (e.g., only one out of five content words can be deleted, or the learner is presented with the fragment of a text or sentence which he or she has to complete appropriately). Cloze procedures can also be applied for visual tests of comprehension, when empty spaces have to be correctly filled within a picture or a graph. There is disagreement about what kind of comprehension processes are being measured with cloze procedures. Some researchers doubt that

comprehension is being measured at all. The question remains to what extent guessing plays a role since due to pre-existing content and linguistic knowledge a number of empty spaces can be filled without any comprehension of the passage.

3.6 Structure Displays

These testing procedures can be viewed as a variant of the mind-mapping technique. Subsequent to a comprehension process the learner externalizes his or her knowledge through writing concept words on cards and connecting them with a set of given content relations. The procedure has been standardized, but it can easily be modified for various aims (Scheele 1992). Unfortunately, no theory-based set of relations has been developed. The possibilities of quantitative and qualitative criteria of formal and content-related analyses are manifold. Measures for the internal coherence and differentiatedness of the knowledge can be calculated. The concepts can also be categorized using content analysis. Structure displays exhibit coherence relations and can be used for knowledge diagnosis. If the prior knowledge about a certain topic is displayed before learning, then the new conceptual interrelations acquired during teaching can be identified.

3.7 Application

In many cases the application of what has been understood in performing a certain behavior is the most valid method for testing comprehension. Examples of this method include conducting an experiment, using an apparatus, and similar activities. The quality of such a performance can be judged by the number of mistakes, the required amount of time, or other appropriate criteria. The use of video-recording allows repeated observation, also with slow motion. Since this procedure requires individual sessions and since the evaluation is costly in terms of time, practical application as a test for comprehension is accordingly rare. In addition, successful performance can sometimes occur on the basis of procedural knowledge rather than conceptual knowledge. In this case, the person being tested acts correctly although he or she did not grasp the meaning of that action. Therefore, tasks have to be constructed so that they are only solvable with the comprehension of the entire content.

4. Future Perspectives

Further research on teaching and testing for comprehension should analyze more deeply the interaction between cognitive, motivational, emotional, and social aspects of understanding. Furthermore, research should not be restricted to language comprehension, since nonverbal comprehension processes also play an important role in education.

In order to promote comprehension processes, a deeper analysis of the interplay between cognitive and metacognitive processes in the self-regulation of comprehension seems to be promising. Related to this analysis is the question of how direct training of comprehension and learning strategies and indirect support of such strategies should be combined. Another important problem is the optimal combination of the cognitively oriented strategies and the motivationlly oriented supportive strategies for specific learner groups.

The provision of indirect support for comprehension strategies is closely related to the situated learning approach to teaching comprehension since in both cases teaching is tied to authentic social and pragmatic contexts. Formal objective tests for comprehension play a limited role in these approaches since comprehension is constantly being evaluated in the social context (communicative validation). The complexity of the field requires multidisciplinary research from the perspectives of cognitive psychology, psycholinguistics, educational psychology, and instructional design.

References

Anderson R C 1972 How to construct achievement tests to assess comprehension. *Rev. Educ. Res.* 42(2): 145–70

Anderson T H 1979 Study skills and learning strategies. In: O'Neil H F, Spielberger D (eds.) 1979 *Cognitive and Affective Learning Strategies*. Academic Press, New York

Ausubel D P 1968 *Educational Psychology: A Cognitive View*. Holt, Rinehart and Winston, New York

Ballstaedt S-P, Mandl H 1988 The assessment of comprehensibility. In: Ammon U, Dittmar N, Mattheier K J (eds.) 1988 *Sociolinguistics. An International Handbook of the Science of Language and Society*. Walter de Gruyter, Berlin

Bartlett F C 1932 *Remembering. A Study in Experimental and Social Psychology*. Cambridge University Press, Cambridge

Berlyne D E 1960 *Conflict, Arousal, and Curiosity*. McGraw-Hill, New York

Borkowski J G, Weyhing R S, Carr M 1988 Effects of attributional retraining on strategy-based reading comprehension in learning-disabled students. *J. Educ. Psychol.* 80(1): 46–53

Bransford J O 1979 *Human Cognition: Learning, Understanding, and Remembering*. Wadsworth, Belmont, California

Brown A L, Armbruster B B, Baker L 1986 The role of metacognition in reading and studying. In: Orasanu J (ed.) 1986 *Reading Comprehension. From Research to Practice*. Erlbaum, Hillsdale, New Jersey

Collins A, Brown J S, Newman S E 1989 Cognitive apprenticeship: Teaching the crafts of reading, writing, and mathematics. In: Resnick L B (ed.) 1989 *Knowing, Learning, and Instruction*. Erlbaum, Hillsdale, New Jersey

Engelkamp J 1984 Verstehen als Informationsverarbeitung. In: Engelkamp J (ed.) 1984 *Psychologische Aspekte des Verstehens*. Springer, Berlin

Flavell J H 1979 Metacognition and cognitive monitoring: A new area of cognitive-developmental inquiry. *Am. Psychol.* 34(10): 906–11

Glenberg A M, Wilkinson A C, Epstein W 1982 The illusion of knowing: Failure in the self-assessment of comprehension. *Memory and Cognit.* 10(6): 597–602

Graesser A C 1981 *Prose Comprehension Beyond the Word*. Springer, New York

Graesser A C, Black J B (eds.) 1985 *The Psychology of Questions*. Erlbaum, Hillsdale, New Jersey

Hartley J, Davies I K 1976 Preinstructional strategies: The role of pretests, behavioral objectives, overviews and advance organizers. *Rev. Educ. Res.* 46: 239–65

Hörmann H 1978 *Meinen und Verstehen. Grundzuge einer psychologischen Semantik*. Suhrkamp, Frankfurt

Lehtinen E 1992 Lern- und Bewältigungsstrategien im Unterricht. In: Mandl H, Friedrich H F (eds.) 1992

Mandl H, Friedrich H F (eds.) 1992 *Lern- und Denkstrategien*. Hogrefe, Göttingen

Marton F, Wenestram C G 1978 Qualitative differences in understanding and retention of the main points in some texts based on the principle-example structure. In: Gruneberg M M, Morris P E, Sykes R N (eds.) 1978 *Practical Aspects of Memory*. Academic Press, London

McKeachie W J, Pintrich P R, Lin Y G 1985 Learning to learn. In: d'Ydewalle G (ed.) 1985 *Cognition, Information Processing, and Motivation*. North-Holland, Amsterdam

Neisser U 1976 *Cognition and Reality. Principles and Implications of Cognitive Psychology*. Freeman, San Francisco, California

Palincsar A M, Brown A L 1984 Reciprocal teaching of comprehension-fostering and comprehension-monitoring activities. *Cognition and Instruction* 1(2): 117–75

Reigeluth C M (ed.) 1983 *Instructional-design Theories and Models: An Overview of Their Current Status*. Erlbaum, Hillsdale, New Jersey

Rickards J P, Denner P R 1978 Inserted questions as aids to reading text. *Instr. Sci.* 7(3): 313–46

Rothkopf E Z 1970 The concept of mathemagenic activities. *Rev. Educ. Res.* 40(3): 325-36

Scheele B (ed.) 1992 *Struktur-Lege-Verfahren als Dialog-Konsens- Methodik*. Aschendorff, Munster

van Dijk T A 1980 *Macrostructures*. Erlbaum, Hillsdale, New Jersey

Wagenschein M 1989 *Verstehen lehren*. Beltz, Weinheim

Weinstein C E 1988 Assessment and training of student learning strategies. In: Schmeck R R (ed.) 1988 *Learning Strategies and Learning Styles*. Plenum Press, New York

Educational Psychology: Impact on Curriculum

G. D. Haertel

Educational psychology is a field of study that mediates between the discipline of psychology and the profession of education. Scholars have yet to agree upon a single definition of educational psychology. The field is characterized by many theoretical persuasions and diversified scholarship: incorporating knowledge from, learning and cognitive psychology; individual differences; instructional design; measurement, evaluation and statistical analysis; human development; and guidance and counseling. Historically, educational psychology was fostered by such eminent United States psychologists as William James, Edward L Thorndike, James McKeen Cattell, G Stanley Hall, John Dewey, and Lewis Terman. Many of these early psychologists were trained in European laboratories which provided an international forum for scholars from many nations (Walberg and Haertel 1992). Scholarship in educational psychology is conducted internationally. This entry addresses the implications of educational psychology for curriculum, conceived as a range of intended learning outcomes, as a program of planned activities directed at bringing about those outcomes, and as a set of discrete tasks and concepts to be mastered. The influence of educational psychology on curriculum is described in terms of historical movements as well as current research fronts. Four important historical movements in educational psychology—the child development movement, behaviorism, the emergence of instructional design, and the cognitive revolution—are described. Research fronts including research on teaching at-risk of school failure students and assessment practices are briefly addressed.

1. The Emergence of Educational Psychology as a Discipline

Psychology, as the science of the mind, began to appear in United States teacher-training schools at the turn of the twentieth century. Even at that time, there was disagreement in schools of education about what content should be included in undergraduate educational psychology courses (Grinder 1978). Students taking educational psychology typically studied learning tests and measurements, the scientific study of the child, child clinical psychology, and exceptional children.

Since the late 1800s, a number of historical movements have occurred within the evolution of educational psychology. These movements represented distinct perspectives, methods, and philosophical underpinnings. Among these historical movements were positivism (which focused on cataloging and testing human abilities), pragmatism (which focused on educational experimentation, use, and innovation and also fostered progressive democratic objectives), the child study movement (which focused on the scientific study of children's beliefs, opinions, and physical attributes), behaviorism (which rejected mentalistic concepts of thought and used stimulus–response models to explain and predict behavior), and cognitivism (which modelled internal mental states and events). Of these five movements, positivism and pragmatism continue to exert strong direct and indirect influences on educational practices, as does cognitivism. Some of these historical movements will be discussed in greater detail in subsequent sections.

2. Major Conceptions of Curriculum

Schubert (1986) discusses eight views of curriculum. These eight views represent major conceptions of curriculum: curriculum as (a) content or subject matter, (b) cultural reproduction, (c) experience, (d) a program of planned activities, (e) intended learning outcomes, (f) discrete tasks and concepts, (g) an agenda for social reconstruction, and (h) "currere" (interpretation of one's life experiences). Three of these conceptions are of special interest in understanding the impact of educational psychology on curriculum. These are curriculum as a program of planned activities, as intended learning outcomes, and as discrete tasks and concepts.

The first of these conceptions, curriculum as a program of planned activities, incorporates "scope and sequence, interpretation and balance of subject matter, motivational devices, teachings techniques, and anything else that can be planned in advance" (Schubert 1986 p. 27). This conception of curriculum includes the planning for a specific instructional activity as well as the curriculum guide used to plan an entire course of study.

The second conception of curriculum, curriculum as intended learning outcomes, focuses on the products of learning. In this perspective, all activities and teaching are directed at reaching a set of specified ends. The curriculum design would include detailed plans of the materials, instructional activities, and assessments that enable students to reach this intended learning outcome.

The third conception of curriculum, curriculum as discrete tasks and concepts, is often described as task analysis. In a high school geometry class, an example of a discrete task to be mastered might be proving the Pythagorean Theorem. Learners would be pretested to assess their prior knowledge, and the act of proving the theorem would be broken down into carefully defined sequential learning tasks that, when implemented, would culminate in students learning to prove the theorem. As a final step, students would be post-tested to determine their mastery of this task.

3. Psychology and Educational Practice: A Productive Union

Psychologists and educators have cautioned against the uninformed application of psychological constructs, theories, or research results to school learning and instruction (Schwab 1969, Shulman 1974). Many of the applications of psychology to educational practice were the product of middle-range theories and the empirical research generated by these theories. Some of the middle-range theories that have been most germane in shaping educational practices with regular and special students include theories of learning (Shuell 1980), cognition (Greeno 1980), and instruction (Bruner 1966); attribution (Weiner 1979), self-efficacy (Bandura 1977); and self-regulation (Vygotsky 1987). Models of school learning provided another key source of influence on educational thought and practice. Carroll (1963) advanced the first theoretical model of school learning; subsequent models such as Walberg's (1984) model of educational productivity were proposed and utilized in planning school, curricular, and instructional programs.

3.1 The Use of Eclectic, Middle-range Theories Grounded in Practice

Middle-range theories provide theoretical propositions that can be used to shape inquiry and generate further research. When compared to theories that represent general laws of nature or lead to prediction or control of phenomena, middle-range theories are more limited in scope and longevity. Middle-range theories operate at a level of specificity that is more suited to informing educational practice. They are not presented as providing solutions across a wide range of educational problems (Shulman 1974).

Schwab's (1969) work has focused on the role of practical inquiry in curriculum. In curriculum planning Schwab emphasizes the importance of situational needs and interests that emerge from particular students, classrooms, schools, and communities. He has objected strongly to the use of theoretic research results in developing curriculum because they are based on isolated elements rather than on complex, contextual variables that are characteristic of real-life classrooms and schools. Schwab advocates the eclectic use of theory grounded in practice in shaping curriculum, and has admonished against relying on psychological theory alone. Middle-range psychological theories can become one of many eclectic sources

that inform curricular planning, instructional practice and classroom life.

The middle-range theories generated by educational psychologists that are most useful to curriculum planners emerge out of the study of schooling: the school's organization, the students, the teachers, the instructional practices, and the psychology of subject matter. Middle-range theories provide descriptions and interpretations of educational phenomena.

3.2 Theories of Learning, Cognition, and Instruction

In describing the types of theories that are most likely to contribute to curriculum, it is important to distinguish among three broad types of psychological theories: learning, instruction, and cognition. Learning theories explain relationships among variables that account for learning as expressed by changes in an individual's behavior over time (Gagné 1965). More often than not, they comprise the kinds of variables and processes that can readily be studied using the methods of experimental psychology in laboratories rather than naturalistic settings. Learning theories (e.g., stimulus–response theory) focus on changes in manifest behaviors, not internal mental states. When individuals learn, their learning is conceived of as changes that come about through the simple accretion of associations and discriminations.

Theories describing how individuals acquire information are based on the constructs and principles of cognitive psychology Cognitive theories are concerned with the integration of new knowledge and skills with prior knowledge into functional systems for use in mental activities and actions (Snow and Lohman 1989). Information-processing theory from computer science became a metaphor for understanding complex human behaviors. Cognitive theories characterized learners as active constructors of general knowledge structures, frames, scripts, plans, and personal theories. School subjects have provided a range of meaningful learning tasks which are sufficiently complex for cognitive research. A cognitive psychology of school subjects has emerged and invigorated the association between psychology and school learning (Greeno 1980).

Shuell (1980) believes that, even though cognitive psychology has generated models of knowledge acquisition in school subjects, these models are limited in their direct implications for educational practice. Like learning theories, cognitive theories of school subjects often ignore contextual factors important to instruction, such as teacher behaviors, student background characteristics, classroom organization, and the global structure of the curriculum. Instructional theories, in contrast, take into account contextual factors of the classroom and school. They include theories of learning and cognition but also address the range of instructional processes needed to bring about intended learning outcomes in the classroom. The importance of instructional theory has been recognized since the 1960s when the limitations of laws of learning and learning theories became clear (Bruner 1966). One example of an instructional theory is found in the work of Taba (1967). She drew implications from the developmental theories of Piaget (1970) and incorporated them into principles for curriculum and instruction.

3.3 Models of School Learning

Educational psychologists have developed models of school learning since the 1960s, beginning with the work of Carroll (1963). Carroll used six constructs in his model: (a) aptitude, (b) ability to comprehend instruction, (c) perseverance, (d) clarity of instruction, (e) matching the task to student characteristics, and (f) opportunity to learn. These six constructs comprised the major psychological influences on schooling in Carroll's model. Other models were developed by Bloom (1982), Harnischfeger and Wiley (1976), Glaser (1976), and Bennett (1978). All these models centered on student ability and related constructs such as aptitude, prior knowledge, and verbal IQ. Motivation, often described as perseverance, self-concept, or attitudes toward school, was included in most models of school learning. The importance of classroom instructional variables was addressed by including constructs such as instructional events, clarity of instruction, use of cues, feedback, and correctives. More recent models have extended the range of variables considered. For example, Walberg (1984) identified nine theoretical constructs that influenced schooling. These constructs comprise: (a) student age or developmental level, (b) ability (including prior achievement), (c) motivation, (d) quantity of instruction, (e) quality of instruction, (f) classroom climate, (g) home environment, (h) influence of the peer group and (i) exposure to mass media. The model of schooling advanced by Wang and Lindvall (1984) introduced constructs used in adaptive education, such as instructional delivery systems, program design, and implementation.

4. Historical Movements

Among the historical developments in educational psychology; the child study movement, behaviorism, the emergence of instructional design, and the cognitive revolution have had great impact on curriculum development.

4.1 The Child Study Movement

The child study movement attempted to base educational practice on the results of scientific studies of children (Davidson and Benjamin 1987). The psychologist most frequently associated with the child study movement was G. Stanley Hall. Using questionnaires that covered a variety of topics, Hall enquired about children's knowledge of the world, their physical charateristics, and their opinions. The results of these studies were widely disseminated through state-level groups and societies. Handbooks reporting results of studies became popular textbooks for teacher-training programs. Classroom teachers were encouraged to conduct studies in their own classrooms and report the results to other child study enthusiasts. Besides the use of questionnaires, teachers conducted observational studies of their students and collected biographical information. Teachers used the results of these studies to select content and develop instructional techniques that were suited to the physical, verbal, and academic characteristics of their students.

4.2 Behaviorism

Educational psychology has been strongly influenced by behaviorism (Skinner 1954). Skinner, a prominent behaviorist, emphasized the experimental analysis of behavior and helped establish the relationship between an individual's behavior and environmental stimuluses. Skinner, using experimental data collected on single case studies, introduced psychologists and educators to constructs such as reinforcement, punishment, extinction, stimulus control, and discrimination. Skinner did not use hypothetical constructs, but instead explicit behaviors that were discrete and observable in establishing functional relationships between behavior and the subject's environment.

Skinner argued that the instructional practices used in school often impeded learning. From his perspective, teaching machines could guide a student's progress in a content area by individualizing instruction to meet his or her particular needs. Another application of behaviorist principles is the use of token reinforcement systems which employ praise, tangible rewards, or group-based contingencies. Token reinforcement systems have been used to change the academic and social behaviors of children, especially those with special needs.

Curricula that apply these techniques have been developed at all levels of schooling. One of the landmark applications was Keller's (1968) system of personalized instruction. Behavioral principles, such as reinforcement, were utilized extensively in early computer-assisted instruction. Other examples of curricula that apply behaviorist principles include programs to improve the academic skills of students at risk of school failure and to change the social behavior of delinquents in residential settings using token economies. Criterion-referenced assessment, which measures immediate referents rather than hypothetical constructs, is based upon behaviorist principles.

4.3 Instructional Design

With the publication of the *Taxonomy of Educational Objectives* (Bloom et al. 1977), educators became aware of the range of cognitive processes that students use in learning. This volume, which received international acclaim, characterized instructional tasks along the dimensions of content and process. The publication of this first *Taxonomy* ushered in an era of planning systematic instruction. In time, taxonomies of psychomotor and affective domains also appeared. These taxonomies promoted an understanding that student learning outcomes should be clearly specified and systematically evaluated.

In response to the Soviet Union's launch of Sputnik in 1958, the United States embarked upon numerous curriculum development efforts in physics, chemistry, biology, and mathematics. Gagné's (1965) application of hierarchical analysis linked subject matter content to the domains of learning and the events of instruction and, in doing so, laid the conceptual groundwork for instructional designers. New curricula were developed based on hierarchical analysis, and employed techniques such as self-paced instruction, linear programming, and branching. Gagné (1965) identified events of instruction, including gaining student attention, motivating the student, utilizing hierarchical analysis to guide instruction, providing practice with feedback, and conducting frequent assessments.

About the same time, Mager (1962) published a small volume, *Preparing Instructional Objectives*, that also influenced instructional design. Mager advocated the use of specifying student behaviors, defining the conditions under which they would occur, and setting standards of acceptable performance.

Scriven's (1967) hallmark paper on formative and summative evaluation was welcomed by instructional designers. It recommended the collection of formative data to improve curricular programs, materials, and instructional activities as they are being developed. Summative evaluation was used to determine the effectiveness of the completed curriculum for the benefit of an external audience or decision-maker.

By the late 1960s, new systems of instruction and curricula appeared that classified tasks along dimensions of content and process, employed hierchical analysis, specified behavioral objectives, and applied formative and summative evaluations.

4.4 The Cognitive Revolution

Cognitive psychology has contributed to educational practice. Shulman (1974) called for a renaissance of the psychology of school subjects. He argued for a "modern" psychology based on the results of cognitive studies conducted in each school subject, rather than a general psychology that does not reflect the structure of the knowledge base within each content area. Shulman's position is in contrast to the position held by earlier researchers who worked to locate and describe a general cognitive system. In the past, cognitive understandings were believed to be content blind. More recent research provides evidence that different types of content are processed in different ways: language processing may occur quite differently from the processing of spatial images. Cognitive research has produced three types of information: the way knowledge is acquired, stored, and retrieved; information about different types of errors and knowledge deficits; and information about self-appraisal, self-regulation, and correction mechanisms. Some key cognitive psychological constructs are described and their implications for curriculum are presented.

Three key constructs, declarative, procedural and prior knowledge, describe the content and organization of knowledge structures. These higher-order structures are used to organize an individual's information in all content areas. Declarative knowledge is a semantic network of facts, ideas, and relations among concepts. A student's ability to retrieve information is directly related to the organization of his or her declarative knowledge. Procedural knowledge is knowledge of certain processes or routines. As knowledge becomes proceduralized it increases in automaticity. Proceduralized knowledge does not demand conscious attention on the part of a student. Prior knowledge refers to the units of knowledge and skills a student brings to the instructional setting. Prior knowledge also includes a student's preconceptions, misconceptions, and personal belief systems. Results of research on knowledge structures suggest that teachers need to present facts, principles, ideas, and concepts to students as part of an organized knowledge base that takes into account the student's prior knowledge and experience. In particular, student's idiosyncratic knowledge structures must be identified and remediated through appropriate instruction.

One of the most fruitful areas of cognitive research has been the study of expert versus novice performance (Snow and Lohman 1989). Experts and novices perform learning tasks differently: experts possess more complex knowledge structures than novices; experts organize their knowledge structures according to higher-order principles; experts pay less attention to the surface characteristics of the problem; experts carefully monitor problem-solving performance; and experts generate rich problem representations as a guide to solution and search (Glaser 1991). Strategies used by experts to solve problems are usually domain-specific. Problems developed as part of instructional activities in various knowledge domains differ dramatically in the way they are structured. Some content domains, such as mathematics, have well-defined and well-structured problems; problem in the social sciences can be described as ill-structured and poorly specified. Curriculum developers should construct instructional programs using problem-solving strategies and advanced skills that are specific to a given content area.

Cognitive researchers have indentified a wide variety of types of error that students systematically make. Among these types of error are: flawed algorithms, misconceptions, misdefinitions, overgeneralizations, faulty analogies, and naive theories. Cognitive researchers have emphasized the importance of identifying student errors in order to provide appropriate instructional remediation. For example, "naive theories" is a term used to describe a personal belief system that is not publicly affirmed. Naive theories vary in comprehensiveness, and may explain isolated concepts or cover a wide range of events (Osborne and Gilbert 1980). Naive theories are constructed by students themselves and are very resistant to remediation. They are not the product of instruction and can impede a student's progress in acquiring new information. Curriculum developers and cognitive psychologists have begun to work together to provide diagnostic assessments that can identify types of errors that students make and to specify the instructional activities needed for instructional remediation. Computer diagnosis of student errors and remediation via computer tutorials has become a fruitful area of research.

Perkins and Simmons (1988) studied patterns of misunderstanding in the content areas of science, mathematics, and computer programming. They developed a model based upon four interlocking levels of knowledge that students need in order to acquire deep understanding in these content areas. The four types of knowledge students need for deep understanding comprise: (a) a content frame that includes facts, definitions, algorithms and metacognitive strategies used to access and recall domain-specific information; (b) a problem-solving frame that includes domain-specific strategies; (c) an epistemic frame that includes domain-specific and general norms and strategies used to validate claims, for example, provide evidence and explain rationales; and (d) an inquiry frame used to challenge knowledge through critical and creative thinking. Educational psychological research aids curriculum developers in identifying the types of knowledge that teachers need to develop students' deep understanding in content domains.

Metacognition is a critical information-processing skill that has provided educators with many practical applications. It is the ability to identify activities and strategies that are needed to understand and perform a learning task (Brown et al. 1981). Metacognitive processes are among the most transferable cognitive skills. They are responsible for the planning, activating, monitoring, evaluating, and modifying of lower-order skills. Reading comprehension and written composition are two curricular areas that have particularly benefited from the study of metacognitive processes. In these areas students are encouraged to set goals, monitor their own progress, and employ new strategies when needed. One widely used curriculum to develop metacognitive skills is the Informed Strategies for Learning program developed by Paris and his colleagues (Cross and Paris 1988). This program "features direct explanation of reading strategies, group discussions about the use of strategies, metaphors to communicate and describe thinking strategies, and the gradual transfer of control from teacher to student" (Cross and Paris 1988 p. 141).

Cognitive research has encouraged educators to view students as active constructors of meaning. As a student integrates his or her prior knowledge with new material provided through schooling, each student's knowledge structure is modified, hence, research on knowledge structures is a practical priority. The full impact of cognitive psychology on curriculum is still unclear. However, because there are many cognitive skills and processes which are specific to content domains, there are ample opportunities for curriculum developers to produce new curricula based on cognitive principles.

Metacognitive processes go beyond students' self-appraised knowledge. They include both the self-regulation of an individual's thinking and his or her own self-evaluations. Students evaluate their own competencies. Students' sense of control and self-evaluation of their own competencies are related to their success in school. Self-evaluations help regulate student's choice of behavior and the amount of effort they expend on school tasks (McCombs 1991). McCombs believes that a student's negative self-evaluation can impede his or her learning. If a student possesses both an internal locus of control and a positive academic self-concept, he or she will be able to access deep-learning processes needed for successful academic achievement. The role of the self is responsible for positive self-perceptions, expectations, affective reactions, self-regulation processes and intrinsic motivation.

Cognitive researchers have addressed the motivational orientation of students through attribution theory, self-efficacy theory, and self-regulated learning theory. Weiner (1979) adapted a three-faceted categorization of internality (internal vs. external), stability (fixed vs. variable), and controllability (controllable vs. uncontrollable), to explain how thought influences behavior. Within Weiner's classification, ability is viewed as internal, fixed, and uncontrollable. Effort is viewed as internal, variable and controllable. The difficulty of the task being mastered is seen as external, fixed, and uncontrollable. These attributions affect students' expectancies for future performance, their persistence, their choice of tasks, and the study strategies they select. Bandura (1977) explicated in his cognitive theory of self-efficacy, that a student's confidence is enhanced through mastery of new experiences. As students become convinced that they can influence their own learning outcomes, they work harder to overcome difficulties. One of the best-known theories of self-regulated learning has been developed by Vygotsky (1987). Vygotsky's theory of verbal self-regulation is characterized as purposeful, self-directed speech used by the individual to promote the accomplishment of his or her own goals. Theories of self-regulated learning stress the active role that students must play. Some of the classroom habits in which self-regulated learners engage, include: starting assignments on time, seeking help on tasks, persisting on assignements, and completing work on time.

All of the theories related to students' motivational orientations have been applied in cognitive self-instruction, a process used in classrooms to teach students how to become active, responsible, self-motivated, and self-managed learners (Manning 1991). The full impact of cognitive-based theories of motivation and self-regulation on curriculum has not been established. However, more curricula are being developed which include components devoted to cognitive self-instruction.

Cognitive psychology has also influenced curriculum through the epistemology of constructivism. Wood (1995 p. 336) reports that from a constructivist perspective learning is "a process of personal construction of meaning." The constructivist perspective has implications for the role of the teacher and the nature of instructional activities. A curriculum designed by constructivists would provide numerous learning experiences that engage students in literacy, mathematical, and scientific activities. Students would have ample opportunities to engage in dialogue, written communication, and problem solving. Instructional activities that involve communal practices allow teachers to link students' construction of ideas, which are based on their cognitive understandings they develop in their daily activities, with more formal school instruction. This interpretation of teaching and learning is compatible with constructivism. The epistemology of constructivism has suggested significant changes in teachers' roles, instructional strategies, and in the content and learning activities included in curricula.

5. Active Research Fronts

Since the late 1980s, a number of active research fronts have generated empirical findings that have influenced the development of curriculum. Some of these research fronts are research on teaching, research on at-risk students, and research on assessment practices.

There are many other active research areas in the discipline of educational psychology, these three have been selected because of their salience to curriculum development.

5.1 Research on Teaching

A variety of research approaches have been employed in identifying explicit information about the process and outcomes of teaching. One of the more popular approaches has been structured observations of classroom processes. Overt teacher behaviors have been correlated with student, teacher, school, and community characteristics, as well as student outcomes. Some of the teacher behaviors correlated with student achievement have included "warmth, businesslike orientation, enthusiasm, organization, variety in materials and academic activities, and high frequencies of clarity, structuring comments, probing questions asked as follow-up to initial questions, and focus on academic activities" (Brophy and Good 1986 p. 330). This type of research has been labeled "process–product research."

A second broad approach to the study of teaching relies upon qualitative methods and is referred to "participant–observer research" (Erickson 1986). This approach uses fieldwork to establish the immediate and local meanings of actions. The research is characterized by heavy involvement in the field setting, collecting extensive notes and documentation, and systematic reflection on the documentary record. Sociolinguistic research exemplifies the participant—observer approach, utilizes verbal exchange as the unit of analysis, and examines verbal and nonverbal communications that occur in the classroom. Sociolinguists believe that communications establish and maintain classroom goals and expectations. This research approach emphasizes the context, history, and meaning of classroom goals and expectations. This research approach emphasizes the context, history, and meaning of classroom interactions.

Research on teaching has influenced curriculum development by identifying the relationships among teacher and student behaviors and outcomes. Researchers have identified effective teacher actions and the learning outcomes with which they are associated. Particular attention has been paid to teacher and student social and academic interactions: questioning, praise and criticism, lesson structure, use of cues, and quantity of instruction. This research has informed the way curriculum developers compose units of instruction, plan instructional activities, and identify desirable student outcomes.

5.2 Educating At-risk of School Failure Students

During the 1980s educators and policymakers focused attention on teaching advanced skills to educationally disadvantaged students who are at risk for academic failure. In the past the prototypical remedial program has been a compensatory education program that emphasized basic skills instruction. Rather than improving children's academic skills, traditional compensatory education programs often contributed to the learning problems of the educationally disadvantaged. Research results have documented that compensatory education programs have provided at-risk students with less instruction to meet their greater-than-usual learning needs. Some of the compensatory programs have delivered radically different content to at-risk students, content that did not emphasize higher-order, advanced skills. For example, at-risk students are often pulled out of regular reading classes and are drilled in phonics, word attack skills, and vocabulary, as compared to advantaged students whose reading instruction focuses on comprehension and higher-order thought processes. Compensatory mathematics instruction for at-risk students frequently stressed drills on basic arithmetic operations, rather than emphasizing problem-solving and higher-order reasoning. In addition, teachers of compensatory education programs have often used instructional approaches that underestimate what students with special needs can do. Often teachers have delayed the introduction of more advanced content and have not provided students with a motivating context for instruction (Means and Knapp 1991).

Means and Knapp (1991) have identified three sets of principles that characterize new instructional programs and curricula targeted at at-risk students. These programs provide a strong motivating context. They recognize the importance of students' prior knowledge and focus on building students' strengths, not just remediating weaknesses. New curricula distinguish between cultural diversity and deficits. Other curricular innovations include a focus on complex, real-life problems, embedding basic skills instruction within complex problems, and relating new content to students' prior knowledge and cultural background.

5.3 Assessment Practices

Historically, the assessment of achievement has served several purposes in the educational system: (a) the diagnosis of student skills, knowledge, and learning difficulties; (b) the support of instructional adaptation on an episodic, daily, weekly, and monthly basis; (c) the provision of placement and certification information; and (d) monitoring and comparing the level of achievement for groups, programs, schools, districts, states, and nations (Resnick and Resnick 1989, Snow and Lohman 1989). In the past, commercially produced achievement tests, both criterion and norm-referenced tests, as well as teacher-constructed classroom tests, were used to fulfill the four purposes listed above. These types of testing were aligned with behaviorist learning theories. In behaviorism, learning is defined as the absorption of incremental information, and the goal of instruction is to enlarge a student's repertoire of facts, principles, and formulas. Traditional multiple-choice tests employ items that expect students to recall facts or to apply simple, unelaborated routines that students have learned through instruction. Even items that measure higher-order thought processes may only demand that students recall a formula and perform simple substitutions in order to get a correct answer. The scoring of traditional achievement tests usually requires summing the number of correct items. Cognitive understandings of how students learn are not reflected in the traditional achievement tests. Advances in assessment include the use of performance tests that employ a variety of item types beyond the multiple-choice item format. New

conceptions of validity and reliability are being developed to reflect cognitive principles of learning (Linn et al. 1991). Assessment practices are being integrated with curriculum into adaptive instruction systems that can provide targeted remediation for students with learning difficulties (Wang 1987).

See also: Cognition and Learning; Human Development: Research and Educational Practice

References

Bandura A 1977 Self-efficacy: Toward a unifying theory of behavioral change. *Psychol. Rev.* 84: 191–215

Bennett S N 1978 Recent research on teaching: A dream, a belief and a model. *Br. J. Educ. Psychol* 48: 127–47

Bloom B S 1982 *Human Characteristics and School Learning.* McGraw Hill, New York

Bloom B S, Engelhart M D, Furst E J, Hill W H, Krathwohl D R 1977 *Taxonomy of Educational Objectives: The Classification of Educational Goals: Handbook I. Cognitive Domain.* Longmans Green, New York

Brophy J E, Good T L 1986 Teacher behavior and student achievement. In: Wittrock M C (ed.) 1986 *Handbook of Research on Teaching,* 3rd edn. Macmillan Inc., New York

Brown A Campione J, Day J E 1981 Psychological theory and the study of learning disabilities. *Educ. Researcher* 19(2): 119–22

Bruner J S 1966 *Toward a Theory of Instruction.* Belknap Press of Harvard University, Cambridge, Massachusetts

Carroll J B 1963 A model of school learning. *Teach. Coll. Rec.* 64: 723–33

Cross D R, Paris S G 1988 Developmental and instructional analyses of children's metacognition and reading comprehension. *J Educ. Psychol.* 80(2): 131–42

Davidson E S, Benjamin L T 1987 A history of the child study movement in America. In: Glover J A, Ronning R R (eds.) 1987 *Historical Foundations of Educational Psychology.* Plenum Press, New York

Erickson F 1986 Qualitative methods in research on teaching. In: Wittrock M C (ed.) 1986 *Handbook of Research on Teaching,* 3rd edn. Macmillan Inc., New York

Gagné R M 1965 *The Conditions of Learning.* Holt, Rinehart and Winston, New York

Glaser R 1976 Components of a psychology theory of instruction: Toward a science of design. *Rev. Educ. Res.* 46: 1–24

Glaser R 1991 Expertise and assessment. In: Wittrock M C, Baker E L (eds.) 1991 *Testing and Cognition.* Prentice Hall, Englewood Cliffs, New Jersey

Greeno J G 1980 Psychology of learning 1960–1980: One participant's observations. *Am. Psychol.* 35: 713–28

Grinder R E 1978 What 200 years tells us about professional priorities in educational psychology. *Educ. Psychol.* 12: 284–89

Harnischfeger A, Wiley D E 1976 The teaching—learning process in elementary schools: A synoptic view. *Curric. Inq.* 6: 5–43

Keller F 1968 Goodbye, teacher . . . *J. Appl. Behav. Anal.* 1: 79–89

Linn R L, Baker E L, Dunbar S B 1991 Complex, performance-based assessment: Expectations and validation criteria. *Educ. Researcher* 20(8): 15–21

Mager R F 1962 *Preparing Instructional Objectives.* Pitman Learning, Belmont, California

Manning B H 1991 *Cognitive Self-Instruction for Classroom Processes.* State University of New York Press, Albany, New York

McCombs B L 1991 The definition and measurement of primary motivational processes. In: Wittrock M C, Baker E L (eds.) 1991

Means B, Knapp M S (eds.) 1991 *Teaching Advanced Skills to Educationally Disadvantaged Students* (Final Report, Contract No. LC89089001). United States Department of Education, Washington, DC

Osborne R J, Gilbert J K 1980 A method for investigating concept understanding in science. *Eur. J. Sci. Educ.* 2(3): 311–21

Perkins D N, Simmons R 1988 Patterns of misunderstanding: An integrative model for science, math and programming. *Rev. Educ. Res.* 59(3): 303–26

Piaget J 1970 *Science of Education and Psychology of the Child.* Orion, New York

Resnick L B, Resnick D F 1989 Tests as standards of achievement in school. In: *Proc. of the 1989 Educational Testing Service Invitational Conf.: The Uses of Standardized Tests in American Education.* Educational Testing Service, Princeton, New Jersey

Schubert W H 1986 *Curriculum: Perspective, Paradigm, and Possibility.* Macmillan Inc., New York

Schwab J J 1969 The practical: A language for curriculum. *Sch. Rev.* 78: 1–23

Scriven M 1967 The methodology of curriculum evaluation. In: Tyler R, Gagné R M, Scriven M (eds.) 1967 *Perspectives of Curriculum Evaluation.* Rand McNally, Chicago, Illinois

Shuell T J 1980 Learning theory, instructional theory, and adaptation. In: Snow R E, Federico P A, Montague W E (eds.) 1980 *Aptitude, Learning and Instruction. Vol 2. Cognitive Process Analyses of Learning and Problem Solving.* Erlbaum, Hillsdale, New Jersey

Shulman L 1974 The psychology of school subjects: A premature obituary? *J. Res. Sci. Teach.* 11: 319–39

Skinner B F 1954 The science of learning and the art of teaching. *Harv. Educ. Rev.* 24: 86–97

Snow R E, Lohman D F 1989 Implications of cognitive psychology for educational measurement. In: Linn R L (ed.) 1989 *Educational Measurement,* 3rd edn. Ace and Macmillan, New York

Taba H 1967 *Teacher's Handbook for Elementary Social Studies.* Addison Wesley, Reading, Massachusetts

Vygotsky L S 1987 Thinking and speech. In: *The Collected Works of Vygotsky L S Vol 1 Problems of General Psychology.* Plenum Press, New York

Walberg H J 1984 Improving the productivity of America's schools. *Educ. Leadership* 41: 19–30

Walberg H J, Haertel G D 1992 Educational psychology's first century. *J. Educ. Psychol.* 84(1): 6–19

Wang M C 1987 The wedding of instruction and assessment in the classroom. In: *Proc. of the Educational Testing Service Invitational Conf.* Educational Testing Service, Princeton, New Jersey

Wang M C, Lindvall M 1984 *Individual Differences and School Learning Environments* (Report No. 1984132). University of Pittsburgh Learning Research and Development Center, Pittsburgh, Pennsylvania

Weiner B 1979 A theory of motivation for some classroom experiences. *J. Educ. Psychol.* 71(1): 3–25

Wood T 1995 From alternative epistemologies to practice in education: Rethinking what it means to teach and learn. In: Steffe L P, Gale J (eds.) 1995

Further Reading

Gardner H 1985 *The Mind's New Science: A History of the Cognitive Revolution.* Basic Books, New York

Resnick L 1987 *Education and Learning to Think.* National Academy Press, Washington, DC

Steffe L P, Gale J (eds.) 1995 *Constructivism in Education.* Erlbaum, Hillsdale, New Jersey

Wittrock M C, Baker E L (eds.) 1991 *Testing and Cognition.* Prentice Hall, Englewood Cliffs, New Jersey

Expert Knowledge and Performance

C. M. Zeitz and R. Glaser

Cognitive scientists have studied the phenomenon of expertise in order to understand the effects of acquired knowledge and extensive experience on human competence. As a result of this work there is a growing body of evidence about properties of expert performance. These findings are of particular significance for defining the characteristics of human cognitive attainment that can be acquired through effective educational practice.

1. The Organization of Experts' Knowledge

Experts develop an organization of knowledge that can be understood through examination of their memory performance, pattern recognition, and representation of problems, and by study of their adaptive use of procedures in solving problems in their domain.

1.1 Experts' Memory Performance

In their fields of knowledge, experts' memory is superior to that of novices' and exceeds what is generally accepted as the capacity of human working memory. To surpass this capacity, information must be integrated with structures in long-term memory so that it will be accessible when needed. Although the limits on human storage abilities are unknown, accessing information to which one has been exposed often fails. Experts' apparent circumvention of these limitations on memory has been demonstrated in such diverse domains of knowledge as computer programming, problem-solving in physics, clinical psychology, and electronic troubleshooting and teaching. Superior memory has even been demonstrated by experts who are children (see, for example, Chi et al. 1988).

Experts' exceptional memory abilities are domain-specific; that is, they display superior memory only for information concerning the content of their domain. For example, although Japanese abacus masters can store 16-digit strings in working memory, they demonstrate quite normal memory spans (i.e., of around seven items) for fruit names or English letters presented orally and rapidly (Hatano and Osawa 1983). The key to this paradox is the way experts' knowledge is organized; their knowledge bases are hierarchical and densely interconnected. This organization allows new pieces of information to become well-integrated, which in turn facilitates recall. Novices lack a well-structured system of knowledge from which inferences can be made for the domain; they are easily overwhelmed by new information, because to them it is a large number of weakly connected items.

1.2 Pattern Recognition

The organization of experts' knowledge is also evident in their rapid recognition of patterns, which enables the accurate recall of organized information and the swift integration of complex data. Domain-relevant content must consist of meaningful configurations if it is to engage experts' special pattern-recognition abilities. In a classic experiment involving chess pieces arranged as they might be in the course of an actual game (De Groot 1966; Chase and Simon 1973), experts recalled the positions of many more pieces than novices. However, the experts' recall superiority was disrupted when they were presented with configurations that were impossible or meaningless, according to the rules of chess. Apparently experts' knowledge bases allow them to recode stimuli in their domain; that is, to encode information in a reorganized form that reflects the structure of the domain. Chess experts chunk a number of pieces together into a meaningful pattern, whereas novices' basic unit of recall is a single or few game pieces. When chess pieces are placed randomly on a board, experts' performance deteriorates because they cannot recognize familiar, meaningful patterns.

When an expert recognizes a familiar pattern of information, related knowledge chunks and implications for action are activated to aid in problem-solving. This ability to absorb and evaluate large quantities of information and then generate accurate solutions can happen so rapidly that it appears that the expert has some special intuition or sixth sense (Simon 1981).

1.3 The Extent of Expert knowledge

Simon (1981) estimated that the number of familiar chunks of game-related information in a chess master's long-term memory is approximately 50,000, a number of the same order of magnitude as the number of words a college-educated reader recognizes. Roughly the same number of chunks of information seem to be required for expertise in a variety of domains (e.g., medicine, mathematics, and chemistry), and about 10 years of devoted effort seems to be required to accumulate this large a store of information in a discipline. All chess grandmasters have spent nearly a decade or more achieving this status—a decade of study and practice appears to be necessary to achieve top professional proficiency in other domains as well (Simon 1981).

Although the amount of information to be acquired in a discipline may appear to become increasingly daunting as more and more knowledge is accumulated over time, it may in fact remain relatively constant. According to Simon (1981) "Some of the most important progress in science is the discovery and testing of powerful new theories that allow large numbers of facts to be subsumed under a few general principles. There is a constant competition between the elaboration of knowledge and its compression into more parsimonious form by theories" (p. 109). In fact, experts rely heavily on abstract principles to organize their own large knowledge stores, and this is reflected in experts' problem-solving performance.

1.4 Problem Representation

The degree of organization of an individual's knowledge base determines the quality of that person's initial representation of a problem. (A problem representation is basically a working mental model of a situation.) Experts' experience in their domain results in the development of a hierarchically organized knowledge base with at least two levels. A basic level facilitates literal, detailed representations that are comparable to novices' representations. A second, more abstract, principled level is removed from concrete literal detail. It is this second level that is the source of many differences between expert and novice. In the development of expertise, a shift occurs from a literal, surface-based system of representation to a more abstract one. This parallels a shift that ocurs in child development, from verbatim representations to gist representations (Brainerd and Reyna 1993) Novices' knowledge enables only a surface-based problem representation consisting mostly of the objects and features explicitly presented in the situation. For example, novices classify introductory physics problems as, say, inclined plane problems or pulley problems. Their ability to address problems follows from this representation. Their solution procedures are syntactic and specific—they often attempt to translate given problem statements directly into equations for solution. In contrast, experts' knowledge organization enables them to represent the problem in a deeper way. For example, a mechanics problem for them is characterized by the relevant implicit physics concepts: the forces involved, the relationships among them, and the principles that pertain to these interrelationships. Experts derive these features, which are not mentioned in the problem description, and use them in classifying problems. Because the experts' representations are based on principles, such as conservation of energy or Newton's second law, they entail appropriate and more generalizable solution procedures (Chi et al. 1981).

Although experts are faster problem-solvers overall, they proceed more slowly than novices in initially encoding a problem. For example, in solving textbook physics problems, they translate problem statements into spatial, abstract representations that may be explicitly manifested in the drawing of a free-body diagram (Larkin et al. 1980). In attacking a problem, experts qualitatively assess its nature, building a mental model or representation from which they can make inferences and add constraints to reduce the problem space.

1.5 The Proceduralization of Experts' Knowledge

An expert's knowledge differs from a novice's in that much of it may be proceduralized. Knowledge can be divided into two categories: declarative knowledge, which consists of factual information, and procedural knowledge, which embodies appropriate uses of declarative knowledge. Procedural knowledge takes the following form: "if certain conditions are met, then certain actions should be performed." Experience in using domain knowledge causes experts' declarative knowledge to become linked to information about conditions where it is applicable. In contrast, novices may know a principle, rule, or specialized vocabulary without knowing the conditions where that knowledge applies or how it can be used most efficiently.

After much practice and experience, experts carry out procedures quickly and without draining attentional resources. The benefits of this automaticity in performance of certain aspects of a task are apparent in numerous domains. For example, skilled readers decode words with little conscious thought and, as a result, can devote attention to interpreting the meaning of a text. In general, in the development of proficiency with attention-demanding complex tasks, some component skills become automatic, so that conscious processing capacity can be devoted to reasoning and reflective thought with minimal interference in the overall performance. These component skills are automatically triggered by recurring situations in the expert's own area and help explain why expertise is domain-specific.

All expert performance is comprised partly of these routinized procedures. However, routine execution of automatic task components may comprise a larger or smaller part of different forms of expertise. For example, an expert typist using familiar equipment may rely almost entirely on automatic skills, whereas an expert philosopher trying to develop a new theory may have few applicable routinized procedures available. Moreover, when experts encounter situations that offer variable conditions of performance, they must plan and apply their knowledge in adaptive ways. The adaptability of the competence that individual experts develop is a function of the task demands they have encountered (Hatano and Inagaki 1986).

Through their extensive experience, experts develop a critical set of self-regulatory or metacognitive skills, which controls their performance. For example, expert physicists adroitly monitor their problem-solving by predicting the difficulty of problems, allocating time appropriately, noting their errors or failures to comprehend, and checking questionable solutions (Larkin et al. 1980). Novices lack understanding of task demands in a new domain and how these match their capabilities, and this prevents them from tackling problems in a planned, organized manner. When they reach an intermediate stage in learning, they give many signs of metacognition: they plan steps effortfully and explicitly before executing them and evaluate them afterward (Simon and Simon 1978). By the time they become experts, these self-monitoring skills will be so well-practiced that they are automatic (Brown and DeLoache 1978).

2. Expertise in Ill-structured Domains

The picture of expertise described so far is derived from studies of problem-solving in well-structured domains, which have quantitative, well-defined rules and clear methods for assessing progress as well as criteria for good and poor solutions. Other domains, especially those in the humanities and social sciences, do not entail such rules, methods, or criteria and can be characterized as ill-structured. Experts in these domains apply themselves to open-ended questions, for which agreed-upon solution evaluation procedures do not exist.

Recent work on expertise in less structured domains has produced a number of findings. One general observation is that experts in ill-structured domains appear to impose constraints on problems in order to make them tractable, and then expend extra effort in defending their approaches, because objective methods of evaluation are unavailable. In addition, experts in ill-structured domains excel at building higher-level representations through the detection of relationships and integration of ideas.

2.1 Imposition of Constraints

A thorough initial analysis of a problem, involving the addition of constraints, is critical in domains

507

such as history or political science, where formal principles or laws do not obtain. In the absence of problem representations that imply direct paths to solutions, elaborations of the problem situation guide solution processes. Asked what measures might have increased productivity in the former Soviet Union, the expert political scientist might begin with consideration of political and geographical factors, thereby raising such issues as the requirements of collectivization and the distribution of arable land. This initial analysis constrains the problem space and precludes discussion of inapplicable solutions that would involve private competition or increased cultivation in certain regions (Voss and Post 1988). Thus, the ability to transform ill-defined questions so that they more closely approximate well-defined problems is one of the skills required of experts in ill-structured domains.

2.2 Justification of Solutions

A second important aspect of expertise in ill-structured domains is the justification of proposed solutions. Argumentation skills are an indispensable component of expertise in domains where there are few generally agreed-upon solutions and no algorithmic proof methods. Studies show that social science experts draw on their knowledge to state a history of previous attempts at a solution and use this as a basis for extensive arguments to support their solutions to problems. Novices in the domain, who cannot access and utilize a well-organized knowledge base for the domain, produce weak support for their claims (Voss and Post 1988). Similarly, experts in literature, when analyzing a text, provide extensive evidence to support their interpretations. Unlike novices, who merely offer simple individual assertions to support their claims directly, experts in literature build up complex arguments, presenting ideas that work together to support more general ideas, which are then used to support their opinions (Zeitz 1994).

2.3 Derived Representations

Experts seem to rely heavily on representations that integrate abstract concepts and situation-specific features in ill-structured domains. Schmidt et al. (1989) compared expert and novice strategies for understanding paintings. The analyses of experts subsumed both formal elements and painting subject matter. Novices emphasized the discernible semantic features or content of paintings more than the formal elements (e.g., line, color, shape). Similar findings regarding the differences between the representations of experts and novices come from a study where they expressed their understanding of works of literature. The two levels of experts' representations for literary texts found in this study are analogous to the feature-based and principle-based levels of representation in phys-

ics. Upon reading a literary text, experts and novices both produced *basic* representations of comparable quality that included characters, events, and the relationships between them that were explicitly stated. In contrast, experts' and novices' *derived* representations varied greatly: these entailed higher-level semantic or conceptual structures (termed "macrostructures" by Kintsch and van Dijk 1978) such as themes that organized the text features. Experts' derived representations contained many connections to the basic representation of the text, to the derived representation for other texts, and to more abstract concepts such as themes, style, genre, literary devices, symbol systems, and so forth. By contrast, novices' higher-level representations were sparse and poorly interconnected (Zeitz 1994). These differences in representation are reflected also in the finding that experts have superior memory for sentences that contain meanings beyond those literally stated, although their memories are equivalent to those of novices for simple plot statements. This reliance by experts in ill-structured domains on integrative, conceptual representations that subsume the surface-level features that novices focus on is directly comparable to findings from studies of the problem representations of experts in well-structured domains.

3. Educational Implications

Cognitive analyses of experts' performance suggest ways in which the level of understanding that underlies expertise can be fostered. Three methods of cultivating aspects of expertise are considered here: the development of organized knowledge, the development of usable knowledge through conditions of practice, and innovative approaches to assessment.

3.1 Knowledge Scaffolding

Providing learners with a framework or scaffolding to which they can attach more detailed levels of new information in order to form a coherent, fleshed-out structure can enhance both knowledge organization and proceduralization (Kieras and Bovair 1984). In introducing a domain of knowledge, first a meaningful framework can be provided in the form of an explanation of a key aspect of expert domain knowledge, such as a principled description of a physics problem or a derived theme of a piece of literature. This overarching explanation can then be elaborated upon, one level at a time, until the details have been described. This contrasts with traditional forms of teaching, based on decomposition, in which the attempt is made to build up understanding from explanations of each of the lowest level elements in the system, with the elements being combined at successively higher levels until, eventually, the structure of the entire system or domain has been described. The crucial importance of principled or derived representations in experts' performances suggests that decomposition may not be the best starting point for instruction. In fact, when novice learners are initially presented with an overview of material to be learned, their knowledge is more hierarchically organized and their performance is more automatic than novices who learn the same material in a bottom-up sequence (Zeitz and Spoehr 1989). Too often the bits of information supplied by teacher and textbook explanations in bottom-up fashion do not encourage students to construct organized knowledge that is usable for thinking and principled performance.

3.2 Effective Practice

One sign of successful knowledge structuring is proceduralization. The transmission of procedural knowledge needs to be a goal of education, because it is an essential component of experts' efficient performance. Teaching can be most effective in the context of useful problem-solving, which both emphasizes the conditions of applicability for information and gives students ample opportunities to practice applying new knowledge. Obviously, expert performance is achieved only through a long period of practice. However, practice, as it comes about in the usual course of training, is not necessarily very efficient. The development of expert performance depends on a long process of *deliberate practice* that emphasizes monitoring performance and improving weaknesses (Ericsson et al. 1988). Deliberate practice requires a great deal of effort and attention, and is not inherently enjoyable; instead it is motivated by the goal of improving performance. As the course the course of the emergence of specific aspects of competence is understood, it becomes possible to design ways to present experiences systematically so as to be maximally informative and encourage adaptability.

It is known, for example, that when low-level skills become automatic, it frees the learner to devote more cognitive resources to higher-level processes. As students practice new skills that are candidates for automatic performance, it may be possible, by assessing them when high-level tasks have to be carried out concurrently, to determine whether they can be executed with minimal use of working memory. Guided practice of this kind might be most helpful in domains in which complex patterns must be perceived and where recognition of these patterns implies particular moves and procedures for solution. An organized sequence of increasingly complex pattern-recognition tasks that provides guidance on procedures has been designed for technical training of certain aspects of air traffic control (Schneider 1985), geometry (Koedinger and Anderson 1990), and electronic troubleshooting (Lesgold et al. 1992). Trainees in these fields attain proficiency and automaticity in skills in a small fraction of the hours of practice usually required by training or on-the-job experience.

A major principle underlying the acquisition of competence is a change in the agency for learning as expertise develops and performance improves (Glaser in press). Initially, learning involves a significant degree of external support through environmental scaffolding and apprenticeship arrangements. These arrangements offer guided practice that fosters self-monitoring and the learning of self-regulatory skills, and the identification and discrimination of standards and criteria for high levels of performance. In later phases of competence, much of the design of the learning environment is under the control of the learner as a developing expert. The conditions of practice are arranged so that performers can obtain feedback on their own performance and so that appropriately challenging situations are available or can be designed. There is very selective use of external support with the performer calling upon competitors, performance situations, and the advice of teachers and coaches as particularly needed. To reach the highest levels of performance, experts must learn to create learning environments for themselves that are conducive to practice without the guidance of tutors

3.3 Assessing Level of Understanding

Developing and assessing the components of expertise require the evaluation of a much broader set of activities than is traditionally considered. Instead of focusing only on final solutions, situations in which students make their problem representations explicit might be designed so that assessment of the depth of their understanding is possible (Silver et al. 1990). It is important to discern whether students can represent problems at the basic level only or whether their representations have begun to approximate expert representations through the inclusion of derived features, principles, and themes. An ability to recognize and use underlying principles and patterns appropriately is an indication of developing procedural knowledge, and assessment situations could be designed to capture such evidence. To discourage the rote application of formulas, students could be challenged with ill-structured problems. The thoroughness of their initial analysis and the validity of the constraints they impose on the problem could be scrutinized. Students could be given the opportunity to explain their answers and develop arguments to defend their points of view. Hallmarks of expertise, such as effective support of arguments and the ability to combine observations into coherent themes, could serve as bases for appraising more complete responses. Moreover, assessment exercises can be designed both to communicate the importance of these processes and to provide students with opportunities to practice them.

Expert performance defines the end goals of instruction and therefore informs, to some extent, the nature of instruction required to instill expertise. Of course, entire curricula cannot be based solely on theories of expertise, because students are not just empty experts. Students have certain kinds of initial competence that instruction can build on. Often they have deep-rooted misconceptions that must be discovered and eradicated. For these reasons it is important to acquire more knowledge in future research about the intermediate stages on the road between the learner's "entry situation" and expertise. For example, some research suggests that as expertise develops, as in the course of child development, level of performance may not be a monotone function of experience. In difficult situations, learners at an intermediate stage may perform worse than both experts and learners with much less experience, because of the transitional state of their knowledge structures.

Given the growing body of information about human competence, the emphasis in educational practice is shifting from the accumulation of facts and their reinforcement through didactic instruction to forms of teaching that foster the acquisition of structured and coherent knowledge that can be used in problem-solving, reasoning, and high levels of performance. If education is to reap the benefits of research on human performance, instruction must become responsive to changes in structures and processes that occur as individuals move from beginning to advanced learners. Educational innovations such as teaching in the context of a meaningful framework, fostering proceduralization of knowledge, and accurately assessing knowledge structures may facilitate students' progression toward the expert level of understanding.

See also: Declarative and Procedural Knowledge; Knowledge Representation and Organization; Metacognition; Prior Knowledge and Learning; Problem-solving and Thinking, Development of Learning Skills in; Reasoning; Assessment in the Service of Learning; Memory, Teaching and Testing for; Memory Development

References

Brainerd D J, Reyna R F 1993 Memory independence and memory interference in cognitive development. *Psychol. Rev.* 100:42–67

Brown A L, DeLoache J S 1978 Skills, plans and self-regulation. In: Siegler R (ed.) 1978 *Children's Thinking: What Develops?* Erlbaum, Hillsdale, New Jersey

Chase W G, Simon H A 1973 Perception in chess. *Cognit. Psychol.* 4(1): 55–81

Chi M T H, Feltovich P J, Glaser R 1981 Categorization and representation of physics problems by experts and novices. *Cognit. Sci.* 5: 121–152

Chi M T H, Glaser R, Farr M (eds.) 1988 *The Nature of Expertise.* Erlbaum, Hillsdale, New Jersey

De Groot A 1966 Perception and memory versus thought: Some old ideas and recent findings. In: Kleinmuntz B (ed.) 1966 *Problem Solving: Research, Method, and Theory.* Wiley, New York

Ericsson A, Krampe R Th, Tesch-Romer C 1993 The role of deliberate practice in the acquisition of expert performance. *Psychol. Rev.* 100:363–406

Glaser R in press Changing the agency for learning: Acquiring expert performance. In: Ericsson A (ed.) in press *The Road to Expert Performance: Empirical Evidence from the Arts and Sciences, Sports, and Games.* Erlbaum, Mahwa, New Jersey

Hatano G, Inagaki K 1986 Two courses of expertise. In: Stevenson H, Azuma H, Hakuta K (eds.) 1986 *Child Development and Education in Japan.* W H Freeman, New York

Hatano G, Osawa K 1983 Digit memory of grand experts in abacus-derived mental calculation. *Cognition* 15: 95–110

Kieras D E, Bovair S 1984 The role of a mental model in learning to operate a device. *Cognit. Sci.* 8(3): 255–73

Kintsch W, van Dijk T A 1978 Toward a model of text comprehension and production. *Psychol. Rev.* 85(5): 363–94

Koedinger K R, Anderson J R 1990 Abstract planning and perceptual chunks: Elements of expertise in geometry. *Cognit. Sci.* 14: 511–50

Larkin J H, McDermott J, Simon D P, Simon H A 1980 Expert and novice performance in solving physics problems. *Science* 208: 1335–42

Lesgold A M, Lajoie S P, Logan D, Eggan G 1992 SHERLOCK: A coached practice environment for an electronics troubleshooting job. In: Larkin J, Chabay R (eds.) 1992 *Computer-assisted Instruction and Intelligent Tutoring Systems: Shared Goals and Complimentary Approaches.* Erlbaum, Hillsdale, New Jersey

Schmidt J A, McLaughlin J P, Leighten P 1989 Novice strategies for understanding paintings. *Applied Cognitive Psychol.* 3(1): 65–72

Schneider W 1985 Training high performance skills: Fallacies and guidelines. *Human Factors* 27(3): 285–300

Silver E A, Kilpatrick J, Schlesinger B 1990 *Thinking through Mathematics: Fostering Inquiry and Communication in Mathematics Classrooms.* The College Entrance Examination Board, New York

Simon D P, Simon H A 1978 Individual differences in solving physics problems. In: Siegler R (ed.) 1978 *Children's Thinking: What Develops?* Erlbaum, Hillsdale, New Jersey

Simon H A 1981 *The Sciences of the Artificial*, 2nd edn. MIT Press, Cambridge, Massachusetts

Voss J F, Post T A 1988 On the solving of ill-structured problems. In: Chi M T H, Glaser R, Farr M (eds.) 1988 *The Nature of Expertise.* Erlbaum, Hillsdale, New Jersey

Zeitz C M 1994 Expert–novice differences in memory, abstraction and reasoning in the domain of literature. *Cognition and Instruction.* 12(4): 277–312

Zeitz C M, Spoehr K T 1989 Knowledge organization and the acquisition of procedural expertise. *Applied Cognitive Psychol.* 3(4): 313–36

Foreign Language Acquisition, Process of

M. H. Long

One of the most salient differences between first language acquisition by young children and foreign language acquisition (FLA) by older children or adults is the near-uniform success of the former and the highly variable outcome, frequently amounting to failure, of the latter. The aim of much FLA research is to account for this difference. Why is it that children with IQs ranging from 70 to 130 exhibit normal first language (L1) development, attain similar standards, and do so at roughly the same pace, whereas many intelligent, motivated, and otherwise successful adults seem unable to progress beyond "intermediate" levels in a second or third language, despite the advantage that learning their native tongue might be expected to convey? Why is it, moreover, that large differences in achievement are often observed within a group of foreign language students with similar learning opportunities inside and outside the classroom? Most researchers agree that both phenomena are produced by a combination of learner differences and environmental factors. Exactly which variables are causal is still controversial, however, as are some of the claimed implications for language teaching.

1. FLA and Second Language Acquisition

In much of the literature on child and adult language learning, a distinction is made between *foreign* language acquisition (FLA) and *second* language acquisition (SLA). In FLA, the target language is studied in a formal instructional setting, typically a classroom, in a society in which that language is not normally used as a means of communication (e.g., French in an Australian secondary school, or English at a Japanese university). In SLA, a new language is learned without the aid of formal instruction, through naturalistic exposure, perhaps by long-term residence in a society where the language is spoken (e.g., German by a Japanese child attending a German kindergarden in Munich, or French or English by a Chilean refugee working in Canada). The distinction draws attention to broader sociolinguistic features of the two learning situations, and to factors impinging on pedagogical options and choices in FL and SL settings, such as the likely differences in learners' communicative needs in the new language, in their motivation to learn, and in the types of language practice opportunities available to them outside the classroom.

2. Interlanguage Development

Differences between FLA and SLA notwithstanding, it is important to recognize that when explicit comparisons are made between FL and SL acquisition processes (i.e., how learners in either setting develop knowledge of the new language), similarities are more striking than differences. This has been established on the basis of detailed studies of interlanguage development.

An interlanguage (IL) is the individual FL or SL acquirer's version of the target language, complete with correct and incorrect forms. Interlanguages are systematic (i.e., rule-governed), as shown by errors like "The children*s* go*ed* their houses," but also variable. The variability is diachronic: ILs change over time as the learner's knowledge grows. It is also synchronic: the learner's performance varies at any one time as a function of topic, immediate linguistic context, and interlocutor, and of various dimensions of task difficulty, including familiarity, linguistic and cognitive requirements, processing demands, memory load, and attentional focus (Hulstijn 1989, Preston 1989, Tarone 1988). Acquisition processes are revealed among other ways by IL development are revealed among other ways by the kinds of errors learners make, the developmental sequences they traverse, and the influence of their first language.

2.1 Error Types

In a major comparison of FLA and SLA, Pica (1983) studied IL samples of three groups of adult Spanish speakers: (a) taking English classes in Mexico, (b) learning English while working in the United States, and (c) taking English classes while living in the United States, (i.e., FL, SL, and "mixed" learners, respectively). Pica examined transcripts of the learners' speech during conversations with a native speaker of English. She found that, despite the differences in setting, each group was developing control of a set of grammatical morphemes ("-ing," plural "-s," copula, auxiliary, article, irregular past, regular past "-ed," third person singular "-s," and possessive "'s") in roughly the same order, as evidenced by the accuracy with which they supplied those items in obligatory and nonobligatory contexts (and despite the fact that this was not the order in which the FL group was taught the items). She also found that, whether they had received formal instruction, all learners made errors of three broad types: omission ("The dog chase__the two boy__"), overgeneralization ("He buy*ed* a car yesterday"), and overuse ("I don't understand*ing* this story").

There was some evidence of beneficial effects of instruction for the FL group in Pica's study, however. The classroom learners were more accurate in their suppliance of two of the nine forms, the semantically transparent, monofunctional plural "-s" and third person singular "-s" morphemes. Also, naturalistic (SL) learners omitted obligatory items more frequently, while classroom (FL) learners overapplied morphological marking (through overgeneralization and overuse errors) significantly more often than SL learners at almost all proficiency levels. Mixed learners behaved more like the SL learners at lower proficiency levels, and more like FL learners at higher levels. In sum, it seems that, while formal instruction initially results in higher frequencies of some kinds of errors, instructed learners are at least more aware of the existence of the forms which give rise to the errors. Their attempts to learn how to use them begin earlier. Second language learners take longer to start those aspects of development, and as later studies have shown, may never start unless their attention is drawn to the items through instruction or some other means. Showing that the route of development is little affected by instruction, in other words, does not mean that instruction is not beneficial.

2.2 Developmental Sequences

Both FL and SL acquirers make numerous errors—which is now recognized as an inevitable and continuous part of the foreign language learning (FLL) process, just as it is a crucial part of child L1 acquisition—and errors of the same three basic types. They also all progress through fixed series of stages, known as developmental sequences, in learning particular linguistic subsystems, such as word order, negation, or relative clauses. In learning English negation, for example, when spontaneous, communicative IL samples (rather than test data) are examined, it is seen that both FL and SL learners go through the same four-stage sequence, defined in terms of placement of the utterance negator:

Stage		Sample utterance
1	External	No that one/No you eating here
2	Internal, preverbal	Carlos no/don't have job
3	Auxiliary + negator	I can't sing well
4	Analyzed *don't*	She doesn't like coffee

The sequence is not altered by the fact that teachers and textbooks model the target version (Stage 4) from day one. Nor is it affected by the shape of negation in the learner's L1. Spanish speakers, with preverbal negation, and Japanese learners, with postverbal negation, both go through the same four stages. Turkish speakers, who have postverbal negation, also start with preverbal negation when learning Swedish in a mixed setting, even though Swedish negation is postverbal (Hyltenstam 1977).

The series of stages FL and SL learners traverse has been reported to be the same (i.e., not altered by instruction) by many other researchers. Developmental sequences for negation, interrogatives, and verb phrase morphology exhibited by three Punjabi-speaking children (aged 10–13) learning English in

special language classes in United Kingdom schools were found to be virtually identical to those reported for naturalistic learners. In a secondary school FL setting, similar results were obtained for German secondary school pupils' English negation, interrogatives, sentence types, and pronouns. In adult FLA, Pienemann (1989) and Ellis (1989) reported that students of German in Australian and English universities passed through the same six-stage sequence for German word order, regardless of the instructional sequence for the various word orders, the pedagogic or textbook focus, or the frequency with which they occurred in teacher speech. Once again, however, while not altering the sequence, form-focused instruction was found to be beneficial in another study of mixed learners (Pienemann 1984), speeding up the rate at which 7- to 9- year old Italian children in Munich traversed the sequence, increasing the frequency with which they supplied the structure, and widening the range of contexts in which it was used.

2.3 Role of the Native Language

While not changing the basic stages in developmental sequences, a learner's native language can affect development in other ways. First, the rate of passage through a sequence can be slowed when a developmental stage is similar to an L1 structure, or speeded up when it is not. Spanish speakers take longer than Japanese to abandon the preverbal (Stage 1) negation structure, for example. Second, substages are sometimes added to an otherwise unaffected sequence for the same reason, as when German learners of English, on reaching Stage 3 (auxiliary + negator), extend this to main verbs, producing sentences like "I play not the guitar," which would be grammatical in German.

Relationships between the learner's L1 and the FL can also affect whether particular linguistic features will be problematic, including whether they can be learned by positive evidence alone (i.e., just by exposure to the target language), or whether negative evidence of some kind will be needed. White (1991) points out that in principle, for example, an English speaker can learn that adverbs can be placed between verb and object in French simply by encountering examples of this in the input (positive evidence). A French learner of English, however, already believes verb–adverb–object strings are possible (because they are possible in French), and has to "unlearn" the French option by noticing its absence in English. This rarely, if ever, happens, as evidenced by the persistence of utterances like "I took *very often* the bus" in the ILs of advanced speakers. They will need negative evidence of some kind (e.g., a grammar lesson or overt error correction), if they are to move from a more inclusive L1 rule to a more restrictive FL one. (White found that French-speaking children learning English as a FL in Quebec who received form-focused instruction on the rule improved in accuracy in adverb placement, whereas comparison groups did not.)

The L1 can also influence the range of hypotheses learners will entertain as to what may transfer successfully. Specifically, transfer will depend in part on whether the learner perceives an L1 construction to be "marked" (in the sense of unusual or atypical), or highly idiomatic, and so probably unique to that language. In one study, Dutch learners of English thought more literal Dutch idioms using "break" (e.g., "he broke his leg" and "the waves broke on the rocks") were more likely to be acceptable in English than the more metaphorical "they broke the strike" and "it breaks up the day." Finally, regardless of learner intuitions about markedness, whether an L1 structure actually is more or less marked than the FL equivalent has often been found to determine the degree of difficulty students will have with the structure. Cases where the L1 is unmarked and the L2 marked are more likely to cause error. Contrary to the predictions of the Contrastive Analysis Hypothesis, differences between L1 and FL do not necessarily result in difficulty. As the above examples illustrate, it depends on which one of a language pair is being learned and on the kind of difference involved.

As with error types and frequencies, and developmental sequences, the five categories of L1 influence on interlanguage development apply across acquisition setting (FL, SL, or mixed), and learner age (children or adults). If the similarities are due, as most would accept, to universals in human cognitive processes, perception, memory, and attention, it remains to explain the often wide differences in attainment using these common human abilities. Why should equivalently endowed children and adults achieve differently, and why should there be within-group differences in children or adults learning under the same conditions?

3. Learner Differences

In the domain of learner differences, both cognitive and affective factors are believed to explain variance in foreign language achievement. The most commonly implicated cognitive factors are the learner's age at the time of first exposure to the new language (age of onset), language learning aptitude, and attention, although several cognitive styles have their champions. Affective and social–psychological variables showing some support in the literature are personality traits (especially extroversion and anxiety), social attitudes, and motivation. Little is known about interactions among variables of each type.

3.1 Cognitive Variables

"Age of onset" has been the subject of almost 100 studies in foreign and second language learning. While still a controversial issue, reviews have tended to conclude that if short-term (rate) and long-term (ultimate attainment) studies are distinguished, (a) adults traverse early stages of morphological and syntactic development faster than children (holding time and exposure constant); (b) older children proceed faster than younger children through those stages, again controlling for time and exposure; (c) child starters catch up and outperform adult starters in the long run; and (d) only child starters can attain native-like levels of proficiency in the new language. Just how young the "child" in (c) and (d) must be, and which aspects of language development are affected, are still unclear. For example, it has been claimed that puberty is the cut-off point and that only phonology is affected (Scovel 1988), that there is a series of sensitive periods starting at age 6 for phonology and closing in the mid-teens for syntax (Long 1990), and that age 6 is critical for all linguistic domains (Hyltenstam 1992).

Explanations for age effects are equally diverse, with affective, input, cognitive, and neurobiological differences between younger and older learners each having their supporters. Given periodic announcements of claimed counterevidence to all these claims in the form of superlearners who began a foreign language as adults and yet have supposedly attained native-like proficiency, it is safe to assume that research on the topic will continue. Some late starters can and do attain extremely high proficiency. Such learners are clearly exceptional, however. Hence, if educational goals are ambitious, wider societal factors (e.g., financial and human resources) do not limit choice in any way, and a worthwhile program can be offered, an early start on foreign languages is indicated. In the short run a language may be most efficiently taught, in terms of rate of development, starting at around age 9, but if something close to native-like proficiency is ultimately needed, beginning as early as the first year of elementary school will probably be necessary.

"Aptitude" refers to the potential, or set of special abilities, innate and/or acquired, an individual has for learning or doing something. As measured by the five sections of the Modern Language Aptitude Test (MLAT, Carroll and Sapon 1959), language learning aptitude has four principle components. Phonetic Coding Ability is the ability to discriminate among foreign sounds and associate them with their written representations. Grammatical Sensitivity is the ability to recognize the grammatical functions of words and other linguistic units in sentences. Inductive Language Learning Ability is the ability to discern semantic or syntactic relationships in linguistic input. Rote Learning Ability is the ability to memorize lists of new vocabulary items and their native language equivalents. Over 20 studies have reported positive correlations between scores on these and other aptitude tests or their subtests and performance on a range of linguistically focused and communicative FL tests, typically accounting for between 16 and 36 percent of the variance in the criterion measures (for review, see Skehan 1989). Several FLL researchers have employed aptitude as a successful predictor variable in their work. It has been found to share some common variance with intelligence—as much as 45 percent in one study—but also to have unique variance associated with it, particularly the phonemic coding ability and memory components.

An interesting question concerns the extent to which aptitude is innate or acquired. If acquired, it may be trainable, and thus a means of improving the effectiveness of language teaching. In the early 1990s, the (inadequate) available evidence suggests that aptitude is mostly innate and stable and little influenced by language learning experience (Skehan 1989). There is a need, however, for research to determine whether some dimensions may be improvable, as the proliferation of books on "how to learn a FL," "successful language learning strategies," and "learning to learn" would imply was already known. Meanwhile, the predictive capacity of aptitude measures has led to their common use in some educational settings (e.g., the military) for screening individuals into and out of language courses and/or supposedly easier and harder FLs. Instruction might be improved by grouping learners according to aptitude, thereby allowing the pace of instruction to vary appropriately. It might also be useful to adjust pedagogy and materials according to students' scores on subsections of aptitude tests (e.g., offering more analytically oriented instruction to learners doing well on the Grammatical Sensitivity MLAT subtest; more gestalt-oriented instruction to those scoring high on sections measuring Inductive Language Learning Ability, etc.). This last suggestion is controversial, however. It is not justified by the current state of knowledge concerning aptitude, and all FL learners presumably need to use both analytical and inductive abilities, processes which are not mutually exclusive.

Several cognitive styles have been postulated as relevant to FLL. In contrast to abilities such as intelligence or memory, possession of which are valued positively, styles are stable bipolar traits, such as reflectivity/impulsivity, (narrow/wide) category width, aural/visual, field dependence/independence, and analytic/gestalt, reflecting differences among individuals, but (supposedly) not greater or lesser merit or ability.

Field dependence/independence (FD/FI), the only style to have been subjected to much empirical study in the FL context, concerns differences in the way people approach and process new information, experiences, and problems (e.g., foreign language learning) (for critical review see Chapelle and Green 1992, Griffiths and Sheen 1992). It began as the construct claimed to underlie the ability of pilots in a laboratory setting to perceive the true (gravitational) upright when deliberately disoriented, and was later extended to other aspects of visual perception, including the ability to

separate figure from ground in a visual display. It is assessed by a variety of measures, often of low reliability or validity, frequently the Embedded Figures Test (EFT). People who do well on the EFT and related tests are FI (i.e., analytically oriented), able to distinguish important material from distracting detail. People who are poor at perceiving target shapes in a drawing (spotting monkeys in a tree, a triangle buried in a collage of geometric shapes) are FD (i.e., holistically oriented), less able to attend selectively to incoming stimuli. Personality correlates are sometimes also claimed. People categorized as FI are believed to be more confident, self-reliant, impersonal, detached, demanding, inconsiderate, and less sensitive to others. Individuals classed as FD are claimed to be more sensitive, tactful, outgoing, gregarious, warm, affectionate, uncertain, and dependent on others. (The use of such judgmental terms is not value-free, of course, and the frequent reference to "ability" in defining "style" suggests that, at least in this case, the style/ability distinction may not be tenable.)

Researchers have reported low to moderate positive correlations between FI and performance on various kinds of FL proficiency tests. The association has tended to disappear, however, when some direct or indirect measure (e.g., maths test scores or general scholastic ability) has been used to partial out intelligence, suggesting that the EFT may really be a surrogate intelligence measure. In fact, most psychologists now believe that FI is really a reflection of fluid intelligence, the set of analytic abilities applicable to any new task that is independent of prior knowledge (e.g., the ability to attend to new stimuli while remembering something else, or to find and compare things at speed). Fluid intelligence contrasts with crystallized intelligence (i.e., learned knowledge or abilities in a content area, such as maths or a foreign language). This would make FI/FD an ability, not a style. Everyone is analytic; when confronted with a new task, some people are better at analyzing than others. In sum, uncertainty about the original theoretical underpinnings of FD/FI; the construct's reconceptualization by psychologists as a manifestation of fluid intelligence, and as an ability, not a style; problems with the reliability and validity of the EFT and other measures; and the weak and inconsistent results of FL studies, have combined to produce growing skepticism about the existence of a relationship between FD/FI and FLL (Skehan 1989, Chappelle and Green 1992, Griffiths and Sheen 1992).

3.2 Affective and Social–Psychological Variables

In the affective domain, several personality variables have been claimed to be relevant for FLL, including empathy, self-esteem, sensitivity to rejection, inhibition, tolerance of ambiguity, extroversion, and anxiety. Of these, extroversion and anxiety have received most attention.

Extroversion is generally conceived as involving two broad components, sociability and impulsivity. While introversion has been related to success in other types of learning, approximately 20 FL studies have examined extroversion as more likely to be beneficial, the assumption being that sociability will lead to greater contact with speakers of the target language, and that this in turn will produce more input, interaction, or output, some or all of which theorists consider beneficial to language learning. Results have been very mixed. An effect is found in only about half the studies, and it is weak, accounting for little variance. Skehan (1989) points out that a positive association seems more likely when a study involves children, naturalistic (rather than classroom) learning, observationally based (rather than self-report) personality assessments, and communicative language measures. He further notes that there is some evidence that among the traits defining the sociability component of extroversion, it is talkativeness and responsiveness, both reflecting willingness to engage in conversations, that best predict language learning. These results and nonresults suggest that extroversion, like other personality variables, plays no direct part in FLL, and that its indirect role, if any, is in triggering greater contact with the target language.

Generally weak, negative correlations have been found between classroom FL anxiety (e.g., nervousness about making errors, usually assessed via self-report, questionnaire data) and classroom participation, and between language anxiety and FL processing and attainment (for review see Gardner 1985, Spolsky 1989). In one study, a significant correlation was found between risk-taking and voluntary participation in Spanish lessons, but minimal connection between classroom participation and performance on an oral and written story-retelling task. As Scovel (1978) has noted, however, the effect of anxiety may be nonlinear; some anxiety may facilitate learning, especially in high-ability, more proficient learners, whereas high anxiety may be debilitating, especially for less able, low-proficiency students.

Attitudes and motivation have been the subject of numerous studies, with positive correlations of between .30 and .50 reported, and motivation and aptitude together accounting for between 25 percent and 40 percent of the variance in some cases (e.g., Gardner 1985). Motivation–achievement relationships sometimes evaporate when researchers control for age, however, and negative correlations have also been found in certain populations. As assessed in much of this research, motivation is treated as a state variable and is not a very pure construct (Crookes and Schmidt 1991). Gardner's Attitude Motivation Index, for example, adds scores on 10 measures of attitudes, interest, integrative orientation, motivational intensity, evaluation of FL teaching and teacher(s) experience, and integrative and instrumental orientation, and then subtracts scores on a measure of FL class anxiety. In a more

recent work, Gardner (1988) has provided support for a Socio-educational Model, in which cultural beliefs affect attitudes and integrativeness, which in turn influence motivation; motivation and aptitude then combine to predict FLL.

In addition to the relationship with achievement, "motivation" has been found to be negatively associated with dropout rates in FL study, and positively associated with classroom participation. Suggestions that motivation is the result, not the cause, of FLA (the so-called "resultative hypothesis") have been made on the basis of data showing, for instance, that among English children studying French in primary school, correlations between first-year achievement and second-year attitude scores after first-year attitude had been partialled out, were higher than correlations between first-year attitude and second-year achievement scores after first-year achievement had been partialled out. This has been at least partially countered, however, by data showing no such increase in the second-year integrativeness, motivation, and attitude scores of students who did well in first-year French compared with students who did less well (Gardner 1985).

There is some continuing support for the distinction between integrative and instrumental motivation. Integrative motivation refers to a positive orientation toward speakers of the target language and a wish to integrate into their group, and has generally been found more important in second-language environments. Instrumental motivation refers to an externally induced desire to learn—for instance, as a result of the need to pass an examination, or of the perceived advantages of FL ability for education and employment—and has often been found more important in FL settings. There is some overlap between the constructs, however (and between the items and instruments used to measure them), and some learners can be motivated in both ways. Alternative motivational orientations involving friendship, travel, and knowledge, or understanding, have also been identified, and a context-sensitive model developed which captures interactions among the ethnolinguistic status of the language learning group, sociolinguistic setting, and the various motivational orientations (Clement and Kruidenier 1985).

As state variables, attitudes and motivation are potentially manipulable by teachers and materials designers. High-interest materials and age-, gender-, and culture-appropriate methodology may be expected to affect attitudes positively and increase student desire to learn. There is no evidence that these or any other affect variables have a direct effect on FLA, however. Motivated and unmotivated learners make the same errors and traverse the same developmental sequences, for example, and numerous motivated learners fail while many apparently unmotivated ones succeed. There are clearly other more powerful cognitive and psycholinguistic factors at work. The positive effects on achievement and perseverance in FLA are probably mediated by intervening psychological processes, such as memory, monitoring, planning—especially attention to input—and by such variables as time on task and amount and quality of FL exposure, which motivation may affect. Nevertheless, given the documented indirect contribution of attitudes and motivation to FL achievement (and the fact that these variables, unlike age, aptitude, or intelligence, are often at least partly susceptible to manipulation), it makes sense for classroom teachers to expend effort in these areas, choosing materials and pedagogical options that appeal to more traditional psychological conceptualizations of motivation (without distal attitudes), that is, as a function of learner choice, engagement, and persistence, themselves determined by interest, relevance, expectancy, and outcomes (Crookes and Schmidt 1991).

4. Environmental Factors

Operating separately or in tandem with learner differences, the second major potential explanation for differential achievement in FLA is variation in the linguistic environment. Does the quality and/or quantity of input to the FL learner influence the learning outcome?

4.1 Input and Conversation

Over 60 studies have been conducted of the speech (and in a few cases, the writing) addressed to non-native speakers (NNSs) by native speakers (NSs) of the target language (for review see Larsen-Freeman and Long 1991, Long in press a). Native speakers have been found to make most of the same modifications in the way they speak that have been observed by child language researchers in studies of caretakers talking to young children learning their L1, triggered principally by the effort to communicate, and most specifically, the NS's perception of the NNS's comprehension. Native speakers adjust their speech in several ways, with the frequency and magnitude of adjustments being greater for interlocutors with lower FL proficiency.

Linguistic adjustments include use of shorter, relatively well-formed utterances containing fewer modifiers, less complex syntax, fewer idiomatic expressions, more overt marking of semantic relations, a more restricted vocabulary (lower type–token ratio), more marking of overt grammatical and semantic relations, a higher proportion of questions to statements, and more pauses, clearer articulation, and a slower rate of delivery. Linguistic adjustments are widely observed, but appear to be less pervasive, less consistent, and less important for facilitating communication than a second type of change, conversational adjustments.

Conversational adjustments, or modifications to the interactional structure of conversation, include frequent repetition of NS and NNS utterances, use of comprehension checks, confirmation checks, and clarification requests, expansions, and questions for topic-initiating moves. They also can include reduction of complex subject–predicate constructions to their topic–comment equivalents (decomposition), and choice and briefer treatment of a more predictable, narrower range of topics, and more willing relinquishment of topic-control to the NNS. The frequency of modifications increases when conversational partners attempt to communicate unknown information, or engage in "negotiation for meaning." Rather than simplifying the NNS's task by removing difficult items from the input, this second type of change elaborates the input, attempting to make comprehension easier by building in redundancy of various kinds. Although most studies have focused on the NS's role in NS–NNS conversation, success really depends on collaboration by both parties, NNSs providing the signals of incomprehension, for example, which trigger many of the NS adaptations. The joint collaborative process is known as "negotiation for meaning."

Some theorists have suggested that it is through participation in negotiated conversations of this sort that people learn languages—that knowledge of the grammar of a language evolves out of trying to use it to communicate (Hatch 1978, Sato 1990). (Most traditional FL teaching assumes the opposite—that students must first be taught the L2 grammar, and that they will then be able to use it to communicate.) There is almost no research on the long-term effects of these and other adjustments on FLA, but a number of controlled laboratory studies have shown that modified versions of spoken or written input originally intended for NS audiences achieve higher levels of NNS comprehension than the original texts. Since there is reason to believe that language learners must understand the meaning of new lexical or grammatical forms if they are to learn how to use them correctly (i.e., attach forms to meanings, or functions), modifications which serve to improve the comprehensibility of input play at least an indirect facilitative role in FLA.

The findings on linguistic simplification and elaborative modification have implications for the way teachers might try to talk to students during otherwise more traditional FL lessons, and also for the design of listening and reading comprehension materials. The results of 15 studies (reviewed in Ross et al. 1991) support the use of elaborated, rather than simplified, texts in the teaching of FL listening and reading skills. Linguistic simplification usually improves comprehension, although short, simple sentences alone may not help, and can even hinder understanding by removing redundancy. Elaboration of texts also usually improves comprehension almost as much as simplification. Both simplification and elaboration are more useful to learners of lower FL proficiency. With the possible exception of rate of delivery, single adjustments of either kind, such as shortening of sentences, repetition, or making topics salient, are rarely powerful enough to affect the overall comprehensibility of written texts or lecturettes. Simplified texts achieve improved comprehension by removing most of the unfamiliar lexis and grammatical points students need to learn. Elaborated versions retain the new items in the input, compensating for this through redundancy and explicitness. They also tend to constitute more natural discourse samples.

Work on the role of caretaker talk in first language development suggests that it is the semantic transparency of the caretaker's responses to children's utterances that is particularly important for language development. While this topic is only now being investigated in FLA, it seems reasonable to suppose that the same would be true there. An important feature of conversational, rather than linguistic, modifications is probably that they often allow the learner to hear their "meanings" reformulated correctly by the NS (or teacher). At the moment this happens, the meaning of what the NS says is already clear, since it originated with the NNS, and this plus the redundancy provided by the elaborated input facilitates comprehension (a prerequisite for acquisition) of any new lexis or complex morphology and syntax the responding move contains. The learner's attention is more likely to be on what the NS says, moreover, motivated by the desire to see whether what he or she just said was understood, making noticing of new forms and of mismatches between learner output and NS input more likely.

Studies of FL classroom interaction have shown that teachers make many of the same kinds of adjustments found in noninstructional conversation outside classrooms (Chaudron 1988). There tends to be less negotiation for meaning in formal language lessons, and thus fewer adjustments for the simple reason that many FL lessons involve an almost exclusive preoccupation with the language itself, as in drills and exercises, leaving very little meaning to negotiate. Studies show that the situation generally improves if either the teacher and student(s) or the students in pairs and small groups work on problem-solving tasks of various kinds. Some task types have been found to be better at stimulating negotiation work than others, at increasing the accuracy and complexity of student talk, and at inducing students to attend to and notice new linguistic items in the input surrounding completion of the tasks (Long in press a, b). Until teachers and textbook writers relinquish topic control to students, however, thereby allowing learners to initiate messages more often than traditional teacher-centered classroom discourse typically allows, there will be few opportunities for the semantically transparent, noticed reformulations more common outside the classroom. This suggests a need to restructure classroom discourse to make such exchanges more feasible, perhaps through the use of various kinds of joint problem-solving tasks requiring two-way information exchanges.

4.2 Focus on Form

As noted earlier, there is no evidence to date to suggest that formal instruction in a FL can alter either the developmental sequences through which learners pass or the acquisition processes they employ, as evidenced by the role of the L1 and the types of errors they commit, although the relative frequency of error types does seem to be affected positively. There is abundant evidence, however, of the beneficial effects of classroom instruction on the rate of learning, and less clearly, on the level of ultimate attainment. Classroom instruction here means more than simply provision of target language exposure and production opportunities for the students —although these are important if negotiation work is to occur—with attendant opportunities for grammar to evolve out of conversation. Instruction does not mean a diet of grammatical explanations, structure drills, and exercises, however, as this would be reverting to classroom interaction of the type in which little or no meaning is negotiated. Rather, an intermediate variety is indicated, probably involving some kind of content- or task-based syllabus and materials, but with a focus on form as an integral part of the pedagogy.

The justification for this suggestion is the growing body of work, both theoretical (McLaughlin 1987, Schmidt 1990, in press) and empirical (Doughty 1991, Hulstijn 1992), which suggests strongly that drawing learners' attention to new lexical or grammatical items in spoken or written materials speeds up their noticing of those forms, thereby possibly, but not inevitably, their acquisition of them. In some cases, such as the French speaker's learning of the earlier cited English adverb-placement rule, a focus on form may be essential if noticing is to occur at all, particularly if violation of the rule typically does not cause a communication breakdown which might alert the NNS to the fact that something is wrong. (Research has shown that NS very rarely correct NNS errors in spontaneous conversation.)

The manner in which focus on form is accomplished —error correction, rule statement, vocabulary explanation, highlighting in pedagogic materials—will vary according to the nature of the target linguistic item, the age of the learners, whether they are literate, and so on, but its provision has been shown to improve accuracy of adverb placement (and other rules) where extensive amounts of natural exposure does not (White 1991), provided the item concerned is not too difficult for learners to process at the time the focusing occurs. The research shows that a meaning-oriented pedagogy with a focus on form can be as efficient as more traditional grammar-oriented "rule and drill" approaches in improving students' mastery of complex syntax (e.g., relative clauses in Doughty 1991), and simultaneously allows learners to glean more meaning from the spoken or written input in which the new language items are embedded. As growing numbers of people are either obliged to or choose to undergo education or vocational training delivered through a second or third language, and as more FL programs abandon linguistically focused syllabuses and materials in favor of a variety of task-based, content-based, and immersion programs (Long and Crookes 1992), the possibility of simultaneously learning the new language and some kind of content expressed through that language, is of increasing importance.

5. Conclusion

In the relatively short period during which it has been subjected to intensive study, foreign language acquisition has been revealed to be a complex, multi-dimensional process influenced by both learner and environmental variables. The learner's cognitive contribution is much stronger than was once thought (and than is still implied by much language teaching methodology), with variation in the order and manner of presentation of the target language in the classroom having relatively little impact on students' errors, learning strategies, or sequences of development. Teaching is beneficial, however, most clearly for rate of learning, but also for those aspects of language which demand a focus on form if students are to notice and learn them. Future research is needed better to understand how learner and environmental factors interact and how different kinds of instruction can help different kinds of learner in foreign and second language contexts.

References

Carroll J B, Sapon S 1959 *Modern Language Aptitude Test*. The Psychological Corporation, New York
Chapelle C, Green P 1992 Field independence/dependence in second language acquisition research. *Language Learning* 42(1):47–83
Chaudron C 1988 *Second Language Classrooms: Research on Teaching and Learning*. Cambridge University Press, Cambridge
Clement R, Kruidenier B G 1985 Aptitude, attitude, and motivation in second language proficiency: A test of Clement's model. *Journal of Language and Social Psychology* 4(1):21–37
Crookes G, Schmidt R W 1991 Motivation: Reopening the research agenda. *Language Learning* 41 (4):469–512
Doughty C 1991 Second language instruction does make a difference. Evidence from an empirical study of SL relativization. *Studies in Second Language Acquisition* 13 (4):431–69
Ellis R 1989 Are classroom and naturalistic acquisition the same? A study of the classroom acquisition of German word order rules. *Studies in Second Language Acquisition* 11 (3):305–28
Gardner R C 1985 *Social Psychology and Second Language Learning: The Role of Attitudes and Motivation*. Edward Arnold, London

Gardner R C 1988 The socio-educational model of second language learning: Assumptions, findings and issues. *Language Learning* 38 (1):101–26
Griffiths R, Sheen R 1992 Disembedded figures in the landscape: A reappraisal of L2 research on field dependence/independence. *Applied Linguistics* 13 (2):133–48
Hatch E M 1978 Discourse analysis and second language acquisition. In: Hatch E M (ed.) 1978 *Second Language Acquisition: A Book of Readings*. Newbury House, Rowley, Massachussets
Hulstijn J H 1989 A cognitive view on interlanguage variability. In: Eisenstein M R (ed.) 1989 *The Dynamic Interlanguage. Empirical studies in Second Language Variation*. Plenum, New York
Hulstijn J H 1992 Retention of inferred and given word meanings: Experiments in incidental vocabulary learning. In: Arneaud P, Bejoint H (eds.) 1992 *Vocabulary and Applied Linguistics*. Macmillan, London
Hyltenstam K 1977 Implicational patterns in interlanguage syntax variation. *Language Learning* 27 (2):383–411
Hyltenstam K 1992 Non-native features of near-native speakers. In: Harris R J (ed.) 1992 *Cognitive Processing in Bilinguals*. North Holland, Amsterdam
Larsen-Freeman D, Long M H 1991 *An Introduction to Second Language Acquisition Research*. Longman, Harlow
Long M H 1990 Maturational constraints on language development. *Studies in Second Language Acquisition* 12 (3):251–85
Long M H in press (a) The role of the linguistic environment in second language acquisition. In: Ritchie W, Bhatia T (eds.) in press *Handbook of Research on Language Acquisition. Volume 2: Second Language Acquisition*. Academic Press, New York
Long M H in press (b) *Task-based Language Teaching*. Blackwell, Oxford
Long M H, Crookes G 1992 Three approaches to task-based syllabus design. *TESOL Quarterly* 26 (1): 27–56
McLaughlin B 1987 *Theories of Second Language Learning*. Edward Arnold, London
Pica T 1983 Adult acquisition of English as a second language under different conditions of exposure. *Language Learning* 33 (4):465–97
Pienemann M 1984 Psychological constraints on the teachability of languages. *Studies in Second Language Acquisition* 6 (2):186–214
Pienemann M 1989 Is language teachable? Psycholinguistic experiments and hypotheses. *Applied Linguistics* 10 (1):52–79
Preston D R 1989 *Sociolinguistics and Second Language Acquisition*. Blackwell, Oxford
Ross S, Long M H, Yano Y 1991 Simplification or elaboration? The effects of two types of text modifications on foreign language reading comprehension. *University of Hawaii Working Papers in ESL 10 (2): 1–32*
Sato C J 1990 *The Syntax of Conversation in Interlanguage Development*. Gunter Narr, Tubingen
Schmidt R W 1990 The role of consciousness in second language learning. *Applied Linguistics* 11 (2): 129–58
Schmidt R W in press Psychological mechanisms underlying second language fluency. *Studies in Second Language Acquisition* 14(4)
Scovel T 1978 The effect of affect on foreign language learning: A review of the anxiety research. *Language Learning* 28 (1): 129–42

Scovel T 1988 *A Time to Speak: A Psycholinguistic Inquiry into the Critical Period for Human Speech*. Newbury House, Cambridge
Skehan P 1989 *Individual Differences in Second-language Learning*. Edward Arnold, London
Spolsky B 1989 *Conditions for Second Language Learning: Introduction to a General Theory*. Oxford University Press, Oxford
Tarone E 1988 *Variation in Interlanguage*. Edward Arnold, London
White L 1991 Adverb placement in second language acquisition: Some effects of positive and negative evidence in the classroom. *Second Language Research* 7 (2): 133–61

Further Reading

McDonough S H 1986 *Psychology in Foreign Language Teaching*, 2nd edn. George Allen and Unwin, London
Mohan B 1986 *Language and Content*. Addison-Wesley, Reading, Massachusetts
Parry T S, Stansfield C W (eds.) 1990 *Language Aptitude Reconsidered*. Prentice-Hall Regents, Englewood Cliffs, New Jersey
Swain M 1991 French immersion and its offshoots: Getting two for one. In: Freed B F (ed.) 1991 *Foreign Language Acquisition Research and the Classroom*. Heath, Lexington, Massachusetts

Learning from Text

E. Kintsch and W. Kintsch

Texts, whether in the traditional book format or presented on the screen of a computer, are the main vehicle for communicating knowledge in modern, information dependent societies. Thus, a thorough understanding of how people understand and learn from written text is fundamental to preparing texts in such a way that learning is optimized. However, this understanding is equally important to the task of equipping students with the skills needed to efficiently acquire from a text knowledge that is both usable and easily accessible.

1. Types of Learning

Learning from text refers to the deliberate actions performed by a reader in order to comprehend a textual message and to integrate the information into existing personal knowledge. Therefore this discussion does not include the unconscious acquisition of implicit knowledge that may accompany intentional learning (such as, for example, remembering where on a page a given idea was discussed).

Learning from text is, according to current cognitive theory, intimately connected to the kinds of processes occurring during comprehension. The product of comprehension is a mental representation which reflects qualitative differences in the mental operations performed by the reader. Thus, one may passively read a novel for its entertainment value or dig much deeper in trying to detect some hidden purpose of the author, and to analyze the means by which it is accomplished. Superficial comprehension processes in the former case are sufficient for retelling or summarizing the plot of the novel. However, making inferences about the author's working style and the situation depicted

in the novel serve to tie the content more closely to the reader's existing knowledge, resulting in a much richer representation of the text. This kind of "deep learning" provides usable knowledge, knowledge that can be applied to a new problem or in a different context.

In the text comprehension theory of Kintsch and van Dijk (1978, van Dijk and Kintsch 1983), the mental representation constructed during reading comprises at least three levels of analysis: Readers encode some elements of the *surface structure*—the actual words and phrases in the text and the linguistic relations between them. The semantic content and its rhetorical structure form the *textbase*. A deeper level of understanding is termed the *situation model*—the reader's understanding of the situation depicted by the text. The situation model is composed of the text content which has been elaborated by inferences from the reader's own prior knowledge, with which it becomes integrated. The distinction between mental representation at the level of the textbase and the situation model captures the important difference alluded to above between shallow and deep learning: readers do not always engage in the kind of active, inferential processing that leads to a richly elaborated situation model. Often reading proceeds in a much more passive manner. The content is understood well enough to recall or summarize it, but readers who only understand a text at the level of the textbase will not easily perceive relationships between the newly learned information and other analogous situations. Thus, they may not draw the appropriate inference between related ideas nor be able to work with the information or reason on its basis.

An example from the empirical literature should help to clarify this distinction. In a study by Mannes and Kintsch (1987) college student subjects read a text about the industrial uses of microbes. Before reading the experimental text, the subjects were given an advance organizer outline to read which provided background information about microbes. For half of the subjects the outline followed the same structure as the experimental text. The other half read an outline with a different organization. After reading the text subjects' learning was measured in various ways in order to tease apart the textbase versus situation model distinction. Specifically, cued recall and sentence recognition tasks were used as measures of reproductive knowledge, that is, textbase understanding; the adequacy of the situation model was assessed by asking subjects to use the information about microbes to solve an actual industrial problem. The effect of the advance organizing outline differed according to the learning measure used: subjects who read an outline which agreed with the text structure performed better on texts of reproductive recall than subjects who read a discrepant outline. However, the latter group of subjects had better scores on the problem-solving task which tested their ability to draw inferences. Apparently, the overlap between text structure and outline served to reinforce those subjects' knowledge of the textbase, thus facilitating their recall of the content. In contrast, the discrepancy between text and outline made it more difficult for the other group of subjects to recall the textual content. The textbase formed by these subjects was not as well structured nor as complete. However, the subjects were forced to engage in extra inferential processing to resolve the difference between the two information sources. In so doing they formed more links between elements of text, the outline, and their own prior knowledge. Thus, they constructed a more elaborated situation model which was also more tightly integrated with their prior knowledge. This proved to be more beneficial than an accurate textbase representation when subjects needed to apply the new knowledge to solve inferential problems.

Cognitive research in the 1980s and 1990s has devoted a great deal of effort towards finding ways to make instructional texts easier to comprehend, and in developing instruction that will improve readers' ability to learn textual content. Yet the realization that effective learning requires more than memory for text is quite recent. Coupled with this realization is a growing need to develop new measures of learning that tap more than mere reproductive capability.

2. Cognitive Processes Involved in Comprehending and Learning from Text

In contrast to the traditional conception of learning as knowledge assimilation, current *constructivist theories* conceive of learning as a process of meaning construction, by which readers are encouraged to use their own intelligence, knowledge, goals, and interests to interpret and evaluate what they read. The traditional model has emphasized the acquisition of a body of knowledge, especially factual knowledge, and research has largely focused on how to structure the material into more easily digestible chunks for the learner. Constructivist theories of learning, instead, emphasize the conceptual processes by which understanding is achieved. Thus, constructivism seeks to replace repetition, drills, and overt attempts to memorize textual content in school with effortful thinking processes: generating inferences, reorganizing information, questioning and evaluating ideas, repairing comprehension problems, developing theories and hypotheses about phenomena, reflecting upon and acting upon information. Within this process-oriented instructional context, texts serve as sources for both collaborative and individual knowledge building, for finding specific information to answer a question or support an opinion. They function as resources to support learning rather than repositories of information which is to be learned.

The constructivist model assumes that learning from text, like learning in general, is active and intentional, and should be directed towards meaningful goals. Meaningful here is used in the sense that learners realize the value of what they are to learn, that goals and learning materials have obvious relevance to a real-world situation, unlike rote learning of operations and decontextualized facts whose usefulness is often not apparent. Intentional learning also means learning that extends from the personal knowledge base. Students are encouraged as they read to seek relationships between new ideas and what they already know, to work with the knowledge and consider it from differing perspectives, in other words to construct knowledge rather than to extract it from a text. Intentional, constructive learning also includes the notion that learners should control their own processing. They should develop *metacognitive awareness* of their own mental processes and learn to diagnose and remediate comprehension problems that occur.

3. Factors which Contribute to Effective Learning from Text

The design of good instructional text has long been a goal of cognitive research, continuing the efforts of behavioral research in the 1960s and 1970s to improve learning by optimizing the presentation of learning materials. More recently the focus has broadened to consider also the specific mental processes that result in superior learning. Thus, a number of studies have sought to identify and specify the strategy differences that distinguish expert and nonexpert performance in reading, writing, and problem solving with the goal of helping students to acquire more expert-like strategies. Both directions continue in present-day research on text learning. On the one hand, we continue to explore how a particular content can be broken down, organized, explained, and presented in a manner appropriate to the learner's level of knowledge. Furthermore, we are interested in what a learner must do to comprehend and learn.

3.1 Learner Factors

A particularly important insight from the research on comprehension and learning strategies is an awareness of the degree to which learning from text involves active, strategic, effortful processes which work best when they are under the conscious metacognitive control of the learner. Expert comprehension and learning or study strategies which have been identified include such activities as: (a) using words or imagery to elaborate the content; (b) rereading, paraphrasing, and summarizing in one's own words to clarify the content; (c) reorganizing the content into a hierarchical outline, diagram or graph that shows the important relationships between ideas; (d) consciously seeking relationships between new content and existing knowledge (e.g., by self explaining, forming analogies, hypothesizing, drawing conclusions and predictions, formulating questions, and evaluating the text for internal consistency and with respect to what one knows of the topic); and (e) consciously monitoring one's ongoing comprehension, identifying the source for a breakdown in comprehension and attempting to resolve the problem rather than passively reading on (for reviews of this literature see, e.g., Dansereau 1985, Palinscar and Brown 1984, Weinstein and Meyer 1986).

The common element in these interpretive and elaborative strategies is that they all involve the generation of inferences by means of which the reader expands and enriches the textual content with ideas and concepts from the personal knowledge base. Such active processes of meaning construction have been revealed as an important deficiency among poorly achieving students and learners across the age range. A number of training studies have thus sought to apply these insights from cognitive research in instructional programs designed to make students more efficient, successful, and ultimately more motivated learners. Again the distinction made earlier between textbase and situation model levels of processing enters into this discussion. The initial instructional programs were developed to teach primarily *textbase strategies* in order to improve students' ability to recall textual materials as completely and accurately as possible. These programs were expanded to include *metacognitive strategies* as researchers recognized the importance of readers' ability to keep track of and control their own on-going comprehension (Brown et al. 1983, Garner 1988). More recently interest has shifted to the kinds of *inferential processes* by which readers interpret a textual content in the light of their own knowledge, thereby constructing a situation model. This kind of memory representation is necessary to support later applications of newly acquired knowledge and thus constitutes what is considered to be true learning. Assessment of learning has paralleled this chronological development in assumptions about learning, from an almost exclusive dependence on measures of textbase memory in earlier research (e.g., tasks involving recognition, recall, summarization, or short-answer questions) to tasks requiring demonstrations of conceptual understanding (e.g., inference questions, problem solving, and other novel applications).

3.1.1 Textbase strategies. Many instructional programs were developed to combat the prevalence of low-level, surface oriented reading and writing strategies which had been identified as a widespread problem among students (Brown et al. 1983). Accordingly, students were taught to focus more on main ideas during reading, to use higher-level summarization strategies, such as constructing macropropositions or topic sentences in their own words rather than lifting verbatim statements from the text. In study skills instruction students are typically taught explicit strategies, such as: (a) previewing a text before reading, paying special attention to headings, pre-organizing statements or questions to guide the reading; (b) rereading for specific information, attending to important information by using structural cues; (c) outlining, diagramming, or networking to understand relationships between ideas; and (d) rehearsing and using adjunct questions to test readiness for a test. These techniques can be quite effective in improving recall of textual materials, especially among lower achieving students. However, the direct instruction approach has had only limited success over the long term and in tests of distant transfer (Mandl and Ballstaedt 1982) for one, because it depends heavily on the direction of a teacher, but also because it over-emphasizes ability to reproduce textual content. A more promising approach is to provide students with the responsibility and control over their own learning and with instructional texts and environments that force them to actively construct their own knowledge.

3.1.2 Metacognitive strategies. Metacognition refers to the ability to stand back and oversee one's own thinking processes, for example, consciously using various problem-solving strategies to comprehend difficult text, monitoring on-going comprehension, and knowing how to overcome breakdowns. Having students and teachers think aloud while performing a difficult task is an effective means of making them aware of these hidden thinking processes. It serves to bring them into the open, so that they can be observed, discussed, and practiced by students under the teacher's guidance. This technique forms the basis of a very successful instructional program, known as "reciprocal teaching," developed by Palincsar and Brown (1984). In reciprocal teaching the teacher initially models four general reading comprehension strategies—questioning unclear content, summarizing paragraph by paragraph, clarifying comprehension problems, and predicting forthcoming text, by thinking aloud as he/she reads. Students then practice modelling the strategies themselves, as the teacher guides and shapes their responses. As the students become more adept, the teacher's role diminishes until students are able to use the strategies independently, themselves assuming the role of teacher in small reading groups. Not only do these general level strategies help students become more involved in the meaning during reading, but unlike explicit strategy instruction, reciprocal teaching puts students in control of their own strategic processes, requiring them to set their own learning goals and ask their own questions.

3.1.3 Integrative learning strategies. Active engagement in meaning construction happens all too seldom when students are reading about an unfamiliar topic. However, two recently developed instructional methods have shown promise in making students think about what they are reading. Chi and her colleagues (Chi et al. 1994) taught eighth-grade students to explain to themselves the meaning of each sentence while reading a biology text and found that these students achieved a deeper and more accurate understanding of the topic than those who simply read the text twice. Moreover, reading with the goal of explaining a passage to others promotes deeper understanding than either summarizing or explaining the passage to oneself, according to Coleman (1994) who compared students' performance on difficult inference questions. The summarizers could recall the text better, however, inference scores were higher among students who read the passage in order to teach the material. Presumably explaining and teaching elicit deeper, meaning construction processes than summarizing for which only a coherent representation of the text content (textbase) suffices.

Questioning students about assigned readings has long been the mainstay of classroom instruction. In traditional classrooms these are typically factual questions which direct students to retrieve specific information from the text. Beck et al. (1996) found that changing the nature of these questions to ones that focus on meaning and interpretation became a powerful tool for changing attitudes about reading. Instead of reproducing verbatim text information, in "Questioning the Author" students are asked to think

about the author's intended message, to evaluate how it was conveyed and whether the author was successful. Thinking about why the author chose a particular piece of information to present and how it connects with other ideas challenges students to evaluate the ideas and to relate them to their existing knowledge. Moreover, Beck et al. (1996) have documented impressive changes in the classroom culture with this technique, from one of teacher dominance with largely passive students to more interactive discourse, often initiated by students' spontaneous comments and questions.

Thus, simply knowing what one is supposed to do may not be enough to change behavior, as indicated by attempts to directly instruct expert strategies. Students must also realize the value of such strategies and their appropriate use. Even in the case of self explaining we do not know whether students who are taught this technique will continue to do so in other learning situations. A technique, such as "Questioning the Author," may prove more effective in the long run because it serves as a tool for transforming both the social structure of the classroom and the attitudes of all participants towards learning from text. As students and teachers engage in thought provoking questions, they also become critical readers and thinkers. Every class then has the potential to provide concrete experiences in successful comprehension which ultimately make learning new and difficult content more rewarding.

3.2 Text Factors

3.2.1 Readability aids. What the learner does in order to understand during reading is a crucial component of successful learning, but it is not the whole story. Cognitive psychologists have long emphasized the role that the instructional materials themselves can play in enhancing—or impeding—comprehension and learning. Early attempts to improve the readability of instructional text have focussed on factors such as using easier vocabulary, shorter and less complex sentences, or overt signals to underlying structure and important information, such as headings, subheadings, highlighting of key terms and other macro-signals. In addition, advance organizing questions or introductory statements are frequently inserted to prime readers' background knowledge. In general, although most of these adjuncts do help somewhat to guide reading and studying, they have not solved the problem of helping readers acquire useful knowledge from written materials in a new, unfamiliar domain (Weaver and Kintsch 1990). On the other hand, comprehensibility of a text can be greatly improved by increasing its semantic coherence.

3.2.2 Semantic coherence. Coherence refers to the degree to which relationships between the ideas and concepts in a text are explicitly made. To some extent inferences are a necessary part of reading, and often they are made quite easily and automatically. For example, connecting a pronoun to its referent, or identifying synonymous relationships, or even filling in a missing connective between two sentences requires little effort, providing the reader has sufficient background knowledge about the topic. However, readers who lack such knowledge are greatly helped by a supportive text in which these local relationships and also broader, macro-level relationships are spelled out. A coherent text makes it easier for readers to form a coherent and more accurate representation of the content and to remember it later, according to studies by Britton and Gulgoz (1991) and by Beck and her colleagues (Beck et al. 1991).

On the other hand, a highly coherent text may be less advantageous for readers with moderate or high background knowledge. In a recent study McNamara et al. (1996) manipulated both text coherence and the background knowledge of the readers. Two revisions of a passage from a biology textbook on heart disease were prepared, one in which coherence gaps were filled by making the relations explicit (e.g., supplying pronoun and synonym referents, adding macropropositions and headings, adding sentence connectives and descriptive elaborations to connect familiar and unfamiliar terms). These linguistic cues were deleted in the less coherent version. The coherent version led to better recall among both high- and low-knowledge readers. Performance on inference and problem-solving questions was also better among low-knowledge readers who read the coherent text. However, the opposite was the case for high-knowledge readers who performed better after reading the less coherent text version. It appears that readers who possess adequate knowledge form a better situation model representation when they must draw these connective inferences on their own. This is because readers must draw on their knowledge to generate the inferences and in so doing construct a more elaborated mental model that is well linked with concepts in the personal knowledge base. Such knowledge is more readily available when needed later to solve problems, even though recall of the actual text content may be less accurate.

The form of a text can greatly affect learning, but also its content—whether there is an optimal amount of overlap between the information in the text and the knowledge and skills that the learner possesses. If the overlap is too great, not much can be learned from the text. On the other hand, if there is insufficient overlap, the reader will not have the requisite knowledge to supply the gap-filling inferences and to adequately integrate the content. The result in this case is an isolated memory representation, which may be sufficient for recall or summarizing, but it does not allow the knowledge to be used in other contexts (Kintsch 1994). Thus, successful learning from text involves an intricate interaction between text and reader which poses a challenge for educational research and practitioners when it comes to finding a good match between the two, for clearly there is no optimal text for all learners.

4. Pictures, Examples, and Other Conceptualization Aids to Comprehending Text

When reading a description of a process or a procedure involving spatial information it is often helpful to see a picture. Various other kinds of displays (e.g., graphs, time lines, trees, tables, animations, and simulations) can likewise help to make abstract concepts visible and concrete. Textual elaborations, for instance, describing an analogous situation, or providing examples (e.g., of problem solution) also serve a similar function of helping readers to form a better and more memorable representation of particular kinds of content. However, pictures, graphs, and examples are only helpful to the extent that they increase the meaningfulness of the text description (Mayer and Gallini 1990), whereas they may be distracting if they are superfluous, or misleading if they distort or oversimplify what they are intended to elucidate. Levin and Mayer (1993) specify several conditions under which illustrations can enrich a reader's conceptualization, and which apply broadly to the use of other representation aids. Pictures can help focus attention on important kinds of information, especially the relations between ideas or objects. They can summarize or provide a succinct overview of a complex description. By supplementing text with concrete conceptualizations pictures may make the material more memorable. They may also facilitate readers' conceptualizations by suggesting an interpretation of the textual description, or by suggesting analogies with familiar situations, objects, or processes.

Several caveats are in order here, since not all texts nor all readers are alike. Concrete, narrative passages need little pictorial embellishment, while a visual representation may facilitate understanding of a complex scientific concept. Low-knowledge readers usually benefit more from pictures and other conceptual aids (Levin and Mayer 1993), probably because high-knowledge readers are able to form rich conceptualizations on their own. Most important is that the reader be able to perceive the relationship between text and visual display, example, or analogy, such that both contribute to the construction of a single situation model. That is, text and pictures, etc., must be integrated and explain each other so that the situation model contains aspects of both, rather than two independent and incomplete representations.

5. Conclusion

Acquiring knowledge from texts depends critically on successful integration of knowledge in the text and knowledge in the individual reader's head. Thus, true learning involves constructing a mental model of the situation depicted in a text. Whereas a coherent representation of a text is sufficient to support its reproduction, only situational understanding allows knowledge to be easily accessed and useful later. This kind of representation can only be achieved when enough overlapping elements exist to enable readers to form links between new information and what they already know. To encourage active processing of meaning during reading, learners should be allowed as much as possible to form their own connective inferences to bridge gaps in the coherence structure of a text, they should form their own macrostructure of the text and be encouraged to elaborate the text with their own knowledge. However, the success of active processing depends on having the requisite knowledge to generate appropriate inferences. Learners who are at the beginning stages of acquiring new domain knowledge will learn better from supportive texts which provide the explicit semantic links to enable the formation of a coherent textbase, and, where appropriate, provide various kinds of textual and visual supports to aid difficult conceptualizations.

See also: Assessment in the Service of Learning; Comprehension: Teaching and Assessing; Constructivism and Learning; Metacognition; Reading Comprehension, Learning of

References

Beck I L, McKeown M G, Worthy J, Sandora C, Kucan L 1996 Questioning the author: A year-long implementation to engage students with text. *Elem. Sch. J.* 96(4): 385–414

Beck I L, McKeown M G, Sinatra G M, Loxterman J A 1991 Revising social studies text from a text-processing perspective: Evidence of improved comprehensibility. *Read. Res. Q.* 27: 251–76

Britton B K, Gulgoz S 1991 Using Kintsch's model to improve instructional text: Effects of inference calls on recall and cognitive structures. *J. Educ. Psychol.* 83: 329–45

Brown A L, Bransford J D, Ferrara R A, Campione J C 1983 Learning, remembering, and understanding. In: Flavell J, Markman E M (eds.) 1983 *Handbook of Child Psychology: Child Development*. Wiley, New York

Chi M T H, de Leeuw N, Chiu M-H, LaVancher C 1994 Eliciting self-explanations improves understanding. *Cognit. Sci.* 18: 439–77

Coleman E B 1994 Effects of explanation vs. summarization

of science texts on memory and inference. Paper presented at the meetings of the Winter Text Conference, Jackson, Wyoming

Dansereau D F 1985 Learning strategy research. In: Segal S C J, Glaser R (eds.) 1985 *Thinking and Learning Skills, Vol. 1: Relating Instruction to Research*. Erlbaum, Hillsdale, New Jersey

Garner R 1988 *Metacognition and Reading Comprehension*. Ablex, Norwood, New Jersey

Kintsch W 1994 Text comprehension, memory, and learning. *Am. Psychol.* 49(4): 294–303

Kintsch W, van Dijk T A 1978 Toward a model of test comprehension and production. *Psychol. Rev.* 85: 363–94

Levin J R, Mayer R E 1993 Understanding illustrations in text. In: Britton B K, Woodward A, Binkley M (eds.) 1993 *Learning from Textbooks*. Erlbaum, Hillsdale, New Jersey

Mandl H, Ballstaedt S P 1982 Effects of elaboration on recall of texts. In: Flammer A, Kintsch W (eds.) 1982 *Discourse Processing*. Elsevier, Amsterdam

Mannes S M, Kintsch W 1987 Knowledge organization and text organization. *Cognition and Instruction* 4: 91–115

Mayer R E, Gallini J K 1990 When is an illustration worth ten thousand words? *J. Educ. Psychol.* 82(4): 715–26

McNamara D S, Kintsch E, Songer N B, Kintsch W 1996 Are good texts always better? Interactions of text coherence, background knowledge, and levels of understanding in learning from text. *Cognition and Instruction* 14(1): 1–43

Palinscar A S, Brown A L 1984 Reciprocal teaching of comprehension-fostering and monitoring activities. *Cognition and Instruction* 1(2): 117–75

van Dijk T A, Kintsch W 1983 *Strategies of Discourse Comprehension*. Academic Press, New York

Weaver C A III, Kintsch W 1990 Expository text. In: Barr R, Kamil M L, Rosenthal P B, Pearson P D (eds.) 1990 *Handbook of Reading*. Longman, New York

Weinstein C E, Mayer R E 1986 The teaching of learning strategies. In: Wittrock M C (ed.) 1986 *Handbook of Research on Teaching*. Macmillan, New York

Further Reading

Britton B K, Woodward A, Binkley M (eds.) 1993 *Learning from Textbooks*. Erlbaum, Hillsdale, New Jersey

Kintsch W et al. 1993 A comprehension-based approach to learning and understanding. In: Medin D L (ed.) 1993 *The Psychology of Learning and Motivation*. Academic Press, New York

Mandl H, Levin J R 1989 *Knowledge Acquisition from Texts and Pictures*. Elsevier, Amsterdam

Resnick L B (ed.) 1989 *Knowing, Learning, and Instruction: Essays in Honor of Robert Glaser*. Erlbaum, Hillsdale, New Jersey

Learning Strategies in Second Language Learning

J. M. O'Malley and A. U. Chamot

Learning strategies are methods or techniques that individuals use to improve their comprehension, learning, retention, and retrieval of information (Weinstein and Mayer 1986). Strategies are typically described as mental procedures that assist learning but may also include overt activities. A learning strategy may be a specific technique or tactic, or it may be a general plan for completing a task. The problems regarding learning strategies to which research has been addressed include the description and classification of strategies, their influences on learning with specific types of tasks and learners, and the transfer of strategies to new tasks or contexts. Second language learning, as discussed here, will include: (a) foreign language learning, or learning a second language in a setting where it is not the dominant language; (b) learning a second language in a setting where it is the dominant language, as in learning English as a second language (ESL) or learning German among immigrant groups. While these are very different second language learning contexts, they have sufficient parallels in a discussion of learning strategies to warrant joint consideration.

The significance of learning strategies stems from the observation that learning is an active and dynamic process in which learners approach new tasks strategically, analyze task requirements, apply various mental processes appropriate to the task, and reflect on the success of their attainments. Effective and less effective learners can be differentiated in terms of their strategies, and less effective students can be assisted in developing skill at strategy use through instruction. Furthermore, individuals instructed to use strategies will, under appropriate conditions, transfer the use of strategies to similar tasks and become more independent and autonomous learners. Strategy instruction has the potential to assist learners in becoming more effective and to aid teachers in better understanding and supporting their students' mental processes and learning effectiveness.

1. Learning Strategies: Origins in Second Language Learning

The prevailing notion in second language acquisition through the mid-1970s was that second language learning occurred through a combination of aptitude and opportunity. That is, some individuals are endowed with particular phonetic coding abilities, grammatical sensitivities, memory, and inductive language learning abilities that enable them to learn second languages more readily than other people do (Carroll 1990). These were not thought to be learned abilities. Second language learning opportunities arise particularly when individuals receive intensive second language instruction and at the same time are immersed in settings requiring them to communicate effectively in social, occupational, or other interactive situations. Individuals with high second language aptitudes immersed in such settings can be expected to attain high levels on tests of second language proficiency.

A second prevailing notion in second language acquisition concerned the mental processes that occur in settings with rich opportunities for communicative interactions. Individuals were said to "acquire" a language most effectively through unconscious or unanalyzed mental processes in such settings in contrast to "learning" a language through conscious attention to the forms and structures encountered in typical instructional environments (Krashen 1982). This perspective served to draw attention to the importance of a "natural approach" to the acquisition of second language functions and applications in an era when the dominant instructional methodology, the audiolingual method, concentrated on repetition drills with isolated language components and conscious attention to form. While contributing to a paradigm shift from form to function in communicative settings, and dramatic changes in instructional methods, this perspective also ignored learners' mental processes in natural settings or in classrooms.

A new paradigm shift has emerged as attention has been directed to the active, dynamic mental processes that learners apply to all communicative and learning activities both within and outside classrooms. Learning strategies are an important element in this shift, which views aptitudes in a secondary role to strategies. Drawing in part on developmental theory and in part on her own experience as a second language learner and teacher, Rubin (1975) suggested that the "good language learner" uses special strategies and described some of the strategies identified.

The notion that second language learning ability resided at least in part in the strategies used for learning has been investigated through interviews, questionnaires, and observations of language learners. Research has revealed a number of discrete strategies that appeared to be important for learning second languages (Naiman et al. 1978). Students' mental processes and reported learning strategies have been analyzed in verbal reports or "think aloud" protocols and through instructional research in which high school students of French were taught explicit reading strategies (Hosenfeld et al. 1981). Additionally, anecdotal reports collected from students on the associations they made while learning vocabulary have revealed that students who made associations remembered vocabulary words more effectively than those who did not (Cohen and Aphek 1981).

Rubin (1981) followed her earlier work by conducting interviews with second language students and suggesting a two-part classification scheme consisting of strategies that directly affect learning (e.g., monitoring, memorizing, deductive reasoning, and practice) and processes that contribute indirectly to learning (creating opportunities for practice and production tricks). More recently, others have pursued the classification of learning strategies and have analyzed the types of strategies used with second language tasks. Based on student interviews, a strategy classification scheme was developed to draw on the distinction in cognitive psychology between metacognitive and cognitive strategies while adding a third category for socialaffective strategies (Chamot and Küpper 1989). This tripartite classification scheme, developed initially with ESL students (O'Malley and Chamot 1990), was validated with foreign language learners, including students of Russian and Spanish in the United States (Chamot and Küpper 1989), English as a Foreign Language students in Brazil (Absy 1992), and students of French in Canada (Vandergrift 1992). The distinction between metacognitive and cognitive strategies, while sometimes ambiguous, nevertheless served to produce acceptably reliable strategy classifications (O'Malley and Chamot 1990). Individual strategies within each of the broader categories included metacognitive strategies for planning, monitoring, and evaluating; cognitive strategies for elaboration, grouping, inferencing, and summarizing; and social/affective strategies for questioning, cooperating, and self-talk. Oxford (1990) used questionnaire data to produce a similar strategy classification based on factor analysis which incorporated more than 60 strategies culled from the literature on second language learning. Wenden (1987) focused on the description of students' metacognitive knowledge and strategies that enable them to direct their own learning.

While the majority of descriptive studies of language learning strategies have emphasized the strategies of good language learners, the strategies of less effective language learners have also been of interest. Unsuccessful language learners are not necessarily unaware of strategies, but are less able to determine the appropriateness of a strategy for a specific task (O'Malley and Chamot 1990, Vann and Abraham 1990). More effective students appear to have more metacognitive understanding of task demands than less effective students, and this understanding leads them to select and apply more appropriate strategies.

A broad range of classroom and nonclassroom tasks have been analyzed in interviews on learning strategies with second language students. The tasks represent typical second language classroom activities, such as learning vocabulary and grammar, following directions, listening for information, reading for comprehension, writing, and presenting oral reports, while also representing language used in functional activities outside the classroom (talking on the telephone, applying for a job). Tasks used in "think aloud" interviews include listening to and reading academic content materials such as science and social studies. The students participating in these interviews included students enrolled to study English as a second language and other foreign languages in secondary schools, colleges, or other adult programs.

Empirical verification that strategies influence learning of second languages has been based on correlational work (Padron and Waxman 1988, Politzer and McGroarty 1985) and experimental interventions (O'Malley and Chamot 1990). Both types of study have produced support for the influence of strategies on second language learning tasks. However, the results, while having statistical and practical significance, have not been consistent for all tasks and should be replicated and extended in a broad program of further research. Additionally, little work on strategy interviews and interventions in second language acquisition has been extended to the middle or elementary grades.

2. Typology and Applications of Learning Strategies

The three-way classification of strategies into metacognitive, cognitive, and social/affective strategies subsumes the major strategies that have been discussed in the literature on second language acquisition. A sampling of the more common strategies is presented in Table 1, organized within this typology. Many of these strategies are similar to strategies used with general learning tasks, while some appear to be unique in second language acquisition. Individuals sometimes use individual strategies in learning second languages, but more often they combine strategies within one level of the strategy typology or combine strategies across levels. For example, in learning to read in a second language, one option too commonly applied is to begin with the first word of an unfamiliar passage and look up every unknown word in a dictionary. A strategic approach would be to scan through the passage looking for familiar words to gain an overview of the content, analyze what is already known about the topic, read through the passage inferring the meaning of unfamiliar words from context, decide which additional words are essential to meet the purposes of reading, and only then look up words in the dictionary. The strategic approach combines selective attention for familiar words, elaboration of existing knowledge, inferencing from context, and metacognitive analysis of task demands. A similar strategic approach to listening would substitute reviewing familiar materials on the anticipated topic for scanning through the passage but would otherwise be similar.

3. Parallels in Cognitive Psychology

The tradition of research on learning strategies in cognitive psychology extends back further than the work in second language learning and has a richer empirical foundation. The cognitive research is based in part on the expert–novice distinction in performing cognitive tasks, in part on developmental research, and in part on cognitive theory (Brown et al. 1983). Extensive empirical research has verified the influence of strategies with a variety of direct and complex tasks (e.g., Pressley et al. 1992, Weinstein and Mayer 1986). For example, instruction in reading strategies has significantly improved the reading comprehension of poor readers (Gagné 1985, Palincsar and Brown 1984) and instruction in problem-solving strategies has had a positive effect on student mathematics achievement (Silver and Marshall 1990). This validation of learning strategy instruction has led to the development of instructional models incorporating learning strategies for content instruction (Pressley et al. 1992). Although the cognitive research has been concerned with a broad range of complex tasks, there has been no investigation of second language learning in this literature except for work on vo-

Table 1
Learning strategies typology in second language learning

Strategy Name	Definition
Metacognitive strategies (executive processes used to plan, monitor, and evaluate a learning task)	
Planning	
Directed attention	Deciding to attend to and focus on the learning task
Organizational planning	Identifying the problem and deciding how to accomplish the learning task
Selective attention	Attending to or scanning key words, phrases, linguistic markers, or types of information
Self-management	Seeking or arranging the conditions that assist learning
Monitoring	Checking one's comprehension during listening or reading
Evaluating	Judging how well one has accomplished a learning task
Cognitive strategies (interacting with the material to be learned by manipulating it mentally or physically)	
Grouping	Classifying words, terminology, numbers, or concepts according to their attributes
Note-taking	Writing down key words and concepts in abbreviated verbal, graphic, or numerical form
Summarizing	Making a mental, oral, or written summary of information gained from listening or reading
Deduction/induction	Applying or figuring out rules to understand or produce language or solve a problem
Imagery	Using mental or actual pictures to learn new information or solve a problem
Elaboration	Relating known to new information, relating different parts, or making personal associations
Linguistic transfer	Using what one already knows about language to assist comprehension or retention; e.g., using cognates
Inferencing	Using information in the text to guess meanings of new items or predict upcoming information
Social/affective strategies (interacting with other persons to assist in learning or to gain affective control)	
Questioning for clarification	Getting additional information through questioning from a teacher or other expert
Cooperation	Working with peers to complete a task, pool information, solve a problem, or obtain feedback
Self-talk	Reducing anxiety by improving one's sense of competence

cabulary (e.g., Pressley et al. 1980), an area that hardly touches the complexity of second language acquisition.

Research on learning strategies with complex first language skills has implications for second language learning since many of the tasks and strategies are similar. Support has been reported for both individual strategies and strategy combinations. Research with individual strategies has the benefit of isolating strategy effects experimentally, but the research on strategy combinations may have greater validity for classroom use and be more powerful. For example, substantial immediate and long-term effects on reading comprehension have been found for "reciprocal teaching," a combination of strategies that includes questioning, summarizing, predicting, and cooperative learning (Palincsar and Brown 1984). Similarly, improvements in writing performance have been reported in a series of studies in which learning disabled students were explicitly taught strategies for planning, composing, and revising their writing (Pressley et al. 1992). Strategies have been linked to motivation (Paris and Winograd 1990) and particularly to a sense of self-efficacy leading to positive expectations of learning success (Zimmerman and Pons 1986). Self-control over strategy use can. be enhanced if strategy instruction is combined with metacognitive awareness of the connection between strategy use and learning outcomes. Students with greater metacognitive awareness understand the similarity between the current learning task and previous tasks, know the strategies required for successful problem-solving or learning, and anticipate that deploying these strategies will result in success (Paris and Winograd 1990).

4. Cognitive Theory and Second Language Acquisition

A reasonable connection between cognitive theory and second language acquisition is essential to explain why learning strategies have beneficial effects on second language learning. The foundation for this connection lies in how information is stored in memory, what information is learned, and how learning occurs. Information is stored as declarative knowledge or what people know, and as procedural knowledge or what people know how to do (Anderson 1983). The latter category includes complex cognitive procedures such as problem-solving and learning strategies (Gagné 1985), which may act on and modify or expand declarative knowledge. While there is debate over the form in which knowledge is stored in long-term memory, declarative knowledge can be construed as memory schemata and procedural knowledge can be viewed as a conditional series of "IF–THEN" connections that result in the execution of a complex

skill. Once learned to an acceptable level of mastery, procedural knowledge requires minimal processing capacity and attention is freed for other aspects of a task that require conscious effort.

What makes the distinction between declarative and procedural knowledge important is how each is learned and how they can be used to explain second language acquisition. While new declarative knowledge is learned most effectively through connections with previous memory structures, procedural knowledge seems to be learned best by opportunities for cued practice rather than through learning the rules for executing each step of a procedure (Gagné 1985). This is in contrast to Anderson's (1983) proposal that procedural knowledge is learned through stages beginning with cognitive control over the rules for each step in the procedure, continuing with practice to increase precision and speed, and culminating with refinement until the procedure becomes automatic. Since many language activities consist of procedures and, by implication, of procedural knowledge, Anderson's proposal would require that people gain second language skills by learning the rules at each step of a procedure, a severe difficulty since many of the rules may not be known and the rules that are known are difficult to retain. Whether through rules or cued practice, however, second languages appear to be learned through the gradual integration of skills as controlled processes initially predominate and later become automatic (McLaughlin et al. 1983).

If cued practice is as important for second language acquisition as it is for procedural knowledge, the learning of a second language may be most effective in an instructional setting with high levels of interactive communication and built-in feedback. However, during initial language acquisition, the feedback should be on the function and effectiveness of the communication rather than on structure and form, consistent with the shift toward a more communication-based type of instruction. Since a single teacher may be unable to provide individualized cued practice for all second language students in a typical classroom, cooperative learning and heterogeneous grouping to enhance cued feedback should be integral components of second language programs.

Learning strategies have been described as a special instance of procedural knowledge in the literature on both cognitive procedures and second language acquisition (Gagné 1985, O'Malley and Chamot 1990). Many strategies entail application of complex procedures such as scanning for information or predicting in reading, problem-solving in mathematics, and inferring the meaning of unfamiliar words from context. Like procedural knowledge, learning strategies are difficult to acquire, can conflict with previously learned ways of behaving, are embedded in specific tasks, and are difficult to transfer to new learning situations or tasks (Gagné 1985). Extensive research has nevertheless been conducted successfully showing the benefits of learning strategies with a variety of simple and complex academic tasks (e.g., Pressley et al. 1992), and the problem of transfer appears to be surmountable through direct instruction situated in specific content and metacognitive awareness (Brown et al. 1983, Palincsar and Brown 1984, Pressley et al. 1992). Since many second language learning tasks parallel those in first language learning, the extension of strategy instruction to second language learning should directly follow.

5. Second Language Learning, Learning Strategies, and Content Instruction

In the 1980s and early 1990s concerns were expressed that the most effective way to learn a language may be not through exclusive study of the language but through study of content areas using the second language (Chamot and O'Malley 1993, Mohan 1986). Content area instruction in second language learning has been advocated in both ESL (Crandall 1987, Mohan 1986) and in foreign language settings (Snow et al. 1989). The reasoning behind this notion is that content instruction carries with it inherent interest in meaningful subject matter such as science or literature, but language learning often focuses on less intrinsically interesting topics such as grammar and language mechanics while postponing for the future the functional use of language to achieve interpersonal or academic communication goals. This emphasis on content in second language acquisition has given prominence to what is referred to as cognitive academic language proficiency—the type of language used in learning, thinking, and reasoning with academic subjects. Academic language skills reportedly take far longer to master for students of English as a second language than the type of language used in interpersonal settings. If students previously expected to master the complexities of a second language are now expected to learn in one or more content areas as well, their task may be more interesting but can also be far more difficult.

The connection between second language learning and learning strategies becomes even more important with the emphasis on academic content in second language classrooms. The accumulated evidence supporting the use of learning strategies for tasks undertaken in nonlanguage subjects and the initial evidence supporting the use of learning strategies in second language learning both point to the importance of combining strategy instruction with second language content. There is a need for integrated instructional models in which strategies are combined with content instruction in second language classrooms. Instructional approaches for integrating content instruction

with learning strategies have been developed both in English as a second language (Chamot and O'Malley 1993, Mohan 1986) and foreign language classrooms (Chamot and Küpper 1989, Oxford 1990).

An example of an instructional model that integrates content and learning strategy instruction for second language learners is the Cognitive Academic Language Learning Approach (CALLA; Chamot and O'Malley 1993). This approach was originally designed to help ESL students succeed in school by providing transitional instruction from ESL or bilingual programs to grade-level classrooms, and has also been adapted for foreign language classrooms (Chamot and Küpper 1989, Chamot and O'Malley 1993). The merit of such integrated instructional models is in ensuring that strategy instruction is combined with the academic content with which it will be used, and is presented through direct instruction, accompanied by metacognitive awareness, and repeated at appropriate intervals to ensure transfer to similar tasks in the curriculum.

6. Conclusion

This entry has suggested that the analysis of student mental processes has constituted a paradigm shift in second language acquisition. Studies in cognitive psychology using first language contexts have been linked with research on second language acquisition processes to establish a theoretical foundation for learning strategies in second language acquisition. A substantial amount of research on second language learning strategies needs to be performed to address the many questions remaining in this area. Descriptive studies have provided a fairly comprehensive understanding of the learning strategies used by adolescent and adult second language learners in several different contexts. Expansion of this line of investigation into additional contexts, to cross-cultural learners, and especially to younger language learners, would broaden the understanding of developmental factors in the acquisition and use of learning strategies and metacognition. Research is needed on experimental interventions with strategy instruction in second language classrooms to determine how, when, and in what situations strategies can most effectively be learned. More rigorous methodological approaches than have been previously employed in second language contexts could provide the type of empirical evidence for the effects of strategy instruction that characterize such research in first language contexts.

At least three additional areas of research on second language learning strategies should be pursued: the effects of strategy instruction on student achievement, proficiency, and motivation; the degree and type of transfer of learning strategies from the first language to the second language and from the second language to the first language; and identification of effective staff development approaches to assist second language teachers in implementing strategy instruction.

See also: Learning Strategies and Learning to Learn

References

Absy C A 1992 Variation in approaches to EFL: A performance-based analysis of the learning strategies used by Brazilian students (Doctoral dissertation, Georgetown University, Washington, DC)

Anderson J R 1983 *The Architecture of Cognition.* Harvard University Press, Cambridge, Massachusetts

Brown A L, Bransford J D, Ferrara R A, Campione J C 1983 Learning, remembering, and understanding. In: Mussen P T (ed.) 1983 *Handbook of Child Psychology*, Vol. 3. Wiley, New York

Carroll J B 1990 Cognitive abilities in foreign language aptitude: Then and now. In: Parry T S, Stansfield C W (eds.) 1990 *Language Aptitude Reconsidered.* Prentice-Hall, Englewood Cliffs, New Jersey

Chamot A U, Küpper L 1989 Learning strategies in foreign language instruction. *Foreign Language Annals* 22(1): 13–24

Chamot A U, O'Malley J M 1993 *The CALLA Handbook: How to implement the Cognitive Academic Language Learning Approach.* Addison-Wesley, Reading, Massachusetts

Cohen A D, Aphek E 1981 Easifying second language learning. *Studies in Second Language Learning* 3: 221–36

Crandall J A (ed.) 1987 *ESL Through Content-area Instruction: Mathematics, Science, Social Studies.* Prentice Hall, Englewood Cliffs, New Jersey

Gagné E D 1985 *The Cognitive Psychology of School Learning.* Little, Brown, Boston, Massachusetts

Hosenfeld C, Arnold V, Kirchofer J, Laciura J, Wilson L 1981 Second language reading: A curricular sequence for teaching reading strategies. *Foreign Language Annals* 14(5): 415–22

Krashen S 1982 *Principles and Practice in Second Language Acquisition.* Pergamon Press, Oxford

McLaughlin B, Rossman T, McLeod B 1983 Second language learning: An information-processing perspective. *Language Learning* 33(2): 135–58

Mohan B A 1986 *Language and Content.* Addison-Wesley, Reading, Massachusetts

Naiman N, Fröhlich M, Stern H H, Todesco A 1978 *The Good Language Learner.* Ontario Institute for Studies in Education, Toronto

O'Malley J M, Chamot A U 1990 *Learning Strategies in Second Language Acquisition.* Cambridge University Press, Cambridge

Oxford R L 1990 *Language Learning Strategies: What Every Teacher Should Know.* Newbury House, New York

Padron Y N, Waxman H C 1988 The effects of ESL students' perceptions of their cognitive strategies on reading achievement. *TESOL Quarterly* 22(1): 146–50

Palincsar A S, Brown A L 1984 Reciprocal teaching of comprehension-fostering and comprehension-monitoring activities. *Cognition and Instruction* 1(2): 117–75

Paris S G, Winograd P 1990 How metacognition can promote academic learning and instruction. In: Jones B F, Idol L (eds.) 1990 *Dimensions of Thinking and Cognitive Instruction.* Erlbaum, Hillsdale, New Jersey

Politzer R L, McGroarty M 1985 An exploratory study of learning behaviors and their relationship to gains in linguistic and communicative competence. *TESOL Quarterly* 19(1): 103–23

Pressley M, et al. 1980 The keyword method of foreign vocabulary learning: An investigation of its generalizability. *J. Appl. Psychol.* 65(6): 635–42

Pressley M, Harris K R, Guthrie J T (eds.) 1992 *Promoting Academic Competence and Literacy in Schools.* Academic Press, San Diego

Rubin J 1975 What the "good language learner" can teach us. *TESOL Quarterly* 9(1): 41–51

Rubin J 1981 Study of cognitive processes in second language learning. *Applied Linguistics* 2(2): 117–31

Silver E A, Marshall S P 1990 Mathematical and scientific problem solving: Findings, issues, and instructional implications. In: Jones B F, Idol L (eds.) 1990 *Dimensions of Thinking and Cognitive Instruction.* Erlbaum, Hillsdale, New Jersey

Snow M A, Met M, Genesee F 1989 A conceptual framework for the integration of language and content in second/foreign language instruction. *TESOL Quarterly* 23(2): 201–17

Vandergrift L 1992 The comprehension strategies of second language (French) listeners (Doctoral dissertation, University of Alberta)

Vann R J, Abraham R G 1990 Strategies of unsuccessful language learners. *TESOL Quarterly* 24(2): 177–98

Weinstein C E, Mayer R E 1986 The teaching of learning strategies. In: Wittrock M C (ed.) 1986 *Handbook of Research on Teaching*, 3rd edn. Macmillan Inc., New York

Wenden A 1987 Metacognition: An expanded view on the cognitive abilities of L2 learners. *Language Learning* 37(4): 573–97

Zimmerman B J, Pons M M 1986 Development of a structured interview for assessing student use of self-regulated learning strategies. *Am. Educ. Res. J.* 23(4): 614–28

Further Reading

Anderson J R 1985 *Cognitive Psychology and its Implications*, 2nd edn. Freeman, New York

Brinton D M, Snow M A, Wesche M B 1989 *Content-based Second Language Instruction.* Newbury House, New York

Jones B F, Palincsar A S, Ogle D S, Carr E G 1987 *Strategic Teaching and Learning: Cognitive Instruction in the Content-Areas.* ASCD, Alexandria, Virginia

Pressley M 1990 *Cognitive Strategy Instruction that Really Improves Children's Academic Performance.* Brookline Books, Cambridge, Massachusetts

Wenden A, Rubin J (eds.) 1987 *Learner Strategies in Language Learning.* Prentice-Hall, Englewood Cliffs, New Jersey

Linguistics and Language Learning

B. Spolsky

The intersection of linguistics and language learning has led to several distinct areas of study. The unifying field of educational linguistics examines issues such as the characteristics of the language being taught, the spread of its use in the community in which the learner lives and in which his or her school is located, factors associated with setting goals in foreign language education, and the effectiveness of teaching strategies in attaining various educational goals.

One subarea of educational linguistics is pedagogical grammar, concerning itself with identifying grammatical rules which facilitate the teaching and the learning of a particular language at various phases of its acquisition, in contrast to scientific grammar, which eventually will exhaustively describe the ideal use of a language. Another area of educational linguistics is contrastive analysis, which examines similarities and differences between the mother tongue of the learner and the language being taught, with the aim of predicting difficulties that learners may encounter in the process of mastering a particular language. Finally, error analysis is based on the systematic study of errors that learners commit at various phases of learning a particular language.

1. Educational Linguistics

The scope of educational linguistics is defined both by the areas that it encompasses, such as language education policy; first and second language learning and teaching; reading; literacy; composition; bilingual, immigrant, and minority education; language testing; and by the fields from which it derives its theoretical foundations, including theoretical linguistics, sociolinguistics, psycholinguistics, and anthropological linguistics (Spolsky 1978a). The focus of study may be on the society (e.g., what languages are used for what purposes?) or the individual (e.g., what is the communicative competence of the person whose education is being examined?). A first major distinction arises between rare homogeneous and more common heterogeneous speech communities, where several varieties are in systematically structured alternative use in the same community, resulting in various kinds of societal bilingualism or diglossia, where one variety is used for informal functions usually including school (Lewis 1980, Spolsky 1988). Studies of communicative competence have shown that language education must be concerned with the ability of the learner to participate in a society as a speaking and communicating member. Approaches that are concerned only with a single variety, or with such a narrow issue as the shibboleths or standard grammar rules of a prestigious written variety are unlikely to meet the needs of those being educated. It is necessary to know the patterns of language use in the communities from which children come, the values ascribed to language by different sectors of society, the actual language ability of the children in the various settings in which they are required to communicate, and the modifications in ability that will best fit the children to function as communicating members of the society they are preparing to join.

Second language learning is a complex process that occurs naturally in all children. In normal circumstances, children acquire the socially expected control of the variety or varieties to which they are exposed before coming to school. Educational linguistics stresses the broad range of communicative competence and the full social context in which language operates. Basic is the notion that all living languages offer evidence of comparable complexity and so of comparable potential for cognitive development; there is no linguistic evidence of an inherently inferior language, and no linguistic support for the notion that one language is intrinsically better than another. At the same time, all varieties of language are socially valued, and this social value rather than inherent linguistic value or quality is usually what determines language education policy. In a strongly religious community, the variety of language associated with the religion or the language of its sacred texts is likely to have the highest prestige; in a modern industrialized society, the variety used by the dominant social group is usually the prestige variety; in the academic world the style and variety of writing called academic prose has the highest prestige. Prestige is crucial in the determination of rationales and goals for language education. There have generally only been sketchy descriptions of language situations and inadequate methods of measuring the actual level of language control achieved by children before they begin their education; as a result the development of aims and curricula for language education programs is often misguided.

Rationales for language education might be linguistic (the notion that acquisition of a variety of language is good in itself), psychological (the notion that mastery of a variety of language has value for personal, emotional, or intellectual growth), sociopolitical (the notion that control of a variety of language has value for a social or political unit), cultural (the notion that knowledge of a variety of language provides access to the religious or cultural knowledge of specific bodies), or pedagogical. The existence of many competing sources of pressure provides the potential for conflict. In heterogeneous communities the study of language education becomes a study of political struggle (Phillipson 1992).

There are a number of unfounded opinions about language education which are likely to influence policymakers, parents, and educators. The first of these is the notion that there is a single correct variety of language. In actual fact, sociolinguistic research has shown that all societies have a complex pattern of social values attached to a wide range of registers, varieties, styles, and languages. A second misleading notion is the idea that language education should be concerned with reading and writing alone. Speaking and listening skills are just as important in most communities and deserve full attention from the school, whether in teaching of the mother tongue or of foreign language. A third mistaken notion has already been discussed: there is no evidence of inherent inferiority in any particular language. A fourth notion that has not stood up to empirical testing is the dictum of UNESCO experts and others that reading must be taught in the mother tongue: there are many situations in which high levels of literacy are achieved in a second language. A fifth incorrect notion is the idea that bilingualism is in some way harmful. This notion, derived from the work of psychologists who carried out their studies in societies where bilingualism was stigmatized as a mark of membership of a linguistic minority, has been refuted by studies of cases where bilingualism is a mark of membership of an elite group (Skutnabb-Kangas and Cummins 1988).

A language education policy may choose to extend and improve the variety of language that a child brings from home (mother tongue education, vernacular education, language arts education, teaching of reading and writing), to add another variety for limited use (foreign language or classical language education) or for general use (bilingual education), or to replace the home language with another language immediately (the home–school language switch, submersion, second language education), or later (transitional bilingual education), or temporarily (immersion foreign language teaching). More than one additional or replacement language may be taught. The policy may or may not be congruent with the actual situation: for instance, failing to recognize the actual home or community language situation, a school may use a mother tongue approach when the pupils are in fact learning a foreign or second language.

Fundamental policy questions are starting age and the amount of time to be devoted to language instruction. Assuming that the mother tongue is to be taught, the most general pattern is to teach it first, but in certain colonialist or postcolonialist situations, instruction in the mother tongue has been delayed until secondary school. There is considerable controversy over the age at which second or foreign language instruction should begin. Research suggests that an early start, combined with appropriate methods, leads ultimately to higher levels of mastery.

The amount of time devoted to language instruction is varied. A number of experiences (the United States Armed Services Training Program and the Foreign Services Institute methods that developed from it, the *ulpanim* in Israel, the immersion bilingual programs in Canada, to name a few of the better-known) have made clear the value of intensive programs for learners of all ages, so that it is clear that the attainment of mastery of a second language comparable to that of a first requires comparable exposure. Political and practical considerations usually mean, however, that only a few hours' instruction a week are available.

The implementation of policy covers the full range of language education pedagogy: method, approach, materials, and teachers. More than most fields, this field's pedagogical history is marked by the regular announcement and temporary acceptance of new panaceas for old ills: a list need only be made of some of the labels that have been popular in the various parts of the field:

(a) in reading: phonics, look-see or whole word, speed reading;

(b) in heterogeneous speech communities: mother tongue, vernacular, transitional or maintenance enrichment, compensatory bilingual, or bilingual–bicultural monoliterate or biliterate, second language;

(c) in foreign or second language teaching: new method, natural method, direct method, audiolingual method, immersion, cognitive method, language for special purposes or for academic purposes, notional, functional, or notional–functional, content-based.

Curricula and textbooks have multiplied, sometimes but not always reflecting growth in understanding of the complex learning processes involved. With the increase of modern technology, language education has joined the subjects that are considered to benefit from modern equipment, such as record players, tape recorders, elaborate systems of tape recorders organized into language laboratories, film, television, programmed instruction with or without computer control, and videodisks. All of these technologies have been applied to various aspects of language education, with varying levels of success.

The selection and training of teachers are also matters of considerable variation and dispute. In traditional societies, the status of language teachers has ranged from that of the Greek slave in Rome to that of the priestly scribe in ancient Israel. In modern societies, people who teach the mother tongue or foreign languages usually share the social status of other teachers, although it is generally the case in tertiary education that those who teach use of language have lower status than those who teach about it. The question of who should teach a language —a native speaker of the variety being taught or a native speaker of the learners' variety—is usually resolved on political or economic grounds rather than on pedagogical ones. Similarly, the question of the best training for language teachers depends on who has control of the universities or institutions where they are trained, which thus determines whether the major emphasis of training be on the language to be taught, on its literature, on linguistics, or on general educational theories and practices.

The measurement and evaluation of outcomes of various programs and the testing of individual students are also central concerns of educational linguistics, but are adequately treated elsewhere. Organizationally, the field of educational linguistics remains comparatively unrepresented: educational linguists are found and trained in various parts of the university, most often where there is collaboration between scholars in education, linguistics, anthropology, and language departments.

2. Pedagogic Grammar

A pedagogic grammar is a collection of explicit generalizations about a language, derived generally from one or more scientific grammars to provide practical teaching material. Notwithstanding the systematic relationship between scientific and pedagogic grammars, they differ significantly with respect to two important features: (a) their inherent goals; (b) the manner in which they represent the linguistic rules (Spolsky 1978b).

The major aim or underlying motivation of a scientific grammar is to describe and explain linguistic knowledge. Such a grammar seeks, therefore, to develop the best theoretical model or framework to provide a vocabulary for discussing the elements of language, such as sounds, words, phrases, clauses, sentences, and discourse units, as well as the linguistic rules that define and explain how these elements are used. The writer of a scientific grammar aims to give a systematic account of the idealized linguistic knowledge or competence that underlies the actual use of language in concrete communicative situations.

The goal of a pedagogic grammar is quite different, since its major objective is to impart knowledge. Such a grammar concerns itself with the needs of the learner

and the teacher. A pedagogic grammar is therefore, by definition, prescriptive in nature, since it must guide the learner in using language properly.

In the process of converting linguistic rules into pedagogic generalizations, the writer of a pedagogic grammar has to follow didactic considerations. The ordering of the rules is, therefore, guided by usefulness, frequency, conceptual familiarity, and contrast with the mother tongue of the learners. A careful process of sequencing, grading, and recycling of information needs to be applied to the ordering of the rules, thus rendering a grammar very different in nature from the scientific grammar or grammars upon which it is based. Some of the rules in the pedagogic grammar give only partial information, and therefore violate the true linguistic validity of these rules, but such partial definitions may be the result of careful pedagogic considerations and are therefore necessary for the acquisition process (Allen 1974).

3. Contrastive Linguistics

Contrastive linguistic analysis is a subdiscipline of comparative linguistics concerned with the comparison of two or more languages or subsystems of languages to determine the differences or similarities between them. After some pioneering contrastive studies with a primarily theoretical bias in the early twentieth century, contrastive linguistic analysis received major impetus from attempts in the United States in the 1940s and 1950s to work out effective and economical foreign language teaching methods. The most efficient language teaching materials and techniques were thought to require a scientific description of the language to be taught, carefully compared with a parallel description of the learner's native language (Fries 1945). The underlying theoretical assumption was the idea, expressed by Lado (1957), that the degree of difference between the two languages also correlated with the degree of difficulty. Later on, attention was also called to the similarities between the languages, and it was found that differences and similarities can be equally problematic. In the United States, a series of extensive contrastive linguistic analyses were undertaken in the 1960s between English and a number of other languages, and in Europe several contrastive projects were launched somewhat later (Fisiak 1981). Although the objectives were normally clearly applied, the results applicable for specific purposes have remained minimal, which has given rise to doubts about the validity of contrastive studies.

Contrastive studies nowadays may be theoretical or applied. As well as giving an extensive account of the differences and similarities between the languages compared, theoretical studies provide an adequate model for cross-language comparison and determine how and which elements are comparable. Theoretical contrastive linguistic studies are also useful in adding to the knowledge about the languages contrasted. No claims are made as to the applicability of the results for specific purposes.

Applied contrastive studies aim at gathering contrastive information for specific purposes, such as language teaching, translation, and bilingual education. The major concern is the identification of potential trouble in the use of the target language. The main concern of early applied contrastive studies was to devise a reliable prediction of the learner's difficulties. This was later to be called the strong hypothesis of contrastive analysis. The strong hypothesis did not prove to be valid because similarities and differences between the languages were not the only causes of problems for the learner. Error analysis was therefore offered as an alternative to contrastive studies, and the predictive role of contrastive studies was superseded by an explanatory one in this weak version of the contrastive hypothesis. Despite continued criticism, contrastive analysis remains a useful tool in the search for the sources of potential trouble. It cannot be overlooked either in syllabus design, or in the preparation of textbooks and teaching materials (Fisiak 1981, Sajavaara and Lehtonen 1975).

4. Error Analysis

Correction of errors has always been a common practice in foreign language teaching. A systematic analysis of learners' errors was introduced in the wake of contrastive analysis. Variability in learner performance could not, however, be explained by means of error analysis alone, and the basic problems found in contrastive analysis, such as comparability of specific items and equivalence, remained.

Traditional error analysis consists of five stages. In error recognition, an attempt is made to distinguish systematic competence errors from performance errors; that is, mistakes and lapses easily corrected by the learner when pointed out (Corder 1981). In the following stages, the errors are described according to a model and classified. In the explanation of the errors, three causes are usually distinguished: interlingual errors caused by interference from the mother tongue, intralingual errors caused by the target language system, and teaching-induced errors. At the final stage, the errors are compared with target language norms to assess their influence on the success of communication. The decisions about

the nature of feedback to be provided to learners are crucially dependent on the systematicity of the errors.

More recent approaches to error analysis consider systematic errors to be markers of the learner's progress—the phenomenon has come to be characterized as interlanguage, transitional competence, approximative system, or idiosyncratic dialect. It is characterized as a distinct linguistic system resulting from the learner's attempts to achieve target language norms (Selinker 1972).

The main problem in error analysis is the same as in contrastive analysis. The theory and methodology of linguistics are insufficient to explain the phenomena involved. A wider framework is needed, involving psychological, sociological, neurological, and other related insights into cognitive mechanisms and information processing in the brain and the speech channel as a whole.

See also: Language and Learning in Education

References

Allen J P B 1974 Pedagogic grammar. In: Allen J P B, Corder S P (eds.) 1970 *The Edinburgh Course in Applied Linguistics.* Oxford University Press, London
Corder S P 1981 *Error Analysis and Interlanguage.* Oxford University Press, London
Fisiak J (ed.) 1981 *Contrastive Analysis and the Language Teacher.* Pergamon Press, Oxford
Fries C C 1945 *Teaching and Learning English as a Foreign Language.* University of Michigan Press, Ann Arbor, Michigan
Lado R 1957 *Linguistics Across Cultures: Applied Linguistics for Language Teachers.* University of Michigan Press, Ann Arbor, Michigan
Lewis E G 1980 *Bilingualism and Bilingual Education: A Comparative Study.* University of New Mexico Press, Albuquerque, New Mexico
Phillipson R 1992 *Linguistic Imperialism.* Oxford University Press, Oxford
Sajavaara K, Lehtonen J (eds.) 1975 *A Select Bibliography of Contrastive Analysis.* University of Jyväskylä, Jyväskylä
Selinker L L 1972 Interlanguage. *International Review of Applied Linguistics in Language Teaching* 10(3): 209–31
Skutnabb-Kangas T, Cummins J (eds.) 1988 *Minority Education: From Shame to Struggle.* Multilingual Matters Ltd, Clevedon
Spolsky B 1978a *Educational Linguistics: An Introduction.* Newbury, Rowley, Massachusetts
Spolsky B 1978b The relevance of grammar to second language pedagogy. *The AILA Bulletin* 2(23): 5–14
Spolsky B 1988 Bilingualism. In: Newmeyer F H (ed.) 1988 *Linguistics: The Cambridge Survey.* Cambridge University Press, Cambridge

Mathematics, Learning and Instruction of

E. De Corte, L. Verschaffel and B. Greer

The domain of mathematics learning and teaching is one of the most representative examples of the subject-matter orientation in research on learning and instruction. Since it emerged in the 1970s this domain has produced a vast body of studies which have been excellently reviewed in the *Handbook of Research on Mathematics Teaching and Learning* (Grouws 1992) and in the *International Handbook of Mathematics Education* (Bishop 1996). The two major groups that have been involved in this work are: (a) psychologists, who use mathematics as a field for investigating fundamental issues of learning, development, and teaching; (b) scholars having a primary interest in mathematics education who draw upon the theoretical concepts and the research tools of cognitive psychology. Initially communication between these groups was rather difficult (Fischbein 1990), but the relationship has since developed into an increasingly productive interaction that has been enriched by contributions from other perspectives such as anthropological and cross-cultural work. Within this community, there has developed an enriched conception of mathematics learning as involving the construction of meaning and understanding based on the modeling of reality.

During the same period several important shifts occurred in both conceptual and methodological approaches to mathematics learning and teaching: from a focus on general to domain-specific processes; from a concentration on the individual to a concern for social and cultural factors; from "cold" to "hot" cognition; from the laboratory to the classroom as the primary setting for research; and from a quantitative experimental approach to a more diversified methodological repertoire, including qualitative and interpretative techniques (see, e.g., Steffe et al. 1996)

These developments will be outlined in three sections: a dispositional view of mathematics learning (Sect. 1); mathematics learning as the construction of knowledge in sociocultural contexts (Sect. 2); designing powerful teaching-learning environments (Sect. 3). (see De Corte et al. 1996 for a more detailed discussion).

1. A Dispositional View of Mathematics Learning

This section focuses on what students should learn in order to acquire competence in mathematics. In this respect, the more or less implicit view that prevails in educational practice is that computational and procedural skills are the essential requirements (see, e.g., Gehrke et al. 1992). This contrasts very sharply with the view that has emerged from the research referred to above. Indeed, there is now a broad consensus that the major characteristics underlying mathematical cognition and thinking are the following (see De Corte 1995, Schoenfeld 1992):

(a)   a well-organized and flexibly accessible domain-specific knowledge base involving facts, symbols, conventions, definitions, formulas, algorithms, concepts, and rules that constitute the contents of mathematics as a subject-matter field;

(b)   heuristic methods, that is, search strategies for problem-solving that do not guarantee the finding of the solution, but substantially increase the probability of success because they induce a systematic approach to the task (e.g., carefully analyzing a problem; decomposing a problem into subgoals; visualizing the problem using a diagram or a drawing);

(c)   metacognition, involving knowledge and beliefs concerning one's own cognitive functioning on the one hand (e.g., believing that one's mathematical ability is strong), and skills and strategies relating to the self-monitoring and regulation of one's cognitive processes on the other (e.g., planning a solution process; monitoring an ongoing solution process; evaluating and, if necessary, debugging a solution; reflecting on one's learning and problem-solving activities);

(d)   affective components involving beliefs about mathematics (e.g., believing that solving a math problem requires effort, or believing that it is a matter of luck), attitudes (e.g., liking or disliking story problems), and emotions (e.g., satisfaction when one finds the solution of a difficult problem) (see McLeod and Adams 1989).

It is certainly useful to distinguish these four categories of components, but it is also important to realize that in expert mathematical cognition they are applied integratively and interactively. For example, discovering the applicability of a heuristic to solve a geometry problem is generally based, at least partially, on a person's conceptual knowledge about the geometrical figures involved. A negative illustration is that a belief such as "solving a math problem should not last more than a few minutes" will inhibit a thorough heuristic and metacognitive approach to a difficult problem. In other words, acquiring competence in mathematics involves more than the mere sum of the four components listed above. As a further elaboration of this view the notion of a "mathematical disposition" introduced in the *Curriculum and Evaluation Standards for School Mathematics* (Commission on Standards for School Mathematics of the National Council for Teachers of Mathematics 1989 p. 233) in the United States points to the integrated availability and application of the different components:

> Learning mathematics extends beyond learning concepts, procedures, and their application. It also includes developing a disposition toward mathematics and seeing mathematics as a powerful way for looking at situations. Disposition refers not simply to attitudes but to a tendency to think and to act in positive ways. Students' mathematical dispositions are manifested in the way they approach tasks—whether with confidence, willingness to explore alternatives, perseverance, and interest—and in their tendency to reflect on their own thinking.

According to Perkins (1991) the notion of disposition also involves, besides ability, inclination and sensitivity. Inclination is the tendency to engage in a given behavior because of motivation and habits; sensitivity refers to the feeling for, and alertness to, opportunities for implementing the appropriate behavior. Ability, then, combines both the knowledge and the skill—in other words, most of the characteristics mentioned above—to deploy that behavior. The acquisition of a disposition—especially the sensitivity and inclination aspects—requires extensive experience with the different categories of knowledge and skills in a large variety of situations. As such, the disposition cannot be directly taught, but rather has to develop over an extensive period (see Greeno 1991).

2. Mathematics Learning as the Construction of Meaning in Sociocultural Contexts

The question arises, then, as to what kind of learning processes are conducive to the attainment of the intended mathematical disposition in students. The negative answer seems to be that this disposition cannot be achieved through learning as it occurs in most classrooms. Indeed, the international literature bulges with findings indicating that students in schools are not equipped with the necessary knowledge, skills, beliefs, and motivation to approach new mathematical problems and learning tasks in an efficient and successful way (see, e.g., De Corte 1992). This can largely be accounted for by the prevailing learning activities in schools, which consist mainly of listening, watching, and imitating the teacher and the textbook (Greeno 1991). In other words, the dominant view of learning in the practice of mathematics education is still the information-transmission model, implying that the mathematical knowledge acquired and institutionalized by past generations has to be transmitted as accurately as possible to the next generation (Romberg and Carpenter 1986).

An additional shortcoming of current mathematics education, which is related to the inappropriate view of learning as information-absorption, is that knowledge is often acquired independently from the social and physical contexts from which it derives its meaning and usefulness. This has become very obvious from a substantial amount of research carried out since the mid-1980s on the influence of cultural and situational factors on mathematics learning, and commonly classified under the heading "ethnomathematics and everyday mathematical cognition" (Nunes 1992). For example, a series of investigations on so-called "street mathematics" has shown that there often exists a gap between formal school mathematics and the informal mathematics applied to solve everyday, real-life problems.

The preceding description of the learner as an absorber and consumer of decontextualized mathematical knowledge contrasts sharply with the conception supported by a substantial amount of evidence in the literature showing that learning is an active and constructive process. Learners are not passive recipients of information; rather, they actively construct their mathematical knowledge and skills through interaction with the physical and social environment, and through reorganization of their prior mental structures (see Steffe and Gale 1995).

Although there are conceptual differences along the continuum from radical to realistic constructivism (see *Constructivism and Learning*), the idea is broadly shared that learning is also a social process through which students construct mathematical knowledge and skills cooperatively; opportunities for learning occur during social interaction through collaborative dialogue, explanation and justification, and negotiation of meaning (Cobb and Banersfeld 1995). Research on small-group learning supports this "social constructivist" perspective; cooperative learning can yield positive learning effects in both cognitive and social–emotional respects. However, it has also become obvious that simply putting students in small groups and telling them to work together is not a panacea; it is only under appropriate conditions that small-group learning can be expected to be productive (Good et al. 1992). Moreover, stressing the social dimension of the construction of knowledge does not exclude the possibility that students also develop new knowledge and skills individually. In addition, most scholars share the assumption of the so-called "cultural constructivist" perspective (Scott et al. 1992) that active and constructive learning can be mediated through appropriate guidance by teachers, peers, and cultural artifacts such as educational media.

3. The Design of Powerful Teaching–Learning Environments

Taking into account the view of mathematical learning as the construction of meaning and understanding, and the goal of mathematics education as the acquisition of a mathematical disposition involving the mastery of different categories of knowledge and skills, a challenging task has to be addressed. It consists of elaborating a coherent framework of research-based principles for the design of powerful teaching–learning environments; that is, situations and contexts that can elicit in students the learning activities and processes conducive to the intended mathematical disposition.

A variety of projects attempting the theory-based design of powerful mathematics learning environments has already been carried out (see De Corte et al. 1996 for a selective overview), reflecting the methodological shifts toward the application of teaching experiments in real classrooms and toward the use of a diversity of techniques for data collection and analysis including qualitative and interpretative methods. For example, Lampert (1986) has designed a learning environment that aims at promoting meaning construction and understanding of multiplication in fourth graders by connecting and integrating principled conceptual knowledge (e.g., the principles of additive and multiplicative composition, associativity, commutativity, and the distributive property of multiplication over addition) with their computational skills. She starts from familiar problems, allowing children to use and explore their informal prior knowledge, and practises collaborative instruction whereby she engages in cooperative work and discussion with the whole class. Students are solicited to propose and invent alternative solutions to problems, which are then discussed, including their explanation and justification.

A second and more comprehensive example is Realistic Mathematics Education (RME), which was developed in the Netherlands. RME conceives mathematics learning essentially as doing mathematics starting from the study of phenomena in the real world. This provides topics for mathematical modeling and results in the reinvention of mathematical knowledge. Based on this fundamental conception of doing mathematics, the design of "realistic" learning environments is guided by a set of five interrelated principles: (a) learning mathematics is a constructive activity; (b) progressing toward higher levels of abstraction; (c) encouraging students' free production and reflection; (d) learning through social interaction and cooperation; (e) interconnecting knowledge components and skills (Treffers 1987).

These representative examples illustrate efforts within the domain of research on mathematics learning and teaching to implement innovative educational settings embodying to some degree ideas that have emerged from theoretical and empirical studies, such as the constructivist view of learning, the conception of mathematics as human activity, the crucial role of students' prior—informal as well as formal—knowledge, the orientation toward understanding and problem-solving, the importance of social interaction and collaboration in doing and learning mathematics, and the need to embed mathematics learning into authentic and meaningful contexts. The results of

projects reported so far are promising, as they demonstrate that this kind of learning environment can lead to fundamental changes in the sort of mathematics knowledge, skills, and beliefs that children acquire, and to making them more autonomous learners and problem-solvers. However, these projects also raise questions for future research. For example, there is a strong need for additional theoretical and empirical work aiming at a better understanding and fine-grained analysis of the acquisition processes that this type of learning environment elicits in students, of the precise nature of the knowledge and beliefs they acquire, and of the critical dimensions that can account for the power of this kind of environment.

See also: Mathematics Education, Affective Issues in; Computers and Learning; Constructivism and Learning; Declarative and Procedural Knowledge; Learning Environments; Expert Knowledge and Performance

References

Bishop A J 1996 *International Handbook of Mathematics Education.* Kluwer, Dordrecht

Cobb P, Banersfeld H (eds.) 1995 *The Emergence of Mathematical Meaning.* Erlbaum, Hillsdale, New Jersey

Commission on Standards for School Mathematics of the National Council of Teachers of Mathematics 1989 *Curriculum and Evaluation Standards for School Mathematics.* National Council of Teachers of Mathematics, Reston, Virginia

De Corte E 1992 On the learning and teaching of problem-solving skills in mathematics and LOGO programming. *Appl. Psychol.* 41: 317–31

De Corte E 1995 Fostering cognitive growth: A perspective from research on mathematics learning and instruction. *Educ. Psychol.* 30: 37–46

De Corte E, Greer B, Verschaffel L 1996 Mathematics. In: Berliner D C, Calfee R C (eds.) 1996 *Handbook of Educational Psychology.* Macmillan, New York

Fischbein E 1990 Introduction. In: Nesher P, Kilpatrick J (eds.) 1990 *Mathematics and Cognition: A Research Synthesis by the International Group for the Psychology of Mathematics Education* (ICMI Study Series). Cambridge University Press, Cambridge

Gehrke N J, Knapp M S, Sirotkin K A 1992 In search of the school curriculum. In: Grant G (ed.) 1992 *Review of Research in Education,* Vol. 18. American Educational Research Association, Washington, DC

Good T L, Mulryan C, McCaslin M 1992 Grouping for instruction in mathematics: A call for programmatic research on small-group processes. In: Grouws D A (ed.) 1992

Greeno J G 1991 Number sense as situated knowing in a conceptual domain *J. Res. Math. Educ.* 22(3): 170–218

Grouws D A (ed.) 1992 *Handbook of Research on Mathematics Teaching and Learning.* Macmillan Inc., New York

Lampert M 1986 Knowing, doing, and teaching multiplication. *Cognition and Instruction* 3: 305–42

McLeod D B, Adams V M (eds.) 1989 *Affect and Mathematical Problem Solving. A New Perspective.* Springer-Verlag, New York

Nunes T 1992 Ethnomathematics and everyday cognition. In: Grouws D A (ed.) 1992

Perkins D N 1991 Creativity and its development: A dispositional approach. Address given at the *Congreso Internacional de Psicologia y Education: Intervencion Psicoeducativa*, Madrid

Romberg T A, Carpenter T P 1986 Research on teaching and learning mathematics: Two disciplines of scientific inquiry. In: Wittrock M (ed.) 1986 *Handbook of Research on Teaching*, 3rd edn. Macmillan Inc., New York

Schoenfeld A H 1992 Learning to think mathematically: Problem solving, metacognition, and sense-making in mathematics. In: Grouws D (ed.) 1992

Scott T, Cole M, Engel M 1992 Computers and education: A cultural constructivist perspective In: Grant G (ed.) 1992 *Review of Research in Education*, Vol. 18. American Educational Research Association, Washington, DC

Steffe L, Nesher P, Cobb P, Goldin G, Greer B (eds.) 1996 Theories of mathematical learning. In: Bishop A J 1996

Steffe L P, Gale J (eds.) 1995 *Constructivism in Education*. Erlbaum, Hillsdale, New Jersey

Treffers A 1987 *Three Dimensions: A Model of Goal and Theory Description in Mathematics Instruction—The Wiskobas Project*. Reidel, Dordrecht

Mathematics and Language

D. Pimm

There are many different relationships between language and mathematics. This entry will refer almost exclusively to an area of mathematics education in which such relationships are examined. These considerations can frequently be found under the heading of "the language of mathematics," though this latter phrase can be interpreted in a number of senses. It can mean: (a) the spoken language of the mathematics classroom (including both teacher and pupil talk); (b) the use of particular words for mathematical ends (often referred to as the "mathematics register"); (c) the language of texts (conventional word problems or textbooks, including graphic material and other modes of representation, issues of word frequency and readability); or (d) the language of written symbolic forms. Each of these perspectives will be examined in turn.

It is important to note that "the language of mathematics" can also refer to language used in aid of an individual doing mathematics alone (and therefore include "inner speech" for instance), as well as language employed with the intent of communicating with others. As Barnes (1976) has commented: "Communication is not the only function of language." The Canadian literary critic Frye (1963) has referred to "the language of mathematics, which is really one of the languages of the imagination, along with literature and music."

One area to which "language and mathematics" could refer, but customarily does not, is the mathematical study of language per se, in the sense of linguist Noam Chomsky's syntactic paradigm. (This took the mathematical notions of function, variable, and predicate and used them to formalize a theory of written sentence structure for natural language.) Such activity is more usually subsumed under language studies.

Since Aiken's (1972) seminal research review on language factors in learning mathematics, study of language and mathematics has exploded dramatically —a comprehensive bibliography would run to thousands of entries. In part, this phenomenal growth has paralleled the increasing interest in language and social factors in education in general, after decades of relative underemphasis during what might be called "the Piagetian years." General reviews of the area of language and mathematics can be found in the collections of Cocking and Mestre (1988), Durkin and Shire (1991), Ellerton and Clements (1991), Pimm (1994), and in Laborde et al. (1990).

1. Communicating Mathematically in Classrooms

Within natural language, there are conventionally two main channels, those of speech and writing. It is important, however, not to ignore the particular nature of working with mathematics and either the deaf (e.g., Barham and Bishop 1991) or the visually impaired. The teaching and learning of mathematics involve activities such as listening and discussing, reading and writing. Each of these linguistic aspects of classrooms has engendered considerable work: a few trends in each will be mentioned here.

1.1 Listening and Discussing

Since the early 1980s, discussion in mathematics classrooms and teacher gambits to promote and facilitate it have moved onto educational agendas in some Western countries (in the United Kingdom with the Cockcroft Report—United Kingdom Department of Education and Science 1982), and in the United States with the publication of the NCTM Standards document (1989). Attempts have been made to specify which parts of classroom talk are to count as mathematical discussion. For instance, Pirie and Schwarzenberger (1988 p. 461) offer the specification: "It [mathematical discussion] is purposeful talk on a mathematical subject in which there are genuine pupil contributions and interaction."

Work looking at the question of reporting back on open-ended or problem-solving activity has raised and explored a number of questions about active listening, as well as the linguistic demands placed on all participants when engaged in reporting back to the rest of the class. Questions arising include the following: How can students develop the linguistic skills of reflection and selection of what to report? How can they work on acquiring a sense of audience? To whom is the reporter talking? For a general account of the role of listening in mathematical reasoning, see Davis (1996).

1.2 Reading and Writing

There are important differences between speech and writing, not least with regard to relative permanence and linear or nonlinear flow in time. Moreover, writing provides the possibility for the whole discourse to be seen at one time and thus serves as an aid for reflection. There has been little research on reading in mathematics and on strategies and skills relevant to what can be read (Borasi and Siegel 1990). The acquisition of reading facility involves constructing meaning from written texts, which becomes increasingly central as students progress through the educational system (Laborde et al. 1991).

One area of research on writing has involved looking at student journals. Waywood (1988) has formulated an initial classification of types of secondary-school journal writing as a framework for analyzing how journals provide a vehicle for student learning. His proposed triple, sequential categorization of use is: (a) recount (narrative); (b) summary description; (c) dialogue (between ideas). His aim is one of reflection on learning, and the work has generated the hypothesis that the mode of journal writing reflects a stance toward learning on the part of the student. (For an account of journal work with much younger children see Phillips and Crespo 1996.)

In general, since the mid-1970s techniques of discourse analysis have been used to examine aspects of classroom discourse, among other linguistic contexts, and to highlight certain normative aspects of language use in these particular speech settings. One early "finding" by Sinclair and Coulthard (1975) was the almost incessant repetition of the sequence I(nitiation)—R(esponse)—F(eedback) in teacher—pupil exchanges. (A more detailed account of this IRF sequence, and some transcripts from lessons in which mathematics teachers found ways of escaping from it, are given in Pimm 1987.)

More generally, the third major, developing area of linguistics (in addition to syntax and semantics) called pragmatics is increasingly being drawn upon. Pragmatics deals with how words can be used to do things, to achieve one's ends in the world, and one core source is philosopher Paul Grice's (1989) work on implicatures and discourse coherence. Two instances of pragmatic accounts invoking Grice's work in mathematics education can be found in Rowland (1995) and Gerofsky (1995).

Finally, another general orientation (arising from ethnographic research) has involved the notions of representativeness and voice. Who gets to speak? From whom does one hear and how? And about what? One result of the disciplined ways of research that many fields develop may be that the same voice (or voices) is replicated again and again. It is worth asking these questions of mathematics classrooms. One focus might be on representativeness of the voices of the two sexes, or of various ethnic or social groups. Another might be more on the form and structure of spoken interactions between mathematics teachers and pupils in general.

2. The Mathematics Register

"Register" is a technical linguistic term used to describe meanings that are appropriate to a particular function of language (here, the expressing of mathematical ideas) together with the words and structures that express those meanings. With regard to the mathematics register, Halliday has written (1975 p. 65):

> We can refer to a 'mathematics register', in the sense of the meanings that belong to the language of mathematics (the mathematical use of natural language, that is: not mathematics itself), and that a language must express if it is used for mathematical purposes. [. . .] It is the meanings, including the styles of meaning and modes of argument, that constitute a register, rather than the words and structures as such. We should not think of a mathematical register as solely consisting of terminology, or of the development of a register as simply a process of adding new words. In order to express new meanings, it may be necessary to invent new words; but there are many different ways in which a language can add new meanings and inventing words is only one of them.

Mathematics classes take place in a mixture of "ordinary" language and "mathematical" language, where the latter refers to use of the mother tongue for mathematical purposes. Many confusions occur as a result of differing linguistic interpretations, with pupils endeavoring to use nonmathematical meanings to interpret mathematical terminology.

Walkerdine (1988 p. 97) cited an example from the experience of an infant school teacher, when the teacher had been discussing with her class the notions of odd and even numbers. She proceeded round the room labeling the tables as odd or even according to the number of children at each. One child regularly got up and left the particular table he was at, if it were about to be labeled "odd." A group of children would regularly cheer the even numbers and boo the odd ones. When asked why they did this, they replied:

"We like evens better." (The term "odd" can mean either "peculiar" or "not divisible by two without a remainder," according to the context of the utterance.)

Examples can also be found at secondary and university levels. Cornu (1981) drew attention to problems that French students have with the sense of *limite* and *tends vers* and to the semantic coloration or "contamination" that occurs by imputing aspects of situations where such terms are ordinarily used (e.g., speed limits) to the mathematical setting. A common topological error is to presume that a set which is not open must be closed—because *open* and *closed* are opposites in normal English usage. Thus, it is not just the meanings of isolated terms but the way they are structured in the lexicon of the language into semantic fields that is important when a word or expression is required to develop new senses. For instance, in Swahili, the word *ulalo* was chosen for the concept of diagonal in mathematics, a concept for which previously there was no term. *Ulalo* means "the longest of all" and customarily referred to the rope cord that goes from one corner of a rectangular bed-frame to the opposite one (see Mmari 1975). However, not all polygonal diagonals are "the longest of all" segments. The problem of semantic contamination across fields is one of the most challenging in language and mathematics.

Every language that has been used by its speakers to express technical mathematical ideas will have some form of mathematics register. The history of the English technical mathematics register starts mainly in the sixteenth century with the translation of arithmetic books and Euclidean geometry into English from Latin, Greek, and Arabic. One early instance is Robert Record's systematic attempt in the mid-sixteenth century to produce a series of mathematics books in English covering a range of mathematical topics (see Fauvel 1991). In geometry, Record used the term "prickes" for points and "sharp," "square" (or "right") and "blunt" corners for acute, right, and obtuse angles. He referred to tangents as "touch lines," equilateral triangles as "threelikes" and parallelograms as "likejammes." So he looked for synonyms, although on occasion he did use a series of Latin-derived words. In France, the production of vernacular mathematics texts came in the next century (Descartes was one of the first vernacular authors of mathematics); in Italy, earlier.

More recent examples may also be cited. The Hawaiian language is being used increasingly as a medium of education and must be elaborated in order to take on the expressive potentiality for mathematics. In parts of Africa, an increasing use of local languages for instruction (rather than a colonial one) has necessitated a similarly rapid, focused development of a language (see UNESCO 1975). Part of learning mathematics is acquiring the mathematics register; that is, learning how to speak and, more subtly, how to mean as a mathematician.

The situation with regard to bilingual pupils and increasingly multilingual classrooms (such as in South Africa) is particularly striking (see Adler 1995). One important aspect is that the existence of incommensurate mathematics registers in different languages means that bilingual children are faced with an increasingly complex task, depending on the extent to which they have started to acquire the register in their mother tongue as well as that of the language of instruction. Teachers can only benefit by having some awareness of how mathematical expressions are formed in the languages of the pupils they are teaching. (See, e.g., Khisty in press for Spanish/English students; Orr 1987 for Black English/Standard English students. For a general discussion of a range of issues facing bilingual learners of mathematics, see Dawe 1983.)

3. Mathematics Texts

Considerable attention has been given to the characteristics of arithmetic word problems, particularly in North America. Particular aspects of word problems have encouraged researchers to consider them as texts with different features from straightforward, narrative descriptions—they form their own genre. Whether questions of the type involving "John having more marbles than Sally," or variation problems requiring ideas and techniques of the calculus, ostensibly "real-world" settings for mathematics questions present interesting challenges. These texts, with their distinctive features (such as being self-contained, despite apparently being about the material world), have been the subject of extensive statistical research to assign difficulty levels, based mainly on syntactic properties, implied temporal order of events, complexity and frequency of vocabulary, pronominal usage, and word order (see Nesher and Katriel 1977).

Further salient variables include the relation and degree of explicitness between known and unknown quantities, order of use versus order of mention, the relations between surface structure and semantic connections, use of keywords (such as "more" or "altogether") which can cue but also miscue. For many studies, the pupils themselves were only required in order to generate empirical data on apparent difficulty level: these data were then modeled against features of the questions themselves. Subsequent, more sophisticated, analyses have looked at the nature of the contexts themselves and at other elements of the problems, such as the presuppositions inherent in the questions when seen as texts. (See, e.g., the preliminary paper exploring pragmatic features of such problem texts in relation to Grice's maxims by Gerofsky 1995).

Work on the language of textbooks by Shuard and Rothery (1984) in the United Kingdom has paid particular attention to the role of diagrams, graphs, and figures and the difficulty of applying traditional readability measures to such complex, supplemented prose. With regard to the language of textbooks, there are questions of language use but also audience. For whom were they written? (see Gray 1991; Love and Pimm 1996).

Written mathematical language displays the feature of lack of redundancy. Such language is frequently impersonal, invoking the passive mood (which avoids having to mention an agent; e.g., "two was added to three"), and utilizing complex nominalizations. There is also the added complexity of the possible shift of the grammatical category of words when they enter the mathematics register. (Numerals provide the most straightforward instance, changing from adjectives to nouns; e.g., from seven chairs to seven.) With the latter use, properties of their own may be attributed, such as being prime or a power of three.

4. Written Symbolic Forms

A familiar aspect of mathematics is its writing system, which is broadly unrelated to any particular natural language writing system though its syntax often reflects that of Western European languages. The symbols used in mathematical writing fall into four main classes: first, *logograms* (specially invented signs for whole concepts), such as @ for "at," & for "and" or +, ≠, √; second, *pictograms* (stylized icons in which the symbol is closely related to the meaning), such as Δ; third, *punctuation symbols*, such as .,: or (); fourth, *alphabetic symbols*, commonly drawing on the Greek and Hebrew alphabets as well as the Roman one.

Certain letters have become stylized, such as the logogram ∫, which was originally a large capital S for *Summa*. This process of abbreviation of words in a natural language to derive a single (usually initial) letter supports the illusion that written mathematical language is in a natural language. Thus, reading aloud the equation $P = \pi d$ in English suggests that the system works by abbreviation (particularly if the reader is aware that π is the Greek equivalent of the letter p—hence related to perimeter).

However, this facility is not always avaliable. Mmari (1975) provides an example from Kiswahili. In developing a mathematics register, terms were created for parts of circles, including *kivembe* for circumference and *kipenyo* for diameter, and no separate term for radius, *nusu kipenyo* ("half diameter") being used. Consequently, the perimeter formula became $K = \pi k$. A textbook revision used the term *mzingo* (referring to perimeters in general) and thus the formula became $M = \pi k$. Finally, a decision was made to conform to international practice ($P = \pi d$) and the link between first-letter naming and the concepts themselves became lost.

The surface features systematically exploited to produce symbol clusters are: symbol order, relative size and position, orientation, and repetition. Many students see only a linear, left-to-right string of symbols, such as $2(x^2 + 5)^3 - 9$, and are unable to gain access to the discriminations being marked by the notational devices.

There is a fundamental tension in the teaching of mathematics between a focus on "understanding" and one involving fluency and automaticity in symbol manipulation. While this is actually a false dichotomy, nonetheless there is concern in many Western countries about an overemphasis on formal symbol manipulation. However, one consequence of this drawing away from symbolic manipulative fluency as a goal is that occasions where working directly with symbols prior to exploring possible meanings and applications tend to be ruled out *a priori*. An overemphasis on "understanding" (which usually means concrete reference) can result in pupils failing to be able to exploit the mathematical writing system for what it was designed to do. For a full and detailed explanation of symbolic manipulation in mathematics, see Pimm 1995.

A focus on the symbolic elements of mathematics can be found in justification for teaching mathematics in Islamic cultures:

> The objective is to make the pupils implicitly able to formulate and understand abstractions and be steeped in the area of symbols. It is a good training for the mind so that they may move from the concrete to the abstract, from sense experience to ideation, and from matter-of-factness to symbolisation. It makes them prepare for a much better understanding of how the Universe, which appears to be concrete and matter-of-fact, is actually *ayutullah*: signs of God—a symbol of reality. (Second World conference on Muslim education 1980 pp. 9–10)

5. Conclusion

Exploring mathematics and its teaching in lingustic terms is one key perception that mathematics education has to offer, though the direct claim that mathematics *is* a language is one that requires careful consideration. Mathematics is not a natural language in the sense that French and Arabic are—for instance, there is no group of people for whom mathematics is their mother tongue. Pupils learning mathematics in school in part are attempting to acquire communicative competence in spoken and written mathematical language. Educational linguist Stubbs has claimed (1980 p. 115): "A general principle in teaching any kind of communicative competence, spoken or written, is that the speaking, listening, writing or reading should have some genuine communicative purpose." Yet this is at odds with viewing a mathematics classroom as an avowedly, deliberately unnatural, artificial setting, one in which the structure and organization of the discourse by the teacher has some quite unusual features.

References

Adler J 1995 Dilemmas and a paradox: Secondary mathematics teachers knowledge of their teaching in multilingual classrooms. *Teaching and Teacher Education* 11(3): 263–74

Aiken L 1972 Language factors in learning mathematics. *Rev. Educ. Res.* 42(3): 359–85

Barham J, Bishop A 1991 Mathematics and the deaf child. In: Durkin K, Shire B (eds.) 1991

Barnes D 1976 *From Communication to Curriculum*. Penguin, Harmondsworth

Borasi R, Siegel M 1990 Reading to learn mathematics: New connections, new questions, new challenges. *For the Learning of Mathematics* 10(3): 9–16

Cocking R, Mestre J (eds.) 1988 *Linguistic and Cultural Influences on Learning Mathematics* Erlbaum, Hillsdale, New Jersey

Cornu B 1981 Apprentissage de la notion de limite: Modèles spontanés et modèles propres. *Proc. fifth PME conference*, Grenoble

Davis B 1996 *Teaching Mathematics: Towards a Sound Alternative*.Garland Publishing, New York

Dawe L 1983 Bilingualism and mathematical reasoning in English as a second language. *Educ. Stud. Mathematics* 14(4): 325–53

Durkin K, Shire B 1991 *Language in Mathematical Education*. Open University Press, Milton Keynes

Ellerton N, Clements M 1991 *Mathematics as Language: A Review of Language Factors in Mathematics Learning*. Deakin University Press, Geelong

Fauvel J 1991 Tone and the teacher: Instruction and complicity in mathematics textbooks. In: Pimm D, Love E (eds.) 1991 *Teaching and Learning School Mathematics*. Hodder and Stoughton, London

Frye N 1963 *The Educated Imagination*. CBC Enterprises, Toronto

Gerofsky S 1995 A linguistic view of mathematical word problems. In: Pothier Y (ed.) 1995 *Proceedings of the 1995 Annual meeting of CMESG*. Memorial University, Newfoundland

Grice P 1989 *Studies in the Way of Words*. Harvard University Press, Cambridge, Massachusetts

Gray E 1991 The primary mathematics textbook: Intermediary in the cycle of change. In Pimm D, Love E (eds.) 1991 *Teaching and Learning School Mathematics*. Hodder and Stoughton, London

Halliday M 1975 Some aspects of sociolinguistics. In: 1975 *Interactions between Linguistics and Mathematical Education*. UNESCO, Paris

Khisty L in press Making inequality: Issues of language and meanings in mathematics teaching with Hispanic students. In: Fennema E et al. (eds.) in press *New Direc-*

tions for Equity in Mathematics Education. University of Wisconsin, Madison, Wisconsin

Laborde C, Conroy J, De Corte E, Lee L, Pimm D 1990 Language and mathematics. In: Nesher P, Kilpatrick J (eds.) 1990 *Mathematics and Cognition*. Cambridge University Press, Cambridge

Laborde C et al. 1991 Lecture de textes mathématiques par des élèves (14–15 ans): Une experimentation. *Petit x* 28: 57–90

Love E, Pimm D 1996 "This is so ": A text on texts. In: Bishop A (ed.) 1996 *International Handbook of Mathematics Education*. Kluwer, Dordrecht

Mmari G 1975 Tanzania. In: *Interactions between Linguistics and Mathematical Education*. UNESCO, Paris

NCTM 1989 *Curriculum and Evaluation Standards*. NCTM, Reston, Virginia

Nesher P, Katriel P 1977 Semantic analysis of addition and subtraction word problems in arithmetic. *Educ. Stud. Mathematics* 8(3): 251–69

Orr E 1987 *Twice as Less: Black English and the Performance of Black Students in Mathematics and Science*. Norton, New York

Phillips E, Crespo S 1996 Developing written communication in mathematics through math penpal letters. *For the Learning of Mathematics* 16(1)

Pimm D 1987 *Speaking Mathematically*. Routledge and Kegan Paul, London

Pimm D 1994 Mathematics classroom language: form, function and force. In: Biehler R et al. (eds.) 1994 *Didactics of Mathematics as a Scientific Discipline*. Kluwer, Dordrecht

Pimm D 1995 *Symbols and Meanings in School Mathematics*. Routledge, London

Pirie S, Schwarzenberger R 1988 Mathematical discussion and mathematical understanding. *Educ. Stud. Mathematics* 19(4): 459–70

Recommendations of the Second World Conference on Muslim Education 1980 King Abdulaziz University and Quaid-i-Azam University, Islamabad

Rowland T 1995 Hedges in mathematics talk: Pointers to linguistic uncertainty. *Educational Studies in Mathematics* 29(3)

Shuard H, Rothery A (eds.) 1984 *Children Reading Mathematics*. Murray, London

Sinclair J, Coulthard M 1975 *Towards an Analysis of Discourse*. Oxford University Press, London

Stubbs M 1980 *Language and Literacy*. Routledge and Kegan Paul, London

UNESCO 1975 *Interactions between Linguistics and Mathematical Education*. UNESCO, Paris.

United Kingdom Department of Education and Science 1982 *Mathematics Counts*. Report of the Committee of Inquiry into the Teaching of Mathematics in Schools HMSO, London

Walkerdine V 1988 *The Mastery of Reason*. Routledge, London

Waywood A 1988 Mathematics and language: Reflections on students using mathematics journals. In: Hunting R (ed.) 1988 *Language Issues in Learning and Teaching Mathematics*. La Trobe University, Bundoora

Mathematics Education, Affective Issues in

P. Kloosterman

Affect is a very broad topic in mathematics education and can include factors such as mathematics anxiety and mathophobia, enjoyment of mathematics, self-confidence in learning mathematics, perceived causes of success and failure in mathematics, and beliefs about the existence of a "mathematics mind." Research on affect has focused on how various attitudes and beliefs form and why they influence mathematical achievement. For example, does getting upset while doing a mathematics problem affect the likelihood of finding a correct solution? How does hearing that mathematics is useful in careers influence motivation to learn the subject? This entry outlines the various types of explorations that fall in the category of affective research in mathematics education. Affective research includes studies of gender differences on affective variables, studies relating affective factors and achievement, and cognitive explanations of affect.

1. Defining Affect With Respect to Mathematics Education

Aiken (1985) noted that attitude was a broad concept and that there was a trend toward measurement of attitude as a multidimensional construct. The notion that attitude is multifaceted continues to prevail, and many researchers use the more general terms "affect" and "affective domain" in place of attitude when they describe their work. In addition, many cognitive researchers are considering affective factors in their attempts to understand how children learn mathematics. However, as Hart (1989) has argued, it is important that the affective factors considered in research studies be clearly defined because terms such as "affect," "attitude," "emotion," "anxiety," and "belief system" are not synonymous.

1.1 Affect

McLeod (1992) notes that affective reactions can vary from "hot" to "cool." A hot affective reaction is one which is highly emotional. For example, some secondary school students express great frustration when they are unable to complete a mathematics problem. In contrast, cool affect has little if any emotional component. The belief that a formula can be memorized is a form of self-confidence and thus affective in nature yet it is one that usually carries little emotion and thus would be considered cool affect. Hart (1989) uses the distinction between hot and cool to define affect when she states "Psychologists often use the term *affect* to indicate hot, gut-level emotional reactions. It is often used by educators to mean a wide variety of beliefs, attitudes, and emotions ranging from cold to hot" (p. 41). In other words, educators may use affect to mean relatively emotion free attitudes and beliefs or to mean highly emotional reactions to mathematics such as "I *hate* word problems."

1.2 The Affective Domain

Like affect, affective domain is a general term and can include any of a variety of affect related variables. McLeod (1992) breaks the affective domain in mathematics into three categories of variables which he feels are worthy of study. His first category is beliefs which includes beliefs about mathematics, beliefs about self as a learner of mathematics, beliefs about mathematics teaching, and beliefs about the social context of mathematics. McLeod's second category within the affective domain is attitudes such as liking of mathematics and enjoyment of solving mathematics problems. McLeod's third category is emotions such as joy in solving nonroutine problems or aesthetic appreciation of an elegant mathematical proof. The exact definition of affective domain varies with the individual using the term. Therefore, like affect, it is essential that the definition of affective domain be clearly understood before findings about the affective domain can be properly interpreted.

1.3 Affective Variables

The list of affective variables that have been studied in mathematics education is almost endless. In addition to beliefs, attitudes, and emotions mentioned by McLeod (1992), several additional variables are commonly mentioned in reviews of research on affect in mathematics education (e.g., Leder 1987, McLeod 1992, Reyes 1984). Self-confidence in learning mathematics is commonly included in studies of mathematics learning because it is often shown to correlate about 0.4 with achievement at the secondary level (Reyes 1984). Pajares and Miller (1994) claim that self-efficacy is a more powerful explanatory variable in mathematics, particulary with respect to problem solving. Mathematics anxiety has been the focus of a number of studies, many of which found that high levels of anxiety were related to poor performance on tests and avoidance of the subject (Hembree 1990).

A belief in the usefulness of mathematics is included in many studies of mathematics learning because students' decisions to take optional mathematics classes depend in part on their believing that knowing mathematics will help them in gaining admission to college and careers (Reyes 1984). Finally, attributions of success and failure in mathematics have been studied. The results suggest, as would be expected, that students who believe that success results from high effort are likely to put forth such effort in their mathematics courses (McLeod 1992).

1.4 Affect is Often Content Specific

In addition to variation in the terms that describe the affective domain, it is important to note that affective reactions in mathematics vary with the content of the mathematics being taught. Starting around age 10, children begin to see mathematics as a collection of topics, some of which they like and some of which they may not like (Kloosterman and Cougan 1994). For example, a child may like drill exercises involving fractions and routine word problems involving addition and subtraction yet dislike nonroutine word problems or anything pertaining to geometry. At the secondary level, it is common to find students whose confidence varies depending on whether algebraic or geometric topics are being considered (Hart 1989). In particular, because mathematics instruction is focusing more and more on noncomputational and higher-order skills, one must be careful not to assume that research findings on affect with regard to computational mathematics will automatically apply to learning situations where problem-solving-oriented instruction is taking place.

2. Gender Differences

When gender differences in mathematics achievement are found, they tend to favor males (Leder 1992). Efforts to explain these gender differences often focus on affective factors because gender differences are often found on specific types of affective measures. Meyer and Koehler (1990) summarize a number of quantitative studies of self-confidence by noting that gender differences favoring males are commonly found on self-confidence measures. They also report that in studies of secondary students, when male students have higher achievement they also see mathematics as more useful than female students do. Although females tend to see mathematics as less of a male-oriented domain than males, studies relating students' perception that mathematics is a male domain to achievement in mathematics have found no consistent relation between these two variables (Meyer and Koehler 1990). Attributional style in mathematics is another affective area where small gender differences are often found (Leder 1992). In general, males are more likely than females to attribute their successes to their ability and their failure to lack of effort. Females are more likely than males to attribute their success to effort and to help from others (Leder 1990, Meyer and Koehler 1990).

One area investigated as part of The Second International Mathematics Study was gender stereotyping in mathematics. The overall finding was that, on average, about 15 percent of Population A students (those with about 8 years of formal schooling) and of Population B students (those with 12 to 14 years of schooling) felt that mathematics was more important or useful for males (Kifer and Robitaille 1989). The percentage of students with gender stereotyped beliefs about mathematics was considerably larger in several of the 20 countries involved in this part of the study. For Population A, these countries were Nigeria, Japan, and Swaziland while for Population B, these countries were Thailand, Hong Kong, and Japan (Kifer and Robitaille 1989).

Fennema and Peterson (1985) summarized much of the research on gender differences in affect and achievement by proposing that gender differences in achievement result because males learn to become more autonomous learners than females. These autonomous learning behaviors, according to Fennema and Peterson (1985) result in part from affective factors including self-confidence, perceived usefulness of mathematics, and attributional style. Other models, such as Eccles' model of academic choice, also attempt to explain how gender differences in achievement result in part from affective factors (see Meyer and Koehler 1985). In brief, gender differences in mathematics achievement are often linked to gender differences in affective variables although, similar to achievement, the extent to which there are gender differences on the affective variables depends on the age of the students being studied as well as the specific affective variable being considered. Although much of the gender research has been done in the United States, the gender difference research that has been done in other countries generally agrees with the findings from United States studies (Leder 1990).

3. Affect and Achievement

Many instructional programs have affective components in their goals. Teachers want students to like mathematics and to feel confident that they can learn mathematics. More important than promoting good attitudes, however, is getting children to learn mathematics. As previously noted, self-confidence has a significant positive correlation with mathematics achievement (Reyes 1984). In most of the studies where self-confidence was correlated with achievement, self-confidence was assessed using self-report scales such as the Fennema-Sherman Mathematics Attitude Scales (see Meyer and Koehler 1990) and achievement was measured using standardized achievement tests. Three studies of this nature shed light on this topic. Cheung (1988) compared attitude and achievement data for the 5,644 Hong Kong students who participated in the Second International

Mathematics Study (SIMS). For this sample, self-confidence was the affective variable that correlated most highly with achievement ($r=0.42$), followed by the belief that mathematics was useful in careers ($r=0.37$), and the belief that mathematics required creativity ($r=0.31$). Maqsud and Khalique (1991) reported correlations between scores on a general attitude instrument and achievement of 0.49 for females ($N=65$) and 0.31 for males ($N=44$) at a senior secondary school (ages 17 to 19) in Bophuthatswana. Maqsud and Khalique (1991) also reported on a study of 75 first-year students at the University of Bophuthatswana. For this group, mathematics anxiety was negatively correlated with matriculation examination scores ($r=-0.55$) and grades in a first-year university mathematics course ($r=-0.52$).

Given the limitations of self-report scales in measuring affect, more and more researchers are beginning to use interviews and other qualitative research methodologies to assess the relationship between affect and achievement in mathematics. For example, Kloosterman and Cougan (1994) interviewed 62 students between the ages of 7 and 12 and found that by age 9, students with modest levels of achievement were just as confident of their abilities in mathematics as students who were high achievers. Low achievers, however, tended to have fairly low estimations of their mathematical ability.

4. Cognitive Explanations of Affect

A major limitation of correlational studies of affect and achievement is that such studies do not readily explain how beliefs and emotions influence achievement or vice versa. Cognitive research deals with how individuals think, and with respect to affect, can help provide a stronger theoretical link between affect and achievement. Another reason for integrating cognitive and affective research is that including both types of variables results in a more complete picture of how the learning process occurs (McLeod 1992).

4.1 Emotion and Learning

As previously noted, emotion is considered a hot affective state. In terms of learning, emotion becomes a factor when emotional reactions can change the way in which an individual thinks about a situation. Mandler's theory of mind and emotion has been applied to mathematics learning to explain how emotion influences performance in mathematics (Mandler 1989, McLeod 1989). According to Mandler (1989), emotions are the result of discrepancies between expected and perceived (actual) events. For example, when a student realizes that his or her attempt to solve a problem on a mathematics examination is futile, the student will have an emotional reaction. Assuming that the student felt the strategy used on the problem was

appropriate, the emotion would be negative because the perceived event (failure to solve the problem) was not desired or anticipated. Mandler's work has been in cognitive psychology rather than mathematics education, but when applied to mathematics learning, helps to put the joy and frustration students experience in mathematics in terms of a larger framework of emotion. In particular, Mandler's work gives mathematics educators a better idea of how emotion is part of the cognitive process that influences mathematics learning (McLeod 1989).

4.2 Beliefs and Learning

Although many students experience hot affective reactions in mathematics on certain occasions, cool affective reactions (e.g., beliefs) are also thought to influence mathematics learning on a continual basis. Burton (1987) worked with adults who were returning to school in the United Kingdom. The adults' goal was to enter a teacher training program but they were required to pass a mathematics course first. In the course, Burton taught mathematics but also worked to change the learners' "image of mathematics and of their relationship to it" (p. 306). Burton found it was possible to change the adults' perception of mathematics from rigid and rule oriented to something that was both cooperative and creative. The most important finding, according to Burton, was that the learners felt that they were much more capable of learning mathematics than they originally thought. This improved self-confidence was a key that kept students motivated and helped them to pass the course.

The Second International Mathematics Study included a number of self-report items on beliefs about mathematics and mathematics learning. One of the more interesting findings was that students tended to see checking answers and memorizing rules and formulas as the most important but least enjoyable aspects of mathematics. This finding was consistent for both Population A and Population B students (Kifer and Robitaille 1989). Another finding was that Japanese students were the least likely, by a wide margin, to report that they found mathematics easy or that they enjoyed doing mathematics. Hong Kong students, despite their stronger overall performance, found mathematics moderately difficult and rather enjoyable. Students in all countries reported that their parents wanted them to do well in mathematics and that they believed mathematics was important to learn. United States students, however, had considerably stronger beliefs in the importance of learning mathematics than did students in other countries (Kifer and Robitaille 1989). Finally, considerable differences were found between countries on the extent to which students were confident of their ability to learn mathematics. In Nigeria, for example, about 70 percent of the Population A students were confident of their mathematical abilities while in Japan, only 30 percent of the students reported such confidence. On the surface, this finding makes it appear that Japanese students, despite their strong achievement, had very low confidence. While this is entirely possible, it is also possible that Japanese students were reluctant to appear boastful by reporting high confidence (Kifer and Robitaille 1989).

When considering the data from the Second International Study, it is important to note that most of the beliefs surveyed have the potential to affect students' thinking and achievement. As Kloosterman (in press) points out, students who believe that mathematics learning requires memorization are likely to put their efforts into memorizing as opposed to understanding mathematical formulas and procedures. Students who feel mathematics will help them find a job, are likely to work hard in mathematics regardless of how well they like it.

As evidenced by the Second International Study, motivation to study mathematics is a key to understanding how "cool" affective factors (e.g., self-confidence, enjoyment, and interest) influence student thinking. Such factors influence a student's motivation which in turn influences achievement. Leder (1987) summarizes several of the key cognitive theories of motivation, most of which make some use of the assumption that individuals do things because they believe that their actions will result in achieving a desired goal. Expectancy-value theory, for example, says that high motivation is likely when: (a) an individual expects a plan of action to succeed and (b) the result of that plan of action is highly valued. When applied to learning mathematics, expectancy-value theory implies that students will study hard if: (a) they think that studying will help them learn mathematics and (b) they want to know mathematics. Attribution theory is similar in that motivation varies depending on how an individual attributes successes and failures in mathematics. For example, if success is attributed to effort (i.e., the student believes that effort makes a difference) the student will be motivated and thus will achieve at a higher level than if the student was not motivated. In brief, beliefs were noted by McLeod (1992) as a key element of the affective domain. Many cognitive theories of learning are based on the idea that actions are the direct result of beliefs about mathematics and mathematics learning.

4.3 Teachers' Beliefs

An area in which there has been considerable research is that of teachers' beliefs about knowing and teaching mathematics. In a sense, this is a part of the affective domain in mathematics education and thus worthy of mention. Civil (1990) studied four prospective elementary school teachers and found that they believed mathematics required neatness and speed and that there was usually a best way to solve a problem.

Applying cognitive motivational theories to these beliefs implies that these individuals will teach children to be neat, to work quickly, and to avoid intuitive approaches to solve problems that can be solved using a formula. Thompson (1992), provides a thorough review of studies of teachers' beliefs and how those beliefs influence instruction.

5. Conclusion

The affective domain is an important area in mathematics education both in its own right and because affective factors have considerable influence on learning. A major consideration with respect to the affective domain in mathematics education is simply being clear about what part of the domain is being discussed. Although some correlational research is still going on, most work has a cognitive focus in that it is intended to explain why attitudes and beliefs form and how those attitudes and beliefs influence both motivation and achievement. Research indicates that self-confidence, anxiety, perceived usefulness, and attributions are important affective variables in part because there is a clear intuitive link between these variables and motivation. It is also important to consider the mathematical content being taught or discussed when referring to the affective domain. Students' beliefs and emotions vary depending on the mathematical topic (e.g., algebra vs. geometry) and the level of thinking (e.g., routine vs. nonroutine problems) they are pursuing.

References

Aiken L R 1985 Attitudes towards mathematics. In: Husén T, Postlethwaite T N (eds.) 1985 *The International Encyclopedia of Education*, 1st edn. Pergamon Press, Oxford

Burton L 1987 From failure to success: Changing the experience of adult learners of mathematics. *Educ. Stud. Math.* 18(3): 305–16

Cheung K C 1988 Outcomes of schooling: Mathematics achievement and attitudes towards mathematics learning in Hong Kong. *Educ. Stud. Math.* 19(2): 209–19

Civil M 1990 "You only do math in math": A look at four prospective teachers' views about mathematics. *For the Learning of Mathematics* 10(1): 7–9

Fennema E, Peterson P L 1985 Autonomous learning behavior: A possible explanation of gender-related differences in mathematics. In: Wilkinson L C, Marrett C B (eds.) 1985 *Gender Influences in Classroom Interaction*. Academic Press, Orlando, Florida

Hart L E 1989 Describing the affective domain: Saying what we mean. In: McLeod D B, Adams V M (eds.) 1989 *Affect and Mathematical Problem Solving. A New Perspective*. Springer-Verlag, New York

Hembree R 1990 The nature, effects, and relief of mathematics anxiety. *J. Res. Math. Educ.* 21(1): 33–46

Kifer E, Robitaille D F 1989 Attitudes, preferences and opinions. In: Robitaille D F, Garden R A (eds.) 1989 *The*

IEA Study of Mathematics II: Contexts and Outcomes of School Mathematics. Pergamon Press, Oxford

Kloosterman P in press Students' beliefs about knowing and learning mathematics. In: Carr M (ed.) in press *Motivation in Mathematics.* Hampton Press, Cresskill, New Jersey

Kloosterman P, Cougan M C 1994 Students' beliefs about learning elementary school mathematics. *Elem. Sch. J* 94(4): 375–388

Leder G C 1987 Attitudes towards mathematics. In: Romberg T A, Stewart D M (eds.) 1987 *The Monitoring of School Mathematics, Vol 2: Implications from Psychology.* Wisconsin Center for Educational Research, Madison, Wisconsin

Leder G C 1990 Teacher/student interactions in the mathematics classroom: A different perspective. In: Fennema E, Leder G C 1990 *Mathematics and Gender.* Teachers College Press, New York

Leder G C 1992 Mathematics and gender: Changing perspectives. In: Grouws D A (ed.) 1992 *Handbook of Research on Mathematics Teaching and Learning.* Macmillan, New York

Mandler G 1989 Affect and learning: Causes and consequences of emotional interactions. In: McLeod D B, Adams V M (eds.) 1989 *Affect and Mathematical Problem Solving.* Springer-Verlag, New York

Maqsud M, Khalique C M 1991 Relationships of some socio-personal factors to mathematics achievement of secondary school and university students in Bophuthatswana. *Educ. Stud. Math.* 22(4): 377–90

McLeod D A 1989 The role of affect in mathematical problem solving. In: McLeod D B, Adams V M (eds.) 1989 *Affect and Mathematical Problem Solving.* Springer-Verlag, New York

McLeod D A 1992 Research on affect in mathematics education: A reconceptualization. In: Grouws D A (ed.) 1992 *Handbook of Research on Mathematics Teaching and Learning.* Macmillan, New York

Meyer M R, Koehler M S 1990 Internal influences on gender differences in mathematics. In: Fennema E, Leder G C 1990 *Mathematics and Gender.* Teachers College Press, New York

Pajares F, Miller M D 1994 Role of self-efficacy and self-concept beliefs in mathematical problem solving: A path analysis. *J. Educ. Psychol.* 86(2): 193–203

Reyes L H 1984 Affective variables in mathematics education. *Elem. Sch. J.* 84(5): 558–82

Thompson A 1992 Teachers' beliefs and conceptions: A synthesis of the research. In: Grouws D A (ed.) 1992 *Handbook of Research on Mathematics Teaching and Learning.* Macmillan, New York

Further Reading

Kloosterman P 1990 Attributions, performance following failure, and motivation in mathematics. In: Fennema E, Leder G C 1990 *Mathematics and Gender.* Teachers College Press, New York

McLeod D B 1988 Affective issues in mathematical problem solving: Some theoretical considerations. *J. Res. Math. Educ.* 19(2): 134–41

Schoenfeld A H 1989 Explorations of students' mathematical beliefs and behavior. *J. Res. Math. Educ.* 20(4): 338–55

Motor Skills: Learning and Instruction

J. M. M. Van der Sanden

The term "motor skills" refers to an individual's acquired ability to make accurate, efficient, smooth, and coordinated bodily movements in order to achieve some goal. Bodily movement implies the use, spatio-temporal coordination and control of various muscles and joints. The goal to be achieved may have to do with: (a) moving, balancing, and controlling (certain parts of) the body, as in walking, certain sports, dance (body-related movements); or (b) manipulating objects and tools, as in handwriting, operating equipment and machines, playing musical instruments, and driving a car (object-related movements).

1. Motor Skills Research: Scope and History

Learning motor skills has long been regarded as a matter of merely watching some expert performing skilled movements and then trying to imitate this skilled behavior in a process of trial and error. Medieval and postmedieval on-the-job apprenticeship systems for job-training are clearly based on this approach. When traditional craftsmanship in a predominantly rural society was replaced by large-scale industrial production systems, it became necessary to select and train large numbers of industrial personnel. Scientific research programs were judged necessary to furnish a knowledge base for selection and training. Frederick Winslow Taylor's time-and-motion studies of employees performing work tasks, produced in the early twentieth century, are a well-known example of the so-called "scientific management" approach. This approach required industrial workers to be capable of maximum performance on rather restricted skills, which, in line with prevailing thinking, were seen as stimulus–response chains. Thus, training focused on automatization of limited skills, thereby maximizing speed and minimizing errors.

The Second World War had a major influence on motor skills research. The sudden need for all kinds of military personnel raised difficult problems of selection and training. These problems gave rise

547

to new research programs in the United States and United Kingdom. The main issues in these projects shifted from selection and individual differences in psychomotor abilities to training procedures emphasizing retention and transfer of motor skills. The move away from the behaviorist perspective on learning and instruction allowed cognitive theories to influence motor skills research. Attention was given to the role of motor programs, schemata, and cognitive processes in performing and controlling motor activities.

2. Analysis and Categorization of Motor Skills

Skillful motor behavior is characterized by a focus on the goal, accuracy, and speed; it is not just effective, but also efficient—irrelevant information is ignored, a minimum amount of energy is spent, future situations and problems are anticipated, errors are avoided as far as possible and, if they do occur, are rapidly detected and corrected. Skillful movements are characterized by a remarkable smoothness, indicating optimum coordination between different parts of the body. All of these characteristics hold up under varying conditions: this makes for consistency and adaptability.

All motor skills involve bodily movements, but there are wide differences in these movements. To come to grips with this diversity, several researchers and theorists have tried to analyze and classify motor skills. Fleishman (1975) described four different approaches for classifying (psychomotor) tasks: the behavior description approach, the behavior requirements approach, the ability requirements approach, and the task characteristics approach.

The behavior description approach is characterized by the recording and classification of behavior that can be observed when somebody performs a certain task.

The behavior requirements approach involves the making of an inventory of the cognitive operations that are required to perform a certain (type of) task successfully. Romiszowski's "expanded skill cycle" (see Romiszowski 1981) is an example of this approach. Romiszowski assumed that performing a skilled activity involves a cycle of four stages: (a) perceive relevant stimuli, (b) recall necessary prerequisites, (c) plan necessary actions, and (d) perform actions. Each stage requires three specific cognitive operations. In the planning stage, for instance, these operations are analysis, synthesis, and evaluation. Together these operations make up a list of 12 factors that are, to a greater or lesser extent, required for successful task performance. An important distinction is made between reproductive and productive skills. Reproductive skills are characterized by the application of procedures and algorithms and require little or no conscious planning operations. Productive skills are characterized by the application of principles and strategies and require conscious planning operations.

The ability requirements approach tries to find the relatively stable psychomotor abilities that are necessary for effective performance on a certain (type of) task. Fleishman's (1975) factor-analytic work is an example of this approach. He distinguished 11 psychomotor abilities that could account for the performance differences of some 200 different (merely laboratory) psychomotor tasks. Among these abilities are control precision, multilimb coordination, manual dexterity, finger dexterity, arm–hand steadiness, and reaction time.

The task characteristics approach looks for task and task-situation characteristics that serve as conditioning features for effective task performance. A number of task characteristics have been described in the literature. Perhaps the most important distinction is that between open and closed tasks, which is based on the predictability of the task environment. Closed tasks occur in a predictable environment and can be planned in advance (e.g., writing a letter). Open tasks occur in an unpredictable environment and cannot be fully planned in advance (e.g., playing football). In between are tasks that occur in a semipredictable environment (e.g., driving a car).

3. Learning and Control of Motor Skills

Psychomotor skills differ greatly with regard to the task requirements, task and task-environment characteristics, and psychomotor abilities involved. In spite of this diversity, the learning of many (reproductive) motor skills appears to proceed from a predominantly cognitive phase through an associative phase to an autonomous phase (Fitts and Posner 1969). In the cognitive phase the emphasis is placed on the cognitive activities involved in acquiring knowledge of the skill to be learned, the goals to be reached, and the steps and procedures to be followed. Performance is jerky and inconsistent; responses are executed step by step, each step requiring conscious application of knowledge. Information necessary for initiating and controlling the task performance is supplied almost exclusively by the eyes. Learning curves are steep in this phase. In the associative phase there is a more gradual performance improvement. Movements are becoming more fluid, integrated, consistent, and regular, and error rates decrease. Information from nonvisual channels increasingly plays a regulatory role. In the autonomous phase it can be observed that conscious cognitive control of movements is no longer necessary. Performance has become efficient and consistent. Attention can be given to things other than the movements per se.

Fitts and Posner's (1969) description of the three phases in learning motor skills is generally recognized as a valid picture of the normal course that the learning of reproductive motor skills takes. When it comes to an explanation of the cognitive processes and structures involved, however, there is much less agreement. This situation is evidenced by a number of different theoretical positions. Some major points of disagreement concern the role of feedback and motor programs in the learning and control of skilled movements.

In closed-loop theories (e.g., Adams 1971) it is assumed that motor behavior is controlled by feedback mechanisms. When performing motor actions, proprioceptive feedback becomes available from internal sensory receptors in muscles and joints and from the vestibular apparatus. In addition, there is external feedback from the auditory and visual channels. This information is compared with some internal representation of the desired state to be reached. When discrepancies of a certain magnitude and direction are detected, corrective actions are undertaken subsequently so that the desired state is reached or maintained. Closed-loop theories are particularly suited to explaining relatively slow or continuous motor behavior, such as in tracking tasks (e.g., driving a car). They encounter difficulties, however, when explaining rapid (ballistic) movements, which once initiated cannot be adjusted. Open-loop theories assume that movements are produced and controlled by central commands from motor programs, which do their work without error-detecting and error-correcting mechanisms. Schmidt's schema theory (Schmidt 1975) is a special kind of open-loop theory that postulates schemata instead of programs. A schema is a generalized motor program pertaining to a certain class of motor actions. The schema concept offers a solution for two kinds of problems, which are inherent to the motor program notion: (a) the storage problem: if it is necessary to have a motor program for every conceivable motor action, it seems impossible to store all these programs; (b) the novelty problem: if a motor program is needed for movements to occur it would be impossible for somebody to make new movements.

There is another problem to which neither open-loop nor closed-loop theories can offer acceptable solutions; the so-called "degrees-of-freedom" problem. The elements of the motor system involved in producing movements (muscles, joints, motor units) together have a considerable number of degrees of freedom. Theories of motor control must account for the way all the elements of the motor system are regulated. Turvey (1977) stated that simultaneous control of all the individual elements involved in performing motor acts is an impossible task for the central nervous system. Therefore he postulated so-called "coordinative structures": in other words, relatively autonomous functional combinations of muscles which are tuned to environmental stimulus configurations. In this approach, perception and action systems are seen as functionally inseparable. Coordinative action structures are tuned to and directly influenced by perceptual states instead of being controlled by calculating, homunculus-like central brain structures. Because of the strong emphasis on man-environment interactions and the tendency to use natural research settings

this approach is sometimes referred to as "ecological viewpoint."

4. Instruction and Training of Motor Skills

An issue that continues to provoke debate among researchers and teachers is the question of when to apply discovery and when to apply expository instructional methods. The emphasis in instructional psychology on problem-solving, metacognition, and self-regulated learning has given a new turn to this discussion. Many metacognitive theorists support the notion of expository and direct instruction in strategies for self-regulated discovery learning.

Proponents of Russian activity theory advocate an expository approach to the teaching of motor skills. They emphasize the formation of complete and coherent movement schemata before executing motor activities.

For the training of reproductive skills, Romiszowski (1981) proposed predominantly expository methods, consisting of modeling, massed or distributed practice on increasingly complex tasks, and feedback on results. For the training of productive skills, however, (guided) discovery methods should be added to the expository modeling of basic skills. This is considered important because productive skills require not only procedural knowledge, but also conditional knowledge and planning skills.

According to Anderson (1987), skill learning implies the transformation of declarative into procedural knowledge. Jelsma (1989) has argued that the speed of proceduralization (i.e, automatization) should depend on prevailing transfer conditions. Fast automatization is desirable for skills that are identical in different task situations (near transfer). The process of automatization should be slowed down, however, for skills that vary over task situations (far transfer).

As a consequence of technological developments and changes in the organization of work and production processes (e.g., total quality management) transfer, problem-solving, and autonomous learning are becoming increasingly important in many jobs. Dissatisfaction with traditional trainer-centered training methods led to the development of new trainee-centered methods. In German industry, for instance, the *Leittext* method has been developed. In this autonomous learning and the transfer of productive motor and cognitive skills are fostered by a six-step heuristic, requiring active and constructive, instead of passive and reproductive, learning activities from the trainee.

New theoretical perspectives in instructional psychology, such as functional context training, cognitive apprenticeship, and constructivism, though primarily addressed to the cognitive domain, are of great promise for the field of motor skills. They can provide new insights and tools for designing on-the-job training and informal learning situations. These situations should be designed in such ways that maximum advantage

549

is taken from interactions of trainees with expert performers engaged in authentic and functional job activities. As was pointed out by Collins et al. (1989), modeling, coaching, scaffolding, articulation, reflection, and exploration should be the key instruments in these authentic learning environments.

References

Adams J A 1971 A closed loop theory of motor learning. *Journal of Motor Behavior* 3(2): 111–49

Anderson J R 1987 Skill acquisition: Compilation of weak-method problem situations. *Psychol. Rev.* 94: 192–210

Collins A, Brown J S, Newman S E 1989 Cognitive apprenticeship: Teaching the crafts of reading, writing and mathematics. In: Resnick L B (ed.) 1989 *Knowing, Learning and Instruction: Essays in Honor of Robert Glaser*. Erlbaum, Hillsdale, New Jersey

Fitts P M, Posner M I 1969 *Human Performance*. Brooks/Cole, Belmont, California

Fleishman E A 1975 Toward a taxonomy of human performance. *Am. Psychol.* 30(12): 1127–49

Jelsma O 1989 *Instructional Control of Transfer*. Twente University, Enschede

Romiszowski A J 1981 *Designing Instructional Systems: Decision Making in Course Planning and Curriculum Design*. Kogan Page, London

Schmidt R A 1975 A schema theory of discrete motor skill learning. *Psychol. Rev.* 82(4): 225–60

Turvey M T 1977 Preliminaries to a theory of action with reference to vision. In: Shaw R, Bransford J (eds.) 1977 *Perceiving, Acting and Knowing: Toward an Ecological Psychology*. Erlbaum, Hillsdale, New Jersey

Further Reading

Schmidt R A 1982 *Motor Control and Learning: A Behavioral Emphasis*. Human Kinetics Publishers, Champaign, Illinois

Singer R N 1980 *Motor Learning and Human Performance: An Application to Motor Skills and Movement Behaviors*, 3rd edn. Macmillan Inc., New York

Development of Learning Skills in Problem-solving and Thinking

R. E. Mayer

Problem-solving and thinking are subjects which frequently find themselves in the spotlight of educational reform. In addition to retaining information, students must be able to use what they have learned to solve new problems. A major goal of education is to help students become more effective problem solvers, that is, people who can generate useful and original solutions when they are confronted with problems they have never seen before.

1. Definitions

A *problem* consists of a given state (i.e., a description of the current situation), a goal state (i.e., a description of the desired situation), and a set of operators (i.e., rules or procedures for moving from one state to another). A problem occurs when a situation is in one state, the problem solver wants it to be in another state, and there are obstacles to a smooth transition from one state to the other. Karl Duncker (1945 p.1) defined a problem in the following way: "A problem arises when a living creature has a goal but does not know how this goal is to be reached." Although Duncker's definition is still valid, it must be modernized to include the possibility of problem-solving by machines, and so the term "problem solver" can refer to both living creatures and machines.

Problem-solving occurs when a problem solver engages in cognitive activity aimed at overcoming a problem. Duncker (1945 p.1) noted that "when one cannot go from the given situation to the desired situation simply by action, then there has to be recourse to thinking" and "such thinking has the task of devising some action which may mediate between the existing and the desired situations." Similarly, Polya (1981 p. ix) defined problem-solving as "finding a way out of a difficulty, a way around an obstacle, attaining an aim that was not immediately attainable." In developing computer simulations of problem-solving, Newell and Simon (1972) defined problem-solving as a search for a path between the given and goal states of a problem. Mayer (1990, 1992) has summarized three major aspects of a definition of problem-solving: (a) problem-solving is *cognitive*, because it occurs internally within the problem solver's cognitive system, (b) problem-solving is a *process*, because it involves manipulating or performing operations on the problem solver's knowledge, and (c) problem-solving is *directed*, because the problem solver is attempting to achieve some goal.

What is the relation between problem-solving and other high-level cognitive processes such as thinking and reasoning? Problem-solving is a common and pervasive type of thinking, namely, directed thinking in which the thinker is attempting to achieve some goal; in contrast, nondirected thinking, in which the thinker is not attempting to achieve some goal, includes daydreaming and the abnormal thinking of autistic and schizophrenic people. In general, the terms "problem-solving" and "thinking" can be used interchangeably, with the recognition that nondirected thinking is excluded. Reasoning can be viewed as a type of problem-solving or thinking. In deductive reasoning, the problem solver is given premises and must apply the rules of logic to derive a conclusion. For example, a problem solver who is told that "all four-sided polygons are quadrilaterals and all squares are four-sided polygons" may logically conclude that "all squares are quadrilaterals." In inductive reasoning, the problem solver is given a series of instances or events or examples and must infer a rule. For example, after learning the Spanish words *la casa, el libro, la escuela, el perro, la muchacha,* and *el muchacho,* the problem solver may conclude that the article *la* goes with words ending in "a" and *el* goes before words ending with "o," a grammatical rule that is not without exceptions in Spanish. Finally, critical thinking, which is aimed at generating and evaluating arguments, and creative thinking, which is aimed at generating novel ideas, are both forms of thinking that are sometimes employed more broadly in reference to thinking and problem-solving in general.

2. Types of Problem

A distinction, which is based on the clarity of the problem statement, can be made between well-defined problems and ill-defined problems. A well-defined problem has a clear given state, a clear goal state, and a clear set of allowable operators. For example, finding the value of x in an algebraic equation such as $x^2 + 2x + 4 = 0$ is a well-defined problem, because the given state is the equation, the goal state is a value for x, and the operators are defined by the rules of algebra and arithmetic. In contrast, an ill-defined problem has a poorly specified given state, goal state, and/or operators. For example, giving a persuasive speech is an ill-defined problem because the goal and the allowable operators are not clearly specified. Most of the problems encountered in school are well-defined problems, whereas most of the crucial problems in everyday life are ill-defined.

Another important distinction is that between routine and nonroutine problems, and is based on the knowledge of the problem solver. Routine problems are identical or very similar to problems that the problem solver has already solved, and therefore require reproductive thinking (Wertheimer 1959), reproducing responses that have been produced previously. For example, routine problems for most high school students are "5 + 5 = _" or "The headquarters of the United Nations is in the city of __." In the strictest sense, routine problems do not conform to the definition of problems, since they do not include an obstacle between the given and goal states. In contrast, nonroutine problems are different from any problems that the problem solver has solved previously, and therefore require productive thinking (Wertheimer 1959), that is creating a novel solution. Examples for most high school students include writing a computer program to compute the mean and standard deviation of a sample, or working out why the Spanish explorers waited for several centuries before colonizing California. In school, students often work on routine problems called "exercises"; however, most important problems in everyday life are nonroutine.

A third distinction can be made between problems requiring convergent and divergent thinking. Convergent thinking problems have a single correct answer that can be determined by applying a procedure or retrieving a fact from memory. Examples include arithmetic computation problems and typical multiple-choice items. Divergent thinking problems (Guilford 1967) have many possible answers, and so the problem solver's job is to create as many solutions as possible. Classic examples include uses problems, such as "List all of the possible uses of a brick," and consequences problems, such as "List all of the consequences of humans having six rather than five fingers." Originality and fluency in producing answers to divergent thinking problems are measures of creativity and are taught in instructional programs in critical thinking (Halpern 1989). Although divergent thinking is the hallmark of creativity, most school-based problems emphasize convergent thinking.

3. Processes in Problem-solving

Problem-solving can be subdivided into four basic processes: (a) representing, (b) planning, (c) executing, and (d) controlling. Representing a problem involves converting the problem-as-presented into an internal mental representation. For example, a student may be given a word problem: "Sarah has three marbles. David has two more marbles than Sarah. How many marbles does David have?". To represent the problem, the student must translate each sentence into an internal mental representation, such as "Sarah's marbles = 3" and "David's marbles = Sarah's marbles + 2," and must integrate the information to form a coherent mental representation, such as "David's marbles = 3 + 2." Planning a solution involves determining the operations that must be performed, such as determining that 3 and 2 must be added in the marble problem. Executing a solution involves carrying out the operation(s) that are specified in the plan, such as computing that 5 is the sum of 3 + 2. Finally, controlling refers to the metacognitive process of monitoring and adjusting the other processes, such as detecting that a plan is not working or that a step was incorrectly executed. Although school instruction tends to emphasize execution of basic skills, students' major difficulties are in learning how to represent problems, devise plans, and monitor the problem-solving processes.

4. Rigidity in Thinking

A major obstacle to effective problem-solving is rigidity in thinking. For example, in some problem-solving situations the problem solver must use an object in a new way, such as using a brick as a doorstop or using chewing gum as adhesive. When a problem solver can only conceive of using an object in its most common function, then the problem cannot be solved. Duncker (1945) used the term "functional fixedness" to refer to a situation in which a problem solver cannot think of using an object in a new function that is required to solve the problem. Another example of rigidity occurs when a problem solver uses a well-learned procedure on a problem for which the procedure is inappropriate. For example, if a student has solved a long series of arithmetic story problems that all contain the word "more" and require adding the numbers together, the student may incorrectly carry out this same procedure for a new problem that actually requires subtracting the numbers from one another. Luchins (1942) used the term *einstellung* (or problem-solving set) to refer to this phenomenon. A goal of instruction in problem-solving is to help students avoid rigid thinking.

5. The Distinction Between Meaningful and Rote Learning

Why is it that some people invent clever solutions when confronted with a problem, whereas others do not? The Gestalt psychologist, Max Wertheimer (1959) attempted to answer this question by distinguishing between the two kinds of thinking mentional above, namely productive thinking and reproductive thinking. Productive thinking involves producing a novel solution when confronted with a problem whereas reproductive thinking occurs when problem solvers use solution procedures that they already know as a result of solving previous problems.

For example, Wertheimer (1959) suggested that there are two ways to learn about how to find the area of a parallelogram: learning by rote and learning by understanding. In learning by rote, the problem solver is taught to measure the height, measure the base, and then multiply the height by the base. According to Wertheimer, these problem solvers would perform well on retention tests, such as finding the area of a similar parallelogram, and poorly on transfer tests, such as finding the area of an unusually shaped parallelogram. In contrast, problem solvers who learn by understanding are encouraged to discover that a parallelogram can be converted into a rectangle by cutting the triangle off one end and moving it to the other end. These problem solvers are expected to perform well on retention and transfer. Thus, learning by rote leads to reproductive thinking, as measured by retention tests, whereas learning by understanding leads to productive thinking, as measured by transfer tests.

6. Thinking by Analogy

When confronted with a new problem, where does the idea for a solution come from? According to analogical transfer theory, problem solvers use existing knowledge about previously solved problems (known as the "source domain" or "base domain") to guide solution of the new problem (known as the "target domain"). For analogical transfer to occur, problem solvers must recognize an analog to use as a source domain, abstract the relevant information from the target domain that corresponds to the source domain, and map the solution procedure for the source to the target.

For example, Gentner and Gentner (1983) asked students to solve electrical circuit problems, such as determining whether a circuit with one battery would generate as much current as a circuit with two batteries in serial. Some students used a water-flow analogy to help solve the circuit problems, in which electrons are like water, wires are like pipes, a battery is like a pump, and a resistor is like a constriction in a pipe. Other students used a moving-crowd analogy, in which electrons are like mice, wires are like corridors, a battery is like a loudspeaker, and a resistor is like a gateway in a corridor. Students who used a water-flow analogy as a base domain solved circuit problems about batteries more accurately than students who used a moving crowd analogy, but the opposite pattern occurred for circuit problems involving resistors.

An instructional implication of research on analogical reasoning is that students may need training in how to use familiar systems to help them understand unfamiliar scientific systems. For example, in learning the principles underlying how radar works (i.e., target domain) students can be reminded about their experiences with balls bouncing off of a distant wall (i.e., base domain). Transmitting a radar pulse is like throwing the ball, reflection of the pulse is like a ball bouncing off a remote object, reception of radar is like the ball returning to the thrower, measurement is like counting the time it took for the ball to return, and conversion is like determining that the longer the time the further away the object was. When students are reminded of the bouncing ball analogy, they are better able to use the information in a lesson about radar to solve transfer problems, such as "How could you increase the area under surveillance?" (Mayer 1989).

7. Problem Space and Search Processes

In information-processing theories of how humans and machines solve well-defined problems, problem-solving involves constructing a problem space and searching for a path through the space (Newell and Simon 1972). A well-defined problem can be described as a "problem space," i.e., a representation of the initial state, goal state, and all possible intervening states that can be created by applying a legal operator

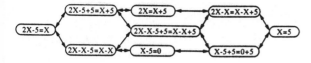

Figure 1
Problem space for an algebra problem

to a state. For example, Fig. 1 shows the problem space for solving the equation, $2X - 5 = X$. The initial state is this equation; the goal state is $X = \_$; and the legal operators are adding, subtracting, multiplying by, or dividing by the same number (operation 1) or variable (operator 2) on both sides of the equation, by carrying out a specified addition, subtraction, multiplication, or division of numbers (operator 3) or variables (operator 4) on either side of the equation. For example, applying operator 1 to the initial state, produces a new state, $2X - 5 + 5 = X + 5$. Similarly applying operator 2 to this state yields $2X = X + 5$. Applying operator 3 to this state yields $2X - X = 5$, and applying operator 4 produces the goal state, $X = 5$.

Once a problem is represented as a problem space, the problem solver's task is to search for a path through the problem space between the initial and goal states. Three possible search strategies are random trial and error, hill-climbing, and means–ends analysis. In random search, the problem solver arbitrarily selects one of several possible paths from the current state, until reaching the goal. A major disadvantage of random search is its inefficiency for complex problem spaces that have many dead end paths. In hill-climbing, the problem solver always selects the operation that will move the problem from its current state to a state that is closer to the goal. A major disadvantage of this approach is that some problems require moving away from the goal in order eventually to solve the problem. Means–ends analysis involves working on one goal at a time; if that goal cannot be achieved directly, then the problem solver sets a new goal of removing the barriers, and so on. This approach has been used in computer programs to simulate human problem-solving, and seems most consistent with the way that beginners solve problems. This approach emphasizes the role of general problem-solving strategies in problem-solving.

8. Cognitive Task Analysis

Well-defined thinking and reasoning tasks can be broken down into component cognitive processes; that is, cognitive processes that are needed to solve the problem (Sternberg 1985). For example, solving a verbal analogy such as "Apple is to fruit as elm is to: (a) maple, (b) leaf, (c) tree, (d) street" requires cognitive processes such as encoding, inferring, applying, and responding. Encoding is mentally representing the A

term (apple), the B term (fruit), the C term (elm), and each of the alternative D terms (maple, leaf, tree, and street). Inferring is determining the relation between the A and B term, such as member-to-category. Applying involves using the relational rule with the C term in order to generate a D term, such as noting that elm is a member of the category of trees. Responding refers to selecting (c) as the correct answer.

Cognitive task analysis can be used to diagnose errors in the problem-solving process of students and to provide instruction in component processes. For example, if students have difficulty in inferring relations, they can be instructed that the major relations include part-to-whole, member-to-category, member-to-member, and others, and be given worked-out practice problems concerning how to determine the relation between two terms. In addition, students may need training in how to coordinate their various cognitive processes (Sternberg 1985). In contrast to the emphasis on general strategies in problem-space analysis, this approach emphasizes the important role of domain-specific knowledge in problem-solving.

9. Historical Overview

The history of scientific research on thinking and problem-solving dates back to 1901, when researchers at the University of Würzburg began publishing their findings concerning the thought processes involved in making free associations concerning words or pairs of words (Humphrey 1963, Mandler and Mandler 1964). The Würzburg researchers generated results that conflicted with the prevailing theories of mental philosophy—such as the finding that thinking sometimes does not involve imagery and that people can control their chain of thought—and stimulated the development of the first theory of thinking in the early 1900s by Otto Selz (Frijda 1981).

Most of the subsequent research on thinking and problem-solving falls within three catagories: associationist, Gestalt, and cognitive (Mayer 1992). The associationist approach, which dominated psychology throughout the first half of the twentieth century, views problem solving as the production of a series of responses until one works. For example, given a problem such as how to escape from a room, a problem solver would try a response that had worked often in the past, such as turning the handle on the door; if that response failed, the problem solver would try the next most common response, such as breaking the window; and if that failed less common responses would be tried, such as crawling through a vent tunnel in the ceiling, until the problem solver hit upon a response that solved the problem. According to this view, problem-solving involves generating responses based on one's past experience with the problem-solving situation. A major criticism of this approach concerns how it can account for creative problem-solving.

The Gestalt approach, developed in Germany in the 1920s and 1930s, views problem solving as mentally reorganizing the elements of the problem so that they fit together in a new way. Thus, the major task in problem-solving is to achieve structural understanding, that is, to see how the given elements mesh with the requirements of the goal. For example, Duncker's (1945 p.1) tumor problem is as follows: "Given a human being with an inoperable stomach tumor, and rays which destroy organic tissue at sufficient intensity, by what procedure can one free him of the tumor by these rays and at the same time avoid destroying the healthy tissue which surrounds it?" According to Duncker, the problem solver must reformulate the givens (e.g., the X rays) or the goal (e.g., destroy the tumor without harming the surrounding tissue) in a new way. First, a problem solver may reformulate the functional requirements of the goal, such as saying that the intensity of X rays must be low through the surrounding tissue and high through the tumor. This reformulated description of the goal leads to a new way of looking at the givens: several weak X rays could be sent through the tumor from different angles forming a lens that converges at the tumor. In this example, problem-solving involves seeing the givens and goals of the problem in a new way. A major criticism of this approach concerns the need for clearly testable theories.

The cognitive view, which began in the late 1950s and evolved into the cognitive science approach by the 1980s, provides for an integration of the positive features of both approaches (Gardner 1985, Mayer 1992). According to this approach, problem solving involves a series of mental computations, so a theory of problem solving must specify the specific mental processes used to solve a problem as well as the methods that problem solvers employ for selecting and controlling their cognitive processes. Computer technology provides a level of clarity and precision that was missing from earlier Gestalt work, and an emphasis on solving real-world problems provides a focus on creative thinking that was missing in associationist work. A major research question concerns the respective roles of domain-specific and domain-general knowledge in problem-solving (Smith 1991).

10. Research on Problem-solving in Real Situations

Since its inception at the start of the twentieth century, the scientific study of problem-solving has focused mainly on how people solve artificial problems and puzzles in well-controlled laboratory situations (Gardner 1985, Humphrey 1963, Mandler and Mandler 1964). However, cognitive-based research towards the end of the twentieth century has begun to shift its focus to problem-solving within more realistic situations including everyday problem-solving, expert problem-solving, and problem-solving within subject areas (Greeno and Simon 1988, Mayer 1992, Osherson and Smith 1990, Sternberg and Smith 1988).

Research on everyday problem-solving reveals that people rarely use school-taught methods to solve problems encountered outside of school (Lave 1988, Nunes, Schliemann, and Carraher 1993, Rogoff and Lave 1984). For example, to determine the best buy for items in a supermarket—such as 90 cents for a 10-ounce can of peanuts versus 45 cents for a 4-ounce can—the school-mathematics method would be to compute the unit price of each item, that is, 9 cents per ounce versus 11.25 cents per ounce, respectively. However, Lave (1988) found that people almost never used the school-taught method; instead, they invented arithmetical procedures better suited to the situation, such as a ratio strategy in which the shopper identifies the first can as the best buy because it costs twice as much as the second but contains more than twice as many ounces. An educational implication is that problem-solving should be taught within more real-world settings.

Another important area of research involves comparing how experts and novices solve problems in domains such as medical diagnosis, computer programming, and physics (Chi et al. 1988), as well as in the game of chess (De Groot 1965). For example, when Larkin (1983) asked experts and novices in physics to think aloud as they solved physics problems, she found that experts were more likely to describe the problem in terms of its physics concepts (such as forces and weights), whereas novices focused on the surface features of the problems (such as pulleys and ropes). Similarly, when Chi et al. (1981) asked experts and novices to sort physics problems into groups, experts sorted problems based on their underlying physics principles (such as conservation of energy), whereas novices sorted the problems based on their surface characteristics (such as inclined planes or springs). Results of expert–novice studies suggest that experts represent and solve problems differently from novices, and so instruction can focus on helping novices to think more like experts.

A third important research area is the study of human problem-solving within subject matter areas such as reading, writing, mathematics, and science, that is, psychologies of subject matter (Mayer 1987). Instead of studying how people think in general, psychologists of subject matter investigate how people think scientifically or mathematically or how people think within the process of reading or writing a passage. For example, in reading comprehension, problem-solving is involved in constructing the meaning of passages; in writing, an important problem-solving activity is the generation of a plan; in mathematical problem-solving, the problem solver must understand the problem; and in scientific problem-solving, the problem solver must overcome preconceptions that he or she brings to the situation. This approach suggests that instruction in subject-matter areas should focus on helping students learn the cognitive processes and strategies required for successful problem-solving.

See also: Computers and Learning; Problem-solving and Learning: Computer Modeling; Computer Programming, Learning and Instruction of; Expert Knowledge and Performance; Metacognition; Problem-solving, Teaching and Assessing; Reasoning; Self-regulation in Learning; Instructional Psychology; Instructional Psychology, Overview; Cognition and Learning; Cognitive Styles and Learning

References

Chi M T H, Feltovich P J, Glaser R 1981 Categorization and representation of physics problems by experts and novices. *Cognit. Sci.* 5: 121–52
Chi M T H, Glaser R, Farr M (eds.) 1988 *The Nature of Expertise.* Erlbaum, Hillsdale, New Jersey
De Groot A D 1965 *Thought and Choice in Chess.* Mouton, The Hague
Duncker K 1945 On problem solving. *Psychological Monographs* 58: 3 (whole No. 270)
Frijda N H (ed.) 1981 *Otto Selz: His Contribution to Psychology.* Mouton, The Hague
Gardner H 1985 *The Mind's New Science: A History of the Cognitive Revolution.* Basic Books, New York
Gentner D, Gentner D R 1983 Flowing waters or teeming crowds: Mental models of electricity. In: Gentner D, Stevens A L (eds.) 1983 *Mental Models.* Erlbaum, Hillsdale, New Jersey
Greeno J G, Simon H A 1988 Problem solving and reasoning. In: Atkinson R C, Hernstein R J, Lindzey G, Luce R D (eds.) 1988 *Stevens' Handbook of Experimental Psychology,* Vol. 2. Wiley, New York
Guilford J P 1967 *The Nature of Human Intelligence.* McGraw-Hill, New York
Halpern D F 1989 *Thought and Knowledge: An Introduction to Critical Thinking,* 2nd edn. Erlbaum, Hillsdale, New Jersey
Humphrey G 1963 *Thinking: An Introduction to its Experimental Psychology.* Wiley, New York
Larkin J H 1983 The role of problem representation in physics. In: Gentner D, Stevens A L (eds.) 1983 *Mental Models.* Erlbaum, Hillsdale, New Jersey
Lave J 1988 *Cognition in Practice: Mind, Mathematics and Culture in Everyday Life.* Cambridge University Press, Cambridge
Luchins A S 1942 Mechanization in problem solving. *Psychological Monographs* 54: 6 (whole No. 248)
Mandler J M, Mandler G 1964 *Thinking: From Association to Gestalt.* Wiley, New York
Mayer R E 1987. *Educational psychology: A Cognitive Approach.* Scott, Harper Collins, New York
Mayer R E 1989 Models for understanding. *Rev. Educ. Res.* 59(1): 43–64
Mayer R E 1990 Problem solving. In: Eysenck M W et al. (eds.) 1990 *The Blackwell Dictionary of Cognitive Psychology.* Blackwell, Oxford
Mayer R E 1992 *Thinking, Problem Solving, Cognition,* 2nd. edn. Freeman, New York
Newell A, Simon H A 1972 *Human Problem Solving.* Prentice-Hall, Englewood Cliffs, New Jersey
Nunes T Schliemann A D Carraher D W 1993 *Street Mathematics and School Mathematics.* Cambridge University Press, New York
Osherson D N, Smith E E (eds.) 1990 *Thinking.* MIT Press, Cambridge, Massachusetts
Polya G 1981 *Mathematical Discovery.* Wiley, New York
Rogoff B, Lave J (eds.) 1984 *Everyday Cognition: Its Development in Social Context.* Harvard University Press, Cambridge, Massachusetts
Smith M U (ed.) 1991 *Toward a Unified Theory of Problem Solving: Views from the Content Domains.* Erlbaum, Hillsdale, New Jersey
Sternberg R J 1985 *Beyond IQ: A Triarchic Theory of Human Intelligence.* Cambridge University Press, Cambridge
Sternberg R J, Smith E E (eds.) 1988 *The Psychology of Human Thought.* Cambridge University Press, Cambridge
Wertheimer M 1959 *Productive Thinking.* Harper and Row, New York

Further Reading

Gilhooly K J 1988 *Thinking: Directed, Undirected, and Creative* 2nd edn. Academic Press, London
Gilhooly K J (ed.) 1989 *Human and Machine Problem Solving.* Plenum Press, London
Halpern D F 1992 *Enhancing Thinking Skills in the Sciences and Mathematics.* Erlbaum Hillsdale, New Jersey
Mayer R E 1992 *Thinking, Problem Solving, Cognition.* Freeman, New York

Problem-solving: Teaching and Assessing

R. E. Mayer

Teaching and testing for problem-solving have become central issues in education. As Charles and Silver (1989) state: "The topics of teaching and evaluating problem solving are high interest topics for teachers, teacher educators, curriculum developers, and administrators . . . . Since 1980, many educators . . . have come to accept the important role problem solving can play in the curriculum" (p.5). National and international assessments of educational progress also have contributed to the interest in evaluating and improving students' ability to solve problems.

1. Teachable Aspects of Problem-solving

The term "problem-solving" has several definitions and has been embedded in a variety of theoretical frameworks. Understanding research on problem-solving is enhanced by viewing modern research within a historical context.

1.1 Definition of Teachable Problem-solving

Teaching of problem-solving can be defined in several different ways. Taking a narrow view, the goal of teaching for problem-solving is to improve students' performance on retention tests that contain routine problems (i.e., problems identical or very similar to those which the students encountered during instruction). For example, drill and practice on solving two-column subtraction problems such as "56 − 43 = ___" may improve students' performance on solving similar problems such as "67 − 52 = ___."

Taking a broader view, the goal of teaching for problem-solving is to improve students' performance on transfer tests containing non-routine problems (i.e., problems they have not solved previously). For example, conceptually based instruction that helps a student develop an understanding of place value may enable the student to transfer what he or she has learned about two-column subtraction problems, such as "56 − 43 = ___," to solving three-column subtraction problems, such as "567 − 423 = ___." This broader view, which could be called "teaching for transfer," is more consistent with the definition of problem-solving than is the narrower view, which could be called "teaching for retention." For this reason, teaching problem-solving is most appropriately defined as teaching students to be able to solve problems they have never solved before.

1.2 Theoretical Framework for Teachable Problem-solving

Mayer (1989, 1992) has summarized three major issues in the design of an effective program for teaching problem-solving: what to teach, how to teach, and where to teach. First, problem solving can be taught as a single, monolithic ability that can be strengthened through training and exercise (e.g., mathematical problem-solving skill or language skill), or as a collection of smaller, component skills that can be specifically taught (e.g., how to represent problems, how to devise solution plans, or how to monitor one's comprehension). Second, problem-solving can be taught by emphasizing the product of problem-solving (namely, getting the right answer), or by emphasizing the process of problem-solving (that is, the method or steps that one goes through to arrive at an answer). Third, problem-solving can be taught in a general, domain-free context in hopes of promoting transfer across many domains or within the context of specific subject domains such as mathematics, science, social studies, or writing, with the expectation that students are generally able to apply a problem-solving strategy only within a particular domain. Although a review of successful and unsuccessful (or undocumented) problem-solving programs does not provide definitive resolutions of these issues, the research suggests that problem-solving is most effectively taught when the focus is on teaching component skills rather than a single general ability, on process rather than product, and on domain-specific rather than context-free settings (Mayer 1989, 1992).

1.3 History of Teachable Problem-solving

A persistent concern of educators has been how to teach problem-solving to students (Chipman et al. 1985, Mayer 1989). In the early eighteenth century, Latin schools were established to provide students with proper "habits of mind" (Rippa 1980); in the 1980s and early 1990s, scholars have developed more modest thinking skills programs. Unfortunately, however, for many of the problem-solving courses, researchers have not been able to produce convincing evidence that attempts to improve problem-solving in one domain transfers well to different domains (Mayer 1987). Overall, attempts to teach transferable problem-solving skills have a disappointing history in educational psychology, leading Mayer (1987) to decry "the elusive search for teachable aspects of problem solving" (p.327). At the same time, however, a review of problem-solving programs sheds light on the characteristics of effective problem-solving instruction.

The first major attempt to teach problem-solving skills to students in school was the Latin School movement (Rippa 1980). The motivating principle of Latin schools was the doctrine of formal discipline, the idea that the study of subjects such as Latin and geometry would improve students' mental discipline and hence improve their thinking in general. Although this remained the prevailing theory through the early part of the twentieth century, research studies conducted by Thorndike and his colleagues (Thorndike and Woodworth 1901) failed to find empirical support for the idea that learning Latin had a positive effect on learning and problem-solving in other domains. Based on these findings, Thorndike proposed the theory of identical elements, the idea that transfer of learning occurs only when specific components that were parts of previously learned material are also parts of new learning (Singley and Anderson 1989).

During the 1930s and 1940s, educators initiated creativity programs in industry (Crawford 1954, Osborn 1963). As early as 1931, Crawford (1954) established a course to teach creative thinking within an industrial setting, including techniques to help designers create new ideas for improving products. Shortly thereafter Osborn (1963) helped to generate creativity courses that emphasized brainstorming, a procedure in which a group tries to generate as many ideas as possible without criticizing any ideas. Unfortunately, there is little scientific data concerning the effectiveness of these kinds of programs (Bouchard 1971, Weisberg 1986), and the preponderance of laboratory-based research studies calls into question the effectiveness of techniques such as brainstorming (Taylor et al. 1958, Weisskopf-Joelson and Eliseo 1961).

During the 1950s, problem-solving programs began to appear in colleges and universities. For example, Bloom and Broder (1950) taught college students how to solve examination problems by having them describe the thought process they used to solve problems from particular domains (e.g., economics), listen to an expert describe his or her process for the same problem, and then compare the two descriptions. The results indicated that the program was successful in improving students' examination performance. In this case the instruction meets the three criteria for successful programs by focusing on component skills, emphasizing process, and teaching within a subject domain.

During the 1960s, problem-solving programs were developed for primary and secondary school students. The Productive Thinking Program (Covington et al. 1974), for example, taught elementary school children skills such as generating ideas, formulating questions, and restating a problem, by asking them to read a series of cartoon-like booklets that presented mystery stories. Students were given a chance to model the thinking process of several characters in the booklets, such as two children and an uncle, who described their thinking processes in trying to solve the mysteries. Evaluation studies have demonstrated that the program improves students' performance on solving problems like those in the booklets but there is less evidence that problem-solving is improved in other domains (Mansfield et al. 1978). Again, this program meets the three criteria of successful programs: a focus on component skills such as "generating hypotheses," a focus on modeling the thinking processes of others, and a focus on improving problem-solving within a limited domain.

Since the 1970s, a variety of programs have been developed for use in schools. They include CORT (DeBono 1985), Instrumental Enrichment (Feuerstein et al. 1985), and Odyssey (Chance 1986). The CORT program teaches specific skills such as how to establish objectives or how to evaluate an idea by describing the skill and giving students guided practice in using the skill on specific problems. Although the program is widely used in schools around the world, including the United Kingdom where it was developed, there is "no adequate evidence . . . and thus no support for the effectiveness of the program" (Polson and Jeffries 1985 p.445). Instrumental Enrichment is a multiyear program, developed in Israel, aimed at entering students who school administrators might label as mentally retarded or slow learners. Through

interaction with an instructor, students learn how to solve a variety of problems that might be found on tests of nonverbal intelligence, including spatial and numerical problems. Although the program requires a major time commitment, evaluation studies reveal that the training has positive effects on students' spatial, mathematical, and nonverbal reasoning.

Finally, Odyssey is an elementary-level program, developed in Venezuela, aimed at teaching specific skills such as inducing a pattern. Through interaction with peers and instructors, as well as working on their own, students learn to solve a series of problems such as determining what would come next in a series of geometric shapes. After a year of training, students performed much better than nontrained students on solving problems like those given during instruction, but only slightly better on solving problems that were unlike the instructed problems. The pattern that emerges from research on thinking skills programs is that it is possible to teach component skills, using process-based methods, within a specific domain.

2. Testable Aspects of Problem-solving

Testing for problem-solving refers either to evaluating the degree to which a person can successfully solve problems or describing the process that a person uses to solve problems. An example of the testing-as-response-evaluation approach is a multiple choice test item in which the student is given an arithmetic story problem and asked to select the correct answer. In general, this approach to testing focuses on the product of problem-solving, on using short items that each require a single response, and on asking questions that do not require a great amount of transfer. An example of the testing-as-process-description approach is a performance test in which a student is given laboratory equipment such as beakers, scales, and eye droppers, and is asked to determine which of three paper towels holds more water (Baxter et al. 1992). In general, this approach focuses on the process of problem-solving, involves realistic problems that require more than a single response, and requires the problem-solver to generate novel solutions (Wiggins 1989).

Three issues in testing for problem-solving concern what to test, how to test, and where to test. First, tests can focus on tabulating the number of correct and incorrect responses or on the cognitive processes and strategies that the problem-solver uses. If the focus is on the product of problem-solving, then the test items call for a final answer. In contrast, if the focus is on the process of problem-solving, then the test items may assess processes such as how the problem-solver represents the problem, plans a solution, and monitors progress toward solving the problem. Second, concerning how to test, tests can present a series of short items measuring separate skills in isolation or can require the problem-solver to engage in higher-level problem-solving on a realistic task in which various skills must be integrated. Third, the issue of where to test concerns whether to rely on routine problems like those presented during instruction or on nonroutine problems that require the problem-solver to invent a novel solution. Although problem-solving tests traditionally have focused on scoring the number of correct responses to short problems that are routine, more recent trends involve describing people's cognitive processes on realistic problems that are nonroutine (Baxter et al. 1992, Frederiksen and Collins 1989).

In general, useful tests of problem-solving are valid, reliable, and objective. Validity means that the test measures what it is intended to measure, so that a test of mathematical problem-solving should not consist entirely of recalling memorized history facts, for example. Performance testing may improve validity by using realistic tasks, whereas traditional, multiple-choice tests may lack validity if they evaluate individual skills in isolation. For this reason, a performance test can be seen as an example of what has been called authentic assessment. Furthermore, the creation of tasks that can change in response to the test taker's actions, such as a hands-on situation or an interactive videodisk system, allow for a performance test to be viewed as an example of dynamic assessment (Campione and Brown 1987, Feuerstein 1979). Reliability means that the test results are consistent; that is, a person will achieve approximately the same score on each administration of the test. Because performance-based tests allow for many alternative methods of solution, they may not be as reliable as traditional methods of tests. This drawback can be partially mitigated by using several different kinds of problems. Objectivity means that different scorers or raters would produce the same result. Although multiple-choice tests are highly objective, well-defined coding procedures can allow performance-based tests to achieve acceptable levels of objectivity.

3. Conclusion

The teaching of problem-solving, which requires an understanding of "what is taught," is intricately tied to testing problem-solving, which requires a specification of "what is learned." If the goal of problem-solving instruction is to improve the cognitive processing of students when they are confronted with a novel problem, then the goal of problem-solving assessment is to describe the cognitive processes they use in their problem-solving. Nickerson (1989) noted that "the need for tests that do a better job of assessing thinking is widely recognized" (p.4). Future developments in the teaching and testing of problem-solving are required to satisfy this educational need. These developments include the design and use of teacher-made tests for higher-order thinking as well as the inclusion of higher-order thinking in large-scale

standardized testing programs (Linn 1991) and the use of tests to diagnose problem-solving processing deficiencies that can be remediated (Bejar 1984, Brown and Burton 1978).

References

Baxter G P, Shavelson R J, Goldman S R, Pine J 1992 Evaluation of procedure-based scoring for hands-on science assessment. *J. Educ. Meas.* 29: 1–17

Bejar I I 1984 Educational diagnostic assessment. *J. Educ. Meas.* 21(2): 175–89

Bloom B S, Broder L J 1950 *Problem-solving Processes of College Students: An Exploratory Investigation.* University of Chicago Press, Chicago, Illinois

Bouchard T J 1971 What ever happened to brainstorming? *J. Creat. Behav.* 5(3): 182–89

Brown J A, Burton R R 1978 Diagnostic models for procedural bugs in basic mathematical skills. *Cognit. Sci.* 2(2): 155–92

Campione J C, Brown A L 1987 Linking dynamic assessment with school achievement. In: Lidz C S (ed.) 1987 *Dynamic Assessment: An Interactional Approach to Evaluation Learning Potential.* Guilford, New York

Chance P 1986 *Thinking in the Classroom: A Survey of Programs.* Teachers College Press, New York

Charles R I, Silver E A (eds.) 1989 *The Teaching and Assessing of Mathematical Problem Solving.* Erlbaum, Lawrence, Hillsdale, New Jersey

Chipman S F, Segal J W, Glaser R (ed.) 1985 *Thinking and Learning Skills. Vol. 2: Research and Open Questions.* Erlbaum, Hillsdale, New Jersey

Covington M V, Crutchfield R S, Davies L B, Olton R M 1974 *The Productive Thinking Program.* Merrill, Columbus, Ohio

Crawford R P 1954 *The Techniques of Creative Thinking.* Hawthorn, New York

DeBono E 1985 The CORT thinking program. In: Segal J W, Chipman S F, Glaser R (eds.) 1985 *Thinking and Learning Skills. Vol. 1: Relating Instruction to Research.* Erlbaum, Hillsdale, New Jersey

Feuerstein R 1979 *The Dynamic Assessment of Retarded Performers: The Learning Potential Assessment Device, Theory, Instruments, and Techniques.* University Park Press, Baltimore, Maryland

Feuerstein R, Jensen M, Hoffman M B, Rand Y 1985 Instrumental enrichment, an intervention program for structural cognitive modifiability: Theory and practice. In: Segal J W, Chipman S F, Glaser R (eds.) 1985 *Thinking and Learning Skills. Vol. 1: Relating Instruction to Research.* Erlbaum, Hillsdale, New Jersey

Frederiksen J R, Collins A 1989 A systems approach to educational testing. *Educ. Res.* 18(9): 27–32

Linn R L 1991 Dimensions of thinking: Implications for testing. In: Idol L, Jones B F (eds.) 1991 *Educational Values and Cognitive Instruction: Implications for Reform.* Erlbaum, Hillsdale, New Jersey

Mansfield R S, Busse T V, Krepelka E J 1978 The effectiveness of creativity training. *Rev. Educ. Res.* 48(4): 517–36

Mayer R E 1987 The elusive search for teachable aspects of problem solving. In: Glover J A, Ronning R R (eds.) 1987 *Historical Foundations of Educational Psychology.* Plenum, New York

Mayer R E 1989 Teaching for thinking: Research on the teachability of thinking skills. In: Cohen I S (ed.) 1989 *The G. Stanley Hall Lecture Series*, Vol. 9. American Psychological Association, Washington, DC

Mayer R E 1992 *Thinking, Problem Solving, Cognition*, 2nd edn. Freeman, New York

Nickerson R S 1989 New directions in educational assessment. *Educ. Researcher* 18(9): 3–7

Osborn A E 1963 *Applied Imagination*. Scribners, New York

Polson P, Jeffries R 1985 Instruction in general problem solving: An analysis of four approaches. In: Segal J W, Chipman S F, Glaser R (eds.) 1985 *Thinking and Learning Skills. Vol. 1: Relating Instruction to Research*. Erlbaum, Hillsdale, New Jersey

Rippa S A 1980 *Education in a Free Society: An American History*. Longman, New York

Singley M K, Anderson J R 1989 *The Transfer of Cognitive Skill*. Harvard University Press, Cambridge, Massachusetts

Taylor D T, Berry P C, Block C H 1958 Does group participation when using brainstorming facilitate or inhibit creative thinking? *Admin. Sci. Q.* 3(1): 23–47

Thorndike E L, Woodworth R S 1901 The influence of improvement in one mental function upon efficiency of other functions. *Psychol. Rev.* 8: 247–61

Weisberg R W 1986 *Creativity: Genius and Other Myths*. Freeman, New York

Weisskopf-Joelson E, Eliseo T S 1961 An experimental study of the effectiveness of brainstorming. *J. Appl. Psychol.* 45: 45–49

Wiggins G 1989 A true test: Toward more authentic and equitable assessment. *Phi Del. Kap.* 70(9): 703–13

Reading, Learning and Instruction of

C. A. Perfetti

Learning to read is the acquisition of a print-accessible lexicon. This simple view has the advantage of not confounding learning to read with other issues of language and cognitive development. From this view, comprehension is not to be accounted for by a theory of learning to read. Comprehension of printed language will approach that of spoken language, once a child learns how to read words.

1. Reading, Speech, and Writing

1.1 Reading and Spoken Language

There are some important differences between print and speech (e.g., Tannen 1982) that seem to derive from basic differences in physical and social design of the two systems (Perfetti 1985). Despite these differences, the central fact for the acquisition of reading competence is that a learner must learn how the writing system encodes language. Whatever else is meant by the term "reading skill," the ability to map print to language, *decoding*, is the fundamental achievement of learning to read.

1.2 Writing Systems

Writing systems, like languages, have variety. However, although a child may biologically know the principles of language design prior to acquiring spoken language (Pinker 1984), there is no parallel for writing systems. Writing systems are a human invention and they vary in how they work even after centuries of convergent development. Reading English, Italian, and Korean involves an alphabetic writing system, in which graphic units associate with phonemes; Chinese involves a logographic system, in which graphic units associate primarily with morphemes; Japanese Kana is a syllabary system, in which graphic units correspond to syllables; Arabic, Hebrew, and Persian involve a modified alphabetic system in which consonants are more reliably represented than are vowels. There is nothing in children's native language endowment to provide constraints for learning their writing system. Whether a child will learn an alphabetic or logographic system, or no system at all, is a matter of cultural and national traditions.

2. The Alphabetic Principle

Reading an alphabetic orthography requires the discovery of the alphabetic principle: a written symbol corresponds to a phoneme, a meaningless speech segment. As widely noted, the invention of the alphabet, and hence the "discovery" of the alphabetic principle, appears to have been a unique cultural achievement, one that came much later than the adaptation of symbols for objects and meanings. It should not be surprising then that learners might have some trouble "replicating" this discovery.

2.1 Phonological Awareness

Young children are likely to have only a dim awareness of the phonological structure of their language. Because phonemes are abstractions over highly variable acoustic events, detecting their status as discreet speech segments is difficult. Thus, the child may have an inadequate representation of phonemes, a critical part of what is needed.

Moreover, children lack advance knowledge about how a writing system might map phonological properties of their language. For example, studies in both English and Swedish (Gleitman and Rozin 1977) suggest that preliterate children do not expect any correspondence between the lengths of printed and spoken words. These results are consistent with the claim that there is no preliterate knowledge concerning writing systems.

Phonemic awareness is even more problematic. A number of studies have confirmed the inability of many preliterate children to demonstrate phonemic awareness in various tasks. Still other studies show a relationship between phonemic awareness and learning to read across alphabetic languages, including English, Italian, Swedish, Dutch, and German (see chapters in Rieben and Perfetti 1991 and Brady and Shankweiler 1991).

A question raised is whether the relationship between phonemic awareness and learning to read is causal. The evidence of training studies gives some support to the causality conclusion, as do longitudinal studies using cross-lag correlations (see Wagner and Torgesen 1987 for a review). It seems correct to conclude that awareness functionally mediates learning how to read in an alphabetic writing system.

There are two additional aspects to this awareness issue. First, phonological abilities have different dimensions that are reflected in different phonemic awareness tasks. Second, the relationship between phonemic awareness and learning to read is not one-directional, but reciprocal. Furthermore, these two facts are linked. Phonemic ability is first promoted through literacy acquisition and then enables further gains in literacy (Perfetti et al. 1987). Some prerequisite phonemic knowledge, however, functions immediately to facilitate the acquisition of reading.

The other side of the phonemic awareness–reading relationship has also received support from studies finding that adult illiterates are very weak in tasks requiring analysis of phonemic structure, while much better at syllable-level and rhyming tasks. Such results suggest the limited level of phonological awareness that can be developed outside of literacy contexts.

2.2 Nonalphabetic Writing Systems

Logographic writing systems present an important comparison with alphabetic systems. Chinese children learn to read characters that, despite potential cues to pronunciation, tend to connect with morphemes more than sublexical phonology. (Note the qualifier "sublexical." Reading characters does involve word pronunciations.) Whereas learning to read an alphabetic system allows a productive (rule-based) process in principle, the logographic system requires this learning to be largely associative. If phonemic awareness depends on alphabetic literacy, readers of Chinese should show little awareness of phonemes. This pre-

diction was confirmed in a study using adults (Read et al. 1986). One group had learned only the traditional system, and one group also learned *pin yin*, a supplemental alphabetic script. Only the *pin yin* group performed the phonemic analysis task successfully.

A more complex picture may hold for learners of Japanese, who learn to read the Kanji system (Chinese characters) and the Kana system, based on syllables. Phonemic awareness is slowed but emerges eventually, perhaps because Kana provides graphic representations for some phonemes (see Alegria and Morais in Rieben and Perfetti 1991).

The overall picture has become reasonably clear, considering evidence from different writing systems. Phonemic awareness is very limited as a spontaneous human ability, but it is important in learning to read in an alphabetic system. Learning to read an alphabetic system promotes awareness of phonemes and, in turn, depends on the emergence of this awareness. In a logographic system, reading is both less dependent on phonemic awareness and does less to promote it.

3. Theories of Learning to Read

What is the form of the learning reader's representation of words and how does the representation system change with learning? Theories of reading acquisition have portrayed broad stages of development (e.g., Chall 1983). Stages can be useful for addressing the representation problem in general terms, although overlapping strategies and individual differences suggest that stages should not be considered all-or-none.

Gough and colleagues (in Rieben and Perfetti 1991) have described a two-stage account of reading, in which the child at first uses various cues to discriminate one word from another, without any decoding knowledge. They refer to this first stage as "selective association," an idiosyncratic connection between some part of a printed word and the name of the word. Under the right circumstances, including an increase in phonological awareness and an intention to encode all the letters of the word, the child can move into the "cipher" stage of true reading.

An alternative stage model comes from Ehri (in Rieben and Perfetti 1991). On her account, children do not begin at a visual-only stage as they do in Gough's account. From the beginning, they use the names of the letters as cues to word identification. Although letter names do not represent the phonemes, they have enough phonetic overlap with phonemes to be useful, as when a child uses the names of the letters J and L to remember the sound of the word "jail." Learning the alphabet, not necessarily the alphabetic principle, is the key that moves a child into the first stage of reading. The acquisition process is the establishment of word representations that have both phonological and orthographic components.

Perfetti (in Gough et al. 1992) gives a third theoretical framework which focuses directly on the acquisition of word representations without postulating stages. Learning to read is the acquisition of increasing numbers of orthographically addressable words (quantity acquisition) and the alteration of individual representations along quality dimensions. The two quality dimensions are "specificity," an increase in the number of position-correct specific letters in a representation, and "redundancy," the increasing establishment of redundant phonemic representations. The redundancy concept rests on the assumption that word pronunciations are part of the child's early representations and that, with learning, phonemes are added in connection with individual letters. These sublexical connections are established as a result of phonemic awareness and context-sensitive decoding knowledge, producing phonological representations at both lexical and phonemic levels. Together, increasing specificity and redundancy allow high-quality word representations that can be reliably activated by orthographic input. As individual words become fully specified and redundant, they move from the functional lexicon, which allows reading, to the autonomous lexicon, which allows resource-cheap reading.

4. Reading Instruction

The central idea of reading instruction is that children can learn to read by being taught, directly or indirectly, the alphabetic principle. Controversies continue to thrive in both North America and Western Europe about "phonics," "language experience," "whole language," and other methods of teaching reading. These controversies center around the relative emphasis to place on decoding instruction. While most instructional programs include some attention to decoding, they vary in the directness of the decoding instruction.

The controversies are less about the relative effectiveness of different teaching methods than about "philosophies" and orienting attitudes. The widespread use of "whole language" instruction represents, according to at least some of its advocates, "an educational paradigm" that takes an ideological stance and addresses fundamental epistemological questions. As an instructional procedure, "whole language" embraces all aspects of language, but rejects the explicit teaching of decoding (Goodman 1986). The assumptions that some whole language advocates make about language and writing systems appear to be fundamentally wrong. In particular, the whole language claim that learning to read can be as natural as learning to speak ignores what has been learned about the biological basis and universality of spoken languages and the relative nonbiological and cultural-invention quality of writing (Liberman and Liberman 1990). The rejection of direct decoding instruction appears to ignore what has been learned through research on language learning and reading. Because there is wide variation in the actual practice, however, many teachers will find a way to teach the code, despite the philosophical proscriptions.

Emphasizing either decoding or meaning is, of course, a false choice. Persuasive demonstrations that the explicit teaching of decoding can be coupled with a focus on meaning are provided by Feitelson (1988) in her discussion of reading instruction in German and English. Adams (1990) presents a balanced analysis of these instructional issues, concluding that the research strongly supports the important role played by phonological processes in reading and learning to read. Instruction can take on some variety. But any instructional system that ignores the alphabetic principle and the critical role it plays in learning how to read has the potential for creating reading failures.

See also: Literacy

References

Adams M J 1990 *Beginning to Read: Thinking and Learning About Print.* MIT Press, Cambridge, Massachusetts

Brady S A, Shankweiler D (eds.)1991 *Phonological Processes in Literacy: A Tribute to Isabelle Y. Liberman.* Erlbaum, Hillsdale, New Jersey

Chall J S 1983 *Learning to Read: The Great Debate.* McGraw-Hill, New York

Feitelson D 1988 *Facts and Fads in Beginning Reading: A Cross-language Perspective.* Ablex, Norwood, New Jersey

Gleitman L R, Rozin P 1977 The structure and acquisition of reading: Relations between orthographies and the structure of language. In: Reber A S, Scarborough D L (eds.) 1977 *Toward a Psychology of Reading: The Proceedings of the CUNY Conference.* Erlbaum, Hillsdale, New Jersey

Goodman K S 1986 *What's the Whole in Whole Language?* Scholastic Educational, Ontario, Canada

Gough P B, Ehri L C, Treiman R 1992 *Reading Acquisition.* Erlbaum, Hillsdale, New Jersey

Liberman I Y, Liberman A M 1990 Whole language vs. code emphasis: Underlying assumptions and their implications for reading instruction. *Annals of Dyslexia* 40: 51–76

Perfetti C A 1985 *Reading Ability.* Oxford University Press, New York

Perfetti C A, Beck I, Bell L, Hughes C 1987 Phonemic knowledge and learning to read are reciprocal: A longitudinal study of first grade children. *Merrill-Palmer Q.* 33(3): 283–319

Pinker S 1984 *Language Learnability and Language Development.* Harvard University Press, Cambridge, Massachusetts

Read C, Zhang Y, Nie H, Ding B 1986 The ability to manipulate speech sounds depends on knowing alphabetic writing *Cog.* 24(1): 31–44

Rieben L, Perfetti C A (eds.) 1991 *Learning to Read: Basic Research and its Implications.* Erlbaum, Hillsdale, New Jersey

Tannen D (ed.) 1982 *Spoken and Written Language: Exploring Orality and Literacy.* Ablex, Norwood, New Jersey

Wagner R K, Torgesen J K 1987 The nature of phonological processing and its causal role in the acquisition of reading skills. *Psych. Bull.* 101(2): 192–212

Reading Comprehension, Learning of

W. Schnotz

In educational settings, understanding of written discourse is a central point in knowledge acquisition. Cognitive research considers reading comprehension as an active, intentional process wherein an individual constructs new knowledge structures on the basis of existing prior knowledge. In contrast to the relatively simple assumptions on mental representations at the beginning of reading comprehension research, scientific approaches since the 1980s presume that such knowledge structures consist of multiple mental representations with several levels. These approaches also emphasize the flexibility of reading comprehension due to the use of different strategies and a metacognitive processing regulation.

1. Reading Comprehension as Construction

According to a widespread view held in everyday life, reading comprehension is an extraction of a certain meaning from a text by the reader. This view was also partially adopted by scientists who considered the sentences of a text as carriers of semantic units, which have to be mentally interconnected by the reader into a coherent whole. Since the 1980s, reading comprehension has no longer been considered as an accumulation of such units: (a) readers are capable of adapting their cognitive processing to the context conditions and expected demands; (b) they can read a text from different perspectives whereby different knowledge structures are acquired; and (c) they can interpret a text differently according to their prior knowledge. Therefore, a reconceptualization of reading comprehension has taken place. According to the new point of view, readers actively construct mental representations during comprehension based on their prior knowledge and certain processing strategies. The text is not a carrier of semantic units, but a trigger of these mental construction processes.

2. Role of Prior Knowledge

In text comprehension readers usually try to make a text as meaningful as possible by relating it to their prior knowledge. Therefore, the mental construction processes afford not only verbal, but also content-specific world knowledge (Bransford 1979). In text recall, individuals try to reconstruct the text content in such a way as to achieve a high correspondence to their overall knowledge. If there are no other knowledge parts that contradict the text information, only a few errors arise. If contradictions occur between prior knowledge and the text information, however, accommodative reconstruction processes ensue: readers try to maintain mental coherence by increasing correspondence between the different knowledge parts, which can result in systematic recall errors. Plausible information that was actually not presented in the text is then often erroneously recognized after reading (Spiro 1980).

Readers can keep the knowledge acquired from a text separate from their prior knowledge in order to recall the text content as exactly as possible. If readers try to update their knowledge about a certain topic, however, then their main objective of text-processing is to achieve a coherent knowledge structure of the subject matter as a whole and not merely a coherent representation of the single text. Readers will then take into account the new information as far as possible, but will not simply give up their prior knowledge altogether: some mismatches between the text information and the overall knowledge will then be accepted to maintain a high coherence of the whole knowledge.

Prior knowledge also contains knowledge about formal text structures, which are often conventionalized in a language culture. Simple narrative texts can often be described in their formal structure through so-called story grammars. Other types of text, as for example, expository texts, do not have such conventionalized structures, but follow rather a more flexible combination of certain structural building blocks. Generally, reading comprehension is facilitated if a reader can easily detect the formal structure of a text.

3. Mental Representations in Reading Comprehension

Research on reading comprehension generally assumed until the 1970s that knowledge acquired from texts is mentally represented in a single format: in terms of semantic units, referred to as "propositions." As far as such propositional representations are constructed during comprehension, a distinction has been made between micropropositions, which represent the semantic content of the text with all details, and macropropositions, which represent the content in a more global way (see Kintsch and van Dijk 1978). Accordingly, comprehension comprises both local and global coherence formation: local coherence formation is concerned with semantic interrelations at the level of micropropositions; global coherence formation refers to semantic interrelations at the level of macropropositions.

Since the 1980s a new generation of comprehension theories has been developed which assume that different levels of mental representations are created during reading. Accordingly, readers construct (a) a mental representation of the text surface; (b) a propositional representation of the semantic content of the text; and (c) a mental model of the subject matter or the situation described in the text, often also referred to as a scenario or a situation model (Johnson-Laird 1983, Sanford and Garrod 1981, van Dijk and Kintsch 1983). These different levels of mental representations serve complementary functions. A mental representation of the text surface allows verbatim recall. A propositional representation preserves the semantic content and, thus, allows recall of what has been said in the text, not necessarily in the original wording, but rather in terms of paraphrases. A mental model is especially suited for drawing inferences. Text recall, however, is less accurate, because the linguistic structure is not encoded here and, therefore, the reproduction has to occur as a new description of the corresponding mental model. These different levels of mental representations correspond to different levels of text-processing, ranging from a superficial processing concerned only with the text surface structure to a deep understanding at the model level.

According to this view, a text serves as a database for the construction of a mental model via other, intermediate levels of representations. In the course of reading, this database is gradually enlarged and the initial model constructed at the beginning becomes more and more elaborated. If longer texts are processed, however, only parts of such a model can be focused at a specific moment due to the limited cognitive processing capacity. Readers have to construct topic-specific (partial) models then, which are carried along from sentence to sentence and become gradually elaborated as long as the respective topic is maintained (see Grosz and Sidner 1986).

4. Strategies in Reading Comprehension

Reading comprehension is an adaptive, dynamic process wherein readers apply different cognitive strategies according to both their aims and the given situational context. They allocate the main focus of their processing differently onto the various levels of mental representation. Cognitive strategies are mental programs which influence the selection and sequencing of different mental operations. They are applied by the reader in order to facilitate or improve comprehension, acquisition, recall, and application of knowledge. If processing concentrates on creating a propositional representation, for example, reproductions become afterwards relatively accurate. This kind of processing corresponds to a recall strategy. If processing concentrates on the formation of a mental model, then this provides a better basis for answering questions requiring insight into the subject matter. This kind of processing corresponds to a comprehension strategy.

Frequently, a distinction is also made between micro- and macrostrategies. A microstrategy is directed toward understanding the subsequent sentences and the interrelations between the respective propositions. A macrostrategy is directed toward grasping the main ideas of a text. Macrostrategies are acquired relatively late in an individual's learning history and accordingly, global coherence formation often proves to be difficult for a reader.

Processing strategies can be activated explicitly by instruction, but also implicitly by means of embedded learning aids, such as advance organizers, questions, marginal notes, and so on. In the so-called reciprocal teaching strategy program developed by Palincsar and Brown (1984), comprehension activities are also embedded in a social context: teachers and learners switch roles and engage in dialogues about text passages just read where they summarize, make predictions, give answers to questions, and provide clarifications. Strategies used by successful readers are described by Pressley et al. (1989).

5. Metacognition in Reading Comprehension

In order to achieve flexible and adaptive text-processing, the available processing strategies have to be selected, coordinated, and monitored according to the specific demands. For that purpose both metacognitive knowledge about comprehension processes (e.g., that application of new knowledge requires deeper understanding than is provided by mere recall) and executive procedures concerning monitoring and control (e.g., for the evaluation of one's own understanding) are necessary (Brown et al. 1985). Regulation of cognitive processing is usually automatized. Only if comprehension problems arise that cannot be resolved by means of such automated procedures, regulation becomes an object of conscious reflection and control.

On the one hand, automation removes some of the load from the cognitive-processing capacity which makes comprehension easier. On the other hand, automation includes the risk that the use of strategies proceeds according to well-established habits of processing which do not correspond to the available metacognitive knowledge. Deficits in metacognitive processing regulation often result from the insufficient criteria readers possess for the evaluation of their own comprehension (Baker 1985). Even experienced readers sometimes do not notice that their understanding of a text is insufficient. As readers usually do not have a complete overview of their knowledge due to a limited cognitive capacity, mental inconsistencies often remain unnoticed.

6. Future Perspectives

The interaction between the different levels of mental representation constructed during reading, from prior knowledge and as a result of the specific aims readers have during text-processing, needs further clarification. To attain this goal a multidisciplinary cooperation of cognitive psychology and psychology of language, linguistics, and artificial intelligence research seems to be most appropriate. Cognitive linguistics is an example for such an integrative approach, where the analysis of language structures and their use are considered as a specific approach to better understanding the structure and functioning of the human cognitive system. Reading comprehension should not only be seen from a cognitive point of view, however. The application of processing strategies certainly depends also on motivational and affective factors, such as attributional beliefs and the individual's self-concept. Up to the early 1990s, there have been hardly any studies about these topics. Finally, although reading comprehension in school settings takes place in social contexts, the embedding of comprehension processes in such social contexts has so far hardly been studied. Apart from basic research, which aims at detailed insights into comprehension processes, a more technologically oriented research is also necessary, to develop and evaluate procedures for the adequate design of written discourse.

See also: Comprehension: Teaching and Assessing; Constructivism and Learning; Knowledge Representation and Organization; Learning Processes and Learning Outcomes; Metacognition; Prior Knowledge and Learning

References

Baker L 1985 How do we know when we don't understand? Standards for evaluating text comprehension. In: Forrest-Pressley D L, MacKinnon G E, Waller T G (eds.) 1985 *Metacognition, Cognition, and Human Performance. Vol. 1: Theoretical Perspectives.* Academic Press, Orlando, Florida

Bransford J D 1979 *Human Cognition: Learning, Understanding, and Remembering.* Wadsworth, Belmont, California

Brown A L, Armbruster B B, Baker L 1985 The role of metacognition in reading and studying. In: Orasanu J (ed.) 1985 *Reading Comprehension: From Research to Practice.* Erlbaum, Hillsdale, New Jersey

Grosz B J, Sidner C L 1986 Attentions, intentions, and the structure of discourse. *Computational Linguistics* 12: 175–204

Johnson-Laird P N 1983 *Mental Models: Towards a Cognitive Science of Language, Inference, and Consciousness.* Cambridge University Press, Cambridge

Kintsch W, van Dijk T A 1978 Toward a model of text comprehension and production. *Psychol. Rev.* 85(5): 363–94

Palincsar A M, Brown A L 1984 Reciprocal teaching of comprehension-fostering and comprehension-monitoring activities. *Cognition and Instruction* 1(2): 117–75

Pressley M, Goodchild F, Fleet J, Zajochowski R, Evans D 1989 The challenges of classroom strategy instruction. *Elem. Sch. J.* 89(3): 301–42

Sanford A J, Garrod S C 1981 *Understanding Written Language: Exploration of Comprehension Beyond the Sentence.* Wiley, New York

Spiro R J 1980 Accommodative reconstruction in prose recall. *J. Verbal Learn. Verbal Behav.* 19(1): 84–95

van Dijk T A, Kintsch W 1983 *Strategies of Discourse Comprehension.* Academic Press, New York

Further Reading

Britton B K, Black J B 1985 *Understanding Expository Text.* Erlbaum, Hillsdale, New Jersey

Pearson P D (ed.) 1984 *Handbook of Reading Research.* Longman, New York

Reading Comprehension in Second and Foreign Language

E. Bialystok

Reading comprehension is one of the most complex forms of cognition in which people routinely engage. It is the result of information from visual, auditory, semantic, conceptual, and linguistic sources combining instantly to provide a rendition of each sentence or fragment. This meaning must be combined with background and inferential information and coordinated with the context and meaning of the whole passage. This process is made more complex if the text is written in a language known only imperfectly, but it is practically paralyzed if the written code on the page is not the same as the one that is used to record the reader's first language. How does comprehension occur when reading in a second language? How do these comprehension processes compare to those used when reading in a first language?

There are normally two situations involving reading comprehension in a second language. The first is the case in which children are taught literacy skills in a language other than their native language. This happens either because of immigration to a new country, or because of selecting a special program of study, such as immersion education. The second is the case in which a literate adult is learning a second language and at the same time learns how to read in that language. The primary focus of this article will be on adults' experiences in reading a second language, but important differences between the two cases will be noted.

1. Interactive Models of Reading

Theoretical models of reading have generally been classified according to a distinction between two kinds of processes: "bottom-up" and "top-down." "Bottom-up" processing consists of the sequential steps involved in identifying and understanding the marks on the page. These include the movements of the eye to take in the next segment of information, the visual pattern recognition to identify the letters, and the reference to syntactic and vocabulary knowledge to understand the individual words and their function. "Top-down" processing is the use of general knowledge to interpret the words and sentences being identified. Some examples are background knowledge of the topic, knowledge of discourse, the ability to make inferences so that information not explicitly stated can be supplied, and general schemata for how knowledge is organized in a particular domain.

1.1 Top-down and Bottom-up in a First Language

If the goal of reading is comprehension, then there is no doubt that both these types of processes are critical to its success. Early models of reading were developed to describe the processing used by skilled readers when reading in their first language. These efforts tended to be somewhat simplistic in that they described processing from only one of the two approaches. The majority of current models, however, assume an interaction between top-down and bottom-up processes (Just and Carpenter 1980, McClelland and Rumelhart 1981). More recently, these models have been applied to the developmental problem of how children learn to read in their first language. In general it is claimed that as readers become more skilled, there is a shift from greater reliance on bottom-up processes to more dependence on top-down processes.

1.2 Top-down and Bottom-up in a Second Language

Both first and second language reading comprehension depend on both top-down and bottom-up processes, but the balance between them is not the same for the two types of reading. Five possible reasons for this asymmetry have been suggested by Carrell (1988). The first is that a second language reader may not be familiar with the cultural assumptions necessary for top-down processing. In different cultural traditions, there are different methods for organizing discourse and for marking rhetorical structure. Familiarity with these conventions is necessary for understanding the text.

The second reason is that these necessary cultural schemata may be present but are simply not activated when needed. If texts are vague or elliptical and the reader is only marginally familiar with the culture, the reader may not realize that some known schema is relevant. The third reason is that second language readers may not have developed sufficient proficiency in the second language necessary for the bottom-up processing. These include the initial letter and word recognition skills that are needed to interact with the top-down schemata. A fourth reason is that readers from different cultural backgrounds may have different conceptions about reading and different ideas about the kinds of strategies that are brought to the task. In some cultures reading may only be done aloud, it may involve only religious or cultural texts, or it may require passive acceptance rather than critical evaluation of the material.

Finally, cognitive style may determine aspects of an individual's balance between top-down and bottom-up processing. Reading in a first language allows for considerable variation in style among readers because of the many sources of information that will lead to a correct interpretation of the text. Reading in a second language may be more restricted in this way because some of the sources of information are simply not available. As a result, certain types of reader may be disadvantaged when reading a second language because their preferred source of information is not sufficiently available.

In summary, the primary difference between first and second language reading comprehension appears to be in the balance between top-down and bottom-up processing that is used. It is likely that second language readers may compensate for weaknesses in one area by relying more heavily on processing from the opposite direction. This flexibility may be the particular advantage of interactive models. In the next two sections of this entry, the top-down and bottom-up processes will be examined more closely for their role in determining second language reading comprehension.

2. Conceptual Resources in Reading Comprehension

Literate adults who learn to read in a second language come to the task with established background knowledge. These resources facilitate top-down processing. What these adults tend to lack are the linguistic resources needed for bottom-up processing. The situation is reversed for children learning to read in their first language. Children have well-developed linguistic resources but need to learn how to read. Children learning to read in a second language may lack both sources of knowledge. To what extent do the background and conceptual knowledge of adults predict their ability to learn to read in a second language?

565

2.1 Reading Skill

If reading skill transfers, then specific linguistic knowledge of the second language will be less important than conceptual knowledge of the topic and general strategies for reading. In this case, the impoverished linguistic resources will not impede reading comprehension. Research studies have examined this question by testing readers in both their first and second languages and measuring the correspondence between these two skills. Although there is an overall correlation between level of reading ability in the first and second language, several factors are important in determining the degree of transfer that can be expected. Cummins (1991) identifies language proficiency in the first language as an important variable in determining the success with which a language learner will read in the second language. The level of difficulty of the text is also important (Alderson 1984). Reading skill levels are the same across languages if the texts are easy, but knowledge of language determines performance if the texts are difficult. A similar interaction is found with the proficiency level of the readers (Barnett 1989). There was more commonality between first and second language reading skill for more advanced learners than for lower-level learners. These results point to the complexity of describing the process of reading comprehension because so many factors need to be considered.

2.2 Background Knowledge

In a review of this literature, Barnitz (1986) shows that the reader's knowledge of cultural schemata, routines, and conventions and the knowledge of the discourse structures used in that cultural tradition significantly predict the level of reading attained. This relation is valid for reading in both a first and a second language.

3. Linguistic Resources in Reading Comprehension

If reading skill does not transfer, then the reader needs to reconstruct the reading process from the bottom up in the second language, just as it was constructed in the first language. Adults reading in a second language, therefore, would use processes similar to those used by children learning to read in their first language. Learners would need to build up a repertoire of linguistic knowledge before there could be much comprehension of the text. In this case, bottom-up processing will be the relevant factor in reading comprehension.

3.1 Syntactic Knowledge

Reading comprehension requires some level of grammatical analysis of the written text. Typically, syntactic information is processed automatically and not even noticed by the reader when reading in a first language (Flores d'Aracais 1986). These syntactic processes may need to become more visible and more salient for reading in a second language. In addition, different languages mark grammatical relations in different ways, leading to differences in the degree of syntactic processing required by various languages in order to achieve comprehension. For example, more grammatical analysis is needed to understand the relations expressed in a language that marks grammatical function through word order rather than through inflections. Therefore, two aspects of syntax will be important in determining the extent to which a reader will be successful in comprehending a second language: the degree to which the reader has mastered the syntax of the second language (Berman 1984), and the similarity between syntactic functions in the two languages (Mitchell et al. 1990).

The role that grammatical knowledge plays in reading comprehension for a second language ultimately depends on deciding whether there is a cognitive mechanism that functions as a universal parser (Mitchell et al. 1990). A cognitive mechanism of this kind would be able to take in strings of words in any language and compute a syntactic structure for that string. The grammatical relations in an utterance, then, would be determined by the same device, irrespective of the rule system used in any particular language. If there is a universal device of this kind, then grammar is not a factor in determining a reader's ability to comprehend a second language. However, in the more likely case that no such device is responsible for parsing, readers would need to determine a great deal of syntactic information about the second language string before comprehension was possible.

3.2 Vocabulary

The possibility of a universal device cannot explain the word identification skills that readers need to establish in order to read in a second language. Irrespective of the assistance of top-down processing, at some point simple knowledge of vocabulary and semantics is needed to interpret the text. The role that vocabulary knowledge plays in determining second language reading comprehension has been demonstrated by Williams and Dallas (1984).

3.3 Automaticity

Another possibility is that the bottom-up processing responsible for interpreting the grammatical and semantic information in the text is the same for both first and second language reading, but that this process works automatically and more efficiently when applied to the first language (McLeod and McLaughlin 1986, Segalowitz 1986). Such low-level skills as word identification and grammatical analysis are carried out more slowly and deliberately in a weak language. This difference in speed between processing the first and second language is evident even at very high levels of proficiency in the second language. On this view a quantitative, as opposed to qualitative, difference in bottom-up processing consistently disadvantages reading in a second language.

4. The Role of Orthography

The issue of whether first language reading skill transfers to the foreign language barely arises if the two languages are written in a different script. Different kinds of scripts are read most efficiently with different reading strategies, and comprehension is a direct result of how efficiently and skillfully the reading is carried out. Henderson (1984) lists three types of scripts, each with different implications for reading: logographic, syllabographic, and alphabetic.

Within these broad classifications, languages differ in terms of what segments they record and what segments they isolate. Some syllabographic languages (e.g., Japanese) represent syllables and mark syllable distinctions visually. Other syllabographic languages (e.g., Korean) represent phonemes but mark syllable distinctions. Alphabetic languages represent phonemes but may or may not mark word boundaries (e.g., English vs. Sanskrit). Obvious processing differences are entailed by each of these scripts. Logographic scripts (e.g., Chinese) that represent higher-order units, such as words or syllables, may require configuration cues to decode, while scripts that represent phonemic units likely require rule systems (Biederman and Tsao 1979).

Even scripts that represent alphabetic characters differ from each other in important ways. Serbo-Croatian is completely regular phonetically, and reading is based on phonological analysis to a degree that would be entirely inappropriate for a language such as English (Turvey et al. 1984). These differences can also be described by a dimension of depth. In Serbo-Croatian the phonology can be generated directly from the print, so this orthography is considered shallow. Hebrew, however, does not represent vowels and so the reader must know something about what the word is before it can be read. This orthography is deep. English is somewhere in between. Frost et al.(1987) have demonstrated how these differences in orthographic depth translate into differences in processing.

5. Implications for Instruction

The variation in emphasis on either top-down or bottom-up processing that characterizes second language reading has direct implications for instruction. To facilitate top-down processing, a foreign language reader would need to become familiar with the content that was being read and with cultural conventions of the text. Conversely, to facilitate bottom-up processing, the reader would need to establish elaborate graphemic, lexical, and syntactic resources for the new language since reading comprehension was built up out of these. It seems clear that complete comprehension of the text can not be attained without some measure of information from both these directions of processing.

The main implication of this body of research, however, is that humans are supremely flexible and able to substitute alternative sources of information quickly to complete processing of a complex cognitive task. At the early stages of second language learning, readers may rely more on general knowledge and reading skill to compensate for their weak linguistic skills. The opposite is true for children beginning to read in their first language who attend assiduously to linguistic information and virtually disregard any conceptual implications. At later stages in the development of the skill, adult second language readers use a broad base of knowledge to understand what they read.

In this way, all of the linguistic and conceptual knowledge amassed by a second language learner ultimately forms the critical resource upon which reading comprehension will proceed. No one kind of information is primary, and no one kind of information is irrelevant.

See also: Language and Learning in Education; Reading, Learning and Instruction of; Reading Comprehension, Learning of

References

Alderson J C 1984 Reading in a foreign language: A reading problem or a language problem? In: Alderson J C, Urquhart A H (eds.) 1984 *Reading in a Foreign Language*. Longman, London

Barnett M A 1989 *More Than Meets the Eye: Foreign Language Learner Reading: Theory and Practice*. Prentice Hall Regents, Englewood Cliffs, New Jersey

Barnitz J G 1986 Toward understanding the effects of cross-cultural schemata and discourse structure on second language reading comprehension. *J. Read. Behav.* 18(2): 95–116

Berman R 1984 Syntactic components of the foreign language reading process. In: Alderson J C, Urquhart A H (eds.) 1984 *Reading in a Foreign Language*. Longman, London

Biederman I, Tsao Y C 1979 On processing Chinese ideographs and English words: Some implications from Stroop-Test results. *Cognit. Psychol.* 11(2): 125–32

Carrell P L 1988 Some causes of text-boundedness and schema interference in ESL reading. In: Carrell P L, Devine J, Eskey D E (eds.) 1988 *Interactive Approaches to Second Language Reading*. Cambridge University Press, Cambridge

Cummins J 1991 Interdependence of first- and second-language proficiency in bilingual children. In: Bialystok E (ed.) 1991 *Language Processing in Bilingual Children*. Cambridge University Press, Cambridge

Flores d'Aracais G B 1986 Syntactic processing during reading for comprehension. In: Coltheart M (ed.) 1986 *Attention and Performance XII: The Psychology of Reading.* Erlbaum, London

Frost R, Katz L, Bentin S 1987 Strategies for visual word recognition and orthographical depth: A multilingual comparison. *J. Exp. Psychol. Hum. Percept. Perform.* 13(1): 104–15

Henderson L 1984 Writing systems and reading processes. In: Henderson L (ed.) 1984 *Orthographies and Reading.* Lawrence Erlbaum, London

Just M A, Carpenter P A 1980 A theory of reading: From eye fixations to comprehension. *Psychol. Rev.* 87(4): 329–54

McClelland J, Rumelhart D 1981 An interactive activation model of context effects in letter perception. *Psychol. Rev.* 88(5): 375–407

McLeod B, McLaughlin B 1986 Restructuring or automaticity? Reading in a second language. *Language Learning* 36(2): 109–23

Mitchell D C, Cuetos F, Zagar D 1990 Reading in different languages: Is there a universal mechanism for parsing sentences? In: Balota D A, Flores d'Aracais G B, Rayner K (eds.) 1990 *Comprehension Processes in Reading.* Erlbaum, Hillsdale, New Jersey

Segalowitz N 1986 Skilled reading in the second language. In: Vaid J (ed.) 1986 *Language Processing in Bilinguals: Psycholinguistic and Neuropsychological Perspectives.* Erlbaum, Hillsdale, New Jersey

Turvey M T, Feldman L B, Lukatela G 1984 The Serbo-Croatian orthography constrains the reader to a phonologically analytic strategy. In: Henderson L (ed.) 1984 *Orthographies and Reading.* Lawrence Erlbaum, London

Williams R, Dallas D 1984 Aspects of vocabulary in readability. In: Alderson J C, Urquhart A H (eds.) 1984 *Reading in a Foreign Language.* Longman, London

Further Reading

Alderson J C, Urquhart A H (eds.) 1984 *Reading in a Foreign Language.* Longman, London

Carrell P L, Devine J, Eskey D E (eds.) 1988 *Interactive Approaches to Second Language Reading.* Cambridge University Press, Cambridge

Carroll J B 1975 *The Teaching of French as a Foreign Language in Eight Countries.* Wiley, New York

Dubin F, Eskey D E, Grabe W (eds.) 1986 *Teaching Second Language Reading for Academic Purposes.* Addison-Wesley Publishing, Reading, Massachusetts

Goodman K S 1973 Psycholinguistic universals of the reading process. In: Smith F (ed.) *Psycholinguistics and Reading.* Holt, Rinehart and Winston, New York

Lewis G E, Massad C E 1975 *The Teaching of English as a Foreign Language in Ten Countries.* Wiley, New York

Mackay R, Barkman B, Jordan R R (eds.) 1978 *Reading in a Second Language: Hypotheses, Organization, and Practice.* Newbury House, Rowley, Massachusetts

Perfetti C A 1985 *Reading Ability.* Oxford University Press, New York

Science, Learning and Instruction of

M. C. Linn and B.-S. Eylon

This entry will summarize a new consensus about the nature of science learning and the characteristics of effective instruction in science. Perspectives on science education that grew out of the fields of developmental psychology, differential psychology, science teaching, and problem-solving are beginning to converge (Eylon and Linn 1988). Debates about science education are joined by experts representing a broad range of relevant areas including classroom teaching, natural science, curriculum development, technology, and cognitive psychology. The complexities of teaching and learning science have been increasingly appreciated while at the same time science has become more and more important in the lives of all citizens. Moreover, science learning is now commonly studied in classroom settings, allowing investigators to examine these complexities more systematically. This new consensus incorporates greater emphasis on the social context of learning, increased understanding of contextual influences on problem-solving, and growing respect for the learner's struggles to make sense of scientific phenomena.

1. Perspectives on Science Education

Four perspectives on science education referred to by Eylon and Linn (1988) as the concept-learning, developmental, differential, and problem-solving perspectives are converging as investigators pay increasing attention to the social context of learning, the learner's construction of knowledge, and the nature of learning in classroom settings.

1.1 Concept-learning Perspective

Studies of the qualitative differences among students' ideas for explaining scientific phenomena follow the concept-learning perspective (Driver et al. 1985, Gentner and Stevens 1983, Pfundt and Duit 1991). At first, the scientific concepts held by students were identified as deficiencies and labeled "misconceptions." More and more researchers see students' concepts as indicative of the struggle necessary to make sense of the world. This construction of knowledge is the focus for those interested in concept-learning. Rather than viewing student ideas as useless, educators are now seeking ways to build on them.

1.1.1 Characteristics of student conceptions. Important consistencies in the concepts students develop have fueled a rethinking of the origin of these ideas. On the one hand, students each follow an idiosyncratic course, developing ideas based on their personal experiences, cultural environment, and instructional programs. On the other hand, the similarities in experiences of scientific phenomena mean that students hold a relatively small number of typical ideas in each scientific domain (Driver et al. 1985, Gentner and Stevens 1983, Pfundt and Duit 1991). For example, students commonly hold the view that "objects released from a curving path will continue on the path," "heat and temperature are the same except that heat is the higher temperatures," and "atoms are small pieces of material that have all the macroscopic features of the material."

In many ways, all students learn science concepts in a similar context. Most students see objects in motion come to rest, experience getting warm when they don a sweater, and observe the sun rise and set. These common experiences motivate students to construct similar ideas. Students tend to construct ideas dominated by their observations. They conclude that the earth must be round like a pancake rather than round like a sphere. They expect that when a ball is thrown, the force of the hand keeps it going. They conclude that electricity comes out of the wall and is consumed by appliances.

In other ways, students learn science in unique or culturally based contexts. Students unfamiliar with snow might have difficulty differentiating "powder" from "ice." Students from cultures where the functionality of objects is emphasized might find it difficult to group objects by abstract criteria such as length (Fensham 1988, Gentner and Stevens 1983). Students convinced that scientific phenomena are governed by magic may reject a rational view of scientific events (Driver et al. 1985, Linn et al. 1991).

Moreover, students may have difficulty generalizing because they expect the context of concept application to be similar to the context of learning. Instead, the context of application is typically much more complex and ambiguous than the context of science instruction. Students may develop scientific ideas associated with classroom science and others associated with their homes rather than seeking coherence across contexts. As a result, teachers may conclude that their students hold inconsistent scientific ideas while students may believe they have a repertoire of alternative ideas.

One final factor in the realization that students'

conceptions may be accomplishments rather than deficiencies is that many of their conceptions are similar to views held by respected scientists of the past, including Aristotle (Gentner and Stevens 1983, McDermott 1984). For example, students often believe that objects released from a curved path will continue to follow a curved trajectory rather than a tangent to its point of release. Subsequent studies have investigated how instruction might build on students' conceptions and modes of learning to bring about a view which is more consistent with established scientific knowledge.

1.1.2 Teaching science concepts. Efforts to help students acquire useful, powerful scientific concepts began by examining experts' reasoning (Larkin et al. 1980, Gentner and Stevens 1983). It became clear that expert reasoning cannot be imposed on students. Instead, students need help in constructing their own ideas. The process of construction can be "scaffolded" by carefully designing the learning environment, but success requires students' active participation (Gentner and Stevens 1983, Resnick 1989). Scaffolding means supporting students as needed, such that they can explore and integrate their repertoire of ideas. Students need evidence that new modes of thinking and behavior are beneficial and warrant their efforts. To reinforce students' efforts to make sense of the world, effective programs must build on student ideas, helping students synthesize and organize their experiences.

1.2 Developmental Perspective

Studies of the development of scientific ideas demonstrate that students gain new concepts slowly and that some ideas commonly precede others (Gentner and Stevens 1983, Linn 1987). Many researchers have found that scientific ideas are developed within specific contexts and are difficult to generalize across contexts. Furthermore, the problem context has come to be seen as a more potent constraint on performance than chronological age. Many studies show that, depending on the context, students might be simultaneously more sophisticated and less sophisticated in their scientific reasoning than their age would suggest (McDermott 1984, Resnick 1989).

The insights of the concept-learning perspective and the developmental perspective jointly suggest that students construct ideas within contexts and that they struggle to generalize their ideas. How do students react to the fleeting coverage of numerous science topics characteristic of many science curricula? Often they cannot make sense of the information presented and resort to memorization instead (Eylon and Linn 1988, Linn et al. 1991).

1.2.1 Teaching for integrated understanding. To help students integrate their knowledge and apply it to new problems and situations, developmentalists point to the power of reflection. Reflection is the process of identifying parallels between diverse ideas, organizing diverse information, and analyzing one's own learning strategies. The challenge is to scaffold this powerful process as part of effective teaching (Resnick 1989).

1.3 Differential Perspective

Researchers from the differential perspective have viewed learners as governed by abilities, such as those characterized as fluid, crystallized, or spatial. They have viewed social experiences based on age, sex, and cultural background as influencing learning. Overall, studies based on these ideas have been disappointing. Some researchers, influenced by the growing interest in context-dependent reasoning, have turned to more precise and situation-specific features of learners and of instruction.

For example, when attempts to make sense of student performance in terms of gender were unsuccessful, researchers examined such variables as "opportunity to learn" as well as the specific interactions of teachers with male and female students. Internationally, these studies revealed that females have fewer opportunities to learn science (Rosier and Keeves 1991).

Furthermore, classroom observation studies showed that teachers treat male and female students differently. Male students are more likely than females to be asked difficult and integrative questions; females when they are asked to contribute at all, are asked more straightforward questions. Moreover, males are praised and females are criticized (Tobin et al. 1990). Teacher behavior in these settings is consistent with the normative view that science is a male domain.

1.4 Problem-solving Perspective

Those following the problem-solving perspective have also shifted from a decontextualized view to a context-rich view. Initially, investigators argued that if students learn basic scientific reasoning processes they could apply the skills in any context and become autonomous science learners. In spite of serious efforts to teach general problem-solving processes, little progress resulted (LaPointe et al. 1989) and researchers turned to teaching problem-solving in much richer domains (Linn et al. in press, Gentner and Stevens 1983).

Early studies compared experts and novices, finding that experts store more information, organize it more efficiently, and can apply it more broadly. For example, experts organize knowledge around central principles, such as conservation of energy, while novices organize knowledge around superficial features such as the apparatus used for the experiment or the name of the variable. Often, however, expert representations are not accessible to students. Instead, novices may benefit from interacting with a series of knowledge representations, designed to help distinguish among a repertoire of ideas.

1.5 Convergence of Perspectives

These four perspectives are converging on a view of science learning as occurring in a rich and socially constructed context. This convergence suggests a view of science instruction that scaffolds students to integrate, organize, and reflect as they learn. In contrast, assessment of the achievements of students in most countries suggests that students acquire little understanding of science concepts at school and generally cannot apply these ideas in solving the complex or ambiguous problems they typically encounter.

2. New Directions

Collaborative groups of investigators are investigating science learning and instruction in classroom settings. This work is characterized by innovative methodologies that shed light on new, more comprehensive questions. Fundamentally, studying problem-solving in a rich context offers insights concerning the goals of science education, the methods of instruction, and the preparation of teachers (Fraser and Tobin in press).

2.1 Goals of Science Education

Students throughout the world need scientific knowledge to cope with an increasingly complex society. Introductory science courses must be both rigorous and relevant to the needs of students who do not plan careers in science. United States programs such as the Physical Science Curriculum Study were intended to meet these dual goals, yet they attracted primarily students who planned to become scientists. Worldwide, few students study physics and those who do often complain that applications of scientific ideas are neglected. Designing programs to meet the dual goals of providing a firm foundation for future scientists while at the same time preparing those who do not plan careers in science to be informed citizens, requires a more relevant and accessible curriculum than is offered in most countries.

Science education reformers have developed examples of courses that meet the dual goals of rigor and relevance (De Corte et al. 1992). These courses eschew quantitative solutions, microscopic models, and formal methods of analysis. And, instead, they feature qualitative reasoning, macroscopic models, and flexible methods of analysis. They emphasize scientific principles that students can apply and scaffold learners as they acquire progressively more abstract views of scientific events. These new approaches to science education emphasize that for any scientific problem there are multiple, qualitatively different explanations and that the most abstract explanation is not necessarily the most appropriate for all learners or all scientists. Just as scientists select the level of explanation to fit the problem, so it is appropriate for educators to select the level of explanation to suit the learner. For example, scientists use molecular-kinetic theory for some problems in thermodynamics and solve others with a qualitative heat-flow model of thermodynamics. By choosing goals for science instruction that are relevant and accessible, students can develop lifelong habits of expanding and integrating their repertoire of ideas, rather than isolating science knowledge.

2.2 Methods of Science Teaching

Scaffolding students as they learn science has become a promising direction for effective teaching (Resnick 1989). This technique has often drawn on technology for its effectiveness. In this case technology is serving as a catalyst for change. Technology as a tool used in conjunction with a sound instructional theory offers substantial promise.

To construct understanding, students need opportunities to elaborate their knowledge, reflect on it, and discuss it in a supportive social context. Technology can often help teachers provide opportunities for elaboration and reflection and free teachers to concentrate on tutoring.

Techniques for scaffolding student understanding are emerging. One successful strategy is to use analogies to provide a bridge between students' intuitive ideas and more abstract notions. Another is to illustrate complex ideas dynamically using technological tools and to allow students to explore the ramifications of these models (De Corte et al. 1992). The strategy of contradicting student ideas and hoping they will construct more comprehensive concepts has not been so successful. Often students adjust their observations to conform to their views. For example, students observing ammeters in series in an electric circuit adjust their recall of the meter readings to fit a model of electricity being consumed.

2.3 Processes of Teacher Education

The new consensus about science learning suggests some effective strategies for educating teachers. In the past, the most comprehensive programs introduced new curricula by having teachers experience the program as a "student." This is not sufficient. Teachers, like students, have difficulty translating ideas from one context to another.

Evaluations revealed that only a few teachers follow new programs. Most adapt new programs to their prior ideas about teaching. In Israel the new physics curriculum emphasized practical work and a laboratory examination. In response, many teachers continued with the "chalk and talk" method and, a few months before the examination, provided a "laboratory session" as preparation for the test. The same scaffolded opportunities for learning as have been successful in science teaching are needed in teacher education. Teachers are constructing knowledge just as students do in science courses. Teachers struggle to gain an understanding of teaching and benefit from scaffolding to connect new practices with prior experience.

As the new goals of science education are incorporated into curricula, the demands on teachers are likely to increase. Teachers need to help all students construct understanding. This requires sophisticated pedagogical and management skills, as well as strong mastery of the subject matter. As was summarized succinctly by Fensham, "Not only is the teacher 'teaching science' but is also teaching learners what it means to be learning science" (Fensham 1988 p.24).

3. Conclusion

The new consensus about learning and teaching science draws on important research in psychology, sociology, education, physical and biological science, and cognitive science. As researchers construct an understanding of science learning and teaching they build on this research base. By integrating results from diverse research projects, reflecting on experiences, and supporting each other, researchers will continue to gain insights into science learning and teaching.

See also: Expert Knowledge and Performance; Preconceptions and Misconceptions; Development of Learning Skills in Problem-solving and Thinking

References

De Corte E, Linn M C, Mandl H, Verschaffel L (eds.) 1992 *Computer-based Learning Environments and Problem Solving.* Springer-verlag, Berlin

Driver R, Guesne E, Tiberghien A (eds.) 1985 *Children's Ideas in Science.* Open University Press, Philadelphia, Pennsylvania

Eylon B, Linn M C 1988 Learning and instruction: An examination of four research perspectives in science education. *Rev. Educ. Res.* 58(3): 251–301

Fensham P (ed.) 1988 *Development and Dilemmas in Science Education.* Falmer, New York

Fraser B J, Tobin K (eds.) in press *International Handbook of Science Education.* Kluwer, The Netherlands

Gentner D, Stevens A L 1983 *Mental Models.* Erlbaum, Hillsdale, New Jersey

LaPointe A E, Mead N A, Phillips G W 1989 *A World of Differences: An International Assessment of Mathematics and Science.* Technical Report No. 19-CAEP-01. Educational Testing Service, Princeton, New Jersey

Larkin J, McDermott J, Simon D P, Simon H A 1980 Expert and novice performance in solving physics problems. *Science* 208(4450): 1335–42

Linn M C 1987 Establishing a research base for science education: Challenges, trends, and recommendations. *J. Res. Sci. Teach.* 24(3): 191–216

Linn M C, Songer N B, Eylon B in press Shifts and convergences in science learning and instruction. In: Calfee R, Berliner D (eds.) *Handbook of Educational Psychology*. Macmillan, Riverside, New Jersey

Linn M C, Songer N B, Lewis E L (eds.) 1991 Students' models and epistemologies of science. *J. Res. Sci. Teach.* 28(9) (special issue)

McDermott L C 1984 Research on conceptual understanding in mechanics. *Physics Today* 37(7): 24–32

Pfundt H, Duit R 1991 *Students' alternative frameworks*. Institut für die Pädagogik der Naturwissenschaften, Uni-

versity of Kiel, Kiel

Resnick L (ed.) 1989 *Knowing, Learning, and Instruction: Essays in Honor of Robert Glaser*. Erlbaum, Hillsdale, New Jersey

Rosier M J, Keeves J P (eds.) 1991 *The International Studies in Educational Achievement Study of Science. Vol. 1: Science Education and Curricula in Twenty-three Countries*. Pergamon Press, Oxford.

Tobin K, Kahle J B, Fraser B J (eds.) 1990 *Windows into Science Classrooms: Problems Associated with Higher-level Cognitive Learning*. Falmer, New York

Social Sciences, Learning and Instruction of

J. F. Voss

The purpose of this entry is to present a summary of cognitive-oriented research conducted in social sciences. The first of two sections considers research in history, economics, and political science, while the concluding section addresses emerging research issues.

1. History, Economics, and Political Science

1.1 History

Research in the study of history has considered history textbooks. Beck et al. (1989) analyzed elementary school history texts in the United States. They concluded that United States texts are difficult to follow because of three factors. First, texts often assume prior knowledge beyond the reader's world knowledge. Second, texts have unclear content goals. Third, the explanations provided are often incomplete. Beck et al. (1989) subsequently demonstrated improvement in knowledge acquisition when texts were accordingly revised. Results of a Spanish study, indicating that 2,000 seventh-grade students reported social sciences as the most difficult subject, suggested that text construction problems may be a general phenomenon (Carretero et al. 1991).

Hallden (1986) argued that the study of history suffers minimal interference from misconceptions and commonsense beliefs: a greater problem is the student's idea of history. To Hallden, students need a better idea of what is explained in a historical explanation. He presented data indicating that students focus upon the actions of individuals and their motives and neglect important event-related conditions. Frisch (1989) also studied the emphasis upon people, by asking students to list individuals in United States history. Many people listed were not noted for historical import but for their symbolic cultural significance, such

as Betsy Ross, the supposed maker of the first United States flag. Frisch (1989) observed that the student's concept of history is reinforced by cultural factors that may be of little historical significance. This conclusion requires further study.

Historical explanation in adolescence has been studied by Carretero et al. (1991). Their results indicated that students of 12 or 14 years had difficulty in establishing causal relations, while older adolescents performed better. Moreover, older humanities students provided more enriched causal explanations than older science students, a result suggesting that causal perception may vary with domain training.

Students also have a poor sense of historical evidence. In an interview study conducted on 167 15-year olds, Shemilt (1987) described four levels of student understanding of historical evidence. The lowest level is "evidence equals knowledge," with the historian viewed as a "memory man." Any uncertainty is due to a lack of knowledge; moreover, no distinction is made between information and evidence. In the second stage the need for evidence is recognized, although students fail to distinguish more and less reliable types of evidence. In the third stage the student differentiates evidence and information, and students realize that some system or set of ideas is needed to determine what constitutes evidence. Moreover, the historian is seen as a person who makes inferences to arrive at conclusions rather than making discoveries. In the fourth stage, history is considered not only as a reconstruction, but also as an interpretation of the past. Even in this stage, however, there is a tendency to view historical knowledge in the limited context of a particular situation and to ignore a broader context. Shemilt (1987) suggested several ways of improving instruction. These included asking students in the first stage to consider alternative answers to questions, thereby getting them to think beyond their simplistic views. Similarly, he suggested that students in the fourth stage should be asked to explore background information and select and determine what evidence contextual information provides.

O'Reilly (1991) has placed student difficulties in learning history in an informal reasoning context. Difficulties include inability to distinguish conclusions from premises, failure to see how arguments are constructed, failure to understand and use terms precisely, and the failure to evaluate ethical claims. In addition, O'Reilly noted the need for teachers not to be constrained in the use of appropriate assessment instruments.

Wineburg (1991) studied student concepts of historical evidence, comparing high school student performance to that of experts (recent history PhDs or graduate students). The task involved evaluating documents and paintings related to the Battle of Lexington during the American Revolution, with respect to their usefulness in historical analysis. Wineburg's comparisons included ascertaining the extent of use of three heuristics: corroboration—comparison of documents with one another; sourcing—examining the source of the document before reading the document; and contextualizing—placing the document in time and place. Use of these heuristics was considerably greater by the historians, and the differences were related to judgments of document reliability. An important point about Wineburg's results is that the historians applied a set of domain-related heuristics they had acquired as historians; their performance did not simply involve the instantiation of some prior knowledge of the Lexington confrontation. A second point is that, since there is a substantial difference between what the historian does and what the student takes to be "history," there is the question of how students may best develop a sense of appreciation for the role of the historian in history.

The nature of teacher explanations provided in teaching high school history classes has also been studied. Leinhardt (1993) has distinguished two types of teacher explanations: blocked and varied repetition. "Blocked" refers to self-contained explanations while "varied repetition" refers to the repeated use of concepts in different historical situations, such as showing how concerns of mercantile and agrarian groups constitute a repeated theme in United States history. Using data from 76 class meetings, Leinhardt demonstrated how blocked and varied repetition explanations occur in different contexts and how they are differentially related to student outcomes, with varied repetition instruction, for example, leading to better thematic understanding.

Studies on the teaching of history have been reviewed by Downey and Levstik (1991), including the use of Piagetian theory and alternative views as bases of historical instruction. The authors essentially conclude that "cultural literacy" as a criterion is essentially superficial, producing only a surface understanding of concepts, and that more research in the learning of history is needed to develop a better idea of how students construct meaning.

1.2 Economics

Research on the learning of economics has been largely focused on the extent to which students understand economic concepts, such as work, money, and means of production. Ajello et al. (1987) postulated that the development of economic concepts at different stages of development involves the child's acquisition of "social scenes," mental representations having economic, political, and social components. Working on a farm, in a factory, or in a shop constitutes such a "scene." Using a curriculum intervention with third-grade children, Ajello et al. found that ease of learning is inversely related to concept complexity, with students, for example, experiencing difficulty in distinguishing the concepts of price and profit. In addition, the authors suggested that personal familiarity with the particular environment is not critical.

Voss et al. (1986) studied the understanding of economic concepts by adults who either had or did not have a college education. Individuals were asked about three concepts, namely, price changes, interest rates, and inflation. Using a number of measures, reasoning and content-based performance was superior for the college-educated individual. Also, differences were not obtained between individuals having and not having college economics.

Efforts to enhance instruction have involved the development of interactive computer environments. One study (Achtenhagen 1991), involving advanced students in the German commercial education system, was designed to have students learn about the relationship of production and costs in the context of jeans manufacturing. Students were required to make decisions about the number of items to be produced, learning to take into account how a number of variables may influence the decision. Other work of this type was that of Shute et al. (1989). In their study individuals learned economic concepts about "Smithtown," a hypothetical community, and then solved problems by requesting information from a database. Performance was then related to variables of inquiry. Results indicated superior performance was characterized by a better understanding of the perceived interrelations of the variables and by the asking of better questions.

The teaching of economics was reviewed by Schug and Walstad (1991). In general, they concluded that research on teaching in economics has developed ways of measuring economic knowledge and attitudes toward economic issues. However, the question of what economics concepts to teach and how they should be taught are still open questions.

1.3 Political Science

While there has been a resurgence of interest in political socialization, little research has been conducted on

573

political science learning. However, one of the more promising approaches, adapted from college political science courses, has consisted of a game format in which different groups of individuals represent respective countries, the groups communicating via computers as a situation evolves. Torney-Purta (1989), in employing such a procedure, reported that not only knowledge was acquired, but that students also developed an appreciation of the political and economic position of the countries the students represented.

2. Research Issues

Research in history suggests that students have a concept of history as a narrative that includes people and important events, but their conception of historical explanation and what the historian does is poor. The challenge is therefore to provide a better understanding of such concepts, via improved texts and improved instruction. Research in economics suggests difficulty in acquiring some economic concepts, but that bringing simulations of real-life situations to the classroom can facilitate learning. However, data also indicate that some people acquire economic concepts with no economic training. It would seem that in each of these domains there is a need to reassess instructional goals as well as a need to increase the avenues of instruction.

In another entry in this *Encyclopedia* (See *Reasoning*), results are presented indicating that informal reasoning skill, such as that found in the social sciences, is a function of ability level, with little evidence to support the contention that schooling helps. There is therefore apparently a strong need to have students acquire knowledge of such ideas on the nature of causal reasoning in history, receiving experience in historical situations.

Interest and motivation, especially in relation to specific content areas, also require study. Little is known about how a student's interest in a particular topic, such as the Second World War, influences learning about that topic, and how to help an uninterested student become interested.

See also: Expert Level of Understanding; Reasoning

References

Achtenhagen F 1991 Development of problem-solving skills in natural settings. In: Carretero M, Pope M, Simons R-J, Pozo J I (eds.) 1991 *Learning and Instruction*, Vol. 3. Pergamon Press, New York

Ajello A M, Bombi A S, Pontecorvo C, Zucc+hermaglio C 1987 Teaching economics in primary school: The concepts of work and profit. *International Journal of Behavioral Development* 10(1): 51–70

Beck I L, McKeown M G, Gromoll E W 1989 Learning from social studies texts. *Cognition and Instruction* 6(2): 99–158

Carretero M, Asensio M, Pozo J I 1991 Cognitive development, historical time representation and causal explanations in adolescence. In: Carretero M, Pope M, Simons R-J, Pozo J I (eds.) 1991 *Learning and Instruction: European Research in an International Context*, Vol. 3 Pergamon Press, Oxford

Downey M T, Levstik L S 1991 Teaching and learning history. In: Shaver J P (ed.) 1991 *Handbook of Research on Social Studies Teaching and Learning*. Macmillan Inc., New York

Frisch M 1989 American history and the structures of collective memory: A modest exercise in empirical iconography. *Journal of American History* 75(4): 1130–55

Hallden O 1986 Learning history. *Oxford Rev. Educ.* 12(1): 53–66

Leinhardt G 1993 Weaving instructional explanations in history. *Br. J. Educ. Psychol.* 63: 46–74

O'Reilly K 1991 Informal reasoning in high-school history. In: Voss J F, Perkins D N, Segal J W (eds.) 1991 *Informal Reasoning and Education*. Erlbaum, Hillsdale, New Jersey

Schug M C, Walstad W B 1991 Teaching and learning economics. In: Shaver J P (ed.) 1991 *Handbook of Research on Social Studies Teaching and Learning*. Macmillan Inc., New York

Shemilt D 1987 Adolescent ideas about evidence and methodology in history. In: Portal C (ed.) 1987 *The History Curriculum for Teachers*. Falmer Press, London

Shute V J, Glaser R, Raghavan K 1989 Inference and discovery in an exploratory laboratory. In: Ackerman P L, Sternberg R J, Glaser R (eds.) 1989 *Learning and Individual Differences*. Freeman, New York

Torney-Purta J 1989 Political cognition and its restructuring in young people. *Hum. Dev.* 32(1) 14–23

Voss J F, Blais J, Means M L, Greene T R, Ahwesh E 1986 Informal reasoning and subject matter knowledge in the solving of economics problems by naive and novice individuals. *Cognition and Instruction* 3(4): 269–302

Wineburg S S 1991 Historical problem solving: A study of cognitive processes used in the evaluation of documentary and pictorial evidence. *J. Educ. Psychol.* 83(1): 73–87

Further Reading

Armento B J 1986 Research on teaching social studies. In: Wittrock M C (ed.) 1986 *Handbook of Research on Teaching*, 3rd edn. Macmillan Inc., New York

Beck I L, McKeown M G 1991 Substantive and methodological considerations for productive textbook analysis. In: Shaver J P (ed.) 1991 *Handbook of Research on Social Studies Teaching and Learning*. Macmillan Inc., New York

Leiser D, Roland-Lévy C, Sevón G (eds.) 1990 *Journal of Economic Psychology* 11(4) (special issue on culture and economic socialization)

Torney-Purta J 1991 Cross-national research in social studies. In: Shaver J P (ed.) 1991 *Handbook of Research on Social Studies Teaching and Learning*. Macmillan Inc., New York

Visual and Performing Arts, Learning and Instruction of

K. Freedman

Instruction in the arts is an important part of all students' schooling, since it provides an understanding of the aesthetic, cultural, and expressive domains of human life. This entry treats the instructional psychology of the visual and performing arts. It includes a brief summary of conditions, and specifically three psychological frameworks that have influenced and continue to shape arts instruction. As part of the most recent framework, contemporary research on arts instruction is summarized. Since most of the research in arts instruction has been about visual art and music, these domains are focused upon here; however, some of the information provided can also be applied to theater and dance education. While the entry will necessarily touch on curriculum by way of example, covering curriculum issues or topics is not its purpose.

1. General Background

In order to understand the influence of psychological research on the field, it is helpful to examine arts instruction in the past. For thousands of years, learning about the arts has been accomplished through the instruction of students trained to become artists and performers by being apprenticed to a master. From the middle of the nineteenth century onward, arts education was a required subject in public schools, taught to those who would not necessarily become professional creative artists as adults. Drawing and music instruction were two of the earliest public school subjects. In the nineteenth century, children learned to draw in school by precisely copying progressively more complex adult drawn images. This early art education was to provide students with industrial work skills and promote discipline. Music and the visual arts were also used at this time in the public schools to provide a moral education and promote the development of good character by illustrating lofty values and proper conduct (Efland 1990).

There are several historical similarities between public school arts education in different countries, in part because ideas on instruction were often imported. For example, the United Kingdom borrowed ideas from Germany on education in the visual arts that were then used in Canada, Australia, Japan, and the United States.

While many ideas have become common to many countries, cultural differences have created different practices and purposes of arts instruction. In the United States, the instructional methods borrowed from the United Kingdom were applied using local materials and were later integrated with ideas from France, Sweden, Japan, and other countries; in Japan, they were combined with instruction in traditional calligraphy skills, materials, and philosophy (Ueno 1989).

There has been variety as well as similarity in the content of international arts instruction. Several Western European and English-speaking countries have focused upon training in the fine arts in their public schools and many have included folk art and popular art. Since the 1960s, some countries such as Sweden and the Netherlands, have focused to a greater extent on the mass media in their arts education (Nordstrom 1988).

2. Psychological Frameworks

Instruction in the arts has been influenced by psychology since the emergence of psychology as a professional domain in the late nineteenth century. The influence has occurred through the use of several psychological perspectives or frameworks for art and learning. These frameworks have focused upon different aspects of student development and been reflected in teaching.

Two frameworks have been particularly influential in the past and continue to shape the field: clinical psychology and developmental psychology. Before the Second World War, arts education shifted its attention from production and performance skills toward a greater focus on self-expression. Educators worked toward the growth of the arts as a means to achieve psychological health. This clinical or therapeutic purpose of the arts in public school grew even stronger in several countries after the Second World War, when a self-expressive character came to be considered an integral part of an archetypal democratic personality.

As part of the effort to understand artistic growth and capabilities, models of artistic development emerged. These models have helped to describe and predict artistic behaviors in children. In spontaneous artistic production, children tend to move from psychomotor, to schematic, to stylized representations as they grow. Children are thought to be uninhibited at young ages, strive toward realism during adolescence, and then have a greater facility for making artistic decisions as they get older.

3. Cognitive Psychology and Contemporary Views

While still influential, earlier psychological views of arts education began to be updated in the late 1970s

575

and 1980s by applying a third framework involving broader sociological and cognitive perspectives. These analyses range from those concerned with the institutional and environmental conditions of art teaching to investigations of the semiotics of artistic knowledge.

One reason for the shift in focus of the frameworks for arts education has been the reconsideration of the portrayal of "the individual" as unique in terms of self-expression and as universal in terms of development. As part of the assessment of the use of psychology in arts education, researchers have reconsidered the implications of its previous assumptions. For example, it has generally been assumed that talent in the visual arts was innate, not greatly influenced by society or education, and characterized by the ability to produce highly realistic images. However, a historical examination of conceptions of artistic talent in children indicates that it was typically male children of a certain racial heritage and socioeconomic class who were typically deemed talented (Freedman 1989). The older conception of talent as a skill in realism has been tempered by a greater concern with characteristics such as interest, immersion, and fluency in a particular art form.

Models of artistic development delineating stages of growth, which have conventionally been based on the assumption that artistic development naturally unfolds as children mature, have been modified as researchers have become increasingly sensitive to socially induced and cultural differences. For example, it has been established that much of children's learning in the arts involves spontaneous copying from a range of mass media and popular arts sources (Wilson and Wilson 1977). Children sometimes revert to an earlier type of artistic behavior and can draw more realistically than developmental models suggest when they are unable to generalize the object they are drawing, such as in the case of autism. Normal children can reduce their tendency to generalize and increase realism by drawing from an upside-down picture. Also, there has been evidence of differences in children's artistic productions in different cultures and historical periods.

4. Artistic Production, Perception, and Response

Developmental research has included studies in artistic production and performance, perception, and responses to works of art. The research indicates that several aspects of artistic behavior are consistent among the children studied. However, these children have typically been from middle range socioeconomic levels in advanced industrial countries. The forces that influence artistic behavior are often culturally specific; they are determined by culture and may differ between cultures. These culturally determined forces include beliefs about what constitutes expressiveness in art, preferred forms of art, and criteria for achievement in art. Researchers are gaining a greater understanding of which aspects of artistic

development are biophysical and which are culturally specific.

Across the groups studied, certain aspects of the ways in which learning in the arts takes place have been established. For example, it is best to start production and performance of the arts in early childhood. To aid in concept development and discrimination, children should be presented at an early age with positive and negative examples of fundamental ideas and skills.

Until adolescence, children typically respond to subject matter and color in visual art before attending to other aspects of the work. During adolescence, children begin to attend more to the style and interpretive aspects of art. Preference influences learning in the arts and children tend to prefer styles of visual art and music with which they are familiar. Young adolescent students prefer faster tempos, rhythmic emphasis, a recognizable melody, and instrumental rather than vocal music. They prefer realistic visual art to the highly abstract. However, children can learn about a wide variety of visual art and musical styles at least by late elementary school and gain a greater appreciation of abstract and unfamiliar styles.

Learning in the visual and performing arts occurs best when children have enough time to practice with a variety of arts experiences, including several modes of study. In the past, arts education in public schools has placed a heavy emphasis on production and performance. Teacher modeling is important for learning in this regard.

However, verbal experiences are also important in arts education, because language aids concept development, understanding, and memory. Although the appropriate amount and type of theoretical and historical arts content in education is currently in debate across the arts, there has been a growing emphasis on written and verbal analysis of works of art in school. Research has supported the view that there are several types of "intelligences" and that several of these types aid artistic production, performance, and appreciation as well as being tied to domains of knowledge óther than the arts (Gardner 1989). While producing and performing art enriches many aspects of student learning, such as kinesthetic and spacial understanding, talking about the art of children and adults helps students understand other aesthetic and critical aspects of art. It also helps to provide an understanding of the professional art community, which forms an important part of artistic knowledge.

See also: Perceptual Development

References

Efland A 1990 *A History of Art Education: Intellectual and Social Currents in Teaching the Visual Arts.* Teachers College Press, New York

Freedman K 1989 Dilemmas of equity in art education: Ideol-
ogies of individualism and cultural capital. In: Secada
W G (ed.) 1989 *Equity in Education.* Falmer Press,
London
Gardner H 1989 Zero-based arts education: An introduction
to ARTS PROPEL. *Studies in Art Education* 30: 71–83
Nordstrom G Z 1988 Art research in the mid-80s. *Bild i
skolan* 59: 14–17
Ueno H 1989 The history of art education in Japan. *International Society for Education Through Art News* 3: 7–15
Wilson B, Wilson M 1977 An iconoclastic view of the imagery sources of the drawing of young people. *Art Education*
30: 5–11

Further Reading

Dissanayake E 1990 *What is Art For?* University of Wash-
ington Press, Seattle, Washington
Eisner E 1982 *Cognition and Curriculum: A Basis for
Deading what to Teach.* Longman, New York
Gardner H 1983 *Frames of Mind: The Theory of Multiple
Intelligences.* Basic Books, New York
Parsons M J 1987 *How We Understand Art: A Cognitive De-
velopment Account of Arsthetic Experience.* Cambridge
University Press, New York
Swanwick K 1988 *Music. Mind. and Education.* Routledge,
London

Writing, Learning and Instruction of

A. Hildyard

Writing is a complex process embedded within complex social relationships. Inclusion of social context
has necessarily led to an increased attention to larger
cultural issues and has required researchers to attend to
issues of instruction. This entry describes advances in
our understanding of the processes involved in learning to write, outlines instructional procedures assumed
to contribute to the achievement of the skills essential
for effective written communication, and finally addresses the issue of the relationship between writing
and thinking.

1. The Writing Process

Various models have been generated in attempts to
understand the specific processes in which a writer
engages. Such models are usually based on the following assumptions: first, that writing involves active and
complex problem-solving; second, that writing consists of several processes—representation, planning,
generation, evaluation, revision—which are invoked
in a recursive manner; third, that differences between
novice and expert writers can appear both at the
level of the problem addressed and in the degree of
interaction of the processes; and lastly, that for effective communication, the strategy of problem-solving
adopted by the writer is intimately related to the nature
and purpose of the writing task.

Bereiter and Scardamalia (1987) have argued that
there are essentially two models of the composing
process. In the "knowledge-telling" model the writer
is assumed to draw upon both content knowledge
and discourse knowledge and essentially tells all he
or she knows in order to execute the written assignment. A knowledge-telling strategy provides an
efficient means of solving a common problem faced

by immature writers, namely a difficulty in generating
texts without the kinds of supports normally available in conversational language. In the "knowledge-
transforming" model, however, the writer transforms
his or her knowledge as the writing proceeds; that
is, the writer actively reworks the content during the
process of writing. While the writer may still draw
upon a knowledge-telling strategy, it is executed within a reflective context, a context in which the writer
formulates and solves problems. A critical difference
between the two models, then, is that the knowledge-
transforming model facilitates development of the
writer's knowledge during the actual writing process.

A number of studies have increased the understanding of the component processes noted above. For
example, Flower et al. (1992) suggested that writers
draw upon three planning strategies: (a) knowledge-
driven planning; (b) schema- or script-driven planning;
(c) constructive planning, which may be invoked individually or in concert. In knowledge-driven planning,
which is equivalent to Bereiter and Scardamalia's
knowledge-telling strategy, the writer essentially tells
all that he or she knows. Although students and teachers traditionally place a high value on "telling what
you know," and it is assumed that people write best
about these areas they know best, there is, in fact, little
research to support this contention. Moreover, while
knowledge-driven strategies may be perfectly appropriate when the knowledge base is conceptualized in a
way that matches the requirements of the writing task,
an individual's knowledge base is not always well-
structured, or may be structured inappropriately for the
task at hand.

Schema- or script-driven planning strategies may be
invoked if writers have sufficient knowledge of the
kinds of elements to be included as well as their
overall arrangement. Schemata are shown to be quite

appropriate for narrative story-telling and some argumentative discourse; however, it would appear that expository writing does not lend itself easily to a schematic approach.

When knowledge-driven and schema-driven strategies are inadequate, effective writers are shown to engage in constructive planning. Constructive planning has five subcomponents. The writer first builds a unique representation of the task, generally at a global and abstract level. (Skilled writers tend to engage in more active and reflective problem-solving, relating the nature of the task, the anticipated audience, and the purpose to be achieved by the written communication.) The writer then generates working goals, which may serve as instructions to the writer or be in the form of criteria or constraints. They may be explicit or tacit. Thirdly, the writer integrates the plans, goals, and knowledge. Such integration can involve the creation of subgoals, monitoring of progress, exploration of ideas, setting intentions, and consolidation. The fourth component involves the instantiation of abstract goals; that is, moving from plans to the actual text. Experienced writers appear to use two techniques to assist them in this regard: code words (pointers), which can be used to integrate already developed units of knowledge, and "how to" elaborations. Finally, in constructive planning, writers resolve the conflicts that may occur when goals contradict each other, when the text appears to be in violation of constraints and so on.

Revision can take place at any time in the process outlined above and involve revisions to the substance of the text per se (i.e., revision to textual entities) or to the ongoing planning of the text (i.e., revisions to internal, mental entities). Further, the nature of the revision will depend upon the way the writer represented the writing task, the product of the writing process, and the rhetorical context.

While it is undeniable that motivation plays a strong role in all cognitive performance, it is not clear exactly what that role might be with respect to writing. It has been suggested that selecting one's own topic for writing will facilitate production, presumably as a result of increased motivation and interest (Englert et al. 1988). Research by Hidi and McLaren (1990) indicated that the issue is not this simple. Working with sixth-grade students, they found that students must have a sufficiently detailed knowledge base from which to write for there to be any motivating impact of interest.

2. The Development of Writing Skills

When looking at the acquisition of writing skills, it is important to keep in mind that even for experts written composition remains a complex and difficult task. Experienced writers are able to draw upon a variety of strategies when engaged in the composition process, including the use of knowledge and schema-driven scripts. Several researchers have looked at the development of such strategies. For example, by the time children begin school, they are able to include many features of narratives in their writing (Applebee 1978). Their mastery of narrative structure continues into middle school, at which time they are able to elaborate on motivation, reactions, and so on. By contrast, for persuasive or argumentative writing there is substantial evidence that, for school-age children, such writing tends to be short, lacking in content, and often exhibits inappropriate structures. It has been suggested that part of the problem may be related to the normally irrelevant nature of school assignments: when children are given the opportunity to write about events that are important to them, evidence then appears of the ability to present arguments.

Research on expert writers shows the critical importance of various cognitive strategies, such as generating information, planning and organizing the material, evaluating and revising the text. Yet research with children frequently points to the slow evolution of appropriate metacognitive strategies. Studies on expert writers indicate that evaluation and revision are critical components of the writing process, with experienced writers focusing upon global aspects of the text. Inexperienced writers, however, tend to focus on "local" problems, such as grammar, syntax, and word choice. Similarly, children often tend to use a simplified composing process with revision at the level of the word.

Another aspect of the developmental process includes gaining an understanding of the relationship between the form and nature of the written communication and the context in which it is embedded. Little is known about children's ability to adjust their writing for different purposes or different audiences, but there is a growing awareness by researchers that even relatively experienced writers face challenges in identifying the needs and expectations of the discourse community within which they are communicating. This view of the writing process essentially builds upon the notion that knowledge is socially constructed —a view that presents a considerable challenge to educators in that it requires them to rethink the relationship between the teacher and the student within the context of learning to write.

What are the implications of this view of the writing process? First of all, there is an obvious need to reexamine the nature of classroom discourse communities, particularly since much of what is written in school is not written for the purpose of communication but as a way to evaluate students. However, if writing is assumed to be one means by which children grow and define themselves, then clearly teachers will need to provide opportunities for students to express emotion, form interpersonal relationships and explore knowledge in contexts where their written products are not subjected to formal evaluation. Such opportunities might be available in peer conferencing and in dialogue journals (Nystrand 1990).

Second, being aware that people operate at all times within a socially determined context—a discourse community—requires teachers to pay closer attention to the relationship between the skills expected to be demonstrated within a specific context and the nature of that context. Heath (1983) has argued that learning to read and write within the context of the school not only teaches students how to read and write, but also imbues them with habits and assumptions that reflect the aims and preferences of the dominant linguistic culture within which they are embedded.

Third, acknowledging the existence of discourse communities necessarily requires a focus on cultural issues. As Heath (1983) has demonstrated, members of mainstream Western culture tend to use "schooled" language both at work and in the home. Heath, in fact, defined mainstream people as relying on formal educational systems to prepare children for participation in literate settings. Members of nonmainstream groups, on the other hand, often enter schools with linguistic and cultural resources that not only differ from, but often conflict with, the school culture.

3. Instructional Facilitation

In an effort to assist young writers in acquiring necessary metacognitive skills, Langer and Applebee (1986) suggested the metaphor of "instructional scaffolding." Instructional scaffolding occurs when the learner interacts with an experienced writer who provides a variety of supports—or scaffolds—for tasks that the learner is not yet able to perform alone. Over time learners internalize the routines, procedures, and strategies such that they eventually become able to perform the task without assistance. Langer and Applebee (1986) have suggested five criteria for effective instructional scaffolding: first, there must be ownership of the written product; second, the tasks must be appropriate in terms of the student's current knowledge; third, the instructional tasks must clearly support a natural sequence of thinking; fourth, the teacher must function as collaborator rather than evaluator; and, finally, the students must internalize the strategies and skills.

Other attempts to facilitate the acquisition of metawriting skills have involved the use of computers in the Language Arts curriculum. A variety of software programs focus on tasks of planning, generating ideas, and providing information—what Bereiter and Scardamalia (1987) have referred to as "procedural facilitation" or the provision of cues and supports that aid the student in carrying out a specific composing process. A review by Cochran-Smith (1991) of research relating to word processing in elementary classrooms warns, however, that while a considerable amount is known about the influence of word processing on students' writing, little is known about the way in which the software is introduced into classrooms or

about its interaction with the social processes at work in the classroom.

4. Writing and Cognition—Writing to Learn

Writing serves at least three pedagogical purposes: first, it is a means of encouraging students to draw upon relevant knowledge and experience in preparing for new activities; second, it is a means of consolidating and reviewing new information and experiences; and third, it is a means of reformulating and extending knowledge. These processes are differentially involved in knowledge-telling and knowledge-transforming approaches to writing and serve to highlight the extent to which writing and thinking are intimately related. Such analyses complement the notion that writing itself is an act of constructive problem-solving and that through writing students may develop a repertoire of cognitive strategies and develop a reflective awareness of these strategies.

Analysis of the knowledge-transforming process in expert writers has led Scardamalia and Bereiter (1991) to argue that in knowledge-transforming, experts engage in a dialectic that "can be represented as taking place between two problem spaces—a content space, in which problems of knowledge and belief are worked out, and a rhetorical space, in which problems of presentation are dealt with" (p. 43). An example of the way in which this dialectic can be supported is provided by CSILE (Computer Supported Intentional Learning Environments), a networked, hypermedia environment in which writing, illustrating, reading, and commenting are integral processes. While the emphasis in CSILE is on knowledge advancement rather than writing per se, data suggest that students also become better writers.

5. Conclusion

Research provides clear evidence that writing is central to the shaping of certain modes of cognition: it is a means of acquiring knowledge; it is a means of learning about oneself; it is a means of belonging to a social group; it is an activity that is under ongoing development. Writing is exceptionally complex and contributes to the construction of knowledge in ways that are not yet fully understood.

See also: Literacy; Metacognition; Social and Communication Skills

References

Applebee A N 1978 *The Child's Concept of Story: Ages Two to Seventeen.* University of Chicago Press, Chicago, Illinois

Bereiter C, Scardamalia M 1987 *The Psychology of Written Composition.* Erlbaum, Hillsdale, New Jersey

Cochran-Smith M 1991 Word processing and writing in elementary classrooms: A critical review of related literature. *Rev. Educ. Res.* 61(1): 107–55

Englert C S, Stewart S R, Hiebert E H 1988 Young writers' use of text structure in expository text generation. *J. Educ. Psychol.* 80(2): 143–51

Flower L, Schriver K A, Carly L, Haas C, Hayes J R 1992 Planning in writing: The cognition of a constructive process. In: Witle S, Nakadak N, Cherry R (eds.) 1992 *A Rhetoric of Doing*. Illinois University Press, Carbondale, Illinois

Heath S B 1983 *Ways with Words: Language, Life and Work in Communities and Classrooms*. Cambridge University Press, Cambridge

Hidi S, McLaren J 1990 The effect of topic and theme interestingness on the production of school expositions. In: Mandl H, De Corte E, Bennett N, Friedrich H F (eds.) 1990 *Learning and Instruction: European Research in an International Context. Vol 2.2: Analysis of Complex Skills and Complex Knowledge Domains*. Pergamon Press, Oxford

Langer J A, Applebee A N 1986 Reading and writing instruction: Toward a theory of teaching and learning. *Rev. Res. Educ.* 13: 171–94

Nystrand M 1990 Sharing words: The effects of readers on developing writers. *Written Communication* 7(1): 3–24

Scardamalia M, Bereiter C 1991 Higher levels of agency for children in knowledge building: A challenge for the design of new knowledge media. *The Journal of the Learning Sciences* 1(1): 37–68

Further Reading

Bryson M, Bereiter C, Scardamalia M, Joram E 1991 Going beyond the problem as given: Problem solving in expert and novice writers. In: Sternberg R J, Frensch P A (eds.) 1991 *Complex Problem Solving: Principles and Mechanisms*. Erlbaum, Hillsdale, New Jersey

Crowhurst M 1990 The development of persuasive/argumentative writing. In: Beach R, Hynds S (eds.) 1990 *Developing Discourse Practices in Adolescence and Adulthood (Advances in Discourse Processes 31)*. Ablex, Norwood, New Jersey

Graves D 1983 *Writing: Teachers and Children at Work*. Heinemann Educational Books, Exeter, New Hampshire

Scardamalia M, Bereiter C, McLean R S, Swallow J, Woodruff 1989 Computer-supported intentional learning environments. *Journal of Educational Computing Research* 5(1): 51–68

Written Composition: Teaching and Assessing

S. W. Freedman

Written composition includes all aspects of writing, from children's earliest efforts to form letters and words, to older students' and adults' increasingly complex and extended pieces for varied audiences (e.g., teachers, self, peers, community members, employers) and for varied purposes (e.g., to display knowledge, to entertain, to learn subject matter across the curriculum, to conduct business). Schools generally are expected to teach and assess multiple aspects of writing although precise values associated with writing and therefore the emphases given to different aspects of writing will vary from one country to another.

In all cases, writing is one aspect of language learning; it relates to talking, listening, and reading. The acquisition of language in general and writing in particular follows a developmental process that educators need to understand and support across time. At any given moment, writers engage in an extended problem-solving process that educators also need to understand and encourage. In setting up instructional environments that facilitate development across time and writers' processes at a given moment, teachers need to work with their students. Together, they must structure writing activities that engage students in writing and motivate them to want to write. Teachers also must arrange for their students to receive helpful feedback as they write.

1. Learning to Write as an Aspect of Learning Language

Writing is learned best when it is taught alongside reading, speaking, and listening; for like them, writing is part of language learning. If literacy is not considered in its full language context, problems that surface in writing are often misunderstood as "literacy problems" when, in fact, they have little to do with literacy per se. For example, garbled writing may be rooted in garbled ideas, not in difficulties with print communication.

Like speaking, writing is a form of language production. Since speech is learned first and does not have to be transcribed, writers sometimes find it helpful to delay transcription and to develop and refine their ideas for writing first by talking, sometimes even by talking to themselves. In fact, very young writers can get started putting their thoughts into print by dictating and thereby bypassing the transcribing process entirely. In classrooms, students gain much by discussing their writing with their teachers in the course of one-on-one conferences, with their friends, in small groups, or during class discussions. As Moffett and Wagner (1992) explain, "Monologue, the basic act of writing, is born of dialogue" (p. 26).

Just as reading and writing develop best when

580

connected to speaking and listening, it is also important to connect reading and writing. In early literacy acquisition, writing often helps students break the print code, and see how sounds and letters relate, thus stimulating progress in both reading and writing. Reading is invariably tied to writing as students read their own writing, for to write well, one must learn to be a careful and sensitive reader of one's own writing. Through reading, writers gain a sense of the sounds and rhythms of written language. Activities that tightly intertwine reading and writing, allowing the skills to build on one another, include dialogue journals between teacher and students or other writing exchanges between students. In these activities readers write and writers read, with writers often modeling their writing on what they have just read. For additional practical suggestions for integrating writing, reading, speaking, and listening inside classrooms, see Britton (1989) and Moffett and Wagner (1992).

2. Writing Development

Young children's writing develops and matures across time, but not all children develop on the same schedule nor do all learn the same way. Children learn to write by building on what they already know about language. They come into school with varied kinds of experiences of and knowledge about language. It is crucial for teachers to understand their knowledge and experiences in order to help them build from what they know.

In the primary grades, for example, stories are usually a staple of children's early exposure to both reading and writing (see Dyson and Freedman 1991). Storytelling is ubiquitous in human culture, and children generally come to school with quite specific ideas about how stories are structured and how they function. However, stories function differently in different cultures and have different forms. Especially in multicultural settings, children may enter school with varied out-of-school experiences with stories (Heath 1983).

During early literacy acquisition teachers need to know how to help children build on the narrative knowledge they bring to school, especially when that knowledge differs from the kind of narratives in school reading books or the kind of narratives children are expected to produce in writing. Since development depends on building on past knowledge, it is critical for teachers to know what their students do know, not just what they do not yet know.

When youngsters are learning to write in a second language, the developmental process becomes more complex. For these writers, it is important for teachers to have specific knowledge about what the writers know about writing in their first language and how they might build on native-language literacy skills (Valdés 1992).

Given that writers approach learning to write with varied but meaningful language experiences, it is difficult to make blanket statements about how writing develops. Furthermore, writing is too complex an enterprise to admit sequences of development. In the first place, most people never fully master any kind of writing. Even professional novelists feel that they could write better narratives, and they know that some of their efforts are more successful than others. Similarly, some business letters require very complex rhetorical moves, and experienced professionals often fail to persuade their readers to accept their ideas. However, many people do reach a point where they can spell most words they need, where they can form complete, if not always elegant, sentences, and where they can write what for them are routine pieces with relative ease.

Whereas the whole of writing is too complex to make statements about development, knowledge about how certain strands develop does exist (Dyson 1987). For example, for languages with alphabetic writing systems, children learn very early that letters and sounds correspond and that letters can be grouped to make words. When children first begin combining sounds with letters, they use "invented spelling." These invented spellings are patterned and provide important clues about children's understandings of sound–symbol relationships. As their ability to compose develops, children gradually come to use conventional spellings.

No particular discourse form is inherently more difficult to acquire than any other; however, within each form there are levels of complexity. That is, stories are not necessarily easier to write than arguments, but young children write much simpler stories and arguments than do older children. Developmentally, writers gradually learn to generalize from their personal experiences, to incorporate into their writing what they read as well as what they experience first-hand, to control increasingly complex and longer sentences, to develop their ideas at some length, and to engage in increasingly more extended decision-making processes.

3. The Processes of Writing

Writing involves thinking through ideas, drafting, and redrafting, with writers moving back and forth among these three aspects of composing as they solve the problems posed by their evolving piece (Hayes and Flower 1980). When students become engaged in this kind of expanded problem-solving process, writing becomes a powerful tool for helping them grapple with complex ideas. Researchers have found that "writing process instruction" goes awry when teachers bypass the complicated problem-solving that is at the heart of an expanded writing process, in favor of relatively rigid sets of procedures for all students to follow (e.g., plan on Monday, draft on Tuesday, revise on Wednesday, edit on Thursday) (see Dyson and Freedman 1991). Such rigid procedures are counter to what is known about the fluid ways in which writers write. Instead of thinking about the process as a set of steps to be followed (plan, draft, revise), it is more productive for teachers to think about the kind of support writers need to engage in this complex problem-solving process.

Studies of the specific nature of this problem-solving process reveal that, even given the same topic, different writers solve different problems. Just as writers develop in different ways, they also compose differently. Although the process may vary from student to student, variation is not idiosyncratic; rather it is patterned. Teachers need to identify the diverse patterns in their classrooms.

4. Teaching Writing

At least two major issues face teachers attempting to set up classrooms to support the teaching and learning of writing. First, they must consider how to get their students to write on topics that are interesting to them, to which they feel in some way connected, and from which they are able to learn. Second, as students write, teachers will need to arrange the kind of support and feedback that will allow them to produce their best work and that will carry over to future writing.

4.1 Setting Up Classrooms

A major difficulty in addressing the first issue is that much writing in school has been restricted in audience and purpose; students write mostly for a teacher or examiner audience and mainly for a grade (Britton et al. 1975). This restricted "school writing" fails to interest many students who write merely to complete a school task, not because they are intellectually or emotionally engaged.

A number of activities can expand the audiences and functions for student writing and can help to engage students. For example, Heath and Mangiola (1991) arranged for 10-year olds who were experiencing difficulty in school to tutor 6-year olds who were just learning to read and write with the goal of interesting the older students in literacy learning. One group of tutors wrote a book for the parents of the 6-year olds explaining how the parents could assist them in their efforts.

In another setting community college students who were not native English speakers studied the languages of their communities and thought explicitly about the varieties of language use and the appropriateness of using particular varieties in particular contexts. Their studies of language in action became the base for their own literacy curriculum. Freedman (1994) describes an audience exchange between inner-city secondary students in the United States and the United Kingdom which involved the students in producing extended pieces for one another—autobiographies, books about their schools and communities, guide books for visiting teenagers, and teenage magazines. Levin et al. (1985) set up a news service on computer networks involving students from around the world.

Even though they were theoretically sound, in no case did these activities in and of themselves create involved and motivated students; rather, what brought the activities to life were the ways they were enacted in particular classrooms. Generally, when these activities were successful, writing was integrated with other language processes; students tackled extended pieces of writing as they engaged in meaningful projects; they were given sufficient time to write; they were involved in planning the writing they did; and they received help as they composed.

The increasing availability of the computer is also beginning to affect the possibilities for interesting students in writing in school. In addition to the international networks that Levin and his colleagues describe, hypermedia programs allow new forms of composition that mix art, sound, and print. Desktop publishing makes school newspapers and other inhouse professional publications possible. Finally, computers can encourage more decentralized classrooms that lead to individualization and collaboration as students write together in class and share computer resources (Greenleaf 1994).

Writing can also be a useful tool to help students learn the content of mathematics, science, social studies, or other subject areas. Writing is particularly useful for helping students understand complex ideas, but not for helping them learn facts (Langer and Applebee 1987). In addition, when students write about new concepts, teachers get feedback on what their students do and do not understand.

4.2 Providing Feedback to Writers

The second issue to be addressed in classrooms that support the teaching and learning of writing is the kind of feedback writers receive as they write. In addition to being genuinely interested in their writing, writers need to grapple with pieces of writing or aspects of a piece of writing that are too challenging for them to manage alone but that they can manage with the help of others. They then are working within what Vygotsky (1978) calls their "zone of proximal development," that developmental area when the learner cannot perform a task alone but can do so with the assistance of a more expert helper. Assuming that writers are working within this zone, it is time to examine the nature of the assistance the more expert helper provides.

The most effective assistance, from the point of view of expert teachers in both the United States and the United Kingdom, is individualized, oral response from the teacher during the writing process (Freedman

1994). Generally, these responses let writers know whether they are communicating what they intended to communicate in the way they intended. Teachers find it difficult, especially when class size is large, to talk to each student about every piece that he or she writes. However, some have demonstrated ways to provide this important kind of response for their students (Freedman 1987, Sperling 1990). Another kind of response during the writing process comes from peers who are often organized by teachers into peer response groups. These groups are most useful when students are generating ideas; they are less reliable for providing feedback on drafts of text (see DiPardo and Freedman 1988).

The traditional form of feedback, the comments teachers write on student papers after a piece of writing is completed, is the least helpful kind of response. These comments normally accompany a grade on the writing. Many a teacher has reported the sinking feeling that comes when a student looks at the grade and tosses a fully annotated piece of writing in the trash can, without even reading the teachers' comments. Analyses of teachers' comments have shown that they often function more to justify the grade than to teach the student (Sommers 1980). Furthermore, when students do read the teachers' comments, they often misinterpret them (Sperling and Freedman 1987).

Other issues have surfaced about the substance of the help that teachers give. There is some debate about how explicit the teaching of writing needs to be, especially when speakers of foreign languages and speakers of nonstandard dialects are learning to write in formal standard varieties of written language. Generally, the recommended time to push for formal correctness is toward the end of the writing process, with fluency most valued during draft writing. However, Delpit (1988) argues that a stress on fluency early in the process often comes at the expense of formal correctness for many speakers of Black English vernacular. Regardless of how this issue is resolved, study after study has shown that having students complete skill exercises in grammar books or workbooks does not help them use correct forms when they write; rather, correctness is best taught by giving students feedback on what they actually write, in the context of their writing (Elley et al. 1979).

5. Assessing Writing

Given the complexity of learning to write, it is no surprise that it is difficult to assess students' writing. The writing portfolio, consisting of a number of varied samples of student writing selected to represent the student's best efforts, provides the most valid data for evaluating an individual's writing abilities and development across time. Portfolios have been used in national assessments (e.g., the General Certificate of Secondary Education in the United Kingdom); in

state and school district assessments (e.g., Vermont's Writing Assessment Program, 1990–91); and in local school assessments that track student progress (e.g., *The Primary Language Record* 1988, Wolf 1989). Constructing portfolios can support good instruction as teachers work together with students to compile the portfolio and as students assess their own progress.

Different approaches have been devised for evaluating portfolios. The GCSE method assigns a single letter grade to the entire portfolio. The Vermont method provides a number of analytic scores, some of them for individual pieces. The PLR uses more descriptive methods, where standardized scores are not required. Unfortunately, there is a tendency to move away from this kind of pedagogically useful assessment approach because it is time-consuming and expensive.

Other approaches to large-scale assessment include collecting and scoring samples of student writing on assigned topics in timed conditions. Examples include the National Assessment of Educational Progress (Applebee et al. 1990) in the United States and the International Education Association Writing Assessment Study in England and Wales (see Gubb et al. 1987). These tests measure a narrow aspect of students' skills as writers and are generally used to assess groups of students for the purpose of informing policy decisions, not for making judgments about individuals.

6. Emergent Trends

In the teaching and assessment of written language there has been much activity in recent years, resulting both in advances in research and changes in practice. This progress will need to continue at a rapid rate. The "global village" is linked by ever-increasing and more immediate communication capacities; writing plays a central role in this global communication (as scripts for satellite television broadcasts; as messages sent over electronic networks; as the text of faxed notes, letters, and other documents; and as much of what runs businesses behind the scenes). As the twenty-first century approaches, writing is taking on ever-widening functions worldwide. Future research will need to examine these changing functions and will have to consider how global schools can best prepare the children of tomorrow to meet global needs.

References

Applebee A et al. 1990 *The Writing Report Card, 1984–88: Findings from the Nation's Report Card.* Educational Testing Service, Princeton, New Jersey
Britton J 1989 Writing and reading in the classroom. In: Dyson A H (ed.) 1989 *Collaboration Through Writing*

and Reading: Exploring Possibilities. National Council of Teachers of English, Urbana, Illinois

Britton J, Burgess T, Martin N, McLeod A, Rosen H 1975 *The Development of Writing Abilities: 11–18.* Macmillan Education Ltd, London

Delpit L 1988 The silenced dialogue: Power and pedagogy in educating other people's children. *Harv. Educ. Rev.* 58: 280–98

DiPardo A, Freedman S W 1988 Peer response groups in the writing classroom: Theoretic foundations and new directions. *Rev. Educ. Res.* 58(2): 119–49

Dyson A H 1987 Individual differences in beginning composing: An orchestral vision of learning to compose. *Written Communication* 4: 411–42

Dyson A H, Freedman S W 1991 Writing. In: Jensen J, Flood J, Lapp D, Squire J (eds.) 1991 *Measures for Research and Teaching the English Language Arts.* Macmillan Inc., New York

Elley W B, Barham I H, Lamb H, Wyllie M 1979 *The Role of Grammar in a Secondary School Curriculum.* New Zealand Council for Educational Research, Wellington

Freedman S W 1987 *Response to Student Writing.* National Council of Teachers of English, Urbana, Illinois

Freedman S W 1994 *Exchanging writing, exchanging cultures: Lessons in School Reform from the United States and Great Britain.* Harvard University Press, Cambridge, Massachusetts

Greenleaf C 1994 Technological indeterminacy: The role of classroom writing practices and pedagogy in shaping student use of the computer. *Written communications* 11: 85–130

Gubb J, Gorman T, Price E 1987 *The Study of Written Composition in England and Wales.* NFER–NELSON, Windsor

Hayes J R, Flower L S 1980 Identifying the organization of writing processes. In: Gregg L W, Steinberg E R (eds.) 1980 *Cognitive Processes in Writing.* Erlbaum, Hillsdale, New Jersey

Heath S B 1983 *Ways with Words.* Cambridge University Press, Cambridge

Heath S B, Mangiola L 1991 *Children of Promise: Literate Activity in Linguistically and Culturally Diverse Classrooms.* National Education Association, Center for the Study of Writing, American Educational Research Association, Washington, DC

Langer J, Applebee A 1987 *How Writing Shapes Thinking.* National Council of Teachers of English, Urbana, Illinois

Levin J, Reil M, Rowe R, Boruta M 1985 Muktuk meets jacuzzi: Computer networks and elementary school writers. In: Freedman S W (ed.) 1985 *The Acquisition of Written Language.* Ablex, Norwood, New Jersey

Moffett J, Wagner B J 1992 *Student-Centered Language Arts, K 12,* 4th edn. Boynton/Cook Heinemann, Portsmouth, New Hampshire

ILEA 1988 *The Primary Language Record: Handbook for Teachers.* ILEA Centre for Language in Primary Education, London

Sommers N I 1980 Revision strategies of student writers and experienced adult writers. *College Composition and Communication* 31(4): 378–87

Sperling M 1990 I want to talk to each of you: Collaboration and the teacher-student writing conference. *Research in the Teaching of English* 24(3): 279–321

Sperling M, Freedman S W 1987 A good girl writes like a good girl: Written response to student writing. *Written Communication* 4(4): 343–69

Valdés G 1992 Bilingual minorities and language issues in writing: Toward professionwide response to a new challenge. *Written Communication* 9(1): 85–136

Vermont's Writing Assessment Program, Pilot Year 1990–1991. The Vermont Department of Education, Vermont

Vygotsky L S 1978 *Mind in Society: The Development of Higher Psychological Processes.* Harvard University Press, Cambridge, Massachusetts

Wolf D P 1989 Portfolio assessment: Sampling student work. *Educ. Leadership* 46(7): 4–10

Further Reading

Daiute C 1985 *Writing and Computers.* Addison-Wesley, Reading, Massachusetts

Hillocks G Jr 1986 *Research on Written Composition: New Directions for Teaching.* ERIC Clearinghouse on Reading and Communication Skills, Urbana, Illinois

Social, Cultural, and Affective Aspects of Learning

Affect, Emotions, and Learning

M. Boekaerts

1. Introduction

It has become evident that effective teaching is not a question of putting information across to a group of students. It is more a question of initiating behavioral change in every student. Many authors have argued that past theories of learning and instruction have focused mainly on knowledge and skill acquisition, and have disregarded complicated but crucial aspects of human learning (e.g., the influence of affective variables on learning, learning in rich and authentic contexts). Indeed, it has become clear that students learn in dynamic social learning environments in which the various interactors continuously influence each other, thereby changing the learning situation itself as well as their own appraisal of the situation. Theories of learning that focus exclusively on information-processing theories cannot grasp this complexity. For this reason, empirical studies have been established to study the effect of affective variables on learning and performance. Such variables include beliefs about the self and about various school subjects, emotions, moods, and behavioral control mechanisms. Findings from these studies are slowly being incorporated in theories of learning and instruction. In this entry, the most important affective variables will be discussed and a model will be outlined to understand the relation between these constructs.

2. Emotions and Moods

At school, learning is embedded in an achievement context and is subject to social pressure and social comparisons. Hence, learning activities may activate specific concerns and a great variety of emotions. Emotions experienced in a classroom context can be categorized as positive (e.g., joy, excitement, pride) or negative (e.g., anxiety, anger, sadness) and as task-related or context-based. Curiously enough, much

evidence is available on the effects of anxiety on learning, whereas little is known about the effect of other emotions such as anger, joy, or sadness on learning and performance. This lack of attention may be due to the fact that until the 1980s, clear theoretical frameworks were missing and measurement of emotions was complicated.

In the 1980s, several authors tried to parse emotional experiences into their separate components and they attributed a central role to the appraisal process. For example, Frijda (1986) argues that emotions are stored in memory along with declarative and procedural knowledge, and this information may be used as a gross discriminator to monitor upcoming and ongoing events in order to identify problematic and nonproblematic situations. Frijda explains that emotions are not present in a situation, but in the individual's appraisal of an event. In other words, events are made meaningful by linking them to internal representations that turn them into satisfiers (nonproblematic, benign–positive situations, associated with positive cognitions and emotions) or into annoyers (problematic, threatening situations that may cause damage, harm, or loss). This means that increased physiological arousal (e.g., increased muscle tension, rapid heartbeat, perspiration) will produce changes in readiness for action, but that the unique interpretation of the arousal, and the event that caused it, will determine the nature of the emotion and its effect on performance. Mandler's theory of mind and body (1984) has already been applied to mathematics learning by McLeod (1989). McLeod describes what happens when students' attempts at solving mathematics problems are interrupted or blocked.

2.1 Anxiety

Test anxiety research has extensively studied the subject's appraisals of achievement situations. A vast amount of evidence illustrates the detrimental effects of test anxiety on cognitive functioning (for a meta-analysis of the data, see Hembree 1988). It was demonstrated in many studies that: (a) anxiety attenuates or blocks task-relevant information processing, (b) grossly overlearned skills are not affected by anxiety, and (c) higher-order cognitive processes are impaired. These findings support the attention-deficit hypothesis of test anxiety, which postulates that anxiety competes with task-relevant information for processing capacity in working memory. This interpretation could also explain the finding that anxious students make use of inappropriate cognitive strategies for achievement. However, the literature is not very consistent here. What is clear is that anxiety acts for all students as a signal that loss of resources is unavoidable, unless something is done. Hence, feelings of increased arousal may occur in students with both high and low test anxiety, but differences occur both in the duration of the increased level of arousal, and in the way students interpret and label it.

2.2 Anger and Mood

In school, students may get angry for a variety of reasons, for example, when they are told off by the teacher, or when they are not allowed to finish an interesting task. Such situations may increase the level of physiological arousal in most students. Nevertheless, some students report only mild irritation while others indicate that they are furious. In an attempt to gain more insight into the types of situations that cause students to be angry in class, Boekaerts (1993) found that in primary and secondary school students, aged from 10 to 14, the situations that provoked most anger were those in which they believed that norms, rules, or rights were violated, and no acceptable excuses were available. However, in class it is not always possible to direct anger openly toward the source of provocation and pupils have to learn to suppress their anger in order to survive in a school context. Intense or frequent anger is often viewed as symptomatic of behavioral problems. Nevertheless, suppressing and controlling anger makes great demands on a person's processing capacity and may interfere with task performance. Moreover, research from health psychology indicates that keeping anger in the arousal system may be a serious health risk.

The effects of sadness, depression, joy, and happiness have not been studied extensively in a classroom context. Nevertheless, it may be assumed that increases in the level of arousal, labeled as sadness or joy, may evoke cognitions and feelings that compete with information-processing capacity. There is some evidence from mainstream psychology on the effect of positive and negative mood states on cognitive processing. Bower conducted many studies (see e.g., Bower 1981) which illustrate that situations that elicit a specific mood may affect the information-processing system. He reported that subjects who are in a positive mood state tend to recall positive experiences and focus on positive details in a text. They spend more time encoding information that matches their mood state, and remember later more positive things about a text. The reverse is true for negative mood states. He also described studies in which positive and negative mood states affect self-perceptions of competence, and influence problem-solving and decision-making processes. These studies allow for the inference that emotions and moods inform students that the environment in which they are working is *unproblematic* or *problematic*, and that they adapt their information processing accordingly.

3. Beliefs about the Self and about School Subjects

During their school career students develop a variety of beliefs about school, about learning and teaching, and about various subject-matter domains. These beliefs may be rather weak at first, but they may become quite strong and resistant to change. Beliefs about the self and about subject-matter domains may be regarded as the basis for motivation, and for the development of positive and negative attitudes. There is a vast literature dealing with students' beliefs about the self and their beliefs about school-related issues.

3.1 Beliefs about the Self

Beliefs about the self have been studied under different headings, including self-concept, self-efficacy, and causal attributions of success and failure. The self-concept can best be seen as a set of beliefs about the self. Important subsets of the self are conceptualizations of physical appearance and ability, emotional stability, social skills, and academic competence. Bandura (1982) argues that when a task is unfamiliar, or when individuals have reason to believe that their personal or social resources have altered in relation to a task, they make efficacy judgments. These self-conceptualizations are based on direct and vicarious experiences, on persuasion, and on self-attributions. The psychological literature offers ample evidence that individuals' beliefs about their competence and control in relation to a domain of knowledge play a major role in their performance. Students with high self-efficacy, reflected in high perceived personal control in a domain of study, score higher on tests of intelligence and on achievement tests, and they also earn better grades. The correlation between self-efficacy and achievement, which is moderately strong, is reciprocal in nature. A longitudinal study by Weinert et al. (1989) detailed that for mathematics this bidirectional relationship emerges in the middle of the sixth grade (age 11–12). Before that age, children's self-efficacy seems not to be consistently related to behavioral outcome, because children may misjudge self-efficacy due to incomplete information about what they need to learn, about their prerequisite skills, and about their ability to guide and monitor their own learning.

Beliefs about the self have also been studied in the context of attributions of success and failure. Weiner (1986) described three dimensions along which causal attributions can be classified: locus of control, stability, and controllability. For example, students who believe that they did poorly on a language test may ascribe their failure to the type of test being used (external, variable, uncontrollable) rather than to low ability (internal, stable, controllable) or lack of effort (internal, variable, controllable). At the start of elementary education children explain success and failure predominantly in terms of effort, or lack of effort, and the second most commonly used factor is ability. Nicholls (1984) presented evidence that young children conceive of ability in a self-referenced manner as "learning through effort." Children do not clearly differentiate effort and ability until age 11. A more mature conception of ability involves a social comparison in which the effort/time required to reach a performance is taken into account. Adolescents conceive of ability as "capacity" relative to others. They determine their capacity within a domain of study by direct experiences, by comparing their performance and effort expenditure with that of their peers, and by the presence or absence of physiological symptoms. Unlike primary school students, adolescents realize that effort may compensate for low ability, thus masking true ability. This belief may lead to hiding effort and to effort avoidance.

3.2 Beliefs about Different School Subjects

Students may develop a variety of beliefs about different subject-matter domains. For example, they may see mathematics assignments as logic-based, important, and relevant, but nevertheless categorize them among the difficult school subjects, in which they have no intrinsic interests. By contrast, text comprehension may be viewed as common-sense based, important, easy to master, and intrinsically interesting. Beliefs about different school subjects have been studied under two main rubrics: attitudes and interests.

Attitudes are defined as relatively stable positive or negative feelings and cognitions about a subject area reflected in students' behavioral responses. Data on attitudes are traditionally collected by means of questionnaires, and they break down factor-analytically into different factors. McLeod (1989) argued that attitudes toward mathematics develop in two distinct ways. First, students may assign an attitude that has already been attached to a memory schema (e.g., geometry) to a new schema (e.g., algebra). Second, negative or positive attitudes may be based on a series of repeated emotional reactions to a set of mathematics tasks. In short, attitudes may be seen as

quasi-automatic reactions to a subject-matter domain, and this property makes them resistant to change and difficult to measure.

Schiefele (1991) drew attention to the fact that people also develop specific relationships with different subject-matter domains, and that this relationship is reflected in their specific interest in that domain. He defines interest in a school subject as content-specific intrinsic motivational orientation, and argued that it should be distinguished from general motivational orientation and attitudes. He demonstrated that students who score high on interest want to become involved in a subject-matter domain for its own sake. For example, students who demonstrated interest in text comprehension not only recalled more information, but their cognitive strategies also reflected deep-level processing (i.e., they rehearse less, elaborate more, seek more information, and engage more in critical thinking than students who display surface-level processing).

4. Appraisals, Effort, and Control Mechanisms

4.1 Appraisals

Drawing on the influential work of Lazarus and Folkman (1984) in stress research, Boekaerts (1991) describes appraisals as nonstop comparison processes between perceived task and situational demands on the one hand, and perceived personal and social resources to meet these demands on the other. She constructed a heuristic model in which appraisals are given a central position. As can be seen in Fig. 1, appraisals draw on three main sources of information. The first source of information is the perception of the task and the physical, social, and didactic context in which it is embedded (component 1). The second source of information is activated domain-specific knowledge and skills relevant to the task (component 2). The third source consists of personality traits, including a subset of the self-concept linked to emotions and attitudes (component 3). Information from these three sources is brought in working memory (WM) and used as a frame of reference to appraise learning situations, and one's own resources to deal with them. Hence, appraisals could be seen as a set of judgments about the task, combining beliefs about the self and beliefs about subject-matter domains. More concretely, students may judge how difficult the task is; how adequate their personal resources are to do the task; how much effort they will have to put in; the quality of the instructional and social context (including available instrumental and emotional support), and how attractive the task is and how eager they are to start. The net outcome of a dynamic appraisal may be expected or perceived gains in resources, expected or perceived losses in resources, or a null operation. When students do not perceive a discrepancy between the task demands and

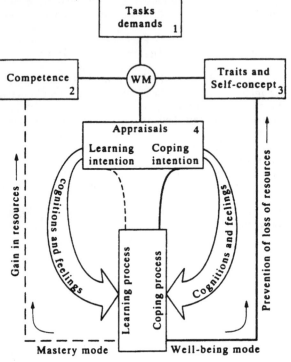

Figure 1
Heuristic model of the affective-learning process

their resources to meet them, they do not expect losses in resources, and their well-being is not at stake; this is known as a null operation. By contrast, when students perceive a discrepancy between the task demands and their resources to meet them, it may elicit a threat (dominantly negative cognitions and emotions) or a challenge (dominantly positive cognitions and emotions).

Much more research is needed to explore the mechanisms whereby appraisals, concerns, interests, and emotions are linked to specific aspects of the learning process. However, it may be assumed that both null operations and challenge appraisals lead to a behavioral intention that starts or continues activity in the mastery mode (left pathway, Fig. 1). This learning-oriented pathway consists of components traditionally used to describe motivated learning. More specifically, a learning intention is formed and translated into actions (cognitive strategies and metacognitive skills) that guide the learning process and result in increased competence or perceived gains in resources. On the other hand, threat appraisals coincide with negative emotions and a decrease in well-being. Such appraisals lead to a coping intention that discontinues action in the mastery mode and starts activity in the well-being mode (right pathway). When learners are on this non-learning-oriented route, their primary concern is to

prevent loss in resources by using preferential coping techniques (problem-focused or emotion-focused coping) to maintain or restore well-being.

4.2 Effort Expenditure

It has been explained that the differentiation of effort and ability as attributional concepts is essential in order to develop a realistic sense of efficacy. Helmke (1989) shed some light on the relation between self-efficacy and effort-expenditure. He reported an indirect relation between self-concept for mathematics and mathematics achievement. At the end of elementary education, students who score high on self-concept of mathematics ability invested qualitative effort which led to better grades. More specifically, these students expended mental effort during the instruction process in order to master the content of the lesson (e.g., attention, cognitive engagement, time-on-task, and school-related virtues such as diligence, circumspection, punctuality, and orderliness). By contrast, students who were low on self-efficacy invested quantitative effort, which was reflected in increasing preparation time for homework and exams. Quantitative effort led to increased anxiety and had a negative effect on mathematics achievement. Self-efficacy seems to create an optimal internal condition for the acquisition of new skills. Students who are self-efficacious believe that they have the necessary and sufficient skills to regulate their own learning process. This result can be linked to other findings, and it may be concluded that optimistic appraisals (Boekaerts 1992), content-specific interest (Schiefele 1991), high perceived task value (Pintrich and De Groot 1990), task orientation (Nicholls 1984), and high self-efficacy (Helmke 1989) should be seen as favorable learning conditions that prompt students to aim their effort at the learning task.

It is important to note, however, that students are not willing to invest effort when they perceive the learning conditions to be less than optimal. Otten and Boekaerts (1990) found that students from the first year of secondary education devoted an average of 3 hours to preparing for a history exam and only 10 minutes to preparing for a literature exam. Further analyses revealed that the students did not find history an attractive subject (attitude), but that they knew how to prepare for the history exam. By contrast, they enjoyed the literature lessons, but did not know how to prepare for the literature exam. When these students were asked to attribute their perceived results on the respective exams, many effort attributions were noted after the history exam, whereas few were observed after the literature exam. After the latter exam, perceived failure was attributed to low ability and to high level of task difficulty. These results seem to indicate that when students believe that effort will not result in mastery, they may refrain from putting in effort and settle for the belief that the subject matter is too difficult (stable, external attribution) or that their personal resources are inadequate (stable, internal attribution). These attributions may protect them from criticism in future, but they also trap them in a vicious circle. Indeed, students who refrain from putting in effort due to low self-efficacy loose their chances of enhancing self-efficacy, interest, and self-regulation.

4.3 Behavioral Control Mechanisms

A distinction between the terms discussed above, and terms coined in the framework of metacognition is needed. Most researchers agree that metacognition can be subdivided into two parts: knowledge of cognitions and regulation of cognitions. However, much conceptual confusion has arisen when data from effort management studies were integrated with data from studies on metacognition. In order to enhance conceptual clarity, Boekaerts (1992, 1996) proposed the term "cognitive strategies" to refer to processing activities that lead directly to learning results (e.g., recognition, recall, analyzing, structuring, elaborating), to reserve the term cognitive regulation for those processes that direct and steer the information-processing flow of the learning process (e.g., orienting, planning, monitoring, reflecting, repairing, evaluating), and to use the name motivational regulation for skills that exert control over behavior in general, and not just over the learning process. She distinguished between several forms of motivational regulation, such as motivation control, action control, and emotion control. These forms of control will be discussed below.

Motivation control refers to cognitive processes involving affect (such as appraisals, beliefs about the self, or content-specific interests). As explained above, cognitive control that involves high intrinsic motivation and high self-efficacy, leads to behavioral intentions that start, or continue activity in the mastery mode, and affect the quantity and quality of effort expenditure. Nevertheless, it is important to note that in a learning context, many behavioral intentions are formed, some of them are enacted, while others fall short of the students' willpower or aspirations. Kuhl (1985) therefore argued that a distinction should be made between subjective control and actual attempts at control. He explained that in order to reach a particular goal, choice of that goal and persistence in striving for it is not enough. A certain amount of effort, or action control, is also necessary to maintain the behavioral intention and to protect it from competing action tendencies.

Kuhl pointed out that behavioral enactment of a learning intention is especially difficult in the presence of attractive behavioral alternatives, or when social pressure undermines a commitment. In such cases, students must actively direct their attention away from competing action tendencies and protect their learning intention. This active mode of control was labeled "action orientation" and contrasted with the passive mode of control, called "state orientation." Individuals

who score high on state orientation are more engaged in exploring their emotional state than in exploring the task. A further distinction was made between students who lack action control in terms of: (a) an inability to initiate intended actions due to indecision, (b) an inability to continue intended actions due to lack of sustained interest, and (c) an inability to continue intended actions due to preoccupation with failure.

Boekaerts (1992) introduced the term "emotion control" to refer to the regulation of emotions. She explained that when well-being is distorted, students will change cognitive and behavioral efforts to restore their well-being. Attempts to regulate emotions may effectively relieve stress by changing the stressful transaction, but they may also temporarily calm down the student, thus only affecting the symptoms and not the underlying causes. As discussed in another entry (see *Stress, Coping, and Learning*), both problem-focused and emotion-focused modes of coping may effectively reduce stress in stressful academic situations. But some forms of coping are more effective for short-term stress, whereas other forms of coping are more effective when threat persists over time. In any case, successful forms of emotion control get the students off the well-being mode, and pave the path for reappraisal and activity in the mastery mode.

See also: Learning Processes and Learning Outcomes; Motivation and Learning; Self-regulation in Learning; Stress, Coping, and Learning

References

Bandura A 1982 Self-efficacy mechanisms in human agency. *Am. Psychol.* 37(2): 122–47

Boekaerts M 1991 Subjective competence, appraisals and self-assessment. *Learning and Instruction* 1(1): 1–17

Boekaerts M 1992 The adaptable learning process: Initiating and maintaining behavioural change. *Appl. Psychol.* 41(4): 375–97

Boekaerts M 1993 Being concerned with well-being and with learning. *Educ. Psychol.* 28(2): 149–67

Boekaerts M 1996 Self-regulated learning at the junction of cognition and motivation. *European Psychologist* 2

Bower G H 1981 Mood and memory. *Am. Psychol.* 36(2): 129–48

Frijda N H 1986 *The Emotions*. Cambridge University Press, Cambridge

Helmke A 1989 Affective student characteristics and cognitive development: Problems, pitfalls, perspectives. *Int. J. Educ. Res.* 13(8): 915–32

Hembree R 1988 Correlates, causes, effects and treatment of test anxiety. *Rev. Educ. Res.* 58(1): 47–77

Kuhl J 1985 Volitional mediators of cognition-behavior consistency: Self-regulatory processes and action versus state orientation. In: Kuhl J, Beckman J (eds.) 1985 *Action Control: From Cognition to Behavior*. Springer-Verlag, Berlin

Lazarus R S, Folkman S 1984 *Stress, Appraisal and Coping*. Springer-Verlag, New York

Mandler G 1984 *Mind and Body: Psychology of Emotion and Stress*. Norton, New York

McLeod D B 1989 Information-processing theories and mathematics learning: The role of affect. *Int. J. Educ. Res.* 14(1): 13–29

Nicholls J G 1984 Achievement motivation: Conceptions of ability, subjective experience, task choice, and performance. *Psychol. Rev.* 91(3): 328–46

Otten R, Boekaerts M 1990 Schoolvakbeleving bij Geschiedenis, Nederlands en wiskunde bij leerlingen in de brugklas. In: Boekaerts M, De Corte E (eds.) 1990 *Onderwijsleerprocessen*. Instituut voor Toegepaste Sociale Wetenschappen, Nijmegen

Pintrich P R, De Groot E V 1990 Motivational and self-regulated learning components of classroom academic performance. *J. Educ. Psychol.* 82(1): 33–41

Schiefele U 1991 Interest, learning, and motivation. *Educ. Psychol.* 26(3/4): 299–323

Weiner B 1986 *An Attributional Theory of Motivation and Emotion*. Springer-Verlag, New York

Weinert F E, Schrader F W, Helmke A 1989 Quality of instruction and achievement outcomes. *Int. J. Educ. Res.* 13(8): 895–912

Further Reading

Boekaerts M (ed.) 1992 Educational psychology (special issue). *Appl. Psychol.* 41(4): whole issue

McLeod D B, Adams V M (eds.) 1989 *Affect and Mathematical Problem Solving: A New Perspective*. Springer-Verlag, New York

Schunk D H (ed.) 1990 Motivation and self-efficacy in education: Research and new directions. *J. Educ. Psychol.* 82(1): 3–91

Culture, Cognition, and Education

E. J. Jacob

Modern educators, facing increasingly heterogeneous student populations, have been concerned about how cultural differences are related to cognition and learning. This entry presents an anthropological perspective on culture and cognition, focusing particular attention on the cultural–historical approach, which was established by the Soviet psychologist, Lev Vygotsky (1896–1934) and his colleagues.

The entry begins by reviewing psychological, anthropological, and early interdisciplinary research in the area of culture and cognition. It then summarizes the Soviet cultural–historical framework and discusses later applications and extensions of the framework. The concluding section examines educational implications of the cultural–historical approach.

As will be shown below, early work viewed culture and cognition as separate entities, with culture influencing cognition in a unidirectional and causal fashion. Many psychological researchers interpreted cognitive differences among cultural groups as reflecting biological differences. Contemporary cultural–historical work, in contrast, views culture and cognition as interdependent influences that create one another in specific contexts. These researchers interpret cognitive differences among cultural groups as being performance differences related to features of particular contexts or as developmental differences reflecting variations in specific prior experiences.

1. Psychological and Anthropological Research

Through the 1960s most scholars interested in culture and cognition operated within the disciplines of psychology or anthropology.

1.1 Psychology

Although some psychologists (e.g., Krewer 1990) have argued that psychology should be conceptualized as a "culture-inclusive science," most psychological studies have not been concerned with culture except in the area of cross-cultural psychology. Cross-cultural psychologists have used experiments as their primary mode of inquiry, treating culture as an independent variable and scores on cognitive tests or tasks as dependent variables. A major goal of this work has been to test the generality of Western theories of cognition (e.g., Berry 1976, Dasen and Heron 1981).

Much of the earliest work compared the performance of a non-Western group to a Western group on tests developed for Western populations, with the result that the non-Western group generally fared worse. Since many of the theories guiding this work viewed cognitive development in terms of universal, context-free processes, scholars often inferred from these studies that the non-Western group was cognitively deficient.

However, in the 1960s studies that compared different groups within a culture began to document differences in cognitive processes *within* non-Western cultures, indicating that the cognitive differences are not biologically based. For example, Greenfield et al. (1966) compared the performance of three groups of Wolof children in Senegal from three settings (unschooled rural, schooled rural, and schooled urban) on classification tasks. They found that although degree of urbanization had some impact on subjects' responses, attendance at school had a more dramatic influence on the children's classifications and the kinds of reasons they gave for the classes they formed, so that schooled children gave more abstract, conceptual answers. Such intracultural comparisons moved the discussion from general comparisons of cultural groups and began to link *particular* cultural features (e.g., social class, Western schooling, urbanization) to various aspects of cognitive development.

These studies, while more informative than general comparisons of different cultural groups, gave minimal attention to the cultural components under study. They rarely reported cultural attitudes and values, aspects of social organization, or daily experiences that were related to the cultural activities under study.

Another deficiency was that many of the cultural features treated as independent variables in the studies were in fact "packaged"; that is, they included "clusters of correlated and often ill-defined traits" (Whiting 1976 p. 305). These variables needed to be "unpackaged" to identify the specific, discrete, and well-defined aspects of culture that accounted for differences in cognition.

A final drawback was that these studies were generally insensitive to contextual influences on cognitive activity. They usually assumed that subjects' test scores reflected underlying ability or competence rather than performance related to the specific context in which they were being tested.

1.2 Anthropology

Although anthropologists have been concerned about the relationships between culture and personality (e.g., Barnouw 1973) and about the cognitive content of culture (e.g., Tyler 1969), few have examined the kinds of cognitive processes that are the primary focus of psychological studies. Anthropologists interested in culture and cognition generally have described naturally occuring cultural practices in which cognitive activities occur and have attempted to show how these practices are linked to larger sociocultural patterns. Using traditional ethnographic research designs, these researchers have used participant observation and informal interviewing as primary methods of data collection and have conducted qualitative analyses of the data.

Such work has focused on the cognitive activities of both children and adults. For example, Fortes (1970), in his study of the Tallensi in Ghana, described children's educational experiences, the social relationships in which these experiences are embedded, and adults' and children's attitudes toward learning. He also examined how children's social relationships, environment, and experiences change as they develop over time, with consequent changes in children's educational experiences.

Bateson (1958) examined the memory skills of learned Iatmul men in New Guinea as part of a larger study of Iatmul culture. He estimated that these men had memorized between 10,000 and 20,000 totemic names for use in debating and other activities. From his observations of men's debates and the order in which the men recited lists of names, Bateson argued that their memory skills were developed through visual and kinaesthetic imagery rather than through rote memorization.

Through this approach, anthropologists documented that non-Western peoples displayed complex and prodigious cognitive skills in everyday life. However, because these studies focused at the level of the cultural group, they did not provide detailed descriptions of the cognitive activities themselves.

Although the psychological and anthropological approaches had strengths, each had serious weaknesses that prevented a rich and detailed study of culture and cognition. Psychological studies were severely limited in their treatment of cultural features, and they relied almost exclusively on data collected in experimental situations. Anthropological studies focused on cultural features and collected data in natural settings, but lacked sufficient detail about cognitive activities.

2. Early Interdisciplinary Research

Although some scholars have continued to work solely within a psychological or anthropological framework, many use a more interdisciplinary approach. In the late 1960s some scholars began conducting research that drew on both traditions. These studies usually compared groups within a culture using tests or experimental tasks, but often developed the tasks and interpreted the results based on anthropological data about the culture.

Cole et al. (1971) pioneered this approach in their study among the Kpelle of Liberia. For general background information on Kpelle culture they drew on previous ethnographic studies. For more detailed information on relevant cultural activities they collected data from observations, conversations, court cases, and school essays. They used the cultural data to develop a variety of experimental tasks in several cognitive areas (e.g., classification, learning, and memory), and to interpret their results from experiments that compared intracultural groups of varying ages, languages, levels of education, and degrees of Westernization. By using multiple tasks to examine the "same" cognitive skill, and by comparing subjects' performance across these tasks and between experimental tasks and everyday life, these researchers found that context influences the use of cognitive skills. For example, in some experiments young children used rote-learning approaches, while in others they responded in terms of stimulus relations.

To provide more detailed understandings of intracultural variation, other interdisciplinary researchers collected a variety of data on individuals, including interviews, surveys, and various kinds of nonparticipant observation data (e.g., Jacob 1983,

Nerlove et al. 1974, Reed and Lave 1979). Sometimes researchers supplemented these focused data with general ethnographic data.

These early interdisciplinary projects presented an increasingly complex picture, demonstrating that cognitive development is related to specific experiences in life, and that factors in the immediate context (e.g., features of an experimental task) influence cognitive performance.

These studies also made some methodological advances. Although tests or experiments were central to almost all studies, some researchers were developing their tasks from previous ethnographic data rather than by importing tasks from outside the culture under study. In addition, researchers gathered focused, individual-level data to relate specific cultural experiences and contexts to specific aspects of cognitive development and performance.

In spite of these methodological advances, much remained to be done. The status of experimental data continued to be a problem. Lave's (1979) observations of arithmetic problem-solving in tailor shops raised questions about the validity even of experimental tasks explicitly derived from everyday life: she found that experimental tasks and everyday situations in the tailor shop tapped quite different problem-solving strategies. In addition, most nonparticipant observations still provided a dearth of information about everyday activities and their sociocultural contexts.

3. Vygotsky and the Soviet Cultural–Historical School

Many of the problems in interdisciplinary research reflected the lack of a theoretical framework that united the social, cultural, contextual, and psychological levels of analysis. In the late 1970s and early 1980s, some researchers turned to the earlier work of Lev Vygotsky and the Soviet cultural–historical school (also called the sociohistorical school) for a possible integrating theoretical framework.

Writing from 1924 until his death 10 years later, Vygotsky developed a theoretical framework that combines history, social institutions, cultural artifacts, cultural meanings, cultural signs (such as language), activities, interpersonal interactions, and cognition. Vygotsky's work, along with that of his colleagues Leont'ev and Luria, brought new life to investigations of culture and cognition.

Vygotsky focused primarily on what he called the higher mental functions (e.g., thinking, reasoning, problem-solving, and voluntary attention), which he saw as characteristics of the mental life of humans and as heavily influenced by sociocultural factors. In Vygotsky's view, society influences the development of higher mental functions both through its history and through immediate interpersonal environments.

At the historical level, society influences cognitive activity through the technical and psychological tools it furnishes for cognitive activity (Vygotsky 1978). Technical tools (e.g., pens, calculators, personal computers) and psychological tools (e.g., language, number sytems, writing) mediate psychological processes; that is, they transform the structure and processes of the action being performed (Vygotsky 1981). For example, editing with a word processor is a different activity from editing with a pen or pencil.

At the level of the immediate personal environment, society influences psychological development through face-to-face interactions. Vygotsky asserted that higher mental functions have their origins in such interactions: "Every function in the child's cultural development appears twice: first, on the social level, and later, on the individual level; first, *between* people (*interpsychological*), and then *inside* the child (*intrapsychological*)" (italics as in original; Vygotsky 1978 p. 57). In Vygotsky's view, the transition from interpsychological to intrapsychological activity is accomplished through language, which is the general mediational means for both interpsychological and intrapsychological activities.

Closely related to the social nature of the development of higher mental functions is the concept of "zone of proximal development," which Vygotsky defined as "*the distance between the actual developmental level as determined by independent problem solving and the level of potential development as determined through problem solving under adult guidance or in collaboration with more capable peers*" (italics as in original; Vygotsky 1978 p. 86). Thus, the zone of proximal development is the dynamic region where an individual moves from interpsychological to intrapsychological functioning.

Although the previous discussion has stressed the influence of society on cognition, Vygotsky did not view the influence as unidirectional. He saw the relationships between society and the individual as dialectical, with both influencing one another (John-Steiner and Souberman 1978).

The cultural–historical school promulgated several important methodological tenets. Vygotsky (1978) argued that it was crucial to focus not just on the products of development, but also on the processes by which psychological development occurs. This contention formed the base of his developmental (or genetic) method, which differed from conventional psychological experiments. This perspective has led to an interest in "microgenesis," the short-term development of psychological processes.

Because Vygotsky did not focus on outcomes but on processes leading to outcomes, his work included narrative descriptions of how individuals accomplished tasks. This aspect of his approach helped to break down barriers between the laboratory of psychologists and the field research of anthropologists.

Vygotsky's framework required a new "holistic" unit of analysis beyond the traditional psychological focus on the individual. His original proposal for this new unit of analysis, that is, the relationship between thinking and speech, was soon seen as inadequate (Wertsch 1985) and replaced by Leont'ev's (1978, 1981) trilevel "activity." The first level, that of "activity," is tied to a socially constructed motive (e.g., getting food, making clothes). The second level, that of "actions," is tied to goals that are instrumental to achieving a motive (e.g., making a weapon or going shopping may be instrumental to the motive of getting food). The third level, that of "operations," involves how an action is carried out (e.g., writing a list or committing items to memory to remember items needed for shopping).

4. Cultural–Historical Work in the 1980s and 1990s

Since the late 1970s, researchers (often termed "neo-Vygotskians") have worked to clarify and extend the theoretical framework of the cultural–historical school and to build a body of empirical research based on its premises. The major contributions of this work have been situating the study of culture and cognition within specific contexts and explicating the mutual influences among culture, context, and cognition, primarily through the mediation of language in social interaction.

Although the framework guiding this work is interdisciplinary, most of the researchers implementing it have been trained within a traditional discipline, with the result that many contemporary studies (like earlier interdisciplinary work) are still heavily influenced by a particular discipline, expecially in their focuses and methodology. Studies dominated by psychology have tended to have an *intra*psychological focus, while studies dominated by anthropology or linguistics have tended to have a more *inter*psychological focus.

4.1 Intrapsychological Studies

Some intrapsychological studies continued the interest in developing and implementing experiments developed from observations. For example, Scribner and Cole (1981) developed experiments based on ethnographic and survey data of Vai literacy behavior in Liberia. They found that literacy affected performance only on tasks whose requirements were similar to literacy activities engaged in by the Vai. Thus, the researchers concluded that nonschool literacy does not produce general cognitive effects; whatever cognitive effects literacy does have are related to specific everyday practices.

Work by Lave and her colleagues (de la Rocha 1985, Lave et al. 1984, Murtaugh 1985) shifted the focus from experimental data to ethnographic observations and interviews. They studied everyday mathematics occurring as part of grocery shopping, dieting, and cooking. Their studies found that the way shoppers

solve problems is related to the way they formulate problems; that dieters' use of precise measurement depended upon features of the environment; and that dieters developed measuring strategies other than the precise measuring encouraged by their program when conflicts arose between their goals for cooking and dieting.

These researchers also explicitly dealt with the role of context in cognitive activities, arguing that context consists of two components. First, a context has physical characteristics, which reflect the larger social order. Second, a context has a mental component, based on how individuals define it as they interact with the physical context and each other.

The intrapsychological studies continued to challenge the view that cognition develops through universal, context-free processes. They presented a picture of everyday cognition in which persons actively construct cognitive practices in specific psychological and physical contexts.

A gap in most of these studies is that few examined the meanings that activities and their related cognitive tasks have for the participants. Moreover, few of the studies dealt with how other persons are resources for an activity, or with the larger social, cultural, and historical contexts in which activities are generated. Recent studies of interpsychological functioning have begun to address these issues.

4.2 Interpsychological Studies

A major area of interest in the cultural–historical approach is how interactions between an expert and a novice (whether mother–child, teacher–student, or student–student) result in cognitive change in the novice. This interest has led to a wide variety of studies focusing on interpsychological (i.e., interactional) processes. With the centrality of interaction in this view, methods of discourse analysis have become increasingly important.

Researchers studying interpsychological functioning have used both experimental and ethnographic designs. In addition, they have implemented a new design (termed "formative experiments"), which combines aspects of the other two approaches.

Experimental studies usually involve two persons jointly accomplishing some task. The researchers record the sessions on videotape to examine the processes that occur during the experiments. Wertsch et al. (1984), for example, compared the instructional processes that mothers and teachers used to instruct children how to construct a copy of a three-dimensional toy barnyard. Wertsch and his colleagues used the three levels of activity theory to explain the differences they found between the way teachers and mothers taught the children. Although Wertsch et al. linked their analyses of adult–child interactions to a discussion of the participants' definitions of the situation and to larger sociocultural contexts, they based their discussion largely on inferences rather than data. Moreover, they treated context as static, and took the context of the experiment for granted.

Several researchers have used the cultural–historical framework to guide ethnographic studies that focus on face-to-face interactions occurring in instructional settings and on the broader sociocultural context. Such studies are particularly useful in showing how larger sociocultural features influence face-to-face interactions. For example, Florio-Ruane (1991) found that the school's definitions of situations, statuses, and roles influenced the nature of interactions that occur in teacher–student writing conferences, often resulting in less than ideal realization. In a similar vein, Jacob (1990) discussed how features of the school, classroom, and peer contexts influenced peer interaction occurring in cooperative learning groups.

While the few ethnographic studies that have been conducted within the cultural–historical framework have linked interpsychological processes to larger sociocultural features, it is exactly this link with existing circumstances that some researchers seek to overcome. These scholars (e.g., Davydov 1988, Griffin et al. 1993, Newman 1990) criticized experiments because they lacked ecological validity. They also criticized naturalistic studies because, while such studies reported the current forms and content of schooling and larger societal influences on schooling, they said little about what *could* be. To address these concerns and to try to improve instruction, some researchers have used "formative experiments," which combine qualitative methods of investigation with interventions in everyday learning situations.

One team of researchers (Moll and Diaz 1987) documented the changes they made in the social organization of instruction to improve the education of minority students. They used ethnographic and microethnographic methods to analyze settings in which minority students were not doing well. They then used cultural–historical theory to reorganize instruction. For example, they examined a bilingual program in which students were not reading well in English. They observed that whereas one teacher gave students a range of tasks in Spanish reading, from decoding to more advanced comprehension activities, the other teacher gave the same students only low-level tasks in English reading. The authors modified the instruction in the English class so that students could discuss English readings in Spanish, with the result that in the new lessons the students showed that they could understand more about the English readings than they could articulate in English. The assistance provided by the researchers allowed the students to display their true English comprehension skills.

Interpsychological studies have contributed to a fuller and more dynamic understanding of cognitive change and of the relationships among culture, context, and cognition. Like intrapsychological studies, these studies present a picture of situated cognitive activities. Moreover, interpsychological studies add a new dimension—a central focus on understanding the interactional processes related to cognitive change. These studies show that cognitive change is often a social process in which language and meanings are central, and that social interactions and their related cognitive processes are in dynamic and dialectical relationships with other sociocultural and historical aspects of the situation.

5. Conclusion

The study of culture and cognition has changed significantly since the 1960s. Many researchers have moved from discipline-based efforts to interdisciplinary efforts that have expanded the work of Vygotsky and the Soviet cultural–historical school. In the cultural–historical view, cognitive development is the product of specific activities in specific contexts. Moreover, culture and cognition are no longer seen as independent and dependent variables, respectively, but as co-creating entities. The field has a fuller understanding of the variety of cultural features that are related to cognition: individuals' definitions of the situation, their goals, their access to and use of technical and psychological tools, their social relations, their co-occurring activities, the physical context, the context created by the participants, and the larger sociocultural and historical factors that influence the routine patterns in a context.

For many researchers the focus of attention has shifted from comparisons of cognitive outcomes among cultural groups to understanding the processes that occur in specific, local contexts. The unit of analysis has shifted from individuals or cultural groups to culturally situated activities in which individuals act, often in concert with other individuals, using available psychological and technical tools.

Although the area of culture and cognition has exhibited tremendous movement and activity, much remains to be done. More work is needed on the role of language as a mediating device and on the links between language and larger sociocultural factors. Wertsch (1991) has contributed to this effort by explicating some ways in which language links the interpsychological and the intrapsychological, and by exploring the link between forms of language and the larger social order, using Bakhtin's notion of "social language."

Another issue that merits further attention is the role of meaning in cognitive processes. Up to the early 1990s scholars have examined meaning primarily in terms of individuals' definition of the situation. Other kinds of meaning come into play, and these need to be explored. For example, cultural meanings are clearly relevant. Cultures not only differ in the kinds of technical and psychological tools they provide, but also in how they evaluate the use of these tools by different groups within a society. Furthermore, relationships between cultural meanings and individual meanings in a particular situation need to be elaborated. There is also a need for a theory of situations or contexts. Such a theory should take into account both physical characteristics and subjective meanings of contexts.

More work is needed on linking interpsychological activity to features of both the immediate context and the larger institutional contexts. Several scholars (e.g., Eckensberger 1990, Lave 1988) have attempted to develop theories that encompass cognition and multiple levels of culture. Other scholars (e.g., Forman et al. 1993) have begun to conduct studies explicitly focused on these issues.

In the methodological arena, contemporary researchers using the cultural–historical framework need to clarify their stance toward experimental data. While some have questioned the acontextual assumptions of traditional experiments, others continue to use traditional experimental designs.

5.1 Educational Implications

When explicitly applied to understanding minority groups, the cultural–historical approach suggests that while cultural groups may exhibit differences in cognition, these differences are related to specific experiences embedded in specific sociocultural and historical contexts, not to deficits in underlying biological capabilities. Moreover, it suggests that there is considerable diversity within cultural groups, which reflects the diversity of experiences and meanings within groups.

The cultural–historical approach has focused attention not only on the past, on what minority students bring with them to school, but also on the present, on the specific contexts in which students are required to perform. Because cognitive performance is related to the specific features of the context, it can no longer be assumed that students' performance in one context (e.g., a standardized testing situation or a monolingual classroom) is an accurate measure of their competence or potential.

Although most educators have been interested in the topic of culture and cognition because of their concerns about educating minority students, cultural–historical theory and research have implications for *all* educational practice. Culture is central to all education. As products of the human mind, all educational theory and practice are socioculturally embedded. Society structures all learning situations through the technical and psychological tools provided, the social organization in which these tools are embedded, and the cultural meanings and values associated with tools and learning contexts. In each immediate context, learning is influenced by the social interaction between teachers and students, the nature of the tasks, the contexts of their engagement, and the meanings these have for participants.

Vygotsky was interested in instruction that could contribute to cognitive development. In his view, instruction should precede development, with the goal of helping a child to develop through zones of proximal development. In Vygotsky's view, the zone of proximal development is determined jointly by a child's developmental level and by the form of instruction involved.

Formative experiments conducted by cultural–historical researchers have demonstrated that different instructional methods can create different zones of proximal development and thereby influence the learning that occurs. These studies provide a model for classroom practice as well as for research. They suggest that teachers, as reflective practitioners, should modify instructional methods, curriculum, and context as needed to facilitate students' movement through their zones of proximal development.

Besides providing a vision of instruction linked to development, the cultural–historical framework has led several scholars to develop educational practices for widespread use. Palincsar and Brown (1984), for example, developed a very effective instructional method for reading–"reciprocal teaching"–which helps students become proficient in four basic reading skills. The teacher and students take turns doing the skills aloud for specific paragraphs. At first, the teacher carries out each activity, modeling expert practice. When the students begin to carry out the activities, the teacher provides assistance by coaching them. As the students become more proficient, the teacher reduces and modifies the assistance he or she provides to support the students' emerging competence.

Building on studies of instructional methods such as reciprocal teaching, Collins et al. (1989) have argued for a cognitive apprenticeship model of teaching, which would focus on helping students acquire the cognitive and metacognitive strategies needed for expert practice in reading, writing, and mathematics. Their model addresses the nature of the social interactions between expert and novice and the social context of learning. Their ideal learning environment embodies the culture of expert practice and utilizes instructional strategies such as coaching and scaffolding. Thus, the cultural–historical approach offers alternatives to traditional, whole-class instruction dominated by the traditional recitation script so widespread in classrooms.

The cultural–historical approach also suggests that traditional assessment measures such as standardized tests are severely limited, presenting a static view of children and documenting only what children are able to do on their own. Drawing on the cultural–historical approach, Brown and Ferrara (1985) have developed and studied "dynamic assessment methods," which offer graduated assistance to children so that the tester is able to evaluate how much the child is able to improve over initial performance.

The cultural–historical approach challenges educators to develop contexts that allow all students to display what they can do and to grow to their potential. It offers not only a critique of existing practices, but also a vision of the future and suggests instructional practices that offer both hope and approaches for change.

See also: Human Learning: Evolution of Anthropological Perspectives; Cognition and Learning; Language and Learning in Education

References

Barnouw V 1973 *Culture and Personality*, rev. edn. Dorsey Press, Homewood, Illinois
Bateson G 1958 *Naven: A Survey of the Problems Suggested by a Composite Picture of the Culture of a New Guinea Tribe Drawn from Three Points of View*, 2nd edn. Stanford University Press, Stanford, California
Berry J W 1976 *Human Ecology and Cognitive Style: Comparative Studies in Cultural and Psychological Adaptation.* Sage, New York
Brown A L, Ferrara R A 1985 Diagnosing zones of proximal development. In: Wertsch J V (ed.) 1985 *Culture, Communication and Cognition: Vygotskian Perspectives.* Cambridge University Press, Cambridge
Cole M, Gay J, Glick J, Sharp D 1971 *The Cultural Context of Learning and Thinking: An Exploration in Experimental Anthropology.* Basic Books, New York
Collins A, Brown J S, Newman S E 1989 Cognitive apprenticeship: Teaching the crafts of reading, writing, and mathematics. In: Resnick L (ed.) 1989 *Knowing, Learning, and Instruction: Essays in Honor of Robert Glaser.* Erlbaum, Hillsdale, New Jersey
Dasen P R, Heron A 1981 Cross-cultural tests of Piaget's theory. In: Triandis H C, Heron A (eds.) 1981 *Handbook of Cross-cultural Psychology. Vol. 4: Developmental Psychology.* Allyn and Bacon, Boston, Massachusetts
Davydov V V 1988 Problems of developmental teaching: The experience of theoretical and experimental psychological research, Part 2. *Soviet Education* 30(9): 3–83
de la Rocha O 1985 The reorganization of arithmetic practice in the kitchen. *Anthropol. Educ. Q.* 16(3): 193–98
Eckensberger L H 1990 From cross-cultural psychology to cultural psychology. *Quarterly Newsletter of the Laboratory of Comparative Human Cognition* 12(1): 37–52
Florio-Ruane S 1991 Instructional conversations in learning to write and learning to teach. In: Jones B F, Idol L (eds.) 1991 *Educational Values and Cognitive Instruction: Implications for Reform*, Vol. 2. Erlbaum, Hillsdale, New Jersey
Forman E A, Minick N, Stone C A 1993 *Contexts for Learning: Sociocultural Dynamics in Children's Development.* Oxford University Press, Oxford
Fortes M 1970 Social and psychological aspects of education in Taleland. In: Middleton J (ed.) 1970 *From Child to Adult: Studies in the Anthropology of Education.* Natural History Press, Garden City, New York
Greenfield P, Reich L, Olver R 1966 On culture and equivalence: II. In: Bruner J, Olver R, Greenfield P (eds.) 1966 *Studies in Cognitive Growth: A Collaboration at the Center for Cognitive Studies.* Wiley, New York
Griffin P, Belyaeva A, Soldatova G 1993 Creating and reconstituting contexts for educational interactions including a computer program. In: Forman E, Minick N, Stone C A (eds.) 1993 *Contexts for Learning: Sociocultural Dynamics in Children's Development.* Oxford University Press, Oxford
Jacob E 1983 Studying Puerto Rican children's informal education at home. In: Rivera C (ed.) 1983 *A Sociolinguistic/Ethnographic Approach to Language Proficiency Assessment.* Multilingual Matters, Clevedon
Jacob E 1990 Studying cooperative learning with minority students: An anthropological perspective. Paper presented at the biennial meeting of the International Association for Cooperation in Education, Baltimore, Maryland
John-Steiner V, Souberman E 1978 Afterword. In: Vygotsky L S 1978
Krewer B 1990 Psyche and culture—Can culture-free psychology take into account the essential features of the species "Homo Sapiens"? *Quarterly Newsletter of the Laboratory of Comparative Human Cognition* 12(1): 24–37
Lave J 1979 A model of mundane arithmetic problem-solving. Paper presented at the Social Science Research Council Conference on Cultural Representations of Knowledge, La Jolla, California
Lave J 1988 *Cognition in Practice: Mind, Mathematics and Culture in Everyday Life.* Cambridge University Press, Cambridge
Lave J, Murtaugh M, de la Rocha O 1984 The dialectic of arithmetic in grocery shopping. In: Rogoff B, Lave J (eds.) 1984 *Everyday Cognition: Its Development in Social Context.* Harvard University Press, Cambridge, Massachusetts
Leont'ev A N 1978 *Activity, Consciousness, and Personality.* Prentice-Hall, Englewood Cliffs, New Jersey
Leont'ev A N 1981 *Problems of the Development of the Mind.* Progress Publishers, Moscow
Moll L, Diaz S 1987 Change as the goal of educational research. *Anthropol. Educ. Q.* 18(4): 300–11
Murtaugh M 1985 The practice of arithmetic by American grocery shoppers. *Anthropol. Educ. Q.* 16(3): 186–92
Nerlove S B, Roberts J M, Klein R E, Yarbrough C, Habicht J-P 1974 Natural indicators of cognitive development: An observational study of rural Guatemalan children. *Ethos* 2: 265–95
Newman D 1990 Opportunities for research on the organizational impact of school computers. *Educ. Researcher* 19(3): 8–13
Palincsar A S, Brown A L 1984 Reciprocal teaching of comprehension-fostering and comprehension-monitoring activities. *Cognition and Instruction* 1: 117–75
Reed H J, Lave J 1979 Arithmetic as a tool for investigating relations between culture and cognition. *American Ethnologist* 6: 568–82
Scribner S Cole M 1981 *The Psychology of Literacy.* Harvard University Press, Cambridge Massachusetts
Tyler S (ed.) 1969 *Cognitive Anthropology.* Holt, Rinehart and Winston, New York
Vygotsky L S 1978 *Mind in Society: The Development of Higher Psychological Processes.* In: Cole M, John-Steiner V, Scribner S, Souberman E (eds.) 1978 Harvard University Press, Cambridge, Massachusetts
Vygotsky L S 1981 The genesis of higher mental functions.

In: Wertsch J V (ed.) 1981 *The Concept of Activity in Soviet Psychology* Sharpe, Armonk, New York

Wertsch J V 1985 *Vygotsky and the Social Formation of Mind*. Harvard University Press, Cambridge, Massachusetts

Wertsch J V 1991 *Voices of the Mind: A Sociocultural Approach to Mediated Action*. Harvester Wheatsheaf, London

Wertsch J V, Minick N, Arns F 1984 The creation of context in joint problem-solving. In: Rogoff B, Lave J (eds.) 1984 *Everyday Cognition: Its Development in Social Context*. Harvard University Press, Cambridge, Massachusetts

Whiting B 1976 The problem of the packaged variable. In: Riegel K F, Meacham J A (eds.) 1976 *The Developing Individual in a Changing World*, Vol. 1. University of Michigan, Ann Arbor, Michigan

Further Reading

Jacob E 1992 Culture, context, and cognition. In: LeCompte M D, Millroy W, Preissle J (eds.) 1992 *The Handbook of Qualititative Research in Education*. Academic Press, San Diego, California

Laboratory of Comparative Human Cognition 1983 Culture and cognitive development. In: Kessen W et al. (eds.) 1983 *Handbook of Child Psychology. Vol 1: History, Theory and Methods*. Wiley, New York

Home Environment and School Learning

A. J. Fuligni and H. W. Stevenson

Among the most important influences on children's academic achievement is their home environment. Until the 1970s, interest centered on determining the relation between school learning and demographic factors, such as gender, socioeconomic status, family size, and birth order. Although demographic factors have remained of interest, the major concern is no longer the description of correlates of school learning but the analysis of the *processes* whereby demographic and other variables exert their effects. When demographic factors are studied, they are likely to be those that are relevant to contemporary families, such as mothers' working status, fathers' presence in the home, and the time spent in different types of parent–child interaction. These changes in interest have led to research that encompasses a broader range of variables than was the case in the past.

1. Perspectives

The study of the effects of home environment on school learning, once almost the exclusive province of sociologists, has captured the attention of increasing numbers of developmental psychologists (see the review by Hess and Holloway 1984). By training and tradition, sociologists are interested in sociostructural variables. Psychologists are more likely to be interested in fine-grained analyses of behavior within the home environment. Both approaches are obviously important, and their combination is leading to a more detailed picture of the rich variety of ways in which the home environment can influence children's performance at school.

Contemporary sociologists such as Marjoribanks (1979) and Alexander and Entwisle (1988) have sought to bridge the gap between sociological and psychological approaches. Supplementing their work are analyses by psychologists of how environmental factors influence psychological processes, such as children's motivation, personality characteristics, attitudes, and beliefs, and how these in turn influence learning. The comprehensive nature of this research is illustrated in the collection of studies edited by Parke (1984).

The field has also benefited from the work of developmental psychologists who have highlighted the importance of the developmental status of the child. The home environment influences learning differentially according to the child's age. Variables affecting a 6- or 7-year old's learning do not necessarily operate in the same manner after the student has been in school for several more years. Moreover, the home environment may change markedly over this period. For example, parent–child interaction declines as children grow older. Parents may spend less than half the time in caretaking and interacting with children during the middle years of childhood than they did during the preschool years (Maccoby 1984). The meaning of other variables, such as paternal absence or parental level of education, may also differ according to the age of the child. By studying academic progress in conjunction with the rest of children's development, studies have yielded a better portrayal of the complex ways in which children may benefit or are impeded in their school learning by different types of home environments.

There has also been a growing interest in examining how home environments influence school learning in different cultures. This interest has its basis in both practical and theoretical concerns. The dramatic differences in academic achievement often found among children in different cultural groups has compelled researchers to look more closely at the environments in which these children live. Of more general theoretical concern is the interest in questions of whether the findings can be generalized across and within different cultural groups. The questions are of the following types: Does the amount of time spent assisting children at home with their schoolwork have an equally positive effect in cultures that place great value on education and in those where formal education is considered to be less important? Are variables that account for differences in achievement across cultures equally effective in explaining differences in achievement within cultures?

2. Changes in the Home Environment

The last half of the twentieth century has witnessed profound changes in family life throughout the world. Transitions from agrarian to industrialized economies, rapid advances in technology and automation, and breakdowns in traditional family structures have had ineradicable effects on the home life of families in both developing and industrialized societies. Stable, hierarchical organizations of family life have in many cultures given way to radical changes in the roles of parents and children. Traditional two-parent families have been replaced by single-parent households. Even in two-parent families, many mothers work full time and are unavailable during the day. The greater independence and at times estrangement of children from their parents is heightened in many societies by the high percentage of children who work in part-time jobs while attending school. As a consequence, factors outside the home come to play more important roles in children's lives. Peers often replace parents as the primary source of values and goals, and children's learning may depend more on their own social world than on what occurs at home.

These dramatic changes have required a new conceptualization of the home environment. Rather than considering the family as a firm structure in which roles are clearly defined and the direction of influence is predominantly from parents to children, the family is viewed as a dynamic system in which there is the potential for mutual influence among all participants. This view has added vitality to research on home influences, but there is only a vague understanding of how the complex interactions among family members influence the processes and outcomes of school learning.

3. Processes of Transmission

The influence of the home environment is transmitted to children in many different ways. These range from the effects of the objective, physical environment in which the child lives to the subjective, psychological environment created by parents through their child-rearing practices. Each of these will be explored in the following sections.

3.1 The Physical Environment

Little attention has been paid to the physical environment of the home as a contributor to school progress. Homes in industrialized countries are typically equipped with reasonable amounts of space, electricity, and other modern amenities. In contrast, homes in many developing countries lack even the most fundamental necessities, including adequate food and fresh water. It is hard to imagine how children living in these unhealthy environments can learn effectively at school. In many developing countries, the dramatic differences between the home environments of rural people, who lack nearly all modern conveniences, and those in the cities are accompanied by striking differences in what children are able to accomplish in school.

Even when economic conditions are not so dire, many parents in developing countries spend significant portions of their limited resources on tuition, books, and school uniforms. Their willingness to do this offers a much stronger indication to children of how their parents value education than is the case in more affluent societies where these expenditures place few limitations on other aspects of family life. Providing space for study imposes little sacrifice on families in industrialized societies, but places severe restrictions on the activities of other family members when the whole family must live in one or two rooms.

Children in economically sound families that do not allocate a quiet place in the home for studying or that fail to provide their children with desks or workbooks demonstrate their family's lack of support for education. Such conditions are less likely to occur in societies where strong emphasis is placed on education than in those where education is given a less central role in children's lives (Stevenson and Lee 1990).

3.2 The Child-rearing Climate

Explorations of the relation between the psychological climate within the family and children's development have a long tradition in research about children. One popular view is that of Baumrind (1973), who describes two important dimensions of family climates: (a) the degree of parental guidance and control; (b) the amount of emotional support and encouragement parents give to their children. A series of studies revealed small but consistent effects of child-rearing practices on children's academic performance during high school (Dornbusch et al. 1987, Steinberg et al. 1991). Students from "authoritative" households (those high in support and control) tended to have the highest grade-point averages. Their performance was better than that of students in either "authoritarian" households (those low in support and high in control) or in "permissive" households (those low in both support and control)

The relation between child-rearing and school performance is assumed to be mediated partly by the effects of child-rearing on other variables. For example, authoritative parenting is predictive of adolescents' self-reliance and feelings of autonomy. Thus, moderate amounts of parental control along with positive emotional support help to produce a sense of competence and confidence in children. These characteristics, in turn, are ones considered to be important for success in school.

Efforts have been made to ascertain whether the effects of authoritative parenting transcend cultural groups. Results from the Dornbusch et al. (1987) study of United States students suggest that the benefits are greatest for children from White households. Authoritative parenting was only slightly predictive of academic success among Hispanic-American adolescents, and not at all predictive among Asian- and African-American adolescents. Hess and Azuma (1991 p. 4) make a distinction between two modes of cultural transmission that influence the family climate: osmosis, where "nurturance, interdependence, and close physical proximity provide exposure to adult values and instill a readiness on the part of the child to imitate, accept, and internalize such values," and teaching, where "direct instruction, injunctions, frequent dialogue, and explanations are used." Japanese parents were much less willing than United States parents to assume the role of teacher. They tended to rely more strongly on modeling as the means of socialization, while parents in the United States depended upon a reward-based training strategy.

Children's success in school may depend, in part, on the extent to which mother–child interaction fits the cultural model and thereby matches the style of instruction in school. Hess and Azuma found, for example, that persistence in children, a highly admired trait among the Japanese, was significantly related to later academic achievement for Japanese children but not for children in the United States. In contrast, early independence, which is fostered in American culture, was a significant predictor for American, but not for Japanese children.

3.3 Parental Involvement

As children with increasingly diverse family backgrounds have begun to attend school, discord between the values and goals espoused by parents and by the schools has increased. For example, parents in many indigenous cultural groups appear to believe that a quiet child is preferable to a talkative one and may rely more closely on modeling and other nonverbal forms of instruction in teaching their children. Teachers at school, on the other hand, expect children to be able to express themselves verbally, and their teaching relies heavily on verbal instruction. In attempts reduce this discord between styles of teaching, ei have been made to involve parents more closely in activities of the school.

The degree of parental involvement varies widely. In some cases, teachers simply want to inform parents about their educational procedures and practices. In other cases, increased parental involvement means that parents are urged to become familiar with their children's daily assignments and progress. This may consist of attending parent–teacher meetings or of communicating daily with the teacher through the notebooks children carry back and forth between home and school. In still other cases, parents are expected to assume direct responsibility for establishing educational policies.

While the benefits of parental involvement in their children's education seem obvious, there has been little research to document the utility of the various forms this can take. Typical of the research that has been reported is the study of Stevenson and Baker (1987), who found that the extent to which parents were involved in school activities, such as parent–teacher organizations and parent–teacher conferences, was positively related to children's school performance. Involvement was greater among parents of younger children and among more highly educated mothers.

3.4 Cognitive Stimulation and Academic Assistance

More direct ways in which the home environment can influence school learning are through cognitive stimulation and assistance with schoolwork. Although in many societies these responsibilities lie with the mother, this is not always the case. In three-generation homes these tasks often become the province of grandparents; in other societies all members of the family, including siblings and other relatives, share these duties.

Despite the potential for cognitive stimulation that exists in all homes, some families do not provide their children with experiences that help assure their success in school. Efforts have been made to remedy these deficiencies by instructing parents about ways in which they can help their children, by talking with them, reading stories, providing toys, and playing games. In some programs, mothers also participate in groups that involve instruction and mutual support. Many of these home-based intervention programs have been found to improve children's later performance in school and, at times, to enhance their cognitive functioning (McCartney and Howley 1992). For example, simply having children read to their parents improves children's reading skills beyond what is achieved through ordinary instruction at school.

Parents' provision of out-of-home experiences, including taking children shopping, visiting zoos, mu-

*n also stimulate cognitive
portunities for informal learn-
day world increase the fund of
on available to the child—a factor
dly been found to be predictive of skill
cts as reading and language arts.
uence of direct assistance by parents on
s schoolwork is little understood. It is gener-
greed that parental involvement and interest are
essary ingredients for academic success, but the
orm they take varies widely. Most parents in industrialized societies are capable of offering direct help
to their children during the early years of elementary
school, but fewer are able to do this when their children
are in the later grades. Because of this, the primary
way in which this interest is expressed is through the
supervision of homework and the creation of an environment conducive to study. The "education moms" in
many societies are distinguished not by direct forms of
teaching but by the intense interest in education they
convey to their children and the support they give to
their children's efforts to achieve.

The value of practicing what has been learned in
school by doing homework is regarded differently in
different cultural groups. This was one of the most
extreme differences found by Stevenson et al. (1990)
in their comparisons of White, Black, and Hispanic
parents. When asked about the value of increasing
the amount of homework for improving elementary
schoolchildren's performance, 88 percent of Black
mothers, 74 percent of Hispanic mothers, but only
46 percent of White mothers answered affirmative-
ly. This occurred despite the fact that, according to
estimates made by the children's teachers, homework
assignments given the previous week to children
enrolled in minority schools required twice as much
time to complete as the assignments given to children
enrolled in all-White schools.

3.5 Beliefs and Attitudes

More subtle in their influence are the beliefs and
attitudes parents hold about ways in which the home
environment can influence school learning. Several
reviews (Goodnow and Collins 1990, Miller 1988)
have documented how beliefs held by family members
affect children's development and how these, in turn,
are related to their success in school.

One focus has been on parental expectations and
their satisfaction with their children's academic progress. In a study of Chinese and American children and
their parents, Chen and Uttal (1988) sought to discover sources of Chinese children's high achievement.
Mothers were asked what score they would expect
their children to obtain on a test with a maximum
score of 100 and an average score of 70. Chinese
and American mothers were equally positive in their
expectations, but when they were asked about the
score with which they would be satisfied, American

mothers reported a score lower than the expected score
and Chinese mothers reported a score higher than
the expected score. High standards are critical in establishing high levels of motivation for achievement;
children cease to be motivated to work harder when
they believe they are already meeting the standards set
by their parents and teachers.

Parents also hold strong beliefs about the relative
contribution of innate ability and effort to children's
achievement. The importance of effort is acknowledged by parents in all cultures. What differs is the
degree to which parents in different cultures believe
innate abilities limit what children are capable of
accomplishing. As part of their cross-cultural studies
of students' achievement, Stevenson and Lee (1990)
examined mothers' beliefs about the roles of ability
and effort in Japan, Taiwan, and the United States.
Japanese and Chinese mothers gave greater emphasis
to effort than did American mothers. Conversely,
American mothers placed greater emphasis on the
importance of innate abilities than the Japanese and
Chinese mothers. A strong belief in innate ability
undermines children's motivation to study hard. Parents, teachers, and children themselves believe that
highly able children do not need to study hard and
that intensive study is not especially
productive for children with low levels of ability.

Beliefs and attitudes about ability and effort are
also related to gender differences in academic achievement, especially in mathematics. Eccles (1983) is
among those who have suggested that the gap in
mathematics achievement between boys and girls in
high school is due primarily to beliefs about their
abilities and to the types of activities and classes
in which they participate. Many parents believe that
boys have innately superior abilities in mathematics.
They believe that boys require less effort to do well
in mathematics than do girls and they hold higher
expectations for boys' performance. This is true even
during the elementary school years, a period when
boys and girls generally perform equally well. These
beliefs about gender differences in mathematics ability
exist in different cultures, even in such achievement-
oriented countries as Japan and Taiwan (Lummis and
Stevenson 1990).

4. Conclusion

The understanding of the relation of home environments to school learning is fragmentary and incomplete, despite its great practical importance to
policymakers. Moreover, what is known comes primarily from studies undertaken in the West, which are
often of little value to policymakers in other societies.
There is great need for further expansion of research.
Refinements in the meaning of categorical variables
such as socioeconomic class have occurred. However,
the means by which the economic and social status of

600

families influence school learning is far from clear. The conceptualization of the home environment has expanded to include important factors such as belief systems and parent involvement, but research dealing with such topics needs to become more systematic and coherent.

Disentangling the direct and indirect ways in which factors within the home environment influence children's learning in school will be a slow process. Nevertheless, the increase in the number of cross-cultural and longitudinal studies, the greater interest in the interplay between children's developmental status and the characteristics of the home, and the trend toward studying variables that mediate between the home environment and school learning should gradually permit more comprehensive statements about this important topic.

References

Alexander K L, Entwisle D R 1988 Achievement in the first two years of school: Patterns and processes. *Monogr. Soc. Res. Child Dev.* 53(2): 1–157

Baumrind D 1973 The development of instrumental competence through socialization. In: Pick A D (ed.) 1973 *Minnesota Symposium on Child Psychology*, Vol. 7. University of Minnesota Press, Minneapolis, Minnesota

Chen C, Uttal D 1988 Cultural values, parents' beliefs, and children's achievement in the United States and China. *Hum. Dev.* 31(6): 351–58

Dornbusch S, Ritter P, Leiderman P, Roberts D, Fraleigh M 1987 The relation of parenting style to adolescent school performance. *Child Dev.* 58(5): 1244–57

Eccles J 1983 Expectancies, values, and academic behaviors. In: Spence J T (ed.) 1983 *Achievement and Achievement Motivation*. Freeman, San Francisco, California

Goodnow J, Collins W A (eds.) 1990 *Development According to Parents: The Nature, Sources, and Consequences of Parents' Ideas*. Erlbaum, Hove

Hess R D, Azuma H 1991 Cultural support for schooling: Contrasts between Japan and the United States. *Educ. Researcher* 20(9): 2–8

Hess R D, Holloway S D 1984 Family and school as educational institutions. In: Parke R D (ed.) 1984

Lummis M, Stevenson H 1990 Gender differences in beliefs and achievement: A cross-cultural study. *Dev. Psychol.* 26(2): 254–63

Maccoby E 1984 Middle childhood in the context of the family In: Collins W A (ed.) 1984 *Development During Middle Childhood: The Years from 6 to 12*. National Academy Press, Washington, DC

Marjoribanks K 1979 *Families and Their Learning Environments: An Empirical Analysis*. Routledge and Kegan Paul, London

McCartney K, Howley E 1992 Parents as instruments of intervention in home-based preschool programs. In: Okagaki L, Steinberg R J (eds.) 1992 *Directors of Development: Influences on the Development of Children's Thinking*. Erlbaum, Hillsdale, New Jersey

Miller S 1988 Parents' beliefs about their children's cognitive development. *Child Dev.* 59(2): 259–85

Parke R D (ed.) 1984 *Review of Child Development Research. Vol. 7: The Family*. University of Chicago Press, Chicago, Illinois

Steinberg L, Mounts N, Lamborn S, Dornbusch S 1991 Authoritative parenting and adolescent adjustment across varied ecological niches. *J. Res. Adol.* 1(1): 19–36

Stevenson D, Baker D 1987 The family–school relation and the child's school performance. *Child Dev.* 58(5): 1348–57

Stevenson H W, Chen C, Uttal D 1990 Beliefs and achievement: A study of Black, White, and Hispanic children. *Child Dev.* 61(2): 508–23

Stevenson H W, Lee S Y 1990 Contexts of achievement: A study of American, Chinese, and Japanese children. *Monogr. Soc. Res. Child Dev.* 55(1,2): 1–116

Further Reading

McAdoo H P, McAdoo J L (eds.) 1985 *Black Children: Social, Educational, and Parental Environments*. Sage, Beverly Hills, California

Mussen P H, Flavell J, Markman E (eds.) 1983 *Handbook of Child Psychology. Vol. 4: Socialization, Personality, and Social Development*. Wiley, New York

Rooparnine J L, Carter D B 1992 *Parent–Child Socialization in Diverse Cultures*. Ablex, Norwood, New Jersey

Stevenson H W, Stigler J W 1992 *The Learning Gap: Why our Schools are Failing and What We Can Learn from Japanese and Chinese Education*. Summit, New York

Learning in School, Sociology of

P. Broadfoot

Most learning is a social activity in which parents, friends, and teachers provide the encouragement and the framework within which learning can take place. This entry explores the social influences which affect learning both within the classroom and outside it.

1. The Nature of Learning

All societies, if they are to endure, must make provision for children to be taught the knowledge, skills, and values which they will need to become competent, adult members of that society. In most traditional societies it seems to have been accepted that the vital tasks of language acquisition, of the development of appropriate modes of behavior, of the learning of necessary skills, and of gaining knowledge and understanding about the world could safely be achieved informally through the child's participation in the daily life of the society. This process of informal learning that sociologists term "socialization" (see *Socialization*) is frequently complemented, however, by more explicit provision for formal instruction or practical training. The nature of such provision has traditionally varied enormously, including, for example, the formal religious schools run by holy men in temples and monasteries which have been a feature of most of the world's major religions, the explicitly vocational training associated with apprenticeships and the attachment of an individual to a particular "master," and those periods of specific training organized by individual tribes as a precursor to initiation into adulthood.

Despite their enormous diversity, however, such traditional forms of educational provision appear to have one feature in common—an acceptance of the process of learning as essentially unproblematic. It is only with the advent of formal educational provision on a mass scale, which is associated with the process of industrialization, that questions have arisen concerning how the necessary learning may most effectively and efficiently be provided.

1.1 Early Studies of Learning Potential

Interest in systematic inquiry into the delivery of education increased dramatically at the end of the nineteenth century and was associated with the very evident differences between individuals in their learning achievement. Such differences were for a long time linked to the search for a physiological explanation of mental capacity. This in turn gave rise to the field of psychometrics and the search for ways of measuring intellectual ability and performance.

When toward the middle of the twentieth century sociologists also began to turn their attention to the empirical study of education the very significant relationship between home background and educational achievement, which studies such as those of Floud et al. (1956), Douglas (1964), and Coleman et al. (1966) were able to document, made it impossible to view differences in student learning outcomes purely as a function of innate intellectual capacity. There followed a protracted debate between leading scholars as to the proportion of intellectual capacity which was genetically determined in the form of an inherited characteristic like eye or hair color and was thus immutable and the degree to which such capacity is a reflection of the environment—especially the social context—to which the individual is exposed which

helps or hinders the development of the intellect (see Husén 1975).

1.2 Social Class and Educational Achievement

The ramifications of the nature–nurture debate have been considerable. The evidence provided by a series of major sociological studies of education since the 1950s associated with, for example, Bernstein, Goldthorpe, and Halsey in the United Kingdom; Bourdieu and Establet in France; Jencks and Bowles and Gintis in the United States; and Connell in Australia has pointed to a powerful relationship between social class and educational achievement. It is clear from the mass of evidence that has been generated that "ability to learn," while being to some extent influenced by heredity, is strongly affected by circumstantial factors rooted in the cultural experiences to which an individual is subject. In addition to social class, it is now recognized that these circumstantial factors include ethnicity and gender which also exercise a strong influence on educational achievement.

1.3 Interactionist Perspectives

The early studies of social inequality in education were largely concerned to demonstrate the existence of a correlation between home background and educational outcomes. It was not until the 1970s that attempts to document how the correlation was actually produced achieved prominence in the rapid growth of interest in interactionist perspectives and associated microsociological studies of the details of educational processes. Although a number of theoretical traditions had long been established under the general umbrella of interactionist perspectives such as symbolic interaction, phenomenology, and ethnomethodology, in the 1970s these perspectives began to be used as the foundation for what could now properly be called a sociology of learning.

Detailed interactionist studies of learning as an interpersonal activity have revealed some of the dynamic factors that affect learning as realized in interaction. Such studies build on quantitative evidence concerning patterns of differential student learning outcomes—according to social groups based on class, race, gender, or geographic location as well as by institution—and seek to explain these in terms of the processes which lie behind such outcomes. By so doing they link the traditional interest of psychologists in individual perspectives and ability and in teaching and learning strategies with the important sociological perspective that a student's ability to respond to a given stimulus or situation is significantly affected by a variety of social factors. These factors include the more or less permanent influence of home background, race, and gender as well as the more ephemeral impact of the classroom, the quality of teaching, and peer group relations.

1.4 Social Theories of Learning

Haste (1987) provides a model of learning which relates these various influences. She identifies three domains of influence—the "intra-individual," the "interpersonal," and the "sociohistorical." The first of these concerns the way in which the individual assimilates experiences and constructs understanding; the second is the domain of social interaction in which meanings are negotiated and through which cultural norms and social conventions are learned; the third concerns the wider sociohistorical context in which learning takes place, its origins, and the circumstances of the learner. This is dealt with later in this entry.

1.4.1 The intra-individual.
One important contribution to the understanding of learning as a social process comes from the work of Vygotsky. Vygotsky emphasizes the central role of language in mediating the culture in which an individual lives by enabling them to make sense of their surroundings by the attribution of concepts and ideas drawn from that culture. Language is thus the mechanism individuals use to make sense of their world and to inform action. There is now a very considerable body of research that explores the relationship between language and the process of learning which is addressed elsewhere in this *Encyclopedia* (see also Barnes 1976).

Vygotsky introduced the concept of the Zone of Proximal Development (ZPD), which distinguishes between the learning which would have taken place given no outside help and the potential development associated with learning under adult guidance or with the support of more capable peers. As Tharp and Gallimore (1988) suggest, social interaction is a crucial part of this process since a deliberate intervention by a teacher or other adult can assist the learners by providing a scaffold for the learners to build across their ZPD.

Vygotsky's emphasis on the interrelatedness of thought, language, and culture as part of a perspective in which social interaction is seen as the central foundation for learning links to the second element in the model—the interpersonal.

1.4.2 The interpersonal.
The emphasis on learning as grounded in the assumption that people need to "make sense" of a given situation so that, through the attribution of meaning, they can incorporate new knowledge into their existing understanding has much in common with the symbolic interactionist perspective which the American social psychologist George Herbert Mead originally popularized in the 1930s. Both this approach and that of Vygotsky stress the crucial role of the individual's own perception of any particular situation and the actions that follow from their perception of the meaning of it. Mead argues that people act together on the basis of meanings which have been generated by their experiences in interac-

tion. These meanings become socially patterned and are sustained through cultures. The same process also produces a perception of oneself—a sense of personal identity which not only influences the way people interact with others, but also, crucially, influences their view of themselves as learners.

This emphasis on the relationship between the social context and student learning is in stark contrast to the concept of learning as a function of innate ability or what Bonniol (1991) refers to as "the old demon of innate IQ." It stresses the dynamic possibilities of any learning situation and thus the need to maximize those social factors which will produce a successful learning environment.

2. The Learning Environment

Most learning is likely to take place in one of three main areas of social life: the home, the school or workplace, or during leisure activities. In relation to each of these settings a number of key concepts may be distinguished which help to explain the nature and significance of the interaction that takes place. Within the fundamental distinction between structure and action, between external reality and the response which is the individual's interpretation of that reality, which characterizes all sociological analysis, influences on learning may be structured in terms of two main groups—the characteristics of the teaching provided and the factors that influence students' response.

2.1 Effective Teaching

A great deal of research has been devoted to identifying the qualities of effective teaching and teachers (Kyriacou 1986). Although significant communalities can be identified in this respect across many different countries (Fraser 1986), variations in the age of the learners and the educational setting, and cultural differences mean that there can be no one recipe for success in this respect. Knowledge of the matter to be taught and being well-organized are two of the variables which consistently appear. Beyond this, however, the emphasis is very much on interactional variables—being able to communicate effectively, being fair, treating learners with respect, having a sense of humor, being approachable. All these commonly identified factors reinforce once again the social nature of the teaching–learning process. In particular they emphasize that the teacher is of major importance in the quality of the opportunity to learn that is provided.

This accords with the social constructivist theory of learning outlined above, which suggests that the teacher needs to provide the means necessary for the learner to traverse the ZPD as effectively as possible by providing instruction and guidance that matches the individual learner's needs in terms of their existing understanding and skill. Teachers must also provide a social setting in which individuals have the confidence to engage in problem-solving activity and to ask the teacher questions, and are motivated to persevere in the face of difficulty.

2.2 The Impact of Evaluation

Evaluation skills are clearly crucial in all these respects. The research of Bennett et al. (1984) in primary schools emphasizes the importance of feedback that highlights what a learner can do to correct unsatisfactory results—a skill that many teachers in conventional classrooms find difficult because of the large numbers of students involved, their lack of knowledge of formative assessment techniques, and the objective constraints of expectations, time, and resources to which they are subject. It is perhaps for these reasons that Tharp and Gallimore find the kind of carefully targeted assistance that learners need to make effective progress is much more common in the one-to-one setting of the parent–child relationship in the home than in the average classroom where there is "too little time for interaction, conversation and joint activity among teacher and children" (1988 p. 80).

A detailed survey of research concerning the impact of evaluation on student learning which was undertaken by Crooks (1988) reinforces the importance of evaluative strategies, suggesting that feedback in the form of global grades or simply confirming correct answers has little effect on subsequent performance. In place of the vague, implicit, and incomplete criteria that teachers frequently use or an emphasis on neatness, conduct, or encouragement which diverts vital intellectual feedback, learners need clear and explicit performance criteria which detail what they are expected to do.

Crooks also highlights the importance of the role played by evaluation and feedback in promoting learning through the affective domain. Self-esteem has long been recognized by psychologists as a major influence on motivation and thus on learning, since students with high self-esteem are likely to try harder and persist longer in the face of difficulties. Of central interest to sociologists is the fact that a major determinant of self-esteem is feedback from significant others. Teachers' evaluations are crucial in this respect, particularly in the early years of schooling when learners are developing their self-image of themselves and of their identity as typically successful or unsuccessful learners.

2.3 Coping Strategies

The kind of one-to-one interactive situation between teacher and taught that often characterizes parent–child or master craftsman and apprentice learning situations makes it relatively easy both to "scaffold" the individual's intellectual progress and to provide the necessary affective conditions which will reinforce the learner's confidence and motivation. In the kind of classroom situation that characterizes most formal educational provision, however, a teacher typically has to deal with a large number of students simultaneously. In this situation a teacher's first priority is to control the class, to impose his or her definition of the situation so that the conditions can be created for some common learning activity to take place. Typically too, the teacher will be obliged to implement external directives concerning what is to be taught and often school-based, or external, policies as to how it should be taught. Limited in time for one-to-one interaction, in resources, and often in the necessary skills needed to diagnose the learning needs of individual students, teachers typically resort to a range of coping strategies which allow them to reconcile the conflicting demands that this kind of formal learning situation inevitably places upon them. Such coping strategies may involve ignoring nondisruptive lapses in discipline, initiating unequal amounts of interaction between more and less demanding pupils, and allowing a whole range of activities to take place which have as their primary function keeping the students occupied and quiet rather than the extension of their learning. Furthermore, given the interactional constraints of the typical classroom situation most teachers feel obliged to pitch their instruction at what they perceive to be the average level; alternatively they may categorize the students into groups according to perceived ability and provide them with differentiated learning tasks. Teachers are often aware of the disadvantages of all these strategies in terms of both students' intellectual progress and their self-concept but feel obliged to adopt these and many other similar compromises between the ideal and the practical if they are to cope with the range of expectations to which they are subject.

2.4 Stereotype Formation

A great deal of the impact of teachers on student learning is not deliberate or overt. Much is embedded in the quality of the routine interaction of the classroom and, in particular, in the process of categorization and, ultimately, stereotyping of individual students. Symbolic interactionist theory emphasizes the need for actors to be able to predict the likely outcome of any given action they may take in order that the desired goal of the action may be achieved. The necessary ability to make such predictions depends on a process of categorization of situations and of individuals according to a range of culturally determined criteria. How a teacher responds to a particular student is thus likely to depend on his or her expectations for that student built upon a range of background information, personal characteristics, and previous evaluations. Teachers' attitudes to and expectations of individual students will be expressed in their varying interactions with students so that individuals and the other members of a particular class quickly come to learn what the teacher thinks of them. Research has shown, for example, that teachers give different feedback to those for whom they have high or low aspirations.

How any one student reacts to this information is certainly influenced by a host of factors including the individual's existing self-image, aspirations, and attitude both to the particular teacher and to learning in general. To the extent that the student accepts a teacher's identification of them as "able," "dull," or "disruptive" and acts accordingly, the initial label will be reinforced and have a compounding effect on all subsequent interactions between that teacher and student. Typically, as a result of both written and verbal reports, impressions will be passed on from teacher to teacher so that the initial stereotype becomes progressively reinforced. It may also be further reinforced by the organizational arrangements of the school in which tracking or streaming provide a structural basis for the grouping together of students who are perceived to have similar learning characteristics. Having been publicly categorized in this way, not only will it be increasingly hard for students to resist accepting and acting upon the imputation of a particular identity, but this identity will tend to be related to preexisting stereotypes of student "types." Teacher actions based on such typification may well ignore important individual characteristics of the learner.

3. Social Differences and Learning

The above schematic account of the process of stereotype formation through interaction tends to imply that students start from an equal baseline, whereas it is now well-known from a wide variety of sociological research studies that this is not so. Structurally determined inequalities of race, class, and gender allow teachers to begin to categorize students almost as soon as they meet them and long before they can make any formal assessment of their intellectual performance. Classroom-based research has found that learners receive different types of feedback according to gender and ethnic group. For example, teachers typically give different kinds of feedback to boys and girls, allowing boys to explain their failure in terms of lack of effort whereas girls are led to attribute their failure to lack of ability. This latter tends to lead to an unwillingness to persist on the part of the learner, which has been termed "learned helplessness." A range of other studies have identified an independent effect of stereotyping operating against working-class children.

To suggest that the process of interaction between student and teacher exerts an independent effect on any individual student's capacity to learn is not to deny the very real differences in ability to profit from schooling and other forms of education and training with which students have been equipped by their previous experience. A substantial body of sociological research has shown that in many ways teachers are justified in expecting the middle-class child to be more "able" since the entire ethos of the school, having its origins in the

dominant culture, tends to reflect that culture in its values, its curriculum, its pedagogy, and its language. It is rather to argue that existing social inequalities are compounded by the differential expectations teachers have of their students. Research into the effects of both the independent and the combined effects of race and gender demonstrate the same tendency for inequalities which exist in the wider society to be reproduced in the process of schooling, not least through the powerful influence of teacher expectation as this influences classroom interaction.

3.1 Cultural Differences in Teacher Expectations

While teacher expectations undoubtedly operate as a powerful influence in all learning situations, there are important cultural differences which inform the nature of those expectations and hence their impact. In Japan, for example, where it has been the tradition in society as a whole to emphasize communality rather than individuality, both teachers and students are more likely to regard differences in educational achievement as a result of relative effort rather than of differences in initial ability and home background. The effect of this appears to be that teachers are able to sustain high expectations of a much greater number of students than in those countries where class and ethnic differential patterns of achievement are more in evidence (White 1987). It is perhaps for this reason that more Japanese students reach the higher levels of the education system than in many other industrialized countries.

Important differences in this respect can also be demonstrated even in near-neighbor countries like the United Kingdom and France. The strong belief in equality of opportunity and national homogeneity that has traditionally informed French education leads to considerably more uniform expectations of students than in the United Kingdom, where a deep-rooted philosophy of responding to the needs of individual learners has at times led to a lowering of teacher expectations and thus of student achievement (Osborn and Broadfoot 1992).

3.2 Cultural Differences in Learning Style

Cultural differences are also an important factor in the creation of successful learning environments. A number of studies have shown that different emphases in child-rearing patterns in terms of, for example, the value placed on students being articulate, or persevering, or docile will influence the kind of learning environment that best suits an individual learner. Comparing the learning behavior of United States and Japanese children, for example, Hess and Azuma (1991) were able to show marked differences, with United States children requiring significantly more regular positive reinforcement in terms of perceived success than their Japanese counterparts who had been socialized to value commitment to the task more than achieving a successful outcome.

Cultural differences such as these may well be intranational as well as international, that is, the product of ethnic or social class differences in cultural style within one country. If this is so, the effect is likely to be far more significant because it leads to the relative disadvantage of particular students who are faced with both uncongenial teaching strategies and the compounding effect of this expressed in negative teacher expectations as discussed above. Cultural differences also find expression in values as well as preferred modes of behavior. Extensive research by Raven in England, Scotland, and Ireland underlines the key role played by values in the motivation of students, leading him to argue that as part of the important task of "scaffolding" individual learning through the ZPD, teachers need to recognize that learners will function most effectively when they themselves value the goals they are striving to achieve (Raven 1991).

3.3 Sources of Cultural Differences

In place of the psychologists' emphasis on individual ability or personality characteristics as the major determinant of learning outcomes, sociological analyses of learning thus take student and teacher perspectives and their often differing attributions of meaning to a given social situation as the starting point for explaining differences in students' problem-solving behavior and hence, learning outcomes. The patterning of such interaction is on the basis of previous social experience. For teachers, the most significant elements in this respect are likely to be their own cultural background including their own experience as a student, their professional training, and their contact with dominant professional and institutional ideologies (Osborn and Broadfoot 1992). For students, their attribution of meaning within social settings, their values, and their preferred modes of behavior are initially, as has been seen, likely to be strongly influenced by ascriptive criteria of gender, race, and socioeconomic background. These variables are likely to influence the "scripts" chosen by individual learners as they come to a definition of their social identity. Classroom studies have shown how students' common cultural understandings, values, and aspirations lead them to adopt a particular "script"—norms of behavior which make the students identifiable as a group in terms of their actions. The relationship between structure and action which is embodied in the concept of "script," highlights the interrelationship of social class, race, and gender in the formation of individual social identities.

3.4 Student Subcultures

Sociologists use the term "subculture" to refer to groups which form on the basis of shared values and modes of social behavior. Although it is clear from the above that many subcultural groups found in schools and colleges are rooted in social experiences outside formal educational settings as a result of common ascribed characteristics such as race or gender or in shared cultural backgrounds, many subcultures are also formed in response to experiences within the process of education itself. The student who is constantly in receipt of negative evaluations either in response to behavior or lack of achievement is likely to try to protect his or her self-esteem by devaluing the goals of the institution and substituting an alternative set of values in which he or she can experience success. Such strategies are likely to be enhanced by the extent to which individuals can group together with other similarly disaffected students, producing the all-too-familiar reality of groups of recalcitrant students typically found in bottom streams. Earlier studies of how the structural organization of the school—notably the impact of streaming—influenced the creation of such subcultural identities have now been complemented by more interactionist accounts which document the creation of more or less enduring subcultures on the basis of the values students bring with them from the outside world. Particularly important in this respect is the influence of elements of youth subculture as this is represented in modes of dress, music, language, and leisure pursuits.

4. Conclusion

Sociological research concerning learning takes as its starting point the idea that learning is an interpersonal activity. The successful promotion of learning thus requires the teacher to be sensitive both to the intellectual needs of the learner and to the role played by the student's own self-image.

Research in the sociology of learning highlights the considerable range of social factors within the classroom, the school, the home, and the peer group which affect the process of learning. It provides insights into the organizational imperatives which determine many of the characteristic features of classroom interaction and thus of the extreme difficulties teachers face in seeking to respond appropriately within such learning contexts to students' individual and social differences. It leads to the conclusion that there is often a deep incompatibility between current forms of formal educational provision and the learning needs of students. The effect of this is that many students turn away from formal education without fulfilling their potential as learners.

See also: Socialization

References

Barnes D 1976 *From Communication to Curriculum.* Penguin Education, Harmondsworth
Bennett N, Desforges C, Cockburn A, Wilkinson B 1984 *The Quality of Pupil Learning Experiences.* Lawrence Erlbaum Associates, London
Bonniol J J 1991 The mechanism regulating the learning

process of pupils. In: Weston P (ed.) 1991 *Assessment of Pupil Achievement, Motivation and School Success*. Council of Europe/Swets and Zeitlinger, Amsterdam

Coleman J S et al. 1966 *Equality of Educational Opportunity*. US Government Printing Office, Washington, DC

Crooks T J 1988 The impact of classroom evaluation practices on students. *Rev. Educ. Res.* 58(4): 438–81

Douglas J W B 1964 *The Home and the School. A Study of Ability and Attainment in the Primary School*. MacGibbon and Kee, London

Floud J, Halsey A H, Martin F M 1956 *Social Class and Educational Opportunity*. Heinemann, London

Fraser B J 1986 *Classroom Environment*. Croom Helm, Sydney

Haste H 1987 Growing into rules. In: Bruner J, Haste H 1987 *Making Sense: The Child's Construction of the World*. Methuen, London

Hess R D, Azuma H 1991 Cultural support for schooling: Contrasts between Japan and the United States. *Educ. Researcher* 20(9): 2–9

Husén T 1975 *Social Influences on Educational Attainment*. Organisation for Economic Co-operation and Development, Paris

Kyriacou C 1986 *Effective Teaching in Schools*. Blackwell, Oxford

Osborn M, Broadfoot P M 1992 A lesson in progress? Primary classrooms observed in England and France. *Oxford Rev. Educ.* 18(1): 3–15

Raven J 1991 *The Tragic Illusion: Educational Testing*. Trillium Press, New York

Tharp R, Gallimore R 1988 *Rousing Minds to Life: Teaching, Learning and Schooling in a Social Context*. Cambridge University Press, Cambridge

White M 1987 *The Japanese Educational Challenge. A Commitment to Children*. The Free Press, New York

Further Reading

Bernstein B 1961 Social class and linguistic development: A theory of social learning. In: Halsey A H, Floud J, Anderson C A (eds.) 1961 *Education, Economy and Society*. The Free Press, New York

Bernstein B 1975 *Class, Codes and Control*, Vol. 3. Routledge and Kegan Paul, London

Bourdieu P 1964 *Les herétiers: Les étudiants et la culture*. Editions de Minuit, Paris

Cashdan A et al. 1972 *Language in Education. A Sourcebook*. Routledge and Kegan Paul, Boston, Massachusetts

Coleman J S 1961 *The Adolescent Society*. The Free Press, Glencoe

Goldthorpe J H 1980 *Social Mobility and Class Structure in Modern Britain*. Clarendon Press, Oxford

Leestma R, Walberg H J 1992 *Japanese Educational Productivity*. Center for Japanese Studies, University of Michigan, Ann Arbor, Michigan

Peer Relations and Learning

W. Damon

Children's communication with their peers has qualities that differ from the qualities of adult–child communication. For example, peer dialogues are usually more equal than conversations between adult and child: children usually listen more respectfully to adults than to peers for information and guidance. Such differences have serious implications for learning. Educators have become aware of these differences and have begun to design classroom strategies that best exploit the learning opportunities provided by both peer and adult–child relations. This entry discusses contemporary methods for applying the special features of children's peer relations to their academic learning.

1. Special Features of Peer Communication

In his work on moral judgment, Piaget introduced the notion that children live within "two social worlds," one of unilateral adult–child commands, the other of mutual peer cooperation (Piaget 1932). Developmental psychologists have elaborated this distinction further (Youniss 1980, Hartup 1985). Whereas adult–child interactions reflect a fundamental asymmetry of power and knowledge, peers interact on an equal footing. This means that adults usually direct and structure the agenda in their conversations with children, whereas children negotiate and "co-construct" the agendas of their peer encounters.

The asymmetry of adult–child interactions creates a context for learning with many advantages: it provides the best available means of transmitting the culture's accumulated store of knowledge and a respect for the existing order of things (Youniss 1980). This unilateral respect, however, may lead to certain cognitive imbalances, such as an uncritical acceptance of the adult word and an overreliance on imitation in the attempt to acquire new skills. Peer relations, in contrast, encourage children to try out new ideas in a relatively supportive and uncritical environment. They create a context for sharing intimate thoughts, for engaging in close collaborative work, for questioning the known, and for attempting the unknown. In terms of their value for children's learning, peer relations offer a context for support and discovery but are not as useful as a forum for imparting basic information, formulas, or skills (Damon and Phelps 1989).

2. Three Types of Peer Learning

Although peer relations are generally more equal than adult–child relations, not all peer engagements are strictly alike. Peer relations themselves can be unequal to various extents. There are three main types of peer learning that have been introduced into classrooms by educational researchers. These have been called "peer tutoring," "cooperative learning," and "peer collaboration" (Damon and Phelps 1989). As in the contrast between adult–child and peer relations, the three distinct forms of peer learning offer different strengths and weaknesses for the educator.

2.1 Cooperative Learning

Cooperative learning, also called "small group learning" or "group work," has been introduced into many schools because the available methods are relatively easy for teachers to adopt. The techniques can be integrated into the normal school day without disruptions in the regular classroom routine. Some cooperative learning programs require as little as an hour or two a week of classroom time.

There are a variety of cooperative learning techniques now in use. All begin by dividing classrooms into small "teams" of no more than four or five children. These teams are generally heterogeneous with respect to students' abilities. The teacher presents a task to the team, and the team sets out to master it. All cooperative learning methods rely on team solidarity and the motivation that it engenders. The assumption is that students will want to perform well for their team and that they will work for the success of their fellow team members and the team as a whole.

Some widely adopted versions of cooperative learning are Aronson's "jigsaw teaching," Sharan's "group investigation," and Slavin's "student teams-achievement divisions" (Slavin 1978). In jigsaw teaching, each member of a student team becomes an expert on one aspect of a larger topic. After studying that aspect in depth, the expert reports back to the team on what he or she has found. The team as a whole is taught by each "specialist" member in turn. In Sharan's method, team members plan and assign themselves specialized roles and prepare detailed reports for each other's edification. Group discussion of the reports is encouraged. Slavin's method establishes competition between opposing teams. It encourages team members to share work and information with one another so that they will perform individually better than members of other teams on quizzes derived from the learning exercises.

Cooperative learning methods vary in the extent to which they encourage individual versus collective activity in the learning groups. In the jigsaw version, team members assume different roles while they are learning about the task. Only then do the team members share the results of their individual work with the rest of the team. In Slavin's version, the team works together to prepare for individual tests or performances that will be given later. Some versions, in contrast, encourage joint planning and discussion throughout the exercise.

Cooperative learning methods also vary in the extent to which they rely on competition between teams as a motivator. Many techniques extrinsically reward strong team performances in order to spur children's interest in the tasks. Rewards are usually allocated on the basis of scores on tests given after the exercise. The explicit message to the team is that they will jointly benefit by beating other teams only if they ensure that all team members master the task. Other cooperative learning approaches spurn this competitive component and rely on intrinsic motivation to engage the learning groups in the exercise.

2.2 Peer Tutoring

In this approach, a child trains another child in skills and subject matter that the first child has mastered. Because the first child has greater information or competence than the second child, the two do not begin the relationship with equal status: rather, the first child is considered an expert and the second child a relative novice. Moreover, the unequal status of the two children is often compounded by other factors as well. Most attempts at peer tutoring pair an older child with a younger child, or a bright child with an educationally disadvantaged one. Peer tutoring, in fact, is often called "cross-age" tutoring, since the tutor is usually two or more years older than the tutee.

Peer tutoring occupies an instructional ground somewhere between adult–child and true peer communication. Like adult–child instruction, peer tutoring is based upon a transmission-of-knowledge model. This model assumes that one party knows the answers and must communicate them to the other party. Knowledge is "passed down" from person to person in a linear fashion rather than co-constructed by persons who are both seeking answers. Unlike adult–child instruction, however, in peer tutoring the expert party is not very far removed from the novice party in authority or knowledge; nor has the expert any special claims to teaching competence. Such differences affect the nature of discourse between tutor and tutee because they place the tutee in less of a passive role than does the adult–child instructional relation. Being closer in knowledge and status, the tutee in a peer relation feels freer to express opinions, ask questions, and risk untested solutions. The interaction between instructor and pupil is more balanced and more lively when the the tutor is a peer (Damon and Phelps 1989).

A theoretical grounding for peer tutoring can be found in L S Vygotsky's idea of the "zone of proximal development." Vygotsky wrote that problem-solving in collaboration with more capable peers could enable children to enter into new areas of potential (Vygotsky 1978). These new areas, which Vygotsky called the "leading edge" of children's intellectual growth, constitute the zone of proximal development; it is created when a child interacts with a more experienced mentor. Because the mentor guides the direction of the interaction in intellectually productive ways, the child's intellectual performance during the interaction surpasses anything that the child has been able to do outside of the interaction. In the course of such experiences, the child retains the ability to reproduce these jointly produced intellectual performances autonomously. When this happens, the achievement becomes part of the child's actual capabilities rather than merely a potential skill that can be realized only through interaction. In this sense, the insights and competencies become internalized. Vygotsky argues that it is not only information that is internalized, but also fundamental cognitive processes that are implicit in the communications. Accordingly, both parties in the communication stand to benefit. The tutee profits from the very acts of questioning, challenging, and providing feedback to the tutor. The tutor profits from the act of reformulating knowledge for transmittal to the tutee, from answering the tutee's questions, and from responding to the tutee's challenges. This is what is meant by the old axiom that one never really knows a subject until one tries to teach it.

When two children enter into a peer-tutoring relationship, they become exposed to new patterns of thought. This is because any peer dialogue is a cooperative, consensual, and nonauthoritarian exchange of ideas. As such, it relies on rationality for its maintenance and emulates several key features of critical thinking. In particular, beliefs must be justified and verified rather than merely asserted by force of mandate. This requires significant intellectual effort for both parties. It calls for skill in symbolically representing ideas as well as the ability to notice and resolve logical contradictions. These are central areas of cognitive competence, areas in which children at all levels and ages have room for improvement.

Of the three types of peer learning, it was peer tutoring that first made inroads into actual school settings. In the 1970s, a number of educators experimented with peer tutoring as an alternative form of instruction. Generally they found it to be effective in stimulating the educational progress of both tutor and tutee (Gartner et al. 1971).

From these and subsequent research programs, the following picture has emerged. Peer tutoring, when carried out over a substantial period of time with carefully trained and supervised tutors, is educationally valuable for its participants. It is also surprisingly cost-effective when compared with other instructional techniques. When done well, it can aid children's acquisition of both verbal and quantitative skills as well as substantive curriculum topics such as history, physics, and social studies. Finally, peer tutoring can also yield personal benefits for both tutor and tutee. Children's self-esteem, educational motivation, school adjustment, and altruistic inclinations all improve in the course of peer tutoring.

2.3 Peer Collaboration

In peer collaboration, a pair of novices work together to solve difficult tasks. This method differs from peer tutoring because the children begin at roughly the same levels of competence. It also differs from cooperative learning, because children work jointly on the same problem rather than individually on separate components of the problem. In actual practice, however, peer collaboration bears some resemblance to other types of peer learning. Even in peer collaboration, one child may assume the lead spontaneously; and the collaborators may separate for independent work.

Peer collaboration encourages children to communicate about strategies and solutions. It simulates the challenge of discovery learning, but places this challenge in a context of peer assistance and support. Like discovery learning, its promise lies in provoking deep conceptual insights and basic developmental shifts on the part of its participants. This is because it encourages experimentation with new and untested ideas and demands a critical reexamination of old assumptions. However, unlike discovery learning done alone, the child does not feel like an isolated incompetent. Rather, peer collaboration provides a sympathetic forum for the creative risk-taking that discovery learning can provoke. As the child works with a fellow novice, the insufficiencies in his or her own knowledge become less discouraging and the unknown becomes less forbidding.

As an educational intervention method, peer collaboration originally emerged from Piagetian studies in Europe and the United States. The studies focused on spatial and physical conversations, notions that had proven resistant to training through standard instructional techniques. Among the innovative experimental methods that developmentalists tried was asking children to work jointly with peers. The strategy of placing novices together on a difficult task and expecting them to come up with a productive approach initially seemed so odd that articles had such titles as "When two wrongs make a right" (Ames and Murray 1982). But peer collaboration proved to be the most consistently effective means of helping children acquire conversation and the basic reasoning skills underlying it.

The dominant rationale for the strategy of teaming novices together has been the Genevan construct of "sociocognitive conflict" (Doise and Mugny 1984).

The idea is that social interactions between peers will lead to disagreements that present the participants with both a social and a cognitive conflict. Such conflicts lead children to a number of important realizations. First, they become aware that there are points of view other than their own. Second, they reexamine their own points of view and reassess their validity. Third, they learn that they must justify their own opinions and communicate them thoroughly if others are to accept them as valid.

In this way, children benefit both cognitively and socially from peer collaboration. The social benefits include their improved communication skills and their sharper sense of other persons' perspectives. The cognitive benefits derive from their forced reexamination of their own conceptions under the guidance of a peer's feedback. Piaget believed that these social and cognitive benefits were directly related in that improved social communication instigates progressive change. When people feel the need to explain and justify their beliefs to others, they realize that these beliefs must be rationalized as fully as possible. This sense of "social responsibility" in communication ultimately leads to improvements in the logical quality of one's reasoning. The Genevan explanation of peer collaboration, therefore, posits a clash of ideas that triggers a need to reexamine, rework, and justify one's understanding of the world.

Some questions have been raised about whether the notion of conflict alone is sufficient to account for the learning that follows from experiences of peer collaboration. There is increasing theoretical emphasis on the constructive or "coconstructive" aspects of peer collaboration. In this view, children learn through peer interaction because it introduces them to the possibilities of cooperative activity (Youniss 1980, Krappman 1992). In a truly cooperative effort, children devise plans together, share ideas, and mutually validate one another's initiatives. Not only is this a powerful procedure for generating new insights, it also yields solutions that are superior to those arrived at by an individual in isolation (Damon and Phelps 1989, Krappman 1992).

Unfortunately there have been very few studies that have attempted to identify the peer interaction processes leading to progressive change. This requires lengthy and complex videotape analyses of the sort not always available in experimental studies. The initial studies favor the co-construction process model over the sociocognitive conflict one.

In these initial studies, children who disagree with one another the most seem the least likely to progress, whereas children who accept one another's views and work positively with them are the most likely to change (Damon and Killen 1982, Damon and Phelps 1989). Constructive rather than conflictual interaction was clearly the key facilitator. Another analysis of children's peer interactions during task engagement found such interactions to be heavily loaded with

"transactive" activity (Kruger and Tomasello 1986). Such activity is a constructive and compromising form of social discourse especially suited for joint exploration into unknown areas of thought.

Finally, a study of children's helping behavior with peers found that peer interactions indeed can provide a unique context for learning many important intellectual skills, provided that such interactions are well-balanced and mutual. The author concluded: "These collaborative efforts of peers, mostly friends, presented almost the only situations in which we found the capacities that the educational system promises to promote—exploration of different aspects of a problem, change of perspectives, experimentation with ideas, reconstruction of failed processes, analyses of mistakes, verification of the indubitable, search for criteria of good solutions—co-constructively developed and jointly applied" (Krappman 1992 p. 179).

Despite its promise, peer collaboration has been used less frequently in educational programs than have the other two forms of peer learning. This is probably because peer collaboration as a technique has its roots in experimental developmental psychology rather than in educational research. As yet, there are no systematic curricula designed around principles of peer collaboration. Still, some promising initial attempts have been made to apply techniques from developmental research on peer relations to actual educational settings (Damon and Phelps 1989, Krappman 1992).

3. Conclusion

During the 1970s and 1980s, educators have made increasing use of children's peer relations in the classroom. Because communication within a peer relation tends to be egalitarian, reciprocal, and lively, it offers a context of intellectual stimulation and social support for children's learning. Although peer learning cannot substitute for adult instruction, it can supplement it in unique ways.

Peer collaboration is perhaps the most promising method of promoting basic conceptual development in children, but there is still much to learn about its nature and its potential. In particular, under what interactional conditions does peer collaboration flourish? To what extent does sociocognitive conflict describe these conditions? To what extent do ideas such as "coconstruction" and "transaction" best describe them? What are the limits of peer collaboration in relation to other forms of peer learning, and what are its special strengths? How may peer collaboration be integrated with the other peer learning approaches?

References

Ames G, Murray F B 1982 When two wrongs make a right: Promoting cognitive change through social conflict. *Dev. Psychol.* 18(6): 894–97

Damon W, Killen M 1982 Peer interaction and the process

of change in children's moral reasoning. *Merrill-Palmer Q*. 28(3): 347–67

Damon W, Phelps E 1989 Critical distinctions among three approaches to peer education. *Int. J. Educ. Res.* 13(1): 9–19

Doise W, Mugny G 1984 *The Social Development of the Intellect.* Pergamon Press, New York

Gartner A, Kohler W, Riessman F 1971 *Children Teaching Children: Learning by Teaching.* Harper & Row, New York

Hartup W W 1985 Relationships and their significance in cognitive development. In: Hinde R A, Perret-Clermont A, Stevenson-Hinde J (eds.) 1985 *Social Relationships and Cognitive Development.* Oxford University Press, Oxford

Krappman L 1992 On the social embedding of learning processes in the classroom. In: Oser F, Dick A, Patry J-L (eds.) 1992 *Effective and Responsible Teaching.* Jossey-Bass, San Francisco, California

Kruger A C, Tomasello M 1986 Transactive discussions with peers and adults. *Dev. Psychol.* 22(5): 681–85

Piaget J 1932 *The Moral Judgment of the Child.* Free Press, New York

Slavin R 1978 Student teams and comparison among equals: Effects on academic performance and student attitudes. *J. Educ. Psychol.* 70(4): 532–38

Vygotsky L S 1978 *Mind in Society: The Development of Higher Psychological Processes.* Harvard University Press, Cambridge, Massachusetts

Youniss J 1980 *Parents and Peers in Social Development: A Sullivan–Piaget Perspective.* University of Chicago Press, Chicago, Illinois

Further Reading

Damon W 1990 Social relations and children's thinking skills. In: Kuhn D (ed.) 1990 *Developmental Perspectives on Teaching and Learning Thinking Skills.* Karger, Basel

Perret-Clermont A-N 1980 *Social Interaction and Cognitive Development in Children.* Academic Press, New York

Personality, School, and Social Environment as Learning Determinants

H. J. Walberg

In the domains of personality, school, and social environments three sets of psychological variables may be divided into nine factors that have shown powerful and consistent influences on affective, behavioral, and cognitive learning in research on schooling. These variables are as follows: (a) in the personality domain, student aptitude includes (i) ability or prior achievement as indexed by tests prior to learning, (ii) development as indexed by chronological age or stage of maturation, and (iii) motivation or self-concept as indicated by questionnaire or personality tests or the student's willingness to persevere intensively on learning tasks; (b) within the school domain, instruction includes (iv) the amount of time students engage in learning, and (v) the quality or appropriateness of the instructional experience including psychological and curricular aspects; (c) within the social environment are (vi) the home environment or psychological support and academic stimulation provided by parents, (vii) classroom climate or educationally constructive morale of the classroom group, (viii) peer group or educational encouragement by students of one another outside school, and (ix) mass media, particularly minimum leisure-time television viewing.

constructive roles. Through various research methods in laboratories and classrooms, psychologists have demonstrated factors that lead to important differences in learner outcomes. Their findings have been used by policymakers and practicing educators to improve the effectiveness and efficiency of curricula, instruction, and other aspects of school programs.

Because of their usual research approach, however, psychologists have sometimes overemphasized one, two, or several methods or solutions. This has encouraged a partisan, narrow, or short-sighted perspective on the improvement of learning. Psychology can learn from its fellow disciplines anthropology, economics, and sociology about the multiple determinants of human behavior—and especially about learning. Educational psychologists, for example, have focused on personality and school determinants of learning, but other social or cultural factors are enormously influential, since students through age 18 spend only about 13 percent of their waking hours in school (Walberg 1984). Therefore, environments in which children spend their time—the family, peer group, and mass media—require consideration and possible changes in policies and practices.

1. Disciplinary Approaches to Education

The chief task of education is to promote learning. In identifying and constructively altering its determinants, psychology has played influential and

2. Research Approaches

In the promotion of learning, psychology and the social sciences are potentially complementary. In-

611

structional psychologists, for example, have typically employed randomization in the experimental study of educational methods to isolate the effects of a single factor at a time. To illustrate: contrasting groups of students might be assigned to a new and a conventional teaching method with a flip of a coin to compare their respective effects in promoting learning gains. Deriving from agricultural and medical field trials, the experimental approach yields relatively confident inferences about the causal efficacy of methods, since differences in groups are attributable to differences in methods and calculable chance factors.

In quasi-experimental methods, groups that happened to have used different methods are compared, but many pre-existing differences in students, teachers, or conditions rather than the methods may have caused the differences. Statistical adjustments such as covariance analysis may be made to compensate for such differences, but such adjustments may be not be completely convincing.

Though intensive experiments (and, to some extent, quasi-experiments) are strong on causality, their effects may be attributable to novelty or the enthusiasm of students and teachers for new methods, which might not be sustained. In addition, few experiments are national or international in scope; most analyze only one or two of the factors and sample limited grade-levels and demographic groups within a local community. They are often strong on observational technique, measurement, verification, and random assignment to treatments—in short, they are strong on internal validity, but are often weak on generalizability or on external validity since they do not rigorously sample from large, well-defined populations (Cook and Campbell 1979).

Survey research, which is often employed by economists and sociologists has complementary strengths and weaknesses: it gathers information from ordinary or natural rather than contrived conditions. It often draws large, stratified, random samples of national or even international populations and it frequently measures more factors while sacrificing internal validity, since the factors are usually measured cross-sectionally (and perhaps superficially because they measure only a few items). Survey research can statistically control to some extent for multiple causes; other things being equal, it can be as convincing as quasi-experiments controlled only for one or two covariates.

3. Research Findings

The complementarity of intensive and extensive studies, however, is important. In principle, consistent, powerful effects should consistently emerge from either form of research as well as from case studies. Robust findings give a more reliable basis for educational policy and practice. In fact, approximately 120 syntheses of about 8,000 intensive studies support the consistent effects or correlations of the nine "productivity factors" or their more specific aspects (Walberg 1984, Fraser et al. 1987, Walberg 1991). In addition, a synthesis of nine regression studies of extensive survey data on 15,802 13- and 17-year old students tested in mathematics, science, social studies, and reading by the American National Assessment of Educational Achievement supports these findings (Walberg 1986). Although the correlations of the factors with achievement and subject-matter interest as learning outcomes varied from −0.45 to +0.68, 83 (or 91 %) of the 91 correlations were in the expected direction. Moreover, when the factors were controlled for one another in multiple regressions, 58 (or 91 %) of the 64 coefficients were signed as expected.

Although the magnitudes of the correlations depend slightly on the type of learning outcome (achievement or attitude), subject matter, and productivity factor, they average +0.19 and most range between +0.05 and +0.40. The regression weights were fairly uniform (nonsignificantly different) across age, subject matter, type of outcome, and productivity factor. The results also revealed collinearity among the factors: students advantaged on one also tend to be advantaged on the others. The results suggest further that no single factor is dominant in determining learning outcomes (although ability or prior achievement might have been if socioeconomic status and grades had not been frequently used as a proxy for this factor).

Paschal and Stariha (1992) compiled the results of further analyses of other data sets including the following national samples from the United States High School and Beyond; the Scholastic Achievement Tests; School Health Educational Evaluation; and the Study of Mathematically Precocious Youth. Another large survey included was the mathematics study of primary and secondary students in 12 countries carried out by the International Association for the Evaluation of Educational Achievement. Also included were several smaller, localized surveys: Chicago preschoolers, Brazilian 12-year olds, and community college students. Paschal and Starhia summarized the results of 23 studies of about 250,000 students in six subjects of study. Of the 341 regression weights, 303 or 88.8 percent were in the hypothesized directions.

4. Educational Theory

The first five factors of student aptitude and instruction (shown in Table 1) are prominent in the educational models of Benjamin S Bloom, Jerome Bruner, John B Carroll, Robert Glaser, and others (see Haertel et al. 1983, for a comparative analysis). Each factor appears to be necessary for learning in school; without at least a small amount of each, the student can learn little. Large amounts of instruction and high

Table 1
Nine educational productivity factors

Student aptitude	*Ability*, or preferably prior achievement, as measured by the usual learning tests
	Development, as indexed by chronological age or stage of maturation
	Motivation, or self-concept, as indicated by personality tests or the student's willingness to persevere intensively on learning tasks
Instruction	*Amount* of time students engage in learning
	Quality of the instructional experience, including method (psychological) and curricular (content) aspects
Psychological environments	*"Curriculum of the home"*
	Morale, or climate of the classroom social group
	Peer group outside school
	Television (minimum leisure-time viewing)

degrees of ability, for example, may count for little if students are unmotivated or instruction is unsuitable. These five essential factors, however, are only partly alterable by educators. For example, the curriculum in terms of lengths of time devoted to various subjects and activities is partly determined by diverse economic, political, and social forces. Ability and motivation, moreover, are influenced by parents, by prior learning, and by the students themselves. Thus educators are unlikely to raise achievement substantially by their own efforts alone.

The remaining factors (the psychological climate of the classroom group; the enduring affection and academic stimulation from adults at home; and an out-of-school peer group with learning interests, goals, and activities) influence learning in two ways: students learn from them directly, and these factors indirectly benefit learning by raising student ability, motivation, and responsiveness to instruction. In addition, about 10 weekly hours of television viewing (not the more typical greater number in the US) seem optimal for learning, perhaps because more television time displaces homework and other educationally and developmentally constructive activities outside school.

The major causal influences flow from aptitudes, instruction, and the psychological environment to learning. In addition, however, these factors also influence one another, and are also influenced in turn by how much students learn, since those who begin well learn faster (Walberg 1984).

The first five essential factors may substitute, compensate, or trade-off for one another at diminishing rates of return. Immense quantities of time, for example, may be required for a moderate amount of learning if motivation, ability, or instructional quality is minimal. Thus, no single essential factor overwhelms the others; all appear important.

Although the other factors are consistent statistically controlled or experimentally demonstrated influences of academic learning, they may directly supplement as well as indirectly influence the essential classroom factors. In either case, the powerful influence of out-of-school factors, especially the home environment, must be considered.

5. Reductionistic Challenges

Just as biology, chemistry, and medicine can be partly reduced to physics, so the theory of educational productivity is reductionistic: it assumes that academic learning is a fundamentally psychological activity that takes place mainly in the social context of the classroom group as well as in the settings of the home, mass media, and peer group. Within its purview, school and community economic, political, and sociological conditions are less relevant to learning because their influences are less alterable, direct, and observable. They are not substitutes for the nine factors, but more distant forces that can support or interfere with them.

More and less productive classes, moreover, may be expected in the same school. It is misleading to characterize a whole school, community, or nation as effective, just as it is less than accurate to characterize an optimal condition for plant growth as the average annual rate of rainfall in a state or farm rather than the amount of water that must reach the roots of a single plant in a given time period. The educational productivity theory is oversimplified because learning is clearly affected by school and community characteristics as well as by many economic, sociological, and political forces at school, community, state, and national levels. An analysis of 228 such factors in 179 reviews of research shows their relative influence (Wang et al. 1990). Yet these characteristics and forces (such as the sex, ethnicity, and socioeconomic status of the student, the size and expenditure levels of schools and districts, and their political and sociological organization) are less alterable in democratic, pluralistic societies. They are less consistently and powerfully linked to learning and appear to operate mainly through the nine factors in the determination of achievement. Thus, the theory is offered not as a threat to those who see the efficacy of other factors but as a collegial invitation to demonstrate their effects on the nine factors or directly on the outcomes of schooling.

6. Magnitudes of Effects and Correlations

Tables 2–4 show the numerical results of quantita-

Table 2
Influences of aptitudes on learning

Aptitude	Correlation	Size[a]
Ability		
IQ	.71	× × × × × × ×
IQ (science)	.48	× × × × ×
Development		
Piagetian stage	.47	× × × × ×
Piagetian stage (science)	.40	× × × ×
Motivation		
Motivation	.34	× × ×
Self-concept	.18	× ×

a The × symbols represent the sizes of the correlation coefficients in numbers of tenths

Table 4
Home, peer, class morale, and media effects on learning

Method	Effect	Size[a]
Graded homework	.79	× × × × × × × ×
Class morale	.60	× × × × × ×
Home interventions	.50	× × × × ×
Home environment	.37	× × × ×
Assigned homework	.28	× × ×
Socioeconic status	.25	× × ×
Peer group	.24	× ×
Television	−.05	×.

a The × symbols represent the sizes of effects in tenths of standard deviations or correlations

tive syntheses (or meta-analyses) of the productivity effects in about 3,000 studies of academic learning conducted from about 1950 through 1980. These may be considered first-order estimates of the magnitudes of the effects and influences of specific manifestations of the nine factors. The tables contain both effects and correlations, and the correlations assume a one-standard deviation rise in the independent variable. On the basis of the burgeoning literature synthesizing effects, Fraser et al. (1987) compiled similar magnitude estimates, which were further updated and summarized (Walberg 1991).

Table 3
Instructional quality and time effects on learning

Method	Effect	Size[a]
Reinforcement	1.17	× × × × × × × × × × × ×
Acceleration	1.00	× × × × × × × × × ×
Reading training	.97	× × × × × × × × × ×
Cues and feedback	.97	× × × × × × × × × ×
Science mastery	.81	× × × × × × × ×
Cooperative programs	.76	× × × × × × × ×
Reading experiments	.60	× × × × × ×
Personalized instruction	.57	× × × × × ×
Adaptive instruction	.45	× × × × ×
Tutoring	.40	× × × ×
Individualized science	.35	× × × ×
Higher-order questions	.34	× × ×
Diagnostic prescription	.33	× × ×
Individualized instruction	.32	× × ×
Individualized mathematics	.32	× × ×
New science curricula	.31	× × ×
Teacher expectation	.28	× × ×
Computer assisted instruction	.24	× ×
Sequenced lessons	.24	× ×
Advanced organizers	.23	× ×
New mathematics curricula	.18	× ×
Inquiry biology	.16	× ×
Homogenous groups	.10	×
Programmed instruction	−.03	−.
Class size	−.09	−×.
Mainstreaming	−.12	−×.
Instructional Time	.38	.× × × ×

a The × symbols represent the sizes of effects in tenths of standard deviations

7. Conclusion

Synthesis of educational and psychological research in ordinary schools shows that improving the amount and quality of instruction can result in vastly more effective and efficient academic learning. Educators can do even more by also enlisting families as partners and by engaging them directly and indirectly in their efforts. Peer groups and exposure to mass media outside school also have important influences on academic learning. They might also be constructively altered in the interest of increased learning.

This entry's overview of a vast amount of research cannot substitute for selective reading of about 120 quantitative syntheses, nearly 200 research reviews, and the roughly 8,000 original studies conducted since the 1940s. Since many details have of necessity been omitted from the present account, reading the original material might promote a more complete and critical understanding of specific factors and methods. For example, although the factors that have large effects are robustly positive, exceptional conditions can reduce their effectiveness. In addition, more syntheses and replications of those already conducted as well as new empirical tests are needed.

See also: Abilities and Aptitudes; Human Development, Learning and Instruction; Teachers' Expectations; Home Environment and School Learning; Intelligence, Learning, and Instruction; Motivation and Learning; Peer Relations and Learning; Prior Knowledge and Learning

References

Cook T D, Campbell D T 1979 *Quasi-Experimentation: Design and Analysis Issues for Field settings*. Rand-McNally, Chicago, Illinois

Fraser B J, Walberg H J, Welch W W, Hattie J A 1987 Syntheses of educational productivity research. *Int. J. Educ. Res.* 11(2): 73–145

Haertel G D, Walberg H J, Weinstein T 1983 Psychological models of educational performance: A theoretical synthesis of constructs. *Rev. Educ. Res.* 53: 75–92

Paschal R A, Stariha W E 1992 Educational productivity studies: A quantitative synthesis. In: Waxman H C (ed.) 1992 *Study of Learning Environments Monographs*, Vol. 5. Curtin University Centre on Science Education, Perth

Walberg H J 1984 Improving the productivity of America's schools. *Educ. Leadership* 41(8): 19–30

Walberg H J 1986 Synthesis of research on teaching. In: Wittrock M C (ed.) 1986 *Handbook of Research on Teaching*. Project of the American Educational Research Association. Macmillan, New York

Walberg H J 1991 Productive teaching and instruction: Assessing the knowledge base. In: Waxman H C, Walberg H J (eds.) 1991

Wang M C, Haertel G D, Walberg H J 1990 What influences learning? A content analysis of review literature. *J. Educ. Res.* 84: 30–43

Further Reading

Walberg H J (ed.) 1979 *Educational Environments and Effects: Evaluation, Policy, and Productivity*. McCutchan, Berkeley, California

Waxman H C, Walberg H J (eds.) 1991 *Effective Teaching: Current Research*. McCutchan, Berkeley, California

Social and Communication Skills

C. Pontecorvo

Social skills enable an individual to initiate and maintain contacts and relationships with other people and to cooperate effectively with them. Communication skills allow an effective exchange of information with others and are closely linked to language acquisition. They are also the main tools for social development and for understanding social reality.

1. Definition of Social and Communication Skills

Looking at social and communication skills from the perspective of instructional psychology means paying attention to the ways in which those skills can be practiced and developed through intervention at school. Three points need to be clarified: (a) From what age does school influence begin? (b) To what extent have

social and communication skills already developed in children before they enter the school system? (c) Is social and communicative development common and generalized, and to what degree is it subject to individual and cultural variability?

The first two questions can be answered together. Educational intervention begins with nursery and kindergarten services, before the beginning of compulsory education. Moreover, the period from 2 to 5 years of age is particularly important for the acquisition of social and communication skills, although essential parts of this development are established during the second year of life. As regards the third question, individual and cultural variability are important aspects to be taken into account from an educational point of view; however, a distinction should be made between universal and specific capabilities.

Social and communicative skills have strong mutual links. Communicative activities start as intersubjective and dialogic processes (Rogoff 1989): a positive social experience within a steady relationship is a crucial factor for their development. Intentional communication depends on the caregiver attributing intentions to the signal movements and expressive acts of young infants and attuning his or her discourse to the child's growing abilities. Communication does not mean "making common" of something that was previously the possession of only one party, or transmission from one to another. Communicating corresponds to the production of shared meanings through effective interactions in recurrent contexts.

Social skills are interactive skills involving increasing knowledge of contexts and the ability to infer the intentions and motives of other participants. Thus communication skills are the main tool for social development and for structuring social reality. Children learn to interact with others and to establish social relationships by grounding their actions on an early understanding of the surrounding social world (Dunn 1988).

A terminological clarification is needed. In this entry "acquisition" is used when referring to broader phenomena in which biological, developmental, and cultural aspects are implied. "Learning" is used for specific social and communicative skills affected by environmental factors.

2. The Acquisition of Social Skills

The word "social" has at least two important different meanings which are interrelated. It can refer to interpersonal and face-to-face relationships. Because these relationships are always embedded within a culture, "social" can also refer to the particular social values that characterize a culture: "Interactions and relationships are affected also by the norms and values of the participants—norms and values which are in part created, transmitted, and transmuted through the agency of dyadic relationships" (Hinde et al. 1986 p. XV).

A sociocultural system of institutions and beliefs affects the social behavior of individuals and introduces elements of variability according to what is considered good for becoming a member of the group.

All children (and also most primates) grow up in a family, interacting first with one or two parents, and then with siblings, relatives, and friends. "Social cognition" must therefore be examined. This includes discovering the existence and the individuality of other persons, considering them as independent centers of thinking, emotions, causality, threats, and so on. In order to be able to establish good relationships with others and to become a person, a child develops, mainly before the third year, a "social understanding" which means "powers of recognizing and sharing

emotional states, of interpreting and anticipating others' reactions, of understanding the relationships between others, of comprehending the sanctions, prohibitions, and accepted practices of their world" (Dunn 1988 p. 5).

Since social skills concern both behavior and knowledge of social rules and values, it is important to understand how children progressively succeed in developing working "theories" about others' actions and intentions. This knowledge is, from a very early age, organized around scripts. A script is an event structure with spatial and temporal features and includes plans, actions, and outcomes. Early scripts are simple and even stereotyped. They develop through frequent repetitions of the same actions and help the acquisition of rule-based knowledge and behavior.

Given that scripts are one of the first forms of conceptual organization, they establish an important link between social and cognitive development. While Piagetian theory has stressed the need for developmental changes in cognitive operations in order to explain changes in children's social judgments, the early development of scriptal knowledge, which is mainly socially based, shows the priority of social settings and contents for children's cognitive development.

Early interaction with caregivers, siblings, relatives, and peers is the main context for the development of social skills. This interaction provides different settings for empathetic and cooperative behavior with peers and adults, opportunity for disputes and arguments, participation in family conversation and in pretend play.

Since social experience is a major factor underlying social development, attention has been paid to the "social-life phases" (Higgins and Parsons 1983), conceived as systematic variations that occur in children's lives such as changes in surrounding socialization agents. These phases correspond to qualitative changes occurring in the social life of children and involve specific social concerns, activities, settings, expectations, and rules for behavior. Entry into elementary school greatly increases children's exposure to different peers and socialization agents, as well as their individual freedom and responsibility. Socialization practices can also vary greatly within the same society as a function of ethnic background, social class, ideology, gender; cooperation and competition are very differently valued in different subcultures.

3. The Acquisition of Communication Skills

During the 1980s a change occurred in the conception of the relationship between communication and language development. Language was no longer presented as an idealized system of syntactic rules but as a complex system of communication. Its first basis is found in children's early communicative interactions, which are mainly prelinguistic. Babies are highly sociable creatures who share a communicative framework of gestures and signals with others: an infant's principal "tool" for achieving its ends is another person (Bruner 1985). Bruner has also shown that infants know a great deal about the cultural conditions for requesting a long time before they learn how to use the grammatical inversion rule for framing a question. Communication settings and interactive processes are now considered to be very important by researchers who challenge the idea that there are strong innate mechanisms in children's language development. Great importance is attributed to the interactive context in which children grow and to the cognitive factors that serve as prerequisites to language development. Context is no longer regarded as a simple elicitor of an innate mechanism. Adults create controlled and facilitating settings for language learning by using a great deal of repetition, a high pitch of voice, and lexical and syntactic simplifications, in order to have children make sense of shared activity. Study of modes of early communication has oriented the understanding of the acquisition of communicative skills in later social-life phases and in new educational contexts.

Research has also examined how children learn to communicate effectively with others once they have acquired the main structures of language. Young children are context-sensitive: their cognitive performance is determined by what they think others want from them. Consequently, most of their answers in typical Piagetian tasks (such as conservation ones) are now interpreted as a function of their being highly sensitive to different aspects of the social and communication setting (Perret-Clermont et al. 1991). Another idea is that children use and develop their communication skills in order to make sense of their environment. This environment is much more social and cultural than physical. Other persons contribute to the communicative development of the child by providing models, support, and cooperation.

There are two main research traditions regarding the acquisition of communication skills in children when school becomes a dominant socialization agent. The experimental tradition, starting from Piaget's early research, is focused on referential communication in artificial tasks. In referential communication a person wants another person to understand unambiguously what he or she is referring to. While Piaget's hypothesis about egocentrism as an explanation for children's communicative failures has not proved to be soundly based, an analytical approach has revealed that referential communication ability includes a number of fairly independent skills, such as composing descriptions, asking questions, and metacommunicating.

A second relevant research trend—the sociolinguistic approach—developed in the 1980s and has been used in descriptive and observational methods for studying the communication of school-age children and their teachers in a variety of classroom settings. In fact, as Wilkinson puts it (1982 p. 3), "learning to

use language in social situations is the focus of the language and communication development of school-age children," who have already acquired structural and functional aspects of language and have to learn to communicate effectively in the classroom. This is both an end in itself and a means of achieving other educational aims, which are both cognitive–academic and social–interpersonal. Once again, the link with social skills emerges, as well as with cognitive development. Moreover, emotional and motivational factors are involved in the development of social and communication skills as well as cognitive ones. Social relationships and communicative competence are always emotionally charged.

4. Learning Social Skills in School

Since it is widely accepted that children have to learn to be communicative and cooperative with others, an important role has been attributed to schools as places in which this can be learned. Neobehaviorist approaches assume that these skills are made up of simpler ones, and consider the mechanism of social reinforcement to be essential for learning. Social reinforcers are responses to the subject's behavior which make this behavior more likely to be repeated and then learned. Most people are sensitive to social reinforcers from early development, since babies are predisposed to learn about sounds and sights that are characteristic features of human persons and to engage in protoconversations. But some children lack social skills: they are unable to interact and cooperate. Autistic-like children are not even able to communicate with others. Some educational programs have succeeded in making them sensitive to social reinforcers and participate effectively in social activities, such as sharing time, symbolic play, social skills practice, and role-taking.

The particular method developed by social learning theory emphasizes the role of modeling: it assumes that children acquire skills by observing and imitating others. Because children prefer to imitate socially desirable models, social reinforcement is the mechanism that supports imitation. Given that children begin to imitate others very early in life, imitation can be considered as the earliest mechanism of social interaction, although it cannot explain the acquisition of novel responses.

5. Classroom Communication

Classroom interaction was studied in the 1970s with a process–product approach, looking for the variables in teachers' verbal behavior that correlate with pupils' learning achievement. This approach was largely dominated by analysis models like that of Flanders

(1970). They use eclectic categories of analysis and do not differentiate verbal behaviors with different communicative functions.

The sociolinguistic approach to classroom interaction is characterized by a more global approach (Cazden 1986) and focuses on the pragmatic dimension of language; that is on how we do things with words within the discourse. It studies social and linguistic interaction in the classroom, which is regarded as a unique communicative context. Results show that cultural and individual differences in communicative patterns can produce breakdowns in communication between teachers and students. This explains unsuccessful interactions, learning difficulties, and underachievement of minority children.

Like any other conversation, classroom conversation is based on "adjacent pairs" such as questions and answers, request and agreement, which enact the principles of conversational cooperativeness. Studies of classroom interaction have discovered that lessons are formally organized activities (Sinclair and Coulthard 1975). They turn around a three-part structure of exchange opened by a teacher's question (which is an assessment one) and followed by a pupil's answer and the teacher's evaluation. Teachers willing to change the traditional interaction pattern have proven able to guide and facilitate children's language and learning through collaborative talk. Wells (1985) reported similarities between learning language and learning through language by using a "semantically contingent" talk which takes over children's ideas, procedures, and knowledge. Teachers can provide opportunities for children to make their judgments explicit and to practice how to negotiate an agreement.

In a study by Orsolini and Pontecorvo (1992), carried out with kindergarten children discussing a narrative and a scientific task with their teacher, interactive exchanges were categorized. Three main sequence patterns (with significant links) were found: "mutual continuations," produced by children and supported by teacher's repetitions and reformulations; "cycles of queries–answers"; and "dispute sequences" in which opposition between children activates a process of giving justifications and explanations which is not affected by the teacher's utterances.

A shared assumption of studies using the sociolinguistic approach is that discursive reasoning operates within a "collective mind" as a social unit formed by at least two persons. This assumption is consistent with Vygotskian theory and explains why pairs or small groups can solve tasks that are beyond the grasp of individual participants.

6. Social Interaction and Cognition

School can be regarded as a natural setting in which social and communication skills develop and contribute to children's cognitive development. The theoretical

perspectives that have stressed the relevance of social interaction processes on cognitive development are linked to two major theories, the Piagetian and the Vygotskian. They have points of convergence and divergence that can be summarized as follows.

(a) Both theories are based on the individual–environment interaction. In Piaget this is mainly physical, but in Vygotsky (1978) it is mainly sociocultural.

(b) As regards the roles of interactants, Piaget (1923) prefers peer interactions, while Vygotsky considers adults or more expert peers to be more effective.

(c) A central role is attributed to the acquisition of metaconsciousness. According to Piaget, this depends on the development of the operational structures, while for Vygotsky it develops from the linguistic and instructional interaction with adults.

(d) The changing factor in the Piagetian theory is the cognitive (or sociocognitive) conflict (Perret-Clermont 1979), which operates if the subject is already near a disequilibrium phase. In the Vygotskian approach the relevant factor is the social support system, enacted by the more competent interactant who is able to operate in the subject's "zone of proximal development."

(e) Both theories refer to the internalization process: for Piaget the child has to internalize an action in order to transform it into an "operation," while for Vygotsky the social relationship and the collaborative activity are internalized.

Although both theories attribute a relevant role to social interaction, the last two points show how their main difference is in the explanatory mechanism, which is an intrapsychological one for Piaget and an interpsychological one for Vygotsky.

Analysis of research carried out using these theories (reviewed in Pontecorvo 1990), shows that the Piagetian approach is valid when judgment tasks are used, while the Vygotskian approach is particularly effective for open problem-solving tasks in which there is room for overt reciprocal regulation, negotiation of meanings, and analysis of alternatives. However, both the sociolinguistic and Vygotskian perspectives have shown that thinking and reasoning are primarily social and collaborative activites. Thus the interactional processes in educational contexts need to be analyzed and better understood.

Many studies have shown that peer tutoring is particularly effective for increasing knowledge acquisition in *tutors*. Palincsar and Brown (1984) reported a positive effect of "reciprocal teaching" on the acquisition of comprehension skills if all children play the teacher role in turn. In their study the child who acts as teacher is requested to tutor the other members of the group overtly by explicitly applying text comprehension strategies modeled first by the teacher. The overt expression of comprehension strategies (such as clarifying, predicting, summarizing, and questioning) which is undertaken in the tutor's role, facilitates the acquisition of comprehension skills in low-ability children.

See also: Group Processes in the Classroom; Peer Relations and Learning; Social Interaction and Learning

References

Bruner J S 1985 *Child's Talk: Learning to Use Language.* Norton, New York
Cazden C B 1986 Classroom discourse. In: Wittrock M C (ed.) 1986 *Handbook of Research on Teaching.* Macmillan Inc., New York
Dunn J 1988 *The Beginnings of Social Understanding.* Harvard University Press, Cambridge, Massachusetts
Flanders N A 1970 *Analyzing Teaching Behavior.* Addison-Wesley, Reading, Massachusetts
Higgins E T, Parsons J E 1983 Social cognition and the social life of the child: Stages as subcultures. In: Higgins E T, Ruble D N, Hartup W W (eds.) 1983 *Social Cognition and Social Development: A Sociocultural Perspective.* Cambridge University Press, Cambridge
Hinde R A, Perret-Clermont A N, Stevenson-Hinde J (eds.) 1986 *Social Relationships and Cognitive Development.* Oxford University Press, New York
Orsolini M, Pontecorvo C 1992 Children's talk in classroom discussion. *Cognition and Instruction* 9(2): 113–36
Palinscar A M, Brown A 1984 Reciprocal teaching of comprehension-fostering and monitoring activities. *Cognition and Instruction* 1(2): 117–75
Perret-Clermont A N 1979 *La construction de l'intelligence dans l'interaction sociale.* Lang, Bern
Perret-Clermont A N, Perret J F, Bell N 1991 The social construction of meaning and cognitive activity in elementary school children. In: Resnick L B, Levine J M, Teasley S D (eds.) 1991 *Perspectives on Socially Shared Cognition.* American Psychological Association, Washington, DC
Piaget J 1923 *Le langage et la pensée chez l'enfant.* Delachaux et Niestlé, Neuchâtel
Pontecorvo C 1990 Social context, semiotic mediation, and forms of discourse in constructing knowledge at school. In: Mandl H, De Corte E, Bennett S N, Friedrich H F (eds.) 1990 *Learning and Instruction. European Research in an International Context.* Pergamon Press, Oxford
Rogoff B 1989 *Apprenticeship in Thinking: Cognitive Development in Social Context.* Oxford University Press, New York
Sinclair J M, Coulthard R M 1975 *Towards an Analysis of Discourse: The English Used by Teachers and Pupils.* Oxford University Press, Oxford
Vygotsky L S 1978 *Mind in Society: The Development of Higher Psychological Processes.* Harvard University Press, Cambridge, Massachusetts
Wells G 1985 *The Meaning Makers: Children Learning Language and Using Language to Learn.* Heinemann Educational Books, Portsmouth, New Hampshire
Wilkinson L C 1982 *Communicating in the Classroom.* Academic Press, New York

Further Reading

Bates E, Benigni L, Bretherton L, Camaioni L, Volterra V 1979 *The Emergence of Symbols: Cognition and Communication in Infancy.* Academic Press, New York
Bruner J S 1987 *Actual Minds, Possible Words.* Harvard University Press, Cambridge, Massachusetts
Dickson P W (ed.) 1981 *Children's Oral Communication Skills.* Academic Press, New York
Flavell J H, Ross L 1981 *Social Cognitive Development: Frontiers and Possible Futures.* Cambridge University Press, Cambridge
Garvey C 1984 *Children's Talk.* Fontana, London
Robinson W P (ed.) 1981 *Communication in Development,* European Monographs in Social Psychology. Vol. 24. Academic Press, New York

Social Interaction and Learning

V. V. Rubtsov

It is important for teaching to consider processes and mechanisms of learning in relation to social interaction. Indeed, efficient interaction is a prerequisite for students' achievements. Learning in the "teacher–student" system depends on the organization of their joint activity. The characteristics of social interaction and learning have been considered in research on the efficiency of pair interaction when engaged in problem-solving ("peer interaction"), in the investigation of characteristic features of joint learning activity and organization in class (involving a teacher and a group of students), and in the study of the influence of computer usage on children's development when they work in groups. The findings resulting from this work may yet form the core of a new approach to the psychology of interaction, and even the basis of a new pedagogical practice differing from the traditional one in both content and methods.

1. Theoretical Basis

The investigation of social interaction and learning was first stimulated by the early works of Vygotsky , Margaret Mead, and Piaget. Though each started from different points, they all put forward a hypothesis about the decisive role of social interaction in personal development. In the cultural–historical theory of Vygotsky, a social situation is considered to be the source of development. According to Vygotsky (1978), "every function in the child's cultural development appears twice, on two levels. First on the social, and later on the psychological level; first between people as an interpsychological category, and then inside the child as an intrapsychological category" (p. 570). Social interaction stimulates undeveloped cognitive processes and enables students to act on a higher cognitive level. The difference between what a student can do independently (the actual level of development) and what a student can do under appropriate guidance is called "the zone of proximal development" (Vygotsky 1978 pp. 84–90). Therefore, according to Vygotsky, learning is successful only if it precedes development; that is, when it stimulates those processes that are still maturing and are situated in the zone of proximal development. Only by stimulating such learning processes can education play an exceptionally important role in development (Newman et al. 1989).

The most important element in Vygotsky's theory is the symbolic context of social interaction. By this Vygotsky meant the way a human being regulates his or her behavior and psychological processes by using signs and symbols as the means for controlling activity. In this regard, a significant difference can be observed between a sign in its instrumental function and a tool. Vygotsky characterized the main difference between a sign and a tool as follows: according to its classical Hegelian meaning, a tool can be placed between a person involved in an operation and an external transforming object to mediate the person's effect on the object of activity; a sign, on the other hand, always mediates the attitude of one person to another (in particular the person's attitude toward himself or herself as another person). In other words, a sign always serves as the means for the organization of action directed toward the regulation of one's own consciousness and personality (Luria 1932, Wertsch 1985).

The symbolic context of social interaction constitutes the basis of Mead's conception of symbolic interactionism. According to Mead, the formation of human "self" occurs in communicative situations. The interiorization of a dialogue becomes in this case the source of person's thinking activity. Interpersonal relations are also "given" in interaction: they determine both the type of interaction emerging in concrete conditions and its extent. In joint activity the emotional basis of interpersonal relations determines various estimations and orientations and gives interaction a certain "coloring." But at the same time this "coloring" cannot utterly predetermine the existence of interaction or its absence: when pulled out of an activity context, interaction makes no sense.

In his early investigations of children's moral judgments, Piaget (1928) considered cooperation during pair interaction as a necessary condition for cognitive changes. However, he developed this into his conclusion about mutual complementarity and reversibility of operational structures and cooperation, and finally to the idea about the parallelism and isomorphism of these two types of structures: "Each grouping internal to the individuals is a system of operations, and cooperation constitutes a system of operations held in common, in a proper sense of 'co-operations.' This type of equilibrium cannot really be considered either as the result of individual thought, nor as an exclusively social product; internal operational activity and external cooperation are only, and in the most precise sense of the words, the two complementary aspects of a single entity, since the equilibrium of each depends on that of the other" (Piaget 1947 p. 177).

Thus, at least two points formulated by Vygotsky, Mead, and Piaget have become cornerstones in the consideration of social interaction and learning, and in the shaping of a corresponding trend in modern psychology. First, the scientific community has realized that social interaction and the development of thinking are not independent processes, Neither are they reversible (i.e., isomorphous) or equivalent, but they are mutually presupposed, because the development and procedures of each depend on the other. Second, the concept of the zone of proximal development introduces a new paradigm of development, and accordingly a new approach to the psychology of learning and teaching. The idea of learning as a natural and individual process dividing the participants of the learning situation into those who teach and those who learn is replaced by the notion of a process of coaction and joint activity. The main mechanism of this process, which makes it cultural and socially determined, is mediation of proper cognitive acts (through interactions) between the participants. In this case both the problem of *what* to teach and the problem *how* to teach, are important; that is the problem of the organization of effective forms of joint learning activity and of the usage of the sign and symbol system.

2. Research on the Influence of Social Interaction on Child Development

The process of cognitive transformations requires active involvement by participants; that is, teachers and students. Therefore the main paradigm of teaching cannot be the idea of imitation. Nor should the learning progress be explained as being a result of a student's interaction with a partner at a higher level (and that any regression is the result of interaction with a partner at a lower level of development). On the basis of the constructivist and interactionist approaches to development created by Piaget and new hypotheses on development formulated by the adherents of the Genevan school of psychology, child development is no longer considered to be "a simple copy of some model. It is an active reconstruction of an examinee during which every piece of knowledge represents a permanent construction carrying an aspect of a new elaboration inside"(Perret-Clermont 1980 p. 118). In this context the most essential aspect of the problem of social interaction as the source of cognitive progress may be a hypothesis about sociocognitive conflict. According to the hypothesis, if interaction is to produce congnitive development there must be a process provoking a conflict between opposite points of view, which will be resolved by creating systems for coordination of these different positions.

To clarify the role of social interaction in children's development it is important to answer the following questions. In what way do emerging social relations affect children's development? How do other people's strategies influence the problem-solving strategy of a particular participant (an examinee)? In addition, it is important to describe the appropriate ways of organizing efficient learning interaction, because not all learning/teaching situations produce development in children's thinking.

The influence of group problem-solving on intellectual development can be investigated by the following means. An experimental group of children is given a pretest to assess their starting level. They then work in small groups (as a rule consisting of two children), attempting to solve together problems similar to those they encountered in the pretest. Then they are given individual advancement. Alongside the experimental group is a control group of children who work on their own and are administered the pretest and the post-test. This method not only helps in discovering the efficiency of group problem-solving as compared to individual work, also reveals the progress in children's intellectual development as a result of their participation in joint activity. Data accumulated by this method of research have shown that there are limits to the idea that imitation of a more advanced model promotes development. On the other hand, these data have confirmed the hypothesis that sociocognitive conflicts between individuals' views do induce thinking processes and affect the development of interaction.

Research has also suggested that in order to change the level of development it is not enough just to place a child (e.g., with an unformed concept of conversation) together with another who possesses a higher level of intellectual development. In such circumstances the first child should be made aware of the *cause* of the conflict between it and its partner. Furthermore, it has been shown that intellectual conflict produces a developmental effect not only on a child with a lower level of intellectual development but also on a child with a higher level as well (Cazden and Forman 1980, Mugny and Doise 1978, Perret-Clermont 1980).

These findings have led to a search for effective forms of joint work. This must consider such components as the distribution of actions and their exchange, mutual understanding, communication, mutual planning, and mutual reflection (Rubtsov 1991). The originality of such a method of organization will lie in modeling interaction situations with the help of symbolic means—so-called "schemes of activity." As a rule these schemes describe the composition of individual actions, the way in which actions are to be distributed between participants, and the sequence in which they are fulfilled. The scheme enables a group of children to organize their communication and collaboration, and describes the changes of methods of cooperation corresponding to different problem-solution strategies.

3. Education Based on Developing Interaction in the Classroom

3.1 Organizing Effective Interaction

In the late 1970s and early 1980s experimental investigations of social interaction learning moved from the laboratory to the classroom. Exponents concentrated on devising effective organizational forms of learning interaction between teachers and schoolchildren and between schoolchildren themselves. In the approach toward learning activity elaborated by the Genevan school, much attention is paid to the concept of pedagogical agreement; in other words, students accept cognitive and social responsibility for constructing their own knowledge, while a teacher has to prepare the appropriate learning conditions that will lead to the gradual acquisition of the knowledge and to its evaluation. Under such conditions, children's work in groups plays a decisive role, while the main function of the pedagogical agreement is to create such communicative conditions that a teacher, with his or her remarks and actions, can participate in the construction of critical situations. These will lead to the analysis and understanding of content and can control the interaction of students with different cognitive abilities. Group work reveals the importance of not immediately choosing a view proposed by the majority of the participants, but of putting in order and coordinating all proposals. While comparing and exchanging views, children enter into sociocognitive conflicts involving the opposition of views.

In this line of research, the organization of children's interaction includes, as a rule, the division of students into small groups, each of them looking for the solution to a problem, followed by discussion between groups of different solution variants and the joint shaping of a correct solution. The role of an adult here is to present the initial problematic situation, to communicate it to the participants, to discuss proposed solution methods with them, and to provide missing information. The instructional efficiency of such joint activity organization is high and provides the opportunity to single out and study the most interesting psychological and pedagogical phenomena, those that are responsible for group efficiency. The results of experiments indicate that such efficiency is derived from a group being able to examine alternative possible solutions. This ability of a group of children is characterized by self-regulation and activity control during problem solution. Children actively discuss means of problem solution, each trying to prove his or her own mode of action and to assess those of the others. The teacher will be confronted with a number of questions relating to the evaluation of different views of group members and the appropriateness of chosen means of joint work organization.

It is important for children to decide not only how to solve a problem, but also to work out how to interact in order to solve it jointly. It means that a series of learning actions already known needs to be prolonged. Apart from the actions of transformation, modeling, control, and estimation of a problem-solution method, a special system of joint actions must be mentioned, for example: including different action models in activity and their mutual coordination; joint planning and modeling of activity organization patterns given by an adult; and communication and mutual understanding in the process of assistance and search for new ways of joint work organization.

3.2 Usage of New Information Technologies

In collaborative learning, special computer and video programs have proven to be extremely useful. In these, every participant fulfils his or her own part of the work on a problem either on a common display unit or at a separate unit and must also interact with his or her partner about actions and their results (Light 1991, Salomon 1989). Research findings in this area are of great importance. They help to explain the psychological mechanisms underlying joint action. The basis of these mechanisms is the mediation of the *contents* of the problem through the participants' interaction: the participants address themselves to the foundations of solving a problem.

The writing of computer learning programs must be based upon sound ways of involving pupils in learning situations. Teachers should demonstrate models of computer use to pupils, and different types of teacher–pupil interactions.

The regulation of cooperation can be achieved by programming different degrees of autonomy in the individual actions required of pupils. These can range from complete independence to significant limitations by mutual influences. The regulation of individual actions within joint action can be accomplished by starting from a consideration of the contents as a symbolic model of the action. This fixes the plan of the future action in relation to the actual means of its realization. The main mechanism of the joint action organization is reflexive analysis, which provides the necessary reconstruction of the action and the realization of the objective conditions of the solution to the problem (Rubtsov 1992).

3.3 From Authoritarian Pedagogy to the Pedagogy of Collaboration

Through participation in joint work, children are involved in and can accomplish the process of real investigation (quasi-research). They also express their own interests and emotional experiences which greatly stimulate their development. At the same time, it is necessary for children's development—although it is not easy to bring about—for teachers to mediate the construction of children's learning communication, that is, communication that elicits the required approach to the learning task, and to organize situations of collective and group learning work leading to the development of ways of interaction and collaboration.

The accumulated experimental data about the role of social interaction in the process of learning reveal new potentials for children's mental development. They constitute a real basis for the improvement of learning contents and methods and, as a result, may lead to the foundation of a new pedagogical approach. Its main principle will be collaboration of children and adults in constructing the conditions for creativity during learning activity and eliminating an authoritarian style of control over children's thoughts.

See also: Group Processes in the Classroom; Learning Activity; Peer Relations and Learning; Development of Learning Skills in Problem Solving and Thinking; Social and Communication Skills; Group Learning; Cooperative Learning

References

Cazden C, Forman E 1980 Exploring the intellectual value of peer interactions. In: *One Issue in Implementing Vygotskian Perspectives in the Classroom.* Chicago, Illinois

Light P 1991 *Learning as a Collaborative Process.* Open University Press, Milton Keynes

Luria A R 1932 *The Nature of Human Conflicts or Emotion, Conflict and Will: An Objective Study of Disorganisation and Control of Human Behavior.* Liveright, New York

Mugny A, Doise W 1978 Socio-cognitive conflict and structuration of individual and collective performance. *European Journal of Social Psychology* 8(2): 181–92

Newman D, Griffin P, Cole M 1989 *The Construction Zone: Working for Cognitive Change in School.* Cambridge University Press, Cambridge, Massachusetts

Perret-Clermont A N 1980 *Social Interaction and Cognitive Development in Children.* Academic Press, London

Piaget J 1928 *Judgement and Reasoning in the Child.* Routledge & Kegan Paul, London

Piaget J 1947 *La psychologie de l'intelligence*. Colin, Paris
Rubtsov V 1991 *Learning in Children: Organization and Development of Cooperative Actions*. Nova Science Publishers, New York
Rubtsov V 1992 How to organize the effective ways of group work with the computer. *Eur. J. Psychol. Educ.* 7
Salomon G 1989 The computer as a zone of proximal development: Internalizing reading-related metacognition from a reading partner. *J. Educ. Psychol.* 81(4): 620–27
Vygotsky L S 1978 *Mind and Society: The Development of Higher Psychological Processes*. Harvard University Press, Cambridge, Massachusetts
Wertsch J V (ed.) 1985 *Culture, Communication and Cognition: Vygotskian Perspectives*. Cambridge University Press, Cambridge, Massachusetts

Further Reading

Cole M, Griffin P 1980 Cultural amplifiers reconsidered. In: Olson D (ed.) 1980 *The Social Foundations of Language and Thought: Essays in Honor of Jerome S Bruner*. Norton, New York
Construction des Savoirs 1989 Obstacles and Conflicts. CIRADE Agence d'ARC. Ottawa
Davydov V V, Lompscher J, Markova A K (eds.) 1982 *Ausbildung der Lerntätigkeit bei Schulern*. Volk und Wissen, Berlin
Flavell J H 1967 Role-talking and communication skills in children. In: Hartup W W, Smothergill N L (eds.) 1967 *The Young Child: Reviews of Research*, Vol. 1. National Association for the Education of Young Children, Washington, DC
Leontyev A N 1981 *The Problem of Activity in Psychology: The Concept of Activity in Soviet Psychology*.
Moll L S (ed.) 1990 *Vygotsky and Education: Instructional Implications and Applications of Socio-historical Psychology*. Cambridge University Press, Cambridge, Massachusetts
Rubtsov V 1989 Organization of joint actions as a factor of child psychological development. *Int. J. Educ. Res.* 13: 622–36

Coping with Stressful Situations in a Learning Context

M. Boekaerts

Two examples of school situations that cause stress are: (a) waiting to take an important exam and discovering that one has studied the wrong material; (b) having a conflict with a teacher and being sent to the school principal. Students know these experiences and can describe how they feel and think, and what they do in such situations. It is a fact, however, that not all students will feel stress in the situations described above, and that those who do will not all react in the same way. When under stress, students report experiencing psychological symptoms such as negative emotions (anger, frustration, anxiety, or sadness), the presence of intrusive and repetitive thoughts about the cause of the stress, and behavioral and bodily changes (e.g., aggressive or passive behavior, increased heart rate, perspiration). Such stress-bound emotions, cognitions, and behavioral changes should be reduced swiftly in order to initiate or maintain adequate functioning.

In the 1980s psychologists studied how individuals of various ages reacted to stressful events (stressors). Numerous studies have examined the relationship between coping techniques and: (a) the way people experience stress (psychological symptoms), and (b) long-term adverse effects of the stress experience (e.g., psychosomatic complaints, absenteeism). The first part of this entry will describe stressful situations. Then the transactional stress model will be presented and a global review provided of the research into coping with stress.

1. Stressful Situations for Children and Adolescents

Before the 1980s stress research in children and adolescents focused on major life events. Difficult existential situations, relating to disease, death, severe loss, or separation, were identified; students' adaptive and nonadaptive reactions were recorded. A vast amount of evidence suggests that psychological and behavioral problems in students of all ages can be related to recent stressful life events. However, considerable differences in students' vulnerability to these life traumas are reported. It seems that it is not so much the stressful impact itself that causes long-term adverse effects on adaptation, development, and health, but the way in which individuals cope with the life stressor.

In the literature, major life events have been distinguished from the irritating, frustrating and anxiety-provoking situations that occur in everyday life. However Perrez and Reicherts (1992) argued that the impact of these repetitive daily burdens on maladjustment may well exceed that of major life events. They defended the view that major life events, for example separation from a loved one, may be seen as a sequence of daily burdens.

Research has yielded evidence that stress at school is a multidimensional construct and that daily frustrations may produce intense and chronic stress in

623

students of all ages. Questionnaires have been constructed to measure the impact of daily frustrations. The data collected indicate that they break down factor-analytically into social conflicts related to criticism, social exposure, and social pressure on the one hand and stressful academic situations on the other. The latter group of stressors includes impediments, overloads, and failures. Any of these daily frustrations may be experienced by a student as a "difficult situation," associated with unpleasant experiences, symptoms of malaise, fatigue, or uncertainty about one's ability to keep the situation under control.

Compas et al. (1989) reported that the relationship between stressful events and psychological symptoms changes with development. In children and young adolescents (up to age 14) family stressors (e.g., pressures and expectations by parents) were most predictive of psychological symptoms. In middle adolescence (age 15–17) only peer stressors were predictive of psychological symptoms. In late adolescence (age 18–20) academic stressors (e.g., doing poorly in an exam or a paper) were the best predictors. A consistent pattern of differences emerged between males and females: females of all ages report more stress than males and are more affected by it; females are also significantly more affected by observing the stress experienced by people in their social network.

2. Two Types of Appraisals

It is important to note, that stress does not lie in a situation but in the way an individual perceives a potential stressor. For this reason stress is defined in terms of an individual's appraisal of a situation. The founder of transactional stress theory, Lazarus, views a person who is experiencing stress as an active organizer of the stress experience and an active responder to the taxing environment. That is, a transaction occurs when the stressor and the person mutually influence each other. Lazarus and Folkman defined stress as "a particular relationship between the person and the environment that is appraised by the person as taxing or exceeding his or her resources and endangering his or her well-being" (1984 p.19). They further explained that any new or unexpected situation calls for two types of appraisals: a primary appraisal which determines the significance of the event and a secondary appraisal which determines whether one's coping options will be sufficient to overcome the perceived or anticipated threat of the situation.

Primary appraisals assess whether a situation is beneficial, negative, or neutral for well-being. When a person does not perceive a discrepancy between the perceived task demands and his or her resources to meet these demands, he or she may feel little stress. By contrast, when an individual assesses situational demands as exceeding his or her resources, the person may experience stress and this will be further differ-

entiated into: (a) actual harm, damage, or loss; (b) anticipated damage or loss (threat); or (c) potential gains, mastery, or benefits that will result from dealing with the event (challenge).

Secondary appraisals assess whether coping resources will be sufficient to overcome the harm, loss, damage, threat, or challenge represented by a stressful situation. The upshot of this is that whether or not stress is experienced depends on the achieved balance between primary appraisals (perception of harm, loss, or threat) and secondary appraisals (perceived coping ability).

3. Coping with Stress

Coping refers to efforts on the part of a student to deal with taxing situations. Lazarus and Folkman defined coping as "constantly changing cognitive and behavioral efforts to manage specific external and/or internal demands that are appraised as taxing or exceeding the resources of the individual" (1984 p.141). Coping is further delineated into two basic, universal ways of dealing with stressors, namely, problem-focused coping and emotion-focused coping. The former coping mode refers to efforts on the part of the learner to act on the source of stress (approach), whereas the latter coping mode alludes to efforts to reduce the emotional distress by moving away from the source of stress either actually or mentally (avoidance). Roth and Cohen (1986) predicted and found that approach and avoidance are highly consistent coping responses within a particular context but that they are not mutually exclusive. On the basis of a meta-analysis on coping with stressful life events, Suls and Fletcher (1986) concluded that approach and avoidance can be seen as habitual or preferential ways of dealing with stressful events, but that neither coping mode is more effective in all situations. Avoidance seems to be more effective to deal with short-term threats, whereas approach is more effective when the threat persists over time, mainly because it allows the individual to engage in cognitive and emotional efforts to deal with long-term stress.

It is important to note that coping in a school context should not be seen as an action executed at a particular moment in time. The relationship between coping and a stressful event is a dynamic process that entails a series of transactions between the student and his or her environment. For example, an open conflict with a teacher in class may produce a variety of coping responses in the same student, ranging from being angry and ignoring the teacher to attempting to make it up or engaging in distracting activities. When perceiving discouragements from fellow-learners, the student may attempt to pacify the teacher, whereas encouragements may increase aggressive behavior. Because of the dynamic nature of the coping construct, it is difficult to typify a student's characteristic coping mode.

Observations of students' coping attempts reveal the existence of many different coping techniques.

3.1 Coping and Learning

Students need multiple attempts before they succeed in performing a new skill swiftly. Constraints are put on their performance by their present ability to perform the skill. When students' initial attempts at mastery fail, or when they fall back several times on older, less adequate skills, they may take this to mean that they are incapable of mastering the new skill. When such a situation arises, students may feel that their personal resources are inadequate to meet the demands of the task. Evidence from mainstream psychology indicates that social exposure, and especially anticipated social comparisons, create a concern with limited personal resources and may cause prolonged physiological arousal, reflected in increased heart rate and variability in blood pressure. Such physiological arousal, and the negative emotions it elicits, signals to the learner that something is wrong and that actions should be undertaken to restore well-being and to prevent stressful experiences from occurring now and in the future.

In the literature on stress and coping, different coping techniques have been described. Unfortunately, most authors have used their own labels to refer to these techniques, which makes it difficult to compare and contrast them. For example, Rost and Schermer (1987) identified four techniques that adolescents use to reduce, accept, or come to terms with threatening academic situations: (a) danger control, (b) anxiety control, (c) anxiety repression, and (d) situation control. Danger control and anxiety control are regarded as preventive ways of coping with anxiety, either cognitively or emotionally. The first way of control refers to adequate preparation in the form of productive study skills. The second way of control refers to strategies that reduce psychic and somatic anxiety symptoms.

Anxiety repression and situation control refer to avoidance; both of these techniques may lead to effective relief of anxiety, but neither of them modifies the underlying causes. Anxiety repression may temporarily calm down the student, whereas situation control may help the student to evade taxing demands in the confrontation phase (e.g., by cheating, or reporting sick).

Seiffge-Krenke (1989) also described the coping techniques adolescents use. She grouped them under three main headings: (a) internal coping, (b) active coping, and (c) withdrawal. The first two labels refer to the problem-focused coping mode. The term "internal coping" is reserved for techniques that are characterized by internal reflection of possible solutions, whereas the term "active coping" is used for responses that reflect active and constructive attempts to solve a problem, by gathering information about the nature of the problem or by eliciting social support. Finally, withdrawal includes defenses such as denial and repression: the student inhibits actions that might produce more stress, are embarrassing, or might get him or her into trouble. Seiffge-Krenke reported that the coping techniques used in adolescence are relatively stable over time, and that the use of internal forms of coping and the willingness to compromise increase with age. She also noted considerable culture and sex differences in the use of coping techniques (for review, see Boekaerts (1995)).

In conclusion, it seems that most students use both the problem- and the emotion-focused coping modes in response to stressful events and that the effectiveness of the selected coping mode depends on the interaction between personal variables and situational demands. A study by Compas, Forsythe and Wagner (1988) supports this view. They found that when there was a match between the student's perception of control and the selected coping mode (e.g., low perceived control and emotion-focused coping, or high perceived control and problem-focused coping) low stress was reported (and vice versa for a mismatch). A further study by Compas, Malcame and Fondacaro (1988) documented that students who demonstrated more flexibility in their coping mode over a four-week period reported lower levels of stress than students who rigidly responded to the changing demands of stressful situations. On the basis of these results intervention programs should provide opportunities for students to extend their coping repertoire. Moreover, students should be prompted to build up conditional knowledge on how, why, and when to use different coping techniques. A specific coping strategy may be adaptive for some students but not for others; it may be effective in one context but not in another; and may be acceptable for younger students but not for older ones. The question is always: Does the coping response take account of the demands and constraints of the concrete situation? Hence, in order to judge the effectiveness and appropriateness of concrete coping strategies, one should have knowledge of the way in which a person construes the stressor and its consequences, about his or her coping intention and the non-availability of coping competencies. A vast number of intervention programs have been designed. Some of these programs concentrate on the use of relaxation techniques, whereas others focus more on problem-solving skills (for an overview, see Compas et al. 1989). Beneficial effects have been reported, including increased self-esteem, enhanced academic performance, ability to handle academic stress, ability to deal with social conflict, and decreased absenteeism.

3.2 Coping, Health, and Development

Educators and teachers often forget that students' participation in classroom activities may also have important implications for their personality development and their health. It has already been pointed out that stressful situations, rooted in perceived academic inadequacy, in social conflict, or in both may hinder students in acquiring new knowledge and skill. When these students' ability to cope with a wide range of stressful daily situations is not enhanced, they are at risk of lagging behind or dropping out. But what is more, stressful experiences may also constitute a health risk. Boekaerts (1991) reported that some coping techniques may be beneficial from the point of view of increasing grade point average but coincide with psychosomatic complaints. Given the significance of coping with stress in the development of educational and health risks, it is crucial that preventive efforts are made to help students understand why certain coping techniques are better than others in different stressful situations. It is important to note, however, that stress and coping with it should be seen as aspects of normal development. Indeed, in major periods of transition, such as for example in the transition from elementary school to junior high school, students are confronted with new challenges, for which their habitual adaptive potential may prove to be inadequate, or unacceptable. Some students may have no trouble in meeting these new challenges, whereas others may find it difficult to bridge the gap between the new stressors and their coping repertoire. Preventive intervention programs aimed at the major transition periods should help students to use new coping techniques. Some promising results have been reported (Elias et al. 1986).

See also: Affect, Emotions, and Learning; Motivation and Learning

References

Boekaerts M 1991 Competitive drive, coping and math achievement: What's so detrimental about avoidance behaviour? In: Hagtvet K (ed.) 1991 *Advances in Test Anxiety Research*, Vol. 7. Swets and Zeitlinger, Lisse
Boekaerts M 1995 Coping with stress in childhood and adolescence. In: Zeidner M, Endler N S (eds.) 1995 *Handbook of Coping*. John Wiley & Sons, New York
Compas B E, Forsythe C J, Wagner B M 1988 Consistency and variability in causal attributions and coping with stress. *Cogni. Therapy and Res.* 12: 305–20
Compas B E, Malcarne V L, Fondacaro K 1988 Coping with stressful events in older children and young adolescents. *J. Consult. Clin. Psychol.* 56(3): 405–11
Compas B E, Phares V, Ledoux N 1989 Stress and coping preventive interventions for children and adolescents. In: Bond L A, Compas B E (eds.) 1989 *Primary Prevention and Promotion in the Schools*. Sage, Newbury Park, California
Elias M J et al. 1986 Impact of a preventive social problem solving intervention on children's coping with middle-school stressors. *Am. J. Community Psychol.* 14: 259–75
Lazarus R S, Folkman S 1984 *Stress, Appraisal and Coping*. Springer-Verlag, New York
Perrez M, Reicherts M 1992 *Stress, Coping, and Health*. Hogrefe & Huber, Seattle, Washington
Rost D H, Schermer F J 1987 Emotion and cognition in coping with test anxiety. *Commun. and Cognition* 20(2/3): 225–44
Roth S, Cohen J 1986 Approach, avoidance and coping with stress. *Am. Psychol.* 41(7): 813–19
Seiffge-Krenke I 1989 Health related behavior and coping with illness in adolescence: A cross-cultural perspective. In: Schmidt L R, Schwenkmezger P, Weinman J, Maes S (eds.) 1989 *Theoretical and Applied Aspects of Health Psychology*. Harwood Academic Publishers, Chur
Suls J, Fletcher B 1986 The relative efficacy of avoidant and nonavoidant coping strategies: A meta-analysis. *Health Psychology* 4: 249–88

Further Reading

Boekaerts M 1993 Being concerned with well-being and with learning. *Educ. Psychol.* 2
Bond A L, Compas B E (eds.) 1989 *Primary Prevention and Promotion in the Schools*. Sage, Newbury Park, California
Bosma H, Jackson S (eds.) 1990 *Coping and Self-concept in Adolescence*. Springer-Verlag, Berlin
Seiffge-Krenke I 1993 Coping behavior in normal and clinical samples: More similarities than differences? *Journal of Adolescence* 16:285–303

Teachers' Expectations

T. L. Good

In the 1960s, an experiment conducted in the United States by Rosenthal and Jacobson (1968) resulted in one of the most exciting and controversial reports in the history of educational research. These investigators presented data suggesting that teachers' experimentally induced expectations for student performance were associated with student performance. That is, students whom teachers expected to achieve at higher levels did in fact achieve at higher levels, even though there was no real basis for these expectations. The study was criticized on several methodological grounds. For example, no observations were conducted in the teachers' classrooms, so there was no basis on which to determine whether teachers interacted differently with the students based on their expectations.

This entry focuses on research on teachers' expectations that has been conducted since the publication of the Rosenthal and Jacobson study. It begins with a definition of teachers' expectations, discusses the major types of research on those expectations and the conceptual frameworks underlying this research, and examines ways in which different expectations are communicated to students, and the perceptions students have of these different teacher behaviors. The entry concludes with a discussion of possible directions for research on teachers' expectations.

1. Defining Teachers' Expectations

Teachers' expectations are inferences that teachers make about the future behavior or academic achievement of their students, based on what they currently know about these students. Teachers' expectations affect student outcomes because of actions that teachers take in response to their expectations. Expectations are an inescapable and important part of daily life (Jussim 1990a), influencing many social issues. Research on expectancies has examined such topics as gender role socialization, affirmative action, political person perception, and equality of educational opportunity. (For discussions of research on the role of expectancies in diverse social areas see Jussim 1990a, 1990b, Oyserman and Markus 1990.)

Cooper and Good (1983) noted that researchers have examined two types of teacher expectation effects. The first is the self-fulfilling prophecy effect, in which an originally erroneous expectation leads to behavior that causes the expectation to become true. The Rosenthal and Jacobson (1968) study deals with this type of expectation effect. In contrast, the sustaining expectation effect occurs when teachers expect students to sustain previously developed behavior patterns to the point that teachers take these patterns for granted and fail to see and capitalize on changes in student potential. Self-fulfilling prophecy effects are more powerful than sustaining expectation effects because they introduce significant change in student behavior (and thinking) instead of merely sustaining established patterns. Self-fulfilling effects can be powerful when they occur, but the more subtle sustaining expectation effects occur more often.

2. Two Types of Research on Teachers' Expectations

To understand the research on teacher expectation effects, two types of studies must be distinguished. The first involves experimental attempts to induce teacher expectations by providing teachers with fictitious information about students. The second type of study uses the expectations that teachers form naturally on the basis of whatever information they have available (e.g., test scores).

Numerous studies have induced expectations in teachers and have explored the consequent effects on student learning (Good and Brophy 1990). Some studies did not produce changes in student outcomes, apparently because the teachers did not acquire the expectations the experimenters were trying to induce. Induced-expectation experiments have produced clear-cut positive results often enough, however, to demonstrate that teacher expectations can have self-fulfilling prophecy effects on student achievement. Such demonstrations are important, because studies of teachers' naturally formed expectations cannot establish cause-and-effect relationships. These experimental studies in classrooms have been enriched by laboratory research in social psychology that has focused on the formation, communication, and interpretation of expectancies (see Jones 1990, Jussim 1990b for reviews).

However, studies linking teachers' naturally formed expectations to their classroom interactions with students are also needed, because they provide information about how teachers' expectations can become self-fulfilling. As Good and Brophy (1990) noted, most studies of teachers' naturally formed expectations have related such expectations to teacher–student interaction rather than to student outcomes. These studies typically demonstrate that many teachers interact differently with students for whom they hold high expectations than they do with students for whom they hold low expectations. They also suggest the mechanisms that mediate sustaining expectation effects.

3. The Brophy–Good Model

In their early research on teacher expectation effects on individual students, Brophy and Good (1970) suggested the following model of the process by which teachers' expectations become self-fulfilling prophecies.

(a) Early in the year, the teacher forms differential expectations for student behavior and achievement.

(b) Consistent with these differential expectations, the teacher behaves differently toward various students.

(c) This treatment tells students how they are expected to behave in the classroom and to perform on academic tasks.

(d) If the teacher's treatment is consistent over time,

and if students do not actively resist or change it, it will likely affect their self-concepts, achievement motivation, levels of aspiration, classroom conduct, and interactions with the teacher.

(e) These effects generally will compliment and reinforce the teacher's expectations, so that students will conform to these expectations more than they might otherwise have done.

(f) Ultimately this reciprocal process will affect student achievement and other outcomes. High-expectation students will achieve at or near their potential, but low-expectation students will not gain as much as they could have if taught differently.

The model begins with the assumption that teachers form differential achievement expectations for various students at the beginning of the school year. Teachers use many cues for forming expectations, including track or group placement, classroom conduct, physical appearance, race, socioeconomic status, ethnicity, gender, speech characteristics, and various diagnostic labels (e.g., see Baron et al. 1985, Jussim 1989).

Self-fulfilling prophecy effects of teacher expectations can occur only when all elements in the model are present (Good and Brophy 1990). Often, however, one or more elements is missing. The teacher may not have clear-cut expectations about every student, or those expectations may change continually. Even when expectations are consistent, the teacher may not necessarily communicate them through consistent behavior. Finally, students might prevent expectations from becoming self-fulfilling by counteracting their effects or resisting them.

4. Communicating Differential Expectations

Given that teachers form differential expectations, how do they express those expectations to students in ways that might influence students' behavior? On the basis of several literature reviews, Good and Brophy (1990) suggested that the following behaviors sometimes indicate differential teacher treatment of high and low achievers: (a) waiting less time for "lows" to answer questions before giving the answer or calling on someone else; (b) giving lows answers or calling on someone else rather than trying to improve their responses by giving clues or repeating or rephrasing questions; (c) providing inappropriate reinforcement (e.g., rewarding inappropriate behavior or incorrect answers by lows); (d) criticizing lows more often for failure; (e) praising lows less often for success; (e) failing to give feedback to the public responses of lows; (f) paying less attention to lows or interacting with them less frequently; (g) calling on lows less often to respond to questions, or asking them only easier, nonanalytical questions; (h) seating lows further from the teacher; (i) demanding less from lows (e.g.,

teaching them less content; accepting lower quality or even incorrect responses from lows; providing excessive sympathy or unneeded help); (j) interacting with lows more privately than publicly, and monitoring and structuring their activities more closely; (k) grading tests or assignments differently (e.g., highs but not lows are given the benefit of the doubt in borderline cases), (l) engaging in less friendly interaction with lows, including less smiling and fewer other nonverbal indicators of support; (m) providing briefer and less informative feedback to questions of lows; (n) using less eye contact and other nonverbal communication of attention and responsiveness (forward lean, positive head nodding) in interactions with lows; (o) using less effective and time-consuming instructional methods with lows when time is limited; (p) accepting and using lows' ideas less often; and (q) exposing lows to an impoverished curriculum (e.g. limited and repetitive information, emphasis on factual recitation).

Three points should be noted when considering these forms of differential treatment. First, these teacher behaviors do not occur in all classrooms. Some teachers do not communicate low expectations; some provide appropriate expectations for all or most students. Second, some of the differences are due to students rather than to the teacher. For example, if lows volunteer less often, it is difficult for teachers to be sure that lows get as many response opportunities as highs. Third, some forms of differential treatment are necessary at times and may even represent appropriate individualizing of instruction rather than inappropriate projection of negative expectations. Low-achieving students in elementary schools appear to require more private structuring of their activities and closer monitoring of their work than do their peers.

When several of these differential communication patterns are observed in a classroom, however, and if the differentiation is significant, the teacher may be communicating inappropriately low expectations to some students. This is especially the case if the differential treatment directly affects students' opportunity to learn. For example, if lows receive less new information and feedback about their performance, they are almost certain to make less progress than highs, regardless of whether lows are aware of such differential treatment.

While research has focused on inappropriately low expectations, teachers can hold too high or too "narrow" expectations so that some students are pushed to do more but not allowed to take time to understand or enjoy academic work. The key is to challenge and guide students in appropriate ways to do more than they are at that time able to achieve (Vygotsky 1978).

5. The Importance of Teachers' Expectations

The effects of teachers' expectations on student learning have often been exaggerated. Indeed, in the popular press the effects have sometimes been touted as almost magical. For example, Good and Brophy (1977) lampooned an advertisement that appeared in *Reader's Digest*: "Just make a wish. Read about how it can come True." Although there is no clear way to predict with certainty the effects of teachers' expectancies on student learning, there is growing consensus among experts that expectancy effects are usually modest (e.g., Jussim 1990b estimates an average effect size of 0.2 to 0.3 standard deviations), but important (Brophy 1983). Even an effect size of 0.2 suggests that 10 percent of students who receive high expectations will show notable improvement, and that 10 percent of students exposed to low expectations will exhibit a significant decline in performance (Jussim 1990b).

There is no doubt that expectancies are common. Rosenthal and Rubin (1978) reported that some type of teacher expectancy effect occurred in about two-thirds of the 345 studies they reviewed. Although the potential importance of expectancies is shown by such reviews (and expectancy effects may compound over time), most students do not receive "average effects"; students are likely to be in classrooms where effects are very high, moderate, or nonexistent.

6. Students' Perceptions of Teachers' Differential Behavior

Unfortunately, many studies that have assessed the effects of teacher expectancies on student performance have not included process or interview data to determine students' perceptions of differential teacher behavior. In addition to expectation effects that occur directly through differences in exposure to content, indirect effects may occur as a result of teacher behavior that affects students' self-concepts, performance expectations, or motivation. Although numerous studies have examined students' achievement motivation and aspirations in classrooms, little of this research has studied these affective variables in relation to teacher behavior. Thus, little is known about how students interpret teacher behaviors and how those behaviors influence students' motivation and effort.

Studies that have been conducted suggest that students are aware of differences in teachers' patterns of interaction with students. Interview and questionnaire data indicate that elementary students see their teachers as projecting higher achievement expectations and offering increased opportunity and choice to high achievers, while structuring the activities of low achievers more closely and providing them with additional help and with more negative feedback about their academic work and classroom conduct (Cooper and Good 1983).

Furthermore, students are more aware of such differentiation in classes in which it occurs frequently (Weinstein et al. 1987). Brattesani et al. (1984) compared classrooms where the students described the teachers as differentiating considerably in their treatment of high and low achievers with classrooms in which students reported little such differentiation. They found that including teacher-expectation measures added from 9 to 18 percent to the variance in year-end achievement beyond what could have been predicted from prior achievement in the high-differentiation classes, but added only 1 to 5 percent in the low-differentiation classes.

7. Good's Passivity Model

Some students receive low expectations so consistently that they appear to internalize these expectations. Studies of expectations have increasingly emphasized how students internalize teachers' expectations, and models have been developed for exploring mediation effects (e.g., Cooper 1985). Good's (1981) passivity model suggested that certain forms of teacher treatment induce passivity in low-achieving students. Over time, differences in the ways teachers treat low achievers (e.g., in the third grade a student is praised or finds teacher acceptance for virtually any verbalization, but in the fourth grade the same student is seldom praised and is criticized frequently) may reduce the efforts of lows and contribute to a passive learning style. Other teacher behaviors may compound this problem. Low-achieving students who are called on frequently one year but infrequently the following year may find it confusing to adjust to different role definitions. Ironically, those students who have the least capacity to adapt may be asked to make the most adjustments as they move from classroom to classroom.

Greater variation among teachers in their interaction with low achievers may occur because teachers agree less about how to respond to students who do not learn readily. Teachers may treat lows inconsistently over the course of the school year as they try one approach after another in an attempt to find something that works.

When teachers provide fewer chances for lower achievers to participate in public discussion, wait less time for them to respond when they are called on (even though these students may need more time to think and form an answer), or criticize lows more per incorrect answer and praise them less per correct answer, the implications are similar. It seems that a good strategy for students who face such conditions would be not to volunteer or not to respond when called on. Students are discouraged from taking risks under such an instructional system (Good 1981). To the extent that students are motivated to reduce risk and ambiguity— and many argue that students are strongly motivated to do so (Doyle 1983)—students would likely become more passive in order to reduce the risk of critical teacher feedback.

Good et al. (1987) found that low achievers were just as likely to ask questions as other students in kindergarten classes, but that lows asked significantly fewer questions than their classmates in upper-elementary and secondary classes. Similarly, in a study involving grades two, four, and six, Newman and Goldin (1990) found that among sixth-graders, the lowest achievers had both the greatest perceived need for help and the greatest resistance to asking for help. Students' ambivalence about asking questions or getting help from teachers becomes especially acute during adolescence, when they are both more concerned about how they are perceived by peers and more sensitive to the costs as well as the benefits of seeking help.

8. Variation in Teachers' Expectations Over Time

Relatively little research has focused on students' classroom experiences over consecutive years, and no study examined students' reactions to differential teacher expectations over consecutive years prior to the work of Midgley et al. (1989). Midgley et al. conducted a longitudinal study in the United States of 1,329 elementary and junior high students, examining their self- and task-related beliefs in mathematics as a function of teachers' efficacy beliefs. They found that students who moved from high- to low-efficacy mathematics teachers during the transition from elementary to junior high school ended the junior high year with the lowest expectancies in perceived performance (even lower than students who had low-efficacy teachers both years) and the highest perceptions of task difficulty. Furthermore, the differences in pre- and post-transitional teachers' views of their efficacy had more of an effect on low-achieving than on high-achieving students' beliefs about mathematics.

9. Increasing Expectations

There is growing evidence that when (a) low achievers are allowed to enroll in more challenging courses or (b) course content is altered to include more challenging material that is traditionally not available to low-performing students, student performance improves. The decision to allow students to engage in more challenging academic work (e.g., move to a higher reading group) is potentially a powerful strategy for increasing teacher and student performance expectations.

Mason et al. (1992) described a study in which 34 average-achieving eighth-grade mathematics students in an urban junior high were assigned to prealgebra classes rather than placed in traditional general mathematics classes. Results showed that students placed in prealgebra classes benefited from advanced placement in comparison to average-achieving eighth-graders from the previous year who took general mathematics (the cohort comparison group). Specifically, prealgebra students outperformed the comparison co-

hort group on a concepts subtest while maintaining equivalent performance on the problem-solving and computation subtests of the Comprehensive Assessment Program Achievement Series Test. Particularly important was that prealgebra students, in comparison with the cohort of general mathematics students, subsequently enrolled in more advanced mathematics classes during high school and obtained higher grades in these classes. Moreover, the presence of average achievers in prealgebra classes did not lower the performance of higher-achieving students in these classes.

Mason et al. qualified their findings. For example, the school in which the study took place was implementing a comprehensive school-improvement plan (higher expectations, active mathematics teaching). Hence, it was impossible to determine what instructional, curriculum, or peer effects were most influential in improving student performance. Further, the authors were aware of potential selection and history effects that can occur in a cross-sectional cohort design. Other investigators, however, have obtained similar results. Peterson (1989) found that remedial students who were placed in a prealgebra program for accelerated students achieved significantly higher results on all three mathematics subtests of the California Test of Basic Skills than did comparable students who were assigned to remedial and general mathematics classes. Such results strongly argue the need for educators to assess carefully the standards they use for assigning students to courses, since current standards may limit unnecessarily many students' access to mathematical knowledge, and potentially their access to future careers and advanced study.

Efforts to change low expectations for student performance can go beyond altering the practices of one teacher or a few teachers to include an entire school. For example, Weinstein et al. (1991) reported positive findings from a comprehensive intervention program designed to raise expectations for student achievement. This quasi-experimental field study involved collaboration between university researchers and teachers and administrators at an urban high school. The cooperating teachers attended university classes that focused on ways in which teachers can inadvertently maintain low expectations, and on the special motivational problems of low-achieving students. Teachers and researchers collaborated to develop a program for preventing and remediating low expectations.

The eight areas of the intervention program are: (a) task and curriculum (minimize tasks that heighten ability comparisons, give low achievers frequent opportunities to work on higher-order thinking and application of knowledge); (b) grouping (minimize ability grouping, make use of heterogeneous grouping and cooperative learning activities); (c) evaluation (emphasize qualitative evaluation, provide private feedback that stresses continuous progress achieved through a combination of ability and effort); (d) motivational climate (minimize competition, stress intrinsic rewards in addition to extrinsic rewards); (e) student role in learning (provide opportunities for students to make choices and to assume increasing responsibility for managing their own learning); (f) class relationships (develop a sense of community among the students that includes valuing diversity); (g) parent–teacher communication (emphasize students' positive attributes and progress rather than their deficiencies or problems); and (h) school-level supports (with cooperation from school administrators, establish increased and varied opportunities for low achievers to participate in school activities and get recognition for their achievements in and out of the classroom). The research procedures and organizational issues associated with this complex and innovative intervention cannot be presented here. However, both a rich description of the project (Weinstein et al. 1991) and an extensive analysis of the program (Weinstein 1991) are available.

The program has had some notable positive effects. For example, teachers were able to implement procedures designed to increase communication of positive expectations to low achievers. Project teachers' expectations for students, as well as their attitudes toward their colleagues, became more positive. Project teachers also expanded their roles and worked to change school tracking practices. Positive changes were also evident for the 158 project students. In contrast to 154 comparison students, project students had improved grades, fewer disciplinary referrals, and increased retention in school one year later. Weinstein et al. (1991) noted, however, that progress was not uniform. Students' absences rose and their improved academic performance was not maintained over the 9-month period of the study. According to the researchers, the limited length and breadth of the intervention and evaluation (students' performance was evaluated only in English and history), although sufficient to retain students, may have been insufficient to affect students' attendance and performance. Moreover, some teachers left the project because of excessive time requirements and lack of administrative support.

10. Directions for Research

Expectations research can be expanded in many ways to enhance understanding of classroom teaching and learning. Two of the most promising research areas are teachers' decisions about content assignments and teachers' knowledge of subject matter.

10.1 Selection of Curriculum Content

Many educators have contended that textbooks define the curriculum, although some research challenges this simplistic view and suggests that teachers act as decision-makers, modifying the curriculum in re-

lation to factors such as teachers' beliefs about students' aptitude, their instructional intentions, and their subject-matter knowledge. If teachers influence the curriculum, then their decisions about curriculum partially determine performance expectations for students, just as teacher behaviors and activity structures do.

According to Freeman and Porter (1989), teachers make many decisions that influence how much content students receive. For example, teachers decide how much time to spend on mathematics on a certain day, what topics should be taught, how much time should be allocated for each topic, whether all students are taught the same topics, and in what order topics should be presented. The time spent on instruction and the focus of instruction (e.g., concepts, skills, applications) seem prime ways in which expectations might be communicated. Subsequent research could profitably attempt to integrate teachers' decisions about how much and what type of content to present with teachers' expectations for students (e.g., how students are likely to learn).

10.2 Teachers' Subject-matter Knowledge

Teachers' subject-matter knowledge is likely an important factor affecting the performance expectations they communicate to students. Because some teachers know more about some subjects or concepts than others, teachers' beliefs about subject matter and how to present it to students would probably affect whether or not they set appropriate performance expectations for students. Carlsen (1991) documented the effects of four novice biology teachers' subject-matter knowledge on discourse in their classrooms as they taught eight science lessons. The findings imply that choice of instructional activity affects students' participation in classroom discussion. Teachers used lectures and laboratory activities, which are characterized by high rates of student questioning, with topics about which they were knowledgeable. They tended to use classroom activities that involved few student questions when they were unfamiliar with the subject matter.

Carlsen's results are especially intriguing in that they illustrate that, because all teachers, and especially novice teachers, have inadequate knowledge in some areas, teachers must develop strategies for teaching content that they are still learning themselves. These strategies might include using sources additional to the textbook, bringing in guest teachers who are more knowledgeable, telling students that this is an area about which they are still learning, and presenting to students the questions that the teachers are using to structure the unit (and their own learning).

Research that examines teachers' performance expectations for individual students along with teachers' subject-matter knowledge would be profitable. When teachers instruct students in topics about which teachers have little knowledge, they may exaggerate differential treatment (i.e., avoid unpredictable questions by low achievers; overly depend on students believed to be more capable). Furthermore, the accountability systems and task structures that teachers select may be a function of their subject-matter knowledge.

11. Conclusion

Research on teacher expectancies in the classroom was a rich and exciting area in the 1970s and 1980s and many useful constructs have been derived from this work. Although the importance of teacher expectation effects have sometimes been overstated, it is clear that they are important, especially when considered with other teaching abilities and other general variables (e.g., home–school correspondence). In the 1980s there has been growing interest in the active role that students play in interpreting, internalizing, or rejecting expectations that are conveyed through teacher behavior or classroom structures. In the 1990s and beyond researchers need to study teacher expectancies and student mediation simultaneously. Such work will be enriched if researchers are also willing to explore how curriculum content and teachers' and students' knowledge of content mediate both the communication and interpretation of performance expectations.

References

Baron R, Tom D, Cooper H 1985 Social class, race and teacher expectations. In: Dusek J (ed.) 1985 *Teacher Expectancies*. Erlbaum, Hillsdale, New Jersey

Brattesani K, Weinstein R, Marshall H 1984 Student perceptions of differential teacher treatment as moderators of teacher expectation effects. *J. Educ. Psychol.* 76(2): 236–47

Brophy J 1983 Research on the self-fulfilling prophecy and teacher expectations. *J. Educ. Psychol.* 75: 631–61

Brophy J, Good T 1970 The Brophy–Good System (dyadic teacher-child interaction). In: Simon A, Boyer E (eds.) 1970 *Mirrors for Behavior: An Anthology of Observation Instruments Continued, 1970 Supplement*, Vols. A and B. Research for Better Schools, Inc., Philadelphia, Pennsylvania

Carlsen W 1991 Subject-matter knowledge and science teaching: A pragmatic perspective. In: Brophy J (ed.) 1991 *Advances in Research on Teaching*, Vol. 2. JAI Press, Greenwich, Connecticut

Cooper H 1985 Models of teacher expectation communication. In: Dusek J (ed.) 1985 *Teacher Expectancies*. Erlbaum, Hillsdale, New Jersey

Cooper H, Good T 1983 *Pygmalion Grows Up: Studies in the Expectation Communication Process*. Longman, New York

Doyle W 1983 Academic work. *Rev. Educ. Res.* 53(2): 159–200

Freeman D, Porter A 1989 Do textbooks dictate the content of mathematics instruction in elementary schools? *Am. Educ. Res. J.* 26(3): 403–21

Good T 1981 Teacher expectations and student perceptions: A decade of research. *Educ. Leadership* 38(5): 415–23

Good T, Brophy J 1977 *Educational Psychology: A Realistic Approach*. Holt, New York

Good T, Brophy J 1990 *Looking in Classrooms*, 5th edn. Harper and Collins, New York

Good T, Slavings R, Harel K, Emerson H 1987 Student passivity: A study of student question-asking in K-12 classrooms. *Sociol. Educ.* 60(4): 181–99

Jones E 1990 *Interpersonal Perception*. Freeman, New York

Jussim L 1989 Teacher expectations: Self-fulfilling prophecies, perceptual biases, and accuracy. *J. Pers. Soc. Psychol.* 57(3): 469–80

Jussim L 1990a Expectancies and social issues: Introduction. *J. Soc. Issues* 46(2): 1–8

Jussim L 1990b Social reality and social problems: The role of expectancies. *J. Soc. Issues* 46(2): 9–34

Mason D, Schroeter D, Combs R, Washington K 1992 Assigning average-achieving eighth graders to advance mathematics classes in an urban junior high. *Elem. Sch. J.* 92(5): 587–99

Midgley C, Feldlaufer H, Eccles J 1989 Change in teacher efficacy and students' self- and task-related beliefs in mathematics during the transition to junior high school. *J. Educ. Psychol.* 81(2): 247–58

Newman R, Goldin L 1990 Children's reluctance to seek help with school work. *J. Educ. Psychol.* 82: 92–100

Oyserman D, Markus H 1990 Possible selves in balance: Implications for delinquency. *J. Soc. Issues* 46(2) 141–58

Peterson J 1989 Remediation is no remedy. *Educ. Leadership* 46(6): 24–25

Rosenthal R, Jacobson L 1968 *Pygmalion in the Classroom: Teacher Expectation and Pupil's Intellectual Development*. Holt, Rinehart, and Winston, New York

Rosenthal R, Rubin D 1978 Interpersonal expectancy effects: The first 345 studies. *The Behavioral and Brain Sciences* 1(3): 377–86

Vygotsky L 1978 *Mind in Society: The Development of Higher Psychological Processes*. Harvard University Press, Cambridge, Massachusetts

Weinstein R 1991 Caught between paradigms: Obstacle or opportunity—a comment on the commentaries. *American Journal of Community Psychology* 19(3): 395–404

Weinstein R, Marshall H, Sharp L, Botkin M 1987 Pygmalion and the student: Age and classroom differences in children's awareness of teacher expectations. *Child Dev.* 58(4): 1079–93

Weinstein R et al. 1991 Expectations and high school change: Teacher–researcher collaboration to prevent school failure. *American Journal of Community Psychology* 19(3): 333–64

Further Reading

Blanck P D 1993 *Interpersonal Expectations Theory, Research, and Applications*. Cambridge University Press, Cambridge

SECTION XII

Individual Differences and Learning and Instruction

Abilities and Aptitudes

J. W. Pellegrino

In typical educational practice, the terms "abilities" and "aptitudes" are used synonymously to denote an individual's potential for acquiring new knowledge or skill. Information about a person's potential may be useful in setting reasonable expectations for what he or she can accomplish, designing effective learning environments, and in diagnosing learning difficulties that individuals may exhibit.

1. Aptitudes, Learning, and Achievement

It is commonly accepted that individuals vary with regard to their specific mental abilities. An individual may show superior linguistic or verbal ability while being relatively weak at spatial and mechanical reasoning tasks. The converse is also a common ability pattern. Such variations among individuals have been of concern to those interested in developing theories and tests of aptitude, as well as educational practitioners wishing to optimize the outcomes of formal instruction. Unfortunately, there is no universally accepted theory of aptitude. It is not known how many specific mental abilities there are nor their degree of independence. There are, however, a number of tests which attempt to measure individual differences in general and specific aptitudes.

Aptitudes are psychological constructs about individual differences in learning or performance in situations where individuals are required to learn from instruction. For a test to be an acceptable measure of verbal or spatial aptitude it must be shown that individual differences in mental test performance are predictive of an individual's ability to learn in some specific instructional setting.

A distinction is drawn, not without controversy, between aptitude and achievement measures. While both may predict an individual's ability to profit from a program or course, the two types of tests are often quite different in content. The essential difference between achievement and aptitude tests is that the former attempts to measure abilities an individual has acquired as a result of specific study in a given instructional sequence. In contrast, an aptitude test attempts to measure what an individual has acquired as a result of more general experience. Both can serve to predict an individual's ability to acquire new knowledge or skill in a given area such as mathematics, mechanics, or foreign language learning. While prior achievement in an area such as mathematics is a better predictor of subsequent learning and performance, often no formal instruction has previously occurred. In such cases, only aptitude assessment is possible.

2. Theories and Tests

Theories of aptitude have been intimately tied to trends and developments in the area of mental testing. Historically there have been two contrasting viewpoints which emphasize general mental ability versus specific abilities. A combination of both viewpoints is represented in hierarchical theories of aptitude and intelligence such as those advocated by Cattell (1971) and Vernon (1979). An interesting point is that the database for all theories is essentially the same. It is derived from performance scores on a number of specific mental tests administered to a large sample of individuals. Individuals' scores on each test are then correlated with scores on all other tests in the battery, resulting in a large intercorrelation matrix. The values in the matrix indicate how strongly individual differences on one test are related to individual differences on all other tests. Factor–analytic and other multivariate techniques are then used to attempt a mathematical reduction of this data matrix. The goal of such multivariate analysis methods is to represent the underlying factors or aptitudes responsible for the entire pattern of correlations.

Within this analysis framework a distinction is often

drawn between general aptitudes such as verbal and quantitative ability, inductive reasoning ability, and spatial ability and much more specific abilities such as perceptual speed, memory span, clerical speed, and numerical fluency. Consistent with this is the fact that there are both general-purpose scholastic aptitude tests and more broad-range differential aptitude tests. Scholastic aptitude tests, often referred to as "general intelligence tests," include the Binet and Wechsler individual intelligence tests and numerous intelligence and aptitude tests designed for group administration. General scholastic aptitude tests emphasize measures of both G_c and G_f, the crystallized and fluid intelligence factors of Cattell's (1971) theory. Such tests yield the highest correlations with measures of typical academic achievement. Differential aptitude batteries sample a broader range of skills. An example is the Differential Aptitude Test (DAT). The DAT reports scores for eight subtests measuring verbal reasoning, numerical ability, abstract reasoning, clerical speed and accuracy, mechanical reasoning, spatial relations, spelling, and language usage. In addition to multiple aptitude batteries, tests have been developed for other areas such as musical aptitude and foreign language learning.

The ultimate goal of differential aptitude testing is to provide information that would be of more help in educational and vocational planning and guidance. To some extent this has been realized. For example, success in occupations such as engineering and dentistry has been found to be significantly related to spatial aptitude. However, the attempt to further differentiate aptitude patterns that are related to school performance has been largely unsuccessful. In 1964, McNemar undertook a careful analysis of the validity coefficients of certain widely used differential aptitude batteries, and concluded:

> Aside from tests of numerical ability having differential value for predicting school grades in math, it seems safe to conclude that the worth of multitest batteries as differential predictors of achievement in school has not been demonstrated . . . It is far from clear that tests of general intelligence have been outmoded by the multitest batteries as the more useful predictors of school achievement. (McNemar 1964 p. 875)

More recent work reaffirms McNemar's conclusion (Carroll 1978).

3. Aptitudes and Instructional Treatments

Although the measurement of aptitude and intelligence has always been tied to instructional settings, the question about what underlies such relationships has been a persistent theoretical and practical problem. Woodrow (1946) was among the first to demonstrate that while the correlation between scholastic aptitude and achievement measures was substantial, gains in achievement scores from year to year seemed to be negligibly related to aptitude. Subsequently, it was demonstrated that when the easiest items are eliminated from achievement tests, gains on such tests are significantly related to the complexity of the material that is mastered rather than total amount.

Psychologists and educational researchers have continued to be concerned about the relationship between measures of individual differences and learning variables (see Ackerman 1987 for a thorough discussion of the issues). To a large extent, this work was heralded by the 1957 book by Cronbach and Gleser entitled *Psychological Tests and Personnel Decisions* and its second edition in 1965. This book developed a decision-theory model for the selection and placement of individuals into various "treatments." The word "treatment" was given a broad meaning, referring to what is done with an individual in an institutional setting. In education it refers to the particular programs or instructional methods a student is assigned to or has the opportunity to select. This theoretical analysis pointed out that aptitude information is useful in modifying and selecting treatments only when aptitude and treatment can be shown to interact. Such research is different from differential aptitude testing in which emphasis is placed on determining the relationship between measured aptitudes and learning outcomes resulting from relatively fixed curricula. In ATI (aptitude–treatment–interaction) research, the emphasis is on determining whether aptitudes can predict which of several different learning methods might help different individuals attain similar educational outcomes.

Cronbach and Snow (1977) carried out a very extensive review and analysis of many of the ramifications of the ATI research area. They conclude that, with a few notable exceptions, ATI effects have not been solidly demonstrated. The frequency of studies in which the appropriate interactions have been found is low, and the empirical evidence found in favor of such interactions in often not very convincing. In those occasional instances when positive results have been obtained, no general principles have emerged because of the lack of consistent findings in replication studies and in transfer to new subject matter areas.

Such results certainly do not recommend that standardized tests be abandoned as inappropriate measures in ATI research; the fault in these efforts appears to be in the absence of adequate theories of test performance rather than in the tests themselves. Traditional psychometric instruments need to be accompanied by careful analyses of processes that relate aptitude, treatment, and the knowledge or skills to be learned. Testable theories are required that describe abilities measured in the pretest, abilities required for competent task performance, and treatment procedures that connect the two (Snow 1980). Generally used aptitude constructs are not very productive dimensions for measuring individual differences that interact with different ways of learning. Such measures, derived from a psychometric selection-oriented tradition, do not appear to relate to the processes of learning and performance that have been under investigation in cognitive and developmental psychology. Furthermore, the treatments investigated in many ATI studies have not been generated by any systematic analysis of the kinds of psychological processes called upon in particular instructional methods, and individual differences have not been assessed in terms of related cognitive processes.

4. Cognitive Psychological Approaches

In 1957, Cronbach suggested that, "Constructs originating in differential psychology are now being tied to experimental variables. As a result, the whole theoretical picture in such an area as human abilities is changing. . . . It now becomes possible . . . ultimately to unite this psychology of intelligence with the psychology of learning" (p. 682). The point was reiterated in 1972 by Glaser who called for research on the "new aptitudes" that would be interpreted in terms of process constructs. Since the mid-1970s research has focused on conceptualizing individual differences in aptitudes in terms of the structure, process, and knowledge constructs of contemporary theories of human cognition and cognitive development.

Within this area of aptitude research, there have been two general research approaches (Pellegrino and Glaser 1979). The *cognitive correlates* approach seeks to specify the information-processing abilities that are differentially related to high and low levels of aptitude. Tests of aptitude or intelligence are used to identify subgroups that are compared on laboratory tasks that have cognitive processing characteristics defined by prior experimental and theoretical research. The *cognitive components* approach is task-analytic and attempts to directly identify the information-processing components of performance on tasks that have been generally used to assess mental abilities. Performance on standardized tests of aptitude and intelligence becomes the object of theoretical and empirical analysis, and the goal is to develop models of task performance and apply such models to individual differences analysis. The two approaches are tied to prevalent theories of human cognition, and both attempt to understand the mental structures and activities that contribute to individual differences as measured by psychometric instruments. Pellegrino and Glaser (1979) have discussed the advantages of each approach, noting that the analysis of knowledge and component processes within test tasks circumvents the need to establish a link between performance differences and aptitude test scores.

5. Analyses of Verbal Ability

Process analyses of verbal aptitude have largely emphasized the cognitive correlates type of approach. This is best typified by the work of Hunt (1978), who asked a series of questions about the differences between high and low verbal ability groups that relate to structures, processes, and parameters of the human information-processing system. An extensive series of experiments suggested that university students who score high on a verbal ability battery show, in contrast to lower scoring individuals, faster performance on tasks that require accessing information in long-term memory and manipulating information in short-term memory. In general, Hunt and his co-workers concluded that verbal intelligence tests directly tap a person's knowledge of language, such as the meaning of words, syntactic rules, and semantic relations between concepts denoted by words, and that these tests also indirectly assess more fundamental or elementary information-processing capacities.

Hunt argued that a complex set of factors beyond processing speed may be required to account for individual differences in verbal ability. He suggested three different sources of individual differences: knowledge, information-free mechanistic processes, and general strategies. The mechanics of information processing are divided by Hunt into two components: automatic and controlled attention-demanding processes. The automatic processes appear to be stable individual traits, particularly over the wide range represented by brain-damaged and retarded groups through high verbal ability adults and outstanding mnemonists. The controlled processes, on the other hand, are more labile and thus are not effective long-term predictors of cognitive performance. General strategies include such cognitive performances as rehearsal strategies and metacognitive activities such as the planning, monitoring, and checking involved in problem-solving. Carroll and Maxwell (1979) and Perfetti (1985) should be consulted for a more extensive discussion of related research on individual differences in verbal ability, including research that focuses on individual differences in reading ability.

6. Analyses of Spatial Ability

Process analyses of spatial aptitude have largely emphasized the cognitive components type of approach. This work has benefited greatly from two major reviews of factor analytic research on spatial aptitude (Lohman 1979, McGee 1979). Both note that all major factor analytic studies have identified mechanical/spatial factors that are distinct from other general and specific aptitudes. Lohman (1979) reanalyzed the data from several major studies and delineated two distinct factors labeled *spatial relations* and *spatial visualization*. The spatial relations factor appears to involve the ability to engage rapidly and accurately in mental rotation processes. Spatial relations tasks can be found in test batteries such as the Primary Mental Abilities Test. The spatial visualization factor is defined by tests that are relatively unspeeded and complex. Such tasks frequently require a manipulation in which there is movement among the internal parts of a stimulus configuration or the folding and unfolding of flat patterns. Spatial visualization tasks can be found in test batteries such as the Differential Aptitude Test.

The differences between and among spatial relations and visualization tasks seem to reflect two complementary dimensions of performance. One of these is the speed–power dimension. Individual spatial relations problems are solved more rapidly than spatial visualization problems and the tests themselves are administered in a format that emphasizes speed in the former case and both speed and accuracy in the latter case. The second dimension involves stimulus complexity. Spatial relations problems, although varying among themselves in complexity, involve less complex stimuli than do spatial visualization problems.

Considerable attention has been given to a cognitive components analysis of performance on spatial relations tasks (see Pellegrino and Kail 1982). Studies have examined sources of sex, individual, and developmental differences in performance on simple mental rotation problems. The results are quite consistent in showing that substantial speed differences exist in the encoding and comparison of unfamiliar two-dimensional stimuli and in the execution of a rotation or transformation process that operates on the internal stimulus representation. Adult individual differences exist in all these components of processing and individual differences mirror overall developmental trends. Analyses of age changes in sources of individual differences further suggest that individual differences initially relate to encoding and comparison processes, and that the rotation process subsequently becomes an increasingly important source of individual differences.

A further potential source of individual differences involves the strategy for task execution. It appears that spatial aptitude is associated with the ability to establish sufficiently precise and stable mental representations of unfamiliar visual stimuli that can be subsequently transformed or operated on with a minimal information loss. In spatial relations and visualization tasks, speed of encoding and comparison is significantly related to skill. In more complex tasks, accuracy of encoding and comparison is also significantly related to skill. Differences between spatial relations and spatial visualization tasks (factors) may reflect a difference in emphasis on coding versus transformation processes within the information processing system. Another difference between the two factors may involve single versus sequential transformations and the ability to coordinate and monitor the latter within a working memory structure.

7. Analyses of Inductive Reasoning Ability

The most extensive application of the cognitive components approach to aptitude analysis has been to inductive reasoning tasks. Spearman (1923) and others have argued that inductive reasoning is central to the concept and measurement of intelligence and scholastic aptitude. Greeno (1978) has classified inductive reasoning tasks as a major form of human problem-solving activity. The importance of inductive thought processes has also been emphasized in science, mathematics, and in classroom learning processes.

Major inductive reasoning tasks include series completion, classification, analogy, and matrix completion problems. Various types of content are used to create individual items including letters, numbers, words, and geometric shapes. One or more induction tasks representing verbal and nonverbal content can be found on virtually every test of scholastic aptitude at every developmental level. All induction tasks have the same generic structure. The individual is presented with a set of elements and the task is to induce the rule structure relating the elements so that the pattern can be completed or extended. An example is a letter series completion problem of the form LQAKRCJSEI—. Process models and theories have been developed for virtually all the major inductive reasoning tasks and have been utilized in analyses of developmental and individual differences in inductive reasoning ability (see Pellegrino 1985).

Both qualitative and quantitative changes occur in the inductive reasoning abilities of elementary school-age children. Qualitative changes refer to the strategies used for task solution and the understanding of task demands and constraints. Quantitative changes generally refer to the efficiency with which a process such as inference, comparison, or evaluation of relations is executed. From studies of analogy and classification tasks using verbal, numerical, figural, and geometric stimuli, it can be concluded that the development of inductive reasoning involves all of the aforementioned loci of change. The hallmark of mature inductive reasoning involves the ability to infer, coordinate, and compare multiple relationships that constitute part of a systematic and higher order relational structure. Studies of adult individual differences focusing on both speed and accuracy of processing support the general conclusion that ability differences are primarily associated with processing efficiency. While speed differences are relatively small among college-age individuals, they are nonetheless significant and co-occur with substantial accuracy differences. Studies of individual differences in high-school and elementary-school populations indicate that, like adults, substantial speed and accuracy differences exist among individuals. Less skilled reasoners have difficulties in coordinating and comparing multiple relations among elements of a pattern. In contrast, skilled reasoners are able to manipulate second and third order relationships among elements. A major source of variance involves qualitative differences in the strategy used to solve problems and general understanding of the formal constraints on problem solution.

Studies of developmental and individual differences

in inductive reasoning ability indicate that there are impressive parallels in the sources of variability between and within age groups. The processes that are problematic for younger children also appear to be the primary problem areas for older individuals. Processes that deal with multiple relationship comparison and evaluation are consistent sources of differences between high and low ability reasoners. This problem manifests itself somewhat differently in adults than in children. Differences among adults are largely efficiency differences. Among children, qualitative differences emerge when comparison and evaluation become extremely difficult. Appropriate inductive reasoning seems to be replaced by a more global associative reasoning process. Goldman and Pellegrino (1984) should be consulted for a more detailed treatment of theories, models, and data on inductive reasoning abilities.

8. Future Directions

When standardized aptitude tests are viewed as samples of the knowledge and skills necessary or helpful in contexts such as school learning or job performance, then research can attempt to specify what skills are being assessed, how individuals differ, how such skills are acquired and how they might be affected by instruction. In contrast to previous psychometric approaches to aptitudes and abilities, a cognitive psychological conception of aptitude provides a dynamic account of individual differences in processes, strategies, and knowledge rather than a static account of amount of a hypothesized entity. Studies of individual differences in specific cognitive abilities have already led to new and productive lines of research on assessment and cognitive process training (Brown et al. 1992, Detterman and Sternberg 1982).

A cognitive conception of aptitude can also lead to forms of assessment that would use existing tests in different ways. It should be possible to distinguish between two levels of performance: a level that individuals can independently achieve on tests and a level that they can achieve with aid and assistance during the course of testing. Such an approach has been important in diagnostic testing based on Vygotsky's developmental theory (see Lidz 1988). Thus, rather than viewing an aptitude score as a fixed measure of one's ability to learn, the independent level would provide a sample of the individual's cognitive resources, the assisted level would provide diagnostic information about learning potential, and the differences between the two would be indicative of the areas that should become the focus of instruction.

In summary, the conception of aptitudes and abilities being developed by cognitive and developmental research is that it is possible to identify the components of individual differences in mental abilities in terms of dynamic process and knowledge structure concepts. Simple and complex performances

demanded on aptitude tests, and that assist in the acquisition of academic knowledge and job skill, are being analyzed in terms of the intellectual components involved in problem-solving, language development and understanding, thinking, memory, imagery, and knowledge representation. These efforts should provide the missing theoretical basis for understanding, assessing, and developing mental abilities.

See also: Assessment in the Service of Learning; Individual Differences and Instruction; Intelligence, Learning, and Instruction; Learning Potential and Learning Potential Tests; Metacognition; Teaching: Aptitude–Treatment Interaction Model; An Overview of Cognitive Development

Refrences

Ackerman P L 1987 Individual differences in skill learning: An integration of psychometric and information processing perspectives. *Psychol. Bull.* 102(1): 3–27

Brown A L, Campione J C, Webber L S, McGilly K 1992 Interactive learning environments: A new look at assessment and instruction. In: Gifford B R, O'Connor M C (eds.) 1992 *Changing Assessments: Alternative Views of Aptitude, Achievement and Instruction*. Kluwer, Boston, Massachusetts

Carroll J B 1978 On the theory-practice interface in the measurement of intellectual abilities. In: Suppes P (ed.) 1978 *Impact of Research on Education: Some Case Studies*. National Academy of Education, Washington, DC

Carroll J B, Maxwell S E 1979 Individual differences in cognitive abilities. *Annu. Rev. Psychol.* 30: 603–40

Cattell R B 1971 *Abilities: Their Structure, Growth and Action*. Houghton Mifflin, Boston, Massachusetts

Cronbach L J 1957 The two disciplines of scientific psychology. *Am. Psychol.* 12: 671–84

Cronbach L J, Gleser C C 1957 *Psychological Tests and Personnel Decisions*. University of Illinois Press, Urbana, Illinois

Cronbach L J, Snow R E 1977 *Aptitudes and Instructional Methods: A Handbook for Research on Interactions*. Irvington, New York

Detterman D K, Sternberg R J 1982 *How and How Much Can Intelligence be Increased*. Ablex, Norwood, New Jersey

Glaser R 1972 Individuals and learning: The new aptitudes. *Educ. Res.* 1: 5–13

Goldman S R, Pellegrino J W 1984 Deductions about induction: Analyses of developmental and individual differences. In: Sternberg R J (ed.) 1984 *Advances in the Psychology of Human Intelligence*, Vol. 2. Erlbaum, Hillsdale, New Jersey

Greeno J G 1978 Natures of problem-solving abilities. In: Estes W K (ed.) 1978 *Handbook of Learning and Cognitive Process*. Erlbaum, Hillsdale, New Jersey

Hunt E 1978 Mechanics of verbal ability. *Psychol. Rev.* 85(2): 109–30

Lidz D (ed.) 1988 *Dynamic Assessment: Foundations and Fundamentals*. Guilford Press, New York

Lohman D F 1979 Spatial ability: A review and reanalysis of the correlational literature (Technical Report No. 8). Aptitude Research Project, School of Education, Stanford University, Stanford, California

McGee M G 1979 Human spatial abilities: Psychometric studies and environmental, genetic, hormonal, and neurological influences. *Psychol. Bull.* 86(5): 889–918

McNemar Q 1964 Lost: Our intelligence? Why? *Am. Psychol.* 19: 871–82

Pellegrino J W 1985 Inductive reasoning ability. In: Sternberg R J (ed.) 1985 *Human Abilities: An Information Processing Approach.* W H Freeman, New York

Pellegrino J W, Glaser R 1979 Cognitive correlates and components in the analysis of individual differences. *Intelligence* 3(3): 187–214

Pellegrino J W, Kail R V 1982 Process analyses of spatial aptitude. In: Sternberg R J (ed.) 1982 *Advances in the Psychology of Human Intelligence*, Vol. 1. Erlbaum, Hillsdale, New Jersey

Perfetti C A 1985 *Reading Ability.* Oxford University Press, New York

Spearman C E 1923 *The Nature of Intelligence and the Principles of Cognition.* Macmillan, London

Snow R E 1980 Aptitude and achievement. *New Directions in Testing and Measurement* 5: 39–59

Vernon P E 1979 *The Structure of Human Abilities*, 2nd edn. Greenwood, Westport, Connecticut

Vygotsky L S 1978 *Mind in Society.* Harvard University Press, Cambridge, Massachusetts

Woodrow H 1946 The ability to learn. *Psychol. Rev.* 53: 147–58

Further Reading

Carroll J B 1993 *Human Cognitive Abilities.* Cambridge University Press, New York

Cognitive Styles and Learning

S. Messick

Cognitive styles are usually conceptualized as characteristic modes of perceiving, remembering, thinking, and problem-solving, reflective of information-processing regularities that develop in congenial ways around underlying personality trends. They are inferred from consistent individual differences in ways of organizing and processing information and experience.

Describing cognitive styles as self-consistent regularities implies that to some degree they are both integrative and pervasive. Yet they are pervasive not just in the sense of individual consistencies cutting across activities *within* broad domains such as thinking or interpersonal functioning, but often also in the sense of cutting *across* broad domains. As an instance, the cognitive style of field independence versus field dependence embraces personal/social and not merely cognitive consistencies: the field-independent person is characterized as analytical, self-referent, and impersonal in orientation, the field-dependent person as global, socially sensitive, and interpersonal in orientation (Witkin and Goodenough 1981).

1. Historical Roots

The idea that different individuals have contrasting personalities that differentially influence their modes of cognition and behavioral expression can be traced back to ancient classifications of temperament and physique. The idea is more closely linked to early twentieth-century European notions of type, as exemplified by Jung's conception of extroverted versus introverted types and thinking versus feeling types.

More recently, three major research traditions have contributed directly to work on cognitive styles. The first was differential psychology, especially the factor analysis of perceptual and intellective task performance as exemplified by the studies of Thurstone and Cattell, both of whom uncovered factorial dimensions similar to field-independence. Indeed, the first succinct formulation of the cognitive-style thesis was provided by Thurstone (1944 p. 6): "The attitudes which the subject adopts spontaneously in making the perceptual judgments in these experiments reflect in some way the parameters that characterize him as a person."

The second tradition was psychoanalytic ego psychology, wherein cognitive styles were viewed as organizing and regulating variables in ego adaptation to the environment (Gardner et al. 1959). Within this tradition, Thurstone's notion of "perceptual attitudes" was generalized first to "cognitive attitudes" and then to "cognitive controls," which are adaptive regulatory mechanisms for coping with cognitive environmental demands. The even more general term "cognitive style," which stresses organizing as well as controlling functions, was first used by Gardner (1953).

The third research tradition was the experimental psychology of cognition, with an emphasis on regularities in information-processing. Within cognitive psychology, the Gestalt movement's focus on issues of form in cognition was particularly influential because it led cognitive-style theorists such as Witkin to view individual consistencies in the manner or form of perceiving and thinking as critical psychological phenomena.

Over time, cognitive styles have been characterized in a number of distinct but overlapping ways (Messick 1984). One way, as was seen, is to view cognitive styles as self-consistent characteristic modes of cognition. Another way views them as individual differences in structural properties of the cognitive system itself, such as degree of differentiation, of discrimination or articulation, and of hierarchic integration of cognitive units, which together comprise the style of cognitive complexity versus simplicity (Messick 1976). Another viewpoint conceives of styles as consistent intra-individual contrasts of abilities or of cognitive controls, as in converging versus diverging styles of thinking (Hudson 1968). Still other conceptions define cognitive styles as enduring preferences for different ways of conceptualizing and organizing the stimulus world; as preferred or habitual decision-making strategies; or, as differential preference (or facility) for processing different forms of information. As a final instance, cognitive styles are viewed as cognitive manifestations of underlying personality structures.

Since these various characterizations are overlapping rather than mutually exclusive, a core conceptualization is derived by playing down some features and emphasizing others in accord with empirical findings and theoretical rationales. This core conceptualization is best described by contrasting cognitive styles with intellective abilities and cognitive strategies so as to highlight their differential implications for learning.

2. Cognitive Styles versus Abilities and Strategies

In contrast with intellective abilities, which refer to the content and level of cognition (the questions of What? and How much?), cognitive styles refer to the manner or mode of cognition (the question of How?). Moreover, abilities are unipolar and value-directional (high amounts of ability are always preferable to low amounts and are uniformly more adaptive), while cognitive styles are typically bipolar and value-differentiated (each pole of a style dimension has different adaptive implications). Cognitive styles also differ from abilities in their breadth of coverage and pervasiveness of application. By and large, an ability is specific to a particular domain of content or function, such as verbal, numerical, or spatial ability or fluency and memory ability. A cognitive style, in contrast, cuts across domains of ability, personality, and interpersonal functioning.

In contrast with cognitive strategies, which refer to conscious decisions among alternative approaches

as a function of task requirements and situational constraints, cognitive styles are spontaneously applied without conscious consideration or choice in a wide variety of situations having similar information-processing requirements. In comparison to styles, which tend to be stable and relatively pervasive across diverse areas, strategies are likely to be more amenable to change through instruction and training. Individuals may not only learn to use a variety of problem-solving and learning strategies that are consonant with their cognitive styles but, with effort, also learn to shift to less congenial strategies that are more effective for a particular task.

The bipolarity, pervasiveness, and value differentiation of cognitive styles are idealized properties of the core conceptualization. However, there is considerable variation in the extent to which these properties characterize particular cognitive styles in empirical research (Kogan 1983, Messick 1984). There is also controversy over whether some cognitive styles are value directional rather than value differentiated. In particular, although field-dependent persons may be interpersonally oriented as Witkin claimed, there is sparse evidence that such an orientation translates into interpersonal skill.

More generally, one might expect evidence of cross-situational generality and of value differentiation (i.e., optimal matches between styles and tasks) to be equivocal and complex. This follows because the critical match is not between the style and the task but between the style and the perception of the task and because task goals, and hence optimal strategies, vary both across people and for a given person over time. This raises the problem of the match between cognitive styles and learning tasks or contexts as well as the attendant need for stylistic flexibility in learning, which is addressed in Sect. 5.

3. Cognitive Styles and Information Processing

In addition to field independence versus field dependence and cognitive complexity versus simplicity, other cognitive styles having implications for learning include:

(a) reflection versus impulsivity, the tendency to evaluate alternative solution hypotheses versus the tendency to respond quickly with the first seemingly reasonable answer;

(b) focused scanning versus unfocused scanning or sharp-focus versus broad-focus scanning, a dimension of individual differences in the intensity and extensiveness of attention deployment;

(c) broad versus narrow categorizing, consistent preferences for broad inclusiveness as opposed to narrow exclusiveness in establishing the acceptable range for specified categories (also referred to as "category width" or "equivalence range");

(d) conceptualizing styles, individual consistencies in the utilization of particular kinds of stimulus properties and relationships as bases for forming concepts, such as the preferred use of thematic or functional relations among stimuli (thematic–relational conceptualizing) as opposed to the analysis of descriptive attributes (analytic–descriptive conceptualizing) or the inference of class membership (categorical–inferential conceptualizing);

(e) leveling versus sharpening, the tendency to minimize as opposed to exaggerate stimulus differences in memory and perception;

(f) converging versus diverging, an individual's relative reliance on convergent thinking (pointed toward logical conclusions and uniquely correct or conventionally best outcomes) as contrasted with divergent thinking (pointed toward variety, quantity, and originality of relevant output).

For further descriptions and references, see Kogan (1983) and Messick (1976, 1984). The two most widely studied cognitive styles, field independence versus field dependence and reflection versus impulsivity, continue to sustain vigorous research interest (Bertini et al. 1986, Globerson and Zelniker 1989, Wapner and Demick 1991).

These various cognitive styles can be distinguished from one another in a number of ways, but the most critical distinction relates styles to different phases of an input–output sequence of information-processing or problem-solving. For example, focused scanning versus unfocused scanning is implicated in information search, category width and conceptualizing styles in encoding, leveling versus sharpening in memory storage and retrieval, cognitive complexity versus simplicity in problem representation, field independence versus field dependence in problem-structuring and restructuring, converging versus diverging in hypothesis generation, and reflection versus impulsivity in strategy selection and decision-making. But such association is by no means one-to-one, because some cognitive styles appear to influence information-processing sequences at several points. As an instance, intensity and extensiveness of scanning affects information search of both external stimulus fields and internal fields of memory, meaning, and knowledge.

4. Learning Styles and Orientations Toward Instruction

Although acknowledged to be manifestations of cognitive styles and personality in learning and studying,

a number of learning styles have been identified that are more closely tied to learning tasks than to underlying personality structures. (For references to research in this section, see Schmeck 1988.) In particular, three major learning styles or orientations have been delineated in different research programs. In Entwistle's (1981) program, the three learning styles are labeled "meaning," "reproducing," and "achieving" orientations. They entail, respectively, a search for personal understanding, memorization, and whatever is required to attain high grades. Students with a meaning orientation are intrinsically motivated, those with a reproducing orientation are externally motivated by fear of failure, while those with an achieving style are extrinsically motivated by hope for success. Three similar dimensions isolated by Biggs (1987) are labeled "internalizing," "utilizing," and "achieving" approaches.

In related research by Pask (1976), two learning strategies and associated learning styles have been exhibited by students who were asked to learn principles and procedures well enough to teach them back to others. One strategy is labeled "holist"; consistency in its use indicates a style of comprehension learning. Comprehension learners adopt a global task approach, have a wide range of attention, rely on analogies and illustrations, and tend to construct an overall concept before filling in details. The contrasting learning strategy is labeled "serialist" and the associated style is operation learning. Operation learners adopt a linear task approach and focus attention on operational details and sequential procedures. Students who flexibly employ both strategies are called "versatile" learners.

Similar distinctions have been made by Marton (Marton and Säljö 1976), emphasizing a conclusion-oriented deep-processing approach to learning as opposed to a description-oriented shallow-processing approach. In conclusion-oriented learning, the student's intention is to understand the material and a deep-processing approach is adopted that relates arguments to evidence and ideas to personal experience. In description-oriented learning the student's intention is to memorize the material, and a shallow-processing approach is adopted focusing on discrete facts and disconnected information learned by rote.

In the terms used by Biggs (1987), Entwistle (1981), and Pask (1976), individuals with a meaning or internalizing orientation tend to adopt a deep-processing approach or a holist strategy, or both; students with a reproducing or utilizing orientation tend to adopt a shallow-processing approach or a serialist strategy, or both; and, those with an achieving orientation employ any approach that leads to high grades, deep-processing if understanding is rewarded or shallow-processing if reproduction is rewarded. Biggs demurs on the latter point, however, holding that achieving students develop a shallow approach even under conditions that should foster deep processing.

640

Although these learning styles clearly reflect stylistic consistencies in learning, Entwistle prefers the term orientation to refer to this style-like consistency. This usage serves to highlight his belief that stylistic consistencies in learning are heavily influenced by the student's perception of the situation, mediated by his or her motives.

5. Optimal Learning and the Problem of the Match

Accumulating research evidence indicates that at least some cognitive styles variously influence how students learn, how teachers teach, how students and teachers interact, and how educational and vocational choices are made. For example, teachers and students who are similar in cognitive style tend to view each other with greater mutual esteem than do those who are dissimilar. They also tend to communicate more effectively, as if they were on the same wavelength.

Cognitive styles might thus provide a basis for tailoring the mode of presentation as well as the nature and degree of substantive structure to stylistic characteristics of learners. Student style and instructional mode would be matched so as to develop, compensate for, or capitalize upon student style for the optimization of subject-matter learning. Contrariwise, depending on the educational goals, students might be deliberately confronted with instructional demands that are uncongenial to their cognitive styles so as to stimulate growth and flexibility.

There is thus a continuing tension over the relative value of matching educational treatments to learner characteristics as opposed to mismatching them. Although matching may be facilitative when the aim is to enhance immediate subject-matter achievement, mismatching may be needed when the aim is to promote flexibility and creative thinking. Such trade-offs are the essence of the problem of the match between learner styles on the one hand and the methods and materials of instruction as well as the conditions of learning on the other.

In this connection, because each direction of a cognitive style dimension has adaptive value under different circumstances, attention can be given to the possibility of effectively utilizing the positive features of both poles—as in Pask's (1976) "versatile" learners who combine comprehension and operation learning, in Hudson's (1968) "all-rounders" or intellectual "labiles" who combine converging and diverging, and in the "bicognitive" development of both field independence and field sensitivity espoused by Ramírez and Castañeda (1974). In this regard, Entwistle (1981) stressed the advantages of systematically alternating learning conditions that foster complementary modes of thought. This suggests that an important educational goal should be to develop and enhance flexibility in modes of thinking, thereby reducing to some extent the restrictiveness and preemptiveness of habitual or stylistic thought.

References

Bertini M, Pizzamiglio L, Wapner S 1986 *Field Dependence in Psychological Theory, Research, and Application.* Erlbaum, Hillsdale, New Jersey

Biggs J B 1987 *Student Approaches to Learning and Studying.* Australian Council for Educational Research, Hawthorn

Entwistle N 1981 *Styles of Learning and Teaching: An Integrated Outline of Educational Psychology for Students, Teachers, and Lecturers.* Wiley, New York

Gardner R W 1953 Cognitive styles in categorizing behavior. *J. Pers.* 22: 214–33

Gardner R W, Holzman P S, Klein G S, Linton H B, Spence D 1959 Cognitive control: A study of individual consistencies in cognitive behavior. *Psychol. Iss.* 1(4): 1–186

Globerson T, Zelniker T (eds.) 1989 *Cognitive Style and Cognitive Development.* Ablex, Norwood, New Jersey

Hudson L 1968 *Contrary Imaginations: A Psychological Study of the English Schoolboy.* Penguin, Harmondsworth

Kogan N 1983 Stylistic variation in childhood and adolescence: Creativity, metaphor, and cognitive style. In: Mussen P H, Flavell J H, Markman E M (eds.) 1983 *Handbook of Child Psychology. Vol. 3: Cognitive Development.* Wiley, New York

Marton F, Säljö R 1976 On qualitative differences in learning: I, Outcome and processes. *Br. J. Educ. Psychol.* 46(1): 4–11

Messick S 1976 Personality consistencies in cognition and creativity. In: Messick S (ed.) 1976 *Individuality in Learning: Implications of Cognitive Styles and Creativity for Human Development.* Jossey-Bass, San Francisco, California

Messick S 1984 The nature of cognitive styles: Problems and promise in educational practice. *Educ. Psychol.* 19(2): 59–74

Pask G 1976 Styles and strategies of learning. *Br. J. Educ. Psychol.* 46(2): 128–48

Ramírez M, Castañeda A 1974 *Cultural Democracy, Bicognitive Development, and Education.* Academic Press, New York

Schmeck R R (ed.) 1988 *Learning Strategies and Learning Styles.* Plenum, New York

Thurstone L L 1944 *A Factorial Study of Perception.* University of Chicago Press, Chicago, Illinois

Wapner S, Demick J 1991 *Field Dependence–Independence: Cognitive Style Across the Life Span.* Erlbaum, Hillsdale, New Jersey

Witkin H A, Goodenough D R 1981 *Cognitive Styles: Essence and Origins—Field Dependence and Field Independence.* International Universities Press, New York

Gender and School Learning: Mathematics

S. F. Chipman

The topic of gender differences in mathematics performance has attracted a great deal of research attention, especially in the United States. Indeed, the amount of research attention seems out of proportion to the phenomenon. Although the belief that males outperform females in mathematics is widespread, the data do not necessarily support this belief, even for United States populations (Chipman and Thomas 1985, Hyde, Fennema and Lamon 1990). Large studies of probability samples of student populations in the United States tend to find little or no gender difference in overall mathematics performance prior to the secondary school years when study of mathematics often becomes optional in the United States. Worldwide, comparable studies in some countries show females outperforming males, and some show males outperforming females (Hanna 1989, Ethington 1990).

Whatever the outcome of a particular population sample in a particular country, it is most important to recognize that reported gender differences in performance are very small in relation to the range of individual differences: an individual's gender has essentially nil value in predicting mathematical performance.

One can be easily misled by the "statistically significant" results that the enormous populations of mass testing programs provide. Despite apparent statistical significance, these results could shift direction because of factors like subtle social influences on the rates of participation of each gender in the populations sampled (persons enrolled in schools, persons voluntarily taking the Scholastic Aptitude Test exam) or idiosyncratic performance of even a single test item.

1. More Detailed Findings

The intense research attention to this topic in the United States has provided many details, but some of the findings may be specific to the particular country or culture. Within the overall picture of no gender difference in mathematics performance in the early school years, in the United States it is sometimes reported that girls perform better on computational items and boys perform better on some types of word problem items (e.g., Marshall 1984). However, a meta-analysis concluded that there are no such differences evident prior to secondary school (Hyde et al. 1990). Similarly, a detailed analysis of gender differences in relation to the content of items in the International Association for the Evaluation of Educational Achievement (IEA) Second International Mathematics Study (Ethington 1990) came to the conclusion that, "within no content area were males found to persistently outperform females across countries or vice versa" (p. 79). These

data refer to students at age 13, when mathematics is still a nearly universal component of the curriculum in all participating countries. In contrast to the general picture of equality, searches for mathematically talented youths have generated reports that extremely high levels of mathematical performance on the SAT at a young age are much more frequently found in males (Benbow and Stanley 1980, 1983). However, these results are not necessarily based on representative samples. By the end of secondary school in the United States, gender differences in mathematics test performance favoring males are usually reported, and the performance differences seem to arise from problem-solving tests or items (Hyde et al. 1990). Evidently, similar gender differences are observed in West Germany (Klieme 1986, 1989).

2. Course-taking as a Critical Variable

An analysis of data from a major United States survey sample collected in the 1960s, when there were very substantial gender differences in secondary school mathematics course enrollment, showed that course enrollments statistically accounted for nearly all of the gender difference in mathematics performance at the end of secondary school (Wise 1985). In the 1980s, the gap in the number of mathematics courses taken by male and female students had narrowed, but the performance difference of about 0.4 of a standard deviation on tests like the SAT, a widely used but noncompulsory test for college and university admission, remains. However, it is also true that large gender differences remain in the enrollments for the more advanced and optional secondary school mathematics courses, such as calculus and statistics and probability. Similar differences in enrollment patterns seem to exist in many countries, such as Israel, Ireland, and New Zealand (Schildkamp-Kündiger 1982). Since the mid-1960s, female participation in college and university level study has risen from about 25 percent to over 50 percent in the United States. Consequently, it is likely that more female students are taking the secondary school mathematics courses which are routinely expected for admission to tertiary institutions, but it is still true that relatively few are committed to career directions which intrinsically require intensive mathematical preparation.

3. School, Classroom, and Teacher Influences

Although one frequently hears anecdotes about the beneficial effects of teacher encouragement or the adverse effects of teacher discouragement, it has proved difficult to demonstrate such effects in research. At one time, there were reports that teachers had lower expectations for the mathematical achievement of girls; in the 1990s teachers in the United States will no longer admit to such beliefs. Extensive classroom observations, accompanied by very thorough efforts at analysis, have been unsuccessful in identifying characteristics of classroom interaction that predict the success of female students or their likelihood of persisting in the study of advanced mathematics. However, there certainly is great variation from school to school in the representation of female students in advanced mathematics classes. No doubt some explanation for this variation could be found in features of the school and faculty, in the surrounding community context, or perhaps in historical accident that has affected local expectations. One study (Casserly and Rock 1985) directed at this question did find that a strong academic tracking system in secondary school favored the persistence of female students in the study of mathematics. Given that male and female test scores in mathematics at the beginning of secondary school are comparable, that a strong tracking system results in a strong expectation for course enrollments, and that female students perform well in mathematics courses when they take them, this result is not surprising.

4. Effects of the Performance Measures Used

Different measures of mathematical performance give different pictures of gender differences. In contrast to standardized tests, course performance measures consistently favor females (Kimball 1989). Similarly, the results of some studies tend to indicate that examinations which are closely tied to the instructed curriculum, like the New York State Regents Exam (Felson and Trudeau 1991) or the IEA Mathematics content which is well-represented in the "implemented curriculum" (Hanna 1989), are more likely to favor females. In a large-scale study, it was shown that when males and females were matched by a university mathematics course taken and the performance grade received, females had received scores nearly 50 points lower (0.5 s.d.) on the SAT examination (Wainer and Steinberg 1992). Such results raise the possibility that gender differences in performance on the standardized tests of mathematics primarily reflect differences in responding to the testing situation itself (Becker 1990), or that they may arise from extracurricular differences in experience that are related to the content of some such tests.

Quite a number of analyses of gender differences in performance on particular test items of the SAT or similar tests have been done. Individual test items can be found that show very large gender differences, but the reasons for those differences are not obvious, and there has been little or no consistency in the apparent nature of such items from one study to the next. Occasionally these analyses have appeared to confirm hypotheses

that gender differences might be concentrated in items with geometric or spatial content, but this has not been consistently true. Such hypotheses originate in the belief that there are substantial gender differences in spatial ability. This belief is also much more weakly supported by the evidence than generally believed (Linn and Petersen 1985), and even where gender differences in both mathematical and spatial ability have been found, the latter do not seem to be able to account for the former (Klieme 1986). In several studies of the SAT, a class of mathematics items ("data sufficiency items") which ask whether sufficient data are available to answer the question, did consistently favor females; such items are no longer used. An experimental study (Chipman et al. 1991) did not confirm the popular hypothesis that sex-stereotyped content of mathematics word problems would affect performance.

5. Broad Social Implications

Because of the important role that the SAT exam plays in influencing access to educational opportunities, including both admission to selective tertiary institutions and scholarship support, the pronounced gender differences in performance on this examination —especially in contrast with the course performance it is intended to predict—have provoked considerable controversy in the United States (Rosser 1989). Apparently similar controversy has surrounded the German examinations for admission to medical school (Klieme 1989), where gender differences of about 0.5 standard deviation have also been observed.

Although the hypothesis has been advanced that the desire to avoid mathematics may account for the low rates of participation of women in scientific and engineering fields requiring mathematics, analysis of the demographic facts of United States women's participation in the advanced study of mathematics yields surprising results. The representation of women among recipients of BA degrees in mathematics has run just below their representation in the total population of BA recipients: no other field has been closer to proportional representation. Mathematics itself seems to be relatively attractive to women; therefore the low rates of participation in engineering and the physical sciences probably should not be attributed to the mathematical component of those fields. At more advanced levels of education, however, United States women have both lower rates of participation in the entire student population and proportionately lower rates of participation in mathematics study. It seems that a similar picture may prevail in Israel (Lewy 1982).

6. Role of Affective Responses to Mathematics

A large number of studies indicate that female students in the United States like mathematics as much as male students do; however, they do tend to have somewhat less confidence in their ability to succeed in mathematics (Chipman and Wilson 1985, Hyde et al. 1990). It seems likely that prevailing social stereotypes account for that gender difference. For example, the extensive and somewhat distorted popular press attention to Benbow and Stanley (1980) had a negative impact on the expectations that girls and their parents had for their achievement in mathematics (Eccles and Jacobs 1986). Headlines at the time read: "Do males have a math gene?" (*Newsweek*); "A new study says males may be naturally abler than females." (*TIME*); "Are girls born with less ability?" (*Science*). In addition, there are still substantial gender differences both in specific vocational interests and plans and in general interest patterns (such as interest in things as contrasted to people) which predict vocational choices. Therefore it is likely that lower rates of participation by females in advanced study of mathematics, and perhaps less intense engagement in the courses that are taken, result from lack of interest in or expectation of pursuing careers in which mathematics is useful or necessary. A report from Israel (Lewy 1982), for example, noted that mathematics performance among kibbutzim children was found to be very strongly related to sex ($r = 0.40$), attributing this fact to the very traditional occupational roles of women in the kibbutzim. The Terman study of gifted children gives some indication of the possible significance of vocationally related interests, even though it is now a look at the past. Women differed from men in both the direction and the breadth of their interests; furthermore, for men, breadth of interest was a negative predictor of career success (Terman and Oden 1947). One should not necessarily attribute differences in achievements to differences in cognitive abilities. Eccles et al. (1985) have been pursuing a research program focused on the motivational aspects of mathematics enrollment and achievement, within the framework provided by the expectation-value theory of human choice.

7. A Larger Context of Interpretation

The interpretation of those gender differences in mathematics performance that may be observed must be considered in a large historical and social perspective which is often forgotten. Within a relatively short span of years, many countries have moved from the presumption that women would never do anything in which mathematical knowledge was relevant, to a situation in which emerging female interest in traditionally masculine fields was blocked by formal barriers, to a situation in which—at least nominally —all fields are considered open to women. As late as the 1940s females were barred from the study of advanced mathematics and physics in some United States secondary schools. In the 1960s, the US National Science Foundation sponsored special summer programs for secondary school students in physics to which female students were not admitted. Similarly,

until 1969, different curricular expectations in mathematics for males and females were institutionalized in the regulations of the Irish government (McGuinness and Oldham 1982). As late as the 1950s, a large proportion of the women who were recognized as creative mathematicians in the United States were unemployed (Helson 1971). Yet, suddenly, "explanations" for low rates of female participation in fields from which they were formerly barred are sought in presumed gender differences in inherent mathematical ability. Any such interpretation is premature. No deep theoretical understanding of the nature of mathematical ability exists that would provide any scientific basis for such an interpretation; all purported tests of mathematical ability (such as the SAT) are also measures of achieved learning. Gender differences in other relevant variables, such as vocational interests and social role expectations, are much larger in magnitude than any reported gender differences in mathematics performance and therefore are also much better candidates for an explanatory role in determining women's career destinies.

See also: Gender and School Learning: Science; Gender Roles

References

Becker B J 1990 Item characteristics and gender differences on the SAT-M for mathematically able youths. *Am. Educ. Res. J.* 27(1): 65–87

Benbow C P, Stanley J C 1980 Sex differences in mathematical ability: Fact or artifact? *Science* 210: 1262–64

Benbow C P, Stanley J C 1983 Sex differences in mathematical reasoning ability: More facts. *Science* 222: 1029–31

Casserly P L, Rock D 1985 Factors related to young women's persistence and achievement in advanced placement mathematics. In: Chipman S F, Brush L R, Wilson D M (eds.) 1985

Chipman S F, Marshall S P, Scott P A 1991 Content effects on word problem performance: A possible source of test bias? *Am. Educ. Res. J.* 28(4): 897–915

Chipman S F, Thomas V G 1985 Women's participation in mathematics: Outlining the problem. In: Chipman S F, Brush L R, Wilson D M (eds.) 1985

Chipman S F, Wilson D M 1985 Understanding mathematics course enrollment and mathematics achievement: A synthesis of the research. In: Chipman S F, Brush L R, Wilson D M (eds.) 1985

Eccles J S et al. 1985 Self-perceptions, task perceptions, socializing influences, and the decision to enroll in mathematics. In: Chipman S F, Brush L R, Wilson D M (eds.) 1985

Eccles J S, Jacobs J E 1986 Social forces shape math attitudes and performance. *Signs* 11(2): 367–80

Ethington C A 1990 Gender differences in mathematics: An international perspective. *J. Res. Math. Educ.* 21(1): 74–80

Felson R B, Trudeau L 1991 Gender differences in mathematics performance. *Soc. Psychol. Q.* 54(2): 113–26

Hanna G 1989 Mathematics achievement of girls and boys in

grade eight: Results from twenty countries. *Educ. Stud. Math.* 20(2): 225–32

Helson R 1971 Women mathematicians and the creative personality. *J. Consult. Clin. Psychol.* 36(2): 210–20

Hyde J S, Fennema E, Lamon S J 1990 Gender differences in mathematics performance: A meta-analysis. *Psychol. Bull.* 107(2): 139–55

Hyde J S, Fennema E, Ryan M, Frost L A, Hopp C 1990 Gender difference of mathematics attitude and affect: A meta-analysis. *Psychol. Women Q.* 14(3): 299–324

Kimball M M 1989 A new perspective on women's math achievement. *Psychol. Bull.* 105(2): 198–214

Klieme E 1986 Bildliches Denken als Mediator fur Geschlectsunterscheiden beim Lösen mathematischer Probleme In: Steiner H G (ed.) *Grundfragen der Entwicklung mathematischer Fähigkeiten.* Aulis, Cologne

Klieme E 1989 *Mathematisches Problemlösen als Testleistung.* Peter Lang, Frankfurt

Lewy A 1982 Gender and mathematics in Israel. In: Schildkamp-Kündiger E (ed.) 1982

Linn M C, Petersen A C 1985 Emergence and characterization of sex differences in spatial ability: A meta-analysis. *Child Dev.* 56(6): 1479–98

Marshall S P 1984 Sex differences in children's mathematics achievement: Solving computations and story problems. *J. Educ. Psychol.* 76(2): 194–204

McGuinness P J, Oldham E E 1982 Gender and mathematics in Ireland. In: Schildkamp-Kündiger (ed.) 1982

Rosser P 1989 *The SAT Gender Gap: Identifying the Causes.* Center for Women Policy Studies, Washington, DC

Schildkamp-Kündiger E (ed.) 1982 *An International Review of Gender and Mathematics.* ERIC Clearinghouse for Science, Mathematics, and Environmental Education, Columbus Ohio (ERIC # ED222326, SE039181)

Terman L M, Oden M H 1947 *Genetic Studies of Genius: The Gifted Child Grows Up: Twenty-five Years' Follow-up of a Superior Group*, Vol. 4. Stanford University Press, Stanford, California

Wainer H, Steinberg L S 1992 Sex differences in performance on the mathematics section of the Scholastic Aptitude Test: A bidirectional validity study. *Harv. Educ. Rev.* 62:323–36

Wise L L 1985 Project TALENT: Mathematics course participation in the 1960s and its career consequences. In: Chipman S F, Brush L R, Wilson D M (eds.) 1985

Further Reading

Chipman S F, Brush L R, Wilson D M (eds.) 1985 *Women and Mathematics: Balancing the Equation.* Erlbaum, Hillsdale, New Jersey

Chipman S F, Thomas V G 1987 The participation of women and minorities in mathematical, scientific, and technical fields. *Rev. Res. Educ.* 14: 387–430

Gender and School Learning: Science

M. C. Linn

The goal of equal opportunity for males and females in school science, informal science learning experiences, and science careers is gradually gaining ground internationally. In all countries women have struggled for access to primary, secondary, and higher education and for opportunities to study science. In most countries the first changes in women's access to science came in fields associated with the home. The benefits of women studying child development, botany, or home economics are easiest to understand. Broader opportunities often follow and in the 1990s in many countries, women comprise a third to a half of the medical doctors and make contributions in scientific endeavors. Nevertheless, even when years of experience are controlled, there is a gap between salaries for men and women in scientific fields (Wellesley College Center for Research on Women 1992) and many women lack the opportunity to learn science.

Patterns of achievement, opportunity, and inclination to learn science tell part of the story. These patterns can only be understood, however, in the context of the society in which individuals live. The mechanisms that govern these patterns, including subtle influences such as the recently publicized tendency of researchers in the health professions to study the health of males more than the health of females, or the differences in the way science teachers treat males and females, are the key to achieving equity.

Overall, the gender gap in participation and success in school science is narrowing slightly. Female participation in science careers is also increasing although there is a tendency toward a leveling off in many technical areas. In order to attract more women to science, changes in both courses and careers is necessary. In addition, broader societal changes are needed to alter the norms and expectations for males and females in science.

1. Is the Gender Gap in Science Achievement Closing?

The achievement of males and females in school science can be assessed by comparing knowledge of scientific information, understanding of scientific concepts, grades in science classes, and students' beliefs about the nature of scientific knowledge. Ideally, achievement would be assessed among those with an equal opportunity to learn. Realistically, since many learning opportunities are informal, occurring in families, at science centers, in libraries, and in apprenticeship programs, such analyses are impossible.

The general narrowing of the gender gap in academic achievement is less apparent in science than in verbal ability, spatial ability, and mathematical ability (Hyde and Linn 1986, Linn and Hyde 1991). Overall, the gap is narrowing more for understanding of scientific concepts than for knowledge of scientific information.

1.1 Knowledge of Scientific Information

Most national and international assessments measure students' ability either to discriminate or recall scientific information. Tests typically cover all major domains of science including physics, chemistry, biology, geology, earth science, and health science. These assessments feature multiple-choice items requiring students to discriminate among reasonably complex scientific ideas. For example, one seventh grade item from the National Assessment of Educational Progress asked students, "Which of the following best explains why water, when heated, takes up more space: (a) the water molecules have become bigger; (b) the average space between the water molecules has increased; (c) water molecules from the air have condensed into the beaker; or (d) many of the water molecules have split, making new gases."

International assessments reveal large discrepancies in performance between students from different countries as well as a gender gap in knowledge of science, with males outperforming females. In the 1988 International Assessment of Mathematics and Science, 13-year old males significantly outperformed females in all countries except the United States and the United Kingdom (LaPointe et al. 1989).

National assessments in the United States reveal that the magnitude of the gender gap varies with scientific domain. Differences are largest for physics, and smallest for biology and health science. The gap also varies with age, getting larger as students become older (Jacobson and Doran 1985, National Assessment of Educational Progress 1988, Keeves 1992, Postlethwaite and Wiley 1992, Rosier and Keeves 1991). Thus, the gender gap in science achievement is smaller in the United States than in other countries, but still larger in physical science and among 17-year old students.

1.2 Understanding of Science Concepts

Research studies often assess understanding of scientific concepts such as "isolation of variables" or "interpretation of experiments." Students may be asked to evaluate an experiment or to use information supplied by the experimenter to reach a conclusion. Understanding of concepts is commonly measured with short answer or essay questions. Meta-analyses reveal few gender differences in performance (Hyde and Linn 1986, Steinkamp and Maehr 1984, NAEP 1988). An exception is that scientific concepts involving the computation of ratios, such as density, are easier for males than females, consistent with the gender gap in mathematics performance.

This pattern of male success on multiple-choice science information tests and female success on short answer science concept tests recurs regularly. For example, on the American Advanced Placement Biology test, females are more successful on the essay, and males are more successful on the multiple-choice questions. Both the essay results and the multiple-choice results are predictive of subsequent grades in science (Linn 1992). One explanation for this pattern is that essay questions draw on integrated knowledge of a topic by the examinee, while multiple-choice items draw on examinees' understanding of all the topics in the field. The multiple-choice items might tap informal, out-of-school learning where males are advantaged. The essay may tap in-school learning as well as verbal skills where females are slightly advantaged.

1.3 Course Experience and Grades in School

Females earn higher science grades than males at all levels of school science from elementary to college (Grandy 1987). Ideally, school grades assess science understanding as well as recall of information taught in class. Yet, among students who take the same courses, males still outperform females on multiple choice assessments (NAEP 1988, Postlethwaite and Wiley 1992, Rosier and Keeves 1991). Whatever students are learning in science classes, it is not contributing to a narrowing of the gender gap on multiple choice assessments. The gap on multiple choice tests, when course experience is controlled, reinforces the conjecture these tests tap broader, culturally-normed experiences.

1.4 Beliefs About Scientific Knowledge

More and more courses are including, among their objectives, the goal of imparting a realistic view of science. Ideally, students would understand the relevance of science to their lives: the implications of science ideas presented in school for complex scientific problems such as waste disposal and air pollution. In addition, students would understand that science is an ongoing, intellectual enterprise, that debate and controversy are components of scientific exploration, and that scientific advance is a complex process involving the weighing of evidence, the construction of theories, and the funding of research. Students would also realize that understanding science is more useful than memorizing scientific ideas.

Investigations of students' beliefs about scientific

knowledge reveal large individual differences. Some students have a realistic view of science and recognize the relationship between scientific knowledge and complex scientific problems. Other students believe that the best way to learn science is to memorize rather than to understand, and see no relationship between the science they study in their science classes and scientific debates in newspapers and on the radio (Linn et al. 1991).

Assessments reveal that males and females are equally aware of the nature of science (NAEP 1988). Females may understand the nature of science in part because they are more likely than males to view science as socially constructed (Gilligan 1982, Keller 1986).

In summary, the gender gap in science information remains large internationally, the gap for understanding science concepts is small and declining, and science grades traditionally favor females rather than males. In scientific information, gender differences are larger in physics than in other domains, and for older rather than younger students. In addition, when beliefs about scientific knowledge are measured, gender differences are not typically found. These patterns of achievement are consistent with formal and informal opportunities to learn science.

2. Opportunity and Inclination to Learn Science and Participate in Science Careers

Historically, in all countries males have had more opportunities than females to learn science (Rossiter 1982). In almost all cultures, males were admitted to science courses before females and males hold positions of power and leadership in science. This situation has led to the widespread view that science is a male domain and that science courses are more useful for males than females. In assessments where students are asked whether science is a male domain, large differences between males and females are frequently found (Zimmerer and Bennett 1987). Males believe that science is a male domain, and females disagree. There are differences between countries and between the sexes in views about the usefulness of science. For example, 82 percent of North Korean students compared to 50 percent of United States students indicated that much of what is learnt in science classes is useful. Similarly, within the United States population, 54 percent of males compared to 47 percent of females expect science to be useful to them (NAEP 1988). Presumably, those who expect to follow science careers view current courses as more useful.

2.1 Course Experience

Participation in science courses is increasing internationally. In some countries, females are gaining access to science instruction for the first time. In other countries, students are enrolling in more advanced courses.

For example, in the United States, female high school students took an average of 2.13 courses in 1982 and 2.53 in 1987. Males took 2.25 courses in 1982 and 2.66 courses in 1987 (Westat Inc. 1988). In spite of these increases the magnitude of the gender gap remains unchanged.

A big problem is the lack of participation of both males and females in advanced science courses. For example, in the United States, only about 20 percent of high school students take courses in physics, and at least two-thirds are male. One remedy is to encourage students to take advanced courses, yet existing science courses often fail to meet the needs of students. These courses convince many students that learning science consists of memorizing scientific facts, and that complex and ambiguous problems in society are not likely to respond to scientific investigation. The goals of improving science courses and increasing participation in these courses must be addressed simultaneously.

Furthermore, courses should prepare all students to be citizens as well as potential scientists. For example, rather than limiting courses on maternal and child health to women, these courses should be required for all students. Similarly, courses that prepare citizens to participate in national scientific debates should be available to all.

Courses will not provide equal experiences for males and females unless the expectations of teachers and peers change. Much research indicates that teachers are more likely to ask males rather than females to answer complex questions, and to give positive feedback to males, but negative feedback to females. Such behavior reinforces the view that science is a male domain and stands in the way of effective and equitable course experience for males and females (Kahle 1990, Tobin 1987, Tobin et al. 1990).

2.2 Informal Learning Experience

The discrepant experiences in school science of males and females are intensified in informal learning. When voluntary courses are available at science centers, museums, and schools, males are more likely than females to participate. Families are more likely to send male children to science camps, to buy computers for male children, and to encourage males to read science books. As a result, even among 9-year olds, when students are asked about experiences with scientific equipment and material, there are large gender differences. For example, in the United States 58 percent of males at age 9 report having used a telescope compared to 45 percent of females (NAEP 1988).

2.3 Career Participation

Participation in scientific careers is much more common for males than females. Furthermore, female participation in some scientific careers has peaked and is declining (Pearl et al. 1990). Historically, many degree programs denied access to women. As access has been granted, women have encountered more subtle barriers to advancement and success.

Many fields have been constructed exclusively by males. As a result, the research agenda and the standards for participation reflect the nature of the participants. Philosophers of science have begun to document the implications of excluding one gender from the development of scientific domains (Keller 1986, Longino 1990). For example, it is likely that the research agenda in the health sciences would be different if the decision makers had included more women. In addition, the aggressive discourse characteristic of many scientific debates often excludes women who are either labeled as "difficult" if they participate or "dumb" if they remain silent.

Increasing participation of females in science requires that both courses and careers be made more inviting.

3. Equitable and Effective Science Courses

Equity and effectiveness go hand in hand in science courses. To teach science to all students, courses should (a) emphasize understanding, not memorization; (b) respect student ideas rather than labeling them misconceptions; and (c) instill a view of science as dynamic rather than static.

3.1 Science Understanding

Current science courses often stand in the way of understanding by featuring fleeting coverage of numerous topics, a barrage of esoteric vocabulary, and tests that assess isolated scientific information. Furthermore, students may fail to achieve understanding because their science courses overemphasize microscopic models of phenomena and formal methods of analysis and also fail to integrate everyday and scientific reasoning. Scientists often complain that science is simpler than it appears to students. Yet from the standpoint of students that simplicity is illusory. Scientists point out that formal, microscopic models such as molecular-kinetic theory are parsimonious and easy to apply to abstract problems while students describe these same models as irrelevant and incomprehensible. Even scientists often use qualitative models such as heat flow to explain complex and ambiguous everyday events. To impart understanding the goals of science courses must be changed to reflect the needs and perspectives of students.

3.2 Building on Student Ideas

Science instructors can discourage students by labeling their ideas as "misconceptions" rather than recognizing these ideas as attempts to construct understanding of complex events. Rather than rejecting a student's view that aluminum foil could keep a drink cold because "metals impart cold," instructors might instead help students differentiate their observations about metals feeling cold from their observations about good and poor insulators. This approach builds on existing observations and reinforces student efforts to make sense of scientific events.

Helping students construct more powerful ideas rather than telling students to substitute scientists' ideas for their own builds lasting knowledge but takes instructional time. Instructors often resort to telling students the "correct" scientific ideas because there is no time to explain or because the explanations in the textbook are inaccessible to students. As a result, few students gain understanding of science and most resort to memorization.

This knowledge-telling approach to instruction combined with the observed propensity of teachers to give more positive and constructive feedback to males than to females is likely to encourage males to memorize science information and females to avoid science.

Often peers interacting in groups reinforce these influential views by encouraging males and criticizing females. Group learning experiences can further undermine the confidence of females in science if not carefully engineered. Instructors using group learning need to help students learn how to respect the ideas of others and avoid stereotyped responses such as "You're wrong. Girls can't do science."

3.3 Imparting a Dynamic View of Science

Understanding of science concepts includes insight into the nature of scientific knowledge. Students need to distinguish established from controversial ideas, to understand how evidence is used to support conjectures, and to recognize that scientific discourse includes heated debate. Courses featuring knowledge telling obscure these scientific processes.

Thus, science courses could be modified to better serve the needs of all students. Such changes would be particularly beneficial for women. Studies of those who drop out of science programs reinforce the view that current courses discourage women. Women who drop out of science are just as successful as those who remain. Women often leave science courses and careers not because of lack of success or poor grades but because they feel undervalued and unwelcome in these courses and careers.

In summary, it is not sufficient to attract women to scientific courses and careers. It is necessary in addition to modify those courses and careers such that they meet the needs of all who could participate. Until these changes occur, it will be more likely that males participate in science courses and careers than females. The extreme of this trend is apparent in statistics showing that foreign male students are more likely to enter advanced training programs in engineering and physics than are native-born women in many countries where advanced training is available.

See also: Gender and School Learning: Mathematics; Sex Differences in Behavior and Behavioral Development

References

Gilligan C 1982 In a different voice: Psychological theory and women's development. *Harv. Educ. Rev.* 47(7): 481–517

Grandy J 1987 *Ten-year Trends in SAT Scores and other Characteristics of High School Seniors Taking the SAT and Planning to Study Mathematics, Science, or Engineering.* Educational Testing Service, Princeton, New Jersey

Hyde J S, Linn M C (eds.) 1986 *The Psychology of Gender: Advances through the Meta-analysis.* Johns Hopkins University Press, Baltimore, Maryland

Jacobson W J, Doran R L 1985 The Second International Science Study US results. *Phi Del. Kap.* 66(6): 414–17

Kahle J B 1990 Real students take chemistry and physics: Gender issues. In: Tobin K, Kahle J B, Fraser B J (eds.) 1990

Keeves J P 1992 *Learning Science in a Changing World.* International Association for the Evaluation of Educational Achievement, The Hague

Keller E F 1986 *Reflections on Gender and Science.* Yale University Press, New Haven, Connecticut

LaPointe A E, Mead N A, Phillips G W 1989 *A World of Differences: An International Assessment of Mathematics and Science Tech.* Report No. 19-CAEP-01. Educational Testing Service, Princeton, New Jersey

Linn M C 1992 Gender differences in educational achievement. In: Pfleiderer J (ed.) 1992 *Sex Equity in Educational Opportunity, Achievement, and Testing.* Proc. 1991 Educational Testing Service Invitational Conference. Educational Testing Service, Princeton, New Jersey

Linn M C, Hyde J S 1991 Trends in cognitive and psychosocial gender differences. In: Lerner R M, Petersen A C, Brooks-Gunn J (eds.) 1991 *Encyclopedia of Adolescence.* Garland Publishing, New York

Linn M C, Songer N B, Lewis E L 1991 Overview: Students' models and epistemologies of science. *J. Res. Sci. Teach.* 28(9): 729–32

Longino H E 1990 *Science as Social Knowledge: Values and Objectivity in Scientific Inquiry.* Princeton University Press, Princeton, New Jersey

National Assessment of Educational Progress (NAEP) 1988 *The Science Report Card: Elements of Risk and Recovery. Trends and Achievement Based on the 1986 National Assessment.* Educational Testing Service, Princeton, New Jersey

Pearl A, Pollack M, Riskin E, Thomas B, Wolf E, Wu A 1990 Becoming a computer scientist. *Comm. ACM* 33(11): 48–57

Postlethwaite T N, Wiley D E 1992 *The International Studies in Educational Achievement (IEA) Study of Science II: Science Education and Curricula in Twenty-three Countries.* Pergamon Press, Oxford

Rosier M J, Keeves J P 1991 *The International Studies in Educational Achievement (IEA) Study of Science I: Science Education and Curricula in Twenty-three Countries.* Pergamon Press, Oxford

Rossiter M W 1982 *Women Scientists in America: Struggles and Strategies to 1940.* Johns Hopkins University Press, Baltimore, Maryland

Steinkamp M W, Maehr M L (eds.) 1984 *Women in Science.* JAI Press, Greenwich, Connecticut

Tobin K 1987 Gender differences in science: They don't happen here! In: Fraser B, Giddings G (eds.) 1987 *Gender Issues in Science Education.* Curtin University of Technology, Perth

Tobin K, Kahle J B, Fraser B J (eds.) 1990 *Windows into Science Classrooms: Problems Associated with Higher-level Cognitive Learning.* Falmer Press, New York

Wellesley College Center for Research on Women 1992 *How Schools Shortchange Girls.* American Association of University Women Educational Foundation, Washington, DC

Westat Inc. 1988 *High School Transcript Study: 1987 Graduates.* United States Department of Education, Washington, DC

Zimmerer L K, Bennett S M 1987 *Gender Differences on the California Statewide Assessment of Attitudes and Achievement in Science.* American Association of University Women Educational Foundation, Washington, DC

Individual Differences, Learning, and Instruction

R. E. Snow

Individual differences among learners present a pervasive, profound problem to educators. At the outset of instruction in any topic, students of any age and in any culture will differ from one another in various intellectual and psychomotor abilities, in both general and specialized prior knowledge, in interests and motives, and in personal styles of thought and work during learning. These differences, in turn, often relate directly to differences in students learning progress. These relations identify individual predispositions that somehow condition students' readiness to profit from the particular instructional conditions provided. Educational theorists and practitioners have long noted these relations; some have sought to adapt instruction to individual differences so as to reduce the relations. However, in most places and in most times actual instructional practice has remained basically fixed and nonadaptive. Students usually must fit the system; some learn more, some less, some not at all, and some drop out, no matter what instructional system is chosen.

As one of its central concerns, research on instruction seeks to understand the sources, development, malleability, and manifestations of individual differences in learning, to recommend and help develop improvements in education for all students. Psychology's first major contribution to education—the technology of mental testing—was motivated by this goal. Ability tests remain one of its most successful and influential but also most controversial and criticized contributions. Unfortunately, the controversies often overshadow not only the value of mental tests when properly used and interpreted, and the importance of continuing research with them, but also psychology's contribution to the measurement and understanding of the many other kinds of individual differences important in education.

This entry examines the state of knowledge about student individual differences, emphasizing the substantive understanding, management, and use of such differences in relation to instruction. It also notes further research that is needed. It does not review the technology of testing, the controversies surrounding it, or many other issues concerning measurement of individual differences in education.

1. Categories of Individual Difference Constructs

The psychology of individual differences is a diverse field, addressing a variety of problems in different contexts using an assortment of methods. Cronbach (1957) likened it to the Holy Roman Empire: a loose network of far-flung provinces containing many subcultures, often with insufficient contact. Differential psychologists study intelligence; a variety of special abilities and talents; creativity; cognitive, motivational, and learning styles and strategies; interests; values; attitudes; and all of human personality, both "normal" and "abnormal." They also study physical, sensory, perceptual, and psychomotor skills, as well as biological and biochemical variations. Differences associated with gender, ethnicity, and socioeconomic status have also been a focus of study. Furthermore, psychologists who compare age groups, cultures, or different sorts of brain damage, or experts and novices in some field would not call themselves "differential psychologists," but they nonetheless contribute to the psychology of individual differences.

To amass the full catalog of distinguishable individual differences of potential relevance to some aspect of instruction would require a cumulative review across a great many sources (e.g., Anastasi 1958, Carroll 1993, Cattell 1971, Cronbach and Snow 1977, Eysenck and Eysenck 1985, Flammer 1975, Guilford 1959, 1967, Jäger 1984, Meili 1981, Pervin and Lewis 1978). There are literally hundreds of individual difference constructs. Also, some topics that come

under "individual differences" need separate special treatment; for example, developmental disabilities and special needs education.

This entry concentrates on the categories of individual differences judged most important for research and development in education: cognitive abilities and prior knowledge, learning strategies and styles, and achievement-related motivation, volition, and interest. Some related kinds of differences are discussed within each of these categories and a catchall category is added to note briefly many other constructs, both new and old, that also deserve assessment and research attention. It then examines how improved understanding of such differences leads to instructional improvements.

For short, but also for theoretical reasons, all individual-difference constructs relevant to learning from instruction are here called "aptitudes," to signify aspects of the present state of a person that are propaedeutic, that is, needed as preparation for some future learning project (Snow 1992). Education is viewed as an aptitude development program in the sense that its primary concern is human preparedness for later states of life. The educational improvements of most importance, therefore, are those that make education adaptive to aptitude differences at the start of instruction and promotive of aptitude developments through and beyond it (Corno and Snow 1986).

2. Cognitive Abilities and Prior Knowledge

2.1 A Taxonomy of Ability Factors

Because an early priority in any science is taxonomy, much research in the twentieth century has sought to build a taxonomy of human abilities, based on intercorrelations among the many cognitive measurements that have been collected. Contemporary studies and reanalyses of old data using modern methods now give a coherent picture (see Carroll 1993, Gustafsson 1984). The distinguishable ability factors emerging from this research can be arranged in three levels of hierarchical order.

General intelligence (G) is at the top of the hierarchy (the third order), implying that this central ability is involved in all cognitive test performances. Three firmly demonstrated second-order factors are linked directly beneath G: fluid intelligence (G_f), or analytic reasoning ability; crystallized intelligence (G_c), or generalized educational achievement; and general visual perception (G_v), reflecting ability in cognitive tasks that impose figural–spatial imagery demands. Also on this second level is general idea production (G_i), retrieval, or fluency, the ability factor most closely associated with creative intellectual performance. Three other second-order factors represent auditory perception, memory, and speed; these factors have been less studied and are therefore less well-understood in relation to learning from instruction, but they should not be ignored. Beneath each second-order factor, the names of its subordinate, first-order ability factors could be listed. Under G_c, for example, such primary factors as verbal comprehension, word knowledge, and grammatical sensitivity would appear. Under G_v, spatial relations, visualization, and the closure factors would be distinguished. G_f would include inductive and deductive reasoning factors; there is also strong evidence that G, G_f, and Thurstone's primary induction factor are identical in a hierarchical model (see also Gustafsson 1984). The primary level distinctions are not further discussed here (see Carroll 1993).

2.2 Ability–Learning Relation

The research evidence indicates many relations between the major abilities and learning performance. G and G_c are most often found to be highly correlated with learning from conventional instruction. Different subjects call different mixes of ability into play, and the mixes change as students progress in a subject. For example, mathematics may require visual perceptual discriminations as well as memory facilities in the early stages. Reasoning skills are also demanded, together with verbal comprehension and word knowledge, when instruction emphasizes explanation and problem-solving. Most learning demands both G_f and G_c abilities. Especially as learning tasks and teaching methods build closely on prior instruction, crystallized ability and prior knowledge will predominate as aptitude. Whether more general crystallized knowledge or more specific prior knowledge is the dominant factor is often disputed; some research seeks to improve the assessment of prior knowledge and to pin down the conditions under which general versus specific aptitudes are important (Dochy 1992, Schneider and Weinert 1990). Clearly there are subject-matter differences as well as student differences in the degree to which given instructional material will be novel versus familiar. Novel content seems to call more general knowledge and fluid reasoning into play. Visual–spatial abilities appear to move in and out of relevance as spatial reasoning and other operations with visual images are required by chosen materials, problems, or forms of teaching. Visual–spatial abilities have been associated with learning in art, architecture, dentistry, and technical courses, such as carpentry, mechanics, and engineering design. Whether such ability is relevant to problem-solving in mathematical topics, such as geometry, or in aspects of science, depends on topic but also on individual teacher or learner strategy; average correlations here are rarely strong. It is important to realize that superficially spatial–figural tasks do not necessarily require spatial ability.

Instructional method differences can also moderate the correlation between cognitive measures and achievement. There is substantial evidence that less

able learners do better when instruction is tightly structured, lessons are broken down into a sequence of simplified units, and teachers or instructional conditions exercise control over minute-to-minute activities and provide frequent feedback. Less able learners do less well in conventional instruction or in environments in which independent activity by learners is required to fill in gaps left by incomplete or less structured teaching; discovery learning would be an example. In these situations, more able learners excel; they often do not benefit particularly from tightly structured teaching (Snow 1982, Snow and Lohman 1984). Again, novelty challenges more able and taxes less able learners. Unfortunately most research does not explicitly distinguish stages of learning and instruction in these terms, and ability–learning relations change with experience in the learning situation. Aptitude differences need to be studied in relation to instructional structure and novelty, as well as other learning task variables, across time and familiarity in particular instructional situations.

In short, general measures of ability regarded as indicators of aptitude correlate strongly with learning achievement and appear to correlate more strongly in some instructional environments than in others: notably those characterized as relatively novel, unstructured, and incomplete. More specialized ability constructs also show some differential validity across different subjects or instructional methods. Just what conditions generate each of these kinds of aptitude-treatment interactions is difficult to determine; there are many subtle variations across situations (Cronbach and Snow 1977, Snow 1977). It is clear that cognitive aptitude differences among learners must be included in evaluation studies to gain a full view of instructional effects.

2.3 Ability Development

Although genetic factors influence ability development, no ability delineated above should be regarded as fixed. The development and differentiation of abilities is significantly a function of the accumulation and specialization of experience before and during education and work (Anastasi 1970). Substantial advances have been made in analyzing the nature of nurture, particularly with respect to general intellectual development. However, the conditions under which particular abilities develop and the means for promoting such development are not well understood. Research is attacking this need, and bringing differential, developmental, and instructional research into intersection (Case and Edelstein 1993). Two programs provide examples. In one, longitudinal patterns of ability differences (Demetriou and Efklides 1987) are related to differences in learning activities and interests (Undheim and Gustafsson 1989), to direct training and transfer effects (Gustafsson et al. 1989), and to different domains of educational achievement (Balke-

Aurell 1982, Gustafsson and Balke-Aurell 1989). The results, though complicated, support Ferguson's (1954, 1956) theory of differential ability development through specializations of learning and transfer over time. G is here interpreted as reflecting cognitive processing complexity; a view consistent with other theories (Snow and Lohman 1984). The other program studies cognitive, motivational, and social development and individual differences longitudinally across a number of years (Weinert and Schneider 1991). Of particular concern are interactions among aptitudes, knowledge, and strategies within particular instructional contexts (Schneider and Weinert 1990).

Distinctions between fluid and crystallized abilities or verbal and spatial abilities appear in the developmental evidence. G_c appears to develop through formal educational experience in learning and transfer of organized knowledge, skills, and processing strategies. Fluid ability presumably develops more through experience in adapting to novelty in the natural world. One theory suggests that fluid ability develops earlier in life and then is invested in formal instructional learning to produce crystallized ability (Horn 1978). Verbal-crystallized ability does appear more influenced by verbal emphasis in educational programs whereas spatial ability is promoted by more technical instruction (Balke-Aurell 1982). In general, less is known about the development of visual–spatial abilities; one hypothesis suggests that early emphasis on verbalization inhibits growth in these abilities.

Direct attempts to improve abilities through instruction have met with mixed but promising results. Some broad interventions have had positive effects on ability development. Some have shown initial improvements that later diminish. Some appear to have positive effects on crystallized skills and negative effects on fluid skills (Detterman and Sternberg 1982, Snow 1982). Some important successes have come from extremely early or intensive interventions (Feuerstein 1979, McKay et al. 1978). Other successes are based on detailed analyses of constituent thinking and reasoning skills and strategies involved in performance (see Baron and Sternberg 1987, Chipman et al. 1985, Nickerson et al. 1985, Resnick 1987, Segal et al. 1985). Examples of success in training G_f skills directly are available (Budoff 1987, Campione and Brown 1987, 1990, DeLeeuw et al. 1987, Feuerstein et al. 1987, Klauer 1990). G_v skills also seem to be trainable (Ben-Chaim 1988, Lajoie 1986). Components of verbal and reading abilities can also be trained (Calfee 1982, Frederiksen and Warren 1987, Perfetti 1985).

2.4 Content and Process Analyses

Cognitive psychology provided new methods for analyzing ability differences to reach more detailed models of information processing for each task. This helped build theories of abilities that identify component processes, metacognitive skills and stra-

tegies, knowledge structures, and sequences of such components involved in individual performance, and thus new interpretations of individual differences in ability.

Initially focused were tasks like those used to represent ability factors; many of these have now been studied. The results provide process models of various reasoning and problem-solving abilities, verbal and reading abilities, mathematical and spatial abilities, and second-language learning abilities (Sternberg 1985a, 1985b). More comprehensive, process-based theories of the cognitive ability hierarchy now seem possible. This supports related research steps. First, analyses of ability task performance suggest how improved assessment measures might be designed. Conventional cognitive tests have not been notably useful for diagnostic purposes. Second, this work supports new attempts at direct training by focusing on diagnosed constituent processes, as suggested in the previous section. Third, research can trace the role of these constituent processes, skills, and strategies in learning particular subject matters. Students clearly differ in strategy selection and adaptation of processing during complex cognitive performance; the problem is to understand this processing in interaction with domain knowledge and the subject matter and instructional context. Finally, developmental studies can track the emergence of component processes involved in various abilities across ages, so ability development may also be describable in process terms. (For reviews of related work see Lohman 1989, Snow and Swanson 1992, Ackerman 1989, Kyllonen and Christal 1990, Frederiksen et al. 1990, Lidz 1987, Snow and Lohman 1989).

Analysis of individual differences in particular subject matter domains is most advanced in mathematics and increasingly in natural science. Mayer (1985) showed mathematical problem-solving to involve individual differences in knowledge related to problem representation, translation, and schema identification; strategy differences in solution planning; and computation automaticity in reaching solutions. Resnick and Omanson (1987) reviewed research on arithmetic understanding to emphasize interplay between reflection on principles, invention, and automatization of procedure. De Corte and Verschaffel (1987) identified many component skills and strategies already apparent among first graders. Gelman and Greeno (1989) analyzed preschool mathematical competence to suggest that children bring implicit principles as initial states to instruction. Thus, although components of mathematical performance have been regarded as skills to be trained onto everybody's blank slate, some children clearly have intuitive concepts of counting, numbers, and sets even before school begins; this early principled knowledge tunes selective attention and allows learning to be generative, not just receptive, from the start. In effect, early principles are constraints that help some learners assemble and monitor successful performance plans, including novel plans. New meanings and principles can be built onto this basic structure, allowing broader transfer as new tasks appear. Other learners clearly start without this basic structure. It follows that assessment of initial states in mathematics should be geared to detect understanding of these principles; new instruction should relate to them meaningfully when they are present, and construct them when they are not. Such assessment and instruction concerns not just what students already know; it also addresses what students can perceive in novel situations and generate as mental models for reasoning therein. Also important is work that identifies the perceptual and spatial thinking skills involved in such situations (Leushina 1991, Yakimanskaya 1991).

3. Learning Strategies and Styles

3.1 Learning Strategies

Ability and knowledge differences are presumably manifested in observable differences in learning strategies and tactics. Thus, when direct training supplants ineffective strategies with effective ones, the hope is that deeper inaptitudes, or at least their effects, are being removed. Dozens of learning strategy constructs have now been defined. Many reflect rehearsal, elaboration, organizational, monitoring, or motivational activities during learning or studying. Some concern use of global planning, heuristic, or mnemonic devices; some are mapping and structuring tactics using cues detected in reading or listening; and some promote metacognitive processes of comprehension monitoring or hypothesis generating and testing while learning. An important general distinction concerns whether individual strategies lead to deep (versus surface) processing during learning (Marton et al. 1984, Entwistle 1987, Ferguson-Hessler and deJong 1990). Depth of processing may be a core construct to which ability and knowledge, as well as many surface strategy distinctions, connect.

3.2 Strategy Development

Strategies can be directly trained, although such training can sometimes be situation or treatment specific. It also can be dysfunctional; for learners with some ability profiles, the new strategy to be learned is (at least temporarily) in conflict with strategies already automatic. Lohman (1986) explained these interference effects using a production system account of skill acquisition, and predicted failure for skill and strategy training whenever it ignores the particulars of G_f or G_c strengths.

Training design clearly requires careful analysis of poor learning strategies in comparison with able learners to allow point by point incrementation toward more effective performance (Case and Bereiter 1984). Learners can be helped through a graduated scaffold of tutorial hints and demonstrations to model and eventually internalize the learning strategies of able performers (Campione and Brown 1990). If done well the result is a repertoire of multiple strategies, skill in their use, and flexibility in adaptation to instructional opportunities and demands. Research shows that some learners develop multiple strategies for a task and shift among them during performance (Kyllonen et al. 1984, Ohlsson 1984a, 1984b). Flexible strategy shifting seems to be a hallmark of able learning, whereas rigid strategies or random shifting suggest low ability. Work on learning strategies for arithmetic (Siegler and Campbell 1990) further suggests that confidence in retrieved answers is a key individual difference controlling strategy use.

3.3 Styles

When strategic differences appear deeply rooted in learner personality, they may be conceptualized as more pervasive learning or cognitive styles (Schmeck 1988). Some style constructs may capture important ability–personality interactions. Some may reflect cognitive organizational differences between subject-matter domains. For example, Pask and Scott (1972) distinguish holist and serialist styles of knowledge organization; although persons habitually prefer one or the other style, it also seems that domains like physics and mathematics call for serialist structure, whereas history is better served by holist structure.

The list of style constructs and associated assessment instruments is lengthy and unorganized (Keefe 1987, Schmeck 1988); it includes many hypothesized habits and preferences as distinct styles, as well as traditional ability and personality constructs. In the 1990s, evidence is still inadequate to judge the validity of style measures or their usefulness in adapting instruction to individuals; some have been called into serious question (Tiedeman 1989).

4. Achievement-related Motivation, Volition, and Interest

Adding style constructs as aptitudes for learning introduces the complex categories of conative and affective individual differences including many kinds of personal needs, motives, goals, and interests relevant to learning. However, these differences have been less well studied and understood in relation to adult learning. Only a few prominent constructs are reviewed here.

There are attempts to bring disparate aspects of motivational and volitional differences together, consider them jointly with cognitive abilities in learning, and derive adaptive instructional design implications.

Most notable are programs by Lepper (1988, Lepper et al. 1990) and Kanfer and Ackerman (1989). Lepper integrated various contrasting student orientations under the general heading of intrinsic versus extrinsic motivation and devised principles for promoting intrinsic motivation in learning. Of particular interest are findings that expert tutors use these principles subtly and adaptively while preserving the student's sense of control. The Kanfer–Ackerman model of ability–motivation interaction concerns attention resource capacity differences. Results show that motivational interventions can impede learning by diverting attention to self-regulatory activities in early stages of skill acquisition depending on ability; in later stages, the same interventions can facilitate performance. Much work in the early 1990s focuses on improving the measurement of cognitive motivational interaction in learning.

4.1 Anxiety and Achievement Motivation

Test anxiety is the most studied motivational aptitude. It interacts with instructional treatment just as G does; high structure is best for more anxious and low structure is best for less anxious students, but ability and anxiety also interact (Snow 1989). Research continues on the information-processing model of anxiety effects in learning, the development of anxiety, and its amelioration by direct intervention.

As Rand et al. (1989) point out, however, test anxiety (or fear of failure) is but half of the traditional theory of achievement motivation and should be studied together with need for achievement as well as ability measures. Lens's (1983) research has shown that need for achievement and anxiety measures can both yield curvilinear relations with instructional achievement. Thus an intermediate level of both kinds of need provides optimal performance; too much or too little of each can be counterproductive. Lens and DeCruyenaere (1991) have also shown that different measures of achievement motivation, anxiety, intrinsic motivation, causal attributions, and expectancy-value instrumentality all yield similar, strong relations with judgments of learning motivation. Boekaerts (1987), however, notes that general measures can miss important situation and task differences.

Also noteworthy are differences in goal orientations and attitudes toward the future. Van Calster et al. (1987) found interactions suggesting that achievement and study motivation depend on future attitudes about goals as well as perceived instrumentality of performance for goals. Dweck and Leggett (1988) found that learners differ in their conceptions about ability development, which then influence motivational orientation to learning; mastery-oriented students believe ability improves with learning and direct their actions toward this end, whereas performance-oriented students think of ability as fixed and direct their actions toward teacher evaluations. Performance goal orientation lim-

its achievement, particularly for learners with low self-perceived ability.

4.2 Interest

A closely related line focuses on interest as both aptitude and task characteristic. Some effects of interest differences on learning rival those of ability differences. There are also qualitative differences in cognitive processing in learning that accrue from interest (see Hidi 1990, Renninger et al. 1992), and related content motivations (see Nenniger 1987). Research aimed at detailing the kinds of variation in subject-specific interests that influence adult learning could be uniquely important for improving instruction.

4.3 Self-efficacy and Effort Investment

Self-perceptions of ability are known to influence choice of learning activities, strategies, and effort investment, as well as short-term achievement. Such differences among self-efficacy also have direct effects on effort investment across semester-long courses (MacIver et al. 1991). Other work shows long-range relations among self-concept of ability, effort, and achievement (Boekaerts 1988). Self-concept research ought to be integrated with the constructs of self-efficacy, effort, and metacognitive strategy. Metacognitive strategy in learning also implies awareness or mindfulness; mindful learning in turn requires the investment of mental effort (Salomon and Globerson 1987). Individual differences in effort investment can appear in the extreme as pathological effort avoidance (Rollett 1987).

4.4 Self-regulation and Action Control

Self-regulation is action control, but the category includes other volitional constructs reflecting purposive striving and persistence. Some learners display state orientation, wherein attention perseverates on present concerns; failures lead to an inability to concentrate on intentions to continue work and perform well. The contrast is action orientation, in which attention is focused on strong intention–action relationships. Action-oriented learners use control strategies to protect their intention–action sequence from competing tendencies; they persist in learning despite momentary difficulties and distractions (Kuhl 1990, Corno 1986, McCombs and Whisler 1989, Simons and Beukhof 1987).

4.5 Achievement via Independence and Achievement via Conformity

Still another construct contrasts persons who are motivated toward learning achievement through independence, who describe themselves as self-sufficient and mature, versus those motivated toward learning achievement through conformity, who characterize themselves as responsible, organized, and attentive to others' expectations. Conforming students show higher achievement when instruction is highly structured with imposed objectives and procedures, whereas students high in independence are better off with low-structure instruction where they can exercise their own initiative (Snow 1977).

5. Other Individual Difference Constructs

Many other individual difference constructs might be included here. In any particular instructional situation, unique combinations of student differences may come into play. Although instructional situations often call upon the major aptitudes discussed above, other differences may illuminate or qualify their functioning in higher-order interactions. Thus, individuality in learning is rich with structure, and there are many faceted contrasts yet to be explored in a systematic, coordinated way in relation to instruction. Some of the personal constructs that deserve such attention are self-perceptions as a learner in relation to perceptions of different instructional environments; interpersonal styles and social competence; the qualitative character of one's conceptions and misconceptions about the physical and social world; and all of the temperaments, attitudes, and emotions that may be connected to these conceptions or to educational conditions directly.

6. Instructional Research, Development, and Evaluation

There are many uses for individual difference information in the study of instruction and the pursuit of its improvement. Those considered here are student selection, instructional system adaptation, individual teacher adaptation, and instructional evaluation in general.

6.1 Student Selection and Advanced Placement

Measures of ability predict future academic achievement and so are used in conjunction with other information to select students for admission to advanced instructional programs. Available evidence supports the validity of this use; it benefits both institutions and individuals by reducing failure rates. Selection by ability is particularly valued where educational resources are scarce or expensive, or where prior academic record is an inadequate predictor. However, selection based only on ability or prior achievement neglects the need for advanced programs to diversify student talents and personal qualities. This argues for a larger future role for research on individual differences in relation to in-

struction. Optimal diversity of personal qualities in university and college environments has not been a research target.

Ability measures are also used to identify students for development of special aptitudes. Programs for pre-university students who show advanced mathematical abilities offer one example (Stanley et al. 1978, Stanley and Benbow 1983). Many universities also now use special assessments for advanced course placements. These uses contribute to instructional systems aimed at individual goal attainment.

6.2 Instructional System Adaptations

Although these uses are important, the achievement of common goals for all students is the major concern for much instructional research, development, and evaluation. This requires adapting instruction to student differences. Many teacher and instructional system adaptations to individual differences have been studied, operating on minute-to-minute, unit-to-unit, month-to-month, or year-to-year bases. It is easiest to imagine first an ideal system and then to examine some instructional designs and teacher adaptations as examples.

Ideally, an adaptive system aimed at enabling all students to reach common goals includes two kinds of instruction. One provides direct aptitude development for students in need of focused training or remediation as preparation for regular further instruction. The other provides alternative instructional paths toward the same common goals, with paths designed to circumvent present inaptitudes by capitalizing on present aptitudes. Periodic assessments decide the alternation of direct aptitude training and instruction that proceeds toward goals by circumventing inaptitudes. Both aspects of instruction are designed and evaluated with particular kinds of student need as targets (Glaser 1977).

For example, students low initially in reading comprehension skills might receive direct training on these skills while in parallel they pursue goals in mathematics or science instruction that do not place heavy demands on such skills. Perhaps this instructional alternative capitalizes instead on visual–spatial abilities by substituting work with concrete, figural–pictorial materials in place of complex verbiage. Similarly, students high in test anxiety might be given direct help in reducing its debilitating effects while also pursuing instruction designed to provide clear, tight, encouraging structure with minimum stress. Although all possible treatments cannot be provided for all possible individuals in such a system, adaptations for the most important aptitude problems can be planned, and some treatments might reasonably serve more than one kind of student. For example, given previous evidence, a highly structured instructional path might serve students low in crystallized ability, or high in anxiety, or low in independence relative to conformity. A less structured path might serve students with the opposite profile. Students could switch paths or move to still other treatments as their progress indicated.

Some instructional systems exist that incorporate parts of this ideal. Among them are the Adaptive Learning Environments models, Individually Guided Education, Mastery Learning and the Program for Learning in Accordance with Needs (see Corno and Snow 1986 for detailed references). These systems individualize instructional pace as well as activities and materials. They do not reach the ideal, and have not been sufficiently evaluated with respect to the major aptitudes discussed here, but existing evidence suggests them as starting forms to which other kinds of adaptation and increasingly detailed knowledge about individual differences in learning can be added. Future research should provide detailed analyses, particularly of ability, anxiety, achievement motivation, and subject-specific interests, in close connection with the sorts of direct training and alternative instructional conditions possible in these or similar systems.

New forms of adaptive instructional design and aptitude assessment aim at bringing deeper and more diagnostic perspectives into instructional research. Some new systems use computer-based intelligent tutoring to adapt subsequent instruction to the details of previous performance. Another approach involves a hint hierarchy and transfer tasks with human tutors to gauge learning differences and provide instruction simultaneously. So far, these assessments and adaptations do not use aptitude information from outside their instructional systems. (See Frederiksen et al. 1990, Glaser and Bassok 1989, Snow and Swanson 1992 for details on these and other systems.)

6.3 Individual Teacher Adaptations

Individual teachers adapt to individual differences whenever they tailor choices of group learning activities, reading materials, or personal handling of different students, based on knowledge of student characteristics. This knowledge may come from formal assessments, but effective teachers also gauge each student's strengths and weaknesses, interests, styles of thought, and prior relevant knowledge through careful observation outside as well as inside the classroom. Some teachers devise alternative learning projects to help discover students' particular strengths and weaknesses. Others may use student learning style questionnaires. These are forms of aptitude assessment, though they may not be standardized or systematic. Based on them, alternative instructional treatments may be chosen or designed to use students' strengths to help overcome students' weaknesses.

Research on teaching has identified teacher decisions and actions that appear to influence average student learning. But few studies focus on differential teaching styles as adaptations to different student characteristics. Some studies match teacher styles and student characteristics that work well or poorly by influencing teacher expectations (Brophy and Evertson 1981). Hummel-Rossi (1981) identified eliciting–permissive versus directing–monitoring styles that teachers applied with success to students who appeared to differ in ability and anxiety. There are methods teachers use to adapt repetition and tutoring time for students differing in ability (Fisher and Berliner 1985). Tutoring has also been studied to define adaptive interactions that work well (see Snow and Swanson 1992). Cole (1985) gave examples of adaptive teaching in culturally diverse classrooms. Styles of discourse already part of a person's culture outside of the learning environment can be used as a bridge to shape the learning encounter.

6.4 Instructional Evaluations

Beyond helping to invent adaptations of instruction to individual differences, differential approaches can test whether existing educational practices are maladaptive and can suggest alternatives. The classic example is ability grouping.

In school education, but not usually in adult basic and secondary education, student abilities reflected in test scores, grades, or teacher observations are used to classify students into homogeneous ability groups or tracks for different instructional treatments. This practice may be maladaptive unless all students' chances to reach the common goals of instruction are improved thereby. Although the intent may be to adapt instruction to different ability levels, such grouping often results in slower pace and lower goals for lower ability students. Placement in lower ability groups can diminish student achievement by reducing opportunities to learn (see Peterson et al. 1984).

Ability tracking may pose more serious problems than within-class grouping. Individual teachers can create and change temporary groups as learning progresses, and they can use observed differences in interests or anxiety as well as ability to form groups. Assignment to different educational programs based on ability, however, may make the disadvantages of homogeneous grouping permanent. Yet ability tracking based on career choice is very common in adult education and training. Classification based on career interests is not problematic, so long as ability and interest development have not been foreclosed prematurely by inadequate earlier instruction or counseling. Such classification may be maladaptive if it forces lower common goals on students in slower tracks. The point is controversial. Some research suggests that the effects of ability grouping and tracking are essentially zero. But this conclusion is contrary to much literature indicating the low quality of instruction in low achievement groups and the negative impact of ability grouping on the motivation and self-esteem of students assigned to low groups. Unfortunately most research on ability grouping still leaves the nature of instruction in different groups out of consideration and fails to evaluate outcomes with respect to initial ability differences (Cronbach and Snow 1977).

Work on cooperative and open learning has suggested alternative ways to use ability grouping to advantage. Webb (1982) showed that using ability information to create systematically heterogeneous groups helps both the more and the less able learners when they are grouped together, especially if the able students act as tutors and the less able students are prompted to ask questions. Other forms of peer cooperative learning in groups and cross-age tutoring have also been found to be effective, though these are not often evaluated with respect to individual differences. Continuing research on the interaction of aptitudes and teacher grouping practices may yet turn prevalent maladaptations into effective adaptations (see Snow and Swanson 1992).

7. Conclusion

The broad review attempted here cannot be briefly summarized. It does support the conclusion that research on individual differences has made and can continue to make important contributions to instructional improvement for children and adult learners. To promote more and better improvements in the future, research needs to integrate knowledge about the many kinds of important individual differences and connect it directly to the design of adaptive educational systems, teacher training programs, and diagnostic assessment devices. Many examples used here identify important points for research and development investment in this connection.

However important the contribution of research on individual differences may be to the design and implementation of particular instructional procedures, the most lasting contribution may be in the enriched conceptions of human diversity it provides to educators who care about evaluating their efforts in this light. A demonstration that a particular procedure is maladaptive for some students may be as important in this regard as a demonstration that some other procedure works well for others. Implicit in this review is the idea that aptitude differences are a function of person–situation interaction, both in the instant and over time; they are thus particular to local conditions. Aptitudes do not simply reside inside individuals as a list of independent, fixed, ever-present traits. Rather, they are exhibited in consort as resultant strengths or weaknesses relative to present and past conditions. Educators who can adopt this view will investigate success and failure in the person–situation interaction, rather than attributing either to the person alone, and manipulate conditions and envi-

ronments for learning accordingly. Fully articulated, studied, and applied, such a view would represent a true paradigm shift in educational theory, research, and practice with respect to individual differences in learning.

See also: Human Development in the Lifespan; Learning Environments; Group Learning; Learning to Learn; Adult Education; Self-directed Adult Learning; Instructional Design Theories

References

Ackerman P 1989 Individual differences and skill acquisition. In: Ackerman P L, Sternberg R J, Glaser R (eds.) 1989 *Learning and Individual Differences*. Freeman, New York
Anastasi P 1958 *Differential Psychology*. Macmillan, New York
Anastasi P 1970 On the formation of psychological traits. *Am. Psychol.* 25: 899–910
Balke-Aurell G 1982 *Changes in Ability as Related to Educational and Occupational Experience*. Acta Universitatis Gothoburgensis, Goteborg
Baron J, Sternberg R J 1987 *Teaching Thinking Skills*. Freeman, New York
Ben-Chaim D, Homang R T, Lappan G 1988 The effect of instruction on spatial visualization skills of middle school boys and girls. *Am. Educ. Res. J.* 25(1): 51–71
Boekaerts M 1987 Situation-specific judgments of a learning task versus overall measures of motivational orientation. In: De Corte E, Lodewijks H, Parmentier R, Span P (eds.) 1987 *Learning and Instruction. European Research in an International Context*, Vol. 1. Pergamon Press, Oxford
Boekaerts M 1988 Emotion, motivation, and learning. *Int. J. Educ. Res.* 12(3): 227–345
Brophy J E, Everston C M 1981 *Student Characteristics and Teaching*. Longman, New York
Budoff M 1987 The validity of learning potential assessment. In: Lidz C S (ed.) 1987
Calfee R C 1982 Cognitive models of reading: Implications for assessment and treatment of reading disability. In: Malatesha R N, Aaron P G (eds.) 1982 *Reading Disorders: Varieties and Treatments*. Academic Press, New York
Campione J C, Brown A L 1987 Linking dynamic assessment with school achievement. In: Lidz C S (ed.) 1987
Campione J C, Brown A L 1990 Guided learning and transfer: Implications for approaches to assessment. In: Frederiksen N, Glaser R, Lesgold A, Shafto M (eds.) 1990
Carroll J B 1993 *Human Cognitive Abilities*. Cambridge University Press, Cambridge
Case R, Bereiter C 1984 From behaviorism to cognitive behaviorism to cognitive development: Steps in the evolution of instructional design. *Instructional Science* 13: 141–58
Case R, Edelstein W (ed.) 1993 *The New Structuralism in Cognitive Development: Contributions to Human Development*, Vol. 23. Karger, Basel
Cattell R B 1971 *Abilities: Their Structure, Growth and Action*. Houghton Mifflin, Boston, Massachusetts
Chipman S F, Segal J W, Glaser R (eds.) 1985 *Thinking and*

Learning Skills, Vol. 2. Erlbaum, Hillsdale, New Jersey

Cole M 1985 Mind as a cultural achievement: Implications for I Q testing. In: Eisner E (ed.) 1985 *Learning and Teaching the Ways of Knowing*. National Society for the Study of Education, Chicago, Illinois

Corno L 1986 The metacognitive control components of self-regulated learning. *Contemp. Educ. Psychol.* 11(4): 333–46

Corno L, Snow R E 1986 Adapting teaching to individual differences among learners. In: Wittrock M C (ed.) 1986 *Handbook of Research on Teaching*. Macmillan, New York

Cronbach L J 1957 The two disciplines of scientific psychology. *Am. Psychol.* 12: 671–84

Cronbach L J, Snow R E 1977 *Aptitudes and Instructional Methods: A Handbook for Research on Interactions*. Irvington, New York

De Corte E, Verschaffel L 1987 Children's problem-solving skills and processes with respect to elementary arithmetic word problems. In: De Corte E, Lodewijks H, Parmentier R, Span P (eds.) 1987 *Learning and Instruction. European Research in an International Context*, Vol. 1. Pergamon Press, Oxford

DeLeeuw L, Van Daalen H, Beishuizen J J 1987 Problem-solving and individual differences: Adaptation to and assessment of student characteristics by computer-based instruction. In: De Corte E, Lodewijks H, Parmentier R, Span P (eds.) 1987 *European Research in an International Context*, Vol. 1. Pergamon Press, Oxford

Demetriou A, Efklides A 1987 Towards a determination of the dimensions and domains of individual differences in cognitive development. In: De Corte E, Lodewijks H, Parmentier R, Span P (eds.) 1987 *Learning and Instruction. European Research in an International context*, Vol. 1. Pergamon Press, Oxford

Detterman D K, Sternberg R J (eds.) 1982 *How and How Much Can Intelligence Be Increased*. Ablex, Norwood, New Jersey

Dochy F R C 1992 *Assessment of Prior Knowledge as a Determinant for Future Learning*. Uitgeverij Lemma B V, Utrecht

Dweck C S, Leggett E L 1988 A social-cognitive approach to motivation and personality *Psychol. Rev.* 95(2): 256–73

Entwistle N 1987 Explaining individual differences in school learning. In: De Corte E, Lodewijks H, Parmentier R, Span P (eds.) 1987 *Learning and Instruction: European Research in an International Context*, Vol. 1. Pergamon Press, Oxford

Eysenck H J, Eysenck M W 1985 *Personality and Individual Differences: A Natural Science Approach*. Plenum Press, New York

Ferguson G A 1954 On learning and human ability. *Canadian Journal of Psychology* 8: 95–112

Ferguson G A 1956 On transfer and the abilities of man. *Canadian Journal of Psychology* 10: 121–31

Ferguson-Hessler M G M, deJong T 1990 Studying physics texts: Differences in study processes between good and poor performers. *Cognition and Instruction* 7(1): 41–54

Feuerstein R 1979 *The Dynamic Assessment of Retarded Performers: The Learning Potential Assessment Device, Theory, Instruments, and Techniques*. University Park Press, Baltimore, Maryland

Feuerstein R, Rand Y, Jensen M R, Kaniel S, Tzuriel D 1987 Prerequisites for assessment of learning potential: The LPAD model. In: Lidz C S (ed.) 1987

Fisher C W, Berliner D C (eds.) 1985 *Perspectives on Instructional Time*. Longman, New York

Flammer A 1975 *Individual Unterschiede im Lernen*. Beltz Verlag, Weinheim

Frederiksen J R, Warren B M 1987 A cognitive framework for developing expertise in reading. In: Glaser R (ed.) 1987 *Advances in Instructional Psychology*, Vol. 3. Erlbaum, Hillsdale, New Jersey

Frederiksen N, Glaser R, Lesgold A, Shafto M 1990 *Diagnostic Monitoring of Skill and Knowledge Acquisition*. Erlbaum, Hillsdale, New Jersey

Gelman R, Greeno J G 1989 On the nature of competence: Principles for understanding in a domain. In: Resnick L B (ed.) 1989 *Knowing, Learning, and Instruction: Essays in Honor of Robert Glaser*. Erlbaum, Hillsdale, New Jersey

Glaser R 1977 *Adaptive Education: Individual Diversity and Learning*. Holt, Rinehart and Winston, New York

Glaser R, Bassok M 1989 Learning theory and the study of instruction. *Annu. Rev. Psychol.* 40: 631–66

Guilford J P 1959 *Personality*. McGraw-Hill, New York

Guilford J P 1967 *The Nature of Human Intelligence*. McGraw-Hill, New York

Gustafsson J-E 1984 A unifying model for the structure of intellectual abilities. *Intelligence* 8: 179–203

Gustafsson J-E, Balke-Aurell G 1989 General and special abilities in the prediction of school achievement. (Unpublished manuscript, University of Goteborg)

Gustafsson J-E, Demetriou A, Efklides A 1989 Organization of cognitive abilities: Training effects. Paper presented at the European Association for Research on Learning and Instruction, Madrid

Hidi S 1990 Interest and its contribution as a mental resource for learning. *Rev. Educ. Res.* 60: 549–71

Horn J L 1978 Human ability systems. In: Baltes P B (ed.) 1978 *Lifespan Development and Behavior*, Vol. 1. Academic Press, New York

Hummel-Rossi B 1981 Aptitudes as predictors of achievement moderated by teacher effect. *Measuring Human Abilities: New Directions for Testing and Measurement.* 12: 59–86

Jäger A O 1984 Intelligenzstrukturforschung: Konkurrierende Modelle, neue Entwicklungen, Perspektiven *Psychol. Rundsch.* 35(1): 21–35

Kanfer R, Ackerman P L 1989 Motivation and cognitive abilities: An integrative/aptitude-treatment interaction approach to skill acquisition. *J. Appl. Psychol. Monogr.* 74(4): 657–90

Keefe J W 1987 *Learning Style Theory and Practice*. National Association of Secondary School Principals, Reston, Virginia

Klauer K J 1990 Paradigmatic teaching of inductive teaching. In: Mandl et al. (eds.) 1990 *Learning and Instruction: European Research in an International Context*. Pergamon Press, Oxford

Kuhl J 1990 Self-regulation: A new theory for old applications. Invited address to the International Congress of Applied Psychology, Kyoto

Kyllonen P C, Christal R E 1990 Reasoning ability is (little more than) working-memory capacity? *Intelligence* 14(4): 389–433

Kyllonen P C, Lohman D F, Woltz D J 1984 Componential modeling of alternative strategies for performing spatial tasks. *J. Educ. Psychol.* 76(6): 1325–45

Lajoie S P 1986 Individual differences in spatial ability:

A computerized tutor for orthographic projection tasks. (Unpublished doctoral dissertation, Stanford University, Stanford, California)

Lens W 1983 Achievement motivation, test anxiety, and academic achievement. *Psychol. Rep.*

Lens W, DeCruyenaere M 1991 Motivation and demotivation in secondary education: Student characteristics. *Learning and Instruction.* 1(2): 145–59

Lepper M R 1988 Motivational considerations in the study of instruction. *Cognition and Instruction* 5: 289–309

Lepper M R, Aspinwall L C, Mumme D L Chabay R W 1990 Self-perception and social perception processes in tutoring: Subtle social control strategies of expert tutors. In: Olson J, Zanna M P (eds.) 1990 *Self Inference Processes: The Ontario Symposium*, Vol. 6. Erlbaum, Hillsdale, New Jersey

Leushina A M (ed.) 1991 *Soviet Studies in Mathematics Education, Vol. 4: The Development of Elementary Mathematical Concepts in Preschool Children.* National Council of Teachers of Mathematics, Reston, Virginia

Lidz C S (ed.) 1987 *Dynamic Assessment.* Guilford Press, New York

Lohman D F 1986 Predicting mathemathanic effects in the teaching of higher-order thinking skills. *Educ. Psychol.* 21(3): 191–208

Lohman D F 1989 Human intelligence: An introduction to advances in theory and research. *Rev. Educ Res* 59(4): 333–73

MacIver D J, Stipek D J, Daniels D H 1991 Explaining within-semester changes in student effort in junior high school and senior high school courses. *J. Educ. Psychol.* 83(2): 201–11

Marton F, Hounsell D, Entwistle N 1984 *The Experience of Learning.* Scottish Academic Press, Edinburgh

Mayer R E 1985 Mathematical ability. In: Sternberg R J (ed.) 1985b

McCombs B L, Whisler J S 1989 The role of affective variables in autonomous learning. *Educ. Psychol.* 24(3): 277–306

McKay H, Sinisterra L, McKay A, Gomez H, Lloreda P 1978 Improving cognitive ability in chronically deprived children. *Science* 200(4339): 270–78

Meili R 1981 *Struktur der Intelligenz: Faktorenanalytische und denkpsychologische Untersuchungen.* Huber, Bern

Nenniger P 1987 How stable is motivation by contents? In: De Corte E, Lodewijks H, Parmentier R, Span P (eds.) 1987 *Learning and Instruction: European Research in an International Context*, Vol. 1. Pergamon Press, Oxford

Nickerson R S, Perkins D N, Smith E E 1985 *The Teaching of Thinking.* Erlbaum, Hillsdale, New Jersey

Ohlsson S 1984a Attentional heuristics in human thinking. *Proc. 6th Conf. Cognitive Science Society.* Boulder, Colorado

Ohlsson S 1984b Induced strategy shifts in spatial reasoning. *Acta Psychol.* 57: 47–67

Pask G, Scott B C E 1972 Learning strategies and individual competence. *International Journal of Man-Machine Studies* 4(3): 217–53

Perfetti C A 1985 *Reading Ability.* Oxford University Press, New York

Pervin L A, Lewis M 1978 *Perspectives in Interactional Psychology.* Plenum Press, New York

Peterson P, Wilkinson L C, Hallinan M (eds.) 1984 *The Social Context of Instruction: Group Organization and Group Processes.* Academic Press, New York

Rand P, Lens W, Decock B 1989 *Negative Motivation is Half the Story: Achievement Motivation Combines Positive and Negative Motivation.* Report No. 2. Institute for Educational Research, University of Oslo

Renninger K A, Hidi S, Krapp A (eds.) 1992 *The Role of Interest in Learning and Development.* Erlbaum, Hillsdale, New Jersey

Resnick L B 1987 *Education and Learning to Think.* National Academy Press, Washington, DC

Resnick L B, Omanson S F 1987 Learning to understand arithmetic. In: Glaser R (ed.) 1987 *Advances in Instructional Psychology.* Erlbaum, Hillsdale, New Jersey

Rollett B A 1987 Effort avoidance and learning. In: De Corte E, Lodewijks H, Parmentier R, Span P (eds.) 1987 *Learning and Instruction: European Research in an International Context*, Vol. 1. Pergamon Press, Oxford

Salomon G, Globerson T 1987 Skill may not be enough: The role of mindfulness in learning and transfer. *Int. J. Educ. Res.* 11(6): 623–37

Schmeck R R (ed.) 1988 *Learning Strategies and Learning Styles.* Plenum Press, New York

Schneider W, Weinert F E (eds.) 1990 *Interactions Among Aptitudes, Strategies, and Knowledge in Cognitive Performance.* Springer-Verlag, New York

Segal J W, Chipman S F, Glaser R (eds.) 1985 *Thinking and Learning Skills*, Vol. 1. Erlbaum, Hillsdale, New Jersey

Siegler R S, Campbell J 1990 Diagnosing individual differences in strategy choice procedures. In: Frederiksen N, Glaser R, Lesgold A, Shafto M (eds.) 1990

Simons P R J, Beukhof G (eds.) 1987 *Regulation of Learning.* Instituut voor Onderzoek van Het Onderwijs SVO, The Hague

Snow R E 1977 Research on aptitudes: A progress report. In: Shulman L S (ed.) 1977 *Rev. of Research in Education*, Vol. 4. Peacock, Itasca, Illinois

Snow R E 1982 Education and intelligence. In: Sternberg R J (ed.) 1982 *Handbook of Human Intelligence.* Cambridge University Press, London

Snow R E 1989 Aptitude–treatment interaction as a framework for research on individual differences in learning. In: Ackerman P L, Sternberg R J, Glaser R (eds.) 1989 *Learning and Individual Differences: Advances in Theory and Research.* Freeman, New York

Snow R E 1992 Aptitude theory: Yesterday, today, and tomorrow. *Educ. Psychol.* 27(1): 5–32

Snow R E, Lohman D F 1984 Toward a theory of cognitive aptitude for learning from instruction. *J. Educ. Psychol.* 76: 347–76

Snow R E, Lohman D F 1989 Implications of cognitive psychology for educational measurement. In: Linn R L (ed.) 1989 *Educational Measurement*, 3rd edn. Macmillan, New York

Snow R E, Swanson J 1992 Instructional psychology: Aptitude, adaptation, and assessment *Annu. Rev. Psychol.* 43: 583–626

Stanley J C, Stanley W C, Solono C H (eds.) 1978 *Educational Programs and Intellectual Prodigies.* Johns Hopkins University, Baltimore, Maryland

Stanley J C, Benbow C P 1983 *Academic Precocity, Aspects of its Development.* Johns Hopkins University, Baltimore, Maryland

Sternberg R J 1985a *Beyond IQ: A Triarchic Theory of Human Intelligence.* Cambridge University Press, Cambridge

Sternberg R J (ed.) 1985b *Human Abilities: An Information Processing Approach.* Freeman, New York

Tiedeman J 1989 Measures of cognitive styles: A critical review. *Educ. Psychol.* 24: 261–75

Undheim J O, Gustafsson J-E 1989 Development of broad and narrow factors of intelligence as a function of verbal interests and activities. Paper presented at the European Association for Research on Learning and Instruction, Madrid

Van Calster K, Lens W, Nuttin J 1987 Affective attitude toward the personal future: Impact on motivation in high school boys. *American Journal of Psychology* 100(1): 1–13

Webb N M 1982 Group composition, group interaction, and achievement in cooperative small groups. *J. Educ. Psychol.* 74: 475–84

Weinert F E, Schneider W (eds.) 1991 *The Munich Longitudinal Study on the Genesis of Individual Competencies (LOGIC) Report No. 7: Assessment Procedures and Results of Wave Four.* Max-Planck-Institute for Psychological Research, Munich

Yakimanskaya I S 1991 *Soviet Studies in Mathematics Education, Vol. 3: The Development of Spatial Thinking in School Children.* National Council of Teachers of Mathematics, Reston, Virginia

Intelligence, Learning, and Instruction

D. F. Lohman

Understanding the nature of human intelligence and devising methods to assess it have been central problems in psychology since its inception. However, as is often the case with psychological terms that originate in the broader culture, the word "intelligence" has diverse meanings. This complicates enormously the task of understanding what intelligence might be, for example, is intelligence best viewed as an innate characteristic or an acquired set of competencies? Those who believe that intelligence is innate have searched for measures of cognitive capacity that are not greatly influenced by education or training. However, measures of physiological or elementary psychological processes must always be validated against some other measure of accomplishment, such as school achievement. Such criterion behaviors invariably show improvements with experience and exercise. Because of this, and also because physiological and elementary psychological measures are not easily interpreted, some have argued that an experience-free measure of intelligence is impossible (Thorndike et al. 1927). Theorists who view intelligence as an acquired set of competencies are more likely to view it as behavior rather than as cognitive power, and thus are more likely to study the growth of intelligence by examining the increasing sophistication in thinking brought about by education and experience.

Is learning a reflection of intelligence? Or is intelligence in some measure the product of learning? How do instructional manipulations moderate the influence of intelligence on learning and of learning on intelligence? These are the main questions to be addressed.

1. Historical Notes

Although the first useful intelligence test was devised by the French psychologist Alfred Binet, and some of the best early work in differential psychology was conducted by the German psychologist Stern, it was British and American researchers who quickly came to dominate the field. There are many reasons for this. The leading German psychologist of the day, Wilhelm Wundt, was not interested in the problem of individual differences. Binet was never accepted by academics in the French universities. In the United States, on the other hand, Binet's fledgling intelligence scale was translated and independently applied by several investigators, most notably by Lewis M Terman at Stanford. In England, Cyril Burt embarked on a similar effort to standardize the Binet scales.

However, the problem of defining intelligence was not left entirely to the test developers. In England, C E Spearman advanced a two-factor theory for intelligence in which he argued that performance on any mental task could be explained by two factors: a general (g) factor common to all intellectual activities, and a specific factor uniquely required by each task. Spearman showed how his theory could account for individual differences in achievement in several age-heterogenous samples. In America, E L Thorndike was not convinced. His data on more homogeneous samples led him to believe that there were many independent abilities, not a single general ability.

The controversy continued through the next two generations of psychologists. In America, Thorndike's position was supported by Kelley, and then by Lewis

L Thurstone, and finally by J P Guilford. All advocated multiple-factor theories of intelligence and downplayed or dismissed the role of the general factor. In England, Burt and then P E Vernon advanced Spearman's case, although modifying it to include other factors arranged in a hierarchy that was dominated by the *g* factor.

1.1 Crystallized and Fluid Intelligences

The controversy continues in muted form today. Some researchers, such as A R Jensen, emphasize the *g* factor whereas others, such as Horn, deny that it is a psychologically meaningful construct. However, the most popular current theory of intelligence contains features of both the British hierarchical theory and the American multiple-factor theory. This new theory was originally proposed in 1941 by R B Cattell, a British-born psychologist who studied for his doctorate under Spearman, completed a postdoctoral fellowship with E L Thorndike, and conducted research with both Burt and Thurstone. In the early 1940s, shortly after taking up permanent residence in the United States, Cattell proposed a quasi-hierarchical theory with two general factors at the apex (see Cattell 1943). Each of these factors was defined by several of the primary factors Thurstone had identified in his research. The two general factors were labeled fluid intelligence (*Gf*) and crystallized intelligence (*Gc*). Fluid intelligence was thought to represent the ability to see relations between ideas. This ability was hypothesized to increase until adolescence and then decline, and to be required by tests composed of unfamiliar problems that had to be solved under time pressure. Crystallized intelligence, on the other hand, was hypothesized to represent those discriminatory habits acquired through the investment of fluid intelligence in particular learning environments. As such, crystallized intelligence was hypothesized to show continued but small improvements over the life span, at least for those individuals who continued to exercise the relevant abilities.

Modern statements of the theory of fluid and crystallized abilities differ somewhat from Cattell's early formulation. Some theorists now posit several higher-order intelligences rather than the two originally hypothesized by Cattell. For example, Horn (1985) claimed to have identified 10 such factors. Other theorists have accepted Cattell's emphasis on fluid and crystallized abilities, and some have even accepted the investment theory of aptitude, but they do so without assuming that fluid ability represents something more fundamental or innate than crystallized abilities. Studies that report equal heritabilities for fluid and crystallized abilities have supported this claim. Indeed, some see fluid abilities as the product of education and experience (see Snow and Yalow 1982). On this view, crystallized abilities are seen as the direct product of learning organized bodies of knowledge and skill, whereas fluid abilities are seen as the indirect product of solving new problems or of applying old knowledge and skills in new contexts.

1.2 Tests of Fluid and Crystallized Intelligence

Although the theory of fluid and crystallized abilities has been the object of much research, only in the 1980s has it been used as a framework for the development of intelligence tests. The most extensive effort to incorporate the theory into a test is that of Woodcock and Johnson (1989). Their test allows estimation of fluid ability, crystallized ability, and five additional broad group factors identified in Horn's (1985) theory. The Stanford–Binet test was also revised along the lines of the Cattell–Horn theory. Although not developed to reflect *Gf–Gc* theory, D Wechsler's verbal–performance distinction bears at least a strong family resemblance to it. Indeed, the Block Design subtest has long been considered an excellent marker for fluid ability and the Information Comprehension, Arithmetic, and Vocabulary subtests together estimate *Gc*. Among group administered tests, B H Raven's Progressive Matrices test is often used to estimate fluid intelligence, and measures of academic achievement are used to estimate crystallized intelligence.

2. From Trait to Process

Modern research on human intelligence differs from earlier research in that researchers are now more concerned with the processes of intelligent thinking than with the organization of traits that define it. This shift from trait to process was a consequence of the cognitive revolution in psychology that began in the late 1950s and which, by the early 1970s, had supplanted behaviorism as the dominant perspective in psychology in the United States and other countries. Cognitively oriented theorists have sought to understand ability constructs by modeling the strategies examinees use to solve ability tests or by correlating performance on ability tests with performance on tasks designed to measure elementary cognitive processes.

2.1 Process Research on Intelligence

In one of the early attempts to develop an information-processing theory of intelligence, Sternberg (1977) developed a method called componential analysis which he then applied to reasoning tasks such as those found on mental tests. Results generally showed that process models could be devised that well accounted for performance on the tasks. By fitting different models to each subject's data, Sternberg could also determine whether different individuals solved the same task in different ways. Later, other researchers extended Sternberg's methods to test whether each subject used the same strategy to solve all items or instead shifted among strategies for different items on the same task. These analyses sometimes showed interesting differences between younger and older, and between lower- and higher-scoring subjects, particularly on complex reasoning and spatial problem-solving tasks. In general, older and more able subjects showed more flexibility in their problem-solving—see Snow and Lohman (1989) for a review.

Decomposing individual differences has proved to be more difficult. For example, in a series of studies, Hunt (1978) and his colleagues sought to understand the nature of verbal ability. However, instead of decomposing performance on verbal ability tests, Hunt administered a variety of laboratory tasks used by experimental psychologists. On each task, one or more process scores were estimated for each subject. These scores were hypothesized to represent the speed or accuracy with which subjects could execute elementary cognitive processes such as speed of retrieval, comparison, or transformation of cognitive units. Hunt then correlated these process scores with the ability test scores. Some correlations were significant and theoretically interesting, although most were small. For example, several analyses suggested that high verbal subjects were better able to keep track of the order of entry of information into working memory than were low verbal subjects. They were also slightly faster in retrieving name codes for stimuli than were their low verbal counterparts.

Another line of research has sought to find measures of intelligence that are less influenced by culture. Choice reaction time and inspection time have been particularly popular measures. Although correlations between reaction time or inspection time and g vary widely, replicable correlations are generally in the range of $r = -0.2$ to $r = -0.4$. Interpretation of these correlations is made difficult by the fact that a measure of individual variability in reaction time over trials shows similar relationships. Carroll (1987) concluded that attentional control may be more important than speed of reaction in these studies.

2.2 Triarchic Theory

Much of the modern research on intelligence has focused rather narrowly on particular tasks rather than on patterns of performance across tasks. Because of this, general theories of intelligence have been relatively rare. One notable exception is the work of Gardner (1983), who hypothesized seven different intelligences (linguistic, logical–mathematical, spatial, musical, bodily–kinesthetic, and two personal intelligences). Although Gardner's theory has received considerable popular attention, Sternberg's (1984) Triarchic Theory is perhaps closer to the mainstream of modern research on intelligence.

Sternberg's theory of intelligence is composed of three subtheories: a contextual subtheory, an experiential subtheory, and a componential subtheory. The contextual subtheory attempts to specify which behaviors will be considered intelligent in different cultures.

Sternberg has argued that, in any culture, contextually intelligent behavior involves purposeful adaptation to the present environment, selection of an optimal environment, or shaping of the present environment to fit better one's skills, interests, and values. Different cultures value as intelligent different skills, such as hunting, navigation, or academic learning. In Western cultures, the prevailing contextual theory of intelligence involves problem- solving (or fluid) abilities, knowledge-based (or crystallized) abilities, and social and practical abilities.

However, even if a particular task is thought to require intelligence, contextually appropriate behavior is not considered equally intelligent at all points along the continuum of experience with that class of tasks. According to the experiential subtheory, intelligence is best demonstrated when the task or situation is relatively novel or when learners are attempting to automatize their responses.

Finally, the componential subtheory specifies the cognitive structures and processes that underlie all intelligent behavior. Contextually appropriate behavior at relevant points in the experiential continuum is said to be intelligent to the extent to which it involves certain types of processes. Three types of processes are hypothesized: metacomponents, which control processing and enable a person to evaluate it; performance components, which execute the plans assembled by the metacomponents; and knowledge acquisition components, which selectively encode and combine new information and selectively compare new information to old information.

The implications of the Triarchic Theory for testing are that tests should allow the examiner to model each examinee's performance on tasks that represent fluid and crystallized abilities, so that component scores and solution strategy may be estimated for each individual. Further, tasks should also be included that require practical or "real world" intelligence.

3. General Theories of Thinking

Intelligence is an individual difference construct. Although there have been occasional complaints about this state of affairs, it was not until the advent of the computer that it became possible to develop and test theories of intelligence that were grounded in process and structure rather than in individual differences. Efforts to develop artificially intelligent systems have thus produced many interesting hypotheses about human intelligence.

The program devised by A Newell and H A Simon, known as the General Problem Solver, was the first real process theory of general reasoning or intelligence. A more recent effort is that of Anderson (1983) on a system he calls Adaptive Control of Thought (ACT*). Anderson claims that all cognitive processes are different manifestations of the same underlying system. Knowledge is represented in two forms in ACT*: as a tangled hierarchy of factual or declarative knowledge, and as systems of skills or procedural knowledge.

Declarative knowledge can be represented in several different ways. The dominant code is one that simply preserves the meaning of an event. The general factor that is often equated with intelligence may in part estimate individual differences in the ability to create, transform, and retain information coded in this way. However, several peripheral encoding systems produce memory representations that are perception-based rather than meaning-based. Examples include images (that preserve information about configuration) and temporal strings (that preserve information about temporal order). Spatial tasks often require the ability to generate, transform, and retain image-coded information. Similarly, specific verbal tasks (e.g., spelling, fluency) may depend on knowledge coded as temporal strings. Some learning disabilities may be caused by dysfunction in one or more of the peripheral systems that encode information from the environment or decode the products of thinking into particular responses.

Aspects of Anderson's theory which describe how procedural knowledge is acquired can explain why the same task can require general problem-solving abilities for the inexperienced subject and specific problem-solving skills for the more experienced subject. The theory thus predicts that more ability factors will be required to explain individual differences among adults than among children.

Kyllonen and Christal (1989) have incorporated Anderson's theory into a general framework for the assessment of individual differences. They argue that individual differences on cognitive tasks arise from four sources: cognitive processing speed, working memory capacity, breadth and pattern of declarative knowledge, and breadth and pattern of procedural knowledge. The theory has served as a framework for a comprehensive cognitive assessment battery and has guided several research programs on learning and skill acquisition.

4. Intelligence and Learning

Binet, Thorndike, and other early theorists presumed that intelligence reflected, at least in part, the ability to learn. Thus, it came as some surprise when, in a series of studies, Woodrow showed that intelligence did not predict either amount or rate of learning. Studies in which general intelligence was decomposed into several group factors also failed to find much relationship between ability factors and estimates of learning. However, in all of these studies, learning was estimated by performance gains on simple laboratory tasks. Later work has shown somewhat stronger relationships between intelligence and learning as learning tasks increase in meaningfulness and complexity.

However, high correlations have not been obtained, neither is it likely that future studies will obtain them.

Why is this so? The construct "intelligence" is defined by variability between persons in overall performance, usually the total number of items answered correctly. The construct "learning" is defined by within-person changes in performance across conditions. When these two scores are estimated on the *same* task, they will be independent. When they are estimated on different tasks, however, there may be some relationship between them, although it is unlikely to be large. Put another way, individuals differ in amount learned, which generates some variability in learning between persons. Attempts to correlate intelligence and learning thus aim to explain a construct defined by between- persons variability (i.e., intelligence) using the between-persons *portion* of the variability of a construct defined by within-person gains. Thus, intelligence cannot be correlated with learning, only with individual differences in learning.

Similar reasoning applies to attempts to model the growth of intelligence. Some have argued that growth is random, and thus unrelated to initial or final status. Cronbach and Snow (1977) pointed out that this occurs only if intelligence is estimated by IQ scores, which constrain the variability in scores to be equal at all ages. If intellectual development is indexed by mental age (MA), which shows an increase in variability with age, then the correlation between initial MA and gain in MA can be large, especially when computed over long intervals and when scores are corrected for unreliability.

5. Dimensions of Learning

5.1 Correlational Studies

Just as researchers have argued over the dimensions of intelligence, so too there has been controversy over the dimensions of learning. There have been some attempts to investigate patterns of individual differences across learning tasks. However, several hours may be required to complete a single learning task, and so the number of learning tasks used in a given study is typically much smaller than the number of ability tests used in an investigation of the factorial structure of intelligence. Several themes are apparent, though. First, intercorrelations among verbal memory tasks show a strong general associative learning factor and weaker factors representing type of learning task (Underwood et al. 1978). Second, other dimensions emerge when a broader array of learning tasks are chosen. In particular, Snow et al. (1984) have shown that learning tasks can also be arrayed along a novel-to-familiar dimension, with fluid intelligence more strongly related to performance on novel (or inductive) learning tasks and crystallized intelligence more strongly related to performance on familiar (or rote) learning tasks. Furthermore, performance on more complex tasks shows stronger relationships with performance on other learning tasks and with performance on ability tests than does performance on simpler tasks. Thus, relationships between intelligence and learning are moderated by many factors, particularly task complexity, task novelty, and transfer (Ackerman 1987).

Anderson's ACT* theory suggests one explanation for these regularities. Anderson claimed that, when learning to perform unfamiliar tasks, subjects must apply general problem-solving skills. This can severely tax working memory, and so initial performance is slow, error prone, and must be constantly monitored by the learner. Performance at this stage of learning often correlates best with some measure of general fluid ability. With practice, task-specific procedures can be created that bypass this effortful application of general procedural knowledge. Performance at intermediate stages of practice shows higher correlations with task-specific abilities (or crystallized knowledge) and, with further practice, with measures of perceptual speed and psychomotor speed. Performance on familiar learning tasks may thus involve the retrieval of already compiled procedures or the application of fact learning mechanisms (Kyllonen and Shute 1989).

5.2 Learning Taxonomies

Because of the limitations imposed by task duration on correlational research on the dimensions of learning, several theorists have proposed rational taxonomies of learning tasks. A W Melton proposed an early scheme that distinguished conditioning, rote learning, probability-learning, skill-learning, concept-learning, and problem-solving. R M Gagné advanced a more popular scheme. He distinguished among intellectual skills, cognitive strategies, verbal information, motor skills, and attitudes. This scheme has been widely used in instructional design. More recently, Kyllonen and Shute (1989) proposed a four-dimensional taxonomy that derives from information-processing psychology and machine learning research. They distinguish knowledge type, instructional environment, domain (or subject matter), and learning style. By including a learning-style dimension, they acknowledge that it is impossible to define a learning task without also specifying how the learner interacts with the task. This point has been much emphasized since the late 1980s in discussions of situated cognition. Instructional environments are distinguished primarily in terms of learner control. This dimension has shown consistent interactions with intelligence, with low control environments placing greater demands on prior ability (Cronbach and Snow 1977). The dimension of learning content acknowledges the domain-specific character of much learning, and predicts transfer relations among knowledge and skill within a more general domain space, defined by the universe of specifiable jobs, courses of study, etc.

6. Intelligence and Instruction

Laboratory investigations of the relationships between learning and intelligence show a much more complex picture than early theorists seem to have envisioned. Interpretation is made easier, however, if intelligence tests are understood as measures of scholastic aptitude rather than of some all-pervasive cognitive power. Although intelligence tests are often used to make broader inferences, it is clear that they were initially devised to predict, and have subsequently been validated against measures of academic learning. Thus, when viewed from the perspective of instruction, the empirical and theoretical links between scholastic aptitude and learning are now more clearly understood than ever before.

Research on the relationships between laboratory learning and intelligence has emphasized the important roles of task complexity, task familiarity, type of learning, content, and amount of learner control. All of these factors have been shown to influence academic learning as well. Incompleteness of instruction along one or more of these dimensions places greater information processing burdens on learners. In such situations, learners must invariably induce some portion of the instructional message for themselves. Intelligence becomes, then, the ability to profit from incomplete instruction (Snow and Yalow 1982). Instructional treatments that increase these burdens on learners tend to show higher correlations between measures of achievement and intelligence than do instructional treatments that simplify or structure learning. Thus, correlations between estimates of intelligence and achievement vary widely. They are lowest ($r = 0.3$ to 0.5) when intelligence is estimated by an individually administered performance test, achievement is estimated by school grades, and instructional treatments simplify and support learning. Correlations are highest ($r = 0.5$ to 0.8) when intelligence is estimated by a group administered test that emphasizes vocabulary and verbal reasoning, achievement is estimated by standardized achievement tests, and the instructional treatment provides minimal support for student learning.

The concepts of fluid and crystallized intelligence provide a further elaboration of this theme. Snow and Yalow (1982) interpreted crystallized intelligence as assemblies of knowledge and skill that can be retrieved as a system and applied in situations similar to those experienced in the past. Fluid intelligence is seen as the ability to assemble a new performance program or strategy in order to respond to relatively novel situations. Instructional environments that place greater demands on learning new skills will thus show greater dependence on fluid abilities whereas instructional environments that require application and extension of old knowledge will show greater dependence on crystallized abilities. These effects are also moderated by other aptitude, task, and outcome variables (Cronbach and Snow 1977).

Finally, both fluid and crystallized intelligence must be understood as products of education, not merely as predictors of success in that medium (Snow and Yalow 1982). This can be obscured by scoring schemes (such as IQ) that eliminate age-related improvements in intellectual accomplishments. On this view, education must aim to develop not only organized bodies of factual and skill knowledge in different domains, but must also develop the ability to apply this knowledge in unfamiliar situations.

See also: Abilities and Aptitudes; Declarative and Procedural Knowledge; Individual Differences and Instruction; Learning Potential and Learning Potential Assessment; Learning Processes and Learning Outcomes; Development of Learning Skills in Problem-solving and Thinking; Transfer of Learning; Development of Learning across the Lifespan

References

Ackerman P L 1987 Individual differences in skill learning: An integration of psychometric and information processing perspectives. *Psych. Bull.* 102(1): 3–27

Anderson J R 1983 *The Architecture of Cognition.* Harvard University Press, Cambridge, Massachusetts

Carroll J B 1987 Jensen's mental chronometry: Some comments and questions. In: Modgil S, Modgil C (eds.) 1987 *Arthur Jensen: Consensus and Controversy.* Falmer Press, New York

Cattell R B 1943 The measurement of adult intelligence. *Psych. Bull.* 40(3): 153–93

Cronbach L J, Snow R E 1977 *Aptitudes and Instructional Methods: A Handbook for Research on Interactions.* Irvington, New York

Gardner H 1983 *Frames of Mind: The Theory of Multiple Intelligences.* Basic Books, New York

Horn J L 1985 Remodeling old models of intelligence. In: Wolman B B (ed.) 1985 *Handbook of Intelligence.* Wiley, New York

Hunt E B 1978 Mechanics of verbal ability. *Pyschol. Rev.* 85(2): 109–30

Kyllonen P C, Christal R E 1989 Cognitive modeling of learning abilities: A status report of LAMP. In: Dillon R, Pellegrino J W (eds.) 1989 *Testing: Theoretical and Applied Perspectives.* Praeger, New York

Kyllonen P C, Shute V J 1989 A taxonomy of learning skills. In: Ackerman P L, Sternberg R J, Glaser R (eds.)

1989 *Learning and Intelligence: Advances in Theory and Research.* Freeman, New York

Snow R E, Yalow E 1982 Education and intelligence. In: Sternberg R J (ed.) 1982 *Handbook of Human Intelligence.* Cambridge University Press, Cambridge, Massachusetts

Snow R E, Kyllonen P C, Marshalek B 1984 The topography of learning and ability correlations. In: Sternberg R J (ed.) 1984 *Advances in the Psychology of Human Intelligence, Vol. 2.* Erlbaum, Hillsdale, New Jersey

Snow R E, Lohman D F 1989 Implications of cognitive psychology for educational measurement. In: Linn R (ed.) 1979 *Educational Measurement,* 3rd edn. Macmillan, New York

Sternberg R J 1977 *Intelligence, Information Processing, and Analogical Reasoning: The Componential Analysis of Human Abilities.* Erlbaum, Hillsdale, New Jersey

Sternberg R J 1984 *Beyond IQ: A Triarchic Theory of Human Intelligence.* Cambridge University Press, Cambridge, Massachusetts

Thorndike E L, Bregman E O, Cobb M V, Woodyard E 1927 *The Measurement of Intelligence.* Teachers College/Columbia University Bureau of Publications, New York

Underwood B J, Boruch R F, Malmi R A 1978 Composition of episodic memory. *J. Exp. Psychol. Gen.* 107(4): 393–419

Woodcock R W, Johnson M B 1989 *Woodcock–Johnson Tests of Cognitive Ability: Standard and Supplemental Batteries.* DLM/Teaching Resources, Allen, Texas

Further Reading

Sternberg R J, Wagner R K (eds.) 1994 *Mind in context: Interactionist Perspectives on Human Intelligence.* Cambridge University Press, Cambridge, Massachusetts

Butcher H J 1968 *Human Intelligence: Its Nature and Assessment.* Methuen, London

Lohman D F 1989 Human intelligence: An introduction to advances in theory and research. *Rev. Educ. Res.* 59(4): 333–73

Sternberg R J (ed.) 1982 *Handbook of Human Intelligence.* Cambridge University Press, Cambridge, Massachusetts

Sternberg R J, Detterman D K (eds.) 1986 *What is Intelligence? Contemporary Viewpoints on its Nature and Definition.* Ablex, Norwood, New Jersey

Wolman B B (ed.) 1985 *Handbook of Intelligence.* Wiley, New York

Student Diversity and Classroom Teaching

M. C. Wang

Advances in theory and research, particularly since the 1970s, have generated substantial conceptual changes in the understanding of the process of learning and increased recognition that certain student characteristics can be altered through schooling. Among the most important of these characteristics are family characteristics, such as parental expectation and family involvement (Comer 1986); cognition (or the processes of learning; de Bono 1976, Feuerstein 1980); intelligence (or the ability to learn; Husén and Tuijnman 1991); and student motivation (or the willingness to learn; Zimmerman 1986). The recognition of the alterability of these characteristics has led researchers to study ways of modifying the psychological processes and cognitive operations used by the individual learner, as well as modifying learning environments and instructional strategies to accommodate learner differences (Wang 1992). Findings from research, along with the practical wisdom culled from implementing innovative school programs, have significantly contributed to the current understanding of what constitutes effective practice and how the learning of diverse students can be enhanced in the same classroom.

Although research has identified numerous variables that are related to differences in student learning and achievement, the sheer number of these variables has posed a perplexing challenge to researchers, policymakers, and practitioners. To begin to address this challenge, these variables can be divided into two groups; those internal to students (e.g., ability and motivation) and those external to students (e.g., quality of instruction and task demands).

1. Models of School Learning

Carroll (1963) introduced educational researchers to the concept of a model of school learning. In his model, he put forth six constructs. Three of these constructs pertained to student differences (aptitude, ability to understand instruction, and perseverance), while the remaining three constructs applied to the classroom environment (clarity of instruction, task appropriateness, and opportunity to learn). These constructs became a point of departure for other models of school learning that were developed during the late 1960s and 1970s (Bennett 1978, Bloom 1976, Bruner 1966, Glaser 1976). Bloom's model specifically differentiated between two types of student characteristics: cognitive entry behaviors and affective entry characteristics.

In retrospect, all of these models recognized both types of entry characteristics. With respect to cognitive entry characteristics, for example, they included constructs such as aptitude, prior knowledge, and home background. With respect to affective entry characteristics, they included perseverance, self-concept, and attitudes toward school and specific subject matters. This acknowledgement of differences among students stood in contrast to more narrow psychological studies of influences on learning, which generally treated individual differences as a source of error, and focused instead on instructional treatment variables.

In addition to student variables, each of these models of school learning gave salience to constructs related to the classroom environment. These constructs varied in generality, some being as broad as "instructional events" or "clarity of instruction," and others as narrow as "use of cues" or "feedback and correctives." Although later models brought some refinement in the ways in which individual difference variables and instructional treatment variables were defined and the ways in which they were related to one another, the primary contributions of more recent models have been in extending the range of influences considered.

The evolution of models of school learning was further advanced with the introduction of models of adaptive instruction (Corno and Snow 1986, Glaser 1976, Wang 1992). School-based implementation of models of adaptive instruction was designed to help schools create classroom environments that maximized each student's opportunities for success in school. Particular attention was paid to new variables associated with instructional delivery systems, program design, and implementation. In particular, attention was given to those features that Glaser (1982) referred to as the "large practical variables," which included efficient allocation and use of teacher and student time, a practical classroom management system, systematic teacher feedback and reinforcement of student learning behavior and progress, instructional interactions based on the diagnosed learning needs of individual students, and flexible administrative and organizational patterns responsive to program implementation and staffing needs.

Another contribution to models of school learning came from researchers concerned with the identification and characterization of effective schools. Edmonds (1979) is most strongly associated with this identification of variables for exceptionally effective schools, especially for the urban poor. Significant contributions to effective school models were also made by Brookover (1979), Brookover and Lezotte (1979), and Rutter et al. (1979). Illustrations of the types of variables characterizing effective schools include degree of curriculum articulation and organization, school-wide staff development, parental involvement and support, school-wide recognition of academic success, maximized learning time, district support, clear goals and high expectations, orderly and disciplined school environment, and principal leadership characterized by attention to quality of instruction (Purkey and Smith 1983).

These various models of school learning have contributed greatly to the understanding of the relative contributions of different influences on student achievement and practical strategies for maximizing educational outcomes across a range of educational conditions and settings. The following section provides a synthesis of the research bases that undergird the design of these models of school learning. Although individual researchers and practitioners may focus their work on particular variables or constructs, the discussion in this section is intended to provide

Table 1
Variable categories of influences on learning with illustrative examples

Category/subcategory[a]	Illustrative variable

Category 1: State and district variables are associated with state- and district-level school governance and administration, including state curriculum and textbook policies, testing and graduation requirements, teacher licensure, specific provisions in teacher contracts, and some district-level administrative and fiscal variables.

District-Level demographics and marker variables	School district size
State-level policy variables	Teacher licensure requirements

Category 2: Out-of-school contextual variables are associated with the home and community contexts within which schools function. They include community demographics, peer culture, parental support and involvement, and the amount of time students spend out of school on activities such as television viewing, leisure reading, and homework.

Community variables	Socioeconomic level of community
Peer group variables	Level of peers' academic aspirations
Home environment and parental support variables	Parental involvement in ensuring completion of homework
Student use of out-of-school time variables	Student participation in clubs and extracurricular school activities

Category 3: School-level variables are associated with school-level demographics, culture, climate, policies, and practices. They include demographics of the student body, whether the school is public or private, and levels of funding for specific categorical programs; school-level decision-making variables; and specific school-level policies and practices, including policies on parental involvement in the school.

Demographic and marker variables	Size of school
Teacher-administrator decision-making variables	Principal actively concerned with instructional program
School culture variables (ethos conducive to teaching and learning)	School-wide emphasis on and recognition of academic achievement
School-wide policy and organization variables	Explicit school-wide discipline policy
Accessibility variables	Accessibility of educational program (overcoming architectural, communication, and environmental barriers)
Parental involvement variables	Parental involvement in improvement and operation of instructional programs

Category 4: Student variables are those associated with students, including demographics; academic history; and a variety of social, behavioral, motivational, cognitive, and affective characteristics.

Demographic and marker variables	Gender
Placement history variables	Prior grade retentions
Social and behavioral variables	Positive, nondisruptive behavior
Motivational and affective variables	Attitude toward subject matter instructed
Cognition variables	Level of specific academic knowledge in subject area instructed
Metacognition variables	Comprehension monitoring (plan, monitor effectiveness of attempted actions, monitor outcomes of actions)
Psychomotor variables	Psychomotor skills specific to area instructed

Category 5: Program design variables are associated with instruction as designed, and with the physical arrangements for its delivery. They include the instructional strategies specified by the curriculum and characteristics of instructional materials.

Demographic and marker variables	Size of instructional group (whole class, small group, one-on-one instruction)
Curriculum and instruction variables	Alignment among goals, contents, instruction, assignments, and evaluation
Curriculum design variables	Materials employ advance organizers

Category 6: Implementation, classroom instruction, and climate variables are associated with the implementation of the curriculum and the instructional program, including classroom routines and practices, characteristics of instruction as delivered, classroom management, monitoring of student progress, quality and quantity of instruction provided, student–teacher interactions, and classroom climate.

Classroom support variables	Establishing efficient classroom routines and communicating rules and procedures
Classroom instruction variables	Use of clear and organized direct instruction
Quantity of instruction variables	Time on task (amount of time students are actively engaged in learning)
Classroom assessment variables	Use of assessment as a frequent, integral component of instruction
Classroom management variables	Group alerting (teacher uses questioning/recitation strategies that maintain active participation by all students)
Student and teacher interactions: social variables	Student responds positively to questions from other students and from teacher
Student and teacher interactions: academic variables	Frequent calls for extended, substantive oral and written responses (not one-word answers)
Classroom climate variables	Cohesiveness (members of class are friends who share common interests and values and emphasize cooperative goals)

a Subcategories are listed below the description of each major category and are each illustrated with representative variables. For example, the first major category includes two subcategories, "District-level demographics and marker variables" and "State-level policy variables" a synoptic view of the entire canopy of influences of learning.

2. The Knowledge Base of School Learning

Focusing on identifying variables related to processes of learning and student achievement, Wang et al. (1993) completed a knowledge base review. The data sources for this review were the consensus ratings from 61 educational research experts, results from 91 quantitative research syntheses, and findings in 179 handbook chapters and narrative reviews published since 1975. Thus, findings from this "meta-review" constitute a distillation of understandings and results from large numbers of primary research studies, quantitative research syntheses, and narrative reviews. They indicate a substantial agreement on the categories of variables that exert influence on student learning, as well as those that had little influence. Table 1 provides a summary list of factors that influence student learning and selected examples of each factor. The factors are placed into one of six major categories and 30 subcategories.

Of the six major categories (see Table 1), the highest ratings overall were assigned to "Program design variables," followed by "Out-of-school contextual variables." The category reflecting the quality of instruction, "Implementation, classroom instruction, and climate variables," ranked third in importance, closely followed by "Student variables." The last two categories, "School-level variables" and "State and district variables," received markedly lower ratings overall.

In the following section, the categories that received exceptionally high ratings are highlighted. The categories representing instruction as designed and instruction as delivered are discussed first. These are followed by out-of-school context and student characteristics.

2.1 Program Design Variables

This category includes instruction as designed and the physical arrangements for its delivery. Variables included in the program design category (Category 5 in Table 1) are organized into three subcategories. The first subcategory, "Demographic and marker variables," was rated the highest of the three. Furthermore, within this subcategory, the most highly rated variables are "size of instructional group (whole class, small group, or one-on-one instruction)," "number of classroom aides," and "resources needed." Thus, the most important aspect of program design appears to be the intensity of educational services provided to each learner. More aides, smaller groups, or increased material resources are associated with significantly higher learning outcomes.

Ratings on the "Curriculum and instruction variables" suggest that the key to effective instructional design is the flexible and appropriate use of a variety of instructional strategies while maintaining an orderly classroom environment. The highest overall rating in this subcategory was for "use of classroom management techniques to control classroom disruptiveness." This variable was followed by "use of prescriptive instruction combined with aspects of informal or open education" and "presence of information in the curriculum on individual differences and commonalities," both of which explicitly relate to student diversity and individualization. Other highly rated variables referred to specific instructional strategies, including "use of mastery-learning techniques," "instructional cues, engagement, and corrective feedback," "use of cooperative learning strategies," and "use of diagnostic–prescriptive methods."

High ratings in the "Curriculum design variables" were given to the variables of "materials employ alternative modes of representation" and "degree of structure in curriculum accommodates needs of different learners," both of which reinforce the importance of offering a variety of instructional materials and approaches to accommodate individual differences. The importance of the organization of curriculum content is revealed by the two highest rated items in this subcategory: "materials employ learning hierarchies" and "material is presented in a cognitively efficient manner."

2.2 Implementation, Classroom Instruction, and Climate Variables

This category includes support of the curriculum and the instructional program; classroom routines; specific instructional, assessment, and classroom-management practices; quantity of instruction; academic and nonacademic student–teacher interaction; and classroom climate. It is by far the largest of the six major categories.

High ratings in the areas of implementation, classroom instruction, and climate point to the importance of maintaining an orderly classroom environment and providing clear, well-organized instruction appropriate to the needs of individual learners. In the overall ranking of all 30 subcategories, classroom management ranked second. Its most critical items were "group alerting (teacher uses questioning/recitation strategies that maintain active participation by all students)" and "learner accountability (teacher maintains student awareness of learning goals and expectations)." Smooth transitions from one instructional activity to another, minimal disruptions, and teacher awareness of what is going on in the classroom at all times also received relatively high ratings.

Quantity of instruction was also highly rated. This subcategory includes time spent in direct instruction, especially direct instruction on basic skills; time spent on homework; and length of the school day and school year. The importance accorded to quantity of instruction is not surprising since it has appeared in many of the most widely cited models of school learning.

Student and teacher interactions were ranked highly, as were classroom climate variables. Taken together, the highly rated items in these two subcategories characterize a classroom in which teachers interact with students frequently for instructional purposes, and where students work with classmates, share common interests and values, and pursue cooperative goals. Students are actively engaged in learning and are involved in some classroom decisions. At the same time, the class is well-organized and well-planned, with a clear academic focus. Objectives of learning activities are specific and explicit, with the pacing of instruction appropriate for the majority.

High ratings were also given to the quality of the instruction provided to students, namely, the use of advanced organizers, the direction of students' attention to the content to be learned, the provision of clear and organized direct instruction, the systematic sequencing of lesson events, and the use of clear lesson transitions. Other highly rated variables included corrective feedback in case of student error, frequent academic questions, and accurate measurement of skills. Finally, the literature strongly supports the teaching of skills in the context of meaningful application, use of good examples and analogies, and teaching for meaningful understanding, together with explicit promotion of student self-monitoring of comprehension and gradual transfer of responsibility for learning from the teacher to the student.

2.3 Out-of-school Contextual Variables

This category includes variables associated with the home and community contexts within which schools function. Variables receiving high ratings under this category include peers' educational and occupational aspirations, parental involvement in ensuring completion of homework, parental participation in school conferences and related activities, and parental interest in students' schoolwork. The educational environment of the home (e.g., number of books and magazines) was also cited in numerous reference sources and received consistently high ratings. Student participation in clubs and extracurricular school activities and time spent on leisure reading were also moderately related to learning outcomes.

2.4 Student Variables

"Metacognition variables" was among the subcategories that received highest mean ratings. Highly rated variables in this subcategory include "comprehension monitoring (planning; monitoring effectiveness of attempted actions; testing, revising, and evaluating learning strategies)," "self-regulatory, self-control strategies (e.g., control of attention)," and

"positive strategies to facilitate generalization of concepts." Other highly rated student variables include positive behavior and ability to make friends with peers, motivation for continual learning, and perseverance on learning tasks. These variables fall under the rubric of affective entry characteristics. Highly rated variables related to cognitive entry characteristics included general mental abilities, levels of basic skills sufficient to profit from instruction, and prior knowledge in the subject area instructed.

3. Implications for Improving Practice

Classroom teachers must respond to a multitude of influences interacting in kaleidoscopic patterns (Lockheed and Hanushek 1988, Purves 1989, Stevenson and Stigler 1992). While a large number of variables are moderately related to learning outcomes, few, if any, single variables are very strongly related to learning. Authors of original research studies and of reviews and syntheses are appropriately cautious in stating the importance of particular variables. Nonetheless, taken together, the extant research base suggests some powerful interactive effects on school learning.

Two sets of implications are particularly noteworthy. First, in contrast to the prevailing conception of the important influence of distal variables (notably, policy, demographic, and organizational), the extant research base suggests that these distal variables are relatively unimportant. One explanation of the limited impact of policy and organizational variables is that they are at least one step removed from the daily learning experiences of teachers and students. Simply implementing any one policy, such as the "extended school day," does not guarantee that students in a given classroom will receive instruction from a teacher who plans lessons with special attention to eliminating poor management practices and inefficient use of class time. Effective school policies require effective implementation by teachers at the classroom and student levels.

A second significant finding of the accumulated knowledge base on school learning is the consistent evidence of the impact of the home environment, classroom management, and metacognitive processes on student learning. There is an increasing research base that prescribes metacognitive processes and functions, such as comprehension monitoring, strategies to facilitate generalization of concepts, and self-regulatory and self-control strategies, and effective interventions, to teach metacognitive skills. Similarly, teachers must use a variety of instructional techniques, activities, and behaviors in their efforts to control classrooms and enhance learning. Examples include group alerting, learner accountability, smooth transitions, and teacher "with-it-ness." Finally, studies supporting the importance of the home environment have identified characteristics and behaviors of parents and extended family members that support student achievement. Parent behaviors such as attendance at school functions, interest in children's schoolwork, monitoring television viewing, engaging in conversations with children, and ensuring completion of homework and regular school attendance have positive effects on student achievement.

References

Bennett S N 1978 Recent research on teaching: A dream, a belief and a model. *Br. J. Educ. Psychol.* 48: 127–47

Bloom B S 1976 *Human Characteristics and School Learning.* McGraw-Hill, New York

Brookover W B (ed.) 1979 *School Social Systems and Student Achievement: Schools Can Make a Difference.* Praeger, New York

Brookover W B, Lezotte L W 1979 *Changes in School Characteristics Coincident with Changes in Student Achievement.* Michigan State University, Institute for Research on Teaching, East Lansing, Michigan

Bruner J S 1966 *Toward a Theory of Instruction.* Norton, New York

Carroll J B 1963 A model of school learning. *Teach. Coll. Rec.* 64: 723–33

Comer J P 1986 Parent participation in the schools. *Phi Del. Kap.* 67: 442–44

Corno L, Snow R E 1986 Adapting teaching to individual differences among learners. In: Wittrock M C (ed.) 1986 *Handbook of Research on Teaching*, 3rd edn. Macmillan Inc., New York

de Bono E 1976 *Teaching Thinking.* Temple Smith, London

Edmonds R 1979 Effective schools for the urban poor. *Educ. Leadership* 37(1): 15–27

Feuerstein R 1980 *Instrumental Enrichment: An Intervention Program for Cognitive Modifiability.* College Park Press, Baltimore, Maryland

Glaser R 1976 Components of a psychological theory of instruction: Toward a science of design. *Rev. Educ. Res.* 46: 1–24

Glaser R 1982 Instructional psychology: Past, present, and future. *Am. Psychol.* 37: 292–305

Husén T, Tuijnman A 1991 The contribution of formal schooling to the increase in intellectual capital. *Educ. Researcher* 20(7): 10–25

Lockheed M E, Hanushek E 1988 Improving educational efficiency in developing countries: What do we know? *Compare* 18(1): 21–38

Purkey S C, Smith M S 1983 Effective schools: A review. *Elementary Sch. J.* 83: 427–52

Purves A C (ed.) 1989 *International Comparisons and Educational Reform.* Association for Supervision and Curriculum Development, Cucamonga, California

Rutter M, Maughan B, Mortimore P, Ouston J, Smith A 1979 *Fifteen Thousand Hours: Secondary Schools and their Effects on Children.* Harvard University Press, Cambridge, Massachusetts

Stevenson H W, Stigler J W 1992 *The Learning Gap.* Summit Books, New York

Wang M C 1992 *Adaptive Education Strategies: Building on Diversity.* Brookes Publishing, Baltimore, Maryland

Wang M C, Haertel G D, Walberg H J 1993 Toward a knowledge base for school learning. *Rev. Educ. Res.* 63(3): 249–94

Zimmerman B J (ed.) 1986 Discussions of role subprocesses in student self-regulated learning . *Contemp. Educ. Psychol.* 11(4)

Teaching: Aptitude–Treatment Interaction Model

R. E. Snow

An aptitude–treatment interaction (ATI) occurs when the characteristics of persons moderate the effects of instructional conditions on those persons. Conversely, ATI implies that the importance of personal characteristics in relation to valued educational outcomes depends on what instructional conditions are administered. The study of aptitude–treatment interactions in education aims at understanding when, how, and why different kinds of persons benefit from different kinds of instruction, so that educational conditions for individual learners can be improved. An adaptive instructional system with respect to individual differences among persons is the goal.

Aptitude–treatment interaction research is a special case of the scientific study of person–environment interaction. The possibility of interactions has long been routinely acknowledged in the physical scien-

tist's qualifier "other things being equal ... " and in the social scientist's question "Can we generalize to other groups (communities, cultures, etc.)?" Evolutionary biology is basically interactionist. Interactions have been put to practical use in medicine; for example, the physician's choice of antibiotic depends on the patient's answer to the test question: "Have you ever had an allergic reaction to penicillin?"

Cronbach (1957, 1975), recognized that person–environment interaction was both a fundamental concept and a fundamental problem for psychology. Interactional research has accumulated in a variety of fields of psychology (Dance and Neufeld 1988, Endler and Magnusson 1976, Magnusson and Allen 1983, Pervin and Lewis 1978, Snow 1991). Although interactional thinking has been evident in educational philosophies since ancient times, the full implications of aptitude–

treatment interaction for education have been systematically addressed only since the 1970s (Cronbach and Snow 1977, Snow 1989).

1. Substantive Definition and Implications for Education

In education, many kinds of individual differences among learners can be observed and measured. When such measures predict individual differences in learning from instruction, they are interpreted as indicators of aptitude, that is, readiness to profit from instruction. When aptitude measures provide differential predictions for learning under different instructional conditions, a conclusion of aptitude–treatment interaction is justified.

Many kinds of aptitude differences among students have been studied, including general and special cognitive abilities, personality and motivational attributes, and cognitive styles. Many kinds of instructional treatments have also been compared. Since ATI findings often occur, there is no doubt that ATI exists in education (Cronbach and Snow 1977). Theoretical and practical understanding of ATI is not, in the early 1990s, sufficient to allow routine use of ATI in educational planning or instructional design.

It is clear, however, that routine use of ATI is both possible and necessary in educational evaluation. Aptitude–treatment interaction methodology is a requisite part of any evaluation study aimed at comparing alternative teaching methods or environments because the evaluation question is never simply which treatment is best on average? It is always which treatment is best for each of the individual learners to be served?

Aptitude–treatment interactions are of interest theoretically because they demonstrate construct validity for aptitude and learning measures in a new way: they show how aptitude–learning relations can be experimentally manipulated and thus understood in a causal rather than only a correlational framework. Neither aptitude constructs nor educational learning processes can be fully understood without reference to one another. Therefore, it is possible that common psychological processes underlie both aptitude and learning differences.

Furthermore, as interactions have appeared ubiquitous in education, they show the need to understand not only persons and situations, but their interface. Learning and aptitude come to be seen as operating in the person–situation union, not just in the heads of persons, thus posing a new theoretical and philosophical problem (Snow 1992).

Practical interest stems from the possibility that ATI can be used to adapt instruction to fit different learners optimally. Many attempts at individualizing instruction have failed to eliminate individual differences in learning outcome because they adapted only to limited aspects of individual performance; for example, by allowing differences in pace. The hope is that research on ATI can provide decision rules that indicate how to vary instructional conditions in ways that mesh with particular learner strengths while avoiding particular learner weaknesses. A related hope is that such research will indicate how best to develop aptitudes directly for persons with different initial aptitude profiles.

Again, the general question for research, and for evaluation studies, is which of the available or conceivable teaching methods, media, or environments is most likely to provide equality of educational opportunity to each individual learner, for his or her aptitude development and educational achievement. The commitment to optimal diversity of educational opportunity (e.g., truly to provide adaptive education as defined by Glaser 1977), demands that educational environments be chosen or invented and evaluated within an ATI perspective (Corno and Snow 1986).

At the same time, however, ATI research has shown that interactions are complex. No simple or general principles for matching students and teachers, teaching methods, or school environments have emerged. Part of the problem stems from the difficulty of conducting ATI research and a widespread lack of understanding of appropriate methods, but part also can be attributed to the multidimensional, dynamic, and often local and even transient character of the person–environment interface. Results to date suggest that work toward instructional theories that seek to optimize instruction for individuals in real school settings will need to be built up from continuous local diagnosis, description, and evaluation activities; local instructional models rather than general educational theory seem to be the more realizable goal (Snow 1991).

2. Statistical Definition and Methodology

Normally, ATI is defined as a statistical interaction: the multiplicative combination of at least one person variable and one treatment variable in affecting one dependent or instructional outcome variable. The interaction exists whenever the regression of an instructional outcome from one treatment upon some personal characteristic of learners differs in slope from the regression of that outcome from another treatment on the same characteristic.

Figure 1 gives the basic patterns of possible relationships. Each graph assumes that student aptitude scores taken before instruction and student outcome scores taken after instruction have been plotted, on the abscissa and ordinate respectively, to form a bivariate distribution for each treatment under investigation. Linear regression slopes have been fitted to each distribution and treatment average effects have been identified (the heavy centered dots). In Fig. 1(a), labeled

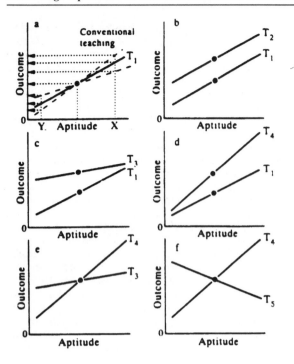

Figure 1
Possible effects of alternative instructional treatments (T) on outcome averages and outcome-on-aptitude regressions

"conventional teaching," the solid slope (T_1) depicts an aptitude–outcome relationship corresponding to a correlation coefficient of 0.50; the dashed slopes depict variation in this relationship between coefficients of 0.30 and 0.70. These data approximate what has often been found in United States public schools, using general intelligence or prior achievement tests as aptitude measures and cognitive achievement measures to reflect instructional outcomes. Note that a student with aptitude score at X is predicted (dotted arrows) to obtain outcome scores above the mean while a student with aptitude score at Y is predicted to obtain outcome scores below the mean.

An important aim of educational research is to improve upon this state of affairs by finding or devising instructional treatments such as T_2 in Fig. 1(b) that raise the average outcome for everyone over that expected from T_1. When such regression slopes are parallel, as shown here, there is no ATI; T_2 is the better treatment for all students regardless of aptitude. Unfortunately, many educational studies have looked only for such average treatment differences, assuming that aptitude slopes were parallel without investigating them.

The pattern in Fig. 1(c) schematizes the goal of special education and of much research on individualized instruction, where it is hoped that a treatment T_3 can be found to improve achievement of lower aptitude students while maintaining the high achievements of

higher aptitude students. However, in searching for generally improved treatments the result shown in Fig. 1 (d) can also be obtained; treatments such as T_4 turn out to be most beneficial for the higher aptitude students rather than for the lower aptitude students. One can think of T_4 as the goal of special programs for the gifted.

The T_3 result has at times been obtained for programmed instruction in comparison to conventional instruction T_1, while the T_4 result has sometimes been obtained in studies of discovery or inductive teaching. This leads to the possibility of combined results such as those in Fig. 1(e). Here, alternative treatments produce improvements for different kinds of students; it is apparent that T_4 should be given to high aptitude students, while T_3 should be given to low aptitude students. In the extreme, if optimal instructional treatments could be found or devised for students like X and Y, the result depicted in Fig. 1(f) might be expected. Negative slopes approximating T_5 do occur at times using cognitive measures, but are more likely when personality or attitudinal characteristics rather than cognitive abilities are used as aptitudes.

Research on ATI seeks to detect nonparallel regression slopes of the sorts shown in Fig. 1 and to understand how instructional treatments can be designed to produce such effects. To the extent that stable interactions like those of Fig. 1(e) and 1(f) can be established, they can be used as suggested above to form decision rules for the assignment of students to optimally different treatments. The regression slopes cross to define the point on the aptitude continuum where persons should be divided to achieve optimal outcome in different instructional treatments. The same regression slope expectations apply to compensatory education programs or to other attempts to develop aptitude directly. The same patterns can be used to interpret evaluation results not aimed at adapting instruction to individual differences. For example, an evaluation that obtained a pattern like that of Fig 1(e) might suggest a revision of T_4 that would improve it specifically for learners below the aptitude mean.

Beyond the simplest cases shown in Fig. 1, there are many technical complications involved in particular study designs and data analyses. Aptitude, treatment, and outcome variables can be multiple; regressions can be nonlinear. Special problems in ATI research attach to the disattenuation of measurements, the evaluation of power of statistical inferences, and the disentangling of regression effects at different levels of aggregation (e.g., individual student, classroom, and school). Since an adaptive instructional system based on ATI would presumably involve periodic aptitude monitoring and reclassification of students, there are also technical issues involved in the sequential assessment of aptitudes and outcomes, and the evaluation of utilities in placement decisions. On these and related topics, see Cronbach and Snow (1977) and Cronbach (1982, 1991).

3. Examples of Instructional Systems

An adaptive instructional system such as that envisioned by Glaser (1977, see also Corno and Snow 1986) could be based on ATI. It would contain at least two alternative instructional routes to successful attainment of some criterion achievement level. The route or treatment taken by each learner would depend on an initial diagnosis of aptitude for learning in each available treatment. Also available in such a system would be at least one form of compensatory, direct training of aptitude for learners diagnosed as unready for any of the available instructional treatments.

A variety of alternative instructional treatments have been evaluated using measures of prior ability and generalized achievement as aptitudes. From a summary of that research (Snow 1989), it appears that instructional treatments differ in the information-processing burdens they place on, or remove from, the responsibility of the learner, and the regressions of achievement outcome on scholastic ability become steeper or shallower, respectively, as a result. As learners are required to puzzle things out for themselves, organize their own study, and build their own comprehension, more able learners do well—they can capitalize on their strengths profitably—while less able learners do poorly. However, as instructional treatments relieve learners from difficult reading and inferencing or analyzing of complex concepts on their own, the more such treatments seem to compensate for or circumvent less able learners' weaknesses. Unfortunately, the structured and simplified treatments that seem to help less able learners are suboptimal for able learners, relative to the more burdensome treatments where they excel. The ATI results from a variety of studies of this hypothesis often approximate the pattern shown in Fig. 1(e), and occasionally that in Fig. 1(f).

For some courses of instruction, then, alternative treatment T4 might be designed to provide relatively unstructured and minimal guidance and to encourage learner self-direction in a discovery-oriented approach. The teacher might guide the inductive process, but instruction would clearly be student centered. In contrast, T3 might be designed to break down the learning task to give clear step-by-step guidance, feedback, and correction through a series of small units, with frequent summary and review, and simplified demonstrations of the concepts to be learned. Students would be assigned to either T3 or T4 on the basis of prior scholastic ability scores taken at the start of instruction. Periodic aptitude and achievement assessments would show the degree to which outcome criterion levels were being achieved for each learner in the particular treatment assigned.

For those students who might not be expected to profit from either alternative, compensatory aptitude training would be assigned. This training might consist of directed work on academic learning or reading skills, study habits, self-management skills, and so on. The aim of this training would be to develop readiness for entry into treatment T3 as soon as possible.

Student anxiety might also be considered as an aptitude in this adaptive instructional system. It has often been found that more anxious students do relatively poorly under unstructured or student-centered forms of instruction, as compared to teacher-structured conditions. In contrast, less anxious students often appear not to need teacher structure. Furthermore, ability and anxiety appear to combine in higher order interaction in relation to this treatment contrast.

The initial placement decision in the instructional system would thus depend on both prior ability and anxiety indices. Able learners showing little anxiety would be assigned to treatment T4. The more anxious, able learners and the less able, less anxious learners would receive treatment T3. The least able and the most anxious students might be given compensatory training adapted to their particular needs: cognitive skills training focused on ability deficits and therapeutic interventions designed to alleviate the effects of anxiety. Periodic monitoring would need to be designed to indicate when particular learners should be switched to alternative treatment assignments.

While these examples provide a hypothetical demonstration, no such system can be properly designed in the abstract. Local conditions must be considered, aptitude measures and alternative treatment designs must be adjusted to these conditions, and periodic evaluation must be relied upon to realize an effective system.

4. Prospects for Research and Development

It is noteworthy that much research in instructional psychology contrasts two treatments without evaluating ATI. Voluminous research on teaching has compared direct teacher-centered instruction with guided discovery. Now research on new instructional technology considers essentially the same contrast in arguments about mastery-oriented computerized tutoring versus discovery learning in computerized microworlds (Glaser and Bassok 1989), again without evaluating ATI. Also, a large number of learning style hypotheses have been developed for use by teachers in adapting classroom instruction to student differences; each such style construct produces an ATI hypothesis, though none have been evaluated as such. Thus, one important prospect for further work is to conduct evaluative research on these developments from an ATI perspective (Cronbach 1982)

A second important line for further research aims at improved analysis of the many different kinds of aptitude constructs and measures that have been used in ATI work (Gustafsson 1989). Several lines of cognitive information processing research have provided analyses of cognitive ability constructs, identifying the underlying component processes and strategies on which individuals may differ (Lohman 1989, Snow 1989, Sternberg 1985a, 1985b).

Another approach has been to examine the differences in learning strategies students engage in during instruction that appear to mediate aptitude–outcome relations. Task analyses of instructional conditions also suggest mediational differences among alternative treatments that may control aptitude–outcome relations. Important new work is investigating prior knowledge differences in relation to cognitive and affective aptitudes for instruction (Schneider and Weinert 1989). There are also important advances in research on cognitive and affective aptitudes (Heckhausen et al. 1985, Kuhl and Kraska 1989).

Finally, more intensive analysis on outcome measures may help diagnose in detail the particular kinds of cognitive effects that derive from particular aptitude–treatment combinations (Snow and Lohman 1984, 1989). Future research on all these fronts in instructional psychology can be brought together within the ATI framework (Snow and Swanson 1992).

References

Corno L, Snow R E 1986 Adapting teaching to individual differences among learners. In: Wittrock M C (ed.) 1986 *Handbook of Research on Teaching*, 3rd edn. Macmillan, New York

Cronbach L J 1957 The two disciplines of scientific psychology. *Am. Psychol.* 12(11): 671–84

Cronbach L J 1975 Beyond the two disciplines of scientific psychology. *Am. Psychol.* 30(2): 116–27

Cronbach L J 1982 *Designing Evaluations of Educational and Social Programs.* Jossey-Bass, San Francisco, California

Cronbach L J 1991 Emerging views on methodology. In: Wachs T D, Plomin R (eds.) 1991 *Conceptualization and Measurement of Organism–Environment Interaction.* American Psychological Association, Washington, DC

Cronbach L J, Snow R E 1977 *Aptitudes and Instructional Methods: A Handbook for Research on Interactions.* Irvington, New York

Dance K A, Neufeld R W J 1988 Aptitude–treatment interaction research in the clinical setting: A review of attempts to dispel the "patient uniformity" myth. *Psych. Bull.* 104(2): 192–213

Endler N S, Magnusson D (eds.) 1976 *Interactional Psychology and Personality.* Hemisphere, Washington, DC

Glaser R 1977 *Adaptive Education: Individual Diversity and Learning.* Holt, Rinehart, and Winston, New York

Glaser R, Bassok M 1989 Learning theory and the study of instruction. *Ann. Rev. Psychol.* 40: 631–66

Gustafsson J E 1989 Broad and narrow abilities in research on learning and instruction. In: Kanfer R, Ackerman P L, Cudeck R (eds.) 1989 *Abilities, Motivation, and Methodology.* Erlbaum, Hillsdale, New Jersey

Heckhausen H, Schmalt H D, Schneider K 1985 *Achievement Motivation in Perspective.* Academic Press, Orlando, Florida

Kuhl J, Kraska K 1989 Self-regulation and metamotivation: Computational mechanisms development and assessment. In: Kanfer R, Ackerman P L, Cudeck R (eds.) 1989 *Abilities, Motivation, and Methodology: The Minnesota Symposium on Learning and Individual Differences.* Erlbaum, Hillsdale, New Jersey

Lohman D F 1989 Human intelligence: An introduction to advances in theory and research. *Rev. Educ. Res.* 59(4): 333–73

Magnusson D, Allen V L (eds.) 1983 *Human Development: An Interactional Perspective.* Academic Press, New York

Pervin L A, Lewis M (eds.) 1978 *Perspectives in Interactional Psychology.* Plenum Press, New York

Schneider W, Weinert F E (eds.) 1989 *Interactions Among Aptitudes, Strategies, and Knowledge in Cognitive Performance.* Springer-Verlag, New York

Snow R E 1989 Aptitude-treatment interaction as a framework for research on individual differences in learning. In: Ackerman P L, Sternberg R J, Glaser R (eds.) 1989 *Learning and Individual Differences.* Freeman, New York

Snow R E 1991 The concept of aptitude. In: Snow R E, Wiley D E (eds.) 1991 *Improving Inquiry in Social Science.* Erlbaum, Hillsdale, New Jersey

Snow R E 1992 Aptitude theory: Yesterday, today, and tomorrow. *Educ. Psychol.* 27(1): 5–32

Snow R E, Lohman D F 1984 Toward a theory of cognitive aptitude for learning from instruction. *J. Educ. Psychol.* 76(3): 347–76

Snow R E, Lohman D F 1989 Implications of cognitive psychology for educational measurement. In: Linn R L (ed.) 1989 *Educational Measurement*, 3rd edn. Macmillan, New York

Snow R E, Swanson J 1992 Instructional psychology: Aptitude, adaptation, and assessment. *Annu. Rev. Psychol.* 43: 583–626

Sternberg R J 1985a *Beyond IQ: A Triarchic Theory of Human Intelligence.* Cambridge University Press, Cambridge

Sternberg R J 1985b (ed.) *Human Abilities: An Information Processing Approach.* Freeman, New York

Further Reading

Snow R E 1982 Education and intelligence. In: Sternberg R J (ed.) 1982 *Handbook of Human Intelligence.* Cambridge University Press, New York

SECTION XIII

Classroom Learning Environments

Academic Learning Time

C. W. Fisher

Academic learning time is a psychological construct intended to capture learning as it occurs in the context of day-to-day activities undertaken by students during classroom instruction. The term is also identified with a model of classroom learning in which the influences of classroom instructional processes and environment (including teaching functions and behaviors) on student achievement are mediated by academic learning time. While it is sometimes difficult to separate the construct from the model, for present purposes the former is emphasized over the latter.

Academic learning time emerged in the mid-1970s as a potential solution to problems encountered in attempts to model, and empirically verify, mechanisms through which classroom teachers facilitate knowledge acquisition among their students. Many of the teaching actions being studied at that time, especially those performed when teachers interacted with students, fluctuated relatively rapidly. That is, teachers changed questioning strategies, grouping for instruction, or task requirements from lesson to lesson and often within a single lesson. However, student learning traditionally had been assessed by paper and pencil tests that were somewhat sensitive to substantial changes in knowledge occurring over semesters or years, but were notably insensitive to minute by minute or daily changes. Even if this were not the case, the intrusiveness of repeated administrations of paper and pencil tests rendered this approach impracticable. Any attempt to quantify relationships among narrowly defined, rapidly changing teaching behaviors and broadly defined, slowly changing achievement test scores appeared problematic.

An even greater problem was inherent in attempting to relate teaching actions directly to achievement test scores. Since students learn through their own actions, whether overt or covert, then if teaching actions are to affect student learning, they must first mediate students' actions and thoughts during (and after) the instructional events. To understand relationships between day-to-day teaching actions and student learning it is necessary to have some representation of students' thoughts and actions that is, at least

approximately, coextensive in time with the teaching event. Attempts to relate teaching actions directly to student achievement test scores leave student action and thought unrepresented and, therefore, the mechanisms of teaching effects inaccessible. Academic learning time, advanced as an index of learning as it occurs, was intended to address these and other issues in research on classroom teaching and learning.

1. Definition

Academic learning time is defined as the amount of time that a student spends engaged in an academic task that he or she can perform with high success (Fisher et al. 1980). On a given schoolday, a particular amount of time is set aside for, or allocated to, a curricular area. This allocation, in United States schools, is made primarily by classroom teachers within guidelines set by district and state educational agencies. For students, the amount of time allocated to a content area constitutes an upper limit on the amount of academic learning time in that content area for that schoolday. For a variety of reasons, a given student will be engaged in the academic task at hand for a portion of the allocated time and, of the engaged time, only a portion will be spent on tasks that the student can complete successfully. It is this latter portion of instructional time, when the student is engaged in tasks at a high rate of success, that is referred to as academic learning time. The more time a student spends in these conditions, the more academic learning time is accumulated, and the more the student learns.

Academic learning time can be thought of as the product of allocated time, student engagement rate, and student success rate on academic tasks. In most United States schools, time allocations tend to vary between classes, but with the exception of variations due to student absences from school, allocations tend to be similar for students in the same class. Engagement rates and success rates on academic tasks vary considerably from student to student within a class and the class distributions of these rates also vary considerably from class to class. As a result, academic learning time, being the product of these three factors, shows remarkable variability both within and between classes.

Academic learning time, as outlined above, is a generic concept in the sense that it is not dependent on subject matter considerations. However, in most cases, educators are interested in learning in some particular domain, say mathematics, and relating this learning to teaching actions during classroom mathematics instruction, measures of outcomes in mathematics (i.e., achievement test scores or performance measures), or both. Academic learning time in mathematics would be a function of time allocated to mathematics, engagement rate during mathematics tasks, and success rate on those tasks. If one were interested in a very specific learning domain, say addition of two-digit numbers, then academic learning time on addition of two-digit numbers could be obtained by restricting the time allocation, engagement, and success rate components accordingly.

As academic learning time in a specified domain is accumulated day after day and week after week, differences among students on this measure of classroom learning are reflected in student achievement test scores in that domain. Since academic learning time has been restricted to classroom instruction, achievement in subject matter areas on which students spent substantial amounts of time in informal education or other out-of-school learning environments would be expected to have relatively weak relationships with time-based measures of classroom learning.

2. Related Concepts

The development and application of time variables, that is, the use of duration of events or conditions to characterize aspects of learning and learning environments, built directly on the seminal work of John Carroll (1963, 1985). While there were earlier applications of time variables to educational issues (e.g., Morrison 1926), most modern interest can be traced to Carroll's model of school learning. In this model, originally developed in the context of foreign language learning and later applied to a wide variety of learning settings, Carroll proposed five constructs, of which three were expressed as durations of time.

Two of these variables, opportunity to learn and perseverance, have been used directly or modified in some way by a considerable number of researchers. Opportunity to learn was originally defined as the amount of time allowed for learning a task (Carroll 1963) and seems equivalent to allocated time as used here. Opportunity to learn and allocated time

are differentiated from a similar concept, content covered, by the latter's specific, as opposed to general, focus on the subject matter dealt with during instruction.

Perseverance or the amount of time the learner is willing to engage actively in learning appears to be similar to engaged time, active learning time, and time-on-task (see Anderson 1984, Berliner 1990, Carroll 1985, Harnischfeger and Wiley 1985 for more detailed discussions of these and other time variables). Time-on-task, a term frequently used by educators, is sometimes confused with academic learning time. Academic learning time differs from time-on-task and its aliases in that academic learning time includes only that part of time-on-task which is spent on tasks the learner can perform at a high rate of success. In other words, academic learning time is a subset of time-on-task.

Time-on-task, by connotation more than denotation, leaves the task unspecified. In educational practice there seems to be a tendency to accord more importance to the quantity of time and to diminish the importance of the quality of the task or tasks on which the time was spent. It is all too easy, though erroneous, to assume either that all learning tasks are of equal quality, or that task quality is somehow subordinate to simple duration.

Inclusion of success rate as a component in the definition of academic learning time was intended to incorporate at least one index, though a crude one, of task quality (Marliave and Filby 1985). Adding the success rate component increased the complexity of the overall concept and amounted to a departure from the elegance, if not the spirit, of the Carroll model. Carroll maintained that what was important was not simply the amount of time spent but the amount of time spent in appropriate circumstances. By including success rate in the definition of academic learning time, a deliberate attempt was made to capture some aspect of task quality. In the process, academic learning time incorporated and confounded aspects of what in the Carroll model had been represented separately as quality of instruction and the learner's ability to understand instruction.

Success rate, reflecting both teacher decisions about which tasks to pursue and the learner's understanding of the instructional tasks, was intended to index task appropriateness for that learner. Hence, different students would have different success rates on the same task or set of tasks. As a result, academic learning time combined, in one concept, aspects of quality of teaching, learner characteristics, and curriculum. Combining three of the four commonplaces of schooling in this manner was considered a liability by many (Harnischfeger and Wiley 1985). However, it maintained the spirit of Carroll's model, though this was not a consideration at the time, by providing a rough estimate of "time actually spent" (the numerator in Carroll's deceptively simple and elegant equation).

In formulating academic learning time in this way, the intention was to create a dynamic index of learning itself, an index which could be, on the one hand, related to narrowly defined teaching actions, and on the other, "integrated" over time, so to speak, to approximate traditional measures of achievement. Though the research team that developed academic learning time conceptualized the construct as a unified entity, they tried to have their cake and eat it too, in that, in empirical work, the various components were typically measured and entered into analyses separately (Fisher et al. 1978). (Due to various measurement problems, academic learning time was not assessed directly as a single variable. Components of the construct were measured directly.)

There is a second aspect of success rate as a component of academic learning time that bears elaboration. Success rate was partitioned into three broadly defined categories. High success characterized situations where students had a good grasp of the task and made only occasional errors. Low success described situations where students did not understand the task and made correct responses at about the chance level. Medium success, reflecting partial understanding of the task, included situations between low and high success. The definition of academic learning time suggests that more time spent on tasks with high success represents more learning. However, this does not necessarily imply that all of a learner's time be spent on tasks with high success. If a learner works only on tasks that are so easy (for that student) that he or she is not challenged by new material, then little learning is likely to occur. Generally, some balance between high and medium success tasks produces the most learning, while low success tasks are detrimental to learning.

This issue of balance in the distribution of tasks is not obvious from a cursory examination of the academic learning time concept, yet it is critically important since the balance is likely to be different depending upon the students, subject matter, and context in which the instruction occurs. The balancing of more and less challenging tasks can also be thought of in terms of curriculum pacing or providing appropriate amounts of independent practice on a task before introducing one or more novel tasks.

3. Research

A variety of procedures has been used for measuring the components of academic learning time. Typically, allocated time has been estimated using teacher logs, one-time survey items, or direct observation. Measurements of engagement rates have relied primarily on direct observation while indexes of success rates have been derived from direct observation and scoring of student responses on paper and pencil curriculum materials. Measures of allocated time are, in general,

easier to obtain and are characterized by somewhat higher reliabilities than either engagement or success rates. The latter two variables are particularly difficult to assess during portions of classroom lessons when students make few overt responses.

By the early 1990s, several dozen studies, mostly conducted in the process–product framework with an increasing number in the case study and descriptive traditions, have presented data on allocated and engaged times. A small subset of these studies has included data on success rates. The vast majority of these studies have been conducted in the United States and therefore reflect American elementary and secondary education practices. The general findings that are outlined below are summarized from a variety of journal articles, chapters, and books (see, e.g., Anderson 1984, Fisher and Berliner 1985, Wittrock 1986).

3.1 Distributional Aspects of the Components of Academic Learning Time

Descriptive studies have yielded information on the components of academic learning time, most often in elementary classrooms. Perhaps the most striking results are the sizes of variations found between classes on allocated time for practically all subject matter areas and, both between and within classes, on engagement and success rates. It is apparently not unusual to find time allocations to a school subject matter area that differ by a factor of three or more for students at the same grade level.

Elementary school students are typically engaged in school tasks about three-fourths of the time with class averages sometimes exceeding 0.90 as well as dipping below 0.50. Variation in engagement rates within classes is usually somewhat greater. In a number of studies, engagement rates have been shown to vary from one organizational arrangement to another within the same class. For example, engagement rates in teacher-led groups are consistently higher than those in independent work groups.

Even general statements about success rates, or error rates as they are more commonly called, must be very tenuous indeed because there seems to be surprisingly little data from ordinary classroom instruction and when there are data, differences in measurement procedures and classroom contexts make comparisons less than straightforward. From the original studies of academic learning time examining basic skills instruction in elementary schools in California, the proportion of time on high success tasks to medium success tasks was approximately one to one.

3.2 Academic Learning Time and Achievement

Since learning occurs over time and since zero time results in no learning, logic maintains that the correlation between time spent trying to learn and achievement in a given domain will be nonnegative. This logical relationship notwithstanding, a considerable number of researchers from several countries have studied the connection between measures of student achievement and allocated time, engaged time, or some variant of these entities. Using a variety of correlational analyses, measures of opportunity to learn and measures of time spent trying to learn have shown positive relationships with student achievement. The consistency of this finding over a wide variety of settings and subject matters has been the inevitable conclusion of a number of sizable reviews giving the finding widespread credence.

For academic learning time per se, its relationship with student achievement was estimated by the research group who developed the construct in the context of basic skills learning in elementary schools in California. Generally speaking, the components of academic learning time, taken together, accounted uniquely for approximately 10 percent of the variation in scores on paper and pencil achievement tests. This estimate represents the contribution of academic learning time after accounting for entering achievement scores but without attempting to make adjustments for errors of measurement. The apparent size and robustness of the relationship between academic learning time (and, generally speaking, other estimates of instructional time) and student achievement is unusual. Within this research framework, few, if any, single measures of classroom instructional phenomena, other than entering achievement level, have shown as much promise.

3.3 Academic Learning Time and Teaching Process Variables

While academic learning time is influenced by a number of different sources, its relationships with teaching process variables have received by far the most attention. In general, student engagement rates have been shown to vary with the amount of substantive interaction between teachers and students. For example, academic monitoring and academic feedback seem to have consistently positive associations with student engagement. Relationships between student success rates and both preactive and interactive teaching process variables have been examined in a number of studies; however, the findings have been somewhat inconsistent.

4. Future Research

Much of the earlier work on academic learning time and many other time-based constructs was done in the context of direct instruction and other pedagogies that rely primarily on "telling" as a metaphor for the teacher–student relationship in classroom learning. As educators in many countries begin to broaden their views on pedagogy, especially to include models based on constructivist principles, some may lose interest in time-based constructs. However, to the extent that students learn what they do in classrooms, academic learning time continues to be a useful construct.

One of its distinctive features, student success rate, was an attempt to include classroom task characteristics directly in studies of classroom learning. While this facet of academic learning time pointed in a useful direction and studies of mediated learning have made substantial progress in this area, educators need more and better understandings of classroom tasks. Ways must be found to conceptualize both the cognitive and social aspects of learning as it occurs in the context of classroom tasks. Doyle's (1983) conceptualization of academic work continues to offer insights in this arena and studies of classroom tasks and task structures (e.g., Fisher and Hiebert 1990, Mergendoller 1988, Stodolsky 1988) shed some light on the conditions in which students and teachers pursue classroom learning. At this point, the mainstream of research on classroom teaching and learning focuses on conceptualizations of, and relationships among, the thoughts and actions of students and teachers. In suggesting a broader and deeper consideration of classroom tasks, the point is to balance this focus with information on the social and cognitive tasks that students and teachers engage in and the contexts in which these thoughts, actions, and tasks are embedded.

See also: Time, Allocated and Instructional

References

Anderson L W (ed.) 1984 *Time and School Learning*. St. Martin's Press, New York

Berliner D C 1990 What's all the fuss about instructional time? In: Ben-Peretz M, Bromme R (eds.) 1990 *The Nature of Time in Schools*. Teachers College Press, New York

Carroll J B 1963 A model of school learning. *Teach. Coll. Rec.* 64:723–33

Carroll J B 1985 The model of school learning: Progress of an idea. In: Fisher C, Berliner D (eds.) 1985

Doyle W 1983 Academic work. *Rev. Educ. Res.* 53:159–99

Fisher C et al. 1978 *Teaching Behaviors, Academic Learning Time, and Student Achievement: Final Report of Phase III-B, Beginning Teacher Evaluation Study*. Far West Laboratory for Educational Research and Development, San Francisco, California

Fisher C et al. 1980 Teaching behaviors, academic learning time, and student achievement: An overview. In Denham C, Lieberman A (eds.) 1980 *Time to Learn*. National Institute of Education, Washington, DC

Fisher C W, Berliner D C 1985 *Perspectives on Instructional Time*. Longman, New York

Fisher C, Hiebert E 1990 Characteristics of tasks in two approaches to literacy instruction. *Elem. Sch. J.* 91:1–13

Harnischfeger A, Wiley D 1985 Origins of active learning time. In: Fisher C, Berliner D (eds.) 1985

Marliave R, Filby N N 1985 Success rate: A measure of task appropriateness. In: Fisher C, Berliner D (eds.) 1985

Mergendoller J (ed.) 1988 Schoolwork and academic tasks. *Elem. Sch. J.* 88 (special issue)

Morrison H C 1926 *The Practice of Teaching in the Secondary School.* University of Chicago Press, Chicago, Illinois

Stodolsky S S 1988 *The Subject Matters.* University of Chicago Press, Chicago, Illinois

Wittrock M C (ed.) 1986 *Handbook of Research on Teaching,* 3rd edn. Macmillan, New York

Further Reading

Bennett N, Desforges C, Cockburn A, Wilkinson B 1984 *The Quality of Pupil Learning Experiences.* Erlbaum, London

Ben-Peretz M, Bromme R (eds.) 1990 *The Nature of Time in Schools.* Teachers College Press, New York

Classroom Environments

B. J. Fraser

The environment, climate, atmosphere, tone, ethos, or ambience of a classroom is believed to exert a powerful influence on student behavior, attitudes, and achievement. Although classroom environment is a somewhat subtle concept, remarkable progress has been made over the last quarter of the twentieth century in its conceptualization and assessment, which has led to an increased understanding of its determinants and effects.

1. An Historical Perspective on the Assessment of Classroom Environments

Murray (1938) introduced the term "alpha press" to describe the environment as assessed by a detached observer and "beta press" to describe the environment as perceived by those who inhabit it. Over the years, both observational instruments and questionnaires have been used to study the classroom environment.

Several structured observation schedules for coding classroom communication and events have been reviewed by Rosenshine and Stevens (1986) and Good and Brophy (1991). One of the most widely-known is Flander's Interaction Analysis System (FIAS) which records classroom behavior at three-second intervals using 10 categories (e.g., praising and encouraging, asking questions, student-initiated talk). Medley and Mitzel constructed an omnibus instrument called OSCAR (Observation Schedule And Record) which includes 14 categories (e.g., pupil leadership activities, manifest teacher hostility, emotional climate, verbal emphasis, and social organization). Other systematic observation schemes are the Emmer Observation System, the Brophy–Good Dyadic Interaction System, and Blumenfeld and Miller's method of coding vocabulary (Good and Brophy 1991).

Since the 1970s, numerous questionnaires have been developed to assess student perceptions of their classroom environments (Fraser 1986; Fraser and Walberg 1991). Advantages claimed for questionnaires are that they can be more economical than classroom observation techniques; they are based on students' experiences over many lessons; they involve the pooled judgments of all students in a class; they can be more important than observed behaviors because they are the determinants of student behavior; and they have been found to account for more variance in student learning outcomes than have directly observed variables.

One of the most widely used questionnaires, the Learning Environment Inventory, was developed as part of the research and evaluation activities of Harvard Project Physics (Welch and Walberg 1972). About the same time, Moos began developing numerous social climate scales which ultimately resulted in the development of the well-known Classroom Environment Scale (Moos and Trickett 1987). Both of these questionnaires built upon the theoretical, conceptual, and measurement foundations laid by pioneers such as Lewin (1936), Murray (1938), and their followers (e.g., Stern 1970). Furthermore, research using these instruments was influenced by prior studies using structured observation instruments.

A more recent approach to studying educational environments involves the application of techniques of naturalistic inquiry, ethnography, and case study. In the early 1990s there is a growing acceptance of a combination of qualitative and quantitative methods (based on observation or student perceptions) in the study of classroom environment (Fraser and Tobin 1991).

2. A Summary of Questionnaires for Assessing Classroom Environments

Table 1 summarizes several questionnaires commonly used to assess student perceptions of classroom

Table 1
Overview of scales contained in seven classroom environment instruments (LEI, CES, ICEQ, MCI, CUCEI, SLEI, and QTI)

Instrument	Level	Items per scale	Scale classified according to Moos's Scheme		
			Relationship dimensions	Personal development dimensions	System maintenance and change dimensions
Learning Environment Inventory (LEI)	secondary	7	cohesiveness friction favoritism cliqueness satisfaction apathy	speed difficulty competitiveness	diversity formality material environment goal direction disorganization democracy
Classroom Environment Scale (CES)	secondary	10	involvement affiliation teacher support	task orientation competition	order and organization rule clarity teacher control innovation
Individualised Classroom Environment Questionnaire (ICEQ)	secondary	10	personalization participation	independence investigation	differentiation
My class Inventory (MCI)	elementary	6–9	cohesiveness friction satisfaction	difficulty competitiveness	
College and University Classroom Environment Inventory (CUCEI)	higher education	7	personalization involvement student cohesiveness satisfaction	task orientation	innovation individualization
Science Laboratory Environment Inventory (SLEI)	upper secondary higher education	7	student cohesiveness	open-endedness integration	rule clarity material environment
Questionnaire on Teacher Interaction (QTI)	secondary elementary	8-10	helpful/friendly understanding dissatisfied admonishing		leadership student responsibility and freedom uncertain strict

learning environment. Each questionnaire is suitable for convenient group administration, can be scored either by hand or computer, and has been shown to be reliable in extensive field trials. All questionnaires include multiple variables or scales. For example, the My Class Inventory contains five scales: cohesiveness, friction, satisfaction, difficulty, and competitiveness. A distinctive feature of most of these instruments is that, in addition to a form that measures perceptions of actual classroom environment, there is another form to measure perceptions of preferred classroom environment. The preferred forms are concerned with goals

and value orientations and measure perceptions of the ideal classroom environment.

Table 1 includes the name of each scale contained in each instrument, the school level (elementary, secondary, or higher education) for which each instrument is suited, the number of items contained in each scale, and the classification of each scale according to Moos's (1974) scheme for classifying human environments. Moos's three basic dimensions are: Relationship (which identify the nature and intensity of personal relationships within the environment and assess the extent to which people are involved in the environment and support and help each other); Personal Development (which assess basic directions along which personal growth and self-enhancement tend to occur); and System Maintenance and System Change (which involve the extent to which the environment is orderly, clear in expectations, maintains control, and is responsive to change).

As mentioned above, the development of the Learning Environment Inventory (LEI) began in the late 1960s in conjunction with the evaluation and research on Harvard Project Physics (Fraser et al. 1982). The LEI contains 105 statements (seven per scale) with response alternatives of "Strongly Disagree," "Disagree," "Agree," and "Strongly Agree." The scoring direction (or polarity) is reversed for some items. A typical item contained in the "Cohesiveness" scale is: "All students know each other very well."

The Classroom Environment Scale (CES) grew out of a comprehensive program of research involving perceptual measures of a variety of human environments including psychiatric hospitals, prisons, university residences, and work milieus (Moos 1974). Moos and Trickett's (1987) final version contains nine scales with 10 true–false items in each scale. Published materials include a test manual, a questionnaire, an answer sheet, and a transparent hand scoring key. A typical item in the CES is: "The teacher takes a personal interest in the students" (Teacher Support).

The Individualized Classroom Environment Questionnaire (ICEQ) differs from other classroom environment scales in that it assesses those dimensions which distinguish individualized classrooms from conventional ones. The final published version (Fraser 1990) contains 50 items with an equal number of items belonging to each of the five scales. Each item is responded to on a five-point scale with the alternatives of "Almost Never," "Seldom," "Sometimes," "Often," and "Very Often." A typical item is: "Different students use different books, equipment, and materials" (Differentiation). The published form consists of a handbook and test master sets from which unlimited numbers of copies of the questionnaires and response sheets may be made.

The LEI has been simplified to form the My Class Inventory (MCI) which is suitable for children in the 8–12 years age range (Fraser et al. 1982) and students in the junior high school, especially those who might experience reading difficulties with the LEI. The MCI differs from the LEI in four ways. First, in order to minimize fatigue among younger children, the MCI contains only five of the LEI's original 15 scales. Second, item wording has been simplified to enhance readability. Third, the LEI's four-point response format has been reduced to a two-point (Yes–No) response format. Fourth, students answer on the questionnaire itself instead of on a separate response sheet to avoid errors in transferring responses from one place to another. The final form contains 38 items. A typical item is: "Children are always fighting with each other" (Friction).

The College and University Classroom Environment Inventory (CUCEI) was developed for small classes (but not for lectures or laboratory classes) (Fraser and Treagust 1986) as a result of the fact that little work had been done in higher education classrooms parallel to the traditions of classroom environment research at the secondary and elementary school levels. The final form of the CUCEI contains seven-item scales. Each item has four responses ("Strongly Agree," "Agree," "Disagree," "Strongly Disagree") and polarity is reversed for approximately half the items. A typical item is: "Activities in this class are clearly and carefully planned" (Task Orientation).

An instrument specifically suited to assessing the environment of science laboratory classes at the senior high school or higher education levels was developed (Fraser et al. 1992) as a result of the critical importance and uniqueness of laboratory settings in science education. The Science Laboratory Environment Inventory (SLEI) has five scales and the response alternatives for each item are "Almost Never," "Seldom," "Sometimes," "Often," and "Very Often." A typical item includes: "We know the results that we are supposed to get before we commence a laboratory activity" (Open-endedness). A noteworthy feature of the validation procedures employed is that the SLEI was field tested simultaneously in six countries (the US, Canada, England, Israel, Australia, and Nigeria).

In the Netherlands a learning environment questionnaire was developed to enable teacher educators to give preservice and inservice teachers advice about the nature and quality of the interaction between teachers and students (Wubbels and Levy in press). Drawing upon a theoretical model of proximity (Cooperation–Opposition) and influence (Dominance–Submission), the Questionnaire of Teacher Interaction (QTI) was developed to assess eight scales: Leadership, Helpful/Friendly, Understanding, Student Responsibility and Freedom, Uncertain, Dissatisfied, Admonishing, and Strict Behavior. The QTI has 77 items altogether (approximately 10 per scale), and each item is responded to on a 5-point scale ranging from Never to Always. A typical item is "she or he gets angry" (Admonishing behavior). The validity and reliability of the QTI have been established for secondary school students in the Netherlands, the United States, and Australia (Wubbels and Levy in press).

3. Classroom Environment Research

The strongest tradition in classroom environment research in several countries has involved investigation of associations between students' cognitive and affective learning outcomes and their perceptions of their classroom environments (Fraser 1993). Numerous studies have shown that student perceptions account for appreciable amounts of variance in learning outcomes often beyond that which can be attributed to student background characteristics. For example, better student achievement on a variety of outcome measures was found consistently in classes perceived as having greater cohesiveness and goal direction, and less disorganization and friction (Haertel et al. 1981)

Classroom environment measures were employed as dependent variables in curriculum evaluation studies, investigations of differences between student and teacher perceptions of classroom environment and studies involving other independent variables (e.g. different subject matters). The significance of curriculum evaluation studies is that classroom environment differed markedly between curricula, even when various achievement outcome measures showed negligible differences. Research involving teachers and students informs educators that teachers are likely to perceive the classroom environment more favorably than their students in the same classrooms. Research studies involving the use of classroom environment as a criterion variable have identified how the classroom environment varies with such factors as teacher personality, class size, grade level, subject matter, the nature of the school-level environment, and the type of school.

4. Practical Uses of Classroom Environment Information

Knowledge of student perceptions can be employed as a basis for reflection upon, discussion of, and systematic attempts to improve classroom environments. For example, Fraser and Fisher's (1986) attempt to improve classroom environments made use of the CES with a class of 22 Grade 9 boys and girls of mixed ability studying science at a government school in Tasmania. The procedure incorporated five fundamental steps.

First, the actual and preferred forms of the CES were administered to all students in the class. Second, the teacher was provided with profiles representing the class means of students' actual and preferred environment scores. Third, the teacher engaged in private reflection and informal discussion about the profiles in order to provide a basis for a decision about whether an attempt would be made to change the environment in terms of some of the CES's dimensions. In fact, the teacher decided to introduce an intervention aimed at increasing the levels of teacher support and order and organization in the classroom. Fourth, the teacher used the intervention for approximately two months. For example, enhancing teacher support involved the teacher moving around the class more to mix with students, providing assistance to students and talking with them more than previously. Fifth, the actual form of the scales was readministered at the end of the intervention to see whether students were perceiving their classroom environment differently from before.

The results showed that some change in student perceptions occurred during the time of the intervention.

Pretest–post-test differences were statistically significant only for teacher support, task orientation, and order and organization. These findings are noteworthy because two of the dimensions on which appreciable changes were recorded were those on which the teacher had attempted to promote change. Also, there appears to be a side effect in that the intervention could have resulted in the classroom becoming more task oriented than the students would have preferred. Overall, this case study suggests the potential usefulness of teachers employing classroom environment instruments to provide meaningful information about their classrooms and a tangible basis to guide improvements in classroom environments.

5. Future Research

Assessment involving students' perceptions of classrooms can involve either individual students' perceptions or the intersubjective perceptions of all students in the same class. This distinction in past classroom environment research has often been important when choosing an appropriate unit of statistical analysis (e.g., individual student scores or class mean scores; see Fraser 1986). The advances in multilevel analysis mean that more sophisticated techniques are available for analyzing the typical data (e.g., with students nested within classes) found in much research on classroom environments.

Although only limited progress has been made toward the desirable goal of combining quantitative and qualitative methods within the same study, the fruitfulness of this objective is illustrated in several studies (Tobin et al. 1990, Fraser and Tobin 1991). For example, in a study of higher-level cognitive learning, six researchers intensively studied the Grade 10 science classes of two teachers over a 10-week period (Tobin et al. 1990). Each lesson was observed by several researchers, interviewing of students and teachers took place on a daily basis, and students' written work was examined. The study also involved quantitative information from questionnaires assessing student perceptions of their classroom environments. An important finding was that students' perceptions of the environment within each classroom were consistent with the observers' field records of the patterns of learning activities and engagements in each classroom. For example, the high level of personalization perceived in one teacher's classroom matched the large proportion of time that she spent in small-group activities during which she constantly moved about the classroom interacting with students.

6. Conclusion

Positive classroom environments are generally assumed to be educationally desirable ends in their own right. Moreover, comprehensive evidence from past research establishes that classroom environments have a potent influence on how well students achieve a range of desired educational outcomes. Consequently, educators need not feel that they must choose between striving to achieve constructive classroom environments and attempting to enhance student achievement of cognitive and affective aims. Rather, constructive educational climates can be viewed both as means to valuable ends and as worthy ends in themselves.

References

Fraser B J 1986 *Classroom Environment*. Croom Helm, London

Fraser B J 1990 *Individualized Classroom Environment Questionnaire*. Australian Council for Educational Research, Melbourne

Fraser B J 1993 Classroom and school climate. In: Gabel D (ed.) 1993 *Handbook of Research on Science Teaching and Learning*. Macmillan, New York

Fraser B J, Anderson G J, Walberg H J 1982 *Assessment of Learning Environments: Manual for Learning Environment Inventory (LEI) and My Class Inventory (MCI)* (3rd version). Western Australian Institute of Technology, Perth

Fraser B J, Fisher D L 1986 Using short forms of classroom climate instruments to assess and improve classroom psychosocial environment. *J. Res. Sci. Teach.* 5: 387–413

Fraser B J, Giddings G J, McRobbie C J 1992 Science laboratory classroom environments at schools and universities: A cross-national study. Paper presented at the annual meeting of the National Association for Research in Science Teaching, Boston, Massachusetts

Fraser B J, Tobin K 1991 Combining qualitative and quantitative methods in classroom environment research. In:

Fraser B J, Walberg H J (eds.) 1991 *Educational Environments: Evaluation, Antecedents and Consequences*. Pergamon Press, Oxford

Fraser B J, Treagust D F 1986 Validity and use of an instrument for assessing classroom psychosocial environment in higher education. *High. Educ.* 15: 37–57

Fraser B J, Walberg H J (eds.) 1991 *Educational Environments: Evaluation, Antecedents and Consequences*. Pergamon Press, Oxford

Good T L, Brophy J 1991 *Looking in Classrooms*, 5th edn. Harper Collins, New York

Haertel G D, Walberg H J, Haertel E H 1981 Sociopsychological environments and learning: A quantitative synthesis. *Br. Educ. Res. J.* 7: 27–36

Lewin K 1936 *Principles of Topological Psychology*. McGraw, New York

Moos R H 1974 *The Social Climate Scales: An Overview*. Consulting Psychologists Press, Palo Alto, California

Moos R H, Trickett E J 1987 *Classroom Environment Scale Manual*, 2nd. edn. Consulting Psychologists Press, Palo Alto, California

Murray H A 1938 *Explorations in Personality*. Oxford University Press, New York

Rosenshine B, Stevens R 1986 Teaching functions. In: Wittrock M C (ed.) 1986 *Handbook of Research on Teaching*, 3rd. edn. Macmillan, New York

Stern G G 1970 *People in Context: Measuring Person-Environment Congruence in Education and Industry*. Wiley, New York

Tobin K, Kahle J B, Fraser B J (eds.) 1990 *Windows into Science Classrooms: Problems Associated with Higher-Level Cognitive Learning*. Falmer Press, London

Welch W W, Walberg H J 1972 A national experiment in curriculum evaluation. *Am. Educ. Res. J.* 9: 373–83

Wubbels T, Levy J (eds.) in press. *Do You Know How You Look? Interpersonal Reationships in Education*. Falmer Press, London

Group Processes in the Classroom

N. Bennett

It has been argued that cooperation is central to human existence, but of all the prominent institutions of society, schools seem least characterized by cooperative activity. Nevertheless there is a developing interest in the use of cooperative groups as effective learning contexts in classrooms. This interest has been fueled by the increasing realization that learning is a function of social interaction (i.e., talk drives learning). As such, there is a move to the implementation of cooperative grouping to achieve a better balance between whole class, individual, and group teaching. This entry sets out the rationale for grouping and describes several group models before considering group processes, including the types talk, that are most effective for learning, and what factors can aid or hinder these.

1. Rationale for Cooperative Grouping

The current interest in children learning in groups has largely been fueled by two differing theoretical perspectives—the developmental approach, drawn from cognitive psychology, and the motivational, derived from social psychology.

Conceptions of the learner in developmental psychology shifted in the 1980s from that of a "lone scientist" to that of a "social being" (Bruner and Haste 1987). The "social being" learns through interactions with others, acquiring a framework for interpreting experience. In other words, intelligence and learning develop as functions of social interaction.

Vygotsky (1962, 1978) has emphasized most the so-

683

cial nature of cognition, arguing that learning awakens a variety of internal developmental processes that are able to operate only when learners are interacting with people in their environment and in cooperation with their peers. His notion of the zone of proximal development identifies the gap between what an individual can do alone and unaided, and what can be achieved with the help of more knowledgeable others. "What a child can do today in cooperation, tomorrow he will be able to do on his own" (Vygotsky 1962). Such aid is often referred to as "scaffolded" instruction.

Whereas the developmental approach focuses primarily on the quality of interactions during collaborative activities, motivational perspectives emphasize the reward or goal structures under which members of the group operate. This approach, which has developed from early work on cooperative, competitive, and individualistic goal structures, maintains that if cooperative learning increases student achievement, it is because the use of cooperative reward structures creates peer norms and sanctions supporting individual efforts (Slavin 1987).

2. Types of Cooperative Groups

The developmental and motivational perspectives have given rise to a plethora of cooperative group models embodying a diversity of goals and assumptions. It is not possible to encompass the full range here; three are described below to illustrate the range.

2.1 Student Teams–Achievement Divisions (STAD)

Pupils are assigned to teams of four or five that are as heterogeneous as can be arranged in terms of ability, sex, and where appropriate, race. Following a class presentation by the teacher, the group works together to master the material of the learning unit. Most often the team members quiz each other working from worksheets that consist of facts, skills, or information to be mastered.

Pupils are evaluated on mastery by individual quizzes. Quiz scores are transformed into team scores using a weighting system for individual scores based on prior performances. Rewards or recognition are provided to teams for high weekly performance and/or high cumulative standings.

2.2 Group Investigation (GI)

This model was designed to provide pupils with broad and diverse learning experiences, in contrast to the STAD approach. It consists of six stages. Pupils identify subtopics within an area identified by the teacher, and organize themselves into heterogeneous groups of some three to six children. The group plans the learning task, usually a complex problem-solving task, and determines the goal(s) and how it is to be studied.

The necessary information is collected, analyzed and evaluated before the final report, event, or summary is prepared. This is then presented to the class, and evaluated by their peers and teacher.

2.3 Reciprocal Teaching

Reciprocal teaching involves a highly structured group discussion with the teacher or students providing the leadership role. The dialogue is structured in four steps: (a) the leader frames a question to which the group responds, (b) the leader summarizes the answer and the group responds, (c) any issues raised are clarified, and (d) the leader solicits predictions about the next step. In summary, reciprocal teaching is an interactive teaching procedure based closely on the ideas of Vygotsky in which the teacher and students collaborate in the construction of meaning (Palincsar and Brown 1984).

The marked differences between group models can be gauged from Sharan's (1980) detailed comparison of what he called a "team-learning methods." Sharan identified differences in the nature of the learning tasks, in interpersonal relations and communication, in the nature of the product and its evaluation, and in classroom organization.

3. Studies of Cooperative Grouping

Changing classroom practice always presents challenges, irrespective of the quality of the theoretical and empirical underpinnings. Thus the implementation and acceptance of cooperative group models have been variable across countries, mediated in part by the cultures and ideologies supporting contemporary practice. In the United States and Israel, for example, didactic teaching is the norm. Consequently the research effort has been directed toward the implementation of experimental grouping programs, with a view to changing the contexts of learning in the classroom from a single to a multiple social system. In the United Kingdom, on the other hand, the immediate social context for learning, in the great majority of primary classrooms at least, is usually a small group of four to six children. The research problem here has not been to change contexts, but to improve them, since typical group practice is not cooperative, and suffers from large amounts of off-task interaction, poor quality on-task interaction, and marked gender effects (Bennett 1991).

Differences in the aims of these studies are reflected in their design. The United States and Israeli studies have tended to be input–output evaluations of grouping models, designed to ascertain their effectiveness, rather than to ascertain how groups work effectively. Group processes have been largely ignored. The United Kingdom (and later United States) studies, on the other hand, have tended to focus on processes.

4. Product Studies

The claims made for the role of cooperative grouping in achievement and social development are generally impressive. Whether the comparison has been with competitive or individualistic goal structures (Johnson and Johnson 1985) with whole class didactic teaching (Sharan and Shachar 1988), or across curriculum areas (Slavin 1987), the conclusion has been that cooperative grouping is associated with, or promotes, higher achievement.

The findings in the area of social and affective development are equally strong. Most reviewers conclude that cooperative grouping increases interpersonal attraction, enhances student self-esteem, and improves social relations between students, particularly with different ethnic groups and with mainstreamed students (Slavin 1985, Cowie and Rudduck 1990).

There appears to be little disagreement that cooperative groups are effective in these terms; the disputes that arise relate to such issues as which group model works best with what kind of task structure in what kind of context with what age of children.

5. Studies of Group Processes

It is only since the late 1980s that studies began to address such central questions as what group interactive processes relate to effective outcomes. However, although some investigations have provided detailed analyses of group talk, and others have presented indications of relationships between types of talk and achievement, the studies undertaken so far are not, as a group, coherent or cumulative. This can be seen clearly in the schemes developed for the analysis of group talk.

5.1 Category Systems

The systems developed or adopted for the categorization of group interactions reflect both the purposes of the study and an explicit or implicit theory of what aspects of interaction are worthy of categorization. However, few systems of categorizing talk appear to have been used other than by their developers, and frequently the same researcher will develop a new system for each study.

The theoretical perspectives underpinning systems development have also varied widely. Some have utilized "grounded" theory approaches (i.e., inductively derived categories from repeated readings of the data) (Barnes and Todd 1977, Bennett et al. 1984). Others have utilized deductive approaches using existing theory. The focuses have included sociolinguistic theory, helping behavior, interpersonal attraction, and theories of children's conversations.

Attempts to create coherence from such diversity

present problems; what follows is an interim statement of what is known about group processes and the influences that appear to operate upon them.

5.2 Group Interaction Variables

The most frequent interaction variable studied is helping behavior. However, these studies have tended to be from the United States, on mathematics tasks, and of short duration. Here it has been necessary to distinguish between receiving and giving help. For receiving help to be effective for learning there must be an understandable explanation (rather than a straight answer) provided in response to the receiving pupil's needs. It has been suggested that the effectiveness of help received may constitute a continuum—receiving explanations is sometimes helpful, receiving information has mixed effects, and receiving the answer may actually be harmful (Webb 1989). For example, receiving an explanation which has been requested is only useful for learning if the explanation provided was relevant, understood, and applied by the receiver. Receiving information is likely to be helpful more often since it is easier for the helper to frame an adequate response, and for the receiver to understand it. However, receiving only the answer is unlikely to enhance the receiver's understanding.

What does the giver gain from the helping interaction? When the first peer tutoring system was set up some 200 years ago, it was argued that the benefit to the tutor resided in the principle *Qui docet indoctos docet se* "by teaching he is best taught." Most modern studies affirm this—giving explanations is positively related to achievement. In explaining to someone the giver must clarify, organize, and often reorganize the material conceptually. Further, if the initial explanation is not understood, reformulation is necessary, perhaps utilizing different terminology, examples or analogies, or representations. All of these, it is claimed, will consolidate or expand the giver's understanding.

The provision and receipt of information and explanations is not the only key to successful group interaction. Practice, feedback, and turn-taking are other variables which can mediate achievement effects. In addition, attempts are being made in the 1990s to operationalize for classrooms the concept of cognitive conflict or controversy. This is based on Piaget's view that progress in cognitive development often occurs when cognitive conflict arises with someone who can be seen as comparable to the self but who offers a discrepant solution. Much laboratory-based research has developed this argument (see Perret-Clermont 1980, Doise and Mugny 1984) but few studies in schools utilizing normal classroom tasks have so far been undertaken.

Finally, although not strictly an interactive variable, it is worth noting the increasing evidence of enhanced pupil involvement when working in cooperative groups. When comparisons have been made between time-on-task in groups and in whole class activity it has been substantially less in whole classes (see Hertz-Lazorowitz 1990). Similarly, when comparisons have been made between cooperative groups and normal classroom groups, pupil involvement in the former has been substantially higher (Bennett and Dunne 1992).

5.3 Noninteraction Variables

The nature and quality of group interactive processes are mediated by several noninteractive variables including the composition of the group, task structures, and training.

5.3.1 Group composition. Under this heading is considered the mix or composition of groups in terms of ability or attainment level, sex, race, and personality.

Studies comparing groups which are homogeneous or heterogeneous in terms of children's ability or attainment level present a consistent picture. The quality of interactive processes is substantially different in each type of group. Of particular concern are homogeneous groups of low-ability children. Compared to high-ability groups, these devote substantially less of their time to interactions concerning academic content, fewer of their requests concerning academic and procedural issues are responded to appropriately, and few explanations are offered. Not surprisingly, children in these groups show poor understanding of the task in outcome measures (Bennett and Cass 1988).

High-ability children, however, appear to perform well irrespective of the type of group they are placed in. They tend to talk more, and more of that talk is academic in content. They are the main sources of help in groups, and provide most of the explanations.

Differential experiences for girls and boys in groups have been reported from studies of noncooperative and cooperative groups. One study found that over 80 percent of interactions were between members of the same sex, even when they were seated in mixed-sex groups.

The sex mix of a group appears to influence the amount and level of interaction. Studies in both the United States and the United Kingdom have found that girls are substantially affected in groups in which they are outnumbered by boys. They speak less and at a lower level of reasoning, and are often ignored by boys. In such groups boys are more successful than girls in obtaining help (Bennett and Dunne 1992, Webb 1989).

Two aspects of group composition that are regarded as particularly important by teachers—race and personality—have attracted little systematic attention. There have been several product studies on race, as indicated earlier, but these have not reported on process variables. The impact of personality has also been ig-

nored, perhaps because of difficulties associated with the measurement of personality variables.

5.3.2. Task structures There is agreement that the task characteristics are important and powerful mediators of group processes, but as yet little is known of these effects. Too often studies provide insufficient detail of the tasks used and the demands made on the groups. Nevertheless, various conceptualizations of task or problem type have been suggested, including open to closed, tight and loose, and simple to complex. Although the labels are different, these distinctions are similar in meaning, with the closed, tight, simple end of the continuum defining tasks which are clearly specified, having one correct solution, and requiring low-level thinking. An alternative conceptualization of task demand has been in terms of abstract and action talk, which clearly distinguished between typical mathematics and language tasks in classrooms. The former demanded only action talk whereas the latter demanded that problems be solved verbally, that meaning be searched for, and that decisions unrelated to action be made (Bennett and Dunne 1992). As yet, however, there is no indication of how task types and demands relate to learning outcomes.

5.3.3. Training It is often assumed that the implementation of cooperative grouping in the classroom is a relatively unproblematic process. Groups are composed and children told to cooperate. This is unlikely to be totally effective, however, and unless handled with care children can devise such work avoidance strategies as the "free riders," "suckers," and "gangers" described by Salomon and Globerson (1989). The quality of group processes is therefore likely to be mediated by training (Cohen 1986), but exhortation has not so far been matched by systematic attempts to evaluate the impact of differing kinds of training on group functioning.

6. Conclusion

The initial research effort on cooperative classroom groups was characterized by input–output designs concentrating on outcomes, to the exclusion of processes. Second generation studies have focused less on basic effects and more on investigating the interactive processes involved in effective group functioning. However, attempts to categorize these processes have been theoretically eclectic, and no unified strategy or perspective has yet emerged.

Interestingly, more effort has been expended on delineating the impact of noninteractive mediating variables, but even here the evidence on many of these is sparse. For example, although the range and variety of group models is well-documented, there have been few, if any, systematic attempts to compare these in terms of interactive processes. Similarly, although there have been tentative attempts to classify tasks and their demands, there is a paucity of research linking tasks and patterns of interaction, and how task types and task demands relate to learning outcomes. This must be a priority for future research, but progress in this area will depend on the development of more sophisticated conceptualizations of task demands.

Progress in accounting for group processes in terms of personality characteristics must also await clearer conceptualization and measurement of potentially relevant personality variables.

However, perhaps the most important area to be tackled in the future is effective implementation in the classroom, concentrating in particular on the crucial role of the teacher. The teacher's role has largely been ignored, but the quality of group processes and outcomes lies in their hands. Teachers create the classroom management system, including the composition of the groups; they select, prepare, and present the tasks; they decide on the frequency and manner of their interventions; and they decide what and when to assess. Clearly, without appropriate guidance and training for both teacher and student, the potential for cooperative groupwork as an effective context for learning will not be fully realized.

See also: Cooperative Learning; Classroom Environments

References

Barnes D, Todd F 1977 *Communications and Learning in Small Groups.* Routledge and Kegan Paul, London
Bennett N 1991 Cooperative learning in classrooms: processes and outcomes (The Emanuel Miller Memorial Lecture 1990) *J. Child Psychol. Psychiatry* 32(4): 581–94
Bennett N, Desforges C, Cockburn A, Wilkinson B 1984 *The Quality of Pupil Learning Experiences.* Erlbaum Associates, London
Bennett N, Cass A 1988 The effects of group composition on group interactive processes and pupil understanding. *Br. Educ. Res. J.* 15: 19–32
Bennett N, Dunne E 1992 *Managing Classroom Groups.* Simon and Shuster, London
Bruner J, Haste H 1987 *Making Sense.* Methuen, London
Cohen E G 1986 *Designing Groupwork: Strategies for the Heterogeneous Classroom.* Teachers College Press, New York
Cowie H, Rudduck J 1990 *Cooperative Group Work in the Multi-Ethnic Classroom.* BP Educational Service, London
Doise W, Mugny G 1984 *The Social Development of the Intellect.* Pergamon Press, Oxford
Hertz-Lazorowitz R 1990 An integrative model of the classroom: The enhancement of cooperation in learning. Paper presented at the American Educational Research Association Conference, Boston, Massachusetts
Johnson D W, Johnson R T 1985 The internal dynamics of cooperative learning groups. In: Slavin R E (ed.) 1985 *Learning to Cooperate, Cooperating to Learn.* Plenum Press, New York
Palincsar A S, Brown A L 1984 Reciprocal teaching of comprehension fostering and comprehension-monitoring activities. *Cognition and Instruction* 1(2): 117–75
Perret-Clermont A N 1980 *Social Interaction and Cognitive Development in Children.* Academic Press, New York
Salomon G, Globerson T 1989 When teams do not function the way they ought to. *Int. J. Educ. Res.* 13: 89–99
Sharan S 1980 Cooperative learning in small groups: Recent methods and effects on achievement, attitudes and ethnic relations. *Rev. Educ. Res.* 50(2): 241–71
Sharan S, Shachar H 1988 *Language and Learning in the Cooperative Classroom.* Springer-Verlag, New York
Slavin R E 1985 Cooperative learning: Applying contact theory in desegregated schools. *J. Soc. Iss.* 41(3): 45–62
Slavin R E 1987 Developmental and motivational perspectives on cooperative learning: a reconciliation. *Child Dev.* 58(5): 1161–67
Vygotsky L S (ed.) 1962 *Thought and Language.* MIT Press, Cambridge, Massachusetts
Vygotsky L S 1978 *Mind in Society: The Development of Higher Psychological Processes.* Harvard University Press, Cambridge, Massachusetts
Webb N M 1989 Peer interaction and learning in small groups. *Int. J. Educ. Res.* 13: 21–39

Environments for Learning

A. Collins, J. G. Greeno and L. B. Resnick

There has been a shift in perspective in educational psychology from teaching to learning. The change is subtle and reflects a move away from an information transmission view to a constructivist view of education. Because of the shift in perspective, this entry is called environments for learning rather than teaching methods. Another shift in perspective involves recognizing that learning and work are not separate activities. In fact, learning takes place both in and out of school, and students' activity in school is a form of work. Resnick (1987) pointed out four contrasts between typical in-school and out-of-school learning: (a) individual cognition in school versus shared cognition outside; (b) pure mentation in school versus tool manipulation outside; (c) symbol manipulation in school versus contextualized reasoning outside; (d) generalized learning in school versus situation-specific competencies outside. The discussion of learning environments will consider those outside as well as within schools, keeping in mind the characteristics to which Resnick has called attention.

In looking broadly at different kinds of learning environments, there are three observable general functions that support different environments: (a) participating in discourse; (b) participating in activities; (c) presenting examples of work to be evaluated. Environments themselves may be divided into six kinds, two relevant to each general function:

(a) (i) communication environments, where learners participate in discourse by actively constructing goals, problems, meanings, information, and criteria of success;

  (ii) information transmission environments, where learners participate in discourse by receiving information;

(b) (i) problem-solving environments, where learners work on projects and problems;

  (ii) training environments, where learners practice exercises to improve specific skills and knowledge;

(c) (i) evaluative performance environments, where learners perform for an audience;

  (ii) recitation and testing environments, where learners demonstrate their ability to work problems or answer questions.

Most teaching and learning environments contain elements of all six types. The most effective learning environments combine the advantages of each type. Each of the following sections will discuss a particular type of environment.

1. Communication Environments

Constructivist views of education stress communication among students. In communication environments the goal is for people jointly to construct understandings of different ideas. Four kinds of communication environments can be distinguished, based on the following activities: discussion, argumentation, inquiry teaching, and brainstorming.

Discussion occurs when groups talk about some topic. In the context of schooling and adult education, discussions often take place concerning a text everyone has read or a video everyone has seen. Discussions are probably the most powerful medium for learning. Some discussions that are formally constituted, such as business meetings, convey information about social roles, provide occasions for individuals to report results of their work and to present proposals, and

often result in shared commitments to action. Informal discussions by groups of friends are occasions for constructing shared attitudes, opinions, understandings, and norms of behavior (see *Group Learning*).

The Computer Supported Intentional Learning Environment (CSILE) developed by Scardamalia and Bereiter (1991) is a discussion environment where learners communicate in writing over a computer network. They first formulate questions they want to investigate (e.g., "Why can humans speak when apes cannot?") and then each learner in the group makes a conjecture. Then they all begin to investigate the question, finding whatever relevant information they can from source materials and typing it into the system for others in the group to read. Through written discussions, they refine their theories for publication in the system. Other experimenters are exploring the potential for students at remote locations to learn through exchanges of electronic messages.

Argumentation is another important learning method. It has had limited use in school, even though it is pervasive in business, law, and adult education and training. Argumentation involves making a case for a particular idea or decision, and counterarguments against possible alternatives. Debate teams foster argumentation in school settings, but debates are usually an extracurricular activity. Presentations of arguments are an integral part of activity in some discussion environments, including the Itakura method (Hatano and Inagaki 1991) and Lampert's (1990) conversational teaching. Being persuasive is an important skill. Argumentation as a learning experience may be mistakenly undervalued.

Inquiry teaching is characterized by a teacher asking questions to help students construct a theory or design. The theory constructed may be one the teacher already had in mind, or it may be a novel theory. Inquiry teachers use systematic strategies for selecting cases (e.g., counterexamples) and for asking questions (Collins and Stevens 1983). The goal of inquiry teaching is to foster thinking and understanding by the learners.

Brainstorming is common in business and academia, but often missing from school and adult education. The goal is for a group to generate ideas without trying to critique the ideas. Participants try to generate new ideas and to reformulate, extend, and synthesize other people's ideas. Brainstorming is a powerful learning method for adult education and training.

2. Information Transmission Environments

Traditional schooling stressed the transmission of knowledge and skills to students. These information transmission environments include reading and lectures as well as newer media formats such as broadcast radio and television, videotape, and film.

Reading is probably one of the two most common

ways to learn through acquiring information (the other is television). Widespread schooling and self-directed learning are built upon the book: printing changed the ways by which humans understand the world, because of the permanence and transportability of the printed word. It is probably the most effective way to become exposed to a wide variety of viewpoints, and has played a crucial role in movements of social change. At the same time, however, reading faces competition from the visual media, because of higher bandwidth and their wider scope.

Attending lectures differs from reading in that the sequence and pace are controlled by a speaker rather than the learner, and the information is spoken rather than written. Active interaction with a text includes rereading and searching for specific information. It is often possible to ask questions of a lecturer, although it is much more common for conversational interactions to be limited to the lecturer presenting questions to students to monitor their attention and understanding. Like reading, lecturing may ultimately be replaced by visual media.

Broadcast television and radio are the most passive of the information transmission media, but television has higher bandwidth than reading or lecturing. This allows it to capture significant aspects of the context of a situation, which can be critical to understanding. If a person is confused, however, it is not possible to ask questions (except to other viewers). It is not even possible to stop and resume study later unless an electronic record is made—a feature television shares with lectures. For this reason, it is much less likely to become an important learning environment than the next two media to be considered. Nevertheless, television shows have been major vehicles for learning around the world.

Videotape and film have the wide bandwidth of television, but also have the flexibility for stopping or replaying sections of the tape. They are under the learner's or teacher's control, and so can be scheduled whenever time allows. Stopping allows a group of viewers to mix discussion with viewing. Replaying allows the group to clarify misunderstandings, look for specific information, and call attention to items of information that support alternative interpretations of the material. Much of the world's collected knowledge will eventually be stored on film, so this is likely to be one of the most important learning environments of the future.

Interactive video, based on laserdisc technology, has the wide bandwidth of the visual media, together with the capability to access any piece of the video instantaneously. Two seminal uses of this technology are the Aspen video, with which a person can simulate a drive around the town of Aspen, Colorado, turning right or left at any cross street, and the Palenque video, with which one can walk through the Mayan ruin at Palenque in Mexico and ask for guidance at different points from an anthropologist. Interactive video is merging with intelligent tutoring system technology to provide even more powerful learning environments.

3. Problem-solving Environments

With the renewed emphasis on thinking in the curriculum, there has been a stress on creating different kinds of problem-solving environments. There are several kinds of environments where problem-solving is the focus; namely, environments dedicated to problem-solving, apprenticeship, and adult learning projects.

Problem-solving in school differs from problem-solving in other activities. Lave (1988) pointed out that school problems tend to be well-defined, have one correct answer, and a correct solution method. Problems that arise in life, which Lave called dilemmas, tend to be ill-defined, often unrecognized as problems, and have many possible solutions and solution methods. Schoenfeld (1985) identified many beliefs that students derive from school math problems: for example, that if the answer is not an integer, it is probably wrong; that all the problems at the end of a chapter use the methods introduced in the chapter; that if you cannot solve the problem in five minutes, you are not using the correct method, etc. Schoenfeld argued that most of these beliefs are counterproductive for problem-solving in life.

Apprenticeship occurs in work environments where apprentices are supervised by masters. In successful apprenticeship learning, masters teach by showing apprentices how to do a task (modeling), and then helping them as they try to do it on their own (coaching and fading). Lave and Wenger (1991) described four cases of apprenticeship and emphasized how productive apprenticeship depends on opportunities for the apprentice to participate legitimately, albeit peripherally, in work activities. Becoming a more central participant in a community of practice can provide a powerful motivation for learning, although what is learned in apprenticeship may not generalize easily to other contexts. Collins et al. (1989) characterized how the modeling, coaching, and fading paradigm of apprenticeship might be applied to learning the cognitive subjects of school in an approach they term "cognitive apprenticeship."

Simulation environments are an attempt to create situations that have significant features of authentic problem-solving. There have long been attempts to create simulated learning environments. For example, in one Massachusetts school, students spend half of each day running a legislature, courts, businesses, and media. This serves as a context for learning the skills of citizenship, reading, writing, calculating, and thinking.

Video and computer technology have enhanced the ability to create simulation environments where students are learning skills in context. A novel use of video technology is the Jasper series developed by the Cognition and Technology Group (1990) at Vanderbilt

University. In a series of six 15-minute videos, students are put into various problem-solving contexts. The problems reflect the complex problem-solving and planning that occur in real life.

There has been a proliferation of computer simulation environments for learning. For example, simulations let students control objects in a simulated Newtonian world without friction or gravity, or prices in a simulated economy. One series of simulations allows students to run a city, a planet, or an ant colony. Simulation allows students to gain knowledge and skills in contexts in which they could never participate naturally, to see features that are invisible in real environments (e.g., the center of mass, the inside of the human body), and to control variables that cannot be controlled in life.

4. Training Environments

People engage in adult education and training to develop skills they believe are valuable, either in themselves or as components of some other activity. In the traditional training environments—drill, rehearsal, and practice—there is an emphasis on skills and procedures rather than ideas, facts, concepts, and theories. Three kinds of training environments that focus on the skills of solving problems are programmed instruction, homework, and intelligent tutoring systems.

Drill involves repetitive training designed to achieve automaticity in a particular skill (Schneider and Shiffrin 1977). It is most commonly used to teach arithmetic and phonics, though Schneider has shown that it can be used to teach other skills, such as recognizing electrical circuits. Repetition helps master routine parts of performance, freeing capacity to concentrate on decision-making aspects of performance.

Rehearsal involves practicing scripted activities in preparation for a performance. While it teaches strategies for mounting a polished performance, the rehearsed activities may not be applicable beyond the performance, which limits the value of rehearsal as a general learning approach.

Practice emphasizes the conceptual and strategic as well as the routine, and can be carried out with or without a coach watching and guiding the practice. Practice is critical to gaining expertise, and successful techniques such as Reciprocal Teaching (Palincsar and Brown 1984) embody a strong practice component. Central to the whole notion of practice, however, is an ultimate performance. The major motivation for practice in school is to do well on tests, but many young people show growing aversion to tests.

Programmed instruction was developed by Skinner and reflects his emphasis on training and positive reinforcement. The tasks given are easy at first, so that students are likely to succeed and be reinforced for their success. There is an emphasis on repetition with variation to ensure practice, but more complex material is slowly introduced to ensure that students are dealing with new problems and tasks.

Intelligent tutoring systems are the latest attempt to create environments that combine training and problem-solving. For example, the geometry, algebra, and computer language tutors developed by Anderson and his colleagues (e.g., Anderson et al. 1985) start students with easy problems and slowly increase the complexity. Though the domain of intelligent tutoring systems may appear limited, they can be built on top of any simulation program (see above) to provide appropriate tasks and guidance for the learners. They are, however, expensive to build and it remains to be seen whether they will be cost effective.

5. Performance Environments

Learning takes place not just in practicing for performances, but also during performances themselves. Most performances can be distinguished from contests such as sporting events. Performances are high-stakes events where there is an audience, either live or present via a communication medium. Because the stakes are high, people are motivated to do well; performance, therefore, is the stimulus for most practice. To the degree teachers encourage performance, it is likely to provide a powerful motivation for students. The wide availability of recording technology makes performances easier to produce and to reflect upon. For example, students can now produce their own news broadcasts, musical performances, or plays, either on audiotape, videotape, or cable television. Furthermore, they can play these back, reflect upon them, and edit them until they are polished. One of the best examples of the use of technology for recording performances has been in Arts Propel (Gardner 1991) with its cycle of performing, reflecting upon the performance in terms of a set of criteria, and then reperforming.

Contests differ from performances in that winning or losing provides an ultimate criterion for judging performance. Films and statistics are important ways to track performance during contests. As well as providing the basis for making important decisions with regard to future contests (who to start, where they should play), they help to guide practice. By designating certain characteristics to track, statistics provide important indicators of what is valued.

6. Conclusion

Participation in discourse, participation in activities, and presentation of work for evaluation are all essential to learning. Traditional schooling has emphasized reading and the lecture, problem-solving, drill and practice, homework, and recitation and testing as learning environments. In the shift from traditional learning environments to more constructivist learning environments, there has been a parallel shift to incorporate some of the characteristics of work environments, such as shared cognition, tool manipulation, and contextualized reasoning (Resnick 1987).

See also: Adult Learning: Overview; Experiential and Open Learning: Adult Education; Group Learning; Learning to Learn

References

Anderson J R, Boyle C F, Reiser B J 1985 Intelligent tutoring systems. *Science* 228: 456–62
Cognition and Technology Group at Vanderbilt 1990 Anchored instruction and its relationship to situated cognition. *Educ. Researcher* 19(6): 2–10
Collins A, Brown J S, Newman S 1989 Cognitive apprenticeship: Teaching the crafts of reading, writing, and mathematics. In: Resnick L B (ed.) 1989 *Knowing, Learning, and Instruction: Essays in Honor of Robert Glaser.* Erlbaum, Hillsdale, New Jersey
Collins A, Stevens A L 1983 A cognitive theory of inquiry teaching. In: Reigeluth C M (ed.) 1983 *Instructional Design Theories and Models: An Overview of Their Current Status.* Erlbaum, Hillsdale, New Jersey
Gardner H 1991 Assessment in context: The alternative to standardized testing. In: Gifford B, O'Connor C (eds.) 1991 *Future Assessments: Changing Views of Aptitude, Achievement, and Instruction.* Kluwer, Boston, Massachusetts

Hatano G, Inagake K 1991 Sharing cognition through collective comprehension activity. In: Resnick L, Levin J, Teasley S D (eds.) 1991 *Perspectives on Socially Shared Cognition.* American Psychological Association, Washington, DC
Lampert M 1990 When the problem is not the question and the solution is not the answer: Mathematical knowing and teaching. *Am. Educ. Res. J.* 27(1): 29–63
Lave J 1988 *Cognition in Practice: Mind, Mathematics, and Culture in Everyday Life.* Cambridge University Press, Cambridge, Massachusetts
Lave J, Wenger E 1991 *Situated Learning: Legitimate Peripheral Participation.* Cambridge University Press, Cambridge
Palincsar A S, Brown A L 1984 Reciprocal teaching of comprehension-fostering and monitoring activities. *Cognition and Instruction* 1(2): 117–75
Resnick L B 1987 The 1987 Presidential address: Learning in school and out. *Educ. Researcher* 16(9): 13–20
Scardamalia M, Bereiter C 1991 Higher levels of agency for children in knowledge building: A challenge for the design of new knowledge media. *Journal of the Learning Sciences* 1(1): 37–68
Schneider W, Shiffrin R M 1977 Controlled and automatic human information processing, I: Detection, search, and attention. *Psychol. Rev.* 84(1): 1–66
Schoenfeld A H 1985 *Mathematical Problem Solving.* Academic Press, New York

Time, Allocated and Instructional

L. W. Anderson

Among the many resources that impact on the quality of education provided to students, time is among the most important. At the most general level, the way in which time is allocated and used in schools informs students of what educators believe to be important. Furthermore, the allocation and use of time has been found to be consistently related to the type and amount of student learning that occurs in schools.

1. Allocated Time

Allocated time refers to the amount of time devoted to schooling or to particular aspects of schooling (e.g., reading, mathematics, art, physical education). Allocated time can be enhanced by including the amount of time that students spend on school-related academic matters outside of school (e.g., homework).

For the most part, allocated time can be determined by looking at schedules, calendars, and policies. School may be scheduled to begin at 9:00 a.m. and end at 3:00 p.m. In this case, six hours would be allocated to the school day. In the northern hemisphere, the school calendar may indicate that school begins in early September and ends in late May or early June. When vacations and holidays are taken into consideration, approximately 180 days might be allocated to the school year. Federal, regional or state, or local policies may dictate that students attend school from the age of six until the age of 16. Students also may be required to complete three years of high school mathematics. Therefore, a minimum of 11 years would be allocated to the school career, with a minimum of three years allocated to high school mathematics for those receiving a high school diploma.

1.1 Descriptive Studies of Allocated Time

Countries differ in the number of days per year that students attend school, the number of hours per day and number of years devoted to the study of specific subject areas, and the total number of hours per year devoted to specific topics or goals within a subject area. The average student in the average country is in school for 192 days per year. The apparent range is from 125 days per year in Ghana (World Bank

1990) to 240 days per year in Japan (Walberg and Fredrick 1991).

There are also between-country differences in the number of hours per day that students are in school. Japanese students are in school for just over nine hours per day, while United States students are in school for slightly more than seven hours per day (Stigler and Stevenson 1991). German students may be in school for as little as five hours per day (Flood 1991). Large within-country differences in the number of hours students spend in school also have been noted (Mortimore et al. 1988).

When in school, the World Bank (1990) estimates that in developing countries twice as much time is spent on literacy as numeracy. In primary schools in Western countries, this difference may be even greater (Anderson 1994). In this regard, Anderson et al. (1989) found that the time spent per day on mathematics instruction across countries was quite small, ranging from 20 minutes to 50 minutes.

Finally, within specific subject matters different amounts of time are devoted to different goals, objectives, and/or topics. Porter (1989), for example, found that three-fourths of the time that United States' students were studying mathematics, the instruction focused on the teaching of mathematical operations involving addition, subtraction, multiplication, and division. Relatively little time was allocated to understanding mathematical concepts or solving mathematical problems. Similarly, based on her research, Durkin (1978–79) concluded that little time in the teaching of reading was spent on comprehension; rather, most of the time was spent on phonics, word recognition skills, and so on.

1.2 Increasing Allocated Time Through Homework

As mentioned above, allocated time may or may not include homework. There is little doubt that homework can increase the amount of time that students spend on school-related, academic matters. The question remains as to how much homework does increase allocated time.

Leone and Richards (1989) estimated that upper elementary and lower secondary students spent, on average, about 6.4 hours per week on homework. Walberg and Fredrick (1991) reported that the average upper secondary student in the United States spent slightly less than five hours per week on homework. Anderson et al. (1989) found that few teachers, typically fewer than 40 percent across eight countries, assigned homework four or five times per week.

Based on these estimates, it seems reasonable to conclude that students spend no more than seven hours per week on homework. This figure represents somewhat less than 20 percent of the total time that students spend in school. That is, for every five hours students spend in school, they devote approximately one hour to homework. From a slightly different perspective, this figure is approximately one-fifth of the time that United States students spend watching television (Walberg and Fredrick 1991).

1.3 Allocated Time and Student Achievement

While the relationship between allocated time and student achievement is consistently positive, the magnitude of this relationship tends to depend on the measure of allocated time used in the study. Summarizing a series of studies conducted under the auspices of the International Association for the Evaluation of Educational Achievement (IEA), Anderson and Postlethwaite (1989) found that the relationship between the number of years spent studying a specific subject matter and achievement in that subject matter was positive. In contrast, the relationship between the number of days per year spent on a subject matter and achievement in that subject matter was essentially zero.

While the former statement has received corroboration (Welsh et al. 1982), the latter has been contradicted by some other reviews. Walberg and Fredrick (1991), for example, found that adding to the length of the school year was positively correlated with student achievement in 10 of 11 studies summarized, with a mean correlation between allocated time and achievement of 0.22. Similarly, Smythe (1985) summarized 26 studies and found that adding to the length of the school day or school week was positively related to student achievement in 23 of the studies, with a mean correlation between allocated time and achievement of 0.40.

The results of using homework to increase the amount of time allocated to schooling and academics have been uniformly positive. In 12 of 14 studies conducted in eight developing countries, Fuller (1987) found the relationship of homework and student achievement to be positive. Similarly, Smythe (1987) found the relationship between homework and achievement to be positive in 88 percent of 43 studies, with a mean correlation of 0.23. Finally, Cooper (1989) found that positive relationships between homework and student achievement existed in 14 of 20 studies, with the results being more pronounced at the secondary school level.

2. Instructional Time

Instructional time is a composite of that portion of the school day during which students receive instruction and that portion of classroom time during which the teacher is teaching. With respect to the school day, lunch, recess, and movement from classroom to classroom are not counted as instructional time. In terms of the classroom, taking attendance, disciplining students, cleaning up and putting away materials, and movement from activity to activity (referred to as "transitions") detract from instructional time.

2.1 Descriptive Studies of Instructional Time

A report issued by the World Bank (1990) illustrates how easily allocated time can slip away in many developing countries. "The school day often began late, teachers frequently were absent on Tuesday and Friday (market days), and 48 public holidays were celebrated" (p. 19). Industrialized countries have the same problem. In the United States, approximately one-fourth of the allocated time in elementary schools is spent on recess, lunch, and similar activities (Walberg and Fredrick 1991). In the United Kingdom, the estimate of the percentage of allocated time that is instructional time is virtually identical (Mortimore et al. 1988).

In the classroom, between 7 and 27 percent of the time is spent on noninstructional matters. Figures less than 10 percent appear to be found only in Asian countries (Anderson et al. 1989, Stigler and Stevenson 1991). Figures above 15 percent occur in Australia, Canada, and the United States (Anderson et al. 1989, Sanford and Evertson 1983).

2.2 Attendance and the Loss of Instructional Time

Both teachers and students are in school and in their classrooms more than 90 percent of the time (Anderson et al. 1989). Nonetheless, variations in attendance consistently are related to variations in student achievement. Fogelman (1978) found a significant relationship between student attendance and student achievement after controlling for the socioeconomic status of the students. Monk and Ibrahim (1984) concluded that student absences accounted for from 32 to 48 percent of the variation in mathematics achievement. Finally, Reynolds and Walberg (1991) found that multiple correlations of attendance and homework (see section above) with science achievement averaged 0.53, which was higher than all other factors included in their predictive model.

2.3 Instructional Time and Student Achievement

The relationship between instructional time and achievement is generally stronger than that between allocated time and achievement (Walberg and Fredrick 1991). For example, Fredrick (1980) found that in high-achieving schools the difference between allocated and instructional time was 25 percent, while in low-achieving schools the difference was almost 50 percent.

3. Conclusions and Recommendations

The way in which time is allocated and used in schools and classrooms communicates to students what educators value and influences what and how much they learn. The way in which time is allocated to various subjects and activities should be carefully examined. Is literacy twice as important as numeracy? Are the fine arts and physical education really "second class citizens" in curricula throughout the world?

Once decisions concerning allocated time have been made, attention must be turned to using as much of that allocated time for instructional purposes as is possible. Most of the suggestions for improvement in this regard are relatively straightforward and easy to implement. They perhaps can be best summed up by a set of recommendations offered by the World Bank (1990).

> Maintaining instructional time requires administrative and/or parental interventions to ensure that (a) schools are open during official hours and children are in attendance, (b) teachers are present and teaching during the official instructional periods, (c) temporary distractions, such as administrative or visitor interruptions, are avoided, and (d) appropriate arrangements are made for continuing instruction under routine inclement weather conditions. (p. 20)

References

Anderson L W 1994 What time tells us. In: Anderson L W, Walberg H J (eds.) 1994 *Time Piece: Extending and Enhancing Learning Time*. National Association of Secondary School Principals, Reston, Virginia
Anderson L W, Postlethwaite T N 1989 What IEA studies say about teachers and teaching. In: Purves A C (ed.) 1989 *International Comparisons and Educational Reform*. Association for Supervision and Curriculum Development, Reston, Virginia
Anderson L W, Ryan D W, Shapiro B J 1989 *The IEA Classroom Environment Study*. Pergamon Press, Oxford
Cooper H 1989 Synthesis of research on homework. *Educ. Leadership* 47(3): 85–91
Durkin D 1978–79 What classroom observations reveal about reading comprehension instruction. *Reading Res. Q.* 14(4): 481–533
Flood R 1991 Are you being served? *The Economist* 320 (7722): 8
Fogelman K 1978 School attendance, attainment, and behaviour. *Br. J. Educ. Psychol.* 48: 148–58
Fredrick W C 1980 Instructional time. *Eval. Educ.* 4: 117–18
Fuller B 1987 What factors raise achievement in the third world? *Rev. Educ. Res.* 57: 255–92
Leone C M, Richards M H 1989 Classwork and homework in early adolescence: The ecology of achievement. *J. Youth Adolescence* 18(6): 531–48
Monk D H, Ibrahim M A 1984 Patterns of absence and pupil achievement. *Am. Educ. Res. J.* 21: 295–310
Mortimore P, Sammons P, Stoll L, Lewis D, Ecob R 1988 *School Matters. The Junior Years*. Open Books, Wells
Porter A 1989 A curriculum out of balance: The case of elementary school mathematics. *Educ. Researcher* 18(5): 9–15
Reynolds A J, Walberg H J 1991 A structural model of science achievement. *J. Educ. Psychol.* 83(1): 97–107
Sanford J P, Evertson C M 1983 Time use and activities in junior high classes. *J. Educ. Res.* 76(3): 140–47
Smythe W J 1987 Time. In: Dunkin M J (ed.) 1987 *The International Encyclopedia of Teaching and Teacher Education*. Pergamon Press, Oxford

Stigler J W, Stevenson H W 1991 How Asian teachers polish each lesson to perfection. *American Educator* 15(1): 12–20, 43–47

Walberg H J, Fredrick W C 1991 *Extending Learning Time.* United States Department of Education Office of Educational Research and Improvement, Washington, DC

Welsh W W, Anderson R E, Harris L J 1982 The effects of schooling on mathematics achievement. *Am. Educ. Res. J.* 19: 145–53

World Bank 1990 *Primary Education.* The International Bank for Reconstruction and Development, Washington, DC

Further Reading

Ben-Peretz M, Bromme R (eds.) 1990 *The Nature of Time in Schools. Theoretical Concepts, Practitioner Perceptions.* Teachers College Press, New York

Fisher C W, Berliner D C (eds.) 1985 *Perspectives on Instructional Time.* Longman, New York

Computers, Media, and Learning

Computers and Learning

E. De Corte, L. Verschaffel and J. Lowyck

The introduction of computers in schools in the early 1980s was accompanied by high expectations about the potential of this new technology for improving student learning at school. However, by the end of the decade, these high expectations, which were raised for various forms of educational computer use, had not been fulfilled. In this entry, expectations, research outcomes, and new developments will be considered in relation to three prevailing educational computer applications; i.e. computer-assisted learning, word processing, and computer programming.

1. Computers and Learning: Expectations and Reality

Computer programs can fulfill a variety of functions in teaching–learning processes, such as: (a) drill and practice, (b) tutorials, (c) instructional computer games, (d) simulations, (e) spreadsheet, (f) word processing, (g) database management, and (h) computer programming (Makrakis 1988, Taylor 1980). In Taylor's (1980) well-known classification schema, the first four types involve the computer as a *tutor*; in types (e) to (g) the computer is used as a *tool*, while in type (h) the computer is considered as a *tutee*. These different computer uses can be ranked in a hierarchical order from low to high, according to several dimensions: the level of cognitive/mental thinking evoked, the degree of learner–computer interaction, and the amount of learner initiative allowed (Makrakis 1988, Scott et al. 1992). As will be demonstrated, these categories tended to merge from the late 1980s onward (Kaput 1992).

In 1989 the International Association for the Evaluation of Educational Achievement (IEA) conducted a survey about the use of computers in education in 20 countries (Pelgrum and Plomp 1991). While big differences between countries were reported, there were also some remarkable similarities. Some overall trends, based on Becker's (1991) survey of the situation in the United States—a country that has played and still plays a pioneering role in the use of computers in education—can be summarized as follows. In the early

1980s educational computer use was largely restricted to drill-and-practice programs, playing instructional games (mostly in mathematics and language), and learning to write simple programs in BASIC. Because most schools at that time had few computers, students had only a limited amount of computer experience. By the end of the decade, systematic and regular hands-on computer experience had become somewhat more common. Especially in middle and high schools, there was an increase in computer applications that score high in terms of the major dimensions of evoked cognitive level and student–computer interaction, such as simulations, word processing, and database management. Learning to program (in BASIC), however, was the only curriculum area where a decline became evident by the end of the 1980s.

From the beginning, the effects of various forms of computer use on students' learning, motivation, and social behavior have been a source of heated debate and a topic of continuing research (Lepper and Gurtner 1989). However, questions about the impact of computers on students' learning and thinking have not always been clearly asked. According to Salomon (1992), one must distinguish between two different ways in which computers can affect human learning and intellect. One way concerns the changes in performance that people display *while* being equipped with a technology; for example, the quality of the student's thinking while using a computer-based graphic tool for solving word problems, or the level of sophistication in the writing process when using a word processor. It has been argued that in these and many other cases, working with a computer affects what one does and how well one does it. A second category of effects concerns relatively lasting changes in people's capacities, as a *cognitive residue* of interaction with a computer (i.e., transfer effects). A typical example here is whether learning to solve word problems or to compose text with the computer will have beneficial effects on those activities when carried out without the technology. Salomon (1992) referred to the former as cognitive effects *with* technology and to the latter as cognitive effects *of* the technology.

It is impossible to give a complete overview here of the state of the art concerning the effects on learning of the whole range of potential applications of computers in education. The entry will therefore focus on three major applications that differ widely in terms of the major educational computer uses in a hierarchical order, namely: (a) computer-assisted learning and intelligent tutoring, (b) the computer as a learning tool, and (c) computer programming.

2. Computer-assisted Learning and Intelligent Tutoring

The oldest and still the most common educational application of the computer is computer-assisted learning (CAL), especially the use of the computer to drill and practice particular concepts or skills in traditional school subjects such as mathematics or language. In typical drill-and-practice programs, the computer generates a set of tasks and provides immediate feedback about the correctness of the student's answer. Many programs also contain stored comments or help of one kind or another associated with different response options.

In some sense, traditional CAL changed little, and is rather an add-on to an existing and unchanged classroom setting. It was, nevertheless, expected that this shift would affect student learning very positively. As long ago as 1966, Suppes (1966 p.206) predicted that "in a few more years millions of school children will have access to what Philip of Macedon enjoyed as a royal prerogative: the personal services of a tutor as well-informed and responsive as Aristotle."

There is some research evidence supporting this claim. Based on a meta-analysis of almost 200 studies on effects of CAL, Kulik and Kulik (1987, 1991) concluded that it has positive effects: students generally learned more in classes where they received help from computers, they learned their lessons with less instructional time, they enjoyed their classes more when they received computer help, and they developed more positive attitudes toward computers. However, even with respect to this most intensively studied educational computer use, the literature is less than compelling. Indeed, many of the studies reporting moderate or strong effects of CAL can be seriously criticized on methodological grounds (Clark 1985, Kulik and Kulik 1987, Lepper and Gurtner 1989). Moreover, it has been argued that what accounts for the observed learning advantages of CAL is the superior instructional quality of the CAL materials as compared to traditional teaching (Fletcher-Flinn and Gravatt 1995). Furthermore, researchers as well as practitioners raised severe criticisms of the CAL programs that prevailed and still prevail in educational practice. A first criticism stresses the lack of individualization of instruction in traditional CAL, because of the limited "intelligence" built into the computer system. A second major criticism involves the mismatch between the content and organization of the CAL programs, on the one hand, and the new developments within the different subject-matter areas of the school curriculum and pedagogy, on the other. Both criticisms have stimulated new developments aiming at overcoming those shortcomings.

Dissatisfaction with the lack of individualization in traditional CAL was one of the major incentives to design a new generation of programs, originally called "intelligent computer-assisted instruction" (ICAI) or "intelligent tutoring systems" (ITS). In contrast to traditional software, these programs are not static, preprogrammed systems; on the contrary, the computer's decisions about what problem or what information to present next to the learner, and when and how exactly to intervene, are *generated*, taking into account a set of built-in components, namely: (a) knowledge about the cognitive structures and solution strategies underlying expertise in that particular domain (i.e., the expert modeling component); (b) a model of the student's knowledge and skills at a given moment in comparison to the expert system, derived from his or her answers and reactions on the previous problems (i.e., the student modeling component); (c) a set of principles about how to control and influence the student's learning process (i.e., the tutorial component); and (d) knowledge about how to organize the interface with the student (i.e., the communication component).

Intelligent tutoring systems have been developed for a variety of topics, such as learning classical mechanics, geometric optics, economic rules, elementary algebra, arithmetic place value, grammar, computer programming, and so on (see Sleeman and Brown 1982, Wenger 1987). In contrast to traditional CAL, systematic data about the achievements of the ITS approach are scarce. Moreover, they are mostly "soft" in character, compared to the hard and quantitative nature of the research findings for traditional CAI (Scott et al. 1992).

While fascinating research and developmental work relating to ITS continues, there is already some opposition to this approach. First, there is the question of how far one *can* go in building the necessary simulation components of the ITS. As was argued above, intelligent tutoring is only possible if the system accurately understands what the student is actually doing when he or she either solves the problem correctly or commits an error. Building such a simulation is not always possible. Take, for example, the processes involved in understanding and solving college algebra word problems. According to Kintsch (1991), the real-world situations described in college algebra problems are so numerous and so varied that only a system that knows essentially as much about the world as students do, would be able to simulate these problem-solving processes. But if simulation is impossible, then so is intelligent tutoring.

A second issue is not whether computer-based tutoring systems can, but rather whether they *should* aim at building a perfect and detailed model of the student's knowledge and skills as a basis for diagnosis and for taking decisions about instructional interventions. Indeed, this can easily lead to a preponderance of highly structured and directive learning situations lacking sufficient opportunity for active and constructive learner involvement and participation—a learning principle that is heavily stressed in instructional theory. Anderson's *Geometry Tutor* (Anderson et al. 1985), one of the most frequently quoted examples of an ITS, is an illustration of such a directive system. As was remarked by Kaput (1992), suggested attempts to make this tutor more flexible and educationally adjustable will not change its underlying educational philosophy: "the knowledge and the underlying authority of the tutor reside in the computer" (p. 545). Paraphrasing Papert (1990), who opposed "constructivism" to "instructionism," one could say that the *Geometry Tutor* will continue to reflect an "instructivist" rather than a "constructivist" view of learning. In this respect, Kintsch (1991) has launched the idea of unintelligent tutoring: "A tutor should not provide the intelligence to guide learning, it should not do all the planning and monitoring of the student's progress, because those are the very activities the students must perform themselves in order to learn. What a tutor should do is to provide a temporary support for learners that allows them to perform at a level just beyond their current ability level" (p. 245). Kintsch (1991) and many others (see, e.g., Scardamalia et al. 1989) have argued that computers are also ideally suited for this type of cognitive scaffolding, which accords better with the constructivist view of learning and teaching.

Traditional CAL has also been severely criticized because of the dated views about learning goals, content, and learning and teaching of the disciplines embedded in these programs. In the domain of mathematics, for example, the large majority of the available software aims mainly at exercising computational skills, replacing in this respect traditional worksheets (Kaput 1992). In other words, computers are mainly used to reproduce—or sometimes even to restore—the traditional, mechanistic approach toward mathematics education. (This also holds for most ITS programs.) But this mechanistic approach toward mathematics education has already been sharply criticized, and major efforts have been made to transform mathematical learning and teaching from the individual absorption and memorization of a fixed body of decontextualized and fragmented concepts and procedural skills transmitted by the teacher into the collaborative, teacher-mediated construction of meaningful and useful knowledge and problem-solving skills based on mathematical modeling of authentic, real-life situations and contexts (De Corte et al. in press, Kaput 1992). In the domain of language, no less than in mathematics, the bulk of available software—also the ICAI—focuses on practicing rules from spelling and grammar, instead of supporting the more essential aspects of reading and writing, namely, comprehension and communication. Therefore, several authors have pleaded for implementing technology in line with reformed objectives, contents, and learning and teaching principles.

3. The Computer as a Learning Tool

Another important category of computer use in classroom instruction comprises the manifold ways in which the computer can serve as a tool in the hands of the student to facilitate the accomplishment of certain academic or creative goals. Typical examples of types of computing are word processors, calculators, spreadsheets, database programs, drawing and music composition programs. Contrary to CAL programs, such tool programs have originated outside of education. However, once available, they were often expected to be equally useful for supporting learning processes at school, such as cognitive learning, creative expression, and communication skills. The underlying idea is that computer tools will significantly affect the quality of students' thinking and learning processes, because these tools assume part of the intellectual burden, free students from lower-level operations, and trace states and processes. In line with Salomon's (1992) distinction mentioned above, some of these qualitative changes in students' cognitive processes have been assumed to occur not only while they are equipped *with* the computerized tool, but also when they do not have it at their disposal (*cognitive residue*).

As an example, word processing will be discussed. Compared with the other tools, it has been used most often in schools, albeit that much more time is devoted to learning how to use a word-processing program rather than to improving writing itself (Becker 1991).

It is no surprise that because of its peculiar features, word processing is perceived to be a powerful vehicle for language learning in schools. Indeed, composing text is essentially subjected to a cyclical control of its quality during a series of steps, such as planning, production, revision and editing at the textual levels of word, sentence, and structure. Moreover, word processing is compatible with a process view on writing, in contrast with the earlier emphasis on the written product (see Fitzgerald 1987, Lepper and Gurtner 1989).

In line with the enthusiasm of professional writers regarding the potential power of word processing compared to the laborious writing activity with paper and pencil, it was initially expected that word processing as an open learning tool could substantially improve students' writing effectiveness (Cochran-Smith 1991). However, there is almost no evidence to show that word processing in schools has clear-cut effects on text quality, length of text, amount and quality of revision, differences between revision with and without computers, and overall writing improvement (Cochran-Smith 1991). A clear example derives from research on revision. Although word processing seems most suitable for this subprocess, it remains unclear whether it affects the amount of students' revision (Cochran-Smith 1991, Fitzgerald 1987). Some reports indicate more revision activities with word processors than with pens or typewriters, while others indicate the reverse. Moreover, the quality of revisions seems not to fit with the expectations. Indeed, more surface revisions are made with word processors and more expanded revisions may occur with pens (Fitzgerald 1987).

It became clear that effectiveness of word processing tools highly depends upon the quality of the support available in a specific context. Consequently, the question is not whether mere word processing is effective, but how word processing interrelates with instructional goals, target groups, organizational and social structures of schools, curricula, teachers and concrete learning contexts (Cochran-Smith 1991). In order to make the tools powerful for learning, explicit support by teachers, peers, and/or supplementary computer programs is needed. In most cases, word-processing programs are accompanied by computerized tools or writing aids, such as text-analysis programs (spelling checker, vocabulary control, style analysis) and prompting programs (writing coaches, text help) which all offer additional support and comfort (Piolat and Blaye 1989). For instance, it is expected that text planners may help students to organize their thoughts before and during the writing process, and revision facilities may elicit and support control strategies.

If computer-based learning environments, and more specifically word processing programs, aim at supporting the active and constructive learning processes in students, both cognitive-oriented writing tools for students must be designed (Salomon 1992, Scardamalia and Bereiter 1991) and additional support for teachers offered (Cochran-Smith 1991). Moreover, the systematic development of tools for knowledge construction needs to be considered, be it for individual use or in computer network systems (Salomon 1992, Scardamalia and Bereiter 1991, 1992). Developments along those lines should aim at linking and integrating in a flexible way several computer tools, in which databases of text and graphics will support the organization of knowledge of individuals and groups (see Scardamalia and Bereiter 1991, 1992), and in which writing processes are embedded in specific subject-matter domains. Another important development is that computers are equally used in computer-mediated communication (CMC) in open and distance learning settings (Romiszowski 1993). It represents the integration of all instructional functions, such as information delivery, learning support, and communication facilitation in a combined use of telecommunication and multimedia, provided by the Internet and the WWW (Lauzon and Moore 1992). These opportunities created by networking facilities, support increasingly cooperative learning (Riel 1990).

4. Computer Programming and Learning to Think

A third major educational computer use is computer programming. In this case the computer is a tutee. As was mentioned above, learning to program a computer (in BASIC) was one of the foremost applications in the early days of computers in education. It was mostly considered as a crucial aspect of acquiring computer literacy. But another argument for learning and teaching programming was the so-called "cognitive effects hypothesis"; that is, the claim that this experience would result in lasting positive changes in students' thinking and problem-solving skills as a cognitive residue of interaction with this programming language (De Corte et al. 1992, Salomon 1992). In this sense, learning to program was seen as a substitute for Latin and Greek, where learning the particulars of the language leads to the acquisition of general thinking skills which can be transferred to other content domains.

In connection with the second argument, the Logo computing language was very popular in the 1980s. Logo originates from an AI approach to educational computing that is at right angles not only to traditional CAL, but also to the early stages of ITS. Indeed, according to Papert (1982), Logo should be acquired in a constructive and self-discovering way, which he called "learning without curriculum."

Despite the evident enthusiasm of many practitioners and investigators in this area, a series of studies about the effects of Logo programming on children's problem-solving skills conducted in the early 1980s did not report any positive results supporting the cognitive effects hypothesis (De Corte et al. 1992). Interestingly, these investigations have not led to a rejection of this hypothesis, a major reason being the poor quality of the Logo learning environments that were designed and implemented in those studies: systematic and direct intervention was kept to a minimum, and it was hoped that the acquisition of the programming skill would somehow "happen" to the pupils as a result of the unique characteristics of the Logo language. In the second half of the 1980s the latter viewpoint was largely abandoned, and most researchers agreed that Logo learning environments should involve systematic guidance and mediation aiming at the acquisition of problem-solving skills in programming and, eventually, at their transfer to other contexts and situations. Most investigations that attempted to overcome the shortcomings of the earlier work have reported more positive results (De Corte et al. 1992).

Taken as a whole, the available research evidence suggests that Logo is not in itself a genuine vehicle for learning to think, but that it can be a very useful device for the acquisition of thinking skills, if embedded in a powerful teaching–learning environment that aims particularly at the mastery and transfer of these skills (De Corte 1993, Hoyles and Noss 1992). This instructional support can, of course, be provided by the teacher in the form of prepared written materials and assignments, explicit task requirements, individual help, and so forth. But part of this support can also be built into the Logo software itself. Therefore, several attempts have been made to enrich the original Logo software with computer-based tool kits and coaching devices that support the development of problem-solving skills. These developments with respect to Logo can also be considered as indicative of the trend toward integration between the different categories of educational computer applications: tutor, tool, and tutee.

5. Conclusion

When microcomputers began to be introduced in schools in the early 1980s, it was predicted that this new interactive and dynamic medium would significantly change the quality and the outcomes of school learning, even before the end of the decade. However, neither traditional computer-assisted instruction nor intelligent tutoring systems have been able to fulfill these initial high expectations. A critical examination of these prevailing forms of educational computer applications, based on findings of media research and on the understanding of the constructive and social nature of the learning process, has shown that this is not at all surprising. Indeed, underlying these educational uses of computers—albeit often implicitly—are both the wrong assumption that computers will by themselves elicit effective learning, and a conception of learning as a rather passive and highly individual process of knowledge absorption and accumulation. Initial disappointing results were also obtained with respect to the other two major forms of educational computer use, namely the computer as a tool (e.g., word-processing) and the computer as a tutee (e.g., Logo). For these applications it also quickly became obvious that the mere "add-on strategy" of computer use in schools cannot produce the improvements in the quality and the outcomes of learning that were originally anticipated. By the early 1990s, it was accepted that the productive educational application of computers requires that they be embedded in powerful teaching–learning environments, that is, instructional settings that elicit from students the acquisition processes necessary to attain worthwhile and desirable educational objectives in different curriculum domains. Embedding means that the computer is not just an "add-on," but is judiciously integrated in the environment, capitalizing on its specific strengths and potential to present, represent, and transform information, and to induce

effective forms of interaction and cooperation. In this new conception, the role of the computer has changed from an authoritarian and directive tutor toward a supportive system that is less structured and less directive, that encompasses student-controlled tools for the acquisition of knowledge and skills, and that attempts to integrate both tools and coaching strategies in collaborative learning environments (Kaput 1992, Scardamalia et al. 1989, Vosniadou et al. 1996).

See also: Computer-assisted Learning; Computer Programming, Learning and Instruction of; Constructivism and Learning; Learning Environments; Media and Learning; Learning Strategies and Learning to Learn

References

Anderson J R, Boyle C F, Reiser B J 1985 Intelligent tutoring systems. *Science* 228: 456–662
Becker H J 1991 How computers are used in the United States schools: Basic data from the 1989 IEA Computers in Education survey. *Journal of Educational Computing Research* 7(4): 385–406
Clark R E 1985 Confounding in educational computing research. *Journal of Educational Computing Research* 1(1): 28–44
Cochran-Smith M 1991 Word processing and writing in elementary classrooms: A critical review of related literature. *Rev. Educ. Res.* 61(1): 107–55
De Corte E 1993 Toward embedding enriched Logo-based learning environments in the school curriculum. In: Georgiadis P, Gyftodimos G, Kotsanis Y, Kynigos C (eds.) 1993 *Logo-like Learning Environments: Reflection and Prospect. Proceedings of the Fourth European Logo Conference University of Athens, Department of Informatics. 28–31 August 1993, Athens, Greece.* Doukas School, Athens
De Corte E, Greer B, Verschaffel L in press Mathematics learning and teaching. In: Berliner D, Calfee R (eds.) in press *Handbook of Educational Psychology.* Macmillan Inc., New York
De Corte E, Verschaffel L, Schrooten H 1992 Cognitive effects of learning to program in Logo: A one-year study with sixth-graders. In: De Corte E, Linn M C, Mandl H, Verschaffel L (eds.) 1992 *Computer-based Learning Environments and Problem Solving* (NATO ASI Series F: Computer and Systems Sciences Vol. 84). Springer-Verlag, Berlin
Fitzgerald J 1987 Research on revision in writing. *Rev. Educ. Res.* 57(4): 481–506
Fletcher-Flinn C M, Gravatt B 1995 The efficacy of computer assisted instruction (CAI): A meta-analysis. *Journal of Educational Computing Research* 12(3): 219-41
Hoyles C, Noss R (eds.) 1992 *Learning Mathematics and Logo.* The MIT Press, Cambridge, Massachusetts
Kaput J J 1992 Technology and mathematics education. In: Grouws D A (ed.) 1992 *Handbook of Research on Mathematics Teaching and Learning.* Macmillan Inc., New York
Kintsch W 1991 A theory of discourse comprehension: Implications for a tutor for word algebra problems. In: Carretero M, Pope M, Simons R J, Pozo J I (eds.)

1991 *Learning and Instruction: European Research in an International Context*, Vol. 3. Pergamon Press, Oxford

Kulik C-L C, Kulik J A 1991 The effectiveness of computer-based instruction: An updated analysis. *Computers in Human Behavior* 7: 75–94

Kulik J A, Kulik C-L C 1987 Review of recent research literature on computer-based instruction. *Contemp. Educ. Psychol.* 12(3): 222–30

Lauzon A C, Moore G A B 1992 A fourth generation distance education system: Integrating computer-assisted learning and computer conferencing. In: Moore M G (ed.) 1992 *Readings in Distance Education,* Vol. 3. American Centre for the Study of Distance Education, Pennsylvania State University, University Park, Pennsylvania

Lepper M R, Gurtner J L 1989 Children and computers: Approaching the twenty-first century. *Am. Psychol.* 44(2): 170–78

Makrakis V 1988 *Computers in School Education: The Cases of Sweden and Greece*. Institute of International Education, University of Stockholm, Stockholm

Papert S 1982 *Mindstorms: Children, Computers, and Powerful ideas*. Basic Books, New York

Papert S 1990 An introduction to the fifth anniversary collection. In: Harel I (ed.) 1990 *Constructionist Learning: A Fifth Anniversary Collection of Papers*. MIT Media Laboratory, Cambridge, Massachusetts

Pelgrum W J, Plomp T 1991 *The Use of Computers in Education Worldwide*. Pergamon Press, Oxford

Piolat A, Blaye A 1989 Effects of word processing and writing aids on revision processes. Paper presented at the Third Conference of the European Association for Research on Learning and Instruction, Madrid

Riel M 1990 Cooperative learning across classrooms in electronic learning circles. *Instructional Science* 19(2): 445–66

Romiszowski A 1993 *Telecommunications and Distance Education*. Syracuse University, Syracuse, New York

Salomon G 1992 Effects *with* and *of* computers and the study of computer-based learning environments. In: De Corte E, Linn M C, Mandl H, Verschaffel L (eds.) 1992 *Computer-based Learning Environments and Problem Solving* (NATO ASI Series F: Computer and Systems Sciences Vol. 84). Springer-Verlag, Berlin

Scardamalia M, Bereiter C 1991 Higher levels of agency for children in knowledge building: A challenge for the design of new knowledge media. *The Journal of the Learning Sciences* 1: 37–68

Scardamalia M, Bereiter C 1992 An architecture for collaborative learning. In: De Corte E, Linn M C, Mandl H, Verschaffel L (eds.) 1992 *Computer-based Learning Environments and Problem Solving* (NATO ASI Series F: Computer and Systems Science Vol. 84). Springer-Verlag, Berlin

Scardamalia M, Bereiter C, McLean R S, Swallow J, Woodruff E 1989 Computer-supported intentional learning environments. *Journal of Educational Computing Research* 5(1): 51–68

Scott T, Cole M, Engel M 1992 Computers and education: A cultural constructivist perspective. In: Grant G (ed.) 1992 *Review of Research in Education*, Vol. 18. American Educational Research Association, Washington, DC

Sleeman D, Brown J S (eds.) 1982 *Intelligent Tutoring Systems*. Academic Press, London

Suppes P 1966 The uses of computers in education. *Scientific American* 215(3): 206–21

Taylor R 1980 *The Computer in the School: Tutor, Tool, Tutee*. Teachers College Press, New York

Vosniadou S, De Corte E, Mandl H, Glaser R (eds.) 1996 *International Perspectives on the Design of Technology-supported Learning Environments*. Lawrence Erlbaum Associates, Mahwah, New York

Wenger E 1987 *Artificial Intelligence and Tutoring Systems: Computational and Cognitive Approaches to the Communication of Knowledge*. Morgan Kaufmann, Los Altos, California

Computer Assisted Learning

D. M. Watson

Computer Assisted Learning (CAL) covers the various ways in which the computer is used for learning. Thus drill and practice exercises, tutorial packages, statistical routines, modeling, simulations, word processing, desktop publishing, art packages, exploring with Logo, manipulating satellite images—all come within the umbrella of CAL. The main attraction of CAL for education is the direct interaction between the software and the user; thus it is an active rather than a passive resource. Its main weakness is that, as with other educational tools, its value critically depends on the environment in which it is used. Its potential as a medium for making learning more active and learner-oriented has always excited educational innovators, while the technically oriented promote CAL because they believe it heralds a new age of Information Technology. Despite substantial attention and investment, the amount of CAL that actually takes place in educational institutions is modest. Moreover, the evidence of its effectiveness is relatively sparse.

1. Classification of CAL by Type of Program

1.1 Drill and Practice

This program requires learners to perform specified tasks, gives feedback on their performance, and graduates the sequence and difficulty of tasks according to their performance. For example, arithmetic tests are set asking students to perform subtractions. If the learners provide the correct answer, the program moves on to harder tasks; if the learner does poorly, and repeatedly produces the wrong answers, the program selects a simpler set of subtractions. Some programs may recognize a pattern of failure, and present a series of tasks geared to this problem.

These programs, by focusing on the learner's recall of particular segments and sequencing of knowledge, are of most value where accurate content is important, such as in language translation. As an accuracy-learning and testing environment for individual students, their value lies in the freeing of the teacher, enabling them to concentrate on other learning activities.

1.2 Tutorial

The tutorial program extends the drill and practice type by first providing information or a demonstration to learners, and then requiring them to perform some input. It also provides feedback on that input. For example, to teach the operation of a piece of equipment, the program shows an animation of the equipment being assembled, asks learners the sequence required, analyzes the learner's input, and tells them if they have got it right or what kind of mistake they are making.

1.3 Simulation

This program simulates an environment. Built around a model of a system, it allows learners to change the values of parameters in the system, and provides feedback in the form of graphical or diagrammatic display of how the system's behavior changes. For example, in a simulation based on a model of a pond with three main inhabitants, phytoplankton, herbivores, and fish, the learners may change the numbers of one or more populations and see the effect on the others.

Simulations provide a means for learning about an environment that may otherwise not be available to learners to explore, for reasons of safety, time, expense, or general practicality. A simulation focuses on exploration and discovery learning; it is not an exercise that necessarily has a fixed or correct solution, and the route to a solution may be varied.

Simulations may be based on models of known relationships as in the scientific world, on theoretical models as in economics, or on models of the past as in history. Concepts in many subjects are so lacking in concreteness that their definitions often need to be constructed around models of some kind. Teachers have long searched for methods of describing models in a way that makes them accessible and useful to learners. Complex relationships can often only be explored through simplification. A computer simulation offers the opportunity for relationships to be explored and exposed by the student's direct manipulation of the variables in the model.

1.4 Games

Some simulations are designed as a game, often including role-playing. For example, in a simulation based on a model of the world's wind zones, the learner adopts the role of a sailing ship's captain, selecting their starting and finishing ports, and responding to the wind patterns they meet by steering their ship to their destination. In other simulations, a group of learners may adopt different roles in order to take decisions about what actions to take. For example, in a simulation of a planning inquiry, different roles might include representing a local amenities society, a group of farmers, a property developer, an environmental protection agency, and the local planning officer. Sometimes a competitive element is introduced and learners compete to produce a solution.

In such simulations the program focuses not only on the underlying model but also on the way in which the learner interacts with the model. Learning may be built up by discovery and conjecture; the simulation encourages learning by inquiry and decision-making. Role-playing simulations may stimulate learners' interest in underlying problems through this indirect exposure to the model.

1.5 Modeling

These programs allow learners to build up models for themselves and explore their properties. They are a natural extension of the use of models for simulations, and enable the learner to experience and manipulate the fundamental structures and dynamism of models in order to appreciate their behavior and the role of models in organizing concepts of knowledge. The increase in the availability of modeling tools with sophisticated user-interfaces has brought modeling out of computer laboratories and into the range of normal classrooms.

1.6 General Purpose Packages

Packages such as word-processing, data-interrogation, and spreadsheets are more than single programs. They consist of two parts: (a) the program, which contains a variety of routines that enable data to be manipulated and displayed; (b) the data files, which are used to store the data, thus making it available for interrogation. These are often called utilities or open-ended packages; though used for CAL, these may be similar or even identical to packages used in the world of business and commerce.

The database is the raw material of an inquiry in the same way that a model is for a simulation. Previously teachers could only present learners with an organized synopsis of evidence; now the evidence itself is made available for students to explore, search for patterns, and analyze for themselves. The interrogation design enables them to set up inquiries by sorting the data into subsets, to use routes for seeking matches across fields, and to produce graphical representation of the results. Large data sets, such as census returns, parish records, United Nations and Government national and regional statistics, can be used to test hypotheses such as "Countries with low populations per doctor are the wealthiest."

These programs encourage the collecting and encoding of data from local field studies or experiments. Learning from direct experience through locally collected data is as important as sorting through large sets from other sources. Many subjects are evidence-based, placing equal weight on the value of the collection of data and on the subsequent interrogation. They demand the basic skills associated with information acquisition and measuring, sorting and classifying, leading to higher-order skills of enquiry and data-analysis.

1.7 Tools for Specific Purposes

There are packages designed for specific purposes, such as desktop publishing, synthesizing music, and capturing and encoding satellite images. These reflect, but are usually simpler than, the same style of package as is used in the adult world. Thus in Logo, which is essentially an authoring programming language, the educational function is drive a symbolic turtle around the screen. In learning the commands that control the turtle the learner is exposed to complexity in the notation and actuality of geometry as well as to programming principles.

2. Classification of CAL by Type of Use

Another way of considering and understanding the nature of CAL is through a classification of use. Some such classifications are based on the the role that the computer plays. Taylor (1980) suggested three roles: tutor, tool, and tutee. The computer is a tutor when it leads the learner step by step through the program; for example, in drill and practice packages, where the learning is clearly driven by the tight framework of the software. The computer is a tool when used with content-free, general-purpose software such as word-processing or data-interrogation; the learner defines the agenda for use. The computer is a tutee when it is programmed by the learner in order to gain understanding, such as with Logo, or real-time control of experiments.

An alternative perception is that of Kemmis et al. (1977), who devised a framework that focused on student interactions when using CAL. It is based on four paradigms of learning: instructional, revelatory, conjectural, and emancipatory. The instructional draws on the ideas of programmed learning and is manifested in drill and practice exercises. The revelatory guides the learner through the process of learning by discovery: the content, key concepts, and related theory are revealed by progress through the software. Computer simulations provide a classic example of this paradigm.

The conjectural paradigm centers on the student learning through exploring explanations of any topic, assisting the articulation, and testing ideas and hypotheses. This suggests use of modeling and data-interrogation, through both general purpose and specific tools. The emancipatory hinges on the concept of the computer reducing the amount of inauthentic labor, thus releasing students from mental drudgery for the more significant work. This paradigm more often stands in conjuction *with*, rather than separate from, the others.

3. Evidence of Use

Evidence of how CAL is actually used (and the value that can be ascribed to its use) is mixed and uneven. Some evidence derives from systematic academic research and analysis using a variety of methods; other evidence comes from publications in which practicing teachers describe what has worked for them.

3.1 Cognitive Gains

Much academic research has been based on measurable cognitive gains (Roblyer et al. 1988). Niemiec and Walberg (1992) concluded from a comprehensive literature survey that focuses entirely on quantitative research that CAL is moderately effective in enhancing student outcomes; their survey suggested that such a conclusion has been reached many times. Collis (1988) supported this, though questioned the validity of some of the studies. Most studies in these surveys have focused on content, usually using instructional programs, often concentrating on lower-level skills.

Some studies however, focusing on particular populations and subjects, have been concerned with higher order thinking skills. Driver and Scanlon (1989) concluded that the development of an enhanced understanding of difficult concepts in science is possible through the revelation and conjecture of simulations, while Hoyles et al. (1989) argued for pupil achievements in their own cognitive goals from using Logo. Collections of readings such as Boyd-Barrett and Scanlon (1991) have reported a wide range of individual studies. Particular subjects (science and mathematics and languages) and particular packages (such as Logo and wordprocessing) have dominated this work.

3.2 Social and Cultural Dimensions

A different range of studies has emerged that focuses more on the social and cultural dimensions of using CAL. Discourse among students when working on and around a task has emerged as an important dimension associated with CAL (Chatterton 1985). This is related to the value of group work and in particular to learner cooperation and collaboration on task. Johnson et al. (1985) showed the benefits of work in groups: learners in collaborative groups achieved more. Pea and Sheingold (1987) supported this in their long-term studies at one institution. A component related to group collaboration and discourse is the level of intrinsic interest and motivation that CAL appears to generate from learners. A variety of case studies (Blomeyer and Martin 1991, Watson 1992), often using ethnographic rather than quantitative research methods, have focused on the positive learning environment generated, rather than attempting to measure specific cognitive gains.

3.3 CAL and the Teacher

A third and growing area of research is the exploration of the combination of factors that appears to influence the take-up of CAL. Some studies focused on the style of teaching and attitude of the teacher who does use CAL. Olson (1988) firmly focused on the role of the teacher for whom CAL either supports their style, and so is acceptable, or threatens it, and so is rejected. Others have considered the organizational and management problems associated with CAL. Moonen and Collis (1992) concluded that even in a technologically rich environment, incremental change with the use of CAL will be slow and complex. Van den Akker et al. (1992) concluded that the disappointing experiences of using CAL are related to poor and ill-considered introduction strategies—indeed, the failure to consider the complexity inherent in the use of such a technological innovation.

4. Agreed Attributes of CAL

Drawing from this research evidence and large scale reports (United States Congress, Office of Technology Assessment 1988) a number of known or potential beneficial effects for CAL can be listed:

(a) developing skills in: (i) problem-solving; (ii) the observation, collection, classification, analysis, interpretation, and appropriate representation of data; (iii) language competence;

(b) encouraging: (i) creative work; (ii) the collection of fieldwork data; (iii) using data from a wider variety of sources; (iv) individual attainment amongst those with special needs;

(c) promoting: (i) inquiries in the humanities; (ii) conceptual understanding in the sciences and mathematics; (iii) logical thinking with Logo; (iv) predictive and deductive work with databases; (v) creative explorations with new tools; (vi) collaboration and social skills; (vii) focused discourse.

Computer Assisted Learning can also be used in-appropriately. Word processors are often used as a method of producing fair copy, and data packages for graphical representations of simplistic analysis that is equally well-done manually. It can be used to reinforce less desirable aspects of learning: the use of drills and repetitive exercises may simply replicate tedious classwork of little proven value.

5. Concluding Issues

Examples of successful use of CAL are rare. Pelgrum and Plomp (1991) have clearly shown that in most countries only a small percentage of teachers are using computers, and the pedagogic aspects of using computers are mentioned by them the least.

Part of this problem can be attributed to a confusion as to why computers have been introduced into education. Hawkridge (1990) has identified four rationales for the introduction of computers into schools: social, vocational, pedagogic, and catalytic. The role of CAL is often perceived to be vocational (i.e., used in schools to prepare learners for the use of IT in the adult world) rather than pedagogic (i.e., to facilitate learning itself). The catalytic is predicated on the assumption that using computers will facilitate a complete change in the nature of learning and educational institutions; a message similar to that espoused by Papert (1980). This is in direct contradiction to the work that claims disinterest in CAL to be due to the poor integration within educational institutions and existing pedagogy.

A much greater corpus of research is needed to enable the picture to be sounder than it is at present. One of the biggest problems facing research communities is that if CAL produces a new and unique interactive environment, it is less easy to chart its benefits because it is not amenable to standard forms of research. This is compounded by the fact that benefits of CAL appear to be in the development of higher order thinking skills, with the outcomes being process-rather than product-oriented.

References

Blomeyer R L, Martin D (eds.) 1991 *Case Studies of Computer Aided Learning.* Falmer Press, London

Boyd-Barrett O, Scanlon E 1991 *Computers and Learning: A Reader.* Addison Wesley, Wokingham

Chatterton J L 1985 Evaluating CAL in the classroom. In: Reid I, Rushtoon J (eds.) *Teachers, Computers and the Classroom.* Manchester University Press, Manchester

Collis B 1988 *Computers, Curriculum and Whole Class Instruction: Issues and Ideas.* Wadsworth, Belmont, California

Driver R, Scanlon E 1989 Conceptual change in science. *Journal of Computer Assisted Learning* 5(1): 25–36

Hawkridge D 1990 Who needs computers in schools and why? *Comput. Educ.* 15(1–3): 1–6

Hoyles C, Noss R, Sutherland R 1989 Designing a Logo-based microworld for ratio and proportion. *Journal of Computer Assisted Learning* 5(4): 208–23

Johnson R T, Johnson D W, Stanne M B 1985 Effects of cooperative, competitive and individualistic goal structures in computer assisted instruction. *J. Educ. Psychol.* 77(6): 668–77

Kemmis S, Atkin R, Wright E 1977 *How do Students Learn? Working Papers on Computer Assisted Learning.* Centre for Applied Research in Education, University of East Anglia, Norwich

Moonen J, Collis B 1992 Changing the school: Experiences from a Dutch technology-enriched school project. *Education and Computing* 8(1–2): 97–102

Niemiec R P, Walberg H J 1992 The effects of computers on learning. *Int. J. Educ. Res.* 17(1): 99–107

Olson J 1988 *Schoolworlds—Microworlds: Computers and the Culture of the Classroom.* Pergamon Press, Oxford

Papert S 1980 *Mindstorms: Children, Computers and Powerful Ideas.* Basic Books, New York

Pea R D, Sheingold K (eds.) 1987 *Mirrors of Mind: Patterns of Excellence in Educational Computing.* Ablex, Norwood, New Jersey

Pelgrum W J, Plomp T 1991 *The Use of Computers in Education Worldwide.* Pergamon Press, Oxford

Roblyer M D, Castine W H, King F J 1988 Assessing the impact of computer based instruction: A review of recent research. *Computers in Schools* 5(3–4)

Taylor R P 1980 *The Computer in the School: Tutor, Tool, Tutee.* Teachers College Press, New York

United States Congress, Office of Technology Assessment 1988 *Power On! New Tools for Teaching and Learning.* United States Government Printing Office, Washington, DC

van den Akker J, Keursten P, Plomp T 1992 The integration of computer use in education. *Int. J. Educ. Res.* 17(1): 65–76

Watson D M 1992 Case studies of classroom processes using geography simulations. In: Plomp T J, Pieters J M, Feteris A (eds.) 1992 *European Conference on Educational Research.* University of Twente, Enschede

Further Reading

McDougall A, Dowling C (eds.) 1990 *Computers in Education.* North Holland/Elsevier, Amsterdam

Tinsley J D, van Weert T J (eds.) 1995 *Computers in Education.* Chapman and Hall, London

Underwood J D M, Underwood G 1990 *Computers and Learning: Helping Children to Acquire Thinking Skills.* Blackwell, Oxford

Watson D, Tinsley D (eds.) 1995 *Integrating Information Technology into Education.* Chapman and Hall, London

Computer-managed Learning

P. K. Komoski

This entry addresses the practice of managing instruction and individual student learning using networked computers. The entry provides a brief history of computer-managed learning in the United States from early computer-assisted instruction (CAI) to growing use of integrated learning systems (ILS) and describes the characteristics of such systems. It also discusses international applications of computer-managed learning, its further evolution, and the paucity of systematic research of its effect on learners, teachers, and curriculum.

1. Nature and Origins of Computer-managed Learning

Computer-managed learning is an evolving pedagogical practice in which networked computers are used to provide individual learners with access to instructional software, productivity software, and electronic information resources. The defining characteristics of such systems are: (a) integration of computer-based instruction and other learning-related software applications; (b) capability to manage a flow of information related to use of the system by individual learners; (c) system-generated progress reports on student progress and achievement.

The origins of computer-managed learning are traceable to the development and use of computer-assisted instruction at a few universities, military training centers, and corporations in the United States during the 1960s. These early efforts were designed as means for providing individualized, interactive instruction to many learners simultaneously. Such systems employed mainframe computers and a network of terminals to store, distribute, and manage instructional programming and a flow of information required to sustain individualized electronic teaching and learning.

2. Growth and Evolution

During the first two decades of school-based application of computer-managed learning, the 1960s and 1970s, it was restricted to a prescriptive, linear approach to teaching basic mathematics and language skills. Although experimental applications in some universities went beyond such limited applications,

Table 1
Functions and features of integrated learning systems

Distribution of software	
Instructional software	Sequential lessons (supplied with system)
	– preset sequencing of lessons
	– resequencing of lessons and teacher lesson planning
	Nonsequential supplemental lessons (added by users)
Tool software	Word processing, spell checker, note pad, etc.
	Database or filing system
	Calculator
	Spreadsheet
Reference software	Electronic encyclopedia, dictionary, etc.
	Research database
System access and security	
Hierarchical access	By students, teachers, systems managers
Passwords	Required, optional, or unavailable
Backup of system-generated data	On system's hard disk or on tape
Student testing	
Diagnostic	
Achievement	
Report generation	
Individual student, by lesson	Percentage completed/percentage correct
	Time spent
	Text of student's responses
	Analysis of responses to lessons
	Aggregate performance on multiple lessons
Progress report to parents	
Reports on class, multiple classes and special groups	
Reports on whole school or multiple schools	
Integrated computer-management of all of above	

those experiments had little effect on the type of applications available to school users.

In United States schools, the growth and evolution of computer-managed learning have been shaped by a complex mix of technical, economic, social, and educational realities. Throughout the 1970s, when school applications still required the use of costly mainframe or minicomputers, plus a level of technical expertise that made most educators wary, the growth in applications of computer-managed learning systems in United States schols was slow. However, during the 1980s cost and technical barriers were lowered considerably by the appearance of lower cost, technically less daunting, networkable microcomputers. This was followed by a significant increase in the number of commercial providers of computer-managed learning systems. This increase coincided with metaresearch findings (Kulik 1985) indicating that CAI was often equal to, or superior to, conventional teaching.

The initial markets for these commercially developed systems were schools and job-training centers looking to improve: (a) remedial instruction in basic skills, and (b) instructional accountability. In time a wider market developed among schools and colleges interested in innovative approaches to teaching through the use of technology. In response to this wider market, such systems have begun to address learning that goes beyond instruction in basic skills. As a result, the number of installations of computer-managed learning in the United States schools grew from a few thousand in the early 1980s to an estimated 20,000 in the early 1990s.

2.1 Integrated Learning Systems

Most installations of computer-managed learning in the United States have been commercially marketed to schools as "integrated learning systems"—a name

Table 2
Networked computers installed in schools in Japan

Type of school	Percentage with installations	Numbers of schools
Primary (age 6-12)	6.3	1,529 of 24,267
Secondary (age 13-15)	28.4	2,998 of 10,551
High (age 16-18)	37.5	1,554 of 4,144
All schools	15.6	6,081 of 38,962

Source: Japanese Ministry of Education

used by those in marketing to indicate that such systems, in addition to delivering CAI, may also include other applications such as word-processing, electronic encyclopedias, and other productivity and research tools. As of the mid-1990s, the term "integrated" in such systems refers to a system's capability to integrate and to manage the use of a variety of computer software applications in addition to each system's distinguishing proprietary instructional software. However, such integration does not usually imply an integrated approach to curriculum and learning across content areas.

Although integrated learning systems vary in complexity and sophistication, as well as in quality of instruction and management, their common functions and features may be outlined as in Table 1.

3. International Applications of Computer-managed Learning

As of 1993, in addition to the United States, countries with a significant base of networked computers installed in schools were Israel, Japan, and Sweden. However, among these only Israeli schools had a significant amount of computer-managed learning installed and in use.

Computer-managed learning in Israel began in the mid-1970s, when rights for the use of a system developed in the United States were granted to an Israeli university. That resulted in the employment of computer-managed learning in a few Israeli schools, and led to a continuing expansion of computer-managed learning in Israel. This acceptance prompted commercial development of a number of systems, two of which are marketed in both Israel and the United States. Although the percentage of Israeli schools using computer-managed learning is estimated to be comparable to use in United States schools, official government statistics are not available for either country.

In Sweden, national education authorities estab-

lished a national policy during the 1980s that called for the use of networked (rather than stand-alone) computers in schools throughout the country. Since then, responsibility for education management has been decentralized, but the policy on networked computers has resulted in the widespread use of networks to provide students with access to software for carrying out writing, computation, and other productivity tasks. There has been only modest development of curriculum-related software by a few commercial publishers. No official statistics are available on the use of software in Swedish schools.

The only country for which detailed statistics exist on the use of networked computers in schools is Japan. The figures in Table 2 from the Japanese Ministry of Education, provide a profile of the base of networked computers installed in schools throughout Japan as of 31 March 1992. It is important to note that these figures pertain only to the presence of networked computers, and not to whether those networks are being used to implement computer-managed learning. The Japan Council for Educational Software reports that appropriate software is still in the early stages of development. The objective is to create networkable software that will meet the requirements of the national curriculum that is widely followed by Japanese schools.

Other applications of computer-managed learning internationally seem to be at much earlier stages of development. In Australia, for example, the use of such learning seems to be limited to the schools secondary level utilizing mainframe computers. Schools in most other countries lack both networked computers and sources of appropriate software. However, if conditions similar to those that have fostered growth of computer-managed learning in the United States develop in other countries, international use of computer-managed learning may increase. Among these conditions are: (a) willingness of education authorities and/or teachers to use networkable computers to individualize instruction; (b) availability of computer networks in schools; (c) sources of appropriate and sufficient educational software; (d) financial resources necessary to implement computer-managed learning; and (e) a concern about accountability for learning.

4. Questions about Future Development

There is little doubt that computer-managed learning will continue to evolve and develop. However, because so much of its evolution has been dependent on the development and marketing to schools of proprietary computer-managed learning systems that are installed, maintained, and updated by commercial vendors, is it to be assumed that future evolution will be as heavily dependent on commercial development of similar proprietary systems? If such systems continue to be based on the use of one vendor's proprietary software, how technically and pedagogically open will such systems be to the integration of other competing proprietary software?

As has been noted, current state-of-the-art computer-managed learning evolved from the CAI systems of the 1960s and 1970s. Although ILS systems now go well beyond early CAI, they retain enough of CAI's well-ordered, diagnostic–prescriptive, sequential approach to individualizing instruction to put them in sharp contrast with current constructivist views about learning. To what extent will constructivist ideas about learning and teaching affect the ongoing evolution of computer-managed learning?

All computer-managed learning is "managed" through the use of management software. Such software is at the heart of all current ILSs. It not only manages the system, but it enables a teacher to plan and adapt the use of the system by learners. To what extent will future computer-managed learning systems enable learners themselves to plan and adapt a system to their personal learning needs and interests? How will the increasing use of non-ILS-related, instructional management systems, and the increasing availability of large amounts of networkable, non-ILS-related educational software by schools affect the evolution of computer-managed learning?

5. Paucity of Research and Evaluation

All of the above questions suggest a need for systematic research on many aspects on computer-managed learning. Extant research says little about the effects of computer-managed learning on learning and teaching, and on learners and teachers. Most relevant research has addressed the effectiveness of CAI as measured by standard tests of performance of basic skills.

A comparative evaluative report on the eight major ILSs used in United States schools as of 1990 found broad user acceptance of computer-managed learning, but many specific criticisms of particular systems by both teachers and learners (EPIE 1990). It also found wide variation in the quality of instructional software and management systems.

As of 1992, only one multiyear, international research study existed (Hativa 1991, Hativa and Lesgold 1991). The study is an integration of findings from the use of four commercially developed ILSs (two United States and two Israeli) in United States and Israeli schools over a period of six years. The research was limited to "arithmetic practice." The research concluded that all four systems fell short of meeting the curricular and instructional management needs of school users. Given such findings, it is evident that a broad base of ongoing systematic research is needed to shape future development of computer-managed learning in educationally productive ways. However, it remains to be seen whether continuing research or continuing market forces will play the major role in such future development.

See also: Computers and Learning

References

EPIE Institute/Komoski P K 1990 *The Integrated Instructional Systems (IIS) Report: A Comparative Evaluation Report on Eight Integrated Learning Systems.* EPIE Institute, Hampton Bays, New York

Hativa N 1991 Cognitive, affective, and social impacts of arithmetic practice with ILS: An integration of findings from six-years qualitative and quantitative studies. ERIC Document Reproduction Service No. ED 336 060, Washington, DC

Hativa N, Lesgold A 1991 The computer as tutor: Can it adapt to the individual learner? ERIC Document Reproduction Service No. EJ 43 1610, Washington, DC

Kulik J A 1985 Consistencies in findings on computer-based education. ERIC Document Reproduction Service No. ED 269 012, Washington, DC

Further Reading

McLaughlin P 1990 Computer-based education: The best of ERIC 1989. ERIC Document Reproduction Service No. ED 341 386, Washington, DC

Plomp T, Moonen J (eds.) 1991 Implementation of computers in education. ERIC Document Reproduction Service No. EJ 436 930, Washington, DC

Computer Networking for Education

L. M. Harasim

The use of computer networks for educational activity at all levels—primary, secondary, tertiary, adult, and distance education—has introduced new options to enhance and transform teaching and learning opportunities and outcomes. Since the late 1960s computer networks (electronic mail, bulletin board services, and computer conferencing) have been adopted and adapted by educators to enhance the curriculum by expanding access to expertise and educational resources, to increase student interaction and peer collaboration both within and between classrooms, and for the delivery of credit and noncredit courses and programs. Computer networks enhance traditional forms of face-to-face and distance education and enable new and unprecedented educational interactions, creating the basis for a new paradigm: network learning.

The new opportunities, however, also introduce new challenges for educators and learners. This entry describes this emerging field and provides examples from around the world to illustrate the applications, outcomes, and issues involved in computer networking for education.

1. Background and Overview

Human communication and interaction are the major uses of computer networks. Educational uses of computer networks on time-sharing computers can be traced to the late 1960s (i.e., the PLATO system) while the application of e-mail networks for course activities and information exchange began in the early 1970s (Hunter 1992). Computer conferencing and bulletin board systems, first developed in the early 1970s, were used for educational communication from the 1970s and by 1981 computer conferencing was used for course delivery (Feenberg 1993, Harasim et al. 1995).

1.1 Classroom Adjunct

One of the earliest educational applications of computer networking was the use of electronic mail to complement traditional face-to-face classroom activities by expanding opportunities for class discussion (Quinn et al. 1983). Computer conferencing and bulletin board systems were also adopted for information exchange and collaborative projects among learning peers, for sharing assignments, communicating with the instructor, and to access expertise and resources beyond what was available locally. As early as 1969, Stanford University began delivering mathematics education to low-income students in Mississippi, Kentucky, and California via computer networks (Hunter 1992). The use of computer networks as a classroom adjunct has been adopted at all levels of education.

1.2 Networked Classrooms

The networked classroom approach links classes in different geographical locations (local and global) for information exchange and group activities (Harasim et al. 1995). One of the earliest examples was a network of secondary schools linked by Dartmouth's time-sharing computer in 1969 (Hunter 1992). The InterCultural Learning Network (ICLN), implemented in 1983, used email to link schoolchildren in San Diego, California, with peers in Alaska and other American states and eventually Japan, Mexico, Puerto Rico, and Israel (Levin et al. 1990). The Canadian RAPPI network (1985–87) linked schoolchildren and teachers in over 70 different schools in Canada, France, Italy and the United Kingdom, to facilitate information exchange with peers in different regions and countries (Hart 1987). Other notable examples of school-level networks are the National Geographic KIDSNet, the AT&T Learning Network, Australia's Computer Pals Across the World, Canada's Southern Interior Telecommunication's Project (Teles and Duxbury 1992), and the Japan-based APICnet. University examples include the European Campus 2000 (Mason 1993) and BESTnet and AFRINet which link university students and courses in the United States, Canada, Latin America, and Africa (Bellman et al. 1993).

1.3 Online Courses and Programs

Since the mid-1980s, networks have been used to deliver credit and noncredit courses. This application is primarily employed by university and adult education institutions. Graduate schools such as the Ontario Institute for Studies in Education (OISE is a graduate school of education affiliated with the University of Toronto) and Connected Education (affiliated with the New School for Social Research, New York) began to offer graduate-level courses entirely on-line in late 1985. Other institutions—such as those associated with the Virtual Classroom Project—developed the use of computer conferencing for undergraduate course delivery (Hiltz 1990, 1994). Full degree or professional programs are offered entirely on-line. Training programs are also adopting networks for on-line course delivery.

1.4 Distance Education and Open Learning

Distance education institutions and programs use computer conferencing and networking in adjunct and full course delivery mode. The American Open University began using computer conferencing in 1984 to supplement learner—tutor communication and to provide a forum for group discussion. In 1989 the British Open University introduced the first mass-based distance education course that incorporated computer conferencing (Mason and Kaye 1989). European initiatives in computer networking provide valuable models and lessons for open and distance education opportunities (Mason 1993, Collis 1991).

1.5 Professional Development Networks

Networks are also used within a broader educational framework, not restricted to curriculum integration. Thousands of specialist forums and user groups on networks such as the Internet, bulletin boards, and commercial services (CompuServe, America Online) support professional collaboration among teachers and educators and provide teacher education and enhancement. Electronic newsletters are published and disseminated over the networks. Professional development activities in the form of mini courses, special lecture seminars, workshops, and formal courses are also available on-line.

1.6 Community Learning

Networks offer a variety of community education and support services. The Big Sky Telegraph network, launched in Montana in 1988, serves rural schools, communities, and cooperatives. Public free-nets are active. The Cleveland Free-Net (the National Public Telecomputing Network) was established in 1986 as a community computer service to offer free networking services in areas such as health, education, technology, government, arts, recreation, and the law. The menu is built around a metaphor of a community which includes an administration building, a public square, a library, and a university circle. GeoNet supports a consortium of Electronic Village Halls throughout Europe (Mason 1993). Computer networks are also used to link the home and school, to enhance educational opportunities for students and in some cases to provide for parent involvement and education as well.

2. Theoretical Framework

2.1 Overview

The use of computer networking in education has been referred to variously as on-line education (Harasim 1990), the virtual classroom (Hiltz 1994), and learning networks (Harasim et al. 1995). The paradigm underlying educational networking should be distinguished from other educational applications of computing: (a) computer-based education, such as computer-assisted instruction (CAI), computer-managed instruction (CMI), computer-based training (CBT), and other like terms, which broadly represent those uses of the computer in which the student is tutored by the computer; (b) programming, in which the student designs instructions that tell a computer how to carry out a particular processing task; and (c) the use of the computer as a tool, exemplified in such applications as word processing, spreadsheets, or database management. These application involve an individualized interaction between the student and the computer and do not facilitate human communication and interaction among members of an educational community (see *Computer-assisted Learning; Computer-managed Learning*). Learning networks are characterized by human communication and require attention to instructional design to organize the message-based computer networks into an educational environment.

2.2 A New Paradigm: Network Learning

Computer networking for educational purposes represents a new learning paradigm: network learning. Network learning shares certain fundamental characteristics with the face-to-face educational environment; that is, interactive group communication. However, participants are geographically separated and thus network learning also shares attributes common to distance education. However, distance education is based on a transmittal model (Burge 1988) which in theory and practice emphasizes individual rather than group learning. The unique combination of place-independent, asynchronous interaction among groups of people linked by a network system yields the new educational model and set of learning outcomes called network learning.

The attributes of the networking environment present unique opportunities as well as constraints for learning. The first attribute is that networking technology supports group communication. Electronic mail networks enable one-to-one (interpersonal) and one-to-many (broadcast) communication, while a group mail facility or distribution list supports some group communication activities. Computer conferencing and some bulletin boards support personal and broadcast modes but provide system features specifically designed to support many-to-many (group) communication.

As a group communication system, the networking environment is in certain respects familiar territory. Topics are discussed, teachers introduce new subjects, and "spaces" may be created to facilitate various types of learning activities. Learners network with peers, experts, and mentors to ask questions, share information, and engage in discussion, debates, apprenticeship, or collaborative work. Learners may work together in groups of 2 or 20 to discuss a topic, undertake a joint research project, create a newspaper, or compose a short story.

There are also significant and fundamental differences to learning on-line. Among the most obvious is that the group interaction is place-independent. Users are not limited by where they live. By using networks, learners and teachers can form linkages with counterparts in other parts of the world with relative ease, to access ideas, perspectives, cultures, and information beyond the local resources (teacher, library, textbook, etc.).

Time-independence or asynchronicity is a third characteristic of most learning networks. While a few networks support synchronous mode (i.e., real-time systems such as audiographics, videoconferencing, and audioconferencing) most computer networks operate primarily as asynchronous communication environments. The asynchronous network is always "open," and class discussions and interaction can occur at any time, 24 hours a day, seven days a week.

Currently, most networks are text-based although multimedia networking is becoming increasingly available. The text-based nature of communication on the network encourages articulation and exchange of ideas. Participants must formulate a comment in order to be "present" and once the idea is entered into the group forum, it invites response and group interaction. The availability of a text-based archive, moreover, provides a form of group memory and also enables retrospective analysis of the proceedings.

The final characteristic is computer-mediation. The mediation of the computer enables the first four attributes and introduces new tools to enhance communication and intellectual work. The computer enables the storage, retrieval, processing, and manipulation of data. Various software programs, from spell checkers to hypertext and information management systems, can be applied to computer networks. Educational software programs can assist the user in structuring messages and with interconnecting new ideas with previous ones to support the creation of personal and group knowledge bases.

3. Design and Implementation of Learning Networks

Attention to design of the applications is one of the single most critical factors in successful learning networks, whether course activity is delivered totally on-line or in adjunct mode. Network learning, just as face-to-face education, involves intervention by a content and/or process expert (the instructor) to organize the content, sequence the instructional activities, structure task and group interaction, and evaluate the process.

3.1 Learning Approaches used in Computer Networks

Six main types of learning approaches are found in educational computer networks (Harasim et al. 1995): (a) ask-an-expert, (b) mentorship, (c) tutor support, (d) peer interaction, (e) structured group activity, (f) access to relevant information. The first three approaches require on-line resource persons such as mentors, experts, and instructors to support student work. The latter three are student-centered. The choice of model depends on the content area and course design. These approaches seem to be most successful when structures and roles are well-defined, or when the information accessed is relevant to a particular learning task.

3.1.1 Ask-an-expert. Learning networks facilitate access, local or global, to subject area experts (scientists, writers, professionals, etc.). Teachers first establish a list of experts willing to undertake this role and set up a set of procedures for undertaking that activity. Students send questions to the expert on a given area and obtain responses in a few days. The main benefits of this model are quick access to up-to-date relevant information and the positive feedback of receiving an answer.

3.1.2 Mentorship. Mentorship is a time-honored educational approach. An on-line mentor is a professional in a particular subject area who provides ongoing feedback until the apprentice masters the learning task. At that point the mentor "fades" away and the apprentice engages in the exploration of expert practice. For example, a student submits a poem or a short story to an on-line mentor who provides coaching in how better to craft the writing. The student–mentor interaction may continue over several weeks or even months as the student submits or resubmits the work and obtains ongoing feedback from the mentor. On-line mentorship is a technique used in the humanities and sciences.

3.1.3 Tutor support. Learners at all levels can be provided with tutoring to support educational activities. Tutoring complements face-to-face and on-line classes, while in distance mode on-line tutors provide the primary source of instructional support and interaction.

3.1.4 Peer interaction. Peer interaction is based on principles of collaborative learning, and has been effective in on-line environments (Harasim 1990). There are two types of peer interaction: informal and structured. Informal peer interaction may take various forms: "electronic pen pals"; special interest group discussions (i.e., newsgroups and distribution lists); and social interaction, as in a "virtual cafe" or public square on the free-nets set up for informal socializing. Often, interactions initiated through such public spaces then move on to the exchange of personal email messages, as learners find peers with similar interests. These forms are common to most learning networks. Structured peer interaction is discussed below under structured group activity.

3.1.5 Structured group activity. This is a curriculum-based approach designed to be implemented within deadlines for submissions and responses. There are many types of curriculum group activity: long and very structured, short and less structured, based on peer interaction and guided coaching.

Group learning structures that have been effectively reformulated for network environments include: seminars, small group discussions, learning partnerships and dyads, small work groups, learning circles, simulations and role plays, and debating teams. In addition, such group spaces as a "virtual cafe" or student lounge and a mutual "assist" space where students help one another with technical and other problems are valuable.

3.1.6 Access to network resources. Global networks such as the Internet, provide access to on-line databases and archives (data files), libraries, as well as to thousands of special interest forums, on topics ranging from nuclear physics to environmental issues.

4. Educational Outcomes

4.1 Active Learning

The network environment has been found to support active participation as well as active contruction of meaning. In order to be "present" on-line, students must formulate and send a message. Articulating that idea and sharing it in a group forum has important cognitive benefits and the ongoing group interaction on the idea can enhance the knowledge building process. Research indicates that with an appropriate course design, most students actively and regularly message on-line (Riel 1992, Harasim 1989) and that the volume of communication is distributed fairly evenly (Harasim 1989). Several factors are cited by users. The opportunity to control the pace, place, and time of participation enables increased participation. Asynchronicity reduces competition for airtime. Moreover, such features as the opportunity to edit a message as well as the anonymity afforded by text-based communication further contribute to students taking a more active role in on-line discussions (Bellman et al. 1993).

Networking can also contribute to facilitating active construction of meaning (Harasim 1990). Group interaction on a network generates a database of ideas and responses. The exposure to positive and negative feedback on one's ideas stimulates cognitive restructuring in response to new information and perspectives. Cognitive learning strategies such as making multiple passes or directed searches through the rich corpus

of ideas are rewarding. Moreover, access to real audiences is more motivational and has been found to contribute to improved writing skills (Cohen and Riel 1989).

4.2 Achievement and User Characteristics

Research on user characteristics has been conducted primarily on on-line course delivery for university students. Hiltz (1990, 1994) found that outcomes for the virtual classroom are at least as good as outcomes for traditional face-to-face courses. The average student reported that both access to and quality of the educational experience were improved. Research indicates high levels of student satisfaction, with a high percentage reporting that they would take another course on-line (Hiltz 1990, Phelps et al. 1991).

Hiltz (1990) found that improved outcomes were generally contingent upon providing adequate access to equipment, instructional effort and skill in teaching with networks, and student characteristics. Students who were motivated to explore the learning network environment were self-disciplined, and those who had average or better verbal skills were likely to experience superior outcomes, compared with achievement on traditional courses. Students who lacked this motivation and basic college-level skills, or who had to travel to use a computer for access, were more likely to drop out of an on-line course, to participate more irregularly, and to perform more poorly than they would in a traditional course.

4.3 Global Education

Computer networks facilitate communication across national boundaries, to enable learners to "meet" and interact with peers and experts from other cultures. Cross-cultural communication and understanding and the perception of the interconnectivity of the world's population can be enhanced by global networks. Students can network to discuss or gather geographically and socially significant data about today's problems and to explore ways to resolve them.

Global education via networks also poses challenges. Conducting group work among people who are geographically separate can be difficult. Issues related to cross-cultural communication, choice of language of communication and different curricula need to be resolved (Mason 1993). Differing cultural and economic perspectives on an event (e.g., a war) or activity (e.g., whaling) challenge as well as enrich global education (Riel 1993, Teles 1993).

4.4 Teacher Revitalization

Teachers who use computer networks report a sense of revitalization as a result of the enhanced learning opportunities that they can offer their students as well as the opportunities for teacher networking (Teles and Duxbury 1992, Riel 1992). Network access to peer support and teacher resources also facilitate teacher adoption of educational change and modification of teaching approaches (Lenk 1992).

5. Research Directions

Despite its short history, significant research has been conducted on educational computer networking, especially with regard to learner participation (i.e., frequency, volume, distribution of communication), learner satisfaction, impacts on teaching, and issues in curriculum design and implementation. The data gathered have proven the viability of this pioneering new field and have illuminated critical organizational and pedagogical issues. There is a need now for systematic study of learning processes in on-line environments, examining patterns of human interaction in decision-making, problem-solving, and knowledge building. Such research is valuable for the purposes of designing software that supports network learning, for instructional design of on-line environments, and for understanding the cognitive and affective processes in learning networks. Computer mediation enables an archive of the proceedings to be established, enabling retrospective content and interaction analysis of the transcript.

As networks become increasingly multimedia, there is a need for research into the relationship between different forms of learning and media. Studies are needed on such issues as the fit between specific educational tasks and media form and content, teaching and learning approaches in multimedia networks, and determining the relative costs and effectiveness of the different media. Finally, there is a critical need for theory building regarding educational technologies such as computer networking. Theories from education or communication or which, like the concept of network learning, build on field experience and research are needed to guide developments in computer networking for education.

6. Conclusion

Rapid progress in the technology of computer networking (email and conferencing) has enabled new educational opportunities that transcend geographic and temporal boundaries. Educators around the world, at all levels of education, have adopted computer networking. A new paradigm for education has emerged: network learning. This entry has described network learning applications and attributes and has outlined instructional design and implementation issues. Network learning, based upon group collaboration in knowledge building, collectively shared goals, active participation, and cross-cultural communication will offer important training for life in the twenty-first century.

See also: Computers and Learning; Computer Assisted Learning

References

Bellman B, Tindimubona A, Arias A Jr 1993 Technology transfer in global networking: Capacity building in Africa and Latin America. In: Harasim L M (ed.) 1993 *Global Networks: Computers and International Communication.* MIT Press, Cambridge, Massachusetts

Burge L 1988 Beyond andragogy: Some explorations for distance learning design. *Journal of Distance Education* 3(1): 5–23

Cohen M, Riel M 1989 The effect of distant audiences on students' writing. *Am. Educ. Res. J.* 26(2): 143–59

Collis B 1991 Telecommunications-based training in Europe: A state-of-the-art report. *Am. J. Distance Educ.* 5(2): 31–40

Feenberg A 1993 Building a global network. In: Harasim L M (ed.) 1993 *Global Networks: Computers and International Communication.* MIT Press, Cambridge, Massachusetts

Harasim L M 1989 On-line education: A new domain. In: Mason R, Kaye T (eds.) 1989

Harasim L M 1990 Online education: An environment for collaboration and intellectual amplification. In: Harasim L M (ed.) 1990 *Online Education: Perspectives on a New Environment.* Praeger, New York

Harasim L M, Hiltz S R, Teles L, Turoff M 1995 *Learning Networks: A Field Guide to Teaching and Learning Online.* MIT Press, Cambridge, Massachusetts

Hart R 1987 Towards a third generation distributed conferring system. *Canadian Journal of Educational Communication* 16(2): 137–52

Hiltz S R 1990 Evaluating the virtual classroom. In: Harasim L M (ed.) 1990 *Online Education: Perspectives on a New Environment.* Praeger, New York

Hiltz S R 1994 *The Virtual Classroom.* Ablex, Norwood, New Jersey

Hunter B 1992 Linking for learning: Computer-and-communications network support for nationwide innovations in education. *Journal of Science Education and Technology* 1(1)

Lenk C 1992 The network science experience: Learning from three major projects. In: Tinker R F, Kapisovsky P M (eds.) 1992

Levin J, Kim H, Riel M 1990 Analyzing instructional interactions on electronic message networks. In: Harasim L M (ed.) 1990 *Online Education: Perspectives on a New Environment.* Praeger, New York

Mason R 1993 Computer conferencing and the new Europe. In: Harasim L M (ed.) 1993 *Global Networks: Computers and International Communication.* MIT Press, Cambridge, Massachusetts

Mason R, Kaye T (eds.) 1989 *Mindweave: Communication, Computers, and Distance Education.* Pergamon Press, Oxford

Phelps R, Wells R, Ashworth R, Hahn H 1991 Effectiveness and costs of distance education using computer-mediated communication. *Am. J. Distance Educ.* 5(3): 7–19

Quinn C N, Mehan H, Levin J A, Black S D 1983 Real education in non-real time: The use of electronic message systems for instruction. *Instructional Science* 11(4): 313–27

Riel M 1992 Learning Circles: A functional analysis of educational telecomputing. *Interactive Learning Environments* 2: 15–30

Riel M 1993 Global education through learning circles. In: Harasim L M (ed.) 1993 *Global Networks: Computers and International Communication*. MIT Press, Cambridge, Massachusetts

Teles L 1993 Cognitive Apprenticeship on Global Networks. In: Harasim L M (ed.) 1993 *Global Networks: Computers and International Communication*. MIT Press, Cambridge, Massachusetts

Teles L, Duxbury N 1992 *The Networked Classroom*. Simon Fraser University, Burnaby

Further Reading

Canadian Journal of Educational Communication 1987 16(2): Spring (issue devoted to computer-mediated communication in education)

Roberts N, Blakeslee G, Brown M, Lenk C 1990 *Integrating Telecommunications into Education*. Prentice-Hall, Englewood Cliffs, New Jersey

Tinker R F, Kapisovsky P M (eds.) 1992 *Prospects for Educational Telecomputing: Selected Readings*. TERC Publication, Cambridge, Massachusetts

Waggoner M D (ed.) 1992 *Empowering Networks: Computer Conferencing in Education*. Educational Technology Publications, Englewood Cliffs, New Jersey

Computer Programming, Learning and Instruction of

R. E. Mayer

A computer program is a list of formal instructions to a computer to make it accomplish a goal. Computer programming is a problem-solving activity that includes creating, comprehending, modifying, and debugging computer programs. In creating a program, the originator produces computer code that solves a problem stated in natural language. In comprehending a program, the user describes in natural language what a given computer program accomplishes. Modifying a program occurs when a person changes an existing program to accomplish a different goal from the one it was originally designed to accomplish. Debugging involves detecting and correcting errors in a program.

During the 1980s, computers became commonplace in elementary and secondary schools—increasing 50-fold over 10 years in some countries. To a lesser extent, computer programming became a major new subject-matter area for many students (Becker 1991, Pelgrum and Plomp 1991). Research also began in this period on how people learn and use computer programming languages and developed into one of the most active psychologies of subject matter (Mayer 1988a, Soloway and Spohrer 1989). Although there are over 1,000 programming languages, the languages most commonly taught in schools and studied by educational researchers are Logo, BASIC, and Pascal.

This entry addresses three major lines of research on the educational psychology of computer programming: (a) how to teach computer programming to novices, (b) what novices learn from instruction in computer programming, and (c) how expert programmers differ from novices.

1. Teaching Computer Programming

One of the major research issues concerns how to teach computer programming. Should students be free to discover how to use creatively a computer programming language in a "hands-on" environment or should teachers also provide more guidance concerning the learning and use of a programming language? In spite of strong claims for the power of allowing students to learn programming on their own, educational researchers have found that students often fail to discover even the fundamentals of programming on their own in nondirective, hands-on instructional programs (Linn 1985, Pea and Kurland 1984). For example, an analysis of students who learned to program by discovery revealed that "students often produced programs without really comprehending how the programs worked" (Nickerson et al. 1985 p. 277). In contrast, teaching that emphasizes structure and mediated guidance results in better learning and transfer than unstructured and nondirected teaching methods (Lehrer and Littlefield 1991, van Merrienboer 1990). Structuring insures that the learner receives the basic information in a useful order whereas mediation insures that the learner connects the presented information with relevant existing knowledge. In a review, Mayer (1988a p. 5) concluded that "the overwhelming consensus . . . is that, for most children, a hands-on discovery environment should be complemented with direct instruction and mediation by a teacher."

Students' ability to use a programming language to solve problems can be enhanced by instructional methods that help the student build a mental model of the computing system. A mental model of a computing system is a simplified representation of the major locations (such as memory space or output screen), objects (such as data or pointers), and actions (such as find or erase) within the computer. For example, when low-ability students are taught to understand BASIC instructions (such as LET A = B + 1) in terms of the underlying activity within the computer (such as "find the number in space B, add 1 to that number, put the result in space A") they build more accurate mental models of the BASIC machine and are better able to solve novel programming problems than comparable students who are given conventional training (Bayman and Mayer 1988).

2. Learning Computer Programming

A second major issue concerns the cognitive consequences of learning to program. Does learning to program affect the way a student thinks? Soloway and Sleeman (1986 p. 1) noted that "some claim that programming is the new Latin of our times" so that "learning to program develops general intellectual skills that are needed in all endeavors." The search for transfer of programming skills to other domains has often yielded disappointing results (Linn 1985, Mayer 1988a, Pea and Kurland 1984). However, transfer has been achieved in some cases, especially when students successfully learned to solve programming problems, instruction emphasized the transferability of the learned programming skills, and the transfer tests were analogous to the programming problems (Clements 1990, Clements and Gullo 1984, De Corte et al. 1992, Mayer and Fay 1987, Mayer et al. 1986, Salomon and Perkins 1987).

Building on Linn's (1985) model of the "chain of cognitive accomplishments," Mayer and Fay (1987) proposed a "chain of cognitive changes" theory to account for the conditions under which learning to program will transfer to nonprogramming domains. The theory asserts that learning the fundamentals of a programming language is a prerequisite for learning to solve programming problems, and that learning to think about programming problems is a prerequisite for solving similar kinds of problems outside the domain of programming. For example, students who learned the underlying syntax and semantics of Logo showed a pretest to posttest improvement in their ability to generate and comprehend English-language instructions for how to navigate with a map, whereas students who did not show improvements in learning the syntax and semantics of Logo did not show signs of transfer (Mayer and Fay 1987). Similarly, students who were able to transfer from learning of BASIC to other domains showed gains on near transfer, such as comprehending English-language instructions, but not on far transfer, such as general reasoning (Mayer et al. 1986).

3. Expertise in Computer Programming

A third research issue concerns the knowledge required to become an expert computer programmer. A cognitive analysis revealed four kinds of programming knowledge: syntactic, semantic, schematic, and strategic (Mayer 1985, 1992). Syntactic knowledge is knowledge of the language units (such as keywords and variable names) and rules for combining language units (such as the legal placement of a line number on a line of code). Semantic knowledge refers to a person's mental model of how the computing system works. Schematic knowledge represents categories of program types (such as various routines for sorting or looping). Finally, strategic knowledge includes methods for devising and monitoring plans (such as breaking a programming task into meaningful parts).

What does an expert know about programming that a novice does not know? Expert and novice programmers differ in their syntactic, semantic, schematic, and strategic knowledge of computer programming (Mayer 1988b). Differences in syntactic knowledge have been investigated by asking students to judge whether or not a line of programming code is grammatically correct. Novices are slow and have to expend mental effort in order to recognize grammatically incorrect code; in contrast, experts make judgments rapidly and effortlessly, suggesting that they have automatized their recognition processes (Wiedenbeck 1985). Differences in semantic knowledge can be measured by asking students to describe what happens inside the computer when it carries out an instruction. The protocols of novices suggest the lack of useful mental models, whereas experts' protocols display the effective use of mental models of the computing system (Bayman and Mayer 1988). Differences in schematic knowledge have been evaluated by asking students to recall programs that are presented in normal or scrambled order. Experts and novices do not differ greatly in recall of scrambled programs, whereas experts perform much better than novices in recall of normal programs (McKeithen et al. 1981). Paralleling earlier research on expert–novice differences in memory for chess pieces on a chess board (De Groot 1965), expert programmers may possess a repertoire of typical combinations of statements that enable them to cluster the lines of a program into several meaningful chunks. Finally, expert–novice differences in strategic knowledge have been measured by asking students to think aloud as they solve programming problems. Experts tend to break a problem into finer parts than novices, are more likely to consider alternative ways to solve a programming problem than are novices, and engage in broader planning before beginning to write a program than do novices (Davies 1991, Soloway and Erhrlich 1984, Vessey 1985).

See also: Computers and Learning; Development of Learning Skills in Problem-solving and Thinking

References

Bayman P, Mayer R E 1988 Using conceptual models to teach BASIC computer programming. *J. Educ. Psychol.* 80(3):291–98

Becker H J 1991 How computers are used in United States schools: Basic data from the 1989 IEA computers in education survey. *J. Educ. Computing Res.* 7(4):385–406

Clements D H 1990 Metacomponential development in a Logo programming environment. *J. Educ. Psychol.* 82(1):141–[2u]49

Clements D H, Gullo D F 1984 Effects of computer programming on young children's cognition. *J. Educ. Psychol.* 76(6):1051–58

Davies S P 1991 Characterizing the program design activity: Neither strictly top-down nor globally opportunistic. *Behaviour & Information Technology* 10:173–90

De Corte E, Verschaffel L, Schrooten H 1992 Transfer of cognitive skills through powerful Logo-based teaching—learning environments. In: De Corte E, Linn M, Mandl H, Verschaffel L (eds.) 1992

De Groot A D 1965 *Thought and Choice in Chess*. Mouton, The Hague

Lehrer R, Littlefield J 1991 Misconceptions and errors in Logo: The role of instruction. *J. Educ. Psychol.* 83(1):124–33

Linn M C 1985 The cognitive consequences of programming instruction in classrooms. *Educ. Researcher* 14(5):14–16, 25–29

Mayer R E 1985 Learning in complex domains: A cognitive analysis of computer programming. In: Bower G (ed.) 1985 *The Psychology of Learning and Motivation*, Vol. 19. Academic Press, San Diego, California

Mayer R E (ed.) 1988a *Teaching and Learning Computer Programming: Multiple Research Perspectives*. Erlbaum, Hillsdale, New Jersey

Mayer R E 1988b From novice to expert. In: Helander M (ed.) 1988 *Handbook of Human–computer Interaction*. North-Holland, Amsterdam

Mayer R E 1992 Psychology of learning and teaching computer programming. In: De Corte E, Linn M, Mandl H, Verschaffel L (eds.) 1992

Mayer R E, Dyck J, Vilberg W 1986 Learning to program and learning to think: What's the connection? *Communications of the ACM 29(2): 605–10*

Mayer R E Fay A L 1987 A chain of cognitive changes with learning to program in Logo. *J. Educ. Psychol.* 79: 269–79

McKeithen K B, Reitman J S, Rueter H H, Hurtle S C 1981 Knowledge organization and skill differences in computer programmers. *Cognitive Psychol.* 13(3): 307–25

Nickerson R S, Perkins D N, Smith E E 1985 *The Teaching of Thinking*. Erlbaum, Hillsdale, New Jersey

Pea R D, Kurland D M 1984 On the cognitive effects of learning computer programming. *New Ideas in Psychology* 2 137–68

Pelgrum W J, Plomp T 1991 *The use of Computers Around the World: Results from the IEA "Computers in Education" Survey in 19 Educational Systems*. Pergamon Press, Oxford

Salomon G, Perkins D N 1987 Transfer of cognitive skills from programming: When and how? *J. Educ. Computing Res.* 3(2):149–69

Soloway E, Erhrlich K 1984 Empirical studies of programming knowledge. IEEE Transactions on Software Engineering 10(5):595–609

Soloway E, Sleeman D 1986 Introduction to special issue on novice programming. *J. Educ. Computing Res.* 2(1):1–3

Soloway E, Spohrer J C (eds.) 1989 *Studying the Novice Programmer*. Erlbaum, Hillsdale, New Jersey

van Merrienboer J J G 1990 Strategies for programming instruction in high school: Program completion vs. program generation. *J. Educ. Computing Res.* 6(3):265–85

Vessey I 1985 Expertise in debugging computer programs: A process analysis. *Int. J. Man–Machine Studies* 23(5):459–94

Wiedenbeck S 1985 Novice/expert differences in programming skills. *Int. J. Man–Machine Studies* 23(4):383–90

Further Reading

Carroll J M (ed.) 1987 *Interfacing Thought: Cognitive Aspects of Human–computer Interaction*. MIT Press, Cambridge, Massachusetts

De Corte E, Linn M, Mandl H, Verschaffel L (eds.) 1992 *Computer-based Learning Environments and Problem Solving*. Springer-Verlag, Berlin

Helander M (ed.) 1988 *Handbook of Human–computer Interaction*. Elsevier, Amsterdam

Mayer R E (ed.) 1988 *Teaching and Learning Computer Programming: Multiple Research Perspectives*. Erlbaum, Hillsdale, New Jersey

Instructional Design Theories

C. M. Reigeluth

Instructional design (ID) is concerned with discerning the methods of instruction that are most likely to work best for different situations. This entry will begin by exploring the idea of ID. Elaborations of the definition will include a description of the conditions–methods–outcomes nature of ID theories and contrasts between ID and learning theories, between prescriptive and descriptive theories, between pragmatic (or eclectic) and ideological views of instruction, between validity and superiority as criteria for judging ID theory, between general and detailed theories, and between ID theories and ID process models. The entry will then present a brief history of ID theories and project their future evolution to meet the needs of a post industrial, information-based society. Finally, there will be a discussion of trends and issues relating to the emergence of a new paradigm of instruction to meet the needs of the information-age society, including the need to develop prescriptions for the use of adaptive strategies, advanced technologies, constructivist strategies, minimalist instruction, affective learning, and systemic change.

Any attempt to understand education is enlightened by the recognition that education is a system; namely, that it is comprised of many interacting elements, and that the effects of each element are dependent to a great extent upon other elements of the system. Banathy (1991) has identified four levels of educational systems: (a) the learning-experience level; (b) the instructional system that implements those learning experiences; (c) the administrative system that supports the instructional system; and (d) the governance system that owns, rules, and funds the entire educational or training enterprise. Separate fields have arisen for each level, including learning theory, instructional and curriculum and counseling theories, administrative studies, and policy studies, respectively. Interdisciplinary linkages are woefully deficient in most cases. This entry will focus on the instructional level of educational systems.

Within the instructional level, there are many theoretical approaches, each oriented around a different type of decision-oriented activity. Curriculum theory and theories of front-end analysis inform decisions about what to teach. Instructional design theory addresses decisions about how to teach it. Instructional mediation (or instructional development) theory is concerned with how to take the designs (or blueprints) for the instruction and make them a reality on the most appropriate media. There are also theories for instructional evaluation, dissemination/implementation/change, and management. This entry only addresses instructional design theory.

1. Characteristics of ID Theories

An ID theory is a set of guidelines that indicate what methods of instruction are most likely to work best for different situations. Just as a carpenter uses different tools for different situations, so a person who creates instruction must use different tools to facilitate learning under different situations. ID theory is accumulated knowledge about which methods work best for which situations.

1.1 Conditions–Methods–Outcomes

It is helpful to think of two aspects of the teaching "situation" that will influence which methods will work best: desired instructional outcomes and instructional conditions. Desired instructional outcomes include the effectiveness of the instruction (which is based on learning outcomes), the efficiency of the

instruction (as indicated by learning time and/or cost of the instruction), and the appeal of the instruction (the extent to which the learner enjoys it).

Instructional conditions include some aspects of the learner (such as relevant prior knowledge, ability, motivation, and learning styles), some aspects of what is to be learned (such as whether it requires application, understanding, or simple memorization), some aspects of the learning environment (such as instructional resource and time constraints), and even some aspects of the instructional development process (such as development resource and time constraints).

Of course, different aspects of an instructional situation will influence how well different kinds of methods, or "tools," will work. Hence the basic form of instructional theory is "if–then" statements—often called "prescriptions" or "guidelines"—in which a method appears in the "then" part and relevant aspects of a situation appear in the "if" part of the statement. If a prescription is very narrow, prescribing a single method variable, it is usually called a "principle of instruction." A theory is much broader in scope: an integrated set of method variables—a package deal—is prescribed, rather than just a single method variable.

A few additional distinctions will assist in clarifying what ID theory includes and excludes.

1.2 Instruction versus Learning

ID theory is different from, but related to, learning theory. ID theory focuses on methods of instruction and facilitation—what the teacher or other learning resource does—whereas learning theory focuses on the learning process—what happens inside the learner.

1.3 Prescriptive versus Descriptive

Simon (1969) has distinguished between the natural sciences, which are descriptive, and the design sciences (or sciences of the artificial), which are prescriptive. The natural and design sciences are usually closely related, as in the case of biology and medicine, physics and engineering, and learning and instruction. Banathy (1991) made the same distinction under the rubrics of conclusion-oriented and decision-oriented disciplines.

ID theory, as a design science, is prescriptive, or decision-oriented, but it is closely related to learning theory. There is a common misconception that descriptive theory must precede prescriptive theory—that learning theory must precede ID theory. In reality, throughout the history of science, from the steam engine to superconductivity, the prescriptive has often preceded the descriptive. Someone has discovered that a certain technique (or tool or method) works; others then set about trying to determine why. Although this has often been true with ID theory, it is also true that instructional tools have been invented and prescriptions have been developed based on a new learning theory.

1.4 Pragmatic (Eclectic) versus Ideological

It seems fair to say that all descriptive theories contribute something useful, no matter how inadequate they may be overall. As Snelbecker (1987) has pointed out, descriptive theorists strive for theoretical purity, adopt a single perspective or view of the world, and put their theories up to compete against other theories. Their primary concern is whether their theory is ideologically pure and conceptually consistent.

But practitioners need to address all aspects of a problem and multiple kinds of problems. Their primary concern is how well a prescriptive theory attains their practical goals. Therefore, they need multiple perspectives, and frequently develop solutions that are based on, or can be explained by, several different descriptive theories. Therefore, prescriptive theorists tend to take a pragmatic view that integrates useful contributions from a variety of theoretical perspectives.

1.5 Validity versus Superiority

For descriptive theories, the major scientific concern is validity—how well they describe reality. But for prescriptive theories, since they are goal-oriented, the major scientific concern is superiority (or optimality) —how well they attain the goal. There are usually many ways to attain a single goal, but some are better than others. The goal of prescriptive theory is not to find out if a given method works; it is not just to identify a method that "satisfices," but to identify the method that is better than the other known alternatives for each set of conditions. Of course, the efficiency (based on time and/or money) and appeal of a method are important criteria, as well as its effectiveness. The goal of prescriptive theory is also to improve the best available methods continually. This is significant, because it requires a completely different paradigm of research than does descriptive theory—a paradigm that is coming to be called "formative research" (Newman 1990, Reigeluth 1989).

1.6 Level of Detail or Generality

Prescriptive theories, like descriptive theories, can be very detailed, very general, or anywhere between. The more general an ID theory is, the broader it will be (i.e., the more situations in which it will apply), but the guidance it will provide to an instructional designer will be reduced. For example, "To improve learning and motivation, have the learner actively engaged," applies to almost all instructional situations, but it provides little guidance to a designer or teacher as to exactly what the instruction should be like for their particular situation. More guidance makes the designer's work easier and quicker, but it also takes more time and effort for the designer to learn initially.

If a designer does not have formal training in instructional theory, he or she will invent their own, but it may differ considerably from the accumulated experience of researchers and practitioners as represented by the current knowledge base of prescriptive theory.

1.7 Product versus Process

Finally, it is helpful to consider the distinction between ends and means, or product and process. ID theory is that knowledge base that deals with the ends or products (using that term loosely)—what the instruction should be like (after it has been designed). Instructional development models, on the other hand, deal with the means or process—what an instructional designer should do to plan and create the "products." Typical development models specify activities for a developer to perform to analyze (needs, tasks, content, learners, and more), design, produce, evaluate, implement, and manage an instructional system or "product." ID theories specify instructional methods for a teacher (or other learning resource) to use to help a learner learn. This is a very important, yet often overlooked, distinction.

For a concise description of some modern ID theories see Reigeluth (1983), in which eight theorists describe their respective ID theories. In another volume (Reigeluth (1987) the same theorists illustrate their theories through a sample lesson.

2. History of ID Theories

Like most fields, ID theory began by investigating general instructional variables, such as expository vs. discovery, lecture vs. discussion, and media-based vs. traditional methods. It was soon realized that two discovery methods could differ more from each other than do a discovery and an expository method. The field then gradually entered an analysis phase in its development (which began to gain visibility in the late 1950s with B F Skinner's work). The research objective was to break a method down into elementary components and discover which ones made a difference. Instructional researchers then proceeded to build a considerable knowledge base of validated prescriptions, primarily for the simpler types of learning, for which the behaviorist paradigm was fairly adequate.

Researchers have since found that the effects of each component are often influenced considerably by which other components happen to be present in the instruction. Furthermore, researchers have realized that practitioners need to think holistically; in other words, they need to identify the best *combination* of method components for a given situation. Hence, the field entered into a synthesis phase, which began to gain visibility in the 1980s with the publication of Reigeluth's (1983) edited volume *Instructional Design Theories and Models*, in which the focus is on building components into optimal models of instruction for different situations. The research objective is to improve a given model or theory.

Industrial age	Information age
Adversarial relationships	Cooperative relationships
Bureaucratic organization	Team organization
Autocratic leadership	Shared leadership
Centralized control	Autonomy with accountability
Autocracy	Democracy
Representative democracy	Participative democracy
Compliance	Initiative
One-way communications	Networking
Compartmentalization (division of labor)	Holism (integration of tasks)

Aside from this developmental process that most fields and disciplines seem to go through, another historical trend has strongly influenced the development of ID theories: the ongoing transformation from the industrial age to the global information age. Certain general characteristics prevailed during the industrial age that are giving way to new characteristics in the information age (Reigeluth 1992a). Some of those changes have particularly important implications for a new paradigm of education (see Table 1).

Perelman (1987) documented many characteristics of the current paradigm systems of education. In the United States and many other industrialized countries, consolidated districts are highly bureaucratic, centrally controlled autocracies in which students receive little preparation for participating in a democratic society. They frequently exhibit adversarial relationships, not only between teachers and administrators but also between teachers and students, and even between teachers and parents. Leadership is vested in individuals according to a hierarchical management structure, and all those lower in the hierarchy are expected to obey those above. Learning is highly compartmentalized into subject areas. Students are often treated as if they are all the same and are all expected to do the same things at the same time. They are also usually forced to be passive learners and passive members of their school community. These characteristics are all incompatible with society's needs in the emerging information age, and changes in this paradigm are beginning to emerge. Those changes will have very important implications for ID theory.

3. Emergent Trends and Issues

Most current ID theories were developed for the industrial-age paradigm of education and training. Just as mass production in business is giving way to customized production (Reich 1991) and mass marketing is giving way to targeted marketing (Toffler 1991), so mass teaching is giving way to personalized teaching. These changes in all of these sectors (and others) are made possible by information technology. Every year teachers are acquiring more and more powerful tools with which to facilitate learning. Those tools require the use of new instructional methods to take full advantage of their expanded capabilities. Hence, ID theories must offer guidance for the use of such new instructional methods. These information-age ID theories are likely to incorporate prescriptions for the use of adaptive strategies, advanced technologies, constructivist strategies, minimalist instruction, and systemic change, to name but a few of the emerging ideas. Each of these will be briefly described.

3.1 Adaptive Strategies

Whereas conformity was one of the general characteristics of the industrial age, diversity is emerging as a hallmark of the information age. Different students increasingly have very different learning needs, interests, goals, abilities, prior knowledge, and so forth. It is therefore increasingly important to adapt instruction —both content and methods—to each learner's needs and interests. Advanced technologies are gradually providing more powerful and cost-effective means for such adaptations.

3.2 Advanced Technologies

There are two important ways in which advanced technologies are influencing the future development of ID theories: through their use as tutors and tools for learners and their use as tools for instructional designers.

As tutors new technologies offer new capabilities that require new instructional strategies to take appropriate advantage of them. Dynamic media require guidelines as to when and how to use motion in instruction. Interactive media require prescriptions as to what kinds of learner activities to elicit when, and when and how to respond to each kind of learner activity. Massive memory storage capabilities require guidelines as to when and how to utilize them best in instruction. Hypertext and hypermedia require guidelines as to when and how their unique capabilities can best be utilized to facilitate learning. Multimedia, expert systems, artificial intelligence, computer-based simulations, and virtual reality represent but a few of the additional technologies for which guidelines are sorely needed. The increasingly more powerful and cost-effective capabilities of these advanced technologies all require guidelines as to when and how best to use them to facilitate learning.

3.3 Constructivist Strategies

Constructivism offers some practical instructional strategies that have much to contribute to the new paradigm of education for the information age. Some of its strategies are fairly uniformly applicable to most kinds of learning, but others are only applicable to higher-level learning in ill-structured domains.

At the heart of constructivism is the belief that each learner must construct his or her own knowledge and therefore that instruction must create an active role for the learner (see, e.g., Brown et al. 1989, Perkins 1992). It also prescribes that learning should be situated in authentic activities. Slightly less broadly applicable is the prescription that instruction should facilitate the construction of meaning, or sense making. This is accomplished primarily through such strategies as learning in context, modeling, and coaching, but it is not appropriate for all learning situations.

Perhaps the most valuable contributions of constructivism are considerably less broadly applicable: those for facilitating higher-level learning in ill-structured domains. Some useful instructional strategies include: generative tasks, learner exploration, analogical transfer, and the fostering of multiple perspectives.

3.4 Minimalist Instruction

Carroll (1990) has developed the idea of "minimalist instruction" for teaching people "what they need to learn in order to do what they wish to do" (p. 3). It is similar to the notions of just-in-time training and on-line help systems. At its heart is the idea of not teaching people things that they do not yet have to know. This seems most appropriate for training situations, such as training people to use desktop computer systems, where it is relatively easy to determine what one needs to learn at a given point in time. Another important aspect of minimalist instruction is "to design instruction to suit the learning strategies people spontaneously adopt" (p. 3) and the relevant knowledge they have already acquired. Both of these require that the instruction be highly adaptive, and utilize advanced technology and some constructivist strategies.

Specific instructional prescriptions include the following. First, all instruction should occur with real tasks that are meaningful to the learner, so that the learner is motivated. Second, the "training wheels" approach should be used so as to pick a version of the meaningful task that is simple enough not to overwhelm the beginner. For example, a real word-processing task might be selected that requires the use of only a small subset of the capabilities of the system. This is similar to the Elaboration Theory's "simplifying conditions method" approach to sequencing (Reigeluth 1992b). Some artificial simplifying conditions can also be instituted, such as disabling certain functions of the system, so that the learner cannot yet make certain types of errors. As the learner progresses, the meaningful tasks become gradually more complex until the learner has mastered all that he or she needs to learn.

Third, the learner should be helped to understand meaningfully what he or she is doing. Reasoning is very important for this process, and the learner's prior knowledge must be diagnosed and utilized. Fourth, reading materials and other passive activities should be reduced to a minimum, and largely replaced with discovery activities. The reading materials should be designed for random access and to be read in any order, and they should have strong linkages to different parts of the real, meaningful task. Fifth, emphasis should be placed on helping the learner to recognize and recover from errors so that errors become triggers for positive learning experiences.

3.5 Affective Learning

The affective domain (Krathwohl et al. 1964) has received relatively little attention from instructional theorists, but it is emerging as an important area of human development for the information age. Martin and Briggs (1986) conducted a comprehensive review of ID theories in this domain, and identified three major dimensions that appear to require different models of instruction: attitudes and values, morals and ethics, and self-development. They also identified a variety of other dimensions of the affective domain: emotional development and feelings, interest and motivation, social development and group dynamics, and attributions. The most advanced ID theories are in the dimension of attitudes and values and include the Yale Communication and Attitude Change Program, Dissonance Theory, Cognitive Balancing Theory, Social Judgment Theory, and Social Learning Theory (see Martin and Briggs 1986 for a summary).

One of the most promising new developments in this domain is an ID theory for attitudes being developed by Kamradt and Kamradt (in press). Based on the notion that attitudes have a tripartite composition of feelings, cognitions, and behaviors, they have developed a set of guidelines for systemically influencing all three through a systematic process that moves the learner just outside of his or her comfort zone one step at a time in the direction of the desired attitude. First, role-playing is used to force a new behavior more consistent with the target attitude. This creates a dissonance or discomfort which serves as a trigger event

719

to influence the cognitive element through discussion and persuasion. Finally, reinforcement techniques are used to change the feelings associated with the new behavior and new thinking. After this small shift in attitude has been consolidated, the learner is ready for another round of this three-part strategy. Ethical issues are particularly important in the affective domain, and the Kamradts advocate that no attempts be made to change a learner's attitude without the knowledge and consent of the learner.

3.6 Systemic Change

It seems highly likely, given the different educational needs of the information age, that ID theories will adapt to meet the needs of a new paradigm of education and training, and that those changes will incorporate the use of adaptive strategies, advanced technologies, constructivist strategies, and minimalist instruction. However, this new paradigm of instruction will be of little value if the larger system within which it is embedded remains rooted in the industrial age. Referring back to Banathy's (1991) four levels of educational (and training) systems (learning-experience, instructional, administrative, and governance), this entry has focused on theory for prescribing the instructional system that will support a new paradigm of learning to meet the radically different education and training needs and conditions of the emerging information society. But unless a compatible paradigm shift is also effected at the administrative and governance levels, the new instructional paradigm will be ineffective and short-lived. Instructional designers and ID theorists alike must begin to view themselves as concerned with educational systems design—spanning all four levels of the system—not just with instructional systems design—focusing on just one of those levels. (For further information, see, e.g., Reigeluth and Garfinkle 1992.)

4. Conclusion

ID theory is still a relatively young field. Much remains to be learned about how to facilitate learning, especially more complex kinds of learning in ill-defined domains (including thinking skills) and the affective domain (including attitudes and values). In addition, massive changes in society are forcing the development of a new paradigm in ID theory for even the least complex kinds of learning. The need for more adaptive instruction, combined with the development of far more powerful technological tools for learning, have created entirely new horizons for ID theory.

See also: Individual Differences, Learning, and Instruction

References

Banathy B H 1991 *Systems Design of Education*. Educational Technology Publications, Englewood Cliffs, New Jersey

Brown J S, Collins A, Duguid P 1989 Situated cognition and the culture of learning. *Educ. Researcher* 18(1): 32–42

Carroll J M 1990 *The Nürnberg Funnel: Designing Minimalist Instruction for Practical Computer Skill*. MIT Press, Cambridge, Massachusetts

Kamradt E M, Kamradt T F in press A systematic approach for attitude development. *Educ. Technol.*

Krathwohl D R, Bloom B S, Masia B B 1964 *Taxonomy of Educational Objectives: The Classification of Educational Goals. Handbook II: Affective Domain*. McKay, New York

Martin B L, Briggs L J 1986 *The Affective and Cognitive Domains: Integration for Instruction and Research*. Educational Technology Publications, Englewood Cliffs, New Jersey

Newman D 1990 Opportunities for research on the organizational impact of school computers. *Educ. Researcher* 19(3): 8–13

Perelman L J 1987 *Technology and Transformation of Schools*. National School Boards Association, Alexandria, Virginia

Perkins D N 1992 Technology meets constructivism: Do they make a marriage? In: Duffy T M, Jonassen D H (eds.) 1992 *Constructivism and the Technology of Instruction*. Erlbaum, Hillsdale, New Jersey

Reich R B 1991 *The Work of Nations*. Knopf, New York

Reigeluth C M (ed.) 1983 *Instructional-Design Theories and Models: An Overview of their Current Status*. Erlbaum, Hillsdale, New Jersey

Reigeluth C M (ed.) 1987 *Instructional Strategies in Action: Lessons Illustrating Selected Theories and Models*. Erlbaum, Hillsdale, New Jersey

Reigeluth C M 1989 Educational technology at the crossroads: New mindsets and new directions. *Educ. Tech. Res. Dev.* 37(1): 67–80

Reigeluth C M 1992a The imperative for systemic change. *Educ. Technol.* 32(11): 9–13

Reigeluth C M 1992b Elaborating the elaboration theory. *Educ. Tech. Res. Dev.* 40(3): 80–86

Reigeluth C M, Garfinkle R J (eds.) 1992 Systemic change in education (special issue). *Educ. Technol.* 32(11)

Simon H A 1969 *The Sciences of the Artificial*. MIT Press, Cambridge, Massachusetts

Snelbecker G E 1987 Contrasting and complementary approaches to instructional design. In: Reigeluth C M (ed.) 1987

Toffler A 1991 *Power Shift*. Bantam Books, New York

Further Reading

Bloom B S (ed.) 1956 *Taxonomy of Educational Objectives: The Classification of Educational goals. Handbook I: Cognitive Domain*. McKay, New York

Gagné R M, Briggs L J, Wager W W 1988 *Principles of Instructional Design*, 3rd edn. Holt, Rinehart, and Winston, New York

Skinner B F 1965 Reflections on a decade of teaching machines. In: Glaser R (ed.) 1965 *Teaching Machines and Programmed Learning, II*. National Education Association, Washington, DC

Instructional Psychology

J. Lowyck and J. Elen

This entry provides a discussion of the relationship between instructional psychology and instructional design. Instructional design can be conceived as a field of study or as an activity. Authors approaching instructional design as a field of study strive for the scientific foundation of instructional design decisions and show a privileged relationship with instructional psychology. Advocates of instructional design as an activity systematically describe the sequence of activities that instructional designers engage in. They are strongly influenced by the systems theory (Reigeluth 1983), although in the light of empirical research the focus is on "psychological" rather than on "logical" design processes.

The contribution of instructional psychology to instructional design is most apparent in the case of a field of study aiming at the translation of descriptive research findings into valid prescriptions for regular instructional settings (Lowyck and Elen 1993).

In the first section, the complex relationship between instructional psychology and instructional design is explored. It is argued that this relationship is a problematic one due to both the emergence of cognitive views on learning and instruction, and the lasting problem of the transition between description and prescription. In the second section different contributions of instructional psychology to instructional design are reviewed. Changes that occurred to design parameters and design procedures as well as the revised conceptualization of the design process will be briefly reviewed.

1. Relationship between Instructional Psychology and Instructional Design

Instructional design has been conceptualized above as a field of study focusing on instructional design decision-making. Instructional design, then, can be described as an applied field of study aiming at the application of descriptive research outcomes in regular instructional settings. This view presupposes a strong relationship of instructional design to descriptive disciplines. Instructional psychology is certainly most influential, as it provides insight into variables that affect learning and gives indications of the effectiveness of instructional interventions. The simple fact that this type of relationship is generally accepted, however, does not imply that it is a direct or an unproblematic one (Bonner 1988). Indeed, evolutions in the conceptualization of learning in instructional psychology, as well as the transition from description to prescription, continue to cause problems.

1.1 From Behaviorism to Constructivism

The relationship between instructional psychology and instructional design has been strongly influenced by the shift in instructional psychology from a behaviorist to a cognitive view of learning.

Instructional design as a field of study emerged during the heyday of behaviorism in psychology. Research on learning was equally research on instruction, given the focus of behaviorists on the influence of external interventions on learning and the overall neglect of mental activities engaged in by the learners themselves. Behaviorists looked for clear-cut ways to ensure effective learning. In this respect they elaborated a systematic and easily applied framework (see Skinner 1968). From this framework, which strongly limited the complexity of learning and instruction, instructional designers could readily derive a number of prescriptions that stressed the importance of information delivery and control activities executed by instructional agents. Instruction was perceived as a set of communications to the learner in order to guarantee that learning would occur. In line with this conceptualization, it was prescribed that objectives were to be formulated in terms of observable (re-)actions, information was to be split up into small units, responses of learners solicited, and direct feedback provided.

This apparently rational approach to learning and instruction was heavily criticized by those with a more cognitive orientation. The occurrence of a cognitive shift in instructional psychology seems to have broken the strong link between this discipline and instructional design. Various reasons are advanced to account for this "divorce." First, as Glaser (1991) contends, the cognitive shift originated a more detailed analysis of the processes involved in competent performance. Far less research attention has been devoted to the processes involved in the transition from one stage of expertise to another. This means that, whereas much is known about the complex processes and mental activities of experts in a great variety of performances, knowledge on learning processes and the conditions that may foster them has hardly increased though such knowledge is highly valuable to instructional design.

Second, the cognitive shift in instructional psychology resulted in a reduction in attention to instructional interventions. The emphasis was on the activities of and processes engaged in by the learners, rather than on ways to enhance and/or optimize them. Moreover, cognitive research on instructional interventions has revealed their problematic nature by pointing to the importance of the interpretation by learners. The cognitive mediational paradigm (Shulman 1986) implies that the effects of instructional interventions mainly depend on the function attributed to them by the learners.

Third, different types of questions are asked by cognitive-oriented instructional psychologists and instructional designers. Bonner (1988) revealed that whereas the former primarily aim at exploring and explaining phenomena, the latter look for possibilities of intervention and control.

The relationship, then, evolved in two different directions. On the one hand, efforts are invested in building and describing so-called "powerful learning environments." This "constructivist" approach aims at the development of mediated and/or computerized learning environments by taking into account learning as a task or performance. It may be expected that these initiatives from a "moderate" constructivist point of view will lead to an elaborate theory of learning in instructional settings which also specifies the conditions that foster learning and, hence, to a renewed relationship between instructional psychology and instructional design. On the other hand, "radical" constructivists argue in favor of the unpredictability of learning outcomes, stress the negative effects of prespecified instructional interventions, and claim that the only tools needed are those that enable learners to decide for themselves when, what, and how they learn (Bednar et al. 1991). Such a conception widens the gulf between instructional psychology and instructional design, since it questions both the value and the validity of any systematic set of rules for defining instructional interventions and, in the end, it rejects any contribution of instruction to learning (Streibel 1991).

1.2 From Description to Prescription

An additional and more fundamental problem of the relationship between instructional psychology and instructional design pertains to a different orientation and, more precisely, to the gap between description and prescription. Whereas instructional psychology aims at revealing and explaining learning in instructional settings, together with the conditions that foster it, instructional design focuses on specifying the adequacy of instructional interventions for the attainment of prespecified learning goals. Instructional psychology, then, can be said to be explanatory-oriented and descriptive, whereas instructional design is intervention-oriented and prescriptive. Though instructional psychology is to be regarded as important for instructional design, it cannot be equated with it. Instructional design as a "technological" field aims precisely at bridging the gap between description and prescription.

In its most general form this problem has been discussed as referring to the tension between theory and practice and as it relates to the call for a "linking science." Various proposals have been formulated as to how best to bring theory and practice, or instructional

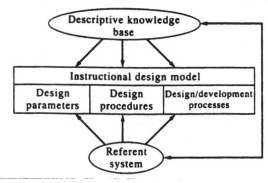

Figure 1
Components of instructional design models

psychology and instructional design, closer together. A first series of proposals pertains to raising the relevance of research questions by the involvement of practitioners in the selection and execution of research projects (Huberman 1990). Within the same realm are calls for an increased communication and dissemination of research outcomes. All these efforts, however, have not resulted in the gap between theory and practice being bridged, but merely in them being brought closer together (De Corte 1991).

In response to this criticism, the need for more prescriptive research has been stressed (Clark 1989). This type of research builds on established descriptive research outcomes and investigates questions with high relevance to practice in order to derive prescriptive rules that may underscore instructional design decision-making.

2. Contributions of Instructional Psychology to Instructional Design

It has been indicated that two major problems threaten the relationship between instructional psychology and instructional design: the cognitive view which has not yet resulted in well-elaborated theories on learning and instruction, and the unsolved problem of the gap between description and prescription. In spite of these problems it should be acknowledged that: (a) implications of the cognitive view on learning and instruction have attracted considerable attention from instructional design researchers, and (b) in many publications on instructional design a cognitive view is (said to be) taken (e.g., Gagné et al. 1988, Tennyson and Rasch 1988).

Elaborated instructional design models consist of two sets of components (Fig. 1). The first two components, the descriptive knowledge base and referent system, determine the content of the models. The last three—design parameters, design procedures, and design processes—specify the content. In this section an overview is provided of the current state-of-the-art of the contributions of instructional psychology to instructional design models. Instructional psychology constitutes one discipline as a part of the descriptive knowledge base of instructional design models. It must be stressed that, though generally very eclectic, the disciplines of the knowledge base hold a cognitive orientation. As to the referent system, no specification is provided in this entry for two reasons: (a) the aim is to provide a global overview and not the particular details of a model, and (b) generally speaking, instructional design models hardly specify their referent system, preferring to claim a broad applicability.

2.1 Design Parameters

Design parameters specify variables of two kinds to be considered in the elaboration of rules for instructional design decision-making. Learner-related parameters are learner characteristics that are important for learning, and instruction-related parameters are elements in the instructional environment that can be changed with respect to learning.

As already indicated, the cognitive shift in instructional psychology resulted in an increased attention being given to processes engaged in and activities executed by learners while fulfilling a particular task. In this respect, many learner-related parameters that affect learners' task performances are identified in the instructional design literature. Motivation (fluid and crystallized, intrinsic and extrinsic), prior knowledge (quality and quantity, declarative, conditional and procedural, misconceptions, factual, conceptual), metacognition (knowledge, skills, self-regulation, monitoring), cognitive and learning skills, and learning conceptions are some of the variables considered. Consequently, instructional psychology has made instructional design more aware of the importance of learner characteristics (Winn 1990).

With regard to instruction-related parameters, instructional psychology has contributed to a drastic change of instructional functions. Instruction is no longer perceived as a mere set of communications to learners in order to guarantee learning, but as an endeavor for enabling and supporting learners in their efforts to learn. In line with this evolution, it is recognized that different types of goals can be distinguished which not only require learners to engage in different activities, but also enhance different kinds of instructional interventions. The focus is on meaningful learning rather than on rote learning, and on problem-solving and learning to learn. Case and Bereiter (1984) in their discussion of the implications of the cognitive shift for instructional design, specified that the major contribution made, especially by Gagné, pertained to the reconceptualization of the "what" rather than of the "how." Far fewer contributions have been made to the instruction-related parameters since no scheme has emerged that clearly identifies important instructional variables and their interrelationships that may enable, support, and foster learning. The literature only provides lists of aspects that could be important

from a limited number of perspectives. Consequently, it is difficult to categorize specific instructional interventions and to synthesize the literature on the effectiveness of such interventions. In this respect one exception may be mentioned. In their influential article on cognitive apprenticeship, Collins et al. (1989) provided a tentative categorization of both learner-related and instruction-related parameters.

The contributions of instructional psychology to instructional design can be summarized by referring to the "cognitive mediational paradigm" (Shulman 1986). In the early 1990s it is accepted, even in the instructional design literature, that the learner is the first person responsible for his or her learning and instructional interventions are only effective if they are adequately interpreted by the learner.

2.2 Design Procedures

Design procedures are of two kinds. First, they enable a thorough diagnosis of elements of the instructional situation (learner- and instruction-related parameters) so as to prepare instructional design decision-making. The outcomes of such procedures are data which enable design decisions to be made on a sound basis. Second, a number of rules are intervention-oriented. These rules specify the relationships between learner-related and instruction-related parameters and, hence, reveal in which situations (given a particular configuration of learner characteristics and features of the instructional situation) specific instructional interventions or approaches seem adequate.

Instructional psychology has influenced diagnostic and intervention rules. With regard to the first kind, instructional psychology contributed to the development of methods for the analysis of instructional aspects and learner-related variables. For instance, concerning task analysis, it has been stressed that, in addition to an analysis of the content of a task, cognitive processes and activities of learners in order to execute the task and to learn it have to be identified (Gagné et al. 1988, Gardner 1985, Resnick 1983). The increased attention to learner characteristics in instructional psychology resulted in the development of many instruments for measurement. The usefulness of some of these instruments for instructional design has been suggested. An example is the Inventory Learning Style (Vermunt 1992) which makes it possible to diagnose cognitive and metacognitive skills as well as learning motivations and conceptions.

Far less advance has been made with regard to intervention-oriented rules. Nevertheless, instructional psychology has contributed by indicating the diversity of learning goals that can be aimed at. Moreover, research on the effects of instructional interventions within the cognitive mediational paradigm, increased the awareness that, in order to adequately support learners, not only the amount but also the quality of the interventions need elaboration in view of learners with different characteristics and a variety of learning goals (Bovy 1981).

In addition to these contributions, instructional psychology—especially endeavors to develop "powerful learning environments"—resulted in the formulation of "design principles." While these principles are mainly descriptions of features of the constructed environments, their validation may in the long run become more formalized and, hence, take the form of intervention rules. Examples of such design principles have been provided by the Cognition and Technology Group at Vanderbilt University (1990) in their "anchored instruction," in which the characteristics of learning and learner variables are more deliberately considered.

2.3 Design Process

Andrews and Goodson (1980) clearly illustrated that most instructional design models are fairly similar as far as the steps or activities embedded in the design process are concerned. These steps and activities result from a rational analysis of what designing as an activity involves. Cognitive instructional psychological research, however, questions the validity of a mere rational design process. Regarding designing as a problem-solving activity, it has been found that designing is not a well-structured but an ill-structured problem (Rowland 1990). Solving ill-structured problems involves a cyclical process and continuous reconceptualization of the problem by taking different perspectives into account.

While more is known about how in reality instruction is designed, this increased knowledge has not yet given rise to a fundamental reconceptualization of the design process in instructional design models. In other words, the gap between description and prescription remains even when instructional design is regarded as an activity.

3. Conclusion

It has been shown that instructional psychology has contributed to instructional design mainly by providing insight into the parameters to be considered and contributing to a reconceptualization of the function of instruction. However, the relationship between instructional psychology and instructional design is rather loose as a consequence of the specific conceptualization of learning and the current research focus in instructional psychology on the one hand, and the difficulties related to the transition from description to prescription on the other. Design principles are worked out, environments are created, and designers' activities are identified. Nevertheless, there are no rules that identify more precisely the conditions under which a particular type of instructional intervention should be selected, and the implications of research in instructional psychology remain vague. A greater focus in instructional psychology on the construction of theories of learning and instruction and increased investments in prescriptive research may help to re-establish a strong link between instructional psychology and instructional design. Instructional design may, then, become a linking science that values the descriptive findings of instructional psychological research and contributes to its development by instrumenting and validating these outcomes in regular settings.

References

Andrews D H, Goodson L A 1980 A comparative analysis of models of instructional design. *J. Instr. Dev.* 3(4): 2–16
Bednar A K, Cunningham D, Duffy T M, Perry J D 1991 Theory into practice. How do we link? In: Anglin G J (ed.) 1991 *Instructional Technology: Past, Present, and Future*. Libraries Unlimited, Englewood, Colorado
Bonner J 1988 Implications of cognitive theory for instructional design: Revisited. *Educ. Comm. & Tech. J.* 36(1): 3–14
Bovy R C 1981 Successful instructional methods: A cognitive information processing approach. *Educ. Comm. & Tech. J.* 29(4): 203–17
Case R, Bereiter C 1984 From behaviorism to cognitive behaviorism to cognitive development: Steps in the evolution of instructional design. *Instructional Science* 13(2): 141–58
Clark R E 1989 Current progress and future directions for research in instructional technology. *Educ. Tech. Res. Dev.* 37(1): 57–66
Cognition and Technology Group at Vanderbilt 1990 Anchored instruction and its relationship to situated cognition. *Educ. Researcher* 19(6): 2–10
Collins A, Brown S J, Newman S E 1989 Cognitive apprenticeship: Teaching the craft of reading, writing, and mathematics. In: Resnick L B (ed.) 1989 *Knowing, Learning, and Instruction. Essays in Honor of Robert Glaser*. Erlbaum, Hillsdale, New Jersey
De Corte E 1991 Bridging the gap between research and educational practice: The case of mathematics. Paper presented at the Fourth European Conference for Research on Learning and Instruction, Turku, Finland. KU Leuven, Leuven
Gagné R M, Briggs L J, Wager W W 1988. *Principles of Instructional Design*, 3rd edn. Holt, Rinehart and Winston, New York
Gardner M K 1985 Cognitive psychological approaches to instructional task analysis. *Rev. Res. Educ.* 12: 157–95
Glaser R 1991 The maturing of the relationship between the science of learning and cognition and educational practice. *Learning and Instruction* 1(2): 129–44
Huberman M 1990 Linkage between researchers and practitioners: A qualitative study. *Am. Educ. Res. J.* 27(2): 363–91
Lowyck J, Elen J 1993 Transitions in the theoretical foundations of constructional design. In: Duffy T M, Lowyck J, Jonassen D H (eds.) 1993 *Designing Environments for Constructive Learning*. Springer-Verlag, Berlin
Reigeluth C M 1983 Instructional design. What is it and why is it? In: Reigeluth C M (ed.) 1983 *Instructional-design Theories and Models: An Overview of their Current Status*. Erlbaum, Hillsdale, New Jersey
Resnick L B 1983 Toward a cognitive theory of instruction.

In: Paris S G, Olson G M, Stevenson H W (eds.) 1983 *Learning and Motivation in the Classroom*. Erlbaum, Hillsdale, New Jersey

Rowland G 1990 *Problem-solving in Instructional Design*. Indiana University, Bloomington, Indiana

Shulman L 1986 Paradigms and research programs in the study of teaching: A contemporary perspective. In: Wittrock M C (ed.) 1986 *Handbook of Research on Teaching*, 3rd edn. Macmillan, New York

Skinner B F 1968 *The Technology of Teaching*. Appleton-Century-Crofts, New York

Streibel M J 1991 Instructional plans and situated learning. The challenge of Suchman's theory of situated action

for instructional designers and instructional systems. In: Anglin G J (ed.) 1991 *Instructional Technology: Past, Present, and Future*. Libraries Unlimited, Englewood, Colorado

Tennyson R D, Rasch M 1988 Linking cognitive learning theory to instructional prescriptions. *Instructional Science* 17(4): 369–85

Vermunt J D H M 1992 *Leerstijlen en sturen van leerprocessen in het hoger onderwijs. Naar procesgerichte instructie in zelfstandig denken*. Swets and Zeitlinger, Lisse

Winn W D 1990 Some implications of cognitive theory for instructional design. *Instructional Science* 19(1): 53–69

Media and Learning

R. E. Clark

The development of media to support learning is the subject of considerable research attention and of widespread interest to publics and governments. The conditions under which media can be made to influence learning optimally are being explored from at least five perspectives: (a) media as technology or machines, (b) media as tutors or teachers, (c) media as socializing agents, (d) media as motivators for learning, and (e) media as mental tools for thinking and problem-solving. A key point that distinguishes these five areas from one another are five different definitions of media. This entry attempts to provide the most representative definition of media and the results of research in each of the five areas.

1. Media as Technology and Machines

Until the 1980s it was common for educational researchers to define a medium as its technology, that is: "the mechanical and electronic aspects that determine its function and, to some extent, its shape and other physical features. These are the characteristics that are commonly used to classify a medium such as a television, a radio, and so on" (Kozma 1991 p. 180). For many decades, researchers used this technocratic definition to study whether one medium produced more learning than another medium, or whether one medium was better than another for certain curriculum content or types of students. These studies were generally not guided by any theoretical explanation for why it should be expected that the technology of one medium should produce more learning than the technology of another.

During the 1980s it became obvious after many hundreds of such atheoretical comparison studies that learning from media had little to do with technological

or mechanical aspects. This view is gradually being accepted. (For reviews of the research and related issues see, for example, Clark and Salomon 1986, Hannifin 1985, Hooper and Hannifin 1991, Kozma 1991, Ross and Morrison 1990, and Salomon and Gardner 1986.) An often-quoted conclusion from reviews of this technocentric research is that media, defined as technology or machines, "are mere vehicles that deliver instruction but do not influence student achievement any more than the truck that delivers our groceries causes changes in our nutrition" (Clark 1983 p.457). The point of the grocery truck analogy is that when media are defined only by their form or machines (and not by the "content" they deliver or the "context" in which they operate), then no learning benefit can be expected from them. School and government policies, however, often reflect a different view. Money allocated for the purchase of school media such as television or computers is often rationalized by the expectation that instruction and learning will improve as a result (Clark and Salomon 1986). Technocentric research would strongly suggest that public policymakers must turn their attention to the content of the media being used for instruction and to the ways in which they are utilized in schools.

2. Media as Tutors

Another common application of media is as a substitute for, or an augmentation of, the classroom teacher. In this approach, a medium is defined as technology plus its instructional content and the context in which it is provided. The goal of technology as tutor is to provide additional teaching resources to schools limited by large class size, inadequate budgets to provide a rich curriculum, isolation, and/or the individual tutoring requirements of students with special needs. Research in this area tends to take the form of large-scale surveys in which systematic counts are made of factors such as: (a) the number of units of different kinds of media technology in use over time, (b) the types of subject matter being taught by different media, (c) the funds spent on technology and instructional programs and the source of those funds, (d) the variety and cost of instructional "packages" or "courseware" purchased or developed by schools and currently in use at different levels of schooling, and (e) the training of teachers to integrate computers into classroom activities and school curricula. Because of the scope and logistical problems with descriptive studies, they tend to be specific to one technology. During the 1980s the computer was the focus of many surveys.

2.1 Comparisons of Computer Use in Europe and North America

Sugrue (1991) compared computer applications in schools in Europe and North America and Becker (1986) provided in-depth analysis of computer use in American elementary and secondary schools. Sugrue found some of the similarities between Europe and North America to be as follows:

(a) Local funds for the purchase and use of computers in schools are at least as important as state or national funding.

(b) Teacher training for the use of computers across the school curriculum is minimal, with a few notable exceptions.

(c) Elementary schools lag behind secondary schools in the use of computers for instruction, though the difference between the two levels is greater in Europe than it is in North America.

(d) Secondary schools have tended to use the computer to teach about the computer rather than use the medium as an instructional device.

The differences between European and North American computer use mentioned by Sugrue included the following:

(a) European educational software for the computer tends to be developed within the education sector, most often supported by central government or European Community grants. Educational software in the United States tends to be developed more by private and business initiatives and evaluation is conducted by schools and universities (if at all).

(b) North American schools appear to have about twice as many computers per student when compared with only the largest European states.

(c) There is a much greater diversity of computer hardware and software in European schools than in North America.

Becker's (1986) analysis of large-scale studies of computer use in the United States describes plans to make much more use of computers in the area of word-processing (using the computer to write), mathematics education, and English-language training. He reported that American schools consider their most serious problems with computers to be that teachers' knowledge of computers is too weak and that computer instruction is too difficult to fit into the existing curriculum and classroom activities.

2.2 Disputes about Teaching and Learning with Media

Clark and Sugrue (1989) reviewed a decade of studies in which the learning benefits of different media were compared. In the later 1980s most of these studies compared various uses of computer-based teaching with teacher-based teaching. Most of the meta-analytic surveys of media research demonstrate a typical learning advantage from "newer" media of about one-third to one-half a standard deviation on final examination performance, compared with "conventional" (i.e., teacher-presented) treatments. In the case of computer-based instruction studies in college environments, for example, this advantage translates as an increase from the 50th to the 66th percentile on final examinations in a variety of courses. This seemed to be an impressive accomplishment. However, closer inspection of these reviews has revealed that most of the large effect sizes attributed to computers in these studies may have resulted from poorly designed experiments and confounding (Clark 1983, Clark and Salomon 1986).

According to Clark (1983), the most common sources of confounding in media research during this period were the uncontrolled effects of: (a) instructional method or content differences between treatments compared, (b) a novelty effect for newer media, which tends to disappear over time. Clark (1983) noted that the positive effect for newer media more or less disappeared when the same teacher produced all treatments. He speculated that different teams of instructional designers or different teachers gave different content and instructional methods to the treatments compared. Clark also noted that effect sizes in longer-term studies were considerably less than those in very short-term studies. This suggested that newer media were novel but that the novelty wore off very quickly.

If many of the media comparison studies were confounded, it was not known at the end of the 1980s whether to attribute measured learning advantages to a medium or to differences between the content and method being compared. However, if the effect for media tended to disappear when the same instructor or team designed contrasting treatments, the lack of difference may be due to greater control of nonmedium variables. Clark summed up his conclusion that media do not influence learning directly in an analogy. He suggested that, in instruction, media serve a function similar to the different forms in which prescription medicines are delivered. It would never be claimed that a solid (tablet) or a liquid suspension of a drug altered the effects of the drug on human biological functions (except to make it more or less efficient). Nor is it important, except for efficiency purposes, whether a drug is administered by the medium of injection or by oral ingestion. It is the prescription compound that influences biology, not the medium of delivery. Here, the drug medium (tablet or liquid suspension) is analogous to the instructional medium of computer or teacher in education. It is not the computer that alters learning any more than the tablet influences biological processes in a different way from the liquid form of a drug. Both the choice of drug medium and instructional medium influence the efficiency and the cost of delivering the "active ingredient." In neither case is the essential biology or psychology of the target system influenced. The active compound in a drug is a mixture, analogous to what most people call a combination of instructional method and information. It is the method, not the medium, that influences the psychological processes that support learning.

3. Media as Socializing Agents

In this research area, studies primarily examine the educational and social effects of so-called "mass media" on children. Here media are defined as the contents or programs presented by commercial and entertainment-based mass communication efforts directed at children in their homes or in out-of-school locations. Examples of the media examined in these studies are broadcast television and radio programs, newspapers, magazines, and movies. From the late 1980s the focus of most of these studies was on the effects of broadcast television programs on the behavior, attitudes, and school performance of children. In a review of European (largely German) mass media studies Strittmatter (1990) noted the criticism that in both Europe and the United States, "there is a lamentable deficit in the theoretical groundwork for the research activities" (p. 489).

In the United States a great deal of research effort has been targeted on questions about whether mass media encourage violent attitudes and behavior and/or detract from children's schoolwork. Other questions that have been examined are concerned with the influence of entertainment media on children's learning of values related to areas such as sex roles, work, and equity issues. General results indicate that some aspects of violent behavior and the development of values and behavior are related to entertainment media

use, and that the effect is greater for some children than for others. On the other hand, the parental concern about whether the time their children spend watching television might negatively influence school performance seems not to be supported by existing research.

3.1 Entertainment Television and School Performance

Studies report either no effect or relatively small negative correlations between the number of hours children spend watching entertainment television and their school performance (Vooijs and Van Der Voort 1990). However, the effect of entertainment may be greater for some children than for others. Among children entering school in the United States, the average amount of time spent watching television was estimated to be about two hours each evening and this amount increased as children grew older. It was estimated that by the time most American children left school, they spent more time watching television than being taught by a teacher (Dorr 1986). Yet there were very large individual differences between children in hours spent in front of the television. Approximately one-third of all children watched television constantly whereas 10 percent did not watch at all. These individual differences in viewing time stay very stable over the years during childhood (Dorr 1986). What accounts for these large individual differences? Plomin et al. (1990) have presented interesting evidence that genetic factors unrelated to either children's intelligence or temperament influence the amount of television viewing. They argue that since the genetic factor that influences television viewing is unrelated to aptitudes that have been found to influence achievement in school, television viewing will most likely not be found to detract from school performance. Yet children do appear to learn both positive and negative attitudes and behaviors from entertainment media. Thus, another area of research asks whether it is possible to influence children's learning in positive directions and help to insulate them against the negative influences.

3.2 Curricula for Teaching Children to be Critical of Television

Vooijs and Van Der Voort (1990) have summarized the results of European and American studies of curricula designed to teach children how to watch television in a way that eliminates its negative effects. They report that "there is little evidence that television curricula are capable of changing television's impact on children's attitudes and behavior" (p.550). However, they stress that existing studies may not give the best impression of what future curricula *might* be able to accomplish. They suggest that more theory-based studies of longer duration should be made, focused on the home behavior (as opposed to school-based behavior) of children who are most "at risk" of negative effects.

4. Media As Motivators For Learning

The use of media to encourage students to invest more effort in learning has a long history. Part of the enthusiasm of researchers and policymakers for newer media has been due to the expectation that learning will become "fun" or at least more engaging. The interest in cognitive theories of motivation has stimulated research on the motivating qualities of student's values, beliefs, and attributions in relation to different media (see Salomon 1984). In this motivation research, media are variously defined as technology, as tutors, and as socializing agents. The results of these studies are complex and somewhat counterintuitive. A brief sample of some of the many interesting results from various reviews of this research would include novelty effects, benefits for special students, individual differences in preferences for different media, and the quality of effort invested in media programs.

While there is usually an initial increase in motivation (and therefore in effort to learn) with the introduction of a new instructional medium, motivation tends to decrease over time in elementary and secondary school students until it reaches preintroduction levels. In computer and/or visual instruction studies, for example, the novelty benefit of the computer or television disappears in most studies lasting longer than eight weeks (Clark and Salomon 1986). This novelty effect is not as common in studies of media use in universities.

There may be motivation benefits that are important for minority and special students. For example, Clark and Salomon (1986) reviewed studies in which students were consistently motivated by media that they perceived as less prejudiced and more "reliable and fair" than their teachers.

Salomon (1984) has provided a very interesting model for the study of media motivation based on an integration of cognitive motivation theory. He noted large individual and cultural differences in students' beliefs and attributions about different media. Clark and Sugrue (1989) have noted that individual differences in motivation for one or another medium may be unstable and might change over a relatively short period of instruction.

Clark (1982) has reviewed aptitude–treatment interaction studies in which students chose instructional media programs that they liked but which where consistently found to produce significantly less achievement than media programs they had rejected. Salomon (1984) provided evidence that North American students like television because they perceive it as "easier" and suggested that children give only "mindless" effort to television and other media they perceive as "easy." On the other hand, media such as books are

perceived as more challenging and are therefore liked somewhat less but students are more "mindful" when they learn from books. As a result of this research, it is reasonable to suggest that caution ought to be exercised when decisions are made to adopt instructional media on the expectation that it will increase student motivation to learn over time.

5. Media As Mental Tools For Thinking and Problem-solving

At the beginning of the 1990s research efforts were being directed toward exploring ways in which newer media, such as computers and video disks, might present instruction that taught students to think *in terms* of the tools presented (Salomon 1988, Kozma 1991). These new instructional programs might, for example, simulate expert reasoning about writing and grammar in a symbolic form particularly suited to the way in which students mentally represent such information. The student was not only expected to learn various rules of grammar but also to incorporate the reasoning heuristics of the expert and to be able, in the future, to think in more expert terms about writing. Salomon (1988) called this process the "internalization" of cognitive tools and he provided both research evidence and theoretical support for the approach.

Kozma (1991) noted that the definition of media has been extended considerably in the mental-tool approach to include not only the technology of a medium but also

> the symbol systems it can employ and the processes that can be performed with it. For example, a computer with a graphics board or a speech synthesis board can use different symbols in its presentations than those without those features. Computers with enough memory to run expert systems can process information in different ways than those without enough memory. These additional symbol systems and processes are likely to account for the cognitive effects of these systems, rather than the technology, per se. (p. 181)

Experiments have demonstrated that it is possible, for example, to improve children's ability to notice parts of paintings and other visual displays through exposure to repeated operations of a "zoom" lens on a film or television camera; and changes have been found in cognitive style measures after children have watched animation sequences in which three-dimensional objects were "unwrapped" into two dimensions and different visual perspectives on a single event were examined (Clark and Sugrue 1989, Salomon 1988). These experiments provided compelling evidence that the children who participated actually internalized the symbolic representation of mental processes which increased their ability to attend to cues and change their visual perspective. Kozma (1991) expanded the experimental examples of the mental-tool approach to include some of the tools that are made possible by various forms of the information capabilities of books, computers, and multimedia technologies. Winn (1990) presented an interesting theoretical and empirical extension of the tool approach to learning from graphic displays, including computer graphics.

5.1 Disputes about the Mental-tool Approach

It is important to note that, as with any new area of research, there have been disputes about the mental-tool approach. One argument is that the tool research may ignore the "cognitive impenetrability" of some thinking processes (see, for example, Winn 1990). Another argument has been about whether the technology of media plays any necessary role in the cultivation of the cognitive skills that are the object of this research. Clark and Sugrue (1989) have suggested that there is no media technology that provides a unique symbol system or process that is necessary for learning any particular thinking or problem-solving skill. They acknowledged that treatments such as visual zooming and unwrapping can, under the conditions noted by Salomon (1988), cultivate mental skills. However, they also provided evidence that very different experimental treatments (taken from different symbol systems and processes) can produce the same or similar thinking skills. (For a discussion of these issues, see, for example, Clark and Sugrue 1989 pp. 26–30.) Critics contended that if different media, symbols, and processes produce similar cognitive skills then the independent variables in learning research are not media-based symbols or processes. Instead, it has been claimed that some symbol systems or processes may be more *efficient* for some students and that it is learning efficiency (e.g., speed and cost) that is being influenced by symbols and processes and not learning per se (Clark and Sugrue 1989, Hooper and Hannifin 1991, Hannifin 1985, Ross and Morrison 1990). Since few studies have provided measures of learning efficiency or comparisons of efficiency between different treatments, the critics claim that educators may not be realizing the potential benefit of this new approach.

6. Conclusion

If judged by the sheer number of studies, media inquiry has been one of the most active areas in educational research. Yet by the end of the 1980s it had proceeded largely without the benefit of any theory that directed experiments. Perhaps because of the lack of theory, hundreds of similar studies came to the same unproductive end. This has been most obvious in the technocentric research that provided gross comparisons of, for example, the relative learning results obtained from teachers and television lessons. Yet several conceptual difficulties that plagued the

technocentric research have also been found in the "media as tutor" and "media as socializing agent" studies. The lack of theory in those areas has resulted in a body of experiments that are both difficult to interpret and to apply in schools and communities (Clark and Salomon 1986, Ross and Morrison 1990, Salomon and Gardner 1986).

Much of the research on media motivation is now guided by the very healthy developments in cognitive motivation theory (Salomon 1984). Because the results of experiments in that area are very counter intuitive, they have even greater potential importance when applied to practice. Finally, the development of theory in the "mental-tool" research has proceeded quickly and in an environment of healthy debate and discussion (see Salomon 1988, Kozma 1991). Most observers believe that some of the most vital and interesting future research will be found in the development of mental tools.

See also: Computers and Learning; Computer Programming, Learning and Instruction of

References

Becker M J 1986 *Instructional Uses of School Computers: Reports from the 1985 National Survey.* Center for Social Organization of Schools, Johns Hopkins University, Baltimore, Maryland

Clark R E 1982 Antagonism between achievement and enjoyment in ATI studies. *Educ. Psychol.* 17(2): 92–101

Clark R E 1983 Reconsidering research on learning from media. *Rev. Educ. Res.* 53(4): 445–59

Clark R E, Salomon G 1986 Media in teaching. In: Wittrock M (ed.) 1986 *Handbook of Research on Teaching*, 3rd edn. Macmillan Inc., New York

Clark R E, Sugrue B M 1989 Research on instructional media, 1978–1988. In: Ely D (ed.) 1989 *Educational Media Yearbook 1988–1989.* Libraries Unlimited, Littletown, Colorado

Dorr A 1986 *Television and Children: A Special Medium for a Special Audience.* Sage, Beverly Hills, California

Hannifin M J 1985 Empirical issues in the study of computer-assisted interactive video. *Educ. Comm. & Tech. J.* 33(4): 235–47

Hooper S, Hannifin M J 1991 Psychological perspectives on emerging instructional technologies: A critical analysis. *Educ. Psychol.* 26(1): 69–95

Kozma R B 1991 Learning with media. *Rev. Educ. Res.* 61(2): 179–211

Plomin R, Corley R, DeFries J C, Fulker D W 1990 Individual differences in television viewing in early childhood: Nature as well as nurture. *Psychol. Science* 1(6): 371–77

Ross S M, Morrison G R 1990 In search of a happy medium in instructional technology research: Issues concerning external validity, media replications and learner control. *Educ. Tech. Res. Dev.* 37(1): 19–33

Salomon G 1984 Television is "easy" and print is "tough": The differential investment of mental effort in learning as a function of perceptions and attributions. *J. Educ. Psychol.* 76(4): 647–58

Salomon G 1988 AI in reverse: Computer tools that become cognitive. *J. Educ. Computing Res.* 4(2): 123–34

Salomon G, Gardner H 1986 The computer as educator: Lessons from television research. *Educ. Res.* 15: 13–19

Strittmatter P 1990 European research on media and technology in education: Current status and future directions. *Int. J. Educ. Res.* 14(6): 489–505

Sugrue B M 1991 A comparative review of European and American approaches to computer-based instruction in schools. In: Shlechter T M (ed.) 1991 *Problems and Promises of Computer-based Training*. Ablex, Norwood, New Jersey

Vooijs M W, Van Der Voort T H A 1990 Teaching television: The effects of critical television viewing curricula. *Int. J. Educ. Res.* 14(6): 543–52

Winn W D 1990 A theoretical framework for research on learning from graphics. *Int. J. Educ. Res.* 14(6): 553–64

Further Reading

Clark R E, Sugrue B M 1990 North American disputes about research on learning from media. *Int. J. Educ. Res.* 14(6): 507–20

Cuban L 1986 *Teachers and Machines: The Classroom Uses of Technology Since 1920*. Teachers College Press, New York

Lepper M R, Gurtner J L 1989 Children and computers: Approaching the twenty-first century. *Am. Psychol.* 44(2): 170–78

Spencer K 1991 Modes, media and methods: The search for educational effectiveness. *Br. J. Educ. Technol.* 22(1): 12–22

US Congress, Office of Technology Assessment 1988 *Power On: New Tools For Teaching and Learning* (OTA-SET-379) US Government Printing Office, Washington, DC

Problem-solving and Learning: Computer Modeling

K. Opwis and H. Spada

Computer modeling of problem-solving and learning is an active field of multidisciplinary research in cognitive science. Problem-solving and learning are highly intertwined. Problem-solving refers to the process of finding or constructing a solution to a task for which no ready solution is at hand. Learning leads to a better performance on tasks. Computer models of problem-solving and learning are simulations of the underlying mental activities. The basic assumption of this perspective on cognition is that problem-solving and learning can be regarded as knowledge-based processes (see Johnson-Laird 1988). Computer models are developed because they permit the expression of theories in precise, explicit, and computationally tractable terms so as to demonstrate the sufficiency of a defined set of theoretical concepts, and to provide an explanation for observed human behavior. With regard to instruction, such models can be seen as descriptive but also as prescriptive theories. They are suitable for guiding and evaluating instructions, especially in the field of computerized teaching.

1. Production Systems: A Framework for Knowledge Representation

Many computer models of cognitive processes use an explicit representation of knowledge. Different approaches have been proposed since the 1970s (see Brachman and Levesque 1985). They can be classified as "propositional" (e.g., semantic nets, scripts, and frames), "rule-based" (e.g., production systems), and "analogical representational systems." Connectionist approaches (see Rumelhart 1989), which can be characterized by a parallel distributed processing of implicitly represented information, are not discussed here. This entry will focus on production systems.

Production systems, often more generally called rule-based systems, were introduced by Newell and Simon (1972) as the basic conceptual framework to model human problem-solving. They also underlie well-known theories of cognition such as ACT* (Anderson 1983) and SOAR (Newell 1990), as well as the theory of inductive inference and learning developed by Holland et al. (1986).

The basic architecture of a simple production system consists of storage and processing elements. The system's storage includes components for long-term knowledge (production memory) and short-term data (working memory). The working memory contains a collection of symbolic data representing the actual declarative knowledge of the system. A production memory consists of condition–action rules called "productions" which specify actions the system initiates when certain triggering conditions are fulfilled. The conditions describe patterns of data that might appear in working memory. The actions specify modifications of the contents of working memory or they change the state of the external "world."

The central processing component of a production system is called the "interpreter." It defines the interplay of the two memories in terms of a test–select–act cycle. In the test phase the system determines which rules can be applied. A match process finds all the rules whose conditions are fulfilled by the current state of working memory. In the next step, a conflict resolution process selects one rule for application. Criteria such as "prefer the rule with the most specific conditions" or "prefer the rule most relevant for the actual goal" might be used. In the act phase the system executes the actions of the selected rule. This cycle can be enforced repeatedly. Obviously this description ignores many of the details as well as variations that are possible within this framework (see Klahr et al. 1987).

2. Problem-solving

A problem arises when one has a goal—a state of affairs that one wants to achieve—and it is not immediately apparent how the goal can be attained. The dominant conceptual framework for analyzing such situations distinguishes three components (see Newell and Simon 1972): (a) the initial problem state; (b) operators that transform problem states into new states; (c) operators that test whether a problem state constitutes a solution. The application of a sequence of operators to the initial state and the resulting states leads to a whole space of states. This "problem space" approach regards problem-solving basically as a search process (see VanLehn 1989).

Which strategies do subjects use in their problem-solving activities? A well-known general strategy is called "means–ends analysis." It comprises two distinct weak methods or heuristics which are used recursively: difference reduction and operator subgoaling. Difference reduction starts with the initial state and chooses an operator such that the differences between the actual state and the desired one are maximally reduced. The selected operator is applied, a new state results, and the steps are repeated. "Operator subgoaling" comes into play if an operator is chosen that turns out to be inapplicable because some of its preconditions are not met. Then a subgoal is formed which is to change the current state so that the preconditions are fulfilled. That requires difference reduction.

The computer modeling of such problem strategies within the production system framework is straightforward: states are represented in working memory as declarative information, operators are formulated as production rules, and the interpreter defines which operator to select.

Up to now problem-solving has been described in knowledge-lean task domains such as puzzles (see the "Tower of Hanoi" as a classical example). There, all the relevant information can be obtained directly from the problem instruction. No domain-specific background knowledge is necessary. A famous example of a computer model in this tradition is the General Problem Solver (Newell and Simon 1972).

The picture gets much more complex if problem-solving in knowledge-rich task domains such as physics, geometry, medical diagnosis, or computer-programming is concerned. The mental activities underlying the solution of tasks in such domains are described by VanLehn (1989) as the selection of problem schemata, as their adaptation (instantiation), and as the execution of their procedural parts. Much research has been devoted to the analysis of the acquisition of this type of expertise (see Chi et al. 1988), but it was mostly restricted to novice–experts cross-sectional comparisons. The computer models that were developed in the 1980s merely describe selected aspects of this learning process. For example, Larkin (1981) modeled strategic learning as a shift from backward reasoning—based on means–end analysis—to forward reasoning in connection with physics problems.

3. Computer Modeling of Learning

3.1 Basic Learning Mechanisms

In rule-based systems two fundamental types of changes can be modeled: the revision of existing rules, for instance by changing some of their attributes (i.e., a strength parameter) and the generation of new rules. The most basic mechanisms for rule creation are discrimination, generalization, and composition (see Klahr et al. 1987).

The discrimination mechanism creates a new rule by making the conditions of some parent rule more specific. The basic idea is that this rule should be applicable only to those subsets of situations matched by its parent rule for which its actions are really appropriate.

Generalization and discrimination can be regarded as inverse processes; that is, the generalization mechanism creates a new rule by making the condition part more general. Compared to its parent rule the new rule will be applicable in more situations.

The composition mechanism interlinks rules that have previously been executed sequentially. Multistep operations are transformed into a single-step production in order to model speedup effects due to practice.

A more complex learning mechanism is "learning by chunking "as used in the SOAR system (see Newell 1990).

A successful application of the outlined learning mechanisms to create and modify knowledge structures requires solutions to some tricky and interrelated problems, as follow.

(a) How can the system's knowledge elements that contribute to a successful behavior or to a negative outcome be identified? This question is often discussed as the problem of credit assignment (see the bucket-brigade algorithm proposed by Holland et al. 1986).

(b) How can plausible and useful new rules that extract and exploit experienced regularities be generated and how can the range of application of newly generated rules be restricted to the appropriate circumstances?

(c) How can knowledge structures be created that enable the system to work efficiently, but which remain flexible and adaptive in a changing environment?

3.2 Knowledge-based Learning Systems

No general solutions are known to the problems mentioned above, but there exist several specific proposals realized as knowledge-based learning systems. They set up a framework in which the discussed as well as additional learning mechanisms can be applied successfully. The different systems—often developed under the heading "Machine Learning" (see Carbonell 1989)—can be described according to the dimensions "inductive versus deductive learning" and "similarity-based versus analysis-based learning" (Plötzner & Spada 1994). Most models of just inductive learning (e.g., the discrimination learner by Langley 1987) are applied to knowledge-lean domains. Learning concepts from examples can be subsumed under this category: given a set of positive and negative examples of some concept, a general definition of that concept is to be found. Because learning takes place by detecting similarities in the set of possible examples, as well as by noticing dissimilarities between positive and negative examples, such inductive knowledge acquisition can be regarded as similarity-based learning. This type of learning is not successful and efficient in knowledge-rich domains, because too many examples are needed and many misleading hypotheses are generated.

On the other extreme, learning systems based exclusively on deductive learning normally use rich domain-specific background knowledge. For example, explanation-based generalization (Mitchell et al. 1986) utilizes at least three kinds of information: (a) concept definition describing the concept to be learned (goal concept); (b) an example of the goal concept (training example); (c) a set of rules and facts to be used in explaining the respects in which the training example is an instance of the goal concept (domain theory). Learning means to find a generalization of the training example that is a sufficient definition for the goal concept. Such a generalization is more abstract than the training example itself, but less abstract than the original goal definition. It explains the training example in terms of the domain theory. Proceduralization and rule composition as part of skill acquisition (Anderson 1983) can also be viewed as deductive learning.

Other well-known classes of learning systems, such as analogy-based learning or case-based learning, involve inductive *and* deductive parts (see the contributions in Carbonell 1989). Many of these systems can be described as analysis-based. Domain-specific back-ground knowledge is used to deduce solutions for new problems or to self-explain worked-out instructional examples. Impasses are overcome by inductively generating new knowledge elements. If their application is successful, they become part of the system's stored knowledge. KAGE (*K*nowledge *A*cquisition *G*overned by *E*xperimentation, Plötzner and Spada 1992) is such a learning system. It reconstructs the acquisition of knowledge about functional relationships between physics variables by analysis-based learning mechanisms. Cascade (VanLehn et al. 1992) simulates the learning process that takes place when worked-out physics examples are analyzed. This model is of special interest from an instructional viewpoint, because it explains why some students benefit very positively from worked-out examples while others hardly profit at all.

4. Outlook: Instructional Relevance

The main impact of computer modeling of problem-solving and learning on instruction is reflected in electronic teaching devices, such as "intelligent tutorial systems." In comparison to conventional computerized teaching programs, these systems are characterized by substantially more flexible control structures and more elaborate techniques for representing and communicating information.

The focus of psychological research within this framework is on how to assess and model the process of knowledge acquisition. One objective is to develop self-adapting teaching systems; that is, systems that adjust their behavior to the student's state of knowledge and to its changes during the learning process.

Given such models of knowledge acquisition as KAGE or Cascade it is also possible to determine those types and sequences of instructional material that are optimal, suboptimal, or even misleading with regard to the implemented learning mechanisms. Thus, such systems can be regarded as descriptive theories of student learning but also as prescriptive theories for good instruction. From the second perspective they can also be used to evaluate instructional material: given a defined set of learning mechanisms and a sequence of instructional steps, what can be learned and what cannot?

In general, computer simulation techniques force the researcher to consider the content of their subjects' knowledge in detail and to provide an outstanding format for theorizing about knowledge acquisition.

See also: Architecture of Cognition; Computers and Learning; Expert Knowledge and Performance; Declarative and Procedural Knowledge; Development of Learning Skills in Problem-solving and Thinking; Reasoning

References

Anderson J R 1983 *The Architecture of Cognition.* Harvard

University Press, Cambridge, Massachusetts

Brachman R J, Levesque H J (eds.) 1985 *Readings in Knowledge Representation.* Morgan Kaufmann, Los Altos, California

Carbonell J G (ed.) 1989 *Machine Learning: Paradigms and Methods.* MIT Press, Cambridge, Massachusetts

Chi M T H, Glaser R, Farr M (eds.) 1988 *The Nature of Expertise.* Erlbaum, Hillsdale, New Jersey

Holland J H, Holyoak K J, Nisbett R E, Thagard P R 1986 *Induction: Processes of Inference, Learning, and Discovery.* MIT Press, Cambridge, Massachusetts

Johnson-Laird P N 1988 *The Computer and the Mind. An Introduction to Cognitive Science.* Harvard University Press, Cambridge, Massachusetts

Klahr D, Langley P, Neches R (eds.) 1987 *Production System Models of Learning and Development.* MIT Press, Cambridge, Massachusetts

Langley P 1987 A general theory of discrimination learning. In: Klahr D, Langley P, Neches R (eds.) 1987

Larkin J H 1981 Enriching formal knowledge: A model for learning to solve textbook physics problems. In: Anderson J R (ed.) 1981 *Cognitive Skills and their Acquisition.* Erlbaum, Hillsdale, New Jersey

Mitchell T M, Keller R, Kedar-Cabelli S 1986 Explanation-based generalization: A unifying view. *Machine Learning* 1: 47–80

Newell A 1990 *Unified Theories of Cognition.* Harvard University Press, Cambridge, Massachusetts

Newell A, Simon H A 1972 *Human Problem Solving.* Prentice-Hall, Englewood Cliffs, New Jersey

Plötzner R, Spada H 1992 Analysis-based learning on multiple levels of mental domain representation. In: De Corte E, Linn M C, Mandl H, Verschaffel L (eds.) 1992 *Computer-based Learning Environments and Problem Solving.* Springer, Berlin

Plötzner R, Spada H 1994 Wissenserwerb: Funktionsprinzipien von Lernprozessen. In: Dörner D, van der Meer E (eds.) 1994 *Gedächtnis.* Hogrefe, Göttingen

Rumelhart D E 1989 The architecture of the mind: A connectionist approach. In: Posner M I (ed.) 1989 *Foundations of Cognitive Science.* MIT Press, Cambridge, Massachusetts

VanLehn K 1989 Problem solving and cognitive skill acquisition. In: Posner M I (ed.) 1989 *Foundations of Cognitive Science.* MIT Press, Cambridge, Massachusetts

VanLehn K, Jones R M, Chi M T H 1992 A model of the self-explanation effect. *The Journal of the Learning Sciences* 2: 1–59

Further Reading

Opwis K 1992 *Kognitive Modellierung: Zur Verwendung wissensbasierter Systeme in der psychologischen Theoriebildung.* Huber, Bern

Osherson D N, Smith E E (eds.) 1990 *An Invitation to Cognitive Science. Vol. 3: Thinking.* MIT Press, Cambridge, Massachusetts

Shavlik J W, Dietterich T G (eds.) 1990 *Readings in Machine Learning.* Morgan Kaufmann, San Mateo, California

Strube G, Wender K F (eds.) 1993 *The Cognitive Psychology of Knowledge: The German Wissenspsychologie Project.* Elsevier, Amsterdam

Wenger E 1987 *Artificial Intelligence and Tutoring Systems.* Morgan Kaufmann, Los Altos, California

Programmed Learning

M. Eraut

Outside the field of education, the word "program" has come to mean either: (a) a listing of a series of events, such as the items in a concert or a show; or (b) the series of events themselves, considered collectively; or (c) a definite plan for an intended set of proceedings or performance. Something is said to be programmed if there is a predefined sequence of events that has been planned in advance. In particular, the term is used to describe distinctive segments of radio and television transmissions which have been separately scripted and are capable of being repeated in recorded form —these are called radio or television programs, and distinct sets of instructions for computers to execute —these are called computer programs. In both broadcasting and computing contexts it soon became normal to distinguish between hardware (machines, devices, instruments, etc.) which was the responsibility of engineers, and software (content, instructions, materials, etc.) which was the responsibility of communications specialists or information scientists. A program was a unit of software that was planned as a discrete entity and could be used independently of other programs.

When Skinner and Crowder began to experiment in the mid-1950s with different types of teaching machine, it was natural for them to describe the rolls of paper or film which carried their information for students as programs, and the process of preparing these instructional sequences as programming. So, when Glaser et al. (1960) devised a means of presenting Skinnerian programs in book format, they called their new product a "paper teaching machine," or, sensing that this term might cause some confusion, a programmed textbook. This new term did not resolve the definition problem because, according to the earlier definition, all textbooks could be regarded as programmed in some sense. But nevertheless the term stuck. Hence textbooks that resemble the early experimental products of Skinner, Glaser, and Crowder are called programmed texts, and most other textbooks are not so described. The collective term used to

describe the whole of this newly developing field
—the new kinds of teaching machine, the programs
that fed these machines, and the machine-independent
programmed texts—was "programmed instruction" or
"programmed learning."

Later workers in the field of programmed learning have come to regret this early hardening of its
terminology, but have been largely unsuccessful in
their attempts to change it. The general public and,
indeed, most educators have persisted in identifying
programmed learning with its earliest, most experimental products (rather like identifying geometry only
with Pythagoras and Euclid). Hence educational tech-
nologists have tended to drop the term and to use
new names to describe innovations that incorporate
many of the principles originally developed under the
heading of programmed learning.

This entry takes a historical approach. First, it describes the early developments that gave programmed
learning its "image." Then it explains how many of the
early ideas were modified and new ideas introduced
as a result of further research and practical experience. Finally, it discusses some of the innovations
that grew out of the "programmed learning" field and
indicates where they are covered elsewhere in this
Encyclopedia.

1. Early Developments

Though there had been earlier work of relevance, the
man who brought programmed learning into prominence was B F Skinner, whose publications between
1954 and 1968 commanded the attention of the
scientific and educational communities and even the
general public. Unlike many educational innovations,
Skinner's work was based on a clearly articulated theoretical base—in his case the psychological theory of
operant conditioning. According to this theory, behavior is only learned if it is immediately reinforced, that
is, followed by some pleasurable event such as food,
praise, or attention. So the task of the programmer,
or indeed any teacher, is to arrange the contingencies
of reinforcement so that correct responses to some
question or assignment are immediately rewarded,
while incorrect responses are not rewarded. Skinner
strongly opposed punishment for creating a dysfunctional degree of anxiety, and even urged that incorrect
responses be kept to a minimum so that there was
no danger of developing a negative attitude toward
the learning activity. His earlier work with rats and
pigeons had shown that this theoretical prescription
could be realized in practice by breaking down a
learning sequence into a large number of very small
steps. This kept the error rate down to a minimum
and allowed reinforcement to be frequent and immediate. Certain behaviors could be shaped by slowly
refining the reinforcement contingencies, for example,
rewarding almost any attempt at pronouncing a new

word in the early stages and progressively becoming
stricter about what would count as correct. With verbal
material this shaping process could be accomplished
by giving the student strong prompts at the beginning
(hints, half-completed answers, etc.) then gradually
weakening the strength of the prompts. Clearly, this
whole process needs to be carefully controlled and it
was for this purpose that Skinner invented his first
teaching machine.

Skinner's early teaching machines shared certain
common features. Only one step in the instructional
sequence appeared at a time. This came to be called a
frame, as it appeared in a "frame" or "window" on top
of the machine; and was limited in length by the size of
this window to about 30 words. Each frame demanded
an overt response from the student (writing a word,
punching a hole, or pressing a key, according to the
type of machine) who then discovered if he or she was
correct by comparing the answer with the correct one
when he or she turned the roll or, in the case of punched
responses, by the automatic presentation of the next
frame. The student's responses are nearly always
correct *if* the program has been properly prepared by
good design and testing and revision; and confirmation
of this correctness is assumed to be reinforcing. The
student can work at his or her own pace and gradually
acquires the chunk of knowledge that the program is
designed to teach.

Early programmed texts simulated these machines
in two important respects. First, they divided their
presentation into frames of a similar size and used
similar techniques of shaping and prompting to construct their learning sequences. Second, they sought
to prevent students seeing the answer in advance of
making their own response (a guaranteed feature of
machine presentation) by printing successive frames
on different pages, each new frame beginning with
the answer to the previous frame. In a typical text of
this kind, page 1 might contain frames 1, 6, 11, 16,
and 21 while page 3 presented frames 2, 7, 12, 17,
and 22, thus completing a 25-frame sequence on page
9 and leaving the even-numbered pages for a similar
sequence working through the book backwards.

To summarize, then, the principal features of these
Skinnerian or linear programs (so-called because each
student follows the same linear sequence of frames)
are: (a) division of the subject matter into a logical
sequence of small steps, (b) revision of this sequence
until the error rate is low, (c) overt responding by
the student, (d) immediate presentation of the correct
response, and (e) an individual mode of working which
allows students to proceed at their own rate.

Thirty years earlier Pressey had designed a series
of self-teaching devices based on different principles
from those of Skinner, but these aroused little interest at the time. Pressey had noted that students can
learn from the experience of taking tests, especially
when provided with immediate feedback on their
performance. So he devised a testing machine which

required students to press keys to answer multiple-choice questions, and only presented the next question after the correct key had been pressed. The assumption was that, after students had been exposed to some initial instruction—either written material or a conventional lecture or lesson—they would consolidate their learning by going through an appropriate machine-presented test until they had mastered all the questions and ceased making any mistakes. The crucial distinction between Pressey and Skinner was that while Skinner treated errors as something to be avoided, Pressey regarded them as useful feedback to the student. A further development of Pressey's position was to use errors to direct the student to an appropriate explanation or remedial sequence; and this was initiated by Crowder.

Crowder's background was in training trouble-shooters to find malfunctions in electronic equipment, where he soon found that the "coach and pupil" method was the most successful. However, there was a scarcity of coaches; so Crowder attempted to automate the coaching procedure by devising a simulated tutor. This was achieved by giving the student some information, asking a multiple-choice question and then providing a different response for each answer chosen. Thus students proceeded through a program along different routes or branches and care could be taken to see that they understood each point before they proceeded to the next. By adopting a fairly conversational style, the student could feel that he or she was talking to a remote tutor who paid special attention to diagnosing and remedying his or her own personal misunderstandings. Crowder called his machines "autotutors" and used microfilm to present his programs. The student's responses on the keyboard controlled the movement of the film, so that the appropriate next frame was shown. Soon, these branching programs were also converted into a book format, with one frame on each page and a multiple-choice question directing the student to a different page for each answer. On reaching that page, the student gets feedback that he or she is correct or has made a particular kind of mistake. In the former case the next chunk of information is presented, while in the latter the student may either be sent back to answer the question again or routed through a short remedial sequence.

Typically, Crowder's frames were much longer than Skinner's and he presented new material a paragraph at a time. When he turned to education, he chose topics from secondaryschool mathematics and computing. The approach to instruction was not shaping behavior but explanation and reasoning. This appealed more to sophisticated adults and to brighter students for whom getting easy questions right was more tedious than reinforcing. One disadvantage, however, was that the provision of remedial loops lessened the burden on frame design, making it less likely that poorly written frames would get detected and revised while the program was being developed.

From 1960 researchers embarked on experiments to compare linear with branching programs and to investigate design variables such as step size, error rate, and response mode, while developers concentrated on training programmers and writing programs. Implementing programmed learning in schools and colleges drew attention to the major problems of matching the right student to the right program and managing classes where students did not all proceed at the same rate. After the initial excitement of the pioneering decade from 1954 to 1964, a more mature, reflective, and practical range of approaches developed; and it is these that form the substance of the next three sections.

2. Preparation for Programming

Skinner and Holland (1958) described the initial stages of preparing a program to teach verbal knowledge in the following terms:

> *Specifications of a course.* The programmer must know what verbal behavior the student is to have in his repertoire after completing the course and how precisely and extensively he is to talk about the field.
> *Knowledge previously acquired.* The student is assumed to possess some verbal behavior in the area before he starts the course. This must be stated, and the programmer must not at any time appeal to material not included in the statement or not provided by earlier parts of the program . . .
> *Ordering the knowledge to be acquired.* At each step the programmer must ask, "What behavior must the student have before he can take this step?" A sequence of steps forms a progression from the initially assumed knowledge up to the specified final repertoire. No step should be encountered before the student has mastered everything needed to take it.
> *Listing the terms, etc.* Before writing frames for each set, the programmer should make lists of (a) the terms to be covered, (b) the processes or principles, (c) a wide range of illustrative examples (pp. 163–64).

Each of these stages was reconceptualized during the following decade, and a range of approaches developed to what was still recognized as essentially the same programming process.

What Skinner and Holland described as the intended "verbal behavior" of the student was soon redefined in terms of learning objectives, thus introducing a term which was already familiar to training psychologists, curriculum specialists, and psychometricians without significantly changing the meaning. The notion of objectives was also given a tremendous boost by the popularity of Mager's (1961) *Preparing Objectives for Programmed Instruction* which argued the need for behavioral objectives in a short, witty, programmed book. Soon an explicit statement of objectives in behavioral terms became the standard form of course specification for all programmed learning sequences.

This was to be accompanied by a statement of student prerequisites, which indicated what knowledge a student would need to have previously acquired before starting the course. The careful step-by-step approach of a linear program could only work if students possessed all the necessary prerequisites, and even branching programs were limited in the number of remedial loops they could incorporate to cope with students who were not fully prepared for them. Sometimes this statement of prerequisites was replaced by a pretest, which a prospective student had to pass. But there was also another kind of pretest, covering the material taught in the program, which students were expected to fail. Originally this was used for scientific reasons, that is, for measuring learning gain in terms of the difference in scores between a pretest and an identical or equivalent post-test. But later another, diagnostic, purpose for pretests was discovered. Some students were already competent in the area covered by the program, and passing a pretest could enable them to skip it, and it was only a short step from this to design pretests which enabled knowledgeable students to skip some sections of a program but not others.

These developments were relatively simple extrapolations from Skinner's original procedures, for it was not until the third and fourth stages of program preparation that major problems arose. Here it was soon realized that Skinner's ideas about "ordering the knowledge to be acquired" and "listing terms" provided insufficient guidance for the programming of complex conceptual material. Nor could the stages be readily separated. The term "task analysis" was imported from the industrial training field to describe these difficult but crucial stages of program preparation. Though some authors are prone to present their views without much modesty, task analysis remains an area where there is little general agreement on the appropriate approach, even today. Nevertheless, a range of concepts and strategies has been developed without which any instructional designer would have an impoverished repertoire of possible approaches. In particular, four main ideas have proved seminal—master performer, hierarchy, matrix, and classification by knowledge type.

The idea of a master performer had a double significance: on the one hand it linked with the training psychologists' tradition of job analysis, while on the other hand it was influential in the curriculum reform movements of the 1960s and early 1970s, where the goal of making students more like practicing scholars in the disciplines was widely advocated. The job analysis approach proved useful to programmers working in industrial and military settings but was less directly applicable to education. Nevertheless, it drew attention to the importance of "knowing how" rather than "knowing that" and strengthened the behavioral focus of course specification by learning objectives. The approach through reanalyzing the critical knowledge, skills, and attitudes of subject matter experts was more directly relevant to education, but often proved difficult to realize in practice where it usually conflicted with curricular traditions and conventional modes of assessment. Though some educators saw programmed learning as particularly inappropriate for a curriculum based on thinking processes, there has been some interesting work in this area (see *Task Analysis*).

The hierarchy approach comes closest to Skinner's original conception of sequencing. It assumes that each objective can be broken down into subobjectives. Each subobjective is dependent on the prior learning of other subobjectives to such an extent that it is appropriate to talk of a hierarchy of objectives, which the learner ascends level by level, one subobjective at a time, using each step as a basis for those that follow. This provides an additional theoretical reason for small steps and makes the sequencing of these steps a matter of crucial importance. Ideally, hierarchies need to be empirically verified, but it is generally assumed that programmers can discern them by careful analysis of the subject matter (White and Gagné 1974). Though the general notion of prerequisite knowledge is widely accepted, there is considerable dispute as to whether many areas of knowledge are in fact acquired in such a methodical piecemeal manner. However, this type of analysis provides a useful approach to the problem of sequencing even if some of the individual steps are later combined.

A more flexible, though some would argue less penetrating, approach to sequencing a series of subobjectives or teaching points is the matrix system (Thomas et al. 1963). This begins by listing what Skinner calls terms, principles, and examples along both the horizontal and the vertical axes of a two-dimensional matrix. Then linkages between any two items can be noted by coloring the appropriate square of the matrix. For example a red square might mean that A is an example of principle B, a green square that A and C are examples of the same principle, a blue square that principle B is a prerequisite for principle D, and so on. Careful interpretation of this matrix then suggests possible sequences for the program, leaving it open for the programmer to choose, for example, between deductive (rule → example) and inductive (example → rule) sequencing.

Two quite distinct approaches have evolved to classification by knowledge type: one is based on Bloom's *Taxonomy of Educational Objectives* and various developments of it, many of them subject specific (Bloom et al. 1971); the other is based on the typologies of learning psychologists which seek to differentiate between such categories as discriminations, chains, concepts, and principles (Gagné 1977). There are a very large number of variations for each approach, so most programmers choose a category system that seems to suit the particular problem they are tackling, often introducing their own modifications to adapt it to each specific situation.

3. Frame Design

While task analysis, the identification and sequencing of teaching points, can still be regarded as part of the preparation process, the design of individual frames and the continuity between them is the central task of program writing. So far two distinct approaches to program writing have been identified—linear small-step programming and branching large-step programming —each with its own implications for frame design. But hybrids soon appeared as programmers developed alternative tracks within linear programs and skip-forward arrangements for their more knowledgeable students, and branching programs began to incorporate short linear sequences (Markle 1969). Pressey-type programs were expanded to include short sequences of remedial instruction, and these were often called "adjunct programs" because they were used after material had been introduced in a conventional lesson or lecture. However, when teachers began to use ordinary linear programs in a similar way, this distinction became somewhat artificial.

The most notable change during the 1960s was the gradual removal of the original guiding principles of linear programming, sometimes with advantage and sometimes not. The first to go was the principle of the short frame, which was found to underestimate the cognitive capacities of many learners. Moreover, the original frame size was an artifact of the window size of the early teaching machines, a restriction which was removed as teaching machines were replaced in most educational contexts by cheaper and more flexible programmed texts. In the interests of efficiency, it was argued that students should receive as much information at a time as they could handle. Master performers usually handled a lot of information at once, and dividing it up into too many pieces was delaying, if not actually preventing, the development of mastery in the student. If too much information was included, this would become apparent when the program was tested and appropriate revisions could then be made. Large frames were particularly important when multiple discriminations were being developed, when passages of text were being analyzed, when maps or diagrams were included, or when task analysis revealed procedural knowledge that could be represented in algorithmic form. They also made the task of frame design more difficult and more imaginative, because responses had to be created which required the student to actively process larger and more complex chunks of information. An influential early exponent of this approach was Gilbert, who devised a complex system of task analysis and frame design called "mathetics" and produced some stunningly elegant programs.

Gilbert paved the way for what came to be known as "lean programming," in which programmers tried to use some of the newer large-frame designs to maximize step size and produce programs with as few frames as possible. One approach advocated by this group of programmers was to convert their preliminary list of teaching points into a small number of criterion frames. Each criterion frame, if correctly answered, indicated the achievement of a significant learning objective; so the full set of criterion frames should be, and usually was, similar to the post-test. Having designed these criterion frames, the programmer then attempted to get students to succeed on each of them with as little preliminary instruction as possible. Since sequences that proved to be "too lean" could easily be detected and revised, this was found to be a practical method of working, and it stimulated programmers' creativity much more than writing to a formula.

The process of shaping behavior became more sophisticated as a range of techniques for prompting the correct response was developed (Markle 1969). However, some linear programmers abandoned the idea of shaping in favor of a simulated dialogue with the student which relied more on question-and-answer sequences than on the gradual withdrawal of prompts. This was more attractive to subject experts, but those who were untutored or inexperienced often failed to realize that information which was not needed for working out the answer to a frame was rarely learned. Programmers who indulged in teachers' natural tendency to talk too much were exposed by Holland's (1965) famous blackout technique, for he showed that if those parts of a frame that were unnecessary for finding the correct response were blacked out, the student usually learned just as much. Nevertheless, programmers who understood the importance of active responding were able to make much more use of question-and-answer sequences than Skinner had originally envisaged.

This principle of active responding was a modification of Skinner's original insistence on overt responding. When books were used instead of teaching machines, the benefit of students having to write their responses (and hence render the books nonreusable) was soon questioned. It was found that in many contexts active responding, in which the learner's mind had to process the necessary information in order to answer a question, was sufficient, and no overt manifestation of the response was necessary unless it was needed as evidence for making later modifications to the program. Overt responding, however, was still superior: (a) when the learners were young children, (b) when the material was difficult, and (c) when special terminology was being taught.

The related principle of providing knowledge of results has also been questioned, though evidence suggests it is usually an advantage. In particular, feedback enhances performance: (a) if the learner is motivated, (b) if knowledge of results is informative, and (c) if the learner knows or is told what to do to correct his or her errors. Though no longer applied in so rigid a manner, the principles of active responding and feedback remain important for instructional design, and it is important to note that they are necessary for cognitive as well as for behavioral approaches to learning.

Two further assumptions that were common to both the linear and the branching paradigms were individualized learning and learner-controlled pacing. Neither has been abandoned as a result of research or practical experience, but both have been modified under certain circumstances. One alternative is for pairs of students to work through a program together, the supposition being that they will challenge and assist each other and enjoy each other's company. Comparisons of pairs with individual working have usually given no significant difference (Hartley 1974). However, one would expect such findings to depend on the particular pairings chosen, previous experience of partners working together, and the learning milieu of each particular classroom.

Learner-controlled pacing is often relinquished when fixed-pace media, such as motion pictures or audiotape, are used to present a program, though some programs of this type stop moving whenever a question is asked, allowing the students to start them again as soon as they are ready. Large group presentation with fixed pacing may be necessary if there is insufficient equipment or space for individualized learning, and it has been argued that fixed-pace programming is more efficient on time as well. Once the initial novelty has passed, students who are not very highly motivated tend to follow Parkinson's Law, their rate of work adapts to fit the time available (Hartley 1974).

4. Developmental Testing

Though Skinner's reinforcement theory assigned special priority to maintaining a very low error rate, this particular principle soon diminished in importance, not because the theoretical debate was resolved but because errors acquired a much more practical significance. Skinner's (1958) comment that "an unexpected advantage of machine instruction has proved to be the feedback to the programmer" became the understatement of the decade. Since programmers were dependent on errors for information about where and how to revise, they were much more interested in their distribution pattern than in any overall rate. Particular attention, for example, was given to any error in a criterion frame and the prior sequence of responses would be scrutinized for clues to any mistake. But on less important frames, errors were ignored unless their frequency was high or some obvious improvement in frame design was readily apparent.

The greatest contribution of programmed learning was probably attitudinal. Programmers accepted that it was their responsibility to get their programs to work for any student in their target population. Hence the focus of developmental testing was on course improvement, and it was not until a later validation stage that they sought firm evidence of the effectiveness of their

final version (Markle 1967). Clues for revision were more important in the earlier stages than statistics, and programmers soon found that more useful feedback was gained from intensive work with individual students than from large-scale testing. This allowed them to discuss mistakes and to try out alternative explanations on the spot. Indeed one group of "lean programmers" suggested changing the usual program writing sequence to: (a) prepare a sequence of criterion frames, (b) tutor a few students through these frames, recording the dialogue on audiotape, (c) use this experience to write the first draft of the program.

As people become more aware of the importance of developmental testing and less confident of the validity of the original programming paradigms, they sought to define programmed learning in terms of the developmental process rather than the features of the product. No doubt this change in preferred definition was hastened by the appearance on the market of large numbers of low-quality programs which had not been properly developed but still bore a superficial resemblance to the early programmed texts. But it also represented a genuine change of opinion amongst programmers, albeit one which failed to convert educators in general away from their product-based image of programmed learning. Figure 1 summarizes the sequence of events which most programmers in the late 1960s were accepting as not only describing but also characterizing and defining the programming process.

5. The Move Toward Instructional Systems

When people tried to use programs as part of larger instructional systems with ordinary teachers in ordinary classrooms, a host of new problems arose (Schramm 1964). First, programs were only available for isolated topics; so it was difficult to construct a whole course from published programmed materials. This made them so much more inconvenient (and expensive) than the traditional textbook that only the most dedicated teachers were likely to take the trouble. Second, when whole programmed courses did appear, they showed little influence of the revolution in frame design described earlier and were uniformly dull. Third, teachers were quite unprepared for the difficult job of sifting out programs of genuine quality which had been properly tested and validated from the crowd of poor imitations that flooded the market. While a bad textbook could be tolerated and adapted, a bad program was a total disaster. Many teachers encountered such programs in the 1960s and were effectively inoculated against programmed learning for life.

Even with good programs, cultural and organizational factors hindered proper implementation. Most schools are not designed for individualized learning, either practically or attitudinally. Teachers find it difficult to manage students who finish early or to

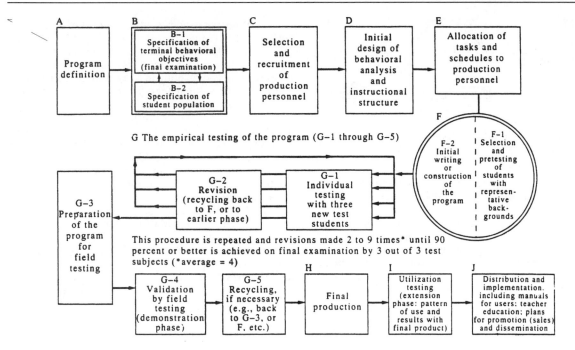

Figure 1
A generalized flowchart of program development
Source: Lange 1967

integrate programs with group activities when all the students are at different stages. Considerable confusion was caused by the plethora of teaching machines and the debate about whether machines were needed at all. Pronouncements about the ineffectiveness of conventional education and talk of machines replacing teachers was highly threatening, and the issue of the teacher's role in a programmed course was handled with an ambivalence that provoked even further anxiety.

It soon became apparent that there were two main alternatives. Programs could be used as supplementary resources on an occasional basis, or the instructional systems which used them would have to be redesigned. The first was nonthreatening but unlikely to succeed. Though using programs for occasional topics and occasional students was compatible with existing classroom practice, the problems of selecting, purchasing, and maintaining teacher awareness of what was available were considerable. There was little real incentive for any teacher who was not specially interested in programmed learning to give the matter any serious attention.

Increasing the scale of the operation from designing programs to designing courses as instructional systems was a much more attractive proposition. The systems approach was becoming an important concept in educational technology and was capable of absorbing the kind of approach to programmed learning described in

Fig. 1. Hence much of the effort of those who pioneered the field of programmed learning was redirected into what came to be called educational or instructional development. Most of the new types of instructional system invented during the late 1960s and early 1970s owed a great deal to programmed learning; but in each case some new name was invented to promote its special characteristics and to avoid association with some of the negative attitudes towards the early examples of programmed learning.

Many of the early instructional systems which evolved at school level in the late 1960s are described in Weisgerber (1971), while more recent work is summarized in other articles in this *Encyclopedia* (see *Mastery Learning*). A system which retained the use of programs that would still be recognized as such by the early pioneers is the Kent Mathematics Project (1978). This has divided the mathematics curriculum for the ages 9 to 16 into seven levels, evolved a clear teacher role in managing and supplementing its instructional materials, and developed a system for assigning students to appropriate tasks. The assignment system and a considerable variety of materials (programmed booklets, audiotapes, and games) have been gradually refined over a period of 10 to 15 years.

Similar developments in higher education are described in Dunkin (1992). The term "module approach" is often used to include both Keller courses (see Keller and Sherman 1974), and those originally

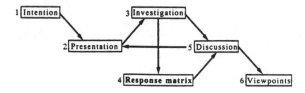

Figure 2
A structural communication study unit
Source: Egan 1976

described as "audiotutorial" (see Postlethwait et al. 1972), because of their frequent use of audiotape. Audiotutorial courses originated independently of programmed learning but later incorporated some of its concepts and techniques. This exchange was mutually beneficial because programmers were encouraged to use a wider range of media and to program practical work as well. Many of these college-level instructional systems built in roles for tutors, some of them managerial, some remedial, and some to involve students in discussion round the topic and to generally encourage intellectual inquiry. For example, a biology course developed at Sussex University, which contains some of the most intellectually demanding programmed texts, supplements these with audiovisual materials, simulations, and tutorials to assist students find connections between different aspects of the subject and to promote an inquiry-oriented approach to their studies (Tribe et al. 1975).

6. Alternative Paradigms

These aims of linkage and inquiry, and helping students to think for themselves and create their own personal maps of the subject matter are accorded special priority in a radically different approach to programming called "structural communication" (Egan 1976). This approach is modular like many of the instructional systems described above, with study units some 10 to 15 pages in length and suitable for about an hour of individual study. The construction of these study units, however, is quite unique. Each unit has six components linked together as in Fig. 2.

The intention provides a short orientation to the topic, while the presentation provides the bulk of the information—it often reads like a rather condensed version of a chapter from a textbook. The investigation then presents the students with four challenges, each designed to penetrate a different aspect of the topic. The student responds to these by selecting a group of four to eight items from a response matrix of 12 to 24 items. Each item consists of a short principle or statement, and the student has to decide which of them are most relevant and which are least relevant to the question posed by the challenge. Having made this selection, he or she consults the discussion guide

—a set of decision rules leading to a set of discussion comments; for example it may include advice such as "If you included item 5 then read comment L" or "If you omitted item 9 or item 16 then read comment P." After reading and reacting to a few assigned discussion comments the student then proceeds to a concluding viewpoints section.

An unusual advantage of this approach is the way it forces students to synthesize a viewpoint of their own, while incidentally processing and remembering a considerable amount of information. It lends itself to use as an adjunct program which can consolidate the teaching of a topic at a far more complex cognitive level than Pressey's multiple-choice testing system.

The idea of learning from multiple-choice testing is used in quite a different way in what came to be called a feedback classroom. In its more sophisticated form each student has a response board for answering multiple-choice questions wired to a master recorder at the teacher's desk, so a teacher can periodically ask a question of the class and receive immediate feedback on the distribution of answers. This keeps students actively involved and ensures that a teacher detects significant misunderstandings at an early enough stage for the lesson to be appropriately modified. An even simpler arrangement used pairs of cardboard disks. One disk is divided into five sectors, marked A, B, C, D, and E on one side and colored on the other side; then a second disk of the same size with one sector cut out is pinned to it centrally. If each student is given a pair of disks he or she can use it to answer a multiple-choice question by putting the chosen sector at the top where the second disk has been cut out. When he or she holds the disks up the teacher will only see the color appropriate to the student's choice, for example, blue, because the other colors will be masked by the rest of the cut-out disk. This enables the teacher to judge the approximate distribution of the students' answers by rapidly assessing the color distribution held up. Used in this way, a planned series of multiple-choice questions, possibly presented by an overhead projector, could be said to constitute programmed teaching.

The most fully developed approach which builds on the notion of programmed teaching is a system called "programmed tutoring." This is a one-to-one method of instruction in which a tutor teaches a student by following carefully structured printed instructions. Often the student will have some kind of workbook and the tutor will be programmed in an adaptive, branching style to respond to a variety of student behaviors. The system is particularly applicable to the teaching of reading and can be adapted to use a teacher aid, parent, or even another student as the tutor (Ellson 1976, Thiagarajan 1976). Sometimes it uses a sequencing technique called "brightening" in which an item is first presented in a relatively difficult form and then later made increasingly easier by the addition of prompts: this process will be familiar to the skillful classroom teacher, but is the exact opposite of the fading or withdrawal of prompting sequences developed by the early linear programmers.

Finally, and probably of greatest significance for the future, come some of the new approaches being developed in computer-assisted learning (CAL) (see *Computer-assisted Learning*). Here, however, it should be noted that it is common for people preparing CAL sequences to be unaware of the developments in instructional design which were made by the more creative exponents of programmed learning. Computers offer great possibilities for new types of program design, but many of the older ideas are still relevant. The same mistakes are being made in CAL as with programmed learning in the 1950s: a failure to realize that instructional design is a highly skilled and time-consuming activity, widespread marketing of low-quality software, and lack of attention to the problems of implementation (see *Computer-managed Learning*).

7. Conclusion

Many people now regard programmed learning as a historical curiosity. Yet some of its products still rank among the most useful and effective materials available. The term is still associated with the low-quality programs that flooded the market in its early days, while many of its ideas have been incorporated into other "new" approaches to individualized learning. The corpus of literature on programmed learning is a major contribution to instructional design, and designers still have much to learn from careful inspection of some of its most successful products.

See also: Computers and Learning; Learning Theories: Historical Overview and Trends

References

Bloom B S, Hastings J T, Madaus G F 1971 *Handbook on Formative and Summative Evaluation of Student Learning.* McGraw-Hill, New York
Dunkin M J 1992 Teaching: University and college. In: Clark B R, Neave G (eds.) 1992 *The Encyclopedia of Higher Education*, Vol. 3. Pergamon Press, Oxford
Egan K 1976 *Structural Communication.* Fearon, Belmont, California
Ellson D G 1976 Tutoring. In: Gage N L (ed.) 1976 *The Psychology of Teaching Methods.* 75th National Society for the Study of Education (NSSE) Yearbook, Part 1. University of Chicago Press, Chicago, Illinois
Gagné R M 1977 *The Conditions of Learning*, 3rd edn. Holt, Rinehart and Winston, New York
Glaser R, Homme L E, Evans J L 1960 An evaluation of textbooks in terms of learning principles. In: Lumsdaine A A, Glaser R (eds.) 1960
Hartley J 1974 Programmed instruction 1954–74: A review. *Program. Learn. Educ. Technol.* 11: 278–91
Holland J G 1965 Research on programming variables. In: Glaser R (ed.) 1965
Keller F S, Sherman J G 1974 *The Keller Plan Handbook.* W A Benjamin, Reading, Massachusetts
Kent Mathematics Project 1978 *Teachers Guide Levels 1–4.* Ward Lock, London
Lange P C (ed.) 1967 *Programmed Instruction.* 66th National Society for the Study of Education (NSSE) Yearbook. University of Chicago Press, Chicago, Illinois
Mager R F 1961 *Preparing Objectives for Programmed Instruction.* Fearon, Belmont, California
Markle S M 1967 Empirical testing of programs. In: Lange P C (ed.) 1967
Markle S M 1969 *Good Frames and Bad: A Grammar of Frame Writing*, 2nd edn. Wiley, New York
Postlethwait S N, Novak J, Murray H T 1972 *The Audio-tutorial Approach to Learning*, 3rd edn. Burgess, Minneapolis, Minnesota
Schramm W L (ed.) 1964 *Four Case Studies of Programmed Instruction.* Fund for the Advancement of Education, New York
Skinner B F 1958 Teaching machines. In: Lumsdaine A A, Glaser R (eds.) 1960
Skinner B F, Holland J G 1958 The use of teaching machines in college instruction. In: Lumsdaine A A, Glaser R (eds.) 1960
Thiagarajan S 1976 *Programmed Instruction for Literacy Workers: A Guide for Developing Self-instructional Materials and Strategies for Adult Learners, Literacy Teachers and Discussion Leaders.* Hulton Educational, Amersham
Thomas C A, Openshaw D, Davies I K, Bird J B 1963 *Programmed Learning in Perspective: A Guide to Program Writing.* Educational Methods, Chicago, Illinois
Tribe M A, Eraut M R, Snook R K 1975 *Basic Biology Course, Tutors' Guide.* Cambridge University Press, Cambridge
Weisgerber R A (ed.) 1971 *Developmental Efforts in Individualized Learning.* Peacock, Itasca, Illinois
White R T, Gagné R M 1974 Past and future research on learning hierarchies. *Educ. Psychol.* 11: 19–28

Further Reading

Davies I K, Hartley J (eds.) 1972 *Contributions to an Educational Technology.* Butterworth, London
Glaser R (ed.) 1965 *Teaching Machines and Programmed Learning: A Source Book. Vol. 2: Data and Directions.* Department of Audiovisual Instruction, National Education Association, Washington, DC
Lumsdaine A A, Glaser R (eds.) 1960 *Teaching Machines and Programmed Learning.* Department of Audiovisual Instruction, National Education Association, Washington, DC

Learning in Adults

Adult Learning: Overview

S. D. Brookfield

Adult learning is frequently spoken of by adult educators as if it were an entirely discrete domain, having little connection to learning in childhood or adolescence. This entry will examine this claim critically by exploring four major research areas: self-directed learning, critical reflection, experiential learning, and learning to learn. Each of these has been proposed as representing a unique and exclusive adult learning process.

1. Issues in Understanding Adult Learning

Despite the plethora of journals, books, and research conferences devoted to adult learning across the world, there is no universal understanding of this process. Even though warnings are frequently issued that at best only a multitude of context and domain-specific theories are likely to result, the energy expended on developing a general theory of adult learning shows no sign of abating. Judged by epistemological, communicative, and critically analytic criteria, theory development in adult learning is weak and is hindered by the persistence of myths that are etched deeply into adult educators' minds (Brookfield 1992). These myths (which, taken together, comprise something of an academic orthodoxy in adult education) hold that adult learning is inherently joyful, that adults are innately self-directed learners, that good educational practice always meets the needs articulated by learners themselves, and that there is a uniquely "adult" learning process as well as a uniquely adult form of practice. This entry argues that it is a grave error to attempt to construct an exclusive theory of adult learning; namely, one that is distinguished wholly by its total exclusion of what is known about learning at other stages in the lifespan. Indeed, a strong case can be made that as learning is examined across the lifespan, the variables of culture, ethnicity, personality, and political ethos assume far greater significance in explaining how learning occurs and is experienced than does the variable of chronological age of the learner.

2. Major Areas of Research on Adult Learning

The four areas discussed below represent the postwar preoccupations of adult learning researchers. Each area has its own internal debates and emphases, yet the concerns and interests of those working within each of them overlap significantly with those of the other three. Indeed, several researchers have made important contributions to more than one of these areas. Considered as a whole, these areas of research constitute an espoused theory of adult learning that informs how many adult educators practice their craft.

2.1 Self-directed Learning

Self-directed learning focuses on the process by which adults take control of their own learning, in particular how they set their own learning goals, locate appropriate resources, decide on which learning methods to use, and evaluate their progress. Work on self-direction is so widespread that it warrants an annual international symposium devoted solely to research and theory in the area (see *Self-directed Adult Learning*). After criticisms that the emphasis on self-directed learning as an adult characteristic was being uncritically advanced, that studies were conducted mostly with middle-class subjects, that issues concerning the quality of self-directed learning projects were being ignored, and that it was treated as disconnected from wider social and political forces, there have been some attempts to inject a more critical tone into work in this area. Meta-analyses of research and theory conducted by Australian, Canadian, and American authors have raised questions about the political dimension to self-directedness and the need to study how deliberation and serendipity intersect in self-directed learning projects (Collins 1988, Candy 1990, Brockett and Hiemstra 1991). There has also been a spirited debate concerning Australian criticism of the reliability and validity of the most widely used scale for assessing readiness for self-directed learning (Field 1991). At least one book, developed in the South African adult educational experience, has argued that self-direction

743

must be seen as firmly in the tradition of emancipatory adult education (Hammond and Collins 1991).

A number of important questions remain regarding the understanding of self-direction as a defining concept for adult learning. For example, the cross-cultural dimension of the concept has been almost completely ignored. More longitudinal and life-history research is needed to understand how periods of self-directedness alternate with more traditional forms of educational participation. Work on gender has criticized the ideal of the independent, self-directed learner as reflecting patriarchal values of division, separation, and competition. The extent to which a disposition to self-directedness is culturally learned, or is tied to personality, is an open issue. Researchers still struggle to understand how various factors—the adult's previous experiences, the nature of the learning task and the domain involved, the political ethos of the time—affect the decision to learn in this manner. There is also a need to know more about how adults engaged in self-directed learning use social networks and peer support groups for emotional sustenance and educational guidance. Finally, work is needed on clarifying the political dimensions of this idea; particularly on the issues of power and control raised by the learner's assuming responsibility for choices and judgments regarding what can be learned, how learning should happen, and whose evaluative judgments regarding the quality and effectiveness of learning should hold sway. If the cultural formation of the self is ignored, it is all too easy to equate self-direction with separateness and selfishness, with a narcissistic pursuit of private ends in disregard to the consequences of this for others and for wider cultural interests. A conception of learning that views adults as self-contained, volitional beings, scurrying around engaged in individual projects, is one that works against cooperative and collective impulses. Citing self-direction, adults can deny the importance of collective action, common interests, and their basic interdependence in favour of an obsessive focus on the self.

2.2 Critical Reflection

Developing critical reflection is probably the main idea for many adult educators who have long been searching for a form and process of learning that could be claimed to be distinctively adult. Evidence that adults are capable of this kind of learning can be found in developmental psychology, where a host of constructs such as embedded logic, dialectical thinking, practical intelligence, reflective judgment, postformal reasoning, and epistemic cognition describe how adults come to think contextually and critically (Brookfield 1987, 1991). As an idea critical reflection focuses on three interrelated processes: (a) the process by which adults question and then replace or reframe an assumption that up to that point has been uncritically accepted as representing

commonsense wisdom; (b) the process through which adults take an alternative perspective on ideas, actions, forms of reasoning and ideologies previously taken for granted; (c) the process by which adults come to recognize the hegemonic aspects of dominant cultural values and to understand how self-evident renderings of the "natural" state of the world actually bolster the power and self-interest of unrepresentative minorities. Writers in this area vary according to the extent to which critical reflection should have a political edge, or the extent to which it can be observed in domains of adult life such as personal relationships and workplace actions. Some confusion is caused by the fact that psychoanalytic and critical social theoretical traditions coexist uneasily in many studies of critical reflection.

The most important work in this area is that of Mezirow (1991). Mezirow's early work (conducted with women returning to higher education) focused on the idea of perspective transformation, which he understood as the learning process by which adults come to recognize and reframe their culturally induced dependency roles and relationships. More recently he has drawn strongly on the work of Jürgen Habermas to propose a theory of transformative learning "that can explain how adult learners make sense or meaning of their experiences, the nature of the structures that influence the way they construe experience, the dynamics involved in modifying meanings, and the way the structures of meaning themselves undergo changes when learners find them to be dysfunctional" (Mezirow 1991 p. xii). Applications of Mezirow's ideas have been made with widely varying groups of adult learners such as displaced homemakers, male spouse abusers, and those suffering ill health, though his work has been criticized by educators in Nigeria, the United States, New Zealand, and Canada for focusing too exclusively on individual transformation (Collard and Law 1989, Ekpenyong 1990, Clark and Wilson 1991).

Many tasks remain for researchers of critical reflection as a dimension of adult learning. A language needs to be found to describe this process to educators which is more accessible than the usual psychoanalytic and critical theory terminology. More understanding of how people experience episodes of critical reflection (viscerally as well as cognitively), and how they deal with the risks of committing cultural suicide that these entail, would help educators respond to fluctuating rhythms of denial and depression in learners. Much research in this area confirms that critical reflection is context- or domain-specific. How is it that the same people can be highly critical regarding, for example, dominant political ideologies, yet show no critical awareness of the existence of repressive features in their personal relationships? Theoretical analyses of critical reflection (frequently drawn from Habermas's work) outweigh to a considerable degree the number of ethnographic, phenomenological studies of how this process is experienced. Contextual factors surrounding the decision to forgo or pursue action after a period of critical reflection are still unclear, as is the extent to which critical reflection is associated with certain personality characteristics.

2.3 Experiential Learning

The emphasis on experience as a defining feature of adult learning was expressed in Lindeman's frequently quoted aphorism that "experience is the adult learner's living textbook" (1926 p. 7) and that adult education was, therefore, "a continuing process of evaluating experiences" (p. 85). This emphasis on experience is central to the concept of andragogy that has evolved to describe adult education practice in societies as diverse as those of the United States, the United Kingdom, France, Hungary, Poland, Russia, Estonia, the former Czechoslovakia, Finland, and the former Yugoslavia (Savicevic 1991, Vooglaid and Marja 1992). The belief that adult teaching should be grounded in adults' experiences, and that these experiences represent a valuable resource, is considered as crucial by adult educators of every conceivable ideological hue (see *Experiential and Open Learning*). Of all the models of experiential learning that have been developed, David Kolb's has probably been the most influential in prompting theoretical work among researchers of adult learning (Jarvis 1987). But almost every textbook on adult education practice affirms the importance of experiential methods such as games, simulations, case studies, psychodrama, role play, and internships, and many universities now grant credit for adults' experiential learning. Not surprisingly, then, the gradual accumulation of experience across the contexts of life is often argued as the chief difference between learning in adulthood and learning at earlier stages in the lifespan. Yet an exclusive reliance on accumulated experience as the defining characteristic of adult learning contains two discernible pitfalls, as follow.

First, experience should not be thought of as an objectively neutral phenomenon, a river of thoughts, perceptions, and sensations into which we decide, occasionally, to dip our toes. Rather, experience is culturally framed and shaped. How events are experienced and the readings made of them are problematic; that is, they change according to the language and categories of analysis used, and according to the cultural, moral, and ideological vantage points from which they are viewed. In a very important sense experience is constructed: how we sense and interpret what happens to us and to the world around us is a function of structures of understanding and perceptual filters that are so culturally embedded that we are scarcely aware of their existence or operation.

Second, the quantity or length of experience is not necessarily connected to its richness or intensity. For example, in an adult educational career spanning 30 years the same one year's experience can, in effect, be repeated 30 times. Indeed, one's "experience" over these 30 years can be interpreted using uncritically assimilated cultural filters in such a way as to prove to oneself that students from certain ethnic groups are lazy or that fear is always the best stimulus to critical thinking. Because of the habitual ways in which meaning is drawn from experiences, these experiences can become evidence for the self-fulfilling prophecies that stand in the way of critical insight. Uncritically affirming people's histories, stories, and experiences risks idealizing and romanticizing them. Experiences are neither innocent nor free from the cultural contradictions that inform them.

2.4 Learning to Learn

The ability of adults to learn how to learn—to become skilled at learning in a range of different situations and through a range of different styles—has often been proposed as an overarching purpose for those educators who work with adults (see *Learning to Learn: Adult Education*). Like its sister term of "metacognition," learning how to learn suffers for lack of a commonly agreed on definition, functioning more as an umbrella term for any attempts by adults to develop insight into their own habitual ways of learning. Most research on this topic has been conducted by Smith (1990) who drew together educators from the United States, Scotland, Australia, Germany, and Sweden to work on theory development in this area. An important body of related work (focusing mostly on young adults) is that of Kitchener and King (1990) who propose the concepts of epistemic cognition and reflective judgment. These authors emphasize that learning how to learn involves an epistemological awareness deeper than simply knowing how one scores on a cognitive-style inventory, or what is one's typical or preferred pattern of learning. Rather, it means that adults possess a self-conscious awareness of how it is they come to know what they know—an awareness of the reasoning, assumptions, evidence, and justifications that underlie our beliefs that something is true.

Studies of learning to learn have been conducted with a range of adult groups and in a range of settings such as adult basic education, the workplace, and religious communities. Yet, of the four areas of adult learning research discussed, learning how to learn has been the least successful in capturing the imagination of the adult educational world and in prompting a dynamic program of follow-up research. This may be because, as several writers have noted, in systems of lifelong education the function of helping people learn how to learn is often claimed as being more appropriate to schools than to adult education. Many books on learning to learn restrict themselves to the applicability of this concept to elementary or secondary school learning. While it is useful to acknowledge the school's foundational and formational role in this area, it is also important to stress that developing this capacity is too difficult to be left solely to primary and secondary education. Learning to learn should be conceived as a lifelong learning project.

Research on learning to learn is also flawed in its emphasis on college students' metacognition and by its lack of attention to how this process manifests itself in the diverse contexts of adult life. That learning to learn is a skill that exists far beyond academic boundaries is evident from the research conducted on practical intelligence and everyday cognition in settings and activities as diverse as grocery shopping and betting shops (Brookfield 1991). The connections between a propensity for learning how to learn and the nature of the learning task or domain also need clarification. Learning how to learn is referred to much more frequently in studies of clearly defined skill development or knowledge acquisition than in studies examining emotional learning or the development of emotional intelligence.

3. Emergent Trends

Three trends in the study of adult learning that have emerged during the 1990s, and that promise to exercise some influence into the twenty-first century, concern: (a) the cross-cultural dimensions of adult learning; (b) adults' engagement in practical theorizing; and (c) the ways in which adults learn within the systems of education that are linked to technological advances (e.g., distance education, computer-assisted instruction, and open learning systems).

3.1 Cross-cultural Adult Learning

Although the literature in the area of cross-cultural adult learning is sparse, there are indications that the variable of ethnicity is being taken with increasing seriousness (Cassara 1990, Ross-Gordon 1991). As China opened its borders to adult educators in the 1980s, research on Chinese conceptions of adult learning started to emerge (Pratt 1992). As literature in this area makes clear, framing discussions of cultural diversity around a simple dichotomy of White and non-White populations vastly oversimplifies a complex reality. Among ethnic groups themselves there are significant intra- and intergroup tensions. In the United States, for example, Black, Hispanic, and Asian workers have points of tension between them. Within each of these broad groupings there is a myriad of overlapping rivalries; between African-Americans and immigrants from the British West Indies; between Colombians, Puerto Ricans, Cubans and Dominicans; between Koreans, Vietnamese, Cambodians, and Hmong tribespeople. Moreover, the tribal cultures of Native Americans cannot be conceptualized as a culturally homogeneous block.

Two important insights for practice have been suggested by early research into cross-cultural adult learning. First, adult educators from the dominant American, European, and Northern cultures will need to examine some of their assumptions, inclinations, and preferences about "natural" adult learning and adult teaching styles (Brookfield 1986). For the Hmong tribespeople from the mountains of Laos who are used to working cooperatively and to looking to their teachers for direction and guidance, ways of working that emphasize self-directedness and that place the locus of control with the individual student will be experienced, initially at least, as dissonant and anxiety-producing (Podeschi 1990). However, their liking for materials that focus on personal concrete experience fits well with the adult education practices that emphasize experiential approaches. Second, "teaching their own" is a common theme in case studies of multicultural learning. In other words, when adults are taught by educators drawn from their own ethnic communities they tend to feel more comfortable and to do better. Ethnocentric theories and assumptions regarding adult learning styles underscore the need for mainstream adult educators to research their own practice with native and aboriginal peoples. This will require a critically responsive stance toward their practice (Brookfield 1990) and a readiness to examine some of their most strongly held, paradigmatic assumptions (Brookfield 1987).

3.2 Practical Theorizing

Practical theorizing is an idea most associated with the work of Usher (Usher and Bryant 1989) who has focused on the ways in which educational practitioners—including adult educators—become critically aware of the informally developed theories that guide their practice. Practical theorizing has its origins in practitioners' attempts to grapple with the dilemmas, tensions, and contradictions of their work. Actions that educators take in these situations often appear instinctual. Yet, on reflection, these apparently instinctive reactions can be understood to be embedded in assumptions, readings, and interpretations that practitioners have evolved over time to make sense of their practice.

Practitioners seem to arrive at a more informed understanding of their informal patterns of reasoning by subjecting these to critical review, drawing on two important sources. First, they compare their emerging informal theories to those of their colleagues. This happens informally in individual conversations and in a more structured way through participation in reflection groups. Colleagues serve as mirrors in these groups; they reflect back to the practitioner readings of his or her behavior that come as an interesting surprise. As they describe their own reactions and experiences dealing with typical crises, colleagues can help the individual worker reframe, broaden, and refine his or her own theories of practice. Second, practitioners also use formal theory as a lens through which to view their own actions and the assumptions that inform these. As well as providing multiple perspectives on familiar situations, formal theory can help educators "name" their practice by illuminating the general elements of what were thought of as idiosyncratic experiences. These two sources—colleagues' experiences and formal theory—intersect continuously in a dialectical interplay of particular and universal perspectives.

3.3 Distance Learning

In contrast to its earlier equation with necessarily limiting correspondence study formats, distance education is now regarded as an important setting within which a great deal of significant adult learning occurs (Gibson 1992). Weekend college formats, multimedia experimentations, and the educational possibilities unleashed by satellite broadcasting have combined to provide learning opportunities for millions of adults across the world. That adult educational themes of empowerment, critical reflection, experience, and collaboration can inform distance learning activities is evident from case studies of practice that have been emerging. Modra (1989) provides an interesting account of how she drew on the work of radical adult educators such as Freire, Shor, and Lovett to use learning journals to encourage adults' critical reflection in an Australian distance education course. Smith and Castle (1992) propose the use of "experiential learning technology, facilitated from a distance, as a method of developing critical thinking skills" with "the scattered, oppressed adult population of South Africa" (p. 191).

4. Further Research

Ten important issues need to be addressed if research on adult learning is to have a greater influence on how the education and training of adults is conducted.

First, much greater definitional clarity is needed when the term "learning" is discussed, particularly as to whether it is being used as a noun or verb and whether it is referring to behavioral change or cognitive development (Brookfield 1986). Many writers speak about adult learning systems when they are really referring to adult educational programs. Although learning often occurs in an adult educational program, it is not a necessary or inevitable consequence of such a program.

Second, the interaction of emotion and cognition in adult learning needs much greater attention. For example, can we speak of the emotional intelligence adults develop? Classificatory schema and conceptual categories dealing with adult learning tend to focus on settings for learning (communities, schools, religious communities, the workplace, and so on), or on externally observable processes (self-directed learning, collaborative learning, and so on). Emotional dimensions to conceptual or instrumental learning, or understanding how adults learn about their own emotional selves, are matters that are rarely addressed. More attention is needed to how making meaning, critical thinking, and entering new cognitive and instrumental domains are viscerally experienced processes.

Third, adult learning needs to be understood much more as a socially embedded and socially constructed phenomenon (Jarvis 1987). Research on adult learning draws almost exclusively from psychologistic sources. It is easy to forget that the "self" in a self-directed learning effort is a socially formed self and that the goals of adults' self-directed learning can therefore be analyzed as culturally framed goals. Learning is a collective process involving the cultural formation and reproduction of symbols and meaning perspectives. It should not be understood or researched as if it were disconnected, idiosyncratic, and wholly autonomous.

Fourth, many more cross-cultural perspectives are needed to break the Eurocentric and North American dominance in research in adult learning and to understand intercultural differences in industrialized societies. Blithe generalizations about "the adult learner," "adults as learners," or "the nature of adult learning" imply that people over 25 form a homogeneous entity simply by virtue of their chronological age. Yet the differences of class, culture, ethnicity, personality, cognitive style, learning patterns, life experiences, and gender among adults are far more significant than the fact that they are not children or adolescents. It is necessary to be much more circumspect when talking about adults as if they were an empirically coherent entity simply by virtue of the fact that they are no longer in school. In particular, it is necessary to challenge the ethnocentrism of much theorizing in this area, which assumes that adult learning as a generic phenomenon or process is synonymous with the learning undertaken in university continuing education classes by White American middle-class adults in the postwar era.

Fifth, the role played by gender in learning is as poorly understood in adulthood as it is at other stages in the lifespan. It is still an open question as to whether the forms of knowing uncovered in some studies of adult women learners are solely a function of gender, are connected to the developmental stages of adulthood, or are culturally constructed.

Sixth, the predominant focus in studies of adult learning on instrumental skill development needs widening to encompass work on spiritual and significant personal learning and to understand the interconnections between these domains. This is particularly so given the fact that in surveys of adult learning most people point to learning in workplaces, families, communities, and recreational societies to be more prevalent and significant than learning undertaken within formal education.

Seventh, a way should be found to grant greater credibility to adults' renderings of the experience of learning from the "inside." Most descriptions of how adults experience learning are rendered by researchers' pens, not learners themselves. More phenomenographic studies of how adults feel their way through learning episodes, given in their own words and using their own interpretations and constructs, would enrich our understanding of the significance of learning to adults.

Eighth, the growing recognition accorded to qualitative studies of adult learning should be solidified. In speaking of research that has influenced their practice, adult educators place much greater emphasis on qualitative studies as compared to survey questionnaires or research through experimental designs.

Ninth, research on adult learning needs to be integrated much more tightly with research on adult development and adult cognition. With a few notable exceptions (Tennant 1988, Merriam and Caffarella 1991) these two strongly related areas exist in separate though parallel compartments, possibly because of adult educators' self-effacing refusal to become involved with what they see as academically "pure" research. There is also a belief held by many adult educators that theirs is a field of applied practice and that questions of theoretical and conceptual import should therefore be left to academics working within universities.

Finally, the links between adult learning and learning at other stages in the lifespan need much more attention (Tuijnman and van Der Kamp 1992). To understand adult learning it is necessary to know about its connections to learning in childhood and adolescence and to the formation during these periods of interpretative filters, cognitive frames, and cultural rules.

See also: Individual Differences, Learning, and Instruction

References

Brockett R G, Hiemstra R 1991 *Self-direction in Adult Learning: Perspectives in Theory, Research, and Practice.* Routledge, New York

Brookfield S D 1986 *Understanding and Facilitating Adult Learning: A Comprehensive Analysis of Principles of Effective Practices.* Jossey-Bass, San Francisco, California

Brookfield S D 1987 *Developing Critical Thinkers: Challenging Adults to Explore Alternative Ways of Thinking and Acting.* Jossey-Bass, San Francisco, California

Brookfield S D 1990 *The Skillful Teacher: On Technique, Trust, and Responsiveness in the Classroom.* Jossey-Bass, San Francisco, California

Brookfield S D 1991 The development of critical reflection in adulthood. *New Educ.* 13(1): 39–48

Brookfield S D 1992 Developing criteria for formal theory building in adult education. *Adult Educ. Q.* 42(2): 79–93

Candy P C 1990 *Self-direction for Lifelong Learning: A Comprehensive Guide to Theory and Practice.* Jossey-Bass, San Francisco, California

Cassara B (ed.) 1990 *Adult Education in a Multicultural Society.* Routledge, New York

Clark M C, Wilson A L 1991 Context and rationality in Mezirow's theory of transformational learning. *Adult Educ. Q.* 41(2): 75–91

Collard S, Law M 1989 The limits of perspective transformation: A critique of Mezirow's theory. *Adult Educ. Q.* 39(2): 99–107

Collins M 1988 Self-directed learning or an emancipatory practice of adult education: Re-thinking the role of the adult educator. *Proc. 29th Annual Adult Education Research Conference.* Faculty of Continuing Education, University of Calgary

Ekpenyong L E 1990 Studying adult learning through the history of knowledge. *Int. J. Lifelong Educ.* 9(3): 161–78

Field L 1991 Guglielmino's self-directed learning readiness scale: Should it continue to be used? *Adult Educ. Q.* 41(2): 100–03

Gibson C C 1992 Distance education: On focus and future. *Adult Educ. Q.* 42(3): 167–79

Hammond M, Collins R 1991 *Self-directed Learning: Critical Practice.* Kogan Page, London

Jarvis P 1987 *Adult Learning in the Social Context.* Croom Helm, London

Kitchener K S, King P M 1990 The reflective judgment model: Transforming assumptions about knowing. In: Mezirow J (ed.) 1990 *Fostering Critical Reflection in Adulthood: A Guide to Transformative and Emancipatory Learning.* Jossey-Bass, San Francisco, California

Lindeman E C L 1926 *The Meaning of Adult Education.* New Republic, New York

Merriam S B, Caffarella R S 1991 *Learning in Adulthood: A Comprehensive Guide.* Jossey-Bass, San Francisco, California

Mezirow J 1991 *Transformative Dimensions of Adult Learning.* Jossey-Bass, San Francisco, California

Modra H 1989 Using journals to encourage critical thinking at a distance. In: Evans T, Nation D (eds.) 1989 *Critical Reflections on Distance Education.* Falmer Press, London

Podeschi R 1990 Teaching their own: Minority challenges to mainstream institutions. In: Ross-Gordon J M, Martin L G, Briscoe D (eds.) 1990 *Serving Culturally Diverse Populations.* Jossey-Bass, San Francisco, California

Pratt D D 1992 Chinese conceptions of learning and teaching: A Westerner's attempt at understanding. *Int. J. Lifelong Educ.* 11(4): 301–20

Ross-Gordon J M 1991 Needed: A multicultural perspective for adult education research. *Adult Educ Q.* 42(1): 1–16

Savicevic D M 1991 Modern conceptions of andragogy: A European framework. *Studies in the Education of Adults* 23(2): 179–201

Smith J E, Castle J 1992 Experiential learning for critical thinking: A viable prospect for distance education in South Africa? *Int. J. Lifelong Educ.* 11(3): 191–98

Smith R M (ed.) 1990 *Learning to Learn Across the Lifespan.* Jossey-Bass, San Francisco, California

Tennant M 1988 *Psychology and Adult Learning.* Routledge, London

Tuijnman A, van Der Kamp M (eds.) 1992 *Learning Across the Lifespan: Theories, Research, Policies.* Pergamon Press, Oxford

Usher R S, Bryant I 1989 *Adult Education as Theory, Practice and Research: The Captive Triangle.* Routledge, New York

Vooglaid Y, Marja T 1992 Andragogical problems of building a democratic society. *Int. J. Lifelong Educ.* 11(4): 321–28

Experiential and Open Learning for Adults

R. H. Paul

The concepts of experiential and open learning are increasingly having an impact on formal education. In university adult education, the previously strong distinctions between "on" and "off" site learning are being blurred as adults return ever more frequently to part-time study, and as institutional programs increasingly integrate off-site and experiential activities into the curriculum. As education increasingly becomes a lifelong activity, flexible and open learning systems become essential means of responding to the tremendous learning needs of the adult population. This entry discusses the principles and applications of open and experiential learning, their importance to adult education, and their implications for educational development.

1. Open Learning

Open learning is a rapidly evolving concept which has had a major impact on the development of new adult education institutions and programs throughout the world since about 1970. In its application to higher and adult education, the term originated and is most widely applied in the United Kingdom.

Open learning is usually characterized by a commitment to assist students, especially adults, in overcoming deterrents to participation in adult education. Examples of such barriers are (Cross 1981, Martindale and Drake 1989):

(a) Prior educational credentials. The following strategies are used in helping adults who lack certified prerequisite knowledge: open admissions policies, accreditation of relevant experience through specific examinations, prior learning assessment, educational contracting, reduced or no requirements, and generous credit transfer arrangements.

(b) Time constraints. These can be overcome by, for example, flexible and individualized timetabling to permit students to study in their own time and at their own pace.

(c) Physical location. Various distance delivery systems are employed to serve the student in his or her own locale (home, workplace, or regional center).

(d) Financial constraints. Apart from instituting special arrangements for reducing the cost burden on adult students, the deterring effect of insufficient financial support can be reduced by using flexible timetabling and distance delivery making it possible for the student to study while working full-time.

(e) Irrelevance of curriculum materials. Open learning strategies are explicitly intended to overcome this barrier by designing learner-centered curricula, putting emphasis on the student's experience and responsibility for his or her own learning, and encouraging that learning needs identified or negotiated by the students are addressed.

(f) Intrinsic personal barriers. The anticipated negative effects may be lessened if the students are encouraged to define their own educational goals, develop self-confidence, and are informed about the advantages of efficient time management and study skills.

(g) Social and cultural bias. A learner-centered focus, which is a common feature of open learning systems, helps in reducing bias by relating to the student's own culture and experience.

In focusing on the removal of barriers, the concept of open learning tends to be critical of traditional forms of educational provision. It takes account of John Dewey's theorizing as to the relationship between personal experience and education.

Unlike learning theories based on research done primarily with children, open learning has received its impetus from adult education. This is not surprising, given its emphasis on prior experience. As such, it is a logical manifestation of available research on adult development and its implications for adult education (see *Adult Learning: Overview*).

Open learning can usefully be thought of as a paradigm against which other approaches to learning can be assessed. A model developed by Lewis (1990) provides nine criteria for assessing the orientation of a learning activity. Lewis takes into account Rumble's (1989) concern that open learning is increasingly being used to describe systems which are anything but open. Hence, one program may be relatively open in access but closed in content, while another may be more restricted as to who is admitted but more flexible as to what is learned.

However, even Lewis's model can hide more subtle barriers to openness, a point central to the work of Harris (1988), who focuses on what he terms the "micro-politics" of open learning. Since formal education commonly involves some assessment of acquired knowledge, the degree of openness of learning systems is by necessity relative, and can vary from student to student. Open learning and experiential learning are related because both emphasize the need of adapting the learning process to social, cultural, and personal variables.

2. Experiential Learning

Like open learning, experiential learning incorporates a wide range of concepts, from highly theoretical ones to the simplicity of "learning by doing." The concept is based on the traditional apprenticeship model. It acquired increased importance in the nineteenth century in response to criticism in the sciences and professions like medicine of the strong emphasis on abstract learning in formal education. Weil and McGill (1989) argue that the concept is being advocated for quite different reasons. Advocates mention the need to shift from an undue emphasis on cognitive aspects to more holistic or humanistic notions of human development, and the necessity of developing cost-efficient and flexible means of offering a relevant education to adult learners.

In the United States, John Dewey (1938) was particularly influential in emphasizing the role of experience in learning, starting from the premise of an intimate and necessary relation between the processes of actual experience and education. The challenge was to find ways to apply the lessons of the past to the problems of the present and future. Recognition of the value of experience became a practical challenge with the return of Second World War veterans who sought to make up for missed educational opportunities. This directed attention to devising processes which encouraged individuals to "make sense" of their experiences in a manner that would facilitate their return to formal education.

Experiential learning received additional impetus from the seminal UNESCO publication *Learning to Be* (Faure et al. 1972), which emphasized lifelong learning as a prerequisite for establishing the knowledge society. A radical idea at the time, lifelong learning has since been widely accepted. A central principle of lifelong learning is to incorporate the student's own experiences and aspirations and to recognise the cultural aspects of learning. As individuals mature, the richness of their experiences provides not only a basis for their own learning but also for assisting others. The challenge for educators is to help the learner to integrate personal experience into current learning activities.

Perhaps the best-known model for experiential learning is that developed by Kolb (1984), which depicts learning as a four-stage cycle. The learner: first, undergoes a concrete personal experience; second, re-examines and reflects on that experience; third, formulates abstract concepts and generalizations; and fourth, tests these in new situations. Individuals have different learning styles and one person may have different styles for different tasks. Hence, the learning cycle can be entered at any of its four stages. Whereas traditional learning models typically start with abstractions which may or may not bear any relationship to the student's experience, experiential learning in adult education emphasizes starting with concrete experience. Although Kolb's (1984) theory of the learning cycle seems relevant, in particular for designing learning environments for adults, it does not yet have an adequate empirical basis in research.

Tough (1971) notes that adults engage in many learning projects, but that formal education is concerned with conscious attempts to learn. In such cases, the challenge is to recognize learning activities through formal assessment. There are a number of responses to this challenge, the best-known being cooperative education, educational contracting, and prior assessment schemes (see Peruniak 1991).

3. Open and Experiential Learning Systems

Examples of "new" approaches to learning since the 1960s are progressive education, deschooling, experiential learning, prior learning assessment, competency-based education, contractual learning, self-directed learning, and cooperative education. These approaches have in common an attempt to democratize formal education and to make it more meaningful or relevant. Perhaps the most universal is the development of open learning systems (Thorpe and Grugeon 1987).

The pioneer in the United Kingdom was the National Extension College, a cost-efficient learning resource centre which provides centrally designed learning materials to institutions throughout the country, notably through its Flexistudy program which enables local authorities to adapt them to local needs. This led the former Manpower Services Commission to introduce its Open Tech program which provided seed money for similar ventures to apply new technologies to various delivery projects in technical and vocational open learning.

The primary motivation for the development of the United Kingdom's Open University (OU) was the democratization of higher education and, while it has been less successful than hoped in attracting students from disadvantaged backgrounds, it has been an international success in establishing the credibility of open education, including open admissions and distance education. It has spurred similar developments in most world regions.

While there is widespread networking across the various open learning institutions, notably through the International Council for Distance Education (ICDE) and similar regional bodies, it would be misleading to suggest that they are replicas of the Open University. In fact, each takes on manifestations of its own culture and rationales and processes vary considerably across national boundaries. Comparisons on Lewis's (1990) scales would reveal strong differences in the extent to which they are truly "open".

The more decentralized and diversified system in the United States has not found it necessary to create open universities, but there are many examples of institutions which provide credit for prior learning and which use new technologies to offer educational accreditation at a distance. The United States has been a leader in correspondence education for a long time, having fostered many entrepreneurial and commercial institutions with a strong emphasis on practical learning schemes. It has also been a pioneer in the application of new technologies to increase the interactive nature of distance delivery through computer-assisted learning, interactive video, and cooperative satellite systems (eg., National Technological University, International Universities Consortium, and University Without Walls).

Institutions in the United States like Antioch, Goddard, and Empire State colleges have been leaders in the development of experiential learning, notably through cooperative education and/or contract learning, which use carefully designed assessment schemes to overcome concerns about the academic value of prior experience. The establishment, in 1974, of the Cooperative Assessment of Experiential Learning (CAEL) has given legitimacy to the concept (Gamson 1989). Now standing for Council for Adult and Experiential Learning, CAEL has evolved into a freestanding nonprofit organization to promote experiential learning as an important component of higher education, primarily through formalized procedures of prior learning assessment. Its 1990 directory listed almost 300 institutional members.

Experiential learning programs have since been adopted not only in highly industrialized countries such as Japan, the United Kingdom, and Sweden and Denmark, but also in parts of Southeast and East Asia and in Eastern Europe.

4. Issues and Trends

Open and experiential learning systems have undoubtedly enhanced adult opportunity to learn. Caution is urged, however, to avoid exaggerated claims for their success. Adult education offerings tend to be mainly directed to the confident, highly motivated, and experienced adult. Many such adults have benefited from open learning institutions, primarily because of open admissions, but the majority of adult learners need far more institutional support and are not necessarily any more successful in open learning institutions than they are in more traditional ones. The real challenge is to find ways of teaching adults how to learn, and how to wean them from dependency on the student support systems which often appear essential to their success.

Moreover, the reliance of open learning systems, particularly those using distance education, on behaviorist principles and centrally controlled course packages can undermine the supposed openness of programs. The theme of putting more control into the hands of the learner is common to many innovative approaches, but controversy over academic credibility remains an important obstacle to realizing open learning.

One danger is that innovative approaches to adult education such as open and experiential learning eventually will become so institutionalized as to represent a "new" orthodoxy and that, despite open admissions and efforts to remove barriers to adult learning, they will simply perpetuate existing educational gaps, whereby those who already have obtained a higher education continue to be those most apt to take advantage of such opportunities. The effective application of new technologies such as computer-assisted learning, and interactive video, and satellite systems, may improve opportunities for interactive learning at a distance, but, again, the educational gap may be widened by the relative inaccessibility of such technologies to the disadvantaged.

5. Suggestions for Research

Much research is needed into topics such as how one encourages "self-directed," "independent," or "interdependent" learners—individuals whose previous exposure to formal education weans them from dependency on such systems in the true spirit of lifelong learning.

Experiential learning has opened up new perspectives on education, as significant differences are found in the ways that individuals perceive the world, notably as influenced by such variables as gender, age, and cultural identity. Further research on gender, in gerontology, and on cross-cultural issues may not only have an impact on adult education strategies but may also affect the way learning processes themselves are interpreted and evaluated.

6. Conclusion

The ideal combination of experience and education held out by Dewey in 1938 remains a laudable goal but its realization is still far from satisfactory. As education to the highest levels is extended to a wide audience, the complexities of overcoming both extrinsic and intrinsic barriers to learning are increasingly recognized. Nevertheless, as more and more adults demonstrate that they can learn when freed from traditional institutional restraints, open learning is gaining more acceptance and credibility.

See also: Adult Learning: Overview; Development of Learning across the Lifespan; Self-directed Adult Learning

References

Cross K P 1981 *Adults as Learners: Increasing Participation and Facilitating Learning*. Jossey-Bass, San Francisco, California

Dewey J 1938 *Experience and Education*. Macmillan, New York

Faure E et al. 1972 *Learning to Be*. UNESCO, Paris

Gamson Z F 1989 *Higher Education and the Real World: The Story of CAEL*. Longwood, Wakefield, New Hampshire

Harris D 1988 The micro-politics of openness. *Open Learning* 3(2): 13–16

Kolb D A 1984 *Experiential Learning: Experience as the Source of Learning and Development*. Prentice-Hall, Englewood Cliffs, New Jersey

Lewis R 1990 Open learning and the misuse of language: A response to Greville Rumble. *Open Learning* 5(1): 3–8

Martindale C J, Drake J B 1989 Factor structure of deterrents to participation in off-duty adult education programs. *Adult Educ. Q.* 39(2): 63–75

Peruniak G S 1991 *Prior learning assessment: Challenges to the integrity of experiential learning*. Paper presented at the 10th Annual Conf. of the Canadian Association for the Study of Adult Education, Kingston, Ontario, June

Rumble G 1989 "Open learning," "distance learning," and the misuse of language. *Open Learning* 4 (2): 28–36

Thorpe M, Grugeon D (eds.) 1987 *Open Learning for Adults*. Longman, London

Tough A M 1971 *The Adult's Learning Projects: A Fresh Approach to Theory and Practice in Adult Learning*. OISE, Toronto

Weil S W, McGill I (eds.) 1989 *Making Sense of Experiential Learning: Diversity in Theory and Practice*. Open University Press, Milton Keynes

Further Reading

Boud D, Keogh R, Walker D (eds.) 1985 *Reflections: Turning Experience into Learning*. Kogan Page, London

Keeton M T (ed.) 1976 *Experiential Learning: Rationale, Characteristics and Assessment*. Jossey-Bass, San Francisco, California

Paul R H 1990 *Open Learning and Open Management: Leadership and Integrity in Distance Education*. Kogan Page, London

Sansregret M 1988 *La Reconnaissance des Acquis*. Hurtubise, Montreal

Torbert W R 1972 *Learning from Experience: Toward Consciousness*. Columbia University, New York

Whitaker U 1989 *Assessing Learning: Standards, Principles and Procedures*. Council for Adult and Experiential Learning, Philadelphia, Pennsylvania

Group Learning

G. G. Darkenwald

This entry deals with the discussion group as a means of facilitating individual learning. Groups concerned with problem-solving or with decision-making are not discussed.

1. Theories of Group Behavior

The goal of establishing a general theory of group behavior has yet to be attained (Levine and Moreland 1990). As Cartwright and Zander noted as far back as 1968 (p. 24), many classificatory schemes have been proposed, typically by selecting a few properties (e.g., size, level of intimacy) "to define 'types' of groups on the basis of whether these properties are present or absent . . . Usually only dichotomies have resulted: formal–informal, primary–secondary, . . . temporary–permanent, consensual–symbiotic." Such classifications seem of little value for furthering our understanding of adult learning in groups.

Theoretical approaches to the study of group dynamics may have greater utility for contributing to our understanding of learning in groups than classification schemes. Among the orientations described by Cartwright and Zander (1968 pp. 26–27), field theory,

interaction theory, and systems theory are particularly germane to a basic understanding of the structure and process dimensions of learning groups. Nonetheless, it must be concluded that neither general theoretical typologies nor orientations offer much in the way of guidance for practitioners concerned with adult learning groups.

2. Learning in Groups

Nearly all organized adult learning occurs in some kind of group—classes, workshops, conferences, symposia, and so on. Each of these forms of group learning is appropriate and effective for achieving certain educational purposes, such as information transmission, problem-solving, and clarifying issues or problems. However, the concern here is with the small, participatory learning group, namely the discussion group. A defining characteristic of the discussion group is mutual education through the free and open sharing of ideas, feelings, and attitudes with respect to a specific issue or topic. Small groups of an instrumental, rather than strictly educational nature, do not fall within the scope of this entry's concerns. They include problem-solving groups, planning groups, and decision-making groups, among others. Admittedly, adults can and do learn through participation in instrumental groups, but learning is incidental to the principal purposes of such groups.

2.1 Affective and Cognitive Learning

Adult learning groups provide opportunities for both affective and cognitive learning. Typically, these two dimensions of learning are intertwined. This is particularly so in discussion groups, where cognitive learning, such as clarification of concepts or issues, is primary and is often accompanied by changes in members' attitudes.

One variant of the discussion group is primarily geared to attitude and behavioral change. Of course, cognitive learning occurs in such groups, but is merely instrumental, not an end in itself. Brookfield (1985 p. 58) makes a critical observation that "discussions of this nature seem to contradict the essential condition of discussion in that they are undertaken in order to achieve previously specified objectives. To this extent, they are not free or open discussions but exercises in attitudinal manipulation."

3. Group Discussion

Bormann (1975 p. 3) defines group discussion as "one or more meetings of a small group of people who thereby communicate, face to face, in order to fulfil a common purpose and achieve a group goal." Zander (1982 p. 30) further observes that "in a group discussion it is assumed that one does not learn from personal experiences simply by having them; one learns from hearing about the lives or ideas of others . . . Each member integrates others' thoughts with his own views in whatever way he finds sensible for him."

The specific aims or purposes of group discussion have been conceived in a variety of ways, but in general such formulations are similar. The following list, proposed by Zander (1982 p. 31), is offered here as illustrative. According to Zander, five purposes are served by group discussion:

(a) It helps members recognize what they do not know but should.

(b) It is an occasion for members to get answers to questions.

(c) It lets members get advice on matters that bother them.

(d) It lets persons share ideas and derive a common wisdom.

(e) It is a way for members to learn about one another as persons.

Other purposes commonly noted in the literature are to clarify complex concepts, issues, or problems, and gain a deeper understanding of them.

One of the principal advantages of learning by discussion is that it aids the participant to "interpret and evaluate the subject matter in terms of his or her own emotional and intellectual experience, and his or her own abilities and needs. . . . Learning achieved through the discussion method is [therefore] not only more complete, but also more immediately usable and more readily retained, because the material has pertained directly to, and become a part of, discussants' lives (Harnack et al. 1977 pp. 27–28).

The degree to which the teacher or leader exerts control over the group is perhaps the most salient factor in determining the nature and outcomes of group activities. Leader control is best conceived as a continuum ranging from virtually complete control —"teaching in which students may raise questions or comment, but the general direction is under the strict control of the teacher" (Bligh 1972 p. 150)—to total abandonment of control, resulting in a self-directed learning group. The definition of group discussion set forth above is incompatible with strict teacher control. The self-directed learning group, on the other hand, comes closer to the ideal. Although doctrinaire, the following observation (Brookfield 1985) bears directly on this issue:

A necessary condition of discussion is that there be no preconceived agenda, no cognitive path to be charted, no previously specified objectives. . . . Hence guided discussion is conceptual nonsense in that discussion is free and open by definition. (p. 57)

The position taken in this entry is that strict leader control is the equivalent of didactic teaching and thus incompatible with the fundamental nature of group discussion. Guided discussion that is not strictly leader controlled does, however, qualify as a variant of the discussion method. Furthermore, as noted below, the discussion leader plays a key role in any discussion group, including those that eventually become totally self-directed.

4. Discussion Leadership

In any kind of group, the leader, if only in the initial stages designed to lead to total group self-direction, must be able to balance initiating behaviors (task orientation) with supportive behaviors (group maintenance or strengthening). The task function involves coordinating and facilitating group activities to enhance goal achievement. The maintenance function is concerned with strengthening relationships among members by "providing warmth, friendliness; conciliating, resolving conflict, relieving tension, providing personal help, counsel, encouragement; showing understanding, tolerance of different points of view . . ." (Newcomb et al. 1965 p. 481).

Thibaut and Kelley (1959) raise the question of whether task and maintenance functions can or should be performed by the same person. They conclude, based on the research evidence, that for most groups, performance of these functions by different individuals enhances group functioning. Pankowski (1984 p. 21) points out that self-directed groups are almost always characterized by a member who presses for task accomplishment and another who performs the maintenance role, pressing for the satisfaction of the emotional/affective needs of group members.

Space precludes a discussion of the literature concerning the specific responsibilities and roles of discussion group leaders. Zander (1982 p. 31) stresses the leader's role in handling three procedural problems: "reluctance of members to take part; members' lack of ideas during discussion; and conditions in the group that restrain ready give and take." With respect to the first procedural problem, Zander (1982 p. 21) points out that "a leader need not try to get everyone talking; generally only 30 percent of those present do most of the commenting in a comfortable and efficient group." One would expect a higher participation rate than 30 percent in leaderless or self-directed discussion groups, unless broader participation is precluded by group size.

Many experts in group discussion methods stress a different perspective on the leader's principal responsibility, which, in short, is gradually to abandon the leadership role and become just another member of a self-directed discussion group. Haiman (1955 p. 9) succinctly summarizes this viewpoint: "The ultimate aim of a discussion leader in a learning situation should be to gain full status as a *member* of the group by working himself out of the leader's role."

The functioning and effectiveness of discussion groups are influenced significantly by factors other than leadership. These factors have to do with variations in the characteristics of attributes of discussion groups as described below.

5. Salient Attributes of Discussion Groups

All groups possess certain general properties or attributes that have profound effects on the manner in which they function and on the quality of group interaction and outcomes. The following attributes are discussed briefly below: composition, size, and cohesion.

5.1 Composition

Homogeneous groups, those whose members share similar characteristics, tend to foster member satisfaction and a group sense. Zander (1982 p. 3) asserts that persons whose values and beliefs "do not fit together will have a hard time forming a strong group." Common sense suggests, however, that too much homogeneity can have the undesirable effect of minimizing the divergent experiences and viewpoints so central to effective group discussion.

5.2 Size

In a research review, Levine and Moreland (1990 p. 593) conclude that "as a group grows larger, it also changes in other ways, generally for the worse. People who belong to a larger group are less satisfied . . ., participate less often . . ., and are less likely to cooperate with one another." Zander (1982 p. 34) notes that "the size of a group greatly affects how often a member can talk and how much he expects others will contribute . . . It is hard to develop a full discussion in a meeting of more than twenty-five members; discussion proceeds better in a group of closer to seven or so." Practical experience suggests that groups of fewer than six or seven are too small to sustain a productive group discussion, whereas seven to twelve seems to be the optimal group size.

5.3 Cohesion

Research has found "group effectiveness to be related to cohesiveness, which is reflected in such things as mutual liking among group members, member satisfaction, and other positive reactions to the group" (Pankowski 1984 p. 18). Zander (1982 pp. 4–5) defines group cohesiveness as "the strength of members' desire to remain members," adding that "as cohesiveness becomes stronger in a group, members talk more readily, listen more carefully, influence one another more often, volunteer more frequently, and adhere to group standards more closely."

Composition, size, and cohesion are interrelated attributes of discussion groups. They reinforce one another to promote or hinder group functioning and outcomes.

6. Problems and Issues

Only one source (Brookfield 1985) could be located that provided a thoughtful critique of the assumptions and practices central to group discussion. According to Brookfield, three cognitive outcomes are generally assumed to result from the use of the discussion method. They are: development of powers of analytic clarity, increased appreciation of the complexity of a topic gained by listening to differing viewpoints, and increased identification with the subject matter through stimulation of interest. Brookfield asserts that these outcomes are seldom realized in actual practice. He argues, for example, that clarification of thought is contingent on discussion occurring under emotionally stable circumstances, but for many adults discussion is extremely threatening. Appreciation of the complexities of a topic or issue is often precluded by the rapid pace of many discussion groups, which can lead to confusion rather than enlightenment. Brookfield's thesis is that many of the claims made with respect to the cognitive outcomes of discussion are unsubstantiated. Other concerns raised by Brookfield (1985) include the often low quality of participants' contributions with respect to their relevance to the topic or issue under consideration, the lack of coherent, cumulative learning over time, and the many dysfunctional aspects of the psychodynamics of discussion groups.

Brookfield (1985) proposes four conditions that, if met, are likely to foster meaningful and productive discussions:

> First, group members need to devise and to subscribe to an appropriate moral culture for group discussion . . . This means that the group must spend some time agreeing upon a set of procedural rules concerning the manner in which equity of participation is to be realized. Second, discussion leaders can exercise a degree of forethought regarding the selection of materials that are to form the substantive focus of group discussions . . . Third, the leader should be well versed both in the subject matter to be covered and in the principles of group dynamics . . . Fourth, discussion participants can be prepared for discussion . . . through the development of reasoning skills (so that inconsistencies and ambiguities in argument can be detected) and through the improvement of communication abilities (so that ideas can be articulated accurately). (p. 65)

Despite the problems and shortcomings identified by Brookfield, group discussion, properly conducted, can be a powerful tool for promoting adult learning. In best practice, as he himself asserts, it may well be the adult education method *par excellence*.

See also: Adult Learning: Overview; Individual Differences, Learning, and Instruction; Self-directed Adult Learning

References

Bormann E 1975 *Discussion and Group Methods: Theory and Practice*. Harper and Row, New York
Bligh D A 1972 *What's the Use of Lecturers?* Penguin, Harmondsworth
Brookfield S D 1985 Discussions as an effective educational method: In: Rosenblum S H (ed.) 1985 *Involving Adults in the Educational Process*. Jossey-Bass, San Francisco, California
Cartwright D, Zander A 1968 *Group Dynamics: Research and Theory*. Harper and Row, New York
Haiman F S 1955 The leader's role. In: Adult Education Association of the USA (eds.) 1955 *How to Lead Discussions*. Adult Education Association of the USA, Washington, DC
Harnack R K, Fest T B, Jones B S 1977 *Group Discussion: Theory and Technique*, 2nd edn. Prentice-Hall, Englewood Cliffs, New Jersey
Levine J, Moreland R 1990 Progress in small group research. *An. Rev. Psychol.* 41:593
Newcomb T M, Turner R H, Converse P E 1965 *Social Psychology: The Study of Human Interaction*. Holt, Rinehart and Winston, New York
Pankowski M L 1984 Creating participatory, task-oriented learning environments. In: Sork T J (ed.) 1984 *Designing and Implementing Effective Workshops*. Jossey-Bass, San Francisco, California
Thibaut J W, Kelley H H 1959 *The Social Psychology of Groups*. Wiley, New York
Zander A 1982 *Making Groups Effective*. Jossey-Bass, San Francisco, California

Further Reading

Berkowitz L (ed.) 1978 *Group Processes: Papers from Advances in Experimental Social Psychology*. Academic Press, New York
Cranton P A 1989 *Planning Instruction for Adult Learners*. Wall & Thompson, Toronto
Hill W F 1969 *Learning thru Discussion*. Sage, Beverly Hills, California
Houle C O 1972 *The Design of Education*. Jossey-Bass, San Francisco, California
Hyman R T 1980 *Improving Discussion Leadership*. Teachers College Press, New York
Legge D 1971 Discussion methods. In: Stephens M D, Roderick G W (eds.) 1971 *Teaching Techniques in Adult Education*. David and Charles, Newton Abbot
Rogers J 1971 *Adults Learning*. Penguin, Harmondsworth
Slavin R E 1983 *Cooperative Learning*. Longman, London

Learning in Industrial Settings

J. Lowyck

This entry reviews briefly the following topics: (a) organizational characteristics and goals; (b) theories of informal learning at work; (c) conceptions of training and development; and (d) training methods and supportive learning environments. These issues evidently are interdependent since environment, human behavior, and behavioral change or learning are strongly interconnected. As industry is influenced by multiple and fast changes in the social, political, ethical, technological, demographic, cultural, and ecological domains, rapid and complex evolutions within industry itself constantly occur, which necessitate corresponding high-level behaviors of individuals and groups. This, in turn, requires increased training and organizational strategies focused on optimal learning output.

1. Organizational Characteristics and Learning

Developing and maintaining competitiveness, managing human capital, optimizing organizational structures, restructuring work, maximizing use of technology, creating effective work environments, improving products and services are all required for the survival of modern industry (Offermann and Gowing 1990). While many routine or repetitive tasks have decreased at the workplace, more complex tasks are left to the employee who needs a more elaborated conceptual framework about the task environment and higher-order cognitive activities (Howell and Cooke 1989). Undoubtedly, evolutions within industrial settings highly influence learning needs, learning processes, and support for learning. If one focuses on learning in industrial settings, it is necessary to consider the complex environment in which both learning and training take place. The training–learning model, then, depends on several characteristics of the organization, such as the availability of a qualified workforce, type of tasks to be executed, personnel and financial conditions for learning support, organizational goals, predictability and constancy of job execution, and training as a management tool. Romiszowski (1990), for example, distinguished the following models of a work organization and the concomitant training requirements.

In a "production-line" model the line manager is equally a trainer who demonstrates the task execution, observes and corrects the trainee's actions, and measures and controls the trainee's performance. It is an apprenticeship-like training. Productivity criteria are derived from extended task analyses defined by means of work studies and meticulous time measurement. Training is highly formulated in terms of lower-level tasks and routinization.

As a result of mechanization and automation the number of repetitive, high-speed manufactory and assembly tasks drastically shrinks. Additionally the multidimensionality of the industrial organization in terms of the participation by workers, job mobility among managers, internationalization, and greater public ownership of industry all necessitate a better preparation of executive staff in order to manage the workforce. Instead of a "production-line" model, a "humanistic" model is promoted, which perceives any organization as the cooperative effort of workers and management toward the attainment of common organizational goals. Optimizing the use of human resources capital and raising social skillfulness become

main functions of management training. However, as Goldstein (1980) observed, "managers only utilized skills developed in training when the organizational climate was favorable" (p.233).

The isolation of individual training efforts from the organization together with the lack of measurement of training effectiveness give rise to an "organization" model. As an answer to the estimated ineffectiveness of management training, organization development starts from a commitment of the top management. By first drawing up a plan for the organization as a whole, goals are subsequently derived for all subparts of the organization. At any level teams and quality circles focus on reaching the organizational goals. Training within this perspective is a very practical, job-related, and process-oriented endeavor. Moreover, in order to keep a "competitive edge" corporations can no longer afford to tolerate suboptimal performance of their human capital and they originate efforts to assess organizational performance carefully. Using performance technology as a strategy, the causes of any under-performance of individuals and groups on specific tasks are diagnosed and multifaceted solutions implemented, such as job redesign, altered reward systems, new information systems, and other recruitment and selection methods (Geis 1986). Training is no longer the exclusive solution for perceived performance shortage.

The introduction of information technology in almost all sectors of industry encourages not only better performance of existing tasks, but even the creation of new activities as a consequence of knowledge handling. It is the "knowledge" model that is now most dominant. As computers take over an increasing part of routine, the focus is on higher-order cognitive processes, such as problem-finding, problem-solving, and decision-making. The metaphor of a "learning organization" has become a powerful perspective on learning in industrial settings, referring to the complex interaction of organization, training, and learning aiming at both innovative processes and the maintenance of identity (see Senge 1990, Pedler et al. 1991).

2. Learning Theories

Although research in educational psychology may be expected to contribute to the foundation of training and development in industrial settings, it has been observed by most reviewers that very little integrative literature is available to work with since both domains exist side by side. Understanding learning theories, however, is essential for any training design and development if at least a systematic and controllable approach is aimed at. Though learning models and theories are developed independently from organizational models, they nevertheless show interesting common characteristics.

2.1 Behaviorist Conceptions

Behaviorist conceptions of learning have been for a long time predominant in training development (Howell and Cooke 1989). Observable behavior is tied to environmental stimuli using reinforcement as the main paradigm. Learning requires the sequential mastery of behavioral elements. Therefore, complex knowledge or skills are subdivided into smaller parts and success in each step of the learning process is conditional for further progress. It is assumed that the accumulation of partial facts and skills can lead to the mastery of more encompassing domain knowledge and skills. Howell and Cooke (1989) observed that "the predominant educational philosophy underlying today's training programs derives from the behavioristic tradition that dominated the psychology of learning until the 1960s" (p.123). When tasks for job execution required relatively limited cognitive activity, and usable tools were available for validating training programs, this strict empiricism was not perceived as a handicap, and some demonstrably successful programs have evolved. The mere use of behaviorist learning principles, however, caused both conceptual and pragmatic problems in contexts involving higher cognitive demands. This forced those responsible for training to accept the importance of cognitive processing in most of the learning processes.

2.2 Cognitive-oriented Conceptions

Cognitive-oriented training conceptions emphasize the continuous and complex interaction between learner characteristics (prior knowledge, cognitive and metacognitive strategies), complex and context-bound tasks, cognitively powerful learning environments, and assessment of learning outcomes in terms of learner control or self-regulation, (meta-) cognitive activity, and transfer. Instead of being seen as a series of elementary subprocesses, learning is conceived in terms of information-processing, interpretation of new information, and reorganization of knowledge by the learner. Moreover, the context or situation is intrinsically part of any learning activity. Learning, within this view, is active, constructive, cumulative, self-regulated, and goal-oriented (Shuell 1986).

"Integrated," "situated," or "active" knowledge highly corresponds with the actual needs of industry since employees need to understand their own behaviors in effectively dealing with complex situations, taking simultaneously technological, organizational, and business aspects into account. This is process-oriented learning and not simply product-oriented learning in terms of isolated outcomes connected to a peculiar situation or task. Knowledge can no longer be perceived as the sum of isolated skills but as a "proactive" competency, oriented toward yet unforeseen situations and tasks (Nyhan 1991). This evidently refers to the problem of transfer.

2.3 Transfer of Training

Training undoubtedly aims at providing usable and adaptive knowledge and skills for future use. However, mainly due to difficulties of measurement, transfer in industrial settings is not well studied. In training for transfer, a distinction is often made between near and far transfer. Near transfer occurs when performance on the job meets the criteria of the task and the setting defined by the training. Far transfer requires the trainee to use learned skills for tasks and settings that differ highly from the training context. As Clark and Voogel (1985) contended, the dilemma is that when one acquires a near-transfer skill it seems to be at the expense of far-transfer generalizability of that skill. Indeed, most training in industrial settings focuses more on procedural and near transfer than on declarative and far transfer, though the importance of far transfer is acknowledged by almost all those responsible for training. This problem of inconsistency increases when emphasis is laid on on-the-job training for specific tasks, since learning of specific procedures on the job is highly contextualized which consequently inhibits transfer.

The outcomes of transfer can be studied from three different angles: (a) the similarity of "the source" and "target" situation (identical elements hypothesis); (b) the significance of general strategies for transfer; and (c) support of transfer by situated cognition. The behaviorist approach of the identical-elements approach raises problems. First, not the surface or objective similarity between "the source" and "the target" is important but the similarity as perceived by the trainee. A second problem is the difficulty of an alignment of the learning context with the functional context due to both the different functions and constraints of both situations and the difficulty of determining exactly all task features of a functional context. Considering the general strategies as defined in the so-called key qualifications, the assumption is that the new requirements of the target situation can be met by means of general or domain-undependent strategies (Mandl et al. 1991). In the case of situated cognition, transfer only takes place under the condition that the learned knowledge and skills are decontextualized by sequencing principles, emphasis on multiple perspectives, and cooperation between trainees and trainers. Examples of methods of training for transfer in industrial settings are the "learning workbench," the "cooperative self-qualification," the "autodidactic learning at the workplace," and "project-oriented learning" (see Mandl et al. 1991).

3. Training and Development: Evolution of the Field

In the *Annual Review of Psychology* an interesting series of reviews on training and development has appeared which reflects the evolution of the domain (Campbell 1971, Goldstein 1980, Wexley 1984, Latham 1988, Tannenbaum and Yukl 1992). Two main observations are the shift from the training of observable behavior to more encompassing, cognitive activities, and the gradual integration of (re-) training efforts in the organization as a whole.

In an early review, Campbell (1971) showed pessimism about the theoretical and empirical basis of training and human resource development: "By and large, the training and human resource development literature is voluminous, nonempirical, nontheoretical, poorly written, and dull" (p.565). In his recommendations, he focused on systematic behavior changes that can result from a systems approach, behavior modification methods, programmed instruction, and differential evaluation techniques.

Goldstein (1980) contended that "while the vast majority of writing in this area is not empirical, theoretical, or thoughtful, there is a small but increasingly significant literature that focuses on important issues" (p.262). In his opinion, more emphasis needs to be given to needs assessment techniques, creative development of evaluation models, embedding training in the organization, and empirical investigations that examine the usefulness of training techniques.

Wexley (1984) pointed to an increasing research effort: since Goldstein's review "much research on training and development has taken place. Training is here defined as a planned effort by an organization to facilitate the learning of job-related behavior on the part of its employees" (p.519). He referred to the shift from training to retraining, mainly due to the impact of new technologies. Moreover, training is not a stand-alone activity, but is highly influenced by internal organizational variables and the changing outside environment. While training currently is designed for well-defined tasks, this becomes problematic since there is a need for open and context-bound competencies and for complex skills in supervision and management. Training is no more perceived in terms of behavioral change, but as the multiplicative result of an individual's ability and motivation.

Latham (1988) restricted his review to scholarly journals. He described the following developments. First, training is increasingly linked to the business strategy of firms. Realizing compatibility between the training plan and the business plan is the responsibility of top management. Second, there is a shift from an almost exclusive focus on the training needs of the individual employees to that of the training needs of specific target groups and work teams. Third, the training has become less determined by the job-specific behaviors of workers and more by their cognitive abilities and judged learning potential. Finally, in terms of content there is now more attention for learning in and about other cultures.

Tannenbaum and Yukl (1992) examined whether insights contributed by cognitive and instructional psychology were being used in the design of training programs. They noted in particular that effective training depends not only on the training program itself but also on pre- and posttraining environments.

4. Training Methods and Learning Environments

Campbell (1988) pointed to the unavailability of precise training guidelines based on well-validated training principles. However, he remarked that the usual practice in industrial training could gain efficiency if the following guidelines were used as heuristics for organizing training: (a) consistency between training methods and learning processes; (b) activation of the trainee in order to reach the required performance level; (c) use of all available sources of feedback; (d) enhancement by instructional processes of the trainee's self-efficacy and self-confidence; and (e) adaptation of training methods to differences in aptitudes and prior knowledge.

Reviewing off-site training, several methods have been elaborated and their effectiveness measured. Campbell (1988) noted that most studies involve comparisons of one single method with another method or with a control condition with no training. However, it has been shown that the effectiveness of a training method is dependent upon training purposes, characteristics of trainees, and effectiveness criteria used. Reviewing more specific training methods, Tannenbaum and Yukl (1992) concluded that: "In summary, some of the same concerns can be expressed regarding the research on simulations, high-technology methods and behavior modeling. Each training method has demonstrated some utility, but more research is needed to determine the types of content for which a training method is appropriate and to discover how different aspects of the training method affect training outcomes" (p.412).

The emphasis on off-site training reveals another problem. Training decisions often focus on short-term effects, claiming that this is quicker, more productive, and more cost-effective. In this case, training is organized in settings that cause training programs to precede, interrupt, conflict with, or follow learning that occurs on the job (see Gery 1989). In short, this kind of training is seldom "just-in-time."

The importance of on-the-job or on-site training is claimed by many companies and it constitutes an important part of the total training effort. In the literature the findings on effectiveness of on-the-job training are often contradictory. Sometimes it is asserted that in the workplace skills are learned faster, retained longer, and result in greater productivity gains than skills learned in classroom settings. Others, on the contrary, contend that on-the-job training is less effective than off-site training. One of the reasons for this controversy is the fact that the unstructured form of on-the-job training often serves as a control condition. It seems as if the criticism about the measurement of effectiveness in off-site training expressed by Tannenbaum and Yukl (1992) applies to studies of on-site training as well. The need for a precise identification of the main dimensions of any training context and function is clear.

5. Conclusion

This review of learning in industrial settings reveals the complexity of the domain. First, learning and training issues focus on the discrepancy between the expected competencies of employees and their actual competence. If there is a mismatch between necessary knowledge, skills, and attitudes, training and learning support seem necessary. Second, training is dependent upon the overall strategy of an industrial organization and it represents only one possibility to solve an organizational problem since other measures such as selection, career development, reward systems, job redesign, and high-technology support are likely to be important for reaching organizational aims. Third, despite some progress in more basic research, mostly in the domain of cognitive psychology, there is a lack of instrumentation of adapted training methods. Indeed, most training design is still embedded in a behaviorist approach for off-site training contexts. Fourth, a developmental approach of learning and training is lacking. In no study are the transition steps from a highly structured environment toward an open environment covered; nor is the adaptation of the environment to the aptitudes of trainees taken seriously. These are consequences of the narrow scope of most training decisions, which focus on one specific type of training. Seldom are combinations of methods and contexts studied, such as systematic support of on-the-job training or explicit trainee-controlled off-site training. Lastly, research on training and development is often blurred by literature of a nonempirical character and there is a lack of conceptual frameworks for communication and cooperation between researchers and practitioners in the field of industrial training.

See also: Adult Learning: Overview

References

Campbell J P 1971 Personnel training and development. *Annu. Rev. Psychol.* 22: 565–602
Campbell J P 1988 Training design for performance improvement. In: Campbell J P, Campbell R J 1988 *Productivity in Organizations: New Perspectives from Industrial and Organizational Psychology.* Jossey-Bass, San Francisco, California
Clark R E, Voogel A 1985 Transfer of training principles for instructional design. *Educ. Comm. & Tech. J.* 33(2): 113–25
Geis G L 1986 Human performance technology: An overview. In: Smith M E (ed.) 1986 *Introduction to Performance Technology.* National Society for Performance and Instruction, Washington, DC
Gery G J 1989 Training vs. performance support: Inadequate training is now insufficient. *Performance Improvement Quarterly* 2: 51–71
Goldstein I L 1980 Training in work organizations. *Annu. Rev. Psychol.* 31: 229–72
Howell W C, Cooke N J 1989 Training the human information processor: A review of cognitive models. In: Goldstein I L et al. (eds.) 1989
Latham G P 1988 Human resource training and development. *Annu. Rev. Psychol.* 39: 545–82
Mandl H, Prenzel M, Gräsel 1991 The problem of transfer in vocational training. Paper presented at the Fourth European Conference for Research on Learning and Instruction, University of Turku
Nyhan B 1991 *Developing People's Ability to Learn: European Perspectives on Self-learning Competency and Technological Change.* European Interuniversity Press, Brussels
Offermann L R, Gowing M K 1990 Organizations of the future: Changes and challenges. *Am. Psychol.* 45(2): 95–108
Pedler M, Burgoyne J, Boydell T 1991 *The Learning Company: A Strategy for Sustainable Development.* McGraw-Hill, London
Romiszowski A J 1990 Trends in corporate training and development. In: Mulder M, Romiszowski A J, van der Sijde P C (eds.) 1990 *Strategic Human Resource Management.* Swets and Zeitlinger, Amsterdam
Senge P M 1990 *The Fifth Discipline: Mastering the Fine Practices of the Learning Organization.* Doubleday, New York
Shuell T J 1986 Cognitive conceptions of learning. *Rev. Educ. Res.* 56(4): 411–36
Tannenbaum S I, Yukl G 1992 Training and development in work organizations. *Annu. Rev. Psychol.* 43: 399–441
Wexley K N 1984 Personnel training. *Annu. Rev. Psychol.* 35: 519–51

Further Reading

Goldstein I L et al. (eds.) 1989 *Training and Development in Organizations.* Jossey-Bass, San Francisco, California
Patrick J 1992 *Training: Research and Practice.* Academic Press, London
Resnick L B 1991 Situations for learning and thinking. Address presented at the Annual Meeting of the American Educational Research Association, Chicago, Illinois

Learning to Learn: Adult Education

R. M. Smith

Long proposed as a major goal for formal education, learning to learn has increasingly become an object of systematic inquiry and experimentation. While much of the expanding body of relevant information pertains to the pre-adult years, the emphasis here is on learning to learn in adulthood.

1. Definition

Learning to learn is understood to be a complex, lifelong process—or a constellation of processes—through which people acquire and modify their skills and capacities for knowledge acquisition, problem-solving, and the extraction of meaning from experience. It refers to learning about learning itself. Conceptually, the idea subsumes the more specific notion of "metacognition" ("knowing about knowing" or "thinking about thinking").

There is no consensus definition of "learning to learn" (nor of "learn how to learn," a frequently used alternative term). Candy (1990) defines it discursively as follows:

(a)　It is a developmental process in which people's conceptions of learning evolve and become consciously available to systematic analysis and review.

(b)　It involves the acquisition of a repertoire of attitudes, understandings, and skills that allow people to become more effective, flexible, and self-organized learners in a variety of contexts.

(c)　It occurs both prior to, and coincidental with, learning endeavors.

(d)　It may be enhanced through processes of formal schooling and the way in which the curriculum is constructed and is therefore a viable—perhaps crucial—objective for educational systems at all levels.

(e)　It involves entering into the deep meaning structures of material to be learned and, in its most advanced forms, may lead to critical awareness of assumptions, rules, conventions, and social expectations that influence how people perceive knowledge and how they think, feel, and act when learning.

(f)　It has both generic and context-specific components.

(g)　It is a multidimensional entity whose meaning varies according to the meaning given to the word learning. (pp. 34–35)

An unresolved issue of definition is the relationship between learning to learn and "critical reflection." Mezirow et al. (1990) states that critical reflection, or critical reflectivity, is a process of testing the validity or justification of one's "taken-for-granted premises" and that adult educators have a special responsibility for its fostering and for helping learners plan to take action. The process is said to involve becoming open to alternative perspectives, recognizing and questioning one's implicit assumptions, and becoming less fearful of change: "becoming reflective of the content, process, and especially the premises of one's prior learning is central to cognition for survival in modern societies" (p. 375). Brookfield (1990 p. 332) posits "reflecting on reflections" as the "same kind of psychological processes as learning to learn." However, there appears to be some danger here of a reductionist point of view that may vitiate the impact of an overall concept of learning to learn that accommodates to such disparate matters, among many, as study skills enhancement, training for independent or collaborative learning, and enhancing holistic learning capacity. There clearly is more to learning to learn than becoming critically reflective.

2. How People Learn to Learn

Learning to learn is a matter of both aptitude and personal experience, and people can typically be said to learn to learn in a relatively haphazard manner. From in-school and out-of-school experience, people constantly acquire new information and behaviors. While so engaged, they gradually develop personal learning strategies and personal knowledge about the optimum conditions for learning. Each person develops a concept of "self-as-learner." The learning to learn process is understood as haphazard because it results not so much from deliberate interventions on the part of teachers or trainers to improve learning capacity and performance as from personal interpretations over time of learning-related experience. These interpretations often prove dysfunctional as far as becoming an active, flexible, confident learner in a variety of contexts is concerned. Hence the growing interest in the deliberate enhancement of learning capacities, dispositions, and strategies through such means as curriculum planning, instruction, and training (Candy 1990).

One perspective on the issue of how people learn to

learn comes from identifying what are believed to be the most important factors leading to effectiveness in lifelong learning. Among these there is considerable agreement about the importance of awareness, reflection, and self-monitoring. The three concepts exhibit an interactive and mutually re-enforcing relationship. "Awareness" refers to insight into self-as-learner and to understandings about education, learning, and learning-related processes.

Effective learners are usually able to describe their preferred ways of taking in and processing information or receiving instruction and undergoing evaluation as well as their preferred environments for learning (i.e., their learning styles). They tend to be more aware of their motives, purposes, and goals for learning. They understand that to learn may be variously to memorize pieces of information, to acquire knowledge for practical application, to abstract meaning from experience, or even to re-interpret reality. They are sensitive to a difference between learning and being taught. They possess reasonably accurate perceptions of the extent of their knowledge and their capabilities. They are also aware of the in- and out-of-school opportunities and resources for learning available to them, which are relatively rich in most industrialized societies. It has also been shown to be useful for the individual to develop something of a sophisticated concept of knowledge, one that acknowledges differences between official, unofficial, and personal knowledge and all that have value—that a person may think relativistically about one domain of knowledge and narrowly or rigidly about others, and that many problems have more than one "correct" answer. People thus learn to learn more effectively as they develop awareness as learners. Self-monitoring and reflection drive this development.

3. Facilitation

Facilitation takes two primary forms: either (a) building a learning to learn dimension into programming and instruction—for example, teaching a subject from a learning to learn stance and perspective; or (b) designing and conducting distinct, discrete events aimed at learning proficiency enhancement—such as a workshop on coping with examinations or on group problem-solving strategies. The latter type of intervention is frequently labeled "training." Approaches and resources for facilitation are discussed in Smith (1982) and Gibbs (1981, 1992).

Facilitators are usually advised to expect resistance and difficulties in helping people to externalize, examine, and modify assumptions and habits related to learning, study, and knowledge. It is recommended that they (a) find ways to make process training palatable and understandable; (b) maintain a climate conducive to behavioral change; (c) carefully adapt approaches and materials to different audiences; and

(d) seek ways of continually strengthening activeness, self-awareness, and reflection in learning (Smith 1982, 1992)

Hammond (1990) describes and evaluates five comprehensive approaches for enhancing effectiveness in learning and states that such programs are likely to be effective and gain acceptance to the extent that they include a credible theoretical base, undergo field testing and evaluation, provide practice and application activity and support in the employment of new behaviors, make available useful materials for both facilitator and learner, and provide training for facilitators if needed.

The role of the facilitator in problem-based learning (Barrows and Tamblyn 1980) has been carefully analyzed and described in Barrows (1988), the principal advocate of an approach intended to place active, independent learning and problem-solving at the center of medical education and continuing education for physicians. Meeting in small groups with a "tutor," participants work at simulated problems drawn from everyday practice:

> The tutor . . . facilitates student learning through guidance at the meta-cognitive level. . . . It is the tutor's expertise in this process, not in the content areas in which the students are studying, that is important. The students are expected to acquire the knowledge they need from content experts . . . who serve as consultants, as well as books, journals, and automated information sources. . . . The tutor guides the students through repeated practices in reasoning and self-directed study, improved through their increasing skills in self-assessment. Although the tutor may be more directive initially and closely models the reasoning processes and information seeking processes he hopes the students will acquire, he eventually withdraws from the group as they learn to take on responsibility for their own learning. (p. 50)

Among the facilitative strategies employed by the tutor with this approach are modeling, climate setting, the asking of probing questions, suggesting resources, challenging group members to substantiate their statements, concensus testing, monitoring of group members' educational progress, and "interventions necessary to maintain an effective group process in which all contribute" (p. 20). Problem-based learning has also been applied in corporate training and faculty development as well as business, professional, and liberal arts courses in higher education institutions (see *Group Learning*).

4. Methods and Applications

There has been considerable interest in the feasibility of helping people to learn more meaningfully—to move from a superficial or "surface" approach (e.g., rote memorization) to the learning of subject matter toward a so-called "deep" approach that results in better understanding of what is learned. Research in several countries has found the use of the surface

761

approach to be common in courses with heavy work-loads, little opportunity for in-depth pursuit, little learner input into topics or methodology, and anxiety-producing assessment systems. Those who employ a deep approach understand more and produce superior written work, remember better, and receive higher marks than those employing a surface approach (Gibbs 1992).

A comprehensive national study in the United Kingdom, the "Improving Student Learning Project," identified nine elements which foster a deep approach. The elements, with some examples of appropriate methods are as follows: (a) encouraging independent learning (learning contracts); (b) supporting personal development (intensive group work); (c) presenting problems (exploring "real world" issues); (d) encouraging reflection (learning diaries or journals); (e) independent group work (peer tutoring); (f) learning by doing (simulations, games); (g) helping learners become more aware of task demands and purposes for learning; (h) project work (individual or group); and (i) fine tuning—minor modifications of conventional methods (making lectures more "interactive").

The above elements emerged from case studies of innovation projects undertaken by volunteer instructors of conventional and extramural courses at 10 colleges under the leadership of the Oxford Centre for Staff Development, which now offers faculty training workshops and consultation to academic departments and institutions. The project demonstrated that significant improvements in the quality of student learning are possible within existing course restraints through appropriate modifications in instructional design and delivery. Optimum results require comprehensive changes involving staff teams, appropriate staff development activity, and usually a modification of assessment systems (Gibbs 1992).

Successful applications of the learning to learn concept in North American colleges and universities are described in Schlossberg et al. (1989). A few institutions have undertaken to integrate learning to learn philosophy and related activity into either the overall college curriculum or in special baccalaureate degree programs for the "returning student." Among these are Alverno College (Milwaukee) and Depaul University (Chicago). Almost 80 percent of 2,600 higher education institutions surveyed in 1985 reported offering a credit or noncredit course on the topic of coping with college—employing such methods as support groups, diagnostic instruments, self-assessment, training in self-monitoring, and autobiographies describing learning experiences. In some instances, substantially superior academic performances of course participants have been documented through research as well as positive effects on intellectual, interpersonal, political, and civic development. In addition, most institutions maintain learning centers or academic support services for students seeking to improve competence in learning.

5. Fostering Autonomy in Learning

The acquisition of learning strategies, listening and viewing comprehension, and the fostering of autonomy and self-direction in learning are among the topics investigated at the Center for Research and Pedagogical Applications at the University of Nancy, France. Holec (1985) states the following with regard to self-direction and autonomy in learning (an "autonomization" process):

> The acquisition of autonomy by the learner is the fundamental goal in the C.R.A.P.E.L. approach, and it is important to underline from the outset that it is a tendency, a dynamic process with a future, not a stable condition, something which develops—hence the neologism "autonomization." This process can be seen from three different points of view: From the point of view of the learner, it is a matter of acquiring those capacities which are necessary to carry out a self-directed learning programme. From the point of view of the teacher, it is a matter of determining those types of intervention which are conducive to the learner's acquiring those capacities. From the institutional point of view, it is a matter of creating those conditions which allow the learner and the teacher to put these aims into practice. (p. 180)

The necessary learner competencies have been found to lay in the defining of objectives, content, materials, and techniques; defining the place, time, and pace of learning; and evaluating what one has learned. Since very few people possess such knowledge and skill, it becomes necessary to learn to learn—a process requiring a radical change in the role of the learners and their perception of that role. Individuals need to be disabused of the notion that they can learn only from experts and usually have to modify their notion of what learning is. Considerable self-examination is involved.

Teachers foster the autonomization process by providing two kinds of support "continuously adapted to the learner's state at any given moment" (Holec 1985 p. 184): technical support and psychosocial support. The former involves providing help as needed in the learner's analysis and making of instrumental decisions and the surfacing of personal "theory" informing one's actions (e.g., in choice of objective, learning resource, or strategy). Psychosocial support takes the form of encouraging learners' commitment to the acquisition of autonomy and to the gradual development of the requisite confidence and skills. Among the potential problems are allowing the learner to become overly dependent on the teacher and the providing of more or less support than is needed. Like the learners, the teachers usually have to examine or modify their conceptions of teaching and learning.

6. Learning to Learn in the Workplace

Interest in learning to learn in the workplace stems from such factors as increased concern for organizational productivity, organizational renewal, and the role of managers as learners and teachers. Mumford (1986 p. 8) carefully examined programs and publications in the area of learning to learn for managers in the United Kingdom and the United States, citing, among others, such potential benefits as the following:

(a) an increase in the capacity of individuals to learn;

(b) a reduction in the frustration of being exposed to inefficient learning processes;

(c) an increase in motivation to learn;

(d) development of learning opportunities well beyond formally created situations;

(e) a multiplier effect for the manager in his or her developmental relationship with his or her subordinates;

(f) the reduction of dependence on an instructor;

(g) the provision of processes which carry through beyond formal programs into on-the-job learning;

(h) the better identification of the role of learning in effective managerial behavior, for example, in problem-solving or team work;

(i) the development of more effective behavior in relation to the crucial subject of change.

Mumford (1986) concluded, however, that the capacity to learn effectively is not a priority for most managers and that learning to learn should be integrated with something they are concerned with, such as developing a specific competence. He found relatively little treatment of the topic of the manager as learner and even less concerning how managers learn to learn, but remained convinced that organizations and human resource personnel cannot afford to ignore this area. Mumford also identified some key factors influencing learning to learn—job content, motivation and personal blockages to learning, influence of superiors and subordinates, and organizational climate—and he provided examples of different approaches to helping managers to learn more effectively.

Marsick (1990) advocates wider use of action learning programs such as those developed at Sweden's Management Institute in Lund in order to foster critical reflectivity, suggesting that these are superior to the quality circles for this purpose. Small group problem-solving workshops through projects linked to taking action on organization-specific issues are central to action learning.

Some publications describe and discuss the broader topic of the relevance of learning to learn initiatives directed to all levels of personnel in the organization and ways to foster development of the "learning organization" (Cheren 1987, 1990, Argyris 1982). Learning to learn efforts include study strategy workshops and interactive video courses; orientation to in-house and outside educational opportunities; and the establishment of corporate learning centers for help with personal learning projects, self-assessment, and answers to reference questions.

Cheren (1990) sees learning to learn applications in the workplace as processes to be built into the formal training activities (e.g., enhancing strategies required for a particular course) and, perhaps more important, a dimension of day-to-day activity. Human resource and training professionals are urged to take the lead in improving problem-solving by individuals and work-station groups, establishing in-house learning resource centers, supporting the employee's personal development plans, and designing record keeping and evaluation systems that credit and reward informal and formal efforts to learn. He suggests "learning management" as a preferred conceptual rubric in the workplace.

7. Conclusion

The viability and utility of the concept of learning to learn now appears to be reasonably well-established despite the complexities of the phenomena involved and the challenges posed by implementation. It seems likely that teaching and learning and learning to learn will henceforth tend to be understood as interacting and interdependent processes. People learn to learn effectively through educational experiences and training that result in flexibility and awareness as well as the development of a repertoire of appropriate strategies for various learning contexts. Self-monitoring and reflective capacities tend to govern people's development as learners and problem-solvers. Theory regarding the facilitation of learning capacities is emerging from research and experience in a variety of contexts, and useful training resources and techniques are becoming available. Dissemination of this information needs to become more systematic and widespread.

See also: Adult Learning: Overview; Experiential and Open Learning for Adults; Learning in Industrial Settings

References

Argyris C 1982 *Reasoning, Learning, and Action: Individual and Organizational.* Jossey-Bass, San Francisco, California

Barrows H S, Tamblyn R M 1980 *Problem-Based Learning: An Approach to Medical Education.* Springer, New York

Barrows H S 1988 *The Tutorial Process.* Southern Illinois School of Medicine, Springfield, Illinois

Brookfield S D 1990 Expanding knowledge about how we learn. In: Smith R M (ed.) 1990

Candy P 1990 How people learn to learn. In: Smith R M (ed.) 1990

Cheren M 1987 *Learning Management: Emerging Directions for Learning to Learn in the Workplace.* National

Center for Research in Vocational Education, Ohio State University, Columbus, Ohio

Cheren M 1990 Prompting active learning in the workplace. In: Smith R M (ed.) 1990

Gibbs G 1981 *Teaching Students to Learn*. Open University Press, Milton Keynes

Gibbs G 1992 *Improving the Quality of Student Learning*. Technical and Educational Services, Bristol

Hammond D 1990 Designing and facilitating learning-to-learn activities. In: Smith R M (ed.) 1990

Holec H 1985 Autonomous learning schemes: Principles and organization. In: Riley P (ed.) 1985 *Discourse and Learning: Papers in Applied Linguistics and Language Learning from the CRAPEL*. Longman, London

Marsick V J 1990 Action learning and reflection in the workplace. In: Mezirow J et al. 1990

Mezirow J et al. 1990 *Fostering Critical Reflection in Adulthood*. Jossey-Bass, San Francisco, California

Mumford A 1986 Learning to learn for managers. *J. European Industrial Training* 10(2): 3–28

Schlossberg N K, Lynch A Q, Chickering A W 1989 *Improving Higher Education Environments for Adults: Responsive Programs and Services From Entry to Departure*. Jossey-Bass, San Francisco, California

Smith R M 1982 *Learning How to Learn: Applied Theory for Adults*. Cambridge University Press, New York

Smith R M 1992 Implementing the learning to learn concept. In: Tuijnman A C, Van Der Kamp M (eds.) *Learning Across the Lifespan: Theories, Research, Policies*. Pergamon Press, Oxford

Further Reading

Boud D J, Keogh R, Walker D (eds.) 1985 *Reflection: Turning Experience into Learning*. Kogan, London

Brown A 1987 Metacognition, executive control, self-regulation and other more mysterious mechanisms. In: Weinert F E, Kluwe R H (eds.) 1987 *Metacognition, Motivation and Understanding*. Lawrence Erlbaum Associates, Hillsdale, New Jersey

Cell E 1984 *Learning to Learn From Experience*. State University of New York Press, Albany, New York

Novak J D, Gowin D B 1984 *Learning How to Learn*. Cambridge University Press, New York

Smith R M (ed.) 1988 *Theory Building for Learning How to Learn*. Educational Studies Press, Northern Illinois University, Department of Leadership and Educational Policy Studies, DeKalb, Illinois

Smith R M (ed.) 1990 *Learning to Learn Across the Lifespan*. Jossey-Bass, San Francisco, California

Lifespan Learning: Implications for Educators

D. Mackeracher and A. C. Tuijnman

Adult learning involves a complex and dynamic interaction among a variety of physiological, personal, and environmental factors. The study of the adult learning process is informed by many theories and findings contributed by different science and social science disciplines ranging from medicine and neurology to psychology and education. This multidisciplinary body of knowledge, while being far from complete, provides useful insights into questions such as whether, why, and how adults change and learn over the lifespan.

The aim of this entry is to describe some important theories, perspectives, and research findings on the adult learning process insofar as these inform the study and practice of adult education. Hence the focus is on the implications for educators and others involved in adult learning, such as administrators, counselors, and program designers.

The topics dealt with include the capacity of adults to learn, learning styles, conditions and factors influencing learning, and motivation. The role of educational technology and open learning networks in facilitating adult learning is also discussed. The entry does not deal, at least not explicitly, with sequential perspectives of adult development over the lifespan, such as functional or structural stage models and postformal theories of cognitive development.

1. The Learning Process

Research studies on the learning of adults generally describe a cyclical sequence of learning activities (Kolb 1984, Brookfield 1986, Mines 1986, Kitchener and King 1990). There is some disagreement on the nature, order, and importance of these learning activities, and on their implications for effective adult learning (Hiemstra 1991). However, there is evidence that the importance of each activity varies with the situation and goals of learning; that the nature and order of activities vary between situations and learners; and that the nature of the learning activity is less important to the learner since the sequence is repetitive, but may be important to the educator in developing strategies for instruction or facilitation (Cross 1981). This interpretation of the adult learning process draws heavily on cognitive and information-processing theories, where the process is viewed as involving a complex interaction among cognitive, affective, psychomotor, and social behaviors and processes.

The basic activities in the learning process include some which are internal to the individual—taking in information, searching for and assigning meaning and value to information, utilizing information, making decisions, acting, and receiving feedback from internal sources on the consequences of actions—

and some which involve the external environment—receiving feedback from external sources about the consequences of actions, interacting with objects and other persons, and having access to additional sources of new information.

The learner takes in information through sensory receptors from both internal and external sources. The richness and accuracy of this information are directly limited by the acuity of the learner's sensory receptors, focus of attention, and personal expectations; and indirectly affected by physical and emotional well-being, cognitive style, and previous experience. The observed information can be selectively controlled by the learner in spite of the quality and quantity of information actually available. By implication, what is learned is not necessarily the same as that presented by the educator. Hence the educator should pay attention to the assessment of learning outcomes.

The learning process continues as the individual searches for and assigns meaning and value to information (Torbert 1972, Hayes 1989). Personal meanings and values are often idiosyncratic and emerge from the ways in which an individual makes sense of direct personal experience. Social meanings and values are acquired throughy socialization and make it possible for the members of the same group to communicate. When created through shared interpersonal activity, meanings and values are both social and personal, and make sense to all individuals who participated in the creation process (Brim and Wheeler 1966). The implication is that learners should be helped to relate new subject matter to previously acquired experience as well as to their current knowledge base.

Information is used in various cognitive activities such as analyzing, comparing, inventing, and organizing. The outcome of these activities is the development of a personal system for making sense of reality and for determining action strategies. The system is flexible, dynamic, and open to change. Conscious cognitive activities involve the use of words, images, sounds, and felt sensations as representational markers for meanings and values. Unconscious activities usually involve nonverbal representational markers and may be raised to consciousness through such processes as thinking, reflecting on experience, and meditating. Emotions modify both conscious and unconscious cognitive activities.

When an individual learns in personal interaction with other persons, whether teachers or learners, there are general social expectations that cognitive and emotional processes will be made explicit, usually by formulating them into words. In this way, the individual's learning activities can be shared with, or assessed by, others.

Information manipulation results in the individual making decisions to act, which may be as unconscious and fleeting as shifting the focus of the eyes, or as conscious and extensive as migrating to a new country. The individual acts in ways which are intended, at least at the conscious level, to be congruent with decisions. Transactions, particularly those intended to change internal conditions, may not be apparent to others, but always provide the individual with new information about the action and its consequences through internal sensory feedback. Actions which involve the external environment provoke a response from persons or objects which, through feedback, also provide the learner with information about the consequences of actions. Responses can vary from silence and immobility to complex dialogues. By this means, an interactive system is established between the learner and both internal and external environments. The educator may be an important component in this interactive system.

The learning process can begin with any activity in the general learning sequence. For example, if the individual is presented with wholly new information, learning may begin with attempts to make sense of information on the basis of personal or social meanings and values. Learning may then occur with changes in information utilization. If the learner receives information or feedback which is contrary to expectations, learning may begin with attempts to develop new strategies for coping and for reducing anxiety associated with the experience.

Educators, those who facilitate the learning process, can do so directly through presenting information of varying quality and quantity at an appropriate speed, allowing for adequate response time, using recognition rather than recall techniques, providing adequate feedback on actions taken by the learner, and interacting with the learner through an exchange of meaning; and indirectly by monitoring internal activities as these are made public by the learner. Facilitation of internal activities is always limited by the learner's willingness to make these public and the ability to describe them accurately.

2. Capacity to Learn

Until the 1970s, it was commonly believed that the learning capacity of people increases until their early twenties, after which there would be a decrease during the remainder of the lifespan. There are different, often hypothesized explanations for this decrease; for example, the speed of peripheral sensory or motor processes would decline with increasing age because of neuronal loss or a general decline in the physiological system, or cognitive performance would decrease because certain functions would be less used with increasing age. Although there is some evidence that cognitive performance declines with increasing age, research studies show that intelligence is not an obstacle to learning at an old age (Peterson 1983). Even though studies have generally demonstrated the ability of most people to learn throughout life, an important role of the educator is to actively encourage a belief in personal learning capacity.

Lohman (1989) summarizes the advances in three traditions of research on human intelligence: trait theories, information-processing theories, and general theories of thinking. Of special interest here is the trait theory of fluid and crystallized abilities (Snow 1981). Crystallized intelligence depends on sociocultural influences; it involves the ability to perceive relations, to engage in formal reasoning, and to understand one's intellectual and cultural heritage. In general, crystallized intelligence continues to grow slowly throughout adulthood as the person acquires increased information and develops an understanding of the relation among various facts and constructs. Fluid intelligence, in contrast, is not closely associated with acculturation. It is generally considered to be independent of instruction or environment and depends more on genetic endowment. It consists of the ability to perceive complex relations, use short-term memory, create concepts, and undertake abstract reasoning. Fluid intelligence involves those abilities that are the most neurophysiological in nature. These are generally assumed to decline after the person reaches maturity.

Lohman and Scheurman (1992) present several conclusions with major implications for adult education:

(a) Intelligence and capacity to learn at all ages are in significant measure the product of education and experience.

(b) Those who view cognitive ability as a reflection of the biological integrity of the organism naturally look for biological causes for the observed decline in general fluid abilities over the lifespan. However, other explanations are equally plausible, including the dispersion in attentional resources brought about by an increase in knowledge, and the relative decline of such abilities through disuse.

(c) Education has traditionally sought only to develop crystallized abilities and has presumed that fluid abilities were unalterable. However, there is some indication that fluidization is encouraged when adults are asked to stretch their knowledge to solve increasingly unfamiliar problems or to organize concepts in new ways.

(d) Fluid abilities are at once both the most important products of education as well as the most important aptitudes for learning in that medium.

(e) Adults continue to develop those abilities that they use; abilities that show decline in the later adult years either emphasize speed or require the solution of novel problems. In both cases, disuse may be a significant factor in explaining the decline.

In conclusion, it appears that learning abilities are determined more by previous experience of education and experience of work than by age. Moreover, differences in learning abilities seem to be larger within than between age cohorts. Older people tend to learn a little slower, but often learn more meticulously and with more intensity than young people.

3. Adult Learning Styles

There are indications that adults exhibit diverse learning styles—that is, the unique ways and means by which they gather, process, and internalize information (see *Individual Differences, Learning, and Instruction*). A theory on the learning styles of adults has been proposed by Kolb (1984). The point of departure is a dialectic model of learning. A two-way matrix is hypothesized based on the following dimensions: concrete versus abstract learning, and active versus reflective learning. Learning is assumed to occur in a field of tension formed by these categories which, according to Kolb, are cyclically arranged. The notion of a "learning circle" is at the heart of the theory. It is postulated that in learning, adults proceed through the four stages of the learning circle. Experience lies at the basis of perception and reflection ("what was good, what was wrong?"). The learner "collects" observations and "translates" them into a "theory." Hypotheses can be derived from this body of ideas, and these are tested in practice by action. This eventually results in new experience.

According to Kolb (1984), four kinds of ability are needed for optimal learning. These are in the domains of experience, reflective observation, abstract concept formation, and active experimenting. However, people usually do not perform equally well in all four domains. One or two may stand out. Adult learning can be particularly effective if the preferred learning ability or mode is employed. Kolb distinguishes four such learning styles, namely: the diverger, the assimilator, the converger, and the accommodator (Van Der Kamp 1992).

The implication could be that the differences in cognitive or learning styles among adults have to be matched with differently designed and paced systems of instruction. Although it is generally assumed that the matching of learning styles with specific instructional methods will enhance both the ability and motivation to learn and, hence, improve learning outcomes, a review of empirical studies by Cohen et al. (1989) found little evidence to support this hypothesis. The apparent absence of a clear link between learning styles, tailored instructional methods, and learning outcomes does not necessarily imply that the concept of learning styles is invalid. Knowledge of the preferred learning modes of adults can be useful in the design of learning environments. There is a realization that good practice in adult education often depends on the application of methods that give attention to individual learner needs and match preferred learning styles.

4. Conditions for Learning

Various writers agree that several conditions are essential for facilitating the learning process. First, the individual must have access to sufficient information from direct experience or secondary sources, with enough variations on themes, presented through a variety of media, to allow similarities and differences to be perceived and patterns of meaning to emerge. Second, the learner must have enough time and freedom from threat to allow learning to proceed naturally, without anxiety or undue stress. Third, the learner must proceed through an appropriate learning "gradient" —the stepwise progression or "pacing" from easy to difficult. Four, effective learning is linked to a positive self-concept and self-evaluation as a learner.

A further condition is assumed to be of importance for adult learners: that sufficient and effective patterns of meaning and strategies for learning must have already developed if the individual is to be a competent learner. While children are usually given the time and assistance needed to develop these basic patterns and strategies, adults are generally assumed to have developed them in earlier years, an assumption which is sometimes false and can create obstacles in the learning process. Learning how to learn is increasingly viewed as an essential component and precondition for competent adult learning. Smith (1990) notes that the concept of "learning to learn" in adult education refers to the knowledge, processes, and procedures that people acquire through assistance to make appropriate educational decisions and carry out instrumental tasks associated with successful lifelong learning (see *Learning to Learn: Adult Education*).

5. Factors Influencing Learning

Factors which influence the learning process include, among others, whether learning occurs when the individual is acting alone, interacting with objects, or engaged in social interaction (Cross 1981); whether learning is based on information from personal experience or from secondary sources, such as opinions of others or factual data (Kolb 1984); whether learning focuses on new meanings, values, skills, or strategies, or on the expansion or transformation of those which already exist (Brim and Wheeler 1966); whether the learner's learning strategies and communicating skills work; and whether the educator's strategies and skills are effective.

Developmental tasks are important factors in adult learning to which educators must be attentive. Havighurst (1953) described the concept as follows:

[A developmental task is] a task which arises at or about a certain period in the life of the individual, successful achievement of which leads to his happiness and to success with later tasks, while failure leads to unhappiness in the individual, disapproval by the society, and difficulty with later tasks. (p. 2)

Developmental tasks can be seen as arising from three sources: physical maturation, cultural pressure resulting from the expectations of the community and society, and aspirations in relation to individual values and needs. These vary according to lifespan phases and the general and specific problems which individuals face during moments of major transition. An elaborate example of the developmental tasks which individuals in Western societies face as they grow older is presented by Fales (1985).

Theories of lifespan development describe one or more additional stages of development that go beyond the level of formal operations described in Piaget's theory. These stages are characterized by an understanding of knowledge as constructed rather than as given, as contextual rather than as absolute, and as mutable rather than as fixed (Lohman and Scheurman 1992). The implications are that, since individual responses vary even in the case where a similar developmental task is confronted, the individual learning needs of adults need to be taken into account in the design of learning environments. Learning activities and instructional approaches should be based on learners' needs and interests, which are not constant but change with advancing age. Moreover, effective learning environments require that educators be conscious of various social or cultural impediments that might affect adult learning activities.

Several additional factors critical to effective adult learning, especially insofar as these have implications for adult educators, are considered below.

5.1 Personal Learning System

Each individual's system of personal structures (such as meanings and values) and information processing capacity can be viewed as having cognitive, affective, and physical components, which determine what information is attended to and taken in, how it is processed and stored, and how selected information is interpreted. These individually based organizing structures and processes may facilitate or inhibit learning. Educators therefore have to pay attention to the individual's preferred cognitive or learning styles, decision-making and problem-solving strategies, action tendencies, and feedback requirements. In general, changing the structures of the learning system is easier than changing the processes. With the passage of time, individuals appear to maintain consistency and continuity in their learning styles (Cross 1981), but do change their interpretation of meanings and values. The major organizing structures of the learning system may change as a consequence of developmental transitions and major life events or crises (Commons et al. 1989, Smith and Baltes 1990).

It follows that adults enter a learning activity with established preconceptions of experience which provide predefined meanings and values even for a wholly new experience. The educator must be prepared to acknowledge each learner's personal system as viable for that individual and as a valued and unique source that influences further learning. Since personal systems become increasingly established as individuals age, older learners may need to be acknowledged and affirmed even more than younger learners (Peterson 1983).

5.2 Feedback

Feedback mechanisms are those processes which provide information to the learner on the actual consequences of personal activity in relation to intended consequences or goals. Feedback may come from three basic sources. First, internal sensory receptors throughout the body provide immediate reflexive feedback about an activity as it occurs. Second, external sensory receptors such as the eyes and ears offer slightly delayed information about the acting self as an object of one's own perception. It may be noted here that older people are more likely than younger people to have difficulty in remembering recently acquired information. Whereas hearing loss appears to be closely associated with difficulties of long-term memory recall, decline in visual perception is more closely associated with problems in short-term memory. Third, other objects and persons in the external environment give delayed feedback by responding to the activity of the learner. As feedback is increasingly delayed, its impact on the learner and potential effect on learning is correspondingly diminished. An individual learner is moreover free either to ignore or attend to any source or type of feedback. The implication is that educators, in designing a learning environment for adults, may well try to appeal to several senses and to incorporate sufficient moments for external feedback.

5.3 Arousal

Arousal is essential to learning and is stimulated by novelty and uncertainty. As arousal levels increase, learning becomes more efficient and effective until optimal conditions are achieved. These conditions are framed by emotions, however, which are arousal states in which both internal and external factors are given meaning based on the current situation, past experience, and expectancy with respect to the future. Thus arousal is accompanied by specific meanings, values, and action tendencies which are learned through experience and conditioned by both the actual learning situation and the learner's expectations as to the outcome. Encouraging the learners to connect new concepts and information with their personal experience, and to intersperse instruction with concrete

examples that have emotional value and are familiar to the learners, are some steps that may be taken to facilitate the learning process. Accordingly, to assist the learner to establish or re-establish connections among personal experiences, meanings, and new information is an essential function of the educator of adults. This may be done by using mindmaps and knowledge bridges often and in different ways.

5.4 Stress, Anxiety, and Resistance

Stress, an arousal state which is nonspecific, is a response to a real or perceived, but identifiable, threat to personal security. Anxiety is a stress-like response in which the threat remains unidentified. Adult learning can be hindered by stress and anxiety, for example, when unpleasant memories of school emerge or when previously acquired knowledge is unsettled. Fear of failure in front of a group is another factor that may lead to resistance and lack of initiative. These examples show that there are not only many external barriers to adult learning, such as high costs or work-specific impediments, but also many personal barriers (see *Experiential and Open Learning*).

Educators should attempt to maintain a learning environment which is free from threat and assist learners to identify unlabeled fears and anxieties. Correspondingly, educators can work to enhance self-confidence in learners by diminishing the possibility to fail or to make grave errors, and by reducing time pressure. Self-pacing may be a desirable method, especially in instructing older adults, because it usually guarantees that the allocation of time for learning is adequate.

Too little information, repetitive and unproductive learning activities, or any condition which reduces the arousal level of the learner can result in sensory deprivation, boredom, and inactivity. Too much information, arousal, or anxiety can result in disorganized learning responses, selective inattention, or distorted perceptions. Optimal levels of arousal and information are individually determined and fluctuate over time and in idiosyncratic ways. Educators must be prepared to respond to individual needs for arousal and information, and to be attuned to changes in these needs over time.

5.5 Motivation and Action Tendencies

"Motivation," as defined by psychologists, generally refers to factors influencing the initiation and direction of behavior. The term thus refers to subjective "sources of organized activity"—drives, urges, emotions, needs, and other states of individuals that impel, move, push, or otherwise make them sensitive to their environment and direct their subsequent behavior (Hewitt 1988). The expectancy/valence theory, as as applied to adult education by Bergsten (1977), provides an explicit formulation of the relationships among variables such as personal meanings and values, self-esteem, context and situation, and expectancy in influencing motivation as a cause of engagement in self-directed learning or of participation in organized adult education.

Apart from expectancy/valence tendencies, orientations which relate to learning can also be described in other terms, such as: "approach/avoidance tendencies," "internal/external locus of control," "achievement/affiliation needs," "active/passive orientations to information use," "coping/irrelevant responses," and so on. A useful way to approach motivation in relation to adult learning is to view learning-associated behaviors as expressions of the individual's wish to master a developmental task or subject and the desire to identify with a group or with significant others.

The task facing the educator is to make sense of motivation to learn and the corresponding action tendencies exhibited by the learners, and to develop a preparedness and strategies for enhancing or blocking specific tendencies. Educators can enhance a desire to learn and mastery by creating high expectations about the learning outcomes, heightening self-esteem, and ensuring respect through accepting and confirming the viability of the learner's self-identity and perceived reality, and through making the learning situation controllable by the individual learner. Using discovery teaching techniques is a useful way to involve and motivate learners. Since many adults are goal-directed, providing explicit instructional objectives is another useful strategy. A third way is to encourage learners to be self-directed in devising their own personal goals, learning approaches and styles, and resource needs (Hiemstra and Sisco 1990) (see *Self-directed Adult Learning*).

In a similar way, educators can enhance action tendencies toward belonging by reducing potentially threatening situations, by utilizing personal biographies and the past experience of learners as resources for learning activities, and by promoting group interactions. Moreover, the educator can use discrepancies between past and current learning experiences as a theme to encourage group interaction, as such interaction has value as a learning motivator and serves a purpose as a means for analyzing individual and group needs (see *Group Learning; Individual Differences, Learning, and Instruction*).

6. New Directions

Some promising innovations in adult education, which to an extent are based on recent insights into the factors that optimize adult learning, are described below. Attention is given, first, to the possible applications of new information technology and, second, to the idea of open learning which is considered to hold great potential for development.

6.1 Personalized Instruction

Personalized systems of instruction that allow the learner to pace the learning encounter are generally considered effective; according to some authors they may increase retention and the satisfaction of adults with the learning encounter. "Computer-based training" is a concept being used at present to denote the entire range of information technologies and programmed instructions applied to adult learning (see *Teaching Methods: Individual Techniques*).

Adult learning through technology makes use of a variety of approaches (for an overview, see Bainbridge and Quintanilla 1989). Examples are "traditional" media, such as broadcasting and audiocassettes; and "innovative" media, such as preprogrammed computer-based learning, computer-based communications, interactive video, tutorial systems, and simulation programs. Interactive videodisk training, for example, is increasingly being used in learning environments where an error in decision-making would be too dangerous or costly. These new educational technologies, which are directed toward the individual learner, offer not only an instructional advantage but may also improve feedback by enhancing the opportunities for self-assessment. New technologies are important, potentially at least, in enhancing learning in the workplace. They not only make further education and training a necessity but also change the context in which learning takes place (Marsick 1987). For example, new information technologies put a demand on the preciseness of the learning task and its objectives, and pose new problems for communication. This has, of course, repercussions also on the competence required of educators.

The new media in education have provided an impetus for the development of new strategies of adult learning. Two examples are "integrated learning" and "accelerated learning." The first refers to a cooperative approach where instructors work in "corporate classrooms." It is essentially based on complete job analysis, after which learning modules for specific skills are developed. Instructors work together with employees in developing activity guides, job-plan sheets, and other instructional materials. Accelerated learning is another innovative concept. Some general principles for achieving accelerated learning can be found in the research literature.

6.2 Open Learning

Open learning refers to a principle of "learner-centeredness" and "open access" to learning opportunities. Paine (1989 p. ix) describes the term as referring to "learning which allows the learner to choose how to learn, where to learn, when to learn and what to learn as far as possible within the resource constraints of any education and training provision."

New directions for open learning have opened up as a consequence of the development of educational technology and its application to adult education, especially by open universities and other institutions for distance learning . However, relying only on the application of educational technology may limit the contribution of the open learning concept to the design of environments for effective adult learning (see *Experiential and Open Learning*). The main characteristics of open learning are (Van Der Zee 1989, Van Der Kamp 1992):

(a) It is learner-centered, rather than institution-centered.

(b) It provides a means of equipping adults for self-directed learning.

(c) It implies informal learning and the use of a wide range of teaching/learner strategies.

(d) It helps in removing barriers to learning, particularly those barriers inherent in the established patterns of education and training.

(e) It gives the adult learner more choice by creating a diversity of individual opportunity.

(f) It is user-friendly, bringing education closer to the learner, who decides on when and how to engage in the learning task.

(g) It is in sharp contrast to a supplier-oriented approach to adult education; hence it has much to offer in designing powerful learning environments.

7. Facilitating Adult Learning: Conclusions

This overview has shown that there is a growing body of information about how to facilitate adult learning and which factors improve the effectiveness of the learning process. It is also evident that the development of powerful learning environments for adults needs to be based in adequate theories, methods of instruction, and new insights into how people organize their own personal learning projects. Promising theories and insights are offered by authors such as Darkenwald and Merriam (1982), Knowles (1984), Brookfield (1986), Caffarella and O'Donnell (1987), Brockett and Hiemstra (1991), Candy (1991), and Van Der Kamp (1992).

Key observations contributed by these authors are: that the readiness and capacity to learn is influenced, both positively and negatively, by previous experiences of learning; that adults generally want to learn, and that they learn most effectively when they have strong intrinsic motivation; that adults generally wish to assume considerable responsibility for their own learning—conversely, they may resist learning when they are told precisely what and how to learn; that adults tend to learn effectively if they consider material relevant to their personal needs and interests; that adults seek to learn what can be applied—they are generally problem-oriented learners; that adults value

information which is meaningful and useful to them—information related to their expectations and previous experience; and that adults want to know the outcomes of their learning efforts—they require positive reinforcement and performance feedback.

See also: Lifespan Development; Adult Learning: Overview

References

Bainbridge L, Quintanilla S A R 1989 *Developing Skills with Information Technology.* Wiley, Chischester

Bergsten U 1977 *Adult Education in Relation to Work and Leisure.* Almqvist and Wiksell, Stockholm

Brim O G, Wheeler S 1966 *Socialization After Childhood: Two Essays.* Wiley, New York

Brockett R G, Hiemstra R 1991 *Self-direction in Adult Learning: Perspectives on Theory, Research and Practice.* Routledge, London

Brookfield S 1986 *Understanding and Facilitating Adult Learning: A Comprehensive Analysis of Principles and Effective Practice.* Jossey-Bass, San Francisco, California

Caffarella R S, O'Donnell J M 1987 Self-directed adult learning: A critical paradigm revisited. *Adult Educ. Q.* 37(4): 199–211

Candy P C 1991 *Self-direction for Lifelong Learning: A Comprehensive Guide to Theory and Practice.* Jossey-Bass, San Francisco, California

Cohen S A, Hyman J S, Ashcroft L, Loveless D 1989 Comparing effects of metacognition, learning styles, and human attributes with allignment. Paper presented at the annual conference of the American Educational Research Association, March

Commons M L, Sinnott J, Richards F A, Armon C (eds.) 1989 *Adult Development: Comparisons and Applications of Developmental Models.* Praeger, New York

Cross K P 1981 *Adults as Learners: Increasing Participation and Facilitating Leaving.* Jossey-Bass, San Francisco, California

Darkenwald G G, Merriam S B 1982 *Adult Education: Foundations of Practice.* Harper and Row, New York

Fales A W 1985 Learning development over the lifespan. In: Husén T, Postlethwaite T N (eds.) 1985 *The International Encyclopedia of Education,* 1st edn. Pergamon Press, Oxford

Havighurst R J 1953 *Human Development and Education,* rev edn. of *Development Tasks and Education.* Longman, New York

Hayes E R 1989 Insights from women's experiences for teaching and learning. In: Hayes E R (ed.) 1989 *Effective Teaching Styles.* Jossey-Bass, San Francisco, California

Hewitt J P 1988 *Self and Society: A Symbolic Interactionist Social Psychology,* 4th edn. Allyn and Bacon, Newton, Massachusetts

Hiemstra R (ed.) 1991 *Creating Environments for Effective Adult Learning.* Jossey-Bass, San Francisco, California

Hiemstra R, Sisco B 1990 *Individualizing Instruction: Making Learning Personal, Empowering and Successful.* Jossey-Bass, San Francisco, California

Kitchener K S, King P M 1990 The reflective judgment model: Ten years of research. In: Commons M L et al. 1990 *Adult Development: Models and Methods in the Study of Adolescent and Adult Thought.* Praeger, New York

Knowles M 1984 *The Adult Learner: A Neglected Species*, 3rd edn. Gulf Publishing, Houston, Texas

Kolb D A 1984 *Experiental Learning*. Prentice-Hall, Englewood Cliffs, New Jersey

Lohman D F 1989 Human intelligence. An introduction to advances in theory and research. *Rev. Educ. Res.* 59(4): 333–73.

Lohman D F, Scheurman G 1992 Fluid abilities and epistemic thinking: Some prescriptions for adult education. In: Tuijnman A C, Van Der Kamp M (eds.) 1992 *Learning Across the Lifespan: Theories, Research, Policies*. Pergamon Press, Oxford.

Marsick V J 1987 *Learning in the Workplace*. Croom Helm, New York

Mines R A (ed.) 1986 *Adult Cognitive Development: Methods and Models*. Praeger, New York

Paine N (ed.) 1989 *Open Learning in Transition. An Agenda for Action*. Kogan Page, London

Peterson D A 1983 *Facilitating Education for Older Learners*. Jossey-Bass, San Francisco, California

Smith J, Baltes P B 1990 Wisdom-related knowledge: Age/cohort differences in response to life-planning problems. *Dev. Psychol.* 26(3): 494–505

Smith R M (ed.) 1990 *Learning to Learn Across the Lifespan*. Jossey-Bass, San Francisco, California

Snow R E 1981 Toward a theory of aptitude for learning: Fluid and crystallized abilities and their correlates. In: Friedman M P, Das J P, O'Connor N (eds.) 1981 *Intelligence and Learning*. Plenum Press, New York

Torbert W 1972 *Learning from Experience: Toward Consciousness*. Columbia University, New York

Van Der Kamp M 1992 Effective adult learning. In: Tuijnman A C, Van Der Kamp M (eds.) 1992 *Learning Across the Lifespan: Theories, Research, Policies*. Pergamon Press, Oxford

Van Der Zee H 1989 Developing the educational potential of public libraries. In: Goffree F, Stroomberg H (eds.) 1989 *Creating Adult Learning*. SMD, Leiden

Further Reading

Boucouvalas M, Krupp J A 1990 Adult development and learning. In: Merriam S B, Cunningham P M (eds.) 1990 *Handbook of Adult and Continuing Education*. Jossey-Bass, San Francisco, California

Birren J E, Schaie K W 1985 *Handbook of the Psychology of Aging*, 2nd edn. Van Nostrand Reinhold, New York

Kohlberg L, Armon C A 1984 Three types of stage models used in the study of adult development. In: Commons M, Richards F A, Armon C A (eds.) 1984 *Beyond Formal Operations: Late Adolescent and Adult Cognitive Development*. Praeger, New York

Merriam S B 1987 Adult learning and theory building: A review. *Adult Educ. Q.* 37(4): 187–98

Weinert F E, Kluwe R H (eds.) 1986 *Metacognition, Motivation, and Understanding*. Erlbaum, Hillsdale, New Jersey

Self-directed Adult Learning

R. Hiemstra

Most adults spend a considerable time acquiring information and learning new skills. The rapidity of change, the continuous creation of new knowledge, and an ever-widening access to information make such acquisitions necessary. Much of this learning takes place at the learner's initiative, even if available through formal settings. A common label given to such activity is self-directed learning. In essence, self-directed learning is seen as any study form in which individuals have primary responsibility for planning, implementing, and even evaluating the effort. Most people, when asked, will proclaim a preference for assuming such responsibility whenever possible.

Interest in self-directed learning considerably increased around the world during the 1980s. Few topics, if any, have received more attention by adult educators than self-directed learning. Numerous new programs, practices, and resources for facilitating self-directed learning have been created, and many studies have been undertaken. This entry extracts some meaning from all this information.

1. What is Self-directed Learning?

Several things are known about self-directed learning:

(a) Individual learners can become empowered to take increasingly more responsibility for various decisions associated with the learning endeavor.

(b) Self-direction is best viewed as a continuum or characteristic that exists to some degree in every person and learning situation.

(c) Self-direction does not necessarily mean that all learning will take place in isolation from others.

(d) Self-directed learners appear able to transfer learning, in terms of both knowledge and study skill, from one situation to another.

(e) Self-directed study can involve various activities and resources, such as self-guided reading, participation in study and tutorial groups, internships, electronic dialogues, and reflective writing activities.

(f) Effective roles for teachers in self-directed learning are possible, such as dialogue with learners, securing resources, evaluating outcomes, and promoting critical thinking.

(g) Some educational institutions are finding ways to support self-directed study through open learning programs, individualized study options, non-traditional course offerings, and other innovative programs.

This latter component—educational institutions developing innovative responses to self-directed learning preferences—has spawned several unique programming efforts. For example, establishment of the Open University in England in 1969 generated similar efforts around the world. St Francis Xavier University (Antigonish, Nova Scotia), Teacher College (Columbia University, New York City), NOVA Southeastern University's nontraditional doctoral program (Fort Lauderdale, Florida), Syracuse University's Instructional Design Program (Syracuse, New York), and the Ontario Institute for Studies in Education (Toronto, Canada) have incorporated self-directed learning principles into various of their adult education efforts. These latter two (Syracuse University and Ontario Institute) have assimilated some computer-mediated instruction into their programs.

Brookfield (1986) describes other higher education efforts where individualized, self-directed learning opportunities exist, including locations in Germany, Denmark, and Eastern Europe. Brockett and Hiemstra (1991) describe several self-directed efforts in China, Indonesia, Japan, Norway, Russia, Saudi Arabia, Sweden, and Tanzania. Knowles (1984) describes various self-directed learning efforts in various government, industry, health, religious, and military settings.

1.1 History of Self-directed Learning

Self-directed learning has existed even from classical antiquity. For example, self-study played an important part in the lives of such Greek philosophers as Socrates, Plato, and Aristotle. Other historical examples of self-directed learners include Alexander the Great, Julius Caesar, Erasmus, and Descartes. Social conditions in countries under foreign rule, in Africa, Asia, and even in colonial America, and a corresponding lack of formal educational institutions necessitated that many people learn on their own.

There were early scholarly efforts to understand self-directed learning in the nineteenth-century United States. Craik (1840) documented and celebrated the self-education efforts of several people. About the same time in the United Kingdom, Smiles (1859) published a book entitled *Self-Help*, that applauded the value of personal development.

However, it is since the 1960s that self-directed learning has become a major research area. Groundwork was laid through the observations of Houle (1961). He interviewed 22 adult learners and classified them into three categories based on reasons for participation in learning: (a) goal-oriented learners, who participate mainly to achieve some end goal; (b) activity-oriented learners, who participate for social or fellowship reasons; and (c) learning-oriented learners, who perceive of learning as an end in itself. It is this latter group that resembles the self-directed learner identified in subsequent research.

The first attempt to understand learning-oriented individuals better was made by Tough, a Canadian researcher and one of Houle's doctoral students. His dissertation effort to analyze self-directed teaching activities and subsequent research with additional subjects resulted in a book called *The Adult's Learning Projects* (Tough 1979). This work has stimulated many similar studies with various populations in different locations.

In parallel scholarship during this same period, Knowles popularized in North America the term "andragogy" with corresponding adult instructional processes. His *Self-directed Learning* (1975) provided foundational definitions and assumptions that guided much subsequent research: (a) self-directed learning assumes that humans grow in capacity and need to be self-directing; (b) learners' experiences are rich resources for learning; (c) individuals learn what is required to perform their evolving life tasks; (d) an adult's natural orientation is task- or problem-centered learning; and (e) self-directed learners are motivated by various internal incentives, such as need for self-esteem, curiosity, desire to achieve, and satisfaction of accomplishment.

Another important research effort was Guglielmino's (1977) Self-directed Learning Readiness Scale (SDLRS), an instrument subsequently used by many researchers to measure self-directed readiness or to compare various self-directed learning aspects with numerous characteristics. Spear and Mocker's (1984) work on organizing circumstances showed how important it is to understand a learner's environmental circumstances in promoting self-directed learning.

Establishment of an annual International Symposium on Self-directed Learning in 1987 by Long and his colleagues completes this historical picture. These symposia have spawned many publications, research projects, and theory-building efforts by researchers throughout the world.

1.2 Competing Concepts

As with the development of many new ideas, self-directed learning has created some confusion in that many related concepts are often used interchangeably or in similar ways. Examples include self-directed education, self-planned learning, learning projects, self-education, self-teaching, autonomous learning, "autodidaxy," independent study, and open learning.

Yet these terms typically offer varied, though sometimes subtly different, emphases. To illustrate some of these differences, some competing terms will be examined. Section 1.4 provides a conceptual model and corresponding definition of self-directed learning.

Self-planned learning. Tough's research on people engaged in learning projects involved obtaining information on "a series of related episodes, adding up to at least seven hours" where "more than half of the person's total motivation is to gain and retain certain fairly clear knowledge and skill, or to produce some other lasting change" (1979 p. 7). Tough used the seven-hour parameter because he felt it approximated a typical working day and separated brief learning activities from more major endeavors. Actually, he and many others have found that most learning projects far exceed the seven-hour minimum. Nearly 100 learning project surveys with various groups in 10 countries have confirmed that approximately 90 percent of adults conduct at least one intentional learning project annually. A typical adult spends about 500 hours a year in such learning with approximately 70 percent planned by the learner. This self-planning predominance spawned considerable research on self-directed learning.

Autonomous learning. Autonomy is often associated with independence of thought, individualized decision-making, and critical intelligence. Gibbs (1979) notes that this concept "is probably the most familiar, for it is part of an individualistic, antiauthoritarian ideology . . . deep-rooted in Western capitalistic democracies" (p. 121). Chene (1983) suggests autonomy stands for psychological and methodological learning dimensions. Boud (1988) provides several ideas on developing student autonomy. Candy (1991) suggests that continuous learning is a process in which adults manifest personality attributes of personal autonomy in self-managing learning efforts. He also profiles various autonomous learner characteristics (pp. 459–66).

Autodidaxy. Candy (1991) urges that self-direction be differentiated as a goal for learner control of decision-making from an educational method in which teachers use processes for promoting self-direction. He proposes "autodidaxy" as a term for referring to self-instruction which takes place outside of formal institutional settings.

Self-education. Self-directed learning can be called something else from country to country or culture to culture. For example, in Russia it is known as self-education:

> The role of self-education naturally increases in adults, for the potential possibilities of the personality are extremely great, and the formed world outlook . . . will make it possible to develop one's abilities more successfully, systematically and comprehensively. This is especially true

since life does not stand still and society is developing scientifically and technically. Anyone who does not engage in self-education, voluntarily or not, lags behind the demands of the time. (Ruvinsky 1986 p. 31)

Ruvinsky also describes several Russians who engage in self-education.

Open learning. Individualized study is often associated with external degree, open learning, or nontraditional programs where most learning takes place outside formal classrooms. One of the most widely known is the United Kingdom's Open University, started in 1969, and emulated since in many countries. Currently, development of many distance education efforts using computer-assisted learning is necessitating new research and understanding regarding how technology can enhance self-directed learning (Hiemstra 1994a) (see *Experimental and Open Learning for Adults*).

Empowerment. A concept gaining cogency in current literature is the notion of an empowered learner, person, or employee who assumes increasing personal responsibility for decisions associated with education, life, or job. For example, business and industrial organizations are beginning to develop self-directed work teams (Osburn et al. 1990) and many efforts to use self-directed learning and the promotion of personal empowerment for enhancing performance in a variety of occupational situations are underway (Durr et al. 1994, Piskurich 1993, 1994).

1.3 Synthesizing Relevant Research

There have been many overviews of self-directed learning research (Brockett and Hiemstra 1991, Caffarella and O'Donnell 1987, Candy 1991, Hiemstra 1992, Merriam and Caffarella 1991).

Confessore and Confessore (1992) conducted a 3-iteration Delphi study involving 22 self-directed learning experts from several countries. Consensus was reached in several areas, such as the most important self-directed learning research findings, research trends, practical applications, and published works.

Based on such literature and research, five major findings can be extracted: (a) several instruments for measuring some self-directed learning aspects have been developed; (b) self-directed learning readiness has been associated with various performance, psychological, and social variables; (c) a majority of self-directed learning research efforts have been qualitative in nature; (d) practice implications and techniques for facilitating self-directed learning are being devised; and (e) a coherent self-directed learning theory has not yet been developed.

1.4 Toward a Theory of Self-directed Learning

Candy (1991) outlines some useful dimensions of a theory and cautions about the often unrecognized dichotomy that exists between self-directed learning as a

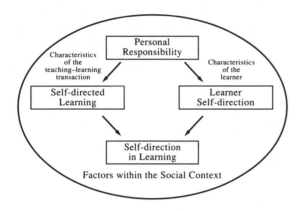

Figure 1
The PRO (Personal Responsibility Orientation) Model (Brockett T
G. Hiemstra R 1991 *Self-direction in Adult Learning.* ©Routledge.
London. Reproduced with permission

process and as a goal. Long (1989) also urges that any self-directed learning theory building be examined in terms of sociological, pedagogical, and psychological dimensions.

Brockett and Hiemstra (1991) synthesized different aspects of knowledge about the topic and conceptualized the Personal Responsibility Orientation (PRO) model. This model recognizes both differences and similarities between self-directed learning as an instructional method and learner self-direction as a set of personality characteristics. As can be seen in Fig. 1, the point of departure for understanding self-direction is personal responsibility. Personal responsibility refers to individuals assuming ownership for their own thoughts and actions. This does not necessarily mean control over all personal life circumstances or environmental conditions, but it does mean people can control how they respond to situations.

In terms of learning, it is the ability or willingness of individuals to take control that determines any potential for self-direction. This means that learners have choices about the directions they pursue. Along with this goes responsibility for accepting any consequences of one's thoughts and actions as a learner.

Brockett and Hiemstra (1991) interpret self-directed learning (see Fig. 1) as an instructional process centering on such activities as assessing needs, securing learning resources, implementing learning activities, and evaluating learning. Hiemstra and Sisco (1990) refer to this process as individualizing instruction, a process focusing on characteristics of the teaching–learning transaction. In essence, this aspect of self-direction centers on those factors external to the individual.

While much early research and seminal thinking (see Sect. 1.1) focused on this process orientation,

more recent research has related to better understanding the various personal or personality characteristics of successful self-directed learners. Self-concept, readiness for self-direction, the role of experience, and learning styles have been some of the characteristics studied. This emphasis on a learner's personal characteristics or internal factors is shown in Fig. 1 as learner self-direction. In essence, learner self-direction refers to those individual characteristics that lead to taking primary responsibility for personal learning.

Consequently, self-direction in learning is a term recognizing both external factors that facilitate a learner taking primary responsibility, and internal factors that predispose an adult accepting responsibility for learning-related thoughts and actions. At the same time there is a strong connection between self-directed learning and learner self-direction. Both internal and external aspects of self-direction can be viewed on a continuum and optimal learning conditions exist when a learner's level of self-direction is balanced with the extent to which self-directed learning opportunities are possible.

The PRO model's final component is represented by the circle in Fig. 1 that encompasses all other elements. While the individual's personality characteristics and the teaching and learning process are starting points for understanding self-direction, the social context provides an arena in which the learning activity or results are created. To fully understand a self-directed learning activity, the interface existing between individual learners, any facilitator or learning resource, and appropriate social dimensions must be recognized. Thus, Brockett and Hiemstra (1991) recommend that self-direction in learning be used as an umbrella definition recognizing those external factors facilitating adults taking primary responsibility for learning and those internal factors or personality characteristics that incline one toward accepting such responsibility.

2. Usefulness of Self-directed Learning Approaches

Formal education and schooling remain highly valued in most societies, and many educators, employers, policymakers, and ordinary citizens find it difficult to place high value on what is learned on their own and outside the formal system. However, adult educators have shown how nontraditional programs, distance education, and self-directed learning efforts can meet many challenges associated with keeping up to date on constantly changing knowledge. Self-directed learning researchers have challenged the assumption that adult learning can take place only in the presence of accredited teachers. In addition, because people can carry out self-directed learning outside of training organizations or formal schools, many administrators are beginning to look toward such learning as a means for stretching scarce education funds.

Several researchers have also demonstrated that giving some learning responsibility back to learners in many instances is more beneficial than other approaches. For example, in the workplace employees with busy schedules can learn necessary skills at their own convenience through self-study. Some technical staff in organizations who must constantly upgrade their knowledge can access new information through an individualized resource center.

Perhaps most important of all, self-directed learning actually works. Many adults succeed as self-directed learners when they could not if personal responsibility for learning decisions had not been possible. Some will even thrive in ways never thought possible when they learn how to take personal responsibility. In many respects, future learners will need to become self-directed throughout their lives just to cope with the huge quantity of information available to them.

3. Self-directed Learning Controversies

There have been several associated controversies. Many sources shown in the bibliography discuss them. Three of the most prominent in the literature will be discussed in this section.

Brookfield (1988) provided several critical reflections on self-directed learning. For example, he suggested that the preoccupation of many adult educators with self-directed learning is unwise because of its inadequate theoretical base. He also suggested that research on self-directed learning up to 1988 had been carried out mainly with middle-class, White subjects. Another concern was his perception that research on self-directed learning had been primarily quantitative in nature.

As discussed elsewhere in this entry there continues to be a need for more adequate theory pertaining to self-directed learning. Brockett and Hiemstra (1991) and others have been working toward that end. Groups traditionally viewed as hard-to-reach or outside the middle-class mainstream have actually been studied more widely than suggested by Brookfield. Regarding his concern about excessive use of quantitative research, Long (1989) and others have discovered that the majority of research efforts in this area have actually been qualitative in nature.

Another major controversy has centered on Guglielmino's (1977) SDLRS, an instrument used in many studies on self-directed learning. It has been criticized as difficult to use with certain groups, without appropriate validation, and both conceptually and methodologically flawed (Bonham 1991; Field 1989, 1991). Guglielmino et al. (1989) and McCune and Guglielmino (1991) are some of the people who have refuted the criticisms in subsequent publications. The instrument appears to have some limitations in terms of with whom and how it is used, but if employed appropriately is helpful for achieving a better understanding of aspects of self-directed learning. However,

additional instruments are needed for future quantitative research.

Candy (1991) suggests that research on self-directed learning has been stalemated in recent years because of the absence of a consistent theoretical base, continued confusion over the term's meaning, and the use of inappropriate research paradigms. His criticisms seem consistent with what others have reported and have already prompted new thinking and research. For example, a staged model has been developed that matches appropriate learning and teaching with self-directed learning abilities (Grow 1991, 1994, Tennant 1992).

4. Emerging Trends and Issues

A number of trends are emerging from the research on self-directed learning. Confessore and Confessore's (1992) Delphi study also obtained consensus views on several trends. Three significant trends are:

(a) research on the feasibility of self-directed learning meeting some job-related training needs in industry (Hiemstra 1994b, Ravid 1987);

(b) efforts to better understand the role of educational technology in self-directed learning and distance education (Hiemstra 1994a);

(c) researchers' focus on enhancing self-directed learning by better understanding environmental factors (Spear and Mocker 1984). For example, Hiemstra (1991) and his colleagues describe various ways physical, social, and psychological aspects of the learning environment can be affected.

4.1 Future Research Issues

Even though several research trends are observable, there still remains much work to be done.

(a) Additional research is required to test conceptual ideas like the PRO model (Brockett and Hiemstra 1991), and other emerging ideas to ensure the evolvement of a theory of self-directed learning.

(b) Ways need to be found whereby organizations and educators can facilitate self-directed learning and enhance critical thinking skills without impinging on the value of self-directed or spontaneous learning (Garrison 1992). For example, Smith (1990) describes how learners can be helped to learn, ask critical questions, and reflect on what they are learning.

(c) It is important that better ways of incorporating computer technology and electronic communication into self-directed learning be determined as more distance education programs are created.

(d) Future research is needed on such issues as expanding the repertoire of design and methodology for studying self-directed learning, how competencies necessary for effective self-directed learning are developed, and how the quality of self-directed learning resources can be measured.

(e) Ways of measuring and maintaining quality in self-directed learning need to be determined.

(f) The most appropriate roles for educators and educational organizations in relation to self-directed learning need to be found.

(g) Ways of better delineating micro-elements of the teaching and learning process so that learners can become self-directed in any part of the process (Hiemstra 1994b).

(h) Finally, ways for learners and others to evaluate the value and effectiveness of self-directed learning need to be developed.

See also: Experiential and Open Learning for Adults; Learning Strategies and Learning to Learn

References

Bonham L A 1991 Guglielmino's self-directed learning readiness scale: What does it measure? *Adult Educ. Q.* 41(2): 92–99

Boud D (ed.) 1988 *Developing Student Autonomy in Learning*, 2nd edn. Kogan Page, London

Brockett R G, Hiemstra R 1991 *Self-direction in Adult Learning: Perspectives in Theory, Research, and Practice.* Routledge, London

Brookfield S D 1986 *Understanding and Facilitating Adult Learning: A Comprehensive Analysis of Principles and Effective Practices.* Jossey-Bass, San Francisco, California

Brookfield S D 1988 Conceptual, methodological and practical ambiguities in self-directed learning. In: Long H B (ed.) 1988 *Self-directed Learning: Application and Theory.* Department of Adult Education, University of Georgia, Athens, Georgia

Caffarella R S, O'Donnell J M 1987 Self-directed adult learning: A critical paradigm revisited. *Adult Educ. Q.* 37(4): 199–211

Candy P C 1991 *Self-direction for Lifelong Learning: A Comprehensive Guide to Theory and Practice.* Jossey-Bass, San Francisco, California

Chene A 1983 The concept of autonomy in adult education: A philosophical discussion. *Adult Educ. Q.* 34(1): 38–47

Confessore G J, Confessore S J 1992 In search of consensus in the study of self-directed learning. In: Long H B (ed.) 1992

Craik G L 1840 *Pursuit of Knowledge Under Difficulties: Its Pleasures and Rewards.* Harper and Brothers, New York

Durr R, Guglielmino L, Guglielmino P 1994 Self-directed learning readiness and job performance at Motorola. In: Long H B (ed.) 1994

Field L 1989 An investigation into the structure, validity, and reliability of Guglielmino's Self-Directed Learning Readiness Scale. *Adult Educ. Q.* 39(3): 125–39

Field L 1991 Guglielmino's self-directed learning readiness scale: Should it continue to be used? *Adult Educ. Q.* 41(2): 100–103

Garrison D R 1992 Critical thinking and self-directed learning in adult education: An analysis of responsibility and control issues. *Adult Educ. Q.* 42(3): 136–148

Gibbs B 1979 Autonomy and authority in education. *J. Phil. Educ.* 13: 119–32

Grow G 1991 Teaching learners to be self-directed. *Adult Educ. Q.* 41(3): 125–149

Grow G 1994 In defense of the staged self-directed learning model. *Adult Educ. Q.* 44(2): 109–114

Guglielmino L M 1977 Development of the self-directed learning readiness scale (Doctoral dissertation, University of Georgia) *Dissertation Abstracts International* 1978 38: 6467A

Guglielmino L M, Long H B, McCune S K 1989 Reactions to Field's investigation into the SDLRS. *Adult Educ. Q.* 39(4): 235–45

Hiemstra R (ed.) 1991 *Creating Environments for Effective Adult Learning.* New Directions for Adult and Continuing Education, No. 50. Jossey-Bass, San Francisco, California

Hiemstra R 1992 Individualizing the instructional process: What we have learned from two decades of research on self-direction in learning. In: Long H B (ed.) 1992

Hiemstra R 1994a Computerized distance education: The role for facilitators. *The MPAEA Journal of Adult Education.* 22(2): 11–22

Hiemstra R 1994b Helping learners take responsibility for self-directed activities. In: Hiemstra R, Brockett R G (eds.) 1994 *Overcoming Resistance to Self-direction in Learning.* New Directions for Adult and Continuing Education, No. 64. Jossey-Bass, San Francisco, California

Hiemstra R, Sisco B 1990 *Individualizing Instruction: Making Learning Personal, Empowering, and Successful.* Jossey-Bass, San Francisco, California

Houle C O 1961 *The Inquiring Mind.* University of Wisconsin Press, Madison, Wisconsin

Knowles M S 1975 *Self-directed Learning: A Guide for Learners and Teachers.* Follett Publishing Co., New York

Knowles M S (ed.) 1984 *Andragogy in Action.* Jossey-Bass, San Francisco, California

Long H B 1989 Self-directed learning: Emerging theory and practice. In: Long H B (ed.) 1989 *Self-directed Learning: Emerging Theory and Practice.* Oklahoma Research Center for Continuing Professional and Higher Education, University of Oklahoma, Norman, Oklahoma

Merriam S B, Caffarella R S 1991 *Learning in Adulthood: A Comprehensive Guide.* Jossey-Bass, San Francisco, California

McCune S L, Guglielmino L M 1991 The validity generalization of Guglielmino's self-directed learning readiness scale. In: Long H B (ed.) 1991

Orsburn J D, Moran L, Musselwhite E, Zenger J H 1990 *Self-directed Work Teams: The New American Challenge.* Business One Irwin, Homewood, Illinois

Piskurich G M 1993 *Self-directed Learning: A Practical Guide to Design, Development, and Implementation.* Jossey-Bass, San Francisco, California

Piskurich G M 1994 The current state of SDL in business and industry. In: Long H B (ed.) 1994

Ravid G 1987 Self-directed learning in industry. In: Marsick

V J (ed.) 1987 *Learning in the Workplace*. Croom Helm, Beckenham

Ruvinsky L I (trans. Sayer J) 1986 *Activeness and Self-education*. Progress Publishers, Moscow

Smiles S 1859 *Self-Help*. John Murray, London

Smith R M (ed.) 1990 *Learning to Learn Across the Life Span*. Jossey-Bass, San Francisco, California

Spear G E, Mocker D W 1984 The organizing circumstance: Environmental determinants in self-directed learning. *Adult Educ. Q.* 35(1): 1–10

Tennant M 1992 The staged self-directed learning model. *Adult Educ. Q.* 42(3): 164–166

Tough A 1979 *The Adult's Learning Projects: A Fresh Approach to Theory and Practice in Adult Learning*, 2nd edn. University Associates (Learning Concepts), San Diego and Ontario Institute for Studies in Education, Toronto

Further Reading

Brockett R G, Hiemstra R 1993 *El aprendizaje autodirigido en la educacion de adultos: Perspectivas teoricas, practicas y de investigacion*. Paidos Ediciones, Barcelona

Confessore G J, Confessore S J (eds.) 1992 *Guideposts to Self-directed Learning*. Organization Design and Development Inc., Pennsylvania

Long H B (ed.) 1990 *Advances in Research and Practice in Self-directed Learning*. Oklahoma Research Center for Continuing Professional and Higher Education, University of Oklahoma, Norman, Oklahoma

Long H B (ed.) 1991 *Self-directed Learning: Consensus and Conflict*. Oklahoma Research Center for Continuing Professional and Higher Education, University of Oklahoma, Norman, Oklahoma

Long H B (ed.) 1992 *Self-directed Learning: Application and Research*. Oklahoma Research Center for Continuing Professional and Higher Education, University of Oklahoma, Norman, Oklahoma

Long H B (ed.) 1993 *Emerging Perspectives of Self-directed Learning*. Oklahoma Research Center for Continuing Professional and Higher Education, University of Oklahoma, Norman, Oklahoma

Long H B (ed.) 1994 *New Ideas about Self-directed Learning*. Oklahoma Research Center for Continuing Professional and Higher Education, University of Oklahoma, Norman, Oklahoma

Long H B, Confessore G J 1992 *Abstracts of Literature in Self-directed Learning 1966–1982*. Oklahoma Research Center for Continuing Professional and Higher Education, University of Oklahoma, Norman, Oklahoma

Long H B, Redding T R 1991 *Self-directed Learning Dissertation Abstracts 1966–1991*. Oklahoma Research Center for Continuing Higher and Professional Education, University of Oklahoma, Norman, Oklahoma

Learning in Children with Special Needs

Cognitive Strategy Instruction: Special Education

Y. M. David and A. S. Palincsar

"Cognitive strategy instruction" refers to instruction that is designed to increase the learner's ability to regulate and monitor his or her own learning activity. There are three types of knowledge generally regarded as essential to self-regulation: (a) knowledge of strategies, or effortful and deliberate activities engaged in for the purpose of accomplishing learning tasks; (b) metacognitive knowledge, or knowledge of one's own learner characteristics as well as knowledge of the task demands, that enables the learner to select, employ, evaluate, and modify strategy use; and (c) real world knowledge. Special educators have been particularly intrigued by cognitive strategy instruction as a response to descriptive research documenting the failure of students experiencing learning difficulties to display the knowledge, beliefs, and behaviors that characterize self-regulated learners (Meltzer et al. 1989).

This entry begins with some historical information regarding cognitive strategy instruction. This is followed by a summary of models of strategy instruction that have attained some prominence in special education (drawn from the reading literature). The entry concludes by identifying enduring issues regarding cognitive strategy instruction.

1. Historical Perspective

Research on cognitive strategy instruction has burgeoned since the 1970s when cognitive psychologists began intensive inquiry into human thought processes. Special educators embraced this model partly because of the disillusionment they were experiencing regarding two other prominent approaches to the instruction of special education students. The first approach—suggested by the underlying ability deficit model—was to teach processes that were assumed to underlie successful academic achievement; for example, auditory memory or visual perception.

This orientation failed to muster support because of its limited usefulness when planning and delivering instruction; when students did demonstrate improvement with the underlying process, this improvement was not reflected in academic performance (Wong 1992). The second approach was the use of operant procedures to modify both social and academic behavior; for example, students would be praised and rewarded for fluency and accuracy in decoding and comprehension. Typically, operant procedures of this nature failed to improve the targeted behavior, or, when improvement was discerned there was little evidence of maintenance of the improvement or generalization to situations different from the one in which the behavior was modified.

In contrast to either of these approaches, a cognitive strategy approach is rooted in theoretical analyses of the task at hand to determine the component skills or procedures underlying successful completion of the designated task, as well as observations of the activity of skilled learners engaged in the academic task of interest. For example, Bereiter and Bird (1985) observed skilled readers who engaged in thinking aloud while reading as a means of sharing the kinds of cognitive activity in which they were engaged. The protocols of these "think alouds" revealed that skillful readers paraphrased as they read, reread for clarification, and predicted in advance of reading. These kinds of observations, in turn, informed the design of strategy instruction programs. For example, reciprocal teaching instruction to improve reading comprehension employs several of the strategies observed with skillful readers in the Bereiter and Bird study. Similarly, in writing, Flower and Hayes (1980) developed a model of writing instruction, informed by the think aloud protocols of skillful writers, which has been successfully employed in the writing instruction work that Englert and her colleagues (Englert and Mariage 1991, Englert et al. 1991); Harris and Graham and their colleagues (Harris and Graham 1985, Graham and Harris 1989) and Wong et al. (1989) have conducted with special education students.

Since the early 1970s, a number of instructional approaches have been designed to teach students problem-solving strategies. These approaches differ in terms of the knowledge and skills that are targeted for instruction, and reflect different assumptions about the role of knowledge and the cognitive processes involved in thinking and problem-solving. Two large categories of approaches will be described: (a) general approaches to enhance thinking and problem-solving independently of academic content, and (b) domain-specific approaches.

A complete review of general thinking-skills approaches that have been developed to teach students a set of thinking skills independent of specific content has been conducted by Nickerson et al. (1985). Generally, this instruction is designed to promote students' general metacognitive and self-monitoring knowledge and skills such as defining the problem goals, identifying relevant facts, and developing a plan to solve the problem. These approaches are based upon two assumptions: (a) that there are general metacognitive skills that can be applied across a wide range of tasks; and (b) that in contrast to good problem-solvers, poor problem-solvers demonstrate a passive approach to problem-solving in which they do not seem to be consciously aware of and use self-monitoring processes (Bloom and Broder 1950). Examples of this approach include: a program developed by Feuerstein et al. (1980) entitled *Instrumental Enrichment*; Whimbey and Lochhead's (1991) program, *Problem Solving and Comprehension*, and The Philosophy for Children Program (Lipman et al. 1980). Data to support the relative effectiveness of these programs are sparse, despite their widespread adoption. Data which do exist suggest that while participants in these programs demonstrate improvement on the kinds of problems encountered in the problem-solving curricula, these improvements do not, in turn, enhance academic achievement.

Alternative models of strategy instruction are domain-specific. The domain-specific nature of strategy use is largely based on research in developmental and cognitive psychology that has demonstrated the importance of examining the ways in which strategies and knowledge interact to enhance problem-solving performance. For example, developmental studies in the area of memory (Chi 1978), examining the role of knowledge on recall performance, have demonstrated that an individual's knowledge influences recall performance as well as the strategies that are employed. Studies conducted to compare the performance of experts and novices within particular domains such as physics (Larkin et al. 1980, Linn 1985), have provided further evidence of the powerful effect that knowledge, not simply the quantity but also the qualitative organization of that knowledge (Chi and Koeske 1983), has on problem-solving performance.

Domain-specific strategy instruction has been a thriving enterprise in special education research since the early 1980s. The reader is referred to the special series of *Journal of Learning Disabilities* (1992) for a representative review of strategy instruction interventions across domains (mathematics, composition, reading). The next section of this entry considers the instructional implications of this research by characterizing and evaluating an array of strategy instruction models that have been implemented with special needs populations in reading.

2. Models of Domain-specific Strategy Instruction in Reading

A considerable amount of the research on cognitive strategy instruction in special education has concentrated on reading, due to the central role reading plays across the curriculum. While reading activities are fundamental, they are differentially employed by students, prompting research efforts to understand these differences in order to develop instructional models to promote greater strategy use across students. The following discussion focuses on six different models of cognitive strategy instruction within the area of reading and these models are used to examine such issues as the role of the teacher and student in strategy instruction, the nature of the context of instruction, and the outcomes of instruction.

2.1 Direct Instruction

Direct instruction is an approach in which the steps of selected strategies are presented by the teacher in a sequential fashion, generally determined through task analysis. Students practice these steps as the teacher provides and eventually fades prompts. A hallmark of direct instruction is the active and directive role assumed by the teacher, who maintains control of the pace, sequence, and content of the lesson.

The effects of direct instruction have been investigated with general and special education students learning an array of comprehension strategies, such as identifying the main idea (Baumann 1984), understanding anaphoric relationships (Baumann 1986), critical reading (Darch and Kameenui 1987, Patching et al. 1983), and study skills (Adams et al. 1982). Typically, the effectiveness of direct instruction approaches has been investigated by comparing them to traditional basal reading instruction methods. The outcomes of these studies suggest that direct instruction is an effective means for teaching specific comprehension strategies to both low and normally achieving students. What is less clear from these studies is the extent to which these students' ability to understand and recall text has been enhanced as a consequence of direct instruction of particular strategies. In part, the results are inconclusive as a function of the measures selected. Those studies that have included measures to evaluate students' generalization beyond the targeted strategies suggest that improvement is typically limited to the specific strategies that were taught; students who have demonstrated mastery of the targeted strategies have neither concurrently demonstrated improvement in their ability to comprehend text nor displayed the flexibility necessary to use the targeted strategies in novel contexts. In other words, the problem of inert knowledge appears prevalent in examining the results of direct instruction.

2.2 Cognitive Behavior Modification

Cognitive behavior modification (CBM) has been used to refer to a broad array of self-instructional programs. Traditional CBM programs are based upon the hypothesis that students can learn to regulate their own performance by means of internalizing a prescribed set of monitoring statements before, during, and after performing a task. The statements, which are developed based upon task analyses, typically assist the student in defining the task, directing attention, reinforcing performance, and coping with difficulties.

The development of CBM has been informed by several different theories of learning including social learning theory and social constructivism, as well as research in the area of verbal mediation (Meichenbaum 1985). Social learning theory emphasized the importance of students' cognitions in facilitating self-control, which directed researchers' attention away from overt behaviors to the ways in which students were mediating those behaviors. Verbal mediation research was informative regarding the importance of teaching individuals to produce and use mediating statements to enhance task comprehension, as well as task completion. A third influence is social constructivist theory, represented by the writings of Vygotsky (1978) and Luria (1976). They were interested in the role of social interactions in cognitive development and the shift of psychological functions from the interpersonal to intrapersonal levels. Luria proposed that this shift occurred in three phases. First, an adult (or more capable person) verbally controls the child's (or a less capable person's) behavior. Second, the child begins to direct his or her own behavior by overt speech. Gradually over time, this speech becomes internalized thus enabling the child to control his or her own behavior.

Within reading, CBM has been used as a means for enhancing students' study skills (Dansereau et al. 1979) and their ability to detect errors in reading passages (Miller et al. 1987). Research indicates that CBM is an effective means of strategy instruction, particularly for above-average learners. This research has, however, not addressed the following matters: flexibility of strategy use, generalized use of instructed strategies, and changes in reading awareness and attitudes following instruction. Similar to direct instruction,

CBM represents strategies as a series of discrete steps, selected and modeled by the teacher with no occasion to evaluate the students' representation of reading activity. Furthermore, there is variability across the CBM studies in terms of the focus on the processes of reading (e.g., how one determines the main idea vs. detail and how one reads for understanding). Finally, Diaz and Berk (1992) critique self-instructional approaches, such as those used in CBM, that were inspired by Vygotskian theories regarding the development of verbal self-regulation. They suggest that the limited success of many of these programs is actually consistent with Vygotsky's theory since they are based upon erroneous assumptions regarding the development of private speech. For example, some approaches are based upon the assumption that children with learning and behavior problems emit less private speech than their normally achieving peers. Yet empirical evidence indicates that this is not the case (Berk and Potts 1991, Copeland 1979, Berk and Landau 1991, Harris 1986). A second erroneous assumption is that simply modeling and asking children to repeat a prescribed set of verbalized instructions will lead children to engage in more spontaneous private speech. Padilla and Diaz (1986) found that adult modeling had no impact on children's private speech or task performance. The authors indicate that modeling does not reflect the kinds of dynamic social interactions that are critical in fostering the emergence of children's spontaneous private speech and the development of self-regulation. Successful interventions that are consistent with Vygotsky's theory are characterized by highly interactive communications among the adult and child in which the child assumes an active role in the problem-solving process. The adult constantly evaluates the child's current level of competence and provides support accordingly. Socially mediated interactions are characterized by a two-way process of appropriation on the part of adult and child (Litowitz 1990), in contrast to modeling which involves little or no reciprocity between the two parties.

2.3 The Strategies Intervention Model

The strategies intervention model, developed at the University of Kansas Institute for Research in Learning Disabilities, has emerged from an extensive research program that investigated the academic performance of students who were identified as either learning disabled or low achieving (Deshler and Schumaker 1986, Lenz et al. 1989). As in direct instruction and cognitive behavior modification, the strategies are taught as a series of steps. Unlike the other models, the strategies intervention model comprises two phases of instruction. In the acquisition phase, students are taught to apply the strategy in a supported setting. In the generalization phase, students learn to apply the strategy in the general education setting. The strategies intervention model is also distinguished by the fact that instruction is preceded by assessment regarding the students' current strategy use in specific contexts. Thereafter, the instructional steps are quite comparable to those used in direct instruction and cognitive behavior modification: modeling and verbal rehearsal of the steps of the strategy, and guided practice and feedback with materials controlled for complexity, length, and difficulty, with the use of mastery criteria to determine when the student can proceed to more difficult materials. Investigations indicate that sustained instruction is successful in improving strategy use, as well as content learning.

2.4 Direct Explanation

Direct explanation (Duffy et al. 1986, 1987) is distinguished from the previous models in several respects. It is an approach in which skills are recast as strategies that serve as tools for understanding text. To make this explicit to students, teachers provide: (a) declarative knowledge (i.e., inform the student about the name of the strategy, the purpose for which it could be useful, and steps in deploying the strategy); (b) procedural knowledge (i.e., teach the students how to use the strategy); and (c) conditional knowledge (i.e., inform the students about when the strategy would be appropriately used). In an effort to teach the skills as tools, the teachers "talk aloud" about the mental processes they use when experiencing difficulty understanding text, the way in which application of the skill can increase comprehension, and the mental steps that should be taken to use the skills strategically. At this point, the steps correspond quite well with those of the learning strategies intervention model, including the use of modeling, guided practice, and independent practice.

Investigations of direct explanation have been conducted by third- and fifth-grade teachers working with their lowest groups of readers. Students in the direct explanation condition showed significantly greater procedural and conditional knowledge of the strategies. In addition, metacognitive interviews indicated greater awareness on the part of the experimental students regarding the strategic nature of reading. The results of reading achievement measures have been somewhat mixed, with experimental students scoring significantly higher on the word study subtest of a reading achievement test, but not on the comprehension subtest of this measure.

2.5 Informed Strategies for Learning

Informed strategies for learning (ISL) is a curricular approach to strategy instruction that was designed to enhance students' reading comprehension (Paris and Oke 1986). It consists of 20 modules addressing 4 comprehension processes: planning for reading, identifying meaning, reasoning while reading, and monitoring comprehension. Each module includes 3 lessons that focus on a specific strategy (e.g., finding

the main idea). These lessons inform students about the usefulness of the strategy, provide metaphors to help students understand the strategy, and offer guided practice, as well as opportunities to apply the strategies to a variety of texts (e.g., science and social studies).

Informed strategies for learning is distinguished from the models of cognitive strategy instruction previously described since it includes an additional component, group dialogues. The purpose of these dialogues is to provide opportunities for teachers and students to discuss their thoughts and feelings about the strategies, and their usefulness, with particular attention paid to personal aspects of strategy use. Although the effectiveness of ISL has been determined with regard to increasing students' awareness of strategies and strategy use, the effects of ISL on reading comprehension with poor readers has been less encouraging.

2.6 Reciprocal Teaching

Reciprocal teaching (Brown and Palincsar 1989, Palincsar and Brown 1984, 1988) features the instruction of four strategies that are taught and practiced as a set of complementary activities to be used flexibly as the text, the needs of the reader, and the demands of the text suggest. In contrast to the previous methods, reciprocal teaching (RT) places less emphasis on teacher explanation or mastery of discrete strategies and greater emphasis on the collaboration of teachers and students to use specific strategies to render the text meaningful.

In RT, teachers and students take turns leading a dialogue about the meaning of the text with which they are working. The discussion focuses on generating questions from the text, summarizing the text, clarifying portions that impair understanding, and predicting upcoming content based on clues that are provided by the content and structure of the text. When these dialogues begin, the teacher assumes principal responsibility for leading and sustaining the discussion, modeling skilled use of the strategies for the purpose of understanding the content. Even from the first day of instruction, however, the children are encouraged to participate in the discussion by generating their own questions, elaborating upon or revising the summary, or suggesting additional predictions. The teacher enables the participation of each student in the dialogue through the use of specific feedback, additional explanation, and modeling.

Investigations of RT have been conducted with at-risk students in the primary grades (as listening comprehension instruction) and with remedial readers in middle school. At both levels, RT has significantly increased students' ability to use the targeted strategies and to attain higher scores on standardized and criterion-referenced comprehension measures. In addition, these gains have been demonstrated to maintain over time and to generalize beyond the experimental setting. Reciprocal Teaching research has not assessed students' conceptions of reading activity or changes in those conceptions with instruction. In addition, the highly interactive nature of RT renders it a difficult model to implement for teachers who are more accustomed to "directive teaching."

3. Challenges of Effectively Implementing Cognitive Strategy Instruction

While there are now a number of models of strategy instruction that have been implemented with special education students, with varying degrees of success, there are still numerous challenges confronting the teacher and researcher concerned with teaching for self-regulation. Some of these challenges are considered below.

3.1 Responding to the Social Context of Education

Alvermann (1992) discusses the importance of engaging in strategy instruction that is culturally sensitive with respect to the norms and values of nonmainstream cultures. Typically, there has been little attention paid to this issue in strategy instruction research. Yet cultural variables may help to explain the differential effects of strategy instruction. Research efforts have been directed toward identifying possible discontinuities between students' native cultures and the school cultures with respect to a number of instructional variables (e.g., discourse modes, participation structures, objectives, and content) that might account for the low academic achievement of some minority groups. This has led to the development of several model programs that are congruent with students' native culture in homogeneous communities (Au 1980, Jordan 1984, 1985). However, additional research is needed since there are still many unanswered questions about how to implement culturally sensitive instruction in culturally diverse communities (Tharp 1989).

Alvermann indicates that for some students, the objectives of strategy instruction may be incongruous with those of their native culture. For example, a commonly identified purpose of this form of instruction is to ensure that each individual can function independently of the teacher. Yet this instructional goal may not be congruent with the values of some cultures that encourage greater interdependence among group members. Alvermann suggests that students who understand the purpose of instruction may value and accept the instructional approach. In culturally diverse classrooms it is important to strike a balance so that one group is not consistently required to compromise its values.

Another possible source of cultural conflict is the nature of instruction. For example, in one replication study of reciprocal teaching, Gaber (1987) raised questions about whether students' lack of participation might be due to cultural differences between their natural discourse modes and the targeted form of discourse. Native Canadian adults, whom Gaber identified as functionally illiterate, were taught to engage in the reciprocal teaching dialogues. While most participants achieved criterion performance on the comprehension assessments, they did not engage in the dialogues among themselves when the teacher was absent from the group. For these students the form of instruction may have been discrepant with their cultural practices, raising questions about whether this form of instruction is appropriate for this particular group.

Another possible reason for the Canadian students' limited participation is their failure to internalize the strategies to the extent that they were able to function independently of the teacher. They might need additional time and teacher support before they become proficient at engaging in the dialogues independently. These issues underscore some of the complexities involved in conducting effective strategy instruction (Duffy and Roehler 1989), as well as emphasizing the way in which knowledge is socially constructed. More effective approaches do not consist of neatly packed instructional programs. Instead, they require skillful instruction in which the teacher mediates the learning of individual students by adjusting the demands of the task in relationship to the students' current knowledge and level of competence. The teachers' role as mediator is an extremely demanding one that requires considerable knowledge regarding development, the use of language in instruction, assessment, and domain knowledge. Duffy and Roehler (1989) suggest that teachers need instructional programs that provide structure and guidance to support the constant decision-making process that is an essential component of effective strategy instruction. This support might be in the form of metascripts (Gallimore and Tharp 1983) or general guidelines that enhance teachers' ability to teach in a responsive and flexible manner.

3.2 The Pursuit of Higher Order Literacies

The question regarding the generality versus domain-specificity of the thinking and problem-solving skills that should constitute the core of curricula continues to be a pressing one. Considerable research is needed to identify those thinking skills that will promote understanding across domains and will have applicability to daily life. One approach to this question is pursued by Perkins and his colleagues (Perkins and Simmons 1988) who examine the teaching of "epistemic forms," which are basic conceptual structures that provide useful ways of organizing knowledge and promoting conceptual understanding. Examples of epistemic forms include "comparison/contrast" and "form fits function." This pursuit will be particularly important when considering the needs of special education students who have, historically, been disenfranchised from the pursuit of higher-order literacy (cf. McGill-Franzen and Allington 1992).

3.3 The Relationship Between Motivation and Strategy Use

Current models of motivation provide a more complete picture of individual and situational variables that account for the learned helplessness approach that characterizes the achievement behavior of many special education students. Dweck and her colleagues developed a social-cognitive model that explains how two factors—students' goal orientation and perceived ability—interact to influence students' patterns of behavior, cognition, and affect (Dweck and Leggett 1988). Two common goal orientations reflect the different concerns or purposes of students: (a) a task orientation reflects a concern with increasing one's understanding and skills; and (b) an ego orientation reflects concern with obtaining favorable ability evaluations and avoiding negative ones. These goal orientations in combination with students' perceived ability level influence students' response to challenging tasks. Performance-oriented students with low ability perceptions typically exhibit a helpless pattern that is characterized by the avoidance of challenge, decreased effort, and decrements in performance. This contrasts with task-focused students who seek challenging tasks, and maintain effective striving when confronted with difficult tasks.

One striking difference that has been observed between task-focused and helpless students is their use of effective problem-solving strategies. In one study, both groups employed effective problem-solving strategies to solve one set of tasks (Diener and Dweck 1978). However, when presented with more challenging tasks, helpless children employed less effective strategies than task-focused children. Additional studies have demonstrated a relationship between students' goal orientations and their valuing and use of effective learning strategies (Nolen 1988, Ames and Archer 1988, Pintrich and DeGroot 1990).

Since a task orientation is more conducive to fostering adaptive problem-solving among students, research has focused on identifying factors that influence the goals students are likely to adopt, including: classroom practices (Epstein 1989, Ames 1992), students' perceptions of classroom goals (Ames and Archer 1988), beliefs about the nature of ability and intelligence (Nicholls 1984, Dweck and Leggett 1988), and valuing of the task. Research indicates that students' goal orientation is not a stable trait but varies across domains and tasks depending upon how important the domain or task is to the student. Other researchers (Maehr and Midgely 1990) have designed interventions to help teachers implement instructional practices that foster a mastery approach to learning that focuses on areas including evaluation, tasks, rewards, and grouping. Results indicate that the children who are most likely to benefit from an enhanced mastery climate are children who are at risk for academic difficulty.

One approach that has been effective in addressing student motivation is combining attributional retraining with strategy instruction (Borkowksi et al. 1988). Current models of motivation suggest that in addition to addressing the maladaptive attributional styles of special education students through attributional retraining, it is important to attend to other individual and classroom variables that influence student performance.

3.4 Restructuring Assessment Practices

It is difficult to overestimate the importance of designing assessment practices in such a manner that they are more closely aligned with instructional goals; in this instance assessment strategies must be consistent with strategic approaches to teaching and learning (Valencia and Pearson 1987). Traditional assessment practices have generally focused on measuring in static ways the outcomes of learning as opposed to the dynamic processes of learning. A movement toward portfolio assessment that is occurring concurrently with the movement toward teaching for self-regulation may advance this agenda (Gifford and O'Connor 1992). In portfolio assessment, there is an emphasis on student and teacher reflection on the learning process as well as the resulting products. Student performance is studied over time, in multiple contexts, with the use of on-line measures, and in a manner that solicits student self-evaluation.

3.5 Supporting Teachers in Instructional Change

The demands of teaching for self-regulation are considerable, suggesting the need to determine ways in which teachers can be supported in their efforts to teach general as well as domain-specific problem-solving activity. Ongoing efforts such as those by Gaskins and Elliot (1991) support the need to: (a) involve faculty in selecting and formulating strategy instruction approaches; (b) provide opportunities to voice the concerns, difficulties, and successes that teachers are experiencing during implementation efforts; (c) support instructional chaining such as peer coaching and peer collaboration; (d) align instructional objectives with assessment; and (e) recognize that change takes time. Based upon their efforts to implement change, Gaskins and Elliot recommend that instructional innovation be phased in over a period of three to five years.

See also: Cognitive Development: Individual Differences; Learning Strategies and Learning to Learn; Learning Strategies: Teaching and Assessing

References

Adams A, Carine D, Gersten R 1982 Instructional strategies for studying content area texts in the intermediate grades. *Read. Res. Q.* 18(1): 27–55

Alvermann D 1992 The influence of sociocultural factors on cognitive strategy instruction: A review of the research. Paper presented at the annual meeting of the American Educational Research Association, San Francisco, California

Ames C 1992 Classrooms: Goals, structures, and student motivation. *J. Educ. Psychol.* 84(3): 261–71

Ames C, Archer J 1988 Achievement goals in the classroom: Student learning strategies and motivation processes. *J. Educ. Psychol.* 80(3): 260–67

Au K H 1980 Participation structures in a reading lesson with Hawaiian children: Analysis of a cultural appropriate instructional event. *Anthropol. Educ. Q.* 11(2): 91–115

Baumann J F 1984 The effectiveness of a direct instruction paradigm for teaching main idea comprehension. *Read. Res. Q.* 20(1): 93–115

Baumann J F 1986 Teaching third-grade students to comprehend anaphoric relationships: The application of a direct instruction model. *Read. Res. Q.* 21(1): 70–90

Bereiter C, Bird M 1985 Use of thinking aloud in identification and teaching of reading comprehension strategies. *Cognition and Instruction* 2(2): 131–56

Berk L E, Landau S 1991 Setting effects on the private speech of learning disabled and normal children. Paper presented at the biennial meeting of the Society for Research in Child Development, Seattle, Washington

Berk L E, Potts M 1991 Developmental and functional significance of private speech among attention-deficit hyperactivity disordered and normal boys. *J. Abnorm. Child Psychol.* 19(3): 357–77

Bloom B S, Broder L J 1950 *Problem-solving Processes of College Students: An Exploratory Investigation*. University of Chicago Press, Chicago, Illinois

Borkowski J G, Weyhing R S, Carr M 1988 Effects of attributional retraining on strategy-based reading comprehension in learning-disabled students. *J. Educ. Psychol.* 80(1): 46–53

Brown A L, Palincsar A S 1989 Guided cooperative learning and individual knowledge acquisition. In: Resnick L (ed.) 1989 *Knowing and Learning: Issues for a Cognitive Psychology of Learning. Essays in Honor of Robert Glaser*. Erlbaum, Hillsdale, New Jersey

Chi M T H 1978 Knowledge structures and memory development. In: Siegler R S (ed.) 1978 *Children's Thinking: What Develops?* Erlbaum, Hillsdale, New Jersey

Chi M T H, Koeske R D 1983 Network representation of a child's dinosaur knowledge. *Dev. Psychol.* 19(1): 29–39

Copeland A P 1979 Types of private speech produced by hyperactive and nonhyperactive boys. *J. Abnorm. Child Psychol.* 7(1): 169–77

Dansereau D F et al. 1979 Development and evaluation of a learning strategy training program. *J. Educ. Psychol.* 71(1): 64–73

Darch C, Kameenui E J 1987 Teaching LD students critical reading skills: A systematic replication. *Learning Disability Quarterly* 10(2): 82–91

Deshler D D, Schumaker J B 1986 Learning strategies: An instructional alternative for low-achieving adolescents. *Excep. Child.* 52(6): 583–90

Diaz R M, Berk L E 1992 Misguided assumptions of self-instructional training. Paper presented at the annual meeting of the American Educational Research Association, San Francisco, California

Diener C I, Dweck C S 1978 An analysis of learned helplessness: Continuous changes in performance, strategy, and achievement cognitions following failure. *J. Pers. Soc. Psychol.* 36(5): 451–62

Duffy G G, Roehler L R 1989 Why strategy instruction is so difficult and what we need to do about it. In: McCormick C B, Miller G E, Pressley M (eds.) 1989 *Cognitive Strategy Research: From Basic Research to Educational Applications*. Springer-Verlag, New York

Duffy G G et al. 1986 The relationship between explicit verbal explanations during reading skill instruction and student awareness and achievement: A study of reading teacher effects. *Read. Res. Q.* 21(3): 237–52

Duffy G G et al. 1987 Effects of explaining the reasoning associated with using reading strategies. *Read. Res. Q.* 22(3): 347–68

Dweck C S, Leggett E L 1988 A social cognitive approach to motivation and personality. *Psychol. Rev.* 95(2): 256–73

Englert C S, Mariage T V 1991 Shared understandings: Structuring the writing experience through dialogue. *J. Learn. Disabil.* 24(6): 330–42

Englert C S, Raphael T M, Anderson L M, Anthony H M 1991 Making strategies and self-talk visible: Writing instruction in regular and special education classrooms. *Am. Educ. Res. J.* 28(2): 337–72

Epstein J 1989 Family structures and student motivation: A developmental perspective. In: Ames C, Ames R (eds.) 1989 *Research on Motivation in Education*, Vol. 3. Academic Press, New York

Feuerstein R, Rand Y, Hoffman M B, Miller R 1980 *Instrumental Enrichment: An Intervention Program for Cognitive Modifiability*. University Park Press, Baltimore, Maryland

Flower L, Hayes J R 1980 The dynamics of composing: Making plans and juggling constraints. In: Gregg L W, Steinberg E R (eds.) 1980 *Cognitive Processes in Writing*. Erlbaum, Hillsdale, New Jersey

Gaber D 1987 The use of reciprocal teaching method to improve the reading comprehension of functionally illiterate adults. Paper presented at the annual meeting of the National Reading Conference, Petersburg, Florida

Gallimore R, Tharp R G 1983 *The Regulatory Functions of Teacher Questions: A Microanalysis of Reading Comprehension Lessons*. Kamehameha Educational Research Institute, The Kamehameha Schools, Honolulu, Hawaii

Gaskins I, Elliot T 1991 *Implementing Cognitive Strategy Training in a School Setting. A How-to Manual for Teachers*. Brookline Books

Gifford B, O'Connor M (eds.) 1992 *Changing Assessment: Alternative Views of Aptitude, Achievement, and Instruction*. Kluwer, Boston, Massachusetts

Graham S, Harris K R 1989 Components analysis of cognitive strategy instruction: Effects on learning disabled students' compositions and self-efficacy. *J. Educ. Psychol.* 81(3): 353–61

Harris K R 1986 The effects of cognitive-behavior modification on the private speech and task performance during problem solving among learning-disabled and normally achieving children. *J. Abnorm. Child Psychol.* 14(1): 63–76

Harris K R, Graham S 1985 Improving learning disabled students' composition skills: Self-control strategy training. *Learning Disabilities Quarterly* 8(1): 27–36

Jordan C 1984 Cultural compatibility and the education of Hawaiian children: Implications for mainland educators. *Educ. Res. Q.* 8(4): 59–71

Jordan C 1985 Translating culture: From ethnographic information to educational program. *Anthropol. Educ. Q.* 16(2): 105–23

Journal of Learning Disabilities 1992 Vol. 25:3–4 (special series)

Larkin J H, McDermott J, Simon D P, Simon H 1980 Expert and novice performance in solving physics problems. *Science* 208(4450): 1335–42

Lenz B, Clark F L, Deshler D D, Schumaker J B 1989 *The Strategies Instructional Approach: A Training Package.* University of Kansas Institute for Research in Learning Disabilities, Lawrence, Kansas

Linn M C 1985 The cognitive consequences of programming instruction in classrooms. *Educ. Researcher* 14: 14–16

Lipman M, Sharp A M, Oscanyan F S 1980 *Philosophy in the Classroom*, 2nd edn. Temple University Press, Philadelphia, Pennsylvania

Litowitz B E 1990 Deconstruction in the zone of proximal development. *The Quarterly Newsletter of the Laboratory of Comparative Human Cognition* 12(4)

Luria A R 1976 *Cognitive Development: Its Cultural and Social Foundations.* Harvard University Press, Cambridge, Massachusetts

Maehr M, Midgely C 1990 Enhancing student motivation: A school-wide approach. Unpublished manuscript. University of Michigan, Ann Arbor, Michigan

McGill-Franzen A Allington R L 1992 The gridlock of low reading achievement: Perspectives on practice and policy. *Rem. Spec. Educ.* 12(3): 20–30

Meichenbaum D 1985 Teaching thinking: A cognitive-behavioral perspective. In: Chipman S F, Segal J W, Glaser R (eds.) 1985 *Thinking and Learning Skills: Vol. 2. Research and Open Questions.* Erlbaum, Hillsdale, New Jersey

Meltzer L J, Solomon B, Fenton R, Levine M D 1989 A developmental study of problem-solving strategies in children with and without learning difficulties. *Journal of Applied Developmental Psychology* 10(2): 171–93

Miller G E, Giovenco A, Rentiers K A 1987 Fostering comprehension monitoring in below average readers through self-instruction training. *J. Read. Behav.* 19(4): 379–93

Nicholls J G 1984 Achievement motivation: Conceptions of ability, subjective experience, task choice, and performance. *Psychol. Rev.* 91(3): 328–46

Nickerson R S, Perkins D N, Smith E E 1985 *The Teaching of Thinking.* Erlbaum, Hillsdale, New Jersey

Nolen S B 1988 Reasons for studying: Motivational orientations and study strategies. *Cognition and Instruction* 5(4): 269–87

Padilla K A, Diaz R M 1986 The training of self-regulatory private speech. Paper presented at the Conference of the Minority Biomedical Research Program, New Orleans, Louisiana

Palincsar A S, Brown A L 1984 Reciprocal teaching of comprehension-fostering and comprehension-monitoring activities. *Cognition and Instruction* 1(2): 117–75

Palincsar A S, Brown A L 1988 Teaching and practicing thinking skills to promote comprehension in the context of group problem solving. *Rem. Spec. Educ.* 9(1): 53–59

Paris S, Oke E 1986 Children's reading strategies, metacognition, and motivation. *Dev. Rev.* 6(1): 25–56

Patching W, Kameenui E, Carnin D, Gersten R, Colvin G 1983 Direct instruction in critical reading skills. *Read. Res. Q.* 18(4): 406–18

Perkins D, Simmons G 1988 Patterns of misunderstanding: An integrative model for science math, and programming. *Rev. Educ. Res.* 58(3): 303–26

Pintrich P, DeGroot E 1990 Motivational and self-regulated learning components of classroom academic performance. *J. Educ. Psychol.* 82(1): 33–40

Tharp R G 1989 Psychocultural variables and constants: Effects of teaching and learning in school. *Am. Psychol.* 44(2): 349–59

Valencia S, Pearson P D 1987 Reading assessment: Time for a change. *Read. Teach.* 40(8): 726–32

Vygotsky L S 1978 *Mind in Society: The Development of Higher Psychological Processes.* Harvard University Press, Cambridge, Massachusetts

Whimbey A, Lochhead J 1991 *Problem Solving and Comprehension*, 5th edn. Erlbaum, Hillsdale, New Jersey

Wong B Y, Wong R, Blenkinsop J 1989 Cognitive and metacognitive aspects of learning disabled adolescents' composing problems. *Learning Disability Quarterly* 12(4): 300–22

Wong B Y (ed.) 1992 *Contemporary Intervention Research in Learning Disabilities: An International Perspective.* Springer-Verlag, New York

Learning Characteristics of Students with Special Needs

M. C. Wang and E. Habelow

Finding ways to create effective and practical learning environments, responsive to the learning needs of each student, has been a challenge throughout the history of school reform. Effective school responses to learner differences have generated increasing international concern, which is expressed in efforts aiming to ensure educational outcomes for all of the increasingly diverse student populations that schools are challenged to serve (Bowman 1986, Ainscow 1991, Lockheed and Verspoor 1992, UNESCO 1991, Wang 1995).

Students differ in interests, learning styles, knowledge, and the speed with which they learn. This entry synthesizes the advances in theory and practice concerning learner differences and the effect of the advances on improving educational practices to ensure the learning success of all students, particularly those with special needs. Discussion is organized under the following headings: (a) learner characteristics and influences, (b) identification and classification of students with special needs, (c) the role of the learner, and (d) a research agenda for establishing a systematic database.

1. Learner Characteristics and Influences

Advances in research on learning and effective instruction reveal many distinct influences on learning characteristics and outcomes of children and youth, as well as methods most likely to maximize learning. These advances have important implications regarding the type of learner characteristics that should be considered in educational planning, in order to improve educational practices to ensure the learning success of students with special needs.

1.1 Alterable Versus Static Variables

There is growing realization that learner characteristics are alterable (Bloom 1981). Learner characteristics are increasingly described by researchers and practitioners in terms of the cognitive and social competencies required to achieve intended learning outcomes. Such information includes the current functing of the individual student in relation to the curriculum, the cognitive and academic skills the student uses to perform specific types of tasks, and the role of the learner in planning and monitoring his or her own learning. These emerging views of learner characteristics and the learning process have greatly improved the possibility that students with varying learning characteristics and needs will achieve learning success, particularly those viewed as the most difficult to motivate and hardest to teach.

These conceptual developments and descriptions of the learner contrast sharply with the traditional view of learning characteristics as static attributes of the individual learner, and with the prevalent practice of classifying and labeling students based on measures, often ill-defined, that provide little, if any, diagnostic information for instructional planning. The ability to provide effective intervention to improve learning outcomes is linked directly to an understanding of the learning process, and to a knowledge of the competencies and attributes needed by individual students to succeed in different types of learning.

1.2 Ethnocultural and Socioeconomic Status

The relationship between students' ethnic and socioeconomic characteristics and the classification and placement of students in special education has been the subject of extensive research. Research findings have brought attention to two related patterns. First, the learning needs of students who are formally classified as disabled and of others who are "low achieving" but not classified as special education students (including students considered "at risk" of school failure or receiving "compensatory" or "remedial" instruction) are very similar (Allington and McGill-Franzen in press, Jenkins et al. 1988). Second, there is a correlation between minority or low socioeconomic status and low achievement. The intersection of these two patterns has resulted in a significant, disproportionate placement of economically disadvantaged children, from ethnic and language minority backgrounds, in special education programs (Brantlinger and Guskin 1987, Heller et al. 1982).

Differences in learning characteristics among students categorized as average, low achieving, economically disadvantaged, or having various mild disabilities (e.g., learning disabilities, mild behavioral disorders, and educable mental retardation) have received increasing attention from researchers and practitioners. Although research findings suggest differences in the characteristics of students classified as mildly disabled and those with "average" levels of performance, findings on differences between students who are low achieving and those with mild disabilities have been equivocal (Reschly 1990, Jenkins et al. 1988). One subject of particular controversy is the apparent lack of major differences in education-related characteristics or outcomes for students classified as learning disabled, having low academic achievement, or otherwise considered to be academically at risk. These findings have important implications for reforming current classification systems and improving instructional practices and programs (Wang and Reynolds 1995).

Students from ethnic and language minority backgrounds may face, for example, biases in grade assignments and teacher expectations, identification and classification of "deviance" behaviors, and referral for special education placement. Biased assessment at any level of the instructional process (e.g., screening, classification, special education placement, and evaluation of individual student/program) can influence the student learning experience. There is a substantial research base suggesting that a significantly greater proportion of students from poor and ethnic minority backgrounds are placed in special education programs as a result of discriminatory counseling and "tracking" practices (O'Neil 1992, National Council on Disability 1989, Kilgore 1991). Tracking, sometimes referred to as ability grouping, has been found to result in inferior education, depriving low-achieving students of self-respect, stimulation by higher-achieving peers, and helpful teacher strategies and achievement expectations. Special education implemented as a second system of education, separate from the regular education curriculum, is in a real sense a tracking practice, because students are segregated and differentiated for instruction according to ability level (Wang et al. 1988).

1.3 Home Environment and Family Influences

Studies supporting the importance of parental involvement and the home environment have shown the positive influence of the family on student achievement, and have identified characteristics and behaviors of parents and extended family members that support student learning (Rutter 1990). The need for care and affection is critical throughout childhood and adolescence. Masten et al. noted that families:

> nurture mastery, motivation, and self-esteem as well as physical growth. Parents provide information, learning opportunities, behavioral models, and connections to other resources. When these transactional protective processes are absent or are severely limited for prolonged periods, a child may be significantly handicapped in subsequent adaptation by low self-esteem, inadequate information or social know-how, a disinclination to learn or interact with the world, and a distrust of people as resources. (Masten et al. 1990 p. 438)

Summarizing findings from a series of studies, Rutter (1990) further suggested that positive, intimate family relationships correlate with a positive self-concept and competence under stress. Research indicates that variables such as the physical environment of the home, the emotional and verbal responsiveness of the parents, parental expectations and their aspirations for the academic achievement of their children, and family cohesiveness and harmony play major roles in enhancing school learning.

1.4 Peer Support and Influence

Student achievement is not only a product of the academic capability of the individual, but also an indication of the quality of the school program and the nurturing of various support networks, including peers. Peer support networks provide a sense of camaraderie and mutual respect that forms important protective mechanisms against stress and adversity and frames attitudes toward academic competence and success in school. Opportunities to interact with students who have high achievement motivation, positive attitudes toward school, and a positive academic self-concept are of particular importance to students with special needs. There is a substantial research base that suggests a positive peer influence through cooperative learning, peer tutoring, and modeling (Johnson et al. 1983).

1.5 Community Connections for Students and Schools

Society educates children and youth for various purposes and through various channels. The ultimate goal of education is to provide individual children and youth with the skills and abilities to function as competent and productive members of society. The community at large (including civic, cultural, and religious institutions, businesses, and governmental, social, and health services agencies) is a central resource in shaping the educational outcomes of children and youth. These multiple levels of intrinsic influences collectively impact on the development and education of children and youth.

On a more macro level, societal expectations serve as important learning standards. Societies with high expectations for education and good citizenship stand out in studies exploring the importance of cultural norms in the development and education of children and youth. Robinson and Tayler (1989), for example, conducted a study in three different countries (England, France, and Japan) to examine the relationship between their national educational expectations and values and actual student development. They found that although the cultures of all three countries place considerable importance on academic effort and success, there are distinct differences. The French and Japanese cultures, for example, have the greatest respect for, and place the highest value on, the individual's overall development. Furthermore, when a student experiences less academic success than his or her peers, the French and Japanese cultures are more likely to focus on the failure of the system than on the failure of the student.

There is growing interest in stimulating closer links among the family, the school, and the community (Center for the Future of Children 1992, Rigsby et al. 1995) as a way to improve the learning outcomes of children with special needs. Children and youth spend large proportions of their waking hours outside of school. To the extent that this time can be made more constructive to their academic, social, and occupational development, their chances for successful lives can be improved.

Educators are enlisting families and communities to engage children in academic activities outside of school to enhance schooling success, particularly for those students requiring exceptional support. Families and other community institutions are increasingly linked, to enhance the chances for learning success, particularly for those with special needs, by broadening their experience and increasing their academic motivation (Center for the Future of Children 1992, US Department of Education 1995, Wang et al. 1995). In the United States exciting new modes of cooperation between schools and communities are being explored across the country (Holzman 1992).

2. Identification and Classification of Students with Special Needs

A fundamental assumption about children and youth with special needs is that their learning characteristics and needs are sufficiently different that they require greater than usual support and "special" intervention. However, findings from research and practice support the argument that the relationships among learner characteristics, classification, placement, and instruction in special education are by no means clear-cut, consistent, and reliable, or even valid (Reynolds et al. 1995). Systems for classifying students with special needs are the products of diverse forces, countervailing trends, historical accident, and compromise among competing constituencies. According to Reschly (1990), for example, extant classification systems incorporate a mixture of models for defining and determining exceptionality. Among the most prominent are the medical and social system models. Reschly further noted that confusion of these two models has led to much questioning about the meaning of exceptionality and the basis for identifying handicaps.

Mercer and Ysseldyke (1977) delineated three characteristics of the medical model. First, the medical model attributes abnormal patterns of behavior or development to underlying biological pathology. Second, the model is crosscultural; that is, it assumes that the same underlying biological abnormalities cause approximately the same deficits in behavior regardless of social status or cultural group. Finally, it is a deficit model that views biological anomalies as inherent. There tends to be little controversy over the classification of students as disabled under the medical model, and there is near universal agreement regarding the importance of early diagnosis and early intervention. Moreover, application of the medical model does not generally result in overrepresentation of economically disadvantaged or minority students. Medical model disabilities can range in severity and are of relatively low prevalence.

In contrast to the medical model, the social system model is based on a strong ecological perspective. Deviant behaviors or abnormal patterns of development are attributed to discrepancies between what is learned in a cultural context and the expectations for normal behavior in specific social roles and settings. Classifications such as mental retardation, emotional disturbance, specific learning disability, and speech impairment, can be regarded as social system model disabilities. The prevalence of such classifications in the United States is very high. For example, more than 80 percent of the students in the United States who are classified as disabled tend to be identified as having social system model conditions; these students have comprised between 7 percent and 9.5 percent of the total school-age population (Algozzine and Korinek 1985).

Similarities have been reported between the behavioral characteristics of students with mild disabilities and those of economically disadvantaged students, who are often members of ethnic or racial minorities (Brantlinger and Guskin 1987). These characteristics include low achievement, inefficient learning, difficulties in correlated processes, such as visual and auditory perception, and social or behavioral difficulties. Furthermore, there is no evidence that the use and effectiveness of different compensatory or remedial education procedures must necessarily depend on a student's classification, particularly if the classification is learning disabled or educable mentally retarded. The same procedures appear to work with students of either classification (Jenkins et al. 1988).

3. The Role of the Learner

The role of the learner may be conceptualized as encompassing two related categories of competence: responsibility for learning behaviors and outcomes, and the ability to be strategic and self-regulating during the learning process. There is a substantial research base that advances the concept of the student as an active participant in the learning process, and as an individual difference variable, with significant implications for developing competence and attitudes that enable students to learn in an active and deliberate manner.

3.1 The Active Learner

Substantial research findings suggest that the student's active learning role holds significant implications, both for understanding the methods that successful and less successful students employ when learning, and for designing effective instruction. The ability of students to assume an active role in learning is generally described as their ability to organize and use knowledge consciously, to know when they do not know, and to know where to seek assistance for learning and problem-solving in future situations.

This active role is also described in cognitive research literature as the metacognitive process, or self-regulated learning (American Psychological Association 1993, Brown 1994, Wang 1992, Wang and Palincsar 1989). When students are involved in active learning, they engage in a continuous process of internal and external adaptation. External adaptation occurs in the ideas and content that are to be learned, and in the modes and forms by which content is presented to the learner. Internal adaptation is on the part of the learner, as new content is assimilated and internal mental structures are modified to accommodate it. Thus, students are active processors, interpreters, and synthesizers of information. They are expected to take responsibility for managing, monitoring, and evaluating their own learning, and for playing an instrumental role in adapting the learning environment to the demands of the instructional learning process.

Both theory and research indicate a close relationship between school achievement and students' belief in their own ability to exert personal control over learning. Students who believe they can influence their learning are more likely to succeed than those who believe learning is controlled by powerful others (e.g., teachers) or that achievement is unaffected by effort. Research suggests that the development of a sense of self-responsibility for learning is particularly critical for students who have histories of academic failure and poor perceptions of self-competence and personal control—characteristics that are frequently associated with students classified as disabled (Keogh 1982).

3.2 Fostering Students' Active Learning Role

Intervention studies that are designed to foster self-responsibility for learning are typified by two major approaches. The first approach is characterized in the research on learned helplessness and attribution retraining (Weiner 1983). It involves interventions aimed at training students to accept responsibility for their learning success and failure. The second major approach to fostering self-responsibility for their learning consists of strategies for training students to monitor their own learning and behavior (Wang and Palincsar 1989). Wang and her associates have used the term "self-instructive skills" to refer to those skills students use when functioning as strategic and self-regulating learners. They define self-instructive skill as the students' ability to access and organize prior knowledge, as well as their ability to seek instructional help for accessing and using the relevant knowledge and skills in new learning. Thus, self-instructive skills involve both knowledge about the learning environment and the subject matter of critical tasks, and the ability to use that knowledge in deliberate learning through strategy planning, self-monitoring and self-assessment, and self-interrogation and clarification.

What students know has been consistently shown to be one of the best predictors of learning performance and outcomes. Knowledge characteristics are generally referred to in the research literature as either subject-matter knowledge or domain-general knowledge. (In research on cognition and learning, domain-general knowledge is discussed most often as "metacognition" or "metacognitive knowledge.") Subject-matter knowledge refers to the specific content of the task to be learned. The relationship between subject-matter knowledge and performance in given domains is well-documented in the literature. Domain-general knowledge, on the other hand, encompasses a broad spectrum of knowledge related to efficient learning. It refers to knowledge about characteristics of the task and the learning environment, perceptions of the knowledge characteristics of the self and others, and knowledge about relevant strategies for effective task performance.

The ability of students to use what they know in learning new tasks and to apply what they know in new situations is considered essential to their active learning role. Earlier work in this area was highly influenced by Flavell's (1970) notion of "production deficiency," which refers to a student's failure to use knowledge spontaneously, even when he or she is aware of the certain prerequisite strategies or behaviors for applying the knowledge to accomplish a goal. Production deficiency has been noted as a frequent problem for students identified as learning disabled (Kauffman and Hallahan 1979). The results from such research on learners with disabilities suggest that children who have difficulty in learning may lack the skills to regulate and coordinate what they know about a task with efficient strategies for task completion.

The extent to which students play an active role in their learning has significant implications for the functioning of successful and less than successful students, and for the design of effective instruction. Partly due to increasing awareness of the research bases in cognitive-instructional psychology, effective instruction, and the processes of learning, both general and special educators have become interested in a variety of instructional strategies or interventions that can enhance students' ability to assume an active role in learning. These interventions, which are typically aimed at training students to use a variety of cognitive strategies, include many programs for teaching thinking skills (Segal et al. 1985, Wang and Palincsar 1989). Cognitive strategy training programs generally focus on ways to enhance the acquisition of knowledge and academic skills in specific subject-matter areas, while also enhancing the development of higher order cognitive skills, such as reasoning and problem-solving.

4. Research Agenda for Establishing a Systematic Database

A major research requirement in the area of learner differences and effective instruction is the establishment of a systematic database for dissemination of learner characteristics that are instructionally relevant or "alterable," and specific intervention strategies for improving each individual student's capacity for learning, particularly those with special needs. Research questions related to this agenda include:

(a) What are the important variables that cause learning? How do some of the salient and commonly agreed-upon variables, such as classroom climate, the principal's leadership, teacher expectations, teacher–student interactions, time on task, and so forth, affect student learning performance, the classroom instructional learning process, academic achievement, and handicap classifications and placement of students with special needs?

(b) What specific aspects of the functioning of students with disabilities and/or students considered to be academically at risk differ from the characteristics of "expert" learners? How do successful and less than successful students differ in terms of their ability to assume an active role in their learning? Are these learner characteristics alterable? What are some of the effective intervention strategies that foster increasing "expertise" in students who are considered academically handicapped or at risk of academic failure?

(c) What are the salient characteristics (features) of programs that appear to develop student self-responsibility and competency in self-instructive skills?

(d) How are certain alterable learner characteristics (e.g., knowledge, students' self-perception of cognitive and/or social competence, temperament, and motivation) related to students' responsiveness to cognitive strategy training and other interventions aimed at developing both subject-matter knowledge and higher order cognitive skills?

(e) Do differences in teacher styles and instructional approaches require differences in levels of student competence for assuming self-responsibility in their learning and the ability to be self-instructive?

(f) How can advances in cognitive-instructional research be incorporated to improve understanding and procedures for diagnosing and monitoring learning processes that are intrinsic to student achievement of subject-matter knowledge and the higher order cognitive skills of reasoning and problem-solving?

(g) What specific steps can be taken to enhance the linkage between assessment (diagnosis of student learning needs and evaluation of learning outcomes) and improvement in instructional effectiveness?

(h) What do teachers need to know about instructionally relevant learner characteristics and state-of-the-art practices to increase their expertise in linking diagnosis and assessment to improve student learning?

Advances in research and program development can provide the foundation for shifting the emphasis on who should be classified as a special education student and by what criteria. This emphasis should be replaced with a focus on introducing and maintaining educational interventions based on the diagnosed instructional and related service needs of individual students. The time and energy that are devoted to determining the eligibility of students for "special" services represent an excessively costly and inefficient use of resources.

Finally, research is needed in the development of effective instructional delivery systems. Experience in a variety of settings has shown that research and program development tend to have little impact on schooling practice unless serious attention is also given to delivery systems that support implementation of innovative improvement practices.

The findings on learner characteristics and the provision of instructional practices that are responsive to learner differences discussed in this entry are causes for optimism for improving learning of students with special needs. Many research-based alternatives to traditional practices are available for further testing and widespread implementation. These alternatives are grounded in the assumption that improved learning can be expected for all students when information on an expanded range of learner characteristics interacts with the design of specific educational interventions for accommodating those characteristics.

See also: Learning Environments

References

Ainscow M (ed.) 1991 *Effective Schools for All.* Fulton, London

Algozzine B, Korinek L 1985 Where is special education for students with high prevalence handicaps going? *Excep. Child.* 51(5): 388–94

Allington R L, McGill-Franzen A in press Individualized planning. In: Wang M C, Reynolds M C, Walberg H J (eds.) in press *Handbook of Special Education: Research and Practice*, 2nd edn. Elsevier Science, Oxford

American Psychological Association 1993 *Learner-centered Psychological Principles: Guidelines for School Redesign and Reform.* Report produced by the Presidential Task Force on Psychology in Education of the American Psychological Association. American Psychological Association, Washington, DC

Bloom B S 1981 *All our Children Learning: A Primer for Parents, Teachers, and Other Educators.* McGraw-Hill, New York

Bowman I 1986 Teacher training and the integration of handicapped pupils: Some findings from a fourteen nation UNESCO study. *Eur. J. Spec. Need. Educ.* 1: 29–38

Brantlinger E A, Guskin S L 1987 Ethnocultural and social psychological effects on learning characteristics of handicapped children. In: Wang M C, Reynolds M C, Walberg H J (eds.) 1987 *Handbook of Special Education: Research and Practice. Vol. 1: Learner Characteristics and Adaptive Education.* Pergamon Press, Oxford

Brown A L 1994 The advancement of learning. *Educ. Researcher* 23(8): 4–12

Center for the Future of Children 1992 School linked services. *The Future of Children* 2(1): 1–117

Flavell J H 1970 Developmental studies of mediated memory. In: Reese H W, Lipsitt L P (eds.) 1970 *Advances in Child Development and Behavior.* Academic Press, New York

Heller K, Holtzman W, Messick S 1982 *Placing Children in Special Education: A Strategy for Equity.* National Academy of Science Press, Washington, DC

Holzman W H (ed.) 1992 *School of the Future.* Hogg Foundation for Mental Health and American Psychological Association, Austin, Texas

Jenkins J R, Pious C G, Peterson D L 1988 Categorical programs for remedial and handicapped students: Issues of validity. *Excep. Child.* 55(2): 147–58

Johnson D W, Johnson R T, Maruyama G 1983 Interdependence and interpersonal attraction among heterogeneous and homogeneous individuals: A theoretical formulation and a meta-analysis of the research. *Rev. Educ. Res.* 53(1): 5–54

Kauffman J M, Hallahan D P 1979 Learning disability and hyperactivity (with comments on minimal brain dysfunction). In: Lahey B B, Kazdin A E (eds.) 1979 *Advances in Clinical Child Psychology*. Plenum, New York

Keogh B K 1982 Children's temperament and teachers' decisions. In: Porter R, Collins G M (eds.) 1982 *Temperamental Differences in Infants and Young Children*. Pittman, London

Kilgore S B 1991 The organizational context of tracking in schools. *Am. Sociol. Rev.* 56(2): 189–203

Lockheed M E, Verspoor A M 1992 *Improving Primary Education in Developing Countries*. Oxford University Press, New York

Masten A S, Best K M, Garmezy N 1990 Resilience and development: Contributions from the study of children who overcome adversity. *Development and Psychopathology* 2(4): 425–44

Mercer J, Ysseldyke J 1977 Designing diagnostic-intervention programs. In: Oakland T (ed.) 1977 *Psychological and Educational Assessment of Minority Children*. Brunner/Mazel, New York

National Council on Disability 1989 *The Education of Students with Disabilities: Where Do We Stand?* National Council on Disability, Washington, DC

O'Neil J 1992 On tracking and individual differences: A conversation with Jeannie Oakes. *Educational Leadership* 50(2): 18–21

Reschly D J 1990 Mild mental retardation: Persistent themes, changing dynamics, and future prospects. In: Wang M C, Reynolds M C, Walberg H J (eds.) 1990 *Special Education Research and Practice: Synthesis of Findings*. Pergamon Press, Oxford

Reynolds M C, Wang M C, Walberg H J 1995 A summary of recommendations. In: M C Wang M C Reynolds (eds) 1995 *Making a Difference for Students at Risk: Trends and Alternatives* Corwin Press, Thousand Oaks, California

Rigsby L C, Reynolds M C, Wang M C (eds.) 1995 *School–Community Connections: Exploring Issues for Research and Practice*. Jossey-Bass, San Francisco California

Robinson W P, Tayler C A 1989 Correlates of low academic attainment in three countries. *Int. J. Educ. Res.* 13(6): 581–95

Rutter M 1990 Psychosocial resilience and protective mechanisms. In: Rolf J, Masten A S, Cicchetti D, Neuchterlein K H, Weintraub S (eds.) 1990 *Risk and Protective Factors in the Development of Psychopathology*. Cambridge University Press, New York

Segal J W, Chipman S F, Glaser R (eds.) 1985 *Thinking and Learning Skills. Vol. 1: Relating Instruction to Research*. Erlbaum, Hillsdale, New Jersey

UNESCO 1991 Special needs outreach. UNESCO *Special Education Newsletter*

US Department of Education 1995 *School-linked Comprehensive Services for Children and Families: What we Know and What we Need to Know*. US Department of Education, Washington, DC

Wang M C 1992 *Adaptive Education Strategies: Building on Diversity*. Paul H Brookes, Baltimore, Maryland

Wang M C 1995 Serving Students with Special Educaton Needs: Equity and access. *Final Report of the World Conference on Special Needs Education: Access and Quality* Ministry of Education and Science, UNESCO, Oviedo

Wang M C, Palincsar A S 1989 Teaching students to assume an active role in their learning. In: Reynolds M C (ed.) 1989 *Knowledge Base for the Beginning Teacher*. Pergamon Press, Oxford

Wang M C, Haertel G D, Walberg H J 1995 The effectiveness of collaborative school-linked services. In: Flaxman E, Passow A H (eds.) 1995 *Changing Populations/Changing Schools: The Ninety-Fourth Yearbook of the National Society for the Study of Education*. University of Chicago Press, Chicago, Illinois

Wang M C, Reynolds M C (eds.) 1995 *Making a Difference for Students at Risk: Trends and Alternatives*. Corwin Press, Thousand Oaks, California

Wang M C, Reynolds M C, Walberg H J 1988 Integrating the children of the second system. *Phi Del. Kap.* 70(3): 248–51

Weiner B A 1983 Speculations regarding the role of affect in achievement-change programs guided by attributional principles. In: Levine J M, Wang M C (eds.) 1983 *Teacher and Student Perceptions: Implications for Learning*. Erlbaum, Hillsdale, New Jersey

Neurological Bases of Learning Problems

G. S. Coles

The study of the neurological bases of learning problems, replete with quantitative, empirical data on brain functioning, seems to lend itself to more agreement than is found in other areas of education. Neurological organization, after all, should be more clear-cut and identifiable than other more complex influences —such as methods of instruction or teacher—student interaction that affect learning. However, this is not so. Although there is a fair amount of agreement on data describing brain processes involved in learning, the meaning of the data, both how and if brain processes cause learning problems, is hotly contended. The intensity of the disputes stems largely from the practical application of theory and research. Since the mid-1960s, conclusions about the neurology of learning problems have shaped schooling, particularly special education, by influencing how students are assessed, classified, and instructed. Many educators and psychologists regard this influence as a scientific achievement and of benefit to children; others consider it spurious and harmful.

An understanding of the knowledge and issues of the relationship between neurological dysfunctions and learning problems requires an overview of definitions, diagnosis, empirical evidence, applications, and paradigms.

1. Definitions

Conceptions of neurologically based learning problems, most commonly called "learning disabilities," share a definition of what constitutes the disorder. These definitions are consistent for United States and international learning disabilities and reading organizations (Hammill et al. 1987).

Although the disabilities may manifest themselves in various intellectual and academic activities—reading, writing, mathematics, listening, or speaking—reading disability is its most commonly identified form in schools and clinics. Whether the nature of the neurological dysfunctions is identified as perceptual, linguistic, attentional, or combinations of these and other abilities, the dysfunction(s) are defined as particular, not general, neurological defects. These defects involve higher order, not sensory functioning —for example, a person might be able to see a group of letters but not be able visually or auditorily to perceive their sequence of sounds. In other words, overall intellectual and sensory abilities are within a normal range, but neurological flaws are thought to impair particular kinds of learning. By definition, these learning disabilities are judged not to be caused by environmental influences (e.g., poor instruction or family problems), though these influences may have a secondary effect.

Although neurological defects are central to the definition, it is important to note that their existence and influence is problematic. Formal definitions of learning disabilities are careful to say that neurological dysfunctions are "presumed" or "suspected" to be, not certain to be, intrinsic to the individual and the cause of the learning disability. It is essential to keep this proviso in mind when assessing the research findings and school applications.

2. Empirical Evidence

Since James Hinshelwood, a Glasgow ophthalmologist, began in 1895 to study and write about "congenital word-blindness," a condition he concluded was caused by a defective language-related area of the brain in otherwise normal children, researchers have attempted to follow his effort to place the diagnosis of a learning problem on a scientific basis. During the first decade of the twentieth century, papers on the condition were published in Holland, Argentina, Germany, France, and the United States (McCready 1926), but the promise of a blossoming area of research was not fulfilled until the mid-1960s.

The burgeoning research since the 1960s has embraced study of a wide array of neurologically based processing problems and use of an even larger array of technological devices. Nonetheless, this research has been minimally fruitful in identifying neurological deficits underlying learning disorders, particularly because of a persistent lack of replication of initial findings and assumptions. For example, the long-held view that perceptual deficits were the primary cause of learning disabilities has been largely abandoned by researchers. In the words of one, the perceptual deficit explanation lacks "conclusive evidence" and "can be questioned on both empirical and theoretical grounds, and in neither context does it fare very well" (Vellutino 1979 p.207). The same may be concluded about other single-deficit explanations, like deficits in attention, memory, and language. Canadian neuropsychologist Byron Rourke, a strong proponent of neurological theories of learning disorders, concluded that these explanations have generally been rubbish, and have mostly been "defended in a manner that can best be characterized as narrow, insular . . . argumentative . . . and self-serving, myopic rationale" (Rourke 1985 pp.vii–viii). However, the claims for "subtyping"—the theory that there is a multiplicity of "subtypes" in a heterogeneous population of children with learning disorders—made by Rourke and others have not been more fruitful (Doehring 1984). Nor has the genetic research using families, twins, or chromosome mapping had any success in documenting the heritability of learning disabilities (Coles 1987 pp.106–17).

New technology has been used in an effort to reconstitute the perceptual deficit explanation. Abnormalities in the pathway of the visual system that aids in perceiving motion and depth and in conveying positional information (the magnocellular system) have also been proposed as the cause of dyslexia (Livingstone et al. 1991). Conclusions are preliminary however, because, as the researchers themselves caution, only five subjects were used in the study. In addition, the meaning of visual-evoked potentials, the technology used in the research, has been questioned in previous reading disabilities research due to measures that are strongly dependent on an individual's attention, motivation, emotional response to the task, and problem-solving skills.

Studies employing positron emission tomography (PET) and magnetic resonance imaging (MRI) have yielded considerable new information about brain function and structure. However, with respect to dyslexia (Flowers 1993), these technologies are hampered by a methodology that fails to demonstrate whether the association between brain function and reading problems are casual or correlational.

Dyslexia studies have also looked at the *planum temporale*, a region involved in analyzing and synthesizing speech sounds. Their findings of a causal connection are controversial because the boundaries of the region are difficult to identify (Steinmetz et al. 1990), and the studies did not control for age and sex (Schultz et al. 1994)

Dissection of "dyslexic" brains in the 1980s offered a promise of better evidence for the neurological thesis. For example, cellular abnormalities in the left cerebral hemisphere were reported (Galaburda et al. 1985, Humphreys et al. 1990). In the left temporal lobe, active in auditory functioning, researchers have identified ectopias (cells out of place) and dysplasias (abnormal tissue forms), particularly polymicrogyria (numerous small, abnormal convolutions). Milder forms of abnormal tissue development were found in other parts of the left hemisphere. Although these abnormalities suggest a dysfunction in the language-related areas in the brains of dyslexics, several considerations caution against drawing firm conclusions from this work. By 1994 only about ten brains had been used in these studies. Most important, the research contains several methodological problems, chief among them being the lack of documentation that the "dyslexics" were in fact dyslexic according to standard criteria. Only brief summary case histories are presented, which raise suspicions about subject selection. For example, for a "dyslexic" male who had a PhD in medical engineering, the sole assessment information provided was an "informal spelling test" given at the age of 14. Another subject was a distinguished psychiatrist who had never had a formal assessment of her educational and psychological abilities.

The medial geniculate, a subsystem involved in the time processing of auditory transmission, has also ben identified as a possible brain site that can create phonological deficits which, in turn, can produce dyslexia (Galaburda et al 1994). However, this finding is questionable because the neuronal differences were analyzed by group average only so that similar neuronal size patterns in individual brains of both dyslexics and normal readers were not explained.

Evidence of neurological defects associated with learning disabilities is available in research on toxic metals, like lead and cadmium; on alcohol and drugs; and on nutrition. There are many ambiguities in determining the influence of lead on academic achievement, but there is a consensus among most investigators in the United States, the United Kingdom, and other European countries that even low levels of lead can impair cognition. Similar conclusions were obtained for other toxic metals. Claims about an extensive influence of diet on children's neurological functioning and learning have not been substantiated by research, but there is a growing consensus that diet could adversely affect the learning of a small, yet undetermined, proportion of children with learning problems (Conners 1989).

Associations between maternal substance abuse during pregnancy and learning difficulties in the offspring have been found, but the extent to which these associations are causal is unclear (Van Dyke and Fox 1990). For example, a study comparing offspring of upper-middle class chronic alcoholic mothers with poor chronic alcoholic mothers found that the cognitive problems of the offspring were bound to many conditions related to socioeconomic deprivation. Fetal alcohol syndrome was "much more prevalent among the low socioeconomic classes," but relatively rare among the offspring of high socioeconomic chronic alcoholic women (Bingol et al. 1987). Although learning disabilities have been identified at a higher rate in alcoholic-dependent than nonalcoholic-dependent adults, these disabilities seem more a consequence of poverty and social class than of alcohol.

The use of alkaloidal cocaine ("crack") during pregnancy can cause neurological and behavioral abnormalities in infants exposed *in utero*, but most of these abnormalities appear to be of short duration, and by the age of two the cognitive scores of these infants on the Bailey Scales of Infant Development are normal. "Generally, then, these children are not intellectually impaired and appear to have good learning ability in structured situations" (Barth 1991 p.131, LeBlanc et al. 1987). Studies of prenatal cocaine exposure suggest that consequences are strongly associated with poverty-related factors like inadequate nutrition and poor prenatal care. Thus, while maternal cocaine use presents risks to the fetus, no simple, linear causal equation can be drawn.

Overall, decades of research have not documented the theory that a substantial number of children identified as "learning disabled"—estimated from 4 to 10 percent of school children—have problems because of minimal neurological dysfunctions. The actual number cannot yet be determined, but research suggests that the number is small—of course, even a small number is consequential. However, because theories and research are not restricted to laboratories and scholarly conferences and because they have their applied side in school and clinical practice, educators and other professionals should be concerned about the disparity between what is actually known about the neurological bases of learning problems and what is presumed known when assessing, classifying, and instructing children. Unfortunately, the majority of research on this topic has been "deficit driven" instead of a search for the relationships, not necessarily causal ones, between neurological functioning and learning.

3. Models of Neurological Functioning and Learning

Implicit in the theory and research on the neurological bases of learning problems is that schooling, instruction, learning, and various social experiences are not causal to the problems. Unsatisfactory conditions (i.e., inadequate instruction or an impoverished community) may worsen a child's neurological deficits but seldom do these conditions cause the problems.

A consequence of these *a priori* assumptions for research has been an absence of close examinations of these conditions. The neurological theory carries with it a methodology in which brain structure and function are considered the primary, and usually the only, causal influences that need to be examined. Seldom has the research included adequate study of interrelationships in classrooms, of alternative modes of instruction, or of the effects of family interactions on learning. This omission is extraordinary because of the huge volume of work worldwide on these issues.

Another paradigmatic matter is the meaning of "bases." Even when learning problems are clearly tied to fetal alcohol syndrome; prenatal drug exposure; or exposure to toxic metals, food additives, or colorings —even when genuine biological abnormalities can be identified—does it make sense to think of these as the "bases" of the learning disorders? It may make more sense to think of cause in terms of social relationships, both direct and indirect, that shape the conditions of the brain. For example, the primary sources of cadmium are food, air, and water. Substance abuse effects come not from within the child but from parents, usually in dire social conditions. Neurological dysfunctions in this inclusive paradigm would be considered conjunctive with, not causal to, learning disorders.

Similarly, what meaning is there in speaking about prenatal drug exposure as a "basis" of learning difficulties? In the words of one research group, "drug abuse is a *symptom* of a much deeper problem faced by tens of millions of individuals with blocked opportunities and severely limited life options" (Rosenbaum 1990 p.18). Again, it makes every kind of sense to use neurological concomitants, not neurological bases, as a category in a theory of learning problems.

Illustrative of the insufficiency of the model is its lack of reference to over three decades of research on how environmental changes can bring about changes in brain anatomy. Referring to research on small animals, Diamond states: "We have learned that every part of the nerve cell from soma to synapse alters its dimensions in response to the environment" (1989 p.156). Environmental stimulation can increase a nerve cell's dendrites and enlarge the dendritic tree; an impoverished environment can produce the reverse effect. Citing the influence of environment on the brain is not a way of suggesting replacing the biological reductionist model with an environmental reductionist one. It is to reject reductionism and to stress the many complex activities and interactions that constitute both the biology and the experience that create, sustain, remediate, and prevent learning dysfunctions.

A related deficiency in the current neurological deficit model is its failure to recognize that a given neurological organization may be regarded as "deficient" not because neurology has a negative influence on all forms of instruction, but because some forms of instruction make particular forms of neural organization "deficient." For example, much of the neurological research uses a "decoding" methodology as its instructional standard. It assumes that children must learn to distinguish between phonemic sounds and to associate sounds and written symbols in order to learn to read. Deficits in these abilities are considered core symptoms of reading disabilities. When children learn to read via this methodology, those whose cognitive and neurological organization is less able to make these associations may indeed be regarded as "disabled" within the confines of the methodology and task.

Reading specialists in various countries have been spearheading a form of literacy instruction that challenges prevailing premises about the cognitive processes most important in learning to read. New Zealand educator Marie M Clay, for example, has rejected "the traditional, older view" that "sees reading as an exact process with an emphasis on letters and words." She notes that "a more recent set of theories sees reading as an inexact process, a search for meaning during which children sample only enough visual information to be satisfied that they have received the message of the text" (Clay 1987 p.1). If the research on neurological deficits were to use the latter standard instead of a decoding standard, a very different interpretation of neurological data would be required.

The need for an adequate paradigm to explain the relationship between neurological organization and learning is one of many similar calls in other areas of the human sciences. Many psychologists and educators seeking new paradigms recognize that the fragmentation of scholarship, the separation of knowledge into discrete "fields," has impaired understanding. For instance, Bruner, talking about the crisis in psychology, observes that the science has been divided into "self-sealing" parts "ever more remote from other inquiries dedicated to the understanding of mind and the human condition" (Bruner 1990 pp.ix— x). He calls for an end to mentalism, reductionism, and determinism, and a beginning of cultural psychology that welds biology within it rather than makes it the predominant shaper of human minds. An even stronger call for the creation of cohesive avenues of inquiry can be garnered from Wallerstein's (1991) entreaty to "unthink" the paradigms of social science. The so-called disciplines, the legacy of nineteenth-century social science, have led to an "intellectual morass" that one can abandon only by more cohesive, integrated approaches to human processes.

4. The Application of Theory and Research

Explanations of neurological disorders underlying learning problems have been incorporated into school and clinical practice through diagnostic procedures and treatment programs. Whatever one's view of the validity of the research, there is little question that practical tools used in assessment have little, if any, validating evidence to demonstrate their power to identify "learning disabled" children. The tests to date are correlated more with low academic achievement than with demonstrated neurological difficulties as such. The lack of a comprehensive research theory carries over to practice in that the emphasis in diagnosis is on cognitive testing out of given social contexts.

The "identification" of neurological impairment has not helped most of the children so categorized. For most of them, whether put in special education classrooms, "resource rooms," or given individual help in classrooms, continued educational failure has been their lot. A major reason is that the neurological explanation has focussed on what is "wrong" within children themselves and not on how instruction and schooling or other contextual influences should be organized to enhance learning. Generally speaking, remediation for reading, the most common learning disability, means a more intensive dosage of what many learning specialists think are the necessary "basics," such as more decoding or more phonics. This approach is endorsed by international organizations like the International Dyslexia Association but has been criticized by many remedial specialists who have proposed different kinds of instruction (Goodman 1990). In any case, to date, when these children are helped, it is because of approaches, materials, and techniques that address their educational and learning problems, not by knowledge of whatever neurological dysfunctions they may have.

5. Conclusion

Work on the relationship between neurological organization and learning has made claims about neurological causation that extend far beyond what research has documented. Of special concern to educators are the practical applications of these claims in schools. These claims have served to organize the thinking of educators and the education of students along narrow lines that have served neither group well.

New paradigms are required that place neurological organization within the full array of the interrelationships and activities that make up individual development. Without them, educators, psychologists, and other professionals will continue the fruitless, and often harmful, pursuit of searching for dysfunctions "within" children.

See also: Brain Development and Human Behavior

References

Barth R P. 1991 Educational implications of prenatally drug-exposed children. *Social Work in Educ.* 13: 130–36

Bingol N et al. 1987 The influence of socioeconomic factors on the occurrence of fetal alcohol syndrome. *Adv. in Alcohol Substance Abuse* 6: 105–18

Bruner J S 1990 *Acts of Meaning*. Harvard University Press, Cambridge, Massachusetts

Clay M M 1987 *Reading: The Patterning of Complex Behavior*. Heinemann, Auckland

Coles G 1987 *The Learning Mystique: A Critical Look at "Learning Disabilities."* Pantheon, New York

Conners C K 1989 *Feeding the Brain: How Foods Affect Children*. Plenum, New York

Diamond M C 1989 *Enriching Heredity: The Impact of the Environment on the Anatomy of the Brain*. Free Press, New York

Doehring D G 1984 Subtypes of reading disorders: Implications for remediation. *Annals of Dyslexia* 34: 205–16

Flowers D L 1993 Brain basis for dyslexia: A summary of work in progress. *Learn. Disabil.* 26: 575–82

Galaburda A M, Menard M T, Rosen G D 1994 Evidence for aberrant auditory anatomy in developmental dyslexia. *Proc. Nat. Acad. Sci* 91: 8010–13

Galaburda A M, Sherman G F, Rosen G D, Aboitiz F, Geschwind N 1985 Developmental dyslexia: Four consecutive patients with cortical anomalies. *Ann. of Neurol.* 18(2): 222–33

Goodman Y M (ed.) 1990 *How Children Construct Literacy: Piagetian Perspectives*. International Reading Association, Newark, Delaware

Hammill D D, Leigh J E, McNutt G, Larsen S C 1987 A new definition of learning disabilities. *J. Learn. Disabil.* 20(2): 109–13

Humphreys P, Kaufmann W E, Galaburda A M 1990 Developmental dyslexia in women: Neuropathological findings in three patients. *Ann. of Neurol.* 28(6): 727–38

LeBlanc P E, Parekh A J, Naso B, Glass L 1987 Effects of intrauterine exposure to alkaloidal cocaine ("crack"). *Amer. J. Dis. Child.* 141(9): 937–38

Livingstone M S, Rosen G D, Drislane F W, Galaburda A M 1991 Physiological and anatomical evidence for a magnocellular defect in developmental dyslexia. *Proc. Nat. Acad. Sci. USA* 88: 7943–47

McCready E B 1926 Defects in the zone of language (word deafness and word-blindness and their influence in education and behavior). *Am. J. Psych.* 6: 267–77

Rosenbaum M 1990 *Just Say What? An Alternative View on Solving America's Drug Problem*. National Council on Crime and Delinquency, San Francisco, California

Rourke B (ed.) 1985 *Neuropsychology of Learning Disabilities: Essentials of Subtype Analysis*. Guilford Press, New York

Schultz R T, Cho N K, Staib L H, Kier L E, Fletcher J M 1994 Brain morphology in normal and dyslexic children: The influence of sex and age. *Brain and Language* 35: 732–42

Steinmetz H et al. 1990 Total surface of temporoparietal intrasylvian cortex: diverging left-right asymmetries. *Brain and Language* 39: 357–372

Van Dyke D C, Fox A A 1990 Fetal drug exposure and its possible implications for learning in the preschool and school-age population. *J. Learn. Disabil.* 23(3): 160–63

Vellutino F R 1979 *Dyslexia: Theory and Research*. MIT Press, Cambridge, Massachusetts

Wallerstein I 1991 *Unthinking Social Science: The Limits of Nineteenth-century Paradigms*. Polity Press, Cambridge

Further Reading

Algozzine B, Ysseldyke J E 1986 The future of the LD field: Screening and diagnosis. *J. Learn. Disabil.* 19(7): 394–98

Bartoli J, Botel M 1988 *Reading/Learning Disability: An Ecological Approach.* Teachers College Press, New York

Clay M M 1991 *Becoming Literate: The Construction of Inner Control.* Heinemann, Auckland

Coles G 1995 *Learning Lessons: The Debate over Literacy.* Hill and Wang, New York

Klatt H 1991 Learning disabilities: a questionable construct. *Educ. Theory.* 41: 47–60

Prior M R 1989 Reading disability: "Normative" or "pathological." *Australian J. Psych.* 41(2): 135–58

Salyer K M, Holmstrom R W, Noshpitz J D 1991 Learning disabilities as a childhood manifestation of severe psychopathology. *Amer. J. Orthopsychiatry.* 61(2): 230–40

Sigmon S B (ed.) 1990 *Critical Voices on Special Education: Problems and Progress Concerning the Mildly Handicapped.* State University of New York Press, Albany, New York

Snowling M J 1987 *Dyslexia: A Cognitive Developmental Perspective.* Basil Blackwell, Oxford

Tarnopol L, Tarnopol M (eds.) 1976 *Reading Disabilities: An International Perspective.* University Park Press, Baltimore, Maryland

Vygotsky L S 1978 *Mind in Society: The Development of Higher Psychological Processes.* Harvard University Press, Cambridge, Massachusetts

Specific Learning Disability

D. J. Palmer and A. Calero-Breckheimer

As an identifiable disability category, learning disabilities is approximately 30 years old. Despite the recent recognition of this disability it is one of the largest and fastest growing disability categories in the United States and Europe. Recent United States estimates indicate that over 2 million school-age students have been identified as learning disabled. Children with this disability have been described as experiencing expressive and receptive language difficulties; perceptual disorders; poor attention and retention of ideas; reading decoding problems; poor listening and reading comprehension; fine and gross motor difficulties; problems in writing and arithmetic; motivational problems; and immature social skills. Due to the range of problems identified with learning disabilities and the multidisciplinary roots of this field there are ongoing controversies regarding the conceptualization, definition, diagnosis, and intervention for the learning disabled student. This summary will provide a brief overview of the history and background, definition, prevalence, diagnostic and intervention programs, current educational directions, and research needs within this field.

1. History and Background

The term "learning disabilities" was proposed by Samuel Kirk in 1963. However, the historical and conceptual roots of learning disabilities may be found in the work of nineteenth- and early twentieth-century physicians in the United States, France, and Germany. Individuals such as John Bouillaud, Pierre Broca, Carl Wernicke, Henry Head, and James Henchelwood sought to identify brain–behavior relationships particularly focusing on brain pathology and written and/or oral language disorders (Wiederholt 1974).

Broca hypothesized that the left side of the brain was endowed with functions that differed from the right side. He attempted to localize speech disorders to specific areas of the cerebral cortex. Wernicke proposed that aphasia came about from interruptions of neural tracks that connected auditory and speech areas of the brain. Much of the early work on disorders of written language was gathered from the study of adults with acquired brain damage. Henchelwood identified a condition in one of his patients as "word blindness." With this condition, the patient may have normal vision but be no longer able to interpret written or printed language. Subsequent autopsy revealed that the patient with this disorder evidenced rather specific brain pathology. Henchelwood believed that adult cases of word blindness had relevance to school-age children with reading disorders. In fact, he labeled these cases "congenital word blindness." Henchelwood proposed that student difficulties in learning to read may be explained by brain defects that affect the storage of visual memories of words and letters. In light of this proposal he suggested a reading instructional program that addressed the remediation of this visual memory deficit. After extensive study of both written and oral language disorders, Samuel Orton in the 1930s proposed that the location of brain pathology was of greater importance than the amount of brain tissue destroyed; he further believed that one side of the brain was all-important for language function. He argued that normal adults used only one side of the brain for reading.

The field of learning disabilities has also been influenced by work on perceptual and motor disorders. A German physician, Kurt Goldstein, engaged in extensive study of brain-injured First World War soldiers. His work provided powerful support for the effects of brain damage on a range of cognitive, perceptual—motor, and affective functions. In turn,

797

his research provided an important conceptual foundation for the work of Alfred Strauss and Heinz Werner with brain-injured mentally retarded children. Working with residentially placed mentally retarded children in the United States, Werner and Strauss distinguished between exogenous and endogenous mental retardation associated with neurological impairments and unspecified familial factors, respectively (Strauss and Lehtinen 1947). They noted similarities in the behavioral characteristics of exogenous children and the characteristics of the brain-injured soldiers described by Goldstein. These characteristics included perceptual disorders, distractibility, uninhibited and less socially acceptable behaviors, and perseveration. Nonretarded children who evidenced this cluster of behaviors were subsequently diagnosed in the 1950s with Strauss' Syndrome. The work of Strauss and his colleagues had a significant influence on the development and implementation of educational programs with an emphasis on perceptual deficits (see Cruickshank et al. 1961, Frostig and Horne 1964, Kephart 1971). Psychiatrists and educators subsequently proposed that the presence of these behavioral, perceptual, and cognitive difficulties may be signs of neurological impairment.

In the spring of 1963 Professor Samuel Kirk, then at the University of Illinois, addressed a meeting of parents and professionals held in Chicago. The purpose of the meeting was to organize an effort to gain educational services for children who were having extensive learning problems in school yet were not retarded, emotionally disturbed, or evidencing sensory handicaps. One of the primary purposes of this meeting was to develop a single, common label to describe children who were identified as having minimal brain damage, perceptual disorders, psychoneurological disorders, Strauss' Syndrome, hyperkinetic disorder, dyslexia, and a host of other terms. Owing to his concern for the potential negative effects of these diagnostic labels on children, Kirk proposed that these various behavioral, cognitive, and perceptual problems be subsumed under a broader behavioral term: "learning disabilities."

The history of learning disabilities reveals a multidisciplinary focus in which medicine played an early and ongoing role in the conceptual development of the field. Much of the understanding of the characteristics of the learning-disabled child grew out of work on adults with diagnosed brain injury and on retarded children. Recognizing the ebb and flow in interest related to brain injury or dysfunction in the history of learning disabilities, there has since been renewed interest by many physicians and neuropsychologists on neurological dysfunctions associated with this disorder. The roots of many of the educational approaches found in the 1990s may be traced to the recommendations physicians made 50 years before, for example, remediation of deficits, multisensory approaches to instruction, and use of stu-

dents' compensatory abilities. The multidisciplinary nature of the field of learning disabilities and the breadth of characteristics subsumed under the label "learning disabilities," has provided a richness of perspectives and data, but has also suffered from a lack of conceptual focus that has affected both research and practice in the field.

2. Definition

In an attempt to define the students whose disorders in language, speech, reading, and associated communication skills he had labeled "learning disabilities," Kirk specifically excluded children who might evidence the previously noted problems but have sensory impairments or mental retardation. One of the first governmental attempts to develop a definition of learning disabilities was initiated in 1967 by the United States National Institute of Neurological Diseases and Blindness (Clements 1966). This definition directly linked learning disabilities to minimal brain dysfunction. A year later the First United States National Advisory Committee on Handicapped Children proposed a definition of learning disabilities which focused on disorders of basic psychological processes and deemphasized the impact of neurological dysfunctions. This definition was subsequently incorporated into the 1969 Children With Specific Learning Disabilities Act and the Education For All Handicapped Children Act in 1975. Disagreements concerning this definition induced the United States Interagency Committee on Learning Disabilities to modify the definition of learning disabilities in 1987. They defined learning disabilities as follows:

Learning disabilities is a generic term that refers to a heterogeneous group of disorders manifested by significant difficulties in the acquisition and use of listening, speaking, reading, writing, reasoning, or mathematical abilities, or of social skills. These disorders are intrinsic to the individual and presumed to be due to central nervous system dysfunction. Even though a learning disability may occur concomitantly with other handicapping conditions (e.g., sensory impairment, mental retardation, social and emotional disturbance), with socio-environmental influences (e.g., cultural differences, insufficient or inappropriate instruction, psychogenic factors), and especially with attention deficit disorder, all of which may cause learning problems, a learning disability is not the direct result of those conditions or influences. (Interagency Committee on Learning Disabilities 1987 p. 222)

Despite differences and disagreements among professionals in the United States regarding the nature and definition of learning disabilities, there is some consensual agreement concerning certain premises. The first premise is that learning-disabled students evidence a discrepancy between their ability and their achievement, that is, they do not achieve at a level commensurate with their overall intellectual ability.

This concept of discrepancy distinguishes learning-disabled students from individuals with academic difficulties, who are identified as retarded or slow learners. While there appears to be consistent support for this definitional marker, there is a great deal of controversy regarding how much discrepancy is necessary to constitute a learning disability, the technical adequacy of assessment instruments to determine a discrepancy, and the appropriateness of various statistical formulas to derive a discrepancy (Swanson 1991). A second premise is that the problems of a learning-disabled child may have a concomitant relationship with but not be caused by other disabilities. Unfortunately, since students with a variety of disabilities may display similar learning and behavior problems it is frequently difficult to determine which disability is primary. Was a learning disability the cause of an emotional or behavioral problem or was a sensory or emotional disorder the cause of the learning disability? The third premise that provides a common marker for learning-disabled students is that the learning problems are due to factors that are internal to the child and as such do not reflect a teaching failure or an experiential deficit. It is unclear, however, what the critical internal characteristics are, for example, neurological status, information processing deficits, cognitive styles, and so on. Moreover, recognition of the transactional nature of development, which requires consideration of both the child and the caregiving or instructional context, has increased. In the United States, premises or general notions of learning disability appear to be held by the general public. Swanson and Christie (1994) report that educated professionals outside the field of special education and even nondisabled children evidence implicit knowledge of the definitions of learning disability that match definitions found in the professional literature.

The Commission of the European Communities Studies (1980) describes children with learning disabilities as children who evidence spelling retardation, word-blindness, dyslexia, dysgraphy, dyscalculism, retarded perception, and "environmentally conditioned" difficulties. Because of these difficulties the children do not benefit sufficiently from ordinary instruction. In Germany, children with learning disabilities are defined as those children who show marked disturbances or impairments concerning learning abilities and who are in need of educational and therapeutical intervention.

In the United Kingdom, learning-disabled children are called "children with learning difficulties," and are described as students who are not able to progress at the same rate as other children their age (Department of Education and Science 1981). In Belgium, France, and Italy, definitions are found for children with learning problems and language delay which have special characteristics that require a special curriculum and educational help (Commission of the European Communities 1980). In many countries, for instance, Algeria, Barbados, Botswana, China, Egypt, Ethiopia, Malawi, Madagascar, Mali, Panama, Saudi Arabia, Senegal, Syria, Tunisia, Uganda, Yugoslavia, and Zaire (UNESCO 1988) learning disablement is not identified as a category of disability at all.

In Europe it is generally assumed that learning disabilities and learning difficulties may be caused by biological and/or environmental factors. Economic, ecologic, and specific cultural factors of the child's environment may cause learning disabilities. Many learning-disabled children come from disadvantaged social and cultural environments (Montogomery 1990). In many cases it is assumed that the school is responsible for the learning difficulties, because moderate learning disabilities become apparent only after the child enters school (Croll and Moses 1985, Hell 1984, Montgomery 1990).

3. Prevalence

According to the United States Department of Education (1995) *Seventeenth Annual Report to Congress*, there were approximately 4.8 million individuals with disabilities between the ages of 6 and 21 for the 1993–94 school year. Over 2.4 million students were identified as learning disabled which accounted for 48.5 percent of the total number of students identified as disabled within the United States. Since 1976–77, the number of students with learning disabilities has grown by 1,623,186 or 208 percent. The relative proportion of these students, as a function of the total number of disabled children served, increased from 23.8 percent in 1976–77 to 51.1 percent in 1993–94. The growth rate in the number of students identified with learning disabilities has exceeded any other disability. Across the 50 states, there was considerable variation in the increase of students identified with learning disabilities, from 1976–77 to 1993–94; nine states reporting less than 100 percent increase and 10 states reporting greater than 300 percent increase. Despite the presumption that learning disabilities are due to factors intrinsic to the individual, a variety of systemic factors including levels of school funding, the ethnicity and socioeconomic background of students, and the variation of assessment procedures and instrumentation may play a significant role in influencing the prevalence of learning-disabled children.

Similar rates and variability of prevalence are also found in Europe. For example, in Germany, states have identified between 2 and 6 percent of schoolchildren as learning disabled (Bildung und Wissenschaft 1985). In Bavaria 2.6 percent of the children are considered to have learning disabilities, in Schleswig-Holstein 4.8 percent (Kerkhoff 1980). In England and Wales learning-disabled children account for approximately 3.6 percent of students in regular schools (Department of Education and Science 1978).

4. Diagnosis and Intervention

The multidisciplinary and multitheoretical nature of the field has resulted in the development and implementation of many varied approaches to the diagnosis of and intervention with learning-disabled students. In the United States a general cognitive (IQ test) measure and an achievement measure are two commonly used assessment tools. These measures are selected primarily to rule out the possibility of mental retardation and to insure that there is a significant ability–achievement discrepancy. While IQ and achievement tests are consistently used, there is a great deal of variability in additional measures that have been used to assist in the diagnosis. It has been estimated that over a thousand different measures have been implemented to assist in the identification of learning-disabled students (Keogh et al. 1982). These measures were designed to reflect particular neurological, perceptual–motor, perceptual, or cognitive processing problems within students.

Educational researchers have determined that assessment primarily plays a confirming role in diagnosing these students (Ysseldyke and Thurlow 1984). Regular classroom teachers are the primary referral agents for these students. The diagnostic and placement process for learning-disabled students begins with recognition by a regular classroom teacher that the student is having significant achievement difficulties that may not be due to a general cognitive deficit. Furthermore, the decision by the teacher to refer reflects teachers' recognition that they can not effectively educate that child within their classrooms. Once a student has been referred, there is a high probability that the referred student will be assessed and subsequently diagnosed as learning disabled. In fact, many students may be identified as learning disabled and placed in special education programs even when the psychometric test results fail to document a severe discrepancy. Furthermore, many of the psychometric measures used do not have adequate reliability or validity to determine the presence or absence of an ability—achievement discrepancy.

Many teachers have expressed concern regarding the limited utility of diagnostic psychometric procedures in planning or implementing an intervention program. These concerns have resulted in the increased use of curriculum-based assessment measures which provide a direct indication of the child's performance on tasks that are relevant to classroom instruction (Shinn 1989). Educators are also recommending assessment procedures that provide insight into students' information-processing activities to include consideration of students' metacognitive characteristics, use of cognitive strategies, and attentional characteristics (Swanson 1984). There is also recent evidence that dynamic assessment procedures may differentiate children with learning disabilities from slow-learning children who evidence similar achievement characteristics (Swanson 1994). Dynamic assessment primarily focuses on the learner's potential for change when provided with assistance (Campione 1989).

With remarkable consistency, similar tests (or test types, such as IQ and achievement tests) and/or test procedures are used to diagnose learning disabilities internationally, even when national test norms are not available (Montgomery 1990, UNESCO 1988). In the majority of countries the decision to provide special education services to a student is made by an interdisciplinary team. This team may include a teacher, doctor, psychologists, other education specialists, and school administration officials. Parents may be included as part of the assessment procedure, but are not always asked for their opinion in the placement of their children in special classes; this is the case in most of the developing countries. Parents are rarely included in the child's educational plan (with the exception of Denmark and the US). In some cases the child is included in the decision (as in France, Denmark, and the US).

Paralleling the diagnostic approaches, a variety of treatment recommendations have been proposed to manage the learning-disabled student effectively (Lloyd 1988). These treatment approaches include the use of medication, modified diet, language-based remediation, developmental visual training, sensory integration training, psychotherapy, behavioral modification procedures, direct instruction, content-based intervention programs, and cognitive strategy programs, among others. In Germany, intervention methods attempt to address students' individual needs and are macropedagogic, that is, they take into consideration the whole person (Baier 1980). Macropedagogic measures include therapy, behavioral intervention, and special classes for subject matters. The intervention approaches developed prior to 1970 were primarily derived from work on disabled children; however, many of the more recent instructional innovations have evolved from programs for educationally at-risk, but not disabled, students. For example, programs in the area of direct instruction were derived, in large part, from work with economically disadvantaged children educated in regular classrooms. These programs have been subsequently tested and implemented with learning-disabled students with some considerable success. In the United States there is a growing consensus that specialized intervention programs may work for small numbers of learning-disabled children with unique problems; however, many children may benefit from the same instructional programs that have been implemented effectively with nondisabled students.

5. Educational Directions

Instructional arrangements for learning-disabled students vary tremendously across the international community (UNESCO 1988). For example, during the 1992–93 school year only 1 percent of students identified as learning disabled in the United States were educated in separate schools while 44 percent were taught in resource room settings in regular public schools, 20 percent in special-class settings, and 35 percent in regular classroom settings (United States Department of Education 1995). In contrast, special schools are the primary education delivery system used to educate students with learning disabilities in Germany. Other countries in Europe, such as Denmark, educate less than 1 percent of their learning-disabled students in special-school settings. Furthermore, while resource-room settings are the primary special education delivery system in the United States, individual states differ in their preference of educational arrangements. Less than 3 percent of learning-disabled students in Vermont are placed in resource rooms, whereas Colorado uses resource rooms to serve approximately 78 percent of those of their students identified as learning disabled. In Vermont almost 95 percent of such students identified as learning disabled are educated in regular classrooms, yet less than 1 percent of the students in Iowa are served in regular classroom settings. Separate-class educational arrangements are used for less than 2 percent of learning-disabled students in four states, while over 44 percent of learning-disabled students in New Jersey and New York are served in separate-class settings.

UNESCO (1988) summarized the following national preferences in the primary instructional arrangements to instruct children with learning difficulties: special day-schools (e.g., in Jordan, Brazil, Costa Rica, Czechoslovakia, Ecuador, El Salvador, Guatemala, Indonesia, Iraq, Israel, Malta, Uruguay, and Zambia); special classes in regular schools (in countries including Chile, Cuba, Denmark, Argentina, Costa Rica, Ecuador, Finland, Guatemala, Israel, Nicaragua, Nigeria, Poland, Sri Lanka, Sweden, Thailand, Venezuela, and Zambia); integrated group units (e.g., in Mexico); and/or support teaching in the regular class (in countries including Ecuador, Denmark, Netherlands, Costa Rica, England, Finland, Guatemala, Indonesia, New Zealand, Poland, Rumania, Sri Lanka, Sweden, Uruguay, Venezuela, Zambia, and Thailand). In Norway learning-disabled children are fully integrated into the normal education system. In Belgium, France, and Italy a large number of the learning-disabled children are provided for in private schools. In Ireland, all children with learning difficulties are provided for in private schools. The variation across states within the United States and internationally may reflect differences in educational philosophy and indicate significant variation in the nature of the students that are served.

Two broad areas in which there have been program development efforts internationally are early intervention with preschool-aged children and the transition of learning-disabled individuals from school to work. The countries of the European Community are attempting to integrate learning-disabled children into preschool educational programs. The United States and the European Community are also moving forward in the provision of assistance, guidance, further training, and vocational placement after learning-disabled children leave compulsory school. Some countries (e.g. Denmark, Germany, Ireland, Chile, Finland, Israel, New Zealand, Nicaragua, Nigeria, Norway, and Venezuela) offer education for the learning disabled after compulsory education in the form of vocational education. In Germany, different governmental departments (e.g. the Department of Work, the Department of Vocational Education, and the Department of Special Schools) try to offer work opportunities to these students. The Department of Work provides a list of offices where learning-disabled persons can find a job after vocational education. Students who complete their education in separate schools for the learning disabled but are not employed are provided vocational education programs by the Ministry of Education and Research. Students who continue to have difficulties in the transition from school to employment will be helped through special classes until they are ready to enter the workforce.

In developing countries (e.g., Jordan and Mexico), educational activities focus on more basic areas of educational planning organization, management, financing, legislation enforcement, training of personnel, and the development of culturally appropriate assessment and diagnostic materials. In many developing countries the education of the learning-disabled child was the responsibility of the family. The development of legislation to support the education of disabled students is a high priority. Developing countries share many educational concerns with industrialized countries, particularly in the areas of integration into regular schools, curriculum development, vocational rehabilitation, and job placement. The social, cultural, and economic characteristics of developing nations influence the development of educational provisions for disabled students. Generally, where resources are limited, children with learning difficulties are not educated at all; in many countries they are excluded from the state educational system.

6. Necessary Research

To further understanding of learning disabilities, and to support the development of efficacious intervention programs for students affected by them, the following recommended areas for research activity are proposed. First, it is recommended that research activities examine the nature and validity of learning disabilities as an independent disability condition. While most educational researchers agree on the existence of learning disabilities, student heterogeneity, definitional confusion, and diagnostic controversy have frustrated the accumulation of a reliable and valid research base.

In turn, controversy continues on basic issues of diagnosis and intervention.

A second area in which research is needed is the interaction of theoretically and empirically based subgroups of learning-disabled students, the nature of instructional tasks, and the design of intervention programs. Information from this program of research may help further define the nature of students' problems within the context of instructional tasks. These research findings would also help in the selection and implementation of instructional activities that are tailored for students.

A third area of research should concern the investigation of contextual variables such as cultural and socioeconomic background variables on students' performance. The majority of the world's children under the age of 5 live in developing countries where infant and preschool mortality rates are similar to those of nineteenth-century Europe. The physical conditions that surround the development of children in these areas clearly reflect the impact of broad cultural factors on at-risk children. Technological advances in Western industrialized societies have led to the survival of many children who would have died at infancy, but have also created additional risk factors for young children, such as lead poisoning. Further, the definition and expression of risk is affected not only by technology in a culture, but also by the demands made on children for education (Werner 1986). While many children in developing countries will leave school after the completion of elementary grades, most children in the United States and Europe are expected to complete high school and possibly receive some additional training to compete for jobs that require an ever-increasing level of mathematical and scientific literacy. There is concern both in the United States and Europe with the impact of broad demographic variables on students' school performance which may subsequently lead to their referral and the identification of learning disability. There is mounting evidence that matching ethnically diverse students on standardized measures of cognitive performance does not indicate cognitive equivalence between ethnic samples (Palmer et al. 1989). Work in this area may provide insight into the possible misidentification of culturally and linguistically diverse children and assist in the development of effective instructional programs for these children.

The fourth area in need of research requires a longitudinal study of learning-disabled students that would focus on the sources of internal and external stresses and support for the learning-disabled student. Such a program of research might increase the understanding of protective factors that may reduce the long-term impact and negative consequences of learning disabilities (Werner and Smith 1992).

See also: Brain Development and Human Behavior; Learning Characteristics of Students with Special Needs; Learning Theories: Historical Overview and Trends

References

Baier H 1980 *Einführung in die Lernbehindertenpädagogik.* Kohlhammer, Stuttgart

Bildung und Wissenschaft 1985 *Education and Research*, Report Nos. 9–10. Inter Nationes, Bonn

Campione J C 1989 Assisted assessment: A taxonomy of approaches and an outline of strengths and weaknesses. *J. Learn. Disabil.* 22(3): 151–65

Clements S D 1966 *Minimal Brain Dysfunction in Children.* National Society for Crippled Children/National Institute of Neurological Diseases and Blindness, Washington, DC

Commission of the European Communities Studies 1980 *Special Education in the European Community*, Education Series No. 11. Collection Studies, Brussels

Croll P, Moses D 1985 *One in Five.* Routledge & Kegan Paul, London

Cruickshank W M, Bentzer F-A, Ratzeberu F H, Tannhausser M T 1961 *A Teaching Method for Brain-injured and Hyperactive Children.* Syracuse University Press, Syracuse, New York

Department of Education and Science 1978 *Special Education Needs* (The Warnock Report). HMSO, London

Department of Education and Science 1981 *Education Act.* HMSO, London

Frostig M, Horne D 1964 *The Frostig Program for the Development of Visual Perception.* Follet, Chicago, Illinois

Hell P 1984 *Differenzierung oder Integration: Ein Beitrag zur adäquaten Beschulung Lernbehinderter aus schulpädagogischer Sicht.* Peter Lang, Frankfurt

Interagency Committee on Learning Disabilities 1987 *A Report to the U.S. Congress.* National Institutes of Health, Bethesda, Maryland

Keogh B K, Major-Kingsley S, Omori-Gordon L, Reid H P 1982 *A System of Marker Variables for the Field of Learning Disabilities.* Syracuse University Press, Syracuse, New York

Kephart N C 1971 *The Slow Learner in the Classroom.* Merrill, Columbus, Ohio

Kerkhoff W 1980 Behinderte in Sonderschulen: Ein statistischer Uberblick. *Sonderpädagogik* 10: 20–33

Lloyd J W 1988 Direct academic intervention in learning disabilities. In: Wang M C, Reynolds M C, Walberg H J (eds.) 1988 *Handbook of Special Education: Research and Practice.* Pergamon Press, New York

Montgomery D 1990 *Children with Learning Difficulties: Special Needs in Ordinary Schools.* Cassell, London

Palmer D J, Olivarez A, Willson V L, Fordyce T 1989 Ethnicity and language dominance—Influence on the prediction of achievement based on intelligence test scores in nonreferred and referred samples. *Learn. Disab. Q.* 12(4): 261–74

Shinn M R (ed.) 1989 *Curriculum-based Measurement, Assessing Special Children.* The Guilford Press, New York

Strauss A A, Lehtinen L E 1947 *Psychopathology and Education of the Brain-injured Child.* Grune & Stratton, New York

Swanson H L 1984 Process assessment of intelligence in learning disabled and mentally retarded children: A multidirectional model. *Educ. Psychol.* 19: 149–62

Swanson H L 1991 Operational definitions and learning disabilities: An overview. *Learn. Disab. Q.* 14(4): 242–54

Swanson H L 1994 The role of working memory and dynamic assessment in the classification of learning disabilities. *Learning Disabilities Research and Practice* 9(4): 190–202

Swanson H L, Christie L 1994 Implicit notions about learning disabilities: Some directions for definitions. *Learning Disabilities Research and Practice.* 9(4): 244–54

UNESCO 1988 UNESCO *Consultation on Special Education, Final Report.* UNESCO, Paris

United States Department of Education 1995 *Seventeenth Annual Report to Congress.* US Department of Education, Washington, DC

Werner E E 1986 The concept of risk from a developmental perspective. In: Keogh B K (ed.) *Advances in Special Education,* Vol. 5. JAI Press, Greenwich, Connecticut

Werner E E, Smith R S 1992 *Overcoming the Odds.* Cornell University Press, New York

Wiederholt J L 1974 Historical perspectives on the education of the learning disabled. In: Mann L, Sabatino D A (eds.) 1974 *The Second Review of Special Education.* JSE Press, Philadelphia, Pennsylvania

Ysseldyke J E, Thurlow M L 1984 Assessment practices in special education: Adequacy and appropriateness. *Educ. Psychol.* 9(3): 123–36.

SECTION XVII

Assessment and Learning

Assessment in the Service of Learning

S. Lane and R. Glaser

Educators, cognitive psychologists, and psychmetricians are reaffirming that the intent of instruction is to promote students' abilities as thinkers, problem-solvers, and inquirers. Underlying this goal is the view that meaningful understanding is based in the active construction of knowledge and often involves shared learning. Assessments, if they are to be aligned with current views on instruction and human learning, must more closely resemble meaningful learning tasks and assess the acquisition of high-level thinking and reasoning abilities as integral to subject-matter knowledge. New conceptual frameworks for the design of assessments require new psychometric theories that reflect current advances in research on cognition and human learning.

1. Traditional Tests and Test Theories

The psychological theory implicit in the design of traditional achievement assessments measuring long-term educational outcomes and growth in the United States has been derived primarily from behavioral theories of the 1960s. These generated behavioral objectives but could not adequately describe complex processes of thought, reasoning, and problem-solving. Tests were generally designed to be administered following instruction, rather than to be integrated with learning. For achievement assessments to inform instruction, analysis of the knowledge and cognitive processes that comprise competency within a subject-matter domain is required, so that assessments reflect the cognitive structures and processes that underlie the complexities of performance.

Techniques for measuring academic achievement have relied on the psychometric technology that emerged in the context of selection and placement testing. Standard test theory characterizes performance in terms of the difficulty level of response–choice items and focuses primarily on measuring the amount of declarative knowledge that students have acquired. This view of performance is at odds with current theories of cognition, which emphasize the meaningful learning that entails reasoning and problem-solving

and involves the active construction of knowledge. Assessments that are integral to instruction and allow students to display the thinking, reasoning, and strategic processes that underlie their competencies can ensure more valid inferences regarding the nature and level of students' understanding.

2. Implications of Cognitive Psychology for Assessment

In conjunction with prevailing views on the acquisition of knowledge and competence, some cognitive psychologists now employ a cognitive-process-oriented assessment approach (Snow and Lohman 1989). Analysis of the structures of knowledge and cognitive processes that reveal degrees of subject-matter competence and descriptions of the differences between expert and novice performance can provide useful information for designing assessments. For example, expert–novice studies indicate that new learners often construct loosely connected knowledge structures that reflect partial understanding of the subject matter. As learning takes place, they broaden, integrate, and restructure their knowledge to accommodate new, qualitatively different information and connections, thus deepening their level of understanding within the subject-matter domain (Glaser and Chi 1988). Assessments should be capable of determining the nature and depth of students' understanding by reflecting the organization and coherence of their knowledge structures.

To promote students' acquisition of coherent knowledge structures, instruction and assessment should emphasize knowledge construction and possibilities for learning in collaborative settings. In classrooms, meaningful knowledge is often constructed through collaborative efforts in the attempt to reach common goals, for instance in discussions reflecting differences in perspective, which in turn lead to self-reflection. Changes in students' knowledge structures are more likely to occur when they are required to explain, elaborate, or justify their position to others, as well as to themselves (Brown and Palincsar 1989).

Such classroom interactions allow for the display of various levels of student understanding and provide a rich environment for assessments of achievement and growth that are integral to learning and teaching.

Assessments should be constructed or selected to ensure their alignment with instructional activities and the results of assessment should be available for formative planning and change. Those that reflect the classroom learning situation can provide valuable information for instructional decision-making before, during, and after instruction. In order to provide an appropriate foundation for instruction, teachers can assess students' prior knowledge and understandings so that instruction can be shaped to meet their needs and abilities. By embedding them within instructional activities that display students' thinking and knowledge, assessments can provide useful information for diagnosing the needs of individual students and for monitoring the success of instructional activities. When administered at the end of instruction, assessments can indicate whether students have acquired subject-matter competencies. Hands-on performance assessments, open-ended tasks, journals, computer simulations of meaningful tasks, and portfolio assessments can all provide valuable information for instructional decision-making and for students' self-evaluation.

3. Considerations for Assessments and Measurement

The changing view of instruction and learning requires new criteria to ensure reliable and valid assessments (Glaser 1990, Frederiksen and Collins 1989, Linn et al. 1991). These criteria should guide the design of both classroom assessments and achievement assessments that measure more long-term educational outcomes and growth.

3.1 Assessments as Access to Educational Opportunities

As Linn (1989) has indicated, the most important challenge for educational assessment and measurement is "to make measurement do a better job of facilitating learning for all individuals" (p. 9). Assessments should be designed to uncover and display ways in which students represent and solve problems so they provide information to facilitate student learning. Underlying the interpretation of scores derived from many traditional tests is the assumption that students have had equivalent or similar educational opportunities. However, students with the same scores on a traditional test may have different understandings of the subject matter and may have employed different strategic processes. Delineating these differences can inform instruction.

Dynamic assessment, for example, a process-oriented approach that can provide information about the nature and depth of a student's understanding,

is also possible. A common feature across differing forms of dynamic assessment is the emphasis on surveying the cognitive processes involved in individual student learning and observing change in the presence of instructional guidance. Dynamic assessment has its roots in Vygotsky's (1978) "zone of proximal development" namely, the level of performance a student can achieve by working initially with other students or with adults. By assessing learning in the zone of proximal development, information can be obtained about the level at which new knowledge and strategies can best be developed.

As a measure of learning potential, dynamic assessment can provide information about the processes and strategies that a student uses to solve problems, the degree to which these enable a student to respond to opportunities to acquire new strategies and knowledge, and the effectiveness of instructional procedures for strengthening the student's strategies (Campione and Brown 1990). In dynamic assessment, the assessment setting is modified in order to evaluate how easily students can improve on their performance level (Campione and Brown 1990). Modification may involve altering task formats, providing feedback, encouraging the use of self-monitoring skills, or providing instruction in domain-specific or general problem-solving strategies. Of importance is students' efficiency in acquiring and implementing these strategies and the resulting improvement in their acquisition of subject-matter knowledge. Dynamic assessment has the potential to identify students who may not have had the opportunity to acquire the knowledge or strategies being assessed, but who would be able to master them if given the opportunity. Therefore, dynamic assessment is particularly important when assessing students with differing educational and experiential backgrounds.

If students understand the criteria for evaluating performance, they can be encouraged to internalize the criteria, to aid each other in attaining them, and to assess their own performances more effectively (Frederikson and Collins 1989). The integration of assessment with instruction in a group environment affords students numerous sources of reflection on their own knowledge and performance. Such enriched self-assessment can help substantially in facilitating students' achievement of specific subject-matter competencies.

In collaborative settings, students and teachers can assess not only students' growing ability to reason and learn but also their facility in adapting to help and guidance. When students' performances are measured so that thought and reasoning processes are apparent, their zone of proximal development becomes clear. As they perform within an appropriate range of competence, teachers or peers can assist with the realization of higher levels of performance.

Assessments that are more representative of meaningful learning may require an entire period or a number of days and may take the form of a task to be undertaken outside the classroom setting. As an example, an extended task in science may require students to plan and conduct a study. Students would need to formulate research questions, to gather data to answer the research questions, to analyze this data, and to develop a report describing their findings. Such an extended task allows for both individual and collaborative work and promotes the display of student thinking.

3.2 Criteria for Valid and Reliable Assessments

Judgments regarding the cognitive significance of an assessment begin with an analysis of the cognitive requirements of the tasks as well as the ways in which students attempt to solve them (Glaser 1990). Although performance assessments may appear to be valid forms of assessment, in that they resemble meaningful learning tasks, these measures may be no more valid than scores derived from response–choice items (Linn et al. 1991). Evidence is needed to assure that assessments require the high-level thought and reasoning processes that they were intended to evoke (e.g., Magone et al. 1994).

Validation involves the examination of the actual and potential consequences of test use and score interpretation, as well as of more traditional empirical evidence (Messick 1989). To validate assessments in terms of their consequential basis, an analysis of the intended and unintended effects of assessments is needed. For example, the type of assessment administered may have direct consequences for instruction. Sole dependence on tests consisting of response–choice items may lead to instruction that emphasizes recall of facts and application of memorized routines and procedures. However, if the assessment requires synthesis of information, divergent thinking, and evaluation, instruction is more likely to include activities that promote these skills.

In line with Messick's conceptualization of consequential validity, Frederiksen and Collins (1989) proposed that assessments have "systemic validity" if they encourage behaviors on the part of teachers and students that promote the learning of valuable skills and knowledge, and allow for issues of transparency and openness, that is access to the criteria for evaluating performance. The collection of evidence on teachers' and students' (and administrators' and policymakers') interpretations of assessment results, as well as on the actions they take as a consequence, should thus be a feature of assessments that are designed for this kind of validity. Changes in instructional and curriculum goals and allocation of time to various instructional activities that enforce desired skills would constitute evidence for validating an assessment.

In interpreting the results of a particular assessment procedure or instrument for various groups of students,

an examination of its differential validity is necessary. For example, group differences in prior knowledge and experiences should be considered when developing assessments. As Messick (1989) has pointed out, to help ensure that one group is not at a disadvantage requires that the assessment fully represents the construct domain being measured and that it does not measure irrelevant constructs (such as reading ability or the context of the problem situation in a mathematics assessment). Differential item functioning (DIF) procedures can be applied to performance assessments, which in turn provide evidence for their fairness. DIF procedures are used to examine whether tasks are functioning the same way for students at the same ability level (as defined by performance on the test or some other criterion) but from different gender/ethnic/racial groups. To apply these procedures, a relatively large number of tasks need to be administered. As was indicated by Linn et al. (1991), the logical examination of the actual assessment tasks and procedures by a panel of professionals, as well as an extensive analysis of the ways in which students from various groups respond to the tasks, are crucial in establishing the fairness of assessments.

The degree to which there can be generalization from performance on an assessment to the larger construct domain is dependent on the breadth of the content represented in the assessment. Performance assessments allow for an extended and rich description of the nature and level of students' understanding of subject-matter knowledge. However, because performance assessments require more time on each task, the breadth of the content covered may be jeopardized. For classroom assessment, using a variety of assessment tasks and procedures that are aligned with instruction will help ensure valid inferences and generalizations regarding students' understanding in subject-matter domains. For achievement assessments at the school level that measure more long-term educational outcomes and growth, a matrix sampling approach (i.e., one in which each student receives a subset of the assessment tasks) will help ensure valid inferences and generalizations regarding school-level outcomes in the subject-matter domain (e.g., Lane et al. 1994).

4. Implications for Test Theory

To provide information useful for instructional decision-making, theories of cognition and performance are being called upon in the design of assessments. Consequently, cognitive models and psychometric technology should be integrated. Despite numerous changes in measurement since the 1970s, models and measurement procedures that capture students' thinking and reasoning and that provide useful information to teachers are at an early stage of development (Linn 1989).

The general principles that led to the development of item response theory (IRT) can provide the foundations of an improved test theory that better reflects the goals of instruction and assessment (Mislevy 1989). IRT models for graded scoring of direct writing assessments have proven to be an effective means of constructing scales from evaluations of open-ended responses (Harris et al. 1988). Using these models, students' abilities can be characterized by parameters that express the probability of scoring at one of a number of continuous levels or discrete states of proficiency. This relationship enables performances on each task to be used to estimate students' ability on the construct being measured.

Harris et al. (1988) have applied partial credit analysis to student responses to a set of narrative writing tasks. Their goals were to identify component skills and knowledge that comprise writing competency and to use a description of these components as the basis of an assessment scheme. In contrast to holistic scoring, which provides a global score, this approach provides information for individual student diagnosis and instructional decision-making. In their study, the students' written stories received a score on each of eight scales (e.g., characterization development and coherence and story structure). Each scale provides a continuum of developing proficiency; a student is assigned to a region on the continuum based on the student's ability estimate. The level of proficiency is the same for students within a region on the continuum. For example, the lowest of the nine score levels of the scale for coherence and story structure indicates that the student's story most probably had "few connections, isolated ideas; reader must make large leaps" (p. 338), whereas the highest level of this scale indicates that there was most probably a "balanced integration of subplots contributing to the story" (p. 338). A student's pattern of scores on the eight scales identifies individual needs and strengths. Further studies of this kind, presenting procedures that successfully integrate cognitive theory and psychometric technology, are needed.

5. Conclusion

The educational goal of enabling students to be effective thinkers and problem-solvers requires a reconceptualization of both instruction and assessment. Traditional didactic instruction and traditional assessments of achievement are not suited to modern educational demands. Instruction that emphasizes student-constructed knowledge and the interactive nature of learning will provide an environment conducive to the acquisition and use of high-level thinking and reasoning abilities in the context of acquiring subject-matter knowledge. Achievement assessments must be an integral part of instruction, in that they should reflect, shape, and improve student learning. This will require that they simulate meaningful learning tasks and be aligned to modern conceptions of

cognition and learning. The merger of cognitive theory and quantitative psychometric models is necessary in the design of performance assessments that reflect meaningful learning tasks.

See also: Prior Knowledge and Learning

References

Brown A L, Palincsar A S 1989 Guided, cooperative learning and individual knowledge acquisition. In: Resnick L (ed.) 1989 *Knowing, Learning, and Instruction: Essays in Honor of Robert Glaser*. Erlbaum, Hillsdale, New Jersey
Campione J C, Brown A L 1990 Guided learning and transfer: Implications for approaches to assessment. In: Frederiksen N, Glaser R, Lesgold A, Shafto M G (eds.) 1990 *Diagnostic Monitoring of Skill and Knowledge Acquisition*. Erlbaum, Hillsdale, New Jersey
Frederiksen J R, Collins A 1989 A system approach to educational testing. *Educ. Researcher* 18(9): 27–32
Glaser R 1990 Testing and assessment: O Tempora! O Mores! Horace Mann Lecture, University of Pittsburgh, LRDC, Pittsburgh, Pennsylvania
Glaser R, Chi M T H 1988 Overview. In: Chi M T H, Glaser R, Farr M J (eds.) 1988 *The Nature of Expertise* Erlbaum, Hillsdale, New Jersey
Harris J, Laan S, Mossenson L 1988 Applying partial credit analysis to the construction of narrative writing tests. *Appl. Measurement in Educ.* 1(4): 335–46
Lane S, Stone C, Ankenmann R, Liu M 1994 Empirical evidence for the reliability and validity of performance assessments. *Int. J. Educ. Res.* 21(3): 247–66
Linn R L 1989 Current perspectives and future directions. In: Linn R L (ed.) 1989 *Educational Measurement*, 3rd edn. Macmillan Inc., New York
Linn R L, Baker E L, Dunbar S B 1991 Complex performance-based assessment: Expectations and validation criteria. *Educ. Researcher* 20(8): 15–21
Magone M, Cai J, Silver E, Wang N 1994 Validity evidence for cognitive complexity of performance assessments: An analysis of selected QUASAR tasks. *Int. J. Educ. Res.* 21(3): 317–40
Messick S 1989 Validity. In: Linn R L (ed.) 1989 *Educational Measurement*, 3rd edn. Macmillan Inc., New York
Mislevy R J 1989 *Foundations of a New Test Theory*, Research Report No. 89–52-ONR. Educational Testing Service, Princeton, New Jersey
Snow R E, Lohman D F 1989 Implications of cognitive psychology for educational measurement. In: Linn R L (ed.) 1989 *Educational Measurement*, 3rd edn. Macmillan Inc., New York
Vygotsky L S 1978 *Mind in Society: The Development of Higher Psychological Processes*. Harvard University Press, Cambridge, Massachusetts

Further Reading

Bennett R E, Ward W C (eds.) 1993 *Construction versus Choice in Cognitive Measurement: Issues in Constructed Response, Performance Testing and Portfolio Assessment*. Erlbanm, Hillsdale, New Jersey

Classroom Assessment

P. W. Airasian

Classroom assessment is the process teachers use when they collect, synthesize, and interpret information to aid them in decision-making. When classroom assessment is viewed from teachers' decision-making perspectives, rather than as the application of particular evidence-gathering techniques, its dimensions are greatly broadened. Both the number of viable assessment purposes and useful information-gathering techniques expand considerably.

The genesis of the teacher-centered view of classroom assessment can be traced over years of close examination of teachers' classroom responsibilities and the decisions needed to carry them out. Teachers' classroom lives have been reported on by Jackson (1990), Lortie (1975), and Bullough (1989). Teachers' thought processes have been studied and described by Calderhead (1987), Clark and Peterson (1986), Elbaz (1991), Feiman-Nemser and Floden (1986), and Schon (1983). General collections on teachers and teaching are also available (Anderson 1989, Wittrock 1986).

A synthesis of this body of research leads to four generalizations that provide a useful perspective for considering the nature and dimensions of classroom assessment. First, classrooms are both social and academic environments. To survive and succeed in classrooms, teachers must know their pupils' social, personal, and emotional characteristics as well as their academic ones. Second, the classroom is an ad hoc, informal, experiential, person-centered environment which calls for constant teacher decision-making. Third, most of the decisions that confront teachers are immediate, practical ones that involve particular students and contexts. Classroom decision-making must invariably take into account the unique qualities of the students and situations involved, thereby requiring teachers to rely on their tacit, practical knowledge of students and the classroom context. Fourth, teachers are both assessors and participants in the classroom society, which has implications for their objectivity in collecting and interpreting assessment information.

Although the general, overriding purpose of classroom assessment is to help teachers make decisions, there are many different decisions and decision contexts that define the nature of classroom assessment. General categorizations of teachers' classroom decisions have been identified. One such organizational schema is based on social/personal, instructional, and bureaucratic teacher decisions (Airasian 1994), while another classifies decisions in terms of whether they occur before, during, or after instruction (American Federation of Teachers National Council on Measurement in Education National Education Association 1990). While there is a great deal of overlap between these two schemata, the categorization based on assessments made before, during, and after instruction will be used in this review.

1. Assessment Before Instruction

Before instruction can begin, teachers must address two assessment needs: (a) learning about their pupils' characteristics, needs, and abilities, and (b) planning their instruction.

1.1 Learning Pupil Characteristics

Before teachers can organize their pupils into classroom societies that are characterized by communication, order, and common goals, they must learn about their pupils' unique strengths, weaknesses, and personalities. This process of "sizing up" others, which occurs in all social settings, is used to form perceptions and expectations that can be used to establish rapport and guide future interactions. Because classrooms are interactive social and academic settings, they require teachers to assess and make decisions about their students' personal, social, and academic characteristics. These decisions produce the perceptions, expectations, interaction patterns, and practical knowledge which teachers rely upon when interacting with, managing, planning for, or instructing students (Feiman-Nemser and Floden 1986, Elbaz 1991).

Many kinds of information are used to inform these "sizing up" decisions, including formal academic pretests in the subject matter, hearsay evidence, students' modes of dress, their friends, and siblings' past performance. Teachers collect this information primarily through naturalistic observation. By the end of a week or two, most classroom teachers can provide detailed descriptions of each student's personal, social, and academic strengths and weaknesses. These initial, tacit perceptions, which remain quite stable over the school year, guide teachers' future academic and social interactions with students.

In spite of their inevitability and the trust teachers place in them, these initial perceptions and expectations often have limited validity and reliability (Airasian 1994). Much of the evidence that teachers use to inform these decisions at the beginning of the year is based upon spontaneous, informal observations which are rarely uniform across either pupils or occurrences. Moreover, the judgments teachers make about students often have little to do with the evidence they observed as, for example, when teachers commonly rely on observations of students' mode of dress, peer group membership, in-class posture, or homework neatness to judge their abilities or motivation. Finally, these initial decisions about pupils' characteristics are, of necessity, made quickly and often on the basis of small samples of behavior, leading to concern about the reliability of the assessment evidence. This concern is especially warranted since the first few days of school often elicit atypical student behavior.

1.2 Planning Instruction

The processes of planning and delivering instruction are important for classroom teachers, partly because they occupy a great deal of their time but mainly because they provide teachers with their chief source of professional satisfaction (Lortie 1975). When teachers plan instruction, they consider information both about student characteristics (such as ability levels, work habits, and readiness) and instructional resources (such as materials, time, space, equipment, and prior teaching experience in the subject area). A synthesis of this information results in a plan which outlines the nature of the instructional activities and goals that will be implemented with students. The primary motive for planning is to help teachers gain control over the instructional process by reducing their uncertainty and anxiety about teaching, reviewing the material to be presented, and identifying ways to get instruction started (Clark and Peterson 1986).

Among the materials teachers consider when planning instruction, none is more important than the textbook, or, more appropriately, the instructional package that is used in a subject area. In most classrooms at most grade levels, the traditional textbook has been replaced by an instructional package, which supplements the textbook with additional instructional and assessment resources such as educational objectives, daily lesson plans, chapter and unit reviews, chapter tests, practice worksheets, motivational activities, follow-up exercises, and so on. The instructional package could conceivably provide all the resources teachers need to plan, carry out, and assess instruction, and studies have shown that a large portion of the elementary school student's learning time and the teacher's instructional time, up to 75 percent, is focused on textbook use (Stodolsky 1988). This heavy reliance on packaged instructional plans and activities is understandable when one considers that many teachers must prepare many daily lesson plans.

Although the instructional package provides virtually all the resources needed to prepare, conduct, and assess a lesson, teachers should determine the appropriateness of these materials for their own particular settings and groups of pupils. Textbooks or instructional packages are intended to have applicability across a range of schools, teachers, and classes. They are not tailored to meet the unique needs and readiness of every group of users. It is, therefore, the responsibility of classroom teachers to assess the appropriateness of the instructional package for their own students and classroom contexts, using criteria such as clarity, comprehensiveness, pertinence, and pupil readiness (Airasian 1994, Brophy and Alleman 1991). Regardless of whether teachers develop lesson plans from scratch or select them from an instructional package, they have a responsibility to collect and examine assessment information both about students' needs, abilities, and work habits and the instructional materials in order to decide which instructional plan is most appropriate.

Thus, even before instruction begins, teachers must carry out considerable assessment and decision-making. They must learn enough about their students' academic and personal characteristics to feel sufficiently familiar with them to create a classroom social setting that encourages communication, order, and learning. Once the classroom society is organized, teachers begin the task of planning their instruction, a task they will repeat daily throughout the school year. In carrying out their planning, teachers consider and meld information about their students and instructional resources into an appropriate plan for instruction.

2. Assessment During Instruction

During instruction, teachers perform two activities. They implement the instructional plans developed or selected during the planning period, and they assess and make decisions about the success of the plan's implementation. As might be expected given the dynamic nature of instruction, teachers rely heavily upon informal observations and questions to collect evidence for their decisions. They focus on pupils' facial expressions, posture, participation, eye contact, deportment, and questions asked or answered to indicate how a lesson is going. They refer to the necessity of "reading" their audience to help them make decisions while teaching (Clark and Peterson 1986, Jackson 1990).

The information teachers collect is used to make decisions about the curriculum, student learning, and class management. Curriculum decisions involve the appropriateness of materials, educational objectives, and activities, as well as the adequacy of their presentation to students. Learning decisions concern whether students understand or follow the main points of instruction. Management decisions monitor whether the students are paying attention or whether they need to be refocused on the lesson.

Assessments during instruction are formative. Their purpose is to monitor and, if necessary, remediate the instructional process. This largely informal approach to assessment during instruction creates two potential problems for the resulting decisions (Airasian 1994). First, classroom teachers may lack objectivity when assessing the adequacy of their teaching and its effects on student learning. Because teachers derive their main professional satisfactions from their instructional successes, it may be hard for them to observe and judge objectively. Every time a favorable judgment about instruction or learning is made, teachers are, in part, rewarding themselves.

Second, the incompleteness of the indicators teachers use in making assessments during instruction also creates a problem. Because instruction is an activity-based, interactive process, it is logical for teachers to focus their assessments on the process itself and students' immediate reactions to it. Such a focus, however, ignores the results of the process on student learning. The fact that students are responsive, attentive, or involved does not necessarily mean that they are learning, although this is a conclusion many teachers make. To increase the validity of assessments made during instruction, information should be collected not only about student reactions to the process, but also about their learning from it. Oral questioning and written assignments (including homework) are the most feasible techniques to utilize in these assessments.

3. Assessment After Instruction

Assessment carried out after the completion of instruction is usually designed to inform decisions about grading, placing, or promoting pupils. Postinstructional assessments focus on summative, bureaucratic decisions that teachers are required to make by virtue of their official positions within the school organization. The preponderance of these decisions are related to assessing students' attainment of the content, skills, and behaviors they were taught during instruction.

Postinstructional assessments lead to decisions that are both public and important. They are recorded in school files, sent home in periodic school reports, and discussed by students, parents, and teachers. They reflect important summative judgments about pupils that can affect their immediate opportunities, future educational placements, and, in some cases, life chances. For these reasons, assessment procedures used to gather evidence about pupil achievement after instruction is completed rely heavily on formal techniques that produce "hard," usually numerical, evidence of performance. This emphasis differs from the reliance on less formal, non-recorded, often impressionistic evidence for most assessments conducted before and during instruction.

Two features of assessments made after the completion of instruction are noteworthy. First, such postinstructional assessments often become the basis for subsequent planning decisions. There is, then, a cycle that unites assessment decisions made before, during, and after instruction. Second, the usefulness of postinstructional, summative assessments of achievement is dependent upon many of the assessments teachers make before and during instruction. To insure valid interpretations and decisions about pupil achievement after instruction, it is necessary that before and during instruction teachers know their students' status and needs, plan instructional activities and outcomes appropriate to these, provide effective instruction, construct or select assessment procedures that assess what their students have been taught, score performance objectively, and assign grades or marks fairly. If there are gaps or inadequacies in one or more of these prerequisite steps, the validity of postinstruction assessments and decisions will likely be diminished.

The primary goal in assessing learning after the completion of instruction is to insure that students are given a fair opportunity to demonstrate how much they have learned from the instruction they were given. A range of formal assessment techniques can be used to attain this goal. These techniques, which are the primary focus of traditional courses and textbooks in educational measurement (Airasian 1991), include teacher-made or textbook-supplied paper-and-pencil tests, performance assessments, and standardized tests. General discussions of assessment topics such as writing test items, observing and rating performance, test scoring, grading and marking, and test administration can be found in many textbooks. It is known that very few classroom teachers have had formal training in these or the other assessment areas described here (Schafer and Lissitz 1987).

The most commonly used postinstructional assessment technique is the teacher-made or textbook-supplied paper-and-pencil achievement test administered at the end of instruction on a unit or chapter of text. Most teacher-made and textbook-supplied tests tend to focus assessment on lower level rote learning, primarily because these are the kinds of behaviors for which it is easiest to construct test items. Although the ready availability of textbook-supplied tests makes them a convenient source of assessment material, these tests should be examined in terms of their appropriateness to teachers' particular classroom objectives and instructional emphases. In general, the more teachers deviate from the textbook during instruction, the less valid a textbook-supplied test is likely to be.

Many classroom achievements are not suitably assessed by paper-and-pencil tests. For example, such methods are not useful for assessing performances such as using a microscope, oral reading or speaking, cutting with scissors, bouncing a ball, or cooperating in group activities. These behaviors are best assessed by formally observing and rating students as they perform them (Burstall 1986). Although much of the assessment that teachers carry out before and during instruction also gathers evidence through teachers' observations of students' performance, these observations are primarily informal, unplanned, and spontaneous, in contrast to the formal, planned observations used to assess achievement after instruction. The use of formal performance assessments is being encouraged to replace perceived overreliance on paper-and-pencil tests in assessing students' learning (National Commission on Testing and Public Policy 1990).

Standardized tests are the third type of formal assessment used to inform postinstructional decisions about students. A standardized test is one which is designed to be used in many different locations and to be administered, scored, and interpreted in the same way no matter when or where it is administered. Most standardized tests provide information about how a given pupil achieved in comparison to his or her peers nationwide. Although the results of these tests are not very influential in teachers' overall assessment repertoires or decision-making, parents, students, and school administrators do take them seriously.

In sum, there are three general domains of assessment: those that occur before, during, and after instruction. Assessments in these domains differ in terms of timing, purpose, evidence-gathering techniques, formality, and record-keeping. All have consequences for student learning and classroom interaction. Taken together, they reflect the richness, complexity, and importance of teachers' classroom assessment activities.

4. Interpreting Classroom Assessments

Before assessment evidence of any kind can be used in decision-making, teachers must interpret it. Interpretation is a subjective process calling for teachers' judgments, and in classrooms, interpretations are heavily influenced by both the sizing-up decisions teachers make of their pupils and teachers' personal theories about children, schools, and learning. Within this framework, a few guidelines can be stated to improve teachers' interpretations and decision-making (Airasian 1994). First, assessment information describes students' learned behaviors and present status. Teachers should not interpret assessment information as representing the fixed "potential" or "capacity" of their students or the way the students necessarily will perform in the future.

Second, all assessment evidence contains some error or imprecision and thus should be interpreted as providing an estimate, not an exact indication, of pupil characteristics or learning. Some assessment error is random and uncontrollable, while other error is related to factors such as teacher bias or inadequate sampling of students' behaviors. Rarely should small differences in students' assessed performance be interpreted as representing significant or meaningful differences.

Third, a single assessment is a poor basis for making important decisions such as grading or promotion. Multiple sources of evidence provide a more valid and reliable indication than single assessments, especially when the decision to be made has significant import for the student. Corroboration of any single source of assessment information is desirable.

Fourth, assessments describe performance; they do not explain it. Assessment that identifies how a student did on a mathematics test or how a learning activity was received by students cannot itself explain why the student and class reacted as they did. To explain

assessment results generally requires the collection of additional evidence.

These guidelines suggest the following teacher behaviors in interpreting assessment information: base interpretations on multiple sources of evidence; recognize the range of cultural and educational factors that can influence a student's performance; consider contextual factors which might provide alternative explanations for students' performance; and recognize that any single assessment provides an estimate of performance that can alter with changes in the student or classroom environment.

5. Ethical Aspects of Classroom Assessment

Teaching is both a practical and moral undertaking. Classroom teachers are professionals who have great autonomy in their classrooms, who possess knowledge their students do not, and who are permitted to make decisions that affect their students' lives. As a consequence, teachers, like other professionals, have ethical responsibilities to their students (Fenstermacher 1990). In the areas of assessment and decision-making, teachers' ethical responsibilities include both the collection and appropriate use of assessment information. Consequently, teachers are responsible for demonstrating behaviors such as respect for student diversity, fairness in grading and judging students, collecting the best evidence possible on which to base decisions, interpreting evidence correctly, and respecting students' privacy.

References

Airasian P W 1991 Perspectives on measurement instruction. *Educ. Meas.: Issues Pract.* 10(1): 13–16
Airasian P W 1994 *Classroom Assessment*. McGraw-Hill, New York
American Federation of Teachers National Council on Measurement in Education National Education Association 1990 Standards for teacher competence in educational assessment of students. *Educ. Meas.: Issues Pract.* 9(4): 30–32
Anderson L W 1989 *The Effective Teacher*. McGraw Hill, New York
Brophy J E, Alleman J 1991 Activities as instructional tools: A framework for analysis and evaluation. *Educ. Res.* 20(4): 9–23
Bullough R 1989 *First-Year Teacher. A Case Study*. Teachers College Press, New York
Burstall C 1986 Innovative forms of assessment: A United Kingdom Perspective. *Educ. Meas.: Issues Pract.* 5(1): 17–22
Calderhead J (ed.) 1987 *Exploring Teachers' Thinking*. Cassel, London
Clark C M, Peterson P L 1986 Teachers' thought processes. In: Wittrock M C (ed.) 1986
Elbaz F 1991 Research on teachers' knowledge: The evolution of discourse. *J. Curric. Stud.* 23(1): 1–19
Feiman-Nemser S, Floden R E 1986 The cultures of teaching. In: Wittrock M C (ed.) 1986
Fenstermacher G D 1990 Some moral considerations in

teaching as a profession. In: Goodlad J L, Soder R, and Sirotnik K A (eds.) 1990 *The Moral Dimensions of Teaching*. Jossey-Bass, San Francisco, California

Jackson P W 1990 *Life in Classrooms*, 2nd edn. Teachers College Press, New York

Lortie D C 1975 *Schoolteacher. A Sociological Study*. University of Chicago Press, Chicago, Illinois

National Commission on Testing and Public Policy 1990 *From Gatekeeper to Gateway: Transforming Testing in America*. Boston College, Chestnut Hill, Massachusetts

Schafer W D, Lissitz R W 1987 Measurement training for school personnel: Recommendations and reality. *J. Teach. Educ.* 38(3): 57–63

Schon D A 1983 *The Reflective Practitioner. How Professionals Think in Action*. Basic Books, New York

Stodolsky S S 1988 *The Subject Matters. Classroom Activity in Math and Social Studies*. University of Chicago Press, Chicago, Illinois

Wittrock M C (ed.) 1986 *Handbook of Research on Teaching*. Macmillan, New York

Learning Potential and Learning Potential Assessment

A. J. J. M. Ruijssenaars and J. H. M. Hamers

Tracing a person's learning potential is important in view of predicting school achievement as well as analyzing weaker or stronger aspects in the actual learning process. The effectiveness of the traditional intelligence test is limited in this context. In accordance with the underlying assumption that intelligence is a more or less stable characteristic, the intelligence test is constructed to maximize this stability. By contrast, in the learning potential test (LPT) an essential characteristic is the possibility of mastering a skill or principle as an effect of training included in the test.

1. Intelligence, Learning Potential, and Learning Potential Tests

Intelligence tests play an important role in explaining and predicting individual differences in learning. The traditional intelligence test assesses the cognitive performances of an individual under standardized conditions that are similar to those of a norm group. In constructing intelligence tests it is (at least implicitly) assumed that the relative position the subject takes compared with a reference group has been the same in the past and will continue to be so in the future. In fact, this implies that, with regard to cognitive development, every person had and will have equal opportunities from which to benefit.

Under these restrictions intelligence is seen as a constant and stable characteristic. Nevertheless, it is assumed that there is a significant relationship between performance on intelligence tests and on learning tasks. Learning, however, by definition cannot be static and constant. In this context Whitely and Dawis (1975) suggested a distinction between the notions "ability" (intelligence as measured in intelligence tests) and "aptitude" (learning potential, which can only be assessed when all environmental conditions have been—and will remain—optimal). In fact this proposal reflects dissatisfaction with the way in which intelligence is usually assessed. For, in educational literature, as in everyday language, intelligence means something like "the ability to learn," including the application and generalization of what has been learned (see Dearborn 1921). There are three ways of overcoming this dissatisfaction, ranging from a radical rejection of tradition to a solution in keeping with it.

The first solution is to dispense completely with the notion of intelligence and the way it is assessed in intelligence tests and to replace it with a new construct, namely, learning potential. Russian psychologists, Kalmykova (1975) for instance, have conceived learning potential as an interaction of abilities such as abstract thinking, reflecting on one's own thinking process, flexible thinking, persistent intensive thinking, and independent thinking. These qualities should be examined in the pupil's problem-solving process during short-term diagnostic teaching experiments. This implies a radical departure from the traditional (mainly Western) conception of a psychometric test. It can be argued, however, that this solution in fact comes very close to what Piaget meant with his statement that intelligence is a process of assimilation and accommodation (Hamers and Ruijssenaars 1984).

The second solution does not question the notion of intelligence as such but the way it is operationalized in intelligence tests. Feuerstein, for instance, has developed a procedure for a "dynamic" assessment of cognitive development, in which an adult, by means of short learning tests, assesses to what degree a child's solution processes change in a great variety of learning tasks (Feuerstein et al. 1979). At first sight there is a striking resemblance between these tasks and the items of regular intelligence tests, but they are manipulated as a learning task by the adult, who is acting as a mediator between environmental stimuli and the learning subject. In this interaction the child acquires an appropriate knowledge base and solution strategies and gives up inadequate behavior. Ideally this "dynamic" assessment phase is followed by a training program to eliminate the cognitive backwardness, which is considered to be temporary. Feuerstein's ideas have often been applied in clinical practice, but the theoretical and empirical (reliability, standardization) foundation is relatively meager (Büchel and Scharnhorst 1993).

The third response to the dissatisfaction about the assessment of the ability to learn in traditional intelligence tests is the design of LPTs that take into account the usual requirements for the construction of tests, such as standardization, norms, objectivity, reliability, and validity. The leading representatives of this school have been Budoff (1975) in the United States and, especially, Guthke (1980) in the former German Democratic Republic. The ban placed on Western intelligence tests by the Communist party in the Soviet Union in 1936 made it necessary after the Second World War for psychologists in the former Eastern bloc to look for alternative diagnostic procedures. Their LPTs can best be compared with the regular intelligence test, preceded by a pretest plus a standardized training phase. In their opinion the posttest score, as a result of learning under optimized conditions, reflects the learning potential. Because this score satisfies the usual requirements of a psychological test, it can be employed to good effect in empirical research. Contrary to the first two solutions, it is possible to examine the degree to which learning potential differs from traditionally assessed intelligence. It should be mentioned, however, that some researchers would rather like to add a weight to this posttest score, reflecting the amount of help needed to obtain results (see Hamers and Ruijssenaars 1984).

2. Issues in Learning Potential Research

2.1 Basic Assumptions

Research on learning potential is not recent and derives directly from Vygotsky's concept of the Zone of Proximal Development (ZPD), originally expounded in 1934, which reflects the difference between the actual and the potential level of the child's cognitive functioning (Vygotsky 1962). Vygotsky argued that education too easily takes off from what pupils are already able to do by themselves (the child's actual level of development). Too little use is made of what the children might be able to do if they were helped (the potential level). In other words, individual differences in cognitive development might be seen as differences in the degree to which children benefit from the adult's help. The dialogue as social contact with the adult has a crucial role in Vygotsky's theory. For diagnostic purposes this means that the ZPD should be mapped by assessing in a dialogue how much information a child needs to acquire to move from being unable to solve a problem to being able (Brown and French 1979). Vygotsky himself stated (Sutton 1974 p. 2):

"The child's greater or lesser degree to transfer from what he can do independently to what he can do with help, proves to be the most sensitive symptom that characterizes the dynamics of the child's development and success."

A second and more recent theory applicable to learning potential research is Sternberg's intelligence theory (1985). Within his theory, Sternberg distinguished between three subtheories: the contextual theory (intelligence cannot be dissociated from the social context in which the person has been educated), the experience theory (one should be able to handle new situations and to automatize relevant processes), and the components theory (analysis and identification of elementary components in information processing). Learning potential research can be considered as an application of the components theory (see, e.g., Campione and Brown 1987): in a standardized training phase, specific strategies and self-regulating skills are taught; then the minimal number of interventions necessary to reach a certain level of performance is defined; afterward, the durability and transfer of the learning effect are checked.

2.2 The Basic Format of the LPT

The LPT format most useful for research and clinical practice consists of a pretest, a training phase, and a posttest. The content and the length of the training phase are systematically changed (see Guthke 1980 for a comprehensive survey). For clinical use the pretest may be omitted, on condition there are norms for scoring the number of prompts in the training phase and for the posttest score. It is increasingly argued that the interventions in the training phase should be adjusted to individual performance. This requires a solid theory of the different levels of relevant solution processes, as well as an adequate psychometric model, an exhaustive item bank, and an answer-dependent decision model (for examples, see Hamers et al. 1993).

2.3 LPT Content

The first attempts to improve intelligence testing concentrated on measurement methods, leaving content largely unchanged. An exception was the work of Soviet researchers, who for their teaching experiments chose the kinds of problems that arose in their educational system, such as solving a physical law or a chess problem. More and more researchers, however, have been arguing for the development of curriculum-related LPTs (see Ruijssenaars et al. 1993), for skills such as reading, spelling, and arithmetic (Tissink 1993) and also for subsidiary skills (e.g., learning to count as a prerequisite for arithmetic or sound-blending as a prerequisite for reading).

2.4 The Use of LPTs

The use of an LPT is certainly advisable when there are doubts about the appropriateness of scores on traditional tests. This has led to the systematic study of its utility for different populations and circumstances, such as:

(a)   when it is suspected that environmental conditions have interfered with development (as with children from ethnic minorities, children with a socially or linguistically deprived background);

(b)   when test results might have been affected by a temporary, strongly negative influence (as with children suffering from a strong fear of failure or impulsive children);

(c)   when there might be interference that has not been assessed but which might exist (e.g., a cerebral lesion);

(d)   when the learning process has yet to begin and a prediction of general or specific readiness is needed;

(e)   when development might stagnate and it is necessary to find out in what way the environment can be optimized.

Surveys of this kind carried out in the United States have been reported by Lidz (1987) and Haywood and Tzuriel (1992), and for Europe in the publications by Hamers et al. (1993), Carlson (1995), and Futhke and Wiedl (1995).

3. Trends, Issues, and Directions for Research

Although the basic idea for the LPT is almost as old as the intelligence test itself, researchers only became really interested in LPTs from the early 1970s onward. Therefore the relatively quick succession in which developments have occurred and the number of questions that remain to be answered should not seem surprising. It is certainly important that some solidly constructed and well-standardized LPTs have been published and have been used in clinical practice as well as in research (e.g., Hegarty 1979, Hamers et al. 1991, Hessels 1993). The most important topics in research on learning potential will be outlined.

3.1 The Validity of LPTs

A major question is whether a traditional intelligence test and an LPT are measuring the same psychological construct (construct validity), and whether there is a difference in the degree to which they correlate with actual or future learning performances (criterion validity).

Several researchers have indicated that an intelligence test and an LPT do not measure an identical psychological construct. It has been argued that LPTs are less sensitive to environmental factors, are more highly correlated with tests of creativity, and reduce the influence of nonintellectual components (e.g., neuroticism) on the test result. Moreover, LPT scores show higher correlations with achievement in strictly controlled learning experiments. Such an opinion is only provisional. Replication studies are still rare and systematic research using the same instrument has also been limited.

There has been a growing number of research projects in which the posttest shows a substantially higher correlation with academic achievement than the pretest or the intelligence test, certainly in pupils who perform poorly on the traditional test. However, this type of research is full of pitfalls and problems, such as the following. How can learning potential be expressed in a single score? What is an appropriate criterion for determining a relationship? Is it performance score or learning progress score? To what degree should predictor and criterion be tuned to each other on the basis of a task analysis? Because there are no generally accepted task models, a simple solution is usually chosen, such as using the posttest score of an LPT as a predictor and the score on a standardized school achievement test as the criterion to be predicted. What is needed is a combination of test construction and task analysis according to basic research principles with the LPT concept (see Brown and French 1979, Sternberg 1985, Lidz 1987).

3.2 Measuring Change

Measuring change and constructing a measure of change are both problematic issues in psychometrics. Because of the limitations of classical test theory, several proposals have been made based on item response theory which permits the tuning of the test score to the cognitive processes that underlie test performance (see e.g., the discussion of the Mokken model and the Rasch model by Sijtsma 1993). There is no doubt that these developments in psychometrics will influence the construction of LPTs and computer-assisted adaptive diagnostic programs. In a critical discussion of Lidz's (1987) publication, Snow (1990) correctly emphasized that learning assessment faces important psychometric problems, and that few methods have been developed specifically for this kind of testing.

3.3 The Relationship between Assessment and Treatment

The question has been raised as to what degree criterion test and predictor must be tuned with respect to content. In intelligence tests this tuning is very limited; in research on learning potential it has received growing attention. The latter is illustrated by a better combination of test construction and task analysis, but also by the development of curriculum-related LPTs (Tissink 1993). Another possibility is to develop so-called prototypic learning tasks (see Ruijssenaars et al. 1993). These simulate a learning process in a learning task on the basis of a task analysis and a process analysis. For instance, memorizing arbitrary auditory–visual associations plays an important role in the process of learning to read. This process can be presented to preschoolers as a learning task, in a version in which names and pictures of children have to be memorized in a number of trials. The aim in this case is to detect at-risk children in time to give them preventive help.

4. Conclusion

Learning potential research is a developing field and has received more and more attention for its attempt to overcome the dissatisfaction that has existed for a long time in clinical practice. However, this type of research remains in its infancy, especially when compared with the long tradition of research on intelligence tests. Nevertheless, the prospects are promising, especially because of the increasing possibilities that test theory offers.

See also: Assessment in the Service of Learning; Intelligence, Learning, and Instruction; Learning Activity

References

Brown A L, French L A 1979 The zone of potential development. Implications for intelligence testing in the year 2000. *Intelligence* 3(3): 255–73

Büchel F P Scharnhorst U 1993 The learning potential assessment device (LPAD): Discussion of theoretical and methodological problems. In: Hamers J H M, Sijtsma K, Ruijssenaars A J J M (eds.) 1993 *Learning Potential Assessment: Theoretical, Methodological and Practical Issues*. Swets & Zeitlinger, Lisse

Budoff M 1975 Measuring learning potential: An alternative to the traditional intelligence test. *Studies in Learning Potential* 3: 39 (whole issue)

Campione J C, Brown A L 1987 Linking dynamic assessment with school achievement. In: Lidz C S (ed.) 1987 *Dynamic Assessment: An Interactional Approach to Evaluating Learning Potential*. Guilford Press, New York

Carlson J S 1995 *Advances in Cognition and Educational Practice*, Vol. 3. JAI Press, Greenwich, Long Island

Dearborn W F 1921 Intelligence and its measurement. *J. Educ. Psychology* 12(4): 210–12

Feuerstein R, Rand Y, Hoffman M B 1979 *The Dynamic Assessment of Retarded Performers: The Learning Potential Assessment Device, Theory, Instruments, and Techniques*. University Park Press, Baltimore, Maryland

Futhke J, Wiedl K H (eds.) 1995 *Dynamisches Testen: Zur Psycho diagnostik inter individueller Variabilität*. Hagrefe, Göttinger

Guthke J 1980 *Ist Intelligenz Messbar?* VEB Deutscher Verlag der Wissenschaften, Berlin

Haywood H C, Tzuriel D 1992 *Interactive Assessment*. Springer-Verlag, New York

Hessets M S P 1993 *Leertest Von et Nische Minolerheden. Theoretiche en Empirische Verant Wording*. Swets & Zeitlinger, Lisee

Hamers J H M, Ruijssenaars A J J M 1984 *Leergeschiktheid en Leertests*. SVO, Nijmegen

Hamers J H M, Hessels M G P, Van Luit J E H 1991 *Leertest voor Etnische Minderheden (LEM). Test en Handleiding*. Swets & Zeitlinger, Lisse

Hamers J H M, Sijtsma K, Ruijssenaars A J J M 1993 *Learning Potential Assessment: Theoretical, Methodological and Practical Issues*. Swets & Zeitlinger, Lisse

Hegarty S 1979 *Manual for the Test of Children's Learning Ability: Individual Version*. NFER, Windsor

Kalmykova Z I 1975 Onderzoek naar de leergeschiktheid. In: Van Parreren C, Van Loon-Vervoorn W A (eds.) 1975 *Denken*. Tjeenk Willink, Groningen

Lidz C S (ed.) 1987 *Dynamic Assessment: An Interactional Approach to Evaluating Learning Potential*. Guilford Press, New York

Ruijssenaars A J J M, Castelijns J H M, Hamers J H M 1993 The validity of learning potential tests. In: Hamers J H M, Sijtsma K, Ruijssenaars A J J M (eds.) 1993 *Learning Potential Assessment: Theoretical, Methodological and Practical Issues*. Swets & Zeitlinger, Lisse

Sijtsma K 1993 Modern test theory and its role in the assessment of learning potential. In: Hamers J H M, Sijtsma K, Ruijssenaars A J J M (eds.) 1993 *Learning Potential Assessment: Theoretical, Methodological and Practical Issues*. Swets & Zeitlinger, Lisse

Snow R E 1990 Progress and propaganda in learning assessment. *Contemporary Psychology* 35: 1134[1u]–36

Sternberg R J 1985 *Beyond IQ: A Triarchic Theory of Human Intelligence*. Cambridge University Press, New York

Sutton A 1974 An introduction to teaching experiment: The Soviet view of the relation between learning, intellectual potential and mental handicap. *Teaching and Research Method Notes*, 3. University of Birmingham, Birmingham

Tissink J 1993 Leertests met curriculum (on) gebouden tahen. Universiteit Utrecht JSOR, Utrecht

Vygotsky L S 1962 *Thought and Language*. MIT Press, Cambridge, Massachusetts

Whitely S E, Dawis R V 1975 A model for psychometrically distinguishing aptitude from ability. *Educational Psychological Measurement* 35(1): 51–66

List of Contributors

Contributors are listed in alphabetical order together with their affiliations. Titles of articles which they have authored follow in alphabetical order, along with the respective page numbers. Where articles are co-authored, this has been indicated by an asterisk preceding the article title.

AINSCROW, M.   (University of Minnesota, Minneapolis, Minnesota, USA)
Children and Youth with Special Needs, Education of   150–60

AIRASIAN, P. W.   (Boston College, Chestnut Hill, Massachusetts, USA)
Classroom Assessment   809–13

ALGOZZINE, B.   (University of North Carolina, Charlotte, North Carolina, USA)
Children and Youth with Special Needs, Diagnosis and Classification of   142–49

ANDERSON, L. W.   (University of South Carolina, Columbia, South Carolina, USA)
Time, Allocated and Instructional   691–94

ASENDORPF, J. B.   (Max Planck Institute, Munich, Germany)
Social Development   217–22

BALLSTAEDT, S.-P.   (University of Tübingen, Tübingen, Germany)
Comprehension: Teaching and Assessing   492–97

BANDURA, A.   (Stanford University, Stanford, California, USA)
Social Learning Theory of Human Development   101–06

BENNETT, N.   (University of Exeter, Exeter, UK)
Group Processes in the Classroom   683–87

BIALYSTOK, E.   (York University, North York, Ontario, Canada)
Reading Comprehension in Second and Foreign Language   564–68

BIJOU, S. W.   (University of Nevada–Reno, Reno, Nevada, USA)
Behaviorist Approaches to Human Development   89–92

BJORKLUND, D. F.   (Florida Atlantic University, Boca Raton, Florida, USA)
Childhood   125–30

BOEKAERTS, M.   (University of Leiden, Leiden, The Netherlands)
Affect, Emotions, and Learning   585–90;
Coping with Stressful Situations in a Learning Context   623–26

BOGIN, B.   (University of Michigan-Dearborn, Dearborn, Michigan, USA)
Human Learning: Evolution of Anthropological Perspectives   334–38

BORKENAU, P.   (Martin-Luther Universität, Halle, Germany)
Genetics and Human Development   171–74

BROADFOOT, P.   (University of Bristol, Bristol, UK)
Learning in School, Sociology of   601–07

BRONFENBRENNER, U.   (Cornell University, Ithaca, New York, USA)
Ecological Models of Human Development   82–86

BROOKFIELD, S. D.   (University of St Thomas, St Paul, Minnesota, USA)
Adult Learning: Overview   743–48

BROOKS-GUNN, J   (Columbia University, New York, USA)
Early Experience and Human Development   243–50

BULLOCK, M.   (Max Planck Institute for Psychological Research, Munich, Germany)
Development of Reasoning Competences in Early and Later Childhood   297–303

BURNS, R. B.   (University of California, Riverside, California, USA)
Models of Learning   327–33

BUTLER, D. L.   (University of British Columbia, Vancouver, British Columbia, Canada)
Student Cognitive Processing and Learning   471–78

CALERO-BRECKHEIMER, A.   (University of Hamburg, Hamburg, Germany)
Specific Learning Disability   797–803

CASSEL, W. S.   (Florida Atlantic University, Boca Raton, Florida, USA)
Childhood   125–30

CHAMOT, A. U.   (Georgetown University, Washington, DC, USA)
Learning Strategies in Second Language Learning   525–30

CHARLESWORTH, W.   (University of Minnesota, Minneapolis, Minnesota, USA)
Socio-biological and Ethological Approaches to Human Development   107–12

CHIPMAN, S. F.   (US Office of Naval Research, Arlington, Virginia, USA)
Gender and School Learning: Mathematics   642–45

CLARK, R. E.   (University of Southern California, Los Angeles, California, USA)
Media and Learning   725–30

COBB, P.   (Vanderbilt University, Nashville, Tennessee, USA)
Constructivism and Learning   338–41

COLES, G. S.   (Robert Wood Johnson Medical School, Piscataway, New Jersey, USA)
Neurological Bases of Learning Problems   792–97

COLLINS, A.   (Bolt Beranek and Newman, Inc., Cambridge, Massachusetts, USA)
Cognition and Learning   377–81;
Environments for Learning   687–91

COPLAN, R. J.   (University of Waterloo, Waterloo, Quebec, Canada)
Play: Developmental Stages, Functions, and Educational Support   306–12

DAMON, W.   (Brown University, Providence, Rhode Island, USA)
Peer Relations and Learning   607–11

DARKENWALD, G. G.   (Rutgers State University, New Brunswick, New Jersey, USA)
Group Learning   752–55

DAVID, Y. M.   (University of Michigan, Ann Arbor, Michigan, USA)
Cognitive Strategy Instruction: Special Education   779–86

DAVIS, W. E.   (University of Maine, Orono, Maine, USA)
Children and Youth at Risk   136–42

DE CORTE, E.   (University of Leuven, Leuven, Belgium)
Computers and Learning   695–700;
Instructional Psychology: Overview   33–43;
Mathematics, Learning and Instruction of   535–38;
Translating Research into Practice   43–50

DEMETRIOU, A.   (Aristotelian University of Thessaloniki, Thessaloniki, Greece)
Human Development: Research and Educational Practice   63–67

DE RIBAUPIERRE, A.   (University of Geneva, Geneva, Switzerland)
Piaget's Theory of Human Development   97–101

DOCHY, F. J. R. C.   (University of Heerlen, Heerlen, The Netherlands)
Prior Knowledge and Learning   459–64

DUIT, R.   (University of Kiel, Kiel, Germany)
Preconceptions and Misconceptions   455–59

DWECK, C.S.   (Columbia University, New York, USA)
Development of Motivation   209–13

D'YDEWALLE, G.   (University of Leuven, Leuven, Belgium.)
Implicit Memory and Learning   399–402

EISENBERG, N. (Arizona State University, Tempe, Arizona, USA)
Development of Prosocial Behavior   206–09

EISNER, J. P.   (University of Pennsylvania, Philadelphia, Pennsylvania, USA)
Self-related Cognition, Learned Helplessness, Learned Optimism, and Human Development   199–202

ELEN, J.   (University of Leuven, Leuven, Belgium)
Instructional Psychology   721–25

ELSHOUT, J.   (University of Amsterdam, Amsterdam, The Netherlands)
Architecture of Cognition   369–72;
Creativity   391–93

ERAUT, M.   (University of Sussex, Brighton, UK)
Programmed Learning   733–41

EYLON, B.-S.   (Weizmann Institute of Science, Rehovot, Israel)
Science, Learning and Instruction of   568–72

FÄGERLIND, I.   (University of Stockholm, Stockholm, Sweden)
Education and Development   17–25

FERGUSON, D. L.   (University of Oregon, Eugene, Oregon, USA)
Developmental Disabilities: Severe   73–76

FISCHER, K. W.   (Harvard University, Cambridge, Massachusetts, USA)
Stages in Human Development   117–21

FISHER, C. W.   (University of Northern Colorado, Greeley, Colorado, USA)
Academic Learning Time   675–79

FRASER, B. J.   (Curtin University of Technology, Perth, Western Australia, Australia)
Classroom Environments   679–83

FREEDMAN, K.   (University of Minnesota, Minneapolis, Minnesota, USA)
Visual and Performing Arts, Learning and Instruction of   575–77

FREEDMAN, S. W.   (University of California, Berkeley, California, USA)
Written Composition: Teaching and Assessing   580–84

FULIGNI, A. J.   (University of Michigan, Ann Arbor, Michigan, USA)
Home Environment and School Learning   597–601

GLASER, R.   (University of Pittsburgh, Pittsburgh, Pennsylvania, USA)
Assessment in the Service of Learning   805–08;
Expert Knowledge and Performance   505–10

GOOD, T. L.   (University of Arizona, Tucson, Arizona, USA)
Teachers' Expectations   626–32

GOTTLIEB, G.   (University of North Carolina, Greensboro, North Carolina, USA)
Prenatal Development   174–77

GREENO, J. G.   (Stanford University, Stanford, California USA)
Environments for Learning   687–91

GREER, B.   (Queens University, Belfast, UK)
Mathematics, Learning and Instruction of   535–38

GRIMM, H.   (University of Bielefeld, Bielefeld, Germany)
Language Development   288–94

GROEBEN, N.   (Heidelberg University, Heidelberg, Germany)
Humanistic Models of Human Development   86–89

GUSKEY, T. R.   (University of Kentucky, Lexington, Kentucky, USA)
Mastery Learning   362–67

HABELOW, E.   (Temple University, Philadelphia, Pennsylvania, USA)
Learning Characteristics of Students with Special Needs   786–92

HAERTEL, G. D.   (Temple University, Philadelphia, Pennsylvania, USA)
Educational Psychology: Impact on Curriculum   498–505

HAKUTA, K.   (Stanford University, Stanford, California, USA)
Bilingualism   375–77

HAMERS, J. H. M.   (University of Utrecht, Utrecht, The Netherlands)
Learning Potential and Learning Potential Assessment   813–16

HARASIM, L. M.   (Simon Fraser University, Burnaby, British Columbia, Canada)
Computer Networking for Education   708–13

HARNISCHFEGER, A.   (Northwestern University, Evanston, Illinois, USA)
Attention and Learning   372–74

HATANO, G.   (Dokkyo University, Saitama, Japan)
Cognitive Development and the Acquisition of Expertise   273–76

HECKHAUSEN, J.   (Max Planck Institute for Human Development and Education, Berlin, Germany)
Lifespan Development   161–63

HELMKE, A.   (University of Landau, Landau, Germany)
Development of the Self-concept   228–32

HENCKE, R.   (Harvard University, Cambridge, Massachusetts, USA)
Stages in Human Development   117–21

HEYMAN, G. D.   (University of Illinois, Champaign, Illinois, USA)
Development of Motivation   209–13

HIEMSTRA, R.   (Syracuse University, Syracuse, New York, USA)
Self-directed Adult Learning   771–77

HILDYARD, A.   (Ontario Institute for Studies in Education, Toronto, Ontario, Canada)
Writing, Learning and Instruction of   577–80

819

HOWE, M. J. A. (University of Exeter, Exeter, UK)
Development of Learning across the Lifespan 313–16

HUTCHINGS, D. E. (New York State Psychiatric Institute, New York, USA)
*Prenatal Development 174–77

JACOB, E. J. (George Mason University, Fairfax, Virginia, USA)
Culture, Cognition, and Education 590–97

JAEGGI, E. (Technische Universität Berlin, Berlin, Germany)
Psychodynamic Theories of Human Development 112–16

KAGAN, S. L. (Yale University, New Haven, Connecticut, USA)
Human Development: Research and Social Policy 59–62

KAIL, R. (Purdue University, West Lafayette, Indiana, USA)
Information-processing Theories of Human Development 92–97

KALVERBOER, A. F. (State University, Groningen, The Netherlands)
Developmental Psychopathology 67–73

KELLER, M (Max Planck Institute, Berlin, Germany)
*Development of Social Cognition 304–06

KILLEN, M. (Wesleyan University, Middleton, Connecticut, USA)
*Development of Social Cognition 304–06

KINTSCH, E. (Institute of Cognitive Science, University of Colorado, Boulder, Colorado, USA)
*Learning from Text 519–24

KINTSCH, W. (Institute of Cognitive Science, University of Colorado, Boulder, Colorado, USA)
*Learning from Text 519–24

KLOOSTERMAN, P. (Indiana University, Bloomington, Indiana, USA)
Mathematics Education, Affective Issues in 543–47

KNOERS, A. (Catholic University of Nijmegen, Nijmegen, The Netherlands)
Paradigms in Instructional Psychology 317–21

KOHNSTAMM, G. A. (University of Leiden, Leiden, The Netherlands)
*Temperament Development 187–91

KOMOSKI, P. K. (EPIE Institute, Hampton Bays, New York, USA)
Computer-managed Learning 704–07

KORNADT, H. J. (University of the Saarland, Saarbrücken, Germany)
*Cross-cultural Approaches to Human Development 51–55

KRASKA, K. (University of Osnabrück, Osnabrück, Germany)
*Self-regulation in Learning 467–71

KUHL, J. (University of Osnabrück, Osnabrück, Germany)
*Self-regulation in Learning 467–71

LANE, S. (University of Pittsburgh, Pittsburgh, Pennsylvania, USA)
*Assessment in the Service of Learning 805–08

LENS, W. (University of Leuven, Leuven, Belgium)
Motivation and Learning 445–51

LERNER, R. M. (Michigan State University, East Lansing, Michigan, USA)
*Adolescence 130–36

LEVY, G. (University of Wyoming, Laramie, Wyoming, USA)
*Gender Roles 239–43

LIAW, F (Columbia University, New York, USA)
*Early Experience and Human Development 243–50

LINN, M. C. (University of California, Berkeley, California, USA)
Gender and School Learning: Science 645–49;
*Science, Learning and Instruction of 568–72

LIPSITT, L. P. (Brown University, Providence, Rhode Island, USA)
Infancy 121–25

LOHMAN, D. F. (University of Iowa, Iowa City, Iowa, USA)
Intelligence, Learning, and Instruction 660–65

LOMPSCHER, J. (Academy of Educational Sciences, Berlin, Germany)
Learning Activity 347–50

LONG, M. H. (University of Hawaii at Manoa, Honolulu, Hawaii, USA)
Foreign Language Acquisition, Process of 511–19

LOWYCK, J. (University of Leuven, Leuven, Belgium)
Computers and Learning 695–700;
Instructional Psychology 721–25;
Learning in Industrial Settings 755–59

MCCAUL, E. J. (University of Maine, Orono, Maine, USA)
Children and Youth at Risk 136–42

MACKERACHER, D. (Ontario Institute for Studies in Education, Toronto, Ontario, Canada)
Lifespan Learning: Implications for Educators 764–71

MAGNUSSON, D. (Stockholm University, Stockholm, Sweden)
Personality Development 233–39

MARKOWITSCH, H. J. (University of Bielefeld, Bielefeld, Germany)
Brain Development and Human Behavior 169–71

MARTIN, C. L. (Arizona State University, Tempe, Arizona, USA)
Gender Roles 239–43

MARTIN, R. P. (University of Georgia, Athens, Georgia, USA)
Temperament Development 187–91

MASON, E. J. (University of Kentucky, Lexington, Kentucky, USA)
Development of Gifted Children 277–80

MAYER, R. E. (University of California, Santa Barbara, California, USA)
Development of Learning Skills in Problem-solving and Thinking 550–55;
Computer Programming, Learning and Instruction of 713–15;
Feedback in Learning 396–98;
History of Instructional Psychology 29–33;
Problem-solving: Teaching and Assessing 555–59

MESSICK, S. (Educational Testing Service, Princeton, New Jersey, USA)
Cognitive Styles and Learning 638–41

MEYER, D. K. (University of Texas, Austin, Texas, USA)
Learning Strategies: Teaching and Assessing 423–27

MÖNKS, F. J. (University of Nijmegen, Nijmegen, The Netherlands)
Development of Gifted Children 277–80

MONTADA, L. (University of Trier, Trier, Germany)
Problems and Crises in Human Development 258–62

MORAN, K. A. (State University of New York, Buffalo, New York, USA)
Learning Theories: Historical Overview and Trends 322–27

NUNNER-WINKLER, G. (Max Plank Institute, Munich, Germany)
Moral Development 222–28

OBIAKOR, F. E. (Emporia State University, Emporia, Kansas, USA)
Children and Youth with Special Needs, Diagnosis and Classification of 142–49

OGBU, J. U. (University of California, Berkeley, California, USA)
Language and Learning in Education 406–08

OHLSSON, S. (University of Pittsburgh, Pittsburgh, Pennsylvania, USA)
Declarative and Procedural Knowledge 394–96

OLSON, D. R. (Ontario Institute for Studies in Education, Toronto, Ontario, Canada)
Literacy 428–31

O'MALLEY, J. M. (Prince William County Schools, Manassas, Virginia, USA)
Learning Strategies in Second Language Learning 525–30

OPWIS, K. (University of Freiburg, Freiburg, Germany)
Problem-solving and Learning: Computer Modeling 730–33

OSER, F. K. (University of Fribourg, Fribourg, Switzerland)
Attitudes and Values, Acquiring 489–92

PALINCSAR, A. S. (University of Michigan, Ann Arbor, Michigan, USA)
Cognitive Strategy Instruction: Special Education 779–86

PALMER, D. J. (Texas A&M University, College Station, Texas, USA)
Specific Learning Disability 797–803

PAUL, R. H. (Laurential University, Sulbury, Ontario, Canada)
Experiential and Open Learning for Adults 749–52

PEKRUN, R. (University of Regensburg, Regensburg, Germany)
Emotional Development 213–17

PELLEGRINO, J. W. (Vanderbilt University, Nashville, Tennessee, USA)
Abilities and Aptitudes 633–38

PERFETTI, C. A.   (University of Pittsburgh, Pittsburgh, Pennsylvania, USA)
Reading, Learning and Instruction of   559–61

PERKINS, D. N.   (Harvard Graduate School of Education, Cambridge, Massachusetts, USA)
*Learning Transfer   483–87

PERNER, J.   (University of Sussex, Brighton, UK)
An Overview of Cognitive Development   263–68

PERRY, D. G.   (Florida Atlantic University, Boca Raton, Florida, USA)
Development and Socialization of Aggression   202–06

PETERSEN, A. C.   (University of Minnesota, Minneapolis-St Paul, Minnesota, USA)
*Sex Differences in Behavior and Development   184–87

PIMM, D.   (Open University, Milton Keynes, UK)
Mathematics and Language   538–42

PONTECORVO, C.   (University of Rome (La Sapienza), Rome, Italy)
Social and Communication Skills   615–19

PRESSLEY, M.   (University of Maryland, College Park, Maryland, USA)
*Memory: Teaching and Assessing   431–36

REIGELUTH, C. M.   (Indiana University, Bloomington, Indiana, USA)
Instructional Design Theories   715–20;
*Task Analysis   478–82

RESNICK, L. B.   (University of Pittsburgh, Pittsburgh, Pennsylvania, USA)
*Cognition and Learning   377–81;
*Environments for Learning   687–91;
Situated Learning   341–47

REYNOLDS, M. C.   (University of Minnesota, Minneapolis, Minnesota, USA)
*Children and Youth with Special Needs, Education of   150–60

RIEBEN, L.   (University of Geneva, Geneva, Switzerland)
*Piaget's Theory of Human Development   97–101

ROCHE, A. F.   (Wright State University, Yellow Springs, Ohio, USA)
Physical Growth and Development: Universal Changes and Individual Differences   178–84

ROWLAND, G.   (Ithaca College, Ithaca, New York, USA)
*Task Analysis   478–82

RUBIN, K. H.   (University of Waterloo, Waterloo, Quebec, Canada)
*Play: Developmental Stages, Functions, and Educational Support   306–12

RUBTSOV, V. V.   (Russian Academy of Education, Moscow, Russia)
Social Interaction and Learning   619–23

RUIJSSENAARS, A. J. J. M.   (University of Leuven, Leuven, Belgium)
*Learning Potential and Learning Potential Assessment   813–16

SAHA, L. J.   (Australian National University, Canberra, ACT, Australia)
*Education and Development   17–25

SALOMON, G.   (University of Haifa, Haifa, Israel)
*Learning Transfer   483–87

SCHAIE, K. W.   (Pennsylvania State University, University Park, Pennsylvania, USA)
Adulthood and Old Age   163–68

SCHNEEWIND, K. A.   (University of Munich, Munich, Germany)
Family Influences on Human Development   250–54

SCHNEIDER, W.   (University of Würzburg, Würzburg, Germany)
Memory Development   294–97

SCHNOTZ, W.   (University of Jena, Jena, Germany)
*Comprehension: Teaching and Assessing   492–97;
Reading Comprehension, Learning of   562–64

SELIGMAN, M.E.P.   (University of Pennsylvania, Philadelphia, Pennsylvania, USA)
*Self-related Cognition, Learned Helplessness, Learned Optimism, and Human Development   199–202

SHUELL, T. J.   (State University of New York, Buffalo, New York, USA)
*Learning Theories: Historical Overview and Trends   322–27

SHUTE, V. J.   (Brooks Air Force Base, Texas, USA)
Learning Processes and Learning Outcomes   409–18

SIMONS, P. R-J.   (University of Nijmegen, Nijmegen, The Netherlands)
Metacognitive Strategies: Teaching and Assessing   441–44;
Metacognition   436–41

SLAVIN, R. E. (Johns Hopkins University, Baltimore, Maryland, USA)
Cooperative Learning 351–55

SMITH, R. M. (Northern Illinois University, De Kalb, Illinois, USA)
Learning to Learn: Adult Education 760–64

SNOW, R. E. (Stanford University, Stanford, California, USA)
Individual Differences, Learning, and Instruction 649–60;
Teaching: Aptitude–Treatment Interaction Model 670–74

SPADA, H. (University of Freiburg, Freiburg, Germany)
Problem-solving and Learning: Computer Modeling 730–33

SPIEL, C. (University of Vienna, Vienna, Austria)
Human Development: Research Methodology 55–59

SPOLSKY, B. (Bar Ilan University, Ramat Gan, Israel)
Linguistics and Language Learning 531–34

STEMMLER, M. (Pennsylvania State University, University Park, Pennsylvania, USA)
Sex Differences in Behavior and Development 184–87

STEVENSON, H. W. (University of Michigan, Ann Arbor, Michigan, USA)
Home Environment and School Learning 597–601

STURMAN, A. (University of Southern Queensland, Toowoomba, Queensland, Australia)
Socialization 193–98

TAMIR, P. (Hebrew University, Jerusalem, Israel)
Discovery Learning and Teaching 355–61

TENNYSON, R. D. (University of Minnesota, Minneapolis, Minnesota, USA)
Concept Learning 381–85; *Concept Learning: Teaching and Assessing* 385–91

THOMAS, R. M. (University of California, Santa Barbara, California, USA)
Cultural and Religious Concepts of Human Development 77–81

TÖRESTAD, B. (Stockholm University, Stockholm, Sweden)
Personality Development 233–39

TROMMSDORFF, G. (University of Konstanz, Konstanz, Germany)
Cross-cultural Approaches to Human Development 51–55

TUIJNMAN, A. C. (OECD, Paris, France)
Lifespan Learning: Implications for Educators 764–71

VAN DER SANDEN, J. M. M. (Tilburg University, Tilburg, The Netherlands)
Motor Skills: Learning and Instruction 547–50

VAN LIESHOUT, C. F. M. (University of Nijmegen, Nijmegen, The Netherlands)
Peer Relations and Development 254–58

VAN MATER STONE, G. (University of Texas, Austin, Texas, USA)
Learning Strategies and Learning to Learn 419–23

VAN METER, P. (University of Maryland, College Park, Maryland, USA)
Memory: Teaching and Assessing 431–36

VERSCHAFFEL, L. (University of Leuven, Leuven, Belgium)
Computers and Learning 695–700;
Mathematics, Learning and Instruction of 535–38

VILLARRUEL, F. A. (Michigan State University, East Lansing, Michigan, USA)
Adolescence 130–36

VON EYE, A. (Michigan State University, East Lansing, Michigan, USA)
Human Development: Research Methodology 55–59

VON HOFSTEN, C. (Umeå University, Umeå, Sweden)
Motor Development and Skill Acquisition 280–84

VOSNIADOU, S. (University of Athens, Athens, Greece)
Knowledge Representation and Organization 402–06

VOSS, J. F. (University of Pittsburgh, Pittsburgh, Pennsylvania, USA)
Reasoning 464–67;
Social Sciences, Learning and Instruction of 572–74

WAGEMANS, J. (University of Leuven, Leuven, Belgium)
Visual Perception 451–55

WALBERG, H. J. (University of Illinois at Chicago, Chicago, Illinois, USA)
Personality, School, and Social Environment as Learning Determinants 611–15

WANG, M. C. (Temple University, Philadelphia, Pennsylvania, USA)
Learning Characteristics of Students with Special Needs 786–92;
Student Diversity and Classroom Teaching 665–70

WATSON, D. M. (King's College, London, UK)
Computer Assisted Learning 700–04

WEINERT, F. E. (Max Planck Institute for Psychological Research, Munich, Germany)
Cognitive Development: Individual Differences 268–72;
Human Development in the Lifespan: Overview 8–17;
Human Development, Learning, and Instruction 25–28;
Translating Research into Practice 43–50

WEINERT, S. (Universität Bielefeld, Bielefeld, Germany.)
History of Developmental Psychology 1–7

WEINSTEIN, C. E. (University of Texas, Austin, Texas, USA)
Learning Strategies and Learning to Learn 419–23;
Learning Strategies: Teaching and Assessing 423–27

WILKENING, F. (University of Tübingen, Tübingen, Germany)
Perceptual Development 284–88

WINNE, P. H. (Simon Fraser University, Burnaby, British Columbia, Canada)
Student Cognitive Processing and Learning 471–78

WONG, B. (Simon Fraser University, Burnaby, British Columbia, Canada)
Children and Youth with Special Needs, Diagnosis and Classification of 142–49

ZEITZ, C. M. (University of Pittsburgh, Pittsburgh, Pennsylvania, USA)
Expert Knowledge and Performance 505–10

Name Index

The Name Index has been compiled so that the reader can proceed directly to the page where an author's work is cited, or to the reference itself in the bibliography. For each name, the page numbers for the bibliographic section are given first, followed by the page number(s) in parentheses where that reference is cited in text. Where a name is referred to only in text, and not in the bibliography, the page number appears only in parentheses.

The accuracy of the spelling of authors' names has been affected by the use of different initials by some authors, or a different spelling of their name in different papers or review articles (sometimes this may arise from a transliteration process), and by those journals which give only one initial to each author.

Abelson R P, 406
Aboitiz F, 796 (794)
Abou-Zeid A W, 183 (181)
Abraham H, 361 (358)
Abraham M R, 459 (456, 458)
Abraham R G, 530 (526)
Abramson L Y, 201 (199, 200), 450 (449)
Absy C A, 530 (526)
Ach N, 267 (263), (318), 471 (468)
Achenbach T M, 221 (221)
Achtenhagen F, 574 (573)
Acioly N M, 467 (466)
Ackerman B P, 303 (297, 299)
Ackerman P L, 272, 374 (373), 418, 637 (634), 657 (652), 658 (654), 665 (664)
Adams A, 785 (780)
Adams F, 160 (152)
Adams G R, 135 (133)
Adams J A, 398 (398), 550 (549)
Adams M J, 561 (561)
Adams V M, 537 (535), 590
Adelson J, 135 (134)
Adey P, 41 (37), 66 (64)
Adler A, 116 (115)
Adler B, 171 (170)
Adler J, 542 (540)
Adoni H, 106 (102)
Aebli H, 272 (269), 396 (394, 395)
Ahwesh E, 574 (573)
Aiken L, 542 (538)
Aiken L R, 546 (543)
Ainscow M, 160 (154, 158, 159), 791 (786)
Ainsworth M D S, 7 (6), 205 (204)
Airasian P W, 812 (809, 810, 811, 812)
Ajello A M, 574 (573)
Alberts J, 177 (175)
Alderson J C, 567–68 (566)
Alexander K L, 601 (597)
Alexander P A, 41 (36), 422–23 (420), 463, 463 (459, 459, 460, 460), 478 (473, 474)
Algozzine B, 149 (142, 145, 146, 147), 791 (789), 796 (795)
Alibali M W, 267 (266)
Allard T, 170 (170)
Allebeck P, 124 (121)
Alleman J, 812 (810)

Allen G E, 149 (147)
Allen J P B, 534 (533)
Allen V L, 674 (670)
Allington R L, 786 (784)
Allport G W, 89 (87), 238 (236), 355 (354), 491 (490)
Almond G A, 24 (20)
Altbach P G, 24 (22)
Althof W, 228 (227), 492
Altmann J, 337 (335)
Alton-Lee A, 327 (326)
Alvermann D, 785 (781, 783)
Amatruda C S, 120 (117)
Amaya-Williams M, 471 (468)
Ames C, 212 (209, 210, 212), 785 (784)
Ames G, 610 (609)
Ammon P, 100 (100)
Amorim M-A, 402 (401)
Amsel E, 303 (299)
Anastasi P, 657 (650, 651)
Andersen H B, 482 (481)
Anderson B, 248–49 (246, 247)
Anderson C A, 24 (23)
Anderson G L, 478 (471), 683 (681)
Anderson J H, 347 (346)
Anderson J R, 43 (37), 97 (95), 371 (369, 370), 396 (394, 395), 418 (410, 411, 413), 422 (422), 435 (434, 435), 510 (509), 530 (528), 550 (549), 559 (556), 665 (662), 691 (690), 699 (697), 732 (730, 732)
Anderson L, 333 (329)
Anderson L M, 785 (779)
Anderson L W, 49 (46), 367 (363), 678 (676, 677), 693 (692, 693), 812 (809)
Anderson R C, 435 (433), 497 (495)
Anderson R E, 694 (692)
Anderson T H, 497 (494)
Andrews D H, 724 (724)
Andrews G R, 212 (212)
Angleitner A, 190 (190)
Angoff W H, 238 (234)
Ankenmann R, 808 (807)
Ankerhus J, 293 (289)
Antaki C, 467
Anthony H M, 785 (779)
Anzai Y, 276 (273)

Aphek E, 530 (526)
Applebee A N, 579–80 (578, 579), 583–84 (582, 583)
Aramburo D, 149 (147)
Archer J, 785 (784)
Argyris C, 763 (763)
Arias A Jr, 712 (708, 711)
Aristotle, (464, 466), (569)
Arlin M, 16 (14)
Armbruster B B, 497 (494), 564 (563)
Armento B J, 574
Armer M, 24 (20)
Armon C, 770 (768)
Arnold V, 530 (526)
Arns F, 597 (593)
Aronson E, 355 (353, 354), (608)
Arredondo D E, 367 (365, 367)
Arthur J, 135 (132)
Asendorpf J B, 221–22 (217, 219, 220)
Asensio M, 574 (572)
Ashcraft M H, 97 (94)
Ashcroft L, 770 (766)
Ashizawa K, 183 (180)
Ashworth R, 712 (711)
Aslin R, 124 (123), 288 (286)
Aspinwall L C, 659 (654)
Astington J, 303 (299)
Atkin R, 704 (702)
Atkinson J W, 450–51 (445, 446, 448)
Au K H, 785 (783)
Austin G A, 398 (397)
Ausubel D P, 361 (356, 357), 463 (459), 497 (493)
Averch H S, 198 (197)
Avis J, 305 (305)
Ayala F J, 111 (107)
Ayles R, 280 (278)
Azuma H, 81, 198 (197), 601 (599), 607 (605)

Baddeley A D, 371 (370), 374 (372), 418 (411)

Badgio P, 303 (302)
Baer D M, 92 (90)
Baeyens F, 402 (400)
Baier H, 802 (800)
Baillaud J, (797)
Bainbridge L, 770
Baird J R, 459 (458)
Baker D, 601 (599)
Baker E L, 504–05 (503, 504), 808 (806, 807)
Baker L, 497 (494), 564 (563)
Baker L A, 174 (172)
Baker-Ward L, 435 (432)
Baldwin J M, (489)
Balke-Aurell G, 657–58 (652)
Ballard K D, 160 (159)
Ball-Rokeach S, 106 (102)
Ballstaedt S-P, 497 (495), 524 (521)
Baltes M M, 163 (162)
Baltes P B, 7 (1, 7), 16 (11), 59 (55, 56, 57, 58), 85 (84), 106 (106), 163 (161, 162), 262 (259), 297 (296, 297), 771 (768)
Banathy B H, 720 (716, 720)
Bandura A, 7 (3), 92, 92 (90, 90), 106 (101, 102, 103, 104, 105), 135 (132, 133), 205 (203, 205), 222 (218), 238 (235, 237), 242 (240), 327, 374 (373), 451 (448, 450), 504 (499, 502), 589 (586)
Banersfeld H, 537 (536)
Bangert-Drowns R L, 49 (47), 367 (362, 366)
Bank L, 206 (204)
Bank-Mikkelsen N, 76 (73)
Baratz J, 408 (407)
Barber P J, 374 (373)
Barham I H, 584 (583)
Barham J, 542 (538)
Barkman B, 568
Barlow G W, 111 (107)
Barnes D, 355 (351), 542 (538), 606 (603), 687 (685)
Barnett L A, 312 (310)
Barnett M A, 567 (566)
Barnett W S, 248 (247)
Barnitz J G, 567 (566)
Barnouw V, 596 (591)
Barocas R, 250 (244, 248)
Baron J, 303 (302), 418 (410, 412), 435 (434), 657 (652)
Baron J B, 467
Baron R, 632 (626, 628)
Barr R, 333 (331)
Barrett K C, 217 (214)
Barro S, 141 (139)
Barron F, 393 (391, 392)
Barrows H S, 763 (761)
Barshis D, 367 (366)
Bar-Tal D, 209 (207)
Barth R P, 796 (794)
Bartholomai F, 86 (82)
Bartholomew D J, 59 (57)
Bartlett F C, 33 (29, 32), 405 (403), 418 (410), 497 (492)
Barton L, 160 (157)
Basel

Basinger K S, 227 (225)
Bassok M, 42 (34, 37), 333 (328), 381 (378), 418 (410, 411), 658 (656), 674 (673)
Bates E, 293 (288, 291), 619
Bates J E, 205 (204)
Bateson G, 312 (308), 596 (591)
Bateson P P G, 72 (69)
Battistich V, 209 (208)
Baudonniere P M, 312 (311)
Bauersfeld H, 341 (340), 459 (456)
Baumann J F, 785 (780)
Baumrind D, 129 (126), 205 (204), 248 (246), 601 (598)
Baxter G P, 558 (557, 558)
Baydar N, 248 (244, 245, 246)
Bayles K, 205 (204)
Bayman P, 715 (714)
Beach R, 478 (475)
Bechinger D, 171 (169)
Beck I L, 524 (522, 523), 561 (560), 574 (572)
Becker B J, 644 (643)
Becker H J, 699 (695, 697), 715 (713)
Becker M J, 729 (726)
Becker P, 89 (87)
Beckmann J, 471 (470)
Beckoff M, 337 (337)
Bednar A K, 724 (722)
Beech J R, 374 (373)
Beecher M D, 111 (107)
Beery R G, 213
Beintema D J, 72 (71)
Beishuizen J J, 658 (652)
Bejar I I, 558 (558)
Bell C, 312 (311)
Bell L, 561 (560)
Bell N, 619 (617)
Bell R Q, 238 (236)
Bellamy G T, 76 (75)
Belle D, 222 (218, 219)
Bellisle F, 184 (180, 181)
Bellman B, 712 (708, 711)
Belmont J M, 435 (435), 487 (485)
Belsky J, 254 (252)
Belyaeva A, 596 (594)
Bem S L, 242 (240)
Benasich A A, 249 (244)
Benavot A, 24 (24)
Benbow C P, 280 (278), 644 (642, 644), 659 (655)
Ben-Chaim D, 657 (652)
Benedict R, 198 (194)
Benigni L, 619
Benjamin L T, 504 (500)
Bennett D S, 205 (204)
Bennett E L, 125 (121), 171
Bennett J M, 427 (425)
Bennett N, 333 (330), 606 (604), 679 (677), 687 (684, 685, 686)
Bennett S M, 649 (647)
Bennett S N, 42 (34), 504 (500), 670 (666)
Ben-Peretz M, 679 (677)
Bentin S, 568 (567)
Bentzer F-A, 802 (798)
Bereiter C, 41–42–43 (37, 38, 40), 380

(380), 391 (388), 408 (406), 579–80 (577, 579), 657 (653), 691 (688), 700, 700 (697, 698, 698, 699), 724 (723), 785 (779)
Berg C A, 97
Bergen D, 312 (311)
Berger, (195)
Bergman A, 116 (113)
Bergman L R, 238 (238)
Bergsten U, 770 (768)
Berk L E, 129 (128), 785 (781)
Berliner D C, 41–42 (34), 49 (46), 658 (656), 678 (676), 694 (692)
Berlyne D E, 312 (308), 497 (494)
Berman R, 567 (566)
Bernard J, 187 (185)
Berndt T J, 258
Bernhard J G, 111 (109, 110)
Bernstein B, 408 (407), 607
Bernstein N, 284 (281, 283)
Berrueta-Clement J R, 248 (247)
Berry D C, 401–02 (401)
Berry J W, 55, 596 (590)
Berry P C, 559 (557)
Bertini M, 641 (640)
Best D L, 297 (296)
Best K M, 792 (788)
Beukhof G, 659 (654)
Beunen G, 183 (182)
Bever T G, 338 (335)
Bialystok E, 377 (376)
Bidell T R, 120 (117, 118)
Biederman I, 567 (567)
Bierman J M, 250 (248)
Biggs J B, 422 (420), 427 (423), 641 (640)
Bigi L, 441 (438)
Bijou S W, 92 (90)
Bill V, 381 (379)
Billing M, 491 (490)
Binet A, 7 (3), 16 (9), 28 (27), (185), 272 (270), (660)
Bingol N, 796 (794)
Binkley M, 524
Birch D, 451 (446)
Birch H, 206 (204)
Bird J B, 741 (736)
Bird M, 785 (779)
Birren J E, 163 (161)
Bisanz J, 97 (93, 95)
Bishop A, 542 (538)
Bishop A J, 537 (535)
Bjork R A, 402
Bjorklund D F, 97, 129 (127, 128, 129), 297 (294, 296)
Black G, 249 (244)
Black J B, 497 (495), 564
Black S D, 713 (708)
Blackburn T C, 81 (79)
Blackford S P, 402 (400)
Blagg N, 28 (27), 49 (47), 272 (271)
Blais J, 574 (573)
Blanc M H A, 377
Blanck G, 116 (115)
Blanck R, 116 (115)
Blaney N T, 355 (353, 354)

Blashfield R K, 148 (142)
Blasi A, 89 (88), 227 (227)
Blatt B, 76 (73)
Blau P, 198 (195)
Blaug M, 24 (19)
Blaxton T A, 401 (400)
Blaye A, 303 (301), 700 (698)
Bleich R P, 402 (400)
Blenkinsop J, 786 (780)
Bligh D A, 755 (753)
Block C H, 559 (557)
Block J, 238 (236)
Block J H, 187 (185), 367 (363, 365, 367)
Blomeyer R L, 703 (703)
Bloom B, 333 (331)
Bloom B S, 49–50 (44), 248 (243), 280,
  367 (362, 363, 365, 367), 463 (460), 504
  (500), 558 (557), (612), 670 (666), 720
  (719), 741 (736), 785 (780), 791 (787)
Blos P, (113)
Blumenfeld, (679)
Blyth D A, 136 (131)
Boas F, (52), 408 (406)
Bock R D, 183 (180)
Bodmer W F, 86 (85)
Boekaerts M, 41 (36, 37, 39), 350 (350),
  589–90 (586, 587, 588, 589), 626, 626
  (625, 625, 626), 657 (654)
Boesch E E, 54 (52)
Boggild-Andersen B, 293 (289)
Bogin B, 337 (336, 337)
Bol E, 350
Boldizar J P, 206 (205)
Boldt D, 171 (170)
Bolles R C, 111 (107), 238 (235)
Bolus R, 232 (230)
Bombi A S, 574 (573)
Bond A L, 626 (625)
Bonham L A, 776 (775)
Bonner J, 724 (721, 722)
Bonner J T, 111 (108), 337 (334, 336)
Bonniol J J, 606 (603)
Booth A, 254
Booth T, 76 (75)
Borasi R, 542 (539)
Borkowski J G, 42 (36), 297 (295, 296),
  422 (420), 435–36 (434, 435), 478 (477),
  497 (495), 785 (784)
Borland J H, 280 (278)
Bormann E, 755 (753)
Bornstein M H, 288 (286, 288), 312 (310)
Boruch R F, 665 (663)
Boruta M, 584 (582)
Bosma H, 626 (625)
Botkin M, 632 (629)
Botkin P T, 306 (304)
Bouchardæ T J, 174 (173)
Bouchard T J, 558 (557)
Bouchard T J Jr, 272 (271)
Boud D, 776 (773)
Bourdieu P, 198 (197), 607
Bovair S, 396 (395), 510 (508)
Bovet M, 100 (99)
Bovy R C, 724 (724)

Bower G H, 33 (30), 371 (369), 398 (397),
  418 (409), 589 (586)
Bower T G R, 288 (285)
Bowerman M, 293 (289, 290)
Bowers J, 401 (400)
Bowlby J, 7 (6), (246)
Bowles S, 24 (19), 198 (196, 198), (602)
Bowman I, 791 (786)
Bowman M J, 24 (23)
Boyd-Barrett O, 703 (702)
Boydell T, 759 (756)
Boyer C B, 135
Boyle C F, 691 (690), 699 (697)
Boyle R A, 42 (35, 36)
Brachman R J, 733 (730)
Bradley R H, 248 (245, 247), 249 (247)
Brady S A, 561 (560)
Braine M D S, 303 (298, 300, 301)
Brainerd C J, 267 (265), 297 (295), 316 (313)
Brainerd D J, 510 (506)
Brakke K E, 338 (335)
Brandstädter J R, 167 (166), 262 (261)
Bransford J D, 41 (36), 380 (377, 378),
  422 (419, 420, 421), 436 (434), 524 (521),
  530 (527, 529), 550 (549), 564 (562)
Bransford J O, 497 (492, 493)
Brantlinger E A, 791 (787, 789)
Brattesani K, 632 (629)
Bray M, 25 (22)
Brazelton T B, 124 (122)
Brecht K, 116 (113)
Bredberg G, 177 (175)
Bregman E O, 665 (660)
Breslow L, 97 (96)
Bretherton I, 222 (218), 293 (288, 291),
  312 (310)
Bretherton L, 619
Breuer K, 385 (383), 391 (389)
Brewer W F, 405 (405)
Bricker W, 206 (204)
Briggs L J, 720 (719), 724 (722, 723)
Brim O G, 167 (166), 198 (194), 770
  (765, 767)
Brim O G Jr., 106 (101), 163 (161), 248 (244)
Brinton D M, 530
Britton B K, 524 (523), 564
Britton J, 355 (351), 583–84 (581, 582)
Broadbent D E, 267 (266), 401 (401)
Broadfoot P M, 607 (605, 606)
Broca P, (797)
Brockett R G, 748 (743), 770 (770), 776–77
Broder L J, 558 (557), 785 (780)
Brody N, 174 (173)
Bromfield R, 272 (270)
Bromme R, 679 (677), 694 (692)
Bronfenbrenner U, 16 (10, 15), 61 (60),
  85–86 (82, 83, 84, 85), 248 (244)
Brook C G D, 183 (181)
Brookfield S D, 748 (743, 744, 746, 747),
  755 (753, 754, 755), 763 (760), 770 (764,
  770), 776 (772, 775)
Brookover W B, 670 (666)
Brooks-Gunn J, 59 (55), 129 (127), 135
  (130), 232 (229, 231), 248–49 (243, 244,

245, 246, 247, 248)
Brophy J E, 190 (189), 504 (503), 632 (627,
  628, 629), 657 (656), 683 (679), 812 (810)
Broughton J M, 288 (285)
Brousseau G, 341 (340)
Brown A, 333 (332), 504 (502), 619 (618)
Brown A L, 41 (37, 38, 40, 41), 49, 49 (48,
  48), 163 (162), 276 (274), 293 (293), 303
  (302), 371 (371), 380–81 (377, 378, 379),
  422 (419, 420, 421), 435–36 (432, 434),
  440–41 (436, 438, 440), 487 (484), 497
  (494, 495), 510 (507), 524, 524 (521, 521,
  522), 530 (527, 528, 529), 558 (558), 564,
  564 (563, 563), 596 (595), 637 (637), 657
  (652, 653), 687 (684), 691 (690), 785–
  86 (782), 791 (789), 808 (805, 806), 816
  (814, 815)
Brown D E, 347 (346)
Brown G W, 72 (71)
Brown J, 267 (265), 333 (332)
Brown J A, 558 (558)
Brown J I, 427 (425)
Brown J S, 41–42 (35, 37, 40), 276 (274),
  321 (319), 326 (323, 324), 381 (380),
  398 (398), 487 (484), 497 (495), 550
  (550), 596 (595), 691 (689), 700 (696),
  720 (719)
Brown L, 149 (145), 160 (154, 157)
Brown M M, 205 (204)
Brown R, 293 (290, 292), 436 (432, 433, 434)
Brown S J, 724 (723)
Bruer J T, 41 (35, 36, 40)
Bruininks R H, 160 (153)
Bruner J, 333 (332), (612), 687 (683)
Bruner J S, 33 (30), 66 (64), 293 (289,
  291), 312 (308), 361 (355, 356, 360), 396
  (395), 398 (397), 478 (471), 504 (499,
  500), 619 (617), 670 (666), 796 (795)
Brunfaut E, 402 (400)
Brush L R, 645 (642)
Bryant B R, 149 (145)
Bryant D M, 249 (248)
Bryant I, 748 (746)
Bryant S L, 436 (432)
Bryk A, 141 (141)
Bryson M, 580
Buchanan C M, 59 (55)
Budoff M, 657 (652), 816 (814)
Bühler C, 7 (2), 163 (161)
Bühler K, (318)
Buka S L, 124 (121)
Bukowski W M, 258 (255, 256)
Bull D, 303 (301)
Bullock D, 120 (118)
Bullock M, 303 (299)
Bullough R, 812 (809)
Burchinal M R, 250 (247)
Burge L, 712 (709)
Burgess T, 584 (582)
Burgoyne J, 759 (756)
Burke W P, 202 (199)
Burns B, 288 (287)
Burns R B, 49 (43, 46), 367 (363)

Burstall C, 812 (811)
Burt C, (660, 661)
Burton L, 546 (545)
Burton R R, 398 (398), 558 (558)
Buschang P H, 183 (182)
Bush D M, 198 (193, 194, 195)
Buss A H, 190 (188), 222 (218), 238 (234)
Busse T V, 558 (557)
Bussey K, 206 (202, 204), 242 (240)
Butcher H J, 665
Butler J A, 76 (75)
Butler R, 212 (212)
Butler R P, 202 (199)
Butterfield E C, 33, 435 (435), 487 (485)
Byard P J, 183 (179, 180)
Byrne R M J, 467
Byrnes J P, 135 (132), 478 (477)

Cabezon E, 367 (366)
Cadwell C, 190 (189)
Caffarella R S, 748 (748), 770 (770), 776 (773)
Cai J, 808 (807)
Cain K M, 201 (200), 212 (211)
Cain R Jr., 249 (246)
Cairns B D, 206 (204)
Cairns R B, 7 (3), 206 (204), 238 (234, 236, 237)
Calderhead J, 812 (809)
Caldwell B, 62 (60)
Caldwell B M, 249 (247)
Calfee R C, 41 (34), 657 (652)
Camaioni L, 293 (293), 619
Campbell D T, 615 (612)
Campbell J, 659 (653)
Campbell J P, 759 (758)
Campione J C, 41 (37, 40, 41), 49 (48), 380–81 (377, 378), 422 (419, 420, 421), 436 (434), 487 (484), 524 (521), 530 (527, 529), 558 (558), 637 (637), 657 (652, 653), 802 (800), 808 (806), 816 (814)
Campos J J, 125 (121), (188), 217 (214), 288 (285)
Campos R G, 217 (214)
Candy P C, 748 (743), 763 (760), 770 (770), 776 (773, 775)
Cannon W B, 239 (234)
Capaldi D, 206 (204)
Carbonell J G, 733 (732)
Carey S, 16 (13), 28 (26), 267 (264, 265), 272 (271), 276 (274, 275), 303 (299), 316 (314, 342), 405
Carey W B, (188)
Carine D, 785 (780)
Carli L L, 187 (186)
Carlisle K E, 482 (480)
Carlsen W, 632 (626, 631)
Carlson J S, 816 (815)
Carly L, 580 (577)
Carnin D, 786 (780)
Carnoy M, 24–25 (18, 19, 24)
Carpenter P A, 568 (565)
Carpenter T P, 341 (339), 538 (536)

Carr E G, 530
Carr M, 478 (477), 497 (495), 785 (784)
Carraher D W, 33 (32), 341 (339), 555 (554)
Carraher T N, 341 (339)
Carrell P L, 567–68 (565)
Carretero M, 41, 43 (34), 574 (572)
Carroll J, 198 (197), 333 (329, 330)
Carroll J B, 49 (46), 504 (499, 500), 518 (513), 530 (525), 568 (612), 637–38 (634, 635), 657 (650, 651), 665 (662), 670 (666), 678 (676)
Carroll J M, 715 (714), 720 (719)
Carstensen L L, 168 (166)
Carter D B, 242–43 (241, 242), 601
Carter K R, 280 (278)
Carter-Saltzman L, 174 (173)
Cartwright D, 755 (752)
Case R, 7 (4), 66 (66), 100–01 (99, 100), 120 (117, 118, 119), 217 (214), 267 (264), 303 (298), 657 (651, 653), 724 (723)
Cashdan A, 607
Cason H, 398 (398)
Cass A, 687 (686)
Cassara B, 748 (746)
Casserly P L, 644 (643)
Cassidy J, 130 (126)
Castañeda A, 641 (641)
Castelijns J H M, 816 (814, 816)
Castelli M C, 293 (293)
Castine W H, 704 (702)
Castle J, 748 (747)
Cattell J M, (498)
Cattell R B, 637 (633, 634), (638), 657 (650), 665 (661)
Catterall J, 141 (137)
Cauley K, 293 (290)
Caverni J P, 467
Cazden C B, 619 (618), 622 (621)
Ceci S J, 86 (82, 84, 85), 272 (271), 297 (295), 316 (314, 315)
Celebuski C, 142 (139)
Cermak L S, 402 (400)
Chall J S, 561 (560)
Chalupa L M, 171
Chamot A U, 530 (526, 528, 529)
Champagne A B, 347 (346), 550 (549)
Chan K S, 367 (366)
Chance P, 558 (557)
Chandler K, 402 (400)
Chandler M, 305 (304)
Chandler M J, 72 (69), 125 (121), 316 (316)
Chapelle C, 518 (514)
Chapman M, 101, 209 (207, 208)
Charles R I, 558 (555)
Charlesworth W, 111 (109)
Chase W G, 276 (273), 316 (313), 510 (506)
Chase-Lansdale P L, 248–49 (244, 246)
Chatterton J L, 703 (702)
Chaudron C, 518 (517)
Chen C, 601 (600)
Chen X, 222 (221)
Chene A, 776 (773)
Cheney D L, 338 (335)

Cheng P W, 303 (300, 302), 381 (379)
Cheren M, 763–64 (763)
Chess S, 191 (188, 189), 206 (204)
Cheung K C, 546 (544)
Chi M T H, 28 (26), 41 (35, 36), 66 (64), 267 (265), 272 (271), 276 (273), 297 (295), 316 (314, 315), 347, 347 (346, 346), 361 (360), 381 (378), 405 (405), 418 (411), 510 (506, 507), 524 (522), 555 (554), 733 (731, 732), 785 (780), 808 (805)
Chiang C, 341 (339)
Chickering A W, 764 (762)
Child I L, 17 (9)
Chipman S F, 558 (556), 644–45 (642, 643, 644), 657, 659 (652), 792 (790)
Chipuer H M, 174 (173)
Chiu M-H, 524 (522)
Chomsky N, 16 (9), (375), 408 (406), (538)
Christ E, 471 (469, 470)
Christal R E, 418 (411, 412, 414), 658 (652), 665 (663)
Christie J F, 312 (310)
Christie L, 803 (799)
Chrzastek-Spruch H M, 183 (182)
Chumlea W C, 183–84 (178, 181)
Church R B, 267 (266)
Cillessen A H N, 258 (256)
Civil M, 546 (546)
Claessens A, 183 (182)
Clanchy M T, 430 (429)
Claparède E, 402 (399)
Clark C M, 812 (809, 810)
Clark F L, 786 (781)
Clark J, 184 (179)
Clark K B, 62 (60)
Clark M C, 748 (744)
Clark M P, 62 (60)
Clark R E, 699 (696), 724 (722), 729–30 (725, 726, 728, 729), 759 (755, 757)
Clarke-Stewart K A, 249 (247)
Clausen J A, 86 (84), 163 (161)
Claxton G, 440 (437)
Clay M M, 796 (795)
Cleeremans A, 402 (401)
Clement J, 347 (346), 398 (397)
Clement R, 518 (515)
Clements D H, 487 (484), 715 (714)
Clements M, 542 (538)
Clements S D, 802 (798)
Clumpner J L, 160 (153)
Cobb M V, 665 (660)
Cobb P, 43 (40), 537–38 (535, 536)
Cochran M, 86 (84)
Cochran-Smith M, 580 (579), 699 (697, 698)
Cockburn A, 606 (604), 679 (677), 687 (685)
Cocking R, 542 (538)
Coelho A M, 337
Cohen A D, 530 (526)
Cohen D K, 62 (60)
Cohen E G, 687 (686)
Cohen J, 626 (624)
Cohen L, 288
Cohen M, 712 (711)
Cohen S A, 770 (766)

Cohn D A, 129 (126)
Cohn R, 89 (87)
Coie J D, 222 (221), 258 (256)
Colby A, 227 (225, 227)
Cole M, 28 (26, 28), 49 (45), 347 (343), 487 (484), 538 (536), 596 (591), 622–23 (620), 658 (656), 700 (695, 696)
Coleman E B, 524 (522)
Coleman J S, 198 (197), 607, 607 (602)
Coleman M R, 280 (277)
Coles G, 796 (793)
Coles M G H, 239 (234)
Collard S, 748 (744)
Collins A, 41–42 (35, 37, 40), 49 (48), 276 (274), 321 (319, 320), 326 (324), 333 (332), 381 (380), 487 (484), 497 (495), 550 (550), 558 (558), 596 (595), 691 (688, 689), 720 (719), 724 (723), 808 (806, 807)
Collins M, 748 (743)
Collins R, 748 (744)
Collins W A, 601 (600)
Collis B, 703–04 (702, 703), 712 (709)
Colvin G, 786 (780)
Combs R, 632 (630)
Comenius J A, (362)
Comer J P, 670 (665)
Commons M L, 770 (768)
Compas B E, 626 (624, 625)
Confessore G J, 776–77, 777 (773, 775)
Confessore S J, 776–77 (773, 775)
Conley J J, 222 (220)
Connell P J, 293 (292)
Connell R, (602)
Conners C K, 221 (221), 796 (794)
Connolly K J, 312 (311)
Conroy J, 542
Conte J R, 254 (251)
Converse P E, 755 (753)
Cook L K, 478 (474)
Cook T, 62 (61)
Cook T D, 615 (612)
Cooke N J, 759 (756, 757)
Cooley C H, 198 (194), 232 (229)
Cooley W, 49 (45)
Coombs P H, 24 (19)
Cooper H, 632 (626, 627, 628, 629), 693 (692)
Cooper L, 355 (354)
Coopersmith S, 232 (230, 232)
Copeland A P, 785 (781)
Coppotelli H, 258 (256)
Corder S P, 534 (534)
Corley R, 729 (727)
Cormier S M, 42 (37)
Cornelius S W, 59 (56)
Corno L, 49 (47), 272 (272), 321, 422 (421), 658 (650, 654, 656), 670 (666), 674 (671, 673)
Cornu B, 542 (540)
Corsaro W, 305 (305)
Costa P T Jr, 16 (15), 168 (166)
Cota-Robles E, 141 (137)
Cougan M C, 547 (544, 545)
Coulmas F, 431 (429)
Coulthard M, 542 (539)

Coulthard R M, 619 (618)
Covington M V, 213, 217 (217), 558 (557)
Cowan P A, 254
Cowie H, 687 (685)
Cowles S, 232 (228)
Cox M, 312 (310)
Cox R, 312 (310)
Craik F I M, 316 (315), 321 (319)
Craik G L, 776 (772)
Crandall J A, 530 (529)
Cravioto J, 183 (179)
Crawford R P, 558 (556)
Crenson M A, 62 (59, 61)
Crespo S, 542 (540)
Crissey B L, 62 (59, 61)
Crist P A, 312 (311)
Crockett L, 187 (184, 186)
Crockett W H, 167 (166)
Croll P, 802 (799)
Cromwell R L, 148 (142)
Cronbach L J, 62 (60), 361 (356), 418, 637 (634, 635), 658 (650, 651, 657), 665 (663, 664), 674 (670, 671, 672, 673)
Cronk C E, 183 (181)
Crook J H, 111 (107)
Crookes G, 518 (515, 516, 518)
Crooks T J, 607 (604)
Cross C, 254 (253)
Cross D R, 42 (34), 440 (438), 504 (502)
Cross K P, 752 (749), 770 (764, 767)
Crowhurst M, 580
Crowley K, 59 (59)
Crowley M J, 174 (173)
Cruickshank W M, 802 (798)
Crutcher R J, 16 (10, 13), 272 (271)
Crutchfield R S, 558 (557)
Csikszentmihalyi M, 222 (218), 316 (316)
Cuban L, 33 (31), 398 (398), 730 (729)
Cubberly E P, 33 (30)
Cudeck R, 418
Cuetos F, 568 (566)
Culligan R C, 167 (166)
Cummings E M, 129 (126)
Cummins J, 149 (147), 377 (376), 534 (532), 567 (566)
Cunningham D, 724 (722)
Cunningham W R, 167 (164)
Cutler G B Jr., 135 (132)
Czyzewska M, 402 (401)

Dagleish M, 312 (309)
Dahllöf U, 333 (330)
Daiute C, 584 (583)
Dale P S, 293 (288, 293)
Dallas D, 568 (566)
Damon W, 227 (227), 232 (229), 305 (305), 610–11 (607, 608, 610)
Dance K A, 674 (670)
Daniels D, 174 (172), 249 (246)
Daniels D H, 659 (654)
Dannefer D, 16 (10)
Dansereau D F, 524 (521), 785 (781)
Danzberger J, 141 (140)

Darch C, 785 (780)
Dark V, 280 (278)
Darkenwald G G, 770 (770)
Darlington R, 249 (247, 248)
Darwin C, 7, 111 (107)
Darwin C R, (213)
Das J P, 33 (32)
Dasen P R, 55, 596 (590)
Datan N, 163 (161)
Daurio S P, 280 (279)
Davidson E S, 504 (500)
Davidson R J, 217
Davidson W, 201 (200)
Davies D P, 183 (179)
Davies I K, 497 (494), 741 (736)
Davies L B, 558 (557)
Davies S P, 715 (714)
Davis B, 542 (539)
Davis E, 149 (147)
Davis W E, 141 (137, 139)
Davydov V V, 33 (32), 42 (34), 350 (347), 596 (594), 623
Dawe L, 542 (540)
Dawis R V, 816 (813)
Dawkins R, 111 (107)
Day J D, 435 (432)
Day J E, 504 (502)
Ben-Peretz M, 694 (692)
McLaughlin P, 341 386, 707 (705)
de Bono E, 670 (666)
de Corte E, 42 (34, 35, 37, 39, 40), 49 (46), 321 (319), 326–27 (326), 350 (350), 463 (460, 463), 537, 537 (535, 535, 536, 537), 542, 571 (570, 571), 658 (652), 699, 699–700 (697, 698, 699, 699), 715 (714), 724 (722)
de Francis J, 431 (429)
De Groot A D, 33 (29), 42 (34), 276 (273), 510 (506), 555 (550, 554), 715 (714)
De Groot E V, 327 (326), 422 (422), 590 (588)
De Haas J H, 184 (178)
De Houwer, 402 (400)
De Jong F P C M, 440 (439, 440), 444 (441, 442)
de la Rocha O, 596 (593)
de Leeuw N, 524 (522)
de Ribaupierre A, 59 (56)
de Villiers J G, 129 (127)
de Villiers P A, 129 (127)
De Vries H, 72 (71)
de Vries J I P, 284 (282)
Dearborn W F, 816 (813)
Deaux K, 187 (185)
DeBarsyshe B D, 258 (257)
DeBono E, 558 (557)
Debus R, 212 (212)
DeCasper A J, 124 (123), 177 (175)
DeCharms R, 451 (449)
Deci E L, 451 (450)
Decock B, 451 (449), 659 (654)
DeCruyenaere M, 659 (654)
Dee Lucas D, 478 (474)
DeFleur M, 106 (102)

DeFries J C, 174 (174), 729 (727)
Degler C N, 111 (108)
DeGroot E, 786 (784)
deJong T, 658 (653)
Delacroix J, 24 (20)
DeLeeuw L, 658 (652)
DeLeon P H, 62 (60)
DeLicardie E, 183 (179)
DeLoache J S, 276 (274), 510 (507)
Delpit L, 584 (583)
Delucchi K L, 209 (208)
Demetriou A, 66 (65, 66), 658 (651)
Demick J, 641 (640)
Dempsey J R, 249 (247)
Dempster F N, 297 (294)
Denn J, 249 (246)
Denner P R, 497 (494)
Denney N W, 16 (11)
Deno S L, 149 (144)
Dent H E, 149 (147)
DePaulo B M, 187 (186)
Derryberry D, (188)
Descartes R, (409), (540)
Desforges C, 606 (604), 679 (677), 687 (685)
Deshler D D, 785–86 (781)
Desiraju T, 171
Detterman D K, 42 (37), 637 (637), 658 (652), 665
Devine J, 568
DeVries D L, 355 (352, 354)
Dewey J, 33 (32), (99), (351), (498), 752 (750, 751)
Diamond M C, 171, 796 (795)
Diamond S, 190 (188)
Diaz R M, 471 (468), 785–86 (781)
Diaz S, 596 (594)
Dichtelmiller M, 249 (248)
Dick A, 49 (46)
Dick W, 42 (34), 333 (329)
Dickson P W, 619
Diener C I, 212 (209, 212), 785 (784)
Dienes Z, 402
Dienstbier R A, 262 (261)
Dietterich T G, 733
Digman J M, 16 (14, 15), 190 (190), 222 (219, 220, 221)
Ding B, 561 (560)
DiPaolo M, 467 (465)
DiPardo A, 584 (583)
Diringer D, 430 (428)
Dissanayake E, 577 (576)
Dittmann-Kohli F, 59 (58)
Dixon R A, 7, 163 (162), 167 (167), 316 (316), 436 (434)
Dobzhansky T, 111 (107)
Docherty D, 183 (182)
Dochy F J R C, 42 (38), 418 (411), 463 (459, 460, 462, 463), 658 (651)
Dodge K A, 206 (205), 258 (255, 256)
Dodson J D, 418 (412)
Doehring D G, 796 (793)
Doise W, 100 (100), 611 (609), 622 (621), 687 (685)
Donaldson M, 267 (263), 316 (313)

Donaldson T S, 198 (197)
Doran R L, 649 (646)
Dornbusch S M, 136, 601 (598, 599)
Dorner D, 396 (395), 440 (438)
Dorr A, 729 (727)
Doughty C, 518 (517)
Douglas J W B, 607 (602)
Douvan E, 135 (134)
Dowling C, 704
Downey J E, 190 (188)
Downey M T, 574 (573)
Doyle A B, 312 (311)
Doyle W, 632 (629), 678 (678)
Drake J B, 752 (749)
Dreeben R, 333 (331)
Dreher B, 171
Dreikurs R, 116 (116)
Drews S, 116 (113)
Drillien C M, 86 (83)
Drislane F W, 796 (793)
Driver R, 361 (355, 359), 459 (458), 571 (568, 569), 703 (702)
Dryfoos J G, 135 (134, 135)
Dubas J S, 187 (185)
Dubin F, 568
Dubin S S, 168 (167)
Dubow E, 249 (247)
DuCette J P, 280 (278)
Duckworth E, 120 (117)
Duffy G G, 785 (782, 783)
Duffy T M, 724 (722)
Dugfy H G, 62 (60)
Duguid P, 41 (35, 37), 276 (274), 321 (319), 326 (324), 381 (380), 487 (484), 720 (719)
Duit R, 459, 572 (568, 569)
Dumais S, 288 (286)
Dunbar S B, 504 (504), 808 (806, 807)
Duncan G J, 249 (246)
Duncan J, 249 (244)
Duncker K, 33, 321 (318), 555 (550, 552, 554)
Dunkin M J, 741 (739)
Dunn J, 72 (69), 254 (252), 267 (265), 467 (464), 619 (616)
Dunn L, 76 (74), 160 (158)
Dunne E, 687 (686)
Dupin J J, 347
Duran R P, 149 (148)
Durden W G, 280 (279)
Durkheim E, (195)
Durkin D, 693 (692)
Durkin K, 542 (538)
Durr R, 776 (773)
Duxbury N, 713 (708, 712)
Dweck C S, 16 (14), 42 (36, 38), 201–02 (200), 212 (209, 210, 211, 212), 441 (437), 451 (446, 447), 658 (654), 785 (784)
Dyck J, 715 (714)
d'Ydewalle G, 402 (400)
Dyke W E, 367 (366)
Dyson A H, 160 (159), 584 (581, 582)

Eagly A H, 187 (186)

Eastenson A, 129 (126)
Easton J Q, 367 (366)
Easton P, 24 (19)
Ebbinghaus H, 33 (29), 418 (409)
Eccles J S, 601 (600), 632 (630), 644 (644)
Eckenrode J, 86 (84)
Eckensberger L H, 54–55 (53, 54), 596 (595)
Ecob R, 693 (692, 693)
Edelstein W, 89 (88), 227 (227), 272 (269), 306 (304, 305), 657 (651)
Edmonds R, 670 (666)
Edwards C P, 222, 243 (241, 242)
Eelen P, 402 (400)
Efklides A, 66 (65, 66), 658 (651)
Efland A, 576 (575)
Egan K, 741 (740)
Eggan G, 510 (509)
Ehn B, 141 (138)
Ehri L C, 561 (560)
Eibl-Eibesfeldt I, 54 (52), 111 (109)
Eimas P D, 288 (286)
Eisen M, 130 (127)
Eisenberg N, 209 (207, 208)
Eisenstadt S N, 7 (1)
Eisenstein E, 430 (429)
Eisner E, 577 (576)
Eisner J P, 201–02 (201)
Eklund G, 124 (121)
Ekman P, 54 (52), 217
Ekpenyong L E, 748 (744)
Elardo R, 249 (247)
Elbaz F, 812 (809)
Elder G H, 106 (101), 254 (253)
Elder G H Jr., 86 (84, 85), 135 (131), 163 (161), 262 (259)
El-Dinary P B, 436 (432, 433, 434)
Elen J, 724 (721)
Elias M J, 626 (626)
Eliseo T S, 559 (557)
Elkind D, 120 (117), 135 (132)
Elkonin D B, (81), 125 (121)
Ellerton N, 542 (538)
Elley W B, 584 (584)
Ellingson R J, 177 (175)
Elliot T, 785 (784)
Elliott G, 136
Elliott-Faust D J, 436 (432)
Ellis R, 518 (512)
Ellson D G, 741 (740)
Elmore R, 385 (383)
El-Nofely A A, 183 (181)
Elster A, 135 (133)
Elwood P C, 183 (179)
Emde R, 116 (114)
Emerson H, 632 (629)
Emminghaus W B, 55 (53)
Endler N S, 239 (233), 674 (670)
Engel M, 49 (45), 538 (536), 700 (695, 696)
Engel R, 177 (175)
Engelhart M D, 504 (500)
Engelkamp J, 497 (493)
Engelmann S, 408 (406)
Engestrom Y, 42 (35), 350 (350)
Englert C S, 580 (578), 785 (779)

Enna B, 201 (200)
Enright R D, 227 (227)
Entin E E, 451 (450)
Entwisle D R, 601 (597)
Entwistle A, 42
Entwistle N J, 42 (35), 42 (38), 321 (319), 422 (420), 427 (423, 425, 427), 641 (640, 641), 658–59 (653)
Epstein A E, 248 (247)
Epstein J, 785 (784)
Epstein J L, 86 (84)
Epstein S, 232 (229)
Epstein W, 497 (494)
Eraut M R, 741 (740)
Erdheim M, 116 (114)
Erhrlich K, 715 (714)
Erickson F, 504 (503)
Ericsson A, 510 (509)
Ericsson K A, 16 (10, 13), 272 (271), 393 (393), 427 (426), 436 (435), 487 (484)
Erikson E H, 16 (10), 116 (114), 163 (161), 167 (165), 198 (194), 201 (200), 222 (217), 262 (259)
Erikson F, 321
Erlbaum, 550, (549)
Eron L D, 206 (202)
Ershler J, 312 (311)
Escalona S, 190 (188)
Eskey D E, 568
Essex M J, 168 (166)
Establet R, (602)
Estes W K, 316 (313)
et al., 201 (199, 200)
Ethington C A, 644 (642)
Euclid, (734)
Evans D, 564 (563)
Evans J L, 741 (733)
Evans J S B T, 467
Everett B A, 62 (61)
Everston C M, 657 (656)
Extra G, 377 (377)
Eylon B S, 288 (287), 571–72 (568, 569, 570)
Eysenck H J, 209 (208), 658 (650)
Eysenck M W, 658 (650)

Fabre J M, 467
Fabricus W V, 303 (301)
Fägerlind I, 24 (17, 18, 23)
Fagot B I, 242 (241)
Fairbairn W R D, (114)
Falconer D S, 174 (173)
Fales A W, 770 (767)
Fantz R L, 288 (286)
Faria L, 212 (210)
Farnish A M, 355 (352)
Faro M J, 28 (26)
Farr M, 41 (35, 36), 510 (506), 555 (554), 733 (731)
Farrar M J, 120 (117, 118, 119)
Faure E, 752 (750)
Fauvel J, 542 (540)
Feather N T, 492
Featherman D L, 163 (161), 249 (245)

Federico P A, 50
Feenberg A, 712 (708)
Feil L A, 250 (246)
Feiman-Nemser S, 812 (809)
Fein G G, 249 (247), 312 (306, 308, 310, 311)
Feitelson D, 561 (561)
Feldhusen J F, 280 (278)
Feldlaufer H, 632 (630)
Feldman L B, 568 (567)
Feldman S, 136
Felson R B, 644 (643)
Feltovich P J, 405 (405), 510 (507), 555 (554)
Fennema E, 341 (339), 546 (544), 645 (642, 644)
Fensham P, 571 (569, 571)
Fenson L, 312 (309)
Fenstermacher G D, 812 (812)
Fenton R, 786 (779)
Ferguson C A, 294 (291, 292)
Ferguson D L, 76 (73)
Ferguson G A, 658 (652)
Ferguson P M, 76 (73)
Ferguson-Hessler M G M, 658 (653)
Ferrara R A, 380 (377, 378), 422 (419, 420, 421), 436 (434), 487 (484), 524 (521), 530 (527, 529), 596 (595)
Ferretti R P, 487 (485)
Feshbach S, 206 (204)
Fest T B, 755 (753)
Feuerstein P, (189)
Feuerstein R, 28 (26), 558 (557, 558), 658 (652), 670 (666), 785 (780), 816 (813)
Field L, 748 (743), 776 (775)
Field T M, 249 (247)
Fielding G D, 491 (491)
Fifer W P, 124 (123)
Fikumotos J S, 62 (60)
Filby N N, 679 (676)
Filipp S H, 17 (15)
Fincham F D, 201 (200)
Fischbein E, 537 (535)
Fischer K W, 59 (59), 100 (99), 120 (117, 118, 119, 120), 272 (268)
Fisher C W, 658 (656), 678, 694 (692)
Fisher D L, 683 (682)
Fisher D M, 284 (282)
Fisher R A, 174 (172)
Fisiak J, 534 (533, 534)
Fitts P M, 550 (548)
Fitzgerald J, 699 (697, 698)
Fitzpatrick M A, 254 (252)
Fivush R, 129 (127)
Flammer A, 658 (650)
Flanders N A, 619 (617)
Flavell E R, 129 (127)
Flavell J H, 33 (29, 32), 120 (119), 129 (127), 297 (294, 295), 306 (304), 418 (414), 436 (431, 432), 441 (436, 437), 497 (494), 619, 623, 791 (790)
Flechsig P, 170 (169)
Fleet J, 564 (563)
Fleischmann T, 467 (465)
Fleishman E A, 550 (548)

Fletcher B, 626 (624)
Fletcher-Flinn C M, 699 (696)
Floden R E, 812 (809)
Flood R, 693 (692)
Flores d'Aracais G B, 568 (566)
Florio-Ruane S, 596 (594)
Floud J, 607 (602)
Flower L, 580 (577), 785 (779)
Flower L S, 584 (581)
Flynn J R, 167 (165), 174 (173)
Flynn M A, 184 (179)
Fodor J A, 267 (263, 264), 391 (388)
Fogel A, 217
Fogelman K, 693 (693)
Fokkema S D, 42 (35)
Folkman S, 589 (587), 626 (624)
Fondacaro K, 626 (625)
Fong G T, 381 (379)
Fontaine A M, 212 (210)
Ford D H, 16 (11)
Ford M E, 222 (218, 220)
Fordyce T, 802 (802)
Forman E, 622 (621)
Forrest-Pressley D L, 436 (432)
Forsythe C J, 626 (625)
Fortes M, 596 (591)
Foster P, 24 (23)
Fowler H S, 361 (360)
Fox A A, 796 (794)
Fox N A, 217
Fox R, 288 (286)
Fox S, 312 (311)
Fraleigh M, 601 (598, 599)
Fraser B J, 49 (46), 571–72 (570), 607 (603), 615 (612, 614), 649 (647), 683 (679, 681, 682)
Frederiksen J R, 418, 558 (558), 658 (652), 808 (806, 807)
Frederiksen N, 463 (463), 658 (652, 656)
Fredrick W C, 693–94 (692, 693)
Freedman K, 577 (576)
Freedman S W, 584 (581, 582, 583)
Freeman D, 54 (52), 632 (631)
Freeze D R, 160 (158)
French F E, 250 (248)
French L A, 163 (162), 816 (814, 815)
Frese M, 217
Freud A, 116 (113)
Freud S, 17 (9), (51), 116 (112), 198 (194), 206 (203), 217 (214), 243 (240), 262 (259), 312 (307)
Frey K S, 243 (240)
Friedman S L, 374 (372)
Friedrich H F, 42 (34), 497 (494)
Friedricks A G, 418 (414)
Fries C C, 534 (533)
Frieze I H, 187 (186)
Frijda N H, 33 (29), 42 (34), 371 (371), 555 (553), 589 (585)
Frisch M, 574 (572)
Fröhlich M, 530 (525)
Fromm E, 89 (88)
Frost L A, 645 (642, 644)
Frost R, 568 (567)

Frostig M, 802 (798)
Fry C L Jr, 306 (304)
Frye N, 542 (538)
Fuhrmann A, 471 (470)
Fulcher G, 76 (74, 75), 160 (154, 159)
Fulker D W, 174 (174), 209 (208), 729 (727)
Fuller B, 25 (24), 198 (197), 693 (692)
Fuller D, 227 (225)
Furst E J, 504 (500)
Furstenberg F F Jr., 248–49 (243, 244, 245, 246, 248)
Fuson K C, 341 (339), 478 (474)
Futhke J, 816 (815)
Futterman A, 149 (147)

Gaber D, 785 (783)
Gadow K D, 72 (70)
Gage N L, 321 (320, 321)
Gagné E D, 530 (527, 528, 529)
Gagné R M, 42 (33, 34), 327 (323), 361 (356), 482 (479, 480, 481), 504 (499, 501), (664), 724 (722, 723), 741 (736)
Gaillard A W K, 239 (234)
Galaburda A M, 796 (793)
Galanter E, 396 (394)
Gale J, 43 (37), 459, 538 (536)
Gardner H, 505 (503)
Gale J 1995
Gardner H, 505 (503)
Gale J, 505 (503)
Gallagher J J, 280 (277, 278)
Gallimore R, 607 (603, 604), 785 (783)
Gallini J K, 524 (523)
Gallistel C R, 129 (128), 303 (299)
Galotti K M, 303 (301)
Gal'perin P Y, 333 (332), 350 (349)
Galton F, (108)
Gamson Z F, 752 (751)
Garden R A, 33 (29)
Gardner H, 33 (31), 66–67 (65), 347 (344), 555 (554), 577 (576), 665 (662), 691 (690), 730 (725, 729)
Gardner M K, 724 (723)
Gardner R C, 377 (376), 518 (515)
Gardner R W, 641 (638)
Garet M S, 62 (60)
Garfinkel H, 198 (195)
Garfinkel I, 249 (246)
Garfinkle R J, 720 (720)
Garmezy N, 124 (121), 222 (221), 249 (244), 792 (788)
Garner R, 391 (388), 427 (426), 441 (436, 438, 439), 524 (521)
Garrison D R, 776 (775)
Garrod A, 66 (65)
Garrod S C, 564 (563)
Gartner A, 141 (140), 160 (158), 611 (609)
Garvey C, 312 (310), 619
Gaskins I W, 303 (302), 785 (784)
Gates A I, 478 (471)
Gaul C A, 183 (182)
Gaur A, 430 (428)
Gay J, 596 (591)

Gayeski D M, 482 (482)
Gecas V, 198 (193, 194, 195, 196, 197)
Gehrke N J, 537 (535)
Geis G L, 759 (756)
Gelb I J, 430 (428)
Gelb S A, 149 (147)
Gelles R J, 254 (251)
Gelman R, 129 (128), 276 (275), 303 (298, 299), 347 (341, 342), 658 (652)
Gelman S A, 276 (275), 303 (298)
Genesee F, 530 (529)
Genishi C, 467 (465)
Gentner D, 303 (302), 555 (552), 571 (568, 569, 570)
George L K, 168 (166)
Geppert U, 217 (215)
Gergen K J, 492
Gerofsky S, 542 (539, 540)
Gersten R, 785–86 (780)
Gertzog W A, 459 (458)
Gery G J, 759 (758)
Geschwind N, 796 (794)
Gesell A, 17 (16), 120 (117), 284 (281)
Geuze R H, 72 (71)
Ghatala E S, 436 (434)
Gibb S, 136
Gibbs B, 776 (773)
Gibbs G, 764 (761, 762)
Gibbs J, 491 (490)
Gibbs J C, 227 (225)
Gibson C C, 748 (747)
Gibson E J, 288 (285)
Gibson J J, 284 (281), 454 (453, 454)
Gibson K R Petersen A C, 187 (186)
Gick M L, 487 (485)
Giddings G J, 683 (681)
Gifford B, 785 (784)
Gilbert J K, 505 (502)
Gilhooly K J, 555
Gilligan C, 187 (184, 185), 227 (226), 649 (647)
Gilligan S G, 371 (369)
Gilly M, 303 (301)
Gilmore G, 213 (211)
Gindis B, 33 (32)
Giovenco A, 786 (781)
Girgus J S, 201 (199, 200, 201)
Girotto V, 303 (301)
Glaser R, 28 (26), 41–42 (34, 35, 36, 37), 49–50 (45), 272, 276 (273), 321, 327 (326), 333 (328), 350, 381 (378), 405 (405), 418 (410, 411), 463 (460, 463), 478 (471), 504 (500, 501), 510 (506, 507, 509), 555 (554), 558 (556), 574 (573), (612), 637–38 (635), 657–59 (652, 655, 656), 670 (665, 666), 674 (671, 673), 700 (699), 724 (721), 733 (731), 741 (733, 736), 792 (790), 808 (805, 806, 807)
Glass G V, 459 (458)
Glass L, 796 (794)
Gleitman L R, 561 (560)
Glenberg A M, 497 (494)
Glenn C L, 141 (136, 137)

Gleser C C, 637 (634)
Glick J, 596 (591)
Gliedman J, 76 (74)
Globerson T, 66 (66), 451 (446), 487 (484), 641 (640), 659 (654), 687 (686)
Goddard H H, 149 (147)
Goetz E T, 423, 435 (433)
Goffman E, 198 (194)
Goldberg L R, 190 (190)
Goldin G, 538 (535)
Goldin L, 632 (630)
Goldman S R, 418 (414), 558 (557, 558), 637 (637)
Goldminz E, 361 (356, 360)
Goldsmith H H, 191 (188)
Goldsteen K, 254 (251)
Goldstein I L, 759 (756, 758)
Goldthorpe J H, 607 (602)
Golinkoff R M, 293 (289, 290)
Gomez H, 659 (652)
Goncu A, 312 (309)
Gonzalez M, 467
Good T, 190 (189), 632 (627, 628, 629)
Good T L, 504 (503), 537 (536), 683 (679)
Goodchild F, 564 (563)
Goodenough D R, 641 (638)
Goodenough F L, 129 (125)
Gooding P, 402 (400)
Goodman D R, 100 (100)
Goodman G S, 125 (121)
Goodman K S, 561 (561), 568
Goodman Y M, 796 (796)
Goodnow J J, 398 (397), 601 (600)
Goodson L A, 724 (724)
Goodstein L P, 482 (481)
Goody J, 431 (430)
Gordon A J, 198 (194)
Gordon L C, 293 (290)
Gore S, 86 (84)
Gorman T, 584 (583)
Gormley W T Jr., 62 (61)
Goslin D A, 17 (9), 198 (196)
Goswami U, 303 (302)
Gottfried A W, 249 (247)
Gottlieb G, 177 (174), 239 (237)
Gottlieb J, 160 (158)
Gough H G, 167 (166)
Gough P B, 561 (560)
Gould S J, 111 (108), 149 (147)
Gowin D B, 459 (456, 458)
Gowing M K, 759 (756)
Goy R W, 187 (186)
Grabe W, 568
Graber J A, 135 (131)
Grabowski B L, 463 (460)
Graesser A C, 497 (495, 496)
Graf P, 402 (400)
Graham S, 785–86 (779)
Grandy J, 649 (646)
Gräsel, 759 (757)
Gravatt B, 699 (696)
Graves D, 580
Graves N B, 209 (207)
Graves T D, 209 (207)

Gray E, 542 (541)
Gray J A, (188)
Gray M A, 89 (87)
Gray O P, 183 (179)
Graziani L J, 177 (174, 175)
Green B L, 129 (129)
Green F L, 129 (127)
Green P, 518 (514)
Greenberger M, 62 (59, 61)
Greene D, 213 (211), 398 (397, 398), 451 (450)
Greene T R, 574 (573)
Greenfield P, 596 (590)
Greenleaf C, 584 (582)
Greeno J G, 42 (35), 347 (345), 381 (379), 487 (484, 485, 486), 504 (499), 537 (536), 555 (554), 637 (636), 658 (652)
Greenspan S, 250 (244, 248)
Greer B, 42 (40), 537–38 (535, 535, 537), 699 (697)
Greer D, 312 (311)
Greer S, 249 (246)
Gregory R L, 454 (453)
Grewe W, 167 (166)
Grice P, 542 (539)
Griffin P, 28 (26, 28), 596 (594), 622–23 (620)
Griffin S, 120 (119)
Griffiths R, 518 (514)
Grimm H, 293 (290, 292)
Grinder R E, 33 (30), 280 (277), 504 (498)
Grochelewsky K, 227 (226)
Gromoll E W, 574 (572)
Gross R T, 249 (246)
Grossmann K, 54 (53), 217
Grosz B J, 564 (563)
Grouws D A, 537 (535)
Grow G, 776 (775)
Grubb N, 62 (61)
Gruber H, 42 (35)
Grugeon D, 752 (750)
Gubb J, 584 (583)
Guckenberg T, 487 (484)
Guerney L, 135 (132)
Guesne E, 571 (568, 569)
Guglielmino L M, 776 (772, 775)
Guglielmino P, 776 (773)
Guic-Robles E, 170 (170)
Guilford J P, 555 (551), 658 (650), (661)
Gulgoz S, 524 (523)
Gullo D F, 487 (484), 715 (714)
Gunnarsson L, 86 (84)
Guntrip H, (114)
Guo G, 249 (248)
Guo S, 183–84 (179, 180, 181, 182)
Gurtner J L, 700 (695, 696, 697), 730 (729)
Guskey T R, 367 (362, 363, 364, 366, 367)
Guskin S L, 791 (787, 789)
Gustafsson J-E, 658, 660 (650, 651, 652), 674 (673)
Guterman E, 487 (484)
Guthke J, 816 (814)
Guthrie J T, 530 (527, 528, 529)
Gutierez Lopez F, 183 (182)

Guttman L, 120 (118)
Guynn M J, 402
Guzzetti B J, 459 (458)

Haan N S, 227 (225)
Haas C, 580 (577)
Habicht J-P, 596 (592)
Habicht J P, 183 (182)
Haddad W D, 25 (18, 24)
Haeckel E, 7 (2)
Haenen J P P, 350
Haertel E H, 683 (682)
Haertel G D, 43 (36), 49 (45), 441 (439), 463 (460), 505 (498), 615 (612, 613), 670 (668), 683 (682)
Hafner A, 141 (140)
Hagen J W, 136
Hagestad G O, 163 (161, 162)
Hagman J D, 42 (37)
Hahn A, 141 (140)
Hahn H, 712 (711)
Haiman F S, 755 (754)
Haith M M, 125 (121)
Haken H, 284 (281)
Hakkarainen P, 42 (35), 350
Hakuta K, 81, 377 (376)
Halisch F, 451 (446)
Hall G S, (498, 500)
Hallahan D P, 792 (790)
Hallden O, 574 (572)
Halliday M, 542 (539)
Hallinan M, 659 (656)
Halpern D F, 555 (551)
Halsey A H, 607 (602)
Halverson C F, 17 (15), 190 (190), 243 (240)
Hamann M S, 97 (94)
Hamers J F, 377
Hamers J H M, 816 (813, 814, 815, 816)
Hamill P V V, 184 (180)
Hamilton S F, 141 (140)
Hammill D D, 149 (145), 796 (793)
Hammond D, 764 (761)
Hammond M, 748 (744)
Hanna R, 427 (425), 644 (642, 643)
Hannifin M J, 729 (725, 729)
Hannum W H, 482 (479, 480, 481)
Hansen E, 293 (289)
Hanushek E, 670 (669)
Harasim L M, 712 (708, 709, 710, 711)
Harber C R, 25 (22)
Hare V C, 478 (473, 474)
Harel K, 632 (629)
Hargreaves D H, 76 (74)
Harman D, 431 (430)
Harnack R K, 755 (753)
Harnischfeger A, 333 (330), 374 (374), 504 (500), 679 (676)
Harnishfeger K K, 129 (128)
Harré R, 391 (388)
Harris D, 361 (355, 356, 361), 752 (749)
Harris J, 808 (808)
Harris J A, 337
Harris K R, 530 (527, 528, 529), 785–86 (779, 781)

Harris L J, 694 (692)
Harris P, 303 (299), 305 (305)
Harris R, 431 (428)
Harris T O, 72 (71)
Harris W V, 431 (428)
Hart B, 92 (91)
Hart D, 232 (229), 306 (305)
Hart L E, 546 (543, 544)
Hart R, 712 (708)
Hart S N, 141 (136, 141)
Harter S, 135 (134), 212 (211), 232 (229, 230)
Hartley J, 497 (494), 741 (736, 738)
Hartley W, 355 (354)
Hartman J, 183 (180)
Hartmann H, (114)
Hartshorne H, 491 (491)
Hartup W W, 129 (126), 206 (202), 243 (241), 258 (255, 256), 312 (311), 611 (607)
Haste H, 607 (603), 687 (683)
Hastings J T, 741 (736)
Hatano G, 276 (274), 436 (432), 510 (506, 507), 691 (688)
Hatch E M, 518 (516)
Hativa N, 707 (707)
Hattie J A, 615 (612, 614)
Hau K, 212 (211)
Hauser R M, 249 (245)
Hauser-Cram P, 250 (247)
Havelock E, 431 (428)
Havighurst R J, 163 (162), 222 (219), 262 (259), 770 (767)
Hawkridge D, 703 (703)
Hayashi T, 55 (53)
Hayes C D, 249 (247)
Hayes E R, 770 (765)
Hayes J R, 316 (313), 487 (484), 580 (577), 584 (581), 785 (779)
Hayes S C, 92 (90, 91)
Hayward S, 217 (214)
Haywood H C, 816 (815)
Hazan C, 125 (121)
Head J, (797)
Heath S B, 580 (579), 584 (581, 582)
Heckhausen H, 17 (14), 217 (215), 374 (372), 451 (446), 674 (674)
Heckhausen J, 163 (162)
Hedegaard M, 42 (35), 350
Hegarty S, 160 (151, 153, 156, 159), 816 (815)
Heibert E H, 367 (366)
Hein K, 135
Heisel B E, 436 (433)
Helander M, 715
Helbing N, 243 (241)
Hell P, 802 (799)
Heller A, 491 (489)
Heller K A, 160 (156), 280 (277)
Helmke A, 28 (27, 28), 42 (36), 50, 50 (46, 46), 232 (231), 272 (272), 589–90 (586, 588)
Helson R, 645 (644)
Helwig C C, 66 (65), 306 (305)
Hembree R, 217 (213, 215, 216), 546 (543), 589 (586)

Henderson C R Jr., 86 (84)
Henderson L, 568 (567)
Henson K T, 361 (356, 357)
Herbart J F, (188), (362)
Hernstein R, 149 (147)
Heron A, 596 (590)
Hersh R H, 491 (491)
Hertzig M E, 72 (68)
Hertz-Lazorowitz R, 687 (686)
Hertzog C, 436 (434)
Herzmark G, 312 (309)
Herzog A R, 168 (166)
Herzog J D, 337 (337)
Herzog W, 89 (88)
Hess R D, 198 (197), 601 (597, 599),
    607 (605)
Hesselink J R, 170 (170)
Hessets M S P, 816 (815)
Hetherington E M, 312 (310)
Hetherington M, 254
Hetzer H, 7 (2), 16 (8)
Hewitt J P, 770 (768)
Hewson P W, 459 (458)
Heyman G D, 212 (211)
Hidi S, 580 (578), 658–59 (654)
Hiebert E H, 580 (578), 678 (678)
Hiebert J, 396 (394)
Hiemstra R, 748 (743), 770 (764, 769, 770),
    776–77 (773, 774, 775, 776)
Higgins A, 228 (227), 492 (491)
Higgins E T, 306 (304), 381 (377, 380),
    619 (616)
Hilgard E R, 33 (30), 49 (45), 333 (328),
    418 (409)
Hill B K, 160 (153)
Hill T, 402 (401)
Hill W H, 504 (500)
Hillocks G Jr., 584 (583)
Hillsdale, 505 (503), 550 (549), 645 (642)
Hiltz S R, 712 (708, 709, 710, 711)
Himes J H, 183–84 (180, 181)
Hinde R A, 249 (244), 254, 258 (255),
    619 (616)
Hinnersmann H, 280 (277)
Hinshelwood J, (793, 794)
Hirsh-Pasek K, 293 (289, 290)
Hobbes T, (409)
Hochapfel G, 116 (115)
Hock E, 249 (246)
Hockey G R, 239 (234)
Hodgkinson H L, 141 (138, 139, 140)
Hoemann H W, 288
Hofer M, 467 (465)
Hoff-Ginsberg E, 293 (289)
Hoffman H, 402 (401)
Hoffman M, 28 (26)
Hoffman M B, 558 (557), 785 (780),
    816 (813)
Hoffman M L, 209 (207, 208), 222 (218),
    227 (227), 306 (304)
Hoffman W L, 171 (170)
Hoffmann S, 116 (115)
Holden D J, 435 (432)
Holec H, 764 (762)

Holland J G, 741 (735, 737)
Holland J H, 467, 733 (730, 731)
Hollingsworth L S, (185)
Holloway S D, 198 (197), 601 (597)
Holtzman W H, 160 (156)
Holyoak K J, 303 (300, 302), 467, 487
    (485), 733 (730, 731)
Holzman P S, 641 (638)
Holzman W H, 791 (788)
Homang R T, 657 (652)
Homans G C, 198 (195)
Homme L E, 741 (733)
Honzik M P, 163 (161)
Hooker D, 177 (174, 175)
Hooper S, 729 (725, 729)
Hopp C, 645 (642, 644)
Hörmann H, 497 (492)
Horn J L, 167 (164), 658 (652), 665 (661)
Horne D, 802 (798)
Horowitz F D, 62 (59)
Hosenfeld C, 530 (526)
Houle C O, 776 (772)
Hounsell D J, 42 (38), 659 (653)
Houser J E, 398 (397)
Howe M J A, 316 (313, 314)
Howell C T, 221 (221)
Howell W C, 759 (756, 757)
Howes C, 249–50 (246, 247), 312 (309)
Howley A A, 280 (277)
Howley C B, 280 (277)
Howley E, 601 (599)
Howlin P, 72 (68), 293 (292)
Hoyles C, 699 (699), 703 (702)
Hoyt J D, 418 (414)
Huba G J, 136 (134)
Hubel D H, 124 (121), 170 (170)
Huberman M, 49 (48), 724 (722)
Hudson J A, 129 (127), 436 (432)
Hudson L, 641 (639, 641)
Huesmann L R, 206 (202)
Hughes C, 561 (560)
Huinink J, 163 (162)
Hull C L, (90)
Hulstijn J H, 518 (511, 517)
Hultsch D F, 167 (167), 316 (316)
Human P G, 341 (340)
Hume D, (409)
Hummel-Rossi B, 658 (656)
Hummert M L, 167 (166)
Humphrey G, 33 (31), 555 (553, 554)
Humphrey T, 177 (175)
Humphreys P, 796 (794)
Hunt E, 637 (635)
Hunt E B, 665 (662)
Hunt J M, 239 (234)
Hunt J V, 249 (243)
Hunter B, 712 (708)
Hunter C St J, 431
Hurst P, 217 (214)
Hurtle S C, 715 (714)
Husén T, 141 (141), 607 (602), 670 (666)
Husseul E G A, (195)
Huston A C, 243 (240, 242), 249 (246, 247)
Hutchins E, 347 (343)

Hyde J S, 17 (15), 187 (185), 645 (642,
    644), 649 (646)
Hyltenstam K, 518 (512, 513)
Hyman J S, 770 (766)
Hymes D, 408 (407)
Hynds S, 478 (475)

Iannotti R J, 129 (126)
Ibrahim M A, 693 (691, 693)
Ichilov O, 25 (21)
Idol L, 423
Ilg F L, 17 (16)
Immelmann K, 111 (107)
Inagaki K, 276 (274), 510 (507)
Ingels S, 141 (140)
Inglehart R, 491 (489)
Inhelder B, 81 (81), 100–01 (99), 120
    (118), 267 (264), 303 (298, 300), 396 (395)
Inkeles A, 25 (20)
Iran-Nejad A, 42, 478 (473)
Izard C E, 217 (213, 214, 215)

Jacklin C N, 130 (126), 187 (185, 186),
    206 (202), 243
Jackson C M, 337
Jackson M, 303 (297, 299)
Jackson P W, 813 (809, 810)
Jackson S, 626 (625)
Jacob E, 596–97 (591, 594)
Jacobs J E, 644 (644)
Jacobson B, 124 (121)
Jacobson L, 632 (626, 627)
Jacobson W J, 649 (646)
Jacoby L L, 402 (400)
Jäger A O, 658 (650)
Jahoda G, 55 (53)
Jakobson R, 293 (289)
James W, 33 (30), 232 (228), 374 (372), (498)
Jamison D T, 25 (18)
Janke R, 355 (354)
Jarvis P, 748 (745, 747)
Jarvis P E, 306 (304)
Jay E, 42
Jeffries R, 559 (557)
Jelsma O, 550 (549)
Jencks C, 198 (197), (602)
Jenkins E, 97 (93), 101 (100)
Jenkins J J, 436 (432)
Jenkins J R, 791 (787, 789)
Jenkins W M, 170 (170)
Jennings A, 183 (181)
Jennings K D, 312 (310)
Jensen A R, 149 (147), 408 (406), (661)
Jensen M, 558 (557)
Jensen M R, 658 (652)
Jensen T S, 293 (289)
Jerison H S, 337 (334)
Jernigan T L, 170 (170)
Jessell T M, 170 (169)
Johanssen D H, 463 (460)
Johansson G, 454 (454)
John O P, 190 (190)

Johnson C J, 436 (433)
Johnson D W, 355 (353, 354), 687 (685),
　704 (703), 791 (788)
Johnson J E, 312 (311)
Johnson J L, 149 (147)
Johnson M, 347 (344)
Johnson M B, 665 (661)
Johnson R T, 355 (353), 687 (685), 704
　(703), 791 (788)
Johnson-Laird P N, 33 (32), 267 (263),
　303 (301), 405 (404), 467, 564 (563),
　733 (730)
John-Steiner V, 280, 596 (592)
Johnston F E, 183 (178, 179, 180)
Johsua S, 347
Jolly A, 337 (334, 335, 336)
Jonas H, 89 (88)
Jonassen D H, 482 (479, 480, 481)
Jones B F, 423, 530
Jones B S, 755 (753)
Jones E, 632 (627)
Jones R M, 733 (732)
Jones T C, 402
Joram E, 580
Jordan C, 786 (783)
Jordan R R, 568
Joyce B, 333 (328)
Judy J E, 41 (36), 422 (420), 463 (460)
Jung C G, 163 (161), (638)
Jung H, 171 (169)
Jusczyk P, 288 (286)
Jussim L, 632 (627, 628, 629)
Just M A, 568 (565)

Kaas J H, 337 (334)
Kagan J, 163 (161), 248 (244)
Kagan S L, 62 (61)
Kahle J B, 572 (570), 649 (647), 683 (682)
Kahn A, 62 (61)
Kahneman D, 374 (372)
Kail R V, 97 (93, 95, 96), 638 (636)
Kalmykova Z I, 816 (813)
Kalverboer A F, 72 (69, 70, 71)
Kameenui E J, 785 (780)
Kamradt E M, 720 (719)
Kamradt T F, 720 (719)
Kandel D, 135 (134)
Kanfer F H, 471 (468)
Kanfer R, 374 (373), 418 (410), 658 (654)
Kaniel S, 658 (652)
Kant E, (409)
Kanter R M, 198 (196)
Kantor J R, 92 (90, 91)
Kaplan B, 239 (236)
Kaplan C A, 372 (369)
Kaplan F, 76 (73)
Kaplan N, 130 (126)
Kaput J J, 49 (46), 699 (695, 697, 699)
Karger, 611 (607, 610)
Karmann G, 89 (88)
Karmiloff-Smith A, 66 (66), 267 (266),
　293 (290, 291)
Karweit N, 355 (354)

Kashiwagi K, 198 (197)
Katchadourian H, 135 (131, 132)
Katona G, 33 (31)
Katriel P, 542 (540)
Katz L, 568 (567)
Kauffman J M, 792 (790)
Kaufmann W E, 796 (794)
Kaye T, 712 (709)
Keane M T, 467
Keating D P, 135 (132)
Kebanuv P K, 249 (246)
Kedar-Cabelli S, 733 (732)
Keefe J W, 658 (653)
Keeves J P, 572 (570), 649 (646)
Keil F C, 267 (264, 265), 276 (274), 303
　(299, 302)
Keith D, 201 (201)
Keller E F, 649 (647, 648)
Keller F, 504 (500)
Keller F S, 741 (739)
Keller M, 227 (227), 272 (269), 306
　(304, 305)
Keller R, 733 (732)
Kelley H H, 755 (754)
Kelley T L, (660)
Kelly G A, 459 (456)
Kemmis S, 704 (702)
Kemper H C G, 183 (182)
Kennard M A, 171 (169)
Kennedy E, 206 (204)
Kennedy R E, 187 (185, 186)
Kent R, 183 (181)
Kenyon G M, 17 (11)
Keogh B K, 190 (188, 189), 792 (790),
　802 (800)
Kephart N C, 802 (798)
Kerckhoff A C, 198 (196, 197)
Kerkhoff W, 802 (799)
Kernberg O, 116 (113)
Keursten P, 704 (703)
Khalique C M, 547 (545)
Khisty L, 542 (540)
Kieras D E, 396 (395), 510 (508)
Kieslar E R, 361 (356, 357)
Kiesling H J, 198 (197)
Kifer E, 546 (544, 545, 546)
Kilgore S B, 792 (787)
Killen M, 66 (65), 306 (305), 610 (610)
Kilpatrick J, 510 (509)
Kim H, 367 (366), 712 (708)
Kimball M M, 243 (241), 645 (643)
Kimchee R, 97 (93)
King F J, 704 (702)
King P M, 748 (745), 770 (764)
Kintsch E, 524 (523)
Kintsch W, 510 (508), 524, 524 (519, 522,
　523), 564 (562, 563), 699 (696, 697)
Kintsch W, 524 (523)
Kirchofer J, 530 (526)
Kitayama S, 55 (54)
Kitchener K S, 748 (745), 770 (764)
Klahr D, 97 (93), 267 (263), 391 (388),
　733 (731)
Klauer K C, 333 (329), 491 (491)

Klauer K J, 658 (652)
Klebanov P K, 249 (246)
Klees S, 24 (19)
Klein G S, 641 (638)
Klein R E, 596 (592)
Kleinginna A M, 217 (213)
Kleinginna P R, 217 (213)
Kliegl R, 59 (58), 163 (162), 297 (296, 297)
Klieme E, 645 (642, 643)
Klinteberg B, 239 (234)
Klivington K A, 374 (372)
Kloosterman P, 547 (544, 545)
Klopfer L E, 347 (346)
Knapp M S, 505 (504), 537 (535)
Knight C, 120 (119, 120)
Knopf M, 163 (162), 297 (296)
Knowles M S, 776 (772)
Kobasa S C, 262 (261)
Kobasigawa A, 436 (434)
Koedinger K R, 510 (509)
Koehler M S, 547 (544)
Koeske R D, 785 (780)
Koffka K, (318), (410)
Kogan N, 167 (166), 641 (639, 640)
Kohlberg L A, 17 (14, 15, 16), (53), 120
　(117, 118), 227–28 (225, 226, 227), 243
　(240), 491–92 (489, 491)
Köhler W, (318), (410), 611 (609)
Kohn M L, 163 (161), 198 (196)
Kohnstamm G A, 17 (15), 190 (189, 190)
Kohut H, 116 (114)
Kolb B, 171 (169, 170)
Kolb D A, 752 (750), 771 (764, 766, 767)
Kolstad A, 141 (139)
Koluchova J, 316 (313)
Komatsu L K, 303 (301)
Komoski P K, 707 (707)
Kopp C B, 471 (468, 470)
Korinek L, 791 (789)
Körkel J, 130 (128), 436 (432)
Kornadt H J, 55 (53)
Kornblau B W, (189)
Kornhuber H H, 171 (169)
Korsakoff S, 402 (399)
Kosslyn S M, 405
Kovacs M, 202
Kozma R B, 42 (34), 729 (725, 728, 729)
Kozol J, 142
Kraemer H C, 249 (246)
Kramlinger T, 482 (480)
Krampe R Th, 510 (509)
Krampen G, 167 (166)
Krantz G C, 160 (153)
Krapp A, 659 (654)
Krappmann L, 306 (305), 611 (610)
Krashen S, 530 (525)
Kraska K, 418 (414), 471 (469, 470, 471),
　674 (674)
Krathwohl D R, 504 (500), 720 (719)
Krause G, 184 (179)
Krause R, 116 (114)
Krepelka E J, 558 (557)
Kreppner K, 254
Krewer B, 596 (590)

Krowitz A, 288 (285)
Kruger A C, 611 (610)
Kruidenier B G, 518 (515)
Kucan L, 524 (522)
Kuhara-Kojima K, 436 (432)
Kuhl J, 213 (210), 418 (414), 451 (446), 471 (468, 469, 470), 589 (589), 658 (654), 674 (674)
Kuhn D, 227 (225), 303 (299), 467 (465)
Kulik C L C, 49 (47), 700, 700 (696, 696)
Kulik J A, 49 (47), 367 (362, 366), 700, 700 (696, 696), 707 (705)
Kulikowich J A, 463 (459)
Külpe O, (318)
Kummer R, 391 (389)
Kupfersmid J H, 66 (65)
Küpper L, 530 (526, 529)
Kurita J A, 436 (433)
Kurland D M, 487 (484), 715 (713, 714)
Kyllonen P C, 418 (411, 412, 414), 658 (652, 653), 665 (663, 664)
Kyriacou C, 607 (603)

Laan S, 808 (808)
Laborde C, 542 (539)
Labouvie-Vief G, 167 (164), 316 (316)
Labov W, 408 (407)
Lachman J L, 33
Lachman M E, 168 (166)
Lachman M F, 167 (166)
Lachman R, 33
Laciura J, 530 (526)
LaCrosse I, 17 (15)
Ladd G W, 258
Lado R, 534 (533)
Lajoie S P, 510 (509), 658 (652)
Lakin K L, 160 (153)
Lamb H, 584 (583)
Lamb M E, 312 (311)
Lambert W E, 377 (376)
Lamborn S D, 59 (59), 601 (598)
Lamm Z, 333 (329)
Lamon S J, 645 (642)
Lampert M L, 341 (341), 537 (537), 691 (688)
Lancaster C S, 337 (337)
Lancaster J B, 337 (337)
Landau S, 785 (781)
Landberg I, 294 (289)
Lane H, 33 (29)
Lane S, 808 (807)
Lange G, 436 (435)
Lange K, 288 (287)
Lange P C, 741
Langeheine R, 367 (366)
Langer A, 288 (285)
Langer E J, 487 (485)
Langer J, 17 (16), 227 (225, 226), 580 (579), 584 (582)
Langley P, 97, 391 (388), 733 (731, 732)
Langlois J H, 206 (204)
LaPointe A E, 571 (570), 649 (646)
Lapp D, 168 (167)

Lappan G, 657 (652)
Lapsley D K, 227 (227)
Larkin J H, 478 (474), 510 (507), 555 (554), 733, (731), 786 (780)
Larner M, 86 (84)
Larsen S C, 796 (793)
Larsen-Freeman D, 518 (516)
Larson R, 222 (218), 316 (316)
Larson-Shapiro N, 478 (475)
Larsson K, 124 (121)
Latham G P, 759 (758)
Latour B, 347 (343)
Latukefu S, 25 (22)
Lau L J, 25 (18)
Laupa M, 306
Laursen B, 129 (126)
Lautrey J, 100 (100)
Lauzon A C, 700 (698)
LaVancher C, 524 (522)
Lave J, 42 (35), 337 (337), 347 (343), 487 (484), 555 (554), 596 (592, 593, 595), 691 (689)
Law L C, 42 (35)
Law M, 748 (744)
Lawson A, 361 (358)
Lawson A E, 459 (456, 458)
Lawson M J, 441 (436, 440)
Lawton S C, 435 (432)
Lazar I, 62 (60), 249 (247, 248)
Lazarus R S, 589 (587), 626 (624)
Leavey M B, 355 (352, 354)
LeBlanc P E, 796 (794)
Lecours A R, 177 (174, 175)
Leder G C, 547 (543, 544, 546)
Ledoux N, 626 (624, 625)
Lee D N, 284 (282)
Lee L, 542
Lee M W, 250 (247)
Lee S Y, 601 (598, 600)
Leekam S R, 267 (265)
Leestma R, 607
Lefevre J, 183 (182)
Lefkowitz B, 141 (140)
Leggett E L, 212 (210, 212), 658 (654), 785 (784)
Lehman D R, 381 (379), 467 (466)
Lehr U, 262 (259)
Lehrer R, 487 (484), 715 (713)
Lehtinen E, 497 (495)
Lehtinen L E, 802 (798)
Lehtonen I, 534 (534)
Leibniz G W von, (409)
Leiderman P, 601 (598, 599)
Leigh J E, 796 (793)
Leighten P, 510 (508)
Leinbach M D, 242 (241)
Leinhardt G, 574 (573)
Leiser D, 574
Lempert R O, 467 (466)
Lemyre L, 72 (71)
Lenk C, 712 (712)
Lennenberg E H, 408 (406)
Lens W, 451 (449, 450), 659–60 (654)
Lenz B, 786 (781)

Leonard L B, 293 (292)
Leone C M, 693 (692)
Leontiev A N, 471 (467), 596 (593)
Leontiev W, (347)
Lepper M R, 213 (211), 398 (397, 398), 451 (447, 450), 659 (654), 700 (695, 696, 697), 730 (729)
Lerner D, 25 (20)
Lerner J V, 190 (188)
Lerner M J, 17 (15)
Lerner R M, 7, 16 (11), 135 (130, 131, 132, 133), 190 (188), 254
Lesgold A M, 42 (35), 418 (410), 463 (463), 510 (509), 658 (652, 656), 707 (707)
Lesgold S, 381 (379)
Leshin C, 482 (480)
Leslie A M, 267 (265)
Lester B M, 124 (122)
Leushina A M, 659 (653)
Levelt W J M, 163 (162)
Levesque H J, 733 (730)
Levin H M, 24 (19), 141 (140)
Levin J, 584 (582), 712 (708)
Levin J A, 713 (708)
Levin J R, 436 (432, 433, 434), 524, 524 (523)
Levine D U, 367 (363)
Levine J, 755 (752, 754)
Levine J M, 381 (377, 380)
Levine M D, 786 (779)
Levinson D J, 163 (161)
Levstik L S, 574 (573)
Levy G D, 243 (241)
Levy J, 683 (681)
Levy V M, 227 (227)
Lewicki P, 402 (401)
Lewin K, 86 (83), 239 (236), 683 (679)
Lewis D, 693 (692, 693)
Lewis E G, 534 (531)
Lewis E L, 572 (569), 649 (647)
Lewis G E, 568
Lewis M, 72 (67), 129 (127), 217 (214), 232 (229, 231), 659 (650), 674 (670)
Lewis M W, 381 (378)
Lewis R, 752 (749, 751)
Lewis R B, 149 (142, 145)
Lewy A, 645 (643, 644)
Lezotte L W, 670 (666)
Liaw F R, 249 (248)
Liben L S, 243
Liberman A M, 561 (561)
Liberman I Y, 561 (561)
Lichtenberg J, 116 (114)
Lidz C S, 659 (652), 816 (815)
Lidz D, 637 (637)
Light L L, 297 (296)
Light P, 303 (301), 622 (622)
Liker J D, 254 (253)
Lin Y G, 497 (494)
Lind G, 227 (226)
Lindblom C E, 62 (60)
Lindeman E C L, 748 (745)
Lindvall M, 505 (500)
Linn M C, 17 (15), 187 (185), 303 (299, 302), 571–72 (568, 569, 570, 571), 645

(643), 649 (646, 647), 715 (713, 714), 786 (780)
Linn R L, 504 (504), 558 (558), 808 (806, 807)
Linsker R, 284 (281)
Linton H B, 641 (638)
Lipman M, 786 (780)
Lipsitt L P, 7 (1, 7), 16 (11), 124–25 (121, 122, 123), 163 (161), 262 (259)
Lipsky D K, 141 (140), 160 (158)
Lipson M Y, 422 (420)
Lissitz R W, 813 (811)
Litowitz B E, 786 (781)
Littlefield J, 715 (713)
Littman R A, 206 (204)
Liu M, 808 (807)
Livingstone M S, 796 (793)
Lloreda P, 659 (652)
Lloyd J W, 802 (800)
Lochhead J, 398 (397), 786 (780)
Locke J, (409)
Lockhart R S, 316 (315), 321 (319)
Lockheed M E, 25 (18), 670 (669), 792 (786)
Lodewijks H, 42 (34, 35)
Lodewijks J G L C, 444 (441)
Loeber R, 258 (257)
Loef M, 341 (339)
Loehlin J C, 174 (173)
Lofti A, 25 (20)
Logan D, 510 (509)
Lohaus A, 243 (241)
Lohman D F, 505 (499, 501, 504), 637 (635), 658–59 (651, 652, 653), 665 (662), 674 (674), 771 (766, 767), 808 (805)
Lompscher J, 350 (347), 623
Long H B, 776–77, 777 (774, 775)
Long M H, 377 (375), 518 (513, 516, 517, 518)
Longino H E, 649 (648)
Longobardi E, 293 (293)
Lonner N, 239 (238)
Lorenz K, 112 (109), 206 (203)
Lortie D C, 813 (809, 810)
Love E, 542 (541)
Loveless D, 770 (766)
Low H, 206 (204)
Low P S, 198 (196)
Löwel S, 171
Lowyck J, 482 (480), 724 (721)
Loxterman J A, 524 (523)
Luchins A S, 555 (552)
Luckman, (195)
Lukatela G, 568 (567)
Lummis M, 601 (600)
Lumsdaine A A, 741 (736)
Lumsden C J, 112 (107, 108)
Lundberg L-J, 294 (289)
Lundgren U, 333 (330)
Lunzer E A, 303
Lupart J, 42 (37)
Luria A R, (347), (467), 487 (485), 622 (620), 786 (781)
Luster T, 249 (247)
Luvia A R, (594)

Lykken D T, 272 (271)
Lynch A Q, 764 (762)

McAdoo H P, 601
McAdoo J L, 601
McCall R B, 183 (180)
McCammon R, 184 (181)
McCandless B R, 125 (122)
McCartney K, 250 (243), 601 (599)
McCaslin M, 537 (536)
McCaul E J, 141 (137, 139)
McClelland D C, 55 (52)
McClelland J L, 267–68 (264), 347 (345), 406, 568 (565)
McClintic S, 213 (211)
Maccoby E E, 62 (61), 130 (126), 187 (185), 206 (202), 243, 249 (246), 601 (597)
McCombs B L, 505 (502), 659 (654)
McCord J, 206 (204)
McCormick C G, 436 (433)
McCormick M C, 249 (244)
McCrae R R, 16 (15), 168 (166)
McCready E B, 796 (793)
McCune L, 312 (309)
McCune S K, 776 (775)
McDermott J, 510 (507), 571 (569), 786 (780)
McDermott L C, 572 (569)
McDill E L, 141 (137, 138, 139)
MacDonald K B, 112 (108)
McDonough D, 288 (287)
McDougall A, 704
McEwen B S, 187 (186)
McGee M G, 638 (635)
McGill I, 752 (750)
McGill-Franzen A, 786 (784)
McGilly K, 637 (637)
McGoldrick J A, 436 (433)
McGraw M B, 124 (122), 284 (281)
McGroarty M, 530 (526)
McGue M, 174 (173), 272 (271)
McGuinness P J, 645 (644)
McGuire W T, (490)
McHugh E L, 81 (78)
McHugh M C, 187 (186)
MacIver D J, 130 (129), 213, 659 (654)
McKay A, 659 (652)
McKay H, 659 (652)
Mackay R, 568
McKeachie W J, 42 (34), 497 (494)
McKeithen K B, 715 (714)
McKeough A, 42 (37)
McKeown M G, 524 (522, 523), 574 (572)
McKey R H, 249 (248)
McKusick V A, 174 (172)
McLanahan S, 249 (246)
McLaren J, 580 (578)
McLaughlin B, 377, 518 (517), 530 (528), 568 (566)
McLaughlin J P, 510 (508)
McLean R S, 580, 700 (697, 699)
McLeod A, 584 (582)
McLeod B, 530 (528), 568 (566)

McLeod D A, 547 (543, 544, 545, 546)
McLeod D B, 537 (535), 547, 590 (585, 587)
McLoughlin J A, 149 (142, 145)
McLoyd V, 249 (246, 247)
McLuhan M, 431 (428)
McNamara D S, 524 (523)
McNemar Q, 638 (634)
McNutt G, 796 (793)
McRobbie C J, 683 (681)
Madaus G F, 741 (736)
Madden N A, 142 (140), 355 (352, 354)
Maehr M L, 213 (211), 649 (646), 786 (784)
Mager R F, 505 (501), 741 (735)
Magnusson D, 17 (11), 72 (69), 136 (131, 134), 239 (233, 234, 235, 236, 237, 238), 674 (670)
Magone M, 808 (807)
Mahapatra M, 306 (305)
Mahler M, 116 (113)
Maier S F, 201 (199)
Main M, 111 (107), 130 (126)
Major-Kingsley S, 802 (800)
Makrakis V, 700 (695)
Malatesta C Z, 217 (213, 214, 215)
Malcarne V L, 626 (625)
Malina R M, 183 (182)
Malinowski B, 55 (51), 81 (79)
Malmi R A, 665 (663)
Malone T W, 451 (447)
Maltby G P, 149 (147, 148)
Mandl H, 42 (34, 35), 418 (410), 497 (494, 495), 524 (521), 571 (570, 571), 700 (699), 715, 759 (757)
Mandler G, 33 (31), 547 (545), 555 (553, 554), 589 (585)
Mandler J M, 33 (31), 267 (266), 555 (553, 554)
Mane S, 106 (102)
Mangiola L, 584 (582)
Mannes S M, 524 (519)
Mannheim K, 198 (194)
Manning B H, 505 (503)
Mansfield R S, 558 (557)
Maqsud M, 547 (545)
Mariage T V, 785 (779)
Marini A, 42 (37)
Marja T, 748 (745)
Marjoribanks K, 601 (597)
Mark M M, 62 (60)
Markle S M, 741 (737, 738)
Markman E M, 293 (289), 303 (301), 601
Markova A K, 623
Markovits H, 303 (301)
Marks I M, 217 (215)
Markus H R, 55 (54), 232 (231), 632 (627)
Markus R L, 168 (166)
Marland S P, (277)
Marler P, 338 (335)
Marliave R, 679 (676)
Marris P, 217 (214)
Marsh H W, 232 (231)
Marshalek B, 665 (663)
Marshall H, 232 (231), 632 (629)
Marshall H H, 327

Marshall S P, 530 (527), 644–45 (642, 643)
Marshall W A, 135 (131, 132)
Marsick V J, 764 (763), 771 (769)
Martin B, 206 (204)
Martin B L, 720 (719)
Martin C L, 243 (240, 241, 242)
Martin D, 703 (703)
Martin F M, 607 (602)
Martin J A, 249 (246)
Martin N, 584 (582)
Martin R P, 17 (15), 190–91 (188, 189, 190)
Martindale C J, 752 (749)
Marton F, 42 (35, 38), 321 (319), 422 (420),
    459 (456, 457), 497 (493), 641 (640),
    659 (653)
Martorell R, 183 (182)
Maruyama G, 791 (788)
Marx K, (196)
Marx R W, 42 (35, 36), 478 (476)
Masia B B, 720 (719)
Maslow A H, 89 (87)
Mason D, 632 (630)
Mason R, 712 (708, 709, 711)
Massad C E, 568
Masten A S, 792 (788)
Matarazzo J D, 168 (164)
Matsuzawa T, 337 (335)
Mattson A, 206 (204)
Maughan B, 670 (666)
Maxwell S E, 637 (635)
May M A, 491 (491)
Mayberry W, 312 (311)
Mayer K-U, 163 (162)
Mayer R E, 33 (29, 31), 321 (319), 398
    (396, 397, 398), 422 (420), 478 (474, 475),
    524, 524 (521, 523, 523), 530 (525, 527),
    555 (550, 552, 553, 554), 558–59 (556),
    659 (652), 715 (713, 714)
Mayes A R, 402 (400)
Mayr E, 112 (107)
Mead G H, 198 (194), 306 (304), 347 (343),
    381 (380), (603)
Mead M, 55 (52), 198 (194)
Mead N A, 571 (570), 649 (646)
Means B, 505 (504)
Means M L, 467 (465), 574 (573)
Medin D L, 405–06 (403)
Medlex, (679)
Meeks S, 168 (166)
Mehan H, 408 (408), 713 (708)
Mehler B, 149 (147)
Meichenbaum D, 471 (468), 786 (781)
Meijer A, 171 (170)
Meijer C J W, 160 (154)
Meili R, 659 (650)
Meisels S J, 249 (248)
Melton A W, (664)
Meltzer L J, 786 (779)
Meltzoff A, 124 (122)
Menyuk P, 293 (289, 290, 291)
Mercer J, 792 (789)
Merenheimo J, 280 (278)
Mergendoller J, 679 (678)
Merriam S B, 748 (748), 770 (770), 776 (773)

Merrill M D, 321, 482 (480)
Merrill P F, 482 (480)
Merzenich M M, 170 (170)
Messer S B, 418 (412)
Messick S, 160 (156), 641 (639, 640),
    808 (807)
Mestre J, 542 (538)
Met M, 530 (529)
Mevarech Z R, 367 (365, 366)
Meyer D K, 427 (425)
Meyer J W, 25 (22), 163 (162)
Meyer L, 160 (154, 157)
Meyer M R, 547 (544)
Meyer R, 120 (117)
Meyer-Probst B, 239 (234)
Meyers E D Jr, 183 (180)
Mezirow J, 748 (744), 764 (760)
Midgley C, 632 (630), 786 (784)
Miles M, 160 (154, 158)
Mill J S, (409)
Millen, (679)
Miller G E, 436 (432)
Miller A, 116 (115)
Miller C A, 467 (464, 465, 466)
Miller G A, 267 (263), 371 (370), 396 (394)
Miller G E, 786 (781)
Miller J G, 306 (305)
Miller J P, 491 (491)
Miller M, 467 (464)
Miller P, 232 (228)
Miller P A, 209 (208)
Miller P H, 130 (128), 441 (438)
Miller R, 28 (26), 785 (780)
Miller S, 601 (600)
Miller S M, 72 (67)
Mills C J, 280 (279)
Minden G von, 116 (113)
Mines R A, 771 (764)
Minick N, 597 (593)
Minkowski M, 177 (175)
Minton H L, 149 (147, 148)
Minuchin P P, 222 (221), 243 (242)
Mirowsky J, 254 (251)
Mischel H N, 471 (468), 492 (489)
Mischel W, 243 (240), 471 (468), 492 (489)
Misiak H, 89 (86)
Mislevy R J, 808 (808)
Mitchell B G, 280 (277, 279)
Mitchell D C, 568 (566)
Mitchell T M, 733 (732)
Mmari D, 542 (540, 541)
Mocker D W, 777 (772, 775)
Modell J, 86 (84)
Modgil C, 492
Modgil S, 492
Modra H, 748 (747)
Moffett J, 584 (580, 581)
Mogilner A, 171 (170)
Mohan B A, 519 (512, 517), 530 (529)
Molenaar P, 121 (119, 120)
Moll L S, 596 (594), 623
Monk D H, 693 (691, 693)
Mönks F J, 280 (278)
Montada L, 17 (15)

Montague W E, 50
Monteiro K P, 371 (369)
Montemayor R, 130 (127)
Montepare J M, 168 (166)
Montessori M, (188), (279)
Montgomery D, 802 (799, 800)
Mook D A, 49 (44)
Moonen J, 704 (703), 707 (705)
Moore B, 209 (208)
Moore G A B, 700 (698)
Moore J L, 381 (379), 487 (484, 485, 486)
Moore M K, 124 (122), 288 (285)
Moos R H, 683 (679, 680, 681)
Moran L, 776 (773)
Moreland R, 755 (752, 754)
Morgan J L, 293 (291)
Morgan M, 106 (102)
Morgan P, 249 (244, 245)
Moroney R M, 62 (61)
Morrison G R, 729 (725, 729)
Morrison H C, 679 (676)
Mortimore P, 670 (666), 693 (692, 693)
Moses D, 802 (799)
Moshman D, 303 (301)
Mossenson L, 808 (808)
Mott F L, 249 (246)
Motulsky A G, 174 (172)
Mounts N, 601 (598)
Mourell M P, 198 (196)
M'Timkulu D, 81 (78)
Mugny A, 622 (621)
Mugny G, 100 (100), 611 (609), 687 (685)
Mukherjee D, 183–84 (180, 181)
Mulopo M M, 361 (360)
Mulryan C, 537 (536)
Mumford A, 764 (763)
Mumme D L Chabay R W, 659 (654)
Munn P, 467 (464)
Munroe R L, 55, 243 (240)
Murphy G L, 405 (403)
Murphy J T, 141 (136, 137, 138)
Murray F B, 610 (609)
Murray H A, 239 (236), 683 (679)
Murray H T, 741 (740)
Murray J C, 341 (340)
Murtaugh M, 596 (593)
Murthy K D, 171
Musgrave P W, 198 (193, 194, 195, 197, 198)
Musselwhite E, 776 (773)
Mussen P H, 209 (207, 208), 601
Myers M, 441 (438)

Nagasaka T, 347 (346)
Nagel R, 190 (189)
Nagel S S, 62 (61)
Naiman N, 530 (525)
Naito M, 130 (128)
Nakamura G V, 436 (433)
Naso B, 796 (794)
Nathan J A, 25 (21, 22)
National Assessment of Educational
    Progress (NAEP), 649 (646, 647)
National Education Association, 741 (736)

Natriello G, 141 (137, 138, 139)
Neal C J, 471 (468)
Neale M C, 209 (208)
Neches R, 97, 391 (388), 733 (731)
Needham J, 431 (428)
Neill A S, 89 (88)
Neisser U, 33 (30, 32), 347 (342), 497 (493)
Nelson K, 436 (432)
Nelson R R, 62 (61)
Nelson S, 201 (200)
Nenniger P, 659 (654)
Nerlove S B, 596 (592)
Nesher P, 538 (535), 542 (540)
Nesselroade J R, 59 (55, 56, 57, 58)
Neufeld R W J, 674 (670)
Neugarten B L, 163 (161, 162)
New D A, 141 (136, 137)
Newcomb A F, 258 (256)
Newcomb T M, 755 (753)
Newell A, 33 (32), 42 (36), 97 (93), 478 (472), 555 (550, 552), (662), 733 (730, 731)
Newman D, 28 (26, 28), 596 (594), 622 (620), 720 (717)
Newman R, 632 (630)
Newman S, 333 (332), 691 (689)
Newman S E, 42 (35, 40), 321, 497 (495), 550 (550), 596 (595), 724 (723)
Nias D K B, 209 (208)
Nicholls J G, 201 (200), 213 (210, 211), 441 (437), 590 (587, 588), 786 (784)
Nichols R C, 174 (173)
Nickerson R S, 559 (558), 659 (652), 715 (713), 786 (780)
Nie H, 561 (560)
Niemiec R P, 49 (45), 704 (702)
Nikhilananda S, 81 (78)
Nirje B, 76 (74)
Nisan M, 227 (227)
Nisbett R E, 213 (211), 303 (302), 381 (379), 398 (397), 467 (466), 733 (730, 731)
Noam G, 89 (88)
Nolen S B, 786 (784)
Nolen-Hoeksema S, 201 (199, 200, 201)
Nordstrom G Z, 577 (575)
Norman D A, 405 (405), 478 (477)
Northfield J R, 459 (458)
Noss R, 699 (699), 703 (702)
Novak J, 459 (456, 458), 741 (740)
Nugent J K, 124 (122)
Nunes T, 33 (32), 537 (536)
Nunner-Winkler G, 89 (88), 227–28 (226)
Nuthall G, 327 (326), 333 (328)
Nuttin J, 451 (450), 660 (654)
Nyberg K, 124 (121)
Nyhan B, 759 (757)
Nystrand M, 580 (578)

Oakhill J, 303 (301)
Obiakor F E, 149 (147, 148)
O'Brien D P, 303 (298, 301)
O'Brien M, 62 (59)
Ochs M T, 170 (170)
Ochse R, 393

O'Connor M, 785 (784)
Oden M H, 645 (644)
O'Donnell J M, 770 (770), 776 (773)
Offer D, 135 (131, 133)
Offermann L R, 759 (756)
Offord K P, 167 (166)
Ogbu J U, 149 (147), 408 (408)
Ogbue R M, 149 (147, 148)
Ogle D S, 530
Ohlsson S, 396 (394, 395), 659 (653)
Ohman A, 72 (69), 239 (235)
Oishi S, 355 (354)
Oke E, 786 (782)
Okun M A, 168 (166)
Oldham E E, 645 (644)
O'Leary D D M, 171 (169)
Oliner P M, 209 (208)
Oliner S P, 209 (208)
Olivarez A, 802 (802)
Oliver L M, 303 (302)
Olivier A I, 341 (340)
Olofsson B, 239 (238)
O'Loughlin M, 303 (299)
Olsen S E, 482 (481)
Olson D R, 303 (299), 431 (429)
Olson J, 704 (703)
Olton R M, 558 (557)
Olver R, 596 (590)
Olweus D, 206 (202, 204, 205), 222 (220), 258 (254, 255, 257)
O'Malley J M, 530 (526, 528, 529)
Omanson S F, 659 (652)
Omori-Gordon L, 802 (800)
Ong W, 431 (428)
Openshaw D, 741 (736)
Opwis K, 733
O'Reilly K, 574 (573)
Ornstein P A, 7 (4), 297 (296), 435 (432)
Orr E, 542 (540)
Orsburn J D, 776 (773)
Orsolini M, 467 (465), 619 (618)
Ortony A, 303, 406, 478 (475)
Osawa K, 510 (506)
Osborn A E, 559 (556)
Osborn M, 607 (605, 606)
Osborne D, 167 (166)
Osborne R J, 505 (502)
Oscanyan F S, 786 (780)
Oser F K, 228 (227), 492 (490)
Osherson D N, 303 (301), 555 (554), 733
Osofsky J D, 125, 249 (246)
Osser H, 408 (406)
Ostendorf F, 190 (190)
Oswalt W H, 81 (79)
Otten R, 590 (588)
Ouston J, 670 (666)
Overbeek B, 72 (71)
Overmier J B, 201 (199)
Overton W F, 17 (10), 135 (132), 303 (300, 302)
Owings J A, 141 (140)
Oxford R L, 530 (526, 529)
Oyserman D, 632 (627)

Padilla K A, 786 (781)
Padron Y N, 530 (526)
Paget K, 190 (189)
Paikoff R L, 59 (55)
Paine N, 771 (769)
Paivio A U, 436 (433)
Palincsar A M, 497 (495), 564 (563)
Palincsar A S, 293 (293), 441 (440), 478 (477), 530 (527, 528, 529), 596 (595), 687 (684), 691 (690), 785–86 (782), 792 (789, 790), 808 (805)
Pallak M S, 62 (60)
Pallas A M, 141 (137, 138, 139)
Palmer D J, 802 (802)
Palmer D R, 427 (425)
Palmer J L, 249 (247)
Palmer S E, 97 (93)
Palti H, 171 (170)
Pankowski M L, 755 (754)
Papert S, 700 (697, 698), 704 (703)
Papousek H, 124 (122), 293 (291)
Papoušek M, 293 (291)
Parekh A J, 796 (794)
Parham I A, 168 (166)
Paris S G, 422 (420), 440–41 (438), 478 (477), 504 (502), 530 (528), 786 (782)
Pařízková J, 183 (181)
Parke R D, 7 (4), 86 (84), 206 (202, 204, 205), 601 (597)
Parker J G, 258 (254)
Parker S, 249 (246)
Parkes C M, 217 (214)
Parmentier R, 42 (34, 35)
Parry T S, 519 (512, 517)
Parseghian P E, 418 (414)
Parsons J E, 619 (616)
Parsons M J, 577 (576)
Parsons T, (195)
Paschal R A, 615 (612)
Pascual-Leone J, 100 (99, 100), 267 (264)
Pask G, 641 (640, 641), 659 (653)
Passeron J C, 198 (197)
Patching W, 786 (780)
Paterson D G, 337
Patry J L, 49 (46)
Pattee L, 258 (255, 256)
Patterson C H, 89 (87)
Patterson G R, 206 (204, 205), 258 (257)
Paul A A, 184 (179)
Paul B, 136
Paul C, 294 (290, 292)
Pavlov I P, (90), (188), (317)
Pea R D, 487 (484), 704 (703), 715 (713, 714)
Pea R W, 381 (380)
Peal E, 377 (376)
Pearl A, 649 (647)
Pearson P D, 564, 786 (784)
Peck C, 160 (154, 157)
Pedersen F A, 249 (246)
Pedler M, 759 (756)
Pédron G, 184 (179)
Pekrun R, 217 (214, 216), 232 (231)
Pelgrum W J, 700 (695), 704 (703), 715 (713)
Pellegrini D, 168 (166), 250 (247)

Pellegrino J W, 42 (35), 418 (414), 637–38 (635, 636, 637)
Pence A R, 86 (84)
Pendarvis E D, 280 (277)
Pepler D J, 206 (205), 258, 312 (309)
Perelman L J, 720 (718)
Perfetti C A, 561 (559, 560), 568, 638 (635), 659 (652)
Periera M E, 337 (335)
Perkins D N, 42 (35, 36, 37), 444 (443), 459 (457), 467 (464, 465), 478 (471, 474, 477), 487 (484, 485, 486), 505 (502), 538 (536), 659 (652), 715 (713, 714), 720 (719), 786 (780)
Perlmutter M, 297 (295)
Perls F S, 89 (87)
Perner J, 130 (128), 267 (265, 267), 306 (304)
Perret J F, 619 (617)
Perret-Clermont A N, 100 (100), 611 (607, 610), 619 (616, 617, 618), 622 (621), 687 (685)
Perrez M, 626 (623)
Perruchet P, 402 (401)
Perry D G, 206 (202, 204, 205)
Perry J D, 724 (722)
Perry L C, 206 (204, 205)
Peruniak G S, 752 (750)
Pervin L A, 239 (233), 659 (650), 674 (670)
Pestalozzi J H, (362)
Petersen A C, 135–36 (130, 131), 187 (184, 185, 186), 645 (643)
Peterson C, 201 (199)
Peterson D A, 771 (765, 768)
Peterson D L, 791 (787, 789)
Peterson D R, 239 (236)
Peterson J, 632 (630)
Peterson P, 659 (656)
Peterson P L, 341 (339), 546 (544), 812 (809, 810)
Peterson R W, 374 (372)
Petrinovich L, 111 (107)
Pettigrew T, 62 (59, 60)
Pettito L A, 338 (335)
Peverly S T, 427 (425)
Pfaffmann C, 124 (123)
Pfundt H, 572 (568, 569)
Phares V, 626 (624, 625)
Phelps E, 611 (608, 610)
Phelps R, 712 (711)
Philippi D L, 81 (77)
Philips S, 408 (407)
Phillips D, 250 (246)
Phillips D H, 249 (246)
Phillips E, 542 (540)
Phillips G W, 571 (570), 649 (646)
Phillipson R, 534 (532)
Piaget J, 7 (5), 17 (9, 10, 13, 14), 28 (25), 42 (34), (53), 81 (81), 100–01 (97, 98, 99), 120 (117, 118, 119), 124 (122, 124), 130 (127), (185), 198 (194), 228 (224), 267 (264, 265), (269), (275), 284 (281, 283), (291), 303 (298, 300), (304), 312 (307), 321 (318), 381 (377), 396 (395), (405), 418 (410), 505 (500), 611 (607),

619 (618), 622–23 (620), (685), (767)
Pica T, 518 (511)
Pichert J W, 435 (433)
Pickles A, 239 (235, 237)
Pienemann M, 518 (512)
Piercy F P, 254 (253)
Pigott T D, 367 (362, 366)
Pijl S J, 160 (154)
Pikowsky B, 467 (465)
Pimm D, 542, 542 (538, 539, 541)
Pincus J, 198 (197)
Pine F, 116 (113)
Pine J, 558 (557, 558)
Pinker S, 561 (559)
Pintrich P R, 42 (34, 35, 36), 327 (326), 422 (421, 422), 427 (423), 497 (494), 590 (588), 786 (784)
Piolat A, 700 (698)
Pious C G, 791 (787, 789)
Pipp S, 120 (118)
Pirie S, 542 (538)
Piskurich G M, 776 (773)
Pizzamiglio L, 641 (640)
Platsidou M, 66 (65)
Plomin R, 17 (12), 174 (171, 172, 173, 174), 190 (188), 206 (204), 238 (234), 249 (246), 254 (251), 272 (271), 729 (727)
Plomp T, 700 (695), 704 (703), 707 (705), 715 (713)
Plötzner R, 733 (732)
Plumer D, 408 (407)
Podeschi R, 748 (746)
Polanyi M, 396 (394), 478 (473)
Politzer R L, 530 (526)
Pollack M, 649 (647)
Pollock J, 482 (480)
Polson P, 559 (557)
Polya G, 555 (550)
Pons M M, 530 (528)
Pontecorvo C, 467 (465), 574 (573), 619 (618)
Poortinga Y H, 55
Pope M, 41 (34)
Porges S W, 72 (70)
Porter A, 632 (631), 693 (692)
Posner G J, 459 (458)
Posner M I, 372 (369), 374 (372), 550 (548)
Post T A, 510 (508)
Postlethwait S N, 741 (740)
Postlethwaite T N, 198 (196), 649 (646), 693 (692)
Potts M, 785 (781)
Power F C, 228 (227), 492 (491)
Pozo J I, 41 (34), 574 (572)
Prader A, 183 (181, 182), 338 (336)
Pratt D D, 748 (746)
Prawat R S, 28 (27), 478 (474)
Prawatt R, 444 (443)
Prechtl H F R, 72 (71), 284 (282)
Prenzel M, 759 (757)
Presley R, 191 (189)
Pressley M, 42 (36), 297 (294, 295, 296), 398 (397), 422 (420), 436 (432, 433, 434), 530 (527, 528, 529), 564 (563)

Preston D R, 518 (511)
Pribram K H, 396 (394)
Price E, 584 (583)
Priest R F, 202 (199)
Prior M R, 171 (170)
Pritzel M, 171 (169)
Psacharopoulos G, 25 (18, 19, 23, 24)
Pullis M E, 190 (189)
Purkey S C, 670 (666)
Purves A C, 670 (669)
Pylyshyn Z W, 267 (264)
Pythagoras, (734)

Quay H C, 221 (221)
Quinn C N, 713 (708)
Quintanilla S A R, 770
Quitmann H, 89 (87, 88)

Radford J, 280
Radke-Yarrow M, 209 (207, 208)
Raghavan K, 574 (573)
Ragin C, 24 (20)
Ramey C T, 249 (248), 250 (247)
Ramírez M, 641 (641)
Rampaul W, 160 (158)
Ramsey E, 258 (257)
Rand P, 451 (449), 659 (654)
Rand Y, 28 (26), 558 (557), 658 (652), 785 (780), 816 (813)
Raphael T M, 785 (779)
Rasch M, 385 (384), 391 (387), 725 (722)
Ratzeberu F H, 802 (798)
Rauch J M, 136 (134)
Raven B H, (661)
Raven J, 607 (606)
Ravid G, 776 (775)
Raynor J O, 451 (450)
Razel M, 288 (287)
Read C, 561 (560)
Reading, 482 (480), 519 (512, 517), 584 (583)
Reber A S, 268 (266), 402 (401)
Recchia S, 213 (211)
Record R, (540)
Redding T R, 777
Reed E S, 284 (283)
Reed H J, 596 (592)
Reed S, 141 (138)
Reed W M, 391 (390)
Rees E, 276 (273), 396 (394, 395), 418 (411)
Rees E T, 66 (64)
Rees J, 72 (69)
Reese H W, 7 (1, 7), 16–17 (10, 11), 59 (55, 56, 57, 58), 106 (106), 163 (161), 262 (259)
Reeve R A, 487 (484)
Regel O, 25 (18, 24)
Reich L, 596 (590)
Reich R B, 720 (718)
Reicherts M, 626 (623)
Reid H P, 802 (800)
Reigeluth C M, 482, 482 (480, 480, 482), 497 (493), 720 (717, 718, 719, 720), 724 (721)

Reil M, 584 (582)
Reimann P, 381 (378)
Reinhart, 361 (356, 357)
Reinisch J M, 206 (204)
Reiser B J, 691 (690), 699 (697)
Reitman J S, 715 (714)
Remy R C, 25 (21, 22)
Rende R, 254 (251)
Renkl A, 42 (35)
Renner G, 167 (166), 262 (261)
Renner J, 361 (358)
Renner J W, 459 (456, 458)
Renninger K A, 659 (654)
Renou L, 81 (77)
Renshaw P D, 258 (255)
Renshon S A, 25 (21)
Renson R, 183 (182)
Rentiers K A, 786 (781)
Repucci N D, 201 (200)
Reschly D J, 792 (787, 789)
Resnick D F, 505 (504)
Resnick L B, 28, 33 (30), 42 (34), 100 (100), 327 (322), 347, 347 (345, 346), 350 (350), 381 (377, 379, 380), 467, 505 (504), 524, 659 (652), 691 (687, 691), 724 (723)
Rest J R, 228 (227)
Reuchlin M, 101 (99)
Revelle W, 418 (412)
Reyes L H, 547 (543, 544)
Reyna R F, 510 (506)
Reynolds A J, 693 (693)
Reynolds M C, 142 (140), 160 (153, 154, 155, 159), 792 (788)
Reynolds R E, 435 (433)
Rheingold H L, 125 (123)
Ricciuti H, 62 (60)
Richards F A, 770 (768)
Richards M H, 693 (692)
Richardson-Klavehn A, 402
Richter J, 250 (247)
Rickards J P, 497 (494)
Ricks D, 17 (15)
Ridge B, 205 (204)
Ridley-Johnson R, 284 (282)
Rieben L, 561 (560)
Riel M, 700 (698), 712–13 (708, 711, 712)
Riesbeck C, 327
Rieser J J, 7 (4)
Riessman F, 611 (609)
Riley D, 86 (84)
Riley E P, 177 (176)
Riley M W, 163 (161)
Rinaldi R, 25 (18, 24)
Rippa S A, 559 (556)
Rips L R, 405 (403)
Riskin E, 649 (647)
Risley T R 1, 92 (91)
Ritmeester J W, 183 (182)
Ritter P, 601 (598, 599)
Rivest L P, 312 (311)
Robbins S P, 198 (196)
Roberts D, 601 (598, 599)

Roberts J, 184 (180)
Roberts J M, 596 (592)
Robinson N M, 160 (158)
Robinson W P, 619, 792 (788)
Robitaille D F, 33 (29), 546 (544, 545, 546)
Roblyer M D, 704 (702)
Roche A F, 183–84 (178, 179, 180, 181, 182)
Rock D, 644 (643)
Rock I, 454 (453)
Rodin J, 168 (166)
Roede M J, 184 (182)
Roediger H L III, 402, 402 (400)
Roehler L R, 785 (783)
Rogers C C, 142 (139)
Rogers C R, 89 (87)
Rogers E M, 106 (103)
Rogoff B, 28, 42 (35), 97 (96), 130 (129), 338 (337), 381 (380), 555 (554), 619 (616)
Rohde-Dachser C, 116 (114)
Rohner R P, 209 (207)
Rohwer W D Jr, 42 (33)
Rokeach M, 492 (490)
Roland-Lévy C, 574
Rolland-Cachera M-F, 184 (179, 180, 181)
Rollett B A, 451 (446), 659 (654)
Romaine S, 377
Romberg T A, 538 (536)
Romiszowski A J, 550 (548, 549), 700 (698), 759 (756)
Rönnqvist L, 284 (282)
Roodin P A, 59 (56)
Roopnarine J L, 312 (311), 601
Rose S, 72 (69)
Rosen G D, 796 (793, 794)
Rosen H, 584 (582)
Rosenbaum M, 796 (795)
Rosenberg M, 232 (229, 230)
Rosenfeld D, 355 (354)
Rosenshine B, 683 (679)
Rosenthal R, 187 (186), 632 (626, 627, 629)
Rosenthal T L, 106 (102, 103)
Rosenzweig M R, 125 (121), 171 (170)
Rosier M J, 572 (570), 649 (646)
Rosinski R R, 288
Rösler H-D, 239 (234)
Ross C E, 254 (251)
Ross D H, 160 (151)
Ross L, 619
Ross S, 518 (516)
Ross S M, 729 (725, 729)
Rosser P, 645 (643)
Ross-Gordon J M, 748 (746)
Rossi P H, 62 (60)
Rossiter M W, 649 (647)
Rossman T, 530 (528)
Rost D H, 626 (625)
Roth E M, 482 (481)
Roth S, 626 (624)
Roth W, 76 (74)
Roth W-M, 459 (456)
Rothbart M K, 191 (188)
Rothery A, 542 (540)
Rothkopf E Z, 497 (494)
Roug L, 294 (289)

Rourke B, 796 (793)
Rovee-Collier C, 125 (122, 123)
Rovine M J, 59 (56, 57), 174 (173)
Rowe R, 584 (582)
Rowland G, 725 (724)
Rowland T, 542 (539)
Roy-Pernot M-P, 184 (179)
Rozin P, 561 (560)
Rubin D C, 187, 632 (629)
Rubin J, 530 (525, 526)
Rubin K H, 206 (205), 222 (219, 221), 258, 312 (306, 308, 310, 311)
Rubinson R, 25 (22)
Ruble D N, 243 (240, 241, 242)
Rubtsov V, 623 (621, 622)
Rudduck J, 687 (685)
Rueda R, 149 (147)
Rueter H H, 715 (714)
Ruffman T, 267 (265, 267)
Ruijssenaars A J J M, 816 (813, 814, 815, 816)
Rumain B, 303 (300, 301)
Rumbaugh D, 338 (335)
Rumble G, 752 (749)
Rumelhart D E, 267–68 (264), 347 (345), 405–06 (405), 478 (477), 568 (565), 733 (730)
Rüppell H, 280 (277)
Rushton J P, 209 (208)
Rust V D, 141 (136)
Rutledge M M, 184 (179)
Rutter M, 72 (67), 124 (121), 202, 222 (221), 239 (235, 237), 249–50 (244, 247), 254 (253), 293 (292), 670 (666), 792 (788)
Rutter R, 142 (140)
Ruvinsky L I, 777 (773)
Ryan D, 333 (329)
Ryan D W, 693 (692, 693)
Ryan M, 645 (642, 644)
Ryan R M, 451 (450)
Rybash J W, 59 (56)
Ryff C D, 106 (101), 168 (166)
Ryle G, 396 (394)

Saarni C, 217 (214)
Saha L J, 24–25 (17, 18, 23, 24)
Sahm W B, 243 (241)
Sajavaara K, 534 (534)
Salapatek P, 288
Salganik L, 142 (139)
Salili F, 212–13 (211)
Salisbury D F, 49 (47)
Säljo R, 321 (319), 441 (437), 467 (465), 641 (640)
Sallis R, 418 (414)
Salomon G, 42 (35, 36, 37, 38), 444 (443), 451 (446), 478 (477), 487 (484, 485, 486), 623 (622), 659 (654), 687 (686), 700 (695, 697, 698), 715 (714), 729–30 (725, 726, 728, 729)
Salthouse T A, 59 (56, 58), 163 (161), 297 (296)
Saltzstein H D, 227 (227)

Salvia J, 149 (142, 145, 147)
Sameroff A J, 72 (69), 125 (121), 239 (236), 250 (244, 246, 247, 248)
Samet J, 268 (264)
Sammons P, 693 (692, 693)
Sampson G, 431 (428)
Samuda R J, 149 (147, 148)
Sancilio L, 487 (484)
Sanders A F, 72 (71)
Sanders R J, 338 (335)
Sandora C, 524 (522)
Sanford A J, 564 (563)
Sanford J P, 693 (693)
Santrock J W, 59 (56)
Sapir E, 408 (406)
Sapon S, 518 (513)
Sarason I G, 217
Sarigiani P A, 187 (185, 186)
Sasaki I, 402 (401)
Sato C J, 518 (516)
Sauer E, 171 (169)
Sautter R C, 141 (138)
Savage-Rumbaugh S, 338 (335)
Savicevic D M, 748 (745)
Savin-Williams R C, 209 (207)
Sayeki Y, 347 (346)
Scanlon E, 703 (702)
Scanlon J W, 62 (60)
Scardamalia M, 41–42–43 (38, 40), 380 (380), 391 (388), 579–80 (577, 579), 691 (688), 700 (697, 698, 699)
Scarr S, 17 (12), 130 (126), 174 (173), 250 (243), 272 (271)
Schack G D, 280 (278)
Schacter D L, 401–02 (400)
Schafer W D, 813 (811)
Schaffer H R, 316 (313)
Schaie K W, 59 (56, 58), 168 (164, 165, 166, 167)
Schaie W, 85 (84)
Schallert D L, 435 (433), 478 (473, 474)
Schalling D, 206 (204)
Schank R, 327
Schank R C, 406
Schaps E, 209 (208)
Schardein J L, 177 (176)
Scheele B, 497 (496)
Scheerenberger R C, 160
Schefft B K, 471 (468)
Scherer K R, 217 (214)
Schermer F J, 626 (625)
Scheurman G, 771 (766, 767)
Schiefele U, 327 (326), 590 (587, 588)
Schildkamp-Kündiger E, 645 (642)
Schiller F, 312 (306)
Schlaefli A, 492 (490)
Schlesinger B, 510 (509)
Schliemann A D, 33 (32), 341 (339), 467 (466), 550 (549)
Schlossberg N K, 764 (762)
Schmalt H D, 674 (674)
Schmeck R R, 641 (640), 659 (653)
Schmidbauer W, 116 (115)
Schmidt H D, 59 (57)

Schmidt J, 293 (289)
Schmidt J A, 510 (508)
Schmidt R A, 550 (549)
Schmidt R W, 518 (515, 516, 517)
Schmitz-Scherzer R, 168 (165)
Schmuller A M, 50 (44)
Schneewind K A, 254 (254)
Schneider B, 141 (140)
Schneider F W, 149 (147, 148)
Schneider G E, 171 (169)
Schneider K, 674 (674)
Schneider W, 42 (36), 130 (128), 163 (162), 239 (238), 297 (294, 295, 296), 422 (420), 436 (432, 434), 510 (509), 659–60 (651, 652), 674 (674), 691 (690)
Schnell S V, 491 (490)
Schoenfeld A H, 43 (40), 441 (438), 538 (535), 547, 691 (689)
Scholnick E, 303 (302)
Schon D A, 813 (809)
Schonfeld W A, 136 (131)
Schooler C, 163 (161), 168 (166), 198 (196)
Schorr L B, 142 (140), 250 (248)
Schrader F W, 28 (27, 28), 50, 50 (46, 46), 272 (272), 590 (586)
Schramm W L, 741 (738)
Schriver K A, 580 (577)
Schröder E, 272 (269)
Schroeter D, 632 (630)
Schrooten H, 699 (698), 715 (714)
Schubert W H, 505 (498)
Schug M C, 574 (573)
Shulman L S, 361 (356, 357)
Schulman P, 201–02 (199, 201)
Schulte A C, 427 (425)
Schultz L H, 121 (118)
Schulze S K, 463 (459)
Schumaker J B, 785–86 (781)
Schunk D H, 43 (38), 327, 374 (373), 422 (419), 427 (423), 590
Schutz A, (195)
Schwab J J, 361 (357, 358, 359), 505 (499)
Schwabe H, 86 (82)
Schwarzenberger R, 542 (538)
Schweinhart L J, 248 (247)
Schwille J, 25 (21)
Scott B C E, 659 (653)
Scott P A, 644 (643)
Scott R, 49 (45)
Scott T, 538 (536), 700 (695, 696)
Scovel T, 518–19 (513, 515)
Scribner S, 487 (484), 596 (593)
Scriven M, 505 (501)
Sealand N, 249 (244)
Seammon R E, 337
Sears R R, 92 (90)
Seattle, 577 (576)
Segal J W, 467 (464), 558 (556), 657, 659 (652), 792 (790)
Segal N L, 272 (271)
Segall M H, 55
Segalowitz N, 568 (566)
Seifer R, 250 (244, 247, 248)

Seiffge-Krenke I, 626 (625)
Sekowski A, 280 (277)
Seligman M E P, 201–02 (199, 200, 201), 450 (449)
Selim M A, 361 (360)
Selinker L L, 534 (534)
Selman R L, 121 (118), 306 (304)
Selz O, 321 (318)
Semmel M I, 160 (158)
Sempé G, 184 (179)
Sempé M, 184 (180, 181)
Senge P M, 759 (756)
Serbin L A, 243 (242)
Sergeant J A, 72 (71)
Sevcik R A, 338 (335)
Sevón G, 574
Sexton V S, 89 (86)
Seyfarth R M, 338 (335)
Shachar C, 355 (351, 354)
Shachar H, 687 (685)
Shaffer D R, 130 (126), 492 (490)
Shaffer J B P, 89 (86, 87, 88)
Shafro M G, 463 (463)
Shafto M, 658 (652, 656)
Shankweiler D, 561 (560)
Shantz C U, 306 (304)
Shapiro A M, 41 (37, 40, 41)
Shapiro B, 333 (329)
Shapiro B J, 693 (692, 693)
Shapiro E K, 222 (221), 243 (242)
Shapiro S, 249 (244)
Shapiro T, 72 (68)
Sharan S, 355 (351, 353, 354), (608), 687 (684, 685)
Sharan Y, 355 (353)
Sharko J, 183 (179)
Sharp A M, 786 (780)
Sharp D, 596 (591)
Sharp L, 632 (629)
Shatz M, 294 (290)
Shavelson R J, 232 (230), 558 (557, 558)
Shavlik J W, 733
Shaw J G, 97 (93)
Shayer M, 41 (37), 66 (64, 65, 66)
Shea S L, 288 (286)
Sheen R, 518 (514)
Sheick J A, 168 (167)
Sheingold K, 704 (703)
Shemilt D, 574 (572)
Shepard T H, 177 (174, 176)
Shepp B E, 288 (287)
Sherman G F, 796 (794)
Sherman G A, 741 (739)
Sherrill L, 303 (297, 299)
Sherrod L R, 163 (161)
Shields S A, 187 (185)
Shiffrin R M, 691 (690)
Shimmin H S, 243 (240)
Shinn M R, 149 (145), 802 (800)
Shire B, 542 (538)
Shonkoff J P, 250 (247)
Shotland R L, 62 (60)
Shrager J, 97 (93)
Shrigley R L, 361 (360)

Shuard H, 542 (540)
Shuell T J, 43 (37), 327 (322, 323, 324, 326), 385 (383), 505 (499), 759 (757)
Shulman L, 505 (499, 501), 725 (721, 723)
Shulman L S, 28 (27), 361 (356, 357, 359)
Shultz T R, 303 (299)
Shuman H H, 249 (247)
Shute V J, 418, 574 (573), 665 (664)
Shweder R A, 55 (52), 306 (305)
Sidner C L, 564 (563)
Sieber R T, 198 (194)
Siegel M, 542 (539)
Siegler I C, 168 (164, 166)
Siegler R S, 7 (3, 4), 17 (13), 28 (27), 59 (59), 97 (93), 101 (100), 297 (294), 659 (653)
Siervogel R M, 183–84 (180, 181, 182)
Sigel I E, 222 (219), 250 (246)
Sigel L S, 250 (246)
Signorella M L, 243
Signorielli N, 106 (102)
Sijtsma K, 816 (814, 815)
Sikes J, 355 (353, 354)
Silver E A, 510 (509), 530 (527), 558 (555), 808 (807)
Silvern L, 272 (268)
Simmons G, 786 (783)
Simmons R, 42 (36, 37), 459 (457), 478 (471, 474, 477), 505 (502)
Simmons R G, 136 (131), 198 (193, 194, 195)
Simon D P, 510 (507), 571 (569), 786 (780)
Simon H, 786 (780)
Simon H A, 33 (32), 42 (36), 97 (93), 276 (273), 316 (313), 372 (369), 427 (426), 436 (435), 441 (436), 487 (484), 510 (506, 507), 555 (550, 552, 554), 571 (569), (662), 720 (716), 733 (731)
Simon T, 7 (3), 16 (9), 28 (27), 272 (270)
Simons H D, 408 (407)
Simons P R J, 444 (441, 442, 443), 659 (654)
Simons R J, 41 (34)
Simonton D K, 316 (314)
Simpson E L, 89 (87), 228 (226)
Sinatra G M, 524 (523)
Sinclair H, 100 (99)
Sinclair J, 542 (539)
Sinclair J M, 619 (618)
Singer D G, 312 (311)
Singer J D, 76 (75)
Singer J L, 312 (311)
Singer R N, 550 (549)
Singer W, 284 (281)
Singley M K, 43 (37), 559 (556)
Sinisterra L, 659 (652)
Sinnott J, 770 (768)
Siqueland E R, 288 (286)
Sirotkin K A, 537 (535)
Sisco B, 770 (769), 776 (774)
Skeels H M, 174 (174)
Skehan P, 519 (514, 515)
Skinner B F, 7 (3), 17 (9, 15), 49 (45), 92 (90), 239 (235), 321 (317, 322, 375), 398 (397, 409), 505 (500), 725 (721), 741 (735, 738)

Skinner E A, 222 (219)
Skodak M, 174 (174)
Skrtic T M, 160 (152, 155, 159)
Skutnabb-Kangas T, 534 (532)
Slaby R G, 206 (202, 204, 205), 243 (240)
Slavin R, 611 (608)
Slavin R E, 28 (28), 49 (47), 142 (140), 272 (271, 272), 355 (351, 352, 353, 354), 367 (366), 451 (448), 687 (684, 685)
Slavings R, 632 (629)
Sleeman D, 700 (696), 715 (714)
Sloboda J, 276 (274)
Slomkowski C, 267 (265)
Smiles S, 777 (772)
Smiley S S, 435 (432)
Smith A, 670 (666)
Smith B H, 338 (336)
Smith D H, 25 (20)
Smith D R, 381 (379), 487 (484, 485, 486)
Smith E E, 406, 467 (466), 555 (554), 659 (652), 715 (713), 733, 786 (780)
Smith J, 163 (162), 297 (296), 393 (393), 487 (484), 771 (768)
Smith J E, 748 (747)
Smith L B, 288 (287)
Smith M S, 670 (666)
Smith M U, 555 (554)
Smith P, 25 (22)
Smith P K, 312 (309, 311)
Smith R M, 748 (745), 764 (761), 771 (767), 777 (775)
Smith R S, 73 (69), 136 (135), 250 (244, 248), 803 (802)
Smith T, 427 (426)
Smull M W, 76 (75)
Smythe W J, 693 (692)
Snapp M, 355 (353)
Snarey J R, 228 (225, 226)
Snelbecker G E, 720 (717)
Snook I, 333 (328)
Snook R K, 741 (740)
Snow C, 294 (291, 292)
Snow M A, 530 (529)
Snow R E, 43 (34), 49–50 (47), 272 (272), 321 (320), 418 (410), 451 (445), 505 (499, 501, 504), 637–38 (634), 658–59 (650, 651, 652, 654, 655, 656, 657), 665 (661, 662, 663, 664, 665), 670 (666), 674 (670, 671, 672, 673, 674), 771 (766), 808 (805), 816 (815)
Snyder L, 293 (288, 291), 385 (383)
Snyder M, 106 (104)
Sodian B, 228 (226), 268 (265), 303 (301)
Sokolov E N, 374 (373)
Soldatova G, 596 (594)
Soled S W, 367 (365)
Solomon B, 786 (779)
Solomon D, 209 (208)
Solono C H, 659 (655)
Soloway E, 715 (713, 714)
Soltz V, 116 (116)
Somerville S C, 303 (301)
Sommers N I, 584 (583)
Songer N B, 524 (523), 572 (569, 570), 649 (647)

Sophian C, 303 (301)
Souberman E, 596 (592)
Sowell E J, 170 (170), 396 (395)
Spada H, 733, 733 (732, 732)
Span P, 42 (34, 35)
Spear G E, 777 (772, 775)
Spearman C E, 638 (636), (660, 661)
Spelke E S, 268 (264), 288, 303 (298)
Spence D, 641, (638)
Spence M J, 177 (175)
Spencer H, 17 (8)
Spencer K, 730 (729)
Sperling M, 584 (583)
Spiker C C, 125 (122)
Spiker D, 249 (246)
Spiro R J, 564 (562)
Spitz R A, 62 (60)
Spoehr K T, 510 (509)
Spohrer J C, 715 (713)
Spolsky B, 519 (515), 534 (531, 533)
Sprenkle D H, 254 (253)
Sroufe L A, 72 (67), 206 (204), 217, 222, 250 (246), 312 (310)
Stainback S, 142 (140), 160 (154, 157)
Stainback W, 142 (140), 160 (154, 157)
Stanhope R, 183 (181)
Stanley J C, 644 (642, 644), 659 (655)
Stanley W C, 659 (655)
Stanne M B, 704 (703)
Stansfield C W, 519 (512, 517)
Stariha W E, 615 (612)
Starko A J, 280 (278)
Stattin H, 136 (131, 134), 239 (234)
Stebbins G L, 111 (107)
Steens G, 183 (182)
Steffe L P, 43 (37), 459 (459), 505 (503), 538 (536)
Stein B S, 41 (36)
Stein N, 467 (464, 465, 466)
Steinbach R, 43 (40)
Steinberg L, 136 (132), 601 (598)
Steinberg L S, 645 (643)
Steinkamp M W, 649 (646)
Steinmetz H, 796 (793, 794)
Stephan C, 206 (204), 355 (353)
Stephan S, 355 (354)
Stepick C D, 183 (182)
Stern D, 116 (114)
Stern G G, 683 (679)
Stern H H, 530 (525)
Stern W, 17 (8), 239 (236), 272 (270), (660)
Sternberg K J, 250 (247)
Sternberg R, 467
Sternberg R J, 33 (31), 42–43 (36, 37), 97, 272 (270), 303, 393, 441 (438), 467 (466), 482 (481), 555 (553, 554), 637 (637), 657–58, 660 (652), 665 (661, 662), 674 (674), 816 (814, 815)
Sternglanz S H, 243 (242)
Stevens A L, 571 (568, 569, 570), 691 (688)
Stevens R, 683 (679)
Stevens R J, 355 (352)
Stevenson D, 141 (140), 601 (599)
Stevenson H, 81, 601 (600)

Stevenson H W, 86 (84), 213 (210, 212), 431 (428), 601 (598, 600), 670 (669), 694 (692, 693)
Stevenson-Hinde J, 217 (214), 249 (244), 254, 619 (616)
Stewart M I, 129 (126)
Stewart S R, 580 (578)
Stigler J W, 86 (84), 601, 670 (669), 694 (692, 693)
Stipek D J, 130 (129), 213 (211), 232 (230), 659 (654)
Stock B, 431 (429)
Stocker C, 254 (252)
Stodolsky S S, 679 (678), 813 (810)
Stoll L, 693 (692, 693)
Stolurow L M, 49 (46)
Stone C, 808 (807)
Stouthamer-Loeber M, 206 (204)
Strauss A A, 802 (798)
Strauss J S, 148 (142)
Streefland L, 43
Street B, 431 (429)
Streibel M J, 725 (722)
Strelau J, 191 (188)
Strike K A, 459 (458)
Striniste N A, 312 (311)
Strittmatter P, 730 (727)
Stromquist N P, 25 (23)
Strube G, 733
Stubbs M, 542 (541)
Sturman A, 198 (197)
Subelman I, 100 (100)
Sugrue B M, 729–30 (726, 728, 729)
Suls J, 626 (624)
Sulzbacher S I, 398 (397)
Sun Y, 222 (221)
Suppes P, 700 (696)
Supplee P L, 280
Susman E J, 187 (186)
Sutherland R, 703 (702)
Sutton A, 816 (814)
Svinicki M D, 427 (425)
Swain M, 519 (512, 517)
Swallow J, 580, 700 (697, 699)
Swanson H L, 280 (278), 802–03 (799, 800)
Swanson J, 43 (34), 451 (445), 659 (652, 656, 657), 674 (674)
Swanwick K, 577 (576)
Sweetnam P M, 183 (179)
Swenson W M, 167 (166)
Sykes R C, 183 (180)
Symons S, 436 (433)

Taba H, 505 (500)
Tachibana Y, 55 (53)
Tait H, 42, 427 (425)
Takanishi R, 62 (60)
Tallal P A, 170 (170), 294 (293)
Talyzina N, 333 (333)
Tamblyn R M, 763 (761)
Tamir P, 361 (356, 357, 359, 360)
Tamis-LeMonda C S, 312 (310)

Tamsky B F, 168 (166)
Tannen D, 561 (559)
Tannenbaum S I, 759 (758, 759)
Tanner J M, 130 (125), 135 (131, 132), 136 (131, 132)
Tannhausser M T, 802 (798)
Tarbot N, 402 (400)
Tarone E, 519 (511)
Tawfik W A, 183 (181)
Tayler C A, 792 (788)
Taylor B, 136 (131)
Taylor C W, 393 (391, 392)
Taylor D T, 559 (557)
Taylor F W, (547)
Taylor M, 361 (355, 356, 361)
Taylor R, 700 (695)
Taylor R P, 704 (702)
Taylor S J, 160 (154)
Teasdale J D, 201 (199, 200), 450 (449)
Teasley S D, 381 (380)
Teichmann H, 239 (234)
Teles L, 712–13 (708, 709, 710, 711, 712)
Tellegen A, 272 (271)
Tennant M, 748 (748), 777 (775)
Tennyson R D, 385 (383, 384), 391 (387), 725 (722)
Terman L, (498)
Terman L M, (185), (277), 645 (644), (660)
Terrace H S, 338 (335)
Tesch-Romer C, 510 (509)
Tesla C, 267 (265)
Tesser A, 492 (490)
Tessmer M, 482 (479, 480, 481)
Tetlock P E, 492 (490)
Thagard P R, 467, 733 (730, 731)
Tharp R G, 607 (603, 604), 785–86 (783)
Thatcher R W, 121 (120)
Thelen E, 217, 284 (282)
Thiagarajan S, 741 (740)
Thibaut J W, 755 (754)
Thissen D, 183–84 (178, 180, 181)
Thoma S J, 228 (226)
Thomae H, 17 (14), 168 (165), 262 (259)
Thomas A, 191 (188, 189), 206 (204)
Thomas B, 649 (647)
Thomas C A, 741 (736)
Thomas R M, 81 (80)
Thomas V G, 644–45 (642)
Thompson A, 547 (546)
Thompson G G, 377 (375)
Thompson H, 120 (117)
Thompson H B, (185)
Thorndike E L, 33 (30, 31), (90), (317), (322), 398, 398 (396, 396), (409), 487 (484), (498), 559 (556), 665 (660)
Thorpe L P, 50 (44)
Thorpe M, 752 (750)
Thum Y M, 141 (141)
Thurlow M L, 149 (142), 803 (800)
Thurstone L L, 187 (185), 272 (270), 418 (414), 641 (638), (661)
Tiberghien A, 571 (568, 569)
Tiedeman J, 660 (653)
Tierney A J, 338 (334)

Tillema H H, 50 (46)
Timiras P S, 338
Tinbergen N, 112 (109)
Tindimubona A, 712 (708, 711)
Tirre W C, 418 (412)
Tisak M, 306 (305)
Tishman S, 42
Tissink J, 816 (814, 815)
Tizard B, 72 (69)
Tobias S, 463 (460)
Tobin K, 571–72 (570, 570), 649 (647), 683 (679, 682)
Tobin-Richards M H, 187 (184, 186)
Todaro M P, 25 (18)
Todd F, 687 (685)
Todesco A, 530 (525)
Toffler A, 720 (718)
Tom D, 632 (626, 628)
Tomasello M, 611 (610)
Tomlinson S, 81 (80), 160 (159)
Tonick I J, 243 (242)
Torbert W, 771 (765)
Törestad B, 239 (236, 237)
Torgesen J K, 561 (560)
Torney-Purta J, 25 (21), 574 (574)
Torrance N, 431 (429)
Tough A M, 752 (750), 777 (772, 773)
Touwen B C L, 72 (71)
Towne B, 184 (182)
Townsend M A R, 435 (432)
Trabasso T R, 398 (397)
Trautner H M, 243 (241)
Treagust D F, 459, 683 (681)
Treffers A, 341 (340), 538 (537)
Treiman R, 561 (560)
Tress B, 171 (170)
Triandis H C, 55 (54)
Tribe M A, 741 (740)
Trickett E J, 683 (679, 681)
Trickett P, 62 (61)
Trommsdorff G, 55 (53, 54)
Trowbridge M H, 398 (398)
Trudeau L, 644 (643)
Tsao Y C, 567 (567)
Tsuang M T, 124 (121)
Tucker J A, 160 (155)
Tuijnman A C, 59 (57), 141 (141), 670 (666), 748 (748)
Tulving E, 268 (266), 316 (315)
Turiel E, 66 (65), 228 (224, 226), 306 (304, 305), 492 (490)
Turner R H, 755 (753)
Turner T, 478 (475)
Turoff M, 712 (708, 709, 710)
Turvey M T, 550 (549), 568 (567)
Tyler S, 596 (591)
Tzuriel D, 658 (652), 816 (815)

Ueno N, 347 (346), 577 (575)
Underwood B J, 209 (208), 374 (372), 665 (663)
Underwood G, 704
Underwood J D M, 704

Undheim J O, 660 (651)
Urquhart A H, 568
Usher R S, 748 (746)
Uttal D, 601 (600)

Vachon R, 303 (301)
Vaessen W, 72 (71)
Valdés G, 584 (581)
Valencia S, 786 (784)
Valentine J W, 111 (107)
Van Avermaet E, 402 (400)
van Aken M A G, 222 (217, 220), 232 (231)
Van Calster K, 451 (450), 660 (654)
Van Daalen H, 658 (652)
Van Dellen T, 72 (71)
van den Akker J, 704 (703)
van Der Kamp M, 748 (748), 771 (766, 770)
van der Maas H, 121 (119, 120)
Van der Meer A L H, 284 (282)
Van der Meere J J, 72 (71)
Van Der Voort T H A, 730 (727)
Van Der Zee H, 771 (770)
van Dijk T A, 497 (496), 510 (508), 524, 524 (519), 564, 564 (562, 563)
Van Dyke D C, 796 (794)
van Geert P, 121, 121 (119, 119)
Van Gelder T, 268 (264)
Van Ijzendoorn H W, 258 (256)
Van Lieshout C F M, 258 (256), 321 (320)
Van Luit J E H, 816 (815)
Van Mater Stone G, 422 (419, 420), 427 (423)
van Merrienboer J J G, 715 (713)
Van Oers B, 350 (350)
Van Parreren C F, 43 (40)
Van Parys M, 120 (119, 120)
Van Rijswijk F, 444 (441)
van Wieringen J C, 184 (178, 182)
vand der Weel F R, 284 (282)
Vandenberg B, 312 (306, 308, 310, 311)
Vandergrift L, 530 (526)
VanLehn K A, 347 (346), 733 (731, 732)
Vann R J, 530 (526)
Vaughn V L, 280 (278)
Veenman S A M, 50 (46)
Vellutino F R, 796 (793)
Verba S, 24 (20)
Verbrugge H P, 184 (178)
Vergnaud G, 396 (396)
Vermunt J D H M, 441 (437, 440), 444 (441), 725 (723)
Vernon P E, 638 (633), (661)
Verschaffel L, 42 (40), 321, 537 (535, 537), 571 (570, 571), 658 (652), 699 (697, 698), 715 (714)
Verschuur R, 183 (182)
Verspoor A M, 792 (786)
Vessey I, 715 (714)
Vigorito J, 288 (286)
Vilberg W, 715 (714)
Visser G H A, 284 (282)
Vogel F, 174 (172)

Vogt E M, 62 (60)
Volterra V, 293 (293), 619
von der Malsburg C, 284 (281)
von Eye A, 59 (56, 57)
von Frisch K, (108)
von Glasersfeld E, 341 (338, 339), 459 (456)
von Hofsten C, 284 (282)
von Zuben M V, 312 (311)
Voogel A, 759 (755, 757)
Vooglaid Y, 748 (745)
Vooijs M W, 730 (727)
Vorhees C V, 177 (176)
Vosniadou S, 43 (36), 303, 405–06 (405), 459 (458), 700 (699)
Voss J F, 43 (34), 467 (464, 465), 510 (508), 574 (573)
Vygotsky L S, 7 (6), 28 (25, 26), 33 (29, 32), 43 (34, 39), (80), 121 (119), 268 (263), 312 (307), 321 (318), (322, 324, 326), 341 (339), 347 (347), 381 (377, 380), (467), 505 (499, 502), 584 (582), 596 (592), (603), 611 (609), 619 (618), 623 (620), 632 (628), 638, 687 (683, 684), 786 (781), 808 (806), 816 (814)

Wachs T D, 288 (288)
Wachtel G F, 293 (289)
Waddington C H, 73 (69)
Wafelbakker F, 184 (178)
Wagenschein M, 497 (493)
Wager W W, 724 (722, 723)
Wagner B J, 584 (580, 581)
Wagner B M, 626 (625)
Wagner D A, 25 (20)
Wagner R K, 561 (560)
Wagoner S, 427 (426)
Wahlen K, 306 (304)
Wainer H, 184 (181), 645 (643)
Wainryb C 1, 306 (305)
Walberg H J, 43 (36), 49, 49 (45, 45, 46), 142 (140), 160 (154), 333 (329), 367 (366), 441 (439), 463 (460), 505 (498, 499, 500), 607, 615 (611, 612, 613, 614), 670 (668), 683 (679, 681, 682), 693–94 (692, 693), 704 (702), 792 (788)
Waldmann M, 272 (270)
Walk R D, 288 (285)
Walker C H, 463 (461)
Walker L J, 228 (225, 226)
Walkerdine V, 542 (539)
Wallerstein I, 796 (795)
Walstad W B, 574 (573)
Walters R H, 92 (90), 106 (103)
Wang M C, 43 (36), 142 (140), 160 (154, 155, 159), 333 (329), 427 (425), 441 (439), 478 (477), 505 (500, 504), 615 (613), 670 (666, 668), 792, 792 (788, 789, 789, 790)
Wang N, 808 (807)
Wapner S, 239 (236), 641 (640)
Warren B M, 658 (652)
Warren D H, 288
Warrington E K, 402 (399)
Washington, 505 (503), 707 (705), 741 (736)

Washburn S L, 338 (337)
Washington, 694 (692)
Washington K, 632 (630)
Wasserman E, 66 (65)
Waters E, 222
Watkins B A, 312 (311)
Watson D M, 704 (703)
Watson J B, 7, 17 (9, 15), 92 (89), (375)
Watson M S, 209 (208)
Waxman H C, 530 (526), 615
Waywood A, 542 (539)
Weaver C A III, 524 (522)
Webb N M, 660 (657), 687 (685, 686)
Webber L S, 637 (637)
Weber M, (195)
Wedenberg E, 177 (175)
Wehing R S, 478 (477)
Wehlage G, 142 (140)
Weikart D P, 248 (247)
Weil M, 333 (328)
Weil S W, 752 (750)
Weiler H N, 25 (19)
Weinberg R A, 250 (243)
Weiner B, 213, 217 (214), 422 (422), 451 (449), 505 (499, 502), 590 (587)
Weiner B A, 792 (790)
Weinert F E, 28 (27, 28), 50 (46), 66 (63), 130 (128), 163 (161, 162), 239 (238), 272 (270, 271), 297 (295), 321 (319), 436 (432), 451 (448), 464 (460, 461), 590 (586), 659–60 (651, 652), 674 (674)
Weinert S, 268 (266)
Weinreich U, 377 (376)
Weinstein C E, 422–23 (419, 420), 427 (423, 425), 478 (475), 497 (494), 524 (521), 530 (525, 527)
Weinstein C S, 43 (34)
Weinstein R, 632 (629, 630, 631)
Weinstein R S, 232 (231)
Weinstein T, 49 (45), 463 (460), 615 (612)
Weisberg R W, 559 (557)
Weisgerber R A, 741 (739)
Weiskrantz L, 402 (399)
Weiss B, 272 (270)
Weiss C H, 62 (60)
Weisskopf-Joelson E, 559 (557)
Weisz J R, 272 (270)
Weitzman E D, 177 (174, 175)
Welch W W, 49 (46), 615 (612, 614), 683 (679)
Wellington J J, 361 (355, 356, 361)
Wellman H M, 130 (128), 276 (275), 297 (295), 303 (298, 301), 306 (305)
Wells G, 619 (618)
Wells R, 712 (711)
Welsh W W, 694 (692)
Weltens B, 377 (377)
Wenden A, 530 (526)
Wender K F, 733
Wenestram C G, 497 (493)
Wenger E, 42, 691 (689), 700 (696), 733
Wentworth W M, 198 (193)
Werebe M J G, 312 (311)
Werker J, 177 (175)

Werner D, 160 (158)
Werner E E, 73 (69), 136 (135), 250 (244, 248), 803 (802)
Werner H, 17 (8)
Wernicke C, (797)
Wertheimer M, 33 (29, 31, 32), 321 (318), (410), 555 (551, 552)
Wertsch J V, 347 (343), 597 (593, 594), 623 (620)
Wesche M B, 530
Westat Inc., 649 (647)
Wexley K N, 759 (758)
Weyhing R S, 497 (495), 785 (784)
Wheeler S, 163 (161), 198 (194), 770 (765, 767)
Whimbey A, 786 (780)
Whishaw I Q, 171 (169, 170)
Whisler J S, 659 (654)
Whitaker J, 312 (311)
White B, 347 (346)
White B L, 316 (313)
White B Y, 43 (40), 418
White L, 377 (375), 519 (512, 517)
White M, 607 (605)
White R T, 741 (736)
White S H, 7 (2)
Whitehead R G, 184 (179)
Whitely S E, 816 (813)
Whiting B B, 55 (53, 54), 209 (207, 208), 222, 243 (241, 242), 597 (591)
Whiting J W M, 55 (53, 54), 209 (207, 208)
Whitley B E, 187 (186)
Whitlock M S, 280 (278)
Wholey J S, 62 (60)
Whorf B, 408 (406)
Wickelgren W A, 372 (370)
Wiedenbeck S, 715 (714)
Wiederholt J L, 803 (797)
Wiedl K H, 816 (815)
Wiegand J, 280 (277)
Wiesel T N, 124 (121)
Wiggins G, 559 (557)
Wijnroks L, 72 (71)
Wilderson F, 355 (354)
Wiley D, 333 (330), 679 (676)
Wiley D E, 374 (374), 504 (500), 649 (646)
Wiley J, 43 (34)
Wilkening F, 288 (287)
Wilkinson A C, 497 (494)
Wilkinson B, 606 (604), 679 (677), 687 (685)
Wilkinson L C, 619 (617), 659 (656)
Will M, 160 (154, 156, 158)
Willett J, 121 (120)
Williams F, 408 (406, 407)
Williams P, 160
Williams R, 568 (566)
Williams W G, 280 (277, 279)
Willis G B, 478 (474)

Willis S L, 59 (58), 168 (164, 165, 167)
Willson V L, 802 (802)
Wilson A, 232 (228)
Wilson A L, 748 (744)
Wilson B, 577 (576)
Wilson C O, 112 (107, 108)
Wilson D M, 644–45 (642, 644)
Wilson E O, 81 (81), 112 (109)
Wilson L, 530 (526)
Wilson M, 577 (576)
Wilson R S, 174 (173, 174)
Wimmer H, 303 (301)
Wineburg S S, 574 (573)
Winkler M, 89 (88)
Winn W D, 725 (723), 730 (729)
Winne P H, 478 (472, 474, 476)
Winnicott D W, (113)
Winograd P, 530 (528)
Winograd T W, 396 (394, 395)
Winston P H, 268 (263)
Wiratchai N, 333 (331)
Wise L L, 645 (642)
Witkin H A, 641 (638)
Witnov S J, 198 (196)
Wittgenstein L, 405 (402)
Wittrock M C, 33 (30), 361 (356, 357), 374 (373, 374), 478 (472), 505 (503), 679 (677), 813 (809)
Wixson K K, 422 (420)
Wohlwill J F, 17 (11), 120 (119)
Wolbarst, 402 (400)
Wolf D P, 584 (583)
Wolf E, 649 (647)
Wolf T H, 33 (29)
Wolfensberger W, 76 (74)
Wolman B B, 665 (660)
Wolters C, 136
Wolters M A, 350
Woltz D J, 658 (653)
Wonderly D, 66 (65)
Wong B Y, 786 (779, 780)
Wong R, 786 (780)
Wood P D P, 183 (179)
Wood R H, 25 (21)
Wood T, 43 (40), 505 (503)
Woodcock R W, 665 (661)
Woodhall M, 25 (18)
Woodhead M, 250 (247)
Woodring P, 33 (30)
Woodruff C, 184 (179)
Woodruff E, 700 (697, 699)
Woods D D, 482 (481)
Woodward A, 524
Woodworth R S, 487 (484), 559 (556)
Woodyard E, 665 (660)
Wooley H T, (185)
Woolsey S, 62 (60)
Worthy J, 524 (522)
Wortman C B, 202
Wright E, 704 (702)

Wright J D, 62 (60)
Wright J W, 306 (304)
Wright T L, 168 (166)
Wu A, 649 (647)
Wubbels T, 683 (681)
Wundt W, 7 (2), 17 (8), (409), (660)
Wurf E, 232 (231)
Wylie R C, 232 (228)
Wyllie M, 584 (583)
Wyndhamna J, 467 (465)

Yackel E, 43 (40)
Yakimanskaya I S, 660 (653)
Yakovlev P I, 177 (174, 175)
Yalow E, 665 (661, 664, 665)
Yamauchi H, 55 (53)
Yanagisawa S, 183 (180)
Yano Y, 518 (516)
Yanok J, 160 (152)
Yarbrough C, 596 (592)
Yates F A, 436 (431)
Yerkes R M, 418 (412)
Yesavage J A, 168 (167)
Yonas A, 288 (285)
Young D R, 62 (61)
Youngblade L, 267 (265)
Youniss J, 306 (305), 611 (607, 610)
Youtz R, 24 (20)
Ysseldyke J E, 149 (142, 145, 146, 147), 792 (789), 796 (795), 803 (800)
Yukl G, 759 (758, 759)
Yule W, 72 (68)

Zagar D, 568 (566)
Zahn-Waxler C, 7 (4), 129 (126), 209 (207, 208)
Zajochowski R, 564 (563)
Zajonc R B, 17 (14)
Zammuner V L, 243 (241), 467 (465)
Zander A, 755 (752, 753, 754)
Zappolo A, 160 (153)
Zaslow M E, 249 (247)
Zax M, 250 (244, 248)
Zeitz C M, 510, 510 (508, 509)
Zelli A, 206 (202)
Zelniker T, 641 (640)
Zemke R, 482 (480)
Zenger J H, 776 (773)
Zhang Y, 561 (560)
Ziegler S, 355 (354)
Zigler E F, 17 (9), 62 (61), 250 (247)
Zill N, 142 (139)
Zimmer J M, 198 (196)
Zimmerer L K, 649 (647)
Zimmerman B J, 43 (38), 106 (102, 103), 327, 374 (373), 422 (419, 420), 427 (423), 441 (438), 478 (476, 477), 530 (528), 670 (666)
Zucchermaglio C, 574 (573)
Zuckerman B, 249 (246)

Subject Index

The Subject Index has been compiled as a guide to the reader who is interested in locating all the references to a particular subject area within the Encyclopedia. Entries may have up to three levels of heading. Where the page numbers appear in bold italic type, this indicates a substantive discussion of the topic. Every effort has been made to index as comprehensively as possible and to standardize the terms used in the index. However, given the diverse nature of the field and the varied use of terms throughout the international community, synonyms and foreign language terms have been included with appropriate cross-references. As a further aid to the reader, cross-references have also been given to terms of related interest.

Ability
    and aptitude *633–38*
    conceptions of 587
    distinguished from aptitude 813
    and energy expenditure 587, 588
        and achievement need 211
        parent attitudes 600
    individual differences 373, *633–38*
    and learning 651
    taxonomy of factors 650
    vs. cognitive style 639
    See also Academic ability; Aptitude;
        Cognitive ability; Gifted; Spatial
        ability; Talent; Verbal ability
Ability grouping
    gifted 279
    and individual differences 656
    interaction
        and academic achievement 686
    and special education placement 787
    steering group learning model 330
Absenteeism *See* Attendance
Abstract reasoning *464–67*, 551
    abstraction
        and transfer of training 485
    concept of 464
    formal and informal 464
    See also Reasoning
Academic ability
    vs. academic achievement
        and learning disabilities 798
Academic achievement
    and age 314
    and attendance 693
    cooperative learning
        teamwork 351
    and family environment *597–601*
    homework 692
    and learning motivation 445
    and learning processes
        research 668
    and network learning 711
    and parent child relationship 598
    and schools
        effects on 197
    and self motivation 467
    sex differences

affective factors 544
    and social class 602
    stress variables 624
    and teacher expectation of students 626
    and television viewing 727
    and test anxiety 216
    and time factors (learning) 692
    and time on task 693
    vs. academic ability
        and learning disabilities 798
Academic aptitude
    and achievement 634
    tests 634
Academic education
    and vocational education for
        development 23
Academic learning time *675–79*
    academic achievement 678
    applications 676
    fundamental concepts of 675
    success rate 676, 677
    task analysis 678
    teacher student relationship 678
    See also Time on task
Acceleration (education)
    for the gifted 278
    high risk students 140
Access to education
    children with disabilities 151
    See also Equal education
Acculturation
    television viewing 103
Achievement
    and conformity 654
    and emotional development 215
    emotions related to 215
    instructional strategies
        equalizing 28
    psychological patterns 199
    and self motivation 654
    sex differences 185
    See also Academic achievement; High
        achievement; Low achievement
Achievement need
    Atkinson's theory 448
    and behavioral objectives 210
    causal attribution approach 211

cross cultural studies 52, 211
    development of *209–13*
    goals approach 209, 212
    social behavior 219
    and test anxiety 448
Achievement tests 633
    and learning disabilities
        diagnosis of 800
    matrix sampling 807
    See also Criterion referenced tests
Action learning *See* Experiential learning
Activity learning *See* Experiential
    learning
Adaptive instruction *See* Adaptive
    teaching
Adaptive teaching
    and learning theories 666
Adjustment (to environment)
    and achievement need 211
    evolutionary processes 108
    individual development *161–63*
        and social cognition *101–06*
    infant behavior
        reflexes 122
    and mental health 189
    personality development 234
    visual perception *451–55*
Admission criteria
    and advanced placement 655
Adolescent development *130–36*
    biological influences 131
    biology 336
    and cognitive development 131
    context effect 130, 134
    developmental stages
        puberty 131
    family influence 132
    identity and role diffusion 259
    individual differences 131, 135
    parent influence 132, 134
    peer influence 132, 134
    and personal autonomy 132
    physical development
        body composition 181
        body height 180
        determinants 181
        menstruation 132

and physical fitness 182
sex differences 181
sexual development 180
social influences 132, 134
stress variables 132
Adolescents
behavior problems
context effect 134
drinking 134
drugs use 133
friendship
and social values 133
mental health
sex differences 186
self actualization 135
sexuality 133
smoking 134
social problems 133
Adopted children
genetic factors in cognitive
development 173, 174
Adoption
quantitative genetic studies 172
Adult development
aging and compensation 162
and aging (individuals) *163–68*
cognitive development 164
age differences 164
developmental stages
expectation 162
Adult education
ethnocentrism in 746
experience of
effects on participation 57
experiential learning *749–52*
independent study *771–77*
learning strategies *760–64*
open education *749–52*, 769
See also Andragogy; Community
education; Distance education;
Independent study; Lifelong
learning
Adult educators
cultural awareness 746
ethnicity
and multicultural education 746
and learning strategies 760
theory practice relationship 746
Adult learning *764–71, 748*
anxiety in 768
cognitive ability 765
cognitive style 766
computer assisted instruction 769
conditions for 767
cross cultural studies 746, 747
developmental tasks 767
distance education 747
effectiveness *760–64*
factors influencing 767
in groups *752–55*
affective and cognitive objectives
753
and human development
research methodology *55–59*
independent study *771–77*

individualized instruction 769
issues in understanding 743
motivation 768
older adults
anxiety in 167
characteristics of 166
research 743
research proposals 747
sex differences 747
socialization 765
trends 746
See also Adult education; Andragogy;
Lifelong learning
Adult literacy
and phoneme grapheme
correspondence 560
See also Functional literacy; Illiteracy
Adults
and child behavior
attribution theory 200
Advanced placement
and admission criteria 655
Aesthetic education
preferences in 576
See also Art education
Affective behavior
cognitive development
and early moral development 226
cognitive psychological explanations
545
effect on learning *585–90*, 412
heuristic model 587
emotional development *213–17*
emotional responses 543
and mathematics education *543–47*
Affective education *See* Humanistic
education
Affective learning *See* Humanistic
education
Africa
special needs students
educational diagnosis 147
Age
and academic achievement 314
effect on learning strategies 315
Aggression *202–06*
biological influences 204
in children
antisocial behavior 208
hostility 202
intervention programs 205
and parent attitudes 204
cross cultural studies 53
developmental patterns 202
changes in form and elicitors of 202
sex differences 202
ethological theory 203
family influences 204
mass media influence 205
peer influence 204
peer relationship 254, 255, 257
psychoanalytic theory 203
and rejection
by peer group 205
sex differences 185

social cognitive theory 203, 205
socialization and 204
stability of 202
Aging (individuals)
and adult development *163–68*
and locus of control 166
and self concept 166
and social change 161
Ainsworth, Mary J. (1913–)
developmental psychology 6
Allocated time *See* Time management
Altruism
children
moral development 208
cross cultural studies 53
young children 207
and moral development 226
Amnesia
dissociation 400
research 399
Andragogy
and experiential learning 745
independent study 772
Androgyny
individual psychology 240
Anger
effect on performance 586
Anorexia nervosa 68
Anthropology
cultural context
and cognitive processes 591
See also Ethnography
Antisocial behavior
aggression 68, *202–06*
peer relationship 254, 255, 257
sociobiological approach 111
Anxiety 68
in adult learning 768
and aptitude treatment interaction 673
effect on learning 585
and stress management 625
See also Mathematics anxiety; Test
anxiety
Appraisal *See* Evaluation
Aptitude *813–16*
and achievement 633
cognitive psychological approaches
635
concept of 813
distinguished from ability 813
future research 637
individual differences *633–38*
and educational improvement
649–60
learning factors in 611, 614
research issues 814
sociology 602
and Sternberg's triarchic theory 814
theories of 633
and time on task 329
and Vygotsky's zone of proximal
development 814
See also Academic aptitude
Aptitude tests 633
basic format 814

content of 814
and curriculum 814, 815
measurement of change 815
predictive measurement *813–16*
use of 814
validity of 815
   See also Academic aptitude, tests;
     Differential aptitude tests
Aptitude treatment interaction (ATI)
   320, 634
definitions of 670
   statistical 671
   substantive 671
evaluation 673
future research 673
and instructional systems
   examples 673
and media research 728
methodology 671
model
   teaching *670–74*
research
   problems 671, 672
Argumentation *See* Persuasive discourse
Arithmetic
skills
   cognitive development 93
Arousal patterns
effect on learning 585
learning processes 768
Art appreciation 576
Art criticism 576
Art education
clinical psychology 575
cognitive psychology 575
cultural differences 575
developmental psychology 575
historical background 575
and mass media 575
psychological frameworks 575
in public schools 575
Art expression
cultural influences 576
Art therapy 575
Artificial intelligence
computer software 662
and declarative and procedural
   knowledge 394, 395
Artistic talent *See* Talent
Assertiveness
children
   prosocial behavior 208
Assessment
criterion-referenced *See* Criterion-
   referenced tests
and learning *805–08*
special needs students
   cultural differences 148
See also Evaluation; Measurement;
   Testing
Association for Persons with Severe
   Handicaps, The (TASH) 73
Associative learning 409, 412
mammalian foundations 334
measurement of 409

and memory 433
problem solving 553
At risk persons
adolescents 134
definitions 137
global approach 136
high risk students *136–42*
Attachment behavior
and aggression
   developmental patterns 204
to child caregiver
   and emotional development 216
cross cultural studies 53
developmental psychology 6
reactive attachment disorder 69
Attendance
and academic achievement 693
Attention *372–74*
and ability
   individual differences 373
in cognitive science 372
concept formation
   cognitive system model 383
conceptual models 372
definition 372
future research trends 374
involuntary arousal 373
and learning 369, 371
and motivation 372, 373
and neurophysiology 372
in observational learning 103
role in short term memory 372
selective strategies 372, 373, 374
voluntary 373
Attention control
age effects 315
in learning 412
metacognition 438
self efficacy
   and academic achievement 373
Attention deficit disorders 373
hyperactivity 68, 70
and personality 189
Attitude change
consciousness raising 491
Attitude measures
multidimensional 543
Attitude scales *See* Attitude measures
Attitudes
definitions of 490
and instructional design theory 719
positive
   and individual development 199
systems approach 490
and values *489–92*
Attribution theory 214
and learning motivation 448
and psychological impact of life
   events 260
self concept *199–202*
and social cognition 304
Audiovisual aids
and programmed instruction 739
Auditory perception
infants 286

language processing 286
and intelligence 650
Auditory stimuli
responses by fetus to 175
Australia
computer managed learning 706
Autism 68
interpersonal relationship
   social reinforcement approach 617
Autodidaxy
use of term 773
Autodidaxy *See* Independent study
Autoinstructional aids
early developments 734
See also Teaching machines
Autonomous learning *See* Independent
   study
Awareness *See* Perception

Baby boomers 164
Baldwin, James Mark (1861–1934)
epistemology 3
Beginning reading
alphabets
   letter names 560
developmental stages theory 560
learning and instruction *559–61*
phoneme grapheme correspondence
   559, 560
vocabulary development 561
Behavior
and brain development *169–71*
developmental psychology 2
and moral development 223
Behavior development
emotional development
   individual differences 214
See also Individual development
Behavior disorders 68
oppositional defiant disorder 68
stereotype/habit disorder 69
See also Behavior problems
Behavior modification
criticisms of 91
to increase attention 374
operant conditioning
   and language 91
and programmed instruction 734, 737
self control
   and learning 589
Behavior problems
antisocial behavior
   disruptive 68
attention deficit disorders 221
externalizing 221
internalizing 221
and peer relationship 221
and self control 470
social development 221
See also Antisocial behavior; Attention
   deficit disorders; Hyperactivity
Behavior theories *See* Attribution theory
Behavioral objectives 446
cognitive strategies 387

contextual skills 386
creative processes 387
intellectual skills 386
and programmed instruction 735, 736
time factors (learning) 387
verbal information 386
Behaviorism *89–92*
    behavior analysis theory 90
        developmental principles 90
        influence of 91
        research methods 91
    child development 3
    feedback
        in learning and instruction 396
    historical background 34
    humanistic psychology view of 86
    individual development 9, 10
    and industrial training 757
    and instructional psychology 721
    interbehavioral psychology 91
    learning theories 317, 409
        Skinner's 317
        Thorndike's 317
    United States 322
    Watson's contribution 89
Behaviorist psychology *See* Behaviorism
Beliefs
    about origins of human race
        religious factors 77
    cultural differences
        and scientific attitudes 79
    cultural influences
        individual development *77–81*
    influence on learning 586
        sex differences 600
    and learning
        Mandler's theory of mind and
            emotion 545
        mathematics education 543, 545
    metacognitive 437
    religious factors
        individual development *77–81*
    and scientific attitudes 79, 81
Bilingualism *375–77*
    attitude and motivation 376
    compound 376
    coordinate 376
    development of 375
        and social cognition 375
    diglossia 531
    effect on cognitive processes 376
    individual differences 376
    and language skill attrition 376
    memory organization in 376
    sociolinguistic circumstances 375
Binet, Alfred (1857–1911)
    child psychology 3
    cognitive development 3
Binet intelligence tests
    historical background 29
Biological influences
    on human development 4
    on human learning *334–38*
Biology
    sex differences 186

Birth defects *See* Congenital impairments
Birth weight
    and child development 246
    physical development 178
Body composition
    assessment of physical development
        178
    Body Mass Index (BMI) 178, 180
Body image
    and aging (individuals) 166
Bowlby, John (1907–90)
    developmental psychology 6
Brain
    development
        in enriched environment 170
        and human behavior *169–71*
        and interactions with environment
            170
        in mammals 169
    sex differences 186
    stimulation
        influence of environment 169
Brain damage *See* Neurological
        impairments
Brain drain
    developing nations
        and modernization 21
Brain hemisphere functions
    and learning disabilities 797
Brain imaging techniques
    and neuropsychological tests 170
Brainstorming 688
    and problem solving 556
Branching 501
    and programmed instruction
        frame design 737
Breastfeeding
    and infant behavior 123
Broadcast communications *See*
        Telecommunications
Broadcast television
    and learning 689
Bulimia 68
Bulletin boards
    and computer networks 708
Bullying *See* Aggression, peer
        relationship

Canada
    institutional support for independent
        study 772
    See also North America
Categorization *See* Classification
Cats
    visual deprivation 4
Causal attributions *See* Attribution theory
Center for Research and Pedagogical
        Applications (CRAPEL) (France)
        762
Character *See* Personality
Chemicals
    producing congenital impairment 176
Child abuse
    and family violence 251

    See also Child neglect
Child care *See* Child rearing; Day care
Child care centers *See* Day care centers
Child development *125–30*
    behaviorism 3
    biology 335
    child language 127
    cognitive development 127
        cultural context 129
        and domain-specific knowledge 26
        learning strategies 128
        problem solving 128
        symbolic learning 127
    cognitive processes
        age differences 128
    cumulative risk model 248
    developmental continuity 118
        individual differences 118
    developmental disabilities
        classification 68
    developmental stages
        characteristics 118
        synchrony in 119
    early experience *243–50*
    ecological model 244
    effect of change on 244
    emotional development 125
    and expert novice differences 274
    and family characteristics 244
    and family environment 597
    family influence *250–54*
    family system model 244
    influence of interpersonal relationships
        620
    metacognition 128
    parent influence 125
    peer relationship 126
    physical development 125
        motor development 125
    prosocial behavior *206–09*
    psychoanalytic theory 3
    research
        historical background 2
    risk and vulnerability model 244
    self concept 126
    skill development
        generalization 119
    social development 125
    Vygotsky's zone of proximal
        development 119
    See also Infants; Piagetian theory
Child health
    nutrition
        global approach 136
Child language 127
    and caregiver speech 291
    cognitive development
        schemata 127
    development of grammar 290
    and grammatical acceptability 290
    interpersonal communication 291
    metalinguistics 290
    and parent child relationship 291
    second language learning 127
    semantics 127

verbal development
  developmental stages 289
Child maltreatment *See* Child abuse
Child neglect
  and social adjustment 256
Child parent relationship *See* Parent
  child relationship
Child psychology
  and developmental psychology 8
  historical background 2
  individual development 51
  research 161
Child rearing
  effect on child development 247
  family environment 598
Childhood *125–30*
  anthropological perspective 129
Children
  aggression 126
  cognitive development
    and concept formation 264
    and theory of mind 265, 267
  empathy 126
  helping relationship 126
  physical development 179
    body composition 180
    body height 179
    determinants 180
    maturity indicators 180
    and physical fitness 180
  prosocial behavior 126
Children's rights 136, 141
Christianity
  beliefs about origin of man 77
Chronemics *See* Time management
Civil rights
  and disabilities 74
  See also Equal education
Class organization
  grouping (instructional purposes)
    and cooperative learning 621
Classification 382
  learning strategies
    memory 296
  and scientific attitudes 80
Classroom communication
  communication skills 617
  discourse analysis
    IRF (initiation, response, feedback)
      sequence 539
  and foreign language learning 517
  interpersonal competence 617
  sociolinguistic approach 618
    disadvantaged children 407
  and writing skills 578
Classroom environment *679–83*
  cooperation
    and cognitive development 806
  evaluation
    alpha press 679
    beta press 679
  evaluation methods *679–83*
    higher education 681
    questionnaires 679
    science laboratories 681

factors affecting 41
factors in learning 611, 613, 614
improvement
  Classroom Environment Scale 682
intervention studies 40
and learning factors 668
and learning theories 666
questionnaires
  Classroom Environment Scale 679
  Learning Environment Inventory
    679
  My Class Inventory 679
  teacher student relationship 681
research
  affective objectives 681
  cognitive objectives 681
  and student attitudes 682
  and teacher expectations of
    students 604
teachers
  coping strategies 604
Classroom Environment Scale (CES) 681
Classroom management *See* Classroom
  techniques
Classroom observation techniques 679
  Flanders Interaction Analysis
    System 679
  Observation Schedule and Record 679
  teacher role
    naturalistic observation 810
  See also Student behavior
Classroom techniques
  and learning factors 668
  learning from texts 522
  See also Discipline; Reinforcement
Classrooms
  and computer networks 708
  peer groups 255
Cognition
  connectionist models 345
  sociohistorical theories of 343
  See also Situated cognition
Cognitive ability
  adult learning 765
  and aging (individuals) 164
  cognitive development
    individual differences 27, 651
  constructs
    and aptitude treatment interaction
      673
  cultural differences
    anthropological perspective *590–97*
    interdisciplinary approach 591
    psychological research 590
  general and specific 66
  generation gap
    cohort analysis 165
  genetic determinants 271
  individual differences 270
    age differences 165
    stability of 27
  and interpersonal relationships 380
  maintenance
    and aging (individuals) 165
  preschool children 298

reasoning
  logical thinking 298
sex differences 185
See also Intelligence; Thinking skills
Cognitive anthropology *See* Ethnography
Cognitive conflict *See* Cognitive
  dissonance
Cognitive development 10, 12
  and acquisition of expertise *273–76*
  children's theories 264
    theory of mind 265, 267
  cognitive ability
    individual differences 27, 651
  cognitive apprenticeship model 320,
    324, 332, 689
  and computer assisted instruction 702
  and conflict resolution 685
  connectionist paradigm 264
  constructivism 520
  and constructivism 3
  contextual approach 96
  contextual influences
    ethnography 592, 593, 595
  cross cultural studies 53
  and cultural deficit theory 590
  cultural historical school 347, 592, 593
    face to face interactions 594
    formative experiments 593, 595
    interpsychological studies 592, 593
    intrapsychological studies 592, 593
  culture and evolution 107
  during childhood and adolescence 336
  and educational practices 63
  and emotional development 214
  and energy expenditure 95
  and expertise 379
    educational implications 275
  genetic factors
    adopted children 173, 174
    twins 173
  grouping (instructional purposes)
    cooperative learning 683
  individual differences *268–72*
    in content-specific knowledge 270
    determinants of 271
    developmental rate 269
    and educational practices 272
    environmental factors 271
    predictive measurement 269
    role of school 271
    types of 268
  infants 122
  influence of domain-specific
    knowledge on 26
  influence of instruction on 26, 27
  influence of learning on *25–28*
  information processing approach
    13, *92–97*
    assumptions 92
    developmental stages 94
    thinking skills 93
  instructional design model 386
  and interpersonal relationship 340, 618
  intra individual differences
    developmental stages 269

and learning strategies 26
mastery learning research 13
maturity (individuals) 25, 27
measurement of
    dynamic model 813
measurement techniques
    academic learning time 675
memory *294–97*
memory systems 386
and moral development 14
and motivation 14
parent student relationship
    helping relationship 599
and perceptual development 284, 287
and personality development 14
Piagetian theory 25, 53, 96, 322
    sex differences 185
and play 309
and pre-existence of concepts 264
prerequisites for 25
psychometric approach 9
reasoning
    in children *297–303*
social cognition 26
and social development 616
and specific life experiences
    ethnography 592
stimulation programs 27
and teaching methods 63
theoretical problems *263–68*
theories of 268
and thinking skills 26
and use of educational media 728
and values education 489
Vygotsky's zone of proximal
    development 26, 318, 603,
    684, 814
    definitions of 592, 620
    determinants of 595
    and dynamic assessment 806
    and learning activity 349
    and learning theories 620
See also Intellectual development;
    Perceptual development
Cognitive dissonance 458
and moral development 225
Cognitive knowledge See Cognitive
    structures
Cognitive linguistics
    reading comprehension 564
Cognitive measurement *805–08*
test validity
    evaluation criteria 807
See also Intelligence tests
Cognitive objectives
    anticipatory outcomes 103
Cognitive processes
    abstract reasoning 350
    and artificial intelligence 662
    and associative learning 94
    classificatory behavior
        discrimination learning 382
        generalization 382, 384
    cognitive control 589
    comprehension

effort after meaning 492
    learning from texts 520
computer simulation *730–33*
concept formation *381–85*
connectionism 404
cultural differences
    intracultural comparisons 590
development of consciousness 266
and discrimination learning 95
ethnography 591
executive functions 371
experimental introspection theory 318
expert performance
    protocol analysis 273
expertise *505–10*
and generalization 94
implications for curriculum
    development 501
information processing approach 93,
    411, 422, 499
and instructional tasks 475
and intelligence 661
and knowledge
    theories of 473
and knowledge acquisition 274
knowledge dependent 378
and learning *377–81*, *478*
learning strategies 319, 422
    older adults 165, 166, 167
and memory
    research 432
metacognition *436–41*, 494
problem solving 551
and radical constructivism 338
and realist constructivism 338
reasoning 299
role of meaning in 594
schematic anticipation theory 318
and social learning theories 90
and student characteristics 472
and task analysis 476, 480
theories
    and second language learning 528
thinking skills *550–55*
use of tools in 380
See also Creative thinking; Critical
    thinking; Learning processes;
    Memory; Metacognition;
    Perception; Problem solving;
    Social cognition
Cognitive psychology 319, 499, 501
    content and process analysis 652
    definitions of learning 323
    feedback
        in learning and instruction 397
    historical background 31
    implications for testing 805
    information processing approach 263
    and instructional design 721
    and learning strategies
        second language learning 527
    and learning theories 322, 410
    and models of learning 328
    problem solving 554
    and psychometrics *805–08*

standard model of cognition *369–72*
Cognitive restructuring 405
    age differences 299
    cognitive strategy instruction 781
    domain-specific 405
    educational programs
        instrumental enrichment 780
    global 405
    and knowledge acquisition 274
    in long term memory 462
    radical 405
    weak 405
Cognitive skills See Thinking skills
Cognitive strategies
    for children
        to reduce aggression 205
    and expertise 378
    See also Learning strategies
Cognitive strategy instruction *779–86*
    cultural differences 783
    definition of 779
    direct explanation 782
    direct instruction 780
    informed strategies for learning 782
    and learning motivation 784
    and portfolio assessment 784
    reading instruction 781
    reciprocal teaching 782
    special education
        historical development 779
        reading 780
    special needs students 790
    strategies intervention model 781
    and teacher support 784
    and thinking skills 783
    types of knowledge in 779, 783
Cognitive structures *369–72*
    analysis of 319
    conceptual change 404
        enrichment 405
    constructivist 359
    and developmental stages 66
    domain specific 96
    and educational strategies 65
    enculturation
        and realist constructivism 339
    evaluation of
        pre-instructional 390
    extent
        experts 506
    individual differences
        and learning 315
    intra individual 269
    and language 406
    and learning 410
    learning processes 274
    and memory 295
    organization
        experts 505, 506
    preconceptions and misconceptions
        about 457
    and prior learning 420
    schemata (cognition) 403
    semantic network 403
    theories of 403

time factors (learning) 379
types of knowledge 501
Cognitive style 412
  adult learning 766
  attention control
    individual differences 639
  classification 639
  cognitive psychology
    Gestalt psychology 638
  concept formation 640
  concepts of 638
    historical development 638
  conceptual tempo 639, 640
  convergent thinking 640
  core conceptualization 639
  cultural differences 378, 605
  Embedded Figures Test 514
  field dependence independence
    638, 640
  foreign language learning 514
  individual differences 653
  and individual psychology 638
  information processing approach
    639, 640
  in learning *638–41*
  and learning strategies 420, 761
  and memory 432
  perception
    discrimination learning 640
  and psychoanalysis
    ego development 638
  and reading processes 565
  and teaching methods 66, 641
  vs. ability 639
  vs. learning strategies 639
Cognitive theory *See* Epistemology
Coherence
  semantic 522
Collaboration
  and situated learning 38
College programs
  problem solving 557
Commission of the European
    Communities
  studies
    and learning disabilities 799
Communication
  and learning 688
Communication apprehension
  classroom environment
    and foreign language learning 515
Communication research
  representativeness and voice 539
Communication skills *615–19*
  definition of 616
  and language acquisition 616
  and social development 616
  sociolinguistic approach 617
Communications media *See* Mass media
Communicative competence (languages)
  language of mathematics 541
  and second language learning 531
Community characteristics
  and learning factors 669
Community education

and computer networks 709
Compensatory education
  high risk students 140
Competence
  evaluation of stages in development
    of 509
  individual differences
    research on expertise 273
  and self motivation 448
  and situated cognition 343
  theories 35
Competition
  and cooperation
    sociobiological approach 110
  and performance
    learning 690
Compliance (psychology)
  social behavior 219
Componential analysis 481, 661
Comprehension
  conceptualization aids 523
  constructive theory 492
  context effort 493
  educational objectives
    teacher guidance 494
  influences
    cognitive processes 492
  learning processes 493
  learning from texts 519
    cognitive processes 520
    tests 519
  and rote learning 552
  situation models 519
  social context
    reciprocal teaching 495
    situated learning 495
  teaching methods *492–97*
    adjunct questions 494
    advance organizers 493
    educational effectiveness 494
    elaboration theory 493
    examples 493
    inquiry-oriented teaching 493
  testing of
    application 496
    cloze procedure 496
    free recall 495
    questioning techniques 495
    structure displays 496
    summarizing 496
    thinking aloud 496
  See also Reading comprehension
Computation
  and affective behavior 544
  sex differences 642
Computer assisted instruction (CAI) 696,
    700–04, 741
  adult learning 769
  attributes of 703
  classification
    by software type 700
    by usage 702
  compared with conventional
    instruction 726
  and computer managed learning 704

and cooperative learning 622
and distance education 773
evidence of use 702, 703
expert systems 696
  evaluation studies 696
independent study 772, 773
individualized instruction 500
media research 725
programmed tutoring 732
role of 703
writing (composition) 582
See also Computer assisted learning
  (CAL); Computer managed
  learning (CML)
Computer assisted learning (CAL) *695–*
  700, 704
  and computer assisted instruction 696
  criticisms of 696, 697
  drills (practice) 696
  research on effects of 696
  See also Computer assisted instruction
    (CAI); Computer managed
    learning (CML)
Computer-based instruction *See*
  Computer assisted instruction
  (CAI)
Computer games
  and computer assisted instruction 701
Computer literacy
  programming *713–15*
    cognitive effects hypothesis 698
Computer managed instruction *See*
  Computer managed learning (CML)
Computer managed learning (CML)
  704–07
  development of 707
  growth and evolution of 704
  international applications of 706
  nature and origins of 704
  and proprietary software 707
  research and evaluation 707
  studies 707
  See also Computer assisted instruction
    (CAI); Computer assisted
    learning (CAL)
Computer networks
  background 708
  and computer managed learning 704
  for education *708–13*
    research directions 712
  and global education 711
  and network learning
    approaches 710
  and outcomes of education 711
  theoretical framework 709
Computer programming *See*
  Programming
Computer programs *See* Computer
  software
Computer simulation
  cognitive processes *730–33*
  and computer assisted instruction 701
  and learning 689
Computer software 713
  for computer assisted instruction 700

and computer managed learning 704
general purpose
    for computer assisted instruction 701
for integrated activities
    features of 706
specific purpose
    for computer assisted instruction 702
task analysis
    SNOWMAN (System for Knowledge
        Management) 482
Computer software development 713
Computer-Supported International
    Learning Environment (CSILE)
    development 40
Computer technology *See* Computers
Computer tutoring systems *See*
    Programmed tutoring
Computer uses in education
    classification of types 695
    and computer assisted instruction 700
    computer networks 708
    effects on learning *695–700*
        cognitive residue 695, 697
    Europe 726
    International Association for the
        Evaluation of Educational
        Achievement survey 695
    North America 726
Computers
    as learning tools 697
    as psychological models 32
Concept formation *385–91*, 415, 455
    abstract reasoning
        in children 382
    affective variables 384
    aids 523
    behavioral objectives 385
    classification 382
    cognitive development 458
        individual differences 314
    cognitive restructuring 458
    complex-dynamic strategies 389
    connectionist learning 264
    contextual knowledge
        and long term memory 384
    decomposition into perceptual
        features 263
    educational strategies 388
    evaluation of
        during instruction 390
        postinstructional 390
    expository strategies
        instructional variables 388
    external sources 382
    innateness theories 264
    internal sources 382
    language of thought theory (Fodor) 263
        compositionality feature 263, 264
    perception
        memory 400
    practice strategies
        instructional variables 389
    preinstructional *455–59*
    problem-oriented strategies 389
    self-directed experiences 390

computer assisted instruction 390
Concept teaching *385–91*
    analogies 346
    behavioral objectives 386
Concepts
    acquisition of
        and hypothesis testing 264
        information processing approach
            263
    classical view 402
    classification of 403
    definition of 381
    nature of 381
    prototype view 403
Conceptual knowledge *See* Declarative
    knowledge
Conceptual rationalism
    biological bases 342
    concept of 341
    and learning 344
    and situated cognition 344
Conceptual tempo 412, 639, 640
Conditioning 90
    and moral development 223
    and programmed instruction 734
Confidence *See* Self esteem
Confluent education *See* Humanistic
    education
Conformity
    and achievement 654
    sex differences 186
Congenital impairments 170
    anoxia during birth 170
    Downs syndrome 170
    fetus
        prenatal influences *174–77*
    fragile-X syndrome 170
    malformations and their causes 175
    See also Downs syndrome
Construct validity
    and aptitude treatment interaction 671
Constructivism
    cognitive development 520
    cognitive development
        learning environments 377
    developmental psychology 64
    and dualism 338, 339, 340
    educational research
        preconceptions and misconceptions
            456
    instructional implications 338
    instructional psychology 32, 722
    learning and *338–41, 691*
    learning theories
        and task analysis 482
    and mathematics learning 536
    radical 339
    realist 338
    research trends 340
    teaching methods
        and cognitive conflict 458
    Vygotsky's views 32
Content analysis
    task analysis 480
Contingency contracts *See* Contingency

management
Contingency management
    feedback in 397
Continuous education *See* Lifelong
    learning
Contract learning *See* Performance
    contracts
Contrastive linguistics
    and error analysis (language) 534
    and second language learning 533
Control *See* Locus of control
Control groups
    composition of
        and metacognition research 443
Conventional instruction
    decomposition method 508
    See also Formal education
Convergent thinking 551
Cooperative education
    and experiential learning 750, 751
Cooperative learning *619–23*, 355
    academic achievement 353
        teamwork 351
    and computer assisted instruction 702
    group investigation 608
    grouping (instructional purposes)
        683–87
    individual differences 657
    integrated activities
        jigsaw method 353, 608
        reading 352
        writing (composition) 352
    learning activities 621
    mastery learning 364
    and network learning 710
    and peer relationship 608, 609
    peer teaching 621
    self-esteem 354
    small group instruction 340
    socio-economic status 354
    student participation 686
    student teams achievement divisions
        608
    teamwork 351
    use of competition 608
Coordination (psychomotor) *See*
    Psychomotor skills
Coping
    control of context 625
    crises
        effectiveness of methods 261
    definition of 624
    health
        and personality development 625
    and learning *623–26*
    life events *258–62*
        protective factors 261
        risk factors 260
    older adults 166
    problem solving 624, 625
    psychological patterns 624
    self control
        and learning 589
    stress management *623–26*
Corporate colleges *See* Corporate

education
Corporate education
　and business strategy 758
Corporate training *See* Industrial training
Correspondence courses *See*
　　Correspondence study
Correspondence study
　United States 751
CoRT thinking program 557
Council for Adult and Experiential
　　Learning (US) 751
Council for the International Evaluation
　　of Educational Achievement *See*
　　International Association for
　　the Evaluation of Educational
　　Achievement (IEA)
Counting *See* Computation
Course evaluation
　and learning strategies
　　teaching of 425
Creationism 77
Creative development 392
Creative thinking 393
　cognitive style
　　and teaching methods 641
　problem solving 551
　teaching of
　　in industry 556
　See also Divergent thinking;
　　Productive thinking
Creativity
　education for 393
　and expertise 393
　individual characteristics 392
　and intelligence 392, 650
　psychological approach *391–93*
　scientific 391
Creativity research *391–93*
Creativity tests 392
Crises (life events) 260
　assessment of developmental
　　consequences 260
　developmental gains 260
　emotional response 260
　individual development *258–62*
　and mental health 260
　use of concept 258
　widespread in population
　　and social attitudes 260, 261
Criterion referenced tests
　and behaviorism 500
　See also Achievement tests
Critical theory
　and context of learning 320
Critical thinking
　adults 744
　problem solving 551
　See also Evaluative thinking
CSILE *See* Computer-Supported
　　International Learning
　　Environment (CSILE)
Cultural awareness
　and reading comprehension 565
　and situated rationalism 346
Cultural context

situated learning 319, 324, 332
　and transfer of training 484, 485
Cultural differences
　cognitive ability *590–97*
　and reading comprehension 565
　in schools
　　and socialization 197
Cultural discontinuities
　and academic achievement 334
Cultural influences
　beliefs
　　individual development *77–81*
　and socialization 193
Cultural transmission
　and family environment 598
　See also Socialization
Culture
　evolutionary theory and education 107
　in other species 108
　use of term 77
Curiosity
　and self motivation 448
Curriculum
　and aptitude tests 814, 815
　cognitive development
　　and expertise 276
　concepts of 498
　learning strategies
　　teaching of 424
　and metacognition
　　instruction 443
　sex bias in 242
　See also Science curriculum; Student
　　centered curriculum
Curriculum-based assessment
　special needs students 144
Curriculum change *See* Curriculum
　　development
Curriculum design
　and cognitive development 63
　and learning factors 668
　and neo-Piagetian theory 100
Curriculum development
　and developmental stages 63
　discovery learning 355
　impact of educational psychology on
　　498–505
　and teacher expectation of students 631
Curriculum improvement *See* Curriculum
　　development
Curriculum materials *See* Instructional
　　materials
Curriculum reform *See* Curriculum
　　development
Curriculum research
　generative curriculum 379

Daily living skills
　stress variables 623
Databases
　and computer assisted instruction 701
Day care
　effect on child development 247
Day care centers

quality
　effect on child development 247
Day care programs *See* Day care
Decision making
　teachers 810
Declarative knowledge *394–96*, 404, 473
　and artificial intelligence 663
　and cognitive development 266
　concept formation
　　and long term memory 384
　definition of 394
　and epistemic structure 395
　examples and characteristics of 394
　experts' use of 507
　learning 415
　learning strategies
　　and second language learning 528
　measurement of 805
Decoding (reading) 559, 561
Deduction 466, 551
　in children 299
　　age differences 299, 300
　　inferences 300
　　cognitive processes 300
　learning processes
　　computer simulation 732
Defining Issues Test (DIT) 225
Delinquency 133
Delinquency prevention 134
Delphi technique
　research on independent study 773, 775
Democratic values
　just communities approach 491
　and nationalism 21
Denmark
　mental retardation 73, 75
Depression (psychology)
　in children
　　and pessimistic explanatory
　　　style 201
　　psychological patterns 199
Depth perception
　infants 285
　　stereogram research 286
Descriptive knowledge *See* Declarative
　　knowledge
Desegregation (disabled students) *See*
　　Mainstreaming
Developing nations
　learning disabilities
　　educational strategies for 801
　　research recommendations 802
Development
　definitions of 18
　and education *17–25*, 15
　and evolutionary processes 108
　as the goal of education 16
　as the prerequisite of education 16
　as a result of education 15
Developmental continuity
　individual development *161–63*
　lifelong learning 162
　　developmental reserve capacity 162
　longitudinal studies 161
Developmental disabilities

behavior disorders 68
interdisciplinary approach 71
longitudinal studies 71
pervasive developmental disorders 68
psychopathology *67–73*
severe disabilities *73–76*
definition of 73
educational discrimination 74
handicap discrimination 74
mainstreaming 74
normalization (handicapped) 73
public policy *73–76*
remedial programs 73
residential care 73
social attitudes 73
social integration 74
special education 73
supported inclusion 75
specific developmental disorders 68
Developmental education
and educational environment 40
Developmental psychology 268
behaviorism *89–92*
biogenetic law 2
change
issues 4
and child psychology 8
comparative studies 2
constructivism in 64
continuity
issues 4
cross sectional studies 9
developmental continuity 161
basic concepts 161
ecological models *82–86*
and educational practices *63–67*
as empirical science 1
empiricism in 64
and environment 2
and evolutionary theory 8
Freud's views 10
growth of 2
historical background 8, *1–7*
individual development 7, 51
individual differences 9, 100
infant cognitive development 122
information processing approach 5
interactional models 259
and interpersonal relationship 6
maturation–degeneration hypothesis 9
mechanistic model 10
objectives 1
organismic model 10
contextualism 11
person-centered approach 11
personality development 190
pluralistic models 11
psychoanalytic theories 6
and psychodynamics 112
responses to crises
individual differences 259
structuralist approaches 99
task analysis 100
theoretical diversity 1
theories of 4, 10

unidirectional models 11
variable-centered approach 11
zone of proximal development 6
Developmental psychopathology *See*
Psychopathology, developmental
disabilities
Developmental research
individual development *55–59*
cohort analysis 57
cross sectional studies 56
designs 56
intervention studies 58
longitudinal studies 56
microdevelopmental studies 58
multivariate developmental
paradigm 55
single case studies 58
time lag studies 57
training studies 58
univariate developmental paradigm
55
Developmental stages
classic theories 117
and curriculum development 63
environmental theories 117
and evolutionary theory 8
individual development *117–21*
interactional theories 117
maturation theories 117
and primary school admission 80
and socialization 194
statistical analysis 119
and time factors (learning) 95
transition crises 259
usefulness of concept 120
See also Child development; Cognitive
development; Piagetian theory
Developmental tasks
adult learning 767
and age 162
Havighurst's sequence 259
and individual development 259
Piagetian theory
criticism of 96
sources of 259
Developmental toxicology 176
and neurological impairment 176
Diagnostic and Statistical Manual of
Mental Disorders (DSM III-R) 67
Diagnostic tests
and cognitive development 637
special needs students 143, 144, 145
Didacticism
conventional instruction
Israel 684
United States 684
Diethylstilbesterol (DES) 176
Differential aptitude tests (DAT) 634
Differential psychology *See* Individual
psychology
Difficulty level
academic learning time 677
Diphenylhydantoin (DPH) 177
Disabilities
categories of 150

in children
social integration 154
and civil rights 74
deficit model 74, 75, 779
definitions of 150
incidence
in children United States 151
legislation
on rights 142
special education *150–60*
See also Developmental disabilities;
Language handicaps; Learning
disabilities; Mental disorders;
Mental retardation; Perceptual
handicaps
Disabled *See* Disabilities
Disadvantaged
definition of 406
language acquisition
and learning *406–08*
See also Economically disadvantaged;
Educationally disadvantaged;
Gifted disadvantaged
Disadvantaged environment
high risk students 137
early intervention 137
Disadvantaged youth
and social change 138
Discipline problems
and personality traits 188
Disciplines (intellectual) *See* Intellectual
disciplines
Discourse analysis
interpsychological studies 593
mathematics instruction 538
Discourse modes
in schools
initiation response evaluation (IRE)
model 408
Discourse participation
and learning experience 688
Discovery learning 332, *355–61*, 393,
academic achievement 359
and aptitude treatment interaction 673
and computer assisted instruction 702
criticisms of 356
deduction 357
discussion (teaching technique) 358
induction 357
instructional effectiveness 360
science curriculum 360
intellectual development 356
learner controlled instruction 358
learning motivation 356
Piagetian theory 318
retention (psychology) 356
Discrimination learning 317
classificatory behavior 382
computer simulation 731
Discussion
cognitive outcomes 754
Discussion (teaching technique)
and computer assisted instruction 702
Discussion groups
adult education *752–55*

attributes of 754
  cohesion 754
  composition 754
  size 754
  and learning 688
Distance education
  and adult learning 747
  and computer assisted instruction 751
  and computer networks 708
  See also Correspondence study
Distance learning *See* Distance education
Divergent thinking 551
  and cognitive style
    gifted 278
Document analysis *See* Content analysis
Downs syndrome
  intelligence quotient 172
Dramatic play 311
Drills (practice)
  computerized 700
  feedback in 398
  and learning 690, 31
Drug use
  in pregnancy
    and congenital impairment 176
Dualism
  and constructivism 338, 339, 340
Dyslexia *792–97*
  and brain hemisphere functions 794
  as congenital impairment 793
  diagnostic problems 794
  as perceptual handicap 793
  remedial reading 796

Early childhood *See* Young children
Early experience
  and cognitive development 12
  effect on infant behavior 121
  individual development *243–50*
  and personality development 12, 14
Early intervention
  disabled children
    effect on child development 247
  disadvantaged children
    effect on child development 247
Eating habits
  disorders 68
Economic development
  definition of 18
  education and 18
    institutionalist approach 19
    neoclassical view 18
    radical perspective 19
  See also Modernization
Economic education *See* Economics
    education
Economic growth *See* Economic
    development
Economically disadvantaged
  and special education placement 787
Economics education
  computer assisted instruction 573
  concept teaching 573
  research on learning in 573

simulation 574
  student understanding of concepts 573
Educable mentally handicapped *See*
    Mild mental retardation
Education
  and development *17–25*
  objectives 37
  and situated rationalism 345
Educational administration
  and learning factors 669
  See also School administration
Educational assessment
  and prior learning 463
Educational computing *See* Computer
    uses in education
Educational diagnosis
  learning disabilities 800
  special needs students *142–49*
    process 143
Educational discrimination
  severe disabilities 74
Educational environment
  models
    cognitive apprenticeship 40
    developmental instruction 40
  objectives 39
  and social development 615
  special needs students 143
  See also Classroom environment;
    Learning environment
Educational history
  developmental psychology *1–7*
  instructional psychology *29–33*
Educational inequality *See* Equal
    education
Educational level *See* Academic
    achievement
Educational management *See*
    Educational administration
Educational materials *See* Instructional
    materials
Educational media
  and learning motivation 728
  mental tool approach 728
  and novelty (stimulus dimension)
    726, 728
  tutoring function 725
  See also Audiovisual aids;
    Autoinstructional aids;
    Instructional materials
Educational objectives
  and cognitive processes 474, 475
  and instructional design theory 717
  and learning strategies 424
  preconceptions and misconceptions
    about 457
  See also Outcomes of education
Educational opportunities
  access to education
    and testing 806
  See also Access to education
Educational policy
  and learning factors 669
Educational practices
  and psychology 499

and research
  translation of *43–50*
Educational psychology
  curriculum development
    influence on *498–505*
    research 503
  emergence as a discipline 498
  factors in learning *612–15*
  and prior learning 459
  and psychoanalytic theory
    ego development 113
  See also Instructional psychology
Educational quality
  and learning factors 669
Educational research
  instructional materials
    texts 520
  instructional psychology *317–21*, 612
  interdisciplinary approach 611
  learning processes
    and student characteristics 665
  meta analysis 614
  outcomes of education
    productivity 614
    regression (statistics) 614
  and practice
    translation into *43–50*
  quasiexperimental design 612
  teacher expectation of students 626
  variables
    classroom environment 682
Educational sociology *See* Sociology
    of education
Educational strategies
  and learning disabilities
    comparative area studies 800
  mastery learning
    formative evaluation 363
Educational technology
  computer networks *708–13*
  and instructional design
    theory of 718
  and learning *725–30*
    measurement of efficiency 729
  mechanical aspects 725
  See also Instructional systems
Educational theories
  aptitude and instruction 612
  productivity 614
Educationally disadvantaged
  at risk persons
    compensatory education 503
  cultural differences 137
  incidence
    United States 140
Effect size
  in teacher expectation of students 629
Effective schools research
  and learning theories 666
Effective teaching *See* Teacher
    effectiveness
Efficiency
  and equal education 24
Effort *See* Energy expenditure
Ego development

psychoanalytic theory 113
Egocentrism
    and social cognition 304
Elderly *See* Older adults
Electric shock treatment
    memory effects 399
Electronic mail
    and computer networks 708
Elementary school curriculum
    problem solving programs 557
Elitism
    education and leadership 22
Email *See* Electronic mail
Embedded Figures Test 514
Emotion
    cognitive theories 214
    conceptualizations 213
    definitions and classification 213
    and learning 545
    psychoanalytic theories 213
    psychobiological approaches 213
    social learning conceptualizations 214
    theories and research traditions 213
Emotional development *213–17*
    and cognitive development 214
    educational implications of research
        216
    future research trends 216
    general principles 214
    integrative approaches 214
    and moral development 215
    primary emotions 214
    self-evaluative emotions 215
Emotional experience
    effect on learning 585
    and motivation
        influence on cognitive processes 371
Emotional problems
    effect on learning 586
Empathy
    cross cultural studies 53
    sex differences 186
    social cognition 304
        and social development 218
    young children 207
Empiricism
    developmental psychology 64
    and learning processes 409, 410
    and scientific attitudes 79
Employment
    See also Work
Empowerment
    concept of 773
    See also Individual power
Encoding (psychology)
    and memorization
        strategies 433
Encopresis *See* Fecal incontinence
Energy expenditure
    and ability
        and achievement need 211
    in learning processes 588
England and Wales
    gifted
        special education for 278

special education legislation 152
See also United Kingdom (UK)
Enrichment
    teaching methods
        mastery learning 364
Enrichment activities
    for the gifted 278
Enuresis *See* Urinary incontinence
Environment
    computer simulation of
        and computer assisted instruction
        701
    and developmental psychology 2
    for learning *687–91*
Epistemology
    genetics
        Piagetian theory 97
    information processing in 472
    learning from texts 519
    theoretical framework 472
Equal education
    and aptitude treatment interaction 671
    and efficiency 24
    sex discrimination
        developing nations 23
Error analysis (language)
    and contrastive linguistics 534
    foreign language instruction 534
    foreign language learning 511
    interlanguage 534
Error correction
    teaching methods
        mastery learning 363
Error patterns
    cognitive psychology research
        and curriculum development 501
Ethical instruction
    moral development
        discussion courses 227
        just communities approach 227
    See also Moral education; Values
        education
Ethnicity
    and adult learning 746
    and high risk students 139
    special needs students 787
    See also Race
Ethnography
    research
        methodology 592
Ethology 52, 108
    and animal ethology 108
    educational research 109
    instinct and learning 109
    naturalistic observation 109
Europe
    behaviorism
        historical background 34
    instructional psychology
        historical background 35
    learning disabilities
        prevalence 799
Evaluation
    impact on learning 604
    See also Educational assessment;

Formative evaluation;
    Measurement; Needs assessment;
    Program evaluation; Summative
    evaluation; Testing
Evaluation research
    and policy 61
Evaluative thinking
    and emotional response
        effect on learning process 585, 587
    self efficacy
        metacognition 105
Evolution
    Darwin's theory 81, 107
    definition of 334
    ecological models 85
    education and culture 107
    and genetics 81
    human foundations of learning 335
    mammalian foundations of learning
        334
    primate foundations of learning 335
    theories of
        and developmental psychology 8
        and individual development *107–12*
    theory of 2
Exceptional persons
    creativity 392
Existentialism
    and humanistic psychology 87
    and the self concept 228, 229
Expectancy *See* Expectation
Expectation
    and cognitive theory of emotion 214
    research 627
    and student development 788
Experience
    effect on learning 314
Experiential learning 763
    adult education *749–52*
    adults 745
        and self fulfilling prophecies 745
    apprenticeship model 750
    and computer networks 711
    concept of 750
    cultural context of 745
    Dewey's contribution 750
    international programs 751
    Kolb's learning cycle 750
Experimental design *See* Research design
Experimental pedagogy *See* Educational
    research
Experimental psychology 9
Experimental schools
    Adler's influence on 115
Expert novice research
    and automaticity of learning 95
    and child development 274
    cognitive development research 271
    cooperative learning 65
    and curriculum development 501
    and developmental psychology 64
    and domain-specific knowledge 26
    effect on memory 296
    and individual differences
        in content-specific knowledge 271

metacognition 65
modeling (psychology) of experts 65
problem solving
    computer simulation 731
    science education 570
transfer of training
    and task analysis 481
Expert systems 732
    analysis-based 732
    and cognitive development 728
    task analysis
        cognitive processes 481
Expertise
    acquisition of
        and cognitive development 27,
            273–76
    in children
        domain-specific 265
        usefulness of training 265
    cognitive development 379
    cognitive psychological research
        505–10
        educational implications 508
    and cognitive strategies 378
    and cognitive structures 378
    and creativity 393
    domain specific 273, 506, 507
    evaluation of component skills 509
    identification of 273
    individual differences 269
    learning strategies 508
    measurement of 273
        and test construction 805
    research on 273
    task analysis 480
    and transfer of training 484
Explanatory learning *See* Discovery
        learning
Explanatory style
    heredity 201
    and individual development *199–202*
        individual differences 199
        optimism 199
        pessimism 199
Extrinsic motivation *See* Incentives
Extroversion introversion
    and foreign language learning 515
    social development 219
Eye movements
    visual perception
        psychological process 452

Faculty development
    learning strategies
        problem solving 761
Failure
    attribution theory
        sex differences 186
    children's perceptions of
        and motivation 211
Family
    definitions of 250
    employed women 598
    and socialization 196

See also One parent family
Family characteristics
    and child development 244
    and learning factors 669
Family counseling 116, 253
Family environment
    and academic achievement *597–
        601*, 788
        cultural differences 597
    changes in 598
    and child rearing 598
    factors in learning 611, 613, 614
    and genetic studies
        individual development 172
    influence on learning in school
        597–601
        age variables 597
        developmental psychology
            perspective 597
        intelligence quotient
            individual differences 173
        and learning factors 669
        physical environment 598
            developing nations 598
Family history
    research 161
Family income
    and child development 246
Family influence
    individual development *250–54*
    and socialization 197
    stress variables 624
Family intervention
    and individual development 253
Family life
    behavior genetics 251
    and health 251
    heredity 251
Family problems
    effect on children's play 310
    prevention 253
Family programs 253
Family relationship 251
    couple relations 252
    intergenerational relations 252
    parent child relationship 252
    sibling relationship 252
Family school relationship
    school community relationship
        and special needs students 788
Family therapy *See* Family counseling
Family violence 251
    and intergenerational relations 253
Farmers
    education of
        and agricultural productivity 18
Fear
    in infants 215
Fecal incontinence 69
Feedback *396–98*
    in behavioral modification 396
    and computer assisted instruction 700
    definition of 396
    educational uses 396
    in instruction

behaviorist views 397
    cognitive psychology views 397
    in learning 396
        behaviorist views 396
        cognitive psychology views 397
    and programmed instruction 734, 737
    in skill development 396
    teaching methods
        mastery learning 363
Feminism
    and sex differences research 185
Fetal alcohol syndrome 176
    and learning disabilities 794
Field dependence independence 638, 640
Firm-based training *See* On the job
        training
First language *See* Native language
Flexible progression
    and tests of prior learning 463
Foreign language instruction
    error analysis (language) 534
    See also Second language instruction
Foreign language learning
    affective and social–psychological
        variables 514
    age effects 513
    attitudes and motivation 515
        Attitude Motivation Index 515
    contextual factors 516
    developmental sequences 512
    individual differences 513
        aptitude 513
        cognitive style 514
    input and conversation 516
    and intelligence 511
    learning processes *511–19*
    learning strategies 525
    motivation 515
    role of native language 512
    See also Second language learning
Forethought *See* Cognitive objectives,
        anticipatory outcomes
Form classes (languages)
    and foreign language learning 517
Formal education
    informal and nonformal
        and development 18
    See also Conventional instruction
Formal operations
    Piagetian theory 98
Formative evaluation
    feedback
        remedial instruction 363
    individualized instruction 363
    mastery learning 363
    student motivation 363
    teaching methods 364
Fostering Communities of Learners
    objectives 40
France
    instructional psychology
        historical background 29
Frankfurt School *See* Critical theory
Freehand drawing 575
Friendship

and social development 256
Functional literacy 428, 430
    and completion of secondary
        education 429
Further education *See* Adult education;
    Vocational education

Games
    puzzles
        transfer of training 484
    See also Computer games
Gender (sex) *See* Sex
Gender differences (sex) *See* Sex
    differences
Generalization
    classificatory behavior 382, 384
    computer simulation 731
Genetics
    and behavior development 173
    disorders
        behavioral consequences 172
    Galton's quantitative paradigm
        171, 172
    individual development *171–74*
    Mendel's paradigm 171
Genotypes
    biological influences 281
Germany
    instructional psychology
        historical background 29
    learning disabilities
        intervention 800
    special education 154
Gerontology 161
Gesell, Arnold (1880–1961)
    developmental psychology 2
Gestalt psychology
    development 31
    historical background 29, 34
    learning theories 318, 322, 410
    problem solving 554
    visual perception theory 452
Gestalt therapy
    and humanistic education 88
Gifted
    academic achievement 277
    child development *277–80*
    cognitive ability 277
    creative development 393
    as human capital 277
    identification
        cultural differences 278
    individual development
        longitudinal studies 278
    minority group children
    personality traits 277
    special education programs 278
        England and Wales 278
    and teacher behavior 278
    teaching methods
        research on 278
Gifted students *See* Gifted
Giftedness
    cognitive development

predictive measures 270
    definitions of 277
    and intelligence quotient 277
    research on 277
        cognitive psychology information
            processing approach 278
    sociocultural model 277
Goal orientation
    problems and crises
        individual development *258–62*
Governance *See* Educational
    administration
Government policy *See* Public policy
Grade point average (GPA)
    and learning strategies
        teaching of 425
Grammar
    pedagogic and scientific 533
    and reading comprehension 566
Grandparents
    influence on individual development
        252
    parent role
        and child development 246
Great Britain *See* United Kingdom (UK)
Group activities
    and cooperative learning 353, 622
    and network learning 711
    problem solving
        and cognitive development 621
Group behavior
    theories of 752
Group discussion 685
    adult education *752–55*
        conditions for productivity 755
        leadership 753
        objectives 753
        problems and issues 754
Group dynamics
    adult education 752
    interaction process analysis 685
        helping relationship 685
    and network learning 709
    teacher role 686
    training in 686
Group instruction
    mastery learning 364
    See also Small group instruction
Group Investigation (GI) method
    and small group instruction 684
Group processes *See* Group dynamics
Grouping (instructional purposes) 362
    and academic achievement
        cognitive psychology approach 683
    cooperative learning *683–87*
        and academic achievement 685
        cross cultural studies 684
        and social development 685
        types of 684
    interaction
        sex differences 686
    intergroup relations 354
    mainstreaming 354
    social psychology approach 683
    See also Ability grouping;

Heterogeneous grouping
Groups
    adult learning in *752–55*
    problem solving in 686
Guidance programs
    for children 115

Hall, G. Stanley (1840–1924)
    developmental psychology 3
Handicap discrimination
    severe disabilities 74
Handicap identification
    at risk persons
        special programs 137
    classification *142–49*
    learning disabilities
        preschool children 801
Handicapped *See* Disabilities
Handicaps *See* Disabilities
Health
    and family life 251
    and marital status 251
Helping relationship
    and learning 610
    young children 207
Helplessness
    and achievement need 209
    explanatory style 199
    in learning 790
Heredity
    congenital impairments 172
    and family life 251
Hermeneutics
    and psychological impact of life
        events 261
Heroin
    use in pregnancy
        effect on newborn infant 177
Heterogeneous grouping
    gifted 279
Heuristics
    and creativity 393
    instruction
        and domain specific knowledge 466
    and procedural knowledge 394
    and skill development 35
High achievement
    learning strategies
        group instruction 362
    and teacher behavior 629
    and teacher expectation of students 628
High risk students
    acceleration (education) 140
    classroom change 140
    community-based learning 140
    cultural deprivation approach 137
    and educational environment 140
    educational programs 140
    indicators 138
    individualized instruction 140
    learning strategies for 419
    and poverty 138
    prevention programs 140
    and race/ethnicity 139

remedial instruction 137, 140
teacher role 141
Hinduism
beliefs about origin of man 77
History
elementary schools
textbook research 572
research on learning of 572
student conceptions and
misconceptions 572
History of education *See* Educational
history
History instruction
concept teaching 574
teacher explanations 573
Holland *See* Netherlands, The
Home environment *See* Family
environment
Homework
academic achievement 692
and parent student relationship 600
Homogeneous grouping
gifted 279
See also Ability grouping
Hormones
sex differences 186
Households *See* Family
Human capital
and economic impact of education 18
rate of return
individual 19
social 19
Human development *8–17*
and adult learning
research methodology *55–59*
behaviorist approaches *89–92*
cross cultural approaches *51–55*
cultural concepts of *77–81*
ecological models *82–86*
Bronfenbrenner's 82
humanistic models *86–89*
religious concepts of *77–81*
research
and educational practice *63–67*
and social policy *59–62*
See also Evolution; Individual
development
Humanistic education
consciousness raising 88
and Gestalt therapy 88
group instruction 87
and self actualization 87
and the human potentials movement 87
and instructional design theory 719
and learner controlled instruction 88
and open education 88
Humanistic psychology
and anti-education 88
assumptions and models 86
and existentialism 87
and individual development *86–89*
and individualism 88
and phenomenology 87
view of behaviorism 86
view of psychiatry 86

Huntington's chorea 172
Hyperactivity
sex differences 189
See also Attention deficit disorders
Hypermedia
as educational environment 40
Hypothesis testing
and moral development 224

Identification (psychology)
and moral development 223
and socialization 194
Ideography
syllabographic languages 567
Illiteracy
and literacy 429
See also Adult literacy; Educationally
disadvantaged; Literacy
Illustrations
learning from texts 523
Imagery
and memorization 433
Imitation
and cultural transmission 108
infant behavior 122
Immigrant children
bilingualism
sociolinguistic studies (US) 375
Impulsiveness *See* Conceptual tempo
Incentives
learning motivation 448
and delay of gratification 450
See also Rewards
Independent learning *See* Independent
study
Independent study *771–77*
adults 743, 747
andragogy 772
computer assisted instruction 772, 773
and conceptual rationalism 342
and empowerment 773
and individual development 772
institutional support 772
learning readiness 772
learning strategies 419, 477
personal responsibility orientation
(PRO) model 774
and programmed instruction 734
promotion of
and cognitive processes 477
related concepts 772
research 772, 773, 775
role of facilitator 761, 762
in schools
problems 738
skills
self-instructive 790
theoretical approaches 773
trends and issues 775
usefulness 774
Individual autonomy *See* Personal
autonomy
Individual development
behavior development

sex differences *184–87*
behaviorist approaches *89–92*
beliefs
about causal forces 79
cultural influences *77–81*
religious factors *77–81*
biological influences 51, 52
biopsychosocial aspects
sex differences 186
cognitive ability 27
cognitive approaches 10
and contextual influences 83
cross cultural studies *51–55*
holistic approach 54
cultural psychology 52
cultural relativism 51
culture and personality school 51
developmental continuity *161–63*
developmental psychology 7
early experience *243–50*
and educational practices *63–67*
educational research *63–67*
objectives 63
emotional development *213–17*
evolutionary theory *107–12*
family influence *250–54*
genetics *171–74*
and heredity
ecological models 85
holistic approach 236
and lifelong learning 237
humanistic models *86–89*
and independent study 772
infants *121–25*
and interpersonal relationships 82
language acquisition *288–94*
lifelong learning *313–16*
memory *294–97*
moral development *222–28*
and narcissism 114
nature nurture controversy 51, 52
and peer relationship *254–58*
personality development *233–39*
physical development *178–84*
problems and crises *258–62*
process–person–context model 83
psychoanalytic theory 9, 114
psychodynamic theories *112–16*
psychological patterns *199–202*
research
ethnocentrism in 51, 52
research methodology *55–59*
self concept *228–32*
sex role *239–43*
social cognition *304–06*
characteristics of 105
theory *101–06*
social development *217–22*
social policy
and research *59–62*
and sociocultural patterns 101
sociological approaches 9
stability and change in 237
vs. maturation 193
See also Adolescent development;

Behavior development; Child
development; Cognitive
development; Creative
development; Emotional
development; Moral development;
Personality development;
Physical development; Skill
development; Social
development; Talent development
Individual differences
    ability *633–38*
    and ability grouping 656
    aptitude *633–38*
    cognitive ability 651
    cognitive development *268–72*
    and developmental psychology 9
    and educational practices 63
    Galton's genetic paradigm 171, 172
    intelligence
        evolutionary approach 108
    and learning 38
    and learning and instruction *649–60*
    and personal narratives 346
    personality development *187–91*
    teaching methods
        mastery learning 363
    See also Sex differences
Individual power
    beliefs about 79
Individual psychology
    individual differences 650
Individualized Classroom Environment
    Questionnaire (ICEQ) 681
Individualized instruction 656
    adult learning 769
    and aptitude treatment interaction
        671, 672
    computer assisted instruction 500
    cooperative learning 352
    mastery learning 362
    pacing 503
    See also Flexible progression
Individuals with Disabilities Education
    Act (IDEA) (US) 74
    1990 amendments 142
Induction 466, 551
    learning processes
        computer simulation 732
    thinking skills 414
        analysis of 636
Industrial restructuring *See* Industrial
    structure
Industrial structure
    characteristics of
        and learning 756
Industrial training
    and cognitive ability 758
    cognitive oriented conceptions 757
    creative thinking 556
    internationalization 758
    learning *755–59*
    learning strategies
        problem solving 761
    methods 758
    See also Job training; On the job

    training
Industrializing countries *See* Developing
    nations
Infant behavior
    approach-avoidance 122, 123
    behavior patterns 123
    change processes 122
    developmental stages *121–25*
    hedonic mediation 122, 123
    implications of research for
        parenting 124
    prosocial 207
    reflexes 122
Infant mortality
    child health 124
    United States 139
Infants
    auditory perception 123
    cognitive development 122
    development
        psychoanalytic theory 114
    developmental psychology 4
    early experience 121
    emotional adjustment 214
    fear in 215
    individual development *121–25*
    learning processes 122
    nature nurture controversy 121
    perception 285
        depth perception 240
    physical development 179
        body composition 179
        and breastfeeding 179
        determinants 180
        maturity indicators 179
        size 179
    Piagetian theory 122, 124
    play 308
    research issues 121, 123
    responses
        genetic factors 121
    self recognition 229
    sensory experience 123
    visual acuity 123
    visual perception 123
Inferences
    and cognitive development
        in children 298
    and learning from texts 521
    logical thinking 298
Information processing
    and developmental psychology 5
    in epistemology 472
Information technology
    and industrial training 756
Inhibition
    shyness
        student behavior 189
Inquiry
    discussion (teaching technique) 358
    teaching method 688
Institutional development *See*
    Organizational development
Institutions
    and socialization 194

Instruction
    cognitive participation in
        variables 472
    factors in learning 611, 614
    feedback in *396–98*
    formative evaluation of
        criticism of 810
    and intelligence 664
    and learning
        interaction 349
        intervention 326
    and learning strategies 761
    planning of
        educational resources 810
        student characteristics 810
    role of
        in development 6
    sequential approach
        the Learning Cycle 358
        science laboratories 358
    summative evaluation of 811
        educational planning 811
        influences 811
    theoretical framework 472
    theories of 329, 332, 499
    See also Pedagogy
Instruction psychology relationship
    dead-end street concept 30
    historical background 29
    one-way street concept 30
    two-way street concept 30
Instructional design
    adaptive strategies 718
    affective learning 719
    constructivist strategies 719
    content analysis 387
    contextual analysis 388
    curriculum design
        and vertical organization 501
    definitions of 715
    and educational objectives 500
    field of study 721
    and Gagné's learning taxonomies 664
    and instructional psychology *721–25*
        contributions 722
        relationship 721
    and learning factors 668
    and learning problems
        from misconceptions and
            preconceptions 457
    minimalist instruction 719
    models
        components of 722
        parameters 723
        procedures 723
        processes 724
    task analysis *478–82*
        selection of technique 480
    theories *715–20*
        attitudes 719
        characteristics of 716
        descriptive vs. prescriptive 722
        effects of information technology
            718
        future trends 720

historical background 717
and learning theories 716
level of detail 717
pragmatic vs. ideological 717
prescriptive vs. descriptive 716
product vs. process 717
trends 718
validity vs. superiority 717
Instructional development 378
models
and instructional design theory 717
Instructional effectiveness
and cognitive development 27
and cognitive processes 475
evaluation methods
paper and pencil tests 811
and misconceptions 456
See also Teacher effectiveness
Instructional improvement
individual differences *649–60*
Instructional materials
attention arousing 374
evaluation
teacher role 810
sex bias in 242
texts
research 520
See also Audiovisual aids; Textbooks
Instructional media *See* Educational
media
Instructional methods *See* Teaching
methods
Instructional processes *See* Teaching
methods
Instructional psychology
and behaviorism 721
cognitive shift in 721
and constructivism 32, 722
criticisms 36
definition of 33
and developmental psychology 320
ecological validity 320
historical background *29–33*, 34
and implicit learning 401
and implicit memory 401
individual differences school 320
influence of Gestalt 318
influence of Vygotsky 318
influence of W rzburg 318
and instructional design *721–25*
relationship 721
international status 29
intervention studies 40
and learning processes 37
learning theories 410
metaphors in 31
and models of learning 328
overview *33–43*
paradigms in *317–21*
quasiexperimental design 320
and research design 320
theories 34
descriptive vs. prescriptive 722
trends and developments 320
Vygotskyian theories 34

See also Educational psychology
Instructional systems
adaptation to individual differences
655
and aptitude treatment interaction
examples 673
and instructional design 716
and programmed instruction 738
Instructional technology *See* Educational
technology
Instructional time *See* Time on task
Instrumental Enrichment Program 557
Integrated activities
Computer Supported Intentional
Learning Environment (CSILE)
579, 688
learning systems
and computer managed learning
704–07
Integration (disabled students) *See*
Mainstreaming
Intellectual development
and cognitive ability 27
and domain specific knowledge 36
influence of learning activities on 80
intelligence tests
predictive validity 270
and interpersonal relationships 621
and literacy 430
measurement
individual differences 663
Intellectual disciplines
interests 587
knowledge of
and teacher expectation of
students 631
Intelligence *660–65*
and aptitude *813–16*
attitudes to
and learning motivation 447
and auditory perception 650
beliefs about
and motivation 210, 212
and biological determinism 147
and cognitive processes 661
correlation with prosocial behavior
in children 208
and creativity 392, 650
crystallized 650, 766
concept of 664
theories of 661
educational implications of research
665
effects of learning on 660
entity theory 437
ethological studies 109
fluid 650, 766
and aging (individuals) 164
concept of 664
theories of 661
general 650
general theories of thinking 662
incremental theory 437
information processing theory 661
and instruction 664

and learning 663
correlational studies 663
taxonomies (Gagné) 664
measurement of 660
and memory 650
metacognitive beliefs about 437
models of multiple (Thurstone) 270
and nature nurture controversy 660
Piaget's definition 98
and prior learning 461
and reaction time 650
Spearman's two factor theory 660
theories of 766
Sternberg's triarchic theory 662, 814
Thorndike's multifactor view 660
training
enrichment activities 26
and visual perception 650
See also Cognitive ability; Mental age
Intelligence differences 662, 663
correlation with learning 663
evolutionary approach 108
verbal ability 662
Intelligence quotient (IQ) 270
effect of education on 173
individual differences
family environment 173
genetic factors 173
influence on social development 220
and intraindividual differences 270
sex differences 185
Intelligence tests 634
adult performance
age differences 164
for children
predictive validity 270
crystallized and fluid intelligence 661
culture fair tests 662
and developmental psychology 9
Embedded Figures Test 514
historical development 660
and learning disabilities
diagnosis of 800
mental age 270
predictive measurement 813
pretests–posttests 814
special needs students 145
See also Cognitive measurement
Intelligent tutoring systems *See*
Computer assisted instruction
(CAI), programmed tutoring
Intentional learning *419–23*
learner controlled instruction 379
and motivation 445
Interaction
and computer assisted instruction 702
uses of 670
See also Aptitude treatment
interaction; Group dynamics
Interaction process analysis
group dynamics 685
Interactionism
and learning 602
Interactive video
and learning 689

Interests
  individual differences
    and motivation 654
Intergroup relations
  peer relationship 255
Interlanguage
  error analysis (language) 534
  skill development 511
International Association for the
    Evaluation of Educational
    Achievement (IEA)
  Computers in Education Study 695
  mathematics studies
    achievement sex differences 642
International Classification of Diseases
    (ICD9-CM) 67
International Conference on Cognitive
    Psychology and Instruction
    (1977) 35
International Council for Distance
    Education (ICDE) 750
Interpersonal competence *615–19*
  and cognitive development
    Piagetian theory 618
    Vygotskyian theory 618
  definitions of 616
  learning in school 617
  modeling (psychology) approach to
    learning 617
  skill development 616
    to reduce aggression 205
  and social development 219
    individual differences 220
    influence of intelligence quotient
      on 220
  social reinforcement approach 617
  and social values 616
Interpersonal interaction *See*
    Interpersonal relationship
Interpersonal relationship
  and child development 620
  and cognitive development 618, 620
  and developmental psychology 6
  egocentrism and altruism
    sociobiological approach 110
  and individual development 620
  and intellectual development 621
  and learning *619–23*
  and preconceptions 455
  social development 218
  and socialization 195
Interpersonal skills *See* Interpersonal
    competence
Intervention
  and instructional design 721
  and instructional psychology 723
  and learning disabilities 800
  and learning strategies
    teaching of 424
  programs
    and teacher expectation of
      students 630
  studies
    instructional psychology 40
Intervention *See* Behavior modification

Interviews
  and learning strategies
    evaluation 426
Intrinsic motivation *See* Self motivation
Invalidity *See* Validity
Inventions
  and creativity 393
Investment in education *See* Human
    capital
IQ *See* Intelligence quotient
Israel
  computer managed learning 706
  physics curriculum 571
  problem solving
    teaching of 557
Italy
  special education 154
Item characteristic curve theory *See*
    Item response theory (IRT)
Item response theory (IRT)
  and programmed instruction 740
  and test theory 807
Itinerant teachers
  special education 153

Japan
  computer managed learning 706
Job development
  task analysis 479
Job training
  psychomotor skill development
    547–50
  See also Off the job training; On the job
    training; Vocational education
Juvenile delinquency *See* Delinquency

Kent Mathematics Project 1978 (UK)
  and programmed instruction 739
Knowledge
  background
    and coherence 523
  biologically preferred 342
  biologically prepared
    vs. culturally elaborated 345
  conceptual 474
  conditional 473
  construction
    learning as 32
  content 474
  content-specific
    individual differences 270
  conversion from declarative to
    procedural 395
  conversion from procedural to
    declarative 395
  discourse 474
  domain specific
    and expertise 274, 275, 378
    and generalization 66
    influence on cognitive development
      26, 27
    and intellectual development 36

    and prior learning 460
    and reasoning 298, 299
  expert
    and performance *505–10*
  experts proceduralization of 507, 509
  explicit 474
  implicit and explicit 266
  and learning strategies 423
  and learning from texts 521
  metacognitive 437, 474
    age differences 438
  organization of *402–06*
  sociocultural 475
  strategy 474
  tacit 473
  task 474
  theories of
    and cognitive processes 473
  transfer of
    research 37
  types of *394–96*
  See also Declarative knowledge;
    Procedural knowledge
Knowledge acquisition
  computer simulation *730–33*
    Cascade model 732
    KAGE model 732
  in context 275
  expertise 273
  learning as 31
  Piagetian theory of internalization 395
  and problem solving 273
Knowledge characteristics
  and learning 790
Knowledge level
  prior learning *459–64*
Knowledge representation *402–06*
  rule-based systems
    computer simulation 730
  symbolic and distributed 404
Knowledge structures *See* Cognitive
    structures
Koranic schools
  and modernization 20

Labeling (of persons)
  special education 155
  special needs students 147
Labor market training *See* Job training
Language
  and cognitive structures 406
  learning
    concept of 401
    and preconceptions 455
  prestige
    and social values 531
  role in learning 603
  and sociocultural factors 594
Language acquisition
  bilingual children 375
  bilingualism
    and connectionist theory 376
  caregiver speech
    and foreign language learning 517

in children
   and implicit and explicit knowledge 266
concept of 401
disadvantaged children
   language deficit theory 406
   language difference theory 406
environmentalist perspectives 406
individual development *288–94*
   developmental stages 289
   prerequisites 291
language handicaps 291
   early identification 292
   specifically language impaired (SLI) children 292
and learning *406–08*
   educational implications 408
nativist perspectives 406
and nature nurture controversy 406
role of mothers 291
writing (composition) 580
Language aptitude
  foreign language learning 513
  learning strategies 514
  Modern Language Aptitude Test 513
Language arts
  computer programs
    writing instruction 579
Language attrition (skills) *See* Language skill attrition
Language development *See* Language acquisition
Language disabilities *See* Language handicaps
Language disorders *See* Language handicaps
Language education
  pedagogy 532
  policy
    beliefs influencing 532
    options 532
    rationales for 531
  technology 532
Language experience approach
  beginning reading 561
Language handicaps
  dysphasia
    and implicit knowledge of artificial grammars 266
  language acquisition 291
  language processing 292
  learning disabilities
    disadvantaged children 406
  and neurological impairments 170
Language processing
  language handicaps 292
Language skill attrition
  in bilingualism 376
    foreign language 377
    native language 377
Language teachers
  teacher education 532
Language usage
  Bernstein paradigm 407
  differences in 407

in mathematics *538–42*
Latent trait theory *See* Item response theory (IRT)
Latin
  studies of
    and transfer of training 483
Latin schools movement
  and problem solving 556
Lead poisoning
  and learning disabilities 794
  and neurological impairment 176
Leadership
  group discussion 753
Leadership responsibility
  education and political socialization 22
Learner characteristics *See* Student characteristics
Learner controlled instruction 422, 324
  and aptitude treatment interaction 673
  and attribution theory 380
  cognitive strategy instruction
    special education *779–86*
  discovery learning 358
  inquiry 358
  intentional learning 379
  and self concept 380
  and socialization 380
Learning
  and ability 651
  acquisition
    and knowledge 477
  activity theory *347–50*
  attention dependent 369, 371
  behaviorism and educational psychology 500
  characteristics of 37
  child study movement 500
  and cognitive processes *377–81*, 478
  cognitive style in *638–41*
  and conceptual rationalism 344
  constructive aspects 37
  and constructivism *338–41*, 691
  cultural differences 605
    sources of 606
  cumulative aspects 37
  deep vs. shallow 519
  definition of 37
  and development 9
  developmental stages
    age differences 313
  domain specific 326
  effect of affective behavior on *585–90*
  environments for *687–91*
  evolution of
    anthropological perspective on *334–38*
  factors affecting 668
  impact of evaluation on 604
  implicit
    characterization 401
    definition of 399
    and instructional psychology 401
    and memory *399–401*
    research 400
    tests 401

individual development *313–16*
individual differences 38, *649–60*
  special needs students *786–92*
and instructional psychology 721, 723
and intelligence 663
by interaction 347, 380
interactionist perspectives 602
as knowledge acquisition 31
and knowledge characteristics 790
as knowledge construction 32
and language acquisition *406–08*
meaningful
  characteristics of 323
  cognitive conceptions 323
and memory 369
metacognitive beliefs about 437
metaphors of 31
modalities 349
models of *327–33*
  Bloom's school learning 331
  Brumer's theory of instruction 332
  Carroll's school learning 329
  Dahll f's steering group 330
  and grouping (instructional purposes) 328
  and prediction 328
  relevance (education) 327
  and teaching methods 328
  validity 327
nature nurture controversy 602
nature of 601
objectives 38
orientations
  and learning strategies 640
and peer relationship *607–11*
personal autonomy in 762
prepared structures 344
psychological patterns 326, *612–15*
and responses 31
role of interpersonal relationship 340
role of language in 603
self-regulation 38
significance for cognitive development 26
and situated rationalism 344
social context of 337
social and cultural context 324
and social and cultural differences 605
social influences *601–07*
social interaction model *601–07*
social theories 603
sociology of *601–07*
stages 399
and symbolic interactionism 603, 604
and teacher effectiveness 603
from texts *519–24*
  factors affecting 520
  integrative learning strategies 522
  metacognitive strategies 521
  textbase strategies 521
theory practice relationship 350, 329
time factors in *See* Time factors (learning)
types of 519
and visual perception *451–55*

in work environment *755–59*
See also Cognitive processes;
    Individual development; Prior
    learning; Situated learning
Learning ability
  and text content 523
Learning activities 347
  and computer managed learning
    704–07
  and learning motivation 447
  participation in 689
Learning characteristics
  alterable vs. static variables 787
  special needs students *786–92*
    community influence 788
    ethnocultural and socio-economic
      status 787
    family environment and influence
      788
    peer influence 788
Learning contracts See Performance
    contracts
Learning difficulties See Learning
    problems
Learning disabilities 150
  comparative area studies 799
  definitions of 793, 798
  diagnosis 800
  educational strategies
    comparative area studies 800
  historical background 797
  intervention 800
  knowledge
    and production deficiency 790
  neurological impairments 170
  prenatal influences 794
  prevalence 799
  research
    recommendations 801
  specific *797–803*
  treatment 800
Learning by doing See Experiential
    learning
Learning environment 377, 380, 603
  communication 688
  Computer Supported Intentional
    Learning Environment (CSILE)
    579, 688
  and distributed cognition 380
  performance 690
  problem solving 689
  and teaching methods *687–91*
  training 690
  See also Educational environment
Learning Environment Inventory
  (LEI) 681
Learning to learn See Learning strategies
Learning materials See Instructional
  materials
Learning motivation 326, *445–51*
  and academic achievement 445
  attention control 446
  and attribution theory 422
  and curriculum development 502
  effort avoidance 446

goal orientation 446
incentives 448
individual development 315
individual power 446
and interest 326
and learning strategies 419, 421
media research 728
  cognitive theories 728
and self efficacy 326, 422
self motivation 448
social sciences 574
and test anxiety 446
See also Self motivation
Learning networks See Network learning
Learning objectives See Behavioral
  objectives
Learning organization 756
  concept of 763
Learning outcomes See Outcomes of
  education
Learning potential See Aptitude
Learning problems
  age differences
    individual development 314
  disadvantaged children
    sociolinguistic research 407
  and misconceptions 457
  neurological impairments *792–97*
    application of theory and
      research 795
    and environmental influences 795
Learning processes 760
  and academic achievement
    research 668
  adult education 764
  analysis and formation 348
  and aptitude treatment interaction 671
  and arousal 412, 768
  as cognitive change 379
  cognitive system model 382
    concept learning model 382
    executive control 383
    long term memory 383
    sensory receptors 383
    short term memory 383
  computer simulation *730–33*
    learning by chunking 731
  concept formation *381–85*
  definition of 412
  discovery processes 356, 359
  dynamics of
    variables 476
  effect of prior learning on *459–64*
  and empiricism 409, 410
  evaluative thinking
    and emotional response 587
  feedback in 768, *396–98*
  functions 324
  guidance 357
  historical background 409
  induction 356
  infants 122
  inquiry 359
  and instructional psychology 37
  Kolb's learning cycle model 750, 766

macrostructure 348
measurement of 435
measurement techniques
  academic learning time 677
and memory
  research 432
misconceptions 477
models of 327
and outcomes of education *409–18*
  instructional psychology model
    412, 416
personal learning system 767
and physical development 314
preconceptions and misconceptions
  resistance to change 456
and prototypic learning tasks 815
and rationalism 409
rationalist views 342
research
  historical background 471
and student characteristics
  research 665
Learning readiness
  independent study 772
Learning strategies 348, 349, *419–23*
  adults 745, *760–64*
    and emotional maturity 746, 747
    epistemic cognition 745
    and lifelong learning 745
    metacognition 746
    reflective judgment 745
  and affective factors 421
  age effects 315
  and aptitude treatment interaction 674
  associative learning 315
  characteristics of expertise 419
  and cognitive development 26, 420
  cognitive mapping 494
  cognitive processes 474
  cognitive style 420
  conclusion-oriented 640
  and context effect 421
  critical reflection 760, 763
  definitions of 525, 760
  description-oriented 640
  developmental stages
    and teaching methods 66
  evaluation 423
    methods 426
  facilitation 761
  group instruction
    high achievers 362
  holistic approach
    comprehension learning 640
  independent study 419
  individual development 315
  individual differences 653, 789
    intervention 790
    research agenda 790
    training in development 653
  informed strategies for learning
    program 502
  integrative 522
  knowledge required 419
  knowledge scaffolding 508

learner controlled instruction 422
mastery learning *362–67*
and memory
   research 432
and metacognition 419, 421, 438,, 442, 789
methods and applications 761
mnemonics 315
models of 424
and motivation 419, 421
phenomenographic approach 319
problem solving *550–55*
proceduralization of knowledge 507, 509
promotion of 495
research 351
and self concept 420
and self efficacy 528
and self evaluation (individuals) 421
serialist approach
   operation learning 640
SMART operations 476
student characteristics 521
and students 423
   characteristics 423
study skills 420
task analysis 420, 480
teaching of *423–27*
   adjunct instruction 424
   case study 425
   course evaluation 425
   courses in 424
   measurement 425
   metacurriculum 425
   types of 423
testing of *423–27*
and theories about intelligence 437
thinking skills *550–55*
training 378
training programs 494
   educational effectiveness 494
transfer of training *483–87*
types of 423
use of metaphors in
   and transfer of training 485
visualization 315
in the work environment 762
See also Study skills
Learning and Study Strategies Inventory (LASSI) 425, 426
Learning style *See* Cognitive style
Learning theories
   accessibility theory 462
   adult learning
      transformative learning 744
   behaviorism *89–92*, 317, 409
      United States 322
   cognitive development
      Piagetian theory 322
   and cognitive psychology 322
   and cognitive restructuring 462
   constructivism
      and task analysis 482
   and curriculum development 499
   elaboration theory 462

experimental psychology 327
and Gagné's types of learning 323, 479
Gal'perin's stage by stage approach 326, 332
Gestalt psychology 318, 322
historical overview *322–27*
Hull's motivational 90
and individualism 322
and industrial training 756
information processing model 322, 462
and instructional design theory 716
instructional psychology 410
models
   of school learning 666
and models of learning 327, 329
and problem solving 322
reflective learning 409
retrieval aid theory 462
selective attention theory 462
social learning theory 90
and student characteristics 471
transfer of training 483
See also Piagetian theory
Learning time *See* Time on task
Learning by using *See* On the job training
Lecture method 689
Liberia
   Vai script
      studies of 484
Life events
   coping 261
   individual development 101
      problems and crises in *258–62*
   and personality development 235
   psychological impact of
      hedonistic value 260
      and subjective interpretations 260
   See also Crises (life events)
Life expectancy
   developed nations 164
Life-span
   beliefs about
      religious traditions 78
Life-span development *See* Individual development
Life-span education *See* Lifelong learning
Life style
   individual psychology 115
Lifelong development *See* Individual development
Lifelong education *See* Lifelong learning
Lifelong learning
   cognitive ability 765
   and developmental continuity 162
   and developmental psychology 7
   developmental stages 767
   effectiveness *760–64*
   implications for educators *764–71*
   independent study 773
   individual development *313–16*
      developmental stages theory 313
   and open education *749–52*
Limited English speaking

high risk students
   United States 139
Linear programming 503
Linguistic competence
   individual differences 269
Linguistics
   scope 531
   second language learning *531–34*
Literacy *428–31*
   definitions of 428
   and development 23
   effect of written language on 429
   environmental 430
   functions of 429
   historical background 428
   and illiteracy 429
   individual differences 80
   levels in relation to length of school attendance 429
   and reading comprehension
      in second languages 564
   and social change 428, 429
   specialization
      development of vocabulary skills 430
      expertise 428, 429, 430
   transfer of training 484, 485
   written language
      cultural differences 428
      historical development 428
   See also Functional literacy; Illiteracy; Scientific literacy
Literacy skills *See* Literacy
Locus of control
   and aging (individuals) 166
   attribution theory
      and helplessness 200
Logic
   and logical thinking 466
Logical thinking *464–67*
   analogical transfer theory 552
   and cognitive structures 300
   inferences 464
   thinking skills 466
LOGO
   and computer assisted instruction 702
   effect on children's problem solving skills 698
Long term memory (LTM) 369
   cognitive restructuring in 462
   concept formation
      contextual knowledge 384
      and declarative knowledge 384
      procedural knowledge 384
      and prior learning 432
Longitudinal studies
   developmental research 56
   teacher expectation of students 630
Low achievement
   ethnocultural and socio-economic status 787
   high risk students 138
   and teacher behavior 629
   and teacher expectation of students 628
      Good's passivity model 629

Low achievers *See* Low achievement

Mainstreaming
    misconceptions about 74
    severe disabilities 74
    special education 153, 154
        developed nations 154
        developing nations 154, 158
Mammals
    brain development 169
Management development
    humanistic model 756
    learning strategies 763
Management training *See* Management
    development
Manpower Services Commission
    (MSC) (UK)
    Open Tech program 750
Manufacturing
    production line model
        training 756
Marital instability
    and child development 252
Marital satisfaction
    and child development 252
Marital status
    and health 251
Marxism
    and socialization 195
Mass communication *See* Mass media
Mass media
    and preconceptions 455
    and socialization 727
    violence in
        and development of aggression in
            children 205
Mastery learning 331, *362–67*
    and academic achievement 362
    and achievement need 209, 212
    evaluative thinking
        and emotional response 588
    group instruction 364
    and individual achievement differences
        28
Mathematical concepts 535
Mathematical enrichment 535, 536
Mathematical vocabulary
    and bilingualism 540
    history of English 540
    language styles
        register 539
Mathematics
    attitudes to 543
    beliefs about 543
    emotional response to 543
    language of *538–42*
    learning motivation 546
        attribution theory 544, 546
        expectancy value theory 546
    and psychology 535
    role of affective behavior
        sex differences 643
    social context
        beliefs about 543

Mathematics achievement
    affective behavior and 544
    individual differences 642
        and prior learning 652
    and self efficacy 543
    and self esteem 543, 544
    sex differences 544, *642–45*
        affective factors 544
        career choice 644
        and educational opportunities 643
    and sex stereotypes 644
Mathematics anxiety 543, 543
    females 643
Mathematics curriculum
    and affective behavior 544
    course selection
        sex differences 642
Mathematics education
    affective behavior and *543–47*
    and cognitive psychology 535
    intervention studies 340
    preconceptions and misconceptions
        455–59
    Realistic Mathematics Education
        (RME) 340, 537
    student attitudes to *543–47*
    and teacher expectation of students 630
Mathematics instruction *535–38*
    beliefs about 543
    classroom communication 538
    cooperative learning 536, 537
    discourse analysis 538
    listening and discussion 538
    reading writing relationship 539
    small group learning 536
Mathematics skills
    affective factors 535
    belief in usefulness 543
    heuristics 535
    learning *535–38*
        cultural constructivism 536
        dispositional view 535
        social constructivism 536
    metacognition 535
Mathematics teachers
    expectations of females 643
Mathematics tests
    scholastic aptitude tests
        sex differences 642, 643
    standardized tests
        sex differences in performance 643
Mathematics textbooks
    language usage 540
Mathophobia *See* Mathematics anxiety
Maturity (individuals)
    and developmental change 4
    psychological characteristics 87, 88
Media (communication) *See* Mass media
Media research
    comparative analysis 726
    and learning *725–30*
Medial geniculate
    studies
        and dyslexia 794
Medicine

role of
    and learning disabilities 798
Meditation 88
Memorization
    and associative learning 370
    encoding strategies
        elaboration 433
        imagery 433
        learning memory 434
        prior knowledge activities 433
        rehearsal 433
        reorganization 433
        retrieval 433
        summarization 433
        transformational mnemonics 433
    hierarchical schemata 370
    and prior learning
        factors 431
Memory
    in bilingualism
        nature of 376
    concept of capacity 294
        older adults 296
    concept formation in 382
    development
        in adults 296
        in children 294
        ethnography 591
    and domain knowledge 295
    evaluation of 434
    expert performance 505, 506
        domain specific 506
    explicit
        definition of 399
        vs. implicit 400
    implicit
        definition of 399
        and instructional psychology 401
        and learning *399–401*
        and priming 266
        research 399
        use of term 399
        vs. explicit 400
    incidental vs. intentional 432
    individual development *294–97*
    and intelligence 650
    and learning 369
        stages 399
    learning strategies 294
    measurement of 434
    and metacognition 295, 296
    in observational learning 103
    in older adults 296
    and prior learning
        role of 432
    scientific study of
        historical background 431
    strategic processing
        coordination 434
        role of 432
    teaching and testing for *431–36*
    tests
        types of 431, 434
    theories
        multiple system approach 400

processing 400
See also Long term memory (LTM);
    Recall (psychology); Recognition
    (psychology); Semantic memory;
    Short term memory (STM)
Menstruation 132
Mental age
  infant cognitive development 122
  intelligence tests 270
Mental disorders
  classification systems 67
    Diagnostic and Statistical Manual
      of (DSM III-R) 67
    International Classification of
      Diseases (ICD) 67
  clinical diagnosis 67
Mental health
  impact of life events on 260
Mental retardation
  children 68
  cognitive development
    predictive measures 270
  genetic disorders 172
  and learning disabilities 797
  See also Mild mental retardation;
    Severe mental retardation
Mental tests *See* Psychological testing
Mentors
  online 710
Metacognition 319, *436–41*, 589
  in children 301
  and cognitive development 414
  and cognitive processes 474
  and cognitive strategies
    second language learning 526
  cognitive strategy instruction 780
  comprehension monitoring 421
  and curriculum development 502
  definition of 441
  development of 458
  and energy expenditure 654
  experts use of 507
  and industrial training 757
  instruction
    choice of students for 442
    content 441
    curriculum issues 443
    evaluation of 443
    future research 443
    guidelines 443
    principles 442
    tasks for 442
    time factors 442
  and learning factors 669
  learning strategies 27, 421, 438,
    760, 789
    activities 419
    learning from texts 521
    and outcomes 528
    research 521
  and memory 295, 296, 437
  and moral development 66
  preconceptions and misconceptions
    457
  processes underlying 414

design 443
  implementation problems 443
  methodological issues 443
  studies 441
  trends 440
self control 436, 438, 469
  problem solving 438
  reading 438
and self efficacy 105, 437
and skill development 35
and social affective strategies
  second language learning 526
strategies 431
  and self-regulation 434
  teaching and assessing *441–44*
thinking skills
  and transfer of training 485
training in 378
and types of knowledge 396
use of concept 436
Metamemory *See* Metacognition
Methadone
  use in pregnancy
    effect on newborn infant 177
Methylmercury
  fetal Minamata disease 176
Migrant education programs
  high risk students 137
Mild disabilities
  learning
    individual differences 787
Mild mental retardation
  and mainstreaming 74
Mildly handicapped *See* Mild disabilities
Mind
  theories of
    and children's cognitive
      development 265, 267
Minimum competencies
  and instructional design theory 719
Minnesota Multiphasic Personality
    Inventory (MMPI)
  age differences 166
Misconceptions *455–59*
  cognitive psychology research
    and curriculum development 502
  definition of 455
  patterns of
    and learning problems 457
  sources of 456
  use of term 455
Mnemonics
  and memorization 433
Model
  use of term 328
Modeling (psychology)
  and cultural transmission 108
  effects of 103
  explanatory style 200
  mass media 102
  and moral development 223
  observational learning 102
  role in social cognition 102
Models
  and computer assisted instruction 701

Modernization
  education and 20
    critique 20
    mass media 20
Montessori method
  for the gifted 279
Moods
  effect on learning 585, 586
Moral development
  and cognitive development 14, 224
    Piagetian theory 224
  and cooperative learning
    Piagetian theory 620
  cross cultural studies 53
  Defining Issues Test (DIT) 225
  and emotional development 215
  factors influencing
    educational implications 227
    individual development *222–28*
  Kohlberg's theory 65, 224
    and citizenship education 65
    developmental stages 224
    and ethnocentrism 226
    evaluation 225
    and feminism 226
    methods of research 225
  learning processes 491
  and metacognition 66
  and motivation 223, 227
  psychoanalytic theories 223
  self motivation 1010
    and disengagement practices 104
  social learning theories 223
  theories of 223
  value judgment
    consistency with action 227
  values education *489–92*
    developmental stages 489
Moral education
  defining objectives 491
  See also Ethical instruction
Moral judgment *See* Moral values, value
    judgment
Moral values 490
  and behavior standards 223
  conventional 490
  definitions of 223
  and individual power 223
  and intention 223
  moral rules 222
  and personal autonomy 491
  and social values 222
  universalism debate 226
  utilitarianism 223
  value judgment
    and moral development 224
    and social cognition 305
Mortality rate
  children 136
Mother tongue *See* Native language
Mothers
  academic achievement
    and child development 245
  employed
    effect on child development 246

knowledge level
  high risk students 139
Motivation
  and academic persistence 446
  achievement need
    development of *209–13*
    individual differences 653
  action orientation 210
  adult education
    expectancy-valence model 768
  adult learning 768
  and attention 372, 373
  attribution theory
    sex differences 200
  and behavior modification 103
  behavior theories 445
  and cognitive development 14
  content theories 445
  developmental issues 210
  and emotional experience
    influence on cognitive processes 371
  and grouping (instructional purposes)
    cooperative learning 684
  hierarchy of needs (Maslow) 87
  and learning strategies 423
    teaching of 426
  and moral development 223
  in observational learning 103
  process theories 445
  psychological patterns in 445
  state orientation 210
  See also Learning motivation; Self
    motivation
Motor development
  and developmental psychology 281
  history of research 281
  origins of 282
    reaching behavior in infants 282
    reflex hypothesis 282
    walking in children 282
  perceptual motor learning *280–84*
  skill development *280–84*
  systems approach 281
Motor skills *See* Psychomotor skills
Movement education
  behaviorist approach 548
  cognitive approach 548
  ecological approach 549
  psychomotor skills *547–50*
Multimedia technology
  and computer networks 712
Multiple choice tests
  and problem solving 557
  and programmed instruction 734, 740
Multiple disabilities 73
Music education 575
  aesthetic preferences in 576
Mutism
  elective 69
My Class Inventory (MCI) 681

Narcissism
  and individual development 114
Narration

writing (composition) 578
National Extension College (UK)
  flexible scheduling 750
Nationalism
  education and 22
Native language
  reading processes 565
Native language instruction
  and language education policy 532
Nature nurture controversy
  cognitive development
    individual differences 271
  developmental psychology 12
  genetics 12
  individual development 51, 52
    cross cultural studies 52
    Mead's views 52
  and language acquisition 406
  and perception in infants 285
  personality development 234
Need gratification
  education and 21
Needs assessment
  and task analysis 482
Negative attitudes
  and individual development 199
Nelson–Denny Reading Comprehension
  Test 425
Nervous system
  development of the brain 169
  Kennard principle of development 169
  myelination process 169
  neural development
    and motor development 281
Netherlands, The
  instructional psychology
    historical background 29
Network learning
  characteristics of 709
  design and implementation 710
Neurological impairments
  and developmental neurotoxicants 176
  diagnostic and clinical problems 796
  influence of environment 169
  and learning disabilities 797
  learning problems *792–97*
    evidence 793
Neurological organization
  brain hemisphere functions 792
  models and learning 794
  stimulation *169–71*
Neurosis 115
New information technology (NIT) *See*
  Information technology
New technology *See* Technological
  advancement
Nigeria
  special needs students 147
Nonverbal behavior *See* Nonverbal
  communication
Nonverbal communication
  and development of language 290
  ethological studies 109
Normalization (handicapped)
  cultural values 74

daily living skills 74
  severe disabilities 73
North America
  instructional psychology
    historical background 29
  learning strategies projects 762
  See also Canada; United States (US)
Norway
  bully/victim research 257
  special education 157

Object relations
  psychoanalytic theory 113
Objective referenced tests *See* Criterion
  referenced tests
Observational learning
  cognitive processes in 103
  mammalian foundations 334
  modeling (psychology) 102
    cognitive processes in 103
    mass media 102
Occupational training *See* Job training
Odyssey (Venezuela)
  problem solving program 557
Oedipal complex 112
  cross cultural studies 51
Off the job training
  evaluation studies 758
Older adults
  adult education 166
  cognitive ability
    maintenance 165, 167
  developmental psychology 7
  educational needs 163, 164, 166
  learning processes 166, 316
  memory 296
On the job training 757
  evaluation studies 758
  evolution in 757
One parent family 598
  and child development 246
  high risk students 139
Online systems
  for courses 708
  user characteristics 711
Ontogeny
  and phylogenesis 8
Open education
  for adults *749–52*, 769
  characteristics of 749
  and computer networks 708
  concepts of 749
  international 750
  issues and trends 751
  research 751
  United Kingdom 750
  United States 751
Open learning *See* Open education
Open schools *See* Open education
Open University (OU) (UK) 750
  and independent study 772, 773
Operant conditioning
  and language 91
  special education 779

Oral language
  and written language 428, 429
Organizational development
  and industrial training 756
Originality *See* Creativity
Orthographic symbols
  role of
    in reading comprehension 567
  types of 567
Outcomes of education
  and aptitude treatment interaction 671
  and computer networks 711
  and instructional design theory 716
  learning processes and *409–18*
  and student characteristics 328, 331

Pacing
  and programmed instruction 738
Paraplegia *See* Neurological impairments
Parent aspiration 600
Parent attitudes
  and aggression
    in children 204
  developing nations 598
  influence on learning 600
  and sex roles 242
Parent child relationship
  and academic achievement 598
  and child development 246, 252
    mothers and 246
Parent influence
  on academic achievement *597–601*
Parent participation
  cultural differences 599
  and learning factors 669
Parent student relationship
  helping relationship
    and cognitive development 599
Parent teacher conferences
  parent participation
    and academic achievement 599
Parent teacher cooperation 599
  sociobiological approach 110
Parenthood
  and health 251
Parenting skills
  and socialization
    via modeling (psychology) 599
Parents
  cognitive ability
    and child development 247
  psychological characteristics
    effect on child development 247
Parents as teachers
  and academic achievement 599
Participant observation
  sociolinguistics 503
Participation
  adult education
    experience factors 57
Pattern recognition 371
  expertise in 506, 509
Payment by results *See* Performance
  contracts

Pedagogy
  authoritarianism 622
  cooperation 622
  See also Instruction
Peer acceptance
  peer groups 255
Peer evaluation
  peer acceptance
    and development 256
  sociometric techniques 255
Peer groups 254
  and socialization 196, 197
Peer influence
  and academic achievement 788
  effect on children's play 311
  factors in learning 611, 613, 614
  and learning in school 598
  personality development
    and genetic factors 172
  special needs students 788
  stress variables 624
Peer relationship
  constructive aspects 610
  and cooperative learning 608, 609
  and discovery learning 609
  helping relationship
    and learning 610
  and individual development *254–58*
  interpersonal communication 607
  and learning *607–11*
  and personality development 256
  problems 254
    intervention programs 257
  and social development 218, 221
  sociobiological approach 110
  and sociocognitive conflict 609
Peer teaching 608, 621
  and cognitive development 618
  critical thinking in 609
  evaluation research 609
  learning experience 685
  peer influence 255
  and Vygotsky's zone of proximal
    development 609
Perception
  concept formation
    cognitive system model 383
    memory 400
  discrimination learning
    and transfer of training 485
  infants 285
  integrative function 371
  sensory experience
    and memory 371
  and spatial ability 371
  visual perception
    and learning *451–55*
Perceptual development *284–88*
  children 287
    separability hypothesis 287
  and cognitive development 284, 287
  depth perception
    infants 240
  enrichment programs 287
    AGAM project (Israel) 287

  and motor development 283
Perceptual handicaps 287
  compensation theory 287
    and attention control 287
  effect on cognitive development 287
  learning disabilities 793, 797
Perceptual motor coordination 283
  feedback in 283
Perceptual motor learning
  development *280–84*
  skill development 283
Perceptual priming
  characteristics of 400
Performance
  automaticity
    in expert 416, 507, 509, 714
    and prior learning 373
  and expert knowledge *505–10*
  as learning experience 690
  and learning motivation 690
  See also Expertise
Performance contracts
  and experiential learning 751
Performance objectives *See* Behavioral
    objectives
Performance tests 504
  and problem solving 557
  reliability 807
  See also Intelligence tests;
    Standardized tests
Performing arts *See* Theater arts
Perinatal influences
  child development 248
  individual characteristics 245
Permanent education *See* Lifelong
    learning
Perseverance *See* Persistence
Persistence
  in children
    Japan 599
  in learning 412
  student behavior 189
Person–environment interaction 670
Person perception *See* Social cognition
Personal autonomy
  in children
    United States 599
  and moral values 491
Personal development *See* Individual
    development
Personal narratives
  and individual differences 346
  and situated rationalism 346
Personality
  and arousal patterns 188
  beliefs about structure of 78
  in children
    research studies 188
  concept of 233
  and educational practices 188
  factors in learning *612–15*
  and heredity 187
  infant behavior 188
  in infants and children
    longitudinal studies 188

sex differences 189
  context effect 190
  and teaching methods 188
Personality assessment
  problems with 189
  by teachers 189
Personality development *233–39*
  in adults 165
    resistance to change 165
  biological factors 234
  and cognitive development 14
  concept of 233
  dynamic interaction theory 235, 237
  ecological model 15
  environmental factors 234, 238
  Erikson's theory 259
  holistic approach 233, 236
  and learning processes 348
  life events 235
  mental system 233
  peer influence
    and genetic factors 172
  and peer relationship 256
  psychological patterns *187–91*
  in social context 14
  and trust (psychology) 200
Personality problems
  narcissism 115
  neurosis 115
Personality rating *See* Personality
    assessment
Personality studies
  attribution theory 14
  five factor model 14, 190
  history
    and conceptual approaches 188
Personality traits
  age differences
    generation gap 165
  cognitive style 638
  and discipline problems 188
  genetic factors 173
  levels of analysis 237
  prosocial behavior 208
  protective factors in life crises 261
  sex differences 185
  and social development 219
Personalized instruction *See*
    Individualized instruction
Personnel selection
  task analysis 479
    recruitment 479
    training 479
Perspective taking
  and social cognition 304
    false belief paradigm 304
Persuasive discourse
  and ability 465
  and graduate study 466
  and instruction 465
  and learning 688
    conversational teaching 688
    Itakura method 688
  logical thinking 464
    in children 465

evaluation studies 465
  role of attitude in 465
Phenomenography
  and instructional psychology 35
Phenomenology
  and humanistic psychology 87
Phenylketonuria 172
Philosophy for children program 780
Phonics
  beginning reading 561
Phylogenesis
  and ontogeny 8
Physical development *178–84*
  methods of assessment 178
    body composition 178
    Body Mass Index (BMI) 178, 180
    maturity indicators 178
Physics
  Physical Science Curriculum Study
    (US) 570
  science curriculum
    Israel 571
Piaget, Jean (1896–1980)
  developmental psychology 4
  self-regulation concept 5
Piagetian theory 12, 64, *97–101*, 318
  cognitive development 25, 53
    causes of 98
    cognitive conflict 98, 100
    conservation experiments 264, 266
  and cognitive psychology 98
  cognitive restructuring 405
  criticisms of 99, 263
  definition of intelligence 98
  developmental stages 13, 98, 117
    criticism of 96, 313
    horizontal *décalages* 269
    infants 122, 124
    moral development 224
  educational principles 99
  egocentrism
    and social cognition 617
  and epistemology 97
  historical background 29
  impact on curriculum design 64, 100
  influence on educational practices 99
  and logical thinking 80
  moral development
    and cooperative learning 620
  of play 307
  and social cognition 304
  and socialization 194
  and testing 64
  theoretical developments 99
Pica (eating disorder)
  and eating habits 68
Pictures *See* Illustrations
Placement
  special education
    options 153
Planum temorale
Play
  and cognitive development 309
  curriculum influences 311
  developmental stages 308

dominance hierarchy 126
ecological influences 311
individual development *306–12*
individual differences 310
  family influence 310
  and parent child relationship 310
  personality traits 310
infants 308
and interpersonal relationships 126
and language development 310
media influence 311
outdoor activities 311
Piagetian theory 307
preschool children 309
psychoanalytic theory 307
sex differences 126
and sex roles 241
and social development 310
theories of 306, 308
toddlers 308
Vygotsky's theory 307
See also Pretend play
Policy
  and evaluation research 61
  See also Educational policy
Policy formation
  and research
    on individual development *59–62*
Policy making *See* Policy formation
Political attitudes
  development and education 21
Political power
  and education 18, 22
Political science
  computer assisted instruction
    computer game format 574
  research on learning 573
Politicalization *See* Political socialization
Polychlorinated biphenyls (PCBs)
  and neurological impairment 177
Poor *See* Economically disadvantaged
Popularity
  peer acceptance
    sociometric techniques 256
Population changes *See* Population trends
Population trends
  baby boomers 164
Portfolio assessment
  and cognitive strategy instruction 784
Posttest scores *See* Pretests–posttests
Poverty
  and child development 248
  and children's well being 246
  and high risk students 138
  See also Economically disadvantaged
Preconceptions *455–59*
  definition of 455
  sources of 455
Pregnancy
  beliefs about 79
  drug abuse
    and learning disabilities 794
  drug use in 177
  substance abuse
    and learning disabilities 794

Premature infants
  auditory sensitivity in 175
  cognitive and social development
    longitudinal studies 71
  responses to visual stimuli 175
Prenatal development
  fetus
    congenital impairments *174–77*
Preschool children
  aggression in 202
  handicap identification
    learning disabilities 801
  play 309
  and prior learning 432
  prosocial behavior 207
Prescriptive knowledge *See* Procedural
    knowledge
Pretend play
  infants 309
  and parent child relationship 310
  preschool children
    behavior development 309
Pretests–posttests
  and programmed instruction 736
Prevention
  and individual development 115
Prewriting 577
Prior knowledge
  and situated rationalism 346
Prior knowledge *See* Prior learning
Prior learning 324, *459–64*
  and academic achievement
    causal models 460
  and aptitude treatment interaction 674
  assessment of 459
  cognitive development
    and expertise 276
  and cognitive structures 460, 462
  concept of 460
  credentials
    adult education 749
  effect on learning processes 461
  influence on learning processes
    individual development 314
  and instruction 455
  and learning strategies
    teaching of 426
  and memorization 431, 433
    strategies 434
  and outcomes of education 460
  preconceptions and misconceptions
    455–59
  and reading achievement 566
  role of
    and memory 432
  and variance in pretest–posttest
    scores 460
Problem solving
  and affective behavior 544
  and cognitive development 384
  cognitive processes 551
  cognitive skills 36
  cognitive strategy instruction 780
  cognitive style 552
  and comprehension program 780

computer simulation *730–33*
  schemata 731
  search process 731
  coping in crises 261
  and creativity 393
  daily living skills 554
  deduction
    in children 299
  definition of 550
  educational research
    historical overview 553
  expert novice research 554
  heuristic models in 318
  information processing approach 552
  instruction
    feedback 397, 398
  intellectual disciplines 554
  learning environments 689
  learning strategies *550–55*
  and learning theories 322
  metacognition
    executive control 438
  problem representation
    evaluation of 509
    expert approach 506, 508
  and programming 713
  research projects 554
  role of facilitator 761
  skills
    effect of LOGO on children's 698
  task analysis 553
  teaching of
    definitions of 556
    history 556
    programs 557
    theoretical framework 556
  teaching and testing for *555–59*
  testable aspects of 557
  tests
    future trends 558
    reliability 558
    validity 558
  use of educational media in 728
  See also Creative thinking; Problems
Problems
  categories 258
  definitions of 550
  individual development *258–62*
  types of 551
  See also Problem solving; Word
    problems (mathematics)
Procedural knowledge *394–96*, 404, 473
  and artificial intelligence 663
  and cognitive development 266
  and cognitive psychology 394
  concept formation
    and long term memory 384
  definition of 394
  examples and characteristics of 394
  experts' use of 507, 509
  and heuristic structure 395
  learning 413
  learning strategies
    and second language learning 528
  skill development 416

  See also Expertise
Productive thinking 551, 552
Productive Thinking Program 557
Professional development
  and computer networks 709
Profiles
  prior learning in 463
Program evaluation 656
  and policy formation 61
Programmed instruction 317, *733–41*
  design
    and feedback 738
    initial stages 735
  developmental testing 738
  early developments 734
  and feedback 397, 734, 737, 740
  frames 734
    design of 737
    large 737
  hierarchy approach 736
  and instructional systems 738
  knowledge classification approach 736
  lean programs 737
  and learning 690
  linear programs 737
  master performer approach 736, 737
  matrix approach 736
  and multiple choice tests 734, 740
  and pacing 738
  prerequisites for 736
  Skinner's work on 734
  structural communication 740
  for task analysis 736
  and teacher attitudes 738
  See also Computer assisted instruction
    (CAI); Programmed tutoring
Programmed instructional materials
  textbooks 733
    and teaching machines 734
Programmed learning *See* Programmed
    instruction
Programmed texts *See* Programmed
    instructional materials, textbooks
Programmed tutoring 740
  feedback in 398
  and skill development 690
Programmers
  attitudes
    and programmed instruction
    design 738
Programming
  and cognitive development 714
  cognitive effects hypothesis 698
  computer literacy *713–15*
  discovery learning 713
  educational psychology *713–15*
  expert novice research 714
  expertise in 714
  instruction in 713
    mental model method 713
  kinds of knowledge required 714
  learning 714
  and procedural knowledge 394
  and thinking skills
    skill development 698

and transfer of training 714, 484
Programming languages 713
Programs
    use of term 733
Propositional knowledge *See* Declarative
        knowledge
Propositions
    knowledge representations 404
Prosocial behavior
    child development *206–09*
    children
        sex differences 208
    correlation with intelligence
        in children 208
    cross cultural studies 53, 207
    developmental continuity 207
    parent influence 208
    peer relationship 254, 255
    personality traits 208
    and socialization 208
    in subcultures 207
    teacher influence 208
Protocol analysis
    cognitive processes 481
    expert performance 273
    verbal 435
Psychiatry
    humanistic psychology view of 86
    See also Psychoanalytic theory
Psychoanalytic theories
    developmental psychology 6
Psychoanalytic theory
    child development 3
    Freud's
        of individual development 9, 112
    Mahler's of child development
        personal autonomy 113
    and moral development 223
    of play 307
Psychodrama 88
Psychodynamics
    and developmental psychology 112
    theories of individual development
        112–16
        Adler's 115
Psychological evaluation
    and learning processes *805–08*
Psychological patterns
    affective behavior
        and learning *585–90*
    cross cultural studies 52
    individual development *199–202*
    and social cognition 304
Psychological processes
    microgenesis 592
Psychological research *See* Psychological
        studies
Psychological testing
    individual differences 650
    multivariate analysis
        factor analysis 633
Psychology
    cross cultural theories of cognition 590
    and educational practices 499
    as empirical science 2

See also Child psychology;
        Developmental psychology;
        Instructional psychology
Psychology instruction relationship
    See Instruction psychology
        relationship
Psychometrics 602
    aptitude tests *813–16*
    cognitive development 9
    and cognitive psychology *805–08*
    intellectual development
        individual differences 270
    and learning disabilities 800
Psychomotor skills
    analysis and categorization 548
    discovery learning
        and direct instruction 549
    handicaps
        and learning disabilities 797
    imitation 547
    instruction and training 549
    learning and control 548
    movement education *547–50*
    patterned responses 547
    perceptual motor coordination 284,
        547–50
    retention and transfer 548
    scope and history of research 547
    skill development
        ability requirements approach 548
        automatization 549
        behavior description approach 548
        behavior requirements approach 548
        degrees of freedom problem 549
        developmental stages 548
        feedback 549
        learner controlled instruction 549
        schema theory 549
        task characteristics approach 548
Psychopathology 214
    developmental disabilities *67–73*
    etiological models 69
        mother infant relations 69
        prenatal and perinatal influences 69
        protective factors 69
        social deprivation 69
    levels of explanation 69
        biochemistry 70
        neuroanatomy 70
        neurophysiology 70
        psychology 71
        social adjustment 71
Psychosexual development
    in adolescents 114
    developmental stages 112
        behavior patterns 113
    Freud's views 112, 114
    theories of
        and socialization 194
Psychotherapy
    and self actualization 87
Puberty 131
Public policy
    links with research *59–62*
Pygmalion effect *See* Self fulfilling

prophecies

Quality of life
    education and 21
    and research on individual
        development *59–62*
    See also Well being

Race
    and high risk students 139
    See also Ethnicity
Radio
    and learning 689
Rationalism
    conceptual 342
    and learning processes 342, 409
    See also Situated rationalism
Reaction time
    and intelligence 650
Readability
    aids
        learning from texts 522
Reading
    basic vocabulary 430
    learning by 689
    learning theories 560
    metacognition
        executive control 438, 439
    metacognitive knowledge
        age differences 438
    models of
        interactive 565
    and speech 559
    See also Beginning reading; Reading
        aloud to others; Remedial reading;
        Speed reading
Reading achievement
    and prior learning 566
Reading aloud to others
    parent audience 599
Reading comprehension *562–64*
    affective factors 564
    and attention control 373
    characteristics of 564
    cognitive linguistics 564
    cognitive processes 562
    cognitive strategies 563
    conceptual resources in 565
    error detection 438
    linguistic resources in 566
    metacognition 563
    motivation 564
    and orthography
        role of 567
    and reading rate 439
    and reciprocal teaching 563, 779
    role of prior learning 562
    schemata in 562
    in second languages *564–68*
        automaticity 566
        instruction implications 567
        role of grammar 566
        utilization 564

and summarization 439
tests
　　Nelson–Denny test 425
text reinspection 439
and text structure 562
Reading consultants
　alternatives to decoding methods 795
Reading difficulties
　decoding (reading)
　　and cognitive processes 795
　disadvantaged children 408
　learning disabilities 793
　See also Dyslexia; Remedial reading
Reading failure
　cultural factors 430
Reading instruction 561
　decoding (reading) 559, 561
　reciprocal teaching method 595
　whole language approach 561
Reading processes
　theories of 565
Reading rate
　and reading comprehension 439
Reading skills
　learning *559–61*
　protocol analysis 779
　second languages
　　and reading comprehension 566
　selective attention strategies 373
　and short term memory 373
　See also Reading comprehension
Reading strategies
　cognitive strategy instruction 781
　　special education 780
Reading writing relationship 559
　learning processes 580
　literacy *428–31*
Reasoning
　analogy
　　age differences 302
　child development
　　age differences 298
　in children
　　analogy 299
　　cognitive development *297–303*
　　developmental stages 301
　　factors influencing 298, 301
　and cognitive style 302
　deduction 299
　definitions of 298
　inference
　　in children 299
　influence of experience on 302
　See also Abstract reasoning;
　　Thinking skills
Reasoning skills *See* Thinking skills
Recall (psychology)
　and children's cognitive development
　　267
　inferential 370
　retrieval aid theory
　　and prior learning 462
　and state dependent memory 369
　tests
　　and memory 434

Reciprocal teaching 332, 684
　and cognitive development 618
　cognitive strategy instruction 782
　cultural differences 783
　objectives 40
　and practice 690
　reading comprehension 563, 779
　reading instruction 595
　second language instruction 528
　and transfer of training 484
Recitation
　and learning 31
Recognition (psychology)
　tests
　　and memory 434
　and visual perception 452, 454
Referral
　special needs students 144
Regression (statistics)
　and aptitude treatment interaction 672
Regular and special education
　　relationship 153
　United States 154
Rehabilitation
　special education
　　community-based programs 158
Rehearsal
　and learning 690
Reinforcement 397
　infant behavior 122
　and programmed instruction 734
　in schools
　　and socialization 197
　token systems 500
Rejection (psychology)
　by peer group
　　and aggression 205
Relaxation training
　stress management 625
Reliability
　problem solving tests 558
Religion
　and beliefs 77
Religious factors
　beliefs
　　individual development *77–81*
Remedial education *See* Remedial
　　instruction
Remedial instruction
　regular and special education
　　relationship 74
　special classes 152
　teaching methods
　　mastery learning 363
Remedial reading
　dyslexia 796
Remediation *See* Remedial instruction
Reproduction (biology)
　demographic trends
　　global consequences of education
　　　111
　and social adjustment
　　sociobiological approach 109
Research
　See also Educational research

Research design
　metacognition 443
Research methodology *See* Scientific
　　methodology
Research practice relationship *See*
　　Theory practice relationship
Research utilization
　social science research
　　and policy formation *59–62*
Residential schools
　special education 153
Resource room programs
　for children with disabilities 153
Response style (tests)
　historical background 31
Responses
　active
　　and programmed instruction 737
Retraining
　technological advancement and 758
Revision (written composition)
　writing processes 578
Rewards
　as incentives 397
　See also Incentives
Rhetoric
　and logical thinking 464
Role playing
　and computer assisted instruction 701
Role taking *See* Perspective taking
Rote learning
　and comprehension 552
Russia
　instructional psychology
　　historical background 29

Scaffolding 379, 508
　and computer assisted learning 697
　science instruction 570, 571
　writing instruction 579
Schemata (cognition) 403, 416
　frames 403
　hierarchical 370
　and language 455
　learning processes 342
　mental images 404
　mental models 404
　modification by new experience 405
　scripts 403
Scholastic aptitude *See* Academic
　　aptitude
School attendance *See* Attendance
School business management *See* School
　　administration
School characteristics *See* Institutional
　　characteristics
School environment *See* Classroom
　　environment; Educational
　　environment
School failure *See* Low achievement
School management *See* School
　　administration
School responsibility
　and socialization 197

School subjects *See* Intellectual
    disciplines
Schools
    independent study in
        problems 738
    and socialization 197
Science *See* Sciences
Science careers
    equal opportunities 647
    female participation 647
Science curriculum
    access to
        equal education 647
    female participation 647
    science programs 570
    sex fairness 648
Science education
    concept learning perspective 568
    developmental perspective 569
    differential perspective 570
    objectives 570
    perspectives on 568
    preconceptions and misconceptions
        455–59
    problem solving perspective 570
Science equipment
    sex differences in informal use 647
Science instruction *568–72*
    observational learning
        preconceptions and misconceptions
        456
    and prior learning 457
    sex fairness *645–49*
    teaching methods 571
        scaffolding 570, 571
Science teachers
    expectations of females 647
    sex bias 570
    teacher education 571
Science tests
    sex differences in performance 646
Sciences
    achievement
        sex differences 645
    learning *568–72*
Scientific attitudes
    cultural influences 77, 79
    sex fairness 648
Scientific concepts
    characteristics of student concepts 569
    concept teaching 569
    learning 568
    misconceptions 569
        and sex bias 648
    sex differences in understanding 646
Scientific literacy
    beliefs about
        sex differences 646
    measurement of
        sex differences 646
    science curriculum 648
Scientific methodology
    cognitive processes 357
    discovery learning 360
    functions 80

Scientific principles 570
Scoring
    partial credit analysis 808
Seatwork
    and cognitive processes 474
Second language instruction
    age of beginning 532
    reciprocal teaching 528
    See also Foreign language instruction
Second language learning
    aptitude and opportunity approach 525
    audiolingual methods 525
    bilingualism
        abstract language properties 375
        age effects 375
        principles of development 375
    cognitive academic language learning
        approach (CALLA) 529
    cognitive academic language
        proficiency (CALP) 529
    compared with foreign language
        instruction 511
    intensive language courses 532
    learning strategies *525–30*
        associative vocabulary learning 526
        classification 526
        and cognitive psychology 527
        and content area instruction 529
        protocol analysis 525
        reading strategies 526
        typology 526
    linguistics *531–34*
    minority groups
        learning strategies 525
    natural approach 525
    See also Foreign language learning
Second languages
    learning strategies 762
    reading comprehension in *564–68*
    reading processes 565
Secondary school students
    in part time employment 598
Self
    as a subject and object 228
Self actualization
    characteristics of 87
    and humanistic psychology 86, 87
    and socialization 88
Self concept
    and aging (individuals) 166
        sex differences 166
    attribution theory *199–202*
        success and failure 587
    child development
        changes in structure 229
    and cognitive processes 474
    cross cultural studies 54
    developmental stages 229
    early development 229
    effect on performance 586
    functional view 229
    individual development *228–32*
    parent influence on development 231
    performance
        and learning motivation 447

    self efficacy 230
        educational strategies 232
        role of classroom environment 231
    and self evaluation 228, 230
        dimensionality 230
        stability issue 230
    and sex role 240
    social cognition
        and social development 218
    and socialization 194
    theoretical view of nature of 228
Self confidence *See* Self esteem
Self control *467–71*
    attention control 469
        individual differences 654
    concept of 5
    and conflict resolution 468
    definition of 467
    and delay of gratification 467, 468
    and emotional response 469
    and individual power 468
    information processing model 468
    and learning 589
    learning strategies 423, 469
    in maturity (individuals) 470
    and metacognition 469
    ontogenetic development theory 468
    and personal autonomy 468, 471
    resistance to temptation 468
        and cognitive restructuring 470
    and self motivation 469
    self regulation test for children 470
    skill development 469
    theory of self regulatory deficit 468
Self determination
    beliefs about 79
    individual power 104
    and self motivation 449
    See also Personal autonomy
Self directed groups
    adult learning 753, 754
Self directed learning *See* Independent
    study
Self efficacy
    and academic achievement 231,
        586, 789,
    attention control
        and academic achievement 373
    and energy expenditure
        individual differences 654
    evaluative thinking 105
    and metacognition 105
    and self concept 230
    and self motivation 449, 450
    social cognition
        and social development 218
    stress variables 624, 625
Self esteem
    and mathematics achievement 543, 544
    and narcissism 115
    and self evaluation 228
Self evaluation (individuals) 502
    cognitive measurement 806
    learning strategies 421, 423
    and metacognition 434

and self esteem 228
Self expression
  art expression 575
Self fulfilling prophecies
  and teacher expectation of students 627
    Brophy–Good model 627
Self instruction *See* Independent study
Self knowledge *See* Self concept
Self motivation
  and academic achievement 467
  and computer assisted instruction 448
  and coping with failure 470
  and feedback 104
  and homogeneous grouping 448
  and learning motivation 448
  and self control 469
  and underachievement 467
Self perception *See* Self concept
Self regulated learning *See* Independent
  study
Self regulation *See* Self control
Semantic memory
  and levels of consciousness 266
  semantic priming 369
Semantics
  coherence 522
  contamination across fields 540
Sensitivity training 88
Sensory experience
  and preconceptions 455
Sensory integration
  neonates
    prenatal influences 174
Separation anxiety 68
Serbocroatian
  orthography of 567
Severe disabilities
  developmental disabilities *73–76*
Severe mental retardation 73
Sex bias
  curriculum 242
  instructional materials 242
  teacher attitudes 242
Sex differences
  behavior development *184–87*
  history of research on 185
  nature nurture controversy 184, 186
  research
    developmental continuity 185
    meta analysis 185
    sex bias in 185
  stereotypes 185
Sex fairness
  educational strategies 242
Sex role
  definitions of 239
  family influence 242
  individual development *239–43*
    cognitive development theories 240
    developmental stages 241
    educational implications 242
    gender schematic processing
      theory 240
    psychoanalytic theory 240
    social influences 241

social learning theories 240
  media influence 241
  peer influence 241
  school influence 242
Sex stereotypes
  and child development 241
  and gender schematic processing
    theory 240
Sexism *See* Sex bias
Sexual identity
  developmental disorders 68
  and identification (psychology) 240
  observational learning 240
  and sex role 240
Sharing behavior
  young children 207
Shinto
  beliefs about origin of man 77
Short term memory (STM) 369
  and accessibility theory 462
  and cognitive processes
    concept formation 383
  and development of memory span 294
  and induction 414
  and learning 411
  processes 472
  role of attention in 372
Shyness
  student behavior 189
Sibling relationship
  and individual development 115, 252
Simulation
  and learning 689
  See also Computer simulation; Role
    playing
Single parent family *See* One
    parent family
Situated cognition
  concept of 341
  and conceptual rationalism 344
  historical background 35
  social bases 342
  tools 343
Situated learning 65, 275, *341–47*
  and collaboration 38
  historical background 35
Situated rationalism
  concept of 343
  and education 345
  and learning 344
Skill analysis
  skills rules and knowledge (SRK) 481
  task analysis 479
    learning hierarchy (Gagné) 479
Skill development
  and automaticity of learning 95
  and learning 690
  motor development *280–84*
  in observational learning 103
  perceptual motor learning 283
  phases 35
  procedural knowledge 416
Small group instruction *351–55*
  cooperative learning 684
  reciprocal teaching 684

student teams achievement divisions
  (STADS) 684
teaching methods
  teamwork 352
and time on task 686
See also Group Investigation (GI)
  method
Social adjustment
  peer relationship 255
Social behavior
  age related changes 217
  individual differences 219
    stability and change 220
  sex differences 185
Social change
  education and 18, 20
Social class
  and academic achievement 602
  effect on children's play 311
Social cognition 306, 380, *619–23*
  and aggression 203, 205
  bilingualism 375
  causal model 101
  cognitive structures 616
  communication skills *615–19*
  individual development *101–06*
  interpersonal competence *615–19*
  learning theories 90
  moral values 305
  observational learning
    cognitive processes in 103
  processes 304
  role of culture 305
  social development 218
  social psychology 304
  social values 305
  symbolic learning 102
  vicarious experiences 102
Social competence *See* Interpersonal
  competence
Social constructivism *See* Constructivism
Social development
  in adolescents 337
  and cognitive development 616
  communication skills *615–19*
  and educational practices 221
  and friendship 256
  individual development *217–22*
    and environmental change 219, 221
  interpersonal competence *615–19*
  and peer relationship 218, 221
  person-oriented view 220
  personality studies 220
  and personality traits 219
  and play 310
  self motivation 104
  social cognition 218
  and social experience
    developmental stages 616
  and social networks 218, 221
  and socialization 616
  Turiel's view of social understanding
    65
Social environment
  changes in

and social development 218
factors in learning *612–15*
and individual development 219
and personality development
    dynamic interaction 237
Social equality
    See also Civil rights
Social experience
    and social development 616
Social indicators
    research utilization 61
Social institutions (organizations) *See*
    Institutions
Social isolation
    effect on development 256
        aggression 257
        behavior problems 257
        peer relationship 255, 256
Social learning *See* Socialization
Social mobility
    factors in developing socio-economic
        status 259
Social networks
    and social development 218, 221
Social organizations
    and socialization 194
Social psychology
    prosocial behavior
        and values 490
Social science research
    individual development
        and policy formation *59–62*
    learning
        issues 574
    and policy formation 60
        contextual factors 61
        measurement of outcomes 61
        values in 60
    and socialization 195
    textbook research 572
Social sciences
    learning and instruction *572–74*
    learning motivation 574
    thinking skills 574
Social skills *See* Interpersonal
    competence
Social values
    conventional 490
    and moral values 222
Socialism
    and education 23
Socialization 198, *601–07*
    achievement need
        in children 211
    agents of 194
    and aggression 204
    and child development
        cultural differences 252
    components of 193
    concept of 193
    conflict approach 195
    contexts of 195, 197
    cooperative learning 351
    definitions of 193
    and developmental psychology 161

and emotional development 214
and family 196
influence of school
    communication skills development
        617
interactive nature of 193
maturation vs. development 193
Mead's views
    and social cognition 304
and moral development 223
occupational 196
organic approach 195
peer groups 196, 197
processes
    in schools 197
and prosocial behavior 208
research 3, 195
role of language in 407
and school context 197
sex role 240, 242
and social development 616
social learning theory
    personality development 235
systems of 194
theory of
    current trends 195
    historical background 194
and values education 489
See also Cultural transmission;
    Political socialization
Sociobiology 109
    and individual development
        adjustment (to environment) 110
        parents' and teachers' roles 110
        peer relationship 110
Sociocultural patterns
    development 18, 20
Socio-economic status (SES)
    special needs students 787
Sociolinguistics
    disadvantaged children
        and language usage 407
    United States 407
Sociology
    age stratification model 161
Sociology of education
    learning *601–07*
Sociometric techniques
    peer evaluation 255
Software *See* Computer software
Spatial ability 651
    process analyses 635
    sex differences 643
    spatial relations 635
    visualization 635
Special classes
    for children with disabilities 153
    and diagnostic tests 142
Special education
    administration 152
    classification 155
        for educational purposes 155
    cognitive strategy instruction *779–86*
    enrollments 151
        developing nations 151

evaluation studies 158
Germany 154
historical development 151
international activities 158
international perspective *150–60*
Italy 154
labeling (of persons) 155
legislation 152
    England and Wales 152
    United States 152
medical model 789
Norway 157
outcomes of education
    and aptitude treatment interaction
        672
policies 152
problems and issues 159
professional organizations 159
provision
    United Kingdom 151
recent trends 152
reconceptualizing
    and supported inclusion 75
research 157
    financial support for 157
    problems of 157
respect for individual differences 159
services
    and learning disabilities 800
    severe disabilities 73
United States 154
Special education personnel 156
    auxiliary professional staff 156
Special education teachers
    burnout 156
    teacher education 156
        curriculum 156
Special needs students
    classification 788
        medical model 789
        social system model 789
    diagnosis and classification
        and cultural differences 147
        issues in 145
        legal considerations 142
        models of 143
        purposes 142
    educational diagnosis *142–49*
        Africa 147
        practices 142
        procedures 145
    identification 788
    intelligence tests 145
    learning characteristics *786–92*
Special programs
    individualized programs 143, 144
Special schools
    for children with disabilities 153
Specific learning disabilities *See*
        Learning disabilities, specific
Speech disorders *See* Speech handicaps
Speech handicaps 69
    cluttering 69
    See also Stuttering
Speech–sound disorders *See* Speech

handicaps
Speed reading
    selective attention strategies 374
Stage theory *See* Developmental stages
Standardized tests
    special needs students
        and cultural differences 147
State policy *See* Public policy
Stereopsis *See* Depth perception
Strategic learning *See* Learning strategies
Streaming *See* Ability grouping
Stress management
    adolescents 625
    attitudes
        transactional stress theory 624
    coping 624
    and learning *623–26*
    in schools 624
Stress variables
    in schools 623
    student responses 189
Structural communication
    programmed instruction 740
Structural linguistics
    mathematics and language 538
Student achievement *See* Academic
        achievement
Student aptitude *See* Academic aptitude
Student attitudes
    expert strategies 522
    to learning 36
    to teacher behavior
        differential 629
Student behavior
    evaluation methods 811
    and teacher expectation of students 628
Student centered curriculum
    differentiated for gifted 279
Student characteristics
    affective entry 666
    and aptitude treatment interaction 671
    cognitive entry 666
    and cognitive processes 472
    and learning factors 669
    and learning from texts 521
    and learning theories 471
    naturalistic observation 809
    teacher evaluation of 809
    and teaching *665–70*
Student differences *See* Student
        characteristics
Student engaged time *See* Time on task
Student evaluation
    data interpretation
        teacher role 812
    ethics 812
    standardized tests 812
    teacher role *809–13*
        decision making 809
Student experience
    and memorization 431
Student improvement
    learning strategies 762
Student outcomes *See* Outcomes of
        education

Student perceptions *See* Student attitudes
Student progress *See* Academic
        achievement
Student reaction
    and teacher behavior
        risks 629
Student responsibility
    and learning strategies 425
Student selection *See* Admission criteria
Student subcultures 606
Students
    learning potential 39
Study skills *419–23*
    and metacognition 442
Study strategies *See* Study skills
Stuttering 69
Subject disciplines *See* Intellectual
        disciplines
Success
    attribution theory
        sex differences 186
Surveys
    research
        strengths and weaknesses 612
Sweden
    computer managed learning 706
Switzerland
    instructional psychology
        historical background 29
Symbolic interactionism
    learning and 603, 604
    Mead's views 620
    and the self concept 229, 231
Symbolic learning
    mammalian foundations 335
    social cognition 102
Symbols (mathematics)
    mathematical formulas 541
Syntax
    and reading comprehension 566
Systems of education
    levels of 716

T groups *See* Sensitivity training
Tachistoscopes
    visual stimuli
        and perception studies 453
Tactile stimuli
    responses by fetus to 175
Talent development
    art education 576
        and cultural differences 576
Taoism
    beliefs about origin of man 78
Tape recordings
    and learning 690
Task analysis
    and cognitive processes 474, 476
    computers in 482
    content analysis 480
    definition of 479
    functions of 479
    information sources 481
    instructional design *478–82*

and instructional psychology 723
    learning theories
        constructivism 482
    procedural 480
        elaboration theory 480, 482
        path analysis 480
    for programmed instruction 736
    research issues and directions 481
    techniques 479
Taxonomy *See* Classification
Teacher attitudes
    and computer networks 711
    and mathematics education 546
    and programmed instruction 738
    sex bias 242
    and student personality traits 189
Teacher behavior
    differential
        student attitudes to 629
    process product research 503
    and teacher expectation of students 628
Teacher effectiveness
    and learning 603
Teacher evaluation
    and aptitude treatment interaction 671
    See also Teacher effectiveness
Teacher expectations of students *626–32*
    definitions of 627
    differential
        and teacher behavior 628
    effects
        types of 627
    explanatory style
        sex differences 200
    future research 632
    importance of 628
    increasing
        effects of 630
    induced 627
    influences 809
    intervention programs 630
        findings 631
    and low achievement
        Good's passivity model 629
    natural 627
    personality traits 189
    preconceptions and misconceptions
        about 457
    research 626
        directions 631
        types of 627
    and self fulfilling prophecies 627
        Brophy–Good model 627
    variations over time 630
    and teacher expectation of students 631
Teacher guidance
    Socratic Method 358
    testing 362
Teacher parent cooperation *See* Parent
        teacher cooperation
Teacher performance *See* Teacher
        effectiveness
Teacher preparation *See* Teacher
        education
Teacher quality *See* Teacher

effectiveness
Teacher response
 individual differences 656
Teacher role
 decision making
  classroom environment 809
Teacher student relationship
 disadvantaged children
  sociolinguistic approach 407
 knowledge acquisition approach 32
 and learning disabilities 800
 and learning strategies 425
Teacher training *See* Teacher education
Teachers
 beliefs of
  See also Teacher attitudes
 and computer assisted instruction 703
 personal autonomy
  in learning 762
Teaching
 aptitude treatment interaction model
  of *670–74*
 classroom
  and student characteristics *665–70*
 cognitive apprenticeship model 595
 See also Reciprocal teaching
Teaching (process) *See* Instruction
Teaching machines 500
 autotutors 735
 characteristics of 734
 and programmed instruction 733
Teaching materials *See* Instructional
  materials
Teaching methods
 ability
  and learning 651
 academic achievement
  academic learning time 675
 and cognitive development 63
 cognitive processes 475
 improvement of
  implications 669
 and instructional design theory 716
 instructional sequencing 358
 and learning environments *687–91*
 and learning factors 668
 learning strategies (strategy
  instruction) 525
 and media research 726
Teaching practices *See* Teaching methods
Teaching styles
 adaptation to student characteristics
  656
Teamwork
 cooperative learning 351
Technological advancement
 and instructional design theory 718
 and psychomotor skill development
  549
Technological change *See* Technological
  advancement
Telecommunications
 between schools 708
Teleconferencing
 and computer networks 708

Television
 sex bias 241
 See also Broadcast television
Television curriculum
 critical viewing 727
Television viewing
 and academic achievement 727
 acculturation 103
 and antisocial behavior 727
 effect on children's play 311
 factors in learning 611, 613, 614
 prosocial behavior 208
 and values 727
 violence
  and development of aggression in
   children 205
Temperament *See* Personality
Teratogens
 and congenital impairments 176
Teratology 176
Terminology *See* Vocabulary
Test administration *See* Testing
Test anxiety 213, 215
 and academic achievement 216
 and achievement need 448, 654
 attention-deficit hypothesis 586
 effect on cognitive processes 586
 therapy 216
Test items
 and problem solving 557
Test taking anxiety *See* Test anxiety
Test theory
 implications of cognitive measurement
  for 807
 standard 805
 See also Item response theory (IRT)
Test use
 grouping (instructional purposes) 362
 learning problems
  remedial instruction 362
Test validity
 differential item functioning 807
 See also Construct validity
Testing
 and cognitive psychology *805–08*
 feedback
  error correction 362
 memory *431–36*
 problem solving *555–59*
 See also Assessment; Educational
  testing; Evaluation; Measurement;
  Psychological testing; Tests
Testing programs
 dynamic 595
Tests
 conventional instruction
  behavioral objectives 805
 prior learning in 463
 See also Achievement tests; Testing
Text processing *See* Word processing
Textbases
 definition 519
 strategies 521
Textbook research
 history 572

social sciences 572
Textbooks 810
 mathematics
  language usage 540
 and programmed instruction 733
Texts
 coherence 522
 comprehension theory 519
 content
  and learning ability 523
 learning from *519–24*
  factors affecting 520, 522
 readability aids 522
 situation models 519
 surface structure 519
 textbases 519
 types of 519
Thalidomide 176
Theater arts
 instructional psychology *575–77*
Theories
 conversion into problem solving
  procedures 395
 and scientific attitudes 79, 80
 See also Hypothesis testing
Theory practice relationship
 declarative and procedural knowledge
  394–96
 education *43–50*
 and instructional design 722
ThinkerTools
 objectives 40
Thinking *See* Cognitive processes
Thinking aloud protocols *See* Protocol
  analysis
Thinking skills *464–67*
 cognitive strategy instruction 780, 783
 effect of educational media on 729
 instruction in
  influence of Piagetian theory 100
 and intellectual disciplines 466
 and intelligence
  general theories 662
 intracultural variation
  ethnography 591
 and knowledge level 466
 learning strategies *550–55*
 and long term memory 370
 reproductive 551, 552
 skill development
  training in 26
 social sciences 574
Third World *See* Developing nations
Tics
 Gilles de la Tourette disorder 68
Time factors (learning) 328, 668, *691–94*
 academic achievement 677, 692
 behavioral objectives 387
 Carroll's model 676
 individual differences 28
 knowledge acquisition 387
 memory systems
  storage 387
 opportunity to learn 676
 research methodology 677

United States 675
Time management
   schools *691–94*
      comparative analysis 691
      homework 692
      literacy 692
      mathematical concepts 692
      policy formation 693
      time on task 692
   See also Time on task
Time on task 676
   and academic achievement 693
   elementary school students 677
   and learning motivation 446
   schools *691–94*
      comparative analysis 692
   See also Academic learning time;
      Time management
Toddlers
   play 308
   prosocial behavior 207
Token economy
   behavior modification
      delinquency 500
Tourette syndrome *See* Tics, Gilles de
   la Tourette disorder
Trace line *See* Item response theory (IRT)
Traditional instruction *See* Conventional
   instruction
Training
   and learning strategies 761
   occupational *See* Job training
   See also Industrial training; Job
      training; Vocational education
Transfer of learning *See* Transfer of
   training
Transfer of training *483–87*
   conditions of 485
   definition of 483
   and industrial training 757
   instruction for 486
   learning strategies 379
   mechanisms of 485
   near vs. far 483, 484
   positive and negative 483
   and problem solving 556
   prospects for 483
Transsexualism 68
Trust (psychology)
   and personality development 200
Tutorial programs
   and computer assisted instruction 701
Twins
   genetic factors in cognitive
      development 173
   personality
      and nature nurture controversy 188
   quantitative genetic studies 172
Typology *See* Classification

Understanding
   and cognitive processes 323
   realist constructivism 339
UNESCO

lifelong learning 750
   special needs in the classroom
      project 158
United Kingdom (UK)
   instructional psychology
      historical background 29
   learning strategies project 762
   mainstreaming
      legislation 74
   special education provision
      historical development 151
   See also England and Wales
United Nations Educational, Scientific,
   and Cultural Organization
      See UNESCO
United States (US)
   computer managed learning 704
   institutional support for independent
      study 772
   learning disabilities
      educational strategies 800
      prevalence 799
   learning strategies
      teaching of 424
   special education 154
      legislation 152
   See also North America
   instructional psychology
      historical background 34
Universal education *See* Equal education
Urinary incontinence 69
Utilitarianism
   moral values 223

Validity
   problem solving tests 558
   See also Construct validity; Test
      validity
Value judgment
   and cultural pluralism 491
Values
   conflicts 490
   contextual factors 491
   See also Democratic values; Moral
      values; Social values
Values clarification 490
Values education *489–92*
   indoctrination vs. value relativism 491
Venezuela
   problem solving
      teaching of 557
Verbal ability
   and aging (individuals) 164
   process analyses 635
   sources of individual differences 635
Verbal communication
   and learning strategies
      evaluation 426
Verbal development
   vocabulary development 289
   production of sentences 289
Verbal learning 409
Vertical mobility *See* Social mobility
Vestibular apparatus

in fetus 175
Veterans education 750
Vision
   system of
      effect of deprivation of stimuli 170
Visual acuity
   infants 286
Visual arts
   aesthetic preferences 576
   instructional psychology *575–77*
   and moral education 575
Visual perception
   cognitive or indirect approach 452
   color
      infants 286
   ecological or direct approach 453
   Gibsonian theory 453
   hypothesis testing theory 453
   illusion research 453
   impoverished stimuli research 453
   and intelligence 650
   and learning *451–55*
   and movement
      optic flow 453
   psychological process 452
   psychological theories
      elementary attributes 452
      Gestalt theory 452
   scanning
      infants 286
   size constancy 453
   See also Depth perception; Visual
      acuity
Visual stimuli
   learning from texts 523
   responses by fetus to 175
Visualization 315, 635
Vitamin A compounds
   and congenital impairment 176
Vocabulary
   second languages
      and reading comprehension 566
Vocational education
   and academic education
      for development 23
   and learning disabilities 801
Vocational training *See* Vocational
   education
Volition *See* Individual power
Vulnerability
   sex differences 186
Vygotsky, Lev Semyonovich
   (1896–1934)
   developmental psychology 4
   theories 5

Warnock Report 1978 (UK)
   mainstreaming 74
Watson, John B. (1878–1958)
   behaviorism 3
Wechsler Adult Intelligence Scale (WAIS)
   age differences 164
Well being
   and aging (individuals) 166

and child development
risk and vulnerability model 244
and evaluative thinking
learning processes 588
Whole language approach
beginning reading 561
Withdrawal (psychology)
and social development 219
Women's rights *See* Feminism
Word associations (reading) *See*
Associative learning
Word blindness *See* Word recognition,
difficulties
Word problems (mathematics)
language usage 540
sex differences 642, 643
Word processing
elementary schools 579
and language skills
writing processes 697
and revision (written composition) 698
Word recognition
difficulties
and learning disabilities 797
Work attitudes
and socialization 196
Work environment
learning in *755–59*
and socialization 196
Working memory *See* Short term
memory (STM)
Workshops
and learning strategies 761
World Conference on Education for All
1990 (WCEFA)
children with no access to
education 151
special education 158

World Health Organisation (WHO)
reports
developmental psychology 6
Writing (composition) *580–84*
cognitive processes 582
discourse modes
and social context 578, 579
feedback 582
teacher response 582
language acquisition 580
learning strategies 580, 582
student motivation 582
metacognition 578
narration 578
persuasive discourse 578
and thinking skills 579
Writing development *See* Writing
improvement
Writing evaluation
methods 583
and writing skills 578
Writing improvement
cognitive development 581
learning processes 581
Writing instruction *577–80*
scaffolding 579
special education
protocol analysis 779
student motivation 582
Writing processes 577
knowledge-telling model 577, 579
knowledge-transforming model
577, 579
problem solving 581
revision (written composition) 578
See also Prewriting
Writing skills
expertise 578, 579

learning *577–80*
skill development 578
Writing strategies
learning disabilities 528
Writing systems *See* Written language
Written composition *See* Writing
(composition)
Written language 559
alphabets
and literacy 428
and reading 559, 560
historical development of functions
429
and historical development of
literacy 428
logographic systems
and literacy 428
and reading 559, 560
phoneme grapheme correspondence
559, 561
syllabary systems
and literacy 428
and reading 559, 560
of Vai
Liberia 484

X-irradiation 176

Yale Clinic of Child Development 2
Young adults
physical development 182
Young children
prosocial behavior 207
See also Infants; Toddlers
Youth problems
and delinquency prevention 134